Collins

BESTSELLING BILINGUAL DICTIONARIES

German
Dictionary

Collins

HarperCollins Publishers
Westerhill Road
Bishopbriggs
Glasgow
G64 2QT
Great Britain

Sixth Edition 2010

Reprint 10 9 8 7 6 5 4 3 2 1

© HarperCollins Publishers 1997, 1999, 2004, 2006, 2007, 2010

ISBN 978-0-00-732316-6

Collins® is a registered trademark of HarperCollins Publishers Limited

Dictionary text prepared by Collins in collaboration with the Langenscheidt Editorial Staff

www.collinslanguage.com

A catalogue record for this book is available from the British Library

HarperCollins Publishers,
10 East 53rd Street,
New York, NY 10022

COLLINS GERMAN CONCISE DICTIONARY.
Fifth US Edition 2010

ISBN 978-0-06-199862-1

www.harpercollins.com

HarperCollins books may be purchased for educational, business, or sales promotional use. For information, please write to: Special Markets Department, HarperCollins Publishers, 10 East 53rd Street, New York, NY 10022

Typeset by Wordcraft, Glasgow

Printed in Italy by
LEGO Spa, Lavis (Trento)

Acknowledgements
We would like to thank those authors and publishers who kindly gave permission for copyright material to be used in the Collins Word Web. We would also like to thank Times Newspapers Ltd for providing valuable data.

Inhalt

Contents

WARENZEICHEN
Wörter, die unseres Wissens eingetragene Warenzeichen darstellen, sind als solche gekennzeichnet. Es ist jedoch zu beachten, dass weder das Vorhandensein noch das Fehlen derartiger Kennzeichnungen die Rechtslage hinsichtlich eingetragener Warenzeichen berührt.

NOTE ON TRADEMARKS
Words, which we have reason to believe constitute trademarks have been designated as such. However, neither the presence nor the absence of such designation should be regarded as affecting the legal status of any trademark.

GESAMTLEITUNG/PUBLISHING DIRECTOR
Rob Scriven

REDAKTIONELLE LEITUNG/EDITORIAL MANAGEMENT
Gaëlle-Amiot Cadey

LEITENDE REDAKTEURIN/SENIOR EDITOR
Susie Beattie

MITARBEITER/CONTRIBUTIONS FROM
Horst Kopleck, Joyce Littlejohn, Dagmar Förtsch, Hildegard Pesch, Veronika Schnorr, Gisela Moohan, Ulrike Seeberger, Elspeth Anderson, Val McNulty, Eva Vennebusch, Robin Sawers, Ilse MacLean, Beate Wengel

DATENVERARBEITUNG/COMPUTING STAFF
Thomas Callan

Einleitung

Sie möchten Englisch lernen oder vielleicht bereits vorhandene Kenntnisse vertiefen. Sie möchten sich auf Englisch ausdrücken, englische Texte lesen oder übersetzen, oder Sie möchten sich ganz einfach mit Englisch sprechenden Menschen unterhalten können. Ganz gleich ob Sie Englisch an der Schule oder an der Universität lernen, in einem Büro oder in einem Unternehmen tätig sind: Sie haben sich den richtigen Begleiter für Ihre Arbeit ausgesucht! Dieses Buch ist der ideale Helfer, wenn Sie sich in englischer Sprache ausdrücken und verständlich machen wollen, ob Sie nun sprechen oder schreiben. Unser Wörterbuch ist ganz bewusst praktisch und modern, es räumt vor allem der Alltagssprache und der Sprache, wie sie Ihnen in Zeitungen und Nachrichten, im Geschäftsleben, im Büro und im Urlaub begegnet, großen Raum ein. Wie in allen unseren Wörterbüchern haben wir das Hauptgewicht auf zeitgenössische Sprache und idiomatische Redewendungen gelegt.

Wie man dieses Buch benutzt

Im Folgenden geben wir einige Erklärungen darüber, wie die Einträge Ihres Wörterbuchs aufgebaut sind. Unser Ziel: Wir wollen Ihnen so viel Information wie möglich bieten, ohne dabei an Klarheit und Verständlichkeit einzubüßen.

Die Wörterbucheinträge

Ein typischer Eintrag in Ihres Wörterbuchs besteht aus folgenden Elementen:

Lautschrift

Wie die meisten modernen Wörterbücher geben wir die Aussprache mit Zeichen an, die zum „internationalen phonetischen Alphabet" gehören. Weiter unten (auf den Seiten xiv) finden Sie eine vollständige Liste der Zeichen, die in diesem System benutzt werden. Die Aussprache englischer Wörter geben wir auf der englisch-deutschen Seite unmittelbar hinter dem jeweiligen Wort in eckigen Klammern an. Die deutsche Aussprache erscheint im deutsch-englischen Teil ebenfalls auf diese Weise unmittelbar hinter den Worteinträgen. Allerdings wird sie nicht immer angegeben, zum Beispiel bei zusammengesetzten Wörtern wie Liebesbrief, deren Bestandteile schon an anderer Stelle im Wörterbuch zu finden sind.

Grammatik-Information

Alle Wörter gehören zu einer der folgenden grammatischen Klassen: Substantiv, Verb, Adjektiv, Pronomen, Artikel, Konjunktion, Präposition, Interjektion, Abkürzung. Substantive können im Deutschen männlich, weiblich oder sächlich sein. Verben können transitiv, intransitiv, reflexiv oder auch unpersönlich sein. Die Wortart folgt auf die Lautschrift und ist in *Kursivschrift* angegeben. Wo bei Übersetzungen eine Geschlechtsangabe erforderlich ist, wird diese ebenfalls in *Kursivschrift* gegeben.

Oft gehören Wörter zu zwei oder mehr grammatischen Klassen. So kann das deutsche Wort **gut** ein Adjektiv („good") oder auch ein Adverb („well") sein, und das englische Wort **spell** ist sowohl ein Substantiv („Zauber") als auch ein Verb („schreiben, buchstabieren"). Das Verb **reden** ist manchmal transitiv, d. h. es hat ein Objekt („sie redet Unsinn"), manchmal intransitiv, d.h. es wird ohne Objekt gebraucht („er redet ständig vom Wetter"). Zur besseren Übersichtlichkeit sind verschiedene Wortarten durch das Symbol ▷ abgegrenzt; alle Beispielsätze werden dann unter den entsprechenden grammatischen Kategorien gegeben.

Bedeutungsunterschiede

Die meisten Wörter haben mehr als eine Bedeutung. So kann z.B. **Rad** einen Teil eines Autos oder Fahrrads bezeichnen, aber auch ein Wort für das Fahrrad selbst sein. Andere Wörter haben je nach Kontext verschiedene Übersetzungen; so bedeutet das Verb **to recede** abhängig vom Subjekt des Satzes entweder „zurückgehen" oder „verschwinden". Damit Sie in jedem Zusammenhang immer die richtige Übersetzung finden, haben wir die Einträge nach Bedeutungen eingeteilt: jede Kategorie wird durch einen „Verwendungshinweis" bestimmt, der *kursiv* gedruckt ist und in

Klammern steht. Die beiden Beispiele von oben sehen dann so aus:

Rad *nt* wheel; (*Fahrrad*) bike
recede *vi* (*tide*) zurückgehen; (*lights etc*) verschwinden

Andere Wörter haben in verschiedenen Sachzusammenhängen unterschiedliche Bedeutungen. Das Wort **Rezept** z. B. bezeichnet eine Koch- oder Backanleitung, bezieht sich in medizinischen Zusammenhängen jedoch auf ärztlich verordnete Medikamente. Wir zeigen Ihnen, welche Übersetzung Sie auswählen sollten, indem wir wieder in Klammern solche Fachgebiete in *kursiven* Buchstaben angeben, mit dem Anfangsbuchstaben großgeschrieben, im vorigen Fall *Koch* als Abkürzung für *Kochen* und *Med* als Abkürzung für *Medizin*:

Rezept *nt* (*Koch*) recipe; (*Med*) prescription

Sie finden eine Liste aller in diesem Wörterbuch benutzten Abkürzungen für solche Sachgebiete auf den Seiten x–xii.

Übersetzungen

Die meisten deutschen Wörter können mit einem einzigen englischen Wort übersetzt werden und umgekehrt. Aber manchmal gibt es eine solche genaue Entsprechung nicht. In diesen Fällen haben wir eine ungefähre Entsprechung angegeben, gekennzeichnet durch ≈. Dies ist z. B. der Fall bei **Gymnasium** mit den englischen bzw. amerikanischen Äquivalenten „grammar school" und „high school", die aufgrund der unterschiedlichen Ausbildungssysteme lediglich ungefähre Entsprechungen sein können.

Gymnasium *nt* ≈ grammar school (*Brit*), high school (*US*)

Manchmal kann man nicht einmal ein ungefähres Äquivalent finden. Besonders oft ist das der Fall beim Essen, insbesondere bei lokalen Spezialitäten wie dieser schottischen Speise:

haggis (*Scot*) *n Gericht aus gehackten Schafsinnereien und Haferschrot, im Schafsmagen gekocht*

Hier wird statt einer Übersetzung (die es einfach gar nicht gibt) eine Erklärung gegeben, die durch *Kursivschrift* als solche kenntlich gemacht ist.

Im Deutschen wissen Sie , in welcher Situation Sie den Ausdruck **ich bin pleite** verwenden würden, wann Sie **ich bin knapp bei Kasse** sagen und wann **ich bin in Geldschwierigkeiten**. Wenn Sie jedoch Englisch verstehen oder selbst sprechen wollen, ist es wichtig zu wissen, welcher Ausdruck etwa höflich ist und welcher nicht. Um Ihnen hierbei zu helfen, haben wir für umgangssprachliche Ausdrücke die Kennzeichnung (*umg*) bzw. (*inf*) verwendet. Besonders anstößige Ausdrücke sind zusätzlich mit einem Ausrufezeichen versehen, also (*umg!*) bzw. (*inf!*), um den Benutzer zu warnen, diese nur mit großer Vorsicht zu verwenden. Angaben wie (*umg*) oder (*inf*) werden bei Übersetzungen in der Regel nicht wiederholt, wenn das Sprachniveau der Zielsprache dem der Ausgangssprache entspricht.

Schlüsselwörter

Im Text als s c h l ü s s e l w ö r t e r hervorgehobene Einträge, wie etwa **to be** und **to do** und ihre deutschen Entsprechungen **sein** und **machen**, werden als Grundelemente der Sprache besonders ausführlich behandelt.

Landeskundliche Informationen

In vom restlichen Text durch eine senkrechte Reihe schattierter Punkte abgesetzten Artikeln werden landeskundliche Aspekte in deutsch- und englischsprachigen Ländern behandelt. Die Themen umfassen Politik, Ausbildung, Medien und Feiertage, z. B. **Bundestag**, **Abitur**, **BBC** und **Hallowe'en**.

Introduction

You may be starting to learn German, or you may wish to extend your knowledge of the language. Perhaps you want to read and study German books, newspapers and magazines, or perhaps simply have a conversation with German speakers. Whatever the reason, whether you're a student, a tourist or want to use German for business, this is the ideal book to help you understand and communicate. This modern, user-friendly dictionary gives priority to everyday vocabulary and the language of current affairs, business and tourism. As in all Collins dictionaries, the emphasis is firmly placed on contemporary language and expressions.

How to use this Dictionary
You will find below an outline of the way in which information is presented in your dictionary. Our aim is to give you the maximum amount of information whilst still providing a text which is clear and user-friendly.

Entries
A typical entry in your dictionary will be made up of the following elements:

Phonetic transcription
Phonetics appear in square brackets immediately after the headword. They are shown using the International Phonetic Alphabet (IPA), and a complete list of the symbols used in this system can be found on pages xiv and xv.

Grammatical information
All words belong to one of the following parts of speech: noun, verb, adjective, adverb, pronoun, article, conjunction, preposition, exclamation, abbreviation. Nouns can be singular or plural and, in German, masculine, feminine or neuter. Verbs can be transitive, intransitive, reflexive or impersonal. Parts of speech appear in *italics* immediately after the phonetic spelling of the headword. The gender of the translation appears in *italics* immediately following the key element of the translation.

Often a word can have more than one part of speech. Just as the English word **next** can be an adjective or an adverb, the German word **gut** can be an adjective ("good") or an adverb ("well"). In the same way the verb **to walk** is sometimes transitive, i.e. it takes an object ("to walk the dog") and sometimes intransitive, i.e. it doesn't take an object ("to walk to school"). To help you find the meaning you are looking for quickly and for clarity of presentation, the different part of speech categories are separated by an open white triangle ▷.

Meaning divisions
Most words have more than one meaning. Take, for example, **punch** which can be, amongst other things, a blow with the fist or an object used for making holes. Other words are translated differently depending on the context in which they are used. The intransitive verb **to recede**, for example, can be translated by "zurückgehen" or "verschwinden" depending on *what* is receding. To help you select the most appropriate translation in every context, entries are divided according to meaning. Each different meaning is introduced by an "indicator" in *italics* and in brackets. Thus, the examples given above will be shown as follows:

> **punch** n (*blow*) Schlag m; (*tool*) Locher m
> **recede** vi (*tide*) zurückgehen; (*lights etc*) verschwinden

Likewise, some words can have a different meaning when used to talk about a specific subject area or field. For example, **bishop**, which in a religious context means a high-ranking clergyman, is also the name of a chess piece. To show English speakers which translation to use, we have added "subject field labels" in italics with initial capitals and in brackets, in this case (*Rel*) and (*Chess*):

bishop *n* (*Rel*) Bischof *m*; (*Chess*) Läufer *m*

Field labels are often shortened to save space. You will find a complete list of abbreviations used in the dictionary on pages x to xii

Translations

Most English words have a direct translation in German and vice versa, as shown in the examples given above. Sometimes, however, no exact equivalent exists in the target language. In such cases we have given an approximate equivalent, indicated by the sign ≈. Such is the case of **high school**, the German equivalent of which is "Oberschule *f*". This is not an exact translation since the systems of the two countries in question are quite different:

high school *n* ≈ Oberschule *f*

On occasion it is impossible to find even an approximate equivalent. This may be the case, for example, with the names of culinary specialities like this German cake:

Streuselkuchen *m cake with crumble topping*

Here the translation (which doesn't exist) is replaced by an explanation. For increased clarity the explanation, or "gloss", is shown in *italics*.

Register

In English you instinctively know when to say **I'm broke** *or* **I'm a bit short of cash** and when to say **I don't have any money**. When you are trying to understand someone who is speaking German, however, or when you yourself try to speak German, it is especially important to know what is polite and what is less so. To help you with this, we have added the register labels (*umg*) and (*inf*) to colloquial or offensive expressions. Those expressions which are particularly vulgar are also given an exclamation mark (*umg!*) or (*inf!*), warning you to use them with extreme care. Please note that the register labels (*umg*) and (*inf*) are not repeated in the target language when the register of the translation matches that of the word or phrase being translated.

Keywords

Words labelled in the text as K E Y W O R D S, such as **be** and **do** or their German equivalents **sein** and **machen**, have been given special treatment because they form the basic elements of the language. This extra help will ensure that you know how to use these complex words with confidence.

Cultural information

Entries which appear separated by a column of dots explain aspects of culture in German- and English-speaking countries. Subject areas covered include politics, education, media and national festivals, for example **Bundestag**, **Abitur**, **BBC** and **Hallowe'en**.

Abkürzungen

Abbreviations

Abkürzung	*abk, abbr*	abbreviation
Adjektiv	*adj*	adjective
Verwaltung	*Admin*	administration
Adverb	*adv*	adverb
Landwirtschaft	*Agr*	agriculture
Akkusativ	*akk, acc*	accusative
Anatomie	*Anat*	anatomy
Architektur	*Archit*	architecture
Artikel	*art*	article
Kunst	*Art*	
Astrologie	*Astrol*	astrology
Astronomie	*Astron*	astronomy
attributiv	*attrib*	attributive
Kraftfahrzeuge	*Aut*	automobiles
Hilfsverb	*aux*	auxiliary
Luftfahrt	*Aviat*	aviation
Bergbau	*Bergb*	mining
besonders	*bes*	especially
Biologie	*Biol*	biology
Botanik	*Bot*	botany
britisch	*Brit*	British
Kartenspiel	*Cards*	
Chemie	*Chem*	chemistry
Film	*Cine*	cinema
Handel	*Comm*	commerce
Komparativ	*comp*	comparative
Computer	*Comput*	computers
Konjunktion	*conj*	conjunction
Bauwesen	*Constr*	building
zusammengesetztes Wort	*cpd*	compound
Kochen und Backen	*Culin*	cooking
Dativ	*dat*	dative
bestimmt	*def*	definite
diminutiv	*dimin*	diminutive
dekliniert	*dekl*	declined
kirchlich	*Eccl*	ecclesiastical
Volkswirtschaft	*Econ*	economics
Eisenbahn	*Eisenb*	railways
Elektrizität	*Elek, Elec*	electricity
besonders	*esp*	especially
und so weiter	*etc*	et cetera
etwas	*etw*	something
Euphemismus	*euph*	euphemism
Ausruf	*excl*	exclamation
Femininum	*f*	feminine
übertragen	*fig*	figurative
Film	*Film*	cinema
Finanzen	*Fin*	finance
formell	*form*	formal
'phrasal verb', bei dem Partikel und Verb nicht getrennt werden können	*fus*	fused: phrasal verb where the particle cannot be separated from the verb
gehoben	*geh*	elevated

x

Genitiv	*gen*	genitive
Geografie	*Geog*	geography
Geologie	*Geol*	geology
Geometrie	*Geom*	geometry
Grammatik	*Gram*	grammar
Geschichte	*Hist*	history
scherzhaft	*hum*	humorous
Imperfekt	*imperf*	imperfect
unpersönlich	*impers*	impersonal
unbestimmt	*indef*	indefinite
umgangssprachlich	*inf*	informal
untrennbares Verb	*insep*	inseparable
Interjektion	*interj*	interjection
Interrogativ	*interrog*	interrogative
unveränderlich	*inv*	invariable
unregelmäßig	*irreg*	irregular
jemand	*jd*	somebody
jemandem	*jdm*	(to) somebody
jemanden	*jdn*	somebody
jemandes	*jds*	somebody's
Rechtswesen	*Jur*	law
Kartenspiel	*Karten*	cards
Kochen und Backen	*Koch*	cooking
Komparativ	*komp*	comparative
Konjunktion	*konj*	conjunction
Rechtswesen	*Law*	law
Sprachwissenschaft	*Ling*	linguistics
wörtlich	*lit*	literal
literarisch	*liter*	literary
Literatur	*Liter*	literature
Maskulinum	*m*	masculine
Mathematik	*Math*	mathematics
Medizin	*Med*	medicine
Meteorologie	*Met*	meteorology
Militärwesen	*Mil*	military
Bergbau	*Min*	mining
Musik	*Mus*	music
Substantiv	*n*	noun
nautisch	*Naut*	nautical
Nominativ	*nom*	nominative
norddeutsch	*Nordd*	North Germany
Neutrum	*nt*	neuter
Zahlwort	*num*	numeral
Objekt	*obj*	object
oder	*od*	or
veraltet	*old*	
sich	*o.s.*	oneself
österreichisch	*Österr*	Austria
Parlament	*Parl*	parliament
pejorativ	*pej*	pejorative
Person/persönlich	*pers*	person/personal
Pharmazie	*Pharm*	pharmacy
Fotografie	*Phot*	photography
Physik	*Phys*	physics
Physiologie	*Physiol*	physiology

Plural	*pl*	plural
Politik	*Pol*	politics
possessiv	*poss*	possessive
Partizip Perfekt	*pp*	past participle
Präfix	*präf, pref*	prefix
Präposition	*präp, prep*	preposition
Präsens	*präs, pres*	present
Pronomen	*pron*	pronoun
Psychologie	*Psych*	psychology
Imperfekt	*pt*	past tense
Radio	*Radio*	radio
Eisenbahn	*Rail*	railways
Religion	*Rel*	religion
Relativ-	*rel*	relative
Rundfunk	*Rundf*	broadcasting
jemand (-en, -em)	*sb*	somebody
Schulwesen	*Sch*	school
Naturwissenschaft	*Sci*	science
Schulwesen	*Scol*	school
schottisch	*Scot*	Scottish
Singular	*sing*	singular
Skisport	*Ski*	skiing
etwas	*sth*	something
Süddeutschland	*Südd*	South German
Suffix	*suff*	suffix
Superlativ	*superl*	superlative
Technik	*Tech*	technology
Telekommunikation	*Tel*	telecommunications
Theater	*Theat*	theatre
Fernsehen	*TV*	television
Typografie	*Typ*	typography
umgangssprachlich	*umg*	colloquial
Universität	*Univ*	university
unpersönlich	*unpers*	impersonal
unregelmäßig	*unreg*	irregular
untrennbar	*untr*	inseparable
unveränderlich	*unver*	invariable
(nord)amerikanisch	*US*	(North)American
gewöhnlich	*usu*	usually
und so weiter	*usw*	et cetera
Verb	*vb*	verb
intransitives Verb	*vi*	intransitive verb
reflexives Verb	*vr*	reflexive verb
transitives Verb	*vt*	transitive verb
Wirtschaft	*Wirts*	economy
Zoologie	*Zool*	zoology
zusammengesetztes Wort	*zW*	compound
ungefähre Entsprechung	≈	cultural equivalent
eingetragene Marke	®	registered trademark

German Noun Endings

After many noun entries on the German-English side of the dictionary, you will find two pieces of grammatical information, separated by commas, to help you with the declension of the noun, e.g. -, -n or -(e)s, -e. The first item shows you the genitive singular form, and the second gives the plural form. The hyphen stands for the word itself and the other letters are endings. Sometimes an umlaut is shown over the hyphen, which means an umlaut must be placed on the vowel of the word, e.g.:

DICTIONARY ENTRY	GENITIVE SINGULAR	PLURAL
Mann m -(e)s, ¨er	**Mannes** or **Manns**	**Männer**
Jacht f -, -en	**Jacht**	**Jachten**

This information is not given when the noun has one of the regular German noun endings below, and you should refer to this table in such cases. Similarly, genitive and plural endings are not shown when the German entry is a compound consisting of two or more words which are to be found elsewhere in the dictionary, since the compound form takes the endings of the LAST word of which it is formed, e.g.:

for **Nebenstraße** see **Straße**
for **Schneeball** see **Ball**

Regular German Noun Endings

NOM	GEN	PL
-ant m	-anten	-anten
-anz f	-anz	-anzen
-ar m	-ar(e)s	-are
-chen nt	-chens	-chen
-ei f	-ei	-eien
-elle f	-elle	-ellen
-ent m	-enten	-enten
-enz f	-enz	-enzen
-ette f	-ette	-etten
-eur m	-eurs	-eure
-euse f	-euse	-eusen
-heit f	-heit	-heiten
-ie f	-ie	-ien
-ik f	-ik	-iken
-in f	-in	-innen
-ine f	-ine	-inen
-ion f	-ion	-ionen
-ist m	-isten	-isten
-ium nt	-iums	-ien
-ius m	-ius	-iusse
-ive f	-ive	-iven
-keit f	-keit	-keiten
-lein nt	-leins	-lein
-ling m	-lings	-linge
-ment nt	-ments	-mente
-mus m	-mus	-men
-schaft f	-schaft	-schaften
-tät f	-tät	-täten
-tor m	-tors	-toren
-ung f	-ung	-ungen
-ur f	-ur	-uren

Phonetic Symbols

Lautschrift

Vowels

Vokale

matt	[a]	
Fahne	[aː]	
Vater	[ər]	
	[ɑː]	calm, part
	[æ]	sat
Rendezvous	[ã]	
Chance	[aː]	
	[ãː]	clientele
Etage	[e]	
Seele, Mehl	[eː]	
Wäsche, Bett	[ɛ]	egg
zählen	[ɛː]	
Teint	[ɛ̃ː]	
mache	[ə]	above
	[əː]	burn, earn
Kiste	[ɪ]	pit, awfully
Vitamin	[i]	
Ziel	[iː]	peat
Oase	[o]	
oben	[oː]	
Champignon	[õ]	
Salon	[õː]	
Most	[ɔ]	cot
	[ɔː]	born, jaw
ökonomisch	[ø]	
blöd	[øː]	
Göttin	[œ]	
	[ʌ]	hut
zuletzt	[u]	put
Mut	[uː]	pool
Mutter	[ʊ]	
Physik	[y]	
Kübel	[yː]	
Sünde	[ʏ]	

Diphthongs		Diphthonge
Styling	[ai]	
weit	[aɪ]	buy, die, my
umbauen	[au]	house, now
Haus	[aʊ]	
	[eɪ]	pay, mate
	[ɛə]	pair, mare
	[əu]	no, boat
	[ɪə]	mere, shear
Heu, Häuser	[ɔʏ]	
	[ɔɪ]	boy, coin
	[uə]	tour, poor

Consonants		Konsonanten
Ball	[b]	ball
mich	[ç]	
	[tʃ]	child
fern	[f]	field
gern	[g]	good
Hand	[h]	hand
ja	[j]	yet, million
	[dʒ]	just
Kind	[k]	kind, catch
links, Pult	[l]	left, little
matt	[m]	mat
Nest	[n]	nest
lang	[ŋ]	long
Paar	[p]	put
rennen	[r]	run
fast, fassen	[s]	sit
Chef, Stein, Schlag	[ʃ]	shall
Tafel	[t]	tab
	[θ]	thing
	[ð]	this
wer	[v]	very
	[w]	wet
Loch	[x]	loch
fix	[ks]	box
singen	[z]	pods, zip
Zahn	[ts]	
genieren	[ʒ]	measure

Other signs		Andere Zeichen
glottal stop	|	Knacklaut
main stress	[']	Hauptton
long vowel	[:]	Längezeichen

German Irregular Verbs

INFINITIV	PRÄSENS 2., 3. SINGULAR	PRÄTERITUM	PARTIZIP PERFEKT
abwägen	wägst ab, wägt ab	wog ab	abgewogen
ausbedingen	bedingst aus, bedingt aus	bedang od bedingte aus	ausbedungen
backen	bäckst, bäckt	backte od buk	gebacken
befehlen	befiehlst, befiehlt	befahl	befohlen
beginnen	beginnst, beginnt	begann	begonnen
beißen	beißt, beißt	biss	gebissen
bergen	birgst, birgt	barg	geborgen
bersten*	birst, birst	barst	geborsten
betrügen	betrügst, betrügt	betrog	betrogen
bewegen	bewegst, bewegt	bewog	bewogen
biegen	biegst, biegt	bog	gebogen
bieten	bietest, bietet	bot	geboten
binden	bindest, bindet	band	gebunden
bitten	bittest, bittet	bat	gebeten
blasen	bläst, bläst	blies	geblasen
bleiben*	bleibst, bleibt	blieb	geblieben
braten	brätst, brät	briet	gebraten
brechen*	brichst, bricht	brach	gebrochen
brennen	brennst, brennt	brannte	gebrannt
bringen	bringst, bringt	brachte	gebracht
denken	denkst, denkt	dachte	gedacht
dreschen	drischst, drischt	drosch	gedroschen
dringen*	dringst, dringt	drang	gedrungen
dürfen	darfst, darf	durfte	gedurft
empfangen	empfängst, empfängt	empfing	empfangen
empfehlen	empfiehlst, empfiehlt	empfahl	empfohlen
empfinden	empfindest, empfindet	empfand	empfunden
erbleichen*	erbleichst, erbleicht	erbleichte	erblichen
erlöschen*	erlischst, erlischt	erlosch	erloschen
erschrecken*	erschrickst, erschrickt	erschrak	erschrocken
erwägen	erwägst, erwägt	erwog	erwogen
essen	isst, isst	aß	gegessen
fahren*	fährst, fährt	fuhr	gefahren
fallen*	fällst, fällt	fiel	gefallen
fangen	fängst, fängt	fing	gefangen
fechten	fichtst, ficht	focht	gefochten
finden	findest, findet	fand	gefunden
flechten	flichtst, flicht	flocht	geflochten
fliegen*	fliegst, fliegt	flog	geflogen
fliehen*	fliehst, flieht	floh	geflohen
fließen*	fließt, fließt	floss	geflossen
fressen	frisst, frisst	fraß	gefressen
frieren	frierst, friert	fror	gefroren
gären*	gärst, gärt	gor	gegoren
gebären	gebierst, gebiert	gebar	geboren
geben	gibst, gibt	gab	gegeben
gedeihen*	gedeihst, gedeiht	gedieh	gediehen
gehen*	gehst, geht	ging	gegangen

INFINITIV	PRÄSENS 2., 3. SINGULAR	PRÄTERITUM	PARTIZIP PERFEKT
gelingen*	–, gelingt	gelang	gelungen
gelten	giltst, gilt	galt	gegolten
genesen*	genest, genest	genas	genesen
genießen	genießt, genießt	genoss	genossen
geraten*	gerätst, gerät	geriet	geraten
geschehen*	–, geschieht	geschah	geschehen
gewinnen	gewinnst, gewinnt	gewann	gewonnen
gießen	gießt, gießt	goss	gegossen
gleichen	gleichst, gleicht	glich	geglichen
gleiten*	gleitest, gleitet	glitt	geglitten
glimmen	glimmst, glimmt	glomm	geglommen
graben	gräbst, gräbt	grub	gegraben
greifen	greifst, greift	griff	gegriffen
haben	hast, hat	hatte	gehabt
halten	hältst, hält	hielt	gehalten
hängen	hängst, hängt	hing	gehangen
hauen	haust, haut	haute	gehauen
heben	hebst, hebt	hob	gehoben
heißen	heißt, heißt	hieß	geheißen
helfen	hilfst, hilft	half	geholfen
kennen	kennst, kennt	kannte	gekannt
klimmen*	klimmst, klimmt	klomm	geklommen
klingen	klingst, klingt	klang	geklungen
kneifen	kneifst, kneift	kniff	gekniffen
kommen*	kommst, kommt	kam	gekommen
können	kannst, kann	konnte	gekonnt
kriechen*	kriechst, kriecht	kroch	gekrochen
laden	lädst, lädt	lud	geladen
lassen	lässt, lässt	ließ	gelassen
laufen*	läufst, läuft	lief	gelaufen
leiden	leidest, leidet	litt	gelitten
leihen	leihst, leiht	lieh	geliehen
lesen	liest, liest	las	gelesen
liegen	liegst, liegt	lag	gelegen
lügen	lügst, lügt	log	gelogen
mahlen	mahlst, mahlt	mahlte	gemahlen
meiden	meidest, meidet	mied	gemieden
melken	melkst, melkt	melkte od molk	gemolken
messen	misst, misst	maß	gemessen
misslingen*	–, misslingt	misslang	misslungen
mögen	magst, mag	mochte	gemocht
müssen	musst, muss	musste	gemusst
nehmen	nimmst, nimmt	nahm	genommen
nennen	nennst, nennt	nannte	genannt
pfeifen	pfeifst, pfeift	pfiff	gepfiffen
preisen	preist, preist	pries	gepriesen
quellen*	quillst, quillt	quoll	gequollen
raten	rätst, rät	riet	geraten
reiben	reibst, reibt	rieb	gerieben

INFINITIV	PRÄSENS 2., 3. SINGULAR	PRÄTERITUM	PARTIZIP PERFEKT
reißen*	reißt, reißt	riss	gerissen
reiten*	reitest, reitet	ritt	geritten
rennen*	rennst, rennt	rannte	gerannt
riechen	riechst, riecht	roch	gerochen
ringen	ringst, ringt	rang	gerungen
rinnen*	rinnst, rinnt	rann	geronnen
rufen	rufst, ruft	rief	gerufen
salzen	salzt, salzt	salzte	gesalzen
saufen	säufst, säuft	soff	gesoffen
saugen	saugst, saugt	sog *od* saugte	-gesogen *od* gesaugt
schaffen	schaffst, schafft	schuf	geschaffen
schallen	schallst, schallt	scholl	geschollen
scheiden*	scheidest, scheidet	schied	geschieden
scheinen	scheinst, scheint	schien	geschienen
scheißen	scheißt, scheißt	schiss	geschissen
schelten	schiltst, schilt	schalt	gescholten
scheren	scherst, schert	schor	geschoren
schieben	schiebst, schiebt	schob	geschoben
schießen	schießt, schießt	schoss	geschossen
schinden	schindest, schindet	schindete	geschunden
schlafen	schläfst, schläft	schlief	geschlafen
schlagen	schlägst, schlägt	schlug	geschlagen
schleichen*	schleichst, schleicht	schlich	geschlichen
schleifen	schleifst, schleift	schliff	geschliffen
schließen	schließt, schließt	schloss	geschlossen
schlingen	schlingst, schlingt	schlang	geschlungen
schmeißen	schmeißt, schmeißt	schmiss	geschmissen
schmelzen*	schmilzt, schmilzt	schmolz	geschmolzen
schneiden	schneidest, schneidet	schnitt	geschnitten
schreiben	schreibst, schreibt	schrieb	geschrieben
schreien	schreist, schreit	schrie	geschrien
schreiten	schreitest, schreitet	schritt	geschritten
schweigen	schweigst, schweigt	schwieg	geschwiegen
schwellen*	schwillst, schwillt	schwoll	geschwollen
schwimmen*	schwimmst, schwimmt	schwamm	geschwommen
schwinden*	schwindest, schwindet	schwand	geschwunden
schwingen	schwingst, schwingt	schwang	geschwungen
schwören	schwörst, schwört	schwor	geschworen
sehen	siehst, sieht	sah	gesehen
sein*	bist, ist	war	gewesen
senden	sendest, sendet	sandte	gesandt
singen	singst, singt	sang	gesungen
sinken*	sinkst, sinkt	sank	gesunken
sinnen	sinnst, sinnt	sann	gesonnen
sitzen	sitzt, sitzt	saß	gesessen
sollen	sollst, soll	sollte	gesollt
speien	speist, speit	spie	gespien
spinnen	spinnst, spinnt	spann	gesponnen
sprechen	sprichst, spricht	sprach	gesprochen
sprießen*	sprießt, sprießt	spross	gesprossen
springen*	springst, springt	sprang	gesprungen

INFINITIV	PRÄSENS 2., 3. SINGULAR	PRÄTERITUM	PARTIZIP PERFEKT
stechen	stichst, sticht	stach	gestochen
stecken	steckst, steckt	steckte *od* stak	gesteckt
stehen	stehst, steht	stand	gestanden
stehlen	stiehlst, stiehlt	stahl	gestohlen
steigen*	steigst, steigt	stieg	gestiegen
sterben*	stirbst, stirbt	starb	gestorben
stinken	stinkst, stinkt	stank	gestunken
stoßen	stößt, stößt	stieß	gestoßen
streichen	streichst, streicht	strich	gestrichen
streiten	streitest, streitet	stritt	gestritten
tragen	trägst, trägt	trug	getragen
treffen	triffst, trifft	traf	getroffen
treiben*	treibst, treibt	trieb	getrieben
treten*	trittst, tritt	trat	getreten
trinken	trinkst, trinkt	trank	getrunken
trügen	trügst, trügt	trog	getrogen
tun	tust, tut	tat	getan
verderben	verdirbst, verdirbt	verdarb	verdorben
verdrießen	verdrießt, verdrießt	verdross	verdrossen
vergessen	vergisst, vergisst	vergaß	vergessen
verlieren	verlierst, verliert	verlor	verloren
verschleißen	verschleißt, verschleißt	verschliss	verschlissen
verschwinden	verschwindest, verschwindet	verschwand	verschwunden
verzeihen	verzeihst, verzeiht	verzieh	verziehen
wachsen*	wächst, wächst	wuchs	gewachsen
wägen	wägst, wägt	wog	gewogen
waschen	wäschst, wäscht	wusch	gewaschen
weben	webst, webt	webte *od* wob	gewoben
weichen*	weichst, weicht	wich	gewichen
weisen	weist, weist	wies	gewiesen
wenden	wendest, wendet	wandte	gewandt
werben	wirbst, wirbt	warb	geworben
werden*	wirst, wird	wurde	geworden
werfen	wirfst, wirft	warf	geworfen
wiegen	wiegst, wiegt	wog	gewogen
winden	windest, windet	wand	gewunden
wissen	weißt, weiß	wusste	gewusst
wollen	willst, will	wollte	gewollt
wringen	wringst, wringt	wrang	gewrungen
zeihen	zeihst, zeiht	zieh	geziehen
ziehen*	ziehst, zieht	zog	gezogen
zwingen	zwingst, zwingt	zwang	gezwungen

Deutsch–Englisch

German–English

Aa

A¹, a [aː] *nt* A, a; **A wie Anton** ≈ A for Andrew, ≈ A for Able (US); **das A und O** the be-all and end-all; (*eines Wissensgebietes*) the basics *pl*; **wer A sagt, muss auch B sagen** (*Sprichwort*) in for a penny, in for a pound (*Sprichwort*)

A² *f abk* (= *Autobahn*) ≈ M (Brit)

a. *abk* = **am**

à [aː] *präp* (*bes Comm*) at

AA *nt abk* (= *Auswärtiges Amt*) F.O. (Brit)

Aachen ['aːxən] (**-s**) *nt* Aachen

Aal [aːl] (**-(e)s, -e**) *m* eel

aalen ['aːlən] (*umg*) *vr*: **sich in der Sonne ~** to bask in the sun

a. a. O. *abk* (= *am angegebenen od angeführten Ort*) loc. cit.

Aas [aːs] (**-es, -e** *od* **Äser**) *nt* carrion; **Aasgeier** *m* vulture

○ SCHLÜSSELWORT

ab [ap] *präp +dat* from; **ab Werk** (*Comm*) ex works; **Kinder ab 12 Jahren** children from the age of 12; **ab morgen** from tomorrow; **ab sofort** as of now

▷ *adv* **1** off; **links ab** to the left; **der Knopf ist ab** the button has come off; **ab nach Hause!** off home with you!; **ab durch die Mitte!** (*umg*) beat it!

2 (*zeitlich*): **von da ab** from then on; **von heute ab** from today, as of today

3 (*auf Fahrplänen*): **München ab 12.20** leaving Munich 12.20

4: **ab und zu** *od* **an** now and then *od* again

abändern ['ap|ɛndərn] *vt*: **~ (in** +akk**)** to alter (to); (*Gesetzentwurf*) to amend (to); (*Strafe, Urteil*) to revise (to)

Abänderung *f* alteration; amendment; revision

Abänderungsantrag *m* (*Parl*) proposed amendment

abarbeiten ['ap|arbaɪtən] *vr* to slave away

Abart ['ap|aːrt] *f* (*Biol*) variety

abartig *adj* abnormal

Abb. *abk* (= *Abbildung*) illus.

Abbau ['apbaʊ] (**-(e)s**) *m* (+gen) dismantling; (*Verminderung*) reduction (in); (*Verfall*) decline (in); (*Min*) mining; (*über Tage*) quarrying; (*Chem*) decomposition

abbaubar *adj*: **biologisch ~** biodegradable

abbauen *vt* to dismantle; (*verringern*) to reduce; (*Min*) to mine; to quarry; (*Chem*) to break down; **Arbeitsplätze ~** to make job cuts

Abbaurechte *pl* mineral rights *pl*

abbeißen ['apbaɪsən] *unreg vt* to bite off

abbekommen ['apbəkɔmən] *unreg vt*: **etwas ~** to get some (of it); (*beschädigt werden*) to get damaged; (*verletzt werden*) to get hurt

abberufen ['apbəruːfən] *unreg vt* to recall

Abberufung *f* recall

abbestellen ['apbəʃtɛlən] *vt* to cancel

abbezahlen ['apbətsaːlən] *vt* to pay off

abbiegen ['apbiːgən] *unreg vi* to turn off; (*Straße*) to bend ▷ *vt* to bend; (*verhindern*) to ward off

Abbiegespur *f* turning lane

Abbild ['apbɪlt] *nt* portrayal; (*einer Person*) image, likeness; **abbilden** ['apbɪldən] *vt* to portray; **Abbildung** *f* illustration; (*Schaubild*) diagram

abbinden ['apbɪndən] *unreg vt* (*Med: Arm, Bein etc*) to ligature

Abbitte ['apbɪtə] *f*: **~ leisten** *od* **tun (bei)** to make one's apologies (to)

abblasen ['apblaːzən] *unreg vt* to blow off; (*fig: umg*) to call off

abblättern ['apblɛtərn] *vi* (*Putz, Farbe*) to flake (off)

abblenden ['apblɛndən] *vt* (*Aut*) to dip (Brit), dim (US) ▷ *vi* to dip (Brit) *od* dim (US) one's headlights

Abblendlicht ['apblɛntlɪçt] *nt* dipped (Brit) *od* dimmed (US) headlights *pl*

abblitzen ['apblɪtsən] (*umg*) *vi*: **jdn ~ lassen** to send sb packing

abbrechen ['apbrɛçən] *unreg vt* to break off; (*Gebäude*) to pull down; (*Zelt*) to take down; (*aufhören*) to stop; (*Comput*) to abort ▷ *vi* to break off; to stop; **sich** *dat* **einen ~** (*umg: sich sehr anstrengen*) to bust a gut

abbrennen ['apbrɛnən] *unreg vt* to burn off; (*Feuerwerk*) to let off ▷ *vi* (*Hilfsverb sein*) to burn down; **abgebrannt sein** (*umg*) to be broke

abbringen ['apbrɪŋən] *unreg vt*: **jdn von etw ~** to dissuade sb from sth; **jdn vom Weg ~** to divert sb; **ich bringe den Verschluss nicht ab** (*umg*) I can't get the top off

abbröckeln ['apbrœkəln] vi to crumble off od away; (Börse: Preise) to ease

Abbruch ['apbrʊx] m (von Verhandlungen etc) breaking off; (von Haus) demolition; (Comput) abort; **jdm/etw ~ tun** to harm sb/sth; **Abbrucharbeiten** pl demolition work sing; **abbruchreif** adj only fit for demolition

abbrühen ['apbry:ən] vt to scald

abbuchen ['apbu:xən] vt to debit; (durch Dauerauftrag): **~ (von)** to pay by standing order (from)

abbürsten ['apbʏrstən] vt to brush off

abbüßen ['apby:sən] vt (Strafe) to serve

ABC-Waffen pl abk (= atomare, biologische und chemische Waffen) ABC weapons (= atomic, biological and chemical weapons)

abdampfen ['apdampfən] vi (fig: umg: losgehen/-fahren) to hit the road

abdanken ['apdaŋkən] vi to resign; (König) to abdicate

Abdankung f resignation; abdication

abdecken ['apdɛkən] vt to uncover; (Tisch) to clear; (Loch) to cover

abdichten ['apdɪçtən] vt to seal; (Naut) to caulk

abdrängen ['apdrɛŋən] vt to push off

abdrehen ['apdre:ən] vt (Gas) to turn off; (Licht) to switch off; (Film) to shoot ▷ vi (Schiff) to change course; **jdm den Hals ~** to wring sb's neck

abdriften ['apdrɪftən] vi to drift (away)

abdrosseln ['apdrɔsəln] vt to throttle; (Aut) to stall; (Produktion) to cut back

Abdruck ['apdrʊk] m (Nachdrucken) reprinting; (Gedrucktes) reprint; (Gipsabdruck, Wachsabdruck) impression; (Fingerabdruck) print; **abdrucken** vt to print

abdrücken ['apdrʏkən] vt to make an impression of; (Waffe) to fire; (umg: Person) to hug, squeeze ▷ vr to leave imprints; (abstoßen) to push o.s. away; **jdm die Luft ~** to squeeze all the breath out of sb

abdüsen ['apdy:sən] (umg) vi to dash od whizz off

abebben ['ap|ɛbən] vi to ebb away

Abend ['a:bənt] **(-s, -e)** m evening; **gegen ~** towards (the) evening; **den ganzen ~ (über)** the whole evening; **zu ~ essen** to have dinner od supper; **heute ~** this evening; **Abendanzug** m dinner jacket (Brit), tuxedo (US); **Abendbrot** nt supper; **Abendessen** nt supper; **abendfüllend** adj taking up the whole evening; **Abendgymnasium** nt night school; **Abendkasse** f (Theat) box office; **Abendkleid** nt evening gown; **Abendkurs** m evening classes pl; **Abendland** nt West; **abendlich** adj evening; **Abendmahl** nt Holy Communion; **Abendrot** nt sunset

abends adv in the evening

Abend- zW: **Abendvorstellung** f evening performance; **Abendzeitung** f evening paper

Abenteuer ['a:bəntɔʏər] **(-s, -)** nt adventure; (Liebesabenteuer) affair; **abenteuerlich** adj adventurous; **Abenteuerspielplatz** m

adventure playground

Abenteurer (-s, -) m adventurer; **Abenteurerin** f adventuress

aber ['a:bər] konj but; (jedoch) however ▷ adv: **oder ~** or else; **bist du ~ braun!** aren't you brown!; **das ist ~ schön** that's really nice; **nun ist ~ Schluss!** now that's enough!; **Aber** nt but

Aberglaube ['a:bərɡlaʊbə] m superstition

abergläubisch ['a:bərɡlɔʏbɪʃ] adj superstitious

aberkennen ['ap|ɛrkɛnən] unreg vt: **jdm etw ~** to deprive sb of sth, take sth (away) from sb

Aberkennung f taking away

abermalig adj repeated

abermals adv once again

Abertausend, abertausend ['a:bərtaʊznt] num: **Tausend und ~** thousands upon thousands

Abf. abk (= Abfahrt) dep.

abfahren ['apfa:rən] unreg vi to leave, depart ▷ vt to take od cart away; (Film) to start; (Film, TV: Kamera) to roll; (Strecke) to drive; (Reifen) to wear; (Fahrkarte) to use; **der Zug ist abgefahren** (lit) the train has left; (fig) we've/you've etc missed the boat; **der Zug fährt um 8.oo von Bremen ab** the train leaves Bremen at 8 o'clock; **jdn ~ lassen** (umg: abweisen) to tell sb to get lost; **auf jdn ~** (umg) to really go for sb

Abfahrt ['apfa:rt] f departure; (Autobahnabfahrt) exit; (Ski) descent; (Piste) run; **Vorsicht bei der ~ des Zuges!** stand clear, the train is about to leave!

Abfahrts- zW: **Abfahrtslauf** m (Ski) downhill; **Abfahrtstag** m day of departure; **Abfahrtszeit** f departure time

Abfall ['apfal] m waste; (von Speisen etc) rubbish (Brit), garbage (US); (Neigung) slope; (Verschlechterung) decline; **Abfalleimer** m rubbish bin (Brit), garbage can (US)

abfallen unreg vi (lit, fig) to fall od drop off; (Pol, vom Glauben) to break away; (sich neigen) to fall od drop away; **wie viel fällt bei dem Geschäft für mich ab?** (umg) how much do I get out of the deal?

abfällig ['apfɛlɪç] adj disparaging, deprecatory

Abfallprodukt nt (lit, fig) waste product

abfangen ['apfaŋən] unreg vt to intercept; (Person) to catch; (unter Kontrolle bringen) to check; (Aufprall) to absorb; (Kunden) to lure away

Abfangjäger m (Mil) interceptor

abfärben ['apfɛrbən] vi (lit) to lose its colour; (Wäsche) to run; (fig) to rub off

abfassen ['apfasən] vt to write, draft

abfeiern ['apfaɪərn] (umg) vt: **Überstunden ~** to take time off in lieu of overtime pay

abfertigen ['apfɛrtɪɡən] vt to prepare for dispatch, process; (an der Grenze) to clear; (Kundschaft) to attend to; **jdn kurz ~** to give sb short shrift

Abfertigung f preparing for dispatch, processing; clearance; (Bedienung: von Kunden) service; (: von Antragstellern): **~ von** dealing with

abfeuern ['apfɔʏərn] *vt* to fire
abfinden ['apfɪndən] *unreg vt* to pay off ▷ *vr* to come to terms; **sich mit jdm ~/nicht ~** to put up with/not to get on with sb; **er konnte sich nie damit ~, dass ...** he could never accept the fact that ...
Abfindung *f* (*von Gläubigern*) payment; (*Geld*) sum in settlement
abflachen ['apflaxən] *vt* to level (off), flatten (out) ▷ *vi* (*fig: sinken*) to decline
abflauen ['apflaʊən] *vi* (*Wind, Erregung*) to die away, subside; (*Nachfrage, Geschäft*) to fall *od* drop off
abfliegen ['apfli:gən] *unreg vi* to take off ▷ *vt* (*Gebiet*) to fly over
abfließen ['apfli:sən] *unreg vi* to drain away; **ins Ausland ~** (*Geld*) to flow out of the country
Abflug ['apflu:k] *m* departure; (*Start*) take-off
Abflugterminal ['apflu:ktœrmɪnəl] (**-s, -s**) *m* departure terminal; **Abflugzeit** *f* departure time
Abfluss ['apflʊs] *m* draining away; (*Öffnung*) outlet; **Abflussrohr** *nt* drainpipe; (*von sanitären Anlagen*) wastepipe
abfragen ['apfra:gən] *vt* to test; (*Comput*) to call up; **jdn etw ~** to question sb on sth
abfrieren ['apfri:rən] *unreg vi*: **ihm sind die Füße abgefroren** his feet got frostbitten, he got frostbite in his feet
abfrühstücken ['apfry:ʃtʏkən] (*umg*) *vt* (*jdn*) to fob off, snub; (*Sache*) to get through with
Abfuhr ['apfu:r] (**-, -en**) *f* removal; (*fig*) snub, rebuff; **sich** *dat* **eine ~ holen** to meet with a rebuff
abführen ['apfy:rən] *vt* to lead away; (*Gelder, Steuern*) to pay ▷ *vi* (*Med*) to have a laxative effect
Abführmittel *nt* laxative, purgative
Abfüllanlage *f* bottling plant
abfüllen ['apfʏlən] *vt* to draw off; (*in Flaschen*) to bottle
Abgabe ['apga:bə] *f* handing in; (*von Ball*) pass; (*Steuer*) tax; (*einer Erklärung*) giving
abgabenfrei *adj* tax-free
abgabenpflichtig *adj* liable to tax
Abgabetermin *m* closing date; (*für Dissertation etc*) submission date
Abgang ['apgaŋ] *m* (*von Schule*) leaving; (*Theat*) exit; (*Med: Ausscheiden*) passing; (*: Fehlgeburt*) miscarriage; (*Abfahrt*) departure; (*der Post, von Waren*) dispatch
Abgangszeugnis *nt* leaving certificate
Abgas ['apga:s] *nt* waste gas; (*Aut*) exhaust
Abgasgrenzwert *m* exhaust emission standard
ABGB *nt abk* (*Österr: = Allgemeines Bürgerliches Gesetzbuch*) Civil Code in Austria
abgeben ['apge:bən] *unreg vt* (*Gegenstand*) to hand *od* give in; (*Ball*) to pass; (*Wärme*) to give off; (*Amt*) to hand over; (*Schuss*) to fire; (*Erklärung, Urteil*) to give; (*darstellen*) to make ▷ *vr*: **sich mit jdm/etw ~** to associate with sb/bother with sth; **„Kinderwagen abzugeben"**

"pram for sale"; **jdm etw ~** (*überlassen*) to let sb have sth
abgebrannt ['apgəbrant] (*umg*) *adj* broke
abgebrüht ['apgəbry:t] (*umg*) *adj* (*skrupellos*) hard-boiled, hardened
abgedroschen ['apgədrɔʃən] *adj* trite; (*Witz*) corny
abgefahren ['apgəfa:rən] *pp von* **abfahren**
abgefeimt ['apgəfaɪmt] *adj* cunning
abgegeben ['apgəge:bən] *pp von* **abgeben**
abgegriffen ['apgəgrɪfən] *adj* (*Buch*) well-thumbed; (*Redensart*) trite
abgehackt ['apgəhakt] *adj* clipped
abgehalftert ['apgəhalftərt] *adj* (*fig: umg*) run-down, dead beat
abgehangen ['apgəhaŋən] *pp von* **abhängen** ▷ *adj*: (**gut**) **~** (*Fleisch*) well-hung
abgehärtet ['apgəhɛrtət] *adj* tough, hardy; (*fig*) hardened
abgehen ['apge:ən] *unreg vi* to go away, leave; (*Theat*) to exit; (*Post*) to go; (*Med*) to be passed; (*sterben*) to die; (*Knopf etc*) to come off; (*abgezogen werden*) to be taken off; (*Straße*) to branch off; (*abweichen*): **von einer Forderung ~** to give up a demand ▷ *vt* (*Strecke*) to go *od* walk along; (*Mil: Gelände*) to patrol; **von seiner Meinung ~** to change one's opinion; **davon gehen 5% ab** 5% is taken off that; **etw geht jdm ab** (*fehlt*) sb lacks sth
abgekämpft ['apgəkɛmpft] *adj* exhausted
abgekartet ['apgəkartət] *adj*: **ein ~es Spiel** a rigged job
abgeklärt ['apgəklɛ:rt] *adj* serene, tranquil
abgelegen ['apgəle:gən] *adj* remote
abgelten ['apgɛltən] *unreg vt* (*Ansprüche*) to satisfy
abgemacht ['apgəmaxt] *adj* fixed; **~!** done!
abgemagert ['apgəma:gərt] *adj* (*sehr dünn*) thin; (*ausgemergelt*) emaciated
abgeneigt ['apgənaɪkt] *adj* averse
abgenutzt ['apgənʊtst] *adj* worn, shabby; (*Reifen*) worn; (*fig: Klischees*) well-worn
Abgeordnete, r ['apgəˌɔrdnətə(r)] *f(m)* elected representative; (*von Parlament*) member of parliament
Abgesandte, r ['apgəzantə(r)] *f(m)* delegate; (*Pol*) envoy
abgeschieden ['apgəʃi:dən] *adv* (*einsam*): **~ leben/wohnen** to live in seclusion
abgeschlagen ['apgəʃla:gən] *adj* (*besiegt*) defeated; (*erschöpft*) exhausted, worn-out
abgeschlossen ['apgəʃlɔsən] *pp von* **abschließen** ▷ *adj attrib* (*Wohnung*) self-contained
abgeschmackt ['apgəʃmakt] *adj* tasteless; **Abgeschmacktheit** *f* lack of taste; (*Bemerkung*) tasteless remark
abgesehen ['apgəze:ən] *adj*: **es auf jdn/etw ~ haben** to be after sb/sth; **~ von ...** apart from ...
abgespannt ['apgəʃpant] *adj* tired out
abgestanden ['apgəʃtandən] *adj* stale; (*Bier*) flat

3

abgestorben ['apgəʃtɔrbən] *adj* numb; (*Biol, Med*) dead

abgestumpft ['apgəʃtʊmpft] *adj* (*gefühllos: Person*) insensitive; (*Gefühle, Gewissen*) dulled

abgetakelt ['apgəta:kəlt] *adj* (*fig*) decrepit, past it

abgetan ['apgəta:n] *adj*: **damit ist die Sache ~** that settles the matter

abgetragen ['apgətra:gən] *adj* worn

abgewinnen ['apgəvɪnən] *unreg vt*: **jdm Geld ~** to win money from sb; **einer Sache etw/ Geschmack ~** to get sth/pleasure from sth

abgewogen ['apgəvo:gən] *adj* (*Urteil, Worte*) balanced

abgewöhnen ['apgəvø:nən] *vt*: **jdm/sich etw ~** to cure sb of sth/give sth up

abgießen ['apgi:sən] *unreg vt* (*Flüssigkeit*) to pour off

Abglanz ['apglants] *m* (*auch fig*) reflection

abgleiten ['apglaɪtən] *unreg vi* to slip, slide

Abgott ['apgɔt] *m* idol

abgöttisch ['apgœtɪʃ] *adj*: **~ lieben** to idolize

abgrasen ['apgra:zən] *vt* (*Feld*) to graze; (*umg: Thema*) to do to death

abgrenzen ['apgrɛntsən] *vt* (*lit, fig*) to mark off; (*Gelände*) to fence off ▷ *vr*: **sich ~ (gegen)** to dis(as)sociate o.s. (from)

Abgrund ['apgrʊnt] *m* (*lit, fig*) abyss

abgründig ['apgrʏndɪç] *adj* unfathomable; (*Lächeln*) cryptic

abgrundtief *adj* (*Hass, Verachtung*) profound

abgucken ['apgʊkən] *vt, vi* to copy

Abguss ['apgʊs] *m* (*Kunst, Metallurgie: Vorgang*) casting; (*: Form*) cast

abhaben ['apha:bən] *unreg* (*umg*) *vt* (*abbekommen*): **willst du ein Stück ~?** do you want a bit?

abhacken ['aphakən] *vt* to chop off

abhaken ['apha:kən] *vt* to tick off (*Brit*), check off (*US*)

abhalten ['aphaltən] *unreg vt* (*Versammlung*) to hold; **jdn von etw ~** (*fernhalten*) to keep sb away from sth; (*hindern*) to keep sb from sth

abhandeln ['aphandəln] *vt* (*Thema*) to deal with; **jdm die Waren/10 Euro ~** to do a deal with sb for the goods/beat sb down 10 euros

abhandenkommen [ap'handən-] *vi* to get lost

Abhandlung ['aphandlʊŋ] *f* treatise, discourse

Abhang ['aphaŋ] *m* slope

abhängen ['aphɛŋən] *unreg vt* (*Bild*) to take down; (*Anhänger*) to uncouple; (*Verfolger*) to shake off ▷ *vi* (*Fleisch*) to hang; **von jdm/etw ~** to depend on sb/sth; **das hängt ganz davon ab** it all depends; **er hat abgehängt** (*Tel: umg*) he hung up (on me *etc*)

abhängig ['aphɛŋɪç] *adj*: **~ (von)** dependent (on); **Abhängigkeit** *f*: **Abhängigkeit (von)** dependence (on)

abhärten ['aphɛrtən] *vt* to toughen up ▷ *vr* to toughen (o.s.) up; **sich gegen etw ~** to harden o.s. to sth

abhauen ['aphaʊən] *unreg vt* to cut off; (*Baum*) to cut down ▷ *vi* (*umg*) to clear off *od* out; **hau ab!** beat it!

abheben ['aphe:bən] *unreg vt* to lift (up); (*Karten*) to cut; (*Masche*) to slip; (*Geld*) to withdraw, take out ▷ *vi* (*Flugzeug*) to take off; (*Rakete*) to lift off; (*Karten*) to cut ▷ *vr*: **sich ~ von** to stand out from, contrast with

abheften ['apheftən] *vt* (*Rechnungen etc*) to file away; (*Nähen*) to tack, baste

abhelfen ['aphɛlfən] *unreg vi +dat* to remedy

abhetzen ['aphɛtsən] *vr* to wear *od* tire o.s. out

Abhilfe ['aphɪlfə] *f* remedy; **~ schaffen** to put things right

abholen ['apho:lən] *vt* (*Gegenstand*) to fetch, collect; (*Person*) to call for; (*am Bahnhof etc*) to pick up, meet

Abholmarkt *m* cash and carry

abholzen ['aphɔltsən] *vt* (*Wald*) to clear, deforest

abhorchen ['aphɔrçən] *vt* (*Med*) to listen to, sound

abhören ['aphø:rən] *vt* (*Vokabeln*) to test; (*Telefongespräch*) to tap; (*Tonband etc*) to listen to; **abgehört werden** (*umg*) to be bugged

Abhörgerät *nt* bug

abhungern ['aphʊŋərn] *vr*: **sich** *dat* **10 Kilo ~** to lose 10 kilos by going on a starvation diet

Abi ['abi] (**-s, -s**) *nt* (*Sch: umg*) = **Abitur**

Abitur [abi'tu:r] (**-s, -e**) *nt* German school-leaving examination, ≈ A-levels *pl* (*Brit*); **(das) ~ machen** to take one's school-leaving exam *od* A-levels; *see culture note*

⊙ **ABITUR**

⊙
⊙ The *Abitur* is the German school-leaving
⊙ examination which is taken at the age of
⊙ 18 or 19 by pupils at a *Gymnasium*. It is taken
⊙ in four subjects and is necessary for entry
⊙ to a university education.

Abiturient, in [abitʊri'ent(ɪn)] *m(f)* candidate for school-leaving certificate

abkämmen ['apkɛmən] *vt* (*Gegend*) to comb, scour

abkanzeln ['apkantsəln] (*umg*) *vt*: **jdn ~** to give sb a dressing-down

abkapseln ['apkapsəln] *vr* to shut *od* cut o.s. off

abkarten ['apkartən] (*umg*) *vt*: **die Sache war von vornherein abgekartet** the whole thing was a put-up job

abkaufen ['apkaʊfən] *vt*: **jdm etw ~** to buy sth from sb

abkehren ['apke:rən] *vt* (*Blick*) to avert, turn away ▷ *vr* to turn away

abklappern ['apklapərn] (*umg*) *vt* (*Kunden*) to call on; (*: Läden, Straße*): **~ (nach)** to scour (for), comb (for)

abklären ['apklɛ:rən] *vt* (*klarstellen*) to clear up, clarify ▷ *vr* (*sich setzen*) to clarify

Abklatsch ['apklatʃ] (**-es, -e**) *m* (*fig*) (poor) copy

abklemmen ['apklɛmən] *vt* (*Leitung*) to clamp

abklingen ['apklɪŋən] *unreg vi* to die away;

(*Rundf*) to fade out

abknallen ['apknalən] (*umg*) *vt* to shoot down

abknöpfen ['apknœpfən] *vt* to unbutton; **jdm etw ~** (*umg*) to get sth off sb

abkochen ['apkɔxən] *vt* to boil; (*keimfrei machen*) to sterilize (by boiling)

abkommandieren ['apkɔmandi:rən] *vt* (*Mil: zu Einheit*) to post; (*zu bestimmtem Dienst*): **~ zu** to detail for

abkommen ['apkɔmən] *unreg vi* to get away; **(vom Thema) ~** to get off the subject, digress; **von der Straße/einem Plan ~** to leave the road/give up a plan

Abkommen (**-s, -**) *nt* agreement

abkömmlich ['apkœmlɪç] *adj* available, free

Abkömmling *m* (*Nachkomme*) descendant; (*fig*) adherent

abkönnen ['apkœnən] *unreg* (*umg*) *vt* (*mögen*): **das kann ich nicht ab** I can't stand it

abkratzen ['apkratsən] *vt* to scrape off ▷ *vi* (*umg*) to kick the bucket

abkriegen ['apkri:gən] (*umg*) *vt* = **abbekommen**

abkühlen ['apky:lən] *vt* to cool down ▷ *vr* (*Mensch*) to cool down *od* off; (*Wetter*) to get cool; (*Zuneigung*) to cool

Abkunft ['apkʊnft] (**-**) *f* origin, birth

abkürzen ['apkʏrtsən] *vt* to shorten; (*Wort*) to abbreviate; **den Weg ~** to take a short cut

Abkürzung *f* abbreviation; short cut

abladen ['apla:dən] *unreg vi* to unload ▷ *vt* to unload; (*fig: umg*): **seinen Ärger (bei jdm) ~** to vent one's anger (on sb)

Ablage ['apla:gə] *f* place to keep/put sth; (*Aktenordnung*) filing; (*für Akten*) tray

ablagern ['apla:gərn] *vt* to deposit ▷ *vr* to be deposited ▷ *vi* to mature

Ablagerung *f* (*abgelagerter Stoff*) deposit

ablassen ['aplasən] *unreg vt* (*Wasser, Dampf*) to let out *od* off; (*vom Preis*) to knock off ▷ *vi*: **von etw ~** to give sth up, abandon sth

Ablauf *m* (*Abfluss*) drain; (*von Ereignissen*) course; (*einer Frist, Zeit*) expiry (Brit), expiration (US); **nach ~ des Jahres/dieser Zeit** at the end of the year/this time

Ablaufdatum *nt* (*Österr*) expiry date; (*von Lebensmitteln*) use-by *od* best-before date

ablaufen ['aplaʊfən] *unreg vi* (*abfließen*) to drain away; (*Ereignisse*) to happen; (*Frist, Zeit, Pass*) to expire ▷ *vt* (*Sohlen*) to wear (down *od* out); **~ lassen** (*abspulen, abspielen: Platte, Tonband*) to play; (*Film*) to run; **sich** *dat* **die Beine** *od* **Hacken nach etw ~** (*umg*) to walk one's legs off looking for sth; **jdm den Rang ~** to steal a march on sb

Ableben ['aple:bən] *nt* (*form*) demise (*form*)

ablegen ['aple:gən] *vt* to put *od* lay down; (*Kleider*) to take off; (*Gewohnheit*) to get rid of; (*Prüfung*) to take, sit (Brit); (*Zeugnis*) to give; (*Schriftwechsel*) to file (away); (*nicht mehr tragen: Kleidung*) to discard, cast off; (*Schwur, Eid*) to swear ▷ *vi* (*Schiff*) to cast off

Ableger (**-s, -**) *m* layer; (*fig*) branch, offshoot

ablehnen ['aple:nən] *vt* to reject; (*missbilligen*)

to disapprove of; (*Einladung*) to decline, refuse ▷ *vi* to decline, refuse

Ablehnung *f* rejection; refusal; **auf ~ stoßen** to meet with disapproval

ableisten ['aplaɪstən] *vt* (*form: Zeit*) to serve

ableiten ['aplaɪtən] *vt* (*Wasser*) to divert; (*deduzieren*) to deduce; (*Wort*) to derive

Ableitung *f* diversion; deduction; derivation; (*Wort*) derivative

ablenken ['aplɛŋkən] *vt* to turn away, deflect; (*zerstreuen*) to distract ▷ *vi* to change the subject; **das lenkt ab** (*zerstreut*) it takes your mind off things; (*stört*) it's distracting

Ablenkung *f* deflection; distraction

Ablenkungsmanöver *nt* diversionary tactic; (*um vom Thema abzulenken*) red herring

ablesen ['aple:zən] *unreg vt* to read; **jdm jeden Wunsch von den Augen ~** to anticipate sb's every wish

ableugnen ['aplɔygnən] *vt* to deny

ablichten ['aplɪçtən] *vt* to photocopy; (*fotografieren*) to photograph

abliefern ['apli:fərn] *vt* to deliver; **etw bei jdm/einer Dienststelle ~** to hand sth over to sb/in at an office

Ablieferung *f* delivery

abliegen ['apli:gən] *unreg vi* to be some distance away; (*fig*) to be far removed

ablisten ['aplɪstən] *vt*: **jdm etw ~** to trick *od* con sb out of sth

ablösen ['aplø:zən] *vt* (*abtrennen*) to take off, remove; (*in Amt*) to take over from; (*Fin: Schuld, Hypothek*) to pay off, redeem; (*Methode, System*) to supersede ▷ *vr* (*auch*: **einander ablösen**) to take turns; (*Fahrer, Kollegen, Wachen*) to relieve each other

Ablösung *f* removal; relieving

abluchsen ['aplʊksən] (*umg*) *vt*: **jdm etw ~** to get *od* wangle sth out of sb

Abluft *f* (*Tech*) used air

ABM *pl abk* (= *Arbeitsbeschaffungsmaßnahmen*) job-creation scheme

abmachen ['apmaxən] *vt* to take off; (*vereinbaren*) to agree; **etw mit sich allein ~** to sort sth out for o.s.

Abmachung *f* agreement

abmagern ['apma:gərn] *vi* to get thinner, become emaciated

Abmagerungskur *f* diet; **eine ~ machen** to go on a diet

Abmarsch ['apmarʃ] *m* departure; **abmarschbereit** *adj* ready to start

abmarschieren ['apmarʃi:rən] *vi* to march off

abmelden ['apmɛldən] *vt* (*Auto*) to take off the road; (*Telefon*) to have disconnected; (*Comput*) to log off ▷ *vr* to give notice of one's departure; (*im Hotel*) to check out; **ein Kind von einer Schule ~** to take a child away from a school; **er/sie ist bei mir abgemeldet** (*umg*) I don't want anything to do with him/her; **jdn bei der Polizei ~** to register sb's departure with the police

abmessen ['apmɛsən] *unreg vt* to measure

Abmessung f measurement; (*Ausmaß*) dimension

abmontieren ['apmɔntiːrən] vt to take off; (*Maschine*) to dismantle

ABM-Stelle f temporary post created as part of a job creation scheme

abmühen ['apmyːən] vr to wear o.s. out

abnabeln ['apnaːbəln] vt: **jdn ~** (*auch fig*) to cut sb's umbilical cord

abnagen ['apnaːgən] vt to gnaw off; (*Knochen*) to gnaw

Abnäher ['apnɛːər] (**-s, -**) m dart

Abnahme ['apnaːmə] f (*+gen*) removal; (*Comm*) buying; (*Verringerung*) decrease (in)

abnehmen ['apneːmən] unreg vt to take off, remove; (*Führerschein*) to take away; (*Prüfung*) to hold; (*Maschen*) to decrease; (*Hörer*) to lift, pick up; (*begutachten: Gebäude, Auto*) to inspect ▷ vi to decrease; (*schlanker werden*) to lose weight; **jdm etw ~** (*Geld*) to get sth out of sb; (*kaufen: auch umg: glauben*) to buy sth from sb; **kann ich dir etwas ~?** (*tragen*) can I take something for you?; **jdm Arbeit ~** to take work off sb's shoulders; **jdm ein Versprechen ~** to make sb promise sth

Abnehmer (**-s, -**) m purchaser, customer; **viele/wenige ~ finden** (*Comm*) to sell well/badly

Abneigung ['apnaɪgʊŋ] f aversion, dislike

abnicken ['apnɪkən] (*umg*) vt: **etw ~** to nod sth through

abnorm [ap'nɔrm] adj abnormal

abnötigen ['apnøːtɪgən] vt: **jdm etw/Respekt ~** to force sth from sb/gain sb's respect

abnutzen ['apnʊtsən] vt to wear out

Abnutzung f wear (and tear)

Abo ['abo] (**-s, -s**) (*umg*) nt = **Abonnement**

Abonnement [abɔn(ə)'maˑ̃ː] (**-s, -s** od **-e**) nt subscription; (*Theaterabonnement*) season ticket

Abonnent, in [abɔ'nɛnt(ɪn)] m(f) subscriber

abonnieren [abɔ'niːrən] vt to subscribe to

abordnen ['apʔɔrdnən] vt to delegate

Abordnung f delegation

Abort [a'bɔrt] (**-(e)s, -e**) m (*veraltet*) lavatory

abpacken ['appakən] vt to pack

abpassen ['appasən] vt (*Person, Gelegenheit*) to wait for; (*warten auf*) to catch; (*jdm auflauern*) to waylay; **etw gut ~** to time sth well

abpausen ['appaʊzən] vt to make a tracing of

abpfeifen ['appfaɪfən] unreg vt, vi (*Sport*): (**das Spiel**) **~** to blow the whistle (for the end of the game)

Abpfiff ['appfɪf] m final whistle

abplagen ['applaːgən] vr to struggle (away)

Abprall ['appral] m rebound; (*von Kugel*) ricochet

abprallen ['appralən] vi to bounce off; to ricochet; **an jdm ~** (*fig*) to make no impression on sb

abputzen ['appʊtsən] vt to clean; (*Nase etc*) to wipe

abquälen ['apkvɛːlən] vr to struggle (away)

abrackern ['aprakərn] (*umg*) vr to slave away

abraten ['apraːtən] unreg vi: **jdm von etw ~** to advise sb against sth, warn sb against sth

abräumen ['aprɔʏmən] vt to clear up od away; (*Tisch*) to clear ▷ vi to clear up od away

abreagieren ['apreagiːrən] vt: **seinen Zorn (an jdm/etw) ~** to work one's anger off (on sb/sth) ▷ vr to calm down; **seinen Ärger an anderen ~** to take it out on others

abrechnen ['apreçnən] vt to deduct, take off ▷ vi (*lit*) to settle up; (*fig*) to get even; **darf ich ~?** would you like your bill (*Brit*) od check (*US*) now?

Abrechnung f settlement; (*Rechnung*) bill; (*Aufstellung*) statement; (*Bilanz*) balancing; (*fig: Rache*) revenge; **in ~ stellen** (*form: Abzug*) to deduct; **~ über +akk** bill/statement for

Abrechnungszeitraum m accounting period

Abrede ['apreːdə] f: **etw in ~ stellen** to deny od dispute sth

abregen ['apreːgən] (*umg*) vr to calm od cool down

abreiben ['apraɪbən] unreg vt to rub off; (*säubern*) to wipe; **jdn mit einem Handtuch ~** to towel sb down

Abreibung (*umg*) f (*Prügel*) hiding, thrashing

Abreise ['apraɪzə] f departure

abreisen vi to leave, set off

abreißen ['apraɪsən] unreg vt (*Haus*) to tear down; (*Blatt*) to tear off ▷ vi: **den Kontakt nicht ~ lassen** to stay in touch

abrichten ['apʀɪçtən] vt to train

abriegeln ['apriːgəln] vt (*Tür*) to bolt; (*Straße, Gebiet*) to seal off

abringen ['aprɪŋən] unreg vt: **sich** dat **ein Lächeln ~** to force a smile

Abriss ['aprɪs] (**-es, -e**) m (*Übersicht*) outline; (*Abbruch*) demolition

abrollen ['aprɔlən] vt (*abwickeln*) to unwind ▷ vi (*vonstattengehen: Programm*) to run; (*: Veranstaltung*) to go off; (*: Ereignisse*) to unfold

Abruf ['apruːf] m: **auf ~** on call

abrufen unreg vt (*Mensch*) to call away; (*Comm: Ware*) to request delivery of; (*Comput*) to recall, retrieve

abrunden ['aprʊndən] vt to round off

abrüsten ['apʀʏstən] vi to disarm

Abrüstung f disarmament

abrutschen ['apʀʊtʃən] vi to slip; (*Aviat*) to sideslip

Abs. abk = **Absender**; (= *Absatz*) par., para

absacken ['apzakən] vi (*sinken*) to sink; (*Boden, Gebäude*) to subside

Absage ['apzaːgə] (**-, -n**) f refusal; (*auf Einladung*) negative reply

absagen vt to cancel, call off; (*Einladung*) to turn down ▷ vi to cry off; (*ablehnen*) to decline; **jdm ~** to tell sb that one can't come

absägen ['apzɛːgən] vt to saw off

absahnen ['apzaːnən] vt (*lit*) to skim; **das Beste für sich ~** (*fig*) to take the cream

Absatz ['apzats] m (*Comm*) sales pl; (*Jur*) section; (*Bodensatz*) deposit; (*neuer Abschnitt*) paragraph; (*Treppenabsatz*) landing;

(*Schuhabsatz*) heel; **Absatzflaute** *f* slump in the market; **Absatzförderung** *f* sales promotion; **Absatzgebiet** *nt* (*Comm*) market; sales territory; **Absatzplus** *nt* increase in sales; **Absatzprognose** *f* sales forecast; **Absatzschwierigkeiten** *pl* sales problems *pl*; **Absatzziffern** *pl* sales figures *pl*

absaufen ['apzaʊfən] *unreg* *vi* (*ertrinken*) to drown; (: *Motor*) to flood; (: *Schiff etc*) to go down

absaugen ['apzaʊgən] *vt* (*Flüssigkeit*) to suck out *od* off; (*Teppich, Sofa*) to hoover®, vacuum

abschaben ['apʃaːbən] *vt* to scrape off; (*Möhren*) to scrape

abschaffen ['apʃafən] *vt* to abolish, do away with

Abschaffung *f* abolition

abschalten ['apʃaltən] *vt, vi* (*lit: umg*) to switch off

abschattieren ['apʃatiːrən] *vt* to shade

abschätzen ['apʃɛtsən] *vt* to estimate; (*Lage*) to assess; (*Person*) to size up

abschätzig ['apʃɛtsɪç] *adj* disparaging, derogatory

Abschaum ['apʃaʊm] **(-(e)s)** *m* scum

Abscheu ['apʃɔy] **(-(e)s)** *m* loathing, repugnance; **abscheuerregend** *adj* repulsive, loathsome; **abscheulich** *adj* abominable

abschicken ['apʃɪkən] *vt* to send off

abschieben ['apʃiːbən] *unreg* *vt* to push away; (*Person*) to pack off; (*ausweisen: Ausländer*) to deport; (*fig: Verantwortung, Schuld*): ~ **(auf** +*akk*) to shift (onto)

Abschied ['apʃiːt] **(-(e)s, -e)** *m* parting; (*von Armee*) discharge; **(von jdm)** ~ **nehmen** to say goodbye (to sb), take one's leave (of sb); **seinen** ~ **nehmen** (*Mil*) to apply for discharge; **zum** ~ on parting

Abschiedsbrief *m* farewell letter

Abschiedsfeier *f* farewell party

abschießen ['apʃiːsən] *unreg* *vt* (*Flugzeug*) to shoot down; (*Geschoss*) to fire; (*umg: Minister*) to get rid of

abschirmen ['apʃɪrmən] *vt* to screen; (*schützen*) to protect ▷ *vr* (*sich isolieren*): **sich** ~ **(gegen)** to cut o.s. off (from)

abschlaffen ['apʃlafən] (*umg*) *vi* to flag

abschlagen ['apʃlaːgən] *unreg* *vt* (*abhacken, Comm*) to knock off; (*ablehnen*) to refuse; (*Mil*) to repel

abschlägig ['apʃlɛːgɪç] *adj* negative; **jdn/etw** ~ **bescheiden** (*form*) to turn sb/sth down

Abschlagszahlung *f* interim payment

abschleifen ['apʃlaɪfən] *unreg* *vt* to grind down; (*Holzboden*) to sand (down) ▷ *vr* to wear off

Abschleppdienst *m* (*Aut*) breakdown service (*Brit*), towing company (*US*)

abschleppen ['apʃlɛpən] *vt* to (take in) tow

Abschleppseil *nt* towrope

abschließen ['apʃliːsən] *unreg* *vt* (*Tür*) to lock; (*beenden*) to conclude, finish; (*Vertrag, Handel*) to conclude; (*Versicherung*) to take out; (*Wette*) to place ▷ *vr* (*sich isolieren*) to cut o.s. off; **mit abgeschlossenem Studium** with a degree;

mit der Vergangenheit ~ to break with the past

abschließend *adj* concluding ▷ *adv* in conclusion, finally

Abschluss ['apʃlʊs] *m* (*Beendigung*) close, conclusion; (*Comm: Bilanz*) balancing; (*von Vertrag, Handel*) conclusion; **zum** ~ in conclusion; **Abschlussfeier** *f* (*Sch*) school-leavers' ceremony; **Abschlussprüfer** *m* accountant; **Abschlussprüfung** *f* (*Sch*) final examination; (*Univ*) finals *pl*; **Abschlussrechnung** *f* final account; **Abschlusszeugnis** *nt* (*Sch*) leaving certificate, diploma (*US*)

abschmecken ['apʃmɛkən] *vt* (*kosten*) to taste; (*würzen*) to season

abschmieren ['apʃmiːrən] *vt* (*Aut*) to grease, lubricate

abschminken ['apʃmɪŋkən] *vt*: **sich** ~ to remove one's make-up

abschmirgeln ['apʃmɪrgəln] *vt* to sand down

abschnallen ['apʃnalən] *vr* to unfasten one's seat belt ▷ *vi* (*umg: nicht mehr folgen können*) to give up; (: *fassungslos sein*) to be staggered

abschneiden ['apʃnaɪdən] *unreg* *vt* to cut off ▷ *vi* to do, come off; **bei etw gut/schlecht** ~ (*umg*) to come off well/badly in sth

Abschnitt ['apʃnɪt] *m* section; (*Mil*) sector; (*Kontrollabschnitt*) counterfoil (*Brit*), stub (*US*); (*Math*) segment; (*Zeitabschnitt*) period

abschnüren ['apʃnyːrən] *vt* to constrict

abschöpfen ['apʃœpfən] *vt* to skim off

abschrauben ['apʃraʊbən] *vt* to unscrew

abschrecken ['apʃrɛkən] *vt* to deter, put off; (*mit kaltem Wasser*) to plunge into cold water

abschreckend *adj* deterrent; **~es Beispiel** warning; **eine abschreckende Wirkung haben**, ~ **wirken** to act as a deterrent

abschreiben ['apʃraɪbən] *unreg* *vt* to copy; (*verloren geben*) to write off; (*Comm*) to deduct; **er ist bei mir abgeschrieben** I'm finished with him

Abschreibung *f* (*Comm*) deduction; (*Wertverminderung*) depreciation

Abschrift ['apʃrɪft] *f* copy

abschuften ['apʃʊftən] (*umg*) *vr* to slog one's guts out (*umg*)

abschürfen ['apʃʏrfən] *vt* to graze

Abschuss ['apʃʊs] *m* (*eines Geschützes*) firing; (*Herunterschießen*) shooting down; (*Tötung*) shooting

abschüssig ['apʃʏsɪç] *adj* steep

Abschussliste *f*: **er steht auf der** ~ (*umg*) his days are numbered

Abschussrampe *f* launch(ing) pad

abschütteln ['apʃʏtəln] *vt* to shake off

abschütten ['apʃʏtən] *vt* (*Flüssigkeit etc*) to pour off

abschwächen ['apʃvɛçən] *vt* to lessen; (*Behauptung, Kritik*) to tone down ▷ *vr* to lessen

abschweifen ['apʃvaɪfən] *vi* to wander; (*Redner*) to digress

Abschweifung *f* digression

abschwellen ['apʃvɛlən] *unreg vi* (*Geschwulst*) to go down; (*Lärm*) to die down

abschwenken ['apʃvɛŋkən] *vi* to turn away

abschwören ['apʃvøːrən] *unreg vi +dat* to renounce

absehbar ['apzeːbaːr] *adj* foreseeable; **in ~er Zeit** in the foreseeable future; **das Ende ist ~** the end is in sight

absehen *unreg vt* (*Ende, Folgen*) to foresee ▷ *vi*: **von etw ~** to refrain from sth; (*nicht berücksichtigen*) to leave sth out of consideration; **jdm etw ~** (*erlernen*) to copy sth from sb

abseilen ['apzaɪlən] *vt* to lower down on a rope ▷ *vr* (*Bergsteiger*) to abseil (down)

Abseits ['apzaɪts] *nt* (*Sport*) offside; **im ~ stehen** to be offside; **im ~ leben** (*fig*) to live in the shadows

abseits *adv* out of the way ▷ *präp +gen* away from

absenden ['apzɛndən] *unreg vt* to send off, dispatch

Absender *m* sender

Absendung *f* dispatch

absetzbar ['apzɛtsbaːr] *adj* (*Beamter*) dismissible; (*Waren*) saleable; (*von Steuer*) deductible

absetzen ['apzɛtsən] *vt* (*niederstellen, aussteigen lassen*) to put down; (*abnehmen; auch Theaterstück*) to take off; (*Comm: verkaufen*) to sell; (*Fin: abziehen*) to deduct; (*entlassen*) to dismiss; (*König*) to depose; (*streichen*) to drop; (*Fußballspiel, Termin*) to cancel; (*hervorheben*) to pick out ▷ *vi*: **er trank das Glas aus, ohne abzusetzen** he emptied his glass in one ▷ *vr* (*sich entfernen*) to clear off; (*sich ablagern*) to be deposited; **das kann man ~** that is tax-deductible

Absetzung *f* (*Fin: Abzug*) deduction; (*Entlassung*) dismissal; (*von König*) deposing; (*Streichung*) dropping

absichern ['apzɪçɐn] *vt* to make safe; (*schützen*) to safeguard ▷ *vr* to protect o.s.

Absicht ['apzɪçt] *f* intention; **mit ~** on purpose; **absichtlich** *adj* intentional, deliberate

absichtslos *adj* unintentional

absinken ['apzɪŋkən] *unreg vi* to sink; (*Temperatur, Geschwindigkeit*) to decrease

absitzen ['apzɪtsən] *unreg vi* to dismount ▷ *vt* (*Strafe*) to serve

absolut [apzoˈluːt] *adj* absolute

Absolutheitsanspruch *m* claim to absolute right

Absolutismus [apzoluˈtɪsmʊs] *m* absolutism

Absolvent, in [apzɔlˈvɛnt(ɪn)] *m(f)*: **die ~en eines Lehrgangs** the students who have completed a course

absolvieren [apzɔlˈviːrən] *vt* (*Sch*) to complete

absonderlich [apˈzɔndɐlɪç] *adj* odd, strange

absondern *vt* to separate; (*ausscheiden*) to give off, secrete ▷ *vr* to cut o.s. off

Absonderung *f* separation; (*Med*) secretion

absorbieren [apzɔrˈbiːrən] *vt* (*lit, fig*) to absorb

abspalten ['apʃpaltən] *vt* to split off

Abspannung ['apʃpanʊŋ] *f* (*Ermüdung*) exhaustion

absparen ['apʃpaːrən] *vt*: **sich** *dat* **etw ~** to scrimp and save for sth

abspecken ['apʃpɛkən] (*umg*) *vt* to shed ▷ *vi* to lose weight

abspeisen ['apʃpaɪzən] *vt* (*fig*) to fob off

abspenstig ['apʃpɛnstɪç] *adj*: (**jdm**) **~ machen** to lure away (from sb)

absperren ['apʃpɛrən] *vt* to block *od* close off; (*Tür*) to lock

Absperrung *f* (*Vorgang*) blocking *od* closing off; (*Sperre*) barricade

abspielen ['apʃpiːlən] *vt* (*Platte, Tonband*) to play; (*Sport: Ball*) to pass ▷ *vr* to happen; **vom Blatt ~** (*Mus*) to sight-read

absplittern ['apʃplɪtɐn] *vt, vi* to chip off

Absprache ['apʃpraːxə] *f* arrangement; **ohne vorherige ~** without prior consultation

absprechen ['apʃprɛçən] *unreg vt* (*vereinbaren*) to arrange ▷ *vr*: **die beiden hatten sich vorher abgesprochen** they had agreed on what to do/say *etc* in advance; **jdm etw ~** to deny sb sth; (*in Abrede stellen: Begabung*) to dispute sb's sth

abspringen ['apʃprɪŋən] *unreg vi* to jump down/off; (*Farbe, Lack*) to flake off; (*Aviat*) to bale out; (*sich distanzieren*) to back out

Absprung ['apʃprʊŋ] *m* jump; **den ~ schaffen** (*fig*) to make the break (*umg*)

abspulen ['apʃpuːlən] *vt* (*Kabel, Garn*) to unwind

abspülen ['apʃpyːlən] *vt* to rinse; **Geschirr ~** to wash up (*Brit*), do the dishes

abstammen ['apʃtamən] *vi* to be descended; (*Wort*) to be derived

Abstammung *f* descent; derivation; **französischer ~** of French extraction *od* descent

Abstand ['apʃtant] *m* distance; (*zeitlich*) interval; **davon ~ nehmen, etw zu tun** to refrain from doing sth; **~ halten** (*Aut*) to keep one's distance; **von etw gewinnen** (*fig*) to distance o.s. from sth; **mit großem ~ führen** to lead by a wide margin; **mit ~ der Beste** by far the best

Abstandssumme *f* compensation

abstatten ['apʃtatən] *vt* (*form: Dank*) to give; (: *Besuch*) to pay

abstauben ['apʃtaʊbən] *vt, vi* to dust; (*umg: mitgehen lassen*) to help oneself to, pinch; (**den Ball**) **~** (*Sport*) to tuck the ball away

Abstauber, in ['apʃtaʊbɐ(ɪn)] (**-s, -**) (*umg*) *m(f)* (*Person*) somebody on the make

abstechen ['apʃtɛçən] *unreg vt* to cut; (*Tier*) to cut the throat of ▷ *vi*: **~ gegen** *od* **von** to contrast with

Abstecher (**-s, -**) *m* detour

abstecken ['apʃtɛkən] *vt* (*Fläche*) to mark out; (*Saum*) to pin

abstehen ['apʃteːən] *unreg vi* (*Ohren, Haare*) to stick out; (*entfernt sein*) to stand away

Absteige *f* cheap hotel

absteigen ['apʃtaɪgən] *unreg vi* (*vom Rad etc*) to

get off, dismount; **in einem Gasthof ~ to** put up at an inn; **(in die Zweite Liga) ~ to be** relegated (to the second division); **auf dem ~den Ast sein** (*umg*) to be going downhill, be on the decline

abstellen ['apʃtɛlən] *vt* (*niederstellen*) to put down; (*entfernt stellen*) to pull out; (*hinstellen: Auto*) to park; (*ausschalten*) to turn *od* switch off; (*Missstand, Unsitte*) to stop; (*abkommandieren*) to order off; (*ausrichten*): **~ auf** *+akk* to gear to; **das lässt sich nicht/lässt sich ~** nothing/something can be done about that

Abstellgleis *nt* siding; **jdn aufs ~ schieben** (*fig*) to cast sb aside

Abstellraum *m* storeroom

abstempeln ['apʃtɛmpəln] *vt* to stamp; (*fig*): **~ zu** *od* **als** to brand as

absterben ['apʃtɛrbən] *unreg vi* to die; (*Körperteil*) to go numb

Abstieg ['apʃtiːk] (**-(e)s, -e**) *m* descent; (*Sport*) relegation; (*fig*) decline

Abstiegskampf *m* (*Sport*) relegation battle

abstimmen ['apʃtɪmən] *vi* to vote ▷ *vt*: **~ (auf** *+akk*) (*Instrument*) to tune (to); (*Interessen*) to match (with); (*Termine, Ziele*) to fit in (with) ▷ *vr* to agree

Abstimmung *f* vote; (*geheime Abstimmung*) ballot

abstinent [apsti'nɛnt] *adj* (*von Alkohol*) teetotal

Abstinenz [apsti'nɛnts] *f* teetotalism

Abstinenzler, in (**-s, -**) *m(f)* teetotaller

abstoßen ['apʃtoːsən] *unreg vt* to push off *od* away; (*anekeln*) to repel; (*Comm: Ware, Aktien*) to sell off

abstoßend *adj* repulsive

abstottern ['apʃtɔtərn] (*umg*) *vt* to pay off in instalments

abstrahieren [apstra'hiːrən] *vt, vi* to abstract

abstrakt [ap'strakt] *adj* abstract ▷ *adv* abstractly, in the abstract

Abstraktion [apstraktsi'oːn] *f* abstraction

Abstraktum [ap'straktʊm] (**-s, Abstrakta**) *nt* abstract concept; (*Gram*) abstract noun

abstrampeln ['apʃtrampəln] *vr* (*fig: umg*) to sweat (away)

abstreifen ['apʃtraɪfən] *vt* (*abtreten: Schuhe, Füße*) to wipe; (*abziehen: Schmuck*) to take off, slip off

abstreiten ['apʃtraɪtən] *unreg vt* to deny

Abstrich ['apʃtrɪç] *m* (*Abzug*) cut; (*Med*) smear; **~e machen** to lower one's sights

abstufen ['apʃtuːfən] *vt* (*Hang*) to terrace; (*Farben*) to shade; (*Gehälter*) to grade

abstumpfen ['apʃtʊmpfən] *vt* (*lit, fig*) to dull, blunt ▷ *vi* to become dulled

Absturz ['apʃtʊrts] *m* fall; (*Aviat*) crash

abstürzen ['apʃtʏrtsən] *vi* to fall; (*Aviat*) to crash

absuchen ['apzuːxən] *vt* to scour, search

absurd [ap'zʊrt] *adj* absurd

Abszess [aps'tsɛs] (**-es, -sse**) *m* abscess

Abt [apt] (**-(e)s, ̈-e**) *m* abbot

Abt. *abk* (= *Abteilung*) dept.

abtasten ['aptastən] *vt* to feel, probe; (*Elek*) to scan; (*bei Durchsuchung*): **~ (auf** *+akk*) to frisk (for)

abtauen ['aptaʊən] *vt, vi* to thaw; (*Kühlschrank*) to defrost

Abtei [ap'taɪ] (**-, -en**) *f* abbey

Abteil [ap'taɪl] (**-(e)s, -e**) *nt* compartment

abteilen ['aptaɪlən] *vt* to divide up; (*abtrennen*) to divide off

Abteilung *f* (*in Firma, Kaufhaus*) department; (*Mil*) unit; (*in Krankenhaus, Jur*) section

Abteilungsleiter, in *m(f)* head of department; (*in Kaufhaus*) department manager(ess)

abtelefonieren ['aptelefoniːrən] (*umg*) *vi* to telephone to say one can't make it

Äbtissin [ɛp'tɪsɪn] *f* abbess

abtönen ['aptøːnən] *vt* (*Phot*) to tone down

abtöten ['aptøːtən] *vt* (*lit, fig*) to destroy, kill (off); (*Nerv*) to deaden

abtragen ['aptraːgən] *unreg vt* (*Hügel, Erde*) to level down; (*Essen*) to clear away; (*Kleider*) to wear out; (*Schulden*) to pay off

abträglich ['aptrɛːklɪç] *adj* (*+dat*) harmful (to)

Abtragung *f* (*Geol*) erosion

Abtransport (**-(e)s, -e**) *m* transportation; (*aus Katastrophengebiet*) evacuation

abtransportieren ['aptransportiːrən] *vt* to transport; to evacuate

abtreiben ['aptraɪbən] *unreg vt* (*Boot, Flugzeug*) to drive off course; (*Kind*) to abort ▷ *vi* to be driven off course; (*Frau*) to have an abortion

Abtreibung *f* abortion

Abtreibungsparagraf *m* abortion law

Abtreibungsversuch *m* attempted abortion

abtrennen ['aptrɛnən] *vt* (*lostrennen*) to detach; (*entfernen*) to take off; (*abteilen*) to separate off

abtreten ['aptreːtən] *unreg vt* to wear out; (*überlassen*) to hand over, cede; (*Rechte, Ansprüche*) to transfer ▷ *vi* to go off; (*zurücktreten*) to step down; **sich** *dat* **die Füße ~** to wipe one's feet; **~!** (*Mil*) dismiss!

Abtritt ['aptrɪt] *m* (*Rücktritt*) resignation

abtrocknen ['aptrɔknən] *vt* to dry ▷ *vi* to do the drying-up

abtropfen ['aptrɔpfən] *vi*: **etw ~ lassen** to let sth drain

abtrünnig ['aptrʏnɪç] *adj* renegade

abtun ['aptuːn] *unreg vt* to take off; (*fig*) to dismiss; **etw kurz ~** to brush sth aside

aburteilen ['apʊrtaɪlən] *vt* to condemn

abverlangen ['apfɛrlaŋən] *vt*: **jdm etw ~** to demand sth from sb

abwägen ['apvɛːgən] *unreg vt* to weigh up

abwählen ['apvɛːlən] *vt* to vote out (of office); (*Sch: Fach*) to give up

abwälzen ['apvɛltsən] *vt*: **~ (auf** *+akk*) (*Schuld, Verantwortung*) to shift (onto); (*Arbeit*) to unload (onto); (*Kosten*) to pass on (to)

abwandeln ['apvandəln] *vt* to adapt

abwandern ['apvandərn] *vi* to move away

Abwärme ['apvɛrmə] *f* waste heat

abwarten ['apvartən] *vt* to wait for ▷ *vi* to wait; **das Gewitter ~** to wait till the storm is

9

over; **~ und Tee trinken** (*umg*) to wait and see; **eine ~de Haltung einnehmen** to play a waiting game

abwärts ['apvɛrts] *adv* down; **mit ihm/dem Land geht es ~** he/the country is going downhill

Abwasch ['apvaʃ] **(-(e)s)** *m* washing-up; **du kannst das auch machen, das ist (dann) ein ~** (*umg*) you could do that as well and kill two birds with one stone

abwaschen *unreg vt* (*Schmutz*) to wash off; (*Geschirr*) to wash (up)

Abwasser ['apvasər] **(-s, -wässer)** *nt* sewage; **Abwasseraufbereitung** *f* sewage treatment; **Abwasserkanal** *m* sewer

abwechseln ['apvɛksəln] *vi, vr* to alternate; (*Personen*) to take turns

abwechselnd *adj* alternate

Abwechslung *f* change; (*Zerstreuung*) diversion; **für ~ sorgen** to provide entertainment

abwechslungsreich *adj* varied

Abweg ['apveːk] *m*: **auf ~e geraten/führen** to go/lead astray

abwegig ['apveːgɪç] *adj* wrong; (*Verdacht*) groundless

Abwehr ['apveːr] **(-)** *f* defence; (*Schutz*) protection; (*Abwehrdienst*) counter-intelligence (service); **auf ~ stoßen** to be repulsed; **abwehren** *vt* to ward off; (*Ball*) to stop; **abwehrende Geste** dismissive gesture; **Abwehrreaktion** *f* (*Psych*) defence (*Brit*) *od* defense (*US*) reaction; **Abwehrstoff** *m* antibody

abweichen ['apvaɪçən] *unreg vi* to deviate; (*Meinung*) to differ; **vom rechten Weg ~** (*fig*) to wander off the straight and narrow

abweichend *adj* deviant; differing

Abweichler **(-s, -)** *m* (*Pol*) maverick

Abweichung *f* (*zeitlich, zahlenmäßig*) allowance; **zulässige ~** (*Tech*) tolerance

abweisen ['apvaɪzən] *unreg vt* to turn away; (*Antrag*) to turn down; **er lässt sich nicht ~** he won't take no for an answer

abweisend *adj* (*Haltung*) cold

abwenden ['apvɛndən] *unreg vt* to avert ▷ *vr* to turn away

abwerben ['apvɛrbən] *unreg vt*: **(jdm) ~** to woo away (from sb)

abwerfen ['apvɛrfən] *unreg vt* to throw off; (*Profit*) to yield; (*aus Flugzeug*) to drop; (*Spielkarte*) to discard

abwerten ['apvɛrtən] *vt* (*Fin*) to devalue

abwertend *adj* pejorative

Abwertung *f* devaluation

abwesend ['apveːzənt] *adj* absent; (*zerstreut*) far away

Abwesenheit ['apveːzənhaɪt] *f* absence; **durch ~ glänzen** (*ironisch*) to be conspicuous by one's absence

abwickeln ['apvɪkəln] *vt* to unwind; (*Geschäft*) to transact, conclude; (*fig: erledigen*) to deal with

Abwicklungskosten ['apvɪklʊŋskɔstən] *pl*

transaction costs *pl*

abwiegen ['apviːgən] *unreg vt* to weigh out

abwimmeln ['apvɪməln] (*umg*) *vt* (*Person*) to get rid of; (: *Auftrag*) to get out of

abwinken ['apvɪŋkən] *vi* to wave it/him *etc* aside; (*fig: ablehnen*) to say no

abwirtschaften ['apvɪrtʃaftən] *vi* to go downhill

abwischen ['apvɪʃən] *vt* to wipe off *od* away; (*putzen*) to wipe

abwracken ['apvrakən] *vt* (*Schiff*) to break (up); **ein abgewrackter Mensch** a wreck (of a person)

Abwurf ['apvʊrf] *m* throwing off; (*von Bomben etc*) dropping; (*von Reiter, Sport*) throw

abwürgen ['apvʏrgən] (*umg*) *vt* to scotch; (*Motor*) to stall; **etw von vornherein ~** to nip sth in the bud

abzahlen ['aptsaːlən] *vt* to pay off

abzählen ['aptsɛːlən] *vt* to count (up); **abgezähltes Fahrgeld** exact fare

Abzählreim ['aptsɛːlraɪm] *m* counting rhyme (*e.g. eeny meeny miney mo*)

Abzahlung *f* repayment; **auf ~ kaufen** to buy on hire purchase (*Brit*) *od* the installment plan (*US*)

abzapfen ['aptsapfən] *vt* to draw off; **jdm Blut ~** to take blood from sb

abzäunen ['aptsɔʏnən] *vt* to fence off

Abzeichen ['aptsaɪçən] *nt* badge; (*Orden*) decoration

abzeichnen ['aptsaɪçnən] *vt* to draw, copy; (*unterschreiben*) to initial ▷ *vr* to stand out; (*fig: bevorstehen*) to loom

Abziehbild *nt* transfer

abziehen ['aptsiːən] *unreg vt* to take off; (*Tier*) to skin; (*Bett*) to strip; (*Truppen*) to withdraw; (*subtrahieren*) to take away, subtract; (*kopieren*) to run off; (*Schlüssel*) to take out, remove ▷ *vi* to go away; (*Truppen*) to withdraw; (*abdrücken*) to pull the trigger, fire

abzielen ['aptsiːlən] *vi*: **~ auf** +*akk* to be aimed at

Abzocke ['aptsɔkə] (*umg*) *f* rip-off

Abzug ['aptsuːk] *m* departure; (*von Truppen*) withdrawal; (*Kopie*) copy; (*Subtraktion*) subtraction; (*Betrag*) deduction; (*Rauchabzug*) flue; (*von Waffen*) trigger; (*Rabatt*) discount; (*Korrekturfahne*) proof; (*Phot*) print; **jdm freien ~ gewähren** to grant sb safe passage

abzüglich ['aptsyːklɪç] *präp* +*gen* less

abzweigen ['aptsvaɪgən] *vi* to branch off ▷ *vt* to set aside

Abzweigung *f* junction

Accessoires [aksɛsoˈaːrs] *pl* accessories *pl*

ach [ax] *interj* oh; **~ so!** I see!; **mit A~ und Krach** by the skin of one's teeth; **~ was** *od* **wo, das ist doch nicht so schlimm!** come on now, it's not that bad!

Achillesferse [aˈxɪlɛsfɛrzə] *f* Achilles heel

Achse ['aksə] **(-, -n)** *f* axis; (*Aut*) axle; **auf ~ sein** (*umg*) to be on the move

Achsel ['aksəl] **(-, -n)** *f* shoulder; **Achselhöhle**

f armpit; **Achselzucken** nt shrug (of one's shoulders)

Achsenbruch m (Aut) broken axle

Achsenkreuz nt coordinate system

Acht¹ [axt] (-, **-en**) f eight; (beim Eislaufen etc) figure (of) eight

Acht² (-) f attention; **hab** ~ (Mil) attention!; ~ **geben = achtgeben; sich in ~ nehmen (vor** +dat) to be careful (of), watch out (for); **etw außer ~ lassen** to disregard sth

acht num eight; ~ **Tage** a week

achtbar adj worthy

achte, r, s adj eighth

Achteck nt octagon

Achtel nt eighth; **Achtelnote** f quaver, eighth note (US)

achten vt to respect ▷ vi: ~ **(auf** +akk) to pay attention (to); **darauf ~, dass ...** to be careful that ...

ächten ['ɛçtən] vt to outlaw, ban

Achterbahn f roller coaster

Achterdeck nt (Naut) afterdeck

achtfach adj eightfold

achtgeben unreg vi: ~ **(auf** +akk) to take care (of); (aufmerksam sein) to pay attention (to)

achtlos adj careless; **viele gehen ~ daran vorbei** many people just pass by without noticing

achtmal adv eight times

achtsam adj attentive

Achtstundentag m eight-hour day

Achtung ['axtʊŋ] f attention; (Ehrfurcht) respect ▷ interj look out!; (Mil) attention!; **alle ~!** good for you/him etc!; ~, **fertig, los!** ready, steady, go!; „~ **Hochspannung!"** "danger, high voltage"; „~ **Lebensgefahr/Stufe!"** "danger/mind the step!"

Achtungserfolg m reasonable success

achtzehn num eighteen

achtzig num eighty; **Achtziger, in** (-s, -) m(f) octogenarian

ächzen ['ɛçtsən] vi: ~ **(vor** +dat) to groan (with)

Acker ['akər] (-s, ⁻) m field; **Ackerbau** m agriculture; **Ackerbau und Viehzucht** farming

ackern vi to plough; (umg) to slog away

a conto [a 'kɔnto] adv (Comm) on account

A. D. abk (= Anno Domini) A.D.

a. D. abk = **außer Dienst**

a. d. abk = **an der** (bei Ortsnamen)

ad absurdum [at ap'zʊrdʊm] adv: ~ **führen** (Argument etc) to reduce to absurdity

ADAC (-) m abk (= Allgemeiner Deutscher Automobil-Club) German motoring organization, ≈ AA (Brit), AAA (US)

ad acta [at 'akta] adv: **etw ~ legen** (fig) to consider sth finished; (Frage, Problem) to consider sth closed

Adam ['a:dam] m: **bei ~ und Eva anfangen** (umg) to start right from scratch od from square one

adaptieren [adap'ti:rən] vt to adapt

adäquat [adɛ'kva:t] adj (Belohnung, Übersetzung) adequate; (Stellung, Verhalten) suitable

addieren [a'di:rən] vt to add (up)

Addis Abeba ['adɪs'a:beba] (-, **-s**) nt Addis Ababa

Addition [aditsi'o:n] f addition

ade interj bye!

Adel ['a:dəl] (-s) m nobility; ~ **verpflichtet** noblesse oblige

adelig adj noble

Adelsstand m nobility

Ader ['a:dər] (-, **-n**) f vein; (fig: Veranlagung) bent

Adhäsionsverschluss [athɛzi'o:nsfɛrʃlʊs] m adhesive seal

Adjektiv ['atjɛkti:f] (-s, **-e**) nt adjective

Adler ['a:dlər] (-s, -) m eagle

adlig adj = **adelig**

Admiral [atmi'ra:l] (-s, **-e**) m admiral

Admiralität f admiralty

adoptieren [adɔp'ti:rən] vt to adopt

Adoption [adɔptsi'o:n] f adoption

Adoptiveltern pl adoptive parents pl

Adoptivkind nt adopted child

Adr. abk (= Adresse) add.

Adressant [adrɛ'sant] m sender

Adressat [adrɛ'sa:t] (-en, **-en**) m addressee

Adressbuch nt directory; (privat) address book

Adresse [a'drɛsə] (-, **-n**) f (auch Comput) address; **an der falschen ~ sein** (umg) to have gone/come to the wrong person; **absolute ~** absolute address; **relative ~** relative address

adressieren [adrɛ'si:rən] vt: ~ **(an** +akk) to address (to)

Adria ['a:dria] (-) f Adriatic Sea

Adriatisches Meer [adri'a:tɪʃəs me:r] nt (form) Adriatic Sea

ADSL m abk (= Asymmetric Digital Subscriber Line) ADSL

Advent [at'vɛnt] (-(e)s, **-e**) m Advent; **der erste ~** the first Sunday in Advent

Advents- zW: **Adventskalender** m Advent calendar; **Adventskranz** m Advent wreath

Adverb [at'vɛrp] nt adverb

adverbial [atvɛrbi'a:l] adj adverbial

aero- [aero] präf aero-

Aerobic [ae'ro:bik] (-s) nt aerobics sing

Affäre [a'fɛ:rə] (-, **-n**) f affair; **sich aus der ~ ziehen** (umg) to get (o.s.) out of it

Affe ['afə] (-n, **-n**) m monkey; (umg: Kerl) berk (Brit)

Affekt (-(e)s, **-e**) m: **im ~ handeln** to act in the heat of the moment

affektiert [afɛk'ti:rt] adj affected

Affen- zW: **affenartig** adj like a monkey; **mit affenartiger Geschwindigkeit** (umg) like a flash; **affengeil** (umg) adj magic, fantastic; **Affenhitze** (umg) f incredible heat; **Affenliebe** f: **Affenliebe (zu)** blind adoration (of); **Affenschande** (umg) f crying shame; **Affentempo** (umg) nt: **in od mit einem Affentempo** at breakneck speed; **Affentheater** (umg) nt: **ein Affentheater aufführen** to make a fuss

affig ['afɪç] adj affected

Afghane [af'ga:nə] (-n, **-n**) m Afghan

Afghanin [afˈgaːnɪn] f Afghan
afghanisch adj Afghan
Afghanistan [afˈgaːnɪstaːn] (-s) nt
Afghanistan
Afrika [ˈaːfrika] (-s) nt Africa
Afrikaans [afriˈkaːns] (-) nt Afrikaans
Afrikaner, in [afriˈkaːnər(ɪn)] (-s, -) m(f)
African
afrikanisch adj African
afroamerikanisch [ˈaːfro|ameriˈkaːnɪʃ] adj
Afro-American
After [ˈaftər] (-s, -) m anus
AG (-) f abk (= Aktiengesellschaft) ≈ plc (Brit), corp.,
inc. (US)
Ägäis [ɛˈgɛːɪs] (-) f Aegean (Sea)
Ägäisches Meer nt Aegean Sea
Agent, in [aˈgɛnt(ɪn)] m(f) agent
Agententätigkeit f espionage
Agentur [agɛnˈtuːr] f agency; **Agenturbericht**
m, **Agenturmeldung** f (news) agency report
Aggregat [agreˈgaːt] (-(e)s, -e) nt aggregate;
(Tech) unit; **Aggregatzustand** m (Phys) state
Aggression [agrɛsiˈoːn] f aggression
aggressiv [agreˈsiːf] adj aggressive
Aggressivität [agrɛsiviˈtɛːt] f aggressiveness
Aggressor [aˈgrɛsoːr] (-s, -en) m aggressor
Agitation [agitatsiˈoːn] f agitation
Agrarpolitik f agricultural policy
Agrarstaat m agrarian state
AGV f abk (= Arbeitsgemeinschaft der
Verbraucherverbände) consumer groups' association
Ägypten [ɛˈgʏptən] (-s) nt Egypt
Ägypter, in (-s, -) m(f) Egyptian
ägyptisch adj Egyptian
aha [aˈhaː] interj aha!
Aha-Erlebnis nt sudden insight
ahd. abk (= althochdeutsch) OHG
Ahn [aːn] (-en, -en) m forebear
ahnden [ˈaːndən] vt (geh: Freveltat, Verbrechen) to
avenge; (Übertretung, Verstoß) to punish
ähneln [ˈɛːnəln] vi +dat to be like, resemble ▷ vr
to be alike od similar
ahnen [ˈaːnən] vt to suspect; (Tod, Gefahr) to
have a presentiment of; **nichts Böses ~** to be
unsuspecting; **du ahnst es nicht!** you have
no idea!; **davon habe ich nichts geahnt** I
didn't have the slightest inkling of it
Ahnenforschung f genealogy
ähnlich [ˈɛːnlɪç] adj (+dat) similar (to); **das
sieht ihm (ganz) ~!** (umg) that's just like
him!, that's him all over!; **Ähnlichkeit** f
similarity
Ahnung [ˈaːnʊŋ] f idea, suspicion; (Vorgefühl)
presentiment
ahnungslos adj unsuspecting
Ahorn [ˈaːhɔrn] (-s, -e) m maple
Ähre [ˈɛːrə] (-, -n) f ear
AHS f abk (Österr: = allgemeinbildende höhere Schule)
≈ secondary school
Aids [eːdz] (-) nt Aids
Airbag [ˈɛːbɛːg] (-s, -s) m (Aut) airbag
Akademie [akadeˈmiː] f academy
Akademiker, in [akaˈdeːmikər(ɪn)] (-s, -) m(f)

university graduate
akademisch adj academic
Akazie [aˈkaːtsiə] (-, -n) f acacia
Akk. abk = **Akkusativ**
akklimatisieren [aklimatiˈziːrən] vr to become
acclimatized
Akkord [aˈkɔrt] (-(e)s, -e) m (Mus) chord; **im
~ arbeiten** to do piecework; **Akkordarbeit** f
piecework
Akkordeon [aˈkɔrdeon] (-s, -s) nt accordion
Akkordlohn m piece wages pl, piece rate
Akkreditiv [akrediˈtiːf] (-s, -e) nt (Comm) letter
of credit
Akku [ˈaku] (-s, -s) (umg) m (Akkumulator) battery
akkurat [akuˈraːt] adj precise; (sorgfältig)
meticulous
Akkusativ [ˈakuzatiːf] (-s, -e) m accusative
(case); **Akkusativobjekt** nt accusative od direct
object
Akne [ˈaknə] (-, -n) f acne
Akribie [akriˈbiː] f (geh) meticulousness
Akrobat, in [akroˈbaːt(ɪn)] (-en, -en) m(f)
acrobat
Akt [akt] (-(e)s, -e) m act; (Kunst) nude
Akte [ˈaktə] (-, -n) f file; **etw zu den ~n legen**
(lit, fig) to file sth away
Akten- zW: **Aktendeckel** m folder; **Aktenkoffer**
m attaché case; **aktenkundig** adj on record;
Aktennotiz f memo(randum); **Aktenordner**
m file; **Aktenschrank** m filing cabinet;
Aktentasche f briefcase; **Aktenzeichen** nt
reference
Aktie [ˈaktsiə] (-, -n) f share; **wie stehen die
~n?** (hum: umg) how are things?
Aktien- zW: **Aktienbank** f joint-stock
bank; **Aktienemission** f share issue;
Aktiengesellschaft f joint-stock company;
Aktienindex m share index; **Aktienkapital** nt
share capital; **Aktienkurs** m share price
Aktion [aktsiˈoːn] f campaign; (Polizeiaktion,
Suchaktion) action
Aktionär, in [aktsioˈnɛːr(ɪn)] (-s, -e) m(f)
shareholder
Aktionismus [aktsioˈnɪsmʊs] m (Pol)
actionism
Aktionsradius [aktsiˈoːnzraːdiʊs] (-, -ien) m
(Aviat, Naut) range; (fig: Wirkungsbereich) scope
aktiv [akˈtiːf] adj active; (Mil) regular; **Aktiv** (-s)
nt (Gram) active (voice)
Aktiva [akˈtiːva] pl assets pl
aktivieren [aktiˈviːrən] vt to activate;
(fig: Arbeit, Kampagne) to step up; (Mitarbeiter) to
get moving
Aktivität [aktiviˈtɛːt] f activity
Aktivposten m (lit, fig) asset
Aktivsaldo m (Comm) credit balance
Aktivurlaub m activity holiday
aktualisieren [aktualiˈziːrən] vt (Comput) to
update
Aktualität [aktualiˈtɛːt] f topicality; (einer
Mode) up-to-dateness
aktuell [aktuˈɛl] adj topical; up-to-date; **eine
~e Sendung** (Rundf, TV) a current affairs

programme

Akupunktur [akupʊŋk'tuːɐr] f acupuncture

Akustik [a'kʊstɪk] f acoustics pl

akustisch [a'kʊstɪʃ] adj acoustic; **ich habe dich rein ~ nicht verstanden** I simply didn't catch what you said (properly)

akut [a'kuːt] adj acute; (Frage) pressing, urgent

AKW nt abk = **Atomkraftwerk**

Akzent [ak'tsɛnt] (**-(e)s, -e**) m accent; (Betonung) stress; **~e setzen** (fig) to bring out od emphasize the main points; **Akzentverschiebung** f (fig) shift of emphasis

Akzept (**-(e)s, -e**) nt (Comm: Wechsel) acceptance

akzeptabel [aktsɛp'taːbl] adj acceptable

akzeptieren [aktsɛp'tiːrən] vt to accept

AL f abk (= Alternative Liste) siehe **alternativ**

Alarm [a'larm] (**-(e)s, -e**) m alarm; (Zustand) alert; **~ schlagen** to give od raise the alarm; **Alarmanlage** f alarm system; **alarmbereit** adj standing by; **Alarmbereitschaft** f stand-by

alarmieren [alar'miːrən] vt to alarm

Alaska [a'laska] (**-s**) nt Alaska

Albaner, in [al'baːnɐr(ɪn)] (**-s, -**) m(f) Albanian

Albanien [al'baːniən] (**-s**) nt Albania

albanisch adj Albanian

albern ['albɐrn] adj silly

Albtraum ['alptraʊm] m nightmare

Album ['albʊm] (**-s, Alben**) nt album

Alcopops ['alkopɔps] pl alcopops pl

Aleuten [ale'uːtən] pl Aleutian Islands pl

Alge ['algə] (**-, -n**) f alga

Algebra ['algebra] (**-**) f algebra

Algerien [al'geːriən] (**-s**) nt Algeria

Algerier, in (**-s, -**) m(f) Algerian

algerisch [al'geːrɪʃ] adj Algerian

Algier ['alʒiːɐr] (**-s**) nt Algiers

ALGOL ['algɔl] (**-(s)**) nt (Comput) ALGOL

alias ['aːlias] adv alias

Alibi ['aːlibi] (**-s, -s**) nt alibi

Alimente [ali'mɛntə] pl alimony sing

Alkohol ['alkohɔl] (**-s, -e**) m alcohol; **unter ~ stehen** to be under the influence (of alcohol); **alkoholarm** adj low alcohol; **Alkoholexzess** m binge drinking; **alkoholfrei** adj non-alcoholic; **Alkoholgehalt** m proof

Alkoholika [alko'hoːlika] pl alcoholic drinks pl, liquor (US)

Alkoholiker, in [alko'hoːlikɐr(ɪn)] (**-s, -**) m(f) alcoholic

alkoholisch adj alcoholic

Alkoholverbot nt ban on alcohol

All [al] (**-s**) nt universe; (Raumfahrt) space; (außerhalb unseres Sternsystems) outer space

allabendlich adj every evening

allbekannt adj universally known

alle adj siehe **alle(r, s)**

alledem ['alədeːm] pron: **bei/trotz** etc **~** with/in spite of etc all that; **zu ~** moreover

Allee [a'leː] (**-, -n**) f avenue

allein [a'laɪn] adj, adv alone; (ohne Hilfe) on one's own, by oneself ▷ konj (geh) but, only; **von ~** by oneself/itself; **nicht ~** (nicht nur) not only; **~ schon der Gedanke**

the very od mere thought ..., the thought alone ...; **alleinerziehend** adj single-parent; **Alleinerziehende, r** f(m), **Alleinerzieher, in** m(f) single parent; **Alleingang** m: **im Alleingang** on one's own; **Alleinherrscher, in** m(f) autocrat; **Alleinhersteller, in** m(f) sole manufacturer

alleinig [a'laɪnɪç] adj sole

allein- zW: **Alleinsein** nt being on one's own; (Einsamkeit) loneliness; **alleinstehend** adj single; **Alleinunterhalter, in** m(f) solo entertainer; **Alleinvertretung** f (Comm) sole agency; **Alleinvertretungsvertrag** m (Comm) exclusive agency agreement

allemal ['alə'maːl] adv (jedes Mal) always; (ohne Weiteres) with no bother; siehe auch **Mal**

allenfalls ['alən'fals] adv at all events; (höchstens) at most

SCHLÜSSELWORT

alle, r, s adj **1** (sämtliche) all; **wir alle** all of us; **alle Kinder waren da** all the children were there; **alle Kinder mögen ...** all children like ...; **alle beide** both of us/them; **sie kamen alle** they all came; **alles Gute** all the best; **alles in allem** all in all; **vor allem** above all; **das ist alles andere als ...** that's anything but ...; **es hat alles keinen Sinn mehr** nothing makes sense any more; **was habt ihr alles gemacht?** what did you get up to?

2 (mit Zeit- oder Maßangaben) every; **alle vier Jahre** every four years; **alle fünf Meter** every five metres

▷ pron everything; **alles was er sagt** everything he says, all that he says; **trotz allem** in spite of everything

▷ adv (zu Ende, aufgebraucht) finished; **die Milch ist alle** the milk's all gone, there's no milk left; **etw alle machen** to finish sth up

allerbeste, r, s ['alɐr'bɛstə(r, s)] adj very best

allerdings ['alɐr'dɪŋs] adv (zwar) admittedly; (gewiss) certainly

Allergie [alɛr'giː] f allergy

allergisch [a'lɛrgɪʃ] adj allergic; **auf etw** akk **~ reagieren** to be allergic to sth

allerhand (umg) adj inv all sorts of; **das ist doch ~!** that's a bit much!; **~!** (lobend) good show!

Allerheiligen nt All Saints' Day; see culture note

ALLERHEILIGEN

Allerheiligen (All Saints' Day) is a public holiday in Germany and in Austria. It is a day in honour of all the saints. *Allerseelen* (All Souls' Day) is celebrated on November 2nd in the Roman Catholic Church. It is customary to visit cemeteries and place lighted candles on the graves of deceased relatives and friends.

aller- zW: **allerhöchste, r, s** adj very highest; **es wird allerhöchste Zeit, dass ...** it's really high time that ...; **allerhöchstens** adv at the very most; **allerlei** adj inv all sorts of; **allerletzte, r, s** adj very last; **der/das ist das Allerletzte** (umg) he's/it's the absolute end!; **allerneueste, allerneuste, r, s** adj very latest

Allerseelen (-s) nt All Soul's Day; siehe auch **Allerheiligen**; **allerseits** adv on all sides; **prost allerseits!** cheers everyone!

Allerwelts- in zW (Durchschnitts-) common; (nichtssagend) commonplace

allerwenigste, r, s adj very least; **die ~n Menschen wissen das** very few people know that

Allerwerteste, r m (hum) posterior (hum)

alles pron everything; siehe auch **alle(r, s)**

allesamt adv all (of them/us etc)

Alleskleber (-s, -) m all-purpose adhesive

Allgäu ['algɔy] nt part of the alpine region of Bavaria

allgegenwärtig adj omnipresent, ubiquitous

allgemein ['algəmaɪn] adj general ▷ adv: **es ist ~ üblich** it's the general rule; **~ verständlich** generally intelligible; **im A~** in general; **im ~en Interesse** in the common interest; **auf ~en Wunsch** by popular request; **Allgemeinbildung** f general od all-round education; **allgemeingültig** adj generally accepted; **Allgemeinheit** f (Menschen) general public; **Allgemeinheiten** pl (Redensarten) general remarks pl; **Allgemeinwissen** nt general knowledge

Allheilmittel [al'haɪlmɪtəl] nt cure-all, panacea (bes fig)

Alliierte, r [ali'i:rtə(r)] f(m) ally

all- zW: **alljährlich** adj annual; **allmächtig** adj all-powerful, omnipotent; **allmählich** adv gradually; **es wird allmählich Zeit** (umg) it's about time; **Allradantrieb** m all-wheel drive; **allseitig** adj (allgemein) general; (ausnahmslos) universal; **Alltag** m everyday life; **alltäglich** adj daily; (gewöhnlich) commonplace; **alltags** adv on weekdays; **Alltagskultur** f everyday culture

Allüren [a'ly:rən] pl odd behaviour (Brit) od behavior (US) sing; (eines Stars etc) airs and graces pl

all- zW: **allwissend** adj omniscient; **Allzeithoch** nt all-time high; **Allzeittief** nt all-time low; **allzu** adv all too; **allzu gern** (mögen) only too much; (bereitwillig) only too willingly; **allzu oft** all too often; **allzu viel** too much

Allzweck- ['altsvɛk-] in zW all-purpose

Alm [alm] (-, -en) f alpine pasture

Almosen ['almo:zən] (-s, -) nt alms pl

Alpen ['alpən] pl Alps pl; **Alpenblume** f alpine flower; **Alpenveilchen** nt cyclamen; **Alpenvorland** nt foothills pl of the Alps

Alphabet [alfa'be:t] (-(e)s, -e) nt alphabet

alphabetisch adj alphabetical

alphanumerisch [alfanu'me:rɪʃ] adj (Comput)

alphanumeric

Alptraum ['alptraʊm] m = **Albtraum**

○ SCHLÜSSELWORT

als [als] konj **1** (zeitlich) when; (gleichzeitig) as; **damals als ...** (in the days) when ...; **gerade als ...** just as ...

2 (in der Eigenschaft) than; **als Antwort** as an answer; **als Kind** as a child

3 (bei Vergleichen) than; **ich kam später als er** I came later than he (did) od later than him; **lieber ... als ...** rather ... than ...; **alles andere als** anything but; **nichts als Ärger** nothing but trouble; **so viel/so weit als möglich** (bei Vergleichen) as much/far as possible

4: als ob/wenn as if

alsbaldig [als'baldɪç] konj: „**zum ~en Verbrauch bestimmt**" "for immediate use only"

also ['alzo:] konj so; (folglich) therefore; **~ wie ich schon sagte** well (then), as I said before; **ich komme ~ morgen** so I'll come tomorrow; **~ gut** od **schön!** okay then; **~, so was!** well really!; **na ~!** there you are then!

Alt [alt] (-s, -e) m (Mus) alto

alt adj old; **ich bin nicht mehr der A~e** I am not the man I was; **alles beim A~en lassen** to leave everything as it was; **ich werde heute nicht ~ (werden)** (umg) I won't last long today/tonight etc; **~ aussehen** (fig: umg) to be in a pickle

Altar [al'ta:r] (-(e)s, -äre) m altar

alt- zW: **Altbau** m old building; **Altbauwohnung** f flat (Brit) od apartment (US) in an old building; **altbekannt** adj well-known; **altbewährt** adj (Methode etc) well-tried; (Tradition etc) long-standing; **Altbier** nt top-fermented German dark beer; **alteingesessen** adj old-established; **Alteisen** nt scrap iron

Altenheim nt old people's home

Altenteil ['altəntaɪl] nt: **sich aufs ~ setzen** od **zurückziehen** (fig) to retire from public life

Alter ['altər] (-s, -) nt age; (hohes) old age; **er ist in deinem ~** he's your age; **im ~ von** at the age of

älter ['ɛltər] adj (comp) older; (Bruder, Schwester) elder; (nicht mehr jung) elderly

altern ['altərn] vi to grow old, age

Alternativ- [alterna'ti:f] in zW alternative

alternativ adj: **A~e Liste** electoral pact between the Greens and alternative parties; **~ leben** to live an alternative way of life

Alternative [alterna'ti:və] f alternative

Alternativ- zW: **Alternativmedizin** f alternative medicine; **Alternativszene** f alternative scene; **Alternativtechnologie** f alternative technology

alters ['altərs] adv (geh): **von** od **seit ~ (her)** from time immemorial

Alters- zW: **Altersarmut** f old-age poverty; **altersbedingt** adj related to a particular age;

caused by old age; **Altersgrenze** f age limit;
flexible Altersgrenze flexible retirement
age; **Altersheim** nt old people's home;
Altersrente f old age pension; **Altersruhegeld**
nt retirement benefit; **altersschwach** adj
(Mensch) old and infirm; (Auto, Möbel) decrepit;
Altersversorgung f provision for old age
Altertum ['altərtuːm] nt antiquity
altertümlich adj (aus dem Altertum) ancient;
(veraltet) antiquated
alt- zW: **altgedient** adj long-serving;
Altglas nt used glass (for recycling),
scrap glass; **Altglascontainer** m bottle
bank; **althergebracht** adj traditional;
Altherrenmannschaft f (Sport) team of players
over thirty; **altklug** adj precocious; **Altlasten** pl
legacy sing of dangerous waste; **Altmaterial** nt
scrap; **Altmetall** nt scrap metal; **altmodisch**
adj old-fashioned; **Altpapier** nt waste paper;
Altstadt f old town
Altstimme f alto
Altwarenhändler m second-hand dealer
Altweibersommer m Indian summer
Alu ['aːlu] (umg) abk = **Arbeitslosen-
unterstützung; Aluminium**
Alufolie ['aːlufoːliə] f tinfoil
Aluminium [alu'miːnium] (-s) nt aluminium,
aluminum (US); **Aluminiumfolie** f tinfoil
Alzheimerkrankheit ['altshaɪmər'kraŋkhaɪt] f
Alzheimer's disease
am [am] = **an dem; am Sterben** on the point
of dying; **am 15. März** on March 15th; **am
letzten Sonntag** last Sunday; **am Morgen/
Abend** in the morning/evening; **am besten/
schönsten** best/most beautiful
Amalgam [amal'gaːm] (-s, -e) nt amalgam
Amateur [ama'tøːr] m amateur
Amazonas [ama'tsoːnas] (-) m Amazon (river)
Ambiente [ambi'entə] (-) nt ambience
Ambition [ambitsi'oːn] f: **~en auf etw** akk
haben to have ambitions of getting sth
Amboss ['ambɔs] (-es, -e) m anvil
ambulant [ambu'lant] adj outpatient
Ameise ['aːmaɪzə] (-, -n) f ant
Ameisenhaufen m anthill
Amerika [a'meːrika] (-s) nt America
Amerikaner [ameri'kaːnər] (-s, -) m American;
(Gebäck) flat iced cake; **Amerikanerin** f American
amerikanisch adj American
Ami ['ami] (-s, -s) (umg) m Yank; (Soldat) GI
Amme ['amə] (-, -n) f (veraltet) foster mother;
(Nährmutter) wet nurse
Ammenmärchen ['amənmɛːrçən] nt fairy tale
od story
Amok ['aːmɔk] m: **~ laufen** to run amok od
amuck
Amortisation [amɔrtizatsi'oːn] f amortization
amortisieren [amɔrti'ziːrən] vr to pay for itself
Ampel ['ampəl] (-, -n) f traffic lights pl
amphibisch [am'fiːbɪʃ] adj amphibious
Ampulle [am'pʊlə] (-, -n) f (Behälter) ampoule
amputieren [ampu'tiːrən] vt to amputate
Amsel ['amzəl] (-, -n) f blackbird

Amsterdam [amstər'dam] nt (-s) Amsterdam
Amt [amt] (-(e)s, ⁻er) nt office; (Pflicht) duty;
(Tel) exchange; **zum zuständigen ~ gehen**
to go to the relevant authority; **von ~s wegen**
(auf behördliche Anordnung hin) officially
amtieren [am'tiːrən] vi to hold office;
(fungieren): **als ... ~** to act as ...
amtierend adj incumbent
amtlich adj official; **~es Kennzeichen**
registration (number), license number (US)
Amtmann (-(e)s, pl **-männer** od **-leute**) m
(Verwaltung) senior civil servant
Amtmännin f (Verwaltung) senior civil servant
Amts- zW: **Amtsarzt** m medical officer;
amtsärztlich adj: **amtsärztlich untersucht
werden** to have an official medical
examination; **Amtsdeutsch, Amtsdeutsche**
nt officialese; **Amtseid** m: **den Amtseid
ablegen** to be sworn in, take the oath of
office; **Amtsgeheimnis** nt (geheime Sache)
official secret; (Schweigepflicht) official
secrecy; **Amtsgericht** nt county (Brit) od
district (US) court; **Amtsmissbrauch** m abuse
of one's position; **Amtsperiode** f term of
office; **Amtsperson** f official; **Amtsrichter**
m district judge; **Amtsschimmel** m (hum)
officialdom; **Amtssprache** f official language;
Amtsstunden pl office hours pl; **Amtsträger**
m office bearer; **Amtswechsel** m change
of office; (in Behörde) rotation (in office);
Amtsweg m: **auf dem Amtsweg** through
official channels; **Amtszeit** f period of office
amüsant [amy'zant] adj amusing
Amüsement [amyzə'maː] nt amusement
amüsieren [amy'ziːrən] vt to amuse ▷ vr to
enjoy o.s.; **sich über etw** akk **~** to find sth
funny; (unfreundlich) to make fun of sth

🔵 SCHLÜSSELWORT

an [an] präp +dat **1** (räumlich: wo?) at; (auf, bei) on;
(nahe bei) near; **an diesem Ort** at this place;
an der Wand on the wall; **zu nahe an etw**
too near to sth; **unten am Fluss** down by the
river; **Köln liegt am Rhein** Cologne is on the
Rhine; **an der gleichen Stelle** at od on the
same spot; **jdn an der Hand nehmen** to take
sb by the hand; **sie wohnen Tür an Tür** they
live next door to one another; **es an der Leber**
etc **haben** (umg) to have liver etc trouble
2 (zeitlich: wann?) on; **an diesem Tag** on this
day; **an Ostern** at Easter
3: arm an Fett low in fat; **jung an Jahren
sein** to be young in years; **an der ganzen
Sache ist nichts** there is nothing in it; **an
etw sterben** to die of sth; **an (und für) sich**
actually
▷ präp +akk **1** (räumlich: wohin?) to; **er ging ans
Fenster** he went (over) to the window; **etw an
die Wand hängen/schreiben** to hang/write
sth on the wall; **an die Arbeit gehen** to get
down to work
2 (zeitlich: woran?): **an etw denken** to think of

sth
3 (*gerichtet an*) to; **ein Gruß/eine Frage an dich** greetings/a question to you
▷ *adv* **1** (*ungefähr*) about; **an die Hundert** about a hundred; **an die 10 Euro** around 10 euros
2 (*auf Fahrplänen*): **Frankfurt an 18.30** arriving Frankfurt 18.30
3 (*ab*): **von dort/heute an** from there/today onwards
4 (*angeschaltet, angezogen*) on; **an sein** (*umg*) to be on; **das Licht ist an** the light is on; **ohne etwas an** with nothing on; *siehe auch* **am**

analog [ana'lo:k] *adj* analogous
Analogie [analo'gi:] *f* analogy
Analogrechner [ana'lo:krɛçnər] *m* analog computer
Analphabet, in [an|alfa'be:t(ɪn)] (**-en, -en**) *m(f)* illiterate (person)
Analyse [ana'ly:zə] (**-, -n**) *f* analysis
analysieren [analy'zi:rən] *vt* to analyse (*Brit*), analyze (*US*)
Anämie [anɛ'mi:] (**-, -n**) *f* anaemia (*Brit*), anemia (*US*)
Ananas ['ananas] (**-, - *od* -se**) *f* pineapple
Anarchie [anar'çi:] *f* anarchy
anarchisch [a'narçɪʃ] *adj* anarchic
Anarchist, in [anar'çɪst(ɪn)] (**-en, -en**) *m(f)* anarchist
Anästhesist, in [an|este'zɪst(ɪn)] (**-en, -en**) *m(f)* anaesthetist (*Brit*), anesthesiologist (*US*)
Anatomie [anato'mi:] *f* anatomy
anbahnen ['anba:nən] *vr* to open up; (*sich andeuten*) to be in the offing; (*Unangenehmes*) to be looming ▷ *vt* to initiate
Anbahnung *f* initiation
anbändeln ['anbɛndəln] (*umg*) *vi* to flirt
Anbau ['anbau] *m* (*Agr*) cultivation; (*Gebäude*) extension
anbauen *vt* (*Agr*) to cultivate; (*Gebäudeteil*) to build on
Anbaugebiet *nt*: **ein gutes ~ für etw** a good area for growing sth
Anbaumöbel *pl* unit furniture *sing*
anbehalten ['anbəhaltən] *unreg vt* to keep on
anbei [an'bai] *adv* enclosed (*form*); **~ schicken wir Ihnen ...** please find enclosed ...
anbeißen ['anbaisən] *unreg vt* to bite into ▷ *vi* (*lit*) to bite; (*fig*) to swallow the bait; **zum A~ aussehen** (*umg*) to look good enough to eat
anbelangen ['anbəlaŋən] *vt* to concern; **was mich anbelangt** as far as I am concerned
anberaumen ['anbəraumən] *vt* (*form*) to fix, arrange
anbeten ['anbe:tən] *vt* to worship
Anbetracht ['anbətraxt] *m*: **in ~** +*gen* in view of
Anbetung *f* worship
anbiedern ['anbi:dərn] (*pej*) *vr*: **sich ~ (bei)** to curry favour (with)
anbieten ['anbi:tən] *unreg vt* to offer ▷ *vr* to volunteer; **das bietet sich als Lösung an** that would provide a solution
anbinden ['anbɪndən] *unreg vt* to tie up;

(*verbinden*) to connect
Anblick ['anblɪk] *m* sight
anblicken *vt* to look at
anbraten ['anbra:tən] *unreg vt* (*Fleisch*) to brown
anbrechen ['anbrɛçən] *unreg vt* to start; (*Vorräte*) to break into ▷ *vi* to start; (*Tag*) to break; (*Nacht*) to fall
anbrennen ['anbrenən] *unreg vi* to catch fire; (*Koch*) to burn
anbringen ['anbrɪŋən] *unreg vt* to bring; (*Ware*) to sell; (*festmachen*) to fasten; (*Telefon etc*) to install
Anbruch ['anbrʊx] *m* beginning; **~ des Tages** dawn; **~ der Nacht** nightfall
anbrüllen ['anbrʏlən] *vt* to roar at
Andacht ['andaxt] (**-, -en**) *f* devotion; (*Versenkung*) rapt interest; (*Gottesdienst*) prayers *pl*; (*Ehrfurcht*) reverence
andächtig ['andɛçtıç] *adj* devout
andauern ['andauərn] *vi* to last, go on
andauernd *adj* continual
Anden ['andən] *pl*: **die ~** the Andes *pl*
Andenken ['andɛŋkən] (**-s, -**) *nt* memory; (*Reiseandenken*) souvenir; (*Erinnerungsstück*) **ein ~ (an** +*akk*) a memento (of), a keepsake (from)
andere, r, s *adj* other; (*verschieden*) different; **am ~n Tage** the next day; **ein ~s Mal** another time; **kein ~r** nobody else; **alles ~ als zufrieden** anything but pleased, far from pleased; **von etwas ~m sprechen** to talk about something else; **es blieb mir nichts ~s übrig als selbst hinzugehen** I had no alternative but to go myself; **unter ~m** among other things; **von einem Tag zum ~n** overnight; **sie hat einen ~n** she has someone else
andererseits *adv* on the other hand
andermal *adv*: **ein ~** some other time
ändern ['ɛndərn] *vt* to alter, change ▷ *vr* to change
andernfalls *adv* otherwise
andernorts ['andərn'ɔrts] *adv* elsewhere
anders *adv*: **~ (als)** differently (from); **wer ~?** who else?; **niemand ~** no-one else; **wie nicht ~ zu erwarten** as was to be expected; **wie könnte es ~ sein?** how could it be otherwise?; **ich kann nicht ~** (*kann es nicht lassen*) I can't help it; (*muss leider*) I have no choice; **~ ausgedrückt** to put it another way; **jemand/irgendwo ~** somebody/somewhere else; **~ aussehen/klingen** to look/sound different; **~ lautend = anderslautend**
andersartig *adj* different
Andersdenkende, r *f(m)* dissident, dissenter
anderseits ['andər'zaits] *adv* = **andererseits**
anders- *zW*: **andersfarbig** *adj* of a different colour; **andersgläubig** *adj* of a different faith; **andersherum** *adv* the other way round; **anderslautend** *adj*: **anderslautende Berichte** reports to the contrary; **anderswo** *adv* elsewhere; **anderswoher** *adv* from elsewhere; **anderswohin** *adv* elsewhere
anderthalb ['andərt'halp] *adj* one and a half

Änderung ['ɛndərʊŋ] f alteration, change

Änderungsantrag ['ɛndərʊŋs|antra:k] m (Parl) amendment

anderweitig ['andər'vaɪtɪç] adj other ▷ adv otherwise; (anderswo) elsewhere

andeuten ['andɔytən] vt to indicate; (Wink geben) to hint at

Andeutung f indication; hint

andeutungsweise adv (als Anspielung, Anzeichen) by way of a hint; (als flüchtiger Hinweis) in passing

andichten ['andɪçtən] vt: **jdm etw ~** (umg: Fähigkeiten) to credit sb with sth

Andorra [an'dɔra] (**-s**) nt Andorra

Andorraner, in [andɔ'ra:nər(ɪn)] m(f) Andorran

Andrang ['andraŋ] m crush

andrehen ['andre:ən] vt to turn od switch on; **jdm etw ~** (umg) to unload sth onto sb

androhen ['andro:ən] vt: **jdm etw ~** to threaten sb with sth

Androhung f: **unter ~ von Gewalt** with the threat of violence

anecken ['an|ɛkən] (umg) vi: **(bei jdm/allen) ~** to rub (sb/everyone) up the wrong way

aneignen ['an|aɪgnən] vt: **sich** dat **etw ~** to acquire sth; (widerrechtlich) to appropriate sth; (sich mit etw vertraut machen) to learn sth

aneinander [an|aɪ'nandər] adv at/on/to etc one another od each other; **aneinanderfügen** vt to put together; **aneinandergeraten** vi to clash; **aneinanderlegen** vt to put together

anekeln ['an|e:kəln] vt to disgust

Anemone [ane'mo:nə] (**-, -n**) f anemone

anerkannt ['an|ɛrkant] adj recognized, acknowledged

anerkennen ['an|ɛrkɛnən] unreg vt to recognize, acknowledge; (würdigen) to appreciate; **das muss man ~** (zugeben) you can't argue with that; (würdigen) one has to appreciate that

anerkennend adj appreciative

anerkennenswert adj praiseworthy

Anerkennung f recognition, acknowledgement; appreciation

anerzogen ['an|ɛrtso:gən] adj acquired

anfachen ['anfaxən] vt (lit) to fan into flame; (fig) to kindle

anfahren ['anfa:rən] unreg vt to deliver; (fahren gegen) to hit; (Hafen) to put into; (umg) to bawl at ▷ vi to drive up; (losfahren) to drive off

Anfahrt ['anfa:rt] f (Anfahrtsweg, Anfahrtszeit) journey; (Zufahrt) approach

Anfall ['anfal] m (Med) attack; **in einem ~ von** (fig) in a fit of

anfallen unreg vt to attack ▷ vi (Arbeit) to come up; (Produkt, Nebenprodukte) to be obtained; (Zinsen) to accrue; (sich anhäufen) to accumulate; **die ~den Kosten/Reparaturen** the costs/repairs incurred

anfällig ['anfɛlɪç] adj delicate; **~ für etw** prone to sth

Anfang ['anfaŋ] (**-(e)s, -fänge**) m beginning, start; **von ~ an** right from the beginning; **zu ~** at the beginning; **~ fünfzig** in one's early fifties; **~ Mai/1994** at the beginning of May/1994

anfangen ['anfaŋən] unreg vt to begin, start; (machen) to do ▷ vi to begin, start; **damit kann ich nichts ~** (nützt mir nichts) that's no good to me; (verstehe ich nicht) it doesn't mean a thing to me; **mit dir ist heute (aber) gar nichts anzufangen!** you're no fun at all today!; **bei einer Firma ~** to start working for a firm

Anfänger, in ['anfɛŋər(ɪn)] (**-s, -**) m(f) beginner

anfänglich ['anfɛŋlɪç] adj initial

anfangs adv at first; **wie ich schon ~ erwähnte** as I mentioned at the beginning; **Anfangsbuchstabe** m initial od first letter; **Anfangsgehalt** nt starting salary; **Anfangsstadium** nt initial stages pl

anfassen ['anfasən] vt to handle; (berühren) to touch ▷ vi to lend a hand ▷ vr to feel

anfechtbar ['anfɛçtba:r] adj contestable

anfechten ['anfɛçtən] unreg vt to dispute; (Meinung, Aussage) to challenge; (Urteil) to appeal against; (beunruhigen) to trouble

anfeinden ['anfaɪndən] vt to treat with hostility

anfertigen ['anfɛrtɪgən] vt to make

anfeuchten ['anfɔyçtən] vt to moisten

anfeuern ['anfɔyərn] vt (fig) to spur on

anflehen ['anfle:ən] vt to implore

anfliegen ['anfli:gən] unreg vt to fly to ▷ vi to fly up

Anflug ['anflu:k] m (Aviat) approach; (Spur) trace

anfordern ['anfɔrdərn] vt to demand; (Comm) to requisition

Anforderung f (+gen) demand (for); (Comm) requisition

Anfrage ['anfra:gə] f inquiry; (Parl) question

anfragen ['anfra:gən] vi to inquire

anfreunden ['anfrɔyndən] vr to make friends; **sich mit etw ~** (fig) to get to like sth

anfügen ['anfy:gən] vt to add; (beifügen) to enclose

anfühlen ['anfy:lən] vt, vr to feel

anführen ['anfy:rən] vt to lead; (zitieren) to quote; (umg: betrügen) to lead up the garden path

Anführer, in (**-s, -**) m(f) leader

Anführung f leadership; (Zitat) quotation

Anführungszeichen pl quotation marks pl, inverted commas pl (Brit)

Angabe ['anga:bə] f statement; (Tech) specification; (umg: Prahlerei) boasting; (Sport) service; **Angaben** pl (Auskunft) particulars pl; **ohne ~ von Gründen** without giving any reasons; **~n zur Person** (form) personal details od particulars

angeben ['ange:bən] unreg vt to give; (anzeigen) to inform on; (bestimmen) to set ▷ vi (umg) to boast; (Sport) to serve

Angeber, in (**-s, -**) (umg) m(f) show-off

Angeberei [ange:bə'raɪ] (umg) f showing off

angeblich ['angeːplɪç] *adj* alleged

angeboren ['angəboːrən] *adj (+dat)* inborn, innate (in); *(Med, fig)*: ~ **(bei)** congenital (to)

Angebot ['angəboːt] *nt* offer; *(Comm)*: ~ **(an** +*dat)* supply (of); **im** ~ *(umg)* on special offer

angeboten ['angəboːtən] *pp von* **anbieten**

Angebotspreis *m* offer price

angebracht ['angəbraxt] *adj* appropriate

angebrannt ['angəbrant] *adv*: **es riecht hier so** ~ there's a smell of burning here

angebrochen ['angəbrɔxən] *adj (Packung, Flasche)* open(ed); **was machen wir mit dem ~en Abend?** *(umg)* what shall we do with the rest of the evening?

angebunden ['angəbʊndən] *adj*: **kurz** ~ **sein** *(umg)* to be abrupt *od* curt

angefangen *pp von* **anfangen**

angegeben *pp von* **angeben**

angegossen ['angəgɔsən] *adj*: **wie** ~ **sitzen** to fit like a glove

angegriffen ['angəgrɪfən] *adj*: **er wirkt** ~ he looks as if he's under a lot of strain

angehalten ['angəhaltən] *pp von* **anhalten** ▷ *adj*: ~ **sein, etw zu tun** to be required *od* obliged to do sth

angehaucht ['angəhauxt] *adj*: **links/rechts** ~ **sein** to have left-/right-wing tendencies *od* leanings

angeheiratet ['angəhaɪratət] *adj* related by marriage

angeheitert ['angəhaɪtərt] *adj* tipsy

angehen ['angeːən] *unreg vt* to concern; *(angreifen)* to attack; *(bitten)*: **jdn** ~ **(um)** to approach sb (for) ▷ *vi (Feuer)* to light; *(umg: beginnen)* to begin; **das geht ihn gar nichts an** that's none of his business; **gegen jdn** ~ *(entgegentreten)* to fight sb; **gegen etw** ~ *(entgegentreten)* to fight sth; *(Missstände, Zustände)* to take measures against sth

angehend *adj* prospective; *(Musiker, Künstler)* budding

angehören ['angəhøːrən] *vi +dat* to belong to

Angehörige, r *f(m)* relative

Angeklagte, r ['angəklaːktə(r)] *f(m)* accused, defendant

angeknackst ['angəknakst] *(umg) adj (Mensch)* uptight; *(: Selbstbewusstsein)* weakened

angekommen ['angəkɔmən] *pp von* **ankommen**

Angel ['angəl] *(-, -n) f* fishing rod; *(Türangel)* hinge; **die Welt aus den ~n heben** *(fig)* to turn the world upside down

Angelegenheit ['angəleːgənhaɪt] *f* affair, matter

angelernt ['angəlɛrnt] *adj (Arbeiter)* semi-skilled

Angelhaken *m* fish hook

angeln ['angəln] *vt* to catch ▷ *vi* to fish; **Angeln** *(-s) nt* angling, fishing

Angelpunkt *m* crucial *od* central point; *(Frage)* key *od* central issue

Angelrute *f* fishing rod

Angelsachse ['angəlzaksə] *(-n, -n) m* Anglo-Saxon

Angelsächsin ['angəlzɛksɪn] *f* Anglo-Saxon

angelsächsisch ['angəlzɛksɪʃ] *adj* Anglo-Saxon

Angelschein *m* fishing permit

angemessen ['angəmɛsən] *adj* appropriate, suitable; **eine der Leistung ~e Bezahlung** payment commensurate with the input

angenehm ['angəneːm] *adj* pleasant; ~! *(bei Vorstellung)* pleased to meet you; **das A~e mit dem Nützlichen verbinden** to combine business with pleasure

angenommen ['angənɔmən] *pp von* **annehmen** ▷ *adj* assumed; *(Kind)* adopted; ~, **wir ...** assuming we ...

angepasst ['angəpast] *adj* conformist

angerufen ['angəruːfən] *pp von* **anrufen**

angesäuselt ['angəzɔʏzəlt] *adj* tipsy, merry

angeschlagen ['angəʃlaːgən] *(umg) adj (Mensch, Aussehen, Nerven)* shattered; *(Gesundheit)* poor

angeschlossen ['angəʃlɔsən] *adj (+dat)* affiliated (to *od* with), associated (with)

angeschmiert ['angəʃmiːrt] *(umg) adj* in trouble; **der/die A~e sein** to have been had

angeschrieben ['angəʃriːbən] *(umg) adj*: **bei jdm gut/schlecht** ~ **sein** to be in sb's good/bad books

angesehen ['angəzeːən] *pp von* **ansehen** ▷ *adj* respected

Angesicht ['angəzɪçt] *nt (geh)* face

angesichts ['angəzɪçts] *präp +gen* in view of, considering

angespannt ['angəʃpant] *adj (Aufmerksamkeit)* close; *(Nerven, Lage)* tense, strained; *(Comm: Markt)* tight, overstretched; *(Arbeit)* hard

Angest. *abk* = **Angestellte(r)**

angestammt ['angəʃtamt] *adj (überkommen)* traditional; *(ererbt: Rechte)* hereditary; *(: Besitz)* inherited

Angestellte, r ['angəʃtɛltə(r)] *f(m)* employee; *(Büroangestellte)* white-collar worker

angestrengt ['angəʃtrɛŋt] *adv* as hard as one can

angetan ['angətaːn] *adj*: **von jdm/etw** ~ **sein** to be taken with sb/sth; **es jdm** ~ **haben** to appeal to sb

angetrunken ['angətrʊŋkən] *adj* inebriated

angewiesen ['angəviːzən] *adj*: **auf jdn/etw** ~ **sein** to be dependent on sb/sth; **auf sich selbst** ~ **sein** to be left to one's own devices

angewöhnen ['angəvøːnən] *vt*: **jdm/sich etw** ~ to accustom sb/become accustomed to sth

Angewohnheit ['angəvoːnhaɪt] *f* habit

angewurzelt ['angəvʊrtsəlt] *adj*: **wie** ~ **dastehen** to be rooted to the spot

angiften ['angɪftən] *(pej: umg) vt* to snap at

angleichen ['anglaɪçən] *unreg vt, vr* to adjust

Angler ['anlər] *(-s, -) m* angler

angliedern ['angliːdərn] *vt*: ~ **(an** +*akk)* *(Verein, Partei)* to affiliate (to *od* with); *(Land)* to annex (to)

Anglist, in [anˈglɪst(ɪn)] *(-en, -en) m(f)* English specialist; *(Student)* English student; *(Professor*

etc) English lecturer/professor
Angola [aŋˈɡoːla] (**-s**) *nt* Angola
angreifen [ˈanɡraɪfən] *unreg vt* to attack;
  (*anfassen*) to touch; (*Arbeit*) to tackle;
  (*beschädigen*) to damage
Angreifer, in (**-s, -**) *m(f)* attacker
angrenzen [ˈanɡrɛntsən] *vi:* **an etw** *akk* **~** to
  border on sth, adjoin sth
Angriff [ˈanɡrɪf] *m* attack; **etw in ~ nehmen** to
  make a start on sth
Angriffsfläche *f:* **jdm/etw eine ~ bieten** (*lit,
  fig*) to provide sb/sth with a target
angriffslustig *adj* aggressive
Angst [aŋst] (**-, ̈e**) *f* fear; **~ haben (vor** +*dat*) to
  be afraid *od* scared (of); **~ um jdn/etw haben**
  to be worried about sb/sth; **jdm ~ einflößen**
  od **einjagen** to frighten sb; **jdm ~ machen**
  to scare sb; **nur keine ~!** don't be scared;
  angst *adj:* **jdm ist angst** sb is afraid *od* scared;
  angstfrei *adj* free of fear; **Angsthase** (*umg*) *m*
  chicken, scaredy-cat
ängstigen [ˈɛŋstɪɡən] *vt* to frighten ▷*vr:* **sich ~
  (vor** +*dat od* **um)** to worry (o.s.) (about)
ängstlich *adj* nervous; (*besorgt*) worried;
  (*schüchtern*) timid; **Ängstlichkeit** *f* nervousness
Angstschweiß *m:* **mir brach der ~ aus** I broke
  out in a cold sweat
angurten [ˈanɡʊrtən] *vt, vr* = **anschnallen**
Anh. *abk* (= *Anhang*) app.
anhaben [ˈanhaːbən] *unreg vt* to have on; **er
  kann mir nichts ~** he can't hurt me
anhaften [ˈanhaftən] *vi* (*lit*): **~ (an** +*dat*) to stick
  (to); (*fig*): **~** +*dat* to stick to, stay with
anhalten [ˈanhaltən] *unreg vt* to stop ▷*vi* to
  stop; (*andauern*) to persist; (*werben*): **um die
  Hand eines Mädchens ~** to ask for a girl's
  hand in marriage; **(jdm) etw ~** to hold sth up
  (against sb); **jdn zur Arbeit/Höflichkeit ~** to
  get sb to work/teach sb to be polite
anhaltend *adj* persistent
Anhalter, in (**-s, -**) *m(f)* hitch-hiker; **per ~
  fahren** to hitch-hike
Anhaltspunkt *m* clue
anhand [anˈhant] *präp* +*gen* with; **~ eines
  Beispiels** by means of an example
Anhang [ˈanhaŋ] *m* appendix; (*Comput*)
  attachment; (*Leute*) family; (*Anhängerschaft*)
  supporters *pl*
anhängen [ˈanhɛŋən] *unreg vt* to hang up;
  (*Wagen*) to couple up; (*Zusatz*) to add (on);
  (*Comput*) to append; **sich an jdn ~** to attach
  o.s. to sb; **eine Datei an eine E-Mail ~**
  (*Comput*) to attach a file to an email; **jdm etw
  ~** (*umg: nachsagen, anlasten*) to blame sb for sth,
  blame sth on sb; (: *Verdacht, Schuld*) to pin sth
  on sb
Anhänger (**-s, -**) *m* supporter; (*Aut*)
  trailer; (*am Koffer*) tag; (*Schmuck*) pendant;
  Anhängerschaft *f* supporters *pl*
Anhängeschloss *nt* padlock
anhängig *adj* (*Jur*) sub judice; **etw ~ machen** to
  start legal proceedings over sth
anhänglich *adj* devoted; **Anhänglichkeit** *f*

devotion
Anhängsel (**-s, -**) *nt* appendage
anhauen [ˈanhaʊən] (*umg*) *vt* (*ansprechen*): **jdn ~
  (um)** to accost sb (for)
anhäufen [ˈanhɔʏfən] *vt* to accumulate, amass
  ▷*vr* to accrue
Anhäufung [ˈanhɔʏfʊŋ] *f* accumulation
anheben [ˈanheːbən] *unreg vt* to lift up; (*Preise*)
  to raise
anheimelnd [ˈanhaɪməlnt] *adj* comfortable,
  cosy
anheimstellen [anˈhaɪmʃtɛlən] *vt:* **jdm etw ~**
  to leave sth up to sb
anheizen [ˈanhaɪtsən] *vt* (*Ofen*) to
  light; (*fig: umg: Wirtschaft*) to stimulate;
  (*verschlimmern: Krise*) to aggravate
anheuern [ˈanhɔʏərn] *vt, vi* (*Naut, fig*) to sign
  on *od* up
Anhieb [ˈanhiːb] *m:* **auf ~** straight off, first go;
  es klappte auf ~ it was an immediate success
anhimmeln [ˈanhɪməln] (*umg*) *vt* to idolize
Anhöhe [ˈanhøːə] *f* hill
anhören [ˈanhøːrən] *vt* to listen to; (*anmerken*)
  to hear ▷*vr* to sound
Anhörung *f* hearing
Animierdame [aniˈmiːrdaːmə] *f* nightclub/
  bar hostess
animieren [aniˈmiːrən] *vt* to encourage, urge on
Anis [aˈniːs] (**-es, -e**) *m* aniseed
Ank. *abk* (= *Ankunft*) arr.
ankämpfen [ˈankɛmpfən] *vi:* **gegen etw ~** to
  fight (against) sth; (*gegen Wind, Strömung*) to
  battle against sth
Ankara [ˈaŋkara] (**-s**) *nt* Ankara
Ankauf [ˈankaʊf] *m:* **~ und Verkauf von ...** we
  buy and sell ...; **ankaufen** *vt* to purchase, buy
Anker [ˈaŋkər] (**-s, -**) *m* anchor; **vor ~ gehen** to
  drop anchor
ankern *vt, vi* to anchor
Ankerplatz *m* anchorage
Anklage [ˈanklaːɡə] *f* accusation; (*Jur*) charge;
  gegen jdn ~ erheben (*Jur*) to bring *od* prefer
  charges against sb; **Anklagebank** *f* dock
anklagen [ˈanklaːɡən] *vt* to accuse; **jdn (eines
  Verbrechens) ~** (*Jur*) to charge sb (with a
  crime)
Anklagepunkt *m* charge
Ankläger, in [ˈanklɛːɡər(ɪn)] (**-s, -**) *m(f)* accuser
Anklageschrift *f* indictment
anklammern [ˈanklamərn] *vt* to clip, staple
  ▷*vr:* **sich an etw** *akk od dat* **~** to cling to sth
Anklang [ˈanklaŋ] *m:* **bei jdm ~ finden** to
  meet with sb's approval
ankleben [ˈankleːbən] *vt:* **„Plakate ~
  verboten!"** "stick no bills"
Ankleidekabine *f* changing cubicle
ankleiden [ˈanklaɪdən] *vt, vr* to dress
anklingen [ˈanklɪŋən] *vi* (*angeschnitten werden*)
  to be touched (up)on; (*erinnern*): **~ an** +*akk* to be
  reminiscent of
anklopfen [ˈanklɔpfən] *vi* to knock
anknipsen [ˈanknɪpsən] *vt* to switch on;
  (*Schalter*) to flick

anknüpfen ['anknʏpfən] vt to fasten od tie on; (Beziehungen) to establish; (Gespräch) to start up ▷ vi (anschließen): ~ **an** +akk to refer to

Anknüpfungspunkt m link

ankommen ['ankɔmən] unreg vi to arrive; (näher kommen) to approach; (Anklang finden): **bei jdm (gut)** ~ to go down well with sb ▷ vi unpers: **er ließ es auf einen Streit/einen Versuch ~** he was prepared to argue about it/to give it a try; **es kommt darauf an** it depends; (wichtig sein) that is what matters; **es kommt auf ihn an** it depends on him; **es darauf ~ lassen** to let things take their course; **gegen jdn/etw ~** to cope with sb/sth; **damit kommst du bei ihm nicht an!** you won't get anywhere with him like that

ankreiden ['ankraɪdən] vt (fig): **jdm etw (dick od übel) ~** to hold sth against sb

ankreuzen ['ankrɔʏtsən] vt to mark with a cross

ankündigen ['ankʏndɪgən] vt to announce

Ankündigung f announcement

Ankunft ['ankʊnft] (-, -künfte) f arrival

Ankunftszeit f time of arrival

ankurbeln ['ankʊrbəln] vt (Aut) to crank; (fig) to boost

Anl. abk (= Anlage) enc(l).

anlachen ['anlaxən] vt to smile at; **sich** dat **jdn ~** (umg) to pick sb up

Anlage ['anla:gə] f disposition; (Begabung) talent; (Park) gardens pl; (Beilage) enclosure; (Tech) plant; (Einrichtung: Mil, Elek) installation(s pl); (Sportanlage etc) facilities pl; (umg: Stereoanlage) (stereo) system; (Fin) investment; (Entwurf) layout; **als ~ od in der ~ erhalten Sie ...** please find enclosed ...; **Anlageberater, in** m(f) investment consultant; **Anlagekapital** nt fixed capital

Anlagenabschreibung f capital allowance

Anlagengeschäft nt investment deal; (Branche) investment banking

Anlagevermögen nt capital assets pl, fixed assets pl

anlangen ['anlaŋən] vi (ankommen) to arrive

Anlass ['anlas] (-es, -lässe) m: ~ **(zu)** cause (for); (Ereignis) occasion; **aus ~** +gen on the occasion of; ~ **zu etw geben** to give rise to sth; **beim geringsten/bei jedem ~** for the slightest reason/at every opportunity; **etw zum ~ nehmen** to take the opportunity of sth

anlassen unreg vt to leave on; (Motor) to start ▷ vr (umg) to start off

Anlasser (-s, -) m (Aut) starter

anlässlich ['anlɛslɪç] präp +gen on the occasion of

anlasten ['anlastən] vt: **jdm etw ~** to blame sb for sth

Anlauf ['anlaʊf] m run-up; (fig: Versuch) attempt, try

anlaufen unreg vi to begin; (Film) to be showing; (Sport) to run up; (Fenster) to mist up; (Metall) to tarnish ▷ vt to call at; **rot ~** to turn od go red; **gegen etw ~** to run into od up against sth;

angelaufen kommen to come running up

Anlauf- zW: **Anlaufstelle** f place to go (with one's problems); **Anlaufzeit** f (fig) time to get going od started

anläuten ['anlɔʏtən] vi to ring

anlegen ['anle:gən] vt to put; (anziehen) to put on; (gestalten) to lay out; (Kartei, Akte) to start; (Comput: Datei) to create; (Geld) to invest ▷ vi to dock; (Naut) to berth; **etw an etw** akk ~ to put sth against od on sth; **ein Gewehr ~ (auf** +akk) to aim a weapon (at); **es auf etw** akk ~ to be out for sth/to do sth; **strengere Maßstäbe ~ (bei)** to lay down od impose stricter standards (in); **sich mit jdm ~** (umg) to quarrel with sb

Anlegeplatz m landing place

Anleger, in (-s, -) m(f) (Fin) investor

Anlegestelle f landing place

anlehnen ['anle:nən] vt to lean; (Tür) to leave ajar; **(sich) an etw** akk ~ to lean on od against sth

Anlehnung f (Imitation): **in ~ an jdn/etw** following sb/sth

Anlehnungsbedürfnis nt need of loving care

anleiern ['anlaɪərn] (umg) vt to get going

Anleihe ['anlaɪə] (-, -n) f (Fin) loan; (Wertpapier) bond

anleiten ['anlaɪtən] vt to instruct

Anleitung f instructions pl

anlernen ['anlɛrnən] vt to teach, instruct

anlesen ['anle:zən] unreg vt (aneignen): **sich** dat **etw ~** to learn sth by reading

Anliegen ['anli:gən] (-s, -) nt matter; (Wunsch) wish

anliegen unreg vi (Kleidung) to cling

anliegend adj adjacent; (beigefügt) enclosed

Anlieger (-s, -) m resident; ~ **frei** no thoroughfare – residents only

anlocken ['anlɔkən] vt to attract; (Tiere) to lure

anlügen ['anly:gən] unreg vt to lie to

Anm. abk (= Anmerkung) n.

anmachen ['anmaxən] vt to attach; (Elektrisches) to put on; (Salat) to dress; **jdn ~** (umg) to try and pick sb up

anmalen ['anma:lən] vt to paint ▷ vr (pej: schminken) to paint one's face od o.s.

Anmarsch ['anmarʃ] m: **im ~ sein** to be advancing; (hum) to be on the way; **im ~ sein auf** +akk to be advancing on

anmaßen ['anma:sən] vt: **sich** dat **etw ~** to lay claim to sth

anmaßend adj arrogant

Anmaßung f presumption

Anmeldeformular ['anmɛldəfɔrmʊla:r] nt registration form

anmelden vt to announce; (geltend machen: Recht, Ansprüche, zu Steuerzwecken) to declare; (Comput) to log on ▷ vr (sich ankündigen) to make an appointment; (polizeilich, für Kurs etc) to register; **ein Gespräch nach Deutschland ~** (Tel) to book a call to Germany

Anmeldung f announcement; appointment; registration; **nur nach vorheriger ~** by appointment only

anmerken ['anmɛrkən] *vt* to observe; (*anstreichen*) to mark; **jdm seine Verlegenheit** *etc* ~ to notice sb's embarrassment *etc*; **sich** *dat* **nichts** ~ **lassen** not to give anything away

Anmerkung *f* note

Anmut ['anmu:t] (-) *f* grace

anmuten *vt* (*geh*): **jdn** ~ to appear *od* seem to sb

anmutig *adj* charming

annähen ['annɛ:ən] *vt* to sew on

annähern ['annɛ:ərn] *vr* to get closer

annähernd *adj* approximate; **nicht** ~ **so viel** not nearly as much

Annäherung *f* approach

Annäherungsversuch *m* advances *pl*

Annahme ['anna:mə] (-, -n) *f* acceptance; (*Vermutung*) assumption; **Annahmestelle** *f* counter; (*für Reparaturen*) reception; **Annahmeverweigerung** *f* refusal

annehmbar ['anne:mba:r] *adj* acceptable

annehmen *unreg vt* to accept; (*Namen*) to take; (*Kind*) to adopt; (*vermuten*) to suppose, assume ▷ *vr* (+*gen*) to take care (of); **jdn an Kindes statt** ~ to adopt sb; **angenommen, das ist so** assuming that is so

Annehmlichkeit *f* comfort

annektieren [anɛk'ti:rən] *vt* to annex

anno ['ano] *adj*: **von** ~ **dazumal** (*umg*) from the year dot

Annonce [a'nõ:sə] (-, -n) *f* advertisement

annoncieren [anõ'si:rən] *vt*, *vi* to advertise

annullieren [anʊ'li:rən] *vt* to annul

Anode [a'no:də] (-, -n) *f* anode

anöden ['an|ø:dən] (*umg*) *vt* to bore stiff

anomal [ano'ma:l] *adj* (*regelwidrig*) unusual, abnormal; (*nicht normal*) strange, odd

anonym [ano'ny:m] *adj* anonymous

Anorak ['anorak] (-s, -s) *m* anorak

anordnen ['an|ɔrdnən] *vt* to arrange; (*befehlen*) to order

Anordnung *f* arrangement; order; **~en treffen** to give orders

anorganisch ['an|ɔrga:nɪʃ] *adj* (*Chem*) inorganic

anpacken ['anpakən] *vt* to grasp; (*fig*) to tackle; **mit** ~ to lend a hand

anpassen ['anpasən] *vt* (*Kleidung*) to fit; (*fig*) to adapt ▷ *vr* to adapt

Anpassung *f* fitting; adaptation

Anpassungsdruck *m* pressure to conform (*to society*)

anpassungsfähig *adj* adaptable

anpeilen ['anpailən] *vt* (*mit Radar, Funk etc*) to take a bearing on; **etw** ~ (*fig: umg*) to have one's sights on sth

Anpfiff ['anpfɪf] *m* (*Sport*) (starting) whistle; (*Spielbeginn: Fußball etc*) kick-off; **einen** ~ **bekommen** (*umg*) to get a rocket (*Brit*)

anpöbeln ['anpø:bəln] *vt* to abuse; (*umg*) to pester

Anprall ['anpral] *m*: ~ **gegen** *od* **an** +*akk* impact on *od* against

anprangern ['anpraŋərn] *vt* to denounce

anpreisen ['anpraizən] *unreg vt* to extol; **sich** ~ **(als)** to sell o.s. (as); **etw** ~ to extol (the virtues of) sth; **seine Waren** ~ to cry one's wares

Anprobe ['anpro:bə] *f* trying on

anprobieren ['anprobi:rən] *vt* to try on

anpumpen ['anpʊmpən] (*umg*) *vt* to borrow from

anquatschen ['ankvatʃən] (*umg*) *vt* to speak to; (: *Mädchen*) to try to pick up

Anrainer ['anrainər] (-s, -) *m* neighbour (*Brit*), neighbor (*US*)

anranzen ['anrantsən] (*umg*) *vt*: **jdn** ~ to tick sb off

anraten ['anra:tən] *unreg vt* to recommend; **auf A~ des Arztes** *etc* on the doctor's *etc* advice *od* recommendation

anrechnen ['anrɛçnən] *vt* to charge; (*fig*) to count; **jdm etw hoch** ~ to think highly of sb for sth

Anrecht ['anrɛçt] *nt*: ~ **auf** +*akk* right (to); **ein** ~ **auf etw haben** to be entitled to sth, have a right to sth

Anrede ['anre:də] *f* form of address

anreden *vt* to address

anregen ['anre:gən] *vt* to stimulate; **angeregte Unterhaltung** lively discussion

anregend *adj* stimulating

Anregung *f* stimulation; (*Vorschlag*) suggestion

anreichern ['anraiçərn] *vt* to enrich

Anreise ['anraizə] *f* journey there/here

anreisen *vi* to arrive

anreißen ['anraisən] *unreg vt* (*kurz zur Sprache bringen*) to touch on

Anreiz ['anraits] *m* incentive

anrempeln ['anrɛmpəln] *vt* (*anstoßen*) to bump into; (*absichtlich*) to jostle

anrennen ['anrɛnən] *unreg vi*: **gegen etw** ~ (*gegen Wind etc*) to run against sth; (*Mil*) to storm sth

Anrichte ['anrɪçtə] (-, -n) *f* sideboard

anrichten *vt* to serve up; **Unheil** ~ to make mischief; **da hast du aber etwas angerichtet!** (*umg: verursacht*) you've started something there all right!; (: *angestellt*) you've really made a mess there!

anrüchig ['anryçɪç] *adj* dubious

anrücken ['anrʏkən] *vi* to approach; (*Mil*) to advance

Anruf ['anru:f] *m* call; **Anrufbeantworter** *m* (telephone) answering machine, answerphone

anrufen *unreg vt* to call out to; (*bitten*) to call on; (*Tel*) to ring up, phone, call

anrühren ['anry:rən] *vt* to touch; (*mischen*) to mix

ans [ans] = **an das**

Ansage ['anza:gə] *f* announcement

ansagen *vt* to announce ▷ *vr* to say one will come

Ansager, in (-s, -) *m(f)* announcer

ansammeln ['anzaməln] *vt* to collect ▷ *vr* to accumulate; (*fig: Wut, Druck*) to build up

Ansammlung *f* collection; (*Leute*) crowd

ansässig ['anzɛsɪç] *adj* resident

Ansatz ['anzats] *m* start; (*Haaransatz*) hairline; (*Halsansatz*) base; (*Verlängerungsstück*) extension; (*Veranschlagung*) estimate; **die ersten Ansätze zu etw** the beginnings of sth; **Ansatzpunkt** *m* starting point; **Ansatzstück** *nt* (*Tech*) attachment

anschaffen ['anʃafən] *vt* to buy, purchase ▷ *vi*: ~ **gehen** (*umg: durch Prostitution*) to be on the game; **sich** *dat* **Kinder** ~ (*umg*) to have children

Anschaffung *f* purchase

anschalten ['anʃaltən] *vt* to switch on

anschauen ['anʃauən] *vt* to look at

anschaulich *adj* illustrative

Anschauung *f* (*Meinung*) view; **aus eigener** ~ from one's own experience

Anschauungsmaterial *nt* illustrative material

Anschein ['anʃaɪn] *m* appearance; **allem** ~ **nach** to all appearances; **den** ~ **haben** to seem, appear

anscheinend *adj* apparent

anschieben ['anʃiːbən] *unreg vt* (*Fahrzeug*) to push

Anschiss ['anʃɪs] (*umg*) *m*: **einen** ~ **bekommen** to get a telling-off *od* ticking-off (*bes Brit*)

Anschlag ['anʃlaːk] *m* notice; (*Attentat*) attack; (*Comm*) estimate; (*auf Klavier*) touch; (*auf Schreibmaschine*) keystroke; **einem** ~ **zum Opfer fallen** to be assassinated; **ein Gewehr im** ~ **haben** (*Mil*) to have a rifle at the ready; **Anschlagbrett** *nt* notice board (*Brit*), bulletin board (*US*)

anschlagen ['anʃlaːgən] *unreg vt* to put up; (*beschädigen*) to chip; (*Akkord*) to strike; (*Kosten*) to estimate ▷ *vi* to hit; (*wirken*) to have an effect; (*Glocke*) to ring; (*Hund*) to bark; **einen anderen Ton** ~ (*fig*) to change one's tune; **an etw** *akk* ~ to hit against sth

anschlagfrei *adj*: **~er Drucker** non-impact printer

Anschlagzettel *m* notice

anschleppen ['anʃlɛpən] (*umg*) *vt* (*unerwünscht mitbringen*) to bring along

anschließen ['anʃliːsən] *unreg vt* to connect up; (*Sender*) to link up; (*in Steckdose*) to plug in; (*fig: hinzufügen*) to add ▷ *vi*: **an etw** *akk* ~ (*zeitlich*) to follow sth ▷ *vr*: **sich jdm/etw** ~ to join sb/sth; (*beipflichten*) to agree with sb/sth; **sich an etw** *akk* ~ (*angrenzen*) to adjoin sth

anschließend *adj* adjacent; (*zeitlich*) subsequent ▷ *adv* afterwards; **~ an** +*akk* following

Anschluss ['anʃlʊs] *m* (*Elek, Eisenb, Tel*) connection; (*weiterer Apparat*) extension; (*von Wasser etc*) supply; (*Comput*) port; **im** ~ **an** +*akk* following; ~ **finden** to make friends; ~ **bekommen** to get through; **kein** ~ **unter dieser Nummer** number unobtainable; **den** ~ **verpassen** (*Eisenb etc*) to miss one's connection; (*fig*) to miss the boat

anschmiegen ['anʃmiːgən] *vr*: **sich an jdn/etw** ~ (*Kind, Hund*) to snuggle *od* nestle up to *od* against sb/sth

anschmiegsam ['anʃmiːkzaːm] *adj* affectionate

anschmieren ['anʃmiːrən] *vt* to smear; (*umg*) to take in

anschnallen ['anʃnalən] *vt* to buckle on ▷ *vr* to fasten one's seat belt

Anschnallpflicht *f*: **für Kinder besteht** ~ children must wear seat belts

anschnauzen ['anʃnautsən] (*umg*) *vt* to yell at

anschneiden ['anʃnaɪdən] *unreg vt* to cut into; (*Thema*) to introduce

Anschnitt ['anʃnɪt] *m* first slice

anschreiben ['anʃraɪbən] *unreg vt* to write (up); (*Comm*) to charge up; (*benachrichtigen*) to write to; **bei jdm gut/schlecht angeschrieben sein** to be well/badly thought of by sb, be in sb's good/bad books

anschreien ['anʃraɪən] *unreg vt* to shout at

Anschrift ['anʃrɪft] *f* address

Anschriftenliste *f* mailing list

Anschub *m* (*bei Firmengründung*) start-up (funds *pl*)

Anschuldigung ['anʃʊldɪgʊŋ] *f* accusation

anschwärzen ['anʃvɛrtsən] *vt* (*fig: umg*): **jdn** ~ (**bei**) to blacken sb's name (with)

anschwellen ['anʃvɛlən] *unreg vi* to swell (up)

anschwemmen ['anʃvɛmən] *vt* to wash ashore

anschwindeln ['anʃvɪndəln] (*umg*) *vt* to lie to

ansehen ['anzeːən] *unreg vt* to look at; **jdm etw** ~ to see sth (from sb's face); **jdn/etw als etw** ~ to look on sb/sth as sth; ~ **für** to consider; (**sich** *dat*) **etw** ~ to (have a) look at sth; (*Fernsehsendung*) to watch sth; (*Film, Stück, Sportveranstaltung*) to see sth; **etw (mit)** ~ to watch sth, see sth happening

Ansehen (**-s**) *nt* respect; (*Ruf*) reputation; **ohne** ~ **der Person** (*Jur*) without respect of person

ansehnlich ['anzeːnlɪç] *adj* fine-looking; (*beträchtlich*) considerable

anseilen ['anzaɪlən] *vt*: **jdn/sich** ~ to rope sb/o.s. up

an sein ['anzaɪn] *siehe* **an**

ansetzen ['anzɛtsən] *vt* (*festlegen*) to fix; (*entwickeln*) to develop; (*Fett*) to put on; (*Blätter*) to grow; (*zubereiten*) to prepare ▷ *vi* (*anfangen*) to start, begin; (*Entwicklung*) to set in; (*dick werden*) to put on weight ▷ *vr* (*Rost etc*) to start to develop; ~ **an** +*akk* (*anfügen*) to fit on to; (*anlegen, an Mund etc*) to put to; **zu etw** ~ to prepare to do sth; **jdn/etw auf jdn/etw** ~ to set sb/sth on sb/sth

Ansicht ['anzɪçt] *f* (*Anblick*) sight; (*Meinung*) view, opinion; **zur** ~ on approval; **meiner** ~ **nach** in my opinion

Ansichtskarte *f* picture postcard

Ansichtssache *f* matter of opinion

ansiedeln ['anziːdəln] *vt* to settle; (*Tierart*) to introduce ▷ *vr* to settle; (*Industrie etc*) to get established

ansonsten [an'zɔnstən] *adv* otherwise

anspannen ['anʃpanən] *vt* to harness; (*Muskel*) to strain

Anspannung f strain
Anspiel ['anʃpi:l] nt (Sport) start of play
anspielen vt (Sport) to play the ball etc to
▷ vi: **auf etw** akk **~** to refer od allude to sth
Anspielung f: **~ (auf** +akk**)** reference (to),
allusion (to)
Ansporn ['anʃpɔrn] (**-(e)s**) m incentive
Ansprache ['anʃpra:xə] f (Rede) address
ansprechen ['anʃprɛçən] unreg vt to speak to;
(bitten, gefallen) to appeal to; (Eindruck machen
auf) to make an impression on ▷ vi: **~ auf** +akk
(Patient) to respond (to); (Messgerät) to react (to);
jdn auf etw akk **(hin) ~** to ask sb about sth
ansprechend adj attractive
Ansprechpartner m contact
anspringen ['anʃprɪŋən] unreg vi (Aut) to start
▷ vt (anfallen) to jump; (Raubtier) to pounce (up)
on; (Hund: hochspringen) to jump up at
Anspruch ['anʃprʊx] (**-s, -sprüche**) m (Recht): **~
(auf** +akk**)** claim (to); **den Ansprüchen
gerecht werden** to meet the requirements;
hohe Ansprüche stellen/haben to demand/
expect a lot; **jdn/etw in ~ nehmen** to occupy
sb/take up sth
anspruchslos adj undemanding
anspruchsvoll adj demanding; (Comm)
upmarket
anspucken ['anʃpʊkən] vt to spit at
anstacheln ['anʃtaxəln] vt to spur on
Anstalt ['anʃtalt] (**-, -en**) f institution; **~en
machen, etw zu tun** to prepare to do sth
Anstand ['anʃtant] m decency; (Manieren)
(good) manners pl
anständig ['anʃtɛndɪç] adj decent; (umg)
proper; (groß) considerable; **Anständigkeit** f
propriety, decency
anstandshalber ['anʃtantshalbər] adv out of
politeness
anstandslos adv without any ado
anstarren ['anʃtarən] vt to stare at
anstatt [an'ʃtat] präp +gen instead of ▷ konj: **~
etw zu tun** instead of doing sth
anstauen ['anʃtaʊən] vr to accumulate; (Blut in
Adern etc) to congest; (fig: Gefühle) to build up
anstechen ['anʃtɛçən] unreg vt to prick; (Fass)
to tap
anstecken ['anʃtɛkən] vt to pin on; (Ring) to
put od slip on; (Med) to infect; (Pfeife) to light;
(Haus) to set fire to ▷ vr: **ich habe mich bei
ihm angesteckt** I caught it from him ▷ vi (fig)
to be infectious
ansteckend adj infectious
Ansteckung f infection
anstehen ['anʃte:ən] unreg vi to queue up
(Brit), line up (US); (Verhandlungspunkt) to be on
the agenda
ansteigen ['anʃtaɪgən] unreg vi to rise; (Straße)
to climb
anstelle, an Stelle [an'ʃtɛlə] präp +gen in place
of
anstellen ['anʃtɛlən] vt (einschalten) to turn on;
(Arbeit geben) to employ; (umg: Unfug treiben) to
get up to; (: machen) to do ▷ vr to queue (up)

(Brit), line up (US); (umg) to act; (: sich zieren) to
make a fuss, act up
Anstellung f employment; (Posten) post,
position; **~ auf Lebenszeit** tenure
ansteuern ['anʃtɔyərn] vt to make od steer od
head for
Anstich ['anʃtɪç] m (von Fass) tapping,
broaching
Anstieg ['anʃti:k] (**-(e)s, -e**) m climb; (fig: von
Preisen etc) increase
anstiften ['anʃtɪftən] vt (Unglück) to cause; **jdn
zu etw ~** to put sb up to sth
Anstifter(-s, -) m instigator
Anstiftung f (von Tat) instigation; (von
Mensch): **~ (zu)** incitement (to)
anstimmen ['anʃtɪmən] vt (Lied) to strike up
(with); (Geschrei) to set up ▷ vi to strike up
Anstoß ['anʃto:s] m impetus; (Ärgernis) offence
(Brit), offense (US); (Sport) kick-off; **der erste
~** the initiative; **ein Stein des ~es** (umstrittene
Sache) a bone of contention; **~ nehmen an** +dat
to take offence at
anstoßen unreg vt to push; (mit Fuß) to kick
▷ vi to knock, bump; (mit der Zunge) to lisp;
(mit Gläsern) to drink a toast; **an etw** akk **~**
(angrenzen) to adjoin sth; **~ auf** +akk to drink (a
toast) to
anstößig ['anʃtø:sɪç] adj offensive, indecent;
Anstößigkeit f indecency, offensiveness
anstrahlen ['anʃtra:lən] vt to floodlight;
(strahlend ansehen) to beam at
anstreben ['anʃtre:bən] vt to strive for
anstreichen ['anʃtraɪçən] unreg vt to paint;
(jdm) etw als Fehler ~ to mark sth wrong
Anstreicher, in (-s, -) m(f) painter
anstrengen ['anʃtrɛŋən] vt to strain;
(strapazieren: jdn) to tire out; (: Patienten) to
fatigue; (Jur) to bring ▷ vr to make an effort;
eine Klage ~ (gegen) (Jur) to initiate od
institute proceedings (against)
anstrengend adj tiring
Anstrengung f effort
Anstrich ['anʃtrɪç] m coat of paint
Ansturm ['anʃtʊrm] m rush; (Mil) attack
Ansuchen ['anzu:xən] (**-s, -**) nt request
ansuchen ['anzu:xən] vi: **um etw ~** to apply
for sth
Antagonismus [antago'nɪsmʊs] m
antagonism
antanzen ['antantsən] (umg) vi to turn od show
up
Antarktis [ant'|arktɪs] (**-**) f Antarctic
antarktisch adj Antarctic
antasten ['antastən] vt to touch; (Recht) to
infringe upon; (Ehre) to question
Anteil ['antaɪl] (**-s, -e**) m share; (Mitgefühl)
sympathy; **~ nehmen an** +dat to share in;
(sich interessieren) to take an interest in; **~ an
etw** dat **haben** (beitragen) to contribute to sth;
(teilnehmen) to take part in sth
anteilig adj proportionate, proportional
anteilmäßig adj pro rata
Anteilnahme (-) f sympathy

Antenne [an'tɛnə] (-, -n) f aerial; (Zool) antenna; **eine/keine ~ für etw haben** (fig: umg) to have a/no feeling for sth

Anthrazit [antra'tsi:t] (-s, -e) m anthracite

Anthropologie [antropolo'gi:] (-) f anthropology

Anti- ['anti] in zW anti; **Antialkoholiker** m teetotaller; **antiautoritär** adj anti-authoritarian; **Antibabypille** f (contraceptive) pill; **Antibiotikum** (-s, -ka) nt antibiotic; **Antiheld** m antihero

antik [an'ti:k] adj antique

Antike (-, -n) f (Zeitalter) ancient world; (Kunstgegenstand) antique

Antikörper m antibody

Antilope [anti'lo:pə] (-, -n) f antelope

Antipathie [antipa'ti:] f antipathy

antippen ['antɪpən] vt to tap; (Pedal, Bremse) to touch; (fig: Thema) to touch on

Antiquariat [antikvari'a:t] (-(e)s, -e) nt secondhand bookshop; **modernes ~** remainder bookshop/department

antiquiert [anti'kvi:rt] (pej) adj antiquated

Antiquitäten [antikvi'tɛ:tən] pl antiques pl; **Antiquitätenhandel** m antique business; **Antiquitätenhändler, in** m(f) antique dealer

Antisemitismus [antizemi'tɪsmʊs] m anti-semitism

antiseptisch [anti'zɛptɪʃ] adj antiseptic

Antiviren- adj (Comput) antivirus; **Antivirensoftware** f antivirus software

Antlitz ['antlɪts] (-es, -e) nt (liter) countenance (liter), face

antörnen ['antœrnən] (umg) vt (Drogen, Musik) to turn on ▷ vi: **... törnt an ...** turns you on

Antrag ['antra:k] (-(e)s, -träge) m proposal; (Parl) motion; (Gesuch) application; **einen ~ auf etw** akk **stellen** to make an application for sth; (Jur etc) to file a petition/claim for sth

Antragsformular nt application form

Antragsgegner, in m(f) (Jur) respondent

Antragsteller, in (-s, -) m(f) claimant; (für Kredit etc) applicant

antreffen ['antrɛfən] unreg vt to meet

antreiben ['antraɪbən] unreg vt to drive on; (Motor) to drive; (anschwemmen) to wash up ▷ vi to be washed up; **jdn zur Eile/Arbeit ~** to urge sb to hurry up/to work

Antreiber (-s, -) (pej) m slave-driver (pej)

antreten ['antre:tən] unreg vt (Amt) to take up; (Erbschaft) to come into; (Beweis) to offer; (Reise) to start, begin ▷ vi (Mil) to fall in; (Sport) to line up; (zum Dienst) to report; **gegen jdn ~** to play/fight against sb

Antrieb ['antri:p] m (lit, fig) drive; **aus eigenem ~** of one's own accord

Antriebskraft f (Tech) power

antrinken ['antrɪŋkən] unreg vt (Flasche, Glas) to start to drink from; **sich** dat **Mut/einen Rausch ~** to give o.s. Dutch courage/get drunk; **angetrunken sein** to be tipsy

Antritt ['antrɪt] m beginning, commencement; (eines Amts) taking up

antun ['antu:n] unreg vt: **jdm etw ~** to do sth to sb; **sich** dat **Zwang ~** to force o.s.

anturnen ['antœrnən] (umg) vt = **antörnen**

Antwerpen [ant'vɛrpən] (-s) nt Antwerp

Antwort ['antvɔrt] (-, -en) f answer, reply; **um ~ wird gebeten** RSVP

antworten vi to answer, reply

anvertrauen ['anfɛrtraʊən] vt: **jdm etw ~** to entrust sb with sth; **sich jdm ~** to confide in sb

anvisieren ['anvizi:rən] vt (fig) to set one's sights on

anwachsen ['anvaksən] unreg vi to grow; (Pflanze) to take root

Anwalt ['anvalt] (-(e)s, -wälte) m solicitor; lawyer; (fig: Fürsprecher) advocate

Anwältin ['anvɛltɪn] f siehe **Anwalt**

Anwalts- zW: **Anwaltshonorar** nt retainer, retaining fee; **Anwaltskammer** f professional association of lawyers, ≈ Law Society (Brit); **Anwaltskosten** pl legal expenses pl

Anwandlung ['anvandlʊŋ] f caprice; **eine ~ von etw** a fit of sth

anwärmen ['anvɛrmən] vt to warm up

Anwärter, in ['anvɛrtər(ɪn)] m(f) candidate

anweisen ['anvaɪzən] unreg vt to instruct; (zuteilen) to assign

Anweisung f instruction; (Comm) remittance; (Postanweisung, Zahlungsanweisung) money order

anwendbar ['anvɛntba:r] adj practicable, applicable

anwenden ['anvɛndən] unreg vt to use, employ; (Gesetz, Regel) to apply

Anwenderprogramm ['anvɛndər] nt (Comput) application program

Anwendersoftware f application package

Anwendung f use; (auch Comput) application, app

anwerfen ['anvɛrfən] unreg vt (Tech) to start up

anwesend ['anve:zənt] adj present; **die A~en** those present

Anwesenheit f presence

Anwesenheitsliste f attendance register

anwidern ['anvi:dərn] vt to disgust

Anwohner, in ['anvo:nər(ɪn)] (-s, -) m(f) resident

Anwuchs ['anvu:ks] m growth

Anzahl ['antsa:l] f: **~ (an** +dat) number (of)

anzahlen vt to pay on account

Anzahlung f deposit, payment on account

anzapfen ['antsapfən] vt to tap

Anzeichen ['antsaɪçən] nt sign, indication; **alle ~ deuten darauf hin, dass ...** all the signs are that ...

Anzeige ['antsaɪgə] (-, -n) f (Zeitungsanzeige) announcement; (Werbung) advertisement; (Comput) display; (bei Polizei) report; **gegen jdn ~ erstatten** to report sb to the police

anzeigen vt (zu erkennen geben) to show; (bekannt geben) to announce; (bei Polizei) to report

Anzeigenteil m advertisements pl

anzeigepflichtig adj notifiable

Anzeiger m indicator

a

anzetteln ['antsɛtəln] (umg) vt to instigate
anziehen ['antsi:ən] unreg vt to attract;
(Kleidung) to put on; (Mensch) to dress;
(Schraube, Seil) to pull tight; (Knie) to draw up;
(Feuchtigkeit) to absorb ▷ vr to get dressed
anziehend adj attractive
Anziehung f (Reiz) attraction
Anziehungskraft f power of attraction; (Phys)
force of gravitation
Anzug ['antsu:k] m suit; **im ~ sein** to be
approaching
anzüglich ['antsy:klıç] adj personal; (anstößig)
offensive; **Anzüglichkeit** f offensiveness;
(Bemerkung) personal remark
anzünden ['antsyndən] vt to light
Anzünder m lighter
anzweifeln ['antsvaɪfəln] vt to doubt
AOK (-) f abk (= Allgemeine Ortskrankenkasse) siehe
Ortskrankenkasse; see culture note

AOK

The AOK (Allgemeine Ortskrankenkasse)
forms part of a compulsory medical
insurance scheme for people who are not
members of a private scheme. In every
large town there is an independently run
AOK office. Foreign nationals may also
receive help from these offices if they fall
ill while in Germany.

APA f abk (= Austria Presse-Agentur) Austrian news
agency
apart [a'part] adj distinctive
Apartheid [a'pa:rthaɪt] f apartheid
Apartment [a'partmənt] (-s, -s) nt flat (Brit),
apartment (bes US)
Apathie [apa'ti:] f apathy
apathisch [a'pa:tɪʃ] adj apathetic
Apenninen [apɛ'ni:nən] pl Apennines pl
Apfel ['apfəl] (-s, ¨) m apple; **in den sauren
~ beißen** (fig: umg) to swallow the bitter pill;
etw für einen ~ und ein Ei kaufen (umg) to
buy sth dirt cheap od for a song; **Apfelmus** nt
apple purée; (als Beilage) apple sauce; **Apfelsaft**
m apple juice
Apfelsine [apfəl'zi:nə] (-, -n) f orange
Apfeltasche f apple turnover
Apfelwein m strong cider
apl. abk = **außerplanmäßig**
APO, Apo ['a:po] (-) f abk (= außerparlamentarische
Opposition) extraparliamentary opposition; see culture
note

APO

The APO was an extraparliamentary
opposition group formed in West
Germany in the late 1960's by those who
felt that their interests were not being
sufficiently represented in parliament. It
was disbanded in the 1970's. Some of its
members then formed the RAF, a terrorist

organisation. Some formed the Green
Party (die Grünen).

apolitisch ['apoli:tɪʃ] adj non-political,
apolitical
Apostel [a'pɔstəl] (-s, -) m apostle
Apostroph [apo'stro:f] (-s, -e) m apostrophe
Apotheke [apo'te:kə] (-, -n) f chemist's (shop)
(Brit), drugstore (US); see culture note

APOTHEKE

The Apotheke is a pharmacy where
prescribed drugs and other medicines only
available on prescription are sold. It also
sells toiletries. The pharmacist is qualified
to give advice on medicines and treatment.

Apotheker, in (-s, -) m(f) pharmacist,
(dispensing) chemist (Brit), druggist (US)
Appalachen [apa'laxən] pl Appalachian
Mountains pl
Apparat [apa'ra:t] (-(e)s, -e) m piece of
apparatus; (Fotoapparat) camera; (Telefon)
telephone; (Rundf, TV) set; (Verwaltungsapparat,
Parteiapparat) machinery, apparatus; **am ~**
on the phone; (als Antwort) speaking; **am ~
bleiben** to hold the line
Apparatur [apara'tu:r] f apparatus
Appartement [apart(ə)'ma ̃:] (-s, -s) nt flat
(Brit), apartment (bes US)
Appell [a'pɛl] (-s, -e) m (Mil) muster, parade;
(fig) appeal
appellieren [apɛ'li:rən] vi: **~ (an** +akk) to appeal
(to)
Appetit [ape'ti:t] (-(e)s, -e) m appetite; **guten
~!** enjoy your meal; **appetitlich** adj appetizing;
Appetitlosigkeit f lack of appetite
Applaus [ap'laʊs] (-es, -e) m applause
Appretur [apre'tu:r] f finish;
(Wasserundurchlässigkeit) waterproofing
approbiert [apro'bi:rt] adj (Arzt) registered,
certified
Apr. abk (= April) Apr.
Aprikose [apri'ko:zə] (-, -n) f apricot
April [a'prɪl] (-(s), -e) (pl selten) m April; **jdn in
den ~ schicken** to make an April fool of sb;
siehe auch **September**; **Aprilwetter** nt April
showers pl
apropos [apro'po:] adv by the way, that
reminds me
Aquaplaning [akva'pla:nɪŋ] (-(s)) nt
aquaplaning
Aquarell [akva'rɛl] (-s, -e) nt watercolour (Brit),
watercolor (US)
Aquarium [a'kva:riʊm] nt aquarium
Äquator [ɛ'kva:tɔr] (-s) m equator
Äquivalent [ɛkviva'lɛnt] (-(e)s, -e) nt
equivalent
Ar [a:r] (-s, -e) nt od m (Maß) are (100 m²)
Ära ['ɛ:ra] (-, **Ären**) f era
Araber, in ['a:rabər(ɪn)] (-s, -) m(f) Arab
Arabien [a'ra:biən] (-s) nt Arabia

arabisch adj Arab; (*Arabien betreffend*) Arabian; (*Sprache*) Arabic; **A~er Golf** Arabian Gulf; **A~es Meer** Arabian Sea; **A~e Wüste** Arabian Desert

Arbeit ['arbaıt] (-, -en) f work; (*Stelle*) job; (*Erzeugnis*) piece of work; (*wissenschaftliche*) dissertation; (*Klassenarbeit*) test; **Tag der ~** Labour (*Brit*) od Labor (*US*) Day; **sich an die ~ machen, an die ~ gehen** to get down to work, start working; **jdm ~ machen** (*Mühe*) to put sb to trouble; **das war eine ~** that was a hard job

arbeiten vi to work ▷ vt to make ▷ vr: **sich nach oben/an die Spitze ~** (*fig*) to work one's way up/to the top

Arbeiter, in (-s, -) m(f) worker; (*ungelernt*) labourer (*Brit*), laborer (*US*)

Arbeiter- zW: **Arbeiterfamilie** f working-class family; **Arbeiterkammer** f (*Österr*) Chambers of Labour; **Arbeiterkind** nt child from a working-class family; **Arbeitermitbestimmung** f employee participation; **Arbeiterschaft** f workers pl, labour (*Brit*) od labor (*US*) force; **Arbeiterselbstkontrolle** f workers' control; **Arbeiter-und-Bauern-Staat** m (DDR) workers' and peasants' state; **Arbeiterwohlfahrt** f workers' welfare association

Arbeit- zW: **Arbeitgeber** (-s, -) m employer; **Arbeitnehmer** (-s, -) m employee

Arbeitsagentur f job agency

Arbeits- in zW labour (*Brit*), labor (*US*); **arbeitsam** adj industrious

Arbeits- zW**: **Arbeitsamt** nt employment exchange, Job Centre (*Brit*); **Arbeitsaufwand** m expenditure of energy; (*Industrie*) use of labour (*Brit*) od labor (*US*); **Arbeitsbedingungen** pl working conditions pl; **Arbeitsbeschaffung** f (*Arbeitsplatzbeschaffung*) job creation; **Arbeitserlaubnis** f work permit; **arbeitsfähig** adj fit for work, able-bodied; **Arbeitsgang** m operation; **Arbeitsgemeinschaft** f study group; **Arbeitsgericht** nt industrial tribunal; **arbeitsintensiv** adj labour-intensive (*Brit*), labor-intensive (*US*); **Arbeitskonflikt** m industrial dispute; **Arbeitskraft** f worker; **Arbeitskräfte** pl workers pl, labour (*Brit*), labor (*US*); **arbeitslos** adj unemployed, out-of-work; **Arbeitslosengeld** nt unemployment benefit; **Arbeitslosenhilfe** f supplementary benefit; **Arbeitslosenunterstützung** f unemployment benefit; **Arbeitslosenversicherung** f compulsory insurance against unemployment; **Arbeitslosigkeit** f unemployment; **Arbeitsmarkt** m job market; **Arbeitsmoral** f attitude to work; (*in Betrieb*) work climate; **Arbeitsniederlegung** f walkout; **Arbeitsplatte** f (*Küche*) work-top, work surface; **Arbeitsplatz** m place of work; (*Stelle*) job; **Arbeitsplatzrechner** m (*Comput*) work station; **Arbeitsplatzverlust** m job loss; **Arbeitsrecht** nt industrial law; **arbeitsscheu** adj workshy; **Arbeitsschutz** m maintenance of health and safety standards at work; **Arbeitstag** m work(ing) day; **Arbeitsteilung** f division of labour (*Brit*) od

labor (*US*); **Arbeitstier** nt (*fig: umg*) glutton for work, workaholic; **arbeitsunfähig** adj unfit for work; **Arbeitsunfall** m industrial accident; **Arbeitsverhältnis** nt employee-employer relationship; **Arbeitsvermittler**, in m(f): **(privater) Arbeitsvermittler** employment officer, job placement officer; **Arbeitsvermittlung** f (*Amt*) employment exchange; (*privat*) employment agency; **Arbeitsvertrag** m contract of employment; **Arbeitszeit** f working hours pl; **Arbeitszeitkonto** nt record of hours worked; **Arbeitszeitmodell** nt model of working hours; **Arbeitszeitregelung** f regulation of working hours; **Arbeitszeitverkürzung** f reduction in working hours; **Arbeitszimmer** nt study

Archäologe [arçeo'lo:gə] (-n, -n) m arch(a)eologist

Archäologin [arçeo'lo:gın] f arch(a)eologist

Arche ['arçə] (-, -n) f: **die ~ Noah** Noah's Ark

Architekt, in [arçi'tɛkt(ın)] (-en, -en) m(f) architect

architektonisch [arçitɛk'to:nıʃ] adj architectural

Architektur [arçitɛk'tu:r] f architecture

Archiv [ar'çi:f] (-s, -e) nt archive

ARD f archive; *see culture note*

Arena [a're:na] (-, Arenen) f (*lit, fig*) arena; (*Zirkusarena, Stierkampfarena*) ring

arg [ark] adj bad, awful ▷ adv awfully, very; **es zu ~ treiben** to go too far

Argentinien [argɛn'ti:niən] (-s) nt Argentina, the Argentine

Argentinier, in (-s, -) m(f) Argentine, Argentinian (*Brit*), Argentinean (*US*)

argentinisch [argɛn'ti:nıʃ] adj Argentine, Argentinian (*Brit*), Argentinean (*US*)

Ärger ['ɛrgər] (-s) m (*Wut*) anger; (*Unannehmlichkeit*) trouble; **jdm ~ machen** od **bereiten** to cause sb a lot of trouble od bother; **ärgerlich** adj (*zornig*) angry; (*lästig*) annoying, aggravating

ärgern vt to annoy ▷ vr to get annoyed

Ärgernis (-ses, -se) nt annoyance; (*Anstoß*) offence (*Brit*), offense (*US*), outrage; **öffentliches ~ erregen** to be a public nuisance

arg- zW: **arglistig** adj cunning, insidious;

a

arglistige Täuschung fraud; **arglos** *adj* guileless, innocent; **Arglosigkeit** *f* guilelessness, innocence

Argument [argu'ment] *nt* argument

argumentieren [argumɛn'ti:rən] *vi* to argue

Argusauge ['argʊs|aʊgə] *nt* (*geh*): **mit ~n** eagle-eyed

Argwohn *m* suspicion

argwöhnisch *adj* suspicious

Arie ['a:riə] *f* aria

Aristokrat, in [arɪsto'kra:t(ɪn)] (**-en, -en**) *m(f)* aristocrat

Aristokratie [arɪstokra:'ti:] *f* aristocracy

aristokratisch *adj* aristocratic

arithmetisch [arɪt'me:tɪʃ] *adj* arithmetical; **~es Mittel** arithmetic mean

Arkaden [ar'ka:dən] *pl* (*Bogengang*) arcade *sing*

Arktis ['arktɪs] (**-**) *f* Arctic

arktisch *adj* Arctic

arm [arm] *adj* poor; **~ dran sein** (*umg*) to have a hard time of it

Arm (**-(e)s, -e**) *m* arm; (*Flussarm*) branch; **jdn auf den ~ nehmen** (*fig: umg*) to pull sb's leg; **jdm unter die ~e greifen** (*fig*) to help sb out; **einen langen/die längeren ~ haben** (*fig*) to have a lot of/more pull (*umg*) *od* influence

Armatur [arma'tu:r] *f* (*Elek*) armature

Armaturenbrett *nt* instrument panel; (*Aut*) dashboard

Armband *nt* bracelet; **Armbanduhr** *f* (wrist) watch

Arme, r *f(m)* poor man/woman; **die ~n** the poor

Armee [ar'me:] (**-, -n**) *f* army; **Armeekorps** *nt* army corps

Ärmel ['ɛrməl] (**-s, -**) *m* sleeve; **etw aus dem ~ schütteln** (*fig*) to produce sth just like that

Ärmelkanal *m* (English) Channel

Armenien [ar'me:niən] (**-s**) *nt* Armenia

Armenier, in [ar'me:niər(ɪn)] (**-s, -**) *m(f)* Armenian

armenisch [ar'me:nɪʃ] *adj* Armenian

Armenrecht *nt* (*Jur*) legal aid

Armer *m* siehe **Arme(r)**

Armlehne *f* armrest

Armleuchter (*pej: umg*) *m* (*Dummkopf*) twit (*Brit*), fool

ärmlich ['ɛrmlɪç] *adj* poor; **aus ~en Verhältnissen** from a poor family

armselig *adj* wretched, miserable; (*mitleiderregend*) pathetic, pitiful

Armut ['armu:t] (**-**) *f* poverty

Armutsgrenze *f* poverty line

Armutsrisiko *nt* poverty risk

Armutszeugnis *nt* (*fig*): **jdm/sich ein ~ ausstellen** to show sb's/one's shortcomings

Aroma [a'ro:ma] (**-s, Aromen**) *nt* aroma; **Aromatherapie** *f* aromatherapy

aromatisch [aro'ma:tɪʃ] *adj* aromatic

arrangieren [araˑ'ʒi:rən] *vt* to arrange ▷ *vr* to come to an arrangement

Arrest [a'rɛst] (**-(e)s, -e**) *m* detention

arretieren [are'ti:rən] *vt* (*Tech*) to lock (in place)

arrogant [aro'gant] *adj* arrogant

Arroganz *f* arrogance

Arsch [arʃ] (**-es, ¨e**) (*umg!*) *m* arse (!); **leck mich am ~!** (*lass mich in Ruhe*) get stuffed! (!), fuck off! (!); **am ~ der Welt** (*umg*) in the back of beyond; **Arschkriecher** (*umg!*) *m* arse licker (!), crawler; **Arschloch** (*umg!*) *nt* (*Mensch*) bastard (!)

Arsen [ar'ze:n] (**-s**) *nt* arsenic

Art [a:rt] (**-, -en**) *f* (*Weise*) way; (*Sorte*) kind, sort; (*Biol*) species; **eine ~ (von) Frucht** a kind of fruit; **Häuser aller ~** houses of all kinds; **einzig in seiner ~ sein** to be the only one of its kind, be unique; **auf diese ~ und Weise** in this way; **das ist doch keine ~!** that's no way to behave!; **es ist nicht seine ~, das zu tun** it's not like him to do that; **ich mache das auf meine ~** I do that my (own) way; **Schnitzel nach ~ des Hauses** chef's special escalope

arten *vi*: **nach jdm ~** to take after sb; **der Mensch ist so geartet, dass ...** human nature is such that ...

Artenschutz *m* protection of endangered species

Arterie [ar'te:riə] *f* artery

Arterienverkalkung *f* arteriosclerosis

Artgenosse ['a:rtgənɔsə] *m* animal/plant of the same species; (*Mensch*) person of the same type

Arthritis [ar'tri:tɪs] (**-, -ritiden**) *f* arthritis

artig ['a:rtɪç] *adj* good, well-behaved

Artikel [ar'ti:kəl] (**-s, -**) *m* article

Artillerie [artɪlə'ri:] *f* artillery

Artischocke [arti'ʃɔkə] (**-, -n**) *f* artichoke

Artistik [ar'tɪstɪk] (**-**) *f* artistry; (*Zirkus-/ Varietékunst*) circus/variety performing

Arznei [a:rts'naɪ] *f* medicine; **Arzneimittel** *nt* medicine, medicament

Arzt [a:rtst] (**-es, ¨e**) *m* doctor; **praktischer ~** general practitioner, GP

Ärztekammer *f* ≈ General Medical Council (*Brit*), State Medical Board of Registration (*US*)

Arzthelferin *f* doctor's assistant

Ärztin ['ɛ:rtstɪn] *f* woman doctor; *siehe auch* **Arzt**

ärztlich ['ɛ:rtstlɪç] *adj* medical

Arztpraxis *f* doctor's practice; (*Räume*) doctor's surgery (*Brit*) *od* office (*US*)

As [as] (**-ses, -se**) *nt* (*Mus*) A flat; *siehe auch* **Ass**

Asbest [as'bɛst] (**-(e)s, -e**) *m* asbestos

Asche ['aʃə] (**-, -n**) *f* ash

Aschen- *zW*: **Aschenbahn** *f* cinder track; **Aschenbecher** *m* ashtray; **Aschenbrödel** *nt* (*Liter, fig*) Cinderella; **Aschenputtel** *nt* (*Liter, fig*) Cinderella

Aschermittwoch *m* Ash Wednesday

Aserbaidschan [azɛrbaɪ'dʒa:n] (**-s**) *nt* Azerbaijan

aserbaidschanisch *adj* Azerbaijani

Asiat, in [azi'a:t(ɪn)] (**-en, -en**) *m(f)* Asian

asiatisch *adj* Asian, Asiatic

Asien ['a:ziən] (**-s**) *nt* Asia

asozial ['azotsia:l] *adj* antisocial; (*Familie*) asocial

Asoziale, r (*pej*) *f(m) dekl wie adj* antisocial person; **Asoziale** *pl* antisocial elements

Aspekt [as'pɛkt] (**-(e)s, -e**) *m* aspect

Asphalt [as'falt] (**-(e)s, -e**) *m* asphalt

asphaltieren [asfal'ti:rən] *vt* to asphalt

Asphaltstraße *f* asphalt road

aß *etc* [a:s] *vb siehe* **essen**

Ass [as] (**-es, -e**) *nt* ace

Ass. *abk* = **Assessor**

Assekurant, in [aseku'rant(ɪn)] (**-en, -en**) *m(f)* underwriter

Assemblersprache [ə'sɛmblərʃpra:xə] *f* (*Comput*) assembly language

Assessor, in [a'sɛsɔr, -'so:rɪn] (**-s, -en**) *m(f)* graduate civil servant who has completed his/her traineeship

Assistent, in [asɪs'tɛnt(ɪn)] *m(f)* assistant

Assistenzarzt [asɪs'tɛntsa:rtst] *m* houseman (*Brit*), intern (*US*)

Assoziation [asotsiatsi'o:n] *f* association

assoziieren [asotsi'i:rən] *vt* (*geh*) to associate

Ast [ast] (**-(e)s, ̈-e**) *m* branch; **sich** *dat* **einen ~ lachen** (*umg*) to double up (with laughter)

AStA ['asta] (**-(s), -(s)**) *m abk* (= *Allgemeiner Studentenausschuss*) *students' association*

ästhetisch [ɛs'te:tɪʃ] *adj* aesthetic (*Brit*), esthetic (*US*)

Asthma ['astma] (**-s**) *nt* asthma

Asthmatiker, in [ast'ma:tikər(ɪn)] (**-s, -**) *m(f)* asthmatic

astrein ['astraɪn] *adj* (*fig: umg: moralisch einwandfrei*) straight, on the level; (: *echt*) genuine; (*prima*) fantastic

Astrologe [astro'lo:gə] (**-n, -n**) *m* astrologer

Astrologie [astrolo'gi:] *f* astrology

Astrologin *f* astrologer

Astronaut, in [astro'naʊt(ɪn)] (**-en, -en**) *m(f)* astronaut

Astronautik *f* astronautics

Astronom, in [astro'no:m(ɪn)] (**-en, -en**) *m(f)* astronomer

Astronomie [astrono'mi:] *f* astronomy

ASU *f abk* (= *Arbeitsgemeinschaft selbstständiger Unternehmer*) association of private traders; (= *Abgassonderuntersuchung*) exhaust emission test

ASW *f abk* (= *außersinnliche Wahrnehmung*) ESP

Asyl [a'zy:l] (**-s, -e**) *nt* asylum; (*Heim*) home; (*Obdachlosenasyl*) shelter

Asylant, in [azy'lant(ɪn)] (**-en, -en**) *m(f)* person seeking (political) asylum

Asylrecht *nt* (*Pol*) right of (political) asylum

A.T. *abk* (= *Altes Testament*) O.T.

Atelier [atəli'e:] (**-s, -s**) *nt* studio

Atem ['a:təm] (**-s**) *m* breath; **den ~ anhalten** to hold one's breath; **außer ~** out of breath; **jdn in ~ halten** to keep sb in suspense *od* on tenterhooks; **das verschlug mir den ~** it took my breath away; **einen langen/den längeren ~ haben** to have a lot of staying power; **atemberaubend** *adj* breathtaking;

atemlos *adj* breathless; **Atempause** *f* breather; **Atemwege** *pl* (*Anat*) respiratory tract; **Atemzug** *m* breath

Atheismus [ate'ɪsmʊs] *m* atheism

Atheist, in *m(f)* atheist; **atheistisch** *adj* atheistic

Athen [a'te:n] (**-s**) *nt* Athens

Athener, in (**-s, -**) *m(f)* Athenian

Äther ['ɛ:tər] (**-s, -**) *m* ether

Äthiopien [ɛti'o:piən] (**-s**) *nt* Ethiopia

Äthiopier, in (**-s, -**) *m(f)* Ethiopian

äthiopisch *adj* Ethiopian

Athlet, in [at'le:t(ɪn)] (**-en, -en**) *m(f)* athlete

Athletik *f* athletics *sing*

Atlantik [at'lantɪk] (**-s**) *m* Atlantic

atlantisch *adj* Atlantic; **der A~e Ozean** the Atlantic Ocean

Atlas ['atlas] (**-** *od* **-ses, -se** *od* **Atlanten**) *m* atlas; **Atlasgebirge** *nt* Atlas Mountains *pl*

atmen ['a:tmən] *vt, vi* to breathe

Atmosphäre [atmo'sfɛ:rə] (**-, -n**) *f* atmosphere

atmosphärisch *adj* atmospheric

Atmung ['a:tmʊŋ] *f* respiration

Ätna ['ɛ:tna] (**-(s)**) *m* Etna

Atom [a'to:m] (**-s, -e**) *nt* atom

atomar [ato'ma:r] *adj* atomic, nuclear; (*Drohung*) nuclear

Atom- *zW:* **Atombombe** *f* atom bomb; **Atomenergie** *f* nuclear *od* atomic energy; **Atomgegner** *m:* **Atomgegner sein** to be antinuclear; **Atomkern** *m* atomic nucleus; **Atomkraft** *f* nuclear power; **Atomkraftwerk** *nt* nuclear power station; **Atomkrieg** *m* nuclear *od* atomic war; **Atomlobby** *f* nuclear lobby; **Atommacht** *f* nuclear *od* atomic power; **Atommeiler** *m* nuclear reactor; **Atommüll** *m* nuclear waste; **Atomphysik** *f* nuclear physics *sing*; **Atompilz** *m* mushroom cloud; **Atomsperrvertrag** *m* (*Pol*) nuclear non-proliferation treaty; **Atomsprengkopf** *m* nuclear *od* atomic warhead; **Atomstrom** *m electricity generated by nuclear power*; **Atomtest** *m* nuclear test; **Atomtestgelände** *nt* nuclear testing range; **Atomwaffen** *pl* nuclear *od* atomic weapons *pl*; **atomwaffenfrei** *adj* (*Zone*) nuclear-free; **Atomwirtschaft** *f* nuclear industry; **Atomzeitalter** *nt* atomic age

Attachment [ə'tɛtʃmɛnt] *nt* (*Comput*) attachment

Attacke [a'takə] (**-, -n**) *f* (*Angriff*) attack

Attentat [atɛn'ta:t] (**-(e)s, -e**) *nt:* **~ (auf +akk)** (attempted) assassination (of)

Attentäter, in [atɛn'tɛ:tər(ɪn)] (**-s, -**) *m(f)* (would-be) assassin

Attest [a'tɛst] (**-(e)s, -e**) *nt* certificate

Attraktion [atraktsi'o:n] *f* attraction

attraktiv [atrak'ti:f] *adj* attractive

Attrappe [a'trapə] (**-, -n**) *f* dummy; **bei ihr ist alles ~** everything about her is false

Attribut [atri'bu:t] (**-(e)s, -e**) *nt* (*Gram*) attribute

At-Zeichen ['attsaɪçən] *nt* (*Comput*) at symbol

ätzen ['ɛtsən] *vi* to be caustic

ätzend *adj* (*lit: Säure*) corrosive; (*Geruch*) pungent; (*fig: umg: furchtbar*) dreadful, horrible

a

⊙ SCHLÜSSELWORT

auch [aʊx] *adv* **1** *(ebenfalls)* also, too, as well; **das ist auch schön** that's nice too *od* as well; **er kommt — ich auch** he's coming — so am I *od* me too; **auch nicht** not ... either; **ich auch nicht** nor I, me neither; **oder auch** or; **auch das noch!** not that as well!; **nicht nur ..., sondern auch ...** not only ... but also ...
2 *(selbst, sogar)* even; **auch wenn das Wetter schlecht ist** even if the weather is bad; **ohne auch nur zu fragen** without even asking
3 *(wirklich)* really; **du siehst müde aus — bin ich auch** you look tired — (so) I am; **so sieht es auch aus** (and) that's what it looks like
4 *(auch immer)*: **wer auch** whoever; **was auch** whatever; **wozu auch?** *(emphatisch)* whatever for?; **wie dem auch sei** be that as it may; **wie sehr er sich auch bemühte** however much he tried

Audienz [aʊdiˈɛnts] **(-, -en)** *f (bei Papst, König etc)* audience
Audimax [aʊdiˈmaks] *nt (Univ: umg)* main lecture hall
audiovisuell [aʊdiovizuˈɛl] *adj* audiovisual
Auditorium [aʊdiˈtoːriʊm] *nt (Hörsaal)* lecture hall; *(geh: Zuhörerschaft)* audience

⊙ SCHLÜSSELWORT

auf [aʊf] *präp +dat (wo?)* on; **auf dem Tisch** on the table; **auf der Reise** on the way; **auf der Post/dem Fest** at the post office/party; **auf der Straße** on the road; **auf dem Land/ der ganzen Welt** in the country/the whole world; **was hat es damit auf sich?** what does it mean?
▷ *präp +akk* **1** *(wohin?)* on(to); **auf den Tisch** on(to) the table; **auf die Post gehen** to go to the post office; **auf das Land** into the country; **etw auf einen Zettel schreiben** to write sth on a piece of paper; **auf eine Tasse Kaffee/eine Zigarette(nlänge)** for a cup of coffee/a smoke; **die Nacht (von Montag) auf Dienstag** Monday night; **auf einen Polizisten kommen 1.000 Bürger** there is one policeman to every 1,000 citizens
2: **auf Deutsch** in German; **auf meine/seine Lebenszeit** for my/his lifetime; **bis auf ihn** except for him; **auf einmal** at once; **auf seinen Vorschlag (hin)** at his suggestion
▷ *adv* **1** *(offen)* open; **auf sein** to be open; **das Fenster ist auf** the window is open
2 *(hinauf)* up; **auf und ab** up and down; **auf und davon** up and away; **auf!** *(los!)* come on!; **von klein auf** from childhood onwards
3 *(aufgestanden)* up; **auf sein** *(Person)* to be up; **ist er schon auf?** is he up yet?
▷ *konj*: **auf dass** (so) that

aufarbeiten [ˈaʊf|arbaɪtən] *vt (erledigen: Korrespondenz etc)* to catch up with
aufatmen [ˈaʊf|a:tmən] *vi* to heave a sigh of relief
aufbahren [ˈaʊfba:rən] *vt* to lay out
Aufbau [ˈaʊfbaʊ] *m (Bauen)* building, construction; *(Struktur)* structure; *(aufgebautes Teil)* superstructure
aufbauen [ˈaʊfbaʊən] *vt* to erect, build (up); *(Existenz)* to make; *(gestalten)* to construct; *(gründen)*: **~ (auf +dat)** to found (on), base (on)
▷ *vr*: **sich vor jdm ~** to draw o.s. up to one's full height in front of sb
aufbäumen [ˈaʊfbɔʏmən] *vr* to rear; *(fig)* to revolt, rebel
aufbauschen [ˈaʊfbaʊʃən] *vt* to puff out; *(fig)* to exaggerate
aufbegehren [ˈaʊfbəge:rən] *vi (geh)* to rebel
aufbehalten [ˈaʊfbəhaltən] *unreg vt* to keep on
aufbekommen [ˈaʊfbəkɔmən] *unreg (umg) vt (öffnen)* to get open; (: *Hausaufgaben*) to be given
aufbereiten [ˈaʊfbəraɪtən] *vt* to process; *(Trinkwasser)* to purify; *(Text etc)* to work up
Aufbereitungsanlage *f* processing plant
aufbessern [ˈaʊfbɛsərn] *vt (Gehalt)* to increase
aufbewahren [ˈaʊfbəva:rən] *vt* to keep; *(Gepäck)* to put in the left-luggage office
Aufbewahrung *f* (safe)keeping; *(Gepäckaufbewahrung)* left-luggage office (Brit), baggage check (US); **jdm etw zur ~ geben** to give sb sth for safekeeping
Aufbewahrungsort *m* storage place
aufbieten [ˈaʊfbi:tən] *unreg vt (Kraft)* to summon (up); *(Armee, Polizei)* to mobilize
Aufbietung *f*: **unter ~ aller Kräfte ...** summoning (up) all his/her *etc* strength ...
aufbinden [ˈaʊfbɪndən] *unreg vt*: **lass dir doch so etwas nicht ~** *(fig)* don't fall for that
aufblähen [ˈaʊfblɛ:ən] *vr* to blow out; *(Segel)* to billow out; *(Med)* to become swollen; *(fig: pej)* to puff o.s. up
aufblasen [ˈaʊfbla:zən] *unreg vt* to blow up, inflate ▷ *vr (umg)* to become big-headed
aufbleiben [ˈaʊfblaɪbən] *unreg vi (Laden)* to remain open; *(Person)* to stay up
aufblenden [ˈaʊfblɛndən] *vt (Scheinwerfer)* to turn on full beam
aufblicken [ˈaʊfblɪkən] *vi* to look up; **~ zu** *(lit)* to look up at; *(fig)* to look up to
aufblühen [ˈaʊfbly:ən] *vi* to blossom; *(fig)* to blossom, flourish
aufblühend *adj (Comm)* booming
aufbocken [ˈaʊfbɔkən] *vt (Auto)* to jack up
aufbrauchen [ˈaʊfbraʊxən] *vt* to use up
aufbrausen [ˈaʊfbraʊzən] *vi (fig)* to flare up
aufbrausend *adj* hot-tempered
aufbrechen [ˈaʊfbrɛçən] *unreg vt* to break open, to prise (Brit) *od* pry (US) open ▷ *vi* to burst open; *(gehen)* to start, set off
aufbringen [ˈaʊfbrɪŋən] *unreg vt (öffnen)* to open; *(in Mode)* to bring into fashion; *(beschaffen)* to procure; *(Fin)* to raise; *(ärgern)* to irritate; **Verständnis für etw ~** to be able to

understand sth

Aufbruch ['aʊfbrʊx] m departure

aufbrühen ['aʊfbryːən] vt (Tee) to make

aufbrummen ['aʊfbrʊmən] (umg) vt: **jdm die Kosten** ~ to land sb with the costs

aufbürden ['aʊfbʏrdən] vt: **jdm etw** ~ to burden sb with sth

aufdecken ['aʊfdɛkən] vt to uncover; (Spielkarten) to show

aufdrängen ['aʊfdrɛŋən] vt: **jdm etw** ~ to force sth on sb ▷ vr: **sich jdm** ~ to intrude on sb

aufdrehen ['aʊfdreːən] vt (Wasserhahn etc) to turn on; (Ventil) to open; (Schraubverschluss) to unscrew; (Radio etc) to turn up; (Haar) to put in rollers

aufdringlich ['aʊfdrɪŋlɪç] adj pushy; (Benehmen) obtrusive; (Parfüm) powerful

aufeinander [aʊf|aɪ'nandər] adv on top of one another; (schießen) at each other; (warten) for one another; (vertrauen) each other; **Aufeinanderfolge** f succession, series; **aufeinanderfolgen** vi to follow one another; **aufeinanderfolgend** adj consecutive; **aufeinanderlegen** vt to lay on top of one another; **aufeinanderprallen** vi (Autos etc) to collide; (Truppen, Meinungen) to clash

Aufenthalt ['aʊf|ɛnthalt] m stay; (Verzögerung) delay; (Eisenb: Halten) stop; (Ort) haunt

Aufenthalts- zW: **Aufenthaltserlaubnis** f, **Aufenthaltsgenehmigung** f residence permit; **Aufenthaltsraum** m day room; (in Betrieb) recreation room

auferlegen ['aʊf|ɛrleːgən] vt: **(jdm)** ~ to impose (upon sb)

auferstehen ['aʊf|ɛrʃteːən] unreg vi untr to rise from the dead

Auferstehung f resurrection

aufessen ['aʊf|ɛsən] unreg vt to eat up

auffahren ['aʊffaːrən] unreg vi (herankommen) to draw up; (hochfahren) to jump up; (wütend werden) to flare up; (in den Himmel) to ascend ▷ vt (Kanonen, Geschütz) to bring up; ~ **auf** +akk (Auto) to run od crash into

auffahrend adj hot-tempered

Auffahrt f (Hausauffahrt) drive; (Autobahnauffahrt) slip road (Brit), entrance ramp (US)

Auffahrunfall m pile-up

auffallen ['aʊffalən] unreg vi to be noticeable; **angenehm/unangenehm** ~ to make a good/ bad impression; **jdm** ~ (bemerkt werden) to strike sb

auffallend adj striking

auffällig ['aʊffɛlɪç] adj conspicuous, striking

auffangen ['aʊffaŋən] unreg vt to catch; (Funkspruch) to intercept; (Preise) to peg; (abfangen: Aufprall etc) to cushion, absorb

Auffanglager nt reception camp

auffassen ['aʊffasən] vt to understand, comprehend; (auslegen) to see, view

Auffassung f (Meinung) opinion; (Auslegung) view, conception; (auch: **Auffassungsgabe**)

grasp

auffindbar ['aʊffɪntbaːr] adj to be found

aufflammen ['aʊfflamən] vi (lit, fig: Feuer, Unruhen etc) to flare up

auffliegen ['aʊffliːgən] unreg vi to fly up; (umg: Rauschgiftring etc) to be busted

auffordern ['aʊffɔrdərn] vt to challenge; (befehlen) to call upon, order; (bitten) to ask

Aufforderung f (Befehl) order; (Einladung) invitation

aufforsten ['aʊffɔrstən] vt (Gebiet) to reafforest; (Wald) to restock

auffrischen ['aʊffrɪʃən] vt to freshen up; (Kenntnisse) to brush up; (Erinnerungen) to reawaken ▷ vi (Wind) to freshen

aufführen ['aʊffyːrən] vt (Theat) to perform; (in einem Verzeichnis) to list, specify ▷ vr (sich benehmen) to behave; **einzeln** ~ to itemize

Aufführung f (Theat) performance; (Liste) specification

auffüllen ['aʊffʏlən] vt to fill up; (Vorräte) to replenish; (Öl) to top up

Aufgabe ['aʊfgaːbə] (-, -n) f task; (Sch) exercise; (Hausaufgabe) homework; (Verzicht) giving up; (von Gepäck) registration; (von Post) posting; (von Inserat) insertion; **sich** dat **etw zur** ~ **machen** to make sth one's job od business

aufgabeln ['aʊfgaːbəln] vt (fig: umg: jdn) to pick up; (: Sache) to get hold of

Aufgabenbereich m area of responsibility

Aufgang ['aʊfgaŋ] m ascent; (Sonnenaufgang) rise; (Treppe) staircase

aufgeben ['aʊfgeːbən] unreg vt (verzichten auf) to give up; (Paket etc) to send, post; (Gepäck) to register; (Bestellung) to give; (Inserat) to insert; (Rätsel, Problem) to set ▷ vi to give up

aufgeblasen ['aʊfgəblaːzən] adj (fig) puffed up, self-important

Aufgebot ['aʊfgəboːt] nt supply; (von Kräften) utilization; (Eheaufgebot) banns pl

aufgedonnert ['aʊfgədɔnərt] (pej: umg) adj tarted up

aufgedreht ['aʊfgədreːt] (umg) adj excited

aufgedunsen ['aʊfgədʊnzən] adj swollen, puffed up

aufgegeben ['aʊfgəgeːbən] pp von **aufgeben**

aufgehen ['aʊfgeːən] unreg vi (Sonne, Teig) to rise; (sich öffnen) to open; (Theat: Vorhang) to go up; (Knopf, Knoten etc) to come undone; (klar werden) to become clear; (Math) to come out exactly; ~ **(in** +dat) (sich widmen) to be absorbed (in); **in Rauch/Flammen** ~ to go up in smoke/flames

aufgeilen ['aʊfgaɪlən] (umg) vt to turn on ▷ vr to be turned on

aufgeklärt ['aʊfgəklɛːrt] adj enlightened; (sexuell) knowing the facts of life

aufgekratzt ['aʊfgəkratst] (umg) adj in high spirits, full of beans

aufgelaufen ['aʊfgəlaʊfən] adj: ~**e Zinsen** pl accrued interest sing

Aufgeld nt premium

aufgelegt ['aʊfgəleːkt] adj: **gut/schlecht** ~

sein to be in a good/bad mood; **zu etw ~ sein** to be in the mood for sth

aufgenommen ['aʊfgənɔmən] *pp von* **aufnehmen**

aufgeregt ['aʊfgəreːkt] *adj* excited

aufgeschlossen ['aʊfgəʃlɔsən] *adj* open, open-minded

aufgeschmissen ['aʊfgəʃmɪsən] (*umg*) *adj* in a fix, stuck

aufgeschrieben ['aʊfgəʃriːbən] *pp von* **aufschreiben**

aufgestanden ['aʊfgəʃtandən] *pp von* **aufstehen**

aufgetakelt ['aʊfgətaːkəlt] *adj* (*fig: umg*) dressed up to the nines

aufgeweckt ['aʊfgəvɛkt] *adj* bright, intelligent

aufgießen ['aʊfgiːsən] *unreg vt* (*Wasser*) to pour over; (*Tee*) to infuse

aufgliedern ['aʊfgliːdərn] *vr*: **sich ~ (in** +*akk*) to (sub)divide (into), break down (into)

aufgreifen ['aʊfgraɪfən] *unreg vt* (*Thema*) to take up; (*Verdächtige*) to pick up, seize

aufgrund, auf Grund [aʊf'grʊnt] *präp +gen*: **~ von** on the basis of; (*wegen*) because of

Aufgussbeutel ['aʊfgʊsbɔʏtəl] *m* sachet (containing coffee/herbs *etc*) for brewing; (*Teebeutel*) tea bag

aufhaben ['aʊfhaːbən] *unreg vt* (*Hut etc*) to have on; (*Arbeit*) to have to do

aufhalsen ['aʊfhalzən] (*umg*) *vt*: **jdm etw ~** to saddle *od* lumber sb with sth

aufhalten ['aʊfhaltən] *unreg vt* (*Person*) to detain; (*Entwicklung*) to check; (*Tür, Hand*) to hold open; (*Augen*) to keep open ▷ *vr* (*wohnen*) to live; (*bleiben*) to stay; **jdn (bei etw) ~** (*abhalten, stören*) to hold *od* keep sb back (from sth); **sich über etw/jdn ~** to go on about sth/sb; **sich mit etw ~** to waste time over sth; **sich bei etw ~** (*sich befassen*) to dwell on sth

aufhängen ['aʊfhɛŋən] *unreg vt* (*Wäsche*) to hang up; (*Menschen*) to hang ▷ *vr* to hang o.s.

Aufhänger (**-s, -**) *m* (*am Mantel*) hook; (*fig*) peg

Aufhängung *f* (*Tech*) suspension

aufheben ['aʊfheːbən] *unreg vt* (*hochheben*) to raise, lift; (*Sitzung*) to wind up; (*Urteil*) to annul; (*Gesetz*) to repeal, abolish; (*aufbewahren*) to keep; (*ausgleichen*) to offset, make up for ▷ *vr* to cancel itself out; **viel A~(s) machen (von)** to make a fuss (about); **bei jdm gut aufgehoben sein** to be well looked after at sb's

aufheitern ['aʊfhaɪtərn] *vt, vr* (*Himmel, Miene*) to brighten; (*Mensch*) to cheer up

Aufheiterungen *pl* (*Met*) bright periods *pl*

aufheizen ['aʊfhaɪtsən] *vt*: **die Stimmung ~** to stir up feelings

aufhelfen ['aʊfhɛlfən] *unreg vi* (*lit: beim Aufstehen*): **jdm ~** to help sb up

aufhellen ['aʊfhɛlən] *vt, vr* to clear up; (*Farbe, Haare*) to lighten

aufhetzen ['aʊfhɛtsən] *vt* to stir up

aufheulen ['aʊfhɔʏlən] *vi* to howl; (*Sirene*) to (start to) wail; (*Motor*) to (give a) roar

aufholen ['aʊfhoːlən] *vt* to make up ▷ *vi* to catch up

aufhorchen ['aʊfhɔrçən] *vi* to prick up one's ears

aufhören ['aʊfhøːrən] *vi* to stop; **~, etw zu tun** to stop doing sth

aufkaufen ['aʊfkaʊfən] *vt* to buy up

aufklappen ['aʊfklapən] *vt* to open; (*Verdeck*) to fold back

aufklären ['aʊfklɛːrən] *vt* (*Geheimnis etc*) to clear up; (*Person*) to enlighten; (*sexuell*) to tell the facts of life to; (*Mil*) to reconnoitre ▷ *vr* to clear up

Aufklärung *f* (*von Geheimnis*) clearing up; (*Unterrichtung, Zeitalter*) enlightenment; (*sexuell*) sex education; (*Mil, Aviat*) reconnaissance

Aufklärungsarbeit *f* educational work

aufkleben ['aʊfkleːbən] *vt* to stick on

Aufkleber (**-s, -**) *m* sticker

aufknöpfen ['aʊfknœpfən] *vt* to unbutton

aufkochen ['aʊfkɔxən] *vt* to bring to the boil

aufkommen ['aʊfkɔmən] *unreg vi* (*Wind*) to come up; (*Zweifel, Gefühl*) to arise; (*Mode*) to start; **für jdn/etw ~** to be liable *od* responsible for sb/sth; **für den Schaden ~** to pay for the damage; **endlich kam Stimmung auf** at last things livened up

aufkreuzen ['aʊfkrɔʏtsən] (*umg*) *vi* (*erscheinen*) to turn up *od* show up

aufkündigen ['aʊfkʏndɪgən] *vt* (*Vertrag etc*) to terminate

aufladen ['aʊflaːdən] *unreg vt* to load ▷ *vr* (*Batterie etc*) to be charged; (*neu aufladen*) to be recharged; **jdm/sich etw ~** (*fig*) to saddle sb/o.s. with sth

Auflage ['aʊflaːgə] *f* edition; (*Zeitung*) circulation; (*Bedingung*) condition; **jdm etw zur ~ machen** to make sth a condition for sb

Auflagehöhe, Auflagenhöhe *f* (*von Buch*) number of copies published; (*von Zeitung*) circulation

auflassen ['aʊflasən] *unreg* (*umg*) *vt* (*offen*) to leave open; (*: aufgesetzt*) to leave on; **die Kinder länger ~** to let the children stay up (longer)

auflauern ['aʊflaʊərn] *vi*: **jdm ~** to lie in wait for sb

Auflauf ['aʊflaʊf] *m* (*Koch*) pudding; (*Menschenauflauf*) crowd

auflaufen *unreg vi* (*auf Grund laufen: Schiff*) to run aground; **jdn ~ lassen** (*umg*) to drop sb in it

Auflaufform *f* (*Koch*) ovenproof dish

aufleben ['aʊfleːbən] *vi* to revive

auflegen ['aʊfleːgən] *vt* to put on; (*Hörer*) to put down; (*Typ*) to print ▷ *vi* (*Tel*) to hang up

auflehnen ['aʊfleːnən] *vt* to lean on ▷ *vr* to rebel

Auflehnung *f* rebellion

auflesen ['aʊfleːzən] *unreg vt* to pick up

aufleuchten ['aʊflɔʏçtən] *vi* to light up

aufliegen ['aʊfliːgən] *unreg vi* to lie on; (*Comm*) to be available

auflisten ['aʊflɪstən] *vt* (*auch Comput*) to list

auflockern ['aʊflɔkərn] vt to loosen; (fig: Eintönigkeit etc) to liven up; (entspannen, zwangloser machen) to make relaxed; (Atmosphäre) to make more relaxed, ease

auflösen ['aʊfløːzən] vt to dissolve; (Missverständnis) to sort out; (Konto) to close; (Firma) to wind up; (Haushalt) to break up; **in Tränen aufgelöst sein** to be in tears

Auflösung f dissolving; (fig) solution; (Bildschirm) resolution

aufmachen ['aʊfmaxən] vt to open; (Kleidung) to undo; (zurechtmachen) to do up ▷ vr to set out

Aufmacher m (Presse) lead

Aufmachung f (Kleidung) outfit, get-up; (Gestaltung) format

aufmerksam ['aʊfmɛrkzaːm] adj attentive; **auf etw** akk **~ werden** to become aware of sth; **jdn auf etw** akk **~ machen** to point sth out to sb; **(das ist) sehr ~ von Ihnen** (zuvorkommend) (that's) most kind of you; **Aufmerksamkeit** f attention, attentiveness; (Geschenk) token (gift)

aufmöbeln ['aʊfmøːbəln] (umg) vt (Gegenstand) to do up; (: beleben) to buck up, pep up

aufmucken ['aʊfmʊkən] (umg) vi: **~ gegen** to protest at od against

aufmuntern ['aʊfmʊntərn] vt (ermutigen) to encourage; (erheitern) to cheer up

aufmüpfig ['aʊfmʏpfɪç] (umg) adj rebellious

Aufnahme ['aʊfnaːmə] (-, -n) f reception; (Beginn) beginning; (in Verein etc) admission; (in Liste etc) inclusion; (Notieren) taking down; (Phot) shot; (auf Tonband etc) recording; **Aufnahmeantrag** m application for membership od admission; **aufnahmefähig** adj receptive; **Aufnahmeleiter** m (Film) production manager; (Rundf, TV) producer; **Aufnahmeprüfung** f entrance test; **Aufnahmestopp** m (für Flüchtlinge etc) freeze on immigration

aufnehmen ['aʊfneːmən] unreg vt to receive; (hochheben) to pick up; (beginnen) to take up; (in Verein etc) to admit; (in Liste etc) to include; (fassen) to hold; (begreifen) to take in, grasp; (beim Stricken: Maschen) to increase, make; (notieren) to take down; (fotografieren) to photograph; (auf Tonband, Platte) to record; (Fin: leihen) to take out; **es mit jdm ~ können** to be able to compete with sb

aufnötigen ['aʊfnøːtɪgən] vt: **jdm etw ~ to** force sth on sb

aufoktroyieren ['aʊfʔɔktroajiːrən] vt: **jdm etw ~** (geh) to impose od force sth on sb

aufopfern ['aʊfʔɔpfərn] vt to sacrifice ▷ vr to sacrifice o.s.

aufopfernd adj selfless

aufpassen ['aʊfpasən] vi (aufmerksam sein) to pay attention; **auf jdn/etw ~** to look after od watch sb/sth; **aufgepasst!** look out!

Aufpasser, in (-s, -) (pej) m(f) (Aufseher, Spitzel) spy, watchdog; (Beobachter) supervisor; (Wächter) guard

aufpflanzen ['aʊfpflantsən] vr: **sich vor jdm ~** to plant o.s. in front of sb

aufplatzen ['aʊfplatsən] vi to burst open

aufplustern ['aʊfpluːstərn] vr (Vogel) to ruffle (up) its feathers; (Mensch) to puff o.s. up

aufprägen ['aʊfprɛːgən] vt: **jdm/etw seinen Stempel ~** (fig) to leave one's mark on sb/sth

Aufprall ['aʊfpral] (-(e)s, -e) m impact

aufprallen vi to hit, strike

Aufpreis ['aʊfpraɪs] m extra charge

aufpumpen ['aʊfpʊmpən] vt to pump up

aufputschen ['aʊfpʊtʃən] vt (aufhetzen) to inflame; (erregen) to stimulate

Aufputschmittel nt stimulant

aufraffen ['aʊfrafən] vr to rouse o.s.

aufräumen ['aʊfrɔʏmən] vt, vi (Dinge) to clear away; (Zimmer) to tidy up

Aufräumungsarbeiten pl clearing-up operations pl

aufrecht ['aʊfrɛçt] adj (lit, fig) upright

aufrechterhalten unreg vt to maintain

aufregen ['aʊfreːgən] vt to excite; (ärgerlich machen) to irritate, annoy; (nervös machen) to make nervous; (beunruhigen) to disturb ▷ vr to get excited

aufregend adj exciting

Aufregung f excitement

aufreiben ['aʊfraɪbən] unreg vt (Haut) to rub raw; (erschöpfen) to exhaust; (Mil: völlig vernichten) to wipe out, annihilate

aufreibend adj strenuous

aufreihen ['aʊfraɪən] vt (in Linie) to line up; (Perlen) to string

aufreißen ['aʊfraɪsən] unreg vt (Umschlag) to tear open; (Augen) to open wide; (Tür) to throw open; (Straße) to take up; (umg: Mädchen) to pick up

Aufreißer (-s, -) m (Person) smooth operator

aufreizen ['aʊfraɪtsən] vt to incite, stir up

aufreizend adj exciting, stimulating

aufrichten ['aʊfrɪçtən] vt to put up, erect; (moralisch) to console ▷ vr to rise; (moralisch): **sich ~ (an +dat)** to take heart (from); **sich im Bett ~** to sit up in bed

aufrichtig ['aʊfrɪçtɪç] adj sincere; honest; **Aufrichtigkeit** f sincerity

aufrollen ['aʊfrɔlən] vt (zusammenrollen) to roll up; (Kabel) to coil od wind up; siehe auch **wiederaufrollen**

aufrücken ['aʊfrʏkən] vi to move up; (beruflich) to be promoted

Aufruf ['aʊfruːf] m summons; (zur Hilfe) call; (des Namens) calling out

aufrufen unreg vt (Namen) to call out; (auffordern): **jdn ~ (zu)** to call upon sb (for); **einen Schüler ~** to ask a pupil (to answer) a question

Aufruhr ['aʊfruːr] (-(e)s, -e) m uprising, revolt; **in ~ sein** to be in uproar

Aufrührer ['aʊfryːrər] (-s, -) m(f) rabble-rouser

aufrührerisch ['aʊfryːrərɪʃ] adj rebellious

aufrunden ['aʊfrʊndən] vt (Summe) to round up

aufrüsten ['aʊfrʏstən] vt, vi to arm

Aufrüstung f rearmament

aufrütteln ['aʊfrʏtəln] *vt* (*lit, fig*) to shake up

aufs [aʊfs] = **auf das**

aufsagen ['aʊfzaːgən] *vt* (*Gedicht*) to recite; (*geh: Freundschaft*) to put an end to

aufsammeln ['aʊfzaməln] *vt* to gather up

aufsässig ['aʊfzɛsɪç] *adj* rebellious

Aufsatz ['aʊfzats] *m* (*Geschriebenes*) essay, composition; (*auf Schrank etc*) top

aufsaugen ['aʊfzaʊgən] *unreg vt* to soak up

aufschauen ['aʊfʃaʊən] *vi* to look up

aufscheuchen ['aʊfʃɔʏçən] *vt* to scare, startle

aufschichten ['aʊfʃɪçtən] *vt* to stack, pile up

aufschieben ['aʊfʃiːbən] *unreg vt* to push open; (*verzögern*) to put off, postpone

Aufschlag ['aʊfʃlaːk] *m* (*Ärmelaufschlag*) cuff; (*Jackenaufschlag*) lapel; (*Hosenaufschlag*) turn-up (*Brit*), cuff (*US*); (*Aufprall*) impact; (*Preisaufschlag*) surcharge; (*Tennis*) service

aufschlagen ['aʊfʃlaːgən] *unreg vt* (*öffnen*) to open; (*verwunden*) to cut; (*hochschlagen*) to turn up; (*aufbauen: Zelt, Lager*) to pitch, erect; (*Wohnsitz*) to take up ▷ *vi* (*aufprallen*) to hit; (*teurer werden*) to go up; (*Tennis*) to serve; **schlagt Seite 111 auf** open your books at page 111

aufschließen ['aʊfʃliːsən] *unreg vt* to open up, unlock ▷ *vi* (*aufrücken*) to close up

Aufschluss ['aʊfʃlʊs] *m* information

aufschlüsseln ['aʊfʃlʏsəln] *vt:* ~ **(nach)** to break down (into); (*klassifizieren*) to classify (according to)

aufschlussreich *adj* informative, illuminating

aufschnappen ['aʊfʃnapən] *vt* (*umg*) to pick up ▷ *vi* to fly open

aufschneiden ['aʊfʃnaɪdən] *unreg vt* to cut open; (*Brot*) to cut up; (*Med: Geschwür*) to lance ▷ *vi* (*umg*) to brag

Aufschneider (**-s, -**) *m* boaster, braggart

Aufschnitt ['aʊfʃnɪt] *m* (slices of) cold meat

aufschnüren ['aʊfʃnyːrən] *vt* to unlace; (*Paket*) to untie

aufschrauben ['aʊfʃraʊbən] *vt* (*festschrauben*) to screw on; (*lösen*) to unscrew

aufschrecken ['aʊfʃrɛkən] *vt* to startle ▷ *vi* (*unreg*) to start up

Aufschrei ['aʊfʃraɪ] *m* cry

aufschreiben ['aʊfʃraɪbən] *unreg vt* to write down

aufschreien *unreg vi* to cry out

Aufschrift ['aʊfʃrɪft] *f* (*Inschrift*) inscription; (*Etikett*) label

Aufschub ['aʊfʃuːp] (**-(e)s, -schübe**) *m* delay, postponement; **jdm ~ gewähren** to grant sb an extension

aufschürfen ['aʊfʃʏrfən] *vt:* **sich** *dat* **die Haut/ das Knie ~** to graze *od* scrape o.s./one's knee

aufschütten ['aʊfʃʏtən] *vt* (*Flüssigkeit*) to pour on; (*Kohle*) to put on (the fire); (*Damm, Deich*) to throw up; **Kaffee ~** to make coffee

aufschwatzen ['aʊfʃvatsən] (*umg*) *vt:* **jdm etw ~** to talk sb into (getting/having *etc*) sth

Aufschwung ['aʊfʃvʊŋ] *m* (*Elan*) boost; (*wirtschaftlich*) upturn, boom; (*Sport: an Gerät*) mount

aufsehen ['aʊfzeːən] *unreg vi* to look up; ~ **zu** (*lit*) to look up at; (*fig*) to look up to; **Aufsehen** (**-s**) *nt* sensation, stir; **aufsehenerregend** *adj* sensational

Aufseher, in (**-s, -**) *m(f)* guard; (*im Betrieb*) supervisor; (*Museumsaufseher*) attendant; (*Parkaufseher*) keeper

auf sein ['aʊfzaɪn] *siehe* **auf**

aufseiten, auf Seiten [aʊfˈzaɪtn] *präp +gen:* ~ **von** on the part of

aufsetzen ['aʊfzɛtsən] *vt* to put on; (*Flugzeug*) to put down; (*Dokument*) to draw up ▷ *vr* to sit upright ▷ *vi* (*Flugzeug*) to touch down

Aufsicht ['aʊfzɪçt] *f* supervision; **die ~ haben** to be in charge; **bei einer Prüfung ~ führen** to invigilate (*Brit*) *od* supervise an exam

Aufsichtsrat *m* board (of directors)

aufsitzen ['aʊfzɪtsən] *unreg vi* (*aufgerichtet sitzen*) to sit up; (*aufs Pferd, Motorrad*) to mount, get on; (*Schiff*) to run aground; **jdn ~ lassen** (*umg*) to stand sb up; **jdm ~** (*umg*) to be taken in by sb

aufspalten ['aʊfʃpaltən] *vt* to split

aufspannen ['aʊfʃpanən] *vt* (*Netz, Sprungtuch*) to stretch *od* spread out; (*Schirm*) to put up, open

aufsparen ['aʊfʃpaːrən] *vt* to save (up)

aufsperren ['aʊfʃpɛrən] *vt* to unlock; (*Mund*) to open wide; **die Ohren ~** (*umg*) to prick up one's ears

aufspielen ['aʊfʃpiːlən] *vr* to show off; **sich als etw ~** to try to come on as sth

aufspießen ['aʊfʃpiːsən] *vt* to spear

aufspringen ['aʊfʃprɪŋən] *unreg vi* (*hochspringen*) to jump up; (*sich öffnen*) to spring open; (*Hände, Lippen*) to become chapped; ~ **auf** +*akk* to jump onto

aufspüren ['aʊfʃpyːrən] *vt* to track down, trace

aufstacheln ['aʊfʃtaxəln] *vt* to incite

aufstampfen ['aʊfʃtampfən] *vi:* **mit dem Fuß ~** to stamp one's foot

Aufstand ['aʊfʃtant] *m* insurrection, rebellion

aufständisch ['aʊfʃtɛndɪʃ] *adj* rebellious, mutinous

aufstauen ['aʊfʃtaʊən] *vr* to collect; (*fig: Ärger*) to be bottled up

aufstechen ['aʊfʃtɛçən] *unreg vt* to prick open, puncture

aufstecken ['aʊfʃtɛkən] *vt* to stick on; (*mit Nadeln*) to pin up; (*umg*) to give up

aufstehen ['aʊfʃteːən] *unreg vi* to get up; (*Tür*) to be open; **da musst du früher** *od* **eher ~!** (*fig: umg*) you'll have to do better than that!

aufsteigen ['aʊfʃtaɪgən] *unreg vi* (*hochsteigen*) to climb; (*Rauch*) to rise; ~ **auf** +*akk* to get onto; **in jdm ~** (*Hass, Verdacht, Erinnerung etc*) to well up in sb

Aufsteiger (**-s, -**) *m* (*Sport*) promoted team; (**sozialer**) ~ social climber

aufstellen ['aʊfʃtɛlən] *vt* (*aufrecht stellen*) to put up; (*Maschine*) to install; (*aufreihen*) to line up; (*Kandidaten*) to nominate; (*Forderung, Behauptung*) to put forward; (*formulieren: Programm etc*) to draw up;

(*leisten: Rekord*) to set up

Aufstellung *f* (*Sport*) line-up; (*Liste*) list

Aufstieg ['aʊfʃtiːk] (**-(e)s, -e**) *m* (*auf Berg*) ascent; (*Fortschritt*) rise; (*beruflich, Sport*) promotion

Aufstiegschance *f* prospect of promotion

aufstöbern ['aʊfʃtøːbərn] *vt* (*Wild*) to start, flush; (*umg: entdecken*) to run to earth

aufstocken ['aʊfʃtɔkən] *vt* (*Vorräte*) to build up

aufstoßen ['aʊfʃtoːsən] *unreg vt* to push open ▷ *vi* to belch

aufstrebend ['aʊfʃtreːbənd] *adj* ambitious; (*Land*) striving for progress

Aufstrich ['aʊfʃtrɪç] *m* spread

aufstülpen ['aʊfʃtʏlpən] *vt* (*Ärmel*) to turn up; (*Hut*) to put on

aufstützen ['aʊfʃtʏtsən] *vt* (*Körperteil*) to prop, lean; (*Person*) to prop up ▷ *vr*: **sich ~ auf** +*akk* to lean on

aufsuchen ['aʊfzuːxən] *vt* (*besuchen*) to visit; (*konsultieren*) to consult

auftakeln ['aʊftaːkəln] *vt* (*Naut*) to rig (out) ▷ *vr* (*pej: umg*) to deck o.s. out

Auftakt ['aʊftakt] *m* (*Mus*) upbeat; (*fig*) prelude

auftanken ['aʊftaŋkən] *vi* to get petrol (*Brit*) *od* gas (*US*) ▷ *vt* to refuel

auftauchen ['aʊftaʊxən] *vi* to appear; (*gefunden werden, kommen*) to turn up; (*aus Wasser etc*) to emerge; (*U-Boot*) to surface; (*Zweifel*) to arise

auftauen ['aʊftaʊən] *vt* to thaw ▷ *vi* to thaw; (*fig*) to relax

aufteilen ['aʊftaɪlən] *vt* to divide up; (*Raum*) to partition

Aufteilung *f* division; partition

auftischen ['aʊftɪʃən] *vt* to serve (up); (*fig*) to tell

Auftr. *abk* = **Auftrag**

Auftrag ['aʊftraːk] (**-(e)s, -träge**) *m* order; (*Anweisung*) commission; (*Aufgabe*) mission; **etw in ~ geben (bei)** to order/commission sth (from); **im ~ von** on behalf of; **im ~** *od* **i. A. J. Burnett** *pp* J. Burnett

auftragen ['aʊftraːgən] *unreg vt* (*Essen*) to serve; (*Farbe*) to put on; (*Kleidung*) to wear out ▷ *vi* (*dick machen*): **die Jacke trägt auf** the jacket makes one look fat; **jdm etw ~** to tell sb sth; **dick ~** (*umg*) to exaggerate

Auftraggeber, in (**-s, -**) *m(f)* client; (*Comm*) customer

Auftragsbestätigung *f* confirmation of order

auftreiben ['aʊftraɪbən] *unreg* (*umg*) *vt* (*beschaffen*) to raise

auftrennen ['aʊftrɛnən] *vt* to undo

auftreten ['aʊftreːtən] *unreg vt* to kick open ▷ *vi* to appear; (*mit Füßen*) to tread; (*sich verhalten*) to behave; (*fig: eintreten*) to occur; (*Schwierigkeiten etc*) to arise; **als Vermittler** *etc* **~** to act as intermediary *etc*; **geschlossen ~** to put up a united front

Auftreten (**-s**) *nt* (*Vorkommen*) appearance; (*Benehmen*) behaviour (*Brit*), behavior (*US*)

Auftrieb ['aʊftriːp] *m* (*Phys*) buoyancy, lift; (*fig*) impetus

Auftritt ['aʊftrɪt] *m* (*des Schauspielers*) entrance; (*lit, fig: Szene*) scene

auftrumpfen ['aʊftrʊmpfən] *vi* to show how good one is; (*mit Bemerkung*) to crow

auftun ['aʊftuːn] *unreg vt* to open ▷ *vr* to open up

auftürmen ['aʊftʏrmən] *vr* (*Gebirge etc*) to tower up; (*Schwierigkeiten*) to pile *od* mount up

aufwachen ['aʊfvaxən] *vi* to wake up

aufwachsen ['aʊfvaksən] *unreg vi* to grow up

Aufwand ['aʊfvant] (**-(e)s**) *m* expenditure; (*Kosten*) expense; (*Luxus*) show; **bitte, keinen ~!** please don't go out of your way

aufwändig ['aʊfvɛndɪç] *adj, adv* costly

Aufwandsentschädigung *f* expense allowance

aufwärmen ['aʊfvɛrmən] *vt* to warm up; (*alte Geschichten*) to rake up

aufwarten ['aʊfvartən] *vi* (*zu bieten haben*): **mit etw ~** to offer sth

aufwärts ['aʊfvɛrts] *adv* upwards; **es geht ~** things are looking up; **Aufwärtsentwicklung** *f* upward trend

aufwecken ['aʊfvɛkən] *vt* to wake(n) up

aufweichen ['aʊfvaɪçən] *vt* to soften; (*Brot*) to soak

aufweisen ['aʊfvaɪzən] *unreg vt* to show

aufwenden ['aʊfvɛndən] *unreg vt* to expend; (*Geld*) to spend; (*Sorgfalt*) to devote

aufwendig ['aʊfvɛndɪç] *adj, adv* costly

aufwerfen ['aʊfvɛrfən] *unreg vt* (*Fenster etc*) to throw open; (*Probleme*) to throw up, raise ▷ *vr*: **sich zu etw ~** to make o.s. out to be sth

aufwerten ['aʊfvɛrtən] *vt* (*Fin*) to revalue; (*fig*) to raise in value

Aufwertung *f* revaluation

aufwickeln ['aʊfvɪkəln] *vt* (*aufrollen*) to roll up; (*umg: Haar*) to put in curlers; (*lösen*) to untie

aufwiegeln ['aʊfviːgəln] *vt* to stir up, incite

aufwiegen ['aʊfviːgən] *unreg vt* to make up for

Aufwind ['aʊfvɪnt] *m* up-current; **neuen ~ bekommen** (*fig*) to get new impetus

aufwirbeln ['aʊfvɪrbəln] *vt* to whirl up; **Staub ~** (*fig*) to create a stir

aufwischen ['aʊfvɪʃən] *vt* to wipe up

aufwühlen ['aʊfvyːlən] *vt* (*lit: Erde, Meer*) to churn (up); (*Gefühle*) to stir

aufzählen ['aʊftsɛːlən] *vt* to count out

aufzeichnen ['aʊftsaɪçnən] *vt* to sketch; (*schriftlich*) to jot down; (*auf Band*) to record

Aufzeichnung *f* (*schriftlich*) note; (*Tonbandaufzeichnung, Filmaufzeichnung*) recording

aufzeigen ['aʊftsaɪgən] *vt* to show, demonstrate

aufziehen ['aʊftsiːən] *unreg vt* (*hochziehen*) to raise, draw up; (*öffnen*) to pull open; (*: Reißverschluss*) to undo; (*Gardinen*) to draw (back); (*Uhr*) to wind; (*großziehen: Kinder*) to raise, bring up; (*Tiere*) to rear; (*umg: necken*) to tease; (*: veranstalten*) to set up; (*: Fest*) to arrange ▷ *vi* (*Gewitter, Wolken*) to gather

Aufzucht ['aʊftsʊxt] *f* (*das Großziehen*) rearing, raising

a

Aufzug ['aʊftsuːk] m (Fahrstuhl) lift (Brit), elevator (US); (Aufmarsch) procession, parade; (Kleidung) get-up; (Theat) act

aufzwingen ['aʊftsvɪŋən] unreg vt: **jdm etw ~** to force sth upon sb

Aug. abk (= August) Aug.

Augapfel ['aʊk|apfəl] m eyeball; (fig) apple of one's eye

Auge ['aʊgə] (-s, -n) nt eye; (Fettauge) globule of fat; **unter vier ~n** in private; **vor aller ~n** in front of everybody, for all to see; **jdn/ etw mit anderen ~n (an)sehen** to see sb/ sth in a different light; **ich habe kein ~ zugetan** I didn't sleep a wink; **ein ~/beide ~n zudrücken** (umg) to turn a blind eye; **jdn/ etw aus den ~n verlieren** to lose sight of sb/ sth; (fig) to lose touch with sb/sth; **etw ins ~ fassen** to contemplate sth; **das kann leicht ins ~ gehen** (fig: umg) it might easily go wrong

Augenarzt m eye specialist, ophthalmologist

Augenblick m moment; **im ~** at the moment; **im ersten ~** for a moment; **augenblicklich** adj (sofort) instantaneous; (gegenwärtig) present

Augen- zW: **Augenbraue** f eyebrow; **Augenhöhe** f: **in Augenhöhe** at eye level; **Augenmerk** nt (Aufmerksamkeit) attention; **Augenschein** m: **jdn/etw in Augenschein nehmen** to have a close look at sb/sth; **augenscheinlich** adj obvious; **Augenweide** f sight for sore eyes; **Augenwischerei** f (fig) eye-wash; **Augenzeuge** m eye witness; **Augenzeugin** f eye witness

August [aʊ'gʊst] (-(e)s od -, -e) (pl selten) m August; siehe auch **September**

Auktion [aʊktsiˈoːn] f auction

Auktionator [aʊktsioˈnaːtɔr] m auctioneer

Aula ['aʊla] (-, **Aulen** od -s) f assembly hall

Aus [aʊs] (-) nt (Sport) outfield; **ins ~ gehen** to go out

⬤ SCHLÜSSELWORT

aus [aʊs] präp +dat **1** (räumlich) out of; (von … her) from; **er ist aus Berlin** he's from Berlin; **aus dem Fenster** out of the window

2 (gemacht/hergestellt aus) made of; **ein Herz aus Stein** a heart of stone

3 (auf Ursache deutend) out of; **aus Mitleid** out of sympathy; **aus Erfahrung** from experience; **aus Spaß** for fun

4: aus ihr wird nie etwas she'll never get anywhere

▷ adv **1** (zu Ende) finished, over; **aus sein** to be over; **es ist aus mit ihm** he is finished, he has had it; **aus und vorbei** over and done with

2 (ausgeschaltet, ausgezogen) off; **aus sein** to be out; **Licht aus!** lights out!

3 (in Verbindung mit von): **von Rom aus** from Rome; **vom Fenster aus** out of the window; **von sich aus** (selbstständig) of one's own accord; **von mir aus** as far as I'm concerned

4: aus und ein gehen to come and go; (bei jdm) to visit frequently; **weder aus noch ein wissen** to be at one's wits' end; **auf etw akk aus sein** to be after sth

ausarbeiten ['aʊs|arbaɪtən] vt to work out

ausarten ['aʊs|artən] vi to degenerate; (Kind) to become overexcited

ausatmen ['aʊs|aːtmən] vi to breathe out

ausbaden ['aʊsbaːdən] (umg) vt: **etw ~ müssen** to carry the can for sth

Ausbau ['aʊsbaʊ] m extension, expansion; removal

ausbauen vt to extend, expand; (herausnehmen) to take out, remove

ausbaufähig adj (fig) worth developing

ausbedingen ['aʊsbədɪŋən] unreg vt: **sich** dat **etw ~** to insist on sth

ausbeißen ['aʊsbaɪsən] unreg vr: **sich** dat **an etw** dat **die Zähne ~** (fig) to have a tough time of it with sth

ausbessern ['aʊsbɛsərn] vt to mend, repair

Ausbesserungsarbeiten pl repair work sing

ausbeulen ['aʊsbɔʏlən] vt to beat out

Ausbeute ['aʊsbɔʏtə] f yield; (Gewinn) profit, gain; (Fische) catch

ausbeuten vt to exploit; (Min) to work

ausbezahlen ['aʊsbətsaːlən] vt (Geld) to pay out

ausbilden ['aʊsbɪldən] vt to educate; (Lehrling, Soldat) to instruct, train; (Fähigkeiten) to develop; (Geschmack) to cultivate

Ausbilder, in (-s, -) m(f) instructor, instructress

Ausbildung f education; training, instruction; development; cultivation; **er ist noch in der ~** he's still a trainee; he hasn't finished his education

Ausbildungs- zW: **Ausbildungsförderung** f (provision of) grants for students and trainees; (Stipendium) grant; **Ausbildungsplatz** m (Stelle) training vacancy

ausbitten ['aʊsbɪtən] unreg vt: **sich** dat **etw ~** (geh: erbitten) to ask for sth; (verlangen) to insist on sth

ausblasen ['aʊsblaːzən] unreg vt to blow out; (Ei) to blow

ausbleiben ['aʊsblaɪbən] unreg vi (Personen) to stay away, not come; (Ereignisse) to fail to happen, not happen; **es konnte nicht ~, dass …** it was inevitable that …

ausblenden ['aʊsblɛndən] vt, vi (TV etc) to fade out

Ausblick ['aʊsblɪk] m (lit, fig) prospect, outlook, view

ausbomben ['aʊsbɔmbən] vt to bomb out

ausbooten ['aʊsboːtən] (umg) vt (jdn) to kick od boot out

ausbrechen ['aʊsbrɛçən] unreg vi to break out ▷ vt to break off; **in Tränen/Gelächter ~ to** burst into tears/out laughing

Ausbrecher, in (-s, -) m(f) (Gefangener) escaped prisoner, escapee

ausbreiten ['aʊsbraɪtən] vt to spread (out); (Arme) to stretch out ▷ vr to spread; **sich über**

35

ein Thema ~ to expand od enlarge on a topic

ausbrennen ['aʊsbrɛnən] unreg vt to scorch; (Wunde) to cauterize ▷ vi to burn out

ausbringen ['aʊsbrɪŋən] unreg vt (ein Hoch) to propose

Ausbruch ['aʊsbrʊx] m outbreak; (von Vulkan) eruption; (Gefühlsausbruch) outburst; (von Gefangenen) escape

ausbrüten ['aʊsbry:tən] vt (lit, fig) to hatch

Ausbuchtung ['aʊsbʊxtʊŋ] f bulge; (Küste) cove

ausbügeln ['aʊsby:gəln] vt to iron out; (umg: Fehler, Verlust) to make good

ausbuhen ['aʊsbu:ən] vt to boo

Ausbund ['aʊsbʊnt] m: **ein ~ an** od **von Tugend/Sparsamkeit** a paragon of virtue/a model of thrift

ausbürgern ['aʊsbʏrgərn] vt to expatriate

ausbürsten ['aʊsbʏrstən] vt to brush out

Ausdauer ['aʊsdaʊər] f stamina; (Beharrlichkeit) perseverance

ausdauernd adj persevering

ausdehnen ['aʊsde:nən] vt, vr (räumlich) to expand; (zeitlich, auch Gummi) to stretch; (Nebel, fig: Macht) to extend

ausdenken ['aʊsdɛŋkən] unreg vt (zu Ende denken) to think through; **sich** dat **etw ~** to think sth up; **das ist nicht auszudenken** (unvorstellbar) it's inconceivable

ausdiskutieren ['aʊsdɪskuti:rən] vt to talk out

ausdrehen ['aʊsdre:ən] vt to turn od switch off

Ausdruck ['aʊsdrʊk] (**-s, -drücke**) m expression, phrase; (Kundgabe, Gesichtsausdruck) expression; (Fachausdruck) term; (Comput) hard copy; **mit dem ~ des Bedauerns** (form) expressing regret

ausdrucken vt (Text) to print out

ausdrücken ['aʊsdrʏkən] vt (auch vr: formulieren, zeigen) to express; (Zigarette) to put out; (Zitrone) to squeeze

ausdrücklich adj express, explicit

Ausdrucks- zW: **Ausdrucksfähigkeit** f expressiveness; (Gewandtheit) articulateness; **ausdruckslos** adj expressionless, blank; **ausdrucksvoll** adj expressive; **Ausdrucksweise** f mode of expression

Ausdünstung ['aʊsdʏnstʊŋ] f (Dampf) vapour (Brit), vapor (US); (Geruch) smell

auseinander [aʊs|aɪ'nandər] adv (getrennt) apart; **weit ~** far apart

auseinander- zW: **auseinanderbringen** unreg vt to separate; **auseinanderfallen** unreg vi to fall apart; **auseinandergehen** unreg vi (Menschen) to separate; (Meinungen) to differ; (Gegenstand) to fall apart; (umg: dick werden) to put on weight; **auseinanderhalten** unreg vt to tell apart; **auseinanderklaffen** vi to gape open; (fig: Meinungen) to be far apart, diverge (wildly); **auseinanderlaufen** unreg vi (Menge) to disperse; (umg: sich trennen) to break up; **auseinanderleben** vr to drift apart; **auseinandernehmen** unreg vt to take to pieces, dismantle; **auseinanderschreiben** unreg vt to write as separate words; **auseinandersetzen** unreg vt to set forth, explain ▷ vr (sich verständigen) to come to terms, settle; (sich befassen) to concern o.s.; **sich mit jdm auseinandersetzen** to talk with sb; (sich streiten) to argue with sb; **Auseinandersetzung** f argument

auserkoren ['aʊs|ɛrko:rən] adj (liter) chosen, selected

auserlesen ['aʊs|ɛrle:zən] adj select, choice

ausersehen ['aʊs|ɛrze:ən] unreg vt (geh): **dazu ~ sein, etw zu tun** to be chosen to do sth

ausfahrbar adj extendable; (Antenne, Fahrgestell) retractable

ausfahren ['aʊsfa:rən] unreg vi to drive out; (Naut) to put out (to sea) ▷ vt to take out; (Aut) to drive flat out; (ausliefern: Waren) to deliver; **ausgefahrene Wege** rutted roads

Ausfahrt f (des Zuges etc) leaving, departure; (Autobahnausfahrt, Garagenausfahrt) exit, way out; (Spazierfahrt) drive, excursion

Ausfall ['aʊsfal] m loss; (Nichtstattfinden) cancellation; (das Versagen: Tech, Med) failure; (von Motor) breakdown; (Produktionsstörung) stoppage; (Mil) sortie; (Fechten) lunge; (radioaktiv) fallout

ausfallen ['aʊsfalən] unreg vi (Zähne, Haare) to fall od come out; (nicht stattfinden) to be cancelled; (wegbleiben) to be omitted; (Person) to drop out; (Lohn) to be stopped; (nicht funktionieren) to break down; (Resultat haben) to turn out; **wie ist das Spiel ausgefallen?** what was the result of the game?; **die Schule fällt morgen aus** there's no school tomorrow

ausfallend adj impertinent

Ausfallstraße f arterial road

Ausfallzeit f (Maschine) downtime

ausfegen ['aʊsfe:gən] vt to sweep out

ausfeilen ['aʊsfaɪlən] vt to file out; (Stil) to polish up

ausfertigen ['aʊsfɛrtɪgən] vt (form) to draw up; (Rechnung) to make out; **doppelt ~** to duplicate

Ausfertigung f (form) drawing up; making out; (Exemplar) copy; **in doppelter/dreifacher ~** in duplicate/triplicate

ausfindig ['aʊsfɪndɪç] adj: **~ machen** to discover

ausfliegen ['aʊsfli:gən] unreg vi to fly away ▷ vt to fly out; **sie sind ausgeflogen** (umg) they're out

ausfließen ['aʊsfli:sən] unreg vi: **~ (aus)** (herausfließen) to flow out (of); (auslaufen: Öl etc) to leak (out of); (Eiter etc) to be discharged (from)

ausflippen ['aʊsflɪpən] (umg) vi to freak out

Ausflucht ['aʊsflʊxt] (**-, -flüchte**) f excuse

Ausflug ['aʊsflu:k] m excursion, outing

Ausflügler, in ['aʊsfly:klər(ɪn)] (**-s, -**) m(f) tripper (Brit), excursionist (US)

Ausfluss ['aʊsflʊs] m outlet; (Med) discharge

ausfragen ['aʊsfra:gən] vt to interrogate, question

ausfransen ['aʊsfranzən] vi to fray

ausfressen ['aʊsfrɛsən] *unreg* (*umg*) *vt* (*anstellen*) to be up to

Ausfuhr ['aʊsfuːr] (**-, -en**) *f* export, exportation; (*Ware*) export ▷ *in zW* export

ausführbar ['aʊsfyːrbaːr] *adj* feasible; (*Comm*) exportable

ausführen ['aʊsfyːrən] *vt* (*verwirklichen*) to carry out; (*Person*) to take out; (*Hund*) to take for a walk; (*Comm*) to export; (*erklären*) to give details of; **die ~de Gewalt** (*Pol*) the executive

Ausfuhrgenehmigung *f* export licence

ausführlich *adj* detailed ▷ *adv* in detail; **Ausführlichkeit** *f* detail

Ausführung *f* execution, performance; (*von Waren*) design; (*von Thema*) exposition; (*Durchführung*) completion; (*Herstellungsart*) version; (*Erklärung*) explanation

Ausfuhrzoll *m* export duty

ausfüllen ['aʊsfʏlən] *vt* to fill up; (*Fragebogen etc*) to fill in; (*Beruf*) to be fulfilling for; **jdn (ganz) ~** (*Zeit in Anspruch nehmen*) to take (all) sb's time

Ausg. *abk* (= *Ausgabe*) ed.

Ausgabe ['aʊsgaːbə] *f* (*Geld*) expenditure, outlay; (*Aushändigung*) giving out; (*Schalter*) counter; (*Ausführung*) version; (*Buch*) edition; (*Nummer*) issue

Ausgang ['aʊsgaŋ] *m* way out, exit; (*Ende*) end; (*Ausgangspunkt*) starting point; (*Ergebnis*) result; (*Ausgehtag*) free time, time off; **ein Unfall mit tödlichem ~** a fatal accident; **kein ~** no exit

Ausgangs- *zW*: **Ausgangsbasis** *f* starting point; **Ausgangspunkt** *m* starting point; **Ausgangssperre** *f* curfew

ausgeben ['aʊsgeːbən] *unreg vt* (*Geld*) to spend; (*austeilen*) to issue, distribute; (*Comput*) to output ▷ *vr*: **sich für etw/jdn ~** to pass o.s. off as sth/sb; **ich gebe heute Abend einen aus** (*umg*) it's my treat this evening

ausgebeult ['aʊsgəbɔʏlt] *adj* (*Kleidung*) baggy; (*Hut*) battered

ausgebucht ['aʊsgəbuːxt] *adj* fully booked

Ausgeburt ['aʊsgəbuːrt] (*pej*) *f* (*der Fantasie etc*) monstrous product *od* invention

ausgedehnt ['aʊsgədeːnt] *adj* (*breit, groß, fig: weitreichend*) extensive; (*Spaziergang*) long; (*zeitlich*) lengthy

ausgedient ['aʊsgədiːnt] *adj* (*Soldat*) discharged; (*verbraucht*) no longer in use; **~ haben** to have come to the end of its useful life

ausgefallen ['aʊsgəfalən] *adj* (*ungewöhnlich*) exceptional

ausgefuchst ['aʊsgəfʊkst] (*umg*) *adj* clever; (*listig*) crafty

ausgegangen ['aʊsgəgaŋən] *pp von* **ausgehen**

ausgeglichen ['aʊsgəglıçən] *adj* (well-) balanced; **Ausgeglichenheit** *f* balance; (*von Mensch*) even-temperedness

Ausgehanzug *m* good suit

ausgehen ['aʊsgeːən] *unreg vi* (*auch Feuer, Ofen, Licht*) to go out; (*zu Ende gehen*) to come to an end; (*Benzin*) to run out; (*Haare, Zähne*) to fall *od* come out; (*Strom*) to go off; (*Resultat haben*) to

turn out; (*spazieren gehen*) to go (out) for a walk; (*abgeschickt werden: Post*) to be sent off; **mir ging das Benzin aus** I ran out of petrol (*Brit*) *od* gas (US); **auf etw** *akk* **~** to aim at sth; **von etw ~** (*wegführen*) to lead away from sth; (*herrühren*) to come from sth; (*zugrunde legen*) to proceed from sth; **wir können davon ~, dass ...** we can proceed from the assumption that ..., we can take as our starting point that ...; **leer ~** to get nothing; **schlecht ~** to turn out badly

ausgehungert ['aʊsgəhʊŋərt] *adj* starved; (*abgezehrt: Mensch etc*) emaciated

Ausgehverbot *nt* curfew

ausgeklügelt ['aʊsgəklyːgəlt] *adj* ingenious

ausgekocht ['aʊsgəkɔxt] (*pej: umg*) *adj* (*durchtrieben*) cunning; (*fig*) out-and-out

ausgelassen ['aʊsgəlasən] *adj* boisterous, high-spirited, exuberant; **Ausgelassenheit** *f* boisterousness, high spirits *pl*, exuberance

ausgelastet ['aʊsgəlastət] *adj* fully occupied

ausgeleiert ['aʊsgəlaıərt] *adj* worn; (*Gummiband*) stretched

ausgelernt ['aʊsgəlɛrnt] *adj* trained, qualified

ausgemacht ['aʊsgəmaxt] *adj* settled; (*umg: Dummkopf etc*) out-and-out, downright; **es gilt als ~, dass ...** it is settled that ...; **es war eine ~e Sache, dass ...** it was a foregone conclusion that ...

ausgemergelt ['aʊsgəmɛrgəlt] *adj* (*Gesicht*) emaciated, gaunt

ausgenommen ['aʊsgənɔmən] *konj* except; **Anwesende sind ~** present company excepted

ausgepowert ['aʊsgəpoːvərt] *adj*: **~ sein** (*umg*) to be tired, be exhausted

ausgeprägt ['aʊsgəprɛːkt] *adj* prominent; (*Eigenschaft*) distinct

ausgerechnet ['aʊsgərɛçnət] *adv* just, precisely; **~ du** you of all people; **~ heute** today of all days

ausgeschlossen ['aʊsgəʃlɔsən] *pp von* **ausschließen** ▷ *adj* (*unmöglich*) impossible, out of the question; **es ist nicht ~, dass ...** it cannot be ruled out that ...

ausgeschnitten ['aʊsgəʃnıtən] *adj* (*Kleid*) low-necked

ausgesehen ['aʊsgəzeːən] *pp von* **aussehen**

ausgesprochen ['aʊsgəʃprɔxən] *adj* (*Faulheit, Lüge etc*) out-and-out; (*unverkennbar*) marked ▷ *adv* decidedly

ausgestorben ['aʊsgəʃtɔrbən] *adj* (*Tierart*) extinct; (*fig*) deserted

ausgewogen ['aʊsgəvoːgən] *adj* balanced; (*Maß*) equal

ausgezeichnet ['aʊsgətsaıçnət] *adj* excellent

ausgiebig ['aʊsgiːbıç] *adj* (*Gebrauch*) full, good; (*Essen*) generous, lavish; **~ schlafen** to have a good sleep

ausgießen ['aʊsgiːsən] *unreg vt* (*aus einem Behälter*) to pour out; (*Behälter*) to empty; (*weggießen*) to pour away

Ausgleich ['aʊsglaıç] (**-(e)s, -e**) *m* balance; (*von Fehler, Mangel*) compensation; (*Sport*): **den ~ erzielen** to equalize; **zum ~** +*gen* in order to offset sth; **das ist ein guter ~** (entspannend) that's very relaxing

ausgleichen ['aʊsglaɪçən] unreg vt to balance (out); (Konflikte) to reconcile; (Höhe) to even up ▷ vi (Sport) to equalize; **~de Gerechtigkeit** poetic justice

Ausgleichssport m keep-fit activity

Ausgleichstor nt equalizer

ausgraben ['aʊsgraːbən] unreg vt to dig up; (Leichen) to exhume; (fig) to unearth

Ausgrabung f excavation

ausgrenzen ['aʊsgrɛntsən] vt to shut out, separate

Ausgrenzung f shut-out, separation

Ausguck ['aʊsgʊk] m look-out

Ausguss ['aʊsgʊs] m (Spüle) sink; (Abfluss) outlet; (Tülle) spout

aushaben ['aʊshaːbən] unreg (umg) vt (Kleidung) to have taken off; (Buch) to have finished

aushalten ['aʊshaltən] unreg vt to bear, stand; (umg: Geliebte) to keep ▷ vi to hold out; **das ist nicht zum A~** that is unbearable; **sich von jdm ~ lassen** to be kept by sb

aushandeln ['aʊshandəln] vt to negotiate

aushändigen ['aʊshɛndɪgən] vt: **jdm etw ~** to hand sth over to sb

Aushang ['aʊshaŋ] m notice

aushängen ['aʊshɛŋən] unreg vt (Meldung) to put up; (Fenster) to take off its hinges ▷ vi to be displayed ▷ vr to hang out

Aushängeschild nt (shop) sign; (fig): **als ~ für etw dienen** to promote sth

ausharren ['aʊsharən] vi to hold out

aushäusig ['aʊshɔʏzɪç] adj gallivanting around, on the tiles

ausheben ['aʊsheːbən] unreg vt (Erde) to lift out; (Grube) to hollow out; (Tür) to take off its hinges; (Diebesnest) to clear out; (Mil) to enlist

aushecken ['aʊshɛkən] (umg) vt to concoct, think up

aushelfen ['aʊshɛlfən] unreg vi: **jdm ~** to help sb out

Aushilfe ['aʊshɪlfə] f help, assistance; (Person) (temporary) worker

Aushilfs- zW: **Aushilfskraft** f temporary worker; **Aushilfslehrer, in** m(f) supply teacher; **aushilfsweise** adv temporarily, as a stopgap

aushöhlen ['aʊshøːlən] vt to hollow out; (fig: untergraben) to undermine

ausholen ['aʊshoːlən] vi to swing one's arm back; (zur Ohrfeige) to raise one's hand; (beim Gehen) to take long strides; **zum Gegenschlag ~** (lit, fig) to prepare for a counter-attack

aushorchen ['aʊshɔrçən] vt to sound out, pump

aushungern ['aʊshʊŋərn] vt to starve out

auskennen ['aʊskɛnən] unreg vr to know a lot; (an einem Ort) to know one's way about; (in Fragen etc) to be knowledgeable; **man kennt sich bei ihm nie aus** you never know where you are with him

auskippen ['aʊskɪpən] vt to empty

ausklammern ['aʊsklamərn] vt (Thema) to exclude, leave out

Ausklang ['aʊsklaŋ] m (geh) end

ausklappbar ['aʊsklapbaːr] adj: **dieser Tisch ist ~** this table can be opened out

auskleiden ['aʊsklaɪdən] vr (geh) to undress ▷ vt (Wand) to line

ausklingen ['aʊsklɪŋən] unreg vi to end; (Ton, Lied) to die away; (Fest) to come to an end

ausklinken ['aʊsklɪŋkən] vt (Bomben) to release ▷ vi (umg) to flip one's lid

ausklopfen ['aʊsklɔpfən] vt (Teppich) to beat; (Pfeife) to knock out

auskochen ['aʊskɔxən] vt to boil; (Med) to sterilize

auskommen ['aʊskɔmən] unreg vi: **mit jdm ~** to get on with sb; **mit etw ~** to get by with sth; **Auskommen (-s)** nt: **sein Auskommen haben** to get by; **mit ihr ist kein Auskommen** she's impossible to get on with

auskosten ['aʊskɔstən] vt to enjoy to the full

auskramen ['aʊskraːmən] (umg) vt to dig out, unearth; (fig: alte Geschichten etc) to bring up

auskratzen ['aʊskratsən] vt (auch Med) to scrape out

auskugeln ['aʊskuːgəln] vr: **sich** dat **den Arm ~** to dislocate one's arm

auskundschaften ['aʊskʊntʃaftən] vt to spy out; (Gebiet) to reconnoitre (Brit), reconnoiter (US)

Auskunft ['aʊskʊnft] (-, -künfte) f information; (nähere) details pl, particulars pl; (Stelle) information office; (Tel) inquiries; **jdm ~ erteilen** to give sb information

auskuppeln ['aʊskʊpəln] vi to disengage the clutch

auskurieren ['aʊskuriːrən] (umg) vt to cure

auslachen ['aʊslaxən] vt to laugh at, mock

ausladen ['aʊslaːdən] unreg vt to unload; (umg: Gäste) to cancel an invitation to ▷ vi (Äste) to spread

ausladend adj (Gebärden, Bewegung) sweeping

Auslage ['aʊslaːgə] f shop window (display)

Auslagen pl outlay sing, expenditure sing

Ausland ['aʊslant] nt foreign countries pl; **im ~** abroad; **ins ~** abroad

Ausländer, in ['aʊslɛndər(ɪn)] (-s, -) m(f) foreigner

Ausländerfeindlichkeit f hostility to foreigners, xenophobia

ausländisch adj foreign

Auslands- zW: **Auslandsaufenthalt** m stay abroad; **Auslandsgespräch** nt international call; **Auslandskorrespondent, in** m(f) foreign correspondent; **Auslandsreise** f trip abroad; **Auslandsschutzbrief** m international travel cover; **Auslandsvertretung** f agency abroad; (von Firma) foreign branch

auslassen ['aʊslasən] unreg vt to leave out; (Wort etc) to omit; (Fett) to melt; (Kleidungsstück) to let out ▷ vr: **sich über etw** akk **~** to speak one's mind about sth; **seine Wut** etc **an jdm ~** to vent one's rage etc on sb

Auslassung f omission

Auslassungszeichen nt apostrophe

auslasten ['auslastən] vt (Fahrzeug) to make full use of; (Maschine) to use to capacity; (jdn) to occupy fully

Auslauf ['auslauf] m (für Tiere) run; (Ausfluss) outflow, outlet

auslaufen unreg vi to run out; (Behälter) to leak; (Naut) to put out (to sea); (langsam aufhören) to run down

Ausläufer ['auslɔyfər] m (von Gebirge) spur; (Pflanze) runner; (Met: von Hoch) ridge; (: von Tief) trough

ausleeren ['auslerən] vt to empty

auslegen ['auslergən] vt (Waren) to lay out; (Köder) to put down; (Geld) to lend; (bedecken) to cover; (Text etc) to interpret

Ausleger (-s, -) m (von Kran etc) jib, boom

Auslegung f interpretation

Ausleihe ['auslaɪə] (-, -n) f issuing; (Stelle) issue desk

ausleihen ['auslaɪən] unreg vt (verleihen) to lend; **sich** dat **etw ~** to borrow sth

auslernen ['auslɛrnən] vi (Lehrling) to finish one's apprenticeship; **man lernt nie aus** (Sprichwort) you live and learn

Auslese ['auslerzə] (-, -n) f selection; (Elite) elite; (Wein) choice wine

auslesen ['auslerzən] unreg vt to select; (umg: zu Ende lesen) to finish

ausliefern ['auslirfərn] vt to hand over; (Comm) to deliver ▷ vr: **sich jdm ~** to give o.s. up to sb; **~ (an** +akk**)** to deliver (up) (to), hand over (to); (an einen Staat) to extradite (to); **jdm/etw ausgeliefert sein** to be at the mercy of sb/sth

Auslieferungsabkommen nt extradition treaty

ausliegen ['auslirgən] unreg vi (zur Ansicht) to be displayed; (Zeitschriften etc) to be available (to the public); (Liste) to be up

auslöschen ['auslœʃən] vt to extinguish; (fig) to wipe out, obliterate

auslosen ['auslorzən] vt to draw lots for

auslösen ['auslørzən] vt (Explosion, Schuss) to set off; (hervorrufen) to cause, produce; (Gefangene) to ransom; (Pfand) to redeem

Auslöser (-s, -) m trigger; (Phot) release; (Anlass) cause

ausloten ['auslortən] vt (Naut: Tiefe) to sound; (fig geh) to plumb

ausmachen ['ausmaxən] vt (Licht, Radio) to turn off; (Feuer) to put out; (entdecken) to make out; (vereinbaren) to agree; (beilegen) to settle; (Anteil darstellen, betragen) to represent; (bedeuten) to matter; **das macht ihm nichts aus** it doesn't matter to him; **macht es Ihnen etwas aus, wenn ...?** would you mind if ...?

ausmalen ['ausmarlən] vt to paint; (fig) to describe; **sich** dat **etw ~** to imagine sth

Ausmaß ['ausmars] nt dimension; (fig) scale

ausmerzen ['ausmɛrtsən] vt to eliminate

ausmessen ['ausmɛsən] unreg vt to measure

ausmisten ['ausmɪstən] vt (Stall) to muck out;

(fig: umg: Schrank etc) to tidy out; (: Zimmer) to clean out

ausmustern ['ausmʊstərn] vt (Maschine, Fahrzeug etc) to take out of service; (Mil: entlassen) to invalid out

Ausnahme ['ausnarmə] (-, -n) f exception; **eine ~ machen** to make an exception; **Ausnahmeerscheinung** f exception, one-off example; **Ausnahmefall** m exceptional case; **Ausnahmezustand** m state of emergency

ausnahmslos adv without exception

ausnahmsweise adv by way of exception, for once

ausnehmen ['ausnermən] unreg vt to take out, remove; (Tier) to gut; (Nest) to rob; (umg: Geld abnehmen) to clean out; (ausschließen) to make an exception of ▷ vr to look, appear

ausnehmend adj exceptional

ausnüchtern ['ausnʏçtərn] vt, vi to sober up

Ausnüchterungszelle f drying-out cell

ausnutzen ['ausnʊtsən] vt (Zeit, Gelegenheit) to use, turn to good account; (Einfluss) to use; (Mensch, Gutmütigkeit) to exploit

auspacken ['auspakən] vt to unpack ▷ vi (umg: alles sagen) to talk

auspfeifen ['auspfaɪfən] unreg vt to hiss/boo at

ausplaudern ['ausplaudərn] vt (Geheimnis) to blab

ausposaunen ['auspozaunən] (umg) vt to tell the world about

ausprägen ['ausprɛrgən] vr (Begabung, Charaktereigenschaft) to reveal od show itself

auspressen ['ausprɛsən] vt (Saft, Schwamm etc) to squeeze out; (Zitrone etc) to squeeze

ausprobieren ['ausprobirən] vt to try (out)

Auspuff ['auspʊf] (-(e)s, -e) m (Tech) exhaust; **Auspuffrohr** nt exhaust (pipe); **Auspufftopf** m (Aut) silencer (Brit), muffler (US)

ausquartieren ['auskvartirən] vt to move out

ausquetschen ['auskvetʃən] vt (Zitrone etc) to squeeze; (umg: ausfragen) to grill; (: aus Neugier) to pump

ausradieren ['ausradirən] vt to erase, rub out

ausrangieren ['ausraˈʒirən] (umg) vt to chuck out; (Maschine, Auto) to scrap

ausrauben ['ausraubən] vt to rob

ausräumen ['ausrɔymən] vt (Dinge) to clear away; (Schrank, Zimmer) to empty; (Bedenken) to put aside

ausrechnen ['ausreçnən] vt to calculate, reckon

Ausrechnung f calculation, reckoning

Ausrede ['ausrerdə] f excuse

ausreden ['ausrerdən] vi to have one's say ▷ vt: **jdm etw ~** to talk sb out of sth; **er hat mich nicht mal ~ lassen** he didn't even let me finish (speaking)

ausreichen ['ausraɪçən] vi to suffice, be enough

ausreichend adj sufficient, adequate; (Sch) adequate

Ausreise ['ausraɪzə] f departure; **bei der ~** when leaving the country; **Ausreiseerlaubnis**

f exit visa

ausreisen ['aʊsraɪzən] *vi* to leave the country

ausreißen ['aʊsraɪsən] *unreg vt* to tear *od* pull out ▷ *vi (Riss bekommen)* to tear; *(umg)* to make off, scram; **er hat sich** *dat* **kein Bein ausgerissen** *(umg)* he didn't exactly overstrain himself

ausrenken ['aʊsrɛŋkən] *vt* to dislocate

ausrichten ['aʊsrɪçtən] *vt (Botschaft)* to deliver; *(Gruß)* to pass on; *(Hochzeit etc)* to arrange; *(in gerade Linie bringen)* to get in a straight line; *(angleichen)* to bring into line; *(Typ etc)* to justify; **etwas/nichts bei jdm ~** to get somewhere/nowhere with sb; **jdm etw ~** to take a message for sb; **ich werde es ihm ~** I'll tell him

ausrotten ['aʊsrɔtən] *vt* to stamp out, exterminate

ausrücken ['aʊsrʏkən] *vi (Mil)* to move off; *(Feuerwehr, Polizei)* to be called out; *(umg: weglaufen)* to run away

Ausruf ['aʊsruːf] *m (Schrei)* cry, exclamation; *(Verkünden)* proclamation

ausrufen *unreg vt* to cry out, exclaim; to call out; **jdn ~ (lassen)** *(über Lautsprecher etc)* to page sb

Ausrufezeichen *nt* exclamation mark

ausruhen ['aʊsruːən] *vt, vi, vr* to rest

ausrüsten ['aʊsrʏstən] *vt* to equip, fit out

Ausrüstung *f* equipment

ausrutschen ['aʊsrʊtʃən] *vi* to slip

Ausrutscher (-s, -) *(umg) m (lit, fig)* slip

Aussage ['aʊsza:gə] *(-, -n) f (Jur)* statement; **der Angeklagte/Zeuge verweigerte die ~** the accused/witness refused to give evidence

aussagekräftig *adj* expressive, full of expression

aussagen ['aʊsza:gən] *vt* to say, state ▷ *vi (Jur)* to give evidence

Aussatz ['aʊszats] *(-es) m (Med)* leprosy

aussaugen ['aʊszaʊgən] *vt (Saft etc)* to suck out; *(Wunde)* to suck the poison out of; *(fig: ausbeuten)* to drain dry

ausschalten ['aʊsʃaltən] *vt* to switch off; *(fig)* to eliminate

Ausschank ['aʊsʃaŋk] *(-(e)s, -schänke) m* dispensing, giving out; *(Comm)* selling; *(Theke)* bar

Ausschankerlaubnis *f* licence *(Brit)*, license *(US)*

Ausschau ['aʊsʃaʊ] *f*: **~ halten (nach)** to look out (for), watch (for)

ausschauen *vi*: **~ (nach)** to look out (for), be on the look-out (for)

ausscheiden ['aʊsʃaɪdən] *unreg vt (aussondern)* to take out; *(Med)* to excrete ▷ *vi*: **~ (aus)** to leave; *(aus einem Amt)* to retire (from); *(Sport)* to be eliminated (from), be knocked out (of); **er scheidet für den Posten aus** he can't be considered for the job

Ausscheidung *f (Aussondern)* removal; *(Med)* excretion; *(Sport)* elimination

ausschenken ['aʊsʃɛŋkən] *vt* to pour out; *(am*

Ausschank) to serve

ausscheren ['aʊsʃe:rən] *vi (Fahrzeug)* to leave the line *od* convoy; *(zum Überholen)* to pull out

ausschildern ['aʊsʃɪldərn] *vt* to signpost

ausschimpfen ['aʊsʃɪmpfən] *vt* to scold, tell off

ausschlachten ['aʊsʃlaxtən] *vt (Auto)* to cannibalize; *(fig)* to make a meal of

ausschlafen ['aʊsʃla:fən] *unreg vi, vr* to sleep late ▷ *vt* to sleep off; **ich bin nicht ausgeschlafen** I didn't have *od* get enough sleep

Ausschlag ['aʊsʃla:k] *m (Med)* rash; *(Pendelausschlag)* swing; *(von Nadel)* deflection; **den ~ geben** *(fig)* to tip the balance

ausschlagen ['aʊsʃla:gən] *unreg vt* to knock out; *(auskleiden)* to deck out; *(verweigern)* to decline ▷ *vi (Pferd)* to kick out; *(Bot)* to sprout; *(Zeiger)* to be deflected

ausschlaggebend *adj* decisive

ausschließen ['aʊsʃli:sən] *unreg vt* to shut *od* lock out; *(Sport)* to disqualify; *(Fehler, Möglichkeit etc)* to rule out; *(fig)* to exclude; **ich will mich nicht ~** myself not excepted

ausschließlich *adj* exclusive ▷ *adv* exclusively ▷ *präp +gen* excluding, exclusive of

ausschlüpfen ['aʊsʃlʏpfən] *vi* to slip out; *(aus Ei, Puppe)* to hatch out

Ausschluss ['aʊsʃlʊs] *m* exclusion; **unter ~ der Öffentlichkeit stattfinden** to be closed to the public; *(Jur)* to be held in camera

ausschmücken ['aʊsʃmʏkən] *vt* to decorate; *(fig)* to embellish

ausschneiden ['aʊsʃnaɪdən] *unreg vt* to cut out; *(Büsche)* to trim

Ausschnitt ['aʊsʃnɪt] *m (Teil)* section; *(von Kleid)* neckline; *(Zeitungsausschnitt)* cutting *(Brit)*, clipping *(US)*; *(aus Film etc)* excerpt

ausschöpfen ['aʊsʃœpfən] *vt* to ladle out; *(fig)* to exhaust; **Wasser** *etc* **aus etw ~** to ladle water *etc* out of sth

ausschreiben ['aʊsʃraɪbən] *unreg vt (ganz schreiben)* to write out (in full); *(Scheck, Rechnung etc)* to write (out); *(Stelle, Wettbewerb etc)* to announce, advertise

Ausschreibung *f (Bekanntmachung: von Wahlen)* calling; *(: von Stelle)* advertising

Ausschreitung ['aʊsʃraɪtʊŋ] *f* excess

Ausschuss ['aʊsʃʊs] *m* committee, board; *(Abfall)* waste, scraps *pl*; *(Comm: auch:* **Ausschussware)** reject

ausschütten ['aʊsʃʏtən] *vt* to pour out; *(Eimer)* to empty; *(Geld)* to pay ▷ *vr* to shake (with laughter)

Ausschüttung *f (Fin)* distribution

ausschwärmen ['aʊsʃvɛrmən] *vi (Bienen, Menschen)* to swarm out; *(Mil)* to fan out

ausschweifend ['aʊsʃvaɪfənt] *adj (Leben)* dissipated, debauched; *(Fantasie)* extravagant

Ausschweifung *f* excess

ausschweigen ['aʊsʃvaɪgən] *unreg vr* to keep silent

ausschwitzen ['aʊsʃvɪtsən] *vt* to sweat out

aussehen ['aʊsze:ən] *unreg vi* to look; **gut ~** to look good/well; **wie siehts aus?** *(umg: wie* *stehts?*) how's things?; **das sieht nach nichts aus** that doesn't look anything special; **es sieht nach Regen aus** it looks like rain; **es sieht schlecht aus** things look bad; **Aussehen (-s)** *nt* appearance

aus sein ['aʊsaɪn] *siehe* **aus**

außen ['aʊsən] *adv* outside; (*nach außen*) outwards; **~ ist es rot** it's red (on the) outside

Außen- *zW*: **Außenantenne** *f* outside aerial; **Außenarbeiten** *pl* work*sing* on the exterior; **Außenaufnahme** *f* outdoor shot; **Außenbezirk** *m* outlying district; **Außenbordmotor** *m* outboard motor

aussenden ['aʊszɛndən] *unreg vt* to send out, emit

Außen- *zW*: **Außendienst** *m* outside *od* field service; (*von Diplomat*) foreign service; **Außenhandel** *m* foreign trade; **Außenminister** *m* foreign minister; **Außenministerium** *nt* foreign office; **Außenpolitik** *f* foreign policy; **Außenseite** *f* outside; **Außenseiter, in (-s, -)** *m(f)* outsider; **Außenspiegel** *m* (*Aut*) outside mirror; **Außenstände** *pl* (*bes Comm*) outstanding debts *pl*, arrears *pl*; **Außenstehende, r** *f(m)* outsider; **Außenstelle** *f* branch; **Außenwelt** *f* outside world

außer ['aʊsər] *präp+dat* (*räumlich*) out of; (*abgesehen von*) except ▷ *konj* (*ausgenommen*) except; **~ Gefahr sein** to be out of danger; **~ Zweifel** beyond any doubt; **~ Betrieb** out of order; **~ sich** *dat* **sein/geraten** to be beside o.s.; **~ Dienst** retired; **~ Landes** abroad; **~ wenn** unless; **~ dass** except; **außeramtlich** *adj* unofficial, private

außerdem *konj* besides, in addition ▷ *adv* anyway

außerdienstlich *adj* private

äußere, r, s ['ɔysərə(r,s)] *adj* outer, external; **Äußere, s** *nt* exterior; (*fig: Aussehen*) outward appearance

außer- *zW*: **außerehelich** *adj* extramarital; **außergewöhnlich** *adj* unusual; **außerhalb** *präp+gen* outside ▷ *adv* outside; **außerirdisch** *adj* extraterrestrial; **Außerkraftsetzung** *f* repeal

äußerlich *adj* external; **rein ~ betrachtet** on the face of it; **Äußerlichkeit** *f* (*fig*) triviality; (*Oberflächlichkeit*) superficiality; (*Formalität*) formality

äußern *vt* to utter, express; (*zeigen*) to show ▷ *vr* to give one's opinion; (*sich zeigen*) to show itself

außer- *zW*: **außerordentlich** *adj* extraordinary; **außerplanmäßig** *adj* unscheduled; **außersinnlich** *adj*: **außersinnliche Wahrnehmung** extrasensory perception

äußerst ['ɔysərst] *adv* extremely, most

außerstande, außer Stande [aʊsər'ʃtandə] *adv* (*nicht in der Lage*) not in a position; (*nicht fähig*) unable

Äußerste, s *nt*: **bis zum ~n gehen** to go to extremes

äußerste, r, s *adj* utmost; (*räumlich*) farthest;

(*Termin*) last possible; (*Preis*) highest; **mein ~s Angebot** my final offer

äußerstenfalls *adv* if the worst comes to the worst

Äußerung *f* (*Bemerkung*) remark, comment; (*Behauptung*) statement; (*Zeichen*) expression

aussetzen ['aʊszɛtsən] *vt* (*Kind, Tier*) to abandon; (*Boote*) to lower; (*Belohnung*) to offer; (*Urteil, Verfahren*) to postpone ▷ *vi* (*aufhören*) to stop; (*Pause machen*) to have a break; **jdn/sich einer Sache** *dat* **~** to lay sb/o.s. open to sth; **jdm/etw ausgesetzt sein** to be exposed to sb/sth; **was haben Sie daran auszusetzen?** what's your objection to it?; **an jdm/etw etwas ~** to find fault with sb/sth

Aussicht ['aʊszɪçt] *f* view; (*in Zukunft*) prospect; **in ~ sein** to be in view; **etw in ~ haben** to have sth in view; **jdm etw in ~ stellen** to promise sb sth

Aussichts- *zW*: **aussichtslos** *adj* hopeless; **Aussichtspunkt** *m* viewpoint; **aussichtsreich** *adj* promising; **Aussichtsturm** *m* observation tower

Aussiedler, in ['aʊsziːdlər(ɪn)] **(-s, -)** *m(f)* (*Auswanderer*) emigrant; *see culture note*

● AUSSIEDLER

Aussiedler are people of German origin from East and South-East Europe who have resettled in Germany. Many come from the former Soviet Union. They are given free German language tuition and receive financial help. The number of *Aussiedler* increased dramatically in the early 1990s.

aussöhnen ['aʊszøːnən] *vt* to reconcile ▷ *vr* (*einander*) to become reconciled; **sich mit jdm/etw ~** to reconcile o.s. with sb/to sth

Aussöhnung *f* reconciliation

aussondern ['aʊszɔndərn] *vt* to separate off, select

aussorgen ['aʊszɔrgən] *vi*: **ausgesorgt haben** to have no more money worries

aussortieren ['aʊszɔrtiːrən] *vt* to sort out

ausspannen ['aʊsʃpanən] *vt* to spread *od* stretch out; (*Pferd*) to unharness; (*umg: Mädchen*): **jdm jdn ~** to steal sb from sb ▷ *vi* to relax

aussparen ['aʊsʃpaːrən] *vt* to leave open

aussperren ['aʊsʃpɛrən] *vt* to lock out

Aussperrung *f* (*Industrie*) lock-out

ausspielen ['aʊsʃpiːlən] *vt* (*Karte*) to lead; (*Geldprämie*) to offer as a prize ▷ *vi* (*Karten*) to lead; **ausgespielt haben** to be finished; **jdn gegen jdn ~** to play sb off against sb

Ausspielung *f* (*im Lotto*) draw

ausspionieren ['aʊsʃpioniːrən] *vt* (*Pläne etc*) to spy out; (*Person*) to spy on

Aussprache ['aʊsʃpraːxə] *f* pronunciation; (*Unterredung*) (frank) discussion

aussprechen ['aʊsʃprɛçən] *unreg vt* to pronounce; (*zu Ende sprechen*) to speak; (*äußern*) to say, express ▷ vr (sich äußern): **sich ~ (über +akk)** to speak (about); (sich anvertrauen) to unburden o.s. (about od on); (diskutieren) to discuss ▷ vi (zu Ende sprechen) to finish speaking; **der Regierung das Vertrauen ~** to pass a vote of confidence in the government

Ausspruch ['aʊsʃprʊx] m remark; (geflügeltes Wort) saying

ausspucken ['aʊsʃpʊkən] vt to spit out ▷ vi to spit

ausspülen ['aʊsʃpyːlən] vt to wash out; (Mund) to rinse

ausstaffieren ['aʊsʃtafiːrən] vt to equip, kit out; (Zimmer) to furnish

Ausstand ['aʊsʃtant] m strike; **in den ~ treten** to go on strike; **seinen ~ geben** to hold a leaving party

ausstatten ['aʊsʃtatən] vt (Zimmer etc) to furnish; **jdn mit etw ~** to equip sb od kit sb out with sth

Ausstattung f (Ausstatten) provision; (Kleidung) outfit; (Aussteuer) dowry; (Aufmachung) make-up; (Einrichtung) furnishing

ausstechen ['aʊsʃtɛçən] unreg vt (Torf, Kekse) to cut out; (Augen) to gouge out; (übertreffen) to outshine

ausstehen ['aʊsʃteːən] unreg vt to stand, endure ▷ vi (noch nicht da sein) to be outstanding

aussteigen ['aʊsʃtaɪgən] unreg vi to get out, alight; **alles ~!** (von Schaffner) all change!; **aus der Gesellschaft ~** to drop out (of society)

Aussteiger, in (umg) m(f) dropout

ausstellen ['aʊsʃtɛlən] vt to exhibit, display; (umg: ausschalten) to switch off; (Rechnung etc) to make out; (Pass, Zeugnis) to issue

Aussteller, in m(f) (auf Messe) exhibitor; (von Scheck) drawer

Ausstellung f exhibition; (Fin) drawing up; (einer Rechnung) making out; (eines Passes etc) issuing

Ausstellungsdatum nt date of issue

Ausstellungsstück nt (in Ausstellung) exhibit; (in Schaufenster etc) display item

aussterben ['aʊsʃtɛrbən] unreg vi to die out; **Aussterben** nt extinction

Aussteuer ['aʊsʃtɔyər] f dowry

aussteuern ['aʊsʃtɔyərn] vt (Verstärker) to adjust

Ausstieg ['aʊsʃtiːk] (-(e)s, -e) m (Ausgang) exit; **~ aus der Atomenergie** abandonment of nuclear energy

ausstopfen ['aʊsʃtɔpfən] vt to stuff

ausstoßen ['aʊsʃtoːsən] unreg vt (Luft, Rauch) to give off, emit; (aus Verein etc) to expel, exclude; (herstellen: Teile, Stückzahl) to turn out, produce

ausstrahlen ['aʊsʃtraːlən] vt, vi to radiate; (Rundf) to broadcast

Ausstrahlung f radiation; (fig) charisma

ausstrecken ['aʊsʃtrɛkən] vt, vr to stretch out

ausstreichen ['aʊsʃtraɪçən] unreg vt to cross out; (glätten) to smooth out

ausstreuen ['aʊsʃtrɔyən] vt to scatter; (fig: Gerücht) to spread

ausströmen ['aʊsʃtrøːmən] vi (Gas) to pour out, escape ▷ vt to give off; (fig) to radiate

aussuchen ['aʊszuːxən] vt to select, pick out

Austausch ['aʊstaʊʃ] m exchange; **austauschbar** adj exchangeable

austauschen vt to exchange, swop

Austauschmotor m replacement engine; (gebraucht) factory-reconditioned engine

Austauschstudent, in m(f) exchange student

austeilen ['aʊstaɪlən] vt to distribute, give out

Auster ['aʊstər] (-, -n) f oyster

austoben ['aʊstoːbən] vr (Kind) to run wild; (Erwachsene) to let off steam; (sich müde machen) to tire o.s. out

austragen ['aʊstraːgən] unreg vt (Post) to deliver; (Streit etc) to decide; (Wettkämpfe) to hold; **ein Kind ~** (nicht abtreiben) to have a child

Austräger ['aʊstrɛːgər] m delivery boy; (Zeitungsausträger) newspaper boy

Austragungsort m (Sport) venue

Australien ['aʊstraːliən] (-s) nt Australia

Australier, in (-s, -) m(f) Australian

australisch adj Australian

austreiben ['aʊstraɪbən] unreg vt to drive out, expel; (Teufel etc) to exorcize; **jdm etw ~** to cure sb of sth; (bes durch Schläge) to knock sth out of sb

austreten ['aʊstreːtən] unreg vi (zur Toilette) to be excused ▷ vt (Feuer) to tread out, trample; (Schuhe) to wear out; (Treppe) to wear down; **aus etw ~** to leave sth

austricksen ['aʊstrɪksən] (umg) vt (Sport, fig) to trick

austrinken ['aʊstrɪŋkən] unreg vt (Glas) to drain; (Getränk) to drink up ▷ vi to finish one's drink, drink up

Austritt ['aʊstrɪt] m emission; (aus Verein, Partei etc) retirement, withdrawal

austrocknen ['aʊstrɔknən] vt, vi to dry up

austüfteln ['aʊstyftəln] (umg) vt to work out; (ersinnen) to think up

ausüben ['aʊsyːbən] vt (Beruf) to practise (Brit), practice (US), carry out; (innehaben: Amt) to hold; (Funktion) to perform; (Einfluss) to exert; **einen Reiz auf jdn ~** to hold an attraction for sb; **eine Wirkung auf jdn ~** to have an effect on sb

Ausübung f practice, exercise; **in ~ seines Dienstes/seiner Pflicht** (form) in the execution of his duty

ausufern ['aʊsuːfərn] vi (fig) to get out of hand; (Konflikt etc): **~ (zu)** to escalate (into)

Ausverkauf ['aʊsfɛrkaʊf] m sale; (fig: Verrat) sell-out

ausverkaufen vt to sell out; (Geschäft) to sell up

ausverkauft adj (Karten, Artikel) sold out; (Theat: Haus) full

auswachsen ['aʊsvaksən] unreg vi: **das ist (ja) zum A~** (umg) it's enough to drive you mad

Auswahl ['aʊsvaːl] f: **eine ~ (an +dat)** a selection (of), a choice (of)

auswählen ['aʊsvɛːlən] vt to select, choose

Auswahlmöglichkeit f choice

Auswanderer ['aʊsvandərər] (**-s, -**) m emigrant

Auswanderin ['aʊsvandərın] f emigrant

auswandern vi to emigrate

Auswanderung f emigration

auswärtig ['aʊsvɛrtıç] adj (nicht am/vom Ort) out-of-town; (ausländisch) foreign; **das A~e Amt** the Foreign Office (Brit), the State Department (US)

auswärts ['aʊsvɛrts] adv outside; (nach außen) outwards; **~ essen** to eat out; **Auswärtsspiel** nt away game

auswaschen ['aʊsvaʃən] unreg vt to wash out; (spülen) to rinse (out)

auswechseln ['aʊsvɛksəln] vt to change, substitute

Ausweg ['aʊsveːk] m way out; **der letzte ~** the last resort; **ausweglos** adj hopeless

ausweichen ['aʊsvaɪçən] unreg vi: **jdm/etw ~** (lit) to move aside od make way for sb/sth; (fig) to sidestep sb/sth; **jdm/einer Begegnung ~** to avoid sb/a meeting

ausweichend adj evasive

Ausweichmanöver nt evasive action

ausweinen ['aʊsvaɪnən] vr to have a (good) cry

Ausweis ['aʊsvaɪs] (**-es, -e**) m identity card; passport; (Mitgliedsausweis, Bibliotheksausweis etc) card; **~, bitte** your papers, please

ausweisen ['aʊsvaɪzən] unreg vt to expel, banish ▷ vr to prove one's identity

Ausweis- zW: **Ausweiskarte** f identity papers pl; **Ausweiskontrolle** f identity check; **Ausweispapiere** pl identity papers pl

Ausweisung f expulsion

ausweiten ['aʊsvaɪtən] vt to stretch

auswendig ['aʊsvɛndıç] adv by heart; **~ lernen** to learn by heart

auswerfen ['aʊsvɛrfən] unreg vt (Anker, Netz) to cast

auswerten ['aʊsvɛrtən] vt to evaluate

Auswertung f evaluation, analysis; (Nutzung) utilization

auswickeln ['aʊsvıkəln] vt (Paket, Bonbon etc) to unwrap

auswirken ['aʊsvırkən] vr to have an effect

Auswirkung f effect

auswischen ['aʊsvıʃən] vt to wipe out; **jdm eins ~** (umg) to put one over on sb

Auswuchs ['aʊsvuːks] m (out)growth; (fig) product; (Missstand, Übersteigerung) excess

auswuchten ['aʊsvʊxtən] vt (Aut) to balance

auszacken ['aʊstsakən] vt (Stoff etc) to pink

auszahlen ['aʊstsaːlən] vt (Lohn, Summe) to pay out; (Arbeiter) to pay off; (Miterben) to buy out ▷ vr (sich lohnen) to pay

auszählen ['aʊstsɛːlən] vt (Stimmen) to count; (Boxen) to count out

auszeichnen ['aʊstsaıçnən] vt to honour (Brit), honor (US); (Mil) to decorate; (Comm) to price ▷ vr to distinguish o.s.; **der Wagen zeichnet sich durch ... aus** one of the car's main features is ...

Auszeichnung f distinction; (Comm) pricing;

(Ehrung) awarding of decoration; (Ehre) honour (Brit), honor (US); (Orden) decoration; **mit ~** with distinction

ausziehen ['aʊstsiːən] unreg vt (Kleidung) to take off; (Haare, Zähne, Tisch etc) to pull out ▷ vi to undress ▷ vi (aufbrechen) to leave; (aus Wohnung) to move out

Auszubildende, r ['aʊstsʊbıldəndə(r)] f(m) trainee; (als Handwerker) apprentice

Auszug ['aʊstsuːk] m (aus Wohnung) removal; (aus Buch etc) extract; (Kontoauszug) statement; (Ausmarsch) departure

autark [aʊˈtark] adj self-sufficient (auch fig); (Comm) autarkical

Auto ['aʊto] (**-s, -s**) nt (motor-)car, automobile (US); **mit dem ~ fahren** to go by car; **~ fahren** to drive

Autoatlas m road atlas

Autobahn f motorway (Brit), expressway (US); see culture note

○ **AUTOBAHN**
○
○ Autobahn is the German for a motorway.
○ In the former West Germany there is an
○ widespread network but in the former
○ DDR the motorways are somewhat less
○ extensive. There is no overall speed
○ limit but a limit of 130 km per hour
○ is recommended and there are lower
○ mandatory limits on certain stretches of
○ road. As yet there are no tolls payable on
○ German Autobahns.

Autobahndreieck nt motorway (Brit) od expressway (US) junction

Autobahnkreuz nt motorway (Brit) od expressway (US) intersection

Autobahnzubringer m motorway feeder od access road

Autobiografie [aʊtobiograˈfiː] f autobiography

Auto- zW: **Autobombe** f car bomb; **Autobus** m bus; (Reisebus) coach (Brit), bus (US); **Autofähre** f car ferry; **Autofahrer, in** m(f) motorist, driver; **Autofahrt** f drive; **Autofriedhof** (umg) m car dump

autogen [aʊtoˈgeːn] adj autogenous; **~es Training** (Psych) relaxation through self-hypnosis

Autogramm [aʊtoˈgram] nt autograph

Automat (**-en, -en**) m machine

Automatik [aʊtoˈmaːtık] f automatic mechanism (auch fig); (Gesamtanlage) automatic system; (Aut) automatic transmission

automatisch adj automatic

Automatisierung [aʊtomatiˈziːrʊŋ] f automation

Automobilausstellung [aʊtomoˈbiːlaʊsʃtɛlʊŋ] f motor show

autonom [aʊtoˈnoːm] adj autonomous

Autopsie [aʊtɔˈpsiː] f post-mortem, autopsy

Autor ['aʊtɔr] (**-s, -en**) m author

Auto- zW: **Autoradio** nt car radio; **Autoreifen** m car tyre (Brit) od tire (US); **Autoreisezug** m motorail train; **Autorennen** nt motor race; (Sportart) motor racing

Autorin [aʊˈtoːrɪn] f author(ess)

autoritär [aʊtoriˈtɛːr] adj authoritarian

Autorität f authority

Auto- zW: **Autoschalter** m drive-in bank (counter); **Autotelefon** nt car phone; **Autounfall** m car od motor accident;

Autoverleih m, **Autovermietung** f car hire (Brit) od rental (US)

AvD (-) m abk (= Automobilclub von Deutschland) German motoring organization, ≈ AA (Brit), AAA (US)

Axt [akst] (-, ⸚e) f axe (Brit), ax (US)

AZ, Az. abk (= Aktenzeichen) ref.

Azoren [aˈtsoːrən] pl (Geog) Azores pl

Azteke [atsˈteːkə] (-n, -n) m Aztec

Azubi [aˈtsuːbi] (-s, -s) (umg) f(m) abk = **Auszubildende(r)**

Bb

B¹, b [be:] *nt* (*letter*) B, b; **B wie Bertha** ≈ B for Benjamin, B for Baker (*US*); **B-Dur/b-Moll** (the key of) B flat major/minor

B² [be:] *f abk* = **Bundesstraße**

Baby ['be:bi] (**-s, -s**) *nt* baby; **Babyausstattung** *f* layette; **Babyklappe** *f anonymous drop-off point for unwanted babies*; **Babyraum** *m* (*Flughafen etc*) nursing room; **babysitten** *vi* to babysit; **Babysitter** ['be:bisitər] (**-s, -**) *m* baby-sitter; **Babyspeck** (*umg*) *m* puppy fat

Bach [bax] (**-(e)s, ¨e**) *m* stream, brook

Backblech *nt* baking tray

Backbord (**-(e)s, -e**) *nt* (*Naut*) port

Backe (**-, -n**) *f* cheek

backen ['bakən] *unreg vt, vi* to bake; **frisch/ knusprig gebackenes Brot** fresh/crusty bread

Backenbart *m* sideboards *pl*

Backenzahn *m* molar

Bäcker, in ['bɛkər(ın)] (**-s, -**) *m(f)* baker

Bäckerei [bɛkəˈraı] *f* bakery; (*Bäckerladen*) baker's (shop)

Bäckerjunge *m* (*Lehrling*) baker's apprentice

Back- *zW*: **Backfisch** *m* fried fish; (*veraltet*) teenager; **Backform** *f* baking tin (*Brit*) *od* pan (*US*); **Backhähnchen** *nt* fried chicken in breadcrumbs; **Backobst** *nt* dried fruit; **Backofen** *m* oven; **Backpflaume** *f* prune; **Backpulver** *nt* baking powder; **Backstein** *m* brick

bäckt [bɛkt] *vb siehe* **backen**

Bad [ba:t] (**-(e)s, ¨er**) *nt* bath; (*Schwimmen*) bathing; (*Ort*) spa

Bade- *zW*: **Badeanstalt** *f* swimming pool; **Badeanzug** *m* bathing suit; **Badehose** *f* bathing *od* swimming trunks *pl*; **Badekappe** *f* bathing *od* swimming cap; **Bademantel** *m* bath(ing) robe; **Bademeister** *m* swimming pool attendant

baden ['ba:dən] *vi* to bathe, have a bath ▷ *vt* to bath; **~ gehen** (*fig: umg*) to come a cropper

Bade- *zW*: **Badeort** *m* spa; **Badesachen** *pl* swimming things *pl*; **Badetuch** *nt* bath towel; **Badewanne** *f* bath(tub); **Badezimmer** *nt* bathroom

baff [baf] *adj*: **~ sein** (*umg*) to be flabbergasted

BAföG, Bafög [ba:føk] *nt abk* = **Bundesausbildungsförderungsgesetz**; *see culture note*

Bafög is the system which awards grants for living expenses to students at universities and certain training colleges. The amount is based on parental income. Part of the grant must be paid back a few years after graduating.

BAG (**-**) *nt abk* (= *Bundesarbeitsgericht*) *German industrial tribunal*

Bagatelle [baga'tɛlə] (**-, -n**) *f* trifle

Bagdad ['bakdat] (**-s**) *nt* Baghdad

Bagger ['bagər] (**-s, -**) *m* excavator; (*Naut*) dredger

baggern *vt, vi* to excavate; (*Naut*) to dredge

Baggersee *m* (flooded) gravel pit

Bahamas [ba'ha:mas] *pl*: **die ~** the Bahamas *pl*

Bahn [ba:n] (**-, -en**) *f* railway (*Brit*), railroad (*US*); (*Weg*) road, way; (*Spur*) lane; (*Rennbahn*) track; (*Astron*) orbit; (*Stoffbahn*) length; **mit der ~** by train *od* rail/tram; **frei ~** (*Comm*) carriage free to station of destination; **jdm/ etw die ~ ebnen** (*fig*) to clear the way for sb/ sth; **von der rechten ~ abkommen** to stray from the straight and narrow; **jdn aus der ~ werfen** (*fig*) to shatter sb; **Bahnbeamte, r** *m* railway (*Brit*) *od* railroad (*US*) official; **bahnbrechend** *adj* pioneering; **Bahnbrecher, in** (**-s, -**) *m(f)* pioneer; **Bahndamm** *m* railway embankment

bahnen *vt*: **sich einen Weg ~** to clear a way

Bahnfahrt *f* railway (*Brit*) *od* railroad (*US*) journey

Bahnhof *m* station; **auf dem ~** at the station; **ich verstehe nur ~** (*hum: umg*) it's all Greek to me

Bahnhofshalle *f* station concourse

Bahnhofsmission *f charitable organization for helping rail travellers; see culture note*

The *Bahnhofsmission* is a charitable organization set up by and run jointly by various churches. They have an office at

railway stations in most big cities to which
people in need of advice and help can go.

Bahnhofswirtschaft *f* station restaurant
Bahn- *zW:* **bahnlagernd** *adj* (*Comm*) to
be collected from the station; **Bahnlinie**
f (railway (*Brit*) *od* railroad (*US*)) line;
Bahnschranke *f* level (*Brit*) *od* grade (*US*)
crossing barrier; **Bahnsteig** *m* platform;
Bahnsteigkarte *f* platform ticket;
Bahnstrecke *f* railway (*Brit*) *od* railroad (*US*)
line; **Bahnübergang** *m* level (*Brit*) *od* grade
(*US*) crossing; **beschrankter Bahnübergang**
crossing with gates; **unbeschrankter**
Bahnübergang unguarded crossing;
Bahnwärter *m* signalman
Bahrain [baˈraɪn] (-s) *nt* Bahrain
Bahre [ˈbaːrə] (-, -n) *f* stretcher
Baiser [bɛˈzeː] (-s, -s) *nt* meringue
Baisse [ˈbɛːsə] (-, -n) *f* (*Börse*) fall; (*plötzlich*)
slump
Bajonett [bajoˈnɛt] (-(e)s, -e) *nt* bayonet
Bakelit® [bakeˈliːt] (-s) *nt* Bakelite®
Bakterien [bakˈteːriən] *pl* bacteria *pl*
Balance [baˈlãːsə] (-, -n) *f* balance, equilibrium
balancieren *vt, vi* to balance
bald [balt] *adv* (*zeitlich*) soon; (*beinahe*) almost;
~ ... ~ ... now ... now ...; ~ **darauf** soon
afterwards; **bis ~!** see you soon
baldig [ˈbaldɪç] *adj* early, speedy
baldmöglichst *adv* as soon as possible
Baldrian [ˈbaldriaːn] (-s, -e) *m* valerian
Balearen [baleˈaːrən] *pl:* **die ~** the Balearics *pl*
Balg [balk] (-(e)s, ¨er) (*pej: umg*) *m od nt* (*Kind*)
brat
balgen [ˈbalgən] *vr:* **sich ~ (um)** to scrap (over)
Balkan [ˈbalkaːn] *m:* **der ~** the Balkans *pl*
Balken [ˈbalkən] (-s, -) *m* beam; (*Tragbalken*)
girder; (*Stützbalken*) prop
Balkon [balˈkõː] (-s, -s *od* -e) *m* balcony; (*Theat*)
(dress) circle
Ball [bal] (-(e)s, ¨e) *m* ball; (*Tanz*) dance, ball
Ballade [baˈlaːdə] (-, -n) *f* ballad
Ballast [ˈbalast] (-(e)s, -e) *m* ballast; (*fig*)
weight, burden; **Ballaststoffe** *pl* (*Med*)
roughage *sing*
Ballen [ˈbalən] (-s, -) *m* bale; (*Anat*) ball
ballen *vt* (*formen*) to make into a ball; (*Faust*) to
clench ▷ *vr* to build up; (*Menschen*) to gather
ballern [ˈbalərn] (*umg*) *vi* to shoot, fire
Ballett [baˈlɛt] (-(e)s, -e) *nt* ballet;
Balletttänzer, in *m(f)* ballet dancer
Ballistik [baˈlɪstɪk] *f* ballistics *sing*
Balljunge *m* ball boy
Ballkleid *nt* evening dress
Ballon [baˈlõː] (-s, -s *od* -e) *m* balloon
Ballspiel *nt* ball game
Ballung [ˈbalʊŋ] *f* concentration; (*von Energie*)
build-up
Ballungs- *zW:* **Ballungsgebiet** *nt*,
Ballungsraum *m* conurbation;
Ballungszentrum *nt* centre (*Brit*) *od* center (*US*)
(*of population, industry etc*)

Balsam [ˈbalzaːm] (-s, -e) *m* balsam; (*fig*) balm
Balte [ˈbaltə] (-n, -n) *m* Balt; **er ist ~** he comes
from the Baltic
Baltikum [ˈbaltikʊm] (-s) *nt:* **das ~** the Baltic
States *pl*
baltisch *adj* Baltic *attrib*
Balz [balts] (-, -en) *f* (*Paarungsspiel*) courtship
display; (*Paarungszeit*) mating season
Bambus [ˈbambʊs] (-ses, -se) *m* bamboo;
Bambusrohr *nt* bamboo cane
Bammel [ˈbaməl] (-s) (*umg*) *m:* **(einen) ~ vor**
jdm/etw haben to be scared of sb/sth
banal [baˈnaːl] *adj* banal
Banalität [banaliˈtɛːt] *f* banality
Banane [baˈnaːnə] (-, -n) *f* banana
Bananenschale *f* banana skin
Bananenstecker *m* jack plug
Banause [baˈnaʊzə] (-n, -n) *m* philistine
Band¹ [bant] (-(e)s, ¨e) *m* (*Buchband*) volume;
das spricht Bände that speaks volumes
Band² (-(e)s, ¨er) *nt* (*Stoffband*) ribbon, tape;
(*Fließband*) production line; (*Fassband*) hoop;
(*Zielband, Tonband*) tape; (*Anat*) ligament; **etw**
auf ~ aufnehmen to tape sth; **am laufenden**
~ (*umg*) non-stop
Band³ (-(e)s, -e) *nt* (*Freundschaftsband etc*) bond
Band⁴ [bɛnt] (-, -s) *f* band, group
band *etc* [bant] *vb siehe* **binden**
Bandage [banˈdaːʒə] (-, -n) *f* bandage
bandagieren *vt* to bandage
Bandbreite *f* (*von Meinungen etc*) range
Bande [ˈbandə] (-, -n) *f* band; (*Straßenbande*)
gang
bändigen [ˈbɛndɪgən] *vt* (*Tier*) to tame; (*Trieb,*
Leidenschaft) to control, restrain
Bandit [banˈdiːt] (-en, -en) *m* bandit
Band- *zW:* **Bandmaß** *nt* tape measure;
Bandnudeln *pl* tagliatelle *pl*; **Bandsäge**
f band saw; **Bandscheibe** *f* (*Anat*) disc;
Bandscheibenschaden *m* slipped disc;
Bandwurm *m* tapeworm
bange [ˈbaŋə] *adj* scared; (*besorgt*) anxious;
jdm wird es ~ sb is becoming scared; **jdm B~**
machen to scare sb; **Bangemacher** (-s, -) *m*
scaremonger
bangen *vi:* **um jdn/etw ~** to be anxious *od*
worried about sb/sth
Bangkok [ˈbaŋkɔk] (-s) *nt* Bangkok
Bangladesch [baŋglaˈdɛʃ] (-s) *nt* Bangladesh
Banjo [ˈbanjo, ˈbɛndʒo] (-s, -s) *nt* banjo
Bank¹ [baŋk] (-, ¨e) *f* (*Sitzbank*) bench; (*Sandbank*
etc) (sand)bank, (sand)bar; **etw auf die lange**
~ schieben (*umg*) to put sth off
Bank² (-, -en) *f* (*Geldbank*) bank; **bei der ~** at the
bank; **Geld auf der ~ haben** to have money
in the bank; **Bankanweisung** *f* banker's
order; **Bankautomat** *m* cash dispenser;
Bankbeamte, r *m* bank clerk; **Bankeinlage** *f*
(bank) deposit
Bankett [banˈkɛt] (-(e)s, -e) *nt* (*Essen*) banquet;
(*Straßenrand*) verge (*Brit*), shoulder (*US*)
Bank- *zW:* **Bankfach** *nt* (*Schließfach*) safe-
deposit box; **Bankgebühr** *f* bank charge;

Bankgeheimnis *nt* confidentiality in banking
Bankier [baŋki'eː] (**-s, -s**) *m* banker
Bank- *zW*: **Bankkonto** *nt* bank account;
Bankleitzahl *f* bank code number; **Banknote** *f* banknote; **Bankraub** *m* bank robbery
bankrott [baŋ'krɔt] *adj* bankrupt; **Bankrott** (**-(e)s, -e**) *m* bankruptcy; **Bankrott machen** to go bankrupt; **den Bankrott anmelden** *od* **erklären** to declare o.s. bankrupt; **Bankrotterklärung** *f* (*lit*) declaration of bankruptcy; (*fig*: *umg*) declaration of failure
Banküberfall *m* bank raid
Bann [ban] (**-(e)s, -e**) *m* (*Hist*) ban; (*Kirchenbann*) excommunication; (*fig*: *Zauber*) spell; **bannen** *vt* (*Geister*) to exorcize; (*Gefahr*) to avert; (*bezaubern*) to enchant; (*Hist*) to banish
Banner (**-s, -**) *nt* banner, flag
Bar [baːr] (**-, -s**) *f* bar
bar *adj* (+*gen*) (*unbedeckt*) bare; (*frei von*) lacking (in); (*offenkundig*) utter, sheer; **~e(s) Geld** cash; **etw (in) ~ bezahlen** to pay sth (in) cash; **etw für ~e Münze nehmen** (*fig*) to take sth at face value; **~ aller Hoffnung** (*liter*) devoid of hope, completely without hope
Bär [bɛːr] (**-en, -en**) *m* bear; **jdm einen ~en aufbinden** (*umg*) to have sb on
Baracke [ba'rakə] (**-, -n**) *f* hut
barbarisch [bar'baːrɪʃ] *adj* barbaric, barbarous
Barbestand *m* money in hand
Bardame *f* barmaid
Bärenhunger (*umg*) *m*: **einen ~ haben** to be famished
bärenstark (*umg*) *adj* strapping, strong as an ox; (*fig*) terrific
barfuß *adj* barefoot
barg *etc* [bark] *vb siehe* **bergen**
Bargeld *nt* cash, ready money
bargeldlos *adj* non-cash; **~er Zahlungsverkehr** non-cash *od* credit transactions *pl*
barhäuptig *adj* bareheaded
Barhocker *m* bar stool
Bariton ['baːritɔn] *m* baritone
Barkauf *m* cash purchase
Barkeeper ['baːrkiːpər] (**-s, -**) *m* barman, bartender
Barkredit *m* cash loan
Barmann (**-(e)s, *pl* -männer**) *m* barman
barmherzig [barm'hɛrtsɪç] *adj* merciful, compassionate; **Barmherzigkeit** *f* mercy, compassion
Barock [ba'rɔk] (**-s** *od* **-**) *nt od m* baroque
Barometer [baro'meːtər] (**-s, -**) *nt* barometer; **das ~ steht auf Sturm** (*fig*) there's a storm brewing
Baron [ba'roːn] (**-s, -e**) *m* baron
Baronesse [baro'nɛsə] (**-, -n**) *f* baroness
Baronin *f* baroness
Barren ['barən] (**-s, -**) *m* parallel bars *pl*; (*Goldbarren*) ingot
Barriere [bari'ɛːrə] (**-, -n**) *f* barrier
Barrikade [bari'kaːdə] (**-, -n**) *f* barricade
Barsch [barʃ] (**-(e)s, -e**) *m* perch

barsch [barʃ] *adj* brusque, gruff; **jdn ~ anfahren** to snap at sb
Barschaft *f* ready money
Barscheck *m* open *od* uncrossed cheque (*Brit*), open check (*US*)
barst *etc* [barst] *vb siehe* **bersten**
Bart [baːrt] (**-(e)s, ̈-e**) *m* beard; (*Schlüsselbart*) bit
bärtig ['bɛːrtɪç] *adj* bearded
Barvermögen *nt* liquid assets *pl*
Barzahlung *f* cash payment
Basar [ba'zaːr] (**-s, -e**) *m* bazaar
Base ['baːzə] (**-, -n**) *f* (*Chem*) base; (*Cousine*) cousin
Basel ['baːzəl] (**-s**) *nt* Basle
Basen *pl von* **Base**; **Basis**
basieren [ba'ziːrən] *vt* to base ▷ *vi* to be based
Basilikum [ba'ziːlikʊm] (**-s**) *nt* basil
Basis ['baːzɪs] (**-, *pl* Basen**) *f* basis; (*Archit, Mil, Math*) base; **~ und Überbau** (*Pol, Soziologie*) foundation and superstructure; **die ~** (*umg*) the grass roots
basisch ['baːzɪʃ] *adj* (*Chem*) alkaline
Basisgruppe *f* action group
Baske ['baskə] (**-n, -n**) *m* Basque
Baskenland *nt* Basque region
Baskenmütze *f* beret
Baskin *f* Basque
Bass [bas] (**-es, ̈-e**) *m* bass
Bassin [ba'sɛ̃ː] (**-s, -s**) *nt* pool
Bassist [ba'sɪst] *m* bass
Bassschlüssel *m* bass clef
Bassstimme *f* bass voice
Bast [bast] (**-(e)s, -e**) *m* raffia
basta ['basta] *interj*: **(und damit) ~!** (and) that's that!
basteln ['bastəln] *vt* to make ▷ *vi* to do handicrafts; **an etw** *dat* **~** (*an etw herumbasteln*) to tinker with sth
Bastler ['bastlər] (**-s, -**) *m* do-it-yourselfer; (*handwerklich*) handicrafts enthusiast
BAT *m abk* (= *Bundesangestelltentarif*) German salary scale for employees
bat *etc* [baːt] *vb siehe* **bitten**
Bataillon [batal'joːn] (**-s, -e**) *nt* battalion
Batist [ba'tɪst] (**-(e)s, -e**) *m* batiste
Batterie [batə'riː] *f* battery
Bau [bau] (**-(e)s**) *m* (*Bauen*) building, construction; (*Aufbau*) structure; (*Körperbau*) frame; (*Baustelle*) building site; (*pl Baue*: *Tierbau*) hole, burrow; (: *Min*) working(s); (*pl Bauten*: *Gebäude*) building; **sich im ~ befinden** to be under construction; **Bauarbeiten** *pl* (*Straßenbau*) roadworks *pl* (*Brit*), roadwork *sing* (*US*); building *od* construction work *sing*; **Bauarbeiter** *m* building worker
Bauch [baux] (**-(e)s, Bäuche**) *m* belly; (*Anat*) stomach, abdomen; **sich** *dat* **(vor Lachen) den ~ halten** (*umg*) to split one's sides (laughing); **mit etw auf den ~ fallen** (*umg*) to come a cropper with sth; **Bauchansatz** *m* beginning of a paunch; **Bauchfell** *nt* peritoneum
bauchig *adj* bulging

47

Bauch- zW: **Bauchlandung** f: **eine Bauchlandung machen** (fig) to experience a failure, to flop; **Bauchmuskel** m abdominal muscle; **Bauchnabel** m navel, belly-button (umg); **Bauchredner** m ventriloquist; **Bauchschmerzen** pl stomachache sing; **Bauchspeicheldrüse** f pancreas; **Bauchtanz** m belly dance; belly dancing; **Bauchweh** nt stomachache

Baudrate [baʊtˈraːtə] f (Comput) baud rate

bauen [ˈbaʊən] vt to build; (Tech) to construct; (umg: verursachen: Unfall) to cause ▷ vi to build; **auf jdn/etw ~** to depend od count upon sb/sth; **da hast du Mist gebaut** (umg) you really messed that up

Bauer¹ [ˈbaʊər] (-n od -s, -n) m farmer; (Schach) pawn

Bauer² (-s, -) nt od m (Vogelbauer) cage

Bäuerchen [ˈbɔʏərçən] nt (Kindersprache) burp

Bäuerin [ˈbɔʏərɪn] f farmer; (Frau des Bauern) farmer's wife

bäuerlich adj rustic

Bauern- zW: **Bauernbrot** nt black bread; **Bauernfängerei** f deception, confidence trick(s); **Bauernfrühstück** nt bacon and potato omelete (Brit) od omelet (US); **Bauernhaus** nt farmhouse; **Bauernhof** m farm; **Bauernschaft** f farming community; **Bauernschläue** f native cunning, craftiness, shrewdness

Bau- zW: **baufällig** adj dilapidated; **Baufälligkeit** f dilapidation; **Baufirma** f construction firm; **Bauführer** m site foreman; **Baugelände** nt building site; **Baugenehmigung** f building permit; **Baugerüst** nt scaffolding; **Bauherr** m client (of construction firm); **Bauingenieur** m civil engineer

Bauj. abk = **Baujahr**

Bau- zW: **Baujahr** nt year of construction; (von Auto) year of manufacture; **Baukasten** m box of bricks; **Bauklötzchen** nt (building) block; **Baukosten** pl construction costs pl; **Bauland** nt building land; **Bauleute** pl building workers pl; **baulich** adj structural; **Baulöwe** m building speculator; **Baulücke** f undeveloped building plot

Baum [baʊm] (-(e)s, pl Bäume) m tree; **heute könnte ich Bäume ausreißen** I feel full of energy today

Baumarkt m DIY superstore

baumeln [ˈbaʊməln] vi to dangle

bäumen [ˈbɔʏmən] vr to rear (up)

Baum- zW: **Baumgrenze** f tree line; **Baumschule** f nursery; **Baumstamm** m tree trunk; **Baumstumpf** m tree stump; **Baumwolle** f cotton

Bau- zW: **Bauplan** m architect's plan; **Bauplatz** m building site; **Bausachverständige, r** f(m) quantity surveyor; **Bausatz** m construction kit

Bausch [baʊʃ] (-(e)s, pl Bäusche) m (Wattebausch) ball, wad; **in ~ und Bogen** (fig) lock, stock, and barrel

bauschen vt, vi, vr to puff out

bauschig adj baggy, wide

Bau- zW: **bausparen** vi untr to save with a building society (Brit) od a building and loan association (US); **Bausparkasse** f building society (Brit), building and loan association (US); **Bausparvertrag** m savings contract with a building society (Brit) od building and loan association (US); **Baustein** m building stone, freestone; **Baustelle** f building site; **Baustil** m architectural style; **bautechnisch** adj in accordance with building od construction methods; **Bauteil** nt prefabricated part (of building); **Bauten** pl von **Bau**; **Bauunternehmer** m contractor, builder; **Bauweise** f (method of) construction; **Bauwerk** nt building; **Bauzaun** m hoarding

b. a. W. abk (= bis auf Weiteres) until further notice

Bayer, in [ˈbaɪər(ɪn)] (-n, -n) m(f) Bavarian

bayerisch, bayrisch adj Bavarian

Bayern nt Bavaria

Bazillus [baˈtsɪlʊs] (-, pl **Bazillen**) m bacillus

Bd. abk (= Band) vol.

Bde. abk (= Bände) vols.

beabsichtigen [bəˈʔapzɪçtɪgən] vt to intend

beachten [bəˈʔaxtən] vt to take note of; (Vorschrift) to obey; (Vorfahrt) to observe

beachtenswert adj noteworthy

beachtlich adj considerable

Beachtung f notice, attention, observation; **jdm keine ~ schenken** to take no notice of sb

Beamte, r [bəˈʔamtə(r)] (-n, -n) m official; (Staatsbeamte) civil servant; (Bankbeamte etc) employee

Beamtenlaufbahn f: **die ~ einschlagen** to enter the civil service

Beamtenverhältnis nt: **im ~ stehen** to be a civil servant

beamtet adj (form) appointed on a permanent basis (by the state)

Beamtin f siehe **Beamte(r)**

beängstigend [bəˈʔɛŋstɪgənt] adj alarming

beanspruchen [bəˈʔanʃprʊxən] vt to claim; (Zeit, Platz) to take up, occupy; **jdn ~** to take up sb's time; **etw stark ~** to put sth under a lot of stress

beanstanden [bəˈʔanʃtandən] vt to complain about, object to; (Rechnung) to query

Beanstandung f complaint

beantragen [bəˈʔantraːgən] vt to apply for, ask for

beantworten [bəˈʔantvɔrtən] vt to answer

Beantwortung f reply

bearbeiten [bəˈʔarbaɪtən] vt to work; (Material) to process; (Thema) to deal with; (Land) to cultivate; (Chem) to treat; (Buch) to revise; (umg: beeinflussen wollen) to work on

Bearbeitung f processing; cultivation; treatment; revision; **die ~ meines Antrags hat lange gedauert** it took a long time to deal with my claim

Bearbeitungsgebühr f handling charge

beatmen [bə'|a:tmən] vt: **jdn künstlich ~** to give sb artificial respiration

Beatmung [bə'|a:tmʊŋ] f respiration

beaufsichtigen [bə'|aʊfzɪçtɪgən] vt to supervise

Beaufsichtigung f supervision

beauftragen [bə'|aʊftra:gən] vt to instruct; **jdn mit etw ~** to entrust sb with sth

Beauftragte, r f(m) representative

bebauen [bə'baʊən] vt to build on; (Agr) to cultivate

beben ['be:bən] vi to tremble, shake; **Beben (-s, -)** nt earthquake

bebildern [bə'bɪldərn] vt to illustrate

Becher ['bɛçər] (-s, -) m mug; (ohne Henkel) tumbler

bechern ['bɛçərn] (umg) vi (trinken) to have a few (drinks)

Becken ['bɛkən] (-s, -) nt basin; (Mus) cymbal; (Anat) pelvis

Bedacht [bə'daxt] m: **mit ~** (vorsichtig) prudently, carefully; (absichtlich) deliberately

bedacht adj thoughtful, careful; **auf etw akk ~ sein** to be concerned about sth

bedächtig [bə'dɛçtɪç] adj (umsichtig) thoughtful, reflective; (langsam) slow, deliberate

bedanken [bə'daŋkən] vr: **sich (bei jdm) ~** to say thank you (to sb); **ich bedanke mich herzlich** thank you very much

Bedarf [bə'darf] (-(e)s) m need; (Bedarfsmenge) requirements pl; (Comm) demand; supply; **alles für den häuslichen ~** all household requirements; **je nach ~** according to demand; **bei ~** if necessary; **~ an etw** dat **haben** to be in need of sth

Bedarfs- zW: **Bedarfsartikel** m requisite; **Bedarfsdeckung** f satisfaction of sb's needs; **Bedarfsfall** m case of need; **Bedarfshaltestelle** f request stop

bedauerlich [bə'daʊərlɪç] adj regrettable

bedauern [bə'daʊərn] vt to be sorry for; (bemitleiden) to pity; **wir ~, Ihnen mitteilen zu müssen, ...** we regret to have to inform you ...; **Bedauern (-s)** nt regret

bedauernswert adj (Zustände) regrettable; (Mensch) pitiable, unfortunate

bedecken [bə'dɛkən] vt to cover

bedeckt adj covered; (Himmel) overcast

bedenken [bə'dɛŋkən] unreg vt to think over, consider; **ich gebe zu ~, dass ...** (geh) I would ask you to consider that ...; **Bedenken (-s, -)** nt (Überlegen) consideration; (Zweifel) doubt; (Skrupel) scruple; **mir kommen Bedenken** I am having second thoughts

bedenklich adj doubtful; (bedrohlich) dangerous, risky

Bedenkzeit f time to consider; **zwei Tage ~** two days to think about it

bedeuten [bə'dɔʏtən] vt to mean; to signify; (wichtig sein) to be of importance; **das bedeutet nichts Gutes** that means trouble

bedeutend adj important; (beträchtlich) considerable

bedeutsam adj significant; (vielsagend) meaningful

Bedeutung f meaning; significance; (Wichtigkeit) importance

bedeutungslos adj insignificant, unimportant

bedeutungsvoll adj momentous, significant

bedienen [bə'di:nən] vt to serve; (Maschine) to work, operate ▷ vr (beim Essen) to help o.s.; (gebrauchen): **sich jds/einer Sache ~** to make use of sb/sth; **werden Sie schon bedient?** are you being served?; **damit sind Sie sehr gut bedient** that should serve you very well; **ich bin bedient!** (umg) I've had enough

Bedienung f service; (Kellner etc) waiter/waitress; (Zuschlag) service (charge); (von Maschinen) operation

Bedienungsanleitung f operating instructions pl

bedingen [bə'dɪŋən] vt (voraussetzen) to demand, involve; (verursachen) to cause, occasion

bedingt adj limited; (Straferlass) conditional; (Reflex) conditioned; **(nur) ~ gelten** to be (only) partially valid; **~ geeignet** suitable up to a point

Bedingung f condition; (Voraussetzung) stipulation; **mit** od **unter der ~, dass ...** on condition that ...; **zu günstigen ~en** (Comm) on favourable (Brit) od favorable (US) terms

Bedingungsform f (Gram) conditional

bedingungslos adj unconditional

bedrängen [bə'drɛŋən] vt to pester, harass

Bedrängnis [bə'drɛŋnɪs] f (seelisch) distress, torment

Bedrängung f trouble

bedrohen [bə'dro:ən] vt to threaten

bedrohlich adj ominous, threatening

Bedrohung f threat, menace

bedrucken [bə'drʊkən] vt to print on

bedrücken [bə'drʏkən] vt to oppress, trouble

bedürfen [bə'dʏrfən] unreg vi +gen (geh) to need, require; **ohne dass es eines Hinweises bedurft hätte, ...** without having to be asked ...

Bedürfnis [bə'dʏrfnɪs] (-ses, -se) nt need; **das ~ nach etw haben** to need sth; **Bedürfnisanstalt** f (form) public convenience (Brit), comfort station (US); **bedürfnislos** adj frugal, modest

bedürftig adj in need, poor, needy

Beefsteak ['bi:fste:k] (-s, -s) nt steak; **deutsches ~** hamburger

beehren [bə'|e:rən] vt (geh) to honour (Brit), honor (US); **wir ~ uns ...** we have pleasure in ...

beeilen [bə'|aɪlən] vr to hurry

beeindrucken [bə'|aɪndrʊkən] vt to impress, make an impression on

beeinflussen [bə'|aɪnflʊsən] vt to influence

Beeinflussung f influence

beeinträchtigen [bə'|aɪntrɛçtɪgən] vt to affect adversely; (Sehvermögen) to impair; (Freiheit) to infringe upon

beenden [bə'|ɛndən], **beendigen** [bə'|ɛn-dɪgən] vt to end, finish, terminate

Beendung, Beendigung f end(ing), finish(ing)

beengen [bə'|ɛŋən] vt to cramp; (fig) to hamper, inhibit; **~de Kleidung** restricting clothing

beengt adj cramped; (fig) stifled

beerben [bə'|ɛrbən] vt to inherit from

beerdigen [bə'|eːrdɪgən] vt to bury

Beerdigung f funeral, burial

Beerdigungsunternehmer m undertaker

Beere ['beːrə] (-, -n) f berry; (Traubenbeere) grape

Beerenauslese f wine made from specially selected grapes

Beet [beːt] (-(e)s, -e) nt (Blumenbeet) bed

befähigen [bə'fɛːɪgən] vt to enable

befähigt adj (begabt) talented; (fähig): **~ (für)** capable (of)

Befähigung f capability; (Begabung) talent, aptitude; **die ~ zum Richteramt** the qualifications to become a judge

befahl etc [bə'faːl] vb siehe **befehlen**

befahrbar [bə'faːrbaːr] adj passable; (Naut) navigable; **nicht ~ sein** (Straße, Weg) to be closed (to traffic); (wegen Schnee etc) to be impassable

befahren [bə'faːrən] unreg vt to use, drive over; (Naut) to navigate ▷ adj used

befallen [bə'falən] unreg vt to come over

befangen [bə'faŋən] adj (schüchtern) shy, self-conscious; (voreingenommen) bias(s)ed; **Befangenheit** f shyness; bias

befassen [bə'fasən] vr to concern o.s.

Befehl [bə'feːl] (-(e)s, -e) m command, order; (Comput) command; **auf ~ handeln** to act under orders; **zu ~, Herr Hauptmann!** (Mil) yes, sir; **den ~ haben** od **führen (über** +akk**)** to be in command (of)

befehlen unreg vt to order ▷ vi to give orders; **jdm etw ~** to order sb to do sth; **du hast mir gar nichts zu ~** I won't take orders from you

befehligen vt to be in command of

Befehls- zW: **Befehlsempfänger** m subordinate; **Befehlsform** f (Gram) imperative; **Befehlshaber** (-s, -) m commanding officer; **Befehlsnotstand** m (Jur) obligation to obey orders; **Befehlsverweigerung** f insubordination

befestigen [bə'fɛstɪgən] vt to fasten; (stärken) to strengthen; (Mil) to fortify; **~ an** +dat to fasten to

Befestigung f fastening; strengthening; (Mil) fortification

Befestigungsanlage f fortification

befeuchten [bə'fɔʏçtən] vt to damp(en), moisten

befinden [bə'fɪndən] unreg vr to be; (sich fühlen) to feel ▷ vt: **jdn/etw für** od **als etw ~** to deem sb/sth to be sth ▷ vi: **~ (über** +akk**)** to decide (on), adjudicate (on)

Befinden (-s) nt health, condition; (Meinung)

view, opinion

beflecken [bə'flɛkən] vt (lit) to stain; (fig geh: Ruf, Ehre) to besmirch

befliegen [bə'fliːgən] unreg vt (Strecke) to fly

beflügeln [bə'flyːgəln] vt (geh) to inspire

befohlen [bə'foːlən] pp von **befehlen**

befolgen [bə'fɔlgən] vt to comply with, follow

befördern [bə'fœrdərn] vt (senden) to transport, send; (beruflich) to promote; **etw mit der Post/per Bahn ~** to send sth by post/by rail

Beförderung f transport; promotion

Beförderungskosten pl transport costs pl

befragen [bə'fraːgən] vt to question; (um Stellungnahme bitten): **~ (über** +akk**)** to consult (about)

Befragung f poll

befreien [bə'fraɪən] vt to set free; (erlassen) to exempt

Befreier, in (-s, -) m(f) liberator

befreit adj (erleichtert) relieved

Befreiung f liberation, release; (Erlassen) exemption

Befreiungs- zW: **Befreiungsbewegung** f liberation movement; **Befreiungskampf** m struggle for liberation; **Befreiungsversuch** m escape attempt

befremden [bə'frɛmdən] vt to surprise; (unangenehm) to disturb; **Befremden** (-s) nt surprise, astonishment

befreunden [bə'frɔʏndən] vr to make friends; (mit Idee etc) to acquaint o.s.

befreundet adj friendly; **wir sind schon lange (miteinander) ~** we have been friends for a long time

befriedigen [bə'friːdɪgən] vt to satisfy

befriedigend adj satisfactory

Befriedigung f satisfaction, gratification

befristet [bə'frɪstət] adj limited; (Arbeitsverhältnis, Anstellung) temporary

befruchten [bə'frʊxtən] vt to fertilize; (fig) to stimulate

Befruchtung f: **künstliche ~** artificial insemination

Befugnis [bə'fuːknɪs] (-, -se) f authorization, powers pl

befugt adj authorized, entitled

befühlen [bə'fyːlən] vt to feel, touch

Befund [bə'fʊnt] (-(e)s, -e) m findings pl; (Med) diagnosis; **ohne ~** (Med) (results) negative

befürchten [bə'fʏrçtən] vt to fear

Befürchtung f fear, apprehension

befürworten [bə'fyːrvɔrtən] vt to support, speak in favour (Brit) od favor (US) of

Befürworter, in (-s, -) m(f) supporter, advocate

Befürwortung f support(ing), favouring (Brit), favoring (US)

begabt [bə'gaːpt] adj gifted

Begabung [bə'gaːbʊŋ] f talent, gift

begann etc [bə'gan] vb siehe **beginnen**

begatten [bə'gatən] vr to mate ▷ vt to mate od pair (with)

begeben [bə'geːbən] unreg vr (gehen) to proceed; (geschehen) to occur; **sich ~ nach** od

b

zu to proceed to(wards); **sich in ärztliche Behandlung** ~ to undergo medical treatment; **sich in Gefahr** ~ to expose o.s. to danger; **Begebenheit** f occurrence

begegnen [bə'ge:gnən] vi: **jdm** ~ to meet sb; (behandeln) to treat; **Blicke** ~ **sich** eyes meet

Begegnung f meeting; (Sport) match

begehen [bə'ge:ən] unreg vt (Straftat) to commit; (Weg etc) to use, negotiate; (geh: feiern) to celebrate

begehren [bə'ge:rən] vt to desire

begehrenswert adj desirable

begehrt adj in demand; (Junggeselle) eligible

begeistern [bə'gaɪstərn] vt to fill with enthusiasm; (inspirieren) to inspire ▷ vr: **sich für etw** ~ to get enthusiastic about sth; **er ist für nichts zu** ~ he's not interested in doing anything

begeistert adj enthusiastic

Begeisterung f enthusiasm

Begierde [bə'gi:rdə] (-, -n) f desire, passion

begierig [bə'gi:rɪç] adj eager, keen; (voll Verlangen) hungry, greedy

begießen [bə'gi:sən] unreg vt to water; (mit Fett: Braten etc) to baste; (mit Alkohol) to drink to

Beginn [bə'gɪn] (-(e)s) m beginning; **zu** ~ at the beginning

beginnen unreg vt, vi to start, begin

beglaubigen [bə'glaʊbɪgən] vt to countersign; (Abschrift) to authenticate; (Echtheit, Übersetzung) to certify

Beglaubigung f countersignature

Beglaubigungsschreiben nt credentials pl

begleichen [bə'glaɪçən] unreg vt to settle, pay; **mit Ihnen habe ich noch eine Rechnung zu** ~ (fig) I've a score to settle with you

begleiten [bə'glaɪtən] vt to accompany; (Mil) to escort

Begleiter, in (-s, -) m(f) companion; (zum Schutz) escort; (Mus) accompanist

Begleit- zW: **Begleiterscheinung** f side effect; **Begleitmusik** f accompaniment; **Begleitpapiere** pl (Comm) accompanying documents pl; **Begleitschiff** nt escort vessel; **Begleitschreiben** nt covering letter; **Begleitumstände** pl attendant circumstances

Begleitung f company; (Mil) escort; (Mus) accompaniment

beglücken [bə'glʏkən] vt to make happy, delight

beglückwünschen [bə'glʏkvʏnʃən] vt: ~ **(zu)** to congratulate (on)

begnadet [bə'gna:dət] adj gifted

begnadigen [bə'gna:dɪgən] vt to pardon

Begnadigung f pardon

begnügen [bə'gny:gən] vr: **sich** ~ **mit** to be satisfied with, content o.s. with

Begonie [bə'go:niə] f begonia

begonnen [bə'gɔnən] pp von **beginnen**

begossen [bə'gɔsən] pp von **begießen** ▷ adj: **er stand da wie ein ~er Pudel** (umg) he looked so sheepish

begraben [bə'gra:bən] unreg vt to bury;

(aufgeben: Hoffnung) to abandon; (beenden: Streit etc) to end; **dort möchte ich nicht** ~ **sein** (umg) I wouldn't like to be stuck in that hole

Begräbnis [bə'grɛ:pnɪs] (-ses, -se) nt burial, funeral

begradigen [bə'gra:dɪgən] vt to straighten (out)

begreifen [bə'graɪfən] unreg vt to understand, comprehend

begreiflich [bə'graɪflɪç] adj understandable; **ich kann mich ihm nicht** ~ **machen** I can't make myself clear to him

begrenzen [bə'grɛntsən] vt (beschränken): ~ **(auf** +akk) to restrict (to), limit (to)

Begrenztheit [bə'grɛntsthaɪt] f limitation, restriction; (fig) narrowness

Begriff [bə'grɪf] (-(e)s, -e) m concept, idea; **im** ~ **sein, etw zu tun** to be about to do sth; **sein Name ist mir ein/kein** ~ his name means something/doesn't mean anything to me; **du machst dir keinen** ~ **(davon)** you've no idea; **für meine** ~**e** in my opinion; **schwer von** ~ (umg) slow on the uptake

Begriffsbestimmung f definition

begriffsstutzig adj slow-witted, dense

begrub etc [bə'gru:p] vb siehe **begraben**

begründen [bə'grʏndən] vt (Gründe geben) to justify; **etw näher** ~ to give specific reasons for sth

Begründer, in (-s, -) m(f) founder

begründet adj well-founded, justified; **sachlich** ~ founded on fact

Begründung f justification, reason

begrünen [bə'gry:nən] vt to plant with greenery

begrüßen [bə'gry:sən] vt to greet, welcome

begrüßenswert adj welcome

Begrüßung f greeting, welcome

begünstigen [bə'gʏnstɪgən] vt (Person) to favour (Brit), favor (US); (Sache) to further, promote

Begünstigte, r f(m) beneficiary

begutachten [bə'gu:t|axtən] vt to assess; (umg: ansehen) to have a look at

begütert [bə'gy:tərt] adj wealthy, well-to-do

begütigend adj (Worte etc) soothing; ~ **auf jdn einreden** to calm sb down

behaart [bə'ha:rt] adj hairy

behäbig [bə'hɛ:bɪç] adj (dick) portly, stout; (geruhsam) comfortable

behaftet [bə'haftət] adj: **mit etw** ~ **sein** to be afflicted by sth

behagen [bə'ha:gən] vi: **das behagt ihm nicht** he does not like it; **Behagen** (-s) nt comfort, ease; **mit Behagen essen** to eat with relish

behaglich [bə'ha:klɪç] adj comfortable, cosy; **Behaglichkeit** f comfort, cosiness

behält [bə'hɛlt] vb siehe **behalten**

behalten [bə'haltən] unreg vt to keep, retain; (im Gedächtnis) to remember; ~ **Sie (doch) Platz!** please don't get up!

Behälter [bə'hɛltər] (-s, -) m container,

receptacle

behämmert [bə'hɛmərt] (umg) adj screwy, crazy

behandeln [bə'handəln] vt to treat; (Thema) to deal with; (Maschine) to handle; **der ~de Arzt** the doctor in attendance

Behändigkeit [bə'hɛndɪçkaɪt] f agility, quickness

Behandlung f treatment; (von Maschine) handling

behängen [bə'hɛŋən] vt to decorate

beharren [bə'harən] vi: **auf etw** dat ~ to stick od keep to sth

beharrlich [bə'harlɪç] adj (ausdauernd) steadfast, unwavering; (hartnäckig) tenacious, dogged; **Beharrlichkeit** f steadfastness; tenacity

behaupten [bə'haʊptən] vt to claim, assert, maintain; (sein Recht) to defend ▷ vr to assert o.s.; **von jdm ~, dass ...** to say (of sb) that ...; **sich auf dem Markt ~** to establish itself on the market

Behauptung f claim, assertion

Behausung [bə'haʊzʊŋ] f dwelling, abode; (armselig) hovel

beheben [bə'he:bən] unreg vt (beseitigen) to remove; (Missstände) to remedy; (Schaden) to repair; (Störung) to clear

beheimatet [bə'haɪma:tət] adj: ~ (in +dat) domiciled (at/in); (Tier, Pflanze) native (to)

beheizen [bə'haɪtsən] vt to heat

Behelf [bə'hɛlf] (-(e)s, -e) m expedient, makeshift; **behelfen** unreg vr: **sich mit etw behelfen** to make do with sth

behelfsmäßig adj improvised, makeshift; (vorübergehend) temporary

behelligen [bə'hɛlɪgən] vt to trouble, bother

Behendigkeit [bə'hɛndɪçkaɪt] f siehe **Behändigkeit**

beherbergen [bə'hɛrbɛrgən] vt (lit, fig) to house

beherrschen [bə'hɛrʃən] vt (Volk) to rule, govern; (Situation) to control; (Sprache, Gefühle) to master ▷ vr to control o.s.

beherrscht adj controlled; **Beherrschtheit** f self-control

Beherrschung f rule; control; mastery; **die ~ verlieren** to lose one's temper

beherzigen [bə'hɛrtsɪgən] vt to take to heart

beherzt adj spirited, brave

behielt etc [bə'hi:lt] vb siehe **behalten**

behilflich [bə'hɪlflɪç] adj helpful; **jdm ~ sein (bei)** to help sb (with)

behindern [bə'hɪndərn] vt to hinder, impede

Behinderte, r f(m) disabled person

Behinderung f hindrance; (Körperbehinderung) handicap

Behörde [bə'hø:rdə] (-, -n) f authorities pl; (Amtsgebäude) office(s pl)

behördlich [bə'hø:rtlɪç] adj official

behüten [bə'hy:tən] vt to guard; **jdn vor etw** dat ~ to preserve sb from sth

behütet adj (Jugend etc) sheltered

behutsam [bə'hu:tza:m] adj cautious, careful; **man muss es ihr ~ beibringen** it will have

to be broken to her gently; **Behutsamkeit** f caution, carefulness

 SCHLÜSSELWORT

bei [baɪ] präp +dat **1** (nahe bei) near; (zum Aufenthalt) at, with; (unter, zwischen) among; **bei München** near Munich; **bei uns** at our place; **beim Friseur** at the hairdresser's; **bei seinen Eltern wohnen** to live with one's parents; **bei einer Firma arbeiten** to work for a firm; **etw bei sich haben** to have sth on one; **jdn bei sich haben** to have sb with one; **bei Goethe** in Goethe; **beim Militär** in the army

2 (zeitlich) at, on; (während) during; (Zustand, Umstand) in; **bei Nacht** at night; **bei Nebel** in fog; **bei Regen** if it rains; **bei solcher Hitze** in such heat; **bei meiner Ankunft** on my arrival; **bei der Arbeit** when I'm etc working; **beim Fahren** while driving; **bei offenem Fenster schlafen** to sleep with the window open; **bei Feuer Scheibe einschlagen** in case of fire break glass; **bei seinem Talent** with his talent

beibehalten ['baɪbəhaltən] unreg vt to keep, retain

Beibehaltung f keeping, retaining

Beiblatt ['baɪblat] nt supplement

beibringen ['baɪbrɪŋən] unreg vt (Beweis, Zeugen) to bring forward; (Gründe) to adduce; **jdm etw ~** (zufügen) to inflict sth on sb; (zu verstehen geben) to make sb understand sth; (lehren) to teach sb sth

Beichte ['baɪçtə] f confession

beichten vt to confess ▷ vi to go to confession

Beichtgeheimnis nt secret of the confessional

Beichtstuhl m confessional

beide ['baɪdə] pron, adj both; **meine ~n Brüder** my two brothers, both my brothers; **die ersten ~n** the first two; **wir ~** we two; **einer von ~n** one of the two; **alles ~s** both (of them); **~ Mal** both times

beider- zW: **beiderlei** adj inv of both; **beiderseitig** adj mutual, reciprocal; **beiderseits** adv mutually ▷ präp +gen on both sides of

beidhändig ['baɪthɛndɪç] adj ambidextrous

beidrehen ['baɪdre:ən] vi to heave to

beidseitig ['baɪtsaɪtɪç] adj (auf beiden Seiten) on both sides

beieinander [baɪʔaɪ'nandər] adv together; **gut ~ sein** (umg: gesundheitlich) to be in good shape; (: geistig) to be all there

Beifahrer, in ['baɪfa:rər(ɪn)] (-s, -) m(f) passenger; **Beifahrerairbag** m (Aut) passenger airbag; **Beifahrersitz** m passenger seat

Beifall ['baɪfal] (-(e)s) m applause; (Zustimmung) approval; **~ heischend** fishing for applause/ approval

beifällig ['baɪfɛlɪç] adj approving; (Kommentar) favourable (Brit), favorable (US)

Beifilm ['baɪfɪlm] m supporting film

b

beifügen ['baɪfyːɡən] vt to enclose

Beigabe ['baɪɡaːbə] f addition

beige ['beːʒ] adj beige

beigeben ['baɪɡeːbən] unreg vt (zufügen) to add; (mitgeben) to give ▷ vi: **klein ~** (nachgeben) to climb down

Beigeschmack ['baɪɡəʃmak] m aftertaste

Beihilfe ['baɪhɪlfə] f aid, assistance; (Studienbeihilfe) grant; (Jur) aiding and abetting; **wegen ~ zum Mord** (Jur) because of being an accessory to the murder

beikommen ['baɪkɔmən] unreg vi +dat to get at; (einem Problem) to deal with

Beil [baɪl] (-(e)s, -e) nt axe (Brit), ax (US), hatchet

Beilage ['baɪlaːɡə] f (Buchbeilage etc) supplement; (Koch) accompanying vegetables; (getrennt serviert) side dish

beiläufig ['baɪlɔʏfɪç] adj casual, incidental ▷ adv casually, by the way

beilegen ['baɪleːɡən] vt (hinzufügen) to enclose, add; (beimessen) to attribute, ascribe; (Streit) to settle

beileibe [baɪ'laɪbə] adv: **~ nicht** by no means

Beileid ['baɪlaɪt] nt condolence, sympathy; **herzliches ~** deepest sympathy

beiliegend ['baɪliːɡənt] adj (Comm) enclosed

beim [baɪm] = **bei dem**

beimessen ['baɪmɛsən] unreg vt to attribute, ascribe

Bein [baɪn] (-(e)s, -e) nt leg; **jdm ein ~ stellen** (lit, fig) to trip sb up; **wir sollten uns auf die ~e machen** (umg) we ought to be making tracks; **jdm ~e machen** (umg: antreiben) to make sb get a move on; **die ~e in die Hand nehmen** (umg) to take to one's heels; **sich** dat **die ~e in den Bauch stehen** (umg) to stand about until one is fit to drop; **etw auf die ~e stellen** (fig) to get sth off the ground

beinah [baɪ'naː], **beinahe** [baɪ'naːə] adv almost, nearly

Beinbruch m fracture of the leg; **das ist kein ~** (fig: umg) it could be worse

beinhalten [bə'|ɪnhaltən] vt to contain

beipflichten ['baɪpflɪçtən] vi: **jdm/etw ~** to agree with sb/sth

Beiprogramm ['baɪproɡram] nt supporting programme (Brit) od program (US)

Beirat ['baɪraːt] m advisory council; (Elternbeirat) parents' council

beirren [bə'|ɪrən] vt to confuse, muddle; **sich nicht ~ lassen** not to let o.s. be confused

Beirut [baɪ'ruːt] (-s) nt Beirut

beisammen [baɪ'zamən] adv together; **beisammenhaben** unreg vt: **er hat (sie) nicht alle beisammen** (umg) he's not all there; **Beisammensein** (-s) nt get-together

Beischlaf ['baɪʃlaːf] m (Jur) sexual intercourse

Beisein ['baɪzaɪn] (-s) nt presence

beiseite [baɪ'zaɪtə] adv to one side, aside; (stehen) on one side, aside; **Spaß ~!** joking apart!; **beiseitelegen** vt (sparen) to put by; **beiseiteschaffen** vt to get rid of

beisetzen ['baɪzɛtsən] vt to bury

Beisetzung f funeral

Beisitzer, in ['baɪzɪtsər(ɪn)] (-s, -) m(f) (Jur) assessor; (bei Prüfung) observer

Beispiel ['baɪʃpiːl] (-(e)s, -e) nt example; **mit gutem ~ vorangehen** to set a good example; **sich** dat **an jdm ein ~ nehmen** to take sb as an example; **zum ~** for example; **beispielhaft** adj exemplary; **beispiellos** adj unprecedented

beispielsweise adv for instance, for example

beispringen ['baɪʃprɪŋən] unreg vi +dat to come to the aid of

beißen ['baɪsən] unreg vt, vi to bite; (stechen: Rauch, Säure) to burn ▷ vr (Farben) to clash

beißend adj biting, caustic; (Geruch) pungent, sharp; (fig) sarcastic

Beißzange ['baɪstsaŋə] f pliers pl

Beistand ['baɪʃtant] (-(e)s, ̈-e) m support, help; (Jur) adviser; **jdm ~ leisten** to give sb assistance/one's support

beistehen ['baɪʃteːən] unreg vi: **jdm ~** to stand by sb

Beistelltisch ['baɪʃtɛltɪʃ] m occasional table

beisteuern ['baɪʃtɔʏərn] vt to contribute

beistimmen ['baɪʃtɪmən] vi +dat to agree with

Beistrich ['baɪʃtrɪç] m comma

Beitrag ['baɪtraːk] (-(e)s, ̈-e) m contribution; (Zahlung) fee, subscription; (Versicherungsbeitrag) premium; **einen ~ zu etw leisten** to make a contribution to sth

beitragen ['baɪtraːɡən] unreg vt, vi: **~ (zu)** to contribute (to); (mithelfen) to help (with)

Beitrags- zW: **beitragsfinanziert** adj financed by fees/contributions; **beitragsfrei** adj non-contributory; **beitragspflichtig** adj contributory; **beitragspflichtig sein** (Mensch) to have to pay contributions; **Beitragszahler, in** m(f) contributor

beitreten ['baɪtreːtən] unreg vi +dat to join

Beitritt ['baɪtrɪt] m joining; membership

Beitrittserklärung f declaration of membership

Beitrittsland nt (zu EU etc) acceding country

Beiwagen ['baɪvaːɡən] m (Motorradbeiwagen) sidecar; (Straßenbahnbeiwagen) extra carriage

beiwohnen ['baɪvoːnən] vi (geh): **einer Sache** dat **~** to attend od be present at sth

Beiwort ['baɪvɔrt] nt adjective

Beize ['baɪtsə] (-, -n) f (Holzbeize) stain; (Koch) marinade

beizeiten [baɪ'tsaɪtən] adv in time

bejahen [bə'jaːən] vt (Frage) to say yes to, answer in the affirmative; (gutheißen) to agree with

bejahrt [bə'jaːrt] adj elderly, advanced in years

bejammern [bə'jamərn] vt to lament, bewail

bejammernswert adj lamentable

bekakeln [bə'kaːkəln] (umg) vt to discuss

bekam etc [bə'kam] vb siehe **bekommen**

bekämpfen [bə'kɛmpfən] vt (Gegner) to fight; (Seuche) to combat ▷ vr to fight

Bekämpfung f: **~ (+gen)** fight (against),

53

struggle (against)

bekannt [bə'kant] *adj* (well-)known; (*nicht fremd*) familiar; **~ geben** to announce publicly; **mit jdm ~ sein** to know sb; **~ machen** to announce; **jdn mit jdm ~ machen** to introduce sb to sb; **sich mit etw ~ machen** to familiarize o.s. with sth; **das ist mir ~** I know that; **es/sie kommt mir ~ vor** it/she seems familiar; **durch etw ~ werden** to become famous because of sth

Bekannte, r *f(m)* friend, acquaintance

Bekanntenkreis *m* circle of friends

bekanntermaßen *adv* as is known

bekannt- *zW*: **Bekanntgabe** *f* announcement; **Bekanntheitsgrad** *m* degree of fame; **bekanntlich** *adv* as is well known, as you know; **Bekanntmachung** *f* publication; (*Anschlag etc*) announcement; **Bekanntschaft** *f* acquaintance

bekehren [bə'ke:rən] *vt* to convert ▷ *vr* to be *od* become converted

Bekehrung *f* conversion

bekennen [bə'kɛnən] *unreg vt* to confess; (*Glauben*) to profess ▷ *vr*: **sich zu jdm/etw ~** to declare one's support for sb/sth; **Farbe ~** (*umg*) to show where one stands

Bekenntnis [bə'kɛntnɪs] (**-ses, -se**) *nt* admission, confession; (*Religion*) confession, denomination; **ein ~ zur Demokratie ablegen** to declare one's belief in democracy; **Bekenntnisschule** *f* denominational school

beklagen [bə'kla:gən] *vt* to deplore, lament ▷ *vr* to complain

beklagenswert *adj* lamentable, pathetic; (*Mensch*) pitiful; (*Zustand*) deplorable; (*Unfall*) terrible

beklatschen [bə'klatʃən] *vt* to applaud, clap

bekleben [bə'kle:bən] *vt*: **etw mit Bildern ~** to stick pictures onto sth

bekleckern [bə'klɛkərn] (*umg*) *vt* to stain

bekleiden [bə'klaɪdən] *vt* to clothe; (*Amt*) to occupy, fill

Bekleidung *f* clothing; (*form: eines Amtes*) tenure

Bekleidungsindustrie *f* clothing industry, rag trade (*umg*)

beklemmen [bə'klɛmən] *vt* to oppress

Beklemmung *f* oppressiveness; (*Gefühl der Angst*) feeling of apprehension

beklommen [bə'klɔmən] *adj* anxious, uneasy; **Beklommenheit** *f* anxiety, uneasiness

bekloppt [bə'klɔpt] (*umg*) *adj* (*Mensch*) crazy; (: *Sache*) lousy

beknackt [bə'knakt] (*umg*) *adj* = **bekloppt**

beknien [bə'kni:ən] (*umg*) *vt* (*jdn*) to beg

bekommen [bə'kɔmən] *unreg vt* to get, receive; (*Kind*) to have; (*Zug*) to catch, get ▷ *vi*: **jdm ~** to agree with sb; **es mit jdm zu tun ~** to get into trouble with sb; **wohl bekomms!** your health!

bekömmlich [bə'kœmlɪç] *adj* easily digestible

beköstigen [bə'kœstɪɡən] *vt* to cater for

bekräftigen [bə'krɛftɪɡən] *vt* to confirm, corroborate

Bekräftigung *f* corroboration

bekreuzigen [bə'krɔytsɪɡən] *vr* to cross o.s.

bekritteln [bə'krɪtəln] *vt* to criticize, pick holes in

bekümmern [bə'kʏmərn] *vt* to worry, trouble

bekunden [bə'kʊndən] *vt* (*sagen*) to state; (*zeigen*) to show

belächeln [bə'lɛçəln] *vt* to laugh at

beladen [bə'la:dən] *unreg vt* to load

Belag [bə'la:k] (**-(e)s, -̈e**) *m* covering, coating; (*Brotbelag*) spread; (*auf Pizza, Brot*) topping; (*auf Tortenboden, zwischen Brotscheiben*) filling; (*Zahnbelag*) tartar; (*auf Zunge*) fur; (*Bremsbelag*) lining

belagern [bə'la:ɡərn] *vt* to besiege

Belagerung *f* siege

Belagerungszustand *m* state of siege

belämmert [bə'lɛmərt] (*umg*) *adj* sheepish

Belang [bə'laŋ] (**-(e)s**) *m* importance

Belange *pl* interests *pl*, concerns *pl*

belangen *vt* (*Jur*) to take to court

belanglos *adj* trivial, unimportant

Belanglosigkeit *f* triviality

belassen [bə'lasən] *unreg vt* (*in Zustand, Glauben*) to leave; (*in Stellung*) to retain; **es dabei ~** to leave it at that

Belastbarkeit *f* (*von Brücke, Aufzug*) load-bearing capacity; (*von Menschen, Nerven*) ability to take stress

belasten [bə'lastən] *vt* (*lit*) to burden; (*fig: bedrücken*) to trouble, worry; (*Comm: Konto*) to debit; (*Jur*) to incriminate ▷ *vr* to weigh o.s. down; (*Jur*) to incriminate o.s.; **etw (mit einer Hypothek) ~** to mortgage sth

belastend *adj* (*Jur*) incriminating

belästigen [bə'lɛstɪɡən] *vt* to annoy, pester

Belästigung *f* annoyance, pestering; (*körperlich*) molesting

Belastung [bə'lastʊŋ] *f* (*lit*) load; (*fig: Sorge etc*) weight; (*Comm*) charge, debit(ing); (*mit Hypothek*): **~ (+gen)** mortgage (on); (*Jur*) incriminating evidence

Belastungs- *zW*: **Belastungsmaterial** *nt* (*Jur*) incriminating evidence; **Belastungsprobe** *f* capacity test; (*fig*) test; **Belastungszeuge** *m* witness for the prosecution

belaubt [bə'laʊpt] *adj*: **dicht ~ sein** to have thick foliage

belaufen [bə'laʊfən] *unreg vr*: **sich ~ auf** +*akk* to amount to

belauschen [bə'laʊʃən] *vt* to eavesdrop on

beleben [bə'le:bən] *vt* (*anregen*) to liven up; (*Konjunktur, jds Hoffnungen*) to stimulate

belebt [bə'le:pt] *adj* (*Straße*) crowded

Beleg [bə'le:k] (**-(e)s, -e**) *m* (*Comm*) receipt; (*Beweis*) documentary evidence, proof; (*Beispiel*) example

belegen [bə'le:ɡən] *vt* to cover; (*Kuchen, Brot*) to spread; (*Platz*) to reserve, book; (*Kurs, Vorlesung*) to register for; (*beweisen*) to verify, prove

Belegschaft *f* personnel, staff

belegt *adj* (*Zunge*) furred; (*Stimme*) hoarse; (*Zimmer*) occupied; **~e Brote** open sandwiches

belehren [bə'le:rən] *vt* to instruct, teach; **jdn**

eines Besseren ~ to teach sb better; **er ist nicht zu ~** he won't be told
Belehrung f instruction
beleibt [bə'laɪpt] adj stout, corpulent
beleidigen [bə'laɪdɪɡən] vt to insult; to offend
beleidigt adj insulted; (gekränkt) offended; **die ~e Leberwurst spielen** (umg) to be in a huff
Beleidigung f insult; (Jur) slander; (: schriftlich) libel
beleihen [bə'laɪən] unreg vt (Comm) to lend money on
belemmert [bə'lɛmərt] (umg) adj siehe **belämmert**
belesen [bə'le:zən] adj well-read
beleuchten [bə'lɔʏçtən] vt to light, illuminate; (fig) to throw light on
Beleuchter, in (-s, -) m(f) lighting technician
Beleuchtung f lighting, illumination
beleumdet [bə'lɔʏmdət] adj: **gut/schlecht ~ sein** to have a good/bad reputation
beleumundet [bə'lɔʏmʊndət] adj = **beleumdet**
Belgien [bɛlɡiən] (-s) nt Belgium
Belgier, in (-s, -) m(f) Belgian
belgisch adj Belgian
Belgrad ['bɛlɡra:t] (-s) nt Belgrade
belichten [bə'lɪçtən] vt to expose
Belichtung f exposure
Belichtungsmesser m exposure meter
Belieben [bə'li:bən] nt: **(ganz) nach ~** (just) as you wish
belieben vi unpers (geh): **wie es Ihnen beliebt** as you wish
beliebig [bə'li:bɪç] adj any you like, as you like; **~ viel** as much as you like; **in ~er Reihenfolge** in any order whatever; **ein ~es Thema** any subject you like od want
beliebt [bə'li:pt] adj popular; **sich bei jdm ~ machen** to make o.s. popular with sb; **Beliebtheit** f popularity
beliefern [bə'li:fərn] vt to supply
Belize [be'li:z] (-s) nt Belize
bellen ['bɛlən] vi to bark
Belletristik [bɛle'trɪstɪk] f fiction and poetry
belohnen [bə'lo:nən] vt to reward
Belohnung f reward
Belüftung [bə'lʏftʊŋ] f ventilation
belügen [bə'ly:ɡən] unreg vt to lie to, deceive
belustigen [bə'lʊstɪɡən] vt to amuse
Belustigung f amusement
bemächtigen [bə'mɛçtɪɡən] vr: **sich einer Sache** gen ~ to take possession of sth, seize sth
bemalen [bə'ma:lən] vt to paint ▷ vr (pej: schminken) to put on one's war paint (umg)
bemängeln [bə'mɛŋəln] vt to criticize
bemannen [bə'manən] vt to man
Bemannung f manning; (Naut, Aviat etc) crew
bemänteln [bə'mɛntəln] vt to cloak, hide
bemerkbar adj perceptible, noticeable; **sich ~ machen** (Person) to make od get o.s. noticed; (Unruhe) to become noticeable
bemerken [bə'mɛrkən] vt (wahrnehmen) to notice, observe; (sagen) to say, mention; **nebenbei bemerkt** by the way

bemerkenswert adj remarkable, noteworthy
Bemerkung f remark, comment; (schriftlich) comment, note
bemitleiden [bə'mɪtlaɪdən] vt to pity
bemittelt [bə'mɪtəlt] adj well-to-do, well-off
bemühen [bə'my:ən] vr to take trouble; **sich um eine Stelle ~** to try to get a job
bemüht adj: **(darum) ~ sein, etw zu tun** to endeavor (Brit) od endeavor (US) to do sth
Bemühung f trouble, pains pl, effort
bemüßigt [bə'my:sɪçt] adj: **sich ~ fühlen/ sehen** (geh) to feel called upon
bemuttern [bə'mʊtərn] vt to mother
benachbart [bə'naxba:rt] adj neighbouring (Brit), neighboring (US)
benachrichtigen [bə'na:xrɪçtɪɡən] vt to inform
Benachrichtigung f notification
benachteiligen [bə'na:xtaɪlɪɡən] vt to (put at a) disadvantage, victimize
benehmen [bə'ne:mən] unreg vr to behave;
Benehmen (-s) nt behaviour (Brit), behavior (US); **kein Benehmen haben** not to know how to behave
beneiden [bə'naɪdən] vt to envy
beneidenswert adj enviable
Beneluxländer ['be:nelʊkslɛndər] pl Benelux (countries pl)
Beneluxstaaten pl Benelux (countries pl)
benennen [bə'nɛnən] unreg vt to name
Bengel ['bɛŋəl] (-s, -) m (little) rascal od rogue
Benimm [bə'nɪm] (-s) (umg) m manners pl
Benin [be'ni:n] (-s) nt Benin
benommen [bə'nɔmən] adj dazed
benoten [bə'no:tən] vt to mark
benötigen [bə'nø:tɪɡən] vt to need
benutzen [bə'nʊtsən] vt to use
benützen [bə'nʏtsən] vt to use
Benutzer, in (-s, -) m(f) user; **benutzerdefiniert** adj (Comput) user-defined; **benutzerfreundlich** adj user-friendly; **Benutzerkonto** nt (Comput) user account; **Benutzername** m username
Benutzung f utilization, use; **jdm etw zur ~ überlassen** to put sth at sb's disposal
Benzin [bɛnt'si:n] (-s, -e) nt (Aut) petrol (Brit), gas(oline) (US); **Benzineinspritzanlage** f (Aut) fuel injection system; **Benzinkanister** m petrol (Brit) od gas (US) can; **Benzintank** m petrol (Brit) od gas (US) tank; **Benzinuhr** f petrol (Brit) od gas (US) gauge
beobachten [bə'|o:baxtən] vt to observe
Beobachter, in (-s, -) m(f) observer; (eines Unfalls) witness; (Presse, TV) correspondent
Beobachtung f observation
beordern [bə'|ɔrdərn] vt: **jdn zu sich ~** to send for sb
bepacken [bə'pakən] vt to load, pack
bepflanzen [bə'pflantsən] vt to plant
bequatschen [bə'kvatʃən] (umg) vt (überreden) to persuade; **etw ~** to talk sth over
bequem [bə'kve:m] adj comfortable; (Ausrede) convenient; (Person) lazy, indolent
bequemen [bə'kve:mən] vr: **sich ~, etw zu**

tun to condescend to do sth
Bequemlichkeit f convenience, comfort; (*Faulheit*) laziness, indolence
Ber. *abk* = **Bericht; Beruf**
berät [bə'rɛːt] *vb siehe* **beraten**
beraten [bə'raːtən] *unreg vt* to advise; (*besprechen*) to discuss, debate ▷ *vr* to consult; **gut/schlecht ~ sein** to be well/ill advised; **sich ~ lassen** to get advice
beratend *adj* consultative; **jdm ~ zur Seite stehen** to act in an advisory capacity to sb
Berater, in (-s, -) m(f) adviser; **Beratervertrag** m consultancy contract
beratschlagen [bə'raːtʃlaːgən] *vi* to deliberate, confer ▷ *vt* to deliberate on, confer about
Beratung f advice; (*Besprechung*) consultation
Beratungsstelle f advice centre (*Brit*) *od* center (*US*)
berauben [bə'raʊbən] *vt* to rob
berauschen [bə'raʊʃən] *vt* (*lit, fig*) to intoxicate
berauschend *adj:* **das war nicht sehr ~** (*ironisch*) that wasn't very exciting
berechenbar [bə'rɛçənbaːr] *adj* calculable; (*Verhalten*) predictable
berechnen [bə'rɛçnən] *vt* to calculate; (*Comm: anrechnen*) to charge
berechnend *adj* (*Mensch*) calculating, scheming
Berechnung f calculation; (*Comm*) charge
berechtigen [bə'rɛçtɪgən] *vt* to entitle; (*bevollmächtigen*) to authorize; (*fig*) to justify
berechtigt [bə'rɛçtɪçt] *adj* justifiable, justified
Berechtigung f authorization; (*fig*) justification
bereden [bə'reːdən] *vt* (*besprechen*) to discuss; (*überreden*) to persuade ▷ *vr* to discuss
beredt [bə'reːt] *adj* eloquent
Bereich [bə'raɪç] (**-(e)s, -e**) m (*Bezirk*) area; (*Ressort, Gebiet*) sphere; **im ~ des Möglichen liegen** to be within the bounds of possibility
bereichern [bə'raɪçərn] *vt* to enrich ▷ *vr* to get rich; **sich auf Kosten anderer ~** to feather one's nest at the expense of other people
Bereifung [bə'raɪfʊŋ] f (set of) tyres (*Brit*) *od* tires (*US*) *pl*; (*Vorgang*) fitting with tyres (*Brit*) *od* tires (*US*)
bereinigen [bə'raɪnɪgən] *vt* to settle
bereisen [bə'raɪzən] *vt* to travel through; (*Comm: Gebiet*) to travel, cover
bereit [bə'raɪt] *adj* ready, prepared; **zu etw ~ sein** to be ready for sth; **sich ~ erklären** to declare o.s. willing; **(sich) ~ machen** to prepare, to get ready
bereiten *vt* to prepare, make ready; (*Kummer, Freude*) to cause; **einer Sache** *dat* **ein Ende ~** to put an end to sth
bereit- *zW:* **bereithalten** *unreg vt* to keep in readiness; **bereitlegen** *vt* to lay out; **bereitmachen** *vt, vr siehe* **bereit**
bereits *adv* already
bereit- *zW:* **Bereitschaft** f readiness; (*Polizei*) alert; **in Bereitschaft sein** to be on the alert *od* on stand-by; **Bereitschaftsarzt** m

doctor on call; (*im Krankenhaus*) duty doctor; **Bereitschaftsdienst** m emergency service; **bereitstehen** *unreg vi* (*Person*) to be prepared; (*Ding*) to be ready; **bereitstellen** *vt* (*Kisten, Pakete etc*) to put ready; (*Geld etc*) to make available; (*Truppen, Maschinen*) to put at the ready
Bereitung f preparation
bereitwillig *adj* willing, ready; **Bereitwilligkeit** f willingness, readiness
bereuen [bə'rɔʏən] *vt* to regret
Berg [bɛrk] (**-(e)s, -e**) m mountain; (*kleiner*) hill; **mit etw hinterm ~ halten** (*fig*) to keep quiet about sth; **über alle ~e sein** to be miles away; **da stehen einem ja die Haare zu ~e** it's enough to make your hair stand on end; **bergab** *adv* downhill; **bergan** *adv* uphill; **Bergarbeiter** m miner; **bergauf** *adv* uphill; **Bergbahn** f mountain railway (*Brit*) *od* railroad (*US*); **Bergbau** m mining
bergen ['bɛrgən] *unreg vt* (*retten*) to rescue; (*Ladung*) to salvage; (*enthalten*) to contain
Bergführer m mountain guide
Berggipfel m mountain top, peak, summit
bergig ['bɛrgɪç] *adj* mountainous, hilly
Berg- *zW:* **Bergkamm** m crest, ridge; **Bergkette** f mountain range; **Bergkristall** m rock crystal; **Bergmann (-(e)s,** *pl* **-leute)** m miner; **Bergnot** f: **in Bergnot sein/geraten** to be in/get into difficulties while climbing; **Bergpredigt** f (*Rel*) Sermon on the Mount; **Bergrettungsdienst** m mountain rescue service; **Bergrutsch** m landslide; **Bergschuh** m walking boot; **Bergsteigen** nt mountaineering; **Bergsteiger, in** m(f) mountaineer, climber; **Berg-und-Tal-Bahn** f big dipper, roller-coaster
Bergung ['bɛrgʊŋ] f (*von Menschen*) rescue; (*von Material*) recovery; (*Naut*) salvage
Bergwacht f mountain rescue service
Bergwerk nt mine
Bericht [bə'rɪçt] (**-(e)s, -e**) m report, account; **berichten** *vt, vi* to report; **Berichterstatter (-s, -)** m reporter, (*newspaper*) correspondent; **Berichterstattung** f reporting
berichtigen [bə'rɪçtɪgən] *vt* to correct
Berichtigung f correction
berieseln [bə'riːzəln] *vt* to spray with water
Berieselung f watering; **die dauernde ~ mit Musik ...** (*fig*) the constant stream of music ...
Berieselungsanlage f sprinkler (system)
Beringmeer ['beːrɪŋmeːr] nt Bering Sea
beritten [bə'rɪtən] *adj* mounted
Berlin [bɛr'liːn] (**-s**) nt Berlin
Berliner[1] *adj attrib* Berlin
Berliner[2] **(-s, -)** m (*Person*) Berliner; (*Koch*) jam doughnut
Berlinerin f Berliner
berlinerisch (*umg*) *adj* (*Dialekt*) Berlin *attr*
Bermudas [bɛr'muːdas] *pl:* **auf den ~** in Bermuda
Bern [bɛrn] (**-s**) nt Berne
Bernhardiner [bɛrnhar'diːnər] (**-s, -**) m Saint

Bernard (dog)

Bernstein ['bɛrnʃtaɪn] *m* amber

bersten ['bɛrstən] *unreg vi* to burst, split

berüchtigt [bə'rʏçtɪçt] *adj* notorious, infamous

berücksichtigen [bə'rʏkzɪçtɪgən] *vt* to consider, bear in mind

Berücksichtigung *f* consideration; **in** *od* **unter ~ der Tatsache, dass ...** in view of the fact that ...

Beruf [bə'ruːf] (**-(e)s, -e**) *m* occupation, profession; (*Gewerbe*) trade; **was sind Sie von ~?** what is your occupation *etc?*, what do you do for a living?; **seinen ~ verfehlt haben** to have missed one's vocation

berufen *unreg vt* (*in Amt*): **jdn in etw** *akk* **~** to appoint sb to sth ▷ *vr*: **sich auf jdn/etw ~** to refer *od* appeal to sb/sth ▷ *adj* competent, qualified; (*ausersehen*): **zu etw ~ sein** to have a vocation for sth

beruflich *adj* professional; **sie ist ~ viel unterwegs** she is away a lot on business

Berufs- *zW*: **Berufsakademie** *f* college of advanced vocational studies; **Berufsausbildung** *f* vocational *od* professional training; **berufsbedingt** *adj* occupational; **Berufsberater** *m* careers adviser; **Berufsberatung** *f* vocational guidance; **Berufsbezeichnung** *f* job description; **Berufseinsteiger, in** *m(f)* first-time employee; **Berufserfahrung** *f* (professional) experience; **Berufsfeuerwehr** *f* fire service; **Berufsgeheimnis** *nt* professional secret; **Berufskrankheit** *f* occupational disease; **Berufskriminalität** *f* professional crime; **Berufsleben** *nt* professional life; **im Berufsleben stehen** to be working *od* in employment; **berufsmäßig** *adj* professional; **Berufsperspektive** *f* job *od* career prospects *pl*; **Berufsrisiko** *nt* occupational hazard; **Berufsschule** *f* vocational *od* trade school; **Berufssoldat** *m* professional soldier, regular; **Berufssportler** *m* professional (sportsman); **berufstätig** *adj* employed; **berufsunfähig** *adj* unable to work (at one's profession); **Berufsunfall** *m* occupational accident; **Berufsverbot** *nt*: **jdm Berufsverbot erteilen** to ban sb from his/her profession; (*einem Arzt, Anwalt*) to strike sb off; **Berufsverkehr** *m* commuter traffic; **Berufswahl** *f* choice of a job

Berufung *f* vocation, calling; (*Ernennung*) appointment; (*Jur*) appeal; **~ einlegen** to appeal; **unter ~ auf etw** *akk* (*form*) with reference to sth

Berufungsgericht *nt* appeal court, court of appeal

beruhen [bə'ruːən] *vi*: **auf etw** *dat* **~** to be based on sth; **etw auf sich ~ lassen** to leave sth at that; **das beruht auf Gegenseitigkeit** the feeling is mutual

beruhigen [bə'ruːɪgən] *vt* to calm, pacify, soothe ▷ *vr* (*Mensch*) to calm (o.s.) down; (*Situation*) to calm down

beruhigend *adj* (*Gefühl, Wissen*) reassuring;

(*Worte*) comforting; (*Mittel*) tranquillizing

Beruhigung *f* reassurance; (*der Nerven*) calming; **zu jds ~** to reassure sb

Beruhigungsmittel *nt* sedative

Beruhigungspille *f* tranquillizer

berühmt [bə'ryːmt] *adj* famous; **das war nicht ~** (*umg*) it was nothing to write home about; **berühmt-berüchtigt** *adj* infamous, notorious; **Berühmtheit** *f* (*Ruf*) fame; (*Mensch*) celebrity

berühren [bə'ryːrən] *vt* to touch; (*gefühlsmäßig bewegen*) to affect; (*flüchtig erwähnen*) to mention, touch on ▷ *vr* to meet, touch; **von etw peinlich berührt sein** to be embarrassed by sth

Berührung *f* contact

Berührungsbildschirm *m* (*Tech*) touch screen

berührungsempfindlich *adj* touch-sensitive

Berührungspunkt *m* point of contact

bes. *abk* (= *besonders*) esp

besagen [bə'zaːgən] *vt* to mean

besagt *adj* (*form: Tag etc*) in question

besaiten [bə'zaɪtən] *vt*: **neu ~** (*Instrument*) to restring

besänftigen [bə'zɛnftɪgən] *vt* to soothe, calm

besänftigend *adj* soothing

Besänftigung *f* soothing, calming

besaß *etc* [bə'zaːs] *vb siehe* **besitzen**

besät [bə'zɛːt] *adj* covered; (*mit Blättern etc*) strewn

Besatz [bə'zats] (**-es, ⁻e**) *m* trimming, edging

Besatzung *f* garrison; (*Naut, Aviat*) crew

Besatzungsmacht *f* occupying power

Besatzungszone *f* occupied zone

besaufen [bə'zaʊfən] *unreg* (*umg*) *vr* to get drunk *od* stoned

beschädigen [bə'ʃɛːdɪgən] *vt* to damage

Beschädigung *f* damage; (*Stelle*) damaged spot

beschaffen [bə'ʃafən] *vt* to get, acquire ▷ *adj* constituted; **so ~ sein wie ...** to be the same as ...; **Beschaffenheit** *f* constitution, nature; **je nach Beschaffenheit der Lage** according to the situation

Beschaffung *f* acquisition

beschäftigen [bə'ʃɛftɪgən] *vt* to occupy; (*beruflich*) to employ; (*innerlich*): **jdn ~** to be on sb's mind ▷ *vr* to occupy *od* concern o.s.

beschäftigt *adj* busy, occupied; (*angestellt*): (**bei einer Firma**) **~** employed (by a firm)

Beschäftigung *f* (*Beruf*) employment; (*Tätigkeit*) occupation; (*geistige Beschäftigung*) preoccupation; **einer ~ nachgehen** (*form*) to be employed

Beschäftigungsprogramm *nt* employment scheme

Beschäftigungstherapie *f* occupational therapy

beschämen [bə'ʃɛːmən] *vt* to put to shame

beschämend *adj* shameful; (*Hilfsbereitschaft*) shaming

beschämt *adj* ashamed

beschatten [bə'ʃatən] *vt* to shade; (*Verdächtige*) to shadow

beschaulich [bəˈʃaʊlɪç] *adj* contemplative; (*Leben, Abend*) quiet, tranquil

Bescheid [bəˈʃaɪt] (**-(e)s, -e**) *m* information; (*Weisung*) directions *pl*; ~ **wissen (über** +*akk*) to be well-informed (about); **ich weiß** ~ I know; **jdm ~ geben** *od* **sagen** to let sb know; **jdm ordentlich ~ sagen** (*umg*) to tell sb where to go

bescheiden [bəˈʃaɪdən] *unreg vr* to content o.s.
▷ *vt*: **etw abschlägig ~** (*form*) to turn sth down
▷ *adj* modest; **Bescheidenheit** *f* modesty

bescheinen [bəˈʃaɪnən] *unreg vt* to shine on

bescheinigen [bəˈʃaɪnɪgən] *vt* to certify; (*bestätigen*) to acknowledge; **hiermit wird bescheinigt, dass ...** this is to certify that ...

Bescheinigung *f* certificate; (*Quittung*) receipt

bescheißen [bəˈʃaɪsən] *unreg* (*umg!*) *vt* to cheat

beschenken [bəˈʃɛŋkən] *vt* to give presents to

bescheren [bəˈʃeːrən] *vt*: **jdm etw ~** to give sb sth as a present; **jdn ~** to give presents to sb

Bescherung *f* giving of presents; (*umg*) mess; **da haben wir die ~!** (*umg*) what did I tell you!

bescheuert [bəˈʃɔʏɐt] (*umg*) *adj* stupid

beschichten [bəˈʃɪçtən] *vt* (*Tech*) to coat, cover

beschießen [bəˈʃiːsən] *unreg vt* to shoot *od* fire at

beschildern [bəˈʃɪldɐn] *vt* to signpost

beschimpfen [bəˈʃɪmpfən] *vt* to abuse

Beschimpfung *f* abuse, insult

beschirmen [bəˈʃɪrmən] *vt* (*geh: beschützen*) to shield

Beschiss [bəˈʃɪs] (**-es**) (*umg*) *m*: **das ist ~** that is a cheat

beschiss *etc vb siehe* **bescheißen**

beschissen *pp von* **bescheißen** ▷ *adj* (*umg!*) bloody awful, lousy

Beschlag [bəˈʃlaːk] (**-(e)s, ⸚e**) *m* (*Metallband*) fitting; (*auf Fenster*) condensation; (*auf Metall*) tarnish; finish; (*Hufeisen*) horseshoe; **jdn/etw in ~ nehmen** *od* **mit ~ belegen** to monopolize sb/sth

beschlagen [bəˈʃlaːgən] *unreg vt* to cover; (*Pferd*) to shoe; (*Fenster, Metall*) to cover ▷ *vi, vr* (*Fenster etc*) to mist over; ~ **sein (in** *od* **auf** +*dat*) to be well versed (in)

beschlagnahmen *vt* to seize, confiscate

Beschlagnahmung *f* confiscation

beschleunigen [bəˈʃlɔʏnɪgən] *vt* to accelerate, speed up ▷ *vi* (*Aut*) to accelerate

Beschleunigung *f* acceleration

beschließen [bəˈʃliːsən] *unreg vt* to decide on; (*beenden*) to end, close

beschlossen [bəˈʃlɔsən] *pp von* **beschließen** ▷ *adj* (*entschieden*) decided, agreed; **das ist ~e Sache** that's been settled

Beschluss [bəˈʃlʊs] (**-es, ⸚e**) *m* decision, conclusion; (*Ende*) close, end; **einen ~ fassen** to pass a resolution

beschlussfähig *adj*: ~ **sein** to have a quorum

Beschlusslage *f* policy position

beschmieren [bəˈʃmiːrən] *vt* (*Wand*) to bedaub

beschmutzen [bəˈʃmʊtsən] *vt* to dirty, soil

beschneiden [bəˈʃnaɪdən] *unreg vt* to cut; (*stutzen*) to trim; (: *Strauch*) to prune; (*Rel*) to circumcise

beschnuppern [bəˈʃnʊpɐn] *vr* (*Hunde*) to sniff each other; (*fig: umg*) to size each other up

beschönigen [bəˈʃøːnɪgən] *vt* to gloss over; **~der Ausdruck** euphemism

beschränken [bəˈʃrɛŋkən] *vt, vr*: **(sich) ~ (auf** +*akk*) to limit *od* restrict (o.s.) (to)

beschrankt [bəˈʃraŋkt] *adj* (*Bahnübergang*) with barrier

beschränkt [bəˈʃrɛŋkt] *adj* confined, narrow; (*Mensch*) limited, narrow-minded; (*pej: geistig*) dim; **Gesellschaft mit ~er Haftung** limited company (*Brit*), corporation (*US*); **Beschränktheit** *f* narrowness

Beschränkung *f* limitation

beschreiben [bəˈʃraɪbən] *unreg vt* to describe; (*Papier*) to write on

Beschreibung *f* description

beschrieb *etc* [bəˈʃriːp] *vb siehe* **beschreiben**

beschrieben [bəˈʃriːbən] *pp von* **beschreiben**

beschriften [bəˈʃrɪftən] *vt* to mark, label

Beschriftung *f* lettering

beschuldigen [bəˈʃʊldɪgən] *vt* to accuse

Beschuldigung *f* accusation

beschummeln [bəˈʃʊməln] (*umg*) *vt, vi* to cheat

Beschuss [bəˈʃʊs] *m*: **jdn/etw unter ~ nehmen** (*Mil*) to (start to) bombard *od* shell sb/sth; (*fig*) to attack sb/sth; **unter ~ geraten** (*lit, fig*) to come into the firing line

beschützen [bəˈʃytsən] *vt*: ~ **(vor** +*dat*) to protect (from)

Beschützer, in (**-s, -**) *m(f)* protector

Beschützung *f* protection

beschwatzen [bəˈʃvatsən] (*umg*) *vt* (*überreden*) to talk over

Beschwerde [bəˈʃveːrdə] (**-, -n**) *f* complaint; (*Mühe*) hardship; (*Industrie*) grievance; **Beschwerden** *pl* (*Leiden*) trouble; ~ **einlegen** (*form*) to lodge a complaint; **beschwerdefrei** *adj* fit and healthy; **Beschwerdefrist** *f* (*Jur*) *period of time during which an appeal may be lodged*

beschweren [bəˈʃveːrən] *vt* to weight down; (*fig*) to burden ▷ *vr* to complain

beschwerlich *adj* tiring, exhausting

beschwichtigen [bəˈʃvɪçtɪgən] *vt* to soothe, pacify

Beschwichtigung *f* soothing, calming

beschwindeln [bəˈʃvɪndəln] *vt* (*betrügen*) to cheat; (*belügen*) to fib to

beschwingt [bəˈʃvɪŋt] *adj* cheery, in high spirits

beschwipst [bəˈʃvɪpst] *adj* tipsy

beschwören [bəˈʃvøːrən] *unreg vt* (*Aussage*) to swear to; (*anflehen*) to implore; (*Geister*) to conjure up

beseelen [bəˈzeːlən] *vt* to inspire

besehen [bəˈzeːən] *unreg vt* to look at; **genau ~** to examine closely

beseitigen [bəˈzaɪtɪgən] *vt* to remove

Beseitigung *f* removal

Besen [ˈbeːzən] (**-s, -**) *m* broom; (*pej: umg: Frau*) old bag; **ich fresse einen ~, wenn das stimmt** (*umg*) if that's right, I'll eat my hat;

Besenstiel *m* broomstick

besessen [bə'zɛsən] *adj* possessed; (*von einer Idee etc*): ~ **(von)** obsessed (with)

besetzen [bə'zɛtsən] *vt* (*Haus, Land*) to occupy; (*Platz*) to take, fill; (*Posten*) to fill; (*Rolle*) to cast; (*mit Edelsteinen*) to set

besetzt *adj* full; (*Tel*) engaged, busy; (*Platz*) taken; (*WC*) engaged; **Besetztzeichen** *nt* engaged tone (*Brit*), busy signal (*US*)

Besetzung *f* occupation; (*von Stelle*) filling; (*von Rolle*) casting; (*die Schauspieler*) cast; **zweite ~** (*Theat*) understudy

besichtigen [bə'zıçtıgən] *vt* to visit, look at

Besichtigung *f* visit

besiedeln *vt*: **dicht/dünn besiedelt** densely/thinly populated

Besiedelung [bə'zi:dəlʊŋ], **Besiedlung** [bə'zi:dlʊŋ] *f* population

besiegeln [bə'zi:gəln] *vt* to seal

besiegen [bə'zi:gən] *vt* to defeat, overcome

Besiegte, r [bə'zi:ktə(r)] *f(m)* loser

besinnen [bə'zınən] *unreg vr* (*nachdenken*) to think, reflect; (*erinnern*) to remember; **sich anders ~** to change one's mind

besinnlich *adj* contemplative

Besinnung *f* consciousness; **bei/ohne ~ sein** to be conscious/unconscious; **zur ~ kommen** to recover consciousness; (*fig*) to come to one's senses

besinnungslos *adj* unconscious; (*fig*) blind

Besitz [bə'zıts] (**-es**) *m* possession; (*Eigentum*) property; **Besitzanspruch** *m* claim of ownership; (*Jur*) title; **besitzanzeigend** *adj* (*Gram*) possessive

besitzen *unreg vt* to possess, own; (*Eigenschaft*) to have

Besitzer, in (**-s, -**) *m(f)* owner, proprietor

Besitz- *zW*: **Besitzergreifung** *f* seizure; **Besitznahme** *f* seizure; **Besitztum** *nt* (*Grundbesitz*) estate(s *pl*), property; **Besitzurkunde** *f* title deeds *pl*

besoffen [bə'zɔfən] (*umg*) *adj* sozzled

besohlen [bə'zo:lən] *vt* to sole

Besoldung [bə'zɔldʊŋ] *f* salary, pay

besondere, r, s [bə'zɔndərə(r, s)] *adj* special; (*eigen*) particular; (*gesondert*) separate; (*eigentümlich*) peculiar

Besonderheit *f* peculiarity

besonders *adv* especially, particularly; (*getrennt*) separately; **das Essen/der Film war nicht ~** the food/film was nothing special *od* out of the ordinary; **wie gehts dir? — nicht ~** how are you? — not too hot

besonnen [bə'zɔnən] *adj* sensible, level-headed; **Besonnenheit** *f* level-headedness

besorgen [bə'zɔrgən] *vt* (*beschaffen*) to acquire; (*kaufen*) to purchase; (*erledigen: Geschäfte*) to deal with; (*sich kümmern um*) to take care of; **es jdm ~** (*umg*) to sort sb out

Besorgnis (**-, -se**) *f* anxiety, concern; **besorgniserregend** *adj* alarming, worrying

besorgt [bə'zɔrkt] *adj* anxious, worried; **Besorgtheit** *f* anxiety, worry

Besorgung *f* acquisition; (*Kauf*) purchase; (*Einkauf*): **~en machen** to do some shopping

bespannen [bə'ʃpanən] *vt* (*mit Saiten, Fäden*) to string

bespielbar *adj* (*Rasen etc*) playable

bespielen [bə'ʃpi:lən] *vt* (*Tonband, Kassette*) to make a recording on

bespitzeln [bə'ʃpıtsəln] *vt* to spy on

besprechen [bə'ʃprɛçən] *unreg vt* to discuss; (*Tonband etc*) to record, speak onto; (*Buch*) to review ▷ *vr* to discuss, consult

Besprechung *f* meeting, discussion; (*von Buch*) review

bespringen [bə'ʃprıŋən] *unreg vt* (*Tier*) to mount, cover

bespritzen [bə'ʃprıtsən] *vt* to spray; (*beschmutzen*) to spatter

besser ['bɛsər] *adj* better; **nur ein ~er ...** just a glorified ...; **~e Leute** a better class of people; **es geht ihm ~** he feels better; *siehe auch* **besserstehen**

bessern *vt* to make better, improve ▷ *vr* to improve; (*Mensch*) to reform

besserstehen *unreg vr* (*umg*) to be better off

Besserung *f* improvement; **auf dem Weg(e) der ~ sein** to be getting better, be improving; **gute ~!** get well soon!

Besserwisser, in (**-s, -**) *m(f)* know-all (*Brit*), know-it-all (*US*)

Bestand [bə'ʃtant] (**-(e)s, ¨e**) *m* (*Fortbestehen*) duration, continuance; (*Kassenbestand*) amount, balance; (*Vorrat*) stock; **eiserner ~** iron rations *pl*; **~ haben, von ~ sein** to last long, endure

bestand *etc vb siehe* **bestehen**

bestanden *pp von* **bestehen** ▷ *adj*: **nach ~er Prüfung** after passing the exam

beständig [bə'ʃtɛndıç] *adj* (*ausdauernd*) constant; (*auch fig*); (*Wetter*) settled; (*Stoffe*) resistant; (*Klagen etc*) continual

Bestandsaufnahme *f* stocktaking

Bestandsüberwachung *f* stock control, inventory control

Bestandteil *m* part, component; (*Zutat*) ingredient; **sich in seine ~e auflösen** to fall to pieces

bestärken [bə'ʃtɛrkən] *vt*: **jdn in etw** *dat* **~** to strengthen *od* confirm sb in sth

bestätigen [bə'ʃtɛ:tıgən] *vt* to confirm; (*anerkennen, Comm*) to acknowledge; **jdn (im Amt) ~** to confirm sb's appointment

Bestätigung *f* confirmation; acknowledgement

bestatten [bə'ʃtatən] *vt* to bury

Bestatter (-s, -) *m* undertaker

Bestattung *f* funeral

Bestattungsinstitut *nt* undertaker's (*Brit*), mortician's (*US*)

bestäuben [bə'ʃtɔybən] *vt* to powder, dust; (*Pflanze*) to pollinate

beste, r, s ['bɛstə(r, s)] *adj* best; **sie singt am ~n** she sings best; **so ist es am ~n** it's best that way; **am ~n gehst du gleich** you'd better go at once; **jdn zum B~n haben** to pull sb's leg; **einen Witz** *etc* **zum B~n geben** to tell a joke *etc*; **aufs B~** in the best possible way; **zu jds B~** for the benefit of sb; **es steht nicht zum B~n** it does not look too promising

bestechen [bə'ʃtɛçən] *unreg vt* to bribe ▷ *vi* (*Eindruck machen*): **(durch etw) ~** to be impressive (because of sth)

bestechend *adj* (*Schönheit, Eindruck*) captivating; (*Angebot*) tempting

bestechlich *adj* corruptible; **Bestechlichkeit** *f* corruptibility

Bestechung *f* bribery, corruption

Bestechungsgelder *pl* bribe *sing*

Bestechungsversuch *m* attempted bribery

Besteck [bə'ʃtɛk] (**-(e)s, -e**) *nt* knife, fork and spoon, cutlery; (*Med*) set of instruments; **Besteckkasten** *m* cutlery canteen

bestehen [bə'ʃte:ən] *unreg vi* to exist; (*andauern*) to last ▷ *vt* (*Probe, Prüfung*) to pass; (*Kampf*) to win; **~ bleiben** to last, endure; (*Frage, Hoffnung*) to remain; **die Schwierigkeit/das Problem besteht darin, dass …** the difficulty/problem lies in the fact that …, the difficulty/problem is that …; **~ auf** +*dat* to insist on; **~ aus** to consist of; **Bestehen** *nt*: **seit Bestehen der Firma** ever since the firm came into existence *od* has existed

bestehlen [bə'ʃte:lən] *unreg vt* to rob

besteigen [bə'ʃtaɪɡən] *unreg vt* to climb, ascend; (*Pferd*) to mount; (*Thron*) to ascend

Bestellbuch *nt* order book

bestellen [bə'ʃtɛlən] *vt* to order; (*kommen lassen*) to arrange to see; (*nominieren*) to name; (*Acker*) to cultivate; (*Grüße, Auftrag*) to pass on; **wie bestellt und nicht abgeholt** (*hum: umg*) like orphan Annie; **er hat nicht viel/nichts zu ~** he doesn't have much/any say here; **ich bin für 10 Uhr bestellt** I have an appointment for *od* at 10 o'clock; **es ist schlecht um ihn bestellt** (*fig*) he is in a bad way

Bestell- *zW*: **Bestellformular** *nt* purchase order; **Bestellnummer** *f* order number; **Bestellschein** *m* order coupon

Bestellung *f* (*Comm*) order; (*Bestellen*) ordering; (*Ernennung*) nomination, appointment

bestenfalls ['bɛstən'fals] *adv* at best

bestens ['bɛstəns] *adv* very well

besteuern [bə'ʃtɔyərn] *vt* to tax

bestialisch [bɛsti'a:lɪʃ] (*umg*) *adj* awful, beastly

besticken [bə'ʃtɪkən] *vt* to embroider

Bestie ['bɛstiə] *f* (*lit, fig*) beast

bestimmen [bə'ʃtɪmən] *vt* (*Regeln*) to lay down; (*Tag, Ort*) to fix; (*prägen*) to characterize; (*ausersehen*) to mean; (*ernennen*) to appoint; (*definieren*) to define; (*veranlassen*) to induce ▷ *vi*: **du hast hier nicht zu ~** you don't make the decisions here; **er kann über sein Geld allein ~** it is up to him what he does with his money

bestimmend *adj* (*Faktor, Einfluss*) determining, decisive

bestimmt *adj* (*entschlossen*) firm; (*gewiss*)

certain, definite; (*Artikel*) definite ▷ *adv* (*gewiss*) definitely, for sure; **suchen Sie etwas B~es?** are you looking for anything in particular?; **Bestimmtheit** *f* certainty; **in** *od* **mit aller Bestimmtheit** quite categorically

Bestimmung *f* (*Verordnung*) regulation; (*Festsetzen*) determining; (*Verwendungszweck*) purpose; (*Schicksal*) fate; (*Definition*) definition

Bestimmungs- *zW*: **Bestimmungsbahnhof** *m* (*Eisenb*) destination; **bestimmungsgemäß** *adj* as agreed; **Bestimmungshafen** *m* (port of) destination; **Bestimmungsort** *m* destination

Bestleistung *f* best performance

bestmöglich *adj* best possible

Best.-Nr. *abk* = **Bestellnummer**

bestrafen [bə'ʃtra:fən] *vt* to punish

Bestrafung *f* punishment

bestrahlen [bə'ʃtra:lən] *vt* to shine on; (*Med*) to treat with X-rays

Bestrahlung *f* (*Med*) X-ray treatment, radiotherapy

Bestreben [bə'ʃtre:bən] (**-s**) *nt* endeavour (*Brit*), endeavor (*US*), effort

bestrebt [bə'ʃtre:pt] *adj*: **~ sein, etw zu tun** to endeavour (*Brit*) *od* endeavor (*US*) to do sth

Bestrebung [bə'ʃtre:buŋ] *f* = **Bestreben**

bestreichen [bə'ʃtraɪçən] *unreg vt* (*Brot*) to spread

bestreiken [bə'ʃtraɪkən] *vt* (*Industrie*) to black; **die Fabrik wird zur Zeit bestreikt** there's a strike on in the factory at the moment

bestreiten [bə'ʃtraɪtən] *unreg vt* (*abstreiten*) to dispute; (*finanzieren*) to pay for, finance; **er hat das ganze Gespräch allein bestritten** he did all the talking

bestreuen [bə'ʃtrɔyən] *vt* to sprinkle, dust; (*Straße*) to (spread with) grit

Bestseller ['bɛstsɛlər] (**-s, -**) *m* best-seller

bestürmen [bə'ʃtyrmən] *vt* (*mit Fragen, Bitten etc*) to overwhelm, swamp

bestürzen [bə'ʃtyrtsən] *vt* to dismay

bestürzt *adj* dismayed

Bestürzung *f* consternation

Bestzeit *f* (*bes Sport*) best time

Besuch [bə'zu:x] (**-(e)s, -e**) *m* visit; (*Person*) visitor; **einen ~ bei jdm machen** to pay sb a visit *od* call; **~ haben** to have visitors; **bei jdm auf** *od* **zu ~ sein** to be visiting sb

besuchen *vt* to visit; (*Sch etc*) to attend; **gut besucht** well-attended

Besucher, in (**-s, -**) *m(f)* visitor, guest

Besuchserlaubnis *f* permission to visit

Besuchszeit *f* visiting hours *pl*

besudeln [bə'zu:dəln] *vt* (*Wände*) to smear; (*fig: Namen, Ehre*) to sully

betagt [bə'ta:kt] *adj* aged

betasten [bə'tastən] *vt* to touch, feel

betätigen [bə'tɛ:tɪɡən] *vt* (*bedienen*) to work, operate ▷ *vr* to involve o.s.; **sich politisch ~** to be involved in politics; **sich als etw ~** to work as sth

Betätigung *f* activity; (*beruflich*) occupation; (*Tech*) operation

betäuben [bə'tɔybən] vt to stun; (fig: Gewissen) to still; (Med) to anaesthetize (Brit), anesthetize (US); **ein ~der Duft** an overpowering smell

Betäubung f (Narkose): **örtliche ~** local anaesthetic (Brit) od anesthetic (US)

Betäubungsmittel nt anaesthetic (Brit), anesthetic (US)

Bete ['be:tə] (-, -n) f: **Rote ~** beetroot (Brit), beet (US)

beteiligen [bə'taɪlɪgən] vr: **sich (an etw** dat) **~** to take part (in sth), participate (in sth); (an Geschäft: finanziell) to have a share (in sth) ▷ vt: **jdn (an etw** dat) **~** to give sb a share od interest (in sth); **sich an den Unkosten ~** to contribute to the expenses

Beteiligung f participation; (Anteil) share, interest; (Besucherzahl) attendance

Beteiligungsgesellschaft f associated company

beten ['be:tən] vi to pray ▷ vt (Rosenkranz) to say

beteuern [bə'tɔyərn] vt to assert; (Unschuld) to protest; **jdm etw ~** to assure sb of sth

Beteuerung f assertion; protestation; assurance

Beton [be'tõ:] (-s, -s) m concrete

betonen [bə'to:nən] vt to stress

betonieren [beto'ni:rən] vt to concrete

Betonmischmaschine f concrete mixer

betont [bə'to:nt] adj (Höflichkeit) emphatic, deliberate; (Kühle, Sachlichkeit) pointed

Betonung f stress, emphasis

betören [bə'tø:rən] vt to beguile

Betr. abk = **Betreff**

betr. abk (= betreffend, betreffs) re

Betracht [bə'traxt] m: **in ~ kommen** to be concerned od relevant; **nicht in ~ kommen** to be out of the question; **etw in ~ ziehen** to consider sth; **außer ~ bleiben** not to be considered

betrachten vt to look at; (fig) to consider, look at

Betrachter, in (-s, -) m(f) onlooker

beträchtlich [bə'trɛçtlɪç] adj considerable

Betrachtung f (Ansehen) examination; (Erwägung) consideration; **über etw** akk **~en anstellen** to reflect on od considering sth

betraf etc [bə'tra:f] vb siehe **betreffen**

Betrag [bə'tra:k] (-(e)s, ̈e) m amount, sum; **~ erhalten** (Comm) sum received

betragen [bə'tra:gən] unreg vt to amount to ▷ vr to behave

Betragen (-s) nt behaviour (Brit), behavior (US); (bes in Zeugnis) conduct

beträgt [bə'trɛ:kt] vb siehe **betragen**

betrat etc [bə'tra:t] vb siehe **betreten**

betrauen [bə'trauən] vt: **jdn mit etw ~** to entrust sb with sth

betrauern [bə'trauərn] vt to mourn

beträufeln [bə'trɔyfəln] vt: **den Fisch mit Zitrone ~** to sprinkle lemon juice on the fish

Betreff m: **~: Ihr Schreiben vom ...** re od reference your letter of ...

betreffen [bə'trɛfən] unreg vt to concern, affect; **was mich betrifft** as for me

betreffend adj relevant, in question

betreffs [bə'trɛfs] präp +gen concerning, regarding

betreiben [bə'traɪbən] unreg vt (ausüben) to practise (Brit), practice (US); (Politik) to follow; (Studien) to pursue; (vorantreiben) to push ahead; (Tech: antreiben) to drive; **auf jds B~ hin** (form) at sb's instigation

Betreiberfirma [bə'traɪbərfɪrma] f operating company

betreten [bə'tre:tən] unreg vt to enter; (Bühne etc) to step onto ▷ adj embarrassed; „**B~ verboten**" "keep off/out"

betreuen [bə'trɔyən] vt to look after

Betreuer, in (-s, -) m(f) carer; (Kinderbetreuer) child-minder

Betreuung f: **er wurde mit der ~ der Gruppe beauftragt** he was put in charge of the group

Betrieb (-(e)s, -e) m (Firma) firm, concern; (Anlage) plant; (Tätigkeit) operation; (Treiben) bustle; (Verkehr) traffic; **außer ~ sein** to be out of order; **in ~ sein** to be in operation; **eine Maschine in/außer ~ setzen** to start a machine up/stop a machine; **eine Maschine/Fabrik in ~ nehmen** to put a machine/factory into operation; **in den Geschäften herrscht großer ~** the shops are very busy; **er hält den ganzen ~ auf** (umg) he's holding everything up

betrieb etc [bə'tri:p] vb siehe **betreiben**

betrieben [bə'tri:bən] pp von **betreiben**

betrieblich adj company attr ▷ adv (regeln) within the company

Betriebs- zW: Betriebsanleitung f operating instructions pl; Betriebsausflug m firm's outing; Betriebsausgaben pl revenue expenditure sing; betriebseigen adj company attr; Betriebsergebnis nt trading od operating result; Betriebserlaubnis f operating permission/licence (Brit) od license (US); betriebsfähig adj in working order; Betriebsferien pl company holidays pl (Brit) od vacation sing (US); Betriebsführung f management; Betriebsgeheimnis nt trade secret; Betriebskapital nt capital employed; Betriebsklima nt (working) atmosphere; Betriebskosten pl running costs; Betriebsleitung f management; Betriebsrat m workers' council; Betriebsrente f company pension; betriebssicher adj safe, reliable; Betriebsstoff m fuel; Betriebsstörung f breakdown; Betriebssystem nt (Comput) operating system; Betriebsunfall m industrial accident; Betriebswirt m management expert; Betriebswirtschaft f business management

betrifft [bə'trɪft] vb siehe **betreffen**

betrinken [bə'trɪŋkən] unreg vr to get drunk

betritt [bə'trɪt] vb siehe **betreten**

betroffen [bə'trɔfən] pp von **betreffen** ▷ adj (bestürzt) amazed, perplexed; **von etw ~**

werden *od* **sein** to be affected by sth

betrüben [bə'try:bən] *vt* to grieve

betrübt [bə'try:pt] *adj* sorrowful, grieved

Betrug (**-(e)s**) *m* deception; (*Jur*) fraud

betrug *etc* [bə'tru:k] *vb siehe* **betragen**

betrügen [bə'try:gən] *unreg vt* to cheat; (*Jur*) to defraud; (*Ehepartner*) to be unfaithful to ▷ *vr* to deceive o.s.

Betrüger, in (**-s, -**) *m(f)* cheat, deceiver

betrügerisch *adj* deceitful; (*Jur*) fraudulent; **in ~er Absicht** with intent to defraud

betrunken [bə'trʊŋkən] *adj* drunk

Betrunkene, r *f(m)* drunk

Bett [bɛt] (**-(e)s, -en**) *nt* bed; **im ~** in bed; **ins** *od* **zu ~ gehen** to go to bed; **Bettbezug** *m* duvet cover; **Bettdecke** *f* blanket; (*Daunenbettdecke*) quilt; (*Überwurf*) bedspread

bettelarm ['bɛtəl|arm] *adj* very poor, destitute

Bettelei [bɛtə'laɪ] *f* begging

Bettelmönch *m* mendicant *od* begging monk

betteln *vi* to beg

betten *vt* to make a bed for

Bett- *zW:* **Betthupferl** (*Südd*) *nt* bedtime sweet; **bettlägerig** *adj* bedridden; **Bettlaken** *nt* sheet; **Bettlektüre** *f* bedtime reading

Bettler, in ['bɛtlər(ɪn)] (**-s, -**) *m(f)* beggar

Bett- *zW:* **Bettnässer** (**-s, -**) *m* bedwetter; **Bettschwere** (*umg*) *f:* **die nötige Bettschwere haben/bekommen** to be/ get tired enough to sleep; **Betttuch** *nt* sheet; **Bettvorleger** *m* bedside rug; **Bettwäsche** *f* bedclothes *pl*, bedding; **Bettzeug** *nt =* **Bettwäsche**

betucht [bə'tu:xt] (*umg*) *adj* well-to-do

betulich [bə'tu:lɪç] *adj* (*übertrieben besorgt*) fussing *attr*; (*Redeweise*) twee

betupfen [bə'tʊpfən] *vt* to dab; (*Med*) to swab

Beugehaft ['bɔygəhaft] *f* (*Jur*) coercive detention

beugen ['bɔygən] *vt* to bend; (*Gram*) to inflect ▷ *vr* (+*dat*) (*sich fügen*) to bow (to)

Beule ['bɔylə] (**-, -n**) *f* bump

beunruhigen [bə'|ʊnru:ɪgən] *vt* to disturb, alarm ▷ *vr* to become worried

Beunruhigung *f* worry, alarm

beurkunden [bə'|u:rkʊndən] *vt* to attest, verify

beurlauben [bə'|u:rlaʊbən] *vt* to give leave *od* holiday to (*Brit*), grant vacation to (*US*); **beurlaubt sein** to have leave of absence; (*suspendiert sein*) to have been relieved of one's duties

beurteilen [bə'|ʊrtaɪlən] *vt* to judge; (*Buch etc*) to review

Beurteilung *f* judgement; (*von Buch etc*) review; (*Note*) mark

Beute ['bɔytə] (**-**) *f* booty, loot; (*von Raubtieren etc*) prey

Beutel (**-s, -**) *m* bag; (*Geldbeutel*) purse; (*Tabaksbeutel*) pouch

bevölkern [bə'fœlkərn] *vt* to populate

Bevölkerung *f* population

Bevölkerungs- *zW:* **Bevölkerungsexplosion** *f* population explosion; **Bevölkerungsschicht** *f*

social stratum; **Bevölkerungsstatistik** *f* vital statistics *pl*

bevollmächtigen [bə'fɔlmɛçtɪgən] *vt* to authorize

Bevollmächtigte, r *f(m)* authorized agent

Bevollmächtigung *f* authorization

bevor [bə'fo:r] *konj* before; **bevormunden** *vt untr* to dominate; **bevorstehen** *unreg vi:* (**jdm**) **bevorstehen** to be in store (for sb); **bevorstehend** *adj* imminent, approaching; **bevorzugen** *vt untr* to prefer; **bevorzugt** [bə'fo:rtsu:kt] *adv:* **etw bevorzugt abfertigen** *etc* to give sth priority; **Bevorzugung** *f* preference

bewachen [bə'vaxən] *vt* to watch, guard

bewachsen [bə'vaksən] *adj* overgrown

Bewachung *f* (*Bewachen*) guarding; (*Leute*) guard, watch

bewaffnen [bə'vafnən] *vt* to arm

Bewaffnung *f* (*Vorgang*) arming; (*Ausrüstung*) armament, arms *pl*

bewahren [bə'va:rən] *vt* to keep; **jdn vor jdm/ etw ~** to save sb from sb/sth; (**Gott**) **bewahre!** (*umg*) heaven *od* God forbid!

bewähren [bə've:rən] *vr* to prove o.s.; (*Maschine*) to prove its worth

bewahrheiten [bə'va:rhaɪtən] *vr* to come true

bewährt *adj* reliable

Bewährung *f* (*Jur*) probation; **ein Jahr Gefängnis mit ~** a suspended sentence of one year with probation

Bewährungs- *zW:* **Bewährungsfrist** *f* (period of) probation; **Bewährungshelfer** *m* probation officer; **Bewährungsprobe** *f:* **etw einer Bewährungsprobe** *dat* **unterziehen** to put sth to the test

bewaldet [bə'valdət] *adj* wooded

bewältigen [bə'vɛltɪgən] *vt* to overcome; (*Arbeit*) to finish; (*Portion*) to manage; (*Schwierigkeiten*) to cope with

bewandert [bə'vandərt] *adj* expert, knowledgeable

Bewandtnis [bə'vantnɪs] *f:* **damit hat es folgende ~** the fact of the matter is this

bewarb *etc* [bə'varp] *vb siehe* **bewerben**

bewässern [bə'vɛsərn] *vt* to irrigate

Bewässerung *f* irrigation

bewegen [bə've:gən] *vt, vr* to move; **der Preis bewegt sich um die 50 Euro** the price is about 50 euros; **jdn zu etw ~** to induce sb to do sth

Beweggrund *m* motive

beweglich *adj* movable, mobile; (*flink*) quick

bewegt [bə've:kt] *adj* (*Leben*) eventful; (*Meer*) rough; (*ergriffen*) touched

Bewegung *f* movement, motion; (*innere*) emotion; (*körperlich*) exercise; **sich** *dat* **~ machen** to take exercise

Bewegungsfreiheit *f* freedom of movement; (*fig*) freedom of action

bewegungslos *adj* motionless

Beweis [bə'vaɪs] (**-es, -e**) *m* proof; (*Zeichen*) sign; **Beweisaufnahme** *f* (*Jur*) taking *od* hearing of

evidence; **beweisbar** *adj* provable
beweisen *unreg vt* to prove; (*zeigen*) to show;
was zu ~ war QED
Beweis- *zW:* **Beweisführung** *f* reasoning;
(*Jur*) presentation of one's case; **Beweiskraft**
f weight, conclusiveness; **beweiskräftig**
adj convincing, conclusive; **Beweislast** *f*
(*Jur*) onus, burden of proof; **Beweismittel** *nt*
evidence; **Beweisnot** *f* (*Jur*) lack of evidence;
Beweisstück *nt* exhibit
bewenden [bə'vɛndən] *vi*: **etw dabei ~ lassen**
to leave sth at that
bewerben [bə'vɛrbən] *unreg vr*: **sich ~ (um)** to
apply (for)
Bewerber, in (**-s, -**) *m(f)* applicant
Bewerbung *f* application
Bewerbungsfrist *f* application deadline
Bewerbungsmappe *f,* **Bewerbungs-
unterlagen** *pl* application documents *pl*
bewerkstelligen [bə'vɛrkʃtɛlɪgən] *vt* to
manage, accomplish
bewerten [bə've:rtən] *vt* to assess
bewies *etc* [bə'vi:s] *vb siehe* **beweisen**
bewiesen [bə'vi:zən] *pp von* **beweisen**
bewilligen [bə'vɪlɪgən] *vt* to grant, allow
Bewilligung *f* granting
bewirbt [bə'vɪrpt] *vb siehe* **bewerben**
bewirken [bə'vɪrkən] *vt* to cause, bring about
bewirten [bə'vɪrtən] *vt* to entertain
bewirtschaften [bə'vɪrtʃaftən] *vt* to manage
Bewirtung *f* hospitality; **die ~ so vieler Gäste**
catering for so many guests
bewog *etc* [bə'vo:k] *vb siehe* **bewegen**
bewogen [bə'vo:gən] *pp von* **bewegen**
bewohnbar *adj* inhabitable
bewohnen [bə'vo:nən] *vt* to inhabit, live in
Bewohner, in (**-s, -**) *m(f)* inhabitant; (*von Haus*)
resident
bewölkt [bə'vœlkt] *adj* cloudy, overcast
Bewölkung *f* clouds *pl*
Bewölkungsauflockerung *f* break-up of the
cloud
beworben [bə'vɔrbən] *pp von* **bewerben**
Bewunderer, in (**-s, -**) *m(f)* admirer
bewundern [bə'vʊndərn] *vt* to admire
bewundernswert *adj* admirable, wonderful
Bewunderung *f* admiration
bewusst [bə'vʊst] *adj* conscious; (*absichtlich*)
deliberate; **jdm etw ~ machen** to make sb
conscious of sth; **sich** *dat* **etw ~ machen** to
realize sth; **sich** *dat* **einer Sache** *gen* **~ sein** to
be aware of sth; **bewusstlos** *adj* unconscious;
Bewusstlosigkeit *f* unconsciousness; **bis
zur Bewusstlosigkeit** (*umg*) ad nauseam;
Bewusstsein *nt* consciousness; **bei
Bewusstsein** conscious; **im Bewusstsein,
dass ...** in the knowledge that ...
Bewusstseins- *zW:* **Bewusstseinsbildung**
f (*Pol*) shaping of political ideas;
bewusstseinserweiternd
adj: **bewusstseinserweiternde
Drogen** mind-expanding drugs;
Bewusstseinserweiterung *f* consciousness

raising
Bez. *abk* = **Bezirk**
bez. *abk* (= *bezüglich*) re.
bezahlen [bə'tsa:lən] *vt* to pay (for); **es macht
sich bezahlt** it will pay
Bezahlfernsehen *nt* pay TV
Bezahlung *f* payment; **ohne/gegen** *od* **für ~**
without/for payment
bezaubern [bə'tsaʊbərn] *vt* to enchant, charm
bezeichnen [bə'tsaɪçnən] *vt* (*kennzeichnen*) to
mark; (*nennen*) to call; (*beschreiben*) to describe;
(*zeigen*) to show, indicate
bezeichnend *adj*: **~ (für)** characteristic (of),
typical (of)
Bezeichnung *f* (*Zeichen*) mark, sign;
(*Beschreibung*) description; (*Ausdruck*)
expression, term
bezeugen [bə'tsɔʏgən] *vt* to testify to
bezichtigen [bə'tsɪçtɪgən] *vt* (*+gen*) to accuse
(of)
Bezichtigung *f* accusation
beziehen [bə'tsi:ən] *unreg vt* (*mit Überzug*) to
cover; (*Haus, Position*) to move into; (*Standpunkt*)
to take up; (*erhalten*) to receive; (*Zeitung*) to
subscribe to, take ▷ *vr* (*Himmel*) to cloud over;
die Betten frisch ~ to change the beds; **etw
auf jdn/etw ~** to relate sth to sb/sth; **sich ~
auf** *+akk* to refer to
Beziehung *f* (*Verbindung*) connection;
(*Zusammenhang*) relation; (*Verhältnis*)
relationship; (*Hinsicht*) respect;
diplomatische ~en diplomatic relations;
seine ~en spielen lassen to pull strings;
in jeder ~ in every respect; **~en haben**
(*vorteilhaft*) to have connections *od* contacts
Beziehungskiste (*umg*) *f* relationship
beziehungsweise *adv* or; (*genauer gesagt*) that
is, or rather; (*im anderen Fall*) and ... respectively
beziffern [bə'tsɪfərn] *vt* (*angeben*): **~ auf** *+akk od*
mit to estimate at
Bezirk [bə'tsɪrk] (**-(e)s, -e**) *m* district
bezirzen [bə'tsɪrtsən] (*umg*) *vt* to bewitch
bezogen [bə'tso:gən] *pp von* **beziehen**
Bezogene, r [bə'tso:gənə(r)] *f(m)* (*von Scheck etc*)
drawee
Bezug [bə'tsu:k] (**-(e)s, ̈-e**) *m* (*Hülle*) covering;
(*Comm*) ordering; (*Gehalt*) income, salary;
(*Beziehung*): **~ (zu)** relationship (to); **in ~ auf**
+akk with reference to; **mit** *od* **unter ~ auf**
+akk regarding; (*form*) with reference to; **~
nehmen auf** *+akk* to refer to
bezüglich [bə'tsy:klɪç] *präp +gen* concerning,
referring to ▷ *adj* concerning; (*Gram*) relative
Bezugnahme *f*: **~ (auf** *+akk*) reference (to)
Bezugs- *zW:* **Bezugsperson** *f*: **die wichtigste
Bezugsperson des Kleinkindes** the person
to whom the small child relates most closely;
Bezugspreis *m* retail price; **Bezugsquelle** *f*
source of supply
bezuschussen [bə'tsu:ʃʊsən] *vt* to subsidize
bezwecken [bə'tsvɛkən] *vt* to aim at
bezweifeln [bə'tsvaɪfəln] *vt* to doubt
bezwingen [bə'tsvɪŋən] *unreg vt* to conquer;

(*Feind*) to defeat, overcome

bezwungen [bə'tsvʊŋən] *pp von* **bezwingen**

Bf. *abk* = **Bahnhof; Brief**

BfA (-) *f abk* (= *Bundesversicherungsanstalt für Angestellte*) Federal insurance company for employees

BfV (-) *nt abk* (= *Bundesamt für Verfassungsschutz*) Federal Office for Protection of the Constitution

BG (-) *f abk* (= *Berufsgenossenschaft*) professional association

BGB (-) *nt abk* (= *Bürgerliches Gesetzbuch*) *siehe* **bürgerlich**

BGH (-) *m abk* (= *Bundesgerichtshof*) Federal Supreme Court

BGS (-) *m abk* = **Bundesgrenzschutz**

BH (-**s, -**(**s**)) *m abk* (= *Büstenhalter*) bra

Bhf. *abk* = **Bahnhof**

BI *f abk* = **Bürgerinitiative**

Biathlon ['bi:atlɔn] (-**s, -s**) *nt* biathlon

bibbern ['bɪbərn] (*umg*) *vi* (*vor Kälte*) to shiver

Bibel ['bi:bəl] (-**, -n**) *f* Bible

bibelfest *adj* well versed in the Bible

Biber ['bi:bər] (-**s, -**) *m* beaver

Biberbettuch *nt* flannelette sheet

Bibliografie [bibliogra'fi:] *f* bibliography

Bibliothek [biblio'te:k] (-**, -en**) *f* (*auch Comput*) library

Bibliothekar, in [bibliote'ka:r(ɪn)] (-**s, -e**) *m(f)* librarian

biblisch ['bi:blɪʃ] *adj* biblical

bieder ['bi:dər] *adj* upright, worthy; (*pej*) conventional; (*Kleid etc*) plain

Biedermann (-**(e)s**, *pl* -**männer**) (*pej*) *m* (*geh*) petty bourgeois

biegbar ['bi:kba:r] *adj* flexible

Biege *f*: **die ~ machen** (*umg*) to buzz off, split

biegen ['bi:gən] *unreg vt, vr* to bend ▷ *vi* to turn; **sich vor Lachen ~** (*fig*) to double up with laughter; **auf B- oder Brechen** (*umg*) by hook or by crook

biegsam ['bi:kza:m] *adj* supple

Biegung *f* bend, curve

Biene ['bi:nə] (-**, -n**) *f* bee; (*veraltet: umg: Mädchen*) bird (*Brit*), chick (*bes US*)

Bienen- *zW*: **Bienenhonig** *m* honey; **Bienenkorb** *m* beehive; **Bienenstich** *m* (*Koch*) sugar-and-almond coated cake filled with custard or cream; **Bienenstock** *m* beehive; **Bienenwachs** *nt* beeswax

Bier [bi:r] (-**(e)s, -e**) *nt* beer; **zwei ~, bitte!** two beers, please; **Bierbauch** (*umg*) *m* beer belly; **Bierbrauer** *m* brewer; **Bierdeckel** *m* beer mat; **Bierfilz** *m* beer mat; **Bierkrug** *m* beer mug; **Bierschinken** *m* ham sausage; **Bierseidel** *nt* beer mug; **Bierwurst** *f* ham sausage

Biest [bi:st] (-**(e)s, -er**) (*pej: umg*) *nt* (*Mensch*) (little) wretch; (*Frau*) bitch (!)

biestig *adj* beastly

bieten ['bi:tən] *unreg vt* to offer; (*bei Versteigerung*) to bid ▷ *vr* (*Gelegenheit*): **sich jdm ~** to present itself to sb; **sich** *dat* **etw ~ lassen** to put up with sth

Bigamie [biga'mi:] *f* bigamy

Bikini [bi'ki:ni] (-**s, -s**) *m* bikini

Bilanz [bi'lants] *f* balance; (*fig*) outcome; **eine ~ aufstellen** to draw up a balance sheet; **~ ziehen (aus)** to take stock (of); **Bilanzprüfer** *m* auditor

bilateral ['bi:latera:l] *adj* bilateral; **~er Handel** bilateral trade; **~es Abkommen** bilateral agreement

Bild [bɪlt] (-**(e)s, -er**) *nt* (*lit, fig*) picture; photo; (*Spiegelbild*) reflection; (*fig: Vorstellung*) image, picture; **ein ~ machen** to take a photo *od* picture; **im ~e sein (über** +*akk*) to be in the picture (about); **Bildauflösung** *f* (*TV, Comput*) resolution; **Bildband** *m* illustrated book; **Bildbericht** *m* pictorial report; **Bildbeschreibung** *f* (*Sch*) description of a picture; **Bilddatei** *f* picture file

bilden ['bɪldən] *vt* to form; (*erziehen*) to educate; (*ausmachen*) to constitute ▷ *vr* to arise; (*durch Lesen etc*) to improve one's mind; (*erziehen*) to educate o.s.

bildend *adj*: **die ~e Kunst** art

Bilderbuch *nt* picture book

Bilderrahmen *m* picture frame

Bild- *zW*: **Bildfläche** *f* screen; (*fig*) scene; **von der Bildfläche verschwinden** (*fig: umg*) to disappear (from the scene); **bildhaft** *adj* (*Sprache*) vivid; **Bildhauer** *m* sculptor; **bildhübsch** *adj* lovely, pretty as a picture; **bildlich** *adj* figurative; pictorial; **sich** *dat* **etw bildlich vorstellen** to picture sth in one's mind's eye

Bildnis ['bɪltnɪs] *nt* (*liter*) portrait

Bild- *zW*: **Bildplatte** *f* videodisc; **Bildröhre** *f* (*TV*) cathode ray tube; **Bildschirm** *m* (*TV, Comput*) screen; **Bildschirmgerät** *nt* (*Comput*) visual display unit, VDU; **Bildschirmschoner** (-**s, -**) *m* (*Comput*) screen saver; **Bildschirmtext** *m* teletext; ≈ Ceefax®, Oracle®; **bildschön** *adj* lovely

Bildtelefon *nt* videophone

Bildung ['bɪldʊŋ] *f* formation; (*Wissen, Benehmen*) education

Bildungs- *zW*: **Bildungsgang** *m* school (and university/college) career; **Bildungsgut** *nt* cultural heritage; **Bildungslücke** *f* gap in one's education; **Bildungspolitik** *f* educational policy; **Bildungsroman** *m* (*Liter*) Bildungsroman, *novel relating hero's intellectual/ spiritual development*; **Bildungsurlaub** *m* educational holiday; **Bildungsweg** *m*: **auf dem zweiten Bildungsweg** through night school/the Open University *etc*; **Bildungswesen** *nt* education system

Bildweite *f* (*Phot*) distance

Bildzuschrift *f* reply enclosing photograph

Billard ['bɪljart] (-**s, -e**) *nt* billiards; **Billardball** *m* billiard ball; **Billardkugel** *f* billiard ball

billig ['bɪlɪç] *adj* cheap; (*gerecht*) fair, reasonable; **~e Handelsflagge** flag of convenience; **~es Geld** cheap/easy money

billigen ['bɪlɪgən] *vt* to approve of; **etw stillschweigend ~** to condone sth

billigerweise *adv* (*veraltet*) in all fairness,

reasonably

Billig- zW: **Billigflieger** m, **Billigfluglinie** f cheap od low-cost airline; **Billigladen** m discount store; **Billigpreis** m low price; **Billigprodukt** nt low-price product

Billigung f approval

Billion [bɪli'oːn] f billion (Brit), trillion (US)

bimmeln ['bɪməln] vi to tinkle

Bimsstein ['bɪmsʃtaɪn] m pumice stone

bin [bɪn] vb siehe **sein**

binär [bi'nɛːr] adj binary; **Binärzahl** f binary number

Binde ['bɪndə] (-, -n) f bandage; (Armbinde) band; (Med) sanitary towel (Brit) od napkin (US); **sich** dat **einen hinter die ~ gießen** od **kippen** (umg) to put a few drinks away

Binde- zW: **Bindeglied** nt connecting link; **Bindehautentzündung** f conjunctivitis; **Bindemittel** nt binder

binden unreg vt to bind, tie ▷ vr (sich verpflichten): **sich ~ (an** +akk) to commit o.s. (to)

bindend adj binding; (Zusage) definite; **~ für** binding on

Bindestrich m hyphen

Bindewort nt conjunction

Bindfaden m string; **es regnet Bindfäden** (umg) it's sheeting down

Bindung f bond, tie; (Ski) binding

binnen ['bɪnən] präp (+dat od gen) within; **Binnenhafen** m inland harbour (Brit) od harbor (US); **Binnenhandel** m internal trade; **Binnenmarkt** m home market; **Europäischer Binnenmarkt** single European market; **Binnennachfrage** f domestic demand

Binse ['bɪnzə] (-, -n) f rush, reed; **in die ~n gehen** (fig: umg) to be a wash-out

Binsenwahrheit f truism

Bio- [bio-] zW: bio-, organic

Biografie [biogra'fiː] f biography

Bioladen ['biolaːdən] m health food shop (Brit) od store (US); see culture note

Biologe [bio'loːgə] (-n, -n) m biologist

Biologie [biolo'giː] f biology

Biologin f biologist

biologisch [bio'loːgɪʃ] adj biological; **~e Vielfalt** biodiversity; **~e Uhr** biological clock

Bio- [bio-] zW: **Biosphäre** f biosphere; **Biotechnik** [bio'tɛçnɪk] f biotechnology; **Bioterrorismus** m bioterrorism; **Biotreibstoff** ['biːotraipʃtɔf] m biofuel

birgt [bɪrkt] vb siehe **bergen**

Birke ['bɪrkə] (-, -n) f birch

Birma ['bɪrma] (-s) nt Burma

Birnbaum m pear tree

Birne ['bɪrnə] (-, -n) f pear; (Elek) (light) bulb

birst [bɪrst] vb siehe **bersten**

 SCHLÜSSELWORT

b

bis [bɪs] adv, präp +akk **1** (zeitlich) till, until; (bis spätestens) by; **Sie haben bis Dienstag Zeit** you have until od till Tuesday; **bis zum Wochenende** up to od until the weekend; (spätestens) by the weekend; **bis Dienstag muss es fertig sein** it must be ready by Tuesday; **bis wann ist das fertig?** when will that be finished?; **bis auf Weiteres** until further notice; **bis in die Nacht** into the night; **bis bald!/gleich!** see you later/soon

2 (räumlich) (up) to; **ich fahre bis Köln** I'm going as far as Cologne; **bis an unser Grundstück** (right od up) to our plot; **bis hierher** this far; **bis zur Straße kommen** to get as far as the road

3 (bei Zahlen, Angaben) up to; **bis zu** up to; **Gefängnis bis zu 8 Jahren** a maximum of 8 years' imprisonment

4: **bis auf etw** akk (außer) except sth; (einschließlich) including sth

▷ konj **1** (mit Zahlen) to; **10 bis 20** 10 to 20

2 (zeitlich) till, until; **bis es dunkel wird** till od until it gets dark; **von ... bis ...** from ... to ...

Bisamratte ['biːzamratə] f muskrat (beaver)

Bischof ['bɪʃɔf] (-s, ̈-e) m bishop

bischöflich ['bɪʃøːflɪç] adj episcopal

bisexuell [bizɛksu'ɛl] adj bisexual

bisher [bɪs'heːr] adv till now, hitherto

bisherig [bɪs'heːrɪç] adj till now

Biskaya [bɪs'kaːya] f: **Golf von ~** Bay of Biscay

Biskuit [bɪs'kviːt] (-(e)s, -s od -e) m od nt biscuit; **Biskuitgebäck** nt sponge cake(s); **Biskuitteig** m sponge mixture

bislang [bɪs'laŋ] adv hitherto

Biss (-es, -e) m bite

biss etc [bɪs] vb siehe **beißen**

bisschen ['bɪsçən] adj, adv bit

Bissen ['bɪsən] (-s, -) m bite, morsel; **sich** dat **jeden ~ vom** od **am Munde absparen** to watch every penny one spends

bissig ['bɪsɪç] adj (Hund) snappy; vicious; (Bemerkung) cutting, biting; **„Vorsicht, ~er Hund"** "beware of the dog"

bist [bɪst] vb siehe **sein**

bisweilen [bɪs'vaɪlən] adv at times, occasionally

Bit [bɪt] (-(s), -(s)) nt (Comput) bit

Bittbrief m petition

Bitte ['bɪtə] (-, -n) f request; **auf seine ~ hin** at his request; **bitte** interj please; (als Antwort auf Dank) you're welcome; **wie bitte?** (I beg your) pardon?; **bitte schön!** it was a pleasure; **bitte schön?** (in Geschäft) can I help you?; **na bitte!** there you are!

bitten unreg vt to ask ▷ vi (einladen): **ich lasse ~** would you ask him/her etc to come in now?; **~ um** to ask for; **aber ich bitte dich!** not at all;

ich bitte darum *(form)* if you wouldn't mind; **ich muss doch (sehr)** ~! well I must say!

bittend *adj* pleading, imploring

bitter ['bɪtər] *adj* bitter; *(Schokolade)* plain; **etw ~ nötig haben** to be in dire need of sth; **bitterböse** *adj* very angry; **bitterernst** *adj*: **damit ist es mir bitterernst** I am deadly serious *od* in deadly earnest; **Bitterkeit** *f* bitterness; **bitterlich** *adj* bitter ▷ *adv* bitterly

Bittsteller, in (**-s, -**) *m(f)* petitioner

Biwak ['biːvak] (**-s, -s** *od* **-e**) *nt* bivouac

Bj. *abk* = **Baujahr**

Blabla [bla'blaː] (**-s**) *(umg)* *nt* waffle

blähen ['blɛːən] *vt, vr* to swell, blow out ▷ *vi* *(Speisen)* to cause flatulence *od* wind

Blähungen *pl (Med)* wind *sing*

blamabel [bla'maːbəl] *adj* disgraceful

Blamage [bla'maːʒə] (**-, -n**) *f* disgrace

blamieren [bla'miːrən] *vr* to make a fool of o.s., disgrace o.s. ▷ *vt* to let down, disgrace

blank [blaŋk] *adj* bright; *(unbedeckt)* bare; *(sauber)* clean, polished; *(umg: ohne Geld)* broke; *(offensichtlich)* blatant

blanko ['blaŋko] *adv* blank; **Blankoscheck** *m* blank cheque *(Brit) od* check *(US)*; **Blankovollmacht** *f* carte blanche

Bläschen ['blɛːsçən] *nt* bubble; *(Med)* small blister

Blase ['blaːzə] (**-, -n**) *f* bubble; *(Med)* blister; *(Anat)* bladder

Blasebalg *m* bellows *pl*

blasen *unreg vt, vi* to blow; **zum Aufbruch ~** *(fig)* to say it's time to go

Blasenentzündung *f* cystitis

Bläser, in ['blɛːzər(ɪn)] (**-s, -**) *m(f) (Mus)* wind player; **die ~** the wind (section)

blasiert [bla'ziːrt] *(pej) adj (geh)* blasé

Blas- *zW*: **Blasinstrument** *nt* wind instrument; **Blaskapelle** *f* brass band; **Blasmusik** *f* brass band music

blass [blas] *adj* pale; *(Ausdruck)* weak, insipid; *(fig: Ahnung, Vorstellung)* faint, vague; **~ vor Neid werden** to go green with envy

Blässe ['blɛsə] (**-**) *f* paleness, pallor

Blatt [blat] (**-(e)s, ¨er**) *nt* leaf; *(von Papier)* sheet; *(Zeitung)* newspaper; *(Karten)* hand; **vom ~ singen/spielen** to sight-read; **kein ~ vor den Mund nehmen** not to mince one's words

blättern ['blɛtərn] *vi*: **in etw** *dat* **~** to leaf through sth

Blätterteig *m* flaky *od* puff pastry

Blattlaus *f* greenfly, aphid

blau [blau] *adj* blue; *(umg)* drunk, stoned; *(Koch)* boiled; *(Auge)* black; **~er Fleck** bruise; **mit einem ~en Auge davonkommen** *(fig)* to get off lightly; **~er Brief** *(Sch) letter telling parents a child may have to repeat a year*; **er wird sein ~es Wunder erleben** *(umg)* he won't know what's hit him; **blauäugig** *adj* blue-eyed; **Blaubeere** *f* bilberry

Blaue *nt*: **Fahrt ins ~** mystery tour; **das ~ vom Himmel (herunter) lügen** *(umg)* to tell a pack of lies

blau- *zW*: **Blauhelm** *(umg)* *m* UN Soldier; **Blaukraut** *nt* red cabbage; **Blaulicht** *nt* flashing blue light; **blaumachen** *(umg)* *vi* to skive off work; **Blaupause** *f* blueprint; **Blausäure** *f* prussic acid; **Blaustrumpf** *m (fig)* bluestocking

Blech [blɛç] (**-(e)s, -e**) *nt* tin, sheet metal; *(Backblech)* baking tray; **~ reden** *(umg)* to talk rubbish *od* nonsense; **Blechbläser** *pl* the brass (section); **Blechbüchse** *f* tin, can; **Blechdose** *f* tin, can

blechen *(umg)* *vt, vi* to pay

Blechschaden *m (Aut)* damage to bodywork

Blechtrommel *f* tin drum

blecken ['blɛkən] *vt*: **die Zähne ~** to bare *od* show one's teeth

Blei [blaɪ] (**-(e)s, -e**) *nt* lead

Bleibe (**-, -n**) *f* roof over one's head

bleiben *unreg vi* to stay, remain; **bitte, ~ Sie doch sitzen** please don't get up; **wo bleibst du so lange?** *(umg)* what's keeping you?; **das bleibt unter uns** *(fig)* that's (just) between ourselves; **~ lassen** *(aufgeben)* to give up; **etw ~ lassen** *(unterlassen)* to give sth a miss

bleich [blaɪç] *adj* faded, pale; **bleichen** *vt* to bleach; **Bleichgesicht** *(umg)* *nt (blasser Mensch)* pasty-face

bleiern *adj* leaden

Blei- *zW*: **bleifrei** *adj* lead-free; **Bleigießen** *nt* New Year's Eve fortune-telling using lead shapes; **bleihaltig** *adj*: **bleihaltig sein** to contain lead; **Bleistift** *m* pencil; **Bleistiftabsatz** *m* stiletto heel *(Brit)*, spike heel *(US)*; **Bleistiftspitzer** *m* pencil sharpener; **Bleivergiftung** *f* lead poisoning

Blende ['blɛndə] (**-, -n**) *f (Phot)* aperture; *(: Einstellungsposition)* f-stop

blenden *vt* to blind, dazzle; *(fig)* to hoodwink

blendend *(umg)* *adj* grand; **~ aussehen** to look smashing

Blender (**-s, -**) *m* con-man

blendfrei ['blɛntfraɪ] *adj (Glas)* non-reflective

Blick [blɪk] (**-(e)s, -e**) *m (kurz)* glance, glimpse; *(Anschauen)* look, gaze; *(Aussicht)* view; **Liebe auf den ersten ~** love at first sight; **den ~ senken** to look down; **den bösen ~ haben** to have the evil eye; **einen (guten) ~ für etw haben** to have an eye for sth; **mit einem ~** at a glance

blicken *vi* to look; **das lässt tief ~** that's very revealing; **sich ~ lassen** to put in an appearance

Blick- *zW*: **Blickfang** *m* eye-catcher; **Blickfeld** *nt* range of vision *(auch fig)*; **Blickkontakt** *m* visual contact; **Blickpunkt** *m*: **im Blickpunkt der Öffentlichkeit stehen** to be in the public eye

blieb *etc* [bliːp] *vb siehe* **bleiben**

blies *etc* [bliːs] *vb siehe* **blasen**

blind [blɪnt] *adj* blind; *(Glas etc)* dull; *(Alarm)* false; **~er Passagier** stowaway

Blinddarm *m* appendix; **Blinddarmentzündung** *f* appendicitis

b

Blindenhund m guide dog
Blindenschrift f braille
Blind- zW: **Blindgänger** m (Mil, fig) dud;
Blindheit f blindness; **mit Blindheit
geschlagen sein** (fig) to be blind; **blindlings**
adv blindly; **Blindschleiche** f slow worm;
blindschreiben unreg vi to touch-type
blinken ['blɪŋkən] vi to twinkle, sparkle; (Licht)
to flash, signal; (Aut) to indicate ▷ vt to flash,
signal
Blinker (-s, -) m (Aut) indicator
Blinklicht nt (Aut) indicator
blinzeln ['blɪntsəln] vi to blink, wink
Blitz [blɪts] (-es, -e) m (flash of) lightning;
wie ein ~ aus heiterem Himmel (fig) like a
bolt from the blue; **Blitzableiter** m lightning
conductor; (fig) vent od safety valve for
feelings; **blitzen** vi (aufleuchten) to glint, shine;
es blitzt (Met) there's a flash of lightning;
Blitzgerät nt (Phot) flash(gun); **Blitzlicht** nt
flashlight; **blitzsauber** adj spick and span;
blitzschnell adj, adv as quick as a flash;
Blitzwürfel m (Phot) flashcube
Block [blɔk] (-(e)s, ⁻e) m (lit, fig) block; (von
Papier) pad; (Pol: Staatenblock) bloc; (Fraktion)
faction
Blockade [blɔ'ka:də] (-, -n) f blockade
Block- zW: **Blockbuchstabe** m block letter od
capital; **Blockflöte** f recorder; **blockfrei** adj
(Pol) non-aligned; **Blockhaus** nt log cabin;
Blockhütte f log cabin
blockieren [blɔ'ki:rən] vt to block ▷ vi (Räder)
to jam
Block- zW: **Blockschokolade** f cooking
chocolate; **Blockschrift** f block letters pl;
Blockstunde f double period
blöd [blø:t] adj silly, stupid
blödeln ['blø:dəln] (umg) vi to fool around
Blödheit f stupidity
Blödian ['blø:dian] (-(e)s, -e) (umg) m idiot
blöd- zW: **Blödmann** (-(e)s, pl -männer) (umg)
m idiot; **Blödsinn** m nonsense; **blödsinnig** adj
silly, idiotic
Blog (-s, -s) nt (Comput) blog; **bloggen** vi to blog;
Blogging nt blogging
blöken ['blø:kən] vi (Schaf) to bleat
blond [blɔnt] adj blond(e), fair-haired
Blondine [blɔn'di:nə] f blonde

🅞 SCHLÜSSELWORT

bloß [blo:s] adj **1** (unbedeckt) bare; (nackt) naked;
mit der bloßen Hand with one's bare hand;
mit bloßem Auge with the naked eye
2 (alleinig: nur) mere; **der bloße Gedanke** the
very thought; **bloßer Neid** sheer envy
▷ adv only, merely; **lass das bloß!** just don't
do that!; **wie ist das bloß passiert?** how on
earth did that happen?

Blöße ['blø:sə] (-, -n) f bareness; nakedness;
(fig) weakness; **sich** dat **eine ~ geben** (fig) to
lay o.s. open to attack

bloßlegen vt to expose
bloßstellen vt to show up
blühen ['bly:ən] vi (lit) to bloom, be in bloom;
(fig) to flourish; (umg: bevorstehen): **(jdm) ~ to be**
in store (for sb)
blühend adj: **wie das ~ Leben aussehen** to
look the very picture of health
Blume ['blu:mə] (-, -n) f flower; (von Wein)
bouquet; **jdm etw durch die ~ sagen** to say
sth in a roundabout way to sb
Blumen- zW: **Blumenbeet** nt flower bed;
Blumengeschäft nt flower shop, florist's;
Blumenkasten m window box; **Blumenkohl**
m cauliflower; **Blumenstrauß** m bouquet,
bunch of flowers; **Blumentopf** m flowerpot;
Blumenzwiebel f bulb
Bluse ['blu:zə] (-, -n) f blouse
Blut [blu:t] (-(e)s) nt (lit, fig) blood; **(nur)
ruhig ~** keep your shirt on (umg); **jdn/sich
bis aufs ~ bekämpfen** to fight sb/fight
bitterly; **~ stillend** styptic; **blutarm** adj
anaemic (Brit), anemic (US); (fig) penniless;
Blutbahn f bloodstream; **Blutbank** f blood
bank; **blutbefleckt** adj bloodstained; **Blutbild**
nt blood count; **Blutbuche** f copper beech;
Blutdruck m blood pressure
Blüte ['bly:tə] (-, -n) f blossom; (fig) prime
Blutegel ['blu:t|e:gəl] m leech
bluten vi to bleed
Blütenstaub m pollen
Bluter (-s, -) m (Med) haemophiliac (Brit),
hemophiliac (US)
Bluterguss m haemorrhage (Brit), hemorrhage
(US); (auf Haut) bruise
Blütezeit f flowering period; (fig) prime
Blutgerinnsel nt blood clot
Blutgruppe f blood group
blutig adj bloody; (umg: Anfänger) absolute;
(: Ernst) deadly
Blut- zW: **blutjung** adj very young;
Blutkonserve f unit od pint of stored blood;
Blutkörperchen nt blood corpuscle; **Blutprobe**
f blood test; **blutrünstig** adj bloodthirsty;
Blutschande f incest; **Blutsenkung** f
(Med): **eine Blutsenkung machen** to test the
sedimentation rate of the blood; **Blutspender**
m blood donor; **blutstillend** adj styptic;
Blutsturz m haemorrhage (Brit), hemorrhage
(US)
blutsverwandt adj related by blood
Blutübertragung f blood transfusion
Blutung f bleeding, haemorrhage (Brit),
hemorrhage (US)
Blut- zW: **blutunterlaufen** adj suffused with
blood; (Augen) bloodshot; **Blutvergießen** nt
bloodshed; **Blutvergiftung** f blood poisoning;
Blutwurst f black pudding; **Blutzuckerspiegel**
m blood sugar level
BLZ abk = **Bankleitzahl**
BMX-Rad nt BMX
BND (-s, -) m abk = **Bundesnachrichtendienst**
Bö (-, -en) f squall
Bock [bɔk] (-(e)s, ⁻e) m buck, ram; (Gestell)

trestle, support; (*Sport*) buck; **alter ~** (*umg*)
old goat; **den ~ zum Gärtner machen** (*fig*) to
choose the worst possible person for the job;
einen ~ schießen (*fig: umg*) to (make a) boob; **~
haben, etw zu tun** (*umg: Lust*) to fancy doing
sth

Bockbier *nt* bock (beer) (*type of strong beer*)

bocken ['bɔkən] (*umg*) *vi* (*Auto, Mensch*) to play
up

Bocksbeutel *m* wide, rounded (*dumpy*) bottle
containing Franconian wine

Bockshorn *nt*: **sich von jdm ins ~ jagen
lassen** to let sb upset one

Bocksprung *m* leapfrog; (*Sport*) vault

Bockwurst *f* bockwurst (*large frankfurter*)

Boden ['bo:dən] (**-s, ⸚**) *m* ground; (*Fußboden*)
floor; (*Meeresboden, Fassboden*) bottom; (*Speicher*)
attic; **den ~ unter den Füßen verlieren** (*lit*)
to lose one's footing; (*fig: in Diskussion*) to get
out of one's depth; **ich hätte (vor Scham) im
~ versinken können** (*fig*) I was so ashamed, I
wished the ground would swallow me up; **am
~ zerstört sein** (*umg*) to be shattered; **etw aus
dem ~ stampfen** (*fig*) to conjure sth up out
of nothing; (*Häuser*) to build overnight; **auf
dem ~ der Tatsachen bleiben** (*fig: Grundlage*)
to stick to the facts; **zu ~ fallen** to fall to the
ground; **festen ~ unter den Füßen haben**
to be on firm ground, be on terra firma;
Bodenkontrolle *f* (*Raumfahrt*) ground control;
bodenlos *adj* bottomless; (*umg*) incredible;
Bodenpersonal *nt* (*Aviat*) ground personnel *pl*,
ground staff; **Bodensatz** *m* dregs *pl*, sediment;
Bodenschätze *pl* mineral wealth *sing*

Bodensee ['bo:dənze:] *m*: **der ~** Lake Constance

Bodenturnen *nt* floor exercises *pl*

Böe (**-, -n**) *f* squall

bog *etc* [bo:k] *vb siehe* **biegen**

Bogen ['bo:gən] (**-s, -**) *m* (*Biegung*) curve; (*Archit*)
arch; (*Waffe, Mus*) bow; (*Papier*) sheet; **den ~
heraushaben** (*umg*) to have got the hang of
it; **einen großen ~ um jdn/etw machen**
(*meiden*) to give sb/sth a wide berth; **jdn in
hohem ~ hinauswerfen** (*umg*) to fling sb
out; **Bogengang** *m* arcade; **Bogenschütze** *m*
archer

Bohle ['bo:lə] (**-, -n**) *f* plank

Böhme ['bø:mə] (**-n, -n**) *m* Bohemian

Böhmen (**-s**) *nt* Bohemia

Böhmin *f* Bohemian woman

böhmisch ['bø:mɪʃ] *adj* Bohemian; **das sind
für mich ~e Dörfer** (*umg*) that's all Greek to
me

Bohne ['bo:nə] (**-, -n**) *f* bean; **blaue ~** (*umg*)
bullet; **nicht die ~** not one little bit

Bohnen- *zW*: **Bohnenkaffee** *m* real coffee;
Bohnenstange *f* (*fig: umg*) beanpole;
Bohnenstroh *nt*: **dumm wie Bohnenstroh**
(*umg*) (as) thick as two (short) planks

bohnern *vt* to wax, polish

Bohnerwachs *nt* floor polish

bohren ['bo:rən] *vt* to bore; (*Loch*) to drill ⊳ *vi* to
drill; (*fig: drängen*) to keep on; (*peinigen: Schmerz,
Zweifel etc*) to gnaw; **nach Öl/Wasser ~** drill
for oil/water; **in der Nase ~** to pick one's nose

Bohrer (**-s, -**) *m* drill

Bohr- *zW*: **Bohrinsel** *f* oil rig; **Bohrmaschine** *f*
drill; **Bohrturm** *m* derrick

Boiler ['bɔylər] (**-s, -**) *m* water heater

Boje ['bo:jə] (**-, -n**) *f* buoy

Bolivianer, in [bolivi'a:nər(ɪn)] (**-s, -**) *m(f)*
Bolivian

Bolivien [bo'li:viən] *nt* Bolivia

bolivisch [bo'li:vɪʃ] *adj* Bolivian

Bollwerk ['bɔlvɛrk] *nt* (*lit, fig*) bulwark

Bolschewismus [bɔlʃe'vɪsmʊs] (**-**) *m*
Bolshevism

Bolzen ['bɔltsən] (**-s, -**) *m* bolt

bombardieren [bɔmbar'di:rən] *vt* to bombard;
(*aus der Luft*) to bomb

Bombe ['bɔmbə] (**-, -n**) *f* bomb; **wie eine ~
einschlagen** to come as a (real) bombshell

Bomben- *zW*: **Bombenalarm** *m* bomb
scare; **Bombenangriff** *m* bombing
raid; **Bombenanschlag** *m* bomb
attack; **Bombenerfolg** (*umg*) *m* huge
success; **Bombengeschäft** (*umg*) *nt*: **ein
Bombengeschäft machen** to do a roaring
trade; **bombensicher** (*umg*) *adj* dead certain

bombig (*umg*) *adj* great, super

Bon [bɔŋ] (**-s, -s**) *m* voucher; (*Kassenzettel*)
receipt

Bonbon [bɔ̃'bõ:] (**-s, -s**) *nt od m* sweet

Bonn [bɔn] (**-s**) *nt* Bonn

Bonus ['bo:nʊs] (**-, -se**) *m* bonus

Bonusmeile *f* bonus mile

Bonuszahlung *f* bonus payment

Bonze ['bɔntsə] (**-n, -n**) *m* big shot (*umg*)

Bonzenviertel (*umg*) *nt* posh quarter (*of town*)

Boot [bo:t] (**-(e)s, -e**) *nt* boat

Bord [bɔrt] (**-(e)s, -e**) *m* (*Aviat, Naut*) board ⊳ *nt*
(*Brett*) shelf; **über ~ gehen** to go overboard;
(*fig*) to go by the board; **an ~** on board

Bordell [bɔr'dɛl] (**-s, -e**) *nt* brothel

Bordstein ['bɔrtʃtain] (**-(e)s, -e**) *m* kerb(stone)
(*Brit*), curb(stone) (*US*)

borgen ['bɔrgən] *vt* to borrow; **jdm etw ~** to
lend sb sth

Borneo ['bɔrneo] (**-s**) *nt* Borneo

borniert [bɔr'ni:rt] *adj* narrow-minded

Börse ['bœrzə] (**-, -n**) *f* stock exchange;
(*Geldbörse*) purse

Börsen- *zW*: **Börsenmakler** *m* stockbroker;
börsennotiert *adj*: **börsennotierte Firma**
listed company; **Börsennotierung** *f* quotation
(on the stock exchange)

Borste ['bɔrstə] (**-, -n**) *f* bristle

Borte ['bɔrtə] (**-, -n**) *f* edging; (*Band*) trimming

bös [bø:s] *adj* = **böse**; **bösartig** *adj* malicious;
(*Med*) malignant

Böschung ['bœʃʊŋ] *f* slope; (*Uferböschung etc*)
embankment

böse ['bø:zə] *adj* bad, evil; (*zornig*) angry; **das
war nicht ~ gemeint** I/he *etc* didn't mean it
nastily

Bösewicht (*umg*) *m* baddy

boshaft ['bo:shaft] *adj* malicious, spiteful

Bosheit f malice, spite
Bosnien ['bɔsniən] (**-s**) nt Bosnia
Bosnien-Herzegowina ['bɔsniənhɛrtsə-
'goːviːna] (**-s**) nt Bosnia-Herzegovina
Bosnier, in (**-s, -**) m(f) Bosnian
bosnisch adj Bosnian
Boss [bɔs] (**-es, -e**) (umg) m boss
böswillig ['bøːsvɪlɪç] adj malicious
bot etc [boːt] vb siehe **bieten**
Botanik [bo'taːnɪk] f botany
botanisch [bo'taːnɪʃ] adj botanical
Bote ['boːtə] (**-n, -n**) m messenger
Botengang m errand
Botenjunge m errand boy
Botin ['boːtɪn] f messenger
Botschaft f message, news; (Pol) embassy;
die Frohe ~ the Gospel; **Botschafter** (**-s, -**) m
ambassador
Botswana [bɔ'tsvaːna] (**-s**) nt Botswana
Bottich ['bɔtɪç] (**-(e)s, -e**) m vat, tub
Bouillon [bʊ'ljõ:] (**-, -s**) f consommé
Boulevard- [bulə'vaːr] zW: **Boulevardblatt**
(umg) nt tabloid; **Boulevardpresse** f tabloid
press; **Boulevardstück** nt light play/comedy
Boutique [bu'tiːk] (**-, -n**) f boutique
Bowle ['boːlə] (**-, -n**) f punch
Bowlingbahn ['boːlɪŋbaːn] f bowling alley
Box [bɔks] f (Lautsprecherbox) speaker
boxen vi to box
Boxer (**-s, -**) m boxer
Boxhandschuh m boxing glove
Boxkampf m boxing match
Boykott [bɔy'kɔt] (**-(e)s, -s**) m boycott
boykottieren [bɔykɔ'tiːrən] vt to boycott
BR abk (= Bayerischer Rundfunk) German radio station
brach etc [braːx] vb siehe **brechen**
brachial [braxi'aːl] adj: **mit ~er Gewalt** by
brute force
brachliegen ['braːxliːgən] unreg vi (lit, fig) to lie
fallow
brachte etc ['braxtə] vb siehe **bringen**
Branche ['brãː ːʃə] (**-, -n**) f line of business
Branchenführer, in m(f) market leader
Branchenverzeichnis nt trade directory
Brand [brant] (**-(e)s, ⁻e**) m fire; (Med) gangrene
Brandanschlag m arson attack
branden ['brandən] vi to surge; (Meer) to break
Brandenburg ['brandənbʊrk] (**-s**) nt
Brandenburg
Brandherd m source of the fire
brandmarken vt to brand; (fig) to stigmatize
brandneu (umg) adj brand-new
Brand- zW: **Brandsalbe** f ointment for burns;
Brandsatz m incendiary device; **Brandstifter**
m arsonist, fire-raiser; **Brandstiftung** f arson
Brandung f surf
Brandwunde f burn
brannte etc ['brantə] vb siehe **brennen**
Branntwein ['brantvain] m brandy;
Branntweinsteuer f tax on spirits
Brasilianer, in [brazili'aːnər(ɪn)] (**-s, -**) m(f)
Brazilian
brasilianisch adj Brazilian

Brasilien [bra'ziːliən] nt Brazil
brät [brɛt] vb siehe **braten**
Bratapfel m baked apple
braten ['braːtən] unreg vt to roast; (in Pfanne) to
fry; **Braten** (**-s, -**) m roast, joint; **den Braten
riechen** (umg) to smell a rat, suss something
Brat- zW: **Brathähnchen** nt (Südd, Österr)
roast chicken; **Brathendl** nt roast chicken;
Brathuhn nt roast chicken; **Bratkartoffeln** pl
fried/roast potatoes pl; **Bratpfanne** f frying
pan; **Bratrost** m grill
Bratsche ['braːtʃə] (**-, -n**) f viola
Bratspieß m spit
Bratwurst f grilled sausage
Brauch [braux] (**-(e)s, pl Bräuche**) m custom
brauchbar adj usable, serviceable; (Person)
capable
brauchen vt (bedürfen) to need; (müssen) to have
to; (verwenden) to use; **wie lange braucht
man, um ...?** how long does it take to ...?
Brauchtum nt customs pl, traditions pl
Braue ['brauə] (**-, -n**) f brow
brauen ['brauən] vt to brew
Brauerei [brauə'rai] f brewery
braun [braun] adj brown; (von Sonne) tanned; **~
gebrannt** tanned; (pej) Nazi
Bräune ['brɔynə] (**-, -n**) f brownness;
(Sonnenbräune) tan
bräunen vt to make brown; (Sonne) to tan
Braunkohle f brown coal
Braunschweig ['braunʃvaik] (**-s**) nt Brunswick
Brause ['brauzə] (**-, -n**) f shower; (von Gießkanne)
rose; (Getränk) lemonade
brausen vi to roar; (auch vr: duschen) to take a
shower
Brausepulver nt lemonade powder
Brausetablette f lemonade tablet
Braut [braut] (**-, pl Bräute**) f bride; (Verlobte)
fiancée
Bräutigam ['brɔytɪgam] (**-s, -e**) m bridegroom;
(Verlobter) fiancé
Braut- zW: **Brautjungfer** f bridesmaid;
Brautkleid nt wedding dress; **Brautpaar** nt
bride and bridegroom, bridal pair
brav [braːf] adj (artig) good; (ehrenhaft) worthy,
honest; (bieder: Frisur, Kleid) plain; **sei schön ~!**
be a good boy/girl
BRD (**-**) f abk (= Bundesrepublik Deutschland) FRG;
die alte ~ former West Germany; see culture
note

● BRD

● The BRD (Bundesrepublik Deutschland) is
● the official name for the Federal Republic
● of Germany. It comprises 16 Länder (see
● Land). It was the name given to the former
● West Germany as opposed to East Germany
● (the DDR). The two Germanies were
● reunited on 3rd October 1990.

Brechbohne f French bean
Brecheisen nt crowbar

brechen unreg vt, vi to break; (*Licht*) to refract; (*speien*) to vomit; **die Ehe ~** to commit adultery; **mir bricht das Herz** it breaks my heart; **~d voll sein** to be full to bursting

Brechmittel nt: **er/das ist das reinste ~** (*umg*) he/it makes me feel ill

Brechreiz m nausea

Brechung f (*des Lichts*) refraction

Brei [braɪ] (**-(e)s, -e**) m (*Masse*) pulp; (*Koch*) gruel; (*Haferbrei*) porridge (*Brit*), oatmeal (*US*); (*für Kinder, Kranke*) mash; **um den heißen ~ herumreden** (*umg*) to beat about the bush

breit [braɪt] adj broad; (*bei Maßangabe*) wide; **die ~e Masse** the masses pl
▷ adv: **ein ~ gefächertes Angebot** a wide range; **Breitband** nt (*Comput*) broadband; **Breitbandanschluss** m (*Comput*) broadband connection; **breitbeinig** adj with one's legs apart

Breite (**-, -n**) f breadth; (*bei Maßangabe*) width; (*Geog*) latitude

breiten vt: **etw über etw** akk **~** to spread sth over sth

Breitengrad m degree of latitude

Breitensport m popular sport

breit- zW: **breitmachen** unreg (*umg*) vr to spread o.s. out; **breitschlagen** unreg (*umg*) vt: **sich breitschlagen lassen** to let o.s. be talked round; **breitschulterig, breitschultrig** adj broad-shouldered; **breittreten** unreg (*umg*) vt to go on about; **Breitwandfilm** m wide-screen film

Bremen ['breːmən] (**-s**) nt Bremen

Bremsbelag m brake lining

Bremse ['brɛmzə] (**-, -n**) f brake; (*Zool*) horsefly

bremsen vi to brake, apply the brakes ▷ vt (*Auto*) to brake; (*fig*) to slow down ▷ vr: **ich kann mich ~** (*umg*) not likely!

Brems- zW: **Bremsflüssigkeit** f brake fluid; **Bremslicht** nt brake light; **Bremspedal** nt brake pedal; **Bremsschuh** m brake shoe; **Bremsspur** f tyre (*Brit*) od tire (*US*) marks pl; **Bremsweg** m braking distance

brennbar adj inflammable; **leicht ~** highly inflammable

Brennelement nt fuel element

brennen ['brɛnən] unreg vi to burn, be on fire; (*Licht, Kerze etc*) to burn ▷ vt (*Holz etc*) to burn; (*Ziegel, Ton*) to fire; (*Kaffee*) to roast; (*Branntwein*) to distil; **wo brennts denn?** (*fig: umg*) what's the panic?; **darauf ~, etw zu tun** to be dying to do sth

Brenn- zW: **Brennmaterial** nt fuel; **Brennnessel** f nettle; **Brennofen** m kiln; **Brennpunkt** m (*Math, Optik*) focus; **Brennspiritus** m methylated spirits pl; **Brennstoff** m liquid fuel

brenzlig ['brɛntslɪç] adj smelling of burning, burnt; (*fig*) precarious

Bresche ['brɛʃə] (**-, -n**) f: **in die ~ springen** (*fig*) to step into the breach

Bretagne [bre'tanjə] f: **die ~** Brittany

Bretone [bre'toːnə] (**-n, -n**) m Breton

Bretonin [bre'toːnɪn] f Breton

Brett [brɛt] (**-(e)s, -er**) nt board, plank; (*Bord*) shelf; (*Spielbrett*) board; **Bretter** pl (*Ski*) skis pl; (*Theat*) boards pl; **Schwarzes ~** notice board; **er hat ein ~ vor dem Kopf** (*umg*) he's really thick

brettern (*umg*) vi to speed

Bretterzaun m wooden fence

Brezel ['breːtsəl] (**-, -n**) f pretzel

bricht [brɪçt] vb siehe **brechen**

Brief [briːf] (**-(e)s, -e**) m letter; **Briefbeschwerer** (**-s, -**) m paperweight; **Briefdrucksache** f circular; **Brieffreund, in** m(f) pen friend, pen-pal; **Briefkasten** m letter box; (*Comput*) mailbox; **Briefkopf** m letterhead; **brieflich** adj, adv by letter; **Briefmarke** f postage stamp; **Brieföffner** m letter opener; **Briefpapier** nt notepaper; **Briefqualität** f (*Comput*) letter quality; **Brieftasche** f wallet; **Brieftaube** f carrier pigeon; **Briefträger** m postman; **Briefumschlag** m envelope; **Briefwahl** f postal vote; **Briefwechsel** m correspondence

briet etc [briːt] vb siehe **braten**

Brigade [bri'gaːdə] (**-, -n**) f (*Mil*) brigade; (*DDR*) (work) team od group

Brikett [bri'kɛt] (**-s, -s**) nt briquette

brillant [brɪl'jant] adj (*fig*) sparkling, brilliant; **Brillant** (**-en, -en**) m brilliant, diamond

Brille ['brɪlə] (**-, -n**) f spectacles pl; (*Schutzbrille*) goggles pl; (*Toilettenbrille*) (toilet) seat

Brillenschlange f (*hum*) four-eyes

Brillenträger, in m(f): **er ist ~** he wears glasses

bringen ['brɪŋən] unreg vt to bring; (*mitnehmen, begleiten*) to take; (*einbringen: Profit*) to bring in; (*veröffentlichen*) to publish; (*Theat, Film*) to show; (*Rundf, TV*) to broadcast; (*in einen Zustand versetzen*) to get; (*umg: tun können*) to manage; **jdn dazu ~, etw zu tun** to make sb do sth; **jdn zum Lachen/Weinen ~** to make sb laugh/cry; **es weit ~** to do very well, get far; **jdn nach Hause ~** to take sb home; **jdn um etw ~** to make sb lose sth; **jdn auf eine Idee ~** to give sb an idea

brisant [bri'zant] adj (*fig*) controversial

Brisanz [bri'zants] f (*fig*) controversial nature

Brise ['briːzə] (**-, -n**) f breeze

Brite ['briːtə] (**-n, -n**) m Briton, Britisher (*US*); **die ~n** the British

Britin f Briton, Britisher (*US*)

britisch ['briːtɪʃ] adj British; **die B~en Inseln** the British Isles

bröckelig ['brœkəlɪç] adj crumbly

Brocken ['brɔkən] (**-s, -**) m piece, bit; (*Felsbrocken*) lump of rock; **ein paar ~ Spanisch** a smattering of Spanish; **ein harter ~** (*umg*) a tough nut to crack

brodeln ['broːdəln] vi to bubble

Brokat [bro'kaːt] (**-(e)s, -e**) m brocade

Brokkoli ['brɔkoli] pl broccoli

Brombeere ['brɔmbeːrə] f blackberry, bramble (*Brit*)

bronchial [brɔnçi'aːl] adj bronchial

Bronchien ['brɔnçiən] pl bronchial tubes pl

Bronchitis [brɔn'çi:tɪs] **(-, -tiden)** f bronchitis
Bronze ['brõ:sə] **(-, -n)** f bronze
Brosame ['bro:za:mə] **(-, -n)** f crumb
Brosche ['brɔʃə] **(-, -n)** f brooch
Broschüre [brɔ'ʃy:rə] **(-, -n)** f pamphlet
Brot [bro:t] **(-(e)s, -e)** nt bread; (Brotlaib) loaf;
  das ist ein hartes ~ (fig) that's a hard way to
  earn one's living
Brötchen ['brø:tçən] nt roll; **kleine ~ backen**
  (fig) to set one's sights lower; **Brötchengeber**
  m (hum) employer, provider (hum)
brotlos ['bro:tlo:s] adj (Person) unemployed;
  (Arbeit etc) unprofitable
Brotzeit (Südd) f (Pause) ≈ tea break
browsen ['brauzən] vi (Comput) to browse
BRT abk (= Bruttoregistertonne) GRT
Bruch [brʊx] **(-(e)s, -̈e)** m breakage;
  (zerbrochene Stelle) break; (fig) split, breach;
  (Med: Eingeweidebruch) rupture, hernia;
  (Beinbruch etc) fracture; (Math) fraction; **zu ~
  gehen** to get broken; **sich einen ~ heben** to
  rupture o.s.; **Bruchbude** (umg) f shack
brüchig ['brʏçɪç] adj brittle, fragile
Bruch- zW: **Bruchlandung** f crash landing;
  Bruchschaden m breakage; **Bruchstelle** f
  break; (von Knochen) fracture; **Bruchstrich**
  m (Math) line; **Bruchstück** nt fragment;
  Bruchteil m fraction
Brücke ['brʏkə] **(-, -n)** f bridge; (Teppich) rug;
  (Turnen) crab
Bruder ['bru:dər] **(-s, -̈)** m brother; **unter
  Brüdern** (umg) between friends
brüderlich adj brotherly; **Brüderlichkeit** f
  fraternity
Brudermord m fratricide
Brüderschaft f brotherhood, fellowship; **~
  trinken** to agree to use the familiar "du" (over
  a drink)
Brühe ['bry:ə] **(-, -n)** f broth, stock; (pej) muck
brühwarm ['bry:'varm] (umg) adj: **er hat das
  sofort ~ weitererzählt** he promptly spread
  it around
Brühwürfel m stock cube (Brit), bouillon cube
  (US)
brüllen ['brʏlən] vi to bellow, roar
Brummbär m grumbler
brummeln ['brʊməln] vt, vi to mumble
brummen vi (Bär, Mensch etc) to growl; (Insekt,
  Radio) to buzz; (Motor) to roar; (murren) to
  grumble ▷ vt to growl; **jdm brummt der
  Kopf** sb's head is buzzing
Brummer ['brʊmər] **(-s, -)** (umg) m (Lastwagen)
  juggernaut
brummig (umg) adj grumpy
Brummschädel (umg) m thick head
brünett [brʏ'nɛt] adj brunette, brown-haired
Brunnen ['brʊnən] **(-s, -)** m fountain; (tief)
  well; (natürlich) spring; **Brunnenkresse** f
  watercress
Brunst [brʊnst] f (von männlichen Tieren) rut; (von
  weiblichen Tieren) heat; **Brunstzeit** f rutting
  season
brüsk [brʏsk] adj abrupt, brusque

brüskieren [brʏs'ki:rən] vt to snub
Brüssel ['brʏsəl] **(-s)** nt Brussels
Brust [brʊst] **(-, -̈e)** f breast; (Männerbrust) chest;
  einem Kind die ~ geben to breast-feed (Brit)
  od nurse (US) a baby
brüsten ['brʏstən] vr to boast
Brust- zW: **Brustfellentzündung** f pleurisy;
  Brustkasten m chest; **Brustkorb** m (Anat)
  thorax; **Brustschwimmen** nt breast-stroke;
  Brustton m: **im Brustton der Überzeugung**
  in a tone of utter conviction
Brüstung ['brʏstʊŋ] f parapet
Brustwarze f nipple
Brut [bru:t] **(-, -en)** f brood; (Brüten) hatching
brutal [bru'ta:l] adj brutal; **Brutalität** f
  brutality
Brutapparat m incubator
brüten ['bry:tən] vi (auch fig) to brood; **~de
  Hitze** oppressive od stifling heat
Brüter (-s, -) m (Tech): **Schneller ~** fast-breeder
  (reactor)
Brutkasten m incubator
Brutstätte f (+gen) (lit, fig) breeding ground (for)
brutto ['brʊto] adv gross; **Bruttoeinkommen**
  nt gross salary; **Bruttogehalt** nt
  gross salary; **Bruttogewicht** nt gross
  weight; **Bruttogewinn** m gross profit;
  Bruttoinlandsprodukt nt gross domestic
  product; **Bruttolohn** m gross wages pl;
  Bruttosozialprodukt nt gross national
  product
brutzeln ['brʊtsəln] (umg) vi to sizzle away ▷ vt
  to fry (up)
Btx abk = **Bildschirmtext**
Bub [bu:p] **(-en, -en)** m boy, lad
Bube ['bu:bə] **(-n, -n)** m (Schurke) rogue; (Karten)
  jack
Bubikopf m bobbed hair
Buch [bu:x] **(-(e)s, -̈er)** nt book; (Comm) account
  book; **er redet wie ein ~** (umg) he never stops
  talking; **ein ~ mit sieben Siegeln** (fig) a
  closed book; **über etw** akk **~ führen** to keep
  a record of sth; **zu ~(e) schlagen** to make
  a significant difference, tip the balance;
  Buchbinder m bookbinder; **Buchdrucker** m
  printer
Buche (-, -n) f beech tree
buchen vt to book; (Betrag) to enter; **etw als
  Erfolg ~** to put sth down as a success
Bücherbord ['by:çər-] nt bookshelf
Bücherbrett nt bookshelf
Bücherei [by:çə'raɪ] f library
Bücherregal nt bookshelves pl, bookcase
Bücherschrank m bookcase
Bücherwurm (umg) m bookworm
Buchfink ['bu:xfɪŋk] m chaffinch
Buch- zW: **Buchführung** f book-keeping,
  accounting; **Buchhalter, in (-s, -)** m(f)
  book-keeper; **Buchhandel** m book trade;
  im Buchhandel erhältlich available in
  bookshops; **Buchhändler, in** m(f) bookseller;
  Buchhandlung f bookshop; **Buchprüfung** f
  audit; **Buchrücken** m spine

Büchse ['bʏksə] (-, -n) f tin, can; (*Holzbüchse*) box; (*Gewehr*) rifle
Büchsenfleisch nt tinned meat
Büchsenöffner m tin od can opener
Buchstabe (-ns, -n) m letter (of the alphabet)
buchstabieren [bu:xʃtaˈbiːrən] vt to spell
buchstäblich ['buːxʃtɛːplɪç] adj literal
Buchstütze f book end
Bucht ['bʊxt] (-, -en) f bay
Buchung ['buːxʊŋ] f booking; (*Comm*) entry
Buchweizen m buckwheat
Buchwert m book value
Buckel ['bʊkəl] (-s, -) m hump; **er kann mir den ~ runterrutschen** (*umg*) he can (go and) take a running jump
buckeln (*pej*) vi to bow and scrape
bücken ['bʏkən] vr to bend; **sich nach etw ~** to bend down od stoop to pick sth up
Bückling ['bʏklɪŋ] m (*Fisch*) kipper; (*Verbeugung*) bow
Budapest ['buːdapɛst] (-s) nt Budapest
buddeln ['bʊdəln] (*umg*) vi to dig
Bude ['buːdə] (-, -n) f booth, stall; (*umg*) digs pl (*Brit*) od place (*US*); **jdm die ~ einrennen** (*umg*) to pester sb; **Leben in die ~ bringen** to liven up the place
Budget [byˈdʒeː] (-s, -s) nt budget
Büfett [byˈfɛt] (-s, -s) nt (*Anrichte*) sideboard; (*Geschirrschrank*) dresser; **kaltes ~** cold buffet
Büffel ['bʏfəl] (-s, -) m buffalo
büffeln ['bʏfəln] (*umg*) vi to swot, cram ▷ vt (*Lernstoff*) to swot up
Bug [buːk] (-(e)s, -e) m (*Naut*) bow; (*Aviat*) nose
Bügel ['byːgəl] (-s, -) m (*Kleiderbügel*) hanger; (*Steigbügel*) stirrup; (*Brillenbügel*) arm; **Bügelbrett** nt ironing board; **Bügeleisen** nt iron; **Bügelfalte** f crease; **bügelfrei** adj non-iron; (*Hemd*) drip-dry
bügeln vt, vi to iron
Buhmann ['buːman] (*umg*) m bogeyman
Bühne ['byːnə] (-, -n) f stage
Bühnenbild nt set, scenery
Buhruf ['buːruːf] m boo
buk etc [buːk] vb (*veraltet*) siehe **backen**
Bukarest ['buːkarɛst] (-s) nt Bucharest
Bulette [buˈlɛtə] f meatball
Bulgare [bʊlˈgaːrə] (-n, -n) m Bulgarian
Bulgarien (-s) nt Bulgaria
Bulgarin f Bulgarian
bulgarisch adj Bulgarian
Bulimie [buliˈmiː] f (*Med*) bulimia
Bull- zW: **Bullauge** nt (*Naut*) porthole; **Bulldogge** f bulldog; **Bulldozer** ['bʊldoːzər] (-s, -) m bulldozer
Bulle (-n, -n) m bull; **die ~n** (*pej: umg*) the fuzz sing, the cops
Bullenhitze (*umg*) f sweltering heat
Bummel ['bʊməl] (-s, -) m stroll; (*Schaufensterbummel*) window-shopping (expedition)
Bummelant [bʊməˈlant] m slowcoach
Bummelei [bʊməˈlaɪ] f wandering; dawdling; skiving

bummeln vi to wander, stroll; (*trödeln*) to dawdle; (*faulenzen*) to skive (*Brit*), loaf around
Bummelstreik m go-slow (*Brit*), slowdown (*US*)
Bummelzug m slow train
Bummler, in ['bʊmlər(ɪn)] (-s, -) m(f) (*langsamer Mensch*) dawdler (*Brit*), slowpoke (*US*); (*Faulenzer*) idler, loafer
bumsen ['bʊmzən] vi (*schlagen*) to thump; (*prallen, stoßen*) to bump, bang; (*umg: koitieren*) to bonk, have it off (*Brit*)
Bund[1] [bʊnt] (-(e)s, ⁻e) m (*Freundschaftsbund etc*) bond; (*Organisation*) union; (*Pol*) confederacy; (*Hosenbund, Rockbund*) waistband; **den ~ fürs Leben schließen** to take the marriage vows
Bund[2] [bʊnt] (-(e)s, -e) nt bunch; (*Strohbund*) bundle
Bündchen ['bʏntçən] nt ribbing; (*Ärmelbündchen*) cuff
Bündel (-s, -) nt bundle, bale
bündeln vt to bundle
Bundes- ['bʊndəs] in zW Federal; **Bundesagentur** f: **Bundesagentur für Arbeit** ≈ Department of Employment; **Bundesbahn** f: **die Deutsche Bundesbahn** German Federal Railways pl; **Bundesbank** f Federal Bank, Bundesbank; **Bundesbürger** m German citizen; (*vor 1990*) West German citizen; **Bundesgebiet** nt Federal territory; **Bundesgerichtshof** m Federal Supreme Court; **Bundesgrenzschutz** m Federal Border Guard; **Bundeshauptstadt** f Federal capital; **Bundeshaushalt** m (*Pol*) National Budget; **Bundeskanzler** m Federal Chancellor; *see culture note*

Bundes- zW: **Bundesland** nt state, Land; **Bundesliga** f (*Sport*) national league; **Bundesministerium** nt Federal Ministry; **Bundesnachrichtendienst** m Federal Intelligence Service; **Bundespost** f (*früher*): **die (Deutsche) Bundespost** the (German) Federal Post (Office); **Bundespräsident** m *see culture note*

Bundesrat *m see culture note*

The *Bundesrat* is the Upper House of the German Parliament whose 68 members are not elected but determined by the parliaments of the individual *Länder*. Its most important function is the approval of federal laws which concern jurisdiction of the Länder. It can raise objections to all other laws but can be outvoted by the *Bundestag*.

Bundes- *zW:* **Bundesrechnungshof** *m* Federal Audit Office; **Bundesregierung** *f* Federal Government; **Bundesrepublik** *f* Federal Republic (of Germany); **Bundesstaat** *m* Federal state; **Bundesstraße** *f* Federal Highway, main road; **Bundestag** *m see culture note*

The *Bundestag* is the Lower House of the German Parliament, elected by the people. There are 646 MPs, half of them elected directly from the first vote (*Erststimme*), and half from the regional list of parliamentary candidates resulting from the second vote (*Zweitstimme*), and giving proportional representation to the parties. The Bundestag exercises parliamentary control over the government.

Bundes- *zW:* **Bundestagsabgeordnete, r** *f(m)* member of the German Parliament; **Bundestagswahl** *f* (Federal) parliamentary elections *pl*; **Bundesverfassungsgericht** *nt* Federal Constitutional Court; **Bundeswehr** *f* German *od* (*vor 1990*) West German Armed Forces *pl*; *see culture note*

The *Bundeswehr* is the name for the German armed forces. It was established in 1955, first of all for volunteers, but since 1956 there has been compulsory military service for all able-bodied young men of 18 (see *Wehrdienst*). In peacetime the Defence Minister is the head of the Bundeswehr, but in wartime, the *Bundeskanzler* takes over. The Bundeswehr comes under the jurisdiction of NATO.

Bundfaltenhose *f* pleated trousers *pl*
Bundhose *f* knee breeches *pl*
bündig ['bʏndɪç] *adj* (*kurz*) concise
Bündnis ['bʏntnɪs] (**-ses, -se**) *nt* alliance
Bunker ['bʊŋkər] (**-s, -**) *m* bunker; (*Luftschutzbunker*) air-raid shelter
bunt [bʊnt] *adj* coloured (*Brit*), colored (*US*);

(*gemischt*) mixed; **jdm wird es zu ~** it's getting too much for sb; **Buntstift** *m* coloured (*Brit*) *od* colored (*US*) pencil, crayon
Bürde ['bʏrdə] (**-, -n**) *f* (*lit, fig*) burden
Burg [bʊrk] (**-, -en**) *f* castle, fort
Bürge ['bʏrgə] (**-n, -n**) *m* guarantor
bürgen *vi* to vouch; **für jdn ~** (*fig*) to vouch for sb; (*Fin*) to stand surety for sb
Bürger, in (**-s, -**) *m(f)* citizen; member of the middle class; **bürgerfreundlich** *adj* citizen-friendly; **Bürgerinitiative** *f* citizen's initiative; **Bürgerkrieg** *m* civil war; **bürgerlich** *adj* (*Rechte*) civil; (*Klasse*) middle-class; (*pej*) bourgeois; **bürgerliches Gesetzbuch** Civil Code; **Bürgermeister** *m* mayor; **Bürgerrecht** *nt* civil rights *pl*; **Bürgerrechtler, in** *m(f)* civil rights campaigner; **Bürgerschaft** *f* population, citizens *pl*; **Bürgerschaftswahl** *f* metropolitan council election; **Bürgerschreck** *m* bogey of the middle classes; **Bürgersteig** *m* pavement (*Brit*), sidewalk (*US*); **Bürgertum** *nt* citizens *pl*; **Bürgerversicherung** *f* citizens' insurance; **Bürgerwehr** *f* vigilantes *pl*
Burgfriede, Burgfrieden *m* (*fig*) truce
Bürgin *f* guarantor
Bürgschaft *f* surety; **~ leisten** to give security
Burgunder (**-s, -**) *m* (*Wein*) burgundy
Büro [by'roː] (**-s, -s**) *nt* office; **Büroangestellte, r** *f(m)* office worker; **Büroklammer** *f* paper clip; **Bürokraft** *f* (office) clerk
Bürokrat [byro'kraːt] (**-en, -en**) *m* bureaucrat
Bürokratie [byrokra'tiː] *f* bureaucracy
bürokratisch *adj* bureaucratic
Bürokratismus *m* red tape
Büroschluss *m* office closing time
Büroturm *m* office tower
Bursch ['bʊrʃ(ə)] (**-en, -en**) *m* = **Bursche**
Bursche (**-n, -n**) *m* lad, fellow; (*Diener*) servant
Burschenschaft *f* student fraternity
burschikos [bʊrʃi'koːs] *adj* (*jungenhaft*) (*tom*) boyish; (*unbekümmert*) casual
Bürste ['bʏrstə] (**-, -n**) *f* brush
bürsten *vt* to brush
Bus [bʊs] (**-ses, -se**) *m* bus
Busch [bʊʃ] (**-(e)s, ̈-e**) *m* bush, shrub; **bei jdm auf den ~ klopfen** (*umg*) to sound sb out
Büschel ['bʏʃəl] (**-s, -**) *nt* tuft
buschig *adj* bushy
Busen ['buːzən] (**-s, -**) *m* bosom; (*Meerbusen*) inlet, bay; **Busenfreund, in** *m(f)* bosom friend
Bushaltestelle *f* bus stop
Buslinie *f* bus route
Bussard ['bʊsart] (**-s, -e**) *m* buzzard
Buße ['buːsə] (**-, -n**) *f* atonement, penance; (*Geld*) fine
büßen ['byːsən] *vi* to do penance, atone ▷ *vt* to atone for
Bußgeld *nt* fine
Buß- und Bettag *m* day of prayer and repentance
Büste ['bʏstə] (**-, -n**) *f* bust
Büstenhalter *m* bra
Butan [bu'taːn] (**-s**) *nt* butane

Büttenrede | bzw.

Büttenrede ['bʏtənreːdə] f carnival speech
Butter ['bʊtər] (-) f butter; **alles (ist) in ~** (umg) everything is fine od hunky-dory; **Butterberg** (umg) m butter mountain; **Butterblume** f buttercup; **Butterbrot** nt (piece of) bread and butter; **Butterbrotpapier** nt greaseproof paper; **Buttercremetorte** f gateau with buttercream filling; **Butterdose** f butter dish; **Butterkeks** m ≈ Rich Tea® biscuit; **Buttermilch** f buttermilk; **butterweich** adj soft as butter; (fig: umg) soft

Butzen ['bʊtsən] (-s, -) m core
BVG nt abk (= Betriebsverfassungsgesetz) ≈ Industrial Relations Act; ≈ **Bundesverfassungsgericht**
b. w. abk (= bitte wenden) p.t.o
Byte [baɪt] (-s, -s) nt (Comput) byte
Bz. abk = **Bezirk**
bzgl. abk (= bezüglich) re.
bzw. abk = **beziehungsweise**

Cc

C¹, c [tse:] *nt* C, c; **C wie Cäsar** ≈ C for Charlie
C² [tse:] *abk* (= *Celsius*) C
ca. [ka] *abk* (= *circa*) approx.
Cabriolet [kabrio'le:] (-s, -s) *nt* (*Aut*) convertible
Café [ka'fe:] (-s, -s) *nt* café
Cafeteria [kafete'ri:a] (-, -s) *f* cafeteria
cal *abk* (= *Kalorie*) cal
Calais [ka'lɛ:] (-') *nt*: **die Straße von ~** the Straits of Dover
Callcenter ['kɔ:lsɛntər] *nt* call centre (*Brit*), call center (*US*)
Camcorder (-s, -) *m* camcorder
campen ['kɛmpən] *vi* to camp
Camper, in (-s, -) *m(f)* camper
Camping ['kɛmpɪŋ] (-s) *nt* camping; **Campingbus** *m* camper; **Campingplatz** *m* camp(ing) site
Caravan ['karavan] (-s, -s) *m* caravan
Cargo ['kargo] (-s, -s) *m* (*Comm*) cargo
Cäsium ['tsɛ:ziʊm] *nt* caesium (*Brit*), cesium (*US*)
ccm *abk* (= *Kubikzentimeter*) cm³
CD *f abk* (= *Compact Disc*) CD; **CD-Brenner** *m* CD burner; **CD-ROM** (-, -s) *f* CD-ROM; **CD-Spieler** *m* CD player
CDU [tse:de:'|u:] (-) *f abk* (= *Christlich-Demokratische Union (Deutschlands)*) Christian Democratic Union; *see culture note*

> ● **CDU**
>
> The CDU (Christlich-Demokratische
> Union) is a Christian and conservative
> political party founded in 1945. It operates
> in all the *Länder* apart from Bavaria where
> its sister party the *CSU* is active. In the
> *Bundestag* the two parties form a coalition.
> It is the second largest party in Germany
> after the *SPD*, the Social Democratic Party.

Celli *pl von* **Cello**
Cellist, in [tʃɛ'lɪst(ɪn)] *m(f)* cellist
Cello ['tʃɛlo] (-s, -s *od* **Celli**) *nt* cello
Celsius ['tsɛlziʊs] *m* Celsius
Cent [(t)sɛnt] (-(s), -(s)) *m* cent
Ces [tsɛs] (-, -) *nt* (*Mus*) C flat
ces [tsɛs] (-, -) *nt* (*Mus*) C flat
Ceylon ['tsaɪlɔn] (-s) *nt* Ceylon

Chamäleon [ka'mɛ:leɔn] (-s, -s) *nt* chameleon
Champagner [ʃam'panjər] (-s, -) *m* champagne
Champignon ['ʃampɪnjõ] (-s, -s) *m* button mushroom
Chance ['ʃãˑːs(ə)] (-, -n) *f* chance, opportunity
chancengleich *adj* with equal opportunities
Chancengleichheit *f* equality of opportunity
Chaos ['ka:ɔs] (-) *nt* chaos
Chaot, in [ka'o:t(ɪn)] (-en, -en) *m(f)* (*Pol*: *pej*) anarchist (*pej*)
chaotisch [ka'o:tɪʃ] *adj* chaotic
Charakter [ka'raktər] (-s, -e) *m* character; **charakterfest** *adj* of firm character
charakterisieren [karakteri'zi:rən] *vt* to characterize
Charakteristik [karakte'rɪstɪk] *f* characterization
charakteristisch [karakte'rɪstɪʃ] *adj*: **~ (für)** characteristic (of), typical (of)
Charakter- *zW*: **charakterlos** *adj* unprincipled; **Charakterlosigkeit** *f* lack of principle; **Charakterschwäche** *f* weakness of character; **Charakterstärke** *f* strength of character; **Charakterzug** *m* characteristic, trait
charmant [ʃar'mant] *adj* charming
Charme [ʃarm] (-s) *m* charm
Charta ['karta] (-, -s) *f* charter
Charterflug ['tʃartərflu:k] *m* charter flight
Chartermaschine ['tʃartərmaʃi:nə] *f* charter plane
chartern ['tʃartərn] *vt* to charter
Chassis [ʃa'si:] (-, -) *nt* chassis
Chatroom ['tʃɛtru:m] *m* (*Comput*) chatroom
Chauffeur [ʃo'fø:r] *m* chauffeur
Chaussee [ʃo'se:] (-, -n) *f* (*veraltet*) high road
Chauvi ['ʃovi] (-s, -s) (*umg*) *m* male chauvinist
Chauvinismus [ʃovi'nɪsmʊs] *m* chauvinism
Chauvinist [ʃovi'nɪst] *m* chauvinist
checken ['tʃɛkən] *vt* (*überprüfen*) to check; (*umg*: *verstehen*) to get
Chef, in [ʃɛf(ɪn)] (-s, -s) *m(f)* head; (*umg*) boss; **Chefarzt** *m* senior consultant; **Chefetage** *f* executive floor; **Chefredakteur** *m* editor-in-chief; **Chefsekretärin** *f* personal assistant/secretary; **Chefvisite** *f* (*Med*) consultant's round
Chemie [çe'mi:] (-) *f* chemistry; **Chemiefaser** *f*

man-made fibre (Brit) od fiber (US)

Chemikalie [çemi'ka:liə] f chemical

Chemiker, in ['çe:mikər(ın)] (**-s, -**) m(f) (industrial) chemist

chemisch ['çe:mıʃ] adj chemical; **~e Reinigung** dry cleaning

Chemotherapie [çemotera'pi:] f chemotherapy

chic [ʃık] adj inv stylish, chic

Chicorée [ʃiko're:] (**-s**) f od m chicory

Chiffre ['ʃıfrə] (**-, -n**) f (Geheimzeichen) cipher; (in Zeitung) box number

Chiffriermaschine [ʃı'fri:rmaʃi:nə] f cipher machine

Chile ['tʃi:le] (**-s**) nt Chile

Chilene [tʃi'le:nə] (**-n, -n**) m Chilean

Chilenin [tʃi'le:nın] f Chilean

chilenisch adj Chilean

China ['çi:na] (**-s**) nt China

Chinakohl m Chinese leaves pl

Chinese [çi'ne:zə] (**-n, -n**) m Chinaman, Chinese

Chinesin f Chinese woman

chinesisch adj Chinese

Chinin [çi'ni:n] (**-s**) nt quinine

Chipkarte ['tʃıpkartə] f smart card

Chips [tʃıps] pl crisps pl (Brit), chips pl (US)

Chirurg, in [çi'rʊrg(ın)] (**-en, -en**) m(f) surgeon

Chirurgie [çirʊr'gi:] f surgery

chirurgisch adj surgical; **ein ~er Eingriff** surgery

Chlor [klo:r] (**-s**) nt chlorine

Chloroform [kloro'fɔrm] (**-s**) nt chloroform

chloroformieren [klorofor'mi:rən] vt to chloroform

Chlorophyll [kloro'fyl] (**-s**) nt chlorophyll

Cholera ['ko:lera] (**-**) f cholera

Choleriker, in [ko'le:rikər(ın)] (**-s, -**) m(f) hot-tempered person

cholerisch [ko'le:rıʃ] adj choleric

Cholesterin [kolɛste'ri:n] (**-s**) nt cholesterol; **Cholesterinspiegel** [kolɛste'ri:nʃpigəl] m cholesterol level

Chor [ko:r] (**-(e)s, ̈-e**) m choir; (Musikstück, Theat) chorus

Choral [ko'ra:l] (**-s, -äle**) m chorale

Choreograf, in [koreo'gra:f(ın)] (**-en, -en**) m(f) choreographer

Choreografie [koreogra'fi:] f choreography

Chorgestühl nt choir stalls pl

Chorknabe m choirboy

Chose ['ʃo:zə] (**-, -n**) (umg) f (Angelegenheit) thing

Chr. abk = **Christus; Chronik**

Christ [krıst] (**-en, -en**) m Christian; **Christbaum** m Christmas tree

Christenheit f Christendom

Christentum (**-s**) nt Christianity

Christin f Christian

Christkind nt ≈ Father Christmas; (Jesus) baby Jesus

christlich adj Christian

Christus (Christi) m Christ; **Christi Himmelfahrt** Ascension Day

Chrom [kro:m] (**-s**) nt (Chem) chromium; chrome

Chromosom [kromo'zo:m] (**-s, -en**) nt (Biol) chromosome

Chronik ['kro:nık] f chronicle

chronisch adj chronic

Chronologie [kronolo'gi:] f chronology

chronologisch adj chronological

Chrysantheme [kryzan'te:mə] (**-, -n**) f chrysanthemum

CIA ['si:ar'eı] (**-**) f od m abk (= Central Intelligence Agency) CIA

circa ['tsırka] adv (round) about

Cis [tsıs] (**-, -**) nt (Mus) C sharp

cis [tsıs] (**-, -**) nt (Mus) C sharp

City ['sıtı] (**-, -s**) f city centre (Brit); **in der ~** in the city centre (Brit), downtown (US); **die ~ von Berlin** the (city) centre of Berlin (Brit), downtown Berlin (US)

clean [kli:n] adj (Drogen: umg) off drugs

clever ['klɛvər] adj clever; (gerissen) crafty

Clique ['klıkə] (**-, -n**) f set, crowd

Clou [klu:] (**-s, -s**) m (von Geschichte) (whole) point; (von Show) highlight, high spot

Clown [klaʊn] (**-s, -s**) m clown

cm abk (= Zentimeter) cm.

Cockpit ['kɔkpıt] (**-s, -s**) nt cockpit

Cocktail ['kɔkte:l] (**-s, -s**) m cocktail

Code [ko:t] (**-s, -s**) m code

Cola ['ko:la] (**-(s), -s**) nt od f Coke®

Collier [kɔli'e:] (**-s, -s**) nt necklet, necklace

Comicheft ['kɔmıkhɛft] nt comic

Computer [kɔm'pju:tər] (**-s, -**) m computer; **computergesteuert** adj computer-controlled; **computergestützt** adj computer-based; **computergestütztes Design** computer-aided design; **Computerkriminalität** f computer crime; **Computerspiel** nt computer game; **Computerspieler, in** m (f) (Comput) gamer; **Computertechnik** f computer technology

Conférencier [kõferaˉ'si:e:] (**-s, -s**) m compère

Container [kɔn'te:nər] (**-s, -**) m container; **Containerschiff** nt container ship

Contergankind [kɔnter'gankınt] (umg) nt thalidomide child

Cookie ['kuki] (**-s, -s**) (Comput) cookie

cool [ku:l] (umg) adj (gefasst) cool

Cord [kɔrt] (**-(e)s, -e** od **-s**) m corduroy

Cornichon [kɔrni'ʃõ:] (**-s, -s**) nt gherkin

Couch [kaʊtʃ] (**-, -es** od **-en**) f couch; **Couchgarnitur** ['kaʊtʃgarni'tu:r] f three-piece suite

Couleur [ku'lø:r] (**-s, -s**) f (geh) kind, sort

Coupé [ku'pe:] (**-s, -s**) nt (Aut) coupé, sports version

Coupon [ku'põ:, ku'pɔŋ] (**-s, -s**) m coupon, voucher; (Stoffcoupon) length of cloth

Courage [ku'ra:ʒə] (**-**) f courage

Cousin [ku'zɛ̃:] (**-s, -s**) m cousin

Cousine [ku'zi:nə] (**-, -n**) f cousin

Crack [krɛk] (-) *nt* (*Droge*) crack
Creme [kreːm] (-, -s) *f* (*lit, fig*) cream;
(*Schuhcreme*) polish; (*Koch*) mousse;
  cremefarben *adj* cream(-coloured (*Brit*) *od*
  -colored (*US*))
cremig ['kreːmɪç] *adj* creamy
Crux [krʊks] (-) *f* = **Krux**
CSU [tseː|ɛs'|uː] (-) *f abk* (= *Christlich-Soziale Union*)
Christian Social Union; *see culture note*

⬤ **c s u**
⬤
⬤ The *CSU* (Christlich-Soziale Union) is a
⬤ party founded in 1945 in Bavaria. Like its

⬤ sister party the *CDU* it is a Christian, right-
⬤ wing party.

CT-Scanner [tseː'teːskenər] *m* CT scanner
Curriculum [kʊ'riːkulʊm] (-s, -cula) *nt* (*geh*)
  curriculum
Curry ['kari] (-s) *m od nt* curry powder;
  Currypulver ['karipʊlfər] *nt* curry powder;
  Currywurst *f* curried sausage
Cursor ['køːrsər] (-s) *m* (*Comput*) cursor;
  Cursortaste *f* cursor key
Cutter, in ['katər(ɪn)] (-s, -) *m(f)* (*Film*) editor
CVJM [tseː'faʊjɔt'|ɛm] (-) *m abk* (= *Christlicher
Verein Junger Männer*) YMCA

Dd

D, d [de:] *nt* D, d; **D wie Dora** = D for David, D
for Dog (US)

D. *abk* = **Doktor** (*der evangelischen Theologie*)

⊙ SCHLÜSSELWORT

da [da:] *adv* **1** (*örtlich*) there; (*hier*) here; **da
draußen** out there; **da sein** to be there; **ein
Arzt, der immer für seine Patienten da ist**
a doctor who always has time for his patients;
da bin ich here I am; **da hast du dein Geld**
(there you are,) there's your money; **da, wo**
where; **ist noch Milch da?** is there any milk
left?
2 (*zeitlich*) then; (*folglich*) so; **es war niemand
im Zimmer, da habe ich ...** there was
nobody in the room, so I ...
3: da haben wir Glück gehabt we were lucky
there; **was gibts denn da zu lachen?** what's
so funny about that?; **da kann man nichts
machen** there's nothing one can do (in a case
like that)
▷ *konj* (*weil*) as, since

d. Ä. *abk* (= *der Ältere*) Sen., sen.
DAAD (-) *m abk* (= *Deutscher Akademischer
Austauschdienst*) German Academic Exchange Service
dabehalten *unreg vt* to keep
dabei [da'baɪ] *adv* (*räumlich*) close to it; (*noch
dazu*) besides; (*zusammen mit*) with them/it
etc; (*zeitlich*) during this; (*obwohl doch*) but,
however; **~ sein** (*anwesend*) to be present;
(*beteiligt*) to be involved; **ich bin ~!** count
me in!; **was ist schon ~?** what of it?; **es ist
doch nichts ~, wenn ...** it doesn't matter
if ...; **bleiben wir ~** let's leave it at that; **es
soll nicht ~ bleiben** this isn't the end of
it; **es bleibt ~** that's settled; **das Dumme/
Schwierige ~** the stupid/difficult part of
it; **er war gerade ~ zu gehen** he was just
leaving; **hast du ~ etwas gelernt?** did you
learn anything from it?; **~ darf man nicht
vergessen, dass ...** it shouldn't be forgotten
that ...; **die ~ entstehenden Kosten** the
expenses arising from this; **es kommt doch
nichts ~ heraus** nothing will come of it; **ich
finde gar nichts ~** I don't see any harm in it;
dabeistehen *unreg vi* to stand around

Dach [dax] (-(e)s, ¨er) *nt* roof; **unter ~ und
Fach sein** (*abgeschlossen*) to be in the bag (*umg*);
(*Vertrag, Geschäft*) to be signed and sealed; (*in
Sicherheit*) to be safe; **jdm eins aufs ~ geben**
(*umg: ausschimpfen*) to give sb a (good) talking
to; **Dachboden** *m* attic, loft; **Dachdecker** (**-s,
-**) *m* slater, tiler; **Dachfenster** *nt* skylight;
(*ausgestellt*) dormer window; **Dachfirst** *m* ridge
of the roof; **Dachgepäckträger** *m* (*Aut*) roof
rack; **Dachgeschoss** *nt* attic storey (*Brit*) *od*
story (US); (*oberster Stock*) top floor *od* storey
(*Brit*) *od* story (US); **Dachluke** *f* skylight;
Dachpappe *f* roofing felt; **Dachrinne** *f* gutter
Dachs [daks] (**-es, -e**) *m* badger
Dachschaden (*umg*) *m*: **einen ~ haben** to have
a screw loose
dachte *etc* ['daxtə] *vb siehe* **denken**
Dach- *zW*: **Dachterrasse** *f* roof terrace;
Dachverband *m* umbrella organization;
Dachziegel *m* roof tile
Dackel ['dakəl] (**-s, -**) *m* dachshund
dadurch [da'dʊrç] *adv* (*räumlich*) through it;
(*durch diesen Umstand*) thereby, in that way;
(*deshalb*) because of that, for that reason
▷ *konj*: **~, dass** because
dafür [da'fy:r] *adv* for it; (*anstatt*) instead; (*zum
Ausgleich*): **in Latein ist er schlecht, ~ kann
er gut Fußball spielen** he's bad at Latin but
he makes up for it at football; **er ist bekannt
~** he is well-known for that; **was bekomme
ich ~?** what will I get for it?; **~ ist er immer
zu haben** he never says no to that; **~ bin ich
ja hier** that's what I'm here for; **er kann
nichts ~ (, dass ...)** he can't help it (that ...);
Dafürhalten (**-s**) *nt* (*geh*): **nach meinem
Dafürhalten** in my opinion
DAG *f abk* (= *Deutsche Angestellten-Gewerkschaft*)
Clerical and Administrative Workers' Union
dagegen [da'ge:gən] *adv* against it; (*im Vergleich
damit*) in comparison with it; (*bei Tausch*) for it
▷ *konj* however; **haben Sie etwas ~, wenn ich
rauche?** do you mind if I smoke?; **ich habe
nichts ~** I don't mind; **ich war ~** I was against
it; **ich hätte nichts ~ (einzuwenden)** that's
okay by me; **~ kann man nichts tun** one
can't do anything about it; **dagegenhalten**
unreg vt (*vergleichen*) to compare with it;
(*entgegnen*) to put forward as an objection

daheim [da'haɪm] *adv* at home; **bei uns** ~ back home; **Daheim (-s)** *nt* home

daher [da'he:r] *adv* from there; (*Ursache*) from that ▷ *konj* (*deshalb*) that's why; **das kommt ~, dass ...** that is because ...; ~ **kommt er auch** that's where he comes from too; ~ **die Schwierigkeiten** that's what is causing the difficulties; **dahergelaufen** *adj*: **jeder dahergelaufene Kerl** any Tom, Dick or Harry; **daherreden** *vi* to talk away ▷ *vt* to say without thinking

dahin [da'hɪn] *adv* (*räumlich*) there; (*zeitlich*) then; (*vergangen*) gone; **ist es noch weit bis ~?** is there still far to go?; ~ **gehend** on this matter; **das tendiert ~** it is tending towards that; **er bringt es noch ~, dass ich ...** he'll make me ...; **dahingegen** *konj* on the other hand; **dahingehen** *unreg vi* (*Zeit*) to pass; **dahingestellt** *adv*: **dahingestellt bleiben** to remain to be seen; **etw dahingestellt sein lassen** to leave sth open *od* undecided; **dahinschleppen** *vr* (*lit: sich fortbewegen*) to drag o.s. along; (*fig: Verhandlungen, Zeit*) to drag on; **dahinschmelzen** *vi* to be enthralled

dahinten [da'hɪntən] *adv* over there

dahinter [da'hɪntər] *adv* behind it; **sich ~ klemmen** *od* **knien** (*umg*) to put one's back into it; ~ **kommen** (*umg*) to find out

dahinvegetieren [da'hɪnvege'ti:rən] *vi* to vegetate

Dahlie ['da:liə] **(-, -n)** *f* dahlia

DAK (-) *f abk* (= *Deutsche Angestellten-Krankenkasse*) health insurance company for employees

Dakar ['dakar] **(-s)** *nt* Dakar

dalassen ['da:lasən] *unreg vt* to leave (behind)

dalli ['dali] (*umg*) *adv*: ~, ~! on (*Brit*) *od* at (*US*) the double!

damalig ['da:ma:lɪç] *adj* of that time, then

damals ['da:ma:ls] *adv* at that time, then

Damaskus [da'maskʊs] *nt* Damascus

Damast [da'mast] **(-(e)s, -e)** *m* damask

Dame ['da:mə] **(-, -n)** *f* lady; (*Schach, Karten*) queen; (*Spiel*) draughts (*Brit*), checkers (*US*)

Damen- *zW*: **Damenbesuch** *m* lady visitor *od* visitors; **Damenbinde** *f* sanitary towel (*Brit*) *od* napkin (*US*); **damenhaft** *adj* ladylike; **Damensattel** *m*: **im Damensattel reiten** to ride side-saddle; **Damenwahl** *f* ladies' excuse-me

Damespiel *nt* draughts (*Brit*), checkers (*US*)

damit [da'mɪt] *adv* with it; (*begründend*) by that ▷ *konj* in order that *od* to; **was meint er ~?** what does he mean by that?; **was soll ich ~?** what am I meant to do with that?; **muss er denn immer wieder ~ ankommen?** must he keep on about it?; **was ist ~?** what about it?; **genug ~!** that's enough!; ~ **basta!** and that's that!; ~ **eilt es nicht** there's no hurry

dämlich ['dɛ:mlɪç] (*umg*) *adj* silly, stupid

Damm [dam] **(-(e)s, ¨e)** *m* dyke (*Brit*), dike (*US*); (*Staudamm*) dam; (*Hafendamm*) mole; (*Bahndamm, Straßendamm*) embankment

dämmen ['dɛmən] *vt* (*Wasser*) to dam up; (*Schmerzen*) to keep back

dämmerig *adj* dim, faint

Dämmerlicht *nt* twilight; (*abends*) dusk; (*Halbdunkel*) half-light

dämmern ['dɛmərn] *vi* (*Tag*) to dawn; (*Abend*) to fall; **es dämmerte ihm, dass ...** (*umg*) it dawned on him that ...

Dämmerung *f* twilight; (*Morgendämmerung*) dawn; (*Abenddämmerung*) dusk

Dämmerzustand *m* (*Halbschlaf*) dozy state; (*Bewusstseinstrübung*) semi-conscious state

Dämmung *f* insulation

Dämon ['dɛ:mɔn] **(-s, -en)** *m* demon

dämonisch [dɛ'mo:nɪʃ] *adj* demonic

Dampf [dampf] **(-(e)s, ¨e)** *m* steam; (*Dunst*) vapour (*Brit*), vapor (*US*); **jdm ~ machen** (*umg*) to make sb get a move on; ~ **ablassen** (*lit, fig*) to let off steam; **dampfen** *vi* to steam

dämpfen ['dɛmpfən] *vt* (*Koch*) to steam; (*bügeln*) to iron with a damp cloth; (*mit Dampfbügeleisen*) to steam iron; (*fig*) to dampen, subdue

Dampfer ['dampfər] **(-s, -)** *m* steamer; **auf dem falschen ~ sein** (*fig*) to have got the wrong idea

Dämpfer (-s, -) *m* (*Mus: bei Klavier*) damper; (*bei Geige, Trompete*) mute; **er hat einen ~ bekommen** (*fig*) it dampened his spirits

Dampf- *zW*: **Dampfkochtopf** *m* pressure cooker; **Dampfmaschine** *f* steam engine; **Dampfschiff** *nt* steamship; **Dampfwalze** *f* steamroller

Damwild ['damvɪlt] *nt* fallow deer

danach [da'na:x] *adv* after that; (*zeitlich*) afterwards; (*gemäß*) accordingly; (*laut diesem*) according to which *od* that; **mir war nicht ~ (zumute)** I didn't feel like it; **er griff schnell ~** he grabbed at it; ~ **kann man nicht gehen** you can't go by that; **er sieht ~ aus** he looks it

Däne ['dɛ:nə] **(-n, -n)** *m* Dane, Danish man/boy

daneben [da'ne:bən] *adv* beside it; (*im Vergleich*) in comparison; ~ **sein** (*umg*) to be completely confused; **danebenbenehmen** *unreg vr* to misbehave; **danebengehen** *unreg vi* to miss; (*Plan*) to fail; **danebengreifen** *unreg vi* to miss; (*fig: mit Schätzung etc*) to be wide of the mark

Dänemark ['dɛ:nəmark] **(-s)** *nt* Denmark

Dänin ['dɛ:nɪn] *f* Dane, Danish woman *od* girl

dänisch *adj* Danish

Dank [daŋk] **(-(e)s)** *m* thanks *pl*; **vielen** *od* **schönen ~** many thanks; **jdm ~ sagen** to thank sb; **mit (bestem) ~ zurück!** many thanks for the loan; **dank** *präp* (+*dat od gen*) thanks to; **dankbar** *adj* grateful; (*Aufgabe*) rewarding; (*haltbar*) hard-wearing; **Dankbarkeit** *f* gratitude

danke *interj* thank you, thanks; ~ **schön** *od* **sehr** thank you very much

danken *vi* +*dat* to thank; **nichts zu ~!** don't mention it; **~d erhalten/ablehnen** to receive/decline with thanks

dankenswert *adj* (*Arbeit*) worthwhile; rewarding; (*Bemühung*) kind

Dank- *zW*: **Dankgottesdienst** *m* service of

79

thanksgiving; **danksagen** vi to express one's thanks; **Dankschreiben** nt letter of thanks

dann [dan] adv then; ~ **und wann** now and then; ~ **eben nicht** well, in that case (there's no more to be said); **erst ~, wenn** ... only when ...; ~ **erst recht nicht!** in that case no way (umg)

dannen ['danən] adv: **von** ~ (liter: weg) away

daran [da'ran] adv on it; (stoßen) against it; **es liegt ~, dass** ... the cause of it is that ...; **gut/schlecht ~ sein** to be well/badly off; **das Beste/Dümmste ~** the best/stupidest thing about it; **ich war nahe ~, zu** ... I was on the point of ...; **im Anschluss ~** (zeitlich: danach anschließend) following that od this; **wir können nichts ~ machen** we can't do anything about it; **es ist nichts ~** (ist nicht fundiert) there's nothing in it; (ist nichts Besonderes) it's nothing special; **er ist ~ gestorben** he died from od of it; **darangehen** unreg vi to start; **daranmachen** (umg) vr: **sich daranmachen, etw zu tun** to set about doing sth; **daransetzen** vt to stake; **er hat alles darangesetzt, von Glasgow wegzukommen** he has done his utmost to get away from Glasgow

darauf [da'rauf] adv (räumlich) on it; (zielgerichtet) towards it; (danach) afterwards; ~ **folgend** following; **es kommt ganz ~ an, ob** ... it depends whether ...; **seine Behauptungen stützen sich ~, dass** ... his claims are based on the supposition that ...; **wie kommst du ~?** what makes you think that?; **die Tage ~** the days following od thereafter; **am Tag ~** the next day; **darauffolgend** adj (Tag, Jahr) next, following; **daraufhin** adv (im Hinblick darauf) in this respect; (aus diesem Grund) as a result; **wir müssen es daraufhin prüfen, ob** ... we must test it to see whether ...; **darauflegen** vt to lay od put on top

daraus [da'raus] adv from it; **was ist ~ geworden?** what became of it?; ~ **geht hervor, dass** ... this means that ...

darbieten ['da:rbi:tən] vt (vortragen: Lehrstoff) to present ▷ vr to present itself

Darbietung f performance

Dardanellen [darda'nɛlən] pl Dardanelles pl

darein- präf = **drein-**

Daressalam [daresa'la:m] nt Dar-es-Salaam

darf [darf] vb siehe **dürfen**

darin [da'rın] adv in (there), in it; **der Unterschied liegt ~, dass** ... the difference is that ...

darlegen ['da:rle:gən] vt to explain, expound, set forth

Darlegung f explanation

Darlehen, Darlehn (-s, -) nt loan

Darm [darm] (**-(e)s, -̈e**) m intestine; (Wurstdarm) skin; **Darmausgang** m anus; **Darmgrippe** f gastric influenza

darstellen ['da:rʃtɛlən] vt (abbilden, bedeuten) to represent; (Theat) to act; (beschreiben) to describe ▷ vr to appear to be

Darsteller, in (-s, -) m(f) actor, actress

darstellerisch adj: **eine ~e Höchstleistung** a magnificent piece of acting

Darstellung f portrayal, depiction

darüber [da'ry:bər] adv (räumlich) over/above it; (fahren) over it; (mehr) more; (währenddessen) meanwhile; (sprechen, streiten) about it; ~ **hinweg sein** (fig) to have got over it; ~ **hinaus** over and above that; ~ **geht nichts** there's nothing like it; **seine Gedanken ~** his thoughts about od on it; ~ **liegen** (fig) to be higher

darum [da'rʊm] adv (räumlich) round it ▷ konj that's why; ~ **herum** round about (it); **er bittet ~** he is pleading for it; **es geht ~, dass** ... the thing is that ...; ~ **geht es mir/ geht es mir nicht** that's my point/that's not the point for me; **er würde viel ~ geben, wenn** ... he would give a lot to ...; siehe auch **drum**

darunter [da'rʊntər] adv (räumlich) under it; (dazwischen) among them; (weniger) less; **ein Stockwerk ~** one floor below (it); **was verstehen Sie ~?** what do you understand by that?; ~ **kann ich mir nichts vorstellen** that doesn't mean anything to me; ~ **fallen** to be included; ~ **mischen** (Mehl) to mix in; **sich ~ mischen** to mingle; ~ **setzen** (Unterschrift) to put to it

das [das] pron that ▷ def art the; siehe auch **der**; ~ **heißt** that is; ~ **und ~** such and such

Dasein ['da:zaɪn] (**-s**) nt (Leben) life; (Anwesenheit) presence; (Bestehen) existence

da sein unreg vi siehe **da**

Daseinsberechtigung f right to exist

Daseinskampf m struggle for survival

dass [das] konj that

dasselbe [das'zɛlbə] nt pron the same

dastehen ['da:ʃte:ən] unreg vi to stand there; (fig): **gut/schlecht ~** to be in a good/bad position; **allein ~** to be on one's own

Dat. abk = **Dativ**

Datei [da'taɪ] f (Comput) file; **Dateimanager** m file manager; **Dateiname** m file name; **Dateiverwaltung** f file management

Daten ['da:tən] pl (Comput) data; (Angaben) data pl, particulars; siehe auch **Datum**; **Datenabgleich** m data comparison; **Datenautobahn** f information (super) highway; **Datenbank** f database; **Datendiebstahl** m (Wirts, Comput) data theft; **Datenerfassung** f data capture; **Datenleitung** f data line; **Datenmüll** m (aus dem Internet) Internet buildup; (auf Festplatte) hard disk clutter; **Datennetz** nt data network; **Datensatz** m record; **Datenschutz** m data protection; **Datensichtgerät** nt visual display unit, VDU; **Datenträger** m data carrier; **Datenübertragung** f data transmission; **Datenverarbeitung** f data processing; **Datenverarbeitungsanlage** f data processing equipment, DP equipment

datieren [da'ti:rən] vt to date

Dativ ['da:ti:f] (**-s, -e**) *m* dative; **Dativobjekt** *nt* (*Gram*) indirect object

dato ['da:to] *adv*: **bis ~** (*Comm*: *umg*) to date

Dattel ['datəl] (**-, -n**) *f* date

Datum ['da:tʊm] (**-s, Daten**) *nt* date; **das heutige ~** today's date

Datumsgrenze *f* (*Geog*) (international) date line

Dauer ['daʊər] (**-, -n**) *f* duration; (*gewisse Zeitspanne*) length; (*Bestand, Fortbestehen*) permanence; **es war nur von kurzer ~** it didn't last long; **auf die ~** in the long run; (*auf längere Zeit*) indefinitely; **Dauerauftrag** *m* standing order; **dauerhaft** *adj* lasting, durable; **Dauerhaftigkeit** *f* durability; **Dauerkarte** *f* season ticket; **Dauerlauf** *m* long-distance run

dauern *vi* to last; **es hat sehr lang gedauert, bis er ...** it took him a long time to ...

dauernd *adj* constant

Dauer- *zW*: **Dauerobst** *nt* fruit suitable for storing; **Dauerredner** (*pej*) *m* long-winded speaker; **Dauerregen** *m* continuous rain; **Dauerschlaf** *m* prolonged sleep; **Dauerstellung** *f* permanent position; **Dauerwelle** *f* perm, permanent wave; **Dauerwurst** *f* German salami; **Dauerzustand** *m* permanent condition

Daumen ['daʊmən] (**-s, -**) *m* thumb; **jdm die ~ drücken** *od* **halten** to keep one's fingers crossed for sb; **über den ~ peilen** to guess roughly; **Daumenlutscher** *m* thumb-sucker

Daune ['daʊnə] (**-, -n**) *f* down

Daunendecke *f* down duvet

davon [da'fɔn] *adv* of it; (*räumlich*) away; (*weg von*) away from it; (*Grund*) because of it; (*mit Passiv*) by it; **das kommt ~!** that's what you get; **~ abgesehen** apart from that; **wenn wir einmal ~ absehen, dass ...** if for once we overlook the fact that ...; **~ sprechen/wissen** to talk/know of *od* about it; **was habe ich ~?** what's the point?; **~ betroffen werden** to be affected by it; **davongehen** *unreg vi* to leave, go away; **davonkommen** *unreg vi* to escape; **davonlassen** *unreg vt*: **die Finger davonlassen** (*umg*) to keep one's hands *od* fingers off (it); **davonlaufen** *unreg vi* to run away; **davonmachen** *vr* to make off; **davontragen** *unreg vt* to carry off; (*Verletzung*) to receive

davor [da'fo:r] *adv* (*räumlich*) in front of it; (*zeitlich*) before (that); **~ warnen** to warn about it

dazu [da'tsu:] *adv* (*legen, stellen*) by it; (*essen*) with it; **und ~ noch** and in addition; **ein Beispiel/seine Gedanken ~** one example for/his thoughts on this; **wie komme ich denn ~?** why should I?; **... aber ich bin nicht ~ gekommen ...** but I didn't get around to it; **das Recht ~** the right to do it; **~ bereit sein, etw zu tun** to be prepared to do sth; **~ fähig sein** to be capable of it; **sich ~ äußern** to say something on it; **dazugehören** *vi* to belong

to it; **das gehört dazu** (*versteht sich von selbst*) it's all part of it; **es gehört schon einiges dazu, das zu tun** it takes a lot to do that; **dazugehörig** *adj* appropriate; **dazukommen** *unreg vi* (*Ereignisse*) to happen too; (*an einen Ort*) to come along; **kommt noch etwas dazu?** will there be anything else?; **dazulernen** *vt*: **schon wieder was dazugelernt!** you learn something (new) every day!; **dazumal** ['da:tsuma:l] *adv* in those days; **dazutun** *unreg vt* to add; **er hat es ohne dein Dazutun geschafft** he managed it without your doing *etc* anything

dazwischen [da'tsvɪʃən] *adv* in between; (*zusammen mit*) among them; **der Unterschied ~** the difference between them; **dazwischenfahren** *unreg vi* (*eingreifen*) to intervene; **dazwischenfunken** (*umg*) *vi* (*eingreifen*) to put one's oar in; **dazwischenkommen** *unreg vi* (*hineingeraten*) to get caught in it; **es ist etwas dazwischengekommen** something (has) cropped up; **dazwischenreden** *vi* (*unterbrechen*) to interrupt; (*sich einmischen*) to interfere; **dazwischentreten** *unreg vi* to intervene

DB *f abk* (= *Deutsche Bahn*) German railways

DBP *f abk* (*früher*) = **Deutsche Bundespost**

DDR (**-**) *f abk* (*früher:* = *Deutsche Demokratische Republik*) GDR; *see culture note*

◉ **DDR**
◉
◉ The DDR (Deutsche Demokratische
◉ Republik) was the name by which the
◉ former Communist German Democratic
◉ Republic was known. It was founded in
◉ 1949 from the Soviet-occupied zone. After
◉ the building of the Berlin Wall in 1961 it
◉ was virtually sealed off from the West
◉ until mass demonstrations and demands
◉ for reform forced the opening of the
◉ borders in 1989. It then merged in 1990
◉ with the BRD.

DDT® *nt abk* DDT

Dealer, in ['di:lər(ɪn)] (**-s, -**) (*umg*) *m(f)* pusher

Debatte [de'batə] (**-, -n**) *f* debate; **das steht hier nicht zur ~** that's not the issue

debattieren [deba'ti:rən] *vt* to debate

Debet ['de:bɛt] (**-s, -s**) *nt* (*Fin*) debits *pl*

Debüt [de'by:] (**-s, -s**) *nt* debut

dechiffrieren [deʃɪ'fri:rən] *vt* to decode; (*Text*) to decipher

Deck [dɛk] (**-(e)s, -s** *od* **-e**) *nt* deck; **an ~ gehen** to go on deck

Deckbett *nt* feather quilt

Deckblatt *nt* (*Schutzblatt*) cover

Decke (**-, -n**) *f* cover; (*Bettdecke*) blanket; (*Tischdecke*) tablecloth; (*Zimmerdecke*) ceiling; **unter einer ~ stecken** to be hand in glove; **an die ~ gehen** to hit the roof; **mir fällt die ~ auf den Kopf** (*fig*) I feel really claustrophobic

Deckel (**-s, -**) *m* lid; **du kriegst gleich eins auf**

den ~ (umg) you're going to catch it

Deckelung f capping

decken vt to cover ▷ vr to coincide ▷ vi to lay the table; **mein Bedarf ist gedeckt** I have all I need; (fig) I've had enough; **sich an einen gedeckten Tisch setzen** (fig) to be handed everything on a plate

Deckmantel m: **unter dem ~ von** under the guise of

Deckname m assumed name

Deckung f (das Schützen) covering; (Schutz) cover; (Sport) defence (Brit), defense (US); (Übereinstimmen) agreement; **zur ~ seiner Schulden** to meet his debts

deckungsgleich adj congruent

Decoder m (TV) decoder

de facto [de: 'fakto] adv de facto

Defekt [de'fɛkt] (-(e)s, -e) m fault, defect; **defekt** adj faulty

defensiv [defɛn'si:f] adj defensive

Defensive f: **jdn in die ~ drängen** to force sb onto the defensive

definieren [defi'ni:rən] vt to define

Definition [definitsi'o:n] f definition

definitiv [defini'ti:f] adj definite

Defizit ['de:fitsɪt] (-s, -e) nt deficit

defizitär [defitsi'tɛ:r] adj: **eine ~e Haushaltspolitik führen** to follow an economic policy which can only lead to deficit

Deflation [deflatsi'o:n] f (Econ) deflation

deflationär [deflatsio'nɛ:r] adj deflationary

deftig ['dɛftɪç] adj (Essen) large; (Witz) coarse

Degen ['de:gən] (-s, -) m sword

degenerieren [degene'ri:rən] vi to degenerate

degradieren [degra'di:rən] vt to degrade

dehnbar ['de:nba:r] adj elastic; (fig: Begriff) loose; **Dehnbarkeit** f elasticity; looseness

dehnen vt, vr to stretch

Dehnung f stretching

Deich [daɪç] (-(e)s, -e) m dyke (Brit), dike (US)

Deichsel ['daɪksəl] (-, -n) f shaft

deichseln vt (fig: umg) to wangle

dein [daɪn] pron your; (adjektivisch): **herzliche Grüße, D~e Elke** with best wishes, yours od (herzlicher) love, Elke

deine, r, s poss pron yours

deiner gen von **du** pron of you

deinerseits adv on your part

deinesgleichen pron people like you

deinetwegen ['daɪnət've:gən] adv (für dich) for your sake; (wegen dir) on your account

deinetwillen ['daɪnət'vɪlən] adv: **um ~ = deinetwegen**

deinige pron: **der/die/das D~** yours

dekadent [deka'dɛnt] adj decadent

Dekadenz f decadence

Dekan [de'ka:n] (-s, -e) m dean

deklassieren [dekla'si:rən] vt (Soziologie: herabsetzen) to downgrade; (Sport: übertreffen) to outclass

Deklination [deklinatsi'o:n] f declension

deklinieren [dekli'ni:rən] vt to decline

Dekolleté, Dekolletee [dekɔl'te:] (-s, -s) nt low neckline

dekomprimieren vt (Comput) to decompress

Dekor [de'ko:r] (-s, -s od -e) m od nt decoration

Dekorateur, in [dekora'tø:r(ɪn)] m(f) window dresser

Dekoration [dekoratsi'o:n] f decoration; (in Laden) window dressing

dekorativ [dekora'ti:f] adj decorative

dekorieren [deko'ri:rən] vt to decorate; (Schaufenster) to dress

Dekostoff ['de:koʃtɔf] m (Textil) furnishing fabric

Dekret [de'kre:t] (-(e)s, -e) nt decree

Delegation [delegatsi'o:n] f delegation

delegieren [dele'gi:rən] vt: **~ (an** +akk) to delegate (to)

Delegierte, r f(m) delegate

Delfin [dɛl'fi:n] (-s, -e) m dolphin

Delfinschwimmen nt butterfly (stroke)

Delhi ['dɛlɪ] (-s) nt Delhi

delikat [deli'ka:t] adj (zart, heikel) delicate; (köstlich) delicious

Delikatesse [delika'tɛsə] (-, -n) f delicacy

Delikatessengeschäft nt delicatessen (shop)

Delikt [de'lɪkt] (-(e)s, -e) nt (Jur) offence (Brit), offense (US)

Delinquent [delɪŋ'kvɛnt] m (geh) offender

Delirium [de'li:riʊm] nt: **im ~ sein** to be delirious; (umg: betrunken) to be paralytic

Delle ['dɛlə] (-, -n) (umg) f dent

Delphin etc [dɛl'fi:n] (-s, -e) m = **Delfin** etc

Delta ['dɛlta] (-s, -s) nt delta

dem [de(:)m] art dat von **der; das; wie ~ auch sei** be that as it may

Demagoge [dema'go:gə] (-n, -n) m demagogue

Demarkationslinie [demarkatsi'o:nzli:niə] f demarcation line

Dementi [de'mɛnti] (-s, -s) nt denial

dementieren [demɛn'ti:rən] vt to deny

dem- zW: **dementsprechend** adj appropriate ▷ adv correspondingly; (demnach) accordingly; **demgemäß** adv accordingly; **demnach** adv accordingly; **demnächst** adv shortly

Demo ['de:mo] (-s, -s) (umg) f demo

Demografie [demogra'fi:] f demography

Demokrat, in [demo'kra:t(ɪn)] (-en, -en) m(f) democrat

Demokratie [demokra'ti:] f democracy; **Demokratieverständnis** nt understanding of (the meaning of) democracy

demokratisch adj democratic

demokratisieren [demokrati'zi:rən] vt to democratize

demolieren [demo'li:rən] vt to demolish

Demonstrant, in [demɔn'strant(ɪn)] m(f) demonstrator

Demonstration [demɔnstratsi'o:n] f demonstration

demonstrativ [demɔnstra'ti:f] adj demonstrative; (Protest) pointed

demonstrieren [demɔn'stri:rən] vt, vi to demonstrate

Demontage [demɔn'ta:ʒə] (-, -n) f (lit, fig)

dismantling

demontieren [demɔn'tiːrən] vt (lit, fig) to dismantle; (Räder) to take off

demoralisieren [demorali'ziːrən] vt to demoralize

Demoskopie [demosko'piː] f public opinion research

demselben dat von **derselbe; dasselbe**

Demut ['deːmuːt] (-) f humility

demütig ['deːmyːtɪç] adj humble

demütigen ['deːmyːtɪgən] vt to humiliate

Demütigung f humiliation

demzufolge ['deːmtsu'fɔlgə] adv accordingly

den [deˑ(ː)n] art akk von **der**

denen ['deːnən] pron dat pl von **der; die; das**

Denk- zW: **Denkanstoß** m: **jdm Denkanstöße geben** to give sb food for thought; **Denkart** f mentality; **denkbar** adj conceivable

denken ['dɛŋkən] unreg vi to think ▷ vt: **für jdn/etw gedacht sein** to be intended od meant for sb/sth ▷ vr (vorstellen): **das kann ich mir ~** I can imagine; (beabsichtigen): **sich** dat **etw bei etw ~** to mean sth by sth; **wo ~ Sie hin!** what an idea!; **ich denke schon** I think so; **an jdn/etw ~** to think of sb/sth; **daran ist gar nicht zu ~** that's (quite) out of the question; **ich denke nicht daran, das zu tun** there's no way I'm going to do that (umg)

Denken (-s) nt thinking

Denker, in (-s, -) m(f) thinker; **das Volk der Dichter und ~** the nation of poets and philosophers

Denk- zW: **Denkfähigkeit** f intelligence; **denkfaul** adj mentally lazy; **Denkfehler** m logical error; **Denkhorizont** m mental horizon

Denkmal (-s, ⁻er) nt monument; **Denkmalschutz** m: **etw unter Denkmalschutz stellen** to classify sth as a historical monument

Denk- zW: **Denkpause** f: **eine Denkpause einlegen** to have a break to think things over; **Denkschrift** f memorandum; **Denkvermögen** nt intellectual capacity; **denkwürdig** adj memorable; **Denkzettel** m: **jdm einen Denkzettel verpassen** to teach sb a lesson

denn [dɛn] konj for; (konzessiv): **es sei ~, (dass)** unless ▷ adv then; (nach Komparativ) than

dennoch ['dɛnɔx] konj nevertheless ▷ adv: **und ~, ...** and yet ...

denselben akk von **derselbe** ▷ dat von **dieselben**

Denunziant, in [denʊntsi'ant(ɪn)] m(f) informer

denunzieren [denʊn'tsiːrən] vt to inform against

Deospray ['deːoʃpreɪ] nt od m deodorant spray

Depesche [de'pɛʃə] (-, -n) f dispatch

deplatziert [depla'tsiːrt] adj out of place

Deponent, in [depo'nɛnt(ɪn)] m(f) depositor

Deponie f dump, disposal site

deponieren [depo'niːrən] vt (Comm) to deposit

deportieren [depɔr'tiːrən] vt to deport

Depot [de'poː] (-s, -s) nt warehouse; (Busdepot, Eisenb) depot; (Bankdepot) strongroom (Brit), safe (US)

Depp [dɛp] (-en, -en) m (Dialekt: pej) twit

Depression [depresi'oːn] f depression

depressiv adj depressive; (Fin) depressed

deprimieren [depri'miːrən] vt to depress

 SCHLÜSSELWORT

der [deˑ(ː)r] (f **die**, nt **das**, gen **des, der, des**, dat **dem, der, dem**, akk **den**) def art the; **der Rhein** the Rhine; **der Klaus** (umg) Klaus; **die Frau** (im Allgemeinen) women; **der Tod/das Leben** death/life; **der Fuß des Berges** the foot of the hill; **gib es der Frau** give it to the woman; **er hat sich** dat **die Hand verletzt** he has hurt his hand
▷ rel pron (bei Menschen) who, that; (bei Tieren, Sachen) which, that; **der Mann, den ich gesehen habe** the man who od whom od that I saw
▷ demon pron he/she/it; (jener, dieser) that; (pl) those; **der/die war es** it was him/her; **der mit der Brille** the one with the glasses; **ich will den (da)** I want that one

derart ['deːr'aːrt] adv (Art und Weise) in such a way; (Ausmaß: vor adj) so; (: vor vb) so much

derartig adj such, this sort of

derb [dɛrp] adj sturdy; (Kost) solid; (grob) coarse; **Derbheit** f sturdiness; solidity; coarseness

deren ['deːrən] rel pron (gen sing von die) whose; (von Sachen) of which; (gen pl von der, die, das) their; whose; of whom

derentwillen ['deːrənt'vɪlən] adv: **um ~** (rel) for whose sake; (von Sachen) for the sake of which

dergestalt adv (geh): **~, dass ...** in such a way that ...

der- zW: **dergleichen** pron such; (substantivisch): **er tat nichts dergleichen** he did nothing of the kind; **und dergleichen (mehr)** and suchlike; **derjenige** pron he; she; it; (rel) the one (who); that (which); **dermaßen** adv to such an extent, so; **derselbe** m pron the same; **derweil, derweilen** adv in the meantime; **derzeit** adv (jetzt) at present, at the moment; (damalig) then

des [dɛs] art gen von **der**

Des [dɛs] (-) nt (Mus: auch: **des**) D flat

Deserteur [dezɛr'tøːr] m deserter

desertieren [dezɛr'tiːrən] vi to desert

desgl. abk = **desgleichen**

desgleichen ['dɛs'glaɪçən] pron the same

deshalb ['dɛs'halp] adv, konj therefore, that's why

Design [di'zaɪn] (-s, -s) nt design

designiert [dezi'gniːrt] adj attrib: **der ~e Vorsitzende/Nachfolger** the chairman designate/prospective successor

Desinfektion [dezɪnfɛktsi'oːn] f disinfection

Desinfektionsmittel nt disinfectant

desinfizieren [dezɪnfi'tsiːrən] vt to disinfect

Desinteresse [dɛs|ɪntə'rɛsə] (-s) nt: **~ (an** +dat**)**

d

lack of interest (in)

desinteressiert [dɛs|ɪntərə'si:rt] adj
uninterested

desselben gen von **derselbe; dasselbe**

dessen ['dɛsən] pron gen von **der; das**; ~
ungeachtet nevertheless, regardless

Dessert [dɛ'se:r] (-s, -s) nt dessert

Dessin [dɛ'sɛ̃:] (-s, -s) nt (Textil) pattern, design

Destillation [dɛstɪlatsi'o:n] f distillation

destillieren [dɛstɪ'li:rən] vt to distil

desto ['dɛsto] adv all od so much the; ~ **besser**
all the better

destruktiv [dɛstrʊk'ti:f] adj destructive

deswegen ['dɛs've:gən] konj therefore, hence

Detail [de'tai] (-s, -s) nt detail

detaillieren [deta'ji:rən] vt to specify, give
details of

Detektiv [detɛk'ti:f] (-s, -e) m detective;
Detektivroman m detective novel

Detektor [de'tɛktɔr] m (Tech) detector

Detonation [detonatsi'o:n] f explosion, blast

Deut m: (um) **keinen** ~ not one iota od jot

deuten ['dɔytən] vt to interpret; (Zukunft) to
read ▷ vi: ~ **(auf** +akk) to point (to od at)

deutlich adj clear; (Unterschied) distinct; **jdm
etw ~ zu verstehen geben** to make sth
perfectly clear od plain to sb; **Deutlichkeit** f
clarity; distinctness

deutsch [dɔytʃ] adj German; ~**e Schrift**
Gothic script; **auf D~** in German; **auf gut
D~ (gesagt)** (fig: umg) = in plain English; **D~e
Demokratische Republik** (Hist) German
Democratic Republic

Deutsche, r f(m): **er ist ~r** he is (a) German

Deutschland nt Germany; **Deutschlandlied**
nt German national anthem; **Deutschlandpolitik**
f home od domestic policy; (von fremdem Staat)
policy towards Germany

deutschsprachig adj (Bevölkerung, Gebiete)
German-speaking; (Zeitung, Ausgabe) German-
language; (Literatur) German

deutschstämmig adj of German origin

Deutung f interpretation

Devise [de'vi:zə] (-, -n) f motto, device;
Devisen pl (Fin) foreign currency od exchange

Devisenausgleich m foreign exchange offset

Devisenkontrolle f exchange control

Dez. abk (= Dezember) Dec.

Dezember [de'tsɛmbər] (-(s), -) m December;
siehe auch **September**

dezent [de'tsɛnt] adj discreet

Dezentralisation [detsɛntralizatsi'o:n] f
decentralization

Dezernat [detsɛr'na:t] (-(e)s, -e) nt (Verwaltung)
department

Dezibel [detsi'bɛl] (-s, -) nt decibel

dezidiert [detsi'di:rt] adj firm, determined

dezimal [detsi'ma:l] adj decimal;
Dezimalbruch m decimal (fraction);
Dezimalsystem nt decimal system

dezimieren [detsi'mi:rən] vt (fig) to decimate
▷ vr to be decimated

DFB m abk (= Deutscher Fußball-Bund) German

Football Association

DFG f abk (= Deutsche Forschungsgemeinschaft)
German Research Council

DGB m abk (= Deutscher Gewerkschaftsbund) ≈ TUC

dgl. abk = **dergleichen**

d. h. abk (= das heißt) i.e.

Di. abk = **Dienstag**

Dia ['di:a] (-s, -s) nt = **Diapositiv**

Diabetes [dia'be:tɛs] (-, -) m (Med) diabetes

Diabetiker, in [dia'be:tikər(ɪn)] (-s, -) m(f)
diabetic

Diagnose [dia'gno:zə] (-, -n) f diagnosis

diagnostizieren [diagnɔsti'tsi:rən] vt, vi
(Med, fig) to diagnose

diagonal [diago'na:l] adj diagonal

Diagonale (-, -n) f diagonal

Diagramm [dia'gram] nt diagram

Diakonie [diako'ni:] f (Rel) social welfare work

Dialekt [dia'lɛkt] (-(e)s, -e) m dialect;
Dialektausdruck m dialect expression od
word; **dialektfrei** adj without an accent

dialektisch adj dialectal; (Logik) dialectical

Dialog [dia'lo:k] (-(e)s, -e) m dialogue

Diamant [dia'mant] m diamond

Diapositiv [diapozi'ti:f] (-s, -e) nt (Phot) slide,
transparency

Diaprojektor m slide projector

Diät [di'ɛ:t] (-) f diet; **Diäten** pl (Pol) allowance
sing; ~ **essen** to eat according to a diet; **(nach
einer)** ~ **leben** to be on a special diet

dich [dɪç] akk von **du** ▷ pron you ▷ refl pron yourself

dicht [dɪçt] adj dense; (Nebel) thick; (Gewebe)
close; (undurchlässig) (water)tight; (fig) concise;
(umg: zu) shut, closed ▷ adv: ~ **an/bei** close
to; **er ist nicht ganz** ~ (umg) he's crackers; ~
machen to make watertight/airtight; ~
hintereinander right behind one another; ~
bevölkert densely od heavily populated; siehe
auch **dichtmachen**

Dichte (-, -n) f density; thickness; closeness;
(water)tightness; (fig) conciseness

dichten vt (dicht machen) to make watertight; to
seal; (Naut) to caulk; (Liter) to compose, write
▷ vi (Liter) to compose, write

Dichter, in (-s, -) m(f) poet; (Autor) writer;
dichterisch adj poetical; **dichterische
Freiheit** poetic licence (Brit) od license (US)

dichthalten unreg (umg) vi to keep one's mouth
shut

dichtmachen (umg) vt (Geschäft) to wind up
▷ vi (Person) to close one's mind; siehe auch
dicht

Dichtung f (Tech) washer; (Aut) gasket;
(Gedichte) poetry; (Prosa) (piece of) writing; ~
und Wahrheit (fig) fact and fantasy

dick [dɪk] adj thick; (fett) fat; **durch ~ und
dünn** through thick and thin; **Dickdarm** m
(Anat) colon

Dicke (-, -n) f thickness; fatness

dickfellig adj thick-skinned

dickflüssig adj viscous

Dickicht (-s, -e) nt thicket

dick- zW: **Dickkopf** m mule; **Dickmilch** f soured

milk; Dickschädel m = **Dickkopf**
die [di:] def art the; siehe auch **der**
Dieb, in [di:p, 'di:bɪn] (**-(e)s, -e**) m(f) thief;
haltet den ~! stop thief!; diebisch adj
thieving; (umg) immense; Diebstahl m theft;
diebstahlsicher adj theft-proof
diejenige ['di:je:nɪgə] pron siehe **derjenige**
Diele ['di:lə] (**-, -n**) f (Brett) board; (Flur) hall,
lobby; (Eisdiele) ice-cream parlour (Brit) od
parlor (US)
dienen ['di:nən] vi: (jdm) ~ to serve (sb); **womit
kann ich Ihnen ~?** what can I do for you?; (in
Geschäft) can I help you?
Diener (**-s, -**) m servant; (umg: Verbeugung) bow;
Dienerin f (maid)servant
dienern vi (fig): ~ (**vor** +dat) to bow and scrape
(to)
Dienerschaft f servants pl
dienlich adj useful, helpful
Dienst [di:nst] (**-(e)s, -e**) m service; (Arbeit,
Arbeitszeit) work; ~ **am Kunden** customer
service; **jdm zu ~en stehen** to be at sb's
disposal; **außer ~** retired; ~ **haben** to be on
duty; ~ **habend** = **diensthabend**; ~ **tuend**
= **diensttuend**; **der öffentliche ~** the civil
service
Dienstag m Tuesday; **am ~** on Tuesday; ~ **in
acht Tagen** od **in einer Woche** a week on
Tuesday, Tuesday week; ~ **vor einer Woche**
od **acht Tagen** a week (ago) last Tuesday
dienstags adv on Tuesdays
Dienst- zW: Dienstalter nt length of service;
dienstbeflissen adj zealous; Dienstbote
m servant; Dienstboteneingang m
tradesmen's od service entrance; diensteifrig
adj zealous; dienstfrei adj off duty;
Dienstgebrauch m (Mil, Verwaltung): **nur
für den Dienstgebrauch** for official use
only; Dienstgeheimnis nt professional
secret; Dienstgespräch nt business call;
Dienstgrad m rank; diensthabend adj (Arzt,
Offizier) on duty; Dienstleistung f service;
Dienstleistungsbereich m service sector od
industry; Dienstleistungsbetrieb m service
industry business; Dienstleistungsgewerbe
nt service industries pl; Dienstleistungssektor
m service sector od industry; dienstlich adj
official; (Angelegenheiten) business attrib;
Dienstmädchen nt domestic servant;
Dienstplan m duty rota; Dienstreise
f business trip; Dienststelle f office;
diensttuend adj on duty; Dienstvorschrift f
service regulations pl; Dienstwagen m (von
Beamten) official car; Dienstweg m official
channels pl; Dienstzeit f office hours pl; (Mil)
period of service
diesbezüglich adj (Frage) on this matter
diese, r, s pron this (one) ▷ adj this; ~ **Nacht**
tonight
Diesel ['di:zəl] (**-s**) m (Kraftstoff) diesel fuel
dieselbe [di:'zɛlbə] f pron the same
dieselben [di:'zɛlbən] pl pron the same
Dieselöl ['di:zələ:l] nt diesel oil

diesig adj drizzly
dies- zW: diesjährig adj this year's; diesmal adv
this time; Diesseits (-) nt this life; diesseits
präp +gen on this side
Dietrich ['di:trɪç] (**-s, -e**) m picklock
Diffamierungskampagne
[dɪfa'mi:rʊŋskampanjə] f smear campaign
differential etc [dɪferɛntsi'a:l] adj = **differenzial**
etc
Differenz [dɪfe'rɛnts] f difference;
Differenzbetrag m difference, balance
differenzial [dɪferɛntsi'a:l] adj differential;
Differenzialgetriebe nt differential gear;
Differenzialrechnung f differential calculus
differenzieren [dɪferɛn'tsi:rən] vt to
make distinctions in ▷ vi: ~ (**bei**) to make
distinctions (in)
differenziert adj complex
diffus [dɪ'fu:s] adj (Gedanken etc) confused
Digital- [digi'ta:l-] zW: Digitalanzeige f
digital display; Digitalfernsehen nt digital
TV; Digitalrechner m digital computer;
Digitaluhr f digital watch
Diktafon, Diktaphon [dɪkta'fo:n] nt
dictaphone®
Diktat [dɪk'ta:t] (**-(e)s, -e**) nt dictation;
(fig: Gebot) dictate; (Pol) diktat, dictate
Diktator [dɪk'ta:tɔr] m dictator; diktatorisch
[-a'to:rɪʃ] adj dictatorial
Diktatur [dɪkta'tu:r] f dictatorship
diktieren [dɪk'ti:rən] vt to dictate
Diktion [dɪktsi'o:n] f style
Dilemma [di'lɛma] (**-s, -s** od **-ta**) nt dilemma
Dilettant [dile'tant] m dilettante, amateur;
dilettantisch adj dilettante
Dimension [dimɛnzi'o:n] f dimension
DIN f abk (= Deutsche Industrie-Norm) German
Industrial Standard; ~ **A4** A4
Ding [dɪŋ] (**-(e)s, -e**) nt thing; object; **das ist
ein ~ der Unmöglichkeit** that is totally
impossible; **guter ~e sein** to be in good
spirits; **so wie die ~e liegen, nach Lage
der ~e** as things are; **es müsste nicht mit
rechten ~en zugehen, wenn ...** it would be
more than a little strange if ...; **ein krummes
~ drehen** to commit a crime; to do something
wrong; dingfest adj: **jdn dingfest machen** to
arrest sb; dinglich adj real, concrete
Dings (-) (umg) nt thingummyjig (Brit)
Dingsbums ['dɪŋsbʊms] (-) (umg) nt
thingummybob (Brit)
Dingsda (-) (umg) nt thingummyjig (Brit)
Dinosaurier [dino'zauriər] m dinosaur
Diözese [diø'tse:zə] (**-, -n**) f diocese
Diphtherie [dɪfte'ri:] f diphtheria
Dipl.-Ing. abk = **Diplom-Ingenieur**
Diplom [di'plo:m] (**-(e)s, -e**) nt diploma;
(Hochschulabschluss) degree; Diplomarbeit f
dissertation
Diplomat [diplo'ma:t] (**-en, -en**) m diplomat
Diplomatie [diploma'ti:] f diplomacy
diplomatisch [diplo'ma:tɪʃ] adj diplomatic
Diplom-Ingenieur m academically qualified

engineer

dir [diːr] *dat von* **du** ▷*pron* (to) you

direkt [diˈrɛkt] *adj* direct; **~ fragen** to ask outright *od* straight out

Direktion [dirɛktsiˈoːn] *f* management; (*Büro*) manager's office

Direktmandat *nt* (*Pol*) direct mandate

Direktor, in *m(f)* (*von Hochschule*) principal; (*von Schule*) principal, head (teacher) (*Brit*)

Direktorium [direkˈtoːriʊm] *nt* board of directors

Direktübertragung *f* live broadcast

Direktverkauf *m* direct selling

Dirigent, in [diriˈgɛnt(ɪn)] *m(f)* conductor

dirigieren [diriˈgiːrən] *vt* to direct; (*Mus*) to conduct

Dirne [ˈdɪrnə] (**-, -n**) *f* prostitute

Dis [dɪs] (**-, -**) *nt* (*Mus*) D sharp

dis [dɪs] (**-, -**) *nt* (*Mus*) D sharp

Disco [ˈdɪsko] (**-, -s**) *f* disco

Disharmonie [dɪsharmoˈniː] *f* (*lit, fig*) discord

Diskette [dɪsˈkɛtə] *f* disk, diskette

Diskettenlaufwerk *nt* disk drive

Disko [ˈdɪsko] (**-, -s**) *f* disco

Diskont [dɪsˈkɔnt] (**-s, -e**) *m* discount; **Diskontsatz** *m* rate of discount

Diskothek [dɪskoˈteːk] (**-, -en**) *f* disco(theque)

diskreditieren [dɪskrediˈtiːrən] *vt* (*geh*) to discredit

Diskrepanz [dɪskreˈpants] *f* discrepancy

diskret [dɪsˈkreːt] *adj* discreet

Diskretion [dɪskretsiˈoːn] *f* discretion; **strengste ~ wahren** to preserve the strictest confidence

diskriminieren [dɪskrimiˈniːrən] *vt* to discriminate against

Diskriminierung *f:* **~ (von)** discrimination (against)

Diskussion [dɪskʊsiˈoːn] *f* discussion; **zur ~ stehen** to be under discussion

Diskussionsbeitrag *m* contribution to the discussion

Diskuswerfen [ˈdɪskʊsvɛrfən] *nt* throwing the discus

diskutabel [dɪskuˈtaːbəl] *adj* debatable

diskutieren [dɪskuˈtiːrən] *vt, vi* to discuss; **darüber lässt sich ~** that sounds like something we could talk about

disponieren [dɪspoˈniːrən] *vi* (*geh: planen*) to make arrangements

Disposition [dɪspozitsiˈoːn] *f* (*geh: Verfügung*): **jdm zur** *od* **zu jds ~ stehen** to be at sb's disposal

disqualifizieren [dɪskvalifiˈtsiːrən] *vt* to disqualify

dissen [ˈdɪsən] (*umg*) *vt* to slag off (*Brit*), to diss (*esp US*)

Dissertation [dɪsɛrtatsiˈoːn] *f* dissertation; doctoral thesis

Dissident, in [dɪsiˈdɛnt(ɪn)] *m(f)* dissident

Distanz [dɪsˈtants] *f* distance; (*fig: Abstand, Entfernung*) detachment; (*Zurückhaltung*) reserve

distanzieren [dɪstanˈtsiːrən] *vr:* **sich von jdm/etw ~** to dissociate o.s. from sb/sth

distanziert *adj* (*Verhalten*) distant

Distel [ˈdɪstəl] (**-, -n**) *f* thistle

Disziplin [dɪstsiˈpliːn] (**-, -en**) *f* discipline

Disziplinarverfahren [dɪstsipliˈnarfɛrfaːrən] *nt* disciplinary proceedings *pl*

dito [ˈdiːto] *adv* (*hum, Comm*) ditto

Diva [ˈdiːva] (**-, -s**) *f* star; (*Film*) screen goddess

divers [diˈvɛrs] *adj* various

Diverses *pl* sundries *pl*; **„~"** "miscellaneous"

Dividende [diviˈdɛndə] (**-, -n**) *f* dividend

dividieren [diviˈdiːrən] *vt:* **~ (durch)** to divide (by)

d. J. *abk* (= *der Jüngere*) jun.

Djakarta [dʒaˈkarta] *nt* Jakarta

DJH *nt abk* (= *Deutsches Jugendherbergswerk*) German Youth Hostel Association

DKP *f abk* (= *Deutsche Kommunistische Partei*) German Communist Party

DLV *m abk* (= *Deutscher Leichtathletik-Verband*) German track and field association

DM *f abk* (*Hist:* = *Deutsche Mark*) DM

d. M. *abk* (= *dieses Monats*) inst.

D-Mark [ˈdeːmark] (**-, -**) *f* (*Hist*) deutschmark

DNS *f abk* (= *Desoxyribo(se)nukleinsäure*) DNA

Do. *abk* = **Donnerstag**

 SCHLÜSSELWORT

doch [dɔx] *adv* **1** (*dennoch*) after all; (*sowieso*) anyway; **er kam doch noch** he came after all; **du weißt es ja doch besser** you know more about it (than I do) anyway; **es war doch ganz interessant** it was actually quite interesting; **und doch, ...** and yet ...

2 (*als bejahende Antwort*) yes I do/it does *etc*; **das ist nicht wahr — doch!** that's not true — yes it is!

3 (*auffordernd*): **komm doch** do come; **lass ihn doch** just leave him; **nicht doch!** oh no!

4: **sie ist doch noch so jung** but she's still so young; **Sie wissen doch, wie das ist** you know how it is(, don't you?); **wenn doch** if only

▷ *konj* (*aber*) but; (*trotzdem*) all the same; **und doch hat er es getan** but still he did it

Docht [dɔxt] (**-(e)s, -e**) *m* wick

Dock [dɔk] (**-s, -s** *od* **-e**) *nt* dock; **Dockgebühren** *pl* dock dues *pl*

Dogge [ˈdɔgə] (**-, -n**) *f* bulldog; **Deutsche ~** Great Dane

Dogma [ˈdɔgma] (**-s, -men**) *nt* dogma

dogmatisch [dɔˈgmaːtɪʃ] *adj* dogmatic

Dohle [ˈdoːlə] (**-, -n**) *f* jackdaw

Doktor [ˈdɔktɔr] (**-s, -en**) *m* doctor; **den ~ machen** (*umg*) to do a doctorate *od* Ph.D.

Doktorand, in [dɔktɔˈrant (-dɪn)] (**-en, -en**) *m(f)* Ph.D. student

Doktor- *zW:* **Doktorarbeit** *f* doctoral thesis; **Doktortitel** *m* doctorate; **Doktorvater** *m* supervisor

doktrinär [dɔktri'nɛːr] *adj* doctrinal; *(stur)* doctrinaire

Dokument [doku'mɛnt] *nt* document

Dokumentar- *zW*: **Dokumentarbericht** *m* documentary; **Dokumentarfilm** *m* documentary (film); **dokumentarisch** *adj* documentary; **Dokumentarspiel** *nt* docudrama

Dokumentationszentrum *nt* documentation centre *(Brit) od* center *(US)*

dokumentieren [dokumɛn'tiːrən] *vt* to document; *(fig: zu erkennen geben)* to reveal, show

Dolch [dɔlç] *(-(e)s, -e) m* dagger; **Dolchstoß** *m* *(bes fig)* stab

dolmetschen ['dɔlmɛtʃən] *vt, vi* to interpret

Dolmetscher, in *(-s, -) m(f)* interpreter

Dolomiten [dolo'miːtən] *pl (Geog)*: **die ~** the Dolomites *pl*

Dom [doːm] *(-(e)s, -e) m* cathedral

Domäne [do'mɛːnə] *(-, -n) f (fig)* domain, province

dominieren [domi'niːrən] *vt* to dominate ▷ *vi* to predominate

Dominikanische Republik [domini'kaːnɪʃə-repu'bliːk] *f* Dominican Republic

Dompfaff ['doːmpfaf] *(-en, -en) m* bullfinch

Dompteur [dɔmp'tøːr] *m (Zirkus)* trainer

Dompteuse [dɔmp'tøːzə] *f (Zirkus)* trainer

Donau ['doːnau] *f*: **die ~** the Danube

Donner ['dɔnər] *(-s, -) m* thunder; **wie vom ~ gerührt** *(fig)* thunderstruck

donnern *vi unpers* to thunder ▷ *vt (umg)* to slam, crash

Donnerschlag *m* thunderclap

Donnerstag *m* Thursday; *siehe auch* **Dienstag**

Donnerwetter *nt* thunderstorm; *(fig)* dressing-down ▷ *interj* good heavens!; *(anerkennend)* my word!

doof [doːf] *(umg) adj* daft, stupid

Dopingkontrolle ['doːpɪŋkɔntrɔlə] *f (Sport)* dope check

Doppel ['dɔpəl] *(-s, -) nt* duplicate; *(Sport)* doubles; **Doppelband** *m (von doppeltem Umfang)* double-sized volume; *(zwei Bände)* two volumes *pl*; **Doppelbett** *nt* double bed; **doppelbödig** *adj (fig)* ambiguous; **doppeldeutig** *adj* ambiguous; **Doppelfenster** *nt* double glazing; **Doppelgänger, in** *(-s, -) m(f)* double; **doppelklicken** *vi* to double-click; **Doppelkorn** *m type of schnapps*; **Doppelpunkt** *m* colon; **doppelseitig** *adj* double-sided; *(Lungenentzündung)* double; **doppelseitige Anzeige** double-page advertisement; **doppelsinnig** *adj* ambiguous; **Doppelstecker** *m* two-way adaptor; **Doppelstunde** *f (Sch)* double period

doppelt *adj* double; *(Comm: Buchführung)* double-entry; *(Staatsbürgerschaft)* dual ▷ *adv*: **die Karte habe ich ~** I have two of these cards; **~ gemoppelt** *(umg)* saying the same thing twice over; **in ~er Ausführung** in duplicate

Doppel- *zW*: **Doppelverdiener** *pl* two-income

family; **Doppelzentner** *m* 100 kilograms; **Doppelzimmer** *nt* double room

Dorf [dɔrf] *(-(e)s, ¨er) nt* village; **Dorfbewohner** *m* villager

dörflich ['dœrflɪç] *adj* village *attrib*

Dorn¹ [dɔrn] *(-(e)s, -en) m (Bot)* thorn; **das ist mir ein ~ im Auge** *(fig)* it's a thorn in my flesh

Dorn² [dɔrn] *(-(e)s, -e) m (Schnallendorn)* tongue, pin

dornig *adj* thorny

Dornröschen *nt* Sleeping Beauty

dörren ['dœrən] *vt* to dry

Dörrobst ['dœroːpst] *nt* dried fruit

dort [dɔrt] *adv* there; **~ drüben** over there; **dorther** *adv* from there; **dorthin** *adv* (to) there

dortig *adj* of that place; in that town

Dose ['doːzə] *(-, -n) f* box; *(Blechdose)* tin, can; **in ~n** *(Konserven)* canned, tinned *(Brit)*

Dosen *pl von* **Dose; Dosis**

dösen ['døːzən] *(umg) vi* to doze

Dosenmilch *f* evaporated milk

Dosenöffner *m* tin *(Brit) od* can opener

Dosenpfand *nt* deposit on drink cans; *(allgemein: Einwegpfand)* deposit on drink cans and disposable bottles

dosieren [do'ziːrən] *vt (lit, fig)* to measure out

Dosis ['doːzɪs] *(-, Dosen) f* dose

Dotierung [do'tiːruŋ] *f* endowment; *(von Posten)* remuneration

Dotter ['dɔtər] *(-s, -) m* egg yolk

Double ['duːbəl] *(-s, -s) nt (Film etc)* stand-in

Download ['daunloːd] *m (Comput)* download

downloaden ['daunloːdən] *vti (Comput)* to download

Downsyndrom *nt no pl (Med)* Down's Syndrome

Doz. *abk =* **Dozent(in)**

Dozent, in [do'tsɛnt(ɪn)] *(-en, -en) m(f)*: **~ (für)** lecturer (in), professor (of) *(US)*

dpa *(-) f abk (= Deutsche Presse-Agentur)* German Press Agency

Dr. *abk =* **Doktor**

Drache ['draxə] *(-n, -n) m (Tier)* dragon

Drachen *(-s, -) m* kite; **einen ~ steigen lassen** to fly a kite; **drachenfliegen** *vi* to hang-glide; **Drachenfliegen** *nt (Sport)* hang-gliding

Dragee, Dragée [dra'ʒeː] *(-s, -s) nt (Pharm)* dragee, sugar-coated pill

Draht [draːt] *(-(e)s, ¨e) m* wire; **auf ~ sein** to be on the ball; **Drahtesel** *m (hum)* trusty bicycle; **Drahtgitter** *nt* wire grating; **drahtlos** *adj* cordless; *(Telefon)* mobile; **Drahtseil** *nt* cable; **Nerven wie Drahtseile** *(umg)* nerves of steel; **Drahtseilbahn** *f* cable railway; **Drahtzange** *f* pliers *pl*; **Drahtzieher, in** *m(f) (fig)* wire-puller

Drall *m (fig: Hang)* tendency; **einen ~ nach links haben** *(Aut)* to pull to the left

drall [dral] *adj* strapping; *(Frau)* buxom

Drama ['draːma] *(-s, Dramen) nt* drama

Dramatiker, in [dra'maːtikər(ɪn)] *(-s, -) m(f)* dramatist

dramatisch [dra'maːtɪʃ] *adj* dramatic

Dramaturg, in [drama'tʊrk (-gɪn)] *(-en, -en)*

m(f) artistic director; (TV) drama producer

dran [dran] *(umg) adv (an der Reihe)*: **jetzt bist du ~** it's your turn now; **früh/spät ~ sein** to be early/late; **ich weiß nicht, wie ich (bei ihm) ~ bin** I don't know where I stand (with him); *siehe auch* **daran**; **dranbleiben** *unreg (umg) vi* to stay close; **dranbleiben** *unreg (umg) vi* to stay close;

Drang **(-(e)s, ¨)** *m (Trieb)* urge, yearning; (*Druck*) pressure; **~ nach** urge *od* yearning for

drang *etc* [draŋ] *vb siehe* **dringen**

drängeln ['drɛŋəln] *vt, vi* to push, jostle

drängen ['drɛŋən] *vt (schieben)* to push, press; (*antreiben*) to urge ▷ *vi (eilig sein)* to be urgent; (*Zeit*) to press; **auf etw** *akk* **~** to press for sth

drangsalieren [draŋza'liːrən] *vt* to pester, plague

dranhalten *(umg) vr* to get a move on

drankommen *(umg: unreg: vi (an die Reihe kommen)* to have one's turn; (*Sch: beim Melden)* to be called; (*Frage, Aufgabe etc*) to come up

drannehmen *(umg: unreg: vt (Schüler)* to ask

drastisch ['drastɪʃ] *adj* drastic

drauf [drauf] *(umg) adv*: **~ und dran sein, etw zu tun** to be on the point of doing sth; *siehe auch* **darauf**; **Draufgänger (-s, -)** *m* daredevil; **draufgehen** *unreg vi (verbraucht werden)* to be used up; (*kaputtgehen*) to be smashed up; **draufhaben** *(umg) unreg vt*: **etw draufhaben** (*können*) to be able to do sth just like that; (*Kenntnisse*) to be well up on sth; **draufzahlen** *vi (fig: Einbußen erleiden)* to pay the price

draußen ['drausən] *adv* outside, out-of-doors

Drechsler, in ['drɛkslər(ɪn)] **(-s, -)** *m(f)* (wood) turner

Dreck [drɛk] **(-(e)s)** *m* mud, dirt; **~ am Stecken haben** (*fig*) to have a skeleton in the cupboard; **das geht ihn einen ~ an** *(umg)* that's none of his business

dreckig *adj* dirty, filthy; **es geht mir ~** *(umg)* I'm in a bad way

Dreckskerl *(umg!) m* dirty swine (!)

Dreh [dreː] *m*: **den ~ raushaben** *od* **weghaben** *(umg)* to have got the hang of it

Dreh- *zW*: **Drehachse** *f* axis of rotation; **Dreharbeiten** *pl (Film)* shooting *sing*; **Drehbank** *f* lathe; **drehbar** *adj* revolving; **Drehbuch** *nt (Film)* script

drehen *vt* to turn, rotate; (*Zigaretten*) to roll; (*Film*) to shoot ▷ *vi* to turn, rotate ▷ *vr* to turn; (*handeln von*): **sich um etw ~** to be about sth; **ein Ding ~** *(umg)* to play a prank

Dreher, in **(-s, -)** *m(f)* lathe operator

Dreh- *zW*: **Drehorgel** *f* barrel organ; **Drehort** *m (Film)* location; **Drehscheibe** *f (Eisenb)* turntable; **Drehtür** *f* revolving door

Drehung *f (Rotation)* rotation; (*Umdrehung, Wendung*) turn

Dreh- *zW*: **Drehwurm** *(umg) m*: **einen Drehwurm haben/bekommen** to be/ become dizzy; **Drehzahl** *f* rate of revolution; **Drehzahlmesser** *m* rev(olution) counter

drei [draɪ] *num* three; **~ viertel** three quarters; **aller guten Dinge sind ~!**

(*Sprichwort*) all good things come in threes!; (*nach zwei missglückten Versuchen*) third time lucky!; **Dreieck** *nt* triangle; **dreieckig** *adj* triangular; **Dreiecksverhältnis** *nt* eternal triangle; **dreieinhalb** *num* three and a half; **Dreieinigkeit** [-ˈaɪnɪçkaɪt] *f* Trinity

dreierlei *adj inv* of three kinds

drei- *zW*: **dreifach** *adj* triple, treble ▷ *adv* three times; **die dreifache Menge** three times the amount; **Dreifaltigkeit** *f* trinity; **Dreifuß** *m* tripod; (*Schemel*) three-legged stool; **Dreigangschaltung** *f* three-speed gear; **dreihundert** *num* three hundred; **Dreikäsehoch** *(umg) m* tiny tot; **Dreikönigsfest** *nt* Epiphany; **dreimal** *adv* three times, thrice; **dreimalig** *adj* three times

dreinblicken ['draɪnblɪkən] *vi*: **traurig** *etc* **~** to look sad *etc*

dreinreden ['draɪnreːdən] *vi*: **jdm ~** (*dazwischenreden*) to interrupt sb; (*sich einmischen*) to interfere with sb

Dreirad *nt* tricycle

Dreisprung *m* triple jump

dreißig ['draɪsɪç] *num* thirty

dreist [draɪst] *adj* bold, audacious

Dreistigkeit *f* boldness, audacity

drei- *zW*: **Dreiviertelstunde** *f* three-quarters of an hour; **Dreivierteltakt** *m*: **im Dreivierteltakt** in three-four time; **dreizehn** *num* thirteen; **jetzt schlägts dreizehn!** *(umg)* that's a bit much

dreschen ['drɛʃən] *unreg vt* to thresh; **Skat ~** *(umg)* to play skat

Dresden ['dreːsdən] **(-s)** *nt* Dresden

dressieren [drɛˈsiːrən] *vt* to train

Dressur [drɛˈsuːr] *f* training; (*für Dressurreiten*) dressage

Dr. h. c. *abk (= Doktor honoris causa)* honorary doctor

driften ['drɪftən] *vi (Naut, fig)* to drift

Drillbohrer *m* light drill

drillen ['drɪlən] *vt (bohren)* to drill, bore; (*Mil*) to drill; (*fig*) to train; **auf etw** *akk* **gedrillt sein** (*fig: umg*) to be practised (*Brit*) *od* practiced (*US*) at doing sth

Drilling *m* triplet

drin [drɪn] *(umg) adv*: **bis jetzt ist noch alles ~** everything is still quite open; *siehe auch* **darin**

dringen ['drɪŋən] *unreg vi (Wasser, Licht, Kälte)*: **~ (durch/in +akk)** to penetrate (through/into); **auf etw** *akk* **~** to insist on sth; **in jdn ~** (*geh*) to entreat sb

dringend ['drɪŋənt] *adj* urgent; **~ empfehlen** to recommend strongly

dringlich ['drɪŋlɪç] *adj* = **dringend**

Dringlichkeit *f* urgency

Dringlichkeitsstufe *f* priority; **~ 1** top priority

drinnen ['drɪnən] *adv* inside, indoors

drinstecken ['drɪnʃtɛkən] *(umg) vi*: **da steckt eine Menge Arbeit drin** a lot of work has gone into it

drischt [drɪʃt] *vb siehe* **dreschen**

dritt *adv*: **wir kommen zu ~** three of us are

coming together

dritte, r, s adj third; **D~ Welt** Third World; **im Beisein D~r** in the presence of a third party

Drittel (-s, -) nt third

drittens adv thirdly

drittklassig adj third-rate, third-class

Dr. jur. abk (= Doktor der Rechtswissenschaften) ≈ L.L.D.

DRK (-) nt abk (= Deutsches Rotes Kreuz) ≈ R.C.

Dr. med. abk (= Doktor der Medizin) ≈ M.D.

droben ['dro:bən] adv above, up there

Droge ['dro:gə] (-, -n) f drug

dröge ['drøgə] (Nordd) adj boring

Drogen- zW: **drogenabhängig** adj addicted to drugs; **Drogenhändler, in** m(f) peddler, pusher; **drogensüchtig** adj addicted to drugs

Drogerie [drogə'ri:] f chemist's shop (Brit), drugstore (US); see culture note

● **DROGERIE**

The Drogerie as opposed to the Apotheke sells medicines not requiring a prescription. It tends to be cheaper and also sells cosmetics, perfume and toiletries.

Drogist, in [dro'gɪst(ɪn)] m(f) pharmacist, chemist (Brit)

Drohbrief m threatening letter

drohen ['dro:ən] vi: **(jdm) ~** to threaten (sb)

Drohgebärde f (lit, fig) threatening gesture

Drohne ['dro:nə] (-, -n) f drone

dröhnen ['drø:nən] vi (Motor) to roar; (Stimme, Musik) to ring, resound

Drohung ['dro:ʊŋ] f threat

drollig ['drɔlɪç] adj droll

Drops [drɔps] (-, -) m od nt fruit drop

drosch etc [drɔʃ] vb siehe **dreschen**

Droschke ['drɔʃkə] (-, -n) f cab

Droschkenkutscher m cabman

Drossel ['drɔsəl] (-, -n) f thrush

drosseln ['drɔsəln] vt (Motor etc) to throttle; (Heizung) to turn down; (Strom, Tempo, Produktion etc) to cut down

Dr. phil. abk (= Doktor der Geisteswissenschaften) ≈ Ph.D.

Dr. theol. abk (= Doktor der Theologie) ≈ D.D.

drüben ['dry:bən] adv over there, on the other side

drüber ['dry:bər] (umg) adv = **darüber**

Druck [drʊk] (-(e)s, -e) m (Zwang, Phys) pressure; (Typ: Vorgang) printing; (: Produkt) print; (fig: Belastung) burden, weight; **~ hinter etw** akk **machen** to put some pressure on sth; **Druckbuchstabe** m block letter; **in Druckbuchstaben schreiben** to print

Drückeberger ['drʏkəbɛrgər] (-s, -) m shirker, dodger

drucken ['drʊkən] vt, vi (Typ, Comput) to print

drücken ['drʏkən] vt (Knopf, Hand) to press; (zu eng sein) to pinch; (fig: Preise) to keep down; (: belasten) to oppress, weigh down ▷ vi to press; to pinch ▷ vr: **sich vor etw** dat **~** to get out of

(doing) sth; **jdm etw in die Hand ~** to press sth into sb's hand

drückend adj oppressive; (Last, Steuern) heavy; (Armut) grinding; (Wetter, Hitze) oppressive, close

Drucker (-s, -) m printer

Drücker (-s, -) m button; (Türdrücker) handle; (Gewehrdrücker) trigger; **am ~ sein** od **sitzen** (fig: umg) to be the key person; **auf den letzten ~** (fig: umg) at the last minute

Druckerei [drʊkə'raɪ] f printing works, press

Druckerschwärze f printer's ink

Druck- zW: **Druckfahne** f galley(-proof); **Druckfehler** m misprint; **Druckknopf** m press stud (Brit), snap fastener; **Druckkopf** m printhead; **Druckluft** f compressed air; **Druckmittel** nt leverage; **druckreif** adj ready for printing, passed for press; (fig) polished; **Drucksache** f printed matter; **Druckschrift** f printing; (gedrucktes Werk) pamphlet; **Drucktaste** f push button; **Druckwelle** f shock wave

drum [drʊm] (umg) adv around; **mit allem D~ und Dran** with all the bits and pieces pl; (Mahlzeit) with all the trimmings pl

Drumherum nt trappings pl

drunten ['drʊntən] adv below, down there

Drüse ['dry:zə] (-, -n) f gland

DSB (-) m abk (= Deutscher Sportbund) German Sports Association

Dschungel ['dʒʊŋəl] (-s, -) m jungle

DSD nt abk (= Duales System Deutschland) German waste collection and recycling service; see culture note

● **DSD**

The DSD (Duales System Deutschland) is a scheme introduced in Germany for separating domestic refuse into two types so as to reduce environmental damage. Normal refuse is disposed of in the usual way by burning or dumping at land-fill sites; packets and containers with a green spot (Grüner Punkt) imprinted on them are kept separate and are then collected for recycling.

dt. abk = **deutsch**

DTC (-) m abk (= Deutscher Touring Automobil Club) German motoring organization

DTP (-) nt abk (= Desktop publishing) DTP

Dtzd. abk (= Dutzend) doz.

du [du:] pron you; **mit jdm per du sein** to be on familiar terms with sb; **Du** nt: **jdm das Du anbieten** to suggest that sb uses "du", suggest that sb uses the familiar form of address

Dübel ['dy:bəl] (-s, -) m plug; (Holzdübel) dowel

dübeln ['dy:bəln] vt, vi to plug

Dublin ['dablɪn] nt Dublin

ducken ['dʊkən] vt (Kopf) to duck; (fig) to take down a peg or two ▷ vr to duck

Duckmäuser ['dʊkmɔʏzər] (-s, -) m yes-man

Dudelsack ['du:dəlzak] m bagpipes pl

Duell [du'ɛl] **(-s, -e)** nt duel

Duett [du'ɛt] **(-(e)s, -e)** nt duet

Duft [dʊft] **(-(e)s, ̈-e)** m scent, odour (Brit), odor (US); **duften** vi to smell, be fragrant

duftig adj (Stoff, Kleid) delicate, diaphanous; (Muster) fine

Duftnote f (von Parfüm) scent

dulden ['dʊldən] vt to suffer; (zulassen) to tolerate ▷ vi to suffer

duldsam adj tolerant

dumm [dʊm] adj stupid; **das wird mir zu ~** that's just too much; **der D~e sein** to be the loser; **der ~e August** (umg) the clown; **du willst mich wohl für ~ verkaufen** you must think I'm stupid; **sich ~ und dämlich reden** to talk till one is blue in the face; **so etwas D~es** how stupid; what a nuisance; **dummdreist** adj impudent

dummerweise adv stupidly

Dummheit f stupidity; (Tat) blunder, stupid mistake

Dummkopf m blockhead

dumpf [dʊmpf] adj (Ton) hollow, dull; (Luft) close; (Erinnerung, Schmerz) vague; **Dumpfheit** f hollowness, dullness; closeness; vagueness

dumpfig adj musty

Dumpingpreis ['dampɪŋpraɪs] m give-away price

Düne ['dy:nə] **(-, -n)** f dune

Dung [dʊŋ] **(-(e)s)** m manure

düngen ['dyŋən] vt to fertilize

Dünger (-s, -) m fertilizer; (Dung) manure

dunkel ['dʊŋkəl] adj dark; (Stimme) deep; (Ahnung) vague; (rätselhaft) obscure; (verdächtig) dubious, shady; **im D~n tappen** (fig) to grope in the dark

Dünkel ['dyŋkəl] **(-s)** m self-conceit; **dünkelhaft** adj conceited

Dunkelheit f darkness; (fig) obscurity; **bei Einbruch der ~** at nightfall

Dunkelkammer f (Phot) dark room

dunkeln vi unpers to grow dark

Dunkelziffer f estimated number of unnotified cases

dünn [dyn] adj thin ▷ adv: **~ gesät** scarce; **Dünndarm** m small intestine; **dünnflüssig** adj watery, thin; **Dünnheit** f thinness; **Dünnschiss** (umg) m the runs

Dunst [dʊnst] **(-es, ̈-e)** m vapour (Brit), vapor (US); (Wetter) haze; **Dunstabzugshaube** f extractor hood

dünsten ['dynstən] vt to steam

Dunstglocke f haze; (Smog) pall of smog

dunstig ['dʊnstɪç] adj vaporous; (Wetter) hazy, misty

düpieren [dy'pi:rən] vt to dupe

Duplikat [dupli'ka:t] **(-(e)s, -e)** nt duplicate

Dur [du:r] **(-, -)** nt (Mus) major

 SCHLÜSSELWORT

durch [dʊrç] präp +akk **1** (hindurch) through; **durch den Urwald** through the jungle;

durch die ganze Welt reisen to travel all over the world

2 (mittels) through, by (means of); (aufgrund) due to, owing to; **Tod durch Herzschlag/ den Strang** death from a heart attack/by hanging; **durch die Post** by post; **durch seine Bemühungen** through his efforts
▷ adj **1** (hindurch) through; **die ganze Nacht durch** all through the night; **den Sommer durch** during the summer; **8 Uhr durch** past 8 o'clock; **durch und durch** completely; **das geht mir durch und durch** that goes right through me

2 (Koch: umg: durchgebraten) done; **(gut) durch** well-done

durcharbeiten vt, vi to work through ▷ vr: **sich durch etw ~** to work one's way through sth

durchatmen vi to breathe deeply

durchaus [dʊrç'aʊs] adv completely; (unbedingt) definitely; **~ nicht** (in verneinten Sätzen: als Verstärkung) by no means; (: als Antwort) not at all; **das lässt sich ~ machen** that sounds feasible; **ich bin ~ Ihrer Meinung** I quite od absolutely agree with you

durchbeißen unreg vt to bite through ▷ vr (fig) to battle on

durchblättern vt to leaf through

Durchblick ['dʊrçblɪk] m view; (fig) comprehension; **den ~ haben** (fig: umg) to know what's what

durchblicken vi to look through; (umg: verstehen) **~ (bei)** to understand (sth); **etw ~ lassen** (fig) to hint at sth

Durchblutung [dʊrç'blu:tʊŋ] f circulation (of blood)

durchbohren vt untr to bore through, pierce

durchboxen ['dʊrçbɔksən] vr (fig: umg): **sich (durch etw) ~** to fight one's way through (sth)

durchbrechen¹ ['dʊrçbrɛçən] unreg vt, vi to break

durchbrechen² [dʊrç'brɛçən] unreg vt untr (Schranken) to break through

durchbrennen unreg vi (Draht, Sicherung) to burn through; (umg) to run away

durchbringen unreg vt to get through; (Geld) to squander ▷ vr to make a living

Durchbruch ['dʊrçbrʊx] m (Öffnung) opening; (Mil) breach; (von Gefühlen etc) eruption; (der Zähne) cutting; (fig) breakthrough; **zum ~ kommen** to break through

durchdacht [dʊrç'daxt] adj well thought-out

durchdenken unreg vt untr to think out

durch- zW: **durchdiskutieren** vt to talk over, discuss; **durchdrängen** vr to force one's way through; **durchdrehen** vt (Fleisch) to mince ▷ vi (umg) to crack up

durchdringen¹ ['dʊrçdrɪŋən] unreg vi to penetrate, get through

durchdringen² [dʊrç'drɪŋən] unreg vt untr to penetrate

durchdringend adj piercing; (Kälte, Wind) biting; (Geruch) pungent

durchdrücken ['dʊrçdrʏkən] vt (durch Presse) to press through; (Creme, Teig) to pipe; (fig: Gesetz, Reformen etc) to push through; (seinen Willen) to get; (Knie, Kreuz etc) to straighten

durcheinander [dʊrçʔaɪˈnandər] adv in a mess, in confusion; (verwirrt) confused; **Durcheinander (-s)** nt (Verwirrung) confusion; (Unordnung) mess; **durcheinanderbringen** vt to mess up; (verwirren) to confuse; **durcheinanderreden** vi to talk at the same time; **durcheinandertrinken** vi to mix one's drinks; **durcheinanderwerfen** vt to muddle up

durch- zW: **durchfahren** unreg vi: **er ist bei Rot durchgefahren** he jumped the lights ▷ vt: **die Nacht durchfahren** to travel through the night; **Durchfahrt** f transit; (Verkehr) thoroughfare; **Durchfahrt bitte freihalten!** please keep access free; **Durchfahrt verboten!** no through road; **Durchfall** m (Med) diarrhoea (Brit), diarrhea (US); **durchfallen** unreg vi to fall through; (in Prüfung) to fail; **durchfinden** unreg vr to find one's way through; **durchfliegen** unreg (umg) vi (in Prüfung): **(durch etw od in etw dat) durchfliegen** to fail (sth); **Durchflug** m: **Passagiere auf dem Durchflug** transit passengers

durchforschen vt untr to explore

durchforsten [dʊrçˈfɔrstən] vt untr (fig: Akten etc) to go through

durchfragen vr to find one's way by asking

durchfressen unreg vr to eat one's way through

durchführbar adj feasible, practicable

durchführen ['dʊrçfyːrən] vt to carry out; (Gesetz) to implement; (Kursus) to run

Durchführung f execution, performance

Durchgang ['dʊrçgaŋ] m passage(way); (bei Produktion, Versuch) run; (Sport) round; (bei Wahl) ballot; **~ verboten** no thoroughfare

durchgängig ['dʊrçgɛŋɪç] adj universal, general

Durchgangs- zW: **Durchgangshandel** m transit trade; **Durchgangslager** nt transit camp; **Durchgangsstadium** nt transitory stage; **Durchgangsverkehr** m through traffic

durchgeben ['dʊrçgeːbən] unreg vt (Rundf, TV: Hinweis, Wetter) to give; (Lottozahlen) to announce

durchgefroren ['dʊrçgəfroːrən] adj (See) completely frozen; (Mensch) frozen stiff

durchgehen ['dʊrçgeːən] unreg vt (behandeln) to go over od through ▷ vi to go through; (ausreißen: Pferd) to break loose; (Mensch) to run away; **mein Temperament ging mit mir durch** my temper got the better of me; **jdm etw ~ lassen** to let sb get away with sth

durchgehend adj (Zug) through; (Öffnungszeiten) continuous

durchgeschwitzt ['dʊrçgəʃvɪtst] adj soaked in sweat

durch- zW: **durchgreifen** unreg vi to take strong action; **durchhalten** unreg vi to last out ▷ vt to keep up; **Durchhaltevermögen** nt staying power; **durchhängen** unreg vi (lit, fig) to sag; **durchhecheln** (umg) vt to gossip about; **durchkommen** unreg vi to get through; (überleben) to pull through

durchkreuzen vt untr to thwart, frustrate

durchlassen unreg vt (Person) to let through; (Wasser) to let in

durchlässig adj leaky

Durchlaucht ['dʊrçlaʊxt] (-, -en) f: **(Euer) ~** Your Highness

Durchlauf ['dʊrçlaʊf] m (Comput) run

durchlaufen unreg vt untr (Schule, Phase) to go through

Durchlauferhitzer (-s, -) m continuous-flow water heater

Durchlaufzeit f (Comput) length of the run

durch- zW: **durchleben** vt untr (Zeit) to live od go through; (Jugend, Gefühl) to experience; **durchlesen** unreg vt to read through; **durchleuchten** vt untr to X-ray; **durchlöchern** vt untr to perforate; (mit Löchern) to punch holes in; (mit Kugeln) to riddle; **durchmachen** vt to go through; **die Nacht durchmachen** to make a night of it

Durchmarsch m march through

Durchmesser (-s, -) m diameter

durchnässen vt untr to soak (through)

durch- zW: **durchnehmen** unreg vt to go over; **durchnummerieren** vt to number consecutively; **durchorganisieren** vt to organize down to the last detail; **durchpausen** vt to trace; **durchpeitschen** vt (lit) to whip soundly; (fig: Gesetzentwurf, Reform) to force through

durchqueren [dʊrçˈkveːrən] vt untr to cross

durch- zW: **durchrechnen** vt to calculate; **durchregnen** vi unpers: **es regnet durchs Dach durch** the rain is coming through the roof; **Durchreiche (-, -n)** f (serving) hatch, pass-through (US); **Durchreise** f transit; **auf der Durchreise** passing through; (Güter) in transit; **Durchreisevisum** nt transit visa; **durchringen** unreg vr to make up one's mind finally; **durchrosten** vi to rust through; **durchrutschen** vi: **(durch etw) durchrutschen** (lit) to slip through (sth); (bei Prüfung) to scrape through (sth)

durchs [dʊrçs] = **durch das**

Durchsage ['dʊrçzaːgə] f intercom od radio announcement

Durchsatz ['dʊrçzats] m (Produktion, Comput) throughput

durchschauen¹ ['dʊrçʃaʊən] vt, vi (lit) to look od see through

durchschauen² [dʊrçˈʃaʊən] vt untr (Person, Lüge) to see through

durchscheinen ['dʊrçʃaɪnən] unreg vi to shine through

durchscheinend adj translucent

durchschlafen ['dʊrçʃlaːfən] unreg vi to sleep through

Durchschlag ['dʊrçʃlaːk] m (Doppel) carbon copy; (Sieb) strainer

durchschlagen unreg vt (entzweischlagen) to split (in two); (sieben) to sieve ▷ vi (zum Vorschein kommen) to emerge, come out ▷ vr to get by

durchschlagend adj resounding; **(eine) ~e Wirkung haben** to be totally effective

Durchschlagpapier nt flimsy; (Kohlepapier) carbon paper

Durchschlagskraft f (von Geschoss) penetration; (fig: von Argument) decisiveness

durch- zW: **durchschlängeln** vr (durch etw: Mensch) to thread one's way through; **durchschlüpfen** vi to slip through; **durchschneiden** unreg vt to cut through

Durchschnitt ['dʊrçʃnɪt] m (Mittelwert) average; **über/unter dem** ~ above/below average; **im** ~ on average; **durchschnittlich** adj average ▷ adv on average; **durchschnittlich begabt/ groß** etc of average ability/height etc

Durchschnitts- zW: **Durchschnittsgeschwindigkeit** f average speed; **Durchschnittsmensch** m average man, man in the street; **Durchschnittswert** m average

durch- zW: **Durchschrift** f copy; **Durchschuss** m (Loch) bullet hole; **durchschwimmen** unreg vt untr to swim across; **durchsegeln** (umg) vi (nicht bestehen): **durch** od **bei etw durchsegeln** to fail od flunk (umg) (sth); **durchsehen** unreg vt to look through

durchsetzen[1] ['dʊrçzɛtsən] vt to enforce ▷ vr (Erfolg haben) to succeed; (sich behaupten) to get one's way; **seinen Kopf** ~ to get one's own way

durchsetzen[2] [dʊrç'zɛtsən] vt untr to mix

Durchsicht ['dʊrçzɪçt] f looking through, checking

durchsichtig adj transparent; **Durchsichtigkeit** f transparency

durch- zW: **durchsickern** vi to seep through; (fig) to leak out; **durchsieben** vt to sieve; **durchsitzen** unreg vt (Sessel etc) to wear out (the seat of); **durchspielen** vt to go od run through; **durchsprechen** unreg vt to talk over; **durchstehen** unreg vt to live through; **Durchstehvermögen** nt endurance, staying power; **durchstellen** vt (Tel) to put through; **durchstöbern** [-'ʃtøːbərn] vt untr to ransack, search through; **durchstoßen** unreg vt, vi to break through (auch Mil); **durchstreichen** unreg vt to cross out; **durchstylen** vt to ponce up (umg); **durchsuchen** vt untr to search; **Durchsuchung** f search; **Durchsuchungsbefehl** m search warrant; **durchtrainieren** vt (Sportler, Körper): **gut durchtrainiert** in superb condition; **durchtränken** vt untr to soak; **durchtreten** unreg vt (Pedal) to step on; (Starter) to kick; **durchtrieben** adj cunning, wily; **durchwachsen** adj (lit: Speck) streaky; (fig: mittelmäßig) so-so

Durchwahl ['dʊrçvaːl] f (Tel) direct dialling; (bei Firma) extension

durch- zW: **durchweg** adv throughout, completely; **durchwursteln** (umg) vr to muddle through; **durchzählen** vt to count ▷ vi to count od number off; **durchzechen** vt untr: **eine durchzechte Nacht** a night of drinking; **durchziehen** unreg vt (Faden) to draw through ▷ vi to pass through; **eine Sache durchziehen** to finish off sth; **durchzucken** vt untr to shoot od flash through; **Durchzug** m (Luft) draught (Brit), draft (US); (von Truppen, Vögeln) passage; **durchzwängen** vt, vr to squeeze od force through

 SCHLÜSSELWORT

dürfen ['dʏrfən] unreg vi **1** (Erlaubnis haben) to be allowed to; **ich darf das** I'm allowed to (do that); **darf ich?** may I?; **darf ich ins Kino?** can od may I go to the cinema?; **es darf geraucht werden** you may smoke
2 (in Verneinungen): **er darf das nicht** he's not allowed to (do that); **das darf nicht geschehen** that must not happen; **da darf sie sich nicht wundern** that shouldn't surprise her; **das darf doch nicht wahr sein!** that can't be true!
3 (in Höflichkeitsformeln): **darf ich Sie bitten, das zu tun?** may od could I ask you to do that?; **wir freuen uns, Ihnen mitteilen zu dürfen** we are pleased to be able to tell you; **was darf es sein?** what can I get you?
4 (können): **das dürfen Sie mir glauben** you can believe me
5 (Möglichkeit): **das dürfte genug sein** that should be enough; **es dürfte Ihnen bekannt sein, dass ...** as you will probably know ...

durfte etc ['dʊrftə] vb siehe **dürfen**

dürftig ['dʏrftɪç] adj (ärmlich) needy, poor; (unzulänglich) inadequate

dürr [dʏr] adj dried-up; (Land) arid; (mager) skinny

Dürre (-, -n) f aridity; (Zeit) drought

Durst [dʊrst] (-(e)s) m thirst; ~ **haben** to be thirsty; **einen über den** ~ **getrunken haben** (umg) to have had one too many

durstig adj thirsty

Durststrecke f hard times pl

Dusche ['dʊʃə] (-, -n) f shower; **das war eine kalte** ~ (fig) that really brought him/her etc down with a bump

duschen vi, vr to have a shower

Duschgelegenheit f shower facilities pl

Düse ['dyːzə] (-, -n) f nozzle; (Flugzeugdüse) jet

Dusel ['duːzəl] (umg) m: **da hat er (einen) ~ gehabt** he was lucky

Düsen- zW: **Düsenantrieb** m jet propulsion; **Düsenflugzeug** nt jet (plane); **Düsenjäger** m jet fighter

Dussel ['dʊsəl] (-s, -) (umg) m twit, berk

Düsseldorf ['dʏsəldɔrf] nt Dusseldorf

dusselig ['dʊsəlɪç], **dusslig** ['dʊslɪç] (umg) adj stupid

düster | D-Zug

düster ['dy:stər] adj dark; (Gedanken, Zukunft) gloomy; Düsterkeit f darkness, gloom; gloominess

Dutzend ['dʊtsənt] (-s, -e) nt dozen; ~(e) Mal a dozen times; Dutzendware (pej) f (cheap) mass-produced item; dutzendweise adv by the dozen

duzen ['du:tsən] vt to address with the familiar "du" form ▷ vr to address each other with the familiar "du" form; siehe auch **siezen**; see culture note

⊜ DUZEN/SIEZEN
⊜
⊜ There are two different forms of address
⊜ in German: du and Sie. Duzen means
⊜ addressing someone as "du" and siezen
⊜ means addressing someone as "Sie". "Du"

⊜ is used to address children, family and
⊜ close friends. Students almost always use
⊜ "du" to each other. "Sie" is used for all
⊜ grown-ups and older teenagers.

Duzfreund m good friend

DVD (-, -s) f abk (= Digital Versatile Disc) DVD

Dynamik [dy'na:mɪk] f (Phys) dynamics; (fig: Schwung) momentum; (von Mensch) dynamism

dynamisch [dy'na:mɪʃ] adj (lit, fig) dynamic; (rentendynamisch) index-linked

Dynamit [dyna'mi:t] (-s) nt dynamite

Dynamo [dy'na:mo] (-s, -s) m dynamo

dz abk = Doppelzentner

D-Zug ['de:tsu:k] m through train; **ein alter Mann ist doch kein** ~ (umg) I am going as fast as I can

Ee

E¹, e [eː] *nt* E, e; **E wie Emil** ≈ E for Edward, E for Easy (US)

E² [eː] *abk* = **Eilzug; Europastraße**

Ebbe ['ɛbə] (-, -n) *f* low tide; **~ und Flut** ebb and flow

eben ['eːbən] *adj* level; *(glatt)* smooth ▷ *adv* just; *(bestätigend)* exactly; **das ist ~ so** that's just the way it is; **mein Bleistift war doch ~ noch da** my pencil was there (just) a minute ago; **~ deswegen** just because of that

Ebenbild *nt*: **das genaue ~ seines Vaters** the spitting image of his father

ebenbürtig *adj*: **jdm ~ sein** to be sb's peer

Ebene (-, -n) *f* plain; *(Math, Phys)* plane; *(fig)* level

eben- *zW*: **ebenerdig** *adj* at ground level; **ebenfalls** *adv* likewise; **Ebenheit** *f* levelness; *(Glätte)* smoothness; **Ebenholz** *nt* ebony; **ebenso** *adv* just as; **ebenso gut** just as well; **ebenso oft** just as often; **ebenso viel** just as much; **ebenso weit** just as far; **ebenso wenig** just as little

Eber ['eːbər] (-s, -) *m* boar

Eberesche *f* mountain ash, rowan

ebnen ['eːbnən] *vt* to level; **jdm den Weg ~** *(fig)* to smooth the way for sb

Echo ['ɛço] (-s, -s) *nt* echo; **(bei jdm) ein lebhaftes ~ finden** *(fig)* to meet with a lively response (from sb)

Echolot ['ɛçoloːt] *nt* (Naut) echo-sounder, sonar

Echse ['ɛksə] (-, -n) *f* (Zool) lizard

echt [ɛçt] *adj* genuine; *(typisch)* typical; **ich hab ~ keine Zeit** (umg) I really don't have any time; **Echtheit** *f* genuineness

Eckball ['ɛkbal] *m* corner (kick)

Ecke ['ɛkə] (-, -n) *f* corner; (Math) angle; **gleich um die ~** just around the corner; **an allen ~n und Enden sparen** (umg) to pinch and scrape; **jdn um die ~ bringen** (umg) to bump sb off; **mit jdm um ein paar ~n herum verwandt sein** (umg) to be distantly related to sb, be sb's second cousin twice removed (hum)

eckig *adj* angular

Eckzahn *m* eye tooth

Eckzins *m* (Fin) minimum lending rate

Ecstasy ['ɛkstəsi] *nt* (Droge) ecstasy

Ecuador [ekua'doːr] (-s) *nt* Ecuador

edel ['eːdəl] *adj* noble; **Edelganove** *m*

gentleman criminal; **Edelgas** *nt* rare gas; **Edelmetall** *nt* rare metal; **Edelstein** *m* precious stone

Edinburg, Edinburgh ['eːdɪnburk] *nt* Edinburgh

EDV (-) *f abk* (= *elektronische Datenverarbeitung*) EDP

EEG (-) *nt abk* (= *Elektroenzephalogramm*) EEG

Efeu ['eːfɔy] (-s) *m* ivy

Effeff [ɛf'ɛf] (-) (umg) *nt*: **etw aus dem ~ können** to be able to do sth standing on one's head

Effekt [ɛ'fɛkt] (-(e)s, -e) *m* effect

Effekten [ɛ'fɛktən] *pl* stocks *pl*; **Effektenbörse** *f* Stock Exchange

Effekthascherei [ɛfɛkthaʃə'raɪ] *f* sensationalism

effektiv [ɛfɛk'tiːf] *adj* effective, actual

Effet [ɛ'feː] (-s) *m* spin

EG (-) *f abk* (= *Europäische Gemeinschaft*) EC

egal [e'gaːl] *adj* all the same; **das ist mir ganz ~** it's all the same to me

egalitär [egali'tɛːr] *adj* (geh) egalitarian

Egge ['ɛgə] (-, -n) *f* (Agr) harrow

Egoismus [ego'ɪsmʊs] *m* selfishness, egoism

Egoist, in *m(f)* egoist; **egoistisch** *adj* selfish, egoistic

egozentrisch [ego'tsɛntrɪʃ] *adj* egocentric, self-centred (Brit), self-centered (US)

eh [eː] *adv*: **seit eh und je** for ages, since the year dot (umg); **ich komme eh nicht dazu** I won't get around to it anyway

e. h. *abk* = **ehrenhalber**

Ehe ['eːə] (-, -n) *f* marriage; **die ~ eingehen** (form) to enter into matrimony; **sie leben in wilder ~** (veraltet) they are living in sin

ehe *konj* before

Ehe- *zW*: **Ehebrecher** (-s, -) *m* adulterer; **Ehebrecherin** *f* adulteress; **Ehebruch** *m* adultery; **Ehefrau** *f* wife; **Eheleute** *pl* married couple *pl*; **ehelich** *adj* matrimonial; *(Kind)* legitimate

ehemalig *adj* former

ehemals *adv* formerly

Ehe- *zW*: **Ehemann** *m* married man; *(Partner)* husband; **Ehepaar** *nt* married couple; **Ehepartner** *m* husband; **Ehepartnerin** *f* wife

eher ['eːər] *adv* (früher) sooner; (lieber) rather, sooner; (mehr) more; **nicht ~ als** not before;

umso ~, als the more so because

Ehe- zW: **Ehering** m wedding ring; **Ehescheidung** f divorce; **Eheschließung** f marriage; **Ehestand** m: **in den Ehestand treten** (form) to enter into matrimony

eheste, r, s ['e:əstə(r, s)] adj (früheste) first, earliest; **am ~n** (am liebsten) soonest; (meist) most; (am wahrscheinlichsten) most probably

Ehevermittlung f (Büro) marriage bureau

Eheversprechen nt (Jur) promise to marry

ehrbar ['e:rba:r] adj honourable (Brit), honorable (US), respectable

Ehre (-, -n) f honour (Brit), honor (US); **etw in ~n halten** to treasure od cherish sth

ehren vt to honour (Brit), honor (US)

Ehren- zW: **ehrenamtlich** adj honorary; **Ehrenbürgerrecht** nt: **die Stadt verlieh ihr das Ehrenbürgerrecht** she was given the freedom of the city; **Ehrengast** m guest of honour (Brit) od honor (US); **ehrenhaft** adj honourable (Brit), honorable (US); **ehrenhalber** adv: **er wurde ehrenhalber zum Vorsitzenden auf Lebenszeit ernannt** he was made honorary president for life; **Ehrenmann** m man of honour (Brit) od honor (US); **Ehrenmitglied** nt honorary member; **Ehrenplatz** m place of honour (Brit) od honor (US); **Ehrenrechte** pl civic rights pl; **ehrenrührig** adj defamatory; **Ehrenrunde** f lap of honour (Brit) od honor (US); **Ehrensache** f point of honour (Brit) od honor (US); **Ehrensache!** (umg) you can count on me; **Ehrentag** m (Geburtstag) birthday; (großer Tag) big day; **ehrenvoll** adj honourable (Brit), honorable (US); **Ehrenwort** nt word of honour (Brit) od honor (US); **Urlaub auf Ehrenwort** parole

Ehr- zW: **ehrerbietig** adj respectful; **Ehrfurcht** f awe, deep respect; **Ehrfurcht gebietend** awesome; (Stimme) authoritative; **Ehrgefühl** nt sense of honour (Brit) od honor (US); **Ehrgeiz** m ambition; **ehrgeizig** adj ambitious; **ehrlich** adj honest; **ehrlich verdientes Geld** hard-earned money; **ehrlich gesagt ...** quite frankly od honestly ...; **Ehrlichkeit** f honesty; **ehrlos** adj dishonourable (Brit), dishonorable (US)

Ehrung f honour(ing) (Brit), honor(ing) (US)

ehrwürdig adj venerable

Ei [aɪ] **(-(e)s, -er)** nt egg; **Eier** pl (umg!: Hoden) balls pl (!); **jdn wie ein rohes Ei behandeln** (fig) to handle sb with kid gloves; **wie aus dem Ei gepellt aussehen** (umg) to look spruce

ei interj well, well; (beschwichtigend) now, now

Eibe ['aɪbə] **(-, -n)** f (Bot) yew

Eichamt ['aɪç|amt] nt Office of Weights and Measures

Eiche (-, -n) f oak (tree)

Eichel (-, -n) f acorn; (Karten) club; (Anat) glans

eichen vt to calibrate

Eichhörnchen nt squirrel

Eichmaß nt standard

Eichung f standardization

Eid [aɪt] **(-(e)s, -e)** m oath; **eine Erklärung an ~es statt abgeben** (Jur) to make a solemn declaration

Eidechse ['aɪdɛksə] **(-, -n)** f lizard

eidesstattlich adj: **~e Erklärung** affidavit

Eid- zW: **Eidgenosse** m Swiss; **Eidgenossenschaft** f: **Schweizerische Eidgenossenschaft** Swiss Confederation; **eidlich** adj (sworn) upon oath

Eidotter nt egg yolk

Eier- zW: **Eierbecher** m egg cup; **Eierkuchen** m pancake; (Omelett) omelette (Brit), omelet (US); **Eierlikör** m advocaat

eiern ['aɪərn] (umg) vi to wobble

Eier- zW: **Eierschale** f eggshell; **Eierstock** m ovary; **Eieruhr** f egg timer

Eifel ['aɪfəl] **(-)** f Eifel (Mountains)

Eifer ['aɪfər] **(-s)** m zeal, enthusiasm; **mit großem ~ bei der Sache sein** to put one's heart into it; **im ~ des Gefechts** (fig) in the heat of the moment; **Eifersucht** f jealousy; **eifersüchtig** adj: **eifersüchtig (auf** +akk**)** jealous (of)

eifrig ['aɪfrɪç] adj zealous, enthusiastic

Eigelb ['aɪgɛlp] **(-(e)s, -e** od **-)** nt egg yolk

eigen ['aɪgən] adj own; (eigenartig) peculiar; (ordentlich) particular; (übergenau) fussy; **ich möchte kurz in ~er Sache sprechen** I would like to say something on my own account; **mit dem ihm ~en Lächeln** with that smile peculiar to him; **sich** dat **etw zu ~ machen** to make sth one's own; **Eigenart** f (Besonderheit) peculiarity; (Eigenschaft) characteristic; **eigenartig** adj peculiar; **Eigenbau** m: **er fährt ein Fahrrad Marke Eigenbau** (hum: umg) he rides a home-made bike; **Eigenbedarf** m one's own requirements pl; **Eigenbrötler, in (-s, -)** m(f) loner, lone wolf; (komischer Kauz) oddball (umg); **Eigengewicht** nt dead weight; **eigenhändig** adj with one's own hand; **Eigenheim** nt owner-occupied house; **Eigenheit** f peculiarity; **Eigeninitiative** f initiative of one's own; **Eigenkapital** nt personal capital; (von Firma) company capital; **Eigenlob** nt self-praise; **eigenmächtig** adj high-handed; (eigenverantwortlich) taken/done etc on one's own authority; (unbefugt) unauthorized; **Eigenname** m proper name; **Eigennutz** m self-interest

eigens adv expressly, on purpose

eigen- zW: **Eigenschaft** f quality, property, attribute; **Eigenschaftswort** nt adjective; **Eigensinn** m obstinacy; **eigensinnig** adj obstinate; **eigenständig** adj independent; **Eigenständigkeit** f independence

eigentlich adj actual, real ▷ adv actually, really; **was willst du ~ hier?** what do you want here anyway?

eigen- zW: **Eigentor** nt own goal; **Eigentum** nt property; **Eigentümer, in (-s, -)** m(f) owner, proprietor; **eigentümlich** adj peculiar; **Eigentümlichkeit** f peculiarity

Eigentumsdelikt nt (Jur: Diebstahl) theft

Eigentumswohnung f freehold flat
Eigenvorsorge f private provision (*for retirement etc*)
eigenwillig adj with a mind of one's own
eignen ['aɪgnən] vr to be suited
Eignung f suitability
Eignungsprüfung f aptitude test
Eignungstest (-(e)s, -s *od* -e) m aptitude test
Eilbote m courier; **per** *od* **durch ~n** express
Eilbrief m express letter
Eile (-) f haste; **es hat keine ~** there's no hurry
Eileiter ['aɪlaɪtər] m (*Anat*) Fallopian tube
eilen vi (*Mensch*) to hurry; (*dringend sein*) to be urgent
eilends adv hastily
Eilgut nt express goods pl, fast freight (*US*)
eilig adj hasty, hurried; (*dringlich*) urgent; **es ~ haben** to be in a hurry
Eil- zW: **Eiltempo** nt: **etw im Eiltempo machen** to do sth in a rush; **Eilzug** m fast stopping train; **Eilzustellung** f special delivery
Eimer ['aɪmər] (-s, -) m bucket, pail; **im ~ sein** (*umg*) to be up the spout
ein, e ['aɪn(ə)] num one ▷ *indef art* a, an
▷ adv: **nicht ~ noch aus wissen** not to know what to do; **E~/Aus** (*an Geräten*) on/off; **er ist ihr E~ und Alles** he means everything to her; **er geht bei uns ~ und aus** he is always round at our place
einander [aɪ'nandər] pron one another, each other
einarbeiten ['aɪn|arbaɪtən] vr: **sich (in etw** *akk*) **~** to familiarize o.s. (with sth)
Einarbeitungszeit f training period
einarmig ['aɪn|armɪç] adj one-armed
einäschern ['aɪn|ɛʃərn] vt (*Leichnam*) to cremate; (*Stadt etc*) to reduce to ashes
einatmen ['aɪn|a:tmən] vt, vi to inhale, breathe in
einäugig ['aɪn|ɔygɪç] adj one-eyed
Einbahnstraße ['aɪnba:nʃtrasə] f one-way street
Einband ['aɪnbant] m binding, cover
einbändig ['aɪnbɛndɪç] adj one-volume
einbauen ['aɪnbauən] vt to build in; (*Motor*) to install, fit
Einbau- zW: **Einbauküche** f (fully-)fitted kitchen; **Einbaumöbel** pl built-in furniture sing; **Einbauschrank** m fitted cupboard
einbegriffen ['aɪnbəgrɪfən] adj included, inclusive
einbehalten ['aɪnbəhaltən] unreg vt to keep back
einberufen unreg vt to convene; (*Mil*) to call up (*Brit*), draft (*US*)
Einberufung f convocation; call-up (*Brit*), draft (*US*)
Einberufungsbefehl m, **Einberufungs-bescheid** m (*Mil*) call-up (*Brit*) *od* draft (*US*) papers pl
einbetten ['aɪnbɛtən] vt to embed
Einbettzimmer nt single room
einbeziehen ['aɪnbətsi:ən] unreg vt to include

einbiegen ['aɪnbi:gən] unreg vi to turn
einbilden ['aɪnbɪldən] vr: **sich** dat **etw ~** to imagine sth; **sich** dat **viel auf etw** akk **~:** *stolz sein*) to be conceited about sth
Einbildung f imagination; (*Dünkel*) conceit
Einbildungskraft f imagination
einbinden ['aɪnbɪndən] unreg vt to bind (up)
einbläuen ['aɪnblɔyən] (*umg*) vt: **jdm etw ~** to hammer sth into sb
einblenden ['aɪnblɛndən] vt to fade in
Einblick ['aɪnblɪk] m insight; **~ in die Akten nehm** to examine the files; **jdm ~ in etw** akk **gewähren** to allow sb to look at sth
einbrechen ['aɪnbrɛçən] unreg vi (*einstürzen*) to fall in; (*Einbruch verüben*) to break in; **bei ~der Dunkelheit** at nightfall
Einbrecher (-s, -) m burglar
einbringen ['aɪnbrɪŋən] unreg vt to bring in; (*Geld, Vorteil*) to yield; (*mitbringen*) to contribute; **das bringt nichts ein** (*fig*) it's not worth it
einbrocken ['aɪnbrɔkən] (*umg*) vt: **jdm/sich etwas ~** to land sb/o.s. in it
Einbruch ['aɪnbrux] m (*Hauseinbruch*) break-in, burglary; (*des Winters*) onset; (*Einsturz, Fin*) collapse; (*Mil: in Front*) breakthrough; **bei ~ der Nacht** at nightfall
einbruchssicher adj burglar-proof
Einbuchtung ['aɪnbuxtʊŋ] f indentation; (*Bucht*) inlet, bay
einbürgern ['aɪnbyrgərn] vt to naturalize
▷ vr to become adopted; **das hat sich so eingebürgert** that's become a custom
Einbürgerung f naturalization
Einbuße ['aɪnbu:sə] f loss, forfeiture
einbüßen ['aɪnby:sən] vt to lose, forfeit
einchecken ['aɪntʃɛkən] vt, vi to check in
eincremen ['aɪnkre:mən] vt to put cream on
eindämmen ['aɪndɛmən] vt (*Fluss*) to dam; (*fig*) to check, contain
eindecken ['aɪndɛkən] vr: **sich ~ (mit)** to lay in stocks (of) ▷ vt (*umg: überhäufen*): **mit Arbeit eingedeckt sein** to be inundated with work
eindeutig ['aɪndɔytɪç] adj unequivocal
eindeutschen ['aɪndɔytʃən] vt (*Fremdwort*) to Germanize
eindösen ['aɪndø:zən] (*umg*) vi to doze off
eindringen ['aɪndrɪŋən] unreg vi: **~ (in** +akk) to force one's way in(to); (*in Haus*) to break in(to); (*in Land*) to invade; (*Gas, Wasser*) to penetrate; **auf jdn ~** (*mit Bitten*) to pester sb
eindringlich adj forcible, urgent; **ich habe ihn ~ gebeten ...** I urged him ...
Eindringling m intruder
Eindruck ['aɪndruk] m impression
eindrücken ['aɪndrykən] vt to press in
eindrucksfähig adj impressionable
eindrucksvoll adj impressive
eine, r, s pron one; (*jemand*) someone; **wie kann ~r nur so dumm sein!** how could anybody be so stupid!; **es kam ~s zum anderen** it was (just) one thing after another; **sich** dat **~n genehmigen** (*umg*) to have a quick one
einebnen ['aɪn|e:bnən] vt (*lit*) to level (off); (*fig*)

to level out

Einehe ['aɪn|eːə] *f* monogamy

eineiig ['aɪn|aɪɪç] *adj (Zwillinge)* identical

eineinhalb ['aɪn|aɪn'halp] *num* one and a half

einengen ['aɪn|ɛŋən] *vt* to confine, restrict

Einer ['aɪnər] **(-)** *m (Math)* unit; *(Ruderboot)* single scull

Einerlei ['aɪnər'laɪ] **(-s)** *nt* monotony; **einerlei** *adj (gleichartig)* the same kind of; **es ist mir einerlei** it is all the same to me

einerseits *adv* on the one hand

einfach ['aɪnfax] *adj* simple; *(nicht mehrfach)* single ▷ *adv* simply; **Einfachheit** *f* simplicity

einfädeln ['aɪnfɛːdəln] *vt (Nadel)* to thread; *(fig)* to contrive

einfahren ['aɪnfaːrən] *unreg vt* to bring in; *(Barriere)* to knock down; *(Auto)* to run in ▷ *vi* to drive in; *(Zug)* to pull in; *(Min)* to go down

Einfahrt *f (Vorgang)* driving in; pulling in; *(Min)* descent; *(Ort)* entrance; *(von Autobahn)* slip road *(Brit)*, entrance ramp *(US)*

Einfall ['aɪnfal] *m (Idee)* idea, notion; *(Lichteinfall)* incidence; *(Mil)* raid

einfallen *unreg vi (einstürzen)* to fall in, collapse; *(Licht)* to fall; *(Mil)* to raid; *(einstimmen):* **~ (in** +*akk*) to join in (with); **etw fällt jdm ein** sth occurs to sb; **das fällt mir gar nicht ein!** I wouldn't dream of it; **sich** *dat* **etwas ~ lassen** to have a good idea; **dabei fällt mir mein Onkel ein, der ...** that reminds me of my uncle who ...; **es fällt mir jetzt nicht ein** I can't think of it *od* it won't come to me at the moment

einfallslos *adj* unimaginative

einfallsreich *adj* imaginative

einfältig ['aɪnfɛltɪç] *adj* simple(-minded)

Einfaltspinsel ['aɪnfaltspɪnzəl] *(umg) m* simpleton

Einfamilienhaus [aɪnfa'miːliənhaʊs] *nt* detached house

einfangen ['aɪnfaŋən] *unreg vt* to catch

einfarbig ['aɪnfarbɪç] *adj* all one colour *(Brit) od* color *(US)*; *(Stoff etc)* self-coloured *(Brit)*, self-colored *(US)*

einfassen ['aɪnfasən] *vt (Edelstein)* to set; *(Beet, Stoff)* to edge

Einfassung *f* setting; border

einfetten ['aɪnfɛtən] *vt* to grease

einfinden ['aɪnfɪndən] *unreg vr* to come, turn up

einfliegen ['aɪnfliːgən] *unreg vt* to fly in

einfließen ['aɪnfliːsən] *unreg vi* to flow in

einflößen ['aɪnfløːsən] *vt:* **jdm etw ~** *(lit)* to give sb sth; *(fig)* to instil sth into sb

Einfluss ['aɪnflʊs] *m* influence; **~ nehmen** to bring an influence to bear; **Einflussbereich** *m* sphere of influence; **einflussreich** *adj* influential

einflüstern ['aɪnflʏstərn] *vt:* **jdm etw ~** to whisper sth to sb; *(fig)* to insinuate sth to sb

einförmig ['aɪnfœrmɪç] *adj* uniform; *(eintönig)* monotonous; **Einförmigkeit** *f* uniformity; monotony

einfrieren ['aɪnfriːrən] *unreg vi* to freeze (in) ▷ *vt*

to freeze; *(Pol: Beziehungen)* to suspend

einfügen ['aɪnfyːgən] *vt* to fit in; *(zusätzlich)* to add; *(Comput)* to insert

einfühlen ['aɪnfyːlən] *vr:* **sich in jdn ~** to empathize with sb

einfühlsam ['aɪnfyːlzaːm] *adj* sensitive

Einfühlungsvermögen *nt* empathy; **mit großem ~** with a great deal of sensitivity

Einfuhr ['aɪnfuːr] **(-)** *f* import; **Einfuhrartikel** *m* imported article

einführen ['aɪnfyːrən] *vt* to bring in; *(Mensch, Sitten)* to introduce; *(Ware)* to import; **jdn in sein Amt ~** to install sb (in office)

Einfuhr- *zW:* **Einfuhrgenehmigung** *f* import permit; **Einfuhrkontingent** *nt* import quota; **Einfuhrsperre** *f* ban on imports; **Einfuhrstopp** *m* ban on imports

Einführung *f* introduction

Einführungspreis *m* introductory price

Einfuhrzoll *m* import duty

einfüllen ['aɪnfʏlən] *vt* to pour in

Eingabe ['aɪngaːbə] *f* petition; *(Dateneingabe)* input; **~/Ausgabe** *(Comput)* input/output

Eingang ['aɪngaŋ] *m* entrance; *(Comm: Ankunft)* arrival; *(Sendung)* post; **wir bestätigen den ~ Ihres Schreibens vom ...** we acknowledge receipt of your letter of the ...

eingängig ['aɪngɛŋɪç] *adj* catchy

eingangs *adv* at the outset ▷ *präp* +*gen* at the outset of

Eingangs- *zW:* **Eingangsbestätigung** *f* acknowledgement of receipt; **Eingangshalle** *f* entrance hall; **Eingangsstempel** *m (Comm)* receipt stamp

eingeben ['aɪngeːbən] *unreg vt (Arznei)* to give; *(Daten etc)* to enter; *(Gedanken)* to inspire

eingebettet ['aɪngəbɛtət] *adj:* **in** *od* **zwischen Hügeln ~** nestling among the hills

eingebildet ['aɪngəbɪldət] *adj* imaginary; *(eitel)* conceited; **~er Kranker** hypochondriac

Eingeborene, r ['aɪngəboːrənə(r)] *f(m)* native

Eingebung *f* inspiration

eingedenk ['aɪngədɛŋk] *präp* +*gen* bearing in mind

eingefahren ['aɪngəfaːrən] *adj (Verhaltensweise)* well-worn

eingefallen ['aɪngəfalən] *adj (Gesicht)* gaunt

eingefleischt ['aɪngəflaɪʃt] *adj* inveterate; **~er Junggeselle** confirmed bachelor

eingefroren ['aɪngəfroːrən] *adj* frozen

eingehen ['aɪngeːən] *unreg vi (Aufnahme finden)* to come in; *(Sendung, Geld)* to be received; *(Tier, Pflanze)* to die; *(Firma)* to fold; *(schrumpfen)* to shrink ▷ *vt (abmachen)* to enter into; *(Wette)* to make; **auf etw** *akk* **~** to go into sth; **auf jdn ~** to respond to sb; **jdm ~** *(verständlich sein)* to be comprehensible to sb; **auf einen Vorschlag/Plan ~** *(zustimmen)* to go along with a suggestion/plan; **bei dieser Hitze/Kälte geht man ja ein!** *(umg)* this heat/cold is just too much!

eingehend *adj* in-depth, thorough

eingekeilt ['aɪngəkaɪlt] *adj* hemmed in; *(fig)*

trapped

eingekesselt ['aɪngəkesəlt] *adj:* ~ **sein** to be encircled *od* surrounded

Eingemachte, s ['aɪngəma:xtə(s)] *nt* preserves *pl*

eingemeinden ['aɪngəmaɪndən] *vt* to incorporate

eingenommen ['aɪngənɔmən] *adj:* ~ **(von)** fond (of), partial (to); ~ **(gegen)** prejudiced (against)

eingeschnappt ['aɪngəʃnapt] (*umg*) *adj* cross; ~ **sein** to be in a huff

eingeschrieben ['aɪngəʃri:bən] *adj* registered

eingeschworen ['aɪngəʃvo:rən] *adj* confirmed; (*Gemeinschaft*) close

eingesessen ['aɪngəzɛsən] *adj* old-established

eingespannt ['aɪngəʃpant] *adj* busy

eingespielt ['aɪngəʃpi:lt] *adj:* **aufeinander ~ sein** to be in tune with each other

Eingeständnis ['aɪngəʃtɛntnɪs] *nt* admission, confession

eingestehen ['aɪngəʃte:ən] *unreg vt* to confess

eingestellt ['aɪngəʃtɛlt] *adj:* **ich bin im Moment nicht auf Besuch ~** I'm not prepared for visitors

eingetragen ['aɪngətra:gən] *adj* (*Comm*) registered; **~er Gesellschaftssitz** registered office; **~es Warenzeichen** registered trademark

Eingeweide ['aɪngəvaɪdə] (**-s, -**) *nt* innards *pl*, intestines *pl*

Eingeweihte, r ['aɪngəvaɪtə(r)] *f(m)* initiate

eingewöhnen ['aɪngəvø:nən] *vr:* **sich ~ (in** +*dat*) to settle down (in)

eingezahlt ['aɪngətsa:lt] *adj:* **~es Kapital** paid-up capital

eingießen ['aɪngi:sən] *unreg vt* to pour (out)

eingleisig ['aɪnglaɪzɪç] *adj* single-track; **er denkt sehr ~** (*fig*) he's completely single-minded

eingliedern ['aɪngli:dərn] *vt:* ~ **(in** +*akk*) to integrate (into) ▷ *vr:* **sich ~ (in** +*akk*) to integrate o.s. (into)

eingraben ['aɪngra:bən] *unreg vt* to dig in ▷ *vr* to dig o.s. in; **dieses Erlebnis hat sich seinem Gedächtnis eingegraben** this experience has engraved itself on his memory

eingreifen ['aɪngraɪfən] *unreg vi* to intervene, interfere; (*Zahnrad*) to mesh

Eingreiftruppe *f* (*Mil*) strike force

eingrenzen ['aɪngrɛntsən] *vt* to enclose; (*fig: Problem*) to delimit

Eingriff ['aɪngrɪf] *m* intervention, interference; (*Operation*) operation

einhaken ['aɪnha:kən] *vt* to hook in ▷ *vr:* **sich bei jdm ~** to link arms with sb ▷ *vi* (*sich einmischen*) to intervene

Einhalt ['aɪnhalt] *m:* ~ **gebieten** +*dat* to put a stop to

einhalten *unreg vt* (*Regel*) to keep ▷ *vi* to stop

einhämmern ['aɪnhɛmərn] *vt:* **jdm etw ~** (*fig*) to hammer sth into sb

einhandeln ['aɪnhandəln] *vt:* **etw gegen** *od*

für etw ~ to trade sth for sth

einhändig ['aɪnhɛndɪç] *adj* one-handed

einhändigen ['aɪnhɛndɪgən] *vt* to hand in

einhängen ['aɪnhɛŋən] *vt* to hang; (*Telefon: auch vi*) to hang up; **sich bei jdm ~** to link arms with sb

einheimisch ['aɪnhaɪmɪʃ] *adj* native

Einheimische, r *f(m)* local

einheimsen (*umg*) *vt* to bring home

einheiraten ['aɪnhaɪra:tən] *vi:* **in einen Betrieb ~** to marry into a business

Einheit ['aɪnhaɪt] *f* unity; (*Maß, Mil*) unit; **eine geschlossene ~ bilden** to form an integrated whole; **einheitlich** *adj* uniform

Einheits- *zW:* **Einheitsfront** *f* (*Pol*) united front; **Einheitsliste** *f* (*Pol*) single *od* unified list of candidates; **Einheitspreis** *m* uniform price

einheizen ['aɪnhaɪtsən] *vi:* **jdm (tüchtig) ~** (*umg: die Meinung sagen*) to make things hot for sb

einhellig ['aɪnhɛlɪç] *adj* unanimous ▷ *adv* unanimously

einholen ['aɪnho:lən] *vt* (*Tau*) to haul in; (*Fahne, Segel*) to lower; (*Vorsprung aufholen*) to catch up with; (*Verspätung*) to make up; (*Rat, Erlaubnis*) to ask ▷ *vi* (*einkaufen*) to buy, shop

Einhorn ['aɪnhɔrn] *nt* unicorn

einhüllen ['aɪnhylən] *vt* to wrap up

einhundert ['aɪn'hʊndərt] *num* one hundred

einig ['aɪnɪç] *adj* (*vereint*) united; **sich** *dat* ~ **sein** to be in agreement; ~ **werden** to agree

einige, r, s *adj, pron* some ▷ *pl* some; (*mehrere*) several; **mit Ausnahme ~r weniger** with a few exceptions; **vor ~n Tagen** a few days ago; **dazu ist noch ~s zu sagen** there are still one or two things to say about that; ~ **Mal** a few times

einigen *vt* to unite ▷ *vr:* **sich (auf etw** *akk*) ~ to agree (on sth)

einigermaßen *adv* somewhat; (*leidlich*) reasonably

einiges *pron siehe* **einige(r, s)**

einiggehen *unreg vi* to agree

Einigkeit *f* unity; (*Übereinstimmung*) agreement

Einigung *f* agreement; (*Vereinigung*) unification

einimpfen ['aɪn|ɪmpfən] *vt:* **jdm etw ~** to inoculate sb with sth; (*fig*) to impress sth upon sb

einjagen ['aɪnja:gən] *vt:* **jdm Furcht/einen Schrecken ~** to give sb a fright

einjährig ['aɪnjɛ:rɪç] *adj of od* for one year; (*Alter*) one-year-old; (*Pflanze*) annual

einkalkulieren ['aɪnkalkuli:rən] *vt* to take into account, allow for

einkassieren ['aɪnkasi:rən] *vt* (*Geld, Schulden*) to collect

Einkauf ['aɪnkaʊf] *m* purchase; (*Comm: Abteilung*) purchasing (department)

einkaufen *vt* to buy ▷ *vi* to shop; ~ **gehen** to go shopping

Einkäufer, in ['aɪnkɔʏfər(ɪn)] *m(f)* (*Comm*) buyer

Einkaufs- *zW:* **Einkaufsbummel** *m:* **einen**

Einkaufsbummel machen to go on a shopping spree; **Einkaufskorb** m shopping basket; **Einkaufsleiter, in** m(f) (Comm) chief buyer; **Einkaufsnetz** nt string bag; **Einkaufspreis** m cost price, wholesale price; **Einkaufswagen** m trolley (Brit), cart (US); **Einkaufszentrum** nt shopping centre

einkehren ['aɪnke:rən] vi (geh: Ruhe, Frühling) to come; **in einem Gasthof ~** to (make a) stop at an inn

einkerben ['aɪnkɛrbən] vt to notch

einklagen ['aɪnkla:gən] vt (Schulden) to sue for (the recovery of)

einklammern ['aɪnklamərn] vt to put in brackets, bracket

Einklang ['aɪnklaŋ] m harmony

einkleiden ['aɪnklaɪdən] vt to clothe; (fig) to express

einklemmen ['aɪnklɛmən] vt to jam

einknicken ['aɪnknɪkən] vt to bend in; (Papier) to fold ▷ vi (Knie) to give way

einkochen ['aɪnkɔxən] vt to boil down; (Obst) to preserve, bottle

Einkommen ['aɪnkɔmən] (**-s, -**) nt income

einkommensschwach adj low-income attrib

einkommensstark adj high-income attrib

Einkommensteuer, Einkommensteuer f income tax; **Einkommensteuererklärung, Einkommensteuererklärung** f income tax return

Einkommensverhältnisse pl (level of) income sing

einkreisen ['aɪnkraɪzən] vt to encircle

einkriegen ['aɪnkri:gən] (umg) vr: **sie konnte sich gar nicht mehr darüber ~, dass ...** she couldn't get over the fact that ...

Einkünfte ['aɪnkʏnftə] pl income sing, revenue sing

einladen ['aɪnla:dən] unreg vt (Person) to invite; (Gegenstände) to load; **jdn ins Kino ~** to take sb to the cinema

Einladung f invitation

Einlage ['aɪnla:gə] f (Programmeinlage) interlude; (Spareinlage) deposit; (Fin: Kapitaleinlage) investment; (Schuheinlage) insole; (Fußstütze) support; (Zahneinlage) temporary filling; (Koch) noodles, vegetables etc (in clear soup)

einlagern ['aɪnla:gərn] vt to store

Einlass ['aɪnlas] (**-es, ⁻e**) m admission; **jdm ~ gewähren** to admit sb

einlassen unreg vt to let in; (einsetzen) to set in ▷ vr: **sich mit jdm/auf etw** akk **~** to get involved with sb/sth; **sich auf einen Kompromiss ~** to agree to a compromise; **ich lasse mich auf keine Diskussion ein** I'm not having any discussion about it

Einlauf ['aɪnlauf] m arrival; (von Pferden) finish; (Med) enema

einlaufen unreg vi to arrive, come in; (Sport) to finish; (Wasser) to run in; (Stoff) to shrink ▷ vt (Schuhe) to break in ▷ vr (Sport) to warm up; (Motor, Maschine) to run in; **jdm das Haus ~** to invade sb's house; **in den Hafen ~** to enter

the harbour

einläuten ['aɪnlɔytən] vt (neues Jahr) to ring in; (Sport: Runde) to sound the bell for

einleben ['aɪnle:bən] vr to settle down

Einlegearbeit f inlay

einlegen ['aɪnle:gən] vt (einfügen: Blatt, Sohle) to insert; (Koch) to pickle; (in Holz etc) to inlay; (Geld) to deposit; (Pause) to have; (Protest) to make; (Veto) to use; (Berufung) to lodge; **ein gutes Wort bei jdm ~** to put in a good word with sb

Einlegesohle f insole

einleiten ['aɪnlaɪtən] vt to introduce, start; (Geburt) to induce

Einleitung f introduction; induction

einlenken ['aɪnlɛŋkən] vi (fig) to yield, give way

einlesen ['aɪnle:zən] unreg vr: **sich in ein Gebiet ~** to get into a subject ▷ vt: **etw in etw** +akk **~** (Daten) to feed sth into sth

einleuchten ['aɪnlɔyçtən] vi: **(jdm) ~** to be clear od evident (to sb)

einleuchtend adj clear

einliefern ['aɪnli:fərn] vt: **~ (in** +akk**)** to take (into); **jdn ins Krankenhaus ~** to admit sb to hospital

Einlieferungsschein m certificate of posting

einlochen ['aɪnlɔxən] (umg) vt (einsperren) to lock up

einlösen ['aɪnlø:zən] vt (Scheck) to cash; (Schuldschein, Pfand) to redeem; (Versprechen) to keep

einmachen ['aɪnmaxən] vt to preserve

Einmachglas nt bottling jar

einmal ['aɪnma:l] adv once; (erstens) first of all, firstly; (später) one day; **nehmen wir ~ an** just let's suppose; **noch ~** once more; **nicht ~** not even; **auf ~** all at once; **es war ~** once upon a time there was/were; **~ ist keinmal** (Sprichwort) once doesn't count; **waren Sie schon ~ in Rom?** have you ever been to Rome?

Einmaleins nt multiplication tables pl; (fig) ABC, basics pl

einmalig adj unique; (einmal geschehend) single; (prima) fantastic

Einmalzahlung f one-off payment

Einmannbetrieb m one-man business

Einmannbus m one-man-operated bus

Einmarsch ['aɪnmarʃ] m entry; (Mil) invasion

einmarschieren vi to march in

einmengen ['aɪnmɛŋən] vr: **sich (in etw** +akk**) ~** to interfere (with sth)

einmieten ['aɪnmi:tən] vr: **sich bei jdm ~** to take lodgings with sb

einmischen ['aɪnmɪʃən] vr: **sich (in etw** +akk**) ~** to interfere (with sth)

einmotten ['aɪnmɔtən] vt (Kleider etc) to put in mothballs

einmünden ['aɪnmʏndən] vi: **~ in** +akk (subj: Fluss) to flow od run into, join; (: Straße: in Platz) to run into; (: in andere Straße) to run into, join

einmütig ['aɪnmy:tɪç] adj unanimous

einnähen ['aɪnnɛ:ən] vt (enger machen) to take in

99

Einnahme ['aɪnna:mə] (-, -n) f (Geld) takings
pl, revenue; (von Medizin) taking; (Mil) capture,
taking; **~n und Ausgaben** income and
expenditure; **Einnahmeausfall** f (Wirts) drop
in takings od revenue; (von Staat) revenue
shortfall; **Einnahmequelle** f source of income
einnehmen ['aɪnne:mən] unreg vt to take;
(Stellung, Raum) to take up; **~ für/gegen** to
persuade in favour of/against
einnehmend adj charming
einnicken ['aɪnnɪkən] vi to nod off
einnisten ['aɪnnɪstən] vr to nest; (fig) to settle
o.s.
Einöde ['aɪn|ø:də] (-, -n) f desert, wilderness
einordnen ['aɪn|ɔrdnən] vt to arrange, fit in
▷ vr to adapt; (Aut) to get in(to) lane
einpacken ['aɪnpakən] vt to pack (up)
einparken ['aɪnparkən] vt, vi to park
einpauken ['aɪnpaʊkən] (umg) vt: **jdm etw ~** to
drum sth into sb
einpendeln ['aɪnpɛndəln] vr to even out
einpennen ['aɪnpɛnən] (umg) vi to drop off
einpferchen ['aɪnpfɛrçən] vt to pen in; (fig) to
coop up
einpflanzen ['aɪnpflantsən] vt to plant; (Med)
to implant
einplanen ['aɪnpla:nən] vt to plan for
einprägen ['aɪnprɛ:gən] vt to impress,
imprint; (beibringen): **jdm etw ~** to impress sth
on sb; **sich** dat **etw ~** to memorize sth
einprägsam ['aɪnprɛ:kza:m] adj easy to
remember; (Melodie) catchy
einprogrammieren ['aɪnprogrami:rən] vt
(Comput) to feed in
einprügeln ['aɪnpry:gəln] (umg) vt: **jdm etw ~**
to din sth into sb
einquartieren ['aɪnkvarti:rən] vt (Mil) to billet;
Gäste bei Freunden ~ to put visitors up with
friends
einrahmen ['aɪnra:mən] vt to frame
einrasten ['aɪnrastən] vi to engage
einräumen ['aɪnrɔʏmən] vt (ordnend) to put
away; (überlassen: Platz) to give up; (zugestehen)
to admit, concede
einrechnen ['aɪnrɛçnən] vt to include;
(berücksichtigen) to take into account
einreden ['aɪnre:dən] vt: **jdm/sich etw ~** to
talk sb/o.s. into believing sth ▷ vi: **auf jdn ~** to
keep on and on at sb
Einreibemittel nt liniment
einreiben ['aɪnraɪbən] unreg vt to rub in
einreichen ['aɪnraɪçən] vt to hand in; (Antrag)
to submit
einreihen ['aɪnraɪən] vt (einordnen, einfügen) to
put in; (klassifizieren) to classify ▷ vr (Auto) to get
in lane; **etw in etw** akk **~** to put sth into sth
Einreise ['aɪnraɪzə] f entry; **Einreisebe-
stimmungen** pl entry regulations
pl; **Einreiseerlaubnis** f entry permit;
Einreisegenehmigung f entry permit
einreisen ['aɪnraɪzən] vi: **in ein Land ~** to enter
a country
Einreiseverbot nt refusal of entry

Einreisevisum nt entry visa
einreißen ['aɪnraɪsən] unreg vt (Papier) to tear;
(Gebäude) to pull down ▷ vi to tear; (Gewohnheit
werden) to catch on
einrenken ['aɪnrɛŋkən] vt (Gelenk, Knie) to put
back in place; (fig: umg) to sort out ▷ vr (fig: umg)
to sort itself out
einrichten ['aɪnrɪçtən] vt (Haus) to furnish;
(schaffen) to establish, set up; (arrangieren) to
arrange; (möglich machen) to manage ▷ vr (in
Haus) to furnish one's house; **sich ~ (auf**
+akk) (sich vorbereiten) to prepare o.s. (for); (sich
anpassen) to adapt (to)
Einrichtung f (Wohnungseinrichtung) furnishings
pl; (öffentliche Anstalt) organization; (Dienste)
service; (Laboreinrichtung etc) equipment;
(Gewohnheit): **zur ständigen ~ werden** to
become an institution
Einrichtungsgegenstand m item of furniture
einrosten ['aɪnrɔstən] vi to get rusty
einrücken ['aɪnrʏkən] vi (Mil: Soldat) to join
up; (: in Land) to move in ▷ vt (Anzeige) to insert;
(Zeile, Text) to indent
Eins [aɪns] (-, -en) f one; **eins** num one; **es ist
mir alles eins** it's all one to me; **eins zu eins**
(Sport) one all; **eins a** (umg) first-rate
einsalzen ['aɪnzaltsən] vt to salt
einsam ['aɪnza:m] adj lonely, solitary; **~e
Klasse/Spitze** (umg: hervorragend) absolutely
fantastic; **Einsamkeit** f loneliness, solitude
einsammeln ['aɪnzaməln] vt to collect
Einsatz ['aɪnzats] m (Teil) insert; (an Kleid)
insertion; (Tischeinsatz) leaf; (Verwendung) use,
employment; (Spieleinsatz) stake; (Risiko) risk;
(Mil) operation; (Mus) entry; **im ~** in action;
etw unter ~ seines Lebens tun to risk one's
life to do sth; **Einsatzbefehl** m order to go into
action; **einsatzbereit** adj ready for action;
Einsatzkommando nt (Mil) task force
einschalten ['aɪnʃaltən] vt (Elek) to switch
on; (einfügen) to insert; (Pause) to make;
(Aut: Gang) to engage; (Anwalt) to bring in ▷ vr
(dazwischentreten) to intervene
Einschaltquote f (TV) viewing figures pl
einschärfen ['aɪnʃerfən] vt: **jdm etw ~** to
impress sth on sb
einschätzen ['aɪnʃetsən] vt to estimate, assess
▷ vr to rate o.s.
einschenken ['aɪnʃeŋkən] vt to pour out
einscheren ['aɪnʃe:rən] vi to get back (into
lane)
einschicken ['aɪnʃɪkən] vt to send in
einschieben ['aɪnʃi:bən] unreg vt to push in;
(zusätzlich) to insert; **eine Pause ~** to have a
break
einschiffen ['aɪnʃɪfən] vt to ship ▷ vr to
embark, go on board
einschl. abk (= einschließlich) inc.
einschlafen ['aɪnʃla:fən] unreg vi to fall asleep,
go to sleep; (fig: Freundschaft) to peter out
einschläfern ['aɪnʃle:fərn] vt (schläfrig
machen) to make sleepy; (Gewissen) to soothe;
(narkotisieren) to give a soporific to; (töten: Tier)

to put to sleep

einschläfernd *adj* (*Med*) soporific; (*langweilig*) boring; (*Stimme*) lulling

Einschlag ['aɪnʃlaːk] *m* impact; (*Aut*) lock; (*fig: Beimischung*) touch, hint

einschlagen ['aɪnʃlaːɡən] *unreg vt* to knock in; (*Fenster*) to smash, break; (*Zähne, Schädel*) to smash in; (*Steuer*) to turn; (*kürzer machen*) to take up; (*Ware*) to pack, wrap up; (*Weg, Richtung*) to take ▷ *vi* to hit; (*sich einigen*) to agree; (*Anklang finden*) to work, succeed; **es muss irgendwo eingeschlagen haben** something must have been struck by lightning; **gut ~** (*umg*) to go down well, be a big hit; **auf jdn ~** to hit sb

einschlägig ['aɪnʃlɛːɡɪç] *adj* relevant; **er ist ~ vorbestraft** (*Jur*) he has a previous conviction for a similar offence

einschleichen ['aɪnʃlaɪçən] *unreg vr* (*in Haus, fig: Fehler*) to creep in, steal in; (*in Vertrauen*) to worm one's way in

einschleppen ['aɪnʃlɛpən] *vt* (*fig: Krankheit etc*) to bring in

einschleusen ['aɪnʃlɔyzən] *vt:* **~ (in** +*akk*) to smuggle in(to)

einschließen ['aɪnʃliːsən] *unreg vt* (*Kind*) to lock in; (*Häftling*) to lock up; (*Gegenstand*) to lock away; (*Bergleute*) to cut off; (*umgeben*) to surround; (*Mil*) to encircle; (*fig*) to include, comprise ▷ *vr* to lock o.s. in

einschließlich *adv* inclusive ▷ *präp* +*gen* inclusive of, including

einschmeicheln ['aɪnʃmaɪçəln] *vr:* **sich (bei jdm) ~** to ingratiate o.s. (with sb)

einschmuggeln ['aɪnʃmʊɡəln] *vt:* **~ (in** +*akk*) to smuggle in(to)

einschnappen ['aɪnʃnapən] *vi* (*Tür*) to click to; (*fig*) to be touchy; **eingeschnappt sein** to be in a huff

einschneidend ['aɪnʃnaɪdənt] *adj* incisive

einschneien ['aɪnʃnaɪən] *vi:* **eingeschneit sein** to be snowed in

Einschnitt ['aɪnʃnɪt] *m* (*Med*) incision; (*im Tal, Gebirge*) cleft; (*im Leben*) decisive point

einschnüren ['aɪnʃnyːrən] *vt* (*einengen*) to cut into; **dieser Kragen schnürt mir den Hals ein** this collar is strangling me

einschränken ['aɪnʃrɛŋkən] *vt* to limit, restrict; (*Kosten*) to cut down, reduce ▷ *vr* to cut down (on expenditure); **~d möchte ich sagen, dass ...** I'd like to qualify that by saying ...

einschränkend *adj* restrictive

Einschränkung *f* restriction, limitation; reduction; (*von Behauptung*) qualification

Einschreibbrief, Einschreibebrief *m* registered (*Brit*) *od* certified (*US*) letter

einschreiben ['aɪnʃraɪbən] *unreg vt* to write in; (*Post*) to send by registered (*Brit*) *od* certified (*US*) mail ▷ *vr* to register; (*Univ*) to enrol; **Einschreiben** *nt* registered (*Brit*) *od* certified (*US*) letter

einschreiten ['aɪnʃraɪtən] *unreg vi* to step in,

intervene; **~ gegen** to take action against

Einschub ['aɪnʃuːp] (**-(e)s, -̈e**) *m* insertion

einschüchtern ['aɪnʃʏçtərn] *vt* to intimidate

Einschüchterung ['aɪnʃʏçtərʊŋ] *f* intimidation

einschulen ['aɪnʃuːlən] *vt:* **eingeschult werden** (*Kind*) to start school

einschweißen ['aɪnʃvaɪsən] *vt* (*in Plastik*) to shrink-wrap; (*Tech*): **etw in etw** *akk* **~** to weld sth into sth

einschwenken ['aɪnʃvɛŋkən] *vi:* **~ (in** +*akk*) to turn *od* swing in(to)

einsehen ['aɪnzeːən] *unreg vt* (*prüfen*) to inspect; (*Fehler etc*) to recognize; (*verstehen*) to see; **das sehe ich nicht ein** I don't see why; **Einsehen (-s)** *nt* understanding; **ein Einsehen haben** to show understanding

einseifen ['aɪnzaɪfən] *vt* to soap, lather; (*fig: umg*) to take in, con

einseitig ['aɪnzaɪtɪç] *adj* one-sided; (*Pol*) unilateral; (*Ernährung*) unbalanced; (*Diskette*) single-sided; **Einseitigkeit** *f* one-sidedness

einsenden ['aɪnzɛndən] *unreg vt* to send in

Einsender, in (**-s, -**) *m(f)* sender, contributor

Einsendeschluss *m* closing date (for entries)

Einsendung *f* sending in

einsetzen ['aɪnzɛtsən] *vt* to put (in); (*in Amt*) to appoint, install; (*Geld*) to stake; (*verwenden*) to use; (*Mil*) to employ ▷ *vi* (*beginnen*) to set in; (*Mus*) to enter, come in ▷ *vr* to work hard; **sich für jdn/etw ~** to support sb/sth; **ich werde mich dafür ~, dass ...** I will do what I can to see that ...

Einsicht ['aɪnzɪçt] *f* insight; (*in Akten*) look, inspection; **zu der ~ kommen, dass ...** to come to the conclusion that ...

einsichtig *adj* (*Mensch*) judicious; **jdm etw ~ machen** to make sb understand *od* see sth

Einsichtnahme (**-, -n**) *f* (*form*) perusal; **„zur ~"** "for attention"

einsichtslos *adj* unreasonable

einsichtsvoll *adj* understanding

Einsiedler ['aɪnziːdlər] (**-s, -**) *m* hermit

einsilbig ['aɪnzɪlbɪç] *adj* (*lit, fig*) monosyllabic; **Einsilbigkeit** *f* (*fig*) taciturnity

einsinken ['aɪnzɪŋkən] *unreg vi* to sink in

Einsitzer ['aɪnzɪtsər] (**-s, -**) *m* single-seater

einspannen ['aɪnʃpanən] *vt* (*Werkstück, Papier*) to put (in), insert; (*Pferde*) to harness; (*umg: Person*) to rope in; **jdn für seine Zwecke ~** to use sb for one's own ends

einsparen ['aɪnʃpaːrən] *vt* to save, economize on; (*Kosten*) to cut down on; (*Posten*) to eliminate

Einsparung *f* saving

einspeichern ['aɪnʃpaɪçərn] *vt:* **etw (in etw** *akk*) **~** (*Comput*) to feed sth in(to sth)

einsperren ['aɪnʃpɛrən] *vt* to lock up

einspielen ['aɪnʃpiːlən] *vr* (*Sport*) to warm up ▷ *vt* (*Film: Geld*) to bring in; (*Instrument*) to play in; **sich aufeinander ~** to become attuned to each other; **gut eingespielt** running smoothly

101

einsprachig ['aɪnʃpraːxɪç] adj monolingual
einspringen ['aɪnʃprɪŋən] unreg vi (aushelfen) to stand in; (mit Geld) to help out
einspritzen ['aɪnʃprɪtsən] vt to inject
Einspritzmotor m (Aut) injection engine
Einspruch ['aɪnʃprʊx] m protest, objection; ~ **einlegen** (Jur) to file an objection
Einspruchsfrist f (Jur) period for filing an objection
Einspruchsrecht nt veto
einspurig ['aɪnʃpuːrɪç] adj single-lane; (Eisenb) single-track
einst [aɪnst] adv once; (zukünftig) one od some day
Einstand ['aɪnʃtant] m (Tennis) deuce; (Antritt) entrance (to office); **er hat gestern seinen ~ gegeben** yesterday he celebrated starting his new job
einstechen ['aɪnʃtɛçən] unreg vt to pierce
einstecken ['aɪnʃtɛkən] vt to stick in, insert; (Brief) to post, mail (US); (Elek: Stecker) to plug in; (Geld) to pocket; (mitnehmen) to take; (überlegen sein) to put in the shade; (hinnehmen) to swallow
einstehen ['aɪnʃteːən] unreg vi: **für jdn ~** to vouch for sb; **für etw ~** to guarantee sth, vouch for sth; (Ersatz leisten) to make good sth
einsteigen ['aɪnʃtaɪgən] unreg vi to get in od on; (in Schiff) to go on board; (sich beteiligen) to come in; (hineinklettern) to climb in; **~!** (Eisenb etc) all aboard!
Einsteiger (-s, -) (umg) m beginner
einstellbar adj adjustable
einstellen ['aɪnʃtɛlən] vt (in Firma) to employ, take on; (aufhören) to stop; (Geräte) to adjust; (Kamera etc) to focus; (Sender, Radio) to tune in to; (unterstellen) to put ▷ vi to take on staff/workers ▷ vr (anfangen) to set in; (kommen) to arrive; **Zahlungen ~** to suspend payment; **etw auf etw** akk **~** to adjust sth to sth; to focus sth on sth; **sich auf jdn/etw ~** to adapt to sb/prepare o.s. for
einstellig adj (Zahl) single-digit
Einstellplatz m (auf Hof) carport; (in Großgarage) (covered) parking space
Einstellung f (Aufhören) suspension, cessation; (von Gerät) adjustment; (von Kamera etc) focusing; (von Arbeiter etc) appointment; (Haltung) attitude
Einstellungsgespräch nt interview
Einstellungsstopp m halt in recruitment
Einstieg ['aɪnʃtiːk] (-(e)s, -e) m entry; (fig) approach; (von Bus, Bahn) door; **kein ~** exit only
einstig ['aɪnstɪç] adj former
einstimmen ['aɪnʃtɪmən] vi to join in ▷ vt (Mus) to tune; (in Stimmung bringen) to put in the mood
einstimmig adj unanimous; (Mus) for one voice; **Einstimmigkeit** f unanimity
einstmalig adj former
einstmals adv once, formerly
einstöckig ['aɪnʃtœkɪç] adj two-storeyed (Brit), two-storied (US)
einstöpseln ['aɪnʃtœpsəln] vt: **etw (in etw**

+akk) **~:** (Elek) to plug sth in(to sth)
einstudieren ['aɪnʃtudiːrən] vt to study, rehearse
einstufen ['aɪnʃtuːfən] vt to classify
Einstufung f: **nach seiner ~ in eine höhere Gehaltsklasse** after he was put on a higher salary grade
einstündig ['aɪnʃtʏndɪç] adj one-hour attrib
einstürmen ['aɪnʃtʏrmən] vi: **auf jdn ~** to rush at sb; (Eindrücke) to overwhelm sb
Einsturz ['aɪnʃtʊrts] m collapse
einstürzen ['aɪnʃtʏrtsən] vi to fall in, collapse; **auf jdn ~** (fig) to overwhelm sb
Einsturzgefahr f danger of collapse
einstweilen adv meanwhile; (vorläufig) temporarily, for the time being
einstweilig adj temporary; **~e Verfügung** (Jur) temporary od interim injunction
eintägig ['aɪntɛːgɪç] adj one-day
Eintagsfliege ['aɪntaːksfliːgə] f (Zool) mayfly; (fig) nine-day wonder
eintauchen ['aɪntaʊxən] vt to immerse, dip in ▷ vi to dive
eintauschen ['aɪntaʊʃən] vt to exchange
eintausend ['aɪntaʊzənt] num one thousand
einteilen ['aɪntaɪlən] vt (in Teile) to divide (up); (Menschen) to assign
einteilig adj one-piece
eintönig ['aɪntøːnɪç] adj monotonous; **Eintönigkeit** f monotony
Eintopf ['aɪntɔpf] m stew
Eintopfgericht ['aɪntɔpfɡərɪçt] nt stew
Eintracht ['aɪntraxt] (-) f concord, harmony
einträchtig ['aɪntrɛçtɪç] adj harmonious
Eintrag ['aɪntraːk] (-(e)s, ̈-e) m entry; **amtlicher ~** entry in the register
eintragen ['aɪntraːgən] unreg vt (in Buch) to enter; (Profit) to yield ▷ vr to put one's name down; **jdm etw ~** to bring sb sth
einträglich ['aɪntrɛːklɪç] adj profitable
Eintragung f: **~ (in** +akk) entry (in)
eintreffen ['aɪntrɛfən] unreg vi to happen; (ankommen) to arrive; (fig: wahr werden) to come true
eintreiben ['aɪntraɪbən] unreg vt (Geldbeträge) to collect
eintreten ['aɪntreːtən] unreg vi (hineingehen) to enter; (sich ereignen) to occur ▷ vt (Tür) to kick open; **in etw** akk **~** to enter sth; (in Klub, Partei) to join sth; **für jdn/etw ~** to stand up for sb/sth
eintrichtern ['aɪntrɪçtərn] (umg) vt: **jdm etw ~** to drum sth into sb
Eintritt ['aɪntrɪt] m (Betreten) entrance; (in Klub etc) joining; **~ frei** admission free; **„~ verboten"** "no admittance"; **bei ~ der Dunkelheit** at nightfall
Eintritts- zW: **Eintrittsgeld** nt admission charge; **Eintrittskarte** f (admission) ticket; **Eintrittspreis** m admission charge
eintrocknen ['aɪntrɔknən] vi to dry up
eintrudeln ['aɪntruːdəln] (umg) vi to drift in
eintunken ['aɪntʊŋkən] vt (Brot): **etw in etw**

akk ~ **to dunk** sth in sth

einüben ['aɪn|y:bən] vt to practise (Brit), practice (US), drill

einverleiben ['aɪnfɛrlaɪbən] vt to incorporate; (Gebiet) to annex; **sich** dat **etw ~** (fig: geistig) to assimilate sth

Einvernehmen ['aɪnfɛrne:mən] (**-s, -**) nt agreement, understanding

einverstanden ['aɪnfɛrʃtandən] interj agreed ▷ adj: ~ **sein** to agree, be agreed; **sich mit etw ~ erklären** to give one's agreement to sth

Einverständnis ['aɪnfɛrʃtɛntnɪs] (**-ses**) nt understanding; (gleiche Meinung) agreement; **im ~ mit jdm handeln** to act with sb's consent

Einwand ['aɪnvant] (**-(e)s, ¨e**) m objection; **einen ~ erheben** to raise an objection

Einwanderer ['aɪnvandərər] m immigrant

Einwanderin f immigrant

einwandern vi to immigrate

Einwanderung f immigration

einwandfrei adj perfect; **etw ~ beweisen** to prove sth beyond doubt

einwärts ['aɪnvɛrts] adv inwards

Einwegflasche ['aɪnve:gflaʃə] f non-returnable bottle

Einwegpfand nt deposit on non-returnables

Einwegspritze f disposable (hypodermic) syringe

einweichen ['aɪnvaɪçən] vt to soak

einweihen ['aɪnvaɪən] vt (Kirche) to consecrate; (Brücke) to open; (Gebäude) to inaugurate; (Person): **in etw** akk **~** to initiate in sth; **er ist eingeweiht** (fig) he knows all about it

Einweihung f consecration; opening; inauguration; initiation

einweisen ['aɪnvaɪzən] unreg vt (in Amt) to install; (in Arbeit) to introduce; (in Anstalt) to send; (in Krankenhaus): **~ (in** +akk) to admit (to)

Einweisung f installation; introduction; sending

einwenden ['aɪnvɛndən] unreg vt: **etwas ~ gegen** to object to, oppose

einwerfen ['aɪnvɛrfən] unreg vt to throw in; (Brief) to post; (Geld) to put in, insert; (Fenster) to smash; (äußern) to interpose

einwickeln ['aɪnvɪkəln] vt to wrap up; (fig: umg) to outsmart

einwilligen ['aɪnvɪlɪgən] vi: **(in etw** akk) **~** to consent (to sth), agree (to sth)

Einwilligung f consent

einwirken ['aɪnvɪrkən] vi: **auf jdn/etw ~** to influence sb/sth

Einwirkung f influence

Einwohner, in ['aɪnvo:nər(ɪn)] (**-s, -**) m(f) inhabitant; **Einwohnermeldeamt** nt registration office; **sich beim Einwohnermeldeamt (an)melden ~** to register with the police; **Einwohnerschaft** f population, inhabitants pl

Einwurf ['aɪnvʊrf] m (Öffnung) slot; (Einwand) objection; (Sport) throw-in

Einzahl ['aɪntsa:l] f singular

einzahlen vt to pay in

Einzahlung f payment; (auf Sparkonto) deposit

einzäunen ['aɪntsɔʏnən] vt to fence in

einzeichnen ['aɪntsaɪçnən] vt to draw in

Einzel ['aɪntsəl] (**-s, -**) nt (Tennis) singles pl

Einzel- zW: **Einzelaufstellung** f (Comm) itemized list; **Einzelbett** nt single bed; **Einzelblattzuführung** f sheet feed; **Einzelfall** m single instance, individual case; **Einzelgänger, in** m(f) loner; **Einzelhaft** f solitary confinement; **Einzelhandel** m retail trade; **im Einzelhandel erhältlich** available retail; **Einzelhandelsgeschäft** nt retail outlet; **Einzelhandelspreis** m retail price; **Einzelhändler** m retailer; **Einzelheit** f particular, detail; **Einzelkind** nt only child

Einzeller ['aɪntsɛlər] (**-s, -**) m (Biol) single-celled organism

einzeln adj single; (von Paar) odd ▷ adv singly; **~ angeben** to specify; **E~e** some (people), a few (people); **der/die E~e** the individual; **das E~e** the particular; **ins E~e gehen** to go into detail(s); **etw im E~en besprechen** to discuss sth in detail; **~ aufführen** to list separately od individually; **bitte ~ eintreten** please come in one (person) at a time

Einzelteil nt individual part; (Ersatzteil) spare part; **etw in seine ~e zerlegen** to take sth to pieces, dismantle sth

Einzelzimmer nt single room

einziehen ['aɪntsi:ən] unreg vt to draw in, take in; (Kopf) to duck; (Fühler, Antenne, Fahrgestell) to retract; (Steuern, Erkundigungen) to collect; (Mil) to call up, draft (US); (aus dem Verkehr ziehen) to withdraw; (konfiszieren) to confiscate ▷ vi to move in; (Friede, Ruhe) to come; (Flüssigkeit): **~ (in** +akk) to soak in(to)

einzig ['aɪntsɪç] adj only; (ohnegleichen) unique ▷ adv: **~ und allein** solely; **das E~e** the only thing; **der/die E~e** the only one; **kein ~es Mal** not once, not one single time; **kein E~er** nobody, not a single person; **einzigartig** adj unique

Einzug ['aɪntsu:k] m entry, moving in

Einzugsauftrag m (Fin) direct debit

Einzugsbereich m catchment area

Einzugsverfahren nt (Fin) direct debit

Eis [aɪs] (**-es, -**) nt ice; (Speiseeis) ice cream; **~ am Stiel** ice lolly (Brit), popsicle® (US); **Eisbahn** f ice od skating rink; **Eisbär** m polar bear; **Eisbecher** m sundae; **Eisbein** nt pig's trotters pl; **Eisberg** m iceberg; **Eisbeutel** m ice pack; **Eiscafé** nt = **Eisdiele**

Eischnee ['aɪʃne:] m (Koch) beaten white of egg

Eisdecke f sheet of ice

Eisdiele f ice-cream parlour (Brit) od parlor (US)

Eisen ['aɪzən] (**-s, -**) nt iron; **zum alten ~ gehören** (fig) to be on the scrap heap

Eisenbahn f railway, railroad (US); **es ist (aller)höchste ~** (umg) it's high time; **Eisenbahner (-s, -)** m railwayman, railway employee, railroader (US); **Eisenbahnnetz** nt rail network; **Eisenbahnschaffner** m railway guard, (railroad) conductor (US); **Eisenbahnüberführung** f footbridge; **Eisenbahnübergang** m level crossing, grade crossing (US); **Eisenbahnwagen** m railway od railroad (US) carriage; **Eisenbahnwaggon**, **Eisenbahnwagon** m (Güterwagen) goods wagon

Eisen- zW: **Eisenerz** nt iron ore; **eisenhaltig** adj containing iron; **Eisenmangel** m iron deficiency; **Eisenwarenhandlung** f ironmonger's (Brit), hardware store (US)

eisern ['aɪzərn] adj iron; (Gesundheit) robust; (Energie) unrelenting; (Reserve) emergency; **der E~e Vorhang** the Iron Curtain; **in etw dat ~ sein** to be adamant about sth; **er ist ~ bei seinem Entschluss geblieben** he stuck firmly to his decision

Eis- zW: **Eisfach** nt freezer compartment, icebox; **eisfrei** adj clear of ice; **eisgekühlt** adj chilled; **Eishockey** nt ice hockey

eisig ['aɪzɪç] adj icy

Eis- zW: **Eiskaffee** m iced coffee; **eiskalt** adj icy cold; **Eiskunstlauf** m figure skating; **Eislaufen** nt ice-skating; **Eisläufer** m ice-skater; **Eismeer** nt: **Nördliches/Südliches Eismeer** Arctic/Antarctic Ocean; **Eispickel** m ice-axe (Brit), ice-ax (US)

Eisprung ['aɪʃprʊŋ] m ovulation

Eis- zW: **Eisschießen** nt ≈ curling; **Eisscholle** f ice floe; **Eisschrank** m fridge, icebox (US); **Eisstadion** nt ice od skating rink; **Eiswürfel** m ice cube; **Eiszapfen** m icicle; **Eiszeit** f Ice Age

eitel ['aɪtəl] adj vain; **Eitelkeit** f vanity

Eiter ['aɪtər] (-s) m pus

eiterig adj suppurating

eitern vi to suppurate

Ei- zW: **Eiweiß** (-es, -e) nt white of an egg; (Chem) protein; **Eiweißgehalt** m protein content; **Eizelle** f ovum

EKD f abk (= Evangelische Kirche in Deutschland) German Protestant Church

Ekel[1] ['e:kəl] (-s) m nausea, disgust; **vor jdm/etw einen ~ haben** to loathe sb/sth

Ekel[2] ['e:kəl] (-s, -) (umg) nt (Mensch) nauseating person

ekelerregend adj nauseating, disgusting

ekelhaft adj, **ekelig** adj nauseating, disgusting

ekeln vt to disgust ▷ vr: **sich vor etw** dat **~** to be disgusted at sth; **es ekelt ihn** he is disgusted

EKG (-) nt abk (= Elektrokardiogramm) ECG

Eklat [e'kla:] (-s) m (geh: Aufsehen) sensation

eklig adj nauseating, disgusting

Ekstase [ɛk'staːzə] (-, -n) f ecstasy; **jdn in ~ versetzen** to send sb into ecstasies

Ekzem [ɛk'tseːm] (-s, -e) nt (Med) eczema

Elan [e'lã:] (-s) m élan

elastisch [e'lastɪʃ] adj elastic

Elastizität [elastitsi'tɛːt] f elasticity

Elbe ['ɛlbə] f (Fluss) Elbe

Elch [ɛlç] (-(e)s, -e) m elk

Elefant [ele'fant] m elephant; **wie ein ~ im Porzellanladen** (umg) like a bull in a china shop

elegant [ele'gant] adj elegant

Eleganz [ele'gants] f elegance

Elektrifizierung [elɛktrifi'tsiːrʊŋ] f electrification

Elektriker [e'lɛktrikər] (-s, -) m electrician

elektrisch [e'lɛktrɪʃ] adj electric

elektrisieren [elɛktri'ziːrən] vt (lit, fig) to electrify; (Mensch) to give an electric shock to ▷ vr to get an electric shock

Elektrizität [elɛktritsi'tɛːt] f electricity

Elektrizitätswerk nt electric power station

Elektroartikel [e'lɛktro|artɪkəl] m electrical appliance

Elektrode [elɛk'troːdə] (-, -n) f electrode

Elektro- zW: **Elektrogerät** nt electrical appliance; **Elektroherd** m electric cooker; **Elektrokardiogramm** nt (Med) electrocardiogram

Elektrolyse [elektro'lyːzə] (-, -n) f electrolysis

Elektromotor m electric motor

Elektron [e'lɛktrɔn] (-s, -en) nt electron

Elektronengehirn, Elektronenhirn nt electronic brain

Elektronenrechner m computer

Elektronik [elɛk'troːnɪk] f electronics sing; (Teile) electronics pl

elektronisch adj electronic; **~e Post** electronic mail

Elektro- zW: **Elektrorasierer** (-s, -) m electric razor; **Elektroschock** m (Med) electric shock, electroshock; **Elektrotechniker** m electrician; (Ingenieur) electrical engineer

Element [ele'mɛnt] (-s, -e) nt element; (Elek) cell, battery

elementar [elemɛn'taːr] adj elementary; (naturhaft) elemental; **Elementarteilchen** nt (Phys) elementary particle

Elend ['eːlɛnt] (-(e)s) nt misery; **da kann man das heulende ~ kriegen** (umg) it's enough to make you scream; **elend** adj miserable; **mir ist ganz elend** I feel really awful

elendiglich ['eːlɛndɪklɪç] adv miserably; **~ zugrunde gehen** to come to a wretched end

Elendsviertel nt slum

elf [ɛlf] num eleven; **Elf** (-, -en) f (Sport) eleven

Elfe (-, -n) f elf

Elfenbein nt ivory; **Elfenbeinküste** f Ivory Coast

Elfmeter m (Sport) penalty (kick)

Elfmeterschießen nt (Sport) penalty shoot-out

eliminieren [elimi'niːrən] vt to eliminate

elitär [eli'tɛːr] adj elitist ▷ adv in an elitist fashion

Elite [e'liːtə] (-, -n) f elite

Elixier [elɪ'ksiːr] (-s, -e) nt elixir

Ellbogen m = **Ellenbogen**

Elle ['ɛlə] (-, -n) f ell; (Maß) ≈ yard

Ellenbogen m elbow; **die ~ gebrauchen** (umg) to be pushy; **Ellenbogenfreiheit** f (fig) elbow room; **Ellenbogengesellschaft** f dog-eat-dog society

Ellipse [ɛ'lɪpsə] (-, -n) f ellipse

E-Lok ['eːlɔk] (-) f abk (= elektrische Lokomotive)

electric locomotive *od* engine
Elsass ['ɛlzas] *nt*: **das ~** Alsace
Elsässer ['ɛlzɛsər] *adj* Alsatian
Elsässer, in (**-s, -**) *m(f)* Alsatian, inhabitant of Alsace
elsässisch *adj* Alsatian
Elster ['ɛlstər] (**-, -n**) *f* magpie
elterlich *adj* parental
Eltern ['ɛltərn] *pl* parents *pl*; **nicht von schlechten ~ sein** (*umg*) to be quite something; **Elternabend** *m* (*Sch*) parents' evening; **Elternhaus** *nt* home; **elternlos** *adj* orphaned; **Elternsprechtag** *m* open day (for parents); **Elternteil** *m* parent
Email [e'maːj] (**-s, -s**) *nt* enamel
E-Mail ['iːmeːl] (**-, -s**) *f* email; **E-Mail-Adresse** *f* email address
e-mailen ['iːmeːlən] *vt* to email
emaillieren [ema'jiːrən] *vt* to enamel
Emanze (**-, -n**) (*pej*) *f* women's libber (*umg*)
Emanzipation [emantsipatsi'oːn] *f* emancipation
emanzipieren [emantsi'piːrən] *vt* to emancipate
Embargo [ɛm'bargo] (**-s, -s**) *nt* embargo
Embryo ['ɛmbryo] (**-s, -s** *od* **-nen**) *m* embryo
Embryonenforschung *f* embryo research
Emigrant, in [emi'grant(ɪn)] *m(f)* emigrant
Emigration [emigratsi'oːn] *f* emigration
emigrieren [emi'griːrən] *vi* to emigrate
Emissionen *pl* emissions *pl*
emissionsarm [emɪsi'oːnsarm] *adj* low in emissions
Emissionshandel *m* emissions trading
Emissionskurs *m* (*Aktien*) issued price
EMNID *m abk* (= *Erforschung, Meinung, Nachrichten, Informationsdienst*) *opinion poll organization*
emotional [emotsio'naːl] *adj* emotional; (*Ausdrucksweise*) emotive
emotionsgeladen [emotsi'oːnsɡəlaːdən] *adj* emotionally-charged
Empf. *abk* = **Empfänger**
empfahl *etc* [ɛm'pfaːl] *vb siehe* **empfehlen**
empfand *etc* [ɛm'pfant] *vb siehe* **empfinden**
Empfang [ɛm'pfaŋ] (**-(e)s, ̈e**) *m* reception; (*Erhalten*) receipt; **in ~ nehmen** to receive; (**zahlbar**) **nach** *od* **bei ~** +*gen* (payable) on receipt (of)
empfangen *unreg vt* to receive ▷ *vi* (*schwanger werden*) to conceive
Empfänger, in [ɛm'pfɛŋər(ɪn)] (**-s, -**) *m(f)* receiver; (*Comm*) addressee, consignee; **~ unbekannt** (*auf Briefen*) not known at this address
empfänglich *adj* receptive, susceptible
Empfängnis (**-, -se**) *f* conception; **empfängnisverhütend** *adj*: **empfängnisverhütende Mittel** contraceptives *pl*; **Empfängnisverhütung** *f* contraception
Empfangs- *zW*: **Empfangsbestätigung** *f* (acknowledgement of) receipt; **Empfangschef** *m* (*von Hotel*) head porter; **Empfangsdame** *f* receptionist; **Empfangsschein** *m* receipt;

Empfangsstörung *f* (*Rundf, TV*) interference; **Empfangszimmer** *nt* reception room
empfehlen [ɛm'pfeːlən] *unreg vt* to recommend ▷ *vr* to take one's leave
empfehlenswert *adj* recommendable
Empfehlung *f* recommendation; **auf ~ von** on the recommendation of
Empfehlungsschreiben *nt* letter of recommendation
empfiehlt [ɛm'pfiːlt] *vb siehe* **empfehlen**
empfinden [ɛm'pfɪndən] *unreg vt* to feel; **etw als Beleidigung ~** to find sth insulting; **Empfinden** (**-s**) *nt*: **meinem Empfinden nach** to my mind
empfindlich *adj* sensitive; (*Stelle*) sore; (*reizbar*) touchy; **deine Kritik hat ihn ~ getroffen** your criticism cut him to the quick; **Empfindlichkeit** *f* sensitiveness; (*Reizbarkeit*) touchiness
empfindsam *adj* sentimental; (*Mensch*) sensitive
Empfindung *f* feeling, sentiment
empfindungslos *adj* unfeeling, insensitive
empfing *etc* [ɛm'pfɪŋ] *vb siehe* **empfangen**
empfohlen [ɛm'pfoːlən] *pp von* **empfehlen** ▷ *adj*: **~er Einzelhandelspreis** recommended retail price
empfunden [ɛm'pfʊndən] *pp von* **empfinden**
empor [ɛm'poːr] *adv* up, upwards
emporarbeiten *vr* (*geh*) to work one's way up
Empore [ɛm'poːrə] (**-, -n**) *f* (*Archit*) gallery
empören [ɛm'pøːrən] *vt* to make indignant; to shock ▷ *vr* to become indignant
empörend *adj* outrageous
emporkommen *unreg vi* to rise; (*vorankommen*) to succeed
Emporkömmling *m* upstart, parvenu
empört *adj*: **~ (über** +*akk*) indignant (at), outraged (at)
Empörung *f* indignation
emsig ['ɛmzɪç] *adj* diligent, busy
End- = **Endkunde**; **Endauswertung** *f* final analysis; **Endbahnhof** *m* terminus; **Endbetrag** *m* final amount
Ende ['ɛndə] (**-s, -n**) *nt* end; **am ~** at the end; (*schließlich*) in the end; **am ~ sein** to be at the end of one's tether; **~ Dezember** at the end of December; **zu ~ sein** to be finished; **zu ~ gehen** to come to an end; **zu ~ führen** to finish (off); **letzten ~s** in the end, at the end of the day; **ein böses ~ nehmen** to come to a bad end; **ich bin mit meiner Weisheit am ~** I'm at my wits' end; **er wohnt am ~ der Welt** (*umg*) he lives at the back of beyond
Endeffekt *m*: **im ~** (*umg*) when it comes down to it
enden *vi* to end
Endergebnis *nt* final result
endgültig *adj* final, definite
Endivie [ɛn'diːviə] *f* endive
End- *zW*: **Endkunde** *m* end customer *od* consumer; **Endlager** *nt* permanent waste disposal site; **Endlagerung** *f* permanent

e

disposal; **endlich** adj final; (Math) finite
▷ adv finally; **endlich!** at last!; **hör endlich
damit auf!** will you stop that!; **endlos** adj
endless; **Endlospapier** nt continuous paper;
Endprodukt nt end od final product; **Endspiel**
nt final(s); **Endspurt** m (Sport) final spurt;
Endstation f terminus

Endung f ending
Endverbraucher m consumer, end-user
Energie [enɛr'giː] f energy; **Energieaufwand** m
energy expenditure; **Energiebedarf** m energy
requirement; **Energieeinsparung** f energy
saving; **Energiegewinnung** f generation of
energy; **energielos** adj lacking in energy,
weak; **Energiequelle** f source of energy;
Energieversorgung f supply of energy;
Energiewirtschaft f energy industry
energisch [e'nɛrgɪʃ] adj energetic; **~
durchgreifen** to take vigorous od firm action
eng [ɛŋ] adj narrow; (Kleidung) tight;
(fig: Horizont) narrow, limited; (Freundschaft,
Verhältnis) close; **~ an etw** dat close to sth; **in
die ~ere Wahl kommen** to be short-listed
(Brit)
Engadin ['ɛŋgadiːn] (-s) nt: **das ~** the Engadine
Engagement [āgaʒə'mãː] (-s, -s) nt
engagement; (Verpflichtung) commitment
engagieren [āga'ʒiːrən] vt to engage ▷ vr to
commit o.s.; **ein engagierter Schriftsteller**
a committed writer
Enge ['ɛŋə] (-, -n) f (lit, fig) narrowness;
(Landenge) defile; (Meerenge) straits pl; **jdn in
die ~ treiben** to drive sb into a corner
Engel ['ɛŋəl] (-s, -) m angel; **engelhaft** adj
angelic; **Engelmacher, in** (-s, -) (umg) m(f)
backstreet abortionist
Engelsgeduld f: **sie hat eine ~** she has the
patience of a saint
Engelszungen pl: **(wie) mit ~ reden** to use all
one's own powers of persuasion
engherzig adj petty
engl. abk = **englisch**
England ['ɛŋlant] nt England
Engländer ['ɛŋlɛndər] (-s, -) m Englishman;
English boy; **die Engländer** pl the
English, the Britishers (US); **Engländerin** f
Englishwoman; English girl
englisch ['ɛŋlɪʃ] adj English
engmaschig ['ɛŋmaʃɪç] adj close-meshed
Engpass m defile, pass; (fig: Verkehr) bottleneck
en gros [āˈgro] adv wholesale
engstirnig ['ɛŋʃtɪrnɪç] adj narrow-minded
Enkel ['ɛŋkəl] (-s, -) m grandson; **Enkelin** f
granddaughter; **Enkelkind** nt grandchild
en masse [āˈmas] adv en masse
enorm [e'nɔrm] adj enormous; (umg: herrlich,
kolossal) tremendous
en passant [āpaˈsã] adv en passant, in passing
Ensemble [āˈsãbəl] (-s, -s) nt ensemble
entarten [ɛntˈ|aːrtən] vi to degenerate
entbehren [ɛnt'beːrən] vt to do without,
dispense with
entbehrlich adj superfluous

Entbehrung f privation; **~en auf sich
nehmen** to make sacrifices
entbinden [ɛnt'bɪndən] unreg vt (+gen) to release
(from); (Med) to deliver ▷ vi (Med) to give birth
Entbindung f release; (Med) delivery, birth
Entbindungsheim nt maternity hospital
Entbindungsstation f maternity ward
entblößen [ɛnt'bløːsən] vt to denude, uncover;
(berauben): **einer Sache** gen **entblößt** deprived
of sth
entbrennen [ɛnt'brɛnən] unreg vi (liter: Kampf,
Streit) to flare up; (: Liebe) to be aroused
entdecken [ɛnt'dɛkən] vt to discover; **jdm etw
~** to disclose sth to sb
Entdecker, in (-s, -) m(f) discoverer
Entdeckung f discovery
Ente ['ɛntə] (-, -n) f duck; (fig) canard, false
report; (Aut) Citroën 2CV, deux-chevaux
entehren [ɛntˈ|eːrən] vt to dishonour (Brit),
dishonor (US), disgrace
enteignen [ɛntˈ|aɪgnən] vt to expropriate;
(Besitzer) to dispossess
enteisen [ɛntˈ|aɪzən] vt to de-ice; (Kühlschrank)
to defrost
enterben [ɛntˈ|ɛrbən] vt to disinherit
Enterhaken ['ɛntərhaːkən] m grappling iron
od hook
entfachen [ɛnt'faxən] vt to kindle
entfallen [ɛnt'falən] unreg vi to drop, fall;
(wegfallen) to be dropped; **jdm ~** (vergessen) to
slip sb's memory; **auf jdn ~** to be allotted to sb
entfalten [ɛnt'faltən] vt to unfold; (Talente) to
develop ▷ vr to open; (Mensch) to develop one's
potential
Entfaltung f unfolding; (von Talenten)
development
entfernen [ɛnt'fɛrnən] vt to remove;
(hinauswerfen) to expel ▷ vr to go away, retire,
withdraw
entfernt adj distant ▷ adv: **nicht im E~esten!**
not in the slightest!; **weit davon ~ sein, etw
zu tun** to be far from doing sth
Entfernung f distance; (Wegschaffen) removal;
unerlaubte ~ von der Truppe absence
without leave
Entfernungsmesser m (Phot) rangefinder
entfesseln [ɛnt'fɛsəln] vt (fig) to arouse
entfetten [ɛnt'fɛtən] vt to take the fat from
entflammen [ɛnt'flamən] vt (fig) to (a)rouse
▷ vi to burst into flames; (fig: Streit) to flare up;
(: Leidenschaft) to be (a)roused od inflamed
entfremden [ɛnt'frɛmdən] vt to estrange,
alienate
Entfremdung f estrangement, alienation
entfrosten [ɛnt'frɔstən] vt to defrost
Entfroster (-s, -) m (Aut) defroster
entführen [ɛnt'fyːrən] vt to abduct, kidnap;
(Flugzeug) to hijack
Entführer (-s, -) m kidnapper (Brit), kidnaper
(US); hijacker
Entführung f abduction, kidnapping (Brit),
kidnaping (US); hijacking
entgegen [ɛnt'geːgən] präp+dat contrary to,

against ▷ *adv* towards; **entgegenbringen** *unreg* *vt* to bring; (*fig*): **jdm etw entgegenbringen** to show sb sth; **entgegengehen** *unreg* *vi* +*dat* to go to meet, go towards; **Schwierigkeiten entgegengehen** to be heading for difficulties; **entgegengesetzt** *adj* opposite; (*widersprechend*) opposed; **entgegenhalten** *unreg* *vt* (*fig*): **einer Sache** *dat* **entgegenhalten, dass ...** to object to sth that ...; **Entgegenkommen** *nt* obligingness; **entgegenkommen** *unreg* *vi* +*dat* to come towards, approach; (*fig*): **jdm entgegenkommen** to accommodate sb; **das kommt unseren Plänen sehr entgegen** that fits in very well with our plans; **entgegenkommend** *adj* obliging; **entgegenlaufen** *unreg* *vi* +*dat* to run towards *od* to meet; (*fig*) to run counter to; **Entgegennahme** *f* (*form: Empfang*) receipt; (*Annahme*) acceptance; **entgegennehmen** *unreg* *vt* to receive, accept; **entgegensehen** *unreg* *vi* +*dat* to await; **entgegensetzen** *vt* to oppose; **dem habe ich entgegenzusetzen, dass ...** against that I'd like to say that ...; **jdm/etw Widerstand entgegensetzen** to put up resistance to sb/sth; **entgegenstehen** *unreg* *vi*: **dem steht nichts entgegen** there's no objection to that; **entgegentreten** *unreg* *vi* +*dat* (*lit*) to step up to; (*fig*) to oppose, counter; **entgegenwirken** *vi* +*dat* to counteract
entgegnen [ɛnt'geːgnən] *vt* to reply, retort
Entgegnung *f* reply, retort
entgehen [ɛnt'geːən] *unreg* *vi* (*fig*): **jdm ~** to escape sb's notice; **sich** *dat* **etw ~ lassen** to miss sth
entgeistert [ɛnt'gaɪstərt] *adj* thunderstruck
Entgelt [ɛnt'gɛlt] **(-(e)s, -e)** *nt* remuneration
entgelten *unreg* *vt*: **jdm etw ~** to repay sb for sth
entgleisen [ɛnt'glaɪzən] *vi* (*Eisenb*) to be derailed; (*fig: Person*) to misbehave; **~ lassen** to derail
Entgleisung *f* derailment; (*fig*) faux pas, gaffe
entgleiten [ɛnt'glaɪtən] *unreg* *vi*: **jdm ~** to slip from sb's hand
entgräten [ɛnt'grɛːtən] *vt* to fillet, bone
Enthaarungsmittel [ɛnt'haːrʊŋsmɪtəl] *nt* depilatory
enthält [ɛnt'hɛlt] *vb siehe* **enthalten**
enthalten [ɛnt'haltən] *unreg* *vt* to contain ▷ *vr* +*gen* to abstain from, refrain from; **sich (der Stimme) ~** to abstain
enthaltsam [ɛnt'haltzaːm] *adj* abstinent, abstemious; **Enthaltsamkeit** *f* abstinence
enthärten [ɛnt'hɛrtən] *vt* (*Wasser*) to soften; (*Metall*) to anneal
enthaupten [ɛnt'haʊptən] *vt* to decapitate; (*als Hinrichtung*) to behead
enthäuten [ɛnt'hɔʏtən] *vt* to skin
entheben [ɛnt'heːbən] *unreg* *vt*: **jdn einer Sache** *gen* **~** to relieve sb of sth
enthemmen [ɛnt'hɛmən] *vt*: **jdn ~** to free sb from his/her inhibitions
enthielt *etc* [ɛnt'hiːlt] *vb siehe* **enthalten**

enthüllen [ɛnt'hʏlən] *vt* to reveal, unveil
Enthüllung *f* revelation; (*von Skandal*) exposure
Enthusiasmus [ɛntuzi'asmʊs] *m* enthusiasm
entjungfern [ɛnt'jʊŋfərn] *vt* to deflower
entkalken [ɛnt'kalkən] *vt* to decalcify
entkernen [ɛnt'kɛrnən] *vt* (*Kernobst*) to core; (*Steinobst*) to stone
entkleiden [ɛnt'klaɪdən] *vt*, *vr* (*geh*) to undress
entkommen [ɛnt'kɔmən] *unreg* *vi* to get away, escape; **jdm/etw** *od* **aus etw ~** to get away *od* escape from sb/sth
entkorken [ɛnt'kɔrkən] *vt* to uncork
entkräften [ɛnt'krɛftən] *vt* to weaken, exhaust; (*Argument*) to refute
entkrampfen [ɛnt'krampfən] *vt* (*fig*) to relax, ease
entladen [ɛnt'laːdən] *unreg* *vt* to unload; (*Elek*) to discharge ▷ *vr* (*Gewehr, Elek*) to discharge; (*Ärger etc*) to vent itself
entlang [ɛnt'laŋ] *präp* (+*akk od dat*) along ▷ *adv* along; **~ dem Fluss, den Fluss entlang** along the river; **hier ~** this way; **entlanggehen** *unreg* *vi* to walk along
entlarven [ɛnt'larfən] *vt* to unmask, expose
entlassen [ɛnt'lasən] *unreg* *vt* to discharge; (*Arbeiter*) to dismiss; (*nach Stellenabbau*) to make redundant
entlässt [ɛnt'lɛst] *vb siehe* **entlassen**
Entlassung *f* discharge; dismissal; **es gab 20 ~en** there were 20 redundancies
Entlassungswelle *f* wave of redundancies *od* job losses
Entlassungszeugnis *nt* (*Sch*) school-leaving certificate
entlasten [ɛnt'lastən] *vt* to relieve; (*Arbeit abnehmen*) to take some of the load off; (*Angeklagte*) to exonerate; (*Konto*) to clear
Entlastung *f* relief; (*Comm*) crediting
Entlastungszeuge *m* defence (*Brit*) *od* defense (*US*) witness
Entlastungszug *m* relief train
entledigen [ɛnt'leːdɪgən] *vr*: **sich jds/einer Sache ~** to rid o.s. of sb/sth
entleeren [ɛnt'leːrən] *vt* to empty; (*Darm*) to evacuate
entlegen [ɛnt'leːgən] *adj* remote
entließ *etc* [ɛnt'liːs] *vb siehe* **entlassen**
entlocken [ɛnt'lɔkən] *vt*: **jdm etw ~** to elicit sth from sb
entlohnen *vt* to pay; (*fig*) to reward
entlüften [ɛnt'lʏftən] *vt* to ventilate
entmachten [ɛnt'maxtən] *vt* to deprive of power
entmenscht [ɛnt'mɛnʃt] *adj* inhuman, bestial
entmilitarisiert [ɛntmilitari'ziːrt] *adj* demilitarized
entmündigen [ɛnt'mʏndɪgən] *vt* to certify; (*Jur*) to (legally) incapacitate, declare incapable of managing one's own affairs
entmutigen [ɛnt'muːtɪgən] *vt* to discourage
Entnahme [ɛnt'naːmə] **(-, -n)** *f* removal, withdrawal
Entnazifizierung [ɛntnatsifi'tsiːrʊŋ] *f*

e

denazification

entnehmen [ɛntˈneːmən] *unreg vt +dat* to take out of, take from; *(folgern)* to infer from; **wie ich Ihren Worten entnehme, ...** I gather from what you say that ...

entpuppen [ɛntˈpʊpən] *vr (fig)* to reveal o.s., turn out; **sich als etw ~** to turn out to be sth

entrahmen [ɛntˈraːmən] *vt* to skim

entreißen [ɛntˈraɪsən] *unreg vt*: **jdm etw ~** to snatch sth (away) from sb

entrichten [ɛntˈrɪçtən] *vt (form)* to pay

entrosten [ɛntˈrɔstən] *vt* to derust

entrüsten [ɛntˈrʏstən] *vt* to incense, outrage ▷ *vr* to be filled with indignation

entrüstet *adj* indignant, outraged

Entrüstung *f* indignation

Entsafter [ɛntˈzaftər] (**-s, -**) *m* juice extractor

entsagen [ɛntˈzaːgən] *vi +dat* to renounce

entschädigen [ɛntˈʃɛːdɪgən] *vt* to compensate

Entschädigung *f* compensation

entschärfen [ɛntˈʃɛrfən] *vt* to defuse; *(Kritik)* to tone down

Entscheid [ɛntˈʃaɪt] (**-(e)s, -e**) *m (form)* decision

entscheiden *unreg vt, vi, vr* to decide; **darüber habe ich nicht zu ~** that is not for me to decide; **sich für jdn/etw ~** to decide in favour of sb/sth; to decide on sb/sth

entscheidend *adj* decisive; *(Stimme)* casting; **das E~e** the decisive *od* deciding factor

Entscheidung *f* decision; **wie ist die ~ ausgefallen?** which way did the decision go?

Entscheidungs- *zW:* **Entscheidungsbefugnis** *f* decision-making powers *pl;* **entscheidungsfähig** *adj* capable of deciding; **Entscheidungsspiel** *nt* play-off; **Entscheidungsträger** *m* decision-maker

entschied *etc* [ɛntˈʃiːt] *vb siehe* **entscheiden**

entschieden [ɛntˈʃiːdən] *pp von* **entscheiden** ▷ *adj* decided; *(entschlossen)* resolute; **das geht ~ zu weit** that's definitely going too far; **Entschiedenheit** *f* firmness, determination

entschlacken [ɛntˈʃlakən] *vt (Med: Körper)* to purify

entschließen [ɛntˈʃliːsən] *unreg vr* to decide; **sich zu nichts ~ können** to be unable to make up one's mind; **kurz entschlossen** straight away

Entschließungsantrag *m (Pol)* resolution proposal

entschloss *etc* [ɛntˈʃlɔs] *vb siehe* **entschließen**

entschlossen [ɛntˈʃlɔsən] *pp von* **entschließen** ▷ *adj* determined, resolute; **Entschlossenheit** *f* determination

entschlüpfen [ɛntˈʃlʏpfən] *vi* to escape, slip away; *(fig: Wort etc)* to slip out

Entschluss [ɛntˈʃlʊs] *m* decision; **aus eigenem ~ handeln** to act on one's own initiative; **es ist mein fester ~** it is my firm intention

entschlüsseln [ɛntˈʃlʏsəln] *vt* to decipher; *(Funkspruch)* to decode

entschlussfreudig *adj* decisive

Entschlusskraft *f* determination, decisiveness

entschuldbar [ɛntˈʃʊltbaːr] *adj* excusable

entschuldigen [ɛntˈʃʊldɪgən] *vt* to excuse ▷ *vr* to apologize ▷ *vi*: **~ Sie (bitte)!** excuse me; *(Verzeihung)* sorry; **jdn bei jdm ~** to make sb's excuses *od* apologies to sb; **sich ~ lassen** to send one's apologies

entschuldigend *adj* apologetic

Entschuldigung *f* apology; *(Grund)* excuse; **jdn um ~ bitten** to apologize to sb; **~!** excuse me; *(Verzeihung)* sorry

entschwefeln [ɛntˈʃveːfəln] *vt* to desulphurize

Entschwefelungsanlage *f* desulphurization plant

entschwinden [ɛntˈʃvɪndən] *unreg vi* to disappear

entsetzen [ɛntˈzɛtsən] *vt* to horrify ▷ *vr* to be horrified *od* appalled; **Entsetzen** (**-s**) *nt* horror, dismay

entsetzlich *adj* dreadful, appalling

entsetzt *adj* horrified

entsichern [ɛntˈzɪçərn] *vt* to release the safety catch of

entsinnen [ɛntˈzɪnən] *unreg vr +gen* to remember

entsorgen [ɛntˈzɔrgən] *vt*: **eine Stadt ~** to dispose of a town's refuse and sewage

Entsorgung *f* waste disposal; *(von Chemikalien)* disposal

entspannen [ɛntˈʃpanən] *vt, vr (Körper)* to relax; *(Pol: Lage)* to ease

Entspannung *f* relaxation, rest; *(Pol)* détente

Entspannungspolitik *f* policy of détente

Entspannungsübungen *pl* relaxation exercises *pl*

entspr. *abk* = **entsprechend**

entsprach *etc* [ɛntˈʃprax] *vb siehe* **entsprechen**

entsprechen [ɛntˈʃprɛçən] *unreg vi +dat* to correspond to; *(Anforderungen, Wünschen)* to meet, comply with

entsprechend *adj* appropriate ▷ *adv* accordingly ▷ *präp +dat*: **er wird seiner Leistung ~ bezahlt** he is paid according to output

entspricht [ɛntˈʃprɪçt] *vb siehe* **entsprechen**

entspringen [ɛntˈʃprɪŋən] *unreg vi (+dat)* to spring (from)

entsprochen [ɛntˈʃprɔxən] *pp von* **entsprechen**

entstaatlichen [ɛntˈʃtaːtlɪçən] *vt* to denationalize

entstammen [ɛntˈʃtamən] *vi +dat* to stem *od* come from

entstand *etc* [ɛntˈʃtant] *vb siehe* **entstehen**

entstanden [ɛntˈʃtandən] *pp von* **entstehen**

entstehen [ɛntˈʃteːən] *unreg vi*: **~ (aus** *od* **durch)** to arise (from), result (from); **wir wollen nicht den Eindruck ~ lassen, ...** we don't want to give rise to the impression that ...; **für ~den** *od* **entstandenen Schaden** for damages incurred

Entstehung *f* genesis, origin

entstellen [ɛntˈʃtɛlən] *vt* to disfigure; *(Wahrheit)* to distort

Entstellung *f* distortion; disfigurement

entstören [ɛntˈʃtøːrən] *vt (Rundf)* to eliminate

interference from; (*Aut*) to suppress

enttäuschen [ɛnt'tɔʏʃən] *vt* to disappoint

Enttäuschung *f* disappointment

entwachsen [ɛnt'vaksən] *unreg vi +dat* to outgrow, grow out of; (*geh: herauswachsen aus*) to spring from

entwaffnen [ɛnt'vafnən] *vt* (*lit, fig*) to disarm

entwaffnend *adj* disarming

Entwarnung [ɛnt'varnʊŋ] *f* all clear (signal)

entwässern [ɛnt'vɛsərn] *vt* to drain

Entwässerung *f* drainage

entweder [ɛnt've:dər] *konj* either; ~ ... **oder** ... either ... or ...

entweichen [ɛnt'vaɪçən] *unreg vi* to escape

entweihen [ɛnt'vaɪən] *unreg vt* to desecrate

entwenden [ɛnt'vɛndən] *unreg vt* to purloin, steal

entwerfen [ɛnt'vɛrfən] *unreg vt* (*Zeichnung*) to sketch; (*Modell*) to design; (*Vortrag, Gesetz etc*) to draft

entwerten [ɛnt've:rtən] *vt* to devalue; (*stempeln*) to cancel

Entwerter (**-s, -**) *m* (ticket-)cancelling (*Brit*) *od* canceling (*US*) machine

entwickeln [ɛnt'vɪkəln] *vt* to develop (*auch Phot*); (*Mut, Energie*) to show, display ▷ *vr* to develop

Entwickler (**-s, -**) *m* developer

Entwicklung [ɛnt'vɪklʊŋ] *f* development; (*Phot*) developing; **in der** ~ at the development stage; (*Jugendliche etc*) still developing

Entwicklungs- *zW*: **Entwicklungsabschnitt** *m* stage of development; **Entwicklungshelfer**, **in** *m(f)* VSO worker (*Brit*), Peace Corps worker (*US*); **Entwicklungshilfe** *f* aid for developing countries; **Entwicklungsjahre** *pl* adolescence *sing*; **Entwicklungsland** *nt* developing country; **Entwicklungszeit** *f* period of development; (*Phot*) developing time

entwirren [ɛnt'vɪrən] *vt* to disentangle

entwischen [ɛnt'vɪʃən] *vi* to escape

entwöhnen [ɛnt'vø:nən] *vt* to wean; (*Süchtige*): (**einer Sache** *dat od* **von etw**) ~ to cure (of sth)

Entwöhnung *f* weaning; cure, curing

entwürdigend [ɛnt'vʏrdɪgənt] *adj* degrading

Entwurf [ɛnt'vʊrf] *m* outline, design; (*Vertragsentwurf, Konzept*) draft

entwurzeln [ɛnt'vʊrtsəln] *vt* to uproot

entziehen [ɛnt'tsi:ən] *unreg vt* (+*dat*) to withdraw (from), take away (from); (*Flüssigkeit*) to draw (from), extract (from) ▷ *vr* (+*dat*) to escape (from); (*jds Kenntnis*) to be outside of beyond; (*der Pflicht*) to shirk (from); **sich jds Blicken** ~ to be hidden from sight

Entziehung *f* withdrawal

Entziehungsanstalt *f* drug addiction/alcoholism treatment centre (*Brit*) *od* center (*US*)

Entziehungskur *f* treatment for drug addiction/alcoholism

entziffern [ɛnt'tsɪfərn] *vt* to decipher; (*Funkspruch*) to decode

entzücken [ɛnt'tsʏkən] *vt* to delight; **Entzücken** (**-s**) *nt* delight

entzückend *adj* delightful, charming

Entzug [ɛnt'tsu:k] (**-(e)s**) *m* (*einer Lizenz etc, Med*) withdrawal

Entzugserscheinung *f* withdrawal symptom

entzündbar *adj*: **leicht** ~ highly inflammable; (*fig*) easily roused

entzünden [ɛnt'tsʏndən] *vt* to light, set light to; (*fig, Med*) to inflame; (*Streit*) to spark off ▷ *vr* (*lit, fig*) to catch fire; (*Streit*) to start; (*Med*) to become inflamed

Entzündung *f* (*Med*) inflammation

entzwei [ɛnt'tsvaɪ] *adv* in two; broken; **entzweibrechen** *unreg vt, vi* to break in two

entzweien *vt* to set at odds ▷ *vr* to fall out

entzweigehen *unreg vi* to break (in two)

Enzian ['ɛntsia:n] (**-s, -e**) *m* gentian

Enzyklika [ɛn'tsy:klika] (**-, -liken**) *f* (*Rel*) encyclical

Enzyklopädie [ɛntsyklopɛ'di:] *f* encyclop(a)edia

Enzym [ɛn'tsy:m] (**-s, -e**) *nt* enzyme

Epen *pl von* **Epos**

Epidemie [epide'mi:] *f* epidemic

Epilepsie [epile'psi:] *f* epilepsy

episch ['e:pɪʃ] *adj* epic

Episode [epi'zo:də] (**-, -n**) *f* episode

Epoche [e'pɔxə] (**-, -n**) *f* epoch; **epochemachend** *adj* epoch-making

Epos ['e:pɔs] (**-, Epen**) *nt* epic (poem)

Equipe [e'kɪp] (**-, -n**) *f* team

er [e:r] *pron* he; it

erachten [ɛr|'axtən] *vt* (*geh*): ~ **für** *od* **als** to consider (to be); **meines E-s** in my opinion

erarbeiten [ɛr|'arbaɪtən] *vt* to work for, acquire; (*Theorie*) to work out

Erbanlage ['ɛrp|anla:gə] *f* hereditary factor(s *pl*)

erbarmen [ɛr'barmən] *vr* (+*gen*) to have pity *od* mercy (on) ▷ *vt*: **er sieht zum E~ aus** he's a pitiful sight; **Herr, erbarme dich (unser)!** Lord, have mercy (upon us)!; **Erbarmen** (**-s**) *nt* pity

erbärmlich [ɛr'bɛrmlɪç] *adj* wretched, pitiful; **Erbärmlichkeit** *f* wretchedness

Erbarmungs- *zW*: **erbarmungslos** *adj* pitiless, merciless; **erbarmungsvoll** *adj* compassionate; **erbarmungswürdig** *adj* pitiable, wretched

erbauen [ɛr'baʊən] *vt* to build, erect; (*fig*) to edify; **er ist von meinem Plan nicht besonders erbaut** (*umg*) he isn't particularly enthusiastic about my plan

Erbauer (**-s, -**) *m* builder

erbaulich *adj* edifying

Erbauung *f* construction; (*fig*) edification

erbberechtigt *adj* entitled to inherit

erbbiologisch *adj*: ~**es Gutachten** (*Jur*) blood test (*to establish paternity*)

Erbe[1] ['ɛrbə] (**-n, -n**) *m* heir; **jdn zum** *od* **als** ~**n einsetzen** to make sb one's/sb's heir

Erbe[2] ['ɛrbə] (**-s**) *nt* inheritance; (*fig*) heritage

erben vt to inherit; (umg: geschenkt bekommen) to get, be given

erbeuten [ɛrˈbɔytən] vt to carry off; (Mil) to capture

Erb- zW: **Erbfaktor** m gene; **Erbfehler** m hereditary defect; **Erbfeind** m traditional od arch enemy; **Erbfolge** f (line of) succession

Erbin f heiress

erbitten [ɛrˈbɪtən] unreg vt to ask for, request

erbittern [ɛrˈbɪtərn] vt to embitter; (erzürnen) to incense

erbittert [ɛrˈbɪtərt] adj (Kampf) fierce, bitter

erblassen [ɛrˈblasən] vi to (turn) pale

Erblasser, in [ˈɛrblasər(ɪn)] (-s, -) m(f) (Jur) person who leaves an inheritance

erbleichen [ɛrˈblaɪçən] unreg vi to (turn) pale

erblich [ˈɛrplɪç] adj hereditary; **er/sie ist ~ (vor)belastet** it runs in the family

erblichen pp von **erbleichen**

erblicken [ɛrˈblɪkən] vt to see; (erspähen) to catch sight of

erblinden [ɛrˈblɪndən] vi to go blind

Erbmasse [ˈɛrpmasə] f estate; (Biol) genotype

erbosen [ɛrˈboːzən] vt (geh) to anger ▷ vr to grow angry

erbrechen [ɛrˈbrɛçən] unreg vt, vr to vomit

Erbrecht nt hereditary right; (Gesetze) law of inheritance

Erbschaft f inheritance, legacy

Erbschaftssteuer f estate od death duties pl

Erbschleicher, in [ˈɛrpʃlaɪçər(ɪn)] (-s, -) m(f) legacy-hunter

Erbse [ˈɛrpsə] (-, -n) f pea

Erb- zW: **Erbstück** nt heirloom; **Erbsünde** f (Rel) original sin; **Erbteil** nt inherited trait; (Jur) (portion of) inheritance

Erd- zW: **Erdachse** f earth's axis; **Erdapfel** (Österr) m potato; **Erdatmosphäre** f earth's atmosphere; **Erdbahn** f orbit of the earth; **Erdbeben** nt earthquake; **Erdbeere** f strawberry; **Erdboden** m ground; **etw dem Erdboden gleichmachen** to level sth, raze sth to the ground

Erde (-, -n) f earth; **zu ebener ~** at ground level; **auf der ganzen ~** all over the world; **du wirst mich noch unter die ~ bringen** (umg) you'll be the death of me yet

erden vt (Elek) to earth

erdenkbar [ɛrˈdɛŋkbaːr] adj conceivable; **sich** dat **alle ~e Mühe geben** to take the greatest (possible) pains

erdenklich [ɛrˈdɛŋklɪç] adj = **erdenkbar**

Erdg. abk = **Erdgeschoss**

Erd- zW: **Erdgas** nt natural gas; **Erdgeschoss** nt ground floor (Brit), first floor (US); **Erdkunde** f geography; **Erdnuss** f peanut; **Erdoberfläche** f surface of the earth; **Erdöl** nt (mineral) oil; **Erdölfeld** nt oilfield; **Erdölindustrie** f oil industry; **Erdreich** nt soil, earth

erdreisten [ɛrˈdraɪstən] vr to dare, have the audacity (to do sth)

erdrosseln [ɛrˈdrɔsəln] vt to strangle, throttle

erdrücken [ɛrˈdrʏkən] vt to crush; **~de**

Übermacht/~des Beweismaterial overwhelming superiority/evidence

Erd- zW: **Erdrutsch** m landslide; **Erdstoß** m (seismic) shock; **Erdteil** m continent

erdulden [ɛrˈdʊldən] vt to endure, suffer

ereifern [ɛrˈ|aɪfərn] vr to get excited

ereignen [ɛrˈ|aɪɡnən] vr to happen

Ereignis [ɛrˈ|aɪɡnɪs] (-ses, -se) nt event; **ereignislos** adj uneventful; **ereignisreich** adj eventful

Eremit [ere'miːt] (-en, -en) m hermit

erfahren [ɛrˈfaːrən] unreg vt to learn, find out; (erleben) to experience ▷ adj experienced

Erfahrung f experience; **~en sammeln** to gain experience; **etw in ~ bringen** to learn od find out sth

Erfahrungsaustausch m exchange of experiences

erfahrungsgemäß adv according to experience

erfand etc [ɛrˈfant] vb siehe **erfinden**

erfassen [ɛrˈfasən] vt to seize; (fig: einbeziehen) to include, register; (verstehen) to grasp

erfinden [ɛrˈfɪndən] unreg vt to invent; **frei erfunden** completely fictitious

Erfinder, in (-s, -) m(f) inventor; **erfinderisch** adj inventive

Erfindung f invention

Erfindungsgabe f inventiveness

Erfolg [ɛrˈfɔlk] (-(e)s, -e) m success; (Folge) result; **~ versprechend** promising; **viel ~!** good luck!

erfolgen [ɛrˈfɔlɡən] vi to follow; (sich ergeben) to result; (stattfinden) to take place; (Zahlung) to be effected; **nach erfolgter Zahlung** when payment has been made

Erfolg- zW: **erfolglos** adj unsuccessful; **Erfolglosigkeit** f lack of success; **erfolgreich** adj successful

Erfolgserlebnis nt feeling of success, sense of achievement

erfolgversprechend adj siehe **Erfolg**

erforderlich adj requisite, necessary

erfordern [ɛrˈfɔrdərn] vt to require, demand

Erfordernis (-ses, -se) nt requirement, prerequisite

erforschen [ɛrˈfɔrʃən] vt (Land) to explore; (Problem) to investigate; (Gewissen) to search

Erforscher, in (-s, -) m(f) explorer; investigator

Erforschung f exploration; investigation; searching

erfragen [ɛrˈfraːɡən] vt to inquire, ascertain

erfreuen [ɛrˈfrɔyən] vr: **sich ~ an** +dat to enjoy ▷ vt to delight; **sich einer Sache** gen **~** (geh) to enjoy sth; **sehr erfreut!** (form: bei Vorstellung) pleased to meet you!

erfreulich [ɛrˈfrɔylɪç] adj pleasing, gratifying

erfreulicherweise adv happily, luckily

erfrieren [ɛrˈfriːrən] unreg vi to freeze (to death); (Glieder) to get frostbitten; (Pflanzen) to be killed by frost

erfrischen [ɛrˈfrɪʃən] vt to refresh

Erfrischung f refreshment

Erfrischungsraum m snack bar, cafeteria

erfüllen [ɛrˈfʏlən] vt (Raum etc) to fill; (fig: Bitte etc) to fulfil (Brit), fulfill (US) ▷ vr to come true; **ein erfülltes Leben** a full life

Erfüllung f: **in ~ gehen** to be fulfilled

erfunden [ɛrˈfʊndən] pp von **erfinden**

ergab etc [ɛrˈgaːp] vb siehe **ergeben**

ergänzen [ɛrˈgɛntsən] vt to supplement, complete ▷ vr to complement one another

Ergänzung f completion; (Zusatz) supplement

ergattern [ɛrˈgatərn] (umg) vt to get hold of, hunt up

ergaunern [ɛrˈgaʊnərn] (umg) vt: **sich** dat **etw ~** to get hold of sth by underhand methods

ergeben [ɛrˈgeːbən] unreg vt to yield, produce ▷ vr to surrender; (folgen) to result ▷ adj devoted; (demütig) humble; **sich einer Sache** dat **~** (sich hingeben) to give o.s. up to sth, yield to sth; **es ergab sich, dass unsere Befürchtungen** ... it turned out that our fears ...; **dem Trunk ~** addicted to drink; **Ergebenheit** f devotion; humility

Ergebnis [ɛrˈgeːpnɪs] (**-ses, -se**) nt result; **zu einem ~ kommen** to come to od reach a conclusion; **ergebnislos** adj without result, fruitless; **ergebnislos bleiben** od **verlaufen** to come to nothing

ergehen [ɛrˈgeːən] unreg vi (form) to be issued, go out ▷ vi unpers: **es ergeht ihm gut/schlecht** he's faring od getting on well/badly ▷ vr: **sich in etw** dat **~** to indulge in sth; **etw über sich** akk **~ lassen** to put up with sth; **sich (in langen Reden) über ein Thema ~** (fig) to hold forth at length on sth

ergiebig [ɛrˈgiːbɪç] adj productive

ergo [ˈɛrgo] konj therefore, ergo (liter, hum)

Ergonomie [ɛrgonoˈmiː] f ergonomics pl

ergötzen [ɛrˈgœtsən] vt to amuse, delight

ergrauen [ɛrˈgraʊən] vi to turn od go grey (Brit) od gray (US)

ergreifen [ɛrˈgraɪfən] unreg vt (lit, fig) to seize; (Beruf) to take up; (Maßnahmen) to resort to; (rühren) to move; **er ergriff das Wort** he began to speak

ergreifend adj moving, affecting

ergriff etc [ɛrˈgrɪf] vb siehe **ergreifen**

ergriffen pp von **ergreifen** ▷ adj deeply moved

Ergriffenheit f emotion

ergründen [ɛrˈgrʏndən] vt (Sinn etc) to fathom; (Ursache, Motive) to discover

Erguss [ɛrˈgʊs] (**-es, ̈-e**) m discharge; (fig) outpouring, effusion

erhaben [ɛrˈhaːbən] adj (lit) raised, embossed; (fig) exalted, lofty; **über etw** akk **~ sein** to be above sth

Erhalt m: **bei** od **nach ~** on receipt

erhält [ɛrˈhɛlt] vb siehe **erhalten**

erhalten [ɛrˈhaltən] unreg vt to receive; (bewahren) to preserve, maintain; **das Wort ~** to receive permission to speak; **jdn am Leben ~** to keep sb alive; **gut ~** in good condition

erhältlich [ɛrˈhɛltlɪç] adj obtainable, available

Erhaltung f maintenance, preservation

erhängen [ɛrˈhɛŋən] vt, vr to hang

erhärten [ɛrˈhɛrtən] vt to harden; (These) to substantiate, corroborate

erhaschen [ɛrˈhaʃən] vt to catch

erheben [ɛrˈheːbən] unreg vt to raise; (Protest, Forderungen) to make; (Fakten) to ascertain ▷ vr to rise (up); **sich über etw** akk **~** to rise above sth

erheblich [ɛrˈheːplɪç] adj considerable

erheitern [ɛrˈhaɪtərn] vt to amuse, cheer (up)

Erheiterung f exhilaration; **zur allgemeinen ~** to everybody's amusement

erhellen [ɛrˈhɛlən] vt (lit, fig) to illuminate; (Geheimnis) to shed light on ▷ vr (Fenster) to light up; (Himmel, Miene) to brighten (up); (Gesicht) to brighten up

erhielt etc [ɛrˈhiːlt] vb siehe **erhalten**

erhitzen [ɛrˈhɪtsən] vt to heat ▷ vr to heat up; (fig) to become heated od aroused

erhoffen [ɛrˈhɔfən] vt to hope for; **was erhoffst du dir davon?** what do you hope to gain from it?

erhöhen [ɛrˈhøːən] vt to raise; (verstärken) to increase; **erhöhte Temperatur haben** to have a temperature

Erhöhung f (Gehalt) increment

erholen [ɛrˈhoːlən] vr to recover; (entspannen) to have a rest; (fig: Preise, Aktien) to rally, pick up

erholsam adj restful

Erholung f recovery; relaxation, rest

erholungsbedürftig adj in need of a rest, run-down

Erholungsgebiet nt holiday (Brit) od vacation (US) area

Erholungsheim nt convalescent home

erhören [ɛrˈhøːrən] vt (Gebet etc) to hear; (Bitte etc) to yield to

Erika [ˈeːrika] (**-, Eriken**) f heather

erinnern [ɛrˈ|ɪnərn] vt: **~ (an** +akk) to remind (of) ▷ vr: **sich (an etw** akk) **~** to remember (sth)

Erinnerung f memory; (Andenken) reminder; **Erinnerungen** pl (Lebenserinnerung) reminiscences pl; (Liter) memoirs pl; **jdn/ etw in guter ~ behalten** to have pleasant memories of sb/sth

Erinnerungsschreiben nt (Comm) reminder

Erinnerungstafel f commemorative plaque

Eritrea [eriˈtreːa] (**-s**) nt Eritrea

erkalten [ɛrˈkaltən] vi to go cold, cool (down)

erkälten [ɛrˈkɛltən] vr to catch cold; **sich** dat **die Blase ~** to catch a chill in one's bladder

erkältet adj with a cold; **~ sein** to have a cold

Erkältung f cold

erkämpfen [ɛrˈkɛmpfən] vt to win, secure

erkannt [ɛrˈkant] pp von **erkennen**

erkannte etc vb siehe **erkennen**

erkennbar adj recognizable

erkennen [ɛrˈkɛnən] unreg vt to recognize; (sehen, verstehen) to see; **jdm zu ~ geben, dass** ... to give sb to understand that ...

erkenntlich adj: **sich ~ zeigen** to show one's appreciation; **Erkenntlichkeit** f gratitude; (Geschenk) token of one's gratitude

Erkenntnis (-, **-se**) *f* knowledge; (*das Erkennen*) recognition; (*Einsicht*) insight; **zur ~ kommen** to realize

Erkennung *f* recognition

Erkennungsdienst *m* police records department

Erkennungsmarke *f* identity disc

Erker ['ɛrkər] (**-s, -**) *m* bay; **Erkerfenster** *nt* bay window

erklärbar *adj* explicable

erklären [ɛr'klɛːrən] *vt* to explain; (*Rücktritt*) to announce; (*Politiker, Pressesprecher etc*) to say; **ich kann mir nicht ~, warum ...** I can't understand why ...

erklärlich *adj* explicable; (*verständlich*) understandable

erklärt *adj attrib* (*Gegner etc*) professed, avowed; (*Favorit, Liebling*) acknowledged

Erklärung *f* explanation; (*Aussage*) declaration

erklecklich [ɛr'klɛklɪç] *adj* considerable

erklimmen [ɛr'klɪmən] *unreg vt* to climb to

erklingen [ɛr'klɪŋən] *unreg vi* to resound, ring out

erklomm *etc* [ɛr'klɔm] *vb siehe* **erklimmen**

erklommen *pp von* **erklimmen**

erkranken [ɛr'kraŋkən] *vi*: **~ (an** +*dat*) to be taken ill (with); (*Organ, Pflanze, Tier*) to become diseased (with)

Erkrankung *f* illness

erkunden [ɛr'kʊndən] *vt* to find out, ascertain; (*bes Mil*) to reconnoitre (*Brit*), reconnoiter (*US*)

erkundigen *vr*: **sich ~ (nach)** to inquire (about); **ich werde mich ~** I'll find out

Erkundigung *f* inquiry; **~en einholen** to make inquiries

Erkundung *f* (*Mil*) reconnaissance, scouting

erlahmen [ɛr'laːmən] *vi* to tire; (*nachlassen*) to flag, wane

erlangen [ɛr'laŋən] *vt* to attain, achieve

Erlass [ɛr'las] (**-es, -e**) *m* decree; (*Aufhebung*) remission

erlassen *unreg vt* (*Verfügung*) to issue; (*Gesetz*) to enact; (*Strafe*) to remit; **jdm etw ~** to release sb from sth

erlauben [ɛr'laʊbən] *vt* to allow, permit ▷ *vr*: **sich** *dat* **etw ~** (*Zigarette, Pause*) to permit o.s. sth; (*Bemerkung, Verschlag*) to venture sth; (*sich leisten*) to afford sth; **jdm etw ~** to allow *od* permit sb (to do) sth; **~ Sie?** may I?; **~ Sie mal!** do you mind!; **was ~ Sie sich (eigentlich)!** how dare you!

Erlaubnis [ɛr'laʊpnɪs] (**-, -se**) *f* permission

erläutern [ɛr'lɔʏtərn] *vt* to explain

Erläuterung *f* explanation; **zur ~** in explanation

Erle ['ɛrlə] (**-, -n**) *f* alder

erleben [ɛr'leːbən] *vt* to experience; (*Zeit*) to live through; (*miterleben*) to witness; (*noch miterleben*) to live to see; **so wütend habe ich ihn noch nie erlebt** I've never seen *od* known him so furious

Erlebnis [ɛr'leːpnɪs] (**-ses, -se**) *nt* experience

erledigen [ɛr'leːdɪgən] *vt* to take care of, deal

with; (*Antrag etc*) to process; (*umg: erschöpfen*) to wear out; (*ruinieren*) to finish; (*umbringen*) to do in ▷ *vr*: **das hat sich erledigt** that's all settled; **das ist erledigt** that's taken care of, that's been done; **ich habe noch einiges in der Stadt zu ~** I've still got a few things to do in town

erledigt (*umg*) *adj* (*erschöpft*) shattered, done in; (: *ruiniert*) finished, ruined

erlegen [ɛr'leːgən] *vt* to kill

erleichtern [ɛr'laɪçtərn] *vt* to make easier; (*fig: Last*) to lighten; (*lindern, beruhigen*) to relieve

erleichtert *adj* relieved; **~ aufatmen** to breathe a sigh of relief

Erleichterung *f* facilitation; lightening; relief

erleiden [ɛr'laɪdən] *unreg vt* to suffer, endure

erlernbar *adj* learnable

erlernen [ɛr'lɛrnən] *vt* to learn, acquire

erlesen [ɛr'leːzən] *adj* select, choice

erleuchten [ɛr'lɔʏçtən] *vt* to illuminate; (*fig*) to inspire

Erleuchtung *f* (*Einfall*) inspiration

erliegen [ɛr'liːgən] *unreg vi* +*dat* (*lit, fig*) to succumb to; (*einem Irrtum*) to be the victim of; **zum E~ kommen** to come to a standstill

erlischt [ɛr'lɪʃt] *vb siehe* **erlöschen**

erlogen [ɛr'loːgən] *adj* untrue, made-up

Erlös [ɛr'løːs] (**-es, -e**) *m* proceeds *pl*

erlosch *etc* [ɛr'lɔʃ] *vb siehe* **erlöschen**

erlöschen [ɛr'lœʃən] *unreg vi* (*Feuer*) to go out; (*Interesse*) to cease, die; (*Vertrag, Recht*) to expire; **ein erloschener Vulkan** an extinct volcano

erlösen [ɛr'løːzən] *vt* to redeem, save

Erlöser (**-s, -**) *m* (*Rel*) Redeemer; (*Befreier*) saviour (*Brit*), savior (*US*)

Erlösung *f* release; (*Rel*) redemption

ermächtigen [ɛr'mɛçtɪgən] *vt* to authorize, empower

Ermächtigung *f* authorization

ermahnen [ɛr'maːnən] *vt* to admonish, exhort

Ermahnung *f* admonition, exhortation

Ermangelung [ɛr'maŋəlʊŋ], **Ermanglung** [ɛr'maŋlʊŋ] *f*: **in Ermang(e)lung** +*gen* because of the lack of

ermäßigen [ɛr'mɛsɪgən] *vt* to reduce

Ermäßigung *f* reduction

ermessen [ɛr'mɛsən] *unreg vt* to estimate, gauge; **Ermessen** (**-s**) *nt* estimation; discretion; **in jds Ermessen** *dat* **liegen** to lie within sb's discretion; **nach meinem Ermessen** in my judgement

Ermessensfrage *f* matter of discretion

ermitteln [ɛr'mɪtəln] *vt* to determine; (*Täter*) to trace ▷ *vi*: **gegen jdn ~** to investigate sb

Ermittlung [ɛr'mɪtlʊŋ] *f* determination; (*Polizeiermittlung*) investigation; **~en anstellen (über** +*akk*) to make inquiries (about)

Ermittlungsverfahren *nt* (*Jur*) preliminary proceedings *pl*

ermöglichen [ɛr'møːklɪçən] *vt* (+*dat*) to make possible (for)

ermorden [ɛr'mɔrdən] *vt* to murder

Ermordung *f* murder

ermüden [ɛrˈmyːdən] *vt* to tire; (*Tech*) to fatigue ▷ *vi* to tire
ermüdend *adj* tiring; (*fig*) wearisome
Ermüdung *f* fatigue
Ermüdungserscheinung *f* sign of fatigue
ermuntern [ɛrˈmʊntərn] *vt* to rouse; (*ermutigen*) to encourage; (*beleben*) to liven up; (*aufmuntern*) to cheer up
ermutigen [ɛrˈmuːtɪgən] *vt* to encourage
ernähren [ɛrˈnɛːrən] *vt* to feed, nourish; (*Familie*) to support ▷ *vr* to support o.s., earn a living; **sich ~ von** to live on
Ernährer, in (**-s, -**) *m(f)* breadwinner
Ernährung *f* nourishment; (*Med*) nutrition; (*Unterhalt*) maintenance
ernennen [ɛrˈnɛnən] *unreg vt* to appoint
Ernennung *f* appointment
erneuern [ɛrˈnɔyərn] *vt* to renew; (*restaurieren*) to restore; (*renovieren*) to renovate
Erneuerung *f* renewal; restoration; renovation
erneut *adj* renewed, fresh ▷ *adv* once more
erniedrigen [ɛrˈniːdrɪgən] *vt* to humiliate, degrade
Ernst [ɛrnst] (**-es**) *m* seriousness; **das ist mein ~** I'm quite serious; **im ~** in earnest; **~ machen mit etw** to put sth into practice; **ernst** *adj* serious ▷ *adv*: **es steht ernst um ihn** things don't look too good for him; **ernst gemeint** meant in earnest, serious; **Ernstfall** *m* emergency; **ernsthaft** *adj* serious; **Ernsthaftigkeit** *f* seriousness; **ernstlich** *adj* serious
Ernte [ˈɛrntə] (**-, -n**) *f* harvest; **Erntedankfest** *nt* harvest festival
ernten *vt* to harvest; (*Lob etc*) to earn
ernüchtern [ɛrˈnyçtərn] *vt* to sober up; (*fig*) to bring down to earth
Ernüchterung *f* sobering up; (*fig*) disillusionment
Eroberer [ɛrˈ|obərər] (**-s, -**) *m* conqueror
erobern *vt* to conquer
Eroberung *f* conquest
eröffnen [ɛrˈ|œfnən] *vt* to open ▷ *vr* to present itself; **jdm etw ~** (*geh*) to disclose sth to sb
Eröffnung *f* opening
Eröffnungsansprache *f* inaugural *od* opening address
Eröffnungsfeier *f* opening ceremony
erogen [ɛroˈgeːn] *adj* erogenous
erörtern [ɛrˈ|œrtərn] *vt* to discuss (in detail)
Erörterung *f* discussion
Erotik [eˈroːtɪk] *f* eroticism
erotisch *adj* erotic
Erpel [ˈɛrpəl] (**-, -**) *m* drake
erpicht [ɛrˈpɪçt] *adj*: **~ (auf** +*akk*) keen (on)
erpressen [ɛrˈprɛsən] *vt* (*Geld etc*) to extort; (*jdn*) to blackmail
Erpresser (**-s, -**) *m* blackmailer
Erpressung *f* blackmail; extortion
erproben [ɛrˈproːbən] *vt* to test; **erprobt** tried and tested
erraten [ɛrˈraːtən] *unreg vt* to guess
errechnen [ɛrˈrɛçnən] *vt* to calculate, work out

erregbar [ɛrˈreːkbaːr] *adj* excitable; (*reizbar*) irritable; **Erregbarkeit** *f* excitability; irritability
erregen [ɛrˈreːgən] *vt* to excite; (*sexuell*) to arouse; (*ärgern*) to infuriate; (*hervorrufen*) to arouse, provoke ▷ *vr* to get excited *od* worked up
Erreger (**-s, -**) *m* causative agent
Erregtheit *f* excitement; (*Beunruhigung*) agitation
Erregung *f* excitement; (*sexuell*) arousal
erreichbar *adj* accessible, within reach
erreichen [ɛrˈraiçən] *vt* to reach; (*Zweck*) to achieve; (*Zug*) to catch; **wann kann ich Sie morgen ~?** when can I get in touch with you tomorrow?; **vom Bahnhof leicht zu ~** within easy reach of the station
errichten [ɛrˈrɪçtən] *vt* to erect, put up; (*gründen*) to establish, set up
erringen [ɛrˈrɪŋən] *unreg vt* to gain, win
erröten [ɛrˈrøːtən] *vi* to blush, flush
Errungenschaft [ɛrˈrʊŋənʃaft] *f* achievement; (*umg: Anschaffung*) acquisition
Ersatz [ɛrˈzats] (**-es**) *m* substitute; replacement; (*Schadenersatz*) compensation; (*Mil*) reinforcements *pl*; **als ~ für jdn einspringen** to stand in for sb; **Ersatzbefriedigung** *f* vicarious satisfaction; **Ersatzdienst** *m* (*Mil*) alternative service; **Ersatzkasse** *f* private health insurance; **Ersatzmann** *m* replacement; (*Sport*) substitute; **Ersatzmutter** *f* substitute mother; **ersatzpflichtig** *adj* liable to pay compensation; **Ersatzreifen** *m* (*Aut*) spare tyre (*Brit*) *od* tire (*US*); **Ersatzteil** *nt* spare (part); **ersatzweise** *adv* as an alternative
ersaufen [ɛrˈzaufən] *unreg* (*umg*) *vi* to drown
ersäufen [ɛrˈzɔyfən] *vt* to drown
erschaffen [ɛrˈʃafən] *unreg vt* to create
erscheinen [ɛrˈʃainən] *unreg vi* to appear
Erscheinung *f* appearance; (*Geist*) apparition; (*Gegebenheit*) phenomenon; (*Gestalt*) figure; **in ~ treten** (*Merkmale*) to appear; (*Gefühle*) to show themselves
Erscheinungsform *f* manifestation
Erscheinungsjahr *nt* (*von Buch*) year of publication
erschien etc [ɛrˈʃiːn] *vb siehe* **erscheinen**
erschienen *pp von* **erscheinen**
erschießen [ɛrˈʃiːsən] *unreg vt* to shoot (dead)
erschlaffen [ɛrˈʃlafən] *vi* to go limp; (*Mensch*) to become exhausted
erschlagen [ɛrˈʃlaːgən] *unreg vt* to strike dead ▷ *adj* (*umg: todmüde*) worn out, dead beat (*umg*)
erschleichen [ɛrˈʃlaiçən] *unreg vt* to obtain by stealth *od* dubious methods
erschließen [ɛrˈʃliːsən] *unreg vt* (*Gebiet, Absatzmarkt*) to develop, open up; (*Bodenschätze*) to tap
erschlossen [ɛrˈʃlɔsən] *adj* (*Gebiet*) developed
erschöpfen [ɛrˈʃœpfən] *vt* to exhaust
erschöpfend *adj* exhaustive, thorough
erschöpft *adj* exhausted

e

Erschöpfung f exhaustion
erschossen [ɛrˈʃɔsən] (umg) adj: **(völlig) ~ sein** to be whacked, be dead (beat)
erschrak etc [ɛrˈʃraːk] vb siehe **erschrecken²**
erschrecken¹ [ɛrˈʃrɛkən] vt to startle, frighten
erschrecken² [ɛrˈʃrɛkən] unreg vi to be frightened od startled
erschreckend adj alarming, frightening
erschrickt [ɛrˈʃrɪkt] vb siehe **erschrecken²**
erschrocken [ɛrˈʃrɔkən] pp von **erschrecken²**
▷ adj frightened, startled
erschüttern [ɛrˈʃʏtərn] vt to shake; (ergreifen) to move deeply; **ihn kann nichts ~** he always keeps his cool (umg)
erschütternd adj shattering
Erschütterung f (des Bodens) tremor; (tiefe Ergriffenheit) shock
erschweren [ɛrˈʃveːrən] vt to complicate; **~de Umstände** (Jur) aggravating circumstances; **es kommt noch ~d hinzu, dass ...** to compound matters ...
erschwindeln [ɛrˈʃvɪndəln] vt to obtain by fraud
erschwinglich adj affordable
ersehen [ɛrˈzeːən] unreg vt: **aus etw ~, dass ...** to gather from sth that ...
ersehnt [ɛrˈzeːnt] adj longed-for
ersetzbar adj replaceable
ersetzen [ɛrˈzɛtsən] vt to replace; **jdm Unkosten** etc **~** to pay sb's expenses etc
ersichtlich [ɛrˈzɪçtlɪç] adj evident, obvious
ersparen [ɛrˈʃpaːrən] vt (Ärger etc) to spare; (Geld) to save; **ihr blieb auch nichts erspart** she was spared nothing
Ersparnis (-, -se) f saving
ersprießlich [ɛrˈʃpriːslɪç] adj profitable, useful; (angenehm) pleasant

⬤ SCHLÜSSELWORT

erst [eːrst] adv **1** first; **mach erst (ein)mal die Arbeit fertig** finish your work first; **wenn du das erst (ein)mal hinter dir hast** once you've got that behind you
2 (nicht früher als, nur) only; (nicht bis) not till; **erst gestern** only yesterday; **erst morgen** not until tomorrow; **erst als** only when, not until; **wir fahren erst später** we're not going until later; **er ist (gerade) erst angekommen** he's only just arrived
3: **wäre er doch erst zurück!** if only he were back!; **da fange ich erst gar nicht an** I simply won't bother to begin; **jetzt erst recht!** that just makes me all the more determined; **da gings erst richtig los** then things really got going

erstarren [ɛrˈʃtarən] vi to stiffen; (vor Furcht) to grow rigid; (Materie) to solidify
erstatten [ɛrˈʃtatən] vt (Unkosten) to refund; **Anzeige gegen jdn ~** to report sb; **Bericht ~** to make a report
Erstattung f (von Unkosten) reimbursement

Erstaufführung [ˈeːrstʔaʊffyːrʊŋ] f first performance
erstaunen [ɛrˈʃtaʊnən] vt to astonish ▷ vi to be astonished; **Erstaunen** (-s) nt astonishment
erstaunlich adj astonishing
Erstausgabe f first edition
erstbeste, r, s adj first that comes along
erste, r, s adj first; **als E~s** first of all; **in ~r Linie** first and foremost; **fürs E~** for the time being; **E~ Hilfe** first aid; **das ~ Mal** the first time
erstechen [ɛrˈʃtɛçən] unreg vt to stab (to death)
erstehen [ɛrˈʃteːən] unreg vt to buy ▷ vi to (a)rise
ersteigen [ɛrˈʃtaɪgən] unreg vt to climb, ascend
ersteigern [ɛrˈʃtaɪgərn] vt to buy at an auction
erstellen [ɛrˈʃtɛlən] vt to erect, build
erstens adv firstly, in the first place
erstere, r, s pron (the) former; **der/die/das E~** the former
ersticken [ɛrˈʃtɪkən] vt (lit, fig) to stifle; (Mensch) to suffocate; (Flammen) to smother ▷ vi (Mensch) to suffocate; (Feuer) to be smothered; **mit erstickter Stimme** in a choked voice; **in Arbeit ~** to be snowed under with work
Erstickung f suffocation
erst- zW: **erstklassig** adj first-class; **Erstkommunion** f first communion; **erstmalig** adj; **erstmals** adv for the first time; **erstrangig** adj first-rate
erstrebenswert [ɛrˈʃtreːbənsveːrt] adj desirable, worthwhile
erstrecken [ɛrˈʃtrɛkən] vr to extend, stretch
Erststimme f first vote; see culture note

⬤ ERSTSTIMME/ZWEITSTIMME

The *Erststimme* and *Zweitstimme* (first and second vote) system is used to elect MPs to the *Bundestag*. Each elector is given two votes. The first is to choose a candidate in his constituency; the candidate with the most votes is elected MP. The second is to choose a party. All the second votes in each *Land* are counted and a proportionate number of MP's from each party is sent to the *Bundestag*.

Ersttagsbrief m first-day cover
Ersttagsstempel m first-day (date) stamp
erstunken [ɛrˈʃtʊŋkən] adj: **das ist ~ und erlogen** (umg) that's a pack of lies
Erstwähler (-s, -) m first-time voter
ersuchen [ɛrˈzuːxən] vt to request
ertappen [ɛrˈtapən] vt to catch, detect
erteilen [ɛrˈtaɪlən] vt to give
ertönen [ɛrˈtøːnən] vi to sound, ring out
Ertrag [ɛrˈtraːk] (-(e)s, ⁻e) m yield; (Gewinn) proceeds pl
ertragen unreg vt to bear, stand
erträglich [ɛrˈtrɛːklɪç] adj tolerable, bearable
ertragreich adj (Geschäft) profitable, lucrative
ertrank etc [ɛrˈtraŋk] vb siehe **ertrinken**
ertränken [ɛrˈtrɛŋkən] vt to drown

erträumen [ɛr'trɔʏmən] *vt:* **sich** *dat* **etw ~** to dream of sth, imagine sth

ertrinken [ɛr'trɪŋkən] *unreg vi* to drown; **Ertrinken (-s)** *nt* drowning

ertrunken [ɛr'trʊŋkən] *pp von* **ertrinken**

erübrigen [ɛr'|yːbrɪgən] *vt* to spare ▷ *vr* to be unnecessary

erwachen [ɛr'vaxən] *vi* to awake; **ein böses E~** (*fig*) a rude awakening

erwachsen [ɛr'vaksən] *adj* grown-up ▷ *vi unreg:* **daraus erwuchsen ihm Unannehmlichkeiten** that caused him some trouble

Erwachsene, r *f(m)* adult

Erwachsenenbildung *f* adult education

erwägen [ɛr'vɛːgən] *unreg vt* to consider

Erwägung *f* consideration; **etw in ~ ziehen** to take sth into consideration

erwähnen [ɛr'vɛːnən] *vt* to mention

erwähnenswert *adj* worth mentioning

Erwähnung *f* mention

erwarb *etc* [ɛr'varp] *vb siehe* **erwerben**

erwärmen [ɛr'vɛrmən] *vt* to warm, heat ▷ *vr* to get warm, warm up; **sich ~ für** to warm to

erwarten [ɛr'vartən] *vt* to expect; (*warten auf*) to wait for; **etw kaum ~ können** to hardly be able to wait for sth

Erwartung *f* expectation; **in ~ Ihrer baldigen Antwort** (*form*) in anticipation of your early reply

erwartungsgemäß *adv* as expected

erwartungsvoll *adj* expectant

erwecken [ɛr'vɛkən] *vt* to rouse, awake; **den Anschein ~** to give the impression; **etw zu neuem Leben ~** to resurrect sth

erwehren [ɛr've:rən] *vr +gen* (*geh*) to fend off, ward off; (*des Lachens etc*) to refrain from

erweichen [ɛr'vaiçən] *vt* to soften; **sich nicht ~ lassen** to be unmoved

erweisen [ɛr'vaizən] *unreg vt* to prove ▷ *vr:* **sich ~ als** to prove to be; **jdm einen Gefallen/ Dienst ~** to do sb a favour/service; **sich jdm gegenüber dankbar ~** to show one's gratitude to sb

erweitern [ɛr'vaitərn] *vt, vr* to widen, enlarge; (*Geschäft*) to expand; (*Med*) to dilate; (*fig: Kenntnisse*) to broaden; (*Macht*) to extend

Erweiterung *f* expansion

Erwerb [ɛr'vɛrp] **(-(e)s, -e)** *m* acquisition; (*Beruf*) trade

erwerben [ɛr'vɛrbən] *unreg vt* to acquire; **er hat sich** *dat* **große Verdienste um die Firma erworben** he has done great service for the firm

Erwerbs- *zW:* **erwerbsfähig** *adj* (*form*) capable of gainful employment; **Erwerbsgesellschaft** *f* acquisitive society; **erwerbslos** *adj* unemployed; **Erwerbsquelle** *f* source of income; **erwerbstätig** *adj* (gainfully) employed; **erwerbsunfähig** *adj* unable to work

erwidern [ɛr'vi:dərn] *vt* to reply; (*vergelten*) to return

Erwiderung *f:* **in ~ Ihres Schreibens vom ...** (*form*) in reply to your letter of the ...

erwiesen [ɛr'vi:zən] *adj* proven

erwirbt [ɛr'vɪrpt] *vb siehe* **erwerben**

erwirtschaften [ɛr'vɪrtʃaftən] *vt* (*Gewinn etc*) to make by good management

erwischen [ɛr'vɪʃən] (*umg*) *vt* to catch, get; **ihn hats erwischt!** (*umg: verliebt*) he's got it bad; (*: krank*) he's got it; **kalt ~** (*umg*) to catch off-balance

erworben [ɛr'vɔrbən] *pp von* **erwerben**

erwünscht [ɛr'vʏnʃt] *adj* desired

erwürgen [ɛr'vʏrgən] *vt* to strangle

Erz [e:rts] **(-es, -e)** *nt* ore

erzählen [ɛr'tsɛːlən] *vt, vi* to tell; **dem werd ich was ~!** (*umg*) I'll have something to say to him; **~de Dichtung** narrative fiction

Erzähler, in **(-s, -)** *m(f)* narrator

Erzählung *f* story, tale

Erzbischof *m* archbishop

Erzengel *m* archangel

erzeugen [ɛr'tsɔʏgən] *vt* to produce; (*Strom*) to generate

Erzeuger(-s, -) *m* producer; **Erzeugerpreis** *m* manufacturer's price

Erzeugnis (-ses, -se) *nt* product, produce

Erzeugung *f* production; generation

Erzfeind *m* arch enemy

erziehbar *adj:* **ein Heim für schwer ~e Kinder** a home for difficult children

erziehen [ɛr'tsi:ən] *unreg vt* to bring up; (*bilden*) to educate, train

Erzieher, in **(-s, -)** *m(f)* educator; (*in Kindergarten*) nursery school teacher

Erziehung *f* bringing up; (*Bildung*) education

Erziehungs- *zW:* **Erziehungsberechtigte, r** *f(m)* parent, legal guardian; **Erziehungsgeld** *nt* payment for new parents; **Erziehungsheim** *nt* community home; **Erziehungsurlaub** *m* leave for a new parent

erzielen [ɛr'tsi:lən] *vt* to achieve, obtain; (*Tor*) to score

erzkonservativ ['ɛrtskɔnzɛrva'ti:f] *adj* ultraconservative

erzog *etc* [ɛr'tso:k] *vb siehe* **erziehen**

erzogen [ɛr'tso:gən] *pp von* **erziehen**

erzürnen [ɛr'tsʏrnən] *vt* (*geh*) to anger, incense

erzwingen [ɛr'tsvɪŋən] *unreg vt* to force, obtain by force

Es [ɛs] **(-)** *nt* (*Mus: Dur*) E flat

es [ɛs] *nom, akk pron* it

Esche ['ɛʃə] **(-, -n)** *f* ash

Esel ['e:zəl] **(-s, -)** *m* donkey, ass; **ich ~!** (*umg*) silly me!

Eselsbrücke *f* (*Gedächtnishilfe*) mnemonic, aide-mémoire

Eselsohr *nt* dog-ear

Eskalation [ɛskalatsi'o:n] *f* escalation

eskalieren [ɛska'li:rən] *vt, vi* to escalate

Eskimo ['ɛskimo] **(-s, -s)** *m* eskimo

Eskorte [ɛs'kɔrtə] **(-, -n)** *f* (*Mil*) escort

eskortieren [ɛskɔr'ti:rən] *vt* (*geh*) to escort

Espenlaub ['ɛspənlaʊp] *nt:* **zittern wie ~** to shake like a leaf

essbar ['ɛsbaːr] adj eatable, edible

Essecke f dining area

essen ['ɛsən] unreg vt, vi to eat; **~ gehen** (auswärts) to eat out; **~ Sie gern Äpfel?** do you like apples?; **Essen (-s, -)** nt (Mahlzeit) meal; (Nahrung) food; **Essen auf Rädern** meals on wheels

Essens- zW: **Essensausgabe** f serving of meals; (Stelle) serving counter; **Essensmarke** f meal voucher; **Essenszeit** f mealtime

Essgeschirr nt dinner service

Essig ['ɛsɪç] (-s, -e) m vinegar; **damit ist es ~** (umg) it's all off; **Essiggurke** f gherkin

Esskastanie f sweet chestnut

Essl. abk (= Esslöffel) tbsp.

Ess- zW: **Esslöffel** m tablespoon; **Esstisch** m dining table; **Esswaren** pl foodstuffs pl; **Esszimmer** nt dining room

Establishment [ɪsˈtæblɪʃmənt] **(-s, -s)** nt establishment

Este ['ɛstə] **(-n, -n)** m, **Estin** f Estonian

Estland ['eːstlant] nt Estonia

estnisch ['eːstnɪʃ] adj Estonian

Estragon ['ɛstragɔn] **(-s)** m tarragon

Estrich ['ɛstrɪç] **(-s, -e)** m stone/clay etc floor

etablieren [eta'bliːrən] vr to establish o.s.; (Comm) to set up

Etage [e'taːʒə] **(-, -n)** f floor, storey (Brit), story (US)

Etagenbetten pl bunk beds pl

Etagenwohnung f flat (Brit), apartment (US)

Etappe [e'tapə] **(-, -n)** f stage

etappenweise adv step by step, stage by stage

Etat [e'taː] **(-s, -s)** m budget; **Etatjahr** nt financial year; **Etatposten** m budget item

etc abk (= et cetera) etc.

etepetete [eːtəpe'teːtə] (umg) adj fussy

Ethik ['eːtɪk] f ethics sing

ethisch ['eːtɪʃ] adj ethical

ethnisch ['ɛtnɪʃ] adj ethnic; **~e Säuberung** ethnic cleansing

Etikett [eti'kɛt] **(-(e)s, -e)** nt (lit, fig) label

Etikette f etiquette, manners pl

Etikettenschwindel m (Pol): **es ist reinster ~, wenn ...** it is just playing od juggling with names if ...

etikettieren [etikɛ'tiːrən] vt to label

etliche, r, s ['ɛtlɪçə(r, s)] adj quite a lot of ▷ pron pl some, quite a few; **~s** quite a lot

Etüde [e'tyːdə] **(-, -n)** f (Mus) étude

Etui [ɛt'viː] **(-s, -s)** nt case

etwa ['ɛtva] adv (ungefähr) about; (vielleicht) perhaps; (beispielsweise) for instance; (entrüstet, erstaunt): **hast du ~ schon wieder kein Geld dabei?** don't tell me you haven't got any money again! ▷ adv (zur Bestätigung): **Sie kommen doch, oder ~ nicht?** you are coming, aren't you?; **nicht ~** by no means; **willst du ~ schon gehen?** (surely) you don't want to go already?

etwaig ['ɛtvaɪç] adj possible

etwas pron something; (fragend, verneinend) anything; (ein wenig) a little ▷ adv a little; **er**

kann ~ he's good; **Etwas** nt: **das gewisse Etwas** that certain something

Etymologie [etymolo'giː] f etymology

EU [eːˈluː] (-) f abk (= Europäische Union) EU

euch [ɔyç] pron (akk von ihr) you; yourselves; (dat von ihr) (to/for) you ▷ re, pron yourselves

euer ['ɔyər] pron gen von **ihr** of you ▷ adj your

EU-Erweiterung f enlargement of the EU

EU-Kommissar, in m(f) EU commissioner

EU-Kommission f EU commission

Eule ['ɔylə] **(-, -n)** f owl

EU-Osterweiterung f eastward expansion of the EU

Euphemismus [ɔyfe'mɪsmʊs] m euphemism

Eurasien [ɔy'raːziən] nt Eurasia

Euratom [ɔyra'toːm] f abk (= Europäische Atomgemeinschaft) Euratom

eure, r, s ['ɔyrə(r, s)] pron yours

eurerseits adv on your part

euresgleichen pron people like you

euretwegen ['ɔyrət'veːgən] adv (für euch) for your sakes; (wegen euch) on your account

euretwillen ['ɔyrət'vɪlən] adv: **um ~ =** **euretwegen**

eurige pron: **der/die/das E~** (geh) yours

Euro ['ɔyro] **(-, -s)** m (Fin) euro

Eurocent m euro cent

Eurokrat [ɔyro'kraːt] **(-en, -en)** m eurocrat

Europa [ɔy'roːpa] **(-s)** nt Europe

Europäer, in [ɔyro'pɛːər(ɪn)] **(-s, -)** m(f) European

europäisch adj European; **das E~e Parlament** the European Parliament; **E~e Union** European Union; **E~e (Wirtschafts)gemeinschaft** European (Economic) Community, Common Market

Europa- zW: **Europameister** m European champion; **Europarat** m Council of Europe; **Europastraße** f Euroroute

Euter ['ɔytər] **(-s, -)** nt udder

Euthanasie [ɔytana'ziː] f euthanasia

EU-Verfassung f EU constitution

E. V., e. V. abk (= eingetragener Verein) registered association

ev. abk = **evangelisch**

evakuieren [evaku'iːrən] vt to evacuate

evangelisch [evaŋ'geːlɪʃ] adj Protestant

Evangelium [evaŋ'geːliʊm] nt Gospel

Evaskostüm nt: **im ~** in her birthday suit

eventuell [evɛntu'ɛl] adj possible ▷ adv possibly, perhaps

Evolution [evolutsi'oːn] f evolution

Evolutionstheorie f theory of evolution

evtl. abk = **eventuell**

EWG [eːveːˈgeː] (-) f abk (früher: = Europäische Wirtschaftsgemeinschaft) EEC

ewig ['eːvɪç] adj eternal ▷ adv: **auf ~** forever; **ich habe Sie ~ lange nicht gesehen** (umg) I haven't seen you for ages; **Ewigkeit** f eternity; **bis in alle Ewigkeit** forever

EWS (-) nt abk (= Europäisches Währungssystem) EMS

EWU (-) f abk (= Europäische Währungsunion) EMU

ex [ɛks] *(umg) adv:* **etw ex trinken** to drink sth down in one

exakt [ɛ'ksakt] *adj* exact

exaltiert [ɛksal'tiːrt] *adj* exaggerated, effusive

Examen [ɛ'ksaːmən] (**-s, -** *od* **Examina**) *nt* examination

Examensarbeit *f* dissertation

Exekutionskommando [ɛksekutsi'oːnskɔmando] *nt* firing squad

Exekutive [ɛkseku'tiːvə] *f* executive

Exempel [ɛ'ksɛmpəl] (**-s, -**) *nt* example; **die Probe aufs ~ machen** to put it to the test

Exemplar [ɛksɛm'plaːr] (**-s, -e**) *nt* specimen; (*Buchexemplar*) copy; **exemplarisch** *adj* exemplary

exerzieren [ɛksɛr'tsiːrən] *vi* to drill

Exhibitionist [ɛkshibitsio'nɪst] *m* exhibitionist

Exil [ɛ'ksiːl] (**-s, -e**) *nt* exile

existentiell [ɛksɪstɛntsi'ɛl] *adj* = **existenziell**

Existenz [ɛksɪs'tɛnts] *f* existence; (*Unterhalt*) livelihood, living; (*pej: Mensch*) character; **Existenzberechtigung** *f* right to exist; **Existenzgrundlage** *f* basis of one's livelihood

existenziell [ɛksɪstɛntsi'ɛl] *adj:* **von ~er Bedeutung** of vital significance

Existenzkampf *m* struggle for existence

Existenzminimum (**-s, -ma**) *nt* subsistence level

existieren [ɛksɪs'tiːrən] *vi* to exist

exkl. *abk* = **exklusive**

exklusiv [ɛksklu'ziːf] *adj* exclusive; **Exklusivbericht** *m* (*Presse*) exclusive report

exklusive [ɛksklu'ziːvə] *präp+gen* exclusive of, not including ▷ *adv* exclusive of, excluding

Exkursion [ɛkskurzi'oːn] *f* (study) trip

Exmatrikulation [ɛksmatrikulatsi'oːn] *f* (*Univ*): **bei seiner ~** when he left university

exorzieren [ɛksɔr'tsiːrən] *vt* to exorcize

exotisch [ɛ'ksoːtɪʃ] *adj* exotic

expandieren [ɛkspan'diːrən] *vi* (*Econ*) to expand

Expansion [ɛkspanzi'oːn] *f* expansion

expansiv [ɛkspan'ziːf] *adj* expansionist; (*Wirtschaftszweige*) expanding

Expedition [ɛkspeditsi'oːn] *f* expedition; (*Comm*) forwarding department

Experiment [ɛksperi'mɛnt] *nt* experiment

experimentell [ɛksperimɛn'tɛl] *adj* experimental

experimentieren [ɛksperimɛn'tiːrən] *vi* to experiment

Experte [ɛks'pɛrtə] (**-n, -n**) *m* expert, specialist; **Expertenkommission** *f* think tank; **Expertenmeinung** *f* expert opinion

Expertin [ɛks'pɛrtɪn] *f* expert, specialist

explodieren [ɛksplo'diːrən] *vi* to explode

Explosion [ɛksplozi'oːn] *f* explosion

explosiv [ɛksplo'ziːf] *adj* explosive

Exponent [ɛkspo'nɛnt] *m* exponent

exponieren [ɛkspo'niːrən] *vt:* **an exponierter Stelle stehen** to be in an exposed position

Export [ɛks'pɔrt] (**-(e)s, -e**) *m* export

Exportartikel *m* export

Exporteur [ɛkspɔr'tøːr] *m* exporter

Exporthandel *m* export trade

Exporthaus *nt* export house

exportieren [ɛkspɔr'tiːrən] *vt* to export

Exportkaufmann *m* exporter

Exportland *nt* exporting country

Exportvertreter *m* export agent

Exportwirtschaft *f* export business *od* sector

Expressgut [ɛks'prɛsguːt] *nt* express goods *pl od* freight

Expressionismus [ɛksprɛsio'nɪsmʊs] *m* expressionism

Expresszug *m* express (train)

extra ['ɛkstra] *adj inv* (*umg: gesondert*) separate; (*besondere*) extra ▷ *adv* (*gesondert*) separately; (*speziell*) specially; (*absichtlich*) on purpose; (*vor Adjektiven, zusätzlich*) extra; **Extra** (**-s, -s**) *nt* extra; **Extraausgabe** *f* special edition; **Extrablatt** *nt* special edition

Extrakt [ɛks'trakt] (**-(e)s, -e**) *m* extract

Extratour *f* (*fig: umg*): **sich dat ~en leisten** to do one's own thing

extravagant [ɛkstrava'gant] *adj* extravagant; (*Kleidung*) flamboyant

Extrawurst (*umg*) *f* (*Sonderwunsch*): **er will immer eine ~ (gebraten haben)** he always wants something different

Extrem [ɛks'treːm] (**-s, -e**) *nt* extreme; **extrem** *adj* extreme; **Extremfall** *m* extreme (case)

Extremist, in *m(f)* extremist

Extremistenerlass [ɛkstre'mɪstən|ɛrlas] *m* *law(s) governing extremism*

extremistisch [ɛkstre'mɪstɪʃ] *adj* (*Pol*) extremist

Extremitäten [ɛkstremi'tɛːtən] *pl* extremities *pl*

extrovertiert [ɛkstrover'tiːrt] *adj* extrovert

Exzellenz [ɛkstsɛ'lɛnts] *f* excellency

exzentrisch [ɛks'tsɛntrɪʃ] *adj* eccentric

Exzess [ɛks'tsɛs] (**-es, -e**) *m* excess

Ff

F, f¹ [ɛf] (-, -) *nt* F, f; **F wie Friedrich** ≈ F for Frederick, F for Fox (*US*); **nach Schema F** (*umg*) in the usual old way

f² *abk* (= *feminin*) fem.

Fa. *abk* (= *Firma*) co.

Fabel ['faːbəl] (-, -n) *f* fable; **fabelhaft** *adj* fabulous, marvellous (*Brit*), marvelous (*US*)

Fabrik [fa'briːk] *f* factory; **Fabrikanlage** *f* plant; (*Gelände*) factory premises *pl*

Fabrikant [fabri'kant] *m* (*Hersteller*) manufacturer; (*Besitzer*) industrialist

Fabrikarbeiter, in *m(f)* factory worker

Fabrikat [fabri'kaːt] (-(e)s, -e) *nt* product; (*Marke*) make

Fabrikation [fabriːkatsi'oːn] *f* manufacture, production

Fabrikbesitzer *m* factory owner

Fabrikgelände *nt* factory site

fabrizieren [fabri'tsiːrən] *vt* (*geistiges Produkt*) to produce; (*Geschichte*) to concoct, fabricate

Fach [fax] (-(e)s, -̈er) *nt* compartment; (*in Schrank, Regal etc*) shelf; (*Sachgebiet*) subject; **ein Mann/eine Frau vom ~** an expert; **Facharbeiter** *m* skilled worker; **Facharzt** *m* (medical) specialist; **Fachausdruck** *m* technical term; **Fachbereich** *m* (special) field; (*Univ*) school, faculty; **Fachbuch** *nt* reference book

Fächer ['fɛçər] (-s, -) *m* fan

Fach- *zW*: **Fachfrau** *f* expert; **Fachgebiet** *nt* (special) field; **Fachgeschäft** *nt* specialist shop (*Brit*) *od* store (*US*); **Fachhändler** *m* stockist; **Fachhochschule** *f* college; **Fachidiot** (*umg*) *m* narrow-minded specialist; **Fachkraft** *f* qualified employee; **Fachkräftemangel** *m* lack of skilled *od* qualified personnel; **Fachkreise** *pl*: **in Fachkreisen** among experts; **fachkundig** *adj* expert, specialist; **Fachlehrer** *m* specialist subject teacher; **fachlich** *adj* technical; (*beruflich*) professional; **Fachmann** (-(e)s, *pl* **-leute**) *m* expert; **fachmännisch** *adj* professional; **Fachrichtung** *f* subject area; **Fachschule** *f* technical college; **fachsimpeln** *vi* to talk shop; **fachspezifisch** *adj* technical; **Fachverband** *m* trade association; **Fachwelt** *f* profession; **Fachwerk** *nt* timber frame; **Fachwerkhaus** *nt* half-timbered house

Fackel ['fakəl] (-, -n) *f* torch

fackeln (*umg*) *vi* to dither

Fackelzug *m* torchlight procession

fad, fade *adj* insipid; (*langweilig*) dull; (*Essen*) tasteless

Faden ['faːdən] (-s, -̈) *m* thread; **der rote ~** (*fig*) the central theme; **alle Fäden laufen hier zusammen** this is the nerve centre (*Brit*) *od* center (*US*) of the whole thing; **Fadennudeln** *pl* vermicelli *sing*; **fadenscheinig** *adj* (*lit, fig*) threadbare

Fagott [fa'gɔt] (-(e)s, -e) *nt* bassoon

fähig ['fɛːɪç] *adj*: **~ (zu** *od* +*gen*) capable (of); able (to); **zu allem ~ sein** to be capable of anything; **Fähigkeit** *f* ability

Fähnchen ['fɛːnçən] *nt* pennon, streamer

fahnden ['faːndən] *vi*: **~ nach** to search for

Fahndung *f* search

Fahndungsliste *f* list of wanted criminals, wanted list

Fahne ['faːnə] (-, -n) *f* flag; standard; **mit fliegenden ~n zu jdm/etw überlaufen** to go over to sb/sth; **eine ~ haben** (*umg*) to smell of drink

Fahnenflucht *f* desertion

Fahrausweis *m* (*form*) ticket

Fahrbahn *f* carriageway (*Brit*), roadway

fahrbar *adj*: **~er Untersatz** (*hum*) wheels *pl*

Fähre ['fɛːrə] (-, -n) *f* ferry

fahren ['faːrən] *unreg vt* to drive; (*Rad*) to ride; (*befördern*) to drive, take; (*Rennen*) to drive in ▷ *vi* (*sich bewegen*) to go; (*Schiff*) to sail; (*abfahren*) to leave; **mit dem Auto/Zug ~** to go *od* travel by car/train; **mit dem Aufzug ~** to take the lift, ride the elevator (*US*); **links/rechts ~** to drive on the left/right; **gegen einen Baum ~** to drive *od* go into a tree; **die U-Bahn fährt alle fünf Minuten** the underground goes *od* runs every five minutes; **mit der Hand ~ über** +*akk* to pass one's hand over; **(bei etw) gut/schlecht ~** (*zurechtkommen*) to do well/ badly (with sth); **was ist (denn) in dich ge~?** what's got (*Brit*) *od* gotten (*US*) into you?; **einen ~ lassen** (*umg*) to fart (!)

fahrend *adj*: **~es Volk** travelling people

Fahrer, in ['faːrər(ɪn)] (-s, -) *m(f)* driver; **Fahrerflucht** *f* hit-and-run driving

Fahr- *zW*: **Fahrgast** *m* passenger; **Fahrgeld** *nt* fare; **Fahrgelegenheit** *f* transport; **Fahrgestell**

nt chassis; (*Aviat*) undercarriage

fahrig ['fa:rɪç] *adj* nervous; (*unkonzentriert*) distracted

Fahr- *zW:* **Fahrkarte** *f* ticket; **Fahrkartenausgabe** *f* ticket office; **Fahrkartenautomat** *m* ticket machine; **Fahrkartenschalter** *m* ticket office

fahrlässig *adj* negligent; **~e Tötung** manslaughter; **Fahrlässigkeit** *f* negligence

Fahr- *zW:* **Fahrlehrer** *m* driving instructor; **Fahrplan** *m* timetable; **fahrplanmäßig** *adj* (*Eisenb*) scheduled; **Fahrpraxis** *f* driving experience; **Fahrpreis** *m* fare; **Fahrprüfung** *f* driving test; **Fahrrad** *nt* bicycle; **Fahrradweg** *m* cycle path; **Fahrrinne** *f* (*Naut*) shipping channel, fairway; **Fahrschein** *m* ticket; **Fahrschule** *f* driving school; **Fahrschüler** *m* learner (driver); **Fahrspur** *f* lane; **Fahrstuhl** *m* lift (*Brit*), elevator (*US*); **Fahrstunde** *f* driving lesson

Fahrt [fa:rt] (**-, -en**) *f* journey; (*kurz*) trip; (*Aut*) drive; (*Geschwindigkeit*) speed; **gute ~!** safe journey!; **volle ~ voraus!** (*Naut*) full speed ahead!

fährt [fɛ:rt] *vb siehe* **fahren**

fahrtauglich ['fa:rtaʊklɪç] *adj* fit to drive

Fährte ['fɛ:rtə] (**-, -n**) *f* track, trail; **jdn auf eine falsche ~ locken** (*fig*) to put sb off the scent

Fahrtenschreiber *m* tachograph

Fahrtkosten *pl* travelling expenses *pl*

Fahrtrichtung *f* course, direction

Fahr- *zW:* **fahrtüchtig** ['fa:rtʏçtɪç] *adj* fit to drive; **Fahrverhalten** *nt* (*von Fahrer*) behaviour (*Brit*) *od* behavior (*US*) behind the wheel; (*von Wagen*) road performance; **Fahrzeug** *nt* vehicle; **Fahrzeughalter** (**-s, -**) *m* owner of a vehicle; **Fahrzeugpapiere** *pl* vehicle documents *pl*

Faible ['fɛ:bl] (**-s, -s**) *nt* (*geh*) liking; (*Schwäche*) weakness; (*Vorliebe*) penchant

fair [fɛ:r] *adj* fair

Fäkalien [fɛ'ka:liən] *pl* faeces *pl*

Faksimile [fak'zi:mile] (**-s, -s**) *nt* facsimile

faktisch ['faktɪʃ] *adj* actual

Faktor *m* factor

Faktum (**-s, -ten**) *nt* fact

fakturieren [faktu'ri:rən] *vt* (*Comm*) to invoice

Fakultät [fakʊl'tɛ:t] *f* faculty

Falke ['falkə] (**-n, -n**) *m* falcon

Falklandinseln ['falklant'ɪnzəln] *pl* Falkland Islands, Falklands

Fall [fal] (**-(e)s, ⁻e**) *m* (*Sturz*) fall; (*Sachverhalt, Jur, Gram*) case; **auf jeden ~, auf alle Fälle** in any case; (*bestimmt*) definitely; **gesetzt den ~** assuming (that); **jds ~ sein** (*umg*) to be sb's cup of tea; **klarer ~!** (*umg*) sure thing!, you bet!; **das mache ich auf keinen ~** there's no way I'm going to do that

Falle (**-, -n**) *f* trap; (*umg: Bett*) bed; **jdm eine ~ stellen** to set a trap for sb

fallen *unreg vi* to fall; (*im Krieg*) to fall, be killed; **etw ~ lassen** to drop sth; (*Bemerkung*) to make

sth; (*Plan*) to abandon sth, to drop sth

fällen ['fɛlən] *vt* (*Baum*) to fell; (*Urteil*) to pass

fällig ['fɛlɪç] *adj* due; (*Wechsel*) mature(d); **längst ~** long overdue; **Fälligkeit** *f* (*Comm*) maturity

Fallobst *nt* fallen fruit, windfall

falls *adv* in case, if

Fall- *zW:* **Fallschirm** *m* parachute; **Fallschirmjäger** *m* paratrooper; **Fallschirmspringer, in** *m(f)* parachutist; **Fallschirmtruppe** *f* paratroops *pl*; **Fallstrick** *m* (*fig*) trap, snare; **Fallstudie** *f* case study

fällt [fɛlt] *vb siehe* **fallen**

Falltür *f* trap door

fallweise *adj* from case to case

falsch [falʃ] *adj* false; (*unrichtig*) wrong; **ein ~es Spiel (mit jdm) treiben** to play (sb) false; **etw ~ verstehen** to misunderstand sth, get sth wrong; *siehe auch* **falschliegen**

fälschen ['fɛlʃən] *vt* to forge

Fälscher, in (**-s, -**) *m(f)* forger

Falschgeld *nt* counterfeit money

Falschheit *f* falsity, falseness; (*Unrichtigkeit*) wrongness

fälschlich *adj* false

fälschlicherweise *adv* mistakenly

falschliegen *unreg vi* to be wrong; **~ bei/mit** to be wrong about/in

Falschmeldung *f* (*Presse*) false report

Fälschung *f* forgery

fälschungssicher *adj* forgery-proof

Faltblatt *nt* leaflet; (*in Zeitschrift etc*) insert

Fältchen ['fɛltçən] *nt* crease, wrinkle

Falte ['faltə] (**-, -n**) *f* (*Knick*) fold, crease; (*Hautfalte*) wrinkle; (*Rockfalte*) pleat

falten *vt* to fold; (*Stirn*) to wrinkle

faltenlos *adj* without folds; without wrinkles

Faltenrock *m* pleated skirt

Falter ['faltər] (**-s, -**) *m* (*Tagfalter*) butterfly; (*Nachtfalter*) moth

faltig ['faltɪç] *adj* (*Haut*) wrinkled; (*Rock usw*) creased

falzen ['faltsən] *vt* (*Papierbogen*) to fold

Fam. *abk* = **Familie**

familiär [famili'ɛ:r] *adj* familiar

Familie [fa'mi:liə] *f* family; **~ Otto Francke** (*als Anschrift*) Mr & Mrs Otto Francke and family; **zur ~ gehören** to be one of the family

Familien- *zW:* **Familienanschluss** *m:* **Unterkunft mit Familienanschluss** *accommodation where one is treated as one of the family*; **Familienkreis** *m* family circle; **Familienmitglied** *nt* member of the family; **Familienname** *m* surname; **Familienpackung** *f* family(-size) pack; **Familienplanung** *f* family planning; **Familienstand** *m* marital status; **Familienunternehmen** *nt* family business; **Familienvater** *m* head of the family; **Familienverhältnisse** *pl* family circumstances *pl*

Fanatiker, in [fa'na:tikər(ɪn)] (**-s, -**) *m(f)* fanatic

fanatisch *adj* fanatical

Fanatismus | FDP

Fanatismus [fana'tɪsmʊs] m fanaticism
fand etc [fant] vb siehe **finden**
Fang [faŋ] (-(e)s, ⁻e) m catch; (Jagen) hunting; (Kralle) talon, claw
fangen unreg vt to catch ▷ vr to get caught; (Flugzeug) to level out; (Mensch: nicht fallen) to steady o.s.; (fig) to compose o.s.; (in Leistung) to get back on form
Fangfrage f catch od trick question
Fanggründe pl fishing grounds pl
fängt [fɛŋkt] vb siehe **fangen**
Fantasie [fanta'zi:] f imagination; **in seiner ~** in his mind; **Fantasiegebilde** nt (Einbildung) figment of the imagination; **fantasielos** adj unimaginative
fantasieren [fanta'zi:rən] vi to fantasize; (Med) to be delirious
fantasievoll adj imaginative
Fantast [fan'tast] (-en, -en) m dreamer
fantastisch adj fantastic
Farb- zW: **Farbabzug** m coloured (Brit) od colored (US) print; **Farbaufnahme** f colour (Brit) od color (US) photograph; **Farbband** nt typewriter ribbon
Farbe ['fa:rbə] (-, -n) f colour (Brit), color (US); (zum Malen etc) paint; (Stofffarbe) dye; (Karten) suit
farbecht ['farp|ɛçt] adj colourfast (Brit), colorfast (US)
färben ['fɛrbən] vt to colour (Brit), color (US); (Stoff, Haar) to dye
farben- zW: **farbenblind** adj colour-blind (Brit), color-blind (US); **farbenfroh** adj colourful (Brit), colorful (US); **farbenprächtig** adj colourful (Brit), colorful (US)
Farbfernsehen nt colour (Brit) od color (US) television
Farbfilm m colour (Brit) od color (US) film
Farbfoto nt colour (Brit) od color (US) photo
farbig adj coloured (Brit), colored (US)
Farbige, r f(m) coloured (Brit) od colored (US) person
Farb- zW: **Farbkasten** m paintbox; **farblos** adj colourless (Brit), colorless (US); **Farbstift** m coloured (Brit) od colored (US) pencil; **Farbstoff** m dye; (Lebensmittelfarb) (artificial) colouring (Brit) od coloring (US); **Farbton** m hue, tone
Färbung ['fɛrbʊŋ] f colouring (Brit), coloring (US); (Tendenz) bias
Farn [farn] (-(e)s, -e) m fern; (Adlerfarn) bracken
Farnkraut [farn] nt = **Farn**
Färöer [fɛ'rø:ər] pl Faeroe Islands pl
Fasan [fa'za:n] (-(e)s, -e(n)) m pheasant
Fasching ['faʃɪŋ] (-s, -e od -s) m carnival
Faschismus [fa'ʃɪsmʊs] m fascism
Faschist, in m(f) fascist
faschistisch [fa'ʃɪstɪʃ] adj fascist
faseln ['fa:zəln] vi to talk nonsense, drivel
Faser ['fa:zər] (-, -n) f fibre
Fass [fas] (-es, ⁻er) nt vat, barrel; (für Öl) drum; **Bier vom ~** draught beer; **ein ~ ohne Boden** (fig) a bottomless pit
Fassade [fa'sa:də] f (lit, fig) façade

fassbar adj comprehensible
Fassbier nt draught beer
fassen ['fasən] vt (ergreifen) to grasp, take; (inhaltlich) to hold; (Entschluss etc) to take; (verstehen) to understand; (Ring etc) to set; (formulieren) to formulate, phrase ▷ vr to calm down; **nicht zu ~** unbelievable; siehe auch **kurzfassen**
fasslich ['faslɪç] adj comprehensible
Fasson [fa'sõ:] (-, -s) f style; (Art und Weise) way; **aus der ~ geraten** (lit) to lose its shape
Fassung ['fasʊŋ] f (Umrahmung) mounting; (Lampenfassung) socket; (Wortlaut) version; (Beherrschung) composure; **jdn aus der ~ bringen** to upset sb; **völlig außer ~ geraten** to lose all self-control
fassungslos adj speechless
Fassungsvermögen nt capacity; (Verständnis) comprehension
fast [fast] adv almost, nearly; **~ nie** hardly ever
fasten ['fastən] vi to fast; **Fasten** (-s) nt fasting; **Fastenzeit** f Lent
Fastnacht f Shrovetide carnival
faszinieren [fastsi'ni:rən] vt to fascinate
fatal [fa'ta:l] adj fatal; (peinlich) embarrassing
fauchen ['fauxən] vt, vi to hiss
faul [faul] adj rotten; (Person) lazy; (Ausreden) lame; **daran ist etwas ~** there's something fishy about it
faulen vi to rot
faulenzen ['faulɛntsən] vi to idle
Faulenzer, in (-s, -) m(f) idler, loafer
Faulheit f laziness
faulig adj putrid
Fäulnis ['fɔylnɪs] (-) f decay, putrefaction
Faulpelz (umg) m lazybones sing
Faust [faust] (-, Fäuste) f fist; **das passt wie die ~ aufs Auge** (passt nicht) it's all wrong; **auf eigene ~** (fig) on one's own initiative
Fäustchen ['fɔystçən] nt: **sich** dat **ins ~ lachen** to laugh up one's sleeve
faustdick (umg) adj: **er hat es ~ hinter den Ohren** he's a crafty one
Fausthandschuh m mitten
Faustregel f rule of thumb
Favorit, in [favo'ri:t(ɪn)] (-en, -en) m(f) favourite (Brit), favorite (US)
Fax [faks] (-, -e) nt fax; **faxen** vt to fax
Faxen ['faksən] pl: **~ machen** to fool around
Fazit ['fa:tsɪt] (-s, -s od -e) nt: **wenn wir aus diesen vier Jahren das ~ ziehen** if we take stock of these four years
FCKW (-s, -s) m abk (= Fluorchlorkohlenwasserstoff) CFC
FdH (umg) abk (= Friss die Hälfte) eat less
FDP, F.D.P. f abk (= Freie Demokratische Partei) Free Democratic Party; see culture note

● **FDP**
●
● The FDP (Freie Demokratische Partei) was
● founded in 1948 and is Germany's centre
● party. It is a liberal party which has formed

governing coalitions with both the SPD and the CDU/CSU at times, both in the regions and in the *Bundestag*.

Feb. *abk* (= *Februar*) Feb.

Februar ['fe:brua:r] **(-(s), -e)** (*pl selten*) *m* February; *siehe auch* **September**

fechten ['fɛçtən] *unreg vi* to fence

Feder ['fe:dər] **(-, -n)** *f* feather; (*Schreibfeder*) pen nib; (*Tech*) spring; **in den ~n liegen** (*umg*) to be/stay in bed; **Federball** *m* shuttlecock; **Federballspiel** *nt* badminton; **Federbett** *nt* continental quilt; **federführend** *adj* (*Behörde*): **federführend (für)** in overall charge (of); **Federhalter** *m* pen; **federleicht** *adj* light as a feather; **Federlesen** *nt*: **nicht viel Federlesens mit jdm/etw machen** to make short work of sb/sth

federn *vi* (*nachgeben*) to be springy; (*sich bewegen*) to bounce ▷ *vt* to spring

Federung *f* suspension

Federvieh *nt* poultry

Federweiße, r *m* new wine

Federzeichnung *f* pen-and-ink drawing

Fee [fe:] **(-, -n)** *f* fairy

feenhaft ['fe:ənhaft] *adj* (*liter*) fairylike

Fegefeuer ['fe:gəfɔyər] *nt* purgatory

fegen ['fe:gən] *vt* to sweep

fehl [fe:l] *adj*: **~ am Platz** *od* **Ort** out of place; **Fehlanzeige** (*umg*) *f* dead loss

fehlen *vi* to be wanting *od* missing; (*abwesend sein*) to be absent ▷ *vi unpers*: **es fehlte nicht viel und ich hätte ihn verprügelt** I almost hit him; **etw fehlt jdm** sb lacks sth; **du fehlst mir** I miss you; **was fehlt ihm?** what's wrong with him?; **der/das hat mir gerade noch gefehlt!** (*ironisch*) he/that was all I needed; **weit gefehlt!** (*fig*) you're way out! (*umg*); (*ganz im Gegenteil*) far from it!; **mir ~ die Worte** words fail me; **wo fehlt es?** what's the trouble?, what's up? (*umg*)

Fehlentscheidung *f* wrong decision

Fehlentwicklung *f* mistake

Fehler (-s, -) *m* mistake, error; (*Mangel, Schwäche*) fault; **ihr ist ein ~ unterlaufen** she's made a mistake; **Fehlerbeseitigung** *f* (*Comput*) debugging; **fehlerfrei** *adj* faultless; without any mistakes; **fehlerhaft** *adj* incorrect; faulty; **fehlerlos** *adj* = **fehlerfrei**; **Fehlermeldung** *f* (*Comput*) error message; **Fehlersuchprogramm** *nt* (*Comput*) debugger

fehl- *zW*: **Fehlgeburt** *f* miscarriage; **fehlgehen** *unreg vi* to go astray; **Fehlgriff** *m* blunder; **Fehlkonstruktion** *f*: **eine Fehlkonstruktion sein** to be badly designed; **Fehlleistung** *f*: **freudsche Fehlleistung** Freudian slip; **Fehlschlag** *m* failure; **fehlschlagen** *unreg vi* to fail; **Fehlschluss** *m* wrong conclusion; **Fehlstart** *m* (*Sport*) false start; **Fehltritt** *m* false move; (*fig*) blunder, slip; (: *Affäre*) indiscretion; **Fehlurteil** *nt* miscarriage of justice; **Fehlzündung** *f* (*Aut*) misfire, backfire

Feier ['faɪər] **(-, -n)** *f* celebration; **Feierabend**

Feb. | **Feministin**

m time to stop work; **Feierabend machen** to stop, knock off; **was machst du am Feierabend?** what are you doing after work?; **jetzt ist Feierabend!** that's enough!

feierlich *adj* solemn; **das ist ja nicht mehr ~** (*umg*) that's beyond a joke; **Feierlichkeit** *f* solemnity; **Feierlichkeiten** *pl* festivities *pl*

feiern *vt, vi* to celebrate

Feiertag *m* holiday

feig *adj* cowardly

Feige ['faɪgə] **(-, -n)** *f* fig

feige *adj* cowardly

Feigheit *f* cowardice

Feigling *m* coward

Feile ['faɪlə] **(-, -n)** *f* file

feilen *vt, vi* to file

feilschen ['faɪlʃən] *vi* to haggle

fein [faɪn] *adj* fine; (*vornehm*) refined; (*Gehör etc*) keen; **~!** great!; **er ist ~ raus** (*umg*) he's sitting pretty; **sich ~ machen** to get all dressed up

Feind, in [faɪnt, 'faɪndɪn] **(-(e)s, -e)** *m(f)* enemy; **Feindbild** *nt* concept of an/the enemy; **feindlich** *adj* hostile; **Feindschaft** *f* enmity; **feindselig** *adj* hostile; **Feindseligkeit** *f* hostility

Fein- *zW*: **feinfühlend** *adj* sensitive; **feinfühlig** *adj* sensitive; **Feingefühl** *nt* delicacy, tact; **Feinheit** *f* fineness; refinement; keenness; **Feinkostgeschäft** *nt* delicatessen (shop), deli; **Feinschmecker (-s, -)** *m* gourmet; **Feinwaschmittel** *nt* mild(-action) detergent

feist [faɪst] *adj* fat

feixen ['faɪksən] (*umg*) *vi* to smirk

Feld [fɛlt] **(-(e)s, -er)** *nt* field; (*Schach*) square; (*Sport*) pitch; **Argumente ins ~ führen** to bring arguments to bear; **das ~ räumen** (*fig*) to bow out; **Feldarbeit** *f* (*Agr*) work in the fields; (*Geog etc*) fieldwork; **Feldblume** *f* wild flower; **Feldherr** *m* commander; **Feldjäger** *pl* (*Mil*) the military police; **Feldlazarett** *nt* (*Mil*) field hospital; **Feldsalat** *m* lamb's lettuce; **Feldstecher** *m* (pair of) binoculars *pl od* field glasses *pl*

Feld-Wald-und-Wiesen- (*umg*) *in zW* common-or-garden

Feld- *zW*: **Feldwebel (-s, -)** *m* sergeant; **Feldweg** *m* path; **Feldzug** *m* (*lit, fig*) campaign

Felge ['fɛlgə] **(-, -n)** *f* (wheel) rim

Felgenbremse *f* caliper brake

Fell [fɛl] **(-(e)s, -e)** *nt* fur; coat; (*von Schaf*) fleece; (*von toten Tieren*) skin; **ein dickes ~ haben** to be thick-skinned, have a thick skin; **ihm sind die ~e weggeschwommen** (*fig*) all his hopes were dashed

Fels [fɛls] **(-en, -en)** *m* = **Felsen**

Felsen ['fɛlzən] **(-s, -)** *m* rock; (*Klippe*) cliff; **felsenfest** *adj* firm

felsig *adj* rocky

Felsspalte *f* crevice

Felsvorsprung *m* ledge

feminin [femi'ni:n] *adj* feminine; (*pej*) effeminate

Feministin [femi'nɪstɪn] *f* feminist

121

Fenchel ['fɛnçəl] (**-s**) m fennel

Fenster ['fɛnstər] (**-s, -**) nt window; **weg vom ~** (umg) out of the game, finished; **Fensterbrett** nt windowsill; **Fensterladen** m shutter; **Fensterleder** nt chamois, shammy (leather); **Fensterplatz** m window seat; **Fensterputzer** (**-s, -**) m window cleaner; **Fensterscheibe** f windowpane; **Fenstersims** m windowsill

Ferien ['fe:riən] pl holidays pl, vacation (US); **die großen ~** the summer holidays (Brit), the long vacation (US Univ); **~ haben** to be on holiday; **Ferienhaus** nt holiday home; **Ferienkurs** m holiday course; **Ferienreise** f holiday; **Ferienwohnung** f holiday flat (Brit), vacation apartment (US); **Ferienzeit** f holiday period

Ferkel ['fɛrkəl] (**-s, -**) nt piglet

fern [fɛrn] adj, adv far-off, distant; **~ von hier** a long way (away) from here; siehe auch **fernhalten, fernliegen**; **Fernbedienung** f remote control; **fernbleiben** unreg vi: **fernbleiben (von** od +dat) to stay away (from)

Ferne (**-, -n**) f distance

ferner adj, adv further; (weiterhin) in future; **unter „~ liefen" rangieren** (umg) to be an also-ran

fern- zW: **Fernfahrer** m long-distance lorry (Brit) od truck driver; **Fernflug** m long-distance flight; **Ferngespräch** nt long-distance call (Brit), toll call (US); **ferngesteuert** adj remote-controlled; (Rakete) guided; **Fernglas** nt binoculars pl; **fernhalten** unreg vt to keep away; **Fernkopie** f fax; **Fernkopierer** m fax machine; **Fernkurs, Fernkursus** m correspondence course; **Fernlenkung** f remote control; **Fernlicht** nt (Aut): **mit Fernlicht fahren** to drive on full beam; **fernliegen** unreg vi: **jdm fernliegen** to be far from sb's mind

Fernmelde- in zW telecommunications; (Mil) signals

fern- zW: **Fernost** aus/in **Fernost** from/in the Far East; **fernöstlich** adj Far Eastern attrib; **Fernrohr** nt telescope; **Fernschreiben** nt telex; **Fernschreiber** m teleprinter; **fernschriftlich** adj by telex

Fernsehapparat m television (set)

Fernsehduell nt TV duel od debate

fernsehen ['fɛrnze:ən] unreg vi to watch television; **Fernsehen** (**-s**) nt television; **im Fernsehen** on television

Fernseher (**-s, -**) m television (set)

Fernseh- zW: **Fernsehgebühr** f television licence (Brit) od license (US) fee; **Fernsehgerät** nt television set; **Fernsehprogramm** nt (Kanal) channel, station (US); (Sendung) programme (Brit), program (US); (Fernsehzeitschrift) (television) programme (Brit) od program (US) guide; **Fernsehsendung** f television programme (Brit) od program (US); **Fernsehüberwachungsanlage** f closed-circuit television; **Fernsehzuschauer** m (television) viewer

Fern- zW: **Fernsprecher** m telephone;

Fernsprechzelle f telephone box (Brit) od booth (US); **Fernsteuerung** f remote control

Fernstudium nt multimedia course, ≈ Open University course (Brit); see culture note

Fernverkehr m long-distance traffic

Fernweh nt wanderlust

Ferse ['fɛrzə] (**-, -n**) f heel

Fersengeld nt: **~ geben** to take to one's heels

fertig ['fɛrtɪç] adj (bereit) ready; (beendet) finished; (gebrauchsfertig) ready-made; **~ ausgebildet** fully qualified; **mit jdm/etw ~ werden** to cope with sb/sth; **mit den Nerven ~ sein** to be at the end of one's tether; **~ bringen** od **machen** (beenden) to finish; **sich ~ machen** to get ready; **~ essen/lesen** to finish eating/reading; **~ stellen** to complete; **Fertigbau** m prefab(ricated house)

fertigbringen unreg vt (fähig sein) to manage, be capable of; (beenden) to finish

fertigen ['fɛrtɪgən] vt to manufacture

Fertig- zW: **Fertiggericht** nt ready-to-serve meal; **Fertighaus** nt prefab(ricated house); **Fertigkeit** f skill; **fertigmachen** (umg) vt (Person) to finish; (körperlich) to exhaust; (moralisch) to get down; siehe auch **fertig**; **fertigstellen** vt to complete

Fertigung f production

Fertigungs- in zW production; **Fertigungsstraße** f production line

Fertigware f finished product

fertigwerden unreg vi siehe **fertig**

fesch [fɛʃ] (umg) adj (modisch) smart; (: hübsch) attractive

Fessel ['fɛsəl] (**-, -n**) f fetter

fesseln vt to bind; (mit Fesseln) to fetter; (fig) to grip; **ans Bett gefesselt** (fig) confined to bed

fesselnd adj gripping

Fest [fɛst] (**-(e)s, -e**) nt (Feier) celebration; (Party) party; **man soll die ~e feiern wie sie fallen** (Sprichwort) make hay while the sun shines

fest adj firm; (Nahrung) solid; (Gehalt) regular; (Gewebe, Schuhe) strong, sturdy; (Freund(in)) steady ▷ adv (schlafen) soundly; **~ angestellt** employed on a permanent basis; **~ entschlossen sein** to be absolutely determined; **~ umrissen** clearcut; **~e Kosten** (Comm) fixed costs pl

Festbeleuchtung f illumination

festbinden unreg vt to tie, fasten

festbleiben *unreg vi* to stand firm
Festessen *nt* banquet
festfahren *unreg vr* to get stuck
Festgeldkonto *nt* time-deposit account
festhalten *unreg vt* to seize, hold fast; (*Ereignis*)
 to record ▷ *vr:* **sich ~ (an** +*dat*) to hold on (to)
festigen *vt* to strengthen
Festigkeit *f* strength
fest- *zW:* **festklammern** *vr:* **sich
 festklammern (an** +*dat*) to cling on (to);
 festklemmen *vt* to wedge fast; **Festkomma** *nt*
 (*Comput*) fixed point; **Festland** *nt* mainland;
 festlegen *vt* to fix ▷ *vr* to commit o.s.; **jdn auf
 etw** *akk* **festlegen** (*festnageln*) to tie sb (down)
 to sth; (*verpflichten*) to commit sb to sth
festlich *adj* festive
fest- *zW:* **festliegen** *unreg vi* (*Fin: Geld*) to be tied
 up; **festmachen** *vt* to fasten; (*Termin etc*) to
 fix; **festnageln** *vt:* **jdn festnageln (auf** +*akk*)
 (*fig: umg*) to pin sb down (to); **Festnahme** (**-, -n**)
 f capture; **festnehmen** *unreg vt* to capture,
 arrest; **Festnetztelefon** *nt* fixed-line phone;
 Festplatte *f* (*Comput*) hard disk; **Festpreis** *m*
 (*Comm*) fixed price
Festrede *f* speech, address
festschnallen *vt* to strap down ▷ *vr* to fasten
 one's seat belt
festsetzen *vt* to fix, settle
Festspiel *nt* festival
fest- *zW:* **feststehen** *unreg vi* to be certain;
 feststellbar *adj* (*herauszufinden*) ascertainable;
 feststellen *vt* to establish; (*sagen*) to remark;
 (*Tech*) to lock (fast); **Feststellung** *f:* **die
 Feststellung machen, dass ...** to realize
 that ...; (*bemerken*) to remark *od* observe that ...;
 Festtag *m* holiday
Festung *f* fortress
festverzinslich *adj* fixed-interest *attrib*
Festwertspeicher *m* (*Comput*) read-only
 memory
Festzelt *nt* marquee
Fête [ˈfɛːtə] (**-, -n**) *f* party
Fett [fɛt] (**-(e)s, -e**) *nt* fat, grease; **fett** *adj* fat;
 (*Essen etc*) greasy; **fett gedruckt** bold-type;
 fettarm *adj* low fat; **fetten** *vt* to grease;
 Fettfleck *m* grease spot *od* stain; **fettfrei** *adj*
 fat-free; **Fettgehalt** *m* fat content; **fettig**
 adj greasy, fatty; **Fettnäpfchen** *nt:* **ins
 Fettnäpfchen treten** to put one's foot in it;
 Fettpolster *nt* (*hum: umg*): **Fettpolster haben**
 to be well-padded
Fetzen [ˈfɛtsən] (**-s, -**) *m* scrap; **..., dass die ~
 fliegen** (*umg*) ... like mad
feucht [fɔyçt] *adj* damp; (*Luft*) humid;
 feuchtfröhlich *adj* (*hum*) boozy
Feuchtigkeit *f* dampness; humidity
Feuchtigkeitscreme *f* moisturizer
feudal [fɔyˈdaːl] *adj* (*Pol, Hist*) feudal; (*umg*)
 plush
Feuer [ˈfɔyər] (**-s, -**) *nt* fire; (*zum Rauchen*) a
 light; (*fig: Schwung*) spirit; **für jdn durchs ~
 gehen** to go through fire and water for sb;
 ~ und Flamme (für etw) sein (*umg*) to be

dead keen (on sth); **~ für etw/jdn fangen**
 (*fig*) to develop a great interest in sth/sb;
 Feueralarm *m* fire alarm; **Feuereifer** *m* zeal;
 feuerfest *adj* fireproof; **Feuergefahr** *f* danger
 of fire; **bei Feuergefahr** in the event of fire;
 feuergefährlich *adj* inflammable; **Feuerleiter**
 f fire escape ladder; **Feuerlöscher** (**-s, -**) *m* fire
 extinguisher; **Feuermelder** (**-s, -**) *m* fire alarm
feuern *vt, vi* (*lit, fig*) to fire
Feuer- *zW:* **feuerpolizeilich** *adj* (*Bestimmungen*)
 laid down by the fire authorities; **Feuerprobe**
 f acid test; **feuerrot** *adj* fiery red
Feuersbrunst *f* (*geh*) conflagration
Feuer- *zW:* **Feuerschlucker** *m* fire-eater;
 Feuerschutz *m* (*Vorbeugung*) fire prevention;
 (*Mil: Deckung*) covering fire; **feuersicher** *adj*
 fireproof; **Feuerstein** *m* flint; **Feuerstelle**
 f fireplace; **Feuertreppe** *f* fire escape;
 Feuerversicherung *f* fire insurance;
 Feuerwaffe *f* firearm; **Feuerwehr** *f* fire
 brigade; **Feuerwehrauto** *nt* fire engine;
 Feuerwerk *nt* fireworks *pl*; **Feuerwerkskörper**
 m firework; **Feuerzangenbowle** *f* red wine
 punch containing rum which has been flamed off;
 Feuerzeug *nt* (cigarette) lighter
Feuilleton [fœjəˈtõː] (**-s, -s**) *nt* (*Presse*) feature
 section; (*Artikel*) feature (article)
feurig [ˈfɔyrɪç] *adj* fiery
Fiche [fiːʃ] (**-s, -s**) *m od nt* (micro)fiche
ficht [fɪçt] *vb siehe* **fechten**
Fichte [ˈfɪçtə] (**-, -n**) *f* spruce
ficken [ˈfɪkən] (*umg!*) *vt, vi* to fuck (!)
fickerig [ˈfɪkərɪç], **fickrig** [ˈfɪkrɪç] (*umg*) *adj*
 fidgety
fidel [fiˈdeːl] (*umg*) *adj* jolly
Fidschi-Inseln, Fidschiinseln [ˈfɪdʒiˈɪnzəln]
 pl Fiji Islands
Fieber [ˈfiːbər] (**-s, -**) *nt* fever, temperature;
 (*Krankheit*) fever; **~ haben** to have a
 temperature; **fieberhaft** *adj* feverish;
 Fiebermesser *m* thermometer;
 Fieberthermometer *nt* thermometer
fiel *etc* [fiːl] *vb siehe* **fallen**
fies [fiːs] (*umg*) *adj* nasty
Figur [fiˈguːr] (**-, -en**) *f* figure; (*Schachfigur*)
 chessman, chess piece; **eine gute/schlechte/
 traurige ~ abgeben** to cut a good/poor/sorry
 figure
fiktiv [fɪkˈtiːf] *adj* fictitious
Filet [fiˈleː] (**-s, -s**) *nt* (*Koch*) fillet; (*Rinderfilet*)
 fillet steak; (*zum Braten*) piece of sirloin *od*
 tenderloin (*US*)
Filiale [filiˈaːlə] (**-, -n**) *f* (*Comm*) branch
Filipino [filiˈpiːno] (**-s, -s**) *m* Filipino
Film [fɪlm] (**-(e)s, -e**) *m* film, movie (*bes US*);
 da ist bei mir der ~ gerissen (*umg*) I had a
 mental blackout; **Filmaufnahme** *f* shooting
Filmemacher, in *m(f)* film-maker
filmen *vt, vi* to film
Film- *zW:* **Filmfestspiele** *pl* film festival *sing*;
 Filmkamera *f* cine-camera; **Filmriss** (*umg*) *m*
 mental blackout; **Filmschauspieler, in** *m(f)*
 film *od* movie (*bes US*) actor, film *od* movie

actress; **Filmverleih** m film distributors pl; **Filmvorführgerät** nt cine-projector
Filter ['fıltər] (**-s, -**) m filter; **Filterkaffee** m filter od drip (US) coffee; **Filtermundstück** nt filter tip
filtern vt to filter
Filterpapier nt filter paper
Filz [fılts] (**-es, -e**) m felt
filzen vt (umg) to frisk ▷ vi (Wolle) to mat
Filzstift m felt-tip (pen)
Fimmel ['fıməl] (**-s, -**) (umg) m: **du hast wohl einen ~!** you're crazy!
Finale [fi'na:lə] (**-s, -(s)**) nt finale; (Sport) final(s pl)
Finanz [fi'nants] f finance; **Finanzen** pl finances pl; **das übersteigt meine ~en** that's beyond my means; **Finanzamt** nt ≈ Inland Revenue Office (Brit), Internal Revenue Office (US); **Finanzbeamte, r** f(m) revenue officer; **Finanzdienstleister, in** m(f) (Bank etc) financial services provider
finanziell [finantsi'el] adj financial
finanzieren [finan'tsi:rən] vt to finance, to fund
Finanzierung f financing, funding
Finanz- zW: **Finanzminister** m ≈ Chancellor of the Exchequer (Brit), Minister of Finance; **finanzschwach** adj financially weak; **Finanzwesen** nt financial system; **Finanzwirtschaft** f public finances pl
finden ['fındən] unreg vt to find; (meinen) to think ▷ vr to be (found); (sich fassen) to compose o.s. ▷ vi: **ich finde schon allein hinaus** I can see myself out; **ich finde nichts dabei, wenn ...** I don't see what's wrong if ...; **das wird sich ~** things will work out
Finder, in (**-s, -**) m(f) finder; **Finderlohn** m reward (for the finder)
findig adj resourceful
fing etc [fıŋ] vb siehe **fangen**
Finger ['fıŋər] (**-s, -**) m finger; **mit ~n auf jdn zeigen** (fig) to look askance at sb; **das kann sich jeder an den (fünf) ~n abzählen** (umg) it sticks out a mile; **sich** dat **etw aus den ~n saugen** (umg) to conjure sth up; **lange ~ machen** (umg) to be light-fingered; **Fingerabdruck** m fingerprint; **Fingerhandschuh** m glove; **Fingerhut** m thimble; (Bot) foxglove; **Fingernagel** m fingernail; **Fingerring** m ring; **Fingerspitze** f fingertip; **Fingerspitzengefühl** nt sensitivity; **Fingerzeig** (**-(e)s, -e**) m hint, pointer
fingieren [fıŋ'gi:rən] vt to feign
fingiert adj made-up, fictitious
Fink ['fıŋk] (**-en, -en**) m finch
Finne ['fınə] (**-n, -n**) m Finn
Finnin ['fının] f Finn
finnisch adj Finnish
Finnland nt Finland
finster ['fınstər] adj dark, gloomy; (verdächtig) dubious; (verdrossen) grim; (Gedanke) dark; **jdn ~ ansehen** to give sb a black look; **Finsternis** (**-**) f darkness, gloom

Finte ['fıntə] (**-, -n**) f feint, trick
Firlefanz ['fırləfants] (umg) m (Kram) frippery; (Albernheit): **mach keinen ~** don't clown around
Firma (**-, -men**) f firm; **die ~ dankt** (hum) much obliged (to you)
Firmen- zW: **Firmeninhaber** m proprietor (of firm); **Firmenregister** nt register of companies; **Firmenschild** nt (shop) sign; **Firmenübernahme** f takeover; **Firmenwagen** m company car; **Firmenzeichen** nt trademark
Firmung f (Rel) confirmation
Firnis ['fırnıs] (**-ses, -se**) m varnish
Fis [fıs] (**-, -**) nt (Mus) F sharp
Fisch [fıʃ] (**-(e)s, -e**) m fish; **Fische** pl (Astrol) Pisces sing; **das sind kleine ~e** (fig: umg) that's child's play; **Fischbestand** m fish population
fischen vt, vi to fish
Fischer (**-s, -**) m fisherman
Fischerei [fıʃə'raı] f fishing, fishery
Fisch- zW: **Fischfang** m fishing; **Fischgeschäft** nt fishmonger's (shop); **Fischgräte** f fishbone; **Fischgründe** pl fishing grounds pl, fisheries pl; **Fischstäbchen** nt fish finger (Brit), fish stick (US); **Fischzucht** f fish-farming; **Fischzug** m catch of fish
Fisimatenten [fizima'tεntən] (umg) pl (Ausflüchte) excuses pl; (Umstände) fuss sing
Fiskus ['fısku s] m (fig: Staatskasse) Treasury
fit [fıt] adj fit
Fitness ['fıtnəs] nt fitness
Fitnesstrainer, in m(f) fitness trainer, personal trainer
Fittich ['fıtıç] (**-(e)s, -e**) m (liter): **jdn unter seine ~e nehmen** (hum) to take sb under one's wing
fix [fıks] adj (flink) quick; (Person) alert, smart; **~e Idee** obsession, idée fixe; **~ und fertig** finished; (erschöpft) done in; **jdn ~ und fertig machen** (nervös machen) to drive sb mad
fixen (umg) vi (Drogen spritzen) to fix
Fixer, in ['fıksər(ın)] (umg) m(f) junkie (inf); **Fixerstube** (umg) f junkies' centre (inf)
fixieren [fı'ksi:rən] vt to fix; (anstarren) to stare at; **er ist zu stark auf seine Mutter fixiert** (Psych) he has a mother fixation
Fixkosten pl (Comm) fixed costs pl
FKK abk = **Freikörperkultur**
flach [flax] adj flat; (Gefäß) shallow; **auf dem ~en Land** in the middle of the country
Fläche ['flεçə] (**-, -n**) f area; (Oberfläche) surface
Flächeninhalt m surface area
Flach- zW: **flachfallen** unreg (umg) vi to fall through; **Flachheit** f flatness; shallowness; **Flachland** nt lowland; **flachliegen** unreg (umg) vi to be laid up; **Flachmann** (**-(e)s, **pl** -männer**) (umg) m hip flask
flachsen ['flaksən] (umg) vi to kid around
flackern ['flakərn] vi to flare, flicker
Fladen- ['fla:dən] (**-s, -**) m (Koch) round flat dough-cake; (umg: Kuhfladen) cowpat
Flagge ['flagə] (**-, -n**) f flag; **~ zeigen** (fig) to nail one's colours to the mast

flaggen vi to fly flags od a flag
flagrant [fla'grant] adj flagrant; **in ~i** red-handed
Flak [flak] **(-s, -)** f (= Flug(zeug)abwehrkanone) anti-aircraft gun; (Einheit) anti-aircraft unit
flambieren [flam'bi:rən] vt (Koch) to flambé
Flame ['fla:mə] **(-n, -n)** m Fleming
Flämin ['flɛ:mɪn] f Fleming
flämisch ['flɛ:mɪʃ] adj Flemish
Flamme ['flamə] **(-, -n)** f flame; **in ~n stehen/ aufgehen** to be in/go up in flames
Flandern ['flandərn] nt Flanders sing
Flanell [fla'nɛl] **(-s, -e)** m flannel
Flanke ['flaŋkə] **(-, -n)** f flank; (Sport: Seite) wing
Flasche ['flaʃə] **(-, -n)** f bottle; (umg: Versager) wash-out; **zur ~ greifen** (fig) to hit the bottle
Flaschen- zW: **Flaschenbier** nt bottled beer; **Flaschenöffner** m bottle opener; **Flaschenwein** m bottled wine; **Flaschenzug** m pulley
flatterhaft adj flighty, fickle
flattern ['flatərn] vi to flutter
flau [flau] adj (Brise, Comm) slack; **jdm ist ~ (im Magen)** sb feels queasy
Flaum [flaum] **(-(e)s)** m (Feder) down
flauschig ['flauʃɪç] adj fluffy
Flausen ['flauzən] pl silly ideas pl; (Ausflüchte) weak excuses pl
Flaute ['flautə] **(-, -n)** f calm; (Comm) recession
Flechte ['flɛçtə] **(-, -n)** f (Med) dry scab; (Bot) lichen
flechten unreg vt to plait; (Kranz) to twine
Fleck [flɛk] **(-(e)s, -e)** m (Schmutzfleck) stain; (Farbfleck) patch; (Stelle) spot; **nicht vom ~ kommen** (lit, fig) not to get any further; **sich nicht vom ~ rühren** not to budge; **vom ~ weg** straight away
Fleckchen nt: **ein schönes ~ (Erde)** a lovely little spot
Flecken **(-s, -)** m = **Fleck; fleckenlos** adj spotless; **Fleckenmittel** nt stain remover; **Fleckenwasser** nt stain remover
fleckig adj marked; (schmutzig) stained
Fledermaus ['fle:dərmaus] f bat
Flegel ['fle:gəl] **(-s, -)** m flail; (Person) lout; **flegelhaft** adj loutish, unmannerly; **Flegeljahre** pl adolescence sing
flegeln vr to loll, sprawl
flehen ['fle:ən] vi (geh) to implore
flehentlich adj imploring
Fleisch ['flaɪʃ] **(-(e)s)** nt flesh; (Essen) meat; **sich** dat od akk **ins eigene ~ schneiden** to cut off one's nose to spite one's face (Sprichwort); **es ist mir in ~ und Blut übergegangen** it has become second nature to me; **Fleischbrühe** f meat stock
Fleischer **(-s, -)** m butcher
Fleischerei [flaɪʃə'raɪ] f butcher's (shop)
fleischig adj fleshy
Fleisch- zW: **Fleischkäse** m meat loaf; **fleischlich** adj carnal; **Fleischpastete** f meat pie; **Fleischsalat** m diced meat salad with mayonnaise; **Fleischvergiftung** f food poisoning (from meat); **Fleischwolf** m mincer; **Fleischwunde** f flesh wound; **Fleischwurst** f pork sausage
Fleiß ['flaɪs] **(-es)** m diligence, industry; **ohne ~ kein Preis** (Sprichwort) success never comes easily
fleißig adj diligent, industrious; **~ studieren/ arbeiten** to study/work hard
flektieren [flɛk'ti:rən] vt to inflect
flennen ['flɛnən] (umg) vi to cry, blubber
fletschen ['flɛtʃən] vt (Zähne) to show
Fleurop® ['flɔyrɔp] f ≈ Interflora®
flexibel [flɛ'ksi:bəl] adj flexible
Flexibilität [flɛksibili'tɛ:t] f flexibility
flicht [flɪçt] vb siehe **flechten**
Flicken ['flɪkən] **(-s, -)** m patch
flicken vt to mend
Flickschusterei ['flɪkʃu:stəraɪ] f: **das ist ~** that's a patch-up job
Flieder ['fli:dər] **(-s, -)** m lilac
Fliege ['fli:gə] **(-, -n)** f fly; (Schlips) bow tie; **zwei ~n mit einer Klappe schlagen** (Sprichwort) to kill two birds with one stone; **ihn stört die ~ an der Wand** every little thing irritates him
fliegen unreg vt, vi to fly; **auf jdn/etw ~** (umg) to be mad about sb/sth; **aus der Kurve ~** to skid off the bend; **aus der Firma ~** (umg) to get the sack
fliegend adj attrib flying; **~e Hitze** hot flushes pl
Fliegengewicht nt (Sport, fig) flyweight
Fliegenklatsche ['fli:gənklatʃə] f fly-swat
Fliegenpilz m fly agaric
Flieger **(-s, -)** m flier, airman; **Fliegeralarm** m air-raid warning
fliehen ['fli:ən] unreg vi to flee
Fliehkraft ['fli:kraft] f centrifugal force
Fliese ['fli:zə] **(-, -n)** f tile
Fließband ['fli:sbant] nt assembly od production line; **am ~ arbeiten** to work on the assembly od production line; **Fließbandarbeit** f production-line work; **Fließbandproduktion** f assembly-line production
fließen unreg vi to flow
fließend adj flowing; (Rede, Deutsch) fluent; (Übergang) smooth
Fließ- zW: **Fließheck** nt fastback; **Fließkomma** nt (Comput) ≈ floating point; **Fließpapier** nt blotting paper (Brit), fleece paper (US)
Flimmerkasten (umg) m (Fernsehen) box
Flimmerkiste (umg) f (Fernsehen) box
flimmern ['flɪmərn] vi to glimmer; **es flimmert mir vor den Augen** my head's swimming
flink [flɪŋk] adj nimble, lively; **mit etw ~ bei der Hand sein** to be quick (off the mark) with sth; **Flinkheit** f nimbleness, liveliness
Flinte ['flɪntə] **(-, -n)** f shotgun; **die ~ ins Korn werfen** to throw in the sponge
Flirt [flœrt] **(-s, -s)** m flirtation; **einen ~ (mit jdm) haben** flirt (with sb)
flirten ['flɪrtən] vi to flirt

Flittchen (*pej: umg*) *nt* floozy
Flitter (**-s, -**) *m* (*Flitterschmuck*) sequins *pl*
Flitterwochen *pl* honeymoon *sing*
flitzen ['flɪtsən] *vi* to flit
Flitzer (**-s, -**) (*umg*) *m* (*Auto*) sporty car
floaten ['floːtən] *vt, vi* (*Fin*) to float
flocht *etc* [flɔxt] *vb siehe* **flechten**
Flocke ['flɔkə] (**-, -n**) *f* flake
flockig *adj* flaky
flog *etc* [floːk] *vb siehe* **fliegen**
Floh [floː] (**-(e)s, ̈e**) *m* flea; **jdm einen ~ ins Ohr setzen** (*umg*) to put an idea into sb's head
floh *etc vb siehe* **fliehen**
Flohmarkt *m* flea market
Flora ['floːra] (**-, -ren**) *f* flora
Florenz [floˈrɛnts] *nt* Florence
florieren [floˈriːrən] *vi* to flourish
Florist, in *m(f)* florist
Floskel ['flɔskəl] (**-, -n**) *f* set phrase; **floskelhaft** *adj* cliché-ridden, stereotyped
Floß [floːs] (**-es, ̈e**) *nt* raft
floss *etc* [flɔs] *vb siehe* **fließen**
Flosse ['flɔsə] (**-, -n**) *f* fin; (*Taucherflosse*) flipper; (*umg: Hand*) paw
Flöte ['fløːtə] (**-, -n**) *f* flute; (*Blockflöte*) recorder
flöten gehen ['fløːtəngeːən] (*umg*) *unreg vi* to go for a burton
Flötist, in [fløˈtɪst(ɪn)] *m(f)* flautist, flutist (*bes US*)
flott [flɔt] *adj* lively; (*elegant*) smart; (*Naut*) afloat
Flotte (**-, -n**) *f* fleet
Flottenstützpunkt *m* naval base
flottmachen *vt* (*Schiff*) to float off; (*Auto, Fahrrad etc*) to put back on the road
Flöz [fløːts] (**-es, -e**) *nt* layer, seam
Fluch [fluːx] (**-(e)s, ̈e**) *m* curse; **fluchen** *vi* to curse, swear
Flucht [flʊxt] (**-, -en**) *f* flight; (*Fensterflucht*) row; (*Reihe*) range; (*Zimmerflucht*) suite; (*geglückt*) flight, escape; **jdn/etw in die ~ schlagen** to put sb/sth to flight
fluchtartig *adj* hasty
flüchten ['flʏçtən] *vi* to flee ▷ *vr* to take refuge
Fluchthilfe *f*: **~ leisten** to aid an escape
flüchtig *adj* fugitive; (*Chem*) volatile; (*oberflächlich*) cursory; (*eilig*) fleeting; **~er Speicher** (*Comput*) volatile memory; **jdn ~ kennen** to have met sb briefly; **Flüchtigkeit** *f* transitoriness; volatility; cursoriness; **Flüchtigkeitsfehler** *m* careless slip
Flüchtling *m* refugee
Flüchtlingslager *nt* refugee camp
Flucht- *zW*: **Fluchtversuch** *m* escape attempt; **Fluchtweg** *m* escape route
Flug [fluːk] (**-(e)s, ̈e**) *m* flight; **im ~** airborne, in flight; **wie im ~(e)** (*fig*) in a flash; **Flugabwehr** *f* anti-aircraft defence; **Flugbahn** *f* flight path; (*Kreisbahn*) orbit; **Flugbegleiter, in** *m(f)* (*Aviat*) flight attendant; **Flugblatt** *nt* pamphlet
Flügel ['flyːgəl] (**-s, -**) *m* wing; (*Mus*) grand piano; **Flügeltür** *f* double door

flugfähig *adj* able to fly; (*Flugzeug: in Ordnung*) airworthy
Fluggast *m* airline passenger
flügge ['flʏgə] *adj* (fully-)fledged; **~ werden** (*lit*) to be able to fly; (*fig*) to leave the nest
Flug- *zW*: **Fluggeschwindigkeit** *f* flying *od* air speed; **Fluggesellschaft** *f* airline (company); **Flughafen** *m* airport; **Flughöhe** *f* altitude (of flight); **Flugkarte** *f* airline ticket; **Fluglotse** *m* air traffic *od* flight controller; **Flugplan** *m* flight schedule; **Flugplatz** *m* airport; (*klein*) airfield; **Flugreise** *f* flight
flugs [flʊks] *adv* speedily
Flug- *zW*: **Flugsand** *m* drifting sand; **Flugschein** *m* pilot's licence (*Brit*) *od* license (*US*); **Flugschreiber** *m* flight recorder; **Flugschrift** *f* pamphlet; **Flugsteig** *m* gate; **Flugstrecke** *f* air route; **Flugverkehr** *m* air traffic; **Flugwesen** *nt* aviation
Flugzeug (**-(e)s, -e**) *nt* plane, aeroplane (*Brit*), airplane (*US*); **Flugzeugentführung** *f* hijacking of a plane; **Flugzeughalle** *f* hangar; **Flugzeugträger** *m* aircraft carrier
fluktuieren [flʊktuˈiːrən] *vi* to fluctuate
Flunder ['flʊndər] (**-, -n**) *f* flounder
flunkern ['flʊŋkərn] *vi* to fib, tell stories
Fluor ['fluːɔr] (**-s**) *nt* fluorine
Flur¹ [fluːr] (**-(e)s, -e**) *m* hall; (*Treppenflur*) staircase
Flur² [fluːr] (**-, -en**) *f* (*geh*) open fields *pl*; **allein auf weiter ~ stehen** (*fig*) to be out on a limb
Fluss [flʊs] (**-es, ̈e**) *m* river; (*Fließen*) flow; **im ~ sein** (*fig*) to be in a state of flux; **etw in ~ bringen** *akk* to get sth moving; **flussab, flussabwärts** *adv* downstream; **flussauf, flussaufwärts** *adv* upstream; **Flussdiagramm** *nt* flow chart
flüssig ['flʏsɪç] *adj* liquid; (*Stil*) flowing; **~es Vermögen** (*Comm*) liquid assets *pl*; **Flüssigkeit** *f* liquid; (*Zustand*) liquidity; **flüssigmachen** *vt* (*Geld*) to make available
Flussmündung *f* estuary
Flusspferd *nt* hippopotamus
flüstern ['flʏstərn] *vt, vi* to whisper
Flüsterpropaganda *f* whispering campaign
Flut [fluːt] (**-, -en**) *f* (*lit, fig*) flood; (*Gezeiten*) high tide; **fluten** *vi* to flood; **Flutlicht** *nt* floodlight
flutschen ['flʊtʃən] (*umg*) *vi* (*rutschen*) to slide; (*funktionieren*) to go well
Flutwelle *f* tidal wave
fl. W. *abk* (= *fließendes Wasser*) running water
focht *etc* [fɔxt] *vb siehe* **fechten**
föderativ [føderaˈtiːf] *adj* federal
Fohlen ['foːlən] (**-s, -**) *nt* foal
Föhn [føːn] (**-(e)s, -e**) *m* foehn, *warm dry alpine wind*; (*Haartrockner*) hairdryer
föhnen *vt* to blow-dry
Föhre ['føːrə] (**-, -**) *f* Scots pine
Folge ['fɔlgə] (**-, -n**) *f* series, sequence; (*Fortsetzung*) instalment (*Brit*), installment (*US*); (*TV, Rundf*) episode; (*Auswirkung*) result; **in rascher ~** in quick succession; **etw zur ~ haben** to result in sth; **~n haben** to have

consequences; **einer Sache** dat ~ **leisten** to comply with sth; **Folgeerscheinung** f result, consequence

folgen vi +dat to follow ▷ vi (gehorchen) to obey; **jdm ~ können** (fig) to follow od understand sb; **daraus folgt, dass ...** it follows from this that ...

folgend adj following; **im F~en** in the following; (schriftlich) below

folgendermaßen ['fɔlgəndər'maːsən] adv as follows, in the following way

folgenreich adj momentous

folgenschwer adj momentous

folgerichtig adj logical

folgern vt: ~ **(aus)** to conclude (from)

Folgerung f conclusion

folgewidrig adj illogical

folglich ['fɔlklɪç] adv consequently

folgsam ['fɔlkzaːm] adj obedient

Folie ['foːliə] (-, -n) f foil

Folienschweißgerät nt shrink-wrap machine

Folklore ['fɔlkloːər] (-) f folklore

Folter ['fɔltər] (-, -n) f torture; (Gerät) rack; **jdn auf die ~ spannen** (fig) to keep sb on tenterhooks

foltern vt to torture

Fön® [føːn] (-(e)s, -e) m hairdryer

Fonds [fõː] (-, -) m (lit, fig) fund; (Fin: Schuldverschreibung) government bond; **Fondsmanager, in** m(f) fund manager

fönen vt siehe **föhnen**

Fono-, fono- in zW = **Phono-, phono-**

Fontäne [fɔn'tɛːnə] (-, -n) f fountain

foppen ['fɔpən] vt to tease

forcieren [fɔr'siːrən] vt to push; (Tempo) to force; (Konsum, Produktion) to push od force up

Förderband ['fœrdərbant] nt conveyor belt

Förderer (-s, -) m patron

Fördergebiet nt development area

Förderin f patroness

Förderkorb m pit cage

Förderleistung f (Min) output

förderlich adj beneficial

fordern ['fɔrdərn] vt to demand; (fig: kosten: Opfer) to claim; (: herausfordern) to challenge

fördern ['fœrdərn] vt to promote; (unterstützen) to help; (Kohle) to extract; (finanziell: Projekt) to sponsor; (jds Talent, Neigung) to encourage, foster

Förderplattform f production platform

Förderstufe f (Sch) first stage of secondary school where abilities are judged

Förderturm m (Min) winding tower; (auf Bohrstelle) derrick

Forderung ['fɔrdərʊŋ] f demand

Förderung ['fœrdərʊŋ] f promotion; help; extraction

Forelle [fo'rɛlə] f trout

Form [fɔrm] (-, -en) f shape; (Gestaltung) form; (Gussform) mould; (Backform) baking tin; **in ~ von** in the shape of; **in ~ sein** to be in good form od shape; **die ~ wahren** to observe the proprieties; **in aller ~** formally

formal [fɔr'maːl] adj formal; (Besitzer, Grund) technical

formalisieren [fɔrmali'ziːrən] vt to formalize

Formalität [fɔrmalɪ'tɛːt] f formality; **alle ~en erledigen** to go through all the formalities

Format [fɔr'maːt] (-(e)s, -e) nt format; (fig) quality

formatieren [fɔrma'tiːrən] vt (Text, Diskette) to format

Formation [fɔrmatsi'oːn] f formation

formbar adj malleable

Formblatt nt form

Formel (-, -n) f formula; (von Eid etc) wording; (Floskel) set phrase; **formelhaft** adj (Sprache, Stil) stereotyped

formell [fɔr'mɛl] adj formal

formen vt to form, shape

Formfehler m faux pas, gaffe; (Jur) irregularity

Formfleisch nt pressed meat

formieren [fɔr'miːrən] vt to form ▷ vr to form up

förmlich ['fœrmlɪç] adj formal; (umg) real; **Förmlichkeit** f formality

formlos adj shapeless; (Benehmen etc) informal; (Antrag) unaccompanied by a form od any forms

Formsache f formality

Formular [fɔrmu'laːr] (-s, -e) nt form

formulieren [fɔrmu'liːrən] vt to formulate

Formulierung f wording

formvollendet adj perfect; (Vase etc) perfectly formed

forsch [fɔrʃ] adj energetic, vigorous

forschen [fɔrʃən] vi to search; (wissenschaftlich) to (do) research; ~ **nach** to search for

forschend adj searching

Forscher (-s, -) m research scientist; (Naturforscher) explorer

Forschung ['fɔrʃʊŋ] f research; ~ **und Lehre** research and teaching; ~ **und Entwicklung** research and development

Forschungsreise f scientific expedition

Forst [fɔrst] (-(e)s, -e) m forest; **Forstarbeiter** m forestry worker

Förster ['fœrstər] (-s, -) m forester; (für Wild) gamekeeper

Forstwesen nt forestry

Forstwirtschaft f forestry

fort [fɔrt] adv away; (verschwunden) gone; (vorwärts) on; **und so ~** and so on; **in einem ~** incessantly; **fortbestehen** unreg vi to continue to exist; **fortbewegen** vt, vr to move away; **fortbilden** vr to continue one's education; **Fortbildung** f further education; **fortbleiben** unreg vi to stay away; **fortbringen** unreg vt to take away; **Fortdauer** f continuance; **fortdauernd** adj continuing; (in der Vergangenheit) continued ▷ adv constantly, continuously; **fortfahren** unreg vi to depart; (fortsetzen) to go on, continue; **fortführen** vt to continue, carry on; **Fortgang** m (Verlauf) progress; (Weggang): **Fortgang (aus)** departure (from); **fortgehen** unreg vi to go away;

fortgeschritten adj advanced; **fortkommen** unreg vi to get on; (wegkommen) to get away; **fortkönnen** unreg vi to be able to get away; **fortlassen** vt (auslassen) to leave out, omit; (weggehen lassen): **jdn fortlassen** to let sb go; **fortlaufend** adj: **fortlaufend nummeriert** consecutively numbered; **fortmüssen** unreg vi to have to go; **fortpflanzen** vr to reproduce; **Fortpflanzung** f reproduction

FORTRAN ['fɔrtran] nt FORTRAN

Forts. abk = **Fortsetzung**

fortschaffen vt to remove

fortschreiten unreg vi to advance

Fortschritt ['fɔrtʃrɪt] m advance; ~e **machen** to make progress; **dem ~ dienen** to further progress; **fortschrittlich** adj progressive

fortschrittsgläubig adj believing in progress

fort- zW: **fortsetzen** vt to continue; **Fortsetzung** f continuation; (folgender Teil) instalment (Brit), installment (US); **Fortsetzung folgt** to be continued; **Fortsetzungsroman** m serialized novel; **fortwährend** adj incessant, continual; **fortwirken** vi to continue to have an effect; **fortziehen** unreg vt to pull away ▷ vi to move on; (umziehen) to move away

Foto ['foːto] (-s, -s) nt photo(graph); **ein ~ machen** to take a photo(graph); **Fotoalbum** nt photograph album; **Fotoapparat** m camera; **Fotograf, in** (-en, -en) m(f) photographer; **Fotografie** f photography; (Bild) photograph; **fotografieren** vt to photograph ▷ vi to take photographs; **Fotohandy** nt camera phone; **Fotokopie** f photocopy; **fotokopieren** vt to photocopy; **Fotokopierer** m photocopier; **Fotokopiergerät** nt photocopier

Foul [faʊl] (-s, -s) nt foul

Foyer [foa'jeː] (-s, -s) nt foyer; (in Hotel) lobby, foyer

FPÖ (-) f abk (= Freiheitliche Partei Österreichs) Austrian Freedom Party

Fr. abk (= Frau) Mrs, Ms

Fracht [fraxt] (-, -en) f freight; (Naut) cargo; (Preis) carriage; ~ **zahlt Empfänger** (Comm) carriage forward; **Frachtbrief** m consignment note, waybill

Frachter (-s, -) m freighter

Fracht- zW: **frachtfrei** adj (Comm) carriage paid od free; **Frachtgut** nt freight; **Frachtkosten** pl (Comm) freight charges pl

Frack [frak] (-(e)s, -̈e) m tails pl, tail coat

Frage ['fraːgə] (-, -n) f question; **jdm eine ~ stellen** to ask sb a question, put a question to sb; **das ist gar keine ~, das steht außer ~** there's no question about it; siehe auch **infrage**; **Fragebogen** m questionnaire

fragen vt, vi to ask ▷ vr to wonder; **nach Arbeit/Post** ~ to ask whether there is/was any work/mail; **da fragst du mich zu viel** (umg) I really couldn't say; **nach** od **wegen** (umg) **jdn** ~ to ask for sb; (nach jds Befinden) to ask after sb; **ohne lange zu** ~ without asking a lot of questions

Fragerei [fraːgə'raɪ] f questions pl

Fragestunde f (Parl) question time

Fragezeichen nt question mark

fraglich adj questionable, doubtful; (betreffend) in question

fraglos adv unquestionably

Fragment [fra'gmɛnt] nt fragment

fragmentarisch [fragmɛn'taːrɪʃ] adj fragmentary

fragwürdig ['fraːkvʏrdɪç] adj questionable, dubious

Fraktion [fraktsi'oːn] f parliamentary party

Fraktionsvorsitzende, r f(m) (Pol) party whip

Fraktionszwang m requirement to obey the party whip

Franchisekette ['frɛnʃaɪskɛtə] f franchise chain

frank [fraŋk] adj frank, candid

Franken¹ ['fraŋkən] nt Franconia

Franken² ['fraŋkən] (-, -) m: **(Schweizer) ~** (Swiss) Franc

Frankfurt ['fraŋkfʊrt] (-s) nt Frankfurt

Frankfurter, in m(f) native of Frankfurt ▷ adj Frankfurt; **Frankfurter Würstchen** pl frankfurters

frankieren [fraŋ'kiːrən] vt to stamp, frank

Frankiermaschine f franking machine

fränkisch ['fraŋkɪʃ] adj Franconian

franko adv carriage paid; (Post) post-paid

Frankreich ['fraŋkraɪç] (-s) nt France

Franse ['franzə] (-, -n) f fringe

fransen vi to fray

franz. abk = **französisch**

Franzbranntwein m alcoholic liniment

Franzose [fran'tsoːzə] (-n, -n) m Frenchman; French boy

Französin [fran'tsœːzɪn] f Frenchwoman; French girl

französisch adj French; ~**es Bett** double bed

Fräse ['frɛːzə] (-, -n) f (Werkzeug) milling cutter; (für Holz) moulding cutter

Fraß (-es, -e) (pej: umg) m (Essen) muck

fraß etc [fraːs] vb siehe **fressen**

Fratze ['fratsə] (-, -n) f grimace; **eine ~ schneiden** to pull od make a face

Frau [fraʊ] (-, -en) f woman; (Ehefrau) wife; (Anrede) Mrs, Ms; ~ **Doktor** Doctor

Frauen- zW: **Frauenarzt** m gynaecologist (Brit), gynecologist (US); **Frauenbewegung** f feminist movement; **frauenfeindlich** adj anti-women, misogynous; **Frauenhaus** nt women's refuge; **Frauenquote** f recommended proportion of women (employed); **Frauenrechtlerin** f feminist; **Frauenzentrum** nt women's advice centre; **Frauenzimmer** (pej) nt female, broad (US)

Fräulein ['frɔylaɪn] nt young lady; (Anrede) Miss; (Verkäuferin) assistant (Brit), sales clerk (US); (Kellnerin) waitress

fraulich ['fraʊlɪç] adj womanly

frech [frɛç] adj cheeky, impudent; ~ **wie Oskar sein** (umg) to be a little monkey; **Frechdachs** m cheeky monkey; **Frechheit** f cheek, impudence; **sich** *dat* **(einige) Frechheiten erlauben** to be a bit cheeky (*bes Brit*) *od* fresh (*bes US*)

Fregatte [freˈɡatə] (**-, -n**) *f* frigate

frei [fraɪ] *adj* free; (*Stelle*) vacant; (*Mitarbeiter*) freelance; (*Geld*) available; (*unbekleidet*) bare; **aus ~en Stücken** *od* **~em Willen** of one's own free will; **~ nach ...** based on ...; **für etw ~e Fahrt geben** (*fig*) to give sth the go-ahead; **der Film ist ~ ab 16 (Jahren)** the film may be seen by people of 16 years (of age) and over; **unter ~em Himmel** in the open (air); **morgen/Mittwoch ist ~** tomorrow/Wednesday is a holiday; **„Zimmer ~"** "vacancies"; **auf ~er Strecke** (*Eisenb*) between stations; (*Aut*) on the road; **~er Wettbewerb** fair/open competition; **~ Haus** (*Comm*) carriage paid; **~ Schiff** (*Comm*) free on board; **~e Marktwirtschaft** free market economy; **von etw ~ sein** to be free of sth; **im F~en** in the open air; **~ halten** (*Ausfahrt etc*) to keep free; **~ sprechen** to talk without notes; **Freibad** *nt* open-air swimming pool; **freibekommen** *unreg vt*: **jdn/einen Tag freibekommen** to get sb freed/get a day off; **freiberuflich** *adj* self-employed; **Freibetrag** *m* tax allowance

Freier (**-s, -**) *m* suitor

Frei- *zW*: **Freiexemplar** *nt* free copy; **freigeben** *unreg vt*: **etw zum Verkauf freigeben** to allow sth to be sold on the open market; **freigebig** *adj* generous; **Freigebigkeit** *f* generosity; **Freihafen** *m* free port; **freihalten** *unreg vt* (*bezahlen*) to pay for; *siehe auch* **frei**; **Freihandel** *m* free trade; **Freihandelszone** *f* free trade area; **freihändig** *adv* (*fahren*) with no hands

Freiheit *f* freedom; **sich** *dat* **die ~ nehmen, etw zu tun** to take the liberty of doing sth; **freiheitlich** *adj* liberal; (*Verfassung*) based on the principle of liberty; (*Demokratie*) free

Freiheits- *zW*: **Freiheitsberaubung** *f* (*Jur*) wrongful deprivation of personal liberty; **Freiheitsdrang** *m* urge/desire for freedom; **Freiheitskampf** *m* fight for freedom; **Freiheitskämpfer, in** *m(f)* freedom fighter; **Freiheitsrechte** *pl* civil liberties *pl*; **Freiheitsstrafe** *f* prison sentence

frei- *zW*: **freiheraus** *adv* frankly; **Freikarte** *f* free ticket; **freikaufen** *vt*: **jdn/sich freikaufen** to buy sb's/one's freedom; **freikommen** *unreg vi* to get free; **Freikörperkultur** *f* nudism; **freilassen** *unreg vt* to (set) free; **Freilauf** *m* freewheeling; **freilaufend** *adj* (*Hühner*) free-range; **freilegen** *vt* to expose; **freilich** *adv* certainly, admittedly; **ja freilich!** yes of course; **Freilichtbühne** *f* open-air theatre; **freimachen** *vt* (*Post*) to frank ▷ *vr* to arrange to be free; **Tage freimachen** to take days off; **sich freimachen** (*beim Arzt*) to take one's clothes off, strip; **Freimaurer** *m* Mason, Freemason

freimütig [ˈfraɪmyːtɪç] *adj* frank, honest

Frei- *zW*: **freinehmen** *vt*: **sich** *dat* **einen Tag freinehmen** to take a day off; **Freiraum** *m*: **Freiraum (zu)** (*fig*) freedom (for); **freischaffend** *adj attrib* freelance; **Freischaltcode** *m* (*Tel*) connecting *od* enabling code; **Freischärler** (**-s, -**) *m* guerrilla; **freischwimmen** *vr* (*fig*) to learn to stand on one's own two feet; **freisetzen** *vt* (*Energien*) to release; **freisinnig** *adj* liberal; **Freisprechanlage** *f* hands-free (headset); (*im Auto*) hands-free (car kit); **freisprechen** *unreg vt*: **freisprechen (von)** to acquit (of); **Freispruch** *m* acquittal; **freistehen** *unreg vi*: **es steht dir frei, das zu tun** you are free to do so; **das steht Ihnen völlig frei** that is completely up to you; **freistellen** *vt*: **jdm etw freistellen** to leave sth (up) to sb; **Freistoß** *m* free kick; **Freistunde** *f* free hour; (*Sch*) free period

Freitag *m* Friday; *siehe auch* **Dienstag**

freitags *adv* on Fridays

Frei- *zW*: **Freitod** *m* suicide; **Freiübungen** *pl* (physical) exercises *pl*; **Freiumschlag** *m* reply-paid envelope; **Freiwild** *nt* (*fig*) fair game; **freiwillig** *adj* voluntary; **Freiwillige, r** *f(m)* volunteer; **Freizeichen** *nt* (*Tel*) ringing tone; **Freizeit** *f* spare *od* free time; **Freizeitgestaltung** *f* organization of one's leisure time; **freizügig** *adj* liberal, broad-minded; (*mit Geld*) generous

fremd [frɛmt] *adj* (*unvertraut*) strange; (*ausländisch*) foreign; (*nicht eigen*) someone else's; **etw ist jdm ~** sth is foreign to sb; **ich bin hier ~** I'm a stranger here; **sich ~ fühlen** to feel like a stranger; **fremdartig** *adj* strange

Fremde (**-**) *f* (*liter*): **die ~** foreign parts *pl*

Fremde, r *f(m)* stranger; (*Ausländer*) foreigner

Fremden- *zW*: **Fremdenführer** *m* (tourist) guide; (*Buch*) guide (book); **Fremdenlegion** *f* foreign legion; **Fremdenverkehr** *m* tourism; **Fremdenzimmer** *nt* guest room

fremd- *zW*: **fremdgehen** *unreg* (*umg*) *vi* to be unfaithful; **Fremdkapital** *nt* loan capital; **Fremdkörper** *m* foreign body; **fremdländisch** *adj* foreign; **Fremdling** *m* stranger; **Fremdsprache** *f* foreign language; **Fremdsprachenkorrespondentin** *f* bilingual secretary; **fremdsprachig** *adj attrib* foreign-language; **Fremdwort** *nt* foreign word

frenetisch [freˈneːtɪʃ] *adj* frenetic

Frequenz [freˈkvɛnts] *f* (*Rundf*) frequency

Fresse (**-, -n**) (*umg!*) *f* (*Mund*) gob; (*Gesicht*) mug

fressen [ˈfrɛsən] *unreg vt, vi* to eat ▷ *vr*: **sich satt ~** to gorge o.s.; **einen Narren an jdm/etw gehaben** to dote on sb/sth

Freude [ˈfrɔʏdə] (**-, -n**) *f* joy, delight; **~ an etw** *dat* **haben** to get *od* derive pleasure from sth; **jdm eine ~ machen** *od* **bereiten** to make sb happy

Freudenhaus *nt* (*veraltet*) house of ill repute

Freudentanz *m*: **einen ~ aufführen** to dance with joy

freudestrahlend *adj* beaming with delight

freudig *adj* joyful, happy

f

freudlos adj joyless

freuen ['frɔʏən] vt unpers to make happy od pleased ▷vr to be glad od happy; **sich auf etw** akk **~** to look forward to sth; **sich über etw** akk **~** to be pleased about sth; **sich zu früh ~** to get one's hopes up too soon

Freund ['frɔʏnt] (**-(e)s, -e**) m friend; (Liebhaber) boyfriend; **ich bin kein ~ von so etwas** I'm not one for that sort of thing; **Freundin** f friend; (Liebhaberin) girlfriend; **freundlich** adj kind, friendly; **bitte recht freundlich!** smile please!; **würden Sie bitte so freundlich sein und das tun?** would you be so kind as to do that?; **freundlicherweise** adv kindly; **Freundlichkeit** f friendliness, kindness; **Freundschaft** f friendship; **freundschaftlich** adj friendly

Frevel ['fre:fəl] (**-s, -**) m: **~ (an** +dat) crime od offence (against); **frevelhaft** adj wicked

Frieden ['fri:dən] (**-s, -**) m peace; **im ~ in** peacetime; **~ schließen** to make one's peace; (Pol) to make peace; **um des lieben ~s willen** (umg) for the sake of peace and quiet; **ich traue dem ~ nicht** (umg) something (fishy) is going on

Friedens- zW: **Friedensbewegung** f peace movement; **Friedensrichter** m justice of the peace; **Friedensschluss** m peace agreement; **Friedenstruppe** f peace-keeping force; **Friedensverhandlungen** pl peace negotiations pl; **Friedensvertrag** m peace treaty; **Friedenszeit** f peacetime

fried- zW: **friedfertig** adj peaceable; **Friedhof** m cemetery; **friedlich** adj peaceful; **etw auf friedlichem Wege lösen** to solve sth by peaceful means

frieren ['fri:rən] unreg vi to freeze ▷vt unpers to freeze ▷vi unpers: **heute Nacht hat es gefroren** it was below freezing last night; **ich friere, es friert mich** I am freezing, I'm cold; **wie ein Schneider ~** (umg) to be od get frozen to the marrow

Fries [fri:s] (**-es, -e**) m (Archit) frieze

Friese ['fri:zə] (**-n, -n**) m Fri(e)sian

Friesin ['fri:zɪn] f Fri(e)sian

frigid, frigide adj frigid

Frikadelle [frika'dɛlə] f meatball

frisch [frɪʃ] adj fresh; (lebhaft) lively; **~ gestrichen!** wet paint!; **sich ~ machen** to freshen (o.s.) up; **jdn auf ~er Tat ertappen** to catch sb red-handed od in the act

Frische (**-**) f freshness; liveliness; **in alter ~** (umg) as always

Frischhaltebeutel m airtight bag

Frischhaltefolie f clingfilm

frischweg adv (munter) straight out

Friseur [fri'zø:r] m hairdresser

Friseuse [fri'zø:zə] f hairdresser

frisieren [fri'zi:rən] vt (Haar) to do; (fig: Abrechnung) to fiddle, doctor ▷vr to do one's hair; **jdn ~, jdm das Haar ~** to do sb's hair

Frisiersalon m hairdressing salon

Frisiertisch m dressing table

Frisör [fri'zø:r] (**-s, -e**) m = **Friseur**

frisst [frɪst] vb siehe **fressen**

Frist [frɪst] (**-, -en**) f period; (Termin) deadline; **eine ~ einhalten/verstreichen lassen** to meet a deadline/let a deadline pass; (bei Rechnung) to pay/not to pay within the period stipulated; **jdm eine ~ von vier Tagen geben** to give sb four days' grace

fristen vt (Dasein) to lead; (kümmerlich) to eke out

Fristenlösung f abortion law (permitting abortion in the first three months)

fristgerecht adj within the period stipulated

fristlos adj (Entlassung) instant

Frisur [fri'zu:r] f hairdo, hairstyle

Fritteuse [fri'tø:zə] (**-, -n**) f chip pan (Brit), deep fat fryer

frittieren [fri'ti:rən] vt to deep fry

frivol [fri'vo:l] adj frivolous

Frl. abk (= Fräulein) Miss

froh [fro:] adj happy, cheerful; **ich bin ~, dass ...** I'm glad that ...

fröhlich ['frø:lɪç] adj merry, happy; **Fröhlichkeit** f merriment, gaiety

frohlocken vi (geh) to rejoice; (pej) to gloat

Frohsinn m cheerfulness

fromm [frɔm] adj pious, good; (Wunsch) idle

Frömmelei [frœmə'laɪ] f false piety

Frömmigkeit f piety

frönen ['frø:nən] vi +dat to indulge in

Fronleichnam [fro:n'laɪçna:m] (**-(e)s**) m Corpus Christi

Front [frɔnt] (**-, -en**) f front; **klare ~en schaffen** (fig) to clarify the position

frontal [frɔn'ta:l] adj frontal; **Frontalangriff** m frontal attack

fror etc [fro:r] vb siehe **frieren**

Frosch [frɔʃ] (**-(e)s, "-e**) m frog; (Feuerwerk) squib; **sei kein ~!** (umg) be a sport!; **Froschmann** m frogman; **Froschperspektive** f: **etw aus der Froschperspektive sehen** to get a worm's-eye view of sth; **Froschschenkel** m frog's leg

Frost [frɔst] (**-(e)s, "-e**) m frost; **frostbeständig** adj frost-resistant; **Frostbeule** f chilblain

frösteln ['frœstəln] vi to shiver

frostig adj frosty

Frostschutzmittel nt anti-freeze

Frottee, Frotté [frɔ'te:] (**-(s), -s**) nt od m towelling

frottieren [frɔ'ti:rən] vt to rub, towel

Frottierhandtuch nt towel

Frottiertuch nt towel

frotzeln ['frɔtsəln] (umg) vt, vi to tease

Frucht [fruxt] (**-, "-e**) f (lit, fig) fruit; (Getreide) corn; (Embryo) foetus; **fruchtbar** adj fruitful, fertile; **Fruchtbarkeit** f fertility; **Fruchtbecher** m fruit sundae

Früchtchen ['frʏçtçən] (umg) nt (Tunichtgut) good-for-nothing

fruchten vi to be of use

fruchtlos adj fruitless

Fruchtsaft m fruit juice

früh [fry:] adj, adv early; **heute ~** this morning;

von ~ auf from an early age; **Frühaufsteher (-s, -)** *m* early riser; **Frühdienst** *m*: **Frühdienst haben** to be on early shift

Frühe (-) *f* early morning; **in aller ~** at the crack of dawn

früher *adj* earlier; *(ehemalig)* former ▷ *adv* formerly; **~ war das anders** that used to be different; **~ oder später** sooner or later

frühestens *adv* at the earliest

Frühgeburt *f* premature birth; *(Kind)* premature baby

Frühjahr *nt* spring

Frühjahrsmüdigkeit *f* springtime lethargy

Frühjahrsputz *m* spring-cleaning

Frühling *m* spring; **im ~** in spring

früh- *zW*: **frühreif** *adj* precocious; **Frührentner** *m* person who has retired early; **Frühschicht** *f* early shift; **Frühschoppen** *m* morning/lunchtime drink; **Frühsport** *m* early morning exercise; **Frühstück** *nt* breakfast; **frühstücken** *vi* to (have) breakfast; **Frühwarnsystem** *nt* early warning system; **frühzeitig** *adj* early; *(vorzeitig)* premature

Frust (-(e)s) *(umg)* *m* frustration

frustrieren [frʊs'triːrən] *vt* to frustrate

frz. *abk* = **französisch**

FSV *abk* (= *Fußball-Sportverein*) F.C.

FU (-) *f abk* (= *Freie Universität Berlin*) Berlin University

Fuchs [fʊks] **(-es, ̈-e)** *m* fox

fuchsen *(umg)* *vt* to rile, annoy ▷ *vr* to be annoyed

Füchsin ['fʏksɪn] *f* vixen

fuchsteufelswild *adj* hopping mad

Fuchtel ['fʊxtl] **(-, -n)** *f* (fig: *umg*): **unter jds ~** under sb's control *od* thumb

fuchteln ['fʊxtəln] *vi* to gesticulate wildly

Fuge ['fuːɡə] **(-, -n)** *f* joint; *(Mus)* fugue

fügen ['fyːɡən] *vt* to place, join ▷ *vr unpers* to happen ▷ *vr*: **sich ~ (in** +*akk*) to be obedient (to); *(anpassen)* to adapt o.s. (to)

fügsam ['fyːkzaːm] *adj* obedient

fühlbar *adj* perceptible, noticeable

fühlen ['fyːlən] *vt, vi, vr* to feel

Fühler (-s, -) *m* feeler

Fühlung *f*: **mit jdm in ~ bleiben/stehen** to stay/be in contact *od* touch with sb

fuhr *etc* [fuːr] *vb siehe* **fahren**

Fuhre (-, -n) *f* (*Ladung*) load

führen ['fyːrən] *vt* to lead; *(Geschäft)* to run; *(Name)* to bear; *(Buch)* to keep; *(im Angebot haben)* to stock ▷ *vi* to lead ▷ *vr* to behave; **was führt Sie zu mir?** *(form)* what brings you to me?; **Geld/seine Papiere bei sich ~** *(form)* to carry money/one's papers on one's person; **das führt zu nichts** that will come to nothing

Führer, in ['fyːrər(ɪn)] **(-s, -)** *m(f)* leader; *(Fremdenführer)* guide; **Führerhaus** *nt* cab; **Führerschein** *m* driving licence *(Brit)*, driver's license *(US)*; **den Führerschein machen** *(Aut)* to learn to drive; *(die Prüfung ablegen)* to take one's (driving) test; **Führerscheinentzug** *m* disqualification from driving

Fuhrmann ['fuːrman] **(-(e)s,** *pl* **-leute)** *m* carter

Führung ['fyːrʊŋ] *f* leadership; *(eines Unternehmens)* management; *(Mil)* command; *(Benehmen)* conduct; *(Museumsführung)* conducted tour

Führungs- *zW*: **Führungskraft** *f* executive; **Führungsstab** *m* (*Mil*) command; *(Comm)* top management; **Führungsstil** *m* management style; **Führungszeugnis** *nt* certificate of good conduct

Fuhrunternehmen *nt* haulage business

Fuhrwerk *nt* cart

Fülle ['fʏlə] **(-)** *f* wealth, abundance

Füllen (-s, -) *nt* foal

füllen *vt* to fill; *(Koch)* to stuff ▷ *vr* to fill (up)

Füller (-s, -) *m* fountain pen

Füllfederhalter *m* fountain pen

Füllgewicht *nt* (*Comm*) weight at time of packing; *(auf Dosen)* net weight

füllig ['fʏlɪç] *adj* (*Mensch*) corpulent, portly; *(Figur)* ample

Füllung *f* filling; *(Holzfüllung)* panel

fummeln ['fʊməln] *(umg)* *vi* to fumble

Fund [fʊnt] **(-(e)s, -e)** *m* find

Fundament [fʊnda'mɛnt] *nt* foundation

fundamental *adj* fundamental

Fundamentalismus *m* fundamentalism

Fundbüro *nt* lost property office, lost and found *(US)*

Fundgrube *f* (*fig*) treasure trove

fundieren [fʊn'diːrən] *vt* to back up

fundiert *adj* sound

fündig ['fʏndɪç] *adj* (*Min*) rich; **~ werden** to make a strike; *(fig)* to strike it lucky

Fundsachen *pl* lost property *sing*

fünf [fʏnf] *num* five; **seine ~ Sinne beisammen haben** to have all one's wits about one; **~(e) gerade sein lassen** *(umg)* to turn a blind eye; **fünfhundert** *num* five hundred; **fünfjährig** *adj* (*Frist, Plan*) five-year; *(Kind)* five-year-old; **Fünfkampf** *m* pentathlon

Fünfprozentklausel *f* (*Parl*) clause debarring parties with less than 5% of the vote from Parliament; see culture note

Fünftagewoche *f* five-day week

fünfte, r, s *adj* fifth

Fünftel (-s, -) *nt* fifth

fünfzehn *num* fifteen

fünfzig *num* fifty

fungieren [fʊŋ'giːrən] *vi* to function; *(Person)* to act

Funk [fʊŋk] **(-s)** *m* radio, wireless *(Brit old)*;

Funkausstellung f radio and television exhibition

Funke (-ns, -n) m (lit, fig) spark

funkeln vi to sparkle

funkelnagelneu (umg) adj brand-new

Funken (-s, -) m = **Funke**

funken vt to radio

Funker (-s, -) m radio operator

Funk- zW: **Funkgerät** nt radio set; **Funkhaus** nt broadcasting centre; **Funkkolleg** nt educational radio broadcasts pl; **Funkrufempfänger** m (Telec) pager, paging device; **Funkspot** m advertisement on the radio; **Funksprechgerät** nt radio telephone; **Funkspruch** m radio signal; **Funkstation** f radio station; **Funkstille** f (fig) ominous silence; **Funkstreife** f police radio patrol; **Funktaxi** nt radio taxi; **Funktelefon** nt cell phone; **Funktelefonnetz** nt radio telephone network

Funktion [fʊŋktsio'oːn] f function; **in ~ treten/ sein** to come into/be in operation

Funktionär, in [fʊŋktsio'nɛːr(ɪn)] (-s, -e) m(f) functionary, official

funktionieren [fʊŋktsio'niːrən] vi to work, function

Funktions- zW: **Funktionsbekleidung** f functional wear; **funktionsfähig** adj working; **Funktionstaste** f (Comput) function key; **funktionstüchtig** adj in working order

Funzel [funtsəl] (-, -n) (umg) f dim lamp

für [fyːr] präp +akk for; **was ~** what kind od sort of; **~ Erste** for the moment; **was Sie da sagen, hat etwas ~ sich** there's something in what you're saying; **Tag ~ Tag** day after day; **Schritt ~ Schritt** step by step; **das F~ und Wider** the pros and cons pl; **Fürbitte** f intercession

Furche ['fʊrçə] (-, -n) f furrow

furchen vt to furrow

Furcht [fʊrçt] (-) f fear; **furchtbar** adj terrible, awful

fürchten ['fyrçtən] vt to be afraid of, fear
▷ vr: **sich ~ (vor** +dat) to be afraid (of)

fürchterlich adj awful

furchtlos adj fearless

furchtsam adj timorous

füreinander [fyːr|aɪ'nandər] adv for each other

Furie ['fuːriə] (-, -n) f (Mythologie) fury; (fig) hellcat

Furnier [fʊr'niːr] (-s, -e) nt veneer

Furore [fu'roːrə] f od nt: **~ machen** (umg) to cause a sensation

fürs [fyːrs] = **für das**

Fürsorge ['fyːrzɔrgə] f care; (Sozialfürsorge) welfare; **von der ~ leben** to live on social security (Brit) od welfare (US); **Fürsorgeamt** nt welfare office

Fürsorger, in (-s, -) m(f) welfare worker

Fürsorgeunterstützung f social security

(Brit), welfare benefit (US)

fürsorglich adj caring

Fürsprache f recommendation; (um Gnade) intercession

Fürsprecher m advocate

Fürst [fyrst] (-en, -en) m prince

Fürstentum nt principality

Fürstin f princess

fürstlich adj princely

Furt [fʊrt] (-, -en) f ford

Furunkel [fu'rʊŋkəl] (-s, -) nt od m boil

Fürwort ['fyːrvɔrt] nt pronoun

furzen ['fʊrtsən] (umg!) vi to fart (!)

Fusion [fuzi'oːn] f amalgamation; (von Unternehmen) merger; (von Atomkernen, Zellen) fusion

fusionieren [fuzio'niːrən] vt to amalgamate

Fuß [fuːs] (-es, ̈e) m foot; (von Glas, Säule etc) base; (von Möbel) leg; **zu ~** on foot; **bei ~!** heel!; **jdm etw vor die Füße werfen** (lit) to throw sth at sb; (fig) to tell sb to keep sth; **(festen) ~ fassen** (lit, fig) to gain a foothold; (sich niederlassen) to settle down; **mit jdm auf gutem ~ stehen** to be on good terms with sb; **auf großem ~ leben** to live the high life

Fußball m football; **Fußballplatz** m football pitch; **Fußballspiel** nt football match; **Fußballspieler** m footballer (Brit), football player (US); **Fußballtoto** m od nt football pools pl

Fußboden m floor; **Fußbodenheizung** f underfloor heating

Fußbremse f (Aut) foot brake

fusselig ['fʊsəlɪç] adj: **sich** dat **den Mund ~ reden** (umg) to talk till one is blue in the face

fusseln ['fʊsəln] vi (Stoff, Kleid etc) to go bobbly (umg)

fußen vi: **~ auf** +dat to rest on, be based on

Fuß- zW: **Fußende** nt foot; **Fußgänger, in** (-s, -) m(f) pedestrian; **Fußgängerüberführung** f pedestrian bridge; **Fußgängerzone** f pedestrian precinct; **Fußleiste** f skirting board (Brit), baseboard (US); **Fußnagel** m toenail; **Fußnote** f footnote; **Fußpfleger** m chiropodist; **Fußpilz** m (Med) athlete's foot; **Fußspur** f footprint; **Fußstapfen** (-s, -) m: **in jds Fußstapfen treten** (fig) to follow in sb's footsteps; **Fußtritt** m kick; (Spur) footstep; **Fußvolk** nt (fig): **das Fußvolk** the rank and file; **Fußweg** m footpath

futsch [fʊtʃ] (umg) adj (weg) gone, vanished

Futter ['fʊtər] (-s, -) nt fodder, feed; (Stoff) lining

Futteral [fʊtə'raːl] (-s, -e) nt case

futtern ['fʊtərn] vi (hum: umg) to stuff o.s. ▷ vt to scoff

füttern ['fʏtərn] vt to feed; (Kleidung) to line; **„F~ verboten"** "do not feed the animals"

Futur [fu'tuːr] (-s, -e) nt future

Gg

G, g[1] [ge:] nt G, g; **G wie Gustav** ≈ G for George; **G-8** f abk (Pol) (= Group of Eight) G8; **G-20** f abk (Pol) (= Group of Twenty) G20

g[2] abk (Österr) = **Groschen**; (= Gramm) g

gab etc [ga:p] vb siehe **geben**

Gabe ['ga:bə] (-, -n) f gift

Gabel ['ga:bəl] (-, -n) f fork; (Tel) rest, cradle; **Gabelfrühstück** nt mid-morning light lunch; **gabeln** vr to fork; **Gabelstapler** (-s, -) m fork-lift truck; **Gabelung** f fork

Gabentisch ['ga:bəntɪʃ] m table for Christmas or birthday presents

Gabun [ga'bu:n] nt Gabon

gackern ['gakərn] vi to cackle

gaffen ['gafən] vi to gape

Gag [gɛk] (-s, -s) m (Filmgag) gag; (Werbegag) gimmick

Gage ['ga:ʒə] (-, -n) f fee

gähnen ['gɛ:nən] vi to yawn; **~de Leere** total emptiness

GAL (-) f abk (= Grün-Alternative Liste) electoral pact of Greens and alternative parties

galant [ga'lant] adj gallant, courteous

Galavorstellung f (Theat) gala performance

Galerie [galə'ri:] f gallery

Galgen ['galgən] (-s, -) m gallows pl; **Galgenfrist** f respite; **Galgenhumor** m macabre humour (Brit) od humor (US); **Galgenstrick** (umg) m, **Galgenvogel** (umg) m gallows bird

Galionsfigur [gali'o:nsfigu:r] f figurehead

gälisch ['gɛ:lɪʃ] adj Gaelic

Galle ['galə] (-, -n) f gall; (Organ) gall bladder; **jdm kommt die ~ hoch** sb's blood begins to boil

Galopp [ga'lɔp] (-s, -s od -e) m gallop; **im ~** (lit) at a gallop; (fig) at top speed

galoppieren [galɔ'pi:rən] vi to gallop

galt etc [galt] vb siehe **gelten**

galvanisieren [galvani'zi:rən] vt to galvanize

Gamasche [ga'maʃə] (-, -n) f gaiter; (kurz) spat

Gameboy® ['ge:mbɔy] m games console

Gamer, in ['ge:mər] (-s, -) m(f) (Comput) gamer

Gameshow ['ge:mʃo:] (-, -s) f game show

Gammastrahlen ['gamaʃtra:lən] pl gamma rays pl

gamm(e)lig ['gam(ə)lɪç] (umg) adj (Kleidung) tatty

gammeln ['gaməln] (umg) vi to loaf about

Gammler, in ['gamlər(ɪn)] (-s, -) m(f) dropout

Gämse ['gɛmzə] (-, -n) f chamois

Gang[1] [gaŋ] (-(e)s, ⸚e) m walk; (Botengang) errand; (Gangart) gait; (Abschnitt eines Vorgangs) operation; (Essensgang, Ablauf) course; (Flur etc) corridor; (Durchgang) passage; (Aut, Tech) gear; (in Kirche, Theat, Aviat) aisle; **den ersten ~ einlegen** to engage first (gear); **einen ~ machen/tun** to go on an errand/for a walk; **den ~ nach Canossa antreten** (fig) to eat humble pie; **seinen gewohnten ~ gehen** (fig) to run its usual course; **in ~ bringen** to start up; (fig) to get off the ground; **in ~ sein** to be in operation; (fig) to be under way

Gang[2] [gɛŋ] (-, -s) f gang

gang adj: **~ und gäbe** usual, normal

Gangart f way of walking, walk, gait; (von Pferd) gait; **eine härtere ~ einschlagen** (fig) to apply harder tactics

gangbar adj passable; (Methode) practicable

Gängelband ['gɛŋəlbant] nt: **jdn am ~ halten** (fig) to spoon-feed sb

gängeln vt to spoonfeed; **jdn ~** to treat sb like a child

gängig ['gɛŋɪç] adj common, current; (Ware) in demand, selling well

Gangschaltung f gears pl

Gangway ['gæŋweɪ] f (Naut) gangway; (Aviat) steps pl

Ganove [ga'no:və] (-n, -n) (umg) m crook

Gans [gans] (-, ⸚e) f goose

Gänse- zW: **Gänseblümchen** nt daisy; **Gänsebraten** m roast goose; **Gänsefüßchen** (umg) pl inverted commas pl (Brit), quotes pl; **Gänsehaut** f goose pimples pl; **Gänsemarsch** m: **im Gänsemarsch** in single file

Gänserich (-s, -e) m gander

ganz [gants] adj whole; (vollständig) complete ▷ adv quite; (völlig) completely; (sehr) really; (genau) exactly; **~ Europa** all Europe; **im (Großen und) G~en genommen** on the whole, all in all; **etw wieder ~ machen** to mend sth; **sein ~es Geld** all his money; **~ gewiss!** absolutely!; **ein ~ klein wenig** just a tiny bit; **das mag ich ~ besonders gern(e)** I'm particularly fond of that; **sie ist ~ die Mutter** she's just od exactly like her mother; **~ und gar nicht** not at all

Ganze, s nt: **es geht ums ~** everything's at

stake; **aufs ~ gehen** to go for the lot

Ganzheitsmethode ['gantshaɪtsmetoːdə] f (Sch) look-and-say method

gänzlich ['gɛntslɪç] adj complete, entire ▷ adv completely, entirely

ganztägig ['gantstɛːgɪç] adj all-day attrib

ganztags adv (arbeiten) full time; **Ganztagsschule** f all-day school; **Ganztagsstelle** f full-time job

gar [gaːr] adj cooked, done ▷ adv quite; ~ **nicht/nichts/keiner** not/nothing/nobody at all; ~ **nicht schlecht** not bad at all; ~ **kein Grund** no reason whatsoever od at all; **er wäre ~ zu gern noch länger geblieben** he would really have liked to stay longer

Garage [gaˈraːʒə] (-, -n) f garage

Garantie [garanˈtiː] f guarantee; **das fällt noch unter die ~** that's covered by the guarantee

garantieren vt to guarantee

garantiert adv guaranteed; (umg) I bet

Garantieschein m guarantee

Garaus ['gaːraus] (umg) m: **jdm den ~ machen** to do sb in

Garbe ['garbə] (-, -n) f sheaf; (Mil) burst of fire

Garde ['gardə] (-, -n) f guard(s); **die alte ~** the old guard

Garderobe [gardəˈroːbə] (-, -n) f wardrobe; (Abgabe) cloakroom (Brit), checkroom (US); (Kleiderablage) hall stand; (Theat: Umkleideraum) dressing room

Garderobenfrau f cloakroom attendant

Garderobenständer m hall stand

Gardine [garˈdiːnə] (-, -n) f curtain

Gardinenpredigt (umg) f: **jdm eine ~ halten** to give sb a talking-to

Gardinenstange f curtain rail; (zum Ziehen) curtain rod

garen ['gaːrən] vt, vi (Koch) to cook

gären ['gɛːrən] unreg vi to ferment

Garn [garn] (-(e)s, -e) nt thread; (Häkelgarn, fig) yarn

Garnele [garˈneːlə] (-, -n) f shrimp, prawn

garnieren [garˈniːrən] vt to decorate; (Speisen) to garnish

Garnison [garniˈzoːn] (-, -en) f garrison

Garnitur [garniˈtuːr] f (Satz) set; (Unterwäsche) set of (matching) underwear; **erste ~** (fig) top rank; **zweite ~** second rate

garstig ['garstɪç] adj nasty, horrid

Garten ['gartən] (-s, ⁻) m garden; **Gartenarbeit** f gardening; **Gartenbau** m horticulture; **Gartenfest** nt garden party; **Gartengerät** nt gardening tool; **Gartenhaus** nt summerhouse; **Gartenkresse** f cress; **Gartenlaube** f (Gartenhäuschen) summerhouse; **Gartenlokal** nt beer garden; **Gartenschere** f pruning shears pl; **Gartentür** f garden gate; **Gartenzaun** m garden fence; **Gartenzwerg** m garden gnome; (pej: umg) squirt

Gärtner, in ['gɛrtnər(ɪn)] (-s, -) m(f) gardener

Gärtnerei [gɛrtnəˈraɪ] f nursery; (Gemüsegärtnerei) market garden (Brit), truck farm (US)

gärtnern vi to garden

Gärung ['gɛːrʊŋ] f fermentation

Gas [gaːs] (-es, -e) nt gas; ~ **geben** (Aut) to accelerate, step on the gas

Gas- zW: **Gasflasche** f bottle of gas, gas canister; **gasförmig** adj gaseous; **Gashahn** m gas tap; **Gasherd** m gas cooker; **Gaskocher** m gas cooker; **Gasleitung** f gas pipeline; **Gasmaske** f gas mask; **Gaspedal** nt accelerator, gas pedal (US); **Gaspistole** f gas pistol

Gasse ['gasə] (-, -n) f lane, alley

Gassenhauer (-s, -) (veraltet: umg) m popular melody

Gassenjunge m street urchin

Gast [gast] (-es, ⁻e) m guest; **bei jdm zu ~ sein** to be sb's guest(s); **Gastarbeiter** m foreign worker

Gäste- zW: **Gästebett** nt spare bed; **Gästebuch** nt visitors' book; **Gästezimmer** nt guest room

Gast- zW: **gastfreundlich** adj hospitable; **Gastfreundlichkeit** f hospitality; **Gastfreundschaft** f hospitality; **Gastgeber, in** (-s, -) m(f) host(ess); **Gasthaus** nt hotel, inn; **Gasthof** m hotel, inn; **Gasthörer, in** m(f) (Univ) observer, auditor (US)

gastieren [gasˈtiːrən] vi (Theat) to (appear as a) guest

Gast- zW: **Gastland** nt host country; **gastlich** adj hospitable; **Gastlichkeit** f hospitality; **Gastrolle** f (Theat) guest role; **eine Gastrolle spielen** to make a guest appearance

Gastronomie [gastronoˈmiː] f (form: Gaststättengewerbe) catering trade

gastronomisch [gastroˈnoːmɪʃ] adj gastronomic(al)

Gast- zW: **Gastspiel** nt (Sport) away game; **ein Gastspiel geben** (Theat) to give a guest performance; (fig) to put in a brief appearance; **Gaststätte** f restaurant; (Trinklokal) pub; **Gastwirt** m innkeeper; **Gastwirtschaft** f hotel, inn; **Gastzimmer** nt guest room

Gas- zW: **Gasvergiftung** f gas poisoning; **Gasversorgung** f (System) gas supply; **Gaswerk** nt gasworks sing od pl; **Gaszähler** m gas meter

Gatte ['gatə] (-n, -n) m (form) husband, spouse; **die ~n** husband and wife

Gatter ['gatər] (-s, -) nt grating; (Tür) gate

Gattin f (form) wife, spouse

Gattung ['gatʊŋ] f (Biol) genus; (Sorte) kind

GAU [gau] m abk (= größter anzunehmender Unfall) MCA, maximum credible accident

Gaudi ['gaudi] (Südd, Österr: umg) nt od f fun

Gaukler ['gauklər] (-s, -) m (liter) travelling entertainer; (Zauberkünstler) conjurer, magician

Gaul [gaul] (-(e)s, Gäule) (pej) m nag

Gaumen ['gaumən] (-s, -) m palate

Gauner ['gaunər] (-s, -) m rogue

Gaunerei [gaunəˈraɪ] f swindle

Gaunersprache f underworld jargon

Gaze ['gaːzə] (-, -n) f gauze

Geäst [gəˈɛst] nt branches pl

geb. *abk* = **geboren**

Gebäck [gə'bɛk] (**-(e)s, -e**) *nt* (*Kekse*) biscuits *pl* (Brit), cookies *pl* (US); (*Teilchen*) pastries *pl*

gebacken [gə'bakən] *pp von* **backen**

Gebälk [gə'bɛlk] (**-(e)s**) *nt* timberwork

gebannt [gə'bant] *adj* spellbound

gebar *etc* [gə'baːr] *vb siehe* **gebären**

Gebärde [gə'bɛːrdə] (**-, -n**) *f* gesture

gebärden *vr* to behave

Gebaren [gə'baːrən] (**-s**) *nt* behaviour (Brit), behavior (US); (*Geschäftsgebaren*) conduct

gebären [gə'bɛːrən] *unreg vt* to give birth to

Gebärmutter *f* uterus, womb

Gebäude [gə'bɔydə] (**-s, -**) *nt* building; **Gebäudekomplex** *m* (building) complex; **Gebäudereinigung** *f* (*das Reinigen*) commercial cleaning; (*Firma*) cleaning contractors *pl*

Gebein [gə'baɪn] (**-(e)s, -e**) *nt* bones *pl*

Gebell [gə'bɛl] (**-(e)s**) *nt* barking

geben [ˈgeːbən] *unreg vt, vi* to give; (*Karten*) to deal ▷ *vt unpers*: **es gibt** there is/are; there will be ▷ *vr* (*sich verhalten*) to behave, act; (*aufhören*) to abate; **jdm etw ~** to give sb sth *od* sth to sb; **in die Post ~** to post; **das gibt keinen Sinn** that doesn't make sense; **er gibt Englisch** he teaches English; **viel/nicht viel auf etw** *akk* **~** to set great store/not much store by sth; **etw von sich ~** (*Laute etc*) to utter; **ein Wort gab das andere** one angry word led to another; **ein gutes Beispiel ~** to set a good example; **~ Sie mir bitte Herrn Braun** (*Tel*) can I speak to Mr Braun please?; **ein Auto in Reparatur ~** to have a car repaired; **was gibts?** what's the matter?, what's up?; **was gibts zum Mittagessen?** what's for lunch?; **das gibts doch nicht!** that's impossible!; **sich geschlagen ~** to admit defeat; **das wird sich schon ~** that'll soon sort itself out

Geberkonferenz [ˈgeːbər-] *f* (*Pol*) donor conference

Gebet [gə'beːt] (**-(e)s, -e**) *nt* prayer; **jdn ins ~ nehmen** (*fig*) to take sb to task

gebeten [gə'beːtən] *pp von* **bitten**

gebeugt [gə'bɔykt] *adj* (*Haltung*) stooped; (*Kopf*) bowed; (*Schultern*) sloping

gebiert [gə'biːrt] *vb siehe* **gebären**

Gebiet [gə'biːt] (**-(e)s, -e**) *nt* area; (*Hoheitsgebiet*) territory; (*fig*) field

gebieten *unreg vt* to command, demand

Gebieter (**-s, -**) *m* master; (*Herrscher*) ruler; **Gebieterin** *f* mistress; **gebieterisch** *adj* imperious

Gebietshoheit *f* territorial sovereignty

Gebilde [gə'bɪldə] (**-s, -**) *nt* object, structure

gebildet *adj* cultured, educated

Gebimmel [gə'bɪməl] (**-s**) *nt* (continual) ringing

Gebirge [gə'bɪrgə] (**-s, -**) *nt* mountains *pl*

gebirgig *adj* mountainous

Gebirgs- *zW*: **Gebirgsbahn** *f* railway crossing a mountain range; **Gebirgskette** *f*, **Gebirgszug** *m* mountain range

Gebiss [gə'bɪs] (**-es, -e**) *nt* teeth *pl*; (*künstlich*) dentures *pl*

gebissen *pp von* **beißen**

Gebläse [gə'blɛːzə] (**-s, -**) *nt* fan, blower

geblasen [gə'blaːzən] *pp von* **blasen**

geblichen [gə'blɪçən] *pp von* **bleichen**

geblieben [gə'bliːbən] *pp von* **bleiben**

geblümt [gə'blyːmt] *adj* flowered; (*Stil*) flowery

Geblüt [gə'blyːt] (**-(e)s**) *nt* blood, race

gebogen [gə'boːgən] *pp von* **biegen**

geboren [gə'boːrən] *pp von* **gebären** ▷ *adj* born; (*Frau*) née; **wo sind Sie ~?** where were you born?

geborgen [gə'bɔrgən] *pp von* **bergen** ▷ *adj* secure, safe

geborsten [gə'bɔrstən] *pp von* **bersten**

Gebot (**-(e)s, -e**) *nt* (*Gesetz*) law; (*Rel*) commandment; (*bei Auktion*) bid; **das ~ der Stunde** the needs of the moment

gebot *etc* [gə'boːt] *vb siehe* **gebieten**

geboten [gə'boːtən] *pp von* **bieten; gebieten** ▷ *adj* advisable; (*: notwendig*) necessary; (*: dringend geboten*) imperative

Gebr. *abk* (= *Gebrüder*) Bros., bros.

gebracht [gə'braxt] *pp von* **bringen**

gebrannt [gə'brant] *pp von* **brennen** ▷ *adj*: **ein ~es Kind scheut das Feuer** (*Sprichwort*) once bitten twice shy (*Sprichwort*)

gebraten [gə'braːtən] *pp von* **braten**

Gebräu [gə'brɔy] (**-(e)s, -e**) *nt* brew, concoction

Gebrauch [gə'braux] (**-(e)s, Gebräuche**) *m* use; (*Sitte*) custom; **zum äußerlichen/innerlichen ~** for external use/to be taken internally

gebrauchen *vt* to use; **er/das ist zu nichts zu ~** he's/that's (of) no use to anybody

gebräuchlich [gə'brɔyçlɪç] *adj* usual, customary

Gebrauchs- *zW*: **Gebrauchsanweisung** *f* directions *pl* for use; **Gebrauchsartikel** *m* article of everyday use; **gebrauchsfertig** *adj* ready for use; **Gebrauchsgegenstand** *m* commodity

gebraucht [gə'brauxt] *adj* used; **Gebrauchtwagen** *m* second-hand *od* used car

gebrechlich [gə'brɛçlɪç] *adj* frail; **Gebrechlichkeit** *f* frailty

gebrochen [gə'brɔxən] *pp von* **brechen**

Gebrüder [gə'bryːdər] *pl* brothers *pl*

Gebrüll [gə'brʏl] (**-(e)s**) *nt* (*von Mensch*) yelling; (*von Löwe*) roar

gebückt [gə'bʏkt] *adj*: **eine ~e Haltung** a stoop

Gebühr [gə'byːr] (**-, -en**) *f* charge; (*Postgebühr*) postage *no pl*; (*Honorar*) fee; **zu ermäßigter ~** at a reduced rate; **~ (be)zahlt Empfänger** postage to be paid by addressee; **nach ~** suitably; **über ~** excessively

gebühren *vi* (*geh*): **jdm ~** to be sb's due *od* due to sb ▷ *vr* to be fitting

gebührend *adj* (*verdient*) due; (*angemessen*) suitable

Gebühren- *zW*: **Gebühreneinheit** *f* (*Tel*) tariff unit; **Gebührenerlass** *m* remission of fees; **Gebührenermäßigung** *f* reduction of fees; **gebührenfrei** *adj* free of charge;

g

Gebührenmanager *m* tariff meter;
gebührenpflichtig *adj* subject to charges;
gebührenpflichtige Verwarnung (*Jur*) fine
gebunden [gə'bʊndən] *pp von* **binden**
▷ *adj*: **vertraglich ~ sein** to be bound by
contract
Geburt [gə'buːrt] (-, -en) *f* birth; **das war eine
schwere ~!** (*fig: umg*) that took some doing
Geburten- *zW*: **Geburtenkontrolle** *f* birth
control; **Geburtenregelung** *f* birth control;
Geburtenrückgang *m* drop in the birth rate;
geburtenschwach *adj* (*Jahrgang*) with a low
birth rate; **Geburtenziffer** *f* birth rate
gebürtig [gə'bʏrtɪç] *adj* born in, native of; **~e
Schweizerin** native of Switzerland, Swiss-
born woman
Geburts- *zW*: **Geburtsanzeige** *f* birth notice;
Geburtsdatum *nt* date of birth; **Geburtsfehler**
m congenital defect; **Geburtshelfer** *m* (*Arzt*)
obstetrician; **Geburtshelferin** *f* (*Ärztin*)
obstetrician; (*Hebamme*) midwife; **Geburtshilfe** *f* (*als Fach*) obstetrics *sing*; (*von Hebamme*)
midwifery; **Geburtsjahr** *nt* year of birth;
Geburtsort *m* birthplace; **Geburtstag** *m*
birthday; **herzlichen Glückwunsch zum
Geburtstag!** happy birthday!, many happy
returns (of the day)!; **Geburtsurkunde** *f* birth
certificate
Gebüsch [gə'bʏʃ] (-(e)s, -e) *nt* bushes *pl*
gedacht [gə'daxt] *pp von* **denken; gedenken**
gedachte *etc vb siehe* **gedenken**
Gedächtnis [gə'dɛçtnɪs] (-ses, -se) *nt* memory;
wenn mich mein ~ nicht trügt if my
memory serves me right; **Gedächtnisfeier** *f*
commemoration; **Gedächtnishilfe** *f* memory
aid, mnemonic; **Gedächtnisschwund** *m* loss
of memory; **Gedächtnisverlust** *m* amnesia
gedämpft [gə'dɛmpft] *adj* (*Geräusch*) muffled;
(*Farben, Instrument, Stimmung*) muted; (*Licht,
Freude*) subdued
Gedanke [gə'daŋkə] (-ns, -n) *m* thought; (*Idee,
Plan, Einfall*) idea; (*Konzept*) concept; **sich über
etw** *akk* **~n machen** to think about sth; **jdn
auf andere ~n bringen** to make sb think
about other things; **etw ganz in ~n** *dat* **tun**
to do sth without thinking; **auf einen ~n
kommen** to have *od* get an idea
Gedanken- *zW*: **Gedankenaustausch** *m*
exchange of ideas; **Gedankenfreiheit**
f freedom of thought; **gedankenlos**
adj thoughtless; **Gedankenlosigkeit** *f*
thoughtlessness; **Gedankensprung** *m*
mental leap; **Gedankenstrich** *m* dash;
Gedankenübertragung *f* thought
transference, telepathy; **gedankenverloren**
adj lost in thought; **gedankenvoll** *adj*
thoughtful
Gedärme [gə'dɛrmə] *pl* intestines *pl*
Gedeck [gə'dɛk] (-(e)s, -e) *nt* cover(ing); (*Menü*)
set meal; **ein ~ auflegen** to lay a place
gedeckt *adj* (*Farbe*) muted
Gedeih *m*: **auf ~ und Verderb** for better or for
worse

gedeihen [gə'daɪən] *unreg vi* to thrive, prosper;
die Sache ist so weit gediehen, dass ... the
matter has reached the point *od* stage where ...
gedenken [gə'dɛŋkən] *unreg vi* +*gen* (*geh: denken
an*) to remember; (*beabsichtigen*) to intend;
Gedenken *nt*: **zum Gedenken an jdn** in
memory *od* remembrance of sb
Gedenk- *zW*: **Gedenkfeier** *f* commemoration;
Gedenkminute *f* minute's silence;
Gedenkstätte *f* memorial; **Gedenktag** *m*
remembrance day
Gedicht [gə'dɪçt] (-(e)s, -e) *nt* poem
gediegen [gə'diːgən] *adj* (good) quality;
(*Mensch*) reliable; (*rechtschaffen*) honest;
Gediegenheit *f* quality; reliability; honesty
gedieh *etc* [gə'diː] *vb siehe* **gedeihen**
gediehen *pp von* **gedeihen**
gedr. *abk* = **gedruckt**
Gedränge [gə'drɛŋə] (-s) *nt* crush, crowd; **ins ~
kommen** (*fig*) to get into difficulties
gedrängt *adj* compressed; **~ voll** packed
gedroschen [gə'drɔʃən] *pp von* **dreschen**
gedruckt [gə'drʊkt] *adj* printed; **lügen wie ~**
(*umg*) to lie left, right and centre
gedrungen [gə'drʊŋən] *pp von* **dringen** ▷ *adj*
thickset, stocky
Geduld [gə'dʊlt] (-) *f* patience; **mir reißt die
~, ich verliere die ~** my patience is wearing
thin, I'm losing my patience
gedulden [gə'dʊldən] *vr* to be patient
geduldig *adj* patient
Geduldsprobe *f* trial of (one's) patience
gedungen [gə'dʊŋən] (*pej*) *adj* (*geh: Mörder*)
hired
gedunsen [gə'dʊnzən] *adj* bloated
gedurft [gə'dʊrft] *pp von* **dürfen**
geehrt [gə'eːrt] *adj*: **Sehr ~e Damen und
Herren!** Ladies and Gentlemen!; (*in Briefen*)
Dear Sir or Madam
geeignet [gə'|aɪgnət] *adj* suitable; **im ~en
Augenblick** at the right moment
Gefahr [gə'faːr] (-, -en) *f* danger; **~ laufen,
etw zu tun** to run the risk of doing sth; **auf
eigene ~** at one's own risk; **außer ~** (*nicht
gefährdet*) not in danger; (*nicht mehr gefährdet*)
out of danger; (*Patienten*) off the danger list
gefährden [gə'fɛːrdən] *vt* to endanger
gefahren [gə'faːrən] *pp von* **fahren**
Gefahren- *zW*: **Gefahrenquelle** *f* source
of danger; **Gefahrenschwelle** *f* threshold
of danger; **Gefahrenstelle** *f* danger spot;
Gefahrenzulage *f* danger money
gefährlich [gə'fɛːrlɪç] *adj* dangerous
Gefährte [gə'fɛːrtə] (-n, -n) *m* companion
Gefährtin [gə'fɛːrtɪn] *f* companion
Gefälle [gə'fɛlə] (-s, -) *nt* (*von Land, Straße*) slope;
(*Neigungsgrad*) gradient; **starkes ~!** steep hill
Gefallen[1] [gə'falən] (-s, -) *m* favour; **jdm etw
zu ~ tun** to do sth to please sb
Gefallen[2] [gə'falən] (-s) *nt* pleasure; **an etw** *dat*
~ finden to derive pleasure from sth; **an jdm
~ finden** to take to sb
gefallen *pp von* **fallen; gefallen** ▷ *vi* (*unreg*): **jdm**

~ to please sb; **er/es gefällt mir** I like him/ it; **das gefällt mir an ihm** that's one thing I like about him; **sich** *dat* **etw ~ lassen** to put up with sth

Gefallene, r *m* soldier killed in action

gefällig [gə'fɛlɪç] *adj* (*hilfsbereit*) obliging; (*erfreulich*) pleasant; **sonst noch etwas ~?** (*veraltet, ironisch*) will there be anything else?; **Gefälligkeit** *f* favour (*Brit*), favor (*US*); helpfulness; **etw aus Gefälligkeit tun** to do sth as a favour (*Brit*) *od* favor (*US*)

gefälligst (*umg*) *adv* kindly; **sei ~ still!** will you kindly keep your mouth shut!

gefällt [gə'fɛlt] *vb siehe* **gefallen**

gefangen [gə'faŋən] *pp von* **fangen** ▷ *adj* captured; (*fig*) captivated; **~ halten** to keep prisoner; **~ nehmen** to capture

Gefangene, r *f(m)* prisoner, captive

Gefangenenlager *nt* prisoner-of-war camp

Gefangen- *zW:* **Gefangennahme (-, -n)** *f* capture; **Gefangenschaft** *f* captivity

Gefängnis [gə'fɛŋnɪs] **(-ses, -se)** *nt* prison; **zwei Jahre ~ bekommen** to get two years' imprisonment; **Gefängnisstrafe** *f* prison sentence; **Gefängniswärter** *m* prison warder (*Brit*) *od* guard

gefärbt [gə'fɛrpt] *adj* (*fig: Bericht*) biased; (*Lebensmittel*) coloured (*Brit*), colored (*US*)

Gefasel [gə'fa:zəl] **(-s)** *nt* twaddle, drivel

Gefäß [gə'fɛ:s] **(-es, -e)** *nt* vessel (*auch Anat*), container

gefasst [gə'fast] *adj* composed, calm; **auf etw** *akk* **~ sein** to be prepared *od* ready for sth; **er kann sich auf etwas ~ machen** (*umg*) I'll give him something to think about

Gefecht [gə'fɛçt] **(-(e)s, -e)** *nt* fight; (*Mil*) engagement; **jdn/etw außer ~ setzen** (*lit, fig*) to put sb/sth out of action

gefedert [gə'fe:dərt] *adj* (*Matratze*) sprung

gefeiert [gə'faɪərt] *adj* celebrated

gefeit [gə'faɪt] *adj:* **gegen etw ~ sein** to be immune to sth

gefestigt [gə'fɛstɪçt] *adj* (*Charakter*) steadfast

Gefieder [gə'fi:dər] **(-s, -)** *nt* plumage, feathers *pl*

gefiedert *adj* feathered

gefiel *etc* [gə'fi:l] *vb siehe* **gefallen**

Geflecht [gə'flɛçt] **(-(e)s, -e)** *nt* (*lit, fig*) network

gefleckt [gə'flɛkt] *adj* spotted; (*Blume, Vogel*) speckled

Geflimmer [gə'flɪmər] **(-s)** *nt* shimmering; (*Film, TV*) flicker(ing)

geflissentlich [gə'flɪsəntlɪç] *adj* intentional ▷ *adv* intentionally

geflochten [gə'flɔxtən] *pp von* **flechten**

geflogen [gə'flo:gən] *pp von* **fliegen**

geflohen [gə'flo:ən] *pp von* **fliehen**

geflossen [gə'flɔsən] *pp von* **fließen**

Geflügel [gə'fly:gəl] **(-s)** *nt* poultry

Geflügelpest *f* poultry plague

geflügelt *adj:* **~e Worte** familiar quotations

Geflüster [gə'flʏstər] **(-s)** *nt* whispering

gefochten [gə'fɔxtən] *pp von* **fechten**

Gefolge [gə'fɔlgə] **(-s, -)** *nt* retinue

Gefolgschaft [gə'fɔlkʃaft] *f* following

Gefolgsmann (-(e)s, *pl* **-leute)** *m* follower

gefragt [ge'fra:kt] *adj* in demand

gefräßig [gə'frɛ:sɪç] *adj* voracious

Gefreite, r [gə'fraɪtə(r)] *m* (*Mil*) lance corporal (*Brit*), private first class (*US*); (*Naut*) able seaman (*Brit*), seaman apprentice (*US*); (*Aviat*) aircraftman (*Brit*), airman first class (*US*)

gefressen [gə'frɛsən] *pp von* **fressen** ▷ *adj:* **den hab(e) ich ~** (*umg*) I'm sick of him

gefrieren [gə'fri:rən] *unreg vi* to freeze

Gefrier- *zW:* **Gefrierfach** *nt* freezer compartment; **Gefrierfleisch** *nt* frozen meat; **gefriergetrocknet** *adj* freeze-dried; **Gefrierpunkt** *m* freezing point; **Gefrierschutzmittel** *nt* antifreeze; **Gefriertruhe** *f* deep-freeze

gefror *etc* [gə'fro:r] *vb siehe* **gefrieren**

gefroren [gə'fro:rən] *pp von* **frieren, gefrieren**

Gefüge [gə'fy:gə] **(-s, -)** *nt* structure

gefügig *adj* submissive; (*gehorsam*) obedient

Gefühl [gə'fy:l] **(-(e)s, -e)** *nt* feeling; **etw im ~ haben** to have a feel for sth; **gefühllos** *adj* unfeeling; (*Glieder*) numb

Gefühls- *zW:* **gefühlsbetont** *adj* emotional; **Gefühlsduselei** [-du:zə'laɪ] (*pej*) *f* mawkishness; **Gefühlsleben** *nt* emotional life; **gefühlsmäßig** *adj* instinctive; **Gefühlsmensch** *m* emotional person

gefühlvoll *adj* (*empfindsam*) sensitive; (*ausdrucksvoll*) expressive; (*liebevoll*) loving

gefüllt [gə'fʏlt] *adj* (*Koch*) stuffed; (*Pralinen*) with soft centres

gefunden [gə'fʊndən] *pp von* **finden** ▷ *adj:* **das war ein ~es Fressen für ihn** that was handing it to him on a plate

gegangen [gə'gaŋən] *pp von* **gehen**

gegeben [gə'ge:bən] *pp von* **geben** ▷ *adj* given; **zu ~er Zeit** in due course

gegebenenfalls [gə'ge:bənənfals] *adv* if need be

 SCHLÜSSELWORT

gegen ['ge:gən] *präp +akk* **1** against; **nichts gegen jdn haben** to have nothing against sb; **X gegen Y** (*Sport, Jur*) X versus Y; **ein Mittel gegen Schnupfen** something for colds
2 (*in Richtung auf*) towards; **gegen Osten** to(wards) the east; **gegen Abend** towards evening; **gegen einen Baum fahren** to drive into a tree
3 (*ungefähr*) round about; **gegen 3 Uhr** around 3 o'clock
4 (*gegenüber*) towards; (*ungefähr*) around; **gerecht gegen alle** fair to all
5 (*im Austausch für*) for; **gegen bar** for cash; **gegen Quittung** against a receipt
6 (*verglichen mit*) compared with

Gegen- *zW:* **Gegenangriff** *m* counter-attack; **Gegenbesuch** *m* return visit; **Gegenbeweis** *m*

g

counter-evidence

Gegend ['ge:gənt] (-, -en) f area, district

Gegen- zW: **Gegendarstellung** f (Presse) reply; **gegeneinander** adv against one another; **Gegenfahrbahn** f opposite carriageway; **gegenfinanzieren** vt to counterfinance; **Gegenfinanzierung** f financing of state expenditure by means of cuts, tax increases etc; **Gegenfrage** f counterquestion; **Gegengewicht** nt counterbalance; **Gegengift** nt antidote; **Gegenkandidat** m rival candidate; **gegenläufig** adj contrary; **Gegenleistung** f service in return; **Gegenlichtaufnahme** f back lit photograph; **Gegenliebe** f requited love; (fig: Zustimmung) approval; **Gegenmaßnahme** f countermeasure; **Gegenmittel** nt: **Gegenmittel (gegen)** (Med) antidote (to); **Gegenprobe** f cross-check

Gegensatz (-es, -̈e) m contrast; **Gegensätze überbrücken** to overcome differences **gegensätzlich** adj contrary, opposite; (widersprüchlich) contradictory

Gegen- zW: **Gegenschlag** m counter-attack; **Gegenseite** f opposite side; (Rückseite) reverse; **gegenseitig** adj mutual, reciprocal; **sich gegenseitig helfen** to help each other; **in gegenseitigem Einverständnis** by mutual agreement; **Gegenseitigkeit** f reciprocity; **Gegenspieler** m opponent; **Gegensprechanlage** f (two-way) intercom; **Gegenstand** m object; **gegenständlich** adj objective, concrete; (Kunst) representational; **gegenstandslos** adj (überflüssig) irrelevant; (grundlos) groundless; **Gegenstimme** f vote against; **Gegenstoß** m counterblow; **Gegenstück** nt counterpart; **Gegenteil** nt opposite; **im Gegenteil** on the contrary; **das Gegenteil bewirken** to have the opposite effect; (Mensch) to achieve the exact opposite; **ganz im Gegenteil** quite the reverse; **ins Gegenteil umschlagen** to swing to the other extreme; **gegenteilig** adj opposite, contrary; **ich habe nichts Gegenteiliges gehört** I've heard nothing to the contrary

gegenüber [ge:gən'|y:bər] präp +dat opposite; (zu) to(wards); (in Bezug auf) with regard to; (im Vergleich zu) in comparison with; (angesichts) in the face of ▷ adv opposite; **mir ~ hat er das nicht geäußert** he didn't say that to me; **Gegenüber (-s, -)** nt person opposite; (bei Kampf) opponent; (bei Diskussion) opposite number; **gegenüberliegen** unreg vr to face each other; **gegenüberstehen** unreg vr to be opposed (to each other); **gegenüberstellen** vt to confront; (fig) to contrast; **Gegenüberstellung** f confrontation; (fig) contrast; (: Vergleich) comparison; **gegenübertreten** unreg vi +dat to face

Gegen- zW: **Gegenveranstaltung** f counter-meeting; **Gegenverkehr** m oncoming traffic; **Gegenvorschlag** m counterproposal

Gegenwart ['ge:gənvart] f present; **in ~ von** in the presence of

gegenwärtig adj present ▷ adv at present; **das ist mir nicht mehr ~** that has slipped my mind

gegenwartsbezogen adj (Roman etc) relevant to present times

Gegen- zW: **Gegenwert** m equivalent; **Gegenwind** m headwind; **Gegenwirkung** f reaction; **gegenzeichnen** vt to countersign; **Gegenzug** m countermove; (Eisenb) corresponding train in the other direction

gegessen [gə'gɛsən] pp von **essen**

geglichen [gə'glıçən] pp von **gleichen**

gegliedert [gə'gli:dərt] adj jointed; (fig) structured

geglitten [gə'glıtən] pp von **gleiten**

geglommen [gə'glɔmən] pp von **glimmen**

geglückt [gə'glʏkt] adj (Feier) successful; (Überraschung) real

Gegner, in ['ge:gnər(ın)] (-s, -) m(f) opponent; **gegnerisch** adj opposing; **Gegnerschaft** f opposition

gegolten [gə'gɔltən] pp von **gelten**

gegoren [gə'go:rən] pp von **gären**

gegossen [gə'gɔsən] pp von **gießen**

gegr. abk (= gegründet) estab.

gegraben [gə'gra:bən] pp von **graben**

gegriffen [gə'grıfən] pp von **greifen**

Gehabe [gə'ha:bə] (-s) (umg) nt affected behaviour (Brit) od behavior (US)

gehabt [gə'ha:pt] pp von **haben**

Gehackte, s [ge'haktə(s)] nt mince(d meat) (Brit), ground meat (US)

Gehalt¹ [gə'halt] (-(e)s, -e) m content

Gehalt² [gə'halt] (-(e)s, -̈er) nt salary

gehalten [gə'haltən] pp von **halten** ▷ adj: **~ sein, etw zu tun** (form) to be required to do sth

Gehalts- zW: **Gehaltsabrechnung** f salary statement; **Gehaltsempfänger** m salary earner; **Gehaltserhöhung** f salary increase; **Gehaltsklasse** f salary bracket; **Gehaltskonto** nt current account (Brit), checking account (US); **Gehaltszulage** f salary increment

gehaltvoll [gə'haltfɔl] adj (Speise, Buch) substantial

gehandicapt, gehandikapt [gə'hɛndikɛpt] adj handicapped

gehangen [gə'haŋən] pp von **hängen**

geharnischt [gə'harnıʃt] adj (fig) forceful, sharp

gehässig [gə'hɛsıç] adj spiteful, nasty; **Gehässigkeit** f spite(fulness)

gehäuft [gə'hɔʏft] adj (Löffel) heaped

Gehäuse [gə'hɔʏzə] (-s, -) nt case; (Radiogehäuse, Uhrgehäuse) casing; (von Apfel etc) core

gehbehindert ['ge:behındərt] adj disabled

Gehege [gə'he:gə] (-s, -) nt enclosure, preserve; **jdm ins ~ kommen** (fig) to poach on sb's preserve

geheim [gə'haım] adj secret; (Dokumente) classified; **streng ~** top secret; **~ halten** to keep secret; **Geheimdienst** m secret service, intelligence service; **Geheimfach** nt secret compartment

Geheimnis (**-ses, -se**) *nt* secret; (*rätselhaftes Geheimnis*) mystery; **Geheimniskrämer** *m* mystery-monger; **geheimnisvoll** *adj* mysterious

Geheim- *zW*: **Geheimnummer** *f* (*Tel*) secret number; **Geheimpolizei** *f* secret police; **Geheimrat** *m* privy councillor; **Geheimratsecken** *pl*: **er hat Geheimratsecken** he is going bald at the temples; **Geheimschrift** *f* code, secret writing; **Geheimtipp** *m* (personal) tip

Geheiß [gə'haɪs] (**-es**) *nt* (*geh*) command; **auf jds ~** *akk* at sb's bidding

geheißen [gə'haɪsən] *pp von* **heißen**

gehemmt [gə'hɛmt] *adj* inhibited

gehen ['ge:ən] *unreg vi* (*auch Auto, Uhr*) to go; (*zu Fuß gehen*) to walk; (*funktionieren*) to work; (*Teig*) to rise ▷ *vt* to go; to walk ▷ *vi unpers*: **wie geht es dir?** how are you *od* things?; **~ nach** (*Fenster*) to face; **in sich** *akk* **~** to think things over; **nach etw ~** (*urteilen*) to go by sth; **sich ~ lassen** to lose one's self-control; (*nachlässig sein*) to let o.s. go; **wie viele Leute ~ in deinen Wagen?** how many people can you get in your car?; **nichts geht über** +*akk* **...** there's nothing to beat ..., there's nothing better than ...; **schwimmen/schlafen ~** to go swimming/to bed; **in die Tausende ~** to run into (the) thousands; **mir/ihm geht es gut** I'm/he's (doing) fine; **geht das?** is that possible?; **gehts noch?** can you manage?; **es geht** not too bad, O.K.; **das geht nicht** that's not on; **es geht um etw** it concerns sth, it's about sth; **lass es dir gut ~** look after yourself, take care of yourself; **so geht das, das geht so** that/this is how it's done; **darum geht es (mir) nicht** that's not the point; (*spielt keine Rolle*) that's not important to me; **morgen geht es nicht** tomorrow's no good; **wenn es nach mir ginge ...** if it were *od* was up to me ...

gehetzt [gə'hɛtst] *adj* harassed

geheuer [gə'hɔʏər] *adj*: **nicht ~** eerie; (*fragwürdig*) dubious

Geheul [gə'hɔʏl] (**-(e)s**) *nt* howling

Gehilfe [gə'hɪlfə] (**-n, -n**) *m* assistant

Gehilfin [gə'hɪlfɪn] *f* assistant

Gehirn [gə'hɪrn] (**-(e)s, -e**) *nt* brain; **Gehirnerschütterung** *f* concussion; **Gehirnschlag** *m* stroke; **Gehirnwäsche** *f* brainwashing

gehoben [gə'ho:bən] *pp von* **heben** ▷ *adj*: **~er Dienst** professional and executive levels of the civil service

geholfen [gə'hɔlfən] *pp von* **helfen**

Gehör [gə'hø:r] (**-(e)s**) *nt* hearing; **musikalisches ~** ear; **absolutes ~** perfect pitch; **~ finden** to gain a hearing; **jdm ~ schenken** to give sb a hearing

gehorchen [gə'hɔrçən] *vi* +*dat* to obey

gehören [gə'hø:rən] *vi* to belong ▷ *vr unpers* to be right *od* proper; **das gehört nicht zur Sache** that's irrelevant; **dazu gehört (schon) einiges** *od* **etwas** that takes some doing (*umg*); **er gehört ins Bett** he should be in bed

gehörig *adj* proper; **~ zu** *od* +*dat* (*geh*) belonging to

gehörlos *adj* (*form*) deaf

gehorsam [gə'ho:rza:m] *adj* obedient; **Gehorsam** (**-s**) *m* obedience

Gehörsinn *m* sense of hearing

Gehsteig ['ge:ʃtaɪk] *m*, **Gehweg** ['ge:vɛk] *m* pavement (*Brit*), sidewalk (*US*)

Geier ['gaɪər] (**-s, -**) *m* vulture; **weiß der ~!** (*umg*) God knows

geifern ['gaɪfərn] *vi* to slaver; (*fig*) to be bursting with venom

Geige ['gaɪgə] (**-, -n**) *f* violin; **die erste/zweite ~ spielen** (*lit*) to play first/second violin; (*fig*) to call the tune/play second fiddle

Geiger, in (**-s, -**) *m(f)* violinist

Geigerzähler *m* geiger counter

geil [gaɪl] *adj* randy (*Brit*), horny (*US*); (*pej*: *lüstern*) lecherous; (*umg*: *gut*) fantastic

Geisel ['gaɪzəl] (**-, -n**) *f* hostage; **Geiselnahme** (**-**) *f* taking of hostages

Geißel ['gaɪsəl] (**-, -n**) *f* scourge, whip; **geißeln** *vt* to scourge

Geist [gaɪst] (**-(e)s, -er**) *m* spirit; (*Gespenst*) ghost; (*Verstand*) mind; **von allen guten ~ern verlassen sein** (*umg*) to have taken leave of one's senses; **hier scheiden sich die ~er** this is the parting of the ways; **den** *od* **seinen ~ aufgeben** to give up the ghost

Geister- *zW*: **Geisterfahrer** (*umg*) *m* ghost-driver (*US*), *person driving in the wrong direction*; **geisterhaft** *adj* ghostly; **Geisterhand** *f*: **wie von Geisterhand** as if by magic

Geistes- *zW*: **geistesabwesend** *adj* absent-minded; **Geistesakrobat** *m* mental acrobat; **Geistesblitz** *m* brain wave; **Geistesgegenwart** *f* presence of mind; **geistesgegenwärtig** *adj* quick-witted; **geistesgestört** *adj* mentally disturbed; (*stärker*) (mentally) deranged; **Geisteshaltung** *f* mental attitude; **geisteskrank** *adj* mentally ill; **Geisteskranke, r** *f(m)* mentally ill person; **Geisteskrankheit** *f* mental illness; **Geistesstörung** *f* mental disturbance; **Geistesverfassung** *f* frame of mind; **Geisteswissenschaften** *pl* arts (subjects) *pl*; **Geisteszustand** *m* state of mind; **jdn auf seinen Geisteszustand untersuchen** to give sb a psychiatric examination

geistig *adj* intellectual; (*Psych*) mental; (*Getränke*) alcoholic; **~ behindert** mentally handicapped; **~-seelisch** mental and spiritual

geistlich *adj* spiritual; (*religiös*) religious; **Geistliche, r** *m* clergyman; **Geistlichkeit** *f* clergy

geist- *zW*: **geistlos** *adj* uninspired, dull; **geistreich** *adj* intelligent; (*witzig*) witty; **geisttötend** *adj* soul-destroying; **geistvoll** *adj* intellectual; (*weise*) wise

Geiz [gaɪts] (**-es**) *m* miserliness, meanness; **geizen** *vi* to be miserly; **Geizhals** *m* miser

g

geizig adj miserly, mean

Geizkragen m miser

gekannt [gə'kant] pp von **kennen**

Gekicher [gə'kıçər] (**-s**) nt giggling

Geklapper [gə'klapər] (**-s**) nt rattling

Geklimper [gə'klımpər] (**-s**) (umg) nt (Klaviergeklimper) tinkling; (: stümperhaft) plonking; (von Geld) jingling

geklungen [gə'klʊŋən] pp von **klingen**

geknickt [gə'knıkt] adj (fig) dejected

gekniffen [gə'knıfən] pp von **kneifen**

gekommen [gə'kɔmən] pp von **kommen**

gekonnt [gə'kɔnt] pp von **können** ▷ adj skilful (Brit), skillful (US)

Gekritzel [gə'krıtsəl] (**-s**) nt scrawl, scribble

gekrochen [gə'krɔxən] pp von **kriechen**

gekünstelt [ge'kynstəlt] adj artificial; (Sprache, Benehmen) affected

Gel [ge:l] (**-s, -e**) nt gel

Gelaber [gə'la:bər], **Gelabere** [gə'la:bərə] (**-s**) (umg) nt prattle

Gelächter [gə'lɛçtər] (**-s, -**) nt laughter; **in ~ ausbrechen** to burst out laughing

gelackmeiert [gə'lakmaıərt] (umg) adj conned

geladen [ge'la:dən] pp von **laden** ▷ adj loaded; (Elek) live; (fig) furious

Gelage [gə'la:gə] (**-s, -**) nt feast, banquet

gelagert [gə'la:gərt] adj: **in anders/ähnlich ~en Fällen** in different/similar cases

gelähmt [gə'lɛ:mt] adj paralysed

Gelände [gə'lɛndə] (**-s, -**) nt land, terrain; (von Fabrik, Sportgelände) grounds pl; (Baugelände) site; **Geländefahrzeug** nt cross-country vehicle; **geländegängig** adj able to go cross-country; **Geländelauf** m cross-country race

Geländer [gə'lɛndər] (**-s, -**) nt railing; (Treppengeländer) banister(s)

gelang etc vb siehe **gelingen**

gelangen [gə'laŋən] vi: **~ an** +akk od **zu** to reach; (erwerben) to attain; **in jds Besitz** akk **~** to come into sb's possession; **in die richtigen/falschen Hände ~** to fall into the right/wrong hands

gelangweilt adj bored

gelassen [gə'lasən] pp von **lassen** ▷ adj calm; (gefasst) composed; **Gelassenheit** f calmness; composure

Gelatine [ʒela'ti:nə] f gelatine

gelaufen [gə'laʊfən] pp von **laufen**

geläufig [gə'lɔyfıç] adj (üblich) common; **das ist mir nicht ~** I'm not familiar with that; **Geläufigkeit** f commonness; familiarity

gelaunt [gə'laʊnt] adj: **schlecht/gut ~** in a bad/good mood; **wie ist er ~?** what sort of mood is he in?

Geläut [gə'lɔyt] (**-(e)s**) nt ringing; (Läutwerk) chime

Geläute (**-s**) nt ringing

gelb [gɛlp] adj yellow; (Ampellicht) amber (Brit), yellow (US); **~e Seiten** Yellow Pages; **gelblich** adj yellowish

Gelbsucht f jaundice

Geld [gɛlt] (**-(e)s, -er**) nt money; **etw zu ~ machen** to sell sth off; **er hat ~ wie Heu** (umg) he's stinking rich; **am ~ hängen** od **kleben** to be tight with money; **staatliche/ öffentliche ~er** state/public funds pl od money; **Geldadel** m: **der Geldadel** the moneyed aristocracy; (hum: die Reichen) the rich; **Geldanlage** f investment; **Geldautomat** m cash dispenser; **Geldautomatenkarte** f cash card; **Geldbeutel** m purse; **Geldbörse** f purse; **Geldeinwurf** m slot; **Geldgeber** (**-s, -**) m financial backer; **geldgierig** adj avaricious; **Geldinstitut** nt financial institution; **Geldmittel** pl capital sing, means pl; **Geldquelle** f source of income; **Geldschein** m banknote; **Geldschrank** m safe, strongbox; **Geldstrafe** f fine; **Geldstück** nt coin; **Geldverlegenheit** f: **in Geldverlegenheit sein/kommen** to be/run short of money; **Geldverleiher** m moneylender; **Geldwäsche** f moneylaundering; **Geldwechsel** m exchange (of money); „**Geldwechsel**" "bureau de change"; **Geldwert** m cash value; (Fin: Kaufkraft) currency value

geleckt [gə'lɛkt] adj: **wie ~ aussehen** to be neat and tidy

Gelee [ʒe'le:] (**-s, -s**) nt od m jelly

gelegen [gə'le:gən] pp von **liegen** ▷ adj situated; (passend) convenient, opportune; **etw kommt jdm ~** sth is convenient for sb; **mir ist viel/ nichts daran ~** (wichtig) it matters a great deal/doesn't matter to me

Gelegenheit [gə'le:gənhaıt] f opportunity; (Anlass) occasion; **bei ~** some time (or other); **bei jeder ~** at every opportunity

Gelegenheits- zW: **Gelegenheitsarbeit** f casual work; **Gelegenheitsarbeiter** m casual worker; **Gelegenheitskauf** m bargain

gelegentlich [gə'le:gəntlıç] adj occasional ▷ adv occasionally; (bei Gelegenheit) some time (or other) ▷ präp +gen on the occasion of

gelehrig [gə'le:rıç] adj quick to learn

gelehrt adj learned; **Gelehrte, r** f(m) scholar; **Gelehrtheit** f scholarliness

Geleise [gə'laızə] (**-s, -**) nt = **Gleis**

Geleit [gə'laıt] (**-(e)s, -e**) nt escort; **freies** od **sicheres ~** safe conduct; **geleiten** vt to escort; **Geleitschutz** m escort

Gelenk [gə'lɛŋk] (**-(e)s, -e**) nt joint

gelenkig adj supple

gelernt [gə'lɛrnt] adj skilled

gelesen [gə'le:zən] pp von **lesen**

Geliebte f sweetheart; (Liebhaberin) mistress

Geliebte, r m sweetheart; (Liebhaber) lover

geliefert [gə'li:fərt] adj: **ich bin ~** (umg) I've had it

geliehen [gə'li:ən] pp von **leihen**

gelind [gə'lınt] adj = **gelinde**

gelinde [gə'lındə] adj (geh) mild; **~ gesagt** to put it mildly

gelingen [gə'lıŋən] unreg vi to succeed; **die Arbeit gelingt mir nicht** I'm not doing very well with this work; **es ist mir gelungen, etw zu tun** I succeeded in doing sth; **Gelingen**

nt (geh: Glück) success; (: erfolgreiches Ergebnis) successful outcome

gelitten [gə'lɪtən] pp von **leiden**

gellen ['gɛlən] vi to shrill

gellend adj shrill, piercing

geloben [gə'lo:bən] vt, vi to vow, swear; **das Gelobte Land** (Rel) the Promised Land

gelogen [gə'lo:gən] pp von **lügen**

gelten ['gɛltən] unreg vt (wert sein) to be worth ▷ vi (gültig sein) to be valid; (erlaubt sein) to be allowed ▷ vb unpers (geh): **es gilt, etw zu tun** it is necessary to do sth; **was gilt die Wette?** do you want a bet?; **das gilt nicht!** that doesn't count!; (nicht erlaubt) that's not allowed; **etw gilt bei jdm viel/wenig** sb values sth highly/ doesn't value sth very highly; **jdm viel/ wenig ~** to mean a lot/not mean much to sb; **jdm ~** (gemünzt sein auf) to be meant for od aimed at sb; **etw ~ lassen** to accept sth; **für diesmal lasse ichs ~** I'll let it go this time; **als** od **für etw ~** to be considered to be sth; **jdm** od **für jdn ~** (betreffen) to apply to sb

geltend adj (Preise) current; (Gesetz) in force; (Meinung) prevailing; **etw ~ machen** to assert sth; **sich ~ machen** to make itself/o.s. felt; **einen Einwand ~ machen** to raise an objection

Geltung ['gɛltʊŋ] f: **~ haben** to have validity; **sich/etw** dat **~ verschaffen** to establish o.s./ sth; **etw zur ~ bringen** to show sth to its best advantage; **zur ~ kommen** to be seen/heard etc to its best advantage

Geltungsbedürfnis nt desire for admiration

geltungssüchtig adj craving admiration

Gelübde [gə'lʏpdə] (-s, -) nt vow

gelungen [gə'lʊŋən] pp von **gelingen** ▷ adj successful

Gem. abk = **Gemeinde**

gemächlich [gə'mɛːçlɪç] adj leisurely

gemacht [gə'maxt] adj (gewollt, gekünstelt) false, contrived; **ein ~er Mann sein** to be made

Gemahl [gə'ma:l] (-(e)s, -e) m (geh, form) spouse, husband

gemahlen [gə'ma:lən] pp von **mahlen**

Gemahlin f (geh, form) spouse, wife

Gemälde [gə'mɛːldə] (-s, -) nt picture, painting

gemasert [gə'ma:zərt] adj (Holz) grained

gemäß [gə'mɛːs] präp +dat in accordance with ▷ adj +dat appropriate to

gemäßigt adj moderate; (Klima) temperate

Gemauschel [gə'mauʃəl] (-s) (umg) nt scheming

Gemecker [gə'mɛkər] (-s) nt (von Ziegen) bleating; (umg: Nörgelei) moaning

gemein [gə'maɪn] adj common; (niederträchtig) mean; **etw ~ haben (mit)** to have sth in common (with)

Gemeinde [gə'maɪndə] (-, -n) f district; (Bewohner) community; (Pfarrgemeinde) parish; (Kirchengemeinde) congregation; **Gemeindeabgaben** pl rates and local taxes pl; **Gemeindebau** m (Österr) subsidized housing; (Gebäude) subsidized house;

Gemeindeordnung f by(e) laws pl, ordinances pl (US); **Gemeinderat** m district council; (Mitglied) district councillor; **Gemeindeschwester** f district nurse (Brit); **Gemeindesteuer** f local rates pl; **Gemeindeverwaltung** f local administration; **Gemeindevorstand** m local council; **Gemeindewahl** f local election

Gemein- zW: **Gemeineigentum** nt common property; **gemeingefährlich** adj dangerous to the public; **Gemeingut** nt public property; **Gemeinheit** f (Niedertracht) meanness; **das war eine Gemeinheit** that was a mean thing to do/to say; **gemeinhin** adv generally; **Gemeinkosten** pl overheads pl; **Gemeinnutz** m public good; **gemeinnützig** adj of benefit to the public; (wohltätig) charitable; **Gemeinplatz** m commonplace, platitude; **gemeinsam** adj joint, common (auch Math) ▷ adv together; **gemeinsame Sache mit jdm machen** to be in cahoots with sb; **der Gemeinsame Markt** the Common Market; **gemeinsames Konto** joint account; **etw gemeinsam haben** to have sth in common; **Gemeinsamkeit** f common ground; **Gemeinschaft** f community; **in Gemeinschaft mit** jointly od together with; **eheliche Gemeinschaft** (Jur) matrimony; **Gemeinschaft Unabhängiger Staaten** Commonwealth of Independent States; **gemeinschaftlich** adj = **gemeinsam**; **Gemeinschaftsantenne** f party aerial (Brit) od antenna (US); **Gemeinschaftsarbeit** f teamwork; **Gemeinschaftsbesitz** m collective ownership; **Gemeinschaftserziehung** f coeducation; **Gemeinschaftskunde** f social studies pl; **Gemeinschaftsraum** m common room; **Gemeinschaftswährung** f common od single currency; (innerhalb der EU) single European currency; **Gemeinsinn** m public spirit; **gemeinverständlich** adj generally comprehensible; **Gemeinwesen** nt community; **Gemeinwohl** nt common good

Gemenge [gə'mɛŋə] (-s, -) nt mixture; (Handgemenge) scuffle

gemessen [gə'mɛsən] pp von **messen** ▷ adj measured

Gemetzel [gə'mɛtsəl] (-s, -) nt slaughter, carnage

gemieden [gə'mi:dən] pp von **meiden**

Gemisch [gə'mɪʃ] (-es, -e) nt mixture

gemischt adj mixed

gemocht [gə'mɔxt] pp von **mögen**

gemolken [gə'mɔlkən] pp von **melken**

Gemse ['gɛmzə] (-, -n) f siehe **Gämse**

Gemunkel [gə'mʊŋkəl] (-s) nt gossip

Gemurmel [gə'mʊrməl] (-s) nt murmur(ing)

Gemüse [gə'my:zə] (-s, -) nt vegetables pl; **Gemüsegarten** m vegetable garden; **Gemüsehändler** m greengrocer (Brit), vegetable dealer (US); **Gemüseplatte** f (Koch): **eine Gemüseplatte** assorted vegetables

gemusst [gə'mʊst] pp von **müssen**

gemustert [gə'mʊstərt] *adj* patterned

Gemüt [gə'my:t] (**-(e)s, -er**) *nt* disposition, nature; *(fig: Mensch)* person; **sich** *dat* **etw zu ~e führen** *(umg)* to indulge in sth; **die ~er erregen** to arouse strong feelings; **wir müssen warten, bis sich die ~er beruhigt haben** we must wait until feelings have cooled down

gemütlich *adj* comfortable, cosy; *(Person)* good-natured; **wir verbrachten einen ~en Abend** we spent a very pleasant evening; **Gemütlichkeit** *f* comfortableness, cosiness; amiability

Gemüts- *zW*: **Gemütsbewegung** *f* emotion; **gemütskrank** *adj* emotionally disturbed; **Gemütsmensch** *m* sentimental person; **Gemütsruhe** *f* composure; **in aller Gemütsruhe** *(umg)* (as) cool as a cucumber; *(gemächlich)* at a leisurely pace; **Gemütszustand** *m* state of mind

gemütvoll *adj* warm, tender

Gen [ge:n] (**-s, -e**) *nt* gene

Gen. *abk* = **Genossenschaft**; (= *Genitiv*) gen.

gen. *abk* (= *genannt*) named, called

genannt [gə'nant] *pp von* **nennen**

genas *etc* [gə'na:s] *vb siehe* **genesen**

genau [gə'naʊ] *adj* exact, precise ▷ *adv* exactly, precisely; **etw ~ nehmen** to take sth seriously; **~ genommen** strictly speaking; **G~eres** further details *pl*; **etw ~ wissen** to know sth for certain; **~ auf die Minute, auf die Minute genau** exactly on time

Genauigkeit *f* exactness, accuracy

genauso [gə'naʊzo:] *adv (vor Adjektiv)* just as; *(allein stehend)* just *od* exactly the same

genehm [gə'ne:m] *adj* agreeable, acceptable

genehmigen *vt* to approve, authorize; **sich** *dat* **etw ~** to indulge in sth

Genehmigung *f* approval, authorization

geneigt [gə'naɪkt] *adj (geh)* well-disposed, willing; **~ sein, etw zu tun** to be inclined to do sth

Genera *pl von* **Genus**

General [gene'ra:l] (**-s, -e** *od* **-̈e**) *m* general; **Generaldirektor** *m* chairman (Brit), president (US); **Generalkonsulat** *nt* consulate general; **Generalprobe** *f* dress rehearsal; **Generalsekretär** *m* secretary-general; **Generalstabskarte** *f* ordnance survey map; **Generalstreik** *m* general strike; **generalüberholen** *vt* to overhaul thoroughly; **Generalvertretung** *f* sole agency

Generation [generatsi'o:n] *f* generation

Generationskonflikt *m* generation gap

Generator [gene'ra:tɔr] *m* generator, dynamo

generell [genə'rɛl] *adj* general

genesen [ge'ne:zən] *unreg vi (geh)* to convalesce, recover

Genesende, r *f(m)* convalescent

Genesung *f* recovery, convalescence

Genetik [ge'ne:tɪk] *f* genetics

genetisch [ge'ne:tɪʃ] *adj* genetic

Genf ['gɛnf] (**-s**) *nt* Geneva

Genfer *adj attrib*: **der ~ See** Lake Geneva; **die ~ Konvention** the Geneva Convention

genial [geni'a:l] *adj* brilliant

Genialität [geniali'tɛ:t] *f* brilliance, genius

Genick [gə'nɪk] (**-(e)s, -e**) *nt* (back of the) neck; **jdm/etw das ~ brechen** *(fig)* to finish sb/sth; **Genickstarre** *f* stiff neck

Genie [ʒe'ni:] (**-s, -s**) *nt* genius

genieren [ʒe'ni:rən] *vr* to be embarrassed ▷ *vt* to bother; **geniert es Sie, wenn ...?** do you mind if ...?

genießbar *adj* edible; *(trinkbar)* drinkable

genießen [gə'ni:sən] *unreg vt* to enjoy; *(essen)* to eat; *(trinken)* to drink; **er ist heute nicht zu ~** *(umg)* he is unbearable today

Genießer, in (**-s, -**) *m(f)* connoisseur; *(des Lebens)* pleasure-lover; **genießerisch** *adj* appreciative ▷ *adv* with relish

Genitalien [geni'ta:liən] *pl* genitals *pl*

Genitiv ['ge:niti:f] *m* genitive

Genmais *m* GM maize

genmanipuliert *adj* genetically modified

genommen [gə'nɔmən] *pp von* **nehmen**

genoss *etc* [gə'nɔs] *vb siehe* **genießen**

Genosse [gə'nɔsə] (**-n, -n**) *m* comrade *(bes Pol)*, companion

genossen *pp von* **genießen**

Genossenschaft *f* cooperative (association)

Genossin [gə'nɔsɪn] *f* comrade *(bes Pol)*, companion

genötigt [gə'nø:tɪçt] *adj*: **sich ~ sehen, etw zu tun** to feel obliged to do sth

Genre [ʒãˑ:rə] (**-s, -s**) *nt* genre

Gent [gɛnt] (**-s**) *nt* Ghent

Gentechnik *f*, **Gentechnologie** *f* gene technology

Genua ['ge:nua] (**-s**) *nt* Genoa

genug [gə'nu:k] *adv* enough; **jetzt ist(s) aber ~!** that's enough!

Genüge [gə'ny:gə] *f*: **jdm/etw ~ tun** *od* **leisten** to satisfy sb/sth; **etw zur ~ kennen** to know sth well enough; *(abwertender)* to know sth only too well

genügen *vi* to be enough; *(den Anforderungen etc)* to satisfy; **jdm ~** to be enough for sb

genügend *adj* enough, sufficient; *(befriedigend)* satisfactory

genügsam [gə'ny:kza:m] *adj* modest, easily satisfied; **Genügsamkeit** *f* moderation

Genugtuung [gə'nu:ktu:ʊŋ] *f* satisfaction

Genus ['ge:nʊs] (**-, Genera**) *nt* *(Gram)* gender

Genuss [gə'nʊs] (**-es, -̈e**) *m* pleasure; *(Zusichnehmen)* consumption; **etw mit ~ essen** to eat sth with relish; **in den ~ von etw kommen** to receive the benefit of sth

genüsslich [gə'nʏslɪç] *adv* with relish

Genussmittel *pl* (semi-)luxury items *pl*

geöffnet [gə'œfnət] *adj* open

Geograf [geo'gra:f] (**-en, -en**) *m* geographer

Geografie [geogra'fi:] *f* geography

Geografin *f* geographer

geografisch *adj* geographical

Geologe [geo'lo:gə] (**-n, -n**) *m* geologist

Geologie [geolo:'gi:] f geology
Geologin f geologist
Geometrie [geome'tri:] f geometry
geordnet [gə'ɔrdnət] adj: **in ~en Verhält-nissen leben** to live a well-ordered life
Georgien [ge'ɔrgiən] (**-s**) nt Georgia
Gepäck [gə'pɛk] (**-(e)s**) nt luggage, baggage; **mit leichtem ~ reisen** to travel light; **Gepäckabfertigung** f luggage desk/office; **Gepäckannahme** f (Bahnhof) baggage office; (Flughafen) baggage check-in; **Gepäckaufbewahrung** f left-luggage office (Brit), baggage check (US); **Gepäckausgabe** f (Bahnhof) baggage office; (Flughafen) baggage reclaim; **Gepäcknetz** nt luggage rack; **Gepäckschein** m luggage od baggage ticket; **Gepäckstück** nt piece of baggage; **Gepäckträger** m porter; (Fahrrad) carrier; **Gepäckwagen** m luggage van (Brit), baggage car (US)
Gepard ['ge:part] (**-(e)s, -e**) m cheetah
gepfeffert [gə'pfɛfərt] (umg) adj (Preise) steep; (Fragen, Prüfung) tough; (Kritik) biting
gepfiffen [gə'pfɪfən] pp von **pfeifen**
gepflegt [gə'pfle:kt] adj well-groomed; (Park etc) well looked after; (Atmosphäre) sophisticated; (Ausdrucksweise, Sprache) cultured
Gepflogenheit [gə'pflo:gənhaɪt] f (geh) custom
Geplapper [gə'plapər] (**-s**) nt chatter
Geplauder [gə'plaʊdər] (**-s**) nt chat(ting)
Gepolter [gə'pɔltər] (**-s**) nt din
gepr. abk (= geprüft) tested
gepriesen [gə'pri:zən] pp von **preisen**
gequält [gə'kvɛ:lt] adj (Lächeln) forced; (Miene, Ausdruck) pained; (Gesang, Stimme) strained
Gequatsche [gə'kvatʃə] (**-s**) (pej: umg) nt gabbing; (Blödsinn) twaddle
gequollen [gə'kvɔlən] pp von **quellen**
Gerade [gə'ra:də] (**-n, -n**) f straight line

○ SCHLÜSSELWORT

gerade [gə'ra:də] adj straight; (aufrecht) upright; **eine gerade Zahl** an even number
▷ adv 1 (genau) just, exactly; (speziell) especially; **gerade deshalb** that's just od exactly why; **das ist es ja gerade!** that's just it; **gerade du** you especially; **warum gerade ich?** why me (of all people)?; **jetzt gerade nicht!** not now!; **gerade neben** right next to; **nicht gerade schön** not exactly beautiful; **gerade biegen** to straighten out; **gerade stehen** (aufrecht) to stand up straight
2 (eben, soeben) just; **er wollte gerade aufstehen** he was just about to get up; **da wir gerade von Geld sprechen** ... talking of money ...; **gerade erst** only just; **gerade noch** (only) just

gerade- zW: **geradeaus** adv straight ahead; **geradebiegen** unreg vt (fig) to straighten out; **geradeheraus** adv straight out, bluntly
gerädert [gə'rɛ:dərt] adj: **wie ~ sein, sich wie**

~ **fühlen** to be od feel (absolutely) whacked (umg)
geradeso adv just so; ~ **dumm** etc just as stupid etc; ~ **wie** just as
geradestehen unreg vi: **für jdn/etw ~** (fig) to answer od be answerable for sb/sth
geradezu adv (beinahe) virtually, almost
geradlinig adj straight
gerammelt [gə'raməlt] adv: ~ **voll** (umg) (jam-)packed
Geranie [ge'ra:niə] f geranium
gerannt [gə'rant] pp von **rennen**
Gerät [gə'rɛ:t] (**-(e)s, -e**) nt device; (Apparat) gadget; (elektrisches Gerät) appliance; (Werkzeug) tool; (Sport) apparatus; (Zubehör) equipment no pl
gerät [gə'rɛ:t] vb siehe **geraten**
geraten [gə'ra:tən] unreg pp von **raten; geraten**
▷ vi (gedeihen) to thrive; (gelingen): (**jdm**) ~ to turn out well (for sb); (zufällig gelangen): ~ **in** +akk to get into; **gut/schlecht ~** to turn out well/badly; **an jdn ~** to come across sb; **an den Richtigen/Falschen ~** to come to the right/wrong person; **in Angst ~** to get frightened; **nach jdm ~** to take after sb
Geräteturnen nt apparatus gymnastics
Geratewohl [gəra:tə'vo:l] nt: **aufs ~** on the off chance; (bei Wahl) at random
geraum [gə'raʊm] adj: **seit ~er Zeit** for some considerable time
geräumig [gə'rɔʏmɪç] adj roomy
Geräusch [gə'rɔʏʃ] (**-(e)s, -e**) nt sound; (unangenehm) noise; **geräuscharm** adj quiet; **Geräuschkulisse** f background noise; (Film, Rundf, TV) sound effects pl; **geräuschlos** adj silent; **Geräuschpegel** m sound level; **geräuschvoll** adj noisy
gerben ['gɛrbən] vt to tan
Gerber (**-s, -**) m tanner
Gerberei [gɛrbə'raɪ] f tannery
gerecht [gə'rɛçt] adj just, fair; **jdm/etw ~ werden** to do justice to sb/sth; **gerechtfertigt** adj justified
Gerechtigkeit f justice, fairness
Gerechtigkeits- zW: **Gerechtigkeitsfanatiker** m justice fanatic; **Gerechtigkeitsgefühl** nt sense of justice; **Gerechtigkeitssinn** m sense of justice
Gerede [gə're:də] (**-s**) nt talk; (Klatsch) gossip
geregelt [gə're:gəlt] adj (Arbeit, Mahlzeiten) regular; (Leben) well-ordered
gereizt [gə'raɪtst] adj irritable; **Gereiztheit** f irritation
Gericht [gə'rɪçt] (**-(e)s, -e**) nt court; (Essen) dish; **jdn/einen Fall vor ~ bringen** to take sb/a case to court; **mit jdm ins ~ gehen** (fig) to judge sb harshly; **über jdn zu ~ sitzen** to sit in judgement on sb; **das Jüngste ~** the Last Judgement; **gerichtlich** adj judicial, legal
▷ adv judicially, legally; **ein gerichtliches Nachspiel haben** to finish up in court; **gerichtlich gegen jdn vorgehen** to take legal proceedings against sb

Gerichts- zW: **Gerichtsakten** pl court records pl; **Gerichtsbarkeit** f jurisdiction; **Gerichtshof** m court (of law); **Gerichtskosten** pl (legal) costs pl; **gerichtsmedizinisch** adj forensic medical attrib; **Gerichtssaal** m courtroom; **Gerichtsstand** m court of jurisdiction; **Gerichtsverfahren** nt legal proceedings pl; **Gerichtsverhandlung** f court proceedings pl; **Gerichtsvollzieher** m bailiff

gerieben [gə'riːbən] pp von **reiben** ▷ adj grated; (umg: schlau) smart, wily

geriet etc [gə'riːt] vb siehe **geraten**

gering [gə'rɪŋ] adj slight, small; (niedrig) low; (Zeit) short ▷ adv: ~ **achten** to think little of; **geringfügig** adj slight, trivial; **geringfügig Beschäftigte** ≈ part-time workers pl; **geringschätzig** adj disparaging; **Geringschätzung** f disdain

geringste, r, s adj slightest, least; **nicht im G~n** not in the least od slightest

Geringverdiener, in m(f) low-income earner

gerinnen [gə'rɪnən] unreg vi to congeal; (Blut) to clot; (Milch) to curdle

Gerinnsel [gə'rɪnzəl] (**-s, -**) nt clot

Gerippe [gə'rɪpə] (**-s, -**) nt skeleton

gerissen [gə'rɪsən] pp von **reißen** ▷ adj wily, smart

geritten [gə'rɪtən] pp von **reiten**

geritzt [gə'rɪtst] (umg) adj: **die Sache ist** ~ everything's fixed up od settled

Germanist, in [gɛrma'nɪst(ɪn)] m(f) Germanist, German specialist; (Student) German student

Germanistik f German (studies pl)

gern [gɛrn] adv willingly, gladly; **(aber)** ~! of course!; ~ **mögen** to like; **etw** ~ **tun** to like doing sth; ~ **geschehen!** you're welcome!, not at all!; **ein** ~ **gesehener Gast** a welcome visitor; **ich hätte** od **möchte** ~ ... I would like ...; siehe auch **gernhaben**

gerne ['gɛrnə] adv = **gern**

Gernegroß (**-, -e**) m show-off; **gernhaben** unreg vt to like; **du kannst mich mal gernhaben!** (umg) (you can) go to hell!

gerochen [gə'rɔxən] pp von **riechen**

Geröll [gə'rœl] (**-(e)s, -e**) nt scree

geronnen [gə'rɔnən] pp von **rinnen; gerinnen**

Gerste ['gɛrstə] (**-, -n**) f barley

Gerstenkorn nt (im Auge) stye

Gerte ['gɛrtə] (**-, -n**) f switch, rod

gertenschlank adj willowy

Geruch [gə'rʊx] (**-(e)s, ̈e**) m smell, odour (Brit), odor (US); **geruchlos** adj odourless (Brit), odorless (US)

Geruchssinn m sense of smell

Gerücht [gə'rʏçt] (**-(e)s, -e**) nt rumour (Brit), rumor (US)

geruchtilgend adj deodorant

gerufen [gə'ruːfən] pp von **rufen**

geruhen [gə'ruːən] vi to deign

geruhsam [gə'ruːzaːm] adj peaceful; (Spaziergang etc) leisurely

Gerümpel [gə'rʏmpəl] (**-s**) nt junk

gerungen [gə'rʊŋən] pp von **ringen**

Gerüst [gə'rʏst] (**-(e)s, -e**) nt (Baugerüst) scaffold(ing); (fig) framework

Ges. abk (= Gesellschaft) Co., co.

gesalzen [gə'zaltsən] pp von **salzen** ▷ adj (fig: umg: Preis, Rechnung) steep, stiff

gesamt [gə'zamt] adj whole, entire; (Kosten) total; (Werke) complete; **im G~en** all in all; **Gesamtauflage** f gross circulation; **Gesamtausgabe** f complete edition; **Gesamtbetrag** m total (amount); **gesamtdeutsch** adj all-German; **Gesamteindruck** m general impression; **Gesamtheit** f totality, whole

Gesamthochschule f polytechnic (Brit); see culture note

> GESAMTHOCHSCHULE
>
> A Gesamthochschule is an institution combining several different kinds of higher education organizations eg. a university, teacher training college and institute of applied science. Students can study for various degrees within the same subject area and it is easier to change course than it is in an individual institution.

Gesamt- zW: **Gesamtmasse** f (Comm) total assets pl; **Gesamtnachfrage** f (Comm) composite demand; **Gesamtschaden** m total damage

Gesamtschule f ≈ comprehensive school; see culture note

> GESAMTSCHULE
>
> The Gesamtschule is a comprehensive school teaching pupils who have different aims. Traditionally pupils would go to one of three different schools, the Gymnasium, Realschule or Hauptschule, depending on ability. The Gesamtschule seeks to avoid the elitist element prevalent in many Gymnasium, but in Germany these schools are still very controversial. Many parents still prefer the traditional system.

Gesamtwertung f (Sport) overall placings pl

gesandt pp von **senden**

Gesandte, r [gə'zantə(r)] f(m) envoy

Gesandtschaft [gə'zantʃaft] f legation

Gesang [gə'zaŋ] (**-(e)s, ̈e**) m song; (Singen) singing; **Gesangbuch** nt (Rel) hymn book

Gesäß [gə'zɛːs] (**-es, -e**) nt seat, bottom

gesättigt [gə'zɛtɪçt] adj (Chem) saturated

gesch. abk (= geschieden) div.

Geschädigte, r [gə'ʃɛːdɪçtə(r)] f(m) victim

geschaffen [gə'ʃafən] pp von **schaffen**

Geschäft [gə'ʃɛft] (**-(e)s, -e**) nt business; (Laden) shop; (Geschäftsabschluss) deal; **mit jdm ins** ~ **kommen** to do business with sb; **dabei**

hat er ein ~ gemacht he made a profit by it; **im ~** at work; *(im Laden)* in the shop; **sein ~ verrichten** to do one's business *(euph)*
Geschäftemacher *m* wheeler-dealer
geschäftig *adj* active, busy; *(pej)* officious
geschäftlich *adj* commercial ▷ *adv* on business; **~ unterwegs** away on business
Geschäfts- *zW:* **Geschäftsabschluss** *m* business deal *od* transaction; **Geschäftsaufgabe** *f* closure of a/the business; **Geschäftsauflösung** *f* closure of a/the business; **Geschäftsbedingungen** *pl* terms of business; **Geschäftsbereich** *m* *(Parl)* responsibilities *pl*; **Minister ohne Geschäftsbereich** minister without portfolio; **Geschäftsbericht** *m* financial report; **Geschäftsbeziehungen** *pl* business relations; **Geschäftscomputer** *m* business computer; **Geschäftsessen** *nt* business lunch; **Geschäftsführer** *m* manager; *(Klub)* secretary; **Geschäftsgeheimnis** *nt* trade secret; **Geschäftsinhaber** *m* owner; **Geschäftsjahr** *nt* financial year; **Geschäftslage** *f* business conditions *pl*; **Geschäftsleitung** *f* management; **Geschäftsmann (-(e)s,** *pl* **-leute)** *m* businessman; **geschäftsmäßig** *adj* businesslike; **Geschäftsordnung** *f* standing orders *pl*; **eine Frage zur Geschäftsordnung** a question on a point of order; **Geschäftspartner** *m* partner; **Geschäftsreise** *f* business trip; **Geschäftsschluss** *m* closing time; **Geschäftssinn** *m* business sense; **Geschäftsstelle** *f* office(s *pl*), place of business; **geschäftstüchtig** *adj* business-minded; **Geschäftsviertel** *nt* shopping centre *(Brit) od* center *(US)*; *(Banken etc)* business quarter, commercial district; **Geschäftswagen** *m* company car; **Geschäftswesen** *nt* business; **Geschäftszeit** *f* business hours *pl*; **Geschäftszweig** *m* branch (of a business)
geschah *etc* [gə'ʃa:] *vb siehe* **geschehen**
geschehen [gə'ʃe:ən] *unreg vi* to happen; **das geschieht ihm (ganz) recht** it serves him (jolly well *(umg))* right; **was soll mit ihm/damit ~?** what is to be done with him/it?; **es war um ihn ~** that was the end of him
gescheit [gə'ʃait] *adj* clever; *(vernünftig)* sensible
Geschenk [gə'ʃɛŋk] **(-(e)s, -e)** *nt* present, gift; **Geschenkartikel** *m* gift; **Geschenkgutschein** *m* gift voucher; **Geschenkpackung** *f* gift pack; **Geschenksendung** *f* gift parcel
Geschichte [gə'ʃɪçtə] **(-, -n)** *f* story; *(Sache)* affair; *(Historie)* history
Geschichtenerzähler *m* storyteller
geschichtlich *adj* historical; *(bedeutungsvoll)* historic
Geschichtsfälschung *f* falsification of history
Geschichtsschreiber *m* historian
Geschick [gə'ʃɪk] **(-(e)s, -e)** *nt* skill; *(geh: Schicksal)* fate
Geschicklichkeit *f* skill, dexterity
Geschicklichkeitsspiel *nt* game of skill

geschickt *adj* skilful *(Brit)*, skillful *(US)*; *(taktisch)* clever; *(beweglich)* agile
geschieden [gə'ʃi:dən] *pp von* **scheiden** ▷ *adj* divorced
geschieht [gə'ʃi:t] *vb siehe* **geschehen**
geschienen [gə'ʃi:nən] *pp von* **scheinen**
Geschirr [gə'ʃɪr] **(-(e)s, -e)** *nt* crockery; *(Küchengeschirr)* pots and pans *pl*; *(Pferdegeschirr)* harness; **Geschirrspülmaschine** *f* dishwasher; **Geschirrtuch** *nt* tea towel *(Brit)*, dishtowel *(US)*
geschissen [gə'ʃɪsən] *pp von* **scheißen**
geschlafen [gə'ʃla:fən] *pp von* **schlafen**
geschlagen [gə'ʃla:gən] *pp von* **schlagen**
geschlaucht [gə'ʃlauxt] *adv:* **~ sein** *(umg)* to be exhausted *od* knackered
Geschlecht [gə'ʃlɛçt] **(-(e)s, -er)** *nt* sex; *(Gram)* gender; *(Cattung)* race; *(Abstammung)* lineage; **geschlechtlich** *adj* sexual
Geschlechts- *zW:* **Geschlechtskrankheit** *f* sexually-transmitted disease; **geschlechtsreif** *adj* sexually mature; **geschlechtsspezifisch** *adj* *(Soziologie)* sex-specific; **Geschlechtsteil** *nt od m* genitals *pl*; **Geschlechtsverkehr** *m* sexual intercourse; **Geschlechtswort** *nt* *(Gram)* article
geschlichen [gə'ʃlɪçən] *pp von* **schleichen**
geschliffen [gə'ʃlɪfən] *pp von* **schleifen**
geschlossen [gə'ʃlɔsən] *pp von* **schließen** ▷ *adj:* **~e Gesellschaft** *(Fest)* private party ▷ *adv:* **~ hinter jdm stehen** to stand solidly behind sb; **~e Ortschaft** built-up area
geschlungen [gə'ʃlʊŋən] *pp von* **schlingen**
Geschmack [gə'ʃmak] **(-(e)s, ̈-e)** *m* taste; **nach jds ~** to sb's taste; **~ an etw** *dat* **finden** to (come to) like sth; **je nach ~** to one's own taste; **er hat einen guten ~** *(fig)* he has good taste; **geschmacklos** *adj* tasteless; *(fig)* in bad taste
Geschmacks- *zW:* **Geschmackssache** *f* matter of taste; **Geschmackssinn** *m* sense of taste; **Geschmacksverirrung** *f:* **unter Geschmacksverirrung leiden** *(ironisch)* to have no taste
geschmackvoll *adj* tasteful
Geschmeide [gə'ʃmaidə] **(-s, -)** *nt* jewellery *(Brit)*, jewelry *(US)*
geschmeidig *adj* supple; *(formbar)* malleable
Geschmeiß *nt* vermin *pl*
Geschmiere [gə'ʃmi:rə] **(-s)** *nt* scrawl; *(Bild)* daub
geschmissen [gə'ʃmɪsən] *pp von* **schmeißen**
geschmolzen [gə'ʃmɔltsən] *pp von* **schmelzen**
Geschnetzelte, s [gə'ʃnɛtsəltə(s)] *nt* *(Koch)* meat cut into strips and stewed to produce a thick sauce
geschnitten [gə'ʃnɪtən] *pp von* **schneiden**
geschoben [gə'ʃo:bən] *pp von* **schieben**
geschollen [gə'ʃɔlən] *pp von* **schallen**
gescholten [gə'ʃɔltən] *pp von* **schelten**
Geschöpf [gə'ʃœpf] **(-(e)s, -e)** *nt* creature
geschoren [gə'ʃo:rən] *pp von* **scheren**
Geschoss [gə'ʃɔs] **(-es, -e)** *nt*, **Geschoß** [gə'ʃo:s] **(-sses, -sse)** *(Österr)* *nt* *(Mil)* projectile; *(Rakete)* missile; *(Stockwerk)* floor
geschossen [gə'ʃɔsən] *pp von* **schießen**

g

145

geschraubt [gəˈʃraʊpt] *adj* stilted, artificial
Geschrei [gəˈʃraɪ] (**-s**) *nt* cries *pl*, shouting;
(*fig: Aufheben*) noise, fuss
geschrieben [gəˈʃriːbən] *pp von* **schreiben**
geschrieen [gəˈʃriːən], **geschrien** [gəˈʃriːn] *pp von* **schreien**
geschritten [gəˈʃrɪtən] *pp von* **schreiten**
geschunden [gəˈʃʊndən] *pp von* **schinden**
Geschütz [gəˈʃʏts] (**-es, -e**) *nt* gun, piece of
artillery; **ein schweres ~ auffahren** (*fig*)
to bring out the big guns; **Geschützfeuer** *nt*
artillery fire, gunfire
geschützt *adj* protected; (*Winkel, Ecke*)
sheltered
Geschw. *abk* = **Geschwister**
Geschwader [gəˈʃvaːdər] (**-s, -**) *nt* (*Naut*)
squadron; (*Aviat*) group
Geschwafel [gəˈʃvaːfəl] (**-s**) *nt* silly talk
Geschwätz [gəˈʃvɛts] (**-es**) *nt* chatter; (*Klatsch*)
gossip
geschwätzig *adj* talkative; **Geschwätzigkeit** *f*
talkativeness
geschweige [gəˈʃvaɪgə] *adv*: **~ (denn)** let alone,
not to mention
geschwiegen [gəˈʃviːgən] *pp von* **schweigen**
geschwind [gəˈʃvɪnt] *adj* quick, swift
Geschwindigkeit [gəˈʃvɪndɪçkaɪt] *f* speed,
velocity
Geschwindigkeits- *zW*: **Geschwindig-**
keitsbegrenzung *f*, **Geschwindigkeits-**
beschränkung *f* speed limit;
Geschwindigkeitsmesser *m* (*Aut*)
speedometer; **Geschwindigkeitsüber-**
schreitung *f* speeding
Geschwister [gəˈʃvɪstər] *pl* brothers and sisters
pl
geschwollen [gəˈʃvɔlən] *pp von* **schwellen** ▷ *adj*
pompous
geschwommen [gəˈʃvɔmən] *pp von*
schwimmen
geschworen [gəˈʃvoːrən] *pp von* **schwören**
Geschworene, r *f(m)* juror; **die**
Geschworenen *pl* the jury
Geschwulst [gəˈʃvʊlst] (**-, ̈-e**) *f* growth, tumour
geschwunden [gəˈʃvʊndən] *pp von* **schwinden**
geschwungen [gəˈʃvʊŋən] *pp von* **schwingen**
▷ *adj* curved
Geschwür [gəˈʃvyːr] (**-(e)s, -e**) *nt* ulcer;
(*Furunkel*) boil
gesehen [gəˈzeːən] *pp von* **sehen**
Geselle [gəˈzɛlə] (**-n, -n**) *m* fellow;
(*Handwerksgeselle*) journeyman
gesellen *vr*: **sich zu jdm ~** to join sb
Gesellenbrief *m* articles *pl*
Gesellenprüfung *f* examination to become a
journeyman
gesellig *adj* sociable; **~es Beisammensein** get-
together; **Geselligkeit** *f* sociability
Gesellschaft *f* society; (*Begleitung, Comm*)
company; (*Abendgesellschaft etc*) party; (*pej*)
crowd (*umg*); (*Kreis von Menschen*) group of
people; **in schlechte ~ geraten** to get into
bad company; **geschlossene ~** private party;

jdm ~ leisten to keep sb company
Gesellschafter, in (**-s, -**) *m(f)* shareholder;
(*Partner*) partner
gesellschaftlich *adj* social
Gesellschafts- *zW*: **Gesellschaftsanzug** *m*
evening dress; **gesellschaftsfähig** *adj* socially
acceptable; **Gesellschaftsordnung** *f* social
structure; **Gesellschaftsreise** *f* group tour;
Gesellschaftsschicht *f* social stratum;
Gesellschaftssystem *nt* social system
gesessen [gəˈzɛsən] *pp von* **sitzen**
Gesetz [gəˈzɛts] (**-es, -e**) *nt* law; (*Parl*) act;
(*Satzung, Regel*) rule; **vor dem ~** in (the eyes
of the) law; **nach dem ~** under the law; **das**
oberste ~ (der Wirtschaft etc) the golden rule
(of industry etc); **Gesetzblatt** *nt* law gazette;
Gesetzbuch *nt* statute book; **Gesetzentwurf**
m bill
Gesetzeshüter *m* (*ironisch*) guardian of the law
Gesetzesvorlage *f* bill
Gesetz- *zW*: **gesetzgebend** *adj* legislative;
Gesetzgeber (**-s, -**) *m* legislator; **Gesetz-**
gebung *f* legislation; **gesetzlich** *adj* legal,
lawful; **Gesetzlichkeit** *f* legality, lawfulness;
gesetzlos *adj* lawless; **gesetzmäßig** *adj* lawful
gesetzt *adj* (*Mensch*) sedate ▷ *konj*: **~ den Fall ...**
assuming (that) ...
gesetzwidrig *adj* illegal; (*unrechtmäßig*)
unlawful
ges. gesch. *abk* (= *gesetzlich geschützt*) reg.
Gesicht [gəˈzɪçt] (**-(e)s, -er**) *nt* face; **das**
Zweite ~ second sight; **das ist mir nie zu ~**
gekommen I've never laid eyes on that; **jdn**
zu ~ bekommen to clap eyes on sb; **jdm etw**
ins ~ sagen to tell sb sth to his face; **sein**
wahres ~ zeigen to show (o.s. in) one's true
colours; **jdm wie aus dem ~ geschnitten**
sein to be the spitting image of sb
Gesichts- *zW*: **Gesichtsausdruck** *m* (facial)
expression; **Gesichtsfarbe** *f* complexion;
Gesichtspackung *f* face pack; **Gesichtspunkt**
m point of view; **Gesichtswasser** *nt* face
lotion; **Gesichtszüge** *pl* features *pl*
Gesindel [gəˈzɪndəl] (**-s**) *nt* rabble
gesinnt [gəˈzɪnt] *adj* disposed, minded
Gesinnung [gəˈzɪnʊŋ] *f* disposition; (*Ansicht*)
views *pl*
Gesinnungs- *zW*: **Gesinnungsgenosse** *m*
like-minded person; **Gesinnungslosigkeit** *f*
lack of conviction; **Gesinnungsschnüffelei**
(*pej*) *f*: **Gesinnungsschnüffelei betreiben**
to pry into people's political convictions;
Gesinnungswandel *m* change of opinion
gesittet [gəˈzɪtət] *adj* well-mannered
gesoffen [gəˈzɔfən] *pp von* **saufen**
gesogen [gəˈzoːgən] *pp von* **saugen**
gesollt [gəˈzɔlt] *pp von* **sollen**
gesondert [gəˈzɔndərt] *adj* separate
gesonnen [gəˈzɔnən] *pp von* **sinnen**
gespalten [gəˈʃpaltən] *adj* (*Bewusstsein*) split;
(*Lippe*) cleft
Gespann [gəˈʃpan] (**-(e)s, -e**) *nt* team; (*umg*)
couple

gespannt adj tense, strained; (neugierig) curious; (begierig) eager; **ich bin ~, ob** I wonder if od whether; **auf etw/jdn ~ sein** to look forward to sth/to meeting sb; **ich bin ~ wie ein Flitzebogen** (hum: umg) I'm on tenterhooks

Gespenst [gə'ʃpɛnst] (-(e)s, -er) nt ghost; (fig: Gefahr) spectre (Brit), specter (US); **~er sehen** (fig: umg) to imagine things

gespensterhaft, gespenstisch adj ghostly

gespieen [gəʃpi:ən], **gespien** [gəʃpi:n] pp von **speien**

gespielt [gə'ʃpi:lt] adj feigned

gesponnen [gəʃpɔnən] pp von **spinnen**

Gespött [gə'ʃpœt] (-(e)s) nt mockery; **zum ~ werden** to become a laughing stock

Gespräch [gə'ʃprɛːç] (-(e)s, -e) nt conversation; (Diskussion) discussion; (Anruf) call; **zum ~ werden** to become a topic of conversation; **ein ~ unter vier Augen** a confidential od private talk; **mit jdm ins ~ kommen** to get into conversation with sb; (fig) to establish a dialogue with sb

gesprächig adj talkative; **Gesprächigkeit** f talkativeness

Gesprächs- zW: **Gesprächseinheit** f (Tel) unit; **Gesprächsgegenstand** m topic; **Gesprächspartner** m: **mein Gesprächspartner bei den Verhandlungen** my opposite number at the talks; **Gesprächsstoff** m topics pl; **Gesprächsthema** nt subject od topic (of conversation)

gesprochen [gə'ʃprɔxən] pp von **sprechen**

gesprossen [gəʃprɔsən] pp von **sprießen**

gesprungen [gə'ʃprʊŋən] pp von **springen**

Gespür [gə'ʃpy:r] (-s) nt feeling

gest. abk (= gestorben) dec.

Gestalt [gə'ʃtalt] (-, -en) f form, shape; (Person) figure; (Liter: pej: Mensch) character; **in ~ von** in the form of; **~ annehmen** to take shape

gestalten vt (formen) to shape, form; (organisieren) to arrange, organize ⊳ vr: **sich ~ (zu)** to turn out (to be); **etw interessanter etc ~ to make sth more interesting** etc

Gestaltung f formation; organization

gestanden [gəʃtandən] pp von **stehen**; **gestehen**

geständig [gə'ʃtɛndıç] adj: **~ sein** to have confessed

Geständnis [gə'ʃtɛntnıs] (-ses, -se) nt confession

Gestank [gə'ʃtaŋk] (-(e)s) m stench

gestatten [gə'ʃtatən] vt to permit, allow; **~ Sie?** may I?; **sich** dat **~, etw zu tun** to take the liberty of doing sth

Geste ['gɛstə] (-, -n) f gesture

Gesteck [gə'ʃtɛk] (-(e)s, -e) nt flower arrangement

gestehen [gəʃte:ən] unreg vt to confess; **offen gestanden** quite frankly

Gestein [gə'ʃtaın] (-(e)s, -e) nt rock

Gestell [gə'ʃtɛl] (-(e)s, -e) nt stand; (Regal) shelf; (Bettgestell, Brillengestell) frame

gestellt adj (unecht) posed

gestern ['gɛstərn] adv yesterday; **~ Abend/Morgen** yesterday evening/morning; **er ist nicht von ~** (umg) he wasn't born yesterday

gestiefelt [gə'ʃti:fəlt] adj: **der G~e Kater** Puss-in-Boots

gestiegen [gəʃti:gən] pp von **steigen**

Gestik (-) f gestures pl

gestikulieren [gɛstiku'li:rən] vi to gesticulate

Gestirn [gə'ʃtırn] (-(e)s, -e) nt star

gestoben [gə'ʃto:bən] pp von **stieben**

Gestöber [gə'ʃtø:bər] (-s, -) nt flurry; (länger) blizzard

gestochen [gə'ʃtɔxən] pp von **stechen** ⊳ adj (Handschrift) clear, neat

gestohlen [gə'ʃto:lən] pp von **stehlen** ⊳ adj: **der/das kann mir ~ bleiben** (umg) he/it can go hang

gestorben [gə'ʃtɔrbən] pp von **sterben**

gestört [gə'ʃtø:rt] adj disturbed; (Rundfunkempfang) poor, with a lot of interference

gestoßen [gə'ʃto:sən] pp von **stoßen**

Gestotter [gə'ʃtɔtər] (-s) nt stuttering, stammering

Gesträuch [gə'ʃtrɔyç] (-(e)s, -e) nt shrubbery, bushes pl

gestreift [gə'ʃtraıft] adj striped

gestrichen [gə'ʃtrıçən] pp von **streichen** ⊳ adj: **~ voll** (genau voll) level; (sehr voll) full to the brim; **ein ~er Teelöffel voll** a level teaspoon(ful)

gestrig ['gɛstrıç] adj yesterday's

gestritten [gə'ʃtrıtən] pp von **streiten**

Gestrüpp [gə'ʃtrʏp] (-(e)s, -e) nt undergrowth

gestunken [gə'ʃtʊŋkən] pp von **stinken**

Gestüt [gə'ʃty:t] (-(e)s, -e) nt stud farm

Gesuch [gə'zu:x] (-(e)s, -e) nt petition; (Antrag) application

gesucht adj (begehrt) sought after

gesund [gə'zʊnt] adj healthy; **wieder ~ werden** to get better; **~ und munter** hale and hearty; **Gesundheit** f health; (Sportlichkeit, fig) healthiness; **Gesundheit!** bless you!; **bei guter Gesundheit** in good health; **gesundheitlich** adj health attrib, physical ⊳ adv physically; **wie geht es Ihnen gesundheitlich?** how's your health?

Gesundheits- zW: **Gesundheitsamt** nt public health department; **Gesundheitsapostel** m (ironisch) health freak (umg); **Gesundheitsfarm** f health farm; **Gesundheitsfürsorge** f health care; **Gesundheitsreform** f health service reforms pl; **Gesundheitsrisiko** nt health hazard; **gesundheitsschädlich** adj unhealthy; **Gesundheitssystem** nt health (care) system; **Gesundheitswesen** nt health service; **Gesundheitszeugnis** nt health certificate; **Gesundheitszustand** m state of health

gesundschreiben unreg vt: **jdn ~** to certify sb (as) fit

gesungen [gə'zʊŋən] pp von **singen**

gesunken [gə'zʊŋkən] pp von **sinken**

getan [gə'ta:n] pp von **tun** ⊳ adj: **nach ~er**

Arbeit when the day's work is done

Getier [gə'tiːər] (**-(e)s, -e**) *nt* (*Tiere, bes Insekten*) creatures *pl*; (*einzelnes*) creature

Getöse [gə'tøːzə] (**-s**) *nt* din, racket

getragen [gə'traːgən] *pp von* **tragen**

Getränk [gə'trɛŋk] (**-(e)s, -e**) *nt* drink

Getränkeautomat *m* drinks machine *od* dispenser

Getränkekarte *f* (*in Café*) list of beverages; (*in Restaurant*) wine list

getrauen [gə'trauən] *vr* to dare

Getreide [gə'traidə] (**-s, -**) *nt* cereal, grain; **Getreidespeicher** *m* granary

getrennt [gə'trɛnt] *adj* separate; **~ leben** to be separated, live apart

getreten [gə'treːtən] *pp von* **treten**

getreu [gə'trɔy] *adj* faithful

Getriebe [gə'triːbə] (**-s, -**) *nt* (*Leute*) bustle; (*Aut*) gearbox

getrieben *pp von* **treiben**

Getriebeöl *nt* transmission oil

getroffen [gə'trɔfən] *pp von* **treffen**

getrogen [gə'troːgən] *pp von* **trügen**

getrost [gə'troːst] *adv* confidently; **~ sterben** to die in peace; **du kannst dich ~ auf ihn verlassen** you need have no fears about relying on him

getrunken [gə'truŋkən] *pp von* **trinken**

Getto ['gɛto] (**-s, -s**) *nt* ghetto

Gettoblaster ['gɛtoblaːstər] (**-s, -s**) *m* ghettoblaster

Getue [gə'tuːə] (**-s**) *nt* fuss

Getümmel [gə'tʏməl] (**-s**) *nt* turmoil

geübt [gə'yːpt] *adj* experienced

GEW (**-**) *f abk* (= *Gewerkschaft Erziehung und Wissenschaft*) *union of employees in education and science*

Gew. *abk* = **Gewerkschaft**

Gewächs [gə'vɛks] (**-es, -e**) *nt* growth; (*Pflanze*) plant

gewachsen [gə'vaksən] *pp von* **wachsen**
▷ *adj*: **jdm/etw ~ sein** to be sb's equal/equal to sth

Gewächshaus *nt* greenhouse

gewagt [gə'vaːkt] *adj* daring, risky

gewählt [gə'vɛːlt] *adj* (*Sprache*) refined, elegant

gewahr [gə'vaːr] *adj*: **eine** *od* **einer Sache** *gen* **~ werden** to become aware of sth

Gewähr [gə'vɛːr] (**-**) *f* guarantee; **keine ~ übernehmen für** to accept no responsibility for; **die Angabe erfolgt ohne ~** this information is supplied without liability

gewähren *vt* to grant; (*geben*) to provide; **jdn ~ lassen** not to stop sb

gewährleisten *vt* to guarantee

Gewährleistungspflicht *f* warranty obligation

Gewahrsam [gə'vaːrzaːm] (**-s, -e**) *m* safekeeping; (*Polizeigewahrsam*) custody

Gewährsmann *m* informant, source

Gewährung *f* granting

Gewalt [gə'valt] (**-, -en**) *f* power; (*große Kraft*) force; (*Gewalttaten*) violence; **mit aller ~** with all one's might; **die ausübende/gesetzgebende/richterliche ~** the executive/legislature/judiciary; **elterliche ~** parental authority; **höhere ~** acts/an act of God;

Gewaltanwendung *f* use of force

Gewaltenteilung *f* separation of powers

Gewaltherrschaft *f* tyranny

gewaltig *adj* tremendous; (*Irrtum*) huge; **sich ~ irren** to be very much mistaken

Gewalt- zW: gewaltlos *adj* non-violent ▷ *adv* without force/violence; **Gewaltmarsch** *m* forced march; **Gewaltmonopol** *nt* monopoly on the use of force; **gewaltsam** *adj* forcible; **gewalttätig** *adj* violent; **Gewaltverbrechen** *nt* crime of violence; **Gewaltverzicht** *m* non-aggression

Gewand [gə'vant] (**-(e)s, ̈-er**) *nt* garment

gewandt [gə'vant] *pp von* **wenden** ▷ *adj* deft, skilful (*Brit*), skillful (*US*); (*erfahren*) experienced; **Gewandtheit** *f* dexterity, skill

gewann *etc* [gə'van] *vb siehe* **gewinnen**

gewaschen [gə'vaʃən] *pp von* **waschen**

Gewässer [gə'vɛsər] (**-s, -**) *nt* waters *pl*

Gewebe [gə'veːbə] (**-s, -**) *nt* (*Stoff*) fabric; (*Biol*) tissue

Gewehr [gə'veːr] (**-(e)s, -e**) *nt* (*Flinte*) rifle; (*Schrotbüchse*) shotgun; **Gewehrlauf** *m* rifle barrel; barrel of a shotgun

Geweih [gə'vai] (**-(e)s, -e**) *nt* antlers *pl*

Gewerbe [gə'vɛrbə] (**-s, -**) *nt* trade, occupation; **Handel und ~** trade and industry; **fahrendes ~** mobile trade; *siehe auch* **gewerbetreibend**; **Gewerbeaufsichtsamt** *nt* ≈ factory inspectorate; **Gewerbepark** *m* trading estate, business park; **Gewerbeschein** *m* trading licence; **Gewerbeschule** *f* technical school

gewerbetreibend *adj* carrying on a trade

gewerblich *adj* industrial

gewerbsmäßig *adj* professional

Gewerbszweig *m* line of trade

Gewerkschaft [gə'vɛrkʃaft] *f* trade *od* labor (*US*) union

Gewerkschafter, Gewerkschaftler, in *m(f)* trade *od* labor (*US*) unionist

gewerkschaftlich *adj*: **wir haben uns ~ organisiert** we organized ourselves into a union

Gewerkschaftsbund *m* federation of trade *od* labor (*US*) unions, ≈ Trades Union Congress (*Brit*), Federation of Labor (*US*)

gewesen [gə'veːzən] *pp von* **sein**

gewichen [gə'viçən] *pp von* **weichen**

Gewicht [gə'viçt] (**-(e)s, -e**) *nt* weight; (*fig*) importance

gewichten *vt* to evaluate

Gewichtheben (**-s**) *nt* (*Sport*) weight-lifting

gewichtig *adj* weighty

Gewichtsklasse *f* (*Sport*) weight (category)

gewieft [gə'viːft] (*umg*) *adj* shrewd, cunning

gewiesen [gə'viːzən] *pp von* **weisen**

gewillt [gə'vɪlt] *adj* willing, prepared

Gewimmel [gə'vɪməl] (**-s**) *nt* swarm; (*Menge*) crush

Gewinde [gə'vɪndə] (**-s, -**) nt (Kranz) wreath; (von Schraube) thread

Gewinn [gə'vɪn] (**-(e)s, -e**) m profit; (bei Spiel) winnings pl; **~ bringend** profitable; **etw mit ~ verkaufen** to sell sth at a profit; **aus etw ~ schlagen** (umg) to make a profit out of sth; **Gewinnanteil** m (Comm) dividend; **Gewinnausschüttung** f prize draw; **Gewinnbeteiligung** f profit-sharing; **gewinnbringend** adj profitable; **Gewinnchancen** pl (beim Wetten) odds pl; **Gewinneinbruch** m slump in profits

gewinnen unreg vt to win; (erwerben) to gain; (Kohle, Öl) to extract ▷ vi to win; (profitieren) to gain; **jdn (für etw) ~** to win sb over (to sth); **an etw** dat **~** to gain in sth

gewinnend adj winning, attractive

Gewinner, in (**-s, -**) m(f) winner

Gewinn- zW: **Gewinnmitnahme** f profit-taking; **Gewinnnummer** f winning number; **Gewinnspanne** f profit margin; **Gewinnsucht** f love of gain; **Gewinn- und Verlustrechnung** f profit and loss account

Gewinnung f (von Kohle etc) mining; (von Zucker etc) extraction

Gewinnwarnung f (Comm) profit warning

Gewirr [gə'vɪr] (**-(e)s, -e**) nt tangle; (von Straßen) maze

gewiss [gə'vɪs] adj certain ▷ adv certainly; **in ~em Maße** to a certain extent

Gewissen [gə'vɪsən] (**-s, -**) nt conscience; **jdm ins ~ reden** to have a serious talk with sb; **gewissenhaft** adj conscientious; **Gewissenhaftigkeit** f conscientiousness; **gewissenlos** adj unscrupulous

Gewissens- zW: **Gewissensbisse** pl pangs of conscience pl, qualms pl; **Gewissensfrage** f matter of conscience; **Gewissensfreiheit** f freedom of conscience; **Gewissenskonflikt** m moral conflict

gewissermaßen [gəvɪsər'ma:sən] adv more or less, in a way

Gewissheit f certainty; **sich** dat **~ verschaffen** to find out for certain

gewisslich adv surely

Gewitter [gə'vɪtər] (**-s, -**) nt thunderstorm

gewittern vi unpers: **es gewittert** there's a thunderstorm

gewitterschwül adj sultry and thundery

Gewitterwolke f thundercloud; (fig: umg) storm cloud

gewitzt [gə'vɪtst] adj shrewd, cunning

gewoben [gə'vo:bən] pp von **weben**

gewogen [gə'vo:gən] pp von **wiegen** ▷ adj (+dat) well-disposed (towards)

gewöhnen [gə'vø:nən] vt: **jdn an etw** akk **~** to accustom sb to sth; (erziehen zu) to teach sb sth ▷ vr: **sich an etw** akk **~** to get used od accustomed to sth

Gewohnheit [gə'vo:nhaɪt] f habit; (Brauch) custom; **aus ~** from habit; **zur ~ werden** to become a habit; **sich** dat **etw zur ~ machen** to make a habit of sth

Gewohnheits- in zW habitual; **Gewohnheitsmensch** m creature of habit; **Gewohnheitsrecht** nt common law; **Gewohnheitstier** (umg) nt creature of habit

gewöhnlich [gə'vø:nlɪç] adj usual; (durchschnittlich) ordinary; (pej) common; **wie ~** as usual

gewohnt [gə'vo:nt] adj usual; **etw ~ sein** to be used to sth

Gewöhnung f: **~ (an** +akk) getting accustomed (to); (das Angewöhnen) training (in)

Gewölbe [gə'vœlbə] (**-s, -**) nt vault

gewollt [gə'vɔlt] pp von **wollen** ▷ adj forced, artificial

gewonnen [gə'vɔnən] pp von **gewinnen**

geworben [gə'vɔrbən] pp von **werben**

geworden [gə'vɔrdən] pp von **werden**

geworfen [gə'vɔrfən] pp von **werfen**

gewrungen [gə'vrʊŋən] pp von **wringen**

Gewühl [gə'vy:l] (**-(e)s**) nt throng

gewunden [gə'vʊndən] pp von **winden**

gewunken [gə'vʊŋkən] pp von **winken**

Gewürz [gə'vʏrts] (**-es, -e**) nt spice; (Pfeffer, Salz) seasoning; **Gewürzgurke** f pickled gherkin; **Gewürznelke** f clove

gewusst [gə'vʊst] pp von **wissen**

gez. abk (= gezeichnet) signed

gezackt [gə'tsakt] adj (Fels) jagged; (Blatt) serrated

gezähnt [gə'tsɛ:nt] adj serrated, toothed

gezeichnet [gə'tsaɪçnət] adj marked

Gezeiten [gə'tsaɪtən] pl tides pl

Gezeter [gə'tse:tər] (**-s**) nt nagging

gezielt [gə'tsi:lt] adj (Frage, Maßnahme) specific; (Hilfe) well-directed; (Kritik) pointed

geziemen [gə'tsi:mən] vr unpers to be fitting

geziemend adj proper

geziert [gə'tsi:rt] adj affected; **Geziertheit** f affectation

gezogen [gə'tso:gən] pp von **ziehen**

Gezwitscher [gə'tsvɪtʃər] (**-s**) nt twitter(ing), chirping

gezwungen [gə'tsvʊŋən] pp von **zwingen** ▷ adj forced; (Atmosphäre) strained

gezwungenermaßen adv of necessity; **etw ~ tun** to be forced to do sth, do sth of necessity

GG abk = **Grundgesetz**

ggf. abk = **gegebenenfalls**

Ghetto ['geto] (**-s, -s**) nt = **Getto**

Gibraltar [gi'braltar] (**-s**) nt Gibraltar

gibst [gi:pst] vb siehe **geben**

gibt vb siehe **geben**

Gicht [gɪçt] (**-**) f gout; **gichtisch** adj gouty

Giebel ['gi:bəl] (**-s, -**) m gable; **Giebeldach** nt gable(d) roof; **Giebelfenster** nt gable window

Gier [gi:r] (**-**) f greed

gierig adj greedy

Gießbach m torrent

gießen ['gi:sən] unreg vt to pour; (Blumen) to water; (Metall) to cast; (Wachs) to mould ▷ vi unpers: **es gießt in Strömen** it's pouring down

Gießerei [gi:sə'raɪ] f foundry

149

Gießkanne f watering can

Gift [gɪft] (**-(e)s, -e**) nt poison; **das ist ~ für ihn** (umg) that is very bad for him; **darauf kannst du ~ nehmen** (umg) you can bet your life on it; **giftgrün** adj bilious green

giftig adj poisonous; (fig: boshaft) venomous

Giftler, in ['gɪftlər] m(f) (Österr: umg) junkie

Gift- zW: **Giftmüll** m toxic waste; **Giftpilz** m poisonous toadstool; **Giftstoff** m toxic substance; **Giftwolke** f poisonous cloud; **Giftzahn** m fang; **Giftzwerg** (umg) m spiteful little devil

Gigabyte ['gɪgabaɪt] nt (Comput) gigabyte

Gilde ['gɪldə] (**-, -n**) f guild

gilt [gɪlt] vb siehe **gelten**

ging etc [gɪŋ] vb siehe **gehen**

Ginseng ['gɪnzɛŋ] (**-s, -s**) m ginseng

Ginster ['gɪnstər] (**-s, -**) m broom

Gipfel ['gɪpfəl] (**-s, -**) m summit, peak; (fig) height; **das ist der ~!** (umg) that's the limit!; **Gipfelkonferenz** f (Pol) summit conference

gipfeln vi to culminate

Gipfeltreffen nt summit (meeting)

Gips [gɪps] (**-es, -e**) m plaster; (Med) plaster (of Paris); **Gipsabdruck** m plaster cast; **Gipsbein** (umg) nt leg in plaster; **gipsen** vt to plaster; **Gipsfigur** f plaster figure; **Gipsverband** m plaster (cast)

Giraffe [gi'rafə] (**-, -n**) f giraffe

Girlande [gɪr'landə] (**-, -n**) f garland

Giro ['ʒiːro] (**-s, -s**) nt giro; **Girokonto** nt current account (Brit), checking account (US)

girren ['gɪrən] vi to coo

Gis [gɪs] (**-, -**) nt (Mus) G sharp

Gischt [gɪʃt] (**-(e)s, -e**) m od f spray, foam

Gitarre [gi'tarə] (**-, -n**) f guitar

Gitter ['gɪtər] (**-s, -**) nt grating, bars pl; (für Pflanzen) trellis; (Zaun) railing(s); **Gitterbett** nt cot (Brit), crib (US); **Gitterfenster** nt barred window; **Gitterzaun** m railing(s)

Glacéhandschuh, Glaceehandschuh [gla'se:hantʃuː] m kid glove

Gladiole [gladi'o:lə] (**-, -n**) f gladiolus

Glanz [glants] (**-es**) m shine, lustre (Brit), luster (US); (fig) splendour (Brit), splendor (US); **Glanzabzug** m (Phot) glossy od gloss print

glänzen ['glɛntsən] vi to shine (also fig), gleam

glänzend adj shining; (fig) brilliant; **wir haben uns ~ amüsiert** we had a marvellous od great time

Glanz- zW: **Glanzlack** m gloss (paint); **Glanzleistung** f brilliant achievement; **glanzlos** adj dull; **Glanzstück** nt pièce de résistance; **Glanzzeit** f heyday

Glas [glaːs] (**-es, ̈-er**) nt glass; (Brillenglas) lens sing; **zwei ~ Wein** two glasses of wine; **Glasbläser** m glass blower; **Glaser** (**-s, -**) m glazier; **Glasfaser** f fibreglass (Brit), fiberglass (US); **Glasfaserkabel** nt optical fibre (Brit) od fiber (US) cable

Glasgow ['glaːsgoʊ] nt Glasgow

glasieren [gla'ziːrən] vt to glaze

glasig adj glassy; (Zwiebeln) transparent

glasklar adj crystal clear

Glasscheibe f pane

Glasur [gla'zuːr] f glaze; (Koch) icing, frosting (bes US)

glatt [glat] adj smooth; (rutschig) slippery; (Absage) flat; (Lüge) downright; (Haar) straight; (Med: Bruch) clean; (pej: allzu gewandt) smooth, slick ▷ adv: ~ **rasiert** (Mann, Kinn) clean-shaven; ~ **streichen** to smooth out; siehe auch **glattgehen**

Glätte ['glɛtə] (**-, -n**) f smoothness; slipperiness

Glatteis nt (black) ice; „**Vorsicht ~!**" "danger, black ice!"; **jdn aufs ~ führen** (fig) to take sb for a ride

glätten vt to smooth out

glattgehen unreg vi to go smoothly

Glatze ['glatsə] (**-, -n**) f bald head; **eine ~ bekommen** to go bald

glatzköpfig adj bald

Glaube ['glaʊbə] (**-ns, -n**) m: ~ (**an** +akk) faith (in); (Überzeugung) belief (in); **den ~n an jdn/ etw verlieren** to lose faith in sb/sth

glauben vt, vi to believe; (meinen) to think; **jdm ~** to believe sb; ~ **an** +akk to believe in; **jdm (etw) aufs Wort ~** to take sb's word (for sth); **wers glaubt, wird selig** (ironisch) a likely story

Glaubens- zW: **Glaubensbekenntnis** nt creed; **Glaubensfreiheit** f religious freedom; **Glaubensgemeinschaft** f religious sect; (christliche) denomination

glaubhaft ['glaʊbhaft] adj credible; **jdm etw ~ machen** to satisfy sb of sth

Glaubhaftigkeit f credibility

gläubig ['glɔʏbɪç] adj (Rel) devout; (vertrauensvoll) trustful; **Gläubige, r** f(m) believer; **die Gläubigen** pl the faithful

Gläubiger, in (**-s, -**) m(f) creditor

glaubwürdig ['glaʊbvvrdɪç] adj credible; (Mensch) trustworthy; **Glaubwürdigkeit** f credibility; trustworthiness

gleich [glaɪç] adj equal; (identisch) (the) same, identical ▷ adv equally; (sofort) straight away; (bald) in a minute; (räumlich): ~ **hinter dem Haus** just behind the house; (zeitlich): ~ **am Anfang** at the very beginning; **es ist mir ~** it's all the same to me; **zu ~en Teilen** in equal parts; **das ~e, aber nicht dasselbe Auto** a similar car, but not the same one; **ganz ~ wer/was** etc no matter who/what etc; **2 mal 2 ~ 4** 2 times 2 is od equals 4; **bis ~!** see you soon!; **wie war doch ~ Ihr Name?** what was your name again?; **es ist ~ drei Uhr** it's very nearly three o'clock; ~ **gesinnt** like-minded; ~ **lautend** identical; **sie sind ~ groß** they are the same size; ~ **nach/an** right after/at; **gleichaltrig** adj of the same age; **gleichartig** adj similar; **gleichbedeutend** adj synonymous; **gleichberechtigt** adj with equal rights; **Gleichberechtigung** f equal rights pl; **gleichbleibend** adj constant; **bei gleichbleibendem Gehalt** when one's salary stays the same

gleichen unreg vi: **jdm/etw ~** to be like sb/sth

▷ *vr* to be alike
gleichermaßen *adv* equally
gleich- *zW:* **gleichfalls** *adv* likewise; **danke gleichfalls!** the same to you; **Gleichförmigkeit** *f* uniformity; **gleichgestellt** *adj:* **rechtlich gleichgestellt** equal in law; **Gleichgewicht** *nt* equilibrium, balance; **jdm aus dem Gleichgewicht bringen** to throw sb off balance; **gleichgültig** *adj* indifferent; (*unbedeutend*) unimportant; **Gleichgültigkeit** *f* indifference; **Gleichheit** *f* equality; (*Identität*) identity; (*Industrie*) parity; **Gleichheitsprinzip** *nt* principle of equality; **Gleichheitszeichen** *nt* (*Math*) equals sign; **gleichkommen** *unreg vi +dat* to be equal to; **gleichlautend** *adj* identical; **Gleichmacherei** *f* egalitarianism, levelling down (*pej*); **gleichmäßig** *adj* even, equal; **Gleichmut** *m* equanimity
Gleichnis (**-ses, -se**) *nt* parable
gleich- *zW:* **gleichrangig** *adj* (*Probleme etc*) equally important; **gleichrangig (mit)** (*Beamte etc*) equal in rank (to), at the same level (as); **gleichsam** *adv* as it were; **gleichschalten** (*pej*) *vt* to bring into line; **Gleichschritt** *m:* **im Gleichschritt, marsch!** forward march!; **gleichsehen** *unreg vi:* **jdm gleichsehen** to be *od* look like sb; **gleichstellen** *vt* (*rechtlich etc*) to treat as equal; **Gleichstrom** *m* (*Elek*) direct current; **gleichtun** *unreg vi:* **es jdm gleichtun** to match sb
Gleichung *f* equation
gleich- *zW:* **gleichviel** *adv* no matter; **gleichwertig** *adj* of the same value; (*Leistung, Qualität*) equal; (*Gegner*) evenly matched; **gleichwohl** *adv* (*geh*) nevertheless; **gleichzeitig** *adj* simultaneous
Gleis [glaɪs] (**-es, -e**) *nt* track, rails *pl*; (*am Bahnhof*) platform (*Brit*), track (*US*)
gleißend ['glaɪsənt] *adj* glistening, gleaming
gleiten *unreg vi* to glide; (*rutschen*) to slide
gleitend ['glaɪtənt] *adj:* **~e Arbeitszeit** flexible working hours *pl*, flex(i)time
Gleit- *zW:* **Gleitflug** *m* glide; **Gleitklausel** *f* (*Comm*) escalator clause; **Gleitkomma** *nt* floating point; **Gleitzeit** *f* flex(i)time
Gletscher ['glɛtʃər] (**-s, -**) *m* glacier; **Gletscherspalte** *f* crevasse
glich *etc* [glɪç] *vb siehe* **gleichen**
Glied [gliːt] (**-(e)s, -er**) *nt* member; (*Arm, Bein*) limb; (*Penis*) penis; (*von Kette*) link; (*Mil*) rank(s); **der Schreck steckt ihr noch in den ~ern** she is still shaking with the shock
gliedern *vt* to organize, structure
Gliederreißen *nt* rheumatic pains *pl*
Gliederschmerz *m* rheumatic pains *pl*
Gliederung *f* structure, organization
Gliedmaßen *pl* limbs *pl*
glimmen ['glɪmən] *unreg vi* to glow
Glimmer (**-s, -**) *m* (*Mineral*) mica
Glimmstängel (*umg*) *m* fag (*Brit*), butt (*US*)
glimpflich ['glɪmpflɪç] *adj* mild, lenient; **~ davonkommen** to get off lightly
glitschig ['glɪtʃɪç] (*umg*) *adj* slippery, slippy

glitt *etc* [glɪt] *vb siehe* **gleiten**
glitzern ['glɪtsərn] *vi* to glitter; (*Stern*) to twinkle
global [glo'baːl] *adj* (*weltweit*) global, worldwide; (*ungefähr, pauschal*) general
Globalisierung [globalɪ'ziːrʊŋ] *f* globalization; **Globalisierungsfalle** *f* globalization trap
Globus ['gloːbʊs] (**- od -ses, Globen** *od* **-se**) *m* globe
Glöckchen ['glœkçən] *nt* (little) bell
Glocke ['glɔkə] (**-, -n**) *f* bell; **etw an die große ~ hängen** (*fig*) to shout sth from the rooftops
Glocken- *zW:* **Glockengeläut** *nt* peal of bells; **Glockenschlag** *m* stroke (of the bell); (*von Uhr*) chime; **Glockenspiel** *nt* chime(s); (*Mus*) glockenspiel; **Glockenturm** *m* belfry, bell-tower
glomm *etc* [glɔm] *vb siehe* **glimmen**
Glorie ['gloːriə] *f* glory; (*von Heiligen*) halo
glorreich ['gloːrraɪç] *adj* glorious
Glossar [glɔ'saːr] (**-s, -e**) *nt* glossary
Glosse ['glɔsə] (**-, -n**) *f* comment
Glotze (**-, -n**) (*umg*) *f* gogglebox (*Brit*), TV set
glotzen ['glɔtsən] (*umg*) *vi* to stare
Glück [glʏk] (**-(e)s**) *nt* luck, fortune; (*Freude*) happiness; **~ haben** to be lucky; **viel ~** good luck; **zum ~** fortunately; **ein ~!** how lucky!, what a stroke of luck!; **auf gut ~** (*aufs Geratewohl*) on the off-chance; (*unvorbereitet*) trusting to luck; (*wahllos*) at random; **sie weiß noch nichts von ihrem ~** (*ironisch*) she doesn't know anything about it yet; **er kann von ~ sagen, dass ...** he can count himself lucky that ...; **Glückauf** *nt:* „**Glückauf"** (*Bergleute*) (cry of) "good luck"
Glucke (**-, -n**) *f* (*Bruthenne*) broody hen; (*mit Jungen*) mother hen
glücken *vi* to succeed; **es glückte ihm, es zu bekommen** he succeeded in getting it
gluckern ['glʊkərn] *vi* to glug
glücklich *adj* fortunate; (*froh*) happy ▷ *adv* happily; (*umg: endlich, zu guter Letzt*) finally, eventually
glücklicherweise *adv* fortunately
glücklos *adj* luckless
Glücksbringer (**-s, -**) *m* lucky charm
glückselig [glʏk'zeːlɪç] *adj* blissful
Glücks- *zW:* **Glücksfall** *m* stroke of luck; **Glückskind** *nt* lucky person; **Glückspilz** *m* lucky beggar (*umg*); **Glückssache** *f* matter of luck; **Glücksspiel** *nt* game of chance; **Glücksstern** *m* lucky star; **Glückssträhne** *f* lucky streak
glückstrahlend *adj* radiant (with happiness)
Glückszahl *f* lucky number
Glückwunsch *m:* **~ (zu)** congratulations *pl* (on), best wishes *pl* (on)
Glühbirne *f* light bulb
glühen ['glyːən] *vi* to glow
glühend *adj* glowing; (*heiß glühend: Metall*) red-hot; (*Hitze*) blazing; (*fig: leidenschaftlich*) ardent; (*: Hass*) burning; (*Wangen*) flushed, burning
Glüh- *zW:* **Glühfaden** *m* (*Elek*) filament;

g

Glühwein m mulled wine; **Glühwürmchen** nt glow-worm

Glut [glu:t] (-, **-en**) f (*Röte*) glow; (*Feuersglut*) fire; (*Hitze*) heat; (*fig*) ardour (*Brit*), ardor (*US*)

GmbH (-, **-s**) f abk (= *Gesellschaft mit beschränkter Haftung*) ≈ Ltd. (*Brit*), plc (*Brit*), Inc. (*US*)

Gnade ['gna:də] (-, **-n**) f (*Gunst*) favour (*Brit*), favor (*US*); (*Erbarmen*) mercy; (*Milde*) clemency; **~ vor Recht ergehen lassen** to temper justice with mercy

gnaden vi: **(dann) gnade dir Gott!** (then) God help you od heaven have mercy on you!

Gnaden- zW: **Gnadenbrot** nt: **jdm/einem Tier das Gnadenbrot geben** to keep sb/an animal in his/her/its old age; **Gnadenfrist** f reprieve; **Gnadengesuch** nt petition for clemency; **gnadenlos** adj merciless; **Gnadenstoß** m coup de grâce

gnädig ['gnɛ:dɪç] adj gracious; (*voll Erbarmen*) merciful; **~e Frau** (*form*) madam, ma'am

Gockel ['gɔkəl] (-s, -) m (*bes Südd*) cock

Gold [gɔlt] (-(e)s) nt gold; **nicht mit ~ zu bezahlen** od **aufzuwiegen sein** to be worth one's weight in gold; **golden** adj golden; **goldene Worte** words of wisdom; **der Tanz ums Goldene Kalb** (*fig*) the worship of Mammon; **Goldfisch** m goldfish; **Goldgrube** f gold mine; **Goldhamster** m (golden) hamster

goldig ['gɔldɪç] adj (*fig: umg*) sweet, cute

Gold- zW: **Goldregen** m laburnum; (*fig*) riches pl; **goldrichtig** (*umg*) adj dead right; **Goldschmied** m goldsmith; **Goldschnitt** m gilt edging; **Goldstandard** m gold standard; **Goldstück** nt piece of gold; (*fig: umg*) treasure; **Goldwaage** f: **jedes Wort auf die Goldwaage legen** (*fig*) to weigh one's words; **Goldwährung** f gold standard

Golf[1] [gɔlf] (-(e)s, -e) m gulf; **der (Persische) ~** the Gulf

Golf[2] [gɔlf] (-s) nt golf; **Golfplatz** m golf course; **Golfschläger** m golf club; **Golfspieler** m golfer

Golfstaaten pl: **die ~** the Gulf States pl

Golfstrom m (*Geog*) Gulf Stream

Gondel ['gɔndəl] (-, **-n**) f gondola; (*von Seilbahn*) cable car

gondeln (*umg*) vi: **durch die Welt ~** to go globetrotting

Gong [gɔŋ] (-s, -s) m gong; (*bei Boxkampf etc*) bell

gönnen ['gœnən] vt: **jdm etw ~** not to begrudge sb sth; **sich** dat **etw ~** to allow o.s. sth

Gönner (-s, -) m patron; **gönnerhaft** adj patronizing; **Gönnerin** f patroness; **Gönnermiene** f patronizing air

googeln ['gu:gəln] vi (*Comput: umg*) to google®

gor etc [go:r] vb siehe **gären**

Gorilla [go'rɪla] (-s, -s) m gorilla; (*umg: Leibwächter*) heavy

goss etc [gɔs] vb siehe **gießen**

Gosse ['gɔsə] (-, **-n**) f gutter

Gote ['go:tə] (-n, -n) m Goth

Gotik ['go:tɪk] f (*Kunst*) Gothic (style); (*Epoche*) Gothic period

Gotin ['go:tɪn] f Goth

Gott [gɔt] (-es, ¨-er) m god; (*als Name*) God; **um ~es Willen!** for heaven's sake!; **~ sei Dank!** thank God!; **grüß ~!** (*bes Südd, Österr*) hello, good morning/afternoon/evening; **den lieben ~ einen guten Mann sein lassen** (*umg*) to take things as they come; **ein Bild für die Götter** (*hum: umg*) a sight for sore eyes; **das wissen die Götter** (*umg*) God (only) knows; **über ~ und die Welt reden** (*fig*) to talk about everything under the sun; **wie ~ in Frankreich leben** (*umg*) to be in clover

Götterspeise f (*Koch*) jelly (*Brit*), jello (*US*)

Gottes- zW: **Gottesdienst** m service; **gottesfürchtig** adj god-fearing; **Gotteshaus** nt place of worship; **Gotteskrieger, in** m(f) religious terrorist; **Gotteslästerung** f blasphemy

Gottheit f deity

Göttin ['gœtɪn] f goddess

göttlich adj divine

Gott- zW: **gottlob** interj thank heavens!; **gottlos** adj godless; **gottverdammt** adj goddamn(ed); **gottverlassen** adj godforsaken; **Gottvertrauen** nt trust in God

Götze ['gœtsə] (-n, -n) m idol

Grab [gra:p] (-(e)s, ¨-er) nt grave

grabbeln ['grabəln] (*Nordd: umg*) vt to rummage

Graben ['gra:bən] (-s, ¨) m ditch; (*Mil*) trench

graben unreg vt to dig

Grabesstille f (*liter*) deathly hush

Grab- zW: **Grabmal** nt monument; (*Grabstein*) gravestone; **Grabrede** f funeral oration; **Grabstein** m gravestone

gräbt vb siehe **graben**

Gracht [graxt] (-, **-en**) f canal

Grad [gra:t] (-(e)s, -e) m degree; **im höchsten ~es** extremely; **Verbrennungen ersten ~es** (*Med*) first-degree burns; **Gradeinteilung** f graduation; **gradlinig** adj straight; **gradweise** adv gradually

Graf [gra:f] (-en, -en) m count, earl (*Brit*)

Grafik ['gra:fɪk] (-, **-en**) f (*Comput, Tech*) graphics; (*Art*) graphic arts pl

Grafiker, in ['gra:fɪkər(ɪn)] (-s, -) m(f) graphic artist; (*Illustrator*) illustrator

Gräfin ['grɛ:fɪn] f countess

grafisch adj ['gra:fɪʃ] ▷ adj graphic; **~e Darstellung** graph

Grafschaft f county

Grahambrot ['gra:hambro:t] nt type of wholemeal (*Brit*) od whole-wheat (*US*) bread

Gralshüter ['gra:lzhy:tər] (-s, -) m (*fig*) guardian

Gram [gra:m] (-(e)s) m (*geh*) grief, sorrow

grämen ['grɛ:mən] vr to grieve; **sich zu Tode ~** to die of grief od sorrow

Gramm [gram] (-s, -e) nt gram(me)

Grammatik [gra'matɪk] f grammar

grammatisch adj grammatical

Grammofon, Grammophon [gramo'fo:n] (-s, -e) nt gramophone

Granat [gra'na:t] (-(e)s, -e) m (*Stein*) garnet; **Granatapfel** m pomegranate

Granate (-, **-n**) *f* (*Mil*) shell; (*Handgranate*) grenade

grandios [gran'dio:s] *adj* magnificent, superb

Granit [gra'ni:t] (**-s, -e**) *m* granite; **auf ~ beißen (bei ...)** to bang one's head against a brick wall (with ...)

grantig ['grantɪç] (*umg*) *adj* grumpy

Graphik *etc* ['gra:fɪk] = **Grafik** *etc*

grapschen ['grapʃən] (*umg*) *vt, vi* to grab; (**sich** *dat*) **etw ~** to grab sth

Gras [gra:s] (**-es, ̈er**) *nt* grass; (*auch umg: Marihuana*) grass; **über etw** *akk* **~ wachsen lassen** (*fig*) to let the dust settle on sth; **grasen** *vi* to graze; **Grashalm** *m* blade of grass

grasig *adj* grassy

Grasnarbe *f* turf

grassieren [gra'si:rən] *vi* to be rampant, rage

grässlich ['grɛslɪç] *adj* horrible

Grat [gra:t] (**-(e)s, -e**) *m* ridge

Gräte ['grɛ:tə] (**-, -n**) *f* fish-bone

Gratifikation [gratifikatsi'o:n] *f* bonus

gratis ['gra:tɪs] *adj, adv* free (of charge); **Gratisprobe** *f* free sample

Grätsche ['grɛ:tʃə] (**-, -n**) *f* (*Sport*) straddle

Gratulant, in [gratu'lant(ɪn)] *m(f)* well-wisher

Gratulation [gratulatsi'o:n] *f* congratulation(s)

gratulieren [gratu'li:rən] *vi*: **jdm (zu etw) ~** to congratulate sb (on sth); **(ich) gratuliere!** congratulations!

Gratwanderung *f* (*fig*) tightrope walk

grau [graʊ] *adj* grey (*Brit*), gray (*US*); **der ~e Alltag** drab reality; **~ meliert** grey-flecked (*Brit*), gray-flecked (*US*); **Graubrot** *nt* = **Mischbrot**

Gräuel ['grɔʏəl] (**-s, -**) *m* horror; (*Gräueltat*) atrocity; **etw ist jdm ein ~** sb loathes sth; **Gräuelpropaganda** *f* atrocity propaganda; **Gräueltat** *f* atrocity

Grauen (**-s**) *nt* horror

grauen *vi* (*Tag*) to dawn ▷ *vi unpers*: **es graut jdm vor etw** sb dreads sth, sb is afraid of sth ▷ *vr*: **sich ~ vor** to dread

grauenhaft, grauenvoll *adj* horrible

grauhaarig *adj* grey-haired (*Brit*), gray-haired (*US*)

gräulich ['grɔʏlɪç] *adj* horrible

Graupelregen ['graʊpəlre:gən] *m* sleet

Graupelschauer *m* sleet

Graupen ['graʊpən] *pl* pearl barley *sing*

grausam ['graʊza:m] *adj* cruel; **Grausamkeit** *f* cruelty

Grausen ['graʊzən] (**-s**) *nt* horror; **da kann man das kalte ~ kriegen** (*umg*) it's enough to give you the creeps

grausen *vb* = **grauen**

Grauzone *f* (*fig*) grey (*Brit*) *od* gray (*US*) area

gravieren [gra'vi:rən] *vt* to engrave

gravierend *adj* grave

Grazie ['gra:tsiə] *f* grace

graziös [gratsi'ø:s] *adj* graceful

Greencard, Green Card ['gri:nka:əd] (**-, -s**) *f* green card

greifbar *adj* tangible, concrete; **in ~er Nähe** within reach

greifen ['graɪfən] *unreg vt* (*nehmen*) to grasp; (*grapschen*) to seize, grab ▷ *vi* (*nicht rutschen, einrasten*) to grip; **nach etw ~** to reach for sth; **um sich ~** (*fig*) to spread; **zu etw ~** (*fig*) to turn to sth; **diese Zahl ist zu niedrig gegriffen** (*fig*) this figure is too low; **aus dem Leben gegriffen** taken from life

Greifer (**-s, -**) *m* (*Tech*) grab

Greifvogel *m* bird of prey

Greis [graɪs] (**-es, -e**) *m* old man

Greisenalter *nt* old age

greisenhaft *adj* very old

Greisin ['graɪzɪn] *f* old woman

grell [grɛl] *adj* harsh

Gremium ['gre:miʊm] *nt* body; (*Ausschuss*) committee

Grenadier [grena'di:ər] (**-s, -e**) *m* (*Mil: Infanterist*) infantryman

Grenzbeamte, r *m* frontier official

Grenze (**-, -n**) *f* border; (*zwischen Grundstücken, fig*) boundary; (*Staatsgrenze*) frontier; (*Schranke*) limit; **über die ~ gehen/fahren** to cross the border; **hart an der ~ des Erlaubten** bordering on the limits of what is permitted

grenzen *vi*: **~ an** +*akk* to border on

grenzenlos *adj* boundless

Grenz- *zW*: **Grenzfall** *m* borderline case; **Grenzgänger** *m* (*Arbeiter*) international commuter (*across a local border*); **Grenzgebiet** *nt* (*lit, fig*) border area; **Grenzkosten** *pl* marginal cost *sing*; **Grenzlinie** *f* boundary; **Grenzübergang** *m* frontier crossing; **Grenzwert** *m* limit; **Grenzzwischenfall** *m* border incident

Gretchenfrage ['gre:tçənfra:gə] *f* (*fig*) crunch question, sixty-four-thousand-dollar question (*umg*)

Greuel *etc* ['grɔʏəl] *siehe* **Gräuel**

greulich ['grɔʏlɪç] *siehe* **gräulich**

Grieche ['gri:çə] (**-n, -n**) *m* Greek

Griechenland *nt* Greece

Griechin ['gri:çɪn] *f* Greek

griechisch *adj* Greek

griesgrämig ['gri:sgrɛ:mɪç] *adj* grumpy

Grieß [gri:s] (**-es, -e**) *m* (*Koch*) semolina; **Grießbrei** *m* cooked semolina

Griff [grɪf] (**-(e)s, -e**) *m* grip; (*Vorrichtung*) handle; (*das Greifen*): **der ~ nach etw** reaching for sth; **jdn/etw in den ~ bekommen** to gain control of sb/sth; **etw in den ~ bekommen** (*geistig*) to get a grasp of sth

griff *etc vb siehe* **greifen**

griffbereit *adj* handy

Griffel ['grɪfəl] (**-s, -**) *m* slate pencil; (*Bot*) style

griffig ['grɪfɪç] *adj* (*Fahrbahn etc*) that has a good grip; (*fig: Ausdruck*) useful, handy

Grill [grɪl] (**-s, -s**) *m* grill; (*Aut*) grille

Grille ['grɪlə] (**-, -n**) *f* cricket; (*fig*) whim

grillen *vt* to grill

Grimasse [gri'masə] (**-, -n**) *f* grimace; **~n schneiden** to make faces

g

grimmig *adj* furious; *(heftig)* fierce, severe
grinsen ['grɪnzən] *vi* to grin; *(höhnisch)* to smirk
Grippe ['grɪpə] (**-, -n**) *f* influenza, flu
Grips [grɪps] (**-es, -e**) *(umg)* m sense
grob [gro:p] *adj* coarse, gross; *(Fehler, Verstoß)* gross; *(brutal, derb)* rough; *(unhöflich)* ill-mannered; **~ geschätzt** at a rough estimate; **Grobheit** *f* coarseness; *(Beschimpfung)* coarse expression
Grobian ['gro:bia:n] (**-s, -e**) *m* ruffian
grobknochig *adj* large-boned
groggy ['grɔgi] *adj (Boxen)* groggy; *(umg: erschöpft)* bushed
grölen ['grø:lən] *(pej)* vt, vi to bawl
Groll [grɔl] (**-(e)s**) *m* resentment; **grollen** *vi* *(Donner)* to rumble; **grollen (mit** *od* +dat) to bear ill will (towards)
Grönland ['grø:nlant] (**-s**) *nt* Greenland
Grönländer, in (**-s, -**) *m(f)* Greenlander
Groschen ['grɔʃən] (**-s, -**) *(umg)* m 10-pfennig piece; *(Österr)* groschen; *(fig)* penny, cent (US); **Groschenroman** *(pej)* m cheap *od* dime (US) novel
groß [gro:s] *adj* big, large; *(hoch)* tall; *(Freude, Werk)* great ▷ *adv* greatly; **im G~en und Ganzen** on the whole; **wie ~ bist du?** how tall are you?; **die G~en** *(Erwachsene)* the grown-ups; **mit etw ~ geworden sein** to have grown up with sth; **die G~en Seen** the Great Lakes *pl*; **~en Hunger haben** to be very hungry; **~e Mode sein** to be all the fashion; **~ angelegt** large-scale, on a large scale; **~ und breit** *(fig: umg)* at great *od* enormous length; *siehe auch* **großschreiben**; **Großabnehmer** *m (Comm)* bulk buyer; **Großalarm** *m* red alert; **großartig** *adj* great, splendid; **Großaufnahme** *f (Film)* close-up; **Großbritannien** (**-s**) *nt* (Great) Britain; **Großbuchstabe** *m* capital (letter)
Größe ['grø:sə] (**-, -n**) *f* size; *(Länge)* height; *(fig)* greatness; **eine unbekannte ~** *(lit, fig)* an unknown quantity
Groß- *zW:* **Großeinkauf** *m* bulk purchase; **Großeinsatz** *m:* **Großeinsatz der Polizei** *etc* large-scale operation by the police *etc*; **Großeltern** *pl* grandparents *pl*
Größenordnung *f* scale; *(Größe)* magnitude; *(Math)* order (of magnitude)
großenteils *adv* for the most part
Größen- *zW:* **Größenunterschied** *m* difference in size; **Größenwahn** *m,* **Größenwahnsinn** *m* megalomania, delusions *pl* of grandeur
Groß- *zW:* **Großformat** *nt* large size; **Großhandel** *m* wholesale trade; **Großhandelspreisindex** *m* wholesale-price index; **Großhändler** *m* wholesaler; **großherzig** *adj* generous; **Großhirn** *nt* cerebrum; **Großindustrielle, r** *f(m)* major industrialist; **großkotzig** *(umg)* adj show-offish, bragging; **Großkundgebung** *f* mass rally; **Großmacht** *f* great power; **Großmaul** *m* braggart; **Großmut** (**-**) *f* magnanimity; **großmütig** *adj* magnanimous; **Großmutter** *f* grandmother; **Großraum** *m:* **der Großraum**

München the Munich area *od* conurbation, Greater Munich; **Großraumbüro** *nt* open-plan office; **Großrechner** *m* mainframe; **Großreinemachen** *nt* thorough cleaning, ≈ spring cleaning; **großschreiben** *unreg* vt: **ein Wort großschreiben** to write a word with a capital; **großgeschrieben werden** *(umg)* to be stressed; **Großschreibung** *f* capitalization; **großspurig** *adj* pompous; **Großstadt** *f* city
größte, r, s [grø:stə(r, s)] *adj superl* von **groß**
größtenteils *adv* for the most part
Groß- *zW:* **Großtuer** (**-s, -**) *m* boaster; **großtun** *unreg* vi to boast; **Großvater** *m* grandfather; **Großverbraucher** *m (Comm)* heavy user; **Großverdiener** *m* big earner; **Großwild** *nt* big game; **großziehen** *unreg* vt to raise; **großzügig** *adj* generous; *(Planung)* on a large scale
grotesk [gro'tɛsk] *adj* grotesque
Grotte ['grɔtə] (**-, -n**) *f* grotto
grub *etc* [gru:p] *vb siehe* **graben**
Grübchen ['gry:pçən] *nt* dimple
Grube ['gru:bə] (**-, -n**) *f* pit; *(Bergwerk)* mine
grübeln ['gry:bəln] *vi* to brood
Grubenarbeiter *m* miner
Grubengas *nt* firedamp
Grübler ['gry:blər] (**-s, -**) *m* brooder; **grüblerisch** *adj* brooding, pensive
Gruft [gruft] (**-, ̈-e**) *f* tomb, vault
grün [gry:n] *adj* green; *(ökologisch)* green; *(Pol)*: **die G~en** the Greens; **~e Minna** *(umg)* Black Maria *(Brit)*, paddy wagon *(US)*; **~e Welle** phased traffic lights; **~e Versicherungskarte** *(Aut)* green card; **sich ~ und blau od gelb ärgern** *(umg)* to be furious; **auf keinen ~en Zweig kommen** *(fig: umg)* to get nowhere; **jdm ~es Licht geben** to give sb the green light; **Grünanlage** *f* park
Grund [grʊnt] (**-(e)s, ̈-e**) *m* ground; *(von See, Gefäß)* bottom; *(fig)* reason; **von ~ auf** entirely, completely; **aus gesundheitlichen** *etc* **Gründen** for health *etc* reasons; **im ~e genommen** basically; **ich habe ~ zu der Annahme, dass ...** I have reason to believe that ...; **einer Sache** *dat* **auf den ~ gehen** *(fig)* to get to the bottom of sth; **in ~ und Boden** *(fig)* utterly, thoroughly; *siehe auch* **aufgrund**; **zugrunde**; **Grundausbildung** *f* basic training; **Grundbedeutung** *f* basic meaning; **Grundbedingung** *f* fundamental condition; **Grundbegriff** *m* basic concept; **Grundbesitz** *m* land(ed property), real estate; **Grundbuch** *nt* land register; **grundehrlich** *adj* thoroughly honest
gründen [grʏndən] *vt* to found ▷ *vr:* **sich ~ auf** +akk to be based on; **~ auf** +akk to base on
Gründer, in (**-s, -**) *m(f)* founder
Grund- *zW:* **grundfalsch** *adj* utterly wrong; **Grundgebühr** *f* basic charge; **Grundgedanke** *m* basic idea; **Grundgesetz** *nt* constitution
Grundierung [grʊn'di:rʊŋ] *f (Farbe)* primer
Grund- *zW:* **Grundkapital** *nt* nominal capital; **Grundkurs** *m* basic course; **Grundlage** *f* foundation; **jeder Grundlage** *gen* **entbehren**

to be completely unfounded; **grundlegend** adj fundamental

gründlich adj thorough; **jdm ~ die Meinung sagen** to give sb a piece of one's mind

Grund- zW: **grundlos** adj (fig) groundless; **Grundmauer** f foundation wall; **Grundnahrungsmittel** nt basic food(stuff)

Gründonnerstag m Maundy Thursday

Grund- zW: **Grundordnung** f: **die freiheitlich-demokratische Grundordnung** (Brd Pol) the German constitution based on democratic liberty; **Grundrechenart** f basic arithmetical operation; **Grundrecht** nt basic od constitutional right; **Grundregel** f basic od ground rule; **Grundriss** m plan; (fig) outline; **Grundsatz** m principle; **grundsätzlich** adj fundamental; (Frage) of principle ▷ adv fundamentally; (prinzipiell) on principle; **das ist grundsätzlich verboten** it is absolutely forbidden; **Grundsatzurteil** nt judgement that establishes a principle

Grundschule f primary (Brit) od elementary school; see culture note

Grund- zW: **Grundsicherung** f (Wirts) guaranteed minimum income; **Grundstein** m foundation stone; **Grundsteuer** f rates pl; **Grundstück** nt plot (of land); (Anwesen) estate; **Grundstücksmakler** m estate agent (Brit), realtor® (US); **Grundstufe** f first stage; (Sch) ≈ junior (Brit) od grade (US) school

Gründung f foundation

Gründungsurkunde f (Comm) certificate of incorporation

Gründungsversammlung f (Aktiengesellschaft) statutory meeting

Grund- zW: **grundverschieden** adj utterly different; **Grundwasser** nt ground water; **Grundwasserspiegel** m water table, ground-water level; **Grundzug** m characteristic; **etw in seinen Grundzügen darstellen** to outline (the essentials of) sth

Grüne (-n) nt: **im ~n** in the open air; **ins ~ fahren** to go to the country

Grüne, r f(m) (Pol) Ecologist, Green; **die Grünen** pl (als Partei) the Greens; see culture note

Grün- zW: **Grünkohl** m kale; **Grünschnabel** m greenhorn; **Grünspan** m verdigris; **Grünstreifen** m central reservation

grunzen ['grʊntsən] vi to grunt

Gruppe ['grʊpə] (-, -n) f group

Gruppen- zW: **Gruppenarbeit** f teamwork; **Gruppendynamik** f group dynamics pl; **Gruppentherapie** f group therapy; **gruppenweise** adv in groups

gruppieren [grʊ'piːrən] vt, vr to group

Gruselfilm m horror film

gruselig adj creepy

gruseln ['gruːzəln] vi unpers: **es gruselt jdm vor etw** sth gives sb the creeps ▷ vr to have the creeps

Gruß [gruːs] (-es, -̈e) m greeting; (Mil) salute; **viele Grüße** best wishes; **Grüße an** +akk regards to; **einen (schönen) ~ an Ihre Frau!** (geh) my regards to your wife; **mit freundlichen Grüßen** (als Briefformel) Yours sincerely

grüßen ['gryːsən] vt to greet; (Mil) to salute; **jdn von jdm ~** to give sb sb's regards; **jdn ~ lassen** to send sb one's regards

Grütze ['grʏtsə] (-, -n) f (Brei) gruel; **rote ~** (type of) red fruit jelly

Guatemala [guate'maːla] (-s) nt Guatemala

Guayana [gua'jaːna] (-s) nt Guyana

gucken ['gʊkən] vi to look

Guckloch nt peephole

Guinea [gi'neːa] (-s) nt Guinea

Gulasch ['guːlaʃ] (-(e)s, -e) nt goulash

gültig ['gʏltɪç] adj valid; **~ werden** to become valid; (Gesetz, Vertrag) to come into effect; (Münze) to become legal tender; **Gültigkeit** f validity; **Gültigkeitsdauer** f period of validity

Gummi ['gʊmi] (-s, -s) nt od m rubber; (Gummiharze) gum; (umg: Kondom) rubber, Durex®; (Gummiband) rubber od elastic band; (Hosengummi) elastic; **Gummiband** nt rubber od elastic band; **Gummibärchen** nt jelly baby; **Gummigeschoss** nt rubber bullet; **Gummiknüppel** m rubber truncheon; **Gummiparagraf** m ambiguous od meaningless law od statute; **Gummistiefel** m rubber boot, wellington (boot) (Brit); **Gummistrumpf** m elastic stocking;

Gummizelle f padded cell
Gunst [gʊnst] (-) f favour (Brit), favor (US); siehe auch **zugunsten**
günstig ['gʏnstɪç] adj favourable (Brit), favorable (US); (Angebot, Preis etc) reasonable, good; **bei ~er Witterung** weather permitting; **im ~sten Fall(e)** with luck
Gurgel ['gʊrgəl] (-, -n) f throat
gurgeln vi to gurgle; (im Rachen) to gargle
Gurke ['gʊrkə] (-, -n) f cucumber; **saure ~** pickled cucumber, gherkin
Gurt [gʊrt] (-(e)s, -e) m belt
Gurtanlegepflicht f (form) obligation to wear a safety belt in vehicles
Gürtel ['gʏrtəl] (-s, -) m belt; (Geog) zone; **Gürtelreifen** m radial tyre; **Gürtelrose** f shingles sing od pl
GUS [geː|uːˈ|ɛs] f abk (= Gemeinschaft Unabhängiger Staaten) CIS
Guss [gʊs] (-es, -e) m casting; (Regenguss) downpour; (Koch) glazing; **Gusseisen** nt cast iron
Gut [guːt] (-(e)s, -er) nt (Besitz) possession; (Landgut) estate; **Güter** pl (Waren) goods pl

○ SCHLÜSSELWORT

gut adj good; **das ist gut gegen** od **für** (umg) **Husten** it's good for coughs; **sei so gut (und) gib mir das** would you mind giving me that; **dafür ist er sich zu gut** he wouldn't stoop to that sort of thing; **das ist ja alles gut und schön, aber ...** that's all very well but ...; **du bist gut!** (umg) you're a fine one!; **alles Gute** all the best; **also gut** all right then
▷ adv well; **gut gehen** to work, come off; **es geht jdm gut** sb's doing fine; **das ist noch einmal gut gegangen** it turned out all right; **gut gehend** thriving; **gut gelaunt** cheerful, in a good mood; **gut gemeint** well meant; **du hast es gut!** you've got it made!; **gut situiert** well-off; **gut unterrichtet** well-informed; **gut, aber ...** OK, but ...; **(na) gut, ich komme** all right, I'll come; **gut drei Stunden** a good three hours; **das kann gut sein** that may well be; **gut und gern** easily; **lass es gut sein** that'll do; siehe auch **guttun**

Gut- zW: **Gutachten** (-s, -) nt report; **Gutachter** (-s, -) m expert; **Gutachterkommission** f quango; **gutartig** adj good-natured; (Med) benign; **gutbürgerlich** adj (Küche) (good) plain; **Gutdünken** nt: **nach Gutdünken** at one's discretion
Güte ['gyːtə] (-) f goodness, kindness;

(Qualität) quality; **ach du liebe** od **meine ~!** (umg) goodness me!; **Güteklasse** f (Comm) grade; **Güteklasseneinteilung** f (Comm) grading
Güter- zW: **Güterabfertigung** f (Eisenb) goods office; **Güterbahnhof** m goods station; **Gütertrennung** f (Jur) separation of property; **Güterverkehr** m freight traffic; **Güterwagen** m goods waggon (Brit), freight car (US); **Güterzug** m goods train (Brit), freight train (US)
Gütesiegel nt (Comm) stamp of quality
gut- zW: **gutgläubig** adj trusting; **Guthaben** (-s) nt credit; **guthaben** unreg vt: **30 Euro (bei jdm) guthaben** to be in credit (with sb) to the tune of 30 euros; **gutheißen** unreg vt to approve (of); **gutherzig** adj kind(-hearted)
gütig ['gyːtɪç] adj kind
gütlich ['gyːtlɪç] adj amicable
gut- zW: **gutmachen** vt (in Ordnung bringen: Fehler) to put right, correct; (Schaden) to make good; **gutmütig** adj good-natured; **Gutmütigkeit** f good nature
Gutsbesitzer, in m(f) landowner
Gut- zW: **Gutschein** m voucher; **gutschreiben** unreg vt to credit; **Gutschrift** f credit
Gutsherr m squire
Gutshof m estate
guttun unreg vi: **jdm ~** to do sb good
Gutverdienende, r f(m) high-income earner
gutwillig adj willing
Gymnasiallehrer, in [gʏmnaziˈaːlleːrər(ɪn)] m(f) ≈ grammar school teacher (Brit), high school teacher (US)
Gymnasium [gʏmˈnaːziʊm] nt ≈ grammar school (Brit), high school (US); see culture note

ⓘ GYMNASIUM

The Gymnasium is a selective secondary school. There are nine years of study at a Gymnasium leading to the Abitur which gives access to higher education. Pupils who successfully complete six years automatically gain the mittlere Reife.

Gymnastik [gʏmˈnastɪk] f exercises pl, keep-fit; **~ machen** to do keep-fit (exercises)/ gymnastics
Gynäkologe [gʏnɛkoˈloːgə] (-n, -n) m gynaecologist (Brit), gynecologist (US)
Gynäkologin [gʏnɛkoˈloːgɪn] f gynaecologist (Brit), gynecologist (US)

Hh

H, h [haː] nt H, h; (Mus) B; **H wie Heinrich** ≈ H for Harry, H for How (US)

ha abk = **Hektar**

Haag [haːk] (-s) m: **Den ~** The Hague

Haar [haːr] (-(e)s, -e) nt hair; **um ein ~** nearly; **~e auf den Zähnen haben** to be a tough customer; **sich die ~e raufen** (umg) to tear one's hair; **sich** dat **in die ~e kriegen** (umg) to quarrel; **das ist an den ~en herbeigezogen** that's rather far-fetched; **Haaransatz** m hairline; **Haarbürste** f hairbrush

haaren vi, vr to lose hair

Haaresbreite f: **um ~** by a hair's-breadth

Haarfestiger (-s, -) m setting lotion

haargenau adv precisely

haarig adj hairy; (fig) nasty

Haar- zW: **Haarklammer** f, **Haarklemme** f hair grip (Brit), barrette (US); **haarklein** adv in minute detail; **haarlos** adj hairless; **Haarnadel** f hairpin; **haarscharf** adv (beobachten) very sharply; (verfehlen) by a hair's breadth; **Haarschnitt** m haircut; **Haarschopf** m head of hair; **Haarsieb** nt fine sieve; **Haarspalterei** f hair-splitting; **Haarspange** f hair slide; **haarsträubend** adj hair-raising; **Haarteil** nt hairpiece; **Haarwaschmittel** nt shampoo; **Haarwasser** nt hair lotion

Hab [haːp] nt: **~ und Gut** possessions pl, belongings pl, worldly goods pl

Habe ['haːbə] (-) f property

haben ['haːbən] unreg vt, hilfsverb to have ▷ vr unpers: **und damit hat es sich** (umg) and that's that; **Hunger/Angst ~** to be hungry/afraid; **da hast du 10 Mark** there's 10 Marks; **die ~s** (ja) (umg) they can afford it; **Ferien ~** to be on holiday; **es am Herzen ~** (umg) to have heart trouble; **sie ist noch zu ~** (umg: nicht verheiratet) she's still single; **für etw ~ sein** to be keen on sth; **sie werden schon merken, was sie an ihm ~** they'll see how valuable he is; **haste was, biste was** (Sprichwort) money brings status; **wie gehabt!** some things don't change; **das hast du jetzt davon** now see what's happened; **woher hast du das?** where did you get that from?; **was hast du denn?** what's the matter (with you)?; **ich habe zu tun** I'm busy

Haben (-s, -) nt (Comm) credit

Habenseite f (Comm) credit side

Habgier f avarice

habgierig adj avaricious

habhaft adj: **jds/einer Sache ~ werden** (geh) to get hold of sb/sth

Habicht ['haːbɪçt] (-(e)s, -e) m hawk

Habilitation [habilitatsiˈoːn] f (Lehrberechtigung) postdoctoral lecturing qualification

Habseligkeiten ['haːpzeːlɪçkaɪtən] pl belongings pl

Habsucht ['haːpzʊxt] f greed

Hachse ['haksə] (-, -n) f (Koch) knuckle

Hackbraten m meat loaf

Hackbrett nt chopping board; (Mus) dulcimer

Hacke ['hakə] (-, -n) f hoe; (Ferse) heel

hacken vt to hack, chop; (Erde) to hoe

Hacker ['hakər] (-s, -) m (Comput) hacker

Hackfleisch nt mince, minced meat, ground meat (US)

Hackordnung f (lit, fig) pecking order

Häcksel ['hɛksəl] (-s) m od nt chopped straw, chaff

hadern ['haːdərn] vi (geh): **~ mit** to quarrel with; (unzufrieden sein) to be at odds with

Hafen ['haːfən] (-s, ̈-) m harbour, harbor (US), port; (fig) haven; **Hafenanlagen** pl docks pl; **Hafenarbeiter** m docker; **Hafendamm** m jetty, mole; **Hafengebühren** pl harbo(u)r dues pl; **Hafenstadt** f port

Hafer ['haːfər] (-s, -) m oats pl; **ihn sticht der ~** (umg) he is feeling his oats; **Haferbrei** m porridge (Brit), oatmeal (US); **Haferflocken** pl rolled oats pl (Brit), oatmeal (US); **Haferschleim** m gruel

Haff [haf] (-(e)s, -s od -e) nt lagoon

Haft [haft] (-) f custody; **Haftanstalt** f detention centre (Brit) od center (US); **haftbar** adj liable, responsible; **Haftbefehl** m warrant (for arrest); **einen Haftbefehl gegen jdn ausstellen** to issue a warrant for sb's arrest

haften vi to stick, cling; **~ für** to be liable od responsible for; **für Garderobe kann nicht gehaftet werden** all articles are left at owner's risk; **~ bleiben (an** +dat) to stick (to)

Häftling ['hɛftlɪŋ] m prisoner

Haft- zW: **Haftpflicht** f liability; **Haftpflichtversicherung** f third party insurance; **Haftrichter** m magistrate

Haftschalen pl contact lenses pl
Haftung f liability
Hagebutte ['ha:gəbutə] (-, -n) f rose hip
Hagedorn m hawthorn
Hagel ['ha:gəl] (-s) m hail; **Hagelkorn** nt hailstone; (Med) eye cyst
hageln vi unpers to hail
Hagelschauer m (short) hailstorm
hager ['ha:gər] adj gaunt
Häher ['hɛ:ər] (-s, -) m jay
Hahn [ha:n] (-(e)s, ̈e) m cock; (Wasserhahn) tap, faucet (US); (Abzug) trigger; ~ **im Korb sein** (umg) to be cock of the walk; **danach kräht kein ~ mehr** (umg) no one cares two hoots about that any more
Hähnchen ['hɛ:nçən] nt cockerel; (Koch) chicken
Hai ['haɪ], **Haifisch** ['haɪfɪʃ] (-(e)s, -e) m shark
Haiti [ha'i:ti] (-s) nt Haiti
Häkchen ['hɛ:kçən] nt small hook
Häkelarbeit f crochet work
häkeln ['hɛ:kəln] vt to crochet
Häkelnadel f crochet hook
Haken ['ha:kən] (-s, -) m hook; (fig) catch; **einen ~ schlagen** to dart sideways; **Hakenkreuz** nt swastika; **Hakennase** f hooked nose
halb [halp] adj half ▷ adv (beinahe) almost; ~ **eins** half past twelve; ~ **offen** half-open; **ein ~es Dutzend** half a dozen; **nichts H~es und nichts Ganzes** neither one thing nor the other; **(noch) ein ~es Kind sein** to be scarcely more than a child; **das ist ~ so schlimm** it's not as bad as all that; **mit jdm ~e-halbe machen** (umg) to go halves with sb
halb- zW: **Halbblut** nt (Tier) crossbreed; **Halbbruder** m half-brother; **Halbdunkel** nt semi-darkness
halber ['halbər] präp +gen (wegen) on account of; (für) for the sake of
Halb- zW: **halbfett** adj medium fat; **Halbfinale** nt semi-final; **Halbheit** f half-measure; **halbherzig** adj half-hearted
halbieren [hal'bi:rən] vt to halve
Halb- zW: **Halbinsel** f peninsula; **halbjährlich** adj half-yearly; **Halbkreis** m semicircle; **Halbkugel** f hemisphere; **halblang** adj: **nun mach mal halblang!** (umg) now wait a minute!; **halblaut** adv in an undertone; **Halbleiter** m (Phys) semiconductor; **halbmast** adv at half-mast; **Halbmond** m half-moon; (fig) crescent; **Halbpension** f half-board (Brit), European plan (US); **Halbschuh** m shoe; **Halbschwester** f half-sister; **halbseiden** adj (lit) fifty per cent silk; (fig: Dame) fast; (: homosexuell) gay; **halbseitig** adj (Anzeige) half-page; **Halbstarke**, r f(m) hooligan, rowdy; **halbtags** adv: **halbtags arbeiten** to work part-time; **Halbtagsarbeit** f part-time work; **Halbtagskraft** f part-time worker; **Halbton** m half-tone; (Mus) semitone; **halbtrocken** adj medium-dry; **Halbwaise** f child/person who has lost one parent; **halbwegs** adv half-

way; **halbwegs besser** more or less better; **Halbwelt** f demimonde; **Halbwertzeit** f half-life; **Halbwüchsige**, r f(m) adolescent; **Halbzeit** f (Sport) half; (Pause) half-time
Halde ['haldə] f tip; (Schlackenhalde) slag heap
half etc [half] vb siehe **helfen**
Hälfte ['hɛlftə] (-, -n) f half; **um die ~ steigen** to increase by half
Halfter¹ ['halftər] (-s, -) m od nt (für Tiere) halter
Halfter² ['halftər] (-, -n od -s, -) f od nt (Pistolenhalfter) holster
Hall [hal] (-(e)s, -e) m sound
Halle ['halə] (-, -n) f hall; (Aviat) hangar
hallen vi to echo, resound
Hallen- in zW indoor; **Hallenbad** nt indoor swimming pool
hallo [ha'lo:] interj hallo
Halluzination [halutsinatsi'o:n] f hallucination
Halm ['halm] (-(e)s, -e) m blade, stalk
Hals [hals] (-es, ̈e) m neck; (Kehle) throat; **sich** dat **nach jdm/etw den ~ verrenken** (umg) to crane one's neck to see sb/sth; **jdm um den ~ fallen** to fling one's arms around sb's neck; **aus vollem ~(e)** at the top of one's voice; ~ **über Kopf** in a rush; **jdn auf dem** od **am ~ haben** (umg) to be lumbered od saddled with sb; **das hängt mir zum ~ raus** (umg) I'm sick and tired of it; **sie hat es in den falschen ~ bekommen** (falsch verstehen) she took it wrongly; **Halsabschneider** (pej: umg) m shark; **Halsband** nt (Hundehalsband) collar; **halsbrecherisch** adj (Tempo) breakneck; (Fahrt) hair-raising; **Halskette** f necklace; **Halskrause** f ruff; **Hals-Nasen-Ohren-Arzt** m ear, nose and throat specialist; **Halsschlagader** f carotid artery; **Halsschmerzen** pl sore throat sing; **halsstarrig** adj stubborn, obstinate; **Halstuch** nt scarf; **Hals- und Beinbruch** interj good luck; **Halsweh** nt sore throat; **Halswirbel** m cervical vertebra
Halt [halt] (-(e)s, -e) m stop; (fester Halt) hold; (innerer Halt) stability; ~!, **halt!** stop!, halt!; ~ **machen** to stop
hält [hɛlt] vb siehe **halten**
Halt- zW: **haltbar** adj durable; (Lebensmittel) non-perishable; (Mil, fig) tenable; **haltbar bis 6.11.** use by 6 Nov.; **Haltbarkeit** f durability; (non-)perishability; tenability; (von Lebensmitteln) shelf life; **Haltbarkeitsdatum** nt best-before date
halten ['haltən] unreg vt to keep; (festhalten) to hold ▷ vi to hold; (frisch bleiben) to keep; (stoppen) to stop ▷ vr (frisch bleiben) to keep; (sich behaupten) to hold out; **den Mund ~** (umg) to keep one's mouth shut; ~ **für** to regard as; ~ **von** to think of; **das kannst du ~ wie du willst** that's completely up to you; **der Film hält nicht, was er verspricht** the film doesn't live up to expectations; **davon halt(e) ich nichts** I don't think much of it; **zu jdm ~** to stand od stick by sb; **an sich** akk ~ to restrain o.s.; **auf sich** akk ~ (auf Äußeres

achten) to take a pride in o.s.; **er hat sich gut gehalten** (*umg*) he's well-preserved; **sich an ein Versprechen** ~ to keep a promise; **sich rechts/links** ~ to keep to the right/left
Halter ['haltər] (**-s, -**) *m* (*Halterung*) holder
Haltestelle *f* stop
Halteverbot *nt*: **absolutes** ~ no stopping; **eingeschränktes** ~ no waiting; **hier ist** ~ you cannot stop here
haltlos *adj* unstable
Haltlosigkeit *f* instability
haltmachen *vi* to stop
Haltung *f* posture; (*fig*) attitude; (*Selbstbeherrschung*) composure; ~ **bewahren** to keep one's composure
Halunke [ha'luŋkə] (**-n, -n**) *m* rascal
Hamburg ['hamburk] (**-s**) *nt* Hamburg
Hamburger (**-s, -**) *m* (*Koch*) burger, hamburger
Hamburger, in (**-s, -**) *m(f)* native of Hamburg
Hameln ['ha:məln] *nt* Hamelin
hämisch ['hɛ:mɪʃ] *adj* malicious
Hammel ['haməl] (**-s, ⁻ od -**) *m* wether; **Hammelfleisch** *nt* mutton; **Hammelkeule** *f* leg of mutton
Hammelsprung *m* (*Parl*) division
Hammer ['hamər] (**-s, ⁻**) *m* hammer; **das ist ein ~!** (*umg: unerhört*) that's absurd!
hämmern ['hɛmərn] *vt, vi* to hammer
Hammondorgel ['hæmənd|ɔrgəl] *f* electric organ
Hämorrhoiden [hɛmɔro'i:dən], **Hämorriden** [hɛmɔ'ri:dən] *pl* piles *pl*, haemorrhoids *pl* (*Brit*), hemorrhoids *pl* (*US*)
Hampelmann ['hampəlman] *m* (*lit, fig*) puppet
Hamster ['hamstər] (**-s, -**) *m* hamster
Hamsterei [hamstə'raɪ] *f* hoarding
Hamsterer (**-s, -**) *m* hoarder
hamstern *vi* to hoard
Hand [hant] (**-, ⁻e**) *f* hand; **etw zur ~ haben** to have sth to hand; (*Ausrede, Erklärung*) to have sth ready; **jdm zur ~ gehen** to lend sb a helping hand; **zu Händen von jdm** for the attention of sb; **in festen Händen sein** to be spoken for; **die ~ für jdn ins Feuer legen** to vouch for sb; **hinter vorgehaltener ~** on the quiet; **~ aufs Herz** cross your heart; **jdn auf Händen tragen** to cherish sb; **bei etw die** *od* **seine ~ im Spiel haben** to have a hand in sth; **eine ~ wäscht die andere** (*Sprichwort*) if you scratch my back I'll scratch yours; **das hat weder ~ noch Fuß** that doesn't make sense; **das liegt auf der ~** (*umg*) that's obvious; **unter der ~** secretly; (*verkaufen*) privately; *siehe auch* **anhand**; **Handarbeit** *f* manual work; (*Nadelarbeit*) needlework; **Handarbeiter** *m* manual worker; **Handball** *m* handball; **Handbesen** *m* brush; **Handbetrieb** *m*: **mit Handbetrieb** hand-operated; **Handbewegung** *f* gesture; **Handbibliothek** *f* (*in Bibliothek*) reference section; (*auf Schreibtisch*) reference books *pl*; **Handbremse** *f* handbrake; **Handbuch** *nt* handbook, manual
Händedruck *m* handshake

Händeklatschen *nt* clapping, applause
Handel¹ ['handəl] (**-s**) *m* trade; (*Geschäft*) transaction; **im ~ sein** to be on the market; (**mit jdm**) ~ **treiben** to trade (with sb); **etw in den ~ bringen/aus dem ~ ziehen** to put sth on/take sth off the market
Handel² (**-s, ⁻**) *m* quarrel
handeln ['handəln] *vi* to trade; (*tätig werden*) to act ▷ *vr unpers*: **sich ~ um** to be a question of, be about; **~ von** to be about; **ich lasse mit mir ~** I'm open to persuasion; (*in Bezug auf Preis*) I'm open to offers
Handeln (**-s**) *nt* action
handelnd *adj*: **die ~en Personen in einem Drama** the characters in a drama
Handels- *zW*: **Handelsbank** *f* merchant bank (*Brit*), commercial bank; **Handelsbilanz** *f* balance of trade; **aktive/passive Handelsbilanz** balance of trade surplus/deficit; **Handelsdelegation** *f* trade mission; **handelseinig** *adj*: **mit jdm handelseinig werden** to conclude a deal with sb; **Handelsgesellschaft** *f* commercial company; **Handelskammer** *f* chamber of commerce; **Handelsklasse** *f* grade; **Handelsmarine** *f* merchant navy; **Handelsmarke** *f* trade name; **Handelsname** *m* trade name; **Handelsrecht** *nt* commercial law; **Handelsregister** *nt* register of companies; **Handelsreisende, r** *f(m)* = **Handlungsreisende(r)** commercial traveller; **Handelssanktionen** *pl* trade sanctions *pl*; **Handelsschule** *f* business school; **Handelsspanne** *f* gross margin, mark-up; **Handelssperre** *f* trade embargo; **handelsüblich** *adj* customary; **Handelsvertreter** *m* sales representative; **Handelsvertretung** *f* trade mission; **Handelsware** *f* commodity
händeringend ['hɛndərɪŋənd] *adv* wringing one's hands; (*fig*) imploringly
Hand- *zW*: **Handfeger** (**-s, -**) *m* brush; **Handfertigkeit** *f* dexterity; **handfest** *adj* hefty; **Handfläche** *f* palm *od* flat (of one's hand); **handgearbeitet** *adj* handmade; **Handgelenk** *nt* wrist; **aus dem Handgelenk** (*umg: ohne Mühe*) effortlessly; (*: improvisiert*) off the cuff; **Handgemenge** *nt* scuffle; **Handgepäck** *nt* hand baggage *od* luggage; **handgeschrieben** *adj* handwritten; **Handgranate** *f* hand grenade; **handgreiflich** *adj* palpable; **handgreiflich werden** to become violent; **Handgriff** *m* flick of the wrist; **Handhabe** *f*: **ich habe gegen ihn keine Handhabe** (*fig*) I have no hold on him; **handhaben** *unreg vt untr* to handle; **Handkarren** *m* handcart; **Handkäse** *m* strong-smelling, round German cheese; **Handkuss** *m* kiss on the hand; **Handlanger** (**-s, -**) *m* odd-job man, handyman; (*fig: Untergeordneter*) dogsbody
Händler ['hɛndlər] (**-s, -**) *m* trader, dealer
handlich ['hantlɪç] *adj* handy
Handlung ['handluŋ] *f* action; (*Tat*) act; (*in*

h

Buch) plot; (*Geschäft*) shop

Handlungs- *zW*: **Handlungsablauf** *m* plot; **Handlungsbevollmächtigte,** r *f(m)* authorized agent; **handlungsfähig** *adj* (*Regierung*) able to act; (*Jur*) empowered to act; **Handlungsfreiheit** *f* freedom of action; **handlungsorientiert** *adj* action-orientated; **Handlungsreisende,** r *f(m)* commercial traveller (*Brit*), traveling salesman (*US*); **Handlungsvollmacht** *f* proxy; **Handlungsweise** *f* manner of dealing

Hand- *zW*: **Handpflege** *f* manicure; **Handschelle** *f* handcuff; **Handschlag** *m* handshake; **keinen Handschlag tun** not to do a stroke (of work); **Handschrift** *f* handwriting; (*Text*) manuscript; **handschriftlich** *adj* handwritten ▷ *adv* (*korrigieren, einfügen*) by hand; **Handschuh** *m* glove; **Handschuhfach** *nt* (*Aut*) glove compartment; **Handtasche** *f* handbag (*Brit*), pocket book (*US*), purse (*US*); **Handtuch** *nt* towel; **Handumdrehen** *nt*: **im Handumdrehen** (*fig*) in the twinkling of an eye

Handwerk *nt* trade, craft; **jdm das ~ legen** (*fig*) to put a stop to sb's game

Handwerker (-s, -) *m* craftsman, artisan; **wir haben seit Wochen die ~ im Haus** we've had workmen in the house for weeks

Handwerkskammer *f* trade corporation

Handwerkszeug *nt* tools *pl*

Handwörterbuch *nt* concise dictionary

Handy ['hɛndi] **(-s, -s)** *nt* (*Tel*) mobile (phone) (*Brit*), cellphone (*US*)

Handzeichen *nt* signal; (*Geste*) sign; (*bei Abstimmung*) show of hands

Handzettel *m* leaflet, handbill

Hanf [hanf] **(-(e)s)** *m* hemp

Hang [haŋ] **(-(e)s, ̈e)** *m* inclination; (*Abhang*) slope

Hänge- ['hɛŋə] *in zW* hanging; **Hängebrücke** *f* suspension bridge; **Hängematte** *f* hammock

Hängen ['hɛŋən] *nt*: **mit ~ und Würgen** (*umg*) by the skin of one's teeth

hängen *unreg vi* to hang ▷ *vt*: **~ (an** +*akk*) to hang (on(to)); **an jdm ~** (*fig*) to be attached to sb; **~ bleiben** to be caught; (*fig*) to remain, stick; **~ bleiben an** +*dat* to catch *od* get caught on; **es bleibt ja doch alles an mir ~** (*fig*: *umg*) in the end it's all down to me anyhow; **~ lassen** (*vergessen*) to leave behind; **sich ~ lassen** to let o.s. go; **den Kopf ~ lassen** (*fig*) to be downcast; **die ganze Sache hängt an ihm** it all depends on him; **sich ~ an** +*akk* to hang on to, cling to

hängend *adj*: **mit ~er Zunge kam er angelaufen** (*fig*) he came running up panting

Hängeschloss *nt* padlock

Hanglage *f*: **in ~** situated on a slope

Hannover [ha'no:fər] **(-s)** *nt* Hanover

Hannoveraner, in [hanovə'ra:nər(ɪn)] **(-s, -)** *m(f)* Hanoverian

hänseln ['hɛnzəln] *vt* to tease

Hansestadt ['hanzəʃtat] *f* Hanseatic *od* Hanse town

Hanswurst [hans'vʊrst] **(-(e)s, -e** *od* **-würste)** *m* clown

Hantel ['hantəl] **(-, -n)** *f* (*Sport*) dumb-bell

hantieren [han'ti:rən] *vi* to work, be busy; **mit etw ~** to handle sth

hapern ['ha:pərn] *vi unpers*: **es hapert an etw** *dat* there is a lack of sth

Happen ['hapən] **(-s, -)** *m* mouthful

happig ['hapɪç] (*umg*) *adj* steep

Harfe ['harfə] **(-, -n)** *f* harp

Harke ['harkə] **(-, -n)** *f* rake

harken *vt, vi* to rake

harmlos ['harmlo:s] *adj* harmless

Harmlosigkeit *f* harmlessness

Harmonie [harmo'ni:] *f* harmony

harmonieren *vi* to harmonize

Harmonika [har'mo:nika] **(-, -s)** *f* (*Ziehharmonika*) concertina

harmonisch [har'mo:nɪʃ] *adj* harmonious

Harmonium [har'mo:nium] **(-s, -nien** *od* **-s)** *nt* harmonium

Harn ['harn] **(-(e)s, -e)** *m* urine; **Harnblase** *f* bladder

Harnisch ['harnɪʃ] **(-(e)s, -e)** *m* armour, armor (*US*); **jdn in ~ bringen** to infuriate sb; **in ~ geraten** to become angry

Harpune [har'pu:nə] **(-, -n)** *f* harpoon

harren ['harən] *vi*: **~ auf** +*akk* to wait for

Harsch [harʃ] **(-(e)s)** *m* frozen snow

harschig *adj* (*Schnee*) frozen

hart [hart] *adj* hard; (*fig*) harsh ▷ *adv*: **das ist ~ an der Grenze** that's almost going too far; **~e Währung** hard currency; **~ bleiben** to stand firm; **~ gekocht** hard-boiled; **~ gesotten** (*Ei*) hard-boiled; **es geht ~ auf ~** it's a tough fight

Härte ['hɛrtə] **(-, -n)** *f* hardness; (*fig*) harshness; **soziale ~n** social hardships; **Härtefall** *m* case of hardship; (*umg*: *Mensch*) hardship case; **Härteklausel** *f* hardship clause

härten *vt, vr* to harden

hart- *zW*: **Hartfaserplatte** *f* hardboard, fiberboard (*US*); **hartgesotten** *adj* (*Kerl*) tough, hard-boiled; **hartherzig** *adj* hard-hearted; **hartnäckig** *adj* stubborn; **Hartnäckigkeit** *f* stubbornness

Harz¹ [ha:rts] **(-es, -e)** *nt* resin

Harz² **(-es)** *m* (*Geog*) Harz Mountains *pl*

Haschee [ha'ʃe:] **(-s, -s)** *nt* hash

haschen ['haʃən] *vt* to catch, snatch ▷ *vi* (*umg*) to smoke hash

Haschisch ['haʃɪʃ] **(-)** *nt* hashish

Hase ['ha:zə] **(-n, -n)** *m* hare; **falscher ~** (*Koch*) meat loaf; **wissen, wie der ~ läuft** (*fig*: *umg*) to know which way the wind blows; **mein Name ist ~(, ich weiß von nichts)** I don't know anything about anything

Haselnuss ['ha:zəlnʊs] *f* hazelnut

Hasenfuß *m* coward

Hasenscharte *f* harelip

Haspel (-, -n) *f* reel, bobbin; (*Winde*) winch

Hass [has] **(-es)** *m* hate, hatred; **einen ~ (auf**

jdn) haben (*umg*: *Wut*) to be really mad (with sb)

hassen ['hasən] *vt* to hate; **etw ~ wie die Pest** (*umg*) to detest sth

hassenswert *adj* hateful

hässlich ['hɛslɪç] *adj* ugly; (*gemein*) nasty; **Hässlichkeit** *f* ugliness; nastiness

Hassliebe *f* love-hate relationship

Hast [hast] (-) *f* haste

hast *vb siehe* **haben**

hasten *vi, vr* to rush

hastig *adj* hasty

hat [hat] *vb siehe* **haben**

hätscheln ['hɛtʃəln] *vt* to pamper; (*zärtlich*) to cuddle

hatte *etc* ['hatə] *vb siehe* **haben**

hätte *etc* ['hɛtə] *vb siehe* **haben**

Haube ['haʊbə] (-, -n) *f* hood; (*Mütze*) cap; (*Aut*) bonnet (*Brit*), hood (*US*); **unter der ~ sein/ unter die ~ kommen** (*hum*) to be/get married

Hauch [haʊx] (-(e)s, -e) *m* breath; (*Lufthauch*) breeze; (*fig*) trace; **hauchdünn** *adj* extremely thin; (*Scheiben*) wafer-thin; (*fig: Mehrheit*) extremely narrow; **hauchen** *vi* to breathe; **hauchfein** *adj* very fine

Haue ['haʊə] (-, -n) *f* hoe; (*Pickel*) pick; (*umg*) hiding

hauen *unreg vt* to hew, cut; (*umg*) to thrash

Hauer ['haʊər] (-s, -) *m* (*Min*) face-worker

Häufchen ['hɔyfçən] *nt*: **ein ~ Unglück** *od* **Elend** a picture of misery

Haufen ['haʊfən] (-s, -) *m* heap; (*Leute*) crowd; **ein ~ (Bücher)** (*umg*) loads *od* a lot (of books); **auf einem ~** in one heap; **etw über den ~ werfen** (*umg: verwerfen*) to chuck sth out; **jdn über den ~ rennen** *od* **fahren** *etc* (*umg*) to knock sb down

häufen ['hɔyfən] *vt* to pile up ▷ *vr* to accumulate

haufenweise *adv* in heaps; in droves; **etw ~ haben** to have piles of sth

häufig ['hɔyfɪç] *adj* frequent ▷ *adv* frequently; **Häufigkeit** *f* frequency

Haupt [haʊpt] (-(e)s, Häupter) *nt* head; (*Oberhaupt*) chief ▷ *in zW* main; **Hauptakteur** *m* (*lit, fig*) leading light; (*pej*) main figure; **Hauptaktionär** *m* major shareholder; **Hauptbahnhof** *m* central station; **hauptberuflich** *adv* as one's main occupation; **Hauptbuch** *nt* (*Comm*) ledger; **Hauptdarsteller, in** *m(f)* leading actor, leading actress; **Haupteingang** *m* main entrance; **Hauptfach** *nt* (*Sch, Univ*) main subject, major (*US*); **etw im Hauptfach studieren** to study sth as one's main subject, major in sth (*US*); **Hauptfilm** *m* main film; **Hauptgericht** *nt* main course; **Hauptgeschäftsstelle** *f* head office; **Hauptgeschäftszeit** *f* peak (shopping) period; **Hauptgewinn** *m* first prize; **einer der Hauptgewinne** one of the main prizes; **Hauptleitung** *f* mains *pl*

Häuptling ['hɔyptlɪŋ] *m* chief(tain)

Haupt- *zW*: **Hauptmahlzeit** *f* main meal; **Hauptmann** (-(e)s, *pl* -leute) *m* (*Mil*) captain; **Hauptnahrungsmittel** *nt* staple food; **Hauptperson** *f* (*im Roman usw*) main character; (*fig*) central figure; **Hauptpostamt** *nt* main post office; **Hauptquartier** *nt* headquarters *pl*; **Hauptrolle** *f* leading part; **Hauptsache** *f* main thing; **in der Hauptsache** in the main, mainly; **hauptsächlich** *adj* chief ▷ *adv* chiefly; **Hauptsaison** *f* peak *od* high season; **Hauptsatz** *m* main clause; **Hauptschlagader** *f* aorta; **Hauptschlüssel** *m* master key

Hauptschule *f* ≈ secondary modern (school) (*Brit*), junior high (school) (*US*); *see culture note*

Haupt- *zW*: **Hauptsendezeit** *f* (*TV*) prime time; **Hauptstadt** *f* capital; **Hauptstraße** *f* main street; **Hauptverkehrsstraße** *f* (*in Stadt*) main street; (*Durchgangsstraße*) main thoroughfare; (*zwischen Städten*) main highway, trunk road (*Brit*); **Hauptverkehrszeit** *f* rush hour; **Hauptversammlung** *f* general meeting; **Hauptwohnsitz** *m* main place of residence; **Hauptwort** *nt* noun

hau ruck ['haʊ 'rʊk] *interj* heave-ho

Haus [haʊs] (-es, Häuser) *nt* house; **nach ~e** home; **zu ~e** at home; **fühl dich wie zu ~e!** make yourself at home!; **ein Freund des ~es** a friend of the family; **~ halten** (*sparen*) to economize; **wir liefern frei ~** (*Comm*) we offer free delivery; **das erste ~ am Platze** (*Hotel*) the best hotel in town; **Hausangestellte** *f* domestic servant; **Hausarbeit** *f* housework; (*Sch*) homework; **Hausarrest** *m* (*im Internat*) detention; (*Jur*) house arrest; **Hausarzt** *m* family doctor; **Hausaufgabe** *f* (*Sch*) homework; **Hausbesetzung** *f* squat; **Hausbesitzer** *m* house-owner; **Hausbesuch** *m* home visit; (*von Arzt*) house call

Häuschen ['hɔysçən] *nt*: **ganz aus dem ~ sein** (*fig: umg*) to be out of one's mind (with excitement/fear *etc*)

Haus *zW*: **Hausdurchsuchung** *f* police raid; **Hausdurchsuchungsbefehl** *m* search warrant

Hauseigentümer *m* house-owner

hausen ['haʊzən] *vi* to live (in poverty); (*pej*) to wreak havoc

Häuser- *zW*: **Häuserblock** *m* block (of houses); **Häusermakler** *m* estate agent (*Brit*), real estate agent (*US*); **Häuserreihe** *f*, **Häuserzeile** *f* row of houses; (*aneinandergebaut*) terrace (*Brit*)

Haus- *zW*: **Hausfrau** *f* housewife; **Hausfreund** *m* family friend; (*umg*) lover; **Hausfriedensbruch** *m* (*Jur*) trespass (*in sb's house*); **Hausgebrauch** *m*: **für den**

h

Hausgebrauch (*Gerät*) for domestic *od* household use; **hausgemacht** *adj* home-made; **Hausgemeinschaft** *f* household (community); **Haushalt** *m* household; (*Pol*) budget; **haushalten** *unreg vi* (*old*) to keep house; (*sparen*) to economize; **Haushälterin** *f* housekeeper

Haushalts- *zW*: **Haushaltsauflösung** *f* dissolution of the household; **Haushaltsbuch** *nt* housekeeping book; **Haushaltsdebatte** *f* (*Parl*) budget debate; **Haushaltsgeld** *nt* housekeeping (money); **Haushaltsgerät** *nt* domestic appliance; **Haushaltshilfe** *f* domestic *od* home help; **Haushaltsjahr** *nt* (*Pol, Wirts*) financial *od* fiscal year; **Haushaltsperiode** *f* budget period; **Haushaltsplan** *m* budget

Haus- *zW*: **Haushaltung** *f* housekeeping; **Hausherr** *m* host; (*Vermieter*) landlord; **haushoch** *adv*: **haushoch verlieren** to lose by a mile

hausieren [hau'ziːrən] *vi* to peddle

Hausierer (**-s, -**) *m* pedlar (*Brit*), peddler (*US*)

hausintern ['haus|ɪntɛrn] *adj* internal company *attrib*

häuslich ['hɔyslɪç] *adj* domestic; **sich irgendwo ~ einrichten** *od* **niederlassen** to settle in somewhere; **Häuslichkeit** *f* domesticity

Hausmacherart ['hausmaxər|aːrt] *f*: **Wurst** *etc* **nach ~** home-made-style sausage *etc*

Haus- *zW*: **Hausmann** (**-(e)s,** *pl* **-männer**) *m* (*den Haushalt versorgender Mann*) househusband; **Hausmarke** *f* (*eigene Marke*) own brand; (*bevorzugte Marke*) favourite (*Brit*) *od* favorite (*US*) brand; **Hausmeister** *m* caretaker, janitor; **Hausmittel** *nt* household remedy; **Hausnummer** *f* house number; **Hausordnung** *f* house rules *pl*; **Hausputz** *m* house cleaning; **Hausratversicherung** *f* (household) contents insurance; **Hausschlüssel** *m* front-door key; **Hausschuh** *m* slipper; **Hausschwamm** *m* dry rot

Hausse ['hoːsə] (**-, -n**) *f* (*Wirts*) boom; (*Börse*) bull market; **~ an** +*dat* boom in

Haus- *zW*: **Haussegen** *m*: **bei ihnen hängt der Haussegen schief** (*hum*) they're a bit short on domestic bliss; **Hausstand** *m*: **einen Hausstand gründen** to set up house *od* home; **Haussuchung** *f* = **Hausdurchsuchung**; **Haussuchungsbefehl** *m* = **Hausdurchsuchungsbefehl**; **Haustier** *nt* domestic animal; **Haustür** *f* front door; **Hausverbot** *nt*: **jdm Hausverbot erteilen** to ban sb from the house; **Hausverwalter** *m* property manager; **Hausverwaltung** *f* property management; **Hauswirt** *m* landlord; **Hauswirtschaft** *f* domestic science; **Haus-zu-haus-Verkauf** *m* door-to-door selling

Haut [haut] (**-, Häute**) *f* skin; (*Tierhaut*) hide; **mit ~ und Haar(en)** (*umg*) completely; **aus der ~ fahren** (*umg*) to go through the roof; **Hautarzt** *m* skin specialist, dermatologist

häuten ['hɔytən] *vt* to skin ▷ *vr* to shed one's skin

hauteng *adj* skintight

Hautfarbe *f* complexion

Hautkrebs *m* (*Med*) skin cancer

Havanna [ha'vana] (**-s**) *nt* Havana

Haxe ['haksə] (**-, -n**) *f* = **Hachse**

Hbf. *abk* = **Hauptbahnhof**

H-Bombe ['haːbɔmbə] *f abk* H-bomb

HDTV *abk* (= *high definition television*: hoch-auflösendes Fernsehen) HDTV

Hebamme ['heːp|amə] *f* midwife

Hebel ['heːbəl] (**-s, -**) *m* lever; **alle ~ in Bewegung setzen** (*umg*) to move heaven and earth; **am längeren ~ sitzen** (*umg*) to have the whip hand

heben ['heːbən] *unreg vt* to raise, lift; (*steigern*) to increase; **einen ~ gehen** (*umg*) to go for a drink

Hebräer *in* [he'brɛːər(ɪn)] (**-s, -**) *m(f)* Hebrew

hebräisch [he'brɛːɪʃ] *adj* Hebrew

Hebriden [he'briːdən] *pl*: **die ~** the Hebrides *pl*

hecheln ['hɛçəln] *vi* (*Hund*) to pant

Hecht [hɛçt] (**-(e)s, -e**) *m* pike; **Hechtsprung** *m* (*beim Schwimmen*) racing dive; (*beim Turnen*) forward dive; (*Fussball: umg*) dive

Heck [hɛk] (**-(e)s, -e**) *nt* stern; (*von Auto*) rear

Hecke ['hɛkə] (**-, -n**) *f* hedge

Heckenrose *f* dog rose

Heckenschütze *m* sniper

Heck- *zW*: **Heckfenster** *nt* (*Aut*) rear window; **Heckklappe** *f* tailgate; **Heckmotor** *m* rear engine

heda ['heːda] *interj* hey there

Heer [heːr] (**-(e)s, -e**) *nt* army

Hefe ['heːfə] (**-, -n**) *f* yeast

Heft ['hɛft] (**-(e)s, -e**) *nt* exercise book; (*Zeitschrift*) number; (*von Messer*) haft; **jdm das ~ aus der Hand nehmen** (*fig*) to seize control *od* power from sb

Heftchen *nt* (*Fahrkartenheftchen*) book of tickets; (*Briefmarkenheftchen*) book of stamps

heften *vt*: **~ (an** +*akk*) to fasten (to); (*nähen*) to tack (on (to)); (*mit Heftmaschine*) to staple *od* fasten (to) ▷ *vr*: **sich an jds Fersen** *od* **Sohlen ~** (*fig*) to dog sb's heels

Hefter (**-s, -**) *m* folder

heftig *adj* fierce, violent; **Heftigkeit** *f* fierceness, violence

Heft- *zW*: **Heftklammer** *f* staple; **Heftmaschine** *f* stapling machine; **Heftpflaster** *nt* sticking plaster; **Heftzwecke** *f* drawing pin (*Brit*), thumb tack (*US*)

hegen ['heːgən] *vt* to nurse; (*fig*) to harbour (*Brit*), harbor (*US*), foster

Hehl [heːl] *m od nt*: **kein(en) ~ aus etw machen** to make no secret of sth

Hehler (**-s, -**) *m* receiver (of stolen goods), fence

Heide[1] ['haɪdə] (**-, -n**) *f* heath, moor; (*Heidekraut*) heather

Heide[2] ['haɪdə] (**-n, -n**) *m* heathen, pagan

Heidekraut *nt* heather

Heidelbeere *f* bilberry

Heiden- *zW*: **Heidenangst** (*umg*) *f*: **eine**

Heidenangst vor etw/jdm haben to be scared stiff of sth/sb; **Heidenarbeit** *(umg)* f real slog; **heidenmäßig** *(umg)* adj terrific; **Heidentum** nt paganism

Heidin f heathen, pagan

heidnisch ['haɪdnɪʃ] adj heathen, pagan

heikel ['haɪkəl] adj awkward, thorny; *(wählerisch)* fussy

Heil [haɪl] **(-(e)s)** nt well-being; *(Seelenheil)* salvation ▷ *interj* hail; **Ski/Petri ~!** good skiing/fishing!

heil adj in one piece, intact; **mit ~er Haut davonkommen** to escape unscathed; **die ~e Welt** an ideal world *(without problems etc)*

Heiland (-(e)s, -e) m saviour *(Brit)*, savior *(US)*

Heil- *zW:* **Heilanstalt** f nursing home; *(für Sucht- oder Geisteskranke)* home; **Heilbad** nt *(Bad)* medicinal bath; *(Ort)* spa; **heilbar** adj curable

Heilbutt ['haɪlbʊt] **(-s, -e)** m halibut

heilen vt to cure ▷ vi to heal; **als geheilt entlassen werden** to be discharged with a clean bill of health

heilfroh adj very relieved

Heilgymnastin f physiotherapist

heilig ['haɪlɪç] adj holy; **jdm ~ sein** *(lit, fig)* to be sacred to sb; **die H~e Schrift** the Holy Scriptures pl; **es ist mein ~er Ernst** I am deadly serious; *siehe auch* **heiligsprechen**; **Heiligabend** m Christmas Eve

Heilige, r f(m) saint

heiligen vt to sanctify, hallow; **der Zweck heiligt die Mittel** the end justifies the means

Heiligenschein m halo

Heiligkeit f holiness

heiligsprechen unreg vt to canonize

Heiligtum nt shrine; *(Gegenstand)* relic

Heilkunde f medicine

heillos adj unholy; *(Schreck)* terrible

Heil- *zW:* **Heilmittel** nt remedy; **Heilpraktiker, in (-s, -)** m(f) non-medical practitioner; **heilsam** adj *(fig)* salutary

Heilsarmee f Salvation Army

Heilung f cure

heim [haɪm] adv home

Heim (-(e)s, -e) nt home; *(Wohnheim)* hostel

Heimarbeit f *(Industrie)* homework, outwork

Heimat ['haɪmaːt] **(-, -en)** f home *(town/ country etc)*; **Heimatfilm** m *sentimental film in idealized regional setting*; **Heimatkunde** f *(Sch)* local history; **Heimatland** nt homeland; **heimatlich** adj native, home attrib; *(Gefühle)* nostalgic; **heimatlos** adj homeless; **Heimatmuseum** nt local history museum; **Heimatort** m home town od area; **Heimatvertriebene, r** f(m) displaced person

heimbegleiten vt to accompany home

Heimchen nt: **~ (am Herd)** *(pej: Frau)* housewife

Heimcomputer m home computer

heimelig ['haɪməlɪç] adj homely

Heim- *zW:* **heimfahren** unreg vi to drive od go home; **Heimfahrt** f journey home; **Heimgang** m return home; *(Tod)* decease;

heimgehen unreg vi to go home; *(sterben)* to pass away; **heimisch** adj *(gebürtig)* native; **sich heimisch fühlen** to feel at home; **Heimkehr (-, -en)** f homecoming; **heimkehren** vi to return home; **Heimkind** nt *child brought up in a home*; **heimkommen** unreg vi to come home; **Heimleiter** m warden of a home/hostel

heimlich adj secret ▷ adv: **~, still und leise** *(umg)* quietly, on the quiet; **Heimlichkeit** f secrecy; **Heimlichtuerei** f secrecy

Heim- *zW:* **Heimreise** f journey home; **Heimspiel** nt home game; **heimsuchen** vt to afflict; *(Geist)* to haunt; **heimtückisch** adj malicious; **heimwärts** adv homewards; **Heimweg** m way home; **Heimweh** nt homesickness; **Heimweh haben** to be homesick; **Heimwerker** m handyman; **heimzahlen** vt: **jdm etw heimzahlen** to pay back sb for sth

Heini ['haɪni] **(-s, -s)** m: **blöder ~** *(umg)* silly idiot

Heirat ['haɪraːt] **(-, -en)** f marriage; **heiraten** vt, vi to marry

Heirats- *zW:* **Heiratsantrag** m proposal *(of marriage)*; **Heiratsanzeige** f *(Annonce)* advertisement for a marriage partner; **Heiratsschwindler** m *person who makes a marriage proposal under false pretences*; **Heiratsurkunde** f marriage certificate

heiser ['haɪzər] adj hoarse; **Heiserkeit** f hoarseness

heiß [haɪs] adj hot; *(Thema)* hotly disputed; *(Diskussion, Kampf)* heated, fierce; *(Begierde, Liebe, Wunsch)* burning; **es wird nichts so ~ gegessen, wie es gekocht wird** *(Sprichwort)* things are never as bad as they seem; **~er Draht** hot line; **~es Eisen** *(fig: umg)* hot potato; **~es Geld** hot money; **~ ersehnt** longed for; **~ umstritten** hotly debated; **jdn/etw ~ und innig lieben** to love sb/sth madly; **heißblütig** adj hot-blooded

heißen ['haɪsən] unreg vi to be called; *(bedeuten)* to mean ▷ vt to command; *(nennen)* to name ▷ vi unpers: **es heißt hier ...** it says here ...; **es heißt, dass ...** they say that ...; **wie ~ Sie?** what's your name?; **... und wie sie alle ~ ...** and the rest of them; **das will schon etwas ~** that's quite something; **jdn willkommen ~** to bid sb welcome; **das heißt** that is; *(mit anderen Worten)* that is to say

Heiß- *zW:* **Heißhunger** m ravenous hunger; **heißlaufen** unreg vi, vr to overheat; **Heißluft** f hot air; **Heißwasserbereiter** m water heater

heiter ['haɪtər] adj cheerful; *(Wetter)* bright; **aus ~em Himmel** *(fig)* out of the blue; **Heiterkeit** f cheerfulness; *(Belustigung)* amusement

heizbar adj heated; *(Raum)* with heating; **leicht ~** easily heated

Heizdecke f electric blanket

heizen vt to heat

Heizer (-s, -) m stoker

Heiz- *zW:* **Heizgerät** nt heater; **Heizkörper**

h

m radiator; **Heizöl** *nt* fuel oil; **Heizsonne** *f* electric fire

Heizung *f* heating

Heizungsanlage *f* heating system

Hektar [hɛk'taːr] (**-s, -e**) *nt od m* hectare

Hektik [['hɛktɪk]] *f* hectic rush; (*von Leben etc*) hectic pace

hektisch ['hɛktɪʃ] *adj* hectic

Hektoliter [hɛkto'liːtər] *m od nt* hectolitre (*Brit*), hectoliter (*US*)

Held [hɛlt] (**-en, -en**) *m* hero; **heldenhaft** ['hɛldənhaft] *adj* heroic; **Heldin** *f* heroine

helfen ['hɛlfən] *unreg vi* to help; (*nützen*) to be of use ▷ *vb unpers*: **es hilft nichts, du musst ...** it's no use, you'll have to ...; **jdm (bei etw) ~ to** help sb (with sth); **sich** *dat* **zu ~ wissen** to be resourceful; **er weiß sich** *dat* **nicht mehr zu ~** he's at his wits' end

Helfer, in (**-s, -**) *m(f)* helper, assistant

Helfershelfer *m* accomplice

Helgoland ['helgolant] (**-s**) *nt* Heligoland

hell [hɛl] *adj* clear; (*Licht, Himmel*) bright; (*Farbe*) light; **~es Bier** ≈ lager; **von etw ~ begeistert sein** to be very enthusiastic about sth; **es wird ~** it's getting light; **hellblau** *adj* light blue; **hellblond** *adj* ash-blond

Helle (**-**) *f* clearness; brightness

Heller (**-s, -**) *m* (*Hist*) farthing; **auf ~ und Pfennig** (down) to the last penny

hellhörig *adj* keen of hearing; (*Wand*) poorly soundproofed

hellicht ['hɛllɪçt] *adj siehe* **helllicht**

Helligkeit *f* clearness; brightness; lightness

helllicht ['hɛllɪçt] *adj*: **am ~en Tage** in broad daylight

hell- *zW*: **Hellraumprojektor** *m* (*Schweiz*) overhead projector; **hellsehen** *vi*: **hellsehen können** to be clairvoyant; **Hellseher, in** *m(f)* clairvoyant; **hellwach** *adj* wide-awake

Helm ['hɛlm] (**-(e)s, -e**) *m* helmet

Helsinki ['hɛlzɪŋki] (**-s**) *nt* Helsinki

Hemd [hɛmt] (**-(e)s, -en**) *nt* shirt; (*Unterhemd*) vest; **Hemdbluse** *f* blouse

Hemdenknopf *m* shirt button

hemdsärmelig *adj* shirt-sleeved; (*fig: umg: salopp*) pally; (*Ausdrucksweise*) casual

Hemisphäre [hemi'sfɛːrə] *f* hemisphere

hemmen ['hɛmən] *vt* to check, hold up; **gehemmt sein** to be inhibited

Hemmschuh *m* (*fig*) impediment

Hemmung *f* check; (*Psych*) inhibition; (*Bedenken*) scruple

hemmungslos *adj* unrestrained, without restraint

Hengst [hɛŋst] (**-es, -e**) *m* stallion

Henkel ['hɛŋkəl] (**-s, -**) *m* handle; **Henkelkrug** *m* jug; **Henkelmann** (*umg*) *m* (*Gefäß*) canteen

henken ['hɛŋkən] *vt* to hang

Henker (**-s, -**) *m* hangman

Henne ['hɛnə] (**-, -n**) *f* hen

Hepatitis [hepa'tiːtɪs] *f* (**-, Hepatitiden**) hepatitis

SCHLÜSSELWORT

her [heːr] *adv* **1** (*Richtung*): **komm her zu mir** come here (to me); **von England her** from England; **von weit her** from a long way away; **her damit!** hand it over!; **wo bist du her?** where do you come from?; **wo hat er das her?** where did he get that from?; **hinter jdm/etw her sein** to be after sb/sth

2 (*Blickpunkt*): **von der Form her** as far as the form is concerned

3 (*zeitlich*): **das ist 5 Jahre her** that was 5 years ago; **ich kenne ihn von früher her** I know him from before

herab [hɛ'rap] *adv* down, downward(s); **herabhängen** *unreg vi* to hang down; **herablassen** *unreg vt* to let down ▷ *vr* to condescend; **herablassend** *adj* condescending; **Herablassung** *f* condescension; **herabsehen** *unreg vi*: **herabsehen (auf +akk)** to look down (on); **herabsetzen** *vt* to lower, reduce; (*fig*) to belittle, disparage; **zu stark herabgesetzten Preisen** at greatly reduced prices; **Herabsetzung** *f* reduction; disparagement; **herabstufen** *vt* to downgrade; **herabstürzen** *vi* to fall off; (*Felsbrocken*) to fall down; **von etw herabstürzen** to fall off sth; to fall down from sth; **herabwürdigen** *vt* to belittle, disparage

heran [hɛ'ran] *adv*: **näher ~!** come closer!; **~ zu mir!** come up to me!; **heranbilden** *vt* to train; **heranbringen** *unreg vt*: **heranbringen (an +akk)** to bring up (to); **heranfahren** *unreg vi*: **heranfahren (an +akk)** to drive up (to); **herangehen** *unreg vi*: **an etw** *akk* **herangehen** (*an Problem, Aufgabe*) to tackle sth; **herankommen** *unreg vi*: (**an jdn/etw**) **herankommen** to approach (sb/sth), come near ((to) sb/sth); **er lässt alle Probleme an sich herankommen** he always adopts a wait-and-see attitude; **heranmachen** *vr*: **sich an jdn heranmachen** to make up to sb; (*umg*) to approach sb; **heranwachsen** *unreg vi* to grow up; **Heranwachsende, r** *f(m)* adolescent; **heranwinken** *vt* to beckon over; (*Taxi*) to hail; **heranziehen** *unreg vt* to pull nearer; (*aufziehen*) to raise; (*ausbilden*) to train; (*zu Hilfe holen*) to call in; (*Literatur*) to consult; **etw zum Vergleich heranziehen** to use sth by way of comparison; **jdn zu etw heranziehen** to call upon sb to help in sth

herauf [hɛ'raʊf] *adv* up, upward(s), up here; **heraufbeschwören** *unreg vt* to conjure up, evoke; **heraufbringen** *unreg vt* to bring up; **heraufsetzen** *vt* to increase; **heraufziehen** *unreg vt* to draw *od* pull up ▷ *vi* to approach; (*Sturm*) to gather

heraus [hɛ'raʊs] *adv* out; **nach vorn ~ wohnen** to live at the front (of the house); **aus dem Gröbsten ~ sein** to be over the worst; **~ mit der Sprache!** out with it!; **herausarbeiten** *vt* to work out; **herausbekommen** *unreg vt* to get out; (*fig*) to find *od* figure out; (*Wechselgeld*) to get back; **herausbringen** *unreg vt* to bring out; (*Geheimnis*) to elicit; **jdn/etw ganz groß herausbringen** (*umg*) to give sb/sth a big build-up; **aus ihm war kein Wort herauszubringen** they couldn't get a single word out of him; **herausfinden** *unreg vt* to find out; **herausfordern** *vt* to challenge; (*provozieren*) to provoke; **Herausforderung** *f* challenge; provocation; **herausgeben** *unreg vt* to give up, surrender; (*Geld*) to give back; (*Buch*) to edit; (*veröffentlichen*) to publish ▷ *vi* (*Wechselgeld geben*): **können Sie (mir) herausgeben?** can you give me change?; **Herausgeber** (**-s, -**) *m* editor; (*Verleger*) publisher; **herausgehen** *unreg vi*: **aus sich herausgehen** to come out of one's shell; **heraushalten** *unreg vr*: **sich aus etw heraushalten** to keep out of sth; **heraushängen** *unreg vt, vi* to hang out; **herausholen** *vt*: **herausholen (aus)** to get out (of); **heraushören** *vt* (*wahrnehmen*) to hear; (*fühlen*): **heraushören (aus)** to detect (in); **herauskehren** *vt* (*fig*): **den Vorgesetzten herauskehren** to act the boss; **herauskommen** *unreg vi* to come out; **dabei kommt nichts heraus** nothing will come of it; **er kam aus dem Staunen nicht heraus** he couldn't get over his astonishment; **es kommt auf dasselbe heraus** it comes (down) to the same thing; **herausnehmen** *unreg vt* to take out; **sich** *dat* **Freiheiten herausnehmen** to take liberties; **Sie nehmen sich zu viel heraus** you're going too far; **herausputzen** *vt*: **sich herausputzen** to get dressed up; **herausreden** *vr* to talk one's way out of it (*umg*); **herausreißen** *unreg vt* to tear out; (*Zahn, Baum*) to pull out; **herausrücken** *vt* (*Geld*) to fork out, hand over; **mit etw herausrücken** (*fig*) to come out with sth; **herausrutschen** *vi* to slip out; **herausschlagen** *unreg vt* to knock out; (*fig*) to obtain; **herausstellen** *vr*: **sich herausstellen (als)** to turn out (to be); **das muss sich erst herausstellen** that remains to be seen; **herausstrecken** *vt* to stick out; **heraussuchen** *vt*: **sich** *dat* **jdn/etw heraussuchen** to pick out sb/ sth; **heraustreten** *unreg vi*: **heraustreten (aus)** to come out (of); **herauswachsen** *unreg vi*: **herauswachsen aus** to grow out of; **herauswinden** *unreg vr* (*fig*): **sich aus etw herauswinden** to wriggle out of sth; **herauswollen** *vi*: **nicht mit etw herauswollen** (*umg*: *sagen wollen*) to not want to come out with sth; **herausziehen** *unreg vt* to pull out, extract

herb [hɛrp] *adj* (slightly) bitter, acid; (*Wein*) dry; (*fig*: *schmerzlich*) bitter; (: *streng*) stern, austere

herbei [hɛr'baɪ] *adv* (over) here; **herbeiführen** *vt* to bring about; **herbeischaffen** *vt* to procure; **herbeisehnen** *vt* to long for

herbemühen ['he:rbəmy:ən] *vr* to take the

trouble to come

Herberge ['hɛrbɛrgə] (**-, -n**) *f* (*Jugendherberge etc*) hostel

Herbergsmutter *f* warden

Herbergsvater *m* warden

herbitten *unreg vt* to ask to come (here)

herbringen *unreg vt* to bring here

Herbst [hɛrpst] (**-(e)s, -e**) *m* autumn, fall (*US*); **im ~** in autumn, in the fall (*US*); **herbstlich** *adj* autumnal

Herd [he:rt] (**-(e)s, -e**) *m* cooker; (*fig, Med*) focus, centre (*Brit*), center (*US*)

Herde ['he:rdə] (**-, -n**) *f* herd; (*Schafherde*) flock

Herdentrieb *m* (*lit, fig: pej*) herd instinct

Herdplatte *f* (*von Elektroherd*) hotplate

herein [hɛ'raɪn] *adv* in (here), here; **~!** come in!; **hereinbitten** *unreg vt* to ask in; **hereinbrechen** *unreg vi* to set in; **hereinbringen** *unreg vt* to bring in; **hereindürfen** *unreg vi* to have permission to enter; **Hereinfall** *m* letdown; **hereinfallen** *unreg vi* to be caught, be taken in; **hereinfallen auf** +*akk* to fall for; **hereinkommen** *unreg vi* to come in; **hereinlassen** *unreg vt* to admit; **hereinlegen** *vt*: **jdn hereinlegen** to take sb in; **hereinplatzen** *vi* to burst in; **hereinschneien** (*umg*) *vi* to drop in; **hereinspazieren** *vi*: **hereinspaziert!** come right in!

her- *zW*: **Herfahrt** *f* journey here; **herfallen** *unreg vi*: **herfallen über** +*akk* to fall upon; **Hergang** *m* course of events, circumstances *pl*; **hergeben** *unreg vt* to give, hand (over); **sich zu etw hergeben** to lend one's name to sth; **das Thema gibt viel/nichts her** there's a lot/nothing to this topic; **hergebracht** *adj*: **in hergebrachter Weise** in the traditional way; **hergehen** *unreg vi*: **hinter jdm hergehen** to follow sb; **es geht hoch her** there are a lot of goings-on; **herhaben** *unreg* (*umg*) *vt*: **wo hat er das her?** where did he get that from?; **herhalten** *unreg vt* to hold out; **herhalten müssen** (*umg*) to have to suffer; **herhören** *vi* to listen; **hör mal her!** listen here!

Hering ['he:rɪŋ] (**-s, -e**) *m* herring; (*Zeltpflock*) (tent) peg

herkommen *unreg vi* to come; **komm mal her!** come here!

herkömmlich *adj* traditional

Herkunft (**-, -künfte**) *f* origin

Herkunftsland *nt* (*Comm*) country of origin

her- *zW*: **herlaufen** *unreg vi*: **herlaufen hinter** +*dat* to run after; **herleiten** *vr* to derive; **hermachen** *vr*: **sich hermachen über** +*akk* to set about *od* upon ▷ *vt* (*umg*): **viel hermachen** to look impressive

Hermelin [hɛrmə'li:n] (**-s, -e**) *m od nt* ermine

hermetisch [hɛr'me:tɪʃ] *adj* hermetic; **~ abgeriegelt** completely sealed off

her- *zW*: **hernach** *adv* afterwards; **hernehmen** *unreg vt*: **wo soll ich das hernehmen?** where am I supposed to get that from?; **hernieder** *adv* down

Heroin [hero'i:n] (**-s**) *nt* heroin; **heroinsüchtig**

adj addicted to heroin; **Heroinsüchtige, r** *f(m)* heroin addict

heroisch [heˈroːɪʃ] *adj* heroic

Herold [ˈheːrɔlt] **(-(e)s, -e)** *m* herald

Herpes [[ˈhɛrpɛs]] *m* **(-)** *(Med)* herpes

Herr [hɛr] **(-(e)n, -en)** *m* master; *(Mann)* gentleman; *(adliger, Rel)* Lord; *(vor Namen)* Mr; **mein ~!** sir!; **meine ~en!** gentlemen!; **Lieber ~ A, Sehr geehrter ~ A** *(in Brief)* Dear Mr A; **„~en"** *(Toilette)* "gentlemen" *(Brit)*, "men's room" *(US)*; **die ~en der Schöpfung** *(hum: Männer)* the gentlemen

Herrchen *(umg)* *nt (von Hund)* master

Herren- *zW:* **Herrenbekanntschaft** *f* gentleman friend; **Herrenbekleidung** *f* menswear; **Herrenbesuch** *m* gentleman visitor *od* visitors; **Herrendoppel** *nt* men's doubles; **Herreneinzel** *nt* men's singles; **herrenlos** *adj* ownerless; **Herrenmagazin** *nt* men's magazine

Herrgott *m:* **~ noch mal!** damn it all!

Herrgottsfrühe *f:* **in aller ~** *(umg)* at the crack of dawn

herrichten [ˈheːrrɪçtən] *vt* to prepare

Herrin *f* mistress

herrisch *adj* domineering

herrje [hɛrˈjeː] *interj* goodness gracious!

herrjemine [hɛrˈjeːmine] *interj* goodness gracious!

herrlich *adj* marvellous *(Brit)*, marvelous *(US)*, splendid; **Herrlichkeit** *f* splendour *(Brit)*, splendor *(US)*, magnificence

Herrschaft *f* power, rule; *(Herr und Herrin)* master and mistress; **meine ~en!** ladies and gentlemen!

herrschen [ˈhɛrʃən] *vi* to rule; *(bestehen)* to prevail, be; **hier ~ ja Zustände!** things are in a pretty state round here!

Herrscher, in **(-s, -)** *m(f)* ruler

Herrschsucht *f* domineeringness

her- *zW:* **herrühren** *vi* to arise, originate; **hersagen** *vt* to recite; **hersehen** *unreg vi:* **hinter jdm/etw hersehen** to follow sb/sth with one's eyes

her sein *siehe* **her**

her- *zW:* **herstammen** *vi* to descend *od* come from; **herstellen** *vt* to make, manufacture; *(zustande bringen)* to establish; **Hersteller (-s, -)** *m* manufacturer; **Herstellung** *f* manufacture; **Herstellungskosten** *pl* manufacturing costs *pl*; **hertragen** *unreg vt:* **etw hinter jdm hertragen** to carry sth behind sb

herüber [heˈryːbər] *adv* over (here), across

herum [hɛˈrʊm] *adv* about, (a)round; **um etw ~** around sth; **herumärgern** *vr:* **sich herumärgern (mit)** to get annoyed (with); **herumblättern** *vi:* **herumblättern in** *+dat* to browse *od* flick through; **herumdoktern** *(umg)* *vi* to fiddle *od* tinker about; **herumdrehen** *vt:* **jdm das Wort im Mund herumdrehen** to twist sb's words; **herumdrücken** *vr (vermeiden):* **sich um etw herumdrücken** to dodge sth; **herumfahren** *unreg vi* to travel around; *(mit Auto)* to drive around; *(sich rasch umdrehen)* to spin (a)round; **herumführen** *vt* to show around; **herumgammeln** *(umg)* *vi* to bum around; **herumgehen** *unreg vi (herumspazieren)* to walk about; **um etw herumgehen** to walk *od* go round sth; **etw herumgehen lassen** to circulate sth; **herumhacken** *vi (fig: umg):* **auf jdm herumhacken** to pick on sb; **herumirren** *vi* to wander about; **herumkommen** *unreg (umg)* *vi:* **um etw herumkommen** to get out of sth; **er ist viel herumgekommen** he has been around a lot; **herumkriegen** *vt* to bring *od* talk round; **herumlungern** *vi* to lounge about; *(umg)* to hang around; **herumquälen** *vr:* **sich mit Rheuma herumquälen** to be plagued by rheumatism; **herumreißen** *unreg vt* to swing around (hard); **herumschlagen** *unreg vr:* **sich mit etw herumschlagen** *(umg)* to tussle with sth; **herumschleppen** *vt:* **etw mit sich herumschleppen** *(Sorge, Problem)* to be troubled by sth; *(Krankheit)* to have sth; **herumsprechen** *unreg vr* to get around, be spread; **herumstochern** *(umg)* *vi:* **im Essen herumstochern** to pick at one's food; **herumtreiben** *unreg vi, vr* to drift about; **Herumtreiber, in (-s, -)** *(pej)* *m(f)* tramp; **herumziehen** *unreg vi, vr* to wander about

herunter [heˈrʊntər] *adv* downward(s), down (there); **mit den Nerven/der Gesundheit ~ sein** *(umg)* to be at the end of one's tether/be run-down; **herunterbrechen** *unreg vt (Zahlen, Kalkulation)* to break down; **herunterfahren** *unreg vti (Comput, Tech)* to shut down; **heruntergekommen** *adj* run-down; **herunterhandeln** *(umg)* *vt (Preis)* to beat down; **herunterhängen** *unreg vi* to hang down; **herunterholen** *vt* to bring down; **herunterkommen** *unreg vi* to come down; *(fig)* to come down in the world; **herunterladbar** *adj (Comput)* downloadable; **herunterladen** *unreg vt (Comput)* to download; **herunterleiern** *(umg)* *vt* to reel off; **heruntermachen** *vt* to take down; *(schlechtmachen)* to run down, knock; **herunterputzen** *(umg)* *vt:* **jdn herunterputzen** to tear sb off a strip; **herunterspielen** *vt* to play down; **herunterwirtschaften** *(umg)* *vt* to bring to the brink of ruin

hervor [hɛrˈfoːr] *adv* out, forth; **hervorbrechen** *unreg vi* to burst forth, break out; **hervorbringen** *unreg vt* to produce; *(Wort)* to utter; **hervorgehen** *unreg vi* to emerge, result; **daraus geht hervor, dass …** from this it follows that …; **hervorheben** *unreg vt* to stress; *(als Kontrast)* to set off; **hervorragend** *adj* excellent; *(lit)* projecting; **hervorrufen** *unreg vt* to cause, give rise to; **hervorstechen** *unreg vi (lit, fig)* to stand out; **hervorstoßen** *unreg vt (Worte)* to gasp (out); **hervortreten** *unreg vi* to come out; **hervortun** *unreg vr* to distinguish o.s.; *(umg: sich wichtigtun)* to show off; **sich mit etw hervortun** to show off sth

Herz [hɛrts] **(-ens, -en)** *nt* heart; *(Karten: Farbe)*

hearts *pl*; **mit ganzem ~en** wholeheartedly; **etw auf dem ~en haben** to have sth on one's mind; **sich** *dat* **etw zu ~en nehmen** to take sth to heart; **du sprichst mir aus dem ~en** that's just what I feel; **es liegt mir am ~en** I am very concerned about it; **seinem ~en Luft machen** to give vent to one's feelings; **sein ~ an jdn/etw hängen** to commit o.s. heart and soul to sb/sth; **ein ~ und eine Seele sein** to be the best of friends; **jdn/etw auf ~ und Nieren prüfen** to examine sb/sth very thoroughly; **Herzanfall** *m* heart attack; **Herzbeschwerden** *pl* heart trouble *sing*

herzen *vt* to caress, embrace

Herzenslust *f*: **nach ~** to one's heart's content

Herz- *zW*: **herzergreifend** *adj* heart-rending; **herzerweichend** *adj* heartrending; **Herzfehler** *m* heart defect; **herzhaft** *adj* hearty

herziehen ['hɛːrtsiːən] *vi*: **über jdn/etw ~** (*umg*) to pull sb/sth to pieces (*fig*)

Herz- *zW*: **Herzinfarkt** *m* heart attack; **Herzklappe** *f* (heart) valve; **Herzklopfen** *nt* palpitation; **herzkrank** *adj* suffering from a heart condition

herzlich *adj* cordial ▷ *adv* (*sehr*): **~ gern!** with the greatest of pleasure!; **~en Glückwunsch** congratulations *pl*; **~e Grüße** best wishes; **Herzlichkeit** *f* cordiality

herzlos *adj* heartless; **Herzlosigkeit** *f* heartlessness

Herzog ['hɛrtsoːk] (**-(e)s, ̈-e**) *m* duke; **Herzogin** *f* duchess; **herzoglich** *adj* ducal; **Herzogtum** *nt* duchy

Herz- *zW*: **Herzschlag** *m* heartbeat; (*Med*) heart attack; **Herzschrittmacher** *m* pacemaker; **herzzerreißend** *adj* heartrending

Hesse ['hɛsə] (**-n, -n**) *m* Hessian

Hessen ['hɛsən] (**-s**) *nt* Hesse

Hessin *f* Hessian

hessisch *adj* Hessian

heterogen [hetero'geːn] *adj* heterogeneous

heterosexuell [heterozɛksu'ɛl] *adj* heterosexual

Hetze ['hɛtsə] *f* (*Eile*) rush

hetzen *vt* to hunt; (*verfolgen*) to chase ▷ *vi* (*eilen*) to rush; **jdn/etw auf jdn/etw ~** to set sb/sth on sb/sth; **~ gegen** to stir up feeling against; **~ zu** to agitate for

Hetzerei [hɛtsə'raɪ] *f* agitation; (*Eile*) rush

Hetzkampagne ['hɛtskampanjə] *f* smear campaign

Heu [hɔʏ] (**-(e)s**) *nt* hay; **Heuboden** *m* hayloft

Heuchelei [hɔʏçə'laɪ] *f* hypocrisy

heucheln ['hɔʏçəln] *vt* to pretend, feign ▷ *vi* to be hypocritical

Heuchler, in [hɔʏçlər(ɪn)] (**-s, -**) *m(f)* hypocrite; **heuchlerisch** *adj* hypocritical

Heuer ['hɔʏər] (**-, -n**) *f* (*Naut*) pay

heuer *adv* this year

heuern ['hɔʏərn] *vt* to sign on, hire

Heugabel *f* pitchfork

Heuhaufen *m* haystack

heulen ['hɔʏlən] *vi* to howl; (*weinen*) to cry; **das**

~de Elend bekommen to get the blues

heurig ['hɔʏrɪç] *adj* this year's

Heuschnupfen *m* hay fever

Heuschrecke *f* grasshopper; (*in heißen Ländern*) locust

heute ['hɔʏtə] *adv* today; **~ Abend/früh** this evening/morning; **~ Morgen** this morning; **~ in einer Woche** a week today, today week; **von ~ auf morgen** (*fig: plötzlich*) overnight, from one day to the next; **das H~** today

heutig ['hɔʏtɪç] *adj* today's; **unser ~es Schreiben** (*Comm*) our letter of today('s date)

heutzutage ['hɔʏttsutaːgə] *adv* nowadays

Hexe ['hɛksə] (**-, -n**) *f* witch

hexen *vi* to practise witchcraft; **ich kann doch nicht ~** I can't work miracles

Hexen- *zW*: **Hexenhäuschen** *nt* gingerbread house; **Hexenkessel** *m* (*lit, fig*) cauldron; **Hexenmeister** *m* wizard; **Hexenschuss** *m* lumbago

Hexerei [hɛksə'raɪ] *f* witchcraft

HG *f abk* = **Handelsgesellschaft**

Hg. *abk* (= *Herausgeber*) ed.

hg. *abk* (= *herausgegeben*) ed.

HGB (**-**) *nt abk* (= *Handelsgesetzbuch*) *statutes of commercial law*

Hieb (**-(e)s, -e**) *m* blow; (*Wunde*) cut, gash; (*Stichelei*) cutting remark; **~e bekommen** to get a thrashing

hieb *etc* [hiːp] *vb* (*veraltet*) *siehe* **hauen**

hieb- und stichfest *adj* (*fig*) watertight

hielt *etc* [hiːlt] *vb siehe* **halten**

hier [hiːr] *adv* here; **~ spricht Dr. Müller** (*Tel*) this is Dr Müller (speaking); **er ist von ~** he's a local (man); *siehe auch* **hierbehalten**; **hierbleiben; hierlassen**

Hierarchie [hierar'çiː] *f* hierarchy

hier- *zW*: **hierauf** *adv* thereupon; (*danach*) after that; **hieraus** *adv*: **hieraus folgt, dass ...** from this it follows that ...; **hierbehalten** *unreg vt* to keep here; **hierbei** *adv* (*bei dieser Gelegenheit*) on this occasion; **hierbleiben** *unreg vi* to stay here; **hierdurch** *adv* by this means; (*örtlich*) through here; **hierher** *adv* this way, here; **hierher gehören** to belong here; (*fig: relevant sein*) to be relevant; **hierlassen** *unreg vt* to leave here; **hiermit** *adv* hereby; **hiermit erkläre ich ...** (*form*) I hereby declare ...; **hiernach** *adv* hereafter; **hiervon** *adv* about this, hereof; **hiervon abgesehen** apart from this; **hierzu** *adv* (*dafür*) for this; (*dazu*) with this; (*außerdem*) in addition to this, moreover; (*zu diesem Punkt*) about this; **hierzulande, hier zu Lande** *adv* in this country

hiesig ['hiːzɪç] *adj* of this place, local

hieß *etc* [hiːs] *vb siehe* **heißen**

Hi-Fi-Anlage ['haɪfianlaːgə] *f* hi-fi set *od* system

Hightechindustrie ['haɪtɛkɪndʊs'triː] *f* high tech *od* hi-tech industry

Hilfe ['hɪlfə] (**-, -n**) *f* help; (*für Notleidende*) aid; **Erste ~** first aid; **jdm ~ leisten** to help sb; **~!** help!; **Hilfeleistung** *f*: **unterlassene**

Hilfeleistung (Jur) denial of assistance; **Hilfestellung** f (Sport, fig) support

Hilf- zW: **hilflos** adj helpless; **Hilflosigkeit** f helplessness; **hilfreich** adj helpful

Hilfs- zW: **Hilfsaktion** f relief action, relief measures pl; **Hilfsarbeiter** m labourer (Brit), laborer (US); **hilfsbedürftig** adj needy; **hilfsbereit** adj ready to help; **Hilfskraft** f assistant, helper; **Hilfsmittel** nt aid; **Hilfsschule** f school for backward children; **Hilfszeitwort** nt auxiliary verb

hilft [hɪlft] vb siehe **helfen**

Himalaja [hi'ma:laja] (**-s**) m: **der ~** the Himalayas pl

Himbeere ['hɪmbeːrə] (**-, -n**) f raspberry

Himmel ['hɪməl] (**-s, -**) m sky; (Rel) heaven; **um ~s willen** (umg) for Heaven's sake; **zwischen ~ und Erde** in midair; **himmelangst** adj: **es ist mir himmelangst** I'm scared to death; **Himmelbett** nt four-poster bed; **himmelblau** adj sky-blue

Himmelfahrt f Ascension

Himmelfahrtskommando nt (Mil: umg) suicide squad; (Unternehmen) suicide mission

Himmelreich nt (Rel) Kingdom of Heaven

himmelschreiend adj outrageous

Himmelsrichtung f direction; **die vier ~en** the four points of the compass

himmelweit adj: **ein ~er Unterschied** a world of difference

himmlisch ['hɪmlɪʃ] adj heavenly

SCHLÜSSELWORT

hin [hɪn] adv **1** (Richtung): **hin und zurück** there and back; **einmal London hin und zurück** a return to London (Brit), a roundtrip ticket to London (US); **hin und her** to and fro; **etw hin und her überlegen** to turn sth over and over in one's mind; **bis zur Mauer hin** up to the wall; **wo ist er hin?** where has he gone?; **nichts wie hin!** (umg) let's go then!; **nach außen hin** (fig) outwardly; **Geld hin, Geld her** money or no money

2 (auf ... hin): **auf meine Bitte hin** at my request; **auf seinen Rat hin** on the basis of his advice; **auf meinen Brief hin** on the strength of my letter

3: hin sein (umg: kaputt sein) to have had it; (Ruhe) to be gone; **mein Glück ist hin** my happiness has gone; **hin und wieder** (every) now and again

hinab [hɪ'nap] adv down; **hinabgehen** unreg vi to go down; **hinabsehen** unreg vi to look down

hinarbeiten ['hɪnarbaɪtən] vi: **auf etw** akk **~** (auf Ziel) to work towards sth

hinauf [hɪ'naʊf] adv up; **hinaufarbeiten** vr to work one's way up; **hinaufsteigen** unreg vi to climb

hinaus [hɪ'naʊs] adv out; **hinten/vorn ~** at the back/front; **darüber ~** over and above this; **auf Jahre ~** for years to come;

hinausbefördern vt to kick od throw out; **hinausfliegen** unreg (umg) vi to be kicked out; **hinausführen** vi: **über etw** akk **hinausführen** (lit, fig) to go beyond sth; **hinausgehen** unreg vi to go out; **hinausgehen über** +akk to exceed; **hinauslaufen** unreg vi to run out; **hinauslaufen auf** +akk to come to, amount to; **hinausschieben** unreg vt to put off, postpone; **hinausschießen** unreg vi: **über das Ziel hinausschießen** (fig) to overshoot the mark; **hinauswachsen** unreg vi: **er wuchs über sich selbst hinaus** he surpassed himself; **hinauswerfen** unreg vt to throw out; **hinauswollen** vi to want to go out; **hoch hinauswollen** to aim high; **hinauswollen auf** +akk to drive at, get at; **hinausziehen** unreg vt to draw out ▷ vr to be protracted; **hinauszögern** vt to delay, put off ▷ vr to be delayed, be put off

hinbekommen unreg (umg) vt: **das hast du gut ~** you've made a good job of it

hinblättern (umg) vt (Geld) to fork out

Hinblick ['hɪnblɪk] m: **in** od **im ~ auf** +akk in view of

hinderlich ['hɪndərlɪç] adj awkward; **jds Karriere** dat **~ sein** to be a hindrance to sb's career

hindern vt to hinder, hamper; **jdn an etw** dat **~** to prevent sb from doing sth

Hindernis (**-ses, -se**) nt obstacle; **Hindernislauf** m, **Hindernisrennen** nt steeplechase

Hinderungsgrund m obstacle

hindeuten ['hɪndɔytən] vi: **~ auf** +akk to point to

Hinduismus [hɪndu'ɪsmʊs] m Hinduism

hindurch [hɪn'dʊrç] adv through; across; (zeitlich) over

hindürfen [hɪn'dʏrfən] unreg vi: **~ (zu)** to be allowed to go (to)

hinein [hɪ'naɪn] adv in; **bis tief in die Nacht ~** well into the night; **hineinfallen** unreg vi to fall in; **hineinfallen in** +akk to fall into; **hineinfinden** unreg vr (fig: sich vertraut machen) to find one's feet; (sich abfinden) to come to terms with it; **hineingehen** unreg vi to go in; **hineingehen in** +akk to go into, enter; **hineingeraten** unreg vi: **hineingeraten in** +akk to get into; **hineinknien** vr (fig: umg): **sich in etw** akk **hineinknien** to get into sth; **hineinlesen** unreg vt: **etw in etw** akk **hineinlesen** to read sth into sth; **hineinpassen** vi to fit in; **hineinpassen in** +akk to fit into; **hineinprügeln** vt: **etw in jdn hineinprügeln** to cudgel sth into sb; **hineinreden** vi: **jdm hineinreden** to interfere in sb's affairs; **hineinstecken** vt: **Geld/Arbeit in etw** akk **hineinstecken** to put money/some work into sth; **hineinsteigern** vr to get worked up; **hineinversetzen** vr: **sich in jdn hineinversetzen** to put o.s. in sb's position; **hineinziehen** unreg vt: **hineinziehen (in** +akk) to pull in (to); **jdn in etw hineinziehen** (in Konflikt, Gespräch) to draw sb into sth

hin- *zW:* **hinfahren** *unreg vi* to go; to drive ▷ *vt* to take; to drive; **Hinfahrt** *f* journey there; **hinfallen** *unreg vi* to fall down; **hinfällig** *adj* frail, decrepit; (*Regel etc*) unnecessary; **hinfliegen** *unreg vi* to fly there; (*umg: hinfallen*) to fall over; **Hinflug** *m* outward flight

hing *etc* [hɪŋ] *vb siehe* **hängen**

hin- *zW:* **Hingabe** *f* devotion; **mit Hingabe tanzen/singen** *etc* (*fig*) to dance/sing *etc* with abandon; **hingeben** *unreg vr +dat* to give o.s. up to, devote o.s. to; **hingebungsvoll** ['hɪŋɡeːbʊŋsfɔl] *adv* (*begeistert*) with abandon; (*lauschen*) raptly

hingegen [hɪn'ɡeːɡən] *konj* however

hin- *zW:* **hingehen** *unreg vi* to go; (*Zeit*) to pass; **gehst du auch hin?** are you going too?; **hingerissen** *adj:* **hingerissen sein** to be enraptured; **hin- und hergerissen sein** (*fig*) to be torn; **ich bin ganz hin- und hergerissen** (*ironisch*) that's absolutely great; **hinhalten** *unreg vt* to hold out; (*warten lassen*) to put off, stall; **Hinhaltetaktik** *f* stalling *od* delaying tactics *pl*

hinhauen ['hɪnhaʊən] *unreg* (*umg*) *vi* (*klappen*) to work; (*ausreichen*) to do

hinhören ['hɪnhøːrən] *vi* to listen

hinken ['hɪŋkən] *vi* to limp; (*Vergleich*) to be unconvincing

hin- *zW:* **hinkommen** *unreg* (*umg*) *vi* (*auskommen*) to manage; (*: ausreichen, stimmen*) to be right; **hinlänglich** *adj* adequate ▷ *adv* adequately; **hinlegen** *vt* to put down ▷ *vr* to lie down; **sich der Länge nach hinlegen** (*umg*) to fall flat; **hinnehmen** *unreg vt* (*fig*) to put up with, take; **hinreichen** *vi* to be adequate ▷ *vt:* **jdm etw hinreichen** to hand sb sth; **hinreichend** *adj* adequate; (*genug*) sufficient; **Hinreise** *f* journey out; **hinreißen** *unreg vt* to carry away, enrapture; **sich hinreißen lassen, etw zu tun** to get carried away and do sth; **hinreißend** *adj* (*Landschaft, Anblick*) enchanting; (*Schönheit, Mensch*) captivating; **hinrichten** *vt* to execute; **Hinrichtung** *f* execution; **hinsehen** *unreg vi:* **bei genauerem Hinsehen** on closer inspection

hin sein ['hɪnzaɪn] *siehe* **hin**

hin- *zW:* **hinsetzen** *vr* to sit down; **Hinsicht** *f:* **in mancher** *od* **gewisser Hinsicht** in some respects *od* ways; **hinsichtlich** *präp +gen* with regard to; **hinsollen** (*umg*) *vi:* **wo soll ich/das Buch hin?** where do I/does the book go?; **Hinspiel** *nt* (*Sport*) first leg; **hinstellen** *vt* to put (down) ▷ *vr* to place o.s.

hinanstellen [hɪnt'|anʃtɛlən] *vt* (*fig*) to ignore

hinten ['hɪntən] *adv* behind; (*rückwärtig*) at the back; **~ und vorn** (*fig: betrügen*) left, right and centre; **das reicht ~ und vorn nicht** that's nowhere near enough; **hintendran** (*umg*) *adv* at the back; **hintenherum** *adv* round the back; (*fig*) secretly

hinter ['hɪntər] *präp* (+*dat od akk*) behind; (*: nach*) after; **~ jdm her sein** to be after sb; **~ die Wahrheit kommen** to get to the truth; **sich ~**

jdn stellen (*fig*) to support sb; **etw ~ sich** *dat* **haben** (*zurückgelegt haben*) to have got through sth; **sie hat viel ~ sich** she has been through a lot; **Hinterachse** *f* rear axle; **Hinterbänkler** (**-s, -**) *m* (*Pol: pej*) backbencher; **Hinterbein** *nt* hind leg; **sich auf die Hinterbeine stellen** to get tough; **Hinterbliebene, r** *f(m)* surviving relative; **hinterdrein** *adv* afterwards

hintere, r, s *adj* rear, back

hinter- *zW:* **hintereinander** *adv* one after the other; **zwei Tage hintereinander** two days running; **hinterfotzig** (*umg*) *adj* underhanded; **hinterfragen** *vt untr* to analyse; **Hintergedanke** *m* ulterior motive; **hintergehen** *unreg vt untr* to deceive; **Hintergrund** *m* background; **hintergründig** *adj* cryptic, enigmatic; **Hintergrundprogramm** *nt* (*Comput*) background program; **Hinterhalt** *m* ambush; **etw im Hinterhalt haben** to have sth in reserve; **hinterhältig** *adj* underhand, sneaky; **hinterher** *adv* afterwards, after; **er ist hinterher, dass ...** (*fig*) he sees to it that ...; **Hinterhof** *m* back yard; **Hinterkopf** *m* back of one's head; **Hinterland** *nt* hinterland; **hinterlassen** *unreg vt untr* to leave; **Hinterlassenschaft** *f* (testator's) estate; **hinterlegen** *vt untr* to deposit; **Hinterlegungsstelle** *f* depository; **Hinterlist** *f* cunning, trickery; (*Handlung*) trick, dodge; **hinterlistig** *adj* cunning, crafty; **Hintermann** (**-(e)s,** *pl* **-männer**) *m* person behind; **die Hintermänner des Skandals** the men behind the scandal

Hintern ['hɪntərn] (**-s, -**) (*umg*) *m* bottom, backside; **jdm den ~ versohlen** to smack sb's bottom

hinter- *zW:* **Hinterrad** *nt* back wheel; **Hinterradantrieb** *m* (*Aut*) rear-wheel drive; **hinterrücks** *adv* from behind; **Hinterteil** *nt* behind; **Hintertreffen** *nt:* **ins Hintertreffen kommen** to lose ground; **hintertreiben** *unreg vt untr* to prevent, frustrate; **Hintertreppe** *f* back stairs *pl*; **Hintertür** *f* back door; (*fig: Ausweg*) escape, loophole; **Hinterwäldler** (**-s, -**) (*umg*) *m* backwoodsman, hillbilly (*bes* US); **hinterziehen** *unreg vt untr* (*Steuern*) to evade (paying)

hintun ['hɪntuːn] *unreg* (*umg*) *vt:* **ich weiß nicht, wo ich ihn ~ soll** (*fig*) I can't (quite) place him

hinüber [hɪ'nyːbər] *adv* across, over; **hinübergehen** *unreg vi* to go over *od* across

hinunter [hɪ'nʊntər] *adv* down; **hinunterbringen** *unreg vt* to take down; **hinunterschlucken** *vt* (*lit, fig*) to swallow; **hinunterspülen** *vt* to flush away; (*Essen, Tablette*) to wash down; (*fig: Ärger*) to soothe; **hinuntersteigen** *unreg vi* to descend

Hinweg ['hɪnveːk] *m* journey out

hinweg- [hɪn'vɛk] *zW:* **hinweggehen** *unreg vi:* **über etw** *akk* **hinweggehen** (*fig*) to pass over sth; **hinweghelfen** *unreg vi:* **jdm**

über etw *akk* **hinweghelfen** to help sb
to get over sth; **hinwegkommen** *unreg vi*
(*fig*): **über etw** *akk* **hinwegkommen** to get
over sth; **hinwegsehen** *unreg vi*: **darüber
hinwegsehen, dass …** to overlook the fact
that …; **hinwegsetzen** *vr*: **sich hinwegsetzen
über** +*akk* to disregard

Hinweis ['hɪnvaɪs] (**-es, -e**) *m* (*Andeutung*) hint;
(*Anweisung*) instruction; (*Verweis*) reference;
sachdienliche ~e relevant information

hinweisen *unreg vi*: **~ auf** +*akk* to point to;
(*verweisen*) to refer to; **darauf ~, dass …** to
point out that …; (*anzeigen*) to indicate that …

Hinweisschild *nt* sign

Hinweistafel *f* sign

hinwerfen *unreg vt* to throw down; **eine
hingeworfene Bemerkung** a casual remark

hinwirken *vi*: **auf etw** *akk* **~** to work towards
sth

Hinz [hɪnts] *m*: **~ und Kunz** (*umg*) every Tom,
Dick and Harry

hinziehen *unreg vr* (*fig*) to drag on

hinzielen *vi*: **~ auf** +*akk* to aim at

hinzu [hɪn'tsuː] *adv* in addition; **hinzufügen** *vt*
to add; **Hinzufügung** *f*: **unter Hinzufügung
von etw** (*form*) by adding sth; **hinzukommen**
unreg vi: **es kommt noch hinzu, dass …** there
is also the fact that …; **hinzuziehen** *unreg vt* to
consult

Hiobsbotschaft ['hiːɔpsboːtʃaft] *f* bad news

Hirn [hɪrn] (**-(e)s, -e**) *nt* brain(s); **Hirngespinst**
(**-(e)s, -e**) *nt* fantasy; **Hirnhautentzündung**
f (*Med*) meningitis; **hirntot** *adj* braindead;
hirnverbrannt *adj* (*umg*) harebrained

Hirsch [hɪrʃ] (**-(e)s, -e**) *m* stag

Hirse ['hɪrzə] (**-, -n**) *f* millet

Hirt ['hɪrt] (**-en, -en**) *m*, **Hirte** (**-n, -n**) *m*
herdsman; (*Schafhirt, fig*) shepherd

Hirtin *f* herdswoman; (*Schafhirtin*) shepherdess

hissen ['hɪsən] *vt* to hoist

Historiker [hɪs'toːrikər] (**-s, -**) *m* historian

historisch [hɪs'toːrɪʃ] *adj* historical

Hit [hɪt] (**-s, -s**) (*umg*) *m* (*Mus, fig*) hit; **Hitparade**
f hit parade

Hitze ['hɪtsə] (**-**) *f* heat; **hitzebeständig** *adj*
heat-resistant; **Hitzefrei** (**-**) *nt*: **Hitzefrei
haben** *to have time off school/work because of
excessive heat*; **Hitzewelle** *f* heat wave

hitzig *adj* hot-tempered; (*Debatte*) heated

Hitz- *zW*: **Hitzkopf** *m* hothead; **hitzköpfig** *adj*
fiery, hot-headed; **Hitzschlag** *m* heatstroke

HIV-negativ *adj* HIV-negative

HIV-positiv *adj* HIV-positive

hl. *abk* = **heilig**

H-Milch ['haːmɪlç] *f* long-life milk, UHT milk

HNO-Arzt *m* ENT specialist

hob *etc* [hoːp] *vb siehe* **heben**

Hobby ['hɔbi] (**-s, -s**) *nt* hobby

Hobel ['hoːbəl] (**-s, -**) *m* plane; **Hobelbank** *f*
carpenter's bench

hobeln *vt, vi* to plane

Hobelspäne *pl* wood shavings *pl*

hoch [hoːx] (*attrib* **hohe(r, s)**) *adj* high ▷ *adv*: **~**

achten to respect; **~ begabt = hochbegabt**;
~ dotiert highly paid; **~ entwickelt** (*Kultur,
Land*) highly developed; (*Geräte, Methoden*)
sophisticated; **wenn es ~ kommt** (*umg*) at
(the) most, at the outside; **das ist mir zu ~**
(*umg*) that's above my head; **ein hohes Tier**
(*umg*) a big fish; **es ging ~ her** (*umg*) we/
they *etc* had a whale of a time; **~ und heilig
versprechen** to promise faithfully; *siehe auch*
hochempfindlich; hochgestellt

Hoch (**-s, -s**) *nt* (*Ruf*) cheer; (*Met, fig*) high

hoch- *zW*: **Hochachtung** *f* respect, esteem; **mit
vorzüglicher Hochachtung** (*form: Briefschluss*)
yours faithfully; **hochachtungsvoll** *adv* yours
faithfully; **hochaktuell** *adj* highly topical;
Hochamt *nt* high mass; **hocharbeiten**
vr to work one's way up; **hochbegabt** *adj*
extremely gifted, aged; **hochbetagt** *adj* very
old, aged; **Hochbetrieb** *m* intense activity;
(*Comm*) peak time; **Hochbetrieb haben** to
be at one's *od* its busiest; **hochbringen** *unreg*
vt to bring up; **Hochburg** *f* stronghold;
Hochdeutsch *nt* High German; **Hochdruck**
m high pressure; **Hochebene** *f* plateau;
hochempfindlich *adj* highly sensitive; (*Film*)
high-speed; **hocherfreut** *adj* highly delighted;
hochfahren *unreg vi* (*erschreckt*) to jump;
(*Comput, Tech*) to start up; **hochfliegend** *adj*
ambitious; (*fig*) high-flown; **Hochform** *f* top
form; **Hochgebirge** *nt* high mountains *pl*;
Hochgefühl *nt* elation; **hochgehen** *unreg* (*umg*)
vi (*explodieren*) to blow up; (*Bombe*) to go off;
Hochgenuss *m* great *od* special treat; (*großes
Vergnügen*) great pleasure; **hochgeschlossen**
adj (*Kleid etc*) high-necked; **hochgestellt** *adj*
(*fig: Persönlichkeit*) high-ranking; **Hochglanz**
m high polish; (*Phot*) gloss; **hochgradig** *adj*
intense, extreme; **hochhalten** *unreg vt* to
hold up; (*fig*) to uphold, cherish; **Hochhaus**
nt multi-storey building; **hochheben** *unreg*
vt to lift (up); **hochkant** *adv*: **jdn hochkant
hinauswerfen** (*fig: umg*) to chuck sb out on
his/her ear; **hochkommen** *unreg vi* (*nach
oben*) to come up; (*fig: gesund werden*) to get
back on one's feet; (*beruflich, gesellschaftlich*)
to come up in the world; **Hochkonjunktur**
f boom; **hochkrempeln** *vt* to roll up;
Hochland *nt* highlands *pl*; **hochleben** *vi*: **jdn
hochleben lassen** to give sb three cheers;
Hochleistungssport *m* competitive sport;
hochmodern *adj* very modern, ultra-modern;
Hochmut *m* pride; **hochmütig** *adj* proud,
haughty; **hochnäsig** *adj* stuck-up, snooty;
hochnehmen *unreg vt* to pick up; **jdn
hochnehmen** (*umg: verspotten*) to pull sb's leg;
Hochofen *m* blast furnace; **hochprozentig**
adj (*Alkohol*) strong; **Hochrechnung** *f*
projected result; **Hochsaison** *f* high season;
Hochschätzung *f* high esteem

Hochschulabschluss *m* degree

Hochschulbildung *f* higher education

Hochschule *f* college; (*Universität*) university

Hochschulreife *f*: **er hat (die) ~ =** he's got

his A-levels (*Brit*), he's graduated from high school (*US*)

hoch- *zW:* **hochschwanger** *adj* heavily pregnant, well advanced in pregnancy; **Hochseefischerei** *f* deep-sea fishing; **Hochsitz** *m* (*Jagd*) (raised) hide; **Hochsommer** *m* middle of summer; **Hochspannung** *f* high tension; **hochspielen** *vt* (*fig*) to blow up; **Hochsprache** *f* standard language; **hochspringen** *unreg vi* to jump up; **Hochsprung** *m* high jump

höchst [høːçst] *adv* highly, extremely

Hochstapler ['hoːxstaːplər] (**-s, -**) *m* swindler

höchste, r, s *adj* highest; (*äußerste*) extreme; **die ~ Instanz** (*Jur*) the supreme court of appeal

höchstens *adv* at the most

Höchst- *zW:* **Höchstform** *f* (*Sport*) top form; **Höchstgeschwindigkeit** *f* maximum speed; **Höchstgrenze** *f* upper limit

Hochstimmung *f* high spirits *pl*

Höchst- *zW:* **Höchstleistung** *f* best performance; (*bei Produktion*) maximum output; **höchstpersönlich** *adv* personally, in person; **Höchstpreis** *m* maximum price; **Höchststand** *m* peak; **höchstwahrscheinlich** *adv* most probably

Hoch- *zW:* **Hochtechnologie** *f* high technology; **hochtechnologisch** *adj* high-tech; **Hochtemperaturreaktor** *m* high-temperature reactor; **Hochtour** *f:* **auf Hochtouren laufen** *od* **arbeiten** to be working flat out; **hochtrabend** *adj* pompous; **Hoch- und Tiefbau** *m* structural and civil engineering; **Hochverrat** *m* high treason; **Hochwasser** *nt* high water; (*Überschwemmung*) floods *pl*; **hochwertig** *adj* high-class, first-rate; **Hochwürden** *m* Reverend; **Hochzahl** *f* (*Math*) exponent

Hochzeit ['hɔxtsaɪt] (**-, -en**) *f* wedding; **man kann nicht auf zwei ~en tanzen** (*Sprichwort*) you can't have your cake and eat it

Hochzeitsreise *f* honeymoon

Hochzeitstag *m* wedding day; (*Jahrestag*) wedding anniversary

hochziehen *unreg vt* (*Rollladen, Hose*) to pull up; (*Brauen*) to raise

Hocke ['hɔkə] (**-, -n**) *f* squatting position; (*beim Turnen*) squat vault; (*beim Skilaufen*) crouch

hocken ['hɔkən] *vi, vr* to squat, crouch

Hocker (**-s, -**) *m* stool

Höcker ['hœkər] (**-s, -**) *m* hump

Hockey ['hɔki] (**-s**) *nt* hockey

Hoden [['hoːdən]] (**-s, -**) *m* testicle

Hodensack *m* scrotum

Hof [hoːf] (**-(e)s, ̈e**) *m* (*Hinterhof*) yard; (*Bauernhof*) farm; (*Königshof*) court; **einem Mädchen den ~ machen** (*veraltet*) to court a girl

hoffen ['hɔfən] *vi:* **~ (auf** +*akk*) to hope (for)

hoffentlich *adv* I hope, hopefully

Hoffnung ['hɔfnʊŋ] *f* hope; **jdm ~en machen** to raise sb's hopes; **sich** *dat* **~en machen** to have hopes; **sich** *dat* **keine ~en machen** not to hold out any hope(s)

Hoffnungs- *zW:* **hoffnungslos** *adj* hopeless; **Hoffnungslosigkeit** *f* hopelessness; **Hoffnungsschimmer** *m* glimmer of hope; **hoffnungsvoll** *adj* hopeful

höflich ['høːflɪç] *adj* courteous, polite; **Höflichkeit** *f* courtesy, politeness

hohe, r, s ['hoːə(r, s)] *adj siehe* **hoch**

Höhe ['høːə] (**-, -n**) *f* height; (*Anhöhe*) hill; **nicht auf der ~ sein** (*fig: umg*) to feel below par; **ein Scheck in ~ von ...** a cheque (*Brit*) *od* check (*US*) for the amount of ...; **das ist doch die ~** (*fig: umg*) that's the limit; **er geht immer gleich in die ~** (*umg*) he always flares up; **auf der ~ der Zeit sein** to be up-to-date

Hoheit ['hoːhaɪt] *f* (*Pol*) sovereignty; (*Titel*) Highness

Hoheits- *zW:* **Hoheitsgebiet** *nt* sovereign territory; **Hoheitsgewalt** *f* (national) jurisdiction; **Hoheitsgewässer** *nt* territorial waters *pl*; **Hoheitszeichen** *nt* national emblem

Höhen- *zW:* **Höhenangabe** *f* altitude reading; (*auf Karte*) height marking; **Höhenflug** *m:* **geistiger Höhenflug** intellectual flight; **Höhenlage** *f* altitude; **Höhenluft** *f* mountain air; **Höhenmesser** *m* altimeter; **Höhensonne** *f* sun lamp; **Höhenunterschied** *m* difference in altitude; **Höhenzug** *m* mountain chain

Höhepunkt *m* climax; (*des Lebens*) high point

höher *adj, adv* higher

hohl [hoːl] *adj* hollow; (*umg: dumm*) hollow(-headed)

Höhle ['høːlə] (**-, -n**) *f* cave; hole; (*Mundhöhle*) cavity; (*fig, Zool*) den

Hohl- *zW:* **Hohlheit** *f* hollowness; **Hohlkreuz** *nt* (*Med*) hollow back; **Hohlmaß** *nt* measure of volume; **Hohlraum** *m* hollow space; (*Gebäude*) cavity; **Hohlsaum** *m* hemstitch; **Hohlspiegel** *m* concave mirror

Hohn [hoːn] (**-(e)s**) *m* scorn; **das ist der reinste ~** it's sheer mockery

höhnen ['høːnən] *vt* to taunt, scoff at

höhnisch *adj* scornful, taunting

Hokuspokus [hoːkʊs'poːkʊs] (**-**) *m* (*Zauberformel*) hey presto; (*fig: Täuschung*) hocus-pocus

hold [hɔlt] *adj* charming, sweet

holen ['hoːlən] *vt* to get, fetch; (*Atem*) to take; **jdn/etw ~ lassen** to send for sb/sth; **sich** *dat* **eine Erkältung ~** to catch a cold

Holland ['hɔlant] (**-s**) *nt* Holland

Holländer ['hɔlɛndər] (**-s, -**) *m* Dutchman

Holländerin *f* Dutchwoman, Dutch girl

holländisch *adj* Dutch

Hölle ['hœlə] (**-, -n**) *f* hell; **ich werde ihm die ~ heißmachen** (*umg*) I'll give him hell

Höllenangst *f:* **eine ~ haben** to be scared to death

Höllenlärm *m* infernal noise (*umg*)

höllisch ['hœlɪʃ] *adj* hellish, infernal

Hologramm [holo'gram] (**-s, -e**) *nt* hologram

holperig ['hɔlpərɪç] *adj* rough, bumpy

holpern ['hɔlpərn] *vi* to jolt

Holunder [ho'lʊndər] (**-s, -**) *m* elder

Holz [hɔlts] (**-es, ÷er**) nt wood; **aus ~** made of wood, wooden; **aus einem anderen/ demselben ~ geschnitzt sein** (fig) to be cast in a different/the same mould; **gut ~!** (Kegeln) have a good game!; **Holzbläser** m woodwind player

hölzern ['hœltsərn] adj (lit, fig) wooden

Holz- zW: **Holzfäller** (**-s, -**) m lumberjack, woodcutter; **Holzfaserplatte** f (wood) fibreboard (Brit) od fiberboard (US); **holzfrei** adj (Papier) wood-free

holzig adj woody

Holz- zW: **Holzklotz** m wooden block; **Holzkohle** f charcoal; **Holzkopf** m (fig: umg) blockhead, numbskull; **Holzscheit** nt log; **Holzschuh** m clog; **Holzweg** m (fig) wrong track; **Holzwolle** f fine wood shavings pl; **Holzwurm** m woodworm

Homecomputer ['hoʊmkɔm'pjuːtər] (**-s, -**) m home computer

Homepage ['hoʊm'paːgə] nt (Comput) home page

Homo-Ehe ['ho:mo|eːə] (umg) f gay marriage

homogen [homo'geːn] adj homogenous

Homöopath [homøo'paːt] (**-en, -en**) m homeopath

Homöopathie [homøopa'tiː] f homeopathy, homeopathic medicine

homosexuell [homozɛksu'ɛl] adj homosexual

Honduras [hɔn'duːras] (**-**) nt Honduras

Hongkong [hɔŋ'kɔŋ] (**-s**) nt Hong Kong

Honig ['ho:nɪç] (**-s, -e**) m honey; **Honiglecken** nt (fig): **das ist kein Honiglecken** it's no picnic; **Honigmelone** f honeydew melon; **Honigwabe** f honeycomb

Honorar [hono'raːr] (**-s, -e**) nt fee

Honoratioren [honoratsi'oːrən] pl dignitaries

honorieren [hono'riːrən] vt to remunerate; (Scheck) to honour (Brit), honor (US)

Hopfen ['hɔpfən] (**-s, -**) m hops pl; **bei ihm ist ~ und Malz verloren** (umg) he's a dead loss

hoppla ['hɔpla] interj whoops

hopsen ['hɔpsən] vi to hop

hörbar adj audible

horch [hɔrç] interj listen

horchen vi to listen; (pej) to eavesdrop

Horcher (**-s, -**) m listener; eavesdropper

Horde ['hɔrdə] (**-, -n**) f horde

hören ['høːrən] vt, vi to hear; **auf jdn/etw ~** to listen to sb/sth; **ich lasse von mir ~** I'll be in touch; **etwas/nichts von sich ~ lassen** to get/not to get in touch; **Hören** nt: **es verging ihm Hören und Sehen** (umg) he didn't know whether he was coming or going

Hörensagen nt: **vom ~** from hearsay

Hörer (**-s, -**) m (Rundf) listener; (Univ) student; (Telefonhörer) receiver

Hörfunk m radio

Hörgerät nt hearing aid

hörig ['høːrɪç] adj: **sie ist ihm (sexuell) ~** he has (sexual) power over her

Horizont [hori'tsɔnt] (**-(e)s, -e**) m horizon; **das geht über meinen ~** (fig) that is beyond me

horizontal [horitsɔ'taːl] adj horizontal

Hormon [hɔr'moːn] (**-s, -e**) nt hormone

Hörmuschel f (Tel) earpiece

Horn [hɔrn] (**-(e)s, ÷er**) nt horn; **ins gleiche** od **in jds ~ blasen** to chime in; **sich** dat **die Hörner abstoßen** (umg) to sow one's wild oats; **Hornbrille** f horn-rimmed spectacles pl

Hörnchen ['hœrnçən] nt (Gebäck) croissant

Hornhaut f horny skin; (des Auges) cornea

Hornisse [hɔr'nɪsə] (**-, -n**) f hornet

Hornochs, Hornochse m (fig: umg) blockhead, idiot

Horoskop [horo'skoːp] (**-s, -e**) nt horoscope

Hör- zW: **Hörrohr** nt ear trumpet; (Med) stethoscope; **Hörsaal** m lecture room; **Hörspiel** nt radio play

Hort [hɔrt] (**-(e)s, -e**) m hoard; (Sch) nursery school; **horten** vt to hoard

Hörweite f: **in/außer ~** within/out of hearing od earshot

Hose ['hoːze] (**-, -n**) f trousers pl, pants pl (US); **in die ~ gehen** (umg) to be a complete flop

Hosen- zW: **Hosenanzug** m trouser suit, pantsuit (US); **Hosenboden** m: **sich auf den Hosenboden setzen** (umg) to get stuck in; **Hosenrock** m culottes pl; **Hosentasche** f trouser pocket; **Hosenträger** pl braces pl (Brit), suspenders pl (US)

Hostie ['hɔstiə] f (Rel) host

Hotel [ho'tɛl] (**-s, -s**) nt hotel; **Hotelfach** nt hotel management; **Hotel garni** nt bed and breakfast hotel

Hotelier [hoteli'eː] (**-s, -s**) m hotelier

Hotspot ['hɔtspɔt] m (wireless) hotspot

Hr. abk (= Herr) Mr

Hrsg. abk (= Herausgeber) ed.

hrsg. abk (= herausgegeben) ed.

HTML abk (= Hyper Text Markup Language) HTML

Hub [huːp] (**-(e)s, ÷e**) m lift; (Tech) stroke

hüben ['hyːbən] adv on this side, over here; **~ und drüben** on both sides

Hubraum m (Aut) cubic capacity

hübsch [hypʃ] adj pretty, nice; **immer ~ langsam!** (umg) nice and easy

Hubschrauber (**-s, -**) m helicopter

Hucke ['hʊkə] (**-, -n**) f: **jdm die ~ vollhauen** (umg) to give sb a good hiding

huckepack ['hʊkəpak] adv piggy-back, pick-a-back

hudeln ['huːdəln] vi to be sloppy

Huf ['huːf] (**-(e)s, -e**) m hoof; **Hufeisen** nt horseshoe; **Hufnagel** m horseshoe nail

Hüfte ['hyftə] (**-, -n**) f hip

Hüftgürtel m girdle

Hüfthalter m girdle

Huftier nt hoofed animal, ungulate

Hügel ['hyːgəl] (**-s, -**) m hill

hügelig, hüglig adj hilly

Huhn [huːn] (**-(e)s, ÷er**) nt hen; (Koch) chicken; **da lachen ja die Hühner** (umg) it's enough to make a cat laugh; **er sah aus wie ein gerupftes ~** (umg) he looked as if he'd been dragged through a hedge backwards

Hühnchen ['hy:nçən] *nt* young chicken; **mit jdm ein ~ zu rupfen haben** (*umg*) to have a bone to pick with sb
Hühner- *zW:* **Hühnerauge** *nt* corn; **Hühnerbrühe** *f* chicken broth; **Hühnerklein** *nt* (*Koch*) chicken trimmings *pl*
Huld [hʊlt] (-) *f* favour (*Brit*), favor (*US*)
huldigen ['hʊldɪgən] *vi:* **jdm ~** to pay homage to sb
Huldigung *f* homage
Hülle ['hylə] (-, -n) *f* cover(ing); (*Zellophanhülle*) wrapping; **in ~ und Fülle** galore; **die ~n fallen lassen** (*fig*) to strip off
hüllen *vt:* **~ (in** +*akk*) to cover (with); to wrap (in)
Hülse ['hylzə] (-, -n) *f* husk, shell
Hülsenfrucht *f* pulse
human [hu'ma:n] *adj* humane
humanistisch [huma'nɪstɪʃ] *adj:* **~es Gymnasium** *secondary school with bias on Latin and Greek*
humanitär [humani'tɛ:r] *adj* humanitarian
Humanität *f* humanity
Humanmedizin *f* (human) medicine
Hummel ['hʊməl] (-, -n) *f* bumblebee
Hummer ['hʊmər] (-s, -) *m* lobster
Humor [hu'mo:r] (-s, -e) *m* humour (*Brit*), humor (*US*); **~ haben** to have a sense of humo(u)r; **Humorist** *in m(f)* humorist; **humoristisch** *adj* humorous; **humorlos** *adj* humourless; **humorvoll** *adj* humorous
humpeln ['hʊmpəln] *vi* to hobble
Humpen ['hʊmpən] (-s, -) *m* tankard
Humus ['hu:mʊs] (-) *m* humus
Hund [hʊnt] (-(e)s, -e) *m* dog; **auf den ~ kommen, vor die Hunde gehen** (*fig: umg*) to go to the dogs; **~e, die bellen, beißen nicht** (*Sprichwort*) empty vessels make most noise (*Sprichwort*); **er ist bekannt wie ein bunter ~** (*umg*) everybody knows him
Hunde- *zW:* **hundeelend** (*umg*) *adj:* **mir ist hundeelend** I feel lousy; **Hundehütte** *f* (dog) kennel; **Hundekuchen** *m* dog biscuit; **Hundemarke** *f* dog licence disc, dog tag (*US*); **hundemüde** (*umg*) *adj* dog-tired
hundert ['hʊndərt] *num* hundred; **Hundert** (-s, -e) *nt* hundred; **Hunderte von Menschen** hundreds of people
Hunderter (-s, -) *m* hundred; (*umg: Geldschein*) hundred (euro/pound/dollar *etc* note)
hundert- *zW:* **Hundertjahrfeier** *f* centenary; **Hundertmeterlauf** *m* (*Sport*): **der/ein Hundertmeterlauf** the/a hundred metres (*Brit*) *od* meters (*US*) *sing*; **hundertprozentig** *adj, adv* one hundred per cent
hundertste, r, s *adj* hundredth; **von H~n ins Tausendste kommen** (*fig*) to get carried away
Hundesteuer *f* dog licence (*Brit*) *od* license (*US*) fee
Hundewetter (*umg*) *nt* filthy weather
Hündin ['hyndɪn] *f* bitch
Hüne ['hy:nə] (-n, -n) *m:* **ein ~ von Mensch** a giant of a man

Hünengrab *nt* megalithic tomb
Hunger ['hʊŋər] (-s) *m* hunger; **~ haben** to be hungry; **ich sterbe vor ~** (*umg*) I'm starving; **Hungerlohn** *m* starvation wages *pl*
hungern *vi* to starve
Hungersnot *f* famine
Hungerstreik *m* hunger strike
Hungertuch *nt:* **am ~ nagen** (*fig*) to be starving
hungrig ['hʊŋrɪç] *adj* hungry
Hunsrück ['hʊnsryk] *m* Hunsruck (Mountains *pl*)
Hupe ['hu:pə] (-, -n) *f* horn
hupen *vi* to hoot, sound one's horn
hupfen ['hʊpfən] *vi* to hop, jump; **das ist gehupft wie gesprungen** (*umg*) it's six of one and half a dozen of the other
hüpfen ['hypfən] *vi* = **hupfen**
Hupkonzert (*umg*) *nt* hooting (of car horns)
Hürde ['hyrdə] (-, -n) *f* hurdle; (*für Schafe*) pen
Hürdenlauf *m* hurdling
Hure ['hu:rə] (-, -n) *f* whore
Hurensohn (*pej: umg!*) *m* bastard (!), son of a bitch (!)
hurra [hʊ'ra:] *interj* hurray, hurrah
hurtig ['hʊrtɪç] *adj* brisk, quick ▷ *adv* briskly, quickly
huschen ['hʊʃən] *vi* to flit, scurry
Husten ['hu:stən] (-s) *m* cough; **husten** *vi* to cough; **auf etw** *akk* **husten** (*umg*) to not give a damn for sth; **Hustenanfall** *m* coughing fit; **Hustenbonbon** *m od nt* cough drop; **Hustensaft** *m* cough mixture
Hut¹ [hu:t] (-(e)s, ¨e) *m* hat; **unter einen ~ bringen** (*umg*) to reconcile; (*Termine etc*) to fit in
Hut² [hu:t] (-) *f* care; **auf der ~ sein** to be on one's guard
hüten ['hy:tən] *vt* to guard ▷ *vr* to watch out; **das Bett/Haus ~** to stay in bed/indoors; **sich ~ zu** to take care not to; **sich ~ vor** +*dat* to beware of; **ich werde mich ~!** not likely!
Hutschnur *f:* **das geht mir über die ~** (*umg*) that's going too far
Hütte ['hytə] (-, -n) *f* hut; (*Holzhütte, Blockhütte*) cabin; (*Eisenhütte*) forge; (*umg: Wohnung*) pad; (*Tech: Hüttenwerk*) iron and steel works
Hüttenindustrie *f* iron and steel industry
Hüttenkäse *m* cottage cheese
Hüttenwerk *nt* iron and steel works
hutzelig ['hʊtsəlɪç] *adj* shrivelled
Hyäne [hy'ɛ:nə] (-, -n) *f* hyena
Hyazinthe [hya'tsɪntə] (-, -n) *f* hyacinth
Hydrant [hy'drant] *m* hydrant
hydraulisch [hy'draʊlɪʃ] *adj* hydraulic
Hydrierung [hy'dri:rʊŋ] *f* hydrogenation
Hygiene [hygi'e:nə] (-) *f* hygiene
hygienisch [hygi'e:nɪʃ] *adj* hygienic
Hymne ['hymnə] (-, -n) *f* hymn, anthem
hyper- ['hypɛr] *präf* hyper-
Hypnose [hyp'no:zə] (-, -n) *f* hypnosis
hypnotisch *adj* hypnotic
Hypnotiseur [hypnoti'zø:r] *m* hypnotist
hypnotisieren [hypnoti'zi:rən] *vt* to

h

hypnotize
Hypotenuse [[hypote'nu:zə]] (-, -n) *f*
hypotenuse
Hypothek [hypo'te:k] (-, -en) *f* mortgage; **eine
~ aufnehmen** to raise a mortgage; **etw mit
einer ~ belasten** to mortgage sth

Hypothese [hypo'te:zə] (-, -n) *f* hypothesis
hypothetisch [hypo'te:tɪʃ] *adj* hypothetical
Hysterie [hyste'ri:] *f* hysteria
hysterisch [hys'te:rɪʃ] *adj* hysterical; **einen
~en Anfall bekommen** (*fig*) to have
hysterics

I, i [i:] *nt* I, i; **I wie Ida** ≈ I for Isaac, I for Item
(US); **das Tüpfelchen auf dem i** (*fig*) the final
touch

i. *abk* = **in; im**

i. A. *abk* (= *im Auftrag*) p.p.

iberisch [i'be:rɪʃ] *adj* Iberian; **die I~e Halbinsel**
the Iberian Peninsula

IC (-) *m abk* = **Intercityzug**

ICE *m abk* (= *Intercity-Expresszug*) inter-city train

ich [ɪç] *pron* I; **~ bins!** it's me!; **Ich** (**-(s), -(s)**)
nt self; (*Psych*) ego; **Ichform** *f* first person;
Ichroman *m* novel in the first person

Ideal [ide'a:l] (**-s, -e**) *nt* ideal; **ideal** *adj* ideal;
Idealfall *m*: **im Idealfall** ideally

Idealismus [idea'lɪsmʊs] *m* idealism

Idealist, in *m(f)* idealist

idealistisch *adj* idealistic

Idealvorstellung *f* ideal

Idee [i'de:] (**-, -n**) *f* idea; (*ein wenig*) shade, trifle;
jdn auf die ~ bringen, etw zu tun to give sb
the idea of doing sth

ideell [ide'ɛl] *adj* ideal

identifizieren [idɛntifi'tsi:rən] *vt* to identify

identisch [i'dɛntɪʃ] *adj* identical

Identität [idɛnti'tɛ:t] *f* identity

Ideologe [ideo'lo:gə] (**-n, -n**) *m* ideologist

Ideologie [ideolo'gi:] *f* ideology

Ideologin [ideo'lo:gɪn] *f* ideologist

ideologisch [ideo'lo:gɪʃ] *adj* ideological

idiomatisch [idio'ma:tɪʃ] *adj* idiomatic

Idiot [idi'o:t] (**-en, -en**) *m* idiot

Idiotenhügel *m* (*hum: umg*) beginners' *od*
nursery slope

idiotensicher (*umg*) *adj* foolproof

Idiotin *f* idiot

idiotisch *adj* idiotic

Idol [i'do:l] *nt* (**-s, -e**) idol

idyllisch [i'dylɪʃ] *adj* idyllic

IG *abk* (= *Industriegewerkschaft*) *industrial trade union*

IGB (-) *m abk* (= *Internationaler Gewerkschaftsbund*)
International Trades Union Congress

Igel [i:gəl] (**-s, -**) *m* hedgehog

igitt [i'gɪt], **igittigitt** [i'gɪti'gɪt] *interj* ugh!

Iglu [i'glu] (**-s, -s**) *m od nt* igloo

Ignorant [ɪgno'rant] (**-en, -en**) *m* ignoramus

ignorieren [ɪgno'ri:rən] *vt* to ignore

IHK *f abk* = **Industrie- und Handelskammer**

ihm [i:m] *pron dat von* **er, es** (to) him, (to) it; **es**

ist ~ nicht gut he doesn't feel well

ihn [i:n] *pron akk von* **er** him; (*bei Tieren, Dingen*) it

ihnen ['i:nən] *pron dat pl von* **sie** (to) them; (*nach
Präpositionen*) them

Ihnen *pron dat von* **Sie** (to) you; (*nach Präpositionen*)
you

ihr [i:r] *pron* **1** (*nom pl*) you; **ihr seid es** it's you
2 (*dat von sie*) (to) her; (*bei Tieren, Dingen*) (to) it;
gib es ihr give it to her; **er steht neben ihr**
he is standing beside her
▷ *poss pron* **1** (*sing*) her; (: *bei Tieren, Dingen*) its;
ihr Mann her husband
2 (*pl*) their; **die Bäume und ihre Blätter** the
trees and their leaves

Ihr *poss pron* your

Ihre, r, s *poss pron* yours; **tun Sie das ~** (*geh*) you
do your bit

ihre, r, s *poss pron* hers; (*eines Tieres*) its; (*von
mehreren*) theirs; **sie taten das I~** (*geh*) they did
their bit

ihrer ['i:rər] *pron gen sing von* **sie** of her; (*pl*) of
them

Ihrer *pron gen von* **Sie** of you

Ihrerseits *adv* for your part

ihrerseits *adv* for her/their part

ihresgleichen *pron* people like her/them; (*von
Dingen*) others like it; **eine Frechheit, die ~
sucht!** an incredible cheek!

ihretwegen *adv* (*für sie*) for her/its/their sake;
(*wegen ihr, ihnen*) on her/its/their account; **sie
sagte, ~ könnten wir gehen** she said that, as
far as she was concerned, we could go

ihretwillen *adv*: **um ~** for her/its/their sake

ihrige ['i:rɪgə] *pron*: **der/die/das ~** *od* **Ihrige**
hers; its; theirs

i. J. *abk* (= *im Jahre*) in (the year)

Ikone [i'ko:nə] (**-, -n**) *f* icon

IKRK *nt abk* (= *Internationales Komitee vom Roten
Kreuz*) ICRC

illegal ['ɪlega:l] *adj* illegal

illegitim ['ɪlegiti:m] *adj* illegitimate

Illusion [ɪluzi'o:n] *f* illusion; **sich** *dat* **~en
machen** to delude o.s.

illusorisch [ɪlu'zo:rɪʃ] *adj* illusory

Illustration [ɪlʊstratsi'oːn] f illustration
illustrieren [ɪlʊs'triːrən] vt to illustrate
Illustrierte (**-n, -n**) f picture magazine
Iltis ['ɪltɪs] (**-ses, -se**) m polecat
im [ɪm] = **in dem** präp: **etw im Liegen/Stehen tun** do sth lying down/standing up
IM (**-s,** no pl) nt abk IM (= instant messaging)
Image ['ɪmɪtʃ] (**-(s), -s**) nt image; **Imagekampagne** ['ɪmɪtʃkampanjə] f image-building campaign; **Imagepflege** ['ɪmɪtʃpfleːgə] (umg) f image-building; **Imageschaden** f damage to one's image
imaginär [imagi'nɛːr] adj imaginary
Imbiss ['ɪmbɪs] (**-es, -e**) m snack; **Imbisshalle** f snack bar; **Imbissstand** m, **Imbissstube** f snack bar
Imissionswert [imisi'oːnsveːrt] m pollution count
imitieren [imi'tiːrən] vt to imitate
Imker ['ɪmkər] (**-s, -**) m beekeeper
immanent [ɪma'nɛnt] adj inherent, intrinsic
Immatrikulation [ɪmatrikulatsi'oːn] f (Univ) registration
immatrikulieren [ɪmatriku'liːrən] vi, vr to register
immer ['ɪmər] adv always; **~ wieder** again and again; **etw ~ wieder tun** to keep on doing sth; **~ noch** still; **~ noch nicht** still not; **für ~** forever; **~ wenn ich …** every time I …; **~ schöner** more and more beautiful; **~ trauriger** sadder and sadder; **was/wer (auch)** **~** whatever/whoever; **immerhin** adv all the same; **immerzu** adv all the time
Immigrant, in [ɪmi'grant(ɪn)] m(f) immigrant
Immobilien [ɪmo'biːliən] pl real property (Brit), real estate (US); (in Zeitungsannoncen) property sing; **Immobilienhändler**, **Immobilienmakler** m estate agent (Brit), realtor (US)
immun [ɪ'muːn] adj immune
immunisieren [ɪmuni'ziːrən] vt to immunize
Immunität [ɪmuni'tɛːt] f immunity
Immunschwäche f immunodeficiency
Immunsystem nt immune system
Imperativ (**-s, -e**) m imperative
Imperfekt ['ɪmpɛrfɛkt] (**-s, -e**) nt imperfect (tense)
Imperialismus [ɪmperia'lɪsmʊs] m imperialism
Imperialist [ɪmperia'lɪst] m imperialist; **imperialistisch** adj imperialistic
impfen ['ɪmpfən] vt to vaccinate
Impf- zW: **Impfpass** m vaccination card; **Impfschutz** m protection given by vaccination; **Impfstoff** m vaccine; **Impfung** f vaccination; **Impfzwang** m compulsory vaccination
implizieren [ɪmpli'tsiːrən] vt to imply
imponieren [ɪmpo'niːrən] vi+dat to impress
Import [ɪm'pɔrt] (**-(e)s, -e**) m import
Importeur [ɪmpɔr'tøːr] (**-s, -e**) m importer
importieren [ɪmpɔr'tiːrən] vt to import
imposant [ɪmpo'zant] adj imposing

impotent ['ɪmpotɛnt] adj impotent
Impotenz ['ɪmpotɛnts] f impotence
imprägnieren [ɪmprɛ'gniːrən] vt to (water)proof
Impressionismus [ɪmprɛsio'nɪsmʊs] m impressionism
Impressum [ɪm'prɛsʊm] (**-s, -ssen**) nt imprint
Improvisation [ɪmprovizatsi'oːn] f improvisation
improvisieren [ɪmprovi'ziːrən] vt, vi to improvise
Impuls [ɪm'pʊls] (**-es, -e**) m impulse; **etw aus einem ~ heraus tun** to do sth on impulse
impulsiv [ɪmpʊl'ziːf] adj impulsive
imstande, im Stande [ɪm'ʃtandə] adj: **~ sein** to be in a position; (fähig) to be able; **er ist zu allem ~** he's capable of anything

 SCHLÜSSELWORT

in [ɪn] präp+akk **1** (räumlich: wohin) in, into; **in die Stadt** into town; **in die Schule gehen** to go to school; **in die Hunderte gehen** to run into (the) hundreds
2 (zeitlich): **bis ins 20. Jahrhundert** into od up to the 20th century
▷ präp+dat **1** (räumlich: wo) in; **in der Stadt** in town; **in der Schule sein** to be at school; **es in sich haben** (umg: Text) to be tough; (: Drink) to have quite a kick
2 (zeitlich: wann): **in diesem Jahr** this year; (in jenem Jahr) in that year; **heute in zwei Wochen** two weeks today

inaktiv ['ɪn|aktiːf] adj inactive; (Mitglied) non-active
Inangriffnahme [ɪn'|angrɪfnaːmə] (**-, -n**) f (form) commencement
Inanspruchnahme [ɪn'|anʃprʊxnaːmə] (**-, -n**) f: **~** (+gen) demands pl (on); **im Falle einer ~ der Arbeitslosenunterstützung** (form) where unemployment benefit has been sought
inbegr. abk (= inbegriffen) enc.
Inbegriff ['ɪnbəgrɪf] m embodiment, personification
inbegriffen adv included
Inbetriebnahme [ɪnbə'triːpnaːmə] (**-, -n**) f (form) commissioning; (von Gebäude, U-Bahn etc) inauguration
inbrünstig ['ɪnbrʏnstɪç] adj ardent
indem [ɪn'deːm] konj while; **~ man etw macht** (dadurch) by doing sth
Inder, in ['ɪndər(ɪn)] (**-s, -**) m(f) Indian
indes [ɪn'dɛs], **indessen** [ɪn'dɛsən] adv meanwhile ▷ konj while
Index ['ɪndɛks] (**-(es), -e** od **Indizes**) m: **auf dem ~ stehen** (fig) to be banned; **Indexzahl** f index number
Indianer, in [ɪndi'aːnər(ɪn)] (**-s, -**) m(f) (American) Indian
indianisch adj (American) Indian
Indien ['ɪndiən] (**-s**) nt India

indigniert [ɪndɪ'gniːrt] *adj* indignant
Indikation [ɪndikatsi'oːn] *f*: **medizinische/
soziale ~** medical/social grounds *pl* for the
termination of pregnancy
Indikativ ['ɪndikatiːf] **(-s, -e)** *m* indicative
indirekt ['ɪndirɛkt] *adj* indirect; **~e Steuer**
indirect tax
indisch ['ɪndɪʃ] *adj* Indian; **I~er Ozean** Indian
Ocean
indiskret ['ɪndɪskreːt] *adj* indiscreet
Indiskretion [ɪndɪskretsi'oːn] *f* indiscretion
indiskutabel ['ɪndɪskutaːbəl] *adj* out of the
question
indisponiert ['ɪndɪsponiːrt] *adj* (*geh*) indisposed
Individualist [ɪndividua'lɪst] *m* individualist
Individualität [ɪndividuali'tɛt] *f* individuality
Individualtourismus *m* individual tourism
individuell [ɪndividu'ɛl] *adj* individual; **etw ~
gestalten** to give sth a personal note
Individuum [ɪndi'viːduʊm] **(-s, -duen)** *nt*
individual
Indiz [ɪn'diːts] **(-es, -ien)** *nt* (*Jur*) clue; **~ (für)**
sign (of)
Indizes ['ɪnditseːz] *pl von* **Index**
Indizienbeweis *m* circumstantial evidence
indizieren [ɪndi'tsiːrən] *vt, vi* (*Comput*) to index
Indochina ['ɪndo'çiːna] **(-s)** *nt* Indochina
indogermanisch ['ɪndogɛr'maːnɪʃ] *adj* Indo-
Germanic, Indo-European
indoktrinieren [ɪndɔktri'niːrən] *vt* to
indoctrinate
Indonesien [ɪndo'neːziən] **(-s)** *nt* Indonesia
Indonesier, in (-s, -) *m(f)* Indonesian
indonesisch [ɪndo'neːzɪʃ] *adj* Indonesian
Indossament [ɪndɔsa'mɛnt] *nt* (*Comm*)
endorsement
Indossant [ɪndɔ'sant] *m* endorser
Indossat [ɪndɔ'saːt] **(-en, -en)** *m* endorsee
indossieren *vt* to endorse
industrialisieren [ɪndʊstriali'ziːrən] *vt* to
industrialize
Industrialisierung *f* industrialization
Industrie [ɪndʊs'triː] *f* industry; **in der ~
arbeiten** to be in industry; **Industriegebiet**
nt industrial area; **Industriegelände**
nt industrial *od* trading estate;
Industriekaufmann *m* industrial manager
industriell [ɪndʊstri'ɛl] *adj* industrial; **~e
Revolution** industrial revolution
Industrielle, r *f(m)* industrialist
Industrie- *zW*: **Industriestaat** *m* industrial
nation; **Industrie- und Handelskammer**
f chamber of industry and commerce;
Industriezone *f* (*bes Österr, Schweiz*) industrial
zone; **Industriezweig** *m* branch of industry
ineinander [ɪn|aɪ'nandər] *adv* in(to) one
another *od* each other; **~ übergehen** to merge
(into each other)
ineinandergreifen *unreg vi* (*lit*) to interlock;
(*Zahnräder*) to mesh; (*fig: Ereignisse etc*) to overlap
Infanterie [ɪnfantə'riː] *f* infantry
Infarkt [ɪn'farkt] **(-(e)s, -e)** *m* coronary
(thrombosis)

Infektion [ɪnfɛktsi'oːn] *f* infection
Infektionsherd *m* focus of infection
Infektionskrankheit *f* infectious disease
Infinitiv ['ɪnfinitiːf] **(-s, -e)** *m* infinitive
infizieren [ɪnfi'tsiːrən] *vt* to infect ▷ *vr*: **sich
(bei jdm) ~** to be infected (by sb)
in flagranti [ɪn fla'granti] *adv* in the act, red-
handed
Inflation [ɪnflatsi'oːn] *f* inflation
inflationär [ɪnflatsio'nɛːr] *adj* inflationary
inflationsbereinigt *adj* inflation-adjusted
Inflationsrate *f* rate of inflation
inflatorisch [ɪnfla'toːrɪʃ] *adj* inflationary
Info ['ɪnfo] **(-s, -s)** (*umg*) *nt* (information) leaflet
Infobrief ['ɪnfo-] *m* info letter
infolge [ɪn'fɔlgə] *präp +gen* as a result of, owing
to; **infolgedessen** *adv* consequently
Informatik [ɪnfɔr'maːtɪk] *f* information
studies *pl*
Informatiker, in (-s, -) *m(f)* computer scientist
Information [ɪnfɔrmatsi'oːn] *f* information *no
pl*; **Informationen** *pl* (*Comput*) data; **zu Ihrer
~** for your information
Informationsabruf *m* (*Comput*) information
retrieval
Informationsgesellschaft *f* information
society
Informationstechnik *f* information
technology
informativ [ɪnfɔrma'tiːf] *adj* informative
informieren [ɪnfɔr'miːrən] *vt*: **~ (über +akk)** to
inform (about) ▷ *vr*: **sich ~ (über +akk)** to find
out (about)
Infotelefon *nt* information line
infrage, in Frage [ɪn'fraːgə] *adv*: **etw ~ stellen**
to question sth; **~ kommend** possible;
(*Bewerber*) worth considering; **nicht ~
kommen** to be out of the question
Infrastruktur ['ɪnfraʃtrʊktuːr] *f* infrastructure
Infusion [ɪnfuzi'oːn] *f* infusion
Ing. *abk* = **Ingenieur**
Ingenieur [ɪnʒeni'øːr] *m* engineer;
Ingenieurschule *f* school of engineering
Ingwer ['ɪŋvər] **(-s)** *m* ginger
Inh. *abk* (= *Inhaber(in)*) prop.; (= *Inhalt*) cont.
Inhaber, in ['ɪnhaːbər(ɪn)] **(-s, -)** *m(f)* owner;
(*Comm*) proprietor; (*Hausinhaber*) occupier;
(*Lizenzinhaber*) licensee, holder; (*Fin*) bearer
inhaftieren [ɪnhaf'tiːrən] *vt* to take into
custody
inhalieren [ɪnha'liːrən] *vt, vi* to inhale
Inhalt ['ɪnhalt] **(-(e)s, -e)** *m* contents *pl*;
(*eines Buchs etc*) content; (*Math: Flächen*) area;
(*: Rauminhalt*) volume; **inhaltlich** *adj* as regards
content
Inhalts- *zW*: **Inhaltsangabe** *f* summary;
Inhaltslos *adj* empty; **Inhaltsreich** *adj* full;
Inhaltsverzeichnis *nt* table of contents;
(*Comput*) directory
inhuman ['ɪnhumaːn] *adj* inhuman
initialisieren [initsia:li'ziːrən] *vt* (*Comput*) to
initialize
Initialisierung *f* (*Comput*) initialization

Initiative [initsia'tiːvə] *f* initiative; **die ~ ergreifen** to take the initiative

Initiator, in [initsi'aːtɔr, -'toːrɪn] *m(f) (geh)* initiator

Injektion [ɪnjɛktsi'oːn] *f* injection

injizieren [ɪnji'tsiːrən] *vt* to inject; **jdm etw ~** to inject sb with sth

Inka ['ɪŋka] (-**(s), -s**) *f(m)* Inca

Inkaufnahme [ɪn'kaʊfnaːmə] *f (form)*: **unter ~ finanzieller Verluste** accepting the inevitable financial losses

inkl. *abk* (= *inklusive*) inc.

inklusive [ɪnklu'ziːvə] *präp +gen* inclusive of
▷ *adv* inclusive

Inklusivpreis *m* all-in rate

inkognito [ɪn'kɔgnito] *adv* incognito

inkonsequent ['ɪnkɔnzekvɛnt] *adj* inconsistent

inkorrekt ['ɪnkɔrɛkt] *adj* incorrect

Inkrafttreten [ɪn'krafttreːtən] (-**s**) *nt* coming into force

Inkubationszeit [ɪnkubatsi'oːnstsaɪt] *f (Med)* incubation period

Inland ['ɪnlant] (-**(e)s**) *nt (Geog)* inland; (*Pol, Comm*) home (country); **im ~ und Ausland** at home and abroad; **Inlandflug** *m* domestic flight

Inlandsporto *nt* inland postage

inmitten [ɪn'mɪtən] *präp +gen* in the middle of; **~ von** amongst

innehaben ['ɪnəhaːbən] *unreg vt* to hold

innehalten ['ɪnəhaltən] *unreg vi* to pause, stop

innen ['ɪnən] *adv* inside; **nach ~** inwards; **von ~** from the inside; **Innenarchitekt** *m* interior designer; **Innenaufnahme** *f* indoor photograph; **Innenbahn** *f (Sport)* inside lane; **Innendienst** *m*: **im Innendienst sein** to work in the office; **Inneneinrichtung** *f* (interior) furnishings *pl*; **Innenleben** *nt (seelisch)* emotional life; (*umg: körperlich*) insides *pl*; **Innenminister** *m* minister of the interior, Home Secretary (*Brit*); **Innenpolitik** *f* domestic policy; **innenpolitisch** *adj* relating to domestic policy, domestic; **Innenstadt** *f* town *od* city centre (*Brit*) *od* center (*US*)

innerbetrieblich *adj* in-house; **etw ~ regeln** to settle sth within the company

innerdeutsch *adj*: **~e(r) Handel** domestic trade in Germany

Innere, s *nt* inside; (*Mitte*) centre (*Brit*), center (*US*); (*fig*) heart

innere, r, s *adj* inner; (*im Körper, inländisch*) internal

Innereien [ɪnə'raɪən] *pl* innards *pl*

inner- *zW*: **innerhalb** *adv* within; (*räumlich*) inside ▷ *prep +dat* within; inside; **innerlich** *adj* internal; (*geistig*) inward; **Innerlichkeit** *f (Liter)* inwardness; **innerparteilich** *adj*: **innerparteiliche Demokratie** democracy (with)in the party structure

Innerste, s *nt* heart; **bis ins ~ getroffen** hurt to the quick

innerste, r, s *adj* innermost

innewohnen ['ɪnəvoːnən] *vi +dat (geh)* to be inherent in

innig ['ɪnɪç] *adj* profound; (*Freundschaft*) intimate; **mein ~ster Wunsch** my dearest wish

Innovation [ɪnovatsi'oːn] *f* innovation

Innung ['ɪnʊŋ] *f* (trade) guild; **du blamierst die ganze ~** (*hum: umg*) you are letting the whole side down

inoffiziell ['ɪnʔofitsiɛl] *adj* unofficial

ins [ɪns] = **in das**

Insasse ['ɪnzasə] (-**n, -n**) *m*, **Insassin** *f (einer Anstalt)* inmate; (*Aut*) passenger

insbesondere [ɪnsbə'zɔndərə] *adv* (e)specially

Inschrift ['ɪnʃrɪft] *f* inscription

Insekt [ɪn'zɛkt] (-**(e)s, -en**) *nt* insect

Insektenvertilgungsmittel *nt* insecticide

Insel ['ɪnzəl] (-**, -n**) *f* island

Inserat [ɪnze'raːt] (-**(e)s, -e**) *nt* advertisement

Inserent [ɪnze'rɛnt] *m* advertiser

inserieren [ɪnze'riːrən] *vt, vi* to advertise

insgeheim [ɪnsgə'haɪm] *adv* secretly

insgesamt [ɪnsgə'zamt] *adv* altogether, all in all

Insiderhandel ['ɪnsaɪdər-] *m* insider dealing *od* trading

Insidertipp ['ɪnsaɪdər-] *m* insider tip

insofern [ɪnzo'fɛrn] *adv* in this respect ▷ *konj* if; (*deshalb*) and so; **~ als** in so far as

insolvent ['ɪnzɔlvɛnt] *adj* bankrupt, insolvent

Insolvenz ['ɪnzɔlvɛnts] *f (Comm)* insolvency; **Insolvenzantrag** *m* application for insolvency proceedings; **Insolvenzverfahren** *nt* insolvency proceedings *pl*; **Insolvenzverwalter, in** *m(f)* official receiver

insoweit *adv, konj* = **insofern**

in spe [ɪn'ʃpeː] (*umg*) *adj*: **unser Schwiegersohn ~** our son-in-law to be, our future son-in-law

Inspektion [ɪnspɛktsi'oːn] *f* inspection; (*Aut*) service

Inspektor, in [ɪn'spɛktɔr, -'toːrɪn] (-**s, -en**) *m(f)* inspector

Inspiration [ɪnspiratsi'oːn] *f* inspiration

inspirieren [ɪnspi'riːrən] *vt* to inspire; **sich von etw ~ lassen** to get one's inspiration from sth

inspizieren [ɪnspi'tsiːrən] *vt* to inspect

Installateur [ɪnstala'tøːr] *m* plumber; (*Elektroinstallateur*) electrician

installieren [ɪnsta'liːrən] *vt* to install (*auch fig, Comput*)

Instandhaltung [ɪn'ʃtanthaltʊŋ] *f* maintenance

inständig [ɪn'ʃtɛndɪç] *adj* urgent; **~ bitten** to beg

Instandsetzung *f* overhaul; (*eines Gebäudes*) restoration

Instant Messaging ['ɪnstənt'mɛsɪdʒɪŋ] (-**, -**) *nt* instant messaging

Instanz [ɪn'stants] *f* authority; (*Jur*) court; **Verhandlung in erster/zweiter ~** first/second court case

Instanzenweg *m* official channels *pl*
Instinkt [ɪn'stɪŋkt] **(-(e)s, -e)** *m* instinct
instinktiv [ɪnstɪŋk'tiːf] *adj* instinctive
Institut [ɪnsti'tuːt] **(-(e)s, -e)** *nt* institute
Institution [ɪnstitutsi'oːn] *f* institution
Instrument [ɪnstru'mɛnt] *nt* instrument
Insulin [ɪnzu'liːn] **(-s)** *nt* insulin
inszenieren [ɪnstse'niːrən] *vt* to direct; *(fig)* to stage-manage
Inszenierung *f* production
intakt [ɪn'takt] *adj* intact
Integralrechnung [ɪnte'graːlrɛçnʊŋ] *f* integral calculus
Integration [ɪntegratsi'oːn] *f* integration
integrieren [ɪnte'griːrən] *vt* to integrate; **integrierte Gesamtschule** comprehensive school *(Brit)*
Integrität [ɪntegri'tɛːt] *f* integrity
Intellekt [ɪnte'lɛkt] **(-(e)s)** *m* intellect
intellektuell [ɪntelɛktu'ɛl] *adj* intellectual
Intellektuelle, r *f(m)* intellectual
intelligent [ɪntɛli'gɛnt] *adj* intelligent
Intelligenz [ɪntɛli'gɛnts] *f* intelligence; *(Leute)* intelligentsia *pl*; **Intelligenzquotient** *m* IQ, intelligence quotient
Intendant [ɪntɛn'dant] *m* director
Intensität [ɪntɛnzi'tɛːt] *f* intensity
intensiv [ɪntɛn'ziːf] *adj* intensive
intensivieren [ɪntɛnzi'viːrən] *vt* to intensify
Intensivkurs *m* intensive course
Intensivstation *f* intensive care unit
interaktiv *adj (Comput)* interactive
Intercityzug [ɪntər'sɪtitsuːk] *m* inter-city train
interessant [ɪntere'sant] *adj* interesting; **sich ~ machen** to attract attention
interessanterweise *adv* interestingly enough
Interesse [ɪnte'rɛsə] **(-s, -n)** *nt* interest; **~ haben an** +*dat* to be interested in
Interessengebiet *nt* field of interest
Interessengegensatz *m* clash of interests
Interessent, in [ɪntere'sɛnt(ɪn)] *m(f)* interested party; **es haben sich mehrere ~en gemeldet** several people have shown interest
interessieren [ɪntere'siːrən] *vt*: **jdn (für etw** *od* **an etw** *dat*) **~** to interest sb (in sth) ▷ *vr*: **sich ~ für** to be interested in
interessiert *adj*: **politisch ~** interested in politics
Interkontinentalrakete [ɪntərkɔntinɛn'taːl-rakeːtə] *f* intercontinental missile
interkulturell *adj* intercultural
intern [ɪn'tɛrn] *adj* internal
Internat [ɪntər'naːt] **(-(e)s, -e)** *nt* boarding school
international [ɪntɛrnatsio'naːl] *adj* international
Internatsschüler, in *m(f)* boarder
Internet ['ɪntɛrnɛt] **(-s)** *nt*: **das ~** the internet; **ins Internet stellen** to put on the internet; **Internetanbieter, in** *m(f)* internet provider; **internetbasiert** *adj* internet-based; **internetbasierte Anwendung** internet-based application; **Internetcafé** *nt* internet

café; **Internethändler, in** *m(f)* online trader *od* dealer; **Internethandy** *nt* mobile phone with internet access, smartphone; **Internetportal** *nt* web *od* internet portal; **Internetseite** *f* web page
internieren [ɪntɛr'niːrən] *vt* to intern
Internierungslager *nt* internment camp
Internist, in *m(f)* internist
Interpol ['ɪntɛrpoːl] **(-)** *f abk (= Internationale Polizei)* Interpol
Interpret [ɪntər'preːt] **(-en, -en)** *m*: **Lieder verschiedener ~en** songs by various singers
Interpretation [ɪntɛrpretatsi'oːn] *f* interpretation
interpretieren [ɪntɛrpre'tiːrən] *vt* to interpret
Interpretin *f siehe* **Interpret**
Interpunktion [ɪntɛrpʊŋktsi'oːn] *f* punctuation
Intervall [ɪntɛr'val] **(-s, -e)** *nt* interval
intervenieren [ɪntɛrve'niːrən] *vi* to intervene
Interview [ɪntər'vjuː] **(-s, -s)** *nt* interview; **interviewen** [-'vjuːən] *vt* to interview
intim [ɪn'tiːm] *adj* intimate; **Intimbereich** *m* *(Anat)* genital area
Intimität [ɪntimi'tɛːt] *f* intimacy
Intimsphäre *f*: **jds ~ verletzen** to invade sb's privacy
intolerant ['ɪntolerant] *adj* intolerant
intransitiv ['ɪntranzitiːf] *adj (Gram)* intransitive
Intrige [ɪn'triːgə] **(-, -n)** *f* intrigue, plot
intrinsisch [ɪn'trɪnzɪʃ] *adj*: **~er Wert** intrinsic value
introvertiert [ɪntrover'tiːrt] *adj*: **~ sein** to be an introvert
intuitiv [ɪntui'tiːf] *adj* intuitive
intus ['ɪntʊs] *adj*: **etw ~ haben** *(umg: Wissen)* to have got sth into one's head; *(Essen, Trinken)* to have got sth down one *(umg)*
Invalide [ɪnva'liːdə] **(-n, -n)** *m* disabled person, invalid
Invalidenrente *f* disability pension
Invasion [ɪnvazi'oːn] *f* invasion
Inventar [ɪnvɛn'taːr] **(-s, -e)** *nt* inventory; *(Comm)* assets and liabilities *pl*
Inventur [ɪnvɛn'tuːr] *f* stocktaking; **~ machen** to stocktake
investieren [ɪnvɛs'tiːrən] *vt* to invest
investiert *adj*: **~es Kapital** capital employed
Investition [ɪnvɛstitsi'oːn] *f* investment
Investitionszulage *f* investment grant
Investmentgesellschaft [ɪn'vɛstməntgəzɛlʃaft] *f* unit trust
inwiefern [ɪnvi'fɛrn] *adv* how far, to what extent
inwieweit [ɪnvi'vait] *adv* how far, to what extent
Inzest [ɪn'tsɛst] **(-(e)s, -e)** *m* incest *no pl*
inzwischen [ɪn'tsvɪʃən] *adv* meanwhile
IOK *nt abk (= Internationales Olympisches Komitee)* IOC
Ion [i'oːn] **(-s, -en)** *nt* ion
ionisch [i'oːnɪʃ] *adj* Ionian; **I~es Meer** Ionian

179

Sea

IP *abk (Comput: = Internet Protocol)* IP

IQ *m abk (= Intelligenzquotient)* IQ

i. R. *abk (= im Ruhestand)* retd

IRA *f abk (= Irisch-Republikanische Armee)* IRA

Irak [i'raːk] (**-s**) *m*: **(der)** ~ Iraq

Iraker, in (**-s, -**) *m(f)* Iraqi

irakisch *adj* Iraqi

Iran [i'raːn] (**-s**) *m*: **(der)** ~ Iran

Iraner, in (**-s, -**) *m(f)* Iranian

iranisch *adj* Iranian

irdisch ['ɪrdɪʃ] *adj* earthly; **den Weg alles I~en gehen** to go the way of all flesh

Ire ['iːrə] (**-n, -n**) *m* Irishman; **die ~n** the Irish

irgend ['ɪrɡənt] *adv* at all; **wann/was/wer ~** whenever/whatever/whoever; **irgendein, e, s** *adj* some, any; **haben Sie (sonst) noch irgendeinen Wunsch?** is there anything else you would like?; **irgendeine, r, s** *pron (Person)* somebody; *(Ding)* something; *(fragend, verneinend)* anybody/anything; **ich will nicht bloß irgendein(e)s** I don't want any old one; **irgendeinmal** *adv* sometime or other; *(fragend)* ever; **irgendetwas** *pron* something; *(fragend, verneinend)* anything; **irgendjemand** *pron* somebody; *(fragend, verneinend)* anybody; **irgendwann** *adv* sometime; **irgendwer** *(umg) pron* somebody; *(fragend, verneinend)* anybody; **irgendwie** *adv* somehow; **irgendwo** *adv* somewhere *(Brit)*, someplace *(US)*; *(fragend, verneinend, bedingend)* anywhere *(Brit)*, any place *(US)*; **irgendwohin** *adv* somewhere *(Brit)*, someplace *(US)*; *(fragend, verneinend, bedingend)* anywhere *(Brit)*, any place *(US)*

Irin ['iːrɪn] *f* Irishwoman; Irish girl

Iris ['iːrɪs] (**-, -**) *f* iris

irisch *adj* Irish; **I~e See** Irish Sea

IRK *nt abk (= Internationales Rotes Kreuz)* IRC

Irland ['ɪrlant] (**-s**) *nt* Ireland; *(Republik Irland)* Eire

Irländer ['ɪrlɛndər] (**-s, -**) *m* = **Ire**; **Irländerin** *f* = **Irin**

Ironie [iro'niː] *f* irony

ironisch [i'roːnɪʃ] *adj* ironic(al)

irre ['ɪrə] *adj* crazy, mad; **~ gut** *(umg)* way out *(umg)*; **Irre, r** *f(m)* lunatic; **irreführen** *vt* to mislead; **Irreführung** *f* fraud

irrelevant ['ɪrelevant] *adj*: **~ (für)** irrelevant (for *od* to)

irremachen *vt* to confuse

irren *vi* to be mistaken; *(umherirren)* to wander, stray ▷ *vr* to be mistaken; **jeder kann**

sich mal ~ anyone can make a mistake; **Irrenanstalt** *f (veraltet)* lunatic asylum; **Irrenhaus** *nt*: **hier geht es zu wie im Irrenhaus** *(umg)* this place is an absolute madhouse

Irrfahrt ['ɪrfaːrt] *f* wandering

irrig ['ɪrɪç] *adj* incorrect, wrong

irritieren [ɪri'tiːrən] *vt (verwirren)* to confuse, muddle; *(ärgern)* to irritate

Irr- *zW*: **Irrlicht** *nt* will-o'-the-wisp; **Irrsinn** *m* madness; **so ein Irrsinn, das zu tun!** what a crazy thing to do!; **irrsinnig** *adj* mad, crazy; *(umg)* terrific; **irrsinnig komisch** incredibly funny; **Irrtum** (**-s, -tümer**) *m* mistake, error; **im Irrtum sein** to be wrong *od* mistaken; **Irrtum!** wrong!; **irrtümlich** *adj* mistaken

ISBN *f abk (= Internationale Standardbuchnummer)* ISBN

Ischias ['ɪʃias] (**-**) *m od nt* sciatica

ISDN-Anlage [iːˈɛsdeːˈɛn-] *m (Tel)* ISDN connection

Islam ['ɪslam] (**-s**) *m* Islam

islamisch [ɪs'laːmɪʃ] *adj* Islamic

Island ['iːslant] (**-s**) *nt* Iceland

Isländer, in ['iːslɛndər(ɪn)] (**-s, -**) *m(f)* Icelander

isländisch *adj* Icelandic

Isolation [izolatsi'oːn] *f* isolation; *(Elek)* insulation; *(von Häftlingen)* solitary confinement

Isolator [izo'laːtɔr] *m* insulator

Isolierband *nt* insulating tape

isolieren [izo'liːrən] *vt* to isolate; *(Elek)* to insulate

Isolierstation *f (Med)* isolation ward

Isolierung *f* isolation; *(Elek)* insulation

Israel ['ɪsraeːl] (**-s**) *nt* Israel

Israeli¹ [ɪsra'eːli] (**-(s), -s**) *m* Israeli

Israeli² [ɪsra'eːli] (**-, -(s)**) *f* Israeli

israelisch *adj* Israeli

isst [ɪst] *vb siehe* **essen**

ist [ɪst] *vb siehe* **sein**

Istanbul ['ɪstambuːl] (**-s**) *nt* Istanbul

Istbestand *m (Geld)* cash in hand; *(Waren)* actual stock

Italien [i'taːliən] (**-s**) *nt* Italy

Italiener, in [itali'eːnər(ɪn)] (**-s, -**) *m(f)* Italian

italienisch *adj* Italian; **die ~e Schweiz** Italian-speaking Switzerland

i. V., I. V. *abk (= in Vertretung)* on behalf of; *(= in Vollmacht)* by proxy

IWF *m abk (= Internationaler Währungsfonds)* IMF

Jj

J, j [jɔt] *nt* J, j; **J wie Julius** ≈ J for Jack, J for Jig (US)

ja [ja:] *adv* **1** yes; **haben Sie das gesehen? — ja** did you see it? — yes(, I did); **ich glaube ja** (yes) I think so; **zu allem Ja und Amen sagen** (*umg*) to accept everything without question
2 (*fragend*) really; **ich habe gekündigt — ja?** I've quit — have you?; **du kommst, ja?** you're coming, aren't you?
3: sei ja vorsichtig do be careful; **Sie wissen ja, dass ...** as you know, ...; **tu das ja nicht!** don't do that!; **sie ist ja erst fünf** (after all) she's only five; **Sie wissen ja, wie das so ist** you know how it is; **ich habe es ja gewusst** I just knew it; **ja, also ...** well you see ...

Jacht [jaxt] (-, -**en**) *f* yacht
Jacke ['jakə] (-, -**n**) *f* jacket; (*Wolljacke*) cardigan
Jacketkrone ['dʒɛ'kɪtkro:nə] *f* (*Zahnkrone*) jacket crown
Jackett [ʒa'kɛt] (-**s**, -**s** *od* -**e**) *nt* jacket
Jagd [ja:kt] (-, -**en**) *f* hunt; (*Jagen*) hunting; **Jagdbeute** *f* kill; **Jagdflugzeug** *nt* fighter; **Jagdgewehr** *nt* sporting gun; **Jagdhund** *m* hunting dog; **Jagdschein** *m* hunting licence (*Brit*) *od* license (*US*); **Jagdwurst** *f* smoked sausage
jagen ['ja:gən] *vi* to hunt; (*eilen*) to race ▷ *vt* to hunt; (*wegjagen*) to drive (off); (*verfolgen*) to chase; **mit diesem Essen kannst du mich ~** (*umg*) I wouldn't touch that food with a barge pole (*Brit*) *od* ten-foot pole (*US*)
Jäger ['jɛ:gər] (-**s**, -) *m* hunter; **Jägerin** *f* huntress, huntswoman; **Jägerlatein** (*umg*) *nt* hunters' tales *pl*; **Jägerschnitzel** *nt* (*Koch*) *cutlet served with mushroom sauce*
jäh [jɛ:] *adj* abrupt, sudden; (*steil*) steep, precipitous; **jählings** *adv* abruptly
Jahr [ja:r] (-(**e**)**s**, -**e**) *nt* year; **im ~(e) 1066** in (the year) 1066; **die Sechzigerjahre** *od* **sechziger ~e** the sixties *pl*; **mit dreißig ~en** at the age of thirty; **in den besten ~en sein** to be in the prime of (one's) life; **nach ~ und Tag** after (many) years; **zwischen den ~en** (*umg*) between Christmas and New Year; **jahraus**

adv: **jahraus, jahrein** year in, year out; **Jahrbuch** *nt* annual, year book
jahrelang *adv* for years
Jahres- *zW*: **Jahresabonnement** *nt* annual subscription; **Jahresabschluss** *m* end of the year; (*Comm*) annual statement of account; **Jahresbeitrag** *m* annual subscription; **Jahresbericht** *m* annual report; **Jahreshauptversammlung** *f* (*Comm*) annual general meeting, AGM; **Jahreskarte** *f* annual season ticket; **Jahrestag** *m* anniversary; **Jahresumsatz** *m* (*Comm*) yearly turnover; **Jahreswechsel** *m* turn of the year; **Jahreszahl** *f* date, year; **Jahreszeit** *f* season
Jahr- *zW*: **Jahrgang** *m* age group; (*von Wein*) vintage; **er ist Jahrgang 1950** he was born in 1950; **Jahrhundert** *nt* century; **Jahrhundertfeier** *f* centenary; **Jahrhundertwende** *f* turn of the century
jährlich ['jɛ:rlɪç] *adj, adv* yearly; **zweimal ~** twice a year
Jahr- *zW*: **Jahrmarkt** *m* fair; **Jahrtausend** *nt* millennium; **Jahrzehnt** *nt* decade
Jähzorn ['jɛ:tsɔrn] *m* hot temper
jähzornig *adj* hot-tempered
Jalousie [ʒalu'zi:] *f* venetian blind
Jamaika [ja'maɪka] (-**s**) *nt* Jamaica
Jammer ['jamər] (-**s**) *m* misery; **es ist ein ~, dass ...** it is a crying shame that ...
jämmerlich ['jɛmərlɪç] *adj* wretched, pathetic; **Jämmerlichkeit** *f* wretchedness
jammern *vi* to wail ▷ *vt unpers*: **es jammert mich** it makes me feel sorry
jammerschade *adj*: **es ist ~** it is a crying shame
Jan. *abk* (= *Januar*) Jan.
Januar ['janua:r] (-**s**, -**e**) (*pl selten*) *m* January; *siehe auch* **September**
Japan ['ja:pan] (-**s**) *nt* Japan
Japaner, in [ja'pa:nər(ɪn)] (-**s**, -) *m(f)* Japanese
japanisch *adj* Japanese
Jargon [ʒar'gõ:] (-**s**, -**s**) *m* jargon
Jasager ['ja:za:gər] (-**s**, -) (*pej*) *m* yes man
Jastimme *f* vote in favour (*Brit*) *od* favor (*US*) (of)
jäten ['jɛ:tən] *vt, vi* to weed
Jauche ['jauxə] *f* liquid manure; **Jauchegrube** *f* cesspool, cesspit
jauchzen ['jauxtsən] *vi* to rejoice, shout (with

joy)

Jauchzer (**-s, -**) m shout of joy

jaulen ['jaʊlən] vi to howl

Jause ['jaʊzə] (Österr) f snack

jawohl adv yes (of course)

Jawort nt consent; **jdm das ~ geben** to consent to marry sb; (bei Trauung) to say "I do"

Jazz [dʒæz] (-) m jazz; **Jazzkeller** m jazz club

⊙ SCHLÜSSELWORT

je [je:] adv 1 (jemals) ever; **hast du so was je gesehen?** did you ever see anything like it?

2 (jeweils) every, each; **sie zahlten je 15 Euro** they paid 15 euros each

▷ konj 1: **je nach** depending on; **je nachdem** it depends; **je nachdem, ob ...** depending on whether ...

2: **je eher, desto** od **umso besser** the sooner the better; **je länger, je lieber** the longer the better

Jeans [dʒi:nz] pl jeans pl; **Jeansanzug** m denim suit

jede, r, s ['je:də(r, s)] adj (einzeln) each; (von zweien) either; (jede von allen) every ▷ indef pron (einzeln) each (one); (jede von allen) everyone, everybody; **ohne ~ Anstrengung** without any effort; **~r Zweite** every other (one); **~s Mal** every time, each time

jedenfalls adv in any case

jedermann pron everyone; **das ist nicht ~s Sache** it's not everyone's cup of tea

jederzeit adv at any time

jedoch [je'dɔx] adv however

jeher ['je:he:r] adv: **von ~** all along

jein [jaɪn] adv (hum) yes no

jemals ['je:ma:ls] adv ever

jemand ['je:mant] indef pron someone, somebody; (bei Fragen, bedingenden Sätzen, Negation) anyone, anybody

Jemen ['je:mən] (-s) m Yemen

Jemenit, in [jeme'ni:t(ɪn)] (-en, -en) m(f) Yemeni

jemenitisch adj Yemeni

Jenaer Glas® ['je:naərgla:s] nt heatproof glass, ≈ Pyrex®

jene, r, s ['je:nə(r, s)] adj that; (pl) those ▷ pron that one; (pl) those; (der Vorherige, die Vorherigen) the former

jenseits ['je:nzaɪts] adv on the other side ▷ präp +gen on the other side of, beyond; **Jenseits** nt: **das Jenseits** the hereafter, the beyond; **jdn ins Jenseits befördern** (umg) to send sb to kingdom come

Jesus ['je:zʊs] (**Jesu**) m Jesus; **~ Christus** Jesus Christ

jetten ['dʒɛtən] (umg) vi to jet (inf)

jetzig ['jɛtsɪç] adj present

jetzt [jɛtst] adv now; **~ gleich** right now

jeweilig adj respective; **die ~e Regierung** the government of the day

jeweils adv: **~ zwei zusammen** two at a time;

zu ~ 10 Euro at 10 euros each; **~ das Erste** the first each time; **~ am Monatsletzten** on the last day of each month

Jg. abk = **Jahrgang**

Jh. abk (= Jahrhundert) cent.

jiddisch ['jɪdɪʃ] adj Yiddish

Job [dʒɔp] (**-s, -s**) (umg) m job

jobben ['dʒɔbən] (umg) vi to work, have a job

Jobcenter ['dʒɔpsɛntər] nt job centre (Brit) od center

Jobmaschine ['dʒɔp-] f (umg) job-creation machine

Joch [jɔx] (**-(e)s, -e**) nt yoke

Jochbein nt cheekbone

Jockey, Jockei ['dʒɔke] (**-s, -s**) m jockey

Jod [jo:t] (**-(e)s**) nt iodine

jodeln ['jo:dəln] vi to yodel

joggen ['dʒɔgən] vi to jog

Joghurt, Jogurt ['jo:gʊrt] (**-s, -s**) m od nt yog(h)urt

Johannisbeere [jo'hanɪsbe:rə] f: **Rote ~** redcurrant; **Schwarze ~** blackcurrant

johlen ['jo:lən] vi to yell

Joint [dʒɔɪnt] (**-s, -s**) (umg) m joint

Joint Venture ['dʒɔɪntventʃə'] (**-, -s**) nt joint venture

Jolle ['jɔlə] (**-, -n**) f dinghy

Jongleur [ʒõ'glø:r] (**-s, -e**) m juggler

jonglieren [ʒõ'gli:rən] vi to juggle

Joppe ['jɔpə] (**-, -n**) f jacket

Jordanien [jɔr'da:niən] (**-s**) nt Jordan

Jordanier, in (**-s, -**) m(f) Jordanian

jordanisch adj Jordanian

Journalismus [ʒʊrna'lɪsmʊs] m journalism

Journalist, in [ʒʊrna'lɪst(ɪn)] m(f) journalist; **journalistisch** adj journalistic

Jubel ['ju:bəl] (**-s**) m rejoicing; **~, Trubel, Heiterkeit** laughter and merriment; **Jubeljahr** nt: **alle Jubeljahre (einmal)** (umg) once in a blue moon

jubeln vi to rejoice

Jubilar, in [jubi'la:r(ɪn)] (**-s, -e**) m(f) person celebrating an anniversary

Jubiläum [jubi'lɛ:ʊm] (**-s, Jubiläen**) nt jubilee; (Jahrestag) anniversary

jucken ['jʊkən] vi to itch ▷ vt: **es juckt mich am Arm** my arm is itching; **das juckt mich** that's itchy; **das juckt mich doch nicht** (umg) I don't care

Juckpulver nt itching powder

Juckreiz m itch

Judaslohn ['ju:daslo:n] m (liter) blood money

Jude ['ju:də] (**-n, -n**) m Jew

Juden- zW: **Judenstern** m star of David; **Judentum** (**-s**) nt (die Juden) Jewry; **Judenverfolgung** f persecution of the Jews

Jüdin ['jy:dɪn] f Jewess

jüdisch adj Jewish

Judo ['ju:do] (**-(s)**) nt judo

Jugend ['ju:gənt] (**-**) f youth; **Jugendamt** nt youth welfare department; **jugendfrei** adj suitable for young people; (Film) U(-certificate), G (US); **Jugendherberge** f youth hostel; **Jugendhilfe** f youth welfare scheme; **Jugendkriminalität** f juvenile crime; **jugendlich** adj youthful; **Jugendliche, r** f(m) teenager, young person; **Jugendliebe** f (Celiebte(r)) love of one's youth; **Jugendrichter** m juvenile court judge; **Jugendschutz** m protection of children and young people; **Jugendstil** m (Kunst) Art Nouveau; **Jugendstrafanstalt** f youth custody centre (Brit); **Jugendsünde** f youthful misdeed; **Jugendzentrum** nt youth centre (Brit) od center (US)

Jugoslawe [jugo'slaːvə] (-n, -n) m Yugoslav

Jugoslawien [jugo'slaːviən] (-s) nt Yugoslavia

Jugoslawin [jugo'slaːvɪn] f Yugoslav

jugoslawisch adj Yugoslav(ian)

Juli ['juːli] (-(s), -s) (pl selten) m July; siehe auch **September**

jun. abk (= junior) jun.

jung [jʊŋ] adj young

Junge (-n, -n) m boy, lad ▷ nt young animal; (pl) young pl

Jünger ['jʏŋər] (-s, -) m disciple

jünger adj younger

Jungfer (-, -n) f: **alte** ~ old maid

Jungfernfahrt f maiden voyage

Jung- zW: **Jungfrau** f virgin; (Astrol) Virgo; **Junggeselle** m bachelor; **Junggesellin** f bachelor girl; (älter) single woman

Jüngling ['jʏŋlɪŋ] m youth

Jungsozialist m (Brd Pol) Young Socialist

jüngst [jʏŋst] adv lately, recently

jüngste, r, s adj youngest; (neueste) latest; **das J~ Gericht** the Last Judgement; **der J~ Tag** Doomsday, the Day of Judgement

Jungwähler, in m(f) young voter

Juni ['juːni] (-(s), -s) (pl selten) m June; siehe auch **September**

Junior ['juːnior] (-s, -en) m junior

Junta ['xʊnta] (-, -ten) f (Pol) junta

jur. abk = **juristisch**

Jura ['juːra] no art (Univ) law

Jurist, in [ju'rɪst(ɪn)] m(f) jurist, lawyer; (Student) law student; **juristisch** adj legal

Juso ['juːzo] (-s, -s) m abk = **Jungsozialist**

just [jʊst] adv just

Justiz [jʊs'tiːts] (-) f justice; **Justizbeamte, r** m judicial officer; **Justizirrtum** m miscarriage of justice; **Justizminister** m minister of justice; **Justizmord** m judicial murder

Juwel [ju've:l] (-s, -en) m od nt jewel

Juwelier [juve'liːr] (-s, -e) m jeweller (Brit), jeweler (US); **Juweliergeschäft** nt jeweller's (Brit) od jeweler's (US) (shop)

Jux [jʊks] (-es, -e) m joke, lark; **etw aus** ~ **tun/ sagen** (umg) to do/say sth in fun

jwd [jɔtve:'de:] adv (hum) in the back of beyond

Kk

K, k [kaː] nt K, k; **K wie Kaufmann** ≈ K for King
Kabarett [kabaˈrɛt] (**-s, -e** od **-s**) nt cabaret;
 Kabarettist, in [kabarɛˈtɪst(ɪn)] m(f) cabaret
 artiste
Kabel [ˈkaːbəl] (**-s, -**) nt (Elek) wire; (stark) cable;
 Kabelanschluss m: **~anschluss haben** to have
 cable television; **Kabelfernsehen** nt cable
 television
Kabeljau [ˈkaːbəljaʊ] (**-s, -e** od **-s**) m cod
kabeln vt, vi to cable
Kabelsalat (umg) m tangle of cable
Kabine [kaˈbiːnə] f cabin; (Zelle) cubicle
Kabinett [kabiˈnɛt] (**-s, -e**) nt (Pol) cabinet;
 (kleines Zimmer) small room ▷ m high-quality
 German white wine
Kabriolett [kabrioˈlɛt] (**-s, -s**) nt (Aut)
 convertible
Kachel [ˈkaxəl] (**-, -n**) f tile
kacheln vt to tile
Kachelofen m tiled stove
Kacke [ˈkakə] (**-, -n**) (umg!) f crap (!)
Kadaver [kaˈdaːvər] (**-s, -**) m carcass
Kader [ˈkaːdər] (**-s, -**) m (Mil, Pol) cadre; (Sport)
 squad; (DDR, Schweiz: Fachleute) group of
 specialists; **Kaderschmiede** f (Pol: umg)
 institution for the training of cadre personnel
Kadett [kaˈdɛt] (**-en, -en**) m cadet
Käfer [ˈkɛːfər] (**-s, -**) m beetle
Kaff [kaf] (**-s, -s**) (umg) nt dump, hole
Kaffee [ˈkafe] (**-s, -s**) m coffee; **zwei ~, bitte!**
 two coffees, please; **das ist kalter ~** (umg)
 that's old hat; **Kaffeekanne** f coffeepot;
 Kaffeeklatsch m, **Kaffeekränzchen** nt
 coffee circle; **Kaffeelöffel** m coffee spoon;
 Kaffeemaschine f coffee maker; **Kaffeemühle**
 f coffee grinder; **Kaffeesatz** m coffee grounds
 pl; **Kaffeetante** f (hum) coffee addict; (in Café)
 old biddy; **Kaffeewärmer** m cosy (for coffeepot)
Käfig [ˈkɛːfɪç] (**-s, -e**) m cage
kahl [kaːl] adj bald; **~ fressen** to strip bare;
 ~ geschoren shaven, shorn; **Kahlheit** f
 baldness; **kahlköpfig** adj bald-headed;
 Kahlschlag m (in Wald) clearing
Kahn [kaːn] (**-(e)s, ̈e**) m boat, barge
Kai [kaɪ] (**-s, -e** od **-s**) m quay
Kairo [ˈkaɪro] (**-s**) nt Cairo
Kaiser [ˈkaɪzər] (**-s, -**) m emperor; **Kaiserin** f
 empress; **kaiserlich** adj imperial; **Kaiserreich**

nt empire; **Kaiserschmarren** [ˈkaɪzərʃmarən]
 m (Koch) sugared, cut-up pancake with raisins;
 Kaiserschnitt m (Med) Caesarean (Brit) od
 Cesarean (US) (section)
Kajak [ˈkaːjak] (**-s, -s**) m or nt kayak
Kajüte [kaˈjyːtə] (**-, -n**) f cabin
Kakao [kaˈkaːo] (**-s, -s**) m cocoa; **jdn durch
 den ~ ziehen** (umg: veralbern) to make fun of sb;
 (: boshaft reden) to run sb down
Kakerlak [ˈkaːkərlak] (**-en, -en**) m cockroach
Kaktee [kakˈteːə] (**-, -n**) f cactus
Kaktus [ˈkaktʊs] (**-, -se**) m cactus
Kalabrien [kaˈlaːbriən] (**-s**) nt Calabria
Kalauer [ˈkaːlaʊər] (**-s, -**) m corny joke;
 (Wortspiel) corny pun
Kalb [kalp] (**-(e)s, ̈er**) nt calf; **kalben** [ˈkalbən]
 vi to calve; **Kalbfleisch** nt veal
Kalbsleder nt calf(skin)
Kalender [kaˈlɛndər] (**-s, -**) m calendar;
 (Taschenkalender) diary
Kali [ˈkaːli] (**-s, -s**) nt potash
Kaliber [kaˈliːbər] (**-s, -**) nt (lit, fig) calibre (Brit),
 caliber (US)
Kalifornien [kaliˈfɔrniən] (**-s**) nt California
Kalk [kalk] (**-(e)s, -e**) m lime; (Biol) calcium;
 Kalkstein m limestone
Kalkül [kalˈkyːl] (**-s, -e**) m od nt (geh) calculation
Kalkulation [kalkulatsiˈoːn] f calculation
Kalkulator [kalkuˈlaːtɔr] m cost accountant
kalkulieren [kalkuˈliːrən] vt to calculate
kalkuliert adj: **~es Risiko** calculated risk
Kalkutta [kalˈkʊta] (**-s**) nt Calcutta
Kalorie [kaloˈriː] (**-, -n**) f calorie
kalorienarm adj low-calorie
kalt [kalt] adj cold; **mir ist (es) ~** I am cold;
 ~e Platte cold meat; **der K~e Krieg** the Cold
 War; **etw ~ stellen** to chill, to put sth to chill;
 die Wohnung kostet ~ 500 Euro the flat
 costs 500 euros without heating; **~ bleiben**
 to be unmoved; **~ lächelnd** (ironisch) cool as
 you please; **kaltblütig** adj cold-blooded; (ruhig)
 cool; **Kaltblütigkeit** f cold-bloodedness;
 coolness
Kälte [ˈkɛltə] (**-**) f coldness; (Wetter) cold;
 Kälteeinbruch m cold spell; **Kältegrad** m
 degree of frost od below zero; **Kältewelle** f cold
 spell
kalt- zW: **kaltherzig** adj cold-hearted;

kaltmachen (*umg*) *vt* to do in; **Kaltmiete** *f* rent exclusive of heating; **Kaltschale** *f* (*Koch*) *cold sweet soup*; **kaltschnäuzig** *adj* cold, unfeeling; **kaltstellen** *vt* (*fig*) to leave out in the cold

Kalzium ['kaltsiʊm] (**-s**) *nt* calcium

kam *etc* [kaːm] *vb siehe* **kommen**

Kambodscha [kam'bɔdʒa] *nt* Cambodia

Kamel [ka'meːl] (**-(e)s, -e**) *nt* camel

Kamera ['kamera] (**-, -s**) *f* camera

Kamerad, in [kamə'raːt, -'raːdɪn] (**-en, -en**) *m(f)* comrade, friend; **Kameradschaft** *f* comradeship; **kameradschaftlich** *adj* comradely

Kamera- *zW:* **Kameraführung** *f* camera work; **Kameramann** (**-(e)s,** *pl* **-männer**) *m* cameraman; **Kamerarekorder** *m* camcorder; **Kameratelefon** *nt* cameraphone

Kamerun ['kaməruːn] (**-s**) *nt* Cameroon

Kamille [ka'mɪlə] (**-, -n**) *f* camomile

Kamillentee *m* camomile tea

Kamin [ka'miːn] (**-s, -e**) *m* (*außen*) chimney; (*innen*) fireside; (*Feuerstelle*) fireplace; **Kaminfeger** (**-s, -**) *m* chimney sweep; **Kaminkehrer** (**-s, -**) *m* chimney sweep

Kamm [kam] (**-(e)s, ̈e**) *m* comb; (*Bergkamm*) ridge; (*Hahnenkamm*) crest; **alle/alles über einen ~ scheren** (*fig*) to lump everyone/everything together

kämmen ['kɛmən] *vt* to comb

Kammer ['kamər] (**-, -n**) *f* chamber; (*Zimmer*) small bedroom; **Kammerdiener** *m* valet; **Kammerjäger** *m* (*Schädlingsbekämpfer*) pest controller; **Kammermusik** *f* chamber music; **Kammerzofe** *f* chambermaid

Kammstück *nt* (*Koch*) shoulder

Kampagne [kam'panjə] (**-, -n**) *f* campaign

Kampf [kampf] (**-(e)s, ̈e**) *m* fight, battle; (*Wettbewerb*) contest; (*fig: Anstrengung*) struggle; **jdm/etw den ~ ansagen** (*fig*) to declare war on sb/sth; **kampfbereit** *adj* ready for action

kämpfen ['kɛmpfən] *vi* to fight; **ich habe lange mit mir ~ müssen, ehe ...** I had a long battle with myself before ...

Kampfer ['kampfər] (**-s**) *m* camphor

Kämpfer, in (**-s, -**) *m(f)* fighter, combatant

Kampf- *zW:* **Kampfflugzeug** *nt* fighter (aircraft); **Kampfgeist** *m* fighting spirit; **Kampfhandlung** *f* action; **Kampfkunst** *f* martial arts *pl*; **kampflos** *adj* without a fight; **kampflustig** *adj* pugnacious; **Kampfplatz** *m* battlefield; (*Sport*) arena, stadium; **Kampfrichter** *m* (*Sport*) referee; **Kampfsport** *m* martial art

Kampuchea [kampʊ'tʃeːa] (**-s**) *nt* Kampuchea

Kanada ['kanada] (**-s**) *nt* Canada

Kanadier, in [ka'naːdiər(ɪn)] (**-s, -**) *m(f)* Canadian

kanadisch [ka'naːdɪʃ] *adj* Canadian

Kanal [ka'naːl] (**-s, Kanäle**) *m* (*Fluss*) canal; (*Rinne*) channel; (*für Abfluss*) drain; **der ~** (*auch:* **der Ärmelkanal**) the (English) Channel

Kanalinseln *pl* Channel Islands *pl*

Kanalisation [kanalizatsi'oːn] *f* sewage system

kanalisieren [kanali'ziːrən] *vt* to provide with a sewage system; (*fig: Energie etc*) to channel

Kanaltunnel *m* Channel Tunnel

Kanarienvogel [ka'naːriənfoːgəl] *m* canary

Kanarische Inseln [ka'naːrɪʃə'ɪnzəln] *pl* Canary Islands *pl*, Canaries *pl*

Kandare [kan'daːrə] (**-, -n**) *f*: **jdn an die ~ nehmen** (*fig*) to take sb in hand

Kandidat, in [kandi'daːt(ɪn)] (**-en, -en**) *m(f)* candidate; **jdn als ~en aufstellen** to nominate sb

Kandidatur [kandida'tuːr] *f* candidature, candidacy

kandidieren [kandi'diːrən] *vi* (*Pol*) to stand, run

kandiert [kan'diːrt] *adj* (*Frucht*) candied

Kandis ['kandɪs], **Kandiszucker** ['kandɪstsʊkər] (**-**) *m* rock candy

Känguru ['kɛŋguru] (**-s, -s**) *nt* kangaroo

Kaninchen [ka'niːnçən] *nt* rabbit

Kanister [ka'nɪstər] (**-s, -**) *m* can, canister

kann [kan] *vb siehe* **können**

Kännchen ['kɛnçən] *nt* pot; (*für Milch*) jug

Kanne ['kanə] (**-, -n**) *f* (*Krug*) jug; (*Kaffeekanne*) pot; (*Milchkanne*) churn; (*Gießkanne*) watering can

Kannibale [kani'baːlə] (**-n, -n**) *m* cannibal

kannte *etc* ['kantə] *vb siehe* **kennen**

Kanon [ka'nɔn] (**-s, -s**) *m* canon

Kanone [ka'noːnə] (**-, -n**) *f* gun; (*Hist*) cannon; (*fig: Mensch*) ace; **das ist unter aller ~** (*umg*) that defies description

Kanonenfutter (*umg*) *nt* cannon fodder

Kant. *abk* = **Kanton**

Kantate [kan'taːtə] (**-, -n**) *f* cantata

Kante ['kantə] (**-, -n**) *f* edge; **Geld auf die hohe ~ legen** (*umg*) to put money by

kantig ['kantɪç] *adj* (*Holz*) edged; (*Gesicht*) angular

Kantine [kan'tiːnə] *f* canteen

Kanton [kan'toːn] (**-s, -e**) *nt* canton

Kantor ['kantɔr] *m* choirmaster

Kanu ['kaːnu] (**-s, -s**) *nt* canoe

Kanzel ['kantsəl] (**-, -n**) *f* pulpit; (*Aviat*) cockpit

Kanzlei [kants'laɪ] *f* chancery; (*Büro*) chambers *pl*

Kanzler, in ['kantslər] (**-s, -**) *m(f)* chancellor

Kanzlerkandidatur *f* candidacy for the chancellorship

Kap [kap] (**-s, -s**) *nt* cape; **das ~ der guten Hoffnung** the Cape of Good Hope

Kapazität [kapatsi'tɛːt] *f* capacity; (*Fachmann*) authority

Kapelle [ka'pɛlə] *f* (*Gebäude*) chapel; (*Mus*) band

Kapellmeister, in *m(f)* director of music; (*Mil, von Tanzkapelle etc*) bandmaster, bandleader

Kaper ['kaːpər] (**-, -n**) *f* caper

kapern *vt* to capture

kapieren [ka'piːrən] (*umg*) *vt, vi* to understand

Kapital [kapi'taːl] (**-s, -e** *od* **-ien**) *nt* capital; **aus etw ~ schlagen** (*pej: lit, fig*) to make capital out of sth; **Kapitalanlage** *f*

k

investment; **Kapitalaufwand** m capital
expenditure; **Kapitalertrag** m capital
gains pl; **Kapitalertragssteuer** f capital
gains tax; **Kapitalflucht** f flight of capital;
Kapitalgesellschaft f (Comm) joint-stock
company; **Kapitalgüter** pl capital goods pl;
kapitalintensiv adj capital-intensive
Kapitalismus [kapita'lɪsmʊs] m capitalism
Kapitalist [kapita'lɪst] m capitalist
kapitalistisch adj capitalist
Kapital- zW: **kapitalkräftig** adj wealthy;
Kapitalmarkt m money market;
kapitalschwach adj financially weak;
kapitalstark adj financially strong;
Kapitalverbrechen nt serious crime; (mit
Todesstrafe) capital crime
Kapitän [kapi'tɛ:n] (**-s, -e**) m captain
Kapitel [ka'pɪtəl] (**-s, -**) nt chapter; **ein
trauriges ~** (Angelegenheit) a sad story
Kapitulation [kapitulatsi'o:n] f capitulation
kapitulieren [kapitu'li:rən] vi to capitulate
Kaplan [ka'pla:n] (**-s, Kapläne**) m chaplain
Kappe ['kapə] (**-, -n**) f cap; (Kapuze) hood; **das
nehme ich auf meine ~** (fig: umg) I'll take the
responsibility for that
kappen vt to cut
Kapsel ['kapsəl] (**-, -n**) f capsule
Kapstadt ['kapʃtat] nt Cape Town
kaputt [ka'pʊt] (umg) adj smashed, broken;
(Person) exhausted, knackered; **etw ~
machen/schlagen** to break/smash sth; **der
Fernseher ist ~** the TV's not working; **ein
~er Typ** a bum; siehe auch **kaputtmachen**;
kaputtgehen unreg vi to break; (Schuhe) to fall
apart; (Firma) to go bust; (Stoff) to wear out;
(sterben) to cop it (umg); **kaputtlachen** vr to
laugh o.s. silly; **kaputtmachen** vt to break;
(Mensch) to exhaust, wear out; **kaputtschlagen**
unreg vt to smash
Kapuze [ka'pu:tsə] (**-, -n**) f hood
Karabiner [kara'bi:nər] (**-s, -**) m (Gewehr)
carbine
Karacho [ka'raxo] (**-s**) nt: **mit ~** (umg) hell for
leather
Karaffe [ka'rafə] (**-, -n**) f carafe; (geschliffen)
decanter
Karambolage [karambo'la:ʒə] (**-, -n**) f
(Zusammenstoß) crash
Karamell [kara'mɛl] (**-s**) m caramel;
Karamellbonbon m od nt toffee
Karat [ka'ra:t] (**-(e)s, -e**) nt carat
Karate (**-s**) nt karate
Karawane [kara'va:nə] (**-, -n**) f caravan
Kardinal [kardi'na:l] (**-s, Kardinäle**) m
cardinal; **Kardinalfehler** m cardinal error;
Kardinalzahl f cardinal number
Karenzzeit [ka'rɛntstsait] f waiting period
Karfreitag [ka:r'fraita:k] m Good Friday
karg [kark] adj scanty, poor; (Mahlzeit)
meagre (Brit), meager (US); **etw ~ bemessen**
to be mean with sth; **Kargheit** f poverty,
scantiness; meagreness (Brit), meagerness (US)
kärglich ['kɛrklɪç] adj poor, scanty

Kargo ['kargo] (**-s, -s**) m (Comm) cargo
Karibik [ka'ri:bɪk] (**-**) f: **die ~** the Caribbean
karibisch adj Caribbean; **das K~e Meer** the
Caribbean Sea
kariert [ka'ri:rt] adj (Stoff) checked (Brit),
checkered (US); (Papier) squared; **~ reden** (umg)
to talk rubbish od nonsense
Karies ['ka:riɛs] (**-**) f caries
Karikatur [karika'tu:r] f caricature;
Karikaturist, in [karikatu:'rɪst(ɪn)] m(f)
cartoonist
karikieren [kari'ki:rən] vt to caricature
karitativ [karita'ti:f] adj charitable
Karneval ['karnəval] (**-s, -e** od **-s**) m carnival;
see culture note

KARNEVAL

Karneval is the name given to the days
immediately before Lent when people
gather to sing, dance, eat, drink and
generally make merry before the fasting
begins. *Rosenmontag*, the day before Shrove
Tuesday, is the most important day of
Karneval on the Rhine. Most firms take
a day's holiday on that day to enjoy the
parades and revelry. In South Germany
Karneval is called "Fasching".

Karnickel [kar'nɪkəl] (**-s, -**) (umg) nt rabbit
Kärnten ['kɛrntən] (**-s**) nt Carinthia
Karo ['ka:ro] (**-s, -s**) nt square; (Karten)
diamonds; **Karoass** nt ace of diamonds
Karosse [ka'rɔsə] (**-, -n**) f coach, carriage
Karosserie [karɔsə'ri:] f (Aut) body(work)
Karotte [ka'rɔtə] (**-, -n**) f carrot
Karpaten [kar'pa:tən] pl Carpathians pl
Karpfen ['karpfən] (**-s, -**) m carp
Karre ['karə] (**-, -n**) f = **Karren**
Karree [ka:'re:] (**-s, -s**) nt: **einmal ums ~ gehen**
(umg) to walk around the block
karren [ka'rən] vt to cart, transport; **Karren**
(**-s, -**) m cart, barrow; **den Karren aus dem
Dreck ziehen** (umg) to get things sorted out
Karriere [kari'ɛ:rə] (**-, -n**) f career; **~ machen** to
get on, get to the top; **Karrieremacher, in** m(f)
careerist
Karsamstag [ka:r'zamsta:k] m Easter
Saturday
Karst [karst] (**-s, -e**) m (Geog, Geol) karst, barren
landscape
Karte ['kartə] (**-, -n**) f card; (Landkarte) map;
(Speisekarte) menu; (Eintrittskarte, Fahrkarte)
ticket; **mit offenen ~n spielen** (fig) to put
one's cards on the table; **alles auf eine ~
setzen** to put all one's eggs in one basket
Kartei [kar'tai] f card index; **Karteikarte** f
index card; **Karteileiche** (umg) f sleeping od
non-active member; **Karteischrank** m filing
cabinet
Kartell [kar'tɛl] (**-s, -e**) nt cartel;
Kartellamt nt monopolies commission;
Kartellgesetzgebung f anti-trust legislation

Karten- zW: **Kartenhaus** nt (lit, fig) house of cards; **Kartenlegen** nt fortune-telling (using cards); **Kartenspiel** nt card game; (Karten) pack (Brit) od deck (US) of cards; **Kartentelefon** nt cardphone; **Kartenvorverkauf** m advance sale of tickets

Kartoffel [kar'tɔfəl] (-, -n) f potato; **Kartoffelbrei** m mashed potatoes pl; **Kartoffelchips** pl potato crisps pl (Brit), potato chips pl (US); **Kartoffelpüree** nt mashed potatoes pl; **Kartoffelsalat** m potato salad

Karton [kar'tõ:] (-s, -s) m cardboard; (Schachtel) cardboard box

kartoniert [karto'ni:rt] adj hardback

Karussell [karu'sɛl] (-s, -s) nt roundabout (Brit), merry-go-round

Karwoche ['ka:rvɔxə] f Holy Week

Karzinom [kartsi'no:m] (-s, -e) nt (Med) carcinoma

Kasachstan [kazaxs'ta:n] (-s) nt (Geog) Kazakhstan

Kaschemme [ka'ʃɛmə] (-, -n) f dive

kaschieren [ka'ʃi:rən] vt to conceal, cover up

Kaschmir ['kaʃmi:r] (-s) nt (Geog) Kashmir

Käse ['kɛ:zə] (-s, -) m cheese; (umg: Unsinn) rubbish, twaddle; **Käseblatt** (umg) nt (local) rag; **Käseglocke** f cheese cover; **Käsekuchen** m cheesecake

Kaserne [ka'zɛrnə] (-, -n) f barracks pl

Kasernenhof m parade ground

käsig ['kɛ:zɪç] adj (fig: umg: Gesicht, Haut) pasty, pale; (vor Schreck) white; (lit) cheesy

Kasino [ka'zi:no] (-s, -s) nt club; (Mil) officers' mess; (Spielkasino) casino

Kaskoversicherung ['kaskofɛrzɪçərʊŋ] f (Aut: Teilkaskoversicherung) ≈ third party, fire and theft insurance; (: Vollkaskoversicherung) fully comprehensive insurance

Kasper ['kaspər] (-s, -) m Punch; (fig) clown

Kasperletheater ['kaspərlətea:tər], **Kasperltheater** ['kaspərltea:tər] nt Punch and Judy (show)

Kaspisches Meer ['kaspɪʃəs'me:r] nt Caspian Sea

Kasse ['kasə] (-, -n) f (Geldkasten) cashbox; (in Geschäft) till, cash register; (Kinokasse, Theaterkasse etc) box office; (Krankenkasse) health insurance; (Sparkasse) savings bank; **die ~ führen** to be in charge of the money; **jdn zur ~ bitten** to ask sb to pay up; **~ machen** to count the money; **getrennte ~ führen** to pay separately; **an der ~** (in Geschäft) at the (cash) desk; **gut bei ~ sein** to be in the money

Kasseler ['kasələr] (-s, -) nt lightly smoked pork loin

Kassen- zW: **Kassenarzt** m ≈ National Health doctor (Brit), ≈ panel doctor (US); **Kassenbestand** m cash balance; **Kassenführer** m (Comm) cashier; **Kassenpatient** m ≈ National Health patient (Brit); **Kassenprüfung** f audit; **Kassenschlager** (umg) m (Theat etc) box-office hit; (: Ware) big seller; **Kassensturz** m: **Kassensturz machen** to check one's money; **Kassenwart** m (von Klub etc) treasurer; **Kassenzettel** m sales slip

Kasserolle [kasə'rɔlə] (-, -n) f casserole

Kassette [ka'sɛtə] f small box; (Tonband, Phot) cassette; (Comput) cartridge, cassette; (Bücherkassette) case

Kassettenrekorder (-s, -) m cassette recorder

Kassiber [ka'si:bər] (-s, -) m (in Gefängnis) secret message

kassieren [ka'si:rən] vt (Gelder etc) to collect; (umg: wegnehmen) to take (away) ▷ vi: **darf ich ~?** would you like to pay now?

Kassierer, in [ka'si:rər(ɪn)] (-s, -) m(f) cashier; (von Klub) treasurer

Kastanie [kas'ta:niə] f chestnut

Kastanienbaum m chestnut tree

Kästchen ['kɛstçən] nt small box, casket

Kaste ['kastə] (-, -n) f caste

Kasten ['kastən] (-s, ¨) m box (auch Sport), case; (Truhe) chest; **er hat was auf dem ~** (umg) he's brainy; **Kastenform** f (Koch) (square) baking tin (Brit) od pan (US); **Kastenwagen** m van

kastrieren [kas'tri:rən] vt to castrate

Kat (-, -s) m abk (Aut) = **Katalysator**

katalanisch [kata'la:nɪʃ] adj Catalan

Katalog [kata'lo:k] (-(e)s, -e) m catalogue (Brit), catalog (US)

katalogisieren [katalogi'zi:rən] vt to catalogue (Brit), catalog (US)

Katalysator [kataly'za:tɔr] m (lit, fig) catalyst; (Aut) catalytic converter; **~-Auto** vehicle fitted with a catalytic converter

Katapult [kata'pʊlt] (-(e)s, -e) nt or m catapult

katapultieren [katapʊl'ti:rən] vt to catapult ▷ vr to catapult o.s.; (Pilot) to eject

Katar ['ka:tar] nt Qatar

Katarrh, Katarr [ka'tar] (-s, -e) m catarrh

Katasteramt [ka'tastəramt] nt land registry

katastrophal [katastro'fa:l] adj catastrophic

Katastrophe [kata'stro:fə] (-, -n) f catastrophe, disaster

Katastrophen- zW: **Katastrophenalarm** m emergency alert; **Katastrophengebiet** nt disaster area; **Katastrophenmedizin** f medical treatment in disasters; **Katastrophenmeldung** f news of a/the catastrophe; **Katastrophenschutz** m disaster control

Katechismus [kate'çɪsmʊs] m catechism

Kategorie [katego'ri:] f category

kategorisch [kate'go:rɪʃ] adj categorical

kategorisieren [kategori'zi:rən] vt to categorize

Kater ['ka:tər] (-s, -) m tomcat; (umg) hangover; **Katerfrühstück** nt breakfast (of pickled herring etc) to cure a hangover

kath. abk = **katholisch**

Katheder [ka'te:dər] (-s, -) nt (Sch) teacher's desk; (Univ) lectern

Kathedrale [kate'dra:lə] (-, -n) f cathedral

Katheter [ka'te:tər] (-s, -) m (Med) catheter

Kathode [ka'to:də] (-, -n) f cathode

Katholik, in [kato'li:k(ɪn)] (-en, -en) m(f) Catholic

k

katholisch [ka'to:lɪʃ] *adj* Catholic
Katholizismus [katoli'tsɪsmʊs] *m* Catholicism
Katode [ka'to:də] (**-, -n**) *f* = **Kathode**
katzbuckeln ['katsbʊkəln] (*pej: umg*) *vi* to bow and scrape
Kätzchen ['kɛtsçən] *nt* kitten
Katze ['katsə] (**-, -n**) *f* cat; **die ~ im Sack kaufen** to buy a pig in a poke; **für die Katz** (*umg*) in vain, for nothing
Katzen- *zW*: **Katzenauge** *nt* cat's-eye (*Brit*); (*am Fahrrad*) rear light; **Katzenjammer** (*umg*) *m* hangover; **Katzenmusik** *f* (*fig*) caterwauling; **Katzensprung** (*umg*) *m* stone's throw, short distance; **Katzentür** *f* cat flap; **Katzenwäsche** *f* a lick and a promise
Kauderwelsch ['kaʊdərvɛlʃ] (**-(s)**) *nt* jargon; (*umg*) double Dutch (*Brit*)
kauen ['kaʊən] *vt, vi* to chew
kauern ['kaʊərn] *vi* to crouch
Kauf [kaʊf] (**-(e)s, Käufe**) *m* purchase, buy; (*Kaufen*) buying; **ein guter ~** a bargain; **etw in ~ nehmen** to put up with sth
kaufen *vt* to buy; **dafür kann ich mir nichts ~** (*ironisch*) what use is that to me!
Käufer, in ['kɔʏfər(ɪn)] (**-s, -**) *m(f)* buyer
Käuferverhalten *nt* buying habits *pl*
Kauf- *zW*: **Kauffrau** *f* businesswoman; (*Einzelhandelskauffrau*) shopkeeper; **kauffreudig** *adj* consumerist; **Kaufhaus** *nt* department store; **Kaufkraft** *f* purchasing power; **Kaufladen** *m* shop, store
käuflich ['kɔʏflɪç] *adj* purchasable, for sale; (*pej*) venal ▷ *adv*: **~ erwerben** to purchase
Kauf- *zW*: **Kauflust** *f* desire to buy things; (*Börse*) buying; **kauflustig** *adj* interested in buying; **Kaufmann** (**-(e)s, pl -leute**) *m* businessman; (*Einzelhandelskaufmann*) shopkeeper; **kaufmännisch** *adj* commercial; **kaufmännischer Angestellter** clerk; **Kaufpreis** *m* purchase price; **kaufsüchtig** *adj*: **kaufsüchtig sein** to be a shopaholic (*umg*); **Kaufvertrag** *m* bill of sale; **Kaufwillige, r** *f(m)* potential buyer; **Kaufzurückhaltung** *f* consumer reticence; **Kaufzwang** *m*: **kein/ ohne Kaufzwang** no/without obligation
Kaugummi ['kaʊgʊmi] *m* chewing gum
Kaukasus ['kaʊkazʊs] *m*: **der ~** the Caucasus
Kaulquappe ['kaʊlkvapə] (**-, -n**) *f* tadpole
kaum [kaʊm] *adv* hardly, scarcely; **wohl ~, ich glaube ~** I hardly think so
Kausalzusammenhang [kaʊ'za:ltsuzamənhaŋ] *m* causal connection
Kaution [kaʊtsi'o:n] *f* deposit; (*Jur*) bail
Kautschuk ['kaʊtʃʊk] (**-s, -e**) *m* India rubber
Kauz [kaʊts] (**-es, Käuze**) *m* owl; (*fig*) queer fellow
Kavalier [kava'li:r] (**-s, -e**) *m* gentleman
Kavaliersdelikt *nt* peccadillo
Kavallerie [kavalə'ri:] *f* cavalry
Kavallerist [kavalə'rɪst] *m* cavalryman
Kaviar ['ka:viar] *m* caviar
KB *nt abk* (= *Kilobyte*) KB, kbyte
Kcal *abk* (= *Kilokalorie*) kcal

keck [kɛk] *adj* daring, bold; **Keckheit** *f* daring, boldness
Kegel ['ke:gəl] (**-s, -**) *m* skittle; (*Math*) cone; **Kegelbahn** *f* skittle alley, bowling alley; **kegelförmig** *adj* conical
kegeln *vi* to play skittles
Kehle ['ke:lə] (**-, -n**) *f* throat; **er hat das in die falsche ~ bekommen** (*lit*) it went down the wrong way; (*fig*) he took it the wrong way; **aus voller ~** at the top of one's voice
Kehl- *zW*: **Kehlkopf** *m* larynx; **Kehlkopfkrebs** *m* cancer of the throat; **Kehllaut** *m* guttural
Kehre ['ke:rə] (**-, -n**) *f* turn(ing), bend
kehren *vt, vi* (*wenden*) to turn; (*mit Besen*) to sweep; **sich an etw** *dat* **nicht ~** not to heed sth; **in sich** *akk* **gekehrt** (*versunken*) pensive; (*verschlossen*) introspective, introverted
Kehricht (**-s**) *m* sweepings *pl*
Kehr- *zW*: **Kehrmaschine** *f* sweeper; **Kehrreim** *m* refrain; **Kehrseite** *f* reverse, other side; (*ungünstig*) wrong *od* bad side; **die Kehrseite der Medaille** the other side of the coin
kehrtmachen *vi* to turn about, about-turn
Kehrtwendung *f* about-turn
keifen ['kaɪfən] *vi* to scold, nag
Keil [kaɪl] (**-(e)s, -e**) *m* wedge; (*Mil*) arrowhead; **keilen** *vt* to wedge ▷ *vr* to fight
Keilerei [kaɪlə'raɪ] (*umg*) *f* punch-up
Keilriemen *m* (*Aut*) fan belt
Keim [kaɪm] (**-(e)s, -e**) *m* bud; (*Med, fig*) germ; **etw im ~ ersticken** to nip sth in the bud
keimen *vi* to germinate
Keim- *zW*: **keimfrei** *adj* sterile; **keimtötend** *adj* antiseptic, germicidal; **Keimzelle** *f* (*fig*) nucleus
kein ['kaɪn], **keine** ['kaɪnə] *pron* none ▷ *adj* no, not any; **~e schlechte Idee** not a bad idea; **~e Stunde/drei Monate** (*nicht einmal*) less than an hour/three months
keine, r, s *indef pron* no one, nobody; (*von Gegenstand*) none
keinerlei ['kaɪnər'laɪ] *adj attrib* no ... whatever
keinesfalls *adv* on no account
keineswegs *adv* by no means
keinmal *adv* not once
Keks [ke:ks] (**-es, -e**) *m od nt* biscuit (*Brit*), cookie (*US*)
Kelch [kɛlç] (**-(e)s, -e**) *m* cup, goblet, chalice
Kelle ['kɛlə] (**-, -n**) *f* ladle; (*Maurerkelle*) trowel
Keller ['kɛlər] (**-s, -**) *m* cellar; **Kellerassel** (**-, -n**) *f* woodlouse
Kellerei [kɛlə'raɪ] *f* wine cellars *pl*; (*Firma*) wine producer
Kellergeschoss *nt* basement
Kellerwohnung *f* basement flat (*Brit*) *od* apartment (*US*)
Kellner, in ['kɛlnər(ɪn)] (**-s, -**) *m(f)* waiter, waitress
kellnern (*umg*) *vi* to work as a waiter/waitress (*Brit*), wait on tables (*US*)
Kelte ['kɛltə] (**-n, -n**) *m* Celt
Kelter (**-, -n**) *f* winepress; (*Obstkelter*) press
keltern ['kɛltərn] *vt* to press

Keltin ['kɛltɪn] f (female) Celt
keltisch adj Celtic
Kenia ['keːnia] (**-s**) nt Kenya
kennen ['kɛnən] unreg vt to know; **~ Sie sich schon?** do you know each other (already)?; **kennst du mich noch?** do you remember me?
kennenlernen vt to get to know ▷ vr to get to know each other; (zum ersten Mal) to meet
Kenner, in (**-s, -**) m(f): **~ (von** od +gen**)** connoisseur (of); expert (on)
Kennkarte f identity card
kenntlich adj distinguishable, discernible; **etw ~ machen** to mark sth
Kenntnis (**-, -se**) f knowledge no pl; **etw zur ~ nehmen** to note sth; **von etw ~ nehmen** to take notice of sth; **jdn in ~ setzen** to inform sb; **über ~se von etw verfügen** to be knowledgeable about sth
Kenn- zW: **Kennwort** nt (Chiffre) code name; (Losungswort) password, code word; **Kennzeichen** nt mark, characteristic; **(amtliches/polizeiliches) Kennzeichen** (Aut) number plate (Brit), license plate (US); **kennzeichnen** vt untr to characterize; **kennzeichnenderweise** adv characteristically; **Kennziffer** f (code) number; (Comm) reference number
kentern ['kɛntərn] vi to capsize
Keramik [keˈraːmɪk] (**-, -en**) f ceramics pl, pottery; (Gegenstand) piece of ceramic work od pottery
Kerbe ['kɛrbə] (**-, -n**) f notch, groove
Kerbel (**-s, -**) m chervil
kerben vt to notch
Kerbholz nt: **etw auf dem ~ haben** to have done sth wrong
Kerker ['kɛrkər] (**-s, -**) m prison
Kerl [kɛrl] (**-s, -e**) (umg) m chap, bloke (Brit), guy; **du gemeiner ~!** you swine!
Kern [kɛrn] (**-(e)s, -e**) m (Obstkern) pip, stone; (Nusskern) kernel; (Atomkern) nucleus; (fig) heart, core; **Kernenergie** f nuclear energy; **Kernfach** nt (Sch) core subject; **Kernfamilie** f nuclear family; **Kernforschung** f nuclear research; **Kernfrage** f central issue; **Kernfusion** f nuclear fusion; **Kerngehäuse** nt core; **kerngesund** adj thoroughly healthy, fit as a fiddle
kernig adj robust; (Ausspruch) pithy
Kern- zW: **Kernkompetenz** f core competence; **Kernkraftwerk** nt nuclear power station; **Kernland** f heartland; **kernlos** adj seedless, pipless; **Kernphysik** f nuclear physics sing; **Kernreaktion** f nuclear reaction; **Kernreaktor** m nuclear reactor; **Kernschmelze** f meltdown; **Kernseife** f washing soap; **Kernspaltung** f nuclear fission; **Kernstück** nt (fig) main item; (von Theorie etc) central part, core; **Kernwaffen** pl nuclear weapons pl; **kernwaffenfrei** adj nuclear-free; **Kernzeit** f core time
Kerze ['kɛrtsə] (**-, -n**) f candle; (Zündkerze) plug
Kerzen- zW: **kerzengerade** adj straight as a die; **Kerzenhalter** m candlestick;

Kerzenständer m candleholder
kess [kɛs] adj saucy
Kessel ['kɛsəl] (**-s, -**) m kettle; (von Lokomotive etc) boiler; (Mulde) basin; (Geog) depression; (Mil) encirclement; **Kesselstein** m scale, fur (Brit); **Kesseltreiben** nt (fig) witch-hunt
Kette ['kɛtə] (**-, -n**) f chain; **jdn an die ~ legen** (fig) to tie sb down
ketten vt to chain
Ketten- zW: **Kettenfahrzeug** nt tracked vehicle; **Kettenhund** m watchdog; **Kettenkarussell** nt merry-go-round (with gondolas on chains); **Kettenladen** m chain store; **Kettenrauchen** nt chain smoking; **Kettenreaktion** f chain reaction
Ketzer, in ['kɛtsər(ɪn)] (**-s, -**) m(f) heretic; **Ketzerei** [kɛtsəˈraɪ] f heresy; **ketzerisch** adj heretical
keuchen ['kɔʏçən] vi to pant, gasp
Keuchhusten m whooping cough
Keule ['kɔʏlə] (**-, -n**) f club; (Koch) leg
Keulung ['kɔʏlʊŋ] f cull, culling
keusch [kɔʏʃ] adj chaste; **Keuschheit** f chastity
Kfm. abk = **Kaufmann**
kfm. abk = **kaufmännisch**
Kfz (**-(s), -(s)**) f abk = **Kraftfahrzeug**
KG (**-, -s**) f abk = **Kommanditgesellschaft**
kg abk (= Kilogramm) kg
kHz abk (= Kilohertz) kHz
Kibbuz [kɪˈbuːts] (**-, Kibbuzim** od **-e**) m kibbutz
kichern ['kɪçərn] vi to giggle
kicken ['kɪkən] vt, vi (Fußball) to kick
kidnappen ['kɪtnɛpən] vt to kidnap
Kidnapper, in (**-s, -**) m(f) kidnapper
Kiebitz ['kiːbɪts] (**-es, -e**) m peewit
Kiefer[1] ['kiːfər] (**-s, -**) m jaw
Kiefer[2] ['kiːfər] (**-, -n**) f pine
Kiefernholz nt pine(wood)
Kiefernzapfen m pine cone
Kieferorthopäde m orthodontist
Kieker ['kiːkər] (**-s, -**) m: **jdn auf dem ~ haben** (umg) to have it in for sb
Kiel [kiːl] (**-(e)s, -e**) m (Federkiel) quill; (Naut) keel; **Kielwasser** nt wake
Kieme ['kiːmə] (**-, -n**) f gill
Kies [kiːs] (**-es, -e**) m gravel; (umg: Geld) money, dough
Kiesel ['kiːzəl] (**-s, -**) m pebble; **Kieselstein** m pebble
Kiesgrube f gravel pit
Kiesweg m gravel path
Kiew ['kiːɛf] (**-s**) nt Kiev
kiffen ['kɪfən] (umg) vt to smoke pot od grass
Kilimandscharo [kilimanˈdʒaːro] (**-s**) m Kilimanjaro
Killer, in ['kɪlər] (**-s, -**) (umg) m killer, murderer; (gedungener) hit man; **Killerin** (umg) f killer, female murderer, murderess
Kilo ['kiːlo] (**-s, -(s)**) nt kilo; **Kilobyte** [kiloˈbaɪt] nt (Comput) kilobyte; **Kilogramm** [kiloˈgram] nt kilogram
Kilometer [kiloˈmeːtər] m kilometre (Brit), kilometer (US); **Kilometerfresser** (umg)

m long-haul driver; **Kilometergeld** *nt* ≈ mileage (allowance); **Kilometerstand** *m* ≈ mileage; **Kilometerstein** *m* ≈ milestone; **Kilometerzähler** *m* ≈ mileometer

Kilowatt [kilo'vat] *nt* kilowatt

Kimme ['kɪmə] (-, -n) *f* notch; (*Gewehr*) back sight

Kind [kɪnt] (-(e)s, -er) *nt* child; **sich freuen wie ein ~** to be as pleased as Punch; **mit ~ und Kegel** (*hum: umg*) with the whole family; **von ~ auf** from childhood

Kinderarzt *m* paediatrician (*Brit*), pediatrician (*US*)

Kinderbett *nt* cot (*Brit*), crib (*US*)

Kinderei [kɪndə'raɪ] *f* childishness

Kindererziehung *f* bringing up of children; (*durch Schule*) education of children

kinderfeindlich *adj* anti-children; (*Architektur, Planung*) not catering for children

Kinderfreibetrag *m* child allowance

Kindergarten *m* nursery school; *see culture note*

Kinder- *zW:* **Kindergärtner, in** *m(f)* nursery-school teacher; **Kindergeld** *nt* child benefit (*Brit*); **Kinderheim** *nt* children's home; **Kinderkrankheit** *f* childhood illness; **Kinderladen** *m* (alternative) playgroup; **Kinderlähmung** *f* polio(myelitis); **kinderleicht** *adj* childishly easy; **kinderlieb** *adj* fond of children; **Kinderlied** *nt* nursery rhyme; **kinderlos** *adj* childless; **Kindermädchen** *nt* nursemaid; **Kinderpflegerin** *f* child minder; **kinderreich** *adj* with a lot of children; **Kinderschuh** *m:* **es steckt noch in den Kinderschuhen** (*fig*) it's still in its infancy; **Kinderspiel** *nt* child's play; **ein Kinderspiel sein** to be a doddle; **Kinderstube** *f:* **eine gute Kinderstube haben** to be well-mannered; **Kindertagesstätte** *f* day-nursery; **Kinderteller** *m* children's dish; **Kinderwagen** *m* pram (*Brit*), baby carriage (*US*); **Kinderzimmer** *nt* child's/children's room; (*für Kleinkinder*) nursery

Kindes- *zW:* **Kindesalter** *nt* infancy; **Kindesbeine** *pl:* **von Kindesbeinen an** from early childhood; **Kindesmisshandlung** *f* child abuse

Kind- *zW:* **kindgemäß** *adj* suitable for a child *od* children; **Kindheit** *f* childhood; **kindisch** *adj* childish; **kindlich** *adj* childlike

kindsköpfig *adj* childish

Kinkerlitzchen ['kɪŋkərlɪtsçən] (*umg*) *pl* knick-knacks *pl*

Kinn [kɪn] (-(e)s, -e) *nt* chin; **Kinnhaken** *m* (*Boxen*) uppercut; **Kinnlade** *f* jaw

Kino ['ki:no] (-s, -s) *nt* cinema (*Brit*), movies (*US*); **Kinobesucher** *m*, **Kinogänger** *m* cinema-goer (*Brit*), movie-goer (*US*); **Kinoprogramm** *nt* film programme (*Brit*), movie program (*US*)

Kiosk [ki'ɔsk] (-(e)s, -e) *m* kiosk

Kippe ['kɪpə] (-, -n) *f* (*umg*) cigarette end; **auf der ~ stehen** (*fig*) to be touch and go

kippen *vi* to topple over, overturn ▷ *vt* to tilt

Kipper ['kɪpər] (-s, -) *m* (*Aut*) tipper, dump(er) truck

Kippschalter *m* rocker switch

Kirche ['kɪrçə] (-, -n) *f* church

Kirchen- *zW:* **Kirchenchor** *m* church choir; **Kirchendiener** *m* churchwarden; **Kirchenfest** *nt* church festival; **Kirchenlied** *nt* hymn; **Kirchenschiff** *nt* (*Längsschiff*) nave; (*Querschiff*) transept; **Kirchensteuer** *f* church tax; **Kirchentag** *m* church congress

Kirch- *zW:* **Kirchgänger, in** (-s, -) *m(f)* churchgoer; **Kirchhof** *m* churchyard; **kirchlich** *adj* ecclesiastical; **Kirchturm** *m* church tower, steeple; **Kirchweih** *f* fair, kermis (*US*)

Kirgistan ['kɪrgista:n] (-s) *nt* (*Geog*) Kirghizia

Kirmes ['kɪrmɛs] (-, -sen) *f* (*Dialekt*) fair, kermis (*US*)

Kirschbaum ['kɪrʃbaum] *m* cherry tree; (*Holz*) cherry (wood)

Kirsche ['kɪrʃə] (-, -n) *f* cherry; **mit ihm ist nicht gut ~n essen** (*fig*) it's best not to tangle with him

Kirschtorte *f:* **Schwarzwälder ~** Black Forest Gateau

Kirschwasser *nt* kirsch

Kissen ['kɪsən] (-s, -) *nt* cushion; (*Kopfkissen*) pillow; **Kissenbezug** *m* pillow case

Kiste ['kɪstə] (-, -n) *f* box; (*Truhe*) chest; (*umg: Bett*) sack; (: *Fernsehen*) box (*Brit*), tube (*US*)

Kita ['kɪta] *f abk* = **Kindertagesstätte**

Kitsch [kɪtʃ] (-(e)s) *m* trash

kitschig *adj* trashy

Kitt [kɪt] (-(e)s, -e) *m* putty

Kittchen (*umg*) *nt* clink

Kittel (-s, -) *m* overall; (*von Arzt, Laborant etc*) (white) coat

kitten *vt* to putty; (*fig*) to patch up

Kitz [kɪts] (-es, -e) *nt* kid; (*Rehkitz*) fawn

kitzelig ['kɪtsəlɪç] *adj* (*lit, fig*) ticklish

kitzeln *vt, vi* to tickle

Kiwi ['ki:vi] (-, -s) *f* kiwi fruit

KKW (-, -s) *nt abk* = **Kernkraftwerk**

Kl. *abk* (= *Klasse*) cl.

Klacks [klaks] (-es, -e) (*umg*) *m* (*von Kartoffelbrei, Sahne*) dollop; (*von Senf, Farbe etc*) blob

Kladde ['kladə] (-, -n) *f* rough book; (*Block*) scribbling pad

klaffen ['klafən] *vi* to gape

kläffen ['klɛfən] *vi* to yelp

Klage ['kla:gə] (-, -n) *f* complaint; (*Jur*) action; **eine ~ gegen jdn einreichen** *od* **erheben** to

institute proceedings against sb; **Klagelied**
nt: **ein Klagelied über jdn/etw anstimmen**
(fig) to complain about sb/sth; **Klagemauer**
f: **die Klagemauer** the Wailing Wall
klagen vi (wehklagen) to lament, wail; (sich
beschweren) to complain; (Jur) to take legal
action; **jdm sein Leid/seine Not ~** to pour
out one's sorrow/distress to sb
Kläger, in ['klɛːgər(ɪn)] (**-s, -**) m(f) (Jur: im
Zivilrecht) plaintiff; (: im Strafrecht) prosecuting
party; (: in Scheidung) petitioner
Klageschrift f (Jur) charge; (bei Scheidung)
petition
kläglich ['klɛːklɪç] adj wretched
Klamauk [kla'maʊk] (**-s**) (umg) m (Albernei)
tomfoolery; (im Theater) slapstick
Klamm [klam] (**-, -en**) f ravine
klamm adj (Finger) numb; (feucht) damp
Klammer ['klamər] (**-, -n**) f clamp; (in Text)
bracket; (Büroklammer) clip; (Wäscheklammer)
peg (Brit), pin (US); (Zahnklammer) brace; **~ auf/
zu** open/close brackets
klammern vr: **sich ~ an** +akk to cling to
klammheimlich [klam'haɪmlɪç] (umg) adj
secret ▷ adv on the quiet
Klamotte [kla'mɔtə] (**-, -n**) f (pej: Film
etc) rubbishy old film etc; **Klamotten** pl
(umg: Kleider) clothes pl; (: Zeug) stuff
Klampfe ['klampfə] (**-, -n**) (umg) f guitar
klang etc [klaŋ] vb siehe **klingen**
Klang (**-(e)s, ⸚e**) m sound
klangvoll adj sonorous
Klappbett nt folding bed
Klappe ['klapə] (**-, -n**) f valve; (an Oboe etc) key;
(Film) clapperboard; (Ofenklappe) damper;
(umg: Mund) trap; **die ~ halten** to shut one's
trap
klappen vi (Geräusch) to click; (Sitz etc) to tip
▷ vt to tip ▷ vi unpers to work; **hat es mit den
Karten/dem Job geklappt?** did you get the
tickets/job O.K.?
Klappentext m blurb
Klapper ['klapər] (**-, -n**) f rattle
klapperig adj run-down, worn-out
klappern vi to clatter, rattle
Klapperschlange f rattlesnake
Klapperstorch m stork; **er glaubt noch an
den ~** he still thinks babies are found under
the gooseberry bush
Klapp- zW: **Klappmesser** nt jackknife;
Klapprad nt collapsible od folding bicycle;
Klappstuhl m folding chair; **Klapptisch** m
folding table
Klaps [klaps] (**-es, -e**) m slap; **einen ~ haben**
(umg) to have a screw loose; **klapsen** vt to slap
klar [klaːr] adj clear; (Naut) ready to sail; (Mil)
ready for action; **bei ~em Verstand sein** to
be in full possession of one's faculties; **sich
dat im K~en sein über** +akk to be clear about;
ins K~e kommen to get clear; **~ sehen** to see
clearly; **sich** dat **über etw** akk **~ werden** to get
sth clear in one's mind
Kläranlage f sewage plant; (von Fabrik)

purification plant
Klare, r (umg) m schnapps
klären vt (Flüssigkeit) to purify; (Probleme) to
clarify ▷ vr to clear (itself) up
Klarheit f clarity; **sich** dat **~ über etw** akk
verschaffen to get sth straight
Klarinette [klari'nɛtə] f clarinet
klar- zW: **klarkommen** unreg (umg) vi: **mit
jdm/etw klarkommen** to be able to cope
with sb/sth; **klarlegen** vt to clear up, explain;
klarmachen vt (Schiff) to get ready for sea;
jdm etw klarmachen to make sth clear to sb;
Klarsichtfolie f transparent film; **klarstellen**
vt to clarify; **Klartext** m: **im Klartext** in clear;
(fig: umg) ≈ in plain English
Klärung ['klɛːrʊŋ] f purification; clarification
Klärungsbedarf m need for clarification
Klasse ['klasə] (**-, -n**) f class; (Sch) class, form;
(auch: **Steuerklasse**) bracket; (Güterklasse) grade
klasse (umg) adj smashing
Klassen- zW: **Klassenarbeit** f test;
Klassenbewusstsein nt class-consciousness;
Klassenbuch nt (Sch) (class) register;
Klassengesellschaft f class society;
Klassenkamerad, in m(f) classmate;
Klassenkampf m class conflict; **Klassenlehrer,
in** m(f) class teacher; **klassenlos** adj classless;
Klassensprecher, in m(f) class spokesperson;
Klassenziel nt: **das Klassenziel nicht
erreichen** (Sch) not to reach the required
standard (for the year); (fig) not to make the
grade; **Klassenzimmer** nt classroom
klassifizieren [klasifi'tsiːrən] vt to classify
Klassifizierung f classification
Klassik ['klasɪk] f (Zeit) classical period; (Stil)
classicism; **Klassiker** (**-s, -**) m classic
klassisch adj (lit, fig) classical
Klassizismus [klasi'tsɪsmʊs] m classicism
Klatsch [klatʃ] (**-(e)s, -e**) m smack, crack;
(Gerede) gossip; **Klatschbase** f gossip(monger)
klatschen vi (tratschen) to gossip; (Beifall spenden)
to applaud, to clap ▷ vt: **(jdm) Beifall ~** to
applaud od clap (sb)
Klatsch- zW: **Klatschmohn** m (corn) poppy;
klatschnass adj soaking wet; **Klatschspalte**
f gossip column; **Klatschtante** (pej: umg) f
gossip(monger)
klauben ['klaʊbən] vt to pick
Klaue ['klaʊə] (**-, -n**) f claw; (umg: Schrift) scrawl
klauen vt to claw; (umg) to pinch
Klause ['klaʊzə] (**-, -n**) f cell; (von Mönch)
hermitage
Klausel ['klaʊzəl] (**-, -n**) f clause; (Vorbehalt)
proviso
Klausur [klaʊ'zuːr] f seclusion; **Klausurarbeit** f
examination paper
Klaviatur [klavia'tuːr] f keyboard
Klavier [kla'viːr] (**-s, -e**) nt piano;
Klavierauszug m piano score
Klebeband nt adhesive tape
Klebemittel nt glue
kleben ['kleːbən] vt, vi: **~ (an** +akk) to stick (to);
jdm eine ~ (umg) to belt sb one

k

191

Klebezettel *m* gummed label
klebrig *adj* sticky
Klebstoff *m* glue
Klebstreifen *m* adhesive tape
kleckern ['klɛkərn] *vi* to slobber
Klecks [klɛks] (**-es, -e**) *m* blot, stain; **klecksen** *vi* to blot; (*pej*) to daub
Klee [kle:] (**-s**) *m* clover; **jdn/etw über den grünen ~ loben** (*fig*) to praise sb/sth to the skies; **Kleeblatt** *nt* cloverleaf; (*fig*) trio
Kleid [klaɪt] (**-(e)s, -er**) *nt* garment; (*Frauenkleid*) dress; **Kleider** *pl* clothes *pl*
kleiden ['klaɪdən] *vt* to clothe, dress ▷ *vr* to dress; **jdn ~** to suit sb
Kleider- *zW*: **Kleiderbügel** *m* coat hanger; **Kleiderbürste** *f* clothes brush; **Kleiderschrank** *m* wardrobe; **Kleiderständer** *m* coat-stand
kleidsam *adj* becoming
Kleidung *f* clothing
Kleidungsstück *nt* garment
Kleie ['klaɪə] (**-, -n**) *f* bran
klein [klaɪn] *adj* little, small; **haben Sie es nicht ~er?** haven't you got anything smaller?; **ein ~es Bier, ein K~es** (*umg*) ≈ half a pint, ≈ a half; **von ~ an** *od* **auf** (*von Kindheit an*) from childhood; (*von Anfang an*) from the very beginning; **das ~ere Übel** the lesser evil; **sein Vater war (ein) ~er Beamter** his father was a minor civil servant; **~ anfangen** to start off in a small way; **~ geschrieben werden** (*umg*) to count for (very) little; **~ hacken** to chop up; **~ schneiden** to chop up; **Kleinanzeige** *f* small ad (*Brit*), want ad (*US*); **Kleinanzeigen** *pl* classified advertising *sing*; **Kleinarbeit** *f*: **in zäher/mühseliger Kleinarbeit** with rigorous/painstaking attention to detail; **Kleinasien** *nt* Asia Minor; **Kleinbürgertum** *nt* petite bourgeoisie; **Kleinbus** *m* minibus
Kleine, r *f(m)* little one
klein- *zW*: **Kleinfamilie** *f* small family, nuclear family (*Soziologie*); **Kleinformat** *nt* small size; **im Kleinformat** small-scale; **Kleingedruckte, s** *nt* small print; **Kleingeld** *nt* small change; **das nötige Kleingeld haben** (*fig*) to have the wherewithal (*umg*); **kleingläubig** *adj* of little faith; **kleinhacken** *vt* to chop up; **Kleinholz** *nt* firewood; **Kleinholz aus jdm machen** to make mincemeat of sb
Kleinigkeit *f* trifle; **wegen** *od* **bei jeder ~** for the slightest reason; **eine ~ essen** to have a bite to eat
klein- *zW*: **kleinkariert** *adj*: **kleinkariert denken** to think small; **Kleinkind** *nt* infant; **Kleinkram** *m* details *pl*; **Kleinkredit** *m* personal loan; **kleinkriegen** (*umg*) *vt* (*gefügig machen*) to bring into line; (*unterkriegen*) to get down; (*körperlich*) to tire out; **kleinlaut** *adj* dejected, quiet; **kleinlich** *adj* petty, paltry; **Kleinlichkeit** *f* pettiness, paltriness; **kleinmütig** *adj* fainthearted
Kleinod ['klaɪno:t] (**-s, -odien**) *nt* gem; (*fig*) treasure
klein- *zW*: **Kleinrechner** *m* minicomputer;

kleinschneiden *unreg vt* to chop up;
kleinschreiben *unreg vt*: **ein Wort kleinschreiben** to write a word with a small initial letter; **Kleinschreibung** *f* use of small initial letters; **Kleinstadt** *f* small town; **kleinstädtisch** *adj* provincial
kleinstmöglich *adj* smallest possible
Kleinwagen *m* small car
Kleister ['klaɪstər] (**-s, -**) *m* paste
kleistern *vt* to paste
Klemme ['klɛmə] (**-, -n**) *f* clip; (*Med*) clamp; (*fig*) jam; **in der ~ sitzen** *od* **sein** (*fig*: *umg*) to be in a fix
klemmen *vt* (*festhalten*) to jam; (*quetschen*) to pinch, nip ▷ *vr* to catch o.s.; (*sich hineinzwängen*) to squeeze o.s. ▷ *vi* (*Tür*) to stick, jam; **sich hinter jdn/etw ~** to get on to sb/get down to sth
Klempner ['klɛmpnər] (**-s, -**) *m* plumber
Kleptomanie [klɛptoma'ni:] *f* kleptomania
Kleriker ['kle:rikər] (**-s, -**) *m* cleric
Klerus ['kle:rʊs] (**-**) *m* clergy
Klette ['klɛtə] (**-, -n**) *f* burr; **sich wie eine ~ an jdn hängen** to cling to sb like a limpet
Kletterer ['klɛtərər] (**-s, -**) *m* climber
Klettergerüst *nt* climbing frame
klettern *vi* to climb
Kletterpflanze *f* creeper
Kletterseil *nt* climbing rope
Klettverschluss *m* Velcro® fastener
klicken ['klɪkən] *vi* to click
Klient, in [kli'ɛnt(ɪn)] *m(f)* client
Klima ['kli:ma] (**-s, -s** *od* **-te**) *nt* climate; **Klimaanlage** *f* air conditioning
Klimaschutz *m* climate protection; **Klimaschutzabkommen** *nt* agreement on climate change
klimatisieren [kli:mati'zi:rən] *vt* to air-condition
klimatisiert *adj* air-conditioned
Klimawechsel *m* change of air
Klimawandel *m* climate change#
Klimbim [klɪm'bɪm] (**-s**) (*umg*) *m* odds and ends *pl*
klimpern ['klɪmpərn] *vi* to tinkle; (*auf Gitarre*) to strum
Klinge ['klɪŋə] (**-, -n**) *f* blade, sword; **jdn über die ~ springen lassen** (*fig*: *umg*) to allow sb to run into trouble
Klingel ['klɪŋəl] (**-, -n**) *f* bell; **Klingelbeutel** *m* collection bag; **Klingelknopf** *m* bell push
klingeln *vi* to ring; **es hat geklingelt** (*an Tür*) somebody just rang the doorbell, the doorbell just rang
Klingelton *m* ringtone
klingen ['klɪŋən] *unreg vi* to sound; (*Gläser*) to clink
Klinik ['kli:nɪk] *f* clinic
klinisch ['kli:nɪʃ] *adj* clinical
Klinke ['klɪŋkə] (**-, -n**) *f* handle
Klinker ['klɪŋkər] (**-s, -**) *m* clinker
Klippe ['klɪpə] (**-, -n**) *f* cliff; (*im Meer*) reef; (*fig*) hurdle

klippenreich adj rocky
klipp und klar ['klɪp|ʊntklaːr] adj clear and concise
Klips [klɪps] (**-es, -e**) m clip; (Ohrklips) earring
klirren ['klɪrən] vi to clank, jangle; (Gläser) to clink; **~de Kälte** biting cold
Klischee [klɪ'ʃeː] (**-s, -s**) nt (Druckplatte) plate, block; (fig) cliché; **Klischeevorstellung** f stereotyped idea
Klitoris ['kliːtorɪs] (**-, -**) f clitoris
Klo [kloː] (**-s, -s**) (umg) nt loo (Brit), john (US)
Kloake [klo'aːkə] (**-, -n**) f sewer
klobig ['kloːbɪç] adj clumsy
Klon [kloːn] (**-s, -e**) m clone
Klonschaf nt cloned sheep
Klopapier (umg) nt toilet paper
klopfen ['klɔpfən] vi to knock; (Herz) to thump ▷ vt to beat; **es klopft** somebody's knocking; **jdm auf die Finger ~** (lit, fig) to give sb a rap on the knuckles; **jdm auf die Schulter ~** to tap sb on the shoulder
Klopfer (**-s, -**) m (Teppichklopfer) beater; (Türklopfer) knocker
Klöppel ['klœpəl] (**-s, -**) m (von Glocke) clapper
klöppeln vi to make lace
Klops [klɔps] (**-es, -e**) m meatball
Klosett [klo'zɛt] (**-s, -e** od **-s**) nt lavatory, toilet; **Klosettbrille** f toilet seat; **Klosettpapier** nt toilet paper
Kloß [kloːs] (**-es, ̈-e**) m (Erdkloß) clod; (im Hals) lump; (Koch) dumpling
Kloster ['kloːstər] (**-s, ̈-**) nt (Männerkloster) monastery; (Frauenkloster) convent; **ins ~ gehen** to become a monk/nun
klösterlich ['kløːstərlɪç] adj monastic; convent
Klotz [klɔts] (**-es, ̈-e**) m log; (Hackklotz) block; **jdm ein ~ am Bein sein** (fig) to be a millstone round sb's neck
Klub [klʊp] (**-s, -s**) m club; **Klubjacke** f blazer; **Klubsessel** m easy chair
Kluft [klʊft] (**-, ̈-e**) f cleft, gap; (Geog) chasm; (Uniform) uniform; (umg: Kleidung) gear
klug [kluːk] adj clever, intelligent; **ich werde daraus nicht ~** I can't make head or tail of it; **Klugheit** f cleverness, intelligence; **Klugscheißer** (umg) m smart-ass
Klümpchen ['klʏmpçən] nt clot, blob
klumpen ['klʊmpən] vi to go lumpy, clot
Klumpen (**-s, -**) m (Koch) lump; (Erdklumpen) clod; (Blutklumpen) clot; (Goldklumpen) nugget
Klumpfuß ['klʊmpfuːs] m club foot
Klüngel ['klʏŋəl] (**-s, -**) (umg) m (Clique) clique
Klunker ['klʊŋkər] (**-s, -**) (umg) m (Schmuck) rock(s pl)
km abk (= Kilometer) km
km/h abk (= Kilometer pro Stunde) km/h
knabbern ['knabərn] vt, vi to nibble; **an etw** dat **~** (fig: umg) to puzzle over sth
Knabe ['knaːbə] (**-n, -n**) m boy
knabenhaft adj boyish
Knäckebrot ['knɛkəbroːt] nt crispbread
knacken ['knakən] vi (lit, fig) to crack ▷ vt (umg: Auto) to break into

knackfrisch (umg) adj oven-fresh, crispy-fresh
knackig adj crisp
Knacks [knaks] (**-es, -e**) m: **einen ~ weghaben** (umg) to be uptight about sth
Knackwurst f type of frankfurter
Knall [knal] (**-(e)s, -e**) m bang; (Peitschenknall) crack; **~ auf Fall** (umg) just like that; **einen ~ haben** (umg) to be crazy od crackers; **Knallbonbon** nt cracker; **Knalleffekt** m surprise effect, spectacular effect; **knallen** vi to bang; to crack ▷ vt: **jdm eine knallen** (umg) to clout sb; **Knallfrosch** m jumping jack; **knallhart** (umg) adj really hard; (: Worte) hard-hitting; (: Film) brutal; (: Porno) hardcore; **Knallkopf** (umg) m dickhead; **knallrot** adj bright red
knapp [knap] adj tight; (Geld) scarce; (kurz) short; (Mehrheit, Sieg) narrow; (Sprache) concise; **meine Zeit ist ~ bemessen** I am short of time; **mit ~er Not** only just; siehe auch **knapphalten**
Knappe (**-n, -n**) m (Edelmann) young knight
knapphalten unreg vt: **jdn (mit etw) ~** to keep sb short (of sth)
Knappheit f tightness; scarcity; conciseness
Knarre ['knarə] (**-, -n**) (umg) f (Gewehr) shooter
knarren vi to creak
Knast [knast] (**-(e)s**) (umg) m clink, can (US)
Knatsch [knaːtʃ] (**-es**) (umg) m trouble
knattern ['knatərn] vi to rattle; (Maschinengewehr) to chatter
Knäuel ['knɔʏəl] (**-s, -**) m od nt (Wollknäuel) ball; (Menschenknäuel) knot
Knauf [knaʊf] (**-(e)s, Knäufe**) m knob; (Schwertknauf) pommel
Knauser ['knaʊzər] (**-s, -**) m miser
knauserig adj miserly
knausern vi to be mean
knautschen ['knaʊtʃən] vt, vi to crumple
Knebel ['kneːbəl] (**-s, -**) m gag
knebeln vt to gag; (Naut) to fasten
Knecht [knɛçt] (**-(e)s, -e**) m servant; (auf Bauernhof) farm labourer (Brit) od laborer (US)
knechten vt to enslave
Knechtschaft f servitude
kneifen ['knaɪfən] unreg vt to pinch ▷ vi to pinch; (sich drücken) to back out; **vor etw** dat **~** to dodge sth
Kneifzange f pliers pl; (kleine) pincers pl
Kneipe ['knaɪpə] (**-, -n**) (umg) f pub (Brit), bar, saloon (US)
Kneippkur ['knaɪpkuːr] f Kneipp cure, type of hydropathic treatment combined with diet, rest etc
Knete ['kneːtə] (umg) f (Geld) dough
kneten vt to knead; (Wachs) to mould (Brit), mold (US)
Knetgummi m od nt Plasticine®
Knetmasse f Plasticine®
Knick [knɪk] (**-(e)s, -e**) m (Sprung) crack; (Kurve) bend; (Falte) fold
knicken vt, vi (springen) to crack; (brechen) to break; (Papier) to fold; **„nicht ~!"** "do not bend"; **geknickt sein** to be downcast

k

Knicks [knɪks] (-es, -e) m curts(e)y; knicksen vi to curts(e)y

Knie [kni:] (-s, -) nt knee; in die ~ gehen to kneel; (fig) to be brought to one's knees; Kniebeuge (-, -n) f knee bend; Kniefall m genuflection; Kniegelenk nt knee joint; Kniekehle f back of the knee

knien vi to kneel ▷ vr: sich in die Arbeit ~ (fig) to get down to (one's) work

Kniescheibe f kneecap

Kniestrumpf m knee-length sock

kniff etc [knɪf] vb siehe kneifen

Kniff (-(e)s, -e) m (Zwicken) pinch; (Falte) fold; (fig) trick, knack

kniffelig adj tricky

knipsen ['knɪpsən] vt (Fahrkarte) to punch; (Phot) to take a snap of, snap ▷ vi (Phot) to take snaps/a snap

Knirps [knɪrps] (-es, -e) m little chap; er hat einen neuen ~® gekauft he has bought a new Knirps® (folding umbrella)

knirschen ['knɪrʃən] vi to crunch; mit den Zähnen ~ to grind one's teeth

knistern ['knɪstərn] vi to crackle; (Papier, Seide) to rustle

Knitterfalte f crease

knitterfrei adj non-crease

knittern vi to crease

knobeln ['kno:bəln] vi (würfeln) to play dice; (um eine Entscheidung) to toss for it

Knoblauch ['kno:plaʊx] (-(e)s) m garlic

Knöchel ['knœçəl] (-s, -) m knuckle; (Fußknöchel) ankle

Knochen ['knɔxən] (-s, -) m bone; Knochenarbeit (umg) f hard work; Knochenbau m bone structure; Knochenbruch m fracture; Knochengerüst nt skeleton; Knochenmark nt bone marrow

knöchern ['knœçərn] adj bone

knochig ['knɔxɪç] adj bony

Knödel ['knø:dəl] (-s, -) m dumpling

Knolle ['knɔlə] (-, -n) f bulb

Knopf [knɔpf] (-(e)s, ¨e) m button; Knopfdruck m touch of a button

knöpfen ['knœpfən] vt to button

Knopfloch nt buttonhole

Knorpel ['knɔrpəl] (-s, -) m cartilage, gristle

knorpelig adj gristly

knorrig ['knɔrɪç] adj gnarled, knotted

Knospe ['knɔspə] (-, -n) f bud

knospen vi to bud

knoten ['kno:tən] vt to knot; Knoten (-s, -) m knot; (Haar) bun; (Bot) node; (Med) lump

Knotenpunkt m junction

knuffen ['knʊfən] (umg) vt to cuff

Knüller ['knʏlər] (-s, -) (umg) m hit; (Reportage) scoop

knüpfen ['knʏpfən] vt to tie; (Teppich) to knot; (Freundschaft) to form

Knüppel ['knʏpəl] (-s, -) m cudgel; (Polizeiknüppel) baton, truncheon; (Aviat) (joy) stick; jdm ~ zwischen die Beine werfen (fig) to put a spoke in sb's wheel; knüppeldick

(umg) adj very thick; (fig) thick and fast; Knüppelschaltung f (Aut) floor-mounted gear change

knurren ['knʊrən] vi (Hund) to snarl, growl; (Magen) to rumble; (Mensch) to mutter

knusperig ['knʊspərɪç], knusprig ['knʊsprɪç] adj crisp; (Keks) crunchy

knutschen ['knu:tʃən] (umg) vt to snog with ▷ vi, vr to snog

k. o. adj (Sport) knocked out; (fig: umg) whacked

Koalition [koalitsi'o:n] f coalition

Koalitionsabsprache f coalition agreement

koalitionsfähig f in a position to form a coalition

Kobalt ['ko:balt] (-s) nt cobalt

Kobold ['ko:bɔlt] (-(e)s, -e) m imp

Kobra ['ko:bra] (-, -s) f cobra

Koch [kɔx] (-(e)s, ¨e) m cook; Kochbuch nt cookery book, cookbook; kochecht adj (Farbe) fast

kochen vi to cook; (Wasser) to boil ▷ vt (Essen) to cook; er kochte vor Wut (umg) he was seething; etw auf kleiner Flamme ~ to simmer sth over a low heat

Kocher (-s, -) m stove, cooker

Köcher ['kœçər] (-s, -) m quiver

Kochgelegenheit f cooking facilities pl

Köchin ['kœçɪn] f cook

Koch- zW: Kochkunst f cooking; Kochlöffel m kitchen spoon; Kochnische f kitchenette; Kochplatte f hotplate; Kochsalz nt cooking salt; Kochtopf m saucepan, pot; Kochwäsche f washing that can be boiled

Kode [ko:t] (-s, -s) m code

Köder ['kø:dər] (-s, -) m bait, lure

ködern vt to lure, entice

Koexistenz [koɛksɪs'tɛnts] f coexistence

Koffein [kɔfe'i:n] (-s) nt caffeine; koffeinfrei adj decaffeinated

Koffer ['kɔfər] (-s, -) m suitcase; (Schrankkoffer) trunk; die ~ packen (lit, fig) to pack one's bags; Kofferkuli m (luggage) trolley (Brit), cart (US); Kofferradio nt portable radio; Kofferraum m (Aut) boot (Brit), trunk (US)

Kognak ['kɔnjak] (-s, -s) m brandy, cognac

Kohl [ko:l] (-(e)s, -e) m cabbage

Kohldampf (umg) m: ~ haben to be famished

Kohle ['ko:lə] (-, -n) f coal; (Holzkohle) charcoal; (Chem) carbon; (umg: Geld): die ~n stimmen the money's right; Kohlehydrat (-(e)s, -e) nt carbohydrate; Kohlekraftwerk nt coal-fired power station

kohlen ['ko:lən] (umg) vi to tell white lies

Kohlen- zW: Kohlenbergwerk nt coal mine, pit, colliery (Brit); Kohlendioxid (-(e)s, -e) nt carbon dioxide; Kohlengrube f coal mine, pit; Kohlenhändler m coal merchant, coalman; Kohlensäure f carbon dioxide; ein Getränk ohne Kohlensäure a non-fizzy od still drink; Kohlenstoff m carbon

Kohlepapier nt carbon paper

Köhler ['kø:lər] (-s, -) m charcoal burner

Kohlestift m charcoal pencil

Kohlezeichnung f charcoal drawing
Kohl- zW: **kohlpechrabenschwarz,**
kohlrabenschwarz adj (Haar) jet-black; (Nacht)
pitch-black; **Kohlrübe** f turnip; **kohlschwarz**
adj coal-black
Koitus ['ko:itʊs] (-, - od -se) m coitus
Koje ['ko:jə] (-, -n) f cabin; (Bett) bunk
Kokain [koka'i:n] (-s) nt cocaine
kokett [ko'kɛt] adj coquettish, flirtatious
kokettieren [kokɛ'ti:rən] vi to flirt
Kokosnuss ['ko:kɔsnʊs] f coconut
Koks [ko:ks] (-es, -e) m coke
Kolben ['kɔlbən] (-s, -) m (Gewehrkolben) butt;
(Keule) club; (Chem) flask; (Tech) piston;
(Maiskolben) cob
Kolchose [kɔl'ço:zə] (-, -n) f collective farm
Kolik ['ko:lɪk] f colic, gripe
Kollaborateur, in [kɔlabora'tøːr(ɪn)] m(f) (Pol)
collaborator
Kollaps [kɔ'laps] (-es, -e) m collapse
Kolleg [kɔl'eːk] (-s, -s od -ien) nt lecture course
Kollege [kɔ'leːgə] (-n, -n) m colleague
kollegial [kɔlegi'aːl] adj cooperative
Kollegin [kɔ'leːgɪn] f colleague
Kollegium nt board; (Sch) staff
Kollekte [kɔ'lɛktə] (-, -n) f (Rel) collection
Kollektion [kɔlɛktsi'o:n] f collection;
(Sortiment) range
kollektiv [kɔlɛk'ti:f] adj collective
Koller ['kɔlər] (-s, -) m (umg) m (Anfall) funny
mood; (Wutanfall) rage; (Tropenkoller,
Gefängniskoller) madness
kollidieren [kɔli'di:rən] vi to collide; (zeitlich)
to clash
Kollier [kɔli'e:] (-s, -s) nt = **Collier**
Kollision [kɔlizi'o:n] f collision; (zeitlich) clash
Kollisionskurs m: **auf ~ gehen** (fig) to be
heading for trouble
Köln [kœln] (-s) nt Cologne
Kölnischwasser nt eau de Cologne
kolonial [koloni'aːl] adj colonial;
Kolonialmacht f colonial power;
Kolonialwarenhändler m grocer
Kolonie [kolo'ni:] f colony
kolonisieren [koloni'zi:rən] vt to colonize
Kolonist, in [kolo'nɪst(ɪn)] m(f) colonist
Kolonne [ko'lɔnə] (-, -n) f column; (von
Fahrzeugen) convoy
Koloss [ko'lɔs] (-es, -e) m colossus
kolossal [kolɔ'saːl] adj colossal
Kolumbianer, in [kolumbi'aːnər(ɪn)] m(f)
Columbian
kolumbianisch adj Columbian
Kolumbien [ko'lumbiən] (-s) nt Columbia
Koma ['ko:ma] (-s, -s od -ta) nt (Med) coma
Kombi ['kɔmbi] (-s, -s) m (Aut) estate (car) (Brit),
station wagon (US)
Kombination [kɔmbinatsi'o:n] f combination;
(Vermutung) conjecture; (Hemdhose)
combinations pl; (Aviat) flying suit
Kombinationsschloss nt combination lock
kombinieren [kɔmbi'ni:rən] vt to combine ⊳ vi
to deduce, work out; (vermuten) to guess

Kombiwagen m (Aut) estate (car) (Brit), station
wagon (US)
Kombizange f (pair of) pliers
Komet [ko'me:t] (-en, -en) m comet
kometenhaft adj (fig: Aufstieg) meteoric
Komfort [kɔm'fo:r] (-s) m luxury; (von Möbel etc)
comfort; (von Wohnung) amenities pl; (von Auto)
luxury features pl; (von Gerät) extras pl
komfortabel [kɔmfɔr'ta:bəl] adj comfortable
Komik ['ko:mɪk] f humour (Brit), humor (US),
comedy; **Komiker (-s, -)** m comedian
komisch ['ko:mɪʃ] adj funny; **mir ist so ~** (umg)
I feel funny od strange od odd; **komischerweise**
['ko:mɪʃər'vaɪzə] adv funnily enough
Komitee [komi'te:] (-s, -s) nt committee
Komm. abk (= Kommission) comm.
Komma ['kɔma] (-s, -s od -ta) nt comma; (Math)
decimal point; **fünf ~ drei** five point three
Kommandant [kɔman'dant] m commander,
commanding officer
Kommandeur [kɔman'dø:r] m commanding
officer
kommandieren [kɔman'di:rən] vt to
command ⊳ vi to command; (Befehle geben) to
give orders
Kommanditgesellschaft
[kɔman'di:tgəzɛlʃaft] f limited partnership
Kommando [kɔ'mando] (-s, -s) nt command,
order; (Truppe) detachment, squad; **auf ~** to
order; **Kommandobrücke** f (Naut) bridge;
Kommandowirtschaft f command economy
kommen ['kɔmən] unreg vi to come; (näher
kommen) to approach; (passieren) to happen;
(gelangen, geraten) to get; (Blumen, Zähne, Tränen
etc) to appear; (in die Schule, ins Gefängnis etc)
to go; **was kommt diese Woche im Kino?**
what's on at the cinema this week? ⊳ vi
unpers: **es kam eins zum anderen** one
thing led to another; **~ lassen** to send for; **in
Bewegung ~** to start moving; **jdn besuchen
~** to come and visit sb; **das kommt davon!**
see what happens?; **du kommst mir gerade
recht** (ironisch) you're just what I need; **das
kommt in den Schrank** that goes in the
cupboard; **an etw** akk **~** (berühren) to touch sth;
(sich verschaffen) to get hold of sth; **auf etw**
akk **~** (sich erinnern) to think of sth; (sprechen über) to
get onto sth; **das kommt auf die Rechnung**
that goes onto the bill; **hinter etw** akk **~**
(herausfinden) to find sth out; **zu sich ~** to come
round od to; **zu etw ~** to acquire sth; **um etw
~** to lose sth; **nichts auf jdn/etw ~ lassen** to
have nothing said against sb/sth; **jdm frech
~** to get cheeky with sb; **auf jeden vierten
kommt ein Platz** there's one place to every
fourth person; **mit einem Anliegen ~** to have
a request (to make); **wer kommt zuerst?**
who's first?; **wer zuerst kommt, mahlt
zuerst** (Sprichwort) first come first served;
unter ein Auto ~ to be run over by a car;
das kommt zusammen auf 20 Euro that
comes to 20 euros altogether; **und so kam es,
dass ...** and that is how it happened that ...;

k

195

daher kommt es, dass ... that's why ...

Kommen (-s) nt coming

kommend adj (Jahr, Woche, Generation) coming; (Ereignisse, Mode) future; (Trend) upcoming; **(am) ~en Montag** next Monday

Kommentar [kɔmɛn'taːr] m commentary; **kein ~** no comment; **kommentarlos** adj without comment

Kommentator [kɔmɛn'taːtɔr] m (TV) commentator

kommentieren [kɔmɛn'tiːrən] vt to comment on; **kommentierte Ausgabe** annotated edition

kommerziell [kɔmɛrtsi'ɛl] adj commercial

Kommilitone [kɔmili'toːnə] **(-n, -n)** m, **Kommilitonin** f fellow student

Kommiss [kɔ'mɪs] **(-es)** m (life in the) army

Kommissar [kɔmɪ'saːr] m police inspector

Kommissbrot nt army bread

Kommission [kɔmɪsi'oːn] f (Comm) commission; (Ausschuss) committee; **in ~ geben** to give (to a dealer) for sale on commission

Kommode [kɔ'moːdə] **(-, -n)** f (chest of) drawers

kommunal [kɔmu'naːl] adj local; (von Stadt) municipal; **Kommunalabgaben** pl local rates and taxes pl; **Kommunalpolitik** f local government politics; **Kommunalverwaltung** f local government; **Kommunalwahlen** pl local (government) elections pl

Kommune [kɔ'muːnə] **(-, -n)** f commune

Kommunikation [kɔmunɪkatsi'oːn] f communication

Kommunikator, in [kɔmuni'kaːtɔr, -'toːrɪn] m(f) communicator

Kommunikee [kɔmyni'keː] **(-s, -s)** nt = **Kommuniqué**

Kommunion [kɔmuni'oːn] f communion

Kommuniqué [kɔmyni'keː] **(-s, -s)** nt communiqué

Kommunismus [kɔmu'nɪsmʊs] m communism

Kommunist, in [kɔmu'nɪst(ɪn)] m(f) communist; **kommunistisch** adj communist

kommunizieren [kɔmuni'tsiːrən] vi to communicate; (Eccl) to receive communion

Komödiant [komødi'ant] m comedian; **Komödiantin** f comedienne

Komödie [ko'møːdiə] f comedy; **~ spielen** (fig) to put on an act

Kompagnon [kɔmpan'jõː] **(-s, -s)** m (Comm) partner

kompakt [kɔm'pakt] adj compact

Kompaktanlage f (Rundf) audio system

Kompanie [kɔmpa'niː] f company

Komparativ ['kɔmparatiːf] **(-s, -e)** m comparative

Kompass ['kɔmpas] **(-es, -e)** m compass

kompatibel [kɔmpa'tiːbəl] adj (auch Comput) compatible

Kompatibilität [kɔmpatibili'tɛːt] f (auch Comput) compatibility

kompensieren [kɔmpɛn'ziːrən] vt to compensate for, offset

kompetent [kɔmpe'tɛnt] adj competent

Kompetenz f competence, authority; **Kompetenzstreitigkeiten** pl dispute over respective areas of responsibility; **Kompetenzverteilung** f distribution of powers; **Kompetenzzentrum** f competence centre (Brit) od center (US)

komplett [kɔm'plɛt] adj complete

komplex [kɔm'plɛks] adj complex; **Komplex** **(-es, -e)** m complex

Komplikation [kɔmplikatsi'oːn] f complication

Kompliment [kɔmpli'mɛnt] nt compliment

Komplize [kɔm'pliːtsə] **(-n, -n)** m accomplice

komplizieren [kɔmpli'tsiːrən] vt to complicate

kompliziert adj complicated; (Med: Bruch) compound

Komplizin [kɔm'pliːtsɪn] f accomplice

Komplott [kɔm'plɔt] **(-(e)s, -e)** nt plot

komponieren [kɔmpo'niːrən] vt to compose

Komponist, in [kɔmpo'nɪst(ɪn)] m(f) composer

Komposition [kɔmpozitsi'oːn] f composition

Kompost [kɔm'pɔst] **(-(e)s, -e)** m compost; **Komposthaufen** m compost heap

Kompott [kɔm'pɔt] **(-(e)s, -e)** nt stewed fruit

Kompresse [kɔm'prɛsə] **(-, -n)** f compress

Kompressor [kɔm'prɛsɔr] m compressor

Kompromiss [kɔmpro'mɪs] **(-es, -e)** m compromise; **einen ~ schließen** to compromise; **kompromissbereit** adj willing to compromise; **Kompromisslösung** f compromise solution

kompromittieren [kɔmprɔmɪ'tiːrən] vt to compromise

Kondensation [kɔndɛnzatsi'oːn] f condensation

Kondensator [kɔndɛn'zaːtɔr] m condenser

kondensieren [kɔndɛn'ziːrən] vt to condense

Kondensmilch f condensed milk

Kondensstreifen m vapour (Brit) od vapor (US) trail

Kondition [kɔnditsi'oːn] f condition, shape; (Durchhaltevermögen) stamina

Konditionalsatz [kɔnditsio'naːlzats] m conditional clause

Konditionstraining nt fitness training

Konditor [kɔn'diːtɔr] m pastry-cook

Konditorei [kɔndito'raɪ] f cake shop; (mit Café) café

kondolieren [kɔndo'liːrən] vi: **jdm ~** to condole with sb, offer sb one's condolences

Kondom [kɔn'doːm] **(-s, -e)** m or nt condom

Konfektion [kɔnfɛktsi'oːn] f (production of) ready-to-wear od off-the-peg clothing

Konfektionsgröße f clothes size

Konfektionskleidung f ready-to-wear od off-the-peg clothing

Konferenz [kɔnfe'rɛnts] f conference; (Besprechung) meeting; **Konferenzschaltung** f (Tel) conference circuit; (Rundf, TV) television od radio link-up

konferieren [kɔnfe'riːrən] *vi* to confer; to have a meeting

Konfession [kɔnfɛsi'oːn] *f* religion; (*christlich*) denomination; **konfessionell** [-'nɛl] *adj* denominational

Konfessions- *zW:* **konfessionsgebunden** *adj* denominational; **konfessionslos** *adj* non-denominational; **Konfessionsschule** *f* denominational school

Konfetti [kɔn'fɛti] **(-(s))** *nt* confetti

Konfiguration [kɔnfiguratsi'oːn] *f* (*Comput*) configuration

Konfirmand, in [kɔnfɪr'mant, -'mandɪn] *m(f)* candidate for confirmation

Konfirmation [kɔnfɪrmatsi'oːn] *f* (*Eccl*) confirmation

konfirmieren [kɔnfɪr'miːrən] *vt* to confirm

konfiszieren [kɔnfɪs'tsiːrən] *vt* to confiscate

Konfitüre [kɔnfi'tyːrə] **(-, -n)** *f* jam

Konflikt [kɔn'flɪkt] **(-(e)s, -e)** *m* conflict; **Konfliktherd** *m* (*Pol*) centre (*Brit*) *od* center (*US*) of conflict; **Konfliktstoff** *m* cause of conflict

konform [kɔn'fɔrm] *adj* concurring; **~ gehen** to be in agreement

Konfrontation [kɔnfrɔntatsi'oːn] *f* confrontation

konfrontieren [kɔnfrɔn'tiːrən] *vt* to confront

konfus [kɔn'fuːs] *adj* confused

Kongo ['kɔŋgo] **(-(s))** *m* Congo

Kongress [kɔn'grɛs] **(-es, -e)** *m* congress

Kongruenz [kɔŋgru'ɛnts] *f* agreement, congruence

König ['køːnɪç] **(-(e)s, -e)** *m* king

Königin ['køːnɪgɪn] *f* queen

königlich *adj* royal ▷ *adv:* **sich ~ amüsieren** (*umg*) to have the time of one's life

Königreich *nt* kingdom

Königtum ['køːnɪçtuːm] **(-(e)s, -tümer)** *nt* kingship; (*Reich*) kingdom

konisch ['koːnɪʃ] *adj* conical

Konj. *abk* (= *Konjunktiv*) conj.

Konjugation [kɔnjugatsi'oːn] *f* conjugation

konjugieren [kɔnju'giːrən] *vt* to conjugate

Konjunktion [kɔnjʊŋktsi'oːn] *f* conjunction

Konjunktiv ['kɔnjʊŋktiːf] **(-s, -e)** *m* subjunctive

Konjunktur [kɔnjʊŋk'tuːr] *f* economic situation; (*Hochkonjunktur*) boom; **steigende/ fallende ~** upward/downward economic trend; **Konjunkturbarometer** *nt* economic indicators *pl*; **Konjunktureinbruch** *m* economic slump; **Konjunkturklima** *nt* economic climate; **Konjunkturloch** *nt* temporary economic dip; **Konjunkturpolitik** *f policies aimed at preventing economic fluctuations*

konkav [kɔn'kaːf] *adj* concave

konkret [kɔn'kreːt] *adj* concrete

Konkurrent, in [kɔnkʊ'rɛnt(ɪn)] *m(f)* competitor

Konkurrenz [kɔnkʊ'rɛnts] *f* competition; **jdm ~ machen** (*Comm, fig*) to compete with sb; **konkurrenzfähig** *adj* competitive; **Konkurrenzkampf** *m* competition; (*umg*) rat race

konkurrieren [kɔnkʊ'riːrən] *vi* to compete

Konkurs [kɔn'kʊrs] **(-es, -e)** *m* bankruptcy; **in ~ gehen** to go into receivership; **~ machen** (*umg*) to go bankrupt; **Konkursverfahren** *nt* bankruptcy proceedings *pl*; **Konkursverwalter** *m* receiver; (*von Gläubigern bevollmächtigt*) trustee

 SCHLÜSSELWORT

können ['kœnən] (*pt* **konnte**, *pp* **gekonnt** *od* (*als Hilfsverb*) **können**) *vt, vi* **1** to be able to; **ich kann es machen** I can do it, I am able to do it; **ich kann es nicht machen** I can't do it, I'm not able to do it; **ich kann nicht ...** I can't ..., I cannot ...; **was können Sie?** what can you do?; **ich kann nicht mehr** I can't go on; **ich kann nichts dafür** I can't help it; **du kannst mich (mal)!** (*umg*) get lost!

2 (*wissen, beherrschen*) to know; **können Sie Deutsch?** can you speak German?; **er kann gut Englisch** he speaks English well; **sie kann keine Mathematik** she can't do mathematics

3 (*dürfen*) to be allowed to; **kann ich gehen?** can I go?; **könnte ich ...?** could I ...?; **kann ich mit?** (*umg*) can I come with you?

4 (*möglich sein*): **Sie könnten recht haben** you may be right; **das kann sein** that's possible; **kann sein** maybe

Können (-s) *nt* ability

Könner (-s, -) *m* expert

Konnossement [kɔnɔsə'mɛnt] *nt* (*Export*) bill of lading

konnte *etc* ['kɔntə] *vb siehe* **können**

konsequent [kɔnze'kvɛnt] *adj* consistent; **ein Ziel ~ verfolgen** to pursue an objective single-mindedly

Konsequenz [kɔnze'kvɛnts] *f* consistency; (*Folgerung*) conclusion; **die ~en tragen** to take the consequences; **(aus etw) die ~en ziehen** to take the appropriate steps

konservativ [kɔnzɛrva'tiːf] *adj* conservative

Konservatorium [kɔnzɛrva'toːriʊm] *nt* academy of music, conservatory

Konserve [kɔn'zɛrvə] **(-, -n)** *f* tinned (*Brit*) *od* canned food

Konservenbüchse *f*, **Konservendose** *f* tin (*Brit*), can

konservieren [kɔnzɛr'viːrən] *vt* to preserve

Konservierung *f* preservation

Konservierungsstoff *m* preservative

Konsole [kɔnzo'leː] *f* games console

konsolidiert [kɔnzoli'diːrt] *adj* consolidated

Konsolidierung *f* consolidation

Konsonant [kɔnzo'nant] *m* consonant

Konsortium [kɔn'zɔrtsiʊm] *nt* consortium, syndicate

konspirativ [kɔnspira'tiːf] *adj:* **~e Wohnung** conspirators' hideaway

konstant [kɔn'stant] *adj* constant

Konstellation [kɔnstɛlatsi'oːn] *f* constellation;

k

(fig) line-up; *(von Faktoren etc)* combination

Konstitution [kɔnstitutsi'oːn] *f* constitution

konstitutionell [kɔnstitutsio'nɛl] *adj* constitutional

konstruieren [kɔnstru'iːrən] *vt* to construct

Konstrukteur, in [kɔnstrʊk'tøːr(ɪn)] *m(f)* designer

Konstruktion [kɔnstrʊktsi'on] *f* construction

Konstruktionsfehler *m (im Entwurf)* design fault; *(im Aufbau)* structural defect

konstruktiv [kɔnstrʊk'tiːf] *adj* constructive

Konsul ['kɔnzʊl] (**-s, -n**) *m* consul

Konsulat [kɔnzʊ'laːt] (**-(e)s, -e**) *nt* consulate

konsultieren [kɔnzʊl'tiːrən] *vt* to consult

Konsum[1] [kɔn'zuːm] (**-s**) *m* consumption

Konsum[2] ['kɔnzuːm] (**-s, -s**) *m (Genossenschaft)* cooperative society; *(Laden)* cooperative store, co-op *(umg)*

Konsumartikel *m* consumer article

Konsument [kɔnzu'mɛnt] *m* consumer

konsumfreudig *f* consumption-oriented, consumerist

Konsumgesellschaft *f* consumer society

konsumieren [kɔnzu'miːrən] *vt* to consume

Konsumtempel *m* temple of consumerism

Konsumterror *m* pressures *pl* of a materialistic society

Konsumzwang *m* compulsion to buy

Kontakt [kɔn'takt] (**-(e)s, -e**) *m* contact; **mit jdm ~ aufnehmen** to get in touch with sb; **Kontaktanzeige** *f* lonely hearts ad; **kontaktarm** *adj* unsociable; **kontaktfreudig** *adj* sociable

kontaktieren [kɔntak'tiːrən] *vt* to contact

Kontakt- *zW:* **Kontaktlinsen** *pl* contact lenses *pl*; **Kontaktmann** (**-(e)s,** *pl* **-männer**) *m (Agent)* contact; **Kontaktsperre** *f* ban on visits and letters *(to a prisoner)*

Konterfei ['kɔntərfaɪ] (**-s, -s**) *nt* likeness, portrait

kontern ['kɔntərn] *vt, vi* to counter

Konterrevolution ['kɔntərrevolutsioːn] *f* counter-revolution

Kontinent [kɔnti'nɛnt] *m* continent

Kontingent [kɔntɪŋ'gɛnt] (**-(e)s, -e**) *nt* quota; *(Truppenkontingent)* contingent

kontinuierlich [kɔntinu'iːrlɪç] *adj* continuous

Kontinuität [kɔntinui'tɛːt] *f* continuity

Konto ['kɔnto] (**-s, Konten**) *nt* account; **das geht auf mein ~** *(umg: ich bin schuldig)* I am to blame for this; *(ich zahle)* this is on me *(umg)*; **Kontoauszug** *m* statement (of account); **Kontoinhaber, in** *m(f)* account holder

Kontor [kɔn'toːr] (**-s, -e**) *nt* office

Kontorist, in [kɔnto'rɪst(ɪn)] *m(f)* clerk, office worker

Kontostand *m* bank balance

kontra ['kɔntra] *präp +akk* against; *(Jur)* versus

Kontra (**-s, -s**) *nt (Karten)* double; **jdm ~ geben** *(fig)* to contradict sb

Kontrabass *m* double bass

Kontrahent [-'hɛnt] *m* contracting party; *(Gegner)* opponent

Kontrapunkt *m* counterpoint

Kontrast [kɔn'trast] (**-(e)s, -e**) *m* contrast

Kontrollabschnitt *m (Comm)* counterfoil, stub

Kontrollampe [kɔn'trɔllampə] *f siehe* **Kontrolllampe**

Kontrolle [kɔn'trɔlə] (**-, -n**) *f* control, supervision; *(Passkontrolle)* passport control

Kontrolleur [kɔntrɔ'løːr] *m* inspector

kontrollieren [kɔntrɔ'liːrən] *vt* to control, supervise; *(nachprüfen)* to check

Kontrolllampe [kɔn'trɔllampə] *f* pilot lamp; *(Aut: für Ölstand etc)* warning light

Kontrollturm *m* control tower

Kontroverse [kɔntro'vɛrzə] (**-, -n**) *f* controversy

Kontur [kɔn'tuːr] *f* contour

Konvention [kɔnvɛntsi'oːn] *f* convention

Konventionalstrafe [kɔnvɛntsio'naːlʃtraːfə] *f* penalty *od* fine *(for breach of contract)*

konventionell [kɔnvɛntsio'nɛl] *adj* conventional

Konversation [kɔnvɛrzatsi'oːn] *f* conversation

Konversationslexikon *nt* encyclopaedia

konvex [kɔn'vɛks] *adj* convex

Konvoi ['kɔnvɔy] (**-s, -s**) *m* convoy

Konzentrat [kɔntsɛn'traːt] (**-s, -e**) *nt* concentrate

Konzentration [kɔntsɛntratsi'oːn] *f* concentration

Konzentrationsfähigkeit *f* power of concentration

Konzentrationslager *nt* concentration camp

konzentrieren [kɔntsɛn'triːrən] *vt, vr* to concentrate

konzentriert *adj* concentrated ▷ *adv (zuhören, arbeiten)* intently

Konzept [kɔn'tsɛpt] (**-(e)s, -e**) *nt* rough draft; *(Plan, Programm)* plan; *(Begriff, Vorstellung)* concept; **jdn aus dem ~ bringen** to confuse sb; **Konzeptpapier** *nt* rough paper

Konzern [kɔn'tsɛrn] (**-s, -e**) *m* combine

Konzert [kɔn'tsɛrt] (**-(e)s, -e**) *nt* concert; *(Stück)* concerto; **Konzertsaal** *m* concert hall

Konzession [kɔntsɛsi'oːn] *f* licence *(Brit)*, license *(US)*; *(Zugeständnis)* concession; **die ~ entziehen** +*dat: Comm)* to disenfranchise

Konzessionär [kɔntsɛsio'nɛːr] (**-s, -e**) *m* concessionaire

konzessionieren [kɔntsɛsio'niːrən] *vt* to license

Konzil [kɔn'tsiːl] (**-s, -e** *od* **-ien**) *nt* council

konzipieren [kɔntsi'piːrən] *vt* to conceive; *(entwerfen)* to design

kooperativ [koǀopera'tiːf] *adj* cooperative

kooperieren [koǀope'riːrən] *vi* to cooperate

koordinieren [koǀɔrdi'niːrən] *vt* to coordinate

Kopenhagen [koːpən'haːgən] (**-s**) *nt* Copenhagen

Kopf [kɔpf] (**-(e)s, ̈-e**) *m* head; **~ hoch!** chin up!; **~ an Kopf** shoulder to shoulder; *(Sport)* neck and neck; **pro ~** per person *od* head; **~ oder Zahl?** heads or tails?; **jdm den ~ waschen** *(fig: umg)* to give sb a piece of one's mind; **jdm über den ~ wachsen** *(lit)* to outgrow sb; (*fig: Sorgen etc*) to be more than sb can cope with; **jdn vor den ~ stoßen** to antagonize sb; **sich** *dat* **an den ~ fassen** (*fig*) to be speechless; **sich** *dat* **über etw** *akk* **den ~ zerbrechen** to rack one's brains over sth; **sich** *dat* **etw durch den ~ gehen lassen** to think about sth; **sich** *dat* **etw aus dem ~ schlagen** to put sth out of one's mind; **... und wenn du dich auf den ~ stellst!** (*umg*) ... no matter what you say/do!; **er ist nicht auf den ~ gefallen** he's no fool; **Kopfbahnhof** *m* terminus station; **Kopfbedeckung** *f* headgear

Köpfchen ['kœpfçən] *nt*: **~ haben** to be brainy

köpfen ['kœpfən] *vt* to behead; (*Baum*) to lop; (*Ei*) to take the top off; (*Ball*) to head

Kopf- *zW*: **Kopfende** *nt* head; **Kopfhaut** *f* scalp; **Kopfhörer** *m* headphone; **Kopfkissen** *nt* pillow; **kopflastig** *adj* (*fig*) completely rational; **kopflos** *adj* panic-stricken; **Kopflosigkeit** *f* panic; **kopfrechnen** *vi* to do mental arithmetic; **Kopfsalat** *m* lettuce; **kopfscheu** *adj*: **jdn kopfscheu machen** to intimidate sb; **Kopfschmerzen** *pl* headache *sing*; **Kopfsprung** *m* header, dive; **Kopfstand** *m* headstand; **Kopfsteinpflaster** *nt*: **eine Straße mit Kopfsteinpflaster** a cobbled street; **Kopfstütze** *f* headrest; (*im Auto*) head restraint; **Kopftuch** *nt* headscarf; **kopfüber** *adv* head-first; **Kopfweh** *nt* headache; **Kopfzerbrechen** *nt*: **jdm Kopfzerbrechen machen** to give sb a lot of headaches

Kopie [ko'piː] *f* copy

kopieren [ko'piːrən] *vt* to copy

Kopierer (**-s, -**) *m* (photo)copier

Kopilot, in ['koːpiloːt(ɪn)] *m(f)* co-pilot

Koppel¹ ['kɔpəl] (**-, -n**) *f* (*Weide*) enclosure

Koppel² ['kɔpəl] (**-s, -**) *nt* (*Gürtel*) belt

koppeln *vt* to couple

Koppelung *f* coupling

Koppelungsmanöver *nt* docking manoeuvre (*Brit*) *od* maneuver (*US*)

Koralle [ko'ralə] (**-, -n**) *f* coral

Korallenkette *f* coral necklace

Korallenriff *nt* coral reef

Korb [kɔrp] (**-(e)s, ̈e**) *m* basket; **jdm einen ~ geben** (*fig*) to turn sb down; **Korbball** *m* basketball

Körbchen ['kœrpçən] *nt* (*von Büstenhalter*) cup

Korbstuhl *m* wicker chair

Kord [kɔrt] (**-(e)s, -e** *od* **-s**) *m* = **Cord**

Kordel ['kɔrdəl] (**-, -n**) *f* cord, string

Korea [ko'reːa] (**-s**) *nt* Korea

Koreaner, in (**-s, -**) *m(f)* Korean

Korfu ['kɔrfu] (**-s**) *nt* Corfu

Korinthe [ko'rɪntə] (**-, -n**) *f* currant

Korinthenkacker [ko'rɪntənkakər] (**-s, -**) (*umg*) *m* fusspot, hair-splitter

Kork [kɔrk] (**-(e)s, -e**) *m* cork

Korken (**-s, -**) *m* stopper, cork; **Korkenzieher** (**-s, -**) *m* corkscrew

Korn¹ [kɔrn] (**-(e)s, ̈er**) *nt* corn, grain

Korn² [kɔrn] (**-(e)s, -e**) *m* (*Gewehr*) sight; **etw aufs ~ nehmen** (*fig: umg*) to hit out at sth

Korn³ [kɔrn] (**-, -s**) *m* (*Kornbranntwein*) corn schnapps

Kornblume *f* cornflower

Körnchen ['kœrnçən] *nt* grain, granule

körnig ['kœrnɪç] *adj* granular, grainy

Kornkammer *f* granary

Körnung ['kœrnʊŋ] *f* (*Tech*) grain size; (*Phot*) granularity

Körper ['kœrpər] (**-s, -**) *m* body; **Körperbau** *m* build; **körperbehindert** *adj* disabled; **Körpergeruch** *m* body odour (*Brit*) *od* odor (*US*); **Körpergewicht** *nt* weight; **Körpergröße** *f* height; **Körperhaltung** *f* carriage, deportment; **körperlich** *adj* physical; **körperliche Arbeit** manual work; **Körperpflege** *f* personal hygiene; **Körperschaft** *f* corporation; **Körperschaft des öffentlichen Rechts** public corporation *od* body; **Körperschaftssteuer** *f* corporation tax; **Körpersprache** *f* body language; **Körperteil** *m* part of the body; **Körperverletzung** *f* (*Jur*): **schwere Körperverletzung** grievous bodily harm

Korps [koːr] (**-, -**) *nt* (*Mil*) corps; (*Univ*) students' club

korpulent [kɔrpu'lɛnt] *adj* corpulent

korrekt [kɔ'rɛkt] *adj* correct; **Korrektheit** *f* correctness

Korrektor, in [kɔ'rɛktɔr, -'toːrɪn] (**-s, -**) *m(f)* proofreader

Korrektur [kɔrɛk'tuːr] *f* (*eines Textes*) proofreading; (*Text*) proof; (*Sch*) marking, correction; **(bei etw) ~ lesen** to proofread (sth); **Korrekturfahne** *f* (*Typ*) proof

Korrespondent, in [kɔrɛspɔn'dɛnt(ɪn)] *m(f)* correspondent

Korrespondenz [kɔrɛspɔn'dɛnts] *f* correspondence; **Korrespondenzqualität** *f* (*Drucker*) letter quality

korrespondieren [kɔrɛspɔn'diːrən] *vi* to correspond

Korridor ['kɔridoːr] (**-s, -e**) *m* corridor

korrigieren [kɔri'giːrən] *vt* to correct; (*Meinung, Einstellung*) to change

Korrosion [kɔrozi'oːn] *f* corrosion

Korrosionsschutz *m* corrosion protection

korrumpieren [kɔrʊm'piːrən] *vt* (*auch Comput*) to corrupt

korrupt [kɔ'rʊpt] *adj* corrupt

Korruption [kɔrʊptsi'oːn] *f* corruption

Korsett [kɔr'zɛt] (**-(e)s, -e**) *nt* corset

Korsika ['kɔrzika] (**-s**) *nt* Corsica

Koseform ['koːzəfɔrm] *f* pet form

kosen *vt* to caress ▷ *vi* to bill and coo

Kosename *m* pet name

Kosewort *nt* term of endearment

Kosmetik [kɔs'meːtɪk] *f* cosmetics *pl*

Kosmetikerin *f* beautician

kosmetisch *adj* cosmetic; (*Chirurgie*) plastic

kosmisch ['kɔsmɪʃ] *adj* cosmic

Kosmonaut [kɔsmo'naʊt] (**-en, -en**) *m* cosmonaut

Kosmopolit [kɔsmopo'liːt] (**-en, -en**) *m*

k

cosmopolitan; **kosmopolitisch** [-po'li:tiʃ] *adj* cosmopolitan

Kosmos ['kɔsmɔs] (-) *m* cosmos

Kost [kɔst] (-) *f* (*Nahrung*) food; (*Verpflegung*) board; **~ und Logis** board and lodging

kostbar *adj* precious; (*teuer*) costly, expensive; **Kostbarkeit** *f* preciousness; costliness, expensiveness; (*Wertstück*) treasure

Kosten *pl* cost(s); (*Ausgaben*) expenses *pl*; **auf ~ von** at the expense of; **auf seine ~ kommen** (*fig*) to get one's money's worth

kosten *vt* to cost; (*versuchen*) to taste ▷ *vi* to taste; **koste es, was es wolle** whatever the cost

Kosten- *zW*: **Kostenanschlag** *m* estimate; **kostendeckend** *adj* cost-effective; **Kostenerstattung** *f* reimbursement of expenses; **Kostenkontrolle** *f* cost control; **kostenlos** *adj* free (of charge); **Kosten-Nutzen-Analyse** *f* cost-benefit analysis; **kostenpflichtig** *adj*: **ein Auto kostenpflichtig abschleppen** to tow away a car at the owner's expense; **Kostenstelle** *f* (*Comm*) cost centre (*Brit*) *od* center (*US*); **Kostenvoranschlag** *m* (costs) estimate

Kostgeld *nt* board

köstlich ['kœstlɪç] *adj* precious; (*Einfall*) delightful; (*Essen*) delicious; **sich ~ amüsieren** to have a marvellous time

Kostprobe *f* taste; (*fig*) sample

kostspielig *adj* expensive

Kostüm [kɔs'ty:m] (-s, -e) *nt* costume; (*Damenkostüm*) suit; **Kostümfest** *nt* fancy-dress party

kostümieren [kɔsty'mi:rən] *vt, vr* to dress up

Kostümprobe *f* (*Theat*) dress rehearsal

Kostümverleih *m* costume agency

Kot [ko:t] (-(e)s) *m* excrement

Kotelett [kotə'lɛt] (-(e)s, -e *od* -s) *nt* cutlet, chop

Koteletten *pl* sideboards *pl* (*Brit*), sideburns *pl* (*US*)

Köter ['kø:tər] (-s, -) *m* cur

Kotflügel *m* (*Aut*) wing

kotzen ['kɔtsən] (*umg!*) *vi* to puke (!), throw up; **das ist zum K~** it makes you sick

KP (-, -s) *f abk* (= *Kommunistische Partei*) C.P.

KPÖ (-) *f abk* (= *Kommunistische Partei Österreichs*) Austrian Communist Party

Kr. *abk* = **Kreis**

Krabbe ['krabə] (-, -n) *f* shrimp

krabbeln *vi* to crawl

Krach [krax] (-(e)s, -s *od* -e) *m* crash; (*andauernd*) noise; (*umg: Streit*) quarrel, argument; **~ schlagen** to make a fuss; **krachen** *vi* to crash; (*beim Brechen*) to crack ▷ *vr* (*umg*) to argue, quarrel

krächzen ['krɛçtsən] *vi* to croak

Kräcker ['krɛkər] (-s, -) *m* (*Koch*) cracker

kraft [kraft] *präp+gen* by virtue of

Kraft (-, ˸e) *f* strength; (*von Stimme, fig*) power, force; (*Arbeitskraft*) worker; **mit vereinten Kräften werden wir ...** if we combine our

efforts we will ...; **nach (besten) Kräften** to the best of one's abilities; **außer ~ sein** (*Jur: Geltung*) to be no longer in force; **in ~ treten** to come into effect

Kraft- *zW*: **Kraftaufwand** *m* effort; **Kraftausdruck** *m* swearword; **Kraftbrühe** *f* beef tea

Kräfteverhältnis ['krɛftəfɛrhɛltnɪs] *nt* (*Pol*) balance of power; (*von Mannschaften etc*) relative strength

Kraftfahrer *m* motor driver

Kraftfahrzeug *nt* motor vehicle; **Kraftfahrzeugbrief** *m* (*Aut*) logbook (*Brit*), motor-vehicle registration certificate (*US*); **Kraftfahrzeugschein** *m* (*Aut*) car licence (*Brit*) *od* license (*US*); **Kraftfahrzeugsteuer** *f* ≈ road tax

kräftig ['krɛftɪç] *adj* strong; (*Suppe, Essen*) nourishing; **kräftigen** ['krɛftɪgən] *vt* to strengthen

Kraft- *zW*: **kraftlos** *adj* weak; powerless; (*Jur*) invalid; **Kraftmeierei** (*umg*) *f showing off of physical strength*; **Kraftprobe** *f* trial of strength; **Kraftrad** *nt* motorcycle; **Kraftstoff** *m* fuel; **Krafttraining** *nt* weight training; **kraftvoll** *adj* vigorous; **Kraftwagen** *m* motor vehicle; **Kraftwerk** *nt* power station; **Kraftwerker** *m* power station worker

Kragen ['kra:gən] (-s, -) *m* collar; **da ist mir der ~ geplatzt** (*umg*) I blew my top; **es geht ihm an den ~** (*umg*) he's in for it; **Kragenweite** *f* collar size; **das ist nicht meine Kragenweite** (*fig: umg*) that's not my cup of tea

Krähe ['krɛ:ə] (-, -n) *f* crow

krähen *vi* to crow

krakeelen [kra'ke:lən] (*umg*) *vi* to make a din

krakelig ['kra:kəlɪç] (*umg*) *adj* (*Schrift*) scrawly, spidery

Kralle ['kralə] (-, -n) *f* claw; (*Vogelkralle*) talon

krallen *vt* to clutch; (*krampfhaft*) to claw

Kram [kra:m] (-(e)s) *m* stuff, rubbish; **den ~ hinschmeißen** (*umg*) to chuck the whole thing; **kramen** *vi* to rummage; **Kramladen** (*pej*) *m* small shop

Krampf [krampf] (-(e)s, ˸e) *m* cramp; (*zuckend*) spasm; (*Unsinn*) rubbish; **Krampfader** *f* varicose vein; **krampfhaft** *adj* convulsive; (*fig: Versuche*) desperate

Kran [kra:n] (-(e)s, ˸e) *m* crane; (*Wasserkran*) tap (*Brit*), faucet (*US*)

Kranich ['kra:nɪç] (-s, -e) *m* (*Zool*) crane

krank [kraŋk] *adj* ill, sick; **das macht mich ~!** (*umg*) it gets on my nerves!, it drives me round the bend!; **sich ~ stellen** to pretend to be ill, malinger

Kranke, r *f(m)* sick person, invalid; (*Patient*) patient

kränkeln ['krɛŋkəln] *vi* to be in bad health

kranken ['kraŋkən] *vi*: **an etw** *dat* **~** (*fig*) to suffer from sth

kränken ['krɛŋkən] *vt* to hurt

Kranken- *zW*: **Krankenbericht** *m* medical

report; **Krankenbesuch** m visit to a sick person; **Krankengeld** nt sick pay; **Krankengeschichte** f medical history; **Krankengymnastik** f physiotherapy; **Krankenhaus** nt hospital; **Krankenkasse** f health insurance; **Krankenpfleger** m orderly; (mit Schwesternausbildung) male nurse; **Krankenpflegerin** f nurse; **Krankenschein** m medical insurance certificate; **Krankenschwester** f nurse; **Krankenversicherung** f health insurance; **Krankenwagen** m ambulance

krankfeiern (umg) vi to be off sick; (vortäuschend) to skive (Brit)

krankhaft adj diseased; (Angst etc) morbid; **sein Geiz ist schon ~** his meanness is almost pathological

Krankheit f illness; disease; **nach langer schwerer ~** after a long serious illness

Krankheitserreger m disease-causing agent

kränklich ['krɛŋklɪç] adj sickly

krankmelden vr to let one's boss etc know that one is ill; (telefonisch) to phone in sick; (bes Mil) to report sick

krankschreiben unreg vt to give sb a medical certificate; (bes Mil) to put sb on the sick list

Kränkung f insult, offence (Brit), offense (US)

Kranz [krants] (-es, ⁻e) m wreath, garland

Kränzchen ['krɛntsçən] nt small wreath; (fig: Kaffeekränzchen) coffee circle

Krapfen ['krapfən] (-s, -) m fritter; (Berliner) doughnut (Brit), donut (US)

krass [kras] adj crass; (Unterschied) extreme

Krater ['kraːtər] (-s, -) m crater

Kratzbürste ['kratsbʏrstə] f (fig) crosspatch

Krätze ['krɛtsə] f (Med) scabies sing

kratzen ['kratsən] vt, vi to scratch; (abkratzen): **etw von etw ~** to scrape sth off sth

Kratzer (-s, -) m scratch; (Werkzeug) scraper

Kraul [kraʊl] (-s) nt (auch: **Kraulschwimmen**) crawl; **kraulen** vi (schwimmen) to do the crawl ▷ vt (streicheln) to tickle

kraus [kraʊs] adj crinkly; (Haar) frizzy; (Stirn) wrinkled

Krause ['kraʊzə] (-, -n) f frill, ruffle

kräuseln ['krɔʏzəln] vt (Haar) to make frizzy; (Stoff) to gather; (Stirn) to wrinkle ▷ vr (Haar) to go frizzy; (Stirn) to wrinkle; (Wasser) to ripple

Kraut [kraʊt] (-(e)s, **Kräuter**) nt plant; (Gewürz) herb; (Gemüse) cabbage; **dagegen ist kein ~ gewachsen** (fig) there's nothing anyone can do about that; **ins ~ schießen** (lit) to run to seed; (fig) to get out of control; **wie ~ und Rüben** (umg) extremely untidy

Kräutertee ['krɔʏtərteː] m herb tea

Krawall [kra'val] (-s, -e) m row, uproar

Krawatte [kra'vatə] (-, -n) f tie

kreativ [krea'tiːf] adj creative

Kreativität [kreativi'tɛːt] f creativity

Kreatur [krea'tuːr] f creature

Krebs [kreːps] (-es, -e) m crab; (Med) cancer; (Astrol) Cancer; **krebserregend** adj carcinogenic; **krebskrank** adj suffering from

cancer; **krebskrank sein** to have cancer; **Krebskranke, r** f(m) cancer victim; (Patient) cancer patient; **krebsrot** adj red as a lobster

Kredit [kre'diːt] (-(e)s, -e) m credit; (Darlehen) loan; (fig) standing; **Kreditdrosselung** f credit squeeze; **kreditfähig** adj creditworthy; **Kreditgrenze** f credit limit; **Kredithai** (umg) m loan-shark; **Kreditkarte** f credit card; **Kreditkonto** nt credit account; **Kreditpolitik** f lending policy; **kreditwürdig** adj creditworthy; **Kreditwürdigkeit** f creditworthiness, credit status

Kreide ['kraɪdə] (-, -n) f chalk; **bei jdm (tief) in der ~ stehen** to be (deep) in debt to sb; **kreidebleich** adj as white as a sheet

Kreis [kraɪs] (-es, -e) m circle; (Stadtkreis etc) district; **im ~ gehen** (lit, fig) to go round in circles; **(weite) ~e ziehen** (fig) to have (wide) repercussions; **weite ~e der Bevölkerung** wide sections of the population; **eine Feier im kleinen ~e** a celebration for a few close friends and relatives

kreischen ['kraɪʃən] vi to shriek, screech

Kreisel ['kraɪzəl] (-s, -) m top; (Verkehrskreisel) roundabout (Brit), traffic circle (US)

kreisen ['kraɪzən] vi to spin; (fig: Gedanken, Gespräch): **~ um** to revolve around

Kreis- zW: **kreisförmig** adj circular; **Kreislauf** m (Med) circulation; (fig: der Natur etc) cycle; **Kreislaufkollaps** m circulatory collapse; **Kreislaufstörungen** pl circulation trouble sing; **Kreissäge** f circular saw

Kreißsaal ['kraɪszaːl] m delivery room

Kreisstadt f ≈ county town

Kreisverkehr m roundabout (Brit), traffic circle (US)

Krematorium [krema'toːriʊm] nt crematorium

Kreml ['kreːml] (-s) m: **der ~** the Kremlin

Krempe ['krɛmpə] (-, -n) f brim

Krempel (-s) (umg) m rubbish

krepieren [kre'piːrən] (umg) vi (sterben) to die, kick the bucket

Krepp [krɛp] (-s, -s od -e) m crêpe

Krepppapier nt crêpe paper

Kreppsohle f crêpe sole

Kresse ['krɛsə] (-, -n) f cress

Kreta ['kreːta] (-s) nt Crete

Kreter, in [kre'tər(ɪn)] (-s, -) m(f) Cretan

kretisch adj Cretan

kreuz [krɔʏts] adj: **~ und quer** all over

Kreuz (-es, -e) nt cross; (Anat) small of the back; (Karten) clubs; (Mus) sharp; (Autobahnkreuz) intersection; **zu ~e kriechen** (fig) to eat humble pie, eat crow (US); **jdn aufs ~ legen** to throw sb on his back; (fig: umg) to take sb for a ride

kreuzen vt to cross ▷ vr to cross; (Meinungen etc) to clash ▷ vi (Naut) to cruise; **die Arme ~** to fold one's arms

Kreuzer (-s, -) m (Schiff) cruiser

Kreuz- zW: **Kreuzfahrt** f cruise; **Kreuzfeuer** nt (fig): **im Kreuzfeuer stehen** to be caught in

the crossfire; **Kreuzgang** *m* cloisters *pl*
kreuzigen *vt* to crucify
Kreuzigung *f* crucifixion
Kreuzotter *f* adder
Kreuzschmerzen *pl* backache *sing*
Kreuzung *f* (*Verkehrskreuzung*) crossing, junction; (*Züchtung*) cross
Kreuz- *zW:* **kreuzunglücklich** *adj* absolutely miserable; **Kreuzverhör** *nt* cross-examination; **ins Kreuzverhör nehmen** to cross-examine; **Kreuzweg** *m* crossroads; (*Rel*) Way of the Cross; **Kreuzworträtsel** *nt* crossword puzzle; **Kreuzzeichen** *nt* sign of the cross; **Kreuzzug** *m* crusade
kribbelig ['krɪbəlɪç], **kribblig** ['krɪblɪç] (*umg*) *adj* fidgety; (*kribbelnd*) tingly
kribbeln ['krɪbəln] *vi* (*jucken*) to itch; (*prickeln*) to tingle
kriechen ['kri:çən] *unreg vi* to crawl, creep; (*pej*) to grovel, crawl
Kriecher (**-s, -**) *m* crawler
kriecherisch *adj* grovelling (*Brit*), groveling (*US*)
Kriechspur *f* crawler lane (*Brit*)
Kriechtier *nt* reptile
Krieg [kri:k] (**-(e)s, -e**) *m* war; **~ führen (mit** *od* **gegen)** to wage war (on)
kriegen ['kri:gən] (*umg*) *vt* to get
Krieger (**-s, -**) *m* warrior; **Kriegerdenkmal** *nt* war memorial; **kriegerisch** *adj* warlike
Kriegführung *f* warfare
Kriegs- *zW:* **Kriegsbeil** *nt:* **das Kriegsbeil begraben** (*fig*) to bury the hatchet; **Kriegsbemalung** *f* war paint; **Kriegsdienstverweigerer** *m* conscientious objector; **Kriegserklärung** *f* declaration of war; **Kriegsfuß** *m:* **mit jdm/etw auf Kriegsfuß stehen** to be at loggerheads with sb/not to get on with sth; **Kriegsgefangene, r** *f(m)* prisoner of war; **Kriegsgefangenschaft** *f* captivity; **Kriegsgericht** *nt* court-martial; **Kriegsrat** *m* council of war; **Kriegsrecht** *nt* (*Mil*) martial law; **Kriegsschauplatz** *m* theatre (*Brit*) *od* theater (*US*) of war; **Kriegsschiff** *nt* warship; **Kriegsschuld** *f* war guilt; **Kriegsverbrecher** *m* war criminal; **Kriegsversehrte, r** *f(m)* person disabled in the war; **Kriegszustand** *m* state of war
Krim [krɪm] *f:* **die ~** the Crimea
Krimi ['kri:mi] (**-s, -s**) (*umg*) *m* thriller
kriminal [krimi'na:l] *adj* criminal; **Kriminalbeamte, r** *m* detective; **Kriminalfilm** *m* crime thriller *od* movie (*esp US*)
Kriminalität [kriminali'tɛ:t] *f* criminality
Kriminalpolizei *f* ≈ Criminal Investigation Department (*Brit*), ≈ Federal Bureau of Investigation (*US*)
Kriminalroman *m* detective story
kriminell [krimi'nɛl] *adj* criminal
Kriminelle, r *f(m)* criminal
Krimskrams ['krɪmskrams] (**-es**) (*umg*) *m* odds and ends *pl*
Kringel ['krɪŋəl] (**-s, -**) *m* (*der Schrift*) squiggle;

(*Koch*) ring
kringelig *adj:* **sich ~ lachen** (*umg*) to kill o.s. laughing
Kripo ['kri:po] (**-, -s**) *f abk* (= *Kriminalpolizei*) ≈ CID (*Brit*), ≈ FBI (*US*)
Krippe ['krɪpə] (**-, -n**) *f* manger, crib; (*Kinderkrippe*) crèche
Krippenspiel *nt* nativity play
Krippentod *m* cot death
Krise ['kri:zə] (**-, -n**) *f* crisis
kriseln *vi:* **es kriselt** there's a crisis looming, there is trouble brewing
Krisen- *zW:* **krisenfest** *adj* stable; **Krisenherd** *m* flash point; trouble spot; **Krisenstab** *m* action *od* crisis committee
Kristall¹ [krɪs'tal] (**-s, -e**) *m* crystal
Kristall² (**-s**) *nt* (*Glas*) crystal; **Kristallzucker** *m* refined sugar crystals *pl*
Kriterium [kri'te:riʊm] *nt* criterion
Kritik [kri'ti:k] *f* criticism; (*Zeitungskritik*) review, write-up; **an jdm/etw ~ üben** to criticize sb/sth; **unter aller ~ sein** (*umg*) beneath contempt
Kritiker, in ['kri:tikər(ɪn)] (**-s, -**) *m(f)* critic
kritiklos *adj* uncritical
kritisch ['kri:tɪʃ] *adj* critical
kritisieren [kriti'zi:rən] *vt, vi* to criticize
kritteln ['krɪtəln] *vi* to find fault, carp
kritzeln ['krɪtsəln] *vt, vi* to scribble, scrawl
Kroate [kro'a:tə] (**-n, -n**) *m* Croat
Kroatien [kro'a:tsiən] (**-s**) *nt* Croatia
Kroatin *f* Croat
kroatisch *adj* Croatian
kroch *etc* [krɔx] *vb siehe* **kriechen**
Krokodil [kroko'di:l] (**-s, -e**) *nt* crocodile
Krokodilstränen *pl* crocodile tears *pl*
Krokus ['kro:kʊs] (**-, -** *od* **-se**) *m* crocus
Krone ['kro:nə] (**-, -n**) *f* crown; (*Baumkrone*) top; **einen in der ~ haben** (*umg*) to be tipsy
krönen ['krø:nən] *vt* to crown
Kron- *zW:* **Kronkorken** *m* bottle top; **Kronleuchter** *m* chandelier; **Kronprinz** *m* crown prince
Krönung ['krø:nʊŋ] *f* coronation
Kronzeuge *m* (*Jur*) person who turns Queen's/King's (*Brit*) *od* State's (*US*) evidence; (*Hauptzeuge*) principal witness
Kropf [krɔpf] (**-(e)s, ̈e**) *m* (*Med*) goitre (*Brit*), goiter (*US*); (*von Vogel*) crop
Krösus ['krø:zʊs] (**-ses, -se**) *m:* **ich bin doch kein ~** (*umg*) I'm not made of money
Kröte ['krø:tə] (**-, -n**) *f* toad; **Kröten** *pl* (*umg: Geld*) pennies *pl*
Krs. *abk* = **Kreis**
Krücke ['krʏkə] (**-, -n**) *f* crutch
Krug [kru:k] (**-(e)s, ̈e**) *m* jug; (*Bierkrug*) mug
Krümel ['kry:məl] (**-s, -**) *m* crumb
krümeln *vt, vi* to crumble
krumm [krʊm] *adj* (*lit, fig*) crooked; (*kurvig*) curved; **keinen Finger ~ machen** (*umg*) not to lift a finger; **ein ~es Ding drehen** (*umg*) to do something crooked; *siehe auch* **krummnehmen**; **krummbeinig** *adj* bandy-legged

krümmen ['krʏmːən] vt to bend ▷ vr to bend, curve

krummlachen (umg) vr to laugh o.s. silly; **sich krumm- und schieflachen** to fall about laughing

krummnehmen unreg (umg) vt: **jdm etw ~** (umg) to take sth amiss

Krümmung f bend, curve

Krüppel ['krʏpəl] (**-s, -**) m cripple

Kruste ['krʊstə] (**-, -n**) f crust

Krux [krʊks] (**-**) f (Schwierigkeit) trouble, problem

Kruzifix [krutsiˈfɪks] (**-es, -e**) nt crucifix

Kt. abk = **Kanton**

Kto. abk (= Konto) a/c

Kuba ['kuːba] (**-s**) nt Cuba

Kubaner, in [kuˈbaːnər(ɪn)] (**-s, -**) m(f) Cuban

kubanisch [kuˈbaːnɪʃ] adj Cuban

Kübel ['kyːbəl] (**-s, -**) m tub; (Eimer) pail

Kubik- [kuˈbiːk] in zW cubic; **Kubikmeter** m cubic metre (Brit) od meter (US)

Küche ['kʏçə] (**-, -n**) f kitchen; (Kochen) cooking, cuisine

Kuchen ['kuːxən] (**-s, -**) m cake; **Kuchenblech** nt baking tray; **Kuchenform** f baking tin (Brit) od pan (US); **Kuchengabel** f pastry fork

Küchen- zW: **Küchengerät** nt kitchen utensil; (elektrisch) kitchen appliance; **Küchenherd** m cooker, stove; **Küchenmaschine** f food processor; **Küchenmesser** nt kitchen knife; **Küchenschabe** f cockroach; **Küchenschrank** m kitchen cabinet

Kuchenteig m cake mixture

Kuckuck ['kʊkʊk] (**-s, -e**) m cuckoo; (umg: Siegel des Gerichtsvollziehers) bailiff's seal (for distraint of goods); **das weiß der ~** heaven (only) knows

Kuckucksuhr f cuckoo clock

Kuddelmuddel ['kʊdəlmʊdəl] (**-s**) (umg) m od nt mess

Kufe ['kuːfə] (**-, -n**) f (Fasskufe) vat; (Schlittenkufe) runner; (Aviat) skid

Kugel ['kuːgəl] (**-, -n**) f ball; (Math) sphere; (Mil) bullet; (Erdkugel) globe; (Sport) shot; **eine ruhige ~ schieben** (umg) to have a cushy number; **kugelförmig** adj spherical; **Kugelkopf** m (Schreibmaschine) golf ball; **Kugelkopfschreibmaschine** f golf-ball typewriter; **Kugellager** nt ball bearing

kugeln vt to roll; (Sport) to bowl ▷ vr (vor Lachen) to double up

Kugel- zW: **kugelrund** adj (Gegenstand) round; (umg: Person) tubby; **Kugelschreiber** m ball-point (pen), Biro®; **kugelsicher** adj bulletproof; **Kugelstoßen** (**-s**) nt shot put

Kuh [kuː] (**-, -̈e**) f cow; **Kuhdorf** (pej: umg) nt one-horse town; **Kuhhandel** (pej: umg) m horse-trading; **Kuhhaut** f: **das geht auf keine Kuhhaut** (fig: umg) that's absolutely incredible

kühl [kyːl] adj (lit, fig) cool; **Kühlanlage** f refrigeration plant

Kühle (**-**) f coolness

kühlen vt to cool

Kühler (**-s, -**) m (Aut) radiator; **Kühlerhaube** f

(Aut) bonnet (Brit), hood (US)

Kühl- zW: **Kühlflüssigkeit** f coolant; **Kühlhaus** nt cold-storage depot; **Kühlraum** m cold-storage chamber; **Kühlschrank** m refrigerator; **Kühltasche** f cool bag; **Kühltruhe** f freezer

Kühlung f cooling

Kühlwagen m (Lastwagen, Eisenb) refrigerator van

Kühlwasser nt coolant

kühn [kyːn] adj bold, daring; **Kühnheit** f boldness

Kuhstall m cow-shed

k. u. k. abk (= kaiserlich und königlich) imperial and royal

Küken ['kyːkən] (**-s, -**) nt chicken; (umg: Nesthäkchen) baby of the family

kulant [kuˈlant] adj obliging

Kulanz [kuˈlants] f accommodating attitude, generousness

Kuli ['kuːli] (**-s, -s**) m coolie; (umg: Kugelschreiber) Biro®

kulinarisch [kuliˈnaːrɪʃ] adj culinary

Kulisse [kuˈlɪsə] (**-, -n**) f scene

Kulissenschieber, in m(f) stagehand

Kulleraugen ['kʊləraʊgən] (umg) pl wide eyes pl

kullern ['kʊlərn] vi to roll

Kult [kʊlt] (**-(e)s, -e**) m worship, cult; **mit etw ~ treiben** to make a cult out of sth

kultivieren [kʊltiˈviːrən] vt to cultivate

kultiviert adj cultivated, refined

Kultstätte f place of worship

Kultstatus m: **~ haben/genießen** to have/ enjoy cult status

Kultur [kʊlˈtuːr] f culture; (Lebensform) civilization; (des Bodens) cultivation; **Kulturbanause** (umg) m philistine, low-brow; **Kulturbetrieb** m culture industry; **Kulturbeutel** m toilet bag (Brit), washbag

kulturell [kʊltuˈrel] adj cultural

Kulturfilm m documentary film

Kulturhauptstadt f: **Europäische ~** European City of Culture

Kulturteil m (von Zeitung) arts section

Kultusminister ['kʊltʊsmɪnɪstər] m minister of education and the arts

Kümmel ['kʏməl] (**-s, -**) m caraway seed; (Branntwein) kümmel

Kummer ['kʊmər] (**-s**) m grief, sorrow

kümmerlich ['kʏmərlɪç] adj miserable, wretched

kümmern vr: **sich um jdn ~** to look after sb ▷ vt to concern; **sich um etw ~** to see to sth; **das kümmert mich nicht** that doesn't worry me

Kumpan, in [kʊmˈpaːn(ɪn)] (**-s, -e**) m(f) mate; (pej) accomplice

Kumpel ['kʊmpəl] (**-s, -**) (umg) m mate

kündbar ['kʏntbaːr] adj redeemable, recallable; (Vertrag) terminable

Kunde¹ ['kʊndə] (**-n, -n**) m customer

Kunde² ['kʊndə] (**-, -n**) f (Botschaft) news

Kunden- zW: **Kundenberatung** f customer

k

advisory service; **Kundendienst** *m* after-sales service; **Kundenfang** *(pej) m:* **auf Kundenfang sein** to be touting for customers; **Kundenfänger** *m* tout *(umg)*; **Kundenkonto** *nt* charge account; **Kundenkreis** *m* customers *pl*, clientele; **kundenorientiert** *m* customer-oriented; **Kundenservice** *f* customer service; **Kundenwerbung** *f* publicity *(aimed at attracting custom or customers)*

Kund- *zW:* **Kundgabe** *f* announcement; **kundgeben** *unreg vt* to announce; **Kundgebung** *f* announcement; *(Versammlung)* rally

kundig *adj* expert, experienced

kündigen ['kʏndɪgən] *vi* to give in one's notice ▷ *vt* to cancel; **jdm** ~ to give sb his notice; **zum 1. April** ~ to give one's notice for April 1st; *(Mieter)* to give notice for April 1st; *(bei Mitgliedschaft)* to cancel one's membership as of April 1st; **(jdm) die Stellung** ~ to give (sb) notice; **sie hat ihm die Freundschaft gekündigt** she has broken off their friendship

Kündigung *f* notice

Kündigungsfrist *f* period of notice

Kündigungsschutz *m* protection against wrongful dismissal

Kundin *f* customer

Kundschaft *f* customers *pl*, clientele

Kundschafter **(-s, -)** *m* spy; *(Mil)* scout

künftig ['kʏnftɪç] *adj* future ▷ *adv* in future

Kunst [kʊnst] **(-, ⁻e)** *f (auch Sch)* art; *(Können)* skill; **das ist doch keine** ~ it's easy; **mit seiner** ~ **am Ende sein** to be at one's wits' end; **das ist eine brotlose** ~ there's no money in that; **Kunstakademie** *f* academy of art; **Kunstdruck** *m* art print; **Kunstdünger** *m* artificial manure; **Kunsterziehung** *f (Sch)* art; **Kunstfaser** *f* synthetic fibre *(Brit) od* fiber *(US)*; **Kunstfehler** *m* professional error; *(weniger ernst)* slip; **Kunstfertigkeit** *f* skilfulness *(Brit)*, skillfulness *(US)*; **Kunstflieger** *m* stunt flyer; **kunstgerecht** *adj* skilful *(Brit)*, skillful *(US)*; **Kunstgeschichte** *f* history of art; **Kunstgewerbe** *nt* arts and crafts *pl*; **Kunstgriff** *m* trick, knack; **Kunsthändler** *m* art dealer; **Kunstharz** *nt* artificial resin; **Kunstleder** *nt* artificial leather

Künstler, in ['kʏnstlər(ɪn)] **(-s, -)** *m(f)* artist; **künstlerisch** *adj* artistic; **Künstlername** *m* pseudonym; *(von Schauspieler)* stage name; **Künstlerpech** *(umg) nt* hard luck

künstlich ['kʏnstlɪç] *adj* artificial; **~e Intelligenz** *(Comput)* artificial intelligence; **sich** ~ **aufregen** *(umg)* to get all worked up about nothing

Kunst- *zW:* **Kunstsammler** *m* art collector; **Kunstseide** *f* artificial silk; **Kunststoff** *m* synthetic material; **Kunststopfen** **(-s)** *nt* invisible mending; **Kunststück** *nt* trick; **das ist kein Kunststück** *(fig)* there's nothing to it; **Kunstturnen** *nt* gymnastics *sing*; **kunstvoll** *adj* artistic; **Kunstwerk** *nt* work of art

kunterbunt ['kʊntərbʊnt] *adj* higgledy-piggledy

Kupee [ku'pe:] **(-s, -s)** *nt* = **Coupé**

Kupfer ['kʊpfər] **(-s, -)** *nt* copper; **Kupfergeld** *nt* coppers *pl*

kupfern *adj* copper ▷ *vt (fig: umg)* to plagiarize, copy, imitate

Kupferstich *m* copperplate engraving

Kupon [ku'põ:] **(-s, -s)** *m* = **Coupon**

Kuppe ['kʊpə] **(-, -n)** *f (Bergkuppe)* top; *(Fingerkuppe)* tip

Kuppel **(-, -n)** *f* cupola, dome

Kuppelei [kʊpə'laɪ] *f (Jur)* procuring

kuppeln *vi (Jur)* to procure; *(Aut)* to operate *od* use the clutch ▷ *vt* to join

Kuppler ['kʊplər] **(-s, -)** *m* procurer; **Kupplerin** *f* procuress

Kupplung *f (auch Tech)* coupling; *(Aut etc)* clutch; **die** ~ **(durch)treten** to disengage the clutch

Kur [ku:r] **(-, -en)** *f (im Kurort)* (health) cure, (course of) treatment; *(Schlankheitskur)* diet; **eine** ~ **machen** to take a cure (in a health resort)

Kür [ky:r] **(-, -en)** *f (Sport)* free exercises *pl*

Kuratorium [kura'to:riʊm] *nt (Vereinigung)* committee

Kurbel ['kʊrbəl] **(-, -n)** *f* crank, winder; *(Aut)* starting handle; **Kurbelwelle** *f* crankshaft

Kürbis ['kʏrbɪs] **(-ses, -se)** *m* pumpkin; *(exotisch)* gourd

Kurde ['kʊrdə] **(-n, -n)** *m*, **Kurdin** *f* Kurd

Kurfürst ['ku:rfʏrst] *m* Elector, electoral prince

Kurgast *m* visitor (to a health resort)

Kurier [ku'ri:r] **(-s, -e)** *m* courier, messenger

kurieren [ku'ri:rən] *vt* to cure

kurios [kuri'o:s] *adj* curious, odd

Kuriosität [kuriozi'tɛːt] *f* curiosity

Kur- *zW:* **Kurkonzert** *nt* concert *(at a health resort)*; **Kurort** *m* health resort; **Kurpfuscher** *m* quack

Kurs [kʊrs] **(-es, -e)** *m* course; *(Fin)* rate; **hoch im** ~ **stehen** *(fig)* to be highly thought of; **einen** ~ **besuchen** *od* **mitmachen** to attend a class; **harter/weicher** ~ *(Pol)* hard/soft line; **Kursänderung** *f (lit, fig)* change of course; **Kursbuch** *nt* timetable

Kürschner, in ['kʏrʃnər(ɪn)] **(-s, -)** *m(f)* furrier

kursieren [kʊr'zi:rən] *vi* to circulate

kursiv *adv* in italics

Kursnotierung *f* quotation

Kursus ['kʊrzʊs] **(-, Kurse)** *m* course

Kurswagen *m (Eisenb)* through carriage

Kurswert *m (Fin)* market value

Kurtaxe *f* spa tax *(paid by visitors)*

Kurve ['kʊrvə] **(-, -n)** *f* curve; *(Straßenkurve)* bend; *(statistisch, Fieberkurve etc)* graph; **die** ~ **nicht kriegen** *(umg)* not to get around to it

kurvenreich *adj:* **„~e Strecke"** "bends"

kurvig *adj (Straße)* bendy

kurz [kʊrts] *adj* short ▷ *adv:* ~ **und bündig** concisely; **zu** ~ **kommen** to come off badly; **den Kürzeren ziehen** to get the worst of it; ~ **und gut** in short; **über** ~ **oder lang** sooner or later; **eine Sache ~ abtun** to dismiss sth out of hand; **~ gefasst** concise; **darf ich mal ~ stören?** could I just interrupt for a moment?; *siehe auch* **kurzfassen; kurzhalten; kurztreten**

Kurzarbeit f short-time work; *see culture note*

kurzärmelig, kurzärmlig adj short-sleeved

kurzatmig adj (fig) feeble, lame; (Med) short-winded

Kürze ['kʏrtsə] (-, -n) f shortness, brevity

kürzen vt to cut short; (in der Länge) to shorten; (Gehalt) to reduce

kurzerhand ['kʊrtsər'hant] adv without further ado; (entlassen) on the spot

kurz- zW: **kurzfassen** vr to be brief; **Kurzfassung** f shortened version; **kurzfristig** adj short-term; **kurzfristige Verbindlichkeiten** current liabilities pl; **Kurzgeschichte** f short story; **kurzhalten** unreg vt to keep short; **kurzlebig** adj short-lived

kürzlich ['kʏrtslɪç] adv lately, recently

Kurz- zW: **Kurzmeldung** f news flash; **Kurzparker** m short-stay parker; **Kurzschluss** m (Elek) short circuit; **Kurzschlusshandlung** f (fig) rash action; **Kurzschrift** f shorthand;

kurzsichtig adj short-sighted; **Kurzstrecken-** in zW short-range; **Kurzstreckenläufer, in** m(f) sprinter; **kurztreten** unreg vi (fig: umg) to go easy; **kurzum** adv in a word

Kürzung f cutback

Kurzwaren pl haberdashery (Brit), notions pl (US)

Kurzwelle f short wave

kuschelig adj cuddly

kuscheln ['kʊʃəln] vr to snuggle up

kuschen ['kʊʃən] vi, vr (Hund etc) to get down; (fig) to knuckle under

Kusine [ku'zi:nə] f cousin

Kuss [kʊs] (-es, -̈e) m kiss

küssen ['kʏsən] vt, vr to kiss

Küste ['kʏstə] (-, -n) f coast, shore

Küsten- zW: **Küstengewässer** pl coastal waters pl; **Küstenschiff** nt coaster; **Küstenwache** f coastguard (station)

Küster ['kʏstər] (-s, -) m sexton, verger

Kutsche ['kʊtʃə] (-, -n) f coach, carriage

Kutscher (-s, -) m coachman

kutschieren [kʊ'tʃiːrən] vi: **durch die Gegend ~** (umg) to drive around

Kutte ['kʊtə] (-, -n) f cowl

Kuvert [ku'vɛrt] (-s, -e od -s) nt envelope; (Gedeck) cover

Kuwait [ku'vait] (-s) nt Kuwait

KV abk (Mus: = Köchelverzeichnis): **KV 280** K. (number) 280

KW abk (= Kurzwelle) SW

kW abk (= Kilowatt) kW

Kybernetik [kybɛr'ne:tɪk] f cybernetics sing

kybernetisch [kybɛr'ne:tɪʃ] adj cybernetic

KZ (-s, -s) nt abk = **Konzentrationslager**

k

L l

L, l¹ [ɛl] *nt* L, l; **L wie Ludwig** = L for Lucy, = L for Love (US)

l² [ɛl] *abk* (= *Liter*) l

laben ['la:bən] *vt* to refresh ▷ *vr* to refresh o.s.; (*fig*): **sich an etw** *dat* ~ to relish sth

labern ['la:bərn] (*umg*) *vi* to prattle (on) ▷ *vt* to talk

labil [la'bi:l] *adj* (*physisch: Gesundheit*) delicate; (: *Kreislauf*) poor; (*psychisch*) unstable

Labor [la'bo:r] (-s, -e *od* -s) *nt* lab(oratory)

Laborant, in [labo'rant(ɪn)] *m(f)* lab(oratory) assistant

Laboratorium [labora'to:riʊm] *nt* lab(oratory)

Labyrinth [laby'rɪnt] (-s, -e) *nt* labyrinth

Lache ['laxə] (-, -n) *f* (*Wasser*) pool, puddle; (*umg: Gelächter*) laugh

lächeln ['lɛçəln] *vi* to smile; **Lächeln** (-s) *nt* smile

lachen ['laxən] *vi* to laugh; **mir ist nicht zum L~ (zumute)** I'm in no laughing mood; **dass ich nicht lache!** (*umg*) don't make me laugh!; **das wäre doch gelacht** it would be ridiculous; **Lachen** *nt*: **dir wird das Lachen schon noch vergehen!** you'll soon be laughing on the other side of your face

Lacher (-s, -) *m*: **die ~ auf seiner Seite haben** to have the last laugh

lächerlich ['lɛçərlɪç] *adj* ridiculous; **Lächerlichkeit** *f* absurdity

Lach- *zW*: **Lachgas** *nt* laughing gas; **lachhaft** *adj* laughable; **Lachkrampf** *m*: **einen Lachkrampf bekommen** to go into fits of laughter

Lachs [laks] (-es, -e) *m* salmon

Lachsalve ['laxzalvə] *f* burst *od* roar of laughter

Lachsschinken *m* smoked, rolled fillet of ham

Lack [lak] (-(e)s, -e) *m* lacquer, varnish; (*von Auto*) paint

lackieren [la'ki:rən] *vt* to varnish; (*Auto*) to spray

Lackierer [la'ki:rər] (-s, -) *m* varnisher

Lackleder *nt* patent leather

Lackmus ['lakmʊs] (-) *m od nt* litmus

Lade ['la:də] (-, -n) *f* box, chest; **Ladebaum** *m* derrick; **Ladefähigkeit** *f* load capacity; **Ladefläche** *f* load area; **Ladegewicht** *nt* tonnage; **Ladehemmung** *f*: **das Gewehr hat Ladehemmung** the gun is jammed

Laden ['la:dən] (-s, ⸚) *m* shop; (*Fensterladen*) shutter; (*umg: Betrieb*) outfit; **der ~ läuft** (*umg*) business is good

laden ['la:dən] *unreg vt* (*Lasten, Comput*) to load; (*Jur*) to summon; (*einladen*) to invite; **eine schwere Schuld auf sich** *akk* ~ to place o.s. under a heavy burden of guilt

Laden- *zW*: **Ladenaufsicht** *f* shopwalker (*Brit*), floorwalker (*US*); **Ladenbesitzer** *m* shopkeeper; **Ladendieb** *m* shoplifter; **Ladendiebstahl** *m* shoplifting; **Ladenhüter** (-s, -) *m* unsaleable item; **Ladenöffnungszeit** *f* shop opening hours *pl*; **Ladenpreis** *m* retail price; **Ladenschluss** *m*, **Ladenschlusszeit** *f* closing time; **Ladentisch** *m* counter

Laderampe *f* loading ramp

Laderaum *m* (*Naut*) hold

lädieren [lɛ'di:rən] *vt* to damage

lädt [lɛ:t] *vb siehe* **laden**

Ladung ['la:dʊŋ] *f* (*Last*) cargo, load; (*Beladen*) loading; (*Jur*) summons; (*Einladung*) invitation; (*Sprengladung*) charge

lag *etc* [la:k] *vb siehe* **liegen**

Lage ['la:gə] (-, -n) *f* position, situation; (*Schicht*) layer; **in der ~ sein** to be in a position; **eine gute/ruhige ~ haben** to be in a good/ peaceful location; **Herr der ~ sein** to be in control of the situation; **Lagebericht** *m* report; (*Mil*) situation report; **Lagebeurteilung** *f* situation assessment

lagenweise *adv* in layers

Lager ['la:gər] (-s, -) *nt* camp; (*Comm*) warehouse; (*Schlaflager*) bed; (*von Tier*) lair; (*Tech*) bearing; **etw auf ~ haben** to have sth in stock; **Lagerarbeiter** *m* storehand; **Lagerbestand** *m* stocks *pl*; **Lagerfeuer** *nt* camp fire; **Lagergeld** *nt* storage (charges *pl*); **Lagerhaus** *nt* warehouse, store

Lagerist, in [la:gə'rɪst(ɪn)] *m(f)* storeman, storewoman

lagern ['la:gərn] *vi* (*Dinge*) to be stored; (*Menschen*) to camp; (*auch vr: rasten*) to lie down ▷ *vt* to store; (*betten*) to lay down; (*Maschine*) to bed

Lager- *zW*: **Lagerraum** *m* storeroom; (*in Geschäft*) stockroom; **Lagerschuppen** *m* store shed; **Lagerstätte** *f* resting place

Lagerung *f* storage

Lagune [la'guːnə] (-, -n) f lagoon

lahm [laːm] adj lame; (umg: langsam, langweilig) dreary, dull; (Geschäftsgang) slow, sluggish; **eine ~e Ente sein** (umg) to have no zip; siehe auch **lahmlegen; lahmarschig** ['laːm|arʃɪç] (umg) adj bloody od damn (!) slow

lahmen vi to be lame, limp

lähmen ['lɛːmən], **lahmlegen** vt to paralyse (Brit), paralyze (US)

Lähmung f paralysis

Lahn [laːn] (-) f (Fluss) Lahn

Laib [laɪp] (-s, -e) m loaf

Laich [laɪç] (-(e)s, -e) m spawn; **laichen** vi to spawn

Laie ['laɪə] (-n, -n) m layman; (fig, Theat) amateur

laienhaft adj amateurish

Lakai [la'kaɪ] (-en, -en) m lackey

Laken ['laːkən] (-s, -) nt sheet

Lakritze [la'krɪtsə] (-, -n) f liquorice

lala ['la'la] (umg) adv: **so ~** so-so, not too bad

lallen ['lalən] vt, vi to slur; (Baby) to babble

Lama ['laːma] (-s, -s) nt llama

Lamelle [la'mɛlə] f lamella; (Elek) lamina; (Tech) plate

lamentieren [lamɛn'tiːrən] vi to lament

Lametta [la'mɛta] (-s) nt tinsel

Lamm [lam] (-(e)s, ¨er) nt lamb; **Lammfell** nt lambskin; **lammfromm** adj like a lamb; **Lammwolle** f lambswool

Lampe ['lampə] (-, -n) f lamp

Lampenfieber nt stage fright

Lampenschirm m lampshade

Lampion [lampi'öː] (-s, -s) m Chinese lantern

Land [lant] (-(e)s, ¨er) nt land; (Nation, nicht Stadt) country; (Bundesland) state; **auf dem ~(e)** in the country; **an ~ gehen** to go ashore; **endlich sehe ich ~** (fig) at last I can see the light at the end of the tunnel; **einen Auftrag an ~ ziehen** (umg) to land an order; **aus aller Herren Länder** from all over the world; siehe auch **hierzulande**; see culture note

> **LAND**
>
> A Land (plural Länder) is a member state of the BRD. There are 16 Länder, namely Baden-Württemberg, Bayern, Berlin, Brandenburg, Bremen, Hamburg, Hessen, Mecklenburg-Vorpommern, Niedersachsen, Nordrhein-Westfalen, Rheinland-Pfalz, Saarland, Sachsen, Sachsen-Anhalt, Schleswig-Holstein and Thüringen. Each Land has its own parliament and constitution.

Landarbeiter m farm od agricultural worker

Landbesitz m landed property

Landbesitzer m landowner

Landebahn f runway

Landeerlaubnis f permission to land

landeinwärts [lant'|aɪnvɛrts] adv inland

landen ['landən] vt, vi to land; **mit deinen**

Komplimenten kannst du bei mir nicht ~ your compliments won't get you anywhere with me

Ländereien [lɛndə'raɪən] pl estates pl

Länderspiel nt international (match)

Landes- zW: **Landesfarben** pl national colours pl (Brit) od colors pl (US); **Landesgrenze** f (national) frontier; (von Bundesland) state boundary; **Landesinnere, s** nt inland region; **Landeskind** nt native of a German state; **Landeskunde** f regional studies pl; **Landestracht** f national costume; **landesüblich** adj customary; **Landesverrat** m high treason; **Landesverweisung** f banishment; **Landeswährung** f national currency; **landesweit** adj countrywide

Landeverbot nt refusal of permission to land

Land- zW: **Landflucht** f emigration to the cities; **Landgut** nt estate; **Landhaus** nt country house; **Landkarte** f map; **Landkreis** m administrative region; **landläufig** adj customary

ländlich ['lɛntlɪç] adj rural

Land- zW: **Landrat** m head of administration of a Landkreis; **Landschaft** f countryside; (Kunst) landscape; **die politische Landschaft** the political scene; **landschaftlich** adj scenic; (Besonderheiten) regional

Landsmann (-(e)s, pl -leute) m compatriot, fellow countryman

Landsmännin f compatriot, fellow countrywoman

Land- zW: **Landstraße** f country road; **Landstreicher** (-s, -) m tramp; **Landstrich** m region; **Landtag** m (Pol) regional parliament

Landung ['landʊŋ] f landing

Landungs- zW: **Landungsboot** nt landing craft; **Landungsbrücke** f jetty, pier; **Landungsstelle** f landing place

Landurlaub m shore leave

Landvermesser m surveyor

landw. abk (= landwirtschaftlich) agricultural

Land- zW: **Landwirt** m farmer; **Landwirtschaft** f agriculture; **Landwirtschaft betreiben** to farm; **Landzunge** f spit

lang [laŋ] adj long; (umg: Mensch) tall ▷ adv: **~ anhaltender Beifall** prolonged applause; **~ ersehnt** longed-for; **hier wird mir die Zeit nicht ~** I won't get bored here; **er machte ein ~es Gesicht** his face fell; **~ und breit** at great length; **langatmig** adj long-winded

lange adv for a long time; (dauern, brauchen) a long time; **~ nicht so ...** not nearly as ...; **wenn der das schafft, kannst du das schon ~** if he can do it, you can do it easily

Länge ['lɛŋə] (-, -n) f length; (Geog) longitude; **etw der ~ nach falten** to fold sth lengthways; **etw in die ~ ziehen** to drag sth out (umg); **der ~ nach hinfallen** to fall flat (on one's face)

langen ['laŋən] vi (ausreichen) to do, suffice; (fassen): **~ nach** to reach for; **es langt mir** I've had enough; **jdm eine ~** (umg) to give sb a clip on the ear

Längengrad m longitude
Längenmaß nt linear measure
Langeweile f boredom
lang- zW: **langfristig** adj long-term ▷ adv in the long term; (planen) for the long term; **langfristige Verbindlichkeiten** long-term liabilities pl; **langjährig** adj (Freundschaft, Gewohnheit) long-standing; (Erfahrung, Verhandlungen) many years of; (Mitarbeiter) of many years' standing; **Langlauf** m (Ski) cross-country skiing; **langlebig** adj long-lived; **langlebige Gebrauchsgüter** consumer durables pl
länglich adj longish
Langmut f forbearance, patience
langmütig adj forbearing
längs [lɛŋs] präp (+gen od dat) along ▷ adv lengthways
langsam adj slow; **immer schön ~!** (umg) easy does it!; **ich muss jetzt ~ gehen** I must be getting on my way; **~ (aber sicher) reicht es mir** I've just about had enough; **Langsamkeit** f slowness
Langschläfer m late riser
Langspielplatte f long-playing record
längsseit, längsseits adv alongside ▷ präp +gen alongside
längst [lɛŋst] adv: **das ist ~ fertig** that was finished a long time ago, that has been finished for a long time
längste, r, s adj longest
Langstrecken- in zw long-distance; **Langstreckenflugzeug** nt long-range aircraft
Languste [laŋ'ɡʊstə] (-, -n) f crayfish, crawfish (US)
lang- zW: **langweilen** vt untr to bore ▷ vr untr to be od get bored; **Langweiler** (-s, -) m bore; **langweilig** adj boring, tedious; **Langwelle** f long wave; **langwierig** adj lengthy, long-drawn-out
Lanze ['lantsə] (-, -n) f lance
Lanzette [lan'tsɛtə] f lancet
Laos ['la:ɔs] (-) nt Laos
Laote [la'o:tə] (-n, -n) m, **Laotin** f Laotian
laotisch [la'o:tɪʃ] adj Laotian
lapidar [lapi'da:r] adj terse, pithy
Lappalie [la'pa:liə] f trifle
Lappe ['lapə] (-n, -n) m Lapp, Laplander
Lappen (-s, -) m cloth, rag; (Anat) lobe; **jdm durch die ~ gehen** (umg) to slip through sb's fingers
läppern ['lɛpərn] (umg) vr unpers: **es läppert sich zusammen** it (all) mounts up
Lappin ['lapɪn] f Lapp, Laplander
läppisch ['lɛpɪʃ] adj foolish
Lappland ['laplant] (-s) nt Lapland
Lappländer, in ['laplɛndər(ɪn)] (-s, -) m(f) Lapp, Laplander
lappländisch adj Lapp
Lapsus ['lapsʊs] (-, -) m slip
Laptop ['lɛptɔp] (-s, -s) m laptop
Lärche ['lɛrçə] (-, -n) f larch
Lärm [lɛrm] (-(e)s) m noise; **Lärmbelästigung** f noise nuisance; **Lärmemission** f noise emission; (stärker) noise pollution; **lärmen** vi to be noisy, make a noise
Larve ['larfə] (-, -n) f mask; (Biol) larva
las etc [la:s] vb siehe **lesen**
Lasagne [la'zanjə] pl lasagne sing
lasch [laʃ] adj slack; (Geschmack) tasteless
Lasche ['laʃə] (-, -n) f (Schuhlasche) tongue; (Eisenb) fishplate
Laser ['le:zər] (-s, -) m laser; **Laserdrucker** m laser printer

 SCHLÜSSELWORT

lassen ['lasən] (pt **ließ**, pp **gelassen** od (als Hilfsverb) **lassen**) vt **1** (unterlassen) to stop; (momentan) to leave; **lass das (sein)!** don't (do it)!; (hör auf) stop it!; **lass mich!** leave me alone!; **lassen wir das!** let's leave it; **er kann das Trinken nicht lassen** he can't stop drinking; **tu, was du nicht lassen kannst!** if you must, you must!
2 (zurücklassen) to leave; **etw lassen, wie es ist** to leave sth (just) as it is
3 (erlauben) to let, allow; **lass ihn doch** let him; **jdn ins Haus lassen** to let sb into the house; **das muss man ihr lassen** (zugestehen) you've got to grant her that
▷ vi: **lass mal, ich mache das schon** leave it, I'll do it
▷ hilfsverb **1** (veranlassen): **etw machen lassen** to have od get sth done; **jdn etw machen lassen** to get sb to do sth; (durch Befehl usw) to make sb do sth; **er ließ mich warten** he kept me waiting; **mein Vater wollte mich studieren lassen** my father wanted me to study; **sich** dat **etw schicken lassen** to have sth sent (to one)
2 (zulassen): **jdn etw wissen lassen** to let sb know sth; **das Licht brennen lassen** to leave the light on; **einen Bart wachsen lassen** to grow a beard; **lass es dir gut gehen!** take care of yourself!
3: lass uns gehen let's go
▷ vr: **das lässt sich machen** that can be done; **es lässt sich schwer sagen** it's difficult to say

lässig ['lɛsɪç] adj casual; **Lässigkeit** f casualness
lässlich ['lɛslɪç] adj pardonable, venial
lässt [lɛst] vb siehe **lassen**
Last [last] (-, -en) f load; (Traglast) burden; (Naut, Aviat) cargo; (meist pl: Gebühr) charge; **jdm zur ~ fallen** to be a burden to sb; **Lastauto** nt lorry (Brit), truck
lasten vi: **~ auf** +dat to weigh on
Lastenaufzug m hoist, goods lift (Brit) od elevator (US)
Lastenausgleichsgesetz nt law on financial compensation for losses suffered in WWII
Laster ['lastər] (-s, -) nt vice ▷ m (umg) lorry (Brit), truck
Lästerer ['lɛstərər] (-s, -) m mocker;

(*Gotteslästerer*) blasphemer
lasterhaft adj immoral
lästerlich adj scandalous
lästern ['lɛstərn] vt, vi (*Gott*) to blaspheme; (*schlecht sprechen*) to mock
Lästerung f jibe; (*Gotteslästerung*) blasphemy
lästig ['lɛstɪç] adj troublesome, tiresome; **(jdm) ~ werden** to become a nuisance (to sb); (*zum Ärgernis werden*) to get annoying (to sb)
Last- zW: **Lastkahn** m barge; **Lastkraftwagen** m heavy goods vehicle; **Lastschrift** f debiting; (*Eintrag*) debit item; **Lasttier** nt beast of burden; **Lastträger** m porter; **Lastwagen** m lorry (*Brit*), truck; **Lastzug** m truck and trailer
Latein [la'taɪn] (**-s**) nt Latin; **mit seinem ~ am Ende sein** (*fig*) to be stumped (*umg*); **Lateinamerika** nt Latin America; **lateinamerikanisch** adj Latin-American; **lateinisch** adj Latin
latent [la'tɛnt] adj latent
Laterne [la'tɛrnə] (**-**, **-n**) f lantern; (*Straßenlaterne*) lamp, light
Laternenpfahl m lamppost
Latinum [la'tiːnʊm] (**-s**) nt: **kleines/großes ~** ≈ Latin O-/A-level exams (*Brit*)
Latrine [la'triːnə] f latrine
Latsche ['latʃə] (**-**, **-n**) f dwarf pine
Latschen ['laːtʃən] (*umg*) m (*Hausschuh*) slipper; (*pej: Schuh*) worn-out shoe
latschen (*umg*) vi (*gehen*) to wander, go; (*lässig*) to slouch
Latte ['latə] (**-**, **-n**) f lath; (*Sport*) goalpost; (*quer*) crossbar
Lattenzaun m lattice fence
Latz [lats] (**-es**, **ⁱe**) m bib; (*Hosenlatz*) front flap
Lätzchen ['lɛtsçən] nt bib
Latzhose f dungarees pl
lau [laʊ] adj (*Nacht*) balmy; (*Wasser*) lukewarm; (*fig: Haltung*) half-hearted
Laub [laʊp] (**-(e)s**) nt foliage; **Laubbaum** m deciduous tree
Laube ['laʊbə] (**-**, **-n**) f arbour (*Brit*), arbor (*US*); (*Gartenhäuschen*) summerhouse
Laub- zW: **Laubfrosch** m tree frog; **Laubsäge** f fretsaw; **Laubwald** m deciduous forest
Lauch [laʊx] (**-(e)s**, **-e**) m leek
Lauer ['laʊər] f: **auf der ~ sein** od **liegen** to lie in wait
lauern vi to lie in wait; (*Gefahr*) to lurk
Lauf [laʊf] (**-(e)s**, **Läufe**) m run; (*Wettlauf*) race; (*Entwicklung, Astron*) course; (*Gewehrlauf*) barrel; **im ~e des Gesprächs** during the conversation; **sie ließ ihren Gefühlen freien ~** she gave way to her feelings; **einer Sache** dat **ihren ~ lassen** to let sth take its course; **Laufbahn** f career; **eine Laufbahn einschlagen** to embark on a career; **Laufbursche** m errand boy
laufen ['laʊfən] unreg vi to run; (*umg: gehen*) to walk; (*Uhr*) to go; (*funktionieren*) to work; (*Elektrogerät: eingeschaltet sein*) to be on; (*gezeigt werden: Film, Stück*) to be on; (*Bewerbung, Antrag*) to be under consideration ▷ vt to run; **es lief**

mir eiskalt über den Rücken a chill ran up my spine; **ihm läuft die Nase** he's got a runny nose; **~ lassen** (*Person*) to let go; **die Dinge ~ lassen** to let things slide; **die Sache ist ge~** (*umg*) it's in the bag; **das Auto läuft auf meinen Namen** the car is in my name; **Ski/Schlittschuh/Rollschuh** etc **~** to ski/ skate/rollerskate etc
laufend adj running; (*Monat, Ausgaben*) current; **auf dem L-en sein/halten** to be/keep up to date; **am ~en Band** (*fig*) continuously; **~e Nummer** serial number; (*von Konto*) number; **~e Kosten** running costs pl
Läufer ['lɔʏfər] (**-s**, **-**) m (*Teppich, Sport*) runner; (*Fußball*) half-back; (*Schach*) bishop
Lauferei [laʊfə'raɪ] (*umg*) f running about
Läuferin f (*Sport*) runner
Lauf- zW: **lauffähig** adj (*Comput*): **das Programm is unter Windows lauffähig** the program can be run under Windows; **Lauffeuer** nt: **sich wie ein Lauffeuer verbreiten** to spread like wildfire; **Laufkundschaft** f passing trade; **Laufmasche** f run, ladder (*Brit*); **Laufpass** m: **jdm den Laufpass geben** (*umg*) to give sb his/ her marching orders; **Laufschritt** m: **im Laufschritt** at a run; **Laufstall** m playpen; **Laufsteg** m catwalk
läuft [lɔʏft] vb siehe **laufen**
Lauf- zW: **Laufwerk** nt running gear; (*Comput*) drive; **Laufzeit** f (*von Wechsel, Vertrag*) period of validity; (*von Maschine*) life; **Laufzettel** m circular
Lauge ['laʊɡə] (**-**, **-n**) f soapy water; (*Chem*) alkaline solution
Laune ['laʊnə] (**-**, **-n**) f mood, humour (*Brit*), humor (*US*); (*Einfall*) caprice; (*schlechte Laune*) temper
launenhaft adj capricious, changeable
launisch adj moody
Laus [laʊs] (**-**, **Läuse**) f louse; **ihm ist (wohl) eine ~ über die Leber gelaufen** (*umg*) something's biting him; **Lausbub** m rascal, imp
Lauschangriff m: **~ (gegen)** bugging operation (on)
lauschen ['laʊʃən] vi to eavesdrop, listen in
Lauscher, in (**-s**, **-**) m(f) eavesdropper
lauschig ['laʊʃɪç] adj snug
Lausejunge (*umg*) m little devil; (*wohlwollend*) rascal
lausen ['laʊzən] vt to delouse
lausig ['laʊzɪç] (*umg*) adj lousy; (*Kälte*) perishing ▷ adv awfully
laut [laʊt] adj loud ▷ adv loudly; (*lesen*) aloud ▷ präp (+gen od dat) according to
Laut (**-(e)s**, **-e**) m sound
Laute ['laʊtə] (**-**, **-n**) f lute
lauten ['laʊtən] vi to say; (*Urteil*) to be
läuten ['lɔʏtən] vt, vi to ring, sound; **er hat davon (etwas) ~ hören** (*umg*) he has heard something about it
lauter ['laʊtər] adj (*Wasser*) clear, pure;

(Wahrheit, Charakter) honest ▷ adj inv (Freude, Dummheit etc) sheer ▷ adv (nur) nothing but, only; **Lauterkeit** f purity; honesty, integrity
läutern ['lɔʏtərn] vt to purify
Läuterung f purification
laut- zW: **lauthals** adv at the top of one's voice; **lautlos** adj noiseless, silent; **lautmalend** adj onomatopoeic; **Lautschrift** f phonetics pl; **Lautsprecher** m loudspeaker; **Lautsprecheranlage** f: **öffentliche Lautsprecheranlage** public-address od PA system; **Lautsprecherwagen** m loudspeaker van; **lautstark** adj vociferous; **Lautstärke** f (Rundf) volume
lauwarm ['laʊvarm] adj (lit, fig) lukewarm
Lava ['la:va] (-, **Laven**) f lava
Lavendel [la'vɛndəl] (-s, -) m lavender
Lawine [la'vi:nə] f avalanche
Lawinengefahr f danger of avalanches
lax [laks] adj lax
Layout, Lay-out ['le:|aʊt] (-s, -s) nt layout
Lazarett [latsa'rɛt] (-(e)s, -e) nt (Mil) hospital, infirmary
Ldkrs. abk = **Landkreis**
leasen ['li:zən] vt to lease
Leasing ['li:zɪŋ] (-s, -s) nt (Comm) leasing
Lebehoch nt three cheers pl
Lebemann (-(e)s, pl **-männer**) m man about town
Leben ['le:bən] (-s, -) nt life; **am ~ sein/ bleiben** to be/stay alive; **ums ~ kommen** to die; **etw ins ~ rufen** to bring sth into being; **seines ~s nicht mehr sicher sein** to fear for one's life; **etw für sein ~ gern tun** to love doing sth
leben vt, vi to live
lebend adj living; **~es Inventar** livestock
lebendig [le'bɛndɪç] adj living, alive; (lebhaft) lively; **Lebendigkeit** f liveliness
Lebens- zW: **Lebensabend** m old age; **Lebensalter** nt age; **Lebensanschauung** f philosophy of life; **Lebensart** f way of life; **lebensbejahend** adj positive; **Lebensdauer** f life (span); (von Maschine) life; **Lebenserfahrung** f experience of life; **Lebenserwartung** f life expectancy; **lebensfähig** adj able to live; **lebensfroh** adj full of the joys of life; **Lebensgefahr** f: **Lebensgefahr!** danger!; **in Lebensgefahr** critically od dangerously ill; **lebensgefährlich** adj dangerous; (Krankheit, Verletzung) critical; **Lebensgefährte** m: **ihr Lebensgefährte** the man she lives with; **Lebensgefährtin** f: **seine Lebensgefährtin** the woman he lives with; **Lebensgröße** f: **in Lebensgröße** life-size(d); **Lebenshaltungskosten** pl cost of living sing; **Lebensinhalt** m purpose in life; **Lebensjahr** nt year of life; **Lebenskünstler** m master in the art of living; **Lebenslage** f situation in life; **lebenslänglich** adj (Strafe) for life; **Lebenslauf** m curriculum vitae, CV; **lebenslustig** adj cheerful, lively; **Lebensmittel** pl food sing; **Lebensmittelgeschäft** nt

grocer's; **Lebensmittelvergiftung** f food poisoning; **lebensmüde** adj tired of life; **Lebenspartnerschaft** f long-term relationship; **eingetragene Lebenspartnerschaft** registered or civil (Brit) partnership; **Lebensqualität** f quality of life; **Lebensraum** m (Pol) Lebensraum; (Biol) biosphere; **Lebensretter** m lifesaver; **Lebensstandard** m standard of living; **Lebensstellung** f permanent post; **Lebensstil** m life style; **Lebensunterhalt** m livelihood; **Lebensversicherung** f life insurance; **Lebenswandel** m way of life; **Lebensweise** f way of life, habits pl; **Lebensweisheit** f maxim; (Lebenserfahrung) wisdom; **lebenswichtig** adj vital; **Lebenszeichen** nt sign of life; **Lebenszeit** f lifetime; **Beamter auf Lebenszeit** permanent civil servant
Leber ['le:bər] (-, -n) f liver; **frei** od **frisch von der ~ weg reden** (umg) to speak out frankly; **Leberfleck** m mole; **Leberkäse** m ≈ meat loaf; **Lebertran** m cod-liver oil; **Leberwurst** f liver sausage
Lebewesen nt creature
Lebewohl nt farewell, goodbye
leb- zW: **lebhaft** adj lively, vivacious; **Lebhaftigkeit** f liveliness, vivacity; **Lebkuchen** m gingerbread; **leblos** adj lifeless; **Lebtag** m (fig): **das werde ich mein Lebtag nicht vergessen** I'll never forget that as long as I live; **Lebzeiten** pl: **zu jds Lebzeiten** (Leben) in sb's lifetime
lechzen ['lɛçtsən] vi: **nach etw ~** to long for sth
leck [lɛk] adj leaky, leaking; **Leck** (-(e)s, -e) nt leak
lecken¹ vi (Loch haben) to leak
lecken² vt, vi (schlecken) to lick
lecker ['lɛkər] adj delicious, tasty; **Leckerbissen** m dainty morsel; **Leckermaul** nt: **ein Leckermaul sein** to enjoy one's food
led. abk = **ledig**
Leder ['le:dər] (-s, -) nt leather; (umg: Fußball) ball; **Lederhose** f leather trousers pl; (von Tracht) leather shorts pl
ledern adj leather
Lederwaren pl leather goods pl
ledig ['le:dɪç] adj single; **einer Sache** gen **~ sein** to be free of sth; **lediglich** adv merely, solely
leer [le:r] adj empty; (Blick) vacant; **~ gefegt** (Straße) deserted; **~ stehend** empty
Leere (-) f emptiness; **(eine) gähnende ~** a gaping void
leeren vt to empty ▷ vr to (become) empty
Leer- zW: **Leergewicht** nt unladen weight; **Leergut** nt empties pl; **Leerlauf** m (Aut) neutral; **Leertaste** f (Schreibmaschine) space-bar
Leerung f emptying; (Post) collection
legal [le'ga:l] adj legal, lawful
legalisieren [legali'zi:rən] vt to legalize
Legalität [legali'tɛ:t] f legality; **(etwas) außerhalb der ~** (euph) (slightly) outside the law
Legasthenie [legaste'ni:] f dyslexia

Legastheniker, in [legas'te:nikər(ın)] **(-s, -)** *m(f)* dyslexic

Legebatterie *f* laying battery

legen ['le:gən] *vt* to lay, put, place; *(Ei)* to lay ▷ *vr* to lie down; *(fig)* to subside; **sich ins Bett ~** to go to bed

Legende [le'gɛndə] **(-, -n)** *f* legend

leger [le'ʒɛːr] *adj* casual

legieren [le'gi:rən] *vt* to alloy

Legierung *f* alloy

Legislative [legısla'ti:və] *f* legislature

Legislaturperiode [legısla'tu:rperio:də] *f* parliamentary *(Brit)* od congressional *(US)* term

legitim [legi'ti:m] *adj* legitimate

Legitimation [legiti:matsi'o:n] *f* legitimation

legitimieren [legiti:'mi:rən] *vt* to legitimate ▷ *vr* to prove one's identity

Legitimität [legitimi'tɛ:t] *f* legitimacy

Lehm [le:m] **(-(e)s, -e)** *m* loam

lehmig *adj* loamy

Lehne ['le:nə] **(-, -n)** *f* arm; *(Rückenlehne)* back

lehnen *vt, vr* to lean

Lehnstuhl *m* armchair

Lehr- *zW*: **Lehramt** *nt* teaching profession; **Lehrbefähigung** *f* teaching qualification; **Lehrbrief** *m* indentures *pl*; **Lehrbuch** *nt* textbook

Lehre ['le:rə] **(-, -n)** *f* teaching, doctrine; *(beruflich)* apprenticeship; *(moralisch)* lesson; *(Tech)* gauge; **bei jdm in die ~ gehen** to serve one's apprenticeship with sb

lehren *vt* to teach

Lehrer, in **(-s, -)** *m(f)* teacher; **Lehrerausbildung** *f* teacher training; **Lehrerkollegium** *nt* teaching staff; **Lehrerzimmer** *nt* staff room

Lehr- *zW*: **Lehrgang** *m* course; **Lehrgeld** *nt*: **Lehrgeld für etw zahlen müssen** *(fig)* to pay dearly for sth; **Lehrjahre** *pl* apprenticeship *sing*; **Lehrkraft** *f* *(form)* teacher; **Lehrling** *m* apprentice; trainee; **Lehrmittel** *nt* teaching aid; **Lehrplan** *m* syllabus; **Lehrprobe** *f* demonstration lesson, crit *(umg)*; **lehrreich** *adj* instructive; **Lehrsatz** *m* proposition; **Lehrstelle** *f* apprenticeship; **Lehrstuhl** *m* chair; **Lehrzeit** *f* apprenticeship

Leib [laıp] **(-(e)s, -er)** *m* body; **halt ihn mir vom ~!** keep him away from me!; **etw am eigenen ~(e) spüren** to experience sth for o.s.

leiben ['laıbən] *vi*: **wie er leibt und lebt** to a T *(umg)*

Leibes- *zW*: **Leibeserziehung** *f* physical education; **Leibeskräfte** *pl*: **aus Leibeskräften schreien** *etc* to shout *etc* with all one's might; **Leibesübung** *f* physical exercise; **Leibesvisitation** *f* body search

Leibgericht *nt* favourite *(Brit)* od favorite *(US)* meal

Leib- *zW*: **leibhaftig** *adj* personified; *(Teufel)* incarnate; **leiblich** *adj* bodily; *(Vater etc)* natural; **Leibrente** *f* life annuity; **Leibwache** *f* bodyguard

Leiche ['laıçə] **(-, -n)** *f* corpse; **er geht über ~n**

(umg) he'd stick at nothing

Leichen- *zW*: **Leichenbeschauer (-s, -)** *m* doctor conducting a post-mortem; **Leichenhalle** *f* mortuary; **Leichenhemd** *nt* shroud; **Leichenträger** *m* bearer; **Leichenwagen** *m* hearse

Leichnam ['laıçna:m] **(-(e)s, -e)** *m* corpse

leicht [laıçt] *adj* light; *(einfach)* easy ▷ *adv*: **~ zerbrechlich** very fragile; **es sich** *dat* **~ machen** to make things easy for o.s.; *(nicht gewissenhaft sein)* to take the easy way out; **~ verletzt** slightly injured; **nichts ~er als das!** nothing (could be) simpler!; *siehe auch* **leichtfallen; leichtnehmen; Leichtathletik** *f* athletics *sing*; **leichtfallen** *unreg vi*: **jdm leichtfallen** to be easy for sb; **leichtfertig** *adj* thoughtless; **leichtgläubig** *adj* gullible, credulous; **Leichtgläubigkeit** *f* gullibility, credulity; **leichthin** *adv* lightly

Leichtigkeit *f* easiness; **mit ~** with ease

leicht- *zW*: **leichtlebig** *adj* easy-going; **Leichtmatrose** *m* ordinary seaman; **Leichtmetall** *nt* light alloy; **leichtnehmen** *unreg vt* to take lightly; **Leichtsinn** *m* carelessness; **sträflicher Leichtsinn** criminal negligence; **leichtsinnig** *adj* careless

Leid [laıt] **(-(e)s)** *nt* grief, sorrow; **jdm sein ~ klagen** to tell sb one's troubles

leid *adj*: **etw ~ haben** od **sein** to be tired of sth; *siehe auch* **leidtun**

leiden ['laıdən] *unreg vt* to suffer; *(erlauben)* to permit ▷ *vi* to suffer; **jdn/etw nicht ~ können** not to be able to stand sb/sth; **Leiden (-s, -)** *nt* suffering; *(Krankheit)* complaint

Leidenschaft *f* passion; **leidenschaftlich** *adj* passionate

Leidens- *zW*: **Leidensgenosse** *m*, **Leidensgenossin** *f* fellow sufferer; **Leidensgeschichte** *f*: **die Leidensgeschichte (Christi)** *(Rel)* Christ's Passion

leider ['laıdər] *adv* unfortunately; **ja, ~** yes, I'm afraid so; **~ nicht** I'm afraid not

leidig ['laıdıç] *adj* miserable, tiresome

leidlich [laıtlıç] *adj* tolerable ▷ *adv* tolerably

Leidtragende, r *f(m)* bereaved; *(Benachteiligter)* one who suffers

leidtun *unreg vi*: **es tut mir/ihm leid** I am/he is sorry; **er/das tut mir leid** I am sorry for him/about it; **sie kann einem ~** you can't help feeling sorry for her

Leidwesen *nt*: **zu jds ~** to sb's dismay

Leier ['laıər] **(-, -n)** *f* lyre; *(fig)* old story

Leierkasten *m* barrel organ

leiern *vt (Kurbel)* to turn; *(umg: Gedicht)* to rattle off ▷ *vi (drehen)*: **~ an** +*dat* to crank

Leih- *zW*: **Leiharbeit** *f* subcontracted labour; **Leiharbeiter, in** *m(f)* subcontracted worker; **Leihbibliothek** *f*, **Leihbücherei** *f* lending library

leihen ['laıən] *unreg vt* to lend; **sich** *dat* **etw ~** to borrow sth

Leih- *zW*: **Leihgabe** *f* loan; **Leihgebühr** *f* hire charge; **Leihhaus** *nt* pawnshop;

211

Leihmutter f surrogate mother; **Leihschein** m pawn ticket; (*in der Bibliothek*) borrowing slip; **Leihunternehmen** nt hire service; (*Arbeitsmarkt*) temp service; **Leihwagen** m hired car (*Brit*), rental car (*US*); **leihweise** adv on loan

Leim [laɪm] (**-(e)s, -e**) m glue; **jdm auf den ~ gehen** to be taken in by sb; **leimen** vt to glue

Leine ['laɪnə] (**-, -n**) f line, cord; (*Hundeleine*) leash, lead; **~ ziehen** (*umg*) to clear out

Leinen (**-s, -**) nt linen; (*grob, segeltuchartig*) canvas; (*als Bucheinband*) cloth

leinen adj linen

Lein- zW: **Leinsamen** m linseed; **Leintuch** nt linen cloth; (*Bettuch*) sheet; **Leinwand** f (*Kunst*) canvas; (*Film*) screen

leise ['laɪzə] adj quiet; (*sanft*) soft, gentle; **mit ~r Stimme** in a low voice; **nicht die ~ste Ahnung haben** not to have the slightest (idea)

Leisetreter (*pej: umg*) m pussyfoot(er)

Leiste ['laɪstə] (**-, -n**) f ledge; (*Zierleiste*) strip; (*Anat*) groin

leisten ['laɪstən] vt (*Arbeit*) to do; (*Gesellschaft*) to keep; (*Ersatz*) to supply; (*vollbringen*) to achieve; **sich** dat **etw ~** to allow o.s. sth; (*sich gönnen*) to treat o.s. to sth; **sich** dat **etw ~ können** to be able to afford sth

Leistenbruch m (*Med*) hernia, rupture

Leistung f performance; (*gute*) achievement; (*eines Motors*) power; (*von Krankenkasse etc*) benefit; (*Zahlung*) payment

Leistungs- zW: **Leistungsabfall** m (*in Bezug auf Qualität*) drop in performance; (*in Bezug auf Quantität*) drop in productivity; **Leistungsbeurteilung** f performance appraisal; **Leistungsdruck** m pressure; **leistungsfähig** adj efficient; **Leistungsfähigkeit** f efficiency; **Leistungsgesellschaft** f meritocracy; **Leistungskurs** m (*Sch*) set; **Leistungskürzung** f reduction of benefit; **leistungsorientiert** adj performance-orientated; **Leistungsprinzip** nt achievement principle; **Leistungssport** m competitive sport; **Leistungszulage** f productivity bonus

Leitartikel m leader

Leitbild nt model

leiten ['laɪtən] vt to lead; (*Firma*) to manage; (*in eine Richtung*) to direct; (*Elek*) to conduct; **sich von jdm/etw ~ lassen** (*lit, fig*) to let o.s. be guided by sb/sth

leitend adj leading; (*Gedanke, Idee*) dominant; (*Stellung, Position*) managerial; (*Ingenieur, Beamter*) in charge; (*Phys*) conductive; **~er Angestellter** executive

Leiter¹ ['laɪtər] (**-s, -**) m leader, head; (*Elek*) conductor

Leiter² ['laɪtər] (**-, -n**) f ladder

Leiterin f leader, head

Leiterplatte f (*Comput*) circuit board

Leit- zW: **Leitfaden** m guide; **Leitfähigkeit** f conductivity; **Leitgedanke** m central idea;

Leitmotiv nt leitmotiv; **Leitplanke** f crash barrier; **Leitspruch** m motto

Leitung f (*Führung*) direction; (*Film, Theat etc*) production; (*von Firma*) management; directors pl; (*Wasserleitung*) pipe; (*Kabel*) cable; **eine lange ~ haben** to be slow on the uptake; **da ist jemand in der ~** (*umg*) there's somebody else on the line

Leitungs- zW: **Leitungsdraht** m wire; **Leitungsmast** m telegraph pole; **Leitungsrohr** nt pipe; **Leitungswasser** nt tap water

Leitwerk nt (*Aviat*) tail unit

Leitzins m (*Fin*) base rate

Lektion [lɛktsi'oːn] f lesson; **jdm eine ~ erteilen** (*fig*) to teach sb a lesson

Lektor, in ['lɛktɔr, lɛk'toːrɪn] m(f) (*Univ*) lector; (*Verlag*) editor

Lektüre [lɛk'tyːrə] (**-, -n**) f (*Lesen*) reading; (*Lesestoff*) reading matter

Lende ['lɛndə] (**-, -n**) f loin

Lendenbraten m roast sirloin

Lendenstück nt fillet

lenkbar ['lɛŋkbaːr] adj (*Fahrzeug*) steerable; (*Kind*) manageable

lenken vt to steer; (*Kind*) to guide; (*Gespräch*) to lead; **~ auf** +akk (*Blick, Aufmerksamkeit*) to direct at; (*Verdacht*) to throw on(to); (*: auf sich*) to draw onto

Lenkrad nt steering wheel

Lenkstange f handlebars pl

Lenkung f steering; (*Führung*) direction

Lenz [lɛnts] (**-es, -e**) m (*liter*) spring; **sich** dat **einen (faulen) ~ machen** (*umg*) to laze about, swing the lead

Leopard [leo'part] (**-en, -en**) m leopard

Lepra ['leːpra] (**-**) f leprosy; **Leprakranke, r** f(m) leper

Lerche ['lɛrçə] (**-, -n**) f lark

lernbegierig adj eager to learn

lernbehindert adj educationally handicapped (*Brit*) od handicaped (*US*)

lernen vt to learn ▷ vi: **er lernt bei der Firma Braun** he's training at Braun's

Lernhilfe f educational aid

lesbar ['leːsbaːr] adj legible

Lesbierin ['lɛsbiərɪn] f lesbian

lesbisch adj lesbian

Lese ['leːzə] (**-, -n**) f (*Weinlese*) harvest

Lesebuch nt reading book, reader

lesen unreg vt to read; (*ernten*) to gather, pick ▷ vi to read; **~/schreiben** (*Comput*) to read/write

Leser, in (**-s, -**) m(f) reader

Leseratte ['leːzəratə] (*umg*) f bookworm

Leser- zW: **Leserbrief** m reader's letter; **„Leserbriefe"** "letters to the editor"; **Leserkreis** m readership; **leserlich** adj legible

Lese- zW: **Lesesaal** m reading room; **Lesestoff** m reading material; **Lesezeichen** nt bookmark; **Lesezirkel** m magazine club

Lesotho [le'zoːto] (**-s**) nt Lesotho

Lesung ['leːzʊŋ] f (*Parl*) reading; (*Eccl*) lesson

lethargisch [le'targɪʃ] adj (*Med, fig*) lethargic

Lette ['lɛtə] (**-n, -n**) m, **Lettin** f Latvian

lettisch adj Latvian
Lettland ['letlant] (**-s**) nt Latvia
Letzt f: **zu guter ~** finally, in the end
letzte, r, s ['letstə(r, s)] adj last; (neueste) latest;
der L~ Wille the last will and testament; **bis zum L~n** to the utmost; **zum ~n Mal** for the last time; **in ~r Zeit** recently
Letzte, s nt: **das ist ja das ~!** (umg) that really is the limit!
letztens adv lately
letztere, r, s adj the latter
letztlich adv in the end
Leuchte ['lɔyçtə] (**-, -n**) f lamp, light; (umg: Mensch) genius
leuchten vi to shine, gleam
Leuchter (**-s, -**) m candlestick
Leucht- zW: **Leuchtfarbe** f fluorescent colour (Brit) od color (US); **Leuchtfeuer** nt beacon; **Leuchtkäfer** m glow-worm; **Leuchtkugel** f flare; **Leuchtpistole** f flare pistol; **Leuchtrakete** f flare; **Leuchtreklame** f neon sign; **Leuchtröhre** f strip light; **Leuchtturm** m lighthouse; **Leuchtzifferblatt** nt luminous dial
leugnen ['lɔygnən] vt, vi to deny
Leugnung f denial
Leukämie [lɔykɛ'mi:] f leukaemia (Brit), leukemia (US)
Leukoplast® [lɔyko'plast] (**-(e)s, -e**) nt Elastoplast®
Leumund ['lɔymʊnt] (**-(e)s, -e**) m reputation
Leumundszeugnis nt character reference
Leute ['lɔytə] pl people pl; **kleine ~** (fig) ordinary people; **etw unter die ~ bringen** (umg: Gerücht etc) to spread sth around
Leutnant ['lɔytnant] (**-s, -s** od **-e**) m lieutenant
leutselig ['lɔytzeːlɪç] adj affable; **Leutseligkeit** f affability
Leviten [le'viːtən] pl: **jdm die ~ lesen** (umg) to haul sb over the coals
lexikalisch [lɛksi'kaːlɪʃ] adj lexical
Lexikografie [lɛksikograˈfiː] f lexicography
Lexikon ['lɛksikɔn] (**-s, Lexiken** od **Lexika**) nt encyclopedia
lfd. abk = **laufend**
Libanese [liba'neːzə] (**-n, -n**) m, **Libanesin** f Lebanese
libanesisch adj Lebanese
Libanon ['liːbanɔn] (**-s**) m: **der ~** the Lebanon
Libelle [li'bɛlə] (**-, -n**) f dragonfly; (Tech) spirit level
liberal [libe'raːl] adj liberal
Liberale, r f(m) (Pol) Liberal
Liberalisierung [liberaliˈziːrʊŋ] f liberalization
Liberalismus [libera'lɪsmʊs] m liberalism
Liberia [li'beːria] (**-s**) nt Liberia
Liberianer, in [liberi'aːnər(ɪn)] (**-s, -**) m(f) Liberian
liberianisch adj Liberian
Libero ['liːbero] (**-s, -s**) m (Fussball) sweeper
Libyen ['liːbyən] (**-s**) nt Libya
Libyer, in (**-s, -**) m(f) Libyan

libysch adj Libyan
Licht [lɪçt] (**-(e)s, -er**) nt light; **~ machen** (anschalten) to turn on a light; (anzünden) to light a candle etc; **mir geht ein ~ auf** it's dawned on me; **jdn hinters ~ führen** (fig) to lead sb up the garden path
licht adj light, bright
Licht- zW: **Lichtbild** nt photograph; (Dia) slide; **Lichtblick** m cheering prospect; **lichtempfindlich** adj sensitive to light
lichten ['lɪçtən] vt to clear; (Anker) to weigh ▷ vr (Nebel) to clear; (Haar) to thin
lichterloh ['lɪçtərˈloː] adv: **~ brennen** to blaze
Licht- zW: **Lichtgeschwindigkeit** f speed of light; **Lichtgriffel** m (Comput) light pen; **Lichthupe** f flashing of headlights; **Lichtjahr** nt light year; **Lichtmaschine** f dynamo; **Lichtmess** (**-**) f Candlemas; **Lichtpause** f photocopy; (bei Blaupausverfahren) blueprint; **Lichtschalter** m light switch; **lichtscheu** adj averse to light; (fig: Gesindel) shady
Lichtung f clearing, glade
Lid [liːt] (**-(e)s, -er**) nt eyelid; **Lidschatten** m eyeshadow
lieb [liːp] adj dear; (viele) **~e Grüße, Deine Silvia** love, Silvia; **Liebe Anna, ~er Klaus! ...** Dear Anna and Klaus, ...; **am ~sten lese ich Kriminalromane** best of all I like detective novels; **den ~en langen Tag** (umg) all the livelong day; **sich bei jdm ~ Kind machen** (pej) to suck up to sb (umg); **~ gewinnen** to get fond of; **~ haben** to love; (weniger stark) to be (very) fond of
liebäugeln ['liːpˌɔygəln] vi untr: **mit dem Gedanken ~, etw zu tun** to toy with the idea of doing sth
Liebe ['liːbə] (**-, -n**) f love; **liebebedürftig** adj: **liebebedürftig sein** to need love
Liebelei f flirtation
lieben ['liːbən] vt to love; (weniger stark) to like; **etw ~d gern tun** to love to do sth
liebens- zW: **liebenswert** adj loveable; **liebenswürdig** adj kind; **liebenswürdigerweise** adv kindly; **Liebenswürdigkeit** f kindness
lieber ['liːbər] adv rather, preferably; **ich gehe ~ nicht** I'd rather not go; **ich trinke ~ Wein als Bier** I prefer wine to beer; **bleib ~ im Bett** you'd better stay in bed
Liebes- zW: **Liebesbrief** m love letter; **Liebesdienst** m good turn; **Liebeskummer** m: **Liebeskummer haben** to be lovesick; **Liebespaar** nt courting couple, lovers pl; **Liebesroman** m romantic novel
liebevoll adj loving
lieb- zW: **Liebhaber, in** (**-s, -**) m(f) lover; (Sammler) collector; **Liebhaberei** f hobby; **liebkosen** vt untr to caress; **lieblich** adj lovely, charming; (Duft, Wein) sweet
Liebling m darling
Lieblings- in zw favourite (Brit), favorite (US)
lieblos adj unloving
Liebschaft f love affair

Liechtenstein ['lɪçtənʃtaɪn] (-s) nt
Liechtenstein

Lied [li:t] (-(e)s, -er) nt song; (Eccl) hymn;
davon kann ich ein ~ singen (fig) I could tell
you a thing or two about that (umg)

Liederbuch nt songbook; (Rel) hymn book

liederlich ['li:dərlɪç] adj slovenly; (Lebenswandel)
loose, immoral; **Liederlichkeit** f slovenliness;
immorality

lief etc [li:f] vb siehe **laufen**

Lieferant [li:fə'rant] m supplier

Lieferanteneingang m tradesmen's entrance;
(von Warenhaus etc) goods entrance

lieferbar adj (vorrätig) available

Lieferbedingungen pl terms of delivery

Lieferfrist f delivery period

liefern ['li:fərn] vt to deliver; (versorgen mit) to
supply; (Beweis) to produce

Lieferschein m delivery note

Liefertermin m delivery date

Lieferung f delivery; (Versorgung) supply

Lieferwagen m (delivery) van, panel truck (US)

Lieferzeit f delivery period; **~ 6 Monate**
delivery six months

Liege ['li:gə] (-, -n) f bed; (Campingliege) camp
bed (Brit), cot (US); **Liegegeld** nt (Hafen,
Flughafen) demurrage

liegen ['li:gən] unreg vi to lie; (sich befinden) to
be (situated); **mir liegt nichts/viel daran** it
doesn't matter to me/it matters a lot to me;
es liegt bei Ihnen, ob ... it rests with you
whether ...; **Sprachen ~ mir nicht** languages
are not my line; **woran liegt es?** what's the
cause?; **so, wie die Dinge jetzt ~** as things
stand at the moment; **an mir soll es nicht
~, wenn die Sache schiefgeht** it won't be my
fault if things go wrong; **~ bleiben** (Person) to
stay in bed; (nicht aufstehen) to stay lying down;
(Ding) to be left (behind); (nicht ausgeführt
werden) to be left (undone); **~ lassen** (vergessen)
to leave behind; **Liegenschaft** f real estate

Liege- zW: **Liegeplatz** m (auf Schiff, in Zug etc)
berth; (Ankerplatz) moorings pl; **Liegesitz** m
(Aut) reclining seat; **Liegestuhl** m deck chair;
Liegestütz m (Sport) press-up (Brit), push-up
(US); **Liegewagen** m (Eisenb) couchette car;
Liegewiese f lawn (for sunbathing)

lieh etc [li:] vb siehe **leihen**

ließ etc [li:s] vb siehe **lassen**

liest [li:st] vb siehe **lesen**

Lift [lɪft] (-(e)s, -e od -s) m lift

Liga ['li:ga] (-, Ligen) f (Sport) league

liieren [li:'i:rən] vt: **liiert sein** (Firmen etc) to be
working together; (ein Verhältnis haben) to have
a relationship

Likör [li'kø:r] (-s, -e) m liqueur

lila ['li:la] adj inv purple; **Lila** (-s, -s) nt (Farbe)
purple

Lilie ['li:liə] f lily

Liliputaner, in [lilipu'ta:nər(ɪn)] (-s, -) m(f)
midget

Limit ['lɪmɪt] (-s, -s od -e) nt limit; (Fin) ceiling

Limonade [limo'na:də] (-, -n) f lemonade

lind [lɪnt] adj gentle, mild

Linde ['lɪndə] (-, -n) f lime tree, linden

lindern ['lɪndərn] vt to alleviate, soothe

Linderung f alleviation

lindgrün adj lime green

Lineal [line'a:l] (-s, -e) nt ruler

linear [line'a:r] adj linear

Linguist, in [lɪŋgu'ɪst(ɪn)] m(f) linguist

Linguistik f linguistics sing

Linie ['li:niə] f line; **in erster ~** first and
foremost; **auf die ~ achten** to watch one's
figure; **fahren Sie mit der ~ 2** take the
number 2 (bus etc)

Linien- zW: **Linienblatt** nt ruled sheet;
Linienbus m service bus; **Linienflug** m
scheduled flight; **Linienrichter** m (Sport)
linesman; **linientreu** adj loyal to the (party)
line

linieren [li'ni:rən], **liniieren** [lini'i:rən] vt to
line

Link [lɪŋk] (-s, -s) m (Comput) link

Linke ['lɪŋkə] (-, -n) f left side; left hand; (Pol)
left

Linke, r f(m) (Pol) left-winger, leftie (pej)

linke, r, s adj left; **~ Masche** purl

linkisch adj awkward, gauche

links adv left; to od on the left; **~ von mir** on
od to my left; **~ von der Mitte** left of centre;
jdn ~ liegen lassen (fig: umg) to ignore sb;
das mache ich mit ~ (umg) I can do that with
my eyes shut; **Linksabbieger** m motorist/
vehicle turning left; **Linksaußen** (-s, -) m
(Sport) outside left; **Linkshänder, in** (-s, -) m(f)
left-handed person; **Linkskurve** f left-hand
bend; **linkslastig** adj: **linkslastig sein** to list od
lean to the left; **linksradikal** adj (Pol) radically
left-wing; **Linksrutsch** m (Pol) swing to the
left; **Linkssteuerung** f (Aut) left-hand drive;
Linksverkehr m driving on the left

Linse ['lɪnzə] (-, -n) f lentil; (optisch) lens

linsen (umg) vi to peek

Lippe ['lɪpə] (-, -n) f lip

Lippenbekenntnis nt lip service

Lippenstift m lipstick

Liquidation [likvidatsi'o:n] f liquidation

Liquidationswert m break-up value

liquid [lik'vi:t], **liquide** [lik'vi:də] adj (Firma)
solvent

Liquidator [likvi'da:tɔr] m liquidator

liquidieren [likvi'di:rən] vt to liquidate

Liquidität [likvidi'tɛ:t] f liquidity

lispeln ['lɪspəln] vi to lisp

Lissabon ['lɪsabɔn] nt Lisbon

List [lɪst] (-, -en) f cunning; (Plan) trick, ruse;
mit ~ und Tücke (umg) with a lot of coaxing

Liste ['lɪstə] (-, -n) f list

Listenplatz m (Pol) place on the party list

Listenpreis m list price

listig adj cunning, sly

Litanei [lita'naɪ] f litany

Litauen ['li:tavən] (-s) nt Lithuania

Litauer, in (-s, -) m(f) Lithuanian

litauisch adj Lithuanian

Liter ['li:tər] **(-s, -)** m od nt litre (Brit), liter (US)
literarisch [lɪte'raːrɪʃ] adj literary
Literatur [lɪtera'tuːr] f literature;
  Literaturpreis m award od prize for literature;
  Literaturwissenschaft f literary studies pl
literweise ['li:tərvaɪzə] adv (lit) by the litre (Brit)
  od liter (US); (fig) by the gallon
Litfaßsäule ['lɪtfaszɔyle] f advertising (Brit) od
  advertizing (US) pillar
Lithografie [litogra'fiː] f lithography
litt etc [lɪt] vb siehe **leiden**
Liturgie [litʊr'giː] f liturgy
liturgisch [li'tʊrgɪʃ] adj liturgical
Litze ['lɪtsə] **(-, -n)** f braid; (Elek) flex
live [laɪf] adj, adv (Rundf, TV) live
Livree [li'vreː] **(-, -n)** f livery
Lizenz [li'tsɛnts] f licence (Brit), license
  (US); **Lizenzausgabe** f licensed edition;
  Lizenzgebühr f licence fee; (im Verlagswesen)
  royalty
Lkw, LKW (-(s), -(s)) m abk = **Lastkraftwagen**
Lkw-Maut, LKW-Maut f toll for trucks
Lob [loːp] **(-(e)s** nt praise
Lobby ['lɔbi] **(-, -s)** f lobby
loben ['loːbən] vt to praise; **das lob ich mir**
  that's what I like (to see/hear etc)
lobenswert adj praiseworthy
löblich ['løːplɪç] adj praiseworthy, laudable
Loblied nt: **ein ~ auf jdn/etw singen** to sing
  sb's/sth's praises
Lobrede f eulogy
Loch [lɔx] **(-(e)s, ̈er)** nt hole; **lochen** vt to
  punch holes in; **Locher (-s, -)** m punch
löcherig ['lœçərɪç] adj full of holes
löchern (umg) vt: **jdn ~** to pester sb with
  questions
Loch- zW: **Lochkarte** f punch card; **Lochzange**
  f punch
Locke ['lɔkə] **(-, -n)** f lock, curl
locken vt to entice; (Haare) to curl
lockend adj tempting
Lockenwickler (-s, -) m curler
locker ['lɔkər] adj loose; (Kuchen, Schaum)
  light; (umg) cool; **lockerlassen** unreg vi: **nicht
  lockerlassen** not to let up
lockern vt to loosen ▷ vr (Atmosphäre) to get
  more relaxed
Lockerungsübung f loosening-up exercise;
  (zum Warmwerden) limbering-up exercise
lockig ['lɔkɪç] adj curly
Lockmittel nt lure
Lockruf m call
Lockung f enticement
Lockvogel m decoy, bait; **Lockvogelangebot** nt
  (Comm) loss leader
Lodenmantel ['loːdənmantəl] m thick woollen
  coat
lodern ['loːdərn] vi to blaze
Löffel ['lœfəl] **(-s, -)** m spoon
löffeln vt to spoon
löffelweise adv by the spoonful
log etc [loːk] vb siehe **lügen**
Logarithmentafel [loga'rɪtmənta:fəl] f

log(arithm) tables pl
Logarithmus [loga'rɪtmʊs] m logarithm
Loge ['loːʒə] **(-, -n)** f (Theat) box; (Freimaurerloge)
  (masonic) lodge; (Pförtnerloge) office
logieren [lo'ʒiːrən] vi to lodge, stay
Logik ['loːgɪk] f logic
Logis [lo'ʒiː] **(-, -)** nt: **Kost und ~** board and
  lodging
logisch ['loːgɪʃ] adj logical; (umg: selbstverständlich): **gehst du auch hin? — ~** are you going
  too? — of course
logo ['loːgo] (umg) interj obvious!
Logopäde [logo'pɛːdə] **(-n, -n)** m speech
  therapist
Logopädin [logo'pɛːdɪn] f speech therapist
Lohn [loːn] **(-(e)s, ̈e)** m reward; (Arbeitslohn)
  pay, wages pl; **Lohnabrechnung** f wages slip;
  Lohnausfall m loss of earnings; **Lohnbüro**
  nt wages office; **Lohndiktat** nt wage
  dictate; **Lohndumping** nt wage dumping;
  Lohnempfänger m wage earner
lohnen ['loːnən] vt (liter): **jdm etw ~** to reward
  sb for sth ▷ vr unpers to be worth it
lohnend adj worthwhile
Lohn- zW: **Lohnerhöhung** f wage increase,
  pay rise; **Lohnforderung** f wage claim;
  Lohnfortzahlung f continued payment of
  wages; **Lohnfortzahlungsgesetz** nt law on
  continued payment of wages; **Lohngefälle** nt wage
  differential; **Lohnkosten** pl labour (Brit) od
  labor (US) costs; **Lohnpolitik** f wages policy;
  Lohnrunde f pay round; **Lohnsteuer** f income
  tax; **Lohnsteuerjahresausgleich** m income
  tax return; **Lohnsteuerkarte** f (income) tax
  card; **Lohnstopp** m pay freeze; **Lohnstreifen** m
  pay slip; **Lohntüte** f pay packet
Lok [lɔk] **(-, -s)** f abk (= Lokomotive) loco (umg)
lokal [lo'kaːl] adj local
Lokal (-(e)s, -e) nt pub(lic house) (Brit)
Lokalblatt (umg) nt local paper
lokalisieren [lokali'ziːrən] vt to localize
Lokalisierung f localization
Lokalität [lokali'tɛːt] f locality; (Raum)
  premises pl
Lokal- zW: **Lokalpresse** f local press; **Lokalteil**
  m (Zeitung) local section; **Lokaltermin** m (Jur)
  visit to the scene of the crime
Lokomotive [lokomo'tiːvə] **(-, -n)** f locomotive
Lokomotivführer m engine driver (Brit),
  engineer (US)
lol abk (Internet, Tel) lol (= Lautes Lachen) laugh
  out loud
Lombardei [lɔmbar'daɪ] f Lombardy
London ['lɔndɔn] **(-s)** nt London
Londoner adj attrib London
Londoner, in (-s, -) m(f) Londoner
Lorbeer ['lɔrbeːr] **(-s, -en)** m (lit, fig) laurel;
  Lorbeerblatt nt (Koch) bay leaf
Lore ['loːrə] **(-, -n)** f (Min) truck
Los [loːs] **(-es, -e)** nt (Schicksal) lot, fate; (in der
  Lotterie) lottery ticket; **das große ~ ziehen**
  (lit, fig) to hit the jackpot; **etw durch das ~
  entscheiden** to decide sth by drawing lots

los *adj* loose ▷ *adv*: ~! go on!; **etw** ~ **sein** to be rid of sth; **was ist** ~? what's the matter?; **dort ist nichts/viel** ~ there's nothing/a lot going on there; **ich bin mein ganzes Geld** ~ (*umg*) I'm cleaned out; **irgendwas ist mit ihm** ~ there's something wrong with him; **wir wollen früh** ~ we want to be off early; **nichts wie** ~! let's get going; **losbinden** *unreg vt* to untie; **losbrechen** *unreg vi* (*Sturm, Gewitter*) to break

losch *etc* [lɔʃ] *vb siehe* **löschen**

Löschblatt ['lœʃblat] *nt* sheet of blotting paper

löschen ['lœʃən] *vt* (*Feuer, Licht*) to put out, extinguish; (*Durst*) to quench; (*Comm*) to cancel; (*Tonband*) to erase; (*Fracht*) to unload; (*Comput*) to delete; (*Tinte*) to blot ▷ *vi* (*Feuerwehr*) to put out a fire; (*Papier*) to blot

Lösch- *zW*: **Löschfahrzeug** *nt* fire engine; **Löschgerät** *nt* fire extinguisher; **Löschpapier** *nt* blotting paper; **Löschtaste** *f* (*Comput*) delete key

Löschung *f* extinguishing; (*Comm*) cancellation; (*Fracht*) unloading

lose ['lo:zə] *adj* loose

Lösegeld *nt* ransom

losen ['lo:zən] *vi* to draw lots

lösen ['lø:zən] *vt* to loosen; (*Handbremse*) to release; (*Husten, Krampf*) to ease; (*Rätsel etc*) to solve; (*Verlobung*) to call off; (*Chem*) to dissolve; (*Partnerschaft*) to break up; (*Fahrkarte*) to buy ▷ *vr* (*aufgehen*) to come loose; (*Schuss*) to go off; (*Zucker etc*) to dissolve; (*Problem, Schwierigkeit*) to (re)solve itself

los- *zW*: **losfahren** *unreg vi* to leave; **losgehen** *unreg vi* to set out; (*anfangen*) to start; (*Bombe*) to go off; **jetzt gehts los!** here we go!; **nach hinten losgehen** (*umg*) to backfire; **auf jdn losgehen** to go for sb; **loskaufen** *vt* (*Gefangene, Geiseln*) to pay ransom for; **loskommen** *unreg vi* (*sich befreien*) to free o.s.; **von etw loskommen** to get away from sth; **loslassen** *unreg vt* (*Seil etc*) to let go of; **der Gedanke lässt mich nicht mehr los** the thought haunts me; **loslaufen** *unreg vi* to run off; **loslegen** (*umg*) *vi*: **nun leg mal los und erzähl(e)** ... now come on and tell me/us ...

löslich ['lø:slɪç] *adj* soluble; **Löslichkeit** *f* solubility

loslösen *vt* to free ▷ *vr*: **sich (von etw)** ~ to detach o.s. (from sth)

losmachen *vt* to loosen; (*Boot*) to unmoor ▷ *vr* to get free

Losnummer *f* ticket number

los- *zW*: **lossagen** *vr*: **sich von jdm/etw lossagen** to renounce sb/sth; **losschießen** *unreg vi*: **schieß los!** (*fig: umg*) fire away!; **losschrauben** *vt* to unscrew; **lossprechen** *unreg vt* to absolve; **losstürzen** *vi*: **auf jdn/etw losstürzen** to pounce on sb/sth

Losung ['lo:zʊŋ] *f* watchword, slogan

Lösung ['lø:zʊŋ] *f* (*Lockermachen*) loosening; (*eines Rätsels, Chem*) solution

Lösungsmittel *nt* solvent

loswerden *unreg vt* to get rid of

losziehen *unreg vi* (*sich aufmachen*) to set out; **gegen jdn** ~ (*fig*) to run sb down

Lot [lo:t] (*-(e)s, -e*) *nt* plumbline; (*Math*) perpendicular; **im** ~ vertical; (*fig*) on an even keel; **die Sache ist wieder im** ~ things have been straightened out; **loten** *vt* to plumb, sound

löten ['lø:tən] *vt* to solder

Lothringen ['lo:trɪŋən] (*-s*) *nt* Lorraine

Lötkolben *m* soldering iron

Lotse ['lo:tsə] (*-n, -n*) *m* pilot; (*Aviat*) air traffic controller

lotsen *vt* to pilot; (*umg*) to lure

Lotterie [lɔtə'ri:] *f* lottery

Lotterleben ['lɔtərle:bən] (*umg*) *nt* dissolute life

Lotto ['lɔto] (*-s, -s*) *nt* ≈ National Lottery

Lottozahlen *pl* winning Lotto numbers *pl*

Löwe ['lø:və] (*-n, -n*) *m* lion; (*Astrol*) Leo

Löwen- *zW*: **Löwenanteil** *m* lion's share; **Löwenmaul** *nt*, **Löwenmäulchen** *nt* antirrhinum, snapdragon; **Löwenzahn** *m* dandelion

Löwin ['lø:vɪn] *f* lioness

loyal [loa'ja:l] *adj* loyal

Loyalität [loajali'tɛ:t] *f* loyalty

LP (*-, -s*) *f abk* (= *Langspielplatte*) LP

LSD (*-(s)*) *nt abk* (= *Lysergsäurediäthylamid*) LSD

lt. *abk* = **laut**

Luchs [lʊks] (*-es, -e*) *m* lynx

Lücke ['lʏkə] (*-, -n*) *f* gap; (*Gesetzeslücke*) loophole; (*in Versorgung*) break

Lücken- *zW*: **Lückenbüßer** (*-s, -*) *m* stopgap; **lückenhaft** *adj* full of gaps; (*Versorgung*) deficient; **lückenlos** *adj* complete

lud *etc* [lu:t] *vb siehe* **laden**

Luder ['lu:dər] (*-s, -*) (*pej*) *nt* (*Frau*) hussy; (*bedauernswert*) poor wretch

Luft [lʊft] (*-, ⁻e*) *f* air; (*Atem*) breath; **die** ~ **anhalten** (*lit*) to hold one's breath; **seinem Herzen** ~ **machen** to get everything off one's chest; **in der** ~ **liegen** to be in the air; **dicke** ~ (*umg*) a bad atmosphere; **(frische)** ~ **schnappen** (*umg*) to get some fresh air; **in die** ~ **fliegen** (*umg*) to explode; **diese Behauptung ist aus der** ~ **gegriffen** this statement is (a) pure invention; **die** ~ **ist rein** (*umg*) the coast is clear; **jdn an die (frische)** ~ **setzen** (*umg*) to show sb the door; **er ist** ~ **für mich** I'm not speaking to him; **jdn wie** ~ **behandeln** to ignore sb; **Luftangriff** *m* air raid; **Luftaufnahme** *f* aerial photo; **Luftballon** *m* balloon; **Luftblase** *f* air bubble; **Luftbrücke** *f* airlift; **luftdicht** *adj* airtight; **Luftdruck** *m* atmospheric pressure; **luftdurchlässig** *adj* pervious to air

lüften ['lʏftən] *vt* to air; (*Hut*) to lift, raise ▷ *vi* to let some air in

Luft- *zW*: **Luftfahrt** *f* aviation; **Luftfeuchtigkeit** *f* humidity; **Luftfracht** *f* air cargo; **luftgekühlt** *adj* air-cooled; **Luftgewehr** *nt* air rifle

luftig *adj* (*Ort*) breezy; (*Raum*) airy; (*Kleider*)

summery

Luft- zW: **Luftkissenfahrzeug** nt hovercraft;
Luftkrieg m war in the air, aerial warfare;
Luftkurort m health resort; **luftleer**
adj: **luftleerer Raum** vacuum; **Luftlinie** f: **in
der Luftlinie** as the crow flies; **Luftloch** nt
air hole; (Aviat) air pocket; **Luftmatratze** f
Lilo® (Brit), air mattress; **Luftpirat** m hijacker;
Luftpost f airmail; **Luftpumpe** f (für Fahrrad)
(bicycle) pump; **Luftraum** m air space;
Luftröhre f (Anat) windpipe; **Luftschlange**
f streamer; **Luftschloss** nt (fig) castle in
the air; **Luftschutz** m anti-aircraft defence
(Brit) od defense (US); **Luftschutzbunker**
m, **Luftschutzkeller** m air-raid shelter;
Luftsprung m (fig): **einen Luftsprung
machen** to jump for joy

Lüftung ['lʏftʊŋ] f ventilation

Luft- zW: **Luftveränderung** f change of air;
Luftverkehr m air traffic; **Luftverschmutzung**
f air pollution; **Luftwaffe** f air force; **Luftweg**
m: **etw auf dem Luftweg befördern** to
transport sth by air; **Luftzufuhr** f air supply;
Luftzug m draught (Brit), draft (US)

Lüge ['ly:gə] (-, -n) f lie; **jdn/etw ~n strafen** to
give the lie to sb/sth

lügen ['ly:gən] unreg vi to lie; **wie gedruckt ~**
(umg) to lie like mad

Lügendetektor ['ly:gəndetɛktor] m lie detector

Lügner, in (-s, -) m(f) liar

Luke ['lu:kə] (-, -n) f hatch; (Dachluke) skylight

lukrativ [lukra'ti:f] adj lucrative

Lümmel ['lʏməl] (-s, -) m lout

lümmeln vr to lounge (about)

Lump [lʊmp] (-en, -en) m scamp, rascal

lumpen ['lʊmpən] vt: **sich nicht ~ lassen** not
to be mean

Lumpen (-s, -) m rag

Lumpensammler m rag and bone man

lumpig ['lʊmpɪç] adj shabby; **~e 10 Euro** (umg)
10 measly euros

Lüneburger Heide ['ly:nəbʊrgər 'haɪdə] f
Lüneburg Heath

Lunge ['lʊŋə] (-, -n) f lung

Lungen- zW: **Lungenentzündung** f
pneumonia; **lungenkrank** adj suffering from a
lung disease; **Lungenkrankheit** f lung disease

lungern ['lʊŋərn] vi to hang about

Lunte ['lʊntə] (-, -n) f fuse; **~ riechen** to smell
a rat

Lupe ['lu:pə] (-, -n) f magnifying glass; **unter
die ~ nehmen** (fig) to scrutinize

lupenrein adj (lit: Edelstein) flawless

Lupine [lu'pi:nə] f lupin

Lurch [lʊrç] (-(e)s, -e) m amphibian

Lust [lʊst] (-, ⁻e) f joy, delight; (Neigung) desire;
(sexuell) lust (pej); **~ haben zu** od **auf etw** akk/
etw zu tun to feel like sth/doing sth; **hast du
~?** how about it?; **er hat die ~ daran verloren**
he has lost all interest in it; **je nach ~ und
Laune** just depending on how I od you etc feel;
lustbetont adj pleasure-orientated

lüstern ['lʏstərn] adj lustful, lecherous

Lustgefühl nt pleasurable feeling

Lustgewinn m pleasure

lustig ['lʊstɪç] adj (komisch) amusing, funny;
(fröhlich) cheerful; **sich über jdn/etw ~
machen** to make fun of sb/sth

Lüstling m lecher

Lust- zW: **lustlos** adj unenthusiastic;
Lustmord m sex(ual) murder; **Lustprinzip**
nt (Psych) pleasure principle; **Lustspiel** nt
comedy; **lustwandeln** vi to stroll about

luth. abk = **lutherisch**

Lutheraner, in [lʊtə'ra:nər(ɪn)] m(f) Lutheran

lutherisch ['lʊtərɪʃ] adj Lutheran

lutschen ['lʊtʃən] vt, vi to suck; **am Daumen ~**
to suck one's thumb

Lutscher (-s, -) m lollipop

Luxemburg ['lʊksəmbʊrk] (-s) nt Luxembourg

Luxemburger, in ['lʊksəmburgər(ɪn)] (-s, -)
m(f) citizen of Luxembourg, Luxembourger

luxemburgisch adj Luxembourgian

luxuriös [lʊksuri'ø:s] adj luxurious

Luxus ['lʊksʊs] (-) m luxury; **Luxusartikel** pl
luxury goods pl; **Luxusausführung** f de luxe
model; **Luxusdampfer** m luxury cruise ship;
Luxushotel nt luxury hotel; **Luxussteuer** f tax
on luxuries

LVA (-) f abk (= Landesversicherungsanstalt) county
insurance company

LW abk (= Langwelle) LW

Lycra ['ly:kra] (-(s)) no pl nt Lycra®

Lymphe ['lʏmfə] (-, -n) f lymph

Lymphknoten m lymph(atic) gland

lynchen ['lʏnçən] vt to lynch

Lynchjustiz f lynch law

Lyrik ['ly:rɪk] f lyric poetry; **Lyriker, in** (-s, -)
m(f) lyric poet

lyrisch ['ly:rɪʃ] adj lyrical

M, m¹ [ɛm] *nt* M, m; **M wie Martha** = M for
Mary, = M for Mike (US)
m² *abk* (= *Meter*) m; (= *männlich*) m.
M. *abk* = **Monat**
MA. *abk* = **Mittelalter**
Maat [maːt] (**-s, -e** *od* **-en**) *m* (*Naut*) (ship's)
mate
Machart *f* make
machbar *adj* feasible
Machbarkeitsstudie *f* feasibility study
Mache (**-**) (*umg*) *f* show, sham; **jdn in der ~
haben** to be having a go at sb

 SCHLÜSSELWORT

machen ['maxən] *vt* **1** to do; **was machst du
da?** what are you doing there?; **das ist nicht
zu machen** that can't be done; **was machen
Sie (beruflich)?** what do you do for a living?;
mach, dass du hier verschwindest! (you
just) get out of here!; **mit mir kann mans ja
machen!** (*umg*) the things I put up with!; **das
lässt er nicht mit sich machen** he won't
stand for that; **eine Prüfung machen** to take
an exam
2 (*herstellen*) to make; **das Radio leiser
machen** to turn the radio down; **aus Holz
gemacht** made of wood; **das Essen machen**
to get the meal; **Schluss machen** to finish
(off)
3 (*verursachen, bewirken*) to make; **jdm Angst
machen** to make sb afraid; **das macht die
Kälte** it's the cold that does that
4 (*ausmachen*) to matter; **das macht nichts**
that doesn't matter; **die Kälte macht mir
nichts** I don't mind the cold
5 (*kosten: ergeben*) to be; **3 und 5 macht 8** 3 and
5 is *od* are 8; **was** *od* **wie viel macht das?** how
much does that come to?
6: was macht die Arbeit? how's the work
going?; **was macht dein Bruder?** how is your
brother doing?; **das Auto machen lassen** to
have the car done; **machs gut!** take care!; (*viel
Glück*) good luck!
▷ *vi:* **mach schnell!** hurry up!; **mach schon!**
come on!; **jetzt macht sie auf große Dame**
(*umg*) she's playing the lady now; **lass mich
mal machen** (*umg*) let me do it; (*ich bringe das in*

Ordnung) I'll deal with it; **groß/klein machen**
(*umg*: *Notdurft*) to do a big/little job; **sich** *dat*
in die Hose machen to wet o.s.; **ins Bett
machen** to wet one's bed; **das macht müde**
it makes you tired; **in etw** *dat* **machen** to be
od deal in sth
▷ *vr* to come along (nicely); **sich an etw** *akk*
machen to set about sth; **sich verständlich
machen** to make o.s. understood; **sich** *dat*
viel aus jdm/etw machen to like sb/sth;
mach dir nichts daraus don't let it bother
you; **sich auf den Weg machen** to get going;
sich an etw *akk* **machen** to set about sth

Machenschaften *pl* wheelings and dealings *pl*
Macher (**-s, -**) (*umg*) *m* man of action
Macho ['matʃo] (*umg*) *adj* macho
Macho (**-s, -s**) (*umg*) *m* macho type
Macht [maxt] (**-**, **ᵋe**) *f* power; **mit aller ~** with
all one's might; **an der ~ sein** to be in power;
alles in unserer ~ Stehende everything
in our power; **Machtergreifung** *f* seizure of
power; **Machthaber** (**-s, -**) *m* ruler
mächtig ['mɛçtɪç] *adj* powerful, mighty;
(*umg*: *ungeheuer*) enormous
Macht- *zW*: **machtlos** *adj* powerless;
Machtprobe *f* trial of strength;
Machtstellung *f* position of power;
Machtwort *nt*: **ein Machtwort sprechen** to
lay down the law
Machwerk *nt* work; (*schlechte Arbeit*) botched
job
Macke ['makə] (**-, -n**) (*umg*) *f* (*Tick, Knall*) quirk;
(*Fehler*) fault
Macker (**-s, -**) (*umg*) *m* fellow, guy
MAD (**-**) *m abk* (= *Militärischer Abschirmdienst*) = MI5
(*Brit*), = CIA (US)
Madagaskar [mada'gaskar] (**-s**) *nt* Madagascar
Mädchen ['mɛːtçən] *nt* girl; **ein ~ für alles**
(*umg*) a dogsbody; (*im Büro etc*) a girl Friday;
mädchenhaft *adj* girlish; **Mädchenname** *m*
maiden name
Made ['maːdə] (**-, -n**) *f* maggot
Madeira¹ [ma'deːra] (**-s**) *nt* (*Geog*) Madeira
Madeira² (**-s, -s**) *m* (*Wein*) Madeira
Mädel ['mɛːdl] (**-s, -(s)**) *nt* (*Dialekt*) lass, girl
madig ['maːdɪç] *adj* maggoty; **madigmachen**
vt: **jdm etw madigmachen** to spoil sth for sb

Madrid [ma'drɪt] (**-s**) *nt* Madrid
mag [maːk] *vb siehe* **mögen**
Mag. *abk* = **Magister**
Magazin [maga'tsiːn] (**-s, -e**) *nt* (*Zeitschrift, am Gewehr*) magazine; (*Lager*) storeroom; (*Bibliotheksmagazin*) stockroom
Magd [maːkt] (**-, ̈-e**) *f* maid(servant)
Magen ['maːɡən] (**-s, - od ̈-**) *m* stomach; **jdm auf den ~ schlagen** (*umg*) to upset sb's stomach; (*fig*) to upset sb; **sich** *dat* **den ~ verderben** to upset one's stomach; **Magenbitter** *m* bitters *pl*; **Magengeschwür** *nt* stomach ulcer; **Magenschmerzen** *pl* stomach-ache *sing*; **Magenverstimmung** *f* stomach upset
mager ['maːɡər] *adj* lean; (*dünn*) thin; **Magerkeit** *f* leanness; thinness; **Magermilch** *f* skimmed milk; **Magerquark** *m* low-fat soft cheese; **Magersucht** *f* (*Med*) anorexia; **magersüchtig** *adj* anorexic
Magie [ma'giː] *f* magic
Magier ['maːɡiər] (**-s, -**) *m* magician
magisch ['maːɡɪʃ] *adj* magical
Magister [ma'ɡɪstər] (**-s, -**) *m* (*Univ*) M.A., Master of Arts
Magistrat [maɡɪs'traːt] (**-(e)s, -e**) *m* municipal authorities *pl*
Magnat [ma'ɡnaːt] (**-en, -en**) *m* magnate
Magnet [ma'ɡneːt] (**-s od -en, -en**) *m* magnet; **Magnetbahn** *f* magnetic railway; **Magnetband** *nt* (*Comput*) magnetic tape; **magnetisch** *adj* magnetic
magnetisieren [maɡneti'ziːrən] *vt* to magnetize
Magnetnadel *f* magnetic needle
Magnettafel *f* magnetic board
Mahagoni [maha'ɡoːni] (**-s**) *nt* mahogany
Mähdrescher (**-s, -**) *m* combine (harvester)
mähen ['mɛːən] *vt, vi* to mow
Mahl [maːl] (**-(e)s, -e**) *nt* meal
mahlen *unreg vt* to grind
Mahlstein *m* grindstone
Mahlzeit *f* meal ▷ *interj* enjoy your meal!
Mahnbrief *m* reminder
Mähne ['mɛːnə] (**-, -n**) *f* mane
mahnen ['maːnən] *vt* to remind; (*warnend*) to warn; (*wegen Schuld*) to demand payment from; **jdn zur Eile/Geduld** *etc* **~** (*auffordern*) to urge sb to hurry/be patient *etc*
Mahn- *zW*: **Mahngebühr** *f* reminder fee; **Mahnmal** *nt* memorial; **Mahnschreiben** *nt* reminder
Mahnung *f* admonition, warning; (*Mahnbrief*) reminder
Mähre ['mɛːrə] (**-, -n**) *f* mare
Mähren ['mɛːrən] (**-s**) *nt* Moravia
Mai [maɪ] (**-(e)s, -e**) (*pl selten*) *m* May; *siehe auch* **September**; **Maibaum** *m* maypole; **Maibowle** *f* white wine punch (*flavoured with woodruff*); **Maiglöckchen** *nt* lily of the valley; **Maikäfer** *m* cockchafer
Mail [meːl] (**-, -s**) *f* (*Comput*) email
Mailand ['maɪlant] (**-s**) *nt* Milan

Main [maɪn] (**-(e)s**) *m* (*Fluss*) Main
Mais [maɪs] (**-es, -e**) *m* maize, corn (US); **Maiskolben** *m* corncob
Majestät [majɛs'tɛːt] *f* majesty
majestätisch *adj* majestic
Majestätsbeleidigung *f* lese-majesty
Majonäse [majo'nɛːzə] (**-, -n**) *f* mayonnaise
Major [ma'joːr] (**-s, -e**) *m* (*Mil*) major; (*Aviat*) squadron leader
Majoran [majo'raːn] (**-s, -e**) *m* marjoram
makaber [ma'kaːbər] *adj* macabre
Makedonien [make'doːniən] (**-s**) *nt* Macedonia
makedonisch *adj* Macedonian
Makel ['maːkəl] (**-s, -**) *m* blemish; (*moralisch*) stain; **ohne ~** flawless; **makellos** *adj* immaculate, spotless
mäkeln ['mɛːkəln] *vi* to find fault
Make-up [meːkˈʔap] (**-s, -s**) *nt* make-up; (*flüssig*) foundation
Makkaroni [maka'roːni] *pl* macaroni *sing*
Makler ['maːklər] (**-s, -**) *m* broker; (*Grundstücksmakler*) estate agent (*Brit*), realtor (*US*); **Maklergebühr** *f* broker's commission, brokerage
Makrele [ma'kreːlə] (**-, -n**) *f* mackerel
Makro- *in zw* macro-
Makrone [ma'kroːnə] (**-, -n**) *f* macaroon
Makroökonomie *f* macroeconomics *sing*
Mal [maːl] (**-(e)s, -e**) *nt* mark, sign; (*Zeitpunkt*) time; **ein für alle ~** once and for all; **mit einem ~(e)** all of a sudden; **das erste ~** the first time; **jedes ~** every time, each time; **zum letzten ~** for the last time; **ein paar ~** a few times
mal *adv* times
-mal *suff* -times
Malaie [ma'laɪə] (**-n, -n**) *m*, **Malaiin** *f* Malay
malaiisch *adj* Malayan
Malawi [ma'laːvi] (**-s**) *nt* Malawi
Malaysia [ma'laɪzia] (**-s**) *nt* Malaysia
Malaysier, in (**-s, -**) *m(f)* Malaysian
malaysisch *adj* Malaysian
Malediven [male'diːvən] *pl*: **die ~** the Maldive Islands
malen *vt, vi* to paint
Maler (**-s, -**) *m* painter
Malerei [maːlə'raɪ] *f* painting
malerisch *adj* picturesque
Malkasten *m* paintbox
Mallorca [ma'jɔrka, ma'lɔrka] (**-s**) *nt* Majorca
Mallorquiner, in [majɔr'kiːnər(ɪn), malɔr'kiːnər(ɪn)] (**-s, -**) *m(f)* Majorcan
mallorquinisch *adj* Majorcan
malnehmen *unreg vt, vi* to multiply
Malta ['malta] (**-s**) *nt* Malta
Malteser, in [mal'teːzər(ɪn)] (**-s, -**) *m(f)* Maltese
Malteser-Hilfsdienst *m* ≈ St. John's Ambulance Brigade (*Brit*)
maltesisch *adj* Maltese
malträtieren [maltrɛ'tiːrən] *vt* to ill-treat, maltreat
Malz [malts] (**-es**) *nt* malt; **Malzbonbon** *nt or m* cough drop; **Malzkaffee** *m* coffee substitute made

m

219

from malt barley

Mama ['maːmaː] (-, -s) (*umg*) *f* mum(my) (*Brit*), mom(my) (*US*)

Mami ['mami] (-, -s) *f* = **Mama**

Mammografie [mamɔgraˈfiː] *f* (*Med*) mammography

Mammut ['mamʊt] (-s, -e *od* -s) *nt* mammoth ▷ *in zw* mammoth, giant; **Mammutanlagen** *pl* (*Industrie*) mammoth plants

mampfen ['mampfən] (*umg*) *vt, vi* to munch, chomp

man [man] *pron* one, you, people *pl*; ~ **hat mir gesagt ...** I was told ...

managen ['mɛnɪdʒən] *vt* to manage; **ich manage das schon!** (*umg*) I'll fix it somehow!

Manager, in (-s, -) *m(f)* manager

manch [manç] *pron*: ~ **ein(e) ...** many a ...; ~ **eine(r)** many a person

manche, r, s *adj* many a; (*pl*) a number of ▷ *pron* some

mancherlei [mançərˈlaɪ] *adj inv* various ▷ *pron* a variety of things

manchmal *adv* sometimes

Mandant, in [manˈdant(ɪn)] *m(f)* (*Jur*) client

Mandarine [mandaˈriːnə] *f* mandarin, tangerine

Mandat [manˈdaːt] (-(e)s, -e) *nt* mandate; **sein ~ niederlegen** (*Parl*) to resign one's seat

Mandel ['mandəl] (-, -n) *f* almond; (*Anat*) tonsil; **Mandelentzündung** *f* tonsillitis

Mandschurei (-) [mandʒuˈraɪ] *f*: **die ~** Manchuria

Manege [maˈneːʒə] (-, -n) *f* ring, arena

Mangel[1] ['maŋəl] (-, -n) *f* mangle; **durch die ~ drehen** (*fig: umg*) to put through it; (*Prüfling etc*) to put through the mill

Mangel[2] ['maŋəl] (-s, ⁻) *m* lack; (*Knappheit*) shortage; (*Fehler*) defect, fault; ~ **an** +*dat* shortage of

Mängelbericht ['mɛŋəlbərɪçt] *m* list of faults

Mangelerscheinung *f* deficiency symptom

mangelhaft *adj* poor; (*fehlerhaft*) defective, faulty; (*Schulnote*) unsatisfactory

mangeln *vi unpers*: **es mangelt jdm an etw** *dat* sb lacks sth ▷ *vt* (*Wäsche*) to mangle

mangels *präp* +*gen* for lack of

Mangelware *f* scarce commodity

Manie [maˈniː] *f* mania

Manier [maˈniːr] (-) *f* manner; (*Stil*) style; (*pej*) mannerism

Manieren *pl* manners *pl*; (*pej*) mannerisms *pl*

manieriert [maniˈriːrt] *adj* mannered, affected

manierlich *adj* well-mannered

Manifest [maniˈfɛst] (-es, -e) *nt* manifesto

Maniküre [maniˈkyːrə] (-, -n) *f* manicure

maniküren *vt* to manicure

Manipulation [manipulatsiˈoːn] *f* manipulation; (*Trick*) manoeuvre (*Brit*), maneuver (*US*)

manipulieren [manipuˈliːrən] *vt* to manipulate

Manko ['maŋko] (-s, -s) *nt* deficiency; (*Comm*) deficit

Mann [man] (-(e)s, ⁻er *od* (*Naut*) **Leute**) *m* man; (*Ehemann*) husband; (*Naut*) hand; **pro** ~ per head; **mit** ~ **und Maus untergehen** to go down with all hands; (*Passagierschiff*) to go down with no survivors; **seinen** ~ **stehen** to hold one's own; **etw an den** ~ **bringen** (*umg*) to get rid of sth; **einen kleinen** ~ **im Ohr haben** (*hum: umg*) to be crazy

Männchen ['mɛnçən] *nt* little man; (*Tier*) male; ~ **machen** (*Hund*) to (sit up and) beg

Mannequin [manəˈkɛ̃ː] (-s, -s) *nt* fashion model

Männersache ['mɛnərzaxə] *f* (*Angelegenheit*) man's business; (*Arbeit*) man's job

mannigfaltig ['manɪçfaltɪç] *adj* various, varied; **Mannigfaltigkeit** *f* variety

männlich ['mɛnlɪç] *adj* (*Biol*) male; (*fig, Gram*) masculine

Mannsbild *nt* (*veraltet: pej*) fellow

Mannschaft *f* (*Sport, fig*) team; (*Naut, Aviat*) crew; (*Mil*) other ranks *pl*

Mannschaftsgeist *m* team spirit

Mannsleute (*umg*) *pl* menfolk *pl*

Mannweib (*pej*) *nt* mannish woman

Manometer [manoˈmeːtər] *nt* (*Tech*) pressure gauge; ~! (*umg*) wow!

Manöver [maˈnøːvər] (-s, -) *nt* manoeuvre (*Brit*), maneuver (*US*)

manövrieren [manøˈvriːrən] *vt, vi* to manoeuvre (*Brit*), maneuver (*US*)

Mansarde [manˈzardə] (-, -n) *f* attic

Manschette [manˈʃɛtə] *f* cuff; (*Papiermanschette*) paper frill; (*Tech*) sleeve

Manschettenknopf *m* cufflink

Mantel ['mantəl] (-s, ⁻) *m* coat; (*Tech*) casing, jacket; **Manteltarif** *m* general terms of employment; **Manteltarifvertrag** *m* general agreement on conditions of employment

Manuskript [manuˈskrɪpt] (-(e)s, -e) *nt* manuscript

Mappe ['mapə] (-, -n) *f* briefcase; (*Aktenmappe*) folder

Marathonlauf ['maːratɔnlaʊf] *m* marathon

Märchen ['mɛːrçən] *nt* fairy tale; **märchenhaft** *adj* fabulous; **Märchenprinz** *m* prince charming

Marder ['mardər] (-s, -) *m* marten

Margarine [margaˈriːnə] *f* margarine

Marge ['marʒə] (-, -n) *f* (*Comm*) margin

Maria [maˈriːa] (-) *f* Mary

Marienbild *nt* picture of the Virgin Mary

Marienkäfer *m* ladybird

Marihuana [marihuˈaːna] (-s) *nt* marijuana

Marinade [mariˈnaːdə] (-, -n) *f* (*Koch*) marinade; (*Soße*) mayonnaise-based sauce

Marine [maˈriːnə] *f* navy; **marineblau** *adj* navy-blue

marinieren [mariˈniːrən] *vt* to marinate

Marionette [marioˈnɛtə] *f* puppet

Mark[1] [mark] (-, -) *f* (*Hist: Geld*) mark

Mark[2] [mark] (-(e)s) *nt* (*Knochenmark*) marrow; **jdn bis ins** ~ **treffen** (*fig*) to cut sb to the quick; **jdm durch** ~ **und Bein gehen** to go right through sb

markant [mar'kant] *adj* striking

Marke ['markə] (-, -n) *f* mark; (*Warensorte*) brand; (*Fabrikat*) make; (*Rabattmarke, Briefmarke*) stamp; (*Essen(s)marke*) luncheon voucher; (*aus Metall etc*) token, disc

Marken- *zW:* **Markenartikel** *m* proprietary article; **markenbewusst** *adj* brand conscious; **Markenbutter** *f* best quality butter; **Markenkleidung** *f* designer clothes; **Markenzeichen** *nt* trademark

Marketing ['marketɪŋ] (-s) *nt* marketing

markieren [mar'ki:rən] *vt* to mark; (*umg*) to act ▷ *vi* (*umg*) to act it

Markierung *f* marking

markig ['markɪç] *adj* (*fig*) pithy

Markise [mar'ki:zə] (-, -n) *f* awning

Markstück *nt* (*Hist*) one-mark piece

Markt [markt] (-(e)s, ⁻e) *m* market; **Marktanalyse** *f* market analysis; **Marktanteil** *m* market share; **marktfähig** *adj* marketable; **Marktforschung** *f* market research; **marktgängig** *adj* marketable; **marktgerecht** *adj* geared to market requirements; **Marktlücke** *f* gap in the market; **Marktmacht** *f* market power; **Marktplatz** *m* market place; **Marktpotenzial, Marktpotential** *nt* market potential; **Marktpreis** *m* market price; **Marktwert** *m* market value; **Marktwirtschaft** *f* market economy; **marktwirtschaftlich** *adj* free enterprise

Marmelade [marmə'la:də] (-, -n) *f* jam

Marmor ['marmɔr] (-s, -e) *m* marble

marmorieren [marmo'ri:rən] *vt* to marble

Marmorkuchen *m* marble cake

marmorn *adj* marble

Marokkaner, in [marɔ'ka:nər(ɪn)] (-s, -) *m(f)* Moroccan

marokkanisch *adj* Moroccan

Marokko [ma'rɔko] (-s) *nt* Morocco

Marone [ma'ro:nə] (-, -n) *f* chestnut

Marotte [ma'rɔtə] (-, -n) *f* fad, quirk

Marsch¹ [marʃ] (-, -en) *f* marsh

Marsch² (-(e)s, ⁻e) *m* march; **jdm den ~ blasen** (*umg*) to give sb a rocket; **marsch!** *interj* march!; **marsch ins Bett!** off to bed with you!

Marschbefehl *m* marching orders *pl*

marschbereit *adj* ready to move

marschieren [mar'ʃi:rən] *vi* to march

Marschverpflegung *f* rations *pl*; (*Mil*) field rations *pl*

Marseille [mar'sɛːj] (-s) *nt* Marseilles

Marsmensch ['marsmɛnʃ] *m* Martian

Marter ['martər] (-, -n) *f* torment

martern *vt* to torture

Martinshorn ['marti:nshɔrn] *nt* siren (*of police etc*)

Märtyrer, in ['mɛrtyrər(ɪn)] (-s, -) *m(f)* martyr

Martyrium [mar'ty:rium] *nt* (*fig*) ordeal

Marxismus [mar'ksɪsmus] *m* Marxism

März [mɛrts] (-(es), -e) (*pl selten*) *m* March; *siehe auch* **September**

Marzipan [martsi'pa:n] (-s, -e) *nt* marzipan

Masche ['maʃə] (-, -n) *f* mesh; (*Strickmasche*) stitch; **das ist die neueste ~** that's the latest dodge; **durch die ~n schlüpfen** to slip through the net

Maschendraht *m* wire mesh

maschenfest *adj* runproof

Maschine [ma'ʃi:nə] *f* machine; (*Motor*) engine; **~ schreiben** to type

maschinell [maʃi'nɛl] *adj* machine(-), mechanical

Maschinen- *zW:* **Maschinenausfallzeit** *f* machine downtime; **Maschinenbauer** *m* mechanical engineer; **Maschinenführer** *m* machinist; **maschinengeschrieben** *adj* typewritten; **Maschinengewehr** *nt* machine gun; **maschinenlesbar** *adj* (*Comput*) machine-readable; **Maschinenpistole** *f* submachine gun; **Maschinenraum** *m* plant room; (*Naut*) engine room; **Maschinensaal** *m* machine shop; **Maschinenschaden** *m* mechanical fault; **Maschinenschlosser** *m* fitter; **Maschinenschrift** *f* typescript; **Maschinensprache** *f* (*Comput*) machine language

Maschinerie [maʃinə'ri:] *f* (*fig*) machinery

Maschinist, in [maʃi'nɪst(ɪn)] *m(f)* engineer

Maser ['ma:zər] (-, -n) *f* grain

Masern *pl* (*Med*) measles *sing*

Maserung *f* grain(ing)

Maske ['maskə] (-, -n) *f* mask

Maskenball *m* fancy-dress ball

Maskenbildner, in *m(f)* make-up artist

Maskerade [maskə'ra:də] *f* masquerade

maskieren [mas'ki:rən] *vt* to mask; (*verkleiden*) to dress up ▷ *vr* to disguise o.s., dress up

Maskottchen [mas'kɔtçən] *nt* (lucky) mascot

Maskulinum [masku'li:num] (-s, **Maskulina**) *nt* (*Gram*) masculine noun

Masochist [mazo'xɪst] (-en, -en) *m* masochist

Maß¹ [ma:s] (-es, -e) *nt* measure; (*Mäßigung*) moderation; (*Grad*) degree, extent; **über alle ~en** (*liter*) extremely, beyond measure; **~ halten = maßhalten**; **mit zweierlei messen** (*fig*) to operate a double standard; **sich** *dat* **etw nach ~ anfertigen lassen** to have sth made to measure *od* order (US); **in besonderem ~e** especially; **das ~ ist voll** (*fig*) that's enough of (that)

Maß² (-, -(e)) *f* litre (*Brit*) *od* liter (US) of beer

maß *etc vb siehe* **messen**

Massage [ma'sa:ʒə] (-, -n) *f* massage

Massaker [ma'sa:kər] (-s, -) *nt* massacre

Maßanzug *m* made-to-measure suit

Maßarbeit *f* (*fig*) neat piece of work

Masse ['masə] (-, -n) *f* mass; **eine ganze ~** (*umg*) a great deal

Maßeinheit *f* unit of measurement

Massen- *zW:* **Massenartikel** *m* mass-produced article; **Massenblatt** *nt* tabloid; **Massengrab** *nt* mass grave; **massenhaft** *adj* masses of; **Massenmedien** *pl* mass media *pl*; **Massenproduktion** *f* mass production; **Massenveranstaltung** *f* mass meeting;

m

Massenvernichtungswaffen pl weapons of mass destruction; **Massenware** f mass-produced article; **massenweise** adv in huge numbers

Masseur [ma'søːr] m masseur

Masseuse [ma'søːzə] f masseuse

Maß- zW: **maßgebend** adj authoritative; **maßgebende Kreise** influential circles; **maßgeblich** adj definitive; **maßgeschneidert** adj (Anzug) made-to-measure, made-to-order (US), custom attrib (US); **maßhalten** unreg vi to exercise moderation

massieren [ma'siːrən] vt to massage; (Mil) to mass

massig ['masɪç] adj massive; (umg) a massive amount of

mäßig ['mɛːsɪç] adj moderate; **mäßigen** ['mɛːsɪgən] vt to restrain, moderate; **sein Tempo mäßigen** to slacken one's pace; **Mäßigkeit** f moderation

massiv [ma'siːf] adj solid; (fig) heavy, rough; **~ werden** (umg) to turn nasty; **Massiv (-s, -e)** nt massif

Maß- zW: **Maßkrug** m tankard; **maßlos** adj (Verschwendung, Essen, Trinken) excessive, immoderate; (Enttäuschung, Ärger etc) extreme; **Maßnahme (-, -n)** f measure, step; **maßregeln** vt untr to reprimand

Maßstab m rule, measure; (fig) standard; (Geog) scale; **als ~ dienen** to serve as a model

maßstabgetreu, maßstabsgetreu adj (true) to scale

maßvoll adj moderation

Mast [mast] **(-(e)s, -e(n))** m mast; (Elek) pylon

Mastdarm m rectum

mästen ['mɛstən] vt to fatten

masturbieren [masturˈbiːrən] vi to masturbate

Material [materiˈaːl] **(-s, -ien)** nt material(s); **Materialfehler** m material defect

Materialismus [materiaˈlɪsmus] m materialism

Materialist, in m(f) materialist; **materialistisch** adj materialistic

Materialkosten pl cost sing of materials

Materialprüfung f material(s) control

Materie [maˈteːriə] f matter, substance

materiell [materiˈɛl] adj material

Mathe ['matə] **(-)** f (Sch: umg) maths (Brit), math (US)

Mathematik [matemaˈtiːk] f mathematics sing; **Mathematiker, in** [mateˈmaːtɪkər(ɪn)] **(-s, -)** m(f) mathematician

mathematisch [mateˈmaːtɪʃ] adj mathematical

Matjeshering ['matjəsheːrɪŋ] (umg) m salted young herring

Matratze [maˈtratsə] **(-, -n)** f mattress

Matrixdrucker m dot-matrix printer

Matrixzeichen nt matrix character

Matrize [maˈtriːtsə] **(-, -n)** f matrix; (zum Abziehen) stencil

Matrose [maˈtroːzə] **(-n, -n)** m sailor

Matsch [matʃ] **(-(e)s)** m mud; (Schneematsch) slush

matschig adj muddy; slushy

matt [mat] adj weak; (glanzlos) dull; (Phot) matt; (Schach) mate; **jdn ~ setzen** (lit) to checkmate sb; siehe auch **mattsetzen; Matt (-s, -s)** nt (Schach) checkmate

Matte ['matə] **(-, -n)** f mat; **auf der ~ stehen** (am Arbeitsplatz etc) to be in

Mattigkeit f weakness; dullness

Mattscheibe f (TV) screen; **~ haben** (umg) to be not quite with it

mattsetzen vt (fig) to checkmate

Matura [maˈtuːra] **(-)** (Österr, Schweiz) f = **Abitur**

Mätzchen ['mɛtsçən] (umg) nt antics pl; **~ machen** to fool around

mau [mau] (umg) adj poor, bad

Mauer ['mauər] **(-, -n)** f wall; **Mauerblümchen** (umg) nt (fig) wallflower

mauern vi to build, lay bricks ▷ vt to build

Mauer- zW: **Mauerschwalbe** f swift; **Mauersegler** m swift; **Mauerwerk** nt brickwork; (Stein) masonry

Maul [maul] **(-(e)s, Mäuler)** nt mouth; **ein loses od lockeres ~ haben** (umg: frech sein) to be an impudent so-and-so; (: indiskret sein) to be a blabbermouth; **halts ~!** (umg) shut your face! (!); **darüber werden sich die Leute das ~ zerreißen** (umg) that will start people's tongues wagging; **dem Volk** od **den Leuten aufs ~ schauen** (umg) to listen to what ordinary people say; **maulen** (umg) vi to grumble; **Maulesel** m mule; **Maulkorb** m muzzle; **Maulsperre** f lockjaw; **Maultier** nt mule; **Maul- und Klauenseuche** f (Tiere) foot-and-mouth disease

Maulwurf m mole

Maulwurfshaufen m molehill

Maurer ['maurər] **(-s, -)** m bricklayer; **pünktlich wie die ~** (hum) super-punctual

Mauretanien [maurəˈtaːniən] **(-s)** nt Mauritania

Maus [maus] **(-, Mäuse)** f (auch Comput) mouse; **Mäuse** pl (umg: Geld) bread sing, dough sing

mauscheln ['mauʃəln] (umg) vt, vi (manipulieren) to fiddle

mäuschenstill ['mɔysçənˈʃtɪl] adj very quiet

Mausefalle f mousetrap

mausen vt (umg) to pinch ▷ vi to catch mice

mausern vr to moult (Brit), molt (US)

mausetot adj stone dead

mausgesteuert adj (Comput) mouse-driven

Mausklick [ˈmausklɪk] nt (Comput) (mouse) click

Maut [maut] **(-, -en)** f toll; **Mautsystem** nt toll system

max. abk (= maximal) max.

maximal [maksiˈmaːl] adj maximum

Maxime [maˈksiːmə] **(-, -n)** f maxim

maximieren [maksiˈmiːrən] vt to maximize

Maximierung f (Wirts) maximization

Maximum ['maksimum] **(-s, Maxima)** nt maximum

Mayonnaise [majɔˈnɛːzə] **(-, -n)** f mayonnaise

Mazedonien [matse'do:niən] (**-s**) *nt* Macedonia

Mäzen [mɛ'tse:n] (**-s, -e**) *m* (*gen*) patron, sponsor

MdB *nt abk* (= *Mitglied des Bundestages*) member of the *Bundestag*, ≈ MP

MdL *nt abk* (= *Mitglied des Landtages*) member of the *Landtag*

m. E. *abk* (= *meines Erachtens*) in my opinion

Mechanik [me'ça:nɪk] *f* mechanics *sing*; (*Getriebe*) mechanics *pl*; **Mechaniker** (**-s, -**) *m* mechanic, engineer

mechanisch *adj* mechanical

Mechanisierung *f* mechanization

Mechanismus [meça'nɪsmʊs] *m* mechanism

meckern [mɛkərn] *vi* to bleat; (*umg*) to moan

Mecklenburg ['me:klənbʊrk] (**-s**) *nt* Mecklenburg

Mecklenburg-Vorpommern (**-s**) *nt* (state of) Mecklenburg-Vorpommern

Medaille [me'daljə] (**-, -n**) *f* medal

Medaillon [medal'jõ:] (**-s, -s**) *nt* (*Schmuck*) locket

Medien ['me:diən] *pl* media *pl*; **Medienbericht** *m* (*meist pl*) media report; **Medienberichten zufolge** according to reports in the media; **Medienforschung** *f* media research; **Mediengesellschaft** *f* media society; **Medienmogul** *m* media mogul; **medienübergreifend** *adj* cross-media *attrib*; **Medienvielfalt** *f* mixture of media

Medikament [medika'mɛnt] *nt* medicine

Meditation [meditatsi'o:n] *f* meditation

meditieren [medi'ti:rən] *vi* to meditate

Medium ['me:diʊm] *nt* medium

Medizin [medi'tsi:n] (**-, -en**) *f* medicine

Mediziner, in (**-s, -**) *m(f)* doctor; (*Univ*) medic (*umg*)

medizinisch *adj* medical; **~-technische Assistentin** medical assistant

Meer [me:r] (**-(e)s, -e**) *nt* sea; **am ~(e)** by the sea; **ans ~ fahren** to go to the sea(side); **Meerbusen** *m* bay, gulf; **Meerenge** *f* straits *pl*

Meeres- *zW*: **Meeresfrüchte** *pl* seafood; **Meeresklima** *nt* maritime climate; **Meeresspiegel** *m* sea level

Meer- *zW*: **Meerjungfrau** *f* mermaid; **Meerrettich** *m* horseradish; **Meerschweinchen** *nt* guinea pig; **Meerwasser** *nt* sea water

Mega-, mega- [mɛga-] *in zw* mega-; **Megabyte** [mega'baɪt] *nt* megabyte; **Megafon, Megaphon** [mega'fo:n] (**-s, -e**) *nt* megaphone; **Megawatt** [mɛga'vat] *nt* megawatt

Mehl [m'e:l] (**-(e)s, -e**) *nt* flour

mehlig *adj* floury

Mehlschwitze *f* (*Koch*) roux

mehr [me:r] *adv* more; **nie ~** never again, nevermore (*liter*); **es war niemand ~ da** there was no one left; **nicht ~ lange** not much longer; **Mehraufwand** *m* additional expenditure; **Mehrbelastung** *f* excess load; (*fig*) additional burden; **mehrdeutig** *adj* ambiguous

mehrere *indef pron* several; (*verschiedene*) various; **~s** several things

mehrfach *adj* multiple; (*wiederholt*) repeated

Mehrheit *f* majority

Mehrheitsprinzip *nt* principle of majority rule

Mehrheitswahlrecht *nt* first-past-the-post voting system

mehr- *zW*: **mehrjährig** *adj attrib* of several years; **Mehrkosten** *pl* additional costs *pl*; **mehrmalig** *adj* repeated; **mehrmals** *adv* repeatedly; **Mehrparteiensystem** *nt* multi-party system; **Mehrplatzsystem** *nt* (*Comput*) multi-user system; **Mehrprogrammbetrieb** *m* (*Comput*) multiprogramming; **mehrsprachig** *adj* multilingual; **mehrstimmig** *adj* for several voices; **mehrstimmig singen** to harmonize; **Mehrwegflasche** *f* returnable bottle; **Mehrwertsteuer** *f* value added tax, VAT; **Mehrzahl** *f* majority; (*Gram*) plural

Mehrzweck- *in zw* multipurpose

meiden ['maɪdən] *unreg vt* to avoid

Meile ['maɪlə] (**-, -n**) *f* mile; **das riecht man drei ~n gegen den Wind** (*umg*) you can smell that a mile off

Meilenstein *m* milestone

meilenweit *adj* for miles

mein [maɪn] *pron* my

meine, r, s *poss pron* mine

Meineid ['maɪn|aɪt] *m* perjury

meinen ['maɪnən] *vt* to think; (*sagen*) to say; (*sagen wollen*) to mean ▷ *vi* to think; **wie Sie ~!** as you wish; **damit bin ich gemeint** that refers to me; **das will ich ~** I should think so

meiner *gen von* **ich** ▷ *pron of* me

meinerseits *adv* for my part

meinesgleichen ['maɪnəs'glaɪçən] *pron* people like me

meinetwegen ['maɪnət've:gən] *adv* (*für mich*) for my sake; (*wegen mir*) on my account; (*von mir aus*) as far as I'm concerned; (*ich habe nichts dagegen*) I don't care *od* mind

meinetwillen ['maɪnət'vɪlən] *adv*: **um ~ = meinetwegen**

meinige *pron*: **der/die/das ~** *od* **Meinige** mine

meins [maɪns] *pron* mine

Meinung ['maɪnʊŋ] *f* opinion; **meiner ~ nach** in my opinion; **einer ~ sein** to think the same; **jdm die ~ sagen** to give sb a piece of one's mind

Meinungs- *zW*: **Meinungsaustausch** *m* exchange of views; **Meinungsbildungsprozess** *f* opinion-forming process; **Meinungsforscher, in** *m(f)* pollster; **Meinungsforschungsinstitut** *nt* opinion research institute; **Meinungsfreiheit** *f* freedom of speech; **Meinungsumfrage** *f* opinion poll; **Meinungsverschiedenheit** *f* difference of opinion

Meise ['maɪzə] (**-, -n**) *f* tit(mouse); **eine ~ haben** (*umg*) to be crackers

Meißel ['maɪsəl] (**-s, -**) *m* chisel

meißeln *vt* to chisel

meist [maɪst] *adj* most ▷ *adv* mostly;

m

Meistbegünstigungsklausel f (Comm) most-favoured-nation clause; **meistbietend** adj: **meistbietend versteigern** to sell to the highest bidder

meiste, r, s superl von **viel**

meistens adv mostly

Meister ['maɪstər] (-s, -) m master; (Sport) champion; **seinen ~ machen** to take one's master craftsman's diploma; **es ist noch kein ~ vom Himmel gefallen** (Sprichwort) no one is born an expert; **Meisterbrief** m master craftsman's diploma; **meisterhaft** adj masterly

Meisterin f (auf einem Gebiet) master, expert; (Sport) (woman) champion

meistern vt to master; **sein Leben ~** to come to grips with one's life

Meister- zW: **Meisterschaft** f mastery; (Sport) championship; **Meisterstück** nt masterpiece; **Meisterwerk** nt masterpiece

meistgekauft adj attrib best-selling

Mekka ['mɛka] (-s, -s) nt (Geog, fig) Mecca

Melancholie [melaŋko'li:] f melancholy

melancholisch [melaŋ'ko:lɪʃ] adj melancholy

Meldebehörde f registration authorities pl

Meldefrist f registration period

melden vt to report; (registrieren) to register ▷ vr to report; to register; (Sch) to put one's hand up; (freiwillig) to volunteer; (auf etw, am Telefon) to answer; **nichts zu ~ haben** (umg) to have no say; **wen darf ich ~?** who shall I say (is here)?; **sich ~ bei** to report to; to register with; **sich auf eine Anzeige ~** to answer an advertisement; **es meldet sich niemand** there's no answer; **sich zu Wort ~** to ask to speak

Meldepflicht f obligation to register with the police

Meldestelle f registration office

Meldung ['mɛldʊŋ] f announcement; (Bericht) report

meliert [me'li:rt] adj mottled, speckled

melken ['mɛlkən] unreg vt to milk

Melodie [melo'di:] f melody, tune

melodisch [me'lo:dɪʃ] adj melodious, tuneful

melodramatisch [melodra'ma:tɪʃ] adj (auch fig) melodramatic

Melone [me'lo:nə] (-, -n) f melon; (Hut) bowler (hat)

Membran [mem'bra:n] (-, -en) f (Tech) diaphragm; (Anat) membrane

Memme ['mɛmə] (-, -n) (umg) f cissy, yellow-belly

Memoiren [memo'a:rən] pl memoirs pl

Menge ['mɛŋə] (-, -n) f quantity; (Menschenmenge) crowd; (große Anzahl) lot (of); **jede ~** (umg) masses pl, loads pl

mengen vt to mix ▷ vr: **sich ~ in** +akk to meddle with

Mengen- zW: **Mengeneinkauf** m bulk buying; **Mengenlehre** f (Math) set theory; **Mengenrabatt** m bulk discount

Menorca [me'nɔrka] (-s) nt Menorca

Mensa ['mɛnza] (-, -s od **Mensen**) f (Univ) refectory (Brit), commons (US)

Mensch [mɛnʃ] (-en, -en) m human being, man; (Person) person; **kein ~** nobody; **ich bin auch nur ein ~!** I'm only human; **~ ärgere dich nicht** nt (Spiel) ludo

Menschen- zW: **Menschenalter** nt generation; **Menschenfeind** m misanthrope; **menschenfreundlich** adj philanthropical; **Menschengedenken** nt: **der kälteste Winter seit Menschengedenken** the coldest winter in living memory; **Menschenhandel** m slave trade; (Jur) trafficking in human beings; **Menschenkenner** m judge of human nature; **Menschenkenntnis** f knowledge of human nature; **menschenleer** adj deserted; **Menschenliebe** f philanthropy; **Menschenmasse** f crowd (of people); **Menschenmenge** f crowd (of people); **menschenmöglich** adj humanly possible; **Menschenrechte** pl human rights pl; **menschenscheu** adj shy; **Menschenschlag** (umg) m kind of people; **Menschenseele** f: **keine Menschenseele** (fig) not a soul

Menschenskind interj good heavens!

Menschen- zW: **menschenunwürdig** adj degrading; **Menschenverachtung** f contempt for human beings od of mankind; **Menschenverstand** m: **gesunder Menschenverstand** common sense; **Menschenwürde** f human dignity; **menschenwürdig** adj (Behandlung) humane; (Unterkunft) fit for human habitation

Mensch- zW: **Menschheit** f humanity, mankind; **menschlich** adj human; (human) humane; **Menschlichkeit** f humanity

Menstruation [mɛnstruatsi'o:n] f menstruation

Mentalität [mentali'tɛ:t] f mentality

Menü [me'ny:] (-s, -s) nt (auch Comput) menu; **Menüführung** f (Comput) menu assistance; **menügesteuert** adj (Comput) menu-driven

Merkblatt nt instruction sheet od leaflet

merken ['mɛrkən] vt to notice; **sich** dat **etw ~** to remember sth; **sich** dat **eine Autonummer ~** to make a (mental) note of a licence (Brit) od license (US) number

merklich adj noticeable

Merkmal nt sign, characteristic

merkwürdig adj odd

meschugge [me'ʃʊgə] (umg) adj nuts, meshuga (US)

Mess- zW: **Messband** nt tape measure; **messbar** adj measurable; **Messbecher** m measuring cup

Messbuch nt missal

Messdiener m (Rel) server, acolyte (form)

Messe ['mɛsə] (-, -n) f fair; (Eccl) mass; (Mil) mess; **auf der ~** at the fair; **Messegelände** nt exhibition centre (Brit) od center (US)

messen unreg vt to measure ▷ vr to compete

Messer (-s, -) nt knife; **auf des ~s Schneide stehen** (fig) to hang in the balance; **jdm**

ins offene ~ laufen (fig) to walk into a trap; **messerscharf** adj (fig): **messerscharf schließen** to conclude with incredible logic (ironisch); **Messerspitze** f knife point; (in Rezept) pinch; **Messerstecherei** f knife fight
Messestadt f (town with an) exhibition centre (Brit) od center (US)
Messstand m exhibition stand
Messgerät nt measuring device, gauge
Messgewand nt chasuble
Messing ['mεsɪŋ] (-s) nt brass
Messstab m (Aut: Ölmessstab etc) dipstick
Messung f (das Messen) measuring; (von Blutdruck) taking; (Messergebnis) measurement
Messwert m measurement; (Ableseergebnis) reading
Metall [me'tal] (-s, -e) nt metal; **die ~ verarbeitende Industrie** the metal-processing industry; **metallen** adj metallic; **metallisch** adj metallic
Metallurgie [metalʊr'giː] f metallurgy
Metapher [me'tafər] (-, -n) f metaphor
metaphorisch [meta'foːrɪʃ] adj metaphorical
Metaphysik [metafy'ziːk] f metaphysics sing
Metastase [meta'staːzə] (-, -n) f (Med) secondary growth
Meteor [mete'oːr] (-s, -e) m meteor
Meteorologe [meteoro'loːgə] (-n, -n) m meteorologist
Meter ['meːtər] (-s, -) m od nt metre (Brit), meter (US); **in 500 ~ Höhe** at a height of 500 metres; **Metermaß** nt tape measure; **Meterware** f (Textil) piece goods
Methode [me'toːdə] (-, -n) f method
Methodik [me'toːdɪk] f methodology
methodisch [me'toːdɪʃ] adj methodical
Metier [meti'eː] (-s, -s) nt (hum) job, profession
metrisch ['meːtrɪʃ] adj metric, metrical
Metropole [metro'poːlə] (-, -n) f metropolis
Mettwurst ['mεtvʊrst] f (smoked) sausage
Metzger ['mεtsgər] (-s, -) m butcher
Metzgerei [mεtsgə'raɪ] f butcher's (shop)
Meuchelmord ['mɔʏçəlmɔrt] m assassination
Meute ['mɔʏtə] (-, -n) f pack
Meuterei [mɔʏtə'raɪ] f mutiny
meutern vi to mutiny
Mexikaner, in [mεksi'kaːnər(ɪn)] (-s, -) m(f) Mexican
mexikanisch adj Mexican
Mexiko ['mεksiko] (-s) nt Mexico
MEZ abk (= mitteleuropäische Zeit) C.E.T.
MFG abk = **Mitfahrgelegenheit**
MfG abk (= mit freundlichen Grüßen) (with) best wishes
MG (-(s), -(s)) nt abk = **Maschinengewehr**
mg abk (= Milligramm) mg
mhd. abk (= mittelhochdeutsch) MHG
MHz abk (= Megahertz) MHz
Mi. abk = **Mittwoch**
miauen [mi'aʊən] vi to miaow
mich [mɪç] akk von **ich** ▷ pron me; (reflexiv) myself
mickerig ['mɪkərɪç], **mickrig** ['mɪkrɪç] (umg)

adj pathetic; (altes Männchen) puny
mied etc [miːt] vb siehe **meiden**
Miederwaren ['miːdərvaːrən] pl corsetry sing
Mief [miːf] (-s) (umg) m fug; (muffig) stale air; (Gestank) stink, pong (Brit)
miefig (umg) adj smelly, pongy (Brit)
Miene ['miːnə] (-, -n) f look, expression; **gute ~ zum bösen Spiel machen** to grin and bear it
Mienenspiel nt facial expressions pl
mies [miːs] (umg) adj lousy
Miese ['miːzə] (umg) pl: **in den ~n sein** to be in the red
Miesmacher, in (umg) m(f) killjoy
Mietauto nt hired car (Brit), rental car (US)
Miete ['miːtə] (-, -n) f rent; **zur ~ wohnen** to live in rented accommodation od accommodations (US)
mieten vt to rent; (Auto) to hire (Brit), rent
Mieter, in (-s, -) m(f) tenant; **Mieterschutz** m rent control
Mietshaus nt tenement, block of flats (Brit) od apartments (US)
Miet- zW: **Mietverhältnis** nt tenancy; **Mietvertrag** m tenancy agreement; **Mietwagen** m = **Mietauto**; **Mietwucher** m the charging of exorbitant rent(s)
Mieze ['miːtsə] (-, -n) (umg) f (Katze) pussy; (Mädchen) chick, bird (Brit)
Migräne [mi'grɛːnə] (-, -n) f migraine
migrieren [mi'griːrən] vi to migrate
Mikado [mi'kaːdo] (-s) nt (Spiel) pick-a-stick
Mikro- ['miːkro] in zW micro-
Mikrobe [mi'kroːbə] (-, -n) f microbe
Mikro- zW: **Mikrochip** m microchip; **Mikrocomputer** m microcomputer; **Mikrofiche** m od nt microfiche; **Mikrofilm** m microfilm
Mikrofon [mikro'foːn] (-s, e) nt microphone
Mikroökonomie f microeconomics pl
Mikrophon [mikro'foːn] (-s, -e) nt microphone
Mikroprozessor (-s, -oren) m microprocessor
Mikroskop [mikro'skoːp] (-s, -e) nt microscope; **mikroskopisch** adj microscopic
Mikrowelle ['miːkrovεlə] f microwave
Mikrowellenherd m microwave (oven)
Milbe ['mɪlbə] (-, -n) f mite
Milch [mɪlç] (-) f milk; (Fischmilch) milt, roe; **Milchdrüse** f mammary gland; **Milchglas** nt frosted glass
milchig adj milky
Milch- zW: **Milchkaffee** m white coffee; **Milchmixgetränk** nt milk shake; **Milchpulver** nt powdered milk; **Milchstraße** f Milky Way; **Milchtüte** f milk carton; **Milchzahn** m milk tooth
mild [mɪlt] adj mild; (Richter) lenient; (freundlich) kind, charitable
Milde ['mɪldə] (-, -n) f mildness; leniency
mildern vt to mitigate, soften; (Schmerz) to alleviate; **~de Umstände** extenuating circumstances
Milieu [mili'øː] (-s, -s) nt background, environment; **milieugeschädigt** adj

m

maladjusted

militant [mili'tant] *adj* militant

Militär [mili'tɛ:r] (**-s**) *nt* military, army;
Militärdienst *m* military service;
Militäreinsatz *m* use of troops;
(*Kampfhandlung*) military action; **Militärgericht**
nt military court; **militärisch** *adj* military

Militarismus [milita'rɪsmʊs] *m* militarism

militaristisch *adj* militaristic

Militärpflicht *f* (compulsory) military service

Mill. *abk* (= *Million(en)*) m

Milli- *in zw* milli-

Milliardär, in [miliar'dɛ:r(ɪn)] (**-s, -e**) *m(f)*
multimillionaire

Milliarde [mili'ardə] (**-, -n**) *f* milliard, billion
(*bes US*); **Milliardengrab** *nt* (*fig*) money burner,
white elephant

Millimeter *m* millimetre (*Brit*), millimeter (*US*);
Millimeterpapier *nt* graph paper

Million [mili'o:n] (**-, -en**) *f* million

Millionär, in [milio'nɛ:r(ɪn)] (**-s, -e**) *m(f)*
millionaire

millionenschwer (*umg*) *adj* worth a few
million

Milz [mɪlts] (**-, -en**) *f* spleen

Mimik ['mi:mɪk] *f* mime

Mimose [mi'mo:zə] (**-, -n**) *f* mimosa; (*fig*)
sensitive person

minder ['mɪndər] *adj* inferior ▷ *adv* less;
minderbegabt *adj* less able; **minderbemittelt**
adj: **geistig minderbemittelt** (*ironisch*)
intellectually challenged

Minderheit *f* minority

Minderheitsbeteiligung *f* (*Aktien*) minority
interest

Minderheitsregierung *f* minority
government

minderjährig *adj* minor; **Minderjährige, r** *f(m)*
minor; **Minderjährigkeit** *f* minority

mindern *vt, vr* to decrease, diminish

minderqualifiziert *adj* less qualified;
Minderqualifizierte, r *f(m)* less qualified
person

Minderung *f* decrease

minder- *zW*: **minderwertig** *adj* inferior;
Minderwertigkeitsgefühl *nt* inferiority
complex; **Minderwertigkeitskomplex** (**-es, -e**)
m inferiority complex

Mindestalter *nt* minimum age

Mindestbetrag *m* minimum amount

mindeste, r, s *adj* least

mindestens *adv* at least

Mindest- *zW*: **Mindestlohn** *m* minimum
wage; **Mindestmaß** *nt* minimum;
Mindeststand *m* (*Comm*) minimum stock;
Mindeststudiendauer *nt* (*Österr*) minimum
length of study; **Mindestumtausch** *m*
minimum obligatory exchange

Mine ['mi:nə] (**-, -n**) *f* mine; (*Bleistiftmine*) lead;
(*Kugelschreibermine*) refill

Minenfeld *nt* minefield

Minensuchboot *nt* minesweeper

Mineral [mine'ra:l] (**-s, -e** *od* **-ien**) *nt* mineral;

mineralisch *adj* mineral; **Mineralölsteuer**
f tax on oil and petrol (*Brit*) *od* gasoline (*US*);
Mineralwasser *nt* mineral water

Miniatur [minia'tu:r] *f* miniature

Minigolf ['mɪnigɔlf] *nt* miniature golf

minimal [mini'ma:l] *adj* minimal

Minimum ['mi:nimʊm] (**-s, Minima**) *nt*
minimum

Minirock ['mɪnirɔk] *m* miniskirt

Minister, in [mi'nɪstər(ɪn)] (**-s, -**) *m(f)* (*Pol*)
minister

ministeriell [minɪsteri'ɛl] *adj* ministerial

Ministerium [minɪs'te:riʊm] *nt* ministry

Ministerpräsident, in *m(f)* prime minister

Minna ['mɪna] *f*: **jdn zur ~ machen** (*umg*) to
give sb a piece of one's mind

minus ['mi:nʊs] *adv* minus; **Minus** (**-, -**)
nt deficit; **Minuspol** *m* negative pole;
Minuszeichen *nt* minus sign

Minute [mi'nu:tə] (**-, -n**) *f* minute; **auf die ~**
(*genau od* **pünktlich**) (right) on the dot

Minutenzeiger *m* minute hand

Mio. *abk* (= *Million(en)*) m

mir [mi:r] *dat von ich* ▷ *pron* (to) me; **von ~ aus!**
I don't mind; **wie du ~, so ich dir** (*Sprichwort*)
tit for tat (*umg*); (*als Drohung*) I'll get my own
back; **~ nichts, dir nichts** just like that

Mirabelle [mira'bɛlə] *f* mirabelle, *small yellow
plum*

Misch- *zW*: **Mischbatterie** *f* mixer tap;
Mischbrot *nt* *bread made from more than one kind of
flour*; **Mischehe** *f* mixed marriage

mischen *vt* to mix; (*Comput: Datei, Text*) to
merge; (*Karten*) to shuffle ▷ *vi* (*Karten*) to
shuffle

Misch- *zW*: **Mischfinanzierung** *m* (*Wirts*) mixed
financing; **Mischkonzern** *m* conglomerate;
Mischling *m* half-caste; **Mischmasch** (*umg*) *m*
hotchpotch; (*Essen*) concoction; **Mischpult** *nt*
(*Rundf, TV*) mixing panel

Mischung *f* mixture

Mischwald *m* mixed (deciduous and
coniferous) woodland

miserabel [mizə'ra:bəl] (*umg*) *adj* lousy;
(*Gesundheit*) wretched; (*Benehmen*) dreadful

Misere [mi'ze:rə] (**-, -n**) *f* (*von Leuten, Wirtschaft
etc*) plight; (*von Hunger, Krieg etc*) misery,
miseries *pl*

Miss- *zW*: **missachten** *vt untr* to disregard;
Missachtung *f* disregard; **Missbehagen**
nt uneasiness; (*Missfallen*) discontent;
Missbildung *f* deformity; **missbilligen** *vt untr*
to disapprove of; **Missbilligung** *f* disapproval;
Missbrauch *m* abuse; (*falscher Gebrauch*)
misuse; **missbrauchen** *vt untr* to abuse; to
misuse; (*vergewaltigen*) to assault; **jdn zu** *od*
für etw missbrauchen to use sb for *od* to do
sth; **missdeuten** *vt untr* to misinterpret

missen *vt* to do without; (*Erfahrung*) to miss

Misserfolg *m* failure

Missernte *f* crop failure

Missetat ['mɪsəta:t] *f* misdeed

Missetäter *m* criminal; (*umg*) scoundrel

Miss- zW: **missfallen** unreg vi untr: **jdm missfallen** to displease sb; **Missfallen (-s)** nt displeasure; **Missgeburt** f freak; (fig) failure; **Missgeschick** nt misfortune; **missglücken** vi untr to fail; **jdm missglückt etw** sb does not succeed with sth; **missgönnen** vt untr: **jdm etw missgönnen** to (be)grudge sb sth; **Missgriff** m mistake; **Missgunst** f envy; **missgünstig** adj envious; **misshandeln** vt untr to ill-treat; **Misshandlung** f ill-treatment; **Misshelligkeit** f: **Misshelligkeiten haben** to be at variance

Mission [misi'o:n] f mission

Missionar, in [misio'na:r(in)] m(f) missionary

Missklang m discord

Misskredit m discredit

misslang etc [mis'laŋ] vb siehe **misslingen**

missliebig adj unpopular

misslingen [mis'liŋən] unreg vi untr to fail; **Misslingen (-s)** nt failure

misslungen [mis'luŋən] pp von **misslingen**

Miss- zW: **Missmut** m bad temper; **missmutig** adj cross; **missraten** unreg vi untr to turn out badly ▷ adj ill-bred; **Missstand** m deplorable state of affairs; **Missstimmung** f discord; (Missmut) ill feeling

misst vb siehe **messen**

Miss- zW: **misstrauen** vi untr to mistrust; **Misstrauen (-s)** nt: **Misstrauen (gegenüber)** distrust (of), suspicion (of); **Misstrauensantrag** m (Pol) motion of no confidence; **Misstrauensvotum** nt (Pol) vote of no confidence; **misstrauisch** adj distrustful, suspicious; **Missverhältnis** nt disproportion; **missverständlich** adj unclear; **Missverständnis** nt misunderstanding; **missverstehen** unreg vt untr to misunderstand

Misswahl ['misva:l] f beauty contest

Misswirtschaft f mismanagement

Mist [mist] **(-(e)s)** m dung; (umg) rubbish; **~!** (umg) blast!; **das ist nicht auf seinem ~ gewachsen** (umg) he didn't think that up himself

Mistel (-, -n) f mistletoe

Mist- zW: **Mistgabel** f pitchfork (used for shifting manure); **Misthaufen** m dungheap; **Miststück** (umg!) nt, **Mistvieh** (umg!) nt (Mann) bastard (!); (Frau) bitch (!)

mit [mit] präp +dat with; (mittels) by ▷ adv along, too; **~ der Bahn** by train; **~ dem nächsten Flugzeug/Bus kommen** to come on the next plane/bus; **~ Bleistift schreiben** to write in pencil; **~ Verlust** at a loss; **er ist ~ der Beste in der Gruppe** he is among the best in the group; **wie wärs ~ einem Bier?** (umg) how about a beer?; **~ 10 Jahren** at the age of 10; **wollen Sie ~?** do you want to come along?

Mitarbeit ['mit|arbait] f cooperation; **mitarbeiten** vi: **mitarbeiten (an** +dat**)** to cooperate (on), collaborate (on)

Mitarbeiter, in m(f) (an Projekt) collaborator; (Kollege) colleague; (Angestellter) member of staff ▷ pl staff; **Mitarbeiterstab** m staff

mit- zW: **mitbekommen** unreg vt to get od be given; (umg: verstehen) to get; **mitbestimmen** vi: **(bei etw) mitbestimmen** to have a say (in sth) ▷ vt to have an influence on; **Mitbestimmung** f participation in decision-making; (Pol) determination; **mitbringen** unreg vt to bring along; **Mitbringsel** ['mitbriŋzəl] **(-s, -)** nt (Geschenk) small present; (Andenken) souvenir; **Mitbürger, in** m(f) fellow citizen; **mitdenken** unreg vi to follow; **du hast ja mitgedacht!** good thinking!; **mitdürfen** unreg vi: **wir durften nicht mit** we weren't allowed to go along; **Miteigentümer** m joint owner

miteinander [mit|ai'nandər] adv together, with one another

miterleben vt to see, witness

Mitesser ['mit|ɛsər] **(-s, -)** m blackhead

mit- zW: **mitfahren** unreg vi: **(mit jdm) mitfahren** to go (with sb); (auf Reise auch) to go od travel (with sb); **Mitfahrerzentrale** f agency for arranging lifts; **Mitfahrgelegenheit** f lift; **mitfühlen** vi: **mit jdm/etw mitfühlen** to sympathize with sb/sth; **mitfühlend** adj sympathetic; **mitführen** vt (Papiere, Ware etc) to carry (with one); (Fluss) to carry along; **mitgeben** unreg vt to give; **Mitgefühl** nt sympathy; **mitgehen** unreg vi to go od come along; **etw mitgehen lassen** (umg) to pinch sth; **mitgenommen** adj done in, in a bad way; **Mitgift** f dowry

Mitglied ['mitgli:t] nt member

Mitgliedsbeitrag m membership fee, subscription

Mitgliedschaft f membership

mit- zW: **mithaben** unreg vt: **etw mithaben** to have sth (with one); **mithalten** unreg vi to keep up; **mithelfen** vi unreg to help, lend a hand; **bei etw mithelfen** to help with sth; **Mithilfe** f help, assistance; **mithören** vt to listen in to; **mitkommen** unreg vi to come along; (verstehen) to keep up, follow; **Mitläufer** m hanger-on; (Pol) fellow traveller

Mitleid nt sympathy; (Erbarmen) compassion

Mitleidenschaft f: **in ~ ziehen** to affect

mitleidig adj sympathetic

mitleidslos adj pitiless, merciless

mit- zW: **mitmachen** vt to join in, take part in; (umg: einverstanden sein): **da macht mein Chef nicht mit** my boss won't go along with that; **Mitmensch** m fellow man; **mitmischen** (umg) vi (sich beteiligen): **mitmischen (in** +dat od **bei)** to be involved (in); (sich einmischen) to interfere (in); **mitnehmen** unreg vt to take along od away; (anstrengen) to wear out, exhaust; **mitgenommen aussehen** to look the worse for wear; **mitreden** vi (Meinung äußern): **(bei etw) mitreden** to join in (sth); (mitbestimmen) to have a say (in sth) ▷ vt: **Sie haben hier nichts mitzureden** this is none of your concern; **mitreißen** vt unreg to sweep away; (fig: begeistern) to carry away; **mitreißend** adj (Rhythmus) infectious; (Reden) rousing; (Film,

m

227

Fußballspiel) thrilling, exciting
mitsamt [mɪtˈtsamt] *präp +dat* together with
mitschneiden *vt unreg* to record
Mitschnitt [ˈmɪtʃnɪt] **(-(e)s, -e)** *m* recording
mitschreiben *unreg vt* to write *od* take down ▷ *vi*
to take notes
Mitschuld *f* complicity
mitschuldig *adj:* ~ **(an** +*dat)* implicated (in); *(an
Unfall)* partly responsible (for)
Mitschuldige, r *f(m)* accomplice
mit- *zW:* **Mitschüler, in** *m(f)* schoolmate;
mitspielen *vi* to join in, take part; **er hat ihr
übel** *od* **hart mitgespielt** *(Schaden zufügen)*
he has treated her badly; **Mitspieler, in** *m(f)*
partner; **Mitspracherecht** *nt* voice, say
Mittag [ˈmɪtaːk] **(-(e)s, -e)** *m* midday, noon,
lunchtime; **morgen** ~ tomorrow at lunchtime
od noon; ~ **machen** to take one's lunch hour;
(zu) ~ **essen** to have lunch; **Mittagessen** *nt*
lunch, dinner
mittags *adv* at lunchtime *od* noon
Mittags- *zW:* **Mittagspause** *f* lunch break;
Mittagsruhe *f* period of quiet (after lunch);
(in Geschäft) midday closing; **Mittagsschlaf**
m early afternoon nap, siesta; **Mittagszeit**
f: **während** *od* **in der Mittagszeit** at
lunchtime
Mittäter, in [ˈmɪttɛːtər(ɪn)] *m(f)* accomplice
Mitte [ˈmɪtə] **(-, -n)** *f* middle; **aus unserer** ~
from our midst
mitteilen [ˈmɪttaɪlən] *vt:* **jdm etw** ~ to inform
sb of sth, communicate sth to sb ▷ *vr:* **sich
(jdm)** ~ to communicate (with sb)
mitteilsam *adj* communicative
Mitteilung *f* communication; **jdm (eine)** ~
von etw machen *(form)* to inform sb of sth;
(bekannt geben) to announce sth to sb
Mitteilungsbedürfnis *nt* need to talk to other
people
Mittel [ˈmɪtəl] **(-s, -)** *nt* means; *(Methode)*
method; *(Math)* average; *(Med)* medicine;
kein ~ **unversucht lassen** to try everything;
als letztes ~ as a last resort; **ein** ~ **zum
Zweck** a means to an end; **Mittelalter** *nt*
Middle Ages *pl;* **mittelalterlich** *adj* medieval;
Mittelamerika *nt* Central America (and the
Caribbean); **mittelamerikanisch** *adj* Central
American; **mittelbar** *adj* indirect; **Mittelding**
nt (Mischung) cross; **Mitteleuropa** *nt* Central
Europe; **Mitteleuropäer, in** *m(f)* Central
European; **mitteleuropäisch** *adj* Central
European; **mittelfristig** *adj (Finanzplanung,
Kredite)* medium-term; **Mittelgebirge** *nt* low
mountain range; **mittelgroß** *adj* medium-
sized; **mittellos** *adj* without means;
Mittelmaß *nt:* **das (gesunde) Mittelmaß** the
happy medium; **mittelmäßig** *adj* mediocre,
middling; **Mittelmäßigkeit** *f* mediocrity;
Mittelmeer *nt* Mediterranean (Sea);
mittelprächtig *adj* not bad; **Mittelpunkt** *m*
centre *(Brit),* center *(US);* **im Mittelpunkt
stehen** to be centre-stage
mittels *präp +gen* by means of

Mittelschicht *f* middle class
Mittelsmann (-(e)s, *pl* **Mittelsmänner** *od*
Mittelsleute) *m* intermediary
Mittel- *zW:* **Mittelstand** *m* middle class;
Mittelstreckenrakete *f* medium-range
missile; **Mittelstreifen** *m* central reservation
(Brit), median strip *(US);* **Mittelstufe** *f (Sch)*
middle school *(Brit),* junior high *(US);*
Mittelstürmer *m* centre forward; **Mittelweg**
m middle course; **Mittelwelle** *f (Rundf)*
medium wave; **Mittelwert** *m* average value,
mean
mitten [ˈmɪtən] *adv* in the middle; ~ **auf der
Straße/in der Nacht** in the middle of the
street/night; **mittendrin** *adv* (right) in the
middle of it; **mittendurch** *adv* (right) through
the middle
Mitternacht [ˈmɪtərnaxt] *f* midnight
mittlere, r, s [ˈmɪtlərə(r, s)] *adj* middle;
(durchschnittlich) medium, average; **der M~
Osten** the Middle East; **~s Management**
middle management; ~ **Reife**; *see culture note*

mittlerweile [ˈmɪtlərvaɪlə] *adv* meanwhile
Mittwoch [ˈmɪtvɔx] **(-(e)s, -e)** *m* Wednesday;
siehe auch **Dienstag**
mittwochs *adv* on Wednesdays
mitunter [mɪtˈʔʊntər] *adv* occasionally,
sometimes
mit- *zW:* **mitverantwortlich** *adj* also
responsible; **mitverdienen** *vi* to (go out to)
work as well; **Mitverfasser** *m* co-author;
Mitverschulden *nt* contributory negligence;
mitwirken *vi:* **(bei etw) mitwirken** to
contribute (to sth); *(Theat)* to take part (in
sth); **Mitwirkende, r** *f(m):* **die Mitwirkenden**
(Theat) the cast; **Mitwirkung** *f* contribution;
participation; **unter Mitwirkung von** with
the help of; **Mitwisser (-s, -)** *m:* **Mitwisser
(einer Sache** *gen)* **sein** to be in the know
(about sth); **jdn zum Mitwisser machen** to
tell sb (all) about it
Mixer [ˈmɪksər] **(-s, -)** *m (Barmixer)* cocktail
waiter; *(Küchenmixer)* blender; *(Rührmaschine,
Rundf, TV)* mixer
ml *abk (= Milliliter)* ml
mm *abk (= Millimeter)* mm
MMS® *m (= Multimedia Messaging Service)* MMS
Mnemonik [mneˈmoːnɪk] *f* mnemonic
Mo. *abk* = **Montag**
mobben [ˈmɔbən] *vt* to bully (at work)
Mobbing [ˈmɔbɪŋ] **(-s)** *nt* workplace bullying
Möbel [ˈmøːbəl] **(-s, -)** *nt* (piece of) furniture;

Möbelpacker m removal man (Brit), (furniture) mover (US); **Möbelwagen** m furniture od removal van (Brit), moving van (US)

mobil [mo'biːl] adj mobile; (Internet, Tel) ~e **Internetnutzung** mobile internet use; ~es **Internet** mobile web; (Mil) mobilized

Mobilfunk m cellular telephone service

Mobiliar [mobili'aːr] (-s, -e) nt movable assets pl

mobilisieren [mobili'ziːrən] vt (Mil) to mobilize

Mobilmachung f mobilization

Mobiltelefon nt (Telec) mobile phone

möbl. abk = **möbliert**

möblieren [mø'bliːrən] vt to furnish; **möbliert wohnen** to live in furnished accommodation

mochte etc ['mɔxtə] vb siehe **mögen**

Möchtegern- ['mœçtəgɛrn] in zw (ironisch) would-be

Modalität [modali'tɛːt] f (von Plan, Vertrag etc) arrangement

Mode ['moːdə] (-, -n) f fashion; **Modefarbe** f in colour (Brit) od color (US); **Modeheft** nt fashion magazine; **Modejournal** nt fashion magazine

Modell [mo'dɛl] (-s, -e) nt model; **Modelleisenbahn** f model railway; (als Spielzeug) train set; **Modellfall** m textbook case

modellieren [modɛ'liːrən] vt to model

Modellversuch m (bes Sch) pilot scheme

Modem ['moːdɛm] (-s, -s) nt (Comput) modem

Modenschau f fashion show

Modepapst m high priest of fashion

Moder ['moːdər] (-s) m mustiness; (Schimmel) mildew

moderat [mode'raːt] adj moderate

Moderator, in [mode'raːtɔr, -a'toːrɪn] m(f) presenter

moderieren [mode'riːrən] vt, vi (Rundf, TV) to present

modern [mo'dɛrn] adj modern; (modisch) fashionable

modernisieren [modɛrni'ziːrən] vt to modernize

Mode- zW: **Modeschmuck** m fashion jewellery (Brit) od jewelry (US); **Modeschöpfer, in** m(f) fashion designer; **Modewort** nt fashionable word

modifizieren [modifi'tsiːrən] vt to modify

modisch ['moːdɪʃ] adj fashionable

Modul ['moːdʊl] (-s, -n) nt (Comput) module

Modus ['moːdʊs] (-, Modi) m way; (Gram) mood; (Comput) mode

Mofa ['moːfa] (-s, -s) nt (= Motorfahrrad) small moped

Mogadischu (-s) [moga'dɪʃu] nt Mogadishu

mogeln ['moːgəln] (umg) vi to cheat

 SCHLÜSSELWORT

mögen ['møːgən] (pt **mochte**, pp **gemocht** od (als Hilfsverb) **mögen**) vt, vi to like; **magst du/mögen Sie ihn?** do you like him?; **ich möchte ...** I would like ..., I'd like ...; **er möchte in die Stadt** he'd like to go into town; **ich möchte nicht, dass du ...** I wouldn't like you to ...; **ich mag nicht mehr** I've had enough; (bin am Ende) I can't take any more; **man möchte meinen, dass ...** you would think that ...

▷ hilfsverb to like to; (wollen) to want; **möchtest du etwas essen?** would you like something to eat?; **sie mag nicht bleiben** she doesn't want to stay; **das mag wohl sein** that may very well be; **was mag das heißen?** what might that mean?; **Sie möchten zu Hause anrufen** could you please call home?

möglich ['møːklɪç] adj possible; **er tat sein M~stes** he did his utmost

möglicherweise adv possibly

Möglichkeit f possibility; **nach ~** if possible

möglichst adv as ... as possible

Mohikaner [mohi'kaːnər] (-s, -) m: **der letzte ~** (hum: umg) the very last one

Mohn [moːn] (-(e)s, -e) m (Mohnblume) poppy; (Mohnsamen) poppy seed

Möhre ['møːrə] (-, -n) f carrot

Mohrenkopf ['moːrənkɔpf] m chocolate-covered marshmallow

Mohrrübe f carrot

mokieren [mo'kiːrən] vr: **sich über etw** akk ~ to make fun of sth

Mokka ['mɔka] (-s) m mocha, strong coffee

Moldau ['mɔldau] f: **die ~** the Vltava

Moldawien [mɔl'daːviən] (-s) nt Moldavia

moldawisch adj Moldavian

Mole ['moːlə] (-, -n) f (Naut) mole

Molekül [mole'kyːl] (-s, -e) nt molecule

molk etc [mɔlk] vb siehe **melken**

Molkerei [mɔlkə'raɪ] f dairy; **Molkereibutter** f blended butter

Moll [mɔl] (-, -) nt (Mus) minor (key)

mollig adj cosy; (dicklich) plump

Molotowcocktail ['moːlotɔfkɔkteːl] m Molotov cocktail

Moment [mo'mɛnt] (-(e)s, -e) m moment ▷ nt factor, element; **im ~** at the moment; **~ mal!** just a minute!; **im ersten ~** for a moment

momentan [momɛn'taːn] adj momentary ▷ adv at the moment

Monaco [mo'nako, 'moːnako] (-s) nt Monaco

Monarch [mo'narç] (-en, -en) m monarch

Monarchie [monar'çiː] f monarchy

Monat ['moːnat] (-(e)s, -e) m month; **sie ist im sechsten ~ (schwanger)** she's five months pregnant; **was verdient er im ~?** how much does he earn a month?

monatelang adv for months

monatlich adj monthly

Monats- zW: **Monatsblutung** f menstrual period; **Monatskarte** f monthly ticket; **Monatsrate** f monthly instalment (Brit) od installment (US)

Mönch [mœnç] (-(e)s, -e) m monk

Mond [moːnt] (**-(e)s, -e**) *m* moon; **auf** *od*
hinter dem ~ leben (*umg*) to be behind
the times; **Mondfähre** *f* lunar (excursion)
module; **Mondfinsternis** *f* eclipse of the
moon; **mondhell** *adj* moonlit; **Mondlandung**
f moon landing; **Mondschein** *m* moonlight;
Mondsonde *f* moon probe

Monegasse [mone'gasə] (**-n, -n**) *m*
Monegasque

Monegassin [mone'gasɪn] *f* Monegasque

monegassisch *adj* Monegasque

Monetarismus [moneta'rɪsmʊs] *m* (*Econ*)
monetarism

Monetarist *m* monetarist

Moneten [mo'neːtən] (*umg*) *pl* (*Geld*) bread *sing*,
dough *sing*

Mongole [mɔŋ'goːlə] (**-n, -n**) *m* Mongolian,
Mongol

Mongolei [mɔŋgo'laɪ] *f*: **die ~** Mongolia

Mongolin *f* Mongolian, Mongol

mongolisch [mɔŋ'goːlɪʃ] *adj* Mongolian

mongoloid [mɔŋgolo'iːt] *adj* (*Med*) mongoloid

monieren [mo'niːrən] *vt* to complain about ▷ *vi*
to complain

Monitor ['moːnitɔr] *m* (*Bildschirm*) monitor

Mono- [mono] *in zw* mono

monogam [mono'gaːm] *adj* monogamous

Monogamie [monoga'miː] *f* monogamy

Monolog [mono'loːk] (**-s, -e**) *m* monologue

Monopol (**-s, -e**) *nt* monopoly

monopolisieren [monopoli'ziːrən] *vt* to
monopolize

Monopolstellung *f* monopoly

monoton [mono'toːn] *adj* monotonous

Monotonie [monoto'niː] *f* monotony

Monstrum ['mɔnstrʊm] (**-s, Monstren**) *nt* (*lit,
fig*) monster; **ein ~ von einem/einer** ... a
hulking great ...

Monsun [mɔn'zuːn] (**-s, -e**) *m* monsoon

Montag ['moːntaːk] (**-(e)s, -e**) *m* Monday; *siehe
auch* **Dienstag**

Montage [mɔn'taːʒə] (**-, -n**) *f* (*Phot etc*)
montage; (*Tech*) assembly; (*Einbauen*) fitting

montags *adv* on Mondays

Montanindustrie [mɔn'taːnɪndʊstriː] *f* coal
and steel industry

Montblanc [mõ'blãː] *m* Mont Blanc

Monte Carlo ['mɔntə 'karlo] (**-s**) *nt* Monte
Carlo

Montenegro [mɔnte'neːgro] (**-s**) *nt*
Montenegro

Monteur [mɔn'tøːr] *m* fitter, assembly man

montieren [mɔn'tiːrən] *vt* to assemble, set up

Montur [mɔn'tuːr] (*umg*) *f* (*Spezialkleidung*) gear,
rig-out

Monument [monu'mɛnt] *nt* monument

monumental [monumɛn'taːl] *adj*
monumental

Moor [moːr] (**-(e)s, -e**) *nt* moor; **Moorbad** *nt*
mud bath

Moos [moːs] (**-es, -e**) *nt* moss

Moped ['moːpɛt] (**-s, -s**) *nt* moped

Mops [mɔps] (**-es, ̈-e**) *m* (*Hund*) pug

Moral [mo'raːl] (**-, -en**) *f* morality; (*einer
Geschichte*) moral; (*Disziplin: von Volk, Soldaten*)
morale; **Moralapostel** *m* upholder of moral
standards; **moralisch** *adj* moral; **einen** *od* **den
moralischen haben** (*umg*) to have (a fit of)
the blues

Moräne [mo'rɛːnə] (**-, -n**) *f* moraine

Morast [mo'rast] (**-(e)s, -e**) *m* morass, mire

morastig *adj* boggy

Mord [mɔrt] (**-(e)s, -e**) *m* murder; **dann gibt es
~ und Totschlag** (*umg*) there'll be hell to pay;
Mordanschlag *m* murder attempt

Mörder ['mœrdər] (**-s, -**) *m* murderer; **Mörderin**
f murderess

mörderisch *adj* (*fig: schrecklich*) dreadful,
terrible; (*Preise*) exorbitant; (*Konkurrenzkampf*)
cut-throat ▷ *adv* (*umg: entsetzlich*) dreadfully,
terribly

Mordkommission *f* murder squad

Mords- *zW*: **Mordsding** (*umg*) *nt* whopper;
Mordsglück (*umg*) *nt* amazing luck; **Mordskerl**
(*umg*) *m* (*verwegen*) hell of a guy; **mordsmäßig**
(*umg*) *adj* terrific, enormous; **Mordsschreck**
(*umg*) *m* terrible fright

Mord- *zW*: **Mordverdacht** *m* suspicion of
murder; **Mordversuch** *m* murder attempt;
Mordwaffe *f* murder weapon

morgen ['mɔrgən] *adv* tomorrow; **bis ~!** see
you tomorrow!; **~ in acht Tagen** a week
(from) tomorrow; **~ um diese Zeit** this
time tomorrow; **~ früh** tomorrow morning;
Morgen (**-s, -**) *m* morning; (*Maß*) ≈ acre; **am
Morgen** in the morning; **guten Morgen!**
good morning!

Morgen- *zW*: **Morgengrauen** *nt* dawn,
daybreak; **Morgenmantel** *m* dressing gown;
Morgenrock *m* dressing gown; **Morgenrot** *nt*,
Morgenröte *f* dawn

morgens *adv* in the morning; **von ~ bis
abends** from morning to night

Morgenstunde *f*: **Morgenstund(e) hat Gold
im Mund(e)** (*Sprichwort*) the early bird catches
the worm (*Sprichwort*)

morgig ['mɔrgɪç] *adj* tomorrow's; **der ~e Tag**
tomorrow

Morphium ['mɔrfiʊm] *nt* morphine

morsch [mɔrʃ] *adj* rotten

Morsealphabet ['mɔrzəʔalfabeːt] *nt* Morse
code

morsen *vi* to send a message by Morse code

Mörser ['mœrzər] (**-s, -**) *m* mortar (*auch Mil*)

Mörtel ['mœrtəl] (**-s, -**) *m* mortar

Mosaik [moza'iːk] (**-s, -en** *od* **-e**) *nt* mosaic

Mosambik [mosam'biːk] (**-s**) *nt* Mozambique

Moschee [mɔ'ʃeː] (**-, -n**) *f* mosque

Mosel¹ ['moːzəl] *f* (*Geog*) Moselle

Mosel² (**-s, -**) *m* (*auch*: **Moselwein**) Moselle
(wine)

mosern ['moːzərn] (*umg*) *vi* to gripe, bellyache

Moskau ['mɔskaʊ] (**-s**) *nt* Moscow

Moskauer *adj* Moscow *attrib*

Moskauer, in (**-s, -**) *m(f)* Muscovite

Moskito [mɔs'kiːto] (**-s, -s**) *m* mosquito

Moslem ['mɔslɛm] (**-s, -s**) *m* Muslim
moslemisch [mɔs'le:mɪʃ] *adj* Muslim
Most [mɔst] (**-(e)s, -e**) *m* (unfermented) fruit juice; (*Apfelwein*) cider
Motel [mo'tel] (**-s, -s**) *nt* motel
Motiv [mo'ti:f] (**-s, -e**) *nt* motive; (*Mus*) theme
Motivation [motivatsi'o:n] *f* motivation
motivieren [moti'vi:rən] *vt* to motivate
Motivierung *f* motivation
Motor ['mo:tɔr] (**-s, -en**) *m* engine; (*bes Elek*) motor; **Motorboot** *nt* motorboat
Motorenöl *nt* engine oil
Motorhaube *f* (*Aut*) bonnet (*Brit*), hood (*US*)
motorisch *adj* (*Physiologie*) motor *attrib*
motorisieren [motori'zi:rən] *vt* to motorize
Motor- *zW*: **Motorrad** *nt* motorcycle; **Motorradfahrer** *m* motorcyclist; **Motorroller** *m* motor scooter; **Motorschaden** *m* engine trouble *od* failure; **Motorsport** *m* motor sport
Motte ['mɔtə] (**-, -n**) *f* moth
Motten- *zW*: **mottenfest** *adj* mothproof; **Mottenkiste** *f*: **etw aus der Mottenkiste hervorholen** (*fig*) to dig sth out; **Mottenkugel** *f* mothball
Motto ['mɔto] (**-s, -s**) *nt* motto
motzen ['mɔtsən] (*umg*) *vi* to grouse, beef
Mountainbike *nt* mountain bike
Möwe ['møːvə] (**-, -n**) *f* seagull
MP (**-**) *f abk* = **Maschinenpistole**
MP3 *abk* (*Comput*) MP3
MP3-Spieler *m* (*Comput*) MP3 player
Mrd. *abk* = **Milliarde(n)**
MS *abk* (= *Motorschiff*) motor vessel, MV; (= *multiple Sklerose*) MS
MTA (**-, -s**) *f abk* (= *medizinisch-technische Assistentin*) medical assistant
mtl. *abk* = **monatlich**
Mucke ['mʊkə] (**-, -n**) *f* (*meist pl*) caprice; (*von Ding*) snag, bug; **seine ~n haben** to be temperamental
Mücke ['mʏkə] (**-, -n**) *f* midge, gnat; **aus einer ~ einen Elefanten machen** (*umg*) to make a mountain out of a molehill
Muckefuck ['mʊkəfʊk] (**-s**) (*umg*) *m* coffee substitute
mucken *vi*: **ohne zu ~** without a murmur
Mückenstich *m* midge *od* gnat bite
Mucks [mʊks] (**-es, e**) *m*: **keinen ~ sagen** not to make a sound; (*nicht widersprechen*) not to say a word
mucksen (*umg*) *vr* to budge; (*Laut geben*) to open one's mouth
mucksmäuschenstill ['mʊks'mɔʏsçənʃtɪl] (*umg*) *adj* (as) quiet as a mouse
müde ['myːdə] *adj* tired; **nicht ~ werden, etw zu tun** never to tire of doing something
Müdigkeit ['myːdɪçkaɪt] *f* tiredness; **nur keine ~ vorschützen!** (*umg*) don't (you) tell me you're tired!
Muff [mʊf] (**-(e)s, -e**) *m* (*Handwärmer*) muff
Muffel (**-s, -**) (*umg*) *m* killjoy, sourpuss
muffig *adj* (*Luft*) musty
Mühe ['myːə] (**-, -n**) *f* trouble, pains *pl*; **mit**

Müh(e) und Not with great difficulty; **sich** *dat* **~ geben** to go to a lot of trouble; **mühelos** *adj* effortless, easy
muhen ['muːən] *vi* to low, moo
mühevoll *adj* laborious, arduous
Mühle ['myːlə] (**-, -n**) *f* mill; (*Kaffeemühle*) grinder; (*Mühlespiel*) nine men's morris
Mühlrad *nt* millwheel
Mühlstein *m* millstone
Mühsal (**-, -e**) *f* tribulation
mühsam *adj* arduous, troublesome ▷ *adv* with difficulty
mühselig *adj* arduous, laborious
Mulatte [mu'latə] (**-, -n**) *m* mulatto
Mulattin *f* mulatto
Mulde ['mʊldə] (**-, -n**) *f* hollow, depression
Mull [mʊl] (**-(e)s, -e**) *m* thin muslin
Müll [mʏl] (**-(e)s**) *m* refuse, rubbish, garbage (*US*); **Müllabfuhr** *f* refuse *od* garbage (*US*) collection; (*Leute*) dustmen *pl* (*Brit*), garbage collectors *pl* (*US*); **Müllabladeplatz** *m* rubbish dump; **Müllbeutel** *m* bin liner (*Brit*), trashcan liner (*US*)
Mullbinde *f* gauze bandage
Mülldeponie *f* waste disposal site, rubbish tip
Mülleimer *m* rubbish bin (*Brit*), garbage can (*US*)
Müller (**-s, -**) *m* miller
Müll- *zW*: **Müllhalde** *f*, **Müllhaufen** *m* rubbish *od* garbage (*US*) heap; **Müllmann** (**-(e)s, *pl* Müllmänner**) (*umg*) *m* dustman (*Brit*), garbage collector (*US*); **Müllsack** *m* rubbish *od* garbage (*US*) bag; **Müllschlucker** *m* waste (*Brit*) *od* garbage (*US*) disposal unit; **Mülltonne** *f* dustbin (*Brit*), trashcan (*US*); **Müllverbrennung** *f* rubbish *od* garbage (*US*) incineration; **Müllverbrennungsanlage** *f* incinerator, incinerating plant; **Müllwagen** *m* dustcart (*Brit*), garbage truck (*US*)
mulmig ['mʊlmɪç] *adj* rotten; (*umg*) uncomfortable; **jdm ist ~** sb feels funny
Multi ['mʊlti] (**-s, -s**) (*umg*) *m* multinational (organization)
multi- *in zw* multi; **multilateral** *adj*: **multilateraler Handel** multilateral trade; **multinational** *adj* multinational; **multinationaler Konzern** multinational organization
multiple Sklerose [mʊl'ti:plə skle'ro:zə] *f* multiple sclerosis
multiplizieren [mʊltipli'tsi:rən] *vt* to multiply
Mumie ['mu:miə] *f* (*Leiche*) mummy
Mumm [mʊm] (**-s**) (*umg*) *m* gumption, nerve
Mumps [mʊmps] (**-**) *m od f* mumps *sing*
München ['mʏnçən] *nt* Munich
Münchener, Münchner, in (**-s, -**) *m(f)* person from Munich
Mund [mʊnt] (**-(e)s, ̈er**) *m* mouth; **den ~ aufmachen** (*fig*: *seine Meinung sagen*) to speak up; **sie ist nicht auf den ~ gefallen** (*umg*) she's never at a loss for words; **Mundart** *f* dialect
Mündel ['mʏndəl] (**-s, -**) *nt* (*Jur*) ward

m

münden ['mʏndən] *vi*: **in etw** *akk* ~ to flow into sth

Mund- *zW*: **mundfaul** *adj* uncommunicative; **mundgerecht** *adj* bite-sized; **Mundgeruch** *m* bad breath; **Mundharmonika** *f* mouth organ

mündig ['mʏndɪç] *adj* of age; **Mündigkeit** *f* majority

mündlich ['mʏntlɪç] *adj* oral; **~e Prüfung** oral (exam); **~e Verhandlung** (*Jur*) hearing; **alles Weitere ~!** let's talk about it more when I see you

Mund- *zW*: **Mundraub** *m* (*Jur*) theft of food for personal consumption; **Mundstück** *nt* mouthpiece; (*von Zigarette*) tip; **mundtot** *adj*: **jdn mundtot machen** to muzzle sb

Mündung ['mʏndʊŋ] *f* estuary; (*von Fluss, Rohr etc*) mouth; (*Gewehrmündung*) muzzle

Mund- *zW*: **Mundwasser** *nt* mouthwash; **Mundwerk** *nt*: **ein großes Mundwerk haben** to have a big mouth; **Mundwinkel** *m* corner of the mouth; **Mund-zu-mund-Beatmung** *f* mouth-to-mouth resuscitation

Munition [munitsi'o:n] *f* ammunition

Munitionslager *nt* ammunition dump

munkeln ['mʊŋkəln] *vi* to whisper, mutter; **man munkelt, dass ...** there's a rumour (*Brit*) *od* rumor (*US*) that ...

Münster ['mʏnstər] (**-s, -**) *nt* minster

munter ['mʊntər] *adj* lively; (*wach*) awake; (*aufgestanden*) up and about; **Munterkeit** *f* liveliness

Münzanstalt *f* mint

Münzautomat *m* slot machine

Münze ['mʏntsə] (**-, -n**) *f* coin

münzen *vt* to coin, mint; **auf jdn gemünzt sein** to be aimed at sb

Münzfernsprecher ['mʏntsfɛrnʃprɛçər] *m* callbox (*Brit*), pay phone (*US*)

Münzwechsler *m* change machine

mürb ['mʏrb], **mürbe** ['mʏrbə] *adj* (*Gestein*) crumbly; (*Holz*) rotten; (*Gebäck*) crisp; **jdn ~(e) machen** to wear sb down

Mürbeteig, Mürbteig *m* shortcrust pastry

Murmel ['mʊrməl] (**-, -n**) *f* marble

murmeln *vt, vi* to murmur, mutter

Murmeltier ['mʊrməlti:r] *nt* marmot; **schlafen wie ein ~** to sleep like a log

murren ['mʊrən] *vi* to grumble, grouse

mürrisch ['mʏrɪʃ] *adj* sullen

Mus [mu:s] (**-es, -e**) *nt* purée

Muschel ['mʊʃəl] (**-, -n**) *f* mussel; (*Muschelschale*) shell; (*Telefonmuschel*) receiver

Muse ['mu:zə] (**-, -n**) *f* muse

Museum [mu'ze:ʊm] (**-s, Museen**) *nt* museum

museumsreif *adj*: **~ sein** to be almost a museum piece

Musik [mu'zi:k] *f* music; (*Kapelle*) band

musikalisch [muzi'ka:lɪʃ] *adj* musical

Musikbox *f* jukebox

Musiker, in ['mu:zikər(ɪn)] (**-s, -**) *m(f)* musician

Musik- *zW*: **Musikhochschule** *f* music school; **Musikinstrument** *nt* musical instrument; **Musikkapelle** *f* band; **Musikstück** *nt* piece of

music; **Musikstunde** *f* music lesson

musisch ['mu:zɪʃ] *adj* artistic

musizieren [muzi'tsi:rən] *vi* to make music

Muskat [mʊs'ka:t] (**-(e)s, -e**) *m* nutmeg

Muskel ['mʊskəl] (**-s, -n**) *m* muscle; **Muskeldystrophie** *f* muscular dystrophy; **Muskelkater** *m*: **einen Muskelkater haben** to be stiff; **Muskelpaket** (*umg*) *nt* muscleman; **Muskelzerrung** (*umg*) *f* pulled muscle

Muskulatur [mʊskula'tu:r] *f* muscular system

muskulös [mʊsku'lø:s] *adj* muscular

Müsli ['my:sli] (**-s, -**) *nt* muesli

Muss [mʊs] (**-**) *nt* necessity, must

muss *vb siehe* **müssen**

Muße ['mu:sə] (**-**) *f* leisure

⊙ SCHLÜSSELWORT

müssen ['mʏsən] (*pt* **musste**, *pp* **gemusst** *od* (*als Hilfsverb*) **müssen**) *vi* **1** (*Zwang*) must (*nur im Präsens*), to have to; **ich muss es tun** I must do it, I have to do it; **ich musste es tun** I had to do it; **er muss es nicht tun** he doesn't have to do it; **muss ich?** must I?, do I have to?; **wann müsst ihr zur Schule?** when do you have to go to school?; **der Brief muss heute noch zur Post** the letter must be posted (*Brit*) *od* mailed (*US*) today; **er hat gehen müssen** he (has) had to go; **muss das sein?** is that really necessary?; **wenn es (unbedingt) sein muss** if it's absolutely necessary; **ich muss mal** (*umg*) I need to go to the loo (*Brit*) *od* bathroom (*US*)

2 (*sollen*): **das musst du nicht tun!** you oughtn't to *od* shouldn't do that; **das müsstest du eigentlich wissen** you ought to *od* you should know that; **Sie hätten ihn fragen müssen** you should have asked him

3: **es muss geregnet haben** it must have rained; **es muss nicht wahr sein** it needn't be true

Mussheirat (*umg*) *f* shotgun wedding

müßig ['my:sɪç] *adj* idle; **Müßiggang** *m* idleness

musst [mʊst] *vb siehe* **müssen**

musste etc ['mʊstə] *vb siehe* **müssen**

Muster ['mʊstər] (**-s, -**) *nt* model; (*Dessin*) pattern; (*Probe*) sample; **~ ohne Wert** free sample; **Musterbeispiel** *nt* classic example; **mustergültig** *adj* exemplary; **musterhaft** *adj* exemplary

mustern *vt* (*betrachten, Mil*) to examine; (*Truppen*) to inspect

Musterprozess *m* test case

Musterschüler *m* model pupil

Musterung *f* (*von Stoff*) pattern; (*Mil*) inspection

Mut [mu:t] *m* courage; **nur ~!** cheer up!; **jdm ~ machen** to encourage sb; **~ fassen** to pluck up courage

mutig *adj* courageous

mutlos *adj* discouraged, despondent

mutmaßen *vt untr* to conjecture ▷ *vi untr* to conjecture

mutmaßlich ['muːtmaːslɪç] *adj* presumed ▷ *adv* probably

Mutprobe *f* test of courage

Mutter¹ ['mʊtər] (-, -n) *f* (*Schraubenmutter*) nut

Mutter² ['mʊtər] (-, ⸚) *f* mother; **Mutterfreuden** *pl* the joys *pl* of motherhood; **Muttergesellschaft** *f* (*Comm*) parent company; **Mutterkuchen** *m* (*Anat*) placenta; **Mutterland** *nt* mother country; **Mutterleib** *m* womb

mütterlich ['mʏtərlɪç] *adj* motherly

mütterlicherseits *adv* on the mother's side

Mutter- *zW:* **Mutterliebe** *f* motherly love; **Muttermal** *nt* birthmark; **Muttermilch** *f* mother's milk

Mutterschaft *f* motherhood

Mutterschaftsgeld *nt* maternity benefit

Mutterschaftsurlaub *m* maternity leave

Mutter- *zW:* **Mutterschutz** *m* maternity regulations *pl*; **mutterseelenallein** *adj* all alone; **Muttersprache** *f* native language; **Muttertag** *m* Mother's Day

Mutti (-, -s) (*umg*) *f* mum(my) (*Brit*), mom(my) (*US*)

mutwillig ['muːtvɪlɪç] *adj* deliberate

Mütze ['mʏtsə] (-, -n) *f* cap

MV *f abk* (= *Mitgliederversammlung*) general meeting

MW *abk* (= *Mittelwelle*) MW

MwSt, Mw.-St. *abk* (= *Mehrwertsteuer*) VAT

mysteriös [mʏsteri'øːs] *adj* mysterious

Mystik ['mʏstɪk] *f* mysticism

Mystiker, in (-s, -) *m(f)* mystic

mystisch ['mʏstɪʃ] *adj* mystical; (*rätselhaft*) mysterious

Mythologie [mytoloˈgiː] *f* mythology

Mythos ['myːtɔs] (-, **Mythen**) *m* myth

m

Nn

N¹, n [ɛn] *nt* N, n; **N wie Nordpol** ≈ N for Nellie, N for Nan (*US*)
N² [ɛn] *abk* (= *Norden*) N
na [na] *interj* well; **na gut** (*umg*) all right, OK; **na also!** (well,) there you are (then)!; **na so was!** well, I never!; **na und?** so what?
Nabel ['naːbəl] (**-s, -**) *m* navel; **der ~ der Welt** (*fig*) the hub of the universe; **Nabelschnur** *f* umbilical cord

⊙ SCHLÜSSELWORT

nach [naːx] *präp +dat* **1** (*örtlich*) to; **nach Berlin** to Berlin; **nach links/rechts** (to the) left/right; **nach oben/hinten** up/back; **er ist schon nach London abgefahren** he has already left for London
2 (*zeitlich*) after; **einer nach dem anderen** one after the other; **nach Ihnen!** after you!; **zehn (Minuten) nach drei** ten (minutes) past *od* after (*US*) three
3 (*gemäß*) according to; **nach dem Gesetz** according to the law; **die Uhr nach dem Radio stellen** to put a clock right by the radio; **ihrer Sprache nach (zu urteilen)** judging by her language; **dem Namen nach** judging by his/her name; **nach allem, was ich weiß** as far as I know
▷ *adv*: **ihm nach!** after him!; **nach und nach** gradually, little by little; **nach wie vor** still

nachäffen ['naːxˌɛfən] *vt* to ape
nachahmen ['naːxˌaːmən] *vt* to imitate
nachahmenswert *adj* exemplary
Nachahmung *f* imitation; **etw zur ~ empfehlen** to recommend sth as an example
Nachbar, in ['naxbaːr(ɪn)] (**-s, -n**) *m(f)* neighbour (*Brit*), neighbor (*US*); **Nachbarhaus** *nt*: **im Nachbarhaus** next door; **nachbarlich** *adj* neighbourly (*Brit*), neighborly (*US*); **Nachbarschaft** *f* neighbourhood (*Brit*), neighborhood (*US*); **Nachbarstaat** *m* neighbouring (*Brit*) *od* neighboring (*US*) state
nach- *zW*: **Nachbehandlung** *f* (*Med*) follow-up treatment; **nachbestellen** *vt* to order again; **Nachbestellung** *f* (*Comm*) repeat order; **nachbeten** (*pej*: *umg*) *vt* to repeat parrot-fashion; **nachbezahlen** *vt* to pay; (*später*) to

pay later; **nachbilden** *vt* to copy; **Nachbildung** *f* imitation, copy; **nachblicken** *vi* to look *od* gaze after; **nachdatieren** *vt* to postdate
nachdem [naːxˈdeːm] *konj* after; (*weil*) since; **je ~ (ob)** it depends (whether)
nach- *zW*: **nachdenken** *unreg vi*: **über etw** *akk* **nachdenken** to think about sth; **darüber darf man gar nicht nachdenken** it doesn't bear thinking about; **Nachdenken** *nt* reflection, meditation; **nachdenklich** *adj* thoughtful, pensive; **nachdenklich gestimmt sein** to be in a thoughtful mood
Nachdruck ['naːxdrʊk] *m* emphasis; (*Typ*) reprint, reproduction; **besonderen ~ darauf legen, dass ...** to stress *od* emphasize particularly that ...
nachdrücklich ['naːxdrʏklɪç] *adj* emphatic; **~ auf etw** *dat* **bestehen** to insist firmly (up) on sth
nacheifern ['naːxˌaɪfərn] *vi*: **jdm ~** to emulate sb
nacheinander [naːxˌaɪˈnandər] *adv* one after the other; **kurz ~** shortly after each other; **drei Tage ~** three days running, three days on the trot (*umg*)
nachempfinden ['naːxˌɛmpfɪndən] *unreg vt*: **jdm etw ~** to feel sth with sb
nacherzählen ['naːxˌɛrtsɛːlən] *vt* to retell
Nacherzählung *f* reproduction (of a story)
Nachf. *abk* = **Nachfolger**
Nachfahr ['naːxfaːr] (**-en, -en**) *m* descendant
Nachfolge ['naːxfɔlɡə] *f* succession; **die/jds ~ antreten** to succeed/succeed sb
nachfolgen *vi* (*lit*): **jdm/etw ~** to follow sb/sth
nachfolgend *adj* following
Nachfolger, in (**-s, -**) *m(f)* successor
nachforschen *vt, vi* to investigate
Nachforschung *f* investigation; **~en anstellen** to make enquiries
Nachfrage ['naːxfraːɡə] *f* inquiry; (*Comm*) demand; **es besteht eine rege ~** (*Comm*) there is a great demand; **danke der ~** (*form*) thank you for your concern; (*umg*) nice of you to ask; **nachfragemäßig** *adj* according to demand
nachfragen *vi* to inquire
nach- *zW*: **nachfühlen** *vt* = **nachempfinden**; **nachfüllen** *vt* to refill; **nachgeben** *unreg vi* to give way, yield

Nachgebühr f surcharge; (Post) excess postage
Nachgeburt f afterbirth
nachgehen ['na:xge:ən] unreg vi (+dat) to follow; (erforschen) to inquire (into); (Uhr) to be slow; **einer geregelten Arbeit ~** to have a steady job
Nachgeschmack ['na:xgəʃmak] m aftertaste
nachgiebig ['na:xgi:bɪç] adj soft, accommodating; **Nachgiebigkeit** f softness
nachgrübeln ['na:xgry:bəln] vi: **über etw** akk **~** to think about sth; (sich Gedanken machen) to ponder on sth
nachgucken ['na:xgʊkən] vt, vi = **nachsehen**
nachhaken ['na:xha:kən] (umg) vi to dig deeper
Nachhall ['na:xhal] m resonance
nachhallen vi to resound
nachhaltig ['na:xhaltɪç] adj lasting; (Widerstand) persistent
nachhängen ['na:xhɛŋən] unreg vi: **seinen Erinnerungen ~** to lose o.s. in one's memories
nachhause adv home
Nachhauseweg [na:x'haʊzəve:k] m way home
nachhelfen ['na:xhɛlfən] unreg vi: **jdm ~** to help od assist sb; **er hat dem Glück ein bisschen nachgeholfen** he engineered himself a little luck
nachher [na:x'he:r] adv afterwards; **bis ~** see you later!
Nachhilfe ['na:xhɪlfə] f (auch: **Nachhilfeunterricht**) extra (private) tuition
Nachhinein ['na:xhɪnaɪn] adv: **im ~** afterwards; (rückblickend) in retrospect
Nachholbedarf m: **einen ~ an etw** dat **haben** to have a lot of sth to catch up on
nachholen ['na:xho:lən] vt to catch up with; (Versäumtes) to make up for
Nachkomme ['na:xkɔmə] (**-n, -n**) m descendant
nachkommen unreg vi to follow; (einer Verpflichtung) to fulfil; **Sie können Ihr Gepäck ~ lassen** you can have your luggage sent on (after)
Nachkommenschaft f descendants pl
Nachkriegs- ['na:xkri:ks] in zw postwar; **Nachkriegszeit** f postwar period
Nach- zW: **Nachlass** (**-es, -lässe**) m (Comm) discount, rebate; (Erbe) estate; **nachlassen** unreg vt (Strafe) to remit; (Summe) to take off; (Schulden) to cancel ▷ vi to decrease, ease off; (Sturm) to die down; (schlechter werden) to deteriorate; **er hat nachgelassen** he has got worse; **nachlässig** adj negligent, careless; **Nachlässigkeit** f negligence, carelessness; **Nachlasssteuer** f death duty; **Nachlassverwalter** m executor
nachlaufen ['na:xlaʊfən] unreg vi: **jdm ~** to run after od chase sb
nachliefern ['na:xli:fərn] vt (später liefern) to deliver at a later date; (zuzüglich liefern) to make a further delivery of
nachlösen ['na:xlø:zən] vi to pay on the train/ when one gets off; (zur Weiterfahrt) to pay the extra

nachm. abk (= nachmittags) p.m.
nachmachen ['na:xmaxən] vt to imitate, copy; (fälschen) to counterfeit; **jdm etw ~** to copy sth from sb; **das soll erst mal einer ~!** I'd like to see anyone else do that!
Nachmieter, in ['na:xmi:tər(ɪn)] m(f): **wir müssen einen ~ finden** we have to find someone to take over the flat etc
Nachmittag ['na:xmɪta:k] m afternoon; **am ~** in the afternoon; **gestern/heute ~** yesterday/ this afternoon
nachmittags adv in the afternoon
Nachmittagsvorstellung f matinée (performance)
Nachn. abk = **Nachnahme**
Nachnahme (**-, -n**) f cash on delivery (Brit), collect on delivery (US); **per ~** C.O.D.
Nachname m surname
Nachporto nt excess postage
nachprüfbar ['na:xpry:fba:r] adj verifiable
nachprüfen ['na:xpry:fən] vt to check, verify
nachrechnen ['na:xrɛçnən] vt to check
Nachrede ['na:xre:də] f: **üble ~** (Jur) defamation of character
nachreichen ['na:xraɪçən] vt to hand in later
Nachricht ['na:xrɪçt] (**-, -en**) f (piece of) news sing; (Mitteilung) message
Nachrichten pl news sing; **Nachrichtenagentur** f news agency; **Nachrichtendienst** m (Mil) intelligence service; **Nachrichtensatellit** m (tele)communications satellite; **Nachrichtensperre** f news blackout; **Nachrichtensprecher, in** m(f) newsreader; **Nachrichtentechnik** f telecommunications sing
nachrücken ['na:xrʏkən] vi to move up
Nachruf ['na:xru:f] m obituary (notice)
nachrüsten ['na:xrʏstən] vt (Kraftwerk etc) to modernize; (Auto etc) to refit; (Waffen) to keep up to date ▷ vi (Mil) to deploy new arms
nachsagen ['na:xza:gən] vt to repeat; **jdm etw ~** to say sth of sb; **das lasse ich mir nicht ~!** I'm not having that said of me!
Nachsaison ['na:xzɛzõ:] f off season
nachschenken ['na:xʃɛŋkən] vt, vi: **darf ich Ihnen noch (etwas) ~?** may I top up your glass?
nachschicken ['na:xʃɪkən] vt to forward
nachschlagen ['na:xʃla:gən] unreg vt to look up ▷ vi: **jdm ~** to take after sb
Nachschlagewerk nt reference book
Nachschlüssel m master key
nachschmeißen ['na:xʃmaɪsən] unreg (umg) vt: **das ist ja nachgeschmissen!** it's a real bargain!
Nachschrift ['na:xʃrɪft] f postscript
Nachschub ['na:xʃu:p] m supplies pl; (Truppen) reinforcements pl
nachsehen ['na:xze:ən] unreg vt (prüfen) to check ▷ vi (erforschen) to look and see; **jdm etw ~** to forgive sb sth; **jdm ~** to gaze after sb
Nachsehen nt: **das ~ haben** to be left empty-handed

nachsenden ['na:xzɛndən] *unreg vt* to send on, forward

Nachsicht ['na:xzɪçt] (-) *f* indulgence, leniency

nachsichtig *adj* indulgent, lenient

Nachsilbe ['na:xzɪlbə] *f* suffix

nachsitzen ['na:xzɪtsən] *unreg vi* (*Sch*) to be kept in

Nachsorge ['na:xzɔrgə] *f* (*Med*) aftercare

Nachspann ['na:xʃpan] *m* credits *pl*

Nachspeise ['na:xʃpaɪzə] *f* dessert, sweet (*Brit*)

Nachspiel ['na:xʃpi:l] *nt* epilogue; (*fig*) sequel

nachspionieren ['na:xʃpioni:rən] (*umg*) *vi*: **jdm ~** to spy on sb

nachsprechen ['na:xʃprɛçən] *unreg vt*: **(jdm) ~** to repeat (after sb)

nächst [nɛ:çst] *präp +dat* (*räumlich*) next to; (*außer*) apart from; **nächstbeste, r, s** *adj* first that comes along; (*zweitbeste*) next-best

Nächste, r, s *f(m)* neighbour (*Brit*), neighbor (*US*)

nächste, r, s *adj* next; (*nächstgelegen*) nearest; **aus ~r Nähe** from close by; (*betrachten*) at close quarters; **Ende ~n Monats** at the end of next month; **am ~n Tag** (the) next day; **bei ~r Gelegenheit** at the earliest opportunity; **in ~r Zeit** some time soon; **der ~ Angehörige** the next of kin

nachstehen ['na:xʃte:ən] *unreg vi*: **jdm in nichts ~** to be sb's equal in every way

nachstehend *adj attrib* following

nachstellen ['na:xʃtɛlən] *vi*: **jdm ~** to follow sb; (*aufdringlich umwerben*) to pester sb

Nächstenliebe *f* love for one's fellow men

nächstens *adv* shortly, soon

nächstliegend *adj* (*lit*) nearest; (*fig*) obvious

nächstmöglich *adj* next possible

nachsuchen ['na:xzu:xən] *vi*: **um etw ~** to ask *od* apply for sth

Nacht [naxt] (-, ̈-e) *f* night; **gute ~!** good night!; **heute ~** tonight; **in der ~** at night; **in der ~ auf Dienstag** during Monday night; **in der ~ vom 12. zum 13. April** during the night of April 12th to 13th; **über ~** (*auch fig*) overnight; **bei ~ und Nebel** (*umg*) at dead of night; **sich** *dat* **die ~ um die Ohren schlagen** (*umg*) to stay up all night; (*mit Feiern, arbeiten*) to make a night of it

Nachtdienst *m* night duty

Nachteil ['na:xtaɪl] *m* disadvantage; **im ~ sein** to be at a disadvantage

nachteilig *adj* disadvantageous

Nachtfalter *m* moth

Nachthemd *nt* (*Herrennachthemd*) nightshirt; nightdress (*Brit*), nightgown

Nachtigall ['naxtɪgal] (-, -en) *f* nightingale

Nachtisch ['na:xtɪʃ] *m* = **Nachspeise**

Nachtleben *nt* night life

nächtlich ['nɛçtlɪç] *adj* nightly

Nacht- *zW*: **Nachtlokal** *nt* night club; **Nachtmensch** ['naxtmɛnʃ] *m* night person; **Nachtportier** *m* night porter

nach- *zW*: **Nachtrag** ['na:xtra:k] (-(e)s, -träge) *m* supplement; **nachtragen** *unreg*

vt (*zufügen*) to add; **jdm etw nachtragen** to carry sth after sb; (*fig*) to hold sth against sb; **nachtragend** *adj* resentful; **nachträglich** *adj* later, subsequent; (*zusätzlich*) additional ▷ *adv* later, subsequently; (*zusätzlich*) additionally; **nachtrauern** *vi*: **jdm/etw nachtrauern** to mourn the loss of sb/sth

Nachtruhe ['naxtru:ə] *f* sleep

nachts *adv* by night

Nachtschicht *f* night shift

Nachtschwester *f* night nurse

nachtsüber *adv* during the night

Nacht- *zW*: **Nachttarif** *m* off-peak tariff; **Nachttisch** *m* bedside table; **Nachttopf** *m* chamber pot; **Nachtwache** *f* night watch; (*im Krankenhaus*) night duty; **Nachtwächter** *m* night watchman

Nach- *zW*: **Nachuntersuchung** *f* checkup; **nachvollziehen** *unreg vt* to understand, comprehend; **nachwachsen** *unreg vi* to grow again; **Nachwahl** *f* ≈ by-election (*bes Brit*); **Nachwehen** *pl* afterpains *pl*; (*fig*) aftereffects *pl*; **nachweinen** *vi +dat* to mourn ▷ *vt*: **dieser Sache** *dat* **weine ich keine Träne nach** I won't shed any tears over that

Nachweis ['na:xvaɪs] (-es, -e) *m* proof; **den ~ für etw erbringen** *od* **liefern** to furnish proof of sth; **nachweisbar** *adj* provable, demonstrable; **nachweisen** ['na:xvaɪzən] *unreg vt* to prove; **jdm etw nachweisen** to point sth out to sb; **nachweislich** *adj* evident, demonstrable

nach- *zW*: **Nachwelt** *f*: **die Nachwelt** posterity; **nachwinken** *vi*: **jdm nachwinken** to wave after sb; **nachwirken** *vi* to have aftereffects; **Nachwirkung** *f* aftereffect; **Nachwort** *nt* appendix; **Nachwuchs** *m* offspring; (*beruflich etc*) new recruits *pl*; **nachzahlen** *vt, vi* to pay extra; **nachzählen** *vt* to count again; **Nachzahlung** *f* additional payment; (*zurückdatiert*) back pay

nachziehen ['na:xtsi:ən] *unreg vt* (*Linie*) to go over; (*Lippen*) to paint; (*Augenbrauen*) to pencil in; (*hinterherziehen*): **etw ~** to drag sth behind one

Nachzügler(-s, -) *m* straggler

Nackedei ['nakədaɪ] (-(e)s, -e *od* -s) *m* (*hum: umg: Kind*) little bare monkey

Nacken ['nakən] (-s, -) *m* nape of the neck; **jdm im ~ sitzen** (*umg*) to breathe down sb's neck

nackt [nakt] *adj* naked; (*Tatsachen*) plain, bare; **Nacktheit** *f* nakedness; **Nacktkultur** *f* nudism

Nadel ['na:dəl] (-, -n) *f* needle; (*Stecknadel*) pin; **Nadelbaum** *m* conifer; **Nadelkissen** *nt* pincushion; **Nadelöhr** *nt* eye of a needle; **Nadelwald** *m* coniferous forest

Nagel ['na:gəl] (-s, ̈-) *m* nail; **sich** *dat* **etw unter den ~ reißen** (*umg*) to pinch sth; **etw an den ~ hängen** (*fig*) to chuck sth in (*umg*); **Nägel mit Köpfen machen** (*umg*) to do the job properly; **Nagelbürste** *f* nailbrush; **Nagelfeile** *f* nailfile; **Nagelhaut** *f* cuticle;

Nagellack *m* nail varnish (*Brit*) *od* polish;
Nagellackentferner (**-s, -**) *m* nail polish
remover
nageln *vt, vi* to nail
nagelneu *adj* brand-new
Nagelschere *f* nail scissors *pl*
nagen ['na:gən] *vt, vi* to gnaw
Nagetier ['na:gəti:r] *nt* rodent
nah *adj* = **nahe**
Nahaufnahme *f* close-up
Nahe *f* (*Fluss*) Nahe
nahe *adj* (*räumlich*) near(by); (*Verwandte*) near,
close; (*Freunde*) close; (*zeitlich*) near, close
▷ *adv*: **von nah und fern** from near and far
▷ *präp +dat* near (to), close to; **von N~m** at close
quarters; **der N~ Osten** the Middle East; **jdm**
~ kommen to get close to sb; **~ stehend** close;
jdm zu ~ treten (*fig*) to offend sb; **mit jdm ~**
verwandt sein to be closely related to sb; *siehe*
auch **naheliegen; nahestehen** *etc*
Nähe ['nɛ:ə] (**-**) *f* nearness, proximity;
(*Umgebung*) vicinity; **in der ~** close by; at hand;
aus der ~ from close to
nahebei *adv* nearby
nahebringen *unreg vt* (*fig*): **jdm etw ~** to bring
sth home to sb
nahegehen *unreg vi* (*fig*): **jdm ~** to grieve sb
nahelegen *vi* (*fig*): **jdm etw ~** to suggest sth
to sb
naheliegen *unreg vi* (*fig*) to be obvious; **der**
Verdacht liegt nahe, dass ... it seems
reasonable to suspect that ...; **~d** obvious
nahen *vi, vr* to approach, draw near
nähen ['nɛ:ən] *vt, vi* to sew
näher *adj* nearer; (*Erklärung, Erkundigung*) more
detailed ▷ *adv* nearer; in greater detail; **~**
kommen to get closer; **ich kenne ihn nicht ~**
I don't know him well
Nähere, s *nt* details *pl*, particulars *pl*
Näherei [nɛ:ə'raɪ] *f* sewing, needlework
Naherholungsgebiet *nt* recreational area
(*close to a centre of population*)
Näherin *f* seamstress
nähern *vr* to approach
Näherungswert *m* approximate value
nahestehen *unreg vi* (*fig*): **jdm ~** to be close to
sb; **einer Sache ~** to sympathize with sth
nahezu *adv* nearly
Nähgarn *nt* thread
Nahkampf *m* hand-to-hand fighting
Nähkasten *m* workbox, sewing basket
nahm *etc* [na:m] *vb siehe* **nehmen**
Nähmaschine *f* sewing machine
Nähnadel *f* (sewing) needle
Nahost [na:'ɔst] *m*: **aus ~** from the Middle East
Nährboden *m* (*lit*) fertile soil; (*fig*) breeding
ground
nähren ['nɛ:rən] *vt* to feed ▷ *vr* (*Person*) to feed
o.s.; (*Tier*) to feed; **er sieht gut genährt aus**
he looks well fed
Nährgehalt ['nɛ:rgəhalt] *m* nutritional value
nahrhaft ['na:rhaft] *adj* (*Essen*) nourishing
Nährstoffe *pl* nutrients *pl*

Nahrung ['na:rʊŋ] *f* food; (*fig*) sustenance
Nahrungs- *zW*: **Nahrungsaufnahme**
f: **die Nahrungsaufnahme verweigern**
to refuse food; **Nahrungskette** *f* food
chain; **Nahrungsmittel** *nt* food(stuff);
Nahrungsmittelindustrie *f* food industry;
Nahrungssuche *f* search for food
Nährwert *m* nutritional value
Naht [na:t] (**-, ⁻e**) *f* seam; (*Med*) suture; (*Tech*)
join; **aus allen Nähten platzen** (*umg*) to be
bursting at the seams; **nahtlos** *adj* seamless;
nahtlos ineinander übergehen to follow
without a gap
Nahverkehr *m* local traffic
Nahverkehrszug *m* local train
Nähzeug *nt* sewing kit, sewing things *pl*
Nahziel *nt* immediate objective
naiv [na'i:f] *adj* naïve
Naivität [naivi'tɛ:t] *f* naïveté, naïvety
Name ['na:mə] (**-ns, -n**) *m* name; **im ~n von**
on behalf of; **dem ~n nach müsste sie**
Deutsche sein judging by her name she must
be German; **die Dinge beim ~n nennen** (*fig*)
to call a spade a spade; **ich kenne das Stück**
nur dem ~n nach I've heard of the play but
that's all
namens *adv* by the name of
Namensänderung *f* change of name
Namenstag *m* name day, saint's day; *see culture*
note

● **NAMENSTAG**
●
●
● In Catholic areas of Germany the *Namenstag*
● is often a more important celebration than
● a birthday. It is the day dedicated to the
● saint after whom a person is called, and
● on that day the person receives presents
● and invites relatives and friends round to
● celebrate.

namentlich ['na:məntlɪç] *adj* by name ▷ *adv*
particularly, especially
namhaft ['na:mhaft] *adj* (*berühmt*) famed,
renowned; (*beträchtlich*) considerable; **~**
machen to name, identify
Namibia [na'mi:bia] (**-s**) *nt* Namibia
nämlich ['nɛ:mlɪç] *adv* that is to say, namely;
(*denn*) since; **der/die/das N~e** the same
nannte *etc* ['nantə] *vb siehe* **nennen**
nanu [na'nu:] *interj* well I never!
Napalm ['na:palm] (**-s**) *nt* napalm
Napf [napf] (**-(e)s, ⁻e**) *m* bowl, dish;
Napfkuchen *m* ≈ ring-shaped pound cake
Narbe ['narbə] (**-, -n**) *f* scar
narbig ['narbɪç] *adj* scarred
Narkose [nar'ko:zə] (**-, -n**) *f* anaesthetic (*Brit*),
anesthetic (*US*)
Narr [nar] (**-en, -en**) *m* fool; **jdn zum ~en**
halten to make a fool of sb; **narren** *vt* to fool
Narrenfreiheit *f*: **sie hat bei ihm ~** he gives
her (a) free rein
narrensicher *adj* foolproof

Narrheit f foolishness
Närrin ['nɛrɪn] f fool
närrisch adj foolish, crazy; **die ~en Tage**
Fasching and the period leading up to it
Narzisse [nar'tsɪsə] (-, -n) f narcissus
narzisstisch [nar'tsɪstɪʃ] adj narcissistic
NASA ['na:za] (-) f abk (= National Aeronautics and
Space Administration) NASA
naschen ['naʃən] vt to nibble; (heimlich) to eat
secretly ▷ vi to nibble sweet things; **~ von** od
an +dat to nibble at
naschhaft adj sweet-toothed
Nase ['na:zə] (-, -n) f nose; **sich** dat **die ~**
putzen to wipe one's nose; (sich schnäuzen)
to blow one's nose; **jdm auf der ~**
herumtanzen (umg) to play sb up; **jdm etw**
vor der ~ wegschnappen (umg) to just beat
sb to sth; **die ~ vollhaben** (umg) to have
had enough; **jdm etw auf die ~ binden**
(umg) to tell sb all about sth; **(immer) der ~**
nachgehen (umg) to follow one's nose; **jdn an**
der ~ herumführen (als Täuschung) to lead sb
by the nose; (als Scherz) to pull sb's leg
Nasen- zW: **Nasenbluten** (-s) nt nosebleed;
Nasenloch nt nostril; **Nasenrücken** m bridge
of the nose; **Nasentropfen** pl nose drops pl
naseweis adj pert, cheeky; (neugierig) nosey
Nashorn ['na:shɔrn] nt rhinoceros
nass [nas] adj wet
Nassauer ['nasauər] (-s, -) (umg) m scrounger
Nässe ['nɛsə] (-) f wetness
nässen vt to wet
nasskalt adj wet and cold
Nassrasur f wet shave
Nation [natsi'o:n] f nation
national [natsio'na:l] adj national;
Nationalelf f international (football) team;
Nationalfeiertag m national holiday;
Nationalhymne f national anthem
nationalisieren [natsiona:li'zi:rən] vt to
nationalize
Nationalisierung f nationalization
Nationalismus [natsiona:'lɪsmʊs] m
nationalism
nationalistisch [natsiona:'lɪstɪʃ] adj
nationalistic
Nationalität [natsionali'tɛ:t] f nationality
National- zW: **Nationalmannschaft** f
international team; **Nationalsozialismus**
m National Socialism; **Nationalsozialist** m
National Socialist
NATO, Nato ['na:to] (-) f abk: **die ~** NATO
Natrium ['na:triʊm] (-s) nt sodium
Natron ['na:trɔn] (-s) nt soda
Natter ['natər] (-, -n) f adder
Natur [na'tu:r] f nature; (körperlich)
constitution; (freies Land) countryside; **das**
geht gegen meine ~ it goes against the grain
Naturalien [natu'ra:liən] pl natural produce
sing; **in ~** in kind
Naturalismus [natura'lɪsmʊs] m naturalism
Naturell [natu'rɛl] (-s, -e) nt temperament,
disposition

Natur- zW: **Naturerscheinung** f natural
phenomenon od event; **naturfarben** adj
natural-coloured (Brit) od -colored (US);
Naturforscher m natural scientist;
Naturfreak (-s, -s) (umg) m back-to-
nature freak; **naturgemäß** adj natural;
Naturgeschichte f natural history;
Naturgesetz nt law of nature; **naturgetreu**
adj true to life; **Naturheilverfahren** nt
natural cure; **Naturkatastrophe** f natural
disaster; **Naturkostladen** m health food shop;
Naturkunde f natural history; **Naturlehrpfad**
m nature trail
natürlich [na'ty:rlɪç] adj natural ▷ adv
naturally; **eines ~en Todes sterben** to die of
natural causes
natürlicherweise [na'ty:rlɪçər'vaɪzə] adv
naturally, of course
Natürlichkeit f naturalness
Natur- zW: **Naturprodukt** nt natural product;
naturrein adj natural, pure; **Naturschutz**
m: **unter Naturschutz stehen** to be legally
protected; **Naturschutzgebiet** nt nature
reserve (BRIT), national park (US); **Naturtalent**
nt natural prodigy; **naturverbunden** adj
nature-loving; **Naturwissenschaft** f natural
science; **Naturwissenschaftler** m scientist;
Naturzustand m natural state
Nautik ['nautɪk] f nautical science, navigation
nautisch ['nautɪʃ] adj nautical
Navelorange ['na:vəlorã:ʒə] f navel orange
Navigation [navigatsi'o:n] f navigation
Navigationsfehler m navigational error
Navigationsinstrumente pl navigation
instruments pl
Nazi ['na:tsi] (-s, -s) m Nazi
NB abk (= nota bene) NB
n. Br. abk (= nördlicher Breite) northern latitude
NC m abk (= numerus clausus) siehe **Numerus**
Nchf. abk = **Nachfolger**
n. Chr. abk (= nach Christus) A.D.
NDR (-) m abk (= Norddeutscher Rundfunk) North
German Radio
Neapel [ne'a:pəl] (-s) nt Naples
Neapolitaner, in [neapoli'ta:nər(ɪn)] (-s, -)
m(f) Neapolitan
neapolitanisch [neapoli'ta:nɪʃ] adj Neapolitan
Nebel ['ne:bəl] (-s, -) m fog, mist
nebelig adj foggy, misty
Nebel- zW: **Nebelleuchte** f (Aut) rear fog-
light; **Nebelscheinwerfer** m fog-lamp;
Nebelschlussleuchte f (Aut) rear fog-light
neben ['ne:bən] präp +akk next to ▷ präp +dat
next to; (außer) apart from, besides; **nebenan**
[ne:bən|'an] adv next door; **Nebenanschluss** m
(Tel) extension; **Nebenausgaben** pl incidental
expenses pl; **nebenbei** [ne:bən'baɪ] adv at
the same time; (außerdem) additionally;
(beiläufig) incidentally; **nebenbei bemerkt**
od **gesagt** by the way, incidentally;
Nebenberuf m second occupation; **er ist im**
Nebenberuf ... he has a second job as a ...;
Nebenbeschäftigung f sideline; (Zweitberuf)

extra job; **Nebenbuhler, in (-s, -)** *m(f)* rival;
nebeneinander [neːbənaɪˈnandər] *adv* side by
side; **nebeneinanderlegen** *vt* to put next to
each other; **Nebeneingang** *m* side entrance;
Nebeneinkünfte *pl*, **Nebeneinnahmen**
pl supplementary income *sing*;
Nebenerscheinung *f* side effect; **Nebenfach**
nt subsidiary subject; **Nebenfluss** *m* tributary;
Nebengeräusch *nt* (*Rundf*)
pl, interference; **Nebenhandlung** *f* (*Liter*)
subplot; **nebenher** [neːbənˈheːr] *adv* (*zusätzlich*)
besides; (*gleichzeitig*) at the same time;
(*daneben*) alongside; **nebenherfahren** *unreg vi*
to drive alongside; **Nebenkläger** *m* (*Jur*) joint
plaintiff; **Nebenkosten** *pl* extra charges *pl*,
extras *pl*; **Nebenmann (-(e)s,** *pl* **-männer)**
m: **Ihr Nebenmann** the person next to you;
Nebenprodukt *nt* by-product; **Nebenrolle**
f minor part; **Nebensache** *f* trifle, side
issue; **nebensächlich** *adj* minor, peripheral;
Nebensaison *f* low season; **Nebensatz** *m*
(*Gram*) subordinate clause; **nebenstehend**
adj: **nebenstehende Abbildung** illustration
opposite; **Nebenstraße** *f* side street;
Nebenstrecke *f* (*Eisenb*) branch *od* local
line; **Nebenverdienst** *m* secondary income;
Nebenzimmer *nt* adjoining room
neblig [ˈneːblɪç] *adj* = **nebelig**
nebst [neːpst] *präp +dat* together with
Necessaire [neseˈseːr] **(-s, -s)** *nt* (*Nähnecessaire*)
needlework box; (*Nagelnecessaire*) manicure
case
Neckar [ˈnɛkar] **(-s)** *m* (*Fluss*) Neckar
necken [ˈnɛkən] *vt* to tease
Neckerei [nɛkəˈraɪ] *f* teasing
neckisch *adj* coy; (*Einfall, Lied*) amusing
nee [neː] (*umg*) *adv* no, nope
Neffe [ˈnɛfə] **(-n, -n)** *m* nephew
negativ [ˈneːgatiːf] *adj* negative; **Negativ (-s,
-e)** *nt* (*Phot*) negative
Neger [ˈneːgər] **(-s, -)** (*pej*) *m* negro (*pej*); **Negerin**
(*pej*) *f* negress (*pej*)
negieren [neˈgiːrən] *vt* (*bestreiten*) to deny;
(*verneinen*) to negate
nehmen [ˈneːmən] *unreg vt, vi* to take; **etw zu
sich ~** to take sth, partake of sth (*liter*); **jdm
etw ~** to take sth (away) from sb; **sich ernst
~** to take o.s. seriously; **~ Sie sich doch bitte**
help yourself; **man nehme ...** (*Koch*) take ...;
wie mans nimmt depending on your point
of view; **die Mauer nimmt einem die ganze
Sicht** the wall blocks the whole view; **er ließ
es sich** *dat* **nicht ~, es persönlich zu tun** he
insisted on doing it himself
Nehrung [ˈneːrʊŋ] *f* (*Geog*) spit (of land)
Neid [naɪt] **(-(e)s)** *m* envy
Neidhammel (*umg*) *m* envious person
neidisch *adj* envious, jealous
Neige (-, -n) *f* (*geh: Ende*): **die Vorräte gehen
zur ~** the provisions are fast becoming
exhausted
neigen [ˈnaɪgən] *vt* to incline, lean; (*Kopf*) to
bow ▷ *vi*: **zu etw ~** to tend to sth

Neigung *f* (*des Geländes*) slope; (*Tendenz*)
tendency, inclination; (*Vorliebe*) liking;
(*Zuneigung*) affection
Neigungswinkel *m* angle of inclination
nein [naɪn] *adv* no
Nelke [ˈnɛlkə] **(-, -n)** *f* carnation, pink;
(*Gewürznelke*) clove
nennen [ˈnɛnən] *unreg vt* to name; (*mit Namen*)
to call; **das nenne ich Mut!** that's what I call
courage!
nennenswert *adj* worth mentioning
Nenner (-s, -) *m* denominator; **etw auf einen
~ bringen** (*lit, fig*) to reduce sth to a common
denominator
Nennung *f* naming
Nennwert *m* nominal value; (*Comm*) par
neokonservativ *adj* neo-conservative, neo-con
(*umg*)
neoliberal *adj* neo-liberal, neo-lib (*umg*)
Neon [ˈneːɔn] **(-s)** *nt* neon
Neonazi [neoˈnaːtsi] *m* Neonazi
Neon- *zW*: **Neonlicht** *nt* neon light;
Neonreklame *f* neon sign; **Neonröhre** *f* neon
tube
Nepal [ˈneːpal] **(-s)** *nt* Nepal
Nepp [nɛp] **(-s)** (*umg*) *m*: **der reinste ~** daylight
robbery, a rip-off
Nerv [nɛrf] **(-s, -en)** *m* nerve; **die ~en sind
mit ihm durchgegangen** he lost control, he
snapped (*umg*); **jdm auf die ~en gehen** to get
on sb's nerves
nerven (*umg*) *vt*: **jdn ~** to get on sb's nerves
Nerven- *zW*: **Nervenaufreibend** *adj*
nerve-racking; **Nervenbündel** *nt* bundle
of nerves; **Nervengas** *nt* (*Mil*) nerve
gas; **Nervenheilanstalt** *f* psychiatric
hospital; **Nervenklinik** *f* psychiatric clinic;
nervenkrank *adj* mentally ill; **Nervensäge**
(*umg*) *f* pain (in the neck); **Nervenschwäche**
f neurasthenia; **Nervensystem** *nt* nervous
system; **Nervenzusammenbruch** *m* nervous
breakdown
nervig [ˈnɛrvɪç] (*umg*) *adj* exasperating,
annoying
nervös [nɛrˈvøːs] *adj* nervous
Nervosität [nɛrvoziˈtɛːt] *f* nervousness
nervtötend *adj* nerve-racking; (*Arbeit*) soul-
destroying
Nerz [nɛrts] **(-es, -e)** *m* mink
Nessel [ˈnɛsəl] **(-, -n)** *f* nettle; **sich in die ~n
setzen** (*fig: umg*) to put o.s. in a spot
Nessessär [nɛsɛˈsɛːr] **(-s, -s)** *nt* = **Necessaire**
Nest [nɛst] **(-(e)s, -er)** *nt* nest; (*umg: Ort*) dump;
(*fig: Bett*) bed; (: *Schlupfwinkel*) hide-out, lair;
da hat er sich ins warme ~ gesetzt (*umg*)
he's got it made; **Nestbeschmutzung** (*pej*) *f*
running-down (*umg*) *od* denigration (of one's
family/country)
nesteln *vi*: **an etw** *+dat* **~** to fumble *od* fiddle
about with sth
Nesthäkchen [ˈnɛsthɛːkçən] *nt* baby of the
family
Netiquette [netɪˈkɛtə] **(-, *no pl*)** *f* (*Internet*)

Netiquette

nett [nɛt] *adj* nice; **sei so ~ und räum auf!** would you mind clearing up?

netterweise ['nɛtərvaɪzə] *adv* kindly

netto *adv* net; **Nettoeinkommen** *nt* net income; **Nettogewicht** *nt* net weight; **Nettogewinn** *m* net profit; **Nettogewinnspanne** *f* net margin; **Nettolohn** *m* take-home pay; **Nettozahler** *m* (*Land etc*) net contributor

Netz [nɛts] (**-es, -e**) *nt* net; (*Gepäcknetz*) rack; (*Einkaufsnetz*) string bag; (*Spinnennetz*) web; (*System, Comput*) network; (*Stromnetz*) mains *sing od pl*; **das soziale ~** the social security network; **jdm ins ~ gehen** (*fig*) to fall into sb's trap; **Netzanbieter** *m* (*Comput*) Internet provider; **Netzanschluss** *m* mains connection; **Netzbetreiber** *m* (*Comput*) Internet provider; **Netzcomputer** *m* network computer; **Netzhaut** *f* retina; **Netzkarte** *f* (*Eisenb*) runabout ticket (*Brit*); **Netzplantechnik** *f* network analysis; **Netzspannung** *f* mains voltage; **Netzwerken** *nt* (social) networking; **Netzzugang** *m* (*Comput*) network access

neu [nɔy] *adj* new; (*Sprache, Geschichte*) modern; **der/die N~e** the new person, the newcomer; **seit N~estem** (since) recently; **~ schreiben** to rewrite, write again; **auf ein N~es!** (*Aufmunterung*) let's try again!; **was gibts N~es?** (*umg*) what's the latest?; **von N~em** (*von vorn*) from the beginning; (*wieder*) again; **sich ~ einkleiden** to buy o.s. a new set of clothes; **~ eröffnet** newly-opened; (*wieder geöffnet*) reopened; **Neuankömmling** *m* newcomer; **Neuanschaffung** *f* new purchase *od* acquisition; **neuartig** *adj* new kind of; **Neuauflage** *f* new edition; **Neuausgabe** *f* new edition; **Neubau** (**-(e)s, -ten**) *m* new building; **Neubauwohnung** *f* newly-built flat; **Neubearbeitung** *f* revised edition; (*das Neubearbeiten*) revision, reworking; **Neudruck** *m* reprint; **Neuemission** *f* (*Aktien*) new issue

neuerdings *adv* (*kürzlich*) (since) recently; (*von Neuem*) again

Neuerscheinung *f* (*Buch*) new publication; (*Schallplatte*) new release

Neuerung *f* innovation, new departure

Neufassung *f* revised version

Neufundland [nɔy'fʊntlant] *nt* Newfoundland; **Neufundländer, in** (**-s, -**) *m(f)* Newfoundlander; **neufundländisch** *adj* Newfoundland *attrib*

neugeboren *adj* newborn; **sich wie ~ fühlen** to feel (like) a new man/woman

Neugier *f* curiosity

Neugierde (**-**) *f*: **aus ~** out of curiosity

neugierig *adj* curious

Neuguinea [nɔygi'ne:a] (**-s**) *nt* New Guinea

Neuheit *f* novelty; (*neuartige Ware*) new thing

Neuigkeit *f* news *sing*

neu- *zW*: **Neujahr** *nt* New Year; **Neuland** *nt* virgin land; (*fig*) new ground; **neulich** *adv* recently, the other day; **Neuling** *m*

novice; **neumodisch** *adj* fashionable; (*pej*) newfangled; **Neumond** *m* new moon

neun [nɔyn] *num* nine; **Neun** (**-, -en**) *f* nine; **ach du grüne Neune!** (*umg*) well I'm blowed!

neunmalklug *adj* (*ironisch*) smart-aleck *attrib*

neunzehn *num* nineteen

neunzig *num* ninety

Neuregelung, Neureglung *f* adjustment

neureich *adj* nouveau riche; **Neureiche, r** *f(m)* nouveau riche

Neurologie [nɔyrolo'gi:] *f* neurology

neurologisch [nɔyro'lo:gɪʃ] *adj* neurological

Neurose [nɔy'ro:zə] (**-, -n**) *f* neurosis

Neurotiker, in [nɔy'ro:tikər(ɪn)] (**-s, -**) *m(f)* neurotic

neurotisch *adj* neurotic

Neu- *zW*: **Neuschnee** *m* fresh snow; **Neuseeland** [nɔy'ze:lant] *nt* New Zealand; **Neuseeländer, in** (**-s, -**) *m(f)* New Zealander; **neuseeländisch** *adj* New Zealand *attrib*; **neusprachlich** *adj*: **neusprachliches Gymnasium** grammar school (*Brit*) *od* high school (*bes US*) stressing modern languages

neutral [nɔy'tra:l] *adj* neutral

neutralisieren [nɔytrali'zi:rən] *vt* to neutralize

Neutralität [nɔytrali'tɛ:t] *f* neutrality

Neutron ['nɔytron] (**-s, -en**) *nt* neutron

Neutrum ['nɔytrʊm] (**-s, Neutra** *od* **Neutren**) *nt* neuter

Neu- *zW*: **Neuwert** *m* purchase price; **neuwertig** *adj* as new; **Neuzeit** *f* modern age; **neuzeitlich** *adj* modern, recent

N. H. *abk* (= *Normalhöhenpunkt*) normal peak (level)

nhd. *abk* (= *neuhochdeutsch*) NHG

Nicaragua [nika'ra:gua] (**-s**) *nt* Nicaragua; **Nicaraguaner, in** [nikaragu'a:nər(ɪn)] (**-s, -**) *m(f)* Nicaraguan; **nicaraguanisch** [nikaragu'a:nɪʃ] *adj* Nicaraguan

⊙ SCHLÜSSELWORT

nicht [nɪçt] *adv* **1** (*Verneinung*) not; **er ist es nicht** it's not him, it isn't him; **nicht rostend** stainless; **er raucht nicht** (*gerade*) he isn't smoking; (*gewöhnlich*) he doesn't smoke; **ich kann das nicht — ich auch nicht** I can't do it — neither *od* nor can I; **es regnet nicht mehr** it's not raining any more; **nicht mehr als** no more than

2 (*Bitte, Verbot*): **nicht!** don't!, no!; **nicht berühren!** do not touch!; **nicht doch!** don't!

3 (*rhetorisch*): **du bist müde, nicht (wahr)?** you're tired, aren't you?; **das ist schön, nicht (wahr)?** it's nice, isn't it?

4: **was du nicht sagst!** the things you say!

▷ *präf* non-

Nicht- *zW*: **Nichtachtung** *f* disregard; **Nichtanerkennung** *f* repudiation; **Nichtangriffspakt** *m* non-aggression pact

Nichte ['nɪçtə] (**-, -n**) *f* niece

Nicht- *zW*: **Nichteinhaltung** *f* (*+gen*) noncompliance (with); **Nichteinmischung** *f* (*Pol*) nonintervention; **Nichtgefallen** *nt:* **bei Nichtgefallen (zurück)** if not satisfied (return)

nichtig ['nɪçtɪç] *adj* (*ungültig*) null, void; (*wertlos*) futile; **Nichtigkeit** *f* nullity, invalidity; (*Sinnlosigkeit*) futility

Nichtraucher *m* nonsmoker; **ich bin ~** I don't smoke

nichts [nɪçts] *pron* nothing; **~ ahnend** unsuspecting; **~ sagend** meaningless; **~ als** nothing but; **~ da!** (*ausgeschlossen*) nothing doing (*umg*); **~ wie raus/hin** *etc* (*umg*) let's get out/over there *etc* (on the double); **für ~ und wieder nichts** for nothing at all; **Nichts (-s)** *nt* nothingness; (*pej: Person*) nonentity

Nichtschwimmer (-s, -) *m* nonswimmer

nichts- *zW:* **nichtsdestotrotz** *adv* notwithstanding (*form*), nonetheless; **nichtsdestoweniger** *adv* nevertheless; **Nichtsnutz (-es, -e)** *m* good-for-nothing; **nichtsnutzig** *adj* worthless, useless; **nichtssagend** *adj* meaningless; **Nichtstun (-s)** *nt* idleness

Nichtzutreffende, s *nt:* **~s (bitte) streichen** (please) delete as applicable

Nickel ['nɪkəl] **(-s)** *nt* nickel; **Nickelbrille** *f* metal-rimmed glasses *pl*

nicken ['nɪkən] *vi* to nod

Nickerchen ['nɪkərçən] *nt* nap; **ein ~ machen** (*umg*) to have forty winks

Nicki ['nɪki] **(-s, -s)** *m* velours pullover

nie [niː] *adv* never; **~ wieder** *od* **mehr** never again; **~ und nimmer** never ever; **fast ~** hardly ever

nieder ['niːdər] *adj* low; (*gering*) inferior ▷ *adv* down; **niederdeutsch** *adj* (*Ling*) Low-German; **Niedergang** *m* decline; **niedergedrückt** *adj* depressed; **niedergehen** *unreg vi* to descend; (*Aviat*) to come down; (*Regen*) to fall; (*Boxer*) to go down; **niedergeschlagen** *adj* depressed, dejected; **Niedergeschlagenheit** *f* depression, dejection; **Niederkunft** *f* (*veraltet*) delivery, giving birth; **Niederlage** *f* defeat

Niederlande ['niːdərlandə] *pl:* **die ~** the Netherlands *pl*

Niederländer, in ['niːdərlɛndər(ɪn)] **(-s, -)** *m(f)* Dutchman, Dutchwoman

niederländisch *adj* Dutch, Netherlands *attrib*

nieder- *zW:* **niederlassen** *unreg vr* (*sich setzen*) to sit down; (*an Ort*) to settle (down); (*Arzt, Rechtsanwalt*) to set up in practice; **Niederlassung** *f* settlement; (*Comm*) branch; **niederlegen** *vt* to lay down; (*Arbeit*) to stop; (*Amt*) to resign; **niedermachen** *vt* to mow down; **Niederösterreich** *nt* Lower Austria; **Niederrhein** *m* Lower Rhine; **niederrheinisch** *adj* Lower Rhine *attrib*; **Niedersachsen** *nt* Lower Saxony; **Niederschlag** *m* (*Chem*) precipitate; (*Bodensatz*) sediment; (*Met*) precipitation (*form*), rainfall; (*Boxen*) knockdown; **radioaktiver Niederschlag** (radioactive) fallout; **niederschlagen** *unreg*

vt (*Gegner*) to beat down; (*Gegenstand*) to knock down; (*Augen*) to lower; (*Jur: Prozess*) to dismiss; (*Aufstand*) to put down ▷ *vr* (*Chem*) to precipitate; **sich in etw** *dat* **niederschlagen** (*Erfahrungen etc*) to find expression in sth; **niederschlagsfrei** ['niːdərʃlaːksfraɪ] *adj* dry, without precipitation (*form*); **niederschmetternd** *adj* (*Nachricht, Ergebnis*) shattering; **niederschreiben** *unreg vt* to write down; **Niederschrift** *f* transcription; **niedertourig** *adj* (*Motor*) low-revving; **niederträchtig** *adj* base, mean; **Niederträchtigkeit** *f* despicable *od* malicious behaviour

Niederung *f* (*Geog*) depression

niederwalzen ['niːdərvaltsən] *vt:* **jdn/etw ~** (*umg*) to mow sb/sth down

niederwerfen ['niːdərvɛrfən] *unreg vt* to throw down; (*fig*) to overcome; (*Aufstand*) to suppress

niedlich ['niːtlɪç] *adj* sweet, nice, cute

niedrig ['niːdrɪç] *adj* low; (*Stand*) lowly, humble; (*Gesinnung*) mean

Niedriglohnsektor *m* low-wage sector

niemals ['niːmaːls] *adv* never

niemand ['niːmant] *pron* nobody, no-one

Niemandsland ['niːmantslant] *nt* no-man's-land

Niere ['niːrə] **(-, -n)** *f* kidney; **künstliche ~** kidney machine

Nierenentzündung *f* kidney infection

nieseln ['niːzəln] *vi* to drizzle

Nieselregen *m* drizzle

niesen ['niːzən] *vi* to sneeze

Niespulver *nt* sneezing powder

Niet [niːt] **(-(e)s, -e)** *m* (*Tech*) rivet

Niete ['niːtə] **(-, -n)** *f* (*Tech*) rivet; (*Los*) blank; (*Reinfall*) flop; (*Mensch*) failure

nieten *vt* to rivet

Nietenhose *f* (pair of) studded jeans *pl*

niet- und nagelfest (*umg*) *adj* nailed down

Niger¹ ['niːgər] **(-s)** *nt* (*Staat*) Niger

Niger² ['niːgər] **(-s)** *m* (*Fluss*) Niger

Nigeria [ni'geːria] **(-s)** *nt* Nigeria; **Nigerianer, in** [nigeri'aːnər(ɪn)] *m(f)* Nigerian; **nigerianisch** [nigeri'aːnɪʃ] *adj* Nigerian

Nihilismus [nihi'lɪsmʊs] *m* nihilism

Nihilist [nihi'lɪst] *m* nihilist; **nihilistisch** *adj* nihilistic

Nikolaus ['niːkolaʊs] **(-, -e** *od* (*hum: umg*) **-läuse)** *m* ≈ Santa Claus, ≈ Father Christmas

Nikosia [niko'ziːa] **(-s)** *nt* Nicosia

Nikotin [niko'tiːn] **(-s)** *nt* nicotine; **nikotinarm** *adj* low-nicotine

Nil [niːl] **(-s)** *m* Nile; **Nilpferd** *nt* hippopotamus

Nimbus ['nɪmbʊs] **(-, -se)** *m* (*Heiligenschein*) halo; (*fig*) aura

nimmersatt ['nɪmərzat] *adj* insatiable; **Nimmersatt (-(e)s, -e)** *m* glutton

Nimmerwiedersehen (*umg*) *nt:* **auf ~!** I never want to see you again

nimmt [nɪmt] *vb siehe* **nehmen**

nippen ['nɪpən] *vt, vi* to sip

Nippes ['nɪpəs] *pl* knick-knacks *pl*, bric-a-brac

sing

Nippsachen ['nɪpzaxən] pl knick-knacks pl

nirgends ['nɪrgənts] adv nowhere; **überall und** ~ here, there and everywhere

nirgendwo ['nɪrgəntvo] adv = **nirgends**

nirgendwohin adv nowhere

Nische ['niːʃə] (-, -n) f niche

nisten ['nɪstən] vi to nest

Nitrat [ni'traːt] (-(e)s, -e) nt nitrate

Niveau [ni'voː] (-s, -s) nt level; **diese Schule hat ein hohes** ~ this school has high standards; **unter meinem** ~ beneath me

Nivellierung [nivɛ'liːrʊŋ] f (Ausgleichung) levelling out

nix [nɪks] (umg) pron = **nichts**

Nixe ['nɪksə] (-, -n) f water nymph

Nizza ['nɪtsa] (-s) nt Nice

n. J. abk (= nächsten Jahres) next year

n. M. abk (= nächsten Monats) next month

NN abk (= Normalnull) m.s.l.

N. N. abk = **NN**

NO abk (= Nordost) NE

no. abk (= netto) net

nobel ['noːbəl] adj (großzügig) generous; (elegant) posh (umg)

Nobelpreis [no'bɛlpraɪs] m Nobel prize; **Nobelpreisträger, in** m(f) Nobel prize winner

 SCHLÜSSELWORT

noch [nɔx] adv 1 (weiterhin) still; **noch nicht** not yet; **noch nie** never (yet); **noch immer** od **immer noch** still; **bleiben Sie doch noch** stay a bit longer; **ich gehe kaum noch aus** I hardly go out any more

2 (in Zukunft) still, yet; (irgendwann einmal) one day; **das kann noch passieren** that might still happen; **er wird noch kommen** he'll come (yet); **das wirst du noch bereuen** you'll come to regret it (one day)

3 (nicht später als): **noch vor einer Woche** only a week ago; **noch am selben Tag** the very same day; **noch im 19. Jahrhundert** as late as the 19th century; **noch heute** today

4 (zusätzlich): **wer war noch da?** who else was there?; **noch (ein)mal** once more, again; **noch dreimal** three more times; **noch einer** another one; **und es regnete auch noch** and on top of that it was raining

5 (bei Vergleichen): **noch größer** even bigger; **das ist noch besser** that's better still; **und wenn es noch so schwer ist** however hard it is

6: Geld noch und noch heaps (and heaps) of money; **sie hat noch und noch versucht, ...** she tried again and again to ...

▷ konj: **weder A noch B** neither A nor B

nochmal, nochmals adv siehe **noch**

nochmalig adj repeated

Nockenwelle ['nɔkənvɛlə] f camshaft

NOK nt abk (= Nationales Olympisches Komitee)

National Olympic Committee

Nom. abk = **Nominativ**

Nominalwert [nomi'naːlveːrt] m (Fin) nominal od par value

Nominativ ['noːminatiːf] (-s, -e) m nominative

nominell [nomi'nɛl] adj nominal

nominieren [nomi'niːrən] vt to nominate

Nonne ['nɔnə] (-, -n) f nun

Nonnenkloster nt convent

Nonplusultra [nɔnplʊs'|ʊltra] (-s) nt ultimate

Non-Profit-Unternehmen, Nonprofitunternehmen [nɔn'prɔfit-] nt non-profit company

Nord [nɔrt] (-s) m north; **Nordafrika** ['nɔrt |aːfrika] nt North Africa; **Nordamerika** nt North America; **nordamerikanisch** ['nɔrt |ameriˈkaːnɪʃ] adj North American

nordd. abk = **norddeutsch**

norddeutsch adj North German

Norddeutschland nt North(ern) Germany

Norden ['nɔrdən] m north

Nord- zW: **Nordengland** nt the North of England; **Nordirland** nt Northern Ireland, Ulster; **nordisch** adj northern; **nordische Kombination** (Ski) nordic combination; **Nordkap** nt North Cape; **Nordkorea** ['nɔrtkoˈreːa] nt North Korea

nördlich ['nœrtlɪç] adj northerly, northern ▷ präp +gen (to the) north of; **der ~e Polarkreis** the Arctic Circle; **N~es Eismeer** Arctic Ocean; ~ **von** north of

Nord- zW: **Nordlicht** nt northern lights pl, aurora borealis; **Nord-Ostsee-Kanal** m Kiel Canal; **Nordpol** m North Pole; **Nordpolargebiet** nt Arctic (Zone)

Nordrhein-Westfalen ['nɔrtraɪnvɛst'faːlən] (-s) nt North Rhine-Westphalia

Nordsee f North Sea

nordwärts adv northwards

Nörgelei [nœrgə'laɪ] f grumbling

nörgeln vi to grumble

Nörgler, in (-s, -) m(f) grumbler

Norm [nɔrm] (-, -en) f norm; (Leistungssoll) quota; (Größenvorschrift) standard (specification)

normal [nɔr'maːl] adj normal; **bist du noch** ~? (umg) have you gone mad?; **Normalbenzin** nt two-star petrol (Brit veraltet), regular gas (US)

normalerweise adv normally

Normalfall m: **im** ~ normally

Normalgewicht nt normal weight; (genormt) standard weight

normalisieren [nɔrmali'ziːrən] vt to normalize ▷ vr to return to normal

Normalzeit f (Geog) standard time

Normandie [nɔrman'diː] f Normandy

normen vt to standardize

Norwegen ['nɔrveːgən] (-s) nt Norway

Norweger, in (-s, -) m(f) Norwegian

norwegisch adj Norwegian

Nostalgie [nɔstal'giː] f nostalgia

Not [noːt] (-, ¨-e) f need; (Mangel) want; (Mühe) trouble; (Zwang) necessity; ~ **leidend** needy;

zur ~ if necessary; (*gerade noch*) just about; **wenn** ~ **am Mann ist** if you/they *etc* are short (*umg*); (*im Notfall*) in an emergency; **er hat seine liebe** ~ **mit ihr/damit** he really has problems with her/it; **in seiner** ~ in his hour of need

Notar, in [no'taːr(ɪn)] (**-s, -e**) *m(f)* notary; **notariell** *adj* notarial; **notariell beglaubigt** attested by a notary

Not- *zW*: **Notarzt** *m* doctor on emergency call; **Notausgang** *m* emergency exit; **Notbehelf** *m* stopgap; **Notbremse** *f* emergency brake; **Notdienst** *m*: **Notdienst haben** (*Apotheke*) to be open 24 hours; (*Arzt*) to be on call; **notdürftig** *adj* scanty; (*behelfsmäßig*) makeshift; **sich notdürftig verständigen können** to be able to communicate to some extent

Note ['noːtə] (**-, -n**) *f* note; (*Sch*) mark (*Brit*), grade (*US*); **Noten** *pl* (*Mus*) music *sing*; **eine persönliche** ~ a personal touch

Noten- *zW*: **Notenbank** *f* issuing bank; **Notenblatt** *nt* sheet of music; **Notenschlüssel** *m* clef; **Notenständer** *m* music stand

Not- *zW*: **Notfall** *m* (case of) emergency; **notfalls** *adv* if need be; **notgedrungen** *adj* necessary, unavoidable; **etw notgedrungen machen** to be forced to do sth; **Notgroschen** ['noːtɡrɔʃən] *m* nest egg

notieren [no'tiːrən] *vt* to note; (*Comm*) to quote **Notierung** *f* (*Comm*) quotation

nötig ['nøːtɪç] *adj* necessary ▷ *adv* (*dringend*): **etw** ~ **brauchen** to need sth urgently; **etw** ~ **haben** to need sth; **das habe ich nicht** ~! I can do without that!

nötigen *vt* to compel, force; **nötigenfalls** *adv* if necessary

Nötigung *f* compulsion, coercion (*Jur*)

Notiz [no'tiːts] (**-, -en**) *f* note; (*Zeitungsnotiz*) item; ~ **nehmen** to take notice; **Notizblock** *m* notepad; **Notizbuch** *nt* notebook; **Notizzettel** *m* piece of paper

Not- *zW*: **Notlage** *f* crisis, emergency; **notlanden** *vi* to make a forced *od* emergency landing; **Notlandung** *f* forced *od* emergency landing; **Notlösung** *f* temporary solution; **Notlüge** *f* white lie

notorisch [no'toːrɪʃ] *adj* notorious

Not- *zW*: **Notruf** *m* emergency call; **Notrufsäule** *f* emergency telephone; **notschlachten** *vt* (*Tiere*) to destroy; **Notstand** *m* state of emergency; **Notstandsgebiet** *nt* (*wirtschaftlich*) depressed area; (*bei Katastrophen*) disaster area; **Notstandsgesetz** *nt* emergency law; **Notunterkunft** *f* emergency accommodation; **Notverband** *m* emergency dressing; **Notwehr** (**-**) *f* self-defence; **notwendig** *adj* necessary; **Notwendigkeit** *f* necessity; **Notzucht** *f* rape.

Nov. *abk* (= *November*) Nov.

Novelle [no'vɛlə] (**-, -n**) *f* novella; (*Jur*) amendment

November [no'vɛmbər] (**-(s), -**) *m* November;

siehe auch **September**

Novum ['noːvʊm] (**-s, Nova**) *nt* novelty

NPD (**-**) *f abk* (= *Nationaldemokratische Partei Deutschlands*) National Democratic Party

Nr. *abk* (= *Nummer*) no.

NRW *abk* = **Nordrhein-Westfalen**

NS *abk* = **Nachschrift; Nationalsozialismus**

NS- *in zw* Nazi

N. T. *abk* (= *Neues Testament*) N.T.

Nu [nuː] *m*: **im Nu** in an instant

Nuance [ny'ãːsə] (**-, -n**) *f* nuance; (*Kleinigkeit*) shade

nüchtern ['nʏçtərn] *adj* sober; (*Magen*) empty; (*Urteil*) prudent; **Nüchternheit** *f* sobriety

Nudel ['nuːdəl] (**-, -n**) *f* noodle; (*umg: Mensch: dick*) dumpling; ((: *komisch*) character; **Nudelholz** *nt* rolling pin

Nugat ['nuːɡat] (**-s, -s**) *m od nt* nougat

nuklear [nukle'aːr] *adj attrib* nuclear

null [nʊl] *num* zero; (*Fehler*) no; ~ **Uhr** midnight; **in** ~ **Komma nichts** (*umg*) in less than no time; **die Stunde** ~ the new starting point; **gleich** ~ **sein** to be absolutely nil; ~ **und nichtig** null and void; **Null** (**-, -en**) *f* nought, zero; (*pej: Mensch*) dead loss; **nullachtfünfzehn** (*umg*) *adj* run-of-the-mill; **Nulldiät** *f* starvation diet; **Nulllösung** *f* (*Pol*) zero option; **Nullpunkt** *m* zero; **auf dem Nullpunkt** at zero; **Nulltarif** *m* (*für Verkehrsmittel*) free travel; **zum Nulltarif** free of charge

numerieren [nume'riːrən] *vt siehe* **nummerieren**

numerisch [nu'meːrɪʃ] *adj* numerical; ~**es Tastenfeld** (*Comput*) numeric pad

Numerus ['nuːmerʊs] (**-, Numeri**) *m* (*Gram*) number; ~ **clausus** (*Univ*) restricted entry

Nummer ['nʊmər] (**-, -n**) *f* number; **auf** ~ **sicher gehen** (*umg*) to play (it) safe

nummerieren [nume'riːrən] *vt* to number

Nummern- *zW*: **Nummernkonto** *nt* numbered bank account; **Nummernscheibe** *f* telephone dial; **Nummernschild** *nt* (*Aut*) number *od* license (*US*) plate

nun [nuːn] *adv* now ▷ *interj* well

nur [nuːr] *adv* just, only; **nicht** ~ ..., **sondern auch** ... not only ... but also ...; **alle,** ~ **ich nicht** everyone but me; **ich hab das** ~ **so gesagt** I was just talking

Nürnberg ['nʏrnbɛrk] (**-s**) *nt* Nuremberg

nuscheln ['nʊʃəln] (*umg*) *vt, vi* to mutter, mumble

Nuss [nʊs] (**-, ̈-e**) *f* nut; **eine doofe** ~ (*umg*) a stupid twit; **eine harte** ~ a hard nut (to crack); **Nussbaum** *m* walnut tree; **Nussknacker** (**-s, -**) *m* nutcracker

Nüster ['nyːstər] (**-, -n**) *f* nostril

Nutte ['nʊtə] (**-, -n**) *f* tart (*Brit*), hooker (*US*)

nutz [nʊts] *adj* = **nütze; nutzbar** *adj*: **nutzbar machen** to utilize; **Nutzbarmachung** *f* utilization; **nutzbringend** *adj* profitable; **etw nutzbringend anwenden** to use sth to good effect, put sth to good use

n

nütze ['nʏtsə] *adj*: **zu nichts ~ sein** to be useless

nutzen *vi* to be of use ▷ *vt*: **(zu etw) ~** to use (for sth); **was nutzt es?** what's the use?, what use is it?; **Nutzen (-s)** *m* usefulness; (*Gewinn*) profit; **von Nutzen** useful

nützen *vt, vi* = **nutzen**

Nutz- *zW*: **Nutzfahrzeug** *nt* farm *od* military vehicle *etc*; (*Comm*) commercial vehicle; **Nutzfläche** *f* us(e)able floor space; (*Agr*) productive land; **Nutzlast** *f* maximum load, payload

nützlich ['nʏtslɪç] *adj* useful; **Nützlichkeit** *f* usefulness

Nutz- *zW*: **nutzlos** *adj* useless; (*unnötig*) needless; **Nutzlosigkeit** *f* uselessness; **Nutznießer (-s, -)** *m* beneficiary

Nutzung *f* (*Gebrauch*) use; (*das Ausnutzen*) exploitation

NW *abk* (= *Nordwest*) NW

Nylon ['naɪlɔn] **(-s)** *nt* nylon

Nymphe ['nʏmfə] **(-, -n)** *f* nymph

Oo

O¹, o [oː] *nt* O, o; **O wie Otto** ≈ O for Olive, ≈ O for Oboe (US)

O² [oː] *abk* (= *Osten*) E

o. Ä. *abk* (= *oder Ähnliche(s)*) or similar

Oase [o'aːzə] (**-, -n**) *f* oasis

OB (**-s, -s**) *m abk* = **Oberbürgermeister**

ob [ɔp] *konj* if, whether; **ob das wohl wahr ist?** can that be true?; **ob ich (nicht) lieber gehe?** maybe I'd better go; **(so) tun als ob** (*umg*) to pretend; **und ob!** you bet!

Obacht ['oːbaxt] *f*: **~ geben** to pay attention

Obdach ['ɔpdax] (**-(e)s**) *nt* shelter, lodging; **obdachlos** *adj* homeless; **Obdachlosenasyl** *nt* hostel *od* shelter for the homeless; **Obdachlosenheim** *nt* = **Obdachlosenasyl**; **Obdachlose, r** *f(m)* homeless person

Obduktion [ɔpduktsi'oːn] *f* postmortem

obduzieren [ɔpdu'tsiːrən] *vt* to do a postmortem on

O-Beine ['oːbaɪnə] *pl* bow *od* bandy legs *pl*

oben ['oːbən] *adv* above; (*in Haus*) upstairs; (*am oberen Ende*) at the top; **~ erwähnt, ~ genannt** above-mentioned; **nach ~** up; **von ~** down; **siehe ~** see above; **ganz ~** right at the top; **~ ohne** topless; **die Abbildung ~ links** *od* **links oben** the illustration in the top left-hand corner; **jdn von ~ herab behandeln** to treat sb condescendingly; **jdn von ~ bis unten ansehen** to look sb up and down; **Befehl von ~** orders from above; **die da ~** (*umg: die Vorgesetzten*) the powers that be; **oben'an** *adv* at the top; **oben'auf** *adv* up above, on the top ▷ *adj* (*munter*) in form; **oben'drein** *adv* into the bargain; **oben'hin** *adv* cursorily, superficially

Ober ['oːbər] (**-s, -**) *m* waiter

Ober- *zW*: **Oberarm** *m* upper arm; **Oberarzt** *m* senior physician; **Oberaufsicht** *f* supervision; **Oberbayern** *nt* Upper Bavaria; **Oberbefehl** *m* supreme command; **Oberbefehlshaber** *m* commander-in-chief; **Oberbegriff** *m* generic term; **Oberbekleidung** *f* outer clothing; **Oberbett** *nt* quilt; **Oberbürgermeister** *m* lord mayor; **Oberdeck** *nt* upper *od* top deck

obere, r, s *adj* upper; **die O-n** the bosses; (*Eccl*) the superiors; **die ~n Zehntausend** (*umg*) high society

Ober- *zW*: **Oberfläche** *f* surface; **oberflächlich** *adj* superficial; **bei oberflächlicher Betrachtung** at a quick glance; **jdn (nur) oberflächlich kennen** to know sb (only) slightly; **Obergeschoss** *nt* upper storey *od* story (US); **im zweiten Obergeschoss** on the second floor (*Brit*), on the third floor (US); **oberhalb** *adv* above ▷ *präp +gen* above; **Oberhand** *f* (*fig*): **die Oberhand gewinnen (über** +*akk*) to get the upper hand (over); **Oberhaupt** *nt* head, chief; **Oberhaus** *nt* (*in Großbritannien*) upper house, House of Lords; **Oberhemd** *nt* shirt; **Oberherrschaft** *f* supremacy, sovereignty

Oberin *f* matron; (*Eccl*) Mother Superior

Ober- *zW*: **oberirdisch** *adj* above ground; (*Leitung*) overhead; **Oberitalien** *nt* Northern Italy; **Oberkellner** *m* head waiter; **Oberkiefer** *m* upper jaw; **Oberkommando** *nt* supreme command; **Oberkörper** *m* upper part of body; **Oberlauf** *m*: **am Oberlauf des Rheins** in the upper reaches of the Rhine; **Oberleitung** *f* (*Elek*) overhead cable; **Oberlicht** *nt* skylight; **Oberlippe** *f* upper lip; **Oberösterreich** *nt* Upper Austria; **Oberprima** *f* (*früher*) *final year of German secondary school*; **Oberschenkel** *m* thigh; **Oberschicht** *f* upper classes *pl*; **Oberschule** *f* grammar school (*Brit*), high school (US); **Oberschwester** *f* (*Med*) matron; **Oberseite** *f* top (side); **Obersekunda** *f* (*früher*) *seventh year of German secondary school*

Oberst ['oːbərst] (**-en** *od* **-s, -en** *od* **-e**) *m* colonel

oberste, r, s *adj* very top, topmost

Ober- *zW*: **Oberstübchen** (*umg*) *nt*: **er ist nicht ganz richtig im Oberstübchen** he's not quite right up top; **Oberstufe** *f* upper school; **Oberteil** *nt* upper part; **Obertertia** *f* (*früher*) *fifth year of German secondary school*; **Oberwasser** *nt*: **Oberwasser haben/bekommen** to be/get on top (of things); **Oberweite** *f* bust *od* chest measurement

obgleich [ɔp'glaɪç] *konj* although

Obhut ['ɔphuːt] (**-**) *f* care, protection; **in jds ~ dat sein** to be in sb's care

obig ['oːbɪç] *adj* above

Objekt [ɔp'jɛkt] (**-(e)s, -e**) *nt* object

objektiv [ɔpjɛk'tiːf] *adj* objective

Objektiv (**-s, -e**) *nt* lens *sing*

Objektivität [ɔpjɛktivi'tɛːt] *f* objectivity

Oblate [o'blaːtə] (**-, -n**) *f* (*Gebäck*) wafer; (*Eccl*)

o

host

obligatorisch [obliga'to:rɪʃ] *adj* compulsory, obligatory

Oboe [o'bo:ə] (**-, -n**) *f* oboe

Obrigkeit ['o:brɪçkaɪt] *f* (*Behörden*) authorities *pl*, administration; (*Regierung*) government

Obrigkeitsdenken *nt* acceptance of authority

obschon [ɔp'ʃo:n] *konj* although

Observatorium [ɔpzɛrva'to:riʊm] *nt* observatory

obskur [ɔps'ku:r] *adj* obscure; (*verdächtig*) dubious

Obst [o:pst] (**-(e)s**) *nt* fruit; **Obstbau** *m* fruit-growing; **Obstbaum** *m* fruit tree; **Obstgarten** *m* orchard; **Obsthändler** *m* fruiterer (*Brit*), fruit merchant; **Obstkuchen** *m* fruit tart; **Obstsaft** *m* fruit juice; **Obstsalat** *m* fruit salad

obszön [ɔps'tsø:n] *adj* obscene

Obszönität [ɔpstøni'tɛ:t] *f* obscenity

Obus ['o:bʊs] (**-ses, -se**) (*umg*) *m* trolleybus

obwohl [ɔp'vo:l] *konj* although

Ochse ['ɔksə] (**-n, -n**) *m* ox; (*umg: Dummkopf*) twit; **er stand da wie der ~ vorm Berg** (*umg*) he stood there utterly bewildered

ochsen (*umg*) *vt, vi* to cram, swot (*Brit*)

Ochsenschwanzsuppe *f* oxtail soup

Ochsenzunge *f* ox tongue

Ocker ['ɔkər] (**-s, -**) *m od nt* ochre (*Brit*), ocher (*US*)

öd [ø:t(ə)] *adj* = **öde**

öde *adj* (*Land*) waste, barren; (*fig*) dull; **~ und leer** dreary and desolate

Öde (**-, -n**) *f* desert, waste(land); (*fig*) tedium

oder ['o:dər] *konj* or; **entweder ... ~** either ... or; **du kommst doch, ~?** you're coming, aren't you?

Ofen ['o:fən] (**-s, ⸚**) *m* oven; (*Heizofen*) fire, heater; (*Kohleofen*) stove; (*Hochofen*) furnace; (*Herd*) cooker, stove; **jetzt ist der ~ aus** (*umg*) that does it!; **Ofenrohr** *nt* stovepipe

offen ['ɔfən] *adj* open; (*aufrichtig*) frank; (*Stelle*) vacant; (*Bein*) ulcerated; (*Haare*) loose; **~er Wein** wine by the carafe od glass; **auf ~er Strecke** (*Straße*) on the open road; (*Eisenb*) between stations; **Tag der ~en Tür** open day (*Brit*), open house (*US*); **~e Handelsgesellschaft** (*Comm*) general od ordinary (*US*) partnership; **~ bleiben** (*Fenster*) to stay open; **~ halten** to keep open; **~ lassen** to leave open; **~ stehen** to be open; **seine Meinung ~ sagen** to speak one's mind; **ein ~es Wort mit jdm reden** to have a frank talk with sb; **~ gesagt** to be honest; *siehe auch* **offenbleiben; offenstehen**

offenbar *adj* obvious; (*vermutlich*) apparently

offenbaren [ɔfən'ba:rən] *vt* to reveal, manifest

Offenbarung *f* (*Rel*) revelation

Offenbarungseid *m* (*Jur*) oath of disclosure

Offen- *zW*: **offenbleiben** *unreg vi* (*fig: Frage, Entscheidung*) to remain open; *siehe auch* **offen**; **Offenheit** *f* candour (*Brit*), candor (*US*), frankness; **offenherzig** *adj* candid, frank; (*hum: Kleid*) revealing; **Offenherzigkeit** *f*

frankness; **offenkundig** *adj* well-known; (*klar*) evident; **offensichtlich** *adj* evident, obvious

offensiv [ɔfɛn'zi:f] *adj* offensive

Offensive (**-, -n**) *f* offensive

offenstehen *unreg vi* (*fig: Rechnung*) to be unpaid; **es steht Ihnen offen, es zu tun** you are at liberty to do it; **die (ganze) Welt steht ihm offen** he has the (whole) world at his feet; *siehe auch* **offen**

öffentlich ['œfəntlɪç] *adj* public; **die ~e Hand** (central/local) government; **Anstalt des ~en Rechts** public institution; **Ausgaben der ~en Hand** public spending *sing*

Öffentlichkeit *f* (*Leute*) public; (*einer Versammlung etc*) public nature; **in aller ~** in public; **an die ~ dringen** to reach the public ear; **unter Ausschluss der ~** in secret; (*Jur*) in camera

Öffentlichkeitsarbeit *f* public relations work

öffentlich-rechtlich *adj attrib* (under) public law

offerieren [ɔfe'ri:rən] *vt* to offer

Offerte [ɔ'fɛrtə] (**-, -n**) *f* offer

offiziell [ɔfitsi'ɛl] *adj* official

Offizier [ɔfi'tsi:r] (**-s, -e**) *m* officer

Offizierskasino *nt* officers' mess

öffnen ['œfnən] *vt, vr* to open; **jdm die Tür ~** to open the door for sb

Öffner ['œfnər] (**-s, -**) *m* opener

Öffnung ['œfnʊŋ] *f* opening

Öffnungsklausel *f* (*Jur*) escape clause; (*fig: Schlupfloch*) loophole

Öffnungszeiten *pl* opening times *pl*

Offsetdruck ['ɔfsɛtdrʊk] *m* offset (printing)

oft [ɔft] *adv* often

öfter ['œftər] *adv* more often *od* frequently; **des Öfteren** quite frequently; **~ mal was Neues** (*umg*) variety is the spice of life (*Sprichwort*)

öfters *adv* often, frequently

oftmals *adv* often, frequently

o. G. *abk* (= *ohne Gewähr*) without liability

OHG *f abk* (= *offene Handelsgesellschaft*) *siehe* **offen**

ohne ['o:nə] *präp +akk, konj* without; **das Darlehen ist ~ Weiteres bewilligt worden** the loan was granted without any problem; **das kann man nicht ~ Weiteres voraussetzen** you can't just assume that automatically; **das ist nicht ~** (*umg*) it's not bad; **~ Weiteres** without a second thought; (*sofort*) immediately; **ohnedies** *adv* anyway; **ohneeinander** [o:nəⁱaɪˈnandər] *adv* without each other; **ohnegleichen** *adj* unsurpassed, without equal; **ohnehin** *adv* anyway, in any case; **es ist ohnehin schon spät** it's late enough already

Ohnmacht ['o:nmaxt] *f* faint; (*fig*) impotence; **in ~ fallen** to faint

ohnmächtig ['o:nmɛçtɪç] *adj* in a faint, unconscious; (*fig*) weak, impotent; **sie ist ~** she has fainted; **ohnmächtige Wut, ~er Zorn** helpless rage; **einer Sache** *dat* **~ gegenüberstehen** to be helpless in the face of sth

Ohr [oːr] **(-(e)s, -en)** *nt* ear; (*Gehör*) hearing; **sich aufs ~ legen** *od* **hauen** (*umg*) to kip down; **jdm die ~en lang ziehen** (*umg*) to tweak sb's ear(s); **jdm in den ~en liegen** to keep on at sb; **jdn übers ~ hauen** (*umg*) to pull a fast one on sb; **auf dem ~ bin ich taub** (*fig*) nothing doing (*umg*); **schreib es dir hinter die ~en** (*umg*) will you (finally) get that into your (thick) head!; **bis über die** *od* **beide ~en verliebt sein** to be head over heels in love; **viel um die ~en haben** (*umg*) to have a lot on (one's plate); **halt die ~en steif!** keep a stiff upper lip!

Öhr [øːr] **(-(e)s, -e)** *nt* eye

Ohren- *zW*: **Ohrenarzt** *m* ear specialist; **ohrenbetäubend** *adj* deafening; **Ohrensausen** *nt* (*Med*) buzzing in one's ears; **Ohrenschmalz** *nt* earwax; **Ohrenschmerzen** *pl* earache *sing*; **Ohrenschützer** **(-s, -)** *m* earmuff

Ohr- *zW*: **Ohrfeige** *f* slap on the face; (*als Strafe*) box on the ears; **ohrfeigen** *vt untr*: **jdn ohrfeigen** to slap sb's face; to box sb's ears; **ich könnte mich selbst ohrfeigen, dass ich das gemacht habe** I could kick myself for doing that; **Ohrläppchen** *nt* ear lobe; **Ohrringe** *pl* earrings *pl*; **Ohrwurm** *m* earwig; (*Mus*) catchy tune

o. J. *abk* (= *ohne Jahr*) no year given

okkupieren [ɔku'piːrən] *vt* to occupy

Öko- [ˈøko-] *in zw* eco-, ecological; **Ökofonds** [ˈøːkofɔː] *m* eco-fund, green fund; **Ökoladen** [ˈøːkolaːdən] *m* wholefood shop

Ökologie [økolo'giː] *f* ecology

ökologisch [øko'loːgɪʃ] *adj* ecological, environmental

Ökonometrie [økonome'triː] *f* econometrics *pl*

Ökonomie [økono'miː] *f* economy; (*als Wissenschaft*) economics *sing*

ökonomisch [øko'noːmɪʃ] *adj* economical

Öko- *zW*: **Ökopax** [øko'paks] **(-en, -e)** (*umg*) *m* environmentalist; **Ökostrom** *m* green electricity; **Ökosystem** [ˈøːkozysteːm] *nt* ecosystem

Okt. *abk* (= *Oktober*) Oct.

Oktan [ɔk'taːn] **(-s, -e)** *nt* octane; **Oktanzahl** *f* octane rating

Oktave [ɔk'taːvə] **(-, -n)** *f* octave

Oktober [ɔk'toːbər] **(-(s), -)** *m* October; *siehe auch* **September**

Oktoberfest *nt see culture note*

⬭ **OKTOBERFEST**

⬭ The annual October beer festival, the
⬭ *Oktoberfest*, takes place in Munich on a huge
⬭ field where beer tents, roller coasters and
⬭ many other amusements are set up. People
⬭ sit at long wooden tables, drink beer from
⬭ enormous litre beer mugs, eat pretzels and
⬭ listen to brass bands. It is a great attraction
⬭ for tourists and locals alike.

ökumenisch [øku'meːnɪʃ] *adj* ecumenical

Öl [øːl] **(-(e)s, -e)** *nt* oil; **auf Öl stoßen** to strike oil

Öl- *zW*: **Ölbaum** *m* olive tree; **ölen** *vt* to oil; (*Tech*) to lubricate; **wie ein geölter Blitz** (*umg*) like greased lightning; **Ölfarbe** *f* oil paint; **Ölfeld** *nt* oilfield; **Ölfilm** *m* film of oil; **Ölheizung** *f* oil-fired central heating

ölig *adj* oily

Oligopol [oligo'poːl] **(-s, -e)** *nt* oligopoly

oliv [o'liːf] *adj* olive-green

Olive [o'liːvə] **(-, -n)** *f* olive

Olivenöl *nt* olive oil

Öljacke *f* oilskin jacket

oll [ɔl] (*umg*) *adj* old; **das sind ~e Kamellen** that's old hat

Öl- *zW*: **Ölmessstab** *m* dipstick; **Ölpest** *f* oil pollution; **Ölplattform** *f* oil rig; **Ölsardine** *f* sardine; **Ölscheich** *m* oil sheik; **Ölstand** *m* oil level; **Ölstandanzeiger** *m* (*Aut*) oil level indicator; **Öltanker** *m* oil tanker; **Ölteppich** *m* oil slick

Ölung *f* oiling; (*Eccl*) anointment; **die Letzte ~** Extreme Unction

Ölwanne *f* (*Aut*) sump (*Brit*), oil pan (*US*)

Ölwechsel *m* oil change

Olymp [o'lʏmp] **(-s)** *m* (*Berg*) Mount Olympus

Olympiade [olʏmpi'aːdə] **(-, -n)** *f* Olympic Games *pl*

Olympiasieger, in [o'lʏmpiaziːɡər(ɪn)] *m(f)* Olympic champion

olympisch [o'lʏmpɪʃ] *adj* Olympic

Ölzeug *nt* oilskins *pl*

Oma [ˈoːma] **(-, -s)** (*umg*) *f* granny

Oman [o'maːn] **(-s)** *nt* Oman

Omelett [ɔm(ə)'lɛt] **(-(e)s, -s)** *nt* omelette (*Brit*), omelet (*US*)

Omelette [ɔm(ə)'lɛt] *f* = **Omelett**

Omen [ˈoːmɛn] **(-s,** *od* **Omina)** *nt* omen

Omnibus [ˈɔmnibʊs] *m* (omni)bus

Onanie [ona'niː] *f* masturbation

onanieren [ona'niːrən] *vi* to masturbate

ondulieren [ɔndu'liːrən] *vt, vi* to crimp

Onkel [ˈɔŋkəl] **(-s, -)** *m* uncle

online [ˈɔnlaɪn] *adj* (*Comput*) on-line

Onlineauktion *f* on-line auction

Onlinedienst *m* (*Comput*) on-line service

OP *m abk* = **Operationssaal**

Opa [ˈoːpa] **(-s, -s)** (*umg*) *m* grandpa

Opal [o'paːl] **(-s, -e)** *m* opal

Oper [ˈoːpər] **(-, -n)** *f* opera; (*Opernhaus*) opera house

Operation [operatsi'oːn] *f* operation

Operationssaal *m* operating theatre (*Brit*) *od* theater (*US*)

operativ [opəra'tiːf] *adv* (*Med*): **eine Geschwulst ~ entfernen** to remove a growth by surgery

Operette [ope'rɛtə] *f* operetta

operieren [ope'riːrən] *vt, vi* to operate; **sich ~ lassen** to have an operation

Opern- *zW*: **Opernglas** *nt* opera glasses *pl*; **Opernhaus** *nt* opera house; **Opernsänger, in** *m(f)* opera singer

Opfer [ˈɔpfər] **(-s, -)** *nt* sacrifice; (*Mensch*)

victim; **Opferbereitschaft** f readiness to make sacrifices
opfern vt to sacrifice
Opferstock m (Eccl) offertory box
Opferung f sacrifice; (Eccl) offertory
Opium ['oːpiʊm] (-s) nt opium
opponieren [ɔpoˈniːrən] vi: **gegen jdn/etw ~** to oppose sb/sth
opportun [ɔpɔrˈtuːn] adj opportune;
  Opportunismus [-ˈnɪsmʊs] m opportunism;
  Opportunist, in [-ˈnɪst(ɪn)] m(f) opportunist
Opposition [ɔpozitsiˈoːn] f opposition
oppositionell [ɔpozitsioˈnɛl] adj opposing
Oppositionsführer m leader of the opposition
optieren [ɔpˈtiːrən] vi (Pol: form): **~ für** to opt for
Optik ['ɔptɪk] f optics sing
Optiker, in (-s, -) m(f) optician
optimal [ɔptiˈmaːl] adj optimal, optimum
Optimismus [ɔptiˈmɪsmʊs] m optimism
Optimist, in [ɔptiˈmɪst(ɪn)] m(f) optimist;
  optimistisch adj optimistic
optisch ['ɔptɪʃ] adj optical; **~e Täuschung** optical illusion
Orakel [oˈraːkəl] (-s, -) nt oracle
Orange [oˈrãːʒə] (-, -n) f orange; **orange** adj orange
Orangeade [orãˈʒaːdə] (-, -n) f orangeade
Orangeat [orãˈʒaːt] (-s, -e) nt candied peel
Orangen- zW: **Orangenmarmelade** f marmalade; **Orangensaft** m orange juice;
  Orangenschale f orange peel
Oratorium [oraˈtoːriʊm] nt (Mus) oratorio
Orchester [ɔrˈkɛstər] (-s, -) nt orchestra
Orchidee [ɔrçiˈdeːə] (-, -n) f orchid
Orden ['ɔrdən] (-s, -) m (Eccl) order; (Mil) decoration
Ordensgemeinschaft f religious order
Ordensschwester f nun
ordentlich ['ɔrdəntlɪç] adj (anständig) decent, respectable; (geordnet) tidy, neat; (umg: annehmbar) not bad; (: tüchtig) real, proper; (Leistung) reasonable; **~es Mitglied** full member; **~er Professor** (full) professor; **eine ~e Tracht Prügel** a proper hiding; **~ arbeiten** to be a thorough and precise worker;
  Ordentlichkeit f respectability; tidiness
Order (-, -s od -n) f (Comm: Auftrag) order
ordern vt (Comm) to order
Ordinalzahl [ɔrdiˈnaːltsaːl] f ordinal number
ordinär [ɔrdiˈnɛːr] adj common, vulgar
Ordinarius [ɔrdiˈnaːriʊs] (-, **Ordinarien**) m (Univ): **~ (für)** professor (of)
ordnen ['ɔrdnən] vt to order, put in order
Ordner (-s, -) m steward; (Comm) file
Ordnung f order; (Ordnen) ordering; (Geordnetsein) tidiness; **geht in ~** (umg) that's all right od OK (umg); **~ schaffen, für ~ sorgen** to put things in order, tidy things up; **jdn zur ~ rufen** to call sb to order; **bei ihm muss alles seine ~ haben** (räumlich) he has to have everything in its proper place; (zeitlich) he has to do everything according to a fixed schedule; **das Kind braucht seine ~** the child needs a

routine
Ordnungs- zW: **Ordnungsamt** nt ≈ town clerk's office; **ordnungsgemäß** adj proper, according to the rules; **ordnungshalber** adv as a matter of form; **Ordnungsliebe** f tidiness, orderliness; **Ordnungsstrafe** f fine; **ordnungswidrig** adj contrary to the rules, irregular; **Ordnungswidrigkeit** f infringement (of law or rule); **Ordnungszahl** f ordinal number
ORF (-) m abk (= Österreichischer Rundfunk)
Organ [ɔrˈgaːn] (-s, -e) nt organ; (Stimme) voice
Organisation [ɔrganizatsiˈoːn] f organization
Organisationstalent nt organizing ability; (Person) good organizer
Organisator [ɔrganiˈzaːtɔr] m organizer
organisch [ɔrˈgaːnɪʃ] adj organic; (Erkrankung, Leiden) physical
organisieren [ɔrganiˈziːrən] vt to organize, arrange; (umg: beschaffen) to acquire ▷ vr to organize
Organismus [ɔrgaˈnɪsmʊs] m organism
Organist [ɔrgaˈnɪst] m organist
Organspender m donor (of an organ)
Organspenderausweis m donor card
Organverpflanzung f transplantation (of an organ)
Orgasmus [ɔrˈgasmʊs] m orgasm
Orgel ['ɔrgəl] (-, -n) f organ; **Orgelpfeife** f organ pipe; **wie die Orgelpfeifen stehen** to stand in order of height
Orgie ['ɔrgiə] f orgy
Orient ['oːriɛnt] (-s) m Orient, east; **der Vordere ~** the Near East
Orientale [oːriɛnˈtaːlə] (-n, -n) m Oriental
Orientalin [oːriɛnˈtaːlɪn] f Oriental
orientalisch adj oriental
orientieren [oːriɛnˈtiːrən] vt (örtlich) to locate; (fig) to inform ▷ vr to find one's way od bearings; (fig) to inform o.s.
Orientierung [oːriɛnˈtiːrʊŋ] f orientation; (fig) information; **die ~ verlieren** to lose one's bearings
Orientierungssinn m sense of direction
Orientierungsstufe m see culture note

ORIENTIERUNGSSTUFE

The Orientierungsstufe is the name given to the first two years spent in a Realschule or Gymnasium, during which a child is assessed as to his or her suitability for the school. At the end of the two years it may be decided to transfer the child to a school more suited to his or her ability.

original [origiˈnaːl] adj original; **~ Meißener Porzellan** genuine Meissen porcelain; **Original** (-s, -e) nt original; (Mensch) character; **Originalausgabe** f first edition; **Originalfassung** f original version
Originalität [originaliˈtɛːt] f originality
Originalübertragung f live broadcast
originell [origiˈnɛl] adj original

Orkan [ɔr'kaːn] (-(e)s, -e) m hurricane;
orkanartig adj (Wind) gale-force; (Beifall)
thunderous

Orkneyinseln ['ɔːknɪ|ɪnzəln] pl Orkney Islands
pl, Orkneys pl

Ornament [ɔrna'mɛnt] nt decoration,
ornament

ornamental [ɔrnamɛn'taːl] adj decorative,
ornamental

Ornithologe [ɔrnito'loːgə] (-n, -n) m
ornithologist

Ornithologin [ɔrnito'loːgɪn] f ornithologist

Ort[1] [ɔrt] (-(e)s, -e) m place; **an ~ und
Stelle** on the spot; **am ~** in the place; **am
angegebenen ~** in the place quoted, loc. cit.;
~ der Handlung (Theat) scene of the action;
das ist höheren ~(e)s entschieden worden
(hum: form) the decision came from above

Ort[2] [ɔrt] (-(e)s, ¨er) m: **vor ~** at the (coal) face;
(auch fig) on the spot

Örtchen ['œrtçən] (umg) nt loo (Brit), john (US)

orten vt to locate

orthodox [ɔrto'dɔks] adj orthodox

Orthografie [ɔrtogra'fiː] f spelling,
orthography

orthografisch [ɔrto'graːfɪʃ] adj orthographic

Orthopäde [ɔrto'pɛːdə] (-n, -n) m orthopaedic
(Brit) od orthopedic (US) specialist,
orthopaedist (Brit), orthopedist (US)

Orthopädie [ɔrtopɛ'diː] f orthopaedics sing
(Brit), orthopedics sing (US)

orthopädisch adj orthopaedic (Brit),
orthopedic (US)

örtlich ['œrtlɪç] adj local; **jdn ~ betäuben** to
give sb a local anaesthetic (Brit) od anesthetic
(US); **Örtlichkeit** f locality; **sich mit den
Örtlichkeiten vertraut machen** to get to
know the place

Ortsangabe f (name of the) town; **ohne ~**
(Buch) no place of publication indicated

ortsansässig adj local

Ortschaft f village, small town; **geschlossene
~** built-up area

Orts- zW: **ortsfremd** adj nonlocal; **Ortsfremde,
r** f(m) stranger; **Ortsgespräch** nt local (phone)
call; **Ortsgruppe** f local branch od group;
Ortskenntnis f: **(gute) Ortskenntnisse
haben** to know one's way around (well);
Ortskrankenkasse f: **Allgemeine
Ortskrankenkasse** compulsory medical insurance
scheme; **ortskundig** adj familiar with the
place; **ortskundig sein** to know one's way
around; **Ortsname** m place name; **Ortsnetz**
nt (Tel) local telephone exchange area;
Ortsnetzkennzahl f (Tel) dialling (Brit) od area
(US) code; **Ortsschild** nt place name sign;
Ortssinn m sense of direction; **Ortstarif** m
(Tel) charge for local calls; **Ortsvorschriften**
pl by(e)-laws pl; **Ortszeit** f local time;
Ortszuschlag m (local) weighting allowance

Ortung f locating

öS. abk (= österreichischer Schilling)

Öse ['øːzə] (-, -n) f loop; (an Kleidung) eye

Oslo ['ɔslo] (-s) nt Oslo

Ossi ['ɔsi] (-s, -s) (umg) m East German; see
culture note

● **OSSI**
●
●
● Ossi is a colloquial and rather derogatory
● word used to describe a German from the
● former DDR.

öst. abk (= österreichisch) Aust.

Ost- zW: **Ostafrika** nt East Africa; **ostdeutsch**
adj East German; **Ostdeutsche, Ostdeutscher**
f(m) East German; **Ostdeutschland** nt (Pol:
früher) East Germany; (Geog) Eastern Germany

Osten (-s) m east; **der Ferne ~** the Far East;
der Nahe ~ the Middle East, the Near East

ostentativ [ɔstɛnta'tiːf] adj pointed,
ostentatious

Oster- zW: **Osterei** nt Easter egg; **Osterfest**
nt Easter; **Osterglocke** f daffodil; **Osterhase**
m Easter bunny; **Osterinsel** f Easter Island;
Ostermarsch m Easter demonstration;
Ostermontag m Easter Monday

Ostern (-s, -) nt Easter; **frohe** od **fröhliche ~!**
Happy Easter!; **zu ~** at Easter

Österreich ['øːstəraɪç] (-s) nt Austria

Österreicher, in (-s, -) m(f) Austrian

österreichisch adj Austrian

Ostersonntag m Easter Day od Sunday

Osteuropa nt East(ern) Europe

osteuropäisch adj East European

östlich ['œstlɪç] adj eastern, easterly

Östrogen [œstro'geːn] (-s, -e) nt oestrogen
(Brit), estrogen (US)

Ost- zW: **Ostsee** f Baltic Sea; **ostwärts** adv
eastwards; **Ostwind** m east wind

oszillieren [ɔstsɪ'liːrən] vi to oscillate

Otter[1] ['ɔtər] (-s, -) m otter

Otter[2] ['ɔtər] (-, -n) f (Schlange) adder

ÖTV (-) f abk (= Gewerkschaft öffentliche Dienste,
Transport und Verkehr) ≈ Transport and General
Workers' Union

Ouvertüre [uvɛr'tyːrə] (-, -n) f overture

oval [o'vaːl] adj oval

Ovation [ovatsi'oːn] f ovation

Overall ['oʊvərɔːl] (-s, -s) m (Schutzanzug)
overalls pl

ÖVP (-) f abk (= Österreichische Volkspartei) Austrian
People's Party

Ovulation [ovulatsi'oːn] f ovulation

Oxid, Oxyd [ɔ'ksyːt] (-(e)s, -e) nt oxide

oxidieren, oxydieren [ɔksy'diːrən] vt, vi to
oxidize

Oxidierung, Oxydierung f oxidization

Ozean ['oːtseaːn] (-s, -e) nt ocean;
Ozeandampfer m (ocean-going) liner

Ozeanien [otse'aːniən] (-s) nt Oceania

ozeanisch [otse'aːnɪʃ] adj oceanic; (Sprachen)
Oceanic

Ozeanriese (umg) m ocean liner

Ozon [o'tsoːn] (-s) nt ozone; **Ozonloch** nt hole
in the ozone layer; **Ozonschicht** f ozone layer

O

Pp

P, p [pe:] *nt* P, p; **P wie Peter** = P for Peter

P. *abk* = **Pastor; Pater**

Paar [pa:r] (**-(e)s, -e**) *nt* pair; (*Liebespaar*) couple

paar *adj inv*: **ein ~ a few**; (*zwei oder drei*) a couple of; *siehe auch* **paarmal**

paaren *vt, vr* (*Tiere*) to mate, pair

Paar- *zW*: **Paarhufer** *pl* (*Zool*) cloven-hoofed animals *pl*; **Paarlauf** *m* pair skating; **paarmal** *adv*: **ein paarmal** a few times

Paarung *f* combination; (*von Tieren*) mating

paarweise *adv* in pairs; in couples

Pacht [paxt] (**-, -en**) *f* lease; (*Entgelt*) rent; **pachten** *vt* to lease; **du hast das Sofa doch nicht für dich gepachtet** (*umg*) don't hog the sofa

Pächter, in ['pɛçtər(ɪn)] (**-s, -**) *m(f)* leaseholder; tenant

Pachtvertrag *m* lease

Pack¹ [pak] (**-(e)s, -e** *od* **-e**) *m* bundle, pack

Pack² [pak] (**-(e)s**) (*pej*) *nt* mob, rabble

Päckchen ['pɛkçən] *nt* small package; (*Zigaretten*) packet; (*Postpäckchen*) small parcel

Packeis *nt* pack ice

Packen (**-s, -**) *m* bundle; (*fig: Menge*) heaps (of); **packen** *vt, vi* (*auch Comput*) to pack; (*fassen*) to grasp, seize; (*umg: schaffen*) to manage; (*fig: fesseln*) to grip; **packen wirs!** (*umg: gehen*) let's go

Packer, in (**-s, -**) *m(f)* packer

Packesel *m* pack mule; (*fig*) packhorse

Packpapier *nt* brown paper, wrapping paper

Packung *f* packet; (*Pralinenpackung*) box; (*Med*) compress

Packzettel *m* (*Comm*) packing slip

Pädagoge [peda'go:gə] (**-n, -n**) *m* educationalist

Pädagogik *f* education

Pädagogin [peda'go:gɪn] *f* educationalist

pädagogisch *adj* educational, pedagogical; **~e Hochschule** college of education

Paddel ['padəl] (**-s, -**) *nt* paddle; **Paddelboot** *nt* canoe

paddeln *vi* to paddle

pädophil [pɛdo'fi:l] *adj* paedophile (*Brit*), pedophile (*US*)

Pädophilie [pɛdofi'li:] *f* paedophilia (*Brit*), pedophilia (*US*)

paffen ['pafən] *vt, vi* to puff

Page ['pa:ʒə] (**-n, -n**) *m* page(boy)

Pagenkopf *m* pageboy cut

paginieren [pagi'ni:rən] *vt* to paginate

Paginierung *f* pagination

Paillette [paɪ'jɛtə] *f* sequin

Paket [pa'ke:t] (**-(e)s, -e**) *nt* packet; (*Postpaket*) parcel; **Paketannahme** *f* parcels office; **Paketausgabe** *f* parcels office; **Paketkarte** *f* dispatch note; **Paketpost** *f* parcel post; **Paketschalter** *m* parcels counter

Pakistan ['pa:kɪsta:n] (**-s**) *nt* Pakistan

Pakistaner, in [pakɪs'ta:nər(ɪn)] (**-s, -**) *m(f)* Pakistani

Pakistani [pakɪs'ta:ni] (**-(s), -(s)**) *m* Pakistani

pakistanisch *adj* Pakistani

Pakt [pakt] (**-(e)s, -e**) *m* pact

Paläontologie [palɛɔntolo'gi:] *f* palaeontology (*Brit*), paleontology (*US*)

Palast [pa'last] (**-es, Paläste**) *m* palace

Palästina [palɛ'sti:na] (**-s**) *nt* Palestine

Palästinenser, in [palɛsti'nɛnzər(ɪn)] (**-s, -**) *m(f)* Palestinian

palästinensisch *adj* Palestinian

Palaver [pa'la:vər] (**-s, -**) *nt* (*auch fig: umg*) palaver

Palette [pa'lɛtə] *f* palette; (*fig*) range; (*Ladepalette*) pallet

Palme ['palmə] (**-, -n**) *f* palm (tree); **jdn auf die ~ bringen** (*umg*) to make sb see red

Palmsonntag *m* Palm Sunday

Pampelmuse ['pampəlmu:zə] (**-, -n**) *f* grapefruit

pampig ['pampɪç] (*umg*) *adj* (*frech*) fresh

Panama ['panama] (**-s**) *nt* Panama; **Panamakanal** *m* Panama Canal

Panflöte ['pa:nflø:tə] *f* panpipes *pl*, Pan's pipes *pl*

panieren [pa'ni:rən] *vt* (*Koch*) to coat with egg and breadcrumbs

Paniermehl [pa'ni:rme:l] *nt* breadcrumbs *pl*

Panik ['pa:nɪk] *f* panic; **nur keine ~!** don't panic!; **in ~ ausbrechen** to panic; **Panikkäufe** *pl* panic buying *sing*; **Panikmache** (*umg*) *f* panicmongering

panisch ['pa:nɪʃ] *adj* panic-stricken

Panne ['panə] (**-, -n**) *f* (*Aut etc*) breakdown; (*Missgeschick*) slip; **uns ist eine ~ passiert** we've boobed (*Brit*) (*umg*) *od* goofed (*US*) (*umg*)

Pannendienst m breakdown service
Pannenhilfe f breakdown service
Panorama [pano'ra:ma] (**-s, -men**) nt panorama
panschen ['panʃən] vi to splash about ▷ vt to water down
Panther, Panter ['pantər] (**-s, -**) m panther
Pantoffel [pan'tɔfəl] (**-s, -n**) m slipper; **Pantoffelheld** (umg) m henpecked husband
Pantomime [panto'mi:mə] (**-, -n**) f mime
Panzer ['pantsər] (**-s, -**) m armour (Brit), armor (US); (fig) shield; (Platte) armo(u)r plate; (Fahrzeug) tank; **Panzerfaust** f bazooka; **Panzerglas** nt bulletproof glass; **Panzergrenadier** m armoured (Brit) od armored (US) infantryman
panzern vt to armour (Brit) od armor (US) plate ▷ vr (fig) to arm o.s.
Panzerschrank m strongbox
Panzerwagen m armoured (Brit) od armored (US) car
Papa [pa'pa:] (**-s, -s**) (umg) m dad(dy), pa
Papagei [papa'gaɪ] (**-s, -en**) m parrot
Papier [pa'pi:r] (**-s, -e**) nt paper; (Wertpapier) share; **Papiere** pl (identity) papers pl; (Urkunden) documents pl; **seine ~e bekommen** (entlassen werden) to get one's cards; **Papierfabrik** f paper mill; **Papiergeld** nt paper money; **Papierkorb** m wastepaper basket; **Papierkram** (umg) m bumf (Brit) (umg); **Papierkrieg** m red tape; **Papiertüte** f paper bag; **Papiervorschub** m (Drucker) paper advance
Pappbecher m paper cup
Pappdeckel (**-, -n**) m cardboard
Pappe ['papə] f cardboard; **das ist nicht von ~** (umg) that is really something
Pappeinband m pasteboard
Pappel (**-, -n**) f poplar
pappen (umg) vt, vi to stick
Pappenheimer pl: **ich kenne meine ~** (umg) I know you lot/that lot (inside out)
Pappenstiel (umg) m: **keinen ~ wert sein** not to be worth a thing; **für einen ~ bekommen** to get for a song
papperlapapp [papərla'pap] interj rubbish!
pappig adj sticky
Pappmaschee, Pappmaché [papma'ʃe:] (**-s, -s**) nt papier-mâché
Pappteller m paper plate
Paprika ['paprika] (**-s, -s**) m (Gewürz) paprika; (Paprikaschote) pepper; **Paprikaschote** f pepper; **gefüllte Paprikaschoten** stuffed peppers
Papst [pa:pst] (**-(e)s, ̈e**) m pope
päpstlich ['pɛ:pstlɪç] adj papal; **~er als der Papst sein** to be more Catholic than the Pope
Parabel [pa'ra:bəl] (**-, -n**) f parable; (Math) parabola
Parabolantenne [para'bo:l|antɛnə] f (TV) satellite dish
Parade [pa'ra:də] (**-, -n**) f (Mil) parade, review; (Sport) parry; **Paradebeispiel** nt prime example; **Parademarsch** m march past;

Paradeschritt m goose step
Paradies [para'di:s] (**-es, -e**) nt paradise; **paradiesisch** adj heavenly
Paradox [para'dɔks] (**-es, -e**) nt paradox; **paradox** adj paradoxical
Paraffin [para'fi:n] (**-s, -e**) nt (Chem: Paraffinöl) paraffin (Brit), kerosene (US); (Paraffinwachs) paraffin wax
Paragraf [para'gra:f] (**-en, -en**) m paragraph; (Jur) section
Paragrafenreiter (umg) m pedant
Paraguay [paragu'a:i] (**-s**) nt Paraguay
Paraguayer, in [para'gua:jər(ɪn)] (**-s, -**) m(f) Paraguayan
paraguayisch adj Paraguayan
parallel [para'le:l] adj parallel; **~ schalten** (Elek) to connect in parallel
Parallele (**-, -n**) f parallel
Parameter [pa'ra:metər] m parameter
paramilitärisch [paramili'tɛ:rɪʃ] adj paramilitary
Paranuss ['pa:ranʊs] f Brazil nut
paraphieren [para'fi:rən] vt (Vertrag) to initial
Parasit [para'zi:t] (**-en, -en**) m (lit, fig) parasite
parat [pa'ra:t] adj ready
Pärchen ['pɛ:rçən] nt couple
Parcours [par'ku:r] (**-, -**) m showjumping course; (Sportart) showjumping
Pardon [par'dõ:] (**-s**) (umg) m od nt: **~!** (Verzeihung) sorry!; **kein ~ kennen** to be ruthless
Parfüm [par'fy:m] (**-s, -s** od **-e**) nt perfume
Parfümerie [parfymə'ri:] f perfumery
Parfümflasche f scent bottle
parfümieren [parfy'mi:rən] vt to scent, perfume
parieren [pa'ri:rən] vt to parry ▷ vi (umg) to obey
Paris [pa'ri:s] (**-**) nt Paris
Pariser [pa'ri:zər] (**-s, -**) m Parisian; (umg: Kondom) rubber ▷ adj attrib Parisian, Paris attrib
Pariserin f Parisian
Parität [pari'tɛ:t] f parity; **paritätisch** adj: **paritätische Mitbestimmung** equal representation
Pariwert ['pa:rive:rt] m par value, parity
Park [park] (**-s, -s**) m park
Parka ['parka] (**-(s), -s**) m parka
Parkanlage f park; (um Gebäude) grounds pl
Parkbucht f parking bay
parken vt, vi to park; **„P~ verboten!"** "No Parking"
Parkett [par'kɛt] (**-(e)s, -e**) nt parquet (floor); (Theat) stalls pl (Brit), orchestra (US); **Parketthandel** m (Fin) floor trading
Park- zW: **Parkhaus** nt multistorey car park; **Parklücke** f parking space; **Parkplatz** m car park, parking lot (US); parking place; **Parkscheibe** f parking disc; **Parkuhr** f parking meter; **Parkverbot** nt parking ban
Parlament [parla'mɛnt] nt parliament
Parlamentarier [parlamɛn'ta:riər] (**-s, -**) m parliamentarian

p

parlamentarisch *adj* parliamentary

Parlaments- *zW:* **Parlamentsausschuss** *m* parliamentary committee; **Parlamentsbeschluss** *m* vote of parliament; **Parlamentsferien** *pl* recess *sing;* **Parlamentsmitglied** *nt* Member of Parliament (*Brit*), Congressman (*US*); **Parlamentssitzung** *f* sitting (of parliament)

Parodie [paro'di:] *f* parody

parodieren *vt* to parody

Parodontose [parodɔn'to:zə] (**-, -n**) *f* shrinking gums *pl*

Parole [pa'ro:lə] (**-, -n**) *f* password; (*Wahlspruch*) motto

Partei [par'taɪ] *f* party; (*im Mietshaus*) tenant, party (*form*); **für jdn ~ ergreifen** to take sb's side; **Parteibuch** *nt* party membership book; **Parteiführung** *f* party leadership; **Parteigenosse** *m* party member; **parteiisch** *adj* partial, bias(s)ed; **parteilich** *adj* party *attrib;* **Parteilinie** *f* party line; **parteilos** *adj* neutral; **Parteinahme** (**-, -n**) *f* partisanship; **parteipolitisch** *adj* party political; **Parteiprogramm** *nt* (party) manifesto; **Parteitag** *m* party conference; **Parteivorsitzende, r** *f(m)* party leader

Parterre [par'tɛr] (**-s, -s**) *nt* ground floor; (*Theat*) stalls *pl* (*Brit*), orchestra (*US*)

Partie [par'ti:] *f* part; (*Spiel*) game; (*Ausflug*) outing; (*Mann, Frau*) catch; (*Comm*) lot; **mit von der ~ sein** to join in

partiell [partsi'ɛl] *adj* partial

Partikel [par'ti:kəl] (**-, -n**) *f* particle

Partisan, in [parti'za:n(ɪn)] (**-s** *od* **-en, -en**) *m(f)* partisan

Partitur [parti'tu:r] *f* (*Mus*) score

Partizip [parti'tsi:p] (**-s, -ien**) *nt* participle; **~ Präsens/Perfekt** (*Gram*) present/past participle

Partner, in ['partnər(ɪn)] (**-s, -**) *m(f)* partner; **Partnerschaft** *f* partnership; (*Städtepartnerschaft*) twinning; **partnerschaftlich** *adj* as partners; **Partnerstadt** *f* twin town (*Brit*)

partout [par'tu:] *adv:* **er will ~ ins Kino gehen** he insists on going to the cinema

Party ['pa:rti] (**-, -s**) *f* party

Parzelle [par'tsɛlə] *f* plot, lot

Pascha ['paʃa] (**-s, -s**) *m:* **wie ein ~** like Lord Muck (*Brit*) (*umg*)

Pass [pas] (**-es, ⸚e**) *m* pass; (*Ausweis*) passport

passabel [pa'sa:bəl] *adj* passable, reasonable

Passage [pa'sa:ʒə] (**-, -n**) *f* passage; (*Ladenstraße*) arcade

Passagier [pasa'ʒi:r] (**-s, -e**) *m* passenger; **Passagierdampfer** *m* passenger steamer; **Passagierflugzeug** *nt* airliner

Passah ['pasa], **Passahfest** ['pasafɛst] *nt* (Feast of the) Passover

Passamt *nt* passport office

Passant, in [pa'sant(ɪn)] *m(f)* passer-by

Passbild *nt* passport photo(graph)

passé, passee [pa'se:] *adj:* **diese Mode ist längst ~** this fashion went out long ago

passen ['pasən] *vi* to fit; (*auf Frage, Karten*) to pass; **~ zu** (*Farbe etc*) to go with; **Sonntag passt uns nicht** Sunday is no good for us; **die Schuhe ~ (mir) gut** the shoes are a good fit (for me); **zu jdm ~** (*Mensch*) to suit sb; **das passt mir nicht** that doesn't suit me; **er passt nicht zu dir** he's not right for you; **das könnte dir so ~!** (*umg*) you'd like that, wouldn't you?

passend *adj* suitable; (*zusammenpassend*) matching; (*angebracht*) fitting; (*Zeit*) convenient; **haben Sie es ~?** (*Geld*) have you got the right money?

Passfoto *nt* passport photo(graph)

passierbar [pa'si:rba:r] *adj* passable; (*Fluss, Kanal*) negotiable

passieren *vt* to pass; (*durch Sieb*) to strain ▷ *vi* (*Hilfsverb sein*) to happen; **es ist ein Unfall passiert** there has been an accident

Passierschein *m* pass, permit

Passion [pasi'o:n] *f* passion

passioniert [pasio'ni:rt] *adj* enthusiastic, passionate

Passionsfrucht *f* passion fruit

Passionsspiel *nt* Passion Play

Passionszeit *f* Passiontide

passiv ['pasi:f] *adj* passive; **~es Rauchen** passive smoking; **Passiv** (**-s, -e**) *nt* passive

Passiva [pa'si:va] *pl* (*Comm*) liabilities *pl*

Passivität [pasivi'tɛ:t] *f* passiveness

Passivposten *m* (*Comm*) debit entry

Pass- *zW:* **Passkontrolle** *f* passport control; **Passstelle** *f* passport office; **Passstraße** *f* (mountain) pass; **Passzwang** *m* requirement to carry a passport

Paste ['pastə] (**-, -n**) *f* paste

Pastell [pas'tɛl] (**-(e)s, -e**) *nt* pastel; **Pastellfarbe** *f* pastel colour (*Brit*) *od* color (*US*); **pastellfarben** *adj* pastel-colo(u)red

Pastete [pas'te:tə] (**-, -n**) *f* pie; (*Pastetchen*) vol-au-vent; (: *ungefüllt*) vol-au-vent case

pasteurisieren [pastøri'zi:rən] *vt* to pasteurize

Pastor ['pastɔr] *m* vicar; pastor, minister

Pate ['pa:tə] (**-n, -n**) *m* godfather; **bei etw ~ gestanden haben** (*fig*) to be the force behind sth

Patenkind *nt* godchild

Patenstadt *f* twin town (*Brit*)

patent [pa'tɛnt] *adj* clever

Patent (**-(e)s, -e**) *nt* patent; (*Mil*) commission; **etw als** *od* **zum ~ anmelden** to apply for a patent on sth

Patentamt *nt* patent office

patentieren [patɛn'ti:rən] *vt* to patent

Patent- *zW:* **Patentinhaber** *m* patentee; **Patentlösung** *f* (*fig*) patent remedy; **Patentschutz** *m* patent right; **Patenturkunde** *f* letters patent *pl*

Pater ['pa:tər] (**-s, -** *od* **Patres**) *m* Father

Paternoster [patər'nɔstər] (**-s, -**) *m* (*Aufzug*) paternoster

pathetisch [pa'te:tɪʃ] *adj* emotional

Pathologe [pato'lo:gə] (**-n, -n**) *m* pathologist
Pathologin [pato'lo:gɪn] *f* pathologist
pathologisch *adj* pathological
Pathos ['pa:tɔs] (**-**) *nt* pathos
Patience [pasi'ã:s] (**-, -n**) *f*: **~n legen** to play patience
Patient, in [patsi'ɛnt(ɪn)] *m(f)* patient
Patin ['pa:tɪn] *f* godmother
Patriarch [patri'arç] (**-en, -en**) *m* patriarch
patriarchalisch [patriar'ça:lɪʃ] *adj* patriarchal
Patriot, in [patri'o:t(ɪn)] (**-en, -en**) *m(f)* patriot;
patriotisch *adj* patriotic
Patriotismus [patrio'tɪsmʊs] *m* patriotism
Patron [pa'tro:n] (**-s, -e**) *m* patron; (*Eccl*) patron saint
Patrone (**-, -n**) *f* cartridge
Patronenhülse *f* cartridge case
Patronin *f* patroness; (*Eccl*) patron saint
Patrouille [pa'trʊljə] (**-, -n**) *f* patrol
patrouillieren [patrʊl'ji:rən] *vi* to patrol
patsch [patʃ] *interj* splash!
Patsche (**-, -n**) (*umg*) *f* (*Händchen*) paw; (*Fliegenpatsche*) swat; (*Feuerpatsche*) beater; (*Bedrängnis*) mess, jam
patschen *vi* to smack, slap; (*im Wasser*) to splash
patschnass *adj* soaking wet
Patt [pat] (**-s, -s**) *nt* (*lit, fig*) stalemate
patzen ['patsən] (*umg*) *vi* to boob (*Brit*), goof (*US*)
patzig ['patsɪç] (*umg*) *adj* cheeky, saucy
Pauke ['paʊkə] (**-, -n**) *f* kettledrum; **auf die ~ hauen** to live it up; **mit ~n und Trompeten durchfallen** (*umg*) to fail dismally
pauken *vt, vi* (*Sch*) to swot (*Brit*), cram
Pauker (**-s, -**) (*umg*) *m* teacher
pausbäckig ['paʊsbɛkɪç] *adj* chubby-cheeked
pauschal [paʊ'ʃa:l] *adj* (*Kosten*) inclusive; (*einheitlich*) flat-rate *attrib*; (*Urteil*) sweeping;
die Werkstatt berechnet ~ pro Inspektion 130 Euro the garage has a flat rate of 130 euros per service
Pauschale (**-, -n**) *f* flat rate; (*vorläufig geschätzter Betrag*) estimated amount
Pauschal- *zW*: **Pauschalgebühr** *f* flat rate; **Pauschalpreis** *m* all-in price; **Pauschalreise** *f* package tour; **Pauschalsumme** *f* lump sum; **Pauschalversicherung** *f* comprehensive insurance
Pause ['paʊzə] (**-, -n**) *f* break; (*Theat*) interval; (*das Innehalten*) pause; (*Mus*) rest; (*Kopie*) tracing
pausen *vt* to trace
Pausen- *zW*: **Pausenbrot** *nt* sandwich (*to eat at break*); **Pausenhof** *m* playground, schoolyard (*US*); **pausenlos** *adj* nonstop; **Pausenzeichen** *nt* (*Rundf*) call sign; (*Mus*) rest
pausieren [paʊ'si:rən] *vi* to make a break
Pauspapier ['paʊspapi:r] *nt* tracing paper
Pavian ['pa:via:n] (**-s, -e**) *m* baboon
Paybackkarte ['pe:bɛkkartə] *f* loyalty card
Pay-per-Click ['pe:pərklɪk] (**-s**) *nt* pay-per-click
Pazifik [pa'tsi:fɪk] (**-s**) *m* Pacific
pazifisch *adj* Pacific; **der P-e Ozean** the Pacific (Ocean)

Pazifist, in [patsi'fɪst(ɪn)] *m(f)* pacifist;
pazifistisch *adj* pacifist
PC *m abk* (= *Personal Computer*) PC
PDA *m abk* (*Comput*: = *personal digital assistant*) PDA
PDS *f abk* (= *Partei des Demokratischen Sozialismus*) German Socialist Party; *see culture note*

Pech [pɛç] (**-s, -e**) *nt* pitch; (*fig*) bad luck; **~ haben** to be unlucky; **die beiden halten zusammen wie ~ und Schwefel** (*umg*) the two are inseparable; **~ gehabt!** tough! (*umg*);
pechschwarz *adj* pitch-black; **Pechsträhne** (*umg*) *f* unlucky patch; **Pechvogel** (*umg*) *m* unlucky person
Pedal [pe'da:l] (**-s, -e**) *nt* pedal; **in die ~e treten** to pedal (hard)
Pedant [pe'dant] *m* pedant
Pedanterie [pedantə'ri:] *f* pedantry
pedantisch *adj* pedantic
Peddigrohr ['pɛdɪçro:r] *nt* cane
Pediküre [pedi'ky:rə] (**-, -n**) *f* (*Fußpflege*) pedicure; (*Fußpflegerin*) chiropodist
Pegel ['pe:gəl] (**-s, -**) *m* water gauge; (*Geräuschpegel*) noise level; **Pegelstand** *m* water level
peilen ['paɪlən] *vt* to get a fix on; **die Lage ~** (*umg*) to see how the land lies
Pein [paɪn] (**-**) *f* pain, suffering
peinigen *vt* to torture; (*plagen*) to torment
peinlich *adj* (*unangenehm*) embarrassing, awkward, painful; (*genau*) painstaking; **in seinem Zimmer herrschte ~e Ordnung** his room was meticulously tidy; **er vermied es ~st, davon zu sprechen** he was at pains not to talk about it; **Peinlichkeit** *f* painfulness, awkwardness; (*Genauigkeit*) scrupulousness
Peitsche ['paɪtʃə] (**-, -n**) *f* whip
peitschen *vt* to whip; (*Regen*) to lash
Peitschenhieb *m* lash
Pekinese [peki'ne:zə] (**-n, -n**) *m* Pekinese, peke (*umg*)
Peking ['pe:kɪŋ] (**-s**) *nt* Peking
Pelikan ['pe:lika:n] (**-s, -e**) *m* pelican
Pelle ['pɛlə] (**-, -n**) *f* skin; **der Chef sitzt mir auf der ~** (*umg*) I've got the boss on my back
pellen *vt* to skin, peel
Pellkartoffeln *pl* jacket potatoes *pl*
Pelz [pɛlts] (**-es, -e**) *m* fur
Pendel ['pɛndəl] (**-s, -**) *nt* pendulum
pendeln *vi* (*schwingen*) to swing (to and fro); (*Zug, Fähre etc*) to shuttle; (*Mensch*) to commute; (*fig*) to fluctuate
Pendelverkehr *m* shuttle service;

P

(*Berufsverkehr*) commuter traffic

Pendler, in ['pɛndlər(ɪn)] (**-s, -**) *m(f)* commuter

penetrant [pene'trant] *adj* sharp; (*Person*) pushing; **das schmeckt/riecht ~ nach Knoblauch** it has a very strong taste/smell of garlic

penibel [pe'ni:bəl] *adj* pernickety (*Brit*) (*umg*), persnickety (*US*) (*umg*), precise

Penis ['pe:nɪs] (**-, -se**) *m* penis

Pennbruder ['pɛnbru:dər] (*umg*) *m* tramp (*Brit*), hobo (*US*)

Penne (**-, -n**) (*umg*) *f* (*Sch*) school

pennen (*umg*) *vi* to kip

Penner (**-s, -**) (*pej*: *umg*) *m* tramp (*Brit*), hobo (*US*)

Pension [pɛnzi'o:n] *f* (*Geld*) pension; (*Ruhestand*) retirement; (*für Gäste*) boarding house, guesthouse; **halbe/volle ~** half/full board; **in ~ gehen** to retire

Pensionär, in [pɛnzio'nɛ:r(ɪn)] (**-s, -e**) *m(f)* pensioner

Pensionat (**-(e)s, -e**) *nt* boarding school

pensionieren [pɛnzio'ni:rən] *vt* to pension (off); **sich ~ lassen** to retire

pensioniert *adj* retired

Pensionierung *f* retirement

Pensions- *zW*: **pensionsberechtigt** *adj* entitled to a pension; **Pensionsfonds** *m* pension fund; **Pensionsgast** *m* boarder, paying guest; **pensionsreif** (*umg*) *adj* ready for retirement

Pensum ['pɛnzʊm] (**-s, Pensen**) *nt* quota; (*Sch*) curriculum

Peperoni [pepe'ro:ni] *pl* chillies *pl*

per [pɛr] *präp+akk* by, per; (*pro*) per; (*bis*) by; **~ Adresse** (*Comm*) care of, c/o; **mit jdm ~ du sein** (*umg*) to be on first-name terms with sb

Perfekt ['pɛrfɛkt] (**-(e)s, -e**) *nt* perfect

perfekt [pɛr'fɛkt] *adj* perfect; (*abgemacht*) settled; **die Sache ~ machen** to clinch the deal; **der Vertrag ist ~** the contract is all settled

perfektionieren [pɛrfɛktsio'ni:rən] *vt* to perfect

Perfektionismus [pɛrfɛktsio'nɪsmʊs] *m* perfectionism

perforieren [pɛrfo'ri:rən] *vt* to perforate

Pergament [pɛrga'mɛnt] *nt* parchment; **Pergamentpapier** *nt* greaseproof paper (*Brit*), wax(ed) paper (*US*)

Pergola ['pɛrgola] (**-, Pergolen**) *f* pergola, arbour (*Brit*), arbor (*US*)

Periode [peri'o:də] (**-, -n**) *f* period; **0,33 ~** 0.33 recurring

periodisch [peri'o:dɪʃ] *adj* periodic; (*dezimal*) recurring

Peripherie [perife'ri:] *f* periphery; (*um Stadt*) outskirts *pl*; (*Math*) circumference; **Peripheriegerät** *nt* (*Comput*) peripheral

Perle ['pɛrlə] (**-, -n**) *f* (*lit, fig*) pearl; (*Glasperle, Holzperle, Tropfen*) bead; (*veraltet: umg: Hausgehilfin*) maid

perlen *vi* to sparkle; (*Tropfen*) to trickle

Perlenkette *f* pearl necklace

Perlhuhn *nt* guinea fowl

Perlmutt ['pɛrlmʊt] (**-s**) *nt* mother-of-pearl

Perlon® ['pɛrlɔn] (**-s**) *nt* ≈ nylon

Perlwein *m* sparkling wine

perplex [pɛr'plɛks] *adj* dumbfounded

Perser ['pɛrzər] (**-s, -**) *m* (*Person*) Persian; (*umg*: *Teppich*) Persian carpet

Perserin *f* Persian

Persianer [pɛrzi'a:nər] (**-s, -**) *m* Persian lamb (coat)

Persien ['pɛrziən] (**-s**) *nt* Persia

Persiflage [pɛrzi'fla:ʒə] (**-, -n**) *f*: **~** (+*gen od* **auf** +*akk*) pastiche (of), satire (on)

persisch *adj* Persian; **P~er Golf** Persian Gulf

Person [pɛr'zo:n] (**-, -en**) *f* person; (*pej: Frau*) female; **sie ist Köchin und Haushälterin in einer ~** she is cook and housekeeper rolled into one; **ich für meine ~** personally I

Personal [pɛrzo'na:l] (**-s**) *nt* personnel; (*Bedienung*) servants *pl*; **Personalabbau** *m* staff cuts *pl*; **Personalakte** *f* personal file; **Personalangaben** *pl* particulars *pl*; **Personalausweis** *m* identity card; **Personalbogen** *m* personal record; **Personalbüro** *nt* personnel (department); **Personalchef** *m* personnel manager; **Personal Computer** *m* personal computer

Personalien [pɛrzo'na:liən] *pl* particulars *pl*

Personalität [pɛrzonali'tɛ:t] *f* personality

Personal- *zW*: **Personalkosten** *pl* staff costs; **Personalmangel** *m* staff shortage; **Personalpronomen** *nt* personal pronoun; **Personalreduzierung** *f* staff reduction

personell [pɛrzo'nɛl] *adj* staff attrib; **-e Veränderungen** changes in personnel

Personen- *zW*: **Personenaufzug** *m* lift, elevator (*US*); **Personenbeschreibung** *f* (personal) description; **Personengedächtnis** *nt* memory for faces; **Personengesellschaft** *f* partnership; **Personenkraftwagen** *m* private motorcar, automobile (*US*); **Personenkreis** *m* group of people; **Personenkult** *m* personality cult; **Personennahverkehr** *m*: **öffentlicher Personennahverkehr** local public transport; **Personenschaden** *m* injury to persons; **Personenverkehr** *m* passenger services *pl*; **Personenwaage** *f* scales *pl*; **Personenzug** *m* stopping train; passenger train

personifizieren [pɛrzonifi'tsi:rən] *vt* to personify

persönlich [pɛr'zø:nlɪç] *adj* personal ▷ *adv* in person; personally; (*auf Briefen*) private (and confidential); **~ haften** (*Comm*) to be personally liable; **Persönlichkeit** *f* personality; **Persönlichkeiten des öffentlichen Lebens** public figures

Perspektive [pɛrspɛk'ti:və] *f* perspective; **das eröffnet ganz neue -n für uns** that opens new horizons for us

Pers. Ref. *abk* (= *Persönlicher Referent*) personal representative

Peru [pe'ru:] (**-s**) *nt* Peru

Peruaner, in [peru'a:nər(ɪn)] (**-s, -**) *m(f)* Peruvian

peruanisch *adj* Peruvian

Perücke [pe'rʏkə] (-, -n) *f* wig

pervers [pɛr'vɛrs] *adj* perverse

Perversität [pɛrvɛrzi'tɛ:t] *f* perversity

Pessar [pɛ'sa:r] (-s, -e) *nt* pessary; (*zur Empfängnisverhütung*) cap, diaphragm

Pessimismus [pɛsi'mɪsmʊs] *m* pessimism

Pessimist, in [pɛsi'mɪst(ɪn)] *m(f)* pessimist; **pessimistisch** *adj* pessimistic

Pest [pɛst] (-) *f* plague; **jdn/etw wie die ~ hassen** (*umg*) to loathe (and detest) sb/sth

Petersilie [petər'zi:liə] *f* parsley

Petrochemie [petro:çe'mi:] *f* petrochemistry

Petrodollar [petro'dɔlar] *m* petrodollar

Petroleum [pe'tro:leʊm] (-s) *nt* paraffin (*Brit*), kerosene (*US*)

petzen ['pɛtsən] (*umg*) *vi* to tell tales; **er petzt immer** he always tells

Pf. (*Hist*) *abk* = **Pfennig**

Pfad [pfa:t] (-(e)s, -e) *m* path; **Pfadfinder** *m* Boy Scout; **er ist bei den Pfadfindern** he's in the (Boy) Scouts; **Pfadfinderin** *f* Girl Guide

Pfaffe ['pfafə] (-n, -n) (*pej*) *m* cleric, parson

Pfahl [pfa:l] (-(e)s, ̈-e) *m* post, stake; **Pfahlbau** *m* pile dwelling

Pfalz [pfalts] (-, -en) *f* (*Geog*) Palatinate

Pfälzer, in ['pfɛltsər(ɪn)] (-s, -) *m(f)* person from the Palatinate

pfälzisch *adj* Palatine, of the (Rhineland) Palatinate

Pfand [pfant] (-(e)s, ̈-er) *nt* pledge, security; (*Flaschenpfand*) deposit; (*im Spiel*) forfeit; (*fig: der Liebe etc*) pledge; **Pfandbrief** *m* bond

pfänden ['pfɛndən] *vt* to seize, impound

Pfänderspiel *nt* game of forfeits

Pfand- *zW*: **Pfandhaus** *nt* pawnshop; **Pfandleiher** (-s, -) *m* pawnbroker; **Pfandrecht** *nt* lien; **Pfandschein** *m* pawn ticket

Pfändung ['pfɛndʊŋ] *f* seizure, distraint (*form*)

Pfanne ['pfanə] (-, -n) *f* (frying) pan; **jdn in die ~ hauen** (*umg*) to tear a strip off sb

Pfannkuchen *m* pancake; (*Berliner*) doughnut (*Brit*), donut (*US*)

Pfarrei [pfar'raɪ] *f* parish

Pfarrer (-s, -) *m* priest; (*evangelisch*) vicar; (*von Freikirchen*) minister

Pfarrhaus *nt* vicarage

Pfau [pfaʊ] (-(e)s, -en) *m* peacock

Pfauenauge *nt* peacock butterfly

Pfd. *abk* (= *Pfund*) ≈ lb.

Pfeffer ['pfɛfər] (-s, -) *m* pepper; **er soll bleiben, wo der ~ wächst!** (*umg*) he can take a running jump; **Pfefferkorn** *nt* peppercorn; **Pfefferkuchen** *m* gingerbread; **Pfefferminz** (-es, -e) *nt* peppermint; **Pfefferminze** *f* peppermint (plant); **Pfeffermühle** *f* pepper mill

pfeffern *vt* to pepper; (*umg: werfen*) to fling; **gepfefferte Preise/Witze** steep prices/spicy jokes

Pfeife ['pfaɪfə] (-, -n) *f* whistle; (*Tabakpfeife, Orgelpfeife*) pipe; **nach jds ~ tanzen** to dance to sb's tune

pfeifen *unreg* *vt, vi* to whistle; **auf dem letzten Loch ~** (*umg: erschöpft sein*) to be on one's last legs; (: *finanziell*) to be on one's beam ends; **ich pfeif(e) drauf!** (*umg*) I don't give a damn!; **Pfeifenstopfer** *m* tamper

Pfeifer (-s, -) *m* piper

Pfeifkonzert *nt* catcalls *pl*

Pfeil [pfaɪl] (-(e)s, -e) *m* arrow

Pfeiler ['pfaɪlər] (-s, -) *m* pillar, prop; (*Brückenpfeiler*) pier

Pfennig ['pfɛnɪç] (-(e)s, -e) *m* (*Hist*) pfennig (*one hundredth of a mark*); **Pfennigabsatz** *m* stiletto heel; **Pfennigfuchser** (-s, -) (*umg*) *m* skinflint

pferchen ['pfɛrçən] *vt* to cram, pack

Pferd [pfe:rt] (-(e)s, -e) *nt* horse; **wie ein ~ arbeiten** (*umg*) to work like a Trojan; **mit ihm kann man ~e stehlen** (*umg*) he's a great sport; **auf das falsche/richtige ~ setzen** (*lit, fig*) to back the wrong/right horse

Pferde- *zW*: **Pferdeäpfel** *pl* horse droppings *pl od* dung *sing*; **Pferdefuß** *m*: **die Sache hat aber einen Pferdefuß** there's just one snag; **Pferderennen** *nt* horse-race; (*Sportart*) horse-racing; **Pferdeschwanz** *m* (*Frisur*) ponytail; **Pferdestall** *m* stable; **Pferdestärke** *f* horsepower

Pfiff (-(e)s, -e) *m* whistle; (*Kniff*) trick

pfiff *etc* [pfɪf] *vb siehe* **pfeifen**

Pfifferling ['pfɪfərlɪŋ] *m* yellow chanterelle; **keinen ~ wert** not worth a thing

pfiffig *adj* smart

Pfingsten ['pfɪŋstən] (-, -) *nt* Whitsun

Pfingstrose *f* peony

Pfingstsonntag *m* Whit Sunday, Pentecost (*Rel*)

Pfirsich ['pfɪrzɪç] (-s, -e) *m* peach

Pflanze ['pflantsə] (-, -n) *f* plant

pflanzen *vt* to plant ▷ *vr* (*umg*) to plonk o.s.

Pflanzenfett *nt* vegetable fat

Pflanzenschutzmittel *nt* pesticide

pflanzlich *adj* vegetable

Pflanzung *f* plantation

Pflaster ['pflastər] (-s, -) *nt* plaster; (*Straßenpflaster*) pavement (*Brit*), sidewalk (*US*); **ein teures ~** (*umg*) a pricey place; **ein heißes ~** a dangerous *od* unsafe place; **pflastermüde** *adj* dead on one's feet

pflastern *vt* to pave

Pflasterstein *m* paving stone

Pflaume ['pflaʊmə] (-, -n) *f* plum; (*umg: Mensch*) twit (*Brit*)

Pflaumenmus *nt* plum jam

Pflege ['pfle:gə] (-, -n) *f* care; (*von Idee*) cultivation; (*Krankenpflege*) nursing; **jdn/etw in ~ nehmen** to look after sb/sth; **in ~ sein** (*Kind*) to be fostered out; **pflegebedürftig** *adj* needing care; **Pflegeeltern** *pl* foster parents *pl*; **Pflegefall** *m* case for nursing; **Pflegegeld** *nt* (*für Pflegekinder*) boarding-out allowance; (*für Kranke*) attendance allowance; **Pflegeheim** *nt* nursing home; **Pflegekind** *nt* foster child; **pflegeleicht** *adj* easy-care; **Pflegemutter** *f* foster mother

p

pflegen | Picknick

pflegen vt to look after; (*Kranke*) to nurse; (*Beziehungen*) to foster ▷ vi (*gewöhnlich tun*): **sie pflegte zu sagen** she used to say
Pfleger (**-s, -**) m (*im Krankenhaus*) orderly; (*voll qualifiziert*) male nurse; **Pflegerin** f nurse
Pflegesatz m hospital and nursing charges pl
Pflegevater m foster father
Pflegeversicherung f geriatric care insurance
Pflicht [pflɪçt] (**-, -en**) f duty; (*Sport*) compulsory section; **Rechte und ~en** rights and responsibilities; **pflichtbewusst** adj conscientious; **Pflichtbewusstsein** nt sense of duty; **Pflichtfach** nt (*Sch*) compulsory subject; **Pflichtgefühl** nt sense of duty; **pflichtgemäß** adj dutiful; **pflichtvergessen** adj irresponsible; **Pflichtversicherung** f compulsory insurance
Pflock [pflɔk] (**-(e)s, ̈-e**) m peg; (*für Tiere*) stake
pflog etc [pfloːk] vb (*veraltet*) siehe **pflegen**
pflücken ['pflʏkən] vt to pick
Pflug [pfluːk] (**-(e)s, ̈-e**) m plough (*Brit*), plow (*US*)
pflügen ['pflyːgən] vt to plough (*Brit*), plow (*US*)
Pflugschar f ploughshare (*Brit*), plowshare (*US*)
Pforte ['pfɔrtə] (**-, -n**) f (*Tor*) gate
Pförtner ['pfœrtnər] (**-s, -**) m porter, doorkeeper, doorman
Pförtnerin f doorkeeper, porter
Pfosten ['pfɔstən] (**-s, -**) m post; (*senkrechter Balken*) upright
Pfote ['pfoːtə] (**-, -n**) f paw; (*umg: Schrift*) scrawl
Pfropf [pfrɔpf] (**-(e)s, -e**) m (*Flaschenpfropf*) stopper; (*Blutpfropf*) clot
Pfropfen (**-s, -**) m = **Pfropf**
pfropfen vt (*stopfen*) to cram; (*Baum*) to graft; **gepfropft voll** crammed full
pfui [pfʊɪ] interj ugh!; (*na na*) tut tut!; (*Buhruf*) boo!; **~ Teufel!** (*umg*) ugh!, yuck!
Pfund [pfʊnt] (**-(e)s**) nt (*Gewicht, Fin*) pound; **das ~ sinkt** sterling od the pound is falling
pfundig (*umg*) adj great
Pfundskerl ['pfʊntskɛrl] (*umg*) m great guy
pfundweise adv by the pound
pfuschen ['pfʊʃən] vi to bungle; (*einen Fehler machen*) to slip up
Pfuscher, in ['pfʊʃər(ɪn)] (**-s, -**) (*umg*) m(f) sloppy worker; (*Kurpfuscher*) quack
Pfuscherei [pfʊʃə'raɪ] (*umg*) f sloppy work; (*Kurpfuscherei*) quackery
Pfütze ['pfʏtsə] (**-, -n**) f puddle
PH (**-, -s**) f abk = **pädagogische Hochschule**
Phänomen [fɛno'meːn] (**-s, -e**) nt phenomenon; **phänomenal** [-'naːl] adj phenomenal
Phantasie etc [fanta'ziː] = **Fantasie** etc
phantasieren [fanta'ziːrən] vi = **fantasieren**
phantasievoll adj = **fantasievoll**
Phantast [fan'tast] (**-en, -en**) m = **Fantast**
phantastisch adj = **fantastisch**
Phantom [fan'toːm] (**-s, -e**) nt (*Trugbild*) phantom; **einem ~ nachjagen** (*fig*) to tilt at windmills; **Phantombild** nt Identikit® picture

Pharisäer [fari'zɛːər] (**-s, -**) m (*lit, fig*) pharisee
Pharmazeut, in [farma'tsɔʏt(ɪn)] (**-en, -en**) m(f) pharmacist
pharmazeutisch adj pharmaceutical
Pharmazie f pharmacy, pharmaceutics sing
Phase ['faːzə] (**-, -n**) f phase
Philanthrop [filan'troːp] (**-en, -en**) m philanthropist; **philanthropisch** adj philanthropic
Philatelist, in [filate'lɪst(ɪn)] (**-en, -en**) m(f) philatelist
Philharmoniker [filhar'moːnikər] (**-s, -**) m: **die ~** the philharmonic (orchestra) sing
Philippine [fɪlɪ'piːnə] (**-n, -n**) m Filipino
Philippinen pl Philippines pl, Philippine Islands pl
Philippin f Filipino
philippinisch adj Filipino
Philologe [filo'loːgə] (**-n, -n**) m philologist
Philologie [filolo'giː] f philology
Philologin f philologist
Philosoph, in [filo'zoːf(ɪn)] (**-en, -en**) m(f) philosopher
Philosophie [filozo'fiː] f philosophy
philosophieren [filozo'fiːrən] vi: **~ (über +akk)** to philosophize (about)
philosophisch adj philosophical
Phlegma ['flɛgma] (**-s**) nt lethargy
phlegmatisch [flɛ'gmaːtɪʃ] adj lethargic
Phobie [fo'biː] f: **~ (vor +dat)** phobia (about)
Phonetik [fo'neːtɪk] f phonetics sing
phonetisch adj phonetic
Phonotypistin [fonoty'pɪstɪn] f audiotypist
Phosphat [fɔs'faːt] (**-(e)s, -e**) nt phosphate
Phosphor ['fɔsfɔr] (**-s**) m phosphorus
phosphoreszieren [fɔsforɛs'tsiːrən] vt to phosphoresce
Photo etc [fo'toː] = **Foto** etc
Phrase ['fraːzə] (**-, -n**) f phrase; (*pej*) hollow phrase; **~n dreschen** (*umg*) to churn out one cliché after another
pH-Wert [peː'haːveːrt] m pH value
Physik [fy'ziːk] f physics sing
physikalisch [fyzi'kaːlɪʃ] adj of physics
Physiker, in ['fyːzikər(ɪn)] (**-s, -**) m(f) physicist
Physikum ['fyːzikʊm] (**-s**) nt (*Univ*) preliminary examination in medicine
Physiologe [fyzio'loːgə] (**-n, -n**) m physiologist
Physiologie [fyziolo'giː] f physiology
Physiologin f physiologist
physisch ['fyːzɪʃ] adj physical
Pianist, in [pia'nɪst(ɪn)] m(f) pianist
Piccolo ['pɪkolo] (**-s, -s**) m trainee waiter; (*auch*: **Piccoloflasche**) quarter bottle of champagne; (*Mus*: auch: **Piccoloflöte**) piccolo
picheln ['pɪçəln] (*umg*) vi to booze
Pickel ['pɪkəl] (**-s, -**) m pimple; (*Werkzeug*) pickaxe; (*Bergpickel*) ice axe
pickelig, picklig adj pimply
picken ['pɪkən] vt to peck ▷ vi: **~ (nach)** to peck (at)
Picknick ['pɪknɪk] (**-s, -e** od **-s**) nt picnic; **~ machen** to have a picnic

piekfein ['piːk'faɪn] (umg) adj posh
Piemont [pie'mɔnt] (-s) nt Piedmont
piepen ['piːpən] vi to chirp; (Funkgerät etc) to bleep; **bei dir piepts wohl!** (umg) are you off your head?; **es war zum P-!** (umg) it was a scream!
piepsen ['piːpsən] vi = **piepen**
Piepser (umg) m pager, paging device
Piepsstimme f squeaky voice
Piepton m bleep
Pier [piːər] (-s, -s od -e) m jetty, pier
piesacken ['piːzakən] (umg) vt to torment
Pietät [pie'tɛːt] f piety; reverence; **pietätlos** adj impious, irreverent
Pigment [pɪg'mɛnt] (-(e)s, -e) nt pigment
Pik [piːk] (-s, -s) nt (Karten) spades; **einen ~ auf jdn haben** (umg) to have it in for sb
pikant [pi'kant] adj spicy, piquant; (anzüglich) suggestive
Pike (-, -n) f: **etw von der ~ auf lernen** (fig) to learn sth from the bottom up
pikiert [pi'kiːrt] adj offended
Pikkolo ['pɪkolo] (-s, -s) m = **Piccolo**
Piktogramm [pɪkto'gram] nt pictogram
Pilger, in ['pɪlgər(ɪn)] (-s, -) m(f) pilgrim; **Pilgerfahrt** f pilgrimage
pilgern vi to make a pilgrimage; (umg: gehen) to wend one's way
Pille ['pɪlə] (-, -n) f pill
Pilot, in [pi'loːt(ɪn)] (-en, -en) m(f) pilot; **Pilotenschein** m pilot's licence (Brit) od license (US)
Pils [pɪls] (-, -) nt Pilsner (lager)
Pilsener [pɪlzənər], **Pilsner** [pɪlznər] (-s, -) nt Pilsner (lager)
Pilz [pɪlts] (-es, -e) m fungus; (essbar) mushroom; (giftig) toadstool; **wie ~e aus dem Boden schießen** (fig) to mushroom; **Pilzkrankheit** f fungal disease
Pimmel ['pɪməl] (-s, -) (umg) m (Penis) willie
pingelig ['pɪŋəlɪç] (umg) adj fussy
Pinguin ['pɪŋɡuiːn] (-s, -e) m penguin
Pinie ['piːniə] f pine
Pinkel (-s, -) (umg) m: **ein feiner** od **vornehmer ~** a swell, Lord Muck (Brit) (umg)
pinkeln ['pɪŋkəln] (umg) vi to pee
Pinnwand ['pɪnvant] f pinboard
Pinsel ['pɪnzəl] (-s, -) m paintbrush
pinseln (umg) vt, vi to paint; (pej: malen) to daub
Pinte ['pɪntə] (-, -n) (umg) f (Lokal) boozer (Brit)
Pinzette [pɪn'tsɛtə] f tweezers pl
Pionier [pio'niːr] (-s, -e) m pioneer; (Mil) sapper, engineer; **Pionierarbeit** f pioneering work; **Pionierunternehmen** nt pioneer company
Pipi [pi'piː] (-s, -s) nt od m (Kindersprache) wee(-wee)
Pirat [pi'raːt] (-en, -en) m pirate
Piratensender m pirate radio station
Pirsch [pɪrʃ] (-) f stalking
PISA-Studie ['piːza-] f (Sch) PISA study
pissen ['pɪsən] (umg!) vi to (have a) piss (!); (regnen) to piss down (!)

Pistazie [pɪs'taːtsiə] (-, -n) f pistachio
Piste ['pɪstə] (-, -n) f (Ski) run, piste; (Aviat) runway
Pistole [pɪs'toːlə] (-, -n) f pistol; **wie aus der ~ geschossen** (fig) like a shot; **jdm die ~ auf die Brust setzen** (fig) to hold a pistol to sb's head
pitschenass ['pɪtʃə'nas], **pitschnass** ['pɪtʃ'nas] (umg) adj soaking (wet)
Pizza ['pɪtsa] (-, -s) f pizza
PKW, Pkw (-(s), -(s)) m abk = **Personenkraftwagen**
Pl. abk (= Plural) pl.; (= Platz) Sq.
Plackerei [plakə'raɪ] f drudgery
plädieren [plɛ'diːrən] vi to plead
Plädoyer [plɛdoa'je:] (-s, -s) nt speech for the defence; (fig) plea
Plage ['plaːɡə] (-, -n) f plague; (Mühe) nuisance; **Plagegeist** m pest, nuisance
plagen vt to torment ▷ vr to toil, slave
Plagiat [plagi'aːt] (-(e)s, -e) nt plagiarism
Plakat [pla'kaːt] (-(e)s, -e) nt poster; (aus Pappe) placard
plakativ [plaka'tiːf] adj striking, bold
Plakatwand f hoarding, billboard (US)
Plakette [pla'kɛtə] (-, -n) f (Abzeichen) badge; (Münze) commemorative coin; (an Wänden) plaque
Plan [plaːn] (-(e)s, ̈-e) m plan; (Karte) map; **Pläne schmieden** to make plans; **nach ~ verlaufen** to go according to plan; **jdn auf den ~ rufen** (fig) to bring sb into the arena
Plane (-, -n) f tarpaulin
planen vt to plan; (Mord etc) to plot
Planer, in (-s, -) m(f) planner
Planet [pla'neːt] (-en, -en) m planet
Planetenbahn f orbit (of a planet)
planieren [pla'niːrən] vt to level off
Planierraupe f bulldozer
Planke ['plaŋkə] (-, -n) f plank
Plänkelei [plɛŋkə'laɪ] f skirmish(ing)
plänkeln ['plɛŋkəln] vi to skirmish
Plankton ['plaŋktɔn] (-s) nt plankton
planlos adj (Vorgehen) unsystematic; (Umherlaufen) aimless
planmäßig adj according to plan; (methodisch) systematic; (Eisenb) scheduled
Planschbecken, Plantschbecken ['planʃbɛkən] nt paddling pool
planschen, plantschen vi to splash
Plansoll nt output target
Planstelle f post
Plantage [plan'taːʒə] (-, -n) f plantation
Planung f planning
Planwagen m covered wagon
Planwirtschaft f planned economy
Plappermaul (umg) nt (Kind) chatterbox
plappern ['plapərn] vi to chatter
plärren ['plɛrən] vi (Mensch) to cry, whine; (Radio) to blare
Plasma ['plasma] (-s, Plasmen) nt plasma
Plastik[1] ['plastɪk] f sculpture
Plastik[2] ['plastɪk] (-s) nt (Kunststoff) plastic; **Plastikfolie** f plastic film; **Plastikgeschoss** nt

p

plastic bullet; **Plastiktüte** f plastic bag
Plastilin [plasti'li:n] (**-s**) nt Plasticine®
plastisch ['plastɪʃ] adj plastic; **stell dir das ~ vor!** just picture it!
Platane [pla'ta:nə] (**-, -n**) f plane (tree)
Platin ['pla:ti:n] (**-s**) nt platinum
Platitüde [plati'ty:də] (**-, -n**) f platitude
platonisch [pla'to:nɪʃ] adj platonic
platsch [platʃ] interj splash!
platschen vi to splash
plätschern ['plɛtʃərn] vi to babble
platschnass adj drenched
platt [plat] adj flat; (umg: überrascht) flabbergasted; (fig: geistlos) flat, boring; **einen P~en haben** to have a flat (umg), have a flat tyre (Brit) od tire (US)
plattdeutsch adj Low German
Platte (**-, -n**) f (Speiseplatte, Phot, Tech) plate; (Steinplatte) flag; (Kachel) tile; (Schallplatte) record; **kalte ~** cold dish; **die ~ kenne ich schon** (umg) I've heard all that before
Plätteisen nt iron
plätten vt, vi to iron
Platten- zW: **Plattenleger** (**-s, -**) m paver; **Plattenspieler** m record player; **Plattenteller** m turntable
Plattform f platform; (fig: Grundlage) basis
Plattfuß m flat foot; (Reifen) flat tyre (Brit) od tire (US)
Plattitüde [plati'ty:də] (**-, -n**) f platitude
Platz [plats] (**-es, ̈-e**) m place; (Sitzplatz) seat; (Raum) space, room; (in Stadt) square; (Sportplatz) playing field; **~ machen** to get out of the way; **~ nehmen** to take a seat; **jdm ~ machen** to make room for sb; **~ sparend** space-saving; **auf ~ zwei** in second place; **fehl am ~e sein** to be out of place; **seinen ~ behaupten** to stand one's ground; **das erste Hotel am ~** the best hotel in town; **auf die Plätze, fertig, los!** (beim Sport) on your marks, get set, go!; **einen Spieler vom ~ stellen** od **verweisen** (Sport) to send a player off; **Platzangst** f (Med) agoraphobia; (umg) claustrophobia; **Platzangst haben/bekommen** (umg) to feel/get claustrophobic; **Platzanweiser, in** (**-s, -**) m(f) usher(ette)
Plätzchen ['plɛtsçən] nt spot; (Gebäck) biscuit
platzen vi (Hilfsverb sein) to burst; (Bombe) to explode; (Naht, Hose, Haut) to split; (umg: scheitern: Geschäft) to fall through; (: Freundschaft) to break up; (: Theorie, Verschwörung) to collapse; (: Wechsel) to bounce; **vor Wut ~** (umg) to be bursting with anger
platzieren [pla'tsi:rən] vt to place ▷ vr (Sport) to be placed; (Tennis) to be seeded; (umg: sich setzen, stellen) to plant o.s.
Platz- zW: **Platzkarte** f seat reservation; **Platzkonzert** nt open-air concert; **Platzmangel** m lack of space; **Platzpatrone** f blank cartridge; **Platzregen** m downpour; **platzsparend** adj space-saving; **Platzverweis** m sending-off; **Platzwart** m (Sport) groundsman (Brit), groundskeeper (US);

Platzwunde f cut
Plauderei [plaʊdə'raɪ] f chat, conversation
plaudern ['plaʊdərn] vi to chat, talk
Plausch [plaʊʃ] (**-(e)s, -e**) (umg) m chat
plausibel [plaʊ'zi:bəl] adj plausible
Play-back, Playback ['pleɪbæk] (**-s, -s**) nt (Verfahren: Schallplatte) double-tracking; (TV) miming
plazieren [pla'tsi:rən] vt siehe **platzieren**
Plebejer, in [ple'be:jər(ɪn)] (**-s, -**) m(f) plebeian
plebejisch [ple'be:jɪʃ] adj plebeian
pleite ['plaɪtə] (umg) adj broke; **Pleite** (**-, -n**) f bankruptcy; (umg: Reinfall) flop; **Pleite machen** to go bust
Pleitegeier (umg) m (drohende Pleite) vulture; (Bankrotteur) bankrupt
plemplem [plɛm'plɛm] (umg) adj nuts
Plenarsitzung [ple'na:rzɪtsʊŋ] f plenary session
Plenum ['ple:nʊm] (**-s, Plenen**) nt plenum
Pleuelstange ['plɔʏəlʃtaŋə] f connecting rod
Plissee [plɪ'se:] (**-s, -s**) nt pleat
Plombe ['plɔmbə] (**-, -n**) f lead seal; (Zahnplombe) filling
plombieren [plɔm'bi:rən] vt to seal; (Zahn) to fill
Plotter ['plɔtər] (**-s, -s**) m (Comput) plotter
plötzlich ['plœtslɪç] adj sudden ▷ adv suddenly; **~er Kindstod** SIDS
Pluderhose ['plu:dərho:zə] f harem trousers pl
plump [plʊmp] adj clumsy; (Hände) coarse; (Körper) shapeless; **~e Annäherungsversuche** very obvious advances
plumpsen (umg) vi to plump down, fall
Plumpsklo, Plumpsklosett (umg) nt earth closet
Plunder ['plʊndər] (**-s**) m junk, rubbish
Plundergebäck nt flaky pastry
plündern ['plʏndərn] vt to plunder; (Stadt) to sack ▷ vi to plunder
Plünderung ['plʏndərʊŋ] f plundering, sack, pillage
Plural ['plu:ra:l] (**-s, -e**) m plural; **im ~ stehen** to be (in the) plural
pluralistisch [plura'lɪstɪʃ] adj pluralistic
plus [plʊs] adv plus; **mit ~ minus null abschließen** (Comm) to break even; **Plus** (**-, -**) nt plus; (Fin) profit; (Vorteil) advantage
Plüsch [ply:ʃ] (**-(e)s, -e**) m plush; **Plüschtier** nt ≈ soft toy
Plus- zW: **Pluspol** m (Elek) positive pole; **Pluspunkt** m (Sport) point; (fig) point in sb's favour; **Plusquamperfekt** nt pluperfect
Plutonium [plu'to:nɪʊm] (**-s**) nt plutonium
PLZ abk = **Postleitzahl**
Pneu [pnɔʏ] (**-s, -s**) m abk (= Pneumatik) tyre (Brit), tire (US)
Po [po:] (**-s, -s**) (umg) m bum (Brit), fanny (US)
Pöbel ['pø:bəl] (**-s**) m mob, rabble
Pöbelei [pø:bə'laɪ] f vulgarity
pöbelhaft adj low, vulgar
pochen ['pɔxən] vi to knock; (Herz) to pound; **auf etw akk ~** (fig) to insist on sth

Pocken ['pɔkən] *pl* smallpox *sing*
Pockenimpfung, Pockenschutzimpfung *f*
  smallpox vaccination
Podcast ['pɔtka:st] (**-s, -s**) *m* podcast
Podest [po'dɛst] (**-(e)s, -e**) *nt od m* (*Sockel, fig*)
  pedestal; (*Podium*) platform
Podium ['po:diʊm] *nt* podium
Podiumsdiskussion *f* panel discussion
Poesie [poe'zi:] *f* poetry
Poet [po'e:t] (**-en, -en**) *m* poet; **poetisch** *adj*
  poetic
Pointe [po'ɛ̃:tə] (**-, -n**) *f* point; (*eines Witzes*)
  punch line
pointiert [poɛ̃'ti:rt] *adj* trenchant, pithy
Pokal [po'ka:l] (**-s, -e**) *m* goblet; (*Sport*) cup;
  Pokalspiel *nt* cup tie
Pökelfleisch ['pø:kəlflaɪʃ] *nt* salt meat
pökeln *vt* (*Fleisch, Fisch*) to pickle, salt
Poker ['po:kər] (**-s**) *nt* poker
pokern ['po:kərn] *vi* to play poker
Pol [po:l] (**-s, -e**) *m* pole; **der ruhende ~** (*fig*) the
  calming influence
pol. *abk* = **politisch; polizeilich**
polar [po'la:r] *adj* polar
polarisieren [polari'zi:rən] *vt, vr* to polarize
Polarkreis *m* polar circle; **nördlicher/**
  südlicher ~ Arctic/Antarctic Circle
Polarstern *m* Pole Star
Pole ['po:lə] (**-n, -n**) *m* Pole
Polemik [po'le:mɪk] *f* polemics *sing*
polemisch *adj* polemical
polemisieren [polemi'zi:rən] *vi* to polemicize
Polen ['po:lən] (**-s**) *nt* Poland
Polente (**-**) (*veraltet: umg*) *f* cops *pl*
Police [po'li:s(ə)] (**-, -n**) *f* insurance policy
Polier [po'li:r] (**-s, -e**) *m* foreman
polieren *vt* to polish
Poliklinik [poli'kli:nɪk] *f* outpatients
  (department) *sing*
Polin *f* Pole, Polish woman
Politesse [poli'tɛsə] (**-, -n**) *f* (*Frau*) ≈ traffic
  warden (*Brit*)
Politik [poli'ti:k] *f* politics *sing*; (*eine bestimmte*)
  policy; **in die ~ gehen** to go into politics; **eine**
  ~ verfolgen to pursue a policy
Politiker, in [po'li:tikər(ɪn)] (**-s, -**) *m(f)*
  politician
politisch [po'li:tɪʃ] *adj* political
politisieren [politi'zi:rən] *vi* to talk politics
  ▷ *vt* to politicize; **jdn ~** to make sb politically
  aware
Politur [poli'tu:r] *f* polish
Polizei [poli'tsaɪ] *f* police; **Polizeiaufsicht**
  f: **unter Polizeiaufsicht stehen** to have to
  report regularly to the police; **Polizeibeamte,**
  r *m* police officer; **polizeilich** *adj* police *attrib*;
  sich polizeilich melden to register with
  the police; **polizeiliches Führungszeugnis**
  certificate of "no criminal record" issued by the police;
  Polizeipräsidium *nt* police headquarters *pl*;
  Polizeirevier *nt* police station; **Polizeispitzel**
  m police spy, informer; **Polizeistaat** *m*
  police state; **Polizeistreife** *f* police patrol;

Polizeistunde *f* closing time; **Polizeiwache** *f*
  police station; **polizeiwidrig** *adj* illegal
Polizist, in [poli'tsɪst(ɪn)] (**-en, -en**) *m(f)*
  policeman/-woman
Pollen ['pɔlən] (**-s, -**) *m* pollen
poln. *abk* = **polnisch**
polnisch ['pɔlnɪʃ] *adj* Polish
Polohemd ['po:lohɛmt] *nt* polo shirt
Polster ['pɔlstər] (**-s, -**) *nt* cushion; (*Polsterung*)
  upholstery; (*in Kleidung*) padding; (*fig: Geld*)
  reserves *pl*; **Polsterer** (**-s, -**) *m* upholsterer;
  Polstergarnitur *f* three-piece suite;
  Polstermöbel *pl* upholstered furniture *sing*
polstern *vt* to upholster; (*Kleidung*) to pad; **sie**
  ist gut gepolstert (*umg*) she's well padded;
  (: *finanziell*) she's not short of the odd penny
Polsterung *f* upholstery
Polterabend ['pɔltəra:bənt] *m* party on the eve of
  a wedding
poltern *vi* (*Krach machen*) to crash; (*schimpfen*)
  to rant
Polygamie [polyga'mi:] *f* polygamy
Polynesien [poly'ne:ziən] (**-s**) *nt* Polynesia
Polynesier, in [poly'ne:ziər(ɪn)] (**-s, -**) *m(f)*
  Polynesian
polynesisch *adj* Polynesian
Polyp [po'ly:p] (**-en, -en**) *m* polyp; (*umg*) cop;
  Polypen *pl* (*Med*) adenoids *pl*
Polytechnikum [poly'tɛçnikʊm] (**-s,**
  Polytechnika) *nt* polytechnic, poly (*umg*)
Pomade [po'ma:də] *f* pomade
Pommern ['pɔmərn] (**-s**) *nt* Pomerania
Pommes frites [pɔm'frɪt] *pl* chips *pl* (*Brit*),
  French fried potatoes *pl* (*Brit*), French fries *pl*
  (*US*)
Pomp [pɔmp] (**-(e)s**) *m* pomp
pompös [pɔm'pø:s] *adj* grandiose
Pontius ['pɔntsiʊs] *m*: **von ~ zu Pilatus** from
  pillar to post
Pony ['pɔni] (**-s, -s**) *m* (*Frisur*) fringe (*Brit*), bangs
  pl (*US*) ▷ *nt* (*Pferd*) pony
Pop [pɔp] (**-s**) *m* (*Mus*) pop; (*Kunst*) pop art
Popelin [popə'li:n] (**-s, -e**) *m* poplin
Popeline (**-, -n**) *f* poplin
Popkonzert *nt* pop concert
Popmusik *f* pop music
Popo [po'po:] (**-s, -s**) (*umg*) *m* bottom, bum (*Brit*)
populär [popu'lɛ:r] *adj* popular
Popularität [populari'tɛ:t] *f* popularity
populärwissenschaftlich *adj* popular science
Pore ['po:rə] (**-, -n**) *f* pore
Porno ['pɔrno] (**-s, no pl**) (*umg*) *m* porn
Pornografie [pɔrnogra'fi:] *f* pornography
pornografisch [pɔrno'gra:fɪʃ] *adj* pornographic
porös [po'rø:s] *adj* porous
Porree ['pɔre] (**-s, -s**) *m* leek
Portal [pɔr'ta:l] (**-s, -e**) *nt* portal
Portefeuille [pɔrt(ə)'fø:j] (**-s, -s**) *nt* (*Pol, Fin*)
  portfolio
Portemonnaie [pɔrtmo'ne:] (**-s, -s**) *nt* purse
Portier [pɔrti'e:] (**-s, -s**) *m* porter; (*Pförtner*)
  porter, doorkeeper, doorman
Portion [pɔrtsi'o:n] *f* portion, helping;

p

259

(*umg: Anteil*) amount; **eine halbe ~**
(*fig: umg: Person*) a half-pint; **eine ~ Kaffee** a
pot of coffee
Portmonee [pɔrtmɔ'neː] (**-s, -s**) *nt* purse
Porto ['pɔrto] (**-s, -s** *od* **Porti**) *nt* postage; **~
zahlt Empfänger** postage paid; **portofrei** *adj*
post-free, (postage) prepaid
Porträt [pɔr'trɛː] (**-s, -s**) *nt* portrait
porträtieren [pɔrtrɛ'tiːrən] *vt* to paint (a
portrait of); (*fig*) to portray
Portugal ['pɔrtugal] (**-s**) *nt* Portugal
Portugiese [pɔrtu'giːzə] (**-n, -n**) *m* Portuguese
Portugiesin *f* Portuguese
portugiesisch *adj* Portuguese
Portwein ['pɔrtvaɪn] *m* port
Porzellan [pɔrtsɛ'laːn] (**-s, -e**) *nt* china,
porcelain; (*Geschirr*) china
Posaune [po'zaʊnə] (**-, -n**) *f* trombone
Pose ['poːzə] (**-, -n**) *f* pose
posieren [po'ziːrən] *vi* to pose
Position [pozitsi'oːn] *f* position; (*Comm: auf
Liste*) item
Positionslichter *pl* navigation lights *pl*
Positionspapier *nt* position paper
positiv ['poːzitiːf] *adj* positive; **~ zu etw
stehen** to be in favour (*Brit*) *od* favor (*US*) of sth;
Positiv (**-s, -e**) *nt* (*Phot*) positive
Positur [pozi'tuːr] *f* posture, attitude; **sich in ~
setzen** *od* **stellen** to adopt a posture
Posse ['pɔsə] (**-, -n**) *f* farce
possessiv ['pɔsɛsiːf] *adj* possessive; **Possessiv**
(**-s, -e**) *nt*, **Possessivpronomen** *nt* possessive
pronoun
possierlich [pɔ'siːrlɪç] *adj* funny
Post [pɔst] (**-, -en**) *f* post (office); (*Briefe*) post,
mail; **ist ~ für mich da?** are there any letters
for me?; **mit getrennter ~** under separate
cover; **etw auf die ~ geben** to post (*Brit*)
od mail sth; **auf die** *od* **zur ~ gehen** to go
to the post office; **Postamt** *nt* post office;
Postanweisung *f* postal order (*Brit*), money
order; **Postbote** *m* postman (*Brit*), mailman (*US*)
Posten (**-s, -**) *m* post, position; (*Comm*) item;
(: *Warenmenge*) quantity, lot; (*auf Liste*) entry;
(*Mil*) sentry; (*Streikposten*) picket; **~ beziehen**
to take up one's post; **nicht ganz auf dem ~
sein** (*nicht gesund sein*) to be off-colour (*Brit*) *od*
off-color (*US*)
posten ['poːstən] *vt* (*ins Internet*) to post
Poster ['poːstər] (**-s, -(s)**) *nt* poster
Postf. *abk* (= *Postfach*) PO Box
Post- *zW*: **Postfach** *nt* post office box;
Postkarte *f* postcard; **postlagernd** *adv* poste
restante; **Postleitzahl** *f* postal code
postmodern [pɔstmo'dɛrn] *adj* postmodern
Post- *zW*: **Postscheckkonto** *nt* Post Office Giro
account (*Brit*); **Postsparbuch** *nt* post office
savings book (*Brit*); **Postsparkasse** *f* post office
savings bank; **Poststempel** *m* postmark;
postwendend *adv* by return (of post);
Postwertzeichen *nt* (*form*) postage stamp;
Postwurfsendung *f* direct mail advertising
potent [po'tɛnt] *adj* potent; (*fig*) high-powered

Potential [potɛntsi'aːl] (**-s, -e**) *nt* = **Potenzial**
potentiell [potɛntsi'ɛl] *adj* = **potenziell**
Potenz [po'tɛnts] *f* power; (*eines Mannes*)
potency
Potenzial [potɛntsi'aːl] (**-s, -e**) *nt* potential
potenziell [potɛntsi'ɛl] *adj* potential
potenzieren [potɛn'tsiːrən] *vt* (*Math*) to raise to
the power of
Potpourri ['pɔtpuri] (**-s, -s**) *nt*: **~ (aus)** (*Mus*)
medley (of); (*fig*) assortment (of)
Pott [pɔt] (**-(e)s, ̈e**) (*umg*) *m* pot; **potthässlich**
(*umg*) *adj* ugly as sin
pp., **ppa.** *abk* (= *per procura*) p.p.
Präambel [prɛ'|ambəl] (**-, -n**) *f* (+*gen*) preamble
(to)
Pracht [praxt] (**-**) *f* splendour (*Brit*), splendor
(*US*), magnificence; **es ist eine wahre ~**
it's (really) marvellous; **Prachtexemplar** *nt*
beauty (*umg*); (*fig: Mensch*) fine specimen
prächtig ['prɛçtɪç] *adj* splendid
Prachtstück *nt* showpiece
prachtvoll *adj* splendid, magnificent
prädestinieren [predɛsti'niːrən] *vt* to
predestine
Prädikat [predi'kaːt] (**-(e)s, -e**) *nt* title; (*Gram*)
predicate; (*Zensur*) distinction; **Wein mit ~**
special quality wine
Prag [praːk] (**-s**) *nt* Prague
prägen ['prɛːgən] *vt* to stamp; (*Münze*) to
mint; (*Ausdruck*) to coin; (*Charakter*) to form;
(*kennzeichnen: Stadtbild*) to characterize; **das
Erlebnis prägte ihn** the experience left its
mark on him
prägend *adj* having a forming *od* shaping
influence
pragmatisch [pra'gmaːtɪʃ] *adj* pragmatic
prägnant [prɛ'gnant] *adj* concise, terse
Prägnanz *f* conciseness, terseness
Prägung ['prɛːgʊŋ] *f* minting; forming;
(*Eigenart*) character, stamp
prahlen ['praːlən] *vi* to boast, brag
Prahlerei [praːlə'raɪ] *f* boasting
prahlerisch *adj* boastful
Praktik ['praktɪk] *f* practice
praktikabel [prakti'kaːbəl] *adj* practicable
Praktikant, in [prakti'kant(ɪn)] *m(f)* trainee
Praktikum (**-s, Praktika** *od* **Praktiken**) *nt*
practical training
praktisch ['praktɪʃ] *adj* practical, handy;
~er Arzt general practitioner; **~es Beispiel**
concrete example
praktizieren [prakti'tsiːrən] *vt, vi* to practise
(*Brit*), practice (*US*)
Praline [pra'liːnə] *f* chocolate
prall [pral] *adj* firmly rounded; (*Segel*) taut;
(*Arme*) plump; (*Sonne*) blazing
prallen *vi* to bounce, rebound; (*Sonne*) to blaze
prallvoll *adj* full to bursting; (*Brieftasche*)
bulging
Prämie ['prɛːmiə] *f* premium; (*Belohnung*)
award, prize
prämienbegünstigt *adj* with benefit of
premiums

prämiensparen *vi* to save in a bonus scheme
prämieren [prɛ'mi:rən] *vt* to give an award to
Pranger ['praŋər] **(-s, -)** *m* (*Hist*) pillory; **jdn an den ~ stellen** (*fig*) to pillory sb
Pranke ['praŋkə] **(-, -n)** *f* (*Tierpranke: umg: Hand*) paw
Präparat [prɛpa'ra:t] **(-(e)s, -e)** *nt* (*Biol*) preparation; (*Med*) medicine
präparieren *vt* (*konservieren*) to preserve; (*Med: zerlegen*) to dissect
Präposition [prɛpozitsi'o:n] *f* preposition
Prärie [prɛ'ri:] *f* prairie
Präs. *abk* = **Präsens; Präsident**
Präsens ['prɛ:zɛns] **(-)** *nt* present tense
präsent *adj*: **etw ~ haben** to have sth at hand
präsentieren [prɛzɛn'ti:rən] *vt* to present
Präsenzbibliothek *f* reference library
Präservativ [prɛzɛrva'ti:f] **(-s, -e)** *nt* condom, sheath
Präsident, in [prɛzi'dɛnt(ɪn)] *m(f)* president; **Präsidentschaft** *f* presidency; **Präsidentschaftskandidat** *m* presidential candidate
Präsidium [prɛ'zi:diʊm] *nt* presidency, chairmanship; (*Polizeipräsidium*) police headquarters *pl*
prasseln ['prasəln] *vi* (*Feuer*) to crackle; (*Hagel*) to drum; (*Wörter*) to rain down
prassen ['prasən] *vi* to live it up
Präteritum [prɛ'te:ritʊm] **(-s, Präterita)** *nt* preterite
Pratze ['pratsə] **(-, -n)** *f* paw
Präventiv- [prɛvɛn'ti:f] *in zw* preventive
Praxis ['praksɪs] **(-, Praxen)** *f* practice; (*Erfahrung*) experience; (*Behandlungsraum*) surgery; (*von Anwalt*) office; **die ~ sieht anders aus** the reality is different; **ein Beispiel aus der ~** an example from real life
Präzedenzfall [prɛtse:'dɛntsfal] *m* precedent
präzis [prɛ'tsi:s] *adj* precise
Präzision [prɛtsizi'o:n] *f* precision
PR-Chef *m* PR officer
predigen ['pre:dɪgən] *vt, vi* to preach
Prediger (-s, -) *m* preacher
Predigt ['pre:dɪçt] **(-, -en)** *f* sermon
Preis [praɪs] **(-es, -e)** *m* price; (*Siegespreis*) prize; (*Auszeichnung*) award; **um keinen ~** not at any price; **um jeden ~** at all costs; **Preisangebot** *nt* quotation; **Preisausschreiben** *nt* competition; **Preisbindung** *f* price-fixing; **Preisbrecher** *m* (*Firma*) undercutter
Preiselbeere *f* cranberry
preisempfindlich *adj* price-sensitive
preisen [praɪzən] *unreg vt* to praise; **sich glücklich ~** (*geh*) to count o.s. lucky
Preis- *zW*: **Preisentwicklung** *f* price trend; **Preiserhöhung** *f* price increase; **Preisfrage** *f* question of price; (*Wettbewerb*) prize question
preisgeben *unreg vt* to abandon; (*opfern*) to sacrifice; (*zeigen*) to expose
Preis- *zW*: **Preisgefälle** *nt* price gap; **preisgekrönt** *adj* prizewinning; **Preisgericht** *nt* jury; **preisgünstig** *adj* inexpensive;

Preisindex *m* price index; **Preiskrieg** *m* price war; **Preislage** *f* price range; **preislich** *adj* price *attr*, in price; **Preisliste** *f* price list, tariff; **Preisnachlass** *m* discount; **Preisschild** *nt* price tag; **Preisspanne** *f* price range; **Preissturz** *m* slump; **Preisträger** *m* prizewinner; **preiswert** *adj* inexpensive
prekär [prɛ'kɛ:r] *adj* precarious
Prellbock [prɛlbɔk] *m* buffers *pl*
prellen *vt* to bruise; (*fig*) to cheat, swindle
Prellung *f* bruise
Premiere [prəmi'e:rə] **(-, -n)** *f* premiere
Premierminister, in [prəmɪ'e:mɪnɪstər(ɪn)] *m(f)* prime minister, premier
Presse ['prɛsə] **(-, -n)** *f* press; **Presseagentur** *f* press *od* news agency; **Presseausweis** *m* press pass; **Presseerklärung** *f* press release; **Pressefreiheit** *f* freedom of the press; **Pressekonferenz** *f* press conference; **Pressemeldung** *f* press report
pressen *vt* to press
Presse- *zW*: **Pressesprecher, in** *m(f)* spokesperson, press officer; **Pressestelle** *f* press office; **Presseverlautbarung** *f* press release
pressieren [prɛ'si:rən] *vi* to be in a hurry; **es pressiert** it's urgent
Pressluft ['prɛslʊft] *f* compressed air; **Pressluftbohrer** *m* pneumatic drill
Prestige [prɛs'ti:ʒə] **(-s)** *nt* prestige; **Prestigeverlust** *m* loss of prestige
Preuße ['prɔysə] **(-n, -n)** *m* Prussian
Preußen (-s) *nt* Prussia
Preußin *f* Prussian
preußisch *adj* Prussian
prickeln ['prɪkəln] *vi* to tingle; (*kitzeln*) to tickle; (*Bläschen bilden*) to sparkle, bubble ▷ *vt* to tickle
pries *etc* [pri:s] *vb siehe* **preisen**
Priester ['pri:stər] **(-s, -)** *m* priest
Priesterin *f* priestess
Priesterweihe *f* ordination (to the priesthood)
Prima ['pri:ma] **(-, Primen)** *f* (*früher*) *eighth and ninth year of German secondary school*
prima *adj inv* first-class, excellent
primär [pri'mɛ:r] *adj* primary; **Primärdaten** *pl* primary data *pl*
Primel ['pri:məl] **(-, -n)** *f* primrose
primitiv [primi'ti:f] *adj* primitive
Primzahl ['pri:mtsa:l] *f* prime (number)
Prinz [prɪnts] **(-en, -en)** *m* prince
Prinzessin [prɪn'tsɛsɪn] *f* princess
Prinzip [prɪn'tsi:p] **(-s, -ien)** *nt* principle; **aus ~** on principle; **im ~** in principle
prinzipiell [prɪntsi'piɛl] *adj* on principle
prinzipienlos *adj* unprincipled
Priorität [priori'tɛ:t] *f* priority; **Prioritäten** *pl* (*Comm*) preference shares *pl*, preferred stock *sing* (*US*); **~en setzen** to establish one's priorities
Prise ['pri:zə] **(-, -n)** *f* pinch
Prisma ['prɪsma] **(-s, Prismen)** *nt* prism
privat [pri'va:t] *adj* private; **jdn ~ sprechen** to speak to sb in private; **Privatbesitz** *m* private

p

261

property; **Privatdozent** m outside lecturer;
Privatfernsehen nt commercial television;
Privatgespräch nt private conversation; (am
Telefon) private call

privatisieren [privati'ziːrən] vt to privatize

Privatschule f private school

Privatvorsorge f (fürs Alter) private pension
scheme; (für Gesundheit) health insurance
scheme

Privatwirtschaft f private sector

Privileg [privi'leːk] (-(e)s, -ien) nt privilege

Pro [proː] (-) nt pro

pro präp+akk per; ~ **Stück** each, apiece

Probe ['proːbə] (-, -n) f test; (Teststück) sample;
(Theat) rehearsal; **jdn auf die ~ stellen** to put
sb to the test; **er ist auf ~ angestellt** he's
employed for a probationary period; **zur ~** to
try out; **Probebohrung** f (Öl) exploration well;
Probeexemplar nt specimen copy; **Probefahrt**
f test drive; **Probelauf** m trial run

proben vt to try; (Theat) to rehearse

Probe- zW: **Probestück** nt specimen;
probeweise adv on approval; **Probezeit** f
probation period

probieren [pro'biːrən] vt to try; (Wein, Speise) to
taste, sample ▷ vi to try; to taste

Problem [pro'bleːm] (-s, -e) nt problem; **vor
einem ~ stehen** to be faced with a problem

Problematik [proble'maːtɪk] f problem

problematisch [proble'maːtɪʃ] adj problematic

problemlos adj problem-free

Problemstellung f way of looking at a
problem

Produkt [pro'dʊkt] (-(e)s, -e) nt product; (Agr)
produce no pl

Produktentwicklung f product development

Produktion [prodʊktsi'oːn] f production

Produktionsleiter m production manager

Produktionsstätte f (Halle) shop floor

produktiv [prodʊk'tiːf] adj productive

Produktivität [prodʊktivi'tɛːt] f productivity

Produzent [produ'tsɛnt] m manufacturer;
(Film) producer

produzieren [produ'tsiːrən] vt to produce ▷ vr
to show off

Prof. [prof] abk (= Professor) Prof

profan [pro'faːn] adj (weltlich) secular, profane;
(gewöhnlich) mundane

professionell [profɛsio'nɛl] adj professional

Professor, in [pro'fɛsɔr, profɛ'soːrɪn] m(f)
professor; (Österr: Gymnasiallehrer) grammar
school teacher (Brit), high school teacher (US)

Professur [profɛ'suːr] f: ~ **(für)** chair (of)

Profi ['proːfi] (-s, -s) m abk (= Professional) pro

Profil [pro'fiːl] (-s, -e) nt profile; (fig) image;
(Querschnitt) cross section; (Längsschnitt) vertical
section; (von Reifen, Schuhsohle) tread

profilieren [profi'liːrən] vr to create an image
for o.s.

Profilsohle f sole with a tread

Profit [pro'fiːt] (-(e)s, -e) m profit

profitgeil adj (umg) profit-greedy

profitieren [profi'tiːrən] vi: ~ **(von)** to profit

(from)

Profitmacherei (umg) f profiteering

pro forma adv as a matter of form

Pro-forma-Rechnung f pro forma invoice

Prognose [pro'gnoːzə] (-, -n) f prediction,
prognosis

Programm [pro'gram] (-s, -e) nt programme
(Brit), program (US); (Comput) program;
(TV: Sender) channel; (Kollektion) range; **nach
~** as planned; **Programmfehler** m (Comput)
bug; **programmgemäß** adj according to plan;
Programmhinweis m (Rundf, TV) programme
(Brit) od program (US) announcement

programmieren [progra'miːrən] vt to
programme (Brit), program (US); (Comput) to
program; **auf etw** akk **programmiert sein**
(fig) to be geared to sth

Programmierer, in (-s, -) m(f) programmer

Programmiersprache f (Comput)
programming language

Programmierung f (Comput) programming

Programmvorschau f preview; (Film) trailer

progressiv [progrɛ'siːf] adj progressive

Projekt [pro'jɛkt] (-(e)s, -e) nt project

Projektleiter, in m(f) project manager(ess)

Projektor [pro'jɛktɔr] m projector

projizieren [proji'tsiːrən] vt to project

proklamieren [prokla'miːrən] vt to proclaim

Pro-Kopf-Einkommen nt per capita income

Prokura [pro'kuːra] (-, Prokuren) f (form) power
of attorney

Prokurist, in [proku'rɪst(ɪn)] m(f) attorney

Prolet [pro'leːt] (-en, -en) m prole, pleb

Proletariat [proletari'aːt] (-(e)s, -e) nt
proletariat

Proletarier [prole'taːriər] (-s, -) m proletarian

Prolog [pro'loːk] (-(e)s, -e) nt prologue

Promenade [promə'naːdə] (-, -n) f promenade

Promenadenmischung f (hum) mongrel

Promille [pro'mɪle] (-(s), -) (umg) nt alcohol
level; **Promillegrenze** f legal (alcohol) limit

prominent [promi'nɛnt] adj prominent

Prominenz [promi'nɛnts] f VIPs pl

Promoter [pro'moːtər] (-s, -) m promoter

Promotion [promotsi'oːn] f doctorate, Ph.D.

promovieren [promo'viːrən] vi to receive a
doctorate etc

prompt [prɔmpt] adj prompt

Pronomen [pro'noːmɛn] (-s, -) nt pronoun

Propaganda [propa'ganda] (-) f propaganda

propagieren [propa'giːrən] vt to propagate

Propangas [pro'paːngaːs] nt propane gas

Propeller [pro'pɛlər] (-s, -) m propeller

proper ['prɔpər] (umg) adj neat, tidy

Prophet, in [pro'feːt(ɪn)] (-en, -en) m(f)
prophet(ess)

prophezeien [profe'tsaɪən] vt to prophesy

Prophezeiung f prophecy

prophylaktisch [profy'laktɪʃ] adj prophylactic
(form), preventive

Proportion [proportsi'oːn] f proportion

proportional [proportsio'naːl] adj
proportional; **Proportionalschrift** f (Comput)

proportional printing
proportioniert [proportsio'niːrt] *adj*: **gut/ schlecht** ~ well/badly proportioned
Proporz [pro'pɔrts] **(-es, -e)** *m* proportional representation
Prosa ['proːza] (-) *f* prose
prosaisch [pro'zaːɪʃ] *adj* prosaic
prosit ['proːzɪt] *interj* cheers!; ~ **Neujahr!** happy New Year!
Prospekt [pro'spɛkt] **(-(e)s, -e)** *m* leaflet, brochure
prost [proːst] *interj* cheers!
Prostata ['prɔstata] (-) *f* prostate gland
Prostituierte [prostitu'iːrtə] **(-n, -n)** *f* prostitute
Prostitution [prostitutsi'oːn] *f* prostitution
prot. [prot] *abk* = **protestantisch**
Protektionismus [protɛktsio'nɪsmʊs] *m* protectionism
Protektorat [protɛkto'raːt] **(-(e)s, -e)** *nt* (*Schirmherrschaft*) patronage; (*Schutzgebiet*) protectorate
Protest [pro'tɛst] **(-(e)s, -e)** *m* protest
Protestant, in [protɛs'tant(ɪn)] *m(f)* Protestant; **protestantisch** *adj* Protestant
Protestbewegung *f* protest movement
protestieren [protɛs'tiːrən] *vi* to protest
Protestkundgebung *f* (protest) rally
Protestpartei *f* protest party
Prothese [pro'teːzə] **(-, -n)** *f* artificial limb; (*Zahnprothese*) dentures *pl*
Protokoll [proto'kɔl] **(-s, -e)** *nt* register; (*Niederschrift*) record; (*von Sitzung*) minutes *pl*; (*diplomatisch*) protocol; (*Polizeiprotokoll*) statement; (*Strafzettel*) ticket; **(das) ~ führen** (*bei Sitzung*) to take the minutes; (*bei Gericht*) to make a transcript of the proceedings; **etw zu ~ geben** to have sth put on record; (*bei Polizei*) to say sth in one's statement; **Protokollführer** *m* secretary; (*Jur*) clerk (of the court)
protokollieren [protoko'liːrən] *vt* to take down; (*Bemerkung*) to enter in the minutes
Proton ['proːtɔn] **(-s, -en)** *nt* proton
Prototyp *m* prototype
Protz ['prɔts] **(-es, -e)** *m* swank; **protzen** *vi* to show off
protzig *adj* ostentatious
Proviant [provi'ant] **(-s, -e)** *m* provisions *pl*, supplies *pl*
Provinz [pro'vɪnts] **(-, -en)** *f* province; **das ist finsterste ~** (*pej*) it's a cultural backwater
provinziell [provɪn'tsiɛl] *adj* provincial
Provision [provizi'oːn] *f* (*Comm*) commission
provisorisch [provi'zoːrɪʃ] *adj* provisional
Provisorium [provi'zoːrium] **(-s, -ien)** *nt* provisional arrangement
Provokation [provokatsi'oːn] *f* provocation
provokativ [provoka'tiːf] *adj* provocative, provoking
provokatorisch [provoka'toːrɪʃ] *adj* provocative, provoking
provozieren [provo'tsiːrən] *vt* to provoke
Proz. *abk* (= *Prozent*) pc

Prozedur [protse'duːr] *f* procedure; (*pej*) carry-on; **die ~ beim Zahnarzt** the ordeal at the dentist's
Prozent [pro'tsɛnt] **(-(e)s, -e)** *nt* per cent, percentage; **Prozentrechnung** *f* percentage calculation; **Prozentsatz** *m* percentage
prozentual [protsɛntu'aːl] *adj* percentage *attrib*
Prozess [pro'tsɛs] **(-es, -e)** *m* trial, case; (*Vorgang*) process; **es zum ~ kommen lassen** to go to court; **mit jdm/etw kurzen ~ machen** (*fig: umg*) to make short work of sb/sth; **Prozessanwalt** *m* barrister, counsel; **Prozessführung** *f* handling of a case
prozessieren [protse'siːrən] *vi*: ~ **(mit)** to bring an action (against), go to law (with *od* against)
Prozession [protsɛsi'oːn] *f* procession
Prozesskosten *pl* (legal) costs *pl*
prüde ['pryːdə] *adj* prudish
Prüderie [pryːdə'riː] *f* prudery
prüfen ['pryːfən] *vt* to examine, test; (*nachprüfen*) to check; (*erwägen*) to consider; (*Geschäftsbücher*) to audit; (*mustern*) to scrutinize
Prüfer, in **(-s, -)** *m(f)* examiner
Prüfling *m* examinee
Prüfstein *m* touchstone
Prüfung *f* (*Sch, Univ*) examination, exam; (*Überprüfung*) checking; **eine ~ machen** to take *od* sit (*Brit*) an exam(ination); **durch eine ~ fallen** to fail an exam(ination)
Prüfungs- *zW*: **Prüfungsausschuss** *m* examining board; **Prüfungskommission** *f* examining board; **Prüfungsordnung** *f* exam(ination) regulations *pl*
Prügel ['pryːgəl] **(-s, -)** *m* cudgel ▷ *pl* beating *sing*
Prügelei [pryːgə'laɪ] *f* fight
Prügelknabe *m* scapegoat
prügeln *vt* to beat ▷ *vr* to fight
Prügelstrafe *f* corporal punishment
Prunk [prʊŋk] **(-(e)s)** *m* pomp, show; **prunkvoll** *adj* splendid, magnificent
prusten ['pruːstən] (*umg*) *vi* to snort
PS *abk* (= *Pferdestärke*) hp; (= *Postskript(um)*) PS
Psalm [psalm] **(-s, -en)** *m* psalm
pseudo- [psɔʏdo] *in zW* pseudo
Psychiater [psy'çiaːtər] **(-s, -)** *m* psychiatrist
Psychiatrie [psyçia'triː] *f* psychiatry
psychiatrisch [psy'çiaːtrɪʃ] *adj* psychiatric; **~e Klinik** mental *od* psychiatric hospital
psychisch ['psyːçɪʃ] *adj* psychological; ~ **gestört** emotionally *od* psychologically disturbed
Psychoanalyse [psyçoana'lyːzə] *f* psychoanalysis
Psychologe [psyço'loːgə] **(-n, -n)** *m* psychologist
Psychologie *f* psychology
Psychologin *f* psychologist
psychologisch *adj* psychological
Psychotherapie *f* psychotherapy
PTT (*Schweiz*) *abk* (= *Post, Telefon, Telegraf*) postal and telecommunication services
Pubertät [pubɛr'tɛːt] *f* puberty
publik [pu'bliːk] *adj*: ~ **werden** to become

P

public knowledge

Publikum ['puːblikʊm] (**-s**) *nt* audience; (*Sport*) crowd; **das ~ in dieser Bar ist sehr gemischt** you get a very mixed group of people using this bar

Publikumserfolg *m* popular success

Publikumsverkehr *m*: „**heute kein ~**" "closed today for public business"

publizieren [publi'tsiːrən] *vt* to publish

Pudding ['pʊdɪŋ] (**-s, -e** *od* **-s**) *m* blancmange; **Puddingpulver** *nt* custard powder

Pudel ['puːdəl] (**-s, -**) *m* poodle; **das also ist des ~s Kern** (*fig*) that's what it's really all about

pudelwohl (*umg*) *adj*: **sich ~ fühlen** to feel on top of the world

Puder ['puːdər] (**-s, -**) *m* powder; **Puderdose** *f* powder compact

pudern *vt* to powder

Puderzucker *m* icing sugar (*Brit*), confectioner's sugar (*US*)

Puerto Ricaner, in [pʊɛrtori'kaːnər(ɪn)] (**-s, -**) *m(f)* Puerto Rican

puerto-ricanisch *adj* Puerto Rican ·

Puerto Rico [pu'ɛrto'riːko] (**-s**) *nt* Puerto Rico

Puff[1] [pʊf] (**-(e)s, -e**) *m* (*Wäschepuff*) linen basket; (*Sitzpuff*) pouf

Puff[2] (**-(e)s, ⁻e**) (*umg*) *m* (*Stoß*) push

Puff[3] (**-s, -s**) (*umg*) *m od nt* (*Bordell*) brothel

Puffer (**-s, -**) *m* (*auch Comput*) buffer; **Pufferspeicher** (*Comput*) cache; **Pufferstaat** *m* buffer state; **Pufferzone** *f* buffer zone

Puffreis *m* puffed rice

Pulle ['pʊlə] (**-, -n**) (*umg*) *f* bottle; **volle ~ fahren** (*umg*) to drive flat out

Pulli ['pʊli] (**-s, -s**) (*umg*) *m* sweater, jumper (*Brit*)

Pullover [pʊ'loːvər] (**-s, -**) *m* sweater, jumper (*Brit*)

Pullunder [pʊ'lʊndər] (**-s, -**) *m* slipover

Puls [pʊls] (**-es, -e**) *m* pulse; **Pulsader** *f* artery; **sich** *dat* **die Pulsader(n) aufschneiden** to slash one's wrists

pulsieren [pʊl'ziːrən] *vi* to throb, pulsate

Pult [pʊlt] (**-(e)s, -e**) *nt* desk

Pulver ['pʊlfər] (**-s, -**) *nt* powder; **Pulverfass** *nt* powder keg; **(wie) auf einem Pulverfass sitzen** (*fig*) to be sitting on (top of) a volcano

pulverig *adj* powdery

pulverisieren [pʊlveri'ziːrən] *vt* to pulverize

Pulverkaffee *m* instant coffee

Pulverschnee *m* powdery snow

pummelig ['pʊməlɪç] *adj* chubby

Pump (**-(e)s**) (*umg*) *m*: **auf ~ kaufen** to buy on tick (*Brit*) *od* credit

Pumpe ['pʊmpə] (**-, -n**) *f* pump; (*umg: Herz*) ticker

pumpen *vt* to pump; (*umg*) to lend; (: *entleihen*) to borrow

Pumphose *f* knickerbockers *pl*

puncto ['pʊŋkto] *präp +gen*: **in ~ X** where X is concerned

Punkt [pʊŋkt] (**-(e)s, -e**) *m* point; (*bei Muster*) dot; (*Satzzeichen*) full stop, period (*bes US*); **~ 12**

Uhr at 12 o'clock on the dot; **nun mach aber mal einen ~!** (*umg*) come off it!; **punktgleich** *adj* (*Sport*) level

punktieren [pʊŋk'tiːrən] *vt* to dot; (*Med*) to aspirate

pünktlich ['pʏŋktlɪç] *adj* punctual; **Pünktlichkeit** *f* punctuality

Punkt- *zW*: **Punktmatrix** *f* dot matrix; **Punktrichter** *m* (*Sport*) judge; **Punktsieg** *m* victory on points; **Punktwertung** *f* points system; **Punktzahl** *f* score

Punsch [pʊnʃ] (**-(e)s, -e**) *m* (hot) punch

Pupille [pu'pɪlə] (**-, -n**) *f* (*im Auge*) pupil

Puppe ['pʊpə] (**-, -n**) *f* doll; (*Marionette*) puppet; (*Insektenpuppe*) pupa, chrysalis; (*Schaufensterpuppe, Übungspuppe*) dummy; (*umg: Mädchen*) doll, bird (*bes Brit*)

Puppen- *zW*: **Puppenhaus** *nt* doll's house, dollhouse (*US*); **Puppenspieler** *m* puppeteer; **Puppenstube** *f* (single-room) doll's house *od* dollhouse (*US*); **Puppentheater** *nt* puppet theatre (*Brit*) *od* theater (*US*); **Puppenwagen** *m* doll's pram

pupsen ['puːpsən] (*umg*) *vi* to make a rude noise/smell

pur [puːr] *adj* pure; (*völlig*) sheer; (*Whisky*) neat

Püree [py'reː] (**-s, -s**) *nt* purée; (*Kartoffelpüree*) mashed potatoes *pl*

Purpur ['pʊrpʊr] (**-s**) *m* crimson

Purzelbaum ['pʊrtsəlbaʊm] *m* somersault

purzeln *vi* to tumble

Puste ['puːstə] (**-**) (*umg*) *f* puff; (*fig*) steam

Pusteblume (*umg*) *f* dandelion

Pustel ['pʊstəl] (**-, -n**) *f* pustule

pusten ['puːstən] (*umg*) *vi* to puff

Pute ['puːtə] (**-, -n**) *f* turkey hen

Puter (**-s, -**) *m* turkey cock; **puterrot** *adj* scarlet

Putsch [pʊtʃ] (**-(e)s, -e**) *m* revolt, putsch; **putschen** *vi* to revolt; **Putschist** *m* rebel; **Putschversuch** *m* attempted coup (d'état)

Putte ['pʊtə] (**-, -n**) *f* (*Kunst*) cherub

Putz [pʊts] (**-es**) *m* (*Mörtel*) plaster, roughcast; **eine Mauer mit ~ verkleiden** to roughcast a wall

putzen *vt* to clean; (*Nase*) to wipe, blow ▷ *vr* to clean o.s.; (*veraltet: sich schmücken*) to dress o.s. up

Putzfrau *f* cleaning lady, charwoman (*Brit*)

putzig *adj* quaint, funny

Putzlappen *m* cloth

putzmunter (*umg*) *adj* full of beans

Putz- *zW*: **Putztag** *m* cleaning day; **Putzteufel** (*umg*) *m* maniac for housework; **Putzzeug** *nt* cleaning things *pl*

Puzzle ['pasəl] (**-s, -s**) *nt* jigsaw (puzzle)

PVC [peːfau'tseː] (**-(s)**) *nt abk* PVC

Pygmäe [pʏ'gmɛːə] (**-n, -n**) *m* Pygmy

Pyjama [pi'dʒaːma] (**-s, -s**) *m* pyjamas *pl* (*Brit*), pajamas *pl* (*US*)

Pyramide [pyra'miːdə] (**-, -n**) *f* pyramid

Pyrenäen [pyre'nɛːən] *pl*: **die ~** the Pyrenees *pl*

Python ['pyːtɔn] (**-s, -s**) *m* python; **Pythonschlange** *f* python

Qq

Q, q [kuː] *nt* Q, q; **Q wie Quelle** ≈ Q for Queen
qcm *abk* (= *Quadratzentimeter*) cm²
qkm *abk* (= *Quadratkilometer*) km²
qm *abk* (= *Quadratmeter*) m²
quabbelig ['kvabəlɪç], **quabblig** ['kvablɪç] *adj*
 wobbly; (*Frosch*) slimy
Quacksalber ['kvakzalbər] (**-s, -**) *m* quack
 (doctor)
Quader ['kvaːdər] (**-s, -**) *m* square stone block;
 (*Math*) cuboid
Quadrat [kva'draːt] (**-(e)s, -e**) *nt* square;
 quadratisch *adj* square; **Quadratlatschen**
 pl (*hum: umg: Schuhe*) clodhoppers *pl*;
 Quadratmeter *m* square metre (*Brit*) *od* meter
 (*US*)
quadrieren [kva'driːrən] *vt* to square
quaken ['kvaːkən] *vi* to croak; (*Ente*) to quack
quäken ['kvɛːkən] *vi* to screech
quäkend *adj* screeching
Quäker, in (**-s, -**) *m(f)* Quaker
Qual [kvaːl] (**-, -en**) *f* pain, agony; (*seelisch*)
 anguish; **er machte ihr das Leben zur ~** he
 made her life a misery
quälen ['kvɛːlən] *vt* to torment ▷ *vr* (*sich*
 abmühen) to struggle; (*geistig*) to torment o.s.;
 ~de Ungewissheit agonizing uncertainty
Quälerei [kvɛːləˈraɪ] *f* torture, torment
Quälgeist (*umg*) *m* pest
Qualifikation [kvalifikatsiˈoːn] *f* qualification
qualifizieren [kvalifiˈtsiːrən] *vt* to qualify;
 (*einstufen*) to label ▷ *vr* to qualify
qualifiziert *adj* (*Arbeiter, Nachwuchs*) qualified;
 (*Arbeit*) professional; (*Pol: Mehrheit*) requisite
Qualität [kvaliˈtɛːt] *f* quality; **von**
 ausgezeichneter ~ (of) top quality
qualitativ [kvalitaˈtiːf] *adj* qualitative
Qualitätskontrolle *f* quality control
Qualitätsstandard *m* quality standard
Qualitätsware *f* article of high quality
Qualle ['kvalə] (**-, -n**) *f* jellyfish
Qualm [kvalm] (**-(e)s**) *m* thick smoke
qualmen *vt, vi* to smoke
qualvoll ['kvaːlfɔl] *adj* painful; (*Schmerzen*)
 excruciating, agonizing
Quantensprung *m* quantum leap
Quantentheorie ['kvantənteoriː] *f* quantum
 theory
Quantität [kvantiˈtɛːt] *f* quantity

quantitativ [kvantitaˈtiːf] *adj* quantitative
Quantum ['kvantʊm] (**-s, Quanten**) *nt*
 quantity, amount
Quarantäne [karanˈtɛːnə] (**-, -n**) *f* quarantine
Quark¹ [kvark] (**-s**) *m* curd cheese, quark; (*umg*)
 rubbish
Quark² [kvark] (**-s, -s**) *nt* (*Phys*) quark
Quarta ['kvarta] (**-, Quarten**) *f* (*früher*) third year
 of German secondary school
Quartal [kvarˈtaːl] (**-s, -e**) *nt* quarter (year);
 Kündigung zum ~ quarterly notice date
Quartett [kvarˈtɛt] (**-(e)s, -e**) *nt* (*Mus*) quartet;
 (*Karten*) set of four cards; (: *Spiel*) ≈ happy
 families
Quartier [kvarˈtiːr] (**-s, -e**) *nt* accommodation
 (*Brit*), accommodations *pl* (*US*); (*Mil*) quarters
 pl; (*Stadtquartier*) district
Quarz [kvaːrts] (**-es, -e**) *m* quartz
quasi ['kvaːzi] *adv* virtually ▷ *präf* quasi
quasseln ['kvasəln] (*umg*) *vi* to natter
Quaste ['kvastə] (**-, -n**) *f* (*Troddel*) tassel; (*von*
 Pinsel) bristles *pl*
Quästur [kvɛsˈtuːr] *f* (*Univ*) bursary
Quatsch [kvatʃ] (**-es**) (*umg*) *m* rubbish,
 hogwash; **hört doch endlich auf mit dem ~!**
 stop being so stupid!; **~ machen** to mess about
quatschen *vi* to chat, natter
Quatschkopf (*umg*) *m* (*pej: Schwätzer*) windbag;
 (*Dummkopf*) twit (*Brit*)
Quecksilber ['kvɛkzɪlbər] *nt* mercury
Quelle ['kvɛlə] (**-, -n**) *f* spring; (*eines*
 Flusses, Computer) source; **an der ~ sitzen** (*fig*)
 to be well placed; **aus zuverlässiger ~** from a
 reliable source
quellen *vi* (*hervorquellen*) to pour *od* gush forth;
 (*schwellen*) to swell
Quellenangabe *f* reference
Quellsprache *f* source language
Quengelei [kvɛŋəˈlaɪ] (*umg*) *f* whining
quengelig (*umg*) *adj* whining
quengeln (*umg*) *vi* to whine
quer [kveːr] *adv* crossways, diagonally;
 (*rechtwinklig*) at right angles; **~ gestreift**
 horizontally striped; **~ auf dem Bett** across
 the bed; *siehe auch* **querlegen**; **Querbalken** *m*
 crossbeam; **Querdenker** *m* maverick
Quere ['kveːrə] (**-**) *f*: **jdm in die ~ kommen** to
 cross sb's path

q

quer- zW: **querfeldein** adv across country; **Querfeldeinrennen** nt cross-country; (mit Motorrädern) motocross; (Radrennen) cyclo-cross; **Querflöte** f flute; **Querformat** nt oblong format; **Querkopf** m awkward customer; **querlegen** vr (fig: umg) to be awkward; **Querschiff** nt transept; **Querschläger** (umg) m ricochet; **Querschnitt** m cross section; **querschnittsgelähmt** adj paraplegic, paralysed below the waist; **Querschnittslähmung** f paraplegia; **Querstraße** f intersecting road; **Querstrich** m (horizontal) stroke od line; **Quersumme** f (Math) sum of digits of a number; **Quertreiber** (-s, -) m obstructionist

Querulant, in [kveru'lant(ɪn)] (-en, -en) m(f) grumbler

Querverbindung f connection, link

Querverweis m cross-reference

quetschen ['kvɛtʃən] vt to squash, crush; (Med) to bruise ▷ vr (sich klemmen) to be caught; (sich zwängen) to squeeze (o.s.)

Quetschung f bruise, contusion (form)

Queue [kø:] (-s, -s) nt (Billiard) cue

quicklebendig ['kvɪkle'bɛndɪc] (umg) adj (Kind) lively, active; (ältere Person) spry

quieken ['kvi:kən] vi to squeak

quietschen ['kvi:tʃən] vi to squeak

quietschvergnügt ['kvi:tʃfɛrgny:kt] (umg) adj happy as a sandboy

quillt [kvɪlt] vb siehe **quellen**

Quinta ['kvɪnta] (-, **Quinten**) f (früher) second year in German secondary school

Quintessenz ['kvɪntɛsɛnts] f quintessence

Quintett [kvɪn'tɛt] (-(e)s, -e) nt quintet

Quirl [kvɪrl] (-(e)s, -e) m whisk

quirlig ['kvɪrlɪç] adj lively, frisky

quitt [kvɪt] adj quits, even

Quitte (-, -n) f quince

quittieren [kvɪ'ti:rən] vt to give a receipt for; (Dienst) to leave

Quittung f receipt; **er hat seine ~ bekommen** he's paid the penalty od price

Quiz [kvɪs] (-, -) nt quiz

quoll etc [kvɔl] vb siehe **quellen**

Quote ['kvo:tə] (-, -n) f proportion; (Rate) rate

Quotenbringer m (TV: umg) ratings booster

Quotenregelung f quota system (for ensuring adequate representation of women)

Quotierung [kvo'ti:rʊŋ] f (Comm) quotation

Rr

R¹, r nt R, r; **R wie Richard** = R for Robert, R for Roger (US)

R², r abk (= Radius) r.

r. abk (= rechts) r.

Rabatt [ra'bat] (-(e)s, -e) m discount

Rabatte (-, -n) f flower bed, border

Rabattmarke f trading stamp

Rabatz [ra'bats] (-es) (umg) m row, din

Rabe ['ra:bə] (-n, -n) m raven

Rabenmutter f bad mother

rabenschwarz adj pitch-black

rabiat [rabi'a:t] adj furious

Rache ['raxə] (-) f revenge, vengeance

Rachen (-s, -) m throat

rächen ['reçən] vt to avenge, revenge ▷ vr to take (one's) revenge; **das wird sich ~** you'll pay for that

Rachitis [ra'xi:tɪs] (-) f rickets sing

Rachsucht f vindictiveness

rachsüchtig adj vindictive

Racker ['rakər] (-s, -) m rascal, scamp

Rad [ra:t] (-(e)s, ̈-er) nt wheel; (Fahrrad) bike; **~ fahren** to cycle; **unter die Räder kommen** (umg) to fall into bad ways; **das fünfte ~ am Wagen sein** (umg) to be in the way

Radar ['ra:da:r] (-s) m od nt radar; **Radarfalle** f speed trap; **Radarkontrolle** f radar-controlled speed check

Radau [ra'dau] (-s) (umg) m row; **~ machen** to kick up a row; (Unruhe stiften) to cause trouble

Raddampfer m paddle steamer

radebrechen ['ra:dəbreçən] vi untr: **Deutsch** etc **~** to speak broken German etc

radeln vi (Hilfsverb sein) to cycle

Rädelsführer ['re:dəlsfy:rər] (-s, -) m ringleader

Rad- zW: **Radfahrer** m cyclist; (pej: umg) crawler; **Radfahrweg** m cycle track od path

radieren [ra'di:rən] vt to rub out, erase; (Art) to etch

Radiergummi m rubber (Brit), eraser (bes US)

Radierung f etching

Radieschen [ra'di:sçən] nt radish

radikal [radi'ka:l] adj radical; **~ gegen etw vorgehen** to take radical steps against sth

Radikale, r f(m) radical

Radikalisierung [radikali'zi:rʊŋ] f radicalization

Radikalkur (umg) f drastic remedy

Radio ['ra:dio] (-s, -s) nt radio, wireless (bes Brit); **im ~** on the radio; **radioaktiv** adj radioactive; **radioaktiver Niederschlag** (radioactive) fallout; **Radioaktivität** f radioactivity; **Radioapparat** m radio (set); **Radiorekorder** m radio-cassette recorder

Radium ['ra:diʊm] (-s) nt radium

Radius ['ra:diʊs] (-, **Radien**) m radius

Radkappe f (Aut) hub cap

Radler, in (-s, -) m(f) cyclist

Rad- zW: **Radrennbahn** f cycling (race)track; **Radrennen** nt cycle race; (Sportart) cycle racing; **Radsport** m cycling

RAF (-) f abk (= Rote Armee Fraktion) Red Army Faction

raffen ['rafən] vt to snatch, pick up; (Stoff) to gather (up); (Geld) to pile up, rake in; (umg: verstehen) to catch on to

Raffgier f greed, avarice

Raffinade [rafi'na:də] f refined sugar

Raffinesse [rafi'nɛsə] (-) f (Feinheit) refinement; (Schlauheit) cunning

raffinieren [rafi'ni:rən] vt to refine

raffiniert adj crafty, cunning; (Zucker) refined

Rage ['ra:ʒə] (-) f (Wut) rage, fury

ragen ['ra:gən] vi to tower, rise

Rahm [ra:m] (-s) m cream

Rahmen (-s, -) m frame(work); **aus dem ~ fallen** to go too far; **im ~ des Möglichen** within the bounds of possibility; **rahmen** vt to frame; **Rahmenhandlung** f (Liter) background story; **Rahmenplan** m outline plan; **Rahmenrichtlinien** pl guidelines pl

rahmig adj creamy

räkeln ['re:kln] vr = **rekeln**

Rakete [ra'ke:tə] (-, -n) f rocket; **ferngelenkte ~** guided missile

Raketenstützpunkt m missile base

Rallye ['rali] (-, -s) f rally

rammdösig ['ramdø:zɪç] (umg) adj giddy, dizzy

rammen ['ramən] vt to ram

Rampe ['rampə] (-, -n) f ramp

Rampenlicht nt (Theat) footlights pl; **sie möchte immer im ~ stehen** (fig) she always wants to be in the limelight

ramponieren [rampo'ni:rən] (umg) vt to damage

r

Ramsch [ramʃ] (-(e)s, -e) m junk
ran [ran] (umg) adv = **heran**
Rand [rant] (-(e)s, ̈er) m edge; (von Brille, Tasse etc) rim; (Hutrand) brim; (auf Papier) margin; (Schmutzrand, unter Augen) ring; (fig) verge, brink; **außer ~ und Band** wild; **am ~e bemerkt** mentioned in passing; **am ~e der Stadt** on the outskirts of the town; **etw am ~e miterleben** to experience sth from the sidelines
randalieren [randa'liːrən] vi to (go on the) rampage
Rand- zW: **Randbemerkung** f marginal note; (fig) odd comment; **Randerscheinung** f unimportant side effect, marginal phenomenon; **Randfigur** f minor figure; **Randgebiet** nt (Geog) fringe; (Pol) border territory; (fig) subsidiary; **Randstreifen** m (der Straße) verge (Brit), berm (US); (der Autobahn) hard shoulder (Brit), shoulder (US); **randvoll** adj full to the brim
rang etc [ran] vb siehe **ringen**
Rang (-(e)s, ̈e) m rank; (Stand) standing; (Wert) quality; (Theat) circle; **ein Mann ohne ~ und Namen** a man without any standing; **erster/ zweiter ~** dress/upper circle
Rangabzeichen nt badge of rank
Rangälteste, r m senior officer
rangeln ['raŋəln] (umg) vi to scrap; (um Posten): ~ **(um)** to wrangle (for)
Rangfolge f order of rank (bes MIL)
Rangierbahnhof [rãˈʒiːrbaːnhoːf] m marshalling yard
rangieren vt (Eisenb) to shunt, switch (US) ▷ vi to rank, be classed
Rangiergleis nt siding
Rangliste f (Sport) ranking list, rankings pl
Rangordnung f hierarchy; (Mil) rank
Rangunterschied m social distinction; (Mil) difference in rank
rank [raŋk] adj: ~ **und schlank** (liter) slender and supple
Ranke ['raŋkə] (-, -n) f tendril, shoot
Ränke ['rɛŋkə] pl intrigues pl
ranken ['raŋkən] vr to trail, grow; **sich um etw ~** to twine around sth
Ränkeschmied m (liter) intriguer
ränkevoll adj scheming
ranklotzen ['raŋklɔtsən] (umg) vi to put one's nose to the grindstone
ranlassen unreg (umg) vt: **jdn ~** to let sb have a go
rann etc [ran] vb siehe **rinnen**
rannte etc ['rantə] vb siehe **rennen**
Ranzen ['rantsən] (-s, -) m satchel; (umg: Bauch) belly, gut
ranzig ['rantsɪç] adj rancid
Rappe ['rapə] (-n, -n) m black horse
Rappel ['rapəl] (-s, -) (umg) m (Fimmel) craze; (Wutanfall): **einen ~ kriegen** to throw a fit
Rappen ['rapən] (-s, -) (Schweiz) m (Geld) centime, rappen
Raps [raps] (-es, -e) m (Bot) rape; **Rapsöl** nt

rapeseed oil
rar [raːr] adj rare; siehe auch **rarmachen**
Rarität [rariˈtɛːt] f rarity; (Sammelobjekt) curio
rarmachen (umg) vr to stay away
rasant [raˈzant] adj quick, rapid
rasch [raʃ] adj quick
rascheln vi to rustle
rasen ['raːzən] vi to rave; (sich schnell bewegen) to race
Rasen (-s, -) m grass; (gepflegt) lawn
rasend adj furious; **~e Kopfschmerzen** a splitting headache
Rasen- zW: **Rasenmäher** (-s, -) m lawnmower; **Rasenmähmaschine** f lawnmower; **Rasenplatz** m lawn; **Rasensprenger** m (lawn) sprinkler
Raserei [raːzəˈraɪ] f raving, ranting; (Schnelle) reckless speeding
Rasier- zW: **Rasierapparat** m shaver; **Rasiercreme** f shaving cream; **rasieren** vt, vr to shave; **Rasierklinge** f razor blade; **Rasiermesser** nt razor; **Rasierpinsel** m shaving brush; **Rasierseife** f shaving soap od stick; **Rasierwasser** nt aftershave
raspeln ['raspəln] vt to grate; (Holz) to rasp
Rasse ['rasə] (-, -n) f race; (Tierrasse) breed; **Rassehund** m thoroughbred dog
Rassel (-, -n) f rattle, clatter
rasseln vi to rattle, clatter
Rassenhass m race od racial hatred
Rassentrennung f racial segregation
rassig ['rasɪç] adj (Pferd, Auto) sleek; (Frau) vivacious; (Wein) spirited, lively
Rassismus [raˈsɪsmʊs] (-) m racialism, racism
rassistisch [raˈsɪstɪʃ] adj racialist, racist
Rast [rast] (-, -en) f rest; **rasten** vi to rest
Raster ['rastər] (-s, -) m (Archit) grid; (Phot: Gitter) screen; (TV) raster; (fig) framework
Rast- zW: **Rasthaus** nt (Aut) service area, services pl; **Rasthof** m (motorway) motel; (mit Tankstelle) service area (with a motel); **rastlos** adj tireless; (unruhig) restless; **Rastplatz** m (Aut) lay-by (Brit); **Raststätte** f service area, services pl
Rasur [raˈzuːr] f shave; (das Rasieren) shaving
Rat [raːt] (-(e)s, -schläge) m (piece of) advice; **jdm mit ~ und Tat zur Seite stehen** to support sb in (both) word and deed; **sich ~ suchend an jdn wenden** to turn to sb for advice; **(sich dat) keinen ~ wissen** not to know what to do; siehe auch **zurate**
rät [rɛːt] vb siehe **raten**
Rate (-, -n) f instalment (Brit), installment (US); **auf ~n kaufen** to buy on hire purchase (Brit) od on the installment plan (US); **in ~n zahlen** to pay in instalments (Brit) od installments (US)
raten unreg vt, vi to guess; (empfehlen): **jdm ~ to** advise sb; **dreimal darfst du ~** I'll give you three guesses (auch ironisch)
ratenweise adv by instalments (Brit) od installments (US)
Ratenzahlung f hire purchase (Brit),

installment plan (US)

Ratespiel nt guessing game; (TV) quiz; (: *Beruferaten etc*) panel game

Ratgeber (-s, -) m adviser

Rathaus nt town hall; (*einer Großstadt*) city hall (bes US)

ratifizieren [ratifi'tsiːrən] vt to ratify

Ratifizierung f ratification

Ration [ratsi'oːn] f ration

rational [ratsio'naːl] adj rational

rationalisieren [ratsionali'ziːrən] vt to rationalize

rationell [ratsio'nɛl] adj efficient

rationieren [ratsio'niːrən] vt to ration

ratlos adj at a loss, helpless

Ratlosigkeit f helplessness

rätoromanisch [rɛtoro'maːnɪʃ] adj Rhaetian

ratsam adj advisable

Ratschlag m (piece of) advice

Rätsel ['rɛːtsəl] (-s, -) nt puzzle; (*Worträtsel*) riddle; **vor einem ~ stehen** to be baffled; **rätselhaft** adj mysterious; **es ist mir rätselhaft** it's a mystery to me; **rätseln** vi to puzzle; **Rätselraten** nt guessing game

Ratsherr m councillor (Brit), councilor (US)

Ratskeller m town-hall restaurant

Ratte ['ratə] (-, -n) f rat

Rattenfänger (-s, -) m rat-catcher

rattern ['ratərn] vi to rattle, clatter

rau [rau] adj rough, coarse; (*Wetter*) harsh; **in ~en Mengen** (umg) by the ton, galore

Raub [raup] (-(e)s) m robbery; (*Beute*) loot, booty; **Raubbau** m overexploitation; **Raubdruck** m pirate(d) edition

raubeinig adj rough-and-ready

rauben ['raubən] vt to rob; (*jdn*) to kidnap, abduct

Räuber ['rɔybər] (-s, -) m robber; **räuberisch** adj thieving

Raub- zW: **Raubfisch** m predatory fish; **raubgierig** adj rapacious; **Raubkassette** f pirate cassette; **Raubmord** m robbery with murder; **Raubtier** nt predator; **Raubüberfall** m robbery with violence; **Raubvogel** m bird of prey

Rauch [raux] (-(e)s) m smoke; **Rauchabzug** m smoke outlet

rauchen vt, vi to smoke; **mir raucht der Kopf** (fig) my head's spinning; **„R- verboten"** "no smoking"

Raucher, in (-s, -) m(f) smoker; **Raucherabteil** nt (Eisenb) smoker

räuchern ['rɔyçərn] vt to smoke, cure

Räucherspeck m ≈ smoked bacon

Räucherstäbchen nt joss stick

Rauch- zW: **Rauchfahne** f smoke trail; **Rauchfang** m chimney hood; **Rauchfleisch** nt smoked meat

rauchig adj smoky

Rauchschwaden pl drifts of smoke pl

räudig ['rɔydɪç] adj mangy

rauf [rauf] (umg) adv = **herauf; hinauf**

Raufasertapete f woodchip paper

Raufbold (-(e)s, -e) m thug, hooligan

raufen vt (*Haare*) to pull out ▷ vi, vr to fight

Rauferei [raufə'rai] f brawl, fight

rauflustig adj ready for a fight, pugnacious

rauh etc siehe **rau** etc

rauhaarig adj wire-haired

Raum [raum] (-(e)s, **Räume**) m space; (*Zimmer, Platz*) room; (*Gebiet*) area; **~ sparend** space-saving; **eine Frage im ~ stehen lassen** to leave a question unresolved; **Raumausstatter, in** m(f) interior decorator

räumen ['rɔymən] vt to clear; (*Wohnung, Platz*) to vacate, move out of; (*verlassen: Gebäude, Gebiet*) to evacuate; (*wegbringen*) to shift, move; (*in Schrank etc*) to put away

Raum- zW: **Raumfähre** f space shuttle; **Raumfahrer** m astronaut; (*sowjetisch*) cosmonaut; **Raumfahrt** f space travel

Räumfahrzeug ['rɔymfaːrtsɔyk] nt bulldozer; (*für Schnee*) snow-clearer

Rauminhalt m cubic capacity, volume

Raumkapsel f space capsule

räumlich ['rɔymlɪç] adj spatial; **Räumlichkeiten** pl premises pl

Raum- zW: **Raummangel** m lack of space; **Raummaß** nt unit of volume; cubic measurement; **Raummeter** m cubic metre (Brit) od meter (US); **Raumnot** f shortage of space; **Raumordnung** f environmental planning; **Raumpflegerin** f cleaner; **Raumschiff** nt spaceship; **Raumschifffahrt** f space travel; **Raumstation** f space station; **Raumtransporter** m space shuttle

Räumung ['rɔymʊŋ] f clearing (away); (*von Haus etc*) vacating; (*wegen Gefahr*) evacuation; (*unter Zwang*) eviction

Räumungs- zW: **Räumungsbefehl** m eviction order; **Räumungsklage** f action for eviction; **Räumungsverkauf** m clearance sale

raunen ['raunən] vt, vi to whisper

Raupe ['raupə] (-, -n) f caterpillar; (*Raupenkette*) (caterpillar) track

Raupenschlepper m caterpillar tractor

Raureif ['raurai f] m hoarfrost

raus [raus] (umg) adv = **heraus; hinaus**

Rausch [rauʃ] (-(e)s, pl **Räusche**) m intoxication; **einen ~ haben** to be drunk

rauschen vi (*Wasser*) to rush; (*Baum*) to rustle; (*Radio etc*) to hiss; (*Mensch*) to sweep, sail

rauschend adj (*Beifall*) thunderous; (*Fest*) sumptuous

Rauschgift nt drug; **Rauschgifthandel** m drug traffic; **Rauschgifthändler, in** m(f) drug trafficker; **Rauschgiftsüchtige, r** f(m) drug addict

rausfliegen unreg (umg) vi to be chucked out

räuspern ['rɔyspərn] vr to clear one's throat

Rausschmeißer ['rausʃmaisər] (-s, -) (umg) m bouncer

Raute ['rautə] (-, -n) f diamond; (*Math*) rhombus

rautenförmig adj rhombic

Razzia ['ratsia] (-, **Razzien**) f raid

r

Reagenzglas [rea'gɛntsglaːs] nt test tube
reagieren [rea'giːrən] vi: **~ (auf** +akk**)** to react (to)
Reaktion [reaktsi'oːn] f reaction
reaktionär [reaktsio'nɛːr] adj reactionary
Reaktionsfähigkeit f reactions pl
Reaktionsgeschwindigkeit f speed of reaction
Reaktor [re'aktɔr] m reactor; **Reaktorkern** m reactor core; **Reaktorunglück** nt nuclear accident
real [re'aːl] adj real, material; **Realeinkommen** nt real income
realisierbar [reali'ziːrbaːr] adj practicable, feasible
Realismus [rea'lɪsmʊs] m realism
Realist, in [rea'lɪst(ɪn)] m(f) realist; **realistisch** adj realistic
Realität [reali'tɛːt] f reality; **Realitäten** pl (Gegebenheiten) facts pl
realitätsfremd adj out of touch with reality
Realpolitik f political realism
Realschule f ≈ middle school (Brit), junior high school (US); see culture note

Realzeit f real time
Rebe ['reːbə] (-, -n) f vine
Rebell, in [re'bɛl(ɪn)] (-en, -en) m(f) rebel
rebellieren [rebɛ'liːrən] vi to rebel
Rebellion [rebɛli'oːn] f rebellion
rebellisch [re'bɛlɪʃ] adj rebellious
Rebensaft m wine
Reb- [rep] zW: **Rebhuhn** nt partridge; **Reblaus** f vine pest; **Rebstock** m vine
Rechen ['rɛçən] (-s, -) m rake; **rechen** vt, vi to rake
Rechen- zW: **Rechenaufgabe** f sum, mathematical problem; **Rechenfehler** m miscalculation; **Rechenmaschine** f adding machine
Rechenschaft f account; **jdm über etw** akk **~ ablegen** to account to sb for sth; **jdn zur ~ ziehen (für)** to call sb to account (for od over); **jdm ~ schulden** to be accountable to sb
Rechenschaftsbericht m report
Rechenschieber m slide rule
Rechenzentrum nt computer centre (Brit) od center (US)
recherchieren [reʃer'ʃiːrən] vt, vi to investigate
rechnen ['rɛçnən] vt, vi to calculate; (veranschlagen) to estimate, reckon; **jdn/etw zu etw ~** to count sb/sth among sth; **~ mit** to reckon with; **~ auf** +akk to count on

Rechnen nt arithmetic; (bes Sch) sums pl
Rechner (-s, -) m calculator; (Comput) computer; **rechnerfern** adj (Comput) remote; **rechnerisch** adj arithmetical
Rechnung f calculation(s); (Comm) bill (Brit), check (US); **auf eigene ~** on one's own account; **(jdm) etw in ~ stellen** to charge (sb) for sth; **jdm/etw ~ tragen** to take sb/sth into account
Rechnungs- zW: **Rechnungsbuch** nt account book; **Rechnungshof** m ≈ Auditor-General's office (Brit), audit division (US); **Rechnungsjahr** nt financial year; **Rechnungsprüfer** m auditor; **Rechnungsprüfung** f audit(ing)
recht [rɛçt] adj right ▷ adv (vor Adjektiv) really, quite; **das ist mir ~** that suits me; **jetzt erst ~** now more than ever; **alles, was ~ ist** (empört) fair's fair; (anerkennend) you can't deny it; **nach dem R~en sehen** to see that everything's O.K.; **~ haben** to be right; **jdm ~ geben** to agree with sb, admit that sb is right; **du kommst gerade ~, um ...** you're just in time to ...; **gehe ich ~ in der Annahme, dass ...?** am I correct in assuming that ...?; **~ herzlichen Dank** thank you very much indeed
Recht (-(e)s, -e) nt right; (Jur) law; **~ sprechen** to administer justice; **mit** od **zu ~** rightly, justly; **von ~s wegen** by rights; **zu seinem ~ kommen** (lit) to gain one's rights; (fig) to come into one's own; **gleiches ~ für alle!** equal rights for all!
Rechte f right (hand); (Pol) Right
Rechte, r, s f(m) (Pol) right-winger ▷ nt right thing; **etwas/nichts ~s** something/nothing proper
rechte, r, s adj right; (Pol) right-wing
recht- zW: **Rechteck** (-(e)s, -e) nt rectangle; **rechteckig** adj rectangular; **rechtfertigen** vt untr to justify ▷ vr untr to justify o.s.; **Rechtfertigung** f justification; **rechthaberisch** adj dogmatic; **rechtlich** adj legal, lawful; **rechtlich nicht zulässig** not permissible in law, illegal; **rechtmäßig** adj legal, lawful
rechts [rɛçts] adv od to the right; **~ stehen** od **sein** (Pol) to be right-wing; **~ stricken** to knit (plain); **Rechtsabbieger** (-s, -) m: **die Spur für Rechtsabbieger** the right-hand turn-off lane; **Rechtsanspruch** m: **einen Rechtsanspruch auf etw** akk **haben** to be legally entitled to sth; **Rechtsanwalt** m, **Rechtsanwältin** f lawyer, barrister; **Rechtsaußen** (-, -) m (Sport) outside right; **Rechtsbeistand** m legal adviser
rechtschaffen adj upright
Rechtschreibung f spelling
Rechts- zW: **Rechtsdrehung** f clockwise rotation; **Rechtsextremismus** m right-wing extremism; **Rechtsextremist** m right-wing extremist; **Rechtsfall** m (law) case; **Rechtsfrage** f legal question; **rechtsgültig**

adj legally valid; **Rechtshänder, in (-s, -)**
m(f) right-handed person; **rechtskräftig** *adj*
valid, legal; **Rechtskurve** *f* right-hand bend;
Rechtslage *f* legal position; **rechtslastig** *adj*
listing to the right; *(fig)* leaning to the right;
Rechtspflege *f* administration of justice;
Rechtspfleger *m* *official with certain judicial
powers*
Rechtsprechung ['rɛçtʃprɛçʊŋ] *f*
(Gerichtsbarkeit) jurisdiction; *(richterliche
Tätigkeit)* dispensation of justice
Rechts- *zW:* **rechtsradikal** *adj* *(Pol)* extreme
right-wing; **Rechtsschutz** *m* legal protection;
Rechtsspruch *m* verdict; **Rechtsstaat** *m* state
under the rule of law; **Rechtsstreit** *m* lawsuit;
Rechtstitel *m* title; **rechtsverbindlich**
adj legally binding; **Rechtsverkehr** *m*
driving on the right; **Rechtsweg** *m:* **der
Rechtsweg ist ausgeschlossen** ≈ the judges'
decision is final; **rechtswidrig** *adj* illegal;
Rechtswissenschaft *f* jurisprudence
rechtwinklig *adj* right-angled
rechtzeitig *adj* timely ▷ *adv* in time
Reck [rɛk] **(-(e)s, -e)** *nt* horizontal bar
recken *vt, vr* to stretch
recyceln [riːˈsaɪkəln] *vt* to recycle
Recycling [riːˈsaɪklɪŋ] **(-s)** *nt* recycling
Red. *abk* = **Redaktion;** (= *Redakteur(in))* ed
Redakteur, in [redakˈtøːr(ɪn)] *m(f)* editor
Redaktion [redaktsiˈoːn] *f* editing; *(Leute)*
editorial staff; *(Büro)* editorial office(s *pl*)
Redaktionsschluss *m* time of going to press;
(Einsendeschluss) copy deadline
Rede ['reːdə] **(-, -n)** *f* speech; *(Gespräch)* talk;
jdn zur ~ stellen to take sb to task; **eine
~ halten** to make a speech; **das ist nicht
der ~ wert** it's not worth mentioning;
davon kann keine ~ sein it's out of the
question; **Redefreiheit** *f* freedom of speech;
redegewandt *adj* eloquent
Reden (-s) *nt* talking, speech
reden *vi* to talk, speak ▷ *vt* to say; *(Unsinn
etc)* to talk; **(viel) von sich ~ machen** to
become (very much) a talking point; **darüber
lässt sich ~** that's a possibility; *(über Preis,
Bedingungen)* I think we could discuss that;
er lässt mit sich ~ he could be persuaded;
(in Bezug auf Preis) he's open to offers;
(gesprächsbereit) he's open to discussion
Redensart *f* set phrase
Redeschwall *m* torrent of words
Redewendung *f* expression, idiom
redlich ['reːtlɪç] *adj* honest; **Redlichkeit** *f*
honesty
Redner, in (-s, -) *m(f)* speaker, orator
redselig ['reːtzeːlɪç] *adj* talkative, loquacious;
Redseligkeit *f* talkativeness, loquacity
redundant [redʊnˈdant] *adj* redundant
Redundanz [redʊnˈdants] **(-)** *f* redundancy
reduzieren [reduˈtsiːrən] *vt* to reduce
Reduzierung *f* reduction
Reede ['reːdə] **(-, -n)** *f* protected anchorage
Reeder (-s, -) *m* shipowner

Reederei [reːdəˈraɪ] *f* shipping line *od* firm
reell [reˈɛl] *adj* fair, honest; *(Preis)* fair;
(Comm: Geschäft) sound; *(Math)* real
Reetdach ['reːtdax] *nt* thatched roof
Ref. *abk* = **Referendar(in); Referent(in)**
Referat [refeˈraːt] **(-(e)s, -e)** *nt* report; *(Vortrag)*
paper; *(Gebiet)* section; *(Verwaltung: Ressort)*
department; **ein ~ halten** to present a
seminar paper
Referendar, in [referenˈdaːr(ɪn)] *m(f)* trainee
(in civil service); *(Studienreferendar)* trainee
teacher; *(Gerichtsreferendar)* articled clerk
Referendum [refeˈrendʊm] **(-s, Referenden)** *nt*
referendum
Referent, in [refeˈrɛnt(ɪn)] *m(f)* speaker;
(Berichterstatter) reporter; *(Sachbearbeiter)* expert
Referenz [refeˈrɛnts] *f* reference
referieren [refeˈriːrən] *vi:* **~ über** +*akk* to speak
od talk on
reflektieren [reflɛkˈtiːrən] *vt, vi* to reflect; **~
auf** +*akk* to be interested in
Reflex [reˈflɛks] **(-es, -e)** *m* reflex;
Reflexbewegung *f* reflex action
reflexiv [reflɛˈksiːf] *adj* *(Gram)* reflexive
Reform [reˈfɔrm] **(-, -en)** *f* reform
Reformation [refɔrmatsiˈoːn] *f* reformation
Reformator [refɔrˈmaːtɔr] *m* reformer;
reformatorisch *adj* reformatory, reforming
reform- *zW:* **reformbedürftig** *adj* in need of
reform; **reformfreudig** *adj* avid for reform;
Reformhaus *nt* health food shop
reformieren [refɔrˈmiːrən] *vt* to reform
Refrain [rəˈfrɛ̃ː] **(-s, -s)** *m* refrain, chorus
Reg. *abk* = *Regierungs-* gov.; (= *Register)* reg
Regal [reˈgaːl] **(-s, -e)** *nt* (book)shelves *pl*,
bookcase; *(Typ)* stand, rack
Regatta [reˈgata] **(-, Regatten)** *f* regatta
Reg.-Bez. *abk* = Regierungsbezirk
rege ['reːgə] *adj* lively, active; *(Geschäft)* brisk
Regel ['reːgəl] **(-, -n)** *f* rule; *(Med)* period; **in
der ~** as a rule; **nach allen ~n der Kunst** *(fig)*
thoroughly; **sich** *dat* **etw zur ~ machen** to
make a habit of sth; **regellos** *adj* irregular,
unsystematic; **regelmäßig** *adj* regular;
Regelmäßigkeit *f* regularity
regeln *vt* to regulate, control; *(Angelegenheit)*
to settle ▷ *vr:* **sich von selbst ~** to take care
of itself; **gesetzlich geregelt sein** to be laid
down by law
regelrecht *adj* proper, thorough
Regelung *f* regulation; settlement
regelwidrig *adj* irregular, against the rules
regen ['reːgən] *vt* to move ▷ *vr* to move, stir
Regen (-s, -) *m* rain; **vom ~ in die Traufe
kommen** *(Sprichwort)* to jump out of the frying
pan into the fire *(Sprichwort)*
Regenbogen *m* rainbow; **Regenbogenhaut**
f *(Anat)* iris; **Regenbogenpresse** *f* trashy
magazines *pl*
regenerieren [regeneˈriːrən] *vr* *(Biol)* to
regenerate; *(fig)* to revitalize *od* regenerate o.s.
od itself; *(nach Anstrengung, Schock etc)* to recover
Regen- *zW:* **Regenguss** *m* downpour;

r

Regenmantel *m* raincoat, mac(kintosh);
Regenmenge *f* rainfall; **Regenschauer** *m*
shower (of rain); **Regenschirm** *m* umbrella
Regent, in [re'gɛnt(ɪn)] *m(f)* regent
Regentag *m* rainy day
Regentropfen *m* raindrop
Regentschaft *f* regency
Regen- *zW:* **Regenwald** *m* (*Geog*) rain forest;
Regenwetter *nt:* **er macht ein Gesicht wie
drei** *od* **sieben Tage Regenwetter** (*umg*)
he's got a face as long as a month of Sundays;
Regenwurm *m* earthworm; **Regenzeit** *f* rainy
season, rains *pl*
Regie [re'ʒiː] *f* (*Film etc*) direction; (*Theat*)
production; **unter der ~ von** directed *od*
produced by; **Regieanweisung** *f* (stage)
direction
regieren [re'giːrən] *vt, vi* to govern, rule
Regierung *f* government; (*Monarchie*) reign; **an
die ~ kommen** to come to power
Regierungs- *zW:* **Regierungsbezirk** *m* ≈ county
(*Brit, US*), ≈ region (*Scot*); **Regierungserklärung**
f inaugural speech; (*in Großbritannien*) Queen's/
King's Speech; **Regierungsmannschaft** *f*
government team; **Regierungssprecher** *m*
government spokesman; **Regierungsvorlage**
f government bill; **Regierungswechsel** *m*
change of government; **Regierungszeit** *f*
period in government; (*von König*) reign
Regiment [regi'mɛnt] (**-s, -er**) *nt* regiment
Region [regi'oːn] *f* region
Regionalplanung [regio'naːlplaːnʊŋ] *f*
regional planning
Regionalprogramm *nt* (*Rundf, TV*) regional
programme (*Brit*) *od* program (*US*)
Regisseur, in [reʒɪ'søːr(ɪn)] *m(f)* director;
(*Theat*) (stage) producer
Register [re'gɪstər] (**-s, -**) *nt* register; (*in Buch*)
table of contents, index; **alle ~ ziehen** (*fig*)
to pull out all the stops; **Registerführer** *m*
registrar
Registratur [regɪstra'tuːr] *f* registry, records
office
registrieren [regɪs'triːrən] *vt* to register;
(*umg: zur Kenntnis nehmen*) to note
Registrierkasse *f* cash register
Regler [re'glər] (**-s, -**) *m* regulator, governor
reglos [re'kloːs] *adj* motionless
regnen [re'gnən] *vi unpers* to rain ▷ *vt unpers:* **es
regnet Glückwünsche** congratulations
are pouring in; **es regnet in Strömen** it's
pouring (with rain)
regnerisch *adj* rainy
Regress [re'grɛs] (**-es, -e**) *m* (*Jur*) recourse,
redress; **Regressanspruch** *m* (*Jur*) claim for
compensation
regsam [re'kzaːm] *adj* active
regulär [regu'lɛːr] *adj* regular
regulieren [regu'liːrən] *vt* to regulate; (*Comm*)
to settle; **sich von selbst ~** to be self-
regulating
Regulierungsbehörde [regu'liːrəʊŋsbəhøːrdə]
f regulatory body *od* authority

Regung ['reːgʊŋ] *f* motion; (*Gefühl*) feeling,
impulse
regungslos *adj* motionless
Reh [reː] (**-(e)s, -e**) *nt* deer; (*weiblich*) roe deer
rehabilitieren [rehabili'tiːrən] *vt* to
rehabilitate; (*Ruf, Ehre*) to vindicate ▷ *vr* to
rehabilitate (*form*) *od* vindicate o.s.
Rehabilitierung *f* rehabilitation
Reh- *zW:* **Rehbock** *m* roebuck; **Rehbraten** *m*
roast venison; **Rehkalb** *nt* fawn; **Rehkitz** *nt*
fawn
Reibach ['raɪbax] (**-s**) *m:* **einen ~ machen**
(*umg*) to make a killing
Reibe ['raɪbə] (**-, -n**) *f* grater
Reibeisen ['raɪp|aɪzən] *nt* grater
Reibekuchen *m* (*Koch*) ≈ potato waffle
reiben *unreg vt* to rub; (*Koch*) to grate
Reiberei [raɪbə'raɪ] *f* friction *no pl*
Reibfläche *f* rough surface
Reibung *f* friction
reibungslos *adj* smooth; **~ verlaufen** to go off
smoothly
Reich [raɪç] (**-(e)s, -e**) *nt* empire, kingdom; (*fig*)
realm; **das Dritte ~** the Third Reich
reich *adj* rich ▷ *adv:* **eine ~ ausgestattete
Bibliothek** a well-stocked library
reichen *vi* to reach; (*genügen*) to be enough
od sufficient ▷ *vt* to hold out; (*geben*) to
pass, hand; (*anbieten*) to offer; **so weit das
Auge reicht** as far as the eye can see; **jdm ~**
(*genügen*) to be enough *od* sufficient for sb; **mir
reichts!** I've had enough!
reich- *zW:* **reichhaltig** *adj* ample, rich;
reichlich *adj* ample, plenty of; **Reichtum** (**-s,
-tümer**) *m* wealth; **Reichweite** *f* range; **jd ist
in Reichweite** sb is nearby
reif [raɪf] *adj* ripe; (*Mensch, Urteil*) mature; **für
etw ~ sein** (*umg*) to be ready for sth
Reif¹ (**-(e)s**) *m* hoarfrost
Reif² (**-(e)s, -e**) *m* (*Ring*) ring, hoop
Reife (**-**) *f* ripeness; maturity; **mittlere ~**
(*Sch*) *first public examination in secondary school*, ≈
O-Levels *pl* (*Brit*)
Reifen (**-s, -**) *m* ring, hoop; (*Fahrzeugreifen*) tyre
(*Brit*), tire (*US*)
reifen *vi* to mature; (*Obst*) to ripen
Reifen- *zW:* **Reifendruck** *m* tyre (*Brit*) *od* tire
(*US*) pressure; **Reifenpanne** *f* puncture, flat;
Reifenprofil *nt* tyre (*Brit*) *od* tire (*US*) tread;
Reifenschaden *m* puncture, flat
Reifeprüfung *f* school-leaving exam
Reifezeugnis *nt* school-leaving certificate
reiflich ['raɪflɪç] *adj* thorough, careful
Reihe ['raɪə] (**-, -n**) *f* row; (*von Tagen
etc: umg: Anzahl*) series *sing*; **eine ganze ~ (von)**
(*unbestimmte Anzahl*) a whole lot (of); **der ~
nach** in turn; **er ist an der ~** it's his turn; **an
die ~ kommen** to have one's turn; **außer der
~ out** of turn; (*ausnahmsweise*) out of the usual
way of things; **aus der ~ tanzen** (*fig: umg*) to
be different; (*gegen Konventionen verstoßen*) to
step out of line; **ich kriege heute nichts auf
die ~** I can't get my act together today

reihen vt to set in a row; to arrange in series; (Perlen) to string
Reihen- zW: **Reihenfolge** f sequence; **alphabetische Reihenfolge** alphabetical order; **Reihenhaus** nt terraced (Brit) od row (US) house; **Reihenuntersuchung** f mass screening; **reihenweise** adv (in Reihen) in rows; (fig: in großer Anzahl) by the dozen
Reiher (-s, -) m heron
reihum [raɪ'ʊm] adv: **etw ~ gehen lassen** to pass sth around
Reim [raɪm] (-(e)s, -e) m rhyme; **sich** dat **einen ~ auf etw** akk **machen** (umg) to make sense of sth; **reimen** vt to rhyme
rein¹ [raɪn] (umg) adv = **herein; hinein**
rein² [raɪn] adj pure; (sauber) clean ▷ adv purely; **~ waschen** to clear o.s.; **das ist die ~ste Freude/der ~ste Hohn** etc it's pure of sheer joy/mockery etc; **etw ins R~e schreiben** to make a fair copy of sth; **etw ins R~e bringen** to clear sth up; **~en Tisch machen** (fig) to get things straight; **~ unmöglich** (umg: ganz, völlig) absolutely impossible
Rein- in zw (Comm) net(t)
Reinemachefrau f cleaning lady, charwoman (Brit)
reineweg (umg) adv completely, absolutely
rein- zW: **Reinfall** (umg) m let-down; (Misserfolg) flop; **reinfallen** vi: **auf jdn/etw reinfallen** to be taken in by sb/sth; **Reingewinn** m net profit; **Reinheit** f purity; cleanness
reinigen ['raɪnɪɡən] vt to clean; (Wasser) to purify
Reiniger (-s, -) m cleaner
Reinigung f cleaning; purification; (Geschäft) cleaner's; **chemische ~** dry-cleaning; (Geschäft) dry-cleaner's
Reinigungsmittel nt cleansing agent
rein- zW: **reinlich** adj clean; **Reinlichkeit** f cleanliness; **Reinmachefrau** f = **Reinemachefrau; reinrassig** adj pedigree; **reinreiten** unreg vt: **jdn reinreiten** to get sb into a mess; **Reinschrift** f fair copy; **Reinvermögen** nt net assets pl
reinweg (umg) adv = **reineweg**
Reis¹ [raɪs] (-es, -e) m rice
Reis² [raɪs] (-es, -er) nt twig, sprig
Reise ['raɪzə] (-, -n) f journey; (Schiffsreise) voyage; **Reisen** pl travels pl; **gute ~!** bon voyage!, have a good journey!; **auf ~n sein** to be away (travelling (Brit) od traveling (US)); **er ist viel auf ~n** he does a lot of travelling (Brit) od traveling (US); **Reiseandenken** nt souvenir; **Reiseapotheke** f first-aid kit; **Reisebericht** m account of one's journey; (Buch) travel story; (Film) travelogue (Brit), travelog (US); **Reisebüro** nt travel agency; **Reisediplomatie** f shuttle diplomacy; **Reiseerleichterungen** pl easing sing of travel restrictions; **reisefertig** adj ready to start; **Reisefieber** nt (fig) travel nerves pl; **Reiseführer** m guide(book); (Mensch) (travel) guide; **Reisegepäck** nt luggage; **Reisegesellschaft** f party of travellers (Brit)

od travelers (US); **Reisekosten** pl travelling (Brit) od traveling (US) expenses pl; **Reiseleiter** m courier; **Reiselektüre** f reading for the journey; **Reiselust** f wanderlust
reisen vi to travel; **~ nach** to go to
Reisende, r f(m) traveller (Brit), traveler (US)
Reise- zW: **Reisepass** m passport; **Reisepläne** pl plans pl for a od the journey; **Reiseproviant** m provisions pl for the journey; **Reiseroute** f itinerary; **Reisescheck** m traveller's cheque (Brit), traveler's check (US); **Reiseschreibmaschine** f portable typewriter; **Reisetasche** f travelling (Brit) od traveling (US) bag od case; **Reisethrombose** f deep vein thrombosis, economy-class syndrome (umg); **Reiseveranstalter** m tour operator; **Reiseverkehr** m tourist od holiday traffic; **Reisewetter** nt holiday weather; **Reiseziel** nt destination
Reisig ['raɪzɪç] (-s) nt brushwood
Reißaus m: **~ nehmen** to run away, flee
Reißbrett nt drawing board; **Reißbrettstift** m drawing pin (Brit), thumbtack (US)
reißen ['raɪsən] unreg vt to tear; (ziehen) to pull, drag; (Witz) to crack ▷ vi to tear; to pull, drag; **etw an sich ~** to snatch sth up; (fig) to take sth over; **sich um etw ~** to scramble for sth; **wenn alle Stricke ~** (fig: umg) if the worst comes to the worst; siehe auch **hingerissen**
Reißen nt (Gewichtheben: Disziplin) snatch; (umg: Gliederreißen) ache
reißend adj (Fluss) torrential; (Comm) rapid; **~en Absatz finden** to sell like hot cakes (umg)
Reißer (-s, -) (umg) m thriller; **reißerisch** adj sensational
Reiß- zW: **Reißleine** f (Aviat) ripcord; **Reißnagel** m drawing pin (Brit), thumbtack (US); **Reißschiene** f T-square; **Reißverschluss** m zip (fastener) (Brit), zipper (US); **Reißwolf** m shredder; **durch den Reißwolf geben** (Dokumente) to shred; **Reißzeug** nt geometry set; **Reißzwecke** f = **Reißnagel**
reiten ['raɪtən] unreg vt, vi to ride
Reiter (-s, -) m rider; (Mil) cavalryman, trooper
Reiterei [raɪtə'raɪ] f cavalry
Reiterin f rider
Reit- zW: **Reithose** f riding breeches pl; **Reitpferd** nt saddle horse; **Reitschule** f riding school; **Reitstiefel** m riding boot; **Reitturnier** nt horse show; **Reitweg** m bridle path; **Reitzeug** nt riding outfit
Reiz [raɪts] (-es, -e) m stimulus; (angenehm) charm; (Verlockung) attraction
reizbar adj irritable; **Reizbarkeit** f irritability
reizen vt to stimulate; (unangenehm) to irritate; (verlocken) to appeal to, attract; (Karten) to bid ▷ vi: **zum Widerspruch ~** to invite contradiction
reizend adj charming
Reiz- zW: **Reizgas** nt tear gas, CS gas; **Reizhusten** m chesty cough; **reizlos** adj unattractive; **reizvoll** adj attractive; **Reizwäsche** f sexy underwear; **Reizwort** nt

r

273

emotive word

rekapitulieren [rekapitu'li:rən] vt to recapitulate

rekeln ['re:kəln] vr to stretch out; (lümmeln) to lounge od loll about

Reklamation [reklamatsi'o:n] f complaint

Reklame [re'kla:mə] (-, -n) f advertising; (Anzeige) advertisement; **mit etw ~ machen** (pej) to show off about sth; **für etw ~ machen** to advertise sth; **Reklametrommel** f: **die Reklametrommel für jdn/etw rühren** (umg) to beat the (big) drum for sb/sth; **Reklamewand** f notice (Brit) od bulletin (US) board

reklamieren [rekla'mi:rən] vi to complain ▷ vt to complain about; (zurückfordern) to reclaim

rekonstruieren [rekɔnstru'i:rən] vt to reconstruct

Rekonvaleszenz [rekɔnvales'tsɛnts] f convalescence

Rekord [re'kɔrt] (-(e)s, -e) m record; **Rekordleistung** f record performance

Rekrut [re'kru:t] (-en, -en) m recruit

rekrutieren [rekru'ti:rən] vt to recruit ▷ vr to be recruited

Rektor ['rɛktɔr] m (Univ) rector, vice-chancellor; (Sch) head teacher (Brit), principal (US)

Rektorat [rɛktɔ'rat] (-(e)s, -e) nt rectorate, vice-chancellorship; headship (Brit), principalship (US); (Zimmer) rector's etc office

Rektorin [rɛk'to:rɪn] f (Sch) head teacher (Brit), principal (US)

Rel. abk (= Religion) rel.

Relais [rə'lɛ:] (-, -) nt relay

Relation [relatsi'o:n] f relation

relativ [rela'ti:f] adj relative

Relativität [relativi'tɛ:t] f relativity

Relativpronomen nt (Gram) relative pronoun

relevant [rele'vant] adj relevant

Relevanz f relevance

Relief [reli'ɛf] (-s, -s) nt relief

Religion [religi'o:n] f religion

Religions- zW: **Religionsfreiheit** f freedom of worship; **Religionslehre** f religious education; **Religionsunterricht** m religious education

religiös [religi'ø:s] adj religious

Relikt [re'lɪkt] (-(e)s, -e) nt relic

Reling ['re:lɪŋ] (-, -s) f (Naut) rail

Reliquie [re'li:kviə] f relic

Reminiszenz [reminɪs'tsɛnts] f reminiscence, recollection

Remis [rə'mi:] (-, - od -en) nt (Schach, Sport) draw

Remittende [remɪ'tɛndə] (-, -n) f (Comm) return

Remittent m (Fin) payee

remittieren vt (Comm: Waren) to return; (Geld) to remit

Remmidemmi ['remi'dɛmi] (-s) (umg) nt (Krach) row, rumpus; (Trubel) rave-up

Remoulade [remu'la:də] (-, -n) f remoulade

rempeln ['rempəln] (umg) vt to jostle, elbow; (Sport) to barge into; (foulen) to push

Ren [re:n, rɛn] (-s, -s od -e) nt reindeer

Renaissance [rənɛ'sā:s] (-, -n) f (Hist) renaissance; (fig) revival, rebirth

Rendezvous [rāde'vu:] (-, -) nt rendezvous

Rendite [rɛn'di:tə] (-, -n) f (Fin) yield, return on capital

Rennbahn f racecourse; (Aut) circuit, racetrack

rennen ['rɛnən] unreg vt, vi to run, race; **um die Wette ~** to have a race; **Rennen** (-s, -) nt running; (Wettbewerb) race; **das Rennen machen** (lit, fig) to win (the race)

Renner (-s, -) (umg) m winner, worldbeater

Renn- zW: **Rennfahrer** m racing driver (Brit), race car driver (US); **Rennpferd** nt racehorse; **Rennplatz** m racecourse; **Rennrad** nt racing cycle; **Rennsport** m racing; **Rennwagen** m racing car (Brit), race car (US)

renommiert [renɔ'mi:rt] adj: ~ **(wegen)** renowned (for), famous (for)

renovieren [reno'vi:rən] vt to renovate

Renovierung f renovation

rentabel [rɛn'ta:bəl] adj profitable, lucrative

Rentabilität [rentabili'tɛ:t] f profitability

Rente ['rɛntə] (-, -n) f pension

Renten- zW: **Rentenbasis** f annuity basis; **Rentenempfänger** m pensioner; **Rentenpapier** nt (Fin) fixed-interest security; **Rentenversicherung** f pension scheme; **Rentenversicherungsträger** m pension provider

Rentier ['rɛnti:r] nt reindeer

rentieren [rɛn'ti:rən] vi, vr to pay, be profitable; **das rentiert (sich) nicht** it's not worth it

Rentner, in ['rɛntnər(ɪn)] (-s, -) m(f) pensioner

Reparation [reparatsi'o:n] f reparation

Reparatur [repara'tu:r] f repairing; repair; **etw in ~ geben** to have sth repaired; **reparaturbedürftig** adj in need of repair; **Reparaturwerkstatt** f repair shop; (Aut) garage

reparieren [repa'ri:rən] vt to repair

Repertoire [repɛrto'a:r] (-s, -s) nt repertoire

Reportage [repɔr'ta:ʒə] (-, -n) f report

Reporter, in [re'pɔrtər(ɪn)] (-s, -) m(f) reporter, commentator

Repräsentant, in [reprɛzɛn'tant(ɪn)] m(f) representative

repräsentativ [reprɛzɛnta'ti:f] adj representative; (Geschenk etc) prestigious; **die ~en Pflichten eines Botschafters** the social duties of an ambassador

repräsentieren [reprɛzɛn'ti:rən] vt to represent ▷ vi to perform official duties

Repressalien [reprɛ'sa:liən] pl reprisals pl

reprivatisieren [reprivati'zi:rən] vt to denationalize

Reprivatisierung f denationalization

Reproduktion [reprodʊktsi'o:n] f reproduction

reproduzieren [reprodu'tsi:rən] vt to reproduce

Reptil [rep'ti:l] (-s, -ien) nt reptile

Republik [repu'bli:k] f republic

Republikaner [republi'ka:nər] (**-s, -**) *m* republican

republikanisch *adj* republican

Requisiten *pl* (*Theat*) props *pl*, properties *pl* (*form*)

Reservat [rezɛr'va:t] (**-(e)s, -e**) *nt* reservation

Reserve [re'zɛrvə] (**-, -n**) *f* reserve; **jdn aus der ~ locken** to bring sb out of his/her shell; **Reserverad** *nt* (*Aut*) spare wheel; **Reservespieler** *m* reserve; **Reservetank** *m* reserve tank

reservieren [rezɛr'vi:rən] *vt* to reserve

reserviert *adj* (*Platz, Mensch*) reserved

Reservist [rezɛr'vɪst] *m* reservist

Reservoir [rezɛrvo'a:r] (**-s, -e**) *nt* reservoir

Residenz [rezi'dɛnts] *f* residence, seat

residieren [rezi'di:rən] *vi* to reside

Resignation [rezɪgnatsi'o:n] *f* resignation

resignieren [rezɪ'gni:rən] *vi* to resign

resolut [rezo'lu:t] *adj* resolute

Resolution [rezolutsi'o:n] *f* resolution; (*Bittschrift*) petition

Resonanz [rezo'nants] *f* (*lit, fig*) resonance; **Resonanzboden** *m* sounding board; **Resonanzkasten** *m* soundbox

Resopal® [rezo'pa:l] (**-s**) *nt* Formica®

resozialisieren [rezotsiali'zi:rən] *vt* to rehabilitate

Resozialisierung *f* rehabilitation

Respekt [re'spɛkt] (**-(e)s**) *m* respect; (*Angst*) fear; **bei allem ~ (vor jdm/etw)** with all due respect (to sb/for sth)

respektabel [respɛk'ta:bəl] *adj* respectable

respektieren [respɛk'ti:rən] *vt* to respect

respektlos *adj* disrespectful

Respektsperson *f* person commanding respect

respektvoll *adj* respectful

Ressentiment [resãti'mã:] (**-s, -s**) *nt* resentment

Ressort [rɛ'so:r] (**-s, -s**) *nt* department; **in das ~ von jdm fallen** (*lit, fig*) to be sb's department

Ressourcen [rɛ'sʊrsən] *pl* resources *pl*

Rest [rɛst] (**-(e)s, -e**) *m* remainder, rest; (*Überrest*) remains *pl*; **Reste** *pl* (*Comm*) remnants *pl*; **das hat mir den ~ gegeben** (*umg*) that finished me off

Restaurant [rɛsto'rã:] (**-s, -s**) *nt* restaurant

Restauration [rɛstaʊratsi'o:n] *f* restoration

restaurieren [rɛstaʊ'ri:rən] *vt* to restore

Restaurierung *f* restoration

Rest- *zW*: **Restbetrag** *m* remainder, outstanding sum; **Restlaufzeit** *f* (*Wirts*) unexpired term; **restlich** *adj* remaining; **restlos** *adj* complete; **Restmüll** *m* non-recyclable waste; **Restposten** *m* (*Comm*) remaining stock

Resultat [rezʊl'ta:t] (**-(e)s, -e**) *nt* result

Retorte [re'tɔrtə] (**-, -n**) *f* retort; **aus der ~** (*umg*) synthetic

Retortenbaby *nt* test-tube baby

retour [re'tu:r] *adv* (*veraltet*) back

Retouren *pl* (*Waren*) returns *pl*

retten ['rɛtən] *vt* to save, rescue ▷ *vr* to escape; **bist du noch zu ~?** (*umg*) are you out of your mind?; **sich vor etw** *dat* **nicht mehr ~ können** (*fig*) to be swamped with sth

Retter, in (**-s, -**) *m(f)* rescuer, saviour (*Brit*), savior (*US*)

Rettich ['rɛtɪç] (**-s, -e**) *m* radish

Rettung *f* rescue; (*Hilfe*) help; **seine letzte ~** his last hope

Rettungs- *zW*: **Rettungsaktion** *f* rescue operation; **Rettungsboot** *nt* lifeboat; **Rettungsdienst** *m* rescue service; **Rettungsgürtel** *m* lifebelt, life preserver (*US*); **rettungslos** *adj* hopeless; **Rettungsring** *m* = **Rettungsgürtel**; **Rettungsschwimmer** *m* lifesaver; (*am Strand*) lifeguard; **Rettungswagen** *m* ambulance

Return-Taste [ri'tø:rntastə] *f* (*Comput*) return key

retuschieren [retʊ'ʃi:rən] *vt* (*Phot*) to retouch

Reue ['rɔʏə] (**-**) *f* remorse; (*Bedauern*) regret

reuen *vt*: **es reut ihn** he regrets it, he is sorry about it

reuig ['rɔʏɪç] *adj* penitent

reumütig *adj* remorseful; (*Sünder*) contrite

Reuse ['rɔʏzə] (**-, -n**) *f* fish trap

Revanche [re'vã:ʃə] (**-, -n**) *f* revenge; (*Sport*) return match

revanchieren [revã'ʃi:rən] *vr* (*sich rächen*) to get one's own back, have one's revenge; (*erwidern*) to reciprocate, return the compliment

Revers [re'vɛ:r] (**-, -**) *nt or m* lapel

revidieren [revi'di:rən] *vt* to revise; (*Comm*) to audit

Revier [re'vi:r] (**-s, -e**) *nt* district; (*Min: Kohlenrevier*) (coal)mine; (*Jagdrevier*) preserve; (*Polizeirevier*) police station, station house (*US*); (*Dienstbereich*) beat (*Brit*), precinct (*US*); (*Mil*) sick bay

Revision [revizi'o:n] *f* revision; (*Comm*) auditing; (*Jur*) appeal

Revisionsverhandlung *f* appeal hearing

Revisor [re'vi:zɔr] (**-s, -en**) *m* (*Comm*) auditor

Revolte [re'vɔltə] (**-, -n**) *f* revolt

Revolution [revolutsi'o:n] *f* revolution

revolutionär [revolutsio'nɛ:r] *adj* revolutionary

Revolutionär, in [revolutsio'nɛ:r(ɪn)] (**-s, -e**) *m(f)* revolutionary

revolutionieren [revolutsio'ni:rən] *vt* to revolutionize

Revoluzzer [revo'lʊtsər] (**-s, -**) (*pej*) *m* would-be revolutionary

Revolver [re'vɔlvər] (**-s, -**) *m* revolver

Revue [rə'vy:] (**-, -n**) *f*: **etw ~ passieren lassen** (*fig*) to pass sth in review

Reykjavik ['raɪkjavi:k] (**-s**) *nt* Reykjavik

Rezensent [retsɛn'zɛnt] *m* reviewer, critic

rezensieren [retsɛn'zi:rən] *vt* to review

Rezension *f* review

Rezept [re'tsɛpt] (**-(e)s, -e**) *nt* (*Koch*) recipe; (*Med*) prescription

Rezeption [retsɛptsi'o:n] *f* (*von Hotel: Empfang*)

r

reception

rezeptpflichtig *adj* available only on prescription

Rezession [retsɛsi'oːn] *f (Fin)* recession

rezitieren [retsi'tiːrən] *vt* to recite

R-Gespräch ['ɛrɡəʃprɛːç] *nt (Tel)* reverse charge call *(Brit)*, collect call *(US)*

Rh *abk (= Rhesus(faktor) positiv)* Rh positive

rh *abk (= Rhesus(faktor) negativ)* Rh negative

Rhabarber [ra'barbər] **(-s)** *m* rhubarb

Rhein [raɪn] **(-(e)s)** *m* Rhine

rhein. *abk = rheinisch*

Rheingau *m* wine-growing area along the Rhine

Rheinhessen *nt* wine-growing area along the Rhine

rheinisch *adj attrib* Rhenish, Rhineland

Rheinland *nt* Rhineland

Rheinländer, in *m(f)* Rhinelander

Rheinland-Pfalz *nt* Rhineland-Palatinate

Rhesusfaktor ['reːzusfaktɔr] *m* rhesus factor

Rhetorik [re'toːrɪk] *f* rhetoric

rhetorisch [re'toːrɪʃ] *adj* rhetorical

Rheuma ['rɔyma] **(-s)** *nt* rheumatism

Rheumatismus [rɔyma'tɪsmʊs] *m* rheumatism

Rhinozeros [ri'noːtserɔs] **(- od -ses, -se)** *nt* rhinoceros; *(umg: Dummkopf)* fool

Rhld. *abk = Rheinland*

Rhodesien [ro'deːziən] **(-s)** *nt* Rhodesia

Rhodos ['roːdɔs] **(-)** *nt* Rhodes

rhythmisch ['rytmɪʃ] *adj* rhythmical

Rhythmus *m* rhythm

RIAS ['riːas] **(-)** *m abk (= Rundfunk im amerikanischen Sektor (Berlin))* broadcasting station in the former American sector of Berlin

Richtantenne ['rɪçt|antɛnə] **(-, -n)** *f* directional aerial *(bes Brit) od* antenna

richten ['rɪçtən] *vt* to direct; *(Waffe)* to aim; *(einstellen)* to adjust; *(instand setzen)* to repair; *(zurechtmachen)* to prepare, get ready; *(adressieren: Briefe, Anfragen)* to address; *(Bitten, Forderungen)* to make; *(in Ordnung bringen)* to do, fix; *(bestrafen)* to pass judgement on ▷ *vr:* **sich ~ nach** to go by; **~ an** +akk to direct at; *(fig)* to direct to; *(Briefe etc)* to address to; *(Bitten etc)* to make to; **~ auf** +akk to aim at; **wir ~ uns ganz nach unseren Kunden** we are guided entirely by our customers' wishes

Richter, in **(-s, -)** *m(f)* judge; **sich zum ~ machen** *(fig)* to set (o.s.) up in judgement; **richterlich** *adj* judicial

Richtgeschwindigkeit *f* recommended speed

richtig *adj* right, correct; *(echt)* proper ▷ *adv* correctly, right; *(umg: sehr)* really; **der/die R~e** the right one *od* person; **das R~e** the right thing; **die Uhr geht ~** the clock is right; **Richtigkeit** *f* correctness; **das hat schon seine Richtigkeit** it's right enough; **richtigstellen** *vt* to correct; **Richtigstellung** *f* correction, rectification

Richt- *zW:* **Richtlinie** *f* guideline; **Richtpreis** *m* recommended price; **Richtschnur** *f (fig: Grundsatz)* guiding principle

Richtung *f* direction; *(Tendenz)* tendency,

orientation; **in jeder ~** each way

Richtungstaste *f* arrow key

Richtungsstreit *m (Pol)* factional dispute

richtungweisend *adj:* **~ sein** to point the way (ahead)

rieb *etc* [riːp] *vb siehe* **reiben**

riechen ['riːçən] *unreg vt, vi* to smell; **an etw** *dat* **~** to smell sth; **es riecht nach Gas** there's a smell of gas; **ich kann das/ihn nicht ~** *(umg)* I can't stand it/him; **das konnte ich doch nicht ~!** *(umg)* how was I (supposed) to know?

Riecher **(-s, -)** *m:* **einen guten** *od* **den richtigen ~ für etw haben** *(umg)* to have a nose for sth

Ried [riːt] **(-(e)s, -e)** *nt* reed; *(Moor)* marsh

rief *etc* [riːf] *vb siehe* **rufen**

Riege ['riːɡə] **(-, -n)** *f* team, squad

Riegel ['riːɡəl] **(-s, -)** *m* bolt, bar; **einer Sache** *dat* **einen ~ vorschieben** *(fig)* to clamp down on sth

Riemen ['riːmən] **(-s, -)** *m* strap; *(Gürtel, Tech)* belt; *(Naut)* oar; **sich am ~ reißen** *(fig: umg)* to get a grip on o.s.; **Riemenantrieb** *m* belt drive

Riese ['riːzə] **(-n, -n)** *m* giant

rieseln *vi* to trickle; *(Schnee)* to fall gently

Riesen- *zW:* **Riesenerfolg** *m* enormous success; **Riesengebirge** *nt (Geog)* Sudeten Mountains *pl*; **riesengroß** *adj*, **riesenhaft** *adj* colossal, gigantic, huge; **Riesenrad** *nt* big *od* Ferris wheel; **Riesenschritt** *m:* **sich mit Riesenschritten nähern** *(fig)* to be drawing on apace; **Riesenslalom** *m (Ski)* giant slalom

riesig ['riːzɪç] *adj* enormous, huge, vast

Riesin *f* giantess

riet *etc* [riːt] *vb siehe* **raten**

Riff [rɪf] **(-(e)s, -e)** *nt* reef

rigoros [riɡo'roːs] *adj* rigorous

Rille ['rɪlə] **(-, -n)** *f* groove

Rind [rɪnt] **(-(e)s, -er)** *nt* ox; *(Kuh)* cow; *(Koch)* beef; **Rinder** *pl* cattle *pl*; **vom ~** beef

Rinde ['rɪndə] **(-, -n)** *f* rind; *(Baumrinde)* bark; *(Brotrinde)* crust

Rinderbraten *m* roast beef

Rinderwahn ['rɪndərvaːn] *m* mad cow disease

Rindfleisch *nt* beef

Rindvieh *nt* cattle *pl*; *(umg)* blockhead, stupid oaf

Ring [rɪŋ] **(-(e)s, -e)** *m* ring; **Ringbuch** *nt* ring binder

ringeln ['rɪŋəln] *vt (Pflanze)* to (en)twine; *(Schwanz etc)* to curl ▷ *vr* to go curly, curl; *(Rauch)* to curl up(wards)

Ringelnatter *f* grass snake

Ringeltaube *f* wood pigeon

ringen *unreg vi* to wrestle; **nach** *od* **um etw ~** to struggle for sth; **Ringen** **(-s)** *nt* wrestling

Ringer **(-s, -)** *m* wrestler

Ring- *zW:* **Ringfinger** *m* ring finger; **ringförmig** *adj* ring-shaped; **Ringkampf** *m* wrestling bout; **Ringrichter** *m* referee

rings *adv:* **~ um** round; **ringsherum** *adv* round about

Ringstraße *f* ring road

ringsum, ringsumher adv (rundherum) round about; (überall) all round
Rinne ['rɪnə] (-, -n) f gutter, drain
rinnen unreg vi to run, trickle
Rinnsal (-s, -e) nt trickle of water
Rinnstein m gutter
Rippchen ['rɪpçən] nt small rib; cutlet
Rippe ['rɪpə] (-, -n) f rib
Rippen- zW: **Rippenfellentzündung** f pleurisy; **Rippenspeer** m od nt (Koch): **Kasseler Rippenspeer** slightly cured pork spare rib; **Rippenstoß** m dig in the ribs
Risiko ['riːziko] (-s, -s od **Risiken**) nt risk; **risikobehaftet** adj fraught with risk; **Risikoinvestition** f sunk cost
riskant [rɪs'kant] adj risky, hazardous
riskieren [rɪs'kiːrən] vt to risk
riss etc [rɪs] vb siehe **reißen**
Riss (-es, -e) m tear; (in Mauer, Tasse etc) crack; (in Haut) scratch; (Tech) design
rissig ['rɪsɪç] adj torn; cracked; scratched
ritt etc [rɪt] vb siehe **reiten**
Ritt (-(e)s, -e) m ride
Ritter (-s, -) m knight; **jdn zum ~ schlagen** to knight sb; **arme ~** pl (Koch) sweet French toast, made with bread soaked in milk; **ritterlich** adj chivalrous; **Ritterschlag** m knighting; **Rittertum** (-s) nt chivalry; **Ritterzeit** f age of chivalry
rittlings adv astride
Ritual [ritu'aːl] (-s, -e od -ien) nt (lit, fig) ritual
rituell [ritu'ɛl] adj ritual
Ritus ['riːtʊs] (-, **Riten**) m rite
Ritze ['rɪtsə] (-, -n) f crack, chink
ritzen vt to scratch; **die Sache ist geritzt** (umg) it's all fixed up
Rivale [ri'vaːlə] (-n, -n) m, **Rivalin** f rival
rivalisieren [rivali'ziːrən] vi: **mit jdm ~ to** compete with sb
Rivalität [rivali'tɛːt] f rivalry
Riviera [rivi'eːra] (-) f Riviera
Rizinusöl ['riːtsinʊs|øːl] nt castor oil
r.-k. abk (= römisch-katholisch) R.C.
Robbe ['rɔbə] (-, -n) f seal
robben ['rɔbən] vi (Hilfsverb sein: auch Mil) to crawl (using elbows)
Robbenfang m seal hunting
Robe ['roːbə] (-, -n) f robe
Roboter ['rɔbɔtər] (-s, -) m robot; **Robotertechnik** f robotics sing
Robotik ['rɔbɔtɪk] f robotics sing
robust [ro'bʊst] adj (Mensch, Gesundheit) robust; (Material) tough
roch etc [rɔx] vb siehe **riechen**
Rochade [rɔ'xaːdə] (-, -n) f (Schach): **die kleine/große ~** castling king's side/queen's side
röcheln ['rœçəln] vi to wheeze; (Sterbender) to give the death rattle
Rock¹ [rɔk] (-(e)s, ⁻e) m skirt; (Jackett) jacket; (Uniformrock) tunic
Rock² [rɔk] (-(s), -(s)) m (Mus) rock; **Rockmusik** f rock music
Rockzipfel m: **an Mutters ~ hängen** (umg) to cling to (one's) mother's skirts
Rodel ['roːdəl] (-s, -) m toboggan; **Rodelbahn** f toboggan run
rodeln vi to toboggan
roden ['roːdən] vt, vi to clear
Rogen ['roːgən] (-s, -) m roe
Roggen ['rɔgən] (-s, -) m rye; **Roggenbrot** nt rye bread; (Vollkornbrot) black bread
roh [roː] adj raw; (Mensch) coarse, crude; **~e Gewalt** brute force; **Rohbau** m shell of a building; **Roheisen** nt pig iron; **Rohfassung** f rough draft; **Rohkost** f raw fruit and vegetables pl; **Rohling** m ruffian; **Rohmaterial** nt raw material; **Rohöl** nt crude oil
Rohr [roːr] (-(e)s, -e) nt pipe, tube; (Bot) cane; (Schilf) reed; (Gewehrrohr) barrel; **Rohrbruch** m burst pipe
Röhre ['røːrə] (-, -n) f tube, pipe; (Rundf etc) valve; (Backröhre) oven
Rohr- zW: **Rohrgeflecht** nt wickerwork; **Rohrleger** (-s, -) m plumber; **Rohrleitung** f pipeline; **Rohrpost** f pneumatic post; **Rohrspatz** m: **schimpfen wie ein Rohrspatz** (umg) to curse and swear; **Rohrstock** m cane; **Rohrstuhl** m basket chair; **Rohrzucker** m cane sugar
Rohseide f raw silk
Rohstoff m raw material
Rokoko ['rɔkoko] (-s) nt rococo
Rolladen m siehe **Rollladen**
Rollbahn f (Aviat) runway
Rollbrett nt skateboard
Rolle ['rɔlə] (-, -n) f roll; (Theat, Soziologie) role; (Garnrolle etc) reel, spool; (Walze) roller; (Wäscherolle) mangle, wringer; **bei od in etw** dat **eine ~ spielen** to play a part in sth; **aus der ~ fallen** (fig) to forget o.s.; **keine ~ spielen** not to matter
rollen vi to roll; (Aviat) to taxi ▷ vt to roll; (Wäsche) to mangle, put through the wringer; **den Stein ins R~ bringen** (fig) to start the ball rolling
Rollen- zW: **Rollenbesetzung** f (Theat) cast; **Rollenkonflikt** m (Psych) role conflict; **Rollenspiel** nt role-play; **Rollentausch** m exchange of roles; (Soziologie) role reversal
Roller (-s, -) m scooter; (Welle) roller
Roll- zW: **Rollfeld** nt runway; **Rollkragen** m roll od polo neck; **Rollladen** m shutter; **Rollmops** m pickled herring
Rollo ['rɔlo] (-, -s) nt (roller) blind
Roll- zW: **Rollschrank** m roll-fronted cupboard; **Rollschuh** m roller skate; **Rollschuhlaufen** nt roller skating; **Rollsplitt** m grit; **Rollstuhl** m wheelchair; **Rolltreppe** f escalator
Rom [roːm] (-s) nt Rome; **das sind Zustände wie im alten ~** (umg: unmoralisch) it's disgraceful; (: primitiv) it's medieval (umg)
röm. abk = **römisch**
Roman [ro'maːn] (-s, -e) m novel; **(jdm) einen ganzen ~ erzählen** (umg) to give (sb) a long rigmarole; **Romanheft** nt pulp novel
romanisch adj (Volk, Sprache) Romance; (Kunst)

r

277

Romanesque

Romanistik [roma'nɪstɪk] *f* (*Univ*) Romance languages and literature

Romanschreiber *m* novelist

Romanschriftsteller *m* novelist

Romantik [ro'mantɪk] *f* romanticism

Romantiker, in (**-s, -**) *m(f)* romanticist

romantisch *adj* romantic

Romanze [ro'mantsə] (**-, -n**) *f* romance

Römer ['rø:mər] (**-s, -**) *m* wineglass; (*Mensch*) Roman; **Römertopf**® *m* (*Koch*) ≈ (chicken) brick

römisch ['rø:mɪʃ] *adj* Roman; **römisch-katholisch** *adj* Roman Catholic

röm.-kath. *abk* (= *römisch-katholisch*) R.C.

Rommé, Rommee [rɔ'me:] (**-s, -s**) *nt* rummy

röntgen ['rœntɡən] *vt* to X-ray; **Röntgenaufnahme** *f* X-ray; **Röntgenbild** *nt* X-ray; **Röntgenstrahlen** *pl* X-rays *pl*

rosa ['ro:za] *adj inv* pink, rose(-coloured)

Rose ['ro:zə] (**-, -n**) *f* rose

Rosé [ro'ze:] (**-s, -s**) *m* rosé

Rosenkohl *m* Brussels sprouts *pl*

Rosenkranz *m* rosary

Rosenmontag *m* Monday of Shrovetide; *siehe auch* **Karneval**

Rosette [ro'zɛtə] *f* rosette

rosig ['ro:zɪç] *adj* rosy

Rosine [ro'zi:nə] *f* raisin; **(große) ~n im Kopf haben** (*umg*) to have big ideas

Rosmarin ['ro:smari:n] (**-s**) *m* rosemary

Ross [rɔs] (**-es, -e**) *nt* horse, steed; **auf dem hohen ~ sitzen** (*fig*) to be on one's high horse; **Rosskastanie** *f* horse chestnut; **Rosskur** (*umg*) *f* kill-or-cure remedy

Rost [rɔst] (**-(e)s, -e**) *m* rust; (*Gitter*) grill, gridiron; (*Bettrost*) springs *pl*; **Rostbraten** *m* roast(ed) meat, roast; **Rostbratwurst** *f* grilled *od* barbecued sausage

rosten *vi* to rust

rösten ['rø:stən] *vt* to roast; (*Brot*) to toast

rostfrei *adj* (*Stahl*) stainless

rostig *adj* rusty

Röstkartoffeln *pl* fried potatoes *pl*

Rostschutz *m* rustproofing

rot [ro:t] *adj* red; **~ werden, einen roten Kopf bekommen** to blush, go red; **die R~e Armee** the Red Army; **das R~e Kreuz** the Red Cross; **das R~e Meer** the Red Sea

Rotation [rotatsi'o:n] *f* rotation

rot- *zW*: **rotbäckig** *adj* red-cheeked; **Rotbarsch** *m* rosefish; **rotblond** *adj* strawberry blond

Röte ['rø:tə] (**-**) *f* redness

Röteln *pl* German measles *sing*

röten *vt, vr* to redden

rothaarig *adj* red-haired

rotieren [ro'ti:rən] *vi* to rotate

Rot- *zW*: **Rotkäppchen** *nt* Little Red Riding Hood; **Rotkehlchen** *nt* robin; **Rotkohl** *m* red cabbage; **Rotkraut** *nt* red cabbage; **rotsehen** (*umg: unreg*) *vi* to see red, to become angry; **Rotstift** *m* red pencil; **Rotwein** *m* red wine

Rotz [rɔts] (**-es, -e**) (*umg*) *m* snot; **rotzfrech** (*umg*) *adj* cocky; **rotznäsig** (*umg*) *adj* snotty-nosed

Rouge [ru:ʒ] (**-s, -s**) *nt* rouge

Roulade [ru'la:də] (**-, -n**) *f* (*Koch*) beef olive

Roulette, Roulett [ru'lɛt] (**-s, -s**) *nt* roulette

Route ['ru:tə] (**-, -n**) *f* route

Routine [ru'ti:nə] *f* experience; (*Gewohnheit*) routine

routiniert [ruti'ni:ərt] *adj* experienced

Rowdy ['raudi] (**-s, -s**) *m* hooligan; (*zerstörerisch*) vandal; (*lärmend*) rowdy (type)

Ruanda [ru'anda] *nt* Rwanda

ruandisch *adj* Rwandan

rubbeln ['rubəln] (*umg*) *vt, vi* to rub

Rübe ['ry:bə] (**-, -n**) *f* turnip; **Gelbe ~** carrot; **Rote ~** beetroot (*Brit*), beet (*US*)

Rübenzucker *m* beet sugar

Rubin [ru'bi:n] (**-s, -e**) *m* ruby

Rubrik [ru'bri:k] *f* heading; (*Spalte*) column

Ruck [ruk] (**-(e)s, -e**) *m* jerk, jolt; **sich** *dat* **einen ~ geben** (*fig: umg*) to make an effort

ruck *adv*: **das geht ~, zuck** it won't take a second

Rückantwort *f* reply, answer; **um ~ wird gebeten** please reply

ruckartig *adj*: **er stand ~ auf** he shot to his feet

Rück- *zW*: **Rückbesinnung** *f* recollection; **rückbezüglich** *adj* reflexive; **Rückblende** *f* flashback; **rückblenden** *vi* to flash back; **Rückblick** *m*: **im Rückblick auf etw** *akk* looking back on sth; **rückblickend** *adj* retrospective ▷ *adv* in retrospect; **rückdatieren** *vt* to backdate

Rücken (**-s, -**) *m* back; (*Bergrücken*) ridge; **jdm in den ~ fallen** (*fig*) to stab sb in the back

rücken *vt, vi* to move

Rücken- *zW*: **Rückendeckung** *f* backing; **Rückenlage** *f* supine position; **Rückenlehne** *f* back (of chair); **Rückenmark** *nt* spinal cord; **Rückenschwimmen** *nt* backstroke; **Rückenstärkung** *f* (*fig*) moral support; **Rückenwind** *m* following wind

Rück- *zW*: **Rückerstattung** *f* return, restitution; **Rückfahrkarte** *f* return ticket (*Brit*), round-trip ticket (*US*); **Rückfahrt** *f* return journey; **Rückfall** *m* relapse; **rückfällig** *adj* relapsed; **rückfällig werden** to relapse; **Rückflug** *m* return flight; **Rückfrage** *f* question; **nach Rückfrage bei der zuständigen Behörde ...** after checking this with the appropriate authority ...; **rückfragen** *vi* to inquire; (*nachprüfen*) to check; **Rückführung** *f* (*von Menschen*) repatriation, return; **Rückgabe** *f* return; **gegen Rückgabe** (+*gen*) on return (of); **Rückgang** *m* decline, fall; **rückgängig** *adj*: **etw rückgängig machen** (*widerrufen*) to undo sth; (*Bestellung*) to cancel sth; **Rückgewinnung** *f* recovery; (*von Land, Gebiet*) reclaiming; (*aus verbrauchten Stoffen*) recycling

Rückgrat *nt* spine, backbone

Rück- *zW*: **Rückgriff** *m* recourse; **Rückhalt** *m* backing; (*Einschränkung*) reserve; **rückhaltlos**

adj unreserved; **Rückhand** *f* (*Sport*) backhand;
rückkaufbar *adj* redeemable; **Rückkehr**
(-,) *f* return; **Rückkoppelung** *f* feedback;
Rücklage *f* reserve, savings *pl*; **Rücklauf**
m reverse running; (*beim Tonband*) rewind;
(*von Maschinenteil*) return travel; **rückläufig**
adj declining, falling; **eine rückläufige**
Entwicklung a decline; **Rücklicht** *nt*
rear light; **rücklings** *adv* from behind;
(*rückwärts*) backwards; **Rückmeldung** *f* (*Univ*)
reregistration; **Rücknahme** **(-, -n)** *f* taking
back; **Rückporto** *nt* return postage; **Rückreise**
f return journey; (*Naut*) home voyage; **Rückruf**
m recall

Rucksack ['rʊkzak] *m* rucksack

Rück- *zW*: **Rückschau** *f* reflection;
rückschauend *adj* = **rückblickend**; **Rückschlag**
m setback; **Rückschluss** *m* conclusion;
Rückschritt *m* retrogression; **rückschrittlich**
adj reactionary; (*Entwicklung*) retrograde;
Rückseite *f* back; (*von Münze etc*) reverse;
siehe Rückseite see over(leaf); **rücksetzen** *vt*
(*Comput*) to reset

Rücksicht *f* consideration; **~ nehmen auf** +*akk*
to show consideration for; **Rücksichtnahme** *f*
consideration

rücksichtslos *adj* inconsiderate; (*Fahren*)
reckless; (*unbarmherzig*) ruthless

Rücksichtslosigkeit *f* lack of consideration;
(*beim Fahren*) recklessness; (*Unbarmherzigkeit*)
ruthlessness

rücksichtsvoll *adj* considerate

Rück- *zW*: **Rücksitz** *m* back seat; **Rückspiegel**
m (*Aut*) rear-view mirror; **Rückspiel** *nt* return
match; **Rücksprache** *f* further discussion
od talk; **Rücksprache mit jdm nehmen**
to confer with sb; **Rückstand** *m* arrears *pl*;
(*Verzug*) delay; **rückständig** *adj* backward,
out-of-date; (*Zahlungen*) in arrears; **Rückstau**
m (*Aut*) tailback (*Brit*), line of cars; **Rückstoß**
m recoil; **Rückstrahler** **(-s, -)** *m* rear reflector;
Rückstrom *m* (*von Menschen, Fahrzeugen*) return;
Rücktaste *f* (*an Schreibmaschine*) backspace key;
Rücktritt *m* resignation; **Rücktrittbremse**
f backpedal brake; **Rücktrittsklausel** *f*
(*Vertrag*) escape clause; **Rückvergütung** *f*
repayment; (*Comm*) refund; **rückversichern**
vt, vi to reinsure ⊳ *vr* to check (up *od* back);
Rückversicherung *f* reinsurance; **rückwärtig**
adj rear; **rückwärts** *adv* backward(s), back;
Rückwärtsgang *m* (*Aut*) reverse gear; **im**
Rückwärtsgang fahren to reverse; **Rückweg**
m return journey, way back; **rückwirkend**
adj retroactive; **Rückwirkung** *f* repercussion;
eine Zahlung mit Rückwirkung
vom ... a payment backdated to ...; **eine**
Gesetzesänderung mit Rückwirkung
vom ... an amendment made retrospective
to ...; **Rückzahlung** *f* repayment; **Rückzieher**
(*umg*) *m*: **einen Rückzieher machen** to back
out; **Rückzug** *m* retreat; **Rückzugsgefecht** *nt*
(*Mil, fig*) rearguard action

rüde ['ry:də] *adj* blunt, gruff

Rüde **(-n, -n)** *m* male dog

Rudel ['ru:dəl] **(-s, -)** *nt* pack; (*von Hirschen*) herd

Ruder ['ru:dər] **(-s, -)** *nt* oar; (*Steuer*) rudder; **das**
~ fest in der Hand haben (*fig*) to be in control
of the situation; **Ruderboot** *nt* rowing boat;
Ruderer **(-s, -)** *m* rower, oarsman

rudern *vt, vi* to row; **mit den Armen ~** (*fig*) to
flail one's arms about

Ruf [ru:f] **(-(e)s, -e)** *m* call, cry; (*Ansehen*)
reputation; (*Univ: Berufung*) offer of a chair

rufen *unreg vt, vi* to call; (*ausrufen*) to cry; **um**
Hilfe ~ to call for help; **das kommt mir wie**
ge~ that's just what I needed

Rüffel ['rʏfəl] **(-s, -)** (*umg*) *m* telling-off, ticking-
off

Ruf- *zW*: **Rufmord** *m* character assassination;
Rufname *m* usual (first) name; **Rufnummer**
f (tele)phone number; **Rufsäule** *f* (*für*
Taxi) telephone; (*an Autobahn*) emergency
telephone; **Rufzeichen** *nt* (*Rundf*) call sign;
(*Tel*) ringing tone

Rüge ['ry:gə] **(-, -n)** *f* reprimand, rebuke

rügen *vt* to reprimand

Ruhe ['ru:ə] **(-)** *f* rest; (*Ungestörtheit*) peace,
quiet; (*Gelassenheit, Stille*) calm; (*Schweigen*)
silence; **~! be quiet!, silence!; angenehme ~!**
sleep well!; **~ bewahren** to stay cool *od* calm;
das lässt ihm keine ~ he can't stop thinking
about it; **sich zur ~ setzen** to retire; **die ~**
weghaben (*umg*) to be unflappable; **immer**
mit der ~ (*umg*) don't panic; **die letzte ~**
finden (*liter*) to be laid to rest; **Ruhelage** *f* (*von*
Mensch) reclining position; (*Med: bei Bruch*)
immobile position; **ruhelos** *adj* restless

ruhen *vi* to rest; (*Verkehr*) to cease; (*Arbeit*) to
stop, cease; (*Waffen*) to be laid down; (*begraben*
sein) to lie, be buried

Ruhe- *zW*: **Ruhepause** *f* break; **Ruheplatz**
m resting place; **Ruhestand** *m* retirement;
Ruhestätte *f*: **letzte Ruhestätte** final
resting place; **Ruhestörung** *f* breach of the
peace; **Ruhetag** *m* closing day

ruhig ['ru:ɪç] *adj* quiet; (*bewegungslos*) still;
(*Hand*) steady; (*gelassen, friedlich*) calm;
(*Gewissen*) clear; **tu das ~** feel free to do that;
etw ~ mit ansehen (*gleichgültig*) to stand by
and watch sth; **du könntest ~ mal etwas für**
mich tun! it's about time you did something
for me!

Ruhm [ru:m] **(-(e)s)** *m* fame, glory

rühmen ['ry:mən] *vt* to praise ⊳ *vr* to boast

rühmlich *adj* praiseworthy; (*Ausnahme*) notable

ruhmlos *adj* inglorious

ruhmreich *adj* glorious

Ruhr [ru:r] **(-)** *f* dysentery

Rührei ['ry:r|aɪ] *nt* scrambled egg

rühren *vt* (*lit, fig*) to move, stir (*auch Koch*) ⊳ *vr*
(*lit, fig*) to move, stir ⊳ *vi*: **~ von** to come *od* stem
from; **~ an** +*akk* to touch; (*fig*) to touch on

rührend *adj* touching, moving; **das ist ~ von**
Ihnen that is sweet of you

Ruhrgebiet *nt* Ruhr (area)

rührig *adj* active, lively

r

rührselig *adj* sentimental, emotional
Rührung *f* emotion
Ruin [ru'i:n] (-s) *m* ruin; **vor dem ~ stehen** to be on the brink *od* verge of ruin
Ruine (-, -n) *f* (*lit, fig*) ruin
ruinieren [rui'ni:rən] *vt* to ruin
rülpsen ['rʏlpsən] *vi* to burp, belch
Rum [rʊm] (-s, -s) *m* rum
rum (*umg*) *adv* = **herum**
Rumäne [ru'mɛ:nə] (-n, -n) *m* Romanian
Rumänien (-s) *nt* Romania
Rumänin *f* Romanian
rumänisch *adj* Romanian
rumfuhrwerken ['rʊmfu:rvɛrkən] (*umg*) *vt* to bustle around
Rummel ['rʊməl] (-s) (*umg*) *m* hurly-burly; (*Jahrmarkt*) fair; **Rummelplatz** *m* fairground, fair
rumoren [ru'mo:rən] *vi* to be noisy, make a noise
Rumpelkammer ['rʊmpəlkamər] *f* junk room
rumpeln *vi* to rumble; (*holpern*) to jolt
Rumpf [rʊmpf] (-(e)s, ̈-e) *m* trunk, torso; (*Aviat*) fuselage; (*Naut*) hull
rümpfen ['rʏmpfən] *vt* (*Nase*) to turn up
Rumtopf *m* soft fruit in rum
rund [rʊnt] *adj* round ▷ *adv* (*etwa*) around; **~ um etw** round sth; **jetzt gehts ~** (*umg*) this is where the fun starts; **wenn er das erfährt, gehts ~** there'll be a to-do when he finds out; **Rundbogen** *m* Norman *od* Romanesque arch; **Rundbrief** *m* circular
Runde ['rʊndə] (-, -n) *f* round; (*in Rennen*) lap; (*Gesellschaft*) circle; **die ~ machen** to do the rounds; (*herumgegeben werden*) to be passed round; **über die ~n kommen** (*Sport, fig*) to pull through; **eine ~ spendieren** *od* **schmeißen** (*umg: Getränke*) to stand a round
runden *vt* to make round ▷ *vr* (*fig*) to take shape
rund- *zW:* **runderneuert** *adj* (*Reifen*) remoulded (*Brit*), remolded (*US*); **Rundfahrt** *f* (round) trip; **Rundfrage** *f:* **Rundfrage (unter** +*dat*) survey (of)
Rundfunk ['rʊntfʊŋk] (-(e)s) *m* broadcasting; (*bes Hörfunk*) radio; (*Rundfunkanstalt*) broadcasting corporation; **im ~** on the radio; **Rundfunkanstalt** *f* broadcasting corporation; **Rundfunkempfang** *m* reception; **Rundfunkgebühr** *f* licence (*Brit*), license (*US*); **Rundfunkgerät** *nt* radio set; **Rundfunksendung** *f* broadcast, radio programme (*Brit*) *od* program (*US*)
Rund- *zW:* **Rundgang** *m* (*Spaziergang*) walk; (*von Wachmann*) rounds *pl*; (*von Briefträger etc*) round; (*zur Besichtigung*): **Rundgang (durch)** tour (of); **rundheraus** *adv* straight out, bluntly;

rundherum *adv* all round; (*fig: umg: völlig*) totally; **rundlich** *adj* plump, rounded; **Rundreise** *f* round trip; **Rundschreiben** *nt* (*Comm*) circular; **rundum** *adv* all around; (*fig*) completely
Rundung *f* curve, roundness
rundweg *adv* straight out
runter ['rʊntər] (*umg*) *adv* = **herunter;** **hinunter; runterwürgen** (*umg*) *vt* (*Ärger*) to swallow
Runzel ['rʊntsəl] (-, -n) *f* wrinkle
runzelig, runzlig *adj* wrinkled
runzeln *vt* to wrinkle; **die Stirn ~** to frown
Rüpel ['ry:pəl] (-s, -) *m* lout; **rüpelhaft** *adj* loutish
rupfen ['rʊpfən] *vt* to pluck
Rupfen (-s, -) *m* sackcloth
ruppig ['rʊpɪç] *adj* rough, gruff
Rüsche ['ry:ʃə] (-, -n) *f* frill
Ruß [ru:s] (-es) *m* soot
Russe ['rʊsə] (-n, -n) *m* Russian
Rüssel ['rʏsəl] (-s, -) *m* snout; (*Elefantenrüssel*) trunk
rußen *vi* to smoke; (*Ofen*) to be sooty
rußig *adj* sooty
Russin *f* Russian
russisch *adj* Russian; **~e Eier** (*Koch*) egg(s) mayonnaise
Russland (-s) *nt* Russia
rüsten ['rʏstən] *vt, vi, vr* to prepare; (*Mil*) to arm
rüstig ['rʏstɪç] *adj* sprightly, vigorous; **Rüstigkeit** *f* sprightliness, vigour (*Brit*), vigor (*US*)
rustikal [rʊsti'ka:l] *adj:* **sich ~ einrichten** to furnish one's home in a rustic style
Rüstung ['rʏstʊŋ] *f* preparation; (*Mil*) arming; (*Ritterrüstung*) armour (*Brit*), armor (*US*); (*Waffen etc*) armaments *pl*
Rüstungs- *zW:* **Rüstungsgegner** *m* opponent of the arms race; **Rüstungsindustrie** *f* armaments industry; **Rüstungskontrolle** *f* arms control; **Rüstungswettlauf** *m* arms race
Rüstzeug *nt* tools *pl*; (*fig*) capacity
Rute ['ru:tə] (-, -n) *f* rod, switch
Rutsch [rʊtʃ] (-(e)s, -e) *m* slide; (*Erdrutsch*) landslide; **guten ~!** (*umg*) have a good New Year!; **Rutschbahn** *f* slide
rutschen *vi* to slide; (*ausrutschen*) to slip; **auf dem Stuhl hin und her ~** to fidget around on one's chair
rutschfest *adj* non-slip
rutschig *adj* slippery
rütteln ['rʏtəln] *vt, vi* to shake, jolt; **daran ist nicht zu ~** (*fig: umg: an Grundsätzen*) there's no doubt about that
Rüttelschwelle *f* (*Aut*) rumble strips *pl*

Ss

S¹, s¹ [ɛs] *nt* S, s; **S wie Samuel** ≈ S for Sugar
S² [ɛs] *abk* (= *Süden*) S; (= *Seite*) p; (= *Schilling*) S
s² *abk* (= *Sekunde*) sec.; (= *siehe*) v., vid.
Sa. *abk* = **Samstag**
SA (-) *f abk* (= *Sturmabteilung*) SA
s. a. *abk* (= *siehe auch*) see also
Saal [zaːl] (**-(e)s, Säle**) *m* hall; (*für Sitzungen etc*) room
Saarland ['zaːrlant] (**-s**) *nt* Saarland
Saat [zaːt] (**-, -en**) *f* seed; (*Pflanzen*) crop; (*Säen*) sowing; **Saatgut** *nt* seed(s *pl*)
Sabbat ['zabat] (**-s, -e**) *m* sabbath
sabbern ['zabərn] (*umg*) *vi* to dribble
Säbel ['zɛːbəl] (**-s, -**) *m* sabre (*Brit*), saber (*US*); **Säbelrasseln** *nt* sabre-rattling
Sabotage [zabo'taːʒə] (**-, -n**) *f* sabotage
sabotieren [zabo'tiːrən] *vt* to sabotage
Saccharin, Sacharin [zaxa'riːn] (**-s**) *nt* saccharin
Sachanlagen ['zax|anlaːgən] *pl* tangible assets *pl*
Sachbearbeiter, in *m(f)*: ~ (**für**) (*Beamter*) official in charge (of)
Sachbuch *nt* non-fiction book
sachdienlich *adj* relevant, helpful
Sache ['zaxə] (**-, -n**) *f* thing; (*Angelegenheit*) affair, business; (*Frage*) matter; (*Pflicht*) task; (*Thema*) subject; (*Aufgabe*) job; (*Ideal*) cause; (*umg: km/h*): **mit 60/100 ~n** ≈ at 40/60 (mph); **ich habe mir die ~ anders vorgestellt** I had imagined things differently; **er versteht seine ~** he knows what he's doing; **das ist so eine ~** (*umg*) it's a bit tricky; **mach keine ~n!** (*umg*) don't be daft!; **bei der ~ bleiben** (*bei Diskussion*) to keep to the point; **bei der ~ sein** to be with it (*umg*); **das ist ~ der Polizei** this is a matter for the police; **zur ~** to the point; **das ist eine runde ~** that is well-balanced *od* rounded-off
Sachertorte ['zaxərtɔrtə] *f rich chocolate cake*, sachertorte
Sach- *zW:* **sachgemäß** *adj* appropriate, suitable; **Sachkenntnis** *f* (*in Bezug auf Wissensgebiet*) knowledge of the/his *etc* subject; (*in Bezug auf Sachlage*) knowledge of the facts; **sachkundig** *adj* (well-)informed; **sich sachkundig machen** to inform oneself; **Sachlage** *f* situation, state of affairs;

Sachleistung *f* payment in kind; **sachlich** *adj* matter-of-fact; (*Kritik etc*) objective; (*Irrtum, Angabe*) factual; **bleiben Sie bitte sachlich** don't get carried away (*umg*); (*nicht persönlich werden*) please stay objective
sächlich ['zɛxlɪç] *adj* neuter
Sachregister *nt* subject index
Sachschaden *m* material damage
Sachse ['zaksə] (**-n, -n**) *m* Saxon
Sachsen (**-s**) *nt* Saxony; **Sachsen-Anhalt** (**-s**) *nt* Saxony Anhalt
Sächsin ['zɛksɪn] *f* Saxon
sächsisch ['zɛksɪʃ] *adj* Saxon
sacht, sachte *adv* softly, gently
Sach- *zW:* **Sachverhalt** (**-(e)s, -e**) *m* facts *pl* (of the case); **sachverständig** *adj* (*Urteil*) expert; (*Publikum*) informed; **Sachverständige, r** *f(m)* expert; **Sachzwang** *m* force of circumstances
Sack [zak] (**-(e)s, ⁻e**) *m* sack; (*aus Papier, Plastik*) bag; (*Anat, Zool*) sac; (*umg!: Hoden*) balls *pl* (!); (: *Kerl, Bursche*) bastard (!); **mit ~ und Pack** (*umg*) with bag and baggage
sacken *vi* to sag, sink
Sackgasse *f* cul-de-sac, dead-end street (*US*)
Sackhüpfen *nt* sack race
Sadismus [za'dɪsmʊs] *m* sadism
Sadist, in [za'dɪst(ɪn)] *m(f)* sadist; **sadistisch** *adj* sadistic
Sadomasochismus [zadomazɔ'xɪsmʊs] *m* sadomasochism
säen ['zɛːən] *vt, vi* to sow; **dünn gesät** (*fig*) thin on the ground, few and far between
Safari [za'faːri] (**-, -s**) *f* safari
Safe [zeːf] (**-s, -s**) *m od nt* safe
Saft [zaft] (**-(e)s, ⁻e**) *m* juice; (*Bot*) sap; **ohne ~ und Kraft** (*fig*) wishy-washy (*umg*), effete
saftig *adj* juicy; (*Grün*) lush; (*umg: Rechnung, Ohrfeige*) hefty; (*Brief, Antwort*) hard-hitting
Saftladen (*pej: umg*) *m* rum joint
saftlos *adj* dry
Sage ['zaːgə] (**-, -n**) *f* saga
Säge ['zɛːgə] (**-, -n**) *f* saw; **Sägeblatt** *nt* saw blade; **Sägemehl** *nt* sawdust
sagen ['zaːgən] *vt, vi*: **(jdm etw) ~** to say (sth to sb), tell (sb sth); **unter uns gesagt** between you and me (and the gatepost (*hum umg*)); **lass dir das gesagt sein** take it from me; **das hat nichts zu ~** that doesn't mean anything; **sagt**

dir der Name etwas? does the name mean anything to you?; **das ist nicht gesagt** that's by no means certain; **sage und schreibe** (whether you) believe it or not

sägen vt, vi to saw; (hum: umg: schnarchen) to snore, saw wood (US)

sagenhaft adj legendary; (umg) great, smashing

sagenumwoben adj legendary

Sägespäne pl wood shavings pl

Sägewerk nt sawmill

sah etc [zaː] vb siehe **sehen**

Sahara [za'haːra] f Sahara (Desert)

Sahne ['zaːnə] (-) f cream

Saison [zɛ'zõː] (-, -s) f season

saisonal [zɛzo'naːl] adj seasonal

Saisonarbeiter m seasonal worker

saisonbedingt adj seasonal

Saite ['zaɪtə] (-, -n) f string; **andere ~n aufziehen** (umg) to get tough

Saiteninstrument nt string(ed) instrument

Sakko ['zako] (-s, -s) m od nt jacket

Sakrament [zakra'mɛnt] nt sacrament

Sakristei [zakrɪs'taɪ] f sacristy

Salami [za'laːmi] (-, -s) f salami

Salat [za'laːt] (-(e)s, -e) m salad; (Kopfsalat) lettuce; **da haben wir den ~!** (umg) now we're in a fine mess!; **Salatbesteck** nt salad servers pl; **Salatplatte** f salad; **Salatsoße** f salad dressing

Salbe ['zalbə] (-, -n) f ointment

Salbei ['zalbaɪ] (-s) m sage

salben vt to anoint

Salbung f anointing

salbungsvoll adj unctuous

saldieren [zal'diːrən] vt (Comm) to balance

Saldo ['zaldo] (-s, **Salden**) m balance; **Saldoübertrag** m balance brought od carried forward; **Saldovortrag** m balance brought od carried forward

Säle ['zɛːlə] pl von **Saal**

Salmiak [zalmi'ak] (-s) m sal ammoniac; **Salmiakgeist** m liquid ammonia

Salmonellen [zalmo'nɛlən] pl salmonellae pl

Salon [za'lɔŋ, za'lõː] (-s, -s) m salon; **Salonlöwe** m lounge lizard

salopp [za'lɔp] adj casual; (Manieren) slovenly; (Sprache) slangy

Salpeter [zal'peːtər] (-s) m saltpetre (Brit), saltpeter (US); **Salpetersäure** f nitric acid

Salto ['zalto] (-s, -s od **Salti**) m somersault

Salut [za'luːt] (-(e)s, -e) m salute

salutieren [zalu'tiːrən] vi to salute

Salve ['zalvə] (-, -n) f salvo

Salz [zalts] (-es, -e) nt salt; **salzarm** adj (Koch) low-salt; **Salzbergwerk** nt salt mine

salzen unreg vt to salt

salzig adj salty

Salz- zW: **Salzkartoffeln** pl boiled potatoes pl; **Salzsäule** f: **zur Salzsäule erstarren** (fig) to stand rooted to the spot; **Salzsäure** f hydrochloric acid; **Salzstange** f pretzel stick; **Salzstreuer** m salt cellar; **Salzwasser** nt salt water

Sambia ['zambia] (-s) nt Zambia

sambisch adj Zambian

Samen ['zaːmən] (-s, -) m seed; (Anat) sperm; **Samenbank** f sperm bank; **Samenhandlung** f seed shop

sämig ['zɛːmɪç] adj thick, creamy

Sammel- zW: **Sammelanschluss** m (Tel) private (branch) exchange; (von Privathäusern) party line; **Sammelantrag** m composite motion; **Sammelband** m anthology; **Sammelbecken** nt reservoir; (fig): **Sammelbecken (von)** melting pot (for); **Sammelbegriff** m collective term; **Sammelbestellung** f collective order; **Sammelbüchse** f collecting tin; **Sammelmappe** f folder

sammeln vt to collect ▷ vr to assemble, gather; (sich konzentrieren) to collect one's thoughts

Sammelname m collective term

Sammelnummer f (Tel) private exchange number, switchboard number

Sammelsurium [zaməl'zuːriʊm] nt hotchpotch (Brit), hodgepodge (US)

Sammler, in (-s, -) m(f) collector

Sammlung ['zamlʊŋ] f collection; (Konzentration) composure

Samstag ['zamstaːk] m Saturday; siehe auch **Dienstag**

samstags adv (on) Saturdays

samt [zamt] präp +dat (along) with, together with; **~ und sonders** each and every one (of them); **Samt** (-(e)s, -e) m velvet; **in Samt und Seide** (liter) in silks and satins

Samthandschuh m: **jdn mit ~en anfassen** (umg) to handle sb with kid gloves

sämtlich ['zɛmtlɪç] adj (alle) all (the); (vollständig) complete; **Schillers ~e Werke** the complete works of Schiller

Sanatorium [zana'toːriʊm] nt sanatorium (Brit), sanitarium (US)

Sand [zant] (-(e)s, -e) m sand; **das/die gibts wie ~ am Meer** (umg) there are piles of it/ heaps of them; **im ~ verlaufen** to peter out

Sandale [zan'daːlə] (-, -n) f sandal

Sandbank f sandbank

Sandelholz ['zandəlhɔlts] (-es) nt sandalwood

sandig ['zandɪç] adj sandy

Sand- zW: **Sandkasten** m sandpit; **Sandkastenspiele** pl (Mil) sand-table exercises pl; (fig) tactical manoeuvrings pl (Brit) od maneuverings pl (US); **Sandkuchen** m Madeira cake; **Sandmann** m, **Sandmännchen** nt (in Geschichten) sandman; **Sandpapier** nt sandpaper; **Sandstein** m sandstone; **sandstrahlen** vt, vi untr to sandblast

sandte etc ['zantə] vb siehe **senden**

Sanduhr f hourglass; (Eieruhr) egg timer

sanft [zanft] adj soft, gentle; **sanftmütig** adj gentle, meek

sang etc [zaŋ] vb siehe **singen**

Sänger, in ['zɛŋər(ɪn)] (-s, -) m(f) singer

sang-und klanglos (umg) adv without any ado, quietly

Sani ['zani] (-s, -s) (umg) m = **Sanitäter**

sanieren [za'ni:rən] vt to redevelop; (Betrieb) to make financially sound; (Haus) to renovate ▷ vr to line one's pockets; (Unternehmen) to become financially sound

Sanierung f redevelopment; renovation

sanitär [zani'tɛ:r] adj sanitary; **~e Anlagen** sanitation sing

Sanitäter [zani'tɛ:tər] (-s, -) m first-aid attendant; (in Krankenwagen) ambulance man; (Mil) (medical) orderly

Sanitätsauto nt ambulance

sank etc [zaŋk] vb siehe **sinken**

Sanktion [zaŋktsi'o:n] f sanction

sanktionieren [zaŋktsio'ni:rən] vt to sanction

sann etc [zan] vb siehe **sinnen**

Saphir ['za:fi:r] (-s, -e) m sapphire

Sarde ['zardə] (-n, -n) m Sardinian

Sardelle [zar'dɛlə] f anchovy

Sardine [zar'di:nə] f sardine

Sardinien [zar'di:niən] (-s) nt Sardinia

Sardinier, in (-s, -) m(f) Sardinian

sardinisch adj Sardinian

sardisch adj Sardinian

Sarg [zark] (-(e)s, ⸚e) m coffin; **Sargnagel** (umg) m (Zigarette) coffin nail

Sarkasmus [zar'kasmʊs] m sarcasm

sarkastisch [zar'kastɪʃ] adj sarcastic

SARS, Sars [zars] abk (= Schweres Akutes Respiratorisches Syndrom) SARS

saß etc [zas] vb siehe **sitzen**

Satan ['za:tan] (-s, -e) m Satan; (fig) devil

Satansbraten m (hum: umg) young devil

Satellit [zatɛ'li:t] (-en, -en) m satellite

Satelliten- zW: **Satellitenantenne** f satellite dish; **Satellitenfernsehen** nt satellite television; **Satellitenfoto** nt satellite picture; **Satellitenschüssel** f satellite dish; **Satellitenstation** f space station

Satin [za'tɛ̃:] (-s, -s) m satin

Satire [za'ti:rə] (-, -n) f: **~ (auf** +akk) satire (on)

Satiriker [za'ti:rikər] (-s, -) m satirist

satirisch [za'ti:rɪʃ] adj satirical

satt [zat] adj full; (Farbe) rich, deep; (blasiert, übersättigt) well-fed; (selbstgefällig) smug; **jdn/etw ~ sein** to be fed-up with sb/sth; **sich ~ essen** to eat one's fill; **~ machen** to be filling; siehe auch **satthaben; satthören; sattsehen**

Sattel ['zatəl] (-s, ⸚) m saddle; (Berg) ridge; **sattelfest** adj (fig) proficient

satteln vt to saddle

Sattelschlepper m articulated lorry (Brit), artic (Brit umg), semitrailer (US), semi (US umg)

Satteltasche f saddlebag; (Gepäcktasche am Fahrrad) pannier

satthaben unreg vt: **jdn/etw ~** to be fed up with sb/sth

satthören vr: **sich ~ an** +dat to hear enough of

sättigen ['zɛtɪgən] vt to satisfy; (Chem) to saturate

Sattler (-s, -) m saddler; (Polsterer) upholsterer

sattsehen unreg vt: **sich ~ an** +dat to see enough of

Satz [zats] (-es, ⸚e) m (Gram) sentence; (Nebensatz, Adverbialsatz) clause; (Theorem) theorem; (der gesetzte Text) type; (Mus) movement; (Comput) record; (Briefmarken, Zusammengehöriges, Tennis) set; (Kaffeesatz) grounds pl; (Bodensatz) dregs pl; (Spesensatz) allowance; (Comm) rate; (Sprung) jump; **Satzbau** m sentence construction; **Satzgegenstand** m (Gram) subject; **Satzlehre** f syntax; **Satzteil** m constituent (of a sentence)

Satzung f statute, rule; (Firma) (memorandum and) articles of association

satzungsgemäß adj statutory

Satzzeichen nt punctuation mark

Sau [zaʊ] (-, **Säue**) f sow; (umg) dirty pig; **die ~ rauslassen** (fig: umg) to let it all hang out

sauber ['zaʊbər] adj clean; (anständig) honest, upstanding; (umg: großartig) fantastic, great; (: ironisch) fine; **~ sein** (Kind) to be (potty-)trained; (Hund etc) to be house-trained; **~ halten** to keep clean; **~ machen** to clean; **Sauberkeit** f cleanness; (einer Person) cleanliness

säuberlich ['zɔʏbərlɪç] adv neatly

säubern vt to clean; (Pol etc) to purge

Säuberung f cleaning; purge

Säuberungsaktion f cleaning-up operation; (Pol) purge

saublöd (umg) adj bloody (Brit!) od damn (!) stupid

Saubohne f broad bean

Sauce ['zo:sə] (-, -n) f = **Soße**

Sauciere [zosi'e:rə] (-, -n) f sauce boat

Saudi- [zaʊdi-] zW: **Saudi-Araber, in** m(f) Saudi; **Saudi-Arabien** (-s) nt Saudi Arabia; **saudi-arabisch** adj Saudi-(Arabian)

sauer ['zaʊər] adj sour; (Chem) acid; (umg) cross; **saurer Regen** acid rain; **~ werden** (Milch, Sahne) to go sour, turn; **jdm das Leben ~ machen** to make sb's life a misery; **Sauerbraten** m braised beef (marinaded in vinegar), sauerbraten (US)

Sauerei [zaʊə'raɪ] (umg) f rotten state of affairs, scandal; (Schmutz etc) mess; (Unanständigkeit) obscenity

Sauerkirsche f sour cherry

Sauerkraut (-(e)s) nt sauerkraut, pickled cabbage

säuerlich ['zɔʏərlɪç] adj sourish, tart

Sauer- zW: **Sauermilch** f sour milk; **Sauerstoff** m oxygen; **Sauerstoffgerät** nt breathing apparatus; **Sauerteig** m leaven

saufen ['zaʊfən] unreg (umg) vt, vi to drink, booze; **wie ein Loch ~** (umg) to drink like a fish

Säufer, in ['zɔʏfər(ɪn)] (-s, -) (umg) m(f) boozer, drunkard

Sauferei [zaʊfə'raɪ] f drinking, boozing; (Saufgelage) booze-up

Saufgelage (pej: umg) nt drinking bout, booze-up

säuft [zɔʏft] vb siehe **saufen**

saugen ['zaʊgən] unreg vt, vi to suck

S

säugen ['zɔygən] vt to suckle

Sauger ['zaʊgər] (**-s,** -) m dummy (Brit), pacifier (US); (auf Flasche) teat; (Staubsauger) vacuum cleaner, hoover® (Brit)

Säugetier nt mammal

saugfähig adj absorbent

Säugling m infant, baby

Säuglingsschwester f infant nurse

Sau- zW: **Sauhaufen** (umg) m bunch of layabouts; **saukalt** (umg) adj bloody (Brit!) od damn (!) cold; **Sauklaue** (umg) f scrawl

Säule ['zɔylə] (**-, -n**) f column, pillar

Säulengang m arcade

Saum [zaʊm] (**-(e)s, Säume**) m hem; (Naht) seam

saumäßig (umg) adj lousy ▷ adv lousily

säumen ['zɔymən] vt to hem; to seam ▷ vi to delay, hesitate

säumig ['zɔymɪç] adj (geh: Schuldner) defaulting; (Zahlung) outstanding, overdue

Sauna ['zaʊna] (**-, -s**) f sauna

Säure ['zɔyrə] (**-, -n**) f acid; (Geschmack) sourness, acidity; **säurebeständig** adj acid-proof

Saure-Gurken-Zeit (-) f (hum: umg) bad time od period; (in den Medien) silly season

säurehaltig adj acidic

Saurier ['zaʊriər] (**-s, -**) m dinosaur

Saus [zaʊs] (**-es**) m: **in ~ und Braus leben** to live like a lord

säuseln ['zɔyzəln] vi to murmur; (Blätter) to rustle ▷ vt to murmur

sausen ['zaʊzən] vi to blow; (umg: eilen) to rush; (Ohren) to buzz; **etw ~ lassen** (umg) not to bother with sth

Sau- zW: **Saustall** (umg) m pigsty; **Sauwetter** (umg) nt bloody (Brit!) od damn (!) awful weather; **sauwohl** (umg) adj: **ich fühle mich sauwohl** I feel bloody (Brit!) od really good

Saxofon, Saxophon [zakso'foːn] (**-s, -e**) nt saxophone

SB abk = **Selbstbedienung**

S-Bahn f abk (= Schnellbahn) high-speed suburban railway or railroad (US)

SBB abk (= Schweizerische Bundesbahnen) Swiss Railways

s. Br. abk (= südlicher Breite) southern latitude

Schabe ['ʃaːbə] (**-, -n**) f cockroach

schaben vt to scrape

Schaber (**-s, -**) m scraper

Schabernack (**-(e)s, -e**) m trick, prank

schäbig ['ʃɛːbɪç] adj shabby; (Mensch) mean; **Schäbigkeit** f shabbiness

Schablone [ʃa'bloːnə] (**-, -n**) f stencil; (Muster) pattern; (fig) convention

schablonenhaft adj stereotyped, conventional

Schach [ʃax] (**-s, -s**) nt chess; (Stellung) check; **im ~ stehen** to be in check; **jdn in ~ halten** (fig) to stall sb; **Schachbrett** nt chessboard

schachern (pej) vi: **um etw ~** to haggle over sth

Schach- zW: **Schachfigur** f chessman; **schachmatt** adj checkmate; **jdn schachmatt setzen** (lit) to (check)mate sb; (fig) to snooker

sb (umg); **Schachpartie** f game of chess; **Schachspiel** nt game of chess

Schacht [ʃaxt] (**-(e)s, ⁻e**) m shaft

Schachtel (**-, -n**) f box; (pej: Frau) bag, cow (Brit); **Schachtelsatz** m complicated od multi-clause sentence

Schachzug m (auch fig) move

schade ['ʃaːdə] adj a pity od shame ▷ interj (what a) pity od shame; **sich dat für etw zu ~ sein** to consider o.s. too good for sth; **um sie ist es nicht ~** she's no great loss

Schädel ['ʃɛːdəl] (**-s, -**) m skull; **einen dicken ~ haben** (fig: umg) to be stubborn; **Schädelbruch** m fractured skull

Schaden (**-s, ⁻**) m damage; (Verletzung) injury; (Nachteil) disadvantage; **zu ~ kommen** to suffer; (physisch) to be injured; **jdm ~ zufügen** to harm sb

schaden ['ʃaːdən] vi +dat to hurt; **einer Sache ~** to damage sth

Schaden- zW: **Schadenersatz** m compensation, damages pl; **Schadenersatz leisten** to pay compensation; **Schadenersatzanspruch** m claim for compensation; **schadenersatzpflichtig** adj liable for damages; **Schadenfreiheitsrabatt** m (Versicherung) no-claim(s) bonus; **Schadenfreude** f malicious delight; **schadenfroh** adj gloating

schadhaft ['ʃaːthaft] adj faulty, damaged

schädigen ['ʃɛːdɪgən] vt to damage; (Person) to do harm to, harm

Schädigung f damage; harm

schädlich adj: **~ (für)** harmful (to); **Schädlichkeit** f harmfulness

Schädling m pest

Schädlingsbekämpfungsmittel nt pesticide

schadlos ['ʃaːtloːs] adj: **sich ~ halten an** +dat to take advantage of

Schadstoff (**-(e)s, -e**) m pollutant; **schadstoffarm** adj low in pollutants; **schadstoffhaltig** adj containing pollutants

Schaf [ʃaːf] (**-(e)s, -e**) nt sheep; (umg: Dummkopf) twit (Brit), dope; **Schafbock** m ram

Schäfchen ['ʃɛːfçən] nt lamb; **sein ~ ins Trockene bringen** (Sprichwort) to see o.s. all right (umg); **Schäfchenwolken** pl cirrus clouds pl

Schäfer ['ʃɛːfər] (**-s, -**) m shepherd; **Schäferhund** m Alsatian (dog) (Brit), German shepherd (dog) (US); **Schäferin** f shepherdess

Schaffen ['ʃafən] (**-s**) nt (creative) activity

schaffen¹ unreg vt to create; (Platz) to make; **sich dat etw ~** to get o.s. sth; **dafür ist er wie ge-** he's just made for it

schaffen² ['ʃafən] vt (erreichen) to manage, do; (erledigen) to finish; (Prüfung) to pass; (transportieren) to take ▷ vi (tun) to do; (umg: arbeiten) to work; **das ist nicht zu ~** that can't be done; **das hat mich geschafft** it took it out of me; (nervlich) it got on top of me; **ich habe damit nichts zu ~** that has nothing to do with me; **jdm (schwer) zu ~**

machen (*zusetzen*) to cause sb (a lot of) trouble; (*bekümmern*) to worry sb (a lot); **sich** *dat* **an etw** *dat* **zu ~ machen** to busy o.s. with sth

Schaffensdrang *m* energy; (*von Künstler*) creative urge

Schaffenskraft *f* creativity

Schaffner, in ['ʃafnər(ɪn)] **(-s, -)** *m(f)* (*Busschaffner*) conductor, conductress; (*Eisenb*) guard (*Brit*), conductor (*US*)

Schaffung *f* creation

Schafskäse *m* sheep's *od* ewe's milk cheese

Schaft [ʃaft] **(-(e)s, ⁻e)** *m* shaft; (*von Gewehr*) stock; (*von Stiefel*) leg; (*Bot*) stalk; (*von Baum*) tree trunk; **Schaftstiefel** *m* high boot

Schakal [ʃa'kaːl] **(-s, -e)** *m* jackal

Schäker, in ['ʃɛːkər(ɪn)] **(-s, -)** *m(f)* flirt; (*Witzbold*) joker

schäkern *vi* to flirt; to joke

Schal [ʃaːl] **(-s, -s** *od* **-e)** *m* scarf

schal *adj* flat; (*fig*) insipid

Schälchen ['ʃɛːlçən] *nt* bowl

Schale ['ʃaːlə] **(-, -n)** *f* skin; (*abgeschält*) peel; (*Nussschale, Muschelschale, Eierschale*) shell; (*Geschirr*) dish, bowl; **sich in ~ werfen** (*umg*) to get dressed up

schälen ['ʃɛːlən] *vt* to peel; to shell ▷ *vr* to peel

Schalk [ʃalk] **(-s, -e** *od* **⁻e)** *m* (*veraltet*) joker

Schall [ʃal] **(-(e)s, -e)** *m* sound; **Name ist ~ und Rauch** what's in a name?; **schalldämmend** *adj* sound-deadening; **Schalldämpfer** *m* (*Aut*) silencer (*Brit*), muffler (*US*); **schalldicht** *adj* soundproof

schallen *vi* to (re)sound

schallend *adj* resounding, loud

Schall- *zW:* **Schallgeschwindigkeit** *f* speed of sound; **Schallgrenze** *f* sound barrier; **Schallmauer** *f* sound barrier; **Schallplatte** *f* record

schalt *etc* [ʃalt] *vb siehe* **schelten**

Schaltbild *nt* circuit diagram

Schaltbrett *nt* switchboard

schalten ['ʃaltən] *vt* to switch, turn ▷ *vi* (*Aut*) to change (gear); (*umg: begreifen*) to catch on; (*reagieren*) to react; **in Reihe/parallel ~** (*Elek*) to connect in series/in parallel; **~ und walten** to do as one pleases

Schalter (-s, -) *m* counter; (*an Gerät*) switch; **Schalterbeamte, r** *m* counter clerk; **Schalterstunden** *pl* hours of business *pl*

Schalt- *zW:* **Schalthebel** *m* switch; (*Aut*) gear lever (*Brit*), gearshift (*US*); **Schaltjahr** *nt* leap year; **Schaltknüppel** *m* (*Aut*) gear lever (*Brit*), gearshift (*US*); (*Aviat, Comput*) joystick; **Schaltkreis** *m* (switching) circuit; **Schaltplan** *m* circuit diagram; **Schaltpult** *nt* control desk; **Schaltstelle** *f* (*fig*) coordinating point; **Schaltuhr** *f* time switch

Schaltung *f* switching; (*Elek*) circuit; (*Aut*) gear change

Scham [ʃaːm] **(-)** *f* shame; (*Schamgefühl*) modesty; (*Organe*) private parts *pl*

schämen ['ʃɛːmən] *vr* to be ashamed

Scham- *zW:* **Schamgefühl** *nt* sense of shame;

Schamhaare *pl* pubic hair *sing*; **schamhaft** *adj* modest; bashful; **Schamlippen** *pl* labia *pl*, lips *pl* of the vulva; **schamlos** *adj* shameless; (*unanständig*) indecent; (*Lüge*) brazen, barefaced

Schampus ['ʃampʊs] **(-, no pl)** (*umg*) *m* champagne, champers (*Brit*)

Schande ['ʃandə] **(-)** *f* disgrace; **zu meiner ~ muss ich gestehen, dass ...** to my shame I have to admit that ...

schänden ['ʃɛndən] *vt* to violate

Schandfleck ['ʃantflɛk] *m:* **er war der ~ der Familie** he was the disgrace of his family

schändlich ['ʃɛntlɪç] *adj* disgraceful, shameful; **Schändlichkeit** *f* disgracefulness, shamefulness

Schandtat (*umg*) *f* escapade, shenanigan

Schändung *f* violation, defilement

Schänke ['ʃɛŋkə] **(-, -n)** *f* = **Schenke**

Schank- *zW:* **Schankerlaubnis** *f*, **Schankkonzession** *f* (publican's) licence (*Brit*), excise license (*US*); **Schanktisch** *m* bar

Schanze ['ʃantsə] **(-, -n)** *f* (*Mil*) fieldwork, earthworks *pl*; (*Sprungschanze*) ski jump

Schar [ʃaːr] **(-, -en)** *f* band, company; (*Vögel*) flock; (*Menge*) crowd; **in ~en** in droves

Scharade [ʃa'raːdə] **(-, -n)** *f* charade

scharen *vr* to assemble, rally

scharenweise *adv* in droves

scharf [ʃarf] *adj* sharp; (*Verstand, Augen*) keen; (*Kälte, Wind*) biting; (*Protest*) fierce; (*Ton*) piercing, shrill; (*Essen*) hot, spicy; (*Munition*) live; (*Maßnahmen*) severe; (*Bewachung*) close, tight; (*Geruch, Geschmack*) pungent, acrid; (*umg: geil*) randy (*Brit*), horny; (*Film*) sexy, blue *attrib*; **~ nachdenken** to think hard; **~ aufpassen/zuhören** to pay close attention/listen closely; **etw ~ einstellen** (*Bild, Diaprojektor etc*) to bring sth into focus; **mit ~em Blick** (*fig*) with penetrating insight; **auf etw** *akk* **~ sein** (*umg*) to be keen on sth; **~e Sachen** (*umg*) hard stuff

Scharfblick *m* (*fig*) penetration

Schärfe ['ʃɛrfə] **(-, -n)** *f* sharpness; (*Strenge*) rigour (*Brit*), rigor (*US*); (*an Kamera, Fernsehen*) focus

schärfen *vt* to sharpen

Schärfentiefe *f* (*Phot*) depth of focus

Scharf- *zW:* **scharfmachen** (*umg*) *vt* to stir up; **Scharfrichter** *m* executioner; **Scharfschießen** *nt* shooting with live ammunition; **Scharfschütze** *m* marksman, sharpshooter; **Scharfsinn** *m* astuteness, shrewdness; **scharfsinnig** *adj* astute, shrewd

Scharlach ['ʃarlax] **(-s, -e)** *m* scarlet; (*Krankheit*) scarlet fever; **Scharlachfieber** *nt* scarlet fever

Scharlatan ['ʃarlatan] **(-s, -e)** *m* charlatan

Scharmützel [ʃar'mʏtsəl] **(-s, -)** *nt* skirmish

Scharnier [ʃar'niːr] **(-s, -e)** *nt* hinge

Schärpe ['ʃɛrpə] **(-, -n)** *f* sash

scharren ['ʃarən] *vt, vi* to scrape, scratch

Scharte ['ʃartə] **(-, -n)** *f* notch, nick; (*Berg*) wind gap

schartig ['ʃartɪç] *adj* jagged

S

Schaschlik ['ʃaʃlɪk] (**-s, -s**) m od nt (shish) kebab
Schatten ['ʃatən] (**-s, -**) m shadow; (schattige Stelle) shade; **jdn/etw in den ~ stellen** (fig) to put sb/sth in the shade; **Schattenbild** nt silhouette; **schattenhaft** adj shadowy
Schattenmorelle (**-, -n**) f morello cherry
Schatten- zW: **Schattenriss** m silhouette; **Schattenseite** f shady side; (von Planeten) dark side; (fig: Nachteil) drawback; **Schattenwirtschaft** f black economy
schattieren [ʃa'tiːrən] vt, vi to shade
Schattierung f shading
schattig ['ʃatɪç] adj shady
Schatulle [ʃa'tʊlə] (**-, -n**) f casket; (Geldschatulle) coffer
Schatz [ʃats] (**-es, ̈e**) m treasure; (Person) darling; **Schatzamt** nt treasury
schätzbar ['ʃɛtsbaːr] adj assessable
Schätzchen nt darling, love
schätzen vt (abschätzen) to estimate; (Gegenstand) to value; (würdigen) to value, esteem; (vermuten) to reckon; **etw zu ~ wissen** to appreciate sth; **sich glücklich ~** to consider o.s. lucky; **~ lernen** to learn to appreciate
Schatzkammer f treasure chamber od vault
Schatzmeister m treasurer
Schätzung f estimate; estimation; valuation; **nach meiner ~ ...** I reckon that ...
schätzungsweise adv (ungefähr) approximately; (so vermutet man) it is thought
Schätzwert m estimated value
Schau [ʃaʊ] (**-**) f show; (Ausstellung) display, exhibition; **etw zur ~ stellen** to make a show of sth, show sth off; **eine ~ abziehen** (umg) to put on a show; **Schaubild** nt diagram
Schauder ['ʃaʊdər] (**-s, -**) m shudder; (wegen Kälte) shiver; **schauderhaft** adj horrible
schaudern vi to shudder; (wegen Kälte) to shiver
schauen ['ʃaʊən] vi to look; **da schau her!** well, well!
Schauer ['ʃaʊər] (**-s, -**) m (Regenschauer) shower; (Schreck) shudder; **Schauergeschichte** f horror story; **schauerlich** adj horrific, spine-chilling; **Schauermärchen** (umg) nt horror story
Schaufel ['ʃaʊfəl] (**-, -n**) f shovel; (Kehrichtschaufel) dustpan; (von Turbine) vane; (Naut) paddle; (Tech) scoop
schaufeln vt to shovel; (Grab, Grube) to dig ▷ vi to shovel
Schaufenster nt shop window; **Schaufensterauslage** f window display; **Schaufensterbummel** m window-shopping (expedition); **Schaufensterdekorateur, in** m(f) window dresser; **Schaufensterpuppe** f display dummy
Schaugeschäft nt show business
Schaukasten m showcase
Schaukel ['ʃaʊkəl] (**-, -n**) f swing
schaukeln vi to swing, rock ▷ vt to rock; **wir werden das Kind od das schon ~** (fig: umg) we'll manage it
Schaukelpferd nt rocking horse
Schaukelstuhl m rocking chair

Schaulustige, r ['ʃaʊlʊstɪgə(r)] f(m) onlooker
Schaum [ʃaʊm] (**-(e)s, Schäume**) m foam; (Seifenschaum) lather; (von Getränken) froth; (von Bier) head; **Schaumbad** nt bubble bath
schäumen ['ʃɔymən] vi to foam
Schaumgummi m foam (rubber)
schaumig adj frothy, foamy
Schaum- zW: **Schaumkrone** f whitecap; **Schaumschläger** m (fig) windbag; **Schaumschlägerei** f (fig: umg) hot air; **Schaumstoff** m foam material; **Schaumwein** m sparkling wine
Schauplatz m scene
Schauprozess m show trial
schaurig adj horrific, dreadful
Schauspiel nt spectacle; (Theat) play
Schauspieler, in m(f) actor, actress; **schauspielerisch** adj (Können, Leistung) acting
schauspielern vi untr to act
Schauspielhaus nt playhouse, theatre (Brit), theater (US)
Schauspielschule f drama school
Schausteller ['ʃaʊʃtɛlər] (**-s, -**) m person who owns or runs a fairground ride/sideshow etc
Scheck [ʃɛk] (**-s, -s**) m cheque (Brit), check (US); **Scheckbuch** nt, **Scheckheft** nt cheque book (Brit), check book (US)
scheckig adj dappled, piebald
Scheckkarte f cheque (Brit) od check (US) card, banker's card
scheel [ʃeːl] (umg) adj dirty; **jdn ~ ansehen** to give sb a dirty look
scheffeln ['ʃefəln] vt to amass
Scheibe ['ʃaɪbə] (**-, -n**) f disc (Brit), disk (US); (Brot etc) slice; (Glasscheibe) pane; (Mil) target; (Eishockey) puck; (Töpferscheibe) wheel; (umg: Schallplatte) disc (Brit), disk (US); **von ihm könntest du dir eine ~ abschneiden** (fig: umg) you could take a leaf out of his book
Scheiben- zW: **Scheibenbremse** f (Aut) disc brake; **Scheibenkleister** interj (euph: umg) sugar!; **Scheibenwaschanlage** f (Aut) windscreen (Brit) od windshield (US) washers pl; **Scheibenwischer** m (Aut) windscreen (Brit) od windshield (US) wiper
Scheich [ʃaɪç] (**-s, -e** od **-s**) m sheik(h)
Scheide ['ʃaɪdə] (**-, -n**) f sheath; (Anat) vagina
scheiden unreg vt to separate; (Ehe) to dissolve ▷ vi to depart; (sich trennen) to part ▷ vr (Wege) to divide; (Meinungen) to diverge; **sich ~ lassen** to get a divorce; **von dem Moment an waren wir (zwei) geschiedene Leute** (umg) after that it was the parting of the ways for us; **aus dem Leben ~** to depart this life
Scheideweg m (fig) crossroads sing
Scheidung f (Ehescheidung) divorce; **die ~ einreichen** to file a petition for divorce
Scheidungsgrund m grounds pl for divorce
Scheidungsklage f divorce suit
Schein [ʃaɪn] (**-(e)s, -e**) m light; (Anschein) appearance; (Geldschein) (bank)note; (Bescheinigung) certificate; **den ~ wahren** to keep up appearances; **etw zum ~ tun**

to pretend to do sth, make a pretence (*Brit*) *od* pretense (*US*) of doing sth; **scheinbar** *adj* apparent

scheinen *unreg vi* to shine; (*Anschein haben*) to seem

Schein- *zW*: **scheinheilig** *adj* hypocritical; **Scheintod** *m* apparent death; **Scheinwerfer** (**-s, -**) *m* floodlight; (*Theat*) spotlight; (*Suchscheinwerfer*) searchlight; (*Aut*) headlight

Scheiß [ʃaɪs] (**-, *no pl***) (*umg!*) *m* bullshit (!)

Scheiß- ['ʃaɪs-] (*umg!*) *in zw* bloody (*Brit!*); **Scheißdreck** (*umg!*) *m* shit (!), crap (!); **das geht dich einen Scheißdreck an** it's got bugger-all to do with you (!)

Scheiße ['ʃaɪsə] (**-**) (*umg!*) *f* shit (!)

scheißegal (*umg!*) *adj*: **das ist mir doch ~!** I don't give a shit (!)

scheißen (*umg!*) *vi* to shit (!)

scheißfreundlich (*pej: umg*) *adj* as nice as pie (*ironisch*)

Scheißkerl (*umg!*) *m* bastard (!), son-of-a-bitch (*US!*)

Scheit [ʃaɪt] (**-(e)s, -e** *od* **-er**) *nt* log

Scheitel ['ʃaɪtəl] (**-s, -**) *m* top; (*Haar*) parting (*Brit*), part (*US*)

scheiteln *vt* to part

Scheitelpunkt *m* zenith, apex

Scheiterhaufen ['ʃaɪtərhaufən] *m* (funeral) pyre; (*Hist: zur Hinrichtung*) stake

scheitern ['ʃaɪtərn] *vi* to fail

Schelle ['ʃɛlə] (**-, -n**) *f* small bell

schellen *vi* to ring; **es hat geschellt** the bell has gone

Schellfisch ['ʃɛlfɪʃ] *m* haddock

Schelm [ʃɛlm] (**-(e)s, -e**) *m* rogue

Schelmenroman *m* picaresque novel

schelmisch *adj* mischievous, roguish

Schelte ['ʃɛltə] (**-, -n**) *f* scolding

schelten *unreg vt* to scold

Schema ['ʃeːma] (**-s, -s** *od* **-ta**) *nt* scheme, plan; (*Darstellung*) schema; **nach ~ F** quite mechanically

schematisch [ʃeˈmaːtɪʃ] *adj* schematic; (*pej*) mechanical

Schemel ['ʃeːməl] (**-s, -**) *m* (foot)stool

schemenhaft *adj* shadowy

Schenke (**-, -n**) *f* tavern, inn

Schenkel ['ʃɛŋkəl] (**-s, -**) *m* thigh; (*Math: von Winkel*) side

schenken ['ʃɛŋkən] *vt* (*lit, fig*) to give; (*Getränk*) to pour; **ich möchte nichts geschenkt haben!** (*lit*) I don't want any presents!; (*fig: bevorzugt werden*) I don't want any special treatment!; **sich** *dat* **etw ~** (*umg*) to skip sth; **jdm etw ~** (*erlassen*) to let sb off sth; **ihm ist nie etwas geschenkt worden** (*fig*) he never had it easy; **das ist geschenkt!** (*billig*) that's a giveaway!; (*nichts wert*) that's worthless!

Schenkung *f* gift

Schenkungsurkunde *f* deed of gift

scheppern ['ʃɛpərn] (*umg*) *vi* to clatter

Scherbe ['ʃɛrbə] (**-, -n**) *f* broken piece, fragment; (*archäologisch*) potsherd

Schere ['ʃeːrə] (**-, -n**) *f* scissors *pl*; (*groß*) shears *pl*; (*Zool*) pincer; (*von Hummer, Krebs etc*) pincer, claw; **eine ~** a pair of scissors

scheren *unreg vt* to cut; (*Schaf*) to shear; (*stören*) to bother ▷ *vr* (*sich kümmern*) to care; **scher dich (zum Teufel)!** get lost!

Scherenschleifer (**-s, -**) *m* knife grinder

Scherenschnitt *m* silhouette

Schererei [ʃeːrəˈraɪ] *f* bother, trouble

Scherflein ['ʃɛrflaɪn] *nt* mite, bit

Scherz [ʃɛrts] (**-es, -e**) *m* joke; fun; **scherzen** *vi* to joke; (*albern*) to banter; **Scherzfrage** *f* conundrum; **scherzhaft** *adj* joking, jocular

Scheu [ʃɔy] (**-**) *f* shyness; (*Ehrfurcht*) awe; (*Angst*): **~ (vor** +*dat*) fear (of)

scheu [ʃɔy] *adj* shy

Scheuche (**-, -n**) *f* scarecrow

scheuchen ['ʃɔyçən] *vt* to scare (off)

scheuen *vr*: **sich ~ vor** +*dat* to be afraid of, shrink from ▷ *vt* to shun ▷ *vi* (*Pferd*) to shy; **weder Mühe noch Kosten ~** to spare neither trouble nor expense

Scheuer ['ʃɔyər] (**-, -n**) *f* barn

Scheuer- *zW*: **Scheuerbürste** *f* scrubbing brush; **Scheuerlappen** *m* floorcloth (*Brit*), scrubbing rag (*US*); **Scheuerleiste** *f* skirting board

scheuern *vt* to scour; (*mit Bürste*) to scrub ▷ *vr*: **sich** *akk* **(wund) ~** to chafe o.s.; **jdm eine ~** (*umg*) to clout sb one

Scheuklappe *f* blinker

Scheune ['ʃɔynə] (**-, -n**) *f* barn

Scheunendrescher (**-s, -**) *m*: **er frisst wie ein ~** (*umg*) he eats like a horse

Scheusal ['ʃɔyzaːl] (**-s, -e**) *nt* monster

scheußlich ['ʃɔyslɪç] *adj* dreadful, frightful; **Scheußlichkeit** *f* dreadfulness

Schi [ʃiː] *m* = **Ski**

Schicht [ʃɪçt] (**-, -en**) *f* layer; (*Klasse*) class, level; (*in Fabrik etc*) shift; **Schichtarbeit** *f* shift work

schichten *vt* to layer, stack

Schichtwechsel *m* change of shifts

schick [ʃɪk] *adj* = **chic**

schicken [ʃɪk] *vt* to send ▷ *vr*: **sich ~ (in** +*akk*) to resign o.s. (to) ▷ *vb unpers* (*anständig sein*) to be fitting

Schickeria [ʃɪkəˈriːa] *f* (*ironisch*) in-people *pl*

Schicki ['ʃɪki], **Schickimicki** ['ʃɪkiˈmɪki] (**-s, -s**) (*umg*) *m* trendy

schicklich *adj* proper, fitting

Schicksal (**-s, -e**) *nt* fate

schicksalhaft *adj* fateful

Schicksalsschlag *m* great misfortune, blow

Schickse ['ʃɪksə] (**-, -n**) (*umg*) *f* floozy, shiksa (*US*)

Schiebedach *nt* (*Aut*) sunroof, sunshine roof

schieben ['ʃiːbən] *unreg vt* (*auch Drogen*) to push; (*Schuld*) to put; (*umg: handeln mit*) to traffic in; **die Schuld auf jdn ~** to put the blame on (to) sb; **etw vor sich** *dat* **her ~** (*fig*) to put sth off

Schieber (**-s, -**) *m* slide; (*Besteckteil*) pusher; (*Person*) profiteer; (*umg: Schwarzhändler*) black marketeer; (: *Waffenschieber*) gunrunner;

S

287

(: *Drogenschieber*) pusher

Schiebetür f sliding door

Schieblehre f (*Math*) calliper (*Brit*) od caliper (*US*) rule

Schiebung f fiddle; **das war doch ~** (*umg*) that was rigged od a fix

schied etc [ʃiːt] vb siehe **scheiden**

Schieds- zW: **Schiedsgericht** nt court of arbitration; **Schiedsmann** (-(e)s, pl -**männer**) m arbitrator; **Schiedsrichter** m referee, umpire; (*Schlichter*) arbitrator; **schiedsrichtern** vi untr to referee, umpire; to arbitrate; **Schiedsspruch** m (arbitration) award; **Schiedsverfahren** nt arbitration

schief [ʃiːf] adj crooked; (*Ebene*) sloping; (*Turm*) leaning; (*Winkel*) oblique; (*Blick*) wry; (*Vergleich*) distorted ▷ adv crookedly; (*ansehen*) askance; **auf die ~e Bahn geraten** (*fig*) to leave the straight and narrow; **etw ~ stellen** to slope sth; siehe auch **schiefgehen; schiefliegen**

Schiefer ['ʃiːfər] (-s, -) m slate; **Schieferdach** nt slate roof; **Schiefertafel** f (child's) slate

schiefgehen (*umg*: unreg) vi to go wrong; **es wird schon ~!** (*hum*) it'll be OK

schieflachen (*umg*) vr to kill o.s. laughing

schiefliegen (*umg*: unreg) vi to be wrong, be on the wrong track (*umg*)

schielen ['ʃiːlən] vi to squint; **nach etw ~** (*fig*) to eye sth up

schien etc [ʃiːn] vb siehe **scheinen**

Schienbein nt shinbone

Schiene ['ʃiːnə] f rail; (*Med*) splint

schienen vt to put in splints

Schienenbus m railcar

Schienenstrang m (*Eisenb etc*) (section of) track

schier [ʃiːr] adj pure; (*fig*) sheer ▷ adv nearly, almost

Schießbude f shooting gallery

Schießbudenfigur (*umg*) f clown, ludicrous figure

schießen ['ʃiːsən] unreg vi to shoot; (*Salat etc*) to run to seed ▷ vt to shoot; (*Ball*) to kick; (*Geschoss*) to fire; **~ auf** +akk to shoot at; **aus dem Boden ~** (*lit, fig*) to spring od sprout up; **jdm durch den Kopf ~** (*fig*) to flash through sb's mind

Schießerei [ʃiːsəˈraɪ] f shoot-out, gun battle

Schieß- zW: **Schießgewehr** nt (*hum*) gun; **Schießhund** m: **wie ein Schießhund aufpassen** (*umg*) to watch like a hawk; **Schießplatz** m firing range; **Schießpulver** nt gunpowder; **Schießscharte** f embrasure; **Schießstand** m rifle od shooting range

Schiff [ʃɪf] (-(e)s, -e) nt ship, vessel; (*Kirchenschiff*) nave

Schiffahrt f siehe **Schifffahrt**

Schiff- zw**: schiffbar** adj navigable; **Schiffbau** m shipbuilding; **Schiffbruch** m shipwreck; **Schiffbruch erleiden** (*lit*) to be shipwrecked; (*fig*) to fail; (*Unternehmen*) to founder; **schiffbrüchig** adj shipwrecked

Schiffchen nt small boat; (*Weben*) shuttle; (*Mütze*) forage cap

Schiffer (-s, -) m boatman, sailor; (*von Lastkahn*) bargee

Schiff- zW: **Schifffahrt** f shipping; (*Reise*) voyage; **Schifffahrtslinie** f shipping route; **Schiffschaukel** f swing boat

Schiffs- zW: **Schiffsjunge** m cabin boy; **Schiffskörper** m hull; **Schiffsladung** f cargo, shipload; **Schiffsplanke** f gangplank; **Schiffsschraube** f ship's propeller

Schiit [ʃiˈiːt] (-en, -en) m Shiite; **schiitisch** adj Shiite

Schikane [ʃiˈkaːnə] (-, -n) f harassment; dirty trick; **mit allen ~n** with all the trimmings; **das hat er aus reiner ~ gemacht** he did it out of sheer bloody-mindedness

schikanieren [ʃikaˈniːrən] vt to harass; (*Ehepartner*) to mess around; (*Mitschüler*) to bully

schikanös [ʃikaˈnøːs] adj (*Mensch*) bloody-minded; (*Maßnahme etc*) harassing

Schild¹ [ʃɪlt] (-(e)s, -e) m shield; (*Mützenschild*) peak, visor; **etwas im ~e führen** to be up to something

Schild² [ʃɪlt] (-(e)s, -er) nt sign; (*Namensschild*) nameplate; (*an Monument, Haus, Grab*) plaque; (*Etikett*) label

Schildbürger m duffer, blockhead

Schilddrüse f thyroid gland

schildern ['ʃɪldərn] vt to describe; (*Menschen etc*) to portray; (*skizzieren*) to outline

Schilderung f description; portrayal

Schildkröte f tortoise; (*Wasserschildkröte*) turtle

Schildkrötensuppe f turtle soup

Schilf [ʃɪlf] (-(e)s, -e) nt, **Schilfrohr** nt (*Pflanze*) reed; (*Material*) reeds pl, rushes pl

Schillerlocke ['ʃɪlərlɔkə] f (*Gebäck*) cream horn; (*Räucherfisch*) strip of smoked rock salmon

schillern ['ʃɪlərn] vi to shimmer

schillernd adj iridescent; (*fig: Charakter*) enigmatic

Schilling ['ʃɪlɪŋ] (-s, - od (*Schillingstücke*) -e) (*Österr*) m schilling

schilt [ʃɪlt] vb siehe **schelten**

Schimmel ['ʃɪməl] (-s, -) m mould (*Brit*), mold (*US*); (*Pferd*) white horse

schimmelig adj mouldy (*Brit*), moldy (*US*)

schimmeln vi to go mouldy (*Brit*) od moldy (*US*)

Schimmer ['ʃɪmər] (-s) m glimmer; **keinen (blassen) ~ von etw haben** (*umg*) not to have the slightest idea about sth

schimmern vi to glimmer; (*Seide, Perlen*) to shimmer

schimmlig adj = **schimmelig**

Schimpanse [ʃɪmˈpanzə] (-n, -n) m chimpanzee

Schimpf [ʃɪmpf] (-(e)s, -e) m disgrace; **mit ~ und Schande** in disgrace

schimpfen vi (*sich beklagen*) to grumble; (*fluchen*) to curse

Schimpfkanonade f barrage of abuse

Schimpfwort nt term of abuse

Schindel ['ʃɪndəl] (-, -n) f shingle

schinden ['ʃɪndən] unreg vt to maltreat, drive

too hard ▷ vr: **sich ~ (mit)** to sweat and strain (at), toil away (at); **Eindruck ~** (umg) to create an impression

Schinder (-s, -) m knacker; (fig) slave driver

Schinderei [ʃɪndəˈraɪ] f grind, drudgery

Schindluder [ˈʃɪntluːdər] nt: **mit etw ~ treiben** to muck od mess sth about; (Vorrecht) to abuse sth

Schinken [ˈʃɪŋkən] (-s, -) m ham; (gekocht und geräuchert) gammon; (pej: umg: Theaterstück etc) hackneyed and clichéd play etc; **Schinkenspeck** m bacon

Schippe [ˈʃɪpə] (-, -n) f shovel; **jdn auf die ~ nehmen** (fig: umg) to pull sb's leg

schippen vt to shovel

Schirm [ʃɪrm] (-(e)s, -e) m (Regenschirm) umbrella; (Sonnenschirm) parasol, sunshade; (Wandschirm, Bildschirm) screen; (Lampenschirm) (lamp)shade; (Mützenschirm) peak; (Pilzschirm) cap; **Schirmbildaufnahme** f X-ray; **Schirmherr, in** m(f) patron(ess); **Schirmherrschaft** f patronage; **Schirmmütze** f peaked cap; **Schirmständer** m umbrella stand

Schiss m: **~ haben** (umg) to be shit scared (!)

schiss etc [ʃɪs] vb siehe **scheißen**

schizophren [ʃitsoˈfreːn] adj schizophrenic

Schizophrenie [ʃitsofreˈniː] f schizophrenia

schlabbern [ˈʃlabərn] (umg) vt, vi to slurp

Schlacht [ʃlaxt] (-, -en) f battle

schlachten vt to slaughter, kill

Schlachtenbummler (umg) m visiting football fan

Schlachter (-s, -) m butcher

Schlacht- zW: **Schlachtfeld** nt battlefield; **Schlachtfest** nt country feast at which freshly slaughtered meat is served; **Schlachthaus** nt, **Schlachthof** m slaughterhouse, abattoir (Brit); **Schlachtopfer** nt sacrifice; (Mensch) human sacrifice; **Schlachtplan** m battle plan; (fig) plan of action; **Schlachtruf** m battle cry, war cry; **Schlachtschiff** nt battleship; **Schlachtvieh** nt animals pl kept for meat

Schlacke [ˈʃlakə] (-, -n) f slag

schlackern (umg) vi to tremble; (Kleidung) to hang loosely, be baggy; **mit den Ohren ~** (fig) to be (left) speechless

Schlaf [ʃlaːf] (-(e)s) m sleep; **um seinen ~ kommen** od **gebracht werden** to lose sleep; **Schlafanzug** m pyjamas pl (Brit), pajamas pl (US)

Schläfchen [ˈʃlɛːfçən] nt nap

Schläfe (-, -n) f (Anat) temple

schlafen unreg vi to sleep; (umg: nicht aufpassen) to be asleep; **~ gehen** to go to bed; **bei jdm ~** to stay overnight with sb; **Schlafengehen** nt going to bed

Schlafenszeit f bedtime

Schläfer, in [ˈʃlɛːfər(ɪn)] (-s, -) m(f) sleeper

schlaff [ʃlaf] adj slack; (Haut) loose; (Muskeln) flabby; (energielos) limp; (erschöpft) exhausted; **Schlaffheit** f slackness; looseness; flabbiness; limpness; exhaustion

Schlafgelegenheit f place to sleep

Schlafittchen [ʃlaˈfɪtçən] (umg) nt: **jdn am** od **beim ~ nehmen** to take sb by the scruff of the neck

Schlaf- zW: **Schlafkrankheit** f sleeping sickness; **Schlaflied** nt lullaby; **schlaflos** adj sleepless; **Schlaflosigkeit** f sleeplessness, insomnia; **Schlafmittel** nt sleeping drug; (fig, ironisch) soporific; **Schlafmütze** (umg) f dope

schläfrig [ˈʃlɛːfrɪç] adj sleepy

Schlaf- zW: **Schlafrock** m dressing gown; **Apfel im Schlafrock** baked apple in puff pastry; **Schlafsaal** m dormitory; **Schlafsack** m sleeping bag

schläft [ʃlɛːft] vb siehe **schlafen**

Schlaf- zW: **Schlaftablette** f sleeping pill; **schlaftrunken** adj drowsy, half-asleep; **Schlafwagen** m sleeping car, sleeper; **schlafwandeln** vi untr to sleepwalk; **Schlafwandler, in** (-s, -) m(f) sleepwalker; **Schlafzimmer** nt bedroom

Schlag [ʃlaːk] (-(e)s, ⁻e) m (lit, fig) blow; (auch Med) stroke; (Pulsschlag, Herzschlag) beat; (Elek) shock; (Blitzschlag) bolt, stroke; (Glockenschlag) chime; (Autotür) car door; (umg: Portion) helping; (: Art) kind, type; **Schläge** pl (Tracht Prügel) beating sing; **~ acht Uhr** (umg) on the stroke of eight; **mit einem ~** all at once; **~ auf Schlag** in rapid succession; **die haben keinen ~ getan** (umg) they haven't done a stroke (of work); **ich dachte, mich trifft der ~** (umg) I was thunderstruck; **vom gleichen ~ sein** to be cast in the same mould (Brit) od mold (US); (pej) to be tarred with the same brush; **ein ~ ins Wasser** (umg) a wash-out; **Schlagabtausch** m (Boxen) exchange of blows; (fig) (verbal) exchange; **Schlagader** f artery; **Schlaganfall** m stroke; **schlagartig** adj sudden, without warning; **Schlagbaum** m barrier; **Schlagbohrer** m percussion drill

Schlägel [ˈʃlɛːgl] (-s, -) m drumstick; (Hammer) hammer

schlagen [ˈʃlaːgən] unreg vt to strike, hit; (wiederholt schlagen, besiegen) to beat; (Glocke) to ring; (Stunde) to strike; (Kreis, Bogen) to describe; (Purzelbaum) to do; (Sahne) to whip; (Schlacht) to fight; (einwickeln) to wrap ▷ vi to strike, hit; to beat; to ring; to strike ▷ vr to fight; **um sich ~** to lash out; **ein Ei in die Pfanne ~** to crack an egg into the pan; **eine ge~e Stunde** a full hour; **na ja, ehe ich mich ~ lasse!** (hum: umg) I suppose you could twist my arm; **nach jdm ~** (fig) to take after sb; **sich gut ~** (fig) to do well; **sich nach links/Norden ~** to strike out to the left/(for the) north; **sich auf jds Seite** akk **~** to side with sb; (die Fronten wechseln) to go over to sb

schlagend adj (Beweis) convincing; **~e Wetter** (Min) firedamp

Schlager [ˈʃlaːgər] (-s, -) m (Mus, fig) hit

Schläger [ˈʃlɛːgər] (-s, -) m brawler; (Sport) racket; (Tennis etc) racket; (Golf) club; (Hockeyschläger) hockey stick

S

Schlägerei [ʃlɛːgəˈraɪ] f fight, punch-up

Schlagersänger m pop singer

Schlägertyp (umg) m thug

Schlag- zW: **schlagfertig** adj quick-witted; **Schlagfertigkeit** f ready wit, quickness of repartee; **Schlaginstrument** nt percussion instrument; **Schlagkraft** f (lit, fig) power; (Mil) strike power; (Boxen) punch(ing power); **schlagkräftig** adj powerful; (Beweise) clear-cut; **Schlagloch** nt pothole; **Schlagobers** (-, -) (Österr) nt, **Schlagrahm** m, **Schlagsahne** f (whipped) cream; **Schlagseite** f (Naut) list; **Schlagstock** m (form) truncheon (Brit), nightstick (US)

schlägt [ʃlɛːkt] vb siehe **schlagen**

Schlag- zW: **Schlagwort** nt slogan, catch phrase; **Schlagzeile** f headline; **Schlagzeilen machen** (umg) to hit the headlines; **Schlagzeug** nt drums pl; (in Orchester) percussion; **Schlagzeuger** (-s, -) m drummer; percussionist

schlaksig [ˈʃlaːksɪç] (umg) adj gangling, gawky

Schlamassel [ʃlaˈmasəl] (-s, -) (umg) m mess

Schlamm [ʃlam] (-(e)s, -e) m mud

schlammig adj muddy

Schlampe [ˈʃlampə] (-, -n) (umg) f slattern, slut

schlampen (umg) vi to be sloppy

Schlamperei [ʃlampəˈraɪ] (umg) f disorder, untidiness; (schlechte Arbeit) sloppy work

schlampig (umg) adj slovenly, sloppy

schlang etc [ʃlaŋ] vb siehe **schlingen**

Schlange [ˈʃlaŋə] (-, -n) f snake; (Menschenschlange) queue (Brit), line (US); ~ **stehen** to (form a) queue (Brit), stand in line (US); **eine falsche** ~ a snake in the grass

schlängeln [ˈʃlɛŋəln] vr to twist, wind; (Fluss) to meander

Schlangen- zW: **Schlangenbiss** m snake bite; **Schlangengift** nt snake venom; **Schlangenlinie** f wavy line

schlank [ʃlaŋk] adj slim, slender; **Schlankheit** f slimness, slenderness; **Schlankheitskur** f diet

schlapp [ʃlap] adj limp; (locker) slack; (umg: energielos) listless; (nach Krankheit etc) run-down

Schlappe (-, -n) (umg) f setback

Schlappen (-s, -) (umg) m slipper

schlapp- zW: **Schlappheit** f limpness; slackness; **Schlapphut** m slouch hat; **schlappmachen** (umg) vi to wilt, droop; **Schlappschwanz** (pej: umg) m weakling, softy

Schlaraffenland [ʃlaˈrafənlant] nt land of milk and honey

schlau [ʃlaʊ] adj crafty, cunning; **ich werde nicht** ~ **aus ihm** I don't know what to make of him; **Schlauberger** (-s, -) (umg) m clever Dick

Schlauch [ʃlaʊx] (-(e)s, **Schläuche**) m hose; (in Reifen) inner tube; (umg: Anstrengung) grind; **auf dem** ~ **stehen** (umg) to be in a jam od fix; **Schlauchboot** nt rubber dinghy

schlauchen (umg) vt to tell on, exhaust

schlauchlos adj (Reifen) tubeless

Schläue [ˈʃlɔyə] (-) f cunning

Schlaufe [ˈʃlaʊfə] (-, -n) f loop; (Aufhänger) hanger

Schlauheit f cunning

Schlaukopf m clever Dick

Schlawiner [ʃlaˈviːnər] (-s, -) m (hum: umg) villain, rogue

schlecht [ʃlɛçt] adj bad; (ungenießbar) bad, off (Brit) ▷ adv: **jdm geht es** ~ sb is in a bad way; **heute geht es** ~ today is not very convenient; **er kann** ~ **Nein sagen** he finds it hard to say no, he can't say no; **jdm ist** ~ sb feels sick od ill; ~ **und recht** after a fashion; **auf jdn** ~ **zu sprechen sein** not to have a good word to say for sb; **er hat nicht** ~ **gestaunt** (umg) he wasn't half surprised; siehe auch **schlechtmachen**

schlechterdings adv simply

Schlecht- zW: **Schlechtheit** f badness; **schlechthin** adv simply; **der Dramatiker schlechthin** THE playwright

Schlechtigkeit f badness; (Tat) bad deed

schlechtmachen vt to run down, denigrate

schlecken [ˈʃlɛkən] vt, vi to lick

Schlegel [ˈʃleːgəl] (-s, -) m (Koch) leg; siehe auch **Schlägel**

schleichen [ˈʃlaɪçən] unreg vi to creep, crawl

schleichend adj creeping; (Krankheit, Gift) insidious

Schleichweg m: **auf ~en** (fig) on the quiet

Schleichwerbung f: **eine** ~ a plug

Schleie [ˈʃlaɪə] (-, -n) f tench

Schleier [ˈʃlaɪər] (-s, -) m veil; **Schleiereule** f barn owl; **schleierhaft** (umg) adj: **jdm schleierhaft sein** to be a mystery to sb

Schleife [ˈʃlaɪfə] (-, -n) f (auch Comput) loop; (Band) bow; (Kranzschleife) ribbon

schleifen¹ vt to drag; (Mil: Festung) to raze ▷ vi to drag; **die Kupplung** ~ **lassen** (Aut) to slip the clutch

schleifen² unreg vt to grind; (Edelstein) to cut; (Mil: Soldaten) to drill

Schleifmaschine f sander; (in Fabrik) grinding machine

Schleifstein m grindstone

Schleim [ʃlaɪm] (-(e)s, -e) m slime; (Med) mucus; (Koch) gruel; **Schleimhaut** f mucous membrane

schleimig adj slimy

schlemmen [ˈʃlɛmən] vi to feast

Schlemmer, in (-s, -) m(f) gourmet, bon vivant

Schlemmerei [ʃlɛməˈraɪ] f feasting

schlendern [ˈʃlɛndərn] vi to stroll

Schlendrian [ˈʃlɛndriaːn] (-(e)s) m sloppy way of working

Schlenker [ˈʃlɛŋkər] (-s, -) m swerve

schlenkern vt, vi to swing, dangle

Schleppe [ˈʃlɛpə] (-, -n) f train

schleppen vt to drag; (Auto, Schiff) to tow; (tragen) to lug

schleppend adj dragging; (Bedienung, Abfertigung) sluggish, slow

Schlepper (-s, -) m tractor; (Schiff) tug

Schleppkahn m (canal) barge

Schlepptau nt towrope; **jdn ins ~ nehmen** (fig) to take sb in tow

Schlesien ['ʃleːziən] (-s) nt Silesia

Schlesier, in (-s, -) m(f) Silesian

schlesisch adj Silesian

Schleswig-Holstein ['ʃleːsvɪçˈhɔlʃtaɪn] (-s) nt Schleswig-Holstein

Schleuder ['ʃlɔydər] (-, -n) f catapult; (Wäscheschleuder) spin-dryer; (Zentrifuge) centrifuge; **Schleuderhonig** m extracted honey

schleudern vt to hurl; (Wäsche) to spin-dry ▷ vi (Aut) to skid; **ins S~ kommen** (Aut) to go into a skid; (fig: umg) to run into trouble

Schleuder- zW: **Schleuderpreis** m give-away price; **Schleudersitz** m (Aviat) ejector seat; (fig) hot seat; **Schleuderware** f cut-price (Brit) od cut-rate (US) goods pl

schleunig ['ʃlɔynɪç] adj prompt, speedy; (Schritte) quick

schleunigst adv straight away

Schleuse ['ʃlɔyzə] (-, -n) f lock; (Schleusentor) sluice

schleusen vt (Schiffe) to pass through a lock, lock; (Wasser) to channel; (Menschen) to filter; (fig: heimlich) to smuggle

Schlich (-(e)s, -e) m dodge, trick; **jdm auf die ~e kommen** to get wise to sb

schlich etc [ʃlɪç] vb siehe **schleichen**

schlicht [ʃlɪçt] adj simple, plain

schlichten vt to smooth; (beilegen) to settle; (Streit: vermitteln) to mediate, arbitrate

Schlichter, in (-s, -) m(f) mediator, arbitrator

Schlichtheit f simplicity, plainness

Schlichtung f settlement; arbitration

Schlick [ʃlɪk] (-(e)s, -e) m mud; (Ölschlick) slick

schlief etc [ʃliːf] vb siehe **schlafen**

Schließe ['ʃliːsə] (-, -n) f fastener

schließen ['ʃliːsən] unreg vt to close, shut; (beenden) to close; (Freundschaft, Bündnis, Ehe) to enter into; (Comput: Datei) to close; (folgern): **~ (aus)** to infer (from) ▷ vi, vr to close, shut; **auf etw** akk **~ lassen** to suggest sth; **jdn/etw in sein Herz ~** to take sb/sth to one's heart; **etw in sich ~** to include sth; **„geschlossen"** "closed"

Schließfach nt locker

schließlich adv finally; (schließlich doch) after all

Schliff (-(e)s, -e) m cut(ting); (fig) polish; **einer Sache den letzten ~ geben** (fig) to put the finishing touch(es) to sth

schliff etc [ʃlɪf] vb siehe **schleifen**

schlimm [ʃlɪm] adj bad; **das war ~** that was terrible; **das ist halb so ~!** that's not so bad!; **schlimmer** adj worse; **schlimmste, r, s** adj worst

schlimmstenfalls adv at (the) worst

Schlinge ['ʃlɪŋə] (-, -n) f loop; (an Galgen) noose; (Falle) snare; (Med) sling

Schlingel (-s, -) m rascal

schlingen unreg vt to wind ▷ vi (essen) to bolt one's food, gobble

schlingern vi to roll

Schlingpflanze f creeper

Schlips [ʃlɪps] (-es, -e) m tie, necktie (US); **sich auf den ~ getreten fühlen** (fig: umg) to feel offended

Schlitten ['ʃlɪtən] (-s, -) m sledge, sled; (Pferdeschlitten) sleigh; **mit jdm ~ fahren** (umg) to give sb a rough time; **Schlittenbahn** f toboggan run; **Schlittenfahren** (-s) nt tobogganing

schlittern ['ʃlɪtərn] vi to slide; (Wagen) to skid

Schlittschuh ['ʃlɪtʃuː] m skate; **~ laufen** to skate; **Schlittschuhbahn** f skating rink; **Schlittschuhläufer** m skater

Schlitz [ʃlɪts] (-es, -e) m slit; (für Münze) slot; (Hosenschlitz) flies pl; **schlitzäugig** adj slant-eyed; **schlitzen** vt to slit; **Schlitzohr** nt (fig) sly fox

schlohweiß ['ʃloːˈvaɪs] adj snow-white

Schlokal nt gourmet restaurant

Schloss (-es, -"er) nt lock, padlock; (an Schmuck etc) clasp; (Bau) castle; (Palast) palace; **ins ~ fallen** to lock (itself)

schloss etc [ʃlɔs] vb siehe **schließen**

Schlosser ['ʃlɔsər] (-s, -) m (Autoschlosser) fitter; (für Schlüssel etc) locksmith

Schlosserei [slɔsəˈraɪ] f metal(working) shop

Schlosshund m: **heulen wie ein ~** to howl one's head off

Schlot [ʃloːt] (-(e)s, -e) m chimney; (Naut) funnel

schlottern ['ʃlɔtərn] vi to shake; (vor Angst) to tremble; (Kleidung) to be baggy

Schlucht [ʃlʊxt] (-, -en) f gorge, ravine

schluchzen ['ʃlʊxtsən] vi to sob

Schluck [ʃlʊk] (-(e)s, -e) m swallow; (größer) gulp; (kleiner) sip; (ein bisschen) drop

Schluckauf (-s) m hiccups pl

schlucken vt to swallow; (umg: Alkohol, Benzin) to guzzle; (: verschlingen) to swallow up ▷ vi to swallow

Schlucker (-s, -) (umg) m: **armer ~** poor devil

Schluckimpfung f oral vaccination

schluderig ['ʃluːdərɪç], **schludrig** ['ʃluːdrɪç] (umg) adj slipshod

schludern ['ʃluːdərn] (umg) vi to do slipshod work

schlug etc [ʃluːk] vb siehe **schlagen**

Schlummer ['ʃlʊmər] (-s) m slumber

schlummern vi to slumber

Schlund [ʃlʊnt] (-(e)s, "e) m gullet; (fig) jaw

schlüpfen ['ʃlʏpfən] vi to slip; (Vogel etc) to hatch (out)

Schlüpfer ['ʃlʏpfər] (-s, -) m panties pl, knickers pl

Schlupfloch ['ʃlʊpflɔx] nt hole; (Versteck) hide-out; (fig) loophole

schlüpfrig ['ʃlʏpfrɪç] adj slippery; (fig) lewd; **Schlüpfrigkeit** f slipperiness; lewdness

Schlupfwinkel m hiding place; (fig) quiet corner

schlurfen ['ʃlʊrfən] vi to shuffle

schlürfen ['ʃlʏrfən] vt, vi to slurp

Schluss [ʃlʊs] (-es, -"e) m end; (Schlussfolgerung)

S

conclusion; **am ~** at the end; **~ für heute!** that'll do for today; **~ jetzt!** that's enough now!; **~ machen mit** to finish with

Schlüssel ['ʃlʏsəl] **(-s, -)** m (lit, fig) key; (Schraubschlüssel) spanner, wrench; (Mus) clef; **Schlüsselbein** nt collarbone; **Schlüsselblume** f cowslip, primrose; **Schlüsselbund** m bunch of keys; **Schlüsselerlebnis** nt (Psych) crucial experience; **Schlüsselkind** nt latchkey child; **Schlüsselloch** nt keyhole; **Schlüsselposition** f key position; **Schlüsselwort** nt safe combination; (Comput) keyword

Schlussfolgerung f conclusion, inference

Schlussformel f (in Brief) closing formula; (bei Vertrag) final clause

schlüssig ['ʃlʏsɪç] adj conclusive; **sich** dat **(über etw** akk**) ~ sein** to have made up one's mind (about sth)

Schluss- zW: **Schlusslicht** nt rear light (Brit), taillight (US); (fig) tail ender; **Schlussstrich** m (fig) final stroke; **einen Schlussstrich unter etw** akk **ziehen** to consider sth finished; **Schlussverkauf** m clearance sale; **Schlusswort** nt concluding words pl

Schmach [ʃmaːx] **(-)** f disgrace, ignominy

schmachten ['ʃmaxtən] vi to languish; **nach jdm ~** to pine for sb

schmächtig ['ʃmɛçtɪç] adj slight

schmachvoll adj ignominious, humiliating

schmackhaft ['ʃmakhaft] adj tasty; **jdm etw ~ machen** (fig) to make sth palatable to sb

schmähen ['ʃmɛːən] vt to abuse, revile

schmählich adj ignominious, shameful

Schmähung f abuse

schmal [ʃmaːl] adj narrow; (Person, Buch etc) slender, slim; (karg) meagre (Brit), meager (US); **schmalbrüstig** adj narrow-chested

schmälern ['ʃmɛːlərn] vt to diminish; (fig) to belittle

Schmalfilm m cine (Brit) od movie (US) film

Schmalspur f narrow gauge

Schmalspur- (pej) in zw small-time

Schmalz [ʃmalts] **(-es, -e)** nt dripping; (Schweineschmalz) lard; (fig) sentiment, schmaltz

schmalzig adj (fig) schmaltzy, slushy

schmarotzen [ʃma'rɔtsən] vi (Biol) to be parasitic; (fig) to sponge

Schmarotzer (-s, -) m (auch fig) parasite

Schmarren ['ʃmarən] **(-s, -)** m (Österr) small pieces of pancake; (fig) rubbish, tripe

schmatzen ['ʃmatsən] vi to eat noisily

Schmaus [ʃmaʊs] **(-es, Schmäuse)** m feast; **schmausen** vi to feast

schmecken ['ʃmɛkən] vt, vi to taste; **es schmeckt ihm** he likes it; **schmeckt es Ihnen?** is it good?, are you enjoying your food od meal?; **das schmeckt nach mehr!** (umg) it's very moreish (hum); **es sich ~ lassen** to tuck in

Schmeichelei [ʃmaɪçə'laɪ] f flattery

schmeichelhaft ['ʃmaɪçəlhaft] adj flattering

schmeicheln vi to flatter

Schmeichler, in (-s, -) m(f) flatterer

schmeißen ['ʃmaɪsən] unreg (umg) vt to throw, chuck; (spendieren): **eine Runde** od **Lage ~** to stand a round

Schmeißfliege f bluebottle

Schmelz [ʃmɛlts] **(-es, -e)** m enamel; (Glasur) glaze; (von Stimme) melodiousness; **schmelzbar** adj fusible

schmelzen unreg vt to melt; (Erz) to smelt ⊳ vi to melt

Schmelz- zW: **Schmelzhütte** f smelting works pl; **Schmelzkäse** m cheese spread; (in Scheiben) processed cheese; **Schmelzofen** m melting furnace; (für Erze) smelting furnace; **Schmelzpunkt** m melting point; **Schmelztiegel** m (lit, fig) melting pot; **Schmelzwasser** nt melted snow

Schmerbauch ['ʃmeːrbaʊx] (umg) m paunch, potbelly

Schmerz [ʃmɛrts] **(-es, -en)** m pain; (Trauer) grief no pl; **~en haben** to be in pain; **schmerzempfindlich** adj sensitive to pain

schmerzen vt, vi to hurt

Schmerzensgeld nt compensation

Schmerz- zW: **schmerzhaft** adj painful; **schmerzlich** adj painful; **schmerzlindernd** adj pain-relieving; **schmerzlos** adj painless; **Schmerzmittel** nt painkiller, analgesic; **schmerzstillend** adj pain-killing, analgesic; **Schmerztablette** f pain-killing tablet

Schmetterling ['ʃmɛtərlɪŋ] m butterfly

Schmetterlingsstil m (Schwimmen) butterfly stroke

schmettern ['ʃmɛtərn] vt to smash; (Melodie) to sing loudly, bellow out ⊳ vi to smash (SPORT); (Trompete) to blare

Schmied [ʃmiːt] **(-(e)s, -e)** m blacksmith

Schmiede ['ʃmiːdə] **(-, -n)** f smithy, forge; **Schmiedeeisen** nt wrought iron

schmieden vt to forge; (Pläne) to devise, concoct

schmiegen ['ʃmiːgən] vt to press, nestle ⊳ vr: **sich ~ an** +akk to cuddle up to, nestle up to

schmiegsam ['ʃmiːkzaːm] adj flexible, pliable

Schmiere ['ʃmiːrə] f grease; (Theat) greasepaint, make-up; (pej: schlechtes Theater) fleapit; **~ stehen** (umg) to be the look-out

schmieren vt to smear; (ölen) to lubricate, grease; (bestechen) to bribe ⊳ vi (schreiben) to scrawl; **es läuft wie geschmiert** it's going like clockwork; **jdm eine ~** (umg) to clout sb one

Schmierenkomödiant (pej) m ham (actor)

Schmier- zW: **Schmierfett** nt grease; **Schmierfink** m messy person; **Schmiergeld** nt bribe; **Schmierheft** nt jotter

schmierig adj greasy

Schmiermittel nt lubricant

Schmierseife f soft soap

schmilzt [ʃmɪltst] vb siehe **schmelzen**

Schminke ['ʃmɪŋkə] **(-, -n)** f make-up

schminken vt, vr to make up

schmirgeln ['ʃmɪrgəln] vt to sand (down)

Schmirgelpapier (-s) nt emery paper
Schmiss (-es, -e) m (Narbe) duelling (Brit) od dueling (US) scar; (veraltet: Schwung) dash, élan
schmiss etc [ʃmɪs] vb siehe **schmeißen**
Schmöker ['ʃmøːkər] (-s, -) (umg) m (trashy) old book
schmökern vi to bury o.s. in a book; (umg) to browse
schmollen ['ʃmɔlən] vi to pout; (gekränkt) to sulk
schmollend adj sulky
Schmollmund m pout
schmolz etc [ʃmɔlts] vb siehe **schmelzen**
Schmorbraten m stewed od braised meat
schmoren ['ʃmoːrən] vt to braise
Schmu [ʃmuː] (-s) (umg) m cheating
Schmuck [ʃmʊk] (-(e)s, -e) m jewellery (Brit), jewelry (US); (Verzierung) decoration
schmücken ['ʃmʏkən] vt to decorate
Schmuck- zW: **schmucklos** adj unadorned, plain; **Schmucklosigkeit** f simplicity; **Schmucksachen** pl jewels pl, jewellery sing (Brit), jewelry sing (US); **Schmuckstück** nt (Ring etc) piece of jewellery (Brit) od jewelry (US); (fig: Prachtstück) gem
schmuddelig ['ʃmʊdəlɪç], **schmuddlig** ['ʃmʊdlɪç] adj messy; (schmutzig) dirty; (schmierig, unsauber) filthy
Schmuggel ['ʃmʊgəl] (-s) m smuggling
schmuggeln vt, vi to smuggle
Schmuggelware f contraband
Schmuggler, in (-s, -) m(f) smuggler
schmunzeln ['ʃmʊntsəln] vi to smile benignly
schmusen ['ʃmuːzən] (umg) vi (zärtlich sein) to cuddle; **mit jdm ~** to cuddle sb
Schmutz [ʃmʊts] (-es) m dirt; (fig) filth; **schmutzen** vi to get dirty; **Schmutzfink** m filthy creature; **Schmutzfleck** m stain
schmutzig adj dirty; **~e Wäsche waschen** (fig) to wash one's dirty linen in public
Schnabel ['ʃnaːbəl] (-s, ¨) m beak, bill; (Ausguss) spout; (umg: Mund) mouth; **reden, wie einem der ~ gewachsen ist** to say exactly what comes into one's head; (unaffektiert) to talk naturally
schnacken ['ʃnakən] (Nordd: umg) vi to chat
Schnake ['ʃnaːkə] (-, -n) f crane fly; (Stechmücke) gnat
Schnalle ['ʃnalə] (-, -n) f buckle; (an Handtasche, Buch) clasp
schnallen vt to buckle
schnalzen ['ʃnaltsən] vi to snap; (mit Zunge) to click
Schnäppchen ['ʃnɛpçən] (umg) nt bargain, snip
schnappen ['ʃnapən] vt to grab, catch; (umg: ergreifen) to snatch ▷ vi to snap
Schnappschloss nt spring lock
Schnappschuss m (Phot) snapshot
Schnaps [ʃnaps] (-es, ¨e) m schnapps; (umg: Branntwein) spirits pl; **Schnapsidee** (umg) f crackpot idea; **Schnapsleiche** (umg) f drunk
schnarchen ['ʃnarçən] vi to snore
schnattern ['ʃnatərn] vi to chatter; (zittern) to

shiver
schnauben ['ʃnaʊbən] vi to snort ▷ vr to blow one's nose
schnaufen ['ʃnaʊfən] vi to puff, pant
Schnaufer (-s, -) (umg) m breath
Schnauzbart ['ʃnaʊtsbaːrt] m moustache (Brit), mustache (US)
Schnauze (-, -n) f snout, muzzle; (Ausguss) spout; (umg) gob; **auf die ~ fallen** (fig) to come a cropper (umg); **etw frei nach ~ machen** to do sth any old how
schnäuzen ['ʃnɔʏtsən] vr to blow one's nose
Schnecke ['ʃnɛkə] (-, -n) f snail; (Nacktschnecke) slug; (Koch: Gebäck) ≈ Chelsea bun; **jdn zur ~ machen** (umg) to give sb a real bawling out
Schneckenhaus nt snail's shell
Schneckentempo (umg) nt: **im ~** at a snail's pace
Schnee [ʃneː] (-s) m snow; (Eischnee) beaten egg white; **~ von gestern** old hat; water under the bridge; **Schneeball** m snowball; **Schneebesen** m (Koch) whisk; **Schneefall** m snowfall; **Schneeflocke** f snowflake; **Schneegestöber** nt snowstorm; **Schneeglöckchen** nt snowdrop; **Schneegrenze** f snowline; **Schneekette** f (Aut) snow chain; **Schneekönig** m: **sich freuen wie ein Schneekönig** to be as pleased as Punch; **Schneemann** m snowman; **Schneepflug** m snowplough (Brit), snowplow (US); **Schneeregen** m sleet; **Schneeschmelze** f thaw; **Schneetreiben** nt driving snow; **Schneewehe** f snowdrift; **Schneewittchen** nt Snow White
Schneid [ʃnaɪt] (-(e)s) (umg) m pluck
Schneidbrenner (-s, -) m (Tech) oxyacetylene cutter
Schneide ['ʃnaɪdə] (-, -n) f edge; (Klinge) blade
schneiden unreg vt to cut; (Film, Tonband) to edit; (kreuzen) to cross, intersect ▷ vr to cut o.s.; (umg: sich täuschen): **da hat er sich aber geschnitten!** he's very much mistaken; **die Luft ist zum S~** (fig: umg) the air is very bad
schneidend adj cutting
Schneider (-s, -) m tailor; **frieren wie ein ~** (umg) to be frozen to the marrow; **aus dem ~ sein** (fig) to be out of the woods
Schneiderei [ʃnaɪdəˈraɪ] f tailor's shop; (einer Schneiderin) dressmaker's shop
Schneiderin f dressmaker
schneidern vt to make ▷ vi to be a tailor
Schneidersitz (-es) m: **im ~ sitzen** to sit cross-legged
Schneidezahn m incisor
schneidig adj dashing; (mutig) plucky
schneien ['ʃnaɪən] vi to snow; **jdm ins Haus ~** (umg: Besuch) to drop in on sb; (: Rechnung, Brief) to come in the post (Brit) od mail (US)
Schneise ['ʃnaɪzə] (-, -n) f (Waldschneise) clearing
schnell [ʃnɛl] adj quick, fast ▷ adv quick(ly), fast; **das ging ~** that was quick; **Schnellboot** nt speedboat
Schnelle (-) f: **etw auf die ~ machen** to do sth in a rush

S

schnellen vi to shoot

Schnellgericht nt (Jur) summary court; (Koch) convenience food

Schnellhefter m loose-leaf binder

Schnelligkeit f speed

Schnell- zW: **Schnellimbiss** m (Essen) (quick) snack; (Raum) snack bar; **Schnellkochtopf** m (Dampfkochtopf) pressure cooker; **Schnellreinigung** f express cleaner's

schnellstens adv as quickly as possible

Schnellstraße f expressway

Schnellzug m fast od express train

schneuzen ['ʃnɔytsən] vr siehe **schnäuzen**

Schnickschnack ['ʃnɪkʃnak] (-(e)s) (umg) m twaddle

Schnippchen ['ʃnɪpçən] nt: **jdm ein ~ schlagen** to play a trick on sb

schnippeln ['ʃnɪpəln] (umg) vt to snip; (mit Messer) to hack ▷ vi: **~ an** +dat to snip at; to hack at

schnippen ['ʃnɪpən] vi: **mit den Fingern ~** to snap one's fingers

schnippisch ['ʃnɪpɪʃ] adj sharp-tongued

Schnipsel ['ʃnɪpsəl] (-s, -) (umg) m od nt scrap; (Papierschnipsel) scrap of paper

Schnitt (-(e)s, -e) m cut(ting); (Schnittpunkt) intersection; (Querschnitt) (cross) section; (Durchschnitt) average; (Schnittmuster) pattern; (Ernte) crop; (an Buch) edge; (umg: Gewinn) profit; **~: L. Schwarz** (Film) editor – L. Schwarz; **im ~** on average

schnitt etc [ʃnɪt] vb siehe **schneiden**

Schnittblumen pl cut flowers pl

Schnittbohnen pl French od green beans pl

Schnitte (-, -n) f slice; (belegt) sandwich

schnittfest adj (Tomaten) firm

Schnittfläche f section

schnittig ['ʃnɪtɪç] adj smart; (Auto, Formen) stylish

Schnitt- zW: **Schnittlauch** m chive; **Schnittmuster** nt pattern; **Schnittpunkt** m (point of) intersection; **Schnittstelle** f (Comput) interface; **Schnittwunde** f cut

Schnitzarbeit f wood carving

Schnitzel (-s, -) nt scrap; (Koch) escalope; **Schnitzeljagd** f paperchase

schnitzen ['ʃnɪtsən] vt to carve

Schnitzer (-s, -) m carver; (umg) blunder

Schnitzerei [ʃnɪtsəˈraɪ] f wood carving

schnodderig ['ʃnɔdərɪç] (umg) adj snotty

schnöde ['ʃnøːdə] adj base, mean

Schnorchel ['ʃnɔrçəl] (-s, -) m snorkel

schnorcheln vi to go snorkelling

Schnörkel ['ʃnœrkəl] (-s, -) m flourish; (Archit) scroll

schnorren ['ʃnɔrən] vt, vi to cadge (Brit)

Schnorrer (-s, -) (umg) m cadger (Brit)

Schnösel ['ʃnøːzəl] (-s, -) (umg) m snotty(-nosed) little upstart

schnuckelig ['ʃnʊkəlɪç] (umg) adj (gemütlich) snug, cosy; (Person) sweet

schnüffeln ['ʃnʏfəln] vi to sniff; (fig: umg: spionieren) to snoop around;

Schnüffeln nt (von Klebstoff etc) glue-sniffing etc

Schnüffler, in (-s, -) m(f) snooper

Schnuller ['ʃnʊlər] (-s, -) m dummy (Brit), pacifier (US)

Schnulze ['ʃnʊltsə] (-, -n) (umg) f schmaltzy film/book/song

Schnupfen ['ʃnʊpfən] (-s, -) m cold

Schnupftabak m snuff

schnuppe ['ʃnʊpə] (umg) adj: **jdm ~ sein** to be all the same to sb

schnuppern ['ʃnʊpərn] vi to sniff

Schnur [ʃnuːr] (-, ¨e) f string; (Kordel) cord; (Elek) flex

Schnürchen ['ʃnyːrçən] nt: **es läuft** od **klappt (alles) wie am ~** everything's going like clockwork

schnüren ['ʃnyːrən] vt to tie

schnurgerade adj straight (as a die od an arrow)

Schnurrbart ['ʃnʊrbaːrt] m moustache (Brit), mustache (US)

schnurren ['ʃnʊrən] vi to purr; (Kreisel) to hum

Schnürschuh m lace-up (shoe)

Schnürsenkel m shoelace

schnurstracks adv straight (away); **~ auf jdn/etw zugehen** to make a beeline for sb/sth (umg)

schob etc [ʃoːp] vb siehe **schieben**

Schock [ʃɔk] (-(e)s, -e) m shock; **unter ~ stehen** to be in (a state of) shock

schocken (umg) vt to shock

Schocker (-s, -) (umg) m shocking film/novel, shocker

schockieren vt to shock, outrage

Schöffe ['ʃœfə] (-n, -n) m lay magistrate

Schöffengericht nt magistrates' court

Schöffin f lay magistrate

Schokolade [ʃokoˈlaːdə] (-, -n) f chocolate

scholl etc [ʃɔl] vb siehe **schallen**

Scholle ['ʃɔlə] (-, -n) f clod; (Eisscholle) ice floe; (Fisch) plaice

Scholli ['ʃɔlɪ] (umg) m: **mein lieber ~!** (drohend) now look here!

 SCHLÜSSELWORT

schon [ʃoːn] adv **1** (bereits) already; **er ist schon da** he's there/here already, he's already there/here; **ist er schon da?** is he there/here yet?; **warst du schon einmal dort?** have you ever been there?; **ich war schon einmal dort** I've been there before; **das war schon immer so** that has always been the case; **hast du schon gehört?** have you heard?; **schon 1920** as early as 1920; **schon vor 100 Jahren** as far back as 100 years ago; **er wollte schon die Hoffnung aufgeben, als ...** he was just about to give up hope when ...; **wartest du schon lange?** have you been waiting (for) long?; **wie schon so oft** as so often (before); **was, schon wieder?** what – again?

2 (bestimmt) all right; **du wirst schon sehen** you'll see (all right); **das wird schon noch**

gut gehen that should turn out OK (in the end)
3 (*bloß*) just; **allein schon das Gefühl** ... just the very feeling ...; **schon der Gedanke** the mere *od* very thought; **wenn ich das schon höre** I only have to hear that
4 (*einschränkend*): **ja schon, aber** ... yes (well), but ...
5: **das ist schon möglich** that's quite possible; **schon gut** OK; **du weißt schon** you know; **komm schon** come on; **hör schon auf damit!** will you stop that!; **was macht das schon, wenn ...?** what does it matter if ...?; **und wenn schon!** (*umg*) so what?

schön [ʃøːn] *adj* beautiful; (*Mann*) handsome; (*nett*) nice ▷ *adv*: **sich ganz ~ ärgern** to be very angry; **da hast du etwas S~es angerichtet** you've made a fine *od* nice mess; **sich ~ machen** to make o.s. look nice; **~e Grüße** best wishes; **~en Dank** (many) thanks; **~ weich/warm** nice and soft/warm
schonen ['ʃoːnən] *vt* to look after; (*jds Nerven*) to spare; (*Gegner, Kind*) to be easy on; (*Teppich, Füße*) to save ▷ *vr* to take it easy
schonend *adj* careful, gentle; **jdm etw ~ beibringen** to break sth to sb gently
Schoner ['ʃoːnər] (**-s, -**) *m* (*Naut*) schooner; (*Sesselschoner*) cover
Schönfärberei *f* (*fig*) glossing things over
Schonfrist *f* period of grace
Schöngeist *m* cultured person, aesthete (*Brit*), esthete (*US*)
Schönheit *f* beauty
Schönheits- *zW*: **Schönheitsfehler** *m* blemish, flaw; **Schönheitsoperation** *f* cosmetic surgery; **Schönheitswettbewerb** *m* beauty contest
Schonkost (**-**) *f* light diet
Schönschrift *f*: **in ~** in one's best (hand)writing
schöntun *unreg vi*: **jdm ~** (*schmeicheln*) to flatter *od* soft-soap sb, play up to sb
Schonung *f* good care; (*Nachsicht*) consideration; (*Forst*) plantation of young trees
schonungslos *adj* ruthless, harsh
Schonzeit *f* close season
Schopf [ʃɔpf] (**-(e)s, ¨e**) *m*: **eine Gelegenheit beim ~ ergreifen** *od* **fassen** to seize *od* grasp an opportunity with both hands
schöpfen ['ʃœpfən] *vt* to scoop; (*Suppe*) to ladle; (*Mut*) to summon up; (*Luft*) to breathe in; (*Hoffnung*) to find
Schöpfer (**-s, -**) *m* creator; (*Gott*) Creator; (*umg: Schöpfkelle*) ladle; **schöpferisch** *adj* creative
Schöpfkelle *f* ladle
Schöpflöffel *m* skimmer, scoop
Schöpfung *f* creation
Schoppen ['ʃɔpən] (**-s, -**) *m* (*Glas Wein*) glass of wine; **Schoppenwein** *m* wine by the glass
schor *etc* [ʃoːr] *vb siehe* **scheren**

Schorf [ʃɔrf] (**-(e)s, -e**) *m* scab
Schorle ['ʃɔrlə] (**-, -n**) *f* spritzer, *wine and soda water or lemonade*
Schornstein ['ʃɔrnʃtaɪn] *m* chimney; (*Naut*) funnel; **Schornsteinfeger** (**-s, -**) *m* chimney sweep
Schose ['ʃoːzə] (**-, -n**) *f* = **Chose**
Schoß (**-es, ¨e**) *m* lap; (*Rockschoß*) coat tail; **im ~ der Familie** in the bosom of one's family
schoss *etc* [ʃɔs] *vb siehe* **schießen**
Schoßhund *m* lapdog
Schössling ['ʃœslɪŋ] *m* (*Bot*) shoot
Schote ['ʃoːtə] (**-, -n**) *f* pod
Schotte ['ʃɔtə] (**-n, -n**) *m* Scot, Scotsman
Schottenrock ['ʃɔtənrɔk] *m* kilt; (*für Frauen*) tartan skirt
Schotter ['ʃɔtər] (**-s**) *m* gravel; (*im Straßenbau*) road metal; (*Eisenb*) ballast
Schottin ['ʃɔtɪn] *f* Scot, Scotswoman
schottisch ['ʃɔtɪʃ] *adj* Scottish, Scots; **das ~e Hochland** the Scottish Highlands *pl*
Schottland (**-s**) *nt* Scotland
schraffieren [ʃraˈfiːrən] *vt* to hatch
schräg [ʃrɛːk] *adj* slanting; (*schief, geneigt*) sloping; (*nicht gerade od parallel*) oblique ▷ *adv*: **~ gedruckt** in italics; **etw ~ stellen** to put sth at an angle; **~ gegenüber** diagonally opposite
Schräge ['ʃrɛːgə] (**-, -n**) *f* slant
Schräg- *zW*: **Schrägkante** *f* bevelled (*Brit*) *od* beveled (*US*) edge; **Schrägschrift** *f* italics *pl*; **Schrägstreifen** *m* bias binding; **Schrägstrich** *m* oblique stroke
Schramme ['ʃramə] (**-, -n**) *f* scratch
schrammen *vt* to scratch
Schrank [ʃraŋk] (**-(e)s, ¨e**) *m* cupboard (*Brit*), closet (*US*); (*Kleiderschrank*) wardrobe
Schranke (**-, -n**) *f* barrier; (*fig: Grenze*) limit; (: *Hindernis*) barrier; **jdn in seine ~n (ver)weisen** (*fig*) to put sb in his place
schrankenlos *adj* boundless; (*zügellos*) unrestrained
Schrankenwärter *m* (*Eisenb*) level-crossing (*Brit*) *od* grade-crossing (*US*) attendant
Schrankkoffer *m* wardrobe trunk
Schrankwand *f* wall unit
Schraube ['ʃraubə] (**-, -n**) *f* screw
schrauben *vt* to screw; **etw in die Höhe ~** (*fig: Preise, Rekorde*) to push sth up; (: *Ansprüche*) to raise sth
Schraubenschlüssel *m* spanner (*Brit*), wrench (*US*)
Schraubenzieher (**-s, -**) *m* screwdriver
Schraubstock ['ʃraupʃtɔk] *m* (*Tech*) vice (*Brit*), vise (*US*)
Schrebergarten ['ʃreːbərgartən] *m* allotment (*Brit*)
Schreck [ʃrɛk] (**-(e)s, -e**) *m* fright; **o - lass nach!** (*hum: umg*) for goodness' sake!
Schrecken (**-s, -**) *m* terror; (*Schreck*) fright; **schrecken** *vt* to frighten, scare ▷ *vi*: **aus dem Schlaf schrecken** to be startled out of one's sleep
schreckensbleich *adj* as white as a sheet *od*

ghost

Schreckensherrschaft *f* (reign of) terror

Schreck- *zW:* **Schreckgespenst** *nt* nightmare; **schreckhaft** *adj* jumpy, easily frightened; **schrecklich** *adj* terrible, dreadful; **schrecklich gerne!** (*umg*) I'd absolutely love to; **Schreckschraube** (*pej: umg*) *f* (old) battle-axe; **Schreckschuss** *m* shot fired in the air; **Schrecksekunde** *f* moment of shock

Schrei [ʃraɪ] **(-(e)s, -e)** *m* scream; (*Ruf*) shout; **der letzte ~** (*umg*) the latest thing, all the rage

Schreibbedarf *m* writing materials *pl*, stationery

Schreibblock *m* writing pad

schreiben ['ʃraɪbən] *unreg vt* to write; (*mit Schreibmaschine*) to type out; (*berichten: Zeitung etc*) to say; (*buchstabieren*) to spell ▷ *vi* to write; to type; to say; to spell ▷ *vr:* **wie schreibt sich das?** how is that spelt?; **Schreiben (-s, -)** *nt* letter, communication

Schreiber, in (**-s, -**) *m(f)* writer; (*Büroschreiber*) clerk

Schreib- *zW:* **schreibfaul** *adj* lazy about writing letters; **Schreibfehler** *m* spelling mistake; **Schreibkraft** *f* typist; **Schreibmaschine** *f* typewriter; **Schreibpapier** *nt* notepaper; **Schreibschrift** *f* running handwriting; (*Typ*) script; **Schreibschutz** *m* (*Comput*) write-protect; **Schreibstube** *f* orderly room; **Schreibtisch** *m* desk; **Schreibtischtäter** *m* wire *od* string puller

Schreibung *f* spelling

Schreib- *zW:* **Schreibunterlage** *f* pad; **Schreibwaren** *pl* stationery *sing*; **Schreibwarengeschäft** *nt* stationer's (shop) (*Brit*), stationery store (*US*); **Schreibweise** *f* spelling; (*Stil*) style; **schreibwütig** *adj* crazy about writing; **Schreibzentrale** *f* typing pool; **Schreibzeug** *nt* writing materials *pl*

schreien ['ʃraɪən] *unreg vt, vi* to scream; (*rufen*) to shout; **es war zum S~** (*umg*) it was a scream *od* a hoot; **nach etw ~** (*fig*) to cry out for sth

schreiend *adj* (*fig*) glaring; (*: Farbe*) loud

Schreihals (*umg*) *m* (*Baby*) bawler; (*Unruhestifter*) noisy troublemaker

Schreikrampf *m* screaming fit

Schreiner ['ʃraɪnər] (**-s, -**) *m* joiner; (*Zimmermann*) carpenter; (*Möbelschreiner*) cabinetmaker

Schreinerei [ʃraɪnə'raɪ] *f* joiner's workshop

schreiten ['ʃraɪtən] *unreg vi* to stride

schrie *etc* [ʃriː] *vb siehe* **schreien**

Schrieb (**-(e)s, -e**) (*umg*) *m* missive (*hum*)

schrieb *etc* [ʃriːp] *vb siehe* **schreiben**

Schrift [ʃrɪft] (**-, -en**) *f* writing; (*Handschrift*) handwriting; (*Schriftart*) script; (*Typ*) typeface; (*Buch*) work; **Schriftart** *f* (*Handschrift*) script; (*Typ*) typeface; **Schriftbild** *nt* script; (*Comput*) typeface; **Schriftdeutsch** *nt* written German; **Schrifterkennung** *f* optical character recognition, OCR; **Schriftführer** *m* secretary; **schriftlich** *adj* written ▷ *adv* in writing; **das kann ich Ihnen schriftlich geben** (*fig: umg*)

I can tell you that for free; **Schriftprobe** *f* (*Handschrift*) specimen of one's handwriting; **Schriftsatz** *m* (*Typ*) fount (*Brit*), font (*US*); **Schriftsetzer** *m* compositor; **Schriftsprache** *f* written language

Schriftsteller, in (**-s, -**) *m(f)* writer; **schriftstellerisch** *adj* literary

Schrift- *zW:* **Schriftstück** *nt* document; **Schriftverkehr** *m* correspondence; **Schriftwechsel** *m* correspondence

schrill [ʃrɪl] *adj* shrill; **schrillen** *vi* (*Stimme*) to sound shrilly; (*Telefon*) to ring shrilly

Schritt (**-(e)s, -e**) *m* step; (*Gangart*) walk; (*Tempo*) pace; (*von Hose*) crotch, crutch (*Brit*); **auf ~ und Tritt** (*lit, fig*) wherever *od* everywhere one goes; **„~ fahren"** "dead slow"; **mit zehn ~en Abstand** at a distance of ten paces; **den ersten ~ tun** (*fig*) to make the first move; (*: etw beginnen*) to take the first step

schritt *etc* [ʃrɪt] *vb siehe* **schreiten**

Schritt- *zW:* **Schrittmacher** *m* pacemaker; **Schritttempo** *nt:* **im Schritttempo** at a walking pace; **schrittweise** *adv* gradually, little by little

schroff [ʃrɔf] *adj* steep; (*zackig*) jagged; (*fig*) brusque; (*ungeduldig*) abrupt

schröpfen ['ʃrœpfən] *vt* (*fig*) to fleece

Schrot [ʃroːt] (**-(e)s, -e**) *m od nt* (*Blei*) (small) shot; (*Getreide*) coarsely ground grain, groats *pl*; **Schrotflinte** *f* shotgun

Schrott [ʃrɔt] (**-(e)s, -e**) *m* scrap metal; **ein Auto zu ~ fahren** to write off a car; **Schrotthändler** *m* scrap merchant; **Schrotthaufen** *m* scrap heap; **schrottreif** *adj* ready for the scrap heap; **Schrottwert** *m* scrap value

schrubben ['ʃrʊbən] *vt* to scrub

Schrubber (**-s, -**) *m* scrubbing brush

Schrulle ['ʃrʊlə] (**-, -n**) *f* eccentricity, quirk

schrullig *adj* cranky

schrumpfen ['ʃrʊmpfən] *vi* (*Hilfsverb sein*) to shrink; (*Apfel*) to shrivel; (*Leber, Niere*) to atrophy

Schub [ʃuːp] (**-(e)s, ̈-e**) *m* (*Stoß*) push, shove; (*Gruppe, Anzahl*) batch; **Schubfach** *nt* drawer; **Schubkarren** *m* wheelbarrow; **Schublade** *f* drawer

Schubs [ʃuːps] (**-es, -e**) (*umg*) *m* shove, push; **schubsen** (*umg*) *vt, vi* to shove, push

schüchtern ['ʃʏçtərn] *adj* shy; **Schüchternheit** *f* shyness

schuf *etc* [ʃuːf] *vb siehe* **schaffen**

Schuft [ʃʊft] (**-(e)s, -e**) *m* scoundrel

schuften (*umg*) *vi* to graft, slave away

Schuh [ʃuː] (**-(e)s, -e**) *m* shoe; **jdm etw in die ~e schieben** (*fig: umg*) to put the blame for sth on sb; **wo drückt der ~?** (*fig*) what's troubling you?; **Schuhband** *nt* shoelace; **Schuhcreme** *f* shoe polish; **Schuhgröße** *f* shoe size; **Schuhlöffel** *m* shoehorn; **Schuhmacher** *m* shoemaker; **Schuhwerk** *nt* footwear

Schukosteckdose® ['ʃʊkoʃtɛkdoːzə] *f* safety socket

Schukostecker® *m* safety plug
Schul- *zW*: **Schulaufgaben** *pl* homework *sing*;
Schulbank *f*: **die Schulbank drücken** (*umg*)
to go to school; **Schulbehörde** *f* education
authority; **Schulbesuch** *m* school attendance;
Schulbuch *nt* schoolbook; **Schulbuchverlag** *m*
educational publisher
Schuld [ʃʊlt] (**-, -en**) *f* guilt; (*Fin*) debt;
(*Verschulden*) fault; **~ haben (an** *+dat*) to be to
blame (for); **jdm (die) ~ geben, jdm die ~
zuschieben** to blame sb; **ich bin mir keiner
~ bewusst** I'm not aware of having done
anything wrong; **~ und Sühne** crime and
punishment; **ich stehe tief in seiner ~** (*fig*)
I'm deeply indebted to him; **~en machen** to
run up debts; *siehe auch* **zuschulden**; **schuld**
adj: **schuld sein (an** *+dat*) to be to blame (for);
er ist schuld it's his fault
schuldbewusst *adj* (*Mensch*) feeling guilty;
(*Miene*) guilty
schulden [ʃʊldən] *vt* to owe
schuldenfrei *adj* free from debt
Schuldgefühl *nt* feeling of guilt
schuldhaft *adj* (*Jur*) culpable
Schuldienst (**-(e)s**) *m* (school)teaching
schuldig *adj* guilty; (*gebührend*) due; **an etw** *dat*
~ sein to be guilty of sth; **jdm etw ~ sein** *od*
bleiben to owe sb sth; **jdn ~ sprechen** to find
sb guilty; **~ geschieden sein** to be the guilty
party in a divorce; **Schuldigkeit** *f* duty
schuldlos *adj* innocent, blameless
Schuldner, in (**-s, -**) *m(f)* debtor
Schuld- *zW*: **Schuldprinzip** *nt* (*Jur*) principle of
the guilty party; **Schuldschein** *m* promissory
note, IOU; **Schuldspruch** *m* verdict of guilty
Schule [ʃuːlə] (**-, -n**) *f* school; **auf** *od* **in der ~**
at school; **in die ~ kommen/gehen** to start
school/go to school; **~ machen** (*fig*) to become
the accepted thing
schulen *vt* to train, school
Schüler, in [ʃyːlər(ɪn)] (**-s, -**) *m(f)* pupil;
Schülerausweis *m* (school) student card;
Schülerlotse *m* pupil acting as a road-crossing
warden; **Schülermitverwaltung** *f* school *od*
student council
Schul- *zW*: **Schulferien** *pl* school holidays *pl*
(*Brit*) *od* vacation *sing* (*US*); **Schulfernsehen** *nt*
schools' *od* educational television; **schulfrei**
adj: **die Kinder haben morgen schulfrei** the
children don't have to go to school tomorrow;
Schulfunk *m* schools' broadcasts *pl*; **Schulgeld**
nt school fees *pl*, tuition (*US*); **Schulheft**
nt exercise book; **Schulhof** *m* playground,
schoolyard
schulisch [ʃuːlɪʃ] *adj* (*Leistungen, Probleme*) at
school; (*Angelegenheiten*) school *attrib*
Schul- *zW*: **Schuljahr** *nt* school year;
Schuljunge *m* schoolboy; **Schulkind** *nt*
schoolchild; **Schulleiter** *m* headmaster (*bes*
Brit), principal; **Schulleiterin** *f* headmistress
(*bes Brit*), principal; **Schulmädchen** *nt*
schoolgirl; **Schulmedizin** *f* orthodox
medicine; **Schulpflicht** *f* compulsory school

attendance; **schulpflichtig** *adj* of school age;
Schulreife *f*: **die Schulreife haben** to be
ready to go to school; **Schulschiff** *nt* (*Naut*)
training ship; **Schulsprecher, in** *m(f)* head
boy/girl (*Brit*); **Schulstunde** *f* period, lesson;
Schultasche *f* school bag
Schulter [ʃʊltər] (**-, -n**) *f* shoulder; **auf
die leichte ~ nehmen** to take lightly;
Schulterblatt *nt* shoulder blade
schultern *vt* to shoulder
Schultüte *f* bag of sweets given to children on the first
day at school
Schulung *f* education, schooling
Schul- *zW*: **Schulverweigerer, in** *m(f)*
school refuser; **Schulweg** *m* way to school;
Schulwesen *nt* educational system;
Schulzeugnis *nt* school report
schummeln [ʃʊməln] (*umg*) *vi*: **(bei etw) ~** to
cheat (at sth)
schummerig [ʃʊmərɪç], **schummrig** [ʃʊmrɪç]
adj (*Beleuchtung*) dim; (*Raum*) dimly-lit
Schund (**-(e)s**) *m* trash, garbage
schund *etc* [ʃʊnt] *vb siehe* **schinden**
Schundroman *m* trashy novel
Schupo [ʃuːpo] (**-s, -s**) *m abk*
(*veraltet: = Schutzpolizist*) cop
Schuppe [ʃʊpə] (**-, -n**) *f* scale; **Schuppen** *pl*
(*Haarschuppen*) dandruff
Schuppen (**-s, -**) *m* shed; (*umg: übles Lokal*) dive;
siehe auch **Schuppe**
schuppen *vt* to scale ▷ *vr* to peel
schuppig [ʃʊpɪç] *adj* scaly
Schur [ʃuːr] (**-, -en**) *f* shearing
Schüreisen *nt* poker
schüren [ʃyːrən] *vt* to rake; (*fig*) to stir up
schürfen [ʃʏrfən] *vt, vi* to scrape, scratch; (*Min*)
to prospect; to dig
Schürfung *f* abrasion; (*Min*) prospecting
Schürhaken *m* poker
Schurke [ʃʊrkə] (**-n, -n**) *m* rogue
Schurwolle *f*: **„reine ~"** "pure new wool"
Schurz [ʃʊrts] (**-es, -e**) *m* apron
Schürze [ʃʏrtsə] (**-, -n**) *f* apron
Schürzenjäger (*umg*) *m* philanderer, one for
the girls
Schuss [ʃʊs] (**-es, -̈e**) *m* shot; (*Fussball*) kick;
(*Spritzer: von Wein, Essig etc*) dash; (*Weben*) weft;
(gut) in ~ sein (*umg*) to be in good shape *od*
nick; (*Mensch*) to be in form; **etw in ~ halten**
to keep sth in good shape; **weitab vom ~ sein**
(*fig: umg*) to be miles from where the action is;
der goldene ~ ≈ a lethal dose of a drug; **ein ~
in den Ofen** (*umg*) a complete waste of time, a
failure; **Schussbereich** *m* effective range
Schüssel [ʃʏsəl] (**-, -n**) *f* bowl, basin;
(*Servierschüssel, umg: Satellitenschüssel*) dish;
(*Waschschüssel*) basin
schusselig [ʃʊsəlɪç] (*umg*) *adj* (*zerstreut*)
scatterbrained, muddle-headed (*umg*)
Schuss- *zW*: **Schusslinie** *f* line of
fire; **Schussverletzung** *f* bullet
wound; **Schusswaffe** *f* firearm;
Schusswaffengebrauch *m* (*form*) use of

S

firearms; **Schusswechsel** *m* exchange of shots; **Schussweite** *f* range (of fire)

Schuster ['ʃuːstər] (**-s, -**) *m* cobbler, shoemaker

Schutt [ʃʊt] (**-(e)s**) *m* rubbish; (*Bauschutt*) rubble; „**~ abladen verboten**" "no tipping"; **Schuttabladeplatz** *m* refuse dump

Schüttelfrost *m* shivering

schütteln ['ʃʏtəln] *vt* to shake ▷ *vr* to shake o.s.; **sich vor Kälte ~** to shiver with cold; **sich vor Ekel ~** to shudder with *od* in disgust

schütten ['ʃʏtən] *vt* to pour; (*Zucker, Kies etc*) to tip; (*verschütten*) to spill ▷ *vi unpers* to pour (down)

schütter *adj* (*Haare*) sparse, thin

Schutthalde *f* dump

Schutthaufen *m* heap of rubble

Schutz [ʃʊts] (**-es**) *m* protection; (*Unterschlupf*) shelter; **jdn in ~ nehmen** to stand up for sb; **Schutzanzug** *m* overalls *pl*; **schutzbedürftig** *adj* in need of protection; **Schutzbefohlene, r** *f(m)* charge; **Schutzblech** *nt* mudguard; **Schutzbrief** *m* (international) travel cover; **Schutzbrille** *f* goggles *pl*

Schütze ['ʃʏtsə] (**-n, -n**) *m* gunman; (*Gewehrschütze*) rifleman; (*Scharfschütze, Sportschütze*) marksman; (*Astrol*) Sagittarius

schützen ['ʃʏtsən] *vt* to protect ▷ *vr* to protect o.s.; (**sich**) **~ vor** +*dat od* **gegen** to protect (o.s.) from *od* against; **gesetzlich geschützt** registered; **urheberrechtlich geschützt** protected by copyright; **vor Nässe ~!** keep dry

Schützenfest *nt* fair featuring shooting matches

Schutzengel *m* guardian angel

Schützen- *zW*: **Schützengraben** *m* trench; **Schützenhilfe** *f* (*fig*) support; **Schützenverein** *m* shooting club

Schutz- *zW*: **Schutzgebiet** *nt* protectorate; (*Naturschutzgebiet*) reserve; **Schutzgebühr** *f* (token) fee; **Schutzhaft** *f* protective custody; **Schutzheilige, r** *f(m)* patron saint; **Schutzhelm** *m* safety helmet; **Schutzimpfung** *f* immunization

Schützling ['ʃʏtslɪŋ] *m* protégé; (*bes Kind*) charge

Schutz- *zW*: **schutzlos** *adj* defenceless (*Brit*), defenseless (*US*); **Schutzmann** (**-(e)s**, *pl* **-leute** *od* **-männer**) *m* policeman; **Schutzmarke** *f* trademark; **Schutzmaßnahme** *f* precaution; **Schutzpatron** *m* patron saint; **Schutzschirm** *m* (*Tech*) protective screen; **Schutzumschlag** *m* (book) jacket; **Schutzverband** *m* (*Med*) protective bandage *od* dressing; **Schutzvorrichtung** *f* safety device

Schw. *abk* = **Schwester**

schwabbelig ['ʃvab(ə)lɪç] (*umg*) *adj* (*Körperteil*) flabby; (*: Gelee*) wobbly

Schwabe ['ʃvaːbə] (**-n, -n**) *m* Swabian

Schwaben (**-s**) *nt* Swabia

Schwäbin ['ʃvɛːbɪn] *f* Swabian

schwäbisch ['ʃvɛːbɪʃ] *adj* Swabian

schwach [ʃvax] *adj* weak, feeble; (*Gedächtnis, Gesundheit*) poor; (*Hoffnung*) faint; **~ werden** to weaken; **das ist ein ~es Bild** (*umg*) *od* **eine ~e Leistung** (*umg*) that's a poor show; **ein ~er Trost** cold *od* small comfort; **mach mich nicht ~!** (*umg*) don't say that!; **auf ~en Beinen** *od* **Füßen stehen** (*fig*) to be on shaky ground; (*: Theorie*) to be shaky

Schwäche ['ʃvɛçə] (**-, -n**) *f* weakness

schwächen *vt* to weaken

schwach- *zW*: **Schwachheit** *f* weakness; **Schwachkopf** (*umg*) *m* dimwit, idiot; **schwachköpfig** *adj* silly, daft (*Brit*)

schwächlich *adj* weakly, delicate

Schwächling *m* weakling

Schwach- *zW*: **Schwachsinn** *m* (*Med*) mental deficiency, feeble-mindedness (*veraltet*); (*umg: Quatsch*) rubbish; (*fig: umg: unsinnige Tat*) idiocy; **schwachsinnig** *adj* mentally deficient; (*Idee*) idiotic; **Schwachstelle** *f* weak point; **Schwachstrom** *m* weak current

Schwächung ['ʃvɛçʊŋ] *f* weakening

Schwaden ['ʃvaːdən] (**-s, -**) *m* cloud

schwafeln ['ʃvaːfəln] (*umg*) *vi* to blather, drivel; (*in einer Prüfung*) to waffle

Schwager ['ʃvaːɡər] (**-s, ̈**) *m* brother-in-law

Schwägerin ['ʃvɛːɡərɪn] *f* sister-in-law

Schwalbe ['ʃvalbə] (**-, -n**) *f* swallow

Schwall [ʃval] (**-(e)s, -e**) *m* surge; (*Worte*) flood, torrent

Schwamm (**-(e)s, ̈e**) *m* sponge; (*Pilz*) fungus; **~ drüber!** (*umg*) (let's) forget it!

schwamm *etc* [ʃvam] *vb siehe* **schwimmen**

schwammig *adj* spongy; (*Gesicht*) puffy; (*vage: Begriff*) woolly (*Brit*), wooly (*US*)

Schwan [ʃvaːn] (**-(e)s, ̈e**) *m* swan

schwand *etc* [ʃvant] *vb siehe* **schwinden**

schwanen *vi unpers*: **jdm schwant es** sb has a foreboding *od* forebodings; **jdm schwant etwas** sb senses something might happen

schwang *etc* [ʃvaŋ] *vb siehe* **schwingen**

schwanger ['ʃvaŋər] *adj* pregnant

schwängern ['ʃvɛŋərn] *vt* to make pregnant

Schwangerschaft *f* pregnancy

Schwangerschaftsabbruch *m* termination of pregnancy, abortion

Schwank [ʃvaŋk] (**-(e)s, ̈e**) *m* funny story; (*Liter*) merry *od* comical tale; (*Theat*) farce

schwanken *vi* to sway; (*taumeln*) to stagger, reel; (*Preise, Zahlen*) to fluctuate; (*zögern*) to hesitate; (*Überzeugung etc*) to begin to waver; **ins S~ kommen** (*Baum, Gebäude etc*) to start to sway; (*Preise, Kurs etc*) to start to fluctuate *od* vary

Schwankung *f* fluctuation

Schwanz [ʃvants] (**-es, ̈e**) *m* tail; (*umg!: Penis*) prick (!); **kein ~** (*umg*) not a (blessed) soul

schwänzen ['ʃvɛntsən] (*umg*) *vt* (*Stunde, Vorlesung*) to skip ▷ *vi* to play truant

Schwänzer ['ʃvɛntsər] (**-s, -**) (*umg*) *m* truant

schwappen ['ʃvapən] *vi* (*überschwappen*) to splash, slosh

Schwarm [ʃvarm] (**-(e)s, ̈e**) *m* swarm; (*umg*) heart-throb, idol

schwärmen ['ʃvɛrmən] *vi* to swarm; **~ für** to be mad *od* wild about

Schwärmerei [ʃvɛrmə'raɪ] f enthusiasm
schwärmerisch adj impassioned, effusive
Schwarte ['ʃvartə] (-, -n) f hard skin;
(*Speckschwarte*) rind; (*umg: Buch*) tome (*hum*)
Schwartenmagen (-s) m (*Koch*) brawn
schwarz [ʃvarts] adj black; (*umg: ungesetzlich*)
illicit; (: *katholisch*) Catholic, Papist (*pej*); (*Pol*)
Christian Democrat; **ins S~e treffen** (*lit*,
fig) to hit the bull's-eye; **das S~e Brett** the
notice (*Brit*) od bulletin (*US*) board; **~e Liste**
blacklist; **~es Loch** black hole; **das S~e Meer**
the Black Sea; **S~er Peter** (*Karten*) children's
card game; **jdm den ~en Peter zuschieben**
(*fig: die Verantwortung abschieben*) to pass the
buck to sb (*umg*); **dort wählen alle ~** they all
vote conservative there; **in den ~en Zahlen**
in the black; *siehe auch* **schwarzärgern;**
schwarzmalen; schwarzsehen;
Schwarzarbeit f illicit work, moonlighting;
Schwarzarbeiter m moonlighter;
schwarzärgern vr to get extremely annoyed;
Schwarzbrot nt (*Pumpernickel*) black bread,
pumpernickel; (*braun*) brown rye bread
Schwärze ['ʃvɛrtsə] (-, -n) f blackness; (*Farbe*)
blacking; (*Druckerschwärze*) printer's ink
Schwarze, r f(m) (*Neger*) black; (*umg: Katholik*)
Papist; (*Pol: umg*) Christian Democrat
schwärzen vt to blacken
Schwarz- zW: **schwarzfahren** unreg vi to
travel without paying; (*ohne Führerschein*) to
drive without a licence (*Brit*) od license (*US*);
Schwarzfahrer m (*Bus etc*) fare dodger (*umg*);
Schwarzhandel m black market (trade);
Schwarzhändler m black-market operator;
schwarzhören vi to listen to the radio without
a licence (*Brit*) od license (*US*)
schwärzlich ['ʃvɛrtslɪç] adj blackish, darkish
Schwarz- zW: **schwarzmalen** vi to be
pessimistic; **Schwarzmarkt** m black market;
schwarzsehen vi unreg (*TV*) to watch TV
without a licence (*Brit*) od license (*US*); (*umg*) to
see the gloomy side of things; **Schwarzseher**
m pessimist; (*TV*) viewer without a licence
(*Brit*) od license (*US*); **Schwarzwald** m Black
Forest; **Schwarzwälder Kirschtorte** f Black
Forest gâteau; **schwarz-weiß, schwarzweiß**
adj black and white; **Schwarzweiß-** in zw black
and white; **Schwarzwurzel** f (*Koch*) salsify
Schwatz [ʃvats] (-es, -e) m chat
schwatzen ['ʃvatsən] vi to chat; (*schnell,
unaufhörlich*) to chatter; (*über belanglose Dinge*) to
prattle; (*Unsinn reden*) to blether (*umg*)
schwätzen ['ʃvɛtsən] vi = **schwatzen**
Schwätzer, in ['ʃvɛtsər(ɪn)] (-s, -) m(f)
chatterbox; (*Schwafler*) gasbag (*umg*);
(*Klatschbase*) gossip
schwatzhaft adj talkative, gossipy
Schwebe ['ʃve:bə] f: **in der ~** (*fig*) in abeyance;
(*Jur, Comm*) pending
Schwebebahn f overhead railway (*Brit*) od
railroad (*US*)
Schwebebalken m (*Sport*) beam
schweben vi to drift, float; (*hoch*) to soar;

(*unentschieden sein*) to be in the balance; **es
schwebte mir vor Augen** (*Bild*) I saw it in my
mind's eye
schwebend adj (*Tech, Chem*) suspended; (*fig*)
undecided, unresolved; **~es Verfahren** (*Jur*)
pending case
schwed. abk = **schwedisch**
Schwede ['ʃve:də] (-n, -n) m Swede
Schweden (-s) nt Sweden
Schwedin ['ʃve:dɪn] f Swede
schwedisch adj Swedish
Schwefel ['ʃve:fəl] (-s) m sulphur (*Brit*), sulfur
(*US*); **Schwefeldioxid** nt sulphur dioxide
schwefelig adj sulphurous (*Brit*), sulfurous (*US*)
Schwefelsäure f sulphuric (*Brit*) od sulfuric
(*US*) acid
Schweif [ʃvaɪf] (-(e)s, -e) m tail
schweifen vi to wander, roam
Schweigegeld nt hush money
Schweigeminute f one minute('s) silence
schweigen ['ʃvaɪgən] unreg vi to be silent; (*still
sein*) to keep quiet; **kannst du ~?** can you keep
a secret?; **ganz zu ~ von ...** to say nothing
of ...; **Schweigen** (-s) nt silence
schweigend adj silent
Schweigepflicht f pledge of secrecy; (*von
Anwalt etc*) requirement of confidentiality
schweigsam ['ʃvaɪkza:m] adj silent; (*als
Charaktereigenschaft*) taciturn; **Schweigsamkeit**
f silence; taciturnity
Schwein [ʃvaɪn] (-(e)s, -e) nt pig; (*fig: umg*)
(good) luck; **kein ~** (*umg*) nobody, not a single
person
Schweine- zW: **Schweinebraten** m joint of
pork; (*gekocht*) roast pork; **Schweinefleisch**
nt pork; **Schweinegeld** (*umg*) nt: **ein
Schweinegeld** a packet; **Schweinegrippe** f
swine flu; **Schweinehund** (*umg*) m stinker,
swine
Schweinerei [ʃvaɪnə'raɪ] f mess; (*Gemeinheit*)
dirty trick; **so eine ~!** (*umg*) how disgusting!
Schweineschmalz nt dripping; (*als Kochfett*)
lard
Schweinestall m pigsty
schweinisch adj filthy
Schweinsleder nt pigskin
Schweinsohr nt pig's ear; (*Gebäck*) (kidney-
shaped) pastry
Schweiß [ʃvaɪs] (-es) m sweat, perspiration;
Schweißband nt sweatband
Schweißbrenner (-s, -) m (*Tech*) welding torch
schweißen vt, vi to weld
Schweißer (-s, -) m welder
Schweiß- zW: **Schweißfüße** pl sweaty feet pl;
Schweißnaht f weld; **schweißnass** adj sweaty
Schweiz [ʃvaɪts] f: **die ~** Switzerland
schweiz. abk = **schweizerisch**
Schweizer ['ʃvaɪtsər] (-s, -) m Swiss ▷ adj attrib
Swiss; **Schweizerdeutsch** nt Swiss German;
Schweizerin f Swiss; **schweizerisch** adj Swiss
schwelen ['ʃve:lən] vi to smoulder (*Brit*),
smolder (*US*)
schwelgen ['ʃvɛlgən] vi to indulge o.s.; **~ in**

S

+*dat* to indulge in

Schwelle ['ʃvɛlə] (**-, -n**) *f* (*auch fig*) threshold; (*Eisenb*) sleeper (*Brit*), tie (*US*)

schwellen *unreg vi* to swell

Schwellenland *nt* threshold country

Schwellung *f* swelling

Schwemme ['ʃvɛmə] *f*: **eine ~ an** +*dat* a glut of

schwemmen ['ʃvɛmən] *vt* (*treiben: Sand etc*) to wash

Schwengel ['ʃvɛŋəl] (**-s, -**) *m* pump handle; (*Glockenschwengel*) clapper

Schwenk [ʃvɛŋk] (**-(e)s, -s**) *m* (*Film*) pan, panning shot

Schwenkarm *m* swivel arm

schwenkbar *adj* swivel-mounted

schwenken *vt* to swing; (*Kamera*) to pan; (*Fahne*) to wave; (*Kartoffeln*) to toss; (*abspülen*) to rinse ▷ *vi* to turn, swivel; (*Mil*) to wheel

Schwenkung *f* turn; (*Mil*) wheel

schwer [ʃveːr] *adj* heavy; (*schwierig*) difficult, hard; (*schlimm*) serious, bad ▷ *adv* (*sehr*) very (much); (*verletzt etc*) seriously, badly; **~ erziehbar** maladjusted; **jdm/sich etw ~ machen** to make sth difficult for sb/o.s.; **~ verdaulich** indigestible; (*fig*) heavy; **~ verdient** (*Geld*) hard-earned; **~ verletzt** seriously *od* badly injured; **~ verwundet** seriously wounded; **~ erkältet sein** to have a heavy cold; **er lernt ~** he's a slow learner; **er ist ~ in Ordnung** (*umg*) he's a good bloke (*Brit*) *od* guy; **~ hören** to be hard of hearing; *siehe auch* **schwerfallen; schwernehmen; schwertun; schwerwiegend;** **Schwerarbeiter** *m* labourer (*Brit*), laborer (*US*); **Schwerbehinderte, r** *f(m)*, **Schwerbeschädigte, r** *f(m)* (*veraltet*) severely handicapped person

Schwere (**-, -n**) *f* weight; heaviness; (*Phys*) gravity; **schwerelos** *adj* weightless; **Schwerelosigkeit** *f* weightlessness

schwer- *zW*: **schwerfallen** *unreg vi*: **jdm schwerfallen** to be difficult for sb; **schwerfällig** *adj* (*auch Stil*) ponderous; (*Gang*) clumsy, awkward; (*Verstand*) slow; **Schwergewicht** *nt* heavyweight; (*fig*) emphasis; **schwergewichtig** *adj* heavyweight; **schwerhörig** *adj* hard of hearing; **Schwerindustrie** *f* heavy industry; **Schwerkraft** *f* gravity; **Schwerkranke, r** *f(m)* person who is seriously ill; **schwerlich** *adv* hardly; **Schwermetall** *nt* heavy metal; **schwermütig** *adj* melancholy; **schwernehmen** *unreg vt* to take to heart; **Schwerpunkt** *m* centre (*Brit*) *od* center (*US*) of gravity; (*fig*) emphasis, crucial point; **Schwerpunktstreik** *m* pinpoint strike; **schwerreich** (*umg*) *adj attrib* stinking rich

Schwert [ʃveːrt] (**-(e)s, -er**) *nt* sword; **Schwertlilie** *f* iris

schwer- *zW*: **schwertun** *unreg vr*: **sich** *dat od akk* **schwertun** to have difficulties; **Schwerverbrecher** *m* criminal; **Schwerverletzte, r** *f(m)* serious casualty;

schwerwiegend *adj* weighty, important

Schwester ['ʃvɛstər] (**-, -n**) *f* sister; (*Med*) nurse; **schwesterlich** *adj* sisterly

schwieg *etc* [ʃviːk] *vb siehe* **schweigen**

Schwieger- *zW*: **Schwiegereltern** *pl* parents-in-law *pl*; **Schwiegermutter** *f* mother-in-law; **Schwiegersohn** *m* son-in-law; **Schwiegertochter** *f* daughter-in-law; **Schwiegervater** *m* father-in-law

Schwiele ['ʃviːlə] (**-, -n**) *f* callus

schwierig ['ʃviːrɪç] *adj* difficult, hard; **Schwierigkeit** *f* difficulty; **Schwierigkeitsgrad** *m* degree of difficulty

schwillt [ʃvɪlt] *vb siehe* **schwellen**

Schwimmbad *nt* swimming baths *pl*

Schwimmbecken *nt* swimming pool

schwimmen *unreg vi* to swim; (*treiben, nicht sinken*) to float; (*fig: unsicher sein*) to be all at sea; **im Geld ~** (*umg*) to be rolling in money; **mir schwimmt es vor den Augen** I feel dizzy

Schwimmer (**-s, -**) *m* swimmer; (*Angeln*) float

Schwimmerin *f* swimmer

Schwimm- *zW*: **Schwimmflosse** *f* (*von Taucher*) flipper; **Schwimmhaut** *f* (*Ornithologie*) web; **Schwimmlehrer** *m* swimming instructor; **Schwimmsport** *m* swimming; **Schwimmweste** *f* life jacket

Schwindel ['ʃvɪndəl] (**-s**) *m* dizziness; (*Betrug*) swindle, fraud; (*Zeug*) stuff; **in ~ erregender Höhe** at a dizzy height; **schwindelfrei** *adj* free from giddiness

schwindeln *vi* (*umg: lügen*) to fib; **mir schwindelt** I feel dizzy; **jdm schwindelt es** sb feels dizzy

schwinden ['ʃvɪndən] *unreg vi* to disappear; (*Kräfte*) to fade, fail; (*sich verringern*) to decrease

Schwindler (**-s, -**) *m* swindler; (*Hochstapler*) con man, fraud; (*Lügner*) liar

schwindlig *adj* dizzy; **mir ist ~** I feel dizzy

Schwindsucht *f* (*veraltet*) consumption

schwingen ['ʃvɪŋən] *unreg vt* to swing; (*Waffe etc*) to brandish ▷ *vi* to swing; (*vibrieren*) to vibrate; (*klingen*) to sound

Schwinger (**-s, -**) *m* (*Boxen*) swing

Schwingtor *nt* up-and-over door

Schwingtür *f* swing door(s *pl*) (*Brit*), swinging door(s *pl*) (*US*)

Schwingung *f* vibration; (*Phys*) oscillation

Schwips [ʃvɪps] (**-es, -e**) *m*: **einen ~ haben** to be tipsy

schwirren ['ʃvɪrən] *vi* to buzz

Schwitze ['ʃvɪtsə] (**-, -n**) *f* (*Koch*) roux

schwitzen *vi* to sweat, perspire

schwofen ['ʃvoːfən] (*umg*) *vi* to dance

schwoll *etc* [ʃvɔl] *vb siehe* **schwellen**

schwören ['ʃvøːrən] *unreg vt, vi* to swear; **auf jdn/etw ~** (*fig*) to swear by sb/sth

schwul [ʃvuːl] (*umg*) *adj* gay, queer (*pej*)

schwül [ʃvyːl] *adj* sultry, close

Schwule, r (*umg*) *m* gay, queer (*pej*), fag (*US pej*)

Schwüle (**-**) *f* sultriness, closeness

Schwulität [ʃvuliˈtɛːt] (*umg*) *f* trouble, difficulty

Schwulst [ʃvʊlst] **(-(e)s)** m bombast
schwülstig ['ʃvʏlstɪç] adj pompous
Schwund [ʃvʊnt] **(-(e)s)** m (+gen) decrease (in), decline (in), dwindling (of); (Med) atrophy; (Schrumpfen) shrinkage
Schwung [ʃvʊŋ] **(-(e)s, ⁻e)** m swing; (Triebkraft) momentum; (fig: Energie) verve, energy; (umg: Menge) batch; **in ~ sein** (fig) to be in full swing; **~ in die Sache bringen** (umg) to liven things up; **schwunghaft** adj brisk, lively; **Schwungrad** nt flywheel; **schwungvoll** adj vigorous
Schwur (-(e)s, ⁻e) m oath
schwur etc [ʃvuːr] vb siehe **schwören**
Schwurgericht nt court with a jury
SDR (-) m abk (= Süddeutscher Rundfunk) South German Radio
sechs [zɛks] num six; **Sechseck** nt hexagon; **sechshundert** num six hundred
sechste, r, s adj sixth
Sechstel ['zɛkstəl] **(-s, -)** nt sixth
sechzehn ['zɛçtseːn] num sixteen
sechzig ['zɛçtsɪç] num sixty
See¹ [zeː] **(-, -n)** f sea; **an der ~** by the sea, at the seaside; **in ~ stechen** to put to sea; **auf hoher ~** on the high seas
See² [zeː] **(-s, -n)** m lake
See- zW: **Seebad** nt seaside resort; **Seebär** m (hum: umg) seadog; (Zool) fur seal; **Seefahrt** f seafaring; (Reise) voyage; **seefest** adj (Mensch) not subject to seasickness; **Seegang** m (motion of the) sea; **Seegras** nt seaweed; **Seehund** m seal; **Seeigel** m sea urchin; **Seekarte** f chart; **seekrank** adj seasick; **Seekrankheit** f seasickness; **Seelachs** m rock salmon
Seele ['zeːlə] **(-, -n)** f soul; (Mittelpunkt) life and soul; **jdm aus der ~ sprechen** to express exactly what sb feels; **das liegt mir auf der ~** it weighs heavily on my mind; **eine ~ von Mensch** an absolute dear
Seelen- zW: **Seelenamt** nt (Rel) requiem; **Seelenfriede, Seelenfrieden** m peace of mind; **Seelenheil** nt salvation of one's soul; (fig) spiritual welfare; **Seelenruhe** f: **in aller Seelenruhe** calmly; (kaltblütig) as cool as you please; **seelenruhig** adv calmly
Seeleute ['zeːlɔytə] pl seamen pl
Seel- zW: **seelisch** adj mental; (Rel) spiritual; (Belastung) emotional; **Seelsorge** f pastoral duties pl; **Seelsorger (-s, -)** m clergyman
See- zW: **Seemacht** f naval power; **Seemann (-(e)s,** pl **-leute)** m seaman, sailor; **Seemeile** f nautical mile
Seengebiet ['zeːəŋɡəbiːt] nt lakeland district
See- zW: **Seenot** f: **in Seenot** (Schiff etc) in distress; **Seepferd, Seepferdchen** nt sea horse; **Seeräuber** m pirate; **Seerecht** nt maritime law; **Seerose** f waterlily; **Seestern** m starfish; **Seetang** m seaweed; **seetüchtig** adj seaworthy; **Seeversicherung** f marine insurance; **Seeweg** m sea route; **auf dem Seeweg** by sea; **Seezunge** f sole

Segel ['zeːɡəl] **(-s, -)** nt sail; **mit vollen ~n** under full sail od canvas; (fig) with gusto; **die ~ streichen** (fig) to give in; **Segelboot** nt yacht; **Segelfliegen (-s)** nt gliding; **Segelflieger** m glider pilot; **Segelflugzeug** nt glider
segeln vt, vi to sail; **durch eine Prüfung ~** (umg) to flop in an exam, fail (in) an exam
Segel- zW: **Segelschiff** nt sailing vessel; **Segelsport** m sailing; **Segeltuch** nt canvas
Segen ['zeːɡən] **(-s, -)** m blessing
segensreich adj beneficial
Segler ['zeːɡlər] **(-s, -)** m sailor, yachtsman; (Boot) sailing boat
Seglerin f yachtswoman
segnen ['zeːɡnən] vt to bless
sehen ['zeːən] unreg vt, vi to see; (in bestimmte Richtung) to look; (Fernsehsendung) to watch; **sieht man das?** does it show?; **da sieht man(s) mal wieder!** that's typical!; **du siehst das nicht richtig** you've got it wrong; **so ge~** looked at in this way; **sich ~ lassen** to put in an appearance, appear; **das neue Rathaus kann sich ~ lassen** the new town hall is certainly something to be proud of; **siehe oben/unten** see above/below; **da kann man mal ~** that just shows (you) od just goes to show (umg); **mal ~!** we'll see!; **darauf ~, dass ...** to make sure (that) ...; **jdn kommen ~** to see sb coming
sehenswert adj worth seeing
Sehenswürdigkeiten pl sights pl (of a town)
Seher (-s, -) m seer
Sehfehler m sight defect
Sehkraft f (eye)sight
Sehne ['zeːnə] **(-, -n)** f sinew; (an Bogen) string
sehnen vr: **sich ~ nach** to long od yearn for
Sehnenscheidenentzündung f (Med) tendinitis
Sehnerv m optic nerve
sehnig adj sinewy
sehnlich adj ardent
Sehnsucht f longing
sehnsüchtig adj longing; (Erwartung) eager
sehnsuchtsvoll adv longingly, yearningly
sehr [zeːr] adv (vor adj, adv) very; (mit Verben) a lot, (very) much; **zu ~** too much; **er ist ~ dafür/dagegen** he is all for it/very much against it; **wie ~ er sich auch bemühte ...** however much he tried ...
Sehvermögen ['zeːfɛrmøːɡən] **(-s)** nt powers pl of vision
seicht [zaɪçt] adj (lit, fig) shallow
seid [zaɪt] vb siehe **sein**
Seide ['zaɪdə] **(-, -n)** f silk
Seidel (-s, -) nt tankard, beer mug
seiden adj silk; **Seidenpapier** nt tissue paper
seidig ['zaɪdɪç] adj silky
Seife ['zaɪfə] **(-, -n)** f soap
Seifen- zW: **Seifenblase** f soap bubble; (fig) bubble; **Seifenlauge** f soapsuds pl; **Seifenschale** f soap dish; **Seifenschaum** m lather
seifig ['zaɪfɪç] adj soapy

S

301

seihen ['zaɪən] vt to strain, filter
Seil [zaɪl] (-(e)s, -e) nt rope; (Kabel) cable;
 Seilbahn f cable railway; **Seilhüpfen** (-s)
 nt skipping; **Seilspringen** (-s) nt skipping;
 Seiltänzer, in m(f) tightrope walker; **Seilzug**
 m tackle

SCHLÜSSELWORT

sein [zaɪn] (pt **war**, pp **gewesen**) vi **1** to be; **ich
 bin** I am; **du bist** you are; **er/sie/es ist** he/
 she/it is; **wir sind/ihr seid/sie sind** we/
 you/they are; **wir waren** we were; **wir sind
 gewesen** we have been
 2: seien Sie nicht böse don't be angry; **sei so
 gut und ...** be so kind as to ...; **das wäre gut**
 that would od that'd be a good thing; **wenn
 ich Sie wäre** if I were od was you; **das wärs**
 that's all, that's it; **morgen bin ich in Rom**
 tomorrow I'll od I will od I shall be in Rome;
 waren Sie mal in Rom? have you ever been
 to Rome?
 3: wie ist das zu verstehen? how is that to
 be understood?; **er ist nicht zu ersetzen**
 he cannot be replaced; **mit ihr ist nicht zu
 reden** you can't talk to her
 4: mir ist kalt I'm cold; **mir ist, als hätte
 ich ihn früher schon einmal gesehen** I've a
 feeling I've seen him before; **was ist?** what's
 the matter?, what is it?; **ist was?** is something
 the matter?; **es sei denn(, dass ...)** unless ...;
 wie dem auch sei be that as it may; **wie wäre
 es mit ...?** how od what about ...?; **etw sein
 lassen** (aufhören) to stop (doing) sth; (nicht
 tun) to drop sth, leave sth; **lass das sein!** stop
 that!; **es ist an dir, zu ...** it's up to you to ...;
 was sind Sie (beruflich)? what do you do?;
 das kann schon sein that may well be
 ▷ pron his; (bei Dingen) its

Sein (-s) nt: **~ oder Nichtsein** to be or not to be
sein, r, s poss pron his; its; **er ist gut ~ zwei
 Meter** (umg) he's a good two metres (Brit)
 od meters (US); **die S~n** (geh) his family, his
 people; **jedem das S~** to each his own
seiner gen von **er; es** ▷ pron of him; of it
seinerseits adv for his part
seinerzeit adv in those days, formerly
seinesgleichen pron people like him
seinetwegen adv (für ihn) for his sake; (wegen
 ihm) on his account; (von ihm aus) as far as he is
 concerned
seinetwillen adv: **um ~ = seinetwegen**
seinige pron: **der/die/das ~** his
Seismograf [zaɪsmo'graːf] (-en, -en) m
 seismograph
seit [zaɪt] präp +dat since; (Zeitdauer) for, in (bes
 US) ▷ konj since; **er ist ~ einer Woche hier** he
 has been here for a week; **~ Langem** for a long
 time; **seitdem** adv, konj since
Seite ['zaɪtə] (-, -n) f side; (Buchseite) page;
 (Mil) flank; **~ an Seite** side by side; **jdm zur
 ~ stehen** (fig) to stand by sb's side; **jdn zur ~**

nehmen to take sb aside; **auf der einen ~ ...,
 auf der anderen (~) ...** on the one hand ..., on
 the other (hand) ...; **einer Sache** dat **die beste
 ~ abgewinnen** to make the best od most of sth;
 siehe auch **aufseiten; vonseiten**
Seiten- zW: **Seitenairbag** m (Aut) side-impact
 airbag; **Seitenansicht** f side view; **Seitenhieb**
 m (fig) passing shot, dig; **seitenlang** adj several
 pages long, going on for pages; **Seitenruder** nt
 (Aviat) rudder
seitens präp +gen on the part of
Seiten- zW: **Seitenschiff** nt aisle; **Seitensprung**
 m extramarital escapade; **Seitenstechen**
 nt (a) stitch; **Seitenstraße** f side road;
 Seitenstreifen m (der Straße) verge (Brit),
 berm (US); (der Autobahn) hard shoulder
 (Brit), shoulder (US); **seitenverkehrt** adj the
 wrong way round; **Seitenwagen** m sidecar;
 Seitenwind m crosswind; **Seitenzahl** f page
 number; (Gesamtzahl) number of pages
seit- zW: **seither** [zaɪt'heːr] adv, konj since
 (then); **seitlich** adv on one/the side ▷ adj side
 attrib; **seitwärts** adv sideways
sek, Sek. abk (= Sekunde) sec.
Sekretär [zekre'tɛːr] m secretary; (Möbel)
 bureau
Sekretariat [zekretari'aːt] (-(e)s, -e) nt
 secretary's office, secretariat
Sekretärin f secretary
Sekt [zɛkt] (-(e)s, -e) m sparkling wine
Sekte (-, -n) f sect
Sektor ['zɛktɔr] m sector; (Sachgebiet) field
Sekunda [ze'kʊnda] (-, **Sekunden**) f
 (Sch: früher: Untersekunda/Obersekunda) sixth/
 seventh year of German secondary school
sekundär [zekʊn'dɛːr] adj secondary;
 Sekundärliteratur f secondary literature
Sekunde (-, -n) f second
Sekunden- zW: **Sekundenkleber** m superglue;
 Sekundenschnelle f: **in Sekundenschnelle**
 in a matter of seconds; **Sekundenzeiger** m
 second hand
sel. abk = **selig**
selber ['zɛlbər] demon pron = **selbst**;
 Selbermachen nt do-it-yourself, DIY (Brit);
 (von Kleidern etc) making one's own
Selbst [zɛlpst] (-) nt self

SCHLÜSSELWORT

selbst [zɛlpst] pron **1: ich/er/wir selbst** I
 myself/he himself/we ourselves; **sie ist die
 Tugend selbst** she's virtue itself; **er braut
 sein Bier selbst** he brews his own beer; **das
 muss er selbst wissen** it's up to him; **wie
 gehts? — gut, und selbst?** how are things? —
 fine, and yourself?
 2 (ohne Hilfe) alone, on my/his/one's etc own;
 von selbst by itself; **er kam von selbst**
 he came of his own accord; **selbst ist der
 Mann/die Frau!** self-reliance is the name of
 the game (umg); **selbst gemacht** home-made;
 selbst gestrickt hand-knitted; (umg: Methode

etc) homespun, amateurish; **selbst verdientes Geld** money one has earned o.s. ▷ *adv* even; **selbst wenn** even if; **selbst Gott** even God (himself)

Selbstachtung *f* self-respect
selbständig *etc* ['zɛlpʃtɛndɪç] *adj* = **selbstständig** *etc*
Selbst- *zW*: **Selbstanzeige** *f*: **Selbstanzeige erstatten** to come forward oneself; **der Dieb hat Selbstanzeige erstattet** the thief has come forward; **Selbstauslöser** *m* (*Phot*) delayed-action shutter release; **Selbstbedienung** *f* self-service; **Selbstbedienungsmentalität** *f* self-service mentality; **Selbstbefriedigung** *f* masturbation; (*fig*) self-gratification; **Selbstbeherrschung** *f* self-control; **Selbstbestätigung** *f* self-affirmation; **selbstbewusst** *adj* self-confident; (*selbstsicher*) self-assured; **Selbstbewusstsein** *nt* self-confidence; **Selbstbildnis** *nt* self-portrait; **Selbsterhaltung** *f* self-preservation; **Selbsterkenntnis** *f* self-knowledge; **Selbstfahrer** *m* (*Aut*): **Autovermietung für Selbstfahrer** self-drive car hire (*Brit*) *od* rental; **selbstgefällig** *adj* smug, self-satisfied; **selbstgerecht** *adj* self-righteous; **Selbstgespräch** *nt* conversation with o.s.; **selbstgewiss** *adj* confident; **selbstherrlich** *adj* high-handed; (*selbstgerecht*) self-satisfied; **Selbsthilfe** *f* self-help; **zur Selbsthilfe greifen** to take matters into one's own hands; **selbstklebend** *adj* self-adhesive; **Selbstkostenpreis** *m* cost price; **selbstlos** *adj* unselfish, selfless; **Selbstmord** *m* suicide; **Selbstmordanschlag** *m* suicide attack; **Selbstmordattentäter, in** *m(f)* suicide bomber; **Selbstmörder, in** *m(f)* (*Person*) suicide; **selbstmörderisch** *adj* suicidal; **selbstsicher** *adj* self-assured; **Selbstsicherheit** *f* self-assurance; **selbstständig** ['zɛlpstʃtɛndɪç] *adj* independent; **sich selbstständig machen** (*beruflich*) to set up on one's own, start one's own business; **Selbstständigkeit** *f* independence; **Selbststudium** *nt* private study; **selbstsüchtig** *adj* selfish; **selbsttätig** *adj* automatic; **Selbstüberwindung** *f* willpower; **selbstvergessen** *adj* absent-minded; (*Blick*) faraway; **selbstverschuldet** *adj*: **wenn der Unfall selbstverschuldet ist** if there is personal responsibility for the accident; **Selbstversorger** *m*: **Selbstversorger sein** to be self-sufficient *od* self-reliant; **Urlaub für Selbstversorger** self-catering holiday
selbstverständlich *adj* obvious ▷ *adv* naturally; **ich halte das für** ~ I take that for granted
Selbstverständlichkeit *f* (*Unbefangenheit*) naturalness; (*natürliche Voraussetzung*) matter of course
Selbst- *zW*: **Selbstverständnis** *nt*: **nach**

seinem eigenen Selbstverständnis as he sees himself; **Selbstverteidigung** *f* self-defence (*Brit*), self-defense (*US*); **Selbstvertrauen** *nt* self-confidence; **Selbstverwaltung** *f* autonomy, self-government; **Selbstwählferndienst** *m* (*Tel*) automatic dialling service, subscriber trunk dialling (*Brit*), STD (*Brit*), direct distance dialing (*US*); **Selbstwertgefühl** *nt* feeling of one's own worth *od* value, self-esteem; **selbstzufrieden** *adj* self-satisfied; **Selbstzweck** *m* end in itself
selig ['ze:lɪç] *adj* happy, blissful; (*Rel*) blessed; (*tot*) late; **Seligkeit** *f* bliss
Sellerie ['zɛlari:] (**-s, -(s)** *od* **-, -n**) *m od f* celery
selten ['zɛltən] *adj* rare ▷ *adv* seldom, rarely; **Seltenheit** *f* rarity; **Seltenheitswert** (**-(e)s**) *m* rarity value
Selterswasser ['zɛltərsvasər] *nt* soda water
seltsam ['zɛltza:m] *adj* curious, strange
seltsamerweise *adv* curiously, strangely
Seltsamkeit *f* strangeness
Semester [ze'mɛstər] (**-s, -**) *nt* semester; **ein älteres** ~ a senior student
Semi- [zemi] *in zw* semi-
Semikolon [-'ko:lɔn] (**-s, -s**) *nt* semicolon
Seminar [zemi'na:r] (**-s, -e**) *nt* seminary; (*Kurs*) seminar; (*Univ: Ort*) department building
semitisch [ze'mi:tɪʃ] *adj* Semitic
Semmel ['zɛməl] (**-, -n**) *f* roll; **Semmelbrösel, Semmelbröseln** *pl* breadcrumbs *pl*; **Semmelknödel** (*Südd, Österr*) *m* bread dumpling
sen. *abk* (= *senior*) sen.
Senat [ze'na:t] (**-(e)s, -e**) *m* senate
Sendebereich *m* transmission range
Sendefolge *f* (*Serie*) series
senden[1] *unreg vt* to send
senden[2] *vt, vi* (*Rundf, TV*) to transmit, broadcast
Sendenetz *nt* network
Sendepause *f* (*Rundf, TV*) interval
Sender (**-s, -**) *m* station; (*Anlage*) transmitter
Sende- *zW*: **Sendereihe** *f* series (of broadcasts); **Sendeschluss** *m* (*Rundf, TV*) closedown; **Sendestation** *f* transmitting station; **Sendestelle** *f* transmitting station; **Sendezeit** *f* broadcasting time, air time
Sendung ['zɛndʊŋ] *f* consignment; (*Aufgabe*) mission; (*Rundf, TV*) transmission; (*Programm*) programme (*Brit*), program (*US*)
Senegal [ze:negal] (**-s**) *nt* Senegal
Senf [zɛnf] (**-(e)s, -e**) *m* mustard; **seinen ~ dazugeben** (*umg*) to put one's oar in; **Senfkorn** *nt* mustard seed
sengen ['zɛŋən] *vt* to singe ▷ *vi* to scorch
senil [ze'ni:l] (*pej*) *adj* senile
Senior ['ze:niɔr] (**-s, -en**) *m* (*Rentner*) senior citizen; (*Geschäftspartner*) senior partner
Seniorenpass [zeni'o:rənpas] *m* senior citizen's travel pass (*Brit*)
Senkblei ['zɛŋkblaɪ] *nt* plumb
Senke (**-, -n**) *f* depression
Senkel (**-s, -**) *m* (shoe)lace

senken vt to lower; (*Kopf*) to bow; (*Tech*) to sink ▷ vr to sink; (*Stimme*) to drop

Senk- zW: **Senkfuß** m flat foot; **Senkgrube** f cesspit; **senkrecht** adj vertical, perpendicular; **Senkrechte** f perpendicular; **Senkrechtstarter** m (*Aviat*) vertical takeoff plane; (*fig: Person*) high-flier

Senner, in ['zɛnər(ın)] (**-s, -**) m(f) (Alpine) dairyman, dairymaid

Sensation [zenzatsi'oːn] f sensation

sensationell [zenzatsio'nɛl] adj sensational

Sensationsblatt nt sensational paper

Sensationssucht f sensationalism

Sense ['zɛnzə] (**-, -n**) f scythe; **dann ist ~!** (*umg*) that's the end!

sensibel [zɛn'ziːbəl] adj sensitive

sensibilisieren [zɛnzibili'ziːrən] vt to sensitize

Sensibilität [zɛnzibili'tɛːt] f sensitivity

sentimental [zɛntimɛn'taːl] adj sentimental

Sentimentalität [zɛntimɛntali'tɛːt] f sentimentality

separat [zepa'raːt] adj separate; (*Wohnung, Zimmer*) self-contained

Sept. abk (= *September*) Sept.

September [zɛp'tɛmbər] (**-(s), -**) m September; **im ~** in September; **im Monat ~** in the month of September; **heute ist der zweite ~** today is the second of September od September second (*US*); (*geschrieben*) today is 2nd September; **in diesem ~** this September; **Anfang/Ende/Mitte ~** at the beginning/end/in the middle of September

septisch ['zɛptɪʃ] adj septic

sequentiell [zekvɛntsi'ɛl] adj = **sequenziell**

Sequenz [ze'kvɛnts] f sequence

sequenziell [zekvɛntsi'ɛl] adj (*Comput*) sequential; **~er Zugriff** sequential access

Serbe ['zɛrbə] (**-n, -n**) m Serbian

Serbien (**-s**) nt Serbia; **~ und Montenegro** Serbia and Montenegro

Serbin f Serbian

serbisch adj Serbian

Serbokroatisch, e nt Serbo-Croat

Serie ['zeːriə] f series

seriell [zeri'ɛl] adj (*Comput*) serial; **~e Daten** serial data pl; **~er Anschluss** serial port; **~er Drucker** serial printer

Serien- zW: **Serienanfertigung** f, **Serienherstellung** f series production; **serienmäßig** adj (*Ausstattung*) standard; (*Herstellung*) series attrib ▷ adv (*herstellen*) in series; **Seriennummer** f serial number; **serienweise** adv in series

seriös [zeri'øːs] adj serious; (*anständig*) respectable

Serpentine [zɛrpɛn'tiːnə] f hairpin (bend)

Serum ['zeːrʊm] (**-s, Seren**) nt serum

Service¹ [zɛr'viːs] (**-(s), -**) nt (*Gläserservice*) set; (*Geschirr*) service

Service² ['sə:vɪs] (**-, -s**) m (*Comm, Sport*) service

servieren [zɛr'viːrən] vt, vi to serve

Serviererin [zɛr'viːrərin] f waitress

Servierwagen m trolley

Serviette [zɛrvi'ɛtə] f napkin, serviette

Servolenkung f power steering

Servomotor m servo motor

Servus ['zɛrvʊs] (*Österr, Südd*) interj hello; (*beim Abschied*) goodbye, so long (*umg*)

Sesam ['zeːzam] (**-s, -s**) m sesame

Sessel ['zɛsəl] (**-s, -**) m armchair; **Sessellift** m chairlift

sesshaft ['zɛshaft] adj settled; (*ansässig*) resident

Set [zɛt] (**-s, -s**) nt od m set; (*Deckchen*) tablemat

setzen ['zɛtsən] vt to put, place, set; (*Baum etc*) to plant; (*Segel, Typ*) to set ▷ vr (*Platz nehmen*) to sit down; (*Kaffee, Tee*) to settle ▷ vi to leap; (*wetten*) to bet; (*Typ*) to set; **jdm ein Denkmal ~** to build a monument to sb; **sich zu jdm ~** to sit with sb

Setzer ['zɛtsər] (**-s, -**) m (*Typ*) typesetter

Setzerei [zɛtsə'raı] f caseroom; (*Firma*) typesetting firm

Setz- zW: **Setzkasten** m (*Typ*) case; (*an Wand*) ornament shelf; **Setzling** m young plant; **Setzmaschine** f (*Typ*) typesetting machine

Seuche ['zɔʏçə] (**-, -n**) f epidemic

Seuchengebiet nt infected area

seufzen ['zɔʏftsən] vt, vi to sigh

Seufzer ['zɔʏftsər] (**-s, -**) m sigh

Sex [zɛks] (**-(es)**) m sex

Sexta ['zɛksta] (**-, Sexten**) f (*früher*) first year of German secondary school

Sexualerziehung [zɛksu'aːlɛrtsiːʊŋ] f sex education

Sexualität [zɛksuali'tɛːt] f sex, sexuality

Sexual- zW: **Sexualkunde** [zɛksu'aːlkʊndə] f sex education; **Sexualleben** nt sex life; **Sexualobjekt** nt sex object

sexuell [zɛksu'ɛl] adj sexual

Seychellen [ze'ʃɛlən] pl Seychelles pl

sezieren [ze'tsiːrən] vt to dissect

SFB (**-**) m abk (= *Sender Freies Berlin*) Radio Free Berlin

Sfr, sFr. abk (= *Schweizer Franken*) sfr

Shampoo [ʃam'puː] (**-s, -s**) nt shampoo

Shetlandinseln ['ʃɛtlant|ınzəln] pl Shetland, Shetland Isles pl

Shorts [ʃoːrts] pl shorts pl

Showmaster ['ʃouma:stər] (**-s, -**) m compère, MC

siamesisch [zia'meːzıʃ] adj: **~e Zwillinge** Siamese twins

Siamkatze f Siamese (cat)

Sibirien [zi'biːriən] (**-s**) nt Siberia

sibirisch adj Siberian

⊙ SCHLÜSSELWORT

sich [zıç] pron **1** (*akk*): **er/sie/es ... sich** he/she/it ... himself/herself/itself; **sie** pl/**man ... sich** they/one ...themselves/oneself; **Sie ... sich** you ... yourself/yourselves pl; **sich wiederholen** to repeat oneself/itself **2** (*dat*): **er/sie/es ... sich** he/she/it ... to himself/herself/itself; **sie** pl/**man ... sich**

they/one ... to themselves/oneself; **Sie ... sich** you ... to yourself/yourselves *pl*; **sie hat sich einen Pullover gekauft** she bought herself a jumper; **sich die Haare waschen** to wash one's hair

3 *(mit Präposition)*: **haben Sie Ihren Ausweis bei sich?** do you have your pass on you?; **er hat nichts bei sich** he's got nothing on him; **sie bleiben gern unter sich** they keep themselves to themselves

4 *(einander)* each other, one another; **sie bekämpfen sich** they fight each other *od* one another

5: dieses Auto fährt sich gut this car drives well; **hier sitzt es sich gut** it's good to sit here

Sichel ['zɪçəl] (**-, -n**) *f* sickle; *(Mondsichel)* crescent

sicher ['zɪçər] *adj* safe; *(gewiss)* certain; *(Hand, Job)* steady; *(zuverlässig)* secure, reliable; *(selbstsicher)* confident; *(Stellung)* secure ▷ *adv* *(natürlich)*: **du hast dich ~ verrechnet** you must have counted wrongly; **vor jdm/etw ~ sein** to be safe from sb/sth; **sich dat einer Sache/jds ~ sein** to be sure of sth/sb; **~ ist sicher** you can't be too sure

sichergehen *unreg vi* to make sure

Sicherheit ['zɪçərhaɪt] *f* safety; *(auch Fin)* security; *(Gewissheit)* certainty; *(Selbstsicherheit)* confidence; **die öffentliche ~** public security; **~ im Straßenverkehr** road safety; **~ leisten** *(Comm)* to offer security

Sicherheits- *zW*: **Sicherheitsabstand** *m* safe distance; **Sicherheitsbestimmungen** *pl* safety regulations *pl*; *(betrieblich, Pol etc)* security controls *pl*; **Sicherheitseinrichtungen** *pl* security equipment *sing*, security devices *pl*; **Sicherheitsglas** *nt* safety glass; **Sicherheitsgurt** *m* seat belt; **sicherheitshalber** *adv* to be on the safe side; **Sicherheitsnadel** *f* safety pin; **Sicherheitsrat** *m* Security Council; **Sicherheitsschloss** *nt* safety lock; **Sicherheitsspanne** *f* *(Comm)* margin of safety; **Sicherheitsverschluss** *m* safety clasp; **Sicherheitsvorkehrung** *f* safety precaution

sicherlich *adv* certainly, surely

sichern *vt* to secure; *(schützen)* to protect; *(Bergsteiger etc)* to belay; *(Waffe)* to put the safety catch on; *(Comput: Daten)* to back up; **jdm/sich etw ~** to secure sth for sb/o.s.

sicherstellen *vt* to impound; *(garantieren)* to guarantee

Sicherung *f* *(Sichern)* securing; *(Vorrichtung)* safety device; *(an Waffen)* safety catch; *(Elek)* fuse; **da ist (bei) ihm die ~ durchgebrannt** *(fig: umg)* he blew a fuse

Sicherungskopie *f* backup copy

Sicht [zɪçt] (**-**) *f* sight; *(Aussicht)* view; *(Sehweite)* visibility; **auf** *od* **nach ~** *(Fin)* at sight; **auf lange ~** on a long-term basis; **sichtbar** *adj* visible; **Sichtbarkeit** *f* visibility

sichten *vt* to sight; *(auswählen)* to sort out;

(ordnen) to sift through

Sicht- *zW*: **sichtlich** *adj* evident, obvious; **Sichtverhältnisse** *pl* visibility *sing*; **Sichtvermerk** *m* visa; **Sichtweite** *f* visibility; **außer Sichtweite** out of sight

sickern ['zɪkərn] *vi (Hilfsverb sein)* to seep; *(in Tropfen)* to drip

Sie [ziː] *nom, akk pron* you

sie *pron (sing: nom)* she; *(: akk)* her; *(pl: nom)* they; *(: akk)* them

Sieb [ziːp] (**-(e)s, -e**) *nt* sieve; *(Koch)* strainer; *(Gemüsesieb)* colander

sieben¹ ['ziːbən] *vt* to sieve, sift; *(Flüssigkeit)* to strain ▷ *vi*: **bei der Prüfung wird stark gesiebt** *(fig: umg)* the exam will weed a lot of people out

sieben² ['ziːbən] *num* seven; **Siebengebirge** *nt*: **das Siebengebirge** the Seven Mountains *pl (near Bonn)*; **siebenhundert** *num* seven hundred; **Siebenmeter** *m (Sport)* penalty; **Siebensachen** *pl* belongings *pl*; **Siebenschläfer** *m (Zool)* dormouse

siebte, r, s ['ziːptə(r, s)] *adj* seventh

Siebtel (**-s, -**) *nt* seventh

siebzehn ['ziːptseːn] *num* seventeen

siebzig ['ziːptsɪç] *num* seventy

siedeln ['ziːdəln] *vi* to settle

sieden ['ziːdən] *vt, vi* to boil

Siedepunkt *m* boiling point

Siedler (**-s, -**) *m* settler

Siedlung *f* settlement; *(Häusersiedlung)* housing estate *(Brit)* od development *(US)*

Sieg [ziːk] (**-(e)s, -e**) *m* victory

Siegel ['ziːɡəl] (**-s, -**) *nt* seal; **Siegellack** *m* sealing wax; **Siegelring** *m* signet ring

siegen ['ziːɡən] *vi* to be victorious; *(Sport)* to win; **über jdn/etw ~** *(fig)* to triumph over sb/sth; *(in Wettkampf)* to beat sb/sth

Sieger, in (**-s, -**) *m(f)* victor; *(Sport etc)* winner; **Siegerehrung** *f (Sport)* presentation ceremony

siegessicher *adj* sure of victory

Siegeszug *m* triumphal procession

siegreich *adj* victorious

siehe ['ziːə] *imperativ* see; *(siehe da)* behold

siehst [ziːst], **sieht** [ziːt] *vb siehe* **sehen**

Siel [ziːl] (**-(e)s, -e**) *nt od m (Schleuse)* sluice; *(Abwasserkanal)* sewer

siezen ['ziːtsən] *vt* to address as "Sie"; *siehe auch* **duzen**

Signal [zɪ'ɡnaːl] (**-s, -e**) *nt* signal; **Signalanlage** *f* signals *pl*, set of signals

signalisieren [zɪɡnali'ziːrən] *vt (lit, fig)* to signal

Signatur [zɪɡna'tuːr] *f* signature; *(Bibliothekssignatur)* shelf mark

Silbe ['zɪlbə] (**-, -n**) *f* syllable; **er hat es mit keiner ~ erwähnt** he didn't say a word about it

Silber ['zɪlbər] (**-s**) *nt* silver; **Silberbergwerk** *nt* silver mine; **Silberblick** *m*: **einen Silberblick haben** to have a slight squint; **Silberhochzeit** *f* silver wedding

silbern *adj* silver

Silberpapier nt silver paper
Silhouette [zilu'ɛtə] f silhouette
Silikonchip [zili'ko:ntʃɪp] m silicon chip
Silo ['zi:lo] (**-s, -s**) nt od m silo
Silvester [zɪl'vɛstər] (**-s, -**) m or nt New Year's
Eve, Hogmanay (Scot); see culture note

Simbabwe [zɪm'ba:bvə] (**-s**) nt Zimbabwe
SIM-Karte ['zɪm-] f SIM card
simpel ['zɪmpəl] adj simple; **Simpel** (**-s, -**) (umg)
m simpleton
Sims [zɪms] (**-es, -e**) nt od m (Kaminsims)
mantelpiece; (Fenstersims) (window)sill
simsen ['zɪmsən] (umg) vti to text
Simulant, in [zimu'lant(ɪn)] (**-en, -en**) m(f)
malingerer
simulieren [zimu'li:rən] vt to simulate;
(vortäuschen) to feign ▷ vi to feign illness
simultan [zimʊl'ta:n] adj simultaneous;
Simultandolmetscher m simultaneous
interpreter
sind [zɪnt] vb siehe **sein**
Sinfonie [zɪnfo'ni:] f symphony
Singapur ['zɪŋgapu:r] (**-s**) nt Singapore
singen ['zɪŋən] unreg vt, vi to sing
Single¹ ['sɪŋəl] (**-s, -s**) m (Alleinlebender) single
person
Single² ['sɪŋəl] (**-, -s**) f (Mus) single
Singsang m (Gesang) monotonous singing
Singstimme f vocal part
Singular ['zɪŋgula:r] m singular
Singvogel ['zɪŋfo:gəl] m songbird
sinken ['zɪŋkən] unreg vi to sink; (Boden, Gebäude)
to subside; (Fundament) to settle; (Preise etc)
to fall, go down; **den Mut/die Hoffnung ~
lassen** to lose courage/hope
Sinn [zɪn] (**-(e)s, -e**) m mind;
(Wahrnehmungssinn) sense; (Bedeutung) sense,
meaning; **im ~e des Gesetzes** according to
the spirit of the law; **~ für etw** sense of sth;
im ~e des Verstorbenen in accordance with
the wishes of the deceased; **von ~en sein** to
be out of one's mind; **das ist nicht der ~ der
Sache** that is not the point; **das hat keinen ~**
there is no point in that; **Sinnbild** nt symbol;
sinnbildlich adj symbolic
sinnen unreg vi to ponder; **auf etw** akk **~** to
contemplate sth; **über etw** akk **~** to reflect
on sth
Sinnenmensch m sensualist
Sinnes- zW: **Sinnesorgan** nt sense organ;
Sinnestäuschung f illusion; **Sinneswandel** m
change of mind

sinngemäß adj faithful; (Wiedergabe) in one's
own words
sinnig adj apt; (ironisch) clever
Sinn- zW: **sinnlich** adj sensual, sensuous;
(Wahrnehmung) sensory; **Sinnlichkeit**
f sensuality; **sinnlos** adj senseless,
meaningless; **sinnlos betrunken** blind
drunk; **Sinnlosigkeit** f senselessness,
meaninglessness; **sinnverwandt** adj
synonymous; **sinnvoll** adj meaningful;
(vernünftig) sensible
Sinologe [zino'lo:gə] (**-n, -n**) m Sinologist
Sinologie f Sinology
Sinologin f Sinologist
Sintflut ['zɪntflu:t] f Flood; **nach uns die ~**
(umg) it doesn't matter what happens after
we've gone; **sintflutartig** adj: **sintflutartige
Regenfälle** torrential rain sing
Sinus ['zi:nʊs] (**-, - od -se**) m (Anat) sinus; (Math)
sine
Siphon [zi'fõ:] (**-s, -s**) m siphon
Sippe ['zɪpə] (**-, -n**) f (extended) family;
(umg: Verwandtschaft) clan
Sippschaft ['zɪpʃaft] (pej) f tribe; (Bande) gang
Sirene [zi're:nə] (**-, -n**) f siren
Sirup ['zi:rʊp] (**-s, -e**) m syrup
Sit-in [sɪt'|ɪn] (**-(s), -s**) nt: **ein ~ machen** to
stage a sit-in
Sitte ['zɪtə] (**-, -n**) f custom; **Sitten** pl morals pl;
was sind denn das für ~n? what sort of way
is that to behave?
Sitten- zW: **Sittenpolizei** f vice squad;
Sittenstrolch (umg) m sex fiend;
Sittenwächter m (ironisch) guardian of public
morals; **sittenwidrig** adj (form) immoral
Sittich ['zɪtɪç] (**-(e)s, -e**) m parakeet
Sitt- zW: **sittlich** adj moral; **Sittlichkeit** f
morality; **Sittlichkeitsverbrechen** nt sex
offence (Brit) od offense (US); **sittsam** adj
modest, demure
Situation [zituatsi'o:n] f situation
situiert [zitu'i:rt] adj: **gut ~ sein** to be well off
Sitz [zɪts] (**-es, -e**) m seat; (von Firma, Verwaltung)
headquarters pl; **der Anzug hat einen guten
~** the suit sits well
sitzen unreg vi to sit; (Bemerkung, Schlag) to strike
home; (Gelerntes) to have sunk in; (umg: im
Gefängnis sitzen) to be inside; **locker ~** to be
loose; **einen ~ haben** (umg) to have had one
too many; **er sitzt im Kultusministerium**
(umg: sein) he's in the Ministry of Education;
~ bleiben to remain seated; (Sch) to have to
repeat a year; **auf etw** dat **~ bleiben** to be
lumbered with sth; **~ lassen** (Sch) to keep
down a year; (Mädchen) to jilt; (Wartenden) to
stand up; **etw auf sich** dat **~ lassen** to take
sth lying down
sitzend adj (Tätigkeit) sedentary
Sitz- zW: **Sitzfleisch** (umg) nt: **Sitzfleisch
haben** to be able to sit still; **Sitzgelegenheit** f
seats pl; **Sitzordnung** f seating plan; **Sitzplatz**
m seat; **Sitzstreik** m sit-down strike
Sitzung f meeting

Sizilianer, in [zitsili'a:nər(ın)] **(-s, -)** *m(f)*
Sicilian
sizilianisch *adj* Sicilian
Sizilien [zi'tsi:liən] **(-s)** *nt* Sicily
Skala ['ska:la] **(-, Skalen)** *f* scale; *(fig)* range
Skalpell [skal'pɛl] **(-s, -e)** *nt* scalpel
skalpieren [skal'pi:rən] *vt* to scalp
Skandal [skan'da:l] **(-s, -e)** *m* scandal
skandalös [skanda'lø:s] *adj* scandalous
Skandinavien [skandi'na:viən] **(-s)** *nt*
Scandinavia
Skandinavier, in **(-s, -)** *m(f)* Scandinavian
skandinavisch *adj* Scandinavian
Skat [ska:t] **(-(e)s, -e** *od* **-s)** *m (Karten)* skat
Skateboard ['ske:tbɔ:rd] **(-s, -s)** *nt* skateboard;
skateboarden *vi* to skateboard
Skelett [ske'lɛt] **(-(e)s, -e)** *nt* skeleton
Skepsis ['skɛpsɪs] **(-)** *f* scepticism (Brit),
skepticism (US)
skeptisch ['skɛptɪʃ] *adj* sceptical (Brit), skeptical
(US)
Ski [ʃi:] **(-s, -er)** *m* ski; **~ laufen** *od* **fahren** to
ski; **Skifahrer** *m* skier; **Skihütte** *f* ski hut;
Skiläufer *m* skier; **Skilehrer** *m* ski instructor;
Skilift *m* ski lift; **Skispringen** *nt* ski
jumping; **Skistiefel** *m* ski boot; **Skistock** *m*
ski pole
Skizze ['skɪtsə] **(-, -n)** *f* sketch
skizzieren [skɪ'tsi:rən] *vt* to sketch; *(fig: Plan
etc)* to outline ▷ *vi* to sketch
Sklave ['skla:və] **(-n, -n)** *m* slave
Sklaventreiber(-s, -) *(pej)* *m* slave-driver
Sklaverei [skla:və'raɪ] *f* slavery
Sklavin *f* slave
sklavisch *adj* slavish
Skonto ['skɔnto] **(-s, -s)** *nt od m* discount
Skorpion [skɔrpi'o:n] **(-s, -e)** *m* scorpion;
(Astrol) Scorpio
Skrupel ['skru:pəl] **(-s, -)** *m* scruple; **skrupellos**
adj unscrupulous
Skulptur [skʊlp'tu:r] *f* sculpture
skurril [skʊ'ri:l] *adj (geh)* droll, comical
Skype® *(Internet, Tel)* nt Skype®
skypen *(Internet, Tel)* vt to skype
Slalom ['sla:lɔm] **(-s, -s)** *m* slalom
Slawe ['sla:və] **(-n, -n)** *m* Slav
Slawin *f* Slav
slawisch *adj* Slavonic, Slavic
Slip [slɪp] **(-s, -s)** *m* (pair of) briefs *pl*
Slowakei [slova'kaɪ] *f* Slovakia
slowakisch *adj* Slovak
Slowenien [slo've:niən] **(-s)** *nt* Slovenia
slowenisch *adj* Slovene
Smaragd [sma'rakt] **(-(e)s, -e)** *m* emerald
Smoking ['smo:kɪŋ] **(-s, -s)** *m* dinner jacket
(Brit), tuxedo (US)
SMS (-, -) *f abk (= Short Message Service)* SMS;
jdm eine ~ schicken to send sb a text; **SMS-Nachricht** *f* text message
Snob [snɔp] **(-s, -s)** *m* snob
Snowboard ['snɔ:bɔ:rd] **(-s, -s)** *nt* snowboard;
snowboarden *vi* to snowboard
So. *abk* = **Sonntag**

SO *abk (= Südost(en))* SE

 SCHLÜSSELWORT

so [zo:] *adv* **1** *(so sehr)* so; **so groß/schön** *etc* so
big/nice *etc*; **so groß/schön wie ...** as big/
nice as ...; **das hat ihn so geärgert, dass ...**
that annoyed him so much that ...
2 *(auf diese Weise)* like this; **so genannt** so-
called; **mach es nicht so** don't do it like that;
so oder so (in) one way or the other; **... oder
so** something (like that); **und so weiter** and
so on; **so viel (wie)** as much as; **rede nicht
so viel** don't talk so much; **so weit sein** to
be ready; **so weit wie** *od* **als möglich** as far
as possible; **ich bin so weit zufrieden** by
and large I'm quite satisfied; **es ist bald so
weit** it's nearly time; **so wenig (wie)** no more
(than), not any more (than); **so wenig wie
möglich** as little as possible; **so ein ...** such
a ...; **so einer wie ich** somebody like me; **so
(et)was** something like this/that; **na so was!**
well I never!; **das ist gut so** that's fine; **sie ist
nun einmal so** that's just the way she is; **das
habe ich nur so gesagt** I didn't really mean it
3 *(umg: umsonst)*: **ich habe es so bekommen** I
got it for nothing
4 *(als Füllwort: nicht übersetzt)*: **so mancher** a
number of people *pl*
▷ *konj*: **so wie es jetzt ist** as things are at the
moment; *siehe auch* **sodass**
▷ *interj*: **so?** really?; **so, das wärs** right, that's
it then

s. o. *abk (= siehe oben)* see above
sobald [zo'balt] *konj* as soon as
Söckchen ['zœkçən] *nt* ankle sock
Socke ['zɔkə] **(-, -n)** *f* sock; **sich auf die ~n
machen** *(umg)* to get going
Sockel ['zɔkəl] **(-s, -)** *m* pedestal, base
sodass [zo'das] *konj* so that
Sodawasser ['zo:davasər] *nt* soda water
Sodbrennen ['zo:tbrenən] **(-s)** *nt* heartburn
Sodomie [zodo'mi:] *f* bestiality
soeben [zo'|e:bən] *adv* just (now)
Sofa ['zo:fa] **(-s, -s)** *nt* sofa
Sofabett *nt* sofa bed, bed settee
sofern [zo'fɛrn] *konj* if, provided (that)
soff *etc* [zɔf] *vb siehe* **saufen**
sofort [zo'fɔrt] *adv* immediately, at once; **(ich)
komme ~!** (I'm) just coming!; **Soforthilfe** *f*
emergency relief *od* aid; **Soforthilfegesetz** *nt*
law on emergency aid
sofortig *adj* immediate
Sofortmaßnahme *f* immediate measure
Softeis ['sɔft|aɪs] **(-es)** *nt* soft ice-cream
Softie ['zɔfti:] **(-s, -s)** *(umg)* *m* softy
Software ['zɔftwɛːər] **(-, -s)** *f* software;
softwarekompatibel *adj* software compatible
Sog **(-(e)s, -e)** *m* suction; *(von Strudel)* vortex;
(fig) maelstrom
sog *etc* [zo:k] *vb siehe* **saugen**
sog. *abk* = **sogenannt**

S

sogar [zo'ga:r] *adv* even

sogenannt ['zo:gənant] *adj attrib* so-called

sogleich [zo'glaiç] *adv* straight away, at once

Sogwirkung *f* suction; (*fig*) knock-on effect

Sohle ['zo:lə] (-, -n) *f* (*Fußsohle*) sole; (*Talsohle etc*) bottom; (*Min*) level; **auf leisen ~n** (*fig*) softly, noiselessly

Sohn [zo:n] (-(e)s, ⁻e) *m* son

Sojasoße ['zo:jazo:sə] *f* soy *od* soya sauce

solang, solange *konj* as *od* so long as

Solar- [zo'la:r] *in zw* solar; **Solarenergie** *f* solar energy

Solarium [zo'la:rium] *nt* solarium

Solbad ['zo:lba:t] *nt* saltwater bath

solch [zolç] *adj inv* such

solche, r, s *adj* such; **ein ~r Mensch** such a person

Sold [zolt] (-(e)s, -e) *m* pay

Soldat [zol'da:t] (-en, -en) *m* soldier; **soldatisch** *adj* soldierly

Söldner ['zœldnər] (-s, -) *m* mercenary

Sole ['zo:lə] (-, -n) *f* brine, salt water

Solei ['zo:lai] *nt* pickled egg

Soli ['zo:li] *pl von* **Solo**

solid [zo'li:d], **solide** [zo'li:də] *adj* solid; (*Arbeit, Wissen*) sound; (*Leben, Person*) staid, respectable

solidarisch [zoli'da:rɪʃ] *adj* in *od* with solidarity; **sich ~ erklären** to declare one's solidarity

solidarisieren [zolidari'zi:rən] *vr*: **sich ~ mit** to show (one's) solidarity with

Solidarität [zolidari'tɛ:t] *f* solidarity

Solidaritätsstreik *m* sympathy strike

Solist, in [zo'lɪst(ɪn)] *m(f)* (*Mus*) soloist

Soll [zol] (-(s), -(s)) *nt* (*Fin*) debit (side); (*Arbeitsmenge*) quota, target; **~ und Haben** debit and credit

soll *vb siehe* **sollen**

sollen ['zolən] (*pt* **sollte**, *pp* **gesollt** *od* (*als Hilfsverb*) **sollen**) *hilfsverb* **1** (*Pflicht, Befehl*) be supposed to; **du hättest nicht gehen sollen** you shouldn't have gone, you oughtn't to have gone; **er sollte eigentlich morgen kommen** he was supposed to come tomorrow; **soll ich?** shall I?; **soll ich dir helfen?** shall I help you?; **sag ihm, er soll warten** tell him he's to wait; **was soll ich machen?** what should I do?; **mir soll es gleich sein** it's all the same to me; **er sollte sie nie wiedersehen** he was never to see her again

2 (*Vermutung*): **sie soll verheiratet sein** she's said to be married; **was soll das heißen?** what's that supposed to mean?; **man sollte glauben, dass ...** you would think that ...; **sollte das passieren, ...** if that should happen ...

▷ *vt, vi*: **was soll das?** what's all this about *od* in aid of?; **das sollst du nicht** you shouldn't do that; **was solls?** what the hell!

sollte *etc* ['zoltə] *vb siehe* **sollen**

Solo ['zo:lo] (-s, -s *od* **Soli**) *nt* solo

solo *adv* (*Mus*) solo; (*fig*: *umg*) on one's own, alone

solvent [zol'vɛnt] *adj* (*Fin*) solvent

Solvenz [zol'vɛnts] *f* (*Fin*) solvency

Somalia [zo'ma:lia] (-s) *nt* Somalia

somit [zo'mɪt] *konj* and so, therefore

Sommer ['zomər] (-s, -) *m* summer; **~ wie Winter** all year round; **Sommerferien** *pl* summer holidays *pl* (*Brit*) *od* vacation *sing* (*US*); (*Jur, Parl*) summer recess *sing*; **sommerlich** *adj* summer *attrib*; (*sommerartig*) summery; **Sommerloch** *nt* silly season; **Sommerreifen** *m* normal tyre (*Brit*) *od* tire (*US*); **Sommerschlussverkauf** *m* summer sale; **Sommersemester** *nt* (*Univ*) summer semester (*bes US*), ≈ summer term (*Brit*); **Sommersprossen** *pl* freckles *pl*; **Sommerzeit** *f* summertime

Sonate [zo'na:tə] (-, -n) *f* sonata

Sonde ['zondə] (-, -n) *f* probe

Sonder- ['zondər] *in zw* special; **Sonderanfertigung** *f* special model; **Sonderangebot** *nt* special offer; **Sonderausgabe** *f* special edition; **sonderbar** *adj* strange, odd; **Sonderbeauftragte, r** *f(m)* (*Pol*) special emissary; **Sonderbeitrag** *m* (special) feature; **Sonderfahrt** *f* special trip; **Sonderfall** *m* special case; **sondergleichen** *adj inv* without parallel, unparalleled; **eine Frechheit sondergleichen** the height of cheek; **sonderlich** *adj* particular; (*außergewöhnlich*) remarkable; (*eigenartig*) peculiar; **Sonderling** *m* eccentric; **Sondermarke** *f* special issue (stamp); **Sondermüll** *m* dangerous waste

sondern *konj* but ▷ *vt* to separate; **nicht nur ..., ~ auch** not only ..., but also

Sonder- *zW*: **Sonderpreis** *m* special price; **Sonderregelung** *f* special provision; **Sonderschule** *f* special school; **Sondervergünstigungen** *pl* perquisites *pl*, perks *pl* (*bes Brit*); **Sonderwünsche** *pl* special requests *pl*; **Sonderzug** *m* special train

sondieren [zon'di:rən] *vt* to suss out; (*Gelände*) to scout out

Sonett [zo'nɛt] (-(e)s, -e) *nt* sonnet

Sonnabend ['zon|a:bənt] *m* Saturday; *siehe auch* **Dienstag**

Sonne ['zonə] (-, -n) *f* sun; **an die ~ gehen** to go out in the sun

sonnen *vr* to sun o.s.; **sich in etw** *dat* **~** (*fig*) to bask in sth

Sonnen- *zW*: **Sonnenaufgang** *m* sunrise; **sonnenbaden** *vi* to sunbathe; **Sonnenblume** *f* sunflower; **Sonnenbrand** *m* sunburn; **Sonnenbrille** *f* sunglasses *pl*; **Sonnencreme** *f* suntan lotion; **Sonnenenergie** *f* solar energy; **Sonnenfinsternis** *f* solar eclipse; **Sonnenfleck** *m* sunspot; **sonnengebräunt** *adj* suntanned; **sonnenklar** *adj* crystal-clear; **Sonnenkollektor** *m* solar panel; **Sonnenkraftwerk** *nt* solar

power station; **Sonnenmilch** f suntan lotion;
Sonnenöl nt suntan oil; **Sonnenschein** m
sunshine; **Sonnenschirm** m sunshade;
Sonnenschutzmittel nt sunscreen;
Sonnenstich m sunstroke; **du hast wohl
einen Sonnenstich!** (hum: umg) you
must have been out in the sun too long!;
Sonnensystem nt solar system; **Sonnenuhr**
f sundial; **Sonnenuntergang** m sunset;
Sonnenwende f solstice
sonnig ['zɔnɪç] adj sunny
Sonntag ['zɔnta:k] m Sunday; siehe auch
Dienstag
sonntäglich adj attrib: ~ **gekleidet** dressed in
one's Sunday best
sonntags adv (on) Sundays
Sonntagsdienst m: ~ **haben** (Apotheke) to be
open on Sundays
Sonntagsfahrer (pej) m Sunday driver
sonst [zɔnst] adv otherwise; (mit pron, in Fragen)
else; (zu anderer Zeit) at other times; (gewöhnlich)
usually, normally ▷ konj otherwise; **er denkt,
er ist ~ wer** (umg) he thinks he's somebody
special; ~ **gehts dir gut?** (ironisch: umg) are
you feeling okay?; **wenn ich Ihnen ~ noch
behilflich sein kann** if I can help you in
any other way; ~ **noch etwas?** anything
else?; ~ **nichts** nothing else; ~ **jemand**
(umg) anybody (at all); **da kann ja ~ was
passieren** (umg) anything could happen; ~
wo (umg) somewhere else; ~ **woher** (umg) from
somewhere else; ~ **wohin** (umg) somewhere
else
sonstig adj other; **„S~es"** "other"
sooft [zo'ɔft] konj whenever
Sopran [zo'pra:n] (-s, -e) m soprano (voice)
Sopranistin [zopra'nɪstɪn] f soprano (singer)
Sorge ['zɔrgə] (-, -n) f care, worry; **dafür ~
tragen, dass ...** (geh) to see to it that ...
sorgen vi: **für jdn ~** to look after sb ▷ vr: **sich ~
(um)** to worry (about); **für etw ~** to take care
of od see to sth; **dafür ~, dass ...** to see to it
that ...; **dafür ist gesorgt** that's taken care of
Sorgen- zW: **sorgenfrei** adj carefree;
Sorgenkind nt problem child; **sorgenvoll** adj
troubled, worried
Sorgerecht (-(e)s) nt custody (of a child)
Sorgfalt ['zɔrkfalt] (-) f care(fulness); **viel ~
auf etw** akk **verwenden** to take a lot of care
over sth
sorgfältig adj careful
sorglos adj careless; (ohne Sorgen) carefree
sorgsam adj careful
Sorte ['zɔrtə] (-, -n) f sort; (Warensorte) brand;
Sorten pl (Fin) foreign currency sing
sortieren [zɔr'ti:rən] vt to sort (out); (Comput)
to sort
Sortiermaschine f sorting machine
Sortiment [zɔrti'mɛnt] nt assortment
SOS [ɛs|oː'|ɛs] nt abk SOS
sosehr [zo'ze:r] konj as much as
soso [zo'zo:] interj: ~! I see!; (erstaunt) well, well!;
(drohend) well!

Soße ['zoːsə] (-, -n) f sauce; (Bratensoße) gravy
Souffleur [zu'fløːr] m prompter
Souffleuse [zu'fløːzə] f prompter
soufflieren [zu'fliːrən] vt, vi to prompt
soundso ['zoː|ʊnt'zoː] adv: ~ **lange** for such and
such a time
soundsovielte, r, s adj: **am S~n** (Datum) on
such and such a date
Souterrain [zute'rɛ̃:] (-s, -s) nt basement
Souvenir [zuvə'niːr] (-s, -s) nt souvenir
souverän [zuvə'rɛːn] adj sovereign; (überlegen)
superior; (fig) supremely good
soviel [zo'fiːl] konj as far as
sowenig [zo've:nɪç] konj however little
sowie [zo'viː] konj (sobald) as soon as; (ebenso) as
well as
sowieso [zovi'zoː] adv anyway
Sowjetbürger m (früher) Soviet citizen
sowjetisch [zɔ'vjetɪʃ] adj (früher) Soviet
Sowjet- zW (früher): **Sowjetrepublik** f Soviet
Republic; **Sowjetrusse** m Soviet Russian;
Sowjetunion f Soviet Union
sowohl [zo'voːl] konj: ~ ... **als** od **wie auch** ...
both ... and ...
soz. abk = **sozial; sozialistisch**
sozial [zotsi'aːl] adj social; ~ **eingestellt**
public-spirited; ~ **verträglich** socially
acceptable; **~er Wohnungsbau** public-sector
housing (programme); **Sozialabbau** m public-
spending cuts pl; **Sozialabgaben** pl National
Insurance contributions pl (Brit), Social
Security contributions pl (US); **Sozialamt** nt
(social) welfare office; **Sozialarbeiter** m social
worker; **Sozialberuf** m caring profession;
Sozialdemokrat m social democrat;
Sozialhilfe f welfare (aid)
Sozialisation [zotsializatsi'oːn] f (Psych,
Soziologie) socialization
sozialisieren [zotsiali'ziːrən] vt to socialize
Sozialismus [zotsia'lɪsmʊs] m socialism
Sozialist, in [zotsia'lɪst(ɪn)] m(f) socialist
sozialistisch adj socialist
Sozial- zW: **Sozialkunde** f social studies
sing; **Sozialleistungen** pl social security
contributions (from the state and employer);
Sozialplan m redundancy payments
scheme; **Sozialpolitik** f social welfare policy;
Sozialprodukt nt (gross od net) national
product; **Sozialstaat** m welfare state;
Sozialversicherung f national insurance
(Brit), social security (US); **sozialverträglich**
adj siehe **sozial; Sozialwohnung** f ≈ council flat
(Brit), state-subsidized apartment; see culture
note

● **SOZIALWOHNUNG**

●
● A Sozialwohnung is a council house or flat
● let at a fairly low rent to people on low
● income. They are built from public funds.
● People applying for a Sozialwohnung have
● to prove their entitlement.

S

Soziologe [zotsio'lo:gə] (**-n, -n**) *m* sociologist

Soziologie [zotsiolo'gi:] *f* sociology

Soziologin [zotsio'lo:gɪn] *f* sociologist

soziologisch [zotsio'lo:gɪʃ] *adj* sociological

Sozius ['zo:tsiʊs] (**-, -se**) *m* (*Comm*) partner; (*Motorrad*) pillion rider; **Soziussitz** *m* pillion (seat)

sozusagen [zotsu'za:gən] *adv* so to speak

Spachtel ['ʃpaxtəl] (**-s, -**) *m* spatula

spachteln *vt* (*Mauerfugen, Ritzen*) to fill (in) ▷ *vi* (*umg: essen*) to tuck in

Spagat [ʃpa'ga:t] (**-s, -e**) *m* od *nt* splits *pl*

Spaghetti, Spagetti [ʃpa'geti] *pl* spaghetti *sing*

spähen ['ʃpɛ:ən] *vi* to peep, peek

Spalier [ʃpa'li:r] (**-s, -e**) *nt* (*Gerüst*) trellis; (*Leute*) guard of honour (*Brit*) *od* honor (*US*); **~ stehen, ein ~ bilden** to form a guard of honour (*Brit*) *od* honor (*US*)

Spalt [ʃpalt] (**-(e)s, -e**) *m* crack; (*Türspalt*) chink; (*fig: Kluft*) split

Spalte (**-, -n**) *f* crack, fissure; (*Gletscherspalte*) crevasse; (*in Text*) column

spalten *vt, vr* (*lit, fig*) to split

Spaltung *f* splitting

Spam [spɛm] (**-s, -s**) *nt* (*Comput*) spam; **Spamfilter** *m* spam filter *od* blocker

spammen ['spɛmən] *vt, vi* to spam

Span [ʃpa:n] (**-(e)s, ¨e**) *m* shaving

Spanferkel *nt* sucking pig

Spange ['ʃpaŋə] (**-, -n**) *f* clasp; (*Haarspange*) hair slide; (*Schnalle*) buckle; (*Armspange*) bangle

Spaniel ['ʃpa:niəl] (**-s, -s**) *m* spaniel

Spanien ['ʃpa:niən] (**-s**) *nt* Spain

Spanier, in (**-s, -**) *m(f)* Spaniard

spanisch *adj* Spanish; **das kommt mir ~ vor** (*umg*) that seems odd to me; **~e Wand** (folding) screen

Spann (**-(e)s, -e**) *m* instep

spann *etc* [ʃpan] *vb siehe* **spinnen**

Spannbeton (**-s**) *m* prestressed concrete

Spanne (**-, -n**) *f* (*Zeitspanne*) space; (*Differenz*) gap; *siehe auch* **Spann**

spannen *vt* (*straffen*) to tighten, tauten; (*befestigen*) to brace ▷ *vi* to be tight

spannend *adj* exciting, gripping; **machs nicht so ~!** (*umg*) don't keep me *etc* in suspense!

Spanner (**-s, -**) (*umg*) *m* (*Voyeur*) peeping Tom

Spannkraft *f* elasticity; (*fig*) energy

Spannung *f* tension; (*Elek*) voltage; (*fig*) suspense; (*unangenehm*) tension

Spannungsgebiet *nt* (*Pol*) flashpoint, area of tension

Spannungsprüfer *m* voltage detector

Spannweite *f* (*von Flügeln, Aviat*) (wing)span

Spanplatte *f* chipboard

Sparbuch *nt* savings book

Sparbüchse *f* moneybox

sparen ['ʃpa:rən] *vt, vi* to save; **sich** *dat* **etw ~** to save o.s. sth; (*Bemerkung*) to keep sth to o.s.; **mit etw ~** to be sparing with sth; **an etw** *dat* **~** to economize on sth

Sparer, in (**-s, -**) *m(f)* (*bei Bank etc*) saver

Sparflamme *f* low flame; **auf ~** (*fig: umg*) just ticking over

Spargel ['ʃpargəl] (**-s, -**) *m* asparagus

Spar- *zW*: **Spargroschen** *m* nest egg; **Sparkasse** *f* savings bank; **Sparkonto** *nt* savings account

spärlich ['ʃpɛ:rlɪç] *adj* meagre (*Brit*), meager (*US*); (*Bekleidung*) scanty; (*Beleuchtung*) poor

Spar- *zW*: **Sparmaßnahme** *f* economy measure; **Sparpackung** *f* economy size; **sparsam** *adj* economical, thrifty; **sparsam im Verbrauch** economical; **Sparsamkeit** *f* thrift, economizing; **Sparschwein** *nt* piggy bank

Sparte ['ʃpartə] (**-, -n**) *f* field; (*Comm*) line of business; (*Presse*) column

Sparvertrag *m* savings agreement

Spaß [ʃpa:s] (**-es, ¨e**) *m* joke; (*Freude*) fun; **~ muss sein** there's no harm in a joke; **jdm ~ machen** to be fun (for sb); **spaßen** *vi* to joke; **mit ihm ist nicht zu spaßen** you can't take liberties with him

spaßeshalber *adv* for the fun of it

spaßig *adj* funny, droll

Spaß- *zW*: **Spaßmacher** *m* joker, funny man; **Spaßverderber** (**-s, -**) *m* spoilsport; **Spaßvogel** *m* joker

Spastiker, in ['ʃpastikər(ɪn)] *m(f)* (*Med*) spastic

spät [ʃpɛ:t] *adj, adv* late; **heute Abend wird es ~** it'll be a late night tonight

Spaten ['ʃpa:tən] (**-s, -**) *m* spade; **Spatenstich** *m*: **den ersten Spatenstich tun** to turn the first sod

Spätentwickler *m* late developer

später *adj, adv* later; **an ~ denken** to think of the future; **bis ~!** see you later!

spätestens *adv* at the latest

Spätlese *f* late vintage

Spatz [ʃpats] (**-en, -en**) *m* sparrow

spazieren [ʃpa'tsi:rən] *vi* (*Hilfsverb sein*) to stroll; **~ fahren** to go for a drive; **~ gehen** to go for a walk

Spazier- *zW*: **Spaziergang** *m* walk; **einen Spaziergang machen** to go for a walk; **Spaziergänger, in** *m(f)* stroller; **Spazierstock** *m* walking stick; **Spazierweg** *m* path, walk

SPD (**-**) *f abk* (*= Sozialdemokratische Partei Deutschlands*) German Social Democratic Party; *see culture note*

● S P D
●
●
● The SPD (Sozialdemokratische Partei
● Deutschlands), the German Social
● Democratic Party, was newly formed in
● 1945. It is the largest political party in
● Germany.

Specht [ʃpɛçt] (**-(e)s, -e**) *m* woodpecker

Speck [ʃpɛk] (**-(e)s, -e**) *m* bacon; **mit ~ fängt man Mäuse** (*Sprichwort*) you need a sprat to catch a mackerel; **ran an den ~** (*umg*) let's get stuck in

Spediteur [ʃpedi'tø:r] *m* carrier; (*Möbelspediteur*) furniture remover

Spedition [ʃpeditsi'o:n] *f* carriage;

Speer (*Speditionsfirma*) road haulage contractor; (*Umzugsfirma*) removal (*Brit*) *od* moving (*US*) firm

Speer [ʃpeːr] (**-(e)s, -e**) *m* spear; (*Sport*) javelin; **Speerwerfen** *nt*: **das Speerwerfen** throwing the javelin

Speiche [ˈʃpaɪçə] (**-, -n**) *f* spoke

Speichel [ˈʃpaɪçəl] (**-s**) *m* saliva, spit(tle); **Speichellecker** (*pej: umg*) *m* bootlicker

Speicher [ˈʃpaɪçər] (**-s, -**) *m* storehouse; (*Dachspeicher*) attic, loft; (*Kornspeicher*) granary; (*Wasserspeicher*) tank; (*Tech*) store; (*Comput*) memory; **Speicherauszug** *m* (*Comput*) dump

speichern *vt* (*auch Comput*) to store

speien [ˈʃpaɪən] *unreg vt, vi* to spit; (*erbrechen*) to vomit; (*Vulkan*) to spew

Speise [ˈʃpaɪzə] (**-, -n**) *f* food; **kalte und warme ~n** hot and cold meals; **Speiseeis** *nt* ice-cream; **Speisefett** *nt* cooking fat; **Speisekammer** *f* larder, pantry; **Speisekarte** *f* menu

speisen *vt* to feed; to eat ▷ *vi* to dine

Speise- *zW*: **Speiseöl** *nt* salad oil; (*zum Braten*) cooking oil; **Speiseröhre** *f* (*Anat*) gullet, oesophagus (*Brit*), esophagus (*US*); **Speisesaal** *m* dining room; **Speisewagen** *m* dining car; **Speisezettel** *m* menu

Spektakel [ʃpɛkˈtaːkəl] (**-s, -**) *m* (*umg: Lärm*) row ▷ *nt* (**-s, -**) spectacle

spektakulär [ʃpɛktakuˈlɛːr] *adj* spectacular

Spektrum [ˈʃpɛktrʊm] (**-s, -tren**) *nt* spectrum

Spekulant, in [ʃpekuˈlant(ɪn)] *m(f)* speculator

Spekulation [ʃpekulatsiˈoːn] *f* speculation

Spekulatius [ʃpekuˈlaːtsiʊs] (**-, -**) *m* spiced biscuit (*Brit*) *od* cookie (*US*)

spekulieren [ʃpekuˈliːrən] *vi* (*fig*) to speculate; **auf etw** *akk* **~** to have hopes of sth

Spelunke [ʃpeˈlʊŋkə] (**-, -n**) *f* dive

spendabel [ʃpɛnˈdaːbəl] (*umg*) *adj* generous, open-handed

Spende [ˈʃpɛndə] (**-, -n**) *f* donation

spenden *vt* to donate, give; **Spendenkonto** *nt* donations account; **Spendenwaschanlage** *f* donation-laundering organization

Spender, in (**-s, -**) *m(f)* donator; (*Med*) donor

spendieren [ʃpɛnˈdiːrən] *vt* to pay for, buy; **jdm etw ~** to treat sb to sth, stand sb sth

Sperling [ˈʃpɛrlɪŋ] *m* sparrow

Sperma [ˈʃpɛrma] (**-s, Spermen**) *nt* sperm

sperrangelweit [ˈʃpɛrˈʔaŋəlˈvaɪt] *adj* wide-open

Sperrbezirk *m* no-go area

Sperre (**-, -n**) *f* barrier; (*Verbot*) ban; (*Polizeisperre*) roadblock

sperren [ˈʃpɛrən] *vt* to block; (*Comm: Konto*) to freeze; (*Comput: Daten*) to disable; (*Sport*) to suspend, bar; (*: vom Ball*) to obstruct; (*einschließen*) to lock; (*verbieten*) to ban ▷ *vr* to baulk, jibe, jib

Sperr- *zW*: **Sperrfeuer** *nt* (*Mil, fig*) barrage; **Sperrfrist** *f* (*auch Jur*) waiting period; (*Sport*) (period of) suspension; **Sperrgebiet** *nt* prohibited area; **Sperrgut** *nt* bulky freight; **Sperrholz** *nt* plywood

sperrig *adj* bulky

Sperr- *zW*: **Sperrkonto** *nt* blocked account; **Sperrmüll** *m* bulky refuse; **Sperrsitz** *m* (*Theat*) stalls *pl* (*Brit*), orchestra (*US*); **Sperrstunde** *f* closing time; **Sperrzeit** *f* closing time; **Sperrzone** *f* exclusion zone

Spesen [ˈʃpeːzən] *pl* expenses *pl*; **Spesenabrechnung** *f* expense account

Spessart [ˈʃpɛsart] (**-s**) *m* Spessart (Mountains *pl*)

Spezi [ˈʃpeːtsi] (**-s, -s**) (*umg*) *m* pal, mate (*Brit*)

Spezial- [ʃpetsiˈaːl] *in zw* special; **Spezialausbildung** *f* specialized training

spezialisieren [ʃpetsialiˈziːrən] *vr* to specialize

Spezialisierung *f* specialization

Spezialist, in [ʃpetsiaˈlɪst(ɪn)] *m(f)*: **~ (für)** specialist (in)

Spezialität [ʃpetsialiˈtɛːt] *f* speciality (*Brit*), specialty (*US*)

speziell [ʃpetsiˈɛl] *adj* special

Spezifikation [ʃpetsifikatsiˈoːn] *f* specification

spezifisch [ʃpeˈtsiːfɪʃ] *adj* specific

Sphäre [ˈsfɛːrə] (**-, -n**) *f* sphere

spicken [ˈʃpɪkən] *vt* to lard ▷ *vi* (*Sch*) to copy, crib

Spickzettel *m* (*Sch: umg*) crib

spie *etc* [ʃpiː] *vb siehe* **speien**

Spiegel [ˈʃpiːɡəl] (**-s, -**) *m* mirror; (*Wasserspiegel*) level; (*Mil*) tab; **Spiegelbild** *nt* reflection; **spiegelbildlich** *adj* reversed

Spiegelei [ˈʃpiːɡəlʔaɪ] *nt* fried egg

spiegeln *vt* to mirror, reflect ▷ *vr* to be reflected ▷ *vi* to gleam; (*widerspiegeln*) to be reflective

Spiegelreflexkamera *f* reflex camera

Spiegelschrift *f* mirror writing

Spiegelung *f* reflection

spiegelverkehrt *adj* in mirror image

Spiel [ʃpiːl] (**-(e)s, -e**) *nt* game; (*Schauspiel*) play; (*Tätigkeit*) play(ing); (*Karten*) pack (*Brit*), deck (*US*); (*Tech*) (free) play; **leichtes ~ (bei** *od* **mit jdm) haben** to have an easy job of it (with sb); **die Hand** *od* **Finger im ~ haben** to have a hand in affairs; **jdn/etw aus dem ~ lassen** to leave sb/sth out of it; **auf dem ~(e) stehen** to be at stake; **Spielautomat** *m* gambling machine; (*zum Geldgewinnen*) fruit machine (*Brit*); **Spielbank** *f* casino; **Spieldose** *f* musical box (*Brit*), music box (*US*)

spielen *vt, vi* to play; (*um Geld*) to gamble; (*Theat*) to perform, act; **was wird hier gespielt?** (*umg*) what's going on here?

spielend *adv* easily

Spieler, in (**-s, -**) *m(f)* player; (*um Geld*) gambler

Spielerei [ʃpiːləˈraɪ] *f* (*Kinderspiel*) child's play

spielerisch *adj* playful; (*Leichtigkeit*) effortless; **~es Können** skill as a player; (*Theat*) acting ability

Spiel- *zW*: **Spielfeld** *nt* pitch, field; **Spielfilm** *m* feature film; **Spielgeld** *nt* (*Einsatz*) stake; (*unechtes Geld*) toy money; **Spielkarte** *f* playing card; **Spielkonsole** *f* play console; **Spielmannszug** *m* (brass) band; **Spielplan** *m* (*Theat*) programme (*Brit*), program (*US*); **Spielplatz** *m* playground; **Spielraum** *m*

S

room to manoeuvre (Brit) od maneuver (US), scope; **Spielregel** f (lit, fig) rule of the game; **Spielsachen** pl toys pl; **Spielshow** f gameshow; **Spielstand** m score; **Spielstraße** f play street; **Spielsucht** f addiction to gambling; **Spielverderber (-s, -)** m spoilsport; **Spielwaren** pl toys pl; **Spielzeit** f (Saison) season; (Spieldauer) playing time; **Spielzeug** nt toy; (Spielsachen) toys pl

Spieß [ʃpi:s] (-es, -e) m spear; (Bratspieß) spit; (Mil: umg) sarge; **den ~ umdrehen** (fig) to turn the tables; **wie am ~(e) schreien** (umg) to squeal like a stuck pig; **Spießbraten** m joint roasted on a spit

Spießbürger (-s, -) m bourgeois

Spießer (-s, -) m bourgeois

Spikes [spaɪks] pl (Sport) spikes pl; (Aut) studs pl; **Spikesreifen** m studded tyre (Brit) od tire (US)

Spinat [ʃpi'na:t] (-(e)s, -e) m spinach

Spind [ʃpɪnt] (-(e)s, -e) m od nt locker

spindeldürr [ʃpɪndəl'dyr] (pej) adj spindly, thin as a rake

Spinne ['ʃpɪnə] (-, -n) f spider; **spinnefeind** (umg) adj: **sich** od **einander** dat **spinnefeind sein** to be deadly enemies

spinnen unreg vt to spin ▷ vi (umg) to talk rubbish; (verrückt) to be crazy od mad; **ich denk ich spinne** (umg) I don't believe it

Spinnengewebe nt cobweb

Spinner, in (-s, -) m(f) (fig: umg) screwball, crackpot

Spinnerei [ʃpɪnə'raɪ] f spinning mill

Spinn- zW: **Spinngewebe** nt cobweb; **Spinnrad** nt spinning wheel; **Spinnwebe** f cobweb

Spion [ʃpi'o:n] (-s, -e) m spy; (in Tür) spyhole

Spionage [ʃpio'na:ʒə] (-) f espionage; **Spionageabwehr** f counterintelligence; **Spionagesatellit** m spy satellite

spionieren [ʃpio'ni:rən] vi to spy

Spionin f (woman) spy

Spirale [ʃpi'ra:lə] (-, -n) f spiral; (Med) coil

Spirituosen [ʃpiritu'o:zən] pl spirits pl

Spiritus ['ʃpi:ritʊs] (-, -se) m (methylated) spirits pl; **Spirituskocher** m spirit stove

Spitz [ʃpɪts] (-es, -e) m (Hund) spitz

spitz adj pointed; (Winkel) acute; (fig: Zunge) sharp; (: Bemerkung) caustic

Spitz- zW: **spitzbekommen** unreg vt: **etw spitzbekommen** (umg) to get wise to sth; **Spitzbogen** m pointed arch; **Spitzbube** m rogue

Spitze (-, -n) f point, tip; (Bergspitze) peak; (Bemerkung) taunt; (fig: Stichelei) dig; (erster Platz) lead, top; (meist pl: Gewebe) lace; **etw auf die ~ treiben** to carry sth too far

spitze adj inv (umg: prima) great

Spitzel (-s, -) m police informer

spitzen vt to sharpen; (Lippen, Mund) to purse; (lit, fig: Ohren) to prick up

Spitzen- in zw top; **Spitzenleistung** f top performance; **Spitzenlohn** m top wages pl; **Spitzenmarke** f brand leader; **spitzenmäßig** adj really great; **Spitzenposition** f leading

position; **Spitzenreiter** m (Sport) leader; (fig: Kandidat) front runner; (Ware) top seller; (Schlager) number one; **Spitzensportler** m top-class sportsman; **Spitzenverband** m leading organization; **Spitzenverdiener, in** m(f) top earner

Spitzer (-s, -) m sharpener

spitzfindig adj (over)subtle

Spitzmaus f shrew

Spitzname m nickname

Spleen [ʃpli:n] (-s, -e od -s) m (Angewohnheit) crazy habit; (Idee) crazy idea; (Fimmel) obsession

Splitt [ʃplɪt] (-s, -e) m stone chippings pl; (Streumittel) grit

Splitter (-s, -) m splinter; **Splittergruppe** f (Pol) splinter group; **splitternackt** adj stark naked

SPÖ (-) f abk (= Sozialistische Partei Österreichs) Austrian Socialist Party

sponsern ['ʃpɔnzərn] vt to sponsor

Sponsor ['ʃpɔnzɔr] (-s, -en) m sponsor

spontan [ʃpɔn'ta:n] adj spontaneous

sporadisch [ʃpo'ra:dɪʃ] adj sporadic

Sporen ['ʃpo:rən] pl (auch Bot, Zool) spurs pl

Sport [ʃpɔrt] (-(e)s, -e) m sport; (fig) hobby; **treiben Sie ~?** do you do any sport?; **Sportabzeichen** nt sports certificate; **Sportartikel** pl sports equipment sing; **Sportfest** nt sports gala; (Sch) sports day (Brit); **Sportgeist** m sportsmanship; **Sporthalle** f sports hall; **Sportklub** m sports club; **Sportlehrer** m games od P.E. teacher

Sportler, in (-s, -) m(f) sportsman, sportswoman

Sport- zW: **sportlich** adj sporting; (Mensch) sporty; (durchtrainiert) athletic; (Kleidung) smart but casual; **Sportmedizin** f sports medicine; **Sportplatz** m playing od sports field; **Sportschuh** m sports shoe; (sportlicher Schuh) casual shoe

Sportsfreund m (fig: umg) buddy

Sport- zW: **Sportverein** m sports club; **Sportwagen** m sports car; **Sportzeug** nt sports gear

Spot [spɔt] (-s, -s) m commercial, advertisement

Spott [ʃpɔt] (-(e)s) m mockery, ridicule; **spottbillig** adj dirt-cheap; **spotten** vi to mock; **spotten über** +akk to mock (at), ridicule; **das spottet jeder Beschreibung** that simply defies description

spöttisch ['ʃpœtɪʃ] adj mocking

Spottpreis m ridiculously low price

sprach etc [ʃpra:x] vb siehe **sprechen**

sprachbegabt adj good at languages

Sprache (-, -n) f language; **heraus mit der ~!** (umg) come on, out with it!; **zur ~ kommen** to be mentioned; **in französischer ~** in French

Sprachenschule f language school

Sprach- zW: **Sprachfehler** m speech defect; **Sprachfertigkeit** f fluency; **Sprachführer** m phrase book; **Sprachgebrauch** m (linguistic) usage; **Sprachgefühl** nt feeling for language;

Sprachkenntnisse *pl*: **mit englischen Sprachkenntnissen** with a knowledge of English; **Sprachkurs** *m* language course; **Sprachlabor** *nt* language laboratory; **sprachlich** *adj* linguistic; **sprachlos** *adj* speechless; **Sprachrohr** *nt* megaphone; (*fig*) mouthpiece; **Sprachstörung** *f* speech disorder; **Sprachwissenschaft** *f* linguistics *sing*

sprang *etc* [ʃpraŋ] *vb siehe* **springen**

Spray [spreː] **(-s, -s)** *m od nt* spray; **Spraydose** *f* aerosol (can), spray

sprayen *vt, vi* to spray

Sprechanlage *f* intercom

Sprechblase *f* speech balloon

sprechen [ˈʃprɛçən] *unreg vi* to speak, talk ▷ *vt* to say; (*Sprache*) to speak; (*Person*) to speak to; **mit jdm ~** to speak *od* talk to sb; **das spricht für ihn** that's a point in his favour; **frei ~** to extemporize; **nicht gut auf jdn zu ~ sein** to be on bad terms with sb; **es spricht vieles dafür, dass ...** there is every reason to believe that ...; **hier spricht man Spanisch** Spanish spoken; **wir ~ uns noch!** you haven't heard the last of this!

Sprecher, in (-s, -) *m(f)* speaker; (*für Gruppe*) spokesman, spokeswoman; (*Rundf, TV*) announcer

Sprech- *zW*: **Sprechfunkgerät** *nt* radio telephone; **Sprechrolle** *f* speaking part; **Sprechstunde** *f* consultation (hour); (*von Arzt*) (doctor's) surgery (*Brit*); **Sprechstundenhilfe** *f* (doctor's) receptionist; **Sprechzimmer** *nt* consulting room, surgery (*Brit*)

spreizen [ˈʃpraɪtsən] *vt* to spread ▷ *vr* to put on airs

Sprengarbeiten *pl* blasting operations *pl*

sprengen [ˈʃprɛŋən] *vt* to sprinkle; (*mit Sprengstoff*) to blow up; (*Gestein*) to blast; (*Versammlung*) to break up

Spreng- *zW*: **Sprengkopf** *m* warhead; **Sprengladung** *f* explosive charge; **Sprengsatz** *m* explosive device; **Sprengstoff** *m* explosive(s *pl*); **Sprengstoffanschlag** *m* bomb attack

Spreu [ʃprɔʏ] **(-)** *f* chaff

spricht [ʃprɪçt] *vb siehe* **sprechen**

Sprichwort *nt* proverb

sprichwörtlich *adj* proverbial

sprießen [ˈʃpriːsən] *vi* (*aus der Erde*) to spring up; (*Knospen*) to shoot

Springbrunnen *m* fountain

springen [ˈʃprɪŋən] *unreg vi* to jump, leap; (*Glas*) to crack; (*mit Kopfsprung*) to dive; **etw ~ lassen** (*umg*) to fork out sth

springend *adj*: **der ~e Punkt** the crucial point

Springer (-s, -) *m* jumper; (*Schach*) knight

Springreiten *nt* show jumping

Springseil *nt* skipping rope

Sprinkler [ˈʃprɪŋklər] **(-s, -)** *m* sprinkler

Sprit [ʃprɪt] **(-(e)s, -e)** (*umg*) *m* petrol (*Brit*), gas(oline) (*US*), fuel

Spritzbeutel *m* icing bag

Spritze [ˈʃprɪtsə] **(-, -n)** *f* syringe; (*Injektion*)

injection; (*an Schlauch*) nozzle

spritzen *vt* to spray; (*Wein*) to dilute with soda water/lemonade; (*Med*) to inject ▷ *vi* to splash; (*heißes Fett*) to spit; (*herausspritzen*) to spurt; (*aus einer Tube etc*) to squirt; (*Med*) to give injections

Spritzer (-s, -) *m* (*Farbspritzer, Wasserspritzer*) splash

Spritzpistole *f* spray gun

Spritztour (*umg*) *f* spin

spröde [ˈʃprøːdə] *adj* brittle; (*Person*) reserved; (*Haut*) rough

Spross (-es, -e) *m* shoot

spross *etc* [ʃprɔs] *vb siehe* **sprießen**

Sprosse [ˈʃprɔsə] **(-, -n)** *f* rung

Sprossenwand *f* (*Sport*) wall bars *pl*

Sprössling [ˈʃprœslɪŋ] *m* offspring *no pl*

Spruch [ʃprʊx] **(-(e)s, ̈-e)** *m* saying, maxim; (*Jur*) judgement; **Sprüche klopfen** (*umg*) to talk fancy; **Spruchband** *nt* banner

Sprüchemacher [ˈʃprʏçəmaxər] (*umg*) *m* patter-merchant

spruchreif *adj*: **die Sache ist noch nicht ~** it's not definite yet

Sprudel [ˈʃpruːdəl] **(-s, -)** *m* mineral water; (*süß*) lemonade

sprudeln *vi* to bubble

Sprüh- *zW*: **Sprühdose** *f* aerosol (can); **sprühen** *vi* to spray; (*fig*) to sparkle ▷ *vt* to spray; **Sprühregen** *m* drizzle

Sprung [ʃprʊŋ] **(-(e)s, ̈-e)** *m* jump; (*schwungvoll, fig: Gedankensprung*) leap; (*Riss*) crack; **immer auf dem ~ sein** (*umg*) to be always on the go; **jdm auf die Sprünge helfen** (*wohlwollend*) to give sb a (helping) hand; **auf einen ~ bei jdm vorbeikommen** (*umg*) to drop in to see sb; **damit kann man keine großen Sprünge machen** (*umg*) you can't exactly live it up on that; **Sprungbrett** *nt* springboard; **Sprungfeder** *f* spring; **sprunghaft** *adj* erratic; (*Aufstieg*) rapid; **Sprungschanze** *f* ski jump; **Sprungturm** *m* diving platform

Spucke [ˈʃpʊkə] **(-)** *f* spit

spucken *vt, vi* to spit; **in die Hände ~** (*fig*) to roll up one's sleeves

Spucknapf *m* spittoon

Spucktüte *f* sickbag

Spuk [ʃpuːk] **(-(e)s, -e)** *m* haunting; (*fig*) nightmare; **spuken** *vi* to haunt; **hier spukt es** this place is haunted

Spülbecken [ˈʃpyːlbɛkən] *nt* sink

Spule [ˈʃpuːlə] **(-, -n)** *f* spool; (*Elek*) coil

Spüle [ˈʃpyːlə] **(-, -n)** *f* (kitchen) sink

spülen *vt* to rinse; (*Geschirr*) to wash, do; (*Toilette*) to flush ▷ *vi* to wash up (*Brit*), do the dishes; to flush; **etw an Land ~** to wash sth ashore

Spül- *zW*: **Spülmaschine** *f* dishwasher; **Spülmittel** *nt* washing-up liquid (*Brit*), dish-washing liquid; **Spülstein** *m* sink

Spülung *f* rinsing; (*Wasserspülung*) flush; (*Med*) irrigation

Spund [ʃpʊnt] **(-(e)s, -e)** *m*: **junger ~**

S

313

(*veraltet: umg*) young pup

Spur [ʃpuːr] (-, -en) f trace; (*Fußspur, Radspur, Tonbandspur*) track; (*Fährte*) trail; (*Fahrspur*) lane; **jdm auf die ~ kommen** to get onto sb; **(seine) ~en hinterlassen** (*fig*) to leave its mark; **keine ~** (*umg*) not/nothing at all

spürbar *adj* noticeable, perceptible

spuren (*umg*) vi to obey; (*sich fügen*) to toe the line

spüren [ˈʃpyːrən] vt to feel; **etw zu ~ bekommen** (*lit*) to feel sth; (*fig*) to feel the (full) force of sth

Spurenelement nt trace element

Spurensicherung f securing of evidence

Spürhund m tracker dog; (*fig*) sleuth

spurlos *adv* without(a) trace; **~ an jdm vorübergehen** to have no effect on sb

Spurt [ʃpʊrt] (-(e)s, -s *od* -e) m spurt

spurten vi (*Hilfsverb sein: Sport*) to spurt; (*umg: rennen*) to sprint

sputen [ˈʃpuːtən] vr to make haste

Squash [skvɔʃ] (-) nt (*Sport*) squash

SS (-) f *abk* (= *Schutzstaffel*) SS ▷ nt *abk* = **Sommersemester**

s. S. *abk* (= *siehe Seite*) see p.

SSV *abk* = **Sommerschlussverkauf**

st *abk* (= *Stunde*) h.

St. *abk* = **Stück**; (= *Stunde*) h.; (= *Sankt*) St

Staat [ʃtaːt] (-(e)s, -en) m state; (*Prunk*) show; (*Kleidung*) finery; **mit etw ~ machen** to show off *od* parade sth

staatenlos *adj* stateless

staatl. *abk* = **staatlich**

staatlich *adj* state *attrib*; state-run ▷ *adv*: **~ geprüft** state-certified

Staats- *zW*: **Staatsaffäre** f (*lit*) affair of state; (*fig*) major operation; **Staatsangehörige, r** f(m) national; **Staatsangehörigkeit** f nationality; **Staatsanleihe** f government bond; **Staatsanwalt** m public prosecutor; **Staatsbürger** m citizen; **Staatsbürgerschaft** f nationality; **doppelte Staatsbürgerschaft** dual nationality; **Staatsdienst** m civil service; **staatseigen** *adj* state-owned; **Staatseigentum** nt public ownership; **Staatsexamen** nt (*Univ*) degree; **staatsfeindlich** *adj* subversive; **Staatsgeheimnis** nt (*lit, fig hum*) state secret; **Staatshaushalt** m budget; **Staatskosten** pl public expenses pl; **Staatsmann** (-(e)s, pl **-männer**) m statesman; **staatsmännisch** *adj* statesmanlike; **Staatsoberhaupt** nt head of state; **Staatsschuld** f (*Fin*) national debt; **Staatssekretär** m secretary of state; **Staatsstreich** m coup (d'état); **Staatsverschuldung** f national debt

Stab [ʃtaːp] (-(e)s, ̈e) m rod; (*für Stabhochsprung*) pole; (*für Staffellauf*) baton; (*Gitterstab*) bar; (*Menschen*) staff; (*von Experten*) panel

Stäbchen [ˈʃtɛːpçən] nt (*Essstäbchen*) chopstick

Stabhochsprung m pole vault

stabil [ʃtaˈbiːl] *adj* stable; (*Möbel*) sturdy

Stabilisator [ʃtabiliˈzaːtɔr] m stabilizer

stabilisieren [ʃtabiliˈziːrən] vt to stabilize

Stabilisierung f stabilization

Stabilität [ʃtabiliˈtɛːt] f stability

Stabreim m alliteration

Stabsarzt m (*Mil*) captain in the medical corps

stach etc [ʃtaːx] vb siehe **stechen**

Stachel [ˈʃtaxəl] (-s, -n) m spike; (*von Tier*) spine; (*von Insekten*) sting; **Stachelbeere** f gooseberry; **Stacheldraht** m barbed wire

stachelig, stachlig *adj* prickly

Stachelschwein nt porcupine

Stadion [ˈʃtaːdiɔn] (-s, **Stadien**) nt stadium

Stadium [ˈʃtaːdiʊm] nt stage, phase

Stadt [ʃtat] (-, ̈e) f town; (*Großstadt*) city; (*Stadtverwaltung*) (town/city) council; **Stadtbad** nt municipal swimming baths pl; **stadtbekannt** *adj* known all over town; **Stadtbezirk** m municipal district

Städtchen [ˈʃtɛːtçən] nt small town

Städtebau (-(e)s) m town planning

Städter, in (-s, -) m(f) town/city dweller, townie

Stadtgespräch nt: **(das) ~ sein** to be the talk of the town

Stadtguerilla f urban guerrilla

städtisch *adj* municipal; (*nicht ländlich*) urban

Stadt- *zW*: **Stadtkasse** f town/city treasury; **Stadtkern** m = **Stadtzentrum**; **Stadtkreis** m town/city borough; **Stadtmauer** f city wall(s pl); **Stadtmitte** f town/city centre (*Brit*) *od* center (*US*); **Stadtpark** m municipal park; **Stadtplan** m street map; **Stadtrand** m outskirts pl; **Stadtrat** m (*Behörde*) (town/city) council; **Stadtstreicher** m street vagrant; **Stadtstreicherin** f bag lady; **Stadtteil** m district, part of town; **Stadtverwaltung** f (*Behörde*) municipal authority; **Stadtviertel** m district *od* part of a town; **Stadtzentrum** nt town/city centre (*Brit*) *od* center (*US*)

Staffel [ˈʃtafəl] (-, -n) f rung; (*Sport*) relay (team); (*Aviat*) squadron

Staffelei [ʃtafəˈlaɪ] f easel

Staffellauf m relay race

staffeln vt to graduate

Staffelung f graduation

Stagnation [ʃtagnatsiˈoːn] f stagnation

stagnieren [ʃtaˈgniːrən] vi to stagnate

Stahl (-(e)s, ̈e) m steel

stahl etc [ʃtaːl] vb siehe **stehlen**

Stahlhelm m steel helmet

stak etc [ʃtaːk] vb siehe **stecken**

Stall [ʃtal] (-(e)s, ̈e) m stable; (*Kaninchenstall*) hutch; (*Schweinestall*) sty; (*Hühnerstall*) henhouse

Stallung f stables pl

Stamm [ʃtam] (-(e)s, ̈e) m (*Baumstamm*) trunk; (*Menschenstamm*) tribe; (*Gram*) stem; (*Bakterienstamm*) strain; **Stammaktie** f ordinary share, common stock (*US*); **Stammbaum** m family tree; (*von Tier*) pedigree; **Stammbuch** nt book of family events with legal documents

stammeln vt, vi to stammer

stammen vi: **~ von** *od* **aus** to come from

Stamm- zW: **Stammform** f base form; **Stammgast** m regular (customer); **Stammhalter** m son and heir

stämmig ['ʃtɛmɪç] adj sturdy; (Mensch) stocky; **Stämmigkeit** f sturdiness; stockiness

Stamm- zW: **Stammkapital** nt (Fin) ordinary share od common stock (US) capital; **Stammkunde** m, **Stammkundin** f regular (customer); **Stammlokal** nt favourite (Brit) od favorite (US) café/restaurant etc; (Kneipe) local (Brit); **Stammplatz** m usual seat; **Stammtisch** m (Tisch in Gasthaus) table reserved for the regulars; **Stammzelle** f stem cell; **embryonale Stammzellen** embryonic stem cells

stampfen ['ʃtampfən] vi to stamp; (stapfen) to tramp ▷ vt (mit Stampfer) to mash

Stampfer (-s, -) m (Stampfgerät) masher

Stand (-(e)s, ¨e) m position; (Wasserstand, Benzinstand etc) level; (Zählerstand etc) reading; (Stehen) standing position; (Zustand) state; (Spielstand) score; (Messestand etc) stand; (Klasse) class; (Beruf) profession; **bei jdm** od **gegen jdn einen schweren ~ haben** (fig) to have a hard time of it with sb; **etw auf den neuesten ~ bringen** to bring sth up to date; siehe auch **außerstande; imstande; zustande**

stand etc [ʃtant] vb siehe **stehen**

Standard ['ʃtandart] (-s, -s) m standard; **Standardausführung** f standard design

standardisieren [ʃtandardi'ziːrən] vt to standardize

Standarte (-, -n) f (Mil, Pol) standard

Standbild nt statue

Ständchen ['ʃtɛntçən] nt serenade

Ständer (-s, -) m stand

Standes- zW: **Standesamt** nt registry office (Brit), city/county clerk's office (US); **standesamtlich** adj: **standesamtliche Trauung** registry office wedding (Brit), civil marriage ceremony; **Standesbeamte, r** m registrar; **Standesbewusstsein** nt status consciousness; **Standesdünkel** m snobbery; **standesgemäß** adj, adv according to one's social position; **Standesunterschied** m social difference

Stand- zW: **standfest** adj (Tisch, Leiter) stable, steady; (fig) steadfast; **standhaft** adj steadfast; **Standhaftigkeit** f steadfastness; **standhalten** unreg vi: **(jdm/etw) standhalten** to stand firm (against sb/sth), resist (sb/sth)

ständig ['ʃtɛndɪç] adj permanent; (ununterbrochen) constant, continual

Stand- zW: **Standlicht** nt sidelights pl (Brit), parking lights pl (US); **Standort** m location; (Mil) garrison; **Standpauke** (umg) f: **jdm eine Standpauke halten** to give sb a lecture; **Standpunkt** m standpoint; **standrechtlich** adj: **standrechtlich erschießen** to put before a firing squad; **Standspur** f (Aut) hard shoulder (Brit), berm (US)

Stange ['ʃtaŋə] (-, -n) f stick; (Stab) pole; (Querstange) bar; (Zigaretten) carton; **von der ~** (Comm) off the peg (Brit) od rack (US); **eine ~**

Geld quite a packet; **jdm die ~ halten** (umg) to stick up for sb; **bei der ~ bleiben** (umg) to stick at od to sth

Stängel ['ʃtɛŋl] (-s, -) m stalk; **vom ~ fallen** (umg: überrascht sein) to be staggered

Stangenbohne f runner bean

Stangenbrot nt French bread; (Laib) French stick (loaf)

stank etc [ʃtaŋk] vb siehe **stinken**

stänkern ['ʃtɛŋkərn] (umg) vi to stir things up

Stanniol [ʃtani'oːl] (-s, -e) nt tinfoil

Stanze ['ʃtantsə] (-, -n) f stanza; (Tech) stamp

stanzen vt to stamp; (Löcher) to punch

Stapel ['ʃtaːpəl] (-s, -) m pile; (Naut) stocks pl; **Stapellauf** m launch

stapeln vt to pile (up)

Stapelverarbeitung f (Comput) batch processing

stapfen ['ʃtapfən] vi to trudge, plod

Star¹ [ʃtaːr] (-(e)s, -e) m starling; **grauer/ grüner ~** (Med) cataract/glaucoma

Star² [ʃtaːr] (-s, -s) m (Filmstar etc) star

starb etc [ʃtarp] vb siehe **sterben**

stark [ʃtark] adj strong; (heftig, groß) heavy; (Maßangabe) thick; (umg: hervorragend) great ▷ adv very; (beschädigt etc) badly; (vergrößert, verkleinert) greatly; **das ist ein ~es Stück!** (umg) that's a bit much!; **er ist ~ erkältet** he has a bad cold; siehe auch **starkmachen**

Stärke ['ʃtɛrkə] (-, -n) f strength (auch fig); heaviness; thickness; (von Mannschaft) size; (Wäschestärke, Koch) starch; **Stärkemehl** nt (Koch) thickening agent

stärken vt (lit, fig) to strengthen; (Wäsche) to starch; (Selbstbewusstsein) to boost; (Gesundheit) to improve; (erfrischen) to fortify ▷ vi to be fortifying; **~des Mittel** tonic

starkmachen vr: **sich für etw ~** (umg) to stand up for sth

Starkstrom m heavy current

Stärkung ['ʃtɛrkʊŋ] f strengthening; (Essen) refreshment

Stärkungsmittel nt tonic

starr [ʃtar] adj stiff; (unnachgiebig) rigid; (Blick) staring

starren vi to stare; **~ vor** +dat od **von** (voll von) to be covered in; (Waffen) to be bristling with; **vor sich** akk **hin ~** to stare straight ahead

starr- zW: **Starrheit** f rigidity; **starrköpfig** adj stubborn; **Starrsinn** m obstinacy

Start [ʃtart] (-(e)s, -e) m start; (Aviat) takeoff; **Startautomatik** f (Aut) automatic choke; **Startbahn** f runway; **starten** vi to start; (Aviat) to take off ▷ vt to start; **Starter** (-s, -) m starter; **Starterlaubnis** f takeoff clearance; **Starthilfe** f (Aviat) rocket-assisted takeoff; (fig) initial aid; **jdm Starthilfe geben** to help sb get off the ground; **Starthilfekabel** nt jump leads pl (Brit), jumper cables pl (US); **startklar** adj (Aviat) clear for takeoff; (Sport) ready to start; **Startkommando** nt (Sport) starting signal; **Startzeichen** nt start signal

Stasi ['ʃtaːzi] (-) (umg) f abk

S

315

(früher: = Staatssicherheitsdienst der DDR) Stasi; see culture note

@ **STASI**
@
@ Stasi, an abbreviation of
@ Staatssicherheitsdienst, the DDR
@ secret service, was founded in 1950 and
@ disbanded in 1989. The Stasi organized
@ an extensive spy network of full-time
@ and part-time workers who often held
@ positions of trust in both the DDR and the
@ BRD. They held personal files on 6 million
@ people.

Station [ʃtatsi'o:n] f station; (Krankenstation) hospital ward; (Haltestelle) stop; **~ machen** to stop off

stationär [ʃtatsio'nɛ:r] adj stationary; (Med) in-patient attrib

stationieren [ʃtatsio'ni:rən] vt to station; (Atomwaffen etc) to deploy

Stations- zW: **Stationsarzt** m ward doctor; **Stationsärztin** f ward doctor; **Stationsvorsteher** m (Eisenb) stationmaster

statisch ['ʃta:tɪʃ] adj static

Statist, in [ʃta'tɪst(ɪn)] m(f) (Film) extra; (Theat) supernumerary

Statistik f statistic; (Wissenschaft) statistics sing

Statistiker, in (-s, -) m(f) statistician

statistisch adj statistical

Stativ [ʃta'ti:f] (-s, -e) nt tripod

statt konj instead of ▷ präp (+dat od gen) instead of

stattdessen adv instead

Stätte ['ʃtɛtə] (-, -n) f place

statt- zW: **stattfinden** unreg vi to take place; **statthaft** adj admissible; **Statthalter** m governor; **stattlich** adj imposing, handsome; (Bursche) strapping; (Sammlung) impressive; (Familie) large; (Summe) handsome

Statue ['ʃta:tuə] (-, -n) f statue

Statur [ʃta'tu:r] f build

Status ['ʃta:tʊs] (-, -) m status; **Statussymbol** nt status symbol

Statuten [ʃta'tu:tən] pl by(e)-law(s pl)

Stau [ʃtaʊ] (-(e)s, -e) m blockage; (Verkehrsstau) (traffic) jam

Staub [ʃtaʊp] (-(e)s) m dust; **~ saugen** to vacuum; **~ wischen** to dust; **sich aus dem ~ machen** (umg) to clear off

stauben ['ʃtaʊbən] vi to be dusty

Staubfaden m (Bot) stamen

staubig ['ʃtaʊbɪç] adj dusty

Staub- zW: **Staublappen** m duster; **Staublunge** f (Med) dust on the lung; **staubsaugen** (pp **staubgesaugt**) vi untr to vacuum; **Staubsauger** m vacuum cleaner; **Staubtuch** nt duster

Staudamm m dam

Staude ['ʃtaʊdə] (-, -n) f shrub

stauen ['ʃtaʊən] vt (Wasser) to dam up; (Blut) to stop the flow of ▷ vr (Wasser) to become

dammed up; (Verkehr, Med) to become congested; (Menschen) to collect together; (Gefühle) to build up

staunen ['ʃtaʊnən] vi to be astonished; **da kann man nur noch ~** it's just amazing; **Staunen (-s)** nt amazement

Stausee ['ʃtaʊze:] m reservoir; artificial lake

Stauung ['ʃtaʊʊŋ] f (von Wasser) damming-up; (von Blut, Verkehr) congestion

Std. abk (= Stunde) h.

stdl. abk = **stündlich**

Steak [ʃte:k] (-s, -s) nt steak

Stechen ['ʃtɛçən] (-s, -) nt (Sport) play-off; (Springreiten) jump-off; (Schmerz) sharp pain

stechen unreg vt (mit Nadel etc) to prick; (mit Messer) to stab; (mit Finger) to poke; (Biene etc) to sting; (Mücke) to bite; (Karten) to take; (Kunst) to engrave; (Torf, Spargel) to cut ▷ vi (Sonne) to beat down; (mit Stechkarte) to clock in ▷ vr: **sich akk od dat in den Finger ~** to prick one's finger; **es sticht** it is prickly; **in See ~** to put to sea

stechend adj piercing, stabbing; (Geruch) pungent

Stech- zW: **Stechginster** m gorse; **Stechkarte** f clocking-in card; **Stechmücke** f gnat; **Stechpalme** f holly; **Stechuhr** f time clock

Steck- zW: **Steckbrief** m "wanted" poster; **steckbrieflich** adv: **steckbrieflich gesucht werden** to be wanted; **Steckdose** f (wall) socket

stecken ['ʃtɛkən] vt to put; (einführen) to insert; (Nadel) to stick; (Pflanzen) to plant; (beim Nähen) to pin ▷ vi (auch unreg) to be; (festsitzen) to be stuck; (Nadeln) to stick; **etw in etw** akk **~** (umg: Geld, Mühe) to put sth into sth; (: Zeit) to devote sth to sth; **der Schlüssel steckt** the key is in the lock; **wo steckt er?** where has he got to?; **zeigen, was in einem steckt** to show what one is made of; **~ bleiben** to get stuck; **~ lassen** to leave in

Steckenpferd nt hobbyhorse

Stecker (-s, -) m (Elek) plug

Steck- zW: **Stecknadel** f pin; **Steckrübe** f swede, turnip; **Steckschlüssel** m box spanner (Brit) od wrench (US); **Steckzwiebel** f bulb

Steg [ʃte:k] (-(e)s, -e) m small bridge; (Anlegesteg) landing stage

Stegreif m: **aus dem ~** just like that

Stehaufmännchen ['ʃte:|aʊfmɛnçən] nt (Spielzeug) tumbler

stehen ['ʃte:ən] unreg vi to stand; (sich befinden) to be; (in Zeitung) to say; (angehalten haben) to have stopped ▷ vi unpers: **es steht schlecht um ...** things are bad for ... ▷ vr: **sich gut/ schlecht ~** to be well-off/badly off; **zu jdm/ etw ~** to stand by sb/sth; **jdm ~** to suit sb; **ich tue, was in meinen Kräften steht** I'll do everything I can; **es steht 2:1 für München** the score is 2-1 to Munich; **mit dem Dativ ~** (Gram) to take the dative; **auf Betrug steht eine Gefängnisstrafe** the penalty for fraud is imprisonment; **wie ~ Sie dazu?** what are your views on that?; **wie stehts?** how are things?;

(*Sport*) what's the score?; **wie steht es damit?** how about it?; ~ **bleiben** (*Uhr*) to stop; (*Zeit*) to stand still; (*Auto, Zug*) to stand; (*Fehler*) to stay as it is; (*Verkehr, Produktion etc*) to come to a standstill *od* stop; ~ **lassen** to leave; (*Bart*) to grow; **alles ~ und liegen lassen** to drop everything

stehend *adj attrib* (*Fahrzeug*) stationary; (*Gewässer*) stagnant; (*ständig*) (*Heer*) regular

Stehlampe *f* standard lamp (*Brit*), floor lamp (*US*)

stehlen ['ʃteːlən] *unreg vt* to steal

Stehplatz *m*: **ein ~ kostet 15 Euro** a standing ticket costs 15 euros

Stehvermögen *nt* staying power, stamina

Steiermark ['ʃtaɪrmark] *f*: **die ~** Styria

steif [ʃtaɪf] *adj* stiff; ~ **und fest auf etw** *dat* **beharren** to insist stubbornly on sth

Steifftier® ['ʃtaɪftiːr] *nt* soft toy animal

Steifheit *f* stiffness

Steigbügel ['ʃtaɪkbyːgəl] *m* stirrup

Steigeisen *nt* crampon

steigen *unreg vi* to rise; (*klettern*) to climb ▷ *vt* (*Treppen, Stufen*) to climb (up); **das Blut stieg ihm in den Kopf** the blood rushed to his head; ~ **in** +*akk*/**auf** +*akk* to get in/on

Steiger (**-s, -**) *m* (*Min*) pit foreman

steigern *vt* to raise; (*Gram*) to compare ▷ *vi* (*Auktion*) to bid ▷ *vr* to increase

Steigerung *f* raising; (*Gram*) comparison

Steigung *f* incline, gradient, rise

steil [ʃtaɪl] *adj* steep; **Steilhang** *m* steep slope; **Steilpass** *m* (*Sport*) through ball

Stein [ʃtaɪn] (**-(e)s, -e**) *m* stone; (*in Uhr*) jewel; **mir fällt ein ~ vom Herzen!** (*fig*) that's a load off my mind!; **bei jdm einen ~ im Brett haben** (*fig: umg*) to be well in with sb; **jdm ~e in den Weg legen** to make things difficult for sb; **Steinadler** *m* golden eagle; **steinalt** *adj* ancient; **Steinbock** *m* (*Astrol*) Capricorn; **Steinbruch** *m* quarry

steinern *adj* (made of) stone; (*fig*) stony

Stein- *zW*: **Steinerweichen** *nt*: **zum Steinerweichen weinen** to cry heartbreakingly; **Steingarten** *m* rockery; **Steingut** *nt* stoneware; **steinhart** *adj* hard as stone

steinig *adj* stony

steinigen *vt* to stone

Stein- *zW*: **Steinkohle** *f* mineral coal; **Steinmetz** (**-es, -e**) *m* stonemason; **steinreich** (*umg*) *adj* stinking rich; **Steinschlag** *m*: **„Achtung Steinschlag"** "danger – falling stones"; **Steinwurf** *m* (*fig*) stone's throw; **Steinzeit** *f* Stone Age

Steiß [ʃtaɪs] (**-es, -e**) *m* rump; **Steißbein** *nt* (*Anat*) coccyx

Stelle ['ʃtɛlə] (**-, -n**) *f* place; (*Arbeit*) post, job; (*Amt*) office; (*Abschnitt*) passage; (*Textstelle, bes beim Zitieren*) reference; **drei ~n hinter dem Komma** (*Math*) three decimal places; **eine freie** *od* **offene ~** a vacancy; **an dieser ~** in this place, here; **an anderer ~** elsewhere;

nicht von der ~ kommen not to make any progress; **auf der ~** (*fig: sofort*) on the spot; *siehe auch* **anstelle**

stellen *vt* to put; (*Uhr etc*) to set; (*zur Verfügung stellen*) to supply; (*fassen: Dieb*) to apprehend; (*Antrag, Forderung*) to make; (*Aufnahme*) to pose; (*arrangieren: Szene*) to arrange ▷ *vr* (*sich aufstellen*) to stand; (*sich einfinden*) to present o.s.; (*bei Polizei*) to give o.s. up; (*vorgeben*) to pretend (to be); **das Radio lauter/leiser ~** to turn the radio up/down; **auf sich** *akk* **selbst gestellt sein** (*fig*) to have to fend for o.s.; **sich hinter jdn/etw ~** (*fig*) to support sb/sth; **sich einer Herausforderung ~** to take up a challenge; **sich zu etw ~** to have an opinion of sth

Stellen- *zW*: **Stellenangebot** *nt* offer of a post; (*in Zeitung*): **„Stellenangebote"** "vacancies"; **Stellenanzeige** *f* job advertisement *od* ad (*umg*); **Stellengesuch** *nt* application for a post; **„Stellengesuche"** "situations wanted"; **Stellenmarkt** *m* job market; (*in Zeitung*) appointments section; **Stellennachweis** *m* employment agency; **Stellenvermittlung** *f* employment agency; **stellenweise** *adv* in places; **Stellenwert** *m* (*fig*) status

Stellung *f* position; (*Mil*) line; ~ **nehmen zu** to comment on

Stellungnahme *f* comment

stellungslos *adj* unemployed

stellv. *abk* = **stellvertretend**

Stell- *zW*: **stellvertretend** *adj* deputy *attrib*, acting *attrib*; **Stellvertreter** *m* (*von Amts wegen*) deputy, representative; **Stellwerk** *nt* (*Eisenb*) signal box

Stelze ['ʃtɛltsə] (**-, -n**) *f* stilt

stelzen (*umg*) *vi* to stalk

Stemmbogen *m* (*Ski*) stem turn

Stemmeisen *nt* crowbar

stemmen ['ʃtɛmən] *vt* to lift (up); (*drücken*) to press; **sich ~ gegen** (*fig*) to resist, oppose

Stempel ['ʃtɛmpəl] (**-s, -**) *m* stamp; (*Poststempel*) postmark; (*Tech: Prägestempel*) die; (*Bot*) pistil; **Stempelgebühr** *f* stamp duty; **Stempelkissen** *nt* inkpad

stempeln *vt* to stamp; (*Briefmarke*) to cancel ▷ *vi* (*umg: Stempeluhr betätigen*) to clock in/out; ~ **gehen** (*umg*) to be *od* go on the dole (*Brit*) *od* on welfare (*US*)

Stengel ['ʃtɛŋəl] (**-s, -**) *m* siehe **Stängel**

Steno ['ʃteno] (*umg*) *f* shorthand; **Stenograf, in** [-graːf(ɪn)] *m(f)* (*in Büro*) shorthand secretary; **Stenografie** [-graˈfiː] *f* shorthand; **stenografieren** [-graˈfiːrən] *vt, vi* to write (in) shorthand; **Stenogramm** [-ˈgram] *nt* text in shorthand; **Stenotypist, in** [-tyˈpɪst(ɪn)] *m(f)* shorthand typist (*Brit*), stenographer (*US*)

Steppdecke *f* quilt

Steppe (**-, -n**) *f* steppe

steppen ['ʃtɛpən] *vt* to stitch ▷ *vi* to tap-dance

Stepptanz *m* tap-dance

Sterbe- *zW*: **Sterbebett** *nt* deathbed; **Sterbefall** *m* death; **Sterbehilfe** *f* euthanasia; **Sterbekasse** *f* death benefit fund

S

317

sterben ['ʃtɛrbən] *unreg vi* to die; **an einer Krankheit/Verletzung ~** to die of an illness/from an injury; **er ist für mich gestorben** *(fig: umg)* he might as well be dead

Sterben *nt*: **im ~ liegen** to be dying

sterbenslangweilig *(umg) adj* deadly boring

Sterbenswörtchen *(umg) nt*: **er hat kein ~ gesagt** he didn't say a word

Sterbeurkunde *f* death certificate

sterblich ['ʃtɛrplɪç] *adj* mortal; **Sterblichkeit** *f* mortality; **Sterblichkeitsziffer** *f* death rate

stereo- ['ʃteːreo] *in zw* stereo(-); **Stereoanlage** *f* stereo unit; **stereotyp** *adj* stereotyped

steril [ʃteˈriːl] *adj* sterile

sterilisieren [ʃteriliˈziːrən] *vt* to sterilize

Sterilisierung *f* sterilization

Stern [ʃtɛrn] **(-(e)s, -e)** *m* star; **das steht (noch) in den ~en** *(fig)* it's in the lap of the gods; **Sternbild** *nt* constellation; **Sternchen** *nt* asterisk; **Sternenbanner** *nt* Stars and Stripes *sing*; **sternhagelvoll** *(umg) adj* legless; **Sternschnuppe (-, -n)** *f* meteor, falling star; **Sternstunde** *f* historic moment; **Sternwarte** *f* observatory; **Sternzeichen** *nt (Astrol)* sign of the zodiac

stet [ʃteːt] *adj* steady

Stethoskop [ʃtetoˈskoːp] **(-(e)s, -e)** *nt* stethoscope

stetig *adj* constant, continual; *(Math: Funktion)* continuous

stets *adv* continually, always

Steuer¹ ['ʃtɔyər] **(-s, -)** *nt (Naut)* helm; *(Steuerruder)* rudder; *(Aut)* steering wheel; **am ~ sitzen** *(Aut)* to be at the wheel; *(Aviat)* to be at the controls

Steuer² **(-, -n)** *f* tax

Steuer- *zW*: **Steuerbefreiung** *f* tax exemption; **steuerbegünstigt** *adj (Investitionen, Hypothek)* tax-deductible; *(Waren)* taxed at a lower rate; **Steuerberater, in** *m(f)* tax consultant; **Steuerbescheid** *m* tax assessment; **Steuerbord** *nt* starboard; **Steuererhöhung** *f* tax increase; **Steuererklärung** *f* tax return; **steuerfrei** *adj* tax-free; **Steuerfreibetrag** *m* tax allowance; **Steuerhinterziehung** *f* tax evasion; **Steuerjahr** *nt* fiscal *od* tax year; **Steuerkarte** *f* tax notice; **Steuerklasse** *f* tax group; **Steuerknüppel** *m* control column; *(Aviat, Comput)* joystick; **steuerlich** *adj* tax *attrib*; **Steuermann (-(e)s, pl -männer** *od* **-leute)** *m* helmsman

steuern *vt* to steer; *(Flugzeug)* to pilot; *(Entwicklung, Tonstärke)* to control ▷ *vi* to steer; *(in Flugzeug etc)* to be at the controls; *(bei Entwicklung etc)* to be in control

Steuer- *zW*: **Steuernummer** *f* ≈ National Insurance Number *(Brit)*, ≈ Social Security Number *(US)*; **Steuerparadies** *nt* tax haven; **steuerpflichtig** *adj* taxable; *(Person)* liable to pay tax; **Steuerprogression** *f* progressive taxation; **Steuerprüfung** *f* tax inspector's investigation; **Steuerrad** *nt* steering wheel; **Steuerrückvergütung** *f* tax rebate;

Steuersenkung *f* tax cut

Steuerung *f* steering *(auch AUT)*, piloting; control; *(Vorrichtung)* controls *pl*; **automatische ~** *(Aviat)* autopilot; *(Tech)* automatic steering (device)

Steuer- *zW*: **Steuervergünstigung** *f* tax relief; **Steuerzahler** *m* taxpayer; **Steuerzuschlag** *m* additional tax

Steward ['stjuːərt] **(-s, -s)** *m* steward

Stewardess ['stjuːərdɛs] **(-, -en)** *f* stewardess

StGB (-s) *nt abk* = **Strafgesetzbuch**

stibitzen [ʃtiˈbɪtsən] *(umg) vt* to pilfer, pinch *(umg)*

Stich [ʃtɪç] **(-(e)s, -e)** *m (Insektenstich)* sting; *(Messerstich)* stab; *(beim Nähen)* stitch; *(Färbung)* tinge; *(Karten)* trick; *(Art)* engraving; *(fig)* pang; **ein ~ ins Rote** a tinge of red; **einen ~ haben** *(umg: Esswaren)* to be bad *od* off *(Brit)*; *(: Mensch: verrückt sein)* to be nuts; **jdn im ~ lassen** to leave sb in the lurch

Stichel (-s, -) *m* engraving tool, style

Stichelei [ʃtɪçəˈlaɪ] *f* jibe, taunt

sticheln *vi (fig)* to jibe; *(pej: umg)* to make snide remarks

Stich- *zW*: **Stichflamme** *f* tongue of flame; **stichhaltig** *adj* valid; *(Beweis)* conclusive; **Stichprobe** *f* spot check

sticht [ʃtɪçt] *vb siehe* **stechen**

Stichtag *m* qualifying date

Stichwahl *f* final ballot

Stichwort *nt (pl -worte)* cue; *(: für Vortrag)* note *(pl -wörter)* *(in Wörterbuch)* headword; **Stichwortkatalog** *m* classified catalogue *(Brit)* *od* catalog *(US)*; **Stichwortverzeichnis** *nt* index

Stichwunde *f* stab wound

sticken ['ʃtɪkən] *vt, vi* to embroider

Stickerei [ʃtɪkəˈraɪ] *f* embroidery

stickig *adj* stuffy, close

Stickstoff (-(e)s) *m* nitrogen

stieben ['ʃtiːbən] *vi (geh: sprühen)* to fly

Stief- ['ʃtiːf] *in zw* step-

Stiefel ['ʃtiːfəl] **(-s, -)** *m* boot; *(Trinkgefäß)* large boot-shaped beer glass

Stief- *zW*: **Stiefkind** *nt* stepchild; *(fig)* Cinderella; **Stiefmutter** *f* stepmother; **Stiefmütterchen** *nt* pansy; **stiefmütterlich** *adj (fig)*: **jdn/etw stiefmütterlich behandeln** to pay little attention to sb/sth; **Stiefvater** *m* stepfather

stieg *etc* [ʃtiːk] *vb siehe* **steigen**

Stiege ['ʃtiːgə] **(-, -n)** *f* staircase

Stieglitz ['ʃtiːglɪts] **(-es, -e)** *m* goldfinch

stiehlt [ʃtiːlt] *vb siehe* **stehlen**

Stiel [ʃtiːl] **(-(e)s, -e)** *m* handle; *(Bot)* stalk

Stielaugen *pl (fig: umg)*: **er machte ~** his eyes (nearly) popped out of his head

Stier (-(e)s, -e) *m* bull; *(Astrol)* Taurus

stier [ʃtiːr] *adj* staring, fixed

stieren *vi* to stare

Stierkampf *m* bullfight

stieß *etc* [ʃtiːs] *vb siehe* **stoßen**

Stift [ʃtɪft] **(-(e)s, -e)** *m* peg; *(Nagel)* tack; *(Buntstift)* crayon; *(Bleistift)* pencil;

(umg: Lehrling) apprentice (boy)

stiften vt to found; (Unruhe) to cause; (spenden) to contribute; ~ **gehen** to hop it

Stifter, in (**-s, -**) m(f) founder

Stiftung f donation; (Organisation) foundation

Stiftzahn m post crown

Stil [ʃtiːl] (**-(e)s, -e**) m style; (Eigenart) way, manner; **Stilblüte** f howler; **Stilbruch** m stylistic incongruity

stilistisch [ʃtiˈlɪstɪʃ] adj stylistic

still [ʃtɪl] adj quiet; (unbewegt) still; (heimlich) secret; **ich dachte mir im S~en** I thought to myself; **er ist ein ~es Wasser** he's a deep one; **~er Teilhaber** (Comm) sleeping (Brit) od silent (US) partner; **der S~e Ozean** the Pacific (Ocean); ~ **stehen** (unbewegt) to stand still

Stille (**-, -n**) f quietness; stillness; **in aller ~** quietly

Stilleben nt siehe **Stillleben**

Stillegung f siehe **Stilllegung**

stillen vt to stop; (befriedigen) to satisfy; (Säugling) to breast-feed

still- zW: **stillgestanden** interj attention!; **Stillhalteabkommen** nt (Fin, fig) moratorium; **stillhalten** unreg vi to keep still; **Stillleben** nt still life; **stilllegen** vt to close down; **Stilllegung** f (Betrieb) shut-down, closure; **stillliegen** unreg vi (außer Betrieb sein) to be shut down; (lahmgelegt sein) to be at a standstill; **Stillschweigen** nt silence; **stillschweigen** unreg vi to be silent; **stillschweigend** adj silent; (Einverständnis) tacit ▷ adv silently; tacitly; **Stillstand** m standstill; **stillstehen** unreg vi to stand still

Stilmöbel pl reproduction od (antik) period furniture sing

stilvoll adj stylish

Stimm- zW: **Stimmabgabe** f voting; **Stimmbänder** pl vocal cords pl; **stimmberechtigt** adj entitled to vote; **Stimmbruch** m: **er ist im Stimmbruch** his voice is breaking

Stimme [ˈʃtɪmə] (**-, -n**) f voice; (Wahlstimme) vote; (Mus: Rolle) part; **mit leiser/lauter ~** in a soft/loud voice; **seine ~ abgeben** to vote

stimmen vi (richtig sein) to be right; (wählen) to vote ▷ vt (Instrument) to tune; **stimmt so!** that's all right; **für/gegen etw ~** to vote for/against sth; **jdn traurig ~** to make sb feel sad

Stimmen- zW: **Stimmengewirr** nt babble of voices; **Stimmengleichheit** f tied vote; **Stimmenmehrheit** f majority (of votes)

Stimm- zW: **Stimmenthaltung** f abstention; **Stimmgabel** f tuning fork; **stimmhaft** adj voiced

stimmig adj harmonious

Stimm- zW: **stimmlos** adj (Ling) unvoiced; **Stimmrecht** nt right to vote; **stimmrechtslos** adj: **stimmrechtslose Aktien** "A" shares

Stimmung f mood; (Atmosphäre) atmosphere; (Moral) morale; **in ~ kommen** to liven up; **~ gegen/für jdn/etw machen** to stir up (public) opinion against/in favour of sb/sth

Stimmungs- zW: **Stimmungskanone** (umg) f life and soul of the party; **Stimmungsmache** (pej) f cheap propaganda; **stimmungsvoll** adj (Atmosphäre) enjoyable; (Gedicht) full of atmosphere

Stimmzettel m ballot paper

stinken [ˈʃtɪŋkən] unreg vi to stink; **die Sache stinkt mir** (umg) I'm fed-up to the back teeth (with it)

Stink- zW: **stinkfaul** (umg) adj bone-lazy; **stinklangweilig** (umg) adj deadly boring; **Stinktier** nt skunk; **Stinkwut** (umg) f: **eine Stinkwut (auf jdn) haben** to be livid (with sb)

Stipendium [ʃtiˈpɛndiʊm] nt grant; (als Auszeichnung) scholarship

Stippvisite [ˈʃtɪpviˈziːtə] (umg) f flying visit

stirbt [ʃtɪrpt] vb siehe **sterben**

Stirn [ʃtɪrn] (**-, -en**) f forehead, brow; (Frechheit) impudence; **die ~ haben zu ...** to have the nerve to ...; **Stirnband** nt headband; **Stirnhöhle** f sinus; **Stirnrunzeln** (**-s**) nt frown

stob etc [ʃtoːp] vb siehe **stieben**

stöbern [ˈʃtøːbərn] vi to rummage

stochern [ˈʃtɔxərn] vi to poke (about)

Stock¹ [ʃtɔk] (**-(e)s, ¨e**) m stick; (Rohrstock) cane; (Zeigestock) pointer; (Bot) stock; **über ~ und Stein** up hill and down dale

Stock² [ʃtɔk] (**-(e)s, - od -werke**) m storey (Brit), story (US); **im ersten ~** on the first (Brit) od second (US) floor

stock- in zw (vor adj: umg) completely

Stöckelschuh [ˈʃtœkəlʃuː] m stiletto-heeled shoe

stocken vi to stop, pause; (Arbeit, Entwicklung) to make no progress; (im Satz) to break off; (Verkehr) to be held up

stockend adj halting

stockfinster (umg) adj pitch-dark

Stockholm [ˈʃtɔkhɔlm] (**-s**) nt Stockholm

stocksauer (umg) adj pissed-off (!)

stocktaub adj stone-deaf

Stockung f stoppage

Stockwerk nt storey (Brit), story (US), floor

Stoff [ʃtɔf] (**-(e)s, -e**) m (Gewebe) material, cloth; (Materie) matter; (von Buch etc) subject (matter); (umg: Rauschgift) dope

Stoffel (**-s, -**) (pej: umg) m lout, boor

Stoff- zW: **stofflich** adj with regard to subject matter; **Stoffrest** m remnant; **Stofftier** nt soft toy; **Stoffwechsel** m metabolism

stöhnen [ˈʃtøːnən] vi to groan

stoisch [ˈʃtoːɪʃ] adj stoical

Stola [ˈʃtoːla] (**-, Stolen**) f stole

Stollen [ˈʃtɔlən] (**-s, -**) m (Min) gallery; (Koch) stollen, cake eaten at Christmas; (von Schuhen) stud

stolpern [ˈʃtɔlpərn] vi to stumble, trip; (fig: zu Fall kommen) to come a cropper (umg)

stolz [ʃtɔlts] adj proud; (imposant: Bauwerk) majestic; (ironisch: Preis) princely; **Stolz** (**-es**) m pride

stolzieren [ʃtɔlˈtsiːrən] vi to strut

stopfen [ˈʃtɔpfən] vt (hineinstopfen) to stuff;

S

319

(*nähen*) to darn ▷ vi (*Med*) to cause constipation; **jdm das Maul ~** (*umg*) to silence sb

Stopfgarn nt darning thread

Stopp [ʃtɔp] (**-s, -s**) m stop, halt; (*Lohnstopp*) freeze

Stoppel ['ʃtɔpəl] (**-, -n**) f stubble

stoppen vt to stop; (*mit Uhr*) to time ▷ vi to stop

Stoppschild nt stop sign

Stoppuhr f stopwatch

Stöpsel ['ʃtœpsəl] (**-s, -**) m plug; (*für Flaschen*) stopper

Stör [ʃtøːr] (**-(e)s, -e**) m sturgeon

Störaktion f disruptive action

störanfällig adj susceptible to interference od breakdown

Storch [ʃtɔrç] (**-(e)s, "-e**) m stork

Store [ʃtoːr] (**-s, -s**) m net curtain

stören ['ʃtøːrən] vt to disturb; (*behindern, Rundf*) to interfere with ▷ vr: **sich an etw** dat **~** to let sth bother one ▷ vi to get in the way; **was mich an ihm/daran stört** what I don't like about him/it; **stört es Sie, wenn ich rauche?** do you mind if I smoke?; **ich möchte nicht ~** I don't want to be in the way

störend adj disturbing, annoying

Störenfried (**-(e)s, -e**) m troublemaker

Störfall m (*in Kraftwerk etc*) malfunction, accident

stornieren [ʃtɔrˈniːrən] vt (*Comm: Auftrag*) to cancel; (*: Buchungsfehler*) to reverse

Storno ['ʃtɔrno] (**-s**) m od nt (*Comm: von Buchungsfehler*) reversal; (*: von Auftrag*) cancellation (*Brit*), cancelation (*US*)

störrisch ['ʃtœrɪʃ] adj stubborn, perverse

Störsender m jammer, jamming transmitter

Störung f disturbance; interference; (*Tech*) fault; (*Med*) disorder

Störungsstelle f (*Tel*) faults service

Stoß [ʃtoːs] (**-es, "-e**) m (*Schub*) push; (*leicht*) poke; (*Schlag*) blow; (*mit Schwert*) thrust; (*mit Ellbogen*) nudge; (*mit Fuß*) kick; (*Erdstoß*) shock; (*Haufen*) pile; **seinem Herzen einen ~ geben** to pluck up courage; **Stoßdämpfer** m shock absorber

Stößel ['ʃtøːsəl] (**-s, -**) m pestle; (*Aut: Ventilstößel*) tappet

stoßen unreg vt (*mit Druck*) to shove, push; (*mit Schlag*) to knock, bump; (*mit Ellbogen*) to nudge; (*mit Fuß*) to kick; (*mit Schwert*) to thrust; (*anstoßen: Kopf etc*) to bump; (*zerkleinern*) to pulverize ▷ vr to get a knock ▷ vi: **~ an** od **auf** +akk to bump into; (*finden*) to come across; (*angrenzen*) to be next to; **sich ~ an** +dat (*fig*) to take exception to; **zu jdm ~** to meet up with sb

Stoßgebet nt quick prayer

Stoßstange f (*Aut*) bumper

stößt [ʃtøːst] vb siehe **stoßen**

Stoß- zW: **Stoßverkehr** m rush-hour traffic; **Stoßzahn** m tusk; **Stoßzeit** f (*im Verkehr*) rush hour; (*in Geschäft etc*) peak period

Stotterer (**-s, -**) m stutterer

Stotterin f stutterer

stottern ['ʃtɔtərn] vt, vi to stutter

Stövchen ['ʃtøːfçən] nt (*teapot- etc*) warmer

StPO abk = **Strafprozessordnung**

Str. abk (= *Straße*) St.

stracks [ʃtraks] adv straight

Straf- zW: **Strafanstalt** f penal institution; **Strafarbeit** f (*Sch*) lines pl, punishment exercise; **Strafbank** f (*Sport*) penalty bench; **strafbar** adj punishable; **sich strafbar machen** to commit an offence (*Brit*) od offense (*US*); **Strafbarkeit** f criminal nature

Strafe ['ʃtraːfə] (**-, -n**) f punishment; (*Jur*) penalty; (*Gefängnisstrafe*) sentence; (*Geldstrafe*) fine; **... bei ~ verboten ...** forbidden; **100 Dollar ~ zahlen** to pay a $100 fine; **er hat seine ~ weg** (*umg*) he's had his punishment

strafen vt, vi to punish; **mit etw gestraft sein** to be cursed with sth

strafend adj attrib punitive; (*Blick*) reproachful

straff [ʃtraf] adj tight; (*streng*) strict; (*Stil etc*) concise; (*Haltung*) erect

straffällig ['ʃtraːfɛlɪç] adj: **~ werden** to commit a criminal offence (*Brit*) od offense (*US*)

straffen vt to tighten

Straf- zW: **straffrei** adj: **straffrei ausgehen** to go unpunished; **Strafgefangene, r** f(m) prisoner, convict; **Strafgesetzbuch** nt penal code; **Strafkolonie** f penal colony

sträflich ['ʃtreːflɪç] adj criminal ▷ adv (*vernachlässigen etc*) criminally

Sträfling m convict

Straf- zW: **Strafmandat** nt ticket; **Strafmaß** nt sentence; **strafmildernd** adj mitigating; **Strafporto** nt excess postage (*charge*); **Strafpredigt** f severe lecture; **Strafprozessordnung** f code of criminal procedure; **Strafraum** m (*Sport*) penalty area; **Strafrecht** nt criminal law; **strafrechtlich** adj criminal; **Strafstoß** m (*Sport*) penalty (kick); **Straftat** f punishable act; **strafversetzen** vt untr (*Beamte*) to transfer for disciplinary reasons; **Strafvollzug** m penal system; **Strafzettel** (*umg*) m ticket

Strahl [ʃtraːl] (**-(e)s, -en**) m ray, beam; (*Wasserstrahl*) jet

strahlen vi (*Kernreaktor*) to radiate; (*Sonne, Licht*) to shine; (*fig*) to beam

Strahlenbehandlung f radiotherapy

Strahlenbelastung f (effects of) radiation

strahlend adj (*Wetter*) glorious; (*Lächeln, Schönheit*) radiant

Strahlen- zW: **Strahlendosis** f radiation dose; **strahlengeschädigt** adj suffering from radiation damage; **Strahlenopfer** nt victim of radiation; **Strahlenschutz** m radiation protection; **Strahlentherapie** f radiotherapy

Strahlung f radiation

Strähnchen ['ʃtreːnçən] pl strands (of hair); (*gefärbt*) highlights

Strähne ['ʃtreːnə] (**-, -n**) f strand

strähnig adj (*Haar*) straggly

stramm [ʃtram] adj tight; (*Haltung*) erect; (*Mensch*) robust; **strammstehen** unreg vi (*Mil*) to stand to attention

Strampelhöschen nt rompers pl
strampeln ['ʃtrampəln] vi to kick (about), fidget
Strand [ʃtrant] (-(e)s, ⁻e) m shore; (Meeresstrand) beach; **am ~** on the beach; **Strandbad** nt open-air swimming pool; (Badeort) bathing resort
stranden ['ʃtrandən] vi to run aground; (fig: Mensch) to fail
Strandgut nt flotsam and jetsam
Strandkorb m beach chair
Strang [ʃtraŋ] (-(e)s, ⁻e) m (Nervenstrang, Muskelstrang) cord; (Schienenstrang) track; **über die Stränge schlagen** to run riot (umg); **an einem ~ ziehen** (fig) to act in concert
strangulieren [ʃtraŋgu'liːrən] vt to strangle
Strapaze [ʃtra'paːtsə] (-, -n) f strain
strapazieren [ʃtrapa'tsiːrən] vt (Material) to be hard on, punish; (jdn) to be a strain on; (erschöpfen) to wear out, exhaust
strapazierfähig adj hard-wearing
strapaziös [ʃtrapatsi'øːs] adj exhausting, tough
Straßburg ['ʃtraːsbʊrk] (-s) nt Strasbourg
Straße ['ʃtraːsə] (-, -n) f road; (in Stadt, Dorf) street; **auf der ~** in the street; **auf der ~ liegen** (fig: umg) to be out of work; **auf die ~ gesetzt werden** (umg) to be turned out (onto the streets)
Straßen- zW: **Straßenbahn** f tram (Brit), streetcar (US); **Straßenbauarbeiten** pl roadworks pl (Brit), roadwork sing (US); **Straßenbeleuchtung** f street lighting; **Straßenfeger** (-s, -) m roadsweeper; **Straßenglätte** f slippery road surface; **Straßenjunge** (pej) m street urchin; **Straßenkarte** f road map; **Straßenkehrer** (-s, -) m roadsweeper; **Straßenkind** nt child of the streets; **Straßenkreuzer** (umg) m limousine; **Straßenmädchen** nt streetwalker; **Straßenrand** m road side; **Straßensperre** f roadblock; **Straßenüberführung** f footbridge; **Straßenverkehr** m road traffic; **Straßenverkehrsordnung** f Highway Code (Brit); **Straßenzustandsbericht** m road report
Stratege [ʃtra'teːgə] (-n, -n) m strategist
Strategie [ʃtrate'giː] f strategy
strategisch adj strategic
Stratosphäre [ʃtrato'sfɛːrə] (-) f stratosphere
sträuben ['ʃtrɔʏbən] vt to ruffle ▷ vr to bristle; (Mensch): **sich (gegen etw)** to resist (sth)
Strauch [ʃtraʊx] (-(e)s, Sträucher) m bush, shrub
straucheln ['ʃtraʊxəln] vi to stumble, stagger
Strauß¹ [ʃtraʊs] (-es, Sträuße) m (Blumenstrauß) bouquet, bunch
Strauß² [ʃtraʊs] (-es, -e) m ostrich
Strebe ['ʃtreːbə] (-, -n) f strut
Strebebalken m buttress
streben vi to strive, endeavour (Brit), endeavor (US); **~ nach** to strive for; **~ zu** od **nach** (sich bewegen) to make for
Strebepfeiler m buttress

Streber (-s, -) m (pej) pushy person; (Sch) swot (Brit)
strebsam adj industrious; **Strebsamkeit** f industry
Strecke ['ʃtrɛkə] (-, -n) f stretch; (Entfernung) distance; (Eisenb, Math) line; **auf der ~ Paris-Brüssel** on the way from Paris to Brussels; **auf der ~ bleiben** (fig) to fall by the wayside; **zur ~ bringen** (Jagd) to bag
strecken vt to stretch; (Waffen) to lay down; (Koch) to eke out ▷ vr to stretch (o.s.)
streckenweise adv in parts
Streich [ʃtraɪç] (-(e)s, -e) m trick, prank; (Hieb) blow; **jdm einen ~ spielen** (Person) to play a trick on sb
streicheln vt to stroke
streichen unreg vt (berühren) to stroke; (auftragen) to spread; (anmalen) to paint; (durchstreichen) to delete; (nicht genehmigen) to cancel; (Schulden) to write off; (Zuschuss etc) to cut ▷ vi (berühren) to brush past; (schleichen) to prowl; **etw glatt ~** to smooth sth (out)
Streicher pl (Mus) strings pl
Streich- zW: **Streichholz** nt match; **Streichholzschachtel** f matchbox; **Streichinstrument** nt string(ed) instrument; **Streichkäse** m cheese spread
Streifband nt wrapper; **Streifbandzeitung** f newspaper sent at printed paper rate
Streife (-, -n) f patrol
streifen ['ʃtraɪfən] vt (leicht berühren) to brush against, graze; (Blick) to skim over; (Thema, Problem) to touch on; (abstreifen) to take off ▷ vi (gehen) to roam
Streifen (-s, -) m (Linie) stripe; (Stück) strip; (Film) film
Streifendienst m patrol duty
Streifenwagen m patrol car
Streifschuss m graze, grazing shot
Streifzug m scouting trip; (Bummel) expedition; (fig: kurzer Überblick): **~ (durch)** brief survey (of)
Streik [ʃtraɪk] (-(e)s, -s) m strike; **in den ~ treten** to come out on strike, strike; **Streikbrecher** m blackleg (Brit), strikebreaker; **streiken** vi to strike; **der Computer streikt** the computer's packed up (umg), the computer's on the blink (umg); **da streike ich** (umg) I refuse!; **Streikkasse** f strike fund; **Streikmaßnahmen** pl industrial action sing; **Streikposten** m (peaceful) picket
Streit [ʃtraɪt] (-(e)s, -e) m argument; (Auseinandersetzung) dispute
streiten unreg vi, vr to argue; to dispute; **darüber lässt sich ~** that's debatable
Streitfrage f point at issue
Streitgespräch nt debate
streitig adj: **jdm etw ~ machen** to dispute sb's right to sth; **Streitigkeiten** pl quarrel sing, dispute sing
Streit- zW: **Streitkräfte** pl (Mil) armed forces pl; **streitlustig** adj quarrelsome; **Streitpunkt** m contentious issue; **Streitsucht**

S

f quarrelsomeness

streng [ʃtrɛŋ] *adj* severe; (*Lehrer, Maßnahme*) strict; (*Geruch etc*) sharp; **~ geheim** top-secret; **~ genommen** strictly speaking; **~ verboten!** strictly prohibited

Strenge (-) *f* severity; strictness; sharpness

strenggläubig *adj* strict

strengstens *adv* strictly

Stress [ʃtrɛs] (-es, -e) *m* stress

stressen *vt* to put under stress

stressfrei *adj* without stress

stressig *adj* stressful

Streu [ʃtrɔy] (-, -en) *f* litter, bed of straw

streuen *vt* to strew, scatter, spread ▷ *vi* (*mit Streupulver*) to grit; (*mit Salz*) to put down salt

Streuer (-s, -) *m* shaker; (*Salzstreuer*) cellar; (*Pfefferstreuer*) pot

Streufahrzeug *nt* gritter (*Brit*), sander

streunen *vi* to roam about; (*Hund, Katze*) to stray

Streupulver (-s) *nt* grit *od* sand for road

Streuselkuchen ['ʃtrɔyzəlkuːxən] *m* cake with crumble topping

Streuung *f* dispersion; (*Statistik*) mean variation; (*Phys*) scattering

Strich (-(e)s, -e) *m* (*Linie*) line; (*Federstrich, Pinselstrich*) stroke; (*von Geweben*) nap; (*von Fell*) pile; (*Querstrich*) dash; (*Schrägstrich*) oblique, slash (*bes US*); **einen ~ machen durch** (*lit*) to cross out; (*fig*) to foil; **jdm einen ~ durch die Rechnung machen** to thwart *od* foil sb's plans; **einen ~ unter etw** *akk* **machen** (*fig*) to forget sth; **nach ~ und Faden** (*umg*) good and proper; **auf den ~ gehen** (*umg*) to walk the streets; **jdm gegen den ~ gehen** to rub sb up the wrong way

strich *etc* [ʃtrɪç] *vb siehe* **streichen**

Strichcode *m* bar code (*Brit*), universal product code (*US*)

Stricheinteilung *f* calibration

stricheln ['ʃtrɪçəln] *vt*: **eine gestrichelte Linie** a broken line

Strich- *zW*: **Strichjunge** (*umg*) *m* male prostitute; **Strichkode** *m* = **Strichcode**; **Strichmädchen** *nt* streetwalker; **Strichpunkt** *m* semicolon; **strichweise** *adv* here and there; **strichweise Regen** (*Met*) rain in places

Strick [ʃtrɪk] (-(e)s, -e) *m* rope; **jdm aus etw einen ~ drehen** to use sth against sb

stricken *vt, vi* to knit

Strick- *zW*: **Strickjacke** *f* cardigan; **Strickleiter** *f* rope ladder; **Stricknadel** *f* knitting needle; **Strickwaren** *pl* knitwear *sing*

striegeln ['ʃtriːgəln] (*umg*) *vr* to spruce o.s. up

Strieme ['ʃtriːmə] (-, -n) *f* weal

strikt [ʃtrɪkt] *adj* strict

Strippe ['ʃtrɪpə] (-, -n) *f* (*Tel: umg*): **jdn an der ~ haben** to have sb on the line

Stripper, in (-s, -) *m(f)* stripper

stritt *etc* [ʃtrɪt] *vb siehe* **streiten**

strittig ['ʃtrɪtɪç] *adj* disputed, in dispute

Stroh [ʃtroː] (-(e)s) *nt* straw; **Strohblume** *f* everlasting flower; **Strohdach** *nt* thatched roof; **strohdumm** (*umg*) *adj* thick; **Strohfeuer** *nt*: **ein Strohfeuer sein** (*fig*) to be a passing fancy; **Strohhalm** *m* (drinking) straw; **Strohmann** (-(e)s, *pl* -**männer**) *m* (*Comm*) dummy; **Strohwitwe** *f* grass widow; **Strohwitwer** *m* grass widower

Strolch [ʃtrɔlç] (-(e)s, -e) (*pej*) *m* rogue, rascal

Strom [ʃtroːm] (-(e)s, "-e) *m* river; (*fig*) stream; (*Elek*) current; **unter ~ stehen** (*Elek*) to be live; (*fig*) to be excited; **der Wein floss in Strömen** the wine flowed like water; **in Strömen regnen** to be pouring with rain; **stromabwärts** *adv* downstream; **Stromanschluss** *m*: **Stromanschluss haben** to be connected to the electricity mains; **stromaufwärts** *adv* upstream; **Stromausfall** *m* power failure

strömen ['ʃtrøːmən] *vi* to stream, pour

Strom- *zW*: **Stromkabel** *nt* electric cable; **Stromkreis** *m* (electrical) circuit; **stromlinienförmig** *adj* streamlined; **Stromnetz** *nt* power supply system; **Stromrechnung** *f* electricity bill; **Stromschnelle** *f* rapids *pl*; **Stromsperre** *f* power cut; **Stromstärke** *f* amperage

Strömung ['ʃtrøːmʊŋ] *f* current

Stromzähler *m* electricity meter

Strophe ['ʃtroːfə] (-, -n) *f* verse

strotzen ['ʃtrɔtsən] *vi*: **vor** +*dat od* **von** to abound in, be full of

Strudel ['ʃtruːdəl] (-s, -) *m* whirlpool, vortex; (*Koch*) strudel

strudeln *vi* to swirl, eddy

Struktur [ʃtrʊk'tuːr] *f* structure

strukturell [ʃtrʊktu'rɛl] *adj* structural

strukturieren [ʃtrʊktu'riːrən] *vt* to structure

Strumpf [ʃtrʊmpf] (-(e)s, "-e) *m* stocking; **Strumpfband** *nt* garter; **Strumpfhalter** *m* suspender (*Brit*), garter (*US*); **Strumpfhose** *f* (pair of) tights *pl* (*Brit*) *od* pantihose *pl* (*US*)

Strunk [ʃtrʊŋk] (-(e)s, "-e) *m* stump

struppig ['ʃtrʊpɪç] *adj* shaggy, unkempt

Stube ['ʃtuːbə] (-, -n) *f* room; **die gute ~** (*veraltet*) the parlour (*Brit*) *od* parlor (*US*)

Stuben- *zW*: **Stubenarrest** *m* confinement to one's room; (*Mil*) confinement to quarters; **Stubenfliege** *f* (common) housefly; **Stubenhocker** (*umg*) *m* stay-at-home; **stubenrein** *adj* house-trained

Stuck [ʃtʊk] (-(e)s) *m* stucco

Stück [ʃtʏk] (-(e)s, -e) *nt* piece; (*etwas*) bit; (*Theat*) play; **am ~** in one piece; **das ist ein starkes ~!** (*umg*) that's a bit much!; **große ~e auf jdn halten** to think highly of sb; **Stückarbeit** *f* piecework

Stuckateur [ʃtʊka'tøːr] *m* (ornamental) plasterer

Stück- *zw***: **Stückgut** *nt* (*Eisenb*) parcel service; **Stückkosten** *pl* unit cost *sing*; **Stücklohn** *m* piecework rates *pl*; **stückweise** *adv* bit by bit, piecemeal; (*Comm*) individually; **Stückwerk** *nt* bits and pieces *pl*

Student, in [ʃtu'dɛnt(ɪn)] *m(f)* student

Studenten- zW: **Studentenausweis** m student card; **Studentenfutter** nt nuts and raisins pl; **Studentenwerk** nt student administration; **Studentenwohnheim** nt hall of residence (Brit), dormitory (US)

studentisch adj student attrib

Studie ['ʃtuːdiə] f study

Studien- zW: **Studienberatung** f course guidance service; **Studienbuch** nt (Univ) book in which the courses one has attended are entered; **Studienfahrt** f study trip; **Studienplatz** m university place; **Studienrat** m, **Studienrätin** f teacher at a secondary (Brit) od high (US) school; **Studienreform** f university course reform; **Studienzeitverkürzung** f shortening of the course of studies

studieren [ʃtuˈdiːrən] vt, vi to study; **bei jdm ~** to study under sb

Studio ['ʃtuːdio] (-s, -s) nt studio

Studium ['ʃtuːdiʊm] nt studies pl

Stufe ['ʃtuːfə] (-, -n) f step; (Entwicklungsstufe) stage; (Niveau) level

Stufen- zW: **Stufenheck** nt (Aut) notchback; **Stufenleiter** f (fig) ladder; **stufenlos** adj (Tech) infinitely variable; **stufenlos verstellbar** continuously adjustable; **Stufenplan** m graduated plan; **Stufenschnitt** m (Frisur) layered cut; **stufenweise** adv gradually

Stuhl [ʃtuːl] (-(e)s, ⁻e) m chair; **zwischen zwei Stühlen sitzen** (fig) to fall between two stools

Stuhlgang m bowel movement

Stukkateur [ʃtʊkaˈtøːr] m siehe **Stuckateur**

stülpen ['ʃtʏlpən] vt (bedecken) to put; **etw über etw** akk **~** to put sth over sth; **den Kragen nach oben ~** to turn up one's collar

stumm [ʃtʊm] adj silent; (Med) dumb

Stummel (-s, -) m stump; (Zigarettenstummel) stub

Stummfilm m silent film (Brit) od movie (US)

Stümper, in ['ʃtʏmpər(ɪn)] (-s, -) m(f) incompetent, duffer; **stümperhaft** adj bungling, incompetent

stümpern (umg) vi to bungle

Stumpf [ʃtʊmpf] (-(e)s, ⁻e) m stump; **etw mit ~ und Stiel ausrotten** to eradicate sth root and branch

stumpf adj blunt; (teilnahmslos, glanzlos) dull; (Winkel) obtuse

Stumpfsinn (-(e)s) m tediousness

stumpfsinnig adj dull

Stunde ['ʃtʊndə] (-, -n) f hour; (Augenblick, Zeitpunkt) time; (Sch) lesson, period (Brit); **~ um Stunde** hour after hour; **80 Kilometer in der ~ ≈ 50** miles per hour

stunden vt: **jdm etw ~** to give sb time to pay sth

Stunden- zW: **Stundengeschwindigkeit** f average speed (per hour); **Stundenkilometer** pl kilometres (Brit) od kilometers (US) per hour; **stundenlang** adj for hours; **Stundenlohn** m hourly wage; **Stundenplan** m timetable; **stundenweise** adv by the hour; (stündlich) every hour

stündlich ['ʃtʏntlɪç] adj hourly

Stunk [ʃtʊŋk] (-s, no pl) m: **~ machen** (umg) to kick up a stink

stupide [ʃtuˈpiːdə] adj mindless

Stups [ʃtʊps] (-es, -e) (umg) m push

stupsen vt to nudge

Stupsnase f snub nose

stur [ʃtuːr] adj obstinate, stubborn; (Nein, Arbeiten) dogged; **er fuhr ~ geradeaus** he just carried straight on; **sich ~ stellen, auf ~ stellen** (umg) to dig one's heels in; **ein ~er Bock** (umg) a pig-headed fellow

Sturm [ʃtʊrm] (-(e)s, ⁻e) m storm; (Wind) gale; (Mil etc) attack, assault; **~ läuten** to keep one's finger on the doorbell; **gegen etw ~ laufen** (fig) to be up in arms against sth

stürmen ['ʃtʏrmən] vi (Wind) to blow hard, to rage; (rennen) to storm ▷ vt (Mil, fig) to storm ▷ vi unpers: **es stürmt** there's a gale blowing

Stürmer (-s, -) m (Sport) forward

sturmfrei adj (Mil) unassailable; **eine ~e Bude** (umg) a room free from disturbance

stürmisch adj stormy; (fig) tempestuous; (Entwicklung) rapid; (Liebhaber) passionate; (Beifall) tumultuous; **nicht so ~** take it easy

Sturm- zW: **Sturmschritt** m (Mil, fig): **im Sturmschritt** at the double; **Sturmwarnung** f gale warning; **Sturmwind** m gale

Sturz [ʃtʊrts] (-es, ⁻e) m fall; (Pol) overthrow; (in Temperatur, Preis) drop

stürzen ['ʃtʏrtsən] vt (werfen) to hurl; (Pol) to overthrow; (umkehren) to overturn ▷ vr to rush; (hineinstürzen) to plunge ▷ vi to fall; (Aviat) to dive; (rennen) to dash; **jdn ins Unglück ~** to bring disaster upon sb; **„nicht ~"** "this side up"; **sich auf jdn/etw ~** to pounce on sb/sth; **sich in Unkosten ~** to go to great expense

Sturzflug m nose dive

Sturzhelm m crash helmet

Stuss [ʃtʊs] (-es) (umg) m nonsense, rubbish

Stute ['ʃtuːtə] (-, -n) f mare

Stuttgart ['ʃtʊtɡart] (-s) nt Stuttgart

Stützbalken m brace, joist

Stütze ['ʃtʏtsə] (-, -n) f support; (Hilfe) help; **die ~n der Gesellschaft** the pillars of society

stutzen ['ʃtʊtsən] vt to trim; (Ohr, Schwanz) to dock; (Flügel) to clip ▷ vi to hesitate; (argwöhnisch werden) to become suspicious

stützen vt (lit, fig) to support; (Ellbogen etc) to prop up ▷ vr: **sich auf jdn/etw ~** (lit) to lean on sb/sth; (Beweise, Theorie) to be based on sb/sth

stutzig adj perplexed, puzzled; (misstrauisch) suspicious

Stützmauer f supporting wall

Stützpunkt m point of support; (von Hebel) fulcrum; (Mil, fig) base

Stützungskäufe pl (Fin) support buying sing

StVO abk = **Straßenverkehrsordnung**

stylen ['staɪlən] vt to style; (Wohnung) to design

Styling ['staɪlɪŋ] (-s, no pl) nt styling

Styropor® [ʃtyroˈpoːr] (-s) nt (expanded) polystyrene

S

s. u. *abk* (= *siehe unten*) see below

Suaheli [zua'he:li] **(-(s))** *nt* Swahili

Subjekt [zʊp'jɛkt] **(-(e)s, -e)** *nt* subject; (*pej: Mensch*) character (*umg*)

subjektiv [zʊpjɛk'ti:f] *adj* subjective

Subjektivität [zʊpjɛktivi'tɛ:t] *f* subjectivity

Subkultur ['zʊpkʊltu:r] *f* subculture

sublimieren [zubli'mi:rən] *vt* (*Chem, Psych*) to sublimate

Submissionsangebot [zʊpmɪsi'o:ns|angəbo:t] *nt* sealed-bid tender

Subroutine ['zʊpruti:nə] *f* (*Comput*) subroutine

Subskription [zʊpskrɪptsi'o:n] *f* subscription

Substantiv ['zʊpstanti:f] **(-s, -e)** *nt* noun

Substanz [zʊp'stants] *f* substance; **von der ~ zehren** to live on one's capital

subtil [zʊp'ti:l] *adj* subtle

subtrahieren [zʊptra'hi:rən] *vt* to subtract

subtropisch ['zʊptro:pɪʃ] *adj* subtropical

Subunternehmer *m* subcontractor

Subvention [zʊpvɛntsi'o:n] *f* subsidy

subventionieren [zʊpvɛntsio'ni:rən] *vt* to subsidize

subversiv [zʊpvɛr'zi:f] *adj* subversive

Suchaktion *f* search

Suchdienst *m* missing persons tracing service

Suche (-, -n) *f* search

suchen ['zu:xən] *vt* to look for, seek; (*versuchen*) to try ▷ *vi* to seek, search; **du hast hier nichts zu ~** you have no business being here; **nach Worten ~** to search for words; (*sprachlos sein*) to be at a loss for words; **such!** (*zu Hund*) seek!, find!; **~ und ersetzen** (*Comput*) search and replace

Sucher (-s, -) *m* seeker, searcher; (*Phot*) viewfinder

Suchmaschine *f* (*Comput*) search engine

Suchmeldung *f* missing *od* wanted person announcement

Suchscheinwerfer *m* searchlight

Sucht [zʊxt] **(-, ̈-e)** *f* mania; (*Med*) addiction; **Suchtdroge** *f* addictive drug; **suchterzeugend** *adj* addictive

süchtig ['zʏçtɪç] *adj* addicted

Süchtige, r *f(m)* addict

Süd [zy:t] **(-(e)s)** *m* south; **Südafrika** *nt* South Africa; **Südamerika** *nt* South America

Sudan [zu'da:n] **(-s)** *m*: **der ~** the Sudan

Sudanese [zuda'ne:zə] **(-n, -n)** *m* Sudanese

Sudanesin *f* Sudanese

südd. *abk* = **süddeutsch**

süddeutsch *adj* South German

Süddeutschland *nt* South(ern) Germany

Süden ['zy:dən] **(-s)** *m* south

Süd- *zW*: **Südeuropa** *nt* Southern Europe; **Südfrüchte** *pl* Mediterranean fruit; **Südkorea** *nt* South Korea; **südländisch** *adj* southern; (*italienisch, spanisch etc*) Latin; **südlich** *adj* southern; **südlich von** (to the) south of; **Südostasien** *nt* South-East Asia; **Südpol** *m* South Pole; **Südpolarmeer** *nt* Antarctic Ocean; **Südsee** *f* South Seas *pl*, South Pacific; **Südtirol** *nt* South Tyrol; **südwärts** *adv* southwards;

Südwestafrika *nt* South West Africa, Namibia

Sueskanal ['zu:ɛskana:l] **(-s)** *m* Suez Canal

Suff [zʊf] *m*: **etw im ~ sagen** (*umg*) to say sth while under the influence

süffig ['zʏfɪç] *adj* (*Wein*) very drinkable

süffisant [zʏfi'zant] *adj* smug

suggerieren [zʊge'ri:rən] *vt* to suggest

Suggestivfrage [zʊgɛs'ti:ffra:gə] *f* leading question

suhlen ['zu:lən] *vr* (*lit, fig*) to wallow

Sühne ['zy:nə] **(-, -n)** *f* atonement, expiation

sühnen *vt* to atone for, expiate

Sühnetermin *m* (*Jur*) conciliatory hearing

Suite ['svi:tə] *f* suite

Sulfat [zʊl'fa:t] **(-(e)s, -e)** *nt* sulphate (*Brit*), sulfate (*US*)

Sultan ['zʊltan] **(-s, -e)** *m* sultan

Sultanine [zʊlta'ni:nə] *f* sultana

Sülze ['zʏltsə] **(-, -n)** *f* brawn (*Brit*), headcheese (*US*); (*Aspik*) aspic

summarisch [zʊ'ma:rɪʃ] *adj* summary

Sümmchen ['zʏmçən] *nt*: **ein hübsches ~** a tidy sum

Summe (-, -n) *f* sum, total

summen *vi* to buzz ▷ *vt* (*Lied*) to hum

Summer (-s, -) *m* buzzer

summieren [zʊ'mi:rən] *vt* to add up ▷ *vr* to mount up

Sumpf [zʊmpf] **(-(e)s, ̈-e)** *m* swamp, marsh

sumpfig *adj* marshy

Sund [zʊnt] **(-(e)s, -e)** *m* sound, straits *pl*

Sünde ['zʏndə] **(-, -n)** *f* sin

Sünden- *zW*: **Sündenbock** *m* (*fig*) scapegoat; **Sündenfall** *m* (*Rel*) Fall; **Sündenregister** *nt* (*fig*) list of sins

Sünder, in (-s, -) *m(f)* sinner

sündhaft *adj* (*lit*) sinful; (*fig: umg: Preise*) wicked

sündigen ['zʏndɪgən] *vi* to sin; (*hum*) to indulge; **~ an** +*dat* to sin against

Super ['zu:pər] **(-s)** *nt* (*Benzin*) four-star (petrol) (*Brit*), premium (*US*)

super (*umg*) *adj* super ▷ *adv* incredibly well

Superlativ ['zu:pərlati:f] **(-s, -e)** *m* superlative

Supermarkt *m* supermarket

Superstar *m* superstar

Suppe ['zʊpə] **(-, -n)** *f* soup; (*mit Einlage*) broth; (*klare Brühe*) bouillon; (*fig: umg: Nebel*) peasouper (*Brit*), pea soup (*US*); **jdm die ~ versalzen** (*umg*) to put a spoke in sb's wheel

Suppen- *zW*: **Suppenfleisch** *nt* meat for making soup; **Suppengrün** *nt* herbs and vegetables for making soup; **Suppenkasper** (*umg*) *m* poor eater; **Suppenteller** *m* soup plate

Surfbrett ['zø:rfbrɛt] *nt* surfboard

surfen ['zø:rfən] *vi* to surf

Surfer, in *m(f)* surfer

Surrealismus [zʊrea'lɪsmʊs] *m* surrealism

surren ['zʊrən] *vi* to buzz; (*Insekt*) to hum

Surrogat [zʊro'ga:t] **(-(e)s, -e)** *nt* substitute, surrogate

suspekt [zʊs'pɛkt] *adj* suspect

suspendieren [zʊspɛn'di:rən] *vt*: **~ (von)** to suspend (from)

Suspendierung f suspension
süß [zy:s] adj sweet
Süße (-) f sweetness
süßen vt to sweeten
Süßholz nt: **~ raspeln** (fig) to turn on the blarney
Süßigkeit f sweetness; (Bonbon etc) sweet (Brit), candy (US)
süß- zW: **süßlich** adj sweetish; (fig) sugary; **süßsauer** adj sweet-and-sour; (fig: gezwungen: Lächeln) forced; (Gurken etc) pickled; (Miene) artificially friendly; **Süßspeise** f pudding, sweet (Brit); **Süßstoff** m sweetener; **Süßwaren** pl confectionery sing; **Süßwasser** nt fresh water
SV (-) m abk = **Sportverein**
SW abk (= Südwest(en)) SW
Swasiland ['sva:zilant] (-s) nt Swaziland
SWF (-) m abk (früher: = Südwestfunk) South West German Radio
Sylvester [zyl'vɛstər] (-s, -) nt = **Silvester**
Symbol [zym'bo:l] (-s, -e) nt symbol
Symbolik f symbolism
symbolisch adj symbolic(al)
symbolisieren [zymboli'zi:rən] vt to symbolize
Symmetrie [zyme'tri:] f symmetry; **Symmetrieachse** f symmetric axis
symmetrisch [zy'me:trɪʃ] adj symmetrical
Sympathie [zympa'ti:] f liking; sympathy; **er hat sich** dat **alle ~(n) verscherzt** he has turned everyone against him; **Sympathiekundgebung** f demonstration of support; **Sympathiestreik** m sympathy strike
Sympathisant, in m(f) sympathizer
sympathisch [zym'pa:tɪʃ] adj likeable, congenial; **er ist mir ~** I like him
sympathisieren [zympati'zi:rən] vi to sympathize
Symphonie [zymfo'ni:] f = **Sinfonie**
Symptom [zymp'to:m] (-s, -e) nt symptom
symptomatisch [zympto'ma:tɪʃ] adj

symptomatic
Synagoge [zyna'go:gə] (-, -n) f synagogue
synchron [zyn'kro:n] adj synchronous; **Synchrongetriebe** nt synchromesh gearbox (Brit) od transmission (US)
synchronisieren [zynkroni'zi:rən] vt to synchronize; (Film) to dub
Synchronschwimmen nt synchronized swimming
Syndikat [zyndi'ka:t] (-(e)s, -e) nt combine, syndicate
Syndrom [zyn'dro:m] (-s, -e) nt syndrome
Synkope [zyn'ko:pə] (-, -n) f (Mus) syncopation
Synode [zy'no:də] (-, -n) f (Rel) synod
Synonym [zyno'ny:m] (-s, -e) nt synonym; **synonym** adj synonymous
Syntax ['zyntaks] (-, -en) f syntax
Synthese [zyn'te:zə] (-, -n) f synthesis
synthetisch adj synthetic
Syphilis ['zy:filɪs] (-) f syphilis
Syrer, in ['zy:rər(ɪn)] (-s, -) m(f) Syrian
Syrien (-s) nt Syria
syrisch adj Syrian
System [zys'te:m] (-s, -e) nt system; **Systemanalyse** f systems analysis; **Systemanalytiker, in** m(f) systems analyst
Systematik f system
systematisch [zyste'ma:tɪʃ] adj systematic
systematisieren [zystemati'zi:rən] vt to systematize
System- zW: **Systemkritiker** m critic of the system; **Systemplatte** f (Comput) system disk; **Systemvoraussetzung** f (meist pl) system requirement; **Systemzwang** m obligation to conform (to the system)
Szenarium [stse'na:rium] nt scenario
Szene ['stse:nə] (-, -n) f scene; **sich in der ~ auskennen** (umg) to know the scene; **sich in ~ setzen** to play to the gallery
Szenenwechsel m scene change
Szenerie [stsenə'ri:] f scenery

S

325

Tt

T, t[1] [te:] *nt* T, t; **T wie Theodor** ≈ T for Tommy

t[2] *abk* (= *Tonne*) t

Tabak ['ta:bak] **(-s, -e)** *m* tobacco; **Tabakladen** *m* tobacconist's (*Brit*), tobacco store (*US*)

tabellarisch [tabɛ'la:rɪʃ] *adj* tabular

Tabelle **(-, -n)** *f* table

Tabellenführer *m* (*Sport*) top of the table, league leader

Tabernakel [tabɛr'na:kəl] **(-s, -)** *nt* tabernacle

Tabl. *abk* = **Tablette(n)**

Tablett **(-(e)s, -s** *od* **-e)** *nt* tray

Tablette [ta'blɛtə] **(-, -n)** *f* tablet, pill

Tabu [ta'bu:] **(-s, -s)** *nt* taboo

tabuisieren [tabui'zi:rən] *vt* to make taboo

Tabulator [tabu'la:tɔr] *m* tabulator, tab (*umg*)

tabulieren *vt* to tab

Tacho ['taxo] **(-s, -s)** (*umg*) *m* speedo (*Brit*)

Tachometer [taxo'me:tər] **(-s, -)** *m* (*Aut*) speedometer

Tadel ['ta:dəl] **(-s, -)** *m* censure, scolding; (*Fehler*) fault; (*Makel*) blemish; **tadellos** *adj* faultless, irreproachable

tadeln *vt* to scold

tadelnswert *adj* blameworthy

Tadschikistan [ta'dʒi:kista:n] **(-s)** *nt* Tajikistan

Tafel ['ta:fəl] **(-, -n)** *f* (*form: festlicher Speisetisch, Math*) table; (*Festmahl*) meal; (*Anschlagtafel*) board; (*Wandtafel*) blackboard; (*Schiefertafel*) slate; (*Gedenktafel*) plaque; (*Illustration*) plate; (*Schalttafel*) panel; (*Schokoladentafel etc*) bar; **tafelfertig** *adj* ready to serve

täfeln ['tɛ:fəln] *vt* to panel

Tafelöl *nt* cooking oil; salad oil

Täfelung *f* panelling (*Brit*), paneling (*US*)

Tafelwasser *nt* table water

Taft [taft] **(-(e)s, -e)** *m* taffeta

Tag [ta:k] **(-(e)s, -e)** *m* day; (*Tageslicht*) daylight; **am ~** during the day; **für** *od* **auf ein paar ~e** for a few days; **in den ~ hinein leben** to take each day as it comes; **bei ~(e)** (*ankommen*) while it's light; (*arbeiten, reisen*) during the day; **unter ~e** (*Min*) underground; **über ~e** (*Min*) on the surface; **an den ~ kommen** to come to light; **er legte großes Interesse an den ~** he showed great interest; **auf den ~ (genau)** to the day; **auf seine alten ~e** at his age; **guten ~!** good morning/afternoon!; *siehe auch* **zutage**;

tagaus *adv*: **tagaus, tagein** day in, day out;

Tagdienst *m* day duty

Tage- *zW*: **Tagebau** *m* (*Min*) open-cast mining; **Tagebuch** *nt* diary; **Tagedieb** *m* idler; **Tagegeld** *nt* daily allowance; **tagelang** *adv* for days

tagen *vi* to sit, meet ▷ *vi unpers*: **es tagt** dawn is breaking

Tages- *zW*: **Tagesablauf** *m* daily routine; **Tagesanbruch** *m* dawn; **Tagesausflug** *m* day trip; **Tagesdecke** *f* bedspread; **Tagesfahrt** *f* day trip; **Tageskarte** *f* (*Eintrittskarte*) day ticket; (*Speisekarte*) menu of the day; **Tageskasse** *f* (*Comm*) day's takings *pl*; (*Theat*) box office; **Tageslicht** *nt* daylight; **Tagesmutter** *f* child minder; **Tagesordnung** *f* agenda; **an der Tagesordnung sein** (*fig*) to be the order of the day; **Tagesrückfahrkarte** *f* day return (ticket); **Tagessatz** *m* daily rate; **Tagesschau** *f* (*TV*) television news (programme (*Brit*) *od* program (*US*)); **Tagesstätte** *f* day nursery (*Brit*), daycare center (*US*); **Tageswert** *m* (*Fin*) present value; **Tageszeit** *f* time of day; **zu jeder Tages- und Nachtzeit** at all hours of the day and night; **Tageszeitung** *f* daily (paper)

tägl. *abk* = **täglich**

täglich ['tɛ:klɪç] *adj, adv* daily; **einmal ~** once a day

tags [ta:ks] *adv*: **~ darauf** *od* **danach** the next *od* following day; **tagsüber** *adv* during the day

tagtäglich *adj* daily ▷ *adv* every (single) day

Tagung *f* conference

Tagungsort *m* venue (of a conference)

Tahiti [ta'hi:ti] **(-s)** *nt* Tahiti

Taifun [taɪ'fu:n] **(-s, -e)** *m* typhoon

Taille ['taljə] **(-, -n)** *f* waist

tailliert [ta'ji:rt] *adj* waisted, gathered at the waist

Taiwan ['taɪvan] **(-s)** *nt* Taiwan

Takel ['ta:kəl] **(-s, -)** *nt* tackle

takeln ['ta:kəln] *vt* to rig

Takt [takt] **(-(e)s, -e)** *m* tact; (*Mus*) time; **Taktgefühl** *nt* tact

Taktik *f* tactics *pl*

Taktiker, in *m(f)* tactician

taktisch *adj* tactical

Takt- *zW*: **taktlos** *adj* tactless; **Taktlosigkeit** *f* tactlessness; **Taktstock** *m* (conductor's) baton; **Taktstrich** *m* (*Mus*) bar (line); **taktvoll**

adj tactful

Tal [taːl] **(-(e)s, ⸚er)** *nt* valley

Talar [taˈlaːr] **(-s, -e)** *m* (*Jur*) robe; (*Univ*) gown

Talbrücke *f* bridge over a valley

Talent [taˈlɛnt] **(-(e)s, -e)** *nt* talent

talentiert [talɛnˈtiːrt] *adj* talented, gifted

Talfahrt *f* descent; (*fig*) decline

Talg [talk] **(-(e)s, -e)** *m* tallow

Talgdrüse *f* sebaceous gland

Talisman [ˈtaːlɪsman] **(-s, -e)** *m* talisman

Tal- *zW:* **Talsohle** *f* bottom of a valley; **Talsperre** *f* dam; **talwärts** *adv* down to the valley

Tamburin [tambuˈriːn] **(-s, -e)** *nt* tambourine

Tamile [taˈmiːlə] **(-n, -n)** *m*, **Tamilin** *f* Tamil

tamilisch *adj* Tamil

Tampon [ˈtampɔn] **(-s, -s)** *m* tampon

Tamtam [tamˈtam] **(-s, -s)** *nt* (*Mus*) tomtom; (*umg: Wirbel*) fuss, ballyhoo; (*Lärm*) din

Tang [taŋ] **(-(e)s, -e)** *m* seaweed

Tangente [taŋˈgɛntə] **(-, -n)** *f* tangent

Tanger [ˈtaŋər] **(-s)** *nt* Tangier(s)

tangieren [taŋˈgiːrən] *vt* (*Problem*) to touch on; (*fig*) to affect

Tank [taŋk] **(-s, -s)** *m* tank

tanken *vt* (*Wagen etc*) to fill up with petrol (*Brit*) *od* gas (*US*); (*Benzin etc*) to fill up with; (*Aviat*) to (re)fuel; (*umg: frische Luft, neue Kräfte*) to get ▷ *vi* to fill up (with petrol *od* gas); to (re)fuel

Tanker (-s, -) *m* tanker

Tank- *zW:* **Tanklaster** *m* tanker; **Tankschiff** *nt* tanker; **Tankstelle** *f* petrol (*Brit*) *od* gas (*US*) station; **Tankuhr** *f* fuel gauge; **Tankverschluss** *m* fuel cap; **Tankwart** *m* petrol pump (*Brit*) *od* gas station (*US*) attendant

Tanne [ˈtanə] **(-, -n)** *f* fir

Tannenbaum *m* fir tree

Tannenzapfen *m* fir cone

Tansania [tanˈzaːnia] **(-s)** *nt* Tanzania

Tante [ˈtantə] **(-, -n)** *f* aunt; **Tante-Emma-Laden** (*umg*) *m* corner shop

Tantieme [tãtiˈeːmə] **(-, -n)** *f* fee; (*für Künstler etc*) royalty

Tanz [tants] **(-es, ⸚e)** *m* dance

tänzeln [ˈtɛntsəln] *vi* to dance along

tanzen *vt, vi* to dance

Tänzer, in (-s, -) *m(f)* dancer

Tanz- *zW:* **Tanzfläche** *f* (dance) floor; **Tanzlokal** *nt* café/restaurant with dancing; **Tanzschule** *f* dancing school

Tapet [taˈpeːt] (*umg*) *nt:* **etw aufs ~ bringen** to bring sth up

Tapete [taˈpeːtə] **(-, -n)** *f* wallpaper

Tapetenwechsel *m* (*fig*) change of scenery

tapezieren [tapeˈtsiːrən] *vt* to (wall)paper

Tapezierer (-s, -) *m* (interior) decorator

tapfer [ˈtapfər] *adj* brave; **sich ~ schlagen** (*umg*) to put on a brave show; **Tapferkeit** *f* courage, bravery

tappen [ˈtapən] *vi* to walk uncertainly *od* clumsily; **im Dunkeln ~** (*fig*) to grope in the dark

täppisch [ˈtɛpɪʃ] *adj* clumsy

Tara [ˈtaːra] **(-, Taren)** *f* tare

Tarantel [taˈrantəl] **(-, -n)** *f:* **wie von der ~ gestochen** as if stung by a bee

Tarif [taˈriːf] **(-s, -e)** *m* tariff, (scale of) fares/charges; **nach/über/unter ~ bezahlen** to pay according to/above/below the (union) rate(s); **Tarifautonomie** *f* free collective bargaining; **Tarifgruppe** *f* grade; **tariflich** *adj* agreed, union; **Tariflohn** *m* standard wage rate; **Tarifordnung** *f* wage *od* salary scale; **Tarifpartner** *m:* **die Tarifpartner** union and management; **Tarifvereinbarung** *f* labour (*Brit*) *od* labor (*US*) agreement; **Tarifverhandlungen** *pl* collective bargaining *sing;* **Tarifvertrag** *m* pay agreement

tarnen [ˈtarnən] *vt* to camouflage; (*Person, Absicht*) to disguise

Tarnfarbe *f* camouflage paint

Tarnmanöver *nt* (*lit, fig*) feint, covering ploy

Tarnung *f* camouflaging; disguising

Tarock [taˈrɔk] **(-s, s)** *m od nt* tarot

Tasche [ˈtaʃə] **(-, -n)** *f* pocket; (*Handtasche*) handbag; **in die eigene ~ wirtschaften** to line one's own pockets; **jdm auf der ~ liegen** (*umg*) to live off sb

Taschen- *zW:* **Taschenbuch** *nt* paperback; **Taschendieb** *m* pickpocket; **Taschengeld** *nt* pocket money; **Taschenlampe** *f* (electric) torch, flashlight (*US*); **Taschenmesser** *nt* penknife; **Taschenrechner** *m* pocket calculator; **Taschenspieler** *m* conjurer; **Taschentuch** *nt* handkerchief

Tasmanien [tasˈmaːniən] **(-s)** *nt* Tasmania

Tasse [ˈtasə] **(-, -n)** *f* cup; **er hat nicht alle ~n im Schrank** (*umg*) he's not all there

Tastatur [tastaˈtuːr] *f* keyboard

Taste [ˈtastə] **(-, -n)** *f* push-button control; (*an Schreibmaschine*) key

tasten *vt* to feel, touch; (*drücken*) to press ▷ *vi* to feel, grope ▷ *vr* to feel one's way

Tastentelefon *nt* push-button telephone

Tastsinn *m* sense of touch

Tat **(-, -en)** *f* act, deed, action; **in der ~** indeed, as a matter of fact; **etw in die ~ umsetzen** to put sth into action

tat *etc* [taːt] *vb siehe* **tun**

Tatbestand *m* facts *pl* of the case

Tatendrang *m* energy

tatenlos *adj* inactive

Täter, in [ˈtɛːtər(ɪn)] **(-s, -)** *m(f)* perpetrator, culprit; **Täterschaft** *f* guilt

tätig *adj* active; **~er Teilhaber** active partner; **in einer Firma ~ sein** to work for a firm

tätigen *vt* (*Comm*) to conclude; (*geh: Einkäufe, Anruf*) to make

Tätigkeit *f* activity; (*Beruf*) occupation

Tätigkeitsbereich *m* field of activity

tatkräftig *adj* energetic; (*Hilfe*) active

tätlich *adj* violent; **Tätlichkeit** *f* violence; **es kam zu Tätlichkeiten** there were violent scenes

Tatort (-(e)s, -e) *m* scene of the crime

tätowieren [tetoˈviːrən] *vt* to tattoo

t

Tätowierung f tattooing; (*Ergebnis*) tattoo
Tatsache f fact; **jdn vor vollendete ~n
stellen** to present sb with a fait accompli
Tatsachenbericht m documentary (report)
tatsächlich *adj* actual ▷ *adv* really
tatverdächtig *adj* suspected
Tatze ['tatsə] (-, -n) f paw
Tau¹ [tau] (-(e)s, -e) *nt* rope
Tau² -(e)s) m dew
taub [taup] *adj* deaf; (*Nuss*) hollow; **sich ~
stellen** to pretend not to hear
Taube ['taubə] (-, -n) f (*Zool*) pigeon; (*fig*) dove
Taubenschlag m dovecote; **hier geht es zu
wie im ~** (*fig: umg*) it's like Waterloo Station
here (*Brit*), it's like Grand Central Station here
(*US*)
Taubheit f deafness
taubstumm *adj* deaf-mute
tauchen ['tauxən] *vt* to dip ▷ *vi* to dive; (*Naut*)
to submerge
Taucher (-s, -) m diver; **Taucheranzug** m
diving suit
Tauchsieder (-s, -) m portable immersion
heater
Tauchstation f: **auf ~ gehen** (*U-Boot*) to dive
tauen ['tauən] *vt, vi* to thaw ▷ *vi unpers*: **es taut**
it's thawing
Taufbecken *nt* font
Taufe ['taufə] (-, -n) f baptism
taufen *vt* to baptize; (*nennen*) to christen
Tauf- *zW*: **Taufname** m Christian name;
Taufpate m godfather; **Taufpatin** f
godmother; **Taufschein** m certificate of
baptism
taugen ['taugən] *vi* to be of use; **~ für** to do *od*
be good for; **nicht ~** to be no good *od* useless
Taugenichts (-es, -e) m good-for-nothing
tauglich ['tauklıç] *adj* suitable; (*Mil*) fit (for
service); **Tauglichkeit** f suitability; fitness
Taumel ['tauməl] (-s) m dizziness; (*fig*) frenzy
taumelig *adj* giddy, reeling
taumeln *vi* to reel, stagger
Taunus ['taunus] (-) m Taunus (Mountains *pl*)
Tausch [tauʃ] (-(e)s, -e) m exchange; **einen
guten/schlechten ~ machen** to get a good/
bad deal
tauschen *vt* to exchange, swap ▷ *vi*: **ich
möchte nicht mit ihm ~** I wouldn't like to be
in his place
täuschen ['tɔyʃən] *vt* to deceive ▷ *vi* to be
deceptive ▷ *vr* to be wrong; **wenn mich nicht
alles täuscht** unless I'm completely wrong
täuschend *adj* deceptive
Tauschhandel m barter
Täuschung f deception; (*optisch*) illusion
Täuschungsmanöver *nt* (*Sport*) feint; (*fig*) ploy
tausend ['tauzənt] *num* a *od* one thousand;
Tausend (-, -en) f (*Zahl*) thousand
Tausender (-s, -) m (*Geldschein*) thousand
Tausendfüßler (-s, -) m centipede
Tau- *zW*: **Tautropfen** m dew drop; **Tauwetter**
nt thaw; **Tauziehen** *nt* tug-of-war
Taxe ['taksə] (-, -n) f taxi, cab

Taxi ['taksi] (-(s), -(s)) *nt* taxi, cab
taxieren [ta'ksi:rən] *vt* (*Preis, Wert*) to estimate;
(*Haus, Gemälde*) to value; (*mustern*) to look up
and down
Taxi- *zW*: **Taxifahrer** m taxi driver; **Taxistand**
m taxi rank (*Brit*) *od* stand (*US*)
Tb, Tbc f *abk* (= *Tuberkulose*) TB
Teamarbeit ['ti:m|arbaıt] f teamwork
Technik ['tɛçnık] f technology; (*Methode,
Kunstfertigkeit*) technique
Techniker, in (-s -) m(f) technician
technisch *adj* technical; **~e Hochschule** =
polytechnic
Technologie [tɛçnolo'gi:] f technology
technologisch [tɛçno'lo:gıʃ] *adj* technological
Techtelmechtel [tɛçtəl'mɛçtəl] (-s, -) (*umg*) *nt*
(*Liebschaft*) affair, carry-on
TEE *abk* (= *Trans-Europ-Express*) Trans-Europe-
Express
Tee [te:] (-s, -s) m tea; **Teebeutel** m tea bag;
Teekanne f teapot; **Teelicht** *nt* night-light;
Teelöffel m teaspoon; **Teemischung** f blend
of tea
Teer [te:r] (-(e)s, -e) m tar; **teeren** *vt* to tar
Teesieb *nt* tea strainer
Teewagen m tea trolley
Teflon® ['tɛflo:n] (-s) *nt* Teflon®
Teheran ['te:həra:n] (-s) *nt* Teheran
Teich [taıç] (-(e)s, -e) m pond
Teig [taık] (-(e)s, -e) m dough
teigig ['taıgıç] *adj* doughy
Teigwaren *pl* pasta *sing*
Teil [taıl] (-(e)s, -e) m *od nt* part; (*Anteil*) share
▷ *nt* (*Bestandteil*) component, part; (*Ersatzteil*)
spare (part); **zum ~** partly; **ich für mein(en)
~ ...** I, for my part ...; **sich** *dat* **sein ~ denken**
(*umg*) to draw one's own conclusions; **er hat
sein(en) ~ dazu beigetragen** he did his bit
od share; **teilbar** *adj* divisible; **Teilbetrag** m
instalment (*Brit*), installment (*US*); **Teilchen** *nt*
(atomic) particle
teilen *vt* to divide; (*mit jdm*) to share ▷ *vr* to
divide; (*in Gruppen*) to split up
Teil- *zW*: **teilentrahmt** *adj* semi-skimmed;
Teilgebiet *nt* (*Bereich*) branch; (*räumlich*) area;
teilhaben *unreg vi*: **an etw** *dat* **teilhaben**
to share in sth; **Teilhaber** (-s, -) m partner;
Teilkaskoversicherung f third party, fire and
theft insurance
Teilnahme (-, -n) f participation; (*Mitleid*)
sympathy; **jdm seine herzliche ~
aussprechen** to offer sb one's heartfelt
sympathy
teilnahmslos *adj* disinterested, apathetic
teilnehmen *unreg vi*: **an etw** *dat* **~** to take part
in sth
Teilnehmer, in (-s, -) m(f) participant
teils *adv* partly
Teilschaden m partial loss
Teilstrecke f stage; (*von Straße*) stretch; (*bei Bus
etc*) fare stage
Teilung f division
Teil- *zW*: **teilweise** *adv* partially, in part;

Teilzahlung f payment by instalments (Brit) od installments (US); **Teilzeitarbeit** f part-time job od work; **Teilzeitbasis** f: **auf Teilzeitbasis arbeiten** to work part-time; **Teilzeitmodell** nt part-time working arrangements

Teint [tɛ̃:] (**-s, -s**) m complexion

Telearbeit ['te:lɛarbaɪt] f teleworking

Telebanking ['te:lebɛŋkɪŋ] (**-s**) nt telebanking

Telebrief ['te:lebri:f] m facsimile, fax

Telefax ['te:lefaks] (**-**) nt telefax

Telefon [tele'fo:n] (**-s, -e**) nt (tele)phone; **ans ~ gehen** to answer the phone; **Telefonamt** nt telephone exchange; **Telefonanruf** m (tele) phone call

Telefonat [telefo'na:t] (**-(e)s, -e**) nt (tele)phone call

Telefon- zW: **Telefonbuch** nt (tele) phone directory; **Telefongebühr** f call charge; (Grundgebühr) (tele)phone rental; **Telefongespräch** nt (tele)phone call; **Telefonhäuschen** (umg) nt = **Telefonzelle**

telefonieren [telefo'ni:rən] vi to (tele)phone; **bei jdm ~** to use sb's phone; **mit jdm ~** to speak to sb on the phone

telefonisch [tele'fo:nɪʃ] adj telephone; (Benachrichtigung) by telephone; **ich bin ~ zu erreichen** I can be reached by phone

Telefonist, in [telefo'nɪst(ɪn)] m(f) telephonist

Telefon- zW: **Telefonkarte** f phone card; **Telefonnummer** f (tele)phone number; **Telefonseelsorge** f: **die Telefonseelsorge** ≈ the Samaritans; **Telefonverbindung** f telephone connection; **Telefonzelle** f telephone box (Brit) od booth (US), callbox (Brit); **Telefonzentrale** f telephone exchange

Telegraf [tele'gra:f] (**-en, -en**) m telegraph

Telegrafenleitung f telegraph line

Telegrafenmast m telegraph pole

Telegrafie [telegra'fi:] f telegraphy

telegrafieren [telegra'fi:rən] vt, vi to telegraph, cable, wire

telegrafisch [tele'gra:fɪʃ] adj telegraphic; **jdm ~ Geld überweisen** to cable sb money

Telegramm [tele'gram] (**-s, -e**) nt telegram, cable; **Telegrammadresse** f telegraphic address; **Telegrammformular** nt telegram form

Telekolleg ['te:ləkɔle:k] nt ≈ Open University (Brit)

Teleobjektiv ['te:ləɔpjɛkti:f] nt telephoto lens

Telepathie [telepa'ti:] f telepathy

telepathisch [tele'pa:tɪʃ] adj telepathic

Teleskop [tele'sko:p] (**-s, -e**) nt telescope

Telespiel nt video game

Telex ['te:lɛks] (**-, -(e)**) nt telex

Teller ['tɛlər] (**-s, -**) m plate

Tempel ['tɛmpəl] (**-s, -**) m temple

Temperafarbe ['tɛmperafarbə] f distemper

Temperament [tɛmpera'mɛnt] nt temperament; (Schwung) vivacity, vitality; **sein ~ ist mit ihm durchgegangen** he went over the top; **temperamentlos** adj spiritless; **temperamentvoll** adj high-spirited, lively

Temperatur [tɛmpera'tu:r] f temperature; **erhöhte ~ haben** to have a temperature

Tempo¹ ['tɛmpo] (**-s, -s**) nt speed, pace; **~! get a move on!**

Tempo² ['tɛmpo] (**-s, Tempi**) nt (Mus) tempo; **das ~ angeben** (fig) to set the pace; **Tempolimit** nt speed limit

temporär [tɛmpo'rɛ:r] adj temporary

Tempotaschentuch® nt paper handkerchief

Tendenz [tɛn'dɛnts] f tendency; (Absicht) intention

tendenziell [tɛndɛntsi'ɛl] adj: **nur ~e Unterschiede** merely differences in emphasis

tendenziös [tɛndɛntsi'ø:s] adj bias(s)ed, tendentious

tendieren [tɛn'di:rən] vi: **zu etw ~** to show a tendency to(wards) sth, incline to(wards) sth

Teneriffa [tene'rɪfa] (**-s**) nt Tenerife

Tenne ['tɛnə] (**-, -n**) f threshing floor

Tennis ['tɛnɪs] (**-**) nt tennis; **Tennisplatz** m tennis court; **Tennisschläger** m tennis racket; **Tennisspieler** m tennis player

Tenor [te'no:r] (**-s, ⁻e**) m tenor

Teppich ['tɛpɪç] (**-s, -e**) m carpet; **Teppichboden** m wall-to-wall carpeting; **Teppichkehrmaschine** f carpet sweeper; **Teppichklopfer** m carpet beater

Termin [tɛr'mi:n] (**-s, -e**) m (Zeitpunkt) date; (Frist) deadline; (Arzttermin etc) appointment; (Jur: Verhandlung) hearing; **sich** dat **einen ~ geben lassen** to make an appointment; **termingerecht** adj on schedule

terminieren [tɛrmi'ni:rən] vt (befristen) to limit; (festsetzen) to set a date for

Terminkalender m diary, appointments book

Terminologie [tɛrminolo'gi:] f terminology

Termite [tɛr'mi:tə] (**-, -n**) f termite

Terpentin [tɛrpɛn'ti:n] (**-s, -e**) nt turpentine, turps sing

Terrain [tɛ'rɛ̃:] (**-s, -s**) nt land, terrain; (fig) territory; **das ~ sondieren** (Mil) to reconnoitre the terrain; (fig) to see how the land lies

Terrasse [tɛ'rasə] (**-, -n**) f terrace

Terrine [tɛ'ri:nə] f tureen

territorial [tɛritori'a:l] adj territorial

Territorium [tɛri'to:rium] nt territory

Terror ['tɛrɔr] (**-s**) m terror; (Terrorherrschaft) reign of terror; **blanker ~** sheer terror; **Terroranschlag** m terrorist attack

terrorisieren [tɛrori'zi:rən] vt to terrorize

Terrorismus [tɛro'rɪsmʊs] m terrorism

Terrorist, in m(f) terrorist

terroristisch adj terrorist attr

Terrornetz(werk) nt terrorist network

Terrororganisation f terrorist organization

Terrorzelle f terrorist cell

Tertia ['tɛrtsia] (**-, Tertien**) f (Sch: früher: Untertertia/Obertertia) fourth/fifth year of German secondary school

Terz [tɛrts] (**-, -en**) f (Mus) third

Terzett [tɛr'tsɛt] (**-(e)s, -e**) nt (Mus) trio

Tesafilm® ['te:zafɪlm] m Sellotape® (Brit), Scotch tape® (US)

t

Test [tɛst] **(-s, -s)** m test

Testament [tɛsta'mɛnt] nt will, testament; (Rel) Testament; **Altes/Neues** ~ Old/New Testament

testamentarisch [tɛstamɛn'taːrɪʃ] adj testamentary

Testamentsvollstrecker, in (-s, -) m(f) executor (of a will)

Testat [tɛs'taːt] nt **(-(e)s, -e)** nt certificate

Testator [tɛs'taːtɔr] m testator

Test- zW: **Testbild** nt (TV) test card; **testen** vt to test; **Testfall** m test case; **Testperson** f subject (of a test); **Teststoppabkommen** nt nuclear test ban agreement

Tetanus ['teːtanʊs] (-) m tetanus; **Tetanusimpfung** f (anti-)tetanus injection

teuer ['tɔyər] adj dear, expensive; **teures Geld** good money; **das wird ihn** ~ **zu stehen kommen** (fig) that will cost him dear

Teuerung f increase in prices

Teuerungszulage f cost-of-living bonus

Teufel ['tɔyfəl] **(-s, -)** m devil; **den** ~ **an die Wand malen** (schwarzmalen) to imagine the worst; (Unheil heraufbeschwören) to tempt fate od providence; **in ~s Küche kommen** to get into a mess; **jdn zum** ~ **jagen** (umg) to send sb packing

Teufelei [tɔyfə'laɪ] f devilment

Teufels- zW: **Teufelsaustreibung** f exorcism; **Teufelsbrut** (umg) f devil's brood; **Teufelskreis** m vicious circle

teuflisch ['tɔyflɪʃ] adj fiendish, diabolic

Text [tɛkst] **(-(e)s, -e)** m text; (Liedertext) words pl; (: von Schlager) lyrics pl; **Textdichter** m songwriter; **texten** vi to write the words

textil [tɛks'tiːl] adj textile; **Textilbranche** f textile trade

Textilien pl textiles pl

Textilindustrie f textile industry

Textilwaren pl textiles pl

Text- zW: **Textnachrichten** pl (Tel) text messaging; **Textstelle** f passage; **Textverarbeitungssystem** nt word processor

TH (-, -s) f abk (= technische Hochschule) siehe **technisch**

Thailand ['taɪlant] **(-s)** nt Thailand

Thailänder, in ['taɪlɛndər(ɪn)] **(-s, -)** m(f) Thai

Theater [te'aːtər] **(-s, -)** nt theatre (Brit), theater (US); (umg) fuss; **(ein)** ~ **machen** to make a (big) fuss; ~ **spielen** to act; (fig) to put on an act; **Theaterbesucher** m playgoer; **Theaterkasse** f box office; **Theaterstück** nt (stage) play

theatralisch [tea'traːlɪʃ] adj theatrical

Theke ['teːkə] **(-, -n)** f (Schanktisch) bar; (Ladentisch) counter

Thema ['teːma] **(-s, Themen** od **-ta)** nt (Leitgedanke, Mus) theme; topic, subject; **beim** ~ **bleiben/vom** ~ **abschweifen** to stick to/ wander off the subject

thematisch [te'maːtɪʃ] adj thematic

Themenkreis m topic

Themenpark m theme park

Themse ['tɛmzə] f: **die** ~ the Thames

Theologe [teo'loːgə] **(-n, -n)** m theologian

Theologie [teolo'giː] f theology

Theologin f theologian

theologisch [teo'loːgɪʃ] adj theological

Theoretiker, in [teo're:tikər(ɪn)] **(-s, -)** m(f) theorist

theoretisch adj theoretical; ~ **gesehen** in theory, theoretically

Theorie [teo'riː] f theory

Therapeut [tera'pɔyt] **(-en, -en)** m therapist

therapeutisch adj therapeutic

Therapie [tera'piː] f therapy

Thermalbad [tɛr'maːlbaːt] nt thermal bath; (Badeort) thermal spa

Thermalquelle f thermal spring

Thermometer [tɛrmo'meːtər] **(-s, -)** nt thermometer

Thermosflasche® ['tɛrmɔsflaʃə] f Thermos® flask

Thermostat [tɛrmo'staːt] **(-(e)s** od **-en, -e(n))** m thermostat

These ['teːzə] **(-, -n)** f thesis

Thrombose [trɔm'boːsə] **(-, -n)** f thrombosis

Thron [troːn] **(-(e)s, -e)** m throne; **Thronbesteigung** f accession (to the throne)

thronen vi to sit enthroned; (fig) to sit in state

Thronerbe m heir to the throne

Thronfolge f succession (to the throne)

Thunfisch ['tuːnfɪʃ] m tuna (fish)

Thüringen ['tyːrɪŋən] **(-s)** nt Thuringia

Thymian ['tyːmiaːn] **(-s, -e)** m thyme

Tibet ['tiːbɛt] **(-s)** nt Tibet

Tick [tɪk] **(-(e)s, -s)** m tic; (Eigenart) quirk; (Fimmel) craze

ticken vi to tick; **nicht richtig** ~ (umg) to be off one's rocker

Ticket ['tɪkət] **(-s, -s)** nt ticket

tief [tiːf] adj deep; (tiefsinnig) profound; (Ausschnitt, Ton) low; **~er Teller** soup plate; ~ **greifend** far-reaching; ~ **schürfend** profound; **bis** ~ **in die Nacht hinein** late into the night; **Tief** **(-s, -s)** nt (Met) depression; (fig) low; **Tiefbau** m civil engineering (at or below ground level); **Tiefdruck** m (Met) low pressure

Tiefe (-, -n) f depth

Tiefebene ['tiːfʔeːbənə] f plain

Tiefenpsychologie f depth psychology

Tiefenschärfe f (Phot) depth of focus

tief- zW: **tiefernst** adj very grave od solemn; **Tiefflug** m low-level od low-altitude flight; **Tiefgang** m (Naut) draught (Brit), draft (US); (geistig) depth; **Tiefgarage** f underground car park (Brit) od parking lot (US); **tiefgekühlt** adj frozen; **Tiefkühlfach** nt freezer compartment; **Tiefkühlkost** f frozen food; **Tiefkühltruhe** f freezer, deep freeze (US); **Tieflader (-s, -)** m low-loader; **Tiefland** nt lowlands pl; **Tiefparterre** f basement; **Tiefpunkt** m low point; (fig) low ebb; **Tiefschlag** m (Boxen, fig) blow below the belt; **Tiefsee** f deep parts of the sea; **Tiefsinn** m profundity; **tiefsinnig** adj profound; (umg) melancholy; **Tiefstand**

m low level; **tiefstapeln** *vi* to be overmodest;
Tiefstart *m* (*Sport*) crouch start

Tiefstwert *m* minimum *od* lowest value

Tiegel ['ti:gəl] (**-s, -**) *m* saucepan; (*Chem*)
crucible

Tier [ti:r] (**-(e)s, -e**) *nt* animal; **Tierarzt** *m*,
Tierärztin *f* vet(erinary surgeon) (*Brit*),
veterinarian (*US*); **Tierfreund** *m* animal
lover; **Tiergarten** *m* zoo, zoological gardens
pl; **Tierhandlung** *f* pet shop (*Brit*) *od* store (*US*);
tierisch *adj* animal *attrib*; (*lit, fig*) brutish;
(*fig: Ernst etc*) deadly; **Tierkreis** *m* zodiac;
Tierkunde *f* zoology; **tierlieb** *adj*, **tierliebend**
adj fond of animals; **Tierquälerei** *f* cruelty
to animals; **Tierreich** *nt* animal kingdom;
Tierschutz *m* protection of animals;
Tierschutzverein *m* society for the prevention
of cruelty to animals; **Tierversuch** *m* animal
experiment; **Tierwelt** *f* animal kingdom

Tiger ['ti:gər] (**-s, -**) *m* tiger; **Tigerin** *f* tigress

tilgen ['tɪlgən] *vt* to erase; (*Sünden*) to expiate;
(*Schulden*) to pay off

Tilgung *f* erasing, blotting out; expiation;
repayment

Tilgungsfonds *m* (*Comm*) sinking fund

tingeln ['tɪŋgəln] (*umg*) *vi* to appear in small
night clubs

Tinktur [tɪŋk'tu:r] *f* tincture

Tinte ['tɪntə] (**-, -n**) *f* ink

Tinten- *zW*: **Tintenfass** *nt* inkwell; **Tintenfisch**
m cuttlefish; (*achtarmig*) octopus; **Tintenfleck**
m ink stain *od* blot; **Tintenstift** *m* indelible
pencil; **Tintenstrahldrucker** *m* ink-jet printer

Tipp [tɪp] (**-s, -s**) *m* (*Sport, Börse*) tip; (*Andeutung*)
hint; (*an Polizei*) tip-off

Tippelbruder (*umg*) *m* tramp, gentleman of
the road (*Brit*), hobo (*US*)

tippen ['tɪpən] *vi* to tap, touch; (*umg: schreiben*)
to type; (*im Lotto etc*) to bet ▷ *vt* to type; to
bet; **auf jdn ~** (*umg: raten*) to tip sb, put one's
money on sb (*fig*)

Tippfehler (*umg*) *m* typing error

Tippse (**-, -n**) (*umg*) *f* typist

tipptopp ['tɪp'tɔp] (*umg*) *adj* tiptop

Tippzettel *m* (pools) coupon

Tirade [ti'ra:də] (**-, -n**) *f* tirade

Tirol [ti'ro:l] (**-s**) *nt* the Tyrol

Tiroler, in (**-s, -**) *m(f)* Tyrolese, Tyrolean

tirolerisch *adj* Tyrolese, Tyrolean

Tisch [tɪʃ] (**-(e)s, -e**) *m* table; **bitte zu ~!** lunch
od dinner is served; **bei ~** at table; **vor/nach ~**
before/after eating; **unter den ~ fallen** (*fig*)
to be dropped; **Tischdecke** *f* tablecloth

Tischler (**-s, -**) *m* carpenter, joiner

Tischlerei [tɪʃlə'raɪ] *f* joiner's workshop;
(*Arbeit*) carpentry, joinery

Tischlerhandwerk *nt* cabinetmaking

tischlern *vi* to do carpentry *etc*

Tisch- *zW*: **Tischnachbar** *m* neighbour (*Brit*) *od*
neighbor (*US*) at table; **Tischrechner** *m* desk
calculator; **Tischrede** *f* after-dinner speech;
Tischtennis *nt* table tennis; **Tischtuch** *nt*
tablecloth

Titel ['ti:təl] (**-s, -**) *m* title; **Titelanwärter** *m*
(*Sport*) challenger; **Titelbild** *nt* cover (picture);
(*von Buch*) frontispiece; **Titelgeschichte** *f*
headline story; **Titelrolle** *f* title role; **Titelseite**
f cover; (*Buchtitel*) title page; **Titelverteidiger**
m defending champion, title holder

Titte ['tɪtə] (**-, -n**) (*umg*) *f* (*weibliche Brust*) boob,
tit (*umg*)

titulieren [titu'li:rən] *vt* to entitle; (*anreden*) to
address

tja [tja] *interj* well!

Toast [to:st] (**-(e)s, -s** *od* **-e**) *m* toast

toasten *vi* to drink a toast ▷ *vt* (*Brot*) to toast;
auf jdn ~ to toast sb, drink a toast to sb

Toaster (**-s, -**) *m* toaster

toben ['to:bən] *vi* to rage; (*Kinder*) to romp
about

tob- *zW*: **Tobsucht** *f* raving madness;
tobsüchtig *adj* maniacal; **Tobsuchtsanfall** *m*
maniacal fit

Tochter ['tɔxtər] (**-, ̈ -**) *f* daughter;
Tochtergesellschaft *f* subsidiary (company)

Tod [to:t] (**-(e)s, -e**) *m* death; **zu ~e betrübt
sein** to be in the depths of despair; **eines
natürlichen/gewaltsamen ~es sterben**
to die of natural causes/die a violent death;
todernst (*umg*) *adj* deadly serious ▷ *adv* in
dead earnest

Todes- *zW*: **Todesangst** *f* mortal fear;
Todesängste ausstehen (*umg*) to be scared
to death; **Todesanzeige** *f* obituary (notice);
Todesfall *m* death; **Todeskampf** *m* death
throes *pl*; **Todesopfer** *nt* death, casualty,
fatality; **Todesqualen** *pl*: **Todesqualen
ausstehen** (*fig*) to suffer agonies; **Todesstoß**
m deathblow; **Todesstrafe** *f* death
penalty; **Todestag** *m* anniversary of death;
Todesursache *f* cause of death; **Todesurteil**
nt death sentence; **Todesverachtung** *f* utter
disgust

Todfeind *m* deadly *od* mortal enemy

todkrank *adj* dangerously ill

tödlich ['tø:tlɪç] *adj* fatal; (*Gift*) deadly, lethal

tod- *zW*: **todmüde** *adj* dead tired; **todschick**
(*umg*) *adj* smart, classy; **todsicher** (*umg*) *adj*
absolutely *od* dead certain; **Todsünde** *f* deadly
sin; **todtraurig** *adj* extremely sad

Tofu ['to:fu] (**-(s)**) *m* tofu

Togo ['to:go] (**-s**) *nt* Togo

Toilette [toa'lɛtə] *f* toilet, lavatory (*Brit*), john
(*US*); (*Frisiertisch*) dressing table; (*Kleidung*)
outfit; **auf die ~ gehen/auf der ~ sein** to go
to/be in the toilet

Toiletten- *zW*: **Toilettenartikel** *pl* toiletries
pl, toilet articles *pl*; **Toilettenpapier** *nt* toilet
paper; **Toilettentisch** *m* dressing table

toi, toi, toi ['tɔy'tɔy'tɔy] (*umg*) *interj* good luck!
(*unberufen*) touch wood

Tokio ['to:kjo] (**-s**) *nt* Tokyo

tolerant [tole'rant] *adj* tolerant

Toleranz *f* tolerance

tolerieren [tole'ri:rən] *vt* to tolerate

toll [tɔl] *adj* mad; (*Treiben*) wild; (*umg*) terrific

t

331

tollen vi to romp

toll- zW: **Tollheit** f madness, wildness; **Tollkirsche** f deadly nightshade; **tollkühn** adj daring; **Tollwut** f rabies

Tomate [to'ma:tə] (-, -n) f tomato; **du treulose ~!** (umg) you're a fine friend!

Tomatenmark (-(e)s) nt tomato purée

Tombola ['tɔmbola] (-, -s od **Tombolen**) f tombola

Ton¹ [to:n] **(-(e)s, -e)** m (Erde) clay

Ton² [to:n] **(-(e)s, ¨e)** m (Laut) sound; (Mus) note; (Redeweise) tone; (Farbton, Nuance) shade; (Betonung) stress; **keinen ~ herausbringen** not to be able to say a word; **den ~ angeben** (Mus) to give an A; (fig: Mensch) to set the tone; **Tonabnehmer** m pick-up; **tonangebend** adj leading; **Tonarm** m pick-up arm; **Tonart** f (musical) key; **Tonband** nt tape; **Tonbandaufnahme** f tape recording; **Tonbandgerät** nt tape recorder

tönen ['tø:nən] vi to sound ▷ vt to shade; (Haare) to tint

tönern ['tø:nərn] adj clay

Ton- zW: **Tonfall** m intonation; **Tonfilm** m sound film; **Tonhöhe** f pitch

Tonikum (-s, -ika) nt (Med) tonic

Ton- zW: **Toningenieur** m sound engineer; **Tonkopf** m recording head; **Tonkünstler** m musician; **Tonleiter** f (Mus) scale; **tonlos** adj soundless

Tonne ['tɔnə] (-, -n) f barrel; (Maß) ton

Ton- zW: **Tonspur** f soundtrack; **Tontaube** f clay pigeon; **Tonwaren** pl pottery sing, earthenware sing

Topf [tɔpf] **(-(e)s, ¨e)** m pot; **alles in einen ~ werfen** (fig) to lump everything together; **Topfblume** f pot plant

Töpfer, in ['tœpfər(ɪn)] **(-s, -)** m(f) potter

Töpferei [tœpfə'raɪ] f (Töpferware) pottery; (Werkstatt) pottery, potter's workshop

töpfern vi to do pottery

Töpferscheibe f potter's wheel

topfit ['tɔp'fɪt] adj in top form

Topflappen m ovencloth

topografisch [topo'gra:fɪʃ] adj topographic

topp [tɔp] interj O.K.

Tor¹ [to:r] **(-en, -en)** m fool

Tor² **(-(e)s, -e)** nt gate; (Sport) goal; **Torbogen** m archway; **Toreinfahrt** f entrance gate

Toresschluss m: **(kurz) vor ~** right at the last minute

Torf [tɔrf] **(-(e)s)** m peat; **Torfstechen** nt peat-cutting

Torheit f foolishness; (törichte Handlung) foolish deed

Torhüter (-s, -) m goalkeeper

töricht ['tø:rɪçt] adj foolish

torkeln ['tɔrkəln] vi to stagger, reel

torpedieren [tɔrpe'di:rən] vt (lit, fig) to torpedo

Torpedo [tɔr'pe:do] **(-s, -s)** m torpedo

Torschlusspanik ['to:rʃlʊspa:nɪk] (umg) f (von Unverheirateten) fear of being left on the shelf

Torte ['tɔrtə] **(-, -n)** f cake; (Obsttorte) flan, tart

Tortenguss m glaze

Tortenheber m cake slice

Tortur [tɔr'tu:r] f ordeal

Torverhältnis nt goal average

Torwart (-(e)s, -e) m goalkeeper

tosen ['to:zən] vi to roar

Toskana [tɔs'ka:na] f Tuscany

tot [to:t] adj dead; **er war auf der Stelle ~** he died instantly; **~ geboren** stillborn; **sich ~ stellen** to pretend to be dead; **der ~e Winkel** the blind spot; **einen ~en Punkt haben** to be at one's lowest; **das T~e Meer** the Dead Sea

total [to'ta:l] adj total; **Totalausverkauf** m clearance sale

totalitär [totali'tɛ:r] adj totalitarian

Totaloperation f extirpation; (von Gebärmutter) hysterectomy

Totalschaden m (Aut) complete write-off

totarbeiten vr to work o.s. to death

totärgern (umg) vr to get really annoyed

Tote, r f(m) dead person

töten ['tø:tən] vt, vi to kill

Toten- zW: **Totenbett** nt deathbed; **totenblass** adj deathly pale, white as a sheet; **Totengräber (-s, -)** m gravedigger; **Totenhemd** nt shroud; **Totenkopf** m skull; **Totenmesse** f requiem mass; **Totenschein** m death certificate; **Totenstille** f deathly silence; **Totentanz** m danse macabre; **Totenwache** f wake

tot- zW: **totfahren** unreg vt to run over; **totkriegen** (umg) vt: **nicht totzukriegen sein** to go on for ever; **totlachen** (umg) vr to laugh one's head off

Toto ['to:to] **(-s, -s)** m od nt ≈ pools pl

tot- zW: **totsagen** vt: **jdn totsagen** to say that sb is dead; **Totschlag** m (Jur) manslaughter, second degree murder (US); **totschlagen** unreg vt (lit, fig) to kill; **Totschläger** m (Waffe) cosh (Brit), blackjack (US); **totschweigen** unreg vt to hush up; **tottreten** unreg vt to trample to death

Tötung ['tø:tʊŋ] f killing

Touchscreen ['tatʃskri:n] m (Tech) touch screen; **Touchscreen-Handy** nt touch screen mobile; **Touchscreen-Technologie** f touch screen technology

toupieren [tu'pi:rən] vt to backcomb

Tour [tu:r] **(-, -en)** f tour, trip; (Umdrehung) revolution; (Verhaltensart) way; **auf ~en kommen** (Aut) to reach top speed; (fig) to get into top gear; **auf vollen ~en laufen** (lit) to run at full speed; (fig) to be in full swing; **auf die krumme ~** by dishonest means; **in einer ~** incessantly

Tourenzahl f number of revolutions

Tourenzähler m rev counter

Tourismus [tu'rɪsmʊs] m tourism

Tourist, in m(f) tourist

Touristenklasse f tourist class

Touristik [tu'rɪstɪk] f tourism

touristisch adj tourist attr

Tournee [tʊr'ne:] **(-, -s od -n)** f (Theat etc) tour;

auf ~ gehen to go on tour
Trab [traːp] (**-(e)s**) m trot; **auf ~ sein** (umg) to be on the go
Trabant [tra'bant] m satellite
Trabantenstadt f satellite town
traben ['traːbən] vi to trot
Tracht [traxt] (**-, -en**) f (Kleidung) costume, dress; **eine ~ Prügel** a sound thrashing
trachten vi to strive, endeavour (Brit), endeavor (US); **danach ~, etw zu tun** to strive to do sth; **jdm nach dem Leben ~** to seek to kill sb
trächtig ['trɛçtɪç] adj (Tier) pregnant
Tradition [traditsi'oːn] f tradition
traditionell [traditsio'nɛl] adj traditional
traf etc [traːf] vb siehe **treffen**
Tragbahre f stretcher
tragbar adj (Gerät) portable; (Kleidung) wearable; (erträglich) bearable
träge ['trɛːgə] adj sluggish, slow; (Phys) inert
tragen ['traːgən] unreg vt to carry; (Kleidung, Brille) to wear; (Namen, Früchte) to bear; (erdulden) to endure ▷ vi (schwanger sein) to be pregnant; (Eis) to hold; **schwer an etw** dat ~ (lit) to have a job carrying sth; (fig) to find sth hard to bear; **zum T~ kommen** to come to fruition; (nützlich werden) to come in useful
tragend adj (Säule, Bauteil) load-bearing; (Idee, Motiv) fundamental
Träger ['trɛːgər] (**-s, -**) m carrier; wearer; bearer; (Ordensträger) holder; (an Kleidung) (shoulder) strap; (Körperschaft etc) sponsor; (Holzträger, Betonträger) (supporting) beam; (Stahlträger, Eisenträger) girder; (Tech: Stütze von Brücken etc) support
Trägerin f (Person) siehe **Träger**
Träger- zW: **Trägerkleid** nt pinafore dress (Brit), jumper (US); **Trägerrakete** f launch vehicle; **Trägerrock** m skirt with shoulder straps
Tragetasche f carrier bag (Brit), carry-all (US)
Trag- zW: **Tragfähigkeit** f load-bearing capacity; **Tragfläche** f (Aviat) wing; **Tragflügelboot** nt hydrofoil
Trägheit ['trɛːkhaɪt] f laziness; (Phys) inertia
Tragik ['traːgɪk] f tragedy
tragikomisch [tragi'koːmɪʃ] adj tragi-comic
tragisch adj tragic; **etw ~ nehmen** (umg) to take sth to heart
Traglast f load
Tragödie [tra'gøːdiə] f tragedy
trägt [trɛːkt] vb siehe **tragen**
Tragweite f range; (fig) scope; **von großer ~ sein** to have far-reaching consequences
Tragwerk nt wing assembly
Trainer, in ['trɛːnər(ɪn)] (**-s, -**) m(f) (Sport) trainer, coach; (Fussball) manager
trainieren [trɛ'niːrən] vt to train; (Übung) to practise (Brit), practice (US) ▷ vi to train; **Fußball ~** to do football practice
Training (**-s, -s**) nt training
Trainingsanzug m track suit
Trakt [trakt] (**-(e)s, -e**) m (Gebäudeteil) section; (Flügel) wing

Traktat [trak'taːt] (**-(e)s, -e**) m od nt (Abhandlung) treatise; (Flugschrift, religiöse Schrift) tract
traktieren (umg) vt (schlecht behandeln) to maltreat; (quälen) to torment
Traktor ['traktɔr] m tractor; (von Drucker) tractor feed
trällern ['trɛlərn] vt, vi to warble; (Vogel) to trill, warble
trampeln ['trampəln] vt to trample; (abschütteln) to stamp ▷ vi to stamp
Trampelpfad m track, path
Trampeltier nt (Zool) (Bactrian) camel; (fig) clumsy oaf
trampen ['trɛmpən] vi to hitchhike
Tramper, in [trɛmpər(ɪn)] (**-s, -**) m(f) hitchhiker
Trampolin [trampo'liːn] (**-s, -e**) nt trampoline
Tranchierbesteck nt pair of carvers, carvers pl
tranchieren [trã'ʃiːrən] vt to carve
Träne ['trɛːnə] (**-, -n**) f tear
tränen vi to water
Tränengas nt tear gas
tranig ['traːnɪç] (umg) adj slow, sluggish
trank etc [traŋk] vb siehe **trinken**
Tränke ['trɛŋkə] (**-, -n**) f watering place
tränken vt (nass machen) to soak; (Tiere) to water
Transaktion [trans|aktsi'oːn] f transaction
Transchierbesteck nt = **Tranchierbesteck**
transchieren vt = **tranchieren**
Transformator [transfɔr'maːtɔr] m transformer
Transfusion [transfuzi'oːn] f transfusion
Transistor [tran'zistɔr] m transistor
transitiv ['tranzitiːf] adj transitive
Transitverkehr [tran'ziːtfɛrkeːr] m transit traffic
transparent [transpa'rɛnt] adj transparent; **Transparent** (**-(e)s, -e**) nt (Bild) transparency; (Spruchband) banner
transpirieren [transpi'riːrən] vi to perspire
Transplantation [transplantatsi'oːn] f transplantation; (Hauttransplantation) graft(ing)
Transport [trans'pɔrt] (**-(e)s, -e**) m transport; (Fracht) consignment, shipment
transportfähig adj moveable
transportieren [transpɔr'tiːrən] vt to transport
Transport- zW: **Transportkosten** pl transport charges pl, carriage sing; **Transportmittel** nt means sing of transport; **Transportunternehmen** nt carrier
transsexuell [transzɛksu'ɛl] adj transsexual
transusig ['traːnzuːzɪç] (umg) adj sluggish
Transvestit [transvɛs'tiːt] (**-en, -en**) m transvestite
Trapez [tra'peːts] (**-es, -e**) nt trapeze; (Math) trapezium
Trara [tra'raː] (**-s**) nt: **mit viel ~ (um)** (fig: umg) with a great hullabaloo (about)
trat etc [traːt] vb siehe **treten**
Tratsch [traːtʃ] (**-(e)s**) (umg) m gossip
tratschen ['traːtʃən] (umg) vi to gossip

Tratte ['tratə] (-, -n) f (Fin) draft
Traube ['traʊbə] (-, -n) f grape; (ganze Frucht) bunch (of grapes)
Traubenlese f grape harvest
Traubenzucker m glucose
trauen ['traʊən] vi +dat to trust ▷ vr to dare ▷ vt to marry; **jdm/etw** ~ to trust sb/sth
Trauer ['traʊər] (-) f sorrow; (für Verstorbenen) mourning; **Trauerfall** m death, bereavement; **Trauerfeier** f funeral service; **Trauerflor** (-s, -e) m black ribbon; **Trauergemeinde** f mourners pl; **Trauermarsch** m funeral march
trauern vi to mourn; **um jdn** ~ to mourn (for) sb
Trauer- zW: **Trauerrand** m black border; **Trauerspiel** nt tragedy; **Trauerweide** f weeping willow
Traufe ['traʊfə] (-, -n) f eaves pl
träufeln ['trɔʏfəln] vt, vi to drip
traulich ['traʊlɪç] adj cosy, intimate
Traum [traʊm] (-(e)s, Träume) m dream; **aus der** ~! it's all over!
Trauma (-s, -men) nt trauma
traumatisieren [traʊmati'zi:rən] vt to traumatize
Traumbild nt vision
Traumdeutung f interpretation of dreams
träumen ['trɔʏmən] vt, vi to dream; **das hätte ich mir nicht ~ lassen** I'd never have thought it possible
Träumer, in (-s, -) m(f) dreamer
Träumerei [trɔʏmə'raɪ] f dreaming
träumerisch adj dreamy
traumhaft adj dreamlike; (fig) wonderful
Traumtänzer m dreamer
traurig ['traʊrɪç] adj sad; **Traurigkeit** f sadness
Trauring m wedding ring
Trauschein m marriage certificate
Trauung f wedding ceremony
Trauzeuge m witness (to a marriage)
treffen ['trɛfən] unreg vt to strike, hit; (Bemerkung) to hurt; (begegnen) to meet; (Entscheidung etc) to make; (Maßnahmen) to take ▷ vi to hit ▷ vr to meet; **er hat es gut getroffen** he did well; **er fühlte sich getroffen** he took it personally; ~ **auf** +akk to come across, meet; **es traf sich, dass ...** it so happened that ...; **es trifft sich gut** it's convenient
Treffen (-s, -) nt meeting
treffend adj pertinent, apposite
Treffer (-s, -) m hit; (Tor) goal; (Los) winner
trefflich adj excellent
Treffpunkt m meeting place
Treibeis nt drift ice
treiben ['traɪbən] unreg vt to drive; (Studien etc) to pursue; (Sport) to do, go in for ▷ vi (Schiff etc) to drift; (Pflanzen) to sprout; (Koch: aufgehen) to rise; (Medikamente) to be diuretic; **die ~de Kraft** (fig) the driving force; **Handel mit etw/jdm** ~ to trade in sth/with sb; **es zu weit** ~ to go too far; **Unsinn** ~ to fool around; **Treiben** (-s) nt activity

Treib- zW: **Treibgut** nt flotsam and jetsam; **Treibhaus** nt greenhouse; **Treibhauseffekt** m greenhouse effect; **Treibhausgas** nt greenhouse gas; **Treibjagd** f shoot (in which game is sent up); (fig) witchhunt; **Treibsand** m quicksand; **Treibstoff** m fuel
Trend [trɛnt] (-s, -s) m trend; **Trendwende** f new trend
trennbar adj separable
trennen ['trɛnən] vt to separate; (teilen) to divide ▷ vr to separate; **sich** ~ **von** to part with
Trennschärfe f (Rundf) selectivity
Trennung f separation
Trennungsstrich m hyphen
Trennwand f partition (wall)
treppab adv downstairs
treppauf adv upstairs
Treppe ['trɛpə] (-, -n) f stairs pl, staircase; (im Freien) steps pl; **eine** ~ a staircase, a flight of stairs od steps; **sie wohnt zwei ~n hoch/höher** she lives two flights up/higher up
Treppengeländer nt banister
Treppenhaus nt staircase
Tresen ['tre:zən] (-s, -) m (Theke) bar; (Ladentisch) counter
Tresor [tre'zo:r] (-s, -e) m safe
Tretboot nt pedal boat, pedalo
treten ['tre:tən] unreg vi to step; (Tränen, Schweiß) to appear ▷ vt (mit Fußtritt) to kick; (niedertreten) to tread, trample; ~ **nach** to kick at; ~ **in** +akk to step in(to); **in Verbindung** ~ to get in contact; **in Erscheinung** ~ to appear; **der Fluss trat über die Ufer** the river overflowed its banks; **in Streik** ~ to go on strike
Treter ['tre:tər] (umg) pl (Schuhe) casual shoes pl
Tretmine f (Mil) (anti-personnel) mine
Tretmühle f (fig) daily grind
treu [trɔʏ] adj faithful, true; **treudoof** (umg) adj naïve
Treue (-) f loyalty, faithfulness
Treuhand (umg) f, **Treuhandanstalt** f trustee organization (overseeing the privatization of former GDR state-owned firms)
Treuhandanstalt f see culture note

Treuhänder (-s, -) m trustee
Treuhandgesellschaft f trust company
treu- zW: **treuherzig** adj innocent; **treulich** adv faithfully; **treulos** adj faithless; **treulos an**

jdm handeln to fail sb
Triathlon ['triːatlɔn] (**-s, -s**) *nt* triathlon
Tribüne [triˈbyːnə] (**-, -n**) *f* grandstand;
  (*Rednertribüne*) platform
Tribut [triˈbuːt] (**-(e)s, -e**) *m* tribute
Trichter ['trɪçtər] (**-s, -**) *m* funnel;
  (*Bombentrichter*) crater
Trick [trɪk] (**-s, -e** *od* **-s**) *m* trick; **Trickfilm** *m*
  cartoon
Trieb (**-(e)s, -e**) *m* urge, drive; (*Neigung*)
  inclination; (*Bot*) shoot
trieb *etc* [triːp] *vb siehe* **treiben**
Trieb- *zW*: **Triebfeder** *f* (*fig*) motivating force;
  triebhaft *adj* impulsive; **Triebkraft** *f* (*fig*)
  drive; **Triebtäter** *m* sex offender; **Triebwagen**
  m (*Eisenb*) railcar; **Triebwerk** *nt* engine
triefen ['triːfən] *vi* to drip
trifft [trɪft] *vb siehe* **treffen**
triftig ['trɪftɪç] *adj* convincing; (*Grund etc*) good
Trigonometrie [trigonomeˈtriː] *f*
  trigonometry
Trikot [triˈkoː] (**-s, -s**) *nt* vest; (*Sport*) shirt ▷ *m*
  (*Gewebe*) tricot
Triller ['trɪlər] (**-s, -**) *m* (*Mus*) trill
trillern *vi* to trill, warble
Trillerpfeife *f* whistle
Trilogie [triloˈgiː] *f* trilogy
Trimester [triˈmɛstər] (**-s, -**) *nt* term
Trimm-Aktion *f* keep-fit campaign
Trimm-dich-Pfad *m* keep-fit trail
trimmen *vt* (*Hund*) to trim; (*umg: Mensch, Tier*) to
  teach, train ▷ *vr* to keep fit
trinkbar *adj* drinkable
trinken ['trɪŋkən] *unreg vt, vi* to drink
Trinker, in (**-s, -**) *m(f)* drinker
Trink- *zW*: **trinkfest** *adj*: **ich bin nicht**
  sehr trinkfest I can't hold my drink very
  well; **Trinkgeld** *nt* tip; **Trinkhalle** *f* (*Kiosk*)
  refreshment kiosk; **Trinkhalm** *m* (drinking)
  straw; **Trinkmilch** *f* milk; **Trinkspruch** *m*
  toast; **Trinkwasser** *nt* drinking water
Trio ['triːo] (**-s, -s**) *nt* trio
trippeln ['trɪpəln] *vi* to toddle
Tripper ['trɪpər] (**-s, -**) *m* gonorrhoea (*Brit*),
  gonorrhea (*US*)
trist [trɪst] *adj* dreary, dismal; (*Farbe*) dull
tritt [trɪt] *vb siehe* **treten**
Tritt (**-(e)s, -e**) *m* step; (*Fußtritt*) kick
Trittbrett *nt* (*Eisenb*) step; (*Aut*) running board
Trittleiter *f* stepladder
Triumph [triˈʊmf] (**-(e)s, -e**) *m* triumph;
  Triumphbogen *m* triumphal arch
triumphieren [triʊmˈfiːrən] *vi* to triumph;
  (*jubeln*) to exult
trivial [triviˈaːl] *adj* trivial; **Trivialliteratur** *f*
  light fiction
trocken ['trɔkən] *adj* dry; **sich ~ rasieren**
  to use an electric razor; **Trockenautomat**
  m tumble dryer; **Trockendock** *nt* dry dock;
  Trockeneis *nt* dry ice; **Trockenelement** *nt* dry
  cell; **Trockenhaube** *f* hair-dryer; **Trockenheit**
  f dryness; **trockenlegen** *vt* (*Sumpf*) to drain;
  (*Kind*) to put a clean nappy (*Brit*) *od* diaper (*US*)

on; **Trockenmilch** *f* dried milk; **Trockenzeit** *f*
  (*Jahreszeit*) dry season
trocknen *vt, vi* to dry
Trockner (**-s, -**) *m* dryer
Troddel ['trɔdəl] (**-, -n**) *f* tassel
Trödel ['trøːdəl] (**-s**) (*umg*) *m* junk; **Trödelmarkt**
  m flea market
trödeln (*umg*) *vi* to dawdle
Trödler (**-s, -**) *m* secondhand dealer
Trog (**-(e)s, ̈-e**) *m* trough
trog *etc* [troːk] *vb siehe* **trügen**
trollen ['trɔlən] (*umg*) *vr* to push off
Trommel ['trɔməl] (**-, -n**) *f* drum; **die ~ rühren**
  (*fig: umg*) to drum up support; **Trommelfell** *nt*
  eardrum; **Trommelfeuer** *nt* drumfire, heavy
  barrage
trommeln *vt, vi* to drum
Trommelrevolver *m* revolver
Trommelwaschmaschine *f* tumble-action
  washing machine
Trommler, in ['trɔmlər(ɪn)] (**-s, -**) *m(f)*
  drummer
Trompete [trɔmˈpeːtə] (**-, -n**) *f* trumpet
Trompeter (**-s, -**) *m* trumpeter
Tropen ['troːpən] *pl* tropics *pl*; **tropenbeständig**
  adj suitable for the tropics; **Tropenhelm** *m*
  topee, sun helmet
Tropf¹ [trɔpf] (**-(e)s, ̈-e**) (*umg*) *m* rogue; **armer**
  ~ poor devil
Tropf² (**-(e)s**) (*umg*) *m* (*Med: Infusion*) drip (*umg*);
  am ~ hängen to be on a drip
tröpfeln ['trœpfəln] *vi* to drip, trickle
Tropfen (**-s, -**) *m* drop; **ein guter** *od* **edler ~**
  a good wine; **ein ~ auf den heißen Stein**
  (*fig: umg*) a drop in the ocean
tropfen *vt, vi* to drip ▷ *vi unpers*: **es tropft** a few
  raindrops are falling
tropfenweise *adv* in drops
tropfnass *adj* dripping wet
Tropfsteinhöhle *f* stalactite cave
Trophäe [troˈfɛːə] (**-, -n**) *f* trophy
tropisch ['troːpɪʃ] *adj* tropical
Trost [troːst] (**-es**) *m* consolation, comfort;
  trostbedürftig *adj* in need of consolation
trösten ['trøːstən] *vt* to console, comfort
Tröster, in (**-s, -**) *m(f)* comfort(er)
tröstlich *adj* comforting
trost- *zW*: **trostlos** *adj* bleak; (*Verhältnisse*)
  wretched; **Trostpflaster** *nt* (*fig*) consolation;
  Trostpreis *m* consolation prize; **trostreich** *adj*
  comforting
Tröstung ['trøːstʊŋ] *f* comfort, consolation
Trott [trɔt] (**-(e)s, -e**) *m* trot; (*Routine*) routine
Trottel (**-s, -**) (*umg*) *m* fool, dope
trotten *vi* to trot
Trottoir [trɔtoˈaːr] (**-s, -s** *od* **-e**) *nt* (*veraltet*)
  pavement (*Brit*), sidewalk (*US*)
trotz [trɔts] *präp* (+*gen od dat*) in spite of
Trotz (**-es**) *m* pig-headedness; **etw aus ~ tun**
  to do sth just to show them; **jdm zum ~** in
  defiance of sb
Trotzalter *nt* obstinate phase
trotzdem *adv* nevertheless ▷ *konj* although

t

trotzen vi +dat to defy; (der Kälte, dem Klima etc) to withstand; (der Gefahr) to brave; (trotzig sein) to be awkward

trotzig adj defiant; (Kind) difficult, awkward

Trotzkopf m obstinate child

Trotzreaktion f fit of pique

trüb [try:p] adj dull; (Flüssigkeit, Glas) cloudy; (fig) gloomy; **~e Tasse** (umg) drip

Trubel ['tru:bəl] (**-s**) m hurly-burly

trüben ['try:bən] vt to cloud ▷ vr to become clouded

Trübheit f dullness; cloudiness; gloom

Trübsal (**-, -e**) f distress; **~ blasen** (umg) to mope

trüb- zW: **trübselig** adj sad, melancholy; **Trübsinn** m depression; **trübsinnig** adj depressed, gloomy

trudeln ['tru:dəln] vi (Aviat) to (go into a) spin

Trüffel ['trʏfəl] (**-, -n**) f truffle

Trug (**-(e)s**) m (liter) deception; (der Sinne) illusion

trug etc [tru:k] vb siehe **tragen**

trügen ['try:gən] unreg vt to deceive ▷ vi to be deceptive; **wenn mich nicht alles trügt** unless I am very much mistaken

trügerisch adj deceptive

Trugschluss ['tru:gʃlʊs] m false conclusion

Truhe ['tru:ə] (**-, -n**) f chest

Trümmer ['trʏmər] pl wreckage sing; (Bautrümmer) ruins pl; **Trümmerfeld** nt expanse of rubble od ruins; (fig) scene of devastation; **Trümmerfrauen** pl (German) women who cleared away the rubble after the war; **Trümmerhaufen** m heap of rubble

Trumpf [trʊmpf] (**-(e)s, ⁻e**) m (lit, fig) trump; **trumpfen** vt, vi to trump

Trunk [trʊŋk] (**-(e)s, ⁻e**) m drink

trunken adj intoxicated; **Trunkenbold** (**-(e)s, -e**) m drunkard; **Trunkenheit** f intoxication; **Trunkenheit am Steuer** drink-driving

Trunksucht f alcoholism

Trupp [trʊp] (**-s, -s**) m troop

Truppe (**-, -n**) f troop; (Waffengattung) force; (Schauspieltruppe) troupe; **nicht von der schnellen ~ sein** (umg) to be slow

Truppen pl troops pl; **Truppenabbau** m cutback in troop numbers; **Truppenführer** m (military) commander; **Truppenteil** m unit; **Truppenübungsplatz** m training area

Trust [trast] (**-(e)s, -e** od **-s**) m trust

Truthahn ['tru:tha:n] m turkey

Tschad [tʃat] (**-s**) m: **der ~** Chad

Tscheche ['tʃɛçə] (**-n, -n**) m, **Tschechin** f Czech

tschechisch adj Czech; **die T~e Republik** the Czech Republic

Tschechoslowakei [tʃɛçoslova:'kai] f (früher): **die ~** Czechoslovakia

tschüss [tʃʏs] (umg) interj cheerio (Brit), so long (US)

T-Shirt ['ti:ʃə:t] (**-s, -s**) nt T-shirt

TU (**-**) f abk (= technische Universität) ≈ polytechnic

Tuba ['tu:ba] (**-, Tuben**) f (Mus) tuba

Tube ['tu:bə] (**-, -n**) f tube

Tuberkulose [tubɛrku'lo:zə] (**-, -n**) f tuberculosis

Tuch [tu:x] (**-(e)s, ⁻er**) nt cloth; (Halstuch) scarf; (Kopftuch) (head)scarf; (Handtuch) towel; **Tuchfühlung** f physical contact

tüchtig ['tʏçtɪç] adj efficient; (fähig) able, capable; (umg: kräftig) good, sound; **etwas T~es lernen/werden** (umg) to get a proper training/job; **Tüchtigkeit** f efficiency; ability

Tücke ['tʏkə] (**-, -n**) f (Arglist) malice; (Trick) trick; (Schwierigkeit) difficulty, problem; **seine ~n haben** to be temperamental

tückisch adj treacherous; (böswillig) malicious

tüfteln ['tʏftəln] (umg) vi to puzzle; (basteln) to fiddle about

Tugend ['tu:gənt] (**-, -en**) f virtue; **tugendhaft** adj virtuous

Tüll [tʏl] (**-s, -e**) m tulle

Tülle (**-, -n**) f spout

Tulpe ['tʊlpə] (**-, -n**) f tulip

tummeln ['tʊməln] vr to romp (about); (sich beeilen) to hurry

Tummelplatz m play area; (fig) hotbed

Tumor ['tu:mɔr] (**-s, -e**) m tumour (Brit), tumor (US)

Tümpel ['tʏmpəl] (**-s, -**) m pond

Tumult [tu'mʊlt] (**-(e)s, -e**) m tumult

tun [tu:n] unreg vt (machen) to do; (legen) to put ▷ vi to act ▷ vr: **es tut sich etwas/viel** something/a lot is happening; **jdm etw ~** to do sth to sb; **etw tut es auch** sth will do; **das tut nichts** that doesn't matter; **das tut nichts zur Sache** that's neither here nor there; **du kannst ~ und lassen, was du willst** you can do as you please; **so ~, als ob** to act as if; **zu ~ haben** (beschäftigt sein) to be busy, have things od something to do

Tünche ['tʏnçə] (**-, -n**) f whitewash

tünchen vt to whitewash

Tunesien [tu'ne:ziən] (**-s**) nt Tunisia

Tunesier, in (**-s, -**) m(f) Tunisian

tunesisch adj Tunisian

Tunfisch m = **Thunfisch**

Tunke ['tʊŋkə] (**-, -n**) f sauce

tunken vt to dip, dunk

tunlichst ['tu:nlɪçst] adv if at all possible; **~ bald** as soon as possible

Tunnel ['tʊnəl] (**-s, -s** od **-**) m tunnel

Tunte ['tʊntə] (**-, -n**) (pej: umg) f fairy (pej)

Tüpfel ['tʏpfəl] (**-s, -**) m dot; **Tüpfelchen** nt (small) dot

tüpfeln ['tʏpfəln] vt to dab

tupfen ['tʊpfən] vt to dab; (mit Farbe) to dot; **Tupfen** (**-s, -**) m dot, spot

Tupfer (**-s, -**) m swab

Tür [ty:r] (**-, -en**) f door; **an die ~ gehen** to answer the door; **zwischen ~ und Angel** in passing; **Weihnachten steht vor der ~** (fig) Christmas is just around the corner; **mit der ~ ins Haus fallen** (umg) to blurt it od things out; **Türangel** f (door) hinge

Turbine [tʊr'bi:nə] f turbine

turbulent [tʊrbu'lɛnt] adj turbulent

Türke ['tʏrkə] (**-n, -n**) *m* Turk
Türkei [tʏr'kaɪ] *f*: **die ~** Turkey
Türkin *f* Turk
Türkis [tʏr'kiːs] (**-es, -e**) *m* turquoise; **türkis** *adj* turquoise
türkisch *adj* Turkish
Türklinke *f* door handle
Turm [tʊrm] (**-(e)s, -̈e**) *m* tower; (*Kirchturm*) steeple; (*Sprungturm*) diving platform; (*Schach*) castle, rook
türmen ['tʏrmən] *vr* to tower up ▷ *vt* to heap up ▷ *vi* (*umg*) to scarper, bolt
Turmuhr *f* clock (on a tower); (*Kirchturmuhr*) church clock
Turnanzug *m* gym costume
turnen ['tʊrnən] *vi* to do gymnastic exercises; (*herumklettern*) to climb about; (*Kind*) to romp ▷ *vt* to perform; **Turnen** (**-s**) *nt* gymnastics *sing*; (*Sch*) physical education, P.E.
Turner, in (**-s, -**) *m(f)* gymnast
Turnhalle *f* gym(nasium)
Turnhose *f* gym shorts *pl*
Turnier [tʊr'niːr] (**-s, -e**) *nt* tournament
Turn- *zW*: **Turnlehrer, in** *m(f)* gym *od* PE teacher; **Turnschuh** *m* gym shoe; **Turnstunde** *f* gym *od* PE lesson
Turnus ['tʊrnʊs] (**-, -se**) *m* rota; **im ~** in rotation
Turnverein *m* gymnastics club
Turnzeug *nt* gym kit
Türöffner *m* buzzer
turteln ['tʊrtəln] (*umg*) *vi* to bill and coo; (*fig*) to whisper sweet nothings
Tusch [tʊʃ] (**-(e)s, -e**) *m* (*Mus*) flourish
Tusche ['tʊʃə] (**-, -n**) *f* Indian ink
tuscheln ['tʊʃəln] *vt, vi* to whisper
Tuschkasten *m* paintbox
Tussi ['tʊsɪ] (**-, -s**) (*umg*) *f* (*Frau, Freundin*) bird (*Brit*), chick (*US*)

tust [tuːst] *vb siehe* **tun**
tut [tuːt] *vb siehe* **tun**
Tüte ['tyːtə] (**-, -n**) *f* bag; **in die ~ blasen** (*umg*) to be breathalyzed; **das kommt nicht in die ~!** (*umg*) no way!
tuten ['tuːtən] *vi* (*Aut*) to hoot (*Brit*), honk (*US*); **von T~ und Blasen keine Ahnung haben** (*umg*) not to have a clue
TÜV [tʏf] *m abk* (= *Technischer Überwachungs-Verein*) ≈ MOT (*Brit*); **durch den ~ kommen** (*Aut*) to pass its test *od* MOT (*Brit*); *see culture note*

   TÜV

   The TÜV (Technischer Überwachungsverein) is the organization responsible for checking the safety of machinery, particularly vehicles. Cars over three years old have to be examined every two years for their safety and for their exhaust emissions. The TÜV is the German equivalent of the MOT.

TV (**-**) *nt abk* (= *Television*) TV ▷ *m abk* = **Turnverein**
Twen [tvɛn] (**-(s), -s**) *m person in his/her twenties*
Twitter® ['tvɪtər] *nt* Twitter®
Typ [tyːp] (**-s, -en**) *m* type
Type (**-, -n**) *f* (*Typ*) type
Typhus ['tyːfʊs] (**-**) *m* typhoid (fever)
typisch ['tyːpɪʃ] *adj*: **~ (für)** typical (of)
Tyrann [ty'ran] (**-en, -en**) *m(f)* tyrant
Tyrannei [tyra'naɪ] *f* tyranny
Tyrannin *f* tyrant
tyrannisch *adj* tyrannical
tyrannisieren [tyrani'ziːrən] *vt* to tyrannize
tyrrhenisch [ty're:nɪʃ] *adj* Tyrrhenian; **T~es Meer** Tyrrhenian Sea

Uu

U, u [u:] *nt* U, u; **U wie Ulrich** = U for Uncle
u. *abk* = **und**
u. a. *abk* (= *und andere(s)*) and others; (= *unter anderem*) amongst other things
u. Ä. *abk* (= *und Ähnliche(s)*) and similar
u. A. w. g. *abk* (= *um Antwort wird gebeten*) R.S.V.P.
U-Bahn ['u:ba:n] *f abk* (= *Untergrundbahn*) underground (*Brit*), subway (*US*)
übel ['y:bəl] *adj* bad; **jdm ist ~** sb feels sick; **~ gelaunt** bad-tempered, sullen; **jdm eine Bemerkung** *etc* **~ nehmen** to be offended at sb's remark *etc*; *siehe auch* **übelwollend**; **Übel** (**-s, -**) *nt* evil; (*Krankheit*) disease; **zu allem Übel ...** to make matters worse ...; **Übelkeit** *f* nausea; **Übelstand** *m* bad state of affairs; **Übeltäter** *m* wrongdoer; **übelwollend** *adj* malevolent
üben ['y:bən] *vt, vi, vr* to practise (*Brit*), practice (*US*); (*Gedächtnis, Muskeln*) to exercise; **Kritik an etw** *dat* **~** to criticize sth

⊙ SCHLÜSSELWORT

über ['y:bər] *präp +dat* **1** (*räumlich*) over, above; **zwei Grad über null** two degrees above zero
2 (*zeitlich*) over; **über der Arbeit einschlafen** to fall asleep over one's work
▷ *präp +akk* **1** (*räumlich*) over; (*hoch über*) above; (*quer über*) across; **er lachte über das ganze Gesicht** he was beaming all over his face; **Macht über jdn haben** to have power over sb
2 (*zeitlich*) over; **über Weihnachten** over Christmas; **über kurz oder lang** sooner or later
3 (*auf dem Wege*) via; **nach Köln über Aachen** to Cologne via Aachen; **ich habe es über die Auskunft erfahren** I found out from information
4 (*betreffend*) about; **ein Buch über ...** a book about *od* on ...; **über jdn/etw lachen** to laugh about *od* at sb/sth; **ein Scheck über 200 Euro** a cheque for 200 euros
5: Fehler über Fehler mistake after mistake
▷ *adv* **1** (*mehr als*) over, more than; **Kinder über 12 Jahren** children over *od* above 12 years of age; **sie liebt ihn über alles** she loves him more than anything
2: über und über over and over; **den ganzen**

Tag/die ganze Zeit über all day long/all the time; **jdm in etw** *dat* **über sein** to be superior to sb in sth

überall [y:bər'|al] *adv* everywhere; **überallhin** *adv* everywhere
überaltert [y:bər'|altərt] *adj* obsolete
Überangebot ['y:bər|angəbo:t] *nt:* **~ (an +***dat***)** surplus (of)
überanstrengen [y:bər'|anʃtrɛŋən] *vt untr* to overexert ▷ *vr untr* to overexert o.s.
überantworten [y:bər'|antvɔrtən] *vt untr* to hand over, deliver (up)
überarbeiten [y:bər'|arbaɪtən] *vt untr* to revise, rework ▷ *vr untr* to overwork (o.s.)
überaus ['y:bər|aus] *adv* exceedingly
überbacken [y:bər'bakən] *unreg vt untr* to put in the oven/under the grill
Überbau ['y:bərbau] *m* (*Gebäude, Philosophie*) superstructure
überbeanspruchen ['y:bərbə|anʃpruxən] *vt untr* (*Menschen, Körper, Maschine*) to overtax
überbelichten ['y:bərbəlıçtən] *vt untr* (*Phot*) to overexpose
Überbesetzung ['y:bərbəzɛtsʊŋ] *f* overmanning
überbewerten ['y:bərbəve:rtən] *vt untr* (*fig*) to overrate; (*Äußerungen*) to attach too much importance to
überbieten [y:bər'bi:tən] *unreg vt untr* to outbid; (*übertreffen*) to surpass; (*Rekord*) to break ▷ *vr untr:* **sich in etw** *dat* **(gegenseitig) ~** to vie with each other in sth
Überbleibsel ['y:bərblaɪpsəl] (**-s, -**) *nt* residue, remainder
Überblick ['y:bərblɪk] *m* view; (*fig: Darstellung*) survey, overview; (*Fähigkeit*): **~ (über +***akk***)** overall view (of), grasp (of); **den ~ verlieren** to lose track (of things); **sich** *dat* **einen ~ verschaffen** to get a general idea
überblicken [y:bər'blɪkən] *vt untr* to survey; (*fig*) to see; (: *Lage etc*) to grasp
überbringen [y:bər'brɪŋən] *unreg vt untr* to deliver, hand over
Überbringer(-s, -) *m* bearer
Überbringung *f* delivery
überbrücken [y:bər'brʏkən] *vt untr* to bridge
Überbrückung *f:* **100 Euro zur ~** 100 euros to

tide me/him *etc* over
Überbrückungskredit *m* bridging loan
überbuchen ['y:bərbu:xən] *vt* to overbook
überdauern [y:bər'dauərn] *vt untr* to outlast
überdenken [y:bər'dɛŋkən] *unreg vt untr* to think over
überdies [y:bər'di:s] *adv* besides
überdimensional ['y:bərdimɛnziona:l] *adj* oversize
Überdosis ['y:bərdo:zɪs] *f* overdose, OD (*umg*); (*zu große Zumessung*) excessive amount
überdrehen [y:bər'dre:ən] *vt untr* (*Uhr etc*) to overwind
überdreht *adj*: ~ **sein** (*fig*) to be hyped up, be overexcited
Überdruck ['y:bərdrʊk] *m* (*Tech*) excess pressure
Überdruss ['y:bərdrʊs] (**-es**) *m* weariness; **bis zum** ~ ad nauseam
überdrüssig ['y:bərdrʏsɪç] *adj +gen* tired of, sick of
überdurchschnittlich ['y:bərdʊrçʃnɪtlɪç] *adj* above-average ⊳ *adv* exceptionally
übereifrig ['y:bər|aɪfrɪç] *adj* overzealous
übereignen [y:bər'|aɪgnən] *vt untr*: **jdm etw** ~ (*geh*) to make sth over to sb
übereilen [y:bər'|aɪlən] *vt untr* to hurry
übereilt *adj* (over)hasty
übereinander [y:bər|aɪ'nandər] *adv* one upon the other; (*sprechen*) about each other
übereinanderschlagen *unreg vt* (*Arme*) to fold; (*Beine*) to cross
übereinkommen [y:bər'|aɪnkɔmən] *unreg vi* to agree
Übereinkunft [y:bər'|aɪnkʊnft] (**-, -künfte**) *f* agreement
übereinstimmen [y:bər'|aɪnʃtɪmən] *vi* to agree; (*Angaben, Messwerte etc*) to tally; (*mit Tatsachen*) to fit
Übereinstimmung *f* agreement
überempfindlich ['y:bər|ɛmpfɪntlɪç] *adj* hypersensitive
überfahren¹ ['y:bərfa:rən] *unreg vt* to take across ⊳ *vi* to cross, go across
überfahren² [y:bər'fa:rən] *unreg vt untr* (*Aut*) to run over; (*fig*) to walk all over
Überfahrt ['y:bərfa:rt] *f* crossing
Überfall ['y:bərfal] *m* (*Banküberfall, Mil*) raid; (*auf jdn*) assault
überfallen [y:bər'falən] *unreg vt untr* to attack; (*Bank*) to raid; (*besuchen*) to drop in on, descend (up)on
überfällig ['y:bərfɛlɪç] *adj* overdue
Überfallkommando *nt* flying squad
überfliegen [y:bər'fli:gən] *unreg vt untr* to fly over, overfly; (*Buch*) to skim through
Überflieger *m* (*fig*) high-flier
überflügeln [y:bər'fly:gəln] *vt untr* to outdo
Überfluss ['y:bərflʊs] *m*: ~ **(an** +*dat*) (*super*) abundance (of), excess (of); **zu allem** *od* **zum** ~ (*unnötigerweise*) superfluously; (*obendrein*) to crown it all (*umg*); **Überflussgesellschaft** *f* affluent society

überflüssig ['y:bərflʏsɪç] *adj* superfluous
überfluten [y:bər'flu:tən] *vt untr* (*lit*) to flood; (*fig*) to flood, inundate
überfordern [y:bər'fɔrdərn] *vt untr* to demand too much of; (*Kräfte etc*) to overtax
überfragt [y:bər'fra:kt] *adj*: **da bin ich** ~ there you've got me, you've got me there
überführen¹ ['y:bərfy:rən] *vt* to transfer; (*Leiche etc*) to transport
überführen² [y:bər'fy:rən] *vt untr* (*Täter*) to have convicted
Überführung *f* (*siehe vbs*) transfer; transport; conviction; (*Brücke*) bridge, overpass
überfüllt [y:bər'fʏlt] *adj* overcrowded; (*Kurs*) oversubscribed
Übergabe ['y:bərga:bə] *f* handing over; (*Mil*) surrender
Übergang ['y:bərgaŋ] *m* crossing; (*Wandel, Überleitung*) transition
Übergangs- *zW*: **Übergangserscheinung** *f* transitory phenomenon; **Übergangsfinanzierung** *f* (*Fin*) accommodation; **übergangslos** *adj* without a transition; **Übergangslösung** *f* provisional solution, stopgap; **Übergangsstadium** *nt* state of transition; **Übergangszeit** *f* transitional period
übergeben [y:bər'ge:bən] *unreg vt untr* to hand over; (*Mil*) to surrender ⊳ *vr untr* to be sick; **dem Verkehr** ~ to open to traffic
übergehen¹ ['y:bərge:ən] *unreg vi* (*Besitz*) to pass; (*zum Feind etc*) to go over, defect; (*überwechseln*): **(zu etw)** ~ to go on (to sth); ~ **in** +*akk* to turn into
übergehen² [y:bər'ge:ən] *unreg vt untr* to pass over, omit
übergeordnet ['y:bərgə|ɔrdnət] *adj* (*Behörde*) higher
Übergepäck ['y:bərgəpɛk] *nt* excess baggage
übergeschnappt ['y:bərgəʃnapt] (*umg*) *adj* crazy
Übergewicht ['y:bərgəvɪçt] *nt* excess weight; (*fig*) preponderance
übergießen [y:bər'gi:sən] *unreg vt untr* to pour over; (*Braten*) to baste
überglücklich ['y:bərglʏklɪç] *adj* overjoyed
übergreifen ['y:bərgraɪfən] *unreg vi*: ~ **(auf** +*akk*) (*auf Rechte etc*) to encroach (on); (*Feuer, Streik, Krankheit etc*) to spread (to); **ineinander** ~ to overlap
übergroß ['y:bərgro:s] *adj* outsize, huge
Übergröße ['y:bərgrø:sə] *f* oversize
überhaben ['y:bərha:bən] *unreg* (*umg*) *vt* to be fed up with
überhandnehmen [y:bər'hant-] *unreg vi* to gain the ascendancy
überhängen ['y:bərhɛŋən] *unreg vi* to overhang
überhäufen [y:bər'hɔyfən] *vt untr*: **jdn mit Geschenken/Vorwürfen** ~ to heap presents/ reproaches on sb
überhaupt [y:bər'haupt] *adv* at all; (*im Allgemeinen*) in general; (*besonders*) especially; ~ **nicht** not at all; **wer sind Sie** ~? who do you

u

think you are?

überheblich [y:bər'he:plɪç] *adj* arrogant; **Überheblichkeit** *f* arrogance

überhöht [y:bər'hø:t] *adj* (*Forderungen, Preise*) exorbitant, excessive

überholen [y:bər'ho:lən] *vt untr* to overtake; (*Tech*) to overhaul

Überholspur *f* overtaking lane

überholt *adj* out-of-date, obsolete

Überholverbot [y:bər'ho:lfɛrbo:t] *nt* overtaking (*Brit*) *od* passing ban

überhören [y:bər'hø:rən] *vt untr* to not hear; (*absichtlich*) to ignore; **das möchte ich überhört haben!** (I'll pretend) I didn't hear that!

Über-Ich, Überich ['y:bər|ɪç] (**-s**) *nt* superego

überirdisch ['y:bər|ɪrdɪʃ] *adj* supernatural, unearthly

überkapitalisieren ['y:bərkapitali'zi:rən] *vt untr* to overcapitalize

überkochen ['y:bərkɔxən] *vi* to boil over

überkompensieren ['y:bərkɔmpɛnzi:rən] *vt untr* to overcompensate for

überladen [y:bər'ladən] *unreg vt untr* to overload ▷ *adj* (*fig*) cluttered

überlassen [y:bər'lasən] *unreg vt untr:* **jdm etw ~** to leave sth to sb ▷ *vr untr:* **sich einer Sache** *dat* **~** to give o.s. over to sth; **das bleibt Ihnen ~** that's up to you; **jdn sich** *dat* **selbst ~** to leave sb to his/her own devices

überlasten [y:bər'lastən] *vt untr* to overload; (*jdn*) to overtax

überlaufen¹ ['y:bərlaʊfən] *unreg vi* (*Flüssigkeit*) to flow over; (*zum Feind etc*) to go over, defect

überlaufen² [y:bər'laʊfən] *unreg vt untr* (*Schauer etc*) to come over ▷ *adj* overcrowded; **~ sein** to be inundated *od* besieged

Überläufer ['y:bərlɔʏfər] *m* deserter

überleben [y:bər'le:bən] *vt untr* to survive

Überlebende, r *f(m)* survivor

überlebensgroß *adj* larger-than-life

überlegen [y:bər'le:gən] *vt untr* to consider ▷ *adj* superior; **ich habe es mir anders** *od* **noch einmal überlegt** I've changed my mind; **Überlegenheit** *f* superiority

Überlegung *f* consideration, deliberation

überleiten ['y:bərlaɪtən] *vt* (*Abschnitt etc*): **~ in** +*akk* to link up with

überlesen [y:bər'le:zən] *unreg vt untr* (*übersehen*) to overlook, miss

überliefern [y:bər'li:fərn] *vt untr* to hand down, transmit

Überlieferung *f* tradition; **schriftliche ~en** (written) records

überlisten [y:bər'lɪstən] *vt untr* to outwit

überm ['y:bərm] = **über dem**

Übermacht ['y:bərmaxt] *f* superior force, superiority

übermächtig ['y:bərmɛçtɪç] *adj* superior (in strength); (*Gefühl etc*) overwhelming

übermannen [y:bər'manən] *vt untr* to overcome

Übermaß ['y:bərma:s] *nt:* **~ (an** +*dat*) excess (of)

übermäßig ['y:bərmɛ:sɪç] *adj* excessive

Übermensch ['y:bərmɛnʃ] *m* superman; **übermenschlich** *adj* superhuman

übermitteln [y:bər'mɪtəln] *vt untr* to convey

übermorgen ['y:bərmɔrgən] *adv* the day after tomorrow

Übermüdung [y:bər'my:dʊŋ] *f* overtiredness

Übermut ['y:bərmu:t] *m* exuberance

übermütig ['y:bərmy:tɪç] *adj* exuberant, high-spirited; **~ werden** to get overconfident

übernächste, r, s [y:bərnɛ:çstə(r, s)] *adj* next ... but one; (*Woche, Jahr etc*) after next

übernachten [y:bər'naxtən] *vi untr:* **(bei jdm) ~** to spend the night (at sb's place)

übernächtigt [y:bər'nɛçtɪçt] *adj* sleepy, tired

Übernachtung *f:* **~ mit Frühstück** bed and breakfast

Übernahme ['y:bərna:mə] (**-, -n**) *f* taking over *od* on; (*von Verantwortung*) acceptance; **Übernahmeangebot** *nt* takeover bid

übernatürlich ['y:bərnaty:rlɪç] *adj* supernatural

übernehmen [y:bər'ne:mən] *unreg vt untr* to take on, accept; (*Amt, Geschäft*) to take over ▷ *vr untr* to take on too much; (*sich überanstrengen*) to overdo it

überparteilich ['y:bərpartaɪlɪç] *adj* (*Zeitung*) independent; (*Amt, Präsident etc*) above party politics

überprüfen [y:bər'pry:fən] *vt untr* to examine, check; (*Pol: jdn*) to screen

Überprüfung *f* examination

überqueren [y:bər'kve:rən] *vt untr* to cross

überragen [y:bər'ra:gən] *vt untr* to tower above; (*fig*) to surpass

überragend *adj* outstanding; (*Bedeutung*) paramount

überraschen [y:bər'raʃən] *vt untr* to surprise

Überraschung *f* surprise

überreden [y:bər're:dən] *vt untr* to persuade; **jdn zu etw ~** to talk sb into sth

Überredungskunst *f* powers *pl* of persuasion

überregional ['y:bərregiona:l] *adj* national; (*Zeitung, Sender*) nationwide

überreichen [y:bər'raɪçən] *vt untr* to hand over; (*feierlich*) to present

überreichlich *adj* (more than) ample

überreizt [y:bər'raɪtst] *adj* overwrought

Überreste ['y:bərrɛstə] *pl* remains *pl*, remnants *pl*

überrumpeln [y:bər'rʊmpəln] *vt untr* to take by surprise; (*umg: überwältigen*) to overpower

überrunden [y:bər'rʊndən] *vt untr* (*Sport*) to lap

übers ['y:bərs] = **über das**

übersättigen [y:bər'zɛtɪgən] *vt untr* to satiate

Überschall- ['y:bərʃal] *in zw* supersonic; **Überschallflugzeug** *nt* supersonic jet; **Überschallgeschwindigkeit** *f* supersonic speed

überschatten [y:bər'ʃatən] *vt untr* to overshadow

überschätzen [y:bər'ʃɛtsən] *vt untr, vr untr* to overestimate

überschaubar [y:bər'ʃaʊba:r] *adj* (*Plan*) easily comprehensible, clear

überschäumen ['y:bərʃɔʏmən] *vi* to froth over; (*fig*) to bubble over

überschlafen [y:bər'ʃla:fən] *unreg vt untr* (*Problem*) to sleep on

Überschlag ['y:bərʃla:k] *m* (*Fin*) estimate; (*Sport*) somersault

überschlagen¹ [y:bər'ʃla:gən] *unreg vt untr* (*berechnen*) to estimate; (*auslassen: Seite*) to omit ▷ *vr untr* to somersault; (*Stimme*) to crack; (*Aviat*) to loop the loop ▷ *adj* lukewarm, tepid

überschlagen² ['y:bərʃla:gən] *unreg vt* (*Beine*) to cross; (*Arme*) to fold ▷ *vi* (*Hilfsverb sein: Wellen*) to break; (: *Funken*) to flash over; **in etw** *akk* **~** (*Stimmung etc*) to turn into sth

überschnappen ['y:bərʃnapən] *vi* (*Stimme*) to crack; (*umg: Mensch*) to flip one's lid

überschneiden [y:bər'ʃnaɪdən] *unreg vr untr* (*lit, fig*) to overlap; (*Linien*) to intersect

überschreiben [y:bər'ʃraɪbən] *unreg vt untr* to provide with a heading; (*Comput*) to overwrite; **jdm etw ~** to transfer *od* make over sth to sb

überschreiten [y:bər'ʃraɪtən] *unreg vt untr* to cross over; (*fig*) to exceed; (*verletzen*) to transgress

Überschrift ['y:bərʃrɪft] *f* heading, title

überschuldet [y:bər'ʃʊldət] *adj* heavily in debt; (*Grundstück*) heavily mortgaged

Überschuss ['y:bərʃʊs] *m*: **~ (an** +*dat*) surplus (of)

überschüssig ['y:bərʃʏsɪç] *adj* surplus, excess

überschütten [y:bər'ʃʏtən] *vt untr*: **jdn/etw mit etw ~** (*lit*) to pour sth over sb/sth; **jdn mit etw ~** (*fig*) to shower sb with sth

Überschwang ['y:bərʃvaŋ] *m* exuberance

überschwänglich ['y:bərʃvɛŋlɪç] *adj* effusive; **Überschwänglichkeit** *f* effusion

überschwappen ['y:bərʃvapən] *vi* to splash over

überschwemmen [y:bər'ʃvɛmən] *vt untr* to flood

Überschwemmung *f* flood

überschwenglich ['y:bərʃvɛŋlɪç] *adj siehe* **überschwänglich**

Übersee ['y:bərze:] *f*: **nach/in ~** overseas

überseeisch *adj* overseas

übersehbar [y:bər'ze:ba:r] *adj* (*fig: Folgen, Zusammenhänge etc*) clear; (*Kosten, Dauer etc*) assessable

übersehen [y:bər'ze:ən] *unreg vt untr* to look (out) over; (*fig: Folgen*) to see, get an overall view of; (: *nicht beachten*) to overlook

übersenden [y:bər'zɛndən] *unreg vt untr* to send, forward

übersetzen¹ [y:bər'zɛtsən] *vt untr, vi untr* to translate

übersetzen² ['y:bərzɛtsən] *vi* (*Hilfsverb sein*) to cross

Übersetzer, in [y:bər'zɛtsər(ɪn)] (**-s, -**) *m(f)* translator

Übersetzung [y:bər'zɛtsʊŋ] *f* translation; (*Tech*) gear ratio

Übersicht ['y:bərzɪçt] *f* overall view; (*Darstellung*) survey; **die ~ verlieren** to lose track; **übersichtlich** *adj* clear; (*Gelände*) open; **Übersichtlichkeit** *f* clarity, lucidity

übersiedeln¹ ['y:bərzi:dəln] *vi* to move

übersiedeln² [y:bər'zi:dəln] *vi untr* to move

überspannen [y:bər'ʃpanən] *vt untr* (*zu sehr spannen*) to overstretch; (*überdecken*) to cover

überspannt *adj* eccentric; (*Idee*) wild, crazy; **Überspanntheit** *f* eccentricity

überspielen [y:bər'ʃpi:lən] *vt untr* (*verbergen*) to cover (up); (*übertragen: Aufnahme*) to transfer

überspitzt [y:bər'ʃpɪtst] *adj* exaggerated

überspringen [y:bər'ʃprɪŋən] *unreg vt untr* to jump over; (*fig*) to skip

übersprudeln ['y:bərʃpru:dəln] *vi* to bubble over

überstehen¹ [y:bər'ʃte:ən] *unreg vt untr* to overcome, get over; (*Winter etc*) to survive, get through

überstehen² ['y:bərʃte:ən] *unreg vi* to project

übersteigen [y:bər'ʃtaɪgən] *unreg vt untr* to climb over; (*fig*) to exceed

übersteigert [y:bər'ʃtaɪgərt] *adj* excessive

überstimmen [y:bər'ʃtɪmən] *vt untr* to outvote

überstrapazieren ['y:bərʃtrapatsi:rən] *vt untr* to wear out ▷ *vr* to wear o.s. out

überstreifen ['y:bərʃtraɪfən] *vt*: **(sich** *dat*) **etw ~** to slip sth on

überströmen¹ [y:bər'ʃtrø:mən] *vt untr*: **von Blut überströmt sein** to be streaming with blood

überströmen² ['y:bərʃtrø:mən] *vi* (*lit, fig*): **~ (vor** +*dat*) to overflow (with)

Überstunden [y:bər'ʃtʊndən] *pl* overtime *sing*

überstürzen [y:bər'ʃtʏrtsən] *vt untr* to rush ▷ *vr untr* to follow (one another) in rapid succession

überstürzt *adj* (over)hasty

übertariflich ['y:bərtarifliç] *adj, adv* above the agreed *od* union rate

übertölpeln [y:bər'tœlpln] *vt untr* to dupe

übertönen [y:bər'tø:nən] *vt untr* to drown (out)

Übertrag ['y:bərtra:k] (**-(e)s, -träge**) *m* (*Comm*) amount brought forward

übertragbar [y:bər'tra:kba:r] *adj* transferable; (*Med*) infectious

übertragen [y:bər'tra:gən] *unreg vt untr* to transfer; (*Rundf*) to broadcast; (*anwenden: Methode*) to apply; (*übersetzen*) to render; (*Krankheit*) to transmit ▷ *vr untr* to spread ▷ *adj* figurative; **~ auf** +*akk* to transfer to; to apply to; **sich ~ auf** +*akk* to spread to; **jdm etw ~** to assign sth to sb; (*Verantwortung etc*) to give sb sth *od* sth to sb

Übertragung *f* (*siehe vb*) transference; broadcast; rendering; transmission

übertreffen [y:bər'trɛfən] *unreg vt untr* to surpass

übertreiben [y:bər'traɪbən] *unreg vt untr* to exaggerate; **man kann es auch ~** you can overdo things

Übertreibung *f* exaggeration

u

übertreten[1] [y:bər'tre:tən] *unreg vt untr* to cross; (*Gebot etc*) to break

übertreten[2] ['y:bərtre:tən] *unreg vi* (*über Linie, Gebiet*) to step (over); (*Sport*) to overstep; (*zu anderem Glauben*) to be converted; ~ **(in** +*akk*) *Pol*) to go over (to)

Übertretung [y:bər'tre:tʊŋ] *f* violation, transgression

übertrieben [y:bər'tri:bən] *adj* exaggerated, excessive

Übertritt ['y:bərtrɪt] *m* (*zu anderem Glauben*) conversion; (*bes zu anderer Partei*) defection

übertrumpfen [y:bər'trʊmpfən] *vt untr* to outdo; (*Karten*) to overtrump

übertünchen [y:bər'tʏnçən] *vt untr* to whitewash; (*fig*) to cover up, whitewash

übervölkert [y:bər'fœlkərt] *adj* overpopulated

übervoll ['y:bərfɔl] *adj* overfull

übervorteilen [y:bər'fɔrtaɪlən] *vt untr* to dupe, cheat

überwachen [y:bər'vaxən] *vt untr* to supervise; (*Verdächtigen*) to keep under surveillance

Überwachung *f* supervision; surveillance

überwältigen [y:bər'vɛltɪgən] *vt untr* to overpower

überwältigend *adj* overwhelming

überwechseln ['y:bərvɛksəln] *vi:* ~ **(in** +*akk*) to move (to); (*zu Partei etc*): ~ **(zu)** to go over (to)

überweisen [y:bər'vaɪzən] *unreg vt untr* to transfer; (*Patienten*) to refer

Überweisung *f* transfer; (*von Patient*) referral

überwerfen[1] ['y:bərverfən] *unreg vt* (*Kleidungsstück*) to put on; (*sehr rasch*) to throw on

überwerfen[2] [y:bər'verfən] *unreg vr untr:* **sich (mit jdm)** ~ to fall out (with sb)

überwiegen [y:bər'vi:gən] *unreg vi untr* to predominate

überwiegend *adj* predominant

überwinden [y:bər'vɪndən] *unreg vt untr* to overcome ▷ *vr untr:* **sich ~, etw zu tun** to make an effort to do sth, bring o.s. to do sth

Überwindung *f* overcoming; (*Selbstüberwindung*) effort of will

überwintern [y:bər'vɪntərn] *vi untr* to (spend the) winter; (*umg: Winterschlaf halten*) to hibernate

Überwurf ['y:bərvʊrf] *m* wrap

Überzahl ['y:bərtsa:l] *f* superior numbers *pl*, superiority; **in der** ~ **sein** to be numerically superior

überzählig ['y:bərtsɛ:lɪç] *adj* surplus

überzeugen [y:bər'tsɔygən] *vt untr* to convince

überzeugend *adj* convincing

überzeugt *adj attrib* (*Anhänger etc*) dedicated; (*Vegetarier*) strict; (*Christ, Moslem*) devout

Überzeugung *f* conviction; **zu der ~ gelangen, dass ...** to become convinced that ...

Überzeugungskraft *f* power of persuasion

überziehen[1] ['y:bərtsi:ən] *unreg vt* to put on

überziehen[2] [y:bər'tsi:ən] *unreg vt untr* to cover; (*Konto*) to overdraw; (*Redezeit etc*) to overrun

▷ *vr untr* (*Himmel*) to cloud over; **ein Bett frisch** ~ to change a bed, change the sheets (on a bed)

Überziehungskredit *m* overdraft

überzüchten [y:bər'tsʏçtən] *vt untr* to overbreed

Überzug ['y:bərtsu:k] *m* cover; (*Belag*) coating

üblich ['y:plɪç] *adj* usual; **allgemein ~ sein** to be common practice

U-Boot ['u:bo:t] *nt* U-boat, submarine

übrig ['y:brɪç] *adj* remaining; **die Übrigen** the others; **das Übrige** the rest; **im Übrigen** besides; ~ **bleiben** to remain, be left (over); ~ **lassen** to leave (over); **einiges/ viel zu wünschen ~ lassen** (*umg*) to leave something/a lot to be desired; *siehe auch* **übrighaben**

übrigens ['y:brɪgəns] *adv* besides; (*nebenbei bemerkt*) by the way

übrighaben *unreg vi:* **für jdn etwas ~** (*umg*) to be fond of sb

Übung ['y:bʊŋ] *f* practice; (*Turnübung, Aufgabe etc*) exercise; ~ **macht den Meister** (*Sprichwort*) practice makes perfect

Übungsarbeit *f* (*Sch*) mock test

Übungsplatz *m* training ground; (*Mil*) drill ground

u. d. M. *abk* (= *unter dem Meeresspiegel*) below sea level

ü. d. M. *abk* (= *über dem Meeresspiegel*) above sea level

u. E. *abk* (= *unseres Erachtens*) in our opinion

Ufer ['u:fər] (**-s, -**) *nt* bank; (*Meeresufer*) shore; **Uferbefestigung** *f* embankment

uferlos *adj* endless; (*grenzenlos*) boundless; **ins U-e gehen** (*Kosten*) to go up and up; (*Debatte etc*) to go on forever

UFO, Ufo ['u:fo] (**-(s), -s**) *nt abk* (= *unbekanntes Flugobjekt*) UFO, ufo

Uganda [u'ganda] (**-s**) *nt* Uganda

Ugander, in (**-s, -**) *m(f)* Ugandan

ugandisch *adj* Ugandan

U-Haft ['u:haft] *f abk* = **Untersuchungshaft**

Uhr [u:r] (**-, -en**) *f* clock; (*Armbanduhr*) watch; **wie viel ~ ist es?** what time is it?; **um wie viel ~?** at what time?; **1 ~** 1 o'clock; **20 ~** 8 o'clock, 20.00 (twenty hundred) hours; **Uhrband** *nt* watchstrap; **Uhrengehäuse, Uhrgehäuse** *nt* clock case; watch case; **Uhrkette** *f* watch chain; **Uhrmacher** *m* watchmaker; **Uhrwerk** *nt* (*auch fig*) clockwork mechanism; **Uhrzeiger** *m* hand; **Uhrzeigersinn** *m:* **im Uhrzeigersinn** clockwise; **entgegen dem Uhrzeigersinn** anticlockwise; **Uhrzeit** *f* time (of day)

Uhu ['u:hu] (**-s, -s**) *m* eagle owl

Ukraine [ukra'i:nə] *f* Ukraine

Ukrainer, in [ukra'i:nər(ɪn)] (**-s, -**) *m(f)* Ukrainian

ukrainisch *adj* Ukrainian

UKW *abk* (= *Ultrakurzwelle*) VHF

Ulk [ʊlk] (**-s, -e**) *m* lark

ulkig ['ʊlkɪç] *adj* funny

Ulme ['ʊlmə] (**-, -n**) *f* elm

Ulster ['ʊlstər] (**-s**) nt Ulster

Ultimatum [ʊlti'ma:tʊm] (**-s, Ultimaten**) nt ultimatum; **jdm ein ~ stellen** to give sb an ultimatum

Ultra- zW: **Ultrakurzwelle** f very high frequency; **Ultraleichtflugzeug** nt microlight; **Ultraschall** m (Phys) ultrasound; **ultraviolett** adj ultraviolet

⊙ SCHLÜSSELWORT

um [ʊm] präp +akk **1** (um herum) (a)round; **um Weihnachten** around Christmas; **er schlug um sich** he hit about him

2 (mit Zeitangabe) at; **um acht (Uhr)** at eight (o'clock)

3 (mit Größenangabe) by; **etw um 4 cm kürzen** to shorten sth by 4 cm; **um 10% teurer** 10% more expensive; **um vieles besser** better by far; **um nichts besser** not in the least bit better; siehe auch **umso**

4: **der Kampf um den Titel** the battle for the title; **um Geld spielen** to play for money; **es geht um das Prinzip** it's a question of principle; **Stunde um Stunde** hour after hour; **Auge um Auge** an eye for an eye

▷ präp +gen: **um ... willen** for the sake of ...; **um Gottes willen** for goodness od (stärker) God's sake

▷ konj: **um ... zu** (in order) to ...; **zu klug, um zu ...** too clever to ...; siehe auch **umso**

▷ adv **1** (ungefähr) about; **um (die) 30 Leute** about od around 30 people

2 (vorbei): **die zwei Stunden sind um** the two hours are up

umadressieren ['ʊm|adresi:rən] vt untr to readdress

umändern ['ʊm|ɛndərn] vt to alter

Umänderung f alteration

umarbeiten ['ʊm|arbaɪtən] vt to remodel; (Buch etc) to revise, rework

umarmen [ʊm'armən] vt untr to embrace

Umbau ['ʊmbaʊ] (**-(e)s, -e** od **-ten**) m reconstruction, alteration(s pl)

umbauen ['ʊmbaʊən] vt to rebuild, reconstruct

umbenennen ['ʊmbənɛnən] unreg vt untr to rename

umbesetzen ['ʊmbəzɛtsən] vt untr (Theat) to recast; (Mannschaft) to change; (Posten, Stelle) to find someone else for

umbiegen ['ʊmbi:gən] unreg vt to bend (over)

umbilden ['ʊmbɪldən] vt to reorganize; (Pol: Kabinett) to reshuffle

umbinden¹ ['ʊmbɪndən] unreg vt (Krawatte etc) to put on

umbinden² [ʊm'bɪndən] unreg vt untr: **etw mit etw ~** to tie sth round sth

umblättern ['ʊmblɛtərn] vt to turn over

umblicken ['ʊmblɪkən] vr to look around

umbringen ['ʊmbrɪŋən] unreg vt to kill

Umbruch ['ʊmbrʊx] m radical change; (Typ)
make-up (into page)

umbuchen ['ʊmbu:xən] vi to change one's reservation od flight etc ▷ vt to change

umdenken ['ʊmdɛŋkən] unreg vi to adjust one's views

umdisponieren ['ʊmdɪsponi:rən] vi untr to change one's plans

umdrängen [ʊm'drɛŋən] vt untr to crowd round

umdrehen ['ʊmdre:ən] vt to turn (round); (Hals) to wring ▷ vr to turn (round); **jdm den Arm ~** to twist sb's arm

Umdrehung f turn; (Phys) revolution, rotation

umeinander [ʊm|aɪ'nandər] adv round one another; (füreinander) for one another

umerziehen ['ʊm|ɛrtsi:ən] unreg vt (Pol: euph): **jdn (zu etw) ~** to re-educate sb (to become sth)

umfahren¹ ['ʊmfa:rən] unreg vt to run over

umfahren² [ʊm'fa:rən] unreg vt untr to drive round; (die Welt) to sail round

umfallen ['ʊmfalən] unreg vi to fall down od over; (fig: umg: nachgeben) to give in

Umfang ['ʊmfaŋ] m extent; (von Buch) size; (Reichweite) range; (Fläche) area; (Math) circumference; **in großem ~** on a large scale; **umfangreich** adj extensive; (Buch etc) voluminous

umfassen [ʊm'fasən] vt untr to embrace; (umgeben) to surround; (enthalten) to include

umfassend adj comprehensive; (umfangreich) extensive

Umfeld ['ʊmfɛlt] nt: **zum ~ von etw gehören** to be associated with sth

umformatieren ['ʊmfɔrmati:rən] vt untr (Comput) to reformat

umformen ['ʊmfɔrmən] vi to transform

Umformer (**-s, -**) m (Elek) converter

umformulieren ['ʊmfɔrmuli:rən] vt untr to redraft

Umfrage ['ʊmfra:gə] f poll; **~ halten** to ask around

umfüllen ['ʊmfʏlən] vt to transfer; (Wein) to decant

umfunktionieren ['ʊmfʊŋktsioni:rən] vt untr to convert

Umgang ['ʊmgaŋ] m company; (mit jdm) dealings pl; (Behandlung) dealings pl

umgänglich ['ʊmgɛŋlɪç] adj sociable

Umgangs- zW: **Umgangsformen** pl manners pl; **Umgangssprache** f colloquial language; **umgangssprachlich** adj colloquial

umgeben [ʊm'ge:bən] unreg vt untr to surround

Umgebung f surroundings pl; (Milieu) environment; (Personen) people in one's circle; **in der näheren/weiteren ~ Münchens** on the outskirts/in the environs of Munich

umgehen¹ ['ʊmge:ən] unreg vi to go (a)round; **im Schlosse ~** to haunt the castle; **mit jdm/etw ~ können** to know how to handle sb/sth; **mit jdm grob etc ~** to treat sb roughly etc; **mit Geld sparsam ~** to be careful with one's money

u

umgehen² [ʊmˈɡeːən] *unreg vt untr* to bypass; (*Mil*) to outflank; (*Gesetz, Vorschrift etc*) to circumvent; (*vermeiden*) to avoid

umgehend *adj* immediate

Umgehung *f* (*siehe vb*) bypassing; outflanking; circumvention; avoidance

Umgehungsstraße *f* bypass

umgekehrt [ˈʊmɡəkeːrt] *adj* reverse(d); (*gegenteilig*) opposite ▷ *adv* the other way around; **und ~** and vice versa

umgestalten [ˈʊmɡəʃtaltən] *vt untr* to alter; (*reorganisieren*) to reorganize; (*umordnen*) to rearrange

umgewöhnen [ˈʊmɡəvøːnən] *vr* to readapt

umgraben [ˈʊmɡraːbən] *unreg vt* to dig up

umgruppieren [ˈʊmɡrʊpiːrən] *vt untr* to regroup

Umhang [ˈʊmhaŋ] *m* wrap, cape

umhängen [ˈʊmhɛŋən] *vt* (*Bild*) to hang somewhere else; **jdm etw ~** to put sth on sb

Umhängetasche *f* shoulder bag

umhauen [ˈʊmhaʊən] *vt* to fell; (*fig*) to bowl over

umher [ʊmˈheːr] *adv* about, around; **umhergehen** *unreg vi* to walk about; **umherirren** *vi* to wander around; (*Blick, Augen*) to roam about; **umherreisen** *vi* to travel about; **umherschweifen** *vi* to roam about; **umherziehen** *unreg vi* to wander from place to place

umhinkönnen [ʊmˈhɪnkœnən] *unreg vi*: **ich kann nicht umhin, das zu tun** I can't help doing it

umhören [ˈʊmhøːrən] *vr* to ask around

umkämpfen [ʊmˈkɛmpfən] *vt untr* (*Entscheidung*) to dispute; (*Wahlkreis, Sieg*) to contest

Umkehr [ˈʊmkeːr] (-) *f* turning back; (*Änderung*) change

umkehren *vi* to turn back; (*fig*) to change one's ways ▷ *vt* to turn round, reverse; (*Tasche etc*) to turn inside out; (*Gefäß etc*) to turn upside down

umkippen [ˈʊmkɪpən] *vt* to tip over ▷ *vi* to overturn; (*umg: ohnmächtig werden*) to keel over; (*fig: Meinung ändern*) to change one's mind

umklammern [ʊmˈklamərn] *vt untr* (*mit Händen*) to clasp; (*festhalten*) to cling to

umklappen [ˈʊmklapən] *vt* to fold down

Umkleidekabine [ˈʊmklaɪdəkabiːnə] *f* changing cubicle (*Brit*), dressing room (*US*)

Umkleideraum [ˈʊmklaɪdəraʊm] *m* changing room; (*US: Theat*) dressing room

umknicken [ˈʊmknɪkən] *vt* (*Ast*) to snap; (*Papier*) to fold (over) ▷ *vi*: **mit dem Fuß ~** to twist one's ankle

umkommen [ˈʊmkɔmən] *unreg vi* to die, perish; (*Lebensmittel*) to go bad

Umkreis [ˈʊmkraɪs] *m* neighbourhood (*Brit*), neighborhood (*US*); **im ~ von** within a radius of

umkreisen [ʊmˈkraɪzən] *vt untr* to circle (round); (*Satellit*) to orbit

umkrempeln [ˈʊmkrɛmpəln] *vt* to turn up; (*mehrmals*) to roll up; (*umg: Betrieb*) to shake up

umladen [ˈʊmlaːdən] *unreg vt* to transfer, reload

Umlage [ˈʊmlaːɡə] *f* share of the costs

Umlauf *m* (*Geldumlauf*) circulation; (*von Gestirn*) revolution; (*Schreiben*) circular; **in ~ bringen** to circulate; **Umlaufbahn** *f* orbit

umlaufen [ˈʊmlaʊfən] *unreg vi* to circulate

Umlaufkapital *nt* working capital

Umlaufvermögen *nt* current assets *pl*

Umlaut [ˈʊmlaʊt] *m* umlaut

umlegen [ˈʊmleːɡən] *vt* to put on; (*verlegen*) to move, shift; (*Kosten*) to share out; (*umkippen*) to tip over; (*umg: töten*) to bump off

umleiten [ˈʊmlaɪtən] *vt* to divert

Umleitung *f* diversion

umlernen [ˈʊmlɛrnən] *vi* to learn something new; (*fig*) to adjust one's views

umliegend [ˈʊmliːɡənt] *adj* surrounding

ummelden [ˈʊmmɛldən] *vt, vr*: **jdn/sich ~** to notify (the police of) a change in sb's/one's address

Umnachtung [ʊmˈnaxtʊŋ] *f* mental derangement

umorganisieren [ˈʊm|ɔrɡaniziːrən] *vt untr* to reorganize

umpflanzen [ˈʊmpflantsən] *vt* to transplant

umquartieren [ˈʊmkvartiːrən] *vt untr* to move; (*Truppen*) to requarter

umrahmen [ʊmˈraːmən] *vt untr* to frame

umranden [ʊmˈrandən] *vt untr* to border, edge

umräumen [ˈʊmrɔʏmən] *vt* (*anders anordnen*) to rearrange ▷ *vi* to rearrange things, move things around

umrechnen [ˈʊmrɛçnən] *vt* to convert

Umrechnung *f* conversion

Umrechnungskurs *m* rate of exchange

umreißen [ʊmˈraɪsən] *unreg vt untr* to outline

umrennen [ˈʊmrɛnən] *unreg vt* to (run into and) knock down

umringen [ʊmˈrɪŋən] *vt untr* to surround

Umriss [ˈʊmrɪs] *m* outline

umrühren [ˈʊmryːrən] *vt, vi* to stir

umrüsten [ˈʊmrʏstən] *vt* (*Tech*) to adapt; (*Mil*) to re-equip; **~ auf** +*akk* to adapt to

ums [ʊms] = **um das**

umsatteln [ˈʊmzatəln] (*umg*) *vi* to change one's occupation, switch jobs

Umsatz [ˈʊmzats] *m* turnover; **Umsatzbeteiligung** *f* commission; **Umsatzeinbuße** *f* loss of profit; **Umsatzsteuer** *f* turnover tax

umschalten [ˈʊmʃaltən] *vt* to switch ▷ *vi* to push/pull a lever; (*auf anderen Sender*): **~ (auf** +*akk*) to change over (to); (*Aut*): **~ in** +*akk* to change (*Brit*) *od* shift into; **„wir schalten jetzt um nach Hamburg"** "and now we go over to Hamburg"

Umschalttaste *f* shift key

Umschau *f* look(ing) round; **~ halten nach** to look around for

umschauen [ˈʊmʃaʊən] *vr* to look round

Umschlag [ˈʊmʃlaːk] *m* cover; (*Buchumschlag*)

jacket, cover; (Med) compress; (Briefumschlag) envelope; (Gütermenge) volume of traffic; (Wechsel) change; (von Hose) turn-up (Brit), cuff (US)

umschlagen ['ʊmʃlaːɡən] unreg vi to change; (Naut) to capsize ▷ vt to knock over; (Ärmel) to turn up; (Seite) to turn over; (Waren) to transfer

Umschlag- zW: **Umschlaghafen** m port of transshipment; **Umschlagplatz** m (Comm) distribution centre (Brit) od center (US); **Umschlagseite** f cover page

umschlingen [ʊmˈʃlɪŋən] unreg vt untr (Pflanze) to twine around; (jdn) to embrace

umschreiben¹ ['ʊmʃraɪbən] unreg vt (neu umschreiben) to rewrite; (übertragen) to transfer; **~ auf** +akk to transfer to

umschreiben² [ʊmˈʃraɪbən] unreg vt untr to paraphrase; (abgrenzen) to circumscribe, define

Umschuldung ['ʊmʃʊldʊŋ] f rescheduling (of debts)

umschulen ['ʊmʃuːlən] vt to retrain; (Kind) to send to another school

umschwärmen [ʊmˈʃvɛrmən] vt untr to swarm round; (fig) to surround, idolize

Umschweife ['ʊmʃvaɪfə] pl: **ohne ~** without beating about the bush, straight out

umschwenken ['ʊmʃvɛnkən] vi (Kran) to swing out; (fig) to do an about-turn (Brit) od about-face (US); (Wind) to veer

Umschwung ['ʊmʃvʊŋ] m (Gymnastik) circle; (fig: ins Gegenteil) change (around)

umsegeln [ʊmˈzeːɡəln] vt untr to sail around; (Erde) to circumnavigate

umsehen ['ʊmzeːən] unreg vr to look around od about; (suchen): **sich ~ (nach)** to look out (for); **ich möchte mich nur mal ~** (in Geschäft) I'm just looking

umseitig ['ʊmzaɪtɪç] adv overleaf

umsetzen ['ʊmzɛtsən] vt (Waren) to turn over ▷ vr (Schüler) to change places; **etw in die Tat ~** to translate sth into action

Umsicht ['ʊmzɪçt] f prudence, caution

umsichtig adj prudent, cautious

umsiedeln ['ʊmziːdəln] vt to resettle

Umsiedler, in (-s, -) m(f) resettler

umso ['ʊmzo] konj: **~ besser/schlimmer** so much the better/worse; **~ mehr, als ...** all the more considering ...

umsonst [ʊmˈzɔnst] adv in vain; (gratis) for nothing

umspringen ['ʊmʃprɪŋən] unreg vi to change; **mit jdm ~** to treat sb badly

Umstand ['ʊmʃtant] m circumstance; **Umstände** pl (fig: Schwierigkeiten) fuss sing; **in anderen Umständen sein** to be pregnant; **Umstände machen** to go to a lot of trouble; **den Umständen entsprechend** much as one would expect (under the circumstances); **die näheren Umstände** further details; **unter Umständen** possibly; **mildernde Umstände** (Jur) extenuating circumstances

umständehalber adv owing to circumstances

umständlich ['ʊmʃtɛntlɪç] adj (Methode)

cumbersome, complicated; (Ausdrucksweise, Erklärung) long-winded; (ungeschickt) ponderous; **etw ~ machen** to make heavy weather of (doing) sth

Umstandskleid nt maternity dress

Umstandswort nt adverb

umstehend ['ʊmʃteːənt] adj attrib (umseitig) overleaf; **die U~en** pl the bystanders pl

Umsteigekarte f transfer ticket

umsteigen ['ʊmʃtaɪɡən] unreg vi (Eisenb) to change; (fig: umg): **~ (auf** +akk**)** to change over (to), switch (over) (to)

umstellen¹ ['ʊmʃtɛlən] vt (an anderen Ort) to change round, rearrange; (Tech) to convert ▷ vr: **sich ~ (auf** +akk**)** to adapt o.s. (to)

umstellen² [ʊmˈʃtɛlən] vt untr to surround

Umstellung f change; (Umgewöhnung) adjustment; (Tech) conversion

umstimmen ['ʊmʃtɪmən] vt (Mus) to retune; **jdn ~** to make sb change his mind

umstoßen ['ʊmʃtoːsən] unreg vt (lit) to overturn; (Plan etc) to change, upset

umstritten [ʊmˈʃtrɪtən] adj disputed; (fraglich) controversial

Umsturz ['ʊmʃtʊrts] m overthrow

umstürzen ['ʊmʃtʏrtsən] vt (umwerfen) to overturn ▷ vi to collapse, fall down; (Wagen) to overturn

umstürzlerisch adj revolutionary

Umtausch ['ʊmtaʊʃ] m exchange; **diese Waren sind vom ~ ausgeschlossen** these goods cannot be exchanged

umtauschen vt to exchange

Umtriebe ['ʊmtriːbə] pl machinations pl, intrigues pl

umtun ['ʊmtuːn] unreg vr: **sich nach etw ~** to look for sth

umverteilen ['ʊmfɛrtaɪlən] vt untr to redistribute

umwälzend ['ʊmvɛltsənt] adj (fig) radical; (Veränderungen) sweeping; (Ereignisse) revolutionary

Umwälzung f (fig) radical change

umwandeln ['ʊmvandəln] vt to change, convert; (Elek) to transform

umwechseln ['ʊmvɛksəln] vt to change

Umweg ['ʊmveːk] m detour; (fig) roundabout way

Umwelt ['ʊmvɛlt] f environment; **Umweltallergie** f environmental allergy; **Umweltauto** (umg) nt environment-friendly vehicle; **Umweltbelastung** f environmental pollution; **Umweltbewusstsein** nt environmental awareness; **umweltfreundlich** adj environment-friendly; **Umweltkrankheit** f environmental illness; **Umweltkriminalität** f crimes pl against the environment; **Umweltministerium** nt Ministry of the Environment; **umweltschädlich** adj harmful to the environment; **Umweltschutz** m environmental protection; **Umweltschützer (-s, -)** m environmentalist; **Umweltverschmutzung** f pollution (of

u

345

the environment); **umweltverträglich**
adj not harmful to the environment;
Umweltverträglichkeit *f* ecofriendliness
umwenden ['ʊmvɛndən] *unreg vt, vr* to turn
(round)
umwerben [ʊm'vɛrbən] *unreg vt untr* to court,
woo
umwerfen ['ʊmvɛrfən] *unreg vt* (*lit*) to upset,
overturn; (*Mantel*) to throw on; (*fig: erschüttern*)
to upset, throw
umwerfend (*umg*) *adj* fantastic
umziehen ['ʊmtsi:ən] *unreg vt, vr* to change ▷ *vi*
to move
umzingeln [ʊm'tsɪŋəln] *vt untr* to surround,
encircle
Umzug ['ʊmtsu:k] *m* procession;
(*Wohnungsumzug*) move, removal
UN *pl abk* (= *United Nations*): **die UN** the UN *sing*
un- *zW*: **unabänderlich** *adj* irreversible,
unalterable; **unabänderlich feststehen**
to be absolutely certain; **unabdingbar**
adj indispensable, essential; (*Recht*)
inalienable; **unabhängig** *adj* independent;
Unabhängigkeit *f* independence;
unabkömmlich *adj* indispensable; **zur Zeit
unabkömmlich** not free at the moment;
unablässig *adj* incessant, constant;
unabsehbar *adj* immeasurable; (*Folgen*)
unforeseeable; (*Kosten*) incalculable;
unabsichtlich *adj* unintentional;
unabwendbar *adj* inevitable
unachtsam ['ʊn|axtza:m] *adj* careless;
Unachtsamkeit *f* carelessness
un- *zW*: **unanfechtbar** *adj* indisputable;
unangebracht *adj* uncalled-for;
unangefochten *adj* unchallenged;
(*Testament, Wahlkandidat, Urteil*) uncontested;
unangemeldet *adj* unannounced;
(*Besucher*) unexpected; **unangemessen** *adj*
inadequate; **unangenehm** *adj* unpleasant;
(*peinlich*) embarrassing; **unangepasst**
adj nonconformist; **Unannehmlichkeit** *f*
inconvenience; **Unannehmlichkeiten** *pl*
trouble *sing*; **unansehnlich** *adj* unsightly;
unanständig *adj* indecent, improper;
Unanständigkeit *f* indecency, impropriety;
unantastbar *adj* inviolable, sacrosanct
unappetitlich ['ʊn|apeti:tlɪç] *adj* unsavoury
(*Brit*), unsavory (*US*)
Unart ['ʊn|a:rt] *f* bad manners *pl*;
(*Angewohnheit*) bad habit
unartig *adj* naughty, badly behaved
un- *zW*: **unaufdringlich** *adj* unobtrusive;
(*Parfüm*) discreet; (*Mensch*) unassuming;
unauffällig *adj* unobtrusive; (*Kleidung*)
inconspicuous; **unauffindbar** *adj* not to be
found; **unaufgefordert** *adj* unsolicited ▷ *adv*
unasked, spontaneously; **unaufgefordert
zugesandte Manuskripte** unsolicited
manuscripts; **unaufhaltsam** *adj* irresistible;
unaufhörlich *adj* incessant, continuous;
unaufmerksam *adj* inattentive; **unaufrichtig**
adj insincere

un- *zW*: **unausbleiblich** *adj* inevitable,
unavoidable; **unausgeglichen** *adj*
volatile; **unausgegoren** *adj* immature;
(*Idee, Plan*) half-baked; **unausgesetzt** *adj*
incessant, constant; **unausgewogen**
adj unbalanced; **unaussprechlich** *adj*
inexpressible; **unausstehlich** *adj* intolerable;
unausweichlich *adj* inescapable, ineluctable
unbändig ['ʊnbɛndɪç] *adj* extreme, excessive
unbarmherzig ['ʊnbarmhɛrtsɪç] *adj* pitiless,
merciless
unbeabsichtigt ['ʊnbə|apzɪçtɪçt] *adj*
unintentional
unbeachtet ['ʊnbə|axtət] *adj* unnoticed;
(*Warnung*) ignored
unbedacht ['ʊnbədaxt] *adj* rash
unbedarft ['ʊnbədarft] (*umg*) *adj* clueless
unbedenklich ['ʊnbədɛŋklɪç] *adj* unhesitating;
(*Plan*) unobjectionable ▷ *adv* without
hesitation
unbedeutend ['ʊnbədɔʏtənt] *adj*
insignificant, unimportant; (*Fehler*) slight
unbedingt ['ʊnbədɪŋt] *adj* unconditional ▷ *adv*
absolutely; **musst du ~ gehen?** do you really
have to go?; **nicht ~** not necessarily
unbefangen ['ʊnbəfaŋən] *adj* impartial,
unprejudiced; (*ohne Hemmungen*) uninhibited;
Unbefangenheit *f* impartiality;
uninhibitedness
unbefriedigend ['ʊnbəfri:dɪgənd] *adj*
unsatisfactory
unbefriedigt ['ʊnbəfri:dɪçt] *adj* unsatisfied;
(*unzufrieden*) dissatisfied; (*unerfüllt*) unfulfilled
unbefristet ['ʊnbəfrɪstət] *adj* permanent
unbefugt ['ʊnbəfu:kt] *adj* unauthorized; **U~en
ist der Eintritt verboten** no admittance to
unauthorized persons
unbegabt ['ʊnbəga:pt] *adj* untalented
unbegreiflich [ʊnbə'graɪflɪç] *adj* inconceivable
unbegrenzt ['ʊnbəgrɛntst] *adj* unlimited
unbegründet ['ʊnbəgrʏndət] *adj* unfounded
Unbehagen ['ʊnbəha:gən] *nt* discomfort
unbehaglich ['ʊnbəha:klɪç] *adj* uncomfortable;
(*Gefühl*) uneasy
unbeherrscht ['ʊnbəhɛrʃt] *adj* uncontrolled;
(*Mensch*) lacking self-control
unbeholfen ['ʊnbəhɔlfən] *adj* awkward,
clumsy; **Unbeholfenheit** *f* awkwardness,
clumsiness
unbeirrt ['ʊnbə|ɪrt] *adj* imperturbable
unbekannt ['ʊnbəkant] *adj* unknown; **~e
Größe** (*Math, fig*) unknown quantity
unbekannterweise *adv*: **grüß(e) sie ~ von
mir** give her my regards although I don't
know her
unbekümmert ['ʊnbəkʏmərt] *adj*
unconcerned
unbelehrbar [ʊnbə'le:rba:r] *adj* fixed in one's
views; (*Rassist etc*) dyed-in-the-wool *attrib*
unbeliebt ['ʊnbəli:pt] *adj* unpopular;
Unbeliebtheit *f* unpopularity
unbemannt ['ʊnbəmant] *adj* (*Raumflug*)
unmanned; (*Flugzeug*) pilotless

unbemerkt ['ʊnbəmɛrkt] *adj* unnoticed
unbenommen [ʊnbə'nɔmən] *adj (form)*: **es
bleibt** *od* **ist Ihnen ~, zu ...** you are at liberty
to ...
unbequem ['ʊnbəkve:m] *adj (Stuhl)*
uncomfortable; *(Mensch)* bothersome;
(Regelung) inconvenient
unberechenbar [ʊnbə'reçənba:r] *adj*
incalculable; *(Mensch, Verhalten)* unpredictable
unberechtigt ['ʊnbərɛçtɪçt] *adj* unjustified;
(nicht erlaubt) unauthorized
unberücksichtigt [ʊnbə'rʏkzɪçtɪçt] *adj*: **etw ~
lassen** not to consider sth
unberufen [ʊnbə'ru:fən] *interj* touch wood!
unberührt ['ʊnbəry:rt] *adj* untouched; *(Natur)*
unspoiled; **sie ist noch ~** she is still a virgin
unbeschadet [ʊnbə'ʃa:dət] *präp+gen (form)*
regardless of
unbescheiden ['ʊnbəʃaɪdən] *adj*
presumptuous
unbescholten ['ʊnbəʃɔltən] *adj* respectable;
(Ruf) spotless
unbeschrankt ['ʊnbəʃraŋkt] *adj (Bahnübergang)*
unguarded
unbeschränkt [ʊnbə'ʃrɛŋkt] *adj* unlimited
unbeschreiblich [ʊnbə'ʃraɪplɪç] *adj*
indescribable
unbeschwert ['ʊnbəʃve:rt] *adj (sorgenfrei)*
carefree; *(Melodien)* light
unbesehen [ʊnbə'ze:ən] *adv* indiscriminately;
(ohne es anzusehen) without looking at it
unbesonnen ['ʊnbəzɔnən] *adj* unwise, rash,
imprudent
unbesorgt ['ʊnbəzɔrkt] *adj* unconcerned; **Sie
können ganz ~ sein** you can set your mind
at rest
unbespielt ['ʊnbəʃpi:lt] *adj (Kassette)* blank
unbest. *abk* = **unbestimmt**
unbeständig ['ʊnbəʃtɛndɪç] *adj (Mensch)*
inconstant; *(Wetter)* unsettled; *(Lage)* unstable
unbestechlich [ʊnbə'ʃtɛçlɪç] *adj* incorruptible
unbestimmt ['ʊnbəʃtɪmt] *adj* indefinite;
(Zukunft) uncertain; **Unbestimmtheit** *f*
vagueness
unbestritten ['ʊnbəʃtrɪtən] *adj* undisputed
unbeteiligt [ʊnbə'taɪlɪçt] *adj* unconcerned;
(uninteressiert) indifferent
unbeugsam ['ʊnbɔykza:m] *adj* stubborn,
inflexible; *(Wille)* unbending
unbewacht ['ʊnbəvaxt] *adj* unguarded,
unwatched
unbewaffnet ['ʊnbəvafnət] *adj* unarmed
unbeweglich ['ʊnbəve:klɪç] *adj* immovable
unbewegt *adj* motionless; *(fig: unberührt)*
unmoved
unbewohnt ['ʊnbəvo:nt] *adj (Gegend)*
uninhabited; *(Haus)* unoccupied
unbewusst ['ʊnbəvʊst] *adj* unconscious
unbezahlbar [ʊnbə'tsa:lba:r] *adj* prohibitively
expensive; *(fig)* priceless; *(nützlich)* invaluable
unbezahlt ['ʊnbətsa:lt] *adj* unpaid
unblutig ['ʊnblu:tɪç] *adj* bloodless
unbrauchbar ['ʊnbrauxba:r] *adj (nutzlos)*

useless; *(Gerät)* unusable; **Unbrauchbarkeit** *f*
uselessness
unbürokratisch ['ʊnbyrokratɪʃ] *adj* without
any red tape
und [ʊnt] *konj* and; **~ so weiter** and so on
Undank ['ʊndaŋk] *m* ingratitude; **undankbar**
adj ungrateful; **Undankbarkeit** *f* ingratitude
undefinierbar [ʊndefi'ni:rba:r] *adj* indefinable
undenkbar [ʊn'dɛŋkba:r] *adj* inconceivable
undeutlich ['ʊndɔytlɪç] *adj* indistinct; *(Schrift)*
illegible; *(Ausdrucksweise)* unclear
undicht ['ʊndɪçt] *adj* leaky
undifferenziert ['ʊndɪfərentsi:rt] *adj*
simplistic
Unding ['ʊndɪŋ] *nt* absurdity
unduldsam ['ʊndʊldsa:m] *adj* intolerant
un- *zW*: **undurchdringlich** *adj (Urwald)*
impenetrable; *(Gesicht)* inscrutable;
undurchführbar *adj* impracticable;
undurchlässig *adj* impervious;
(wasserundurchlässig) waterproof, impermeable;
undurchschaubar *adj* inscrutable;
undurchsichtig *adj* opaque; *(Motive)* obscure;
(fig: pej: Mensch, Methoden) devious
uneben ['ʊn|e:bən] *adj* uneven
unecht ['ʊn|ɛçt] *adj* artificial, fake;
(pej: Freundschaft, Lächeln) false
unehelich ['ʊn|e:əlɪç] *adj* illegitimate
uneigennützig ['ʊn|aɪgənnʏtsɪç] *adj* unselfish
uneinbringlich [ʊn|aɪn'brɪŋlɪç] *adj*: **~e
Forderungen** *(Comm)* bad debts *pl*
uneingeschränkt ['ʊn|aɪŋɡəʃrɛŋkt] *adj*
absolute, total; *(Rechte, Handel)* unrestricted;
(Zustimmung) unqualified
uneinig ['ʊn|aɪnɪç] *adj* divided; **~ sein** to
disagree; **Uneinigkeit** *f* discord, dissension
uneinnehmbar [ʊn|aɪn'ne:mba:r] *adj*
impregnable
uneins ['ʊn|aɪns] *adj* at variance, at odds
unempfänglich ['ʊn|ɛmpfɛŋlɪç] *adj*: **~ (für)** not
susceptible (to)
unempfindlich ['ʊn|ɛmpfɪntlɪç] *adj*
insensitive; **Unempfindlichkeit** *f* insensitivity
unendlich [ʊn|'ɛntlɪç] *adj* infinite ▷ *adv*
endlessly; *(fig: sehr)* terribly; **Unendlichkeit** *f*
infinity
un- *zW*: **unentbehrlich** *adj* indispensable;
unentgeltlich *adj* free (of charge);
unentschieden *adj* undecided;
unentschieden enden *(Sport)* to end in
a draw; **unentschlossen** *adj* undecided;
(entschlusslos) irresolute; **unentwegt** *adj*
unswerving; *(unaufhörlich)* incessant
un- *zW*: **unerbittlich** *adj* unyielding,
inexorable; **unerfahren** *adj* inexperienced;
unerfreulich *adj* unpleasant; **Unerfreuliches**
(schlechte Nachrichten) bad news *sing*; *(Übles)*
bad things *pl*; **unerfüllt** *adj* unfulfilled;
unergiebig *adj (Quelle, Thema)* unproductive;
(Ernte, Nachschlagewerk) poor; **unergründlich**
adj unfathomable; **unerheblich** *adj*
unimportant; **unerhört** *adj* unheard-of;
(unverschämt) outrageous; *(Bitte)* unanswered;

u

347

unerlässlich adj indispensable; **unerlaubt** adj unauthorized; **unerledigt** adj unfinished; (Post) unanswered; (Rechnung) outstanding; (schwebend) pending; **unermesslich** adj immeasurable, immense; **unermüdlich** adj indefatigable; **unersättlich** adj insatiable; **unerschlossen** adj (Land) undeveloped; (Boden) unexploited; (Vorkommen, Markt) untapped; **unerschöpflich** adj inexhaustible; **unerschrocken** adj intrepid, courageous; **unerschütterlich** adj unshakeable; **unerschwinglich** adj (Preis) prohibitive; **unersetzlich** adj irreplaceable; **unerträglich** adj unbearable; (Frechheit) insufferable; **unerwartet** adj unexpected; **unerwünscht** adj undesirable, unwelcome; **unerzogen** adj ill-bred, rude

unfähig ['ʊnfɛːɪç] adj incapable; (attrib) incompetent; **zu etw ~ sein** to be incapable of sth; **Unfähigkeit** f inability; incompetence

unfair ['ʊnfɛːr] adj unfair

Unfall ['ʊnfal] m accident; **Unfallflucht** f hit-and-run (driving); **Unfallopfer** nt casualty; **Unfallstation** f emergency ward; **Unfallstelle** f scene of the accident; **Unfallversicherung** f accident insurance; **Unfallwagen** m car involved in an accident; (umg: Rettungswagen) ambulance

unfassbar [ʊn'fasbaːr] adj inconceivable

unfehlbar [ʊn'feːlbaːr] adj infallible ▷ adv without fail; **Unfehlbarkeit** f infallibility

unfertig ['ʊnfɛrtɪç] adj unfinished, incomplete; (Mensch) immature

unflätig ['ʊnflɛːtɪç] adj rude

unfolgsam ['ʊnfɔlkzaːm] adj disobedient

unförmig ['ʊnfœrmɪç] adj (formlos) shapeless; (groß) cumbersome; (Füße, Nase) unshapely

unfrankiert ['ʊnfraŋkiːrt] adj unfranked

unfrei ['ʊnfraɪ] adj not free

unfreiwillig adj involuntary

unfreundlich ['ʊnfrɔʏntlɪç] adj unfriendly; **Unfreundlichkeit** f unfriendliness

Unfriede ['ʊnfriːdə], **Unfrieden** ['ʊnfriːdən] m dissension, strife

unfruchtbar ['ʊnfrʊxtbaːr] adj infertile; (Gespräche) fruitless; **Unfruchtbarkeit** f infertility; fruitlessness

Unfug ['ʊnfuːk] (-s) m (Benehmen) mischief; (Unsinn) nonsense; **grober ~** (Jur) gross misconduct

Ungar, in ['ʊŋar(ɪn)] (-n, -n) m(f) Hungarian; **ungarisch** adj Hungarian

Ungarn (-s) nt Hungary

ungeachtet ['ʊŋə|axtət] präp +gen notwithstanding

ungeahndet ['ʊŋə|aːndət] adj (Jur) unpunished

ungeahnt ['ʊŋə|aːnt] adj unsuspected, undreamt-of

ungebeten ['ʊŋəbeːtən] adj uninvited

ungebildet ['ʊŋəbɪldət] adj uncultured; (ohne Bildung) uneducated

ungeboren ['ʊŋəboːrən] adj unborn

ungebräuchlich ['ʊŋəbrɔʏçlɪç] adj unusual, uncommon

ungebraucht ['ʊŋəbraʊxt] adj unused

ungebührlich ['ʊŋəbyːrlɪç] adj: **sich ~ aufregen** to get unduly excited

ungebunden ['ʊŋəbʊndən] adj (Buch) unbound; (Leben) (fancy-)free; (ohne festen Partner) unattached; (Pol) independent

ungedeckt ['ʊŋədɛkt] adj (schutzlos) unprotected; (Scheck) uncovered

Ungeduld ['ʊŋədʊlt] f impatience

ungeduldig ['ʊŋədʊldɪç] adj impatient

ungeeignet ['ʊŋə|aɪgnət] adj unsuitable

ungefähr ['ʊŋəfɛːr] adj rough, approximate ▷ adv roughly, approximately; **so ~!** more or less!; **das kommt nicht von ~** that's hardly surprising

ungefährlich ['ʊŋəfɛːrlɪç] adj not dangerous, harmless

ungehalten ['ʊŋəhaltən] adj indignant

ungeheuer ['ʊŋəhɔʏər] adj huge ▷ adv (umg) enormously; **Ungeheuer (-s, -)** nt monster; **ungeheuerlich** [ʊŋə'hɔʏərlɪç] adj monstrous

ungehindert ['ʊŋəhɪndərt] adj unimpeded

ungehobelt ['ʊŋəhoːbəlt] adj (fig) uncouth

ungehörig ['ʊŋəhøːrɪç] adj impertinent, improper; **Ungehörigkeit** f impertinence

ungehorsam ['ʊŋəhoːrzaːm] adj disobedient; **Ungehorsam** m disobedience

ungeklärt ['ʊŋəklɛːrt] adj not cleared up; (Rätsel) unsolved; (Abwasser) untreated

ungekürzt ['ʊŋəkʏrtst] adj not shortened; (Film) uncut

ungeladen ['ʊŋəlaːdən] adj not loaded; (Elek) uncharged; (Gast) uninvited

ungelegen ['ʊŋəleːgən] adj inconvenient; **komme ich (Ihnen) ~?** is this an inconvenient time for you?

ungelernt ['ʊŋəlɛrnt] adj unskilled

ungelogen ['ʊŋəloːgən] adv really, honestly

ungemein ['ʊŋəmaɪn] adj immense

ungemütlich ['ʊŋəmyːtlɪç] adj uncomfortable; (Person) disagreeable; **er kann ~ werden** he can get nasty

ungenau ['ʊŋənaʊ] adj inaccurate

Ungenauigkeit f inaccuracy

ungeniert ['ʊnʒeniːrt] adj free and easy; (bedenkenlos, taktlos) uninhibited ▷ adv without embarrassment, freely

ungenießbar ['ʊŋəniːsbaːr] adj inedible; (nicht zu trinken) undrinkable; (umg) unbearable

ungenügend ['ʊŋənyːgənt] adj insufficient, inadequate; (Sch) unsatisfactory

ungenutzt ['ʊŋənʊtst] adj: **eine Chance ~ lassen** to miss an opportunity

ungepflegt ['ʊŋəpfleːkt] adj (Garten etc) untended; (Person) unkempt; (Hände) neglected

ungerade ['ʊŋəraːdə] adj odd, uneven (US)

ungerecht ['ʊŋərɛçt] adj unjust

ungerechtfertigt ['ʊŋərɛçtfɛrtɪçt] adj unjustified

Ungerechtigkeit f unfairness, injustice

ungeregelt ['ʊŋəreːgəlt] adj irregular

ungereimt ['ʊŋəraɪmt] adj (Verse) unrhymed;

(fig) inconsistent

ungern ['ʊngɛrn] *adv* unwillingly, reluctantly

ungerufen ['ʊngəru:fən] *adj* without being called

ungeschehen ['ʊngəʃe:ən] *adj:* ~ **machen** to undo

Ungeschicklichkeit ['ʊngəʃɪklɪçkaɪt] *f* clumsiness

ungeschickt *adj* awkward, clumsy

ungeschliffen ['ʊngəʃlɪfən] *adj (Edelstein)* uncut; *(Messer etc)* blunt; *(fig: Benehmen)* uncouth

ungeschmälert ['ʊngəʃmɛ:lərt] *adj* undiminished

ungeschminkt ['ʊngəʃmɪŋkt] *adj* without make-up; *(fig)* unvarnished

ungeschoren ['ʊngəʃo:rən] *adj:* **jdn ~ lassen** *(umg)* to spare sb; *(ungestraft)* to let sb off

ungesetzlich ['ʊngəzɛtslɪç] *adj* illegal

ungestempelt ['ʊngəʃtɛmpəlt] *adj (Briefmarke)* unfranked, mint

ungestört ['ʊngəʃtø:rt] *adj* undisturbed

ungestraft ['ʊngəʃtra:ft] *adv* with impunity

ungestüm ['ʊngəʃty:m] *adj* impetuous; **Ungestüm (-(e)s** *nt* impetuosity

ungesund ['ʊngəzʊnt] *adj* unhealthy

ungetrübt ['ʊngətry:pt] *adj* clear; *(fig)* untroubled; *(Freude)* unalloyed

Ungetüm ['ʊngəty:m] *(-(e)s, -e)* *nt* monster

ungeübt ['ʊngəy:pt] *adj* unpractised *(Brit)*, unpracticed *(US)*; *(Mensch)* out of practice

ungewiss ['ʊngəvɪs] *adj* uncertain; **Ungewissheit** *f* uncertainty

ungewöhnlich ['ʊngəvø:nlɪç] *adj* unusual

ungewohnt ['ʊngəvo:nt] *adj* unusual

ungewollt ['ʊngəvɔlt] *adj* unintentional

Ungeziefer ['ʊngətsi:fər] *(-s)* *nt* vermin *pl*

ungezogen ['ʊngətso:gən] *adj* rude, impertinent; **Ungezogenheit** *f* rudeness, impertinence

ungezwungen ['ʊngətsvʊŋən] *adj* natural, unconstrained

ungläubig ['ʊnglɔʏbɪç] *adj* unbelieving; **ein ~er Thomas** a doubting Thomas; **die U~en** the infidel(s *pl*)

unglaublich ['ʊnglaʊplɪç] *adj* incredible

unglaubwürdig ['ʊnglaʊpvʏrdɪç] *adj* untrustworthy, unreliable; *(Geschichte)* improbable; **sich ~ machen** to lose credibility

ungleich ['ʊnglaɪç] *adj* dissimilar; *(Mittel, Waffen)* unequal ▷ *adv* incomparably; **ungleichartig** *adj* different; **Ungleichbehandlung** *f (von Frauen, Ausländern)* unequal treatment; **Ungleichheit** *f* dissimilarity; inequality; **ungleichmäßig** *adj* uneven; *(Atemzüge, Gesichtszüge, Puls)* irregular

Unglück ['ʊnglʏk] *nt* misfortune; *(Pech)* bad luck; *(Unglücksfall)* calamity, disaster; *(Verkehrsunglück)* accident; **zu allem ~** to make matters worse; **unglücklich** *adj* unhappy; *(erfolglos)* unlucky; *(unerfreulich)* unfortunate; **unglücklicherweise** *adv* unfortunately; **unglückselig** *adj* calamitous; *(Person)*

unfortunate

Unglücksfall *m* accident, mishap

Unglücksrabe *(umg)* *m* unlucky thing

Ungnade ['ʊngna:də] *f:* **bei jdm in ~ fallen** to fall out of favour *(Brit)* od favor *(US)* with sb

ungültig ['ʊngʏltɪç] *adj* invalid; **etw für ~ erklären** to declare sth null and void; **Ungültigkeit** *f* invalidity

ungünstig ['ʊngʏnstɪç] *adj* unfavourable *(Brit)*, unfavorable *(US)*; *(Termin)* inconvenient; *(Augenblick, Wetter)* bad; *(nicht preiswert)* expensive

ungut ['ʊngu:t] *adj (Gefühl)* uneasy; **nichts für ~!** no offence!

unhaltbar ['ʊnhaltba:r] *adj* untenable

unhandlich ['ʊnhantlɪç] *adj* unwieldy

Unheil ['ʊnhaɪl] *nt* evil; *(Unglück)* misfortune; **~ anrichten** to cause mischief; **~ bringend** fatal, fateful

unheilbar ['ʊn'haɪlba:r] *adj* incurable

unheilvoll *adj* disastrous

unheimlich ['ʊnhaɪmlɪç] *adj* weird, uncanny ▷ *adv (umg)* tremendously; **das/er ist mir ~** it/he gives me the creeps *(umg)*

unhöflich ['ʊnhø:flɪç] *adj* impolite; **Unhöflichkeit** *f* impoliteness

unhörbar ['ʊn'hø:rba:r] *adj* silent; *(Frequenzen)* inaudible

unhygienisch ['ʊnhygie:nɪʃ] *adj* unhygienic

Uni ['ʊni] *(-, -s)* *(umg)* *f* university

uni ['yni:] *adj* self-coloured *(Brit)*, self-colored *(US)*

Uniform [uni'fɔrm] *(-, -en)* *f* uniform

uniformiert [unifɔr'mi:rt] *adj* uniformed

Unikum ['u:nɪkʊm] *(-s, -s od Unika) (umg)* *nt* real character

uninteressant ['ʊn|ɪntɛrɛsant] *adj* uninteresting

uninteressiert ['ʊn|ɪntərɛ'si:rt] *adj:* ~ **(an** +*dat)* uninterested (in), not interested (in)

Union [uni'o:n] *f* union

Unionsparteien *pl (BRD Pol)* CDU and CSU parties *pl*

universal [univɛr'za:l] *adj* universal

universell [univɛr'zɛl] *adj* universal

Universität [univɛrzi'tɛ:t] *f* university; **auf die ~ gehen, die ~ besuchen** to go to university

Universum [uni'vɛrzʊm] *(-s)* *nt* universe

unkenntlich ['ʊnkɛntlɪç] *adj* unrecognizable; **Unkenntlichkeit** *f:* **bis zur Unkenntlichkeit** beyond recognition

Unkenntnis ['ʊnkɛntnɪs] *f* ignorance

unklar ['ʊnkla:r] *adj* unclear; **im U~en sein über** +*akk* to be in the dark about; **Unklarheit** *f* unclarity; *(Unentschiedenheit)* uncertainty

unklug ['ʊnklu:k] *adj* unwise

unkompliziert ['ʊnkɔmplitsi:rt] *adj* straightforward, uncomplicated

unkontrolliert ['ʊnkɔntrɔli:rt] *adj* unchecked

unkonzentriert ['ʊnkɔntsɛntri:rt] *adj* lacking in concentration

Unkosten ['ʊnkɔstən] *pl* expense(s *pl*); **sich in**

u

~ **stürzen** (umg) to go to a lot of expense
Unkraut ['ʊnkraʊt] nt weed; weeds pl; ~
  vergeht nicht (Sprichwort) it would take
  more than that to finish me/him etc off;
  Unkrautvertilgungsmittel nt weedkiller
unlängst ['ʊnlɛŋst] adv not long ago
unlauter ['ʊnlaʊtər] adj unfair
unleserlich ['ʊnleːzərlɪç] adj illegible
unleugbar ['ʊnlɔʏkbaːr] adj undeniable,
  indisputable
unlogisch ['ʊnloːgɪʃ] adj illogical
unlösbar [ʊn'løːsbar] adj insoluble
unlöslich [ʊn'løːslɪç] adj insoluble
Unlust ['ʊnlʊst] f lack of enthusiasm
unlustig adj unenthusiastic ▷ adv without
  enthusiasm
unmännlich ['ʊnmɛnlɪç] adj unmanly
Unmasse ['ʊnmasə] (umg) f load
unmäßig ['ʊnmɛːsɪç] adj immoderate
Unmenge ['ʊnmɛŋə] f tremendous number,
  vast number
Unmensch ['ʊnmɛnʃ] m ogre, brute;
  unmenschlich adj inhuman, brutal;
  (ungeheuer) awful
unmerklich [ʊn'mɛrklɪç] adj imperceptible
unmissverständlich ['ʊnmɪsfɛrʃtɛntlɪç] adj
  unmistakable
unmittelbar ['ʊnmɪtəlbaːr] adj immediate;
  ~er Kostenaufwand direct expense
unmöbliert ['ʊnmøbliːrt] adj unfurnished
unmöglich ['ʊnmøːklɪç] adj impossible;
  ich kann es ~ tun I can't possibly do
  it; **~ aussehen** (umg) to look ridiculous;
  Unmöglichkeit f impossibility
unmoralisch ['ʊnmoraːlɪʃ] adj immoral
unmotiviert ['ʊnmotiviːrt] adj unmotivated
unmündig ['ʊnmʏndɪç] adj (minderjährig)
  underage
Unmut ['ʊnmuːt] m ill humour (Brit) od humor
  (US)
unnachahmlich ['ʊnnaːx|aːmlɪç] adj
  inimitable
unnachgiebig ['ʊnnaːxgiːbɪç] adj unyielding
unnahbar [ʊn'naːbaːr] adj unapproachable
unnatürlich ['ʊnnaty:rlɪç] adj unnatural
unnormal ['ʊnnɔrmaːl] adj abnormal
unnötig ['ʊnnøːtɪç] adj unnecessary
unnötigerweise adv unnecessarily
unnütz ['ʊnnʏts] adj useless
UNO ['uːno] f abk (= United Nations
  Organization): **die ~** the UN
unordentlich ['ʊn|ɔrdəntlɪç] adj untidy
Unordnung ['ʊn|ɔrdnʊŋ] f disorder;
  (Durcheinander) mess
unorganisiert ['ʊn|ɔrganiziːrt] adj
  disorganized
unparteiisch ['ʊnpartaɪʃ] adj impartial
Unparteiische, r f(m) umpire; (Fussball) referee
unpassend ['ʊnpasənt] adj inappropriate;
  (Zeit) inopportune
unpässlich ['ʊnpɛslɪç] adj unwell
unpersönlich ['ʊnpɛrzøːnlɪç] adj impersonal
unpolitisch ['ʊnpoliːtɪʃ] adj apolitical

unpraktisch ['ʊnpraktɪʃ] adj impractical,
  unpractical
unproduktiv ['ʊnprodʊktiːf] adj unproductive
unproportioniert ['ʊnprɔpɔrtsioniːrt] adj out
  of proportion
unpünktlich ['ʊnpʏŋktlɪç] adj unpunctual
unqualifiziert ['ʊnkvalifitsiːrt] adj
  unqualified; (Äußerung) incompetent
unrasiert ['ʊnraziːrt] adj unshaven
Unrat ['ʊnraːt] (-(e)s) m (geh) refuse; (fig) filth
unrationell ['ʊnratsionɛl] adj inefficient
unrecht ['ʊnrɛçt] adj wrong; **das ist mir gar
  nicht so ~** I don't really mind; **~ haben** to
  be wrong; **Unrecht** nt wrong; **zu Unrecht**
  wrongly; **nicht zu Unrecht** not without good
  reason; **im Unrecht sein** to be wrong
unrechtmäßig adj unlawful, illegal
unredlich ['ʊnreːtlɪç] adj dishonest;
  Unredlichkeit f dishonesty
unreell ['ʊnreːl] adj unfair; (unredlich)
  dishonest; (Preis) unreasonable
unregelmäßig ['ʊnreːgəlmɛːsɪç] adj irregular;
  Unregelmäßigkeit f irregularity
unreif ['ʊnraɪf] adj (Obst) unripe; (fig) immature
Unreife f immaturity
unrein ['ʊnraɪn] adj not clean; (Ton, Gedanken,
  Taten) impure; (Atem, Haut) bad
unrentabel ['ʊnrɛntaːbəl] adj unprofitable
unrichtig ['ʊnrɪçtɪç] adj incorrect, wrong
Unruh ['ʊnruː] (-, -en) f (von Uhr) balance
Unruhe (-, -n) f unrest; **Unruheherd** m trouble
  spot; **Unruhestifter** m troublemaker
unruhig adj restless; (nervös) fidgety; (belebt)
  noisy; (Schlaf) fitful; (Zeit etc, Meer) troubled
unrühmlich ['ʊnryːmlɪç] adj inglorious
uns [ʊns] pron akk, dat von **wir** us; (reflexiv)
  ourselves
unsachgemäß ['ʊnzaxgəmɛːs] adj improper
unsachlich ['ʊnzaxlɪç] adj not to the point,
  irrelevant; (persönlich) personal
unsagbar [ʊn'zaːkbaːr] adj indescribable
unsäglich [ʊn'zɛːklɪç] adj indescribable
unsanft ['ʊnzanft] adj rough
unsauber ['ʊnzaʊbər] adj (schmutzig) dirty; (fig)
  crooked; (: Klang) impure
unschädlich ['ʊnʃɛːtlɪç] adj harmless; **jdn/etw
  ~ machen** to render sb/sth harmless
unscharf ['ʊnʃarf] adj indistinct; (Bild etc) out of
  focus, blurred
unschätzbar [ʊn'ʃɛtsbaːr] adj incalculable;
  (Hilfe) invaluable
unscheinbar ['ʊnʃaɪnbaːr] adj insignificant;
  (Aussehen, Haus etc) unprepossessing
unschlagbar [ʊn'ʃlaːkbaːr] adj invincible
unschlüssig ['ʊnʃlʏsɪç] adj undecided
unschön ['ʊnʃøːn] adj unsightly; (lit, fig: Szene)
  ugly; (Vorfall) unpleasant
Unschuld ['ʊnʃʊlt] f innocence
unschuldig ['ʊnʃʊldɪç] adj innocent
Unschuldsmiene f innocent expression
unschwer ['ʊnʃveːr] adv easily, without
  difficulty
unselbstständig ['ʊnzɛlpstʃtɛndɪç],

unselbständig ['ʊnzɛlpʃtɛndɪç] *adj* dependent, over-reliant on others

unselig ['ʊnzeːlɪç] *adj* unfortunate; (*verhängnisvoll*) ill-fated

unser ['ʊnzər] *poss pron* our ▷ *pron gen von* **wir** of us

unsere, r, s *poss pron* ours; **wir tun das U~** (*geh*) we are doing our bit

unsereiner *pron* the likes of us

unsereins *pron* the likes of us

unsererseits ['ʊnzərərˈzaɪts] *adv* on our part

unseresgleichen *pron* the likes of us

unserige, r, s *poss pron*: **der/die/das U~** ours

unseriös ['ʊnzeriøːs] *adj* (*unehrlich*) not straight, untrustworthy

unserteils ['ʊnzərˈzaɪts] *adv* = **unsererseits**

unsertwegen ['ʊnzərtˈveːgən] *adv* (*für uns*) for our sake; (*wegen uns*) on our account

unsertwillen ['ʊnzərtˈvɪlən] *adv*: **um ~ = unsertwegen**

unsicher ['ʊnzɪçər] *adj* uncertain; (*Mensch*) insecure; **die Gegend ~ machen** (*fig: umg*) to knock about the district; **Unsicherheit** *f* uncertainty; insecurity

unsichtbar ['ʊnzɪçtbaːr] *adj* invisible; **Unsichtbarkeit** *f* invisibility

Unsinn ['ʊnzɪn] *m* nonsense

unsinnig *adj* nonsensical

Unsitte ['ʊnzɪtə] *f* deplorable habit

unsittlich ['ʊnzɪtlɪç] *adj* indecent; **Unsittlichkeit** *f* indecency

unsolide ['ʊnzoliːdə] *adj* (*Mensch, Leben*) loose; (*Firma*) unreliable

unsozial ['ʊnzotsiaːl] *adj* (*Verhalten*) antisocial; (*Politik*) unsocial

unsportlich ['ʊnʃpɔrtlɪç] *adj* not sporty; (*Verhalten*) unsporting

unsre *etc* ['ʊnzrə] *poss pron* = **unsere** *etc; siehe auch* **unser**

unsrige, r, s ['ʊnzrɪgə(r, s)] *poss pron* = **unserige**

unsterblich ['ʊnʃtɛrplɪç] *adj* immortal; **Unsterblichkeit** *f* immortality

unstet ['ʊnʃteːt] *adj* (*Mensch*) restless; (*wankelmütig*) changeable; (*Leben*) unsettled

Unstimmigkeit ['ʊnʃtɪmɪçkaɪt] *f* inconsistency; (*Streit*) disagreement

Unsumme ['ʊnzʊmə] *f* vast sum

unsympathisch ['ʊnzympaːtɪʃ] *adj* unpleasant; **er ist mir ~** I don't like him

untadelig ['ʊntaːdəlɪç], **untadlig** ['ʊntaːdlɪç] *adj* impeccable; (*Mensch*) beyond reproach

Untat ['ʊntaːt] *f* atrocity

untätig ['ʊntɛːtɪç] *adj* idle

untauglich ['ʊntaʊklɪç] *adj* unsuitable; (*Mil*) unfit; **Untauglichkeit** *f* unsuitability; unfitness

unteilbar [ʊnˈtaɪlbaːr] *adj* indivisible

unten ['ʊntən] *adv* below; (*im Haus*) downstairs; (*an der Treppe etc*) at the bottom; **~ genannt** undermentioned; **siehe ~** see below; **nach ~** down; **~ am Berg** *etc* at the bottom of the mountain *etc*; **er ist bei mir ~ durch** (*umg*) I'm through with him; **untenan** *adv*

(*am unteren Ende*) at the far end; (*lit, fig*) at the bottom

 SCHLÜSSELWORT

unter ['ʊntər] *präp +dat* **1** (*räumlich*) under; (*drunter*) underneath, below
2 (*zwischen*) among(st); **sie waren unter sich** they were by themselves; **einer unter ihnen** one of them; **unter anderem** among other things; **unter der Hand** secretly; (*verkaufen*) privately
▷ *präp +akk* under, below
▷ *adv* (*weniger als*) under; **Mädchen unter 18 Jahren** girls under *od* less than 18 (years of age)

Unter- *zW*: **Unterabteilung** *f* subdivision; **Unterarm** *m* forearm; **unterbelegt** *adj* (*Kurs*) under-subscribed; (*Hotel etc*) not full

unterbelichten ['ʊntərbəlɪçtən] *vt untr* (*Phot*) to underexpose

Unterbeschäftigung ['ʊntərbəʃɛːftɪgʊŋ] *f* underemployment

unterbesetzt ['ʊntərbəzɛtst] *adj* understaffed

Unterbewusstsein ['ʊntərbəvʊstzaɪn] *nt* subconscious

unterbezahlt ['ʊntərbətsaːlt] *adj* underpaid

unterbieten [ʊntərˈbiːtən] *unreg vt untr* (*Comm*) to undercut; (*fig*) to surpass

unterbinden [ʊntərˈbɪndən] *unreg vt untr* to stop, call a halt to

unterbleiben [ʊntərˈblaɪbən] *unreg vi untr* (*aufhören*) to stop; (*versäumt werden*) to be omitted

Unterbodenschutz [ʊntərˈboːdənʃʊts] *m* (*Aut*) underseal

unterbrechen [ʊntərˈbrɛçən] *unreg vt untr* to interrupt

Unterbrechung *f* interruption

unterbreiten [ʊntərˈbraɪtən] *vt untr* (*Plan*) to present

unterbringen ['ʊntərbrɪŋən] *unreg vt* (*in Koffer*) to stow; (*in Zeitung*) to place; (*Person: in Hotel etc*) to accommodate, put up; (*: beruflich*): **~ (bei)** to fix up (with)

unterbuttern ['ʊntərbʊtərn] (*umg*) *vt* (*zuschießen*) to throw in; (*unterdrücken*) to ride roughshod over

unterdessen [ʊntərˈdɛsən] *adv* meanwhile

Unterdruck ['ʊntərdrʊk] *m* (*Tech*) below atmospheric pressure

unterdrücken [ʊntərˈdrykən] *vt untr* to suppress; (*Leute*) to oppress

untere, r, s ['ʊntərə(r, s)] *adj* lower

untereinander [ʊntər|aɪˈnandər] *adv* (*gegenseitig*) each other; (*miteinander*) among themselves *etc*

unterentwickelt ['ʊntər|ɛntvɪkəlt] *adj* underdeveloped

unterernährt ['ʊntər|ɛrnɛːrt] *adj* undernourished

Unterernährung *f* malnutrition

Unterfangen [ʊntərˈfaŋən] *nt* undertaking

u

Unterführung [ʊntərˈfyːrʊŋ] f subway, underpass

Untergang [ˈʊntərɡaŋ] m (down)fall, decline; (Naut) sinking; (von Gestirn) setting; **dem ~ geweiht sein** to be doomed

untergeben [ʊntərˈɡeːbən] adj subordinate

Untergebene, r f(m) subordinate

untergehen [ˈʊntərɡeːən] unreg vi to go down; (Sonne) to set, go down; (Staat) to fall; (Volk) to perish; (Welt) to come to an end; (im Lärm) to be drowned

untergeordnet [ˈʊntərɡəʔɔrdnət] adj (Dienststelle) subordinate; (Bedeutung) secondary

Untergeschoss [ˈʊntərɡəʃɔs] nt basement

Untergewicht [ˈʊntərɡəvɪçt] nt: **(10 Kilo) ~ haben** to be (10 kilos) underweight

untergliedern [ʊntərˈɡliːdərn] vt untr to subdivide

untergraben [ʊntərˈɡraːbən] unreg vt untr to undermine

Untergrund [ˈʊntərɡrʊnt] m foundation; (Pol) underground; **Untergrundbahn** f underground (Brit), subway (US); **Untergrundbewegung** f underground (movement)

unterhaken [ˈʊntərhaːkən] vr: **sich bei jdm ~** to link arms with sb

unterhalb [ˈʊntərhalp] präp +gen below ▷ adv below; **~ von** below

Unterhalt [ˈʊntərhalt] m maintenance; **seinen ~ verdienen** to earn one's living

unterhalten [ʊntərˈhaltən] unreg vt untr to maintain; (belustigen) to entertain; (versorgen) to support; (Geschäft, Kfz) to run; (Konto) to have ▷ vr untr to talk; (sich belustigen) to enjoy o.s.

unterhaltend, unterhaltsam [ʊntərˈhaltzaːm] adj entertaining

Unterhaltskosten pl maintenance costs pl

Unterhaltszahlung f maintenance payment

Unterhaltung f maintenance; (Belustigung) entertainment, amusement; (Gespräch) talk

Unterhaltungskosten pl running costs pl

Unterhaltungsmusik f light music

Unterhändler [ˈʊntərhɛntlər] m negotiator

Unterhaus [ˈʊntərhaus] nt House of Commons (Brit), House of Representatives (US), Lower House

Unterhemd [ˈʊntərhɛmt] nt vest (Brit), undershirt (US)

unterhöhlen [ʊntərˈhøːlən] vt untr (lit, fig) to undermine

Unterholz [ˈʊntərhɔlts] nt undergrowth

Unterhose [ˈʊntərhoːzə] f underpants pl

unterirdisch [ˈʊntərʔɪrdɪʃ] adj underground

unterjubeln [ˈʊntərjuːbəln] (umg) vt: **jdm etw ~** to palm sth off on sb

unterkapitalisiert [ˈʊntərkapitaliˈziːrt] adj undercapitalized

unterkellern [ʊntərˈkɛlərn] vt untr to build with a cellar

Unterkiefer [ˈʊntərkiːfər] m lower jaw

unterkommen [ˈʊntərkɔmən] unreg vi to find

shelter; (Stelle finden) to find work; **das ist mir noch nie untergekommen** I've never met with that; **bei jdm ~** to stay at sb's (place)

unterkriegen [ˈʊntərkriːɡən] (umg) vt: **sich nicht ~ lassen** not to let things get one down

unterkühlt [ʊntərˈkyːlt] adj (Körper) affected by hypothermia; (fig: Mensch, Atmosphäre) cool

Unterkunft [ˈʊntərkʊnft] (-, -künfte) f accommodation (Brit), accommodations pl (US); **~ und Verpflegung** board and lodging

Unterlage [ˈʊntərlaːɡə] f foundation; (Beleg) document; (Schreibunterlage etc) pad

unterlassen [ʊntərˈlasən] unreg vt untr (versäumen) to fail to do; (sich enthalten) to refrain from

unterlaufen [ʊntərˈlaufən] unreg vi untr to happen ▷ adj: **mit Blut ~** suffused with blood; (Augen) bloodshot; **mir ist ein Fehler ~** I made a mistake

unterlegen¹ [ˈʊntərleːɡən] vt to lay od put under

unterlegen² [ʊntərˈleːɡən] adj inferior; (besiegt) defeated

Unterleib [ˈʊntərlaip] m abdomen

unterliegen [ʊntərˈliːɡən] unreg vi untr +dat to be defeated od overcome (by); (unterworfen sein) to be subject (to)

Unterlippe [ˈʊntərlɪpə] f bottom od lower lip

unterm = **unter dem**

untermalen [ʊntərˈmaːlən] vt untr (mit Musik) to provide with background music

Untermalung f: **musikalische ~** background music

untermauern [ʊntərˈmauərn] vt untr (Gebäude, fig) to underpin

Untermiete [ˈʊntərmiːtə] f subtenancy; **bei jdm zur ~ wohnen** to rent a room from sb

Untermieter, in m(f) lodger

untern = **unter den**

unternehmen [ʊntərˈneːmən] unreg vt untr to do; (durchführen) to undertake; (Versuch, Reise) to make; **Unternehmen** (-s, -) nt undertaking, enterprise (auch COMM); (Firma) business

unternehmend adj enterprising, daring

Unternehmensberater m management consultant

Unternehmensplanung f corporate planning, management planning

Unternehmer, in [ʊntərˈneːmər(ɪn)] (-s, -) m(f) (business) employer; (alten Stils) entrepreneur; **Unternehmerverband** m employers' association

Unternehmungsgeist m spirit of enterprise

unternehmungslustig adj enterprising

Unteroffizier [ˈʊntərʔɔfitsiːr] m noncommissioned officer, NCO

unterordnen [ˈʊntərʔɔrdnən] vt: **~ (+dat)** to subordinate (to)

Unterordnung f subordination

Unterprima [ˈʊntərpriːma] f (früher) eighth year of German secondary school

Unterprogramm [ˈʊntərproɡram] nt (Comput) subroutine

Unterredung [ʊntərˈreːdʊŋ] *f* discussion, talk
Unterricht [ˈʊntərrɪçt] (**-(e)s**) *m* teaching;
(*Stunden*) lessons *pl*; **jdm ~ (in etw** *dat*) **geben**
to teach sb (sth)
unterrichten [ʊntərˈrɪçtən] *vt untr* to instruct;
(*Sch*) to teach ▷ *vr untr:* **sich ~ (über** +*akk*)
to inform o.s. (about), obtain information
(about)
Unterrichts- *zW:* **Unterrichtsgegenstand**
m topic, subject; **Unterrichtsmethode**
f teaching method; **Unterrichtsstoff** *m*
teaching material; **Unterrichtsstunde**
f lesson; **Unterrichtszwecke** *pl:* **zu**
Unterrichtszwecken for teaching purposes
Unterrock [ˈʊntərrɔk] *m* petticoat, slip
unters = **unter das**
untersagen [ʊntərˈzaːgən] *vt untr* to forbid;
jdm etw ~ to forbid sb to do sth
Untersatz [ˈʊntərzats] *m* mat; (*für Blumentöpfe*
etc) base
unterschätzen [ʊntərˈʃɛtsən] *vt untr* to
underestimate
unterscheiden [ʊntərˈʃaɪdən] *unreg vt untr* to
distinguish ▷ *vr untr* to differ
Unterscheidung *f* (*Unterschied*) distinction;
(*Unterscheiden*) differentiation
Unterschenkel [ˈʊntərʃɛŋkəl] *m* lower leg
Unterschicht [ˈʊntərʃɪçt] *f* lower class
unterschieben [ˈʊntərʃiːbən] *unreg vt* (*fig*): **jdm**
etw ~ to foist sth on sb
Unterschied [ˈʊntərʃiːt] (**-(e)s, -e**) *m*
difference, distinction; **im ~ zu** as distinct
from; **unterschiedlich** *adj* varying, differing;
(*diskriminierend*) discriminatory
unterschiedslos *adv* indiscriminately
unterschlagen [ʊntərˈʃlaːgən] *unreg vt untr* to
embezzle; (*verheimlichen*) to suppress
Unterschlagung *f* embezzlement; (*von Briefen,*
Beweis) withholding
Unterschlupf [ˈʊntərʃlʊpf] (**-(e)s, -schlüpfe**)
m refuge
unterschlüpfen [ˈʊntərʃlʏpfən] (*umg*) *vi* to take
cover *od* shelter; (*Versteck finden*): (**bei jdm**) **~** to
hide out (at sb's) (*umg*)
unterschreiben [ʊntərˈʃraɪbən] *unreg vt untr* to
sign
Unterschrift [ˈʊntərʃrɪft] *f* signature;
(*Bildunterschrift*) caption
unterschwellig [ˈʊntərʃvɛlɪç] *adj* subliminal
Unterseeboot [ˈʊntərzeːboːt] *nt* submarine
Unterseite [ˈʊntərzaɪtə] *f* underside
Untersekunda [ˈʊntərzekunda] *f* (*früher*) sixth
year of German secondary school
Untersetzer [ˈʊntərzɛtsər] *m* tablemat; (*für*
Gläser) coaster
untersetzt [ʊntərˈzɛtst] *adj* stocky
unterste, r, s [ˈʊntərstə(r, s)] *adj* lowest,
bottom
unterstehen¹ [ʊntərˈʃteːən] *unreg vi untr* +*dat* to
be under ▷ *vr untr* to dare
unterstehen² [ˈʊntərʃteːən] *unreg vi* to shelter
unterstellen¹ [ʊntərˈʃtɛlən] *vt untr* to
subordinate; (*fig*) to impute; **jdm/etw**

unterstellt sein to be under sb/sth; (*in Firma*)
to report to sb/sth
unterstellen² [ˈʊntərʃtɛlən] *vt* (*Auto*) to garage,
park ▷ *vr* to take shelter
Unterstellung *f* (*falsche Behauptung*)
misrepresentation; (*Andeutung*) insinuation
unterstreichen [ʊntərˈʃtraɪçən] *unreg vt untr* (*lit,*
fig) to underline
Unterstufe [ˈʊntərʃtuːfə] *f* lower grade
unterstützen [ʊntərˈʃtʏtsən] *vt untr* to support
Unterstützung *f* support, assistance
untersuchen [ʊntərˈzuːxən] *vt untr* (*Med*) to
examine; (*Polizei*) to investigate; **sich ärztlich**
~ lassen to have a medical (*Brit*) *od* physical
(*US*) (examination), have a check-up
Untersuchung *f* examination; investigation,
inquiry
Untersuchungs- *zW:*
Untersuchungsausschuss *m* committee
of inquiry; **Untersuchungsergebnis** *nt* (*Jur*)
findings *pl*; (*Med*) result of an examination;
Untersuchungshaft *f* custody; **in**
Untersuchungshaft sein to be remanded in
custody; **Untersuchungsrichter** *m* examining
magistrate
Untertagebau [ʊntərˈtaːgəbau] *m*
underground mining
Untertan [ˈʊntərtaːn] (**-s, -en**) *m* subject
untertänig [ˈʊntərtɛːnɪç] *adj* submissive,
humble
Untertasse [ˈʊntərtasə] *f* saucer
untertauchen [ˈʊntərtauxən] *vi* to dive; (*fig*) to
disappear, go underground
Unterteil [ˈʊntərtaɪl] *nt od m* lower part,
bottom
unterteilen [ʊntərˈtaɪlən] *vt untr* to divide up
Untertertia [ˈʊntərtɛrtsia] *f* (*früher*) fourth *year of*
German secondary school
Untertitel [ˈʊntərtiːtəl] *m* subtitle; (*für Bild*)
caption
unterwandern [ʊntərˈvandərn] *vt untr* to
infiltrate
Unterwäsche [ˈʊntərvɛʃə] *f* underwear
unterwegs [ʊntərˈveːks] *adv* on the way; (*auf*
Reisen) away
unterweisen [ʊntərˈvaɪzən] *unreg vt untr* to
instruct
Unterwelt [ˈʊntərvɛlt] *f* (*lit, fig*) underworld
unterwerfen [ʊntərˈvɛrfən] *unreg vt untr* to
subject; (*Volk*) to subjugate ▷ *vr untr* to submit
unterwürfig [ʊntərˈvʏrfɪç] *adj* obsequious
unterzeichnen [ʊntərˈtsaɪçnən] *vt untr* to sign
Unterzeichner *m* signatory
unterziehen [ʊntərˈtsiːən] *unreg vt untr* +*dat* to
subject ▷ *vr untr* +*dat* to undergo; (*einer Prüfung*)
to take
Untiefe [ˈʊntiːfə] *f* shallow
Untier [ˈʊntiːr] *nt* monster
untragbar [ʊnˈtraːkbaːr] *adj* intolerable,
unbearable
untreu [ˈʊntrɔy] *adj* unfaithful; **sich** *dat* **selbst**
~ werden to be untrue to o.s.
Untreue *f* unfaithfulness

u

untröstlich [ʊnˈtrøːstlɪç] *adj* inconsolable
Untugend [ˈʊntuːɡənt] *f* vice; *(Angewohnheit)* bad habit
un- *zW:* **unüberbrückbar** *adj (fig: Gegensätze etc)* irreconcilable; *(Kluft)* unbridgeable; **unüberlegt** *adj* ill-considered ▷ *adv* without thinking; **unübersehbar** *adj (Schaden etc)* incalculable; *(Menge)* vast, immense; *(auffällig: Fehler etc)* obvious; **unübersichtlich** *adj (Gelände)* broken; *(Kurve)* blind; *(System, Plan)* confused; **unübertroffen** *adj* unsurpassed
un- *zW:* **unumgänglich** *adj* indispensable, vital; **unumstößlich** *adj (Tatsache)* incontrovertible; *(Entschluss)* irrevocable; **unumstritten** *adj* undisputed; **unumwunden** [-ʊmˈvʊndən] *adj* candid ▷ *adv* straight out
ununterbrochen [ˈʊn|ʊntərbrɔxən] *adj* uninterrupted
un- *zW:* **unveränderlich** *adj* unchangeable; **unverantwortlich** *adj* irresponsible; *(unentschuldbar)* inexcusable; **unverarbeitet** *adj (lit, fig)* raw; **unveräußerlich** [-fɛrˈɔysərlɪç] *adj* inalienable; *(Besitz)* unmarketable; **unverbesserlich** *adj* incorrigible; **unverbindlich** *adj* not binding; *(Antwort)* curt ▷ *adv (Comm)* without obligation; **unverbleit** [-fɛrblaɪt] *adj (Benzin)* unleaded; **unverblümt** [-fɛrˈblyːmt] *adj* plain, blunt ▷ *adv* plainly, bluntly; **unverdaulich** *adj* indigestible; **unverdorben** *adj* unspoilt; **unverdrossen** *adj* undeterred; *(unermüdlich)* untiring; **unvereinbar** *adj* incompatible; **unverfälscht** [-fɛrfɛlʃt] *adj (auch fig)* unadulterated; *(Dialekt)* pure; *(Natürlichkeit)* unaffected; **unverfänglich** *adj* harmless; **unverfroren** *adj* impudent; **unvergänglich** *adj* immortal; *(Eindruck, Erinnerung)* everlasting; **unvergesslich** *adj* unforgettable; **unvergleichlich** *adj* unique, incomparable; **unverhältnismäßig** *adv* disproportionately; *(übermäßig)* excessively; **unverheiratet** *adj* unmarried; **unverhofft** *adj* unexpected; **unverhohlen** [-fɛrhoːlən] *adj* open, unconcealed; **unverkäuflich** *adj:* „**unverkäuflich**" "not for sale"; **unverkennbar** *adj* unmistakable; **unverletzlich** *adj (fig: Rechte)* inviolable; *(lit)* invulnerable; **unverletzt** *adj* uninjured; **unvermeidlich** *adj* unavoidable; **unvermittelt** *adj (plötzlich)* sudden, unexpected; **Unvermögen** *nt* inability; **unvermutet** *adj* unexpected; **unvernünftig** *adj* foolish; **unverrichtet** *adj:* **unverrichteter Dinge** empty-handed; **unverschämt** *adj* impudent; **Unverschämtheit** *f* impudence, insolence; **unverschuldet** *adj* occurring through no fault of one's own; **unversehens** *adv* all of a sudden; **unversehrt** [-fɛrzeːrt] *adj* uninjured; **unversöhnlich** *adj* irreconcilable; **Unverstand** *m* lack of judgement; *(Torheit)* folly; **unverständlich** *adj* unintelligible; **unversucht** *adj:* **nichts unversucht lassen** to try everything; **unverträglich** *adj* quarrelsome; *(Meinungen, Med)* incompatible;

unverwechselbar *adj* unmistakable, distinctive; **unverwüstlich** *adj* indestructible; *(Mensch)* irrepressible; **unverzeihlich** *adj* unpardonable; **unverzinslich** *adj* interest-free; **unverzüglich** [-fɛrˈtsyːklɪç] *adj* immediate; **unvollendet** *adj* unfinished; **unvollkommen** *adj* imperfect; **unvollständig** *adj* incomplete; **unvorbereitet** *adj* unprepared; **unvoreingenommen** *adj* unbiased; **unvorhergesehen** *adj* unforeseen; **unvorsichtig** *adj* careless, imprudent; **unvorstellbar** *adj* inconceivable; **unvorteilhaft** *adj* disadvantageous
unwahr [ˈʊnvaːr] *adj* untrue; **unwahrhaftig** *adj* untruthful; **Unwahrheit** *f* untruth; **die Unwahrheit sagen** not to tell the truth; **unwahrscheinlich** *adj* improbable, unlikely ▷ *adv (umg)* incredibly; **Unwahrscheinlichkeit** *f* improbability, unlikelihood
unwegsam [ˈʊnveːkzaːm] *adj (Gelände etc)* rough
unweigerlich [ʊnˈvaɪɡərlɪç] *adj* unquestioning ▷ *adv* without fail
unweit [ˈʊnvaɪt] *präp +gen* not far from ▷ *adv* not far
Unwesen [ˈʊnveːzən] *nt* nuisance; *(Unfug)* mischief; **sein ~ treiben** to wreak havoc; *(Mörder etc)* to be at large
unwesentlich *adj* inessential, unimportant; **~ besser** marginally better
Unwetter [ˈʊnvɛtər] *nt* thunderstorm
unwichtig [ˈʊnvɪçtɪç] *adj* unimportant
un- *zW:* **unwiderlegbar** *adj* irrefutable; **unwiderruflich** *adj* irrevocable; **unwiderstehlich** [-viːdərˈʃteːlɪç] *adj* irresistible
unwiederbringlich [ʊnviːdərˈbrɪŋlɪç] *adj (geh)* irretrievable
Unwille [ˈʊnvɪlə], **Unwillen** [ˈʊnvɪlən] *m* indignation
unwillig *adj* indignant; *(widerwillig)* reluctant
unwillkürlich [ˈʊnvɪlkyːrlɪç] *adj* involuntary ▷ *adv* instinctively; *(lachen)* involuntarily
unwirklich [ˈʊnvɪrklɪç] *adj* unreal
unwirksam [ˈʊnvɪrkzaːm] *adj* ineffective
unwirsch [ˈʊnvɪrʃ] *adj* cross, surly
unwirtlich [ˈʊnvɪrtlɪç] *adj* inhospitable
unwirtschaftlich [ˈʊnvɪrtʃaftlɪç] *adj* uneconomical
unwissend [ˈʊnvɪsənt] *adj* ignorant
Unwissenheit *f* ignorance
unwissenschaftlich *adj* unscientific
unwissentlich *adv* unwittingly, unknowingly
unwohl [ˈʊnvoːl] *adj* unwell, ill; **Unwohlsein** (-s) *nt* indisposition
unwürdig [ˈʊnvʏrdɪç] *adj* unworthy
Unzahl [ˈʊntsaːl] *f:* **eine ~ von ...** a whole host of ...
unzählig [ʊnˈtsɛːlɪç] *adj* innumerable, countless
unzeitgemäß [ˈʊntsaɪtɡəmɛːs] *adj (altmodisch)* old-fashioned
un- *zW:* **unzerbrechlich** *adj* unbreakable; **unzerreißbar** *adj* untearable; **unzerstörbar** *adj*

indestructible; **unzertrennlich** *adj* inseparable

Unzucht ['ʊntsʊxt] *f* sexual offence

unzüchtig ['ʊntsʏçtiç] *adj* immoral

un- *zW:* **unzufrieden** *adj* dissatisfied; **Unzufriedenheit** *f* discontent; **unzugänglich** *adj* (*Gegend*) inaccessible; (*Mensch*) inapproachable; **unzulänglich** *adj* inadequate; **unzulässig** *adj* inadmissible; **unzumutbar** *adj* unreasonable; **unzurechnungsfähig** *adj* irresponsible; **jdn für unzurechnungsfähig erklären lassen** (*Jur*) to have sb certified (insane); **unzusammenhängend** *adj* disconnected; (*Äußerung*) incoherent; **unzustellbar** *adj*: **falls unzustellbar, bitte an Absender zurück** if undelivered, please return to sender; **unzutreffend** *adj* incorrect; **„nzutreffendes bitte streichen"** "delete as applicable"; **unzuverlässig** *adj* unreliable

unzweckmäßig ['ʊntsvɛkmɛːsɪç] *adj* (*nicht ratsam*) inadvisable; (*unpraktisch*) impractical; (*ungeeignet*) unsuitable

unzweideutig ['ʊntsvaɪdɔʏtiç] *adj* unambiguous

unzweifelhaft ['ʊntsvaɪfəlhaft] *adj* indubitable

üppig ['ʏpiç] *adj* (*Frau*) curvaceous; (*Essen*) sumptuous, lavish; (*Vegetation*) luxuriant, lush; (*Haar*) thick

Ur- ['uːr] *in zw* original

Urabstimmung ['uːrˌʔapʃtɪmʊŋ] *f* ballot

Ural [u'raːl] (**-s**) *m*: **der ~** the Ural mountains *pl*, the Urals *pl*; **Uralgebirge** *nt* Ural mountains

uralt ['uːrˌalt] *adj* ancient, very old

Uran [u'raːn] (**-s**) *nt* uranium

Uraufführung *f* first performance

urbar *adj*: **die Wüste/Land ~ machen** to reclaim the desert/cultivate land

Urdu ['ʊrdu] (**-**) *nt* Urdu

Ur- *zW:* **Ureinwohner** *m* original inhabitant; **Ureltern** *pl* ancestors *pl*; **Urenkel, in** *m(f)* great-grandchild; **Urfassung** *f* original version; **Urgroßmutter** *f* great-grandmother; **Urgroßvater** *m* great-grandfather

Urheber(**-s, -**) *m* originator; (*Autor*) author; **Urheberrecht** *nt*: **Urheberrecht (an** +*dat*) copyright (on); **urheberrechtlich** *adv*: **urheberrechtlich geschützt** copyright

urig ['uːrɪç] (*umg*) *adj* (*Mensch, Atmosphäre*) earthy

Urin [u'riːn] (**-s, -e**) *m* urine

urkomisch *adj* incredibly funny

Urkunde *f* document; (*Kaufurkunde*) deed

urkundlich ['uːrkʊntliç] *adj* documentary

URL *f abk* (= *uniform resource locator*) URL

Urlader *m* (*Comput*) bootstrap

Urlaub ['uːrlaʊp] (**-(e)s, -e**) *m* holiday(s *pl*) (*Brit*), vacation (*US*); (*Mil etc*) leave; **Urlauber** (**-s, -**) *m* holiday-maker (*Brit*), vacationer (*US*)

Urlaubs- *zW:* **Urlaubsgeld** *nt* holiday (*Brit*) *od* vacation (*US*) money; **Urlaubsort** *m* holiday (*Brit*) *od* vacation (*US*) resort; **urlaubsreif** *adj* in need of a holiday (*Brit*) *od* vacation (*US*)

Urmensch *m* primitive man

Urne ['ʊrnə] (**-, -n**) *f* urn; **zur ~ gehen** to go to the polls

urplötzlich ['uːrˈplœtsliç] (*umg*) *adv* all of a sudden

Ursache ['uːrzaxə] *f* cause; **keine ~!** (*auf Dank*) don't mention it, you're welcome; (*auf Entschuldigung*) that's all right

ursächlich ['uːrzɛçliç] *adj* causal

Urschrei ['uːrʃraɪ] *m* (*Psych*) primal scream

Ursprung ['uːrʃprʊŋ] *m* origin, source; (*von Fluss*) source

ursprünglich ['uːrʃprʏŋliç] *adj* original ▷ *adv* originally

Ursprungsland *nt* (*Comm*) country of origin

Ursprungszeugnis *nt* certificate of origin

Urteil ['ʊrtaɪl] (**-s, -e**) *nt* opinion; (*Jur*) sentence, judgement; **sich** *dat* **ein ~ über etw** *akk* **erlauben** to pass judgement on sth; **ein ~ über etw** *akk* **fällen** to pass judgement on sth; **urteilen** *vi* to judge

Urteilsbegründung *f* (*Jur*) opinion

Urteilsspruch *m* sentence; verdict

Uruguay [uru'guaːi] (**-s**) *nt* Uruguay

Uruguayer, in [uru'guaːi] (**-s, -**) *m(f)* Uruguayan

uruguayisch *adj* Uruguayan

Ur- *zW:* **Urwald** *m* jungle; **urwüchsig** *adj* natural; (*Landschaft*) unspoilt; (*Humor*) earthy; **Urzeit** *f* prehistoric times *pl*

USA [uːˈɛsˈʔaː] *pl abk*: **die ~** the USA *sing*

USB *abk* (= *universal serial bus*) USB

Usbekistan [ʊsˈbeːkistaːn] (**-s**) *nt* Uzbekistan

usw. *abk* (= *und so weiter*) etc.

Utensilien [utɛnˈziːliən] *pl* utensils *pl*

Utopie [uto'piː] *f* pipe dream

utopisch [u'toːpɪʃ] *adj* utopian

u. U. *abk* (= *unter Umständen*) possibly

UV *abk* (= *ultraviolett*) U.V.

u. v. a. *abk* (= *und viele(s) andere*) and much/many more

u. v. a. m. *abk* (= *und viele(s) andere mehr*) and much/many more

u. W. *abk* (= *unseres Wissens*) to our knowledge

Ü-Wagen *m* (*Rundf, TV*) outside broadcast vehicle

uzen ['uːtsən] (*umg*) *vt, vi* to tease, kid

u. zw. *abk* = **und zwar**

u

Vv

V¹, v [faʊ] *nt* V, v; **V wie Viktor** ≈ V for Victor
V² [faʊ] *abk* (= *Volt*) v
VAE *pl abk* (= *Vereinigte Arabische Emirate*) UAE
vag, vage *adj* vague
Vagina [vaˈgiːna] (-, **Vaginen**) *f* vagina
Vakuum [ˈvaːkuʊm] (-s, **Vakua** *od* **Vakuen**)
  nt vacuum; **vakuumverpackt** *adj* vacuum-
  packed
Vandalismus [vandaˈlɪsmʊs] *m* vandalism
Vanille [vaˈnɪljə] (-) *f* vanilla; **Vanillezucker** *m*
  vanilla sugar
Vanillinzucker *m* vanilla sugar
variabel [variˈaːbəl] *adj*: **variable Kosten**
  variable costs
Variable [variˈaːblə] (-, **-n**) *f* variable
Variante [variˈantə] (-, **-n**) *f*: **~ (zu)** variant (on)
Variation [variatsiˈoːn] *f* variation
variieren [variˈiːrən] *vt, vi* to vary
Vase [ˈvaːzə] (-, **-n**) *f* vase
Vater [ˈfaːtər] (-s, **⁻**) *m* father; **~ Staat** (*umg*)
  the State; **Vaterland** *nt* native country; (*bes
  Deutschland*) Fatherland; **Vaterlandsliebe** *f*
  patriotism
väterlich [ˈfɛːtərlɪç] *adj* fatherly
väterlicherseits *adv* on the father's side
Vaterschaft *f* paternity
Vaterschaftsklage *f* paternity suit
Vaterstelle *f*: **~ bei jdm vertreten** to take the
  place of sb's father
Vaterunser (-s, -) *nt* Lord's Prayer
Vati [ˈfaːti] (-s, -s) (*umg*) *m* dad(dy)
Vatikan [vatiˈkaːn] (-s) *m* Vatican
V-Ausschnitt [ˈfaʊˌaʊsʃnɪt] *m* V-neck
VB *abk* (= *Verhandlungsbasis*) o.i.r.o.
v. Chr. *abk* (= *vor Christus*) B.C.
Vegetarier, in [vegeˈtaːriər(ɪn)] (-s, -) *m(f)*
  vegetarian
vegetarisch *adj* vegetarian
Vegetation [vegetatsiˈoːn] *f* vegetation
vegetativ [vegetaˈtiːf] *adj* (*Biol*) vegetative;
  (*Med*) autonomic
vegetieren [vegeˈtiːrən] *vi* to vegetate; (*kärglich
  leben*) to eke out a bare existence
Vehikel [veˈhiːkəl] (-s, -) (*pej: umg*) *nt*
  boneshaker
Veilchen [ˈfaɪlçən] *nt* violet; (*umg: blaues Auge*)
  shiner, black eye
Velours (-, -) *nt* suede; **Veloursleder** *nt* suede

Vene [ˈveːnə] (-, **-n**) *f* vein
Venedig [veˈneːdɪç] (-s) *nt* Venice
Venezianer, in [venetsiˈaːnər(ɪn)] (-s, -) *m(f)*
  Venetian
venezianisch [venetsiˈaːnɪʃ] *adj* Venetian
Venezolaner, in [venetsoˈlaːnər(ɪn)] (-s, -) *m(f)*
  Venezuelan
venezolanisch *adj* Venezuelan
Venezuela [venetsuˈeːla] (-s) *nt* Venezuela
Ventil [vɛnˈtiːl] (-s, **-e**) *nt* valve
Ventilator [vɛntiˈlaːtɔr] *m* ventilator
verabreden [fɛrˈʔapreːdən] *vt* to arrange;
  (*Termin*) to agree upon ▷ *vr* to arrange to
  meet; **sich (mit jdm) ~** to arrange to meet
  (sb); **schon verabredet sein** to have a prior
  engagement (*form*), have something else on
Verabredung *f* arrangement; (*Treffen*)
  appointment; **ich habe eine ~** I'm meeting
  somebody
verabreichen [fɛrˈʔapraɪçən] *vt* (*Tracht Prügel
  etc*) to give; (*Arznei*) to administer (*form*)
verabscheuen [fɛrˈʔapʃɔyən] *vt* to detest,
  abhor
verabschieden [fɛrˈʔapʃiːdən] *vt* (*Gäste*) to say
  goodbye to; (*entlassen*) to discharge; (*Gesetz*) to
  pass ▷ *vr*: **sich ~ (von)** to take one's leave (of)
Verabschiedung *f* (*von Beamten etc*) discharge;
  (*von Gesetz*) passing
verachten [fɛrˈʔaxtən] *vt* to despise; **nicht zu
  ~** (*umg*) not to be scoffed at
verächtlich [fɛrˈʔɛçtlɪç] *adj* contemptuous;
  (*verachtenswert*) contemptible; **jdn ~ machen**
  to run sb down
Verachtung *f* contempt; **jdn mit ~ strafen** to
  treat sb with contempt
veralbern [fɛrˈʔalbərn] (*umg*) *vt* to make fun of
verallgemeinern [fɛrˈʔalgəˈmaɪnərn] *vt* to
  generalize
Verallgemeinerung *f* generalization
veralten [fɛrˈʔaltən] *vi* to become obsolete *od*
  out-of-date
Veranda [veˈranda] (-, **Veranden**) *f* veranda
veränderlich [fɛrˈʔɛndərlɪç] *adj* variable;
  (*Wetter*) changeable; **Veränderlichkeit** *f*
  variability; changeability
verändern *vt, vr* to change
Veränderung *f* change; **eine berufliche ~** a
  change of job

verängstigen [fɛrˈʔɛŋstɪɡən] *vt* (*erschrecken*) to frighten; (*einschüchtern*) to intimidate

verankern [fɛrˈʔaŋkərn] *vt* (*Naut, Tech*) to anchor; (*fig*): ~ **(in** +*dat*) to embed (in)

veranlagen [fɛrˈʔanla:ɡən] *vt*: **etw ~ (mit)** to assess sth (at)

veranlagt *adj*: **praktisch ~ sein** to be practically-minded; **zu** *od* **für etw ~ sein** to be cut out for sth

Veranlagung *f* disposition, aptitude

veranlassen [fɛrˈʔanlasən] *vt* to cause; **Maßnahmen ~** to take measures; **sich veranlasst sehen** to feel prompted; **etw ~** to arrange for sth; (*befehlen*) to order sth

Veranlassung *f* cause; motive; **auf jds ~** *akk* **(hin)** at sb's instigation

veranschaulichen [fɛrˈʔanʃaʊlɪçən] *vt* to illustrate

veranschlagen [fɛrˈʔanʃla:ɡən] *vt* to estimate

veranstalten [fɛrˈʔanʃtaltən] *vt* to organize, arrange

Veranstalter, in (-s, -) *m(f)* organizer; (*Comm: von Konzerten etc*) promoter

Veranstaltung *f* (*Veranstalten*) organizing; (*Veranstaltetes*) event; (*feierlich, öffentlich*) function

verantworten [fɛrˈʔantvɔrtən] *vt* to accept responsibility for; (*Folgen etc*) to answer for ▷ *vr* to justify o.s.; **etw vor jdm ~** to answer to sb for sth

verantwortlich *adj* responsible

Verantwortung *f* responsibility; **jdn zur ~ ziehen** to call sb to account

verantwortungs- *zW*: **verantwortungsbewusst** *adj* responsible; **Verantwortungsgefühl** *nt* sense of responsibility; **verantwortungslos** *adj* irresponsible; **verantwortungsvoll** *adj* responsible

verarbeiten [fɛrˈʔarbaɪtən] *vt* to process; (*geistig*) to assimilate; (*Erlebnis etc*) to digest; **etw zu etw ~** to make sth into sth; **-de Industrie** processing industries *pl*

verarbeitet *adj*: **gut ~** (*Kleid etc*) well finished

Verarbeitung *f* processing; assimilation

verärgern [fɛrˈʔɛrɡərn] *vt* to annoy

verarmen [fɛrˈʔarmən] *vi* (*lit, fig*) to become impoverished

verarschen [fɛrˈʔarʃən] (*umg!*) *vt*: **jdn ~** to take the mickey out of sb

verarzten [fɛrˈʔa:rtstən] *vt* to fix up (*umg*)

verausgaben [fɛrˈʔaʊsɡa:bən] *vr* to run out of money; (*fig*) to exhaust o.s.

veräußern [fɛrˈʔɔysərn] *vt* (*form: verkaufen*) to dispose of

Verb [vɛrp] (**-s, -en**) *nt* verb

Verb. *abk* (= *Verband*) assoc.

Verband [fɛrˈbant] (**-(e)s, ⁻e**) *m* (*Med*) bandage, dressing; (*Bund*) association, society; (*Mil*) unit

verband *etc vb siehe* **verbinden**

Verband- *zW*: **Verbandkasten, Verbandskasten** *m* medicine chest, first-aid box; **Verbandpäckchen, Verbandspäckchen** *nt* gauze bandage; **Verbandstoff** *m* bandage, dressing material; **Verbandzeug** *nt* bandage, dressing material

verbannen [fɛrˈbanən] *vt* to banish

Verbannung *f* exile

verbarrikadieren [fɛrbarika'di:rən] *vt* to barricade ▷ *vr* to barricade o.s. in

verbauen [fɛrˈbaʊən] *vt*: **sich** *dat* **alle Chancen ~** to spoil one's chances

verbergen [fɛrˈbɛrɡən] *unreg vt, vr*: **(sich) ~ (vor** +*dat*) to hide (from)

verbessern [fɛrˈbɛsərn] *vt* to improve; (*berichtigen*) to correct ▷ *vr* to improve; to correct o.s.

verbessert *adj* revised; improved; **eine neue, ~e Auflage** a new revised edition

Verbesserung *f* improvement; correction

verbeugen [fɛrˈbɔyɡən] *vr* to bow

Verbeugung *f* bow

verbiegen [fɛrˈbi:ɡən] *unreg vi* to bend

verbiestert [fɛrˈbi:stərt] (*umg*) *adj* crotchety

verbieten [fɛrˈbi:tən] *unreg vt* to forbid; (*amtlich*) to prohibit; (*Zeitung, Partei*) to ban; **jdm etw ~** to forbid sb to do sth

verbilligen [fɛrˈbɪlɪɡən] *vt* to reduce (the price of) ▷ *vr* to become cheaper, go down

verbinden [fɛrˈbɪndən] *unreg vt* to connect; (*kombinieren*) to combine; (*Med*) to bandage ▷ *vr* to combine (*auch CHEM*), join (together); **jdm die Augen ~** to blindfold sb

verbindlich [fɛrˈbɪntlɪç] *adj* binding; (*freundlich*) obliging; **~ zusagen** to accept definitely; **Verbindlichkeit** *f* obligation; (*Höflichkeit*) civility; **Verbindlichkeiten** *pl* (*Jur*) obligations *pl*; (*Comm*) liabilities *pl*

Verbindung *f* connection; (*Zusammensetzung*) combination; (*Chem*) compound; (*Univ*) club; (*Tel: Anschluss*) line; **mit jdm in ~ stehen** to be in touch *od* contact with sb; **~ mit jdm aufnehmen** to contact sb

Verbindungsmann (-(e)s, *pl* -männer *od* **-leute)** *m* intermediary; (*Agent*) contact

verbissen [fɛrˈbɪsən] *adj* grim; (*Arbeiter*) dogged; **Verbissenheit** *f* grimness; doggedness

verbitten [fɛrˈbɪtən] *unreg vt*: **sich** *dat* **etw ~** not to tolerate sth, not to stand for sth

verbittern [fɛrˈbɪtərn] *vt* to embitter ▷ *vi* to get bitter

verblassen [fɛrˈblasən] *vi* to fade

Verbleib [fɛrˈblaɪp] (**-(e)s**) *m* whereabouts

verbleiben [fɛrˈblaɪbən] *unreg vi* to remain; **wir sind so verblieben, dass wir ...** we agreed to ...

verbleit [fɛrˈblaɪt] *adj* leaded

Verblendung [fɛrˈblɛndʊŋ] *f* (*fig*) delusion

verblöden [fɛrˈblø:dən] *vi* (*Hilfsverb sein*) to get stupid

verblüffen [fɛrˈblʏfən] *vt* to amaze; (*verwirren*) to baffle

Verblüffung *f* stupefaction

verblühen [fɛrˈbly:ən] *vi* to wither, fade

verbluten [fɛrˈblu:tən] *vi* to bleed to death

V

357

verbohren [fɛr'boːrən] (*umg*) *vr*: **sich in etw** *akk* ~ to become obsessed with sth

verbohrt *adj* (*Haltung*) stubborn, obstinate

verborgen [fɛr'bɔrgən] *adj* hidden; **~e Mängel** latent defects *pl*

Verbot [fɛr'boːt] (**-(e)s, -e**) *nt* prohibition, ban

verboten *adj* forbidden; **Rauchen ~!** no smoking; **er sah ~ aus** (*umg*) he looked a real sight

verbotenerweise *adv* though it is forbidden

Verbotsschild *nt* prohibitory sign

verbrämen [fɛr'brɛːmən] *vt* (*fig*) to gloss over; (*Kritik*): ~ (**mit**) to veil (in)

Verbrauch [fɛr'braux] (**-(e)s**) *m* consumption

verbrauchen *vt* to use up; **der Wagen verbraucht 10 Liter Benzin auf 100 km** the car does 10 kms to the litre (*Brit*) *od* liter (*US*)

Verbraucher, in (**-s, -**) *m(f)* consumer; **Verbrauchermarkt** *m* hypermarket; **verbrauchernah** *adj* consumer-friendly; **Verbraucherschutz** *m* consumer protection; **Verbraucherverband** *m* consumer council

Verbrauchsgüter *pl* consumer goods *pl*

verbraucht *adj* used up, finished; (*Luft*) stale; (*Mensch*) worn-out

Verbrechen (**-s, -**) *nt* crime

Verbrecher, in (**-s, -**) *m(f)* criminal; **verbrecherisch** *adj* criminal; **Verbrecherkartei** *f* file of offenders, ≈ rogues' gallery; **Verbrechertum** (**-s**) *nt* criminality

verbreiten [fɛr'braɪtən] *vt* to spread; (*Licht*) to shed; (*Wärme, Ruhe*) to radiate ▷ *vr* to spread; **eine (weit) verbreitete Ansicht** a widely held opinion; **sich über etw** *akk* ~ to expound on sth

verbreitern [fɛr'braɪtərn] *vt* to broaden

Verbreitung *f* spread(ing); shedding; radiation

verbrennbar *adj* combustible

verbrennen [fɛr'brɛnən] *unreg vt* to burn; (*Leiche*) to cremate; (*versengen*) to scorch; (*Haar*) to singe; (*verbrühen*) to scald

Verbrennung *f* burning; (*in Motor*) combustion; (*von Leiche*) cremation

Verbrennungsanlage *f* incineration plant

Verbrennungsmotor *m* internal-combustion engine

verbriefen [fɛr'briːfən] *vt* to document

verbringen [fɛr'brɪŋən] *unreg vt* to spend

Verbrüderung [fɛr'bryːdərʊŋ] *f* fraternization

verbrühen [fɛr'bryːən] *vt* to scald

verbuchen [fɛr'buːxən] *vt* (*Fin*) to register; (*Erfolg*) to enjoy; (*Misserfolg*) to suffer

verbummeln [fɛr'bʊməln] (*umg*) *vt* (*verlieren*) to lose; (*Zeit*) to waste, fritter away; (*Verabredung*) to miss

verbunden [fɛr'bʊndən] *adj* connected; **jdm ~ sein** to be obliged *od* indebted to sb; **ich/er** *etc* **war falsch ~** (*Tel*) it was a wrong number

verbünden [fɛr'bʏndən] *vr* to form an alliance

Verbundenheit *f* bond, relationship

Verbündete, r *f(m)* ally

Verbundglas [fɛr'bʊntglaːs] *nt* laminated glass

verbürgen [fɛr'bʏrgən] *vr*: **sich ~ für** to vouch for; **ein verbürgtes Recht** an established right

verbüßen [fɛr'byːsən] *vt*: **eine Strafe ~** to serve a sentence

verchromt [fɛr'kroːmt] *adj* chromium-plated

Verdacht [fɛr'daxt] (**-(e)s**) *m* suspicion; ~ **schöpfen (gegen jdn)** to become suspicious (of sb); **jdn in ~ haben** to suspect sb; **es besteht ~ auf Krebs** *akk* cancer is suspected

verdächtig *adj* suspicious

verdächtigen [fɛr'dɛçtɪgən] *vt* to suspect

Verdächtigung *f* suspicion

verdammen [fɛr'damən] *vt* to damn, condemn

Verdammnis (**-**) *f* perdition, damnation

verdammt (*umg*) *adj, adv* damned; ~ **noch mal!** bloody hell (*!*), damn (*!*)

verdampfen [fɛr'dampfən] *vt, vi* (*vi Hilfsverb sein*) to vaporize; (*Koch*) to boil away

verdanken [fɛr'daŋkən] *vt*: **jdm etw ~** to owe sb sth

verdarb *etc* [fɛr'darp] *vb siehe* **verderben**

verdattert [fɛr'datərt] (*umg*) *adj, adv* flabbergasted

verdauen [fɛr'dauən] *vt* (*lit, fig*) to digest ▷ *vi* (*lit*) to digest

verdaulich [fɛr'daulɪç] *adj* digestible; **das ist schwer ~** that is hard to digest

Verdauung *f* digestion

Verdauungsspaziergang *m* constitutional

Verdauungsstörung *f* indigestion

Verdeck [fɛr'dɛk] (**-(e)s, -e**) *nt* (*Aut*) soft top; (*Naut*) deck

verdecken *vt* to cover (up); (*verbergen*) to hide

verdenken [fɛr'dɛŋkən] *unreg vt*: **jdm etw ~** to blame sb for sth, hold sth against sb

verderben [fɛr'dɛrbən] *unreg vt* to spoil; (*schädigen*) to ruin; (*moralisch*) to corrupt ▷ *vi* (*Essen*) to spoil, rot; (*Mensch*) to go to the bad; **es mit jdm ~** to get into sb's bad books

Verderben (**-s**) *nt* ruin

verderblich *adj* (*Einfluss*) pernicious; (*Lebensmittel*) perishable

verderbt *adj* (*veraltet*) depraved; **Verderbtheit** *f* depravity

verdeutlichen [fɛr'dɔytlɪçən] *vt* to make clear

verdichten [fɛr'dɪçtən] *vt* (*Phys, fig*) to compress ▷ *vr* to thicken; (*Verdacht, Eindruck*) to deepen

verdienen [fɛr'diːnən] *vt* to earn; (*moralisch*) to deserve ▷ *vi* (*Gewinn machen*): ~ (**an** +*dat*) to make (a profit) (on)

Verdienst [fɛr'diːnst] (**-(e)s, -e**) *m* earnings *pl* ▷ *nt* merit; (*Dank*) credit; (*Leistung*): ~ (**um**) service (to), contribution (to); **verdienstvoll** *adj* commendable

verdient [fɛr'diːnt] *adj* well-earned; (*Person*) of outstanding merit; (*Lohn, Strafe*) rightful; **sich um etw ~ machen** to do a lot for sth

verdirbst [fɛr'dɪrpst] *vb siehe* **verderben**

verdirbt [fɛr'dɪrpt] *vb siehe* **verderben**

verdonnern [fɛr'dɔnərn] (*umg*) *vt* (*zu Haft etc*): ~ (**zu**) to sentence (to); **jdn zu etw ~** to order sb to do sth

verdoppeln [fɛrˈdɔpəln] *vt* to double

Verdoppelung, Verdopplung *f* doubling

verdorben [fɛrˈdɔrbən] *pp von* **verderben** ▷ *adj* spoilt; *(geschädigt)* ruined; *(moralisch)* corrupt

verdorren [fɛrˈdɔrən] *vi* to wither

verdrängen [fɛrˈdrɛŋən] *vt* to oust; *(auch Phys)* to displace; *(Psych)* to repress

Verdrängung *f* displacement; *(Psych)* repression

verdrehen [fɛrˈdreːən] *vt (lit, fig)* to twist; *(Augen)* to roll; **jdm den Kopf ~** *(fig)* to turn sb's head

verdreht *(umg) adj* crazy; *(Bericht)* confused

verdreifachen [fɛrˈdraɪfaxən] *vt* to treble

verdrießen [fɛrˈdriːsən] *unreg vt* to annoy

verdrießlich [fɛrˈdriːslɪç] *adj* peevish, annoyed

verdross *etc* [fɛrˈdrɔs] *vb siehe* **verdrießen**

verdrossen [fɛrˈdrɔsən] *pp von* **verdrießen** ▷ *adj* cross, sulky

verdrücken [fɛrˈdrʏkən] *(umg) vt* to put away, eat ▷ *vr* to disappear

Verdruss [fɛrˈdrʊs] **(-es, -e)** *m* frustration; **zu jds ~** to sb's annoyance

verduften [fɛrˈdʊftən] *vi* to evaporate; *(umg)* to disappear

verdummen [fɛrˈdʊmən] *vt* to make stupid ▷ *vi* to grow stupid

verdunkeln [fɛrˈdʊŋkəln] *vt* to darken; *(fig)* to obscure ▷ *vr* to darken

Verdunkelung, Verdunklung *f* blackout; *(fig)* obscuring

verdünnen [fɛrˈdʏnən] *vt* to dilute

Verdünner (-s, -) *m* thinner

verdünnisieren [fɛrdʏniˈziːrən] *(umg) vr* to make o.s. scarce

verdunsten [fɛrˈdʊnstən] *vi* to evaporate

verdursten [fɛrˈdʊrstən] *vi* to die of thirst

verdutzt [fɛrˈdʊtst] *adj* nonplussed *(Brit)*, nonplused *(US)*, taken aback

verebben [fɛrˈʔɛbən] *vi* to subside

veredeln [fɛrˈʔeːdəln] *vt (Metalle, Erdöl)* to refine; *(Fasern)* to finish; *(Bot)* to graft

verehren [fɛrˈʔeːrən] *vt* to venerate, worship *(auch REL)*; **jdm etw ~** to present sb with sth

Verehrer, in [fɛrˈʔeːrɐ] **(-s, -)** *m(f)* admirer, worshipper *(Brit)*, worshiper *(US)*

verehrt *adj* esteemed; **(sehr) ~e Anwesende/ verehrtes Publikum** Ladies and Gentlemen

Verehrung *f* respect; *(Rel)* worship

vereidigen [fɛrˈʔaɪdɪgən] *vt* to put on oath; **jdn auf etw** *akk* **~** to make sb swear on sth

Vereidigung *f* swearing in

Verein [fɛrˈʔaɪn] **(-(e)s, -e)** *m* club, association; **ein wohltätiger ~** a charity

vereinbar *adj* compatible

vereinbaren [fɛrˈʔaɪnbaːrən] *vt* to agree upon

Vereinbarkeit *f* compatibility

Vereinbarung *f* agreement

vereinfachen [fɛrˈʔaɪnfaxən] *vt* to simplify

Vereinfachung *f* simplification

vereinheitlichen [fɛrˈʔaɪnhaɪtlɪçən] *vt* to standardize

vereinigen [fɛrˈʔaɪnɪgən] *vt, vr* to unite

vereinigt *adj* united; **Vereinigte Arabische Emirate** *pl* United Arab Emirates; **Vereinigtes Königreich** *nt* United Kingdom; **Vereinigte Staaten** *pl* United States

Vereinigung *f* union; *(Verein)* association

vereinnahmen [fɛrˈʔaɪnnaːmən] *vt (geh)* to take; **jdn ~** *(fig)* to make demands on sb

vereinsamen [fɛrˈʔaɪnzaːmən] *vi* to become lonely

vereint [fɛrˈʔaɪnt] *adj* united; **Vereinte Nationen** *pl* United Nations

vereinzelt [fɛrˈʔaɪntsəlt] *adj* isolated

vereisen [fɛrˈʔaɪzən] *vi* to freeze, ice over ▷ *vt (Med)* to freeze

vereiteln [fɛrˈʔaɪtəln] *vt* to frustrate

vereitern [fɛrˈʔaɪtɐn] *vi* to suppurate, fester

Verelendung [fɛrˈʔeːlɛndʊŋ] *f* impoverishment

verenden [fɛrˈʔɛndən] *vi* to perish, die

verengen [fɛrˈʔɛŋən] *vr* to narrow

vererben [fɛrˈʔɛrbən] *vt* to bequeath; *(Biol)* to transmit ▷ *vr* to be hereditary

vererblich [fɛrˈʔɛrplɪç] *adj* hereditary

Vererbung *f* bequeathing; *(Biol)* transmission; **das ist ~** *(umg)* it's hereditary

verewigen [fɛrˈʔeːvɪgən] *vt* to immortalize ▷ *vr (umg)* to leave one's name

Verf. *abk* = **Verfasser**

verfahren [fɛrˈfaːrən] *unreg vi* to act ▷ *vr* to get lost ▷ *adj* tangled; **~ mit** to deal with

Verfahren (-s, -) *nt* procedure; *(Tech)* process; *(Jur)* proceedings *pl*

Verfahrenstechnik *f (Methode)* process

Verfahrensweise *f* procedure

Verfall [fɛrˈfal] **(-(e)s)** *m* decline; *(von Haus)* dilapidation; *(Fin)* expiry

verfallen *unreg vi* to decline; *(Haus)* to be falling down; *(Fin)* to lapse ▷ *adj (Gebäude)* dilapidated, ruined; *(Karten, Briefmarken)* invalid; *(Strafe)* lapsed; *(Pass)* expired; **~ in** +*akk* to lapse into; **~ auf** +*akk* to hit upon; **einem Laster ~ sein** to be addicted to a vice; **jdm völlig ~ sein** to be completely under sb's spell

Verfallsdatum *nt* expiry date; *(der Haltbarkeit)* best-before date

verfänglich [fɛrˈfɛŋlɪç] *adj* awkward, tricky; *(Aussage, Beweismaterial etc)* incriminating; *(gefährlich)* dangerous

verfärben [fɛrˈfɛrbən] *vr* to change colour *(Brit)* od color *(US)*

verfassen [fɛrˈfasən] *vt* to write; *(Gesetz, Urkunde)* to draw up

Verfasser, in (-s, -) *m(f)* author, writer

Verfassung *f* constitution *(auch POL)*; *(körperlich)* state of health; *(seelisch)* state of mind; **sie ist in guter/schlechter ~** she is in good/bad shape

Verfassungs- *zW*: **verfassungsfeindlich** *adj* anticonstitutional; **Verfassungsgericht** *nt* constitutional court; **verfassungsmäßig** *adj* constitutional; **Verfassungsschutz** *m (Aufgabe)* defence of the constitution; *(Amt)*

V

office responsible for defending the constitution;
Verfassungsschützer, in *m(f)* defender of
the constitution; **verfassungswidrig** *adj*
unconstitutional

verfaulen [fɛrˈfaulən] *vi* to rot

verfechten [fɛrˈfɛçtən] *unreg vt* to defend;
(Lehre) to advocate

Verfechter, in [fɛrˈfɛçtər(ɪn)] (**-s, -**) *m(f)*
champion; defender

verfehlen [fɛrˈfeːlən] *vt* to miss; **das Thema ~**
to be completely off the subject

verfehlt *adj* unsuccessful; *(unangebracht)*
inappropriate; **etw für ~ halten** to regard sth
as mistaken

Verfehlung *f (Vergehen)* misdemeanour *(Brit)*,
misdemeanor *(US)*; *(Sünde)* transgression

verfeinern [fɛrˈfaɪnərn] *vt* to refine

Verfettung [fɛrˈfɛtʊŋ] *f (von Organ, Muskeln)*
fatty degeneration

verfeuern [fɛrˈfɔʏərn] *vt* to burn; *(Munition)* to
fire; *(umg)* to use up

verfilmen [fɛrˈfɪlmən] *vt* to film, make a film
of

Verfilmung *f* film (version)

Verfilzung [fɛrˈfɪltsʊŋ] *f (fig: von Firmen, Parteien)*
entanglements *pl*

verflachen [fɛrˈflaxən] *vi* to flatten out;
(fig: Diskussion) to become superficial

verfliegen [fɛrˈfliːgən] *unreg vi* to evaporate;
(Zeit) to pass, fly ▷ *vr* to stray *(past)*

verflixt [fɛrˈflɪkst] *(umg) adj, adv* darned

verflossen [fɛrˈflɔsən] *adj* past, former

verfluchen [fɛrˈfluːxən] *vt* to curse

verflüchtigen [fɛrˈflʏçtɪgən] *vr* to evaporate;
(Geruch) to fade

verflüssigen [fɛrˈflʏsɪgən] *vr* to become liquid

verfolgen [fɛrˈfɔlgən] *vt* to pursue; *(gerichtlich)*
to prosecute; *(grausam, bes Pol)* to persecute

Verfolger, in (**-s, -**) *m(f)* pursuer

Verfolgte, r *f(m) (politisch)* victim of
persecution

Verfolgung *f* pursuit; persecution;
strafrechtliche ~ prosecution

Verfolgungswahn *m* persecution mania

verfrachten [fɛrˈfraxtən] *vt* to ship

verfremden [fɛrˈfrɛmdən] *vt* to alienate,
distance

verfressen [fɛrˈfrɛsən] *(umg) adj* greedy

verfrüht [fɛrˈfryːt] *adj* premature

verfügbar *adj* available

verfügen [fɛrˈfyːgən] *vt* to direct, order ▷ *vr*
to proceed ▷ *vi*: **~ über** *+akk* to have at one's
disposal; **über etw** *akk* **frei ~ können** to be
able to do as one wants with sth

Verfügung *f* direction, order; *(Jur)* writ; **zur
~** at one's disposal; **jdm zur ~ stehen** to be
available to sb

Verfügungsgewalt *f (Jur)* right of disposal

verführen [fɛrˈfyːrən] *vt* to tempt; *(sexuell)* to
seduce; *(die Jugend, das Volk etc)* to lead astray

Verführer *m* tempter; seducer

Verführerin *f* temptress; seductress

verführerisch *adj* seductive

Verführung *f* seduction; *(Versuchung)*
temptation

Vergabe [fɛrˈgaːbə] *f (von Arbeiten)* allocation;
(von Stipendium, Auftrag etc) award

vergällen [fɛrˈgɛlən] *vt (geh)*: **jdm die Freude/
das Leben ~** to spoil sb's fun/sour sb's life

vergaloppieren [fɛrgaloˈpiːrən] *(umg) vr (sich
irren)* to be on the wrong track

vergammeln [fɛrˈgaməln] *(umg) vi* to go to
seed; *(Nahrung)* to go off; *(Zeit)* to waste

vergangen [fɛrˈgaŋən] *adj*
past; **Vergangenheit** *f* past;
Vergangenheitsbewältigung *f* coming to
terms with the past

vergänglich [fɛrˈgɛŋlɪç] *adj* transitory;
Vergänglichkeit *f* transitoriness,
impermanence

vergasen [fɛrˈgaːzən] *vt* to gasify; *(töten)* to gas

Vergaser (**-s, -**) *m (Aut)* carburettor *(Brit)*,
carburetor *(US)*

vergaß *etc* [fɛrˈgaːs] *vb* siehe **vergessen**

vergeben [fɛrˈgeːbən] *unreg vt* to forgive;
(weggeben) to give away; *(fig: Chance)* to throw
away; *(Auftrag, Preis)* to award; *(Studienplätze,
Stellen)* to allocate; **jdm (etw) ~** to forgive sb
(sth); **~ an** *+akk* to award to; to allocate to;
~ sein to be occupied; *(umg: Mädchen)* to be
spoken for

vergebens *adv* in vain

vergeblich [fɛrˈgeːplɪç] *adv* in vain ▷ *adj* vain,
futile

Vergebung *f* forgiveness

vergegenwärtigen [fɛrgeːgənˈvɛrtɪgən]
vr: **sich** *dat* **etw ~** to visualize sth; *(erinnern)* to
recall sth

vergehen [fɛrˈgeːən] *unreg vi* to pass by *od* away
▷ *vr* to commit an offence *(Brit) od* offense
(US); **vor Angst ~** to be scared to death; **jdm
vergeht etw** sb loses sth; **sich an jdm ~**
to (sexually) assault sb; **Vergehen** (**-s, -**) *nt*
offence *(Brit)*, offense *(US)*

vergeigen [fɛrˈgaɪgən] *(umg) vt* to cock up

vergeistigt [fɛrˈgaɪstɪçt] *adj* spiritual

vergelten [fɛrˈgɛltən] *unreg vt*: **jdm etw ~** to
pay sb back for sth, repay sb for sth

Vergeltung *f* retaliation, reprisal

Vergeltungsmaßnahme *f* retaliatory
measure

Vergeltungsschlag *m (Mil)* reprisal

vergesellschaften [fɛrgəˈzɛlʃaftən] *vt (Pol)* to
nationalize

vergessen [fɛrˈgɛsən] *unreg vt* to forget;
Vergessenheit *f* oblivion; **in Vergessenheit
geraten** to fall into oblivion

vergesslich [fɛrˈgɛslɪç] *adj* forgetful;
Vergesslichkeit *f* forgetfulness

vergeuden [fɛrˈgɔʏdən] *vt* to squander, waste

vergewaltigen [fɛrgəˈvaltɪgən] *vt* to rape; *(fig)*
to violate

Vergewaltigung *f* rape

vergewissern [fɛrgəˈvɪsərn] *vr* to make sure;
sich einer Sache *gen od* **über etw** *akk* **~** to
make sure of sth

vergießen [fɛr'giːsən] *unreg vt* to shed
vergiften [fɛr'gɪftən] *vt* to poison
Vergiftung *f* poisoning
vergilbt [fɛr'gɪlpt] *adj* yellowed
Vergissmeinnicht [fɛr'gɪsmaɪnnɪçt] (**-(e)s, -e**) *nt* forget-me-not
vergisst [fɛr'gɪst] *vb siehe* **vergessen**
vergittert [fɛr'gɪtərt] *adj:* ~**e Fenster** barred windows
verglasen [fɛr'glaːzən] *vt* to glaze
Vergleich [fɛr'glaɪç] (**-(e)s, -e**) *m* comparison; (*Jur*) settlement; **einen ~ schließen** (*Jur*) to reach a settlement; **in keinem ~ zu etw stehen** to be out of all proportion to sth; **im ~ mit** *od* **zu** compared with *od* to; **vergleichbar** *adj* comparable
vergleichen *unreg vt* to compare ▷ *vr* (*Jur*) to reach a settlement
vergleichsweise *adv* comparatively
verglühen [fɛr'glyːən] *vi* (*Feuer*) to die away; (*Draht*) to burn out; (*Raumkapsel, Meteor etc*) to burn up
vergnügen [fɛr'gnyːgən] *vr* to enjoy *od* amuse o.s.; **Vergnügen** (**-s, -**) *nt* pleasure; **das war ein teures Vergnügen** (*umg*) that was an expensive bit of fun; **viel Vergnügen!** enjoy yourself!
vergnüglich *adj* enjoyable
vergnügt [fɛr'gnyːkt] *adj* cheerful
Vergnügung *f* pleasure, amusement
Vergnügungs- *zW:* **Vergnügungspark** *m* amusement park; **vergnügungssüchtig** *adj* pleasure-loving; **Vergnügungsviertel** *nt* entertainments district
vergolden [fɛr'gɔldən] *vt* to gild
vergönnen [fɛr'gœnən] *vt* to grant
vergöttern [fɛr'gœtərn] *vt* to idolize
vergraben [fɛr'graːbən] *unreg vt* to bury
vergrämt [fɛr'grɛːmt] *adj* (*Gesicht*) troubled
vergreifen [fɛr'graɪfən] *unreg vr:* **sich an jdm** ~ to lay hands on sb; **sich an etw** *dat* ~ to misappropriate sth; **sich im Ton** ~ to say the wrong thing
vergriffen [fɛr'grɪfən] *adj* (*Buch*) out of print; (*Ware*) out of stock
vergrößern [fɛr'grøːsərn] *vt* to enlarge; (*mengenmäßig*) to increase; (*Lupe*) to magnify
Vergrößerung *f* enlargement; increase; magnification
Vergrößerungsglas *nt* magnifying glass
vergünstigt *adj* (*Lage*) improved; (*Preis*) reduced
Vergünstigung [fɛr'gʏnstɪgʊŋ] *f* concession; (*Vorteil*) privilege
vergüten [fɛr'gyːtən] *vt:* **jdm etw** ~ to compensate sb for sth; (*Arbeit, Leistung*) to pay sb for sth
Vergütung *f* compensation; payment
verh. *abk* = **verheiratet**
verhaften [fɛr'haftən] *vt* to arrest
Verhaftete, r *f(m)* prisoner
Verhaftung *f* arrest
verhallen [fɛr'halən] *vi* to die away
verhalten [fɛr'haltən] *unreg vr* (*Sache*) to be,

stand; (*sich benehmen*) to behave; (*Math*) to be in proportion to ▷ *vr unpers:* **wie verhält es sich damit?** (*wie ist die Lage?*) how do things stand?; (*wie wird das gehandhabt?*) how do you go about it? ▷ *adj* restrained; **sich ruhig** ~ to keep quiet; (*sich nicht bewegen*) to keep still; **wenn sich das so verhält …** if that is the case …; **Verhalten** (**-s**) *nt* behaviour (*Brit*), behavior (*US*)
Verhaltens- *zW:* **Verhaltensforschung** *f* behavioural (*Brit*) *od* behavioral (*US*) science; **verhaltensgestört** *adj* disturbed; **Verhaltensmaßregel** *f* rule of conduct
Verhältnis [fɛr'hɛltnɪs] (**-ses, -se**) *nt* relationship; (*Liebesverhältnis*) affair; (*Math*) proportion, ratio; (*Einstellung*): ~ (**zu**) attitude (to); **Verhältnisse** *pl* (*Umstände*) conditions *pl*; **aus was für ~sen kommt er?** what sort of background does he come from?; **für klare ~se sorgen, klare ~se schaffen** to get things straight; **über seine ~se leben** to live beyond one's means; **verhältnismäßig** *adj* relative, comparative ▷ *adv* relatively, comparatively; **Verhältniswahl** *f* proportional representation; **Verhältniswahlrecht** *nt* (system of) proportional representation
verhandeln [fɛr'handəln] *vi* to negotiate; (*Jur*) to hold proceedings ▷ *vt* to discuss; (*Jur*) to hear; **über etw** *akk* ~ to negotiate sth *od* about sth
Verhandlung *f* negotiation; (*Jur*) proceedings *pl*; **~en führen** to negotiate
Verhandlungspaket *nt* (*Comm*) package deal
Verhandlungstisch *m* negotiating table
verhangen [fɛr'haŋən] *adj* overcast
verhängen [fɛr'hɛŋən] *vt* (*fig*) to impose, inflict
Verhängnis [fɛr'hɛŋnɪs] (**-ses, -se**) *nt* fate; **jdm zum** ~ **werden** to be sb's undoing; **verhängnisvoll** *adj* fatal, disastrous
verharmlosen [fɛr'harmloːzən] *vt* to make light of, play down
verharren [fɛr'harən] *vi* to remain; (*hartnäckig*) to persist
verhärten [fɛr'hɛrtən] *vr* to harden
verhaspeln [fɛr'haspəln] (*umg*) *vr* to get into a muddle *od* tangle
verhasst [fɛr'hast] *adj* odious, hateful
verhätscheln [fɛr'hɛːtʃəln] *vt* to spoil, pamper
Verhau [fɛr'hau] (**-(e)s, -e**) *m* (*zur Absperrung*) barrier; (*Käfig*) coop
verhauen *unreg* (*umg*) *vt* (*verprügeln*) to beat up; (*Prüfung etc*) to muff
verheben [fɛr'heːbən] *unreg vr* to hurt o.s. lifting sth
verheerend [fɛr'heːrənt] *adj* disastrous, devastating
verhehlen [fɛr'heːlən] *vt* to conceal
verheilen [fɛr'haɪlən] *vi* to heal
verheimlichen [fɛr'haɪmlɪçən] *vt:* (**jdm**) **etw** ~ to keep sth secret (from sb)
verheiratet [fɛr'haɪraːtət] *adj* married
verheißen [fɛr'haɪsən] *unreg vt:* **jdm etw** ~ to

V

promise sb sth

verheißungsvoll *adj* promising

verheizen [fɛrˈhaɪtsən] *vt* to burn, use as fuel

verhelfen [fɛrˈhɛlfən] *unreg vi*: **jdm zu etw ~** to help sb to get sth

verherrlichen [fɛrˈhɛrlɪçən] *vt* to glorify

verheult [fɛrˈhɔylt] *adj (Augen, Gesicht)* puffy *(from crying)*

verhexen [fɛrˈhɛksən] *vt* to bewitch; **es ist wie verhext** it's jinxed

verhindern [fɛrˈhɪndərn] *vt* to prevent; **verhindert sein** to be unable to make it; **das lässt sich leider nicht ~** it can't be helped, unfortunately; **ein verhinderter Politiker** *(umg)* a would-be politician

Verhinderung *f* prevention

verhöhnen [fɛrˈhøːnən] *vt* to mock, sneer at

verhohnepipeln [fɛrˈhoːnəpiːpəln] *(umg) vt* to send up *(Brit)*, ridicule

verhökern [fɛrˈhøːkərn] *(umg) vt* to turn into cash

Verhör [fɛrˈhøːr] *(-(e)s, -e) nt* interrogation; *(gerichtlich)* (cross-)examination

verhören *vt* to interrogate; to (cross-)examine ▷ *vr* to mishear

verhüllen [fɛrˈhylən] *vt* to veil; *(Haupt, Körperteil)* to cover

verhungern [fɛrˈhʊŋərn] *vi* to starve, die of hunger

verhunzen [fɛrˈhʊntsən] *(umg) vt* to ruin

verhüten [fɛrˈhyːtən] *vt* to prevent, avert

Verhütung *f* prevention

Verhütungsmittel *nt* contraceptive

verifizieren [verifiˈtsiːrən] *vt* to verify

verinnerlichen [fɛrˈɪnərlɪçən] *vt* to internalize

verirren [fɛrˈɪrən] *vr* to get lost, lose one's way; *(fig)* to go astray; *(Tier, Kugel)* to stray

verjagen [fɛrˈjaːɡən] *vt* to drive away *od* out

verjähren [fɛrˈjɛːrən] *vi* to come under the statute of limitations; *(Anspruch)* to lapse

Verjährungsfrist *f* limitation period

verjubeln [fɛrˈjuːbəln] *(umg) vt (Geld)* to blow

verjüngen [fɛrˈjʏŋən] *vt* to rejuvenate ▷ *vr* to taper

verkabeln [fɛrˈkaːbəln] *vt (TV)* to link up to the cable network

Verkabelung *f (TV)* linking up to the cable network

verkalken [fɛrˈkalkən] *vi* to calcify; *(umg)* to become senile

verkalkulieren [fɛrkalkuˈliːrən] *vr* to miscalculate

verkannt [fɛrˈkant] *adj* unappreciated

verkatert [fɛrˈkaːtərt] *(umg) adj* hung over

Verkauf [fɛrˈkaʊf] *m* sale; **zum ~ stehen** to be up for sale

verkaufen *vt, vi* to sell; **„zu ~"** "for sale"

Verkäufer, in [fɛrˈkɔyfər(ɪn)] *(-s, -) m(f)* seller; *(im Außendienst)* salesman, saleswoman; *(in Laden)* shop assistant *(Brit)*, sales clerk *(US)*

verkäuflich [fɛrˈkɔyflɪç] *adj* saleable

Verkaufs- *zW*: **Verkaufsabteilung** *f* sales department; **Verkaufsautomat** *m* slot machine; **Verkaufsbedingungen** *pl (Comm)* terms and conditions of sale; **Verkaufskampagne** *f* sales drive; **Verkaufsleiter** *m* sales manager; **verkaufsoffen** *adj*: **verkaufsoffener Samstag** *Saturday on which the shops are open all day*; **Verkaufsschlager** *m* big seller; **Verkaufsstelle** *f* outlet; **Verkaufstüchtigkeit** *f* salesmanship

Verkehr [fɛrˈkeːr] *(-s, -e) m* traffic; *(Umgang, bes sexuell)* intercourse; *(Umlauf)* circulation; **aus dem ~ ziehen** to withdraw from service; **für den ~ freigeben** *(Straße etc)* to open to traffic; *(Transportmittel)* to bring into service

verkehren *vi (Fahrzeug)* to ply, run ▷ *vt, vr* to turn, transform; **~ mit** to associate with; **mit jdm brieflich** *od* **schriftlich ~** *(form)* to correspond with sb; **bei jdm ~** to visit sb regularly

Verkehrs- *zW*: **Verkehrsampel** *f* traffic lights *pl*; **Verkehrsamt** *nt* tourist (information) office; **Verkehrsaufkommen** *nt* volume of traffic; **verkehrsberuhigt** *adj* traffic-calmed; **Verkehrsberuhigung** *f* traffic-calming; **Verkehrsbetriebe** *pl* transport services *pl*; **Verkehrsdelikt** *nt* traffic offence *(Brit)* *od* violation *(US)*; **Verkehrserziehung** *f* road safety training; **verkehrsgünstig** *adj* convenient; **Verkehrsinsel** *f* traffic island; **Verkehrsknotenpunkt** *m* traffic junction; **Verkehrsmittel** *nt*: **öffentliche/private Verkehrsmittel** public/private transport *sing*; **Verkehrsschild** *nt* road sign; **verkehrssicher** *adj (Fahrzeug)* roadworthy; **Verkehrssicherheit** *f* road safety; **Verkehrsstockung** *f* traffic jam, stoppage; **Verkehrssünder** *(umg) m* traffic offender; **Verkehrsteilnehmer** *m* road user; **verkehrstüchtig** *adj (Fahrzeug)* roadworthy; *(Mensch)* fit to drive; **Verkehrsunfall** *m* traffic accident; **Verkehrsverein** *m* tourist information office; **verkehrswidrig** *adj* contrary to traffic regulations; **Verkehrszeichen** *nt* road sign

verkehrt *adj* wrong; *(umgekehrt)* the wrong way round

verkennen [fɛrˈkɛnən] *unreg vt* to misjudge; *(unterschätzen)* to underestimate

Verkettung [fɛrˈkɛtʊŋ] *f*: **eine ~ unglücklicher Umstände** an unfortunate chain of events

verklagen [fɛrˈklaːɡən] *vt* to take to court

verklappen [fɛrˈklapən] *vt* to dump (at sea)

verklären [fɛrˈklɛːrən] *vt* to transfigure; **verklärt lächeln** to smile radiantly

verklausulieren [fɛrklaʊzuˈliːrən] *vt (Vertrag)* to hedge in with (restrictive) clauses

verkleben [fɛrˈkleːbən] *vt* to glue up, stick ▷ *vi* to stick together

verkleiden [fɛrˈklaɪdən] *vt* to disguise; *(kostümieren)* to dress up; *(Schacht, Tunnel)* to line; *(vertäfeln)* to panel; *(Heizkörper)* to cover in ▷ *vr* to disguise o.s.; to dress up

Verkleidung *f* disguise; *(Archit)* panelling *(Brit)*, paneling *(US)*

verkleinern [fɛr'klaɪnərn] vt to make smaller, reduce in size

verklemmt [fɛr'klɛmt] adj (fig) inhibited

verklickern [fɛr'klɪkərn] (umg) vt: **jdm etw ~** to make sth clear to sb

verklingen [fɛr'klɪŋən] unreg vi to die away

verknacksen [fɛr'knaksən] (umg) vt: **sich** dat **den Fuß ~** to twist one's ankle

verknallen [fɛr'knalən] (umg) vr: **sich in jdn ~** to fall for sb

verkneifen [fɛr'knaɪfən] (umg) vt: **sich** dat **etw ~** from doing sth; **ich konnte mir das Lachen nicht ~** I couldn't help laughing

verknöchert [fɛr'knœçərt] adj (fig) fossilized

verknüpfen [fɛr'knʏpfən] vt to tie (up), knot; (fig) to connect

Verknüpfung f connection

verkochen [fɛr'kɔxən] vt, vi (Flüssigkeit) to boil away

verkohlen [fɛr'ko:lən] vi to carbonize ⊳ vt to carbonize; (umg): **jdn ~** to have sb on

verkommen [fɛr'kɔmən] unreg vi to deteriorate, decay; (Mensch) to go downhill, come down in the world ⊳ adj (moralisch) dissolute, depraved; **Verkommenheit** f depravity

verkorksen [fɛr'kɔrksən] (umg) vt to ruin, mess up

verkörpern [fɛr'kœrpərn] vt to embody, personify

verköstigen [fɛr'kœstɪgən] vt to feed

verkrachen [fɛr'kraxən] (umg) vr: **sich (mit jdm) ~** to fall out (with sb)

verkracht (umg) adj (Leben) ruined

verkraften [fɛr'kraftən] vt to cope with

verkrampfen [fɛr'krampfən] vr (Muskeln) to go tense

verkrampft [fɛr'krampft] adj (fig) tense

verkriechen [fɛr'kri:çən] unreg vr to creep away, creep into a corner

verkrümeln [fɛr'kry:məln] (umg) vr to disappear

verkrümmt [fɛr'krʏmt] adj crooked

Verkrümmung f bend, warp; (Anat) curvature

verkrüppelt [fɛr'krʏpəlt] adj crippled

verkrustet [fɛr'krʊstət] adj encrusted

verkühlen [fɛr'ky:lən] vr to get a chill

verkümmern [fɛr'kʏmərn] vi to waste away; **emotionell/geistig ~** to become emotionally/intellectually stunted

verkünden [fɛr'kʏndən] vt to proclaim; (Urteil) to pronounce

verkündigen [fɛr'kʏndɪgən] vt to proclaim; (ironisch) to announce; (Evangelium) to preach

verkuppeln [fɛr'kʊpəln] vt: **jdn an jdn ~** (Zuhälter) to procure sb for sb

verkürzen [fɛr'kʏrtsən] vt to shorten; (Wort) to abbreviate; **sich** dat **die Zeit ~** to while away the time; **verkürzte Arbeitszeit** shorter working hours pl

Verkürzung f shortening; abbreviation

Verl. abk (= Verlag) publ.

verladen [fɛr'la:dən] unreg vt to load

Verlag [fɛr'la:k] (-(e)s, -e) m publishing firm

verlagern [fɛr'la:gərn] vt, vr (lit, fig) to shift

Verlagsanstalt f publishing firm

Verlagswesen nt publishing

verlangen [fɛr'laŋən] vt to demand; (wollen) to want ⊳ vi: **~ nach** to ask for; **Sie werden am Telefon verlangt** you are wanted on the phone; **~ Sie Herrn X** ask for Mr X; **Verlangen** (-s, -) nt: **Verlangen (nach)** desire (for); **auf jds Verlangen** akk (hin) at sb's request

verlängern [fɛr'lɛŋərn] vt to extend; (länger machen) to lengthen; (zeitlich) to prolong; (Pass, Abonnement etc) to renew; **ein verlängertes Wochenende** a long weekend

Verlängerung f extension; (Sport) extra time

Verlängerungsschnur f extension cable

verlangsamen [fɛr'laŋza:mən] vt, vr to decelerate, slow down

Verlass [fɛr'las] m: **auf ihn/das ist kein ~** he/it cannot be relied upon

verlassen [fɛr'lasən] unreg vt to leave ⊳ vr: **sich ~ auf** +akk to depend on ⊳ adj desolate; (Mensch) abandoned; **einsam und ~** so all alone; **Verlassenheit** f loneliness (Brit), lonesomeness (US)

verlässlich [fɛr'lɛslɪç] adj reliable

Verlauf [fɛr'lauf] m course; **einen guten/schlechten ~ nehmen** to go well/badly

verlaufen unreg vi (zeitlich) to pass; (Farben) to run ⊳ vr to get lost; (Menschenmenge) to disperse

Verlautbarung f announcement

verlauten [fɛr'lautən] vi: **etw ~ lassen** to disclose sth; **wie verlautet** as reported

verleben [fɛr'le:bən] vt to spend

verlebt [fɛr'le:pt] adj dissipated, worn-out

verlegen [fɛr'le:gən] vt to move; (verlieren) to mislay; (Kabel, Fliesen etc) to lay; (Buch) to publish; (verschieben): **~ (auf** +akk) to postpone (until) ⊳ vr: **sich auf etw** akk **~** to resort to sth ⊳ adj embarrassed; **nicht ~ um** never at a loss for; **Verlegenheit** f embarrassment; (Situation) difficulty, scrape

Verleger [fɛr'le:gər] (-s, -) m publisher

verleiden [fɛr'laɪdən] vt: **jdm etw ~** to put sb off sth

Verleih [fɛr'laɪ] (-(e)s, -e) m hire service; (das Verleihen) renting (out), hiring (out) (Brit); (Filmverleih) distribution

verleihen unreg vt: **etw (an jdn) ~** to lend sth (to sb), lend (sb) sth; (gegen Gebühr) to rent sth (out) (to sb), hire sth (out) (to sb) (Brit); (Kraft, Anschein) to confer sth (on sb), bestow sth (on sb); (Preis, Medaille) to award sth (to sb), award (sb) sth

Verleiher (-s, -) m hire (Brit) od rental firm; (von Filmen) distributor; (von Büchern) lender

Verleihung f lending; (von Kraft etc) bestowal; (von Preis) award

verleiten [fɛr'laɪtən] vt to lead astray; **~ zu** to talk into, tempt into

verlernen [fɛr'lɛrnən] vt to forget, unlearn

verlesen [fɛr'le:zən] unreg vt to read out; (aussondern) to sort out ⊳ vr to make a mistake in reading

V

verletzbar adj vulnerable

verletzen [fɛrˈlɛtsən] vt (lit, fig) to injure, hurt; (Gesetz etc) to violate

verletzend adj (fig: Worte) hurtful

verletzlich adj vulnerable

Verletzte, r f(m) injured person

Verletzung f injury; (Verstoß) violation, infringement

verleugnen [fɛrˈlɔygnən] vt to deny; (Menschen) to disown; **er lässt sich immer (vor ihr) ~** he always pretends not to be there (when she calls)

Verleugnung f denial

verleumden [fɛrˈlɔymdən] vt to slander; (schriftlich) to libel

verleumderisch adj slanderous; libellous (Brit), libelous (US)

Verleumdung f slander; libel

verlieben vr: **sich ~ (in** +akk) to fall in love (with)

verliebt [fɛrˈliːpt] adj in love; **Verliebtheit** f being in love

verlieren [fɛrˈliːrən] unreg vt, vi to lose ▷ vr to get lost; (verschwinden) to disappear; **das/er hat hier nichts verloren** (umg) that/he has no business to be here

Verlierer, in (**-s, -**) m(f) loser

Verlies [fɛrˈliːs] (**-es, -e**) nt dungeon

verloben [fɛrˈloːbən] vr: **sich ~ (mit)** to get engaged (to); **verlobt sein** to be engaged

Verlobte, r [fɛrˈloːptə(r)] f(m): **mein ~r** my fiancé; **meine ~** my fiancée

Verlobung f engagement

verlocken [fɛrˈlɔkən] vt to entice, lure

verlockend adj (Angebot, Idee) tempting

Verlockung f temptation, attraction

verlogen [fɛrˈloːgən] adj untruthful; (Komplimente, Versprechungen) false; (Moral, Gesellschaft) hypocritical; **Verlogenheit** f untruthfulness

verlor etc [fɛrˈloːr] vb siehe **verlieren**

verloren pp von **verlieren** ▷ adj lost; (Eier) poached; **der ~e Sohn** the prodigal son; **auf ~em Posten kämpfen** od **stehen** to be fighting a losing battle; **etw ~ geben** to give sth up for lost; **~ gehen** to get lost; **an ihm ist ein Sänger ~ gegangen** he would have made a (good) singer

verlöschen [fɛrˈlœʃən] vi (Hilfsverb sein) to go out; (Inschrift, Farbe, Erinnerung) to fade

verlosen [fɛrˈloːzən] vt to raffle (off), draw lots for

Verlosung f raffle, lottery

verlottern [fɛrˈlɔtərn] (umg) vi to go to the dogs

verludern [fɛrˈluːdərn] (umg) vi to go to the dogs

Verlust [fɛrˈlʊst] (**-(e)s, -e**) m loss; (Mil) casualty; **mit ~ verkaufen** to sell at a loss; **Verlustanzeige** f "lost" notice; **Verlustgeschäft** nt: **das war ein Verlustgeschäft** I/he etc made a loss; **Verlustzeit** f (Industrie) waiting time

vermachen [fɛrˈmaxən] vt to bequeath, leave

Vermächtnis [fɛrˈmɛçtnɪs] (**-ses, -se**) nt legacy

vermählen [fɛrˈmɛːlən] vr to marry

Vermählung f wedding, marriage

vermarkten [fɛrˈmarktən] vt to market; (fig: Persönlichkeit) to promote

Vermarktung f marketing

vermasseln [fɛrˈmasəln] (umg) vt to mess up

vermehren [fɛrˈmeːrən] vt, vr to multiply; (Menge) to increase

Vermehrung f multiplying; increase

vermeiden [fɛrˈmaidən] unreg vt to avoid

vermeidlich adj avoidable

vermeintlich [fɛrˈmaintlɪç] adj supposed

vermengen [fɛrˈmɛŋən] vt to mix; (fig) to mix up, confuse

Vermenschlichung [fɛrˈmɛnʃlɪçʊŋ] f humanization

Vermerk [fɛrˈmɛrk] (**-(e)s, -e**) m note; (in Ausweis) endorsement

vermerken vt to note

vermessen [fɛrˈmɛsən] unreg vt to survey ▷ vr (falsch messen) to measure incorrectly ▷ adj presumptuous, bold; **Vermessenheit** f presumptuousness

Vermessung f survey(ing)

Vermessungsamt nt land survey(ing) office

Vermessungsingenieur m land surveyor

vermiesen [fɛrˈmiːzən] (umg) vt to spoil

vermieten [fɛrˈmiːtən] vt to let (Brit), rent (out); (Auto) to hire out, rent

Vermieter, in (**-s, -**) m(f) landlord, landlady

Vermietung f letting, renting (out); (von Autos) hiring (out), rental

vermindern [fɛrˈmɪndərn] vt, vr to lessen, decrease

Verminderung f reduction

verminen [fɛrˈmiːnən] vt to mine

vermischen [fɛrˈmɪʃən] vt, vr to mix; (Teesorten etc) to blend; **vermischte Schriften** miscellaneous writings

vermissen [fɛrˈmɪsən] vt to miss; **vermisst sein, als vermisst gemeldet sein** to be reported missing; **wir haben dich bei der Party vermisst** we didn't see you at the party

Vermisste, r f(m) missing person

Vermisstenanzeige f missing persons report

vermitteln [fɛrˈmɪtəln] vi to mediate ▷ vt to arrange; (Gespräch) to connect; (Stelle) to find; (Gefühl, Bild, Idee etc) to convey; (Wissen) to impart; **~de Worte** conciliatory words; **jdm etw ~** to help sb to obtain sth; (Stelle) to find sth for sb

Vermittler, in [fɛrˈmɪtlər(ɪn)] (**-s, -**) m(f) (Comm) agent; (Schlichter) mediator

Vermittlung f procurement; (Stellenvermittlung) agency; (Tel) exchange; (Schlichtung) mediation

Vermittlungsgebühr f commission

vermögen [fɛrˈmøːgən] unreg vt to be capable of; **~ zu** to be able to; **Vermögen** (**-s, -**) nt wealth; (Fähigkeit) ability; **mein ganzes Vermögen besteht aus ...** my entire assets consist of ...; **ein Vermögen kosten** to cost a fortune

vermögend *adj* wealthy
Vermögens- *zW*: **Vermögenssteuer** *f*
property tax, wealth tax; **Vermögenswert**
m asset; **vermögenswirksam** *adj*: **sein Geld**
vermögenswirksam anlegen to invest one's
money profitably; **vermögenswirksame**
Leistungen *employers' contributions to tax-*
deductible savings scheme
vermummen [fɛr'mʊmən] *vr* to wrap up
(warm); (*sich verkleiden*) to disguise
Vermummungsverbot (**-(e)s**) *nt law against*
disguising o.s. at demonstrations
vermurksen [fɛr'mʊrksən] (*umg*) *vt* to make a
mess of
vermuten [fɛr'muːtən] *vt* to suppose;
(*argwöhnen*) to suspect
vermutlich *adj* supposed, presumed ▷ *adv*
probably
Vermutung *f* supposition; suspicion; **die ~**
liegt nahe, dass ... there are grounds for
assuming that ...
vernachlässigen [fɛr'naːxlɛsɪɡən] *vt* to neglect
▷ *vr* to neglect o.s. *od* one's appearance
Vernachlässigung *f* neglect
vernarben [fɛr'narbən] *vi* to heal up
vernarren [fɛr'narən] (*umg*) *vr*: **in jdn/etw**
vernarrt sein to be crazy about sb/sth
vernaschen [fɛr'naʃən] *vt* (*Geld*) to spend on
sweets; (*umg: Mädchen, Mann*) to make it with
vernehmen [fɛr'neːmən] *unreg vt* to hear,
perceive; (*erfahren*) to learn; (*Jur*) to (cross-)
examine; (*Polizei*) to question; **Vernehmen**
nt: **dem Vernehmen nach** from what I/we
etc hear
vernehmlich *adj* audible
Vernehmung *f* (cross-)examination
vernehmungsfähig *adj* in a condition to be
(cross-)examined
verneigen [fɛr'naɪɡən] *vr* to bow
verneinen [fɛr'naɪnən] *vt* (*Frage*) to answer
in the negative; (*ablehnen*) to deny; (*Gram*) to
negate
verneinend *adj* negative
Verneinung *f* negation
vernichten [fɛr'nɪçtən] *vt* to destroy,
annihilate
vernichtend *adj* (*fig*) crushing; (*Blick*)
withering; (*Kritik*) scathing
Vernichtung *f* destruction, annihilation
Vernichtungsschlag *m* devastating blow
verniedlichen [fɛr'niːtlɪçən] *vt* to play down
Vernunft [fɛr'nʊnft] (**-**) *f* reason; **~ annehmen**
to see reason; **Vernunftehe** *f*, **Vernunftheirat**
f marriage of convenience
vernünftig [fɛr'nʏnftɪç] *adj* sensible,
reasonable
Vernunftmensch *m* rational person
veröden [fɛr'|øːdən] *vi* to become desolate ▷ *vt*
(*Med*) to remove
veröffentlichen [fɛr'|œfəntlɪçən] *vt* to publish
Veröffentlichung *f* publication
verordnen [fɛr'|ɔrdnən] *vt* (*Med*) to prescribe
Verordnung *f* order, decree; (*Med*) prescription

verpachten [fɛr'paxtən] *vt* to lease (out)
verpacken [fɛr'pakən] *vt* to pack;
(*verbrauchergerecht*) to package; (*einwickeln*) to
wrap
Verpackung *f* packing; packaging; wrapping
verpassen [fɛr'pasən] *vt* to miss; **jdm eine**
Ohrfeige ~ (*umg*) to give sb a clip round the ear
verpatzen [fɛr'patsən] (*umg*) *vt* to spoil, mess
up
verpennen [fɛr'pɛnən] (*umg*) *vi, vr* to oversleep
verpesten [fɛr'pɛstən] *vt* to pollute
verpetzen [fɛr'pɛtsən] (*umg*) *vt*: **jdn ~ (bei)** to
tell on sb (to)
verpfänden [fɛr'pfɛndən] *vt* to pawn; (*Jur*) to
mortgage
verpfeifen [fɛr'pfaɪfən] *unreg* (*umg*) *vt*: **jdn ~**
(bei) to grass on sb (to)
verpflanzen [fɛr'pflantsən] *vt* to transplant
Verpflanzung *f* transplanting; (*Med*)
transplant
verpflegen [fɛr'pfleːɡən] *vt* to feed, cater for
(*Brit*)
Verpflegung *f* catering; (*Kost*) food; (*in Hotel*)
board
verpflichten [fɛr'pflɪçtən] *vt* to oblige, bind;
(*anstellen*) to engage ▷ *vr* to undertake; (*Mil*)
to sign on ▷ *vi* to carry obligations; **jdm**
verpflichtet sein to be under an obligation
to sb; **sich zu etw ~** to commit o.s. to doing
sth; **jdm zu Dank verpflichtet sein** to be
obliged to sb
verpflichtend *adj* (*Zusage*) binding
Verpflichtung *f* obligation; (*Aufgabe*) duty
verpfuschen [fɛr'pfʊʃən] (*umg*) *vt* to bungle,
make a mess of
verplanen [fɛr'plaːnən] *vt* (*Zeit*) to book up;
(*Geld*) to budget
verplappern [fɛr'plapərn] (*umg*) *vr* to open
one's big mouth
verplempern [fɛr'plɛmpərn] (*umg*) *vt* to waste
verpönt [fɛr'pøːnt] *adj*: **~ (bei)** frowned upon
(by)
verprassen [fɛr'prasən] *vt* to squander
verprügeln [fɛr'pryːɡəln] (*umg*) *vt* to beat up
verpuffen [fɛr'pʊfən] *vi* to (go) pop; (*fig*) to fall
flat
Verputz [fɛr'pʊts] *m* plaster; (*Rauputz*)
roughcast; **verputzen** *vt* to plaster;
(*umg: Essen*) to put away
verqualmen [fɛr'kvalmən] *vt* (*Zimmer*) to fill
with smoke
verquollen [fɛr'kvɔlən] *adj* swollen; (*Holz*)
warped
verrammeln [fɛr'raməln] *vt* to barricade
Verrat [fɛr'raːt] (**-(e)s**) *m* treachery; (*Pol*)
treason; **~ an jdm üben** to betray sb
verraten *unreg vt* to betray; (*fig: erkennen lassen*)
to show; (*Geheimnis*) to divulge ▷ *vr* to give o.s.
away
Verräter, in [fɛr'rɛːtər(ɪn)] (**-s, -**) *m(f)* traitor,
traitress; **verräterisch** *adj* treacherous
verrauchen [fɛr'rauxən] *vi* (*fig: Zorn*) to blow
over

verrechnen [fɛrˈrɛçnən] *vt*: ~ **mit** to set off against ▷ *vr* to miscalculate

Verrechnung *f*: **nur zur** ~ (*auf Scheck*) a/c payee only

Verrechnungsscheck *m* crossed cheque (*Brit*)

verregnet [fɛrˈreːɡnət] *adj* rainy, spoilt by rain

verreisen [fɛrˈraɪzən] *vi* to go away (on a journey); **er ist geschäftlich verreist** he's away on business

verreißen [fɛrˈraɪsən] *unreg vt* to pull to pieces

verrenken [fɛrˈrɛŋkən] *vt* to contort; (*Med*) to dislocate; **sich** *dat* **den Knöchel** ~ to sprain one's ankle

Verrenkung *f* contortion; (*Med*) dislocation

verrennen [fɛrˈrɛnən] *unreg vr*: **sich in etw** *akk* ~ to get stuck on sth

verrichten [fɛrˈrɪçtən] *vt* (*Arbeit*) to do, perform

verriegeln [fɛrˈriːɡəln] *vt* to bolt

verringern [fɛrˈrɪŋərn] *vt* to reduce ▷ *vr* to decrease

Verringerung *f* reduction; decrease

verrinnen [fɛrˈrɪnən] *unreg vi* to run out *od* away; (*Zeit*) to elapse

Verriss [fɛrˈrɪs] *m* slating review

verrohen [fɛrˈroːən] *vi* to become brutalized

verrosten [fɛrˈrɔstən] *vi* to rust

verrotten [fɛrˈrɔtən] *vi* to rot

verrucht [fɛrˈruːxt] *adj* despicable; (*verrufen*) disreputable

verrücken [fɛrˈrʏkən] *vt* to move, shift

verrückt *adj* crazy, mad; **Verrückte, r** *f(m)* lunatic; **Verrücktheit** *f* madness, lunacy

Verruf [fɛrˈruːf] *m*: **in ~ geraten/bringen** to fall/bring into disrepute

verrufen *adj* disreputable

verrutschen [fɛrˈrʊtʃən] *vi* to slip

Vers [fɛrs] (**-es, -e**) *m* verse

versacken [fɛrˈzakən] *vi* (*lit*) to sink; (*fig*: *umg*: *herunterkommen*) to go downhill; (: *lange zechen*) to get involved in a booze-up (*Brit*) *od* a drinking spree

versagen [fɛrˈzaːɡən] *vt*: **jdm/sich etw** ~ to deny sb/o.s. sth ▷ *vi* to fail; **Versagen** (**-s**) *nt* failure; **menschliches Versagen** human error

Versager (**-s, -**) *m* failure

versalzen [fɛrˈzaltsən] *vt* to put too much salt in; (*fig*) to spoil

versammeln [fɛrˈzaməln] *vt, vr* to assemble, gather

Versammlung *f* meeting, gathering

Versammlungsfreiheit *f* freedom of assembly

Versand [fɛrˈzant] (**-(e)s**) *m* dispatch; (*Versandabteilung*) dispatch department; **Versandbahnhof** *m* dispatch station; **Versandhaus** *nt* mail-order firm; **Versandkosten** *pl* transport(ation) costs *pl*; **Versandweg** *m*: **auf dem Versandweg** by mail order

versäumen [fɛrˈzɔʏmən] *vt* to miss; (*Pflicht*) to neglect; (*Zeit*) to lose

Versäumnis (**-ses, -se**) *nt* neglect; (*Unterlassung*) omission

verschachern [fɛrˈʃaxərn] (*umg*) *vt* to sell off

verschachtelt [fɛrˈʃaxtəlt] *adj* (*Satz*) complex

verschaffen [fɛrˈʃafən] *vt*: **jdm/sich etw** ~ to get *od* procure sth for sb/o.s.

verschämt [fɛrˈʃɛːmt] *adj* bashful

verschandeln [fɛrˈʃandəln] (*umg*) *vt* to spoil

verschanzen [fɛrˈʃantsən] *vr*: **sich hinter etw** *dat* ~ to dig in behind sth; (*fig*) to take refuge behind sth

verschärfen [fɛrˈʃɛrfən] *vt* to intensify; (*Lage*) to aggravate; (*strenger machen: Kontrollen, Gesetze*) to tighten up ▷ *vr* to intensify; to become aggravated; to become tighter

Verschärfung *f* intensification; (*der Lage*) aggravation; (*von Kontrollen etc*) tightening

verscharren [fɛrˈʃarən] *vt* to bury

verschätzen [fɛrˈʃɛtsən] *vr* to miscalculate

verschenken [fɛrˈʃɛŋkən] *vt* to give away

verscherzen [fɛrˈʃɛrtsən] *vt*: **sich** *dat* **etw** ~ to lose sth, throw sth away

verscheuchen [fɛrˈʃɔʏçən] *vt* to frighten away

verschicken [fɛrˈʃɪkən] *vt* to send off; (*Sträfling*) to transport

verschieben [fɛrˈʃiːbən] *unreg vt* to shift; (*Eisenb*) to shunt; (*Termin*) to postpone; (*umg*: *Waren, Devisen*) to traffic in

Verschiebung *f* shift, displacement; shunting; postponement

verschieden [fɛrˈʃiːdən] *adj* different; **das ist ganz** ~ (*wird verschieden gehandhabt*) that varies, that just depends; **sie sind** ~ **groß** they are of different sizes; **verschiedenartig** *adj* various, of different kinds; **zwei so verschiedenartige ...** two such differing ...; **Verschiedene** *pron pl* various people; various things *pl*; **Verschiedenes** *pron* various things *pl*; **etwas Verschiedenes** something different; **Verschiedenheit** *f* difference

verschiedentlich *adv* several times

verschiffen [fɛrˈʃɪfən] *vt* to ship; (*Sträfling*) to transport

verschimmeln [fɛrˈʃɪməln] *vi* (*Nahrungsmittel*) to go mouldy (*Brit*) *od* moldy (*US*); (*Leder, Papier etc*) to become mildewed

verschlafen [fɛrˈʃlaːfən] *unreg vt* to sleep through; (*fig*: *versäumen*) to miss ▷ *vi, vr* to oversleep ▷ *adj* sleepy

Verschlag [fɛrˈʃlaːk] *m* shed

verschlagen [fɛrˈʃlaːɡən] *unreg vt* to board up; (*Tennis*) to hit out of play; (*Buchseite*) to lose ▷ *adj* cunning; **jdm den Atem** ~ to take sb's breath away; **an einen Ort** ~ **werden** to wind up in a place

verschlampen [fɛrˈʃlampən] *vi* (*Hilfsverb sein*: *Mensch*) to go to seed (*umg*) ▷ *vt* to lose, mislay

verschlechtern [fɛrˈʃlɛçtərn] *vt* to make worse ▷ *vr* to deteriorate, get worse; (*gehaltlich*) to take a lower-paid job

Verschlechterung *f* deterioration

Verschleierung [fɛrˈʃlaɪərʊŋ] *f* veiling; (*fig*) concealment; (*Mil*) screening

Verschleierungstaktik *f* smoke-screen tactics

pl

Verschleiß [fɛrˈʃlaɪs] (**-es, -e**) *m* wear and tear
verschleißen *unreg vt, vi, vr* to wear out
verschleppen [fɛrˈʃlɛpən] *vt* to carry
off, abduct; (*zeitlich*) to drag out, delay;
(*verbreiten: Seuche*) to spread
verschleudern [fɛrˈʃlɔydərn] *vt* to squander;
(*Comm*) to sell dirt-cheap
verschließbar *adj* lockable
verschließen [fɛrˈʃliːsən] *unreg vt* to lock
▷ *vr:* **sich einer Sache** *dat* ~ to close one's
mind to sth
verschlimmern [fɛrˈʃlɪmərn] *vt* to make worse,
aggravate ▷ *vr* to get worse, deteriorate
Verschlimmerung *f* deterioration
verschlingen [fɛrˈʃlɪŋən] *unreg vt* to devour,
swallow up; (*Fäden*) to twist
verschliss *etc* [fɛrˈʃlɪs] *vb siehe* **verschleißen**
verschlissen [fɛrˈʃlɪsən] *pp von* **verschleißen**
▷ *adj* worn(-out)
verschlossen [fɛrˈʃlɔsən] *adj* locked; (*fig*)
reserved; (*schweigsam*) tight-lipped;
Verschlossenheit *f* reserve
verschlucken [fɛrˈʃlʊkən] *vt* to swallow ▷ *vr*
to choke
Verschluss [fɛrˈʃlʊs] *m* lock; (*von Kleid etc*)
fastener; (*Phot*) shutter; (*Stöpsel*) plug; **unter ~**
halten to keep under lock and key
verschlüsseln [fɛrˈʃlʏsəln] *vt* to encode
verschmachten [fɛrˈʃmaxtən] *vi:* ~ (**vor** +*dat*)
to languish (for); **vor Durst** ~ to be dying of
thirst
verschmähen [fɛrˈʃmɛːən] *vt* to scorn
verschmelzen [fɛrˈʃmɛltsən] *unreg vt, vi* to
merge, blend
verschmerzen [fɛrˈʃmɛrtsən] *vt* to get over
verschmiert [fɛrˈʃmiːrt] *adj* (*Hände*) smeary;
(*Schminke*) smudged
verschmitzt [fɛrˈʃmɪtst] *adj* mischievous
verschmutzen [fɛrˈʃmʊtsən] *vt* to soil;
(*Umwelt*) to pollute
Verschmutzung *f* pollution
verschnaufen [fɛrˈʃnaʊfən] (*umg*) *vi, vr* to have
a breather
verschneiden [fɛrˈʃnaɪdən] *vt* (*Whisky etc*) to
blend
verschneit [fɛrˈʃnaɪt] *adj* covered in snow,
snowed up
Verschnitt [fɛrˈʃnɪt] *m* (*von Whisky etc*) blend
verschnörkelt [fɛrˈʃnœrkəlt] *adj* ornate
verschnupft [fɛrˈʃnʊpft] (*umg*) *adj:* ~ **sein** to
have a cold; (*beleidigt*) to be peeved (*umg*)
verschnüren [fɛrˈʃnyːrən] *vt* to tie up
verschollen [fɛrˈʃɔlən] *adj* lost, missing
verschonen [fɛrˈʃoːnən] *vt:* **jdn mit etw** ~ to
spare sb sth; **von etw verschont bleiben** to
escape sth
verschönern [fɛrˈʃøːnərn] *vt* to decorate;
(*verbessern*) to improve
verschossen [fɛrˈʃɔsən] *adj:* ~ **sein** (*fig: umg*) to
be in love
verschränken [fɛrˈʃrɛŋkən] *vt* to cross; (*Arme*)
to fold

verschreckt [fɛrˈʃrɛkt] *adj* frightened, scared
verschreiben [fɛrˈʃraɪbən] *unreg vt* (*Papier*)
to use up; (*Med*) to prescribe ▷ *vr* to make a
mistake (in writing); **sich einer Sache** *dat* ~
to devote o.s. to sth
verschrieen [fɛrˈʃriːən], **verschrien** [fɛrˈʃriːn]
adj notorious
verschroben [fɛrˈʃroːbən] *adj* eccentric, odd
verschrotten [fɛrˈʃrɔtən] *vt* to scrap
verschüchtert [fɛrˈʃʏçtərt] *adj* subdued,
intimidated
verschulden [fɛrˈʃʊldən] *vt* to be guilty
of ▷ *vi* (*in Schulden geraten*) to get into debt;
Verschulden (**-s**) *nt* fault
verschuldet *adj* in debt
Verschuldung *f* debts *pl*
verschütten [fɛrˈʃʏtən] *vt* to spill; (*zuschütten*)
to fill; (*unter Trümmer*) to bury
verschwand *etc* [fɛrˈʃvant] *vb siehe*
verschwinden
verschweigen [fɛrˈʃvaɪgən] *unreg vt* to keep
secret; **jdm etw** ~ to keep sth from sb
verschwenden [fɛrˈʃvɛndən] *vt* to squander
Verschwender, in (**-s, -**) *m(f)* spendthrift;
verschwenderisch *adj* wasteful; (*Leben*)
extravagant
Verschwendung *f* waste
verschwiegen [fɛrˈʃviːgən] *adj* discreet; (*Ort*)
secluded; **Verschwiegenheit** *f* discretion;
seclusion; **zur Verschwiegenheit**
verpflichtet bound to secrecy
verschwimmen [fɛrˈʃvɪmən] *unreg vi* to grow
hazy, become blurred
verschwinden [fɛrˈʃvɪndən] *unreg vi* to
disappear, vanish; **verschwinde!** clear off!
(*umg*); **Verschwinden** (**-s**) *nt* disappearance
verschwindend *adj* (*Anzahl, Menge*)
insignificant
verschwitzen [fɛrˈʃvɪtsən] *vt* to stain with
sweat; (*umg*) to forget
verschwitzt *adj* (*Kleidung*) sweat-stained;
(*Mensch*) sweaty
verschwommen [fɛrˈʃvɔmən] *adj* hazy, vague
verschworen [fɛrˈʃvoːrən] *adj* (*Gesellschaft*)
sworn
verschwören [fɛrˈʃvøːrən] *unreg vr* to conspire,
plot
Verschwörer, in (**-s, -**) *m(f)* conspirator
Verschwörung *f* conspiracy, plot
verschwunden [fɛrˈʃvʊndən] *pp von*
verschwinden ▷ *adj* missing
versehen [fɛrˈzeːən] *unreg vt* to supply, provide;
(*Pflicht*) to carry out; (*Amt*) to fill; (*Haushalt*) to
keep ▷ *vr* (*fig*) to make a mistake; **ehe er (es)**
sich ~ hatte ... before he knew it ...; **Versehen**
(**-s, -**) *nt* oversight; **aus Versehen** by mistake
versehentlich *adv* by mistake
Versehrte, r [fɛrˈzeːrtə(r)] *f(m)* disabled person
verselbstständigen [fɛrˈzɛlpstʃtɛndɪgən],
verselbständigen [fɛrˈzɛlpʃtɛndɪgən] *vr* to
become independent
versenden [fɛrˈzɛndən] *unreg vt* to send; (*Comm*)
to forward

V

versengen [fɛr'zɛŋən] vt to scorch; (Feuer) to singe; (umg: verprügeln) to wallop

versenken [fɛr'zɛŋkən] vt to sink ▷ vr: **sich ~ in** +akk to become engrossed in

versessen [fɛr'zɛsən] adj: **~ auf** +akk mad about, hellbent on

versetzen [fɛr'zɛtsən] vt to transfer; (verpfänden) to pawn; (umg: vergeblich warten lassen) to stand up; (nicht geradlinig anordnen) to stagger; (Sch: in höhere Klasse) to move up ▷ vr: **sich in jdn** od **in jds Lage ~** to put o.s. in sb's place; **jdm einen Tritt/Schlag ~** to kick/hit sb; **etw mit etw ~** to mix sth with sth; **jdm einen Stich ~** (fig) to cut sb to the quick, wound sb (deeply); **jdn in gute Laune ~** to put sb in a good mood

Versetzung f transfer; **seine ~ ist gefährdet** (Sch) he's in danger of having to repeat a year

verseuchen [fɛr'zɔʏçən] vt to contaminate

Versicherer (-s, -) m insurer; (bei Schiffen) underwriter

versichern [fɛr'zɪçərn] vt to assure; (mit Geld) to insure ▷ vr: **sich ~** +gen to make sure of

Versicherte, r f(m) insured

Versicherung f assurance; insurance

Versicherungs- zW: **Versicherungsbeitrag** m insurance premium; (bei staatlicher Versicherung etc) social security contribution; **Versicherungsgesellschaft** f insurance company; **Versicherungsnehmer** (-s, -) m (form) insured, policy holder; **Versicherungspolice** f insurance policy; **Versicherungsschutz** m insurance cover; **Versicherungssumme** f sum insured; **Versicherungsträger** m insurer

versickern [fɛr'zɪkərn] vi to seep away; (fig: Interesse etc) to peter out

versiegeln [fɛr'zi:gəln] vt to seal (up)

versiegen [fɛr'zi:gən] vi to dry up

versiert [vɛr'zi:rt] adj: **in etw** dat **~ sein** to be experienced od well versed in sth

versilbert [fɛr'zɪlbərt] adj silver-plated

versinken [fɛr'zɪŋkən] unreg vi to sink; **ich hätte im Boden** od **vor Scham ~ mögen** I wished the ground would swallow me up

versinnbildlichen [fɛr'zɪnbɪltlɪçən] vt to symbolize

Version [vɛrzi'o:n] f version

Versmaß ['fɛrsma:s] nt metre (Brit), meter (US)

versohlen [fɛr'zo:lən] (umg) vt to belt

versöhnen [fɛr'zø:nən] vt to reconcile ▷ vr to become reconciled

versöhnlich adj (Ton, Worte) conciliatory; (Ende) happy

Versöhnung f reconciliation

versonnen [fɛr'zɔnən] adj (Gesichtsausdruck) pensive, thoughtful; (träumerisch: Blick) dreamy

versorgen [fɛr'zɔrgən] vt to provide, supply; (Familie etc) to look after ▷ vr to look after o.s.

Versorger, in (-s, -) m(f) (Ernährer) provider, breadwinner; (Belieferer) supplier

Versorgung f provision; (Unterhalt) maintenance; (Altersversorgung etc) benefit, assistance

Versorgungs- zW: **Versorgungsamt** nt pension office; **Versorgungsbetrieb** m public utility; **Versorgungsnetz** nt (Wasserversorgung etc) (supply) grid; (von Waren) supply network

verspannen [fɛr'ʃpanən] vr (Muskeln) to tense up

verspäten [fɛr'ʃpɛ:tən] vr to be late

verspätet adj late

Verspätung f delay; **~ haben** to be late; **mit zwanzig Minuten ~** twenty minutes late

versperren [fɛr'ʃpɛrən] vt to bar, obstruct

verspielen [fɛr'ʃpi:lən] vt, vi to lose; **(bei jdm) verspielt haben** to have had it (as far as sb is concerned)

verspielt [fɛr'ʃpi:lt] adj playful

versponnen [fɛr'ʃpɔnən] adj crackpot

verspotten [fɛr'ʃpɔtən] vt to ridicule, scoff at

versprach etc [fɛr'ʃprax] vb siehe **versprechen**

versprechen [fɛr'ʃprɛçən] unreg vt to promise ▷ vr (etwas Nichtgemeintes sagen) to make a slip of the tongue; **sich** dat **etw von etw ~** to expect sth from sth; **Versprechen** (-s, -) nt promise

Versprecher (-s, -) (umg) m slip (of the tongue)

verspricht [fɛr'ʃprɪçt] vb siehe **versprechen**

verspüren [fɛr'ʃpy:rən] vt to feel, be conscious of

verstaatlichen [fɛr'ʃta:tlɪçən] vt to nationalize

verstaatlicht adj: **~er Industriezweig** nationalized industry

Verstaatlichung f nationalization

Verstand [fɛr'ʃtant] m intelligence; (Intellekt) mind; (Fähigkeit zu denken) reason; **den ~ verlieren** to go out of one's mind; **über jds ~** akk **gehen** to be beyond sb

verstand etc vb siehe **verstehen**

verstanden [fɛr'ʃtandən] pp von **verstehen**

verstandesmäßig adj rational

verständig [fɛr'ʃtɛndɪç] adj sensible

verständigen [fɛr'ʃtɛndɪgən] vt to inform ▷ vr to communicate; (sich einigen) to come to an understanding

Verständigkeit f good sense

Verständigung f communication; (Benachrichtigung) informing; (Einigung) agreement

verständlich [fɛr'ʃtɛntlɪç] adj understandable, comprehensible; (hörbar) audible; **sich ~ machen** to make o.s. understood; (sich klar ausdrücken) to make o.s. clear

verständlicherweise adv understandably (enough)

Verständlichkeit f clarity, intelligibility

Verständnis (-ses, -se) nt understanding; **für etw kein ~ haben** to have no understanding od sympathy for sth; (für Kunst etc) to have no appreciation of sth; **verständnislos** adj uncomprehending; **verständnisvoll** adj understanding, sympathetic

verstärken [fɛr'ʃtɛrkən] vt to strengthen; (Ton) to amplify; (erhöhen) to intensify ▷ vr to intensify

Verstärker (-s, -) m amplifier

Verstärkung f strengthening; (Hilfe) reinforcements pl; (von Ton) amplification

verstaubt [fɛr'ʃtaʊpt] adj dusty; (fig: Ansichten) fuddy-duddy (umg)

verstauchen [fɛr'ʃtaʊxən] vt to sprain

verstauen [fɛr'ʃtaʊən] vt to stow away

Versteck [fɛr'ʃtɛk] (-(e)s, -e) nt hiding (place)

verstecken vt, vr to hide

versteckt adj hidden; (Tür) concealed; (fig: Lächeln, Blick) furtive; (Andeutung) veiled

verstehen [fɛr'ʃteːən] unreg vt, vi to understand; (können, beherrschen) to know ▷ vr (auskommen) to get on; **das ist nicht wörtlich zu ~** that isn't to be taken literally; **das versteht sich von selbst** that goes without saying; **die Preise ~ sich einschließlich Lieferung** prices are inclusive of delivery; **sich auf etw** akk **~** to be an expert at sth

versteifen [fɛr'ʃtaɪfən] vt to stiffen, brace ▷ vr (fig): **sich ~ auf** +akk to insist on

versteigen [fɛr'ʃtaɪɡən] unreg vr: **sie hat sich zu der Behauptung verstiegen, dass ...** she presumed to claim that ...

versteigern [fɛr'ʃtaɪɡərn] vt to auction

Versteigerung f auction

verstellbar adj adjustable, variable

verstellen [fɛr'ʃtɛlən] vt to move, shift; (Uhr) to adjust; (versperren) to block; (fig) to disguise ▷ vr to pretend, put on an act

Verstellung f pretence (Brit), pretense (US)

versteuern [fɛr'ʃtɔʏərn] vt to pay tax on; **zu ~** taxable

verstiegen [fɛr'ʃtiːɡən] adj exaggerated

verstimmt [fɛr'ʃtɪmt] adj out of tune; (fig) cross, put out; (: Magen) upset

Verstimmung f (fig) disgruntled state, peevishness

verstockt [fɛr'ʃtɔkt] adj stubborn; **Verstocktheit** f stubbornness

verstohlen [fɛr'ʃtoːlən] adj stealthy

verstopfen [fɛr'ʃtɔpfən] vt to block, stop up; (Med) to constipate

Verstopfung f obstruction; (Med) constipation

verstorben [fɛr'ʃtɔrbən] adj deceased, late

Verstorbene, r f(m) deceased

verstört [fɛr'ʃtøːrt] adj (Mensch) distraught

Verstoß [fɛr'ʃtoːs] m: **~ (gegen)** infringement (of), violation (of)

verstoßen unreg vt to disown, reject ▷ vi: **~ gegen** to offend against

Verstrebung [fɛr'ʃtreːbʊŋ] f (Strebebalken) support(ing beam)

verstreichen [fɛr'ʃtraɪçən] unreg vt to spread ▷ vi to elapse; (Zeit) to pass (by); (Frist) to expire

verstreuen [fɛr'ʃtrɔʏən] vt to scatter (about)

verstricken [fɛr'ʃtrɪkən] vt (fig) to entangle, ensnare ▷ vr: **sich ~ in** +akk to get entangled in

verströmen [fɛr'ʃtrøːmən] vt to exude

verstümmeln [fɛr'ʃtʏməln] vt to maim, mutilate (auch fig)

verstummen [fɛr'ʃtʊmən] vi to go silent; (Lärm) to die away

Versuch [fɛr'zuːx] (-(e)s, -e) m attempt; (Chem

etc) experiment; **das käme auf einen ~ an** we'll have to have a try

versuchen vt to try; (verlocken) to tempt ▷ vr: **sich an etw** dat **~** to try one's hand at sth

Versuchs- zW: **Versuchsanstalt** f research institute; **Versuchsbohrung** f experimental drilling; **Versuchskaninchen** nt guinea pig; **Versuchsobjekt** nt test object; (fig: Mensch) guinea pig; **Versuchsreihe** f series of experiments; **versuchsweise** adv tentatively

Versuchung f temptation

versumpfen [fɛr'zʊmpfən] vi (Gebiet) to become marshy; (fig: umg) to go to pot; (lange zechen) to get involved in a booze-up (Brit) od drinking spree (US)

versündigen [fɛr'zʏndɪɡən] vr (geh): **sich an** jdm/etw **~** to sin against sb/sth

versunken [fɛr'zʊŋkən] adj sunken; **~ sein in** +akk to be absorbed od engrossed in; **Versunkenheit** f absorption

versüßen [fɛr'zyːsən] vt: **jdm etw ~** (fig) to make sth more pleasant for sb

vertagen [fɛr'taːɡən] vt, vi to adjourn

Vertagung f adjournment

vertauschen [fɛr'taʊʃən] vt to exchange; (versehentlich) to mix up; **vertauschte Rollen** reversed roles

verteidigen [fɛr'taɪdɪɡən] vt to defend ▷ vr to defend o.s.; (vor Gericht) to conduct one's own defence (Brit) od defense (US)

Verteidiger, in (-s, -) m(f) defender; (Anwalt) defence (Brit) od defense (US) lawyer

Verteidigung f defence (Brit), defense (US)

Verteidigungsfähigkeit f ability to defend

Verteidigungsminister m Minister of Defence (Brit), Defense Secretary (US)

verteilen [fɛr'taɪlən] vt to distribute; (Rollen) to assign; (Salbe) to spread

Verteiler (-s, -) m (Comm, Aut) distributor

Verteilung f distribution

Verteuerung [fɛr'tɔʏərʊŋ] f increase in price

verteufeln [fɛr'tɔʏfəln] vt to condemn

verteufelt (umg) adj awful, devilish ▷ adv awfully, devilishly

vertiefen [fɛr'tiːfən] vt to deepen; (Sch) to consolidate ▷ vr: **sich in etw** akk **~** to become engrossed od absorbed in sth

Vertiefung f depression

vertikal [vɛrti'kaːl] adj vertical

vertilgen [fɛr'tɪlɡən] vt to exterminate; (umg) to eat up, consume

Vertilgungsmittel nt weedkiller; (Insektenvertilgungsmittel) pesticide

vertippen [fɛr'tɪpən] vr to make a typing mistake

vertonen [fɛr'toːnən] vt to set to music; (Film etc) to add a soundtrack to

vertrackt [fɛr'trakt] adj awkward, tricky, complex

Vertrag [fɛr'traːk] (-(e)s, ̈e) m contract, agreement; (Pol) treaty

vertragen [fɛr'traːɡən] unreg vt to tolerate, stand ▷ vr to get along; (sich aussöhnen)

V

369

to become reconciled; **viel ~ können**
(*umg: Alkohol*) to be able to hold one's drink;
sich mit etw ~ (*Nahrungsmittel, Farbe*) to go
with sth; (*Aussage, Verhalten*) to be consistent
with sth

vertraglich *adj* contractual

verträglich [fɛr'trɛːklɪç] *adj* good-natured;
(*Speisen*) easily digested; (*Med*) easily tolerated;
Verträglichkeit *f* good nature; digestibility

Vertrags- *zW*: **Vertragsbruch** *m* breach
of contract; **vertragsbrüchig** *adj* in
breach of contract; **vertragsfähig** *adj* (*Jur*)
competent to contract; **vertragsmäßig** *adj,
adv* (as) stipulated, according to contract;
Vertragspartner *m* party to a contract;
Vertragsspieler *m* (*Sport*) player under
contract; **vertragswidrig** *adj, adv* contrary to
contract

vertrauen [fɛr'trauən] *vi*: **jdm ~** to trust
sb; **~ auf** +*akk* to rely on; **Vertrauen (-s)** *nt*
confidence; **jdn ins Vertrauen ziehen** to
take sb into one's confidence; **Vertrauen
zu jdm fassen** to gain confidence in sb;
vertrauenerweckend *adj* inspiring trust

Vertrauens- *zW*: **Vertrauensmann (-(e)
s,** *pl* **-männer** *od* **-leute)** *m* intermediary;
Vertrauenssache *f* (*vertrauliche Angelegenheit*)
confidential matter; (*Frage des Vertrauens*)
question of trust; **vertrauensselig** *adj*
trusting; **vertrauensvoll** *adj* trustful;
Vertrauensvotum *nt* (*Parl*) vote of confidence;
vertrauenswürdig *adj* trustworthy

vertraulich [fɛr'trauliç] *adj* familiar; (*geheim*)
confidential; **Vertraulichkeit** *f* familiarity;
confidentiality

verträumt [fɛr'trɔymt] *adj* dreamy; (*Städtchen
etc*) sleepy

vertraut [fɛr'traut] *adj* familiar; **sich mit dem
Gedanken ~ machen, dass ...** to get used to
the idea that ...

Vertraute, r *f(m)* confidant(e), close friend

Vertrautheit *f* familiarity

vertreiben [fɛr'traibən] *unreg vt* to drive away;
(*aus Land*) to expel; (*Comm*) to sell; (*Zeit*) to pass

Vertreibung *f* expulsion

vertretbar *adj* justifiable; (*Theorie, Argument*)
tenable

vertreten [fɛr'treːtən] *unreg vt* to represent;
(*Ansicht*) to hold, advocate; (*ersetzen*) to replace;
(*Kollegen*) to cover for; (*Comm*) to be the agent
for; **sich** *dat* **die Beine ~** to stretch one's legs

Vertreter, in (-s, -) *m(f)* representative;
(*Verfechter*) advocate; (*Comm: Firma*) agent;
Vertreterprovision *f* agent's commission

Vertretung *f* representation; advocacy; **die ~
übernehmen (für)** to stand in (for)

Vertretungsstunde *f* (*Sch*) cover lesson

Vertrieb [fɛr'triːp] **(-(e)s, -e)** *m* marketing; **den
~ für eine Firma haben** to have the (selling)
agency for a firm

Vertriebene, r [fɛr'triːbənə(r)] *f(m)* exile

Vertriebskosten *pl* marketing costs *pl*

vertrocknen [fɛr'trɔknən] *vi* to dry up

vertrödeln [fɛr'trøːdəln] (*umg*) *vt* to fritter
away

vertrösten [fɛr'trøːstən] *vt* to put off

vertun [fɛr'tuːn] *unreg vt* to waste ▷ *vr* (*umg*) to
make a mistake

vertuschen [fɛr'tuʃən] *vt* to hush *od* cover up

verübeln [fɛr'|yːbəln] *vt*: **jdm etw ~** to be cross
od offended with sb on account of sth

verüben [fɛr'|yːbən] *vt* to commit

verulken [fɛr'|ʊlkən] (*umg*) *vt* to make fun of

verunglimpfen [fɛr'|ʊnglɪmpfən] *vt* to
disparage

verunglücken [fɛr'|ʊnglʏkən] *vi* to have an
accident; (*fig: umg: misslingen*) to go wrong;
tödlich ~ to be killed in an accident

Verunglückte, r *f(m)* accident victim

verunreinigen [fɛr'|ʊnrainɪgən] *vt* to soil;
(*Umwelt*) to pollute

verunsichern [fɛr'|ʊnzɪçərn] *vt* to rattle (*fig*)

verunstalten [fɛr'|ʊnʃtaltən] *vt* to disfigure;
(*Gebäude etc*) to deface

veruntreuen [fɛr'|ʊntrɔyən] *vt* to embezzle

verursachen [fɛr'|uːrzaxən] *vt* to cause

verurteilen [fɛr'|uːrtailən] *vt* to condemn; (*zu
Strafe*) to sentence; (*für schuldig befinden*): **jdn ~
(für)** to convict sb (of)

Verurteilung *f* condemnation; (*Jur*) sentence;
conviction

vervielfachen [fɛr'fiːlfaxən] *vt* to multiply

vervielfältigen [fɛr'fiːlfɛltɪgən] *vt* to
duplicate, copy

Vervielfältigung *f* duplication, copying

vervollkommnen [fɛr'fɔlkɔmnən] *vt* to perfect

vervollständigen [fɛr'fɔlʃtɛndɪgən] *vt* to
complete

verw. *abk* = **verwitwet**

verwachsen [fɛr'vaksən] *adj* (*Mensch*)
deformed; (*verkümmert*) stunted; (*überwuchert*)
overgrown

verwackeln [fɛr'vakəln] *vt* (*Foto*) to blur

verwählen [fɛr'vɛːlən] *vr* (*Tel*) to dial the wrong
number

verwahren [fɛr'vaːrən] *vt* to keep (safe) ▷ *vr* to
protest

verwahrlosen *vi* to become neglected;
(*moralisch*) to go to the bad

verwahrlost *adj* neglected; (*moralisch*)
wayward

Verwahrung *f* (*von Geld etc*) keeping; (*von Täter*)
custody, detention; **jdn in ~ nehmen** to take
sb into custody

verwaist [fɛr'vaist] *adj* orphaned

verwalten [fɛr'valtən] *vt* to manage; (*Behörde*)
to administer

Verwalter, in (-s, -) *m(f)* administrator;
(*Vermögensverwalter*) trustee

Verwaltung *f* management; administration

Verwaltungs- *zW*: **Verwaltungsapparat**
m administrative machinery;
Verwaltungsbezirk *m* administrative district;
Verwaltungsgericht *nt* Administrative Court

verwandeln [fɛr'vandəln] *vt* to change,
transform ▷ *vr* to change

Verwandlung f change, transformation
verwandt [fɛr'vant] adj: ~ **(mit)** related (to);
geistig ~ sein (fig) to be kindred spirits
Verwandte, r f(m) relative, relation
Verwandtschaft f relationship; (Menschen)
relatives pl, relations pl; (fig) affinity
verwarnen [fɛr'varnən] vt to caution
Verwarnung f caution
verwaschen [fɛr'vaʃən] adj faded; (fig) vague
verwässern [fɛr'vɛsərn] vt to dilute, water
down
verwechseln [fɛr'vɛksəln] vt: ~ **mit** to confuse
with; **zum V~ ähnlich** as like as two peas
Verwechslung f confusion, mixing up; **das
muss eine ~ sein** there must be some mistake
verwegen [fɛr've:gən] adj daring, bold;
Verwegenheit f daring, audacity, boldness
verwehren [fɛr've:rən] vt (geh): **jdm etw ~** to
refuse od deny sb sth
Verwehung [fɛr've:ʊŋ] f (Schneeverwehung)
snowdrift; (Sandverwehung) sanddrift
verweichlichen [fɛr'vaiçlıçən] vt to
mollycoddle
verweichlicht adj effeminate, soft
verweigern [fɛr'vaigərn] vt: **jdm etw ~** to
refuse sb sth; **den Gehorsam/die Aussage ~**
to refuse to obey/testify
Verweigerung f refusal
verweilen [fɛr'vailən] vi to stay; (fig): ~ **bei** to
dwell on
verweint [fɛr'vaint] adj (Augen) swollen with
tears od with crying; (Gesicht) tear-stained
Verweis [fɛr'vais] (-es, -e) m reprimand,
rebuke; (Hinweis) reference
verweisen [fɛr'vaizən] unreg vt to refer; **jdn
auf etw** akk/**an jdn ~** (hinweisen) to refer sb to
sth/sb; **jdn vom Platz** od **des Spielfeldes ~**
(Sport) to send sb off; **jdn von der Schule ~** to
expel sb (from school); **jdn des Landes ~** to
deport sb
Verweisung f reference; (Landesverweisung)
deportation
verwelken [fɛr'vɛlkən] vi to fade; (Blumen) to
wilt
verweltlichen [fɛr'vɛltlıçən] vt to secularize
verwendbar [fɛr'vɛndba:r] adj usable
verwenden [fɛr'vɛndən] unreg vt to use; (Mühe,
Zeit, Arbeit) to spend ▷ vr to intercede
Verwendung f use
Verwendungsmöglichkeit f (possible) use
verwerfen [fɛr'vɛrfən] unreg vt to reject;
(Urteil) to quash; (kritisieren: Handlungsweise) to
condemn
verwerflich [fɛr'vɛrflıç] adj reprehensible
verwertbar adj usable
verwerten [fɛr've:rtən] vt to utilize
Verwertung f utilization
verwesen [fɛr've:zən] vi to decay
Verwesung f decomposition
verwickeln [fɛr'vıkəln] vt to tangle (up); (fig) to
involve ▷ vr to get tangled (up); **jdn ~ in** +akk
to involve sb in, get sb involved in; **sich ~ in**
+akk to get involved in

verwickelt adj involved
Verwicklung f entanglement, complication
verwildern [fɛr'vıldərn] vi to run wild
verwildert adj wild; (Garten) overgrown; (jds
Aussehen) unkempt
verwinden [fɛr'vındən] unreg vt to get over
verwirken [fɛr'vırkən] vt (geh) to forfeit
verwirklichen [fɛr'vırklıçən] vt to realize, put
into effect
Verwirklichung f realization
verwirren [fɛr'vırən] vt to tangle (up); (fig) to
confuse
Verwirrspiel nt confusing tactics pl
Verwirrung f confusion
verwischen [fɛr'vıʃən] vt (verschmieren)
to smudge; (lit, fig: Spuren) to cover over;
(fig: Erinnerungen) to blur
verwittern [fɛr'vıtərn] vi to weather
verwitwet [fɛr'vıtvət] adj widowed
verwöhnen [fɛr'vø:nən] vt to spoil, pamper
Verwöhnung f spoiling, pampering
verworfen [fɛr'vɔrfən] adj depraved;
Verworfenheit f depravity
verworren [fɛr'vɔrən] adj confused
verwundbar [fɛr'vʊntba:r] adj vulnerable
verwunden [fɛr'vʊndən] vt to wound
verwunderlich [fɛr'vʊndərlıç] adj surprising;
(stärker) astonishing
verwundern vt to astonish ▷ vr: **sich ~ über**
+akk to be astonished at
Verwunderung f astonishment
Verwundete, r f(m) injured person; **die ~n** the
injured; (Mil) the wounded
Verwundung f wound, injury
verwünschen [fɛr'vʏnʃən] vt to curse
verwurzelt [fɛr'vʊrtsəlt] adj: **(fest) in etw** dat
od **mit etw ~** (fig) deeply rooted in sth
verwüsten [fɛr'vy:stən] vt to devastate
Verwüstung f devastation
Verz. abk = **Verzeichnis**
verzagen [fɛr'tsa:gən] vi to despair
verzagt [fɛr'tsa:kt] adj disheartened
verzählen [fɛr'tsɛ:lən] vr to miscount
verzahnen [fɛr'tsa:nən] vt to dovetail;
(Zahnräder) to cut teeth in
verzapfen [fɛr'tsapfən] (umg) vt: **Unsinn ~** to
talk nonsense
verzaubern [fɛr'tsaʊbərn] vt (lit) to cast a spell
on; (fig: jdn) to enchant
verzehren [fɛr'tse:rən] vt to consume
verzeichnen [fɛr'tsaiçnən] vt to list;
(Niederlage, Verlust) to register
Verzeichnis (-ses, -se) nt list, catalogue (Brit),
catalog (US); (in Buch) index; (Comput) directory
verzeihen [fɛr'tsaiən] unreg vt, vi to forgive;
jdm etw ~ to forgive sb (for) sth; ~ **Sie!** excuse
me!
verzeihlich adj pardonable
Verzeihung f forgiveness, pardon; ~! sorry!,
excuse me!; **(jdn) um ~ bitten** to apologize
(to sb)
verzerren [fɛr'tseɛrən] vt to distort; (Sehne,
Muskel) to strain, pull

V

verzetteln [fɛr'tsɛtəln] vr to waste a lot of time
Verzicht [fɛr'tsɪçt] (-(e)s, -e) m: ~ (auf +akk)
renunciation (of); **verzichten** vi: **verzichten auf** +akk to forego, give up
verziehen [fɛr'tsi:ən] unreg vi (Hilfsverb sein) to move ▷ vt to put out of shape; (Kind) to spoil; (Pflanzen) to thin out ▷ vr to go out of shape; (Gesicht) to contort; (verschwinden) to disappear; **verzogen** (Vermerk) no longer at this address; **keine Miene ~** not to turn a hair; **das Gesicht ~** to pull a face
verzieren [fɛr'tsi:rən] vt to decorate
Verzierung f decoration
verzinsen [fɛr'tsɪnzən] vt to pay interest on
verzinslich adj: **(fest)~ sein** to yield (a fixed rate of) interest
verzogen [fɛr'tso:gən] adj (Kind) spoilt; siehe auch **verziehen**
verzögern [fɛr'tsø:gərn] vt to delay
Verzögerung f delay
Verzögerungstaktik f delaying tactics pl
verzollen [fɛr'tsɔlən] vt to pay duty on; **haben Sie etwas zu ~?** have you anything to declare?
verzücken [fɛr'tsʏkən] vt to send into ecstasies, enrapture
Verzug [fɛr'tsu:k] m delay; (Fin) arrears pl; **mit etw in ~ geraten** to fall behind with sth
verzweifeln [fɛr'tsvaɪfəln] vi to despair
verzweifelt adj desperate
Verzweiflung f despair
verzweigen [fɛr'tsvaɪgən] vr to branch out
verzwickt [fɛr'tsvɪkt] (umg) adj awkward, complicated
Vesper ['fɛspər] (-, -n) f vespers pl
Vesuv [ve'zu:f] (-(s)) m Vesuvius
Veto ['ve:to] (-s, -s) nt veto
Vetter ['fɛtər] (-s, -n) m cousin
vgl. abk (= vergleiche) cf
v. H. abk (= vom Hundert) pc
VHS (-) f abk = **Volkshochschule**
Viadukt [via'dʊkt] (-(e)s, -e) m viaduct
Vibrator [vi'bra:tɔr] m vibrator
vibrieren [vi'bri:rən] vi to vibrate
Video ['vi:deo] (-s, -s) nt video; **Videoaufnahme** f video (recording); **Videokamera** f video camera; **Videorekorder** m video recorder; **Videospiel** nt video game; **Videotext** m teletext
Vieh [fi:] (-(e)s) nt cattle pl; (Nutztiere) livestock; (umg: Tier) animal; **viehisch** adj bestial; **Viehzucht** f (live)stock od cattle breeding
viel [fi:l] adj a lot of, much ▷ adv a lot, much; **in ~em** in many respects; **noch (ein)mal so ~** (Zeit etc) as much (time etc) again; **einer zu ~** one too many; **~ zu wenig** much too little; **~ beschäftigt** very busy; **~ geprüft** (hum) sorely tried; **~ sagend** significant; **~ versprechend** promising; **viele** pl a lot of, many; **gleich viele (Angestellte/Anteile** etc) the same number (of employees/shares etc)
vielerlei adj a great variety of
vielerorts adv in many places
viel- zW: **vielfach** adj, adv many times; **auf**

vielfachen Wunsch at the request of many people; **Vielfache, s** nt (Math) multiple; **um ein Vielfaches** many times over; **Vielfalt** (-) f variety; **vielfältig** adj varied, many-sided; **Vielfraß** m glutton
vielleicht [fi'laɪçt] adv perhaps; (in Bitten) by any chance; **du bist ~ ein Idiot!** (umg) you really are an idiot!
viel- zW: **vielmal, vielmals** adv many times; **danke vielmals** many thanks; **ich bitte vielmals um Entschuldigung!** I do apologize!; **vielmehr** adv rather, on the contrary; **vielsagend** adj significant; **vielschichtig** adj (fig) complex; **vielseitig** adj many-sided; (Ausbildung) all-round attr; (Interessen) varied; (Mensch, Gerät) versatile; **vielversprechend** adj promising; **Vielvölkerstaat** m multinational state
vier [fi:r] num four; **alle ~e von sich strecken** (umg) to stretch out; **Vierbeiner** m (hum) four-legged friend; **Viereck** (-(e)s, -e) nt four-sided figure; (gleichseitig) square; **viereckig** adj four-sided; square; **vierhundert** num four hundred; **vierkant** adj, adv (Naut) square; **vierköpfig** adj: **eine vierköpfige Familie** a family of four; **Viermächteabkommen** nt four-power agreement
viert adj: **wir gingen zu ~** four of us went
Viertaktmotor m four-stroke engine
vierte, r, s ['fi:rtə(r, s)] adj fourth
vierteilen vt to quarter
Viertel ['fɪrtəl] (-s, -) nt quarter; **ein ~ Leberwurst** a quarter of liver sausage; **Viertelfinale** nt quarter finals pl; **Vierteljahr** nt three months pl, quarter (COMM, FIN); **Vierteljahresschrift** f quarterly; **vierteljährlich** adj quarterly; **Viertelnote** f crotchet (Brit), quarter note (US); **Viertelstunde** f quarter of an hour
vier- zW: **viertürig** adj four-door attr; **Vierwaldstättersee** m Lake Lucerne; **vierzehn** ['fɪrtse:n] num fourteen; **in vierzehn Tagen** in a fortnight (Brit), in two weeks (US); **vierzehntägig** adj fortnightly; **vierzehnte, r, s** adj fourteenth
vierzig ['fɪrtsɪç] num forty; **Vierzigstundenwoche** f forty-hour week
Vierzimmerwohnung f four-room flat (Brit) od apartment (US)
Vietnam [viɛt'nam] (-s) nt Vietnam
Vietnamese [viɛtna'me:zə] (-n, -n) m, **Vietnamesin** f Vietnamese
vietnamesisch adj Vietnamese
Vikar [vi'ka:r] (-s, -e) m curate
Villa ['vɪla] (-, **Villen**) f villa
Villenviertel nt (prosperous) residential area
violett [vio'lɛt] adj violet
Violinbogen m violin bow
Violine [vio'li:nə] (-, -n) f violin
Violinkonzert nt violin concerto
Violinschlüssel m treble clef
virtuell [vɪrtu'ɛl] adj (Comput) virtual; **~e Realität** virtual reality

virtuos [vɪrtuˈoːs] *adj* virtuoso *attrib*
Virtuose [vɪrtuˈoːzə] (**-n, -n**) *m* virtuoso
Virtuosin [vɪrtuˈoːzɪn] *f* virtuoso
Virtuosität [vɪrtuoziˈtɛt] *f* virtuosity
Virus [ˈviːrʊs] (**-, Viren**) *m od nt* (*also Comput*) virus
Virus- *in zw* viral: **Virusinfektion** *f* virus infection
Visage [viˈzaːʒə] (**-, -n**) (*pej*) *f* face, (ugly) mug (*umg*)
Visagist, in [vizaˈʒɪst(ɪn)] *m(f)* make-up artist
vis-à-vis, vis-a-vis [vizaˈviː] *adv* (*veraltet*): **~ (von)** opposite (to) ▷ *präp +dat* opposite (to)
Visier [viˈziːr] (**-s, -e**) *nt* gunsight; (*am Helm*) visor
Vision [viziˈoːn] *f* vision
Visite [viˈziːtə] (**-, -n**) *f* (*Med*) visit
Visitenkarte *f* visiting card
visuell [vizuˈɛl] *adj* visual
Visum [ˈviːzʊm] (**-s, Visa** *od* **Visen**) *nt* visa; **Visumzwang** *m* obligation to hold a visa
vital [viˈtaːl] *adj* lively, full of life; (*lebenswichtig*) vital
Vitamin [vitaˈmiːn] (**-s, -e**) *nt* vitamin; **Vitaminmangel** *m* vitamin deficiency
Vitrine [viˈtriːnə] (**-, -n**) *f* (*Schrank*) glass cabinet; (*Schaukasten*) showcase, display case
Vivisektion [vivizɛktsiˈoːn] *f* vivisection
Vize [ˈfiːtsə] *m* (*umg*) number two; (*: Vizemeister*) runner-up ▷ *in zw* vice-
v. J. *abk* (= *vorigen Jahres*) of the previous *od* last year
Vlies [fliːs] (**-es, -e**) *nt* fleece
v. M. *abk* (= *vorigen Monats*) ult.
V-Mann *m abk* = **Verbindungsmann; Vertrauensmann**
VN *pl abk* (= *Vereinte Nationen*) UN
VO *abk* = **Verordnung**
Vogel [ˈfoːɡəl] (**-s, ⸚**) *m* bird; **einen ~ haben** (*umg*) to have bats in the belfry; **den ~ abschießen** (*umg*) to surpass everyone (*ironisch*); **Vogelbauer** *nt* birdcage; **Vogelbeerbaum** *m* rowan (tree); **Vogeldreck** *m* bird droppings *pl*; **Vogelperspektive** *f* bird's-eye view; **Vogelschau** *f* bird's-eye view; **Vogelscheuche** *f* scarecrow; **Vogelschutzgebiet** *nt* bird sanctuary; **Vogel-Strauß-Politik** *f* head-in-the-sand policy
Vogesen [voˈɡeːzən] *pl* Vosges *pl*
Voicemail [ˈvɔɪsmeːl] *f* (*Tel*) voice mail
Vokabel [voˈkaːbəl] (**-, -n**) *f* word
Vokabular [vokabuˈlaːr] (**-s, -e**) *nt* vocabulary
Vokal [voˈkaːl] (**-s, -e**) *m* vowel
Volk [fɔlk] (**-(e)s, ⸚er**) *nt* people; (*Nation*) nation; **etw unters ~ bringen** (*Nachricht*) to spread sth
Völker- *zW*: **Völkerbund** *m* League of Nations; **Völkerkunde** *f* ethnology; **Völkermord** *m* genocide; **Völkerrecht** *nt* international law; **völkerrechtlich** *adj* according to international law; **Völkerverständigung** *f* international understanding; **Völkerwanderung** *f* migration

Volks- *zW*: **Volksabstimmung** *f* referendum; **Volksarmee** *f* People's Army; **Volksbegehren** *nt* petition for a referendum; **Volksdeutsche, r** *f(m) dekl wie adj* ethnic German; **volkseigen** *adj* (*DDR*) nationally-owned; **Volksfeind** *m* enemy of the people; **Volksfest** *nt* popular festival; (*Jahrmarkt*) fair
Volkshochschule *f* adult education classes *pl*; *see culture note*

● **VOLKSHOCHSCHULE**

●
● The *Volkshochschule* (VHS) is an institution
● which offers Adult Education classes. No
● set qualifications are necessary to attend.
● For a small fee adults can attend both
● vocational and non-vocational classes in
● the day-time or evening.

Volks- *zW*: **Volkslauf** *m* fun run; **Volkslied** *nt* folk song; **Volksmund** *m* vernacular; **Volkspolizei** *f* (*DDR*) People's Police; **Volksrepublik** *f* people's republic; **Volksschule** *f* ≈ primary school (*Brit*), ≈ elementary school (*US*); **Volksseuche** *f* epidemic; **Volksstamm** *m* tribe; **Volksstück** *nt* folk play in dialect; **Volkstanz** *m* folk dance; **Volkstrauertag** *m* ≈ Remembrance Day (*Brit*), ≈ Memorial Day (*US*); **volkstümlich** *adj* popular; **Volkswirtschaft** *f* national economy; (*Fach*) economics *sing*, political economy; **Volkswirtschaftler** *m* economist; **Volkszählung** *f* (national) census
voll [fɔl] *adj* full ▷ *adv* fully; (*Tafel*) to cover (with writing); **jdn für ~ nehmen** (*umg*) to take sb seriously; **aus dem V~en schöpfen** to draw on unlimited resources; **in ~er Größe** (*Bild*) life-size(d); (*bei plötzlicher Erscheinung etc*) large as life; **~ sein** (*umg: satt*) to be full (up); (*: betrunken*) to be plastered; **~ und ganz** completely; *siehe auch* **vollmachen; vollschreiben; volltanken**
vollauf [fɔlˈʔaʊf] *adv* amply; **~ zu tun haben** to have quite enough to do
voll- *zW*: **Vollbad** *nt* (proper) bath; **Vollbart** *m* full beard; **Vollbeschäftigung** *f* full employment; **Vollbesitz** *m*: **im Vollbesitz** *+gen* in full possession of; **Vollblut** *nt* thoroughbred; **vollblütig** *adj* full-blooded; **Vollbremsung** *f* emergency stop; **vollbringen** *unreg vt untr* to accomplish; **Volldampf** *m* (*Naut*): **mit Volldampf** at full steam; **vollenden** *vt untr* to finish, complete; **vollendet** *adj* (*vollkommen*) perfect; (*Tänzer etc*) accomplished; **vollends** *adv* completely; **Vollendung** *f* completion
voller *adj* fuller; **~ Flecken/Ideen** full of stains/ideas
Völlerei [fœləˈraɪ] *f* gluttony
Volleyball [ˈvɔlibal] (**-(e)s**) *m* volleyball
voll- *zW*: **vollfett** *adj* full-fat; **Vollgas** *nt*: **mit Vollgas** at full throttle; **Vollgas geben** to step on it
völlig [ˈfœlɪç] *adj* complete ▷ *adv* completely

V

voll- zW: **volljährig** adj of age;
Vollkaskoversicherung f fully comprehensive
insurance; **vollkommen** adj perfect; (völlig)
complete, absolute; **Vollkommenheit** f
perfection; **Vollkornbrot** nt wholemeal
(Brit) od whole-wheat (US) bread; **volllaufen**
unreg vi: **etw volllaufen lassen** to fill sth
up; **vollmachen** vt to fill (up); **Vollmacht** f
authority, power of attorney; **Vollmatrose** m
able-bodied seaman; **Vollmilch** f full-cream
milk; **Vollmond** m full moon; **Vollnarkose**
f general anaesthetic (Brit) od anesthetic
(US); **Vollpension** f full board; **vollschlank**
adj plump, stout; **vollschreiben** unreg vt
(Heft, Seite) to fill; **vollständig** adj complete;
vollstrecken vt untr to execute; **volltanken**
vt, vi to fill up; **Volltreffer** m (lit, fig) bull's-
eye; **Vollversammlung** f general meeting;
Vollwaise f orphan; **vollwertig** adj full attrib;
(Stellung) equal; **Vollwertkost** f wholefoods
pl; **vollzählig** adj complete; (anwesend) in full
number; **vollziehen** unreg vt untr to carry out
▷ vr untr to happen; **Vollzug** m execution
Volontär, in [volɔn'tɛːr(ɪn)] (**-s, -e**) m(f) trainee
Volt [vɔlt] (**-, od -(e)s, -**) nt volt
Volumen [vo'luːmən] (**-s, - od Volumina**) nt
volume
vom [fɔm] = **von dem**

○ SCHLÜSSELWORT

von [fɔn] präp +dat **1** (Ausgangspunkt) from;
von ... bis from ... to; **von morgens bis
abends** from morning till night; **von ...
nach ...** from ... to ...; **von ... an** from ...;
von ... aus from ...; **von dort aus** from there;
etw von sich aus tun to do sth of one's own
accord; **von mir aus** (umg) if you like, I don't
mind; **von wo/wann ...?** where/when ...
from?
2 (Ursache, im Passiv) by; **ein Gedicht von
Schiller** a poem by Schiller; **von etw müde**
tired from sth
3 (als Genitiv) of; **ein Freund von mir** a friend
of mine; **nett von dir** nice of you; **jeweils
zwei von zehn** two out of every ten
4 (über) about; **er erzählte vom Urlaub** he
talked about his holiday
5: von wegen! (umg) no way!

voneinander adv from each other
vonseiten, von Seiten [vɔn'zaɪtn] präp +gen on
the part of
vonstattengehen [fɔn'ʃtatən-] unreg vi to
proceed, go

○ SCHLÜSSELWORT

vor [foːr] präp +dat **1** (räumlich) in front of
2 (zeitlich, Reihenfolge) before; **ich war vor ihm
da** I was there before him; **X kommt vor Y**
X comes before Y; **vor zwei Tagen** two days
ago; **5 (Minuten) vor 4** 5 (minutes) to 4; **vor**
Kurzem a little while ago
3 (Ursache) with; **vor Wut/Liebe** with rage/
love; **vor Hunger sterben** to die of hunger;
vor lauter Arbeit because of work
4: vor allem, vor allen Dingen above all
▷ präp +akk (räumlich) in front of; **vor sich hin
summen** to hum to oneself
▷ adv: **vor und zurück** backwards and
forwards

Vor- zW: **Vorabdruck** m preprint; **Vorabend**
m evening before, eve; **Vorahnung** f
presentiment, premonition
voran [fo'ran] adv before, ahead; **voranbringen**
unreg vt to make progress with; **vorangehen**
unreg vi to go ahead; **einer Sache** dat
vorangehen to precede sth; **vorangehend**
adj previous; **vorankommen** unreg vi to make
progress, come along
Voranschlag ['foːr|anʃlaːk] m estimate
voranstellen [fo'ranʃtɛlən] vt +dat to put in
front (of); (fig) to give precedence (over)
Vorarbeiter ['foːr|arbaɪtər] m foreman
voraus [fo'raʊs] adv ahead; (zeitlich) in
advance; **jdm ~ sein** to be ahead of sb; **im
V~** in advance; **vorausbezahlen** vt to pay
in advance; **vorausgehen** unreg vi to go
(on) ahead; (fig) to precede; **voraushaben**
unreg vt: **jdm etw voraushaben** to have the
edge on sb in sth; **Voraussage** f prediction;
voraussagen vt to predict; **voraussehen**
unreg vt to foresee; **voraussetzen** vt to
assume; (sicher annehmen) to take for granted;
(erfordern: Kenntnisse, Geduld) to require, demand;
vorausgesetzt, dass ... provided that ...;
Voraussetzung f requirement, prerequisite;
unter der Voraussetzung, dass ... on
condition that ...; **Voraussicht** f foresight;
aller Voraussicht nach in all probability;
in der Voraussicht, dass ... anticipating
that ...; **voraussichtlich** adv probably;
Vorauszahlung f advance payment
Vorbau ['foːrbaʊ] (**-(e)s, -ten**) m porch; (Balkon)
balcony
vorbauen ['foːrbaʊən] vt to build up in front
▷ vi +dat to take precautions (against)
Vorbedacht ['foːrbədaxt] m: **mit/ohne ~**
(Überlegung) with/without due consideration;
(Absicht) intentionally/unintentionally
Vorbedingung ['foːrbədɪŋʊŋ] f precondition
Vorbehalt ['foːrbəhalt] m reservation, proviso;
unter dem ~, dass ... with the reservation
that ...
vorbehalten unreg vt: **sich/jdm etw ~** to
reserve sth (for o.s.)/for sb; **alle Rechte ~** all
rights reserved
vorbehaltlich präp +gen (form) subject to
vorbehaltlos adj unconditional ▷ adv
unconditionally
vorbei [fɔr'baɪ] adv by, past; **aus und ~** over
and done with; **damit ist es nun ~** that's
all over now; **vorbeibringen** unreg (umg) vt
to drop off; **vorbeigehen** unreg vi to pass by,

go past; **vorbeikommen** unreg vi: **bei jdm vorbeikommen** to drop od call in on sb; **vorbeireden** vi: **an etw** dat **vorbeireden** to talk around sth

vorbelastet ['foːrbəlastət] adj (fig) handicapped (Brit), handicaped (US)

Vorbemerkung ['foːrbəmɛrkʊŋ] f introductory remark

vorbereiten ['foːrbəraɪtən] vt to prepare

Vorbereitung f preparation

vorbestellen ['foːrbəʃtɛlən] vt to book (in advance), reserve

Vorbestellung f advance booking

vorbestraft ['foːrbəʃtraft] adj previously convicted, with a record

Vorbeugehaft f preventive custody

vorbeugen ['foːrbɔʏgən] vt, vr to lean forward ▷ vi +dat to prevent

vorbeugend adj preventive

Vorbeugung f prevention; **zur ~ gegen** for the prevention of

Vorbild ['foːrbɪlt] nt model; **sich** dat **jdn zum ~ nehmen** to model o.s. on sb; **vorbildlich** adj model, ideal

Vorbildung ['foːrbɪldʊŋ] f educational background

Vorbote ['foːrboːtə] m (fig) herald

vorbringen ['foːrbrɪŋən] unreg vt to voice; (Meinung etc) to advance, state; (umg: nach vorne) to bring to the front

vordatieren ['foːrdatiːrən] vt (Schreiben) to postdate

Vorder- zW: **Vorderachse** f front axle; **Vorderansicht** f front view; **Vorderasien** nt Near East

vordere, r, s adj front

Vorder- zW: **Vordergrund** m foreground; **im Vordergrund stehen** (fig) to be to the fore; **Vordergrundprogramm** nt (Comput) foreground program; **vorderhand** adv for the present; **Vordermann** (-(e)s, pl -**männer**) m man in front; **jdn auf Vordermann bringen** (umg) to get sb to shape up; **Vorderseite** f front (side); **Vordersitz** m front seat

vorderste, r, s adj front

vordrängen ['foːrdrɛŋən] vr to push to the front

vordringen ['foːrdrɪŋən] unreg vi: **bis zu jdm/ etw ~** to get as far as sb/sth

vordringlich adj urgent

Vordruck ['foːrdrʊk] m form

vorehelich ['foːr|eːəlɪç] adj premarital

voreilig ['foːr|aɪlɪç] adj hasty, rash; **~e Schlüsse ziehen** to jump to conclusions

voreinander [foːr|aɪˈnandər] adv (räumlich) in front of each other; (einander gegenüber) face to face

voreingenommen ['foːr|aɪŋgənɔmən] adj bias(s)ed; **Voreingenommenheit** f bias

voreingestellt ['foːr|aɪŋgəʃtɛlt] adj: **~er Parameter** (Comput) default (parameter)

vorenthalten ['foːr|ɛnthaltən] unreg vt: **jdm etw ~** to withhold sth from sb

Vorentscheidung ['foːr|ɛntʃaɪdʊŋ] f preliminary decision

vorerst ['foːr|eːrst] adv for the moment od present

Vorfahr ['foːrfaːr] (-en, -en) m ancestor

vorfahren unreg vi to drive (on) ahead; (vors Haus etc) to drive up

Vorfahrt f (Aut) right of way; „**~ (be)achten**" "give way" (Brit), "yield" (US)

Vorfahrts- zW: **Vorfahrtsregel** f rule of right of way; **Vorfahrtsschild** nt "give way" (Brit) od "yield" (US) sign; **Vorfahrtsstraße** f major road

Vorfall ['foːrfal] m incident

vorfallen unreg vi to occur

Vorfeld ['foːrfɛlt] nt (fig): **im ~ (+gen)** in the run-up (to)

Vorfilm ['foːrfɪlm] m short

vorfinden ['foːrfɪndən] unreg vt to find

Vorfreude ['foːrfrɔʏdə] f anticipation

vorfühlen ['foːrfyːlən] vi (fig) to put out feelers

vorführen ['foːrfyːrən] vt to show, display; (Theaterstück, Kunststücke): **(jdm) etw ~** to perform sth (to od in front of sb); **dem Gericht ~** to bring before the court

Vorgabe ['foːrgaːbə] f (Sport) handicap

Vorgang ['foːrgaŋ] m (Ereignis) event; (Ablauf) course of events; (Chem etc) process

Vorgänger, in ['foːrgɛŋər(ɪn)] (-s, -) m(f) predecessor

vorgaukeln ['foːrgaʊkəln] vt: **jdm etw ~** to lead sb to believe in sth

vorgeben ['foːrgeːbən] unreg vt to pretend, use as a pretext; (Sport) to give an advantage od a start of

Vorgebirge ['foːrgəbɪrgə] nt foothills pl

vorgefasst ['foːrgəfast] adj preconceived

vorgefertigt ['foːrgəfɛrtɪçt] adj prefabricated

Vorgefühl ['foːrgəfyːl] nt anticipation; (etwas Böses) presentiment

vorgehen ['foːrgeːən] unreg vi (voraus) to go (on) ahead; (nach vorn) to go forward; (handeln) to act, proceed; (Uhr) to be fast; (Vorrang haben) to take precedence; (passieren) to go on

Vorgehen (-s) nt action

Vorgehensweise f proceedings pl

vorgerückt ['foːrgərʏkt] adj (Stunde) late; (Alter) advanced

Vorgeschichte ['foːrgəʃɪçtə] f prehistory; (von Fall, Krankheit) past history

Vorgeschmack ['foːrgəʃmak] m foretaste

Vorgesetzte, r ['foːrgəzɛtstə(r)] f(m) superior

vorgestern ['foːrgɛstərn] adv the day before yesterday; **von ~** (fig) antiquated

vorgreifen ['foːrgraɪfən] unreg vi +dat to anticipate; **jdm ~** to forestall sb

vorhaben ['foːrhaːbən] unreg vt to intend; **hast du schon was vor?** have you got anything on?

Vorhaben (-s, -) nt intention

Vorhalle ['foːrhalə] f (Diele) entrance hall; (von Parlament) lobby

vorhalten ['foːrhaltən] unreg vt to hold od put up ▷ vi to last; **jdm etw ~** to reproach sb for

V

375

sth

Vorhaltung f reproach

Vorhand ['fo:rhant] f forehand

vorhanden [fo:r'handən] adj existing; (erhältlich) available; **Vorhandensein (-s)** nt existence, presence

Vorhang ['fo:rhaŋ] m curtain

Vorhängeschloss ['fo:rhɛŋəʃlɔs] nt padlock

Vorhaut ['fo:rhaʊt] f (Anat) foreskin

vorher [fo:r'he:r] adv before(hand); **vorherbestimmen** vt (Schicksal) to preordain; **vorhergehen** unreg vi to precede

vorherig [fo:r'he:rɪç] adj previous

Vorherrschaft ['fo:rhɛrʃaft] f predominance, supremacy

vorherrschen vi to predominate

vorher- zW: **Vorhersage** f forecast; **vorhersagen** vt to forecast, predict; **vorhersehbar** adj predictable; **vorhersehen** unreg vt to foresee

vorhin [fo:r'hɪn] adv not long ago, just now

Vorhinein ['fo:rhɪnaɪn] adv: **im ~** beforehand

Vorhof ['fo:rho:f] m forecourt

vorig ['fo:rɪç] adj previous, last

Vorjahr ['fo:rja:r] nt previous year, year before

vorjährig ['fo:rjɛ:rɪç] adj of the previous year

vorjammern ['fo:rjamərn] vt, vi: **jdm (etwas) ~** to moan to sb (about sth)

Vorkämpfer, in ['fo:rkɛmpfər(ɪn)] m(f) pioneer

Vorkaufsrecht ['fo:rkaʊfsrɛçt] nt option to buy

Vorkehrung ['fo:rke:rʊŋ] f precaution

Vorkenntnis ['fo:rkɛntnɪs] f previous knowledge

vorknöpfen ['fo:rknœpfən] vt (fig: umg): **sich** dat **jdn ~** to take sb to task

vorkommen ['fo:rkɔmən] unreg vi to come forward; (geschehen, sich finden) to occur; (scheinen) to seem (to be); **so was soll ~!** that's life!; **sich** dat **dumm** etc **~** to feel stupid etc

Vorkommen nt occurrence; (Min) deposit

Vorkommnis ['fo:rkɔmnɪs] **(-ses, -se)** nt occurrence

Vorkriegs- ['fo:rkri:ks] in zw pre-war

vorladen ['fo:rla:dən] unreg vt (bei Gericht) to summons

Vorladung f summons

Vorlage ['fo:rla:gə] f model, pattern; (das Vorlegen) presentation; (von Beweismaterial) submission; (Gesetzesvorlage) bill; (Sport) pass

vorlassen ['fo:rlasən] unreg vt to admit; (überholen lassen) to let pass; (vorgehen lassen) to allow to go in front

Vorlauf ['fo:rlaʊf] m (preliminary) heat (of running event)

Vorläufer m forerunner

vorläufig ['fo:rlɔyfɪç] adj temporary; (provisorisch) provisional

vorlaut ['fo:rlaʊt] adj impertinent, cheeky

Vorleben ['fo:rle:bən] nt past (life)

vorlegen ['fo:rle:gən] vt to put in front, present; (Beweismaterial etc) to produce, submit; **jdm etw ~** to put sth before sb

Vorleger (-s, -) m mat

Vorleistung ['fo:rlaɪstʊŋ] f (Fin: Vorausbezahlung) advance (payment); (Vorarbeit) preliminary work; (Pol) prior concession

vorlesen ['fo:rle:zən] unreg vt to read (out)

Vorlesung f (Univ) lecture

Vorlesungsverzeichnis nt lecture timetable

vorletzte, r, s ['fo:rlɛtstə(r, s)] adj last but one, penultimate

Vorliebe ['fo:rli:bə] f preference, special liking; **etw mit ~ tun** to particularly like doing sth

vorliebnehmen [fo:r'li:p-] unreg vi: **~ mit** to make do with

vorliegen ['fo:rli:gən] unreg vi to be (here); **etw liegt jdm vor** sb has sth; **etw liegt gegen jdn vor** sb is charged with sth

vorliegend adj present, at issue

vorm. abk (= vormittags) a.m.; (= vormals) formerly

vormachen ['fo:rmaxən] vt: **jdm etw ~** to show sb how to do sth; **jdm etwas ~** (fig) to fool sb; **mach mir doch nichts vor** don't try and fool me

Vormachtstellung ['fo:rmaxtʃtɛlʊŋ] f supremacy

vormals ['fo:rmals] adv formerly

Vormarsch ['fo:rmarʃ] m advance

vormerken ['fo:rmɛrkən] vt to book; (notieren) to make note of; (bei Bestellung) to take an order for

Vormittag ['fo:rmɪta:k] m morning; **am ~** in the morning

vormittags adv in the morning, before noon

Vormund ['fo:rmʊnt] **(-(e)s, -e** od **-münder)** m guardian

vorn [fɔrn] adv in front; **von ~ anfangen** to start at the beginning; **nach ~** to the front; **er betrügt sie von ~ bis hinten** he deceives her right, left and centre

Vorname ['fo:rna:mə] m first od Christian name

vornan [fɔrn|an] adv at the front

vorne ['fɔrnə] = **vorn**

vornehm ['fo:rne:m] adj distinguished; (Manieren etc) refined; (Kleid) elegant; **in ~en Kreisen** in polite society

vornehmen unreg vt (fig) to carry out; **sich** dat **etw ~** to start on sth; (beschließen) to decide to do sth; **sich** dat **zu viel ~** to take on too much; **sich** dat **jdn ~** to tell sb off

vornehmlich adv chiefly, specially

vorneweg ['fɔrnəvɛk], **vornweg** ['fɔrnvɛk] adv in front; (als Erstes) first

vornherein ['fɔrnhɛraɪn] adv: **von ~** from the start

Vorort ['fo:r|ɔrt] m suburb; **Vorortzug** m commuter train

vorprogrammiert ['fo:rprogrami:rt] adj (Erfolg, Antwort) automatic

Vorrang ['fo:rraŋ] m precedence, priority

vorrangig adj of prime importance, primary

Vorrat ['fo:rra:t] m stock, supply; **solange der ~ reicht** (Comm) while stocks last

vorrätig ['fo:rrɛ:tɪç] adj in stock

Vorratskammer f store cupboard; (für Lebensmittel) larder

Vorraum m anteroom; (Büro) outer office

vorrechnen ['foːrrɛçnən] vt: **jdm etw ~** to calculate sth for sb; (als Kritik) to point sth out to sb

Vorrecht ['foːrrɛçt] nt privilege

Vorrede ['foːrreːdə] f introductory speech; (Theat) prologue (Brit), prolog (US)

Vorrichtung ['foːrrɪçtʊŋ] f device, gadget

vorrücken ['foːrrʏkən] vi to advance ▷ vt to move forward

Vorruhestand ['foːrruːəʃtant] m early retirement

Vorrunde ['foːrrʊndə] f (Sport) preliminary round

Vors. abk = **Vorsitzende(r)**

vorsagen ['foːrzaːɡən] vt to recite; (Sch: zuflüstern) to tell secretly, prompt

Vorsaison ['foːrzɛzõ] f early season, low season

Vorsatz ['foːrzats] m intention; (Jur) intent; **einen ~ fassen** to make a resolution

vorsätzlich ['foːrzɛtslɪç] adj intentional; (Jur) premeditated ▷ adv intentionally

Vorschau ['foːrʃau] f (Rundf, TV) (programme (Brit) od program (US)) preview; (Film) trailer

Vorschein ['foːrʃain] m: **zum ~ kommen** (lit: sichtbar werden) to appear; (fig: entdeckt werden) to come to light

vorschieben ['foːrʃiːbən] unreg vt to push forward; (vor etw) to push across; (fig) to put forward as an excuse; **jdn ~** to use sb as a front

vorschießen ['foːrʃiːsən] unreg (umg) vt: **jdm Geld ~** to advance sb money

Vorschlag ['foːrʃlaːk] m suggestion, proposal

vorschlagen ['foːrʃlaːɡən] unreg vt to suggest, propose

Vorschlaghammer m sledgehammer

vorschnell ['foːrʃnɛl] adj hasty, too quick

vorschreiben ['foːrʃraibən] unreg vt (Dosis) to prescribe; (befehlen) to specify; **(jdm) etw ~** (lit) to write sth out (for sb); **ich lasse mir nichts ~** I won't be dictated to

Vorschrift ['foːrʃrɪft] f regulation(s pl), rule(s pl); (Anweisungen) instruction(s pl); **jdm ~en machen** to give sb orders; **Dienst nach ~** work-to-rule (Brit), slowdown (US)

vorschriftsmäßig adv as per regulations/instructions

Vorschub ['foːrʃuːp] m: **jdm/einer Sache ~ leisten** to encourage sb/sth

Vorschule ['foːrʃuːlə] f nursery school

vorschulisch ['foːrʃuːlɪʃ] adj preschool attr

Vorschuss ['foːrʃʊs] m advance

vorschützen ['foːrʃʏtsən] vt to put forward as a pretext; (Unwissenheit) to plead

vorschweben ['foːrʃveːbən] vi: **jdm schwebt etw vor** sb has sth in mind

vorsehen ['foːrzeːən] unreg vt to provide for; (planen) to plan ▷ vr to take care, be careful

Vorsehung f providence

vorsetzen ['foːrzɛtsən] vt to move forward;

(davor setzen): **~ vor** +akk to put in front of; (anbieten): **jdm etw ~** to offer sb sth

Vorsicht ['foːrzɪçt] f caution, care; **~!** look out!, take care!; (auf Schildern) caution!, danger!; **~ Stufe!** mind the step!; **etw mit ~ genießen** (umg) to take sth with a pinch of salt

vorsichtig adj cautious, careful

vorsichtshalber adv just in case

Vorsichtsmaßnahme f precaution

Vorsilbe ['foːrzɪlbə] f prefix

vorsintflutlich ['foːrzɪntfluːtlɪç] (umg) adj antiquated

Vorsitz ['foːrzɪts] m chair(manship); **den ~ führen** to chair the meeting

Vorsitzende, r f(m) chairman/-woman, chair(person)

Vorsorge ['foːrzɔrɡə] f precaution(s pl); (Fürsorge) provision(s pl)

vorsorgen vi: **~ für** to make provision(s pl) for

Vorsorgeuntersuchung ['foːrzɔrɡə|ʊntɐzuːxʊŋ] f medical check-up

vorsorglich ['foːrzɔrklɪç] adv as a precaution

Vorspann ['voːrʃpan] m (Film, TV) opening credits pl; (Presse) opening paragraph

vorspannen vt (Pferde) to harness

Vorspeise ['foːrʃpaizə] f hors d'œuvre, starter

Vorspiegelung ['foːrʃpiːɡəlʊŋ] f: **das ist (eine) ~ falscher Tatsachen** it's all sham

Vorspiel ['foːrʃpiːl] nt prelude; (bei Geschlechtsverkehr) foreplay

vorspielen vt: **jdm etw ~** (Mus) to play sth to sb; (Theat) to act sth to sb; (fig) to act out a sham of sth in front of sb

vorsprechen ['foːrʃprɛçən] unreg vt to say out loud; (vortragen) to recite ▷ vi (Theat) to audition; **bei jdm ~** to call on sb

vorspringend ['foːrʃprɪŋənt] adj projecting; (Nase, Kinn) prominent

Vorsprung ['foːrʃprʊŋ] m projection; (Felsvorsprung) ledge; (fig) advantage, start

Vorstadt ['foːrʃtat] f suburbs pl

Vorstand ['foːrʃtant] m executive committee; (Comm) board (of directors); (Person) director; (Leiter) head

Vorstandssitzung f (von Firma) board meeting

Vorstandsvorsitzende, r f(m) chairperson

vorstehen ['foːrʃteːən] unreg vi to project; **einer Sache** dat **~** (fig) to be the head of sth

Vorsteher, in (**-s, -**) m(f) (von Abteilung) head; (von Gefängnis) governor; (Bahnhofsvorsteher) stationmaster

vorstellbar adj conceivable

vorstellen ['foːrʃtɛlən] vt to put forward; (vor etw) to put in front; (bekannt machen) to introduce; (darstellen) to represent ▷ vr to introduce o.s.; (bei Bewerbung) to go for an interview; **sich** dat **etw ~** to imagine sth; **stell dir das nicht so einfach vor** don't think it's so easy

Vorstellung f (Bekanntmachen) introduction; (Theat etc) performance; (Gedanke) idea

Vorstellungsgespräch nt interview

Vorstellungsvermögen nt powers of

imagination *pl*

Vorstoß ['foːrʃtoːs] *m* advance; (*fig*: *Versuch*) attempt

vorstoßen *unreg vt, vi* to push forward

Vorstrafe ['foːrʃtraːfə] *f* previous conviction

vorstrecken ['foːrʃtrɛkən] *vt* to stretch out; (*Geld*) to advance

Vorstufe ['foːrʃtuːfə] *f* first step(s *pl*)

Vortag ['foːrtak] *m*: **am ~ einer Sache** *gen* on the day before sth

Vortal ['foːrtaːl] *nt* (*Comput*) vortal

vortasten ['foːrtastən] *vr*: **sich langsam zu etw ~** to approach sth carefully

vortäuschen ['foːrtɔyʃən] *vt* to pretend, feign

Vortäuschung *f*: **unter ~ falscher Tatsachen** under false pretences (*Brit*) *od* pretenses (*US*)

Vorteil ['foːrtaɪl] (**-s, -e**) *m*: **~ (gegenüber)** advantage (over); **im ~ sein** to have the advantage; **die Vor- und Nachteile** the pros and cons; **vorteilhaft** *adj* advantageous; (*Kleider*) flattering; (*Geschäft*) lucrative

Vortr. *abk* = **Vortrag**

Vortrag ['foːrtraːk] (**-(e)s, Vorträge**) *m* talk, lecture; (*Vortragsart*) delivery; (*von Gedicht*) rendering; (*Comm*) balance carried forward; **einen ~ halten** to give a lecture *od* talk

vortragen ['foːrtraːgən] *unreg vt* to carry forward (*auch COMM*); (*fig*) to recite; (*Rede*) to deliver; (*Lied*) to perform; (*Meinung etc*) to express

Vortragsabend *m* lecture evening; (*mit Musik*) recital; (*mit Gedichten*) poetry reading

Vortragsreihe *f* series of lectures

vortrefflich [foːrˈtrɛflɪç] *adj* excellent

vortreten ['foːrtreːtən] *unreg vi* to step forward; (*Augen etc*) to protrude

Vortritt ['foːrtrɪt] *m*: **jdm den ~ lassen** (*lit, fig*) to let sb go first

vorüber [foˈryːbər] *adv* past, over; **vorübergehen** *unreg vi* to pass (by); **vorübergehen an** +*dat* (*fig*) to pass over; **vorübergehend** *adj* temporary, passing

Voruntersuchung ['foːrʊntərzuːxʊŋ] *f* (*Med*) preliminary examination; (*Jur*) preliminary investigation

Vorurteil ['foːrʊrtaɪl] *nt* prejudice

vorurteilsfrei *adj* unprejudiced, open-minded

Vorverkauf ['foːrfɛrkauf] *m* advance booking

Vorverkaufsstelle *f* advance booking office

vorverlegen ['foːrfɛrleːgən] *vt* (*Termin*) to bring forward

Vorw. *abk* = **Vorwort**

vorwagen ['foːrvaːgən] *vr* to venture forward

Vorwahl ['foːrvaːl] *f* preliminary election; (*Tel*) dialling (*Brit*) *od* area (*US*) code

Vorwand ['foːrvant] (**-(e)s, Vorwände**) *m* pretext

Vorwarnung ['foːrvarnʊŋ] *f* (advance) warning

vorwärts ['foːrvɛrts] *adv* forward; **~!** (*umg*) let's go!; (*Mil*) forward march!; *siehe auch* **vorwärtsgehen; vorwärtskommen;**

Vorwärtsgang *m* (*Aut etc*) forward gear;

vorwärtsgehen *unreg vi* to progress;

vorwärtskommen *unreg vi* to get on, make progress

Vorwäsche *f* prewash

Vorwaschgang *m* prewash

vorweg [foːrˈvɛk] *adv* in advance;

Vorwegnahme (**-, -n**) *f* anticipation;

vorwegnehmen *unreg vt* to anticipate

vorweisen ['foːrvaɪzən] *unreg vt* to show, produce

vorwerfen ['foːrvɛrfən] *unreg vt*: **jdm etw ~** to reproach sb for sth, accuse sb of sth; **sich** *dat* **nichts vorzuwerfen haben** to have nothing to reproach o.s. with; **das wirft er mir heute noch vor** he still holds it against me; **Tieren/ Gefangenen etw ~** (*lit*) to throw sth down for the animals/prisoners

vorwiegend ['foːrviːgənt] *adj* predominant ▷ *adv* predominantly

vorwitzig *adj* saucy, cheeky

Vorwort ['foːrvɔrt] (**-(e)s, -e**) *nt* preface

Vorwurf ['foːrvʊrf] (**-(e)s, ˝-e**) *m* reproach; **jdm/ sich Vorwürfe machen** to reproach sb/o.s.

vorwurfsvoll *adj* reproachful

Vorzeichen ['foːrtsaɪçən] *nt* (*Omen*) omen; (*Med*) early symptom; (*Math*) sign

vorzeigen ['foːrtsaɪgən] *vt* to show, produce

Vorzeit ['foːrtsaɪt] *f* prehistoric times *pl*

vorzeitig *adj* premature

vorziehen ['foːrtsiːən] *unreg vt* to pull forward; (*Gardinen*) to draw; (*zuerst behandeln, abfertigen*) to give priority to; (*lieber haben*) to prefer

Vorzimmer ['foːrtsɪmər] *nt* anteroom; (*Büro*) outer office

Vorzug ['foːrtsuːk] *m* preference; (*gute Eigenschaft*) merit, good quality; (*Vorteil*) advantage; (*Eisenb*) relief train; **einer Sache** *dat* **den ~ geben** (*form*) to prefer sth; (*Vorrang geben*) to give sth precedence

vorzüglich [foːrˈtsyːklɪç] *adj* excellent, first-rate

Vorzugsaktien *pl* preference shares (*Brit*), preferred stock (*US*)

vorzugsweise *adv* preferably; (*hauptsächlich*) chiefly

Votum ['voːtʊm] (**-s, Voten**) *nt* vote

Voyeur [voaˈjøːr] (**-s, -e**) *m* voyeur; **Voyeurismus** [voajøˈrɪsmʊs] *m* voyeurism

v. T. *abk* (= *vom Tausend*) per thousand

vulgär [vʊlˈgɛːr] *adj* vulgar

Vulkan [vʊlˈkaːn] (**-s, -e**) *m* volcano; **Vulkanausbruch** *m* volcanic eruption

vulkanisieren [vʊlkaniˈziːrən] *vt* to vulcanize

v. u. Z. *abk* (= *vor unserer Zeitrechnung*) B.C.

Ww

W, w [ve:] *nt* W, w; **W wie Wilhelm** ≈ W for
William

W. *abk* (= *West(en)*) W

w. *abk* = **wenden; werktags; westlich;**
(= *weiblich*) f

Waage ['va:gə] (**-, -n**) *f* scales *pl*; (*Astrol*) Libra;
sich *dat* **die ~ halten** (*fig*) to balance one
another; **waagerecht** *adj* horizontal

Waagschale *f* (scale) pan; (**schwer**) **in die ~
fallen** (*fig*) to carry weight

wabbelig ['vabəlıç], **wabblig** ['vablıç] *adj*
wobbly

Wabe ['va:bə] (**-, -n**) *f* honeycomb

wach [vax] *adj* awake; (*fig*) alert; **~ werden** to
wake up

Wachablösung *f* changing of the guard;
(*Mensch*) relief guard; (*fig: Regierungswechsel*)
change of government

Wache (**-, -n**) *f* guard, watch; **~ halten** to keep
watch; **~ stehen** *od* **schieben** (*umg*) to be on
guard (duty)

wachen *vi* to be awake; (*Wache halten*) to keep
watch; **bei jdm ~** to sit up with sb

wachhabend *adj attrib* duty

Wachhund *m* watchdog, guard dog; (*fig*)
watchdog

Wacholder [va'xɔldər] (**-s, -**) *m* juniper

wachrütteln ['vaxrytəln] *vt* (*fig*) to (a)rouse

Wachs [vaks] (**-es, -e**) *nt* wax

wachsam ['vaxza:m] *adj* watchful, vigilant,
alert; **Wachsamkeit** *f* vigilance

wachsen¹ *unreg vi* to grow

wachsen² *vt* (*Skier*) to wax

Wachsfigurenkabinett *nt* waxworks
(exhibition)

Wachsmalstift, Wachsstift *m* wax crayon

wächst [vɛkst] *vb siehe* **wachsen¹**

Wachtuch ['vakstu:x] *nt* oilcloth

Wachstum ['vakstu:m] (**-s**) *nt* growth

Wachstums- *zW*: **Wachstumsbranche** *f*
growth industry; **Wachstumsgrenze** *f* limits
of growth; **wachstumshemmend** *adj* growth-
inhibiting; **Wachstumsrate** *f* growth rate;
Wachstumsschmerzen *pl* growing pains;
Wachstumsstörung *f* disturbance of growth

Wachtel ['vaxtəl] (**-, -n**) *f* quail

Wächter ['vɛçtər] (**-s, -**) *m* guard; (*Parkwächter*)
warden, keeper; (*Museumswächter,*
Parkplatzwächter) attendant

Wachtmeister *m* officer

Wachtposten *m* guard, sentry

Wachtturm, Wachturm *m* watchtower

Wach- und Schließgesellschaft *f* security
corps

wackelig *adj* shaky, wobbly; **auf ~en Beinen
stehen** to be wobbly on one's legs; (*fig*) to be
unsteady

Wackelkontakt *m* loose connection

wackeln *vi* to shake; (*fig: Position*) to be shaky;
mit den Hüften/dem Schwanz ~ to wiggle
one's hips/wag its tail

wacker ['vakər] *adj* valiant, stout; **sich ~
schlagen** (*umg*) to put up a brave fight

wacklig *adj* = **wackelig**

Wade ['va:də] (**-, -n**) *f* (*Anat*) calf

Waffe ['vafə] (**-, -n**) *f* weapon; **jdn mit seinen
eigenen ~n schlagen** (*fig*) to beat sb at his
own game

Waffel ['vafəl] (**-, -n**) *f* waffle; (*Eiswaffel*) wafer

Waffen- *zW*: **Waffengewalt** *f*: **mit
Waffengewalt** by force of arms; **Waffenlager**
nt (*von Armee*) ordnance depot; (*von Terroristen*)
cache; **Waffenschein** *m* firearms *od*
gun licence (*Brit*), firearms license (*US*);
Waffenschmuggel *m* gunrunning, arms
smuggling; **Waffenstillstand** *m* armistice,
truce

Wagemut ['va:gəmu:t] *m* daring

Wagen ['va:gən] (**-s, -**) *m* vehicle; (*Auto*) car,
automobile (*US*); (*Eisenb*) car, carriage (*Brit*);
(*Pferdewagen*) wag(g)on, cart

wagen *vt* to venture, dare

Wagen- *zW*: **Wagenführer** *m* driver;
Wagenheber (**-s, -**) *m* jack; **Wagenpark**
m fleet of cars; **Wagenrückholtaste** *f*
(*Schreibmaschine*) carriage return (key);
Wagenrücklauf *m* carriage return

Waggon [va'gõ:] (**-s, -s**) *m* wag(g)on;
(*Güterwaggon*) goods van (*Brit*), freight truck
(*US*)

waghalsig ['va:khalzıç] *adj* foolhardy

Wagnis ['va:knıs] (**-ses, -se**) *nt* risk

Wagon (**-s, -s**) *m* = **Waggon**

Wahl [va:l] (**-, -en**) *f* choice; (*Pol*) election; **erste
~** (*Qualität*) top quality; (*Gemüse, Eier*) grade one;
zweite ~ (*Comm*) seconds *pl*; **aus freier ~** of

one's own free choice; **wer die ~ hat, hat die Qual** (*Sprichwort*) he is *od* you are *etc* spoilt for choice; **die ~ fiel auf ihn** he was chosen; **sich zur ~ stellen** (*Pol etc*) to stand (*Brit*) *od* run (for parliament *etc*)

wählbar *adj* eligible

Wahl- *zW*: **wahlberechtigt** *adj* entitled to vote; **Wahlbeteiligung** *f* poll, turnout; **Wahlbezirk** *m* (*Pol*) ward

wählen ['vɛːlən] *vt* to choose; (*Pol*) to elect, vote for; (*Tel*) to dial ▷ *vi* to choose; (*Pol*) to vote; (*Tel*) to dial

Wähler, in (**-s, -**) *m(f)* voter; **Wählerabwanderung** *f* voter drift; **wählerisch** *adj* fastidious, particular; **Wählerschaft** *f* electorate

Wahl- *zW*: **Wahlfach** *nt* optional subject; **wahlfrei** *adj*: **wahlfreier Zugriff** (*Comput*) random access; **Wahlgang** *m* ballot; **Wahlgeschenk** *nt* pre-election vote-catching gimmick; **Wahlheimat** *f* country of adoption; **Wahlhelfer** *m* (*im Wahlkampf*) election assistant; (*bei der Wahl*) polling officer; **Wahlkabine** *f* polling booth; **Wahlkampf** *m* election campaign; **Wahlkreis** *m* constituency; **Wahlleiter** *m* returning officer; **Wahlliste** *f* electoral register; **Wahllokal** *nt* polling station; **wahllos** *adv* at random; (*nicht wählerisch*) indiscriminately; **Wahlrecht** *nt* franchise; **allgemeines Wahlrecht** universal franchise; **das aktive Wahlrecht** the right to vote; **das passive Wahlrecht** eligibility (for political office); **Wahlspruch** *m* motto; **Wahlurne** *f* ballot box; **wahlweise** *adv* alternatively

Wählzeichen *nt* (*Tel*) dialling tone (*Brit*), dial tone (*US*)

Wahn [vaːn] (**-(e)s**) *m* delusion; **Wahnsinn** *m* madness; **wahnsinnig** *adj* insane, mad ▷ *adv* (*umg*) incredibly; **wahnwitzig** *adj* crazy *attrib* ▷ *adv* terribly

wahr [vaːr] *adj* true; **da ist (et)was W~es dran** there's some truth in that

wahren *vt* to maintain, keep

währen ['vɛːrən] *vi* to last

während *präp +gen* during ▷ *konj* while; **währenddessen** *adv* meanwhile

wahr- *zW*: **wahrhaben** *unreg vt*: **etw nicht wahrhaben wollen** to refuse to admit sth; **wahrhaft** *adv* (*tatsächlich*) truly; **wahrhaftig** *adj* true, real ▷ *adv* really

Wahrheit *f* truth; **die ~ sagen** to tell the truth

wahrheitsgetreu *adj* (*Bericht*) truthful; (*Darstellung*) faithful

wahrnehmen *unreg vt* to perceive; (*Frist*) to observe; (*Veränderungen etc*) to be aware of; (*Gelegenheit*) to take; (*Interessen, Rechte*) to look after

Wahrnehmung *f* perception; observing; awareness; taking; looking after

wahrsagen *vi* to predict the future, tell fortunes

Wahrsager *m* fortune-teller

wahrscheinlich [vaːr'ʃaɪnlɪç] *adj* probable ▷ *adv* probably; **Wahrscheinlichkeit** *f* probability; **aller Wahrscheinlichkeit nach** in all probability

Währung ['vɛːrʊŋ] *f* currency

Währungs- *zW*: **Währungseinheit** *f* monetary unit; **Währungspolitik** *f* monetary policy; **Währungsraum** *m* currency area; **Währungsreserven** *pl* official reserves *pl*; **Währungsunion** *f* monetary union

Wahrzeichen *nt* (*Gebäude, Turm etc*) symbol; (*von Stadt, Verein*) emblem

Waise ['vaɪzə] (**-, -n**) *f* orphan

Waisen- *zW*: **Waisenhaus** *nt* orphanage; **Waisenkind** *nt* orphan; **Waisenknabe** *m*: **gegen dich ist er ein Waisenknabe** (*umg*) he's no match for you; **Waisenrente** *f* orphan's allowance

Wal [vaːl] (**-(e)s, -e**) *m* whale

Wald [valt] (**-(e)s, ̈-er**) *m* wood(s *pl*); (*groß*) forest; **Waldbrand** *m* forest fire

Wäldchen ['vɛltçən] *nt* copse, grove

Waldhorn *nt* (*Mus*) French horn

waldig ['valdɪç] *adj* wooded

Wald- *zW*: **Waldlehrpfad** *m* nature trail; **Waldmeister** *m* (*Bot*) woodruff; **Waldsterben** *nt* loss of trees due to pollution

Wald- und Wiesen- (*umg*) *in zw* common-or-garden

Waldweg *m* woodland *od* forest path

Wales [weɪlz] *nt* Wales

Walfang ['vaːlfaŋ] *m* whaling

Walfisch ['valfɪʃ] *m* whale

Waliser, in [va'liːzər(ɪn)] (**-s, -**) *m(f)* Welshman, Welshwoman

walisisch *adj* Welsh

Walkman® ['wɔːkman] (**-s**) *m* Walkman®, personal stereo

Wall [val] (**-(e)s, ̈-e**) *m* embankment; (*Bollwerk*) rampart

wallfahren *vi untr* to go on a pilgrimage

Wallfahrer, in *m(f)* pilgrim

Wallfahrt *f* pilgrimage

Wallis ['valɪs] (**-**) *nt*: **das ~** Valais

Wallone [va'loːnə] (**-n, -n**) *m*, **Wallonin** *f* Walloon

Walnuss ['valnʊs] *f* walnut

Walross ['valrɔs] *nt* walrus

walten ['valtən] *vi* (*geh*): **Vernunft ~ lassen** to let reason prevail

Walzblech (**-(e)s**) *nt* sheet metal

Walze ['valtsə] (**-, -n**) *f* (*Gerät*) cylinder; (*Fahrzeug*) roller

walzen *vt* to roll (out)

wälzen ['vɛltsən] *vt* to roll (over); (*Bücher*) to hunt through; (*Probleme*) to deliberate on ▷ *vr* to wallow; (*vor Schmerzen*) to roll about; (*im Bett*) to toss and turn

Walzer ['valtsər] (**-s, -**) *m* waltz

Wälzer ['vɛltsər] (**-s, -**) (*umg*) *m* tome

Wampe ['vampə] (**-, -n**) (*umg*) *f* paunch

Wand (**-, ̈-e**) *f* wall; (*Trennwand*) partition; (*Bergwand*) precipice; (*Felswand*) (rock) face; (*fig*)

barrier; **weiß wie die** ~ as white as a sheet; **jdn an die** ~ **spielen** to put sb in the shade; (Sport) to outplay sb

wand etc [vant] vb siehe **winden**

Wandel ['vandəl] (**-s**) m change; **wandelbar** adj changeable, variable

Wandelhalle f foyer

wandeln vt, vr to change ▷ vi (gehen) to walk

Wanderausstellung f touring exhibition

Wanderbühne f touring theatre (Brit) od theater (US)

Wanderer (**-s, -**) m hiker, rambler

Wanderin f hiker, rambler

Wanderkarte f hiker's map

Wanderlied nt hiking song

wandern vi to hike; (Blick) to wander; (Gedanken) to stray; (umg: in den Papierkorb etc) to land

Wanderpreis m challenge trophy

Wanderschaft f travelling (Brit), traveling (US)

Wanderung f walk, hike; (von Tieren, Völkern) migration

Wanderweg m trail, (foot)path

Wandgemälde nt mural

Wandlung f change; (völlige Umwandlung) transformation; (Rel) transubstantiation

Wand- zW: **Wandmalerei** f mural painting; **Wandschirm** m (folding) screen; **Wandschrank** m cupboard

wandte etc ['vantə] vb siehe **wenden**

Wandteppich m tapestry

Wandverkleidung f panelling

Wange ['vaŋə] (**-, -n**) f cheek

wankelmütig ['vaŋkəlmy:tıç] adj fickle, inconstant

wanken ['vaŋkən] vi to stagger; (fig) to waver

wann [van] adv when; **seit** ~ **bist/hast du ...?** how long have you been/have you had ...?

Wanne ['vanə] (**-, -n**) f tub

Wanze ['vantsə] (**-, -n**) f (Abhörgerät, Zool) bug

WAP nt abk (Comput: = Wireless Application Protocol) WAP

WAP-Handy nt WAP phone

Wappen ['vapən] (**-s, -**) nt coat of arms, crest; **Wappenkunde** f heraldry

wappnen vr (fig) to prepare o.s.; **gewappnet sein** to be forearmed

war etc [va:r] vb siehe **sein**

warb etc [varp] vb siehe **werben**

Ware ['va:rə] (**-, -n**) f ware; **Waren** pl goods pl

wäre etc ['vɛ:rə] vb siehe **sein**

Waren- zW: **Warenbestand** m stock; **Warenhaus** nt department store; **Warenlager** nt stock, store; **Warenmuster** nt sample; **Warenprobe** f sample; **Warenrückstände** pl backlog sing; **Warensendung** f trade sample (sent by post); **Warenzeichen** nt trademark

warf etc [varf] vb siehe **werfen**

warm [varm] adj warm; (Essen) hot; (umg: homosexuell) queer; **mir ist** ~ I'm warm; **mit jdm** ~ **werden** (umg) to get close to sb; ~ **laufen** (Aut) to warm up; siehe auch **warmhalten**

Wärme ['vɛrmə] (**-, -n**) f warmth; **10 Grad** ~ 10 degrees above zero

wärmen vt, vr to warm (up), heat (up)

Wärmflasche f hot-water bottle

warm- zW: **Warmfront** f (Met) warm front; **warmhalten** unreg vt: **sich** dat **jdn warmhalten** (fig) to keep in with sb; **warmherzig** adj warm-hearted; **Warmwassertank** m hot-water tank

Warnblinkanlage f (Aut) hazard warning lights pl

Warndreieck nt warning triangle

warnen ['varnən] vt to warn

Warnstreik m token strike

Warnung f warning

Warschau ['varʃau] (**-s**) nt Warsaw; **Warschauer Pakt** m Warsaw Pact

Warte (**-, -n**) f observation point; (fig) viewpoint

warten ['vartən] vi to wait ▷ vt (Auto, Maschine) to service; ~ **auf** +akk to wait for; **auf sich** ~ **lassen** to take a long time; **warte mal!** wait a minute!; (überlegend) let me see; **mit dem Essen auf jdn** ~ to wait for sb before eating

Wärter, in ['vɛrtər(ın)] (**-s, -**) m(f) attendant

Wartesaal m (Eisenb) waiting room

Wartezimmer nt waiting room

Wartung f (von Auto, Maschine) servicing; ~ **und Instandhaltung** maintenance

warum [va'rʊm] adv why; ~ **nicht gleich so!** that's better

Warze ['vartsə] (**-, -n**) f wart

was [vas] pron what; (umg: etwas) something; **das,** ~ **...** that which ...; ~ **für ...?** what sort od kind of ...?

Wasch- zW: **Waschanlage** f (für Autos) car wash; **waschbar** adj washable; **Waschbecken** nt washbasin

Wäsche ['vɛʃə] (**-, -n**) f wash(ing); (Bettwäsche) linen; (Unterwäsche) underwear; **dumm aus der** ~ **gucken** (umg) to look stupid

waschecht adj (Farbe) fast; (fig) genuine

Wäsche- zW: **Wäscheklammer** f clothes peg (Brit), clothespin (US); **Wäschekorb** m dirty clothes basket; **Wäscheleine** f washing line (Brit), clothes line (US)

waschen ['vaʃən] unreg vt, vi to wash ▷ vr to (have a) wash; **sich** dat **die Hände** ~ to wash one's hands; ~ **und legen** (Haare) to shampoo and set

Wäscherei [vɛʃə'raı] f laundry

Wäscheschleuder f spin-dryer

Wasch- zW: **Waschgang** m stage of the washing programme (Brit) od program (US); **Waschküche** f laundry room; **Waschlappen** m face cloth od flannel (Brit), washcloth (US); (umg) softy; **Waschmaschine** f washing machine; **Waschmittel** nt detergent; **Waschpulver** nt washing powder; **Waschsalon** m Launderette® (Brit), Laundromat® (US)

wäscht [vɛʃt] vb siehe **waschen**

Waschtisch m washstand

381

Washington ['wɔʃɪŋtən] (-s) nt Washington
Wasser¹ ['vasər] (-s, -) nt water; ~ **abstoßend**
water-repellent; **dort wird auch nur mit
~ gekocht** (fig) they're no different from
anybody else (there); **ins ~ fallen** (fig) to fall
through; **mit allen ~n gewaschen sein** (umg)
to be a shrewd customer; ~ **lassen** (euph) to
pass water; **jdm das ~ abgraben** (fig) to take
the bread from sb's mouth
Wasser² (-s, ⁻) nt (Flüssigkeit) water; (Med)
lotion; (Parfüm) cologne; (Mineralwasser)
mineral water
Wässerchen nt: **er sieht aus, als ob er kein ~
trüben könnte** he looks as if butter wouldn't
melt in his mouth
Wasser- zW: **wasserdicht** adj watertight;
(Stoff, Uhr) waterproof; **Wasserfall** m waterfall;
Wasserfarbe f watercolour (Brit), watercolor
(US); **wassergekühlt** adj (Aut) water-cooled;
Wassergraben m (Sport) water jump; (um Burg)
moat; **Wasserhahn** m tap, faucet (US)
wässerig ['vɛsərɪç] adj watery
Wasser- zW: **Wasserkessel** m kettle; (Tech)
boiler; **Wasserkraftwerk** nt hydroelectric
power station; **Wasserleitung** f water pipe;
(Anlagen) plumbing; **Wassermann** m (Astrol)
Aquarius
wassern vi to land on the water
wässern ['vɛsərn] vt, vi to water
Wasser- zW: **Wasserscheide** f watershed;
wasserscheu adj afraid of water;
Wasserschutzpolizei f (auf Flüssen) river
police; (im Hafen) harbour (Brit) od harbor
(US) police; (auf der See) coastguard service;
Wasserski nt water-skiing; **Wasserspiegel** m
(Oberfläche) surface of the water; (Wasserstand)
water level; **Wasserstand** m water level;
Wasserstoff m hydrogen; **Wasserstoffbombe**
f hydrogen bomb; **Wasserverbrauch** m water
consumption; **Wasserwaage** f spirit level;
Wasserwelle f shampoo and set; **Wasserwerfer**
(-s, -) m water cannon; **Wasserwerk** nt
waterworks; **Wasserzeichen** nt watermark
waten ['va:tən] vi to wade
watscheln ['va:tʃəln] vi to waddle
Watt¹ [vat] (-(e)s, -en) nt mud flats pl
Watt² (-s, -) nt (Elek) watt
Watte (-, -n) f cotton wool (Brit), absorbent
cotton (US)
Wattenmeer (-(e)s) nt mud flats pl
Wattestäbchen nt cotton(-wool) swab
wattieren [va'ti:rən] vt to pad
WC [ve:'tse:] (-s, -s) nt abk (= Wasserklosett) WC
Web [wɛb] nt (Comput): **das ~** the Web; **im ~** on
the Web
Webadresse f (= URL, Internet-Adresse) web
address
weben ['ve:bən] unreg vt to weave
Weber, in (-s, -) m(f) weaver
Weberei [ve:bə'raɪ] f (Betrieb) weaving mill
Webpage ['wɛbpa:gə] nt web page
Webseite ['wɛbzaɪtə] f Web page, web site
Webstuhl ['ve:pʃtu:l] m loom

Wechsel ['vɛksəl] (-s, -) m change;
(Geldwechsel) exchange; (Comm) bill of
exchange; **Wechselbäder** pl alternating
hot and cold baths pl; **Wechselbeziehung**
f correlation; **Wechselforderungen** pl
(Comm) bills receivable pl; **Wechselgeld**
nt change; **wechselhaft** adj (Wetter)
variable; **Wechselinhaber** m bearer;
Wechseljahre pl change of life, menopause;
in die Wechseljahre kommen to start the
change; **Wechselkurs** m rate of exchange;
Wechselkursmechanismus m Exchange Rate
Mechanism, ERM
wechseln vt to change; (Blicke) to exchange ▷ vi
to change; (einander ablösen) to alternate
wechselnd adj changing; (Stimmungen)
changeable; (Winde, Bewölkung) variable
Wechsel- zW: **wechselseitig** adj reciprocal;
Wechselsprechanlage f two-way intercom;
Wechselstrom m alternating current;
Wechselstube f currency exchange, bureau
de change; **Wechselverbindlichkeiten** pl bills
payable pl; **wechselweise** adv alternately;
Wechselwirkung f interaction
wecken ['vɛkən] vt to wake (up); (fig) to arouse;
(Bedarf) to create; (Erinnerungen) to revive
Wecker (-s, -) m alarm clock; **jdm auf den ~
fallen** (umg) to get on sb's nerves
Weckglas® nt preserving jar
Weckruf m (Tel) alarm call
wedeln ['ve:dəln] vi (mit Schwanz) to wag; (mit
Fächer) to fan; (Ski) to wedel
weder ['ve:dər] konj neither; ~ ... **noch** ...
neither ... nor ...
Weg [ve:k] (-(e)s, -e) m way; (Pfad) path; (Route)
route; **sich auf den ~ machen** to be on one's
way; **jdm aus dem ~ gehen** to keep out of
sb's way; **jdm nicht über den ~ trauen** (fig)
not to trust sb an inch; **den ~ des geringsten
Widerstandes gehen** to follow the line of
least resistance; **etw in die ~e leiten** to
arrange sth; **jdm Steine in den ~ legen** (fig)
to put obstacles in sb's way; siehe auch **zuwege**
weg [vɛk] adv away, off; **über etw** akk **~ sein**
to be over sth; **er war schon ~** he had already
left; **nichts wie** od **nur ~ von hier!** let's get
out of here!; ~ **damit!** (mit Schere etc) put it/
them away!; **Finger ~!** hands off!
Wegbereiter (-s, -) m pioneer
wegblasen unreg vt to blow away; **wie
weggeblasen sein** (fig) to have vanished
wegbleiben unreg vi to stay away; **mir bleibt
die Spucke weg!** (umg) I am absolutely
flabbergasted!
wegen ['ve:gən] (umg) präp +gen od +dat because
of; **von ~!** you must be joking!
weg- zW: **wegfahren** unreg vi to drive
away; (abfahren) to leave; **Wegfahrsperre**
f (Aut): **(elektronische) Wegfahrsperre**
(electronic) immobilizer; **wegfallen** unreg vi to
be left out; (Ferien, Bezahlung) to be cancelled;
(aufhören) to cease; **weggehen** unreg vi to go
away, leave; (umg: Ware) to sell; **weghören** vi

to turn a deaf ear; **wegjagen** *vt* to chase away; **wegkommen** *unreg vi*: **(bei etw) gut/schlecht wegkommen** (*umg*) to come off well/badly (with sth); **weglassen** *unreg vt* to leave out; **weglaufen** *unreg vi* to run away *od* off; **das läuft (dir) nicht weg!** (*fig hum*) that can wait; **weglegen** *vt* to put aside; **wegmachen** (*umg*) *vt* to get rid of; **wegmüssen** *unreg* (*umg*) *vi* to have to go; **wegnehmen** *unreg vt* to take away

Wegrand ['veːkrant] *m* wayside

weg- *zW*: **wegräumen** *vt* to clear away; **wegschaffen** *vt* to clear away; **wegschließen** *unreg vt* to lock away; **wegschnappen** *vt*: **(jdm) etw wegschnappen** to snatch sth away (from sb); **wegstecken** *vt* to put away; (*umg: verkraften*) to cope with; **wegtreten** *unreg vi* (*Mil*): **wegtreten!** dismiss!; **geistig weggetreten sein** (*umg: geistesabwesend*) to be away with the fairies; **wegtun** *unreg vt* to put away

wegweisend ['veːɡvaɪzənt] *adj* pioneering *attrib*, revolutionary

Wegweiser ['veːɡvaɪzər] **(-s, -)** *m* road sign, signpost; (*fig: Buch etc*) guide

Wegwerf- ['vɛkvɛrf] *in zw* disposable

weg- *zW*: **wegwerfen** *unreg vt* to throw away; **wegwerfend** *adj* disparaging; **Wegwerfgesellschaft** *f* throw-away society; **wegwollen** *unreg vi* (*verreisen*) to want to go away; **wegziehen** *unreg vi* to move away

weh [veː] *adj* sore

Wehe ['veːə] **(-, -n)** *f* drift

wehe *interj*: **~, wenn du …** you'll regret it if you …; **~ dir!** you dare!

Wehen *pl* (*Med*) contractions *pl*; **in den ~ liegen** to be in labour (*Brit*) *od* labor (*US*)

wehen *vt, vi* to blow; (*Fahnen*) to flutter

weh- *zW*: **wehklagen** *vi untr* to wail; **wehleidig** *adj* oversensitive to pain; (*jammernd*) whiny, whining; **Wehmut** *f* melancholy; **wehmütig** *adj* melancholy

Wehr¹ [veːr] **(-(e)s, -e)** *nt* weir

Wehr² [veːr] **(-, -en)** *f* (*Feuerwehr*) fire brigade (*Brit*) *od* department (*US*) ▷ *in zw* defence (*Brit*), defense (*US*); **sich zur ~ setzen** to defend o.s.

Wehrdienst *m* military service; *see culture note*

Wehrdienstverweigerer *m* ≈ conscientious objector

wehren *vr* to defend o.s.

Wehr- *zW*: **wehrlos** *adj* defenceless (*Brit*), defenseless (*US*); **jdm wehrlos ausgeliefert sein** to be at sb's mercy; **Wehrmacht** *f* armed forces *pl*; **Wehrpflicht** *f* conscription; **wehrpflichtig** *adj* liable for military service; **Wehrübung** *f* reserve duty training exercise

wehtun ['veːtuːn] *unreg vt*: **jdm/sich ~** to hurt sb/o.s.

Wehwehchen (*umg*) *nt* (minor) complaint

Weib [vaɪp] **(-(e)s, -er)** *nt* woman, female (*pej*)

Weibchen *nt* (*Ehefrau*) little woman; (*Zool*) female

weibisch ['vaɪbɪʃ] *adj* effeminate

weiblich *adj* feminine

weich [vaɪç] *adj* soft; (*Ei*) soft-boiled; **~e Währung** soft currency

Weiche **(-, -n)** *f* (*Eisenb*) points *pl*; **die ~n stellen** (*lit*) to switch the points; (*fig*) to set the course

weichen *unreg vi* to yield, give way; **(nicht) von jdm** *od* **von jds Seite ~** (not) to leave sb's side

Weichensteller **(-s, -)** *m* pointsman

weich- *zW*: **Weichheit** *f* softness; **Weichkäse** *m* soft cheese; **weichlich** *adj* soft, namby-pamby; **Weichling** *m* wimp; **Weichspüler** **(-s, -)** *m* fabric conditioner; **Weichteile** *pl* soft parts *pl*; **Weichtier** *nt* mollusc (*Brit*), mollusk (*US*)

Weide ['vaɪdə] **(-, -n)** *f* (*Baum*) willow; (*Gras*) pasture

weiden *vi* to graze ▷ *vr*: **sich an etw** *dat* **~ to** delight in sth

Weidenkätzchen *nt* willow catkin

weidlich ['vaɪtlɪç] *adv* thoroughly

weigern ['vaɪgərn] *vr* to refuse

Weigerung ['vaɪgərʊŋ] *f* refusal

Weihe ['vaɪə] **(-, -n)** *f* consecration; (*Priesterweihe*) ordination

weihen *vt* to consecrate; (*widmen*) to dedicate; **dem Untergang geweiht** (*liter*) doomed

Weiher **(-s, -)** *m* pond

Weihnachten **(-)** *nt* Christmas; **fröhliche ~!** happy *od* merry Christmas!; **weihnachten** *vi unpers*: **es weihnachtet sehr** (*poetisch, ironisch*) Christmas is very much in evidence

weihnachtlich *adj* Christmas(sy)

Weihnachts- *zW*: **Weihnachtsabend** *m* Christmas Eve; **Weihnachtsbaum** *m* Christmas tree; **Weihnachtsgeld** *nt* Christmas bonus; **Weihnachtsgeschenk** *nt* Christmas present; **Weihnachtslied** *nt* Christmas carol; **Weihnachtsmann** *m* Father Christmas (*Brit*), Santa Claus

Weihnachtsmarkt *m* Christmas fair; *see culture note*

W

there, for example, gingerbread and
mulled wine.

Weihnachtstag m: **(erster)** ~ Christmas day;
zweiter ~ Boxing Day (Brit)

Weihwasser nt holy water

weil [vaɪl] konj because

Weile ['vaɪlə] (-) f while, short time

Weiler ['vaɪlər] **(-s, -)** m hamlet

Weimarer Republik ['vaɪmarər repu'bli:k] f
Weimar Republic

Wein [vaɪn] **(-(e)s, -e)** m wine; (Pflanze) vine;
jdm reinen ~ einschenken (fig) to tell sb
the truth; **Weinbau** m cultivation of vines;
Weinbauer m wine-grower; **Weinbeere** f grape;
Weinberg m vineyard; **Weinbergschnecke** f
snail; **Weinbrand** m brandy

weinen vt, vi to cry; **das ist zum W~** it's
enough to make you cry od weep

weinerlich adj tearful

Wein- zW: **Weingegend** f wine-growing area;
Weingeist m (ethyl) alcohol; **Weinglas** nt
wine glass; **Weingut** nt wine-growing estate;
Weinkarte f wine list

Weinkrampf m crying fit

Wein- zW: **Weinlese** f vintage; **Weinprobe** f
wine tasting; **Weinrebe** f vine; **weinrot** adj
(Farbe) claret; **Weinstein** m tartar; **Weinstock**
m vine; **Weinstube** f wine bar; **Weintraube**
f grape

weise ['vaɪzə] adj wise

Weise (-, -n) f manner, way; (Lied) tune; **auf
diese ~** in this way

Weise, r f(m) wise man, wise woman, sage

weisen unreg vt to show; **etw (weit) von sich ~**
(fig) to reject sth (emphatically)

Weisheit ['vaɪshaɪt] f wisdom

Weisheitszahn m wisdom tooth

weismachen ['vaɪsmaxən] vt: **er wollte uns
~, dass ...** he would have us believe that ...

weiß¹ [vaɪs] vb siehe **wissen**

weiß² adj white; **Weißblech** nt tin plate;
Weißbrot nt white bread; **weißen** vt to
whitewash; **Weißglut** f (Tech) incandescence;
jdn zur Weißglut bringen (fig) to make sb
see red; **Weißkohl** m (white) cabbage

Weißrussland nt B(y)elorussia

weißt [vaɪst] vb siehe **wissen**

Weißwandtafel f whiteboard; **interaktive ~**
interactive whiteboard

Weiß- zW: **Weißwaren** pl linen sing; **Weißwein**
m white wine; **Weißwurst** f veal sausage

Weisung ['vaɪzʊŋ] f instruction

weit [vaɪt] adj wide; (Begriff) broad; (Reise,
Wurf) long ▷ adv far; **~ blickend** far-seeing;
~ hergeholt far-fetched; **~ reichend** (fig)
far-reaching; **~ verbreitet** widespread; **~
verzweigt = weitverzweigt; in ~er Ferne**
in the far distance; **wie ~ ist es ...?** how far
is it ...?; **das geht zu ~** that's going too far;
~ und breit for miles around; **~ gefehlt!** far
from it!; **es so ~ bringen, dass ...** to bring
it about that ...; **~ zurückliegen** to be far

behind; **von W~em** from a long way off;
weitab adv: **weitab von** far (away) from;
weitaus adv by far; **Weitblick** m (fig) far-
sightedness; **weitblickend** adj far-seeing

Weite (-, -n) f width; (Raum) space; (von
Entfernung) distance

weiten vt, vr to widen

weiter ['vaɪtər] adj wider; (zusätzlich) further
▷ adv further; **wenn es ~ nichts ist, ...** well,
if that's all (it is), ...; **das hat ~ nichts zu
sagen** that doesn't really matter; **immer
~** on and on; (Anweisung) keep on (going);
~ nichts/niemand nothing/nobody
else; **weiterarbeiten** vi to go on working;
weiterbilden vr to continue one's studies;
Weiterbildung f further education

Weitere, s nt further details pl; **bis auf ~s** for
the time being; **ohne ~s** without further ado,
just like that

weiter- zW: **weiterempfehlen** unreg vt to
recommend (to others); **weitererzählen**
vt (Geheimnis) to pass on; **Weiterfahrt** f
continuation of the journey; **weiterführend**
adj (Schule) secondary (Brit), high (US);
weitergehen unreg vi to go on; **weiterhin**
adv: **etw weiterhin tun** to go on doing
sth; **weiterkommen** unreg vi: **nicht
weiterkommen** (fig) to be bogged down;
weiterleiten vt to pass on; **weitermachen** vt,
vi to continue; **weiterreisen** vi to continue
one's journey; **weitersagen** vt: **nicht
weitersagen!** don't tell anyone!; **weitersehen**
unreg vi: **dann sehen wir weiter** then
we'll see; **weiterverarbeiten** vt to process;
weiterwissen unreg vi: **nicht (mehr)
weiterwissen** (verzweifelt sein) to be at one's
wits' end

weit- zW: **weitgehend** adj considerable ▷ adv
largely; **weithin** adv widely; (weitgehend)
to a large extent; **weitläufig** adj (Gebäude)
spacious; (Erklärung) lengthy; (Verwandter)
distant; **weitreichend** adj (fig) far-reaching;
weitschweifig adj long-winded; **weitsichtig**
adj (lit) long-sighted (Brit), far-sighted
(US); (fig) far-sighted; **Weitsprung** m long
jump; **weitverbreitet** adj widespread;
weitverzweigt adj (Straßensystem) extensive;
Weitwinkelobjektiv nt (Phot) wide-angle lens

Weizen ['vaɪtsən] **(-s, -)** m wheat; **Weizenbier**
nt light, fizzy wheat beer; **Weizenkeime** pl (Koch)
wheatgerm sing

welch [vɛlç] pron: **~ ein(e) ...** what a ...

◯ SCHLÜSSELWORT

welche, r, s interrog pron which; **welcher von
beiden?** which (one) of the two?; **welchen
hast du genommen?** which (one) did you
take?; **welche Freude!** what joy!
▷ indef pron some; (in Fragen) any; **ich habe
welche** I have some; **haben Sie welche?** do
you have any?
▷ rel pron (bei Menschen) who; (bei Sachen) which,

that; **welche(r, s) auch immer** whoever/whichever/whatever

welk [vɛlk] *adj* withered; **welken** *vi* to wither
Wellblech *nt* corrugated iron
Welle ['vɛlə] (-, -n) *f* wave; (*Tech*) shaft; **(hohe) ~n schlagen** (*fig*) to create (quite) a stir
Wellen- *zW:* **Wellenbereich** *m* waveband; **Wellenbrecher** *m* breakwater; **Wellengang** *m:* **starker Wellengang** heavy sea(s) *od* swell; **Wellenlänge** *f* (*lit, fig*) wavelength; **mit jdm auf einer Wellenlänge sein** (*fig*) to be on the same wavelength as sb; **Wellenlinie** *f* wavy line
Wellensittich *m* budgerigar
Wellpappe *f* corrugated cardboard
Welpe ['vɛlpə] (-n, -n) *m* pup, whelp; (*von Wolf etc*) cub
Welt [vɛlt] (-, -en) *f* world; **aus der ~ schaffen** to eliminate; **in aller ~** all over the world; **vor aller ~** in front of everybody; **auf die ~ kommen** to be born; **Weltall** *nt* universe; **Weltanschauung** *f* philosophy of life; **weltberühmt** *adj* world-famous; **weltbewegend** *adj* world-shattering; **Weltbild** *nt* conception of the world; (*jds Ansichten*) philosophy
Weltenbummler, in *m(f)* globetrotter
Weltergewicht ['vɛltərgəvɪçt] *nt* (*Sport*) welterweight
weltfremd *adj* unworldly
Weltgesundheitsorganisation *f* World Health Organization
Welt- *zW:* **weltgewandt** *adj* sophisticated; **Weltkirchenrat** *m* World Council of Churches; **Weltkrieg** *m* world war; **weltlich** *adj* worldly; (*nicht kirchlich*) secular; **Weltliteratur** *f* world literature; **Weltmacht** *f* world power; **weltmännisch** *adj* sophisticated; **Weltmeister** *m* world champion; **Weltmeisterschaft** *f* world *od* world's (*US*) championship; (*Fussball etc*) World Cup; **Weltrang** *m:* **von Weltrang** world-famous; **Weltraum** *m* space; **Weltraumforschung** *f* space research; **Weltraumstation** *f* space station; **Weltreise** *f* trip round the world; **Weltruf** *m* world-wide reputation; **Weltsicherheitsrat** *m* (*Pol*) United Nations Security Council; **Weltstadt** *f* metropolis; **Weltuntergang** *m* (*lit, fig*) end of the world; **weltweit** *adj* worldwide; **Weltwirtschaft** *f* world economy; **Weltwirtschaftskrise** *f* world economic crisis; **Weltwunder** *nt* wonder of the world
wem [ve:m] *dat von* **wer** ▷ *pron* to whom
wen [ve:n] *akk von* **wer** ▷ *pron* whom
Wende ['vɛndə] (-, -n) *f* turn; (*Veränderung*) change; **die ~** (*Pol*) (the) reunification (of Germany); **Wendekreis** *m* (*Geog*) tropic; (*Aut*) turning circle
Wendeltreppe *f* spiral staircase
wenden *unreg vt, vi, vr* to turn; **bitte ~!** please turn over; **sich an jdn ~** to go/come to sb
Wendepunkt *m* turning point

wendig *adj* (*lit, fig*) agile; (*Auto etc*) manoeuvrable (*Brit*), maneuverable (*US*)
Wendung *f* turn; (*Redewendung*) idiom
wenig ['ve:nɪç] *adj, adv* little; **ein ~** a little; **er hat zu ~ Geld** he doesn't have enough money; **ein Exemplar zu ~** one copy too few
wenige ['ve:nɪgə] *pl* few *pl*; **in ~n Tagen** in (just) a few days
weniger *adj* less; (*mit pl*) fewer ▷ *adv* less
Wenigkeit *f* trifle; **meine ~** (*umg*) little me
wenigste, r, s *adj* least
wenigstens *adv* at least
wenn [vɛn] *konj* if; (*zeitlich*) when; **~ auch ...** even if ...; **~ ich doch ...** if only I ...; **~ wir erst die neue Wohnung haben** once we get the new flat
Wenn *nt:* **ohne ~ und Aber** unequivocally
wennschon *adv:* **na ~!** so what?; **~, dennschon!** in for a penny, in for a pound!
wer [ve:r] *pron* who
Werbe- *zW:* **Werbeagentur** *f* advertising agency; **Werbeaktion** *f* advertising campaign; **Werbeantwort** *f* business reply card; **Werbebanner** *nt* banner; **Werbefernsehen** *nt* commercial television; **Werbefilm** *m* promotional film; **Werbegeschenk** *nt* promotional gift, freebie (*umg*); (*zu Gekauftem*) free gift; **Werbegrafiker, in** *m(f)* commercial artist; **Werbekampagne** *f* advertising campaign
werben ['vɛrbən] *unreg vt* to win; (*Mitglied*) to recruit ▷ *vi* to advertise; **um jdn/etw ~** to try to win sb/sth; **für jdn/etw ~** to promote sb/sth
Werbe- *zW:* **Werbespot** *m* commercial; **Werbetexter** (-s, -) *m* copywriter; **Werbetrommel** *f:* **die Werbetrommel (für etw) rühren** (*umg*) to beat the big drum (for sth); **werbewirksam** *adj:* **werbewirksam sein** to be good publicity
Werbung *f* advertising; (*von Mitgliedern*) recruitment; (*TV etc: Werbeblock*) commercial break; **~ um jdn/etw** promotion of sb/sth
Werbungskosten *pl* professional *od* business expenses *pl*
Werdegang ['ve:rdəgaŋ] *m* development; (*beruflich*) career

◯ SCHLÜSSELWORT

werden ['ve:rdən] *unreg* (*pt* **wurde**, *pp* **geworden** *od* **(bei Passiv) worden**) *vi* to become; **was ist aus ihm/aus der Sache geworden?** what became of him/it?; **es ist nichts/gut geworden** it came to nothing/turned out well; **es wird Nacht/Tage** it's getting dark/light; **es wird bald ein Jahr, dass ...** it's almost a year since ...; **er wird am 8. Mai 36** he will be 36 on the 8th May; **mir wird kalt** I'm getting cold; **mir wird schlecht** I feel ill; **Erster werden** to come *od* be first; **das muss anders werden** that will have to change; **rot/zu Eis werden** to turn red/to ice; **was willst**

W

du (mal) werden? what do you want to be?;
die Fotos sind gut geworden the photos
turned out well

▷ *hilfsverb* **1** (*bei Futur*): **er wird es tun** he will *od*
he'll do it; **er wird das nicht tun** he will not
od he won't do it; **es wird gleich regnen** it's
going to rain any moment
2 (*bei Konjunktiv*): **ich würde ...** I would ...; **er
würde gern ...** he would *od* he'd like to ...; **ich
würde lieber ...** I would *od* I'd rather ...
3 (*bei Vermutung*): **sie wird in der Küche sein**
she will be in the kitchen
4 (*bei Passiv*): **gebraucht werden** to be used; **er
ist erschossen worden** he has *od* he's been shot;
mir wurde gesagt, dass ... I was told that ...

werdend *adj*: **~e Mutter** expectant mother
werfen ['vɛrfən] *unreg vt* to throw ▷ *vi* (*Tier*) to
have its young; **„nicht ~"** "handle with care"
Werft [vɛrft] (**-, -en**) *f* shipyard; (*für Flugzeuge*)
hangar
Werk [vɛrk] (**-(e)s, -e**) *nt* work; (*Tätigkeit*) job;
(*Fabrik, Mechanismus*) works *pl*; **ans ~ gehen** to
set to work; **das ist sein ~** this is his doing; **ab
~** (*Comm*) ex works
werkeln ['vɛrkəln] (*umg*) *vi* to potter about
(*Brit*), putter around (*US*)
Werken (**-s**) *nt* (*Sch*) handicrafts *pl*
Werkschutz *m* works security service
Werksgelände *nt* factory premises *pl*
Werk- *zW*: **Werkstatt** (**-, -stätten**) *f* workshop;
(*Aut*) garage; **Werkstoff** *m* material;
Werkstudent *m* self-supporting student;
Werktag *m* working day; **werktags** *adv*
on working days; **werktätig** *adj* working;
Werkzeug *nt* tool; **Werkzeugkasten** *m*
toolbox; **Werkzeugmaschine** *f* machine tool;
Werkzeugschrank *m* tool chest
Wermut ['ve:rmu:t] (**-(e)s, -s**) *m* wormwood;
(*Wein*) vermouth
Wermutstropfen *m* (*fig*) drop of bitterness
Wert [ve:rt] (**-(e)s, -e**) *m* worth; (*Fin*) value; **~
legen auf** +*akk* to attach importance to; **es hat
doch keinen ~** it's useless; **im ~e von** to the
value of
wert [ve:rt] *adj* worth; (*geschätzt*) dear; (*würdig*)
worthy; **das ist nichts/viel ~** it's not worth
anything/it's worth a lot; **das ist es/er mir ~**
it's/he's worth that to me; **ein Auto ist viel ~**
(*nützlich*) a car is very useful
Wertangabe *f* declaration of value
wertbeständig *adj* stable in value
werten *vt* to rate; (*beurteilen*) to judge; (*Sport: als
gültig werten*) to allow; **~ als** to rate as; to judge
to be
Wert- *zW*: **Wertgegenstand** *m* article of
value; **wertlos** *adj* worthless; **Wertlosigkeit**
f worthlessness; **Wertmaßstab** *m* standard;
Wertpapier *nt* security; **faule Wertpapiere**
toxic asset(s); **Wertsteigerung** *f* appreciation
Wertung *f* (*Sport*) score
Wert- *zW*: **wertvoll** *adj* valuable;
Wertvorstellung *f* moral concept;

Wertzuwachs *m* appreciation
Wesen ['ve:zən] (**-s, -**) *nt* (*Geschöpf*) being;
(*Natur, Character*) nature
wesentlich *adj* significant; (*beträchtlich*)
considerable; **im W~en** essentially; (*im Großen*)
in the main
weshalb [vɛs'halp] *adv* why
Wespe ['vɛspə] (**-, -n**) *f* wasp
wessen ['vɛsən] *gen von* **wer** ▷ *pron* whose
Wessi ['vɛsɪ] (**-s, -s**) (*umg*) *m* West German; *see
culture note*

West- *zW*: **westdeutsch** *adj* West German;
Westdeutsche, r *f(m)* West German;
Westdeutschland *nt* (*Pol: früher*) West
Germany; (*Geog*) Western Germany
Weste ['vɛstə] (**-, -n**) *f* waistcoat, vest (*US*); **eine
reine ~ haben** (*fig*) to have a clean slate
Westen (**-s**) *m* west
Westentasche *f*: **etw wie seine ~ kennen**
(*umg*) to know sth like the back of one's hand
Westerwald ['vɛstərvalt] (**-s**) *m* Westerwald
(Mountains *pl*)
Westeuropa *nt* Western Europe
westeuropäisch ['vɛst|ɔʏro'pɛːɪʃ] *adj* West(ern)
European; **~e Zeit** Greenwich Mean Time
Westfale [vɛst'fa:lə] (**-n, -n**) *m* Westphalian
Westfalen (**-s**) *nt* Westphalia
Westfälin [vɛst'fɛ:lɪn] *f* Westphalian
westfälisch *adj* Westphalian
Westindien ['vɛst|ɪndɪən] (**-s**) *nt* West Indies *pl*
westindisch *adj* West Indian; **die W~en
Inseln** the West Indies
west- *zW*: **westlich** *adj* western ▷ *adv* to
the west; **Westmächte** *pl* (*Pol: früher*): **die
Westmächte** the Western powers *pl*;
westwärts *adv* westwards
weswegen [vɛs've:gən] *adv* why
wett [vɛt] *adj* even; **~ sein** to be quits
Wettbewerb *m* competition
Wettbewerbsbeschränkung *f* restraint of
trade
wettbewerbsfähig *adj* competitive
Wette (**-, -n**) *f* bet, wager; **um die ~ laufen** to
run a race (with each other)
Wetteifer *m* rivalry
wetteifern *vi untr*: **mit jdm um etw ~** to
compete with sb for sth
wetten ['vɛtən] *vt, vi* to bet; **so haben wir
nicht gewettet!** that's not part of the
bargain!
Wetter ['vɛtər] (**-s, -**) *nt* weather; (*Min*)
air; **Wetteramt** *nt* meteorological office;
Wetteraussichten *pl* weather outlook

sing; **Wetterbericht** m weather report;
Wetterdienst m meteorological service;
wetterfest adj weatherproof; **wetterfühlig**
adj sensitive to changes in the weather;
Wetterkarte f weather chart; **Wetterlage** f
(weather) situation

wettern ['vɛtərn] vi to curse and swear

Wetter- zW: **Wetterumschlag** m sudden
change in the weather; **Wettervorhersage**
f weather forecast; **Wetterwarte** f weather
station; **wetterwendisch** adj capricious

Wett- zW: **Wettkampf** m contest; **Wettlauf**
m race; **ein Wettlauf mit der Zeit** a race
against time

wettmachen vt to make good

Wett- zW: **Wettrüsten** nt arms race; **Wettspiel**
nt nt match; **Wettstreit** m contest

wetzen ['vɛtsən] vt to sharpen ▷ vi (umg) to
scoot

WEU f abk (= Westeuropäische Union) WEU

WEZ abk (= westeuropäische Zeit) GMT

WG abk = **Wohngemeinschaft**

Whisky ['vɪski] (-s, -s) m whisky (Brit), whiskey
(US, Ireland)

WHO (-) f abk (= World Health Organization) WHO

wich etc [vɪç] vb siehe **weichen**

wichsen ['vɪksən] vt (Schuhe) to polish ▷ vi
(umg!: onanieren) to jerk od toss off (!)

Wichser (umg!) m wanker (!)

Wicht [vɪçt] (-(e)s, -e) m titch; (pej) worthless
creature

wichtig adj important; **sich selbst/etw (zu)**
~ nehmen to take o.s./sth (too) seriously;
Wichtigkeit f importance; **Wichtigtuer, in**
(pej) m(f) pompous ass (umg)

Wicke ['vɪkə] (-, -n) f (Bot) vetch; (Gartenwicke)
sweet pea

wickeln ['vɪkəln] vt to wind; (Haare) to set;
(Kind) to change; **da bist du schief gewickelt!**
(fig: umg) you're very much mistaken; **jdn/etw**
in etw akk **~** to wrap sb/sth in sth

Wickeltisch m baby's changing table

Widder ['vɪdər] (-s, -) m ram; (Astrol) Aries

wider ['vi:dər] präp +akk against

widerfahren unreg vi untr: **jdm ~** to happen to sb

Widerhaken ['vi:dərha:kən] m barb

Widerhall ['vi:dərhal] m echo; **keinen ~**
(bei jdm) finden (Interesse) to meet with no
response (from sb)

widerlegen vt untr to refute

widerlich ['vi:dərlɪç] adj disgusting, repulsive;
Widerlichkeit f repulsiveness

widerrechtlich adj unlawful

Widerrede f contradiction; **keine ~!** don't
argue!

Widerruf ['vi:dərru:f] m retraction;
countermanding; **bis auf ~** until revoked

widerrufen unreg vt untr to retract; (Anordnung)
to revoke; (Befehl) to countermand

Widersacher, in ['vi:dərzaxər(ɪn)] (-s, -) m(f)
adversary

widersetzen vr untr: **sich jdm ~** to oppose sb;
(der Polizei) to resist sb; **sich einer Sache ~** to

oppose sth; (einem Befehl) to refuse to comply
with sth

widerspenstig ['vi:dərʃpɛnstɪç] adj wilful (Brit),
willful (US); **Widerspenstigkeit** f wilfulness
(Brit), willfulness (US)

widerspiegeln ['vi:dərʃpi:gəln] vt to reflect

widersprechen unreg vi untr: **jdm ~** to
contradict sb

widersprechend adj contradictory

Widerspruch ['vi:dərʃprʊx] m contradiction;
ein ~ in sich a contradiction in terms

widersprüchlich ['vi:dərʃprʏçlɪç] adj
contradictory, inconsistent

widerspruchslos adv without arguing

Widerstand ['vi:dərʃtant] m resistance; **der**
Weg des geringsten ~es the line of least
resistance; **jdm/etw ~ leisten** to resist sb/sth

Widerstands- zW: **Widerstandsbewegung**
f resistance (movement); **widerstandsfähig**
adj resistant, tough; **widerstandslos** adj
unresisting

widerstehen unreg vi untr: **jdm/etw ~** to
withstand sb/sth

widerstreben vi untr: **es widerstrebt mir, so**
etwas zu tun I am reluctant to do anything
like that

widerstrebend adj reluctant; (gegensätzlich)
conflicting

Wider- zW: **Widerstreit** m conflict;
widerwärtig adj nasty, horrid; **Widerwille**
m: **Widerwille (gegen)** aversion (to);
(Abneigung) distaste (for); (Widerstreben)
reluctance; **widerwillig** adj unwilling,
reluctant; **Widerworte** pl answering back sing

Widget ['vɪdʒɪt] nt (Comput) widget

widmen ['vɪtmən] vt to dedicate ▷ vr to devote
o.s.

Widmung f dedication

widrig ['vi:drɪç] adj (Umstände) adverse; (Mensch)
repulsive

⊙ SCHLÜSSELWORT

wie [vi:] adv how; **wie groß/schnell?** how
big/fast?; **wie viel** how much; **wie viel**
Menschen how many people; **wie wärs?** how
about it?; **wie wärs mit einem Whisky?**
(umg) how about a whisky?; **wie nennt man**
das? what is that called?; **wie ist er?** what's
he like?; **wie gut du das kannst!** you're very
good at it; **wie bitte?** pardon? (Brit), pardon
me? (US); (entrüstet) I beg your pardon!; **und**
wie! and how!

▷ konj **1** (bei Vergleichen): **so schön wie …** as
beautiful as …; **wie ich schon sagte** as I said;
wie noch nie as never before; **wie du** like you;
singen wie ein … to sing like a …; **wie (zum**
Beispiel) such as (for example)

2 (zeitlich): **wie er das hörte, ging er** when he
heard that he left; **er hörte, wie der Regen**
fiel he heard the rain falling

wieder ['vi:dər] adv again; **~ da sein** to be back

(again); **gehst du schon ~?** are you off again?;
~ ein(e) ... another ...; das ist auch ~ wahr
that's true enough; **da sieht man mal ~ ...**
it just shows ...; **~ finden, ~ gutmachen** etc =
wiederfinden, wiedergutmachen etc

wieder- zW: **Wiederaufbau** [-'|aufbaʊ]
m rebuilding; **wiederaufbereiten** vt
to recycle; (Atommüll) to reprocess;
Wiederaufbereitungsanlage f reprocessing
plant; **Wiederaufnahme** [-'|aufna:mə]
f resumption; **wiederaufnehmen** unreg
vt to resume; (Gedanken, Hobby) to take up
again; (Thema) to revert to; (Jur: Verfahren)
to reopen; **wiederaufrollen** vt (Fall, Prozess)
to reopen; **wiederbekommen** unreg vt to
get back; **wiederbeleben** unreg vt to revive;
wiederbeschreibbar adj (CD, DVD) rewritable;
wiederbringen unreg vt to bring back;
wiedererkennen unreg vt to recognize;
Wiedererstattung f reimbursement;
wiederfinden unreg vt (fig: Selbstachtung etc) to
regain

Wiedergabe f (von Rede, Ereignis) account;
(Wiederholung) repetition; (Darbietung)
performance; (Reproduktion) reproduction;
Wiedergabegerät nt playback unit

wieder- zW: **wiedergeben** unreg vt (zurückgeben)
to return; (Erzählung etc) to repeat; (Gefühle
etc) to convey; **Wiedergeburt** f rebirth;
wiedergutmachen vt to make up for;
(Fehler) to put right; **Wiedergutmachung** f
reparation; **wiederherstellen** vt (Gesundheit,
Gebäude, Ruhe) to restore

wiederholen vt untr to repeat

wiederholt adj: **zum ~en Male** once again

Wiederholung f repetition

Wiederholungstäter, in m(f) (Jur) second-
time offender; (mehrmalig) persistent offender

wieder- zW: **Wiederhören** nt: **auf
Wiederhören** (Tel) goodbye; **wiederkäuen**
vi to ruminate ▷ vt to ruminate; (fig: umg)
to go over again and again; **Wiederkehr** (-)
f return; (von Vorfall) repetition, recurrence;
wiederkehrend adj recurrent; **Wiederkunft**
(-, ¨e) f return; **wiedersehen** unreg vt to see
again; **auf Wiedersehen** goodbye; **wiederum**
adv again; (seinerseits etc) in turn; (andererseits)
on the other hand; **wiedervereinigen** vt to
reunite; **Wiedervereinigung** f reunification;
Wiederverkäufer m distributor; **Wiederwahl**
f re-election

Wiege ['vi:gə] (-, -n) f cradle

wiegen¹ vt (schaukeln) to rock; (Kopf) to shake

wiegen² unreg vt, vi to weigh; **schwer ~** (fig) to
carry a lot of weight; (Irrtum) to be serious

wiehern ['vi:ərn] vi to neigh, whinny

Wien [vi:n] (-s) nt Vienna

Wiener, in (-s, -) m(f) Viennese ▷ adj attrib
Viennese; **~ Schnitzel** Wiener schnitzel

wies etc [vi:s] vb siehe **weisen**

Wiese ['vi:zə] (-, -n) f meadow

Wiesel ['vi:zəl] (-s, -) nt weasel; **schnell** od
flink wie ein ~ quick as a flash

wieso [vi:'zo:] adv why

wievielmal [vi:'fi:lma:l] adv how often

wievielte, r, s adj: **zum ~n Mal?** how many
times?; **den W~n haben wir?** what's the
date?; **an ~r Stelle?** in what place?; **der ~
Besucher war er?** how many visitors were
there before him?

wieweit [vi:'vaɪt] adv to what extent

Wi-Fi ['waɪfi, 'waɪfaɪ] nt Wi-Fi

Wikinger ['vi:kɪŋər] (-s, -) m Viking

wild [vɪlt] adj wild; **~er Streik** unofficial
strike; **in ~er Ehe leben** (veraltet, hum) to live
in sin; **~ entschlossen** (umg) dead set

Wild (-(e)s) nt game

Wild- zW: **Wildbahn** f: **in freier Wildbahn**
in the wild; **Wildbret** nt game; (von Rotwild)
venison; **Wilddieb** m poacher

Wilde, r ['vɪldə(r)] f(m) savage

wildern ['vɪldərn] vi to poach

wild- zW: **Wildfang** m little rascal; **wildfremd**
(umg) adj quite strange od unknown; **Wildheit**
f wildness; **Wildleder** nt suede

Wildnis (-, -se) f wilderness

Wild- zW: **Wildschwein** nt (wild) boar;
Wildwechsel m: **„Wildwechsel"** "wild
animals"; **Wildwestroman** m western

will [vɪl] vb siehe **wollen**

Wille ['vɪlə] (-ns, -n) m will; **jdm seinen ~n
lassen** to let sb have his own way; **seinen
eigenen ~n haben** to be self-willed

willen präp +gen: **um ... ~** for the sake of ...

willenlos adj weak-willed

willens adj (geh): **~ sein** to be willing

willensstark adj strong-willed

willentlich ['vɪləntlɪç] adj wilful (Brit), willful
(US), deliberate

willig adj willing

willkommen [vɪl'kɔmən] adj welcome; **jdn ~
heißen** to welcome sb; **herzlich ~ (in** +dat)
welcome (to); **Willkommen** (-s, -) nt welcome

willkürlich adj arbitrary; (Bewegung) voluntary

willst [vɪlst] vb siehe **wollen**

Wilna ['vɪlna] (-s) nt Vilnius

wimmeln ['vɪməln] vi: **~ (von)** to swarm (with)

wimmern ['vɪmərn] vi to whimper

Wimper ['vɪmpər] (-, -n) f eyelash; **ohne mit
der ~ zu zucken** (fig) without batting an eyelid

Wimperntusche f mascara

Wind [vɪnt] (-(e)s, -e) m wind; **den Mantel**
od **das Fähnchen nach dem ~ hängen** to
trim one's sails to the wind; **etw in den ~
schlagen** to turn a deaf ear to sth

Windbeutel m cream puff; (fig) windbag

Winde ['vɪndə] (-, -n) f (Tech) winch, windlass;
(Bot) bindweed

Windel ['vɪndəl] (-, -n) f nappy (Brit), diaper (US)

windelweich adj: **jdn ~ schlagen** (umg) to beat
the living daylights out of sb

winden¹ ['vɪndən] vi unpers to be windy

winden² unreg vt to wind; (Kranz) to weave;
(entwinden) to twist ▷ vr to wind; (Person) to
writhe; (fig: ausweichen) to try to wriggle out

Windenergie f wind power

Windeseile f: **sich in** od **mit ~ verbreiten** to spread like wildfire

Windhose f whirlwind

Windhund m greyhound; (Mensch) fly-by-night

windig ['vɪndɪç] adj windy; (fig) dubious

Wind- zW: **Windjacke** f windcheater, windbreaker (US); **Windkanal** m (Tech) wind tunnel; **Windkraft** f wind power; **Windkraftanlage** f wind power station; **Windmühle** f windmill; **gegen Windmühlen (an)kämpfen** (fig) to tilt at windmills; **Windpark** m wind farm

Windpocken pl chickenpox sing

Wind- zW: **Windrose** f (Naut) compass card; (Met) wind rose; **Windschatten** m lee; (von Fahrzeugen) slipstream; **Windschutzscheibe** f (Aut) windscreen (Brit), windshield (US); **Windstärke** f wind force; **windstill** adj (Tag) windless; **es ist windstill** there's no wind; **Windstille** f calm; **Windstoß** m gust of wind; **Windsurfen** nt windsurfing

Windung f (von Weg, Fluss etc) meander; (von Schlange, Spule) coil; (von Schraube) thread

Wink [vɪŋk] (-(e)s, -e) m (mit Kopf) nod; (mit Hand) wave; (Tipp, Hinweis) hint; **ein ~ mit dem Zaunpfahl** a broad hint

Winkel ['vɪŋkəl] (-s, -) m (Math) angle; (Gerät) set square; (in Raum) corner; **Winkeladvokat** (pej) m incompetent lawyer; **Winkelmesser** m protractor; **Winkelzug** m: **mach keine Winkelzüge** stop evading the issue

winken ['vɪŋkən] vt, vi to wave; **dem Sieger winkt eine Reise nach Italien** the (lucky) winner will receive a trip to Italy

winseln ['vɪnzəln] vi to whine

Winter ['vɪntər] (-s, -) m winter; **Wintergarten** m conservatory; **winterlich** adj wintry; **Winterreifen** m winter tyre (Brit) od tire (US); **Winterschlaf** m (Zool) hibernation; **Winterschlussverkauf** m winter sale; **Wintersemester** nt (Univ) winter semester (bes US), ≈ autumn term (Brit); **Winterspiele** pl: **(Olympische) Winterspiele** Winter Olympics pl; **Wintersport** m winter sports pl

Winzer, in ['vɪntsər(ɪn)] (-s, -) m(f) wine-grower

winzig ['vɪntsɪç] adj tiny

Wipfel ['vɪpfəl] (-s, -) m treetop

Wippe ['vɪpə] (-, -n) f seesaw

wir [viːr] pron we; **~ alle** all of us, we all

Wirbel ['vɪrbəl] (-s, -) m whirl, swirl; (Trubel) hurly-burly; (Aufsehen) fuss; (Anat) vertebra; **~ um jdn/etw machen** to make a fuss about sb/sth

wirbellos adj (Zool) invertebrate

wirbeln vi to whirl, swirl

Wirbel- zW: **Wirbelsäule** f spine; **Wirbeltier** nt vertebrate; **Wirbelwind** m whirlwind

wirbst vb siehe **werben**

wirbt [vɪrpt] vb siehe **werben**

wird [vɪrt] vb siehe **werden**

wirfst vb siehe **werfen**

wirft [vɪrft] vb siehe **werfen**

wirken ['vɪrkən] vi to have an effect; (erfolgreich sein) to work; (scheinen) to seem ▷ vt (Wunder) to work; **etw auf sich ~ lassen** to take sth in

wirklich ['vɪrklɪç] adj real; **Wirklichkeit** f reality; **wirklichkeitsgetreu** adj realistic

wirksam ['vɪrkzaːm] adj effective; **Wirksamkeit** f effectiveness

Wirkstoff m active substance

Wirkung ['vɪrkʊŋ] f effect

Wirkungs- zW: **Wirkungsbereich** m field (of activity od interest etc); (Domäne) domain; **wirkungslos** adj ineffective; **wirkungslos bleiben** to have no effect; **wirkungsvoll** adj effective

wirr [vɪr] adj confused; (unrealistisch) wild; (Haare etc) tangled

Wirren pl disturbances pl

Wirrwarr ['vɪrvar] (-s) m disorder, chaos; (von Stimmen) hubbub; (von Fäden, Haaren etc) tangle

Wirsing ['vɪrzɪŋ], **Wirsingkohl** ['vɪrzɪŋkoːl] (-s) m savoy cabbage

wirst [vɪrst] vb siehe **werden**

Wirt, in [vɪrt(ɪn)] (-(e)s, -e) m(f) landlord, landlady

Wirtschaft ['vɪrtʃaft] f (Gaststätte) pub; (Haushalt) housekeeping; (eines Landes) economy; (Geschäftsleben) industry and commerce; (umg: Durcheinander) mess; **wirtschaften** vi (sparsam sein): **gut wirtschaften können** to be economical; **Wirtschafter** m (Verwalter) manager; **Wirtschafterin** f (im Haushalt, Heim etc) housekeeper; **wirtschaftlich** adj economical; (Pol) economic; **Wirtschaftlichkeit** f economy; (von Betrieb) viability

Wirtschafts- zW: **Wirtschaftsgeld** nt housekeeping (money); **Wirtschaftsgeografie** f economic geography; **Wirtschaftshilfe** f economic aid; **Wirtschaftskrise** f economic crisis; **Wirtschaftsminister** m minister of economic affairs; **Wirtschaftsordnung** f economic system; **Wirtschaftspolitik** f economic policy; **Wirtschaftsprüfer** m chartered accountant (Brit), certified public accountant (US); **Wirtschaftsspionage** f industrial espionage; **Wirtschaftswachstum** nt economic growth; **Wirtschaftswissenschaft** f economics sing; **Wirtschaftswunder** nt economic miracle; **Wirtschaftszweig** m branch of industry

Wirtshaus nt inn

Wisch [vɪʃ] (-(e)s, -e) m scrap of paper

wischen vt to wipe

Wischer (-s, -) m (Aut) wiper

Wischiwaschi [vɪʃi'vaʃiː] (-s) (pej: umg) nt drivel

Wisent ['viːzɛnt] (-s, -e) m bison

WiSo ['vɪzo] abk (= Wirtschafts- und Sozialwissenschaften) economics and social sciences

wispern ['vɪspərn] vt, vi to whisper

Wiss. abk = **Wissenschaft**

wiss. abk = **wissenschaftlich**

W

Wissbegier ['vɪsbəgiːr], **Wissbegierde** ['vɪsbəgiːrdə] f thirst for knowledge
wissbegierig adj eager for knowledge
wissen ['vɪsən] unreg vt, vi to know; **von jdm/ etw nichts ~ wollen** not to be interested in sb/sth; **sie hält sich für wer weiß wie klug** (umg) she doesn't half think she's clever; **gewusst wie/wo!** etc sheer brilliance!; **ich weiß seine Adresse nicht mehr** (sich erinnern) I can't remember his address; **Wissen (-s)** nt knowledge; **etw gegen (sein) besseres Wissen tun** to do sth against one's better judgement; **nach bestem Wissen und Gewissen** to the best of one's knowledge and belief
Wissenschaft ['vɪsənʃaft] f science
Wissenschaftler, in (-s, -) m(f) scientist; (Geisteswissenschaftler) academic
wissenschaftlich adj scientific; **W~er Assistent** assistant lecturer
wissenswert adj worth knowing
wissentlich adj knowing
wittern ['vɪtərn] vt to scent; (fig) to suspect
Witterung f weather; (Geruch) scent
Witwe ['vɪtvə] (-, -n) f widow
Witwer (-s, -) m widower
Witz [vɪts] (-es, -e) m joke; **der ~ an der Sache ist, dass ...** the great thing about it is that ...; **Witzbold (-(e)s, -e)** m joker
witzeln vi to joke
witzig adj funny
witzlos (umg) adj (unsinnig) pointless, futile
WM (-) f abk = **Weltmeisterschaft**
wo [voː] adv where; (umg: irgendwo) somewhere ▷ konj (wenn) if; **im Augenblick, wo ...** the moment (that) ...; **die Zeit, wo ...** the time when ...
woanders [voː'|andərs] adv elsewhere
wob etc [voːp] vb siehe **weben**
wobei [voː'baɪ] adv (rel) ... in/by/with which; (interrog) how; what ... in/by/with; **~ mir gerade einfällt ...** which reminds me ...
Woche ['vɔxə] (-, -n) f week
Wochenbett nt: **im ~ sterben** to die in childbirth
Wochen- zW: **Wochenende** nt weekend; **Wochenendhaus** nt weekend house; **Wochenkarte** f weekly ticket; **wochenlang** adj lasting weeks ▷ adv for weeks; **Wochenschau** f newsreel; **Wochentag** m weekday
wöchentlich ['vœçəntlɪç] adj, adv weekly
Wochenzeitung f weekly (paper)
Wöchnerin ['vœçnərɪn] f woman who has recently given birth
Wodka ['vɔtka] (-s, -s) m vodka
wodurch [voː'dʊrç] adv (rel) through which; (interrog) what ... through
wofür [voː'fyːr] adv (rel) for which; (interrog) what ... for
wog etc [voːk] vb siehe **wiegen²**
Woge ['voːgə] (-, -n) f wave
wogegen [voː'geːgən] adv (rel) against which; (interrog) what ... against

wogen vi to heave, surge
woher [voː'heːr] adv where ... from; **~ kommt es eigentlich, dass ...?** how is it that ...?
wohin [voː'hɪn] adv where ... to; **~ man auch schaut** wherever you look
wohingegen konj whereas, while
Wohl (-(e)s) nt welfare; **zum ~!** cheers!

 **SCHLÜSSELWORT**

wohl [voːl] adv **1** well; (behaglich) at ease, comfortable; **sich wohl fühlen** siehe **wohlfühlen; wohl gemeint = wohlgemeint; bei dem Gedanken ist mir nicht wohl** I'm not very happy at the thought; **wohl oder übel** whether one likes it or not; **er weiß das sehr wohl** he knows that perfectly well
2 (wahrscheinlich) probably; (vermutlich) I suppose; (gewiss) certainly; (vielleicht) perhaps; **sie ist wohl zu Hause** she's probably at home; **sie wird wohl das Haus verkaufen** I suppose od presumably she's going to sell the house; **das ist doch wohl nicht dein Ernst!** surely you're not serious!; **das mag wohl sein** that may well be; **ob das wohl stimmt?** I wonder if that's true; siehe auch **wohltun**

wohl- zW: **wohlauf** [voːl'|aʊf] adj well, in good health; **Wohlbefinden** nt well-being; **Wohlbehagen** nt comfort; **wohlbehalten** adj safe and sound; **Wohlergehen** nt welfare; **Wohlfahrt** f welfare; **Wohlfahrtsstaat** m welfare state; **wohlfühlen** vr (zufrieden) to feel happy; (gesundheitlich) to feel well; **Wohlgefallen** nt: **sich in Wohlgefallen auflösen** (hum: Gegenstände, Probleme) to vanish into thin air; (zerfallen) to fall apart; **wohlgemeint** adj well-intentioned; **wohlgemerkt** adv mark you; **wohlhabend** adj wealthy
wohlig adj contented; (gemütlich) comfortable
wohl- zW: **Wohlklang** m melodious sound; **wohlmeinend** adj well-meaning; **wohlschmeckend** adj delicious; **Wohlstand** m prosperity; **Wohlstandsgesellschaft** f affluent society; **Wohltat** f (Gefallen) favour (Brit), favor (US); (gute Tat) good deed; (Erleichterung) relief; **Wohltäter** m benefactor; **wohltätig** adj charitable; **Wohltätigkeit** f charity; **wohltuend** adj pleasant; **wohltun** unreg vi: **jdm wohltun** to do sb good; **wohlverdient** adj (Ruhe) well-earned; (Strafe) well-deserved; **wohlweislich** adv prudently; **Wohlwollen (-s)** nt good will; **wohlwollend** adj benevolent
Wohnblock ['voːnblɔk] (-s, -s) m block of flats (Brit), apartment house (US)
wohnen ['voːnən] vi to live
wohn- zW: **Wohnfläche** f living space; **Wohngeld** nt housing benefit; **Wohngemeinschaft** f people sharing a flat (Brit) od apartment (US); (von Hippies) commune; **wohnhaft** adj resident; **Wohnheim**

nt (für Studenten) hall (of residence), dormitory (US); (für Senioren) home; (bes für Arbeiter) hostel; **Wohnkomfort** m: **mit sämtlichem Wohnkomfort** with all mod cons (Brit); **wohnlich** adj comfortable; **Wohnmobil** nt motor caravan (Brit), motor home (US); **Wohnort** m domicile; **Wohnsilo** nt concrete block of flats (Brit) od apartment block (US); **Wohnsitz** m place of residence; **ohne festen Wohnsitz** of no fixed abode

Wohnung f house; (Etagenwohnung) flat (Brit), apartment (US)

Wohnungs- zW: **Wohnungsamt** nt housing office; **Wohnungsbau** m house-building; **Wohnungsmarkt** m housing market; **Wohnungsnot** f housing shortage

wohn- zW: **Wohnviertel** nt residential area; **Wohnwagen** m caravan (Brit), trailer (US); **Wohnzimmer** nt living room

wölben ['vœlbən] vt, vr to curve

Wölbung f curve

Wolf [vɔlf] **(-(e)s, ̈e)** m wolf; (Tech) shredder; (Fleischwolf) mincer (Brit), grinder (US)

Wölfin ['vœlfɪn] f she-wolf

Wolke ['vɔlkə] **(-, -n)** f cloud; **aus allen ~n fallen** (fig) to be flabbergasted (umg)

Wolken- zW: **Wolkenbruch** m cloudburst; **wolkenbruchartig** adj torrential; **Wolkenkratzer** m skyscraper; **Wolkenkuckucksheim** nt cloud-cuckoo-land (Brit), cloudland (US); **wolkenlos** adj cloudless

wolkig ['vɔlkɪç] adj cloudy

Wolle ['vɔlə] **(-, -n)** f wool; **sich mit jdm in die ~ kriegen** (fig: umg) to start squabbling with sb

○ SCHLÜSSELWORT

wollen[1] ['vɔlən] unreg (pt **wollte** od (als Hilfsverb) **wollen**) vt, vi to want; **ich will nach Hause** I want to go home; **er will nicht** he doesn't want to; **sie wollte das nicht** she didn't want it; **wenn du willst** if you like; **ich will, dass du mir zuhörst** I want you to listen to me; **oh, das hab ich nicht gewollt** oh, I didn't mean to do that; **ich weiß nicht, was er will** (verstehe ihn nicht) I don't know what he's on about

▷ Hilfsverb: **er will ein Haus kaufen** he wants to buy a house; **ich wollte, ich wäre ...** I wish I were ...; **etw gerade tun wollen** to be just about to od going to do sth; **und so jemand** od **etwas will Lehrer sein!** (umg) and he calls himself a teacher!; **das will alles gut überlegt sein** that needs a lot of thought

wollen[2] adj woollen (Brit), woolen (US)

Wollsachen pl wool(l)ens pl

wollüstig ['vɔlʏstɪç] adj lusty, sensual

wo- zW: **womit** [vo'mɪt] adv (rel) with which; (interrog) what ... with; **womit kann ich dienen?** what can I do for you?; **womöglich** [vo'møːklɪç] adv probably, I suppose; **wonach** [vo'naːx] adv (rel) after/for which; (interrog)

what ... after

Wonne ['vɔnə] **(-, -n)** f joy, bliss

woran [vo'ran] adv (rel) on/at which; (interrog) what ... on/at; **~ liegt das?** what's the reason for it?

worauf [vo'raʊf] adv (rel) on which; (interrog) what ... on; (zeitlich) whereupon; **~ du dich verlassen kannst** of that you can be sure

woraus [vo'raʊs] adv (rel) from/out of which; (interrog) what ... from/out of

worden ['vɔrdən] vb siehe **werden**

worin [vo'rɪn] adv (rel) in which; (interrog) what ... in

Wort [vɔrt] **(-(e)s, ̈er** od **-e)** nt word; **jdn beim ~ nehmen** to take sb at his word; **ein ernstes ~ mit jdm reden** to have a serious talk with sb; **man kann sein eigenes ~ nicht (mehr) verstehen** you can't hear yourself speak; **jdm aufs ~ gehorchen** to obey sb's every word; **zu ~ kommen** to get a chance to speak; **jdm das ~ erteilen** to allow sb to speak; **Wortart** f (Gram) part of speech; **wortbrüchig** adj not true to one's word

Wörtchen nt: **da habe ich wohl ein ~ mitzureden** (umg) I think I have some say in that

Wörterbuch ['vœrtərbuːx] nt dictionary

Wort- zW: **Wortfetzen** pl snatches pl of conversation; **Wortführer** m spokesman; **wortgetreu** adj true to one's word; (Übersetzung) literal; **wortgewaltig** adj eloquent; **wortkarg** adj taciturn; **Wortlaut** m wording; **im Wortlaut** verbatim

wörtlich ['vœrtlɪç] adj literal

Wort- zW: **wortlos** adj mute; **Wortmeldung** f: **wenn es keine weiteren Wortmeldungen gibt, ...** if nobody else wishes to speak ...; **wortreich** adj wordy, verbose; **Wortschatz** m vocabulary; **Wortspiel** nt play on words, pun; **Wortwechsel** m dispute; **wortwörtlich** adj word-for-word ▷ adv quite literally

worüber [vo'ryːbər] adv (rel) over/about which; (interrog) what ... over/about

worum [vo'rʊm] adv (rel) about/round which; (interrog) what ... about/round; **~ handelt es sich?** what's it about?

worunter [vo'rʊntər] adv (rel) under which; (interrog) what ... under

wo- zW: **wovon** [vo'fɔn] adv (rel) from which; (interrog) what ... from; **wovor** [vo'fɔr] adv (rel) in front of/before which; (interrog) what ... in front of/before what; **wozu** [vo'tsu] adv (rel) to/for which; (interrog) what ... for/to; (warum) why; **wozu soll das gut sein?** what's the point of that?

Wrack [vrak] **(-(e)s, -s)** nt wreck

wrang etc [vraŋ] vb siehe **wringen**

wringen ['vrɪŋən] unreg vt to wring

WS abk = **Wintersemester**

WSV abk = **Winterschlussverkauf**

Wucher ['vuːxər] **(-s)** m profiteering; **Wucherer (-s, -)** m, **Wucherin** f profiteer; **wucherisch** adj profiteering

wuchern vi (Pflanzen) to grow wild
Wucherpreis m exorbitant price
Wucherung f (Med) growth
Wuchs [vu:ks] (-es) m (Wachstum) growth;
(Statur) build
wuchs etc vb siehe **wachsen¹**
Wucht [vʊxt] (-) f force
wuchtig adj massive, solid
wühlen ['vy:lən] vi to scrabble; (Tier) to root;
(Maulwurf) to burrow; (umg: arbeiten) to slave
away ▷ vt to dig
Wühlmaus f vole
Wühltisch m (in Kaufhaus) bargain counter
Wulst [vʊlst] (-es, ⸚e) m bulge; (an Wunde)
swelling
wulstig adj bulging; (Rand, Lippen) thick
wund [vʊnt] adj sore; **sich** dat **die Füße ~
laufen** (lit) to get sore feet from walking; (fig)
to walk one's legs off; **ein ~er Punkt** a sore
point; **Wundbrand** m gangrene
Wunde ['vʊndə] (-, -n) f wound; **alte ~n
wieder aufreißen** (fig) to open up old wounds
Wunder (-s, -) nt miracle; **es ist kein ~** it's
no wonder; **meine Eltern denken ~ was
passiert ist** my parents think goodness
knows what has happened; **wunderbar** adj
wonderful, marvellous (Brit), marvelous (US);
Wunderkerze f sparkler; **Wunderkind** nt child
prodigy; **wunderlich** adj odd, peculiar
wundern vt to surprise ▷ vr: **sich ~ über** +akk to
be surprised at
Wunder- zW: **wunderschön** adj beautiful;
Wundertüte f lucky bag; **wundervoll** adj
wonderful
Wundfieber (-s) nt traumatic fever
Wundstarrkrampf ['vʊntʃtarkrampf] m
tetanus, lockjaw
Wunsch [vʊnʃ] (-(e)s, ⸚e) m wish; **haben
Sie (sonst) noch einen ~?** (beim Einkauf etc)
is there anything else you'd like?; **auf jds
(besonderen/ausdrücklichen) ~ hin** at sb's
(special/express) request; **Wunschdenken** nt
wishful thinking
Wünschelrute ['vʏnʃəlru:tə] f divining
rod
wünschen ['vʏnʃən] vt to wish ▷ vi: **zu
wünschen/viel zu ~ übrig lassen** to leave
something/a great deal to be desired; **sich** dat
etw ~ to want sth, wish for sth; **was ~ Sie?** (in
Geschäft) what can I do for you?; (in Restaurant)
what would you like?
wünschenswert adj desirable
Wunsch- zW: **Wunschkind** nt planned child;
Wunschkonzert nt (Rundf) musical request
programme (Brit) od program (US); **wunschlos**
adj: **wunschlos glücklich** perfectly happy;
Wunschtraum m dream; (unrealistisch) pipe
dream; **Wunschzettel** m list of things one
would like
wurde etc ['vʊrdə] vb siehe **werden**
Würde ['vʏrdə] (-, -n) f dignity; (Stellung)

honour (Brit), honor (US); **unter aller ~ sein**
to be beneath contempt
Würdenträger m dignitary
würdevoll adj dignified
würdig ['vʏrdɪç] adj worthy; (würdevoll)
dignified
würdigen ['vʏrdɪgən] vt to appreciate; **etw
zu ~ wissen** to appreciate sth; **jdn keines
Blickes ~** not to so much as look at sb
Wurf [vʊrf] (-(e)s, ⸚e) m throw; (Junge) litter
Würfel ['vʏrfəl] (-s, -) m dice; (Math) cube; **die
~ sind gefallen** the die is cast; **Würfelbecher**
m (dice) cup
würfeln vi to play dice ▷ vt to dice
Würfelspiel nt game of dice
Würfelzucker m lump sugar
Wurf- zW: **Wurfgeschoss** nt projectile;
Wurfsendung f circular; **Wurfsendungen** pl
(Reklame) junk mail
Würgegriff (-(e)s) m (lit, fig) stranglehold
würgen ['vʏrgən] vt, vi to choke; **mit Hängen
und W~** by the skin of one's teeth
Wurm [vʊrm] (-(e)s, ⸚er) m worm; **da steckt
der ~ drin** (fig: umg) there's something wrong
somewhere; (verdächtig) there's something
fishy about it (umg)
wurmen (umg) vt to rile, nettle
Wurmfortsatz m (Med) appendix
wurmig adj worm-eaten
wurmstichig adj worm-ridden
Wurst [vʊrst] (-, ⸚e) f sausage; **das ist mir ~**
(umg) I don't care, I don't give a damn; **jetzt
geht es um die ~** (fig: umg) the moment of
truth has come
Würstchen ['vʏrstçən] nt frankfurter, hot dog
sausage; **Würstchenbude** f, **Würstchenstand**
m hot dog stall
Württemberg ['vʏrtəmbɛrk] nt Württemberg
Würze ['vʏrtsə] (-, -n) f seasoning
Wurzel ['vʊrtsəl] (-, -n) f root; **~n schlagen** (lit)
to root; (fig) to put down roots; **die ~ aus 4 ist
2** (Math) the square root of 4 is 2
würzen vt to season; (würzig machen) to spice
würzig adj spicy
wusch etc [vu:ʃ] vb siehe **waschen**
wusste etc ['vʊstə] vb siehe **wissen**
Wust [vu:st] (-(e)s) (umg) m (Durcheinander)
jumble; (Menge) pile
wüst [vy:st] adj untidy, messy; (ausschweifend)
wild; (öde) waste; (umg: heftig) terrible; **jdn ~
beschimpfen** to use vile language to sb
Wüste (-, -n) f desert; **die ~ Gobi** the Gobi
Desert; **jdn in die ~ schicken** (fig) to send sb
packing
Wut [vu:t] (-) f rage, fury; **eine ~ (auf jdn/etw)
haben** to be furious (with sb/sth); **Wutanfall**
m fit of rage
wüten ['vy:tən] vi to rage
wütend adj furious, enraged
wutentbrannt adj furious, enraged
Wz abk (= Warenzeichen)®

X, x [ɪks] *nt* X, x; **X wie Xanthippe** ≈ X for Xmas; **jdm ein X für ein U vormachen** to put one over on sb (*umg*)

X-Beine ['ɪksbaɪnə] *pl* knock-knees *pl*

x-beliebig [ɪksbə'li:bɪç] *adj* any (... whatever)

Xerografie [kserogra'fi:] *f* xerography

xerokopieren [kseroko'pi:rən] *vt* to xerox, photocopy

x-fach ['ɪksfax] *adj*: **die ~e Menge** (*Math*) n times the amount

x-mal ['ɪksma:l] *adv* any number of times, n times

XML *abk* (*Comput:* = *extensible markup language*) XML

x-te ['ɪkstə] *adj* (*Math: umg*) nth; **zum ~n Male** (*umg*) for the nth *od* umpteenth time

Xylofon, Xylophon [ksylo'fo:n] (**-s, -e**) *nt* xylophone

Yy

Y, y ['ʏpsilɔn] *nt* Y, y; **Y wie Ypsilon** ≈ Y for Yellow, Y for Yoke (US)

Yen [jɛn] **(-(s), -(s))** *m* yen

Yoga ['joːga] **(-(s))** *m od nt* yoga

Ypsilon ['ʏpsilɔn] **(-(s), -s)** *nt* the letter Y

Zz

Z, z [tsɛt] *nt* Z, z; **Z wie Zacharias** ≈ Z for Zebra
Zack [tsak] *m*: **auf ~ sein** (*umg*) to be on the ball
Zacke ['tsakə] (**-, -n**) *f* point; (*Bergzacke*) jagged peak; (*Gabelzacke*) prong; (*Kammzacke*) tooth
zackig ['tsakɪç] *adj* jagged; (*umg*) smart; (: *Tempo*) brisk
zaghaft ['tsa:khaft] *adj* timid
Zaghaftigkeit *f* timidity
Zagreb ['za:grɛp] (**-s**) *nt* Zagreb
zäh [tsɛ:] *adj* tough; (*Mensch*) tenacious; (*Flüssigkeit*) thick; (*schleppend*) sluggish; **zähflüssig** *adj* viscous; (*Verkehr*) slow-moving
Zähigkeit *f* toughness; tenacity
Zahl [tsa:l] (**-, -en**) *f* number
zahlbar *adj* payable
zahlen *vt, vi* to pay; **~ bitte!** the bill *od* check (*US*) please!
zählen ['tsɛ:lən] *vt* to count ▷ *vi* (*sich verlassen*): **~ auf** +*akk* to count on; **seine Tage sind gezählt** his days are numbered; **~ zu** to be numbered among
Zahlen- *zW*: **Zahlenangabe** *f* figure; **Zahlenkombination** *f* combination of figures; **zahlenmäßig** *adj* numerical; **Zahlenschloss** *nt* combination lock
Zahler (**-s, -**) *m* payer
Zähler (**-s, -**) *m* (*Tech*) meter; (*Math*) numerator; **Zählerstand** *m* meter reading
Zahl- *zW*: **Zahlgrenze** *f* fare stage; **Zahlkarte** *f* transfer form; **zahllos** *adj* countless; **Zahlmeister** *m* (*Naut*) purser; **zahlreich** *adj* numerous; **Zahltag** *m* payday
Zahlung *f* payment; **in ~ geben/nehmen** to give/take in part exchange
Zahlungs- *zW*: **Zahlungsanweisung** *f* transfer order; **Zahlungsaufforderung** *f* request for payment; **zahlungsfähig** *adj* solvent; **Zahlungsmittel** *nt* means *sing* of payment; (*Münzen, Banknoten*) currency; **Zahlungsrückstände** *pl* arrears *pl*; **zahlungsunfähig** *adj* insolvent; **Zahlungsverzug** *m* default
Zahlwort *nt* numeral
zahm [tsa:m] *adj* tame
zähmen ['tsɛ:mən] *vt* to tame; (*fig*) to curb
Zahn [tsa:n] (**-(e)s, ⁻e**) *m* tooth; **die dritten Zähne** (*umg*) false teeth *pl*; **einen ~ draufhaben** (*umg*: *Geschwindigkeit*) to be going

like the clappers (*Brit*) *od* like crazy (*US*); **jdm auf den ~ fühlen** (*fig*) to sound sb out; **einen ~ zulegen** (*fig*) to get a move on; **Zahnarzt** *m*, **Zahnärztin** *f* dentist; **Zahnbelag** *m* plaque; **Zahnbürste** *f* toothbrush; **Zahncreme** *f* toothpaste; **zahnen** *vi* to teethe; **Zahnersatz** *m* denture; **Zahnfäule** (**-**) *f* tooth decay, caries *sing*; **Zahnfleisch** *nt* gums *pl*; **auf dem Zahnfleisch gehen** (*fig*: *umg*) to be all in, be at the end of one's tether; **zahnlos** *adj* toothless; **Zahnmedizin** *f* dentistry; **Zahnpasta** *f*, **Zahnpaste** *f* toothpaste; **Zahnrad** *nt* cog(wheel); **Zahnradbahn** *f* rack railway; **Zahnschmelz** *m* (tooth) enamel; **Zahnschmerzen** *pl* toothache *sing*; **Zahnseide** *f* dental floss; **Zahnspange** *f* brace; **Zahnstein** *m* tartar; **Zahnstocher** (**-s, -**) *m* toothpick; **Zahntechniker**, **in** *m*(*f*) dental technician; **Zahnweh** *nt* toothache
Zaire [za'i:r] (**-s**) *nt* Zaire
Zange ['tsaŋə] (**-, -n**) *f* pliers *pl*; (*Zuckerzange etc*) tongs *pl*; (*Beißzange, Zool*) pincers *pl*; (*Med*) forceps *pl*; **jdn in die ~ nehmen** (*fig*) to put the screws on sb (*umg*)
Zangengeburt *f* forceps delivery
Zankapfel *m* bone of contention
zanken ['tsaŋkən] *vi, vr* to quarrel
zänkisch ['tsɛŋkɪʃ] *adj* quarrelsome
Zäpfchen ['tsɛpfçən] *nt* (*Anat*) uvula; (*Med*) suppository
Zapfen ['tsapfən] (**-s, -**) *m* plug; (*Bot*) cone; (*Eiszapfen*) icicle
zapfen *vt* to tap
Zapfenstreich *m* (*Mil*) tattoo
Zapfsäule *f* petrol (*Brit*) *od* gas (*US*) pump
zappelig ['tsapəlɪç] *adj* wriggly; (*unruhig*) fidgety
zappeln ['tsapəln] *vi* to wriggle; to fidget; **jdn ~ lassen** (*fig*: *umg*) to keep sb in suspense
Zar [tsa:r] (**-en, -en**) *m* tzar, czar
zart [tsa:rt] *adj* (*weich, leise*) soft; (*Braten etc*) tender; (*fein, schwächlich*) delicate; **zartbesaitet** ['tsa:rtbəzaɪtət] *adj* highly sensitive; **zartbitter** *adj* (*Schokolade*) plain (*Brit*), bittersweet (*US*); **Zartgefühl** *nt* tact; **Zartheit** *f* softness; tenderness; delicacy
zärtlich ['tsɛ:rtlɪç] *adj* tender, affectionate; **Zärtlichkeit** *f* tenderness; **Zärtlichkeiten** *pl*

caresses pl

Zäsium ['tsɛːzɪʊm] nt = **Cäsium**

Zäsur [tsɛ'zuːr] f caesura; (fig) break

Zauber ['tsaʊbər] (**-s, -**) m magic; (Zauberbann) spell; **fauler ~** (umg) humbug

Zauberei [tsaʊbə'raɪ] f magic

Zauberer (**-s, -**) m magician; (Zauberkünstler) conjurer

Zauber- zW: **zauberhaft** adj magical, enchanting; **Zauberin** f magician; conjurer; **Zauberkünstler** m conjurer; **Zauberkunststück** nt conjuring trick; **Zaubermittel** nt magical cure; (Trank) magic potion

zaubern vi to conjure, do magic

Zauberspruch m (magic) spell

Zauberstab m magic wand

zaudern ['tsaʊdərn] vi to hesitate

Zaum [tsaʊm] (**-(e)s, Zäume**) m bridle; **etw im ~ halten** to keep sth in check

Zaun [tsaʊn] (**-(e)s, Zäune**) m fence; **vom ~(e) brechen** (fig) to start; **Zaungast** m (Person) mere onlooker; **Zaunkönig** m wren

z. B. abk (= zum Beispiel) e.g.

z. d. A. abk (= zu den Akten) to be filed

ZDF nt see culture note

Zebra ['tseːbra] (**-s, -s**) nt zebra; **Zebrastreifen** m pedestrian crossing (Brit), crosswalk (US)

Zeche ['tsɛçə] (**-, -n**) f (Rechnung) bill, check (US); (Bergbau) mine

zechen vi to booze (umg)

Zechprellerei [tsɛçprɛlə'raɪ] f skipping payment in restaurants etc

Zecke ['tsɛkə] (**-, -n**) f tick

Zeder ['tseːdər] (**-, -n**) f cedar

Zeh [tseː] (**-s, -en**) m toe

Zehe ['tseːə] (**-, -n**) f toe; (Knoblauchzehe) clove

Zehenspitze f: **auf ~n** on tiptoe

zehn [tseːn] num ten

Zehnerpackung f packet of ten

Zehnfingersystem nt touch-typing method

Zehnkampf m (Sport) decathlon

zehnte, r, s adj tenth

Zehntel (**-s, -**) nt tenth (part)

zehren ['tseːrən] vi: **an jdm/etw ~** (an Mensch, Kraft) to wear sb/sth out

Zeichen ['tsaɪçən] (**-s, -**) nt sign; (Comput) character; **jdm ein ~ geben** to give sb a signal; **unser/Ihr ~** (Comm) our/your reference; **Zeichenblock** m sketch pad; **Zeichencode** m (Comput) character code; **Zeichenerklärung** f key; (auf Karten) legend; **Zeichenfolge** f

(Comput) string; **Zeichenkette** f (Comput) character string; **Zeichensatz** m (Comput) character set; **Zeichensetzung** f punctuation; **Zeichentrickfilm** m (animated) cartoon

zeichnen vt to draw; (kennzeichnen) to mark; (unterzeichnen) to sign ▷ vi to draw; to sign

Zeichner, in (**-s, -**) m(f) artist; **technischer ~** draughtsman (Brit), draftsman (US)

Zeichnung f drawing; (Markierung) markings pl

zeichnungsberechtigt adj authorized to sign

Zeigefinger m index finger

zeigen ['tsaɪgən] vt to show ▷ vi to point ▷ vr to show o.s.; **~ auf** +akk to point to; **es wird sich ~ time** will tell; **es zeigte sich, dass ...** it turned out that ...

Zeiger (**-s, -**) m pointer; (Uhrzeiger) hand

Zeile ['tsaɪlə] (**-, -n**) f line; (Häuserzeile) row

Zeilen- zW: **Zeilenabstand** m line spacing; **Zeilenausrichtung** f justification; **Zeilendrucker** m line printer; **Zeilenumbruch** m (Comput) wraparound; **Zeilenvorschub** m (Comput) line feed

zeit [tsaɪt] präp +gen: **~ meines Lebens** in my lifetime

Zeit (**-, -en**) f time; (Gram) tense; **sich** dat **~ lassen** to take one's time; **eine Stunde ~ haben** to have an hour (to spare); **sich** dat **für jdn/etw ~ nehmen** to devote time to sb/sth; **eine ~ lang** a while, a time; **von ~ zu Zeit** from time to time; **~ raubend** = **zeitraubend**; **in letzter ~** recently; **nach ~ bezahlt werden** to be paid by the time; **zu der ~, als ...** (at the time) when ...; siehe auch **zurzeit**

Zeit- zW: **Zeitalter** nt age; **Zeitansage** f (Rundf) time check; (Tel) speaking clock; **Zeitarbeit** f temporary work; **Zeitaufwand** m time (needed for a task); **Zeitbombe** f time bomb; **Zeitdruck** m: **unter Zeitdruck stehen** to be under pressure; **Zeitgeist** m spirit of the times; **zeitgemäß** adj in keeping with the times; **Zeitgenosse** m contemporary; **zeitgenössisch** ['tsaɪtgənœsɪʃ] adj contemporary

zeitig adj, adv early

Zeit- zW: **Zeitkarte** f season ticket; **zeitkritisch** adj (Aufsatz) commenting on contemporary issues; **zeitlebens** adv all one's life; **zeitlich** adj temporal ▷ adv: **das kann sie zeitlich nicht einrichten** she can't find (the) time for that; **das Zeitliche segnen** (euph) to depart this life; **zeitlos** adj timeless; **Zeitlupe** f slow motion; **Zeitlupentempo** nt: **im Zeitlupentempo** at a snail's pace; **Zeitnot** f: **in Zeitnot geraten** to run short of time; **Zeitplan** m schedule; **Zeitpunkt** m moment, point in time; **Zeitraffer** (**-s**) m time-lapse photography; **zeitraubend** adj time-consuming; **Zeitraum** m period; **Zeitrechnung** f time, era; **nach/vor unserer Zeitrechnung** A.D./B.C.; **Zeitschrift** f periodical; **Zeittafel** f chronological table

Zeitung f newspaper

Zeitungs- zW: **Zeitungsanzeige** f newspaper advertisement; **Zeitungsausschnitt** m press cutting; **Zeitungshändler** m newsagent

(Brit), newsdealer (US); **Zeitungspapier** nt newsprint; **Zeitungsstand** m newsstand

Zeit- zW: **Zeitverschwendung** f waste of time; **Zeitvertreib** m pastime, diversion; **zeitweilig** adj temporary; **zeitweise** adv for a time; **Zeitwort** nt verb; **Zeitzeichen** nt (Rundf) time signal; **Zeitzone** f time zone; **Zeitzünder** m time fuse

Zelle ['tsɛlə] (-, -n) f cell; (Telefonzelle) callbox (Brit), booth

Zellkern m cell, nucleus

Zellophan [tsɛlo'faːn] (-s) nt cellophane

Zellstoff m cellulose

Zelt [tsɛlt] (-(e)s, -e) nt tent; **seine ~e aufschlagen/abbrechen** to settle down/pack one's bags; **Zeltbahn** f groundsheet; **zelten** vi to camp; **Zeltlager** nt camp; **Zeltplatz** m camp site

Zement [tse'mɛnt] (-(e)s, -e) m cement

zementieren [tsemɛn'tiːrən] vt to cement

Zementmaschine f cement mixer

Zenit [tse'niːt] (-(e)s) m (lit, fig) zenith

zensieren [tsɛn'ziːrən] vt to censor; (Sch) to mark

Zensur [tsɛn'zuːr] f censorship; (Sch) mark

Zensus ['tsɛnzʊs] (-, -) m census

Zentimeter [tsɛnti'meːtər] m od nt centimetre (Brit), centimeter (US); **Zentimetermaß** nt (metric) tape measure

Zentner ['tsɛntnər] (-s, -) m hundredweight

zentral [tsɛn'traːl] adj central

Zentrale (-, -n) f central office; (Tel) exchange

Zentraleinheit f (Comput) central processing unit

Zentralheizung f central heating

zentralisieren [tsɛntrali'ziːrən] vt to centralize

Zentralverriegelung f (Aut) central locking

Zentrifugalkraft [tsɛntrifu'gaːlkraft] f centrifugal force

Zentrifuge [tsɛntri'fuːgə] (-, -n) f centrifuge; (für Wäsche) spin-dryer

Zentrum ['tsɛntrʊm] (-s, Zentren) nt centre (Brit), center (US)

Zepter ['tsɛptər] (-s, -) nt sceptre (Brit), scepter (US)

zerbrechen unreg vt, vi to break

zerbrechlich adj fragile

zerbröckeln [tsɛr'brœkəln] vt, vi to crumble (to pieces)

zerdeppern [tsɛr'dɛpərn] vt to smash

zerdrücken vt to squash; to crush; (Kartoffeln) to mash

Zeremonie [tseremo'niː] f ceremony

Zeremoniell [tseremoni'ɛl] (-s, -e) nt ceremonial

zerfahren adj scatterbrained, distracted

Zerfall m decay, disintegration; (von Kultur, Gesundheit) decline; **zerfallen** unreg vi to disintegrate, decay; (sich gliedern): **zerfallen in** +akk to fall into

zerfetzen [tsɛr'fɛtsən] vt to tear to pieces

zerfleischen [tsɛr'flaɪʃən] vt to tear to pieces

zerfließen unreg vi to dissolve, melt away

zerfressen unreg vt to eat away; (Motten, Mäuse etc) to eat

zergehen unreg vi to melt, dissolve

zerkleinern [tsɛr'klaɪnərn] vt to reduce to small pieces

zerklüftet [tsɛr'klyftət] adj: **tief ~es Gestein** deeply fissured rock

zerknirscht [tsɛr'knɪrʃt] adj overcome with remorse

zerknüllen [tsɛr'knʏlən] vt to crumple up

zerlaufen unreg vi to melt

zerlegbar [tsɛr'leːkbaːr] adj able to be dismantled

zerlegen vt to take to pieces; (Fleisch) to carve; (Satz) to analyse

zerlumpt [tsɛr'lʊmpt] adj ragged

zermalmen [tsɛr'malmən] vt to crush

zermürben [tsɛr'mʏrbən] vt to wear down

zerpflücken vt (lit, fig) to pick to pieces

zerplatzen vi to burst

zerquetschen vt to squash

Zerrbild ['tsɛrbɪlt] nt (fig) caricature, distorted picture

zerreden vt (Problem) to flog to death

zerreiben unreg vt to grind down

zerreißen unreg vt to tear to pieces ▷ vi to tear, rip

Zerreißprobe f (lit) pull test; (fig) real test

zerren ['tsɛrən] vt to drag ▷ vi: **~ (an** +dat) to tug (at)

zerrinnen unreg vi to melt away; (Geld) to disappear

zerrissen [tsɛr'rɪsən] pp von **zerreißen** ▷ adj torn, tattered; **Zerrissenheit** f tattered state; (Pol) disunion, discord; (innere) disintegration

Zerrspiegel ['tsɛrʃpiːgəl] m (lit) distorting mirror; (fig) travesty

Zerrung f: **eine ~** a pulled ligament/muscle

zerrütten [tsɛr'rʏtən] vt to wreck, destroy

zerrüttet adj wrecked, shattered

Zerrüttungsprinzip nt (bei Ehescheidung) principle of irretrievable breakdown

zerschellen [tsɛr'ʃɛlən] vi (Schiff, Flugzeug) to be smashed to pieces

zerschießen unreg vt to shoot to pieces

zerschlagen unreg vt to shatter, smash; (fig: Opposition) to crush; (: Vereinigung) to break up ▷ vr to fall through

zerschleißen [tsɛr'ʃlaɪsən] unreg vt, vi to wear out

zerschmelzen unreg vi to melt

zerschmettern unreg vt to shatter; (Feind) to crush ▷ vi to shatter

zerschneiden unreg vt to cut up

zersetzen vt, vr to decompose, dissolve

zersetzend adj (fig) subversive

zersplittern [tsɛr'ʃplɪtərn] vt, vi to split (into pieces); (Glas) to shatter

zerspringen unreg vi to shatter ▷ vi (fig) to burst

zerstäuben [tsɛr'ʃtɔʏbən] vt to spray

Zerstäuber (-s, -) m atomizer

zerstören vt to destroy

Zerstörer (-s, -) m (Naut) destroyer

z

Zerstörung f destruction
Zerstörungswut f destructive mania
zerstoßen unreg vt to pound, pulverize
zerstreiten unreg vr to fall out, break up
zerstreuen vt to disperse, scatter; (Zweifel etc) to dispel ▷ vr (sich verteilen) to scatter; (fig) to be dispelled; (sich ablenken) to take one's mind off things
zerstreut adj scattered; (Mensch) absent-minded; **Zerstreutheit** f absent-mindedness
Zerstreuung f dispersion; (Ablenkung) diversion
zerstritten adj: **mit jdm ~ sein** to be on very bad terms with sb
zerstückeln [tsɛrˈʃtykəln] vt to cut into pieces
zerteilen vt to divide into parts
Zertifikat [tsɛrtifiˈkaːt] (-(e)s, -e) nt certificate
zertreten unreg vt to crush underfoot
zertrümmern [tsɛrˈtrymərn] vt to shatter; (Gebäude etc) to demolish
zerwühlen vt to ruffle up, tousle; (Bett) to rumple (up)
Zerwürfnis [tsɛrˈvyrfnɪs] (-ses, -se) nt dissension, quarrel
zerzausen [tsɛrˈtsauzən] vt (Haare) to ruffle up, tousle
zetern [ˈtseːtərn] (pej) vi to clamour (Brit), clamor (US); (keifen) to scold
Zettel [ˈtsɛtəl] (-s, -) m piece od slip of paper; (Notizzettel) note; (Formular) form; „~ **ankleben verboten**" "stick no bills"; **Zettelkasten** m card index (box); **Zettelwirtschaft** (pej) f: **eine Zettelwirtschaft haben** to have bits of paper everywhere
Zeug [tsɔʏk] (-(e)s, -e) (umg) nt stuff; (Ausrüstung) gear; **dummes ~** (stupid) nonsense; **das ~ haben zu** to have the makings of; **sich ins ~ legen** to put one's shoulder to the wheel; **was das ~ hält** for all one is worth; **jdm am ~ flicken** to find fault with sb
Zeuge [ˈtsɔʏɡə] (-n, -n) m witness
zeugen vi to bear witness, testify ▷ vt (Kind) to father; **es zeugt von ...** it testifies to ...
Zeugenaussage f evidence
Zeugenstand m witness box (Brit) od stand (US)
Zeugin f witness
Zeugnis [ˈtsɔʏɡnɪs] (-ses, -se) nt certificate; (Sch) report; (Referenz) reference; (Aussage) evidence, testimony; **~ geben von** to be evidence of, testify to; **Zeugniskonferenz** f (Sch) staff meeting to decide on marks etc
Zeugung [ˈtsɔʏɡuŋ] f procreation
zeugungsunfähig adj sterile
ZH abk = **Zentralheizung**
z. H., z. Hd. abk (= zu Händen) att., attn.
Zicken [ˈtsɪkən] (umg) pl: **~ machen** to make trouble
zickig adj (albern) silly; (prüde) prudish
Zickzack [ˈtsɪktsak] (-(e)s, -e) m zigzag
Ziege [ˈtsiːɡə] (-, -n) f goat; (pej: umg: Frau) cow (!)
Ziegel [ˈtsiːɡəl] (-s, -) m brick; (Dachziegel) tile

Ziegelei [tsiːɡəˈlaɪ] f brickworks
Ziegelstein m brick
Ziegenbock m billy goat
Ziegenleder nt kid
Ziegenpeter m mumps sing
Ziehbrunnen m well
ziehen [ˈtsiːən] unreg vt to draw; (zerren) to pull; (Schach etc) to move; (züchten) to rear ▷ vi to draw; (umziehen, wandern) to move; (Rauch, Wolke etc) to drift; (reißen) to pull ▷ vb unpers: **es zieht** there is a draught (Brit) od draft (US), it's draughty (Brit) od drafty (US) ▷ vr (Gummi) to stretch; (Grenze etc) to run; (Gespräche) to be drawn out; **etw nach sich ~** to lead to sth, entail sth; **etw ins Lächerliche ~** to ridicule sth; **so was zieht bei mir nicht** I don't like that sort of thing; **zu jdm ~** to move in with sb; **mir ziehts im Rücken** my back hurts; **Ziehen** (-s, -) nt (Schmerz) ache; (im Unterleib) dragging pain
Ziehharmonika [ˈtsiːharmoːnika] f concertina
Ziehung [ˈtsiːʊŋ] f (Losziehung) drawing
Ziel [tsiːl] (-(e)s, -e) nt (einer Reise) destination; (Sport) finish; (Mil) target; (Absicht) goal, aim; **jdm/sich ein ~ stecken** to set sb/o.s. a goal; **am ~ sein** to be at one's destination; (fig) to have reached one's goal; **über das ~ hinausschießen** (fig) to overshoot the mark; **zielbewusst** adj purposeful; **zielen** vi: **zielen (auf +akk)** to aim (at); **Zielfernrohr** nt telescopic sight; **Zielfoto** nt (Sport) photo-finish, photograph; **Zielgruppe** f target group; **Ziellinie** f (Sport) finishing line; **ziellos** adj aimless; **Zielort** m destination; **Zielscheibe** f target; **zielstrebig** adj purposeful
ziemen [ˈtsiːmən] vr unpers (geh): **das ziemt sich nicht (für dich)** it is not proper (for you)
ziemlich [ˈtsiːmlɪç] adj attrib (Anzahl) fair ▷ adv quite, pretty (umg); (beinahe) almost, nearly; **eine ~e Anstrengung** quite an effort; **~ lange** quite a long time; **~ fertig** almost od nearly ready
Zierde [ˈtsiːrdə] (-, -n) f ornament, decoration; (Schmuckstück) adornment
zieren [ˈtsiːrən] vr to act coy
Zierleiste f border; (an Wand, Möbeln) moulding (Brit), molding (US); (an Auto) trim
zierlich adj dainty; **Zierlichkeit** f daintiness
Zierstrauch m flowering shrub
Ziffer [ˈtsɪfər] (-, -n) f figure, digit; **römische/ arabische ~n** roman/arabic numerals; **Zifferblatt** nt dial, (clock od watch) face
zig [tsɪk] (umg) adj umpteen
Zigarette [tsigaˈrɛtə] f cigarette
Zigaretten- zW: **Zigarettenautomat** m cigarette machine; **Zigarettenpause** f break for a cigarette; **Zigarettenschachtel** f cigarette packet od pack (US); **Zigarettenspitze** f cigarette holder
Zigarillo [tsigaˈrɪlo] (-s, -s) nt od m cigarillo
Zigarre [tsiˈɡarə] (-, -n) f cigar
Zigeuner, in [tsiˈɡɔʏnər(ɪn)] (-s, -) m(f) gipsy; **Zigeunerschnitzel** nt (Koch) cutlet served in a spicy

sauce with green and red peppers; **Zigeunersprache** f Romany (language)

Zimmer ['tsɪmər] **(-s, -)** *nt* room; **Zimmerantenne** f indoor aerial; **Zimmerdecke** f ceiling; **Zimmerlautstärke** f reasonable volume; **Zimmermädchen** *nt* chambermaid; **Zimmermann** **(-(e)s,** *pl* **-leute)** *m* carpenter

zimmern *vt* to make from wood

Zimmer- *zW:* **Zimmernachweis** *m* accommodation service; **Zimmerpflanze** f indoor plant; **Zimmervermittlung** f accommodation (*Brit*) *od* accommodations (*US*) service

zimperlich ['tsɪmpərlɪç] *adj* squeamish; (*pingelig*) fussy, finicky

Zimt [tsɪmt] **(-(e)s, -e)** *m* cinnamon; **Zimtstange** f cinnamon stick

Zink [tsɪŋk] **(-(e)s)** *nt* zinc

Zinke **(-, -n)** f (*Gabelzinke*) prong; (*Kammzinke*) tooth

Zinken **(-s, -)** (*umg*) *m* (*Nase*) hooter

zinken *vt* (*Karten*) to mark

Zinksalbe f zinc ointment

Zinn [tsɪn] **(-(e)s)** *nt* (*Element*) tin; (*in Zinnwaren*) pewter; **Zinnbecher** *m* pewter tankard

zinnoberrot [tsɪ'no:bərrot] *adj* vermilion

Zinnsoldat *m* tin soldier

Zinnwaren *pl* pewter *sing*

Zins [tsɪns] **(-es, -en)** *m* interest

Zinseszins *m* compound interest

Zins- *zW:* **Zinsfuß** *m* rate of interest; **zinslos** *adj* interest-free; **Zinssatz** *m* rate of interest; **Zinssteuer** f tax on interest

Zionismus [tsio'nɪsmʊs] *m* Zionism

Zipfel ['tsɪpfəl] **(-s, -)** *m* corner; (*von Land*) tip; (*Hemdzipfel*) tail; (*Wurstzipfel*) end; **Zipfelmütze** f pointed cap

zirka ['tsɪrka] *adv* = **circa**

Zirkel ['tsɪrkəl] **(-s, -)** *m* circle; (*Math*) pair of compasses; **Zirkelkasten** *m* geometry set

zirkulieren [tsɪrku'li:rən] *vi* to circulate

Zirkus ['tsɪrkʊs] **(-, -se)** *m* circus; (*umg: Getue*) fuss, to-do

zirpen ['tsɪrpən] *vi* to chirp, cheep

Zirrhose [tsɪ'ro:zə] **(-, -n)** f cirrhosis

zischeln ['tsɪʃəln] *vt, vi* to whisper

zischen ['tsɪʃən] *vi* to hiss; (*Limonade*) to fizz; (*Fett*) to sizzle

Zitat [tsi'ta:t] **(-(e)s, -e)** *nt* quotation, quote

zitieren [tsi'ti:rən] *vt* to quote; (*vorladen, rufen*): ~ **(vor** +*akk*) to summon (before)

Zitronat [tsitro'na:t] **(-(e)s, -e)** *nt* candied lemon peel

Zitrone [tsi'tro:nə] **(-, -n)** f lemon

Zitronen- *zW:* **Zitronenlimonade** f lemonade; **Zitronensaft** *m* lemon juice; **Zitronensäure** f citric acid; **Zitronenscheibe** f lemon slice

zitterig ['tsɪtərɪç], **zittrig** ['tsɪtrɪç] *adj* shaky

zittern ['tsɪtərn] *vi* to tremble; **vor jdm ~** to be terrified of sb

Zitze ['tsɪtsə] **(-, -n)** f teat, dug

Zivi ['tsivi] **(-s, -s)** *m abk* = **Zivildienstleistender**

zivil [tsi'vi:l] *adj* civilian; (*anständig*) civil; (*Preis*) moderate; **~er Ungehorsam** civil disobedience; **Zivil (-s)** *nt* plain clothes *pl*; (*Mil*) civilian clothing; **Zivilbevölkerung** f civilian population; **Zivilcourage** f courage of one's convictions

Zivildienst *m* alternative service (for conscientious objectors); *see culture note*

Zivildienstleistender *m conscientious objector doing alternative community service*

Zivilisation [tsivilizatsi'o:n] f civilization

Zivilisationserscheinung f phenomenon of civilization

Zivilisationskrankheit f disease of civilized man

zivilisieren [tsivili'zi:rən] *vt* to civilize

zivilisiert *adj* civilized

Zivilist [tsivi'lɪst] *m* civilian

Zivilrecht *nt* civil law

ZK (-s, -s) *nt abk* (= *Zentralkomitee*) central committee

Zobel ['tso:bəl] **(-s, -)** *m* (*auch:* **Zobelpelz**) sable (fur)

Zofe ['tso:fə] **(-, -n)** f lady's maid; (*von Königin*) lady-in-waiting

zog *etc* [tso:k] *vb siehe* **ziehen**

zögern ['tsø:gərn] *vi* to hesitate

Zölibat [tsøli'ba:t] **(-(e)s)** *nt od m* celibacy

Zoll¹ [tsɔl] **(-(e)s, -)** *m* (*Maß*) inch

Zoll² **(-(e)s, ¨e)** *m* customs *pl*; (*Abgabe*) duty; **Zollabfertigung** f customs clearance; **Zollamt** *nt* customs office; **Zollbeamte, r** *m* customs official; **Zollerklärung** f customs declaration; **zollfrei** *adj* duty-free; **Zollgutlager** *nt* bonded warehouse; **Zollkontrolle** f customs (check); **zollpflichtig** *adj* liable to duty, dutiable

Zollstock *m* inch rule

Zone ['tso:nə] **(-, -n)** f zone; (*von Fahrkarte*) fare stage

Zoo [tso:] **(-s, -s)** *m* zoo; **Zoohandlung** f pet shop

Zoologe [tsoo'lo:gə] **(-n, -n)** *m* zoologist

Zoologie f zoology

Zoologin f zoologist

zoologisch *adj* zoological

Zoom [zu:m] **(-s, -s)** *nt* zoom shot; (*Objektiv*) zoom lens

Zopf [tsɔpf] **(-(e)s, ¨e)** *m* plait; pigtail; **alter ~** antiquated custom

Zorn [tsɔrn] **(-(e)s)** *m* anger

zornig *adj* angry

Z

399

Zote ['tso:tə] (-, -n) f smutty joke/remark

zottig ['tsɔtıç] adj shaggy

ZPO abk (= Zivilprozessordnung) ≈ General Practice Act (US)

z. T. abk = **zum Teil**

⬤ SCHLÜSSELWORT

zu [tsu:] präp +dat **1** (örtlich) to; **zum Bahnhof/ Arzt gehen** to go to the station/doctor; **zur Schule/Kirche gehen** to go to school/church; **sollen wir zu Euch gehen?** shall we go to your place?; **sie sah zu ihm hin** she looked towards him; **zum Fenster herein** through the window; **zu meiner Linken** to od on my left

2 (zeitlich) at; **zu Ostern** at Easter; **bis zum 1. Mai** until May 1st; (nicht später als) by May 1st; **zu meiner Zeit** in my time

3 (Zusatz) with; **Wein zum Essen trinken** to drink wine with one's meal; **sich zu jdm setzen** to sit down beside sb; **setz dich doch zu uns** (come and) sit with us; **Anmerkungen zu etw** notes on sth

4 (Zweck) for; **Wasser zum Waschen** water for washing; **Papier zum Schreiben** paper to write on; **etw zum Geburtstag bekommen** to get sth for one's birthday; **es ist zu seinem Besten** it's for his own good

5 (Veränderung) into; **zu etw werden** to turn into sth; **jdn zu etw machen** to make sb (into) sth; **zu Asche verbrennen** to burn to ashes

6 (mit Zahlen): **3 zu 2** (Sport) 3-2; **das Stück zu 5 Euro** at 5 euros each; **zum ersten Mal** for the first time

7: zu meiner Freude etc to my joy etc; **zum Glück** luckily; **zu Fuß** on foot; **es ist zum Weinen** it's enough to make you cry

▷ konj to; **etw zu essen** sth to eat; **um besser sehen zu können** in order to see better; **ohne es zu wissen** without knowing it; **noch zu bezahlende Rechnungen** outstanding bills

▷ adv **1** (allzu) too; **zu sehr** too much; **zu viel** too much; (umg: zu viele) too many; **er kriegt zu viel** (umg) he gets annoyed; **zu wenig** too little; (umg: zu wenige) too few

2 (örtlich) toward(s); **er kam auf mich zu** he came towards od up to me

3 (geschlossen) shut; closed; **die Geschäfte haben zu** the shops are closed; **zu sein** to be closed; **auf/zu** (Wasserhahn etc) on/off

4 (umg: los): **nur zu!** just keep at it!; **mach zu!** hurry up!

zuallererst adv first of all

zuallerletzt adv last of all

zubauen ['tsu:bauən] vt (Lücke) to fill in; (Platz, Gebäude) to build up

Zubehör ['tsu:bəhøːr] (-(e)s, -e) nt accessories pl

Zuber ['tsu:bər] (-s, -) m tub

zubereiten ['tsu:bəraıtən] vt to prepare

zubilligen ['tsu:bılıgən] vt to grant

zubinden ['tsu:bındən] unreg vt to tie up; **jdm die Augen ~** to blindfold sb

zubleiben ['tsu:blaıbən] unreg vi to stay shut

zubringen ['tsu:brıŋən] unreg vt to spend; (herbeibringen) to bring, take; (umg: Tür) to get shut

Zubringer (-s, -) m (Tech) feeder, conveyor; (Verkehrsmittel) shuttle; (zum Flughafen) airport bus; **Zubringerbus** m shuttle (bus); **Zubringerstraße** f slip road (Brit), entrance ramp (US)

Zucchini [tsʊ'ki:ni:] pl courgettes pl (Brit), zucchini(s) pl (US)

Zucht [tsʊxt] (-, -en) f (von Tieren) breeding; (von Pflanzen) cultivation; (Rasse) breed; (Erziehung) raising; (Disziplin) discipline; **Zuchtbulle** m breeding bull

züchten ['tsʏçtən] vt (Tiere) to breed; (Pflanzen) to cultivate, grow

Züchter, in (-s, -) m(f) breeder; grower

Zuchthaus nt prison, penitentiary (US)

Zuchthengst m stallion, stud

züchtig ['tsʏçtıç] adj modest, demure

züchtigen ['tsʏçtıgən] vt to chastise

Züchtigung f chastisement; **körperliche ~** corporal punishment

Zuchtperle f cultured pearl

Züchtung f (von Tieren) breeding; (von Pflanzen) cultivation; (Zuchtart: von Tier) breed; (: von Pflanze) strain

zucken ['tsʊkən] vi to jerk, twitch; (Strahl etc) to flicker ▷ vt to shrug; **der Schmerz zuckte (mir) durch den ganzen Körper** the pain shot right through my body

zücken ['tsʏkən] vt (Schwert) to draw; (Geldbeutel) to pull out

Zucker ['tsʊkər] (-s, -) m sugar; (Med) diabetes; **~ haben** (umg) to be a diabetic; **Zuckerdose** f sugar bowl; **Zuckererbse** f mangetout (Brit), sugar pea (US); **Zuckerguss** m icing; **Zuckerhut** m sugar loaf; **zuckerkrank** adj diabetic; **Zuckerkrankheit** f diabetes sing; **Zuckerlecken** nt: **das ist kein Zuckerlecken** it's no picnic

zuckern vt to sugar

Zucker- zW: **Zuckerrohr** nt sugar cane; **Zuckerrübe** f sugar beet; **Zuckerspiegel** m (Med) (blood) sugar level; **zuckersüß** adj sugary; **Zuckerwatte** f candy floss (Brit), cotton candy (US)

Zuckung f convulsion, spasm; (leicht) twitch

zudecken ['tsu:dɛkən] vt to cover (up); (im Bett) to tuck up od in

zudem [tsu'de:m] adv in addition (to this)

zudrehen ['tsu:dre:ən] vt to turn off

zudringlich ['tsu:drıŋlıç] adj forward, pushy; (Nachbar etc) intrusive; **~ werden** to make advances; **Zudringlichkeit** f forwardness; intrusiveness

zudrücken ['tsu:drʏkən] vt to close; **jdm die Kehle ~** to throttle sb; **ein Auge ~** to turn a blind eye

zueinander [tsu|aɪ'nandər] adv to one other; (in Verbverbindung) together

zuerkennen ['tsu:|ɛrkɛnən] unreg vt: **jdm etw ~** to award sth to sb, award sb sth

zuerst [tsu'|eːrst] adv first; (zu Anfang) at first; **~ einmal** first of all

Zufahrt ['tsu:faːrt] f approach; „**keine ~ zum Krankenhaus**" "no access to hospital"

Zufahrtsstraße f approach road; (von Autobahn etc) slip road (Brit), entrance ramp (US)

Zufall ['tsu:fal] m chance; (Ereignis) coincidence; **durch ~** by accident; **so ein ~!** what a coincidence!

zufallen unreg vi to close, shut; (Anteil, Aufgabe): **jdm ~** to fall to sb

zufällig ['tsu:fɛlɪç] adj chance ▷ adv by chance; (in Frage) by any chance

Zufallstreffer m fluke

zufassen ['tsu:fasən] vi (zugreifen) to take hold (of it od them); (fig: schnell handeln) to seize the opportunity; (helfen) to lend a hand

zufliegen ['tsu:fliːgən] unreg vi: **ihm fliegt alles nur so zu** (fig) everything comes so easily to him

Zuflucht ['tsu:flʊxt] f recourse; (Ort) refuge; **zu etw ~ nehmen** (fig) to resort to sth

Zufluchtsort m, **Zufluchtsstätte** f place of refuge

Zufluss ['tsu:flʊs] m (Zufließen) inflow, influx; (Geog) tributary; (Comm) supply

zufolge [tsu'fɔlgə] präp +dat od +gen (laut) according to; (aufgrund) as a result of

zufrieden [tsu'friːdən] adj content(ed); **er ist mit nichts ~** nothing pleases him; **zufriedengeben** unreg vr: **sich mit etw zufriedengeben** to be satisfied with sth; **Zufriedenheit** f contentedness; (Befriedigtsein) satisfaction; **zufriedenlassen** unreg vt: **lass mich damit zufrieden!** (umg) shut up about it!; **zufriedenstellen** vt to satisfy; **zufriedenstellend** adj satisfactory

zufrieren ['tsu:friːrən] unreg vi to freeze up od over

zufügen ['tsu:fyːgən] vt to add; (Leid etc): **jdm etw ~** to cause sb sth

Zufuhr ['tsu:fuːr] (**-, -en**) f (Herbeibringen) supplying; (Met) influx; (Mil) supplies pl

zuführen ['tsu:fyːrən] vt (bringen) to bring; (transportieren) to convey; (versorgen) to supply ▷ vi: **auf etw** akk **~** to lead to sth

Zug [tsuːk] (**-(e)s, ⁻e**) m (Eisenbahnzug) train; (Luftzug) draught (Brit), draft (US); (Ziehen) pull(ing); (Gesichtszug) feature; (Schach etc) move; (Klingelzug) pull; (Schriftzug, beim Schwimmen) stroke; (Atemzug) breath; (Charakterzug) trait; (an Zigarette) puff, pull, drag; (Schluck) gulp; (Menschengruppe) procession; (von Vögeln) migration; (Mil) platoon; **etw in vollen Zügen genießen** to enjoy sth to the full; **in den letzten Zügen liegen** (umg) to be at one's last gasp; **im ~(e)** +gen (im Verlauf) in the course of; **~ um Zug** (fig) step by step; **zum ~(e) kommen** (umg) to get

a look-in; **etw in groben Zügen darstellen** od **umreißen** to outline sth; **das war kein schöner ~ von dir** that wasn't nice of you

Zugabe ['tsu:gaːbə] f extra; (in Konzert etc) encore

Zugabteil nt train compartment

Zugang ['tsu:gaŋ] m entrance; (Zutritt, fig) access

zugänglich ['tsu:gɛŋlɪç] adj accessible; (öffentliche Einrichtungen) open; (Mensch) approachable

Zugangscode m (Comput) access code

Zugbegleiter m (Eisenb) guard (Brit), conductor (US)

Zugbrücke f drawbridge

zugeben ['tsu:geːbən] unreg vt (beifügen) to add, throw in; (zugestehen) to admit; (erlauben) to permit; **zugegeben ...** granted ...

zugegebenermaßen ['tsu:gegəːbənər'maːsən] adv admittedly

zugegen [tsu'geːgən] adv (geh): **~ sein** to be present

zugehen ['tsu:geːən] unreg vi (schließen) to shut ▷ vi unpers (sich ereignen) to go on, happen; **auf jdn/etw ~** to walk towards sb/sth; **dem Ende ~** to be finishing; **er geht schon auf die siebzig zu** he's getting on for seventy; **hier geht es nicht mit rechten Dingen zu** there's something going on here; **dort geht es ... zu** things are ... there

Zugehörigkeit ['tsu:gəhœːrɪçkaɪt] f: **~ (zu)** membership (of), belonging (to)

Zugehörigkeitsgefühl nt feeling of belonging

zugeknöpft ['tsu:gəknœpft] (umg) adj reserved, stand-offish

Zügel ['tsyːgəl] (**-s, -**) m rein, reins pl; (fig) rein, curb; **die ~ locker lassen** to slacken one's hold on the reins; **die ~ locker lassen bei** (fig) to give free rein to

zugelassen ['tsu:gəlasən] adj authorized; (Heilpraktiker) registered; (Kfz) licensed

zügellos adj unrestrained; (sexuell) licentious

Zügellosigkeit f lack of restraint; licentiousness

zügeln vt to curb; (Pferd) to rein in

zugesellen vr: **sich jdm ~** to join sb, join up with sb

Zugeständnis ['tsu:gəʃtɛntnɪs] (**-ses, -se**) nt concession; **~se machen** to make allowances

zugestehen unreg vt to admit; (Rechte) to concede

zugetan ['tsu:gətaːn] adj: **jdm/etw ~ sein** to be fond of sb/sth

Zugewinn (**-(e)s**) m (Jur) property acquired during marriage

Zugezogene, r ['tsu:gətsoːgənə(r)] f(m) newcomer

Zugführer m (Eisenb) chief guard (Brit) od conductor (US); (Mil) platoon commander

zugig adj draughty (Brit), drafty (US)

zügig ['tsyːgɪç] adj speedy, swift

zugkräftig adj (fig: Werbetext, Titel) eye-catching; (Schauspieler) crowd-pulling attr,

z

popular

zugleich [tsu'glaɪç] *adv* (*zur gleichen Zeit*) at the same time; (*ebenso*) both

Zugluft *f* draught (*Brit*), draft (*US*)

Zugmaschine *f* traction engine, tractor

zugreifen ['tsu:ɡraɪfən] *unreg vi* to seize *od* grab it/them; (*helfen*) to help; (*beim Essen*) to help o.s.

Zugriff ['tsu:ɡrɪf] *m* (*Comput*) access; **sich dem ~ der Polizei entziehen** (*fig*) to evade justice

zugrunde, zu Grunde [tsu'ɡrʊndə] *adv*: **~ gehen** to collapse; (*Mensch*) to perish; **er wird daran nicht ~ gehen** he'll survive; (*finanziell*) it won't ruin him; **einer Sache** *dat* **etw ~ legen** to base sth on sth; **einer Sache** *dat* **~ liegen** to be based on sth; **~ richten** to ruin, destroy

zugunsten, zu Gunsten [tsu'ɡʊnstən] *präp* +*gen od* +*dat* in favour (*Brit*) *od* favor (*US*) of

zugutehalten [tsu'ɡu:təhaltən] *unreg vt*: **jdm etw ~** to concede sth to sb

zugutekommen [tsu'ɡu:təkɔmən] *unreg vt*: **jdm ~** to be of assistance to sb

Zug- *zW*: **Zugverbindung** *f* train connection; **Zugvogel** *m* migratory bird; **Zugzwang** *m* (*Schach*) zugzwang; **unter Zugzwang stehen** (*fig*) to be in a tight spot

zuhalten ['tsu:haltən] *unreg vt* to hold shut ▷ *vi*: **auf jdn/etw ~** to make for sb/sth; **sich** *dat* **die Nase ~** to hold one's nose

Zuhälter ['tsu:hɛltər] (**-s, -**) *m* pimp

zuhause [tsu'haʊzə] *adv* at home

Zuhause (**-s**) *nt* home

Zuhilfenahme [tsu'hɪlfəna:mə] *f*: **unter ~ von** with the help of

zuhören ['tsu:hø:rən] *vi* to listen

Zuhörer (**-s, -**) *m* listener; **Zuhörerschaft** *f* audience

zujubeln ['tsu:ju:bəln] *vi*: **jdm ~** to cheer sb

zukehren ['tsu:ke:rən] *vt* (*zuwenden*) to turn

zuklappen ['tsu:klapən] *vt* (*Buch, Deckel*) to close ▷ *vi* (*Hilfsverb sein: Tür etc*) to click shut

zukleben ['tsu:kle:bən] *vt* to paste up

zukneifen ['tsu:knaɪfən] *vt* (*Augen*) to screw up; (*Mund*) to shut tight(ly)

zuknöpfen ['tsu:knœpfən] *vt* to button (up), fasten (up)

zukommen ['tsu:kɔmən] *unreg vi* to come up; **auf jdn ~** to come up to sb; **jdm ~** (*sich gehören*) to be fitting for sb; **diesem Treffen kommt große Bedeutung zu** this meeting is of the utmost importance; **jdm etw ~ lassen** to give sb sth; **die Dinge auf sich** *akk* **~ lassen** to take things as they come

Zukunft ['tsu:kʊnft] (**-**, *no pl*) *f* future

zukünftig ['tsu:kʏnftɪç] *adj* future ▷ *adv* in future; **mein ~er Mann** my husband-to-be

Zukunfts- *zW*: **Zukunftsaussichten** *pl* future prospects *pl*; **Zukunftsmusik** (*umg*) *f* wishful thinking; **Zukunftsroman** *m* science-fiction novel; **zukunftsträchtig** *adj* promising for the future; **zukunftsweisend** *adj* trend-setting

Zulage ['tsu:la:ɡə] *f* bonus

zulande [tsu'landə] *adv*: **bei uns ~** in our country

zulangen ['tsu:laŋən] (*umg*) *vi* (*Dieb, beim Essen*) to help o.s.

zulassen ['tsu:lasən] *unreg vt* (*hereinlassen*) to admit; (*erlauben*) to permit; (*Auto*) to license; (*umg: nicht öffnen*) to keep shut

zulässig ['tsu:lɛsɪç] *adj* permissible, permitted; **~e Höchstgeschwindigkeit** (upper) speed limit

Zulassung *f* (*amtlich*) authorization; (*von Kfz*) licensing; (*als praktizierender Arzt*) registration

Zulauf *m*: **großen ~ haben** (*Geschäft*) to be very popular

zulaufen ['tsu:laʊfən] *unreg vi*: **~ auf** +*akk* to run towards; **jdm ~** (*Tier*) to adopt sb; **spitz ~** to come to a point

zulegen ['tsu:le:ɡən] *vt* to add; (*Geld*) to put in; (*Tempo*) to accelerate, quicken; (*schließen*) to cover over; **sich** *dat* **etw ~** (*umg*) to get oneself sth

zuleide [tsu'laɪdə] *adj*: **jdm etw ~ tun** to harm sb

zuleiten ['tsu:laɪtən] *vt* (*Wasser*) to supply; (*schicken*) to send

Zuleitung *f* (*Tech*) supply

zuletzt [tsu'lɛtst] *adv* finally, at last; **wir blieben bis ~** we stayed to the very end; **nicht ~ wegen** not least because of

zuliebe [tsu'li:bə] *adv*: **jdm ~** (in order) to please sb

Zulieferbetrieb ['tsu:li:fərbətri:p] *m* (*Comm*) supplier

zum [tsʊm] = **zu dem**; **~ dritten Mal** for the third time; **~ Scherz** as a joke; **~ Trinken** for drinking; **bis ~ 15. April** until 15th April; (*nicht später als*) by 15th April; **~ ersten Mal(e)** for the first time; **es ist ~ Weinen** it's enough to make you (want to) weep; **~ Glück** luckily

zumachen ['tsu:maxən] *vt* to shut; (*Kleidung*) to do up, fasten ▷ *vi* to shut; (*umg*) to hurry up

zumal [tsu'ma:l] *konj* especially (as)

zumeist [tsu'maɪst] *adv* mostly

zumessen ['tsu:mɛsən] *unreg vt* (+*dat*) (*Zeit*) to allocate (for); (*Bedeutung*) to attach (to)

zumindest [tsu'mɪndəst] *adv* at least

zumutbar ['tsu:mu:tba:r] *adj* reasonable

zumute [tsu'mu:tə] *adv*: **wie ist ihm ~?** how does he feel?

zumuten ['tsu:mu:tən] *vt*: **(jdm) etw ~** to expect *od* ask sth (of sb); **sich** *dat* **zu viel ~** to take on too much

Zumutung *f* unreasonable expectation *od* demand; (*Unverschämtheit*) impertinence; **das ist eine ~!** that's a bit much!

zunächst [tsu'nɛ:çst] *adv* first of all; **~ einmal** to start with

zunageln ['tsu:na:ɡəln] *vt* (*Fenster etc*) to nail up; (*Kiste etc*) to nail down

zunähen ['tsu:nɛ:ən] *vt* to sew up

Zunahme ['tsu:na:mə] (**-, -n**) *f* increase

Zuname ['tsu:na:mə] *m* surname

zünden ['tsʏndən] *vi* (*Feuer*) to light, ignite;

(*Motor*) to fire; (*fig*) to kindle enthusiasm ▷ *vt* to ignite; (*Rakete*) to fire

zündend *adj* fiery

Zünder (-s, -) *m* fuse; (*Mil*) detonator

Zünd- *ZW:* **Zündholz** *nt* match; **Zündkabel** *nt* (*Aut*) plug lead; **Zündkerze** *f* (*Aut*) spark(ing) plug; **Zündplättchen** *nt* cap; **Zündschlüssel** *m* ignition key; **Zündschnur** *f* fuse wire; **Zündstoff** *m* fuel; (*fig*) dynamite

Zündung *f* ignition

zunehmen ['tsu:ne:mən] *unreg vi* to increase, grow; (*Mensch*) to put on weight

zunehmend *adj:* **mit ~em Alter** with advancing age

zuneigen ['tsu:naɪgən] *vi* to incline, lean; **sich dem Ende ~** to draw to a close; **einer Auffassung ~** to incline towards a view; **jdm zugeneigt sein** to be attracted to sb

Zuneigung *f* affection

Zunft [tsʊnft] **(-, ̈-e)** *f* guild

zünftig ['tsʏnftɪç] *adj* (*Arbeit*) professional; (*umg: ordentlich*) proper, real

Zunge ['tsʊŋə] *f* tongue; (*Fisch*) sole; **böse ~n behaupten, …** malicious gossip has it …

züngeln ['tsʏŋəln] *vi* (*Flammen*) to lick

Zungenbrecher *m* tongue-twister

zungenfertig *adj* glib

Zünglein ['tsʏŋlaɪn] *nt:* **das ~ an der Waage sein** (*fig*) to tip the scales

zunichtemachen [tsu'nɪçtəmaxən] *vt* to ruin, destroy

zunichtewerden [tsu'nɪçtəve:rdən] *unreg vi* to come to nothing

zunutze [tsu'nʊtsə] *adv:* **sich** *dat* **etw ~ machen** to make use of sth

zuoberst [tsu'|o:bərst] *adv* at the top

zuordnen ['tsu:|ɔrdnən] *vt* to assign

zupacken ['tsu:pakən] (*umg*) *vi* (*zugreifen*) to make a grab for it; (*bei der Arbeit*) to get down to it; **mit ~** (*helfen*) to give me/them *etc* a hand

zupfen ['tsʊpfən] *vt* to pull, pick, pluck; (*Gitarre*) to pluck

zur [tsu:r] = **zu der**

zurate, zu Rate [tsu'ra:tə] *adv:* **jdm ~ ziehen** to consult sb

zurechnungsfähig ['tsu:rɛçnʊŋsfɛ:ɪç] *adj* (*Jur*) responsible, of sound mind; **Zurechnungsfähigkeit** *f* responsibility, accountability

zurecht- *ZW:* **zurechtbiegen** *unreg vt* to bend into shape; (*fig*) to twist; **zurechtfinden** *unreg vr* to find one's way (about); **zurechtkommen** *unreg vi* (*rechtzeitig kommen*) to come in time; (*schaffen*) to cope; (*finanziell*) to manage; **zurechtlegen** *vt* to get ready; (*Ausrede etc*) to have ready; **zurechtmachen** *vt* to prepare ▷ *vr* to get ready; (*sich schminken*) to put on one's make-up; **zurechtweisen** *unreg vt* to reprimand; **Zurechtweisung** *f* reprimand, rebuff

zureden ['tsu:re:dən] *vi:* **jdm ~** to persuade sb, urge sb

zureiten ['tsuraɪtən] *unreg vt* (*Pferd*) to break in

Zürich ['tsy:rɪç] **(-s)** *nt* Zurich

zurichten ['tsu:rɪçtən] *vt* (*Essen*) to prepare; (*beschädigen*) to batter, bash up

zürnen ['tsʏrnən] *vi:* **jdm ~** to be angry with sb

zurück [tsu'rʏk] *adv* back; (*mit Zahlungen*) behind; (*fig: zurückgeblieben: von Kind*) backward; **~!** get back!; **zurückbehalten** *unreg vt* to keep back; **er hat Schäden zurückbehalten** he suffered lasting damage; **zurückbekommen** *unreg vt* to get back; **zurückbezahlen** *vt* to repay, pay back; **zurückbleiben** *unreg vi* (*Mensch*) to remain behind; (*nicht nachkommen*) to fall behind, lag; (*Schaden*) to remain; **zurückbringen** *unreg vt* to bring back; **zurückdatieren** *vt* to backdate; **zurückdrängen** *vt* (*Gefühle*) to repress; (*Feind*) to push back; **zurückdrehen** *vt* to turn back; **zurückerobern** *vt* to reconquer; **zurückerstatten** *vt* to refund; **zurückfahren** *unreg vi* to travel back; (*vor Schreck*) to recoil ▷ *vt* to drive back; **zurückfallen** *unreg vi* to fall back; (*in Laster*) to relapse; (*in Leistungen*) to fall behind; (*an Besitzer*): **zurückfallen an** +*akk* to revert to; **zurückfinden** *unreg vi* to find one's way back; **zurückfordern** *vt* to demand back; **zurückführen** *vt* to lead back; **etw auf etw** *akk* **zurückführen** to trace sth back to sth; **zurückgeben** *unreg vt* to give back; (*antworten*) to retort with; **zurückgeblieben** *adj* retarded; **zurückgehen** *unreg vi* to go back; (*fallen*) to go down, fall; (*zeitlich*): **zurückgehen (auf** +*akk***)** to date back (to); **Waren zurückgehen lassen** to send back goods; **zurückgezogen** *adj* retired, withdrawn; **zurückgreifen** *unreg vi:* **zurückgreifen (auf** +*akk***)** (*fig*) to fall back (upon); (*zeitlich*) to go back (to); **zurückhalten** *unreg vt* to hold back; (*Mensch*) to restrain; (*hindern*) to prevent ▷ *vr* (*reserviert sein*) to be reserved; (*im Essen*) to hold back; (*im Hintergrund bleiben*) to keep in the background; (*bei Verhandlung*) to keep a low profile; **zurückhaltend** *adj* reserved; **Zurückhaltung** *f* reserve; **zurückholen** *vt* (*Comput: Daten*) to retrieve; **zurückkehren** *vi* to return; **zurückkommen** *unreg vi* to come back; **auf etw** *akk* **zurückkommen** to return to sth; **zurücklassen** *unreg vt* to leave behind; **zurücklegen** *vt* to put back; (*Geld*) to put by; (*reservieren*) to keep back; (*Strecke*) to cover ▷ *vr* to lie back; **zurückliegen** *unreg vi:* **der Unfall liegt etwa eine Woche zurück** the accident was about a week ago; **zurücknehmen** *unreg vt* to take back; **zurückreichen** *vi* (*Tradition etc*): **zurückreichen (in** +*akk***)** to go back (to); **zurückrufen** *unreg vt, vi* to call back; **etw ins Gedächtnis zurückrufen** to recall sth; **zurückschrauben** *vt:* **seine Ansprüche zurückschrauben** to lower one's sights; **zurückschrecken** *vi:* **zurückschrecken vor** +*dat* to shrink from; **vor nichts zurückschrecken** to stop at nothing; **zurücksetzen** *vt* to put back; (*im Preis*) to reduce; (*benachteiligen*) to put at

Z

a disadvantage ▷ vi (mit Fahrzeug) to reverse, back; **zurückstecken** vt to put back ▷ vi (fig) to moderate one's wishes; **zurückstellen** vt to put back, replace; (aufschieben) to put off, postpone; (Mil) to turn down; (Interessen) to defer; (Ware) to keep; **persönliche Interessen hinter etw** dat **zurückstellen** to put sth before one's personal interests; **zurückstoßen** unreg vt to repulse; **zurückstufen** vt to downgrade; **zurücktreten** unreg vi to step back; (vom Amt) to retire; (von einem Vertrag etc): **zurücktreten (von)** to withdraw (from); **gegenüber** od **hinter etw** dat **zurücktreten** to diminish in importance in view of sth; **bitte zurücktreten!** stand back, please!; **zurückverfolgen** vt (fig) to trace back; **zurückversetzen** vt (in alten Zustand): **zurückversetzen (in** +akk) to restore (to) ▷ vr: **sich zurückversetzen (in** +akk) to think back (to); **zurückweichen** unreg vi: **zurückweichen (vor** +dat) to shrink back (from); **zurückweisen** unreg vt to turn down; (Mensch) to reject; **zurückwerfen** unreg vt (Ball, Kopf) to throw back; (Strahlen, Schall) to reflect; (fig: Feind) to repel; (: wirtschaftlich): **zurückwerfen (um)** to set back (by); **zurückzahlen** vt to pay back, repay; **Zurückzahlung** f repayment; **zurückziehen** unreg vt to pull back; (Angebot) to withdraw ▷ vr to retire

Zuruf ['tsuːruːf] m shout, cry

zurzeit [tsʊrˈtsaɪt] adv at the moment

zus. abk = **zusammen**; **zusätzlich**

Zusage ['tsuːzaːɡə] f promise; (Annahme) consent

zusagen vt to promise ▷ vi to accept; **jdm etw auf den Kopf ~** (umg) to tell sb sth outright; **jdm ~** (gefallen) to appeal to od please sb

zusammen [tsuˈzamən] adv together;
Zusammenarbeit f cooperation;
zusammenarbeiten vi to cooperate;
Zusammenballung f accumulation;
zusammenbauen vt to assemble;
zusammenbeißen unreg vt (Zähne) to clench;
zusammenbleiben unreg vi to stay together;
zusammenbrauen (umg) vt to concoct ▷ vr (Gewitter, Unheil etc) to be brewing;
zusammenbrechen unreg vi (Hilfsverb sein) to collapse; (Mensch) to break down, collapse; (Verkehr etc) to come to a standstill;
zusammenbringen unreg vt to bring od get together; (Geld) to get; (Sätze) to put together;
Zusammenbruch m collapse; (Comput) crash; **zusammenfahren** unreg vi to collide; (erschrecken) to start; **zusammenfallen** unreg vi (einstürzen) to collapse; (Ereignisse) to coincide;
zusammenfassen vt to summarize; (vereinigen) to unite; **zusammenfassend** adj summarizing ▷ adv to summarize; **Zusammenfassung** f summary, résumé; **zusammenfinden** unreg vi, vr to meet (together);
zusammenfließen unreg vi to flow together, meet; **Zusammenfluss** m confluence;

zusammenfügen vt to join (together), unite;
zusammenführen vt to bring together; (Familie) to reunite; **zusammengehören** vi to belong together; (Paar) to match;
Zusammengehörigkeitsgefühl nt sense of belonging; **zusammengesetzt** adj compound, composite; **zusammengewürfelt** adj motley;
zusammenhalten unreg vt to hold together ▷ vi to hold together; (Freunde, fig) to stick together;
Zusammenhang m connection; **im/aus dem Zusammenhang** in/out of context; **etw aus dem Zusammenhang reißen** to take sth out of its context; **zusammenhängen** unreg vi to be connected od linked; **zusammenhängend** adj (Erzählung) coherent; **zusammenhanglos**, **zusammenhangslos** adj incoherent;
zusammenklappbar adj folding, collapsible;
zusammenklappen vt (Messer etc) to fold ▷ vi (umg: Mensch) to flake out; **zusammenknüllen** vt to crumple up; **zusammenkommen** unreg vi to meet, assemble; (sich ereignen) to occur at once od together; **zusammenkramen** vt to gather (together); **Zusammenkunft (-, -künfte)** f meeting; **zusammenlaufen** unreg vi to run od come together; (Straßen, Flüsse etc) to converge, meet; (Farben) to run into one another; **zusammenlegen** vt to put together; (stapeln) to pile up; (falten) to fold; (verbinden) to combine, unite; (Termine, Feste) to combine; (Geld) to collect; **zusammennehmen** unreg vt to summon up ▷ vr to pull o.s. together; **alles zusammengenommen** all in all;
zusammenpassen vi to go well together, match; **Zusammenprall** m (lit) collision; (fig) clash; **zusammenprallen** vi (Hilfsverb sein) to collide; **zusammenreimen** (umg) vt: **das kann ich mir nicht zusammenreimen** I can't make head nor tail of this; **zusammenreißen** unreg vr to pull o.s. together; **zusammenrotten** unreg (pej) vr to gang up; **zusammenschlagen** unreg vt (jdn) to beat up; (Dinge) to smash up; (falten) to fold; (Hände) to clap; (Hacken) to click; **zusammenschließen** unreg vt, vr to join (together); **Zusammenschluss** m amalgamation; **zusammenschmelzen** unreg vi (verschmelzen) to fuse; (zerschmelzen) to melt (away); (Anzahl) to dwindle;
zusammenschrecken unreg vi to start;
zusammenschreiben unreg vt to write together; (Bericht) to put together;
zusammenschrumpfen vi (Hilfsverb sein) to shrink, shrivel up; **Zusammensein (-s)** nt get-together; **zusammensetzen** vt to put together ▷ vr: **sich zusammensetzen aus** to consist of; **Zusammensetzung** f composition;
Zusammenspiel nt teamwork; (von Kräften etc) interaction; **zusammenstellen** vt to put together; **Zusammenstellung** f list; (Vorgang) compilation; **Zusammenstoß** m collision; **zusammenstoßen** unreg vi (Hilfsverb sein) to collide; **zusammenströmen** vi (Hilfsverb sein: Menschen) to flock together; **zusammentragen** unreg vt to collect;

Zusammentreffen nt meeting; (Zufall) coincidence; **zusammentreffen** unreg vi (Hilfsverb sein) to coincide; (Menschen) to meet; **zusammentreten** unreg vi (Verein etc) to meet; **zusammenwachsen** unreg vi to grow together; **zusammenwirken** vi to combine; **zusammenzählen** vt to add up; **zusammenziehen** unreg vt (verengern) to draw together; (vereinigen) to bring together; (addieren) to add up ▷ vr to shrink; (sich bilden) to form, develop; **zusammenzucken** vi (Hilfsverb sein) to start

Zusatz ['tsu:zats] m addition; **Zusatzantrag** m (Pol) amendment; **Zusatzgerät** nt attachment

zusätzlich ['tsu:zɛtslɪç] adj additional

Zusatzmittel nt additive

zuschauen ['tsu:ʃaʊən] vi to watch, look on

Zuschauer (**-s, -**) m spectator ▷ pl (Theat) audience sing

zuschicken ['tsu:ʃɪkən] vt: **jdm etw ~** to send od forward sth to sb

zuschießen ['tsu:ʃi:sən] unreg vt to fire; (Geld) to put in ▷ vi: **~ auf** +akk to rush towards

Zuschlag ['tsu:ʃla:k] m extra charge; (Erhöhung) surcharge; (Eisenb) supplement

zuschlagen ['tsu:ʃla:gən] unreg vt (Tür) to slam; (Ball) to hit; (bei Auktion) to knock down; (Steine etc) to knock into shape ▷ vi (Fenster, Tür) to shut; (Mensch) to hit, punch

zuschlagfrei adj (Eisenb) not subject to a supplement

zuschlagpflichtig adj subject to surcharge

Zuschlagskarte f (Eisenb) supplementary ticket

zuschließen ['tsu:ʃli:sən] unreg vt to lock (up)

zuschmeißen ['tsu:ʃmaɪsən] unreg (umg) vt to slam, bang shut

zuschmieren ['tsu:ʃmi:rən] vt to smear over; (Löcher) to fill in

zuschneiden ['tsu:ʃnaɪdən] unreg vt to cut to size; (Nähen) to cut out; **auf etw** akk **zugeschnitten sein** (fig) to be geared to sth

zuschnüren ['tsu:ʃny:rən] vt to tie up; **die Angst schnürte ihm die Kehle zu** (fig) he was choked with fear

zuschrauben ['tsu:ʃraʊbən] vt to screw shut

zuschreiben ['tsu:ʃraɪbən] unreg vt (fig) to ascribe, attribute; (Comm) to credit; **das hast du dir selbst zu~** you've only got yourself to blame

Zuschrift ['tsu:ʃrɪft] f letter, reply

zuschulden, zu Schulden [tsu:ʃʊldən] adv: **sich** dat **etw ~ kommen lassen** to make o.s. guilty of sth

Zuschuss ['tsu:ʃʊs] m subsidy

Zuschussbetrieb m loss-making concern

zuschütten ['tsu:ʃʏtən] vt to fill up

zusehen ['tsu:ze:ən] unreg vi to watch; (dafür sorgen) to take care; (etw dulden) to sit back (and watch); **jdm/etw ~** to watch sb/sth

zusehends adv visibly

zu sein ['tsu:zaɪn] siehe **zu**

zusenden ['tsu:zɛndən] unreg vt to forward, send on

zusetzen ['tsu:zɛtsən] vt (beifügen) to add; (Geld) to lose ▷ vi: **jdm ~** to harass sb; (Krankheit) to take a lot out of sb; (unter Druck setzen) to lean on sb (umg); (schwer treffen) to hit sb hard

zusichern ['tsu:zɪçərn] vt: **jdm etw ~** to assure sb of sth

Zusicherung f assurance

zusperren ['tsu:ʃpɛrən] vt to bar

zuspielen ['tsu:ʃpi:lən] vt, vi to pass; **jdm etw ~** to pass sth to sb; (fig) to pass sth on to sb; **etw der Presse ~** to leak sth to the press

zuspitzen ['tsu:ʃpɪtsən] vt to sharpen ▷ vr (Lage) to become critical

zusprechen ['tsu:ʃpreçən] unreg vt (zuerkennen): **jdm etw ~** to award sb sth, award sth to sb ▷ vi: **jdm ~** to speak to sb; **jdm Trost ~** to comfort sb; **dem Essen/Alkohol ~** to eat/drink a lot

Zuspruch ['tsu:ʃprʊx] m encouragement; (Anklang) popularity

Zustand ['tsu:ʃtant] m state, condition; **in gutem/schlechtem ~** in good/poor condition; (Haus) in good/bad repair; **Zustände bekommen** od **kriegen** (umg) to have a fit

zustande, zu Stande [tsu'ʃtandə] adv: **~ bringen** to bring about; **~ kommen** to come about

zuständig ['tsu:ʃtɛndɪç] adj competent, responsible; **Zuständigkeit** f competence, responsibility; **Zuständigkeitsbereich** m area of responsibility

zustattenkommen [tsu'ʃtatənkɔmən] unreg vi: **jdm ~** (geh) to come in useful for sb

zustehen ['tsu:ʃte:ən] unreg vi: **jdm ~** to be sb's right

zusteigen ['tsu:ʃtaɪgən] unreg vi: **noch jemand zugestiegen?** (in Zug) any more tickets?

zustellen ['tsu:ʃtɛlən] vt (verstellen) to block; (Post etc) to send

Zustellung f delivery

zusteuern ['tsu:ʃtɔʏərn] vi: **auf etw** akk **~** to head for sth; (beim Gespräch) to steer towards sth ▷ vt (beitragen) to contribute

zustimmen ['tsu:ʃtɪmən] vi to agree

Zustimmung f agreement; (Einwilligung) consent; **allgemeine ~ finden** to meet with general approval

zustoßen ['tsu:ʃto:sən] unreg vi (fig): **jdm ~** to happen to sb

Zustrom ['tsu:ʃtro:m] m (fig: Menschenmenge) stream (of visitors etc); (hineinströmend) influx; (Met) inflow

zustürzen ['tsu:ʃtʏrtsən] vi: **auf jdn/etw ~** to rush up to sb/sth

zutage, zu Tage [tsu'ta:gə] adv: **~ bringen** to bring to light; **~ treten** to come to light

Zutaten ['tsu:ta:tən] pl ingredients pl; (fig) accessories pl

zuteilen ['tsu:taɪlən] vt to allocate, assign

zuteilwerden [tsu'taɪlve:rdən] unreg vi (geh): **jdm wird etw zuteil** sb is granted sth,

Z

sth is granted to sb

zutiefst ['tsu:ti:fst] *adv* deeply

zutragen ['tsu:tra:gən] *unreg vt*: **jdm etw ~** to bring sb sth, bring sth to sb ▷ *vt* (*Klatsch*) to tell sb sth ▷ *vr* to happen

zuträglich ['tsu:trɛ:klɪç] *adj* beneficial

zutrauen ['tsu:trauən] *vt*: **jdm etw ~** to credit sb with sth; **sich** *dat* **nichts ~** to have no confidence in o.s.; **jdm viel ~** to think a lot of sb; **jdm wenig ~** not to think much of sb; **Zutrauen (-s)** *nt*: **Zutrauen (zu)** trust (in); **zu jdm Zutrauen fassen** to begin to trust sb

zutraulich *adj* trusting; (*Tier*) friendly; **Zutraulichkeit** *f* trust

zutreffen ['tsu:trɛfən] *unreg vi* to be correct; (*gelten*) to apply

zutreffend *adj* (*richtig*) accurate; **Z~es bitte unterstreichen** please underline where applicable

zutrinken ['tsu:trɪŋkən] *unreg vi*: **jdm ~** to drink to sb

Zutritt ['tsu:trɪt] *m* access; (*Einlass*) admittance; **kein ~, ~ verboten** no admittance

zutun ['tsu:tu:n] *unreg vt* to add; (*schließen*) to shut

Zutun (-s) *nt* assistance

zuunterst [tsu'ʊntərst] *adv* right at the bottom

zuverlässig ['tsu:fɛrlɛsɪç] *adj* reliable; **Zuverlässigkeit** *f* reliability

Zuversicht ['tsu:fɛrzɪçt] (-) *f* confidence; **zuversichtlich** *adj* confident; **Zuversichtlichkeit** *f* confidence

zu viel [tsu'fi:l] *siehe* **zu**

zuvor [tsu'fo:r] *adv* before, previously

zuvorderst [tsu'fɔrdərst] *adv* right at the front

zuvorkommen *unreg vi +dat* to anticipate; (*Gefahr etc*) to forestall; **jdm ~** to beat sb to it

zuvorkommend *adj* courteous; (*gefällig*) obliging

Zuwachs ['tsu:vaks] (-es) *m* increase, growth; (*umg*) addition

zuwachsen *unreg vi* to become overgrown; (*Wunde*) to heal (up)

Zuwachsrate *f* rate of increase

zuwandern ['tsu:vandərn] *vi* to immigrate

zuwege, zu Wege [tsu've:gə] *adv*: **etw ~ bringen** to accomplish sth; **mit etw ~ kommen** to manage sth; **gut ~ sein** to be (doing) well

zuweilen [tsu'vaɪlən] *adv* at times, now and then

zuweisen ['tsu:vaɪzən] *unreg vt* to assign, allocate

zuwenden ['tsu:vɛndən] *unreg vt +dat* to turn towards ▷ *vr +dat* to turn to; (*sich widmen*) to devote o.s. to; **jdm seine Aufmerksamkeit ~** to give sb one's attention

Zuwendung *f* (*Geld*) financial contribution; (*Liebe*) love and care

zu wenig [tsu've:nɪç] *siehe* **zu**

zuwerfen ['tsu:vɛrfən] *unreg vt*: **jdm etw ~** to throw sth to sb, throw sb sth

zuwider [tsu'vi:dər] *adv*: **etw ist jdm ~** sb loathes sth, sb finds sth repugnant ▷ *präp +dat* contrary to; **zuwiderhandeln** *vi +dat* to act contrary to; **einem Gesetz zuwiderhandeln** to contravene a law; **Zuwiderhandlung** *f* contravention; **zuwiderlaufen** *unreg vi*: **einer Sache** *dat* **zuwiderlaufen** to run counter to sth

zuwinken *vi*: **jdm ~** to wave to sb

zuz. *abk* = **zuzüglich**

zuzahlen ['tsu:tsa:lən] *vt*: **10 Euro ~** to pay another 10 euros

zuziehen ['tsu:tsi:ən] *unreg vt* (*schließen*: Vorhang) to draw, close; (*herbeirufen*: Experten) to call in ▷ *vi* to move in, come; **sich** *dat* **etw ~** (*Krankheit*) to catch sth; (*Zorn*) to incur sth; **sich** *dat* **eine Verletzung ~** (*form*) to sustain an injury

Zuzug ['tsu:tsuk] (-(e)s) *m* (*Zustrom*) influx; (*von Familie etc*): **~ nach** move to

zuzüglich ['tsu:tsy:klɪç] *präp +gen* plus, with the addition of

zuzwinkern ['tsu:tsvɪnkərn] *vi*: **jdm ~** to wink at sb

ZVS *f abk* (= *Zentralstelle für die Vergabe von Studienplätzen*) central body organizing the granting of places at university

Zwang (-(e)s, ¨e) *m* compulsion; (*Gewalt*) coercion; **gesellschaftliche Zwänge** social constraints; **tu dir keinen ~ an** don't feel you have to be polite

zwang *etc* [tsvaŋ] *vb siehe* **zwingen**

zwängen ['tsvɛŋən] *vt, vr* to squeeze

Zwang- *zW*: **zwanghaft** *adj* compulsive; **zwanglos** *adj* informal; **Zwanglosigkeit** *f* informality

Zwangs- *zW*: **Zwangsabgabe** *f* (*Comm*) compulsory levy; **Zwangsarbeit** *f* forced labour (*Brit*) *od* labor (*US*); **Zwangsernährung** *f* force-feeding; **Zwangsjacke** *f* straitjacket; **Zwangslage** *f* predicament, tight corner; **zwangsläufig** *adj* inevitable; **Zwangsmaßnahme** *f* compulsory measure; (*Pol*) sanction; **Zwangsvollstreckung** *f* execution; **Zwangsvorstellung** *f* (*Psych*) obsession; **zwangsweise** *adv* compulsorily

zwanzig ['tsvantsɪç] *num* twenty

zwanzigste, r, s *adj* twentieth

zwar [tsva:r] *adv* to be sure, indeed; **das ist ~ ..., aber ...** that may be ... but ...; **und ~ in** fact, actually; **und ~ am Sonntag** on Sunday to be precise; **und ~ so schnell, dass ...** in fact so quickly that ...

Zweck [tsvɛk] (-(e)s, -e) *m* purpose, aim; **es hat keinen ~, darüber zu reden** there is no point (in) talking about it; **zweckdienlich** *adj* practical; (*nützlich*) useful; **zweckdienliche Hinweise** (any) relevant information

Zwecke (-, -n) *f* hobnail; (*Heftzwecke*) drawing pin (*Brit*), thumbtack (*US*)

Zweck- *zW*: **zweckentfremden** *vt untr* to use for another purpose; **Zweckentfremdung** *f* misuse; **zweckfrei** *adj* (*Forschung etc*) pure; **zwecklos** *adj* pointless; **zweckmäßig** *adj*

suitable, appropriate; **Zweckmäßigkeit** f suitability

zwecks präp +gen (form) for (the purpose of)

zweckwidrig adj unsuitable

zwei [tsvaɪ] num two; **Zweibettzimmer** nt twin-bedded room; **zweideutig** adj ambiguous; (unanständig) suggestive; **Zweidrittelmehrheit** f (Parl) two-thirds majority; **zweieiig** adj (Zwillinge) non-identical

zweierlei ['tsvaɪər'laɪ] adj two kinds od sorts of; **~ Stoff** two different kinds of material; **~ zu tun haben** to have two different things to do

zweifach adj double

Zweifel ['tsvaɪfəl] (-s, -) m doubt; **ich bin mir darüber im ~** I'm in two minds about it; **zweifelhaft** adj doubtful, dubious; **zweifellos** adj doubtless

zweifeln vi: **(an etw** dat) **~** to doubt (sth)

Zweifelsfall m: **im ~** in case of doubt

Zweifrontenkrieg m war(fare) on two fronts

Zweig [tsvaɪk] (-(e)s, -e) m branch; **Zweiggeschäft** nt (Comm) branch

zweigleisig ['tsvaɪglaɪzɪç] adj: **~ argumentieren** to argue along two different lines

Zweigstelle f branch (office)

zwei- zW: **zweihändig** adj two-handed; (Mus) for two hands; **Zweiheit** f duality; **zweihundert** num two hundred; **Zweikampf** m duel; **zweimal** adv twice; **das lasse ich mir nicht zweimal sagen** I don't have to be told twice; **zweimotorig** adj twin-engined; **zweireihig** adj (Anzug) double-breasted; **Zweisamkeit** f togetherness; **zweischneidig** adj (fig) double-edged; **Zweisitzer** (-s, -) m two-seater; **zweisprachig** adj bilingual; **Zweispurgerät**, **Zweispurtonbandgerät** nt twin-track (tape) recorder; **zweispurig** adj (Aut) two-lane; **zweistellig** adj (Zahl) two-digit attrib, with two digits; **zweistimmig** adj for two voices

zweit [tsvaɪt] adv: **zu ~** (in Paaren) in twos

Zweitaktmotor m two-stroke engine

zweitbeste, r, s adj second best

zweite, r, s adj second; **Bürger ~r Klasse** second-class citizen(s)(f)

zweiteilig ['tsvaɪtaɪlɪç] adj (Buch, Film etc) in two parts; (Kleidung) two-piece

zweitens adv secondly

zweit- zW: **zweitgrößte, r, s** adj second largest; **zweitklassig** adj second-class; **zweitletzte, r, s** adj last but one, penultimate; **zweitrangig** adj second-rate; **Zweitschlüssel** m duplicate key; **Zweitstimme** f second vote; siehe auch **Erststimme**

zweitürig ['tsvaɪtyːrɪç] adj two-door

Zweitwagen m second car

Zweitwohnung f second home

zweizeilig adj two-lined; (Typ: Abstand) double-spaced

Zweizimmerwohnung f two-room(ed) flat (Brit) od apartment (US)

Zwerchfell ['tsvɛrçfɛl] nt diaphragm

Zwerg, in [tsvɛrk, 'tsvɛrgɪn] (-(e)s, -e) m(f) dwarf; (fig: Knirps) midget; **Zwergschule** (umg) f village school

Zwetsche ['tsvɛtʃə], **Zwetschge** ['tsvɛtʃgə] (-, -n) f plum

Zwickel ['tsvɪkəl] (-s, -) m gusset

zwicken ['tsvɪkən] vt to pinch, nip

Zwickmühle ['tsvɪkmyːlə] f: **in der ~ sitzen** (fig) to be in a dilemma

Zwieback ['tsviːbak] (-(e)s, -e od -bäcke) m rusk

Zwiebel ['tsviːbəl] (-, -n) f onion; (Blumenzwiebel) bulb; **zwiebelartig** adj bulbous; **Zwiebelturm** m (tower with an) onion dome

Zwie- zW: **Zwiegespräch** nt dialogue (Brit), dialog (US); **Zwielicht** nt twilight; **ins Zwielicht geraten sein** (fig) to appear in an unfavourable (Brit) od unfavorable (US) light; **zwielichtig** adj shady, dubious; **Zwiespalt** m conflict; (zwischen Menschen) rift, gulf; **zwiespältig** adj (Gefühle) conflicting; (Charakter) contradictory; **Zwietracht** f discord, dissension

Zwilling ['tsvɪlɪŋ] (-s, -e) m twin; **Zwillinge** pl (Astrol) Gemini

zwingen ['tsvɪŋən] unreg vt to force

zwingend adj (Grund etc) compelling; (logisch notwendig) necessary; (Schluss, Beweis) conclusive

Zwinger (-s, -) m (Käfig) cage; (Hundezwinger) run

zwinkern ['tsvɪŋkərn] vi to blink; (absichtlich) to wink

Zwirn [tsvɪrn] (-(e)s, -e) m thread

zwischen ['tsvɪʃən] präp (+akk od dat) between; (bei mehreren) among; **Zwischenaufenthalt** m stopover; **Zwischenbemerkung** f (incidental) remark; **zwischenblenden** vt (Film, Rundf, TV) to insert; **Zwischending** nt cross; **Zwischendividende** f interim dividend; **zwischendurch** adv in between; (räumlich) here and there; **Zwischenergebnis** nt intermediate result; **Zwischenfall** m incident; **Zwischenfrage** f question; **Zwischengröße** f in-between size; **Zwischenhandel** m wholesaling; **Zwischenhändler** m middleman, agent; **Zwischenlagerung** f temporary storage; **Zwischenlandung** f (Aviat) stopover; **Zwischenlösung** f temporary solution; **zwischenmahlzeit** f snack (between meals); **zwischenmenschlich** adj interpersonal; **Zwischenprüfung** f intermediate examination; **Zwischenraum** m gap, space; **Zwischenruf** m interjection, interruption; **Zwischenrufe** pl heckling sing; **Zwischensaison** f low season; **Zwischenspeicher** m (Comput) buffer; **Zwischenspiel** nt (Theat, fig) interlude; (Mus) intermezzo; **zwischenstaatlich** adj interstate; (international) international; **Zwischenstation** f intermediate station; **Zwischenstecker** m (Elek) adapter; **Zwischenstück** nt connecting piece; **Zwischensumme** f subtotal; **Zwischenwand** f partition; **Zwischenzeit** f interval; **in der Zwischenzeit** in the interim, meanwhile; **Zwischenzeugnis** nt (Sch) interim report

Zwist [tsvɪst] (-es, -e) m dispute

zwitschern ['tsvɪtʃərn] vt, vi to twitter, chirp; **einen ~** (umg) to have a drink

Zwitter ['tsvɪtər] (-s, -) m hermaphrodite

zwo [tsvoː] num (Tel, Mil) two

zwölf [tsvœlf] num twelve; **fünf Minuten vor ~** (fig) at the eleventh hour

Zwölffingerdarm (-(e)s) m duodenum

Zyankali [tsyaˈnˈkaːli] (-s) nt (Chem) potassium cyanide

Zyklon [tsyˈkloːn] (-s, -e) m cyclone

Zyklus ['tsyːklʊs] (-, Zyklen) m cycle

Zylinder [tsiˈlɪndər] (-s, -) m cylinder; (Hut) top hat; **zylinderförmig** adj cylindrical

Zyniker, in ['tsyːnikər(ɪn)] (-s, -) m(f) cynic

zynisch ['tsyːnɪʃ] adj cynical

Zynismus ['tsyːnɪsmʊs] m cynicism

Zypern ['tsyːpərn] (-s) nt Cyprus

Zypresse [tsyˈprɛsə] (-, -n) f (Bot) cypress

Zypriot, in [tsypriˈoːt(ɪn)] (-en, -en) m(f) Cypriot

zypriotisch adj Cypriot, Cyprian

zyprisch ['tsyːprɪʃ] adj Cypriot, Cyprian

Zyste ['tsʏstə] (-, -n) f cyst

zz., zzt. abk = **zurzeit**

z. Z., z. Zt. abk = **zur Zeit**

English–German

Englisch–Deutsch

Aa

A¹, a [eɪ] *n* (*letter*) A *nt*, a *nt*; (*Scol*) ≈ Eins *f*,
sehr gut *nt*; **A for Andrew, A for Able**
(*US*) ≈ A wie Anton; **A road** (*Brit*: *Aut*)
Hauptverkehrsstraße *f*; **A shares** (*Brit*: *Stock
Exchange*) stimmrechtslose Aktien *pl*
A² [eɪ] *n* (*Mus*) A *nt*, a *nt*

◯ **KEYWORD**

a [ə] (*before vowel and silent h:* **an**) *indef art* **1** ein;
(*before feminine noun*) eine; **a book** ein Buch;
a lamp eine Lampe; **she's a doctor** sie ist
Ärztin; **I haven't got a car** ich habe kein
Auto; **a hundred/thousand** *etc* **pounds**
einhundert/eintausend *etc* Pfund
2 (*in expressing ratios, prices etc*) pro; **3 a day/week**
3 pro Tag/Woche, 3 am Tag/in der Woche; **10
km an hour** 10 km pro Stunde

A2 (*Brit*) *n* (*Scol*) Mit "A2" wird das zweite Jahr der
britischen Sekundarstufe II bezeichnet, in dem die
übrigen drei Wahlpflichtfächer unterrichtet und am
Ende des Schuljahres geprüft werden. Die Note für den
"A level" setzt sich aus den Noten der Jahre "AS" und
"A2" zusammen

AA *n abbr* (*Brit*: = *Automobile Association*)
Autofahrerorganisation, ≈ ADAC *m*; (*US*: = *Associate
in Art*) akademischer Grad für Geisteswissenschaftler;
(= *Alcoholics Anonymous*) Anonyme Alkoholiker
pl, AA *pl*

AAA *n abbr* (= *American Automobile Association*)
Autofahrerorganisation, ≈ ADAC *m*; (*Brit*: = *Amateur
Athletics Association*) Leichtathletikverband der
Amateure

A & E *n abbr* (= *Accident and Emergency*): ~
department Notfallstation *f*, Notaufnahme *f*
abaci [ˈæbəsaɪ] *npl of* **abacus**
aback [əˈbæk] *adv*: **to be taken** ~ verblüfft sein
abacus [ˈæbəkəs] (*pl* **abaci**) *n* Abakus *m*
abandon [əˈbændən] *vt* verlassen; (*child*)
aussetzen; (*give up*) aufgeben ⊳ *n* (*wild
behaviour*): **with** ~ selbstvergessen; **to** ~ **ship**
das Schiff verlassen
abandoned [əˈbændənd] *adj* verlassen; (*child*)
ausgesetzt; (*unrestrained*) selbstvergessen
abase [əˈbeɪs] *vt*: **to** ~ **o.s.** sich erniedrigen;
to ~ **o.s. so far as to do sth** sich dazu

erniedrigen, etw zu tun
abashed [əˈbæʃt] *adj* verlegen
abate [əˈbeɪt] *vi* nachlassen, sich legen
abatement [əˈbeɪtmənt] *n*: **noise** ~ **society**
Gesellschaft *f* zur Lärmbekämpfung
abattoir [ˈæbətwɑːʳ] (*Brit*) *n* Schlachthof *m*
abbey [ˈæbɪ] *n* Abtei *f*
abbot [ˈæbət] *n* Abt *m*
abbreviate [əˈbriːvɪeɪt] *vt* abkürzen; (*essay etc*)
kürzen
abbreviation [əbriːvɪˈeɪʃən] *n* Abkürzung *f*
ABC *n abbr* (= *American Broadcasting Companies*)
Fernsehsender
abdicate [ˈæbdɪkeɪt] *vt* verzichten auf +*acc* ⊳ *vi*
(*monarch*) abdanken
abdication [æbdɪˈkeɪʃən] *n* (*see vb*) Verzicht *m*;
Abdankung *f*
abdomen [ˈæbdəmɛn] *n* Unterleib *m*
abdominal [æbˈdɒmɪnl] *adj* (*pain etc*)
Unterleibs-
abduct [æbˈdʌkt] *vt* entführen
abduction [æbˈdʌkʃən] *n* Entführung *f*
Aberdonian [æbəˈdəʊnɪən] *adj* (*Geog*)
Aberdeener *inv* ⊳ *n* Aberdeener(in) *m(f)*
aberration [æbəˈreɪʃən] *n* Anomalie *f*; **in a
moment of mental** ~ in einem Augenblick
geistiger Verwirrung
abet [əˈbɛt] *vt see* **aid**
abeyance [əˈbeɪəns] *n*: **in** ~ (*law*) außer Kraft;
(*matter*) ruhend
abhor [əbˈhɔːʳ] *vt* verabscheuen
abhorrent [əbˈhɔrənt] *adj* abscheulich
abide [əˈbaɪd] *vt*: **I can't** ~ **it/him** ich kann es/
ihn nicht ausstehen
▶ **abide by** *vt fus* sich halten an +*acc*
abiding [əˈbaɪdɪŋ] *adj* (*memory, impression*)
bleibend
ability [əˈbɪlɪtɪ] *n* Fähigkeit *f*; **to the best of
my** ~ so gut ich es kann
abject [ˈæbdʒɛkt] *adj* (*poverty*) bitter; (*apology*)
demütig; (*coward*) erbärmlich
ablaze [əˈbleɪz] *adj* in Flammen; ~ **with light**
hell erleuchtet
able [ˈeɪbl] *adj* fähig; **to be** ~ **to do sth** etw tun
können
able-bodied [ˈeɪblˈbɒdɪd] *adj* kräftig; ~ **seaman**
(*Brit*) Vollmatrose *m*

ablutions [əˈbluːʃənz] *npl* Waschungen *pl*

ably [ˈeɪblɪ] *adv* gekonnt

ABM *n abbr* (= *antiballistic missile*) Anti-Raketen-Rakete *f*

abnormal [æbˈnɔːməl] *adj* abnorm; (*child*) anormal

abnormality [æbnɔːˈmælɪtɪ] *n* Abnormität *f*

aboard [əˈbɔːd] *adv* (*Naut, Aviat*) an Bord ▷ *prep* an Bord +*gen*; **~ the train/bus** im Zug/Bus

abode [əˈbəʊd] *n* (*Law*): **of no fixed ~** ohne festen Wohnsitz

abolish [əˈbɒlɪʃ] *vt* abschaffen

abolition [æbəˈlɪʃən] *n* Abschaffung *f*

abominable [əˈbɒmɪnəbl] *adj* scheußlich

abominably [əˈbɒmɪnəblɪ] *adv* scheußlich

Aborigine [æbəˈrɪdʒɪnɪ] *n* Ureinwohner(in) *m(f)* Australiens

abort [əˈbɔːt] *vt* abtreiben; (*Med: miscarry*) fehlgebären; (*Comput*) abbrechen

abortion [əˈbɔːʃən] *n* Abtreibung *f*; (*miscarriage*) Fehlgeburt *f*; **to have a ~** abtreiben lassen

abortionist [əˈbɔːʃənɪst] *n* Abtreibungshelfer(in) *m(f)*

abortive [əˈbɔːtɪv] *adj* misslungen

abound [əˈbaʊnd] *vi* im Überfluss vorhanden sein; **to ~ in** *or* **with** reich sein an +*dat*

○ KEYWORD

about [əˈbaʊt] *adv* **1** (*approximately*) etwa, ungefähr; **about a hundred/thousand** *etc* etwa hundert/tausend *etc*; **at about two o'clock** etwa um zwei Uhr; **I've just about finished** ich bin gerade fertig
2 (*referring to place*) herum; **to run/walk** *etc* **about** herumlaufen/-gehen *etc*; **is Paul about?** ist Paul da?
3: to be about to do sth im Begriff sein, etw zu tun; **he was about to cry** er fing fast an zu weinen; **she was about to leave/wash the dishes** sie wollte gerade gehen/das Geschirr spülen
▷ *prep* **1** (*relating to*) über +*acc*; **what is it about?** worum geht es?; (*book etc*) wovon handelt es?; **we talked about it** wir haben darüber geredet; **what** *or* **how about going to the cinema?** wollen wir ins Kino gehen?
2 (*referring to place*) um ... herum; **to walk about the town** durch die Stadt gehen; **her clothes were scattered about the room** ihre Kleider waren über das ganze Zimmer verstreut

about-face [əˈbaʊtˈfeɪs] (*US*) *n* = **about-turn**

about-turn [əˈbaʊtˈtɜːn] (*Brit*) *n* Kehrtwendung *f*

above [əˈbʌv] *adv* oben; (*greater, more*) darüber ▷ *prep* über +*dat*; **to cost ~ £10** mehr als £10 kosten; **mentioned ~** oben genannt; **he's not ~ a bit of blackmail** er ist sich *dat* nicht zu gut für eine kleine Erpressung; **~ all** vor allem

above board *adj* korrekt

abrasion [əˈbreɪʒən] *n* Abschürfung *f*

abrasive [əˈbreɪzɪv] *adj* (*substance*) Scheuer-; (*person, manner*) aggressiv

abreast [əˈbrɛst] *adv* nebeneinander; **three ~** zu dritt nebeneinander; **to keep ~ of** (*fig*) auf dem Laufenden bleiben mit

abridge [əˈbrɪdʒ] *vt* kürzen

abroad [əˈbrɔːd] *adv* (*be*) im Ausland; (*go*) ins Ausland; **there is a rumour ~ that ...** (*fig*) ein Gerücht geht um *or* kursiert, dass ...

abrupt [əˈbrʌpt] *adj* abrupt; (*person, behaviour*) schroff

abruptly [əˈbrʌptlɪ] *adv* abrupt

abscess [ˈæbsɪs] *n* Abszess *m*

abscond [əbˈskɒnd] *vi*: **to ~ with** sich davonmachen mit; **to ~ (from)** fliehen (aus)

abseil [ˈæbseɪl] *vi* sich abseilen

absence [ˈæbsəns] *n* Abwesenheit *f*; **in the ~ of** (*person*) in Abwesenheit +*gen*; (*thing*) in Ermangelung +*gen*

absent [ˈæbsənt] *adj* abwesend, nicht da ▷ *vt*: **to ~ o.s. from** fernbleiben +*dat*; **to be ~** fehlen; **to be ~ without leave** (*Mil*) sich unerlaubt von der Truppe entfernen

absentee [æbsənˈtiː] *n* Abwesende(r) *f(m)*

absenteeism [æbsənˈtiːɪzəm] *n* (*from school*) Schwänzen *nt*; (*from work*) Nichterscheinen *nt* am Arbeitsplatz

absent-minded [ˈæbsəntˈmaɪndɪd] *adj* zerstreut

absent-mindedly [ˈæbsəntˈmaɪndɪdlɪ] *adv* zerstreut; (*look*) abwesend

absent-mindedness [ˈæbsəntˈmaɪndɪdnɪs] *n* Zerstreutheit *f*

absolute [ˈæbsəluːt] *adj* absolut; (*power*) uneingeschränkt

absolutely [æbsəˈluːtlɪ] *adv* absolut; (*agree*) vollkommen; **~!** genau!

absolution [æbsəˈluːʃən] *n* Lossprechung *f*

absolve [əbˈzɒlv] *vt*: **to ~ sb (from)** jdn lossprechen (von); (*responsibility*) jdn entbinden (von)

absorb [əbˈzɔːb] *vt* aufnehmen (*also fig*); (*light, heat*) absorbieren; (*group, business*) übernehmen; **to be ~ed in a book** in ein Buch vertieft sein

absorbent [əbˈzɔːbənt] *adj* saugfähig

absorbent cotton (*US*) *n* Watte *f*

absorbing [əbˈzɔːbɪŋ] *adj* saugfähig; (*book, film, work etc*) fesselnd

absorption [əbˈsɔːpʃən] *n* (*see vb*) Aufnahme *f*; Absorption *f*; Übernahme *f*; (*interest*) Faszination *f*

abstain [əbˈsteɪn] *vi* (*voting*) sich (der Stimme) enthalten; **to ~ (from)** (*eating, drinking etc*) sich enthalten (+*gen*)

abstemious [əbˈstiːmɪəs] *adj* enthaltsam

abstention [əbˈstɛnʃən] *n* (*Stimm*)enthaltung *f*

abstinence [ˈæbstɪnəns] *n* Enthaltsamkeit *f*

abstract [ˈæbstrækt] *adj* abstrakt ▷ *n* (*summary*) Zusammenfassung *f* ▷ *vt*: **to ~ sth (from)** (*summarize*) etw entnehmen (aus); (*remove*) etw entfernen (aus)

abstruse [æb'struːs] *adj* abstrus
absurd [əb'səːd] *adj* absurd
absurdity [əb'səːdɪtɪ] *n* Absurdität *f*
ABTA ['æbtə] *n abbr* (= *Association of British Travel Agents*) *Verband der Reiseveranstalter*
Abu Dhabi ['æbu:'dɑːbɪ] *n* (*Geog*) Abu Dhabi *nt*
abundance [ə'bʌndəns] *n* Reichtum *m*; **an ~ of** eine Fülle von; **in ~** in Hülle und Fülle
abundant [ə'bʌndənt] *adj* reichlich
abundantly [ə'bʌndəntlɪ] *adv* reichlich; **~ clear** völlig klar
abuse [ə'bjuːs] *n* (*insults*) Beschimpfungen *pl*; (*ill-treatment*) Misshandlung *f*; (*misuse*) Missbrauch *m* ▷ *vt* (*see n*) beschimpfen; misshandeln; missbrauchen; **to be open to ~** sich leicht missbrauchen lassen
abuser [ə'bjuːzə'] *n* (*also:* **drug abuser**) *jd, der Drogen missbraucht*; (*also:* **child abuser**) *jd, der Kinder missbraucht oder misshandelt*
abusive [ə'bjuːsɪv] *adj* beleidigend
abysmal [ə'bɪzməl] *adj* entsetzlich; (*ignorance etc*) grenzenlos
abysmally [ə'bɪzməlɪ] *adv* (*see adj*) entsetzlich; grenzenlos
abyss [ə'bɪs] *n* Abgrund *m*
AC *abbr* = **alternating current**; (*US:* = *athletic club*) ≈ SV *m*
a/c *abbr* (*Banking etc*) = **account**; (= *current account*) Girokonto *nt*
academic [ækə'dɛmɪk] *adj* akademisch (*also pej*); (*work*) wissenschaftlich; (*person*) intellektuell ▷ *n* Akademiker(in) *m(f)*
academic year *n* (*university year*) Universitätsjahr *nt*; (*school year*) Schuljahr *nt*
academy [ə'kædəmɪ] *n* Akademie *f*; (*school*) Hochschule *f*; **~ of music** Musikhochschule *f*; **military/naval ~** Militär-/Marineakademie *f*
ACAS ['eɪkæs] (*Brit*) *n abbr* (= *Advisory Conciliation and Arbitration Service*) *Schlichtungsstelle für Arbeitskonflikte*
accede [æk'siːd] *vi*: **to ~ to** zustimmen +*dat*
accelerate [æk'sɛləreɪt] *vt* beschleunigen ▷ *vi* (*Aut*) Gas geben
acceleration [æksɛlə'reɪʃən] *n* Beschleunigung *f*
accelerator [æk'sɛləreɪtə'] *n* Gaspedal *nt*
accent ['æksɛnt] *n* Akzent *m*; (*fig: emphasis, stress*) Betonung *f*; **to speak with an Irish ~** mit einem irischen Akzent sprechen; **to have a strong ~** einen starken Akzent haben
accentuate [æk'sɛntjueɪt] *vt* betonen; (*need, difference etc*) hervorheben
accept [ək'sɛpt] *vt* annehmen; (*fact, situation*) sich abfinden mit; (*risk*) in Kauf nehmen; (*responsibility*) übernehmen; (*blame*) auf sich *acc* nehmen
acceptable [ək'sɛptəbl] *adj* annehmbar
acceptance [ək'sɛptəns] *n* Annahme *f*; **to meet with general ~** allgemeine Anerkennung finden
access ['æksɛs] *n* Zugang *m* ▷ *vt* (*Comput*) zugreifen auf +*dat*; **the burglars gained ~ through a window** die Einbrecher gelangten

durch ein Fenster hinein
accessible [æk'sɛsəbl] *adj* erreichbar; (*knowledge, art etc*) zugänglich
accession [æk'sɛʃən] *n* Antritt *m*; (*of monarch*) Thronbesteigung *f*; (*to library*) Neuanschaffung *f*
accessory [æk'sɛsərɪ] *n* Zubehörteil *nt*; (*Dress*) Accessoire *nt*; (*Law*): **~ to** Mitschuldige(r) *f(m)* an +*dat*; **accessories** *npl* Zubehör *nt*; **toilet accessories** (*Brit*) Toilettenartikel *pl*
access road *n* Zufahrt(sstraße) *f*
access time *n* (*Comput*) Zugriffszeit *f*
accident ['æksɪdənt] *n* Unfall *m*; (*mishap, disaster*) Unfall *m*; **to meet with** *or* **to have an ~** einen Unfall haben, verunglücken; **~s at work** Arbeitsunfälle *pl*; **by ~** zufällig
accidental [æksɪ'dɛntl] *adj* zufällig; (*death, damage*) Unfall-
accidentally [æksɪ'dɛntəlɪ] *adv* zufällig
accident insurance *n* Unfallversicherung *f*
accident-prone ['æksɪdənt'prəun] *adj* vom Pech verfolgt
accident risk *n* Unfallrisiko *f*
acclaim [ə'kleɪm] *n* Beifall *m* ▷ *vt*: **to be ~ed for one's achievements** für seine Leistungen gefeiert werden
acclamation [æklə'meɪʃən] *n* Anerkennung *f*; (*applause*) Beifall *m*
acclimate [ə'klaɪmət] (*US*) *vt* = **acclimatize**
acclimatize [ə'klaɪmətaɪz], (*US*) **acclimate** *vt*: **to become ~d** sich akklimatisieren; **to become ~d to** sich gewöhnen an +*acc*
accolade ['ækəleɪd] *n* (*fig*) Auszeichnung *f*
accommodate [ə'kɔmədeɪt] *vt* unterbringen; (*subj: car, hotel etc*) Platz bieten +*dat*; (*oblige, help*) entgegenkommen +*dat*; **to ~ one's plans to** seine Pläne anpassen an +*acc*
accommodating [ə'kɔmədeɪtɪŋ] *adj* entgegenkommend
accommodation [əkɔmə'deɪʃən] *n* Unterkunft *f*; **accommodations** (*US*) *npl* Unterkunft *f*; **have you any ~?** haben Sie eine Unterkunft?; **"~ to let"** „Zimmer zu vermieten"; **they have ~ for 500** sie können 500 Personen unterbringen; **the hall has seating ~ for 600** (*Brit*) in dem Saal können 600 Personen sitzen
accompaniment [ə'kʌmpənɪmənt] *n* Begleitung *f*
accompanist [ə'kʌmpənɪst] *n* Begleiter(in) *m(f)*
accompany [ə'kʌmpənɪ] *vt* begleiten
accomplice [ə'kʌmplɪs] *n* Komplize *m*, Komplizin *f*
accomplish [ə'kʌmplɪʃ] *vt* vollenden; (*achieve*) erreichen
accomplished [ə'kʌmplɪʃt] *adj* ausgezeichnet
accomplishment [ə'kʌmplɪʃmənt] *n* Vollendung *f*; (*achievement*) Leistung *f*; (*skill: gen pl*) Fähigkeit *f*
accord [ə'kɔːd] *n* Übereinstimmung *f*; (*treaty*) Vertrag *m* ▷ *vt* gewähren; **of his own ~** freiwillig; **with one ~** geschlossen; **to be in ~** übereinstimmen

accordance [əˈkɔːdəns] n: in ~ with in Übereinstimmung mit

according [əˈkɔːdɪŋ] prep: ~ to zufolge +dat; ~ to plan wie geplant

accordingly [əˈkɔːdɪŋlɪ] adv entsprechend; (as a result) folglich

accordion [əˈkɔːdɪən] n Akkordeon nt

accost [əˈkɔst] vt ansprechen

account [əˈkaunt] n (Comm: bill) Rechnung f; (in bank, department store) Konto nt; (report) Bericht m; accounts npl (Comm) Buchhaltung f; (Bookkeeping) (Geschäfts)bücher pl; "~ payee only" (Brit) „nur zur Verrechnung"; to keep an ~ of Buch führen über +acc; to bring sb to ~ for sth/for having embezzled £50,000 jdn für etw/für die Unterschlagung von £50.000 zur Rechenschaft ziehen; by all ~s nach allem, was man hört; of no ~ ohne Bedeutung; on ~ auf Kredit; to pay £5 on ~ eine Anzahlung von £5 leisten; on no ~ auf keinen Fall; on ~ of wegen +gen; to take into account, take ~ of berücksichtigen
▸ account for vt fus erklären; (expenditure) Rechenschaft ablegen für; (represent) ausmachen; all the children were ~ed for man wusste, wo alle Kinder waren; four people are still not ~ed for vier Personen werden immer noch vermisst

accountability [əˈkauntəˈbɪlɪtɪ] n Verantwortlichkeit f

accountable [əˈkauntəbl] adj: ~ (to) verantwortlich (gegenüber +dat); to be held ~ for sth für etw verantwortlich gemacht werden

accountancy [əˈkauntənsɪ] n Buchhaltung f

accountant [əˈkauntənt] n Buchhalter(in) m(f)

accounting [əˈkauntɪŋ] n Buchhaltung f

accounting period n Abrechnungszeitraum m

account number n Kontonummer f

accounts payable npl Verbindlichkeiten pl

accounts receivable npl Forderungen pl

accredited [əˈkrɛdɪtɪd] adj anerkannt

accretion [əˈkriːʃən] n Ablagerung f

accrue [əˈkruː] vi sich ansammeln; to ~ to zufließen +dat

accrued interest n aufgelaufene Zinsen pl

accumulate [əˈkjuːmjuleɪt] vt ansammeln ▸ vi sich ansammeln

accumulation [əkjuːmjuˈleɪʃən] n Ansammlung f

accuracy [ˈækjurəsɪ] n Genauigkeit f

accurate [ˈækjurɪt] adj genau

accurately [ˈækjurɪtlɪ] adv genau; (answer) richtig

accusation [ækjuˈzeɪʃən] n Vorwurf m; (instance) Beschuldigung f; (Law) Anklage f

accusative [əˈkjuːzətɪv] n Akkusativ m

accuse [əˈkjuːz] vt: to ~ sb (of sth) jdn (einer Sache gen) beschuldigen; (Law) jdn (wegen etw dat) anklagen

accused [əˈkjuːzd] n (Law): the ~ der/die Angeklagte

accuser [əˈkjuːzəʳ] n Ankläger(in) m(f)

accusing [əˈkjuːzɪŋ] adj anklagend

accustom [əˈkʌstəm] vt gewöhnen; to ~ o.s. to sth sich an etw acc gewöhnen

accustomed [əˈkʌstəmd] adj gewohnt; (in the habit): ~ to gewohnt an +acc

AC/DC abbr (= alternating current/direct current) WS/GS

ACE [eɪs] n abbr (= American Council on Education) akademischer Verband für das Erziehungswesen

ace [eɪs] n As nt

acerbic [əˈsəːbɪk] adj scharf

acetate [ˈæsɪteɪt] n Acetat nt

ache [eɪk] n Schmerz m ▸ vi schmerzen, wehtun; (yearn): to ~ to do sth sich danach sehnen, etw zu tun; I've got (a) stomach ~ ich habe Magenschmerzen; I'm aching all over mir tut alles weh; my head ~s mir tut der Kopf weh

achieve [əˈtʃiːv] vt (aim, result) erreichen; (success) erzielen; (victory) erringen

achievement [əˈtʃiːvmənt] n (act of achieving) Erreichen nt; (success, feat) Leistung f

Achilles heel [əˈkɪliːz-] n Achillesferse f

acid [ˈæsɪd] adj sauer ▸ n (Chem) Säure f; (inf: LSD) Acid nt

Acid House n Acid House nt, elektronische Funk-Diskomusik

acidic [əˈsɪdɪk] adj sauer

acidity [əˈsɪdɪtɪ] n Säure f

acid rain n saurer Regen m

acid test n (fig) Feuerprobe f

acknowledge [əkˈnɔlɪdʒ] vt (also: acknowledge receipt of) den Empfang +gen bestätigen; (fact) zugeben; (situation) zur Kenntnis nehmen; (person) grüßen

acknowledgement [əkˈnɔlɪdʒmənt] n Empfangsbestätigung f; acknowledgements npl (in book) ≈ Danksagung f

ACLU n abbr (= American Civil Liberties Union) Bürgerrechtsverband

acme [ˈækmɪ] n Gipfel m, Höhepunkt m

acne [ˈæknɪ] n Akne f

acorn [ˈeɪkɔːn] n Eichel f

acoustic [əˈkuːstɪk] adj akustisch

acoustic coupler n (Comput) Akustikkoppler m

acoustics [əˈkuːstɪks] n Akustik f

acoustic screen n Trennwand f zur Schalldämpfung

acquaint [əˈkweɪnt] vt: to ~ sb with sth jdn mit etw vertraut machen; to be ~ed with (person) bekannt sein mit; (fact) vertraut sein mit

acquaintance [əˈkweɪntəns] n Bekannte(r) f(m); (with person) Bekanntschaft f; (with subject) Kenntnis f; to make sb's ~ jds Bekanntschaft machen

acquiesce [ækwɪˈɛs] vi einwilligen; to ~ (to) (demand, arrangement, request) einwilligen (in +acc)

acquire [əˈkwaɪəʳ] vt erwerben; (interest) entwickeln; (habit) annehmen

acquired [əˈkwaɪəd] adj erworben; whisky is an ~ taste man muss sich an Whisky erst gewöhnen

acquisition [ækwɪ'zɪʃən] n (see vb) Erwerb m, Entwicklung f, Annahme f; (thing acquired) Errungenschaft f

acquisitive [ə'kwɪzɪtɪv] adj habgierig; **the ~ society** die Erwerbsgesellschaft

acquit [ə'kwɪt] vt freisprechen; **to ~ o.s. well** seine Sache gut machen

acquittal [ə'kwɪtl] n Freispruch m

acre ['eɪkəʳ] n Morgen m

acreage ['eɪkərɪdʒ] n Fläche f

acrid ['ækrɪd] adj bitter; (smoke: fig) beißend

acrimonious [ækrɪ'məʊnɪəs] adj bitter; (dispute) erbittert

acrimony ['ækrɪmənɪ] n Erbitterung f

acrobat ['ækrəbæt] n Akrobat(in) m(f)

acrobatic [ækrə'bætɪk] adj akrobatisch

acrobatics [ækrə'bætɪks] npl Akrobatik f

acronym ['ækrənɪm] n Akronym nt

Acropolis [ə'krɒpəlɪs] n: **the ~** (Geog) die Akropolis

across [ə'krɒs] prep über +acc; (on the other side of) auf der anderen Seite +gen ▷ adv (direction) hinüber, herüber; (measurement) breit; **to take sb ~ the road** jdn über die Straße bringen; **a road ~ the wood** eine Straße durch den Wald; **the lake is 12 km ~** der See ist 12 km breit; **~ from** gegenüber +dat; **to get sth ~ (to sb)** (jdm) etw klarmachen

acrylic [ə'krɪlɪk] adj (acid, paint, blanket) Acryl- ▷ n Acryl nt; **acrylics** npl: **he paints in ~s** er malt mit Acrylfarbe

ACT® n abbr (= American College Test) Eignungstest für Studienbewerber

act [ækt] n Tat f; (of play) Akt m; (in a show etc) Nummer f; (Law) Gesetz nt ▷ vi handeln; (behave) sich verhalten; (have effect) wirken; (Theat) spielen ▷ vt spielen; **it's only an ~** es ist nur Schau; **~ of God** (Law) höhere Gewalt f; **to be in the ~ of doing sth** dabei sein, etw zu tun; **to catch sb in the ~** jdn auf frischer Tat ertappen; **to ~ the fool** (Brit) herumalbern; **he is only ~ing** er tut (doch) nur so; **to ~ as** fungieren als; **it ~s as a deterrent** es dient zur Abschreckung

▶ **act on** vt: **to ~ on sth** (take action) auf etw +acc hin handeln

▶ **act out** vt (event) durchspielen; (fantasies) zum Ausdruck bringen

acting ['æktɪŋ] adj stellvertretend ▷ n (profession) Schauspielkunst f; (activity) Spielen nt; **~ in my capacity as chairman ...** in meiner Eigenschaft als Vorsitzender ...

action ['ækʃən] n Tat f; (motion) Bewegung f; (Mil) Kampf m, Gefecht nt; (Law) Klage f ▷ vt (Comm) in die Tat umsetzen; **to bring an ~ against sb** (Law) eine Klage gegen jdn anstrengen; **killed in ~** (Mil) gefallen; **out of ~** (person) nicht einsatzfähig; (thing) außer Betrieb; **to take ~** etwas unternehmen; **to put a plan into ~** einen Plan in die Tat umsetzen

action replay n (TV) Wiederholung f

activate ['æktɪveɪt] vt in Betrieb setzen; (Chem, Phys) aktivieren

active ['æktɪv] adj aktiv; (volcano) tätig; **to play an ~ part in sth** sich aktiv an etw dat beteiligen

active duty (US) n (Mil) Einsatz m

actively ['æktɪvlɪ] adv aktiv; (dislike) offen

active partner n (Comm) aktiver Teilhaber m

active service (Brit) n (Mil) Einsatz m

active suspension n (Aut) aktives or computergesteuertes Fahrwerk nt

activist ['æktɪvɪst] n Aktivist(in) m(f)

activity [æk'tɪvɪtɪ] n Aktivität f; (pastime, pursuit) Betätigung f

activity holiday n Aktivurlaub m

actor ['æktəʳ] n Schauspieler m

actress ['æktrɪs] n Schauspielerin f

actual ['æktjʊəl] adj wirklich; (emphatic use) eigentlich

actually ['æktjʊəlɪ] adv wirklich; (in fact) tatsächlich; (even) sogar

actuary ['æktjʊərɪ] n Aktuar m

actuate ['æktjʊeɪt] vt auslösen

acuity [ə'kjuːɪtɪ] n Schärfe f

acumen ['ækjʊmən] n Scharfsinn m; **business ~** Geschäftssinn m

acupuncture ['ækjʊpʌŋktʃəʳ] n Akupunktur f

acute [ə'kjuːt] adj akut; (anxiety) heftig; (mind) scharf; (person) scharfsinnig; (Math: angle) spitz; (Ling): **~ accent** Akut m

AD adv abbr (= Anno Domini) n. Chr. ▷ n abbr (US: Mil) = **active duty**

ad [æd] (inf) n = **advertisement**

adage ['ædɪdʒ] n Sprichwort nt

adamant ['ædəmənt] adj: **to be ~ that ...** darauf bestehen, dass ...; **to be ~ about sth** auf etw dat bestehen

Adam's apple ['ædəmz-] n Adamsapfel m

adapt [ə'dæpt] vt anpassen; (novel etc) bearbeiten ▷ vi: **to ~ (to)** sich anpassen (an +acc)

adaptability [ədæptə'bɪlɪtɪ] n Anpassungsfähigkeit f

adaptable [ə'dæptəbl] adj anpassungsfähig; (device) vielseitig

adaptation [ædæp'teɪʃən] n (of novel etc) Bearbeitung f; (of machine etc) Umstellung f

adapter [ə'dæptəʳ] n (Elec) Adapter m; (: for several plugs) Mehrfachsteckdose f

adaptor [ə'dæptəʳ] n = **adapter**

ADC n abbr (Mil) = **aide-de-camp**; (US: = Aid to Dependent Children) Beihilfe für sozialschwache Familien

add [æd] vt hinzufügen; (figures: also: **add up**) zusammenzählen ▷ vi: **to ~ to** (increase) beitragen zu

▶ **add on** vt (amount) dazurechnen; (room) anbauen

▶ **add up** vt (figures) zusammenzählen ▷ vi (fig): **it doesn't ~ up** es ergibt keinen Sinn; **it doesn't ~ up to much** (fig) das ist nicht berühmt (inf)

addenda [ə'dɛndə] npl of **addendum**

addendum [ə'dɛndəm] (pl **addenda**) n

Nachtrag m

adder ['ædə'] n Kreuzotter f, Viper f

addict ['ædɪkt] n Süchtige(r) f(m); (enthusiast) Anhänger(in) m(f)

addicted [ə'dɪktɪd] adj: **to be ~ to drugs/drink** drogensüchtig/alkoholsüchtig sein; **to be ~ to football** (fig) ohne Fußball nicht mehr leben können

addiction [ə'dɪkʃən] n Sucht f

addictive [ə'dɪktɪv] adj: **to be ~** (drug) süchtig machen; (activity) zur Sucht werden können

adding machine ['ædɪŋ-] n Addiermaschine f

Addis Ababa ['ædɪs'æbəbə] n (Geog) Addis Abeba nt

addition [ə'dɪʃən] n (adding up) Zusammenzählen nt; (thing added) Zusatz m; (: to payment, bill) Zuschlag m; (: to building) Anbau m; **in ~ (to)** zusätzlich (zu)

additional [ə'dɪʃənl] adj zusätzlich

additive ['ædɪtɪv] n Zusatz m

addled ['ædld] adj (Brit: egg) faul; (brain) verwirrt

address [ə'drɛs] n Adresse f; (speech) Ansprache f ▷ vt adressieren; (speak to: person) ansprechen; (: audience) sprechen zu; **form of ~** (Form f der) Anrede f; **what form of ~ do you use for ...?** wie redet man ... an?; **absolute/relative ~** (Comput) absolute/relative Adresse; **to ~ (o.s. to)** (problem) sich befassen mit

address book n Adressbuch nt

addressee [ædrɛ'si:] n Empfänger(in) m(f)

Aden ['eɪdən] n (Geog): **Gulf of ~** Golf m von Aden

adenoids ['ædɪnɔɪdz] npl Rachenmandeln pl

adept ['ædɛpt] adj: **to be ~ at** gut sein in +dat

adequacy ['ædɪkwəsɪ] n (of resources) Adäquatheit f; (of performance, proposals etc) Angemessenheit f

adequate ['ædɪkwɪt] adj ausreichend, adäquat; (satisfactory) angemessen

adequately ['ædɪkwɪtlɪ] adv ausreichend; (satisfactorily) zufriedenstellend

adhere [əd'hɪə'] vi: **to ~ to** haften an +dat; (fig: abide by) sich halten an +acc; (: hold to) festhalten an +dat

adhesion [əd'hi:ʒən] n Haften nt, Haftung f

adhesive [əd'hi:zɪv] adj klebend, Klebe- ▷ n Klebstoff m

adhesive tape n (Brit) Klebstreifen m; (US: Med) Heftpflaster nt

ad hoc [æd'hɔk] adj (committee, decision) Ad-hoc- ▷ adv ad hoc

ad infinitum [ædɪnfɪ'naɪtəm] adv ad infinitum

adjacent [ə'dʒeɪsənt] adj: **~ to** neben +dat

adjective ['ædʒɛktɪv] n Adjektiv nt, Eigenschaftswort nt

adjoin [ə'dʒɔɪn] vt: **the hotel ~ing the station** das Hotel neben dem Bahnhof

adjoining [ə'dʒɔɪnɪŋ] adj benachbart, Neben-

adjourn [ə'dʒə:n] vt vertagen ▷ vi sich vertagen; **to ~ a meeting till the following week** eine Besprechung auf die nächste Woche vertagen; **they ~ed to the pub** (Brit: inf) sie begaben sich in die Kneipe

adjournment [ə'dʒə:nmənt] n Unterbrechung f

Adjt. abbr (Mil) = **adjutant**

adjudicate [ə'dʒu:dɪkeɪt] vt (contest) Preisrichter sein bei; (claim) entscheiden ▷ vi entscheiden; **to ~ on** urteilen bei +dat

adjudication [ədʒu:dɪ'keɪʃən] n Entscheidung f

adjudicator [ə'dju:dɪkeɪtə'] n Schiedsrichter(in) m(f); (in contest) Preisrichter(in) m(f)

adjust [ə'dʒʌst] vt anpassen; (change) ändern; (clothing) zurechtrücken; (machine etc) einstellen; (Insurance) regulieren ▷ vi: **to ~ (to)** sich anpassen (an +acc)

adjustable [ə'dʒʌstəbl] adj verstellbar

adjuster [ə'dʒʌstə'] n see **loss**

adjustment [ə'dʒʌstmənt] n Anpassung f; (to machine) Einstellung f

adjutant ['ædʒətənt] n Adjutant m

ad-lib [æd'lɪb] vi, vt improvisieren ▷ adv: **ad lib** aus dem Stegreif

adman ['ædmæn] (inf: irreg: like **man**) n Werbefachmann m

admin ['ædmɪn] (inf) n = **administration**

administer [əd'mɪnɪstə'] vt (country, department) verwalten; (justice) sprechen; (oath) abnehmen; (Med: drug) verabreichen

administration [ədmɪnɪs'treɪʃən] n (management) Verwaltung f; (government) Regierung f; **the A~** (US) die Regierung

administrative [əd'mɪnɪstrətɪv] adj (department, reform etc) Verwaltungs-

administrator [əd'mɪnɪstreɪtə'] n Verwaltungsbeamte(r) f(m)

admirable ['ædmərəbl] adj bewundernswert

admiral ['ædmərəl] n Admiral m

Admiralty ['ædmərəltɪ] (Brit) n: **the ~** (also: **the Admiralty Board**) das Marineministerium

admiration [ædmə'reɪʃən] n Bewunderung f; **to have great ~ for sb/sth** jdn/etw sehr bewundern

admire [əd'maɪə'] vt bewundern

admirer [əd'maɪərə'] n (suitor) Verehrer m; (fan) Bewunderer m, Bewunderin f

admiring [əd'maɪərɪŋ] adj bewundernd

admissible [əd'mɪsəbl] adj (evidence, as evidence) zulässig

admission [əd'mɪʃən] n (admittance) Zutritt m; (to exhibition, night club etc) Einlass m; (to club, hospital) Aufnahme f; (entry fee) Eintritt(spreis) m; (confession) Geständnis nt; **"~ free"**, **"free admission"** „Eintritt frei"; **by his own ~** nach eigenem Eingeständnis

admit [əd'mɪt] vt (confess) gestehen; (permit to enter) einlassen; (to club, hospital) aufnehmen; (responsibility etc) anerkennen; **"children not ~ted"** „kein Zutritt für Kinder"; **this ticket ~s two** diese Karte ist für zwei Personen; **I must ~ that ...** ich muss zugeben, dass ...; **to ~ defeat** sich geschlagen geben

▶ **admit of** vt fus (interpretation etc) erlauben

▸ **admit to** vt fus (murder etc) gestehen

admittance [əd'mɪtəns] n Zutritt m; **"no ~"** „kein Zutritt"

admittedly [əd'mɪtɪdlɪ] adv zugegebenermaßen

admonish [əd'mɔnɪʃ] vt ermahnen

ad nauseam [æd'nɔːsɪæm] adv (talk) endlos; (repeat) bis zum Gehtnichtmehr (inf)

ado [ə'duː] n: **without (any) more ~** ohne weitere Umstände

adolescence [ædəu'lɛsns] n Jugend f

adolescent [ædəu'lɛsnt] adj heranwachsend; (remark, behaviour) pubertär ▷ n Jugendliche(r) f(m)

adopt [ə'dɔpt] vt adoptieren; (Pol: candidate) aufstellen; (policy, attitude, accent) annehmen

adopted [ə'dɔptɪd] adj (child) adoptiert

adoption [ə'dɔpʃən] n (see vb) Adoption f; Aufstellung f; Annahme f

adoptive [ə'dɔptɪv] adj (parents etc) Adoptiv-; ~ **country** Wahlheimat f

adorable [ə'dɔːrəbl] adj entzückend

adoration [ædə'reɪʃən] n Verehrung f

adore [ə'dɔːʳ] vt (person) verehren; (film, activity etc) schwärmen für

adoring [ə'dɔːrɪŋ] adj (fans etc) ihn/sie bewundernd; (husband/wife) sie/ihn innig liebend

adoringly [ə'dɔːrɪŋlɪ] adv bewundernd

adorn [ə'dɔːn] vt schmücken

adornment [ə'dɔːnmənt] n Schmuck m

ADP n abbr = **automatic data processing**

adrenalin [ə'drɛnəlɪn] n Adrenalin nt; **it gets the ~ going** das bringt einen in Fahrt

Adriatic [eɪdrɪ'ætɪk] n: **the ~ (Sea)** (Geog) die Adria, das Adriatische Meer

adrift [ə'drɪft] adv (Naut) treibend; (fig) ziellos; **to be ~** (Naut) treiben; **to come ~** (boat) sich losmachen; (fastening etc) sich lösen

adroit [ə'drɔɪt] adj gewandt

ADSL n abbr (= asymmetric digital subscriber line) ADSL nt

ADT (US) abbr (= Atlantic Daylight Time) atlantische Sommerzeit

adulation [ædju'leɪʃən] n Verherrlichung f

adult ['ædʌlt] n Erwachsene(r) f(m) ▷ adj erwachsen; (animal) ausgewachsen; (literature etc) für Erwachsene

adult education n Erwachsenenbildung f

adulterate [ə'dʌltəreɪt] vt verunreinigen; (with water) panschen

adulterer [ə'dʌltərəʳ] n Ehebrecher m

adulteress [ə'dʌltərɪs] n Ehebrecherin f

adultery [ə'dʌltərɪ] n Ehebruch m

adulthood ['ædʌlthud] n Erwachsenenalter nt

advance [əd'vɑːns] n (movement) Vorrücken nt; (progress) Fortschritt m; (money) Vorschuss m ▷ vt (money) vorschießen; (theory, idea) vorbringen ▷ vi (move forward) vorrücken; (make progress) Fortschritte machen ▷ adj: ~ **booking** Vorverkauf m; **to make ~s (to sb)** Annäherungsversuche (bei jdm) machen; **in ~** im Voraus; **to give sb ~ notice** jdm frühzeitig Bescheid sagen; **to give sb ~ warning** jdn vorwarnen

advanced [əd'vɑːnst] adj (Scol: studies) für Fortgeschrittene; (country) fortgeschritten; (child) weit entwickelt; (ideas) fortschrittlich; ~ **in years** in fortgeschrittenem Alter

Advanced Higher (Scot) n (Scol) Mit "Advanced Higher" wird das Ausbildungsjahr nach "Higher" bezeichnet, dessen erfolgreicher Abschluss eine Hochschulzugangsberechtigung darstellt

advancement [əd'vɑːnsmənt] n (improvement) Förderung f; (in job, rank) Aufstieg m

advantage [əd'vɑːntɪdʒ] n Vorteil m; **to take ~ of** ausnutzen; (opportunity) nutzen; **it's to our ~ (to)** es ist für uns von Vorteil(, wenn wir)

advantageous [ædvən'teɪdʒəs] adj: ~ **(to)** vorteilhaft (für), von Vorteil (für)

advent ['ædvənt] n (of innovation) Aufkommen nt; (Rel): **A~** Advent m

Advent calendar n Adventskalender m

adventure [əd'vɛntʃəʳ] n Abenteuer nt

adventure playground n Abenteuerspielplatz m

adventurous [əd'vɛntʃərəs] adj abenteuerlustig; (bold) mutig

adverb ['ædvəːb] n Adverb nt

adversarial [ædvə'sɛərɪəl] adj konfliktreich

adversary ['ædvəsərɪ] n Widersacher(in) m(f)

adverse ['ædvəːs] adj ungünstig; **in ~ circumstances** unter widrigen Umständen; ~ **to** ablehnend gegenüber +dat

adversity [əd'vəːsɪtɪ] n Widrigkeit f

advert ['ædvəːt] (Brit) n = **advertisement**

advertise ['ædvətaɪz] vi (Comm) werben; (in newspaper) annoncieren, inserieren ▷ vt (product, event) werben für; (job) ausschreiben; **to ~ for** (staff etc) (per Anzeige) suchen

advertisement [əd'vəːtɪsmənt] n (Comm) Werbung f, Reklame f; (in classified ads) Anzeige f, Inserat nt

advertiser ['ædvətaɪzəʳ] n (in newspaper) Inserent(in) m(f); (on television etc) Firma, die im Fernsehen etc wirbt

advertising ['ædvətaɪzɪŋ] n Werbung f

advertising agency n Werbeagentur f

advertising campaign n Werbekampagne f

advice [əd'vaɪs] n Rat m; (notification) Benachrichtigung f, Avis m or nt (Comm); **a piece of ~** ein Rat(schlag); **to ask sb for ~** jdn um Rat fragen; **to take legal ~** einen Rechtsanwalt zurate ziehen

advice note (Brit) n (Comm) Avis m or nt

advisable [əd'vaɪzəbl] adj ratsam

advise [əd'vaɪz] vt (person) raten +dat; (company etc) beraten; **to ~ sb of sth** jdn von etw in Kenntnis setzen; **to ~ against sth** von etw abraten; **to ~ against doing sth** davon abraten, etw zu tun; **you would be well-/ ill-~d to go** Sie wären gut/schlecht beraten, wenn Sie gingen

advisedly [əd'vaɪzɪdlɪ] adv bewusst

adviser [əd'vaɪzəʳ] n Berater(in) m(f)

advisor [əd'vaɪzəʳ] n = **adviser**

417

advisory [əd'vaɪzərɪ] adj beratend, Beratungs-; **in an ~ capacity** in beratender Funktion

advocate ['ædvəkɪt] vt befürworten ▷ n (Law) (Rechts)anwalt m, (Rechts)anwältin f; (supporter, upholder): **~ of** Befürworter(in) m(f) +gen; **to be an ~ of sth** etw befürworten

advt. abbr = **advertisement**

AEA (Brit) n abbr (= Atomic Energy Authority) britische Atomenergiebehörde; (Brit: Scol: = Advanced Extension Award) eine besondere Qualifikation für leistungsstarke Schüler des "A level"

AEC (US) n abbr (= Atomic Energy Commission) amerikanische Atomenergiebehörde

AEEU (Brit) n abbr (= Amalgamated Engineering and Electrical Union) Gewerkschaft der Ingenieure und Elektriker

Aegean [iː'dʒiːən] n: **the ~ (Sea)** (Geog) die Ägäis, das Ägäische Meer

aegis ['iːdʒɪs] n: **under the ~ of** unter der Schirmherrschaft +gen

aeon ['iːən] n Äon m, Ewigkeit f

aerial ['ɛərɪəl] n Antenne f ▷ adj (view, bombardment etc) Luft-

aero ... ['ɛərə(u)] pref Luft-

aerobatics ['ɛərəʊ'bætɪks] npl fliegerische Kunststücke pl

aerobics [ɛə'rəʊbɪks] n Aerobic nt

aerodrome ['ɛərədrəʊm] (Brit) n Flugplatz m

aerodynamic ['ɛərəʊdaɪ'næmɪk] adj aerodynamisch

aeronautics [ɛərə'nɔːtɪks] n Luftfahrt f, Aeronautik f

aeroplane ['ɛərəpleɪn] (Brit) n Flugzeug nt

aerosol ['ɛərəsɔl] n Sprühdose f

aerospace industry ['ɛərəʊspeɪs-] n Raumfahrtindustrie f

aesthetic [iːs'θɛtɪk] adj ästhetisch

aesthetically [iːs'θɛtɪklɪ] adv ästhetisch

afar [ə'fɑː'] adv: **from ~** aus der Ferne

AFB (US) n abbr (= Air Force Base) Luftwaffenstützpunkt m

affable ['æfəbl] adj umgänglich, freundlich

affair [ə'fɛə'] n Angelegenheit f; (romance: also: **love affair**) Verhältnis nt; **affairs** npl Geschäfte pl

affect [ə'fɛkt] vt (influence) sich auswirken auf +acc; (subj: disease) befallen; (move deeply) bewegen; (concern) betreffen; (feign) vortäuschen; **to be ~ed by sth** von etw beeinflusst werden

affectation [æfɛk'teɪʃən] n Affektiertheit f

affected [ə'fɛktɪd] adj affektiert

affection [ə'fɛkʃən] n Zuneigung f

affectionate [ə'fɛkʃənɪt] adj liebevoll, zärtlich; (animal) anhänglich

affectionately [ə'fɛkʃənɪtlɪ] adv liebevoll, zärtlich

affidavit [æfɪ'deɪvɪt] n (Law) eidesstattliche Erklärung f

affiliated [ə'fɪlɪeɪtɪd] adj angeschlossen

affinity [ə'fɪnɪtɪ] n: **to have an ~ with** or **for** sich verbunden fühlen mit; (resemblance): **to have an ~ with** verwandt sein mit

affirm [ə'fəːm] vt versichern; (profess) sich bekennen zu

affirmation [æfə'meɪʃən] n (of facts) Bestätigung f; (of beliefs) Bekenntnis nt

affirmative [ə'fəːmətɪv] adj bejahend ▷ n: **to reply in the ~** mit "Ja" antworten

affix [ə'fɪks] vt aufkleben

afflict [ə'flɪkt] vt quälen; (misfortune) heimsuchen

affliction [ə'flɪkʃən] n Leiden nt

affluence ['æfluəns] n Wohlstand m

affluent ['æfluənt] adj wohlhabend; **the ~ society** die Wohlstandsgesellschaft

afford [ə'fɔːd] vt sich dat leisten; (time) aufbringen; (provide) bieten; **can we ~ a car?** können wir uns ein Auto leisten?; **I can't ~ the time** ich habe einfach nicht die Zeit

affordable [ə'fɔːdəbl] adj erschwinglich

affray [ə'freɪ] (Brit) n Schlägerei f

affront [ə'frʌnt] n Beleidigung f

affronted [ə'frʌntɪd] adj beleidigt

Afghan ['æfgæn] adj afghanisch ▷ n Afghane m, Afghanin f

Afghanistan [æf'gænɪstæn] n Afghanistan nt

afield [ə'fiːld] adv: **far ~** weit fort; **from far ~** aus weiter Ferne

AFL-CIO n abbr (= American Federation of Labor and Congress of Industrial Organizations) amerikanischer Gewerkschafts-Dachverband

afloat [ə'fləut] adv auf dem Wasser ▷ adj: **to be ~** schwimmen; **to stay ~** sich über Wasser halten; **to keep/get a business ~** ein Geschäft über Wasser halten/auf die Beine stellen

afoot [ə'fut] adv: **there is something ~** da ist etwas im Gang

aforementioned [ə'fɔːmɛnʃənd] adj oben erwähnt

aforesaid [ə'fɔːsɛd] adj = **aforementioned**

afraid [ə'freɪd] adj ängstlich; **to be ~ of** Angst haben vor +dat; **to be ~ of doing sth** or **to do sth** Angst davor haben, etw zu tun; **to be ~ to** sich scheuen, ...; **I am ~ that ...** leider ...; **I am ~ so/not** leider ja/nein

afresh [ə'frɛʃ] adv von Neuem, neu

Africa ['æfrɪkə] n Afrika nt

African ['æfrɪkən] adj afrikanisch ▷ n Afrikaner(in) m(f)

Afrikaans [æfrɪ'kɑːns] n Afrikaans nt

Afrikaner [æfrɪ'kɑːnə'] n Afrika(a)nder(in) m(f)

Afro-American ['æfrəʊə'mɛrɪkən] adj afro-amerikanisch

AFT (US) n abbr (= American Federation of Teachers) Lehrergewerkschaft

aft [ɑːft] adv (be) achtern; (go) nach achtern

after ['ɑːftə'] prep nach +dat; (of place) hinter +dat ▷ adv danach ▷ conj nachdem; **~ dinner** nach dem Essen; **the day ~ tomorrow** übermorgen; **what are you ~?** was willst du; **who are you ~?** wen suchst du?; **the police are ~ him** die Polizei ist hinter ihm her; **to name sb ~ sb** jdn nach jdm nennen; **it's twenty ~ eight** (US) es ist zwanzig nach acht;

to ask ~ sb nach jdm fragen; **~ all** schließlich; **~ you!** nach Ihnen!; **~ he left** nachdem er gegangen war; **~ having shaved** nachdem er sich rasiert hatte

afterbirth ['ɑːftəbəːθ] n Nachgeburt f

aftercare ['ɑːftəkɛəʳ] (Brit) n Nachbehandlung f

aftereffects ['ɑːftərɪfɛkts] npl Nachwirkungen pl

afterlife ['ɑːftəlaɪf] n Leben nt nach dem Tod

aftermath ['ɑːftəmɑːθ] n Auswirkungen pl; **in the ~ of** nach +dat

afternoon ['ɑːftə'nuːn] n Nachmittag m

afternoon market n (Econ) Nachmittagsmarkt m

afters ['ɑːftəz] (Brit: inf) n Nachtisch m

after-sales service [ɑːftə'seɪlz-] (Brit) n Kundendienst m

aftershave ['ɑːftəʃeɪv], **aftershave lotion** n Rasierwasser nt

aftershock ['ɑːftəʃɔk] n Nachbeben nt

aftersun ['ɑːftəsʌn] n After-Sun-Lotion f

aftertaste ['ɑːftəteɪst] n Nachgeschmack m

afterthought ['ɑːftəθɔːt] n: **as an ~** nachträglich; **I had an ~** mir ist noch etwas eingefallen

afterwards, (US) **afterward** ['ɑːftəwəd(z)] adv danach

again [ə'gɛn] adv (once more) noch einmal; (repeatedly) wieder; **not him ~!** nicht schon wieder er!; **to do sth ~** etw noch einmal tun; **to begin ~** noch einmal anfangen; **to see ~** wiedersehen; **he's opened it ~** er hat er schon wieder geöffnet; **~ and again** immer wieder; **now and ~** ab und zu, hin und wieder

against [ə'gɛnst] prep gegen +acc; (leaning on) an +acc; (compared to) gegenüber +dat; **~ a blue background** vor einem blauen Hintergrund; **(as) ~** gegenüber +dat

age [eɪdʒ] n Alter nt; (period) Zeitalter nt ▷ vi altern, alt werden ▷ vt alt machen; **what ~ is he?** wie alt ist er?; **20 years of ~** 20 Jahre alt; **under ~** minderjährig; **to come of ~** mündig werden; **it's been ~s since ...** es ist ewig her, seit ...

aged[1] [eɪdʒd] adj: **~ ten** zehn Jahre alt, zehnjährig

aged[2] ['eɪdʒɪd] npl: **the ~** die Alten pl

age group n Altersgruppe f; **the 40 to 50 ~** die Gruppe der Vierzig- bis Fünfzigjährigen

ageing ['eɪdʒɪŋ] adj (person, population) alternd; (thing) älter werdend; (system, technology) veraltend

ageless ['eɪdʒlɪs] adj zeitlos

age limit n Altersgrenze f

agency ['eɪdʒənsɪ] n Agentur f; (government body) Behörde f; **through** or **by the ~ of** durch die Vermittlung von

agenda [ə'dʒɛndə] n Tagesordnung f

agent ['eɪdʒənt] n (Comm) Vertreter(in) m(f); (representative, spy) Agent(in) m(f); (Chem) Mittel nt; (fig) Kraft f

aggravate ['ægrəveɪt] vt verschlimmern; (inf: annoy) ärgern

aggravating ['ægrəveɪtɪŋ] (inf) adj ärgerlich

aggravation [ægrə'veɪʃən] (inf) n Ärger m

aggregate ['ægrɪgɪt] n Gesamtmenge f ▷ vt zusammenzählen; **on ~** (Sport) nach Toren

aggression [ə'grɛʃən] n Aggression f

aggressive [ə'grɛsɪv] adj aggressiv

aggressiveness [ə'grɛsɪvnɪs] n Aggressivität f

aggressor [ə'grɛsəʳ] n Aggressor(in) m(f), Angreifer(in) m(f)

aggrieved [ə'griːvd] adj verärgert

aggro ['ægrəʊ] (Brit: inf) n (hassle) Ärger m, Theater nt; (aggressive behaviour) Aggressivität f

aghast [ə'gɑːst] adj entsetzt

agile ['ædʒaɪl] adj beweglich, wendig

agility [ə'dʒɪlɪtɪ] n Beweglichkeit f, Wendigkeit f; (of mind) (geistige) Beweglichkeit f

agitate ['ædʒɪteɪt] vt aufregen; (liquid: stir) aufrühren; (: shake) schütteln ▷ vi: **to ~ for/against sth** für/gegen etw agitieren

agitated ['ædʒɪteɪtɪd] adj aufgeregt

agitator ['ædʒɪteɪtəʳ] n Agitator(in) m(f)

AGM n abbr (= annual general meeting) JHV f

agnostic [æg'nɔstɪk] n Agnostiker(in) m(f)

ago [ə'gəʊ] adv: **two days ~** vor zwei Tagen; **not long ~** vor Kurzem; **as long ~ as 1980** schon 1980; **how long ~?** wie lange ist das her?

agog [ə'gɔg] adj gespannt

agonize ['ægənaɪz] vi: **to ~ over sth** sich dat den Kopf über etw acc zermartern

agonizing ['ægənaɪzɪŋ] adj qualvoll; (pain etc) quälend

agony ['ægənɪ] n (pain) Schmerz m; (torment) Qual f; **to be in ~** Qualen leiden

agony aunt (Brit: inf) n Briefkastentante f

agony column n Kummerkasten m

agree [ə'griː] vt (price, date) vereinbaren ▷ vi übereinstimmen; (consent) zustimmen; **to ~ with sb** (subj: person) jdm zustimmen; (: food) jdm bekommen; **to ~ to sth** einer Sache dat zustimmen; **to ~ to do sth** sich bereit erklären, etw zu tun; **to ~ on sth** sich auf etw acc einigen; **to ~ that** (admit) zugeben, dass; **garlic doesn't ~ with me** Knoblauch vertrage ich nicht; **it was ~d that ...** es wurde beschlossen, dass ...; **they ~d on this** sie haben sich in diesem Punkt geeinigt; **they ~d on going** sie einigten sich darauf, zu gehen; **they ~d on a price** sie vereinbarten einen Preis

agreeable [ə'griːəbl] adj angenehm; (willing) einverstanden; **are you ~ to this?** sind Sie hiermit einverstanden?

agreed [ə'griːd] adj vereinbart; **to be ~** sich dat einig sein

agreement [ə'griːmənt] n (concurrence) Übereinstimmung f; (consent) Zustimmung f; (arrangement) Abmachung f; (contract) Vertrag m; **to be in ~ (with sb)** (mit jdm) einer Meinung sein; **by mutual ~** in gegenseitigem Einverständnis

agricultural [ægrɪ'kʌltʃərəl] adj landwirtschaftlich; (show) Landwirtschafts-

agriculture ['ægrɪkʌltʃəʳ] n Landwirtschaft f
aground [ə'graʊnd] adv: **to run ~** auf Grund laufen
ahead [ə'hɛd] adv vor uns/ihnen etc; **~ of** (in advance of) vor +dat; **to be ~ of sb** (in progress, ranking) vor jdm liegen; **to be ~ of schedule** schneller als geplant vorankommen; **~ of time** zeitlich voraus; **to arrive ~ of time** zu früh ankommen; **go right** or **straight ~** gehen/fahren Sie geradeaus; **go ~!** (fig) machen Sie nur!, nur zu!; **they were (right) ~ of us** sie waren (genau) vor uns
AI n abbr (= Amnesty International) AI no art; (Comput) = **artificial intelligence**
AID n abbr (= artificial insemination by donor) künstliche Besamung durch Samenspender; (US: = Agency for International Development) Abteilung zur Koordination von Entwicklungshilfe und Außenpolitik
aid [eɪd] n Hilfe f; (to less developed country) Entwicklungshilfe f; (device) Hilfsmittel nt ▷ vt (help) helfen, unterstützen; **with the ~ of** mithilfe von; **in ~ of** zugunsten +gen; **to ~ and abet** Beihilfe leisten; see also **hearing aid**
aide [eɪd] n Berater(in) m(f); (Mil) Adjutant m
aide-de-camp ['eɪddə'kɔ̃] n (Mil) Adjutant m
AIDS [eɪdz] n abbr (= acquired immune deficiency syndrome) AIDS nt
AIH n abbr (= artificial insemination by husband) künstliche Besamung durch den Ehemann/Partner
ailing ['eɪlɪŋ] adj kränklich; (economy, industry etc) krank
ailment ['eɪlmənt] n Leiden nt
aim [eɪm] vt: **to ~ at** (gun, missile, camera) richten auf +acc; (blow) zielen auf +acc; (remark) richten an +acc ▷ vi (also: **take aim**) zielen ▷ n (objective) Ziel nt; (in shooting) Zielsicherheit f; **to ~ at** zielen auf +acc; (objective) anstreben +acc; **to ~ to do sth** vorhaben, etw zu tun
aimless ['eɪmlɪs] adj ziellos
aimlessly ['eɪmlɪslɪ] adv ziellos
ain't [eɪnt] (inf) = **am not; aren't; isn't**
air [ɛəʳ] n Luft f; (tune) Melodie f; (appearance) Auftreten nt; (demeanour) Haltung f; (of house etc) Atmosphäre f ▷ vt lüften; (grievances, views) Luft machen +dat; (knowledge) zur Schau stellen; (ideas) darlegen ▷ cpd Luft-; **into the ~** in die Luft; **by ~** mit dem Flugzeug; **to be on the ~** (Radio, TV: programme) gesendet werden; (: station) senden; (: person) auf Sendung sein
air base n Luftwaffenstützpunkt m
air bed (Brit) n Luftmatratze f
airborne ['ɛəbɔːn] adj in der Luft; (plane, particles) in der Luft befindlich; (troops) Luftlande-
air cargo n Luftfracht f
air-conditioned ['ɛəkən'dɪʃənd] adj klimatisiert
air conditioning n Klimaanlage f
air-cooled ['ɛəkuːld] adj (engine) luftgekühlt
aircraft ['ɛəkrɑːft] n inv Flugzeug nt
aircraft carrier n Flugzeugträger m
air cushion n Luftkissen nt

airfield ['ɛəfiːld] n Flugplatz m
Air Force n Luftwaffe f
air freight n Luftfracht f
air freshener n Raumspray nt
air gun n Luftgewehr nt
air hostess (Brit) n Stewardess f
airily ['ɛərɪlɪ] adv leichtfertig
airing ['ɛərɪŋ] n: **to give an ~ to** (fig: ideas) darlegen; (: views) Luft machen +dat
air letter (Brit) n Luftpostbrief m
airlift ['ɛəlɪft] n Luftbrücke f
airline ['ɛəlaɪn] n Fluggesellschaft f
airliner ['ɛəlaɪnəʳ] n Verkehrsflugzeug nt
airlock ['ɛəlɔk] n (in pipe etc) Luftblase f; (compartment) Luftschleuse f
air mail n: **by ~** per or mit Luftpost
air mattress n Luftmatratze f
airplane ['ɛəpleɪn] (US) n Flugzeug nt
air pocket n Luftloch nt
airport ['ɛəpɔːt] n Flughafen m
air raid n Luftangriff m
air rifle n Luftgewehr nt
airsick ['ɛəsɪk] adj luftkrank
airspace ['ɛəspeɪs] n Luftraum m
airspeed ['ɛəspiːd] n Fluggeschwindigkeit f
airstrip ['ɛəstrɪp] n Start-und-Lande-Bahn f
air terminal n Terminal m or nt
airtight ['ɛətaɪt] adj luftdicht
airtime ['ɛətaɪm] n (Radio, TV) Sendezeit f
air-traffic control ['ɛətræfɪk-] n Flugsicherung f
air-traffic controller ['ɛətræfɪk-] n Fluglotse m
air waybill n Luftfrachtbrief m
airy ['ɛərɪ] adj luftig; (casual) lässig
aisle [aɪl] n Gang m; (section of church) Seitenschiff nt
aisle seat n Sitz m am Gang
ajar [ə'dʒɑːʳ] adj angelehnt
AK (US) abbr (Post) = **Alaska**
a.k.a. abbr (= also known as) alias
akin [ə'kɪn] adj: **~ to** ähnlich +dat
AL (US) abbr (Post) = **Alabama**
ALA n abbr (= American Library Association) akademischer Verband für das Bibliothekswesen
Ala. (US) abbr (Post) = Alabama
alabaster ['æləbɑːstəʳ] n Alabaster m
à la carte adv à la carte
alacrity [ə'lækrɪtɪ] n Bereitwilligkeit f; **with ~** ohne zu zögern
alarm [ə'lɑːm] n (anxiety) Besorgnis f; (in shop, bank) Alarmanlage f ▷ vt (worry) beunruhigen; (frighten) erschrecken
alarm call n Weckruf m
alarm clock n Wecker m
alarmed [ə'lɑːmd] adj beunruhigt; **don't be ~** erschrecken Sie nicht
alarming [ə'lɑːmɪŋ] adj (worrying) beunruhigend; (frightening) erschreckend
alarmingly [ə'lɑːmɪŋlɪ] adv erschreckend
alarmist [ə'lɑːmɪst] n Panikmacher(in) m(f)
alas [ə'læs] excl leider
Alaska [ə'læskə] n Alaska nt
Albania [æl'beɪnɪə] n Albanien nt

a

Albanian [ælˈbeɪnɪən] *adj* albanisch ▷ *n* (*Ling*) Albanisch *nt*

albatross [ˈælbətrɔs] *n* Albatros *m*

albeit [ɔːlˈbiːɪt] *conj* wenn auch

album [ˈælbəm] *n* Album *nt*

albumen [ˈælbjumɪn] *n* Albumen *nt*

alchemy [ˈælkɪmɪ] *n* Alchimie *f*, Alchemie *f*

alcohol [ˈælkəhɔl] *n* Alkohol *m*

alcoholic [ælkəˈhɔlɪk] *adj* alkoholisch ▷ *n* Alkoholiker(in) *m(f)*

alcoholism [ˈælkəhɔlɪzəm] *n* Alkoholismus *m*

alcove [ˈælkəuv] *n* Alkoven *m*, Nische *f*

Ald. *abbr* = **alderman**

alderman [ˈɔːldəmən] (*irreg: like* **man**) *n* ≈ Stadtrat *m*

ale [eɪl] *n* Ale *nt*

alert [əˈlɜːt] *adj* aufmerksam ▷ *n* Alarm *m* ▷ *vt* alarmieren; **to be ~ to** (*danger, opportunity*) sich *dat* bewusst sein +*gen*; **to be on the ~** wachsam sein; **to ~ sb (to sth)** jdn (vor etw *dat*) warnen

Aleutian Islands [əˈluːʃən-] *npl* Aleuten *pl*

A level (*Brit*) *n* ≈ Abschluss *m* der Sekundarstufe 2, ≈ Abitur *nt*

Alexandria [ælɪgˈzɑːndrɪə] *n* Alexandria *nt*

alfresco [ælˈfreskəu] *adj, adv* im Freien

algebra [ˈældʒɪbrə] *n* Algebra *f*

Algeria [ælˈdʒɪərɪə] *n* Algerien *nt*

Algerian [ælˈdʒɪərɪən] *adj* algerisch ▷ *n* Algerier(in) *m(f)*

Algiers [ælˈdʒɪəz] *n* Algier *nt*

algorithm [ˈælgərɪðəm] *n* Algorithmus *m*

alias [ˈeɪlɪəs] *adv* alias ▷ *n* Deckname *m*

alibi [ˈælɪbaɪ] *n* Alibi *nt*

alien [ˈeɪlɪən] *n* Ausländer(in) *m(f)*; (*extraterrestrial*) außerirdisches Wesen *nt* ▷ *adj:* **~ (to)** fremd (+*dat*)

alienate [ˈeɪlɪəneɪt] *vt* entfremden; (*antagonize*) befremden

alienation [eɪlɪəˈneɪʃən] *n* Entfremdung *f*

alight [əˈlaɪt] *adj* brennend; (*eyes, expression*) leuchtend ▷ *vi* (*bird*) sich niederlassen; (*passenger*) aussteigen

align [əˈlaɪn] *vt* ausrichten

alignment [əˈlaɪnmənt] *n* Ausrichtung *f*; **it's out of ~ (with)** es ist nicht richtig ausgerichtet (nach)

alike [əˈlaɪk] *adj* ähnlich ▷ *adv* (*similarly*) ähnlich; (*equally*) gleich; **to look ~** sich *dat* ähnlich sehen; **winter and summer ~** Sommer wie Winter

alimony [ˈælɪmənɪ] *n* Unterhalt *m*

alive [əˈlaɪv] *adj* (*living*) lebend; (*lively*) lebendig; (*active*) lebhaft; **~ with** erfüllt von; **to be ~ to sth** sich *dat* einer Sache *gen* bewusst sein

alkali [ˈælkəlaɪ] *n* Base *f*, Lauge *f*

alkaline [ˈælkəlaɪn] *adj* basisch, alkalisch

○ **KEYWORD**

all [ɔːl] *adj* alle(r, s); **all day/night** den ganzen Tag/die ganze Nacht (über); **all men are equal** alle Menschen sind gleich; **all five**

came alle fünf kamen; **all the books** die ganzen Bücher, alle Bücher; **all the food** das ganze Essen; **all the time** die ganze Zeit (über); **all his life** sein ganzes Leben (lang)

▷ *pron* **1** alles; **I ate it all, I ate all of it** ich habe alles gegessen; **all of us/the boys went** wir alle/alle Jungen gingen; **we all sat down** wir setzten uns alle; **is that all?** ist das alles?; (*in shop*) sonst noch etwas?

2 (*in phrases*): **above all** vor allem; **after all** schließlich; **all in all** alles in allem

▷ *adv* ganz; **all alone** ganz allein; **it's not as hard as all that** so schwer ist es nun auch wieder nicht; **all the more/the better** um so mehr/besser; **all but** (*all except for*) alle außer; (*almost*) fast; **the score is 2 all** der Spielstand ist 2 zu 2

allay [əˈleɪ] *vt* (*fears*) zerstreuen

all clear *n* Entwarnung *f*

allegation [ælɪˈgeɪʃən] *n* Behauptung *f*

allege [əˈledʒ] *vt* behaupten; **he is ~d to have said that ...** er soll angeblich gesagt haben, dass ...

alleged [əˈledʒd] *adj* angeblich

allegedly [əˈledʒɪdlɪ] *adv* angeblich

allegiance [əˈliːdʒəns] *n* Treue *f*

allegory [ˈælɪgərɪ] *n* Allegorie *f*

all-embracing [ˈɔːlɪmˈbreɪsɪŋ] *adj* (all) umfassend

allergic [əˈlɜːdʒɪk] *adj* (*rash, reaction*) allergisch; (*person*): **~ to** allergisch gegen

allergy [ˈælədʒɪ] *n* Allergie *f*

alleviate [əˈliːvɪeɪt] *vt* lindern

alley [ˈælɪ] *n* Gasse *f*

alleyway [ˈælɪweɪ] *n* Durchgang *m*

alliance [əˈlaɪəns] *n* Bündnis *nt*

allied [ˈælaɪd] *adj* verbündet, alliiert; (*products, industries*) verwandt

alligator [ˈælɪgeɪtər] *n* Alligator *m*

all-important [ˈɔːlɪmˈpɔːtənt] *adj* entscheidend, äußerst wichtig

all in (*Brit*) *adv* inklusive

all-in [ˈɔːlɪn] (*Brit*) *adj* (*price*) Inklusiv-

all-in wrestling *n* (*esp Brit*) Freistilringen *nt*

alliteration [əlɪtəˈreɪʃən] *n* Alliteration *f*

all-night [ˈɔːlˈnaɪt] *adj* (*café, cinema*) die ganze Nacht geöffnet; (*party*) die ganze Nacht dauernd

allocate [ˈæləkeɪt] *vt* zuteilen

allocation [æləuˈkeɪʃən] *n* Verteilung *f*; (*of money, resources*) Zuteilung *f*

allot [əˈlɔt] *vt:* **to ~ (to)** zuteilen (+*dat*); **in the ~ted time** in der vorgesehenen Zeit

allotment [əˈlɔtmənt] *n* (*share*) Anteil *m*; (*garden*) Schrebergarten *m*

all-out [ˈɔːlaut] *adj* (*effort, dedication etc*) äußerste(r, s); (*strike*) total ▷ *adv:* **all out** mit aller Kraft; **to go all out for** sein Letztes *or* Äußerstes geben für

allow [əˈlau] *vt* erlauben; (*behaviour*) zulassen; (*sum, time*) einplanen; (*claim, goal*) anerkennen; (*concede*): **to ~ that** annehmen, dass; **to ~ sb**

to do sth jdm erlauben, etw zu tun; **he is ~ed to ...** er darf ...; **smoking is not ~ed** Rauchen ist nicht gestattet; **we must ~ three days for the journey** wir müssen für die Reise drei Tage einplanen
▸ **allow for** vt fus einplanen, berücksichtigen
allowance [ə'lauəns] n finanzielle Unterstützung f; (welfare payment) Beihilfe f; (pocket money) Taschengeld nt; (tax allowance) Freibetrag m; **to make ~s for** (person) Zugeständnisse machen für; (thing) berücksichtigen
alloy ['ælɔɪ] n Legierung f
all right adv (well) gut; (correctly) richtig; (as answer) okay, in Ordnung
all-rounder [ɔ:l'raundəʳ] n Allrounder m; (athlete etc) Allroundsportler(in) m(f)
allspice ['ɔ:lspaɪs] n Piment m or nt
all-time ['ɔ:l'taɪm] adj aller Zeiten
allude [ə'lu:d] vi: **to ~ to** anspielen auf +acc
alluring [ə'ljuərɪŋ] adj verführerisch
allusion [ə'lu:ʒən] n Anspielung f
alluvium [ə'lu:vɪəm] n Anschwemmung f
ally ['ælaɪ] n Verbündete(r) f(m); (during wars) Alliierte(r) f(m) ▷ vt: **to ~ o.s. with** sich verbünden mit
almighty [ɔ:l'maɪtɪ] adj allmächtig; (tremendous) mächtig
almond ['ɑ:mənd] n Mandel f; (tree) Mandelbaum m
almost ['ɔ:lməust] adv fast, beinahe; **he ~ fell** er wäre beinahe gefallen
alms [ɑ:mz] npl Almosen pl
aloft [ə'lɔft] adv (hold, carry) empor
alone [ə'ləun] adj, adv allein; **to leave sb ~** jdn in Ruhe lassen; **to leave sth ~** die Finger von etw lassen; **let ~ ...** geschweige denn ...
along [ə'lɔŋ] prep entlang +acc ▷ adv: **is he coming ~ with us?** kommt er mit?; **he was hopping/limping ~** er hüpfte/humpelte daher; **~ with** (together with) zusammen mit; **all ~** (all the time) die ganze Zeit
alongside [ə'lɔŋ'saɪd] prep neben +dat; (ship) längsseits +gen ▷ adv (come) nebendran; (be) daneben; **we brought our boat ~** wir brachten unser Boot heran; **a car drew up ~** ein Auto fuhr neben mich/ihn etc heran
aloof [ə'lu:f] adj unnahbar ▷ adv: **to stand ~** abseitsstehen
aloofness [ə'lu:fnɪs] n Unnahbarkeit f
aloud [ə'laud] adv laut
alphabet ['ælfəbɛt] n Alphabet nt
alphabetical [ælfə'bɛtɪkl] adj alphabetisch; **in ~ order** in alphabetischer Reihenfolge
alphanumeric ['ælfənju:'mɛrɪk] adj alphanumerisch
alpine ['ælpaɪn] adj alpin, Alpen-
Alps [ælps] npl: **the ~** die Alpen
already [ɔ:l'rɛdɪ] adv schon
alright ['ɔ:l'raɪt] (Brit) adv = **all right**
Alsace ['ælsæs] n Elsass nt
Alsatian [æl'seɪʃən] (Brit) n (dog) Schäferhund m

also ['ɔ:lsəu] adv (too) auch; (moreover) außerdem
altar ['ɔltəʳ] n Altar m
alter ['ɔltəʳ] vt ändern; (clothes) umändern ▷ vi sich (ver)ändern
alteration [ɔltə'reɪʃən] n Änderung f; (to clothes) Umänderung f; (to building) Umbau m; **alterations** npl (Sewing) Änderungen pl; (Archit) Umbau m
altercation [ɔltə'keɪʃən] n Auseinandersetzung f
alternate [adj ɔl'tə:nɪt, vi 'ɔltəneɪt] adj abwechselnd; (US: alternative: plans etc) Alternativ- ▷ vi: **to ~ (with)** sich abwechseln (mit); **on ~ days** jeden zweiten Tag
alternately [ɔl'tə:nɪtlɪ] adv abwechselnd
alternating current ['ɔltə:neɪtɪŋ-] n Wechselstrom m
alternative [ɔl'tə:nətɪv] adj alternativ; (solution etc) Alternativ- ▷ n Alternative f
alternative energy n Alternativenergie f
alternatively [ɔl'tə:nətɪvlɪ] adv: **~ one could ...** oder man könnte ...
alternative medicine n Alternativmedizin f
alternative society n Alternativgesellschaft f
alternator ['ɔltə:neɪtəʳ] n (Aut) Lichtmaschine f
although [ɔ:l'ðəu] conj obwohl
altitude ['æltɪtju:d] n Höhe f
alto ['æltəu] n Alt m
altogether [ɔ:ltə'gɛðəʳ] adv ganz; (on the whole, in all) im Ganzen, insgesamt; **how much is that ~?** was macht das zusammen?
altruism ['æltruɪzəm] n Altruismus m
altruistic [æltru'ɪstɪk] adj uneigennützig, altruistisch
aluminium [ælju'mɪnɪəm], (US) **aluminum** [ə'lu:mɪnəm] n Aluminium nt
always ['ɔ:lweɪz] adv immer; **we can ~ ...** (if all else fails) wir können ja auch ...
Alzheimer's ['æltshaɪməz], **Alzheimer's disease** n (Med) Alzheimerkrankheit f
AM abbr (= amplitude modulation) AM, ≈ MW ▷ n abbr (Brit: in Wales: Pol: = Assembly Member) Mitglied nt der walisischen Versammlung
am [æm] vb see **be**
a.m. adv abbr (= ante meridiem) morgens; (later) vormittags
AMA n abbr (= American Medical Association) Medizinerverband
amalgam [ə'mælgəm] n Amalgam nt; (fig) Mischung f
amalgamate [ə'mælgəmeɪt] vi, vt fusionieren
amalgamation [əmælgə'meɪʃən] n Fusion f
amass [ə'mæs] vt anhäufen; (evidence) zusammentragen
amateur ['æmətəʳ] n Amateur m ▷ adj (Sport) Amateur-; **~ dramatics** Laientheater nt
amateurish ['æmətərɪʃ] adj laienhaft; (pej) dilettantisch, stümperhaft
amaze [ə'meɪz] vt erstaunen; **to be ~d (at)** erstaunt sein (über +acc)
amazement [ə'meɪzmənt] n Erstaunen nt
amazing [ə'meɪzɪŋ] adj erstaunlich; (bargain,

offer) sensationell

amazingly [ə'meɪzɪŋlɪ] *adv* erstaunlich

Amazon ['æməzən] *n* (*river*) Amazonas *m*; **the ~ basin** das Amazonastiefland; **the ~ jungle** der Amazonas-Regenwald

Amazonian [æmə'zəʊnɪən] *adj* amazonisch

ambassador [æm'bæsədə^r] *n* Botschafter(in) *m(f)*

amber ['æmbə^r] *n* Bernstein *m*; **at ~** (*Brit: traffic lights*) auf Gelb; (*: move off*) bei Gelb

ambidextrous [æmbɪ'dekstrəs] *adj* beidhändig

ambience ['æmbɪəns] *n* Atmosphäre *f*

ambiguity [æmbɪ'gjuːɪtɪ] *n* Zweideutigkeit *f*; (*lack of clarity*) Unklarheit *f*

ambiguous [æm'bɪgjuəs] *adj* zweideutig; (*not clear*) unklar

ambition [æm'bɪʃən] *n* Ehrgeiz *m*; (*desire*) Ambition *f*; **to achieve one's ~** seine Ambitionen erfüllen

ambitious [æm'bɪʃəs] *adj* ehrgeizig

ambivalence [æm'bɪvələns] *n* Ambivalenz *f*

ambivalent [æm'bɪvələnt] *adj* ambivalent

amble ['æmbl] *vi* schleudern

ambulance ['æmbjuləns] *n* Krankenwagen *m*

ambulanceman ['æmbjulənsmən] (*irreg: like* **man**) *n* Sanitäter *m*

ambush ['æmbuʃ] *n* Hinterhalt *m*; (*attack*) Überfall *m* aus dem Hinterhalt ▷ *vt* (aus dem Hinterhalt) überfallen

ameba [ə'miːbə] (*US*) *n* = **amoeba**

ameliorate [ə'miːlɪəreɪt] *vt* verbessern

amen ['ɑːmɛn] *excl* amen

amenable [ə'miːnəbl] *adj*: **~ to** zugänglich +*dat*; (*to flattery etc*) empfänglich für; **~ to the law** dem Gesetz verantwortlich

amend [ə'mɛnd] *vt* ändern; (*habits, behaviour*) bessern

amendment [ə'mɛndmənt] *n* Änderung *f*; (*to law*) Amendement *nt*

amends [ə'mɛndz] *npl*: **to make ~** es wiedergutmachen; **to make ~ for sth** etw wiedergutmachen

amenities [ə'miːnɪtɪz] *npl* Einkaufs-, Unterhaltungs- und Transportmöglichkeiten

amenity [ə'miːnɪtɪ] *n* (Freizeit)einrichtung *f*

America [ə'mɛrɪkə] *n* Amerika *nt*

American [ə'mɛrɪkən] *adj* amerikanisch ▷ *n* Amerikaner(in) *m(f)*

Americanize [ə'mɛrɪkənaɪz] *vt* amerikanisieren

amethyst ['æmɪθɪst] *n* Amethyst *m*

Amex ['æmɛks] *n abbr* (= *American Stock Exchange*) US-Börse; (= *American Express®*) Kreditkarte

amiable ['eɪmɪəbl] *adj* liebenswürdig

amiably ['eɪmɪəblɪ] *adv* liebenswürdig

amicable ['æmɪkəbl] *adj* freundschaftlich; (*settlement*) gütlich

amicably ['æmɪkəblɪ] *adv* (*part, discuss*) in aller Freundschaft; (*settle*) gütlich

amid [ə'mɪd], **amidst** [ə'mɪdst] *prep* inmitten +*gen*

amiss [ə'mɪs] *adj, adv*: **to take sth ~** etw übel nehmen; **there's something ~** da stimmt

ammeter ['æmɪtə^r] *n* Amperemeter *nt*

ammo ['æməʊ] (*inf*) *n* = **ammunition**

ammonia [ə'məʊnɪə] *n* Ammoniak *nt*

ammunition [æmju'nɪʃən] *n* Munition *f*

ammunition dump *n* Munitionslager *nt*

amnesia [æm'niːzɪə] *n* Amnesie *f*, Gedächtnisschwund *m*

amnesty ['æmnɪstɪ] *n* Amnestie *f*; **to grant an ~ to** amnestieren

Amnesty International *n* Amnesty International *no art*

amoeba, (*US*) **ameba** [ə'miːbə] *n* Amöbe *f*

amok [ə'mɔk] *adv*: **to run ~** Amok laufen

among [ə'mʌŋ], **amongst** [ə'mʌŋst] *prep* unter +*dat*

amoral [æ'mɔrəl] *adj* unmoralisch

amorous ['æmərəs] *adj* amourös

amorphous [ə'mɔːfəs] *adj* formlos, gestaltlos

amortization [əmɔːtaɪ'zeɪʃən] *n* Amortisation *f*

amount [ə'maunt] *n* (*quantity*) Menge *f*; (*sum of money*) Betrag *m*; (*total*) Summe *f*; (*of bill etc*) Höhe *f* ▷ *vi*: **to ~ to** (*total*) sich belaufen auf +*acc*; (*be same as*) gleichkommen +*dat*; **the total ~** (*of money*) die Gesamtsumme

amp ['æmp], **ampère** ['æmpɛə^r] *n* Ampere *nt*; **a 3 ~(ère) fuse** eine Sicherung von 3 Ampere; **a 13 ~(ère) plug** ein Stecker mit einer Sicherung von 13 Ampere

ampersand ['æmpəsænd] *n* Et-Zeichen *nt*, Und-Zeichen *nt*

amphetamine [æm'fɛtəmiːn] *n* Amphetamin *nt*

amphibian [æm'fɪbɪən] *n* Amphibie *f*

amphibious [æm'fɪbɪəs] *adj* amphibisch; (*vehicle*) Amphibien-

amphitheatre, (*US*) **amphitheater** ['æmfɪθɪətə^r] *n* Amphitheater *nt*

ample ['æmpl] *adj* (*large*) üppig; (*abundant*) reichlich; (*enough*) genügend; **this is ~** das ist reichlich; **to have ~ time/room** genügend Zeit/Platz haben

amplifier ['æmplɪfaɪə^r] *n* Verstärker *m*

amplify ['æmplɪfaɪ] *vt* verstärken; (*expand: idea etc*) genauer ausführen

amply ['æmplɪ] *adv* reichlich

ampoule, (*US*) **ampule** ['æmpuːl] *n* Ampulle *f*

amputate ['æmpjuteɪt] *vt* amputieren

amputation [æmpju'teɪʃən] *n* Amputation *f*

amputee [æmpju'tiː] *n* Amputierte(r) *f(m)*

Amsterdam ['æmstədæm] *n* Amsterdam *nt*

amt *abbr* = **amount**

amuck [ə'mʌk] *adv* = **amok**

amuse [ə'mjuːz] *vt* (*entertain*) unterhalten; (*make smile*) amüsieren, belustigen; **to ~ o.s. with sth/by doing sth** sich die Zeit mit etw vertreiben/damit vertreiben, etw zu tun; **to be ~d** sich amüsieren über +*acc*; **he was not ~d** er fand das gar nicht komisch *or* zum Lachen

amusement [ə'mjuːzmənt] *n* (*mirth*) Vergnügen *nt*; (*pleasure*) Unterhaltung *f*;

(*pastime*) Zeitvertreib *m*; **much to my ~** zu meiner großen Belustigung

amusement arcade *n* Spielhalle *f*

amusement park *n* Vergnügungspark *m*

amusing [ə'mju:zɪŋ] *adj* amüsant, unterhaltsam

an [æn, ən] *indef art see* **a**

ANA *n abbr* (= *American Newspaper Association*) *amerikanischer Zeitungsverband*; (= *American Nurses Association*) *Verband amerikanischer Krankenschwestern und Krankenpfleger*

anachronism [ə'nækrənɪzəm] *n* Anachronismus *m*

anaemia, (US) **anemia** [ə'ni:mɪə] *n* Anämie *f*

anaemic, (US) **anemic** [ə'ni:mɪk] *adj* blutarm

anaesthetic, (US) **anesthetic** [ænɪs'θetɪk] *n* Betäubungsmittel *nt*; **under (the) ~** unter Narkose; **local ~** örtliche Betäubung *f*; **general ~** Vollnarkose *f*

anaesthetist [æ'ni:sθɪtɪst] *n* Anästhesist(in) *m(f)*

anagram ['ænəgræm] *n* Anagramm *nt*

anal ['eɪnl] *adj* anal, Anal-

analgesic [ænæl'dʒi:sɪk] *adj* schmerzstillend ▷ *n* Schmerzmittel *nt*, schmerzstillendes Mittel *nt*

analogous [ə'næləgəs] *adj*: **~ (to** *or* **with)** analog (zu)

analogue, (US) **analog** ['ænəlɒg] *adj* (*watch, computer*) Analog-

analogy [ə'nælədʒɪ] *n* Analogie *f*; **to draw an ~ between** eine Analogie herstellen zwischen +*dat*; **by ~** durch einen Analogieschluss

analyse, (US) **analyze** ['ænəlaɪz] *vt* analysieren; (*Chem, Med*) untersuchen; (*person*) psychoanalytisch behandeln

analyses [ə'næləsi:z] *npl of* **analysis**

analysis [ə'næləsɪs] (*pl* **analyses**) *n* (*see vb*) Analyse *f*; Untersuchung *f*; Psychoanalyse *f*; **in the last ~** letzten Endes

analyst ['ænəlɪst] *n* Analytiker(in) *m(f)*; (US) Psychoanalytiker(in) *m(f)*

analytic [ænə'lɪtɪk], **analytical** [ænə'lɪtɪkəl] *adj* analytisch

analyze ['ænəlaɪz] (US) *vt* = **analyse**

anarchic [æ'nɑ:kɪk] *adj* anarchisch

anarchist ['ænəkɪst] *adj* anarchistisch ▷ *n* Anarchist(in) *m(f)*

anarchy ['ænəkɪ] *n* Anarchie *f*

anathema [ə'næθɪmə] *n*: **that is ~ to him** das ist ihm ein Gräuel

anatomical [ænə'tɒmɪkl] *adj* anatomisch

anatomy [ə'nætəmɪ] *n* Anatomie *f*; (*body*) Körper *m*

ANC *n abbr* (= *African National Congress*) ANC *m*

ancestor ['ænsɪstə^r] *n* Vorfahr(in) *m(f)*

ancestral [æn'sestrəl] *adj* angestammt; **~ home** Stammsitz *m*

ancestry ['ænsɪstrɪ] *n* Abstammung *f*

anchor ['æŋkə^r] *n* Anker *m* ▷ *vi* (*also*: **to drop anchor**) ankern, vor Anker gehen ▷ *vt* (*fig*) verankern; **to ~ sth to** etw verankern in +*dat*; **to weigh ~** den Anker lichten

anchorage ['æŋkərɪdʒ] *n* Ankerplatz *m*

anchorman [ænkəmæn] (*irreg: like* **man**) *n* (*TV, Radio*) = Moderator *m*

anchor store *n* (*attractive store*) = Magnetbetrieb *m*

anchorwoman [ænkəwʊmən] (*irreg: like* **woman**) *n* (*TV, Radio*) = Moderatorin *f*

anchovy ['æntʃəvɪ] *n* Sardelle *f*, An(s)chovis *f*

ancient ['eɪnʃənt] *adj* alt; (*person, car*) uralt

ancient monument *n* historisches Denkmal *nt*

ancillary [æn'sɪlərɪ] *adj* Hilfs-

and [ænd] *conj* und; **~ so on** und so weiter; **try ~ come please** bitte versuche zu kommen; **better ~ better** immer besser

Andes ['ændi:z] *npl*: **the ~** die Anden *pl*

Andorra [æn'dɔ:rə] *n* Andorra *nt*

anecdote ['ænɪkdəʊt] *n* Anekdote *f*

anemia *etc* [ə'ni:mɪə] (US) = **anaemia** *etc*

anemone [ə'nɛmənɪ] *n* (*Bot*) Anemone *f*, Buschwindröschen *nt*

anesthetic *etc* [ænɪs'θetɪk] (US) = **anaesthetic** *etc*

anew [ə'nju:] *adv* von Neuem

angel ['eɪndʒəl] *n* Engel *m*

angel dust (*inf*) *n* als halluzinogene Droge missbrauchtes Medikament

angelic [æn'dʒɛlɪk] *adj* engelhaft

anger ['æŋgə^r] *n* Zorn *m* ▷ *vt* ärgern; (*enrage*) erzürnen; **red with ~** rot vor Wut

angina [æn'dʒaɪnə] *n* Angina pectoris *f*

angle ['æŋgl] *n* Winkel *m*; (*viewpoint*): **from their ~** von ihrem Standpunkt aus ▷ *vi*: **to ~ for** (*invitation*) aus sein auf +*acc*; (*compliments*) fischen nach ▷ *vt*: **to ~ sth towards** *or* **to** etw ausrichten auf +*acc*

angler ['æŋglə^r] *n* Angler(in) *m(f)*

Anglican ['æŋglɪkən] *adj* anglikanisch ▷ *n* Anglikaner(in) *m(f)*

anglicize ['æŋglɪsaɪz] *vt* anglisieren

angling ['æŋglɪŋ] *n* Angeln *nt*

Anglo- ['æŋgləʊ] *pref* Anglo-, anglo-

Anglo-German ['æŋgləʊdʒə:mən] *adj* englisch-deutsch

Anglo-Saxon ['æŋgləʊ'sæksən] *adj* angelsächsisch ▷ *n* Angelsachse *m*, Angelsächsin *f*

Angola [æn'gəʊlə] *n* Angola *nt*

Angolan [æn'gəʊlən] *adj* angolanisch ▷ *n* Angolaner(in) *m(f)*

angrily ['æŋgrɪlɪ] *adv* verärgert

angry ['æŋgrɪ] *adj* verärgert; (*wound*) entzündet; **to be ~ with sb** auf jdn böse sein; **to be ~ at sth** über etw *acc* verärgert sein; **to get ~** wütend werden; **to make sb ~** jdn wütend machen

anguish ['æŋgwɪʃ] *n* Qual *f*

anguished ['æŋgwɪʃt] *adj* gequält

angular ['æŋgjʊlə^r] *adj* eckig; (*features*) kantig

animal ['ænɪməl] *n* Tier *nt*; (*living creature*) Lebewesen *nt*; (*pej: person*) Bestie *f* ▷ *adj* tierhaft; (*attraction etc*) animalisch

animal spirits *npl* Vitalität *f*

animate [vt 'ænɪmeɪt, adj 'ænɪmɪt] vt beleben
▷ adj lebend

animated ['ænɪmeɪtɪd] adj lebhaft; (film)
Zeichentrick-

animation [ænɪ'meɪʃən] n (liveliness)
Lebhaftigkeit f; (film) Animation f

animosity [ænɪ'mɒsɪtɪ] n Feindseligkeit f

aniseed ['ænɪsiːd] n Anis m

Ankara ['æŋkərə] n Ankara nt

ankle ['æŋkl] n Knöchel m

ankle sock (Brit) n Söckchen nt

annex ['ænɛks] n (also: **annexe**: Brit) Anhang m;
(building) Nebengebäude nt; (extension) Anbau m
▷ vt (take over) annektieren

annexation [ænɛk'seɪʃən] n Annexion f

annihilate [ə'naɪəleɪt] vt (also fig) vernichten

annihilation [ənaɪə'leɪʃən] n Vernichtung f

anniversary [ænɪ'vɜːsərɪ] n Jahrestag m

anno Domini adv anno Domini, nach Christus

annotate ['ænəuteɪt] vt kommentieren

announce [ə'nauns] vt ankündigen; (birth,
death etc) anzeigen; **he ~d that he wasn't
going** er verkündete, dass er nicht gehen
würde

announcement [ə'naunsmənt] n
Ankündigung f; (official) Bekanntmachung f;
(of birth, death etc) Anzeige f; **I'd like to make
an ~** ich möchte etwas bekannt geben

announcer [ə'naunsə'] n Ansager(in) m(f)

annoy [ə'nɔɪ] vt ärgern; **to be ~ed (at sth/
with sb)** sich (über etw/jdn) ärgern; **don't
get ~ed!** reg dich nicht auf!

annoyance [ə'nɔɪəns] n Ärger m

annoying [ə'nɔɪɪŋ] adj ärgerlich; (person, habit)
lästig

annual ['ænjuəl] adj jährlich; (income) Jahres-
▷ n (Bot) einjährige Pflanze f; (book) Jahresband
m

annual general meeting (Brit) n
Jahreshauptversammlung f

annually ['ænjuəlɪ] adv jährlich

annual report n Geschäftsbericht m

annuity [ə'njuːɪtɪ] n Rente f; **life ~** Rente f auf
Lebenszeit

annul [ə'nʌl] vt annullieren; (law) aufheben

annulment [ə'nʌlmənt] n (see vb) Annullierung
f; Aufhebung f

annum ['ænəm] n see **per**

Annunciation [ənʌnsɪ'eɪʃən] n Mariä
Verkündigung f

anode ['ænəud] n Anode f

anodyne ['ænədaɪn] (fig) n Wohltat f ▷ adj
schmerzlos

anoint [ə'nɔɪnt] vt salben

anomalous [ə'nɒmələs] adj anomal

anomaly [ə'nɒmətlɪ] n Anomalie f

anon. [ə'nɒn] abbr = **anonymous**

anonymity [ænə'nɪmɪtɪ] n Anonymität f

anonymous [ə'nɒnɪməs] adj anonym

anorak ['ænəræk] n Anorak m

anorexia [ænə'rɛksɪə] n Magersucht f,
Anorexie f

anorexic [ænə'rɛksɪk] adj magersüchtig

another [ə'nʌðə'] pron (additional) noch eine(r,
s); (different) ein(e) andere(r, s) ▷ adj: **~ book**
(one more) noch ein Buch; (a different one)
ein anderes Buch; **~ drink?** noch etwas zu
trinken?; **in ~ five years** in weiteren fünf
Jahren; see also **one**

ANSI [eɪɛnɛs'aɪ] n abbr (= American National
Standards Institution) amerikanischer
Normenausschuss

answer ['ɑːnsə'] n Antwort f; (to problem)
Lösung f ▷ vi antworten; (Tel) sich melden
▷ vt (reply to: person) antworten +dat; (: letter,
question) beantworten; (problem) lösen; (prayer)
erhören; **in ~ to your letter** in Beantwortung
Ihres Schreibens; **to ~ the phone** ans Telefon
gehen; **to ~ the bell** or **the door** die Tür
aufmachen

▶ **answer back** vi widersprechen; (child) frech
sein

▶ **answer for** vt fus (person) verantwortlich sein
für, sich verbürgen für

▶ **answer to** vt fus (description) entsprechen +dat

answerable ['ɑːnsərəbl] adj: **to be ~ to sb for
sth** jdm gegenüber für etw verantwortlich
sein; **I am ~ to no-one** ich brauche mich vor
niemandem zu verantworten

answering machine ['ɑːnsərɪŋ-] n
Anrufbeantworter m

ant [ænt] n Ameise f

antagonism [æn'tægənɪzəm] n Feindseligkeit
f, Antagonismus m

antagonist [æn'tægənɪst] n Gegner(in) m(f),
Antagonist(in) m(f)

antagonistic [æntægə'nɪstɪk] adj feindselig

antagonize [æn'tægənaɪz] vt gegen sich
aufbringen

Antarctic [ænt'ɑːktɪk] n: **the ~** die Antarktis

Antarctica [ænt'ɑːktɪkə] n Antarktik f

Antarctic Circle n: **the ~** der südliche
Polarkreis

Antarctic Ocean n: **the ~** das Südpolarmeer

ante ['æntɪ] n: **to up the ~** den Einsatz erhöhen

ante ... ['æntɪ] pref vor-

anteater ['æntiːtə'] n Ameisenbär m

antecedent [æntɪ'siːdənt] n Vorläufer m; (of
living creature) Vorfahr m; **antecedents** npl
Herkunft f

antechamber ['æntɪtʃeɪmbə'] n Vorzimmer nt

antelope ['æntɪləup] n Antilope f

antenatal ['æntɪ'neɪtl] adj vor der Geburt,
Schwangerschafts-

antenatal clinic n Sprechstunde f für
werdende Mütter

antenna [æn'tɛnə] (pl **~e**) n (of insect) Fühler m;
(Radio, TV) Antenne f

antennae [æn'tɛniː] npl of **antenna**

anteroom ['æntɪrum] n Vorzimmer nt

anthem ['ænθəm] n: **national ~**
Nationalhymne f

ant hill n Ameisenhaufen m

anthology [æn'θɒlədʒɪ] n Anthologie f

anthropologist [ænθrə'pɒlədʒɪst] n
Anthropologe m, Anthropologin f

425

anthropology [ænθrə'pɔlədʒɪ] n
Anthropologie f
anti ... ['æntɪ] pref Anti-, anti-
anti-aircraft ['æntɪ'eəkrɑːft] adj (gun, rocket)
Flugabwehr-
anti-aircraft defence n Luftverteidigung f
antiballistic ['æntɪbə'lɪstɪk] adj (missile) Anti-
Raketen-
antibiotic ['æntɪbaɪ'ɔtɪk] n Antibiotikum nt
antibody ['æntɪbɒdɪ] n Antikörper m
anticipate [æn'tɪsɪpeɪt] vt erwarten; (foresee)
vorhersehen; (look forward to) sich freuen auf
+acc; (forestall) vorwegnehmen; **this is worse
than I ~d** es ist schlimmer, als ich erwartet
hatte; **as ~d** wie erwartet
anticipation [æntɪsɪ'peɪʃən] n Erwartung
f; (eagerness) Vorfreude f; **thanking you in ~**
vielen Dank im Voraus
anticlimax ['æntɪ'klaɪmæks] n Enttäuschung f
anticlockwise ['æntɪ'klɔkwaɪz] (Brit) adv gegen
den Uhrzeigersinn
antics ['æntɪks] npl Mätzchen pl; (of politicians
etc) Gehabe nt
anticyclone ['æntɪ'saɪkləun] n
Hoch(druckgebiet) nt
antidote ['æntɪdəut] n Gegenmittel nt
antifreeze ['æntɪfriːz] n Frostschutzmittel
nt
anti-globalist [æntɪ'gləubəlɪst] n, **anti-
globalization protester** [æntɪgləublaɪ'zeɪʃn-]
▷ n Globalisierungsgegner(in) m(f)
antihistamine ['æntɪ'hɪstəmɪn] n
Antihistamin nt
Antilles [æn'tɪliːz] npl: **the ~** die Antillen pl
antipathy [æn'tɪpəθɪ] n Antipathie f,
Abneigung f
antiperspirant ['æntɪ'pəːspɪrənt] n
Antitranspirant m
Antipodean [æntɪpə'diːən] adj antipodisch
Antipodes [æn'tɪpədiːz] npl: **the ~** Australien
und Neuseeland nt
antiquarian [æntɪ'kweərɪən] n (collector)
Antiquitätensammler(in) m(f); (seller)
Antiquitätenhändler(in) m(f) ▷ adj: ~
bookshop Antiquariat nt
antiquated ['æntɪkweɪtɪd] adj antiquiert
antique [æn'tiːk] n Antiquität f ▷ adj antik
antique dealer n Antiquitätenhändler(in)
m(f)
antique shop n Antiquitätenladen m
antiquity [æn'tɪkwɪtɪ] n (period) Antike f;
antiquities npl (objects) Altertümer pl
anti-Semitic ['æntɪsɪ'mɪtɪk] adj antisemitisch
anti-Semitism ['æntɪ'sɛmɪtɪzəm] n
Antisemitismus m
antiseptic [æntɪ'sɛptɪk] n Antiseptikum nt
▷ adj antiseptisch
antisocial ['æntɪ'səuʃəl] adj unsozial; (person)
ungesellig
antitank ['æntɪ'tæŋk] adj (gun, fire)
Panzerabwehr-
antitheses [æn'tɪθɪsiːz] npl of **antithesis**
antithesis [æn'tɪθɪsɪs] (pl **antitheses**) n

Gegensatz m; **she's the ~ of a good cook**
sie ist das genaue Gegenteil einer guten
Köchin
antitrust ['æntɪ'trʌst] (US) adj: ~ **legislation**
Kartellgesetzgebung f
antiviral ['æntɪ'vaɪərəl] adj (Med) antiviral
anti-virus [æntɪ'vaɪrəs] adj (Comput) Antiviren-
anti-virus software n Antivirensoftware f
antlers ['æntləz] npl Geweih nt
Antwerp ['æntwəːp] n Antwerpen nt
anus ['eɪnəs] n After m
anvil ['ænvɪl] n Amboss m
anxiety [æŋ'zaɪətɪ] n (worry) Sorge f; (Med)
Angstzustand m; (eagerness): ~ **to do sth**
Verlangen (danach), etw zu tun
anxious ['æŋkʃəs] adj (worried) besorgt;
(situation) Angst einflößend; (question,
moments) bang(e); (keen): **to be ~ to do sth** etw
unbedingt tun wollen; **I'm very ~ about you**
ich mache mir große Sorgen um dich
anxiously ['æŋkʃəslɪ] adv besorgt

🔘 KEYWORD

any ['ɛnɪ] adj **1** (in questions etc): **have you any
butter/children?** haben Sie Butter/Kinder?;
if there are any tickets left falls noch
Karten da sind
2 (with negative) kein(e); **I haven't any money/
books** ich habe kein Geld/keine Bücher
3 (no matter which) irgendein(e); **choose any
book you like** nehmen Sie irgendein Buch or
ein beliebiges Buch
4 (in phrases): **in any case** in jedem Fall; **any
day now** jeden Tag; **at any moment** jeden
Moment; **at any rate** auf jeden Fall; **any
time** (at any moment) jeden Moment; (whenever)
jederzeit
▷ pron **1** (in questions etc): **have you got any?**
haben Sie welche?; **can any of you sing?**
kann (irgend)einer von euch singen?
2 (with negative): **I haven't any (of them)** ich
habe keine (davon)
3 (no matter which one(s)) egal welche; **take
any of those books (you like)** nehmen Sie
irgendwelche von diesen Büchern
▷ adv **1** (in questions etc): **do you want any more
soup/sandwiches?** möchtest du noch Suppe/
Butterbrote?; **are you feeling any better?**
geht es Ihnen etwas besser?
2 (with negative): **I can't hear him any more**
ich kann ihn nicht mehr hören; **don't wait
any longer** warte nicht noch länger

anybody ['ɛnɪbɒdɪ] pron = **anyone**

🔘 KEYWORD

anyhow ['ɛnɪhau] adv **1** (at any rate) sowieso,
ohnehin; **I shall go anyhow** ich gehe auf
jeden Fall
2 (haphazard): **do it anyhow you like** machen
Sie es, wie Sie wollen

⊙ KEYWORD

anyone ['ɛnɪwʌn] *pron* **1** (*in questions etc*) (irgend) jemand; **can you see anyone?** siehst du jemanden?
2 (*with negative*) keine(r); **I can't see anyone** ich kann keinen *or* niemanden sehen
3 (*no matter who*) jede(r); **anyone could do it** das kann jeder

anyplace ['ɛnɪpleɪs] (*US*) *adv* = **anywhere**

⊙ KEYWORD

anything ['ɛnɪθɪŋ] *pron* **1** (*in questions etc*) (irgend)etwas; **can you see anything?** kannst du etwas sehen?
2 (*with negative*) nichts; **I can't see anything** ich kann nichts sehen
3 (*no matter what*) irgendetwas; **you can say anything you like** du kannst sagen, was du willst; **anything between 15 and 20 pounds** (ungefähr) zwischen 15 und 20 Pfund

⊙ KEYWORD

anyway ['ɛnɪweɪ] *adv* **1** (*at any rate*) sowieso, ohnehin; **I shall go anyway** ich gehe auf jeden Fall
2 (*besides*): **anyway, I can't come** jedenfalls kann ich nicht kommen; **why are you phoning, anyway?** warum rufst du überhaupt *or* eigentlich an?

⊙ KEYWORD

anywhere ['ɛnɪwɛəʳ] *adv* **1** (*in questions etc*) irgendwo; **can you see him anywhere?** kannst du ihn irgendwo sehen?
2 (*with negative*) nirgendwo, nirgends; **I can't see him anywhere** ich kann ihn nirgendwo *or* nirgends sehen
3 (*no matter where*) irgendwo; **put the books down anywhere** legen Sie die Bücher irgendwohin

Anzac ['ænzæk] *n abbr* (= *Australia-New Zealand Army Corps*) (*soldier*) australischer/ neuseeländischer Soldat *m*; *siehe Info-Artikel*

⊙ **ANZAC DAY**
⊙
⊙ *Anzac Day*, der 25 April, ist in Australien und
⊙ Neuseeland ein Feiertag zum Gedenken
⊙ an die Landung der australischen und
⊙ neuseeländischen Truppen in Gallipoli im
⊙ Ersten Weltkrieg.

apace [ə'peɪs] *adv*: **to continue ~** (*negotiations, preparations etc*) rasch vorangehen
apart [ə'pɑːt] *adv* (*be*) entfernt; (*move*) auseinander; (*aside*) beiseite; (*separately*)

getrennt; **10 miles ~** 10 Meilen voneinander entfernt; **a long way ~** weit auseinander; **they are living ~** sie leben getrennt; **with one's legs ~** mit gespreizten Beinen; **to take ~** auseinandernehmen; **~ from** (*excepting*) abgesehen von; (*in addition*) außerdem
apartheid [ə'pɑːteɪt] *n* Apartheid *f*
apartment [ə'pɑːtmənt] *n* (*US: flat*) Wohnung *f*; (*room*) Raum *m*, Zimmer *nt*
apartment building (*US*) *n* Wohnblock *m*
apathetic [æpə'θɛtɪk] *adj* apathisch, teilnahmslos
apathy ['æpəθɪ] *n* Apathie *f*, Teilnahmslosigkeit *f*
APB (*US*) *n abbr* (= *all points bulletin*) polizeiliche Fahndung
ape [eɪp] *n* (Menschen)affe *m* ⊳ *vt* nachahmen
Apennines ['æpənaɪnz] *npl*: **the ~** die Apenninen *pl*, der Appenin
apéritif *n* Aperitif *m*
aperture ['æpətʃʊəʳ] *n* Öffnung *f*; (*Phot*) Blende *f*
APEX ['eɪpɛks] *n abbr* (*Aviat, Rail*: = *advance purchase excursion*) APEX
apex ['eɪpɛks] *n* Spitze *f*
aphid ['æfɪd] *n* Blattlaus *f*
aphorism ['æfərɪzəm] *n* Aphorismus *m*
aphrodisiac [æfrəʊ'dɪzɪæk] *adj* aphrodisisch
⊳ *n* Aphrodisiakum *nt*
apiece [ə'piːs] *adv* (*each person*) pro Person; (*each thing*) pro Stück
aplomb [ə'plɔm] *n* Gelassenheit *f*
APO (*US*) *n abbr* (= *Army Post Office*) Poststelle der Armee
apocalypse [ə'pɔkəlɪps] *n* Apokalypse *f*
apolitical [eɪpə'lɪtɪkl] *adj* apolitisch
apologetic [əpɔlə'dʒɛtɪk] *adj* entschuldigend; **to be very ~ (about sth)** sich (wegen etw *gen*) sehr entschuldigen
apologize [ə'pɔlədʒaɪz] *vi*: **to ~ (for sth to sb)** sich (für etw bei jdm) entschuldigen
apology [ə'pɔlədʒɪ] *n* Entschuldigung *f*; **to send one's apologies** sich entschuldigen lassen; **please accept my apologies** ich bitte um Verzeihung
apoplectic [æpə'plɛktɪk] *adj* (*Med*) apoplektisch; (*fig*): **to be ~ with rage** vor Wut fast platzen
apoplexy ['æpəplɛksɪ] *n* Schlaganfall *m*
apostle [ə'pɔsl] *n* Apostel *m*
apostrophe [ə'pɔstrəfɪ] *n* Apostroph *m*, Auslassungszeichen *nt*
app [æp] *n abbr* (*Comput*) = **application**
appal [ə'pɔːl] *vt* entsetzen; **to be ~led by** entsetzt sein über +*acc*
Appalachian Mountains [æpə'leɪʃən-] *npl*: **the ~** die Appalachen *pl*
appalling [ə'pɔːlɪŋ] *adj* entsetzlich; **she's an ~ cook** sie kann überhaupt nicht kochen
apparatus [æpə'reɪtəs] *n* Gerät *nt*; (*in gymnasium*) Geräte *pl*; (*of organization*) Apparat *m*; **a piece of ~** ein Gerät *nt*
apparel [ə'pærəl] (*US*) *n* Kleidung *f*

apparent [əˈpærənt] *adj* (*seeming*) scheinbar; (*obvious*) offensichtlich; **it is ~ that ...** es ist klar, dass ...

apparently [əˈpærəntlɪ] *adv* anscheinend

apparition [æpəˈrɪʃən] *n* Erscheinung *f*

appeal [əˈpiːl] *vi* (*Law*) Berufung einlegen ▷ *n* (*Law*) Berufung *f*; (*plea*) Aufruf *m*; (*charm*) Reiz *m*; **to ~ (to sb) for** (jdn) bitten um; **to ~ to** (*be attractive to*) gefallen +*dat*; **it doesn't ~ to me** es reizt mich nicht; **right of ~** (*Law*) Berufungsrecht *nt*; **on ~** (*Law*) in der Berufung

appealing [əˈpiːlɪŋ] *adj* ansprechend; (*touching*) rührend

appear [əˈpɪə'] *vi* erscheinen; (*seem*) scheinen; **to ~ on TV/in "Hamlet"** im Fernsehen/in „Hamlet" auftreten; **it would ~ that ...** anscheinend ...

appearance [əˈpɪərəns] *n* Erscheinen *nt*; (*look*) Aussehen *nt*; (*in public, on TV*) Auftritt *m*; **to put in** *or* **make an ~** sich sehen lassen; **in** *or* **by order of ~** (*Theat etc*) in der Reihenfolge ihres Auftritts; **to keep up ~s** den (äußeren) Schein wahren; **to all ~s** allem Anschein nach

appease [əˈpiːz] *vt* beschwichtigen

appeasement [əˈpiːzmənt] *n* Beschwichtigung *f*

append [əˈpɛnd] *vt* (*Comput*) anhängen

appendage [əˈpɛndɪdʒ] *n* Anhängsel *nt*

appendices [əˈpɛndɪsiːz] *npl of* **appendix**

appendicitis [əpɛndɪˈsaɪtɪs] *n* Blinddarmentzündung *f*

appendix [əˈpɛndɪks] (*pl* **appendices**) *n* (*Anat*) Blinddarm *m*; (*to publication*) Anhang *m*; **to have one's ~ out** sich *dat* den Blinddarm herausnehmen lassen

appetite [ˈæpɪtaɪt] *n* Appetit *m*; (*fig*) Lust *f*; **that walk has given me an ~** von dem Spaziergang habe ich Appetit bekommen

appetizer [ˈæpɪtaɪzə'] *n* (*food*) Appetithappen *m*; (*drink*) appetitanregendes Getränk *nt*

appetizing [ˈæpɪtaɪzɪŋ] *adj* appetitanregend

applaud [əˈplɔːd] *vi* applaudieren, klatschen ▷ *vt* (*actor etc*) applaudieren +*dat*, Beifall spenden *or* klatschen +*dat*; (*action, attitude*) loben; (*decision*) begrüßen

applause [əˈplɔːz] *n* Applaus *m*, Beifall *m*

apple [ˈæpl] *n* Apfel *m*; **he's the ~ of her eye** er ist ihr Ein und Alles

apple tree *n* Apfelbaum *m*

apple turnover *n* Apfeltasche *f*

appliance [əˈplaɪəns] *n* Gerät *nt*

applicable [əˈplɪkəbl] *adj*: **~ (to)** anwendbar (auf +*acc*); (*on official forms*) zutreffend (auf +*acc*); **the law is ~ from January** das Gesetz gilt ab Januar

applicant [ˈæplɪkənt] *n* Bewerber(in) *m(f)*

application [æplɪˈkeɪʃən] *n* (*for job*) Bewerbung *f*; (*for grant etc*) Antrag *m*; (*hard work*) Fleiß *m*; (*applying: of paint etc*) Auftragen *nt*; (*Comput*) Anwendung *f*; **on ~** auf Antrag

application form *n* (*for a job*) Bewerbungsformular *nt*; (*for a grant etc*) Antragsformular *nt*

application program *n* (*Comput*) Anwendungsprogramm *nt*

applications package *n* (*Comput*) Anwendungspaket *nt*

applied [əˈplaɪd] *adj* angewandt

apply [əˈplaɪ] *vt* anwenden; (*paint etc*) auftragen ▷ *vi*: **to ~ (to)** (*be applicable*) gelten (für); **to ~ the brakes** die Bremse betätigen, bremsen; **to ~ o.s. to sth** sich bei etw anstrengen; **to ~ to** (*ask*) sich wenden an +*acc*; **to ~ for** (*permit, grant*) beantragen; (*job*) sich bewerben um

appoint [əˈpɔɪnt] *vt* ernennen; (*date, place*) festlegen, festsetzen

appointed [əˈpɔɪntɪd] *adj*: **at the ~ time** zur festgesetzten Zeit

appointee [əpɔɪnˈtiː] *n* Ernannte(r) *f(m)*

appointment [əˈpɔɪntmənt] *n* Ernennung *f*; (*post*) Stelle *f*; (*arranged meeting*) Termin *m*; **to make an ~ (with sb)** einen Termin (mit jdm) vereinbaren; **by ~** nach Anmeldung, mit Voranmeldung

apportion [əˈpɔːʃən] *vt* aufteilen; (*blame*) zuweisen; **to ~ sth to sb** jdm etw zuteilen

apposition [æpəˈzɪʃən] *n* Apposition *f*, Beifügung *f*; **A is in ~ to B** A ist eine Apposition zu B

appraisal [əˈpreɪzl] *n* Beurteilung *f*

appraise [əˈpreɪz] *vt* beurteilen

appreciable [əˈpriːʃəbl] *adj* merklich, deutlich

appreciably [əˈpriːʃəblɪ] *adv* merklich

appreciate [əˈpriːʃieɪt] *vt* (*like*) schätzen; (*be grateful for*) zu schätzen wissen; (*understand*) verstehen; (*be aware of*) sich *dat* bewusst sein +*gen* ▷ *vi* (*Comm: currency, shares*) im Wert steigen; **I ~ your help** ich weiß Ihre Hilfe zu schätzen

appreciation [əpriːʃiˈeɪʃən] *n* (*enjoyment*) Wertschätzung *f*; (*understanding*) Verständnis *nt*; (*gratitude*) Dankbarkeit *f*; (*Comm: in value*) (Wert)steigerung *f*

appreciative [əˈpriːʃiətɪv] *adj* dankbar; (*comment*) anerkennend

apprehend [æprɪˈhɛnd] *vt* (*arrest*) festnehmen; (*understand*) verstehen

apprehension [æprɪˈhɛnʃən] *n* (*fear*) Besorgnis *f*; (*arrest*) Festnahme *f*

apprehensive [æprɪˈhɛnsɪv] *adj* ängstlich; **to be ~ about sth** sich *dat* Gedanken *or* Sorgen um etw machen

apprentice [əˈprɛntɪs] *n* Lehrling *m*, Auszubildende(r) *f(m)* ▷ *vt*: **to be ~d to sb** bei jdm in der Lehre sein

apprenticeship [əˈprɛntɪsʃɪp] *n* Lehre *f*, Lehrzeit *f*; **to serve one's ~** seine Lehre machen

appro [ˈæprəʊ] (*Brit: inf*) *abbr* (*Comm: = approval*): **on ~** zur Ansicht

approach [əˈprəʊtʃ] *vi* sich nähern; (*event*) nahen ▷ *vt* (*come to*) sich nähern +*dat*; (*ask, apply to: person*) herantreten an +*acc*, ansprechen; (*situation, problem*) herangehen an +*acc*, angehen ▷ *n* (*advance*) (Heran)nahen *nt*;

a

(*access*) Zugang *m*; (: *for vehicles*) Zufahrt *f*; (*to problem etc*) Ansatz *m*; **to ~ sb about sth** jdn wegen etw ansprechen

approachable [ə'prəʊtʃəbl] *adj* (*person*) umgänglich; (*place*) zugänglich

approach road *n* Zufahrtsstraße *f*

approbation [æprə'beɪʃən] *n* Zustimmung *f*

appropriate [*adj* ə'prəʊprɪɪt, *vt* ə'prəʊprɪeɪt] *adj* (*apt*) angebracht; (*relevant*) entsprechend ▷ *vt* sich *dat* aneignen; **it would not be ~ for me to comment** es wäre nicht angebracht, wenn ich mich dazu äußern würde

appropriately [ə'prəʊprɪɪtlɪ] *adv* entsprechend

appropriation [əprəʊprɪ'eɪʃən] *n* Zuteilung *f*, Zuweisung *f*

approval [ə'pruːvəl] *n* (*approbation*) Zustimmung *f*, Billigung *f*; (*permission*) Einverständnis *f*; **to meet with sb's ~** jds Zustimmung *or* Beifall finden; **on ~** (*Comm*) zur Probe

approve [ə'pruːv] *vt* billigen; (*motion, decision*) annehmen

▶ **approve of** *vt fus* etwas halten von; **I don't ~ of it/him** ich halte nichts davon/von ihm

approved school [ə'pruːvd-] (*Brit*) *n* Erziehungsheim *nt*

approvingly [ə'pruːvɪŋlɪ] *adv* zustimmend

approx. *abbr* = **approximately**

approximate [*adj* ə'prɒksɪmɪt, *vb* ə'prɒksɪmeɪt] *adj* ungefähr ▷ *vt, vi*: **to ~ (to)** nahe kommen +*dat*

approximately [ə'prɒksɪmɪtlɪ] *adv* ungefähr

approximation [ə'prɒksɪ'meɪʃən] *n* Annäherung *f*

APR *n abbr* (= *annual(ized) percentage rate*) Jahreszinssatz *m*

Apr. *abbr* = **April**

apricot ['eɪprɪkɒt] *n* Aprikose *f*

April ['eɪprəl] *n* April *m*; **~ fool!** April, April!; *see also* **July**

apron ['eɪprən] *n* Schürze *f*; (*Aviat*) Vorfeld *nt*

apse [æps] *n* Apsis *f*

Apt. *abbr* = **apartment**

apt [æpt] *adj* (*suitable*) passend, treffend; (*likely*): **to be ~ to do sth** dazu neigen, etw zu tun

aptitude ['æptɪtjuːd] *n* Begabung *f*

aptitude test *n* Eignungstest *m*

aptly ['æptlɪ] *adv* passend, treffend

aqualung ['ækwəlʌŋ] *n* Tauchgerät *nt*

aquarium [ə'kwɛərɪəm] *n* Aquarium *nt*

Aquarius [ə'kwɛərɪəs] *n* Wassermann *m*; **to be ~** (ein) Wassermann sein

aquatic [ə'kwætɪk] *adj* (*plants etc*) Wasser-; (*life*) im Wasser

aqueduct ['ækwɪdʌkt] *n* Aquädukt *m or nt*

AR (US) *abbr* (*Post*) = **Arkansas**

ARA (*Brit*) *n abbr* (= *Associate of the Royal Academy*) Qualifikationsnachweis im künstlerischen Bereich

Arab ['ærəb] *adj* arabisch ▷ *n* Araber(in) *m(f)*

Arabia [ə'reɪbɪə] *n* Arabien *nt*

Arabian [ə'reɪbɪən] *adj* arabisch

Arabian Desert *n*: **the ~** die Arabische Wüste

Arabian Sea *n*: **the ~** das Arabische Meer

Arabic ['ærəbɪk] *adj* arabisch ▷ *n* (*Ling*) Arabisch *nt*

arable ['ærəbl] *adj* (*land*) bebaubar; **~ farm** Bauernhof, der ausschließlich Ackerbau betreibt

ARAM (*Brit*) *n abbr* (= *Associate of the Royal Academy of Music*) Qualifikationsnachweis in Musik

arbiter ['ɑːbɪtəʳ] *n* Vermittler *m*

arbitrary ['ɑːbɪtrərɪ] *adj* willkürlich

arbitrate ['ɑːbɪtreɪt] *vi* vermitteln

arbitration [ɑːbɪ'treɪʃən] *n* Schlichtung *f*; **the dispute went to ~** der Streit wurde vor eine Schlichtungskommission gebracht

arbitrator ['ɑːbɪtreɪtəʳ] *n* Vermittler(in) *m(f)*; (*Industry*) Schlichter(in) *m(f)*

ARC *n abbr* (= *American Red Cross*) ≈ DRK *nt*

arc [ɑːk] *n* Bogen *m*

arcade [ɑː'keɪd] *n* Arkade *f*; (*shopping mall*) Passage *f*

arch [ɑːtʃ] *n* Bogen *m*; (*of foot*) Gewölbe *nt* ▷ *vt* (*back*) krümmen ▷ *adj* schelmisch ▷ *pref* Erz-

archaeological [ɑːkɪə'lɒdʒɪkl] *adj* archäologisch

archaeologist [ɑːkɪ'ɒlədʒɪst] *n* Archäologe *m*, Archäologin *f*

archaeology, (US) **archeology** [ɑːkɪ'ɒlədʒɪ] *n* Archäologie *f*

archaic [ɑː'keɪɪk] *adj* altertümlich; (*language*) veraltet, archaisch

archangel ['ɑːkeɪndʒəl] *n* Erzengel *m*

archbishop [ɑːtʃ'bɪʃəp] *n* Erzbischof *m*

archenemy ['ɑːtʃ'enəmɪ] *n* Erzfeind(in) *m(f)*

archeology *etc* [ɑːkɪ'ɒlədʒɪ] (US) = **archaeology** *etc*

archery ['ɑːtʃərɪ] *n* Bogenschießen *nt*

archetypal ['ɑːkɪtaɪpəl] *adj* (*arche*)typisch

archetype ['ɑːkɪtaɪp] *n* Urbild *nt*, Urtyp *m*

archipelago [ɑːkɪ'pɛlɪgəʊ] *n* Archipel *m*

architect ['ɑːkɪtɛkt] *n* Architekt(in) *m(f)*

architectural [ɑːkɪ'tɛktʃərəl] *adj* architektonisch

architecture ['ɑːkɪtɛktʃəʳ] *n* Architektur *f*

archive file *n* (*Comput*) Archivdatei *f*

archives ['ɑːkaɪvz] *npl* Archiv *nt*

archivist ['ɑːkɪvɪst] *n* Archivar(in) *m(f)*

archway ['ɑːtʃweɪ] *n* Torbogen *m*

ARCM (*Brit*) *n abbr* (= *Associate of the Royal College of Music*) Qualifikationsnachweis in Musik

Arctic ['ɑːktɪk] *adj* arktisch ▷ *n*: **the ~** die Arktis

Arctic Circle *n*: **the ~** der nördliche Polarkreis

Arctic Ocean *n*: **the ~** das Nordpolarmeer

ardent ['ɑːdənt] *adj* leidenschaftlich; (*admirer*) glühend

ardour, (US) **ardor** ['ɑːdəʳ] *n* Leidenschaft *f*

arduous ['ɑːdjuəs] *adj* mühsam

are [ɑːʳ] *vb see* **be**

area ['ɛərɪə] *n* Gebiet *nt*; (*Geom etc*) Fläche *f*; (*dining area etc*) Bereich *m*; **in the London ~** im Raum London

area code (US) *n* Vorwahl(nummer) *f*

arena [ə'riːnə] *n* Arena *f*

aren't [ɑːnt] = **are not**

Argentina [ɑːdʒən'tiːnə] *n* Argentinien *nt*

Argentinian [ɑːdʒən'tɪnɪən] *adj* argentinisch
▷ *n* Argentinier(in) *m(f)*
arguable ['ɑːgjuəbl] *adj*: **it is ~ whether** ... es
ist (noch) die Frage, ob ...; **it is ~ that** ... man
kann (wohl) sagen, dass ...
arguably ['ɑːgjuəbli] *adv* wohl; **it is ~** ... es
dürfte wohl ... sein
argue ['ɑːgjuː] *vi (quarrel)* sich streiten; *(reason)*
diskutieren ▷ *vt (debate)* diskutieren, erörtern;
to ~ that ... den Standpunkt vertreten,
dass ...; **to ~ about sth** sich über etw *acc*
streiten; **to ~ for/against sth** sich für/gegen
etw aussprechen
argument ['ɑːgjumənt] *n (reasons)* Argument
nt; (quarrel) Streit *m*, Auseinandersetzung *f;
(debate)* Diskussion *f;* **~ for/against** Argument
für/gegen; **to have an ~** sich streiten
argumentative [ɑːgju'mɛntətɪv] *adj*
streitlustig
aria ['ɑːrɪə] *n* Arie *f*
ARIBA [ə'riːbə] *(Brit) n abbr (= Associate of the Royal
Institute of British Architects)* Qualifikationsnachweis
in Architektur
arid ['ærɪd] *adj (land)* dürr; *(subject)* trocken
aridity [ə'rɪdɪtɪ] *n* Dürre *f*, Trockenheit *f*
Aries ['ɛərɪz] *n* Widder *m;* **to be ~** (ein) Widder
sein
arise [ə'raɪz] *(pt* **arose***, pp* **~n***) vi (difficulty etc)*
sich ergeben; *(question)* sich stellen; **to ~ from**
sich ergeben aus, herrühren von; **should the
need ~** falls es nötig wird
arisen [ə'rɪzn] *pp of* **arise**
aristocracy [ærɪs'tɔkrəsɪ] *n* Aristokratie *f*,
Adel *m*
aristocrat ['ærɪstəkræt] *n* Aristokrat(in) *m(f)*,
Ad(e)lige(r) *f(m)*
aristocratic [ærɪstə'krætɪk] *adj* aristokratisch,
ad(e)lig
arithmetic [ə'rɪθmətɪk] *n* Rechnen *nt;
(calculation)* Rechnung *f*
arithmetical [ærɪθ'mɛtɪkl] *adj* rechnerisch,
arithmetisch
Ariz. *(US) abbr (Post)* = **Arizona**
ark [ɑːk] *n:* **Noah's A~** die Arche Noah
arm [ɑːm] *n* Arm *m; (of clothing)* Ärmel *m; (of
chair)* Armlehne *f; (of organization etc)* Zweig *m*
▷ *vt* bewaffnen; **arms** *npl (weapons)* Waffen *pl;
(Heraldry)* Wappen *nt*
armaments ['ɑːməmənts] *npl (weapons)* (Aus)
rüstung *f*
armband ['ɑːmbænd] *n* Armbinde *f*
armchair ['ɑːmtʃɛəʳ] *n* Sessel *m*, Lehnstuhl *m*
armed [ɑːmd] *adj* bewaffnet; **the ~ forces** die
Streitkräfte *pl*
armed robbery *n* bewaffneter Raubüberfall *m*
Armenia [ɑː'miːnɪə] *n* Armenien *nt*
Armenian [ɑː'miːnɪən] *adj* armenisch ▷ *n*
Armenier(in) *m(f); (Ling)* Armenisch *nt*
armful ['ɑːmful] *n* Armvoll *m*
armistice ['ɑːmɪstɪs] *n* Waffenstillstand *m*
armour, *(US)* **armor** ['ɑːməʳ] *n (Hist)* Rüstung
f; (also: **armour-plating***)* Panzerplatte *f;
(Mil: tanks)* Panzerfahrzeuge *pl*

armoured car ['ɑːməd-] *n* Panzerwagen *m*
armoury ['ɑːmərɪ] *n (storeroom)* Waffenlager *nt*
armpit ['ɑːmpɪt] *n* Achselhöhle *f*
armrest ['ɑːmrɛst] *n* Armlehne *f*
arms control [ɑːmz-] *n* Rüstungskontrolle *f*
arms race [ɑːmz-] *n:* **the ~** das Wettrüsten
army ['ɑːmɪ] *n* Armee *f*, Heer *nt; (fig: host)* Heer
aroma [ə'rəumə] *n* Aroma *nt*, Duft *m*
aromatherapy [ərəumə'θɛrəpɪ] *n*
Aromatherapie *f*
aromatic [ærə'mætɪk] *adj* aromatisch, duftend
arose [ə'rəuz] *pt of* **arise**
around [ə'raund] *adv (about)* herum; *(in the area)*
in der Nähe ▷ *prep (encircling)* um ... herum;
(near) in der Nähe von; *(fig: about: dimensions)*
etwa; *(: time)* gegen; *(: date)* um; **is he ~?** ist er
da?; **~ £5** um die £5, etwa £5; **~ 3 o'clock** gegen
3 Uhr
arousal [ə'rauzəl] *n (sexual)* Erregung *f; (of
feelings, interest)* Weckung *f*
arouse [ə'rauz] *vt (feelings, interest)* wecken
arpeggio [ɑː'pɛdʒɪəu] *n* Arpeggio *nt*
arrange [ə'reɪndʒ] *vt (meeting etc)* vereinbaren;
(tour etc) planen; *(books etc)* anordnen; *(flowers)*
arrangieren; *(Mus)* arrangieren, bearbeiten
▷ *vi:* **we have ~d for a car to pick you up**
wir haben veranlasst, dass Sie mit dem Auto
abgeholt werden; **it was ~d that** ... es wurde
vereinbart, dass ...; **to ~ to do sth** vereinbaren
or ausmachen, etw zu tun
arrangement [ə'reɪndʒmənt] *n (agreement)*
Vereinbarung *f; (layout)* Anordnung *f;
(Mus)* Arrangement *nt*, Bearbeitung *f;*
arrangements *npl* Pläne *pl; (preparations)*
Vorbereitungen *pl;* **to come to an ~ with
sb** eine Regelung mit jdm treffen; **home
deliveries by ~** nach Vereinbarung Lieferung
ins Haus; **I'll make ~s for you to be met** ich
werde veranlassen, dass Sie abgeholt werden
arrant ['ærənt] *adj (coward, fool etc)* Erz-;
(nonsense) total
array [ə'reɪ] *n:* **an ~ of** *(things)* eine Reihe
von; *(people)* Aufgebot an +*dat; (Math, Comput)*
(Daten)feld *nt*
arrears [ə'rɪəz] *npl* Rückstand *m;* **to be in
~ with one's rent** mit seiner Miete im
Rückstand sein
arrest [ə'rɛst] *vt (person)* verhaften; *(sb's
attention)* erregen ▷ *n* Verhaftung *f;* **under ~**
verhaftet
arresting [ə'rɛstɪŋ] *adj (fig)* atemberaubend
arrival [ə'raɪvl] *n* Ankunft *f; (Comm: of goods)*
Sendung *f;* **new ~** *(person)* Neuankömmling *m;
(baby)* Neugeborene(s) *nt*
arrive [ə'raɪv] *vi* ankommen
▶ **arrive at** *vt fus (fig: conclusion)* kommen zu;
(: situation) es bringen zu
arrogance ['ærəgəns] *n* Arroganz *f*,
Überheblichkeit *f*
arrogant ['ærəgənt] *adj* arrogant, überheblich
arrow ['ærəu] *n* Pfeil *m*
arse [ɑːs] *(Brit: inf!) n* Arsch *m (!)*
arsenal ['ɑːsɪnl] *n* Waffenlager *nt; (stockpile)*

Arsenal nt

arsenic ['ɑːsnɪk] n Arsen nt

arson ['ɑːsn] n Brandstiftung f

art [ɑːt] n Kunst f; **Arts** npl (Scol) Geisteswissenschaften pl; **work of ~** Kunstwerk nt

art and design (Brit) n (Scol) = Kunst und Design

arterial [ɑːˈtɪərɪəl] adj arteriell; **~ road** Fernverkehrsstraße f; **~ line** (Rail) Hauptstrecke f

artery ['ɑːtərɪ] n Arterie f, Schlagader f; (fig) Verkehrsader f

artful ['ɑːtful] adj raffiniert

art gallery n Kunstgalerie f

arthritic [ɑːˈθrɪtɪk] adj arthritisch

arthritis [ɑːˈθraɪtɪs] n Arthritis f

artichoke ['ɑːtɪtʃəuk] n (also: **globe artichoke**) Artischocke f; (also: **Jerusalem artichoke**) Topinambur m

article ['ɑːtɪkl] n Artikel m; (object, item) Gegenstand m; **articles** (Brit) npl (Law) (Rechts)referendarzeit f; **~ of clothing** Kleidungsstück nt

articles of association npl (Comm) Gesellschaftsvertrag m

articulate [adj ɑːˈtɪkjulɪt, vt, vi ɑːˈtɪkjuleɪt] adj (speech, writing) klar; (speaker) redegewandt ▷ vt darlegen ▷ vi artikulieren; **to be ~** (person) sich gut ausdrücken können

articulated lorry (Brit) n Sattelschlepper m

artifice ['ɑːtɪfɪs] n List f

artificial [ɑːtɪˈfɪʃəl] adj künstlich; (manner) gekünstelt; **to be ~** (person) gekünstelt or unnatürlich wirken

artificial insemination [-ɪnsɛmɪˈneɪʃən] n künstliche Besamung f

artificial intelligence n künstliche Intelligenz f

artificial respiration n künstliche Beatmung f

artillery [ɑːˈtɪlərɪ] n Artillerie f

artisan ['ɑːtɪzæn] n Handwerker m

artist ['ɑːtɪst] n Künstler(in) m(f)

artistic [ɑːˈtɪstɪk] adj künstlerisch

artistry ['ɑːtɪstrɪ] n künstlerisches Geschick nt

artless ['ɑːtlɪs] adj arglos

art school n Kunstakademie f, Kunsthochschule f

artwork ['ɑːtwəːk] n (for advert etc, material for printing) Druckvorlage f; (in book) Bildmaterial nt

ARV n abbr (Bible: = American Revised Version) amerikanische revidierte Bibelübersetzung

AS (US) n abbr (= Associate in Science) akademischer Grad in Naturwissenschaften ▷ abbr (Post) = American Samoa

○ KEYWORD

as [æz] conj **1** (referring to time) als; **as the years went by** mit den Jahren; **he came in as I was leaving** als er hereinkam, ging ich gerade; **as from tomorrow** ab morgen

2 (in comparisons): **as big as** so groß wie; **twice as big as** zweimal so groß wie; **as much/ many as** so viel/so viele wie; **as soon as** sobald; **much as I admire her ...** sosehr ich sie auch bewundere ...

3 (since, because) da, weil; **as you can't come I'll go without you** da du nicht mitkommen kannst, gehe ich ohne dich

4 (referring to manner, way) wie; **do as you wish** mach, was du willst; **as she said** wie sie sagte; **he gave it to me as a present** er gab es mir als Geschenk; **as it were** sozusagen

5 (in the capacity of) als; **he works as a driver** er arbeitet als Fahrer

6 (concerning): **as for** or **to that** was das betrifft or angeht

7: as if or **though** als ob; see also **long**; **such**; **well**

ASA n abbr (= American Standards Association) amerikanischer Normenausschuss; (Brit) = Advertising Standards Authority

a.s.a.p. adv abbr (= as soon as possible) baldmöglichst

asbestos [æzˈbɛstəs] n Asbest m

ascend [əˈsɛnd] vt hinaufsteigen; (throne) besteigen

ascendancy [əˈsɛndənsɪ] n Vormachtstellung f; **~ over sb** Vorherrschaft f über jdn

ascendant [əˈsɛndənt] n: **to be in the ~** im Aufstieg begriffen sein

ascension [əˈsɛnʃən] n: **the A~** (Rel) die Himmelfahrt f (Christi)

Ascension Island n Ascension nt

ascent [əˈsɛnt] n Aufstieg m

ascertain [æsəˈteɪn] vt feststellen

ascetic [əˈsɛtɪk] adj asketisch

asceticism [əˈsɛtɪsɪzəm] n Askese f

ASCII ['æskiː] n abbr (Comput: = American Standard Code for Information Interchange) ASCII

ascribe [əˈskraɪb] vt: **to ~ sth to** etw zuschreiben +dat; (cause) etw zurückführen auf +acc

ASCU (US) n abbr (= Association of State Colleges and Universities) Verband staatlicher Bildungseinrichtungen

ASEAN ['æsɪæn] n abbr (= Association of Southeast Asian Nations) ASEAN f (Gemeinschaft südostasiatischer Staaten)

ASH [æʃ] (Brit) n abbr (= Action on Smoking and Health) Antiraucherinitiative

ash [æʃ] n Asche f; (wood, tree) Esche f

ashamed [əˈʃeɪmd] adj beschämt; **to be ~ of** sich schämen für; **to be ~ of o.s. for having done sth** sich schämen, dass man etw getan hat

A shares npl stimmrechtslose Aktien pl

ashen ['æʃən] adj (face) aschfahl

ashore [əˈʃɔːʳ] adv an Land

ashtray ['æʃtreɪ] n Aschenbecher m

Ash Wednesday n Aschermittwoch m

Asia ['eɪʃə] n Asien nt

Asia Minor n Kleinasien nt

Asian ['eɪʃən] *adj* asiatisch ▷ *n* Asiat(in) *m(f)*
Asiatic [eɪsɪ'ætɪk] *adj* asiatisch
aside [ə'saɪd] *adv* zur Seite; *(take)* beiseite ▷ *n*
beiseite gesprochene Worte *pl*; **to brush**
objections ~ Einwände beiseiteschieben
aside from *prep* außer +*dat*
ask [ɑːsk] *vt* fragen; *(invite)* einladen; **to ~ sb**
to do sth jdn bitten, etw zu tun; **to ~ (sb) sth**
(jdn) etw fragen; **to ~ sb a question** jdm eine
Frage stellen; **to ~ sb the time** jdn nach der
Uhrzeit fragen; **to ~ sb about sth** jdn nach
etw fragen; **to ~ sb out to dinner** jdn zum
Essen einladen
▶ **ask after** *vt fus* fragen nach
▶ **ask for** *vt fus* bitten um; *(trouble)* haben
wollen; **it's just ~ing for trouble/it** das
kann ja nicht gut gehen
askance [ə'skɑːns] *adv*: **to look ~ at sb** jdn
misstrauisch ansehen; **to look ~ at sth** etw
mit Misstrauen betrachten
askew [ə'skjuː] *adv* schief
asking price ['ɑːskɪŋ-] *n*: **the ~** der geforderte
Preis
asleep [ə'sliːp] *adj* schlafend; **to be ~** schlafen;
to fall ~ einschlafen
AS level *n abbr* (= *Advanced Subsidiary level*) Mit
"AS level" wird das erste Jahr der Sekundarstufe II
bezeichnet, nach dessen Abschluss Prüfungen in
drei der insgesamt sechs für den "A level" benötigten
Wahlpflichtfächern abgehalten werden
asp [æsp] *n* Natter *f*
asparagus [əs'pærəgəs] *n* Spargel *m*
asparagus tips *npl* Spargelspitzen *pl*
ASPCA *n abbr* (= *American Society for the Prevention of*
Cruelty to Animals) Tierschutzverein
aspect ['æspɛkt] *n* (*of subject*) Aspekt *m*; (*of*
building etc) Lage *f*; (*quality, air*) Erscheinung *f*;
to have a south-westerly ~ nach Südwesten
liegen
aspersions [əs'pəːʃənz] *npl*: **to cast ~ on** sich
abfällig äußern über +*acc*
asphalt ['æsfælt] *n* Asphalt *m*
asphyxiate [æs'fɪksɪeɪt] *vt* ersticken
asphyxiation [æsfɪksɪ'eɪʃən] *n* Erstickung *f*
aspirate ['æspəreɪt] *vt* aspirieren, behauchen
aspirations [æspə'reɪʃənz] *npl* Hoffnungen *pl*;
to have ~ to(wards) sth etw anstreben
aspire [əs'paɪər] *vi*: **to ~ to** streben nach
aspirin ['æsprɪn] *n* Kopfschmerztablette *f*,
Aspirin® *nt*
aspiring [əs'paɪərɪŋ] *adj* aufstrebend
ass [æs] *n* (*also fig*) Esel *m*; (*US: inf!*) Arsch! *m*
assail [ə'seɪl] *vt* angreifen; (*fig*): **to be ~ed by**
doubts von Zweifeln geplagt werden
assailant [ə'seɪlənt] *n* Angreifer(in) *m(f)*
assassin [ə'sæsɪn] *n* Attentäter(in) *m(f)*
assassinate [ə'sæsɪneɪt] *vt* ermorden, ein
Attentat verüben auf +*acc*
assassination [əsæsɪ'neɪʃən] *n* Ermordung *f*,
(geglücktes) Attentat *nt*
assault [ə'sɔːlt] *n* Angriff *m* ▷ *vt* angreifen;
(*sexually*) vergewaltigen; **~ and battery** (*Law*)
Körperverletzung *f*

assemble [ə'sɛmbl] *vt* versammeln;
(*car, machine*) montieren; (*furniture etc*)
zusammenbauen ▷ *vi* sich versammeln
assembly [ə'sɛmblɪ] *n* Versammlung *f*; (*of car,*
machine) Montage *f*; (*of furniture*) Zusammenbau
m
assembly language *n* (*Comput*)
Assemblersprache *f*
assembly line *n* Fließband *nt*
assent [ə'sɛnt] *n* Zustimmung *f* ▷ *vi*: **to ~ (to)**
zustimmen (+*dat*)
assert [ə'səːt] *vt* behaupten; (*innocence*)
beteuern; (*authority*) geltend machen; **to ~ o.s.**
sich durchsetzen
assertion [ə'səːʃən] *n* Behauptung *f*
assertive [ə'səːtɪv] *adj* (*person*) selbstbewusst;
(*manner*) bestimmt
assess [ə'sɛs] *vt* (*situation*) einschätzen; (*abilities*
etc) beurteilen; (*tax*) festsetzen; (*damages,*
property etc) schätzen
assessment [ə'sɛsmənt] *n* (*see vt*)
Einschätzung *f*; Beurteilung *f*; Festsetzung *f*;
Schätzung *f*
assessor [ə'sɛsər] *n* (*Law*) Gutachter(in) *m(f)*
asset ['æsɛt] *n* Vorteil *m*; (*person*) Stütze *f*;
assets *npl* (*property, funds*) Vermögen *nt*; (*Comm*)
Aktiva *pl*
asset-stripping ['æsɛt'strɪpɪŋ] *n* (*Comm*) Aufkauf
von finanziell gefährdeten Firmen und anschließender
Verkauf ihrer Vermögenswerte
assiduous [ə'sɪdjuəs] *adj* gewissenhaft
assign [ə'saɪn] *vt*: **to ~ (to)** (*date*) zuweisen
(+*dat*); (*task*) übertragen (+*dat*); (*person*)
einteilen (für); (*cause*) zuschreiben (+*dat*);
(*meaning*) zuordnen (+*dat*); **to ~ sb to do sth**
jdn damit beauftragen, etw zu tun
assignment [ə'saɪnmənt] *n* Aufgabe *f*
assimilate [ə'sɪmɪleɪt] *vt* aufnehmen;
(*immigrants*) integrieren
assimilation [əsɪmɪ'leɪʃən] *n* (*see vt*) Aufnahme
f; Integration *f*
assist [ə'sɪst] *vt* helfen; (*with money etc*)
unterstützen
assistance [ə'sɪstəns] *n* Hilfe *f*; (*with money etc*)
Unterstützung *f*
assistant [ə'sɪstənt] *n* Assistent(in) *m(f)*;
(*Brit: also*: **shop assistant**) Verkäufer(in) *m(f)*
assistant manager *n* stellvertretender
Geschäftsführer *m*, stellvertretende
Geschäftsführerin *f*
assisted living [əsɪstd'lɪvɪŋ] *n* (*US*) betreutes
Wohnen *nt*
associate [*adj, n* ə'səuʃɪɪt, *vt, vi* ə'səuʃɪeɪt]
adj (*director*) assoziiert; (*member, professor*)
außerordentlich ▷ *n* (*at work*) Kollege *m*,
Kollegin *f* ▷ *vt* in Verbindung bringen ▷ *vi*: **to ~**
with sb mit jdm verkehren
associated company [ə'səuʃɪeɪtɪd-] *n*
Partnerfirma *f*
association [əsəusɪ'eɪʃən] *n* (*group*) Verband *m*;
(*involvement*) Verbindung *f*; (*Psych*) Assoziation
f; **in ~ with** in Zusammenarbeit mit
association football *n* Fußball *m*

assorted [ə'sɔːtɪd] adj gemischt; (various) diverse(r, s); **in ~ sizes** in verschiedenen Größen

assortment [ə'sɔːtmənt] n Mischung f; (of books, people etc) Ansammlung f

Asst abbr = **assistant**

assuage [ə'sweɪdʒ] vt (grief, pain) lindern; (thirst, appetite) stillen, befriedigen

assume [ə'sjuːm] vt annehmen; (responsibilities etc) übernehmen

assumed name [ə'sjuːmd-] n Deckname m

assumption [ə'sʌmpʃən] n Annahme f; (of power etc) Übernahme f; **on the ~ that ...** vorausgesetzt, dass ...

assurance [ə'ʃuərəns] n Versicherung f; (promise) Zusicherung f; (confidence) Zuversicht f; **I can give you no ~s** ich kann Ihnen nichts versprechen

assure [ə'ʃuər] vt versichern; (guarantee) sichern

assured [ə'ʃuəd] adj sicher

AST (US) abbr (= Atlantic Standard Time) Ortszeit in Ostkanada

asterisk ['æstərɪsk] n Sternchen nt

astern [ə'stəːn] adv achtern

asteroid ['æstərɔɪd] n Asteroid m

asthma ['æsmə] n Asthma nt

asthmatic [æs'mætɪk] adj asthmatisch ▷ n Asthmatiker(in) m(f)

astigmatism [ə'stɪgmətɪzəm] n Astigmatismus m

astir [ə'stəːr] adv: **to be ~** (out of bed) auf sein

astonish [ə'stɔnɪʃ] vt erstaunen

astonishing [ə'stɔnɪʃɪŋ] adj erstaunlich; **I find it ~ that ...** es überrascht mich, dass ...

astonishingly [ə'stɔnɪʃɪŋlɪ] adv erstaunlich; **~, ...** erstaunlicherweise ...

astonishment [ə'stɔnɪʃmənt] n Erstaunen nt

astound [ə'staund] vt verblüffen, sehr erstaunen

astounded [ə'staundɪd] adj (höchst) erstaunt

astounding [ə'staundɪŋ] adj erstaunlich

astray [ə'streɪ] adv: **to go ~** (letter) verloren gehen; (fig) auf Abwege geraten; **to lead ~** auf Abwege bringen; **to go ~ in one's calculations** sich verrechnen

astride [ə'straɪd] adv (sit, ride) rittlings; (stand) breitbeinig ▷ prep rittlings auf +dat; breitbeinig über +dat

astringent [əs'trɪndʒənt] adj adstringierend; (fig: caustic) ätzend, beißend ▷ n Adstringens nt

astrologer [əs'trɔlədʒər] n Astrologe m, Astrologin f

astrology [əs'trɔlədʒɪ] n Astrologie f

astronaut ['æstrənɔːt] n Astronaut(in) m(f)

astronomer [əs'trɔnəmər] n Astronom(in) m(f)

astronomical [æstrə'nɔmɪkl] adj (also fig) astronomisch

astronomy [əs'trɔnəmɪ] n Astronomie f

astrophysics ['æstrəu'fɪzɪks] n Astrophysik f

astute [əs'tjuːt] adj scharfsinnig; (operator, behaviour) geschickt

asunder [ə'sʌndər] adv: **to tear ~** auseinanderreißen

ASV n abbr (Bible: = American Standard Version) amerikanische Standard-Bibelübersetzung

asylum [ə'saɪləm] n Asyl nt; (mental hospital) psychiatrische Klinik f; **to seek political ~** um (politisches) Asyl bitten

asymmetrical [eɪsɪ'mɛtrɪkl] adj asymmetrisch

⊙ **KEYWORD**

at [æt] prep **1** (referring to position, direction) an +dat; in +dat; **at the top** an der Spitze; **at home** zu Hause; **at school** in der Schule; **at the baker's** beim Bäcker; **to look at sth** auf etw acc blicken

2 (referring to time): **at four o'clock** um vier Uhr; **at night/dawn** bei Nacht/Tagesanbruch; **at Christmas** zu Weihnachten; **at times** zuweilen

3 (referring to rates, speed etc): **at £2 a kilo** zu £2 pro Kilo; **two at a time** zwei auf einmal; **at 50 km/h** mit 50 km/h

4 (referring to activity): **to be at work** (in office etc) auf der Arbeit sein; **to play at cowboys** Cowboy spielen; **to be good at sth** gut in etw dat sein

5 (referring to cause): **shocked/surprised/annoyed at sth** schockiert/überrascht/verärgert über etw acc; **I went at his suggestion** ich ging auf seinen Vorschlag hin

6: not at all (in answer to question) überhaupt nicht, ganz und gar nicht; (in answer to thanks) nichts zu danken, keine Ursache; **I'm not at all tired** ich bin überhaupt nicht müde; **anything at all** irgendetwas

7 (@ symbol) At-Zeichen nt

ate [eɪt] pt of **eat**

atheism ['eɪθɪɪzəm] n Atheismus m

atheist ['eɪθɪɪst] n Atheist(in) m(f)

Athenian [ə'θiːnɪən] adj Athener ▷ n Athener(in) m(f)

Athens ['æθɪnz] n Athen nt

athlete ['æθliːt] n Athlet(in) m(f)

athletic [æθ'lɛtɪk] adj sportlich; (muscular) athletisch

athletics [æθ'lɛtɪks] n Leichtathletik f

Atlantic [ət'læntɪk] adj atlantisch; (coast etc) Atlantik- ▷ n: **the ~ (Ocean)** der Atlantik

atlas ['ætləs] n Atlas m

Atlas Mountains npl: **the ~** der Atlas, das Atlasgebirge

ATM abbr (= automated teller machine) Geldautomat m

atmosphere ['ætməsfɪər] n Atmosphäre f; (air) Luft f

atmospheric [ætməs'fɛrɪk] adj atmosphärisch

atmospherics [ætməs'fɛrɪks] npl atmosphärische Störungen pl

atoll ['ætɔl] n Atoll nt

atom ['ætəm] n Atom nt

atom bomb n Atombombe f

atomic [ə'tɔmɪk] adj atomar; (energy, weapons) Atom-

atomic bomb n Atombombe f
atomizer ['ætəmaɪzə'] n Zerstäuber m
atone [ə'təun] vi: **to ~ for** büßen für
atonement [ə'təunmənt] n Buße f
A to Z® n Stadtplan m
ATP n abbr (= Association of Tennis Professionals) Tennis-Profiverband
atrocious [ə'trəuʃəs] adj grauenhaft
atrocity [ə'trɒsɪtɪ] n Gräueltat f
atrophy ['ætrəfɪ] n Schwund m, Atrophie f ▷ vt schwinden lassen ▷ vi schwinden, verkümmern
attach [ə'tætʃ] vt befestigen; (document, letter) anheften, beiheften; (employee, troops) zuteilen; (importance etc) beimessen; **to be ~ed to sb/sth** (like) an jdm/etw hängen; (be connected with) mit jdm/etw zu tun haben; **the ~ed letter** der beiliegende Brief; **to ~ a file to an email** eine Datei an eine E-Mail anhängen
attaché [ə'tæʃeɪ] n Attaché m
attaché case n Aktenkoffer m
attachment [ə'tætʃmənt] n (tool) Zubehörteil nt; (love): **~ (to sb)** Zuneigung f (zu jdm); (to email) Attachment nt, Anhang m
attack [ə'tæk] vt angreifen; (subj: criminal) überfallen; (task, problem etc) in Angriff nehmen ▷ n (also fig) Angriff m; (on sb's life) Anschlag m; (of illness) Anfall m; **heart ~** Herzanfall m, Herzinfarkt m
attacker [ə'tækə'] n Angreifer(in) m(f)
attain [ə'teɪn] vt (also: **attain to**) erreichen; (knowledge) erlangen
attainments [ə'teɪnmənts] npl Fähigkeiten pl
attempt [ə'tɛmpt] n Versuch m ▷ vt versuchen; **to make an ~ on sb's life** einen Anschlag auf jdn verüben
attempted [ə'tɛmptɪd] adj versucht; **~ murder/suicide** Mord-/Selbstmordversuch m; **~ theft** versuchter Diebstahl
attend [ə'tɛnd] vt besuchen; (patient) behandeln
  ▶ **attend to** vt fus sich kümmern um; (needs) nachkommen +dat; (customer) bedienen
attendance [ə'tɛndəns] n Anwesenheit f; (people present) Besucherzahl f; (Sport) Zuschauerzahl f
attendant [ə'tɛndənt] n (helper) Begleiter(in) m(f); (in garage) Tankwart m; (in museum) Aufseher(in) m(f) ▷ adj damit verbunden
attention [ə'tɛnʃən] n Aufmerksamkeit f; (care) Fürsorge f ▷ excl (Mil) Achtung!; **attentions** npl (acts of courtesy) Aufmerksamkeiten pl; **for the ~ of ...** zu Händen von ...; **it has come to my ~ that ...** ich bin darauf aufmerksam geworden, dass ...; **to stand to** or **at ~** (Mil) stillstehen
attentive [ə'tɛntɪv] adj aufmerksam
attentively [ə'tɛntɪvlɪ] adv aufmerksam
attenuate [ə'tɛnjueɪt] vt abschwächen ▷ vi schwächer werden
attest [ə'tɛst] vt, vi: **~ (to)** bezeugen
attic ['ætɪk] n Dachboden m
attire [ə'taɪə'] n Kleidung f
attitude ['ætɪtjuːd] n (posture, manner) Haltung

f; (mental): **~ to** or **towards** Einstellung f zu
attorney [ə'təːnɪ] n (US: lawyer) (Rechts)anwalt m, (Rechts)anwältin f; (having proxy) Bevollmächtigte(r) f(m); **power of ~** Vollmacht f
Attorney General n (Brit) ≈ Justizminister(in) m(f); (US) ≈ Generalbundesanwalt m, ≈ Generalbundesanwältin f
attract [ə'trækt] vt (draw) anziehen; (interest) auf sich acc lenken; (attention) erregen
attraction [ə'trækʃən] n Anziehungskraft f; (of house, city) Reiz m; (gen pl: amusements) Attraktion f; (fig): **to feel an ~ towards sb/sth** sich von jdm/etw angezogen fühlen
attractive [ə'træktɪv] adj attraktiv; (price, idea, offer) verlockend, reizvoll
attribute [n 'ætrɪbjuːt, vt ə'trɪbjuːt] n Eigenschaft f ▷ vt: **to ~ sth to** (cause) etw zurückführen auf +acc; (poem, painting) etw zuschreiben +dat; (quality) etw beimessen +dat
attribution [ætrɪ'bjuːʃən] n (see vt) Zurückführung f; Zuschreibung f; Beimessung f
attrition [ə'trɪʃən] n: **war of ~** Zermürbungskrieg m
Atty. Gen. abbr = **Attorney General**
ATV n abbr (= all-terrain vehicle) Geländefahrzeug nt
atypical [eɪ'tɪpɪkl] adj atypisch
aubergine ['əubəʒiːn] n Aubergine f; (colour) Aubergine nt
auburn ['ɔːbən] adj rotbraun
auction ['ɔːkʃən] n (also: **sale by auction**) Versteigerung f, Auktion f ▷ vt versteigern
auctioneer [ɔːkʃə'nɪə'] n Versteigerer m
auction room n Auktionssaal m
audacious [ɔː'deɪʃəs] adj wagemutig, kühn
audacity [ɔː'dæsɪtɪ] n Kühnheit f, Verwegenheit f; (pej: impudence) Dreistigkeit f
audible ['ɔːdɪbl] adj hörbar
audience ['ɔːdɪəns] n Publikum nt; (Radio) Zuhörer pl; (TV) Zuschauer pl; (with queen etc) Audienz f
audiovisual ['ɔːdɪəu'vɪzjuəl] adj audiovisuell
audiovisual aid n audiovisuelles Lehrmittel nt
audit ['ɔːdɪt] vt (Comm) prüfen ▷ n Buchprüfung f, Rechnungsprüfung f
audition [ɔː'dɪʃən] n Vorsprechprobe f ▷ vi: **to ~ (for)** vorsprechen (für)
auditor ['ɔːdɪtə'] n Buchprüfer(in) m(f), Rechnungsprüfer(in) m(f)
auditorium [ɔːdɪ'tɔːrɪəm] n (building) Auditorium nt; (audience area) Zuschauerraum m
AU n abbr = African Union
Aug. abbr = **August**
augment [ɔːg'mɛnt] vt vermehren; (income, diet) verbessern
augur ['ɔːgə'] vi: **it ~s well** das ist ein gutes Zeichen or Omen
August ['ɔːgəst] n August m; see also **July**
august [ɔː'gʌst] adj erhaben

aunt [ɑːnt] *n* Tante *f*

auntie ['ɑːntɪ] *n dimin of* **aunt**

aunty ['ɑːntɪ] *n dimin of* **aunt**

au pair ['əʊ'pɛər] *n (also:* **au pair girl***)* Aupair(mädchen) *nt*, Au-pair(-Mädchen) *nt*

aura ['ɔːrə] *n* Aura *f*

auspices ['ɔːspɪsɪz] *npl:* **under the ~ of** unter der Schirmherrschaft +*gen*

auspicious [ɔːs'pɪʃəs] *adj* verheißungsvoll; *(opening, start)* vielversprechend

austere [ɔs'tɪər] *adj* streng; *(room, decoration)* schmucklos; *(person, lifestyle)* asketisch

austerity [ɔs'tɛrɪtɪ] *n* Strenge *f*; *(of room etc)* Schmucklosigkeit *f*; *(hardship)* Entbehrung *f*

Australasia [ɔːstrə'leɪzɪə] *n* Australien und Ozeanien *nt*

Australasian [ɔːstrə'leɪzɪən] *adj* ozeanisch, südwestpazifisch

Australia [ɔs'treɪlɪə] *n* Australien *nt*

Australian [ɔs'treɪlɪən] *adj* australisch ▷ *n* Australier(in) *m(f)*

Austria ['ɔstrɪə] *n* Österreich *nt*

Austrian ['ɔstrɪən] *adj* österreichisch ▷ *n* Österreicher(in) *m(f)*

AUT (Brit) *n abbr (= Association of University Teachers)* Gewerkschaft der Universitätsdozenten

authentic [ɔː'θɛntɪk] *adj* authentisch

authenticate [ɔː'θɛntɪkeɪt] *vt* beglaubigen

authenticity [ɔːθɛn'tɪsɪtɪ] *n* Echtheit *f*

author ['ɔːθər] *n (of text)* Verfasser(in) *m(f)*; *(profession)* Autor(in) *m(f)*, Schriftsteller(in) *m(f)*; *(creator)* Urheber(in) *m(f)*; *(: of plan)* Initiator(in) *m(f)*

authoritarian [ɔːθɔrɪ'tɛərɪən] *adj* autoritär

authoritative [ɔː'θɔrɪtətɪv] *adj (person, manner)* bestimmt, entschieden; *(source, account)* zuverlässig; *(study, treatise)* maßgeblich, maßgebend

authority [ɔː'θɔrɪtɪ] *n* Autorität *f*; *(government body)* Behörde *f*, Amt *nt*; *(official permission)* Genehmigung *f*; **the authorities** *npl (ruling body)* die Behörden *pl*; **to have the ~ to do sth** befugt sein, etw zu tun

authorization [ɔːθəraɪ'zeɪʃən] *n* Genehmigung *f*

authorize ['ɔːθəraɪz] *vt* genehmigen; **to ~ sb to do sth** jdn ermächtigen, etw zu tun

authorized capital ['ɔːθəraɪzd-] *n* autorisiertes Aktienkapital *nt*

authorship ['ɔːθəʃɪp] *n* Autorschaft *f*, Verfasserschaft *f*

autistic [ɔː'tɪstɪk] *adj* autistisch

auto ['ɔːtəʊ] (US) *n* Auto *nt*, Wagen *m*

autobiographical ['ɔːtəbaɪə'græfɪkl] *adj* autobiografisch

autobiography [ɔːtəbaɪ'ɔgrəfɪ] *n* Autobiografie *f*

autocratic [ɔːtə'krætɪk] *adj* autokratisch

Autocue® ['ɔːtəʊkjuː] *n* Teleprompter *m*

autograph ['ɔːtəgrɑːf] *n* Autogramm *nt* ▷ *vt* signieren

autoimmune [ɔːtəʊɪ'mjuːn] *adj (disease)* Autoimmun-

automat ['ɔːtəmæt] *n* Automat *m*; *(US)* Automatenrestaurant *nt*

automata [ɔː'tɔmətə] *npl of* **automaton**

automate ['ɔːtəmeɪt] *vt* automatisieren

automatic [ɔːtə'mætɪk] *adj* automatisch ▷ *n* *(gun)* automatische Waffe; *(washing machine)* Waschautomat *m*; *(car)* Automatikwagen *m*

automatically [ɔːtə'mætɪklɪ] *adv* automatisch

automatic data processing *n* automatische Datenverarbeitung *f*

automation [ɔːtə'meɪʃən] *n* Automatisierung *f*

automaton [ɔː'tɔmətən] *(pl* **automata***)* *n* Roboter *m*

automobile ['ɔːtəməbiːl] *(US)* *n* Auto(mobil) *nt*

autonomous [ɔː'tɔnəməs] *adj* autonom

autonomy [ɔː'tɔnəmɪ] *n* Autonomie *f*

autopsy ['ɔːtɔpsɪ] *n* Autopsie *f*

autumn ['ɔːtəm] *n* Herbst *m*; **in** ~ im Herbst

autumnal [ɔː'tʌmnəl] *adj* herbstlich

auxiliary [ɔːg'zɪlɪərɪ] *adj (tool, verb)* Hilfs- ▷ *n* *(assistant)* Hilfskraft *f*

AV *n abbr (Bible: = Authorized Version) englische Bibelübersetzung von 1611* ▷ *abbr* = **audiovisual**

avail [ə'veɪl] *vt:* **to ~ o.s. of** Gebrauch machen von ▷ *n:* **to no ~** vergeblich, erfolglos

availability [əveɪlə'bɪlɪtɪ] *n* Erhältlichkeit *f*; *(of staff)* Vorhandensein *nt*

available [ə'veɪləbl] *adj* erhältlich; *(person: unoccupied)* frei, abkömmlich; *(: unattached)* zu haben; *(time)* frei, verfügbar; **every ~ means** alle verfügbaren Mittel; **is the manager ~?** ist der Geschäftsführer zu sprechen?; **to make sth ~ to sb** jdm etw zur Verfügung stellen

avalanche ['ævəlɑːnʃ] *n (also fig)* Lawine *f*

avant-garde ['ævɑ̃ŋ'gɑːd] *adj* avantgardistisch

avarice ['ævərɪs] *n* Habsucht *f*

avaricious [ævə'rɪʃəs] *adj* habsüchtig

avdp. *abbr (= avoirdupois) Handelsgewicht*

Ave *abbr* = **avenue**

avenge [ə'vɛndʒ] *vt* rächen

avenue ['ævənjuː] *n* Straße *f*; *(drive)* Auffahrt *f*; *(means)* Weg *m*

average ['ævərɪdʒ] *n* Durchschnitt *m* ▷ *adj* durchschnittlich, Durchschnitts- ▷ *vt (reach an average of)* einen Durchschnitt erreichen von; **on ~** im Durchschnitt, durchschnittlich; **above/below (the)** ~ über/unter dem Durchschnitt

▸ **average out** *vi:* **to ~ out at** durchschnittlich ausmachen

averse [ə'vɜːs] *adj:* **to be ~ to sth/doing sth** eine Abneigung gegen etw haben/dagegen haben, etw zu tun; **I wouldn't be ~ to a drink** ich hätte nichts gegen einen Drink

aversion [ə'vɜːʃən] *n* Abneigung *f*; **to have an ~ to sb/sth** eine Abneigung gegen jdn/etw haben

avert [ə'vɜːt] *vt (prevent)* verhindern; *(ward off)* abwehren; *(turn away)* abwenden

aviary ['eɪvɪərɪ] *n* Vogelhaus *nt*

aviation [eɪvɪ'eɪʃən] *n* Luftfahrt *f*

avid ['ævɪd] *adj* begeistert, eifrig

avidly ['ævɪdlɪ] *adv* begeistert, eifrig
avocado [ævə'kɑːdəu] (*Brit*) *n* (*also:* **avocado pear**) Avocado *f*
avoid [ə'vɔɪd] *vt* (*person, obstacle*) ausweichen +*dat*; (*trouble*) vermeiden; (*danger*) meiden
avoidable [ə'vɔɪdəbl] *adj* vermeidbar
avoidance [ə'vɔɪdəns] *n* (*of tax*) Umgehung *f*; (*of issue*) Vermeidung *f*
avowed [ə'vaud] *adj* erklärt
AVP (US) *n abbr* (= *assistant vice president*) stellvertretender Vizepräsident
avuncular [ə'vʌŋkjuləʳ] *adj* onkelhaft
AWACS ['eɪwæks] *n abbr* (= *airborne warning and control system*) AWACS
await [ə'weɪt] *vt* warten auf +*acc*; **~ing attention/delivery** zur Bearbeitung/Lieferung bestimmt; **long ~ed** lang ersehnt
awake [ə'weɪk] (*pt* **awoke**, *pp* **awoken** *or* **~d**) *adj* wach ▷ *vt* wecken ▷ *vi* erwachen, aufwachen; **~ to** sich *dat* bewusst werden +*gen*
awakening [ə'weɪknɪŋ] *n* (*also fig*) Erwachen *nt*
award [ə'wɔːd] *n* Preis *m*; (*for bravery*) Auszeichnung *f*; (*damages*) Entschädigung(ssumme) *f* ▷ *vt* (*prize*) verleihen; (*damages*) zusprechen
aware [ə'weəʳ] *adj*: **~ (of)** bewusst (+*gen*); **to become ~ of** sich *dat* bewusst werden +*gen*; **to become ~ that ...** sich *dat* bewusst werden, dass ...; **politically/socially ~** politik-/sozialbewusst; **I am fully ~ that** es ist mir völlig klar *or* bewusst, dass
awareness [ə'weənɪs] *n* Bewusstsein *nt*; **to develop people's ~ of sth** den Menschen etw zu Bewusstsein bringen
awash [ə'wɔʃ] *adj* (*also fig*) überflutet
away [ə'weɪ] *adv* weg, fort; (*position*) entfernt; **two kilometres ~** zwei Kilometer entfernt; **two hours ~ by car** zwei Autostunden entfernt; **the holiday was two weeks ~** es war noch zwei Wochen bis zum Urlaub; **he's ~ for a week** er ist eine Woche nicht da; **he's ~ in Milan** er ist in Mailand; **to take ~ (from)** (*remove*) entfernen (von); (*subtract*) abziehen (von); **to work/pedal** *etc* **~** unablässig arbeiten/strampeln *etc*; **to fade ~** (*colour, light*) verblassen; (*sound*) verhallen; (*enthusiasm*) schwinden
away game *n* Auswärtsspiel *nt*
awe [ɔː] *n* Ehrfurcht *f*

awe-inspiring ['ɔːɪnspaɪərɪŋ] *adj* Ehrfurcht gebietend
awesome ['ɔːsəm] *adj* Ehrfurcht gebietend; (*fig: inf*) überwältigend
awe-struck ['ɔːstrʌk] *adj* von Ehrfurcht ergriffen
awful ['ɔːfəl] *adj* furchtbar, schrecklich; **an ~ lot (of)** furchtbar viel(e)
awfully ['ɔːfəlɪ] *adv* furchtbar, schrecklich
awhile [ə'waɪl] *adv* eine Weile
awkward ['ɔːkwəd] *adj* (*clumsy*) unbeholfen; (*inconvenient, difficult*) ungünstig; (*embarrassing*) peinlich
awkwardness ['ɔːkwədnɪs] *n* (*see adj*) Unbeholfenheit *f*; Ungünstigkeit *f*; Peinlichkeit *f*
awl [ɔːl] *n* Ahle *f*, Pfriem *m*
awning ['ɔːnɪŋ] *n* (*of tent, caravan*) Vordach *nt*; (*of shop etc*) Markise *f*
awoke [ə'wəuk] *pt of* **awake**
awoken [ə'wəukən] *pp of* **awake**
AWOL ['eɪwɒl] *abbr* (*Mil*: = *absent without leave*) *see* **absent**
awry [ə'raɪ] *adv*: **to be ~** (*clothes*) schief sitzen; **to go ~** schiefgehen
axe, (US) **ax** [æks] *n* Axt *f*, Beil *nt* ▷ *vt* (*employee*) entlassen; (*project, jobs etc*) streichen; **to have an ~ to grind** (*fig*) ein persönliches Interesse haben
axes[1] ['æksɪz] *npl of* **axe**
axes[2] ['æksiːz] *npl of* **axis**
axiom ['æksɪəm] *n* Axiom *nt*, Grundsatz *m*
axiomatic [æksɪəu'mætɪk] *adj* axiomatisch
axis ['æksɪs] (*pl* **axes**[2]) *n* Achse *f*
axle ['æksl] *n* (*also:* **axletree**) Achse *f*
aye [aɪ] *excl* (*yes*) ja ▷ *n*: **the ~s** die Jastimmen *pl*
AYH *n abbr* (= *American Youth Hostels*) Jugendherbergsverband, ≈ DJHV *m*
AZ (US) *abbr* (*Post*) = **Arizona**
azalea [ə'zeɪlɪə] *n* Azalee *f*
Azerbaijan [æzəbaɪ'dʒɑːn] *n* Aserbaidschan *nt*
Azerbaijani [æzəbaɪ'dʒɑːnɪ], **Azeri** [ə'zeərɪ] *adj* aserbaidschanisch ▷ *n* Aserbaidschaner(in) *m(f)*
Azores [ə'zɔːz] *npl*: **the ~** die Azoren *pl*
AZT *n abbr* (= *azidothymidine*) AZT *nt*
Aztec ['æztɛk] *adj* aztekisch ▷ *n* Azteke *m*, Aztekin *f*
azure ['eɪʒəʳ] *adj* azurblau, tiefblau

Bb

B¹, b [biː] n (letter) B nt, b nt; (Scol) ≈ Zwei f, ≈ Gut nt; **B for Benjamin, B for Baker** (US) ≈ B wie Bertha; **B road** (Brit) Landstraße f

B² [biː] n (Mus) H nt, h nt

b. abbr = **born**

BA n abbr (= Bachelor of Arts) see **bachelor**; (= British Academy) Verband zur Förderung der Künste und Geisteswissenschaften

babble ['bæbl] vi schwatzen; (baby) plappern; (brook) plätschern ▷ n: **a ~ of voices** ein Stimmengewirr nt

babe [beɪb] n (liter) Kindlein nt; (esp US: address) Schätzchen nt; **~ in arms** Säugling m

baboon [bə'buːn] n Pavian m

baby ['beɪbɪ] n Baby nt; (US: inf: darling) Schatz m, Schätzchen nt

baby carriage (US) n Kinderwagen m

baby grand n (also: **baby grand piano**) Stutzflügel m

babyhood ['beɪbɪhʊd] n frühe Kindheit f

babyish ['beɪbɪɪʃ] adj kindlich

baby-minder ['beɪbɪmaɪndə'] (Brit) n Tagesmutter f

baby-sit ['beɪbɪsɪt] vi babysitten

baby-sitter ['beɪbɪsɪtə'] n Babysitter(in) m(f)

baby wipe n Ölpflegetuch nt

bachelor ['bætʃələ'] n Junggeselle m; **B~ of Arts/Science (degree)** ≈ Magister m der philosophischen Fakultät/der Naturwissenschaften

bachelorhood ['bætʃələhʊd] n Junggesellentum nt

bachelor party (US) n Junggesellenparty f

⊘ **BACHELOR'S DEGREE**

⊘ *Bachelor's Degree* ist der akademische Grad,
⊘ den man nach drei- oder vierjährigem,
⊘ erfolgreich abgeschlossenem
⊘ Universitätsstudium erhält. Die
⊘ am häufigsten verliehenen Grade
⊘ sind *BA* (Bachelor of Arts = Magister
⊘ der Geisteswissenschaften), *BSc*
⊘ (Bachelor of Science = Magister
⊘ der Naturwissenschaften), *BEd*
⊘ (Bachelor of Education = Magister
⊘ der Erziehungswissenschaften) und

⊘ LLB (Bachelor of Laws = Magister der
⊘ Rechtswissenschaften). Siehe auch *master's*
⊘ *degree, doctorate.*

back [bæk] n Rücken m; (of house, page) Rückseite f; (of chair) (Rücken)lehne f; (of train) Ende nt; (Football) Verteidiger m ▷ vt (candidate: also: **back up**) unterstützen; (horse) setzen or wetten auf +acc; (car) zurücksetzen, zurückfahren ▷ vi (also: **back up**: person) rückwärtsgehen; (car etc) zurücksetzen, zurückfahren ▷ cpd (payment, rent) ausstehend ▷ adv hinten; **in the ~ (of the car)** hinten (im Auto); **at the ~ of the book/crowd/audience** hinten im Buch/in der Menge/im Publikum; **~ to front** verkehrt herum; **to break the ~ of a job** (Brit) mit einer Arbeit über den Berg sein; **to have one's ~ to the wall** (fig) in die Enge getrieben sein; **~ room** Hinterzimmer nt; **~ garden** Garten m (hinter dem Haus); **~ seat** (Aut) Rücksitz m; **to take a ~ seat** (fig) sich zurückhalten; **~ wheels** Hinterräder pl; **he's ~** er ist zurück or wieder da; **throw the ball ~** wirf den Ball zurück; **he called ~** er rief zurück; **he ran ~** er rannte zurück; **when will you be ~?** wann kommen Sie wieder?; **can I have it ~?** kann ich es zurückhaben or wiederhaben?

▸ **back down** vi nachgeben

▸ **back on to** vt fus: **the house ~s on to the golf course** das Haus grenzt hinten an den Golfplatz an

▸ **back out** vi (of promise) einen Rückzieher machen

▸ **back up** vt (support) unterstützen; (Comput) sichern

backache ['bækeɪk] n Rückenschmerzen pl

⊘ **BACK BENCH**

⊘ *Back Bench* bezeichnet im britischen
⊘ Unterhaus die am weitesten vom
⊘ Mittelgang entfernten Bänke, im
⊘ Gegensatz zur *front bench*. Auf diesen
⊘ hinteren Bänken sitzen diejenigen
⊘ Unterhausabgeordneten (auch
⊘ backbenchers genannt), die kein

Regierungsamt bzw. keine wichtige
Stellung in der Opposition innehaben.

backbencher ['bæk'bentʃəʳ] (Brit) n
Abgeordnete(r) f(m) (in den hinteren Reihen im
britischen Parlament), Hinterbänkler(in) m(f)
(pej); see also **back bench**
backbiting ['bækbaɪtɪŋ] n Lästern nt
backbone ['bækbəʊn] n (also fig) Rückgrat nt
backchat ['bæktʃæt] (Brit: inf) n Widerrede f
backcloth ['bækklɒθ] (Brit) n Hintergrund m
backcomb ['bækkəʊm] (Brit) vt toupieren
backdate [bæk'deɪt] vt (zu)rückdatieren;
~d pay rise rückwirkend geltende
Gehaltserhöhung f
backdrop ['bækdrɒp] n = **backcloth**
backer ['bækəʳ] n (Comm) Geldgeber m
backfire [bæk'faɪəʳ] vi (Aut) Fehlzündungen
haben; (plans) ins Auge gehen
backgammon ['bækgæmən] n Backgammon
nt
background ['bækgraʊnd] n Hintergrund
m; (basic knowledge) Grundkenntnisse
pl; (experience) Erfahrung f ▷ cpd (music)
Hintergrund-; **family ~** Herkunft f; **~ noise**
Geräuschkulisse f; **~ reading** vertiefende
Lektüre f
backhand ['bækhænd] n (Tennis: also:
backhand stroke) Rückhand f
backhanded [bæk'hændɪd] adj (fig: compliment)
zweifelhaft
backhander [bæk'hændəʳ] (Brit) n
Schmiergeld nt
backing ['bækɪŋ] n (Comm: fig) Unterstützung f;
(Mus) Begleitung f
backlash ['bæklæʃ] n (fig) Gegenreaktion f
backlog ['bæklɒg] n: **to have a ~ of work** mit
der Arbeit im Rückstand sein
back number n alte Ausgabe f or Nummer f
backpack ['bækpæk] n Rucksack m
backpacker ['bækpækəʳ] n Rucksacktourist(in)
m(f)
back pay n Nachzahlung f
back-pedal ['bækpɛdl] vi (fig) einen Rückzieher
machen
back-seat driver n Mitfahrer, der dem Fahrer
dazwischenredet
backside ['bæksaɪd] (inf) n Hintern m
backslash ['bækslæʃ] n Backslash m
backslide ['bækslaɪd] vi rückfällig werden
backspace ['bækspeɪs] vi (in typing) die
Rücktaste betätigen
backstage [bæk'steɪdʒ] adv (Theat) hinter
den Kulissen; (: in dressing-room area) in der
Garderobe
backstreet ['bækstriːt] n Seitenstraße f ▷ cpd: **~
abortionist** Engelmacher(in) m(f)
backstroke ['bækstrəʊk] n
Rückenschwimmen nt
backtrack ['bæktræk] vi (fig) einen Rückzieher
machen
backup ['bækʌp] adj (train, plane) Entlastungs-;
(Comput: copy etc) Sicherungs- ▷ n (support)

Unterstützung f; (Comput: also: **backup disk**,
backup file) Sicherungskopie f, Back-up nt
backward ['bækwəd] adj (movement)
Rückwärts-; (person) zurückgeblieben; (country)
rückständig; **~ and forward movement** Vor-
und Zurückbewegung f; **~ step/glance** Blick
m/Schritt m zurück
backwards ['bækwədz] adv rückwärts; (read)
von hinten nach vorne; (fall) nach hinten; (in
time) zurück; **to know sth ~**, **to know sth ~
and forwards** (US) etw in- und auswendig
kennen
backwater ['bækwɔːtəʳ] n (fig) Kaff nt
back yard n Hinterhof m
bacon ['beɪkən] n (Frühstücks)speck m,
(Schinken)speck m
bacteria [bæk'tɪərɪə] npl Bakterien pl
bacteriology [bæktɪərɪ'ɒlədʒɪ] n Bakteriologie
f
bad [bæd] adj schlecht; (naughty) unartig,
ungezogen; (mistake, accident, injury) schwer;
his ~ leg sein schlimmes Bein; **to go ~**
verderben, schlecht werden; **to have a ~ time
of it** es schwer haben; **I feel ~ about it** es tut
mir leid; **in ~ faith** mit böser Absicht
bad debt n uneinbringliche Forderung f
baddy ['bædɪ] (inf) n Bösewicht m
bade [bæd] pt of **bid**
badge [bædʒ] n Plakette f; (stick-on) Aufkleber
m; (fig) Merkmal m
badger ['bædʒəʳ] n Dachs m ▷ vt zusetzen +dat
bad hair day n (inf) Scheißtag f, Tag m, an dem
alles schiefgeht
badly ['bædlɪ] adv schlecht; **~ wounded** schwer
verletzt; **he needs it ~** er braucht es dringend;
things are going ~ es sieht schlecht or nicht
gut aus; **to be ~ off (for money)** wenig Geld
haben
bad-mannered ['bæd'mænəd] adj ungezogen,
unhöflich
badminton ['bædmɪntən] n Federball m
bad-tempered ['bæd'tɛmpəd] adj schlecht
gelaunt; (by nature) übellaunig
baffle ['bæfl] vt verblüffen
baffling ['bæflɪŋ] adj rätselhaft, verwirrend
bag [bæg] n Tasche f; (made of paper, plastic)
Tüte f; (handbag) (Hand)tasche f; (satchel)
Schultasche f; (case) Reisetasche f; (of hunter)
Jagdbeute f; (pej: woman) Schachtel f; **~s of**
(inf: lots of) jede Menge; **to pack one's ~s** die
Koffer packen; **~s under the eyes** Ringe pl
unter den Augen
bagful ['bægful] n: **a ~ of** eine Tasche/Tüte voll
baggage ['bægɪdʒ] n Gepäck nt
baggage allowance n Freigepäck nt
baggage car (US) n Gepäckwagen m
baggage claim n Gepäckausgabe f
baggy ['bægɪ] adj weit; (out of shape) ausgebeult
Baghdad [bæg'dæd] n Bagdad nt
bag lady (esp US) n Stadtstreicherin f
bagpipes ['bægpaɪps] npl Dudelsack m
bag-snatcher ['bægsnætʃəʳ] (Brit) n
Handtaschendieb(in) m(f)

Bahamas [bəˈhɑːməz] *npl*: **the ~** die Bahamas *pl*, die Bahamainseln *pl*

Bahrain [bɑːˈreɪn] *n* Bahrain *nt*

bail [beɪl] *n* (*Law: payment*) Kaution *f*; (: *release*) Freilassung *f* gegen Kaution ▷ *vt* (*prisoner*) gegen Kaution freilassen; (*boat: also:* **bail out**) ausschöpfen; **to be on ~** gegen Kaution freigelassen sein; **to be released on ~** gegen Kaution freigelassen werden; *see also* **bale**
  ▶ **bail out** *vt* (*prisoner*) gegen Kaution freibekommen; (*firm, friend*) aus der Patsche helfen +*dat*

bailiff [ˈbeɪlɪf] *n* (*Law: Brit*) Gerichtsvollzieher(in) *m(f)*; (: *US*) Gerichtsdiener(in) *m(f)*; (*Brit: factor*) (Guts)verwalter(in) *m(f)*

bait [beɪt] *n* Köder *m* ▷ *vt* (*hook, trap*) mit einem Köder versehen; (*tease*) necken

baize [beɪz] *n* Flausch *m*; **green ~** Billardtuch *nt*

bake [beɪk] *vt* backen; (*clay etc*) brennen ▷ *vi* backen

baked beans [beɪkt-] *npl* gebackene Bohnen *pl* (in Tomatensoße)

baked potato *n* in der Schale gebackene Kartoffel *f*

baker [ˈbeɪkəʳ] *n* Bäcker(in) *m(f)*

baker's dozen *n* dreizehn (Stück)

bakery [ˈbeɪkərɪ] *n* Bäckerei *f*

baking [ˈbeɪkɪŋ] *n* Backen *nt*; (*batch*) Ofenladung *f* ▷ *adj* (*inf: hot*) wie im Backofen

baking powder *n* Backpulver *nt*

baking tin *n* Backform *f*

baking tray *n* Backblech *nt*

balaclava [bæləˈklɑːvə] *n* (*also:* **balaclava helmet**) Kapuzenmütze *f*

balance [ˈbæləns] *n* (*equilibrium*) Gleichgewicht *nt*; (*Comm: sum*) Saldo *m*; (*remainder*) Restbetrag *m*; (*scales*) Waage *f* ▷ *vt* ausgleichen; (*Aut: wheels*) auswuchten; (*pros and cons*) (gegeneinander) abwägen; **on ~** alles in allem; **~ of trade/payments** Handels-/Zahlungsbilanz *f*; **~ carried forward** or **brought forward** (*Comm*) Saldovortrag *m*, Saldoübertrag *m*; **to ~ the books** (*Comm*) die Bilanz ziehen or machen

balanced [ˈbælənst] *adj* ausgeglichen; (*report*) ausgewogen

balance sheet *n* Bilanz *f*

balance wheel *n* Unruh *f*

balcony [ˈbælkənɪ] *n* Balkon *m*; (*in theatre*) oberster Rang *m*

bald [bɔːld] *adj* kahl; (*tyre*) abgefahren; (*statement*) knapp

baldness [ˈbɔːldnɪs] *n* Kahlheit *f*

bale [beɪl] *n* (*Agr*) Bündel *nt*; (*of papers etc*) Packen *m*
  ▶ **bale out** *vi* (*of a plane*) abspringen ▷ *vt* (*water*) schöpfen; (*boat*) ausschöpfen

Balearic Islands [bælɪˈærɪk-] *npl*: **the ~** die Balearen *pl*

baleful [ˈbeɪlful] *adj* böse

balk [bɔːk] *vi*: **to ~ (at)** (*subj: person*) zurückschrecken (vor +*dat*); (: *horse*) scheuen

(vor +*dat*)

Balkan [ˈbɔːlkən] *adj* (*countries etc*) Balkan-
  ▷ *n*: **the ~s** der Balkan, die Balkanländer *pl*

ball [bɔːl] *n* Ball *m*; (*of wool, string*) Knäuel *m* or *nt*; **to set the ~ rolling** (*fig*) den Stein ins Rollen bringen; **to play ~ (with sb)** (*fig*) (mit jdm) mitspielen; **to be on the ~** (*fig: competent*) am Ball sein; (: *alert*) auf Draht or Zack sein; **the ~ is in their court** (*fig*) sie sind am Ball

ballad [ˈbæləd] *n* Ballade *f*

ballast [ˈbæləst] *n* Ballast *m*

ball bearing *npl* Kugellager *nt*; (*individual ball*) Kugellagerkugel *f*

ball cock *n* Schwimmerhahn *m*

ballerina [bæləˈriːnə] *n* Ballerina *f*

ballet [ˈbæleɪ] *n* Ballett *nt*

ballet dancer *n* Balletttänzer(in) *m(f)*

ballistic [bəˈlɪstɪk] *adj* ballistisch

ballistic missile *n* Raketengeschoss *nt*

ballistics [bəˈlɪstɪks] *n* Ballistik *f*

balloon [bəˈluːn] *n* (Luft)ballon *m*; (*hot air balloon*) Heißluftballon *m*; (*in comic strip*) Sprechblase *f*

balloonist [bəˈluːnɪst] *n* Ballonfahrer(in) *m(f)*

ballot [ˈbælət] *n* (geheime) Abstimmung *f*

ballot box *n* Wahlurne *f*

ballot paper *n* Stimmzettel *m*

ballpark [ˈbɔːlpɑːk] (*US*) *n* (*Sport*) Baseballstadion *nt*

ballpark figure (*inf*) *n* Richtzahl *f*

ballpoint [ˈbɔːlpɔɪnt], **ballpoint pen** *n* Kugelschreiber *m*

ballroom [ˈbɔːlrum] *n* Tanzsaal *m*

balls [bɔːlz] (*inf!*) *npl* (*testicles*) Eier *pl* (!); (*courage*) Schneid *m*, Mumm *m* ▷ *excl* red keinen Scheiß! (!)

balm [bɑːm] *n* Balsam *m*

balmy [ˈbɑːmɪ] *adj* (*breeze*) sanft; (*air*) lau, lind; (*Brit: inf*) = **barmy**

BALPA [ˈbælpə] *n abbr* (= *British Airline Pilots' Association*) Flugpilotengewerkschaft

balsa [ˈbɔːlsə], **balsa wood** *n* Balsaholz *nt*

balsam [ˈbɔːlsəm] *n* Balsam *m*

Baltic [ˈbɔːltɪk] *n*: **the ~ (Sea)** die Ostsee

balustrade [bæləsˈtreɪd] *n* Balustrade *f*

bamboo [bæmˈbuː] *n* Bambus *m*

bamboozle [bæmˈbuːzl] (*inf*) *vt* hereinlegen; **to ~ sb into doing sth** jdn durch Tricks dazu bringen, etw zu tun

ban [bæn] *n* Verbot *nt* ▷ *vt* verbieten; **he was ~ned from driving** (*Brit*) ihm wurde Fahrverbot erteilt

banal [bəˈnɑːl] *adj* banal

banana [bəˈnɑːnə] *n* Banane *f*

band [bænd] *n* (*group*) Gruppe *f*, Schar *f*; (*Mus: jazz, rock etc*) Band *f*; (: *military etc*) (Musik)kapelle *f*; (*strip, range*) Band *nt*; (*stripe*) Streifen *m*
  ▶ **band together** *vi* sich zusammenschließen

bandage [ˈbændɪdʒ] *n* Verband *m* ▷ *vt* verbinden

Band-Aid® [ˈbændeɪd] (*US*) *n* Heftpflaster *nt*

B & B *n abbr* = **bed and breakfast**

b

bandit ['bændɪt] n Bandit m
bandstand ['bændstænd] n Musikpavillion m
bandwagon ['bændwægən] n: **to jump on the ~** (fig) auf den fahrenden Zug aufspringen
bandy ['bændɪ] vt (jokes) sich erzählen; (ideas) diskutieren; (insults) sich an den Kopf werfen
▸ **bandy about** vt (word, expression) immer wieder gebrauchen; (name) immer wieder nennen
bandy-legged ['bændɪ'legɪd] adj o-beinig
bane [beɪn] n: **it/he is the ~ of my life** das/er ist noch mal mein Ende
bang [bæŋ] n (of door) Knallen nt; (of gun, exhaust) Knall m; (blow) Schlag m ▷ excl peng ▷ vt (door) zuschlagen, zuknallen; (one's head etc) sich dat stoßen +acc ▷ vi knallen ▷ adv: **to be ~ on time** (Brit: inf) auf die Sekunde pünktlich sein; **to ~ at the door** gegen die Tür hämmern; **to ~ into sth** sich an etw dat stoßen
banger ['bæŋər] (Brit: inf) n (car: also: **old banger**) Klapperkiste f; (sausage) Würstchen nt; (firework) Knallkörper m
Bangkok [bæŋ'kɔk] n Bangkok nt
Bangladesh [bæŋglə'deʃ] n Bangladesch nt
bangle ['bæŋgl] n Armreif(en) m
bangs [bæŋz] (US) npl (fringe) Pony m
banish ['bænɪʃ] vt verbannen
banister ['bænɪstər] n, **banisters** ['bænɪstəz] ▷ npl Geländer nt
banjo ['bændʒəʊ] (pl **banjoes** or **~s**) n Banjo nt
bank [bæŋk] n Bank f; (of river, lake) Ufer nt; (of earth) Wall m; (of switches) Reihe f ▷ vi (Aviat) sich in die Kurve legen; (Comm): **they ~ with Pitt's** sie haben ihr Konto bei Pitt's
▸ **bank on** vt fus sich verlassen auf +acc
bank account n Bankkonto nt
bank balance n Kontostand m
bank card n Scheckkarte f
bank charges (Brit) npl Kontoführungsgebühren pl
bank draft n Bankanweisung f
banker ['bæŋkər] n Bankier m
banker's card (Brit) n = **bank card**
banker's order (Brit) n Dauerauftrag m
bank giro n Banküberweisung f
bank holiday (Brit) n (öffentlicher) Feiertag m; siehe Info-Artikel

● **BANK HOLIDAY**
●
● Als bank holiday wird in Großbritannien
● ein gesetzlicher Feiertag bezeichnet, an
● dem die Banken geschlossen sind. Die
● meisten dieser Feiertage, abgesehen von
● Weihnachten und Ostern, fallen auf
● Montage im Mai und August. An diesen
● langen Wochenenden (bank holiday
● weekends) fahren viele Briten in Urlaub,
● sodass dann auf den Straßen, Flughäfen
● und bei der Bahn sehr viel Betrieb ist.

banking ['bæŋkɪŋ] n Bankwesen nt
banking hours npl Schalterstunden pl

bank loan n Bankkredit m
bank manager n Filialleiter(in) m(f) (einer Bank)
banknote ['bæŋknəʊt] n Geldschein m, Banknote f
bank rate n Diskontsatz m
bankrupt ['bæŋkrʌpt] adj bankrott ▷ n Bankrotteur(in) m(f); **to go ~** Bankrott machen
bankruptcy ['bæŋkrʌptsɪ] n (Comm: fig) Bankrott m
bank statement n Kontoauszug m
banner ['bænər] n Banner nt; (in demonstration) Spruchband nt
banner headline n Schlagzeile f
bannister ['bænɪstər] n, **bannisters** ['bænɪstəz] ▷ n(pl) = **banister; banisters**
banns [bænz] npl Aufgebot nt
banquet ['bæŋkwɪt] n Bankett nt
bantamweight ['bæntəmweɪt] n Bantamgewicht nt
banter ['bæntər] n Geplänkel nt
BAOR n abbr (= British Army of the Rhine) britische Rheinarmee
baptism ['bæptɪzəm] n Taufe f
Baptist ['bæptɪst] n Baptist(in) m(f)
baptize [bæp'taɪz] vt taufen
bar [bɑːʳ] n (for drinking) Lokal nt; (counter) Theke f; (rod) Stange f; (on window etc) (Gitter) stab m; (slab: of chocolate) Tafel f; (fig: obstacle) Hindernis nt; (prohibition) Verbot nt; (Mus) Takt m ▷ vt (road) blockieren, versperren; (window) verriegeln; (person) ausschließen; (activity) verbieten; **~ of soap** Stück nt Seife; **behind ~s** hinter Gittern; **the B~** (Law) die Anwaltschaft; **~ none** ohne Ausnahme
Barbados [bɑː'beɪdɔs] n Barbados nt
barbaric [bɑː'bærɪk] adj barbarisch
barbarous ['bɑːbərəs] adj barbarisch
barbecue ['bɑːbɪkjuː] n Grill m; (meal, party) Barbecue nt
barbed wire ['bɑːbd-] n Stacheldraht m
barber ['bɑːbəʳ] n (Herren)friseur m
barbiturate [bɑː'bɪtjʊrɪt] n Schlafmittel nt, Barbiturat nt
Barcelona [bɑːsə'ləʊnə] n Barcelona nt
bar chart n Balkendiagramm nt
bar code n Strichcode m
bare [beəʳ] adj nackt; (trees, countryside) kahl; (minimum) absolut ▷ vt entblößen; (teeth) blecken; **the ~ essentials, the ~ necessities** das Allernotwendigste; **to ~ one's soul** sein Innerstes entblößen
bareback ['beəbæk] adv ohne Sattel
barefaced ['beəfeɪst] adj (fig) unverfroren, schamlos
barefoot ['beəfʊt] adj barfüßig ▷ adv barfuß
bareheaded [beə'hedɪd] adj barhäuptig ▷ adv ohne Kopfbedeckung
barely ['beəlɪ] adv kaum
Barents Sea ['bærənts-] n: **the ~** die Barentssee
bargain ['bɑːgɪn] n (deal) Geschäft nt; (transaction) Handel m; (good offer)

Sonderangebot nt; (good buy) guter Kauf m
▷ vi: **to ~ (with sb)** (mit jdm) verhandeln;
(haggle) (mit jdm) handeln; **into the ~**
obendrein
▶ bargain for vt fus: **he got more than he ~ed
for** er bekam mehr, als er erwartet hatte
bargaining ['bɑːgənɪŋ] n Verhandeln nt
bargaining position n Verhandlungsposition
f
barge [bɑːdʒ] n Lastkahn m, Frachtkahn m
▶ **barge in** vi (enter) hereinplatzen; (interrupt)
unterbrechen
▶ **barge into** vt fus (place) hereinplatzen;
(person) anrempeln
bargepole ['bɑːdʒpəʊl] n: **I wouldn't touch it
with a ~** (fig) das würde ich nicht mal mit der
Kneifzange anfassen
baritone ['bærɪtəʊn] n Bariton m
barium meal ['bɛərɪəm-] n Kontrastbrei m
bark [bɑːk] n (of tree) Rinde f; (of dog) Bellen nt
▷ vi bellen; **she's ~ing up the wrong tree** (fig)
sie ist auf dem Holzweg
barley ['bɑːlɪ] n Gerste f
barley sugar n Malzbonbon nt or m
barmaid ['bɑːmeɪd] n Bardame f
barman ['bɑːmən] (irreg: like **man**) n Barmann m
barmy ['bɑːmɪ] (Brit: inf) adj bekloppt
barn [bɑːn] n Scheune f
barnacle ['bɑːnəkl] n Rankenfußkrebs m
barn owl n Schleiereule f
barometer [bə'rɒmɪtə'] n Barometer nt
baron ['bærən] n Baron m; **industrial ~**
Industriemagnat m; **press ~** Pressezar m
baroness ['bærənɪs] n (baron's wife) Baronin f;
(baron's daughter) Baroness f, Baronesse f
baronet ['bærənɪt] n Baronet m
barracking ['bærəkɪŋ] n Buhrufe pl
barracks ['bærəks] npl Kaserne f
barrage ['bærɑːʒ] n (Mil) Sperrfeuer nt; (dam)
Staustufe f; (fig: of criticism, questions etc) Hagel m
barrel ['bærəl] n Fass nt; (of oil) Barrel nt; (of gun)
Lauf m
barrel organ n Drehorgel f
barren ['bærən] adj unfruchtbar
barricade [bærɪ'keɪd] n Barrikade f ▷ vt (road,
entrance) verbarrikadieren; **to ~ o.s. (in)** sich
verbarrikadieren
barrier ['bærɪə'] n (at frontier, entrance) Schranke
f; (Brit: also: **crash barrier**) Leitplanke f; (fig)
Barriere f; (: to progress etc) Hindernis nt
barrier cream (Brit) n Hautschutzcreme f
barring ['bɑːrɪŋ] prep außer im Falle +gen
barrister ['bærɪstə'] (Brit) n Rechtsanwalt m,
Rechtsanwältin f; siehe Info-Artikel

⬤ **BARRISTER**

⬤ Barrister oder barrister-at-law ist in England
⬤ die Bezeichnung für einen Rechtsanwalt,
⬤ der seine Klienten vor allem vor Gericht
⬤ vertritt; im Gegensatz zum solicitor, der
⬤ nicht vor Gericht auftritt, sondern einen
⬤ barrister mit dieser Aufgabe beauftragt.

barrow ['bærəʊ] n Schubkarre f, Schubkarren
m; (cart) Karren m
bar stool n Barhocker m
Bart. (Brit) abbr = **baronet**
bartender ['bɑːtɛndə'] (US) n Barmann m
barter ['bɑːtə'] n Tauschhandel m ▷ vt: **to ~ sth
for sth** etw gegen etw tauschen
barter exchange n Tauschbörse f
base [beɪs] n (of tree etc) Fuß m; (of cup, box etc)
Boden m; (foundation) Grundlage f; (centre)
Stützpunkt m, Standort m; (for organization) Sitz
m ▷ adj gemein, niederträchtig ▷ vt: **to ~ sth
on** etw gründen or basieren auf +acc; **to be ~d
at** (troops) stationiert sein in +dat; (employee)
arbeiten in +dat; **I'm ~d in London** ich wohne
in London; **a Paris-~d firm** eine Firma mit
Sitz in Paris; **coffee-~d** auf Kaffeebasis
baseball ['beɪsbɔːl] n Baseball m
baseboard ['beɪsbɔːd] (US) n Fußleiste f
base camp n Basislager nt, Versorgungslager
nt
Basel [bɑːl] n = **Basle**
baseline ['beɪslaɪn] n (Tennis) Grundlinie f;
(fig: standard) Ausgangspunkt m
basement ['beɪsmənt] n Keller m
base rate n Eckzins m, Leitzins m
bases[1] ['beɪsɪz] npl of **base**
bases[2] ['beɪsiːz] npl of **basis**
bash [bæʃ] (inf) vt schlagen, hauen ▷ n: **I'll
have a ~ (at it)** (Brit) ich probier's mal
▶ **bash up** vt (car) demolieren; (Brit: person)
vermöbeln
bashful ['bæʃfʊl] adj schüchtern
bashing ['bæʃɪŋ] (inf) n Prügel pl; **Paki-/
queer-~** Überfälle pl auf Pakistaner/Schwule
BASIC ['beɪsɪk] n (Comput) BASIC nt
basic ['beɪsɪk] adj (method, needs etc)
Grund-; (principles) grundlegend; (problem)
grundsätzlich; (knowledge) elementar;
(facilities) primitiv
basically ['beɪsɪklɪ] adv im Grunde
basic rate n Eingangssteuersatz m
basics ['beɪsɪks] npl: **the ~** das Wesentliche
basil ['bæzl] n Basilikum nt
basin ['beɪsn] n Gefäß nt; (Brit: for food) Schüssel
f; (also: **wash basin**) (Wasch)becken nt; (of river,
lake) Becken nt
basis ['beɪsɪs] (pl **bases**) n Basis f, Grundlage f;
on a part-time ~ stundenweise; **on a trial
~** zur Probe; **on the ~ of what you've said**
aufgrund dessen, was Sie gesagt haben
bask [bɑːsk] vi: **to ~ in the sun** sich sonnen
basket ['bɑːskɪt] n Korb m; (smaller) Körbchen nt
basketball ['bɑːskɪtbɔːl] n Basketball m
basketball player n Basketballspieler(in) m(f)
Basle [bɑːl] n Basel nt
basmati rice [bəz'mæti-] n Basmatireis m
Basque [bæsk] adj baskisch ▷ n Baske m,
Baskin f
bass [beɪs] n Bass m
bass clef n Bassschlüssel m
bassoon [bə'suːn] n Fagott nt

bastard ['bɑːstəd] *n* uneheliches Kind *nt*; (*inf!*) Arschloch *nt* (!)

baste [beɪst] *vt* (*Culin*) (mit Fett und Bratensaft) begießen; (*Sewing*) heften, reihen

bastion ['bæstɪən] *n* Bastion *f*

bat [bæt] *n* (*Zool*) Fledermaus *f*; (*for cricket, baseball etc*) Schlagholz *nt*; (*Brit: for table tennis*) Schläger *m* ▷ *vt*: **he didn't ~ an eyelid** er hat nicht mit der Wimper gezuckt; **off one's own ~** auf eigene Faust

batch [bætʃ] *n* (*of bread*) Schub *m*; (*of letters, papers*) Stoß *m*, Stapel *m*; (*of applicants*) Gruppe *f*; (*of work*) Schwung *m*; (*of goods*) Ladung *f*, Sendung *f*

batch processing *n* (*Comput*) Stapelverarbeitung *f*

bated ['beɪtɪd] *adj*: **with ~ breath** mit angehaltenem Atem

bath [bɑːθ] *n* Bad *nt*; (*bathtub*) (Bade)wanne *f* ▷ *vt* baden; **to have a ~** baden, ein Bad nehmen; *see also* **baths**

bathe [beɪð] *vi*, *vt* (*also fig*) baden

bather ['beɪðə^r] *n* Badende(r) *f(m)*

bathing ['beɪðɪŋ] *n* Baden *nt*

bathing cap *n* Bademütze *f*, Badekappe *f*

bathing costume, (US) **bathing suit** *n* Badeanzug *m*

bath mat *n* Bademattte *f*, Badevorleger *m*

bathrobe ['bɑːθrəub] *n* Bademantel *m*

bathroom ['bɑːθrum] *n* Bad(ezimmer) *nt*

baths [bɑːðz] *npl* (*also*: **swimming baths**) (Schwimm)bad *nt*

bath towel *n* Badetuch *nt*

bathtub ['bɑːθtʌb] *n* (Bade)wanne *f*

batman ['bætmən] (*irreg: like* **man**) (*Brit*) *n* (*Mil*) (Offiziers)bursche *m*

baton ['bætən] *n* (*Mus*) Taktstock *m*; (*Athletics*) Staffelholz *nt*; (*policeman's*) Schlagstock *m*

battalion [bə'tælɪən] *n* Bataillon *nt*

batten ['bætn] *n* Leiste *f*, Latte *f*; (*Naut: on sail*) Segellatte *f*

▶ **batten down** *vt* (*Naut*): **to ~ down the hatches** die Luken dicht machen

batter ['bætə^r] *vt* schlagen, misshandeln; (*subj: rain*) schlagen; (*wind*) rütteln ▷ *n* (*Culin*) Teig *m*; (*for frying*) (Ausback)teig *m*

battered ['bætəd] *adj* (*hat, pan*) verbeult; **~ wife** misshandelte Ehefrau; **~ child** misshandeltes Kind

battering ram ['bætərɪŋ-] *n* Rammbock *m*

battery ['bætərɪ] *n* Batterie *f*; (*of tests, reporters*) Reihe *f*

battery charger *n* (Batterie)ladegerät *nt*

battery farming *n* Batteriehaltung *f*

battle ['bætl] *n* (*Mil*) Schlacht *f*; (*fig*) Kampf *m* ▷ *vi* kämpfen; **that's half the ~** damit ist schon viel gewonnen; **it's a losing ~, we're fighting a losing ~** (*fig*) es ist ein aussichtsloser Kampf

battledress ['bætldres] *n* Kampfanzug *m*

battlefield ['bætlfiːld] *n* Schlachtfeld *nt*

battlements ['bætlmənts] *npl* Zinnen *pl*

battleship ['bætlʃɪp] *n* Schlachtschiff *nt*

batty ['bætɪ] (*inf*) *adj* verrückt

bauble ['bɔːbl] *n* Flitter *m*

baud [bɔːd] *n* (*Comput*) Baud *nt*

baud rate *n* (*Comput*) Baudrate *f*

baulk [bɔːlk] *vi* = **balk**

bauxite ['bɔːksaɪt] *n* Bauxit *m*

Bavaria [bə'veərɪə] *n* Bayern *nt*

Bavarian [bə'veərɪən] *adj* bay(e)risch ▷ *n* Bayer(in) *m(f)*

bawdy ['bɔːdɪ] *adj* derb, obszön

bawl [bɔːl] *vi* brüllen, schreien

bay [beɪ] *n* Bucht *f*; (*Brit: for parking*) Parkbucht *f*; (: *for loading*) Ladeplatz *m*; (*horse*) Braune(r) *m*; **to hold sb at ~** jdn in Schach halten

bay leaf *n* Lorbeerblatt *nt*

bayonet ['beɪənɪt] *n* Bajonett *nt*

bay tree *n* Lorbeerbaum *m*

bay window *n* Erkerfenster *nt*

bazaar [bə'zɑː^r] *n* Basar *m*

bazooka [bə'zuːkə] *n* Panzerfaust *f*

BB (*Brit*) *n abbr* (= *Boys' Brigade*) Jugendorganisation *für Jungen*

BBB (*US*) *n abbr* (= *Better Business Bureau*) *amerikanische Verbraucherbehörde*

BBC *n abbr* BBC *f*; *siehe Info-Artikel*

⬭ **BBC**

⬭
⬭ BBC (Abkürzung für British Broadcasting
⬭ Corporation) ist die staatliche britische
⬭ Rundfunk- und Fernsehanstalt.
⬭ Die Fernsehsender BBC1 und BBC2
⬭ bieten beide ein umfangsreiches
⬭ Fernsehprogramm, wobei BBC1 mehr
⬭ Sendungen von allgemeinem Interesse
⬭ wie z.B. leichte Unterhaltung, Sport,
⬭ Aktuelles, Kinderprogramme und
⬭ Außenübertragungen zeigt. BBC2
⬭ berücksichtigt Reisesendungen, Drama,
⬭ Musik und internationale Filme. Die 5
⬭ landesweiten Radiosender bieten von
⬭ Popmusik bis Kricket etwas für jeden
⬭ Geschmack; dazu gibt es noch 37 regionale
⬭ Radiosender. Der BBC World Service ist auf
⬭ der ganzen Welt auf Englisch oder in einer
⬭ von 35 anderen Sprachen zu empfangen.
⬭ Finanziert wird die BBC vor allem durch
⬭ Fernsehgebühren und ins Ausland
⬭ verkaufte Sendungen. Obwohl die BBC
⬭ dem Parlament gegenüber verantwortlich
⬭ ist, werden die Sendungen nicht vom Staat
⬭ kontrolliert.

BC *adv abbr* (= *before Christ*) v. Chr. ▷ *abbr* (*Canada*: = *British Columbia*) Britisch-Kolumbien *nt*

BCG *n abbr* (= *bacille Calmette-Guérin*) BCG *m*

BD *n abbr* (= *Bachelor of Divinity*) *akademischer Grad in Theologie*

B/D *abbr* = **bank draft**

BDS *n abbr* (= *Bachelor of Dental Surgery*) *akademischer Grad in Zahnmedizin*

B/E *abbr* = **bill of exchange**

○ KEYWORD

be [biː] (pt **was, were**, pp **been**) aux vb **1** (with present participle: forming continuous tenses): **what are you doing?** was machst du?; **it is raining** es regnet; **have you been to Rome?** waren Sie schon einmal in Rom?

2 (with pp: forming passives) werden; **to be killed** getötet werden; **the box had been opened** die Kiste war geöffnet worden

3 (in tag questions): **he's good-looking, isn't he?** er sieht gut aus, nicht (wahr)?; **she's back again, is she?** sie ist wieder da, oder?

4 (+ to + infinitive): **the house is to be sold** das Haus soll verkauft werden; **he's not to open it** er darf es nicht öffnen

▷ vb + complement **1** sein; **I'm tired/English** ich bin müde/Engländer(in); **I'm hot/cold** mir ist heiß/kalt; **2 and 2 are 4** 2 und 2 ist or macht 4; **she's tall/pretty** sie ist groß/hübsch; **be careful/quiet** sei vorsichtig/ruhig **2** (of health): **how are you?** wie geht es Ihnen? **3** (of age): **how old are you?** wie alt bist du?; **I'm sixteen (years old)** ich bin sechzehn (Jahre alt)

4 (cost) kosten; **how much was the meal?** was hat das Essen gekostet?; **that'll be 5 pounds please** das macht 5 Pfund, bitte

▷ vi **1** (exist, occur etc) sein; **there is/are** es gibt; **is there a God?** gibt es einen Gott?; **be that as it may** wie dem auch sei; **so be it** gut (und schön)

2 (referring to place) sein, liegen; **Edinburgh is in Scotland** Edinburgh liegt or ist in Schottland; **I won't be here tomorrow** morgen bin ich nicht da

3 (referring to movement) sein; **where have you been?** wo warst du?

▷ impers vb **1** (referring to time, distance, weather) sein; **it's 5 o'clock** es ist 5 Uhr; **it's 10 km to the village** es sind 10 km bis zum Dorf; **it's too hot/cold** es ist zu heiß/kalt

2 (emphatic): **it's only me** ich bins nur; **it's only the postman** es ist nur der Briefträger

beach [biːtʃ] n Strand m ▷ vt (boat) auf (den) Strand setzen
beach buggy n Strandbuggy m
beachcomber ['biːtʃkəʊməʳ] n Strandgutsammler m
beachwear ['biːtʃwɛəʳ] n Strandkleidung f
beacon ['biːkən] n Leuchtfeuer nt; (marker) Bake f; (also: **radio beacon**) Funkfeuer nt
bead [biːd] n Perle f; **beads** npl (necklace) Perlenkette f
beady ['biːdɪ] adj: ~ **eyes** Knopfaugen pl
beagle ['biːgl] n Beagle m
beak [biːk] n Schnabel m
beaker ['biːkəʳ] n Becher m
beam [biːm] n (Archit) Balken m; (of light) Strahl m; (Radio) Leitstrahl m ▷ vi (smile) strahlen ▷ vt ausstrahlen, senden; **to ~ at sb** jdn

anstrahlen; **to drive on full** or **main** or **high** ~ mit Fernlicht fahren
beaming ['biːmɪŋ] adj strahlend
bean [biːn] n Bohne f; **runner** ~ Stangenbohne f; **broad** ~ dicke Bohne; **coffee** ~ Kaffeebohne f
beanpole ['biːnpəʊl] n (lit, fig) Bohnenstange f
beanshoots ['biːnʃuːts] npl Sojabohnensprossen pl
beansprouts ['biːnsprauts] npl = **beanshoots**
bear [bɛəʳ] (pt **bore**, pp **borne**) n Bär m; (Stock Exchange) Baissier m ▷ vt tragen; (tolerate, endure) ertragen; (examination) standhalten +dat; (traces, signs) aufweisen, zeigen; (Comm: interest) tragen, bringen; (produce: children) gebären; (: fruit) tragen ▷ vi: **to ~ right/left** (Aut) sich rechts/links halten; **to ~ the responsibility of** die Verantwortung tragen für; **to ~ comparison with** einem Vergleich standhalten mit; **I can't ~ him** ich kann ihn nicht ausstehen; **to bring pressure to ~ on sb** Druck auf jdn ausüben
▶ **bear out** vt (person, suspicions etc) bestätigen
▶ **bear up** vi Haltung bewahren; **he bore up well** er hat sich gut gehalten
▶ **bear with** vt fus Nachsicht haben mit; ~ **with me a minute** bitte gedulden Sie sich einen Moment
bearable ['bɛərəbl] adj erträglich
beard [bɪəd] n Bart m
bearded ['bɪədɪd] adj bärtig
bearer ['bɛərəʳ] n (of letter, news) Überbringer(in) m(f); (of cheque, passport, title etc) Inhaber(in) m(f)
bearing ['bɛərɪŋ] n (posture) Haltung f; (air) Auftreten nt; (connection) Bezug m; (Tech) Lager nt; **bearings** npl (also: **ball bearings**) Kugellager nt; **to take a ~ with a compass** den Kompasskurs feststellen; **to get one's ~s** sich zurechtfinden
beast [biːst] n (animal) Tier nt; (inf: person) Biest nt
beastly ['biːstlɪ] adj scheußlich
beat [biːt] (pt ~, pp ~**en**) n (of heart) Schlag m; (Mus) Takt m; (of policeman) Revier nt ▷ vt schlagen; (record) brechen ▷ vi schlagen; **to ~ time** den Takt schlagen; **to ~ it** (inf) abhauen, verschwinden; **that ~s everything** das ist doch wirklich der Gipfel or die Höhe; **to ~ about the bush** um den heißen Brei herumreden; **off the ~en track** abgelegen
▶ **beat down** vt (door) einschlagen; (price) herunterhandeln; (seller) einen niedrigeren Preis aushandeln mit ▷ vi (rain) herunterprasseln; (sun) herunterbrennen
▶ **beat off** vt (attack, attacker) abwehren
▶ **beat up** vt (person) zusammenschlagen; (mixture, eggs) schlagen
beater ['biːtəʳ] n (for eggs, cream) Schneebesen m
beating ['biːtɪŋ] n Schläge pl, Prügel pl; **to take a ~** (fig) eine Schlappe einstecken
beat-up ['biːtʌp] (inf) adj zerbeult, ramponiert
beautician [bjuːˈtɪʃən] n Kosmetiker(in) m(f)
beautiful ['bjuːtɪful] adj schön

443

beautifully ['bjuːtɪflɪ] *adv* (*play, sing, drive etc*) hervorragend; (*quiet, empty etc*) schön
beautify ['bjuːtɪfaɪ] *vt* verschönern
beauty ['bjuːtɪ] *n* Schönheit *f*; (*fig: attraction*) Schöne *nt*; **the ~ of it is that ...** das Schöne daran ist, dass ...
beauty contest *n* Schönheitswettbewerb *m*
beauty queen *n* Schönheitskönigin *f*
beauty salon *n* Kosmetiksalon *m*
beauty sleep *n* (Schönheits)schlaf *m*
beauty spot (*Brit*) *n* besonders schöner Ort *m*
beaver ['biːvəʳ] *n* Biber *m*
becalmed [bɪ'kaːmd] *adj*: **to be ~** (*sailing ship*) in eine Flaute geraten
became [bɪ'keɪm] *pt of* **become**
because [bɪ'kɔz] *conj* weil; **~ of** wegen *+gen or* (*inf*) *+dat*
beck [bɛk] *n*: **to be at sb's ~ and call** nach jds Pfeife tanzen
beckon ['bɛkən] *vt* (*also:* **beckon to**) winken ▷ *vi* locken
become [bɪ'kʌm] (*irreg: like* **come**) *vi* werden; **it became known that** es wurde bekannt, dass; **what has ~ of him?** was ist aus ihm geworden?
becoming [bɪ'kʌmɪŋ] *adj* (*behaviour*) schicklich; (*clothes*) kleidsam
BECTU ['bɛktu] (*Brit*) *n abbr* (= *Broadcasting, Entertainment, Cinematographic and Theatre Union*) *Gewerkschaft für Beschäftigte in der Unterhaltungsindustrie*
BEd *n abbr* (= *Bachelor of Education*) *akademischer Grad im Erziehungswesen*
bed [bɛd] *n* Bett *nt*; (*of coal*) Flöz *nt*; (*of clay*) Schicht *f*; (*of river*) (Fluss)bett *nt*; (*of sea*) (Meeres)boden *m*, (Meeres)grund *m*; (*of flowers*) Beet *nt*; **to go to ~** ins *or* zu Bett gehen
▸ **bed down** *vi* sein Lager aufschlagen
bed and breakfast *n* (*place*) (Frühstücks) pension *f*; (*terms*) Übernachtung *f* mit Frühstück; *siehe Info-Artikel*

○ **BED AND BREAKFAST**
○
○ *Bed and breakfast* bedeutet „Übernachtung
○ mit Frühstück", wobei sich dies in
○ Großbritannien nicht auf Hotels, sondern
○ auf kleinere Pensionen, Privathäuser
○ und Bauernhöfe bezieht, wo man
○ wesentlich preisgünstiger übernachten
○ kann als in Hotels. Oft wird für Bed and
○ Breakfast, auch *B & B* genannt, durch ein
○ entsprechendes Schild im Garten oder an
○ der Einfahrt geworben.

bedbug ['bɛdbʌg] *n* Wanze *f*
bedclothes ['bɛdkləʊðz] *npl* Bettzeug *nt*
bedding ['bɛdɪŋ] *n* Bettzeug *nt*
bedevil [bɪ'dɛvl] *vt* (*person*) heimsuchen; (*plans*) komplizieren; **to be ~led by misfortune/bad luck** vom Schicksal/Pech verfolgt sein
bedfellow ['bɛdfɛləʊ] *n*: **they are strange ~s** (*fig*) sie sind ein merkwürdiges Gespann

bedlam ['bɛdləm] *n* Chaos *nt*
bedpan ['bɛdpæn] *n* Bettpfanne *f*, Bettschüssel *f*
bedpost ['bɛdpəʊst] *n* Bettpfosten *m*
bedraggled [bɪ'drægld] *adj* (*wet*) triefnass, tropfnass; (*dirty*) verdreckt
bedridden ['bɛdrɪdn] *adj* bettlägerig
bedrock ['bɛdrɔk] *n* (*fig*) Fundament *nt*; (*Geog*) Grundgebirge *nt*, Grundgestein *nt*
bedroom ['bɛdrum] *n* Schlafzimmer *nt*
Beds [bɛdz] (*Brit*) *abbr* (*Post*) = *Bedfordshire*
bed settee *n* Sofabett *nt*
bedside ['bɛdsaɪd] *n*: **at sb's ~** an jds Bett; **~ lamp** Nachttischlampe *f*; **~ book** Bettlektüre *f*
bedsit ['bɛdsɪt], **bedsitter** ['bɛdsɪtəʳ] (*Brit*) *n* möbliertes Zimmer *nt*
bedspread ['bɛdsprɛd] *n* Tagesdecke *f*
bedtime ['bɛdtaɪm] *n* Schlafenszeit *f*; **it's ~** es ist Zeit, ins Bett zu gehen
bee [biː] *n* Biene *f*; **to have a ~ in one's bonnet about cleanliness** einen Sauberkeitsfimmel *or* Sauberkeitstick haben
beech [biːtʃ] *n* Buche *f*
beef [biːf] *n* Rind(fleisch) *nt*; **roast ~** Rinderbraten *m*
▸ **beef up** (*inf*) *vt* aufmotzen; (*essay*) auswalzen
beefburger ['biːfbəːgəʳ] *n* Hamburger *m*
beefeater ['biːfiːtəʳ] *n* Beefeater *m*
beehive ['biːhaɪv] *n* Bienenstock *m*
beekeeping ['biːkiːpɪŋ] *n* Bienenzucht *f*, Imkerei *f*
beeline ['biːlaɪn] *n*: **to make a ~ for** schnurstracks zugehen auf *+acc*
been [biːn] *pp of* **be**
beep [biːp] (*inf*) *n* Tut(tut) *nt* ▷ *vi* tuten ▷ *vt*: **to ~ one's horn** hupen
beer [bɪəʳ] *n* Bier *nt*
beer belly (*inf*) *n* Bierbauch *m*
beer can *n* Bierdose *f*
beet [biːt] *n* Rübe *f*; (*US: also:* **red beet**) Rote Bete *f*
beetle ['biːtl] *n* Käfer *m*
beetroot ['biːtruːt] (*Brit*) *n* Rote Bete *f*
befall [bɪ'fɔːl] (*irreg: like* **fall**) *vi* sich zutragen ▷ *vt* widerfahren *+dat*
befit [bɪ'fɪt] *vt* sich gehören für
before [bɪ'fɔːʳ] *prep* *vor +dat*; (*with movement*) vor *+acc* ▷ *conj* bevor ▷ *adv* (*time*) vorher; (*space*) davor; **~ going** bevor er/sie *etc* geht/ging; **~ she goes** bevor sie geht; **the week ~** die Woche davor; **I've never seen it ~** ich habe es noch nie gesehen
beforehand [bɪ'fɔːhænd] *adv* vorher
befriend [bɪ'frɛnd] *vt* sich annehmen *+gen*
befuddled [bɪ'fʌdld] *adj*: **to be ~** verwirrt sein
beg [bɛg] *vi* betteln ▷ *vt* (*food, money*) betteln um; (*favour, forgiveness etc*) bitten um; **to ~ for** (*food etc*) betteln um; (*forgiveness, mercy etc*) bitten um; **to ~ sb to do sth** jdn bitten, etw zu tun; **I ~ your pardon** (*apologizing*) entschuldigen Sie bitte; (*: not hearing*) (wie) bitte?; **to ~ the question** der Frage ausweichen; *see also* **pardon**

b

began [bɪ'gæn] *pt of* **begin**
beggar ['bɛgəʳ] *n* Bettler(in) *m(f)*
begin [bɪ'gɪn] (*pt* **began**, *pp* **begun**) *vt*, *vi*
beginnen, anfangen; **to ~ doing** *or* **to do sth**
anfangen, etw zu tun; **~ning (from) Monday**
ab Montag; **I can't ~ to thank you** ich kann
Ihnen gar nicht genug danken; **we'll have**
soup to ~ with als Vorspeise hätten wir
gern Suppe; **to ~ with, I'd like to know ...**
zunächst einmal möchte ich wissen, ...
beginner [bɪ'gɪnəʳ] *n* Anfänger(in) *m(f)*
beginning [bɪ'gɪnɪŋ] *n* Anfang *m*; **right from**
the ~ von Anfang an
begrudge [bɪ'grʌdʒ] *vt*: **to ~ sb sth** jdm etw
missgönnen *or* nicht gönnen
beguile [bɪ'gaɪl] *vt* betören
beguiling [bɪ'gaɪlɪŋ] *adj* (*charming*)
verführerisch; (*deluding*) betörend
begun [bɪ'gʌn] *pp of* **begin**
behalf [bɪ'hɑːf] *n*: **on ~ of, in ~ of** (*US: as*
representative of) im Namen von; (*for benefit of*)
zugunsten von; **on my/his ~** in meinem/
seinem Namen; zu meinen/seinen Gunsten
behave [bɪ'heɪv] *vi* (*person*) sich verhalten,
sich benehmen; (*thing*) funktionieren;
(*also*: **behave o.s.**) sich benehmen
behaviour, (*US*) **behavior** [bɪ'heɪvjəʳ] *n*
Verhalten *nt*; (*manner*) Benehmen *nt*
behead [bɪ'hɛd] *vt* enthaupten
beheld [bɪ'hɛld] *pt*, *pp of* **behold**
behind [bɪ'haɪnd] *prep* hinter ▷ *adv* (*at/towards*
the back) hinten ▷ *n* (*buttocks*) Hintern *m*,
Hinterteil *nt*; **~ the scenes** (*fig*) hinter den
Kulissen; **we're ~ them in technology** auf
dem Gebiet der Technologie liegen wir hinter
ihnen zurück; **to be ~** (*schedule*) im Rückstand
or Verzug sein; **to leave/stay ~** zurücklassen/-
bleiben
behold [bɪ'həuld] (*irreg: like* **hold**) *vt* sehen,
erblicken
beige [beɪʒ] *adj* beige
Beijing ['beɪ'dʒɪŋ] *n* Peking *nt*
being ['biːɪŋ] *n* (*creature*) (Lebe)wesen *nt*;
(*existence*) Leben *nt*, (Da)sein *nt*; **to come into**
~ entstehen
Beirut [beɪ'ruːt] *n* Beirut *nt*
Belarus [bɛlə'rus] *n* Weißrussland *nt*
Belarussian *adj* belarussisch, weißrussisch
▷ *n* Weißrusse *m*, Weißrussin *f*; (*Ling*)
Weißrussisch *nt*
belated [bɪ'leɪtɪd] *adj* verspätet
belch [bɛltʃ] *vi* rülpsen ▷ *vt* (*also*: **belch**
out: *smoke etc*) ausstoßen
beleaguered [bɪ'liːgɪd] *adj* (*city*) belagert; (*army*)
eingekesselt; (*fig*) geplagt
Belfast ['bɛlfɑːst] *n* Belfast *nt*
belfry ['bɛlfrɪ] *n* Glockenstube *f*
Belgian ['bɛldʒən] *adj* belgisch ▷ *n* Belgier(in)
m(f)
Belgium ['bɛldʒəm] *n* Belgien *nt*
Belgrade [bɛl'greɪd] *n* Belgrad *nt*
belie [bɪ'laɪ] *vt* (*contradict*) im Widerspruch
stehen zu; (*give false impression of*)

hinwegtäuschen über +*acc*; (*disprove*)
widerlegen, Lügen strafen
belief [bɪ'liːf] *n* Glaube *m*; (*opinion*)
Überzeugung *f*; **it's beyond ~** es ist
unglaublich *or* nicht zu glauben; **in the ~**
that im Glauben, dass
believable [bɪ'liːvəbl] *adj* glaubhaft
believe [bɪ'liːv] *vt* glauben ▷ *vi* (an Gott)
glauben; **he is ~d to be abroad** es heißt, dass
er im Ausland ist; **to ~ in** (*God, ghosts*) glauben
an +*acc*; (*method etc*) Vertrauen haben zu; **I**
don't ~ in corporal punishment ich halte
nicht viel von der Prügelstrafe
believer [bɪ'liːvəʳ] *n* (*in idea, activity*)
Anhänger(in) *m(f)*; (*Rel*) Gläubige(r) *f(m)*; **she's**
a great ~ in healthy eating sie ist sehr für
eine gesunde Ernährung
belittle [bɪ'lɪtl] *vt* herabsetzen
Belize [bɛ'liːz] *n* Belize *nt*
bell [bɛl] *n* Glocke *f*; (*small*) Glöckchen *nt*,
Schelle *f*; (*on door*) Klingel *f*; **that rings a ~** (*fig*)
das kommt mir bekannt vor
bell-bottoms ['bɛlbɔtəmz] *npl* Hose *f* mit
Schlag
bellboy ['bɛlbɔɪ] (*Brit*) *n* Page *m*, Hoteljunge *m*
bellhop ['bɛlhɔp] (*US*) *n* = **bellboy**
belligerence [bɪ'lɪdʒərəns] *n* Angriffslust *f*
belligerent [bɪ'lɪdʒərənt] *adj* angriffslustig
bellow ['bɛləu] *vi*, *vt* brüllen
bellows ['bɛləuz] *npl* Blasebalg *m*
bell push (*Brit*) *n* Klingel *f*
belly ['bɛlɪ] *n* Bauch *m*
bellyache ['bɛlɪeɪk] (*inf*) *n* Bauchschmerzen *pl*
▷ *vi* murren
bellybutton ['bɛlɪbʌtn] *n* Bauchnabel *m*
bellyful ['bɛlɪful] (*inf*) *n*: **I've had a ~ of that**
davon habe ich die Nase voll
belong [bɪ'lɔŋ] *vi*: **to ~ to** (*person*) gehören +*dat*;
(*club etc*) angehören +*dat*; **this book ~s here**
dieses Buch gehört hierher
belongings [bɪ'lɔŋɪŋz] *npl* Sachen *pl*,
Habe *f*; **personal ~** persönlicher Besitz *m*,
persönliches Eigentum *nt*
Belorussia [bɛleu'rʌʃə] *n* Weißrussland *nt*
Belorussian [bɛleu'rʌʃən] *adj*, *n* = **Belarussian**
beloved [bɪ'lʌvɪd] *adj* geliebt ▷ *n* Geliebte(r)
f(m)
below [bɪ'ləu] *prep* (*beneath*) unterhalb +*gen*;
(*less than*) unter +*dat* ▷ *adv* (*beneath*) unten;
see ~ siehe unten; **temperatures ~ normal**
Temperaturen unter dem Durchschnitt
belt [bɛlt] *n* Gürtel *m*; (*Tech*) (Treib)riemen *m*
▷ *vt* schlagen ▷ *vi* (*Brit: inf*): **to ~ along** rasen;
to ~ down/into hinunter-/hineinrasen;
industrial ~ Industriegebiet *nt*
  ▶ **belt out** *vt* (*song*) schmettern
  ▶ **belt up** (*Brit: inf*) *vi* den Mund *or* die Klappe
  halten
beltway ['bɛltweɪ] (*US*) *n* Umgehungsstraße
f, Ringstraße *f*; (*motorway*)
Umgehungsautobahn *f*
bemoan [bɪ'məun] *vt* beklagen
bemused [bɪ'mjuːzd] *adj* verwirrt

bench [bɛntʃ] n Bank f; (workbench) Werkbank f; **the B~** (Law: judges) die Richter pl, der Richterstand

benchmark ['bɛntʃmɑːk] n (fig) Maßstab m

bend [bɛnd] (pt, pp **bent**) vt (leg, arm) beugen; (pipe) biegen ▷ vi (person) sich beugen ▷ n (Brit: in road) Kurve f; (in pipe, river) Biegung f; **bends** npl (Med): **the ~s** die Taucherkrankheit
  ▸ **bend down** vi sich bücken
  ▸ **bend over** vi sich bücken

beneath [bɪ'niːθ] prep unter +dat ▷ adv darunter

benefactor ['bɛnɪfæktə'] n Wohltäter m

benefactress ['bɛnɪfæktrɪs] n Wohltäterin f

beneficial [bɛnɪ'fɪʃl] adj (effect) nützlich; (influence) vorteilhaft; **~ (to)** gut (für)

beneficiary [bɛnɪ'fɪʃərɪ] n (Law) Nutznießer(in) m(f)

benefit ['bɛnɪfɪt] n (advantage) Vorteil m; (money) Beihilfe f; (also: **benefit concert, benefit match**) Benefizveranstaltung f ▷ vt nützen +dat, zugutekommen +dat ▷ vi: **he'll ~ from it** er wird davon profitieren

Benelux ['bɛnɪlʌks] n die Beneluxstaaten pl

benevolent [bɪ'nɛvələnt] adj wohlwollend; (organization) Wohltätigkeits-

BEng n abbr (= Bachelor of Engineering) akademischer Grad für Ingenieure

benign [bɪ'naɪn] adj gütig; (Med) gutartig

bent [bɛnt] pt, pp of **bend** ▷ n Neigung f ▷ adj (wire, pipe) gebogen; (inf: dishonest) korrupt; (: pej: homosexual) andersrum; **to be ~ on** entschlossen sein zu

bequeath [bɪ'kwiːð] vt vermachen

bequest [bɪ'kwɛst] n Vermächtnis nt, Legat nt

bereaved [bɪ'riːvd] adj leidtragend ▷ npl: **the ~** die Hinterbliebenen pl

bereavement [bɪ'riːvmənt] n schmerzlicher Verlust m

bereft [bɪ'rɛft] adj: **~ of** beraubt +gen

beret ['bɛreɪ] n Baskenmütze f

Bering Sea ['beɪrɪŋ-] n: **the ~** das Beringmeer

berk [bəːk] (inf) n Dussel m

Berks [bɑːks] (Brit) abbr (Post) = Berkshire

Berlin [bəː'lɪn] n Berlin nt; **East/West ~** (formerly) Ost-/Westberlin nt

berm [bəːm] (US) n Seitenstreifen m

Bermuda [bəː'mjuːdə] n Bermuda nt, die Bermudinseln pl

Bermuda shorts npl Bermudashorts pl

Bern [bəːn] n Bern nt

berry ['bɛrɪ] n Beere f

berserk [bə'səːk] adj: **to go ~** wild werden

berth [bəːθ] n (bed) Bett nt; (on ship) Koje f; (on train) Schlafwagenbett nt; (for ship) Liegeplatz m ▷ vi anlegen; **to give sb a wide ~** (fig) einen großen Bogen um jdn machen

beseech [bɪ'siːtʃ] (pt, pp **besought**) vt anflehen

beset [bɪ'sɛt] (pt, pp ~) vt (subj: difficulties) bedrängen; (: fears, doubts) befallen; **~ with** (problems, dangers etc) voller +dat

beside [bɪ'saɪd] prep neben +dat; (with movement) neben +acc; **to be ~ o.s.** außer sich sein; **that's ~ the point** das hat damit nichts zu tun

besides [bɪ'saɪdz] adv außerdem ▷ prep außer +dat

besiege [bɪ'siːdʒ] vt belagern; (fig) belagern, bedrängen

besmirch [bɪ'sməːtʃ] vt besudeln

besotted [bɪ'sɔtɪd] (Brit) adj: **~ with** vernarrt in +acc

besought [bɪ'sɔːt] pt, pp of **beseech**

bespectacled [bɪ'spɛktɪkld] adj bebrillt

bespoke [bɪ'spəuk] (Brit) adj (garment) maßgeschneidert; (suit) Maß-; **~ tailor** Maßschneider m

best [bɛst] adj beste(r, s) ▷ adv am besten ▷ n: **at ~** bestenfalls; **the ~ thing to do is …** das Beste ist …; **the ~ part of** der größte Teil +gen; **to make the ~ of sth** das Beste aus etw machen; **to do one's ~** sein Bestes tun; **to the ~ of my knowledge** meines Wissens; **to the ~ of my ability** so gut ich kann; **he's not exactly patient at the ~ of times** er ist schon normalerweise ziemlich ungeduldig

best-before date n Mindesthaltbarkeitsdatum nt

bestial ['bɛstɪəl] adj bestialisch

best man n Trauzeuge m (des Bräutigams)

bestow [bɪ'stəu] vt schenken; **to ~ sth on sb** (honour, praise) jdm etw zuteilwerden lassen; (title) jdm etw verleihen

best seller n Bestseller m

bet [bɛt] (pt, pp ~ or **betted**) n Wette f ▷ vi wetten ▷ vt: **to ~ sb sth** mit jdm um etw wetten; **it's a safe ~** (fig) es ist so gut wie sicher; **to ~ money on sth** Geld auf etw acc setzen

Bethlehem ['bɛθlɪhɛm] n Bethlehem nt

betray [bɪ'treɪ] vt verraten; (trust, confidence) missbrauchen

betrayal [bɪ'treɪəl] n Verrat m

better ['bɛtə'] adj, adv besser ▷ vt verbessern ▷ n: **to get the ~ of sb** jdn unterkriegen; (curiosity) über jdn siegen; **I had ~ go** ich gehe jetzt (wohl) besser; **you had ~ do it** tun Sie es lieber; **he thought ~ of it** er überlegte es sich dat anders; **to get ~** gesund werden; **that's ~!** so ist es besser!; **a change for the ~** eine Wendung zum Guten

better off adj (wealthier) bessergestellt; (more comfortable etc) besser dran; (fig): **you'd be ~ this way** so wäre es besser für Sie

betting ['bɛtɪŋ] n Wetten nt

betting shop (Brit) n Wettbüro nt

between [bɪ'twiːn] prep zwischen +dat; (with movement) zwischen +acc; (amongst) unter +acc or dat ▷ adv dazwischen; **the road ~ here and London** die Straße zwischen hier und London; **we only had £5 ~ us** wir hatten zusammen nur £5

bevel ['bɛvəl] n (also: **bevel edge**) abgeschrägte Kante f

bevelled ['bɛvəld] adj: **a ~ edge** eine Schrägkante, eine abgeschrägte Kante

beverage ['bɛvərɪdʒ] n Getränk nt

bevy ['bɛvɪ] n: **a ~ of** eine Schar +gen

b

bewail [bɪ'weɪl] vt beklagen
beware [bɪ'weə^r] vi: **to ~ (of)** sich in Acht nehmen (vor +dat); **"~ of the dog"** „Vorsicht, bissiger Hund"
bewildered [bɪ'wɪldəd] adj verwirrt
bewildering [bɪ'wɪldrɪŋ] adj verwirrend
bewitching [bɪ'wɪtʃɪŋ] adj bezaubernd, hinreißend
beyond [bɪ'jɔnd] prep (in space) jenseits +gen; (exceeding) über +acc ... hinaus; (after) nach; (above) über +dat ▷ adv (in space) dahinter; (in time) darüber hinaus; **it is ~ doubt** es steht außer Zweifel; **~ repair** nicht mehr zu reparieren; **it is ~ my understanding** es übersteigt mein Begriffsvermögen; **it's ~ me** das geht über meinen Verstand
b/f abbr (Comm: = brought forward) Übertr.
BFPO n abbr (= British Forces Post Office) Postbehörde der britischen Armee
bhp n abbr (Aut: = brake horsepower) Bremsleistung f
bi ... [baɪ] pref Bi-, bi-
biannual [baɪ'ænjuəl] adj zweimal jährlich
bias ['baɪəs] n (prejudice) Vorurteil nt; (preference) Vorliebe f
biased, biassed ['baɪəst] adj voreingenommen; **to be bias(s)ed against** voreingenommen sein gegen
biathlon [baɪ'æθlən] n Biathlon nt
bib [bɪb] n Latz m
Bible ['baɪbl] n Bibel f
biblical ['bɪblɪkl] adj biblisch
bibliography [bɪblɪ'ɔɡrəfɪ] n Bibliografie f
bicarbonate of soda [baɪ'kɑ:bənɪt-] n Natron nt
bicentenary [baɪsɛn'ti:nərɪ] n Zweihundertjahrfeier f
bicentennial [baɪsɛn'tɛnɪəl] (US) n = **bicentenary**
biceps ['baɪsɛps] n Bizeps m
bicker ['bɪkə^r] vi sich zanken
bickering ['bɪkərɪŋ] n Zankerei f
bicycle ['baɪsɪkl] n Fahrrad nt
bicycle path n (Fahr)radweg m
bicycle pump n Luftpumpe f
bicycle track n (Fahr)radweg m
bid [bɪd] (pt **bade** or **~**, pp **bidden** or **~**) n (at auction) Gebot nt; (in tender) Angebot nt; (attempt) Versuch m ▷ vi bieten; (Cards) bieten, reizen ▷ vt bieten; **to ~ sb good day** jdm einen Guten Tag wünschen
bidder ['bɪdə^r] n: **the highest ~** der/die Höchstbietende or Meistbietende
bidding ['bɪdɪŋ] n Steigern nt, Bieten nt; (order, command): **to do sb's ~** tun, was jd einem sagt
bide [baɪd] vt: **to ~ one's time** den rechten Augenblick abwarten
bidet ['bi:deɪ] n Bidet nt
bidirectional ['baɪdɪ'rɛkʃənl] adj (Comput) bidirektional
biennial [baɪ'ɛnɪəl] adj zweijährlich ▷ n zweijährige Pflanze f
bifocals [baɪ'fəuklz] npl Bifokalbrille f

big [bɪɡ] adj groß; **to do things in a ~ way** alles im großen Stil tun
bigamist ['bɪɡəmɪst] n Bigamist(in) m(f)
bigamous ['bɪɡəməs] adj bigamistisch
bigamy ['bɪɡəmɪ] n Bigamie f
big dipper [-'dɪpə^r] n Achterbahn f
big end n (Aut) Pleuelfuß m, Schubstangenkopf m
biggish ['bɪɡɪʃ] adj ziemlich groß
bigheaded ['bɪɡ'hɛdɪd] adj eingebildet
big-hearted ['bɪɡ'hɑ:tɪd] adj großherzig
bigot ['bɪɡət] n Eiferer m; (about religion) bigotter Mensch m
bigoted ['bɪɡətɪd] adj (see n) eifernd; bigott
bigotry ['bɪɡətrɪ] n (see n) eifernde Borniertheit f; Bigotterie f
big toe n große Zehe f
big top n Zirkuszelt nt
big wheel n Riesenrad nt
bigwig ['bɪɡwɪɡ] (inf) n hohes Tier nt
bike [baɪk] n (Fahr)rad nt; (motorcycle) Motorrad nt
bike lane n Fahrradspur f
bikini [bɪ'ki:nɪ] n Bikini m
bilateral [baɪ'lætərəl] adj bilateral
bile [baɪl] n Galle(nflüssigkeit) f; (fig: invective) Beschimpfungen pl
bilingual [baɪ'lɪŋɡwəl] adj zweisprachig
bilious ['bɪlɪəs] adj unwohl; (fig: colour) widerlich; **he felt ~** ihm war schlecht or übel
bill [bɪl] n Rechnung f; (Pol) (Gesetz)entwurf m, (Gesetzes)vorlage f; (US: banknote) Banknote f, (Geld)schein m; (of bird) Schnabel m ▷ vt (item) in Rechnung stellen, berechnen; (customer) eine Rechnung ausstellen +dat; **"post no ~s"** „Plakate ankleben verboten"; **on the ~** (Theat) auf dem Programm; **to fit** or **fill the ~** (fig) der/die/das Richtige sein; **~ of exchange** Wechsel m, Tratte f; **~ of fare** Speisekarte f; **~ of lading** Seefrachtbrief m, Konnossement nt; **~ of sale** Verkaufsurkunde f
billboard ['bɪlbɔ:d] n Reklametafel f
billet ['bɪlɪt] (Mil) n Quartier nt ▷ vt einquartieren
billfold ['bɪlfəuld] (US) n Brieftasche f
billiards ['bɪljədz] n Billard nt
billion ['bɪljən] n (Brit) Billion f; (US) Milliarde f
billionaire [bɪljə'nɛə^r] n Milliardär(in) m(f)
billow ['bɪləu] n (of smoke) Schwaden m ▷ vi (smoke) in Schwaden aufsteigen; (sail) sich blähen
billy goat ['bɪlɪ-] n Ziegenbock m
bimbo ['bɪmbəu] (inf: pej) n (woman) Puppe f, Häschen nt
bin [bɪn] n (Brit) Mülleimer m; (container) Behälter m
binary ['baɪnərɪ] adj binär
bind [baɪnd] (pt, pp **bound**) vt binden; (tie together: hands and feet) fesseln; (constrain, oblige) verpflichten ▷ n (inf: nuisance) Last f
▶ **bind over** vt rechtlich verpflichten
▶ **bind up** vt (wound) verbinden; **to be bound up in** sehr beschäftigt sein mit; **to be bound**

up with verbunden or verknüpft sein mit

binder ['baɪndə^r] n (file) Hefter m; (for magazines) Mappe f

binding ['baɪndɪŋ] adj bindend, verbindlich ▷ n (of book) Einband m

binge [bɪndʒ] (inf) n: **to go on a ~** auf eine Sauftour gehen

bingo ['bɪŋɡəʊ] n Bingo nt

bin liner n Müllbeutel m

binoculars [bɪ'nɔkjʊləz] npl Fernglas nt

biochemistry [baɪə'kemɪstrɪ] n Biochemie f

biodegradable ['baɪəʊdɪ'ɡreɪdəbl] adj biologisch abbaubar

biodiversity ['baɪəʊdaɪ'vɜːsɪtɪ] n biologische Vielfalt f

biofuel n Biotreibstoff m

biographer [baɪ'ɔɡrəfə^r] n Biograf(in) m(f)

biographic [baɪə'ɡræfɪk], **biographical** [baɪə'ɡræfɪkl] adj biografisch

biography [baɪ'ɔɡrəfɪ] n Biografie f

biological [baɪə'lɔdʒɪkl] adj biologisch

biological clock n biologische Uhr f

biological waste n Bioabfall m

biologist [baɪ'ɔlədʒɪst] n Biologe m, Biologin f

biology [baɪ'ɔlədʒɪ] n Biologie f

biophysics ['baɪəʊ'fɪzɪks] n Biophysik f

biopic ['baɪəʊpɪk] n Filmbiografie f

biopsy ['baɪɔpsɪ] n Biopsie f

biosphere ['baɪəsfɪə^r] n Biosphäre f

biotechnology ['baɪəʊtek'nɔlədʒɪ] n Biotechnik f

biped ['baɪped] n Zweifüßer m

birch [bɜːtʃ] n Birke f

bird [bɜːd] n Vogel m; (Brit: inf: girl) Biene f

bird of prey n Raubvogel m

bird's-eye view ['bɜːdzaɪ-] n Vogelperspektive f; (overview) Überblick m

bird-watcher ['bɜːdwɔtʃə^r] n Vogelbeobachter(in) m(f)

Biro® ['baɪərəʊ] n Kugelschreiber m, Kuli m (inf)

birth [bɜːθ] n Geburt f; **to give ~ to** (subj: woman) gebären, entbunden werden von; (: animal) werfen

birth certificate n Geburtsurkunde f

birth control n Geburtenkontrolle f, Geburtenregelung f

birthday ['bɜːθdeɪ] n Geburtstag m ▷ cpd Geburtstags-; see also **happy**

birthmark ['bɜːθmɑːk] n Muttermal nt

birthplace ['bɜːθpleɪs] n Geburtsort m; (house) Geburtshaus nt; (fig) Entstehungsort m

birth rate ['bɜːθreɪt] n Geburtenrate f, Geburtenziffer f

Biscay ['bɪskeɪ] n: **the Bay of ~** der Golf von Biskaya

biscuit ['bɪskɪt] n (Brit) Keks m or nt; (US) Brötchen nt

bisect [baɪ'sɛkt] vt halbieren

bisexual ['baɪ'sɛksjʊəl] adj bisexuell ▷ n Bisexuelle(r) f(m)

bishop ['bɪʃəp] n (Rel) Bischof m; (Chess) Läufer m

bistro ['biːstrəʊ] n Bistro nt

bit [bɪt] pt of **bite** ▷ n (piece) Stück nt; (of drill) (Bohr)einsatz m, Bohrer m; (of plane) (Hobel) messer nt; (Comput) Bit nt; (of horse) Gebiss nt; (US): **two/four/six ~s** 25/50/75 Cent(s); **a ~ of** ein bisschen; **a ~ mad** ein bisschen verrückt; **a ~ dangerous** etwas gefährlich; **~ by bit** nach und nach; **to come to ~s** kaputtgehen; **bring all your ~s and pieces** bringen Sie Ihre (Sieben)sachen mit; **to do one's ~** sein(en) Teil tun or beitragen

bitch [bɪtʃ] n (dog) Hündin f; (inf!: woman) Miststück nt

bite [baɪt] (pt **bit**, pp **bitten**) vt, vi beißen; (subj: insect etc) stechen ▷ n (insect bite) Stich m; (mouthful) Bissen m; **to ~ one's nails** an seinen Nägeln kauen; **let's have a ~ (to eat)** (inf) lasst uns eine Kleinigkeit essen

biting ['baɪtɪŋ] adj (wind) schneidend; (wit) scharf

bit part n kleine Nebenrolle f

bitten ['bɪtn] pp of **bite**

bitter ['bɪtə^r] adj bitter; (person) verbittert; (wind, weather) bitterkalt, eisig; (criticism) scharf ▷ n (Brit: beer) halbdunkles obergäriges Bier; **to the ~ end** bis zum bitteren Ende

bitterly ['bɪtəlɪ] adv (complain, weep) bitterlich; (oppose) erbittert; (criticize) scharf; (disappointed) bitter; (jealous) sehr; **it's ~ cold** es ist bitterkalt

bitterness ['bɪtənɪs] n Bitterkeit f

bittersweet ['bɪtəswiːt] adj bittersüß

bitty ['bɪtɪ] (Brit: inf) adj zusammengestoppelt, zusammengestückelt

bitumen ['bɪtjʊmɪn] n Bitumen nt

bivouac ['bɪvʊæk] n Biwak nt

bizarre [bɪ'zɑː^r] adj bizarr

bk abbr = **bank; book**

BL n abbr (= Bachelor of Law) akademischer Grad für Juristen; (= Bachelor of Letters) akademischer Grad für Literaturwissenschaftler; (US: = Bachelor of Literature) akademischer Grad für Literaturwissenschaftler

B/L abbr = **bill of lading**

blab [blæb] (inf) vi quatschen

black [blæk] adj schwarz ▷ vt (Brit: Industry) boykottieren ▷ n Schwarz nt; (person): **B~** Schwarze(r) f(m); **to give sb a ~ eye** jdm ein blaues Auge schlagen; **~ and blue** grün und blau; **there it is in ~ and white** (fig) da steht es schwarz auf weiß; **to be in the ~** in den schwarzen Zahlen sein

▶ **black out** vi (faint) ohnmächtig werden

black belt n (US) Gebiet in den Südstaaten der USA, das vorwiegend von Schwarzen bewohnt wird; (Judo) schwarzer Gürtel m

blackberry ['blækbərɪ] n Brombeere f

blackbird ['blækbɜːd] n Amsel f

blackboard ['blækbɔːd] n Tafel f

black box n (Aviat) Flugschreiber m

black coffee n schwarzer Kaffee m

Black Country (Brit) n: **the ~** Industriegebiet in den englischen Midlands

blackcurrant ['blæk'kʌrənt] n Johannisbeere f

black economy n: **the ~** die

Schattenwirtschaft

blacken ['blækn] vt: **to ~ sb's name/ reputation** (fig) jdn verunglimpfen

Black Forest n: **the ~** der Schwarzwald

blackhead ['blækhɛd] n Mitesser m

black hole n schwarzes Loch nt

black ice n Glatteis nt

blackjack ['blækdʒæk] n (Cards) Siebzehnundvier nt; (US: truncheon) Schlagstock m

blackleg ['blæklɛg] (Brit) n Streikbrecher(in) m(f)

blacklist ['blæklɪst] n schwarze Liste f ▷ vt auf die schwarze Liste setzen

blackmail ['blækmeɪl] n Erpressung f ▷ vt erpressen

blackmailer ['blækmeɪlər] n Erpresser(in) m(f)

black market n Schwarzmarkt m

blackout ['blækaut] n (in wartime) Verdunkelung f; (power cut) Stromausfall m; (TV, Radio) Ausfall m; (faint) Ohnmachtsanfall m

black pepper n schwarzer Pfeffer m

Black Sea n: **the ~** das Schwarze Meer

black sheep n (fig) schwarzes Schaf nt

blacksmith ['blæksmɪθ] n Schmied m

black spot n (Aut) Gefahrenstelle f; (for unemployment etc) Gebiet, in dem ein Problem besonders ausgeprägt ist

bladder ['blædər] n Blase f

blade [bleɪd] n (of knife etc) Klinge f; (of oar, propeller) Blatt nt; **a ~ of grass** ein Grashalm m

Blairite [blɛəraɪt] (Pol) adj blairistisch ▷ n Blair-Anhänger(in) m(f)

blame [bleɪm] n Schuld f ▷ vt: **to ~ sb for sth** jdm die Schuld an etw dat geben; **to be to ~** Schuld daran haben, schuld sein; **who's to ~?** wer hat Schuld or ist schuld?; **I'm not to ~** es ist nicht meine Schuld

blameless ['bleɪmlɪs] adj schuldlos

blanch [blɑːntʃ] vi blass werden ▷ vt (Culin) blanchieren

blancmange [blə'mɒnʒ] n Pudding m

bland [blænd] adj (taste, food) fade

blank [blæŋk] adj (paper) leer, unbeschrieben; (look) ausdruckslos ▷ n (on form) Lücke f; (cartridge) Platzpatrone f; **my mind was a ~** ich hatte ein Brett vor dem Kopf; **we drew a ~** (fig) wir hatten kein Glück

blank cheque n Blankoscheck m; **to give sb a ~ to do sth** (fig) jdm freie Hand geben, etw zu tun

blanket ['blæŋkɪt] n Decke f ▷ adj (statement) pauschal; (agreement) Pauschal-

blanket cover n umfassende Versicherung f

blare [blɛər] vi (brass band) schmettern; (horn) tuten; (radio) plärren

▶ **blare out** vi (radio, stereo) plärren

blasé ['blɑːzeɪ] adj blasiert

blaspheme [blæs'fiːm] vi Gott lästern

blasphemous ['blæsfɪməs] adj lästerlich, blasphemisch

blasphemy ['blæsfɪmɪ] n (Gottes)lästerung f,

Blasphemie f

blast [blɑːst] n (of wind) Windstoß m; (of whistle) Trillern nt; (shock wave) Druckwelle f; (of air, steam) Schwall m; (of explosive) Explosion f ▷ vt (blow up) sprengen ▷ excl (Brit: inf) verdammt!, so ein Mist!; **at full ~** (play music) mit voller Lautstärke; (move, work) auf Hochtouren

▶ **blast off** vi (Space) abheben, starten

blast furnace n Hochofen m

blastoff ['blɑːstɒf] n (Space) Abschuss m

blatant ['bleɪtənt] adj offensichtlich

blatantly ['bleɪtəntlɪ] adv (lie) unverfroren; **it's ~ obvious** es ist überdeutlich

blaze [bleɪz] n (fire) Feuer nt, Brand m; (fig: of colour) Farbenpracht f; (: of glory) Glanz m ▷ vi (fire) lodern; (guns) feuern; (fig: eyes) glühen ▷ vt: **to ~ a trail** (fig) den Weg bahnen; **in a ~ of publicity** mit viel Publicity

blazer ['bleɪzər] n Blazer m

bleach [bliːtʃ] n (also: **household bleach**) ≈ Reinigungsmittel nt ▷ vt bleichen

bleached [bliːtʃt] adj gebleicht

bleachers ['bliːtʃəz] (US) npl unüberdachte Zuschauertribüne f

bleak [bliːk] adj (countryside) öde; (weather, situation) trostlos; (prospect) trüb; (expression, voice) deprimiert

bleary-eyed ['blɪərɪ'aɪd] adj triefäugig

bleat [bliːt] vi (goat) meckern; (sheep) blöken ▷ n Meckern nt; Blöken nt

bled [blɛd] pt, pp of **bleed**

bleed [bliːd] (pt, pp **bled**) vi bluten; (colour) auslaufen ▷ vt (brakes, radiator) entlüften; **my nose is ~ing** ich habe Nasenbluten

bleep [bliːp] n Piepton m ▷ vi piepen ▷ vt (doctor etc) rufen, anpiepen (inf)

bleeper ['bliːpər] n Piepser m (inf), Funkrufempfänger m

blemish ['blɛmɪʃ] n Makel m

blend [blɛnd] n Mischung f ▷ vt (Culin) mischen, mixen; (colours, styles, flavours etc) vermischen ▷ vi (colours etc: also: **blend in**) harmonieren

blender ['blɛndər] n (Culin) Mixer m

bless [blɛs] (pt, pp **~ed** or **blest**) vt segnen; **to be ~ed with** gesegnet sein mit; **~ you!** (after sneeze) Gesundheit!

blessed ['blɛsɪd] adj heilig; (happy) selig; **it rains every ~ day** (inf) es regnet aber auch jeden Tag

blessing ['blɛsɪŋ] n (approval) Zustimmung f; (Rel: fig) Segen m; **to count one's ~s** von Glück sagen können; **it was a ~ in disguise** es war schließlich doch ein Segen

blew [bluː] pt of **blow**

blight [blaɪt] vt zerstören; (hopes) vereiteln; (life) verderben ▷ n (of plants) Brand m

blimey ['blaɪmɪ] (Brit: inf) excl Mensch!

blind [blaɪnd] adj blind ▷ n (for window) Rollo nt, Rouleau nt; (also: **Venetian blind**) Jalousie f ▷ vt blind machen; (dazzle) blenden; (deceive: with facts etc) verblenden; **the blind** npl (blind people) die Blinden pl; **to turn a ~ eye (on** or **to)** ein

Auge zudrücken (bei); **to be ~ to sth** (*fig*) blind für etw sein

blind alley *n* (*fig*) Sackgasse *f*

blind corner (*Brit*) *n* unübersichtliche Ecke *f*

blind date *n* Rendezvous *nt* mit einem/einer Unbekannten

blindfold ['blaɪndfəʊld] *n* Augenbinde *f* ▷ *adj, adv* mit verbundenen Augen ▷ *vt* die Augen verbinden +*dat*

blinding ['blaɪndɪŋ] *adj* (*dazzling*) blendend; (*remarkable*) bemerkenswert

blindly ['blaɪndlɪ] *adv* (*without seeing*) wie blind; (*without thinking*) blindlings

blindness ['blaɪndnɪs] *n* Blindheit *f*

blind spot *n* (*Aut*) toter Winkel *m*; (*fig: weak spot*) schwacher Punkt *m*

blink [blɪŋk] *vi* blinzeln; (*light*) blinken ▷ *n*: **the TV's on the ~** (*inf*) der Fernseher ist kaputt

blinkers ['blɪŋkəz] *npl* Scheuklappen *pl*

blinking ['blɪŋkɪŋ] (*Brit: inf*) *adj*: **this ~ ...** diese(r, s) verflixte ...

blip [blɪp] *n* (*on radar screen*) leuchtender Punkt *m*; (*in a straight line*) Ausschlag *m*; (*fig*) (zeitweilige) Abweichung *f*

bliss [blɪs] *n* Glück *nt*, Seligkeit *f*

blissful ['blɪsfʊl] *adj* (*event, day*) herrlich; (*smile*) selig; **a ~ sigh** ein wohliger Seufzer *m*; **in ~ ignorance** in herrlicher Ahnungslosigkeit

blissfully ['blɪsfəlɪ] *adv* selig; **~ happy** überglücklich; **~ unaware of ...** ohne auch nur zu ahnen, dass ...

blister ['blɪstə*r*] *n* Blase *f* ▷ *vi* (*paint*) Blasen werfen

BLit, BLitt *n abbr* (= *Bachelor of Literature; Bachelor of Letters*) akademischer Grad für Literaturwissenschaftler

blithely ['blaɪðlɪ] *adv* (*unconcernedly*) unbekümmert, munter; (*joyfully*) fröhlich

blithering ['blɪðərɪŋ] (*inf*) *adj*: **this ~ idiot** dieser Trottel

blitz [blɪts] *n* (*Mil*) Luftangriff *m*; **to have a ~ on sth** (*fig*) einen Großangriff auf etw *acc* starten

blizzard ['blɪzəd] *n* Schneesturm *m*

bloated ['bləʊtɪd] *adj* aufgedunsen; (*full*) (über)satt

blob [blɔb] *n* Tropfen *m*; (*sth indistinct*) verschwommener Fleck *m*

bloc [blɔk] *n* (*Pol*) Block *m*

block [blɔk] *n* Block *m*; (*toy*) Bauklotz *m*; (*in pipes*) Verstopfung *f* ▷ *vt* blockieren; (*progress*) aufhalten; (*Comput*) blocken; **~ of flats** (*Brit*) Wohnblock *m*; **3 ~s from here** 3 Blocks or Straßen weiter; **mental ~** geistige Sperre *f*, Mattscheibe *f* (*inf*); **~ and tackle** Flaschenzug *m* ▶ **block up** *vt, vi* verstopfen

blockade [blɔ'keɪd] *n* Blockade *f* ▷ *vt* blockieren

blockage ['blɔkɪdʒ] *n* Verstopfung *f*

block booking *n* Gruppenbuchung *f*

blockbuster ['blɔkbʌstə*r*] *n* Knüller *m*

block capitals *npl* Blockschrift *f*

blockhead ['blɔkhɛd] (*inf*) *n* Dummkopf *m*

block letters *npl* Blockschrift *f*

block release (*Brit*) *n* blockweise Freistellung von Auszubildenden zur Weiterbildung

block vote (*Brit*) *n* Stimmenblock *m*

blog [blɔg] *n* (*Comput*) Blog *m*, Weblog *m* ▷ *vi* bloggen

blogging ['blɔgɪn] *n* (*Comput*) Blogging *nt*

bloke [bləʊk] (*Brit: inf*) *n* Typ *m*

blond, blonde [blɔnd] *adj* blond ▷ *n*: **~(e)** (*woman*) Blondine *f*

blood [blʌd] *n* Blut *nt*; **new ~** (*fig*) frisches Blut *nt*

blood bank *n* Blutbank *f*

blood bath *n* Blutbad *nt*

blood count *n* Blutbild *nt*

bloodcurdling ['blʌdkə:dlɪŋ] *adj* grauenerregend

blood donor *n* Blutspender(in) *m(f)*

blood group *n* Blutgruppe *f*

bloodhound ['blʌdhaund] *n* Bluthund *m*

bloodless ['blʌdlɪs] *adj* (*victory*) unblutig; (*pale*) blutleer

blood-letting ['blʌdlɛtɪŋ] *n* (*also fig*) Aderlass *m*

blood poisoning *n* Blutvergiftung *f*

blood pressure *n* Blutdruck *m*; **to have high/low ~** hohen/niedrigen Blutdruck haben

bloodshed ['blʌdʃɛd] *n* Blutvergießen *nt*

bloodshot ['blʌdʃɔt] *adj* (*eyes*) blutunterlaufen

blood sport *n* Jagdsport *m* (*und andere Sportarten, bei denen Tiere getötet werden*)

bloodstained ['blʌdsteɪnd] *adj* blutbefleckt

bloodstream ['blʌdstri:m] *n* Blut *nt*, Blutkreislauf *m*

blood test *n* Blutprobe *f*

bloodthirsty ['blʌdθə:stɪ] *adj* blutrünstig

blood transfusion *n* Blutübertragung *f*, (*Blut*)transfusion *f*

blood type *n* Blutgruppe *f*

blood vessel *n* Blutgefäß *nt*

bloody ['blʌdɪ] *adj* blutig; (*Brit: inf!*): **this ~ ...** diese(r, s) verdammte ...; **~ strong** (*inf!*) verdammt stark; **~ good** (*inf!*) echt gut

bloody-minded ['blʌdɪ'maɪndɪd] (*Brit: inf*) *adj* stur

bloom [blu:m] *n* Blüte *f* ▷ *vi* blühen; **to be in ~** in Blüte stehen

blooming ['blu:mɪŋ] (*Brit: inf*) *adj*: **this ~ ...** diese(r, s) verflixte ...

blossom ['blɔsəm] *n* Blüte *f* ▷ *vi* blühen; (*fig*): **to ~ into** erblühen or aufblühen zu

blot [blɔt] *n* Klecks *m*; (*fig: on name etc*) Makel *m* ▷ *vt* (*liquid*) aufsaugen; (*make blot on*) beklecksen; **to be a ~ on the landscape** ein Schandfleck in der Landschaft sein; **to ~ one's copy book** (*fig*) sich unmöglich machen ▶ **blot out** *vt* (*view*) verdecken; (*memory*) auslöschen

blotchy ['blɔtʃɪ] *adj* fleckig

blotter ['blɔtə*r*] *n* (Tinten)löscher *m*

blotting paper ['blɔtɪŋ-] *n* Löschpapier *nt*

blotto ['blɔtəʊ] (*inf*) *adj* (*drunk*) sternhagelvoll

blouse [blauz] *n* Bluse *f*

blow [bləʊ] (*pt* **blew**, *pp* **~n**) *n* (*also fig*) Schlag *m* ▷ *vi* (*wind*) wehen; (*person*) blasen ▷ *vt* (*subj*: *wind*) wehen; (*instrument, whistle*) blasen; (*fuse*) durchbrennen lassen; **to come to ~s** handgreiflich werden; **to ~ off course** (*ship*) vom Kurs abgetrieben werden; **to ~ one's nose** sich *dat* die Nase putzen; **to ~ a whistle** pfeifen

▶ **blow away** *vt* wegblasen ▷ *vi* wegfliegen
▶ **blow down** *vt* umwehen
▶ **blow off** *vt* wegwehen ▷ *vi* wegfliegen
▶ **blow out** *vi* ausgehen
▶ **blow over** *vi* sich legen
▶ **blow up** *vi* ausbrechen ▷ *vt* (*bridge*) in die Luft jagen; (*tyre*) aufblasen; (*Phot*) vergrößern

blow-dry ['bləʊdraɪ] *vt* föhnen ▷ *n*: **to have a ~** sich föhnen lassen

blowlamp ['bləʊlæmp] (*Brit*) *n* Lötlampe *f*

blown [bləʊn] *pp of* **blow**

blowout ['bləʊaʊt] *n* Reifenpanne *f*; (*inf*: *big meal*) Schlemmerei *f*; (*of oil-well*) Ölausbruch *m*

blowtorch ['bləʊtɔːtʃ] *n* = **blowlamp**

blow-up ['bləʊʌp] *n* Vergrößerung *f*

blowzy ['blaʊzɪ] (*Brit*) *adj* schlampig

BLS (*US*) *n abbr* (= *Bureau of Labor Statistics*) Amt für Arbeitsstatistik

blubber ['blʌbər] *n* Walfischspeck *m* ▷ *vi* (*pej*) heulen

bludgeon ['blʌdʒən] *vt* niederknüppeln; (*fig*): **to ~ sb into doing sth** jdm so lange zusetzen, bis er etw tut

blue [bluː] *adj* blau; (*depressed*) deprimiert, niedergeschlagen ▷ *n*: **out of the ~** (*fig*) aus heiterem Himmel; **blues** *n* (*Mus*): **the ~s** der Blues; **~ film** Pornofilm *m*; **~ joke** schlüpfriger Witz *m*; **(only) once in a ~ moon** (nur) alle Jubeljahre einmal; **to have the ~s** deprimiert *or* niedergeschlagen sein

blue baby *n* Baby *nt* mit angeborenem Herzfehler

bluebell ['bluːbɛl] *n* Glockenblume *f*

bluebottle ['bluːbɒtl] *n* Schmeißfliege *f*

blue cheese *n* Blauschimmelkäse *m*

blue-chip ['bluːtʃɪp] *adj*: **~ investment** sichere Geldanlage *f*

blue-collar worker ['bluːkɒlər-] *n* Arbeiter(in) *m(f)*

blue jeans *npl* (Blue)jeans *pl*

blueprint ['bluːprɪnt] *n* (*fig*): **a ~ (for)** ein Plan *m or* Entwurf *m* (für)

bluff [blʌf] *vi* bluffen ▷ *n* Bluff *m*; (*cliff*) Klippe *f*; (*promontory*) Felsvorsprung *m*; **to call sb's ~** es darauf ankommen lassen

blunder ['blʌndər] *n* (dummer) Fehler *m* ▷ *vi* einen (dummen) Fehler machen; **to ~ into sb** mit jdm zusammenstoßen; **to ~ into sth** in etw *acc* (hinein)tappen

blunt [blʌnt] *adj* stumpf; (*person*) direkt; (*talk*) unverblümt ▷ *vt* stumpf machen; **~ instrument** (*Law*) stumpfer Gegenstand *m*

bluntly ['blʌntlɪ] *adv* (*speak*) unverblümt

bluntness ['blʌntnɪs] *n* (*of person*) Direktheit *f*

blur [bləːr] *n* (*shape*) verschwommener Fleck *m*; (*scene etc*) verschwommenes Bild *nt*; (*memory*) verschwommene Erinnerung *f* ▷ *vt* (*vision*) trüben; (*distinction*) verwischen

blurb [bləːb] *n* Informationsmaterial *nt*

blurred [bləːd] *adj* (*photograph, TV picture etc*) verschwommen; (*distinction*) verwischt

blurt out [bləːt-] *vt* herausplatzen mit

blush [blʌʃ] *vi* erröten ▷ *n* Röte *f*

blusher ['blʌʃər] *n* Rouge *nt*

bluster ['blʌstər] *n* Toben *nt*, Geschrei *nt* ▷ *vi* toben

blustering ['blʌstərɪŋ] *adj* polternd

blustery ['blʌstərɪ] *adj* stürmisch

Blvd *abbr* = **boulevard**

BM *n abbr* (= *British Museum*) Britisches Museum *nt*; (= *Bachelor of Medicine*) akademischer Grad für Mediziner

BMA *n abbr* (= *British Medical Association*) Dachverband der Ärzte

BMJ *n abbr* (= *British Medical Journal*) vom BMA herausgegebene Zeitschrift

BMus *n abbr* (= *Bachelor of Music*) akademischer Grad für Musikwissenschaftler

BMX *n abbr* (= *bicycle motocross*): **~ bike** BMX-Rad *nt*

bn *abbr* = **billion**

BO *n abbr* (*inf*: = *body odour*) Körpergeruch *m*; = **box office**

boar [bɔːr] *n* (*male pig*) Eber *m*; (*wild pig*) Keiler *m*

board [bɔːd] *n* Brett *nt*; (*cardboard*) Pappe *f*; (*committee*) Ausschuss *m*; (*in firm*) Vorstand *m* ▷ *vt* (*ship*) an Bord +*gen* gehen; (*train*) einsteigen in +*acc*; **on ~** (Naut, Aviat) an Bord; **full/half ~** (*Brit*) Voll-/Halbpension *f*; **~ and lodging** Unterkunft und Verpflegung *f*; **to go by the ~** (*fig*) unter den Tisch fallen; **above ~** (*fig*) korrekt; **across the ~** (*fig*) allgemein; (: *criticize, reject*) pauschal

▶ **board up** *vt* mit Brettern vernageln

boarder ['bɔːdər] *n* Internatsschüler(in) *m(f)*

board game *n* Brettspiel *nt*

boarding card ['bɔːdɪŋ-] *n* (Aviat, Naut) = **boarding pass**

boarding house ['bɔːdɪŋ-] *n* Pension *f*

boarding party ['bɔːdɪŋ-] *n* (Naut) Enterkommando *nt*

boarding pass ['bɔːdɪŋ-] *n* Bordkarte *f*

boarding school ['bɔːdɪŋ-] *n* Internat *nt*

board meeting *n* Vorstandssitzung *f*

boardroom ['bɔːdruːm] *n* Sitzungssaal *m*

boardwalk ['bɔːdwɔːk] (*US*) *n* Holzsteg *m*

boast [bəʊst] *vi* prahlen ▷ *vt* (*fig*: *possess*) sich rühmen +*gen*, besitzen; **to ~ about** *or* **of** prahlen mit

boastful ['bəʊstfʊl] *adj* prahlerisch

boastfulness ['bəʊstfʊlnɪs] *n* Prahlerei *f*

boat [bəʊt] *n* Boot *nt*; (*ship*) Schiff *nt*; **to go by ~** mit dem Schiff fahren; **to be in the same ~** (*fig*) in einem Boot *or* im gleichen Boot sitzen

boater ['bəʊtər] *n* steifer Strohhut *m*, Kreissäge *f* (*inf*)

boating ['bəʊtɪŋ] *n* Bootfahren *nt*

boat people *npl* Bootsflüchtlinge *pl*

boatswain ['bəʊsn] *n* Bootsmann *m*

bob [bɒb] *vi* (*also*: **bob up and down**) sich auf

und ab bewegen ▷ n (Brit: inf) = **shilling**
▶ **bob up** vi auftauchen
bobbin ['bɔbɪn] n Spule f
bobby ['bɔbɪ] (Brit: inf) n Bobby m, Polizist m
bobsleigh ['bɔbsleɪ] n Bob m
bode [bəud] vi: **to ~ well/ill (for)** ein gutes/
schlechtes Zeichen sein (für)
bodice ['bɔdɪs] n (of dress) Oberteil nt
bodily ['bɔdɪlɪ] adj körperlich; (needs) leiblich
▷ adv (lift, carry) mit aller Kraft
body ['bɔdɪ] n Körper m; (corpse) Leiche f; (main
part) Hauptteil m; (of car) Karosserie f; (of
plane) Rumpf m; (group) Gruppe f; (organization)
Organ nt; **ruling ~** amtierendes Organ; **in a ~**
geschlossen
body blow n (fig: setback) schwerer Schlag m
body building n Bodybuilding nt
body double n (Film, TV) Double für Szenen, in
denen Körperpartien in Nahaufnahme gezeigt werden
bodyguard ['bɔdɪgɑːd] n (group) Leibwache f;
(one person) Leibwächter m
body language n Körpersprache f
body repairs npl Karosseriearbeiten pl
body search n Leibesvisitation f
body stocking n Body(stocking) m
bodywork ['bɔdɪwəːk] n Karosserie f
boffin ['bɔfɪn] (Brit) n Fachidiot m
bog [bɔg] n Sumpf m ▷ vt: **to get ~ged down**
(fig) sich verzetteln
bogey ['bəugɪ] n Schreckgespenst nt;
(also: **bogeyman**) Butzemann m, schwarzer
Mann m
boggle ['bɔgl] vi: **the mind ~s** das ist nicht or
kaum auszumalen
bogie ['bəugɪ] n Drehgestell nt; (trolley)
Draisine f
Bogotá [bəugə'taː] n Bogotá nt
bogus ['bəugəs] adj (workman etc) falsch; (claim)
erfunden
Bohemia [bəu'hiːmɪə] n Böhmen nt
Bohemian [bəu'hiːmɪən] adj böhmisch
▷ n Böhme m, Böhmin f; (also: **bohemian**)
Bohemien m
boil [bɔɪl] vt, vi kochen ▷ n (Med) Furunkel nt
or m; **to come to the ~** (Brit), **to come to a ~**
(US) zu kochen anfangen
▶ **boil down to** vt fus (fig) hinauslaufen auf +acc
▶ **boil over** vi überkochen
boiled egg [bɔɪld-] n gekochtes Ei nt
boiled potatoes npl Salzkartoffeln pl
boiler ['bɔɪləʳ] n Boiler m
boiler suit (Brit) n Overall m
boiling ['bɔɪlɪŋ] adj: **I'm ~ (hot)** (inf) mir ist
fürchterlich heiß; **it's ~** es ist eine Affenhitze
(inf)
boiling point n Siedepunkt m
boil-in-the-bag [bɔɪlɪnðə'bæg] adj (meals)
Kochbeutel-
boisterous ['bɔɪstərəs] adj ausgelassen
bold [bəuld] adj (brave) mutig; (pej: cheeky)
dreist; (pattern, colours) kräftig
boldly ['bəuldlɪ] adv (see adj) mutig; dreist;
kräftig

boldness ['bəuldnɪs] n Mut m; (cheekiness)
Dreistigkeit f
bold type n Fettdruck m
Bolivia [bə'lɪvɪə] n Bolivien nt
Bolivian [bə'lɪvɪən] adj bolivisch, bolivianisch
▷ n Bolivier(in) m(f), Bolivianer(in) m(f)
bollard ['bɔləd] (Brit) n Poller m
Bollywood ['bɔlɪwud] n Bollywood nt
bolshy ['bɔlʃɪ] (Brit: inf) adj (stroppy) pampig
bolster ['bəulstəʳ] n Nackenrolle f
▶ **bolster up** vt stützen; (case) untermauern
bolt [bəult] n Riegel m; (with nut) Schraube f; (of
lightning) Blitz(strahl) m ▷ vt (door) verriegeln;
(also: **bolt together**) verschrauben; (food)
hinunterschlingen ▷ vi (run away: person)
weglaufen; (: horse) durchgehen ▷ adv: **~
upright** kerzengerade; **a ~ from the blue**
(fig) ein Blitz m aus heiterem Himmel
bomb [bɔm] n Bombe f ▷ vt bombardieren;
(plant bomb in or near) einen Bombenanschlag
verüben auf +acc
bombard [bɔm'bɑːd] vt (also fig) bombardieren
bombardment [bɔm'bɑːdmənt] n
Bombardierung f, Bombardement nt
bombastic [bɔm'bæstɪk] adj bombastisch
bomb disposal n: **~ unit**
Bombenräumkommando nt; **~
expert** Bombenräumexperte m,
Bombenräumexpertin f
bomber ['bɔməʳ] n Bomber m; (terrorist)
Bombenattentäter(in) m(f)
bombing ['bɔmɪŋ] n Bombenangriff m
bomb scare n Bombenalarm m
bombshell ['bɔmʃɛl] n (fig: revelation) Bombe f
bomb site n Trümmergrundstück nt
bona fide ['bəunə'faɪdɪ] adj echt; **~ offer**
Angebot nt auf Treu und Glauben
bonanza [bə'nænzə] n (Econ) Boom m
bond [bɔnd] n Band nt, Bindung f; (Fin)
festverzinsliches Wertpapier nt, Bond m
bondage ['bɔndɪdʒ] n Sklaverei f
bonded warehouse ['bɔndɪd] n Zolllager nt
bone [bəun] n Knochen m; (of fish) Gräte f ▷ vt
(meat) die Knochen herauslösen aus; (fish)
entgräten; **I've got a ~ to pick with you**
ich habe mit Ihnen (noch) ein Hühnchen zu
rupfen
bone china n ≈ feines Porzellan nt
bone-dry ['bəun'draɪ] adj knochentrocken
bone idle adj stinkfaul
bone marrow n Knochenmark nt
boner ['bəunəʳ] (US) n Schnitzer m
bonfire ['bɔnfaɪəʳ] n Feuer nt
bonk [bɔŋk] (inf) vt, vi (have sex (with)) bumsen
bonkers ['bɔŋkəz] (Brit: inf) adj (mad) verrückt
Bonn [bɔn] n Bonn nt
bonnet ['bɔnɪt] n Haube f; (for baby) Häubchen
nt; (Brit: of car) Motorhaube f
bonny ['bɔnɪ] (Scot, Northern English) adj schön,
hübsch
bonus ['bəunəs] n Prämie f; (on wages) Zulage
f; (at Christmas) Gratifikation f; (fig: additional
benefit) Plus nt

bony ['bəʊnɪ] *adj* knochig; (*Med*) knöchern; (*tissue*) knochenartig; (*meat*) mit viel Knochen; (*fish*) mit viel Gräten

boo [buː] *excl* buh ▷ *vt* auspfeifen, ausbuhen

boob [buːb] (*inf*) *n* (*breast*) Brust *f*; (*Brit: mistake*) Schnitzer *m*

booby prize ['buːbɪ-] *n* Scherzpreis für den schlechtesten Teilnehmer

booby trap ['buːbɪ-] *n* versteckte Bombe *f*; (*fig: joke etc*) als Schabernack versteckt angebrachte Falle

booby-trapped ['buːbɪtræpt] *adj*: **a ~ car** ein Auto *nt*, in dem eine Bombe versteckt ist

book [buk] *n* Buch *nt*; (*of stamps, tickets*) Heftchen *nt* ▷ *vt* bestellen; (*seat, room*) buchen, reservieren lassen; (*subj: traffic warden, policeman*) aufschreiben; (: referee) verwarnen; **books** *npl* (*Comm: accounts*) Bücher *pl*; **to keep the ~s** die Bücher führen; **by the ~** nach Vorschrift; **to throw the ~ at sb** jdn nach allen Regeln der Kunst fertig machen
  ▶ **book in** (*Brit*) *vi* sich eintragen
  ▶ **book up** *vt*: **all seats are ~ed up** es ist bis auf den letzten Platz ausverkauft; **the hotel is ~ed up** das Hotel ist ausgebucht

bookable ['bukəbl] *adj*: **all seats are ~** Karten für alle Plätze können vorbestellt werden

bookcase ['bukkeɪs] *n* Bücherregal *nt*

book ends *npl* Bücherstützen *pl*

booking ['bukɪŋ] (*Brit*) *n* Bestellung *f*; (*of seat, room*) Buchung *f*, Reservierung *f*

booking office (*Brit*) *n* (*Rail*) Fahrkartenschalter *m*; (*Theat*) Vorverkaufsstelle *f*, Vorverkaufskasse *f*

book-keeping ['buk'kiːpɪŋ] *n* Buchhaltung *f*, Buchführung *f*

booklet ['buklɪt] *n* Broschüre *f*

bookmaker ['bukmeɪkə'] *n* Buchmacher *m*

bookmark ['bukmɑːk] *n* Lesezeichen *nt*; (*Comput*) Bookmark *nt* ▷ *vt* (*Comput*) ein Bookmark einrichten für, bookmarken

bookseller ['buksɛlə'] *n* Buchhändler(in) *m(f)*

bookshelf ['bukʃɛlf] *n* Bücherbord *nt*;
  bookshelves *npl* Bücherregal *nt*

bookshop ['bukʃɔp] *n* Buchhandlung *f*

bookstall ['bukstɔːl] *n* Bücher- und Zeitungskiosk *m*

book store *n* = **bookshop**

book token *n* Buchgutschein *m*

book value *n* Buchwert *m*, Bilanzwert *m*

bookworm ['bukwəːm] *n* (*fig*) Bücherwurm *m*

boom [buːm] *n* Donnern *nt*, Dröhnen *nt*; (*in prices, population etc*) rapider Anstieg *m*; (*Econ*) Hochkonjunktur *f*; (*busy period*) Boom *m* ▷ *vi* (*guns*) donnern; (*thunder*) hallen; (*voice*) dröhnen; (*business*) florieren

boomerang ['buːməræŋ] *n* Bumerang *m* ▷ *vi* (*fig*) einen Bumerangeffekt haben

boom town *n* Goldgräberstadt *f*

boon [buːn] *n* Segen *m*

boorish ['buərɪʃ] *adj* rüpelhaft

boost [buːst] *n* Auftrieb *m* ▷ *vt* (*confidence*) stärken; (*sales, economy etc*) ankurbeln; **to give**

a ~ to sb/sb's spirits jdm Auftrieb geben

booster ['buːstə'] *n* (*Med*) Wiederholungsimpfung *f*; (*TV*) Zusatzgleichrichter *m*; (*Elec*) Puffersatz *m*; (*also:* **booster rocket**) Booster *m*, Startrakete *f*

booster seat *n* (*Aut*) Sitzerhöhung *f*

boot [buːt] *n* Stiefel *m*; (*ankle boot*) hoher Schuh *m*; (*Brit: of car*) Kofferraum *m* ▷ *vt* (*Comput*) laden; ... **to ~** (*in addition*) obendrein ...; **to give sb the ~** (*inf*) jdn rauswerfen *or* rausschmeißen

booth [buːð] *n* (*at fair*) Bude *f*, Stand *m*; (*telephone booth*) Zelle *f*; (*voting booth*) Kabine *f*

bootleg ['buːtlɛg] *adj* (*alcohol*) schwarzgebrannt; (*fuel*) schwarz hergestellt; (*tape etc*) schwarz mitgeschnitten

bootlegger ['buːtlɛgə'] *n* Bootlegger *m*, Schwarzhändler *m*

booty ['buːtɪ] *n* Beute *f*

booze [buːz] (*inf*) *n* Alkohol *m* ▷ *vi* saufen

boozer ['buːzə'] (*inf*) *n* (*person*) Säufer(in) *m(f)*; (*Brit: pub*) Kneipe *f*

border ['bɔːdə'] *n* Grenze *f*; (*for flowers*) Rabatte *f*; (*on cloth etc*) Bordüre *f* ▷ *vt* (*road*) säumen; (*another country: also:* **border on**) grenzen an +*acc*; **Borders** *n*: **the B~s** das Grenzgebiet zwischen England und Schottland
  ▶ **border on** *vt fus* (*fig*) grenzen an +*acc*

borderline ['bɔːdəlaɪn] *n* (*fig*): **on the ~** an der Grenze

borderline case *n* Grenzfall *m*

bore [bɔː'] *pt of* **bear** ▷ *vt* bohren; (*person*) langweilen ▷ *n* Langweiler *m*; (*of gun*) Kaliber *nt*; **to be ~d** sich langweilen; **he's ~d to tears** *or* **~d to death** *or* **~d stiff** er langweilt sich zu Tode

boredom ['bɔːdəm] *n* Langeweile *f*; (*boring quality*) Langweiligkeit *f*

boring ['bɔːrɪŋ] *adj* langweilig

born [bɔːn] *adj*: **to be ~** geboren werden; **I was ~ in 1960** ich bin *or* wurde 1960 geboren; **~ blind** blind geboren, von Geburt (an) blind; **a ~ comedian** ein geborener Komiker

born-again [bɔːnə'gɛn] *adj* wiedergeboren

borne [bɔːn] *pp of* **bear**

Borneo ['bɔːnɪəu] *n* Borneo *nt*

borough ['bʌrə] *n* Bezirk *m*, Stadtgemeinde *f*

borrow ['bɔrəu] *vt*: **to ~ sth** etw borgen, sich *dat* etw leihen; (*from library*) sich *dat* etw ausleihen; **may I ~ your car?** kann ich deinen Wagen leihen?

borrower ['bɔrəuə'] *n* (*of loan etc*) Kreditnehmer(in) *m(f)*

borrowing ['bɔrəuɪŋ] *n* Kreditaufnahme *f*

borstal ['bɔːstl] (*Brit*) *n* (*formerly*) Besserungsanstalt *f*

Bosnia ['bɔznɪə] *n* Bosnien *nt*

Bosnia-Herzegovina *n* Bosnien-Herzegowina *nt*

Bosnian ['bɔznɪən] *adj* bosnisch ▷ *n* Bosnier(in) *m(f)*

bosom ['buzəm] *n* Busen *m*; (*fig: of family*) Schoß *m*

453

bosom friend n Busenfreund(in) m(f)
boss [bɔs] n Chef(in) m(f); (leader) Boss
m ▷ vt (also: **boss around, boss about**)
herumkommandieren; **stop ~ing everyone
about!** hör auf mit dem ständigen
Herumkommandieren!
bossy ['bɔsɪ] adj herrisch
bosun ['bəusn] n Bootsmann m
botanical [bə'tænɪkl] adj botanisch
botanist ['bɔtənɪst] n Botaniker(in) m(f)
botany ['bɔtənɪ] n Botanik f
botch [bɔtʃ] vt (also: **botch up**) verpfuschen
both [bəuθ] adj beide ▷ pron beide; (two different
things) beides ▷ adv: ~ **A and B** sowohl A als
auch B; ~ **(of them)** (alle) beide; ~ **of us
went, we ~ went** wir gingen beide; **they
sell ~ the fabric and the finished curtains**
sie verkaufen sowohl den Stoff als auch die
fertigen Vorhänge
bother ['bɔðəʳ] vt Sorgen machen +dat; (disturb)
stören ▷ vi (also: **bother o.s.**) sich dat Sorgen
or Gedanken machen ▷ n (trouble) Mühe f;
(nuisance) Plage f ▷ excl Mist! (inf); **don't ~
phoning** du brauchst nicht anzurufen; **I'm
sorry to ~ you** es tut mir leid, dass ich Sie
belästigen muss; **I can't be ~ed** ich habe
keine Lust; **please don't ~** bitte machen Sie
sich keine Umstände; **don't ~!** lass es!; **it is
a ~ to have to shave every morning** es ist
wirklich lästig, sich jeden Morgen rasieren zu
müssen; **it's no ~** es ist kein Problem
Botswana [bɔt'swɑːnə] n Botswana nt
bottle ['bɔtl] n Flasche f; (Brit: inf: courage)
Mumm m ▷ vt in Flaschen abfüllen;
(fruit) einmachen; **a ~ of wine/milk** eine
Flasche Wein/Milch; **wine/milk ~** Wein-/
Milchflasche f
▶ **bottle up** vt in sich dat aufstauen
bottle bank n Altglascontainer m
bottle-fed ['bɔtlfɛd] adj mit der Flasche
ernährt
bottleneck ['bɔtlnɛk] n (also fig) Engpass m
bottle-opener ['bɔtləupnəʳ] n Flaschenöffner
m
bottom ['bɔtəm] n Boden m; (buttocks) Hintern
m; (of page, list) Ende nt; (of chair) Sitz m; (of
mountain, tree) Fuß m ▷ adj (lower) untere(r, s);
(last) unterste(r, s); **at the ~ of** unten an/in
+dat; **at the ~ of the page/list** unten auf der
Seite/Liste; **to be at the ~ of the class** der/
die Letzte in der Klasse sein; **to get to the
~ of sth** (fig) einer Sache dat auf den Grund
kommen
bottomless ['bɔtəmlɪs] adj (fig) unerschöpflich
bottom line n (of accounts) Saldo m; (fig): **that's
the ~ (of it)** (what it amounts to) darauf läuft es
im Endeffekt hinaus
botulism ['bɔtjulɪzəm] n Botulismus m,
Nahrungsmittelvergiftung f
bough [bau] n Ast m
bought [bɔːt] pt, pp of **buy**
boulder ['bəuldəʳ] n Felsblock m
boulevard ['buːləvɑːd] n Boulevard m

bounce [bauns] vi (auf)springen; (cheque)
platzen ▷ vt (ball) (auf)springen lassen; (signal)
reflektieren ▷ n Aufprall m; **he's got plenty
of ~** (fig) er hat viel Schwung
bouncer ['baunsəʳ] (inf) n Rausschmeißer
m
bouncy castle ['baunsɪ-] n Hüpfburg f
bound [baund] pt, pp of **bind** ▷ n Sprung m; (gen
pl: limit) Grenze f ▷ vi springen ▷ vt begrenzen
▷ adj: ~ **by** gebunden durch; **to be ~ to do sth**
(obliged) verpflichtet sein, etw zu tun; (very
likely) etw bestimmt tun; **he's ~ to fail** es kann
ihm ja gar nicht gelingen; ~ **for** nach; **the
area is out of ~s** das Betreten des Gebiets ist
verboten
boundary ['baundrɪ] n Grenze f
boundless ['baundlɪs] adj grenzenlos
bountiful ['bauntɪful] adj großzügig; (God)
gütig; (supply) reichlich
bounty ['bauntɪ] n Freigebigkeit f; (reward)
Kopfgeld m
bounty hunter n Kopfgeldjäger m
bouquet ['bukeɪ] n (Blumen)strauß m; (of wine)
Bukett nt, Blume f
bourbon ['buəbən] (US) n (also: **bourbon
whiskey**) Bourbon m
bourgeois ['buəʒwɑː] adj bürgerlich, spießig
(pej) ▷ n Bürger(in) m(f), Bourgeois m
bout [baut] n Anfall m; (Boxing etc) Kampf m
boutique [buːˈtiːk] n Boutique f
bow[1] [bəu] n Schleife f; (weapon, Mus) Bogen m
bow[2] [bau] n Verbeugung f; (Naut: also:
bows) Bug m ▷ vi sich verbeugen; (yield): **to
~ to** or **before** sich beugen +dat; **to ~ to the
inevitable** sich in das Unvermeidliche
fügen
bowels ['bauəlz] npl Darm m; (of the earth etc)
Innere nt
bowl [bəul] n Schüssel f; (shallower) Schale
f; (ball) Kugel f; (of pipe) Kopf m; (US: stadium)
Stadion nt ▷ vi werfen
▶ **bowl over** vt (fig) überwältigen
bow-legged ['bəu'lɛgɪd] adj o-beinig
bowler ['bəuləʳ] n Werfer(in) m(f); (Brit: also:
bowler hat) Melone f
bowling ['bəulɪŋ] n Kegeln nt; (on grass)
Bowling nt
bowling alley n Kegelbahn f
bowling green n Bowlingrasen m
bowls [bəulz] n Bowling nt
bow tie [bəu-] n Fliege f
box [bɔks] n Schachtel f; (cardboard box) Karton
m; (crate) Kiste f; (Theat) Loge f; (Brit: Aut) gelb
schraffierter Kreuzungsbereich; (on form) Feld nt
▷ vt (in eine Schachtel etc) verpacken; (fighter)
boxen ▷ vi boxen; **to ~ sb's ears** jdm eine
Ohrfeige geben
▶ **box in** vt einkeilen
▶ **box off** vt abtrennen
boxer ['bɔksəʳ] n (person, dog) Boxer m
box file n Sammelordner m
boxing ['bɔksɪŋ] n Boxen nt
Boxing Day (Brit) n zweiter Weihnachts(feier)

tag m; *siehe Info-Artikel*

BOXING DAY

Boxing Day ist ein Feiertag in Großbritannien. Wenn Weihnachten auf ein Wochenende fällt, wird der Feiertag am nächsten darauffolgenden Wochentag nachgeholt. Der Name geht auf einen alten Brauch zurück; früher erhielten Händler und Lieferanten an diesem Tag ein Geschenk, die sogenannte Christmas Box.

boxing gloves *npl* Boxhandschuhe *pl*
boxing ring *n* Boxring *m*
box number *n* Chiffre *f*
box office *n* Kasse *f*
boxroom ['bɒksrʊm] *n* Abstellraum *m*
boy [bɔɪ] *n* Junge *m*
boycott ['bɔɪkɒt] *n* Boykott *m* ▷ *vt* boykottieren
boyfriend ['bɔɪfrend] *n* Freund *m*
boyish ['bɔɪɪʃ] *adj* jungenhaft; (*woman*) knabenhaft
boy scout *n* Pfadfinder *m*
bp *abbr* = **bishop**
bra [brɑː] *n* BH *m*
brace [breɪs] *n* (*on teeth*) (Zahn)klammer *f*, (Zahn)spange *f*; (*tool*) (Hand)bohrer *m*; (*also*: **brace bracket**) geschweifte Klammer *f* ▷ *vt* spannen; **braces** *npl* (*Brit*) Hosenträger *pl*; **to ~ o.s.** (*for weight*) sich stützen; (*for shock*) sich innerlich vorbereiten
bracelet ['breɪslɪt] *n* Armband *nt*
bracing ['breɪsɪŋ] *adj* belebend
bracken ['brækən] *n* Farn *m*
bracket ['brækɪt] *n* Träger *m*; (*group, range*) Gruppe *f*; (*also*: **round bracket**) (runde) Klammer *f*; (*also*: **brace bracket**) geschweifte Klammer *f*; (*also*: **square bracket**) eckige Klammer *f* ▷ *vt* (*also*: **bracket together**) zusammenfassen; (*word, phrase*) einklammern; **income ~** Einkommensgruppe *f*; **in ~s** in Klammern
brackish ['brækɪʃ] *adj* brackig
brag [bræg] *vi* prahlen
braid [breɪd] *n* Borte *f*; (*of hair*) Zopf *m*
Braille [breɪl] *n* Blindenschrift *f*, Brailleschrift *f*
brain [breɪn] *n* Gehirn *nt*; **brains** *npl* (*Culin*) Hirn *nt*; (*intelligence*) Intelligenz *f*; **he's got ~s** er hat Köpfchen *or* Grips
brainchild ['breɪntʃaɪld] *n* Geistesprodukt *nt*
braindead ['breɪndɛd] *adj* hirntot; (*inf*) hirnlos
brain drain *n* Abwanderung *f* von Wissenschaftlern, Braindrain *m*
brainless ['breɪnlɪs] *adj* dumm
brainstorm ['breɪnstɔːm] *n* (*fig*) Anfall *m* geistiger Umnachtung; (*US*: *brain wave*) Geistesblitz *m*
brainwash ['breɪnwɒʃ] *vt* einer Gehirnwäsche *dat* unterziehen
brain wave *n* Geistesblitz *m*
brainy ['breɪnɪ] *adj* intelligent

braise [breɪz] *vt* schmoren
brake [breɪk] *n* Bremse *f* ▷ *vi* bremsen
brake fluid *n* Bremsflüssigkeit *f*
brake light *n* Bremslicht *nt*
brake pedal *n* Bremspedal *nt*
bramble ['bræmbl] *n* Brombeerstrauch *m*; (*fruit*) Brombeere *f*
bran [bræn] *n* Kleie *f*
branch [brɑːntʃ] *n* Ast *m*; (*of family, organization*) Zweig *m*; (*Comm*) Filiale *f*, Zweigstelle *f*; (: *bank, company etc*) Geschäftsstelle *f* ▷ *vi* sich gabeln
▶ **branch out** *vi* (*fig*): **to ~ out into** seinen (Geschäfts)bereich erweitern auf +*acc*
branch line *n* (*Rail*) Zweiglinie *f*, Nebenlinie *f*
branch manager *n* Zweigstellenleiter(in) *m(f)*, Filialleiter(in) *m(f)*
brand [brænd] *n* (*also*: **brand name**) Marke *f*; (*fig: type*) Art *f* ▷ *vt* mit einem Brandzeichen kennzeichnen; (*fig: pej*): **to ~ sb a communist** jdn als Kommunist brandmarken
brandish ['brændɪʃ] *vt* schwingen
brand name *n* Markenname *m*
brand-new ['brænd'njuː] *adj* nagelneu, brandneu
brandy ['brændɪ] *n* Weinbrand *m*
brash [bræʃ] *adj* dreist
Brasilia [brə'zɪlɪə] *n* Brasilia *nt*
brass [brɑːs] *n* Messing *nt*; **the ~** (*Mus*) die Blechbläser *pl*
brass band *n* Blaskapelle *f*
brassière ['bræsɪəʳ] *n* Büstenhalter *m*
brass tacks *npl*: **to get down to ~** zur Sache kommen
brassy ['brɑːsɪ] *adj* (*colour*) messingfarben; (*sound*) blechern; (*appearance, behaviour*) auffällig
brat [bræt] (*pej*) *n* Balg *m or nt*, Gör *nt*
bravado [brə'vɑːdəʊ] *n* Draufgängertum *nt*
brave [breɪv] *adj* mutig; (*attempt, smile*) tapfer ▷ *n* (indianischer) Krieger *m* ▷ *vt* trotzen +*dat*
bravely ['breɪvlɪ] *adv* (*see adj*) mutig; tapfer
bravery ['breɪvərɪ] *n* (*see adj*) Mut *m*; Tapferkeit *f*
bravo [brɑː'vəʊ] *excl* bravo
brawl [brɔːl] *n* Schlägerei *f* ▷ *vi* sich schlagen
brawn [brɔːn] *n* Muskeln *pl*; (*meat*) Schweinskopfsülze *f*
brawny ['brɔːnɪ] *adj* muskulös, kräftig
bray [breɪ] *vi* schreien ▷ *n* (Esels)schrei *m*
brazen ['breɪzn] *adj* unverschämt, dreist; (*lie*) schamlos ▷ *vt*: **to ~ it out** durchhalten
brazier ['breɪzɪəʳ] *n* (*container*) Kohlenbecken *nt*
Brazil [brə'zɪl] *n* Brasilien *nt*
Brazilian [brə'zɪljən] *adj* brasilianisch ▷ *n* Brasilianer(in) *m(f)*
Brazil nut *n* Paranuss *f*
breach [briːtʃ] *vt* (*defence*) durchbrechen; (*wall*) eine Bresche schlagen in +*acc* ▷ *n* (*gap*) Bresche *f*; (*estrangement*) Bruch *m*; (*breaking*): **~ of contract** Vertragsbruch *m*; **~ of the peace** öffentliche Ruhestörung *f*; **~ of trust** Vertrauensbruch *m*
bread [bred] *n* Brot *nt*; (*inf: money*) Moos *nt*, Kies *m*; **to earn one's daily ~** sein Brot verdienen; **to know which side one's ~ is buttered (on)**

wissen, wo etwas zu holen ist
bread and butter n Butterbrot nt; (fig)
Broterwerb m
bread bin (Brit) n Brotkasten m
breadboard ['brɛdbɔ:d] n Brot(schneide)brett
nt; (Comput) Leiterplatte f
bread box (US) n Brotkasten m
breadcrumbs ['brɛdkrʌmz] npl Brotkrumen pl;
(Culin) Paniermehl nt
breadline ['brɛdlaɪn] n: **to be on the ~** nur das
Allernotwendigste zum Leben haben
breadth [brɛtθ] n (also fig) Breite f
breadwinner ['brɛdwɪnəʳ] n Ernährer(in) m(f)
break [breɪk] (pt **broke**, pp **broken**) vt
zerbrechen; (leg, arm) sich dat brechen; (promise,
record) brechen; (law) verstoßen gegen ▷ vi
zerbrechen, kaputtgehen; (storm) losbrechen;
(weather) umschlagen; (dawn) anbrechen;
(story, news) bekannt werden ▷ n Pause f; (gap)
Lücke f; (fracture) Bruch m; (chance) Chance
f, Gelegenheit f; (holiday) Urlaub m; **to ~ the
news to sb** es jdm sagen; **to ~ even** seine (Un)
kosten decken; **to ~ with sb** mit jdm brechen,
sich von jdm trennen; **to ~ free** or **loose** sich
losreißen; **to take a ~** (eine) Pause machen;
(holiday) Urlaub machen; **without a ~** ohne
Unterbrechung or Pause, ununterbrochen; **a
lucky ~** ein Durchbruch m
▸ **break down** vt (figures, data) aufschlüsseln;
(door etc) einrennen ▷ vi (car) eine Panne
haben; (machine) kaputtgehen; (person,
resistance) zusammenbrechen; (talks) scheitern
▸ **break in** vt (horse) zureiten ▷ vi einbrechen;
(interrupt) unterbrechen
▸ **break into** vt fus einbrechen in +acc
▸ **break off** vi abbrechen ▷ vt (talks) abbrechen;
(engagement) lösen
▸ **break open** vt, vi aufbrechen
▸ **break out** vi ausbrechen; **to ~ out in
spots/a rash** Pickel/einen Ausschlag
bekommen
▸ **break through** vi: **the sun broke through**
die Sonne kam durch ▷ vt fus durchbrechen
▸ **break up** vi (ship) zerbersten; (crowd, meeting,
partnership) sich auflösen; (marriage) scheitern;
(friends) sich trennen; (Scol) in die Ferien
gehen ▷ vt zerbrechen; (journey, fight etc)
unterbrechen; (meeting) auflösen; (marriage)
zerstören
breakable ['breɪkəbl] adj zerbrechlich ▷ n: **~s**
zerbrechliche Ware f
breakage ['breɪkɪdʒ] n Bruch m; **to pay for ~s**
für zerbrochene Ware or für Bruch bezahlen
breakaway ['breɪkəweɪ] adj (group etc) Splitter-
break dancing n Breakdance m
breakdown ['breɪkdaun] n (Aut) Panne
f; (in communications) Zusammenbruch m;
(of marriage) Scheitern nt; (also: **nervous
breakdown**) (Nerven)zusammenbruch m; (of
statistics) Aufschlüsselung f
breakdown service (Brit) n Pannendienst m
breakdown van (Brit) n Abschleppwagen m
breaker ['breɪkəʳ] n (wave) Brecher m

breakeven ['breɪk'i:vn] cpd: **~ chart**
Gewinnschwellendiagramm nt; **~ point**
Gewinnschwelle f
breakfast ['brɛkfəst] n Frühstück nt ▷ vi
frühstücken
breakfast cereal n Getreideflocken pl
break-in ['breɪkɪn] n Einbruch m
breaking and entering ['breɪkɪŋən'entrɪŋ] n
(Law) Einbruch m
breaking point ['breɪkɪŋ-] n (fig): **to reach ~**
völlig am Ende sein
breakthrough ['breɪkθru:] n Durchbruch m
break-up ['breɪkʌp] n (of partnership) Auflösung
f; (of marriage) Scheitern nt
break-up value n (Comm) Liquidationswert m
breakwater ['breɪkwɔ:təʳ] n Wellenbrecher m
breast [brɛst] n Brust f; (of meat) Brust f,
Bruststück nt
breast-feed ['brɛstfi:d] (irreg: like **feed**) vt, vi
stillen
breast pocket n Brusttasche f
breaststroke ['brɛststrəuk] n
Brustschwimmen nt
breath [brɛθ] n Atem m; (a breath) Atemzug
m; **to go out for a ~ of air** an die frische Luft
gehen, frische Luft schnappen gehen; **out of
~** außer Atem, atemlos; **to get one's ~ back**
wieder zu Atem kommen
breathalyse ['brɛθəlaɪz] vt blasen lassen (inf)
Breathalyser® ['brɛθəlaɪzəʳ] n Promillemesser
m
breathe [bri:ð] vt, vi atmen; **I won't ~ a word
about it** ich werde kein Sterbenswörtchen
darüber sagen
▸ **breathe in** vt, vi einatmen
▸ **breathe out** vt, vi ausatmen
breather ['bri:ðəʳ] n Atempause f,
Verschnaufpause f
breathing ['bri:ðɪŋ] n Atmung f
breathing space n (fig) Atempause f,
Ruhepause f
breathless ['brɛθlɪs] adj atemlos, außer Atem;
(Med) an Atemnot leidend; **I was ~ with
excitement** die Aufregung verschlug mir den
Atem
breathtaking ['brɛθteɪkɪŋ] adj atemberaubend
breath test n Atemalkoholtest m
bred [brɛd] pt, pp of **breed**
-bred suff: **well/ill-~** gut/schlecht erzogen
breed [bri:d] (pt, pp **bred**) vt züchten; (fig: give rise
to) erzeugen; (: hate, suspicion) hervorrufen ▷ vi
Junge pl haben ▷ n Rasse f; (type, class) Art f
breeder ['bri:dəʳ] n Züchter(in) m(f);
(also: **breeder reactor**) Brutreaktor m, Brüter m
breeding ['bri:dɪŋ] n Erziehung f
breeding ground n (also fig) Brutstätte f
breeze [bri:z] n Brise f
breeze block (Brit) n Ytong® m
breezy ['bri:zɪ] adj (manner, tone) munter;
(weather) windig
Breton ['brɛtən] adj bretonisch ▷ n Bretone m,
Bretonin f
brevity ['brɛvɪtɪ] n Kürze f

brew [bru:] *vt* (*tea*) aufbrühen, kochen; (*beer*) brauen ▷ *vi* (*tea*) ziehen; (*beer*) gären; (*storm: fig*) sich zusammenbrauen

brewer ['bru:ə^r] *n* Brauer *m*

brewery ['bru:ərɪ] *n* Brauerei *f*

briar ['braɪə^r] *n* Dornbusch *m*; (*wild rose*) wilde Rose *f*

bribe [braɪb] *n* Bestechungsgeld *nt* ▷ *vt* bestechen; **to ~ sb to do sth** jdn bestechen, damit er etw tut

bribery ['braɪbərɪ] *n* Bestechung *f*

bric-a-brac ['brɪkəbræk] *n* Nippes *pl*, Nippsachen *pl*

brick [brɪk] *n* Ziegelstein *m*, Backstein *m*; (*of ice cream*) Block *m*

bricklayer ['brɪkleɪə^r] *n* Maurer(in) *m(f)*

brickwork ['brɪkwə:k] *n* Mauerwerk *nt*

bridal ['braɪdl] *adj* (*gown, veil etc*) Braut-

bride [braɪd] *n* Braut *f*

bridegroom ['braɪdgru:m] *n* Bräutigam *m*

bridesmaid ['braɪdzmeɪd] *n* Brautjungfer *f*

bridge [brɪdʒ] *n* Brücke *f*; (*Naut*) (Kommando) brücke *f*; (*of nose*) Sattel *m*; (*Cards*) Bridge *nt* ▷ *vt* (*river*) eine Brücke schlagen *or* bauen über +*acc*; (*fig*) überbrücken

bridging loan ['brɪdʒɪŋ-] (*Brit*) *n* Überbrückungskredit *m*

bridle ['braɪdl] *n* Zaum *m* ▷ *vt* aufzäumen ▷ *vi*: **to ~ (at)** sich entrüstet wehren (gegen)

bridle path *n* Reitweg *m*

brief [bri:f] *adj* kurz ▷ *n* (*Law*) Auftrag *m*; (*task*) Aufgabe *f* ▷ *vt* instruieren; (*Mil etc*): **to ~ sb (about)** jdn instruieren (über +*acc*); **briefs** *npl* Slip *m*; **in ~ ...** kurz (gesagt) ...

briefcase ['bri:fkeɪs] *n* Aktentasche *f*

briefing ['bri:fɪŋ] *n* Briefing *nt*, Lagebespechung *f*

briefly ['bri:flɪ] *adv* kurz; **to glimpse sth ~** einen flüchtigen Blick von etw erhaschen

Brig. *abbr* = **brigadier**

brigade [brɪ'geɪd] *n* Brigade *f*

brigadier [brɪgə'dɪə^r] *n* Brigadegeneral *m*

bright [braɪt] *adj* (*light, room*) hell; (*weather*) heiter; (*clever*) intelligent; (*lively*) heiter, fröhlich; (*colour*) leuchtend; (*outlook, future*) glänzend; **to look on the ~ side** die Dinge von der positiven Seite betrachten

brighten ['braɪtn] (*also*: **brighten up**) *vt* aufheitern; (*event*) beleben ▷ *vi* (*weather, face*) sich aufheitern; (*person*) fröhlicher werden; (*prospects*) sich verbessern

brightly ['braɪtlɪ] *adv* (*shine*) hell; (*smile*) fröhlich; (*talk*) heiter

brill [brɪl] (*Brit: inf*) *adj* toll

brilliance ['brɪljəns] *n* Strahlen *nt*; (*of person*) Genialität *f*, Brillanz *f*; (*of talent, skill*) Großartigkeit *f*

brilliant ['brɪljənt] *adj* strahlend; (*person, idea*) genial, brillant; (*career*) großartig; (*inf: holiday etc*) fantastisch

brilliantly ['brɪljəntlɪ] *adv* (*see adj*) strahlend; genial, brillant; großartig; fantastisch

brim [brɪm] *n* Rand *m*; (*of hat*) Krempe *f*

brimful ['brɪm'ful] *adj*: **~ (of)** randvoll (mit); (*fig*) voll (von)

brine [braɪn] *n* Lake *f*

bring [brɪŋ] (*pt, pp* **brought**) *vt* bringen; (*with you*) mitbringen; **to ~ sth to an end** etw zu Ende bringen; **I can't ~ myself to fire him** ich kann es nicht über mich bringen, ihn zu entlassen

▶ **bring about** *vt* herbeiführen

▶ **bring back** *vt* (*restore*) wiedereinführen; (*return*) zurückbringen

▶ **bring down** *vt* (*government*) zu Fall bringen; (*plane*) herunterholen; (*price*) senken

▶ **bring forward** *vt* (*meeting*) vorverlegen; (*proposal*) vorbringen; (*Bookkeeping*) übertragen

▶ **bring in** *vt* (*money*) (ein)bringen; (*include*) einbeziehen; (*person*) einschalten; (*legislation*) einbringen; (*verdict*) fällen

▶ **bring off** *vt* (*plan*) durchführen; (*deal*) zustande bringen

▶ **bring out** *vt* herausholen; (*meaning, book, album*) herausbringen

▶ **bring round** *vt* (*after faint*) wieder zu Bewusstsein bringen

▶ **bring up** *vt* heraufbringen; (*educate*) erziehen; (*question, subject*) zur Sprache bringen; (*food*) erbrechen

bring-and-buy sale *n* Basar *m* (*wo mitgebrachte Sachen verkauft werden*)

brink [brɪŋk] *n* Rand *m*; **on the ~ of doing sth** nahe daran, etw zu tun; **she was on the ~ of tears** sie war den Tränen nahe

brisk [brɪsk] *adj* (*abrupt: person, tone*) forsch; (*pace*) flott; (*trade*) lebhaft, rege; **to go for a ~ walk** einen ordentlichen Spaziergang machen; **business is ~** das Geschäft ist rege

bristle ['brɪsl] *n* Borste *f*; (*of beard*) Stoppel *f* ▷ *vi* zornig werden; **bristling with** strotzend von

bristly ['brɪslɪ] *adj* borstig; (*chin*) stoppelig

Brit [brɪt] (*inf*) *n* (= *British person*) Brite *m*, Britin *f*

Britain ['brɪtən] *n* (*also*: **Great Britain**) Großbritannien *nt*

British ['brɪtɪʃ] *adj* britisch ▷ *npl*: **the ~** die Briten *pl*

British Isles *npl*: **the ~** die Britischen Inseln

British Rail *n britische Eisenbahngesellschaft*

British Summer Time *n* britische Sommerzeit *f*

Briton ['brɪtən] *n* Brite *m*, Britin *f*

Brittany ['brɪtənɪ] *n* die Bretagne

brittle ['brɪtl] *adj* spröde; (*glass*) zerbrechlich; (*bones*) schwach

broach [brəʊtʃ] *vt* (*subject*) anschneiden

broad [brɔːd] *adj* breit; (*general*) allgemein; (*accent*) stark ▷ *n* (*US: inf*) Frau *f*; **in ~ daylight** am hellichten Tag; **~ hint** deutlicher Wink *m*

broadband ['brɔːdbænd] (*Comput*) *adj* Breitband- ▷ *n* Breitband *nt*

broad bean *n* dicke Bohne *f*, Saubohne *f*

broadcast ['brɔːdkɑːst] (*pt, pp* **~**) *n* Sendung *f* ▷ *vt, vi* senden

broadcaster ['brɔːdkɑːstə^r] *n* (*Radio, TV*) Rundfunk-/Fernsehpersönlichkeit *f*

broadcasting ['brɔ:dkɑ:stɪŋ] *n* (*Radio*) Rundfunk *m*; (*TV*) Fernsehen *nt*
broadcasting station *n* (*Radio*) Rundfunkstation *f*; (*TV*) Fernsehstation *f*
broaden ['brɔ:dn] *vt* erweitern ▷ *vi* breiter werden, sich verbreitern; **to ~ one's mind** seinen Horizont erweitern
broadly ['brɔ:dlɪ] *adv* (*in general terms*) in großen Zügen; **~ speaking** allgemein *or* generell gesagt
broad-minded ['brɔ:d'maɪndɪd] *adj* tolerant
broadsheet ['brɔ:dʃi:t] *n* (*newspaper*) großformatige Zeitung
broccoli ['brɒkəlɪ] *n* Brokkoli *pl*, Spargelkohl *m*
brochure ['brəʊʃjʊəʳ] *n* Broschüre *f*
brogue [brəʊg] *n* Akzent *m*; (*shoe*) fester Schuh *m*
broil [brɔɪl] (*US*) *vt* grillen
broiler ['brɔɪləʳ] *n* Brathähnchen *nt*
broke [brəʊk] *pt of* **break** ▷ *adj* (*inf*) pleite; **to go ~** pleitegehen
broken ['brəʊkn] *pp of* **break** ▷ *adj* zerbrochen; (*machine: also:* **broken down**) kaputt; (*promise, vow*) gebrochen; **a ~ leg** ein gebrochenes Bein; **a ~ marriage** eine gescheiterte Ehe; **a ~ home** zerrüttete Familienverhältnisse *pl*; **in ~ English/German** in gebrochenem Englisch/Deutsch
broken-down ['brəʊkn'daʊn] *adj* kaputt; (*house*) baufällig
brokenhearted [brəʊkn'hɑ:tɪd] *adj* untröstlich
broker ['brəʊkəʳ] *n* Makler(in) *m(f)*
brokerage ['brəʊkrɪdʒ] *n* (*commission*) Maklergebühr *f*; (*business*) Maklergeschäft *nt*
brolly ['brɒlɪ] (*Brit: inf*) *n* (Regen)schirm *m*
bronchitis [brɒŋ'kaɪtɪs] *n* Bronchitis *f*
bronze [brɒnz] *n* Bronze *f*
bronzed [brɒnzd] *adj* braun, (sonnen)gebräunt
brooch [brəʊtʃ] *n* Brosche *f*
brood [bru:d] *n* Brut *f* ▷ *vi* (*hen*) brüten; (*person*) grübeln
▶ **brood on** *vt fus* nachgrübeln über +*acc*
▶ **brood over** *vt fus* = **brood on**
broody ['bru:dɪ] *adj* (*person*) grüblerisch; (*hen*) brütig
brook [brʊk] *n* Bach *m*
broom [brʊm] *n* Besen *m*; (*Bot*) Ginster *m*
broomstick ['brʊmstɪk] *n* Besenstiel *m*
bros., Bros. *abbr* (*Comm:* = *brothers*) Gebr.
broth [brɒθ] *n* Suppe *f*, Fleischbrühe *f*
brothel ['brɒθl] *n* Bordell *nt*
brother ['brʌðəʳ] *n* Bruder *m*; (*in trade union, society etc*) Kollege *m*
brotherhood ['brʌðəhud] *n* Brüderlichkeit *f*
brother-in-law ['brʌðərɪn'lɔ:] *n* Schwager *m*
brotherly ['brʌðəlɪ] *adj* brüderlich
brought [brɔ:t] *pt, pp of* **bring**
brought forward *adj* (*Comm*) vorgetragen
brow [braʊ] *n* Stirn *f*; (*eyebrow*) (Augen)braue *f*; (*of hill*) (Berg)kuppe *f*
browbeat ['braʊbi:t] *vt*: **to ~ sb (into doing sth)** jdn (so) unter Druck setzen(, dass er etw tut)

brown [braʊn] *adj* braun ▷ *n* Braun *nt* ▷ *vt* (*Culin*) (an)bräunen; **to go ~** braun werden
brown bread *n* Graubrot *nt*, Mischbrot *nt*
Brownie ['braʊnɪ] *n* (*also:* **Brownie Guide**) Wichtel *m*
brownie ['braʊnɪ] (*US*) *n kleiner Schokoladenkuchen*
brown paper *n* Packpapier *nt*
brown rice *n* Naturreis *m*
brown sugar *n* brauner Zucker *m*
browse [braʊz] *vi* (*in shop*) sich umsehen; (*animal*) weiden; (: *deer*) äsen ▷ *vti* (*Comput*) browsen ▷ *n*: **to have a ~ (around)** sich umsehen; **to ~ through a book** in einem Buch schmökern
browser ['braʊzəʳ] *n* (*Comput*) Browser *m*
bruise [bru:z] *n* blauer Fleck *m*, Bluterguss *m*; (*on fruit*) Druckstelle *f* ▷ *vt* (*arm, leg etc*) sich *dat* stoßen; (*person*) einen blauen Fleck schlagen; (*fruit*) beschädigen ▷ *vi* (*fruit*) eine Druckstelle bekommen; **to ~ one's arm** sich *dat* den Arm stoßen, sich *dat* einen blauen Fleck am Arm holen
bruising ['bru:zɪŋ] *adj* (*experience, encounter*) schmerzhaft ▷ *n* Quetschung *f*
Brum [brʌm] (*Brit: inf*) *n abbr* (= *Birmingham*)
Brummie ['brʌmɪ] (*inf*) *n* aus Birmingham stammende oder dort wohnhafte Person, Birminghamer(in) *m(f)*
brunch [brʌntʃ] *n* Brunch *m*
brunette [bru:'nɛt] *n* Brünette *f*
brunt [brʌnt] *n*: **to bear the ~ of** die volle Wucht +*gen* tragen
brush [brʌʃ] *n* Bürste *f*; (*for painting, shaving etc*) Pinsel *m*; (*quarrel*) Auseinandersetzung *f* ▷ *vt* fegen; (*groom*) bürsten; (*teeth*) putzen; (*also:* **brush against**) streifen; **to have a ~ with sb** (*verbally*) sich mit jdm streiten; (*physically*) mit jdm aneinandergeraten; **to have a ~ with the police** mit der Polizei aneinandergeraten
▶ **brush aside** *vt* abtun
▶ **brush past** *vt* streifen
▶ **brush up** *vt* auffrischen
brushed [brʌʃt] *adj* (*steel, chrome etc*) gebürstet; (*denim etc*) aufgeraut; **~ nylon** Nylonvelours *m*
brushoff ['brʌʃɔf] (*inf*) *n*: **to give sb the ~** jdm eine Abfuhr erteilen
brushwood ['brʌʃwʊd] *n* Reisig *nt*
brusque [bru:sk] *adj* brüsk; (*tone*) schroff
Brussels ['brʌslz] *n* Brüssel *nt*
Brussels sprouts *npl* Rosenkohl *m*
brutal ['bru:tl] *adj* brutal
brutality [bru:'tælɪtɪ] *n* Brutalität *f*
brutalize ['bru:təlaɪz] *vt* brutalisieren; (*ill-treat*) brutal behandeln
brute [bru:t] *n* brutaler Kerl *m*; (*animal*) Tier *nt* ▷ *adj*: **by ~ force** mit roher Gewalt
brutish ['bru:tɪʃ] *adj* tierisch
BS (*US*) *n abbr* (= *Bachelor of Science*) akademischer Grad für Naturwissenschaftler
BSA *n abbr* (= *Boy Scouts of America*) amerikanische Pfadfinderorganisation

b

BSc abbr (= Bachelor of Science) akademischer Grad für Naturwissenschaftler

BSE n abbr (= bovine spongiform encephalopathy) BSE f

BSI n abbr (= British Standards Institution) britischer Normenausschuss

BST abbr = **British Summer Time**

Bt (Brit) abbr = **baronet**

btu n abbr (= British thermal unit) britische Wärmeeinheit

bubble ['bʌbl] n Blase f ▷ vi sprudeln; (sparkle) perlen; (fig: person) übersprudeln

bubble bath n Schaumbad nt

bubble gum n Bubblegum m

bubble-jet printer n Bubblejetdrucker m

bubble pack n (Klar)sichtpackung f

bubbly ['bʌblɪ] adj (person) lebendig; (liquid) sprudelnd ▷ n (inf: champagne) Schampus m

Bucharest [bu:kə'rɛst] n Bukarest nt

buck [bʌk] n (rabbit) Rammler m; (deer) Bock m; (US: inf) Dollar m ▷ vi bocken; **to pass the ~** die Verantwortung abschieben; **to pass the ~ to sb** jdm die Verantwortung zuschieben
▶ **buck up** vi (cheer up) aufleben ▷ vt: **to ~ one's ideas up** sich zusammenreißen

bucket ['bʌkɪt] n Eimer m ▷ vi (Brit: inf): **the rain is ~ing (down)** es gießt or schüttet (wie aus Kübeln)

BUCKINGHAM PALACE

Buckingham Palace ist die offizielle Londoner Residenz der britischen Monarchen und liegt am St James Park. Der Palast wurde 1703 für den Herzog von Buckingham erbaut, 1762 von Georg III. gekauft, zwischen 1821 und 1836 von John Nash umgebaut und Anfang des 20. Jahrhunderts teilweise neu gestaltet. Teile des Buckingham Palace sind heute der Öffentlichkeit zugänglich.

buckle ['bʌkl] n Schnalle f ▷ vt zuschnallen; (wheel) verbiegen ▷ vi sich verbiegen
▶ **buckle down** vi sich dahinter klemmen; **to ~ down to sth** sich hinter etw acc klemmen

Bucks [bʌks] (Brit) abbr (Post) = **Buckinghamshire**

bud [bʌd] n Knospe f ▷ vi knospen, Knospen treiben

Budapest [bju:də'pɛst] n Budapest nt

Buddha ['budə] n Buddha m

Buddhism ['budɪzəm] n Buddhismus m

Buddhist ['budɪst] adj buddhistisch ▷ n Buddhist(in) m(f)

budding ['bʌdɪŋ] adj angehend

buddy ['bʌdɪ] (US) n Kumpel m

budge [bʌdʒ] vt (von der Stelle) bewegen; (fig) zum Nachgeben bewegen ▷ vi sich von der Stelle rühren; (fig) nachgeben

budgerigar ['bʌdʒərɪgɑː'] n Wellensittich m

budget ['bʌdʒɪt] n Budget nt, Etat m, Haushalt m ▷ vi Haus halten, haushalten, wirtschaften; **I'm on a tight ~** ich habe nicht viel Geld zur Verfügung; **she works out her ~ every**

month sie macht (sich dat) jeden Monat einen Haushaltsplan; **to ~ for sth** etw kostenmäßig einplanen

budgie ['bʌdʒɪ] n = **budgerigar**

Buenos Aires ['bweɪnɔs'aɪrɪz] n Buenos Aires nt

buff [bʌf] adj gelbbraun ▷ n (inf) Fan m

buffalo ['bʌfələu] (pl ~ or **buffaloes**) n (Brit) Büffel m; (US) Bison m

buffer ['bʌfə'] n Puffer m, (Comput) Zwischenspeicher m, Pufferspeicher m; (Rail) Prellbock m; (fig) Polster nt ▷ vi (Comput) zwischenspeichern

buffering ['bʌfərɪŋ] n (Comput) Pufferung f

buffer state n Pufferstaat m

buffer zone n Pufferzone f

buffet[1] ['bufeɪ] (Brit) n Büfett nt, Bahnhofsrestaurant nt; (food) kaltes Buffet nt

buffet[2] ['bʌfɪt] vt (subj: sea) hin und her werfen; (: wind) schütteln

buffet car (Brit) n Speisewagen m

buffet lunch n Buffet nt

buffoon [bə'fu:n] n Clown m

bug [bʌg] n (esp US) Insekt nt; (Comput: of program) Programmfehler m; (: of equipment) Fehler m; (fig: germ) Bazillus m; (hidden microphone) Wanze f ▷ vt (inf) nerven; (telephone etc) abhören; (room) verwanzen; **I've got the travel ~** (fig) mich hat die Reiselust gepackt

bugbear ['bʌgbeə'] n Schreckgespenst nt

bugger ['bʌgə'] (inf!) n Scheißkerl m, Arschloch nt ▷ vb: **~ off!** hau ab!; **~ (it)!** Scheiße!

buggy ['bʌgɪ] n (for baby) Sportwagen m

bugle ['bju:gl] n Bügelhorn nt

build [bɪld] (pt, pp **built**) n Körperbau m ▷ vt bauen
▶ **build on** vt fus (fig) aufbauen auf +dat
▶ **build up** vt aufbauen; (production) steigern; (morale) stärken; (stocks) anlegen; **don't ~ your hopes up too soon** mach dir nicht zu früh Hoffnungen

builder ['bɪldə'] n Bauunternehmer m

building ['bɪldɪŋ] n (industry) Bauindustrie f; (construction) Bau m; (structure) Gebäude nt, Bau

building contractor n Bauunternehmer m

building industry n Bauindustrie f

building site n Baustelle f

building society (Brit) n Bausparkasse f

building trade n Baubranche f or -gewerbe nt

build-up ['bɪldʌp] n Ansammlung f; (publicity): **to give sb/sth a good ~** jdn/etw ganz groß herausbringen

built [bɪlt] pt, pp of **build** ▷ adj: **~-in** eingebaut, Einbau-; (safeguards) eingebaut; **well-~** gut gebaut

built-up area ['bɪltʌp-] n bebautes Gebiet nt

bulb [bʌlb] n (Blumen)zwiebel f; (Elec) (Glüh)birne f

bulbous ['bʌlbəs] adj knollig

Bulgaria [bʌl'geərɪə] n Bulgarien nt

Bulgarian [bʌl'geərɪən] adj bulgarisch ▷ n Bulgare m, Bulgarin f; (Ling) Bulgarisch nt

bulge [bʌldʒ] n Wölbung f; (in birth rate, sales) Zunahme f ▷ vi (pocket) prall gefüllt sein;

(cheeks) voll sein; (file) (zum Bersten) voll sein;
to be bulging with prall gefüllt sein mit
bulimia [bəˈlɪmɪə] n Bulimie f
bulk [bʌlk] n (of thing) massige Form f; (of person)
massige Gestalt f; **in ~** im Großen, en gros;
the ~ of der Großteil +gen
bulk buying [-ˈbaɪɪŋ] n Mengeneinkauf m,
Großeinkauf m
bulk carrier n Bulkcarrier m
bulkhead [ˈbʌlkhɛd] n Schott nt
bulky [ˈbʌlkɪ] adj sperrig
bull [bʊl] n Stier m; (male elephant or whale)
Bulle m; (Stock Exchange) Haussier m,
Haussespekulant m; (Rel) Bulle f
bulldog [ˈbʊldɒg] n Bulldogge f
bulldoze [ˈbʊldəʊz] vt mit Bulldozern
wegräumen; (building) mit Bulldozern
abreißen; **I was ~d into it** (fig: inf) ich wurde
gezwungen or unter Druck gesetzt, es zu tun
bulldozer [ˈbʊldəʊzəʳ] n Bulldozer m,
Planierraupe f
bullet [ˈbʊlɪt] n Kugel f
bulletin [ˈbʊlɪtɪn] n (TV etc) Kurznachrichten
pl; (journal) Bulletin nt
bulletin board n (Comput) Schwarzes Brett
nt
bulletproof [ˈbʊlɪtpruːf] adj kugelsicher
bullfight [ˈbʊlfaɪt] n Stierkampf m
bullfighter [ˈbʊlfaɪtəʳ] n Stierkämpfer m
bullfighting [ˈbʊlfaɪtɪŋ] n Stierkampf m
bullion [ˈbʊljən] n: **gold/silver ~** Barrengold
nt/-silber nt
bullock [ˈbʊlək] n Ochse m
bullring [ˈbʊlrɪŋ] n Stierkampfarena f
bull's-eye [ˈbʊlzaɪ] n (on a target): **the ~** der
Scheibenmittelpunkt, das Schwarze
bullshit [ˈbʊlʃɪt] (inf!) n Scheiß m, Quatsch m
▷ vi Scheiß erzählen; **~!** Quatsch!
bully [ˈbʊlɪ] n Tyrann m ▷ vt tyrannisieren;
(frighten) einschüchtern
bullying [ˈbʊlɪŋ] n Tyrannisieren nt
bum [bʌm] (inf) n Hintern m; (esp US: good-for-
nothing) Rumtreiber m; (tramp) Penner m
▶ **bum around** (inf) vi herumgammeln
bumblebee [ˈbʌmblbiː] n Hummel f
bumf [bʌmf] (inf) n Papierkram m
bump [bʌmp] n Zusammenstoß m; (jolt)
Erschütterung f; (swelling) Beule f; (on road)
Unebenheit f ▷ vt stoßen; (car) eine Delle
fahren in +acc
▶ **bump along** vi entlangholpern
▶ **bump into** vt fus (obstacle) stoßen gegen;
(inf: person) treffen
bumper [ˈbʌmpəʳ] n Stoßstange f ▷ adj: **~ crop,
~ harvest** Rekordernte f
bumper cars npl Autoskooter pl
bumper sticker n Aufkleber m
bumph [bʌmf] n = **bumf**
bumptious [ˈbʌmpʃəs] adj wichtigtuerisch
bumpy [ˈbʌmpɪ] adj holperig; **it was a ~
flight/ride** während des Fluges/auf der Fahrt
wurden wir tüchtig durchgerüttelt
bun [bʌn] n Brötchen nt; (of hair) Knoten m

bunch [bʌntʃ] n Strauß m; (of keys) Bund m;
(of bananas) Büschel nt; (of people) Haufen m;
bunches npl (in hair) Zöpfe pl; **~ of grapes**
Weintraube f
bundle [ˈbʌndl] n Bündel nt ▷ vt (also: **bundle
up**) bündeln; (put): **to ~ sth into** etw stopfen
or packen in +acc; **to ~ sb into** jdn schaffen
in +acc
▶ **bundle off** vt schaffen
▶ **bundle out** vt herausschaffen
bun fight (Brit: inf) n Festivitäten pl; (tea party)
Teegesellschaft f
bung [bʌŋ] n Spund m, Spundzapfen m ▷ vt
(Brit: inf: also: **bung in**) schmeißen; (also: **bung
up**) verstopfen; **my nose is ~ed up** meine
Nase ist verstopft
bungalow [ˈbʌŋgələʊ] n Bungalow m
bungee jumping [ˈbʌndʒiːˈdʒʌmpɪŋ] n
Bungeespringen nt
bungle [ˈbʌŋgl] vt verpfuschen
bunion [ˈbʌnjən] n entzündeter Ballen m
bunk [bʌŋk] n Bett nt, Koje f; **to do a ~** (inf)
abhauen
▶ **bunk off** (inf) vi abhauen
bunk beds npl Etagenbett nt
bunker [ˈbʌŋkəʳ] n Kohlenbunker m; (Mil, Golf)
Bunker m
bunny [ˈbʌnɪ] n (also: **bunny rabbit**) Hase m,
Häschen nt
bunny girl (Brit) n Häschen nt
bunny hill (US) n (Ski) Anfängerhügel m
bunting [ˈbʌntɪŋ] n (flags) Wimpel pl, Fähnchen
pl
buoy [bɔɪ] n Boje f
▶ **buoy up** vt (fig) Auftrieb geben +dat
buoyancy [ˈbɔɪənsɪ] n (of ship, object)
Schwimmfähigkeit f
buoyant [ˈbɔɪənt] adj (ship, object)
schwimmfähig; (market) fest; (economy)
stabil; (prices, currency) fest, stabil; (person,
nature) heiter
burden [ˈbəːdn] n Belastung f; (load) Last f
▷ vt: **to ~ sb with sth** jdn mit etw belasten; **to
be a ~ to sb** jdm zur Last fallen
bureau [ˈbjʊərəʊ] (pl **~x**) n (Brit: writing desk)
Sekretär m; (US: chest of drawers) Kommode f;
(office) Büro nt
bureaucracy [bjʊəˈrɒkrəsɪ] n Bürokratie f
bureaucrat [ˈbjʊərəkræt] n Bürokrat(in)
m(f)
bureaucratic [bjʊərəˈkrætɪk] adj bürokratisch
bureaux [ˈbjʊərəʊz] npl of **bureau**
burgeon [ˈbəːdʒən] vi hervorsprießen
burger [ˈbəːgəʳ] n (inf) Hamburger m
burglar [ˈbəːgləʳ] n Einbrecher(in) m(f)
burglar alarm n Alarmanlage f
burglarize [ˈbəːgləraɪz] (US) vt einbrechen in
+acc
burglary [ˈbəːglərɪ] n Einbruch m
burgle [ˈbəːgl] vt einbrechen in +acc
Burgundy [ˈbəːgəndɪ] n Burgund nt
burial [ˈbɛrɪəl] n Beerdigung f
burial ground n Begräbnisstätte f

b

burlesque [bəːˈlɛsk] n (parody) Persiflage f; (US: Theat) Burleske f

burly [ˈbəːlɪ] adj kräftig, stämmig

Burma [ˈbəːmə] n Birma nt, Burma nt

Burmese [bəːˈmiːz] adj birmanisch, burmesisch ▷ n inv Birmane m, Burmese m, Birmanin f, Burmesin f ▷ n (Ling) Birmanisch nt, Burmesisch nt

burn [bəːn] (pt, pp **burned** or **~t**) vt verbrennen; (fuel) als Brennstoff verwenden; (food) anbrennen lassen; (house etc) niederbrennen ▷ vi brennen; (food) anbrennen ▷ n Verbrennung f; **the cigarette ~t a hole in her dress** die Zigarette brannte ein Loch in ihr Kleid; **I've ~t myself!** ich habe mich verbrannt!

▸ **burn down** vt abbrennen

▸ **burn out** vt: **to ~ o.s. out** (writer etc) sich völlig verausgaben; **the fire ~t itself out** das Feuer brannte aus

burner [ˈbəːnəʳ] n Brenner m

burning [ˈbəːnɪŋ] adj brennend; (sand, desert) glühend heiß

burnish [ˈbəːnɪʃ] vt polieren

⊚ **BURNS' NIGHT**

⊚ Burns' Night ist der am 25. Januar begangene
⊚ Gedenktag für den schottischen
⊚ Dichter Robert Burns (1759–1796). Wo
⊚ Schotten leben, sei es in Schottland
⊚ oder im Ausland, wird dieser Tag mit
⊚ einem Abendessen gefeiert, bei dem
⊚ es als Hauptgericht haggis gibt, der
⊚ mit Dudelsackbegleitung aufgetischt
⊚ wird. Dazu isst man Steckrüben- und
⊚ Kartoffelpüree und trinkt Whisky.
⊚ Während des Essens werden Burns'
⊚ Gedichte vorgelesen, seine Lieder
⊚ gesungen, bestimmte Reden gehalten und
⊚ Trinksprüche ausgegeben.

burnt [bəːnt] pt, pp of **burn**

burnt sugar (Brit) n Karamell m

burp [bəːp] (inf) n Rülpser m ▷ vt (baby) aufstoßen lassen ▷ vi rülpsen

burrow [ˈbʌrəu] n Bau m ▷ vi graben; (rummage) wühlen

bursar [ˈbəːsəʳ] n Schatzmeister m, Finanzverwalter m

bursary [ˈbəːsərɪ] (Brit) n Stipendium nt

burst [bəːst] (pt, pp **~**) vt zum Platzen bringen, platzen lassen ▷ vi platzen ▷ n Salve f; (also: **burst pipe**) (Rohr)bruch m; **the river has ~ its banks** der Fluss ist über die Ufer getreten; **to ~ into flames** in Flammen aufgehen; **to ~ into tears** in Tränen ausbrechen; **to ~ out laughing** in Lachen ausbrechen; **~ blood vessel** geplatzte Ader f; **to be ~ing** with zum Bersten voll sein mit; (pride) fast platzen vor +dat; **to ~ open** aufspringen; **a ~ of energy** ein Ausbruch m von Energie; **a ~ of enthusiasm** ein

Begeisterungsausbruch m; **a ~ of speed** ein Spurt m; **~ of laughter** Lachsalve f; **~ of applause** Beifallssturm m

▸ **burst in on** vt fus: **to ~ in on sb** bei jdm hereinplatzen

▸ **burst into** vt fus (into room) platzen in +acc

▸ **burst out of** vt fus (of room) stürmen or stürzen aus

bury [ˈbɛrɪ] vt begraben; (at funeral) beerdigen; **to ~ one's face in one's hands** das Gesicht in den Händen vergraben; **to ~ one's head in the sand** (fig) den Kopf in den Sand stecken; **to ~ the hatchet** (fig) das Kriegsbeil begraben

bus [bʌs] n (Auto) Bus m, (Omni)bus m; (double decker) Doppeldecker m (inf)

bus boy (US) n Bedienungshilfe f

bush [buʃ] n Busch m, Strauch m; (scrubland) Busch; **to beat about the ~** um den heißen Brei herumreden

bushed [buʃt] (inf) adj (exhausted) groggy

bushel [ˈbuʃl] n Scheffel m

bushfire n Buschfeuer nt

bushy [ˈbuʃɪ] adj buschig

busily [ˈbɪzɪlɪ] adv eifrig; **to be ~ doing sth** eifrig etw tun

business [ˈbɪznɪs] n (matter) Angelegenheit f; (trading) Geschäft nt; (firm) Firma f, Betrieb m; (occupation) Beruf m; **to be away on ~** geschäftlich unterwegs sein; **I'm here on ~** ich bin geschäftlich hier; **he's in the insurance/transport ~** er arbeitet in der Versicherungs-/Transportbranche; **to do ~ with sb** Geschäfte pl mit jdm machen; **it's my ~ to ...** es ist meine Aufgabe, zu ...; **it's none of my ~** es geht mich nichts an; **he means ~** er meint es ernst

business address n Geschäftsadresse f

business card n (Visiten)karte f

businesslike [ˈbɪznɪslaɪk] adj geschäftsmäßig

businessman [ˈbɪznɪsmən] (irreg: like **man**) n Geschäftsmann m

business trip n Geschäftsreise f

businesswoman [ˈbɪznɪswumən] (irreg: like **woman**) n Geschäftsfrau f

busker [ˈbʌskəʳ] (Brit) n Straßenmusikant(in) m(f)

bus lane (Brit) n Busspur f

bus shelter n Wartehäuschen nt

bus station n Busbahnhof m

bus stop n Bushaltestelle f

bust [bʌst] n Busen m; (measurement) Oberweite f; (sculpture) Büste f ▷ adj (inf) kaputt ▷ vt (inf) verhaften; **to go ~** pleitegehen

bustle [ˈbʌsl] n Betrieb m ▷ vi eilig herumlaufen

bustling [ˈbʌslɪŋ] adj belebt

bust-up [ˈbʌstʌp] (Brit: inf) n Krach m

busty [ˈbʌstɪ] adj (woman) vollbusig

busy [ˈbɪzɪ] adj (person) beschäftigt; (shop, street) belebt; (Tel, esp US) besetzt ▷ vt: **to ~ o.s. with** sich beschäftigen mit; **he's a ~ man** er ist ein viel beschäftigter Mann; **he's ~** er hat (zurzeit) viel zu tun

busybody ['bɪzɪbɔdɪ] *n*: **to be a ~** sich ständig einmischen

busy signal (*US*) *n* (*Tel*) Besetztzeichen *nt*

 KEYWORD

but [bʌt] *conj* **1** (*yet*) aber; **not blue but red** nicht blau, sondern rot; **he's not very bright, but he's hard-working** er ist nicht sehr intelligent, aber er ist fleißig **2** (*however*): **I'd love to come, but I'm busy** ich würde gern kommen, bin aber beschäftigt **3** (*showing disagreement, surprise etc*): **but that's far too expensive!** aber das ist viel zu teuer!; **but that's fantastic!** das ist doch toll!

▷ *prep* (*apart from, except*) außer +*dat*; **nothing but trouble** nichts als Ärger; **no-one but him can do it** keiner außer ihm kann es machen; **but for you** wenn Sie nicht gewesen wären; **but for your help** ohne Ihre Hilfe; **I'll do anything but that** ich mache alles, nur nicht das; **the last house but one** das vorletzte Haus; **the next street but one** die übernächste Straße

▷ *adv* (*just, only*) nur; **she's but a child** sie ist doch noch ein Kind; **I can but try** ich kann es ja versuchen

butane ['bju:teɪn] *n* (*also*: **butane gas**) Butan(gas) *nt*

butch [butʃ] (*inf*) *adj* maskulin

butcher ['butʃəʳ] *n* Fleischer *m*, Metzger *m*; (*pej: murderer*) Schlächter *m* ▷ *vt* schlachten; (*prisoners etc*) abschlachten

butcher's ['butʃəz], **butcher's shop** *n* Fleischerei *f*, Metzgerei *f*

butler ['bʌtləʳ] *n* Butler *m*

butt [bʌt] *n* großes Fass *nt*, Tonne *f*; (*thick end*) dickes Ende *nt*; (*of gun*) Kolben *m*; (*of cigarette*) Kippe *f*; (*Brit: fig: target*) Zielscheibe *f*; (*US: inf!*) Arsch *m* ▷ *vt* (*goat*) mit den Hörnern stoßen; (*person*) mit dem Kopf stoßen

▶ **butt in** *vi* sich einmischen, dazwischenfunken (*inf*)

butter ['bʌtəʳ] *n* Butter *f* ▷ *vt* buttern

buttercup ['bʌtəkʌp] *n* Butterblume *f*

butter dish *n* Butterdose *f*

butterfingers ['bʌtəfɪŋgəz] (*inf*) *n* Schussel *m*

butterfly ['bʌtəflaɪ] *n* Schmetterling *m*; (*Swimming: also*: **butterfly stroke**) Schmetterlingsstil *m*, Butterfly *m*

buttocks ['bʌtəks] *npl* Gesäß *nt*

button ['bʌtn] *n* Knopf *m*; (*US: badge*) Plakette *f* ▷ *vt* (*also*: **button up**) zuknöpfen ▷ *vi* geknöpft werden

buttonhole ['bʌtnhəul] *n* Knopfloch *nt*; (*flower*) Blume *f* im Knopfloch ▷ *vt* zu fassen bekommen, sich *dat* schnappen (*inf*)

buttress ['bʌtrɪs] *n* Strebepfeiler *m*

buxom ['bʌksəm] *adj* drall

buy [baɪ] (*pt, pp* **bought**) *vt* kaufen; (*company*) aufkaufen ▷ *n* Kauf *m*; **that was a good/bad ~** das war ein guter/schlechter Kauf;

to ~ sb sth jdm etw kaufen; **to ~ sth from sb** etw bei jdm kaufen; (*from individual*) jdm etw abkaufen; **to ~ sb a drink** jdm einen ausgeben (*inf*)

▶ **buy back** *vt* zurückkaufen

▶ **buy in** (*Brit*) *vt* einkaufen

▶ **buy into** (*Brit*) *vt fus* sich einkaufen in +*acc*

▶ **buy off** *vt* kaufen

▶ **buy out** *vt* (*partner*) auszahlen; (*business*) aufkaufen

▶ **buy up** *vt* aufkaufen

buyer ['baɪəʳ] *n* Käufer(in) *m(f)*; (*Comm*) Einkäufer(in) *m(f)*

buyer's market ['baɪəz-] *n* Käufermarkt *m*

buyout ['baɪaut] *n* (*of firm: by workers, management*) Aufkauf *m*

buzz [bʌz] *vi* summen, brummen; (*saw*) kreischen ▷ *vt* rufen; (*with buzzer*) (mit dem Summer) rufen; (*Aviat: plane, building*) dicht vorbeifliegen an +*dat* ▷ *n* Summen *nt*, Brummen *nt*; (*inf*): **to give sb a ~** jdn anrufen; **my head is ~ing** mir schwirrt der Kopf

▶ **buzz off** (*inf*) *vi* abhauen

buzzard ['bʌzəd] *n* Bussard *m*

buzzer ['bʌzəʳ] *n* Summer *m*

buzz word (*inf*) *n* Modewort *nt*

 KEYWORD

by [baɪ] *prep* **1** (*referring to cause, agent*) von +*dat*, durch +*acc*; **killed by lightning** vom Blitz *or* durch einen Blitz getötet; **a painting by Picasso** ein Bild von Picasso

2 (*referring to method, manner, means*): **by bus/car/train** mit dem Bus/Auto/Zug; **to pay by cheque** mit *or* per Scheck bezahlen; **by saving hard, he was able to …** indem er eisern sparte, konnte er …

3 (*via, through*) über +*acc*; **we came by Dover** wir sind über Dover gekommen

4 (*close to*) bei +*dat*, an +*dat*; **the house by the river** das Haus am Fluss

5 (*past*) an … *dat* vorbei; **she rushed by me** sie eilte an mir vorbei

6 (*not later than*) bis +*acc*; **by 4 o'clock** bis 4 Uhr; **by this time tomorrow** morgen um diese Zeit

7 (*amount*): **by the kilo/metre** kilo-/meterweise; **to be paid by the hour** stundenweise bezahlt werden

8 (*Math, measure*): **to divide by 3** durch 3 teilen; **to multiply by 3** mit 3 malnehmen; **it missed me by inches** es hat mich um Zentimeter verfehlt

9 (*according to*): **to play by the rules** sich an die Regeln halten; **it's all right by me** von mir aus ist es in Ordnung

10: **(all) by myself/himself** *etc* (ganz) allein

11: **by the way** übrigens

▷ *adv* **1** *see* **go**, **pass** *etc*

2: **by and by** irgendwann

3: **by and large** im Großen und Ganzen

bye ['baɪ], **bye-bye** ['baɪ'baɪ] *excl* (auf) Wiedersehen, tschüss (*inf*)

bye-law ['baɪlɔː] *n see* **by-law**

by-election ['baɪɪlɛkʃən] (*Brit*) *n* Nachwahl *f*

Byelorussia [bjɛləu'rʌʃə] *n* = **Belorussia**

Byelorussian [bjɛləu'rʌʃən] *adj, n* = **Belarussian**

bygone ['baɪgɒn] *adj* (längst) vergangen
▷ *n*: **let ~s be ~s** wir sollten die Vergangenheit ruhen lassen

by-law ['baɪlɔː] *n* Verordnung *f*

bypass ['baɪpɑːs] *n* Umgehungsstraße *f*; (*Med*)

Bypassoperation *f* ▷ *vt* (*also fig*) umgehen

by-product ['baɪprɒdʌkt] *n* Nebenprodukt *nt*

byre ['baɪəʳ] (*Brit*) *n* Kuhstall *m*

bystander ['baɪstændəʳ] *n* Zuschauer(in) *m(f)*

byte [baɪt] *n* (*Comput*) Byte *nt*

byway ['baɪweɪ] *n* Seitenweg *m*

byword ['baɪwəːd] *n*: **to be a ~ for** der Inbegriff +*gen* sein, gleichbedeutend sein mit

by-your-leave ['baɪjɔːˈliːv] *n*: **without so much as a ~** ohne auch nur (um Erlaubnis) zu fragen

Cc

C¹, c¹ [si:] n (letter) C nt, c nt; (Scol) ≈ Drei f, ≈
Befriedigend nt; **C for Charlie** ≈ C wie Cäsar
C² [si:] n (Mus) C nt, c nt
C³ [si:] abbr = **Celsius; centigrade**
c² abbr = **century**; (= circa) ca.; (US etc: = cent(s))
Cent
CA n abbr (Brit) = **chartered accountant** ▷ abbr =
Central America; (US: Post) = California
C/A abbr (Comm) = **capital account; credit
account; current account**
ca. abbr (= circa) ca.
CAA n abbr (Brit) = **Civil Aviation
Authority**; (US: = Civil Aeronautics Authority)
Zivilluftfahrtbehörde
CAB (Brit) n abbr = **Citizens' Advice Bureau**
cab [kæb] n Taxi nt; (of truck, train etc)
Führerhaus nt; (horse-drawn) Droschke f
cabaret ['kæbəreɪ] n Kabarett nt
cabbage ['kæbɪdʒ] n Kohl m
cabbie, cabby ['kæbɪ] n Taxifahrer(in) m(f)
cab driver n Taxifahrer(in) m(f)
cabin ['kæbɪn] n Kabine f; (house) Hütte f
cabin cruiser n Kajütboot nt
cabinet ['kæbɪnɪt] n kleiner Schrank m;
(also: **display cabinet**) Vitrine f; (Pol) Kabinett
nt
cabinet-maker ['kæbɪnɪt'meɪkər] n
Möbeltischler m
cabinet minister n Mitglied nt des Kabinetts,
Minister(in) m(f)
cable ['keɪbl] n Kabel nt ▷ vt kabeln
cable car n (Draht)seilbahn f
cablegram ['keɪblgræm] n (Übersee)
telegramm nt, Kabel nt
cable railway n Seilbahn f
cable television n Kabelfernsehen nt
cable TV n = **cable television**
cache [kæʃ] n Versteck nt, geheimes Lager nt; **a
~ of food** ein geheimes Proviantlager
cackle ['kækl] vi (person: laugh) meckernd
lachen; (hen) gackern
cacti ['kæktaɪ] npl of **cactus**
cactus ['kæktəs] (pl **cacti**) n Kaktus m
CAD n abbr (= computer-aided design) CAD nt
caddie ['kædɪ] n (Golf) Caddie m
caddy ['kædɪ] n = **caddie**
cadence ['keɪdəns] n (of voice) Tonfall m
cadet [kə'dɛt] n Kadett m; **police ~**

Polizeianwärter(in) m(f)
cadge [kædʒ] (inf) vt: **to ~ (from** or **off)**
schnorren (bei or von +dat); **to ~ a lift with sb**
von jdm mitgenommen werden
cadger ['kædʒər] (Brit: inf) n Schnorrer(in) m(f)
cadre ['kædrɪ] n Kader m
Caesarean [si:'zɛərɪən] n: **~ (section)**
Kaiserschnitt m
CAF (Brit) abbr (= cost and freight) cf
café ['kæfeɪ] n Café nt
cafeteria [kæfɪ'tɪərɪə] n Cafeteria f
caffeine, caffein ['kæfi:n] n Koffein nt
cage [keɪdʒ] n Käfig m; (of lift) Fahrkorb m ▷ vt
einsperren
cagey ['keɪdʒɪ] (inf) adj vorsichtig; (evasive)
ausweichend
cagoule [kə'gu:l] n Regenjacke f
cahoots [kə'hu:ts] (inf) n: **to be in ~ with**
unter einer Decke stecken mit
CAI n abbr (= computer-aided instruction) CAI nt
Cairo ['kaɪərəʊ] n Kairo nt
cajole [kə'dʒəʊl] vt: **to ~ sb into doing sth** jdn
bereden, etw zu tun
cake [keɪk] n Kuchen m; (small) Gebäckstück
nt; (of soap) Stück nt; **it's a piece of ~** (inf) das
ist ein Kinderspiel or ein Klacks; **he wants
to have his ~ and eat it (too)** (fig) er will das
eine, ohne das andere zu lassen
caked [keɪkt] adj: **~ with** (mud, blood) verkrustet
mit
cake shop n Konditorei f
Cal. (US) abbr (Post) = California
calamine lotion ['kæləmaɪn-] n Galmeilotion f
calamitous [kə'læmɪtəs] adj katastrophal
calamity [kə'læmɪtɪ] n Katastrophe f
calcium ['kælsɪəm] n Kalzium nt
calculate ['kælkjuleɪt] vt (work out) berechnen;
(estimate) abschätzen
  ▶ **calculate on** vt fus: **to ~ on sth** mit etw
rechnen; **to ~ on doing sth** damit rechnen,
etw zu tun
calculated ['kælkjuleɪtɪd] adj (insult) bewusst;
(action) vorsätzlich; **a ~ risk** ein kalkuliertes
Risiko
calculating ['kælkjuleɪtɪŋ] adj (scheming)
berechnend
calculation [kælkju'leɪʃən] n (see vt)
Berechnung f; Abschätzung f; (sum) Rechnung

f

calculator ['kælkjuleɪtə^r] n Rechner m
calculus ['kælkjuləs] n Infinitesimalrechnung f; **integral/differential ~** Integral-/ Differenzialrechnung f
calendar ['kæləndə^r] n Kalender m; (timetable, schedule) (Termin)kalender m
calendar month n Kalendermonat m
calendar year n Kalenderjahr nt
calf [kɑːf] (pl **calves**) n Kalb nt; (of elephant, seal etc) Junge(s) nt; (also: **calfskin**) Kalb(s)leder nt; (Anat) Wade f
caliber ['kælɪbə^r] (US) n = **calibre**
calibrate ['kælɪbreɪt] vt (gun etc) kalibrieren; (scale of measuring instrument) eichen
calibre, (US) **caliber** ['kælɪbə^r] n Kaliber nt; (of person) Format nt
calico ['kælɪkəu] n (Brit) Kattun m, Kaliko m; (US) bedruckter Kattun
Calif. (US) abbr (Post) = **California**
California [kælɪ'fɔːnɪə] n Kalifornien nt
calipers ['kælɪpəz] (US) npl = **callipers**
call [kɔːl] vt (name, consider) nennen; (shout out, summon) rufen; (Tel) anrufen; (witness, flight) aufrufen; (meeting) einberufen; (strike) ausrufen ▷ vi rufen; (Tel) anrufen; (visit: also: **call in, call round**) vorbeigehen, vorbeikommen ▷ n Ruf m; (Tel) Anruf m; (visit) Besuch m; (for a service etc) Nachfrage f; (for flight etc) Aufruf m; (fig: lure) Ruf m, Verlockung f; **to be ~ed** (named) heißen; **who is ~ing?** (Tel) wer spricht da bitte?; **London ~ing** (Radio) hier ist London; **please give me a ~ at 7** rufen Sie mich bitte um 7 an; **to make a ~** ein (Telefon)gespräch führen; **to pay a ~ on sb** jdn besuchen; **on ~** dienstbereit; **to be on ~** einsatzbereit sein; (doctor etc) Bereitschaftsdienst haben; **there's not much ~ for these items** es besteht keine große Nachfrage nach diesen Dingen
▶ **call at** vt fus (subj: ship) anlaufen; (: train) halten in +dat
▶ **call back** vi (return) wiederkommen; (Tel) zurückrufen ▷ vt (Tel) zurückrufen
▶ **call for** vt fus (demand) fordern; (fetch) abholen
▶ **call in** vt (doctor, expert, police) zurate ziehen; (books, cars, stock etc) aus dem Verkehr ziehen ▷ vi vorbeigehen, vorbeikommen
▶ **call off** vt absagen
▶ **call on** vt fus besuchen; (appeal to) appellieren an +acc; **to ~ on sb to do sth** jdn bitten or auffordern, etw zu tun
▶ **call out** vi rufen ▷ vt rufen; (police, troops) alarmieren
▶ **call up** vt (Mil) einberufen; (Tel) anrufen
Callanetics® n sing Callanetics f
call box (Brit) n Telefonzelle f
call centre n Telefoncenter nt, Callcenter nt
caller ['kɔːlə^r] n Besucher(in) m(f); **hold the line, ~!** (Tel) bitte bleiben Sie am Apparat!
caller ID ['kɔːlə^raɪdiː] n (Tel) Anruferkennung

m; (of email, text message) Absenderkennung m
call girl n Callgirl nt
call-in ['kɔːlɪn] (US) n (Radio, TV) Phone-in nt
calling ['kɔːlɪŋ] n (trade) Beruf m; (vocation) Berufung f
calling card (US) n Visitenkarte f
callipers, (US) **calipers** ['kælɪpəz] npl (Math) Tastzirkel m; (Med) Schiene f
callous ['kæləs] adj herzlos
callousness ['kæləsnɪs] n Herzlosigkeit f
callow ['kæləu] adj unreif
calm [kɑːm] adj ruhig; (unworried) gelassen ▷ n Ruhe f ▷ vt beruhigen; (fears) zerstreuen; (grief) lindern
▶ **calm down** vt beruhigen ▷ vi sich beruhigen
calmly ['kɑːmlɪ] adv (see adj) ruhig; gelassen
calmness ['kɑːmnɪs] n (see adj) Ruhe f; Gelassenheit f
Calor gas® ['kælə-] n Butangas nt
calorie ['kælərɪ] n Kalorie f; **low-~ product** kalorienarmes Produkt nt
calve [kɑːv] vi kalben
calves [kɑːvz] npl of **calf**
CAM n abbr (= computer-aided manufacture) CAM nt
camber ['kæmbə^r] n Wölbung f
Cambodia [kæm'bəudɪə] n Kambodscha nt
Cambodian [kæm'bəudɪən] adj kambodschanisch ▷ n Kambodschaner(in) m(f)
Cambs (Brit) abbr (Post) = **Cambridgeshire**
camcorder ['kæmkɔːdə^r] n Camcorder m, Kamerarekorder m
came [keɪm] pt of **come**
camel ['kæməl] n Kamel nt
cameo ['kæmɪəu] n Kamee f; (Theat, Liter) Miniatur f
camera ['kæmərə] n (Cine, Phot) Kamera f; (also: **cine camera, movie camera**) Filmkamera f; **35 mm ~** Kleinbildkamera f; **in ~** (Law) unter Ausschluss der Öffentlichkeit
cameraman ['kæmərəmæn] (irreg: like **man**) n Kameramann m
camera phone n Kameratelefon nt
Cameroon [kæmə'ruːn] n Kamerun nt
Cameroun [kæmə'ruːn] n = **Cameroon**
camomile ['kæməumaɪl] n Kamille f
camouflage ['kæməflɑːʒ] n Tarnung f ▷ vt tarnen
camp [kæmp] n Lager nt; (barracks) Kaserne f ▷ vi zelten ▷ adj (effeminate) tuntenhaft (inf)
campaign [kæm'peɪn] n (Mil) Feldzug m; (Pol etc) Kampagne f ▷ vi kämpfen; **to ~ for/ against** sich einsetzen für/gegen
campaigner [kæm'peɪnə^r] n: **~ for** Befürworter(in) m(f) +gen; **~ against** Gegner(in) m(f) +gen
camp bed (Brit) n Campingliege f
camper ['kæmpə^r] n (person) Camper m; (vehicle) Wohnmobil nt
camping ['kæmpɪŋ] n Camping nt; **to go ~** zelten gehen, campen
camping site, camp site n Campingplatz m
campus ['kæmpəs] n (Univ)

Universitätsgelände nt, Campus m

camshaft ['kæmʃɑːft] n Nockenwelle f

can¹ [kæn] n Büchse f, Dose f; (for oil, water) Kanister m ▷ vt eindosen, in Büchsen or Dosen einmachen; **a ~ of beer** eine Dose Bier; **he had to carry the ~** (Brit: inf) er musste die Sache ausbaden

 KEYWORD

can² (negative **cannot**, **can't**, conditional and pt **could**) aux vb **1** (be able to, know how to) können; **you can do it if you try** du kannst es, wenn du es nur versuchst; **I can't see you** ich kann dich nicht sehen; **I can swim/drive** ich kann schwimmen/Auto fahren; **can you speak English?** sprechen Sie Englisch?

2 (may) können, dürfen; **can I use your phone?** kann or darf ich Ihr Telefon benutzen?; **could I have a word with you?** könnte ich Sie mal sprechen?

3 (expressing disbelief, puzzlement): **it can't be true!** das darf doch nicht wahr sein!

4 (expressing possibility, suggestion, etc): **he could be in the library** er könnte in der Bibliothek sein

Canada ['kænədə] n Kanada nt

Canadian [kə'neɪdɪən] adj kanadisch ▷ n Kanadier(in) m(f)

canal [kə'næl] n (also Anat) Kanal m

Canaries [kə'nɛərɪz] npl = **Canary Islands**

canary [kə'nɛərɪ] n Kanarienvogel m

Canary Islands [kə'nɛərɪ 'aɪləndz] npl: **the ~** die Kanarischen Inseln pl

Canberra ['kænbərə] n Canberra nt

cancel ['kænsəl] vt absagen; (reservation) abbestellen; (train, flight) ausfallen lassen; (contract) annullieren; (order) stornieren; (cross out) durchstreichen; (stamp) entwerten; (cheque) ungültig machen

▶ **cancel out** vt aufheben; **they ~ each other out** sie heben sich gegenseitig auf

cancellation [kænsə'leɪʃən] n Absage f; (of reservation) Abbestellung f; (of train, flight) Ausfall m; (Tourism) Rücktritt m

cancer ['kænsə^r] n (also: **Cancer**: Astrol) Krebs m; **to be C~** (ein) Krebs sein

cancerous ['kænsrəs] adj krebsartig

cancer patient n Krebskranke(r) f(m)

cancer research n Krebsforschung f

c and f (Brit) abbr (Comm: = cost and freight) cf

candid ['kændɪd] adj offen, ehrlich

candidacy ['kændɪdəsɪ] n Kandidatur f

candidate ['kændɪdeɪt] n Kandidat(in) m(f); (for job) Bewerber(in) m(f)

candidature ['kændɪdətʃə^r] (Brit) n = **candidacy**

candied ['kændɪd] adj kandiert; **~ apple** (US) kandierter Apfel m

candle ['kændl] n Kerze f; (of tallow) Talglicht nt

candleholder ['kændlhəʊldə^r] n see **candlestick**

candlelight ['kændllaɪt] n: **by ~** bei Kerzenlicht

candlestick ['kændlstɪk] n (also, candleholder) Kerzenhalter m; (bigger, ornate) Kerzenleuchter m

candour, (US) **candor** ['kændə^r] n Offenheit f

C & W n abbr = **country and western**

candy ['kændɪ] n (also: **sugar-candy**) Kandis(zucker) m; (US) Bonbon nt or m

candyfloss ['kændɪflɒs] (Brit) n Zuckerwatte f

candy store (US) n Süßwarenhandlung f

cane [keɪn] n Rohr nt; (stick) Stock m; (: for walking) (Spazier)stock m ▷ vt (Brit: Scol) mit dem Stock schlagen

canine ['keɪnaɪn] adj (species) Hunde-

canister ['kænɪstə^r] n Dose f; (pressurized container) Sprühdose f; (of gas, chemicals etc) Kanister m

cannabis ['kænəbɪs] n Haschisch nt; (also: **cannabis plant**) Hanf m, Cannabis m

canned [kænd] adj Dosen-; (inf: music) aus der Konserve; (US: inf: worker) entlassen, rausgeschmissen (inf)

cannibal ['kænɪbəl] n Kannibale m, Kannibalin f

cannibalism ['kænɪbəlɪzəm] n Kannibalismus m

cannibalization [kænɪbəlaɪ'zeɪʃn] n (Econ) Kannibalisierung f

cannon ['kænən] (pl ~ or **cannons**) n Kanone f

cannonball ['kænənbɔːl] n Kanonenkugel f

cannon fodder n Kanonenfutter nt

cannot ['kænɒt] = **can not**

canny ['kænɪ] adj schlau

canoe [kə'nuː] n Kanu nt

canoeing [kə'nuːɪŋ] n Kanusport m

canon ['kænən] n Kanon m; (clergyman) Kanoniker m, Kanonikus m

canonize ['kænənaɪz] vt kanonisieren, heiligsprechen

can-opener ['kænəʊpnə^r] n Dosenöffner m, Büchsenöffner m

canopy ['kænəpɪ] n (also fig) Baldachin m

cant [kænt] n scheinheiliges Gerede nt

can't [kænt] = **can not**

Cantab. (Brit) abbr (in degree titles: = Cantabrigiensis) der Universität Cambridge

cantankerous [kæn'tæŋkərəs] adj mürrisch

canteen [kæn'tiːn] n (in school, workplace) Kantine f; (: mobile) Feldküche f; (Brit: of cutlery) Besteckkasten m

canter ['kæntə^r] vi leicht galoppieren, kantern ▷ n leichter Galopp m, Kanter m

cantilever ['kæntɪliːvə^r] n Ausleger m

canvas ['kænvəs] n Leinwand f; (painting) Gemälde nt; (Naut) Segeltuch nt; **under ~** im Zelt

canvass ['kænvəs] vt (opinions, views) erforschen; (person) für seine Partei zu gewinnen suchen; (place) Wahlwerbung machen in +dat ▷ vi: **to ~ for ...** (Pol) um Stimmen für ... werben

canvasser ['kænvəsə^r] n (Pol) Wahlhelfer(in) m(f)

canvassing ['kænvəsɪŋ] n (Pol) Wahlwerbung f

canyon ['kænjən] n Cañon m

CAP n abbr (= Common Agricultural Policy) gemeinsame Agrarpolitik f der EG

cap [kæp] n Mütze f, Kappe f; (of pen) (Verschluss)kappe f; (of bottle) Verschluss m, Deckel m; (contraceptive: also: **Dutch cap**) Pessar nt; (for toy gun) Zündplättchen nt; (for swimming) Bademütze f, Badekappe f; (Sport) Ehrenkappe, die Nationalspielern verliehen wird ▷ vt (outdo) überbieten; (Sport) für die Nationalmannschaft aufstellen; **~ped with** ... mit ... obendrauf; **and to ~ it all**, ... und obendrein ...

capability [keɪpə'bɪlɪtɪ] n Fähigkeit f; (Mil) Potenzial nt

capable ['keɪpəbl] adj fähig; **to be ~ of doing sth** etw tun können, fähig sein, etw zu tun; **to be ~ of sth** (interpretation etc) etw zulassen

capacious [kə'peɪʃəs] adj geräumig

capacity [kə'pæsɪtɪ] n Fassungsvermögen nt; (of lift etc) Höchstlast f; (capability) Fähigkeit f; (position, role) Eigenschaft f; (of factory) Kapazität f; **filled to ~** randvoll; (stadium etc) bis auf den letzten Platz besetzt; **in his ~ as** ... in seiner Eigenschaft als ...; **this work is beyond my ~** zu dieser Arbeit bin ich nicht fähig; **in an advisory ~** in beratender Funktion; **to work at full ~** voll ausgelastet sein

cape [keɪp] n Kap nt; (cloak) Cape nt, Umhang m

Cape of Good Hope n: **the ~** das Kap der guten Hoffnung

caper ['keɪpər] n (Culin: usu pl) Kaper f; (prank) Eskapade f, Kapriole f

Cape Town n Kapstadt nt

capita ['kæpɪtə] see **per capita**

capital ['kæpɪtl] n (also: **capital city**) Hauptstadt f; (money) Kapital nt; (also: **capital letter**) Großbuchstabe m

capital account n Kapitalverkehrsbilanz f; (of country) Kapitalkonto nt

capital allowance n (Anlage)abschreibung f

capital assets npl Kapitalvermögen nt

capital expenditure n Kapitalaufwendungen pl

capital gains tax n Kapitalertragssteuer f

capital goods npl Investitionsgüter pl

capital-intensive ['kæpɪtlɪn'tensɪv] adj kapitalintensiv

capitalism ['kæpɪtəlɪzəm] n Kapitalismus m

capitalist ['kæpɪtəlɪst] adj kapitalistisch ▷ n Kapitalist(in) m(f)

capitalize ['kæpɪtəlaɪz] vt (Comm) kapitalisieren ▷ vi: **to ~ on** Kapital schlagen aus

capital punishment n Todesstrafe f

capital transfer tax (Brit) n Erbschafts- und Schenkungssteuer f

Capitol ['kæpɪtl] n: **the ~** das Kapitol; siehe

Info-Artikel

○ **CAPITOL**
○
○ Capitol ist das Gebäude in Washington
○ auf dem Capitol Hill, in dem der
○ Kongress der USA zusammentritt.
○ Die Bezeichnung wird in vielen
○ amerikanischen Bundesstaaten auch für
○ das Parlamentsgebäude des jeweiligen
○ Staates verwendet.

capitulate [kə'pɪtjuleɪt] vi kapitulieren

capitulation [kəpɪtju'leɪʃən] n Kapitulation f

capricious [kə'prɪʃəs] adj launisch

Capricorn ['kæprɪkɔ:n] n (Astrol) Steinbock m; **to be ~** (ein) Steinbock sein

caps. [kæps] abbr (= capital letters) Großbuchstaben pl

capsize [kæp'saɪz] vt zum Kentern bringen ▷ vi kentern

capstan ['kæpstən] n Poller m

capsule ['kæpsju:l] n Kapsel f

Capt. abbr (Mil) = **captain**

captain ['kæptɪn] n Kapitän m; (of plane) (Flug) kapitän m; (in army) Hauptmann m ▷ vt (ship) befehligen; (team) anführen

caption ['kæpʃən] n Bildunterschrift f

captivate ['kæptɪveɪt] vt fesseln

captive ['kæptɪv] adj gefangen ▷ n Gefangene(r) f(m)

captivity [kæp'tɪvɪtɪ] n Gefangenschaft f

captor ['kæptər] n: **his ~s** diejenigen, die ihn gefangen nahmen

capture ['kæptʃər] vt (animal) (ein)fangen; (person) gefangen nehmen; (town, country, share of market) erobern; (attention) erregen; (Comput) erfassen ▷ n (of animal) Einfangen nt; (of person) Gefangennahme f; (of town etc) Eroberung f; (also: **data capture**) Erfassung f

car [ka:r] n Auto nt, Wagen m; (Rail) Wagen m; **by ~** mit dem Auto or Wagen

carafe [kə'ræf] n Karaffe f

caramel ['kærəməl] n Karamelle f, Karamellbonbon m or nt; (burnt sugar) Karamell m

carat ['kærət] n Karat nt; **18 ~ gold** achtzehnkarätiges Gold

caravan ['kærəvæn] n (Brit) Wohnwagen m; (in desert) Karawane f

caravan site (Brit) n Campingplatz m für Wohnwagen

caraway seed n Kümmel m

carbohydrate [ka:bəu'haɪdreɪt] n Kohle(n) hydrat nt

carbolic acid [ka:'bɔlɪk-] n Karbolsäure f

car bomb n Autobombe f

carbon ['ka:bən] n Kohlenstoff m

carbonated ['ka:bəneɪtɪd] adj mit Kohlensäure (versetzt)

carbon copy n Durchschlag m

carbon dioxide n Kohlendioxid nt

carbon footprint n ökologischer Fußabdruck

carbon monoxide [mɔ'nɔksaɪd] *n* Kohlenmonoxid *nt*

carbon paper *n* Kohlepapier *nt*

carbon ribbon *n* Kohlefarbband *nt*

car-boot sale *n* auf einem Parkplatz stattfindender Flohmarkt mit dem Kofferraum als Auslage

carburettor, (*US*) **carburetor** [kɑ:bju'rɛtəʳ] *n* Vergaser *m*

carcass ['kɑ:kəs] *n* Kadaver *m*

carcinogenic [kɑ:sɪnə'dʒɛnɪk] *adj* krebserregend, karzinogen

card [kɑ:d] *n* Karte *f*; (*material*) (dünne) Pappe *f*, Karton *m*; (*also*: **record card, index card** *etc*) (Kartei)karte *f*; (*also*: **membership card**) (Mitglieds)ausweis *m*; (*also*: **playing card**) (Spiel)karte *f*; (*also*: **visiting card**) (Visiten) karte *f*; **to play ~s** Karten spielen

cardamom ['kɑ:dəməm] *n* Kardamom *m*

cardboard ['kɑ:dbɔ:d] *n* Pappe *f*

cardboard box *n* (Papp)karton *m*

card-carrying ['kɑ:d'kærɪɪŋ] *adj*: **~ member** eingetragenes Mitglied *nt*

card game *n* Kartenspiel *nt*

cardiac ['kɑ:dɪæk] *adj* (*failure, patient*) Herz-

cardigan ['kɑ:dɪgən] *n* Strickjacke *f*

cardinal ['kɑ:dɪnl] *adj* (*principle, importance*) Haupt- ▷ *n* Kardinal *m*; **~ number** Kardinalzahl *f*; **~ sin** Todsünde *f*

card index *n* Kartei *f*

cardphone *n* Kartentelefon *nt*

cardsharp ['kɑ:dʃɑ:p] *n* Falschspieler *m*

card vote (*Brit*) *n* Abstimmung *f* durch Wahlmänner

CARE [kɛəʳ] *n abbr* (= *Cooperative for American Relief Everywhere*) karitative Organisation

care [kɛəʳ] *n* (*attention*) Versorgung *f*; (*worry*) Sorge *f*; (*charge*) Obhut *f*, Fürsorge *f* ▷ *vi*: **to ~ about** sich kümmern um; **~ of** bei; **"handle with ~"** „Vorsicht, zerbrechlich"; **in sb's ~** in jds *dat* Obhut; **to take ~** aufpassen; **to take ~ to do sth** sich bemühen, etw zu tun; **to take ~ of** sich kümmern um; **the child has been taken into ~** das Kind ist in Pflege genommen worden; **would you ~ to/for ...?** möchten Sie gerne ...?; **I wouldn't ~ to do it** ich möchte es nicht gern tun; **I don't ~** es ist mir egal *or* gleichgültig; **I couldn't ~ less** es ist mir völlig egal *or* gleichgültig

▶ **care for** *vt fus* (*look after*) sich kümmern um; (*like*) mögen

career [kə'rɪəʳ] *n* (*job, profession*) Beruf *m*; (*life*) Laufbahn *f* ▷ *vi* (*also*: **career along**) rasen

career girl *n* Karrierefrau *f*

careers officer [kə'rɪəz-] *n* Berufsberater(in) *m(f)*

career woman *n* Karrierefrau *f*

carefree ['kɛəfri:] *adj* sorglos

careful ['kɛəful] *adj* vorsichtig; (*thorough*) sorgfältig; **(be) ~!** Vorsicht!, pass auf!; **to be ~ with one's money** sein Geld gut zusammenhalten

carefully ['kɛəfəlɪ] *adv* vorsichtig; (*methodically*) sorgfältig

careless ['kɛəlɪs] *adj* leichtsinnig; (*negligent*) nachlässig; (*remark*) gedankenlos

carelessly ['kɛəlɪslɪ] *adv* (*see adj*) leichtsinnig; nachlässig; gedankenlos

carelessness ['kɛəlɪsnɪs] *n* (*see adj*) Leichtsinn *m*; Nachlässigkeit *f*; Gedankenlosigkeit *f*

caress [kə'rɛs] *n* Streicheln *nt* ▷ *vt* streicheln

caretaker ['kɛəteɪkəʳ] *n* Hausmeister(in) *m(f)*

caretaker government (*Brit*) *n* geschäftsführende Regierung *f*

car ferry *n* Autofähre *f*

cargo ['kɑ:gəu] (*pl* **~es**) *n* Fracht *f*, Ladung *f*

cargo boat *n* Frachter *m*, Frachtschiff *nt*

cargo plane *n* Transportflugzeug *nt*

car hire (*Brit*) *n* Autovermietung *f*

Caribbean [kærɪ'bi:ən] *adj* karibisch ▷ *n*: **the ~ (Sea)** die Karibik, das Karibische Meer

caricature ['kærɪkətjuəʳ] *n* Karikatur *f*

caring ['kɛərɪŋ] *adj* liebevoll; (*society, organization*) sozial; (*behaviour*) fürsorglich

carjacking *n* Angriff durch Banditen, die gewaltsam in PKWs eindringen und den Wagen samt Insassen entführen

carnage ['kɑ:nɪdʒ] *n* (*Mil*) Blutbad *nt*, Gemetzel *nt*

carnal ['kɑ:nl] *adj* fleischlich, sinnlich

carnation [kɑ:'neɪʃən] *n* Nelke *f*

carnival ['kɑ:nɪvl] *n* Karneval *m*; (*US: funfair*) Kirmes *f*

carnivorous [kɑ:'nɪvərəs] *adj* fleischfressend

carol ['kærəl] *n*: **(Christmas) ~** Weihnachtslied *nt*

carouse [kə'rauz] *vi* zechen

carousel [kærə'sɛl] (*US*) *n* Karussell *nt*

carp [kɑ:p] *n* Karpfen *m*

▶ **carp at** *vt fus* herumnörgeln an +*dat*

car park *n* Parkplatz *m*; (*building*) Parkhaus *nt*

car-park ticket *n* Parkschein *m*

carpenter ['kɑ:pɪntəʳ] *n* Zimmermann *m*

carpentry ['kɑ:pɪntrɪ] *n* Zimmerhandwerk *nt*; (*school subject, hobby*) Tischlern *nt*

carpet ['kɑ:pɪt] *n* (*also fig*) Teppich *m* ▷ *vt* (mit Teppichen/Teppichboden) auslegen; **fitted ~** (*Brit*) Teppichboden *m*

carpet bombing *n* Flächenbombardierung *f*

carpet slippers *npl* Pantoffeln *pl*

carpet-sweeper ['kɑ:pɪtswi:pəʳ] *n* Teppichkehrer *m*

car phone *n* (*Telec*) Autotelefon *nt*

carport ['kɑ:pɔ:t] *n* Einstellplatz *m*

car rental *n* Autovermietung *f*

carriage ['kærɪdʒ] *n* (*Rail, of typewriter*) Wagen *m*; (*horse-drawn vehicle*) Kutsche *f*; (*of goods*) Beförderung *f*; (*transport costs*) Beförderungskosten *pl*; **~ forward** Fracht zahlt Empfänger; **~ free** frachtfrei; **~ paid** frei Haus

carriage return *n* (*on typewriter*) Wagenrücklauf *m*; (*Comput*) Return *nt*

carriageway ['kærɪdʒweɪ] (*Brit*) *n* Fahrbahn *f*

carrier ['kærɪəʳ] *n* Spediteur *m*, Transportunternehmer *m*; (*Med*) Überträger *m*

carrier bag (*Brit*) *n* Tragetasche *f*, Tragetüte *f*
carrier pigeon *n* Brieftaube *f*
carrion ['kærɪən] *n* Aas *nt*
carrot ['kærət] *n* Möhre *f*, Mohrrübe *f*, Karotte *f*; (*fig*) Köder *m*
carry ['kærɪ] *vt* tragen; (*transport*) transportieren; (*a motion, bill*) annehmen; (*responsibilities etc*) mit sich bringen; (*disease, virus*) übertragen ▷ *vi* (*sound*) tragen; **to get carried away** (*fig*) sich hinreißen lassen; **this loan carries 10% interest** dieses Darlehen wird mit 10% verzinst
▶ **carry forward** *vt* übertragen, vortragen
▶ **carry on** *vi* weitermachen; (*inf: make a fuss*) (ein) Theater machen ▷ *vt* fortführen; **to ~ on with sth** mit etw weitermachen; **to ~ on singing/eating** weitersingen/-essen
▶ **carry out** *vt* (*orders*) ausführen; (*investigation*) durchführen; (*idea*) in die Tat umsetzen; (*threat*) wahr machen
carrycot ['kærɪkɔt] (*Brit*) *n* Babytragetasche *f*
carry-on ['kærɪ'ɔn] (*inf*) *n* Theater *nt*
cart [kɑːt] *n* Wagen *m*, Karren *m*; (*for passengers*) Wagen *m*; (*handcart*) (Hand)wagen *m* ▷ *vt* (*inf*) mit sich herumschleppen
carte blanche ['kɑːt'blɔ̃ʃ] *n*: **to give sb ~** jdm Carte blanche *or* (eine) Blankovollmacht geben
cartel [kɑː'tɛl] *n* Kartell *nt*
cartilage ['kɑːtɪlɪdʒ] *n* Knorpel *m*
cartographer [kɑː'tɔgrəfəʳ] *n* Kartograf(in) *m(f)*
cartography [kɑː'tɔgrəfɪ] *n* Kartografie *f*
carton ['kɑːtən] *n* (Papp)karton *m*; (*of yogurt*) Becher *m*; (*of milk*) Tüte *f*; (*of cigarettes*) Stange *f*
cartoon [kɑː'tuːn] *n* (*drawing*) Karikatur *f*; (*Brit: comic strip*) Cartoon *m*; (*Cine*) Zeichentrickfilm *m*
cartoonist [kɑː'tuːnɪst] *n* Karikaturist(in) *m(f)*
cartridge ['kɑːtrɪdʒ] *n* (*for gun, pen*) Patrone *f*; (*music tape, for camera*) Kassette *f*; (*of record-player*) Tonabnehmer *m*
cartwheel ['kɑːtwiːl] *n* Rad *nt*; **to turn a ~** Rad schlagen
carve [kɑːv] *vt* (*meat*) (ab)schneiden; (*wood*) schnitzen; (*stone*) meißeln; (*initials, design*) einritzen
▶ **carve up** *vt* (*land etc*) aufteilen; (*meat*) aufschneiden
carving ['kɑːvɪŋ] *n* Skulptur *f*; (*in wood etc*) Schnitzerei *f*
carving knife *n* Tran(s)chiermesser *nt*
car wash *n* Autowaschanlage *f*
Casablanca [kæsə'blæŋkə] *n* Casablanca *nt*
cascade [kæs'keɪd] *n* Wasserfall *m*, Kaskade *f*; (*of money*) Regen *m*; (*of hair*) wallende Fülle *f* ▷ *vi* (in Kaskaden) herabfallen; (*hair etc*) wallen; (*people*) strömen
case [keɪs] *n* Fall *m*; (*for spectacles etc*) Etui *nt*; (*Brit: also*: **suitcase**) Koffer *m*; (*of wine, whisky etc*) Kiste *f*; (*Typ*): **lower-/upper ~** klein-/großgeschrieben; **to have a good ~** gute Chancen haben, durchzukommen; **there's a strong ~ for reform** es spricht viel für eine

Reform; **in ~ ... falls ...**; **in ~ of fire** bei Feuer; **in ~ of emergency** im Notfall; **in ~ he comes** falls er kommt; **in any ~** sowieso; **just in ~** für alle Fälle
case-hardened ['keɪshɑːdnd] *adj* (*fig*) abgebrüht (*inf*)
case history *n* (*Med*) Krankengeschichte *f*
case study *n* Fallstudie *f*
cash [kæʃ] *n* (Bar)geld *nt* ▷ *vt* (*cheque etc*) einlösen; **to pay (in) ~** bar bezahlen; **~ on delivery** per Nachnahme; **~ with order** zahlbar bei Bestellung
▶ **cash in** *vt* einlösen
▶ **cash in on** *vt fus* Kapital schlagen aus
cash account *n* Kassenbuch *nt*
cash-and-carry [kæʃən'kærɪ] *n* Abholmarkt *m*
cash-book ['kæʃbuk] *n* Kassenkonto *nt*
cash box *n* (Geld)kassette *f*
cash card (*Brit*) *n* (Geld)automatenkarte *f*
cash crop *n* zum Verkauf bestimmte Ernte *f*
cash desk (*Brit*) *n* Kasse *f*
cash discount *n* Skonto *m or nt*
cash dispenser (*Brit*) *n* Geldautomat *m*
cashew [kæ'ʃuː] *n* (*also*: **cashew nut**) Cashewnuss *f*
cash flow *n* Cashflow *m*
cashier [kæ'ʃɪəʳ] *n* Kassierer(in) *m(f)*
cashmere ['kæʃmɪəʳ] *n* Kaschmir *m*
cash point *n* Geldautomat *m*
cash price *n* Bar(zahlungs)preis *m*
cash register *n* Registrierkasse *f*
cash sale *n* Barverkauf *m*
casing ['keɪsɪŋ] *n* Gehäuse *nt*
casino [kə'siːnəu] *n* Kasino *nt*
cask [kɑːsk] *n* Fass *nt*
casket ['kɑːskɪt] *n* Schatulle *f*; (*US: coffin*) Sarg *m*
Caspian Sea ['kæspɪən-] *n*: **the ~** das Kaspische Meer
casserole ['kæsərəul] *n* Auflauf *m*; (*pot, container*) Kasserolle *f*
cassette [kæ'sɛt] *n* Kassette *f*
cassette deck *n* Kassettendeck *nt*
cassette player *n* Kassettenrekorder *m*
cassette recorder *n* Kassettenrekorder *m*
cast [kɑːst] (*pt, pp* ~) *vt* werfen; (*net, fishing-line*) auswerfen; (*metal, statue*) gießen ▷ *vi* die Angel auswerfen ▷ *n* (*Theat*) Besetzung *f*; (*mould*) (Guss)form *f*; (*also*: **plaster cast**) Gipsverband *m*; **to ~ sb as Hamlet** (*Theat*) die Rolle des Hamlet mit jdm besetzen; **to ~ one's vote** seine Stimme abgeben; **to ~ one's eyes over sth** einen Blick auf etw *acc* werfen; **to ~ aspersions on sb/sth** abfällige Bemerkungen über jdn/etw machen; **to ~ doubts on sth** etw in Zweifel ziehen; **to ~ a spell on sb/sth** jdn/etw verzaubern; **to ~ its skin** sich häuten
▶ **cast aside** *vt* fallen lassen
▶ **cast off** *vi* (*Naut*) losmachen; (*Knitting*) abketten ▷ *vt* abstoßen
▶ **cast on** *vi, vt* (*Knitting*) anschlagen, aufschlagen
castaway ['kɑːstəweɪ] *n* Schiffbrüchige(r) *f(m)*

caste [kɑːst] n Kaste f; *(system)* Kastenwesen nt

caster sugar ['kɑːstə-] *(Brit)* n Raffinade f

casting vote ['kɑːstɪŋ-] *(Brit)* n ausschlaggebende Stimme f

cast iron n Gusseisen nt ▷ adj: **cast-iron** *(fig: will)* eisern; *(: alibi, excuse etc)* hieb- und stichfest

castle ['kɑːsl] n Schloss nt; *(manor)* Herrenhaus nt; *(fortified)* Burg f; *(Chess)* Turm m

cast off n abgelegtes Kleidungsstück nt

castor ['kɑːstə^r] n Rolle f

castor oil n Rizinusöl nt

castrate [kæs'treɪt] vt kastrieren

casual ['kæʒjul] adj *(by chance)* zufällig; *(work etc)* Gelegenheits-; *(unconcerned)* lässig, gleichgültig; *(clothes)* leger; ~ **wear** Freizeitkleidung f

casual labour n Gelegenheitsarbeit f

casually ['kæʒjulɪ] adv lässig; *(glance)* beiläufig; *(dress)* leger; *(by chance)* zufällig

casualty ['kæʒjultɪ] n *(of war etc)* Opfer nt; *(someone injured)* Verletzte(r) f(m); *(someone killed)* Tote(r) f(m); *(Med)* Unfallstation f; **heavy casualties** *(Mil)* schwere Verluste pl

casualty ward *(Brit)* n Unfallstation f

cat [kæt] n Katze f; *(lion etc)* (Raub)katze f

catacombs ['kætəkuːmz] npl Katakomben pl

catalogue, *(US)* **catalog** ['kætəlɔg] n Katalog m ▷ vt katalogisieren

catalyst ['kætəlɪst] n Katalysator m

catalytic converter [kætə'lɪtɪk kən'vɜːtə^r] n *(Aut)* Katalysator m

catapult ['kætəpʌlt] *(Brit)* n Schleuder f; *(Mil)* Katapult nt or m ▷ vi geschleudert or katapultiert werden ▷ vt schleudern, katapultieren

cataract ['kætərækt] n *(Med)* grauer Star m

catarrh [kə'tɑː^r] n Katarrh m

catastrophe [kə'tæstrəfɪ] n Katastrophe f

catastrophic [kætə'strɔfɪk] adj katastrophal

catcalls ['kætkɔːlz] npl Pfiffe und Buhrufe pl

catch [kætʃ] *(pt, pp* **caught)** vt fangen; *(take: bus, train etc)* nehmen; *(arrest)* festnehmen; *(surprise)* erwischen, ertappen; *(breath)* holen; *(attention)* erregen; *(hit)* treffen; *(hear)* mitbekommen; *(illness)* sich dat zuziehen or holen; *(person: also:* **catch up)** einholen ▷ vi *(fire)* (anfangen zu) brennen; *(become trapped)* hängen bleiben ▷ n Fang m; *(trick, hidden problem)* Haken m; *(of lock)* Riegel m; *(game)* Fangen nt; **to ~ sb's attention/eye** jdn auf sich acc aufmerksam machen; **to ~ fire** Feuer fangen; **to ~ sight of** erblicken

▶ **catch on** vi *(grow popular)* sich durchsetzen; **to ~ on (to sth)** (etw) kapieren

▶ **catch out** *(Brit)* vt *(fig)* hereinlegen

▶ **catch up** vi *(fig: with person)* mitkommen; *(: on work)* aufholen ▷ vt: **to ~ sb up, to ~ up with sb** jdn einholen

catch-22 ['kætʃtwɛntɪ'tuː] n: **it's a ~ situation** es ist eine Zwickmühle

catching ['kætʃɪŋ] adj ansteckend

catchment area ['kætʃmənt-] *(Brit)* n Einzugsgebiet nt

catch phrase n Schlagwort nt, Slogan m

catchy ['kætʃɪ] adj *(tune)* eingängig

catechism ['kætɪkɪzəm] n Katechismus m

categoric [kætɪ'gɔrɪk], **categorical** [kætɪ'gɔrɪkəl] adj kategorisch

categorize ['kætɪgəraɪz] vt kategorisieren

category ['kætɪgərɪ] n Kategorie f

cater ['keɪtə^r] vi: **to ~ (for)** die Speisen und Getränke liefern (für)

▶ **cater for** *(Brit)* vt fus *(needs, tastes)* gerecht werden +dat; *(readers, consumers)* eingestellt or ausgerichtet sein auf +acc

caterer ['keɪtərə^r] n Lieferant(in) m(f) von Speisen und Getränken; *(company)* Lieferfirma f für Speisen und Getränke

catering ['keɪtərɪŋ] n Gastronomie f

caterpillar ['kætəpɪlə^r] n Raupe f ▷ cpd *(vehicle)* Raupen-

caterpillar track n Raupenkette f, Gleiskette f

cat flap n Katzentür f

cathedral [kə'θiːdrəl] n Kathedrale f, Dom m

cathode ['kæθəud] n Kat(h)ode f

cathode-ray tube [kæθəud'reɪ-] n Kat(h)-odenstrahlröhre f

Catholic ['kæθəlɪk] adj katholisch ▷ n Katholik(in) m(f)

catholic ['kæθəlɪk] adj vielseitig

CAT scanner n abbr *(Med: = computerized axial tomography scanner)* CAT-Scanner m

Catseye® ['kæts'aɪ] *(Brit)* n Katzenauge nt

catsup ['kætsəp] *(US)* n Ket(s)chup m or nt

cattle ['kætl] npl Vieh nt

catty ['kætɪ] adj gehässig

catwalk ['kætwɔːk] n Steg m; *(for models)* Laufsteg m

Caucasian [kɔː'keɪzɪən] adj kaukasisch ▷ n Kaukasier(in) m(f)

Caucasus ['kɔːkəsəs] n Kaukasus m

caucus ['kɔːkəs] n *(group)* Gremium nt, Ausschuss m; *(US)* Parteiversammlung f; *siehe Info-Artikel*

◉ CAUCUS

◉ *Caucus* bedeutet vor allem in den USA ein
◉ privates Treffen von Parteifunktionären,
◉ bei dem z. B. Kandidaten ausgewählt
◉ oder Grundsatzentscheidungen getroffen
◉ werden. Meist wird ein solches Treffen vor
◉ einer öffentlichen Parteiversammlung
◉ abgehalten. Der Begriff bezieht sich im
◉ weiteren Sinne auch auf den kleinen, aber
◉ mächtigen Kreis von Parteifunktionären,
◉ der beim caucus zusammentrifft.

---

caught [kɔːt] pt, pp of **catch**

cauliflower ['kɔlɪflauə^r] n Blumenkohl m

cause [kɔːz] n Ursache f; *(reason)* Grund m; *(aim)* Sache f ▷ vt verursachen; **there is no ~ for concern** es besteht kein Grund zur Sorge; **to ~ sth to be done** veranlassen, dass etw getan wird; **to ~ sb to do sth** jdn veranlassen, etw zu tun

causeway ['kɔːzweɪ] n Damm m

caustic ['kɔːstɪk] adj ätzend, kaustisch; (remark) bissig

cauterize ['kɔːtəraɪz] vt kauterisieren

caution ['kɔːʃən] n Vorsicht f; (warning) Warnung f; (: Law) Verwarnung f ▷ vt warnen; (Law) verwarnen

cautious ['kɔːʃəs] adj vorsichtig

cautiously ['kɔːʃəslɪ] adv vorsichtig

cautiousness ['kɔːʃəsnɪs] n Vorsicht f

cavalier [kævə'lɪəʳ] adj unbekümmert

cavalry ['kævəlrɪ] n Kavallerie f

cave [keɪv] n Höhle f ▷ vi: **to go caving** auf Höhlenexpedition(en) gehen
▶ **cave in** vi einstürzen; (to demands) nachgeben

caveman ['keɪvmæn] (irreg: like **man**) n Höhlenmensch m

cavern ['kævən] n Höhle f

caviar, caviare ['kævɪɑːʳ] n Kaviar m

cavity ['kævɪtɪ] n Hohlraum m; (in tooth) Loch nt

cavity wall insulation n Schaumisolierung f

cavort [kə'vɔːt] vi tollen, toben

cayenne [keɪ'ɛn] n (also: **cayenne pepper**) Cayennepfeffer m

CB n abbr (= Citizens' Band (Radio)) CB-Funk m

CBC n abbr (= Canadian Broadcasting Corporation) kanadische Rundfunkgesellschaft

CBE (Brit) n abbr (= Commander of (the Order of) the British Empire) britischer Ordenstitel

CBI n abbr (= Confederation of British Industry) britischer Unternehmerverband, ≈ BDI m

CBS (US) n abbr (= Columbia Broadcasting System) Rundfunkgesellschaft

CC (Brit) abbr = **county council**

cc abbr (= cubic centimetre) ccm; = **carbon copy**

CCTV n abbr = **closed-circuit television**

CCU (US) n abbr (= cardiac or coronary care unit) Intensivstation für Herzpatienten

CD abbr (Brit: = Corps Diplomatique) CD ▷ n abbr (Mil: Brit: = Civil Defence (Corps)) Zivilschutz m; (: US: = Civil Defense) Zivilschutz m; (= compact disc) CD f; **CD player** CD-Spieler m

CDC (US) n abbr (= Center for Disease Control) Seuchenkontrollbehörde

Cdr abbr (Mil) = **commander**

CD-ROM n abbr (= compact disc read-only memory) CD-ROM f

CDT (US) abbr (= Central Daylight Time) mittelamerikanische Sommerzeit; (Brit: Scol: = Craft, Design and Technology) Arbeitslehre f

cease [siːs] vt beenden ▷ vi aufhören

ceasefire ['siːsfaɪəʳ] n Waffenruhe f

ceaseless ['siːslɪs] adj endlos, unaufhörlich

CED (US) n abbr (= Committee for Economic Development) Komitee für wirtschaftliche Entwicklung

cedar ['siːdəʳ] n Zeder f; (wood) Zedernholz nt

cede [siːd] vt abtreten

cedilla [sɪ'dɪlə] n Cedille f

CEEB (US) n abbr (= College Entry Examination Board) akademische Zulassungsstelle

ceilidh ['keɪlɪ] (Scott) n Fest mit Volksmusik, Gesang und Tanz

ceiling ['siːlɪŋ] n Decke f; (upper limit) Obergrenze f, Höchstgrenze f

celebrate ['sɛlɪbreɪt] vt feiern; (mass) zelebrieren ▷ vi feiern

celebrated ['sɛlɪbreɪtɪd] adj gefeiert

celebration [sɛlɪ'breɪʃən] n Feier f

celebrity [sɪ'lɛbrɪtɪ] n berühmte Persönlichkeit f

celeriac [sə'lɛrɪæk] n (Knollen)sellerie f

celery ['sɛlərɪ] n (Stangen)sellerie f

celestial [sɪ'lɛstɪəl] adj himmlisch

celibacy ['sɛlɪbəsɪ] n Zölibat nt or m

cell [sɛl] n Zelle f

cellar ['sɛləʳ] n Keller m; (for wine) (Wein)keller m

cellist ['tʃɛlɪst] n Cellist(in) m(f)

cello ['tʃɛləu] n Cello nt

cellophane ['sɛləfeɪn] n Cellophan nt

cellphone n Handy nt, Mobiltelefon nt

cellular ['sɛljuləʳ] adj (Biol) zellular, Zell-; (fabrics) aus porösem Material

Celluloid® ['sɛljulɔɪd] n Zelluloid nt

cellulose ['sɛljuləus] n Zellulose f, Zellstoff m

Celsius ['sɛlsɪəs] adj (scale) Celsius-

Celt [kɛlt] n Kelte m, Keltin f

Celtic ['kɛltɪk] adj keltisch ▷ n (Ling) Keltisch nt

cement [sə'mɛnt] n Zement m; (concrete) Beton m; (glue) Klebstoff m ▷ vt zementieren; (stick, glue) kleben; (fig) festigen

cement mixer n Betonmischmaschine f

cemetery ['sɛmɪtrɪ] n Friedhof m

cenotaph ['sɛnətɑːf] n Ehrenmal nt

censor ['sɛnsəʳ] n Zensor(in) m(f) ▷ vt zensieren

censorship ['sɛnsəʃɪp] n Zensur f

censure ['sɛnʃəʳ] vt tadeln ▷ n Tadel m

census ['sɛnsəs] n Volkszählung f

cent [sɛnt] n Cent m; see also **per cent**

centenary [sɛn'tiːnərɪ] n hundertster Jahrestag m

centennial [sɛn'tɛnɪəl] (US) n = **centenary**

center etc ['sɛntəʳ] (US) = **centre** etc

centigrade ['sɛntɪgreɪd] adj (scale) Celsius-

centilitre, (US) **centiliter** ['sɛntɪliːtəʳ] n Zentiliter m or nt

centimetre, (US) **centimeter** ['sɛntɪmiːtəʳ] n Zentimeter m or nt

centipede ['sɛntɪpiːd] n Tausendfüßler m

central ['sɛntrəl] adj zentral; (committee, government) Zentral-; (idea) wesentlich

Central African Republic n Zentralafrikanische Republik f

Central America n Mittelamerika nt

central heating n Zentralheizung f

centralize ['sɛntrəlaɪz] vt zentralisieren

central processing unit n (Comput) Zentraleinheit f

central reservation (Brit) n Mittelstreifen m

centre, (US) **center** ['sɛntəʳ] n Mitte f; (health centre etc, town centre) Zentrum nt; (of attention, interest) Mittelpunkt m; (of action, belief etc) Kern m ▷ vt zentrieren; (ball) zur Mitte spielen ▷ vi (*concentrate*): **to ~ on** sich konzentrieren auf +*acc*

centrefold, (US) **centerfold** ['sɛntəfəuld] *n* *doppelseitiges Bild in der Mitte einer Zeitschrift*
centre forward *n* Mittelstürmer(in) *m(f)*
centre half *n* Stopper(in) *m(f)*
centrepiece, (US) **centerpiece** ['sɛntəpi:s] *n* Tafelaufsatz *m*; (*fig*) Kernstück *nt*
centre spread (Brit) *n* *Doppelseite in der Mitte einer Zeitschrift*
centre-stage [sɛntə'steɪdʒ] (*fig*) *adv*: **to be ~** im Mittelpunkt stehen ▷ *n*: **to take centre stage** in den Mittelpunkt rücken
centrifugal [sɛn'trɪfjugl] *adj* (*force*) Zentrifugal-
centrifuge ['sɛntrɪfju:ʒ] *n* Zentrifuge *f*, Schleuder *f*
century ['sɛntjurɪ] *n* Jahrhundert *nt*; (*Cricket*) Hundert *f*; **in the twentieth ~** im zwanzigsten Jahrhundert
CEO *n abbr* = **chief executive officer**
ceramic [sɪ'ræmɪk] *adj* keramisch; (*tiles*) Keramik-
ceramics [sɪ'ræmɪks] *npl* Keramiken *pl*
cereal ['si:rɪəl] *n* Getreide *nt*; (*food*) Getreideflocken *pl* (*Cornflakes etc*)
cerebral ['sɛrɪbrəl] *adj* (*Med*) zerebral; (*intellectual*) geistig
ceremonial [sɛrɪ'məunɪəl] *n* Zeremoniell *nt* ▷ *adj* zeremoniell
ceremony ['sɛrɪmənɪ] *n* Zeremonie *f*; (*behaviour*) Förmlichkeit *f*; **to stand on ~** förmlich sein
cert [sə:t] (Brit: *inf*) *n*: **it's a dead ~** es ist todsicher
certain ['sə:tən] *adj* sicher; **a ~ Mr Smith** ein gewisser Herr Smith; **~ days/places** bestimmte Tage/Orte; **a ~ coldness** eine gewisse Kälte; **to make ~ of** sich vergewissern +*gen*; **for ~** ganz sicher, ganz genau
certainly ['sə:tənlɪ] *adv* bestimmt; (*of course*) sicherlich; **~!** (aber) sicher!
certainty ['sə:təntɪ] *n* Sicherheit *f*; (*inevitability*) Gewissheit *f*
certificate [sə'tɪfɪkɪt] *n* Urkunde *f*; (*diploma*) Zeugnis *nt*
certified letter ['sə:tɪfaɪd-] (US) *n* Einschreibebrief *m*
certified mail (US) *n* Einschreiben *nt*
certified public accountant ['sə:tɪfaɪd-] (US) *n* geprüfter Buchhalter *m*, geprüfte Buchhalterin *f*
certify ['sə:tɪfaɪ] *vt* bescheinigen; (*award a diploma to*) ein Zeugnis verleihen +*dat*; (*declare insane*) für unzurechnungsfähig erklären ▷ *vi*: **to ~ to** sich verbürgen für
cervical ['sə:vɪkl] *adj*: **~ cancer** Gebärmutterhalskrebs *m*; **~ smear** Abstrich *m*
cervix ['sə:vɪks] *n* Gebärmutterhals *m*
Cesarean [sɪ'zɛərɪən] (US) *n* = **Caesarean**
cessation [sə'seɪʃən] *n* (*of hostilities etc*) Einstellung *f*, Ende *nt*
cesspit ['sɛspɪt] *n* (*sewage tank*) Senkgrube *f*

CET *abbr* (= *Central European Time*) MEZ
Ceylon [sɪ'lɒn] *n* Ceylon *nt*
cf. *abbr* (= *compare*) vgl.
c/f *abbr* (Comm: = *carried forward*) Übertr.
CFC *n abbr* (= *chlorofluorocarbon*) FCKW *m*
CG (US) *n abbr* = **coastguard**
cg *abbr* (= *centigram*) cg
CH (Brit) *n abbr* (= *Companion of Honour*) britischer Ordenstitel
ch. *abbr* (= *chapter*) Kap.
Chad [tʃæd] *n* Tschad *m*
chafe [tʃeɪf] *vt* (wund) reiben ▷ *vi* (*fig*): **to ~ against** sich ärgern über +*acc*
chaffinch ['tʃæfɪntʃ] *n* Buchfink *m*
chagrin ['ʃægrɪn] *n* Ärger *m*
chain [tʃeɪn] *n* Kette *f* ▷ *vt* (*also*: **chain up**: *prisoner*) anketten; (: *dog*) an die Kette legen
chain reaction *n* Kettenreaktion *f*
chain-smoke ['tʃeɪnsməuk] *vi* eine Zigarette nach der anderen rauchen
chain store *n* Kettenladen *m*
chair [tʃɛəʳ] *n* Stuhl *m*; (*armchair*) Sessel *m*; (*of university*) Lehrstuhl *m*; (*of meeting, committee*) Vorsitz *m* ▷ *vt* den Vorsitz führen bei; **the ~** (US) der elektrische Stuhl
chair lift *n* Sessellift *m*
chairman ['tʃɛəmən] (*irreg: like* **man**) *n* Vorsitzende(r) *f(m)*; (Brit: *of company*) Präsident *m*
chairperson ['tʃɛəpə:sn] *n* Vorsitzende(r) *f(m)*
chairwoman ['tʃɛəwumən] (*irreg: like* **woman**) *n* Vorsitzende *f*
chalet ['ʃæleɪ] *n* Chalet *nt*
chalice ['tʃælɪs] *n* Kelch *m*
chalk [tʃɔ:k] *n* Kalkstein *m*, Kreide *f*; (*for writing*) Kreide *f*
 ▶ **chalk up** *vt* aufschreiben, notieren; (*fig: success etc*) verbuchen
challenge ['tʃælɪndʒ] *n* (*of new job*) Anforderungen *pl*; (*of unknown etc*) Reiz *m*; (*to authority etc*) Infragestellung *f*; (*dare*) Herausforderung *f* ▷ *vt* herausfordern; (*authority, right, idea etc*) infrage stellen; **to ~ sb to do sth** jdn dazu auffordern, etw zu tun; **to ~ sb to a fight/game** jdn zu einem Kampf/ Spiel herausfordern
challenger ['tʃælɪndʒəʳ] *n* Herausforderer *m*, Herausforderin *f*
challenging ['tʃælɪndʒɪŋ] *adj* (*career, task*) anspruchsvoll; (*tone, look etc*) herausfordernd
chamber ['tʃeɪmbəʳ] *n* Kammer *f*; (Brit: Law: *gen pl: of barristers*) Kanzlei *f*; (: *of judge*) Amtszimmer *nt*; **~ of commerce** Handelskammer *f*
chambermaid ['tʃeɪmbəmeɪd] *n* Zimmermädchen *nt*
chamber music *n* Kammermusik *f*
chamber pot *n* Nachttopf *m*
chameleon [kə'mi:lɪən] *n* Chamäleon *nt*
chamois ['ʃæmwɑ:] *n* Gämse *f*; (*cloth*) Ledertuch *nt*, Fensterleder *nt*
chamois leather ['ʃæmɪ-] *n* Ledertuch *nt*, Fensterleder *nt*
champagne [ʃæm'peɪn] *n* Champagner *m*

champers ['ʃæmpəz] (inf) n (champagne) Schampus m

champion ['tʃæmpɪən] n Meister(in) m(f); (of cause, principle) Verfechter(in) m(f); (of person) Fürsprecher(in) m(f) ▷ vt eintreten für, sich engagieren für

championship ['tʃæmpɪənʃɪp] n Meisterschaft f; (title) Titel m

chance [tʃɑːns] n (hope) Aussicht f; (likelihood, possibility) Möglichkeit f; (opportunity) Gelegenheit f; (risk) Risiko nt ▷ vt riskieren ▷ adj zufällig; **the ~s are that ...** aller Wahrscheinlichkeit nach ..., wahrscheinlich ...; **there is little ~ of his coming** es ist unwahrscheinlich, dass er kommt; **to take a ~** es darauf ankommen lassen; **by ~** durch Zufall, zufällig; **it's the ~ of a lifetime** es ist eine einmalige Chance; **to ~ to do sth** zufällig etw tun; **to ~ it** es riskieren

▸ **chance (up)on** vt fus (person) zufällig begegnen +dat, zufällig treffen; (thing) zufällig stoßen auf +acc

chancel ['tʃɑːnsəl] n Altarraum m

chancellor ['tʃɑːnsələʳ] n Kanzler m

Chancellor of the Exchequer (Brit) n Schatzkanzler m, Finanzminister m

chancy ['tʃɑːnsɪ] adj riskant

chandelier [ʃændəˈlɪəʳ] n Kronleuchter m

change [tʃeɪndʒ] vt ändern; (wheel, job, money, baby's nappy) wechseln; (bulb) auswechseln; (baby) wickeln ▷ vi sich verändern; (traffic lights) umspringen ▷ n Veränderung f; (difference) Abwechslung f; (of government, climate, job) Wechsel m; (coins) Kleingeld nt; (money returned) Wechselgeld nt; **to ~ sb into** jdn verwandeln in +acc; **to ~ gear** (Aut) schalten; **to ~ one's mind** seine Meinung ändern, es sich dat anders überlegen; **to ~ hands** den Besitzer wechseln; **to ~ (trains/buses/planes** etc) umsteigen; **to ~ (one's clothes)** sich umziehen; **to ~ into** (be transformed) sich verwandeln in +acc; **she ~d into an old skirt** sie zog einen alten Rock an; **a ~ of clothes** Kleidung f zum Wechseln; **~ of government/climate/job** Regierungs-/Klima-/Berufswechsel m; **small ~** Kleingeld nt; **to give sb ~ for** or **of £10** jdm £10 wechseln; **keep the ~** das stimmt so, der Rest ist für Sie; **for a ~** zur Abwechslung

changeable ['tʃeɪndʒəbl] adj (weather) wechselhaft, veränderlich; (mood) wechselnd; (person) unbeständig

change machine n (Geld)wechselautomat m

changeover ['tʃeɪndʒəuvəʳ] n Umstellung f

changing ['tʃeɪndʒɪŋ] adj sich verändernd

changing room (Brit) n (Umkleide)kabine f; (Sport) Umkleideraum m

channel ['tʃænl] n (TV) Kanal m; (of river, waterway) (Fluss)bett nt; (for boats) Fahrrinne f; (groove) Rille f; (fig: means) Weg m ▷ vt leiten; (fig): **to ~ into** lenken auf +acc; **through the usual ~s** auf dem üblichen Wege; **green ~**

(Customs) „nichts zu verzollen"; **red ~** (Customs) „Waren zu verzollen"; **the (English) C~** der Ärmelkanal; **the C~ Islands** die Kanalinseln pl

channel-hopping ['tʃænlhɒpɪŋ] n (TV) ständiges Umschalten

Channel Tunnel n: **the ~** der Kanaltunnel

chant [tʃɑːnt] n Sprechchor m; (Rel) Gesang m ▷ vt im (Sprech)chor rufen; (Rel) singen ▷ vi Sprechchöre anstimmen; (Rel) singen; **the demonstrators ~ed their disapproval** die Demonstranten machten ihrem Unmut in Sprechchören Luft

chaos ['keɪɒs] n Chaos nt, Durcheinander nt

chaos theory n Chaostheorie f

chaotic [keɪˈɒtɪk] adj chaotisch

chap [tʃæp] (Brit: inf) n Kerl m, Typ m; **old ~** alter Knabe or Junge

chapel ['tʃæpl] n Kapelle f; (Brit: non-conformist chapel) Sektenkirche f; (: of union) Betriebsgruppe innerhalb der Gewerkschaft der Drucker und Journalisten

chaperone ['ʃæpərəun] n Anstandsdame f ▷ vt begleiten

chaplain ['tʃæplɪn] n Pfarrer(in) m(f); (Roman Catholic) Kaplan m

chapped [tʃæpt] adj aufgesprungen, rau

chapter ['tʃæptəʳ] n Kapitel nt; **a ~ of accidents** eine Serie von Unfällen

char [tʃɑːʳ] vt verkohlen ▷ vi (Brit) putzen gehen ▷ n (Brit) = **charlady**

character ['kærɪktəʳ] n Charakter m; (personality) Persönlichkeit f; (in novel, film) Figur f, Gestalt f; (eccentric) Original nt; (letter: also Comput) Zeichen nt; **a person of good ~** ein guter Mensch

character code n (Comput) Zeichencode m

characteristic [kærɪktəˈrɪstɪk] n Merkmal nt ▷ adj: **~ (of)** charakteristisch (für), typisch (für)

characterize ['kærɪktəraɪz] vt kennzeichnen, charakterisieren; (describe the character of): **to ~ (as)** beschreiben (als)

charade [ʃəˈrɑːd] n Scharade f

charcoal ['tʃɑːkəul] n Holzkohle f; (for drawing) Kohle f, Kohlestift m

charge [tʃɑːdʒ] n (fee) Gebühr f; (accusation) Anklage f; (responsibility) Verantwortung f; (attack) Angriff m ▷ vt (customer) berechnen +dat; (sum) berechnen; (battery) (auf)laden; (gun) laden; (enemy) angreifen; (sb with task) beauftragen ▷ vi angreifen; (usu with: up, along etc) stürmen; **charges** npl Gebühren pl; **labour ~s** Arbeitskosten pl; **to reverse the ~s** (Brit: Tel) ein R-Gespräch führen; **is there a ~?** kostet das etwas?; **there's no ~** es ist umsonst, es kostet nichts; **at no extra ~** ohne Aufpreis; **free of ~** kostenlos, gratis; **to take ~ of** (child) sich kümmern um; (company) übernehmen; **to be in ~ of** die Verantwortung haben für; (business) leiten; **they ~d us £10 for the meal** das Essen kostete £10; **how much do you ~?** was verlangen Sie?; **to ~ an expense (up) to sb's**

account eine Ausgabe auf jds Rechnung *acc* setzen; **to ~ sb (with)** (*Law*) jdn anklagen (wegen)

charge account *n* Kunden(kredit)konto *nt*

charge card *n* Kundenkreditkarte *f*

chargé d'affaires *n* Chargé d'affaires *m*

charge hand (*Brit*) *n* Vorarbeiter(in) *m(f)*

charger ['tʃɑːdʒəʳ] *n* (*also:* **battery charger**) Ladegerät *nt*; (*warhorse*) (Schlacht)ross *nt*

chariot ['tʃærɪət] *n* (Streit)wagen *m*

charisma [kæ'rɪsmə] *n* Charisma *nt*

charitable ['tʃærɪtəbl] *adj* (*organization*) karitativ, Wohltätigkeits-; (*remark*) freundlich

charity ['tʃærɪtɪ] *n* (*organization*) karitative Organisation *f*, Wohltätigkeitsverein *m*; (*kindness, generosity*) Menschenfreundlichkeit *f*; (*money, gifts*) Almosen *pl*

charlady ['tʃɑːleɪdɪ] (*irreg: like* **lady**) (*Brit*) *n* Putzfrau *f*, Reinemachefrau *f*

charlatan ['ʃɑːlətən] *n* Scharlatan *m*

charm [tʃɑːm] *n* Charme *m*; (*to bring good luck*) Talisman *m*; (*on bracelet etc*) Anhänger *m* ▷ *vt* bezaubern

charm bracelet *n* Armband *nt* mit Anhängern

charming ['tʃɑːmɪŋ] *adj* reizend, charmant; (*place*) bezaubernd

chart [tʃɑːt] *n* Schaubild *nt*, Diagramm *nt*; (*map*) Karte *f*; (*also:* **weather chart**) Wetterkarte *f* ▷ *vt* (*course*) planen; (*progress*) aufzeichnen; **charts** *npl* (*hit parade*) Hitliste *f*

charter ['tʃɑːtəʳ] *vt* chartern ▷ *n* Charta *f*; (*of university, company*) Gründungsurkunde *f*; **on ~** gechartert

chartered accountant ['tʃɑːtəd-] (*Brit*) *n* Wirtschaftsprüfer(in) *m(f)*

charter flight *n* Charterflug *m*

charwoman ['tʃɑːwumən] (*irreg: like* **woman**) *n* Putzfrau *f*, Reinemachefrau *f*

chary ['tʃɛərɪ] *adj*: **to be ~ of doing sth** zögern, etw zu tun

chase [tʃeɪs] *vt* jagen, verfolgen; (*also:* **chase away**) wegjagen, vertreiben; (*business, job etc*) her sein hinter +*dat* (*inf*) ▷ *n* Verfolgungsjagd *f*

▶ **chase down** (*US*) *vt* = **chase up**

▶ **chase up** (*Brit*) *vt* (*person*) rankriegen (*inf*); (*information*) ranschaffen (*inf*)

chasm ['kæzəm] *n* Kluft *f*

chassis ['ʃæsɪ] *n* Fahrgestell *nt*

chaste [tʃeɪst] *adj* keusch

chastened ['tʃeɪsnd] *adj* zur Einsicht gebracht

chastening ['tʃeɪsnɪŋ] *adj* ernüchternd

chastise [tʃæs'taɪz] *vt* (*scold*) schelten

chastity ['tʃæstɪtɪ] *n* Keuschheit *f*

chat [tʃæt] *vi* (*also:* **have a chat**) plaudern, sich unterhalten; (*Comput*) chatten ▷ *n* Plauderei *f*, Unterhaltung *f*; (*Comput*) Chat

▶ **chat up** (*Brit: inf*) *vt* anmachen

chatline ['tʃætlaɪn] *n* *Telefondienst, der Anrufern die Teilnahme an einer Gesprächsrunde ermöglicht*

chatroom ['tʃætruːm] *n* (*Comput*) Chatroom *m*

chat show (*Brit*) *n* Talkshow *f*

chattel ['tʃætl] *n*: **goods and ~s** *see* **good**

chatter ['tʃætəʳ] *vi* schwatzen; (*monkey*) schnattern; (*teeth*) klappern ▷ *n* (*see vi*) Schwatzen *nt*; Schnattern *nt*; Klappern *nt*; **my teeth are ~ing** mir klappern die Zähne

chatterbox ['tʃætəbɒks] (*inf*) *n* Quasselstrippe *f*

chattering classes ['tʃætərɪŋ 'klɑːsɪz] *npl*: **the ~** die intellektuellen Schwätzer *pl*

chatty ['tʃætɪ] *adj* geschwätzig; (*letter*) im Plauderton

chauffeur ['ʃəufəʳ] *n* Chauffeur *m*, Fahrer *m*

chauvinism ['ʃəuvɪnɪzəm] *n* (*also:* **male chauvinism**) Chauvinismus *m*

chauvinist ['ʃəuvɪnɪst] *n* Chauvinist *m*

chauvinistic [ʃəuvɪ'nɪstɪk] *adj* chauvinistisch

ChE *abbr* (= *chemical engineer*) *Titel für Chemotechniker*

cheap [tʃiːp] *adj* billig; (*reduced*) ermäßigt; (*poor quality*) billig, minderwertig; (*behaviour, joke*) ordinär ▷ *adv*: **to buy/sell sth ~** etw billig kaufen/verkaufen

cheap day return *n* Tagesrückfahrkarte *f* (*zu einem günstigeren Tarif*)

cheapen ['tʃiːpn] *vt* entwürdigen

cheaper ['tʃiːpəʳ] *adj* billiger

cheaply ['tʃiːplɪ] *adv* billig

cheat [tʃiːt] *vi* mogeln (*inf*), schummeln (*inf*) ▷ *n* Betrüger(in) *m(f)* ▷ *vt*: **to ~ sb (out of sth)** jdn (um etw) betrügen; **to ~ on sb** (*inf*) jdn betrügen

cheating ['tʃiːtɪŋ] *n* Mogeln *nt* (*inf*), Schummeln *nt* (*inf*)

check [tʃɛk] *vt* überprüfen; (*passport, ticket*) kontrollieren; (*facts*) nachprüfen; (*enemy, disease*) aufhalten; (*impulse*) unterdrücken; (*person*) zurückhalten ▷ *vi* nachprüfen ▷ *n* Kontrolle *f*; (*curb*) Beschränkung *f*; (*US*) = **cheque**; (: *bill*) Rechnung *f*; (*pattern: gen pl*) Karo(muster) *nt* ▷ *adj* kariert; **to ~ o.s.** sich beherrschen; **to ~ with sb** bei jdm nachfragen; **to keep a ~ on sb/sth** jdn/etw kontrollieren

▶ **check in** *vi* (*at hotel*) sich anmelden; (*at airport*) einchecken ▷ *vt* (*luggage*) abfertigen lassen

▶ **check off** *vt* abhaken

▶ **check out** *vi* (*of hotel*) abreisen ▷ *vt* (*luggage*) abfertigen; (*investigate*) überprüfen

▶ **check up** *vi*: **to ~ up on sth** etw überprüfen; **to ~ up on sb** Nachforschungen über jdn anstellen

checkered ['tʃɛkəd] (*US*) *adj* = **chequered**

checkers ['tʃɛkəz] (*US*) *npl* Damespiel *nt*

check guarantee card (*US*) *n* Scheckkarte *f*

check-in ['tʃɛkɪn], **check-in desk** *n* (*at airport*) Abfertigung *f*, Abfertigungsschalter *m*

checking account ['tʃɛkɪŋ-] (*US*) *n* Girokonto *nt*

check list *n* Prüfliste *f*, Checkliste *f*

checkmate ['tʃɛkmeɪt] *n* Schachmatt *nt*

checkout ['tʃɛkaut] *n* Kasse *f*

checkpoint ['tʃɛkpɔɪnt] *n* Kontrollpunkt *m*

checkroom ['tʃɛkrum] (*US*) *n* (*left-luggage office*) Gepäckaufbewahrung *f*

checkup ['tʃɛkʌp] *n* Untersuchung *f*

cheek [tʃiːk] n Backe f; (impudence) Frechheit f; (nerve) Unverschämtheit f
cheekbone ['tʃiːkbəʊn] n Backenknochen m
cheeky ['tʃiːkɪ] adj frech
cheep [tʃiːp] vi (bird) piep(s)en ▷ n Piep(s) m, Piepser m
cheer [tʃɪəʳ] vt zujubeln +dat; (gladden) aufmuntern, aufheitern ▷ vi jubeln, Hurra rufen ▷ n (gen pl) Hurraruf m, Beifallsruf m; **cheers** npl Hurrageschrei nt, Jubel m; **~s!** prost!
▶ **cheer on** vt anspornen, anfeuern
▶ **cheer up** vi vergnügter or fröhlicher werden ▷ vt aufmuntern, aufheitern
cheerful ['tʃɪəful] adj fröhlich
cheerfulness ['tʃɪəfulnɪs] n Fröhlichkeit f
cheerio [tʃɪərɪ'əʊ] (Brit) excl tschüss (inf)
cheerleader ['tʃɪəliːdəʳ] n jd, der bei Sportveranstaltungen etc die Zuschauer zu Beifallsrufen anfeuert
cheerless ['tʃɪəlɪs] adj freudlos, trüb; (room) trostlos
cheese [tʃiːz] n Käse m
cheeseboard ['tʃiːzbɔːd] n Käsebrett nt; (with cheese on it) Käseplatte f
cheeseburger ['tʃiːzbɜːgəʳ] n Cheeseburger m
cheesecake ['tʃiːzkeɪk] n Käsekuchen m
cheetah ['tʃiːtə] n Gepard m
chef [ʃef] n Küchenchef(in) m(f)
chemical ['kemɪkl] adj chemisch ▷ n Chemikalie f
chemical engineering n Chemotechnik f
chemist ['kemɪst] n (Brit: pharmacist) Apotheker(in) m(f); (scientist) Chemiker(in) m(f)
chemistry ['kemɪstrɪ] n Chemie f
chemist's ['kemɪsts]
chemist's shop (Brit) n Drogerie f; (also: **dispensing chemist's**) Apotheke f
chemotherapy [kiːməʊ'θerəpɪ] n Chemotherapie f
cheque [tʃek] (Brit) n Scheck m; **to pay by ~** mit (einem) Scheck bezahlen
chequebook ['tʃekbuk] n Scheckbuch nt
cheque card (Brit) n Scheckkarte f
chequered, (US) **checkered** ['tʃekəd] adj (fig) bewegt
cherish ['tʃerɪʃ] vt (person) liebevoll sorgen für; (memory) in Ehren halten; (dream) sich hingeben +dat; (hope) hegen
cheroot [ʃə'ruːt] n Stumpen m
cherry ['tʃerɪ] n Kirsche f; (also: **cherry tree**) Kirschbaum m
chervil ['tʃɜːvɪl] n Kerbel m
Ches. (Brit) abbr (Post) = Cheshire
chess [tʃes] n Schach(spiel) nt
chessboard ['tʃesbɔːd] n Schachbrett nt
chessman ['tʃesmən] (irreg: like **man**) n Schachfigur f
chess player n Schachspieler(in) m(f)
chest [tʃest] n Brust f, Brustkorb m; (box) Kiste f, Truhe f; **to get sth off one's ~** (inf) sich dat etw von der Seele reden
chest measurement n Brustweite f,

Brustumfang m
chestnut ['tʃesnʌt] n Kastanie f ▷ adj kastanienbraun
chest of drawers n Kommode f
chesty ['tʃestɪ] adj (cough) tief sitzend
chew [tʃuː] vt kauen
chewing gum ['tʃuːɪŋ-] n Kaugummi m
chic [ʃiːk] adj chic inv, schick
chick [tʃɪk] n Küken nt; (inf: girl) Mieze f
chicken ['tʃɪkɪn] n Huhn nt; (meat) Hähnchen nt; (inf: coward) Feigling m
▶ **chicken out** (inf) vi: **to ~ out of doing sth** davor kneifen, etw zu tun
chicken feed n (inf: money) ein paar Pfennige pl (Hist); (as salary) ein Hungerlohn m
chickenpox ['tʃɪkɪnpɔks] n Windpocken pl
chickpea ['tʃɪkpiː] n Kichererbse f
chicory ['tʃɪkərɪ] n (in coffee) Zichorie f; (salad vegetable) Chicorée f or m
chide [tʃaɪd] vt: **to ~ sb (for)** jdn schelten (wegen)
chief [tʃiːf] n Häuptling m; (of organization, department) Leiter(in) m(f), Chef(in) m(f) ▷ adj Haupt-, wichtigste(r, s)
chief constable (Brit) n Polizeipräsident m, Polizeichef m
chief executive, (US) **chief executive officer** n Generaldirektor(in) m(f)
chiefly ['tʃiːflɪ] adv hauptsächlich
Chief of Staff n Stabschef m
chiffon ['ʃɪfɔn] n Chiffon m
chilblain ['tʃɪlbleɪn] n Frostbeule f
child [tʃaɪld] (pl **children**) n Kind nt; **do you have any children?** haben Sie Kinder?
child benefit (Brit) n Kindergeld nt
childbirth ['tʃaɪldbɜːθ] n Geburt f, Entbindung f
childhood ['tʃaɪldhud] n Kindheit f
childish ['tʃaɪldɪʃ] adj kindisch
childless ['tʃaɪldlɪs] adj kinderlos
childlike ['tʃaɪldlaɪk] adj kindlich
child minder (Brit) n Tagesmutter f
child prodigy n Wunderkind nt
children ['tʃɪldrən] npl of **child**
children's home ['tʃɪldrənz-] n Kinderheim nt
child's play ['tʃaɪldz-] n: **it was ~** es war ein Kinderspiel
Chile ['tʃɪlɪ] n Chile nt
Chilean ['tʃɪlɪən] adj chilenisch ▷ n Chilene m, Chilenin f
chill [tʃɪl] n Kühle f; (illness) Erkältung f ▷ adj kühl; (fig: reminder) erschreckend ▷ vt kühlen; (person) frösteln or frieren lassen; **"serve -ed"** „gekühlt servieren"
chilli, (US) **chili** ['tʃɪlɪ] n Peperoni pl
chilling ['tʃɪlɪŋ] adj (wind, morning) eisig; (fig: effect, prospect etc) beängstigend
chill out (inf) vi sich entspannen, relaxen
chilly ['tʃɪlɪ] adj kühl; (person, response, look) kühl, frostig; **to feel ~** frösteln, frieren
chime [tʃaɪm] n Glockenspiel nt ▷ vi läuten
chimney ['tʃɪmnɪ] n Schornstein m
chimney sweep n Schornsteinfeger(in) m(f)
chimpanzee [tʃɪmpæn'ziː] n Schimpanse m

chin [tʃɪn] n Kinn nt
China ['tʃaɪnə] n China nt
china ['tʃaɪnə] n Porzellan nt
Chinese [tʃaɪ'niːz] adj chinesisch ▷ n inv
Chinese m, Chinesin f; (Ling) Chinesisch nt
chink [tʃɪŋk] n (in door, wall etc) Ritze f, Spalt m;
(of bottles etc) Klirren nt
chintz [tʃɪnts] n Chintz m
chinwag ['tʃɪnwæg] (Brit: inf) n Schwatz m
chip [tʃɪp] n (gen pl) Pommes frites pl; (US: also:
potato chip) Chip m; (of wood) Span m; (of glass,
stone) Splitter m; (in glass, cup etc) abgestoßene
Stelle f; (in gambling) Chip m, Spielmarke f;
(Comput: also: **microchip**) Chip m ▷ vt (cup, plate)
anschlagen; **when the ~s are down** (fig)
wenn es drauf ankommt
  ▶ **chip in** (inf) vi (contribute) etwas beisteuern;
(interrupt) sich einschalten
chip and PIN n: ~ **machine** Chip-und-Pin-
Kartenlesegerät nt
chipboard ['tʃɪpbɔːd] n Spanplatte f
chipmunk ['tʃɪpmʌŋk] n Backenhörnchen nt
chippings ['tʃɪpɪŋz] npl: **loose ~** (on road)
Schotter m

chiropodist [kɪ'rɒpədɪst] (Brit) n Fußpfleger(in)
m(f)
chirp [tʃəːp] vi (bird) zwitschern; (crickets) zirpen
chirpy ['tʃəːpɪ] (inf) adj munter
chisel ['tʃɪzl] n (for stone) Meißel m; (for wood)
Beitel m
chit [tʃɪt] n Zettel m
chitchat ['tʃɪttʃæt] n Plauderei f
chivalrous ['ʃɪvəlrəs] adj ritterlich
chivalry ['ʃɪvəlrɪ] n Ritterlichkeit f
chives [tʃaɪvz] npl Schnittlauch m
chloride ['klɔːraɪd] n Chlorid nt
chlorinate ['klɔːrɪneɪt] vt chloren
chlorine ['klɔːriːn] n Chlor nt
chock [tʃɒk] n Bremskeil m, Bremsklotz m
chock-a-block ['tʃɒkə'blɒk] adj gerammelt voll
chock-full [tʃɒk'ful] adj = **chock-a-block**
chocolate ['tʃɒklɪt] n Schokolade f; (drink)
Kakao m, Schokolade f; (sweet) Praline f
choice [tʃɔɪs] n Auswahl f; (option) Möglichkeit
f; (preference) Wahl f ▷ adj Qualitäts-,
erstklassig; **I did it by** or **from ~** ich habe
es mir so ausgesucht; **a wide ~** eine große
Auswahl
choir ['kwaɪər] n Chor m
choirboy ['kwaɪəbɔɪ] n Chorknabe m
choke [tʃəuk] vi ersticken; (with smoke, dust,

anger etc) keine Luft mehr bekommen ▷ vt
erwürgen, erdrosseln ▷ n (Aut) Choke m,
Starterklappe f; **to be ~d (with)** verstopft sein
(mit)
cholera ['kɒlərə] n Cholera f
cholesterol [kə'lɛstərɒl] n Cholesterin nt
choose [tʃuːz] (pt **chose**, pp **chosen**) vt (aus)
wählen; (profession, friend) sich dat aussuchen
▷ vi: **to ~ between** wählen zwischen +dat,
eine Wahl treffen zwischen +dat; **to ~ from**
wählen aus or unter +dat, eine Wahl treffen
aus or unter +dat; **to ~ to do sth** beschließen,
etw zu tun
choosy ['tʃuːzɪ] adj wählerisch
chop [tʃɒp] vt (wood) hacken; (also: **chop
up**: vegetables, fruit, meat) klein schneiden ▷ n
Kotelett nt; **chops** (inf) npl (of animal) Maul nt;
(of person) Mund m; **to get the ~** (Brit: inf: project)
dem Rotstift zum Opfer fallen; (: be sacked)
rausgeschmissen werden
  ▶ **chop down** vt (tree) fällen
chopper ['tʃɒpər] (inf) n Hubschrauber m
choppy ['tʃɒpɪ] adj (sea) kabbelig, bewegt
chopsticks ['tʃɒpstɪks] npl Stäbchen pl
choral ['kɔːrəl] adj (singing) Chor-; (society)
Gesang-
chord [kɔːd] n Akkord m; (Math) Sehne f
chore [tʃɔːr] n Hausarbeit f; (routine task) lästige
Routinearbeit f; **household ~s** Hausarbeit
choreographer [kɒrɪ'ɒgrəfər] n Choreograf(in)
m(f)
choreography [kɒrɪ'ɒgrəfɪ] n Choreografie f
chorister ['kɒrɪstər] n Chorsänger(in) m(f)
chortle ['tʃɔːtl] vi glucksen
chorus ['kɔːrəs] n Chor m; (refrain) Refrain m; (of
complaints) Flut f
chose [tʃəuz] pt of **choose**
chosen ['tʃəuzn] pp of **choose**
chow [tʃau] n Chow-Chow m
chowder ['tʃaudər] n (sämige) Fischsuppe f
Christ [kraɪst] n Christus m
christen ['krɪsn] vt taufen
christening ['krɪsnɪŋ] n Taufe f
Christian ['krɪstɪən] adj christlich ▷ n
Christ(in) m(f)
Christianity [krɪstɪ'ænɪtɪ] n Christentum nt
Christian name n Vorname m
Christmas ['krɪsməs] n Weihnachten
nt; **Happy** or **Merry ~!** frohe or fröhliche
Weihnachten!
Christmas card n Weihnachtskarte f
Christmas Day n der erste Weihnachtstag
Christmas Eve n Heiligabend m
Christmas Island n Weihnachtsinsel f
Christmas tree n Weihnachtsbaum m,
Christbaum m
chrome [krəum] n = **chromium**
chromium ['krəumɪəm] n Chrom nt;
(also: **chromium plating**) Verchromung f
chromosome ['krəuməsəum] n Chromosom nt
chronic ['krɒnɪk] adj (also fig) chronisch; (severe)
schlimm
chronicle ['krɒnɪkl] n Chronik f

chronological [krɔnə'lɔdʒɪkl] adj
chronologisch

chrysanthemum [krɪ'sænθəməm] n
Chrysantheme f

chubby ['tʃʌbɪ] adj pummelig; ~ **cheeks**
Pausbacken pl

chuck [tʃʌk] (inf) vt werfen, schmeißen;
(Brit: also: **chuck up, chuck in**: job)
hinschmeißen; (: person) Schluss machen mit
▶ **chuck out** vt (person) rausschmeißen; (rubbish
etc) wegschmeißen

chuckle ['tʃʌkl] vi leise in sich acc hineinlachen

chuffed [tʃʌft] (Brit: inf) adj vergnügt und
zufrieden; (flattered) gebauchpinselt

chug [tʃʌg] vi (also: **chug along**) tuckern

chum [tʃʌm] n Kumpel m

chump [tʃʌmp] (inf) n Trottel m

chunk [tʃʌŋk] n großes Stück nt

chunky ['tʃʌŋkɪ] adj (furniture etc) klobig; (person)
stämmig, untersetzt; (knitwear) dick

church [tʃə:tʃ] n Kirche f; **the C~ of England**
die anglikanische Kirche

churchyard ['tʃə:tʃjɑ:d] n Friedhof m

churlish ['tʃə:lɪʃ] adj griesgrämig; (behaviour)
ungehobelt

churn [tʃə:n] n Butterfass nt; (also: **milk churn**)
Milchkanne f
▶ **churn out** vt am laufenden Band
produzieren

chute [ʃu:t] n (also: **rubbish chute**)
Müllschlucker m; (for coal, parcels etc) Rutsche f;
(Brit: slide) Rutschbahn f, Rutsche f

chutney ['tʃʌtnɪ] n Chutney nt

CIA (US) n abbr (= Central Intelligence Agency) CIA
f or m

cicada [sɪ'kɑːdə] n Zikade f

CID (Brit) n abbr = **Criminal Investigation
Department**

cider ['saɪdə'] n Apfelwein m

c.i.f., CIF abbr (Comm: = cost, insurance, and freight)
cif

cigar [sɪ'gɑː'] n Zigarre f

cigarette [sɪgə'rɛt] n Zigarette f

cigarette case n Zigarettenetui nt

cigarette end n Zigarettenstummel m

cigarette holder n Zigarettenspitze f

C in C abbr (Mil) = **commander in chief**

cinch [sɪntʃ] (inf) n: **it's a ~** das ist ein
Kinderspiel or ein Klacks

Cinderella [sɪndə'rɛlə] n Aschenputtel nt,
Aschenbrödel nt

cinders ['sɪndəz] npl Asche f

cine camera ['sɪnɪ-] (Brit) n (Schmal)
filmkamera f

cine film (Brit) n Schmalfilm m

cinema ['sɪnəmə] n Kino nt; (film-making) Film
m

cine projector (Brit) n Filmprojektor m

cinnamon ['sɪnəmən] n Zimt m

cipher ['saɪfə'] n (code) Chiffre f; (fig) Niemand
m; **in ~** chiffriert

circa ['sə:kə] prep circa

circle ['sə:kl] n Kreis m; (in cinema, theatre) Rang

m ▷ vi kreisen ▷ vt kreisen um; (surround)
umgeben

circuit ['sə:kɪt] n Runde f; (Elec) Stromkreis m;
(track) Rennbahn f

circuit board n Platine f, Leiterplatte f

circuitous [sə:'kjuɪtəs] adj umständlich

circular ['sə:kjulə'] adj rund; (route) Rund- ▷ n
(letter) Rundschreiben nt, Rundbrief m; (as
advertisement) Wurfsendung f; ~ **argument**
Zirkelschluss m

circulate ['sə:kjuleɪt] vi (traffic) fließen; (blood,
report) zirkulieren; (news, rumour) kursieren, in
Umlauf sein; (person) die Runde machen ▷ vt
herumgehen or zirkulieren lassen

circulating capital [sə:kju'leɪtɪŋ-] n (Comm)
flüssiges Kapital nt, Umlaufkapital nt

circulation [sə:kju'leɪʃən] n (of traffic) Fluss m;
(of air etc) Zirkulation f; (of newspaper) Auflage f;
(Med: of blood) Kreislauf m

circumcise ['sə:kəmsaɪz] vt beschneiden

circumference [sə'kʌmfərəns] n Umfang m;
(edge) Rand m

circumflex ['sə:kəmflɛks] n (also: **circumflex
accent**) Zirkumflex m

circumscribe ['sə:kəmskraɪb] vt (Math) einen
Kreis umbeschreiben; (fig) eingrenzen

circumspect ['sə:kəmspɛkt] adj umsichtig

circumstances ['sə:kəmstənsɪz] npl Umstände
pl; (financial condition) (finanzielle) Verhältnisse
pl; **in the ~** unter diesen Umständen; **under
no ~** unter (gar) keinen Umständen, auf
keinen Fall

circumstantial [sə:kəm'stænʃl] adj
ausführlich; ~ **evidence** Indizienbeweis m

circumvent [sə:kəm'vɛnt] vt umgehen

circus ['sə:kəs] n Zirkus m; (also: **Circus**: in place
names) Platz m

cirrhosis [sɪ'rəusɪs] n (also: **cirrhosis of the
liver**) Leberzirrhose f

CIS n abbr (= Commonwealth of Independent States)
GUS f

cissy ['sɪsɪ] n, adj see **sissy**

cistern ['sɪstən] n Zisterne f; (of toilet)
Spülkasten m

citation [saɪ'teɪʃən] n Zitat nt; (US) Belobigung
f; (Law) Vorladung f (vor Gericht)

cite [saɪt] vt zitieren; (example) anführen; (Law)
vorladen

citizen ['sɪtɪzn] n Staatsbürger(in) m(f); (of
town) Bürger(in) m(f)

Citizens' Advice Bureau ['sɪtɪznz-] n ≈
Bürgerberatungsstelle f

citizenship ['sɪtɪznʃɪp] n Staatsbürgerschaft f;
(Brit: Scol) Gesellschaftskunde f

citric acid ['sɪtrɪk-] n Zitronensäure f

citrus fruit ['sɪtrəs-] n Zitrusfrucht f

city ['sɪtɪ] n (Groß)stadt f; **the C~** (Fin) die City,
das Londoner Banken- und Börsenviertel

city centre n Stadtzentrum nt, Innenstadt f

City Hall n Rathaus nt; (US: municipal government)
Stadtverwaltung f

civic ['sɪvɪk] adj (authorities etc) Stadt-, städtisch;
(duties, pride) Bürger-, bürgerlich

civic centre (Brit) n Stadtverwaltung f
civil ['sıvıl] adj (disturbances, rights) Bürger-;
(liberties, law) bürgerlich; (polite) höflich
Civil Aviation Authority (Brit) n Behörde f für
Zivilluftfahrt
civil defence n Zivilschutz m
civil disobedience n ziviler Ungehorsam m
civil engineer n Bauingenieur(in) m(f)
civil engineering n Hoch- und Tiefbau m
civilian [sɪ'vɪlɪən] adj (population) Zivil- ▷ n
Zivilist m; ~ **casualties** Verluste pl unter der
Zivilbevölkerung
civilization [sɪvɪlaɪ'zeɪʃən] n Zivilisation f; (a
society) Kultur f
civilized ['sɪvɪlaɪzd] adj zivilisiert; (person)
kultiviert; (place, experience) gepflegt
civil law n Zivilrecht nt, bürgerliches Recht nt
civil liberties n (bürgerliche) Freiheitsrechte pl
civil rights npl Bürgerrechte pl
civil servant n (Staats)beamter m, (Staats)
beamtin f
Civil Service n Beamtenschaft f
civil war n Bürgerkrieg m
civvies ['sɪvɪz] (inf) npl Zivilklamotten pl
cl abbr (= centilitre) cl
clad [klæd] adj: ~ **(in)** gekleidet (in +acc)
claim [kleɪm] vt (assert) behaupten;
(responsibility) übernehmen; (credit) in
Anspruch nehmen; (rights, inheritance)
Anspruch erheben auf +acc; (expenses) sich dat
zurückerstatten lassen; (compensation, damages)
verlangen ▷ vi (for insurance) Ansprüche
geltend machen ▷ n (assertion) Behauptung
f; (for pension, wage rise, compensation) Forderung
f; (right: to inheritance, land) Anspruch m; (for
expenses) Spesenabrechnung f; **(insurance)** ~
(Versicherungs)anspruch m; **to put in a ~ for**
beantragen
claimant ['kleɪmənt] n Antragsteller(in) m(f)
claim form n Antragsformular nt
clairvoyant [kleə'vɔɪənt] n Hellseher(in) m(f)
clam [klæm] n Venusmuschel f
  ▶ **clam up** (inf) vi keinen Piep (mehr) sagen
clamber ['klæmbə'] vi klettern
clammy ['klæmɪ] adj feucht
clamour, (US) **clamor** ['klæmə'] n Lärm m;
(protest) Protest m, Aufschrei m ▷ vi: **to ~ for**
schreien nach
clamp [klæmp] n Schraubzwinge f, Klemme f
▷ vt (two things) zusammenklemmen; (one thing
on another) klemmen; (wheel) krallen
  ▶ **clamp down on** vt fus rigoros vorgehen
gegen
clampdown ['klæmpdaun] n: ~ **(on)** hartes
Durchgreifen nt (gegen)
clan [klæn] n Clan m
clandestine [klæn'dɛstɪn] adj geheim,
Geheim-
clang [klæŋ] vi klappern; (bell) läuten ▷ n (see
vi) Klappern nt; Läuten nt
clanger ['klæŋə'] (Brit: inf) n Fauxpas m; **to
drop a ~** ins Fettnäpfchen treten
clansman ['klænzmən] n (irreg: like **man**)

Clanmitglied nt
clap [klæp] vi (Beifall) klatschen ▷ vt: **to ~
(one's hands)** (in die Hände) klatschen ▷ n: **a
~ of thunder** ein Donnerschlag m
clapping ['klæpɪŋ] n Beifall m
claptrap ['klæptræp] (inf) n Geschwafel nt
claret ['klærət] n roter Bordeaux(wein) m
clarification [klærɪfɪ'keɪʃən] n Klärung f
clarify ['klærɪfaɪ] vt klären
clarinet [klærɪ'nɛt] n Klarinette f
clarity ['klærɪtɪ] n Klarheit f
clash [klæʃ] n (fight) Zusammenstoß m;
(disagreement) Streit m, Auseinandersetzung f;
(of beliefs, ideas, views) Konflikt m; (of colours, styles,
personalities) Unverträglichkeit f; (of events, dates,
appointments) Überschneidung f; (noise) Klirren
nt ▷ vi (fight) zusammenstoßen; (disagree) sich
streiten, eine Auseinandersetzung haben;
(beliefs, ideas, views) aufeinanderprallen;
(colours) sich beißen; (styles, personalities)
nicht zusammenpassen; (two events, dates,
appointments) sich überschneiden; (make noise)
klirrend aneinanderschlagen
clasp [klɑːsp] n Griff m; (embrace)
Umklammerung f; (of necklace, bag) Verschluss
m ▷ vt (er)greifen; (embrace) umklammern
class [klɑːs] n Klasse f; (lesson) (Unterrichts)
stunde f ▷ adj (struggle, distinction) Klassen- ▷ vt
einordnen, einstufen
class-conscious ['klɑːs'kɒnʃəs] adj
klassenbewusst, standesbewusst
class-consciousness ['klɑːs'kɒnʃəsnɪs] n
Klassenbewusstsein nt, Standesbewusstsein
nt
classic ['klæsɪk] adj klassisch ▷ n Klassiker m;
(race) bedeutendes Pferderennen für dreijährige Pferde;
classics npl (Scol) Altphilologie f
classical ['klæsɪkl] adj klassisch
classification [klæsɪfɪ'keɪʃən] n Klassifikation
f; (category) Klasse f; (system) Einteilung f
classified ['klæsɪfaɪd] adj geheim
classified advertisement n Kleinanzeige f
classify ['klæsɪfaɪ] vt klassifizieren, (ein)
ordnen
classless ['klɑːslɪs] adj: ~ **society** klassenlose
Gesellschaft f
classmate ['klɑːsmeɪt] n Klassenkamerad(in)
m(f)
classroom ['klɑːsrum] n Klassenzimmer nt
classroom assistant n Assistenzlehrkraft f
classy ['klɑːsɪ] (inf) adj nobel, exklusiv; (person)
todschick
clatter ['klætə'] n Klappern nt; (of hooves)
Trappeln nt ▷ vi (see n) klappern; trappeln
clause [klɔːz] n (Law) Klausel f; (Ling) Satz m
claustrophobia [klɔːstrə'fəubɪə] n
Klaustrophobie f, Platzangst f
claustrophobic [klɔːstrə'fəubɪk] adj (place,
situation) beengend; (person): **to be/feel ~**
Platzangst haben/bekommen
claw [klɔː] n Kralle f; (of lobster) Schere f,
Zange f
  ▶ **claw at** vt fus sich krallen an +acc

clay [kleɪ] n Ton m; (soil) Lehm m
clean [kli:n] adj sauber; (fight) fair; (record, reputation) einwandfrei; (joke, story) stubenrein, anständig; (edge, fracture) glatt ▷ vt sauber machen; (car, hands, face etc) waschen ▷ adv: **he ~ forgot** er hat es glatt(weg) vergessen; **to have a ~ driving licence, to have a ~ driving record** (US) keine Strafpunkte haben; **to ~ one's teeth** (Brit) sich dat die Zähne putzen; **the thief got ~ away** der Dieb konnte entkommen; **to come ~** (inf) auspacken
▶ **clean off** vt abwaschen, abwischen
▶ **clean out** vt gründlich sauber machen; (inf: person) ausnehmen
▶ **clean up** vt aufräumen; (child) sauber machen; (fig) für Ordnung sorgen in +dat ▷ vi aufräumen, sauber machen; (inf: make profit) absahnen
clean-cut ['kli:n'kʌt] adj gepflegt; (situation) klar
cleaner ['kli:nəʳ] n Raumpfleger(in) m(f); (woman) Putzfrau f; (substance) Reinigungsmittel nt, Putzmittel nt
cleaner's ['kli:nəz] n (also: **dry cleaner's**) Reinigung f
cleaning ['kli:nɪŋ] n Putzen nt
cleaning lady n Putzfrau f, Reinemachefrau f
cleanliness ['klɛnlɪnɪs] n Sauberkeit f, Reinlichkeit f
cleanly ['kli:nlɪ] adv sauber
cleanse [klɛnz] vt (purify) läutern; (face, cut) reinigen
cleanser ['klɛnzəʳ] n (for face) Reinigungscreme f, Reinigungsmilch f
clean-shaven ['kli:n'ʃeɪvn] adj glatt rasiert
cleansing department ['klɛnzɪŋ-] (Brit) n ≈ Stadtreinigung f
clean sweep n: **to make a ~** (Sport) alle Preise einstecken
clean-up ['kli:nʌp] n: **to give sth a ~** etw gründlich sauber machen
clear [klɪəʳ] adj klar; (footprint) deutlich; (photograph) scharf; (commitment) eindeutig; (glass, plastic) durchsichtig; (road, way, floor etc) frei; (conscience, skin) rein ▷ vt (room) ausräumen; (trees) abholzen; (weeds etc) entfernen; (slums etc, stock) räumen; (Law) freisprechen; (fence, wall) überspringen; (cheque) verrechnen ▷ vi (weather, sky) aufklaren; (fog, smoke) sich auflösen; (room etc) sich leeren ▷ adv: **to be ~ of the ground** den Boden nicht berühren ▷ n: **to be in the ~** (out of debt) schuldenfrei sein; (free of suspicion) von jedem Verdacht frei sein; (out of danger) außer Gefahr sein; **~ profit** Reingewinn m; **I have a ~ day tomorrow** ich habe morgen nichts vor; **to make o.s. ~** sich klar ausdrücken; **to make it ~ to sb that ...** es jdm (unmissverständlich) klarmachen, dass ...; **to ~ the table** den Tisch abräumen; **to ~ a space (for sth)** (für etw) Platz schaffen; **to ~ one's throat** sich räuspern; **to ~ a profit** einen Gewinn machen; **to keep ~ of sb** jdm

aus dem Weg gehen; **to keep ~ of sth** etw meiden; **to keep ~ of trouble** allem Ärger aus dem Weg gehen
▶ **clear off** (inf) vi abhauen, verschwinden
▶ **clear up** vt aufräumen; (mystery) aufklären; (problem) lösen ▷ vi (bad weather) sich aufklären; (illness) sich bessern
clearance ['klɪərəns] n (of slums) Räumung f; (of trees) Abholzung f; (permission) Genehmigung f; (free space) lichte Höhe f
clearance sale n Räumungsverkauf m
clear-cut ['klɪə'kʌt] adj klar
clearing ['klɪərɪŋ] n Lichtung f; (Brit: Banking) Clearing nt
clearing bank (Brit) n Clearingbank f
clearing house n (Comm) Clearingstelle f
clearly ['klɪəlɪ] adv klar; (obviously) eindeutig
clearway ['klɪəweɪ] (Brit) n Straße f mit Halteverbot
cleavage ['kli:vɪdʒ] n (of woman's breasts) Dekolleté nt
cleaver ['kli:vəʳ] n Hackbeil nt
clef [klɛf] n (Noten)schlüssel m
cleft [klɛft] n Spalte f
cleft palate n (Med) Gaumenspalte f
clemency ['klɛmənsɪ] n Milde f
clement ['klɛmənt] adj mild
clench [klɛntʃ] vt (fist) ballen; (teeth) zusammenbeißen
clergy ['klə:dʒɪ] n Klerus m, Geistlichkeit f
clergyman ['klə:dʒɪmən] (irreg: like **man**) n Geistliche(r) m
clerical ['klɛrɪkl] adj (job, worker) Büro-; (error) Schreib-; (Rel) geistlich
clerk [klɑ:k, (US) klə:rk] n (Brit) Büroangestellte(r) f(m); (US: sales person) Verkäufer(in) m(f)
Clerk of Court n Protokollführer(in) m(f)
clever ['klɛvəʳ] adj klug; (deft, crafty) schlau, clever (inf); (device, arrangement) raffiniert
cleverly ['klɛvəlɪ] adv geschickt
clew [klu:] (US) n = **clue**
cliché ['kli:ʃeɪ] n Klischee nt
click [klɪk] vi klicken ▷ vt: **to ~ one's tongue** mit der Zunge schnalzen; **to ~ one's heels** die Hacken zusammenschlagen
client ['klaɪənt] n Kunde m, Kundin f; (of bank, lawyer) Klient(in) m(f); (of restaurant) Gast m
clientele [kli:ɑ̃:n'tɛl] n Kundschaft f
cliff [klɪf] n Kliff nt
cliffhanger ['klɪfhæŋəʳ] n spannungsgeladene Szene am Ende einer Filmepisode, Cliffhanger m
climactic [klaɪ'mæktɪk] adj: **~ point** Höhepunkt m
climate ['klaɪmɪt] n Klima nt
climate conference n (Pol) Klimakonferenz f
climax ['klaɪmæks] n (sexual) Höhepunkt m
climb [klaɪm] vi klettern; (plane, sun, prices, shares) steigen ▷ vt (stairs, ladder) hochsteigen, hinaufsteigen; (tree) klettern auf +acc; (hill) steigen auf +acc ▷ n Aufstieg m; (of prices etc) Anstieg m; **to ~ over a wall/into a car** über eine Mauer/in ein Auto steigen or klettern

479

▶ **climb down** (Brit) vi (fig) nachgeben
climb-down ['klaɪmdaʊn] n Nachgeben nt,
Rückzieher m (inf)
climber ['klaɪmə'] n Bergsteiger(in) m(f); (plant)
Kletterpflanze f
climbing ['klaɪmɪŋ] n Bergsteigen nt
clinch [klɪntʃ] vt (deal) perfekt machen;
(argument) zum Abschluss bringen
clincher ['klɪntʃə'] n ausschlaggebender Faktor
m
cling [klɪŋ] (pt, pp **clung**) vi: **to ~ to** (mother,
support) sich festklammern an +dat; (idea, belief)
festhalten an +dat; (subj: clothes, dress) sich
anschmiegen +dat
clingfilm ['klɪŋfɪlm] n, **clingwrap** ['klɪŋræp] n
(US) Frischhaltefolie f
clinic ['klɪnɪk] n Klinik f; (session) Sprechstunde
f; (: Sport) Trainingstunde f
clinical ['klɪnɪkl] adj klinisch; (fig) nüchtern,
kühl; (: building, room) steril
clink [klɪŋk] vi klirren
clip [klɪp] n (also: **paper clip**) Büroklammer f;
(Brit: also: **bulldog clip**) Klammer f; (holding wire,
hose etc) Klemme f; (for hair) Spange f; (TV, Cine)
Ausschnitt m ▷ vt festklemmen; (also: **clip
together**) zusammenheften; (cut) schneiden
clippers ['klɪpəz] npl (for gardening) Schere f;
(also: **nail clippers**) Nagelzange f
clipping ['klɪpɪŋ] n (from newspaper) Ausschnitt
m
clique [kliːk] n Clique f, Gruppe f
clitoris ['klɪtərɪs] n Klitoris f
cloak [kləʊk] n Umhang m ▷ vt (fig) hüllen
cloakroom ['kləʊkrum] n Garderobe f;
(Brit: WC) Toilette f
clobber ['klɒbə'] (inf) n Klamotten pl ▷ vt (hit)
hauen, schlagen; (defeat) in die Pfanne hauen
clock [klɒk] n Uhr f; **round the ~** rund um
die Uhr; **30,000 on the ~** (Brit: Aut) ein
Tachostand von 30.000; **to work against the
~** gegen die Uhr arbeiten
▶ **clock in** (Brit) vi (den Arbeitsbeginn)
stempeln or stechen
▶ **clock off** (Brit) vi (das Arbeitsende) stempeln
or stechen
▶ **clock on** (Brit) vi = **clock in**
▶ **clock out** (Brit) vi = **clock off**
▶ **clock up** vt (miles) fahren; (hours) arbeiten
clockwise ['klɒkwaɪz] adv im Uhrzeigersinn
clockwork ['klɒkwəːk] n Uhrwerk nt ▷ adj
aufziehbar, zum Aufziehen; **like ~** wie am
Schnürchen
clog [klɒg] n Clog m; (wooden) Holzschuh m ▷ vt
verstopfen ▷ vi (also: **clog up**) verstopfen
cloister ['klɔɪstə'] n Kreuzgang m
clone [kləʊn] n Klon m
close¹ [kləʊs] adj (writing, friend, contact) eng;
(texture) dicht, fest; (relative) nahe; (examination)
genau, gründlich; (watch) streng, scharf;
(contest) knapp; (weather) schwül; (room)
stickig ▷ adv nahe; **~ (to)** nahe (+gen); **~ to** in
der Nähe +gen; **~ by, ~ at hand** in der Nähe;
how ~ is Edinburgh to Glasgow? wie weit

ist Edinburgh von Glasgow entfernt?; **a ~
friend** ein guter or enger Freund; **to have a ~
shave** (fig) gerade noch davonkommen; **at ~
quarters** aus der Nähe
close² [kləʊz] vt schließen, zumachen; (sale,
deal, case) abschließen; (speech) schließen,
beenden ▷ vi schließen, zumachen; (door, lid)
sich schließen, zugehen; (end) aufhören ▷ n
Ende nt, Schlus m; **to bring sth to a ~** etw
beenden
▶ **close down** vi (factory) stillgelegt werden;
(magazine etc) eingestellt werden
▶ **close in** vi (night) hereinbrechen; (fog) sich
verdichten; **to ~ in on sb/sth** jdm/etw auf
den Leib rücken; **the days are closing in** die
Tage werden kürzer
▶ **close off** vt (area) abriegeln; (road) sperren
closed [kləʊzd] adj geschlossen; (road) gesperrt
closed-circuit television n
Fernsehüberwachungsanlage f
closed shop n Betrieb m mit
Gewerkschaftszwang
close-knit ['kləʊs'nɪt] adj eng
zusammengewachsen
closely ['kləʊslɪ] adv (examine, watch) genau;
(connected) eng; (related) nah(e); (resemble) sehr;
we are ~ related wir sind nah verwandt;
a ~ guarded secret ein streng gehütetes
Geheimnis
close season ['kləʊs-] n Schonzeit f; (Sport)
Sommerpause f
closet ['klɒzɪt] n Wandschrank m
close-up ['kləʊsʌp] n Nahaufnahme f
closing ['kləʊzɪŋ] adj (stages) Schluss-; (remarks)
abschließend
closing price n (Stock Exchange) Schlusskurs m,
Schlussnotierung f
closing time (Brit) n (in pub) Polizeistunde f,
Sperrstunde f
closure ['kləʊʒə'] n (of factory) Stilllegung f; (of
magazine) Einstellung f; (of road) Sperrung f; (of
border) Schließung f
clot [klɒt] n (blood clot) (Blut)gerinnsel nt;
(inf: idiot) Trottel m ▷ vi gerinnen; (external
bleeding) zum Stillstand kommen
cloth [klɒθ] n (material) Stoff m, Tuch nt; (rag)
Lappen m; (Brit: also: **teacloth**) (Spül)tuch nt;
(also: **tablecloth**) Tischtuch nt, Tischdecke f
clothe [kləʊð] vt anziehen, kleiden
clothes [kləʊðz] npl Kleidung f, Kleider pl; **to
put one's ~ on** sich anziehen; **to take one's ~
off** sich ausziehen
clothes brush n Kleiderbürste f
clothesline ['kləʊðzlaɪn] n Wäscheleine f
clothes peg, (US) **clothes pin** n
Wäscheklammer f
clothing ['kləʊðɪŋ] n = **clothes**
clotted cream ['klɒtɪd-] (Brit) n Sahne aus
erhitzter Milch
cloud [klaʊd] n Wolke f ▷ vt trüben; **every ~
has a silver lining** (proverb) auf Regen folgt
Sonnenschein; **to ~ the issue** es unnötig
kompliziert machen; (deliberately) die

Angelegenheit verschleiern

▶ **cloud over** vi (sky) sich bewölken, sich bedecken; (face, eyes) sich verfinstern

cloudburst ['klaudbə:st] n Wolkenbruch m

cloud-cuckoo-land [klaud'kuku:lænd] (Brit) n Wolkenkuckucksheim nt

cloudy ['klaudɪ] adj wolkig, bewölkt; (liquid) trüb

clout [klaut] vt schlagen, hauen ▷ n (fig) Schlagkraft f

clove [kləuv] n Gewürznelke f; **~ of garlic** Knoblauchzehe f

clover ['kləuvər] n Klee m

cloverleaf ['kləuvəli:f] n Kleeblatt nt

clown [klaun] n Clown m ▷ vi (also: **clown about, clown around**) herumblödeln, herumkaspern

cloying ['klɔɪɪŋ] adj süßlich

club [klʌb] n Klub m, Verein m; (weapon) Keule f, Knüppel m; (also: **golf club**: object) Golfschläger m ▷ vt knüppeln ▷ vi: **to ~ together** zusammenlegen; **clubs** npl (Cards) Kreuz nt

club car (US) n Speisewagen m

club class n Klubklasse f, Businessklasse f

clubhouse ['klʌbhaus] n Klubhaus nt

club soda (US) n (soda water) Sodawasser nt

cluck [klʌk] vi glucken

clue [klu:] n Hinweis m, Anhaltspunkt m; (in crossword) Frage f; **I haven't a ~** ich habe keine Ahnung

clued-up ['klu:dʌp], (US: inf) **clued in** adj: **to be ~ on sth** über etw acc im Bilde sein

clueless ['klu:lɪs] adj ahnungslos, unbedarft

clump [klʌmp] n Gruppe f

clumsy ['klʌmzɪ] adj ungeschickt; (object) unförmig; (effort, attempt) plump

clung [klʌŋ] pt, pp of **cling**

cluster ['klʌstər] n Gruppe f ▷ vi (people) sich scharen; (houses) sich drängen

clutch [klʌtʃ] n Griff m; (Aut) Kupplung f ▷ vt (purse, hand) umklammern; (stick) sich festklammern an +dat ▷ vi: **to ~ at** sich klammern an +acc

clutter ['klʌtər] vt (also: **clutter up**: room) vollstopfen; (: table) vollstellen ▷ n Kram m (inf)

cm abbr (= centimetre) cm

CNAA (Brit) n abbr (= Council for National Academic Awards) Zentralstelle zur Vergabe von Qualifikationsnachweisen

CND (Brit) n abbr (= Campaign for Nuclear Disarmament) Organisation für atomare Abrüstung

CO n abbr = **commanding officer**; (Brit: = Commonwealth Office) Regierungsstelle für Angelegenheiten des Commonwealth ▷ abbr (US: Post) = Colorado

Co. abbr = **company**; **county**

c/o abbr (= care of) bei, c/o

coach [kəutʃ] n (Reise)bus m; (horse-drawn) Kutsche f; (of train) Wagen m; (Sport) Trainer m; (Scol) Nachhilfelehrer(in) m(f) ▷ vt trainieren; (student) Nachhilfeunterricht geben +dat

coach trip n Busfahrt f

coagulate [kəu'ægjuleɪt] vi (blood) gerinnen;

(paint etc) eindicken ▷ vt (blood) gerinnen lassen; (paint) dick werden lassen

coal [kəul] n Kohle f

coalface ['kəulfeɪs] n Streb m

coalfield ['kəulfi:ld] n Kohlenrevier nt

coalition [kəuə'lɪʃən] n (Pol) Koalition f; (of pressure groups etc) Zusammenschluss m

coalman ['kəulmən] (irreg: like **man**) n Kohlenhändler m

coal merchant n = **coalman**

coal mine n Kohlenbergwerk nt, Zeche f

coal miner n Bergmann m, Kumpel m (inf)

coal mining n (Kohlen)bergbau m

coarse [kɔ:s] adj (texture) grob; (vulgar) gewöhnlich, derb; (salt, sand etc) grobkörnig

coast [kəust] n Küste f ▷ vi (im Leerlauf) fahren

coastal ['kəustl] adj Küsten-

coaster ['kəustər] n (Naut) Küstenfahrzeug nt; (for glass) Untersetzer m

coastguard ['kəustgɑ:d] n (officer) Küstenwächter m; (service) Küstenwacht f

coastline ['kəustlaɪn] n Küste f

coat [kəut] n Mantel m; (of animal) Fell nt; (layer) Schicht f; (: of paint) Anstrich m ▷ vt überziehen

coat hanger n Kleiderbügel m

coating ['kəutɪŋ] n (of chocolate etc) Überzug m; (of dust etc) Schicht f

coat of arms n Wappen nt

coauthor ['kəu'ɔ:θər] n Mitautor(in) m(f), Mitverfasser(in) m(f)

coax [kəuks] vt (person) überreden

cob [kɔb] n see **corn**

cobbler ['kɔblər] n Schuster m

cobbles ['kɔblz] npl Kopfsteinpflaster nt

cobblestones ['kɔblstəunz] npl = **cobbles**

COBOL ['kəubɔl] n COBOL nt

cobra ['kəubrə] n Kobra f

cobweb ['kɔbweb] n Spinnennetz nt

cocaine [kə'keɪn] n Kokain nt

cock [kɔk] n Hahn m; (male bird) Männchen nt ▷ vt (gun) entsichern; **to ~ one's ears** (fig) die Ohren spitzen

cock-a-hoop [kɔkə'hu:p] adj ganz aus dem Häuschen

cockerel ['kɔkərl] n junger Hahn m

cock-eyed ['kɔkaɪd] adj (fig) verrückt, widersinnig

cockle ['kɔkl] n Herzmuschel f

cockney ['kɔknɪ] n Cockney m, echter Londoner m; (Ling) Cockney nt

cockpit ['kɔkpɪt] n Cockpit nt

cockroach ['kɔkrəutʃ] n Küchenschabe f, Kakerlak m

cocktail ['kɔkteɪl] n Cocktail m; **fruit ~** Obstsalat m; **prawn ~** Krabbencocktail m

cocktail cabinet n Hausbar f

cocktail party n Cocktailparty f

cocktail shaker [-'ʃeɪkər] n Mixbecher m

cock-up ['kɔkʌp] (inf!) n Schlamassel m

cocky ['kɔkɪ] adj großspurig

cocoa ['kəukəu] n Kakao m

coconut ['kəukənʌt] n Kokosnuss f

cocoon [kə'ku:n] n Puppe f, Kokon m; (fig) schützende Umgebung f

COD abbr (Brit) = **cash on delivery**; (US) = **collect on delivery**

cod [kɔd] n Kabeljau m

code [kəud] n (cipher) Chiffre f; (also: **dialling code**) Vorwahl f; (also: **post code**) Postleitzahl f; ~ **of behaviour** Sittenkodex m; ~ **of practice** Verfahrensregeln pl

codeine ['kəudi:n] n Codein nt

codger ['kɔdʒəʳ] (inf) n: **old** ~ komischer Kauz m

codicil ['kɔdɪsɪl] n (Law) Kodizill nt

codify ['kəudɪfaɪ] vt kodifizieren

cod-liver oil ['kɔdlɪvə-] n Lebertran m

co-driver ['kəu'draɪvəʳ] n Beifahrer(in) m(f)

co-ed ['kəu'ɛd] (Scol) adj abbr = **coeducational** ▷ n abbr (US: female pupil/student) Schülerin/ Studentin an einer gemischten Schule/Universität; (Brit: school) gemischte Schule f

coeducational ['kəuɛdju'keɪʃənl] adj (school) Koedukations-, gemischt

coerce [kəu'ə:s] vt zwingen

coercion [kəu'ə:ʃən] n Zwang m

coexistence ['kəuɪg'zɪstəns] n Koexistenz f

C of C n abbr = **chamber of commerce**

C of E abbr = **Church of England**

coffee ['kɔfɪ] n Kaffee m; **black** ~ schwarzer Kaffee m; **white** ~ Kaffee mit Milch; ~ **with cream** Kaffee mit Sahne

coffee bar (Brit) n Café nt

coffee bean n Kaffeebohne f

coffee break n Kaffeepause f

coffee cake (US) n Kuchen m zum Kaffee

coffee cup n Kaffeetasse f

coffeepot ['kɔfɪpɔt] n Kaffeekanne f

coffee table n Couchtisch m

coffin ['kɔfɪn] n Sarg m

C of I abbr (= Church of Ireland) anglikanische Kirche Irlands

C of S abbr (= Church of Scotland) presbyterianische Kirche in Schottland

cog [kɔg] n (wheel) Zahnrad nt; (tooth) Zahn m

cogent ['kəudʒənt] adj stichhaltig, zwingend

cognac ['kɔnjæk] n Kognak m

cogwheel ['kɔgwi:l] n Zahnrad nt

cohabit [kəu'hæbɪt] vi (formal) in eheähnlicher Gemeinschaft leben; **to ~ (with sb)** (mit jdm) zusammenleben

coherent [kəu'hɪərənt] adj (speech) zusammenhängend; (answer, theory) schlüssig; (person) bei klarem Verstand

cohesion [kəu'hi:ʒən] n Geschlossenheit f

cohesive [kə'hi:sɪv] adj geschlossen

coil [kɔɪl] n Rolle f; (one loop) Windung f; (of smoke) Kringel m; (Aut, Elec) Spule f; (contraceptive) Spirale f ▷ vt aufrollen, aufwickeln

coin [kɔɪn] n Münze f ▷ vt prägen

coinage ['kɔɪnɪdʒ] n Münzen pl; (Ling) Prägung f

coin box (Brit) n Münzfernsprecher m

coincide [kəuɪn'saɪd] vi (events) zusammenfallen; (ideas, views) übereinstimmen

coincidence [kəu'ɪnsɪdəns] n Zufall m

coin-operated ['kɔɪn'ɔpəreɪtɪd] adj Münz-

Coke® [kəuk] n Coca-Cola® nt or f, Coke® nt

coke [kəuk] n Koks m

Col. abbr = **colonel**

COLA (US) n abbr (= cost of living adjustment) Anpassung der Löhne und Gehälter an steigende Lebenshaltungskosten

colander ['kɔləndəʳ] n Durchschlag m

cold [kəuld] adj kalt; (unemotional) kalt, kühl ▷ n Kälte f; (Med) Erkältung f; **it's** ~ es ist kalt; **to be/feel** ~ (person) frieren; (object) kalt sein; **in** ~ **blood** kaltblütig; **to have** ~ **feet** (fig) kalte Füße bekommen; **to give sb the** ~ **shoulder** jdm die kalte Schulter zeigen; **to catch** ~, **to catch a** ~ sich erkälten

cold-blooded ['kəuld'blʌdɪd] adj kaltblütig

cold calling n (Comm: on phone) unaufgeforderte Telefonwerbung; (: visit) unaufgeforderter Vertreterbesuch

cold cream n (halbfette) Feuchtigkeitscreme f

coldly ['kəuldlɪ] adv kalt, kühl

cold-shoulder [kəuld'ʃəuldəʳ] vt die kalte Schulter zeigen +dat

cold sore n Bläschenausschlag m

cold sweat n: **to come out in a** ~ (**about sth**) (wegen etw) in kalten Schweiß ausbrechen

cold turkey n: **to do** ~ Totalentzug machen

Cold War n: **the** ~ der Kalte Krieg

coleslaw ['kəulslɔː] n Krautsalat m

colic ['kɔlɪk] n Kolik f

colicky ['kɔlɪkɪ] adj: **to be** ~ Kolik f or Leibschmerzen pl haben

collaborate [kə'læbəreɪt] vi zusammenarbeiten; (with enemy) kollaborieren

collaboration [kəlæbə'reɪʃən] n (see vb) Zusammenarbeit f; Kollaboration f

collaborator [kə'læbəreɪtəʳ] n (see vb) Mitarbeiter(in) m(f); Kollaborateur(in) m(f)

collage [kɔ'lɑːʒ] n Collage f

collagen ['kɔlədʒən] n Kollagen nt

collapse [kə'læps] vi zusammenbrechen; (building) einstürzen; (plans) scheitern; (government) stürzen ▷ n (see vb) Zusammenbruch m; Einsturz m; Scheitern nt; Sturz m

collapsible [kə'læpsəbl] adj Klapp-, zusammenklappbar

collar ['kɔləʳ] n Kragen m; (of dog, cat) Halsband nt; (Tech) Bund m ▷ vt (inf) schnappen

collarbone ['kɔləbəun] n Schlüsselbein nt

collate [kɔ'leɪt] vt vergleichen

collateral [kə'lætərl] n (Comm) (zusätzliche) Sicherheit f

collateral damage n (Mil) Schäden pl in Wohngebieten; (: casualties) Opfer pl unter der Zivilbevölkerung

collation [kə'leɪʃən] n Vergleich m; (Culin): **a cold** ~ ein kalter Imbiss m

colleague ['kɔliːg] n Kollege m, Kollegin f

collect [kə'lɛkt] vt sammeln; (mail: Brit: fetch) abholen; (debts) eintreiben; (taxes) einziehen

▷ *vi* sich ansammeln ▷ *adv* (US: *Tel*): **to call ~** ein R-Gespräch führen; **to ~ one's thoughts** seine Gedanken ordnen, sich sammeln; **~ on delivery** (US: *Comm*) per Nachnahme

collected [kə'lɛktɪd] *adj*: **~ works** gesammelte Werke *pl*

collection [kə'lɛkʃən] *n* Sammlung *f*; (*from place, person, of mail*) Abholung *f*; (*in church*) Kollekte *f*

collective [kə'lɛktɪv] *adj* kollektiv, gemeinsam ▷ *n* Kollektiv *nt*; **~ farm** landwirtschaftliche Produktionsgenossenschaft *f*

collective bargaining *n* Tarifverhandlungen *pl*

collector [kə'lɛktəʳ] *n* Sammler(in) *m(f)*; (*of taxes etc*) Einnehmer(in) *m(f)*; (*of rent, cash*) Kassierer(in) *m(f)*; **~'s item** or **piece** Sammlerstück *nt*, Liebhaberstück *nt*

college ['kɔlɪdʒ] *n* College *nt*; (*of agriculture, technology*) Fachhochschule *f*; **to go to ~** studieren; **~ of education** pädagogische Hochschule *f*

collide [kə'laɪd] *vi*: **to ~ (with)** zusammenstoßen (mit); (*fig: clash*) eine heftige Auseinandersetzung haben (mit)

collie ['kɔlɪ] *n* Collie *m*

colliery ['kɔlɪərɪ] (*Brit*) *n* (Kohlen)bergwerk *nt*, Zeche *f*

collision [kə'lɪʒən] *n* Zusammenstoß *m*; **to be on a ~ course** (*also fig*) auf Kollisionskurs sein

collision damage waiver *n* (*Insurance*) *Verzicht auf Haftungsbeschränkung bei Unfällen mit Mietwagen*

colloquial [kə'ləukwɪəl] *adj* umgangssprachlich

collusion [kə'lu:ʒən] *n* (geheime) Absprache *f*; **to be in ~ with** gemeinsame Sache machen mit

Colo. (*US*) *abbr* (*Post*) = Colorado

Cologne [kə'ləun] *n* Köln *nt*

cologne [kə'ləun] *n* (*also*: **eau de cologne**) Kölnischwasser *nt*, Eau de Cologne *nt*

Colombia [kə'lɔmbɪə] *n* Kolumbien *nt*

Colombian [kə'lɔmbɪən] *adj* kolumbianisch ▷ *n* Kolumbianer(in) *m(f)*

colon ['kəulən] *n* Doppelpunkt *m*; (*Anat*) Dickdarm *m*

colonel ['kə:nl] *n* Oberst *m*

colonial [kə'ləunɪəl] *adj* Kolonial-

colonize ['kɔlənaɪz] *vt* kolonisieren

colony ['kɔlənɪ] *n* Kolonie *f*

color *etc* ['kʌləʳ] (*US*) = **colour** *etc*

Colorado beetle [kɔlə'rɑ:dəu-] *n* Kartoffelkäfer *m*

colossal [kə'lɔsl] *adj* riesig, kolossal

colour, (*US*) **color** ['kʌləʳ] *n* Farbe *f*; (*skin colour*) Hautfarbe *f*; (*of spectacle etc*) Atmosphäre *f* ▷ *vt* bemalen; (*with crayons*) ausmalen; (*dye*) färben; (*fig*) beeinflussen ▷ *vi* (*blush*) erröten, rot werden ▷ *cpd* Farb-; **colours** *npl* (*of party, club etc*) Farben *pl*; **in ~** (*film*) in Farbe; (*illustrations*) bunt

▸ **colour in** *vt* ausmalen

colour bar *n* Rassenschranke *f*

colour-blind ['kʌləblaɪnd] *adj* farbenblind

coloured ['kʌləd] *adj* farbig; (*photo*) Farb-; (*illustration etc*) bunt

colour film *n* Farbfilm *m*

colourful ['kʌləful] *adj* bunt; (*account, story*) farbig, anschaulich; (*personality*) schillernd

colouring ['kʌlərɪŋ] *n* Gesichtsfarbe *f*, Teint *m*; (*in food*) Farbstoff *m*

colour scheme *n* Farbzusammenstellung *f*

colour supplement (*Brit*) *n* Farbbeilage *f*, Magazin *nt*

colour television *n* Farbfernsehen *nt*; (*set*) Farbfernseher *m*

colt [kəult] *n* Hengstfohlen *nt*

column ['kɔləm] *n* Säule *f*; (*of people*) Kolonne *f*; (*of print*) Spalte *f*; (*gossip/sports column*) Kolumne *f*; **the editorial ~** der Leitartikel

columnist ['kɔləmnɪst] *n* Kolumnist(in) *m(f)*

coma ['kəumə] *n* Koma *nt*; **to be in a ~** im Koma liegen

comb [kəum] *n* Kamm *m* ▷ *vt* kämmen; (*area*) durchkämmen

combat ['kɔmbæt] *n* Kampf *m* ▷ *vt* bekämpfen

combination [kɔmbɪ'neɪʃən] *n* Kombination *f*

combination lock *n* Kombinationsschloss *nt*

combine [*vti* kəm'baɪn, *n* 'kɔmbaɪn] *vt* verbinden ▷ *vi* sich zusammenschließen; (*Chem*) sich verbinden ▷ *n* Konzern *m*; (*Agr*) = **combine harvester**; **~d effort** vereintes Unternehmen

combine harvester *n* Mähdrescher *m*

combo ['kɔmbəu] *n* Combo *f*

combustible [kəm'bʌstɪbl] *adj* brennbar

combustion [kəm'bʌstʃən] *n* Verbrennung *f*

◯ KEYWORD

come [kʌm] (*pt* **came**, *pp* **come**) *vi* **1** (*movement towards*) kommen; **come with me** kommen Sie mit mir; **to come running** angelaufen kommen; **coming!** ich komme!

2 (*arrive*) kommen; **they came to a river** sie kamen an einen Fluss; **to come home** nach Hause kommen

3 (*reach*): **to come to** kommen an +*acc*; **her hair came to her waist** ihr Haar reichte ihr bis zur Hüfte; **to come to a decision** zu einer Entscheidung kommen

4 (*occur*): **an idea came to me** mir kam eine Idee

5 (*be, become*) werden; **I've come to like him** mittlerweile mag ich ihn; **if it comes to it** wenn es darauf ankommt

▸ **come about** *vi* geschehen

▸ **come across** *vt fus* (*find: person, thing*) stoßen auf +*acc*

▷ *vi*: **to come across well/badly** (*idea etc*) gut/ schlecht ankommen; (*meaning*) gut/schlecht verstanden werden

▸ **come along** *vi* (*arrive*) daherkommen; (*make progress*) vorankommen; **come along!** komm schon!

▸ **come apart** vi (break in pieces) auseinandergehen

▸ **come away** vi (leave) weggehen; (become detached) abgehen

▸ **come back** vi (return) zurückkommen; **to come back into fashion** wieder in Mode kommen

▸ **come by** vt fus (acquire) kommen zu

▸ **come down** vi (price) sinken, fallen; (building: be demolished) abgerissen werden; (tree: during storm) umstürzen

▸ **come forward** vi (volunteer) sich melden

▸ **come from** vt fus kommen von, stammen aus; (person) kommen aus

▸ **come in** vi (enter) hereinkommen; (report, news) eintreffen; (on deal etc) sich beteiligen; **come in!** herein!

▸ **come in for** vt fus (criticism etc) einstecken müssen

▸ **come into** vt fus (inherit: money) erben; **to come into fashion** in Mode kommen; **money doesn't come into it** Geld hat nichts damit zu tun

▸ **come off** vi (become detached: button, handle) sich lösen; (succeed: attempt, plan) klappen ▷ vt fus (inf): **come off it!** mach mal halblang!

▸ **come on** vi (pupil, work, project) vorankommen; (lights etc) angehen; **come on!** (hurry up) mach schon!; (encouragement) los!

▸ **come out** vi herauskommen; (stain) herausgehen; **to come out (on strike)** in den Streik treten

▸ **come over** vt fus: **I don't know what's come over him!** ich weiß nicht, was in ihn gefahren ist

▸ **come round** vi (after faint, operation) wieder zu sich kommen; (visit) vorbeikommen; (agree) zustimmen

▸ **come through** vi (survive) durchkommen; (telephone call) (durch)kommen ▷ vt fus (illness etc) überstehen

▸ **come to** vi (regain consciousness) wieder zu sich kommen ▷ vt fus (add up to): **how much does it come to?** was macht das zusammen?

▸ **come under** vt fus (heading) kommen unter +acc; (criticism, pressure, attack) geraten unter +acc

▸ **come up** vi (approach) herankommen; (sun) aufgehen; (problem) auftauchen; (event) bevorstehen; (in conversation) genannt werden; **something's come up** etwas ist dazwischengekommen

▸ **come up against** vt fus (resistance, difficulties) stoßen auf +acc

▸ **come upon** vt fus (find) stoßen auf +acc

▸ **come up to** vt fus: **the film didn't come up to our expectations** der Film entsprach nicht unseren Erwartungen; **it's coming up to 10 o'clock** es ist gleich 10 Uhr

▸ **come up with** vt fus (idea) aufwarten mit; (money) aufbringen

comeback ['kʌmbæk] n (of film star etc) Comeback nt; (reaction, response) Reaktion f

comedian [kə'miːdɪən] n Komiker m

comedienne [kəmiːdɪ'ɛn] n Komikerin f

comedown ['kʌmdaun] (inf) n Enttäuschung f; (professional) Abstieg m

comedy ['kɔmɪdɪ] n Komödie f; (humour) Witz m

comet ['kɔmɪt] n Komet m

comeuppance [kʌm'ʌpəns] n: **to get one's ~** die Quittung bekommen

comfort ['kʌmfət] n (physical) Behaglichkeit f; (material) Komfort m; (solace, relief) Trost m ▷ vt trösten; **comforts** npl (of home etc) Komfort m, Annehmlichkeiten pl

comfortable ['kʌmfətəbl] adj bequem; (room) komfortabel; (walk, climb etc) geruhsam; (income) ausreichend; (majority) sicher; **to be ~** (physically) sich wohlfühlen; (financially) sehr angenehm leben; **the patient is ~** dem Patienten geht es den Umständen entsprechend gut; **I don't feel very ~ about it** mir ist nicht ganz wohl bei der Sache

comfortably ['kʌmfətəblɪ] adv (sit) bequem; (live) angenehm

comforter ['kʌmfətər] (US) n Schnuller m

comfort shopping n Frustkauf m

comfort station (US) n öffentliche Toilette f

comic ['kɔmɪk] adj (also: **comical**) komisch ▷ n Komiker(in) m(f); (Brit: magazine) Comicheft nt

comical ['kɔmɪkl] adj komisch

comic strip n Comicstrip m

coming ['kʌmɪŋ] n Ankunft f, Kommen nt ▷ adj kommend; (next) nächste(r, s); **in the ~ weeks** in den nächsten Wochen

coming and going n, **comings and goings** ▷ npl Kommen und Gehen nt

Comintern ['kɔmɪntɜːn] n (Pol) Komintern f

comma ['kɔmə] n Komma nt

command [kə'mɑːnd] n (also Comput) Befehl m; (control, charge) Führung f; (Mil: authority) Kommando nt, Befehlsgewalt f; (mastery) Beherrschung f ▷ vt (troops) befehligen, kommandieren; (be able to get) verfügen über +acc; (deserve: respect, admiration etc) verdient haben; **to be in ~ of** das Kommando or den (Ober)befehl haben über +acc; **to have ~ of** das Kommando haben über +acc; **to take ~ of** das Kommando übernehmen +gen; **to have at one's ~** verfügen über +acc; **to ~ sb to do sth** jdm befehlen, etw zu tun

commandant ['kɔməndænt] n Kommandant m

command economy n Kommandowirtschaft f

commandeer [kɔmən'dɪər] vt requirieren, beschlagnahmen; (fig) sich aneignen

commander [kə'mɑːndər] n Befehlshaber m, Kommandant m

commander in chief n Oberbefehlshaber m

commanding [kə'mɑːndɪŋ] adj (appearance) imposant; (voice, tone) gebieterisch; (lead) entscheidend; (position) vorherrschend

commanding officer n befehlshabender Offizier m

commandment [kə'mɑːndmənt] n Gebot nt

command module n Kommandokapsel f

commando [kə'mɑːndəu] n Kommando nt, Kommandotrupp m; (soldier) Angehörige(r) m eines Kommando(trupp)s

commemorate [kə'mɛmərеɪt] vt gedenken +gen

commemoration [kəmɛmə'reɪʃən] n Gedenken nt

commemorative [kə'mɛmərətɪv] adj Gedenk-

commence [kə'mɛns] vt, vi beginnen

commend [kə'mɛnd] vt loben; **to ~ sth to sb** jdm etw empfehlen

commendable [kə'mɛndəbl] adj lobenswert

commendation [kɔmɛn'deɪʃən] n Auszeichnung f

commensurate [kə'mɛnʃərɪt] adj: **~ with** or **to** entsprechend +dat

comment ['kɔmɛnt] n Bemerkung f; (on situation etc) Kommentar m ▷ vi: **to ~ (on)** sich äußern (über +acc or zu); (on situation etc) einen Kommentar abgeben (zu); **"no ~"** „kein Kommentar!"; **to ~ that ...** bemerken, dass ...

commentary ['kɔməntərɪ] n Kommentar m; (Sport) Reportage f

commentator ['kɔmənteɪtər] n Kommentator(in) m(f); (Sport) Reporter(in) m(f)

commerce ['kɔmɜːs] n Handel m

commercial [kə'mɜːʃəl] adj kommerziell; (organization) Wirtschafts- ▷ n (advertisement) Werbespot m

commercial bank n Handelsbank f

commercial break n Werbung f

commercial college n Fachschule f für kaufmännische Berufe

commercialism [kə'mɜːʃəlɪzəm] n Kommerzialisierung f

commercialize [kə'mɜːʃəlaɪz] vt kommerzialisieren

commercialized [kə'mɜːʃəlaɪzd] (pej) adj kommerzialisiert

commercial radio n kommerzielles Radio nt

commercial television n kommerzielles Fernsehen nt

commercial traveller n Handelsvertreter(in) m(f)

commercial vehicle n Lieferwagen m

commiserate [kə'mɪzəreɪt] vi: **to ~ with sb** jdm sein Mitgefühl zeigen

commission [kə'mɪʃən] n (order for work) Auftrag m; (Comm) Provision f; (committee) Kommission f; (Mil) Offizierspatent nt ▷ vt (work of art) in Auftrag geben; (Mil) (zum Offizier) ernennen; **out of ~** außer Betrieb; (Naut) nicht im Dienst; **I get 10% ~** ich bekomme 10% Provision; **~ of inquiry** Untersuchungsausschuss m, Untersuchungskommission f; **to ~ sb to do sth** jdn damit beauftragen, etw zu tun; **to ~ sth from sb** jdm etw in Auftrag geben

commissionaire [kəmɪʃə'nɛər] (Brit) n Portier m

commissioner [kə'mɪʃənər] n Polizeipräsident m

commit [kə'mɪt] vt (crime) begehen; (money, resources) einsetzen; (to sb's care) anvertrauen; **to ~ o.s.** sich festlegen; **to ~ o.s. to do sth** sich (dazu) verpflichten, etw zu tun; **to ~ suicide** Selbstmord begehen; **to ~ to writing** zu Papier bringen; **to ~ sb for trial** jdn einem Gericht überstellen

commitment [kə'mɪtmənt] n Verpflichtung f; (to ideology, system) Engagement nt

committed [kə'mɪtɪd] adj engagiert

committee [kə'mɪtɪ] n Ausschuss m, Komitee nt; **to be on a ~** in einem Ausschuss or Komitee sein or sitzen

committee meeting n Ausschusssitzung f

commodity [kə'mɔdɪtɪ] n Ware f; (food) Nahrungsmittel nt

common ['kɔmən] adj (shared by all) gemeinsam; (good) Gemein-; (property) Gemeinschafts-; (usual, ordinary) häufig; (vulgar) gewöhnlich ▷ n Gemeindeland nt; **the Commons** (Brit: Pol) npl das Unterhaus; **in ~ use** allgemein gebräuchlich; **it's ~ knowledge that** es ist allgemein bekannt, dass; **to the ~ good** für das Gemeinwohl; **to have sth in ~ (with sb)** etw (mit jdm) gemein haben

common cold n Schnupfen m

common denominator n (Math: fig) gemeinsamer Nenner m

commoner ['kɔmənər] n Bürgerliche(r) f(m)

common ground n (fig) gemeinsame Basis f

common land n Gemeindeland nt

common law n Gewohnheitsrecht nt

common-law ['kɔmənlɔː] adj: **she is his ~ wife** sie lebt mit ihm in eheähnlicher Gemeinschaft

commonly ['kɔmənlɪ] adv häufig

Common Market n: **the ~** der Gemeinsame Markt

commonplace ['kɔmənpleɪs] adj alltäglich

common room n Aufenthaltsraum m, Tagesraum m

common sense n gesunder Menschenverstand m

Commonwealth ['kɔmənwɛlθ] (Brit) n: **the ~** das Commonwealth; siehe Info-Artikel

- COMMONWEALTH

- Das Commonwealth, offiziell
- Commonwealth of Nations, ist ein
- lockerer Zusammenschluss aus
- souveränen Staaten, die früher unter
- britischer Regierung standen, und
- von Großbritannien abhängigen
- Gebieten. Die Mitgliedstaaten
- erkennen den britischen Monarchen
- als Oberhaupt des Commonwealth an.
- Bei der Commonwealth Conference,
- einem Treffen der Staatsoberhäupter

der Commonwealthländer, werden
Angelegenheiten von gemeinsamem
Interesse diskutiert.

commotion [kə'məʊʃən] n Tumult m
communal ['kɔmjuːnl] adj gemeinsam,
Gemeinschafts-; (life) Gemeinschafts-
commune [n 'kɔmjuːn, vi kə'mjuːn] n
Kommune f ▷ vi: **to ~ with** Zwiesprache
halten mit
communicate [kə'mjuːnɪkeɪt] vt mitteilen;
(idea, feeling) vermitteln ▷ vi: **to ~ (with)** (by
speech, gesture) sich verständigen (mit); (in
writing) in Verbindung or Kontakt stehen (mit)
communication [kəmjuːnɪ'keɪʃən] n
Kommunikation f; (letter, call) Mitteilung f
communication cord (Brit) n Notbremse f
communications network
[kəmjuːnɪ'keɪʃənz-] n Kommunikationsnetz nt
communications satellite n
Kommunikationssatellit m,
Nachrichtensatellit m
communicative [kə'mjuːnɪkətɪv] adj
gesprächig, mitteilsam
communion [kə'mjuːnɪən] n (also: **Holy
Communion**: Catholic) Kommunion f;
(: Protestant) Abendmahl nt
communiqué [kə'mjuːnɪkeɪ] n Kommuniqué
nt, (amtliche) Verlautbarung f
communism ['kɔmjunɪzəm] n Kommunismus
m
communist ['kɔmjunɪst] adj kommunistisch
▷ n Kommunist(in) m(f)
community [kə'mjuːnɪtɪ] n Gemeinschaft f;
(within larger group) Bevölkerungsgruppe f
community centre n Gemeindezentrum nt
community charge (Brit) n (formerly)
Gemeindesteuer f
community chest (US) n Wohltätigkeitsfonds
m, Hilfsfonds m
community health centre n Gemeinde-
Ärztezentrum nt
community home (Brit) n Erziehungsheim nt
community service n Sozialdienst m
community spirit n Gemeinschaftssinn m
commutation ticket [kɔmju'teɪʃən-] (US) n
Zeitkarte f
commute [kə'mjuːt] vi pendeln ▷ vt (Law,
Math) umwandeln
commuter [kə'mjuːtəʳ] n Pendler(in) m(f)
compact [adj kəm'pækt, n 'kɔmpækt] adj
kompakt ▷ n (also: **powder compact**)
Puderdose f
compact disc n Compact Disc f, CD f
compact disc player n CD-Spieler m
companion [kəm'pænjən] n Begleiter(in) m(f)
companionship [kəm'pænjənʃɪp] n
Gesellschaft f
companionway [kəm'pænjənweɪ] n (Naut)
Niedergang m
company ['kʌmpənɪ] n Firma f; (Theat)
(Schauspiel)truppe f; (Mil) Kompanie f;
(companionship) Gesellschaft f; **he's good ~**

seine Gesellschaft ist angenehm; **to keep sb
~** jdm Gesellschaft leisten; **to part ~ with** sich
trennen von; **Smith and C~** Smith & Co
company car n Firmenwagen m
company director n Direktor(in) m(f),
Firmenchef(in) m(f)
company secretary (Brit) n ≈ Prokurist(in)
m(f)
comparable ['kɔmpərəbl] adj vergleichbar
comparative [kəm'pærətɪv] adj relativ; (study,
literature) vergleichend; (Ling) komparativ
comparatively [kəm'pærətɪvlɪ] adv relativ
compare [kəm'peəʳ] vt: **to ~ (with or to)**
vergleichen (mit) ▷ vi: **to ~ (with)** sich
vergleichen lassen (mit); **how do the prices
~?** wie lassen sich die Preise vergleichen?; **~d
with** or **to** im Vergleich zu, verglichen mit
comparison [kəm'pærɪsn] n Vergleich m; **in ~
(with)** im Vergleich (zu)
compartment [kəm'pɑːtmənt] n (Rail) Abteil
nt; (section) Fach nt
compass ['kʌmpəs] n Kompass m; (fig: scope)
Bereich m; **compasses** npl (also: **pair of
compasses**) Zirkel m; **within the ~ of** im
Rahmen or Bereich +gen; **beyond the ~ of** über
den Rahmen or Bereich +gen hinaus
compassion [kəm'pæʃən] n Mitgefühl nt
compassionate [kəm'pæʃənɪt] adj
mitfühlend; **on ~ grounds** aus familiären
Gründen
compassionate leave n (esp Mil) Beurlaubung
wegen Krankheit oder Trauerfall in der Familie
compatibility [kəmpætɪ'bɪlɪtɪ] n (see adj)
Vereinbarkeit f; Zueinanderpassen nt;
Kompatibilität f
compatible [kəm'pætɪbl] adj (ideas etc)
vereinbar; (people) zueinanderpassend;
(Comput) kompatibel
compel [kəm'pɛl] vt zwingen
compelling [kəm'pɛlɪŋ] adj zwingend
compendium [kəm'pɛndɪəm] n Kompendium
nt
compensate ['kɔmpənseɪt] vt entschädigen
▷ vi: **to ~ for** (loss) ersetzen; (disappointment,
change etc) (wieder) ausgleichen
compensation [kɔmpən'seɪʃən] n (see vb)
Entschädigung f; Ersatz m; Ausgleich m;
(money) Schaden(s)ersatz m
compère ['kɔmpeəʳ] n Conférencier m
compete [kəm'piːt] vi (in contest, game)
teilnehmen; (two theories, statements)
unvereinbar sein; **to ~ (with)** (companies, rivals)
konkurrieren (mit)
competence ['kɔmpɪtəns] n Fähigkeit f
competent ['kɔmpɪtənt] adj fähig
competing [kəm'piːtɪŋ] adj konkurrierend
competition [kɔmpɪ'tɪʃən] n Konkurrenz
f; (contest) Wettbewerb m; **in ~ with** im
Wettbewerb mit
competitive [kəm'pɛtɪtɪv] adj (industry, society)
wettbewerbsbetont, wettbewerbsorientiert;
(person) vom Konkurrenzdenken geprägt; (price,
product) wettbewerbsfähig, konkurrenzfähig;

(*sport*) (Wett)kampf-
competitive examination n (*for places*)
Auswahlprüfung f; (*for prizes*) Wettbewerb m
competitor [kəm'pɛtɪtə^r] n Konkurrent(in)
m(f); (*participant*) Teilnehmer(in) m(f)
compilation [kɔmpɪ'leɪʃən] n
Zusammenstellung f
compile [kəm'paɪl] vt zusammenstellen; (*book*)
verfassen
complacency [kəm'pleɪsnsɪ] n
Selbstzufriedenheit f, Selbstgefälligkeit f
complacent [kəm'pleɪsnt] adj selbstzufrieden,
selbstgefällig
complain [kəm'pleɪn] vi (*protest*) sich
beschweren; **to ~ (about)** sich beklagen (über
+acc); **to ~ of** (*headache etc*) klagen über +acc
complaint [kəm'pleɪnt] n Klage f; (*in shop etc*)
Beschwerde f; (*illness*) Beschwerden pl
complement ['kɔmplɪmənt] n Ergänzung f;
(*esp ship's crew*) Besatzung f ▷ vt ergänzen; **to
have a full ~ of** ... (*people*) die volle Stärke
an ... dat haben; (*items*) die volle Zahl an ... dat
haben
complementary [kɔmplɪ'mɛntərɪ] adj
komplementär, einander ergänzend
complete [kəm'pliːt] adj (*total: silence*)
vollkommen; (: *change*) völlig; (: *success*) voll;
(*whole*) ganz; (: *set*) vollständig; (: *edition*)
Gesamt-; (*finished*) fertig ▷ vt fertigstellen;
(*task*) beenden; (*set, group etc*) vervollständigen;
(*fill in*) ausfüllen; **it's a ~ disaster** es ist eine
totale Katastrophe
completely [kəm'pliːtlɪ] adv völlig,
vollkommen
completion [kəm'pliːʃən] n Fertigstellung f;
(*of contract*) Abschluss m; **to be nearing ~** kurz
vor dem Abschluss sein or stehen; **on ~ of the
contract** bei Vertragsabschluss
complex ['kɔmplɛks] adj kompliziert ▷ n
Komplex m
complexion [kəm'plɛkʃən] n Teint m,
Gesichtsfarbe f; (*of event etc*) Charakter m;
(*political, religious*) Anschauung f; **to put a
different ~ on sth** etw in einem anderen
Licht erscheinen lassen
complexity [kəm'plɛksɪtɪ] n Kompliziertheit f
compliance [kəm'plaɪəns] n Fügsamkeit
f; (*agreement*) Einverständnis nt; **~ with**
Einverständnis mit, Zustimmung f zu; **in ~
with** gemäß +dat
compliant [kəm'plaɪənt] adj gefällig,
entgegenkommend
complicate ['kɔmplɪkeɪt] vt komplizieren
complicated ['kɔmplɪkeɪtɪd] adj kompliziert
complication [kɔmplɪ'keɪʃən] n Komplikation
f
complicity [kəm'plɪsɪtɪ] n Mittäterschaft f
compliment [n 'kɔmplɪmənt, vt 'kɔmplɪmɛnt]
n Kompliment nt ▷ vt ein Kompliment/
Komplimente machen; **compliments** npl
(*regards*) Grüße pl; **to pay sb a ~** jdm ein
Kompliment machen; **to ~ sb (on sth)** jdm
Komplimente (wegen etw) machen; **to ~ sb**

on doing sth jdm Komplimente machen,
dass er/sie etw getan hat
complimentary [kɔmplɪ'mɛntərɪ] adj
schmeichelhaft; (*ticket, copy of book etc*) Frei-
compliments slip n Empfehlungszettel m
comply [kəm'plaɪ] vi: **to ~ with** (*law*) einhalten
+acc; (*ruling*) sich richten nach
component [kəm'pəʊnənt] adj einzeln ▷ n
Bestandteil m
compose [kəm'pəʊz] vt (*music*) komponieren;
(*poem*) verfassen; (*letter*) abfassen; **to be ~d of**
bestehen aus; **to ~ o.s.** sich sammeln
composed [kəm'pəʊzd] adj ruhig, gelassen
composer [kəm'pəʊzə^r] n Komponist(in) m(f)
composite ['kɔmpəzɪt] adj zusammengesetzt;
(*Bot*) Korbblütler-; (*Math*) teilbar; (*Bot*): **~ plant**
Korbblütler m
composition [kɔmpə'zɪʃən] n
Zusammensetzung f; (*essay*) Aufsatz m; (*Mus*)
Komposition f
compositor [kəm'pɔzɪtə^r] n (Schrift)setzer(in)
m(f)
compos mentis ['kɔmpɔs 'mɛntɪs] adj
zurechnungsfähig
compost ['kɔmpɔst] n Kompost m;
(*also:* **potting compost**) Blumenerde f
composure [kəm'pəʊʒə^r] n Fassung f,
Beherrschung f
compound [n, adj 'kɔmpaʊnd, vt kəm'paʊnd]
n (*Chem*) Verbindung f; (*enclosure*) umzäuntes
Gebiet or Gelände nt; (*Ling*) Kompositum nt
▷ adj zusammengesetzt; (*eye*) Facetten- ▷ vt
verschlimmern, vergrößern
compound fracture n komplizierter Bruch m
compound interest n Zinseszins m
comprehend [kɔmprɪ'hɛnd] vt begreifen,
verstehen
comprehension [kɔmprɪ'hɛnʃən] n
Verständnis nt
comprehensive [kɔmprɪ'hɛnsɪv] adj
umfassend; (*insurance*) Vollkasko- ▷ n =
comprehensive school
comprehensive school (*Brit*) n Gesamtschule
f; *siehe Info-Artikel*

● **COMPREHENSIVE SCHOOL**
●
● *Comprehensive school* ist in Großbritannien
● eine nicht selektive, weiterführende
● Schule, an der alle Kinder aus einem
● Einzugsgebiet gemeinsam unterrichtet
● werden. An einer solchen Gesamtschule
● können alle Schulabschlüsse gemacht
● werden. Die meisten staatlichen Schulen
● in Großbritannien sind comprehensive
● schools.

compress [vt kəm'prɛs, n 'kɔmprɛs]
vt (*information etc*) verdichten; (*air*)
komprimieren; (*cotton, paper etc*)
zusammenpressen ▷ n (*Med*) Kompresse f
compressed air [kəm'prɛst-] n Druckluft f,
Pressluft f

C

compression [kəm'preʃən] n (see vb) Verdichtung f; Kompression f; Zusammenpressen nt

comprise [kəm'praɪz] vt (also: **be comprised of**) bestehen aus; (constitute) bilden, ausmachen

compromise ['kɔmprəmaɪz] n Kompromiss m ▷ vt (beliefs, principles) verraten; (person) kompromittieren ▷ vi Kompromisse schließen ▷ cpd (solution etc) Kompromiss-

compulsion [kəm'pʌlʃən] n Zwang m; (force) Druck m, Zwang m; **under ~** unter Druck or Zwang

compulsive [kəm'pʌlsɪv] adj zwanghaft; **it makes ~ viewing/reading** das muss man einfach sehen/lesen; **he's a ~ smoker** das Rauchen ist bei ihm zur Sucht geworden

compulsory [kəm'pʌlsərɪ] adj obligatorisch; (retirement) Zwangs-

compulsory purchase n Enteignung f

compunction [kəm'pʌŋkʃən] n Schuldgefühle pl, Gewissensbisse pl; **to have no ~ about doing sth** etw tun, ohne sich schuldig zu fühlen

computer [kəm'pju:tə^r] n Computer m, Rechner m ▷ cpd Computer-; **the process is done by ~** das Verfahren wird per Computer durchgeführt

computer game n Computerspiel nt

computerization [kəmpju:təraɪ'zeɪʃən] n Computerisierung f

computerize [kəm'pju:təraɪz] vt auf Computer umstellen; (information) computerisieren

computer literate adj: **to be ~** Computerkenntnisse haben

computer programmer n Programmierer(in) m(f)

computer programming n Programmieren nt

computer science n Informatik f

computer scientist n Informatiker(in) m(f)

computing [kəm'pju:tɪŋ] n Informatik f; (activity) Computerarbeit f

comrade ['kɔmrɪd] n Genosse m, Genossin f; (friend) Kamerad(in) m(f)

comradeship ['kɔmrɪdʃɪp] n Kameradschaft f

Comsat® ['kɔmsæt] n abbr = **communications satellite**

con [kɔn] vt betrügen; (cheat) hereinlegen ▷ vi Schwindel m; **to ~ sb into doing sth** jdn durch einen Trick dazu bringen, dass er/sie etw tut

concave ['kɔnkeɪv] adj konkav

conceal [kən'si:l] vt verbergen; (information) verheimlichen

concede [kən'si:d] vt zugeben ▷ vi nachgeben; (admit defeat) sich geschlagen geben; **to ~ defeat** sich geschlagen geben; **to ~ a point to sb** jdm in einem Punkt recht geben

conceit [kən'si:t] n Einbildung f

conceited [kən'si:tɪd] adj eingebildet

conceivable [kən'si:vəbl] adj denkbar, vorstellbar; **it is ~ that ...** es ist denkbar, dass ...

conceivably [kən'si:vəblɪ] adv: **he may ~ be**

right es ist durchaus denkbar, dass er recht hat

conceive [kən'si:v] vt (child) empfangen; (plan) kommen auf +acc; (policy) konzipieren ▷ vi **to ~ of sth** sich dat etw vorstellen; **to ~ of doing sth** sich dat vorstellen, etw zu tun

concentrate ['kɔnsəntreɪt] vi sich konzentrieren ▷ vt sich konzentrieren

concentration [kɔnsən'treɪʃən] n Konzentration f

concentration camp n Konzentrationslager nt, KZ nt

concentric [kɔn'sɛntrɪk] adj konzentrisch

concept ['kɔnsɛpt] n Vorstellung f; (principle) Begriff m

conception [kən'sɛpʃən] n Vorstellung f; (of child) Empfängnis f

concern [kən'sə:n] n Angelegenheit f; (anxiety, worry) Sorge f; (Comm) Konzern m ▷ vt Sorgen machen +dat; (involve) angehen; (relate to) betreffen; **to be ~ed (about)** sich dat Sorgen machen (um); **"to whom it may ~"** (on certificate) „Bestätigung"; (on reference) „Zeugnis"; **as far as I am ~ed** was mich betrifft; **to be ~ed with** sich interessieren für; **the department ~ed** (under discussion) die betreffende Abteilung; (involved) die zuständige Abteilung

concerning [kən'sə:nɪŋ] prep bezüglich +gen, hinsichtlich +gen

concert ['kɔnsət] n Konzert nt; **in ~** (Mus) live; (activities, actions etc) gemeinsam

concerted [kən'sə:tɪd] adj gemeinsam

concert hall n Konzerthalle f, Konzertsaal m

concertina [kɔnsə'ti:nə] n Konzertina f ▷ vi sich wie eine Ziehharmonika zusammenschieben

concerto [kən'tʃə:təu] n Konzert nt

concession [kən'sɛʃən] n Zugeständnis nt, Konzession f; (Comm) Konzession; **tax ~** Steuervergünstigung f

concessionaire [kənsɛʃə'nɛə^r] n Konzessionär m

concessionary [kən'sɛʃənrɪ] adj ermäßigt

conciliation [kənsɪlɪ'eɪʃən] n Schlichtung f

conciliatory [kən'sɪlɪətrɪ] adj versöhnlich

concise [kən'saɪs] adj kurz gefasst, prägnant

conclave ['kɔnkleɪv] n Klausur f; (Rel) Konklave f

conclude [kən'klu:d] vt beenden, schließen; (treaty, deal etc) abschließen; (decide) schließen, folgern ▷ vi schließen; (events) **to ~ (with)** enden (mit); **"That," he ~d, "is why we did it"** „Darum", schloss er, „haben wir es getan"; **I ~ that ...** ich komme zu dem Schluss, dass ...

concluding [kən'klu:dɪŋ] adj (remarks etc) abschließend, Schluss-

conclusion [kən'klu:ʒən] n (see vb) Ende nt; Schluss m; Abschluss m; Folgerung f; **to come to the ~ that ...** zu dem Schluss kommen, dass ...

conclusive [kən'klu:sɪv] adj (evidence) schlüssig;

(*defeat*) endgültig

concoct [kən'kɔkt] *vt* (*excuse etc*) sich *dat* ausdenken; (*meal, sauce*) improvisieren

concoction [kən'kɔkʃən] *n* Zusammenstellung *f*; (*drink*) Gebräu *nt*

concord ['kɔŋkɔːd] *n* Eintracht *f*; (*treaty*) Vertrag *m*

concourse ['kɔŋkɔːs] *n* (Eingangs)halle *f*; (*crowd*) Menge *f*

concrete ['kɔŋkriːt] *n* Beton *m* ▷ *adj* (*ceiling, block*) Beton-; (*proposal, idea*) konkret

concrete mixer *n* Betonmischmaschine *f*

concur [kən'kəːʳ] *vi* übereinstimmen; **to ~ with** beipflichten +*dat*

concurrently [kən'kʌrntlɪ] *adv* gleichzeitig

concussion [kən'kʌʃən] *n* Gehirnerschütterung *f*

condemn [kən'dɛm] *vt* verurteilen; (*building*) für abbruchreif erklären

condemnation [kɔndɛm'neɪʃən] *n* Verurteilung *f*

condensation [kɔndɛn'seɪʃən] *n* Kondenswasser *nt*

condense [kən'dɛns] *vi* kondensieren, sich niederschlagen ▷ *vt* zusammenfassen

condensed milk [kən'dɛnst-] *n* Kondensmilch *f*, Büchsenmilch *f*

condescend [kɔndɪ'sɛnd] *vi* herablassend sein; **to ~ to do sth** sich dazu herablassen, etw zu tun

condescending [kɔndɪ'sɛndɪŋ] *adj* herablassend

condition [kən'dɪʃən] *n* Zustand *m*; (*requirement*) Bedingung *f*; (*illness*) Leiden *nt* ▷ *vt* konditionieren; (*hair*) in Form bringen; **conditions** *npl* (*circumstances*) Verhältnisse *pl*; **in good/poor ~** (*person*) in guter/schlechter Verfassung; (*thing*) in gutem/schlechtem Zustand; **a heart ~** ein Herzleiden *nt*; **weather ~s** die Wetterlage; **on ~ that ...** unter der Bedingung, dass ...

conditional [kən'dɪʃənl] *adj* bedingt; **to be ~ upon** abhängen von

conditioner [kən'dɪʃənəʳ] *n* (*for hair*) Pflegespülung *f*; (*for fabrics*) Weichspüler *m*

condo ['kɔndəu] (*US: inf*) *n abbr* = **condominium**

condolences [kən'dəulənsɪz] *npl* Beileid *nt*

condom ['kɔndəm] *n* Kondom *m* or *nt*

condominium [kɔndə'mɪnɪəm] (*US*) *n* Haus *nt* mit Eigentumswohnungen; (*rooms*) Eigentumswohnung *f*

condone [kən'dəun] *vt* gutheißen

conducive [kən'djuːsɪv] *adj*: **~ to** förderlich +*dat*

conduct [*n* 'kɔndʌkt, *vt* kən'dʌkt] *n* Verhalten *nt* ▷ *vt* (*investigation etc*) durchführen; (*manage*) führen; (*orchestra, choir etc*) dirigieren; (*heat, electricity*) leiten; **to ~ o.s.** sich verhalten

conducted tour [kən'dʌktɪd-] *n* Führung *f*

conductor [kən'dʌktəʳ] *n* (*of orchestra*) Dirigent(in) *m(f)*; (*on bus*) Schaffner *m*; (*US: on train*) Zugführer(in) *m(f)*; (*Elec*) Leiter *m*

conductress [kən'dʌktrɪs] *n* (*on bus*) Schaffnerin *f*

conduit ['kɔndjuɪt] *n* (*Tech*) Leitungsrohr *nt*; (*Elec*) Isolierrohr *nt*

cone [kəun] *n* Kegel *m*; (*on road*) Leitkegel *m*; (*Bot*) Zapfen *m*; (*ice cream cornet*) (Eis)tüte *f*

confectioner [kən'fɛkʃənəʳ] *n* (*maker*) Süßwarenhersteller(in) *m(f)*; (*seller*) Süßwarenhändler(in) *m(f)*; (*of cakes*) Konditor(in) *m(f)*

confectioner's [kən'fɛkʃənəz], **confectioner's shop** *n* Süßwarenladen *m*; (*cake shop*) Konditorei *f*

confectionery [kən'fɛkʃənrɪ] *n* Süßwaren *pl*, Süßigkeiten *pl*; (*cakes*) Konditorwaren *pl*

confederate [kən'fɛdrɪt] *adj* verbündet ▷ *n* (*pej*) Komplize *m*, Komplizin *f*; (*US: Hist*): **the C~s** die Konföderierten *pl*

confederation [kənfɛdə'reɪʃən] *n* Bund *m*; (*Pol*) Bündnis *nt*; (*Comm*) Verband *m*

confer [kən'fəːʳ] *vt*: **to ~ sth (on sb)** (jdm) etw verleihen ▷ *vi* sich beraten; **to ~ with sb about sth** sich mit jdm über etw *acc* beraten, etw mit jdm besprechen

conference ['kɔnfərəns] *n* Konferenz *f*; (*more informal*) Besprechung *f*; **to be in ~** in *or* bei einer Konferenz/Besprechung sein

conference room *n* Konferenzraum *m*; (*smaller*) Besprechungszimmer *nt*

confess [kən'fɛs] *vt* bekennen; (*sin*) beichten; (*crime*) zugeben, gestehen ▷ *vi* (*admit*) gestehen; **to ~ to sth** (*crime*) etw gestehen; (*weakness etc*) sich zu etw bekennen; **I must ~ that I didn't enjoy it at all** ich muss sagen, dass es mir überhaupt keinen Spaß gemacht hat

confession [kən'fɛʃən] *n* Geständnis *nt*; (*Rel*) Beichte *f*; **to make a ~** ein Geständnis ablegen

confessor [kən'fɛsəʳ] *n* Beichtvater *m*

confetti [kən'fɛtɪ] *n* Konfetti *nt*

confide [kən'faɪd] *vi*: **to ~ in** sich anvertrauen +*dat*

confidence ['kɔnfɪdns] *n* Vertrauen *nt*; (*self-assurance*) Selbstvertrauen *nt*; (*secret*) vertrauliche Mitteilung *f*, Geheimnis *nt*; **to have ~ in sb/sth** Vertrauen zu jdm/ etw haben; **to have (every) ~ that ...** ganz zuversichtlich sein, dass ...; **motion of no ~** Misstrauensantrag *m*; **to tell sb sth in strict ~** jdm etw ganz im Vertrauen sagen; **in ~** vertraulich

confidence trick *n* Schwindel *m*

confident ['kɔnfɪdənt] *adj* (selbst)sicher; (*positive*) zuversichtlich

confidential [kɔnfɪ'dɛnʃəl] *adj* vertraulich; (*secretary*) Privat-

confidentiality [kɔnfɪdɛnʃɪ'ælɪtɪ] *n* Vertraulichkeit *f*

configuration [kənfɪgjuˈreɪʃən] *n* Anordnung *f*; (*Comput*) Konfiguration *f*

confine [kən'faɪn] *vt* (*shut up*) einsperren; **to ~ (to)** beschränken (auf +*acc*); **to ~ o.s. to sth** sich auf etw *acc* beschränken; **to ~ o.s. to doing sth** sich darauf beschränken, etw zu tun

confined [kən'faɪnd] *adj* begrenzt
confinement [kən'faɪnmənt] *n* Haft *f*
confines ['kɒnfaɪnz] *npl* Grenzen *pl*; (*of situation*) Rahmen *m*
confirm [kən'fəːm] *vt* bestätigen; **to be ~ed** (*Rel*) konfirmiert werden
confirmation [kɒnfə'meɪʃən] *n* Bestätigung *f*; (*Rel*) Konfirmation *f*
confirmed [kən'fəːmd] *adj* (*bachelor*) eingefleischt; (*teetotaller*) überzeugt
confiscate ['kɒnfɪskeɪt] *vt* beschlagnahmen, konfiszieren
confiscation [kɒnfɪs'keɪʃən] *n* Beschlagnahme *f*, Konfiszierung *f*
conflagration [kɒnflə'greɪʃən] *n* Feuersbrunst *f*
conflict ['kɒnflɪkt] *n* Konflikt *m*; (*fighting*) Zusammenstoß *m*, Kampf *m* ▷ *vi*: **to ~ (with)** im Widerspruch stehen (zu)
conflicting [kən'flɪktɪŋ] *adj* widersprüchlich
conform [kən'fɔːm] *vi* sich anpassen; **to ~ to** entsprechen +*dat*
conformist [kən'fɔːmɪst] *n* Konformist(in) *m(f)*
confound [kən'faund] *vt* verwirren; (*amaze*) verblüffen
confounded [kən'faundɪd] *adj* verdammt, verflixt (*inf*)
confront [kən'frʌnt] *vt* (*problems, task*) sich stellen +*dat*; (*enemy, danger*) gegenübertreten +*dat*
confrontation [kɒnfrən'teɪʃən] *n* Konfrontation *f*
confuse [kən'fjuːz] *vt* verwirren; (*mix up*) verwechseln; (*complicate*) durcheinanderbringen
confused [kən'fjuːzd] *adj* (*person*) verwirrt; (*situation*) verworren, konfus; **to get ~** konfus werden
confusing [kən'fjuːzɪŋ] *adj* verwirrend
confusion [kən'fjuːʒən] *n* (*mix-up*) Verwechslung *f*; (*perplexity*) Verwirrung *f*; (*disorder*) Durcheinander *nt*
congeal [kən'dʒiːl] *vi* (*blood*) gerinnen; (*sauce, oil*) erstarren
congenial [kən'dʒiːnɪəl] *adj* ansprechend, sympathisch; (*atmosphere, place, work, company*) angenehm
congenital [kən'dʒenɪtl] *adj* angeboren
conger eel ['kɒŋgər-] *n* Seeaal *m*
congested [kən'dʒestɪd] *adj* (*road*) verstopft; (*area*) überfüllt; (*nose*) verstopft; **his lungs are ~** in seiner Lunge hat sich Blut angestaut
congestion [kən'dʒestʃən] *n* (*Med*) Blutstau *m*; (*of road*) Verstopfung *f*; (*of area*) Überfüllung *f*
congestion charge *n* City-Maut *f*
conglomerate [kən'glɒmərɪt] *n* (*Comm*) Konglomerat *nt*
conglomeration [kənglɒmə'reɪʃən] *n* Ansammlung *f*
Congo ['kɒŋgəu] *n* (*state*) Kongo *m*
congratulate [kən'grætjuleɪt] *vt* gratulieren; **to ~ sb (on sth)** jdm (zu etw) gratulieren
congratulations [kəngrætju'leɪʃənz]

npl Glückwunsch *m*, Glückwünsche *pl*; **~!** herzlichen Glückwunsch!; **~ on** Glückwünsche zu
congregate ['kɒŋgrɪgeɪt] *vi* sich versammeln
congregation [kɒŋgrɪ'geɪʃən] *n* Gemeinde *f*
congress ['kɒŋgres] *n* Kongress *m*; (*US*): **C~** der Kongress; *siehe Info-Artikel*

○ **CONGRESS**

○ Der *Congress* ist die nationale gesetzgebende
○ Versammlung der USA, die in Washington
○ im *Capitol* zusammentritt. Der Kongress
○ besteht aus dem Repräsentantenhaus
○ (435 Abgeordnete, entsprechend den
○ Bevölkerungszahlen auf die einzelnen
○ Bundesstaaten verteilt und jeweils für
○ 2 Jahre gewählt) und dem Senat (100
○ Senatoren, 2 für jeden Bundesstaat, für
○ 6 Jahre gewählt, wobei ein Drittel alle
○ zwei Jahre neu gewählt wird). Sowohl
○ die Abgeordneten als auch die Senatoren
○ werden in direkter Wahl vom Volk
○ gewählt.

---

congressman ['kɒŋgresmən] (*US*) *n* (*irreg: like* **man**) Kongressabgeordnete(r) *m*
congresswoman ['kɒŋgreswumən] (*US*) *n* (*irreg: like* **woman**) *n* Kongressabgeordnete *f*
conical ['kɒnɪkl] *adj* kegelförmig, konisch
conifer ['kɒnɪfər] *n* Nadelbaum *m*
coniferous [kə'nɪfərəs] *adj* Nadel-
conjecture [kən'dʒektʃər] *n* Vermutung *f*, Mutmaßung *f* ▷ *vi* vermuten, mutmaßen
conjugal ['kɒndʒugl] *adj* ehelich
conjugate ['kɒndʒugeɪt] *vt* konjugieren
conjugation [kɒndʒə'geɪʃən] *n* Konjugation *f*
conjunction [kən'dʒʌŋkʃən] *n* Konjunktion *f*; **in ~ with** zusammen mit, in Verbindung mit
conjunctivitis [kəndʒʌŋktɪ'vaɪtɪs] *n* Bindehautentzündung *f*
conjure ['kʌndʒər] *vi* zaubern ▷ *vt* (*also fig*) hervorzaubern
▶ **conjure up** *vt* (*ghost, spirit*) beschwören; (*memories*) heraufbeschwören
conjurer ['kʌndʒərər] *n* Zauberer *m*, Zauberkünstler(in) *m(f)*
conjuring trick ['kʌndʒərɪŋ-] *n* Zaubertrick *m*, Zauberkunststück *nt*
conker ['kɒŋkər] (*Brit*) *n* (Ross)kastanie *f*
conk out [kɒŋk-] (*inf*) *vi* den Geist aufgeben
con man *n* Schwindler *m*
Conn. (*US*) *abbr* (*Post*) = *Connecticut*
connect [kə'nekt] *vt* verbinden; (*Elec*) anschließen; (*Tel: caller*) verbinden; (*: subscriber*) anschließen; (*fig: associate*) in Zusammenhang bringen ▷ *vi*: **to ~ with** (*train, plane etc*) Anschluss haben an +*acc*; **to ~ sth to sth** etw mit einer Sache verbinden; **to be ~ed with** (*associated*) in einer Beziehung or in Verbindung stehen zu; (*have dealings with*) zu tun haben mit; **I am trying to ~ you** (*Tel*) ich versuche, Sie zu verbinden

connection [kə'nɛkʃən] n Verbindung f;
(Elec) Kontakt m; (train, plane etc, Tel: subscriber)
Anschluss m; (fig: association) Beziehung
f, Zusammenhang m; **in ~ with** in
Zusammenhang mit; **what is the ~ between
them?** welche Verbindung besteht zwischen
ihnen?; **business ~s** Geschäftsbeziehungen
pl; **to get/miss one's ~** seinen Anschluss
erreichen/verpassen

connexion [kə'nɛkʃən] (Brit) n = **connection**

conning tower ['kɒnɪŋ-] n Kommandoturm m

connive [kə'naɪv] vi: **to ~ at** stillschweigend
dulden

connoisseur [kɒnɪ'sə:ʳ] n Kenner(in) m(f)

connotation [kɒnə'teɪʃən] n Konnotation f

connubial [kə'nju:bɪəl] adj ehelich

conquer ['kɒŋkəʳ] vt erobern; (enemy, fear,
feelings) besiegen

conqueror ['kɒŋkərəʳ] n Eroberer m

conquest ['kɒŋkwɛst] n Eroberung f

cons [kɒnz] npl see **convenience**, **pro**

conscience ['kɒnʃəns] n Gewissen nt; **to
have a guilty/clear ~** ein schlechtes/gutes
Gewissen haben; **in all ~** allen Ernstes

conscientious [kɒnʃɪ'ɛnʃəs] adj gewissenhaft

conscientious objector n Wehrdienst-
or Kriegsdienstverweigerer m (aus
Gewissensgründen)

conscious ['kɒnʃəs] adj bewusst; (awake) bei
Bewusstsein; **to become ~ of sth** sich dat
einer Sache gen bewusst werden; **to become ~
that ...** sich dat bewusst werden, dass ...

consciousness ['kɒnʃəsnɪs] n Bewusstsein
nt; **to lose ~** bewusstlos werden; **to regain ~**
wieder zu sich kommen

conscript ['kɒnskrɪpt] n Wehrpflichtige(r) m

conscription [kən'skrɪpʃən] n Wehrpflicht f

consecrate ['kɒnsɪkreɪt] vt weihen

consecutive [kən'sɛkjʊtɪv] adj
aufeinanderfolgend; **on three ~ occasions**
dreimal hintereinander

consensus [kən'sɛnsəs] n Übereinstimmung f;
the ~ (of opinion) die allgemeine Meinung

consent [kən'sɛnt] n Zustimmung f
▷ vi: **to ~ to** zustimmen +dat; **age of ~**
Ehemündigkeitsalter nt; **by common ~** auf
allgemeinen Wunsch

consenting [kən'sɛntɪŋ] adj: **between ~
adults** ≈ zwischen Erwachsenen

consequence ['kɒnsɪkwəns] n Folge f; **of ~**
bedeutend, wichtig; **it's of little ~** es spielt
kaum eine Rolle; **in ~** folglich

consequently ['kɒnsɪkwəntlɪ] adv folglich

conservation [kɒnsə'veɪʃən] n Erhaltung f,
Schutz m; (of energy) Sparen nt; (also: **nature
conservation**) Umweltschutz m; (of paintings,
books) Erhaltung f, Konservierung f; **energy ~**
Energieeinsparung f

conservationist [kɒnsə'veɪʃnɪst] n
Umweltschützer(in) m(f)

conservative [kən'sə:vətɪv] adj konservativ;
(cautious) vorsichtig; (Brit: Pol): **C~** konservativ
▷ n (Brit: Pol): **C~** Konservative(r) f(m)

Conservative Party n: **the ~** die Konservative
Partei f

conservatory [kən'sə:vətrɪ] n Wintergarten m;
(Mus) Konservatorium nt

conserve [kən'sə:v] vt erhalten; (supplies, energy)
sparen ▷ n Konfitüre f

consider [kən'sɪdəʳ] vt (study) sich dat
überlegen; (take into account) in Betracht
ziehen; **to ~ that ...** der Meinung sein, dass ...;
to ~ sb/sth as ... jdn/etw für ... halten; **to ~
doing sth** in Erwägung ziehen, etw zu tun;
they ~ themselves to be superior sie halten
sich für etwas Besseres; **she ~ed it a disaster**
sie betrachtete es als eine Katastrophe; **~
yourself lucky** Sie können sich glücklich
schätzen; **all things ~ed** alles in allem

considerable [kən'sɪdərəbl] adj beträchtlich

considerably [kən'sɪdərəblɪ] adv beträchtlich;
(bigger, smaller etc) um einiges

considerate [kən'sɪdərɪt] adj rücksichtsvoll

consideration [kənsɪdə'reɪʃən] n Überlegung
f; (factor) Gesichtspunkt m, Faktor m;
(thoughtfulness) Rücksicht f; (reward) Entgelt
nt; **out of ~ for** aus Rücksicht auf +acc; **to be
under ~** geprüft werden; **my first ~ is my
family** ich denke zuerst an meine Familie

considered [kən'sɪdəd] adj: **~ opinion**
ernsthafte Überzeugung f

considering [kən'sɪdərɪŋ] prep in Anbetracht
+gen; **~ (that)** wenn man bedenkt(, dass)

consign [kən'saɪn] vt: **to ~ to** (object: to
place) verbannen in +acc; (person: to sb's care)
anvertrauen +dat; (: to poverty) verurteilen zu;
(send) versenden an +acc

consignment [kən'saɪnmənt] n Sendung f,
Lieferung f

consignment note n Frachtbrief m

consist [kən'sɪst] vi: **to ~ of** bestehen aus

consistency [kən'sɪstənsɪ] n (of actions etc)
Konsequenz f; (of cream etc) Konsistenz f, Dicke f

consistent [kən'sɪstənt] adj konsequent;
(argument, idea) logisch, folgerichtig; **to be ~
with** entsprechen +dat

consolation [kɒnsə'leɪʃən] n Trost m

console [kən'səul] vt trösten ▷ n (panel)
Schalttafel f

consolidate [kən'sɒlɪdeɪt] vt festigen

consols ['kɒnsɒlz] (Brit) npl (Stock Exchange)
Konsols pl, konsolidierte Staatsanleihen pl

consommé [kən'sɒmeɪ] n Kraftbrühe f,
Consommé f

consonant ['kɒnsənənt] n Konsonant m,
Mitlaut m

consort ['kɒnsɔ:t] n Gemahl(in) m(f), Gatte m,
Gattin f ▷ vi: **to ~ with sb** mit jdm verkehren;
prince ~ Prinzgemahl m

consortium [kən'sɔ:tɪəm] n Konsortium nt

conspicuous [kən'spɪkjuəs] adj auffallend; **to
make o.s. ~** auffallen

conspiracy [kən'spɪrəsɪ] n Verschwörung f,
Komplott nt

conspiratorial [kənspɪrə'tɔ:rɪəl] adj
verschwörerisch

conspire [kən'spaɪə'] vi sich verschwören; (*events*) zusammenkommen

constable ['kʌnstəbl] (*Brit*) n Polizist m; **chief ~** Polizeipräsident m, Polizeichef m

constabulary [kən'stæbjulərɪ] (*Brit*) n Polizei f

constant ['kɔnstənt] adj dauernd, ständig; (*fixed*) konstant, gleichbleibend

constantly ['kɔnstəntlɪ] adv (an)dauernd, ständig

constellation [kɔnstə'leɪʃən] n Sternbild nt

consternation [kɔnstə'neɪʃən] n Bestürzung f

constipated ['kɔnstɪpeɪtɪd] adj: **to be ~** Verstopfung haben, verstopft sein

constipation [kɔnstɪ'peɪʃən] n Verstopfung f

constituency [kən'stɪtjuənsɪ] n (*Pol*) Wahlkreis m; (*electors*) Wähler pl (*eines Wahlkreises*)

constituency party n Parteiorganisation in einem Wahlkreis

constituent [kən'stɪtjuənt] n (*Pol*) Wähler(in) m(f); (*component*) Bestandteil m

constitute ['kɔnstɪtjuːt] vt (*represent*) darstellen; (*make up*) bilden, ausmachen

constitution [kɔnstɪ'tjuːʃən] n (*Pol*) Verfassung f; (*of club etc*) Satzung f; (*health*) Konstitution f, Gesundheit f; (*make-up*) Zusammensetzung f

constitutional [kɔnstɪ'tjuːʃənl] adj (*government*) verfassungsmäßig; (*reform etc*) Verfassungs-

constitutional monarchy n konstitutionelle Monarchie f

constrain [kən'streɪn] vt zwingen

constrained [kən'streɪnd] adj gezwungen

constraint [kən'streɪnt] n Beschränkung f, Einschränkung f; (*compulsion*) Zwang m; (*embarrassment*) Befangenheit f

constrict [kən'strɪkt] vt einschnüren; (*blood vessel*) verengen; (*limit, restrict*) einschränken

constriction [kən'strɪkʃən] n Einschränkung f; (*tightness*) Verengung f; (*squeezing*) Einschnürung f

construct [kən'strʌkt] vt bauen; (*machine*) konstruieren; (*theory, argument*) entwickeln

construction [kən'strʌkʃən] n Bau m; (*structure*) Konstruktion f; (*fig: interpretation*) Deutung f; **under ~** in or im Bau

construction industry n Bauindustrie f

constructive [kən'strʌktɪv] adj konstruktiv

construe [kən'struː] vt auslegen, deuten

consul ['kɔnsl] n Konsul(in) m(f)

consulate ['kɔnsjulɪt] n Konsulat nt

consult [kən'sʌlt] vt (*doctor, lawyer*) konsultieren; (*friend*) sich beraten or besprechen mit; (*reference book*) nachschlagen in +*dat*; **to ~ sb (about sth)** jdn (wegen etw) fragen

consultancy [kən'sʌltənsɪ] n Beratungsbüro nt or -firma f; (*Med: job*) Facharztstelle f

consultant [kən'sʌltənt] n (*Med*) Facharzt m, Fachärztin f; (*other specialist*) Berater(in) m(f) ▷ cpd: **~ engineer** beratender Ingenieur m; **~ paediatrician** Facharzt/-ärztin m/f für Pädiatrie or Kinderheilkunde; **legal/management ~** Rechts-/

Unternehmensberater(in) m(f); **consultants** npl Beratungsbüro nt or -firma f

consultation [kɔnsəl'teɪʃən] n (*Med, Law*) Konsultation f; (*discussion*) Beratung f, Besprechung f; **in ~ with** in gemeinsamer Beratung mit

consultative [kən'sʌltətɪv] adj beratend

consulting room [kən'sʌltɪŋ-] (*Brit*) n Sprechzimmer nt

consume [kən'sjuːm] vt (*food, drink*) zu sich nehmen, konsumieren; (*fuel, energy*) verbrauchen; (*time*) in Anspruch nehmen; (*subj: emotion*) verzehren; (*: fire*) vernichten

consumer [kən'sjuːmə'] n Verbraucher(in) m(f)

consumer credit n Verbraucherkredit m

consumer durables npl (langlebige) Gebrauchsgüter pl

consumer goods npl Konsumgüter pl

consumerism [kən'sjuːmərɪzəm] n Verbraucherschutz m

consumer society n Konsumgesellschaft f

consumer watchdog n Verbraucherschutzorganisation f

consummate ['kɔnsʌmeɪt] vt (*marriage*) vollziehen; (*ambition etc*) erfüllen

consumption [kən'sʌmpʃən] n Verbrauch m; (*of food*) Verzehr m; (*of drinks, buying*) Konsum m; (*Med*) Schwindsucht f; **not fit for human ~** zum Verzehr ungeeignet

cont. abbr (= *continued*) Forts.

contact ['kɔntækt] n Kontakt m; (*touch*) Berührung f; (*person*) Kontaktperson f ▷ vt sich in Verbindung setzen mit; **to be in ~ with sb/sth** mit jdm/etw in Verbindung or Kontakt stehen; (*touch*) jdn/etw berühren; **business ~s** Geschäftsverbindungen pl

contact lenses npl Kontaktlinsen pl

contagious [kən'teɪdʒəs] adj ansteckend

contain [kən'teɪn] vt enthalten; (*growth, spread*) in Grenzen halten; (*feeling*) beherrschen; **to ~ o.s.** an sich acc halten

container [kən'teɪnə'] n Behälter m; (*for shipping etc*) Container m ▷ cpd Container-

containerize [kən'teɪnəraɪz] vt in Container verpacken; (*port*) auf Container umstellen

container ship n Containerschiff nt

contaminate [kən'tæmɪneɪt] vt (*water, food*) verunreinigen; (*soil etc*) verseuchen

contamination [kəntæmɪ'neɪʃən] n (*see vb*) Verunreinigung f; Verseuchung f

cont'd abbr (= *continued*) Forts.

contemplate ['kɔntəmpleɪt] vt nachdenken über +*acc*; (*course of action*) in Erwägung ziehen; (*person, painting etc*) betrachten

contemplation [kɔntəm'pleɪʃən] n Betrachtung f

contemporary [kən'tɛmpərərɪ] adj zeitgenössisch; (*present-day*) modern ▷ n Altersgenosse m, Altersgenossin f; **Samuel Pepys and his contemporaries** Samuel Pepys und seine Zeitgenossen

contempt [kən'tɛmpt] n Verachtung f; **~ of court** (*Law*) Missachtung f (der Würde) des

Gerichts, Ungebühr f vor Gericht; **to have ~ for sb/sth** jdn/etw verachten; **to hold sb in ~** jdn verachten

contemptible [kən'tɛmptəbl] *adj* verachtenswert

contemptuous [kən'tɛmptjuəs] *adj* verächtlich, geringschätzig

contend [kən'tɛnd] *vt*: **to ~ that ...** behaupten, dass ...; **to ~ with** fertig werden mit; **to ~ for** kämpfen um; **to have to ~ with** es zu tun haben mit; **he has a lot to ~ with** er hat viel um die Ohren

contender [kən'tɛndəʳ] *n (Sport)* Wettkämpfer(in) *m(f)*; *(for title)* Anwärter(in) *m(f)*; *(Pol)* Kandidat(in) *m(f)*

content [*adj, vt* kən'tɛnt, *n* 'kɔntɛnt] *adj* zufrieden ▷ *vt* zufriedenstellen ▷ *n* Inhalt *m*; *(fat content, moisture content etc)* Gehalt *m*; **contents** *npl* Inhalt; **(table of) ~s** Inhaltsverzeichnis *nt*; **to be ~ with** zufrieden sein mit; **to ~ o.s. with sth** sich mit etw zufriedengeben *or* begnügen; **to ~ o.s. with doing sth** sich damit zufriedengeben *or* begnügen, etw zu tun

contented [kən'tɛntɪd] *adj* zufrieden

contentedly [kən'tɛntɪdlɪ] *adv* zufrieden

contention [kən'tɛnʃən] *n* Behauptung f; *(disagreement, argument)* Streit *m*; **bone of ~** Zankapfel *m*

contentious [kən'tɛnʃəs] *adj* strittig, umstritten

contentment [kən'tɛntmənt] *n* Zufriedenheit f

contest [*n* 'kɔntɛst, *vt* kən'tɛst] *n (competition)* Wettkampf *m*; *(for control, power etc)* Kampf *m* ▷ *vt (election, competition)* teilnehmen an +*dat*; *(compete for)* kämpfen um; *(statement)* bestreiten; *(decision)* angreifen; *(Law)* anfechten

contestant [kən'tɛstənt] *n (in quiz)* Kandidat(in) *m(f)*; *(in competition)* Teilnehmer(in) *m(f)*; *(in fight)* Kämpfer(in) *m(f)*

context ['kɔntɛkst] *n* Zusammenhang *m*, Kontext *m*; **in ~** im Zusammenhang; **out of ~** aus dem Zusammenhang gerissen

continent ['kɔntɪnənt] *n* Kontinent *m*, Erdteil *m*; **the C~** *(Brit)* (Kontinental)europa *nt*; **on the C~** in (Kontinental)europa, auf dem Kontinent

continental [kɔntɪ'nɛntl] *adj* kontinental; *(European)* europäisch ▷ *n (Brit)* (Festlands) europäer(in) *m(f)*

continental breakfast *n* kleines Frühstück *nt*

continental quilt *(Brit)* *n* Steppdecke f

contingency [kən'tɪndʒənsɪ] *n* möglicher Fall *m*, Eventualität f

contingency plan *n* Plan *m* für den Eventualfall

contingent [kən'tɪndʒənt] *n* Kontingent *nt* ▷ *adj*: **to be ~ upon** abhängen von

continual [kən'tɪnjuəl] *adj* ständig; *(process)* ununterbrochen

continually [kən'tɪnjuəlɪ] *adv (see adj)* ständig;

ununterbrochen

continuation [kəntɪnju'eɪʃən] *n* Fortsetzung f; *(extension)* Weiterführung f

continue [kən'tɪnjuː] *vi* weitermachen, andauern; *(performance, road)* weitergehen; *(person: talking)* fortfahren ▷ *vt* fortsetzen; **to ~ to do sth/doing sth** etw weiter tun; **"to be ~d"** „Fortsetzung folgt"; **"~d on page 10"** „Fortsetzung auf Seite 10"

continuing education [kən'tɪnjuɪŋ-] *n* Erwachsenenbildung f

continuity [kɔntɪ'njuːɪtɪ] *n* Kontinuität f; *(TV, Cine)* Anschluß *m* ▷ *cpd (TV)*: **~ announcer** Ansager(in) *m(f)*; **~ studio** Ansagestudio *nt*

continuous [kən'tɪnjuəs] *adj* ununterbrochen; *(growth etc)* kontinuierlich; **~ form** *(Ling)* Verlaufsform f; **~ performance** *(Cine)* durchgehende Vorstellung f

continuously [kən'tɪnjuəslɪ] *adv* dauernd, ständig; *(uninterruptedly)* ununterbrochen

continuous stationery *n (Comput)* Endlospapier *nt*

contort [kən'tɔːt] *vt (body)* verrenken, verdrehen; *(face)* verziehen

contortion [kən'tɔːʃən] *n* Verrenkung f

contortionist [kən'tɔːʃənɪst] *n* Schlangenmensch *m*

contour ['kɔntuəʳ] *n (also:* **contour line***)* Höhenlinie f; *(shape, outline: gen pl)* Kontur f, Umriss *m*

contraband ['kɔntrəbænd] *n* Schmuggelware f ▷ *adj* Schmuggel-

contraception [kɔntrə'sɛpʃən] *n* Empfängnisverhütung f

contraceptive [kɔntrə'sɛptɪv] *adj* empfängnisverhütend ▷ *n* Verhütungsmittel *nt*

contract [*n, cpd* 'kɔntrækt, *vb* kən'trækt] *n* Vertrag *m* ▷ *vi* schrumpfen; *(metal, muscle)* sich zusammenziehen ▷ *vt (illness)* erkranken an +*dat* ▷ *cpd* vertraglich festgelegt; *(work)* Auftrags-; **~ of employment/service** Arbeitsvertrag *m*; **to ~ to do sth** *(Comm)* sich vertraglich verpflichten, etw zu tun

▶ **contract in** *(Brit)* *vi* beitreten

▶ **contract out** *(Brit)* *vi* austreten

contraction [kən'trækʃən] *n* Zusammenziehen *nt*; *(Ling)* Kontraktion f; *(Med)* Wehe f

contractor [kən'træktəʳ] *n* Auftragnehmer *m*; *(also:* **building contractor***)* Bauunternehmer *m*

contractual [kən'træktʃuəl] *adj* vertraglich

contradict [kɔntrə'dɪkt] *vt* widersprechen +*dat*

contradiction [kɔntrə'dɪkʃən] *n* Widerspruch *m*; **to be in ~ with** im Widerspruch stehen zu; **a ~ in terms** ein Widerspruch in sich

contradictory [kɔntrə'dɪktərɪ] *adj* widersprüchlich

contralto [kən'træltəu] *n (Mus)* Altistin f; *(: voice)* Alt *m*

contraption [kən'træpʃən] *(pej)* *n (device)* Vorrichtung f; *(machine)* Gerät *nt*, Apparat *m*

contrary¹ ['kɔntrərɪ] *adj* entgegengesetzt;

(*ideas, opinions*) gegensätzlich; (*unfavourable*) widrig ▷ *n* Gegenteil *nt*; **~ to what we thought** im Gegensatz zu dem, was wir dachten; **on the ~** im Gegenteil; **unless you hear to the ~** sofern Sie nichts Gegenteiliges hören

contrary² [kən'trɛəri] *adj* widerspenstig

contrast ['kɒntrɑːst] *n* Gegensatz *m*, Kontrast *m* ▷ *vt* vergleichen, gegenüberstellen; **in ~ to** *or* **with** im Gegensatz zu

contrasting [kən'trɑːstɪŋ] *adj* (*colours*) kontrastierend; (*attitudes*) gegensätzlich

contravene [kɒntrə'viːn] *vt* verstoßen gegen

contravention [kɒntrə'vɛnʃən] *n* Verstoß *m*; **to be in ~ of sth** gegen etw verstoßen

contribute [kən'trɪbjuːt] *vi* beitragen ▷ *vt*: **to ~ £10/an article to** £10/einen Artikel beisteuern zu; **to ~ to** (*charity*) spenden für; (*newspaper*) schreiben für; (*discussion, problem etc*) beitragen zu

contribution [kɒntrɪ'bjuːʃən] *n* Beitrag *m*; (*donation*) Spende *f*

contributor [kən'trɪbjutə'] *n* (*to appeal*) Spender(in) *m(f)*; (*to newspaper*) Mitarbeiter(in) *m(f)*

contributory [kən'trɪbjutəri] *adj*: **a ~ cause** ein Faktor, der mit eine Rolle spielt; **it was a ~ factor in ...** es trug zu ... bei

contributory pension scheme (*Brit*) *n* beitragspflichtige Rentenversicherung *f*

contrite ['kɒntraɪt] *adj* zerknirscht

contrivance [kən'traɪvəns] *n* (*scheme*) List *f*; (*device*) Vorrichtung *f*

contrive [kən'traɪv] *vt* (*meeting*) arrangieren ▷ *vi*: **to ~ to do sth** es fertigbringen, etw zu tun

control [kən'trəul] *vt* (*country*) regieren; (*organization*) leiten; (*machinery, process*) steuern; (*wages, prices*) kontrollieren; (*temper*) zügeln; (*disease, fire*) unter Kontrolle bringen ▷ *n* (*of country*) Kontrolle *f*; (*of organization*) Leitung *f*; (*of oneself, emotions*) Beherrschung *f*; (*Sci: also:* **control group**) Kontrollgruppe *f*; **controls** *npl* (*of vehicle*) Steuerung *f*; (*on radio, television etc*) Bedienungsfeld *nt*; (*governmental*) Kontrolle *f*; **to ~ o.s.** sich beherrschen; **to take ~ of** die Kontrolle übernehmen über +*acc*; (*Comm*) übernehmen; **to be in ~ of** unter Kontrolle haben; (*in charge of*) unter sich *dat* haben; **out of/under ~** außer/unter Kontrolle; **everything is under ~** ich habe/wir haben *etc* die Sache im Griff (*inf*); **the car went out of ~** der Fahrer verlor die Kontrolle über den Wagen; **circumstances beyond our ~** unvorhersehbare Umstände

control key *n* (*Comput*) Controltaste *f*, Steuerungstaste *f*

controlled substance *n* veschreibungspflichtiges Medikament

controller [kən'trəulə'] *n* (*Radio, TV*) Intendant(in) *m(f)*

controlling interest [kən'trəulɪŋ-] *n* Mehrheitsanteil *m*

control panel *n* Schalttafel *f*; (*on television*) Bedienungsfeld *nt*

control point *n* Kontrollpunkt *m*, Kontrollstelle *f*

control room *n* (*Naut*) Kommandoraum *m*; (*Mil*) (Operations)zentrale *f*; (*Radio, TV*) Regieraum *m*

control tower *n* Kontrollturm *m*

control unit *n* (*Comput*) Steuereinheit *f*

controversial [kɒntrə'vəːʃl] *adj* umstritten, kontrovers

controversy ['kɒntrəvəːsɪ] *n* Streit *m*, Kontroverse *f*

conurbation [kɒnə'beɪʃən] *n* Ballungsgebiet *nt*, Ballungsraum *m*

convalesce [kɒnvə'lɛs] *vi* genesen

convalescence [kɒnvə'lɛsns] *n* Genesungszeit *f*

convalescent [kɒnvə'lɛsnt] *adj* (*leave etc*) Genesungs-, Kur- ▷ *n* Genesende(r) *f(m)*

convector [kən'vɛktə'] *n* Heizlüfter *m*

convene [kən'viːn] *vt* einberufen ▷ *vi* zusammentreten

convener [kən'viːnə'] *n* (*organizer*) Organisator(in) *m(f)*; (*chairperson*) Vorsitzende(r) *f(m)*

convenience [kən'viːnɪəns] *n* Annehmlichkeit *f*; (*suitability*): **the ~ of this arrangement/ location** diese günstige Vereinbarung/Lage; **I like the ~ of having a shower** mir gefällt, wie angenehm es ist, eine Dusche zu haben; **I like the ~ of living in the city** mir gefällt, wie praktisch es ist, in der Stadt zu wohnen; **at your ~** wann es Ihnen passt; **at your earliest ~** möglichst bald, baldmöglichst; **with all modern ~s, with all mod cons** (*Brit*) mit allem modernen Komfort; *see also* **public convenience**

convenience foods *npl* Fertiggerichte *pl*

convenient [kən'viːnɪənt] *adj* günstig; (*handy*) praktisch; (*house etc*) günstig gelegen; **if it is ~ to you** wenn es Ihnen (so) passt, wenn es Ihnen keine Umstände macht

conveniently [kən'viːnɪəntlɪ] *adv* (*happen*) günstigerweise; (*situated*) günstig

convenor [kən'viːnə'] *n* = **convener**

convent ['kɒnvənt] *n* Kloster *nt*

convention [kən'vɛnʃən] *n* Konvention *f*; (*conference*) Tagung *f*, Konferenz *f*; (*agreement*) Abkommen *nt*

conventional [kən'vɛnʃənl] *adj* konventionell

convent school *n* Klosterschule *f*

converge [kən'vəːdʒ] *vi* (*roads*) zusammenlaufen ▷ *vi* sich einander annähern; **to ~ on sb/a place** (*people*) von überallher zu jdm/an einen Ort strömen

conversant [kən'vəːsnt] *adj*: **to be ~ with** vertraut sein mit

conversation [kɒnvə'seɪʃən] *n* Gespräch *nt*, Unterhaltung *f*

conversational [kɒnvə'seɪʃənl] *adj* (*tone, style*) Unterhaltungs-; (*language*) gesprochen; **~ mode** (*Comput*) Dialogbetrieb *m*

conversationalist [kɔnvəˈseɪʃnəlɪst] *n*
Unterhalter(in) *m(f)*, Gesprächspartner(in)
m(f)

converse [*n* ˈkɔnvəːs, *vi* kənˈvəːs] *n* Gegenteil *nt*
▷ *vi:* **to ~ (with sb) (about sth)** sich (mit jdm)
(über etw) unterhalten

conversely [kɔnˈvəːslɪ] *adv* umgekehrt

conversion [kənˈvəːʃən] *n* Umwandlung *f*; *(of
weights etc)* Umrechnung *f*; (Rel) Bekehrung *f*;
(Brit: of house) Umbau *m*

conversion table *n* Umrechnungstabelle *f*

convert [*vt* kənˈvəːt, *n* ˈkɔnvəːt] *vt* umwandeln;
(person) bekehren; *(building)* umbauen; *(vehicle)*
umrüsten; *(Comm)* konvertieren; *(Rugby)*
verwandeln ▷ *n* Bekehrte(r) *f(m)*

convertible [kənˈvəːtəbl] *adj (currency)*
konvertierbar ▷ *n* (Aut) Kabriolett *nt*

convex [ˈkɔnvɛks] *adj* konvex

convey [kənˈveɪ] *vt (information etc)* vermitteln;
(cargo, traveller) befördern; *(thanks)* übermitteln

conveyance [kənˈveɪəns] *n* Beförderung *f*,
Spedition *f*; *(vehicle)* Gefährt *nt*

conveyancing [kənˈveɪənsɪŋ] *n* (Eigentums)
übertragung *f*

conveyor belt *n* Fließband *nt*

convict [*vt* kənˈvɪkt, *n* ˈkɔnvɪkt] *vt* verurteilen
▷ *n* Sträfling *m*

conviction [kənˈvɪkʃən] *n* Überzeugung *f*;
(Law) Verurteilung *f*

convince [kənˈvɪns] *vt* überzeugen; **to ~ sb (of
sth)** jdn (von etw) überzeugen; **to ~ sb that …**
jdn davon überzeugen, dass …

convinced [kənˈvɪnst] *adj:* **~ (of)** überzeugt
(von); **~ that …** überzeugt davon, dass …

convincing [kənˈvɪnsɪŋ] *adj* überzeugend

convincingly [kənˈvɪnsɪŋlɪ] *adv* überzeugend

convivial [kənˈvɪvɪəl] *adj* freundlich; *(event)*
gesellig

convoluted [ˈkɔnvəluːtɪd] *adj* verwickelt,
kompliziert; *(shape)* gewunden

convoy [ˈkɔnvɔɪ] *n* Konvoi *m*

convulse [kənˈvʌls] *vt:* **to be ~d with
laughter/pain** sich vor Lachen schütteln/
Schmerzen krümmen

convulsion [kənˈvʌlʃən] *n* Schüttelkrampf *m*

coo [kuː] *vi* gurren

cook [kuk] *vt* kochen, zubereiten ▷ *vi (person,
food)* kochen; *(fry, roast)* braten; *(pie)* backen ▷ *n*
Koch *m*, Köchin *f*
▶ **cook up** *(inf) vt* sich *dat* einfallen lassen,
zurechtbasteln

cookbook [ˈkukbuk] *n* Kochbuch *nt*

cook-chill [ˈkuktʃɪl] *adj* durch rasches Kühlen
haltbar gemacht

cooker [ˈkukəʳ] *n* Herd *m*

cookery [ˈkukərɪ] *n* Kochen *nt*, Kochkunst *f*

cookery book (Brit) *n* = **cookbook**

cookie [ˈkukɪ] *(US) n* Keks *m* or *nt*, Plätzchen *nt*;
(Comput) Cookie *m*

cooking [ˈkukɪŋ] *n* Kochen *nt*; *(food)* Essen *nt*
▷ *cpd* Koch-; *(chocolate)* Block-

cookout [ˈkukaut] *(US) n* ≈ Grillparty *f*

cool [kuːl] *adj* kühl; *(dress, clothes)* leicht,
luftig; *(person: calm)* besonnen; (: *unfriendly)*
kühl ▷ *vt* kühlen ▷ *vi* abkühlen; **it's ~** es ist
kühl; **to keep sth ~** or **in a ~ place** etw kühl
aufbewahren
▶ **cool down** *vi* abkühlen; *(fig)* sich beruhigen

coolant [ˈkuːlənt] *n* Kühlflüssigkeit *f*

cool box *n* Kühlbox *f*

cooler [ˈkuːləʳ] *(US) n* = **cool box**

cooling [ˈkuːlɪŋ] *adj (drink, shower)* kühlend;
(feeling, emotion) abkühlend

cooling tower [ˈkuːlɪŋ-] *n* Kühlturm *m*

coolly [ˈkuːlɪ] *adv (calmly)* besonnen, ruhig; *(in
unfriendly way)* kühl

coolness [ˈkuːlnɪs] *n (see adj)* Kühle *f*;
Leichtigkeit *f*, Luftigkeit *f*; Besonnenheit *f*

coop [kuːp] *n (for rabbits)* Kaninchenstall *m*;
(for poultry) Hühnerstall *m* ▷ *vt:* **to ~ up** *(fig)*
einsperren

co-op [ˈkəuɔp] *n abbr* (= *cooperative (society)*)
Genossenschaft *f*

cooperate [kəuˈɔpəreɪt] *vi* zusammenarbeiten;
(assist) mitmachen, kooperieren; **to ~ with sb**
mit jdm zusammenarbeiten

cooperation [kəuɔpəˈreɪʃən] *n (see vb)*
Zusammenarbeit *f*; Mitarbeit *f*, Kooperation *f*

cooperative [kəuˈɔpərətɪv] *adj (farm, business)*
auf Genossenschaftsbasis; *(person)* kooperativ;
(: *helpful)* hilfsbereit ▷ *n* Genossenschaft *f*,
Kooperative *f*

coopt [kəuˈɔpt] *vt:* **to ~ sb onto a committee**
jdn in ein Komitee hinzuwählen or
kooptieren

coordinate [*vt* kəuˈɔːdɪneɪt, *n* kəuˈɔːdɪnət]
vt koordinieren ▷ *n* (Math) Koordinate *f*;
coordinates *npl (clothes)* Kleidung *f* zum
Kombinieren

coordination [kəuɔːdɪˈneɪʃən] *n*
Koordinierung *f*, Koordination *f*

coownership [kəuˈəunəʃɪp] *n* Mitbesitz *m*

cop [kɔp] *(inf) n* Polizist(in) *m(f)*, Bulle *m (pej)*

cope [kəup] *vi* zurechtkommen; **to ~ with**
fertig werden mit

Copenhagen [ˈkəupnˈheɪgən] *n* Kopenhagen *nt*

copier [ˈkɔpɪəʳ] *n (also:* **photocopier**)
Kopiergerät *nt*, Kopierer *m*

copilot [ˈkəupaɪlət] *n* Kopilot(in) *m(f)*

copious [ˈkəupɪəs] *adj* reichlich

copper [ˈkɔpəʳ] *n* Kupfer *nt*; *(Brit: inf)*
Polizist(in) *m(f)*, Bulle *m (pej)*; **coppers** *npl*
(small change, coins) Kleingeld *nt*

coppice [ˈkɔpɪs], **copse** [kɔps] *n* Wäldchen *nt*

copulate [ˈkɔpjuleɪt] *vi* kopulieren

copy [ˈkɔpɪ] *n* Kopie *f*; *(of book, record, newspaper)*
Exemplar *nt*; *(for printing)* Artikel *m* ▷ *vt (person)*
nachahmen; *(idea etc)* nachmachen; *(something
written)* abschreiben; **this murder story will
make good ~** *(Press)* aus diesem Mord kann
man etwas machen
▶ **copy out** *vt* abschreiben

copycat [ˈkɔpɪkæt] *(pej) n* Nachahmer(in) *m(f)*

copyright [ˈkɔpɪraɪt] *n* Copyright *nt*,
Urheberrecht *nt*; **~ reserved** urheberrechtlich
geschützt

copy typist n Schreibkraft f (die mit Textvorlagen arbeitet)

copywriter ['kɔpɪraɪtəʳ] n Werbetexter(in) m(f)

coral ['kɔrəl] n Koralle f

coral reef n Korallenriff nt

Coral Sea n: **the ~** das Korallenmeer

cord [kɔːd] n Schnur f; (string) Kordel f; (Elec) Kabel nt, Schnur f; (fabric) Cord(samt) m; **cords** npl (trousers) Cordhosen pl

cordial ['kɔːdɪəl] adj herzlich ▷ n (Brit) Fruchtsaftkonzentrat nt

cordless ['kɔːdlɪs] adj schnurlos

cordon ['kɔːdn] n Kordon m, Absperrkette f
▶ **cordon off** vt (area) absperren, abriegeln; (crowd) mit einer Absperrkette zurückhalten

corduroy ['kɔːdərɔɪ] n Cord(samt) m

CORE [kɔːʳ] (US) n abbr (= Congress of Racial Equality) Ausschuss für Rassengleichheit

core [kɔːʳ] n Kern m; (of fruit) Kerngehäuse nt ▷ vt das Kerngehäuse ausschneiden aus; **rotten to the ~** durch und durch schlecht

core (business) activity n (Econ) Kerngeschäft nt

Corfu [kɔːˈfuː] n Korfu nt

coriander [kɔrɪˈændəʳ] n Koriander m

cork [kɔːk] n (stopper) Korken m; (substance) Kork m

corkage ['kɔːkɪdʒ] n Korkengeld nt

corked [kɔːkt] adj: **the wine is ~** der Wein schmeckt nach Kork

corkscrew ['kɔːkskruː] n Korkenzieher m

corky ['kɔːkɪ] (US) adj = **corked**

corm [kɔːm] n Knolle f

cormorant ['kɔːmərnt] n Kormoran m

corn [kɔːn] n (Brit) Getreide nt, Korn nt; (US) Mais m; (on foot) Hühnerauge nt; **~ on the cob** Maiskolben m

cornea ['kɔːnɪə] n Hornhaut f

corned beef ['kɔːnd-] n Corned Beef nt

corner ['kɔːnəʳ] n Ecke f; (bend) Kurve f ▷ vt in die Enge treiben; (Comm: market) monopolisieren ▷ vi (in car) die Kurve nehmen; **to cut ~s** (fig) das Verfahren abkürzen

corner flag n Eckfahne f

corner kick n Eckball m

cornerstone ['kɔːnəstəun] n (fig) Grundstein m, Eckstein m

cornet ['kɔːnɪt] n (Mus) Kornett nt; (Brit: for ice cream) Eistüte f

cornflakes ['kɔːnfleɪks] npl Cornflakes pl

cornflour ['kɔːnflauəʳ] (Brit) n Stärkemehl nt

cornice ['kɔːnɪs] n (Ge)sims nt

Cornish ['kɔːnɪʃ] adj kornisch, aus Cornwall

corn oil n (Mais)keimöl nt

cornstarch ['kɔːnstɑːtʃ] (US) n = **cornflour**

cornucopia [kɔːnjuˈkəupɪə] n Fülle f

Cornwall ['kɔːnwəl] n Cornwall nt

corny ['kɔːnɪ] (inf) adj (joke) blöd

corollary [kəˈrɔlərɪ] n (logische) Folge f

coronary ['kɔrənərɪ] n (also: **coronary thrombosis**) Herzinfarkt m

coronation [kɔrəˈneɪʃən] n Krönung f

coroner ['kɔrənəʳ] n Beamter, der Todesfälle untersucht, die nicht eindeutig eine natürliche Ursache haben

coronet ['kɔrənɪt] n Krone f

Corp. abbr = **corporation**; (Mil) = **corporal**

corporal ['kɔːpərl] n Stabsunteroffizier m

corporal punishment n Prügelstrafe f

corporate ['kɔːpərɪt] adj (organization) körperschaftlich; (action, effort, ownership) gemeinschaftlich; (finance) Unternehmens-; (image, identity) Firmen-

corporate hospitality n Empfänge, Diners etc auf Kosten der ausrichtenden Firma

corporation [kɔːpəˈreɪʃən] n (Comm) Körperschaft f; (of town) Gemeinde f, Stadt f

corporation tax n Körperschaftssteuer f

corps [kɔːʳ] (pl **~**) n Korps nt; **the press ~** die Presse

corpse [kɔːps] n Leiche f

corpuscle ['kɔːpʌsl] n Blutkörperchen nt

corral [kəˈrɑːl] n Korral m

correct [kəˈrekt] adj richtig; (proper) korrekt ▷ vt korrigieren; (mistake) berichtigen, verbessern; **you are ~** Sie haben recht

correction [kəˈrekʃən] n (see vb) Korrektur f; Berichtigung f, Verbesserung f

correctly [kəˈrektlɪ] adv (see adj) richtig; korrekt

correlate ['kɔrɪleɪt] vt zueinander in Beziehung setzen ▷ vi: **to ~ with** in einer Beziehung stehen zu

correlation [kɔrɪˈleɪʃən] n Beziehung f, Zusammenhang m

correspond [kɔrɪsˈpɔnd] vi: **to ~ (with)** (write) korrespondieren (mit); (be in accordance) übereinstimmen (mit); **to ~ to** (be equivalent) entsprechen +dat

correspondence [kɔrɪsˈpɔndəns] n Korrespondenz f, Briefwechsel m; (relationship) Beziehung f

correspondence column n Leserbriefspalte f

correspondence course n Fernkurs m

correspondent [kɔrɪsˈpɔndənt] n Korrespondent(in) m(f)

corresponding [kɔrɪsˈpɔndɪŋ] adj entsprechend

corridor ['kɔrɪdɔːʳ] n Korridor m; (in train) Gang m

corroborate [kəˈrɔbəreɪt] vt bestätigen

corrode [kəˈrəud] vt zerfressen ▷ vi korrodieren

corrosion [kəˈrəuʒən] n Korrosion f

corrosive [kəˈrəuzɪv] adj korrosiv

corrugated ['kɔrəgeɪtɪd] adj (roof) gewellt; (cardboard) Well-

corrugated iron n Wellblech nt

corrupt [kəˈrʌpt] adj korrupt; (depraved) verdorben ▷ vt korrumpieren; (morally) verderben; **~ practices** Korruption f

corruption [kəˈrʌpʃən] n Korruption f

corset ['kɔːsɪt] n Korsett nt; (Med) Stützkorsett nt

Corsica ['kɔːsɪkə] n Korsika nt

Corsican ['kɔːsɪkən] adj korsisch ▷ n Korse m, Korsin f

cortège [kɔː'teɪʒ] *n* (*also*: **funeral cortège**) Leichenzug *m*

cortisone ['kɔːtɪzəun] *n* Kortison *nt*

coruscating ['kɒrəskeɪtɪŋ] *adj* sprühend

cosh [kɒʃ] (*Brit*) *n* Totschläger *m*

cosignatory ['kəu'sɪgnətərɪ] *n* Mitunterzeichner(in) *m(f)*

cosiness ['kəuzɪnɪs] *n* Gemütlichkeit *f*, Behaglichkeit *f*

cos lettuce ['kɒs-] *n* römischer Salat *m*

cosmetic [kɒz'mɛtɪk] *n* Kosmetikum *nt* ▷ *adj* kosmetisch; **~ surgery** (*Med*) kosmetische Chirurgie *f*

cosmic ['kɒzmɪk] *adj* kosmisch

cosmonaut ['kɒzmənɔːt] *n* Kosmonaut(in) *m(f)*

cosmopolitan [kɒzmə'pɒlɪtn] *adj* kosmopolitisch

cosmos ['kɒzmɒs] *n*: **the ~** der Kosmos

cosset ['kɒsɪt] *vt* verwöhnen

cost [kɒst] (*pt, pp* **~**) *n* Kosten *pl*; (*fig: loss, damage etc*) Preis *m* ▷ *vt* kosten; (*find out cost of*) (*pt, pp* **~ed**) veranschlagen; **costs** *npl* (*Comm, Law*) Kosten *pl*; **the ~ of living** die Lebenshaltungskosten *pl*; **at all ~s** um jeden Preis; **how much does it ~?** wie viel *or* was kostet es?; **it ~s £5/too much** es kostet £5/ist zu teuer; **what will it ~ to have it repaired?** wie viel kostet die Reparatur?; **to ~ sb time/ effort** jdn Zeit/Mühe kosten; **it ~ him his life/job** es kostete ihn das Leben/seine Stelle

cost accountant *n* Kostenbuchhalter(in) *m(f)*

co-star ['kəustɑːʳ] *n* einer der Hauptdarsteller *m*, eine der Hauptdarstellerinnen *f*; **she was Sean Connery's ~ in ...** sie spielte neben Sean Connery in ...

Costa Rica ['kɒstə'riːkə] *n* Costa Rica *nt*

cost centre *n* Kostenstelle *f*

cost control *n* Kostenkontrolle *f*

cost-effective ['kɒstɪ'fɛktɪv] *adj* rentabel; (*Comm*) kostengünstig

cost-effectiveness ['kɒstɪ'fɛktɪvnɪs] *n* Rentabilität *f*

costing ['kɒstɪŋ] *n* Kalkulation *f*

costly ['kɒstlɪ] *adj* teuer, kostspielig; (*in time, effort*) aufwendig

cost-of-living ['kɒstəv'lɪvɪŋ] *adj* Lebenshaltungskosten-; (*index*) Lebenshaltungs-

cost price (*Brit*) *n* Selbstkostenpreis *m*; **to sell/ buy at ~** zum Selbstkostenpreis verkaufen/ kaufen

costume ['kɒstjuːm] *n* Kostüm *nt*; (*Brit: also*: **swimming costume**) Badeanzug *m*

costume jewellery *n* Modeschmuck *m*

cosy, (*US*) **cozy** ['kəuzɪ] *adj* gemütlich, behaglich; (*bed, scarf, gloves*) warm; (*chat, evening*) gemütlich; **I'm very ~ here** ich fühle mich hier sehr wohl, ich finde es hier sehr gemütlich

cot [kɒt] *n* (*Brit*) Kinderbett *nt*; (*US: campbed*) Feldbett *nt*

cot death *n* Krippentod *m*, plötzlicher Kindstod *m*

Cotswolds ['kɒtswəuldz] *npl*: **the ~** die Cotswolds *pl*

cottage ['kɒtɪdʒ] *n* Cottage *nt*, Häuschen *nt*

cottage cheese *n* Hüttenkäse *m*

cottage industry *n* Heimindustrie *f*

cottage pie *n* Hackfleisch mit Kartoffelbrei überbacken

cotton ['kɒtn] *n* (*fabric*) Baumwollstoff *m*; (*plant*) Baumwollstrauch *m*; (*thread*) (Baumwoll)garn *nt* ▷ *cpd* (*dress etc*) Baumwoll-
▶ **cotton on** (*inf*) *vi*: **to ~ on** es kapieren *or* schnallen; **to ~ on to sth** etw kapieren *or* schnallen

cotton candy (*US*) *n* Zuckerwatte *f*

cotton wool (*Brit*) *n* Watte *f*

couch [kautʃ] *n* Couch *f* ▷ *vt* formulieren

couchette [kuː'ʃɛt] *n* Liegewagen(platz) *m*

couch potato (*esp US: inf*) *n* Dauerglotzer(in) *m(f)*

cough [kɒf] *vi* husten; (*engine*) stottern ▷ *n* Husten *m*

cough drop *n* Hustenpastille *f*

cough mixture *n* Hustensaft *m*

cough syrup *n* = **cough mixture**

could [kud] *pt* = **can²**

couldn't ['kudnt] = **could not**

council ['kaunsl] *n* Rat *m*; **city/town ~** Stadtrat *m*; **C~ of Europe** Europarat *m*

council estate (*Brit*) *n* Siedlung *f* mit Sozialwohnungen

council house (*Brit*) *n* Sozialwohnung *f*

council housing *n* sozialer Wohnungsbau *m*; (*accommodation*) Sozialwohnungen *pl*

councillor ['kaunsləʳ] *n* Stadtrat *m*, Stadträtin *f*

council tax (*Brit*) *n* Gemeindesteuer *f*

counsel ['kaunsl] *n* Rat(schlag) *m*; (*lawyer*) Rechtsanwalt *m*, Rechtsanwältin *f* ▷ *vt* beraten; **to ~ sth** raten *or* empfehlen; **to ~ sb to do sth** jdm raten *or* empfehlen, etw zu tun; **~ for the defence** Verteidiger(in) *m(f)*; **~ for the prosecution** Vertreter(in) *m(f)* der Anklage

counsellor ['kaunsləʳ] *n* Berater(in) *m(f)*; (*US: lawyer*) Rechtsanwalt *m*, Rechtsanwältin *f*

count [kaunt] *vt* zählen; (*include*) mitrechnen, mitzählen ▷ *vi* zählen; (*be considered*) betrachtet *or* angesehen werden ▷ *n* Zählung *f*; (*level*) Zahl *f*; (*nobleman*) Graf *m*; **to ~ (up) to 10** bis 10 zählen; **not ~ing the children** die Kinder nicht mitgerechnet; **10 ~ing him 10**, wenn man ihn mitrechnet; **to ~ the cost of sth** die Folgen von etw abschätzen; **it ~s for very little** es zählt nicht viel; **~ yourself lucky** Sie können sich glücklich schätzen; **to keep ~ of sth** die Übersicht über etw *acc* behalten; **blood ~** Blutbild *nt*; **cholesterol/ alcohol ~** Cholesterin-/Alkoholspiegel *m*
▶ **count on** *vt fus* rechnen mit; (*depend on*) sich verlassen auf +*acc*; **to ~ on doing sth** die feste Absicht haben, etw zu tun
▶ **count up** *vt* zusammenzählen, zusammenrechnen

countdown ['kauntdaun] *n* Countdown *m*

countenance ['kauntɪnəns] n Gesicht nt ▷ vt gutheißen

counter ['kauntəʳ] n (in shop) Ladentisch m; (in café) Theke f; (in bank, post office) Schalter m; (in game) Spielmarke f; (Tech) Zähler m ▷ vt (oppose: sth said, sth done) begegnen +dat; (blow) kontern ▷ adv: ~ **to** gegen +acc; **to buy sth under the** ~ (fig) etw unter dem Ladentisch bekommen; **to** ~ **sth with sth** auf etw acc mit etw antworten; **to** ~ **sth by doing sth** einer Sache damit begegnen, dass man etw tut

counteract ['kauntər'ækt] vt entgegenwirken +dat; (effect) neutralisieren

counterattack ['kauntərə'tæk] n Gegenangriff m ▷ vi einen Gegenangriff starten

counterbalance ['kauntə'bæləns] vt Gegengewicht nt

counterclockwise ['kauntə'klɔkwaɪz] adv gegen den Uhrzeigersinn

counterespionage ['kauntər'ɛspɪənɑːʒ] n Gegenspionage f, Spionageabwehr f

counterfeit ['kauntəfɪt] n Fälschung f ▷ vt fälschen ▷ adj (coin) Falsch-

counterfoil ['kauntəfɔɪl] n Kontrollabschnitt m

counterintelligence ['kauntərɪn'tɛlɪdʒəns] n Gegenspionage f, Spionageabwehr f

countermand ['kauntəmɑːnd] vt aufheben, widerrufen

countermeasure ['kauntəmɛʒəʳ] n Gegenmaßnahme f

counteroffensive ['kauntərə'fɛnsɪv] n Gegenoffensive f

counterpane ['kauntəpeɪn] n Tagesdecke f

counterpart ['kauntəpɑːt] n Gegenüber nt; (of document etc) Gegenstück nt, Pendant nt

counterproductive ['kauntəprə'dʌktɪv] adj widersinnig

counterproposal ['kauntəprə'pəuzl] n Gegenvorschlag m

countersign ['kauntəsaɪn] vt gegenzeichnen

countersink ['kauntəsɪŋk] vt senken

countess ['kauntɪs] n Gräfin f

countless ['kauntlɪs] adj unzählig, zahllos

countrified ['kʌntrɪfaɪd] adj ländlich

country ['kʌntrɪ] n Land nt; (native land) Heimatland nt; **in the** ~ auf dem Land; **mountainous** ~ gebirgige Landschaft f

country and western, country and western music n Country-und-Western-Musik f

country dancing (Brit) n Volkstanz m

country house n Landhaus nt

countryman ['kʌntrɪmən] (irreg: like **man**) n (compatriot) Landsmann m; (country dweller) Landmann m

countryside ['kʌntrɪsaɪd] n Land nt; (scenery) Landschaft f, Gegend f

country-wide ['kʌntrɪ'waɪd] adj, adv landesweit

county ['kauntɪ] n (Brit) Grafschaft f; (US) (Verwaltungs)bezirk m

county council (Brit) n Gemeinderat m (einer Grafschaft)

county town (Brit) n Hauptstadt einer Grafschaft

coup [kuː] (pl ~s) n (also: **coup d'état**) Staatsstreich m, Coup d'Etat m; (achievement) Coup m

coupé [kuːˈpeɪ] n Coupé nt

couple ['kʌpl] n Paar nt; (also: **married couple**) Ehepaar nt ▷ vt verbinden; (vehicles) koppeln; **a** ~ **of** (two) zwei; (a few) ein paar

couplet ['kʌplɪt] n Verspaar nt

coupling ['kʌplɪŋ] n Kupplung f

coupon ['kuːpɔn] n Gutschein m; (detachable form) Abschnitt m; (Comm) Coupon m

courage ['kʌrɪdʒ] n Mut m

courageous [kəˈreɪdʒəs] adj mutig

courgette [kuəˈʒet] (Brit) n Zucchino m

courier ['kurɪəʳ] n (messenger) Kurier(in) m(f); (for tourists) Reiseleiter(in) m(f)

course [kɔːs] n (Scol) Kurs(us) m; (of ship) Kurs m; (of life, events, time etc, of river) Lauf m; (of argument) Richtung f; (part of meal) Gang m; (for golf) Platz m; **of** ~ natürlich; **of** ~**!** (aber) natürlich!, (aber) selbstverständlich!; **(no) of** ~ **not!** natürlich nicht!; **in the** ~ **of the next few days** während or im Laufe der nächsten paar Tage; **in due** ~ zu gegebener Zeit; ~ **(of action)** Vorgehensweise f; **the best** ~ **would be to ...** das Beste wäre es, zu ...; **we have no other** ~ **but to ...** es bleibt uns nichts anderes übrig, als zu ...; ~ **of lectures** Vorlesungsreihe f; ~ **of treatment** (Med) Behandlung f; **first/last** ~ erster/letzter Gang, Vor-/Nachspeise f

court [kɔːt] n Hof m; (Law) Gericht nt; (for tennis, badminton etc) Platz m ▷ vt den Hof machen +dat; (favour, popularity) werben um; (death, disaster) herausfordern; **out of** ~ (Law) außergerichtlich; **to take to** ~ (Law) verklagen, vor Gericht bringen

courteous ['kɜːtɪəs] adj höflich

courtesan [kɔːtɪ'zæn] n Kurtisane f

courtesy ['kɜːtəsɪ] n Höflichkeit f; **(by)** ~ **of** freundlicherweise zur Verfügung gestellt von

courtesy bus, courtesy coach n gebührenfreier Bus m

courtesy light n Innenleuchte f

court fine n Ordnungsgeld nt; **to issue/face a** ~ ein Ordnungsgeld verhängen/zu zahlen haben

courthouse ['kɔːthaus] (US) n Gerichtsgebäude nt

courtier ['kɔːtɪəʳ] n Höfling m

court martial (pl **courts martial**) n Militärgericht nt

court of appeal (pl **courts of appeal**) n Berufungsgericht nt

court of inquiry (pl **courts of inquiry**) n Untersuchungskommission f

courtroom ['kɔːtrum] n Gerichtssaal m

court shoe n Pumps m

courtyard ['kɔːtjɑːd] n Hof m

cousin ['kʌzn] n (male) Cousin m, Vetter m; (female) Cousine f; **first** ~ Cousin(e) ersten Grades

cove [kəuv] n (kleine) Bucht f

covenant ['kʌvənənt] n Schwur m ▷ vt: **to ~ £200 per year to a charity** sich vertraglich verpflichten, £200 im Jahr für wohltätige Zwecke zu spenden

Coventry ['kɔvəntrɪ] n: **to send sb to ~** (fig) jdn schneiden (inf)

cover ['kʌvəʳ] vt bedecken; (distance) zurücklegen; (Insurance) versichern; (topic) behandeln; (include) erfassen; (Press: report on) berichten über +acc ▷ n (for furniture) Bezug m; (for typewriter, PC etc) Hülle f; (of book, magazine) Umschlag m; (shelter) Schutz m; (Insurance) Versicherung f; (fig: for illegal activities) Tarnung f; **to be ~ed in** or **with** bedeckt sein mit; **£10 will ~ my expenses** £10 decken meine Unkosten; **to take ~** (from rain) sich unterstellen; **under ~** geschützt; **under ~ of darkness** im Schutz(e) der Dunkelheit; **under separate ~** getrennt
  ▶ **cover up** vt zudecken; (fig: facts, feelings) verheimlichen; (: mistakes) vertuschen ▷ vi (fig): **to ~ up for sb** jdn decken

coverage ['kʌvərɪdʒ] n Berichterstattung f; **television ~ of the conference** Fernsehberichte pl über die Konferenz; **to give full ~ to** ausführlich berichten über +acc

coveralls ['kʌvərɔːlz] (US) npl Overall m

cover charge n Kosten pl für ein Gedeck

covering ['kʌvərɪŋ] n Schicht f; (of snow, dust etc) Decke f

covering letter, (US) **cover letter** n Begleitbrief m

cover note n (Insurance) Deckungszusage f

cover price n Einzel(exemplar)preis m

covert ['kʌvət] adj versteckt; (glance) verstohlen

cover-up ['kʌvərʌp] n Vertuschung f, Verschleierung f

covet ['kʌvɪt] vt begehren

cow [kau] n (animal, inf!: woman) Kuh f ▷ cpd Kuh- ▷ vt einschüchtern

coward ['kauəd] n Feigling m

cowardice ['kauədɪs] n Feigheit f

cowardly ['kauədlɪ] adj feige

cowboy ['kaubɔɪ] n (in US) Cowboy m; (pej: tradesman) Pfuscher m

cow elephant n Elefantenkuh f

cower ['kauəʳ] vi sich ducken; (squatting) kauern

cowshed ['kauʃed] n Kuhstall m

cowslip ['kauslɪp] n Schlüsselblume f

cox [kɔks] n abbr = **coxswain**

coxswain ['kɔksn] n Steuermann m; (of ship) Boot(s)führer m

coy [kɔɪ] adj verschämt

coyote [kɔɪˈəutɪ] n Kojote m

cozy ['kəuzɪ] (US) adj = **cosy**

CP n abbr (= Communist Party) KP f

cp. abbr (= compare) vgl.

CPA (US) n abbr = **certified public accountant**

CPI n abbr (= Consumer Price Index) (Verbraucher) preisindex m

Cpl abbr (Mil) = **corporal**

CP/M n abbr (= Control Program for Microprocessors)
CP/M nt

cps abbr (Comput, Typ: = characters per second) cps, Zeichen pl pro Sekunde

CPSA (Brit) n abbr (= Civil and Public Services Association) Gewerkschaft im öffentlichen Dienst

CPU n abbr (Comput) = **central processing unit**

cr. abbr = **credit; creditor**

crab [kræb] n Krabbe f, Krebs m; (meat) Krabbe f

crab apple n Holzapfel m

crack [kræk] n (noise) Knall m; (of wood breaking) Knacks m; (gap) Spalte f; (in bone, dish, glass) Sprung m; (in wall) Riss m; (joke) Witz m; (Drugs) Crack nt ▷ vt (whip) knallen mit; (twig) knacken mit; (dish, glass) einen Sprung machen in +acc; (bone) anbrechen; (nut, code) knacken; (wall) rissig machen; (problem) lösen; (joke) reißen ▷ adj erstklassig; **to have a ~ at sth** (inf) etw mal probieren; **to ~ jokes** (inf) Witze reißen; **to get ~ing** (inf) loslegen
  ▶ **crack down on** vt fus hart durchgreifen gegen
  ▶ **crack up** vi durchdrehen, zusammenbrechen

crackdown ['krækdaun] n: **~ (on)** scharfes Durchgreifen nt (gegen)

cracked [krækt] (inf) adj übergeschnappt

cracker ['krækəʳ] n (biscuit) Cracker m; (also: **Christmas cracker**) Knallbonbon nt; (firework) Knallkörper m, Kracher m; **a ~ of a ...** (Brit: inf) ein(e) tolle(r, s) ...; **he's ~s** (Brit: inf) er ist übergeschnappt

crackle ['krækl] vi (fire) knistern, prasseln; (twig) knacken

crackling ['kræklɪŋ] n (of fire) Knistern nt, Prasseln nt; (of twig, on radio, telephone) Knacken nt; (of pork) Kruste f (des Schweinebratens)

crackpot ['krækpɔt] (inf) n Spinner(in) m(f) ▷ adj verrückt

cradle ['kreɪdl] n Wiege f ▷ vt fest in den Armen halten

craft [krɑːft] n (skill) Geschicklichkeit f; (art) Kunsthandwerk nt; (trade) Handwerk nt; (pl inv: boat) Boot nt; (pl inv: plane) Flugzeug nt

craftsman ['krɑːftsmən] (irreg: like **man**) n Handwerker m

craftsmanship ['krɑːftsmənʃɪp] n handwerkliche Ausführung f

crafty ['krɑːftɪ] adj schlau, clever

crag [kræg] n Fels m

craggy ['krægɪ] adj (mountain) zerklüftet; (cliff) felsig; (face) kantig

cram [kræm] vt vollstopfen ▷ vi pauken (inf), büffeln (inf); **to ~ with** vollstopfen mit; **to ~ sth into** etw hineinstopfen in +acc

cramming ['kræmɪŋ] n (for exams) Pauken nt, Büffeln nt

cramp [kræmp] n Krampf m ▷ vt hemmen

cramped [kræmpt] adj eng

crampon ['kræmpən] n Steigeisen nt

cranberry ['krænbərɪ] n Preiselbeere f

crane [kreɪn] n Kran m; (bird) Kranich m
  ▷ vt: **to ~ one's neck** den Hals recken ▷ vi: **to ~ forward** den Hals recken

cranium ['kreɪnɪəm] (pl **crania**) n Schädel m
crank [kræŋk] n Spinner(in) m(f); (handle) Kurbel f
crankshaft ['kræŋkʃɑːft] n Kurbelwelle f
cranky ['kræŋkɪ] adj verrückt
cranny ['krænɪ] n see **nook**
crap [kræp] (inf!) n Scheiße f (!) ▷ vi scheißen (!); **to have a ~** scheißen (!)
crappy ['kræpɪ] (inf!) adj beschissen (!)
crash [kræʃ] n (noise) Krachen nt; (of car) Unfall m; (of plane etc) Unglück nt; (collision) Zusammenstoß m; (of stock market, business etc) Zusammenbruch m ▷ vt (car) einen Unfall haben mit; (plane etc) abstürzen mit ▷ vi (plane) abstürzen; (car) einen Unfall haben; (two cars) zusammenstoßen; (market) zusammenbrechen; (firm) Pleite machen; **to ~ into** krachen or knallen gegen; **he ~ed the car into a wall** er fuhr mit dem Auto gegen eine Mauer
crash barrier (Brit) n Leitplanke f
crash course n Schnellkurs m, Intensivkurs m
crash helmet n Sturzhelm m
crash-landing ['kræʃlændɪŋ] n Bruchlandung f
crass [kræs] adj krass; (behaviour) unfein, derb
crate [kreɪt] n (also inf) Kiste f; (for bottles) Kasten m
crater ['kreɪtər] n Krater m
cravat [krə'væt] n Halstuch nt
crave [kreɪv] vt, vi: **to ~ (for)** sich sehnen nach
craven ['kreɪvən] adj feige
craving ['kreɪvɪŋ] n: **~ (for)** Verlangen nt (nach)
crawl [krɔːl] vi kriechen; (child) krabbeln ▷ n (Swimming) Kraulstil m, Kraul(en) nt; **to ~ to sb** (inf) vor jdm kriechen; **to drive along at a ~** im Schneckentempo or Kriechtempo vorankommen
crawler lane (Brit) n (Aut) Kriechspur f
crayfish ['kreɪfɪʃ] n inv (freshwater) Flusskrebs m; (saltwater) Languste f
crayon ['kreɪən] n Buntstift m
craze [kreɪz] n Fimmel m; **to be all the ~** große Mode sein
crazed [kreɪzd] adj wahnsinnig; (pottery, glaze) rissig
crazy ['kreɪzɪ] adj wahnsinnig, verrückt; **~ about sb/sth** (inf) verrückt or wild auf jdn/etw; **to go ~** wahnsinnig or verrückt werden
crazy paving (Brit) n Mosaikpflaster nt
creak [kriːk] vi knarren
cream [kriːm] n Sahne f, Rahm m (Südd); (artificial cream, cosmetic) Creme f; (élite) Creme f, Elite f ▷ adj cremefarben; **whipped ~** Schlagsahne f
▷ **cream off** vt absahnen (inf)
cream cake n Sahnetorte f; (small) Sahnetörtchen nt
cream cheese n (Doppelrahm)frischkäse m
creamery ['kriːmərɪ] n (shop) Milchgeschäft nt; (factory) Molkerei f
creamy ['kriːmɪ] adj (colour) cremefarben; (taste) sahnig
crease [kriːs] n Falte f; (in trousers) Bügelfalte

f ▷ vt zerknittern; (forehead) runzeln ▷ vi knittern; (forehead) sich runzeln
crease-resistant ['kriːsrɪzɪstənt] adj knitterfrei
create [kriː'eɪt] vt schaffen; (interest) hervorrufen; (problems) verursachen; (produce) herstellen; (design) entwerfen, kreieren; (impression, fuss) machen
creation [kriː'eɪʃən] n (see vb) Schaffung f; Hervorrufen nt; Verursachung f; Herstellung f; Entwurf m, Kreation f; (Rel) Schöpfung f
creative [kriː'eɪtɪv] adj kreativ, schöpferisch
creativity [kriːeɪ'tɪvɪtɪ] n Kreativität f
creator [kriː'eɪtər] n Schöpfer(in) m(f)
creature ['kriːtʃər] n Geschöpf nt; (living animal) Lebewesen nt
creature comforts [-'kʌmfəts] npl Lebensgenüsse pl
crèche [kreʃ] n (Kinder)krippe f; (all day) (Kinder)tagesstätte f
credence ['kriːdns] n: **to lend** or **give ~ to sth** etw glaubwürdig erscheinen lassen or machen
credentials [krɪ'dɛnʃlz] npl Referenzen pl, Zeugnisse pl; (papers of identity) (Ausweis)papiere pl
credibility [krɛdɪ'bɪlɪtɪ] n Glaubwürdigkeit f
credible ['krɛdɪbl] adj glaubwürdig
credit ['krɛdɪt] n (loan) Kredit m; (recognition) Anerkennung f; (Scol) Schein m ▷ adj (Comm: terms etc) Kredit- ▷ vt (Comm) gutschreiben; (believe: also: **give credit to**) glauben; **credits** npl (Cine, TV: at beginning) Vorspann m; (: at end) Nachspann m; **to be in ~** (person) Geld auf dem Konto haben; (bank account) im Haben sein; **on ~** auf Kredit; **it is to his ~ that ...** es ehrt ihn, dass ...; **to take the ~ for** das Verdienst in Anspruch nehmen für; **it does him ~** es spricht für ihn; **he's a ~ to his family** er macht seiner Familie Ehre; **to ~ sb with sth** (fig) jdm etw zuschreiben; **to ~ £5 to sb** jdm £5 gutschreiben
creditable ['krɛdɪtəbl] adj lobenswert, anerkennenswert
credit account n Kreditkonto nt
credit agency (Brit) n Kreditauskunftei f
credit balance n Kontostand m
credit bureau (US) n = **credit agency**
credit card n Kreditkarte f
credit control n Kreditüberwachung f
credit crunch n Kreditklemme f
credit facilities npl (Comm) Kreditmöglichkeiten pl
credit limit n Kreditgrenze f
credit note (Brit) n Gutschrift f
creditor ['krɛdɪtər] n Gläubiger m
credit transfer n Banküberweisung f
creditworthy ['krɛdɪtwɜːðɪ] adj kreditwürdig
credulity [krɪ'djuːlɪtɪ] n Leichtgläubigkeit f
creed [kriːd] n Glaubensbekenntnis nt
creek [kriːk] n (kleine) Bucht f; (US: stream) Bach m; **to be up the ~** (inf) in der Tinte sitzen
creel [kriːl] n (also: **lobster creel**) Hummer(fang)korb m

creep [kri:p] (*pt, pp* **crept**) *vi* schleichen; (*plant: horizontally*) kriechen; (: *vertically*) klettern ▷ *n* (*inf*) Kriecher *m*; **to ~ up on sb** sich an jdn heranschleichen; (*time etc*) langsam auf jdn zukommen; **he's a ~** er ist ein widerlicher *or* fieser Typ; **it gives me the ~s** davon kriege ich das kalte Grausen
creeper ['kri:pə^r] *n* Kletterpflanze *f*
creepers ['kri:pəz] (US) *npl* Schuhe mit weichen Sohlen
creepy ['kri:pı] *adj* gruselig; (*experience*) unheimlich, gruselig
creepy-crawly ['kri:pı'krɔ:lı] (*inf*) *n* Krabbeltier *nt*
cremate [krı'meıt] *vt* einäschern
cremation [krı'meıʃən] *n* Einäscherung *f*, Kremation *f*
crematoria [krɛmə'tɔ:rıə] *npl of* **crematorium**
crematorium [krɛmə'tɔ:rıəm] (*pl* **crematoria**) *n* Krematorium *nt*
creosote ['krıəsəut] *n* Kreosot *nt*
crepe [kreıp] *n* Krepp *m*; (*rubber*) Krepp(gummi) *m*
crepe bandage (*Brit*) *n* elastische Binde *f*
crepe paper *n* Krepppapier *nt*
crepe sole *n* Kreppsohle *f*
crept [krɛpt] *pt, pp of* **creep**
crescendo [krı'ʃɛndəu] *n* Höhepunkt *m*; (*Mus*) Crescendo *nt*
crescent ['krɛsnt] *n* Halbmond *m*; (*street*) halbkreisförmig verlaufende Straße
cress [krɛs] *n* Kresse *f*
crest [krɛst] *n* (*of hill*) Kamm *m*; (*of bird*) Haube *f*; (*coat of arms*) Wappen *nt*
crestfallen ['krɛstfɔ:lən] *adj* niedergeschlagen
Crete [kri:t] *n* Kreta *nt*
crevasse [krı'væs] *n* Gletscherspalte *f*
crevice ['krɛvıs] *n* Spalte *f*
crew [kru:] *n* Besatzung *f*; (*TV, Cine*) Crew *f*; (*gang*) Bande *f*
crew cut *n* Bürstenschnitt *m*
crew neck *n* runder (Hals)ausschnitt *m*
crib [krıb] *n* Kinderbett *nt*; (*Rel*) Krippe *f* ▷ *vt* (*inf: copy*) abschreiben
cribbage ['krıbıdʒ] *n* Cribbage *nt*
crib death (*US*) *n* = **cot death**
crick [krık] *n* Krampf *m*
cricket ['krıkıt] *n* Kricket *nt*; (*insect*) Grille *f*
cricketer ['krıkıtə^r] *n* Kricketspieler(in) *m(f)*
crime [kraım] *n* (*no pl: illegal activities*) Verbrechen *pl*; (*illegal action: fig*) Verbrechen *nt*; **minor ~** kleineres Vergehen *nt*
crime wave *n* Verbrechenswelle *f*
criminal ['krımınl] *n* Kriminelle(r) *f(m)*, Verbrecher(in) *m(f)* ▷ *adj* kriminell; **C~ Investigation Department** Kriminalpolizei *f*
criminal code *n* Strafgesetzbuch *nt*
criminal profile *n* Täterprofil *nt*
crimp [krımp] *vt* kräuseln; (*hair*) wellen
crimson ['krımzn] *adj* purpurrot
cringe [krındʒ] *vi* (*in fear*) zurückweichen; (*in embarrassment*) zusammenzucken
crinkle ['krıŋkl] *vt* (zer)knittern

cripple ['krıpl] *n* Krüppel *m* ▷ *vt* zum Krüppel machen; (*ship, plane*) aktionsunfähig machen; (*production, exports*) lahmlegen, lähmen; **~d with rheumatism** von Rheuma praktisch gelähmt
crippling ['krıplıŋ] *adj* (*disease*) schwer; (*taxation, debts*) erdrückend
crises ['kraısi:z] *npl of* **crisis**
crisis ['kraısıs] (*pl* **crises**) *n* Krise *f*
crisp [krısp] *adj* (*vegetables etc*) knackig; (*bacon etc*) knusprig; (*weather*) frisch; (*manner, tone, reply*) knapp
crisps [krısps] (*Brit*) *npl* Chips *pl*
crisscross ['krıskrɔs] *adj* (*pattern*) Kreuz- ▷ *vt* kreuz und quer durchziehen
criteria [kraı'tıərıə] *npl of* **criterion**
criterion [kraı'tıərıən] (*pl* **criteria**) *n* Kriterium *nt*
critic ['krıtık] *n* Kritiker(in) *m(f)*
critical ['krıtıkl] *adj* kritisch; **to be ~ of sb/sth** jdn/etw kritisieren; **he is in a ~ condition** sein Zustand ist kritisch
critically ['krıtıklı] *adv* kritisch; (*ill*) schwer
criticism ['krıtısızəm] *n* Kritik *f*
criticize ['krıtısaız] *vt* kritisieren
critique [krı'ti:k] *n* Kritik *f*
croak [krəuk] *vi* (*frog*) quaken; (*bird, person*) krächzen
Croat *n* Kroate *m*, Kroatin *f*; (*Ling*) Kroatisch *nt*
Croatia [krəu'eıʃə] *n* Kroatien *nt*
Croatian [krəu'eıʃən] *adj* kroatisch
crochet ['krəuʃeı] *n* (*activity*) Häkeln *nt*; (*result*) Häkelei *f*
crock [krɔk] *n* Topf *m*; (*inf: also:* **old crock**: *vehicle*) Kiste *f*; (: *person*) Wrack *nt*
crockery ['krɔkərı] *n* Geschirr *nt*
crocodile ['krɔkədaıl] *n* Krokodil *nt*
crocus ['krəukəs] *n* Krokus *m*
croft [krɔft] (*Brit*) *n* kleines Pachtgut *nt*
crofter ['krɔftə^r] (*Brit*) *n* Kleinpächter(in) *m(f)*
crone [krəun] *n* alte Hexe *f*
crony ['krəunı] (*inf: pej*) *n* Kumpan(in) *m(f)*
crook [kruk] *n* (*criminal*) Gauner *m*; (*of shepherd*) Hirtenstab *m*; (*of arm*) Beuge *f*
crooked ['krukıd] *adj* krumm; (*dishonest*) unehrlich
crop [krɔp] *n* (*Feld*)frucht *f*; (*amount produced*) Ernte *f*; (*riding crop*) Reitpeitsche *f*; (*of bird*) Kropf *m* ▷ *vt* (*hair*) stutzen; (*subj: animal: grass*) abfressen
▷ **crop up** *vi* aufkommen
cropper ['krɔpə^r] (*inf*) *n*: **to come a ~** hinfallen; (*fig: fail*) auf die Nase fallen
crop spraying [-'spreıın] *n* Schädlingsbekämpfung *f* (*durch Besprühen*)
croquet ['krəukeı] (*Brit*) *n* Krocket *nt*
croquette [krə'kɛt] *n* Krokette *f*
cross [krɔs] *n* Kreuz *nt*; (*Biol, Bot*) Kreuzung *f* ▷ *vt* (*street*) überqueren; (*room etc*) durchqueren; (*cheque*) zur Verrechnung ausstellen; (*arms*) verschränken; (*legs*) übereinanderschlagen; (*animal, plant*) kreuzen; (*thwart: person*) verärgern; (: *plan*) durchkreuzen ▷ *adj*

ärgerlich, böse ▷ vi: **the boat ~es from ...
to ...** das Schiff fährt von ... nach ...; **to ~ o.s.**
sich bekreuzigen; **we have a ~ed line** (*Brit*) es
ist jemand in der Leitung; **they've got their
lines** *or* **wires ~ed** (*fig*) sie reden aneinander
vorbei; **to be/get ~ with sb (about sth)** mit
jdm *or* auf jdn (wegen etw) böse sein/werden
▶ **cross out** vt streichen
▶ **cross over** vi hinübergehen

crossbar ['krɔsbɑːʳ] n (*Sport*) Querlatte f; (*of
bicycle*) Stange f
crossbow n Armbrust f
crossbreed ['krɔsbriːd] n Kreuzung f
cross-Channel ferry ['krɔs'tʃænl-] n
Kanalfähre f
crosscheck ['krɔstʃɛk] n Gegenprobe f ▷ vt
überprüfen
cross-country ['krɔs'kʌntrɪ], **cross-country
race** n Querfeldeinrennen nt
cross-dressing [krɔs'drɛsɪŋ] n (*transvestism*)
Transvestismus m
cross-examination ['krɔsɪgzæmɪ'neɪʃən] n
Kreuzverhör nt
cross-examine ['krɔsɪg'zæmɪn] vt ins
Kreuzverhör nehmen
cross-eyed ['krɔsaɪd] adj schielend; **to be ~**
schielen
crossfire ['krɔsfaɪəʳ] n Kreuzfeuer nt; **to get
caught in the ~** (*also fig*) ins Kreuzfeuer
geraten
crossing ['krɔsɪŋ] n Überfahrt f;
(*also*: **pedestrian crossing**) Fußgängerüberweg m
crossing guard (*US*) n ≈ Schülerlotse m
crossing point n Übergangsstelle f
cross-purposes ['krɔs'pəːpəsɪz] npl: **to be at ~
with sb** jdn missverstehen; **we're (talking)
at ~** wir reden aneinander vorbei
cross-question ['krɔs'kwɛstʃən] vt ins
Kreuzverhör nehmen
cross-reference ['krɔs'rɛfrəns] n (Quer)
verweis m
crossroads ['krɔsrəʊdz] n Kreuzung f
cross section n Querschnitt m
crosswalk ['krɔswɔːk] (*US*) n
Fußgängerüberweg m
crosswind ['krɔswɪnd] n Seitenwind m
crosswise ['krɔswaɪz] adv quer
crossword ['krɔswəːd] n (*also*: **crossword
puzzle**) Kreuzworträtsel nt
crotch [krɔtʃ] n Unterleib m; (*of garment*) Schritt
m
crotchet ['krɔtʃɪt] n Viertelnote f
crotchety ['krɔtʃɪtɪ] adj reizbar
crouch [krautʃ] vi kauern
croup [kruːp] n (*Med*) Krupp m
croupier ['kruːpɪə'] n Croupier m
crouton ['kruːtɔn] n Crouton m
crow [krəʊ] n (*bird*) Krähe f; (*of cock*) Krähen nt
▷ vi krähen; (*fig*) sich brüsten, angeben
crowbar ['krəʊbɑːʳ] n Brechstange f
crowd [kraud] n (Menschen)menge f ▷ vt
(*room, stadium*) füllen ▷ vi: **to ~ round**

sich herumdrängen; **~s of people**
Menschenmassen pl; **the/our ~** (*of friends*)
die/unsere Clique f; **to ~ sb/sth in** jdn/
etw hineinstopfen; **to ~ sb/sth into** jdn
pferchen/etw stopfen in +acc; **to ~ in** sich
hineindrängen
crowded ['kraudɪd] adj überfüllt; (*densely
populated*) dicht besiedelt; **~ with** voll von
crowd scene n Massenszene f
crown [kraun] n (*also of tooth*) Krone f; (*of head*)
Wirbel m; (*of hill*) Kuppe f; (*of hat*) Kopf m ▷ vt
krönen; (*tooth*) überkronen; **the C~** die Krone;
and to ~ it all ... (*fig*) und zur Krönung des
Ganzen ...

● CROWN COURT

Crown Court ist ein Strafgericht, das
in etwa 90 verschiedenen Städten in
England und Wales zusammentritt.
Schwere Verbrechen wie Mord, Totschlag,
Vergewaltigung und Raub werden nur
vor dem crown court unter Vorsitz eines
Richters mit Geschworenen verhandelt.

crowning ['kraunɪŋ] adj krönend
crown jewels npl Kronjuwelen pl
crown prince n Kronprinz m
crow's-feet ['krəuzfiːt] npl Krähenfüße pl
crow's-nest ['krəuznest] n Krähennest nt,
Mastkorb m
crucial ['kruːʃl] adj (*decision*) äußerst wichtig;
(*vote*) entscheidend; **~ to** äußerst wichtig für
crucifix ['kruːsɪfɪks] n Kruzifix nt
crucifixion [kruːsɪ'fɪkʃən] n Kreuzigung f
crucify ['kruːsɪfaɪ] vt kreuzigen; (*fig*) in der Luft
zerreißen
crude [kruːd] adj (*oil, fibre*) Roh-; (*fig: basic*)
primitiv; (: *vulgar*) ordinär ▷ n = **crude oil**
crude oil n Rohöl nt
cruel ['kruəl] adj grausam
cruelty ['kruəltɪ] n Grausamkeit f
cruet ['kruːɪt] n Gewürzständer m
cruise [kruːz] n Kreuzfahrt f ▷ vi (*ship*) kreuzen;
(*car*) (mit Dauergeschwindigkeit) fahren;
(*aircraft*) (mit Reisegeschwindigkeit) fliegen;
(*taxi*) gemächlich fahren
cruise missile n Marschflugkörper m
cruiser ['kruːzə'] n Motorboot nt; (*warship*)
Kreuzer m
cruising speed n Reisegeschwindigkeit f
crumb [krʌm] n Krümel m; (*fig: of information*)
Brocken m; **a ~ of comfort** ein winziger Trost
crumble ['krʌmbl] vt (*bread*) zerbröckeln;
(*biscuit etc*) zerkrümeln ▷ vi (*building, earth
etc*) zerbröckeln; (*plaster*) abbröckeln;
(*fig: opposition*) sich auflösen; (: *belief*) ins
Wanken geraten
crumbly ['krʌmblɪ] adj krümelig
crummy ['krʌmɪ] (*inf*) adj mies
crumpet ['krʌmpɪt] n Teekuchen m (*zum
Toasten*)
crumple ['krʌmpl] vt zerknittern

crunch [krʌntʃ] vt (biscuit, apple etc) knabbern; (underfoot) zertreten ▷ n: **the ~** der große Krach; **if it comes to the ~** wenn es wirklich dahin kommt; **when the ~ comes** wenn es hart auf hart geht

crunchy ['krʌntʃɪ] adj knusprig; (apple etc) knackig; (gravel, snow etc) knirschend

crusade [kru:'seɪd] n Feldzug m ▷ vi: **to ~ for/ against sth** für/gegen etw zu Felde ziehen

crusader [kru:'seɪdəʳ] n Kreuzritter m; (fig): ~ **(for)** Apostel m (+gen)

crush [krʌʃ] n (crowd) Gedränge nt ▷ vt quetschen; (grapes) zerquetschen; (paper, clothes) zerknittern; (garlic, ice) (zer)stoßen; (defeat) niederschlagen; (devastate) vernichten; **to have a ~ on sb** (love) für jdn schwärmen; **lemon ~** Zitronensaftgetränk nt

crush barrier (Brit) n Absperrung f

crushing ['krʌʃɪŋ] adj vernichtend

crust [krʌst] n Kruste f

crustacean [krʌs'teɪʃən] n Schalentier nt, Krustazee f

crusty ['krʌstɪ] adj knusprig

crutch [krʌtʃ] n Krücke f; (support) Stütze f; see also **crotch**

crux [krʌks] n Kern m

cry [kraɪ] vi weinen; (also: **cry out**) aufschreien ▷ n Schrei m; (shout) Ruf m; **what are you ~ing about?** warum weinst du?; **to ~ for help** um Hilfe rufen; **she had a good ~** sie hat sich (mal richtig) ausgeweint; **it's a far ~ from ...** (fig) das ist etwas ganz anderes als ...
▷ **cry off** (inf) vi absagen

crying ['kraɪɪŋ] adj (fig: need) dringend; **it's a ~ shame** es ist ein Jammer

crypt [krɪpt] n Krypta f

cryptic ['krɪptɪk] adj hintergründig, rätselhaft; (clue) verschlüsselt

crystal ['krɪstl] n Kristall m; (glass) Kristall(glas) nt

crystal clear adj glasklar

crystallize ['krɪstəlaɪz] vt (opinion, thoughts) (feste) Form geben +dat ▷ vi (sugar etc) kristallisieren; **~d fruits** (Brit) kandierte Früchte pl

CSA n abbr (= Child Support Agency) Amt zur Regelung von Unterhaltszahlungen für Kinder

CSC n abbr (= Civil Service Commission) Einstellungsbehörde für den öffentlichen Dienst

CSE (Brit) n abbr (formerly: = Certificate of Secondary Education) Schulabschlusszeugnis, ≈ mittlere Reife f

CS gas (Brit) n ≈ Tränengas nt

CST (US) abbr (= Central Standard Time) mittelamerikanische Standardzeit

CT (US) abbr (Post) = Connecticut

ct abbr = **cent; court**

CTC (Brit) n abbr = **city technology college**

CT scanner n abbr (Med: = computerized tomography scanner) CT-Scanner m

cu ['si:ju:] abbr (= see you: in text messages) bis dann, bis später

cu. abbr = **cubic**

cub [kʌb] n Junge(s) nt; (also: **cub scout**)

Wölfling m

Cuba ['kju:bə] n Kuba nt

Cuban ['kju:bən] adj kubanisch ▷ n Kubaner(in) m(f)

cubbyhole ['kʌbɪhəʊl] n (room) Kabuff nt; (space) Eckchen nt

cube [kju:b] n Würfel m; (Math: of number) dritte Potenz f ▷ vt (Math) in die dritte Potenz erheben, hoch drei nehmen

cube farm n (inf) Großraumbüro nt (mit Trennwänden)

cube root n Kubikwurzel f

cubic ['kju:bɪk] adj (volume) Kubik-; ~ **metre** etc Kubikmeter m etc

cubic capacity n Hubraum m

cubicle ['kju:bɪkl] n Kabine f; (in hospital) Bettnische f

cuckoo ['kuku:] n Kuckuck m

cuckoo clock n Kuckucksuhr f

cucumber ['kju:kʌmbəʳ] n Gurke f

cud [kʌd] n: **to chew the ~** (animal) wiederkäuen; (fig: person) vor sich acc hin grübeln

cuddle ['kʌdl] vt in den Arm nehmen, drücken ▷ vi schmusen

cuddly ['kʌdlɪ] adj (toy) zum Liebhaben or Drücken; (person) knuddelig (inf)

cudgel ['kʌdʒl] n Knüppel m ▷ vt: **to ~ one's brains** sich dat das (Ge)hirn zermartern

cue [kju:] n (Sport) Billardstock m, Queue nt; (Theat: word) Stichwort nt; (: action) (Einsatz) zeichen nt; (Mus) Einsatz m

cuff [kʌf] n (of sleeve) Manschette f; (US: of trousers) Aufschlag m; (blow) Klaps m ▷ vt einen Klaps geben +dat; **off the ~** aus dem Stegreif

cuff links npl Manschettenknöpfe pl

cu. in. abbr (= cubic inches) Kubikzoll

cuisine [kwɪ'zi:n] n Küche f

cul-de-sac ['kʌldəsæk] n Sackgasse f

culinary ['kʌlɪnərɪ] adj (skill) Koch-; (delight) kulinarisch

cull [kʌl] vt (zusammen)sammeln; (animals) ausmerzen ▷ n Erlegen überschüssiger Tierbestände

culminate ['kʌlmɪneɪt] vi: **to ~ in** gipfeln in +dat

culmination [kʌlmɪ'neɪʃən] n Höhepunkt m

culottes [kju:'lɔts] npl Hosenrock m

culpable ['kʌlpəbl] adj schuldig

culprit ['kʌlprɪt] n Täter(in) m(f)

cult [kʌlt] n Kult m

cult figure n Kultfigur f

cultivate ['kʌltɪveɪt] vt (land) bebauen, landwirtschaftlich nutzen; (crop) anbauen; (feeling) entwickeln; (person) sich dat warm halten (inf), die Beziehung pflegen zu

cultivation [kʌltɪ'veɪʃən] n (of land) Bebauung f, landwirtschaftliche Nutzung f; (of crop) Anbau m

cultural ['kʌltʃərəl] adj kulturell

culture ['kʌltʃəʳ] n Kultur f

cultured ['kʌltʃəd] adj kultiviert; (pearl) Zucht-

cumbersome ['kʌmbəsəm] adj (suitcase etc) sperrig, unhandlich; (piece of machinery) schwer zu handhaben; (clothing) hinderlich; (process) umständlich

cumin ['kʌmɪn] n Kreuzkümmel m

cumulative ['kju:mjulətɪv] adj (effect, result) Gesamt-

cunning ['kʌnɪŋ] n Gerissenheit f ▷ adj gerissen; (device, idea) schlau

cunt [kʌnt] (inf!) n (vagina) Fotze f (!); (term of abuse) Arsch m (!)

cup [kʌp] n Tasse f; (as prize) Pokal m; (of bra) Körbchen nt; **a ~ of tea** eine Tasse Tee

cupboard ['kʌbəd] n Schrank m

cup final (Brit) n Pokalendspiel nt

cupful ['kʌpful] n Tasse f

Cupid ['kju:pɪd] n Amor m; (figurine) Amorette f

cupidity [kju:'pɪdɪtɪ] n Begierde f, Gier f

cupola ['kju:pələ] n Kuppel f

cuppa ['kʌpə] (Brit: inf) n Tasse f Tee

cup tie (Brit) n Pokalspiel nt

curable ['kjuərəbl] adj heilbar

curate ['kjuərɪt] n Vikar m

curator [kjuə'reɪtəʳ] n Kustos m

curb [kə:b] vt einschränken; (person) an die Kandare nehmen ▷ n Einschränkung f; (US: kerb) Bordstein m

curd cheese n Weißkäse m

curdle ['kə:dl] vi gerinnen

curds [kə:dz] npl ≈ Quark m

cure [kjuəʳ] vt heilen; (Culin: salt) pökeln; (: smoke) räuchern; (: dry) trocknen; (problem) abhelfen +dat ▷ n (remedy) (Heil)mittel nt; (treatment) Heilverfahren nt; (solution) Abhilfe f; **to be ~d of sth** von etw geheilt sein

cure-all ['kjuərɔ:l] n (also fig) Allheilmittel nt

curfew ['kə:fju:] n Ausgangssperre f; (time) Sperrstunde f

curio ['kjuərɪəu] n Kuriosität f

curiosity [kjuərɪ'ɒsɪtɪ] n (see adj) Wissbegier(de) f; Neugier f; Merkwürdigkeit f

curious ['kjuərɪəs] adj (interested) wissbegierig; (nosy) neugierig; (strange, unusual) sonderbar, merkwürdig; **I'm ~ about him** ich bin gespannt auf ihn

curiously ['kjuərɪəslɪ] adv neugierig; (inquisitively) wissbegierig; **~ enough, ...** merkwürdigerweise ...

curl [kə:l] n Locke f; (of smoke etc) Kringel m ▷ vt (hair: loosely) locken; (: tightly) kräuseln ▷ vi sich locken; sich kräuseln; (smoke) sich kringeln
▶ **curl up** vi sich zusammenrollen

curler ['kə:ləʳ] n Lockenwickler m; (Sport) Curlingspieler(in) m(f)

curlew ['kə:lu:] n Brachvogel m

curling ['kə:lɪŋ] n (Sport) Curling nt

curling tongs, (US) **curling irons** npl Lockenschere f, Brennschere f

curly ['kə:lɪ] adj lockig; (tightly curled) kraus

currant ['kʌrnt] n Korinthe f; (blackcurrant, redcurrant) Johannisbeere f

currency ['kʌrnsɪ] n (system) Währung f; (money) Geld nt; **foreign ~** Devisen pl; **to gain ~** (fig) sich verbreiten, um sich greifen

current ['kʌrnt] n Strömung f; (Elec) Strom m; (of opinion) Tendenz f, Trend m ▷ adj gegenwärtig; (expression) gebräuchlich; (idea, custom) verbreitet; **direct/alternating ~** (Elec) Gleich-/Wechselstrom m; **the ~ issue of a magazine** die neueste or letzte Nummer einer Zeitschrift; **in ~ use** allgemein gebräuchlich

current account (Brit) n Girokonto nt

current affairs npl Tagespolitik f

current assets npl (Comm) Umlaufvermögen nt

current liabilities npl (Comm) kurzfristige Verbindlichkeiten pl

currently ['kʌrntlɪ] adv zurzeit

curricula [kə'rɪkjulə] npl of **curriculum**

curriculum [kə'rɪkjuləm] (pl **~s** or **curricula**) n Lehrplan m

curriculum vitae [-'vi:taɪ] n Lebenslauf m

curry ['kʌrɪ] n (dish) Curry(gericht nt ▷ vt: **to ~ favour with** sich einschmeicheln bei

curry powder n Curry m or nt, Currypulver nt

curse [kə:s] vi fluchen ▷ vt verfluchen ▷ n Fluch m

cursor ['kə:səʳ] n (Comput) Cursor m

cursory ['kə:sərɪ] adj flüchtig; (examination) oberflächlich

curt [kə:t] adj knapp, kurz angebunden

curtail [kə:'teɪl] vt einschränken; (visit etc) abkürzen

curtain ['kə:tn] n Vorhang m; (net) Gardine f; **to draw the ~s** (together) die Vorhänge zuziehen; (apart) die Vorhänge aufmachen

curtain call n (Theat) Vorhang m

curtsey, **curtsy** ['kə:tsɪ] vi knicksen ▷ n Knicks m

curvature ['kə:vətʃəʳ] n Krümmung f

curve [kə:v] n Bogen m; (in the road) Kurve f ▷ vi einen Bogen machen; (surface, arch) sich wölben ▷ vt biegen

curved [kə:vd] adj (line) gebogen; (table legs etc) geschwungen; (surface, arch, sides of ship) gewölbt

cushion ['kuʃən] n Kissen nt ▷ vt dämpfen; (seat) polstern

cushy ['kuʃɪ] (inf) adj: **a ~ job** ein gemütlicher or ruhiger Job; **to have a ~ time** eine ruhige Kugel schieben

custard ['kʌstəd] n (for pouring) Vanillesoße f

custard powder (Brit) n Vanillesoßenpulver nt

custodial [kʌs'təudɪəl] adj: **~ sentence** Gefängnisstrafe f

custodian [kʌs'təudɪən] n Verwalter(in) m(f); (of museum etc) Aufseher(in) m(f), Wächter(in) m(f)

custody ['kʌstədɪ] n (of child) Vormundschaft f; (for offenders) (polizeilicher) Gewahrsam m, Haft f; **to take into ~** verhaften; **in the ~ of** unter der Obhut +gen; **the mother has ~ of the children** die Kinder sind der Mutter zugesprochen worden

custom ['kʌstəm] n Brauch m; (habit) (An)gewohnheit f; (Law) Gewohnheitsrecht nt; (Comm) Kundschaft f

customary ['kʌstəmərɪ] adj (conventional) üblich; (habitual) gewohnt; **it is ~ to do it** es ist üblich, es zu tun

custom-built ['kʌstəm'bɪlt] adj speziell angefertigt

customer ['kʌstəmər] n Kunde m, Kundin f; **he's an awkward ~** (inf) er ist ein schwieriger Typ

customer profile n Kundenprofil nt

customized ['kʌstəmaɪzd] adj individuell aufgemacht

custom-made ['kʌstəm'meɪd] adj (shirt etc) maßgefertigt, nach Maß; (car etc) speziell angefertigt

customs ['kʌstəmz] npl Zoll m; **to go through (the) ~** durch den Zoll gehen

Customs and Excise (Brit) n die Zollbehörde f

customs duty n Zoll m

customs officer n Zollbeamte(r) m, Zollbeamtin f

cut [kʌt] (pt, pp **~**) vt schneiden; (text, programme, spending) kürzen; (prices) senken, heruntersetzen, herabsetzen; (supply) einschränken; (cloth) zuschneiden; (road) schlagen, hauen; (inf: lecture, appointment) schwänzen ▷ vi schneiden; (lines) sich schneiden ▷ n Schnitt m; (in skin) Schnittwunde f; (in salary, spending etc) Kürzung f; (of meat) Stück nt; (of jewel) Schnitt m, Schliff m; **to ~ a tooth** zahnen, einen Zahn bekommen; **to ~ one's finger/hand/knee** sich in den Finger/in die Hand/am Knie schneiden; **to get one's hair ~** sich dat die Haare schneiden lassen; **to ~ sth short** etw vorzeitig abbrechen; **to ~ sb dead** jdn wie Luft behandeln; **cold ~s** (US) Aufschnitt m; **power ~** Stromausfall m

▶ **cut back** vt (plants) zurückschneiden; (production) zurückschrauben; (expenditure) einschränken

▶ **cut down** vt (tree) fällen; (consumption) einschränken; **to ~ sb down to size** (fig) jdn auf seinen Platz verweisen

▶ **cut down on** vt fus einschränken

▶ **cut in** vi (Aut) sich direkt vor ein anderes Auto setzen; **to ~ in (on)** (conversation) sich einschalten (in +acc)

▶ **cut off** vt abschneiden; (supply) sperren; (Tel) unterbrechen; **we've been ~ off** (Tel) wir sind unterbrochen worden

▶ **cut out** vt ausschneiden; (an activity etc) aufhören mit; (remove) herausschneiden

▶ **cut up** vt klein schneiden; **it really ~ me up** (inf) es hat mich ziemlich mitgenommen; **to feel ~ up about sth** (inf) betroffen über etw acc sein

cut and dried adj (also: **cut-and-dry**: answer) eindeutig; (: solution) einfach

cutaway ['kʌtəweɪ] n (coat) Cut(away) m; (drawing) Schnittdiagramm nt; (model) Schnittmodell nt; (Cine, TV) Schnitt m

cutback ['kʌtbæk] n Kürzung f

cute [kjuːt] adj süß, niedlich; (clever) schlau

cut glass n geschliffenes Glas nt

cuticle ['kjuːtɪkl] n Nagelhaut f; **~ remover**

Nagelhautentferner m

cutlery ['kʌtlərɪ] n Besteck nt

cutlet ['kʌtlɪt] n Schnitzel nt; (also: **vegetable cutlet, nut cutlet**) Bratling m

cutoff ['kʌtɔf] n (also: **cutoff point**) Trennlinie f

cutoff switch n Ausschaltmechanismus m

cutout ['kʌtaut] n (switch) Unterbrecher m; (shape) Ausschneidemodell nt; (paper figure) Ausschneidepuppe f

cut-price ['kʌt'praɪs] adj (goods) heruntergesetzt; (offer) Billig-

cut-rate ['kʌt'reɪt] (US) adj = **cut-price**

cutthroat ['kʌtθraut] n Mörder(in) m(f) ▷ adj unbarmherzig, mörderisch

cutting ['kʌtɪŋ] adj (edge, remark) scharf ▷ n (Brit: from newspaper) Ausschnitt m; (: Rail) Durchstich m; (from plant) Ableger m

cutting edge n (fig) Spitzenstellung f; **on the ~ (of)** an der Spitze +gen

cuttlefish ['kʌtlfɪʃ] n Tintenfisch m

CV n abbr = **curriculum vitae**

c.w.o. abbr (Comm) = **cash with order**

cwt abbr = **hundredweight**

cyanide ['saɪənaɪd] n Zyanid nt

cybercafé ['saɪbəkæfeɪ] n Internetcafé nt

cybernetics [saɪbə'netɪks] n Kybernetik f

cyclamen ['sɪkləmən] n Alpenveilchen nt

cycle ['saɪkl] n (bicycle) (Fahr)rad nt; (series: of seasons, songs etc) Zyklus m; (: of events) Gang m; (: Tech) Periode f ▷ vi Rad fahren

cycle lane, cycle path n (Fahr)radweg m

cycle race n Radrennen nt

cycle rack n Fahrradständer m

cycling ['saɪklɪŋ] n Radfahren nt; **to go on a ~ holiday** (Brit) Urlaub mit dem Fahrrad machen

cyclist ['saɪklɪst] n (Fahr)radfahrer(in) m(f)

cyclone ['saɪkləun] n Zyklon m

cygnet ['sɪgnɪt] n Schwanjunge(s) nt

cylinder ['sɪlɪndər] n Zylinder m; (of gas) Gasflasche f

cylinder block n Zylinderblock m

cylinder head n Zylinderkopf m

cylinder-head gasket ['sɪlɪndəhed-] n Zylinderkopfdichtung f

cymbals ['sɪmblz] npl (Mus) Becken nt

cynic ['sɪnɪk] n Zyniker(in) m(f)

cynical ['sɪnɪkl] adj zynisch

cynicism ['sɪnɪsɪzəm] n Zynismus m

cypress ['saɪprɪs] n Zypresse f

Cypriot ['sɪprɪət] adj zypriotisch, zyprisch ▷ n Zypriot(in) m(f)

Cyprus ['saɪprəs] n Zypern nt

cyst [sɪst] n Zyste f

cystitis [sɪs'taɪtɪs] n Blasenentzündung f, Zystitis f

CZ (US) n abbr (= Canal Zone) Bereich des Panamakanals

czar [zɑːr] n = **tsar**

Czech [tʃek] adj tschechisch ▷ n Tscheche m, Tschechin f; (language) Tschechisch nt; **the ~ Republic** die Tschechische Republik f

Czechoslovak [tʃekə'sləuvæk] adj, n =

505

Czechoslovakian
Czechoslovakia [tʃɛkəslə'vækɪə] n (formerly) die
Tschechoslowakei f

Czechoslovakian [tʃɛkəslə'vækɪən] (formerly)
adj tschechoslowakisch ▷ n Tschechoslowake
m, Tschechoslowakin f

Dd

D¹, d¹ [di:] n (letter) D nt, d nt; **D for David, D for Dog** (US) ≈ D wie Dora

D² [di:] n (Mus) D nt, d nt

D³ [di:] (US) abbr (Pol) = **Democrat; Democratic**

d² (Brit: formerly) abbr = **penny**

d. abbr (= died): **Henry Jones, d. 1754** Henry Jones, gest. 1754

DA (US) n abbr = **district attorney**

dab [dæb] vt betupfen; (paint, cream) tupfen ▷ n Tupfer m; **to be a ~ hand at sth** gut in etw dat sein; **to be a ~ hand at doing sth** sich darauf verstehen, etw zu tun
  ▶ **dab at** vt betupfen

dabble ['dæbl] vi: **to ~ in** sich (nebenbei) beschäftigen mit

dachshund ['dækshund] n Dackel m

dad [dæd] (inf) n Papa m, Vati m

daddy ['dædɪ] (inf) n = **dad**

daddy-longlegs [dædɪ'lɒŋlɛgz] (inf) n Schnake f

daffodil ['dæfədɪl] n Osterglocke f, Narzisse f

daft [dɑ:ft] (inf) adj doof (inf), blöd (inf); **to be ~ about sb/sth** verrückt nach jdm/etw sein

dagger ['dægəʳ] n Dolch m; **to be at ~s drawn with sb** mit jdm auf Kriegsfuß stehen; **to look ~s at sb** jdn mit Blicken durchbohren

dahlia ['deɪljə] n Dahlie f

daily ['deɪlɪ] adj täglich; (wages) Tages- ▷ n (paper) Tageszeitung f; (Brit: also: **daily help**) Putzfrau f ▷ adv täglich; **twice ~** zweimal täglich or am Tag

dainty ['deɪntɪ] adj zierlich

dairy ['dɛərɪ] n (Brit: shop) Milchgeschäft nt; (company) Molkerei f; (on farm) Milchkammer f ▷ cpd Milch-; (herd, industry, farming) Milchvieh-

dairy farm n auf Milchviehhaltung spezialisierter Bauernhof

dairy products npl Milchprodukte pl, Molkereiprodukte pl

dairy store (US) n Milchgeschäft nt

dais ['deɪɪs] n Podium nt

daisy ['deɪzɪ] n Gänseblümchen nt

daisywheel ['deɪzɪwi:l] n Typenrad nt

daisywheel printer n Typenraddrucker m

Dakar ['dækəʳ] n Dakar nt

dale [deɪl] (Brit) n Tal nt

dally ['dælɪ] vi (herum)trödeln; **to ~ with** (plan, idea) spielen mit

dalmatian [dæl'meɪʃən] n Dalmatiner m

dam [dæm] n (Stau)damm m; (reservoir) Stausee m ▷ vt stauen

damage ['dæmɪdʒ] n Schaden m ▷ vt schaden +dat; (spoil, break) beschädigen; **damages** npl (Law) Schaden(s)ersatz m; **~ to property** Sachbeschädigung f; **to pay £5,000 in ~s** 5000 Pfund Schaden(s)ersatz (be)zahlen

damaging ['dæmɪdʒɪŋ] adj: **~ (to)** schädlich (für)

Damascus [də'mɑ:skəs] n Damaskus nt

dame [deɪm] n Dame f; (US: inf) Weib nt; (Theat) (komische) Alte f (von einem Mann gespielt)

damn [dæm] vt verfluchen; (condemn) verurteilen ▷ adj (inf: also: **damned**) verdammt ▷ n (inf): **I don't give a ~** das ist mir scheißegal (!); **~ (it)!** verdammt (noch mal)!

damnable ['dæmnəbl] adj grässlich

damnation [dæm'neɪʃən] n Verdammnis f ▷ excl (inf) verdammt

damning ['dæmɪŋ] adj belastend

damp [dæmp] adj feucht ▷ n Feuchtigkeit f ▷ vt (also: **dampen**) befeuchten, anfeuchten; (enthusiasm etc) dämpfen

dampcourse ['dæmpkɔ:s] n Dämmschicht f

damper ['dæmpəʳ] n (Mus) Dämpfer m; (of fire) (Luft)klappe f; **to put a ~ on** (fig) einen Dämpfer aufsetzen +dat

dampness ['dæmpnɪs] n Feuchtigkeit f

damson ['dæmzən] n Damaszenerpflaume f

dance [dɑ:ns] n Tanz m; (social event) Tanz(abend) m ▷ vi tanzen; **to ~ about** (herum)tänzeln

dance hall n Tanzsaal m

dancer ['dɑ:nsəʳ] n Tänzer(in) m(f)

dancing ['dɑ:nsɪŋ] n Tanzen nt ▷ cpd (teacher, school, class etc) Tanz-

D and C n abbr (Med: = dilation and curettage) Ausschabung f

dandelion ['dændɪlaɪən] n Löwenzahn m

dandruff ['dændrəf] n Schuppen pl

D and T (Brit) n abbr (Scol) = **Design and Technology**

dandy ['dændɪ] n Dandy m ▷ adj (US: inf) prima

Dane [deɪn] n Däne m, Dänin f

danger ['deɪndʒəʳ] n Gefahr f; **there is ~ of fire/poisoning** es besteht Feuer-/Vergiftungsgefahr; **there is a ~ of sth**

happening es besteht die Gefahr, dass etw geschieht; "~!" „Achtung!"; **in** ~ in Gefahr; **to be in ~ of doing sth** Gefahr laufen, etw zu tun; **out of** ~ außer Gefahr

danger list n: **on the** ~ in Lebensgefahr

dangerous ['deɪndʒrəs] adj gefährlich

dangerously ['deɪndʒrəslɪ] adv gefährlich; (close) bedenklich; ~ **ill** schwer krank

danger zone n Gefahrenzone f

dangle ['dæŋgl] vt baumeln lassen ▷ vi baumeln

Danish ['deɪnɪʃ] adj dänisch ▷ n (Ling) Dänisch nt

Danish pastry n Plundergebäck nt

dank [dæŋk] adj (unangenehm) feucht

Danube ['dænjuːb] n: **the** ~ die Donau

dapper ['dæpəʳ] adj gepflegt

Dardanelles [dɑːdə'nɛlz] npl: **the** ~ die Dardanellen pl

dare [dɛəʳ] vt: **to** ~ **sb to do sth** jdn dazu herausfordern, etw zu tun ▷ vi: **to** ~ **(to) do sth** es wagen, etw zu tun; **I** ~**n't tell him** (Brit) ich wage nicht, es ihm zu sagen; **I** ~ **say** ich nehme an

daredevil ['dɛədɛvl] n Draufgänger m

Dar-es-Salaam ['dɑːrɛssə'lɑːm] n Daressalam nt

daring ['dɛərɪŋ] adj kühn, verwegen; (bold) gewagt ▷ n Kühnheit f

dark [dɑːk] adj dunkel; (look) finster ▷ n: **in the** ~ im Dunkeln; **to be in the** ~ **about** (fig) keine Ahnung haben von; **after** ~ nach Einbruch der Dunkelheit; **it is/is getting** ~ es ist/wird dunkel; ~ **chocolate** Zartbitterschokolade f

Dark Ages npl: **the** ~ das finstere Mittelalter

darken [dɑːkn] vt dunkel machen ▷ vi sich verdunkeln

dark glasses npl Sonnenbrille f

dark horse n (in competition) Unbekannte(r) f(m) (mit Außenseiterchancen); (quiet person) stilles Wasser nt

darkly ['dɑːklɪ] adv finster

darkness ['dɑːknɪs] n Dunkelheit f, Finsternis f

darkroom ['dɑːkrum] n Dunkelkammer f

darling ['dɑːlɪŋ] adj lieb ▷ n Liebling m; **to be the** ~ **of** der Liebling +gen sein; **she is a** ~ sie ist ein Schatz

darn [dɑːn] vt stopfen

dart [dɑːt] n (in game) (Wurf)pfeil m; (in sewing) Abnäher m ▷ vi: **to** ~ **towards** (also: **make a dart towards**) zustürzen auf +acc; **to** ~ **away/along** davon-/entlangflitzen

dartboard ['dɑːtbɔːd] n Dartscheibe f

darts [dɑːts] n Darts nt, Pfeilwurfspiel nt

dash [dæʃ] n (sign) Gedankenstrich m; (rush) Jagd f ▷ vt (throw) schleudern; (hopes) zunichtemachen ▷ vi: **to** ~ **towards** zustürzen auf +acc; **a** ~ **of ...** (small quantity) etwas ..., ein Schuss m ...; **to make a** ~ **for sth** auf etw acc zustürzen; **we'll have to make a** ~ **for it** wir müssen rennen, so schnell wir können

▶ **dash away** vi losstürzen

▶ **dash off** vi = **dash away**

dashboard ['dæʃbɔːd] n Armaturenbrett nt

dashing ['dæʃɪŋ] adj flott

dastardly ['dæstədlɪ] adj niederträchtig

DAT n abbr (= digital audio tape) DAT nt

data ['deɪtə] npl Daten pl

data analysis n Datenanalyse f

database ['deɪtəbeɪs] n Datenbank f

data capture n Datenerfassung f

data processing n Datenverarbeitung f

data projector n Beamer m

data transmission n Datenübertragung f

date [deɪt] n Datum nt; (with friend) Verabredung f; (fruit) Dattel f ▷ vt datieren; (person) ausgehen mit; **what's the** ~ **today?** der Wievielte ist heute?; ~ **of birth** Geburtsdatum nt; **closing** ~ Einsendeschluss m; **to** ~ bis heute; **out of** ~ altmodisch; (expired) abgelaufen; **up to** ~ auf dem neuesten Stand; **to bring up to** ~ auf den neuesten Stand bringen; (person) über den neuesten Stand der Dinge informieren; **a letter** ~**d 5 July** ein vom 5. Juli datierter Brief

dated ['deɪtɪd] adj altmodisch

dateline ['deɪtlaɪn] n (Geog) Datumsgrenze f; (Press) Datumszeile f

date rape n Vergewaltigung f einer Bekannten (mit der der Täter eine Verabredung hatte)

date stamp n Datumsstempel m

dative ['deɪtɪv] n Dativ m

daub [dɔːb] vt schmieren; **to** ~ **with** beschmieren mit

daughter ['dɔːtəʳ] n Tochter f

daughter-in-law ['dɔːtərɪnlɔː] n Schwiegertochter f

daunt [dɔːnt] vt entmutigen

daunting ['dɔːntɪŋ] adj entmutigend

dauntless ['dɔːntlɪs] adj unerschrocken, beherzt

dawdle ['dɔːdl] vi trödeln; **to** ~ **over one's work** bei der Arbeit bummeln or trödeln

dawn [dɔːn] n Tagesanbruch m, Morgengrauen nt; (of period) Anbruch m ▷ vi dämmern; (fig): **it** ~**ed on him that ...** es dämmerte ihm, dass ...; **from** ~ **to dusk** von morgens bis abends

dawn chorus (Brit) n Morgenkonzert nt der Vögel

day [deɪ] n Tag m; (heyday) Zeit f; **the** ~ **before/after** am Tag zuvor/danach; **the** ~ **after tomorrow** übermorgen; **the** ~ **before yesterday** vorgestern; **(on) the following** ~ am Tag darauf; **the** ~ **that ...** (am Tag,) als ...; ~ **by day** jeden Tag, täglich; **by** ~ tagsüber; **paid by the** ~ tageweise bezahlt; **to work an eight hour** ~ einen Achtstundentag haben; **these** ~**s, in the present** ~ heute, heutzutage

daybook ['deɪbuk] (Brit) n Journal nt

dayboy ['deɪbɔɪ] n Externe(r) m

daybreak ['deɪbreɪk] n Tagesanbruch m

day-care centre ['deɪkɛə-] n (for children) (Kinder)tagesstätte f; (for old people) Altentagesstätte f

daydream ['deɪdriːm] vi (mit offenen Augen) träumen ▷ n Tagtraum m, Träumerei f

daygirl ['deɪɡəːl] n Externe f
daylight ['deɪlaɪt] n Tageslicht nt
daylight robbery (inf) n Halsabschneiderei f
daylight-saving time (US) n Sommerzeit f
day release n: **to be on** ~ tageweise (zur Weiterbildung) freigestellt sein
day return (Brit) n Tagesrückfahrkarte f
day shift n Tagschicht f
daytime ['deɪtaɪm] n Tag m; **in the** ~ tagsüber, bei Tage
day-to-day ['deɪtə'deɪ] adj täglich, Alltags-; **on a** ~ **basis** tageweise
day trader n (Stock Exchange) Day-Trader(in) m(f), Tageshändler(in) m(f)
day trip n Tagesausflug m
day-tripper ['deɪ'trɪpəʳ] n Tagesausflügler(in) m(f)
daze [deɪz] vt benommen machen ▷ n: **in a** ~ ganz benommen
dazed [deɪzd] adj benommen
dazzle ['dæzl] vt blenden
dazzling ['dæzlɪŋ] adj (light) blendend; (smile) strahlend; (career, achievements) glänzend
DC abbr = **direct current**
DCC n abbr (= digital compact cassette) DCC f
DD n abbr (= Doctor of Divinity) ≈ Dr. theol.
DD abbr = **direct debit**
D-day ['diːdeɪ] n der Tag X
DDS (US) n abbr (= Doctor of Dental Surgery) ≈ Dr. med. dent.
DDT n abbr (= dichlorodiphenyltrichloroethane) DDT nt
deacon ['diːkən] n Diakon m
dead [dɛd] adj tot; (flowers) verwelkt; (numb) abgestorben, taub; (battery) leer; (place) wie ausgestorben ▷ adv total, völlig; (directly, exactly) genau ▷ npl: **the** ~ die Toten pl; **to shoot sb** ~ jdn erschießen; ~ **silence** Totenstille f; **in the** ~ **centre (of)** genau in der Mitte (+gen); **the line has gone** ~ (Tel) die Leitung ist tot; ~ **on time** auf die Minute pünktlich; ~ **tired** todmüde; **to stop** ~ abrupt stehen bleiben
dead beat (inf) adj (tired) völlig kaputt
deaden [dɛdn] vt (blow) abschwächen; (pain) mildern; (sound) dämpfen
dead end n Sackgasse f
dead-end ['dɛdɛnd] adj: **a** ~ **job** ein Job m ohne Aufstiegsmöglichkeiten
dead heat n: **to finish in a** ~ unentschieden ausgehen
dead letter office n Amt nt für unzustellbare Briefe
deadline ['dɛdlaɪn] n (letzter) Termin m; **to work to a** ~ auf einen Termin hinarbeiten
deadlock ['dɛdlɔk] n Stillstand m; **the meeting ended in** ~ die Verhandlung war festgefahren
dead loss (inf) n: **to be a** ~ ein hoffnungsloser Fall sein
deadly ['dɛdlɪ] adj tödlich ▷ adv: ~ **dull** todlangweilig
deadpan ['dɛdpæn] adj (look) unbewegt; (tone) trocken

Dead Sea n: **the** ~ das Tote Meer
dead season n tote Saison f
deaf [dɛf] adj taub; (partially) schwerhörig; **to turn a** ~ **ear to sth** sich einer Sache dat gegenüber taub stellen
deaf aid (Brit) n Hörgerät nt
deaf-and-dumb ['dɛfən'dʌm] adj taubstumm; ~ **alphabet** Taubstummensprache f
deafen ['dɛfn] vt taub machen
deafening ['dɛfnɪŋ] adj ohrenbetäubend
deaf-mute ['dɛfmjuːt] n Taubstumme(r) f(m)
deafness ['dɛfnɪs] n Taubheit f
deal [diːl] (pt, pp ~**t**) n Geschäft nt, Handel m ▷ vt (blow) versetzen; (card) geben, austeilen; **to strike a** ~ **with sb** ein Geschäft mit jdm abschließen; **it's a** ~! (inf) abgemacht!; **he got a fair/bad** ~ **from them** er ist von ihnen anständig/schlecht behandelt worden; **a good** ~ (a lot) ziemlich viel; **a great** ~ **(of)** ziemlich viel
▶ **deal in** vt fus handeln mit
▶ **deal with** vt fus (person) sich kümmern um; (problem) sich befassen mit; (successfully) fertig werden mit; (subject) behandeln
dealer ['diːləʳ] n Händler(in) m(f); (in drugs) Dealer m; (Cards) Kartengeber(in) m(f)
dealership ['diːləʃɪp] n (Vertrags)händler m
dealings ['diːlɪŋz] npl Geschäfte pl; (relations) Beziehungen pl
dealt [dɛlt] pt, pp of **deal**
dean [diːn] n Dekan m; (US: Scol: administrator) Schul- oder Collegeverwalter mit Beratungs- und Disziplinarfunktion
dear [dɪəʳ] adj lieb; (expensive) teuer ▷ n: **(my)** ~ (mein) Liebling m ▷ excl: ~ **me!** (ach) du liebe Zeit!; **D**~ **Sir/Madam** Sehr geehrte Damen und Herren; **D**~ **Mr/Mrs X** Sehr geehrter Herr/geehrte Frau X; (less formal) Lieber Herr/ Liebe Frau X
dearly ['dɪəlɪ] adv (love) von ganzem Herzen; (pay) teuer
dear money n (Comm) teures Geld nt
dearth [dəːθ] n: **a** ~ **of** ein Mangel m an +dat
death [dɛθ] n Tod m; (fatality) Tote(r) f(m), Todesfall m
deathbed ['dɛθbɛd] n: **to be on one's** ~ auf dem Sterbebett liegen
death certificate n Sterbeurkunde f, Totenschein m
deathly ['dɛθlɪ] adj (silence) eisig ▷ adv (pale etc) toten-
death penalty n Todesstrafe f
death rate n Sterbeziffer f
death row [-'rəu] (US) n Todestrakt m
death sentence n Todesurteil nt
death squad n Todeskommando nt
death toll n Zahl f der Todesopfer or Toten
deathtrap ['dɛθtræp] n Todesfalle f
deb [dɛb] (inf) n abbr = **debutante**
debacle [deɪ'bɑːkl] n Debakel nt
debar [dɪ'bɑːʳ] vt: **to** ~ **sb from doing sth** jdn davon ausschließen, etw zu tun; **to** ~ **sb from**

a club jdn aus einem Klub ausschließen
debase [dɪˈbeɪs] vt (value, quality) mindern, herabsetzen; (person) erniedrigen, entwürdigen
debatable [dɪˈbeɪtəbl] adj fraglich
debate [dɪˈbeɪt] n Debatte f ▷ vt debattieren über +acc; (course of action) überlegen ▷ vi: **to ~ whether** hin und her überlegen, ob
debauchery [dɪˈbɔːtʃərɪ] n Ausschweifungen pl
debenture [dɪˈbentʃəʳ] n Schuldschein m
debilitate [dɪˈbɪlɪteɪt] vt schwächen
debilitating [dɪˈbɪlɪteɪtɪŋ] adj schwächend
debit [ˈdɛbɪt] n Schuldposten m ▷ vt: **to ~ a sum to sb/sb's account** jdn/jds Konto mit einer Summe belasten; see also **direct**
debit balance n Sollsaldo nt, Debetsaldo nt
debit note n Lastschriftanzeige f
debonair adj flott
debrief [diːˈbriːf] vt befragen
debriefing [diːˈbriːfɪŋ] n Befragung f
debris [ˈdɛbriː] n Trümmer pl, Schutt m
debt [dɛt] n Schuld f; (state of owing money) Schulden pl, Verschuldung f; **to be in ~** Schulden haben, verschuldet sein; **bad ~** uneinbringliche Forderung f
debt collector n Inkassobeauftragte(r) f(m), Schuldeneintreiber(in) m(f)
debtor [ˈdɛtəʳ] n Schuldner(in) m(f)
debug [diːˈbʌg] vt (Comput) Fehler beseitigen in +dat
debunk [diːˈbʌŋk] vt (myths, ideas) bloßstellen; (claim) entlarven; (person, institution) vom Sockel stoßen
debut [ˈdeɪbjuː] n Debüt nt
debutante [ˈdɛbjutænt] n Debütantin f
Dec. abbr = **December**
decade [ˈdɛkeɪd] n Jahrzehnt nt
decadence [ˈdɛkədəns] n Dekadenz f
decadent [ˈdɛkədənt] adj dekadent
decaff [ˈdiːkæf] n koffeinfreier Kaffee m
decaffeinated [diːˈkæfɪneɪtɪd] adj koffeinfrei
decamp [dɪˈkæmp] (inf) vi verschwinden, sich aus dem Staub machen
decant [dɪˈkænt] vt umfüllen
decanter [dɪˈkæntəʳ] n Karaffe f
decarbonize [diːˈkɑːbənaɪz] vt entkohlen
decathlon [dɪˈkæθlən] n Zehnkampf m
decay [dɪˈkeɪ] n Verfall m; (of tooth) Fäule f ▷ vi (body) verwesen; (teeth) faulen; (leaves) verrotten; (fig: society etc) verfallen
decease [dɪˈsiːs] n (Law): **upon your ~** bei Ihrem Ableben
deceased [dɪˈsiːst] n: **the ~** der/die Tote or Verstorbene
deceit [dɪˈsiːt] n Betrug m
deceitful [dɪˈsiːtful] adj betrügerisch
deceive [dɪˈsiːv] vt täuschen; (husband, wife etc) betrügen; **to ~ o.s.** sich dat etwas vormachen
decelerate [diːˈsɛləreɪt] vi (car etc) langsamer werden; (driver) die Geschwindigkeit herabsetzen
December [dɪˈsɛmbəʳ] n Dezember m; see also **July**

decency [ˈdiːsənsɪ] n (propriety) Anstand m; (kindness) Anständigkeit f
decent [ˈdiːsənt] adj anständig; **we expect you to do the ~ thing** wir erwarten, dass Sie die Konsequenzen ziehen; **they were very ~ about it** sie haben sich sehr anständig verhalten; **that was very ~ of him** das war sehr anständig von ihm; **are you ~?** (dressed) hast du etwas an?
decently [ˈdiːsəntlɪ] adv anständig
decentralization [ˈdiːsentrəlaɪˈzeɪʃən] n Dezentralisierung f
decentralize [diːˈsentrəlaɪz] vt dezentralisieren
deception [dɪˈsɛpʃən] n Täuschung f, Betrug m
deceptive [dɪˈsɛptɪv] adj irreführend, täuschend
decibel [ˈdɛsɪbɛl] n Dezibel nt
decide [dɪˈsaɪd] vt entscheiden; (persuade) veranlassen ▷ vi sich entscheiden; **to ~ to do sth/that** beschließen, etw zu tun/dass; **to ~ on sth** sich für etw entscheiden; **to ~ on/against doing sth** sich dafür/dagegen entscheiden, etw zu tun
decided [dɪˈsaɪdɪd] adj entschieden; (character) entschlossen; (difference) deutlich
decidedly [dɪˈsaɪdɪdlɪ] adv entschieden; (emphatically) entschlossen
deciding [dɪˈsaɪdɪŋ] adj entscheidend
deciduous [dɪˈsɪdjuəs] adj (tree, woods) Laub-
decimal [ˈdɛsɪməl] adj (system, number) Dezimal- ▷ n Dezimalzahl f; **to three ~ places** auf drei Dezimalstellen
decimalize [ˈdɛsɪməlaɪz] (Brit) vt auf das Dezimalsystem umstellen
decimal point n Komma nt
decimate [ˈdɛsɪmeɪt] vt dezimieren
decipher [dɪˈsaɪfəʳ] vt entziffern
decision [dɪˈsɪʒən] n Entscheidung f; (decisiveness) Bestimmtheit f, Entschlossenheit f; **to make a ~** eine Entscheidung treffen
decisive [dɪˈsaɪsɪv] adj (action etc) entscheidend; (person) entschlussfreudig; (manner, reply) bestimmt, entschlossen
deck [dɛk] n Deck nt; (also: **record deck**) Plattenspieler m; (of cards) Spiel nt; **to go up on ~** an Deck gehen; **below ~** unter Deck; **top ~** (of bus) Oberdeck nt; **cassette ~** Tapedeck nt
deck chair n Liegestuhl m
deck hand n Deckshelfer(in) m(f)
declaration [dɛkləˈreɪʃən] n Erklärung f
declare [dɪˈklɛəʳ] vt erklären; (result) bekannt geben, veröffentlichen; (income etc) angeben; (goods at customs) verzollen
declassify [diːˈklæsɪfaɪ] vt freigeben
decline [dɪˈklaɪn] n Rückgang m; (decay) Verfall m ▷ vt ablehnen ▷ vi (strength) nachlassen; (business) zurückgehen; (old person) abbauen; **~ in/of** Rückgang m +gen; **~ in living standards** Sinken nt des Lebensstandards
declutch [diːˈklʌtʃ] vi auskuppeln
decode [ˈdiːˈkəud] vt entschlüsseln
decoder [diːˈkəudəʳ] n Decoder m

decompose [di:kəm'pəuz] *vi (organic matter)*
sich zersetzen; *(corpse)* verwesen
decomposition [di:kɔmpə'zɪʃən] *n* Zersetzung
f
decompression [di:kəm'prɛʃən] *n*
Dekompression *f*, Druckverminderung *f*
decompression chamber *n*
Dekompressionskammer *f*
decongestant [dən'dʒɛstənt] *n (Med)*
abschwellendes Mittel *nt*; *(: drops)*
Nasentropfen *pl*
decontaminate [di:kən'tæmɪneɪt] *vt*
entgiften
decontrol [di:kən'trəul] *vt* freigeben
décor ['deɪkɔ:ʳ] *n* Ausstattung *f*; *(Theat)* Dekor
m or nt
decorate ['dɛkəreɪt] *vt*: **to ~ (with)** verzieren
(mit); *(tree, building)* schmücken (mit) ▷ *vt*
(room, house: from bare walls) anstreichen und
tapezieren; *(: redecorate)* renovieren
decoration [dɛkə'reɪʃən] *n* Verzierung *f*;
(on tree, building) Schmuck *m*; *(act: see verb)*
Verzieren *nt*; Schmücken *nt*; (An)streichen *nt*;
Tapezieren *nt*; *(medal)* Auszeichnung *f*
decorative ['dɛkərətɪv] *adj* dekorativ
decorator ['dɛkəreɪtəʳ] *n* Maler(in) *m(f)*,
Anstreicher(in) *m(f)*
decorum [dɪ'kɔ:rəm] *n* Anstand *m*
decoy ['di:kɔɪ] *n* Lockvogel *m*; *(object)* Köder
m; **they used him as a ~ for the enemy** sie
benutzten ihn dazu, den Feind anzulocken
decrease ['di:kri:s] *vt* verringern, reduzieren
▷ *vi* abnehmen, zurückgehen ▷ *n*: **~ (in)**
Abnahme *f (+gen)*, Rückgang *m (+gen)*; **to be on
the ~** abnehmen, zurückgehen
decreasing [di:'kri:sɪŋ] *adj* abnehmend,
zurückgehend
decree [dɪ'kri:] *n (Admin, Law)* Verfügung *f*;
(Pol) Erlass *m*; *(Rel)* Dekret *nt* ▷ *vt*: **to ~ (that)**
verfügen(, dass), verordnen(, dass)
decree absolute *n* endgültiges
Scheidungsurteil *nt*
decree nisi [-'naɪsaɪ] *n* vorläufiges
Scheidungsurteil *nt*
decrepit [dɪ'krɛpɪt] *adj (shack)* baufällig; *(person)*
klapprig *(inf)*
decry [dɪ'kraɪ] *vt* schlechtmachen
dedicate ['dɛdɪkeɪt] *vt*: **to ~ to** widmen *+dat*
dedicated ['dɛdɪkeɪtɪd] *adj* hingebungsvoll,
engagiert; *(Comput)* dediziert; **~ word
processor** dediziertes Textverarbeitungssystem *nt*
dedication [dɛdɪ'keɪʃən] *n* Hingabe *f*; *(in book,
on radio)* Widmung *f*
deduce [dɪ'dju:s] *vt*: **to ~ (that)** schließen(,
dass), folgern(, dass)
deduct [dɪ'dʌkt] *vt* abziehen; **to ~ sth (from)**
etw abziehen (von); *(esp from wage etc)* etw
einbehalten (von)
deduction [dɪ'dʌkʃən] *n (act of deducting)* Abzug
m; *(act of deducing)* Folgerung *f*
deed [di:d] *n* Tat *f*; *(Law)* Urkunde *f*; **~ of
covenant** Vertragsurkunde *f*

deem [di:m] *vt (formal)* erachten für, halten
für; **to ~ it wise/helpful to do sth** es für
klug/hilfreich halten, etw zu tun
deep [di:p] *adj* tief ▷ *adv*: **the spectators stood
20 ~** die Zuschauer standen in 20 Reihen
hintereinander; **to be 4 metres ~** 4 Meter tief
sein; **knee-~ in water** bis zu den Knien im
Wasser; **he took a ~ breath** er holte tief Luft
deepen ['di:pn] *vt* vertiefen ▷ *vi (crisis)* sich
verschärfen; *(mystery)* größer werden
deepfreeze ['di:p'fri:z] *n* Tiefkühltruhe *f*
deep-fry ['di:p'fraɪ] *vt* frittieren
deeply ['di:plɪ] *adv (breathe)* tief; *(interested)*
höchst; *(moved, grateful)* zutiefst
deep-rooted ['di:p'ru:tɪd] *adj* tief verwurzelt;
(habit) fest eingefahren
deep-sea ['di:p'si:] *cpd* Tiefsee-; *(fishing)*
Hochsee-
deep-seated ['di:p'si:tɪd] *adj* tief sitzend
deep-set ['di:p'sɛt] *adj* tief liegend
deer [dɪəʳ] *n inv* Reh *nt*; *(male)* Hirsch *m*; **(red) ~**
Rotwild *nt*; **(roe) ~** Reh *nt*; **(fallow) ~** Damwild
nt
deerskin ['dɪəskɪn] *n* Hirschleder *nt*, Rehleder
nt
deerstalker ['dɪəstɔ:kəʳ] *n* ≈ Sherlock-Holmes-
Mütze *f*
deface [dɪ'feɪs] *vt (with paint etc)* beschmieren;
(slash, tear) zerstören
defamation [dɛfə'meɪʃən] *n* Diffamierung *f*,
Verleumdung *f*
defamatory [dɪ'fæmətrɪ] *adj* diffamierend,
verleumderisch
default [dɪ'fɔ:lt] *n (also:* **default value)**
Voreinstellung *f* ▷ *vi*: **to ~ on a debt** einer
Zahlungsverpflichtung nicht nachkommen;
to win by ~ kampflos gewinnen
defaulter [dɪ'fɔ:ltəʳ] *n* säumiger Zahler *m*,
säumige Zahlerin *f*
default option *n* Voreinstellung *f*
defeat [dɪ'fi:t] *vt* besiegen, schlagen ▷ *n*
(failure) Niederlage *f*; *(of enemy)*: **~ (of)** Sieg *m*
(über *+acc*)
defeatism [dɪ'fi:tɪzəm] *n* Defätismus *m*
defeatist [dɪ'fi:tɪst] *adj* defätistisch ▷ *n*
Defätist(in) *m(f)*
defect [*n* 'di:fɛkt, *vi* dɪ'fɛkt] *n* Fehler *m* ▷ *vi*: **to
~ to the enemy** zum Feind überlaufen;
physical/mental ~ körperlicher/geistiger
Schaden *m or* Defekt *m*; **to ~ to the West** sich
in den Westen absetzen
defective [dɪ'fɛktɪv] *adj* fehlerhaft
defector [dɪ'fɛktəʳ] *n* Überläufer(in) *m(f)*
defence, *(US)* **defense** [dɪ'fɛns] *n* Verteidigung
f; *(justification)* Rechtfertigung *f*; **in ~ of** zur
Verteidigung *+gen*; **witness for the ~** Zeuge
m/Zeugin *f* der Verteidigung; **the Ministry
of D~, the Department of Defense** *(US)* das
Verteidigungsministerium
defenceless [dɪ'fɛnslɪs] *adj* schutzlos
defend [dɪ'fɛnd] *vt* verteidigen
defendant [dɪ'fɛndənt] *n* Angeklagte(r) *f(m)*;
(in civil case) Beklagte(r) *f(m)*

d

defender [dɪˈfɛndəʳ] n Verteidiger(in) m(f)

defending champion [dɪˈfɛndɪŋ-] n (Sport) Titelverteidiger(in) m(f)

defending counsel [dɪˈfɛndɪŋ-] n Verteidiger(in) m(f)

defense [dɪˈfɛns] (US) n = **defence**

defensive [dɪˈfɛnsɪv] adj defensiv ▷ n: **on the ~** in der Defensive

defer [dɪˈfəːʳ] vt verschieben

deference [ˈdɛfərəns] n Achtung f, Respekt m; **out of** or **in ~ to** aus Rücksicht auf +acc

deferential [dɛfəˈrɛnʃəl] adj ehrerbietig, respektvoll

defiance [dɪˈfaɪəns] n Trotz m; **in ~ of sth** einer Sache dat zum Trotz, unter Missachtung einer Sache gen

defiant [dɪˈfaɪənt] adj trotzig; (challenging) herausfordernd

defiantly [dɪˈfaɪəntlɪ] adv (see adj) trotzig; herausfordernd

deficiency [dɪˈfɪʃənsɪ] n Mangel m; (defect) Unzulänglichkeit f; (deficit) Defizit nt

deficiency disease n Mangelkrankheit f

deficient [dɪˈfɪʃənt] adj: **sb/sth is ~ in sth** jdm/etw fehlt es an etw dat

deficit [ˈdɛfɪsɪt] n Defizit nt

defile [dɪˈfaɪl] vt (memory) beschmutzen; (statue etc) schänden ▷ n Hohlweg m

define [dɪˈfaɪn] vt (limits, boundaries) bestimmen, festlegen; (word) definieren

definite [ˈdɛfɪnɪt] adj definitiv; (date etc) fest; (clear, obvious) klar, eindeutig; (certain) bestimmt; **he was ~ about it** er war sich dat sehr sicher

definite article n bestimmter Artikel m

definitely [ˈdɛfɪnɪtlɪ] adv bestimmt; (decide) fest, definitiv

definition [dɛfɪˈnɪʃən] n (of word) Definition f; (of photograph etc) Schärfe f

definitive [dɪˈfɪnɪtɪv] adj (account) definitiv; (version) maßgeblich

deflate [diːˈfleɪt] vt (tyre, balloon) die Luft ablassen aus; (person) einen Dämpfer versetzen +dat; (Econ) deflationieren

deflation [diːˈfleɪʃən] n Deflation f

deflationary [diːˈfleɪʃənrɪ] adj deflationistisch

deflect [dɪˈflɛkt] vt (attention) ablenken; (criticism) abwehren; (shot) abfälschen; (light) brechen, beugen

defog [ˈdiːˈfɔg] (US) vt von Beschlag freimachen

defogger [ˈdiːˈfɔgəʳ] (US) n Gebläse nt

deform [dɪˈfɔːm] vt deformieren, verunstalten

deformed [dɪˈfɔːmd] adj deformiert, missgebildet

deformity [dɪˈfɔːmɪtɪ] n Deformität f, Missbildung f

defraud [dɪˈfrɔːd] vt: **to ~ sb (of sth)** jdn (um etw) betrügen

defray [dɪˈfreɪ] vt: **to ~ sb's expenses** jds Unkosten tragen or übernehmen

defrost [diːˈfrɔst] vt (fridge) abtauen; (windscreen) entfrosten; (food) auftauen

defroster [diːˈfrɔstəʳ] (US) n (Aut) Gebläse nt

deft [dɛft] adj geschickt

defunct [dɪˈfʌŋkt] adj (industry) stillgelegt; (organization) nicht mehr bestehend

defuse [diːˈfjuːz] vt entschärfen

defy [dɪˈfaɪ] vt sich widersetzen +dat; (challenge) auffordern; **it defies description** es spottet jeder Beschreibung

degenerate [dɪˈdʒɛnəreɪt] vi degenerieren ▷ adj degeneriert

degradation [dɛgrəˈdeɪʃən] n Erniedrigung f

degrade [dɪˈgreɪd] vt erniedrigen; (reduce the quality of) degradieren

degrading [dɪˈgreɪdɪŋ] adj erniedrigend

degree [dɪˈgriː] n Grad m; (Scol) akademischer Grad m; **10 ~s below (zero)** 10 Grad unter null; **6 ~s of frost** 6 Grad Kälte or unter null; **a considerable ~ of risk** ein gewisses Risiko; **a ~ in maths** ein Hochschulabschluss m in Mathematik; **by ~s** nach und nach; **to some ~, to a certain ~** einigermaßen, in gewissem Maße

dehydrated [diːhaɪˈdreɪtɪd] adj ausgetrocknet, dehydriert; (milk, eggs) pulverisiert, Trocken-

dehydration [diːhaɪˈdreɪʃən] n Austrocknung f, Dehydration f

de-ice [ˈdiːˈaɪs] vt enteisen

de-icer [ˈdiːˈaɪsəʳ] n Defroster m

deign [deɪn] vi: **to ~ to do sth** sich herablassen, etw zu tun

deity [ˈdiːɪtɪ] n Gottheit f

dejected [dɪˈdʒɛktɪd] adj niedergeschlagen, deprimiert

dejection [dɪˈdʒɛkʃən] n Niedergeschlagenheit f, Depression f

Del. (US) abbr (Post) = Delaware

delay [dɪˈleɪ] vt (decision, ceremony) verschieben, aufschieben; (person, plane, train) aufhalten ▷ vi zögern ▷ n Verzögerung f; (postponement) Aufschub m; **to be ~ed** (person) sich verspäten; (departure etc) verspätet sein; (flight etc) Verspätung haben; **without ~** unverzüglich

delayed-action [dɪˈleɪdˈækʃən] adj (bomb, mine) mit Zeitzünder; (Phot): **~ shutter release** Selbstauslöser m

delectable [dɪˈlɛktəbl] adj (person) reizend; (food) köstlich

delegate [ˈdɛlɪgɪt] n Delegierte(r) f(m) ▷ vt delegieren; **to ~ sth to sb** jdm mit etw beauftragen; **to ~ sb to do sth** jdn damit beauftragen, etw zu tun

delegation [dɛlɪˈgeɪʃən] n Delegation f; (group) Abordnung f, Delegation f

delete [dɪˈliːt] vt streichen; (Comput) löschen

Delhi [ˈdɛlɪ] n Delhi nt

deli [ˈdɛlɪ] n Feinkostgeschäft nt

deliberate [adj dɪˈlɪbərɪt, vi dɪˈlɪbəreɪt] adj absichtlich; (action, insult) bewusst; (slow) bedächtig ▷ vi überlegen

deliberately [dɪˈlɪbərɪtlɪ] adv absichtlich, bewusst; (slowly) bedächtig

deliberation [dɪlɪbəˈreɪʃən] n Überlegung f; (usu pl: discussions) Beratungen pl

delicacy ['dɛlɪkəsɪ] n Feinheit f, Zartheit f; (of problem) Delikatheit f; (choice food) Delikatesse f

delicate ['dɛlɪkɪt] adj fein; (colour, health) zart; (approach) feinfühlig; (problem) delikat, heikel

delicately ['dɛlɪkɪtlɪ] adv zart, fein; (act, express) feinfühlig

delicatessen [dɛlɪkə'tɛsn] n Feinkostgeschäft nt

delicious [dɪ'lɪʃəs] adj köstlich; (feeling, person) herrlich

delight [dɪ'laɪt] n Freude f ▷ vt erfreuen; **sb takes (a) ~ in sth** etw bereitet jdm große Freude; **sb takes (a) ~ in doing sth** es bereitet jdm große Freude, etw zu tun; **to be the ~ of** die Freude +gen sein; **she was a ~ to interview** es war eine Freude, sie zu interviewen; **the ~s of country life** die Freuden des Landlebens

delighted [dɪ'laɪtɪd] adj: **~ (at or with)** erfreut (über +acc), entzückt (über +acc); **to be ~ to do sth** etw gern tun; **I'd be ~** ich würde mich sehr freuen

delightful [dɪ'laɪtful] adj reizend, wunderbar

delimit [di:'lɪmɪt] vt abgrenzen

delineate [dɪ'lɪnɪeɪt] vt (fig) beschreiben

delinquency [dɪ'lɪŋkwənsɪ] n Kriminalität f

delinquent [dɪ'lɪŋkwənt] adj straffällig ▷ n Delinquent(in) m(f)

delirious [dɪ'lɪrɪəs] adj: **to be ~** (with fever) im Delirium sein; (with excitement) im Taumel sein

delirium [dɪ'lɪrɪəm] n Delirium nt

deliver [dɪ'lɪvəʳ] vt liefern; (letters, papers) zustellen; (hand over) übergeben; (message) überbringen; (speech) halten; (blow) versetzen; (Med: baby) zur Welt bringen; (warning) geben; (ultimatum) stellen; (free): **to ~ (from)** befreien (von); **to ~ the goods** (fig) halten, was man versprochen hat

deliverance [dɪ'lɪvrəns] n Befreiung f

delivery [dɪ'lɪvərɪ] n Lieferung f; (of letters, papers) Zustellung f; (of speaker) Vortrag m; (Med) Entbindung f; **to take ~ of sth** etw in Empfang nehmen

delivery note n Lieferschein m

delivery van, (US) **delivery truck** n Lieferwagen m

delouse ['di:'laus] vt entlausen

delta ['dɛltə] n Delta nt

delude [dɪ'lu:d] vt täuschen; **to ~ o.s.** sich dat etwas vormachen

deluge ['dɛlju:dʒ] n (of rain) Guss m; (fig: of petitions, requests) Flut f

delusion [dɪ'lu:ʒən] n Irrglaube m; **to have ~s of grandeur** größenwahnsinnig sein

de luxe [də'lʌks] adj (hotel, model) Luxus-

delve [dɛlv] vi: **to ~ into** (subject) sich eingehend befassen mit; (cupboard, handbag) tief greifen in +acc

Dem. (US) abbr (Pol) **= Democrat; Democratic**

demagogue ['dɛməgɔg] n Demagoge m, Demagogin f

demand [dɪ'mɑ:nd] vt verlangen; (rights) fordern; (need) erfordern, verlangen ▷ n Verlangen nt; (claim) Forderung f; (Econ) Nachfrage f; **to ~ sth (from or of sb)** etw (von jdm) verlangen or fordern; **to be in ~** gefragt sein; **on ~** (available) auf Verlangen; (payable) bei Vorlage or Sicht

demand draft n Sichtwechsel m

demanding [dɪ'mɑ:ndɪŋ] adj anspruchsvoll; (work, child) anstrengend

demarcation [di:mɑ:'keɪʃən] n (of area, tasks) Abgrenzung f

demarcation dispute n Streit m um den Zuständigkeitsbereich

demean [dɪ'mi:n] vt: **to ~ o.s.** sich erniedrigen

demeanour, (US) **demeanor** [dɪ'mi:nəʳ] n Benehmen nt, Auftreten nt

demented [dɪ'mɛntɪd] adj wahnsinnig

demerger [di:'mə:dʒəʳ] n (Comm) Abspaltung f, Demerger m

demilitarized zone [di:'mɪlɪtəraɪzd-] n entmilitarisierte Zone f

demise [dɪ'maɪz] n Ende nt; (death) Tod m

demist [di:'mɪst] (Brit) vt (Aut: windscreen) von Beschlag freimachen

demister [di:'mɪstəʳ] (Brit) n (Aut) Gebläse nt

demo ['dɛməu] (inf) n abbr **= demonstration**

demob [di:'mɔb] (inf) vt **= demobilize**

demobilize [di:'məubɪlaɪz] vt aus dem Kriegsdienst entlassen, demobilisieren

democracy [dɪ'mɔkrəsɪ] n Demokratie f

democrat ['dɛməkræt] n Demokrat(in) m(f)

democratic [dɛmə'krætɪk] adj demokratisch

Democratic Party (US) n: **the ~** die Demokratische Partei

demography [dɪ'mɔgrəfɪ] n Demografie f

demolish [dɪ'mɔlɪʃ] vt abreißen, abbrechen; (fig: argument) widerlegen

demolition [dɛmə'lɪʃən] n Abriss m, Abbruch m; (of argument) Widerlegung f

demon ['di:mən] n Dämon m ▷ adj teuflisch gut

demonstrate ['dɛmənstreɪt] vt (theory) demonstrieren; (skill) zeigen, beweisen; (appliance) vorführen ▷ vi: **to ~ (for/against)** demonstrieren (für/gegen)

demonstration [dɛmən'streɪʃən] n Demonstration f; (of gadget, machine etc) Vorführung f; **to hold a ~** eine Demonstration veranstalten or durchführen

demonstrative [dɪ'mɔnstrətɪv] adj demonstrativ

demonstrator ['dɛmənstreɪtəʳ] n Demonstrant(in) m(f); (sales person) Vorführer(in) m(f); (car) Vorführwagen m; (computer etc) Vorführgerät nt

demoralize [dɪ'mɔrəlaɪz] vt entmutigen

demote [dɪ'məut] vt zurückstufen; (Mil) degradieren

demotion [dɪ'məuʃən] n Zurückstufung f; (Mil) Degradierung f

demur [dɪ'mə:ʳ] (form) vi Einwände pl erheben ▷ n: **without ~** widerspruchslos; **they ~red at the suggestion** sie erhoben Einwände gegen den Vorschlag

demure [dɪ'mjuəʳ] adj zurückhaltend; (smile)

höflich; (*dress*) schlicht

demurrage [dɪ'mʌrɪdʒ] *n* Liegegeld *nt*

den [dɛn] *n* Höhle *f*; (*of fox*) Bau *m*; (*room*) Bude *f*

denationalization ['di:næʃnəlaɪ'zeɪʃən] *n* Privatisierung *f*

denationalize [di:'næʃnəlaɪz] *vt* privatisieren

denatured alcohol [di:'neɪtʃəd-] (*US*) *n* vergällter Alkohol *m*

denial [dɪ'naɪəl] *n* Leugnen *nt*; (*of rights*) Verweigerung *f*

denier ['dɛnɪəʳ] *n* Denier *nt*

denigrate ['dɛnɪgreɪt] *vt* verunglimpfen

denim ['dɛnɪm] *n* Jeansstoff *m*; **denims** *npl* (Blue) Jeans *pl*

denim jacket *n* Jeansjacke *f*

denizen ['dɛnɪzn] *n* Bewohner(in) *m(f)*; (*person in town*) Einwohner(in) *m(f)*; (*foreigner*) eingebürgerter Ausländer *m*, eingebürgerte Ausländerin *f*

Denmark ['dɛnma:k] *n* Dänemark *nt*

denomination [dɪnɒmɪ'neɪʃən] *n* (*of money*) Nennwert *m*; (*Rel*) Konfession *f*

denominator [dɪ'nɒmɪneɪtəʳ] *n* Nenner *m*

denote [dɪ'nəut] *vt* (*indicate*) hindeuten auf +*acc*; (*represent*) bezeichnen

denounce [dɪ'nauns] *vt* (*person*) anprangern; (*action*) verurteilen

dense [dɛns] *adj* dicht; (*inf: person*) beschränkt

densely ['dɛnslɪ] *adv* dicht

density ['dɛnsɪtɪ] *n* Dichte *f*; **single/double-~ disk** (*Comput*) Diskette *f* mit einfacher/ doppelter Dichte

dent [dɛnt] *n* Beule *f*; (*in pride, ego*) Knacks *m* ▷ *vt* (*also*: **make a dent in**) einbeulen; (*pride, ego*) anknacksen

dental ['dɛntl] *adj* (*filling, hygiene etc*) Zahn-; (*treatment*) zahnärztlich

dental floss [-flɒs] *n* Zahnseide *f*

dental surgeon *n* Zahnarzt *m*, Zahnärztin *f*

dentifrice ['dɛntɪfrɪs] *n* Zahnpasta *f*

dentist ['dɛntɪst] *n* Zahnarzt *m*, Zahnärztin *f*; (*also*: **dentist's (surgery)**) Zahnarzt *m*, Zahnarztpraxis *f*

dentistry ['dɛntɪstrɪ] *n* Zahnmedizin *f*

dentures ['dɛntʃəz] *npl* Zahnprothese *f*; (*full*) Gebiss *nt*

denuded [di:'nju:dɪd] *adj*: ~ **of** entblößt von

denunciation [dɪnʌnsɪ'eɪʃən] *n* (*of person*) Anprangerung *f*; (*of action*) Verurteilung *f*

deny [dɪ'naɪ] *vt* leugnen; (*involvement*) abstreiten; (*permission, chance*) verweigern; (*country, religion etc*) verleugnen; **he denies having said it** er leugnet *or* bestreitet, das gesagt zu haben

deodorant [di:'əudərənt] *n* Deodorant *nt*

depart [dɪ'pa:t] *vi* (*visitor*) abreisen; (: *on foot*) weggehen; (*bus, train*) abfahren; (*plane*) abfliegen; **to ~ from** (*fig*) abweichen von

departed [dɪ'pa:tɪd] *adj*: **the (dear) ~** der/ die (liebe) Verstorbene *m/f*, die (lieben) Verstorbenen *pl*

department [dɪ'pa:tmənt] *n* Abteilung *f*; (*Scol*) Fachbereich *m*; (*Pol*) Ministerium *nt*; **that's**

not my ~ (*fig*) dafür bin ich nicht zuständig; **D~ of State** (*US*) Außenministerium *nt*

departmental [di:pa:t'mɛntl] *adj* (*budget, costs*) der Abteilung; (*level*) Abteilungs-; **~ manager** Abteilungsleiter(in) *m(f)*

department store *n* Warenhaus *nt*

departure [dɪ'pa:tʃəʳ] *n* (*of visitor*) Abreise *f*; (*on foot, of employee etc*) Weggang *m*; (*of bus, train*) Abfahrt *f*; (*of plane*) Abflug *m*; (*fig*): ~ **from** Abweichen *nt* von; **a new ~** ein neuer Weg *m*

departure lounge *n* Abflughalle *f*

depend [dɪ'pɛnd] *vi*: **to ~ on** abhängen von; (*rely on, trust*) sich verlassen auf +*acc*; (*financially*) abhängig sein von, angewiesen sein auf +*acc*; **it ~s** es kommt darauf an; **~ing on the result ...** je nachdem, wie das Ergebnis ausfällt, ...

dependable [dɪ'pɛndəbl] *adj* zuverlässig

dependant [dɪ'pɛndənt] *n* abhängige(r) (Familien)angehörige(r) *f(m)*

dependence [dɪ'pɛndəns] *n* Abhängigkeit *f*

dependent [dɪ'pɛndənt] *adj*: **to be ~ on** (*person*) abhängig sein von, angewiesen sein auf +*acc*; (*decision*) abhängen von ▷ *n* = **dependant**

depict [dɪ'pɪkt] *vt* (*in picture*) darstellen; (*describe*) beschreiben

depilatory [dɪ'pɪlətrɪ] *n* (*also*: **depilatory cream**) Enthaarungsmittel *nt*

depleted [dɪ'pli:tɪd] *adj* (*reserves*) aufgebraucht; (*stocks*) erschöpft

deplorable [dɪ'plɔ:rəbl] *adj* bedauerlich

deplore [dɪ'plɔ:ʳ] *vt* verurteilen

deploy [dɪ'plɔɪ] *vt* einsetzen

depopulate [di:'pɒpjuleɪt] *vt* entvölkern

depopulation ['di:pɒpju'leɪʃən] *n* Entvölkerung *f*

deport [dɪ'pɔ:t] *vt* (*criminal*) deportieren; (*illegal immigrant*) abschieben

deportation [di:pɔ:'teɪʃən] *n* (*see vb*) Deportation *f*; Abschiebung *f*

deportation order *n* Ausweisung *f*

deportee [di:pɔ:'ti:] *n* Deportierte(r) *f(m)*

deportment [dɪ'pɔ:tmənt] *n* Benehmen *nt*

depose [dɪ'pəuz] *vt* absetzen

deposit [dɪ'pɒzɪt] *n* (*in account*) Guthaben *nt*; (*down payment*) Anzahlung *f*; (*for hired goods etc*) Sicherheit *f*, Kaution *f*; (*on bottle etc*) Pfand *nt*; (*Chem*) Ablagerung *f*; (*of ore, oil*) Lagerstätte *f* ▷ *vt* deponieren; (*subj: river: sand etc*) ablagern; **to put down a ~ of £50** eine Anzahlung von £50 machen

deposit account *n* Sparkonto *nt*

depositary [dɪ'pɒzɪtərɪ] *n* Treuhänder(in) *m(f)*

depositor [dɪ'pɒzɪtəʳ] *n* Deponent(in) *m(f)*, Einzahler(in) *m(f)*

depository [dɪ'pɒzɪtərɪ] *n* (*person*) Treuhänder(in) *m(f)*; (*place*) Lager(haus) *nt*

depot ['dɛpəu] *n* Lager(haus) *nt*; (*for vehicles*) Depot *nt*; (*US: station*) Bahnhof *m*; (: *bus station*) Busbahnhof *m*

depraved [dɪ'preɪvd] *adj* verworfen

depravity [dɪ'prævɪtɪ] *n* Verworfenheit *f*

deprecate ['dɛprɪkeɪt] *vt* missbilligen

deprecating ['dɛprɪkeɪtɪŋ] *adj (disapproving)* missbilligend; *(apologetic)* entschuldigend

depreciate [dɪ'priːʃɪeɪt] *vi* an Wert verlieren; *(currency)* an Kaufkraft verlieren; *(value)* sinken

depreciation [dɪpriːʃɪ'eɪʃən] *n (see vb)* Wertminderung *f*; Kaufkraftverlust *m*; Sinken *nt*

depress [dɪ'prɛs] *vt* deprimieren; *(price, wages)* drücken; *(press down)* herunterdrücken

depressant [dɪ'prɛsnt] *n* Beruhigungsmittel *nt*

depressed [dɪ'prɛst] *adj* deprimiert, niedergeschlagen; *(price)* gesunken; *(industry)* geschwächt; *(area)* Notstands-; **to get ~** deprimiert werden

depressing [dɪ'prɛsɪŋ] *adj* deprimierend

depression [dɪ'prɛʃən] *n (Psych)* Depressionen *pl*; *(Econ)* Wirtschaftskrise *f*; *(Met)* Tief(druckgebiet) *nt*; *(hollow)* Vertiefung *f*

deprivation [dɛprɪ'veɪʃən] *n* Entbehrung *f*, Not *f*; *(of freedom, rights etc)* Entzug *m*

deprive [dɪ'praɪv] *vt*: **to ~ sb of sth** *(liberty)* jdm etw entziehen; *(life)* jdm etw nehmen

deprived [dɪ'praɪvd] *adj* benachteiligt; *(area)* Not leidend

dept *abbr* = **department**

depth [dɛpθ] *n* Tiefe *f*; **in the ~s of** in den Tiefen +*gen*; **in the ~s of despair** in tiefster Verzweiflung; **in the ~s of winter** im tiefsten Winter; **at a ~ of 3 metres** in 3 Meter Tiefe; **to be out of one's ~** *(in water)* nicht mehr stehen können; *(fig)* überfordert sein; **to study sth in ~** etw gründlich *or* eingehend studieren

depth charge *n* Wasserbombe *f*

deputation [dɛpju'teɪʃən] *n* Abordnung *f*

deputize ['dɛpjutaɪz] *vi*: **to ~ for sb** jdn vertreten

deputy ['dɛpjutɪ] *cpd* stellvertretend ▷ *n* (Stell) vertreter(in) *m(f)*; *(Pol)* Abgeordnete(r) *f(m)*; *(US: also:* **deputy sheriff**) Hilfssheriff *m*; **~ head** *(Brit: Scol)* Konrektor(in) *m(f)*

derail [dɪ'reɪl] *vt*: **to be ~ed** entgleisen

derailment [dɪ'reɪlmənt] *n* Entgleisung *f*

deranged [dɪ'reɪndʒd] *adj*: **to be mentally ~** geistesgestört sein

derby ['dəːrbɪ] *n* Derby *nt*; *(US: hat)* Melone *f*

deregulate [dɪ'rɛgjuleɪt] *vt* staatliche Kontrollen aufheben bei

deregulation [dɪ'rɛgju'leɪʃən] *n* Aufhebung *f* staatlicher Kontrollen

derelict ['dɛrɪlɪkt] *adj* verfallen

deride [dɪ'raɪd] *vt* sich lustig machen über +*acc*

derision [dɪ'rɪʒən] *n* Hohn *m*, Spott *m*

derisive [dɪ'raɪsɪv] *adj* spöttisch

derisory [dɪ'raɪsərɪ] *adj* spöttisch; *(sum)* lächerlich

derivation [dɛrɪ'veɪʃən] *n* Ableitung *f*

derivative [dɪ'rɪvətɪv] *n (Ling)* Ableitung *f*; *(Chem)* Derivat *nt* ▷ *adj* nachahmend

derive [dɪ'raɪv] *vt*: **to ~ (from)** gewinnen (aus); *(benefit)* ziehen (aus) ▷ *vi*: **to ~ from** *(originate in)* sich herleiten *or* ableiten von; **to ~ pleasure from** Freude haben an +*dat*

dermatitis [dəːmə'taɪtɪs] *n* Hautentzündung

dermatology [dəːmə'tɒlədʒɪ] *n* Dermatologie *f*

derogatory [dɪ'rɒgətərɪ] *adj* abfällig

derrick ['dɛrɪk] *n (on ship)* Derrickkran *m*; *(on well)* Bohrturm *m*

derv [dəːv] *(Brit)* *n (Aut)* Diesel(kraftstoff) *m*

desalination [diːsælɪ'neɪʃən] *n* Entsalzung *f*

descend [dɪ'sɛnd] *vt* hinuntergehen, hinuntersteigen; *(lift, vehicle)* hinunterfahren; *(road)* hinunterführen ▷ *vi* hinuntergehen; *(lift)* nach unten fahren; **to ~ from** abstammen von; **to ~ to** sich erniedrigen zu; **in ~ing order of importance** nach Wichtigkeit geordnet

▶ **descend on** *vt fus* überfallen; *(subj: misfortune)* hereinbrechen über +*acc*; *(: gloom)* befallen; *(: silence)* sich senken auf +*acc*; **see also visitors ~ed (up)on us** der Besuch hat uns überfallen

descendant [dɪ'sɛndənt] *n* Nachkomme *m*

descent [dɪ'sɛnt] *n* Abstieg *m*; *(origin)* Abstammung *f*

describe [dɪs'kraɪb] *vt* beschreiben

description [dɪs'krɪpʃən] *n* Beschreibung *f*; *(sort)*: **of every ~** aller Art

descriptive [dɪs'krɪptɪv] *adj* deskriptiv

desecrate ['dɛsɪkreɪt] *vt* schänden

desegregate [diː'sɛgrɪgeɪt] *vt* die Rassentrennung aufheben in +*dat*

desert [*n* 'dɛzət, *vb* dɪ'zəːt] *n* Wüste *f* ▷ *vt* verlassen ▷ *vi* desertieren; *see also* **deserts**

deserter [dɪ'zəːtər] *n* Deserteur *m*

desertion [dɪ'zəːʃən] *n* Desertion *f*, Fahnenflucht *f*; *(Law)* böswilliges Verlassen *nt*

desert island *n* einsame *or* verlassene Insel *f*

deserts [dɪ'zəːts] *npl*: **to get one's just ~** bekommen, was man verdient

deserve [dɪ'zəːv] *vt* verdienen

deservedly [dɪ'zəːvɪdlɪ] *adv* verdientermaßen

deserving [dɪ'zəːvɪŋ] *adj* verdienstvoll

desiccated ['dɛsɪkeɪtɪd] *adj* vertrocknet; *(coconut)* getrocknet

design [dɪ'zaɪn] *n* Design *nt*; *(process)* Entwurf *m*, Gestaltung *f*; *(sketch)* Entwurf *m*; *(layout, shape)* Form *f*; *(pattern)* Muster *nt*; *(of car)* Konstruktion *f*; *(intention)* Plan *m*, Absicht *f* ▷ *vt* entwerfen; **to have ~s on** es abgesehen haben auf +*acc*; **well-~ed** mit gutem Design

design and technology *(Brit)* *n (Scol)* ≈ Design und Technologie

designate [*vt* 'dɛzɪgneɪt, *adj* 'dɛzɪgnɪt] *vt* bestimmen, ernennen ▷ *adj* designiert

designation [dɛzɪg'neɪʃən] *n* Bezeichnung *f*

designer [dɪ'zaɪnər] *n* Designer(in) *m(f)*; *(Tech)* Konstrukteur(in) *m(f)*; *(also:* **fashion designer**) Modeschöpfer(in) *m(f)* ▷ *adj (clothes etc)* Designer-

desirability [dɪzaɪərə'bɪlɪtɪ] *n*: **they discussed the ~ of the plan** sie besprachen, ob der Plan wünschenswert sei

desirable [dɪ'zaɪərəbl] *adj (proper)* wünschenswert; *(attractive)* reizvoll, attraktiv

desire [dɪ'zaɪər] *n* Wunsch *m*; *(sexual)* Verlangen *nt*, Begehren *nt* ▷ *vt* wünschen; *(lust after)* begehren; **to ~ to do sth/that** wünschen, etw zu tun/dass

desirous [dɪ'zaɪərəs] *adj:* **to be ~ of doing sth** den Wunsch haben, etw zu tun

desist [dɪ'zɪst] *vi:* **to ~ (from)** absehen (von), Abstand nehmen (von)

desk [dɛsk] *n* Schreibtisch *m*; *(for pupil)* Pult *nt*; *(in hotel)* Empfang *m*; *(at airport)* Schalter *m*; *(Brit: in shop, restaurant)* Kasse *f*

desk job *n* Bürojob *m*

desktop ['dɛsktɒp] *n* Arbeitsfläche *f*

desktop publishing *n* Desktop-Publishing *nt*

desolate ['dɛsəlɪt] *adj* trostlos

desolation [dɛsə'leɪʃən] *n* Trostlosigkeit *f*

despair [dɪs'pɛəʳ] *n* Verzweiflung *f* ▷ *vi:* **to ~ of** alle Hoffnung aufgeben auf *+acc*; **to be in ~** verzweifelt sein

despatch [dɪs'pætʃ] *n, vt* = **dispatch**

desperate ['dɛspərɪt] *adj* verzweifelt; *(shortage)* akut; *(criminal)* zum Äußersten entschlossen; **to be ~ for sth/to do sth** etw dringend brauchen/unbedingt tun wollen

desperately ['dɛspərɪtlɪ] *adv (shout, struggle etc)* verzweifelt; *(ill)* schwer; *(unhappy etc)* äußerst

desperation [dɛspə'reɪʃən] *n* Verzweiflung *f*; **in (sheer) ~** aus (reiner) Verzweiflung

despicable [dɪs'pɪkəbl] *adj (action)* verabscheuungswürdig; *(person)* widerwärtig

despise [dɪs'paɪz] *vt* verachten

despite [dɪs'paɪt] *prep* trotz *+gen*

despondent [dɪs'pɒndənt] *adj* niedergeschlagen, mutlos

despot ['dɛspɒt] *n* Despot *m*

dessert [dɪ'zə:t] *n* Nachtisch *m*, Dessert *nt*

dessertspoon [dɪ'zə:tspu:n] *n* Dessertlöffel *m*

destabilize [di:'steɪbɪlaɪz] *vt* destabilisieren

destination [dɛstɪ'neɪʃən] *n (Reise)ziel *nt*; *(of mail)* Bestimmungsort *m*

destined ['dɛstɪnd] *adj:* **to be ~ to do sth** dazu bestimmt *or* ausersehen sein, etw zu tun; **to be ~ for** bestimmt *or* ausersehen sein für

destiny ['dɛstɪnɪ] *n* Schicksal *nt*

destitute ['dɛstɪtju:t] *adj* mittellos

destroy [dɪs'trɔɪ] *vt* zerstören; *(animal)* töten

destroyer [dɪs'trɔɪəʳ] *n* Zerstörer *m*

destruction [dɪs'trʌkʃən] *n* Zerstörung *f*

destructive [dɪs'trʌktɪv] *adj* zerstörerisch; *(child, criticism etc)* destruktiv

desultory ['dɛsəltərɪ] *adj* flüchtig; *(conversation)* zwanglos

detach [dɪ'tætʃ] *vt (remove)* entfernen; *(unclip)* abnehmen; *(unstick)* ablösen

detachable [dɪ'tætʃəbl] *adj* abnehmbar

detached [dɪ'tætʃt] *adj* distanziert; *(house)* frei stehend, Einzel-

detachment [dɪ'tætʃmənt] *n* Distanz *f*; *(Mil)* Sonderkommando *nt*

detail ['di:teɪl] *n* Einzelheit *f*; *(no pl: in picture, one's work etc)* Detail *nt*; *(trifle)* unwichtige Einzelheit ▷ *vt (einzeln)* aufführen; **in ~** in Einzelheiten; **to go into ~s** auf Einzelheiten eingehen, ins Detail gehen

detailed ['di:teɪld] *adj* detailliert, genau

detain [dɪ'teɪn] *vt* aufhalten; *(in captivity)* in Haft halten; *(in hospital)* festhalten

detainee [di:teɪ'ni:] *n* Häftling *m*

detect [dɪ'tɛkt] *vt* wahrnehmen; *(Med, Tech)* feststellen; *(Mil)* ausfindig machen

detection [dɪ'tɛkʃən] *n* Entdeckung *f*, Feststellung *f*; **crime ~** Ermittlungsarbeit *f*; **to escape ~** *(criminal)* nicht gefasst werden; *(mistake)* der Aufmerksamkeit *dat* entgehen

detective [dɪ'tɛktɪv] *n* Kriminalbeamte(r) *m*; **private ~** Privatdetektiv *m*

detective story *n* Kriminalgeschichte *f*, Detektivgeschichte *f*

detector [dɪ'tɛktəʳ] *n* Detektor *m*

détente [deɪ'tɑ:nt] *n* Entspannung *f*, Détente *f*

detention [dɪ'tɛnʃən] *n (arrest)* Festnahme *f*; *(captivity)* Haft *f*; *(Scol)* Nachsitzen *nt*

deter [dɪ'tə:ʳ] *vt (discourage)* abschrecken; *(dissuade)* abhalten

detergent [dɪ'tə:dʒənt] *n* Reinigungsmittel *nt*; *(for clothes)* Waschmittel *nt*; *(for dishes)* Spülmittel *nt*

deteriorate [dɪ'tɪərɪəreɪt] *vi* sich verschlechtern

deterioration [dɪtɪərɪə'reɪʃən] *n* Verschlechterung *f*

determination [dɪtə:mɪ'neɪʃən] *n* Entschlossenheit *f*; *(establishment)* Festsetzung *f*

determine [dɪ'tə:mɪn] *vt (facts)* feststellen; *(limits etc)* festlegen; **to ~ that** beschließen, dass; **to ~ to do sth** sich entschließen, etw zu tun

determined [dɪ'tə:mɪnd] *adj* entschlossen; *(quantity)* bestimmt; **to be ~ to do sth** (fest) entschlossen sein, etw zu tun

deterrence [dɪ'tɛrəns] *n* Abschreckung *f*

deterrent [dɪ'tɛrənt] *n* Abschreckungsmittel *nt*; **to act as a ~** als Abschreckung(smittel) dienen

detest [dɪ'tɛst] *vt* verabscheuen

detestable [dɪ'tɛstəbl] *adj* abscheulich, widerwärtig

detonate ['dɛtəneɪt] *vi* detonieren ▷ *vt* zur Explosion bringen

detonator ['dɛtəneɪtəʳ] *n* Sprengkapsel *f*

detour ['di:tuəʳ] *n* Umweg *m*; *(US: Aut)* Umleitung *f*

detract [dɪ'trækt] *vi:* **to ~ from** schmälern; *(effect)* beeinträchtigen

detractor [dɪ'træktəʳ] *n* Kritiker(in) *m(f)*

detriment ['dɛtrɪmənt] *n:* **to the ~ of** zum Schaden *+gen*; **without ~ to** ohne Schaden für

detrimental [dɛtrɪ'mɛntl] *adj:* **to be ~ to** schaden *+dat*

deuce [dju:s] *n (Tennis)* Einstand *m*

devaluation [dɪvælju'eɪʃən] *n* Abwertung *f*

devalue ['di:'vælju:] *vt* abwerten

devastate ['dɛvəsteɪt] *vt* verwüsten; *(fig: shock)*: **to be ~d by** niedergeschmettert sein von

devastating ['dɛvəsteɪtɪŋ] *adj* verheerend; *(announcement, news)* niederschmetternd

devastation [dɛvəs'teɪʃən] n Verwüstung f
develop [dɪ'vɛləp] vt entwickeln; (*business*)
erweitern, ausbauen; (*land, resource*)
erschließen; (*disease*) bekommen ▷ vi sich
entwickeln; (*facts*) an den Tag kommen;
(*symptoms*) auftreten; **to ~ a taste for sth**
Geschmack an etw finden; **the machine/car
~ed a fault/engine trouble** an dem Gerät/
dem Wagen trat ein Defekt/ein Motorschaden
auf; **to ~ into** sich entwickeln zu, werden
developer [dɪ'vɛləpə'] n (*also:* **property
developer**) Bauunternehmer und Immobilienmakler
developing country [dɪ'vɛləpɪŋ-] n
Entwicklungsland nt
development [dɪ'vɛləpmənt] n Entwicklung f;
(*of land*) Erschließung f
development area n Entwicklungsgebiet nt
deviant ['di:vɪənt] adj abweichend
deviate ['di:vɪeɪt] vi: **to ~ (from)** abweichen
(von)
deviation [di:vɪ'eɪʃən] n Abweichung f
device [dɪ'vaɪs] n Gerät nt; (*ploy, stratagem*) Trick
m; **explosive ~** Sprengkörper m
devil ['dɛvl] n Teufel m; **go on, be a ~!** nur zu,
riskier mal was!; **talk of the ~!** wenn man
vom Teufel spricht!
devilish ['dɛvlɪʃ] adj teuflisch
devil's advocate ['dɛvlz-] n Advocatus Diaboli
m
devious ['di:vɪəs] adj (*person*) verschlagen;
(*route, path*) gewunden
devise [dɪ'vaɪz] vt sich dat ausdenken; (*machine*)
entwerfen
devoid [dɪ'vɔɪd] adj: **~ of** bar +gen, ohne +acc
devolution [di:və'lu:ʃən] n Dezentralisierung f
devolve [dɪ'vɔlv] vt übertragen ▷ vi: **to ~ (up)
on** übergehen auf +acc
devote [dɪ'vəut] vt: **to ~ sth/o.s. to** etw/sich
widmen +dat
devoted [dɪ'vəutɪd] adj treu; (*admirer*) eifrig;
to be ~ to sb jdn innig lieben; **the book is
~ to politics** das Buch widmet sich ganz der
Politik dat
devotee [dɛvəu'ti:] n (*fan*) Liebhaber(in) m(f);
(*Rel*) Anhänger(in) m(f)
devotion [dɪ'vəuʃən] n (*affection*) Ergebenheit f;
(*dedication*) Hingabe f; (*Rel*) Andacht f
devour [dɪ'vauə'] vt verschlingen
devout [dɪ'vaut] adj fromm
dew [dju:] n Tau m
dexterity [dɛks'tɛrɪtɪ] n Geschicklichkeit f;
(*mental*) Gewandtheit f
dexterous, dextrous ['dɛkstrəs] adj geschickt
DfEE (*Brit*) n abbr (= *Department for Education and
Employment*) ≈ Ministerium nt für Bildung und
Arbeit
dg abbr (= *decigram*) dg
DHSS (*Brit*) n abbr (*formerly:* = *Department of Health
and Social Security*) Ministerium für Gesundheit und
Sozialfürsorge
diabetes [daɪə'bi:ti:z] n Zuckerkrankheit f
diabetic [daɪə'bɛtɪk] adj zuckerkrank;
(*chocolate, jam*) Diabetiker- ▷ n Diabetiker(in)

m(f)
diabolical [daɪə'bolɪkl] (*inf*) adj schrecklich,
fürchterlich
diaeresis [daɪ'ɛrɪsɪs] n Diärese f
diagnose [daɪəg'nəuz] vt diagnostizieren
diagnoses [-si:z] pl of **diagnosis**
diagnosis [daɪəg'nəusɪs] (pl **diagnoses**) n
Diagnose f
diagonal [daɪ'ægənl] adj diagonal ▷ n
Diagonale f
diagram ['daɪəgræm] n Diagramm nt,
Schaubild nt
dial ['daɪəl] n Zifferblatt nt; (*on radio set*)
Einstellskala f; (*of phone*) Wählscheibe f
▷ vt wählen; **to ~ a wrong number** sich
verwählen; **can I ~ London direct?** kann ich
nach London durchwählen?
dial. abbr = **dialect**
dial code (*US*) n = **dialling code**
dialect ['daɪəlɛkt] n Dialekt m
dialling code ['daɪəlɪŋ-], (*US*) **dial code** n
Vorwahl f
dialling tone, (*US*) **dial tone** n Amtszeichen nt
dialogue, (*US*) **dialog** ['daɪəlɔg] n Dialog m;
(*conversation*) Gespräch nt, Dialog m
dial tone (*US*) n = **dialling tone**
dialysis [daɪ'ælɪsɪs] n Dialyse f
diameter [daɪ'æmɪtə'] n Durchmesser m
diametrically [daɪə'mɛtrɪklɪ] adv: **~ opposed
(to)** diametral entgegengesetzt (+dat)
diamond ['daɪəmənd] n Diamant m; (*shape*)
Raute f; **diamonds** npl (*Cards*) Karo nt
diamond ring n Diamantring m
diaper ['daɪəpə'] (*US*) n Windel f
diaphragm ['daɪəfræm] n Zwerchfell nt;
(*contraceptive*) Pessar nt
diarrhoea, (*US*) **diarrhea** [daɪə'ri:ə] n
Durchfall m
diary ['daɪərɪ] n (*Termin*)kalender m; (*daily
account*) Tagebuch nt; **to keep a ~** Tagebuch
führen
diatribe ['daɪətraɪb] n Schmährede f; (*written*)
Schmähschrift f
dice [daɪs] n inv Würfel m ▷ vt in Würfel
schneiden
dicey ['daɪsɪ] (*inf*) adj riskant
dichotomy [daɪ'kɔtəmɪ] n Dichotomie f, Kluft f
dickhead ['dɪkhɛd] (*inf*) n Knallkopf m
Dictaphone® ['dɪktəfəun] n Diktafon nt,
Diktiergerät nt
dictate [dɪk'teɪt] vt diktieren ▷ n Diktat nt;
(*principle*): **the ~s of** die Gebote +gen ▷ vi: **to ~ to**
diktieren +dat; **I won't be ~d to** ich lasse mir
keine Vorschriften machen
dictation [dɪk'teɪʃən] n Diktat nt; **at ~ speed**
im Diktiertempo
dictator [dɪk'teɪtə'] n Diktator m
dictatorship [dɪk'teɪtəʃɪp] n Diktatur f
diction ['dɪkʃən] n Diktion f
dictionary ['dɪkʃənrɪ] n Wörterbuch nt
did [dɪd] pt of **do**
didactic [daɪ'dæktɪk] adj didaktisch
diddle ['dɪdl] (*inf*) vt übers Ohr hauen

517

didn't ['dɪdnt] = **did not**

die [daɪ] n (pl: **dice**) Würfel m; (: dies) Gussform f ▷ vi sterben; (plant) eingehen; (fig: noise) aufhören; (: smile) vergehen; (engine) stehen bleiben; **to ~ of** or **from** sterben an +dat; **to be dying** im Sterben liegen; **to be dying for sth** etw unbedingt brauchen; **to be dying to do sth** darauf brennen, etw zu tun

▸ **die away** vi (sound) schwächer werden; (light) nachlassen

▸ **die down** vi (wind) sich legen; (fire) herunterbrennen; (excitement, noise) nachlassen

▸ **die out** vi aussterben

die-hard ['daɪhɑːd] n Ewiggestrige(r) f(m)

diesel ['diːzl] n (vehicle) Diesel m; (also: **diesel oil**) Diesel(kraftstoff) m

diesel engine n Dieselmotor m

diet ['daɪət] n Ernährung f; (Med) Diät f; (when slimming) Schlankheitskur f ▷ vi (also: **be on a diet**) eine Schlankheitskur machen; **to live on a ~** of sich ernähren von, leben von

dietician [daɪə'tɪʃən] n Diätassistent(in) m(f)

differ ['dɪfər] vi (be different): **to ~ (from)** sich unterscheiden (von); (disagree): **to ~ (about)** anderer Meinung sein (über +acc); **to agree to ~** sich dat verschiedene Meinungen zugestehen

difference ['dɪfrəns] n Unterschied m; (disagreement) Differenz f, Auseinandersetzung f; **it makes no ~ to me** das ist mir egal or einerlei; **to settle one's ~s** die Differenzen or Meinungsverschiedenheiten beilegen

different ['dɪfrənt] adj (various people, things) verschieden, unterschiedlich; **to be ~ (from)** anders sein (als)

differential [dɪfə'renʃəl] n (Math) Differenzial nt; (Brit: in wages) (Einkommens)unterschied m

differentiate [dɪfə'renʃieɪt] vi: **to ~ (between)** unterscheiden (zwischen) ▷ vt: **to ~ A from B** A von B unterscheiden

differently ['dɪfrəntlɪ] adv anders; (shaped, designed) verschieden, unterschiedlich

difficult ['dɪfɪkəlt] adj schwierig; (task, problem) schwer, schwierig; **~ to understand** schwer zu verstehen

difficulty ['dɪfɪkəltɪ] n Schwierigkeit f; **to be in/get into difficulties** in Schwierigkeiten sein/geraten

diffidence ['dɪfɪdəns] n Bescheidenheit f, Zurückhaltung f

diffident ['dɪfɪdənt] adj bescheiden, zurückhaltend

diffuse [dɪ'fjuːs] adj diffus ▷ vt verbreiten

dig [dɪg] (pt, pp **dug**) vt graben; (garden) umgraben ▷ n (prod) Stoß m; (archaeological) (Aus)grabung f; (remark) Seitenhieb m, spitze Bemerkung f; **to ~ one's nails into sth** seine Nägel in etw acc krallen

▸ **dig in** vi (fig: inf: eat) reinhauen ▷ vt (compost) untergraben, eingraben; (knife) hineinstoßen; (claw) festkrallen; **to ~ one's heels in** (fig) sich auf die Hinterbeine stellen (inf)

▸ **dig into** vt fus (savings) angreifen; (snow, soil) ein Loch graben in +acc; **to ~ into one's pockets for sth** in seinen Taschen nach etw suchen or wühlen

▸ **dig out** vt ausgraben

▸ **dig up** vt ausgraben

digest [daɪ'dʒest] vt verdauen ▷ n Digest m or nt, Auswahl f

digestible [dɪ'dʒestəbl] adj verdaulich

digestion [dɪ'dʒestʃən] n Verdauung f

digestive [dɪ'dʒestɪv] adj (system, upsets) Verdauungs- ▷ n Keks aus Vollkornmehl

digit ['dɪdʒɪt] n (number) Ziffer f; (finger) Finger m

digital ['dɪdʒɪtl] adj (watch, display etc) Digital-

digital computer n Digitalrechner m

digital projector n Beamer m

digital TV n Digitalfernsehen nt

dignified ['dɪgnɪfaɪd] adj würdevoll

dignitary ['dɪgnɪtərɪ] n Würdenträger(in) m(f)

dignity ['dɪgnɪtɪ] n Würde f

digress [daɪ'gres] vi: **to ~ (from)** abschweifen (von)

digression [daɪ'greʃən] n Abschweifung f

digs [dɪgz] (Brit: inf) npl Bude f

dike [daɪk] n = **dyke**

dilapidated [dɪ'læpɪdeɪtɪd] adj verfallen

dilate [daɪ'leɪt] vi sich weiten ▷ vt weiten

dilatory ['dɪlətərɪ] adj langsam

dilemma [daɪ'lemə] n Dilemma nt; **to be in a ~** sich in einem Dilemma befinden, in der Klemme sitzen (inf)

diligence ['dɪlɪdʒəns] n Fleiß m

diligent ['dɪlɪdʒənt] adj fleißig; (research) sorgfältig, genau

dill [dɪl] n Dill m

dilly-dally ['dɪlɪ'dælɪ] vi trödeln

dilute [daɪ'luːt] vt verdünnen; (belief, principle) schwächen ▷ adj verdünnt

dim [dɪm] adj schwach; (outline, figure) undeutlich, verschwommen; (room) dämmerig; (future) düster; (prospects) schlecht; (inf: person) schwer von Begriff ▷ vt (light) dämpfen; (US: Aut) abblenden; **to take a ~ view of sth** wenig or nicht viel von etw halten

dime [daɪm] (US) n Zehncentstück nt

dimension [daɪ'menʃən] n (aspect) Dimension f; (measurement) Abmessung f, Maß nt; (also pl: scale, size) Ausmaß nt

-dimensional [dɪ'menʃənl] adj suff -dimensional

diminish [dɪ'mɪnɪʃ] vi sich verringern ▷ vt verringern

diminished responsibility n verminderte Zurechnungsfähigkeit f

diminutive [dɪ'mɪnjutɪv] adj winzig ▷ n Verkleinerungsform f

dimly ['dɪmlɪ] adv schwach; (see) undeutlich, verschwommen

dimmer ['dɪmər] n (also: **dimmer switch**) Dimmer m; (US: Aut) Abblendschalter m

dimmer ['dɪmə]

dimmer switch n (Elec) Dimmer m; (US: Aut) Abblendschalter m

dimmers ['dɪməz] (US) npl (Aut: dipped headlights) Abblendlicht nt; (: parking lights) Parklicht nt

dimple ['dɪmpl] n Grübchen nt

dim-witted ['dɪm'wɪtɪd] (inf) adj dämlich

din [dɪn] n Lärm m, Getöse nt ▷ vt (inf): **to ~ sth into sb** jdm etw einbläuen

dine [daɪn] vi speisen

diner ['daɪnəʳ] n Gast m; (US: restaurant) Esslokal nt

dinghy ['dɪŋgɪ] n (also: **rubber dinghy**) Schlauchboot nt; (also: **sailing dinghy**) Dingi nt

dingy ['dɪndʒɪ] adj schäbig; (clothes, curtains etc) schmuddelig

dining car ['daɪnɪŋ-] (Brit) n Speisewagen m

dining room n Esszimmer nt; (in hotel) Speiseraum m

dinner ['dɪnəʳ] n (evening meal) Abendessen nt; (lunch) Mittagessen nt; (banquet) (Fest)essen nt

dinner jacket n Smokingjackett nt

dinner party n Abendgesellschaft f (mit Essen)

dinner service n Tafelservice nt

dinner time n Essenszeit f

dinosaur ['daɪnəsɔːʳ] n Dinosaurier m

dint [dɪnt] n: **by ~ of** durch +acc

diocese ['daɪəsɪs] n Diözese f

dioxide [daɪ'ɔksaɪd] n Dioxid nt

Dip. (Brit) abbr = **diploma**

dip [dɪp] n Senke f; (in sea) kurzes Bad nt; (Culin) Dip m; (for sheep) Desinfektionslösung f ▷ vt eintauchen; (Brit: Aut) abblenden ▷ vi abfallen

diphtheria [dɪf'θɪərɪə] n Diphtherie f

diphthong ['dɪfθɔŋ] n Diphthong m

diploma [dɪ'pləʊmə] n Diplom nt

diplomacy [dɪ'pləʊməsɪ] n Diplomatie f

diplomat ['dɪpləmæt] n Diplomat(in) m(f)

diplomatic [dɪplə'mætɪk] adj diplomatisch; **to break off ~ relations (with)** die diplomatischen Beziehungen abbrechen (mit)

diplomatic corps n diplomatisches Korps nt

diplomatic immunity n Immunität f

dip rod ['dɪprɔd] (US) n Ölmessstab m

dipstick ['dɪpstɪk] (Brit) n Ölmessstab m

dip switch (Brit) n Abblendschalter m

dire [daɪəʳ] adj schrecklich

direct [daɪ'rɛkt] adj, adv direkt ▷ vt richten; (company, project, programme etc) leiten; (play, film) Regie führen bei; **to ~ sb to do sth** jdn anweisen, etw zu tun; **can you ~ me to ...?** können Sie mir den Weg nach ... sagen?

direct access n (Comput) Direktzugriff m

direct cost n direkte Kosten pl

direct current n Gleichstrom m

direct debit (Brit) n Einzugsauftrag m; (transaction) automatische Abbuchung f

direct dialling n Selbstwahl f

direct hit n Volltreffer m

direction [dɪ'rɛkʃən] n Richtung f; (TV, Radio) Leitung f; (Cine) Regie f; **directions** npl (instructions) Anweisungen pl; **sense of ~** Orientierungssinn m; **~s for use** Gebrauchsanweisung f, Gebrauchsanleitung f; **to ask for ~s** nach dem Weg fragen; **in the ~ of** in Richtung

directional [dɪ'rɛkʃənl] adj (aerial) Richt-

directive [dɪ'rɛktɪv] n Direktive f, Weisung f; **government ~** Regierungserlass m

direct labour n (Comm) Produktionsarbeit f; (Brit) eigene Arbeitskräfte pl

directly [dɪ'rɛktlɪ] adv direkt; (at once) sofort, gleich

direct mail n Werbebriefe pl

direct mailshot (Brit) n Direktwerbung f per Post

directness [daɪ'rɛktnɪs] n Direktheit f

director [dɪ'rɛktəʳ] n Direktor(in) m(f); (of project, TV, Radio) Leiter(in) m(f); (Cine) Regisseur(in) m(f)

Director of Public Prosecutions (Brit) n ≈ Generalstaatsanwalt m, ≈ Generalstaatsanwältin f

directory [dɪ'rɛktərɪ] n (also: **telephone directory**) Telefonbuch nt; (also: **street directory**) Einwohnerverzeichnis nt; (Comput) Verzeichnis nt; (Comm) Branchenverzeichnis nt

directory enquiries, (US) **directory assistance** n (Fernsprech)auskunft f

dirt [dəːt] n Schmutz m; (earth) Erde f; **to treat sb like ~** jdn wie (den letzten) Dreck behandeln

dirt-cheap ['dəːt'tʃiːp] adj spottbillig

dirt road n unbefestigte Straße f

dirty ['dəːtɪ] adj schmutzig; (story) unanständig ▷ vt beschmutzen

dirty bomb n schmutzige Bombe f

dirty trick n gemeiner Trick m

disability [dɪsə'bɪlɪtɪ] n Behinderung f

disability allowance n Behindertenbeihilfe f

disable [dɪs'eɪbl] vt zum Invaliden machen; (tank, gun) unbrauchbar machen

disabled [dɪs'eɪbld] adj behindert ▷ npl: **the ~** die Behinderten pl

disabuse [dɪsə'bjuːz] vt: **to ~ sb (of)** jdn befreien (von)

disadvantage [dɪsəd'vɑːntɪdʒ] n Nachteil m; (detriment) Schaden m; **to be at a ~** benachteiligt or im Nachteil sein

disadvantaged [dɪsəd'vɑːntɪdʒd] adj benachteiligt

disadvantageous [dɪsædvɑːn'teɪdʒəs] adj ungünstig

disaffected [dɪsə'fɛktɪd] adj entfremdet

disaffection [dɪsə'fɛkʃən] n Entfremdung f

disagree [dɪsə'griː] vi nicht übereinstimmen; (to be against, think differently): **to ~ (with)** nicht einverstanden sein (mit); **I ~ with you** ich bin anderer Meinung; **garlic ~s with me** ich vertrage keinen Knoblauch, Knoblauch bekommt mir nicht

disagreeable [dɪsə'griːəbl] adj unangenehm; (person) unsympathisch

disagreement [dɪsə'griːmənt] n Uneinigkeit f; (argument) Meinungsverschiedenheit f; **to have a ~ with sb** sich mit jdm nicht einig sein

disallow ['dɪsə'laʊ] vt (appeal) abweisen; (goal) nicht anerkennen, nicht geben

disappear [dɪsə'pɪə^r] vi verschwinden; (*custom etc*) aussterben

disappearance [dɪsə'pɪərəns] n (*see vi*) Verschwinden nt; Aussterben nt

disappoint [dɪsə'pɔɪnt] vt enttäuschen

disappointed [dɪsə'pɔɪntɪd] adj enttäuscht

disappointing [dɪsə'pɔɪntɪŋ] adj enttäuschend

disappointment [dɪsə'pɔɪntmənt] n Enttäuschung f

disapproval [dɪsə'pru:vəl] n Missbilligung f

disapprove [dɪsə'pru:v] vi dagegen sein; **to ~ of** missbilligen +acc

disapproving [dɪsə'pru:vɪŋ] adj missbilligend

disarm [dɪs'a:m] vt entwaffnen; (*criticism*) zum Verstummen bringen ▷ vi abrüsten

disarmament [dɪs'a:məmənt] n Abrüstung f

disarming [dɪs'a:mɪŋ] adj entwaffnend

disarray [dɪsə'reɪ] n: **in ~** (*army, organization*) in Auflösung (begriffen); (*hair, clothes*) unordentlich; (*thoughts*) durcheinander; **to throw into ~** durcheinanderbringen

disaster [dɪ'za:stə^r] n Katastrophe f; (*Aviat etc*) Unglück nt; (*fig: mess*) Fiasko nt

disaster area n Katastrophengebiet nt; (*fig: person*) Katastrophe f; **my office is a ~** in meinem Büro sieht es katastrophal aus

disastrous [dɪ'za:strəs] adj katastrophal

disband [dɪs'bænd] vt auflösen ▷ vi sich auflösen

disbelief ['dɪsbə'li:f] n Ungläubigkeit f; **in ~** ungläubig

disbelieve ['dɪsbə'li:v] vt (*person*) nicht glauben +dat; (*story*) nicht glauben; **I don't ~ you** ich bezweifle nicht, was Sie sagen

disc [dɪsk] n (*Anat*) Bandscheibe f; (*record*) Platte f; (*Comput*) = **disk**

disc. abbr (*Comm*) = **discount**

discard [dɪs'ka:d] vt ausrangieren; (*fig: idea, plan*) verwerfen

disc brake n Scheibenbremse f

discern [dɪ'sə:n] vt wahrnehmen; (*identify*) erkennen

discernible [dɪ'sə:nəbl] adj erkennbar; (*object*) wahrnehmbar

discerning [dɪ'sə:nɪŋ] adj (*judgement*) scharfsinnig; (*look*) kritisch; (*listeners etc*) anspruchsvoll

discharge [dɪs'tʃa:dʒ] vt (*duties*) nachkommen +dat; (*debt*) begleichen; (*waste*) ablassen; (*Elec*) entladen; (*Med*) ausscheiden, absondern; (*patient, employee, soldier*) entlassen; (*defendant*) freisprechen ▷ n (*of gas*) Ausströmen nt; (*of liquid*) Ausfließen nt; (*Elec*) Entladung f; (*Med*) Ausfluss m; (*of patient, employee, soldier*) Entlassung f; (*of defendant*) Freispruch m; **to ~ a gun** ein Gewehr abfeuern

discharged bankrupt [dɪs'tʃa:dʒd-] n (*Law*) entlasteter Konkursschuldner m, entlastete Konkursschuldnerin f

disciple [dɪ'saɪpl] n Jünger m; (*fig: follower*) Schüler(in) m(f)

disciplinary ['dɪsɪplɪnərɪ] adj (*powers etc*) Disziplinar-; **to take ~ action against sb** ein

Disziplinarverfahren gegen jdn einleiten

discipline ['dɪsɪplɪn] n Disziplin f ▷ vt disziplinieren; (*punish*) bestrafen; **to ~ o.s. to do sth** sich dazu anhalten or zwingen, etw zu tun

disc jockey n Discjockey m

disclaim [dɪs'kleɪm] vt (*knowledge*) abstreiten; (*responsibility*) von sich weisen

disclaimer [dɪs'kleɪmə^r] n Dementi nt; **to issue a ~** eine Gegenerklärung abgeben

disclose [dɪs'kləuz] vt enthüllen, bekannt geben

disclosure [dɪs'kləuʒə^r] n Enthüllung f

disco ['dɪskəu] n = **discotheque**

discolor etc [dɪs'kʌlə^r] (US) = **discolour** etc

discolour [dɪs'kʌlə^r] vt verfärben ▷ vi sich verfärben

discolouration [dɪskʌlə'reɪʃən] n Verfärbung f

discoloured [dɪs'kʌləd] adj verfärbt

discomfort [dɪs'kʌmfət] n (*unease*) Unbehagen nt; (*physical*) Beschwerden pl

disconcert [dɪskən'sə:t] vt beunruhigen, irritieren

disconcerting [dɪskən'sə:tɪŋ] adj beunruhigend, irritierend

disconnect [dɪskə'nɛkt] vt abtrennen; (*Elec, Radio*) abstellen; **I've been ~ed** (*Tel*) das Gespräch ist unterbrochen worden; (*supply, connection*) man hat mir das Telefon/den Strom/das Gas etc abgestellt

disconnected [dɪskə'nɛktɪd] adj unzusammenhängend

disconsolate [dɪs'kɔnsəlɪt] adj niedergeschlagen

discontent [dɪskən'tent] n Unzufriedenheit f

discontented [dɪskən'tentɪd] adj unzufrieden

discontinue [dɪskən'tɪnju:] vt einstellen; **"~d"** (*Comm*) „ausgelaufene Serie"

discord ['dɪskɔ:d] n Zwietracht f; (*Mus*) Dissonanz f

discordant [dɪs'kɔ:dənt] adj unharmonisch

discotheque ['dɪskəutɛk] n Diskothek f

discount [n 'dɪskaunt, vt dɪs'kaunt] n Rabatt m ▷ vt nachlassen; (*idea, fact*) unberücksichtigt lassen; **to give sb a ~ on sth** jdm auf etw acc Rabatt geben; **~ for cash** Skonto nt or m (bei Barzahlung); **at a ~** mit Rabatt

discount house n Diskontbank f; (*also:* **discount store**) Diskontgeschäft nt

discount rate n Diskontsatz m

discourage [dɪs'kʌrɪdʒ] vt entmutigen; **to ~ sb from doing sth** jdm davon abraten, etw zu tun

discouragement [dɪs'kʌrɪdʒmənt] n Mutlosigkeit f; **to act as a ~ to sb** entmutigend für jdn sein

discouraging [dɪs'kʌrɪdʒɪŋ] adj entmutigend

discourteous [dɪs'kə:tɪəs] adj unhöflich

discover [dɪs'kʌvə^r] vt entdecken; (*missing person*) finden; **to ~ that ...** herausfinden, dass ...

discovery [dɪs'kʌvərɪ] n Entdeckung f

discredit [dɪs'krɛdɪt] vt in Misskredit bringen

▷ *n*: **to sb's** ~ zu jds Schande
discreet [dɪsˈkriːt] *adj* diskret; (*unremarkable*)
dezent
discreetly [dɪsˈkriːtlɪ] *adv* diskret;
(*unremarkably*) dezent
discrepancy [dɪsˈkrepənsɪ] *n* Diskrepanz *f*
discretion [dɪsˈkreʃən] *n* Diskretion *f*; **at the**
~ **of** im Ermessen +*gen*; **use your own** ~ Sie
müssen nach eigenem Ermessen handeln
discretionary [dɪsˈkreʃənrɪ] *adj*: ~ **powers**
Ermessensspielraum *m*; ~ **payments**
Ermessenszahlungen *pl*
discriminate [dɪsˈkrɪmɪneɪt] *vi*: **to** ~ **between**
unterscheiden zwischen +*dat*; **to** ~ **against**
diskriminieren +*acc*
discriminating [dɪsˈkrɪmɪneɪtɪŋ] *adj*
anspruchsvoll, kritisch; (*tax, duty*)
Differenzial-
discrimination [dɪskrɪmɪˈneɪʃən]
n Diskriminierung *f*; (*discernment*)
Urteilsvermögen *nt*; **racial** ~
Rassendiskriminierung *f*; **sexual** ~
Diskriminierung aufgrund des Geschlechts
discus [ˈdɪskəs] *n* Diskus *m*; (*event*)
Diskuswerfen *nt*
discuss [dɪsˈkʌs] *vt* besprechen; (*debate*)
diskutieren; (*analyse*) erörtern, behandeln
discussion [dɪsˈkʌʃən] *n* Besprechung *f*; (*debate*)
Diskussion *f*; **under** ~ in der Diskussion
disdain [dɪsˈdeɪn] *n* Verachtung *f* ▷ *vt*
verachten ▷ *vi*: **to** ~ **to do sth** es für unter
seiner Würde halten, etw zu tun
disease [dɪˈziːz] *n* Krankheit *f*
diseased [dɪˈziːzd] *adj* krank; (*tree*) befallen
disembark [dɪsɪmˈbɑːk] *vt* ausschiffen ▷ *vi*
(*passengers*) von Bord gehen
disembarkation [dɪsembɑːˈkeɪʃən] *n*
Ausschiffung *f*
disembodied [ˈdɪsɪmˈbɔdɪd] *adj* (*voice*)
geisterhaft; (*hand*) körperlos
disembowel [ˈdɪsɪmˈbauəl] *vt* die Eingeweide
herausnehmen +*dat*
disenchanted [ˈdɪsɪnˈtʃɑːntɪd] *adj*: ~ **(with)**
enttäuscht (von)
disenfranchise [ˈdɪsɪnˈfræntʃaɪz] *vt* (*Pol*)
das Wahlrecht entziehen +*dat*; (*Comm*) die
Konzession entziehen +*dat*
disengage [dɪsɪnˈgeɪdʒ] *vt* (*Tech*) ausrasten; **to**
~ **the clutch** auskuppeln
disengagement [dɪsɪnˈgeɪdʒmənt] *n* (*Pol*)
Disengagement *nt*
disentangle [dɪsɪnˈtæŋgl] *vt* befreien; (*wool,
wire*) entwirren
disfavour, (*US*) **disfavor** [dɪsˈfeɪvəʳ] *n*
Missfallen *nt*; **to fall into** ~ **(with sb)** (bei
jdm) in Ungnade fallen
disfigure [dɪsˈfɪɡəʳ] *vt* entstellen; (*object, place*)
verunstalten
disgorge [dɪsˈɡɔːdʒ] *vt* (*liquid*) ergießen; (*people*)
ausspeien
disgrace [dɪsˈɡreɪs] *n* Schande *f*; (*scandal*)
Skandal *m* ▷ *vt* Schande bringen über +*acc*
disgraceful [dɪsˈɡreɪsful] *adj* skandalös

disgruntled [dɪsˈɡrʌntld] *adj* verärgert
disguise [dɪsˈɡaɪz] *n* Verkleidung *f* ▷ *vt*: **to** ~
(as) (*person*) verkleiden (als); (*object*) tarnen
(als); **in** ~ (*person*) verkleidet; **there's no
disguising the fact that** ... es kann nicht
geleugnet werden, dass ...; **to** ~ **o.s. as** sich
verkleiden als
disgust [dɪsˈɡʌst] *n* Abscheu *m* ▷ *vt* anwidern;
she walked off in ~ sie ging voller Empörung
weg
disgusting [dɪsˈɡʌstɪŋ] *adj* widerlich
dish [dɪʃ] *n* Schüssel *f*; (*flat*) Schale *f*; (*recipe,
food*) Gericht *nt*; (*also*: **satellite dish**)
Parabolantenne *f*, Schüssel (*inf*); **to do** *or* **wash
the** ~**es** Geschirr spülen, abwaschen
▶ **dish out** *vt* verteilen; (*food, money*) austeilen;
(*advice*) erteilen
▶ **dish up** *vt* (*food*) auftragen, servieren; (*facts,
statistics*) auftischen (*inf*)
dishcloth [ˈdɪʃklɔθ] *n* Spültuch *nt*,
Spüllappen *m*
dishearten [dɪsˈhɑːtn] *vt* entmutigen
dishevelled, (*US*) **disheveled** [dɪˈʃevəld] *adj*
unordentlich; (*hair*) zerzaust
dishonest [dɪsˈɔnɪst] *adj* unehrlich; (*means*)
unlauter
dishonesty [dɪsˈɔnɪstɪ] *n* Unehrlichkeit *f*
dishonor *etc* [dɪsˈɔnəʳ] (*US*) = **dishonour** *etc*
dishonour [dɪsˈɔnəʳ] *n* Schande *f*
dishonourable [dɪsˈɔnərəbl] *adj* unehrenhaft
dish soap (*US*) *n* Spülmittel *nt*
dishtowel [ˈdɪʃtauəl] (*US*) *n* Geschirrtuch *nt*
dishwasher [ˈdɪʃwɔʃəʳ] *n* (*machine*) (Geschirr)
spülmaschine *f*
dishy [ˈdɪʃɪ] (*inf: Brit*) *adj* attraktiv
disillusion [dɪsɪˈluːʒən] *vt* desillusionieren
▷ *n* = **disillusionment**; **to become** ~**ed (with)**
seine Illusionen (über +*acc*) verlieren
disillusionment [dɪsɪˈluːʒənmənt] *n*
Desillusionierung *f*
disincentive [dɪsɪnˈsentɪv] *n* Entmutigung
f; **it's a** ~ es hält die Leute ab; **to be a** ~ **to sb**
jdm keinen Anreiz bieten
disinclined [dɪsɪnˈklaɪnd] *adj*: **to be** ~ **to do
sth** abgeneigt sein, etw zu tun
disinfect [dɪsɪnˈfekt] *vt* desinfizieren
disinfectant [dɪsɪnˈfektənt] *n*
Desinfektionsmittel *nt*
disinflation [dɪsɪnˈfleɪʃən] *n* (*Econ*) Rückgang *m*
einer inflationären Entwicklung
disinformation [dɪsɪnfəˈmeɪʃən] *n*
Desinformation *f*
disingenuous [dɪsɪnˈdʒenjuəs] *adj*
unaufrichtig
disinherit [dɪsɪnˈherɪt] *vt* enterben
disintegrate [dɪsˈɪntɪɡreɪt] *vi* zerfallen;
(*marriage, partnership*) scheitern; (*organization*)
sich auflösen
disinterested [dɪsˈɪntrəstɪd] *adj* (*advice*)
unparteiisch, unvoreingenommen; (*help*)
uneigennützig
disjointed [dɪsˈdʒɔɪntɪd] *adj*
unzusammenhängend

d

disk [dɪsk] n Diskette f; **single-/double-sided** ~ einseitige/zweiseitige Diskette

disk drive n Diskettenlaufwerk nt

diskette [dɪs'kɛt] (US) n = **disk**

disk operating system n Betriebssystem nt

dislike [dɪs'laɪk] n Abneigung f ▷ vt nicht mögen; **to take a ~ to sb/sth** eine Abneigung gegen jdn/etw entwickeln; **I ~ the idea** die Idee gefällt mir nicht; **he ~s it** er kann es nicht leiden, er mag es nicht

dislocate ['dɪsləkeɪt] vt verrenken, ausrenken; **he has ~d his shoulder** er hat sich dat den Arm ausgekugelt

dislodge [dɪs'lɔdʒ] vt verschieben

disloyal [dɪs'lɔɪəl] adj illoyal

dismal ['dɪzml] adj trübe, trostlos; (song, person, mood) trübsinnig; (failure) kläglich

dismantle [dɪs'mæntl] vt (machine) demontieren

dismast [dɪs'mɑ:st] vt (Naut) entmasten

dismay [dɪs'meɪ] n Bestürzung f ▷ vt bestürzen; **much to my ~** zu meiner Bestürzung; **in ~** bestürzt

dismiss [dɪs'mɪs] vt entlassen; (case) abweisen; (possibility, idea) abtun

dismissal [dɪs'mɪsl] n Entlassung f

dismount [dɪs'maunt] vi absteigen

disobedience [dɪsə'bi:dɪəns] n Ungehorsam m

disobedient [dɪsə'bi:dɪənt] adj ungehorsam

disobey [dɪsə'beɪ] vt nicht gehorchen +dat; (order) nicht befolgen

disorder [dɪs'ɔ:dəʳ] n Unordnung f; (rioting) Unruhen pl; (Med) (Funktions)störung f; **civil ~** öffentliche Unruhen pl

disorderly [dɪs'ɔ:dəlɪ] adj unordentlich; (meeting) undiszipliniert; (behaviour) ungehörig

disorderly conduct n (Law) ungebührliches Benehmen nt

disorganize [dɪs'ɔ:gənaɪz] vt durcheinanderbringen

disorganized [dɪs'ɔ:gənaɪzd] adj chaotisch

disorientated [dɪs'ɔ:rɪenteɪtɪd] adj desorientiert, verwirrt

disown [dɪs'əun] vt (action) verleugnen; (child) verstoßen

disparaging [dɪs'pærɪdʒɪŋ] adj (remarks) abschätzig, geringschätzig; **to be ~ about sb/sth** (person) abschätzig or geringschätzig über jdn/etw urteilen

disparate ['dɪspərɪt] adj völlig verschieden

disparity [dɪs'pærɪtɪ] n Unterschied m

dispassionate [dɪs'pæʃənət] adj nüchtern

dispatch [dɪs'pætʃ] vt senden, schicken; (deal with) erledigen; (kill) töten ▷ n Senden nt, Schicken nt; (Press) Bericht m; (Mil) Depesche f

dispatch department n Versandabteilung f

dispatch rider n (Mil) Meldefahrer m

dispel [dɪs'pɛl] vt (myths) zerstören; (fears) zerstreuen

dispensary [dɪs'pensərɪ] n Apotheke f; (in chemist's) Raum in einer Apotheke, wo Arzneimittel abgefüllt werden

dispensation [dɪspən'seɪʃən] n (of treatment) Vergabe f; (special permission) Dispens m; **~ of justice** Rechtsprechung f

dispense [dɪs'pens] vt (medicines) abgeben; (charity) austeilen; (advice) erteilen
  ▶ **dispense with** vt fus verzichten auf +acc

dispenser [dɪs'pensəʳ] n (machine) Automat m

dispensing chemist [dɪs'pensɪŋ-] (Brit) n (shop) Apotheke f

dispersal [dɪs'pə:sl] n (of objects) Verstreuen nt; (of group, crowd) Auflösung f, Zerstreuen nt

disperse [dɪs'pə:s] vt (objects) verstreuen; (crowd etc) auflösen, zerstreuen; (knowledge, information) verbreiten ▷ vi (crowd) sich auflösen or zerstreuen

dispirited [dɪs'pɪrɪtɪd] adj entmutigt

displace [dɪs'pleɪs] vt ablösen

displaced person [dɪs'pleɪst-] n Verschleppte(r) f(m)

displacement [dɪs'pleɪsmənt] n Ablösung f; (of people) Vertreibung f; (Phys) Verdrängung f

display [dɪs'pleɪ] n (in shop) Auslage f; (exhibition) Ausstellung f; (of feeling) Zeigen nt; (pej) Zurschaustellung f; (Comput, Tech) Anzeige f ▷ vt zeigen; (ostentatiously) zur Schau stellen; (results, departure times) aushängen; **on ~** ausgestellt

display advertising n Displaywerbung f

displease [dɪs'pli:z] vt verstimmen, verärgern

displeased [dɪs'pli:zd] adj: **I am very ~ with you** ich bin sehr enttäuscht von dir

displeasure [dɪs'plɛʒəʳ] n Missfallen nt

disposable [dɪs'pəuzəbl] adj (lighter) Wegwerf-; (bottle) Einweg-; (income) verfügbar

disposable nappy (Brit) n Papierwindel f

disposal [dɪs'pəuzl] n (of goods for sale) Loswerden nt; (of property, belongings: by selling) Verkauf m; (: by giving away) Abgeben nt; (of rubbish) Beseitigung f; **at one's ~** zur Verfügung; **to put sth at sb's ~** jdm etw zur Verfügung stellen

dispose [dɪs'pəuz]: **~ of** vt fus (body) aus dem Weg schaffen; (unwanted goods) loswerden; (problem, task) erledigen; (stock) verkaufen

disposed [dɪs'pəuzd] adj: **to be ~ to do sth** (inclined) geneigt sein, etw zu tun; (willing) bereit sein, etw zu tun; **to be well ~ towards sb** jdm wohlwollen

disposition [dɪspə'zɪʃən] n (nature) Veranlagung f; (inclination) Neigung f

dispossess ['dɪspə'zɛs] vt enteignen; **to ~ sb of his/her land** jds Land enteignen

disproportion [dɪsprə'pɔ:ʃən] n Missverhältnis nt

disproportionate [dɪsprə'pɔ:ʃənət] adj unverhältnismäßig; (amount) unverhältnismäßig hoch/niedrig

disprove [dɪs'pru:v] vt widerlegen

dispute [dɪs'pju:t] n Streit m; (also: **industrial dispute**) Auseinandersetzung f zwischen Arbeitgebern und Arbeitnehmern; (Pol, Mil) Streitigkeiten pl ▷ vt bestreiten; (ownership etc) anfechten; **to be in** or **under ~** umstritten sein

disqualification [dɪskwɔlɪfɪˈkeɪʃən]
n: ~ **(from)** Ausschluss *m* (von); (*Sport*)
Disqualifizierung *f* (von); ~ **(from driving)**
(*Brit*) Führerscheinentzug *m*

disqualify [dɪsˈkwɔlɪfaɪ] *vt* disqualifizieren; **to**
~ **sb for sth** jdn für etw ungeeignet machen;
to ~ **sb from doing sth** jdn ungeeignet
machen, etw zu tun; **to** ~ **sb from driving**
(*Brit*) jdm den Führerschein entziehen

disquiet [dɪsˈkwaɪət] *n* Unruhe *f*

disquieting [dɪsˈkwaɪətɪŋ] *adj* beunruhigend

disregard [dɪsrɪˈgɑːd] *vt* nicht beachten,
ignorieren ▷ *n*: ~ **(for)** Missachtung *f* (+*gen*);
(*for danger, money*) Geringschätzung *f* (+*gen*)

disrepair [ˈdɪsrɪˈpɛəʳ] *n*: **to fall into** ~ (*machine*)
vernachlässigt werden; (*building*) verfallen

disreputable [dɪsˈrɛpjʊtəbl] *adj* (*person*)
unehrenhaft; (*behaviour*) unfein

disrepute [ˈdɪsrɪˈpjuːt] *n* schlechter Ruf *m*; **to**
bring/fall into ~ in Verruf bringen/kommen

disrespectful [dɪsrɪˈspɛktful] *adj* respektlos

disrupt [dɪsˈrʌpt] *vt* (*plans*)
durcheinanderbringen; (*conversation,*
proceedings) unterbrechen

disruption [dɪsˈrʌpʃən] *n* Unterbrechung *f*;
(*disturbance*) Störung *f*

disruptive [dɪsˈrʌptɪv] *adj* störend; (*action*) Stör-

dissatisfaction [dɪssætɪsˈfækʃən] *n*
Unzufriedenheit *f*

dissatisfied [dɪsˈsætɪsfaɪd] *adj*: ~ **(with)**
unzufrieden (mit)

dissect [dɪˈsɛkt] *vt* sezieren

disseminate [dɪˈsɛmɪneɪt] *vt* verbreiten

dissent [dɪˈsɛnt] *n* abweichende Meinungen *pl*

dissenter [dɪˈsɛntəʳ] *n* Abweichler(in) *m(f)*

dissertation [dɪsəˈteɪʃən] *n* (*speech*) Vortrag
m; (*piece of writing*) Abhandlung *f*; (*for PhD*)
Dissertation *f*

disservice [dɪsˈsəːvɪs] *n*: **to do sb a** ~ jdm einen
schlechten Dienst erweisen

dissident [ˈdɪsɪdnt] *adj* andersdenkend; (*voice*)
kritisch ▷ *n* Dissident(in) *m(f)*

dissimilar [dɪˈsɪmɪləʳ] *adj*: ~ **(to)** anders (als)

dissipate [ˈdɪsɪpeɪt] *vt* (*heat*) neutralisieren;
(*clouds*) auflösen; (*money, effort*) verschwenden

dissipated [ˈdɪsɪpeɪtɪd] *adj* zügellos,
ausschweifend

dissociate [dɪˈsəʊʃɪeɪt] *vt* trennen; **to** ~ **o.s.**
from sich distanzieren von

dissolute [ˈdɪsəluːt] *adj* zügellos,
ausschweifend

dissolution [dɪsəˈluːʃən] *n* Auflösung *f*

dissolve [dɪˈzɔlv] *vt* auflösen ▷ *vi* sich auflösen;
to ~ **in(to) tears** in Tränen zerfließen

dissuade [dɪˈsweɪd] *vt*: **to** ~ **sb (from sth)** jdn
(von etw) abbringen

distaff [ˈdɪstɑːf] *n*: **the** ~ **side** die mütterliche
Seite

distance [ˈdɪstns] *n* Entfernung *f*; (*in time*)
Abstand *m*; (*reserve*) Abstand, Distanz *f* ▷ *vt*: **to**
~ **o.s. (from)** sich distanzieren (von); **in the**
~ in der Ferne; **what's the** ~ **to London?** wie
weit ist es nach London?; **it's within walking**

~ es ist zu Fuß erreichbar; **at a** ~ **of 2 metres**
in 2 Meter(n) Entfernung; **keep your** ~!
halten Sie Abstand!

distant [ˈdɪstnt] *adj* (*place*) weit entfernt, fern;
(*time*) weit zurückliegend; (*relative*) entfernt;
(*manner*) distanziert, kühl

distaste [dɪsˈteɪst] *n* Widerwille *m*

distasteful [dɪsˈteɪstful] *adj* widerlich; **to be** ~
to sb jdm zuwider sein

Dist. Atty. (*US*) *abbr* = **district attorney**

distemper [dɪsˈtɛmpəʳ] *n* (*paint*) Temperafarbe
f; (*disease of dogs*) Staupe *f*

distend [dɪsˈtɛnd] *vt* blähen ▷ *vi* sich blähen

distended [dɪsˈtɛndɪd] *adj* aufgebläht

distil, (*US*) **distill** [dɪsˈtɪl] *vt* destillieren; (*fig*)
(heraus)destillieren

distillery [dɪsˈtɪlərɪ] *n* Brennerei *f*

distinct [dɪsˈtɪŋkt] *adj* deutlich, klar; (*possibility*)
eindeutig; (*different*) verschieden; **as** ~ **from**
im Unterschied zu

distinction [dɪsˈtɪŋkʃən] *n* Unterschied *m*;
(*honour*) Ehre *f*; (*in exam*) Auszeichnung *f*; **to**
draw a ~ **between** einen Unterschied machen
zwischen +*dat*; **a writer of** ~ ein Schriftsteller
von Rang

distinctive [dɪsˈtɪŋktɪv] *adj* unverwechselbar

distinctly [dɪsˈtɪŋktlɪ] *adv* deutlich, klar; (*tell*)
ausdrücklich; (*unhappy*) ausgeprochen; (*better*)
entschieden

distinguish [dɪsˈtɪŋgwɪʃ] *vt* unterscheiden;
(*details etc*) erkennen, ausmachen; **to** ~
(between) unterscheiden (zwischen +*dat*); **to**
~ **o.s.** sich hervortun

distinguished [dɪsˈtɪŋgwɪʃt] *adj* von hohem
Rang; (*career*) hervorragend; (*in appearance*)
distinguiert

distinguishing [dɪsˈtɪŋgwɪʃɪŋ] *adj*
charakteristisch

distort [dɪsˈtɔːt] *vt* verzerren; (*argument*)
verdrehen

distortion [dɪsˈtɔːʃən] *n* (*see vb*) Verzerrung *f*;
Verdrehung *f*

distract [dɪsˈtrækt] *vt* ablenken

distracted [dɪsˈtræktɪd] *adj* unaufmerksam;
(*anxious*) besorgt, beunruhigt

distraction [dɪsˈtrækʃən] *n*
Unaufmerksamkeit *f*; (*confusion*) Verstörtheit
f; (*sth which distracts*) Ablenkung *f*; (*amusement*)
Zerstreuung *f*; **to drive sb to** ~ jdn zur
Verzweiflung treiben

distraught [dɪsˈtrɔːt] *adj* verzweifelt

distress [dɪsˈtrɛs] *n* Verzweiflung *f* ▷ *vt*
Kummer machen +*dat*; **in** ~ (*ship*) in
Seenot; (*person*) verzweifelt; ~**ed area** (*Brit*)
Notstandsgebiet *nt*

distressing [dɪsˈtrɛsɪŋ] *adj* beunruhigend

distress signal *n* Notsignal *nt*

distribute [dɪsˈtrɪbjuːt] *vt* verteilen; (*profits*)
aufteilen

distribution [dɪstrɪˈbjuːʃən] *n* Vertrieb *m*; (*of*
profits) Aufteilung *f*

distribution costs *npl* Vertriebskosten *pl*

distribution management *n* (*Comm*)

Vertriebscontrolling *nt*
distributor [dɪsˈtrɪbjutəʳ] *n* (*Comm*)
Vertreiber(in) *m(f)*; (*Aut, Tech*) Verteiler *m*
district [ˈdɪstrɪkt] *n* Gebiet *nt*; (*of town*) Stadtteil
m; (*Admin*) (Verwaltungs)bezirk *m*
district attorney (US) *n* Bezirksstaatsanwalt
m, Bezirksstaatsanwältin *f*

⬤ **DISTRICT COUNCIL**

District Council heißt der in jedem
der britischen districts (Bezirke)
alle vier Jahre neu gewählte
Bezirksrat, der für bestimmte
Bereiche der Kommunalverwaltung
(Gesundheitswesen, Wohnungsbeschaffung, Baugenehmigungen,
Müllabfuhr) zuständig ist. Die
district councils werden durch
Kommunalabgaben und durch einen
Zuschuss von der Regierung finanziert.
Ihre Ausgaben werden von einer
unabhängigen Prüfungskommission
kontrolliert, und bei zu hohen Ausgaben
wird der Regierungszuschuss gekürzt.

district nurse (Brit) *n* Gemeindeschwester *f*
distrust [dɪsˈtrʌst] *n* Misstrauen *nt* ▷ *vt*
misstrauen +*dat*
distrustful [dɪsˈtrʌstful] *adj*: ~ **(of)**
misstrauisch (gegenüber +*dat*)
disturb [dɪsˈtəːb] *vt* stören; (*upset*)
beunruhigen; (*disorganize*)
durcheinanderbringen; **sorry to ~ you**
entschuldigen Sie bitte die Störung
disturbance [dɪsˈtəːbəns] *n* Störung *f*; (*political
etc*) Unruhe *f*; (*violent event*) Unruhen *pl*; (*by
drunks etc*) (Ruhe)störung *f*; **to cause a ~**
Unruhe/eine Ruhestörung verursachen; **~ of
the peace** Ruhestörung
disturbed [dɪsˈtəːbd] *adj* beunruhigt; (*childhood*)
unglücklich; **mentally/emotionally ~**
geistig/seelisch gestört
disturbing [dɪsˈtəːbɪŋ] *adj* beunruhigend
disuse [dɪsˈjuːs] *n*: **to fall into ~** nicht mehr
benutzt werden
disused [dɪsˈjuːzd] *adj* (*building*) leer stehend;
(*airfield*) stillgelegt
ditch [dɪtʃ] *n* Graben *m* ▷ *vt* (*inf: partner*)
sitzen lassen; (: *plan*) sausen lassen; (: *car etc*)
loswerden
dither [ˈdɪðəʳ] (*pej*) *vi* zaudern
ditto [ˈdɪtəu] *adv* dito, ebenfalls
divan [dɪˈvæn] *n* (*also:* **divan bed**) Polsterbett *nt*
dive [daɪv] *n* Sprung *m*; (*underwater*) Tauchen
nt; (*of submarine*) Untertauchen *nt*; (*pej: place*)
Spelunke *f* (*inf*) ▷ *vi* springen; (*under water*)
tauchen; (*bird*) einen Sturzflug machen;
(*submarine*) untertauchen; **to ~ into** (*bag, drawer
etc*) greifen in +*acc*; (*shop, car etc*) sich stürzen
in +*acc*
diver [ˈdaɪvəʳ] *n* Taucher(in) *m(f)*; (*also:* **deep-
sea diver**) Tiefseetaucher(in) *m(f)*

diverge [daɪˈvəːdʒ] *vi* auseinandergehen
divergent [daɪˈvəːdʒənt] *adj* unterschiedlich;
(*views*) voneinander abweichend; (*interests*)
auseinandergehend
diverse [daɪˈvəːs] *adj* verschiedenartig
diversification [daɪvəːsɪfɪˈkeɪʃən] *n*
Diversifikation *f*
diversify [daɪˈvəːsɪfaɪ] *vi* diversifizieren
diversion [daɪˈvəːʃən] *n* (*Brit: Aut*) Umleitung *f*;
(*distraction*) Ablenkung *f*; (*of funds*) Umlenkung *f*
diversionary [daɪˈvəːʃənrɪ] *adj*: ~ **tactics**
Ablenkungsmanöver *pl*
diversity [daɪˈvəːsɪtɪ] *n* Vielfalt *f*
divert [daɪˈvəːt] *vt* (*sb's attention*) ablenken;
(*funds*) umlenken; (*re-route*) umleiten
divest [daɪˈvɛst] *vt*: **to ~ sb of office/his
authority** jdn seines Amtes entkleiden/
seiner Macht entheben
divide [dɪˈvaɪd] *vt* trennen; (*Math*) dividieren,
teilen; (*share out*) verteilen ▷ *vi* sich teilen;
(*road*) sich gabeln; (*people, groups*) sich aufteilen
▷ *n* Kluft *f*; **to ~ (between** or **among)** aufteilen
(unter +*dat*); **40 ~d by 5** 40 geteilt or dividiert
durch 5
  ▶ **divide out** *vt*: **to ~ out (between** or **among)**
  aufteilen (unter +*dat*)
divided [dɪˈvaɪdɪd] *adj* geteilt; **to be ~ about** or
over sth geteilter Meinung über etw *acc* sein
divided highway (US) *n* ≈ Schnellstraße *f*
dividend [ˈdɪvɪdɛnd] *n* Dividende *f*; (*fig*): **to pay
~s** sich bezahlt machen
dividend cover *n* (*Comm*) Dividendendeckung *f*
dividers [dɪˈvaɪdəz] *npl* (*Math, Tech*) Stechzirkel
m; (*between pages*) Register *nt*
divine [dɪˈvaɪn] *adj* göttlich ▷ *vt* (*future*)
weissagen, prophezeien; (*truth*) erahnen;
(*water, metal*) aufspüren
diving [ˈdaɪvɪŋ] *n* Tauchen *nt*; (*Sport*)
Kunstspringen *nt*
diving board *n* Sprungbrett *nt*
diving suit *n* Taucheranzug *m*
divinity [dɪˈvɪnɪtɪ] *n* Göttlichkeit *f*; (*god or
goddess*) Gottheit *f*; (*Scol*) Theologie *f*
divisible [dɪˈvɪzəbl] *adj*: ~ **(by)** teilbar (durch);
to be ~ into teilbar sein in +*acc*
division [dɪˈvɪʒən] *n* Teilung *f*; (*Math*)
Teilen *nt*, Division *f*; (*sharing out*) Verteilung
f; (*disagreement*) Uneinigkeit *f*; (*Brit: Pol*)
Abstimmung *f* durch Hammelsprung; (*Comm*)
Abteilung *f*; (*Mil*) Division *f*; (*esp Football*) Liga
f; ~ **of labour** Arbeitsteilung *f*
divisive [dɪˈvaɪsɪv] *adj*: **to be ~** (*tactics*) auf
Spaltung abzielen; (*system*) zu Feindseligkeit
führen
divorce [dɪˈvɔːs] *n* Scheidung *f* ▷ *vt* sich
scheiden lassen von; (*dissociate*) trennen
divorced [dɪˈvɔːst] *adj* geschieden
divorcee [dɪvɔːˈsiː] *n* Geschiedene(r) *f(m)*
divot [ˈdɪvət] *n* vom Golfschläger etc ausgehacktes
Rasenstück
divulge [daɪˈvʌldʒ] *vt* preisgeben
DIY (Brit) *n abbr* = **do-it-yourself**
dizziness [ˈdɪzɪnɪs] *n* Schwindel *m*

dizzy ['dɪzɪ] *adj* schwind(e)lig; *(turn, spell)*
Schwindel-; *(height)* schwindelerregend; **I feel
~** mir ist *or* ich bin schwind(e)lig
DJ *n abbr* = **disc jockey**
dj *n abbr* = **dinner jacket**
Djakarta [dʒə'kɑːtə] *n* Jakarta *nt*
DJIA *(US) n abbr* (= *Dow-Jones Industrial Average*)
Dow-Jones-Index *m*
dl *abbr* (= *decilitre*) dl
DLit, DLitt *n abbr* (= *Doctor of Literature, Doctor of
Letters*) akademischer Grad in Literaturwissenschaft
dm *abbr* (= *decimetre*) dm
DMus *n abbr* (= *Doctor of Music*) Doktor der
Musikwissenschaft
DMZ *n abbr* = **demilitarized zone**
DNA *n abbr* (= *deoxyribonucleic acid*) DNS *f*
DNA test *n* DNS-Test *m*

O KEYWORD

do [duː] *(pt* **did,** *pp* **done)** *aux vb* **1** *(in negative
constructions):* **I don't understand** ich verstehe
nicht
2 *(to form questions):* **didn't you know?** wusstest
du das nicht?; **what do you think?** was
meinst du?
3 *(for emphasis):* **she does seem rather upset**
sie scheint wirklich recht aufgeregt zu sein;
do sit down/help yourself bitte nehmen Sie
Platz/bedienen Sie sich; **oh do shut up!** halte
endlich den Mund!
4 *(to avoid repeating vb):* **she swims better than
I do** sie schwimmt besser als ich; **she lives in
Glasgow — so do I** sie wohnt in Glasgow —
ich auch; **who made this mess? — I did** wer
hat dieses Durcheinander gemacht? — ich
5 *(in question tags):* **you like him, don't you?** du
magst ihn, nicht wahr?; **I don't know him,
do I?** ich kenne ihn nicht, oder?
▷ *vt* **1** *(carry out, perform)* tun, machen; **what are
you doing tonight?** was machen Sie heute
Abend?; **what do you do (for a living)?** was
machen Sie beruflich?; **to do one's teeth/
nails** sich *dat* die Zähne putzen/die Nägel
schneiden
2 *(Aut etc)* fahren; **the car was doing 100** das
Auto fuhr 100
▷ *vi* **1** *(act, behave):* **do as I do** mach es wie ich
2 *(get on, fare):* **he's doing well/badly at
school** er ist gut/schlecht in der Schule; **the
company is doing well** der Firma geht es gut;
how do you do? guten Tag/Morgen/Abend!
3 *(suit, be sufficient)* reichen; **will that do?**
reicht das?; **will this dress do for the party?**
ist dieses Kleid gut genug für die Party?; **will
£10 do?** reichen £10?; **that'll do** das reicht;
(in annoyance) jetzt reichts aber!; **to make do
with** auskommen mit
▷ *n* *(inf: party etc)* Party *f*, Fete *f*; **it was quite a
do** es war ganz schön was los
▶ **do away with** *vt fus (get rid of)* abschaffen
▶ **do for** *(inf) vt fus:* **to be done for** erledigt
sein
▶ **do in** *(inf) vt (kill)* umbringen
▶ **do out of** *(inf) vt (deprive)* bringen um
▶ **do up** *vt fus (laces, dress, buttons)* zumachen;
(renovate: room, house) renovieren
▶ **do with** *vt fus* **1** *(need)* brauchen; **I could do
with some help/a drink** ich könnte Hilfe/
einen Drink gebrauchen
2: **it has to do with money** es hat mit Geld
zu tun
▶ **do without** *vt fus* auskommen ohne

do. *abbr* = **ditto**
DOA *abbr* (= *dead on arrival*) bei Einlieferung ins
Krankenhaus bereits tot
d.o.b. *abbr* = **date of birth**
doc [dɔk] *(inf) n* Doktor *m*
docile ['dəʊsaɪl] *adj* sanft(mütig)
dock [dɔk] *n* Dock *nt*; *(Law)* Anklagebank *f*;
(Bot) Ampfer *m* ▷ *vi* anlegen; *(Space)* docken
▷ *vt*: **they ~ed a third of his wages** sie
kürzten seinen Lohn um ein Drittel; **docks** *npl*
(Naut) Hafen *m*
dock dues [-djuːz] *npl* Hafengebühr *f*
docker ['dɔkəʳ] *n* Hafenarbeiter *m*, Docker *m*
docket ['dɔkɪt] *n* Inhaltserklärung *f*; *(on parcel
etc)* Warenbegleitschein *m*, Laufzettel *m*
dockyard ['dɔkjɑːd] *n* Werft *f*
doctor ['dɔktəʳ] *n* Arzt *m*, Ärztin *f*; *(PhD
etc)* Doktor *m* ▷ *vt*: **to ~ a drink** *etc* einem
Getränk *etc* etwas beimischen; **~'s office** *(US)*
Sprechzimmer *nt*
doctorate ['dɔktərɪt] *n* Doktorwürde *f*; *siehe
Info-Artikel*

◎ DOCTORATE
◎
◎ *Doctorate* ist der höchste akademische
◎ Grad auf jedem Wissensgebiet und
◎ wird nach erfolgreicher Vorlage einer
◎ Doktorarbeit verliehen. Die Studienzeit
◎ (meist mindestens 3 Jahre) und Länge
◎ der Doktorarbeit ist je nach Hochschule
◎ verschieden. Am häufigsten wird der
◎ Titel *PhD* (Doctor of Philosophy) auf
◎ dem Gebiet der Geisteswissenschaften,
◎ Naturwissenschaften und des
◎ Ingenieurwesens verliehen, obwohl es
◎ auch andere Doktortitel (in Musik, Jura
◎ usw.) gibt. Siehe auch *Bachelor's degree,
◎ Master's degree.*

Doctor of Philosophy *n* Doktor *m* der
Philosophie
doctrine ['dɔktrɪn] *n* Doktrin *f*
docudrama ['dɔkjudrɑːmə] *n*
Dokumentarspiel *nt*
document ['dɔkjumənt] *n* Dokument *nt* ▷ *vt*
dokumentieren
documentary [dɔkju'mɛntərɪ] *adj*
dokumentarisch ▷ *n* Dokumentarfilm *m*
documentation [dɔkjumən'teɪʃən] *n*
Dokumentation *f*
DOD *(US) n abbr* (= *Department of Defense*)

d

Verteidigungsministerium *nt*

doddering ['dɔdərɪŋ] *adj (shaky, unsteady)* zittrig

doddery ['dɔdərɪ] *adj* = **doddering**

doddle ['dɔdl] *(inf) n:* **a ~** ein Kinderspiel *nt*

Dodecanese [dəudɪkə'niːz], **Dodecanese Islands** *npl:* **the ~ (Islands)** der Dodekanes

dodge [dɔdʒ] *n* Trick *m* ▷ *vt* ausweichen +*dat*; *(tax)* umgehen ▷ *vi* ausweichen; **to ~ out of the way** zur Seite springen; **to ~ through the traffic** sich durch den Verkehr schlängeln

dodgems ['dɔdʒəmz] *(Brit) npl* Autoskooter *pl*

dodgy ['dɔdʒɪ] *(inf) adj (person)* zweifelhaft; *(plan etc)* gewagt

DOE *n abbr (Brit:* = *Department of the Environment) Umweltministerium; (US:* = *Department of Energy) Energieministerium*

doe [dəu] *n* Reh *nt*, Ricke *f*; *(rabbit)* (Kaninchen)weibchen *nt*

does [dʌz] *vb see* **do**

doesn't ['dʌznt] = **does not**

dog [dɔg] *n* Hund *m* ▷ *vt (subj: person)* auf den Fersen bleiben +*dat*; *(: bad luck, memory etc)* verfolgen; **to go to the ~s** *(inf)* vor die Hunde gehen

dog biscuits *npl* Hundekuchen *pl*

dog collar *n* Hundehalsband *nt*; *(Rel)* Kragen *m* des Geistlichen

dog-eared ['dɔgɪəd] *adj* mit Eselsohren

dog food *n* Hundefutter *nt*

dogged ['dɔgɪd] *adj* beharrlich

doggy ['dɔgɪ] *n* Hündchen *nt*

doggy bag *n* Tüte für Essensreste, die man nach Hause mitnehmen möchte

dogma ['dɔgmə] *n* Dogma *nt*

dogmatic [dɔg'mætɪk] *adj* dogmatisch

do-gooder [duː'gudər] *(pej) n* Weltverbesserer(in) *m(f)*

dogsbody ['dɔgzbɔdɪ] *(Brit: inf) n* Mädchen *nt* für alles

doily ['dɔɪlɪ] *n* Deckchen *nt*

doing ['duɪŋ] *n:* **this is your ~** das ist dein Werk

doings ['duɪŋz] *npl* Treiben *nt*

do-it-yourself ['duːɪtjɔː'sɛlf] *n* Heimwerken *nt*, Do-it-yourself *nt*

doldrums ['dɔldrəmz] *npl:* **to be in the ~** *(person)* niedergeschlagen sein; *(business)* in einer Flaute stecken

dole [dəul] *(Brit) n* Arbeitslosenunterstützung *f*; **on the ~** arbeitslos

▷ **dole out** *vt* austeilen, verteilen

doleful ['dəulful] *adj* traurig

doll [dɔl] *n (toy, also US: inf: woman)* Puppe *f*

dollar ['dɔlər] *(US etc) n* Dollar *m*

dollar area *n* Dollarblock *m*

dolled up *(inf) adj* aufgedonnert

dollop ['dɔləp] *(inf) n* Schlag *m*

dolly ['dɔlɪ] *(inf) n (doll, woman)* Puppe *f*

Dolomites ['dɔləmaɪts] *npl:* **the ~** die Dolomiten *pl*

dolphin ['dɔlfɪn] *n* Delfin *m*

domain [də'meɪn] *n* Bereich *m*; *(empire)* Reich *nt*

dome [dəum] *n* Kuppel *f*

domestic [də'mɛstɪk] *adj (trade)* Innen-; *(situation)* innenpolitisch; *(news)* Inland-, aus dem Inland; *(tasks, appliances)* Haushalts-; *(animal)* Haus-; *(duty, happiness)* häuslich

domesticated [də'mɛstɪkeɪtɪd] *adj (animal)* zahm; *(person)* häuslich

domesticity [dəumɛs'tɪsɪtɪ] *n* häusliches Leben *nt*

domestic servant *n* Hausangestellte(r) *f(m)*

domicile ['dɔmɪsaɪl] *n* Wohnsitz *m*

dominant ['dɔmɪnənt] *adj* dominierend; *(share)* größte(r, s)

dominate ['dɔmɪneɪt] *vt* dominieren, beherrschen

domination [dɔmɪ'neɪʃən] *n* (Vor)herrschaft *f*

domineering [dɔmɪ'nɪərɪŋ] *adj* herrschsüchtig

Dominican Republic [də'mɪnɪkən-] *n:* **the ~** die Dominikanische Republik

dominion [də'mɪnɪən] *n (territory)* Herrschaftsgebiet *nt*; *(authority):* **to have ~ over** Macht haben über +*acc*

domino ['dɔmɪnəu] *(pl* **~es)** *n (block)* Domino(stein) *m*

domino effect *n* Dominoeffekt *m*

dominoes ['dɔmɪnəuz] *n (game)* Domino(spiel) *nt*

don [dɔn] *n (Brit) (Universitäts)dozent *m* *(besonders in Oxford und Cambridge)* ▷ *vt* anziehen

donate [də'neɪt] *vt:* **to ~ (to)** *(organization, cause)* spenden (für)

donation [də'neɪʃən] *n (act of donating)* Spenden *nt*; *(contribution)* Spende *f*

done [dʌn] *pp of* **do**

donkey ['dɔŋkɪ] *n* Esel *m*

donkey-work ['dɔŋkɪwəːk] *(Brit: inf) n* Dreckarbeit *f*

donor ['dəunər] *n* Spender(in) *m(f)*

donor card *n* Organspenderausweis *m*

donor conference *n (Pol, Econ)* Geberkonferenz *f*

donor fatigue *n* Spendenmüdigkeit *f*

don't [dəunt] = **do not**

donut ['dəunʌt] *(US) n* = **doughnut**

doodle ['duːdl] *vi* Männchen malen ▷ *n* Kritzelei *f*

doom [duːm] *n* Unheil *nt* ▷ *vt:* **to be ~ed to failure** zum Scheitern verurteilt sein

doomsday ['duːmzdeɪ] *n* der Jüngste Tag

door [dɔːr] *n* Tür *f*; **to go from ~ to door** von Tür zu Tür gehen

door bell *n* Türklingel *f*

door handle *n* Türklinke *f*; *(of car)* Türgriff *m*

doorman ['dɔːmən] *(irreg: like* **man**) *n* Portier *m*

doormat ['dɔːmæt] *n* Fußmatte *f*; *(fig)* Fußabtreter *m*

doorpost ['dɔːpəust] *n* Türpfosten *m*

doorstep ['dɔːstɛp] *n* Eingangsstufe *f*, Türstufe *f*; **on the ~** vor der Haustür

door-to-door ['dɔːtə'dɔːr] *adj (selling)* von Haus zu Haus; **~ salesman** Vertreter *m*

doorway ['dɔːweɪ] *n* Eingang *m*

dope [dəup] *n (inf)* Stoff *m*, Drogen *pl*; *(: person)* Esel *m*, Trottel *m*; *(: information)* Informationen pl ▷ vt dopen

dopey ['dəupɪ] (inf) adj (groggy) benebelt; (stupid) blöd, bekloppt

dormant ['dɔ:mənt] adj (plant) ruhend; (volcano) untätig; (idea, report etc) to lie ~ schlummern

dormer ['dɔ:mə'] n (also: **dormer window**) Mansardenfenster nt

dormice ['dɔ:maɪs] npl of **dormouse**

dormitory ['dɔ:mɪtrɪ] n Schlafsaal m; (US: building) Wohnheim nt

dormouse ['dɔ:maus] (pl **dormice**) n Haselmaus f

DOS [dɔs] n abbr (Comput: = disk operating system) DOS

dosage ['dəusɪdʒ] n Dosis f; (on label) Dosierung f

dose [dəus] n Dosis f; (Brit: bout) Ration f ▷ vt: **to ~ o.s.** Medikamente nehmen; **a ~ of flu** eine Grippe

dosser ['dɔsə'] (Brit: inf) n Penner(in) m(f)

dosshouse ['dɔshaus] (Brit: inf) n Obdachlosenheim nt

dossier ['dɔsɪeɪ] n Dossier nt

DOT (US) n abbr (= Department of Transportation) ≈ Verkehrsministerium nt

dot [dɔt] n Punkt m ▷ vt: **~ted with** übersät mit; **on the ~** (auf die Minute) pünktlich

dote [dəut]: **~ on** vt fus abgöttisch lieben

dot-matrix printer [dɔt'meɪtrɪks-] n Nadeldrucker m

dotted line ['dɔtɪd-] n punktierte Linie f; **to sign on the ~** (fig) seine formelle Zustimmung geben

dotty ['dɔtɪ] (inf) adj schrullig

double ['dʌbl] adj doppelt; (chin) Doppel- ▷ adv (cost) doppelt so viel ▷ n Doppelgänger(in) m(f) ▷ vt verdoppeln; (paper, blanket) (einmal) falten ▷ vi sich verdoppeln; **~ five two six (5526)** (Brit: Tel) fünfundfünfzig sechsundzwanzig; **it's spelt with a ~ "l"** es wird mit zwei l geschrieben; **an egg with a ~ yolk** ein Ei mit zwei Dottern; **on the ~, at the ~** (Brit: quickly) schnell; (immediately) unverzüglich; **to ~ as ...** (person) auch als ... fungieren; (thing) auch als ... dienen

▶ **double back** vi kehrtmachen, zurückgehen/-fahren

▶ **double up** vi sich krümmen; (share room) sich ein Zimmer teilen

double bass n Kontrabass m

double bed n Doppelbett nt

double bend (Brit) n S-Kurve f

double-blind adj: **~ experiment** Doppelblindversuch m

double-breasted ['dʌbl'brɛstɪd] adj (jacket, coat) zweireihig

double-check ['dʌbl'tʃɛk] vt noch einmal (über)prüfen ▷ vi es noch einmal (über)prüfen

double-clutch ['dʌbl'klʌtʃ] (US) vi mit Zwischengas schalten

double cream (Brit) n Sahne f mit hohem Fettgehalt, ≈ Schlagsahne f

double-cross [dʌbl'krɔs] vt ein Doppelspiel treiben mit

double-decker [dʌbl'dɛkə'] n Doppeldecker m

double-declutch ['dʌbldi:'klʌtʃ] (Brit) vi mit Zwischengas schalten

double exposure n doppelt belichtetes Foto nt

double glazing [-'gleɪzɪŋ] (Brit) n Doppelverglasung f

double-page spread ['dʌblpeɪdʒ-] n Doppelseite f

double-parking [dʌbl'pɑ:kɪŋ] n Parken nt in der zweiten Reihe

double room n Doppelzimmer nt

doubles ['dʌblz] n (Tennis) Doppel nt

double time n doppelter Lohn m

double whammy [-'wæmɪ] (inf) n Doppelschlag m

doubly ['dʌblɪ] adv (ganz) besonders

doubt [daut] n Zweifel m ▷ vt bezweifeln; **without (a) ~** ohne Zweifel; **to ~ sb** jdm nicht glauben; **I ~ it (very much)** das bezweifle ich (sehr), das möchte ich (stark) bezweifeln; **to ~ if** or **whether ...** bezweifeln, dass ...; **I don't ~ that ...** ich bezweifle nicht, dass ...

doubtful ['dautful] adj zweifelhaft; **to be ~ about sth** an etw dat zweifeln; **to be ~ about doing sth** Bedenken haben, ob man etw tun soll; **I'm a bit ~** ich bin nicht ganz sicher

doubtless ['dautlɪs] adv ohne Zweifel, sicherlich

dough [dəu] n Teig m; (inf: money) Kohle f, Knete f

doughnut, (US) **donut** ['dəunʌt] n ≈ Berliner (Pfannkuchen) m

dour [duə'] adj mürrisch, verdrießlich

douse [dauz] vt Wasser schütten über +acc; (extinguish) löschen; **to ~ with** übergießen mit

dove [dʌv] n Taube f

Dover ['dəuvə'] n Dover nt

dovetail ['dʌvteɪl] vi übereinstimmen ▷ n (also: **dovetail joint**) Schwalbenschwanzverbindung f

dowager ['dauədʒə'] n (adlige) Witwe f

dowdy ['daudɪ] adj ohne jeden Schick; (clothes) unmodern

Dow-Jones average ['dau'dʒəunz-] (US) n Dow-Jones-Index m

down [daun] n Daunen pl ▷ adv hinunter, herunter; (on the ground) unten ▷ prep hinunter, herunter; (movement along) entlang ▷ vt (inf: drink) runterkippen; **~ there/here** da/hier unten; **the price of meat is ~** die Fleischpreise sind gefallen; **I've got it ~ in my diary** ich habe es in meinem Kalender notiert; **to pay £2 ~** £2 anzahlen; **England is two goals ~** England liegt mit zwei Toren zurück; **to ~ tools** (Brit) die Arbeit niederlegen; **~ with ...!** nieder mit ...!

down-and-out ['daunəndaut] n Penner(in) m(f) (inf)

down-at-heel ['daunət'hi:l] adj (appearance, person) schäbig, heruntergekommen; (shoes) abgetreten

downbeat ['daunbi:t] n (Mus) erster betonter

527

Taktteil *m* ▷ *adj* zurückhaltend
downcast ['daʊnkɑːst] *adj* niedergeschlagen
downer ['daʊnəʳ] (*inf*) *n* (*drug*)
Beruhigungsmittel *nt*; **to be on a ~**
deprimiert sein
downfall ['daʊnfɔːl] *n* Ruin *m*; (*of dictator etc*)
Sturz *m*, Fall *m*
downgrade ['daʊngreɪd] *vt* herunterstufen
downhearted ['daʊn'hɑːtɪd] *adj*
niedergeschlagen, entmutigt
downhill ['daʊn'hɪl] *adv* bergab ▷ *n* (*Ski: also:*
downhill race) Abfahrtslauf *m*; **to go ~** (*road*)
bergab führen; (*person*) hinuntergehen,
heruntergehen; (*car*) hinunterfahren,
herunterfahren; (*fig*) auf dem absteigenden
Ast sein

DOWNING STREET

Downing Street ist die Straße in London, die
von Whitehall zum St James Park führt
und in der sich der offizielle Wohnsitz
des Premierministers (Nr. 10) und des
Finanzministers (Nr. 11) befindet. Im
weiteren Sinne bezieht sich der Begriff
Downing Street auf die britische
Regierung.

download ['daʊnləʊd] *vt* (*Comput*)
herunterladen, downloaden ▷ *n* Download *m*
downloadable ['daʊnləʊdəbl] *adj* (*Comput*)
herunterladbar
down-market ['daʊn'mɑːkɪt] *adj* (*product*) für
den Massenmarkt
down payment *n* Anzahlung *f*
downplay ['daʊnpleɪ] (*US*) *vt* herunterspielen
downpour ['daʊnpɔːʳ] *n* Wolkenbruch *m*
downright ['daʊnraɪt] *adj* (*liar etc*)
ausgesprochen; (*refusal, lie*) glatt
Downs [daʊnz] (*Brit*) *npl*: **the ~** die Downs *pl*,
Hügellandschaft in Südengland
downscale ['daʊnskeɪl] *adj* (*US*) wenig
anspruchsvoll; (*goods, products*) minderwertig;
(*service*) mangelhaft; (*restaurant, hotel*) der
unteren Preisklasse
downsize ['daʊnsaɪz] *vi* (*Econ: company*) sich
verkleinern
Down's syndrome *n* (*Med*) Downsyndrom *nt*
downstairs ['daʊn'steəz] *adv* unten;
(*downwards*) nach unten
downstream ['daʊnstriːm] *adv* flussabwärts,
stromabwärts
downtime ['daʊntaɪm] *n* Ausfallzeit *f*
down-to-earth ['daʊntuː'əːθ] *adj* (*person*)
nüchtern; (*solution*) praktisch
downtown ['daʊn'taʊn] (*esp US*) *adv* im
Zentrum, in der (Innen)stadt; (*go*) ins
Zentrum, in die (Innen)stadt ▷ *adj*: **~ Chicago**
das Zentrum von Chicago
downtrodden ['daʊntrɔdn] *adj* unterdrückt,
geknechtet
down under *adv* (*be*) in Australien/
Neuseeland; (*go*) nach Australien/Neuseeland

downward ['daʊnwəd] *adj, adv* nach unten; **a ~**
trend ein Abwärtstrend *m*
downwards ['daʊnwədz] *adv* = **downward**
dowry ['daʊrɪ] *n* Mitgift *f*
doz. *abbr* = **dozen**
doze [dəʊz] *vi* ein Nickerchen *nt* machen
▷ **doze off** *vi* einschlafen, einnicken
dozen ['dʌzn] *n* Dutzend *nt*; **a ~ books** ein
Dutzend Bücher; **8op a ~** 80 Pence das
Dutzend; **~s of** Dutzende von
DPh, DPhil *n abbr* (= *Doctor of Philosophy*) ≈ Dr. phil.
DPP (*Brit*) *n abbr* (= *Director of Public Prosecutions*)
DPT *n abbr* = *diphtheria, pertussis, tetanus*)
Diphtherie, Keuchhusten und Tetanus
Dr *abbr* = **doctor**; (*in street names:* = *Drive*) ≈ Str.
dr *abbr* (*Comm*) = **debtor**
drab [dræb] *adj* trist
draft [drɑːft] *n* Entwurf *m*; (*also:* **bank draft**)
Tratte *f*; (*US: call-up*) Einberufung *f* ▷ *vt*
entwerfen; *see also* **draught**
draftsman *etc* ['drɑːftsmən] (*US*) *n* =
draughtsman *etc*
drag [dræg] *vt* schleifen, schleppen; (*river*)
absuchen ▷ *vi* sich hinziehen ▷ *n* (*Aviat*)
Luftwiderstand *m*; (*Naut*) Wasserwiderstand
m; (*inf*): **to be a ~** (*boring*) langweilig sein; (*a*
nuisance) lästig sein; (*women's clothing*): **in ~** in
Frauenkleidung
▷ **drag away** *vt*: **to ~ away (from)**
wegschleppen *or* wegziehen (von)
▷ **drag on** *vi* sich hinziehen
dragnet ['drægnet] *n* Schleppnetz *nt*; (*fig*) groß
angelegte Polizeiaktion *f*
dragon ['drægn] *n* Drache *m*
dragonfly ['drægənflaɪ] *n* Libelle *f*
dragoon [drə'guːn] *n* Dragoner *m* ▷ *vt*: **to ~ sb**
into doing sth (*Brit*) jdn zwingen, etw zu tun
drain [dreɪn] *n* Belastung *f*; (*in street*) Gully
m ▷ *vt* entwässern; (*pond*) trockenlegen;
(*vegetables*) abgießen; (*glass, cup*) leeren ▷ *vi*
ablaufen; **to feel ~ed (of energy/emotion)**
sich ausgelaugt fühlen
drainage ['dreɪnɪdʒ] *n* Entwässerungssystem
nt; (*process*) Entwässerung *f*
draining board ['dreɪnɪŋ-], (*US*) **drainboard**
['dreɪnbɔːd] *n* Ablaufbrett *nt*
drainpipe ['dreɪnpaɪp] *n* Abflussrohr *nt*
drake [dreɪk] *n* Erpel *m*, Enterich *m*
dram [dræm] (*Scot*) *n* (*drink*) Schluck *m*
drama ['drɑːmə] *n* Drama *nt*
dramatic [drə'mætɪk] *adj* dramatisch;
(*theatrical*) theatralisch
dramatically [drə'mætɪklɪ] *adv* dramatisch;
(*say, announce, pause*) theatralisch
dramatist ['dræmətɪst] *n* Dramatiker(in) *m(f)*
dramatize ['dræmətaɪz] *vt* dramatisieren;
(*for TV/cinema*) für das Fernsehen/den Film
bearbeiten
drank [dræŋk] *pt of* **drink**
drape [dreɪp] *vt* drapieren
drapes [dreɪps] (*US*) *npl* Vorhänge *pl*
drastic ['dræstɪk] *adj* drastisch
drastically ['dræstɪklɪ] *adv* drastisch

draught, (US) **draft** [drɑːft] n (Luft)zug m; (Naut) Tiefgang m; (of chimney) Zug m; **on ~** vom Fass

draught beer n Bier nt vom Fass

draughtboard ['drɑːftbɔːd] (Brit) n Damebrett nt

draughts [drɑːfts] (Brit) n Damespiel nt

draughtsman, (US) **draftsman** ['drɑːftsmən] (irreg: like **man**) n Zeichner(in) m(f); (as job) technischer Zeichner m, technische Zeichnerin f

draughtsmanship, (US) **draftsmanship** ['drɑːftsmənʃɪp] n zeichnerisches Können nt; (art) Zeichenkunst f

draw [drɔː] (pt **drew**, pp **~n**) vt zeichnen; (cart, gun, tooth, conclusion) ziehen; (curtain: open) aufziehen; (: close) zuziehen; (admiration, attention) erregen; (money) abheben; (wages) bekommen ▷ vi (Sport) unentschieden spielen ▷ n (Sport) Unentschieden nt; (lottery) Lotterie f; (: picking of ticket) Ziehung f; **to ~ a comparison/distinction (between)** einen Vergleich ziehen/Unterschied machen (zwischen +dat); **to ~ near** näher kommen; (event) nahen; **to ~ to a close** zu Ende gehen
▶ **draw back** vi: **to ~ back (from)** zurückweichen (von)
▶ **draw in** vi (Brit: car) anhalten; (: train) einfahren; (nights) länger werden
▶ **draw on** vt (resources) zurückgreifen auf +acc; (imagination) zu Hilfe nehmen; (person) einsetzen
▶ **draw out** vi länger werden ▷ vt (money) abheben
▶ **draw up** vi (an)halten ▷ vt (chair etc) heranziehen; (document) aufsetzen

drawback ['drɔːbæk] n Nachteil m

drawbridge ['drɔːbrɪdʒ] n Zugbrücke f

drawee [drɔːˈiː] n Bezogene(r) f(m)

drawer [drɔːʳ] n Schublade f

drawing ['drɔːɪŋ] n Zeichnung f; (skill, discipline) Zeichnen nt

drawing board n Reißbrett nt; **back to the ~** (fig) das muss noch einmal neu überdacht werden

drawing pin (Brit) n Reißzwecke f

drawing room n Salon m

drawl [drɔːl] n schleppende Sprechweise f ▷ vi schleppend sprechen

drawn [drɔːn] pp of **draw** ▷ adj abgespannt

drawstring ['drɔːstrɪŋ] n Kordel f zum Zuziehen

dread [dred] n Angst f, Furcht f ▷ vt große Angst haben vor +dat

dreadful ['dredful] adj schrecklich, furchtbar; **I feel ~!** (ill) ich fühle mich schrecklich; (ashamed) es ist mir schrecklich peinlich

dream [driːm] (pt, pp **dreamed** or **~t**) n Traum m ▷ vt, vi träumen; **to have a ~ about sb/sth** von jdm/etw träumen; **sweet ~s!** träume süß!
▶ **dream up** vt sich dat einfallen lassen, sich dat ausdenken

dreamer ['driːməʳ] n Träumer(in) m(f)

dreamt [dremt] pt, pp of **dream**

dream world n Traumwelt f

dreamy ['driːmɪ] adj verträumt; (music) zum Träumen

dreary ['drɪərɪ] adj langweilig; (weather) trüb

dredge [dredʒ] vt ausbaggern
▶ **dredge up** vt ausbaggern; (fig: unpleasant facts) ausgraben

dredger ['dredʒəʳ] n (ship) Schwimmbagger m; (machine) Bagger m; (Brit: also: **sugar dredger**) Zuckerstreuer m

dregs [dregz] npl Bodensatz m; (of humanity) Abschaum m

drench [drentʃ] vt durchnässen; **~ed to the skin** nass bis auf die Haut

dress [dres] n Kleid nt; (no pl: clothing) Kleidung f ▷ vt anziehen; (wound) verbinden ▷ vi sich anziehen; **she ~es very well** sie kleidet sich sehr gut; **to ~ a shop window** ein Schaufenster dekorieren; **to get ~ed** sich anziehen
▶ **dress up** vi sich fein machen; (in fancy dress) sich verkleiden

dress circle (Brit) n (Theat) erster Rang m

dress designer n Modezeichner(in) m(f)

dresser ['dresəʳ] n (Brit) Anrichte f; (US) Kommode f; (also: **window dresser**) Dekorateur(in) m(f)

dressing ['dresɪŋ] n Verband m; (Culin) (Salat) soße f

dressing gown (Brit) n Morgenrock m

dressing room n Umkleidekabine f; (Theat) (Künstler)garderobe f

dressing table n Frisierkommode f

dressmaker ['dresmeɪkəʳ] n (Damen) schneider(in) m(f)

dressmaking ['dresmeɪkɪŋ] n Schneidern nt

dress rehearsal n Generalprobe f

dressy ['dresɪ] (inf) adj elegant

drew [druː] pt of **draw**

dribble ['drɪbl] vi tropfen; (baby) sabbern; (Football) dribbeln ▷ vt (ball) dribbeln mit

dried [draɪd] adj (fruit) getrocknet, Dörr-; **~ egg** Trockenei nt, Eipulver nt; **~ milk** Trockenmilch f, Milchpulver nt

drier ['draɪəʳ] n = **dryer**

drift [drɪft] n Strömung f; (of snow) Schneewehe f; (of questions) Richtung f ▷ vi treiben; (sand) wehen; **to let things ~** die Dinge treiben lassen; **to ~ apart** sich auseinanderleben; **I get or catch your ~** ich verstehe, worauf Sie hinauswollen

drifter ['drɪftəʳ] n: **to be a ~** sich treiben lassen

driftwood ['drɪftwud] n Treibholz nt

drill [drɪl] n Bohrer m; (machine) Bohrmaschine f; (Mil) Drill m ▷ vt bohren; (troops) drillen ▷ vi: **to ~ (for)** bohren (nach); **to ~ pupils in grammar** mit den Schülern Grammatik pauken

drilling ['drɪlɪŋ] n Bohrung f

drilling rig n Bohrturm m; (at sea) Bohrinsel f

drily ['draɪlɪ] adv = **dryly**

drink [drɪŋk] (pt **drank**, pp **drunk**) n Getränk nt;

(*alcoholic*) Glas nt, Drink m; (*sip*) Schluck m ▷ vt,
vi trinken; **to have a ~** etwas trinken; **a ~ of
water** etwas Wasser; **we had ~s before lunch**
vor dem Mittagessen gab es einen Drink;
would you like something to ~? möchten
Sie etwas trinken?
  ▶ **drink in** vt (*fresh air*) einatmen, einsaugen;
(*story, sight*) (begierig) in sich aufnehmen
drinkable ['drɪŋkəbl] adj trinkbar
drink-driving ['drɪŋk'draɪvɪŋ] n Trunkenheit
f am Steuer
drinker ['drɪŋkəʳ] n Trinker(in) m(f)
drinking ['drɪŋkɪŋ] n Trinken nt
drinking fountain n Trinkwasserbrunnen m
drinking water n Trinkwasser nt
drip [drɪp] n Tropfen nt; (*one drip*) Tropfen m;
(*Med*) Tropf m ▷ vi tropfen; (*wall*) triefnass sein
drip-dry ['drɪp'draɪ] adj bügelfrei
drip-feed ['drɪpfiːd] vt künstlich ernähren
  ▷ n: **to be on a ~** künstlich ernährt werden
dripping ['drɪpɪŋ] n Bratenfett nt ▷ adj
triefend; **I'm ~** ich bin klatschnass (*inf*); **~ wet**
triefnass
drive [draɪv] (pt **drove**, pp **~n**) n Fahrt f;
(*also:* **driveway**) Einfahrt f; (*: longer*) Auffahrt
f; (*energy*) Schwung m, Elan m; (*campaign*)
Aktion f; (*Sport*) Treibschlag m; (*Comput: also:*
disk drive) Laufwerk nt ▷ vt fahren; (*Tech*)
antreiben ▷ vi fahren; **to go for a ~** ein
bisschen (raus)fahren; **it's 3 hours' ~ from
London** es ist drei Stunden Fahrt von London
(entfernt); **left-/right-hand ~** Links-/
Rechtssteuerung f; **front-/rear-wheel ~**
Vorderrad-/Hinterradantrieb m; **he ~s a taxi**
er ist Taxifahrer; **to ~ sth into sth** (*nail, stake
etc*) etw in etw schlagen acc; (*animal*) treiben;
(*ball*) weit schlagen; (*incite, encourage: also:* **drive
on**) antreiben; **to ~ sb home/to the airport**
jdn nach Hause/zum Flughafen fahren; **to ~
sb mad** jdn verrückt machen; **to ~ sb to (do)
sth** jdn dazu treiben, etw zu tun; **to ~ at 50
km an hour** mit (einer Geschwindigkeit von)
50 Stundenkilometern fahren; **what are you
driving at?** worauf wollen Sie hinaus?
  ▶ **drive off** vt vertreiben
  ▶ **drive out** vt (*evil spirit*) austreiben; (*person*)
verdrängen
drive-by shooting ['draɪvbaɪ-] n
Schusswaffenangriff aus einem vorbeifahrenden Wagen
drive-in ['draɪvɪn] (*esp US*) adj, n: **~ (cinema)**
Autokino nt; **~ (restaurant)** Autorestaurant nt
drive-in window (*US*) n Autoschalter m
drivel ['drɪvl] (*inf*) n Blödsinn m
driven ['drɪvn] pp of **drive**
driver ['draɪvəʳ] n Fahrer(in) m(f); (*Rail*)
Führer(in) m(f)
driver's license ['draɪvəz-] (*US*) n Führerschein
m
driveway ['draɪvweɪ] n Einfahrt f; (*longer*)
Auffahrt f
driving ['draɪvɪŋ] n Fahren nt ▷ adj: **~ rain**
strömender Regen m; **~ snow** Schneetreiben nt
driving belt n Treibriemen m

driving force n treibende Kraft f
driving instructor n Fahrlehrer(in) m(f)
driving lesson n Fahrstunde f
driving licence (*Brit*) n Führerschein m
driving mirror n Rückspiegel m
driving school n Fahrschule f
driving test n Fahrprüfung f
drizzle ['drɪzl] n Nieselregen m ▷ vi nieseln
droll [drəʊl] adj drollig
dromedary ['drɒmədərɪ] n Dromedar nt
drone [drəʊn] n Brummen nt; (*male bee*)
Drohne f ▷ vi brummen; (*bee*) summen;
(*also:* **drone on**) eintönig sprechen
drool [druːl] vi sabbern; **to ~ over sth/sb** etw/
jdn sehnsüchtig anstarren
droop [druːp] vi (*flower*) den Kopf hängen
lassen; **his shoulders/head ~ed** er ließ die
Schultern/den Kopf herabhängen
drop [drɒp] n Tropfen m; (*lessening*) Rückgang
m; (*distance*) Höhenunterschied m; (*in salary*)
Verschlechterung f; (*also:* **parachute drop**)
(Ab)sprung m ▷ vt fallen lassen; (*voice, eyes,
price*) senken; (*set down from car*) absetzen;
(*omit*) weglassen ▷ vi (herunter)fallen; (*wind*)
sich legen; **drops** npl Tropfen pl; **a 300 ft
~** ein Höhenunterschied von 300 Fuß; **a ~
of 10%** ein Rückgang um 10%; **cough ~s**
Hustentropfen pl; **to ~ anchor** ankern, vor
Anker gehen; **to ~ sb a line** jdm ein paar
Zeilen schreiben
  ▶ **drop in** (*inf*) vi: **to ~ in (on sb)** (bei jdm)
vorbeikommen
  ▶ **drop off** vi einschlafen ▷ vt (*passenger*)
absetzen
  ▶ **drop out** vi (*withdraw*) ausscheiden; (*student*)
sein Studium abbrechen
droplet ['drɒplɪt] n Tröpfchen nt
dropout ['drɒpaʊt] n Aussteiger(in) m(f); (*Scol*)
Studienabbrecher(in) m(f)
dropper ['drɒpəʳ] n Pipette f
droppings ['drɒpɪŋz] npl Kot m
dross [drɒs] n Schlacke f; (*fig*) Schund m
drought [draʊt] n Dürre f
drove [drəʊv] pt of **drive** ▷ n: **~s of people**
Scharen pl von Menschen
drown [draʊn] vt ertränken; (*fig: also:* **drown
out**) übertönen ▷ vi ertrinken
drowse [draʊz] vi (vor sich acc hin) dösen or
dämmern
drowsy ['draʊzɪ] adj schläfrig
drudge [drʌdʒ] n Arbeitstier nt
drudgery ['drʌdʒərɪ] n (stumpfsinnige)
Plackerei f (*inf*); **housework is sheer ~**
Hausarbeit ist eine einzige Plackerei
drug [drʌg] n Medikament nt, Arzneimittel nt;
(*narcotic*) Droge f, Rauschgift nt ▷ vt betäuben;
to be on ~s drogensüchtig sein; **hard/soft ~s**
harte/weiche Drogen pl
drug abuse n Drogenmissbrauch m; **~
prevention** Drogenprävention f
drug addict n Drogensüchtige(r) f(m),
Rauschgiftsüchtige(r) f(m)
druggist ['drʌgɪst] (*US*) n Drogist(in) m(f)

drug peddler n Drogenhändler(in) m(f), Dealer m (inf)

drugstore ['drʌgstɔːʳ] (US) n Drogerie f

drum [drʌm] n Trommel f; (for oil, petrol) Fass nt
▷ vi trommeln; **drums** npl (kit) Schlagzeug nt
▶ **drum up** vt (enthusiasm) erwecken; (support) auftreiben

drummer ['drʌməʳ] n Trommler(in) m(f); (in band, pop group) Schlagzeuger(in) m(f)

drum roll n Trommelwirbel m

drumstick ['drʌmstɪk] n Trommelstock m; (of chicken) Keule f

drunk [drʌŋk] pp of **drink** ▷ adj betrunken ▷ n (also: **drunkard**) Trinker(in) m(f); **to get ~** sich betrinken; **a ~ driving offence** Trunkenheit f am Steuer

drunken ['drʌŋkən] adj betrunken; (party) feucht-fröhlich; **~ driving** Trunkenheit f am Steuer

drunkenness ['drʌŋkənnɪs] n (state) Betrunkenheit f; (habit) Trunksucht f

dry [draɪ] adj trocken ▷ vt, vi trocknen; **on ~ land** auf festem Boden; **to ~ one's hands/ hair/eyes** sich dat die Hände (ab)trocknen/die Haare trocknen/die Tränen abwischen; **to ~ the dishes** (das Geschirr) abtrocknen
▶ **dry up** vi austrocknen; (in speech) den Faden verlieren

dry-clean ['draɪ'kliːn] vt chemisch reinigen

dry-cleaner ['draɪ'kliːnəʳ] n (job) Inhaber(in) m(f) einer chemischen Reinigung; (shop: also: **dry-cleaner's**) chemische Reinigung f

dry-cleaning ['draɪ'kliːnɪŋ] n (process) chemische Reinigung f

dry dock n Trockendock nt

dryer ['draɪəʳ] n Wäschetrockner m; (US: spin-dryer) Wäscheschleuder f

dry goods npl Kurzwaren pl

dry ice n Trockeneis nt

dryly ['draɪlɪ] adv (say, remark) trocken

dryness ['draɪnɪs] n Trockenheit f

dry rot n (Haus)schwamm m, (Holz)schwamm m

dry run n (fig) Probe f

dry ski slope n Trockenskipiste f

DSc n abbr (= Doctor of Science) ≈ Dr. rer. nat.

DSL n abbr (Comput: = digital subscriber line) DSL

DSL connection n (Comput) DSL-Anschluss m

DSS (Brit) n abbr (= Department of Social Security) Ministerium für Sozialfürsorge

DST abbr = **daylight-saving time**

DTI (Brit) n abbr (= Department of Trade and Industry) ≈ Wirtschaftsministerium nt

DTP n abbr (= desktop publishing) DTP nt; see also **desktop publishing**; (= diphtheria, tetanus, pertussis) Diphtherie, Tetanus und Keuchhusten

DT's (inf) npl abbr (= delirium tremens) Delirium tremens nt; **to have the ~** vom Trinken den Tatterich haben (inf)

dual ['djuəl] adj doppelt; (personality) gespalten

dual carriageway (Brit) n ≈ Schnellstraße f

dual nationality n doppelte

Staatsangehörigkeit f

dual-purpose ['djuəl'pəːpəs] adj zweifach verwendbar

dubbed [dʌbd] adj synchronisiert; (nicknamed) getauft

dubious ['djuːbɪəs] adj zweifelhaft; **I'm very ~ about it** ich habe da (doch) starke Zweifel

Dublin ['dʌblɪn] n Dublin nt

Dubliner ['dʌblɪnəʳ] n Dubliner(in) m(f)

duchess ['dʌtʃɪs] n Herzogin f

duck [dʌk] n Ente f ▷ vi (also: **duck down**) sich ducken ▷ vt (blow) ausweichen +dat; (duty, responsibility) aus dem Weg gehen +dat

duckling ['dʌklɪŋ] n Entenküken nt; (Culin) (junge) Ente f

duct [dʌkt] n Rohr nt; (Anat) Röhre f; **tear ~** Tränenkanal m

dud [dʌd] n Niete f (inf); (note) Blüte f (inf)
▷ adj: **~ cheque** (Brit) ungedeckter Scheck m

due [djuː] adj fällig; (attention etc) gebührend; (consideration) reichlich ▷ n: **to give sb his/her ~** jdn gerecht behandeln ▷ adv: **~ north** direkt nach Norden; **dues** npl Beitrag m; (in harbour) Gebühren pl; **in ~ course** zu gegebener Zeit; (eventually) im Laufe der Zeit; **~ to** (owing to) wegen +gen, aufgrund +gen; **to be ~ to do sth** etw tun sollen; **the rent is ~ on the 30th** die Miete ist am 30. fällig; **the train is ~ at 8** der Zug soll (laut Fahrplan) um 8 ankommen; **she is ~ back tomorrow** sie müsste morgen zurück sein; **I am ~ 6 days' leave** mir stehen 6 Tage Urlaub zu

due date n Fälligkeitsdatum nt

duel ['djuəl] n Duell nt

duet [djuː'ɛt] n Duett nt

duff [dʌf] (Brit: inf) adj kaputt
▶ **duff up** vt vermöbeln

duffel bag ['dʌfl-] n Matchbeutel m

duffel coat n Dufflecoat m

duffer ['dʌfəʳ] (inf) n Versager m, Flasche f

dug [dʌg] pt, pp of **dig**

dugout ['dʌgaut] n (canoe) Einbaum m; (shelter) Unterstand m

duke [djuːk] n Herzog m

dull [dʌl] adj trüb; (intelligence, wit) schwerfällig, langsam; (event) langweilig; (sound, pain) dumpf ▷ vt (pain, grief) betäuben; (mind, senses) abstumpfen

duly ['djuːlɪ] adv (properly) gebührend; (on time) pünktlich

dumb [dʌm] adj stumm; (pej: stupid) dumm, doof (inf); **he was struck ~** es verschlug ihm die Sprache
▶ **dumb down** vi an Niveau or Qualität verlieren, verflachen ▷ vt fus verdummen, dumm machen

dumbbell ['dʌmbɛl] n Hantel f

dumbfounded [dʌm'faundɪd] adj verblüfft

dumbing down [dʌmɪŋ'daun] n Verdummung f, Qualitätsverlust m

dummy ['dʌmɪ] n (Schneider)puppe f; (mock-up) Attrappe f; (Sport) Finte f; (Brit: for baby) Schnuller m ▷ adj (firm) fiktiv; **~ bullets**

Übungsmunition f

dummy run n Probe f

dump [dʌmp] n (also: **rubbish dump**)
Abfallhaufen m; (inf: place) Müllkippe f; (Mil)
Depot nt ▷ vt fallen lassen; (get rid of) abladen;
(car) abstellen; (Comput: data) ausgeben; **to be
down in the ~s** (inf) deprimiert or down sein;
"no ~ing" „Schuttabladen verboten"

dumpling ['dʌmplɪŋ] n Kloß m, Knödel m

dumpy ['dʌmpɪ] adj pummelig

dunce [dʌns] n Niete f

dune [djuːn] n Düne f

dung [dʌŋ] n (Agr) Dünger m, Mist m; (Zool)
Dung m

dungarees [dʌŋgə'riːz] npl Latzhose f

dungeon ['dʌndʒən] n Kerker m, Verlies nt

dunk [dʌŋk] vt (ein)tunken

Dunkirk [dʌn'kəːk] n Dünkirchen nt

duo ['djuːəʊ] n Duo nt

duodenal [djuːəʊ'diːnl] adj Duodenal-; **~ ulcer**
Zwölffingerdarmgeschwür nt

duodenum [djuːəʊ'diːnəm] n
Zwölffingerdarm m

dupe [djuːp] n Betrogene(r) f(m) ▷ vt betrügen

duplex ['djuːplɛks] (US) n Zweifamilienhaus
nt; (apartment) zweistöckige Wohnung f

duplicate [n, adj 'djuːplɪkət, vt 'djuːplɪkeɪt] n
(also: **duplicate copy**) Duplikat nt, Kopie f;
(also: **duplicate key**) Zweitschlüssel m ▷ adj
doppelt ▷ vt kopieren; (repeat) wiederholen; **in
~** in doppelter Ausfertigung

duplicating machine ['djuːplɪkeɪtɪŋ-] n
Vervielfältigungsapparat m

duplicator ['djuːplɪkeɪtə'] n
Vervielfältigungsapparat m

duplicity [djuː'plɪsɪtɪ] n Doppelspiel nt

Dur. (Brit) abbr (Post) = Durham

durability [djʊərə'bɪlɪtɪ] n Haltbarkeit f

durable ['djʊərəbl] adj haltbar

duration [djʊə'reɪʃən] n Dauer f

duress [djʊə'rɛs] n: **under ~** unter Zwang

Durex® ['djʊərɛks] (Brit) n Gummi m (inf)

during ['djʊərɪŋ] prep während +gen

dusk [dʌsk] n (Abend)dämmerung f

dusky ['dʌskɪ] adj (room) dunkel; (light)
Dämmer-

dust [dʌst] n Staub m ▷ vt abstauben; (cake
etc): **to ~ with** bestäuben mit
▶ **dust off** vt abwischen, wegwischen; (fig)
hervorkramen

dustbin ['dʌstbɪn] (Brit) n Mülltonne f

dustbin liner (Brit) n Müllsack m

duster ['dʌstə'] n Staubtuch nt

dust jacket n (Schutz)umschlag m

dustman ['dʌstmən] (Brit: irreg: like **man**) n
Müllmann m

dustpan ['dʌstpæn] n Kehrschaufel f,
Müllschaufel f

dusty ['dʌstɪ] adj staubig

Dutch [dʌtʃ] adj holländisch, niederländisch
▷ n Holländisch nt, Niederländisch nt ▷ adv: **to
go ~** (inf) getrennte Kasse machen; **the Dutch**
npl die Holländer pl, die Niederländer pl

Dutch auction n Versteigerung mit stufenweise
erniedrigtem Ausbietungspreis

Dutchman ['dʌtʃmən] (irreg: like **man**) n
Holländer m, Niederländer m

Dutchwoman ['dʌtʃwʊmən] (irreg: like **woman**)
n Holländerin f, Niederländerin f

dutiable ['djuːtɪəbl] adj zollpflichtig

dutiful ['djuːtɪful] adj pflichtbewusst; (son,
daughter) gehorsam

duty ['djuːtɪ] n Pflicht f; (tax) Zoll m; **duties** npl
(functions) Aufgaben pl; **to make it one's ~ to
do sth** es sich dat zur Pflicht machen, etw zu
tun; **to pay ~ on sth** Zoll auf etw acc zahlen;
on/off ~ im/nicht im Dienst

duty-free ['djuːtɪ'friː] adj zollfrei; **~ shop**
Dutyfreeshop m, Duty-free-Shop m

duty officer n Offizier m vom Dienst

duvet ['djuːveɪ] (Brit) n Federbett nt

DV abbr (= Deo volente) so Gott will

DVD n abbr (= digital versatile or video disc)
DVD f

DVLA (Brit) n abbr (= Driver and Vehicle Licensing
Authority) Zulassungsbehörde für Kraftfahrzeuge

DVM (US) n abbr (= Doctor of Veterinary Medicine) =
Dr. med. vet.

dwarf [dwɔːf] (pl **dwarves**) n Zwerg(in) m(f)
▷ vt: **to be ~ed by sth** neben etw dat klein
erscheinen

dwarves [dwɔːvz] npl of **dwarf**

dwell [dwɛl] (pt, pp **dwelt**) vi wohnen, leben
▶ **dwell on** vt fus (in Gedanken) verweilen bei

dweller ['dwɛlə'] n Bewohner(in) m(f); **city ~**
Stadtbewohner(in) m(f)

dwelling ['dwɛlɪŋ] n Wohnhaus nt

dwelt [dwɛlt] pt, pp of **dwell**

dwindle ['dwɪndl] vi abnehmen; (interest)
schwinden; (attendance) zurückgehen

dwindling ['dwɪndlɪŋ] adj (strength, interest)
schwindend; (resources, supplies) versiegend

dye [daɪ] n Farbstoff m; (for hair) Färbemittel nt
▷ vt färben

dyestuffs ['daɪstʌfs] npl Farbstoffe pl

dying ['daɪɪŋ] adj sterbend; (moments, words)
letzte(r, s)

dyke [daɪk] n (Brit: wall) Deich m, Damm m;
(channel) (Entwässerungs)graben m; (causeway)
Fahrdamm m

dynamic [daɪ'næmɪk] adj dynamisch

dynamics [daɪ'næmɪks] n or npl Dynamik f

dynamite ['daɪnəmaɪt] n Dynamit nt ▷ vt
sprengen

dynamo ['daɪnəməʊ] n Dynamo m; (Aut)
Lichtmaschine f

dynasty ['dɪnəstɪ] n Dynastie f

dysentery ['dɪsntrɪ] n (Med) Ruhr f

dyslexia [dɪs'lɛksɪə] n Legasthenie f

dyslexic [dɪs'lɛksɪk] adj legasthenisch ▷ n
Legastheniker(in) m(f)

dyspepsia [dɪs'pɛpsɪə] n Dyspepsie f,
Verdauungsstörung f

dystrophy ['dɪstrəfɪ] n Dystrophie f,
Ernährungsstörung f; **muscular ~**
Muskelschwund m

Ee

E¹, e [iː] n (letter) E nt, e nt; **E for Edward, E for Easy** (US) E wie Emil
E² [iː] n (Mus) E nt, e nt
E³ [iː] abbr (= east) O ▷ n abbr (drug: = Ecstasy) Ecstasy nt
e- pref E-, elektronisch
E111 n abbr (also: **form E111**) E111-Formular nt
ea. abbr = **each**
each [iːtʃ] adj, pron jede(r, s); **~ other** sich, einander; **they hate ~ other** sie hassen sich or einander; **you are jealous of ~ other** ihr seid eifersüchtig aufeinander; **~ day** jeden Tag; **they have 2 books ~** sie haben je 2 Bücher; **they cost £5 ~** sie kosten 5 Pfund das Stück; **~ of us** jede(r, s) von uns
eager ['iːɡəʳ] adj eifrig; **to be ~ to do sth** etw unbedingt tun wollen; **to be ~ for sth** auf etw acc erpicht or aus (inf) sein
eagerly ['iːɡəlɪ] adv eifrig; (awaited) gespannt, ungeduldig
eagle ['iːɡl] n Adler m
ear [ɪəʳ] n Ohr nt; (of corn) Ähre f; **to be up to one's ~s in debt/work** bis über beide Ohren in Schulden/Arbeit stecken; **to be up to one's ~s in paint/baking** mitten im Anstreichen/Backen stecken; **to give sb a thick ~** jdm ein paar hinter die Ohren geben; **we'll play it by ~** (fig) wir werden es auf uns zukommen lassen
earache ['ɪəreɪk] n Ohrenschmerzen pl
eardrum ['ɪədrʌm] n Trommelfell nt
earful ['ɪəful] (inf) n: **to give sb an ~** jdm was erzählen; **to get an ~** was zu hören bekommen
earl [əːl] (Brit) n Graf m
earlier ['əːlɪəʳ] adj, adv früher; **I can't come any ~** ich kann nicht früher or eher kommen
early ['əːlɪ] adv früh; (ahead of time) zu früh ▷ adj früh; (Christians) Ur-; (death, departure) vorzeitig; (reply) baldig; **~ in the morning** früh am Morgen; **to have an ~ night** früh ins Bett gehen; **in the ~ hours** in den frühen Morgenstunden; **in the ~** or **~ in the spring/19th century** Anfang des Frühjahrs/des 19. Jahrhunderts; **take the ~ train** nimm den früheren Zug; **you're ~!** Sie sind früh dran!; **she's in her ~ forties** sie ist Anfang Vierzig; **at your earliest convenience** so

bald wie möglich
early retirement n: **to take ~** vorzeitig in den Ruhestand gehen
early retirement benefits npl Vorruhestandsleistungen pl
early warning system n Frühwarnsystem nt
earmark ['ɪəmaːk] vt: **to ~ (for)** bestimmen (für), vorsehen (für)
earn [əːn] vt verdienen; (interest) bringen; **to ~ one's living** seinen Lebensunterhalt verdienen; **this ~ed him much praise, he ~ed much praise for this** das trug ihm viel Lob ein; **he's ~ed his rest/reward** er hat sich seine Pause/Belohnung verdient
earned income [əːnd-] n Arbeitseinkommen nt
earnest ['əːnɪst] adj ernsthaft; (wish, desire) innig ▷ n (also: **earnest money**) Angeld nt; **in ~** (adv) richtig; (adj): **to be in ~** es ernst meinen; **work on the tunnel soon began in ~** die Tunnelarbeiten begannen bald richtig; **is the Minister in ~ about these proposals?** meint der Minister diese Vorschläge ernst?
earnings ['əːnɪŋz] npl Verdienst m; (of company etc) Ertrag m
ear, nose and throat specialist n Hals-Nasen-Ohren-Arzt m, Hals-Nasen-Ohren-Ärztin f
earphones ['ɪəfəunz] npl Kopfhörer pl
earplugs ['ɪəplʌɡz] npl Ohropax® nt
earring ['ɪərɪŋ] n Ohrring m
earset ['ɪəset] n (Tel) Earset nt, Ohrhörer m
earshot ['ɪəʃɒt] n: **within/out of ~** in/außer Hörweite
earth [əːθ] n Erde f; (of fox) Bau m ▷ vt (Brit: Elec) erden
earthenware ['əːθnwɛəʳ] n Tongeschirr nt ▷ adj Ton-
earthly ['əːθlɪ] adj irdisch; **~ paradise** Paradies nt auf Erden; **there is no ~ reason to think** … es besteht nicht der geringste Grund für die Annahme …
earthquake ['əːθkweɪk] n Erdbeben nt
earthshattering ['əːθʃætərɪŋ] adj (fig) weltbewegend
earth tremor n Erdstoß m
earthworks ['əːθwəːks] npl Erdarbeiten pl
earthworm ['əːθwəːm] n Regenwurm m

earthy [ˈəːθɪ] *adj* (*humour*) derb

earwig [ˈɪəwɪɡ] *n* Ohrwurm *m*

ease [iːz] *n* Leichtigkeit *f*; (*comfort*) Behagen *nt* ▷ *vt* (*problem*) vereinfachen; (*pain*) lindern; (*tension*) verringern; (*loosen*) lockern ▷ *vi* nachlassen; (*situation*) sich entspannen; **to ~ sth in/out** (*push/pull*) etw behutsam hineinschieben/herausziehen; **at ~!** (*Mil*) rührt euch!; **with ~** mit Leichtigkeit; **life of ~** Leben *nt* der Muße; **to ~ in the clutch** die Kupplung behutsam kommen lassen
  ▸ **ease off** *vi* nachlassen; (*slow down*) langsamer werden
  ▸ **ease up** *vi* = **ease off**

easel [ˈiːzl] *n* Staffelei *f*

easily [ˈiːzɪlɪ] *adv* (*see adj*) leicht; ungezwungen; bequem

easiness [ˈiːzɪnɪs] *n* Leichtigkeit *f*; (*of manner*) Ungezwungenheit *f*

east [iːst] *n* Osten *m* ▷ *adj* (*coast, Asia etc*) Ost- ▷ *adv* ostwärts, nach Osten; **the E~** der Osten

Easter [ˈiːstər] *n* Ostern *nt* ▷ *adj* (*holidays etc*) Oster-

Easter egg *n* Osterei *nt*

Easter Island *n* Osterinsel *f*

easterly [ˈiːstəlɪ] *adj* östlich; (*wind*) Ost-

Easter Monday *n* Ostermontag *m*

eastern [ˈiːstən] *adj* östlich; **E~ Europe** Osteuropa *nt*; **the E~ bloc** (*formerly*) der Ostblock

Easter Sunday *n* Ostersonntag *m*

East Germany *n* (*formerly*) die DDR *f*

eastward [ˈiːstwəd], **eastwards** [ˈiːstwədz] *adv* ostwärts, nach Osten

easy [ˈiːzɪ] *adj* leicht; (*relaxed*) ungezwungen; (*comfortable*) bequem ▷ *adv*: **to take it/things ~** (*go slowly*) sich *dat* Zeit lassen; (*not worry*) es nicht so schwernehmen; (*rest*) sich schonen; **payment on ~ terms** Zahlung zu günstigen Bedingungen; **that's easier said than done** das ist leichter gesagt als getan; **I'm ~** (*inf*) mir ist alles recht

easy chair *n* Sessel *m*

easy-going [ˈiːzɪˈɡəʊɪŋ] *adj* gelassen

easy touch (*inf*) *n*: **to be an ~** (*for money etc*) leicht anzuzapfen sein

eat [iːt] (*pt* **ate**, *pp* **~en**) *vt, vi* essen; (*animal*) fressen
  ▸ **eat away** *vt* (*subj: sea*) auswaschen; (: *acid*) zerfressen
  ▸ **eat away at** *vt fus* (*metal*) anfressen; (*savings*) angreifen
  ▸ **eat into** *vt fus* = **eat away at**
  ▸ **eat out** *vi* essen gehen
  ▸ **eat up** *vt* aufessen; **it ~s up electricity** es verbraucht viel Strom

eatable [ˈiːtəbl] *adj* genießbar

eau de Cologne [ˈəʊdəkəˈləʊn] *n* Kölnischwasser *nt*, Eau de Cologne *nt*

eaves [iːvz] *npl* Dachvorsprung *m*

eavesdrop [ˈiːvzdrɒp] *vi* lauschen; **to ~ on** belauschen +*acc*

ebb [ɛb] *n* Ebbe *f* ▷ *vi* ebben; (*fig: also*: **ebb away**) dahinschwinden; (: *feeling*) abebben; **the ~ and flow** (*fig*) das Auf und Ab; **to be at a low ~** (*fig*) auf einem Tiefpunkt angelangt sein

ebb tide *n* Ebbe *f*

ebony [ˈɛbənɪ] *n* Ebenholz *nt*

ebullient [ɪˈbʌlɪənt] *adj* überschäumend, übersprudelnd

EC *n abbr* (= *European Community*) EG *f*

e-card [ˈiːkɑːd] *n abbr* (= *electronic card*) E-Card *nt*, elektronische Grußkarte

ECB *n abbr* (= *European Central Bank*) EZB *f*

eccentric [ɪkˈsɛntrɪk] *adj* exzentrisch ▷ *n* Exzentriker(in) *m(f)*

ecclesiastic [ɪkliːzɪˈæstɪk], **ecclesiastical** [ɪkliːzɪˈæstɪkl] *adj* kirchlich

ECG *n abbr* (= *electrocardiogram*) EKG *nt*

echo [ˈɛkəʊ] (*pl* **~es**) *n* Echo *nt* ▷ *vt* wiederholen ▷ *vi* widerhallen; (*place*) hallen

éclair [eɪˈklɛər] *n* Eclair *nt*

eclipse [ɪˈklɪps] *n* Finsternis *f* ▷ *vt* in den Schatten stellen

eco- [ˈiːkəʊ] *pref* Öko-, öko-

ecofriendly *adj* umweltfreundlich

ecological [iːkəˈlɒdʒɪkəl] *adj* ökologisch; (*damage, disaster*) Umwelt-

ecologist [ɪˈkɒlədʒɪst] *n* Ökologe *m*, Ökologin *f*

ecology [ɪˈkɒlədʒɪ] *n* Ökologie *f*

e-commerce [iːˈkɒmɜːs] *n* E-Commerce *nt*, elektronischer Handel

economic [iːkəˈnɒmɪk] *adj* (*system, policy etc*) Wirtschafts-; (*profitable*) wirtschaftlich

economical [iːkəˈnɒmɪkl] *adj* wirtschaftlich; (*person*) sparsam

economically [iːkəˈnɒmɪklɪ] *adv* wirtschaftlich; (*thriftily*) sparsam

economics [iːkəˈnɒmɪks] *n* Wirtschaftswissenschaften *pl* ▷ *npl* Wirtschaftlichkeit *f*; (*of situation*) wirtschaftliche Seite *f*

economist [ɪˈkɒnəmɪst] *n* Wirtschaftswissenschaftler(in) *m(f)*

economize [ɪˈkɒnəmaɪz] *vi* sparen

economy [ɪˈkɒnəmɪ] *n* Wirtschaft *f*; (*financial prudence*) Sparsamkeit *f*; **economies of scale** (*Comm*) Einsparungen *pl* durch erhöhte Produktion

economy class *n* Touristenklasse *f*

economy size *n* Sparpackung *f*

ecosystem [ˈiːkəʊsɪstəm] *n* Ökosystem *nt*

ecotourism [ˈiːkəʊtʊərɪzm] *n* Ökotourismus *m*

ECSC *n abbr* (= *European Coal and Steel Community*) Europäische Gemeinschaft für Kohle und Stahl

ecstasy [ˈɛkstəsɪ] *n* Ekstase *f*; (*drug*) Ecstasy *nt*; **to go into ecstasies over** in Verzückung geraten über +*acc*; **in ~** verzückt

ecstatic [ɛksˈtætɪk] *adj* ekstatisch

ECT *n abbr* = **electroconvulsive therapy**

Ecuador [ˈɛkwədɔːr] *n* Ecuador *nt*, Ekuador *nt*

ecumenical [iːkjuˈmɛnɪkl] *adj* ökumenisch

eczema [ˈɛksɪmə] *n* Ekzem *nt*

eddy [ˈɛdɪ] *n* Strudel *m*

edge [ɛdʒ] *n* Rand *m*; (*of table, chair*) Kante *f*; (*of lake*) Ufer *nt*; (*of knife etc*) Schneide *f* ▷ *vt* einfassen ▷ *vi*: **to ~ forward** sich nach vorne schieben; **on ~** (*fig*) = **edgy; to have the ~ on** überlegen sein +*dat*; **to ~ away from** sich allmählich entfernen von; **to ~ past** sich vorbeischieben, sich vorbeidrücken

edgeways ['ɛdʒweɪz] *adv*: **he couldn't get a word in ~** er kam überhaupt nicht zu Wort

edging ['ɛdʒɪŋ] *n* Einfassung *f*

edgy ['ɛdʒɪ] *adj* nervös

edible ['ɛdɪbl] *adj* essbar, genießbar

edict ['iːdɪkt] *n* Erlass *m*

edifice ['ɛdɪfɪs] *n* Gebäude *nt*

edifying ['ɛdɪfaɪɪŋ] *adj* erbaulich

Edinburgh ['ɛdɪnbərə] *n* Edinburg(h) *nt*

edit ['ɛdɪt] *vt* (*text*) redigieren; (*book*) lektorieren; (*film, broadcast*) schneiden, cutten; (*newspaper, magazine*) herausgeben; (*Comput*) editieren

edition [ɪ'dɪʃən] *n* Ausgabe *f*

editor ['ɛdɪtə'] *n* Redakteur(in) *m(f)*; (*of newspaper, magazine*) Herausgeber(in) *m(f)*; (*of book*) Lektor(in) *m(f)*; (*Cine, Radio, TV*) Cutter(in) *m(f)*

editorial [ɛdɪ'tɔːrɪəl] *adj* redaktionell; (*staff*) Redaktions- ▷ *n* Leitartikel *m*

EDP *n abbr* (*Comput*: = *electronic data processing*) EDV *f*

EDT (*US*) *abbr* (= *Eastern Daylight Time*) ostamerikanische Sommerzeit

educate ['ɛdjukeɪt] *vt* erziehen; **~d at ...** zur Schule/Universität gegangen in ...

educated ['ɛdjukeɪtɪd] *adj* gebildet

educated guess ['ɛdjukeɪtɪd-] *n* wohl begründete Vermutung *f*

education [ɛdju'keɪʃən] *n* Erziehung *f*; (*schooling*) Ausbildung *f*; (*knowledge, culture*) Bildung *f*; **primary ~, elementary ~** (*US*) Grundschul(aus)bildung *f*; **secondary ~** höhere Schul(aus)bildung *f*

educational [ɛdju'keɪʃənl] *adj* pädagogisch; (*experience*) lehrreich; (*toy*) pädagogisch wertvoll; **~ technology** Unterrichtstechnologie *f*

Edwardian [ɛd'wɔːdɪən] *adj* aus der Zeit Edwards VII

EE *abbr* = **electrical engineer**

EEG *n abbr* (= *electroencephalogram*) EEG *nt*

eel [iːl] *n* Aal *m*

EEOC (*US*) *n abbr* (= *Equal Employment Opportunity Commission*) Kommission für Gleichberechtigung am Arbeitsplatz

eerie ['ɪərɪ] *adj* unheimlich

EET *abbr* (= *Eastern European Time*) OEZ *f*

efface [ɪ'feɪs] *vt* auslöschen; **to ~ o.s.** sich im Hintergrund halten

effect [ɪ'fɛkt] *n* Wirkung *f*, Effekt *m* ▷ *vt* bewirken; (*repairs*) durchführen; **effects** *npl* Effekten *pl*; (*Theat, Cine etc*) Effekte *pl*; **to take ~** (*law*) in Kraft treten; (*drug*) wirken; **to put into ~** in Kraft setzen; **to have an ~ on sb/ sth** eine Wirkung auf jdn/etw haben; **in ~** eigentlich, praktisch; **his letter is to the ~ that ...** sein Brief hat zum Inhalt, dass ...

effective [ɪ'fɛktɪv] *adj* effektiv, wirksam; (*actual*) eigentlich, wirklich; **to become ~** in Kraft treten; **~ date** Zeitpunkt *m* des Inkrafttretens

effectively [ɪ'fɛktɪvlɪ] *adv* effektiv

effectiveness [ɪ'fɛktɪvnɪs] *n* Wirksamkeit *f*, Effektivität *f*

effeminate [ɪ'fɛmɪnɪt] *adj* feminin, effeminiert

effervescent [ɛfə'vɛsnt] *adj* sprudelnd

efficacy ['ɛfɪkəsɪ] *n* Wirksamkeit *f*

efficiency [ɪ'fɪʃənsɪ] *n* (*see adj*) Fähigkeit *f*, Tüchtigkeit *f*; Rationalität *f*; Leistungsfähigkeit *f*

efficiency apartment (*US*) *n* Einzimmerwohnung *f*

efficient [ɪ'fɪʃənt] *adj* fähig, tüchtig; (*organization*) rationell; (*machine*) leistungsfähig

efficiently [ɪ'fɪʃəntlɪ] *adv* gut, effizient

effigy ['ɛfɪdʒɪ] *n* Bildnis *nt*

effluent ['ɛfluənt] *n* Abwasser *nt*

effort ['ɛfət] *n* Anstrengung *f*; (*attempt*) Versuch *m*; **to make an ~ to do sth** sich bemühen, etw zu tun

effortless ['ɛfətlɪs] *adj* mühelos; (*style*) flüssig

effrontery [ɪ'frʌntərɪ] *n* Unverschämtheit *f*; **to have the ~ to do sth** die Frechheit besitzen, etw zu tun

effusive [ɪ'fjuːsɪv] *adj* überschwänglich

EFL *n abbr* (*Scol*: = *English as a Foreign Language*) Englisch *nt* als Fremdsprache

EFTA ['ɛftə] *n abbr* (= *European Free Trade Association*) EFTA *f*

e.g. *adv abbr* (= *exempli gratia*) z. B.

egalitarian [ɪgælɪ'tɛərɪən] *adj* egalitär; (*principles*) Gleichheits- ▷ *n* Verfechter(in) *m(f)* des Egalitarismus

egg [ɛg] *n* Ei *nt*; **hard-boiled/soft-boiled ~** hart/weich gekochtes Ei *nt*
  ▶ **egg on** *vt* anstacheln

egg cup *n* Eierbecher *m*

eggplant ['ɛgplɑːnt] *n* (*esp US*) Aubergine *f*

eggshell ['ɛgʃel] *n* Eierschale *f* ▷ *adj* eierschalenfarben

egg timer *n* Eieruhr *f*

egg white *n* Eiweiß *nt*

egg yolk *n* Eigelb *nt*

ego ['iːgəu] *n* (*self-esteem*) Selbstbewusstsein *nt*

egoism ['ɛgəuɪzəm] *n* Egoismus *m*

egoist ['ɛgəuɪst] *n* Egoist(in) *m(f)*

egotism ['ɛgəutɪzəm] *n* Ichbezogenheit *f*, Egotismus *m*

egotist ['ɛgəutɪst] *n* ichbezogener Mensch *m*, Egotist(in) *m(f)*

ego trip (*inf*) *n* Egotrip *m*

Egypt ['iːdʒɪpt] *n* Ägypten *nt*

Egyptian [ɪ'dʒɪpʃən] *adj* ägyptisch ▷ *n* Ägypter(in) *m(f)*

eiderdown ['aɪdədaun] *n* Federbett *nt*, Daunendecke *f*

eight [eɪt] *num* acht

eighteen [eɪ'tiːn] *num* achtzehn

eighteenth [eɪ'tiːnθ] *num* achtzehnte(r, s)

eighth [eɪtθ] num achte(r, s) ▷ n Achtel nt

eighty ['eɪtɪ] num achtzig

Eire ['eərə] n (Republik f) Irland nt

EIS n abbr (= Educational Institute of Scotland) schottische Lehrergewerkschaft

either ['aɪðə'] adj (one or other) eine(r, s) (von beiden); (both, each) beide pl, jede(r, s) ▷ pron: ~ **(of them)** eine(r, s) (davon) ▷ adv auch nicht ▷ conj: ~ **yes or no** entweder ja oder nein; **on ~ side** (on both sides) auf beiden Seiten; (on one or other side) auf einer der beiden Seiten; **I don't like ~** ich mag beide nicht or keinen von beiden; **no, I don't ~** nein, ich auch nicht; **I haven't seen ~ one or the other** ich habe weder den einen noch den anderen gesehen

ejaculation [ɪdʒækjuˈleɪʃən] n Ejakulation f, Samenerguss m

eject [ɪˈdʒɛkt] vt ausstoßen; (tenant, gatecrasher) hinauswerfen ▷ vi den Schleudersitz betätigen

ejector seat [ɪˈdʒɛktə-] n Schleudersitz m

eke out vt (make last) strecken

EKG (US) n abbr = **electrocardiogram**

el [ɛl] (US: inf) n abbr = **elevated railroad**

elaborate [adj ɪˈlæbərɪt, vb ɪˈlæbəreɪt] adj kompliziert; (plan) ausgefeilt ▷ vt näher ausführen; (refine) ausarbeiten ▷ vi mehr ins Detail gehen; **to ~ on** näher ausführen

elapse [ɪˈlæps] vi vergehen, verstreichen

elastic [ɪˈlæstɪk] n Gummi nt ▷ adj elastisch

elastic band (Brit) n Gummiband nt

elasticity [ɪlæsˈtɪsɪtɪ] n Elastizität f

elated [ɪˈleɪtɪd] adj: **to be ~** hocherfreut or in Hochstimmung sein

elation [ɪˈleɪʃən] n große Freude f, Hochstimmung f

elbow ['ɛlbəʊ] n Ell(en)bogen m ▷ vt: **to ~ one's way through the crowd** sich durch die Menge boxen

elbow grease (inf) n Muskelkraft f

elbowroom ['ɛlbəʊrʊm] n Ellbogenfreiheit f

elder ['ɛldə'] adj älter ▷ n (Bot) Holunder m; (older person: gen pl) Ältere(r) f(m)

elderly ['ɛldəlɪ] adj ältere(r, s) ▷ npl: **the ~** ältere Leute pl

elder statesman n erfahrener Staatsmann m

eldest ['ɛldɪst] adj älteste(r, s) ▷ n Älteste(r) f(m)

elect [ɪˈlɛkt] vt wählen ▷ adj: **the president ~** der designierte or künftige Präsident; **to ~ to do sth** sich dafür entscheiden, etw zu tun

election [ɪˈlɛkʃən] n Wahl f; **to hold an ~** eine Wahl abhalten

election campaign n Wahlkampf m

election débâcle n Wahldebakel nt

electioneering [ɪlɛkʃəˈnɪərɪŋ] n Wahlkampf m

elector [ɪˈlɛktə'] n Wähler(in) m(f)

electoral [ɪˈlɛktərəl] adj Wähler-

electoral college n Wahlmännergremium nt

electorate [ɪˈlɛktərɪt] n Wähler pl, Wählerschaft f

electric [ɪˈlɛktrɪk] adj elektrisch

electrical [ɪˈlɛktrɪkl] adj elektrisch; (appliance) Elektro-; (failure) Strom-

electrical engineer n Elektrotechniker m

electric blanket n Heizdecke f

electric chair (US) n elektrischer Stuhl m

electric cooker n Elektroherd m

electric current n elektrischer Strom m

electric fire (Brit) n elektrisches Heizgerät nt

electrician [ɪlɛkˈtrɪʃən] n Elektriker(in) m(f)

electricity [ɪlɛkˈtrɪsɪtɪ] n Elektrizität f; (supply) (elektrischer) Strom m ▷ cpd Strom-; **to switch on/off the ~** den Strom an-/ abschalten

electricity board (Brit) n Elektrizitätswerk nt

electricity price n Strompreis m

electricity rate n Stromtarif m

electric light n elektrisches Licht nt

electric shock n elektrischer Schlag m, Stromschlag m

electrify [ɪˈlɛktrɪfaɪ] vt (fence) unter Strom setzen; (rail network) elektrifizieren; (audience) elektrisieren

electro ... [ɪˈlɛktrəʊ] pref Elektro-

electrocardiogram [ɪˈlɛktrəˈkɑːdɪəgræm] n Elektrokardiogramm nt

electroconvulsive therapy [ɪˈlɛktrəkənˈvʌlsɪv-] n Elektroschocktherapie f

electrocute [ɪˈlɛktrəkjuːt] vt durch einen Stromschlag töten; (US: criminal) auf dem elektrischen Stuhl hinrichten

electrode [ɪˈlɛktrəʊd] n Elektrode f

electroencephalogram [ɪˈlɛktrəʊenˈsɛfələgræm] n Elektroenzephalogramm nt

electrolysis [ɪlɛkˈtrɒlɪsɪs] n Elektrolyse f

electromagnetic [ɪˈlɛktrəmægˈnɛtɪk] adj elektromagnetisch

electron [ɪˈlɛktrɒn] n Elektron nt

electronic [ɪlɛkˈtrɒnɪk] adj elektronisch

electronic data processing n elektronische Datenverarbeitung f

electronic mail n elektronische Post f

electronics [ɪlɛkˈtrɒnɪks] n Elektronik f

electronic tag n elektronische Fußfessel f

electron microscope n Elektronenmikroskop nt

electroplated [ɪˈlɛktrəˈpleɪtɪd] adj galvanisiert

electrotherapy [ɪˈlɛktrəˈθɛrəpɪ] n Elektrotherapie f

elegance ['ɛlɪgəns] n Eleganz f

elegant ['ɛlɪgənt] adj elegant

element ['ɛlɪmənt] n Element nt; (of heater, kettle etc) Heizelement nt

elementary [ɛlɪˈmɛntərɪ] adj grundlegend; **~ school** Grundschule f; siehe Info-Artikel; **~ education** Elementarunterricht m; **~ maths/ French** Grundbegriffe pl der Mathematik/des Französischen

---

● **ELEMENTARY SCHOOL**

●
● Elementary school ist in den USA und Kanada
● eine Grundschule, an der ein Kind die
● ersten sechs bis acht Schuljahre verbringt.

In den USA heißt diese Schule auch „grade school" oder „grammar school". Siehe auch *high school*.

elephant [ˈɛlɪfənt] *n* Elefant *m*
elevate [ˈɛlɪveɪt] *vt* erheben; *(physically)* heben
elevated railroad [ˈɛlɪveɪtɪd-] *(US) n* Hochbahn *f*
elevation [ɛlɪˈveɪʃən] *n* Erhebung *f*; *(height)* Höhe *f* über dem Meeresspiegel; *(Archit)* Aufriss *m*
elevator [ˈɛlɪveɪtər] *n (US)* Aufzug *m*, Fahrstuhl *m*; *(in warehouse etc)* Lastenaufzug *m*
eleven [ɪˈlɛvn] *num* elf
elevenses [ɪˈlɛvnzɪz] *(Brit) npl* zweites Frühstück *nt*
eleventh [ɪˈlɛvnθ] *num* elfte(r, s); **at the ~ hour** *(fig)* in letzter Minute
elf [ɛlf] *(pl* **elves**) *n* Elf *m*, Elfe *f*; *(mischievous)* Kobold *m*
elicit [ɪˈlɪsɪt] *vt*: **to ~ (from sb)** *(information)* (aus jdm) herausbekommen; *(reaction, response)* (von jdm) bekommen
eligible [ˈɛlɪdʒəbl] *adj (marriage partner)* begehrt; **to be ~ for sth** für etw infrage kommen; **to be ~ for a pension** pensionsberechtigt sein
eliminate [ɪˈlɪmɪneɪt] *vt* beseitigen; *(candidate etc)* ausschließen; *(team, contestant)* aus dem Wettbewerb werfen
elimination [ɪlɪmɪˈneɪʃən] *n (see vb)* Beseitigung *f*; Ausschluss *m*; Ausscheiden *nt*; **by process of ~** durch negative Auslese
élite [eɪˈliːt] *n* Elite *f*
élitist [eɪˈliːtɪst] *(pej) adj* elitär
elixir [ɪˈlɪksər] *n* Elixier *nt*
Elizabethan [ɪlɪzəˈbiːθən] *adj* elisabethanisch
ellipse [ɪˈlɪps] *n* Ellipse *f*
elliptical [ɪˈlɪptɪkl] *adj* elliptisch
elm [ɛlm] *n* Ulme *f*
elocution [ɛləˈkjuːʃən] *n* Sprechtechnik *f*
elongated [ˈiːlɔŋgeɪtɪd] *adj* lang gestreckt; *(shadow)* verlängert
elope [ɪˈləup] *vi* weglaufen
elopement [ɪˈləupmənt] *n* Weglaufen *nt*
eloquence [ˈɛləkwəns] *n (see adj)* Beredtheit *f*, Wortgewandtheit *f*; Ausdrucksfülle *f*
eloquent [ˈɛləkwənt] *adj* beredt, wortgewandt; *(speech, description)* ausdrucksvoll
else [ɛls] *adv* andere(r, s); **something ~** etwas anderes; **somewhere ~** woanders, anderswo; **everywhere ~** sonst überall; **where ~?** wo sonst?; **is there anything ~ I can do?** kann ich sonst noch etwas tun?; **there was little ~ to do** es gab nicht viel anderes zu tun; **everyone ~** alle anderen; **nobody ~ spoke** niemand anders sagte etwas, sonst sagte niemand etwas
elsewhere [ɛlsˈweər] *adv* woanders, anderswo; *(go)* woandershin, anderswohin
ELT *n abbr (Scol:* = *English Language Teaching) Englisch als Unterrichtsfach*
elucidate [ɪˈluːsɪdeɪt] *vt* erläutern
elude [ɪˈluːd] *vt (captor)* entkommen +*dat*;

(capture) sich entziehen +*dat*; **this fact/idea ~d him** diese Tatsache/Idee entging ihm
elusive [ɪˈluːsɪv] *adj* schwer zu fangen; *(quality)* unerreichbar; **he's very ~** er ist sehr schwer zu erreichen
elves [ɛlvz] *npl of* **elf**
emaciated [ɪˈmeɪsɪeɪtɪd] *adj* abgezehrt, ausgezehrt
email [ˈiːmeɪl] *n abbr (= electronic mail)* E-Mail *f*
  ▷ *vt* eine E-Mail schicken +*dat*
emanate [ˈɛməneɪt] *vi*: **to ~ from** stammen von; *(sound, light etc)* ausgehen von
emancipate [ɪˈmænsɪpeɪt] *vt (women)* emanzipieren; *(poor)* befreien; *(slave)* freilassen
emancipation [ɪmænsɪˈpeɪʃən] *n (see vb)* Emanzipation *f*; Befreiung *f*; Freilassung *f*
emasculate [ɪˈmæskjuleɪt] *vt* schwächen
embalm [ɪmˈbɑːm] *vt* einbalsamieren
embankment [ɪmˈbæŋkmənt] *n* Böschung *f*; *(of railway)* Bahndamm *m*; *(of river)* Damm *m*
embargo [ɪmˈbɑːgəu] *(pl* **~es**) *n* Embargo *nt*
  ▷ *vt* mit einem Embargo belegen; **to put** *or* **impose** *or* **place an ~ on sth** ein Embargo über etw *acc* verhängen; **to lift an ~** ein Embargo aufheben
embark [ɪmˈbɑːk] *vt* einschiffen ▷ *vi*: **to ~ (on)** sich einschiffen (auf); **to ~ on** *(journey)* beginnen; *(task)* in Angriff nehmen; *(course of action)* einschlagen
embarkation [ɛmbɑːˈkeɪʃən] *n* Einschiffung *f*
embarkation card *n* Bordkarte *f*
embarrass [ɪmˈbærəs] *vt* in Verlegenheit bringen
embarrassed [ɪmˈbærəst] *adj* verlegen
embarrassing [ɪmˈbærəsɪŋ] *adj* peinlich
embarrassment [ɪmˈbærəsmənt] *n* Verlegenheit *f*; *(embarrassing problem)* Peinlichkeit *f*
embassy [ˈɛmbəsɪ] *n* Botschaft *f*; **the Swiss E~** die Schweizer Botschaft
embedded [ɪmˈbɛdɪd] *adj* eingebettet; *(attitude, belief, feeling)* verwurzelt
embellish [ɪmˈbɛlɪʃ] *vt (account)* ausschmücken; **to be ~ed with** geschmückt sein mit
embers [ˈɛmbəz] *npl* Glut *f*
embezzle [ɪmˈbɛzl] *vt* unterschlagen
embezzlement [ɪmˈbɛzlmənt] *n* Unterschlagung *f*
embezzler [ɪmˈbɛzlər] *n jd, der eine Unterschlagung begangen hat*
embitter [ɪmˈbɪtər] *vt* verbittern
embittered [ɪmˈbɪtəd] *adj* verbittert
emblem [ˈɛmbləm] *n* Emblem *nt*; *(symbol)* Wahrzeichen *nt*
embodiment [ɪmˈbɒdɪmənt] *n* Verkörperung *f*; **to be the ~ of ...** *(subj: thing)* ... verkörpern; *(: person)* ... in Person sein
embody [ɪmˈbɒdɪ] *vt* verkörpern; *(include, contain)* enthalten
embolden [ɪmˈbəuldn] *vt* ermutigen
embolism [ˈɛmbəlɪzəm] *n* Embolie *f*
embossed [ɪmˈbɒst] *adj* geprägt; **~ with a logo**

537

mit geprägtem Logo

embrace [ɪm'breɪs] vt umarmen; (include) umfassen ▷ vi sich umarmen ▷ n Umarmung f

embroider [ɪm'brɔɪdə^r] vt (cloth) besticken; (fig: story) ausschmücken

embroidery [ɪm'brɔɪdərɪ] n Stickerei f; (activity) Sticken nt

embroil [ɪm'brɔɪl] vt: **to become ~ed (in sth)** (in etw acc) verwickelt or hineingezogen werden

embryo ['ɛmbrɪəu] n Embryo m; (fig) Keim m

emcee [ɛm'siː] n Conférencier m

emend [ɪ'mɛnd] vt verbessern, korrigieren

emerald ['ɛmərəld] n Smaragd m

emerge [ɪ'məːdʒ] vi: **to ~ (from)** auftauchen (aus); (from sleep) erwachen (aus); (from imprisonment) entlassen werden (aus); (from discussion etc) sich herausstellen (bei); (new idea, industry, society) entstehen (aus); **it ~s that** (Brit) es stellt sich heraus, dass

emergence [ɪ'məːdʒəns] n Entstehung f

emergency [ɪ'məːdʒənsɪ] n Notfall m ▷ cpd Not-; (repair) notdürftig; **in an ~** im Notfall; **state of ~** Notstand m

emergency cord (US) n Notbremse f

emergency exit n Notausgang m

emergency landing n Notlandung f

emergency lane (US) n Seitenstreifen m

emergency road service (US) n Pannendienst m

emergency services npl: **the ~** der Notdienst

emergency stop (Brit) n Vollbremsung f

emergent [ɪ'məːdʒənt] adj jung, aufstrebend

emeritus [ɪ'mɛrɪtəs] adj emeritiert

emery board ['ɛmərɪ-] n Papiernagelfeile f

emery paper ['ɛmərɪ-] n Schmirgelpapier nt

emetic [ɪ'mɛtɪk] n Brechmittel nt

emigrant ['ɛmɪgrənt] n Auswanderer m, Auswanderin f, Emigrant(in) m(f)

emigrate ['ɛmɪgreɪt] vi auswandern, emigrieren

emigration [ɛmɪ'greɪʃən] n Auswanderung f, Emigration f

émigré ['ɛmɪgreɪ] n Emigrant(in) m(f)

eminence ['ɛmɪnəns] n Bedeutung f

eminent ['ɛmɪnənt] adj bedeutend

eminently ['ɛmɪnəntlɪ] adv ausgesprochen

emirate ['ɛmɪrɪt] n Emirat nt

emission [ɪ'mɪʃən] n Emission f

emissions [ɪ'mɪʃənz] npl Emissionen pl

emit [ɪ'mɪt] vt abgeben; (smell) ausströmen; (light, heat) ausstrahlen

emolument [ɪ'mɔljumənt] n (often pl) Vergütung f; (fee) Honorar nt; (salary) Bezüge pl

emoticon [ɪ'məutɪkən] n (Comput) Emoticon nt

emotion [ɪ'məuʃən] n Gefühl nt

emotional [ɪ'məuʃənl] adj emotional; (exhaustion) seelisch; (scene) ergreifend; (speech) gefühlsbetont

emotionally [ɪ'məuʃnəlɪ] adv emotional; (be involved) gefühlsmäßig; (speak) gefühlvoll; **~ disturbed** seelisch gestört

emotive [ɪ'məutɪv] adj emotional

empathy ['ɛmpəθɪ] n Einfühlungsvermögen nt; **to feel ~ with sb** sich in jdn einfühlen

emperor ['ɛmpərə^r] n Kaiser m

emphasis ['ɛmfəsɪs] (pl **emphases**) n Betonung f; (importance) (Schwer)gewicht nt; **to lay** or **place ~ on sth** etw betonen; **the ~ is on reading** das Schwergewicht liegt auf dem Lesen

emphasize ['ɛmfəsaɪz] vt betonen; (feature) hervorheben; **I must ~ that ...** ich möchte betonen, dass ...

emphatic [ɛm'fætɪk] adj nachdrücklich; (denial) energisch; (person, manner) bestimmt, entschieden

emphatically [ɛm'fætɪklɪ] adv nachdrücklich; (certainly) eindeutig

emphysema [ɛmfɪ'siːmə] n Emphysem nt

empire ['ɛmpaɪə^r] n Reich nt

empirical [ɛm'pɪrɪkl] adj empirisch

employ [ɪm'plɔɪ] vt beschäftigen; (tool, weapon) verwenden; **he's ~ed in a bank** er ist bei einer Bank angestellt

employee [ɪmplɔɪ'iː] n Angestellte(r) f(m)

employer [ɪm'plɔɪə^r] n Arbeitgeber(in) m(f)

employment [ɪm'plɔɪmənt] n Arbeit f; **to find ~** Arbeit or eine (An)stellung finden; **without ~** stellungslos; **your place of ~** Ihre Arbeitsstätte f

employment agency n Stellenvermittlung f

employment exchange (Brit) n Arbeitsamt nt

empower [ɪm'pauə^r] vt: **to ~ sb to do sth** jdn ermächtigen, etw zu tun

empress ['ɛmprɪs] n Kaiserin f

empties ['ɛmptɪz] npl Leergut nt

emptiness ['ɛmptɪnɪs] n Leere f

empty ['ɛmptɪ] adj leer; (house, room) leer stehend; (space) frei ▷ vt leeren; (place, house etc) räumen ▷ vi sich leeren; (liquid) abfließen; (river) münden; **on an ~ stomach** auf nüchternen Magen; **to ~ into** (river) münden or sich ergießen in +acc

empty-handed ['ɛmptɪ'hændɪd] adj mit leeren Händen; **he returned ~** er kehrte unverrichteter Dinge zurück

empty-headed ['ɛmptɪ'hɛdɪd] adj strohdumm

EMS n abbr (= European Monetary System) EWS nt

EMT (US) n abbr (= emergency medical technician) ≈ Sanitäter(in) m(f)

EMU n abbr (= Economic and Monetary Union) EWU f

emu ['iːmjuː] n Emu m

emulate ['ɛmjuleɪt] vt nacheifern +dat

emulsion [ɪ'mʌlʃən] n Emulsion f; (also: **emulsion paint**) Emulsionsfarbe f

enable [ɪ'neɪbl] vt: **to ~ sb to do sth** (permit) es jdm erlauben, etw zu tun; (make possible) es jdm ermöglichen, etw zu tun

enact [ɪ'nækt] vt (law) erlassen; (play) aufführen; (role) darstellen, spielen

enamel [ɪ'næməl] n Email nt, Emaille f; (also: **enamel paint**) Email(le)lack m; (of tooth) Zahnschmelz m

enamoured [ɪ'næməd] adj: **to be ~ of** (person) verliebt sein in +acc; (pastime, idea, belief) angetan sein von

encampment [ɪnˈkæmpmənt] n Lager nt

encased [ɪnˈkeɪst] adj: ~ **in** (shell) umgeben von; **to be ~ in** (limb) in Gips liegen or sein

encash [ɪnˈkæʃ] (Brit) vt einlösen

enchant [ɪnˈtʃɑːnt] vt bezaubern

enchanted [ɪnˈtʃɑːntɪd] adj verzaubert

enchanting [ɪnˈtʃɑːntɪŋ] adj bezaubernd

encircle [ɪnˈsɜːkl] vt umgeben; (person) umringen; (building: police etc) umstellen

encl. abbr (on letters etc: = enclosed, enclosure) Anl.

enclave [ˈɛnkleɪv] n: **an ~ (of)** eine Enklave (+gen)

enclose [ɪnˈkləuz] vt umgeben; (land, space) begrenzen; (with fence) einzäunen; (letter etc): **to ~ (with)** beilegen (+dat); **please find ~d** als Anlage übersenden wir Ihnen

enclosure [ɪnˈkləuʒər] n eingefriedeter Bereich m; (in letter etc) Anlage f

encoder [ɪnˈkəudər] n Codierer m

encompass [ɪnˈkʌmpəs] vt umfassen

encore [ɔŋˈkɔːr] excl Zugabe! ▷ n Zugabe f

encounter [ɪnˈkauntər] n Begegnung f ▷ vt begegnen +dat; (problem) stoßen auf +acc

encourage [ɪnˈkʌrɪdʒ] vt (activity, attitude) unterstützen; (growth, industry) fördern; **to ~ sb (to do sth)** jdn ermutigen(, etw zu tun)

encouragement [ɪnˈkʌrɪdʒmənt] n (see vb) Unterstützung f; Förderung f; Ermutigung f

encouraging [ɪnˈkʌrɪdʒɪŋ] adj ermutigend

encroach [ɪnˈkrəutʃ] vi: **to ~ (up)on** (rights) eingreifen in +acc; (property) eindringen in +acc; (time) in Anspruch nehmen

encrusted [ɪnˈkrʌstɪd] adj: ~ **with** (gems) besetzt mit; (snow, dirt) verkrustet mit

encumber [ɪnˈkʌmbər] vt: **to be ~ed with** beladen sein mit; (debts) belastet sein mit

encyclopaedia, encyclopedia [ɛnsaɪkləuˈpiːdɪə] n Lexikon nt, Enzyklopädie f

end [ɛnd] n Ende nt; (of film, book) Schluss m, Ende nt; (of table) Schmalseite f; (of pointed object) Spitze f; (aim) Zweck m, Ziel nt ▷ vt (also: **bring to an end, put an end to**) beenden ▷ vi enden; **from ~ to end** von einem Ende zum anderen; **to come to an ~** zu Ende gehen; **to be at an ~** zu Ende sein; **in the ~** schließlich; **on ~** hochkant; **to stand on ~** (hair) zu Berge stehen; **for hours on ~** stundenlang ununterbrochen; **for 5 hours on ~** 5 Stunden ununterbrochen; **at the ~ of the street** am Ende der Straße; **at the ~ of the day** (Brit: fig) letztlich; **to this end, with this ~ in view** mit diesem Ziel vor Augen

▶ **end up** vi: **to ~ up in** (place) landen in +dat; **to ~ up in trouble** Ärger bekommen; **to ~ up doing sth** etw schließlich tun

endanger [ɪnˈdeɪndʒər] vt gefährden; **an ~ed species** eine vom Aussterben bedrohte Art

endear [ɪnˈdɪər] vt: **to ~ o.s. to sb** sich bei jdm beliebt machen

endearing [ɪnˈdɪərɪŋ] adj gewinnend

endearment [ɪnˈdɪəmənt] n: **to whisper ~s** zärtliche Worte flüstern; **term of ~** Kosewort

nt, Kosename m

endeavour, (US) **endeavor** [ɪnˈdɛvər] n Anstrengung f, Bemühung f; (effort) Bestrebung f ▷ vi: **to ~ to do sth** (attempt) sich anstrengen or bemühen, etw zu tun; (strive) bestrebt sein, etw zu tun

endemic [ɛnˈdɛmɪk] adj endemisch, verbreitet

ending [ˈɛndɪŋ] n Ende nt, Schluss m; (Ling) Endung f

endive [ˈɛndaɪv] n Endivie f; (chicory) Chicorée f or m

endless [ˈɛndlɪs] adj endlos; (patience, resources, possibilities) unbegrenzt

endorse [ɪnˈdɔːs] vt (cheque) indossieren, auf der Rückseite unterzeichnen; (proposal, plan) billigen; (candidate) unterstützen

endorsee [ɪndɔːˈsiː] n Indossat m

endorsement [ɪnˈdɔːsmənt] n Billigung f; (of candidate) Unterstützung f; (Brit: on driving licence) Strafvermerk m

endow [ɪnˈdau] vt (institution) eine Stiftung machen an +acc; **to be ~ed with** besitzen

endowment [ɪnˈdaumənt] n Stiftung f; (quality) Begabung f

endowment assurance n Versicherung f auf den Erlebensfall, Erlebensversicherung f

endowment mortgage n Hypothek f mit Lebensversicherung

end product n Endprodukt nt; (fig) Produkt nt

end result n Endergebnis nt

endurable [ɪnˈdjuərəbl] adj erträglich

endurance [ɪnˈdjuərəns] n Durchhaltevermögen nt; (patience) Geduld f

endurance test n Belastungsprobe f

endure [ɪnˈdjuər] vt ertragen ▷ vi Bestand haben

enduring [ɪnˈdjuərɪŋ] adj dauerhaft

end user n (Comput) Endbenutzer m

enema [ˈɛnɪmə] n Klistier nt, Einlauf m

enemy [ˈɛnəmɪ] adj feindlich; (strategy) des Feindes ▷ n Feind(in) m(f); **to make an ~ of sb** sich dat jdn zum Feind machen

energetic [ɛnəˈdʒɛtɪk] adj aktiv

energy [ˈɛnədʒɪ] n Energie f; **Department of E~** Energieministerium nt

energy crisis n Energiekrise f

energy-saving [ˈɛnədʒɪˈseɪvɪŋ] adj energiesparend; (policy) energiebewusst

enervating [ˈɛnəveɪtɪŋ] adj strapazierend

enforce [ɪnˈfɔːs] vt (law, rule, decision) Geltung verschaffen +dat

enforced [ɪnˈfɔːst] adj erzwungen

enfranchise [ɪnˈfræntʃaɪz] vt das Wahlrecht geben or erteilen +dat

engage [ɪnˈgeɪdʒ] vt in Anspruch nehmen; (employ) einstellen; (lawyer) sich dat nehmen; (Mil) angreifen ▷ vi (Tech) einrasten; **to ~ the clutch** einkuppeln; **to ~ sb in conversation** jdn in ein Gespräch verwickeln; **to ~ in** sich beteiligen an +dat; **to ~ in commerce** kaufmännisch tätig sein; **to ~ in study** studieren

engaged [ɪnˈgeɪdʒd] adj verlobt; (Brit: busy,

in use) besetzt; **to get ~** sich verloben;
he is ~ in research/a survey er ist mit
Forschungsarbeit/einer Umfrage beschäftigt
engaged tone (*Brit*) *n* Besetztzeichen *nt*
engagement [ɪn'geɪdʒmənt] *n* Verabredung *f*;
(*booking*) Engagement *nt*; (*to marry*) Verlobung *f*;
(*Mil*) Gefecht *nt*, Kampf *m*; **I have a previous ~**
ich habe schon eine Verabredung
engagement ring *n* Verlobungsring *m*
engaging [ɪn'geɪdʒɪŋ] *adj* einnehmend
engender [ɪn'dʒendər] *vt* erzeugen
engine ['endʒɪn] *n* Motor *m*; (*Rail*) Lok(omotive)
f
engine driver *n* (*Rail*) Lok(omotiv)führer(in)
m(f)
engineer [endʒɪ'nɪər] *n* Ingenieur(in) *m(f)*;
(*Brit*: *for repairs*) Techniker(in) *m(f)*; (*US*: *Rail*)
Lok(omotiv)führer(in) *m(f)*; (*on ship*)
Maschinist(in) *m(f)*; **civil/mechanical ~**
Bau-/Maschinenbauingenieur(in) *m(f)*
engineering [endʒɪ'nɪərɪŋ] *n* Technik *f*; (*design,
construction*) Konstruktion *f* ▷ *cpd*: **~ works** *or*
factory Maschinenfabrik *f*
engine failure *n* Maschinenschaden *m*; (*Aut*)
Motorschaden *m*
engine trouble *n* Maschinenschaden *m*; (*Aut*)
Motorschaden *m*
England ['ɪŋglənd] *n* England *nt*
English ['ɪŋglɪʃ] *adj* englisch ▷ *n* Englisch *nt*;
the English *npl* die Engländer *pl*; **an ~ speaker**
jd, der Englisch spricht
English Channel *n*: **the ~** der Ärmelkanal
Englishman ['ɪŋglɪʃmən] (*irreg*: *like* **man**) *n*
Engländer *m*
English-speaking ['ɪŋglɪʃ'spi:kɪŋ] *adj* (*country*)
englischsprachig
Englishwoman ['ɪŋglɪʃwumən] (*irreg*: *like*
woman) *n* Engländerin *f*
engrave [ɪn'greɪv] *vt* gravieren; (*name etc*)
eingravieren; (*fig*) einprägen
engraving [ɪn'greɪvɪŋ] *n* Stich *m*
engrossed [ɪn'grəust] *adj*: **~ in** vertieft in *+acc*
engulf [ɪn'gʌlf] *vt* verschlingen; (*subj*: *panic, fear*)
überkommen
enhance [ɪn'hɑːns] *vt* verbessern; (*enjoyment,
beauty*) erhöhen
enigma [ɪ'nɪgmə] *n* Rätsel *nt*
enigmatic [enɪg'mætɪk] *adj* rätselhaft
enjoy [ɪn'dʒɔɪ] *vt* genießen; (*health, fortune*) sich
erfreuen *+gen*; (*success*) haben; **to ~ o.s.** sich
amüsieren; **I ~ dancing** ich tanze gerne
enjoyable [ɪn'dʒɔɪəbl] *adj* nett, angenehm
enjoyment [ɪn'dʒɔɪmənt] *n* Vergnügen *nt*;
(*activity*) Freude *f*
enlarge [ɪn'lɑːdʒ] *vt* vergrößern; (*scope*)
erweitern ▷ *vi*: **to ~ on** weiter ausführen
enlarged [ɪn'lɑːdʒd] *adj* erweitert; (*Med*)
vergrößert
enlargement [ɪn'lɑːdʒmənt] *n* Vergrößerung *f*
enlighten [ɪn'laɪtn] *vt* aufklären
enlightened [ɪn'laɪtnd] *adj* aufgeklärt
enlightening [ɪn'laɪtnɪŋ] *adj* aufschlussreich
enlightenment [ɪn'laɪtnmənt] *n* (*also*

Hist: *Enlightenment*) Aufklärung *f*
enlist [ɪn'lɪst] *vt* anwerben; (*support, help*)
gewinnen ▷ *vi*: **to ~ in** eintreten in *+acc*; **~ed
man** (*US*: *Mil*) gemeiner Soldat *m*; (*US*: *in navy*)
Matrose *m*
enliven [ɪn'laɪvn] *vt* beleben
enmity ['enmɪtɪ] *n* Feindschaft *f*
ennoble [ɪ'nəubl] *vt* adeln; (*fig*: *dignify*) erheben
enormity [ɪ'nɔːmɪtɪ] *n* ungeheure Größe *f*
enormous [ɪ'nɔːməs] *adj* gewaltig, ungeheuer;
(*pleasure, success etc*) riesig
enormously [ɪ'nɔːməslɪ] *adv* enorm; (*rich*)
ungeheuer
enough [ɪ'nʌf] *adj* genug, genügend ▷ *pron*
genug ▷ *adv*: **big ~** groß genug; **he has not
worked ~** er hat nicht genug *or* genügend
gearbeitet; **have you got ~?** haben Sie genug?;
~ to eat genug zu essen; **will 5 be ~?** reichen
5?; **I've had ~!** jetzt reichts mir aber!; **it's hot
~ (as it is)** es ist heiß genug; **he was kind ~
to lend me the money** er war so gut und hat
mir das Geld geliehen; **~! es reicht!; that's
~, thanks** danke, das reicht *or* ist genug;
I've had ~ of him ich habe genug von ihm;
funnily/oddly ~ ... komischerweise ...
enquire [ɪn'kwaɪər] *vt, vi* = **inquire**
enrage [ɪn'reɪdʒ] *vt* wütend machen
enrich [ɪn'rɪtʃ] *vt* bereichern
enrol, (*US*) **enroll** [ɪn'rəul] *vt* anmelden; (*at
university*) einschreiben, immatrikulieren ▷ *vi*
(*see vt*) sich anmelden; sich einschreiben, sich
immatrikulieren
enrolment, (*US*) **enrollment** [ɪn'rəulmənt]
n (*see vb*) Anmeldung *f*; Einschreibung *f*,
Immatrikulation *f*
en route [ɔn'ruːt] *adv* unterwegs; **~ for** auf
dem Weg nach; **~ from London to Berlin** auf
dem Weg von London nach Berlin
ensconced [ɪn'skɔnst] *adj*: **she is ~ in ...** sie
hat es sich *dat* in ... *dat* gemütlich gemacht
ensemble [ɔn'sɔmbl] *n* Ensemble *nt*
enshrine [ɪn'ʃraɪn] *vt* bewahren; **to be ~d in**
verankert sein in *+dat*
ensue [ɪn'sjuː] *vi* folgen
ensuing [ɪn'sjuːɪŋ] *adj* folgend
ensure [ɪn'ʃuər] *vt* garantieren; **to ~ that**
sicherstellen, dass
ENT *n abbr* (*Med*: = *ear, nose, and throat*) HNO
entail [ɪn'teɪl] *vt* mit sich bringen
entangled [ɪn'tæŋgld] *adj*: **to become ~ (in)**
sich verfangen (in *+dat*)
enter ['entər] *vt* betreten; (*club*) beitreten
+dat; (*army*) gehen zu; (*profession*) ergreifen;
(*race, contest*) sich beteiligen an *+dat*; (*sb for a
competition*) anmelden; (*write down*) eintragen;
(*Comput*: *data*) eingeben ▷ *vi* (*come in*)
hereinkommen; (*go in*) hineingehen
▶ **enter for** *vt fus* anmelden für
▶ **enter into** *vt fus* (*discussion, negotiations*)
aufnehmen; (*correspondence*) treten in *+acc*;
(*agreement*) schließen
▶ **enter up** *vt* eintragen
▶ **enter (up)on** *vt fus* (*career, policy*) einschlagen

enteritis [ɛntəˈraɪtɪs] n
Dünndarmentzündung f
enterprise [ˈɛntəpraɪz] n Unternehmen
nt; (initiative) Initiative f; **free** ~ freies
Unternehmertum nt; **private** ~
Privatunternehmertum nt
enterprising [ˈɛntəpraɪzɪŋ] adj einfallsreich
entertain [ɛntəˈteɪn] vt unterhalten; (invite)
einladen; (idea, plan) erwägen
entertainer [ɛntəˈteɪnəʳ] n Unterhalter(in)
m(f), Entertainer(in) m(f)
entertaining [ɛntəˈteɪnɪŋ] adj amüsant ▷ n: **to
do a lot of** ~ sehr oft Gäste haben
entertainment [ɛntəˈteɪnmənt] n
Unterhaltung f; (show) Darbietung f
entertainment allowance n
Aufwandspauschale f
enthral [ɪnˈθrɔːl] vt begeistern; (story) fesseln
enthralled [ɪnˈθrɔːld] adj gefesselt; **he was** ~
by or **with the book** das Buch fesselte ihn
enthralling [ɪnˈθrɔːlɪŋ] adj fesselnd; (details)
spannend
enthuse [ɪnˈθuːz] vi: **to** ~ **about** or **over**
schwärmen von
enthusiasm [ɪnˈθuːzɪæzəm] n Begeisterung f
enthusiast [ɪnˈθuːzɪæst] n Enthusiast(in) m(f);
he's a jazz/sports ~ er begeistert sich für
Jazz/Sport
enthusiastic [ɪnθuːzɪˈæstɪk] adj begeistert;
(response, reception) enthusiastisch; **to be** ~
about begeistert sein von
entice [ɪnˈtaɪs] vt locken; (tempt) verleiten
enticing [ɪnˈtaɪsɪŋ] adj verlockend
entire [ɪnˈtaɪəʳ] adj ganz
entirely [ɪnˈtaɪəlɪ] adv völlig
entirety [ɪnˈtaɪərətɪ] n: **in its** ~ in seiner
Gesamtheit
entitle [ɪnˈtaɪtl] vt: **to** ~ **sb to sth** jdn zu etw
berechtigen; **to** ~ **sb to do sth** jdn dazu
berechtigen, etw zu tun
entitled [ɪnˈtaɪtld] adj: **a book/film** etc ~ ... ein
Buch/Film etc mit dem Titel ...; **to be** ~ **to do
sth** das Recht haben, etw zu tun
entity [ˈɛntɪtɪ] n Wesen nt
entourage [ɔntuˈrɑːʒ] n Gefolge nt
entrails [ˈɛntreɪlz] npl Eingeweide pl
entrance [n ˈɛntrns, vt ɪnˈtrɑːns] n Eingang
m; (arrival) Ankunft f; (on stage) Auftritt m ▷ vt
bezaubern; **to gain** ~ **to** (building etc) sich
dat Zutritt verschaffen zu; (university) die
Zulassung erhalten zu; (profession etc) Zugang
erhalten zu
entrance examination n Aufnahmeprüfung f
entrance fee n Eintrittsgeld nt
entrance ramp (US) n Auffahrt f
entrancing [ɪnˈtrɑːnsɪŋ] adj bezaubernd
entrant [ˈɛntrnt] n Teilnehmer(in) m(f); (Brit: in
exam) Prüfling m
entreat [ɛnˈtriːt] vt: **to** ~ **sb to do sth** jdn
anflehen, etw zu tun
entreaty [ɛnˈtriːtɪ] n (flehentliche) Bitte f
entrée [ˈɔntreɪ] n Hauptgericht nt
entrenched [ɛnˈtrɛntʃt] adj verankert; (ideas)

festgesetzt
entrepreneur [ˈɔntrəprəˈnəːʳ] n
Unternehmer(in) m(f)
entrepreneurial [ˈɔntrəprəˈnəːrɪəl] adj
unternehmerisch
entrust [ɪnˈtrʌst] vt: **to** ~ **sth to sb** jdm etw
anvertrauen; **to** ~ **sb with sth** (task) jdn
mit etw betrauen; (secret, valuables) jdm etw
anvertrauen
entry [ˈɛntrɪ] n Eingang m; (in competition)
Meldung f; (in register, account book, reference
book) Eintrag m; (arrival) Eintritt m; (to country)
Einreise f; **"no** ~" „Zutritt verboten"; (Aut)
„Einfahrt verboten"; **single/double** ~ **book-
keeping** einfache/doppelte Buchführung f
entry form n Anmeldeformular nt
entry phone (Brit) n Türsprechanlage f
entwine [ɪnˈtwaɪn] vt verflechten
enumerate [ɪˈnjuːməreɪt] vt aufzählen
enunciate [ɪˈnʌnsɪeɪt] vt artikulieren;
(principle, plan etc) formulieren
envelop [ɪnˈvɛləp] vt einhüllen
envelope [ˈɛnvələup] n Umschlag m
enviable [ˈɛnvɪəbl] adj beneidenswert
envious [ˈɛnvɪəs] adj neidisch; **to be** ~ **of sth/
sb** auf etw/jdn neidisch sein
environment [ɪnˈvaɪərnmənt] n
Umwelt f; **Department of the E~** (Brit)
Umweltministerium nt
environmental [ɪnvaɪərnˈmɛntl] adj
(problems, pollution etc) Umwelt-; ~ **expert**
Umweltexperte m, Umweltexpertin f; ~
studies Umweltkunde f
environmentalist [ɪnvaɪərnˈmɛntlɪst] n
Umweltschützer(in) m(f)
Environmental Protection Agency (US) n
staatliche Umweltbehörde der USA
environment-friendly adj umweltfreundlich
envisage [ɪnˈvɪzɪdʒ] vt sich dat vorstellen; **I** ~
that ... ich stelle mir vor, dass ...
envision [ɪnˈvɪʒən] (US) vt = **envisage**
envoy [ˈɛnvɔɪ] n Gesandte(r) f(m)
envy [ˈɛnvɪ] n Neid m ▷ vt beneiden; **to** ~ **sb
sth** jdn um etw beneiden
enzyme [ˈɛnzaɪm] n Enzym nt
eon [ˈiːən] n Äon m, Ewigkeit f
EPA (US) n abbr = **Environmental Protection
Agency**
ephemeral [ɪˈfɛmərl] adj kurzlebig
epic [ˈɛpɪk] n Epos nt ▷ adj (journey) lang und
abenteuerlich
epicentre, (US) **epicenter** [ˈɛpɪsɛntəʳ] n
Epizentrum nt
epidemic [ɛpɪˈdɛmɪk] n Epidemie f
epigram [ˈɛpɪgræm] n Epigramm nt
epilepsy [ˈɛpɪlɛpsɪ] n Epilepsie f
epileptic [ɛpɪˈlɛptɪk] adj epileptisch ▷ n
Epileptiker(in) m(f)
epilogue [ˈɛpɪlɔg] n Epilog m, Nachwort nt
Epiphany [ɪˈpɪfənɪ] n Dreikönigsfest nt
episcopal [ɪˈpɪskəpl] adj bischöflich; **the E~
Church** die Episkopalkirche
episode [ˈɛpɪsəud] n Episode f; (TV, Radio)

541

Folge f

epistle [ɪ'pɪsl] n Epistel f; (Rel) Brief m

epitaph ['ɛpɪtɑːf] n Epitaph nt; (on gravestone etc) Grab(in)schrift f

epithet ['ɛpɪθɛt] n Beiname m

epitome [ɪ'pɪtəmɪ] n Inbegriff m

epitomize [ɪ'pɪtəmaɪz] vt verkörpern

epoch ['iːpɔk] n Epoche f

epoch-making ['iːpɔkmeɪkɪŋ] adj epochal; (discovery) epochemachend

eponymous [ɪ'pɔnɪməs] adj namengebend

equable ['ɛkwəbl] adj ausgeglichen; (reply) sachlich

equal ['iːkwl] adj gleich ▷ n Gleichgestellte(r) f(m) ▷ vt gleichkommen +dat; (number) gleich sein +dat; **they are roughly ~ in size** sie sind ungefähr gleich groß; **the number of exports should be ~ to imports** Export- und Importzahlen sollten gleich sein; **~ opportunities** Chancengleichheit f; **to be ~ to** (task) gewachsen sein +dat; **two times two ~s four** zwei mal zwei ist (gleich) vier

equality [iː'kwɔlɪtɪ] n Gleichheit f; **~ of opportunity** Chancengleichheit f

equalize ['iːkwəlaɪz] vt angleichen ▷ vi (Sport) ausgleichen

equally ['iːkwəlɪ] adv gleichmäßig; (good, bad etc) gleich; **they are ~ clever** sie sind beide gleich klug

Equal Opportunities Commission, (US) **Equal Employment Opportunity Commission** n Ausschuss m für Chancengleichheit am Arbeitsplatz

equal sign, equals sign n Gleichheitszeichen nt

equanimity [ɛkwə'nɪmɪtɪ] n Gleichmut m, Gelassenheit f

equate [ɪ'kweɪt] vt: **to ~ sth with** etw gleichsetzen mit ▷ vt (compare) auf die gleiche Stufe stellen; **to ~ A to B** A und B auf die gleiche Stufe stellen

equation [ɪ'kweɪʃən] n Gleichung f

equator [ɪ'kweɪtər] n Äquator m

equatorial [ɛkwə'tɔːrɪəl] adj äquatorial

Equatorial Guinea n Äquatorial-Guinea nt

equestrian [ɪ'kwɛstrɪən] adj (sport, dress etc) Reit-; (statue) Reiter- ▷ n Reiter(in) m(f)

equilibrium [iːkwɪ'lɪbrɪəm] n Gleichgewicht nt

equinox ['iːkwɪnɔks] n Tagundnachtgleiche f; **the spring/autumn ~** die Frühjahrs-/die Herbst-Tagundnachtgleiche f

equip [ɪ'kwɪp] vt: **to ~ (with)** (person, army) ausrüsten (mit); (room, car etc) ausstatten (mit); **to ~ sb for** jdn vorbereiten auf +acc; **to be well ~ped** gut ausgerüstet sein

equipment [ɪ'kwɪpmənt] n Ausrüstung f

equitable ['ɛkwɪtəbl] adj gerecht

equities ['ɛkwɪtɪz] (Brit) npl Stammaktien pl

equity ['ɛkwɪtɪ] n Gerechtigkeit f

equity capital n Eigenkapital nt

equivalent [ɪ'kwɪvələnt] adj gleich, gleichwertig ▷ n Gegenstück nt; **to be ~ to** or **the ~ of** entsprechen +dat

equivocal [ɪ'kwɪvəkl] adj vieldeutig; (open to suspicion) zweifelhaft

equivocate [ɪ'kwɪvəkeɪt] vi ausweichen, ausweichend antworten

equivocation [ɪkwɪvə'keɪʃən] n Ausflucht f, ausweichende Antwort f

ER (Brit) abbr (= Elizabeth Regina) offizieller Namenszug der Königin

ERA (US) n abbr (Pol: = Equal Rights Amendment) Artikel der amerikanischen Verfassung zur Gleichberechtigung; (Baseball: = earned run average) durch Eigenleistung erzielte Läufe

era ['ɪərə] n Ära f, Epoche f

eradicate [ɪ'rædɪkeɪt] vt ausrotten

erase [ɪ'reɪz] vt (tape: Comput) löschen; (writing) ausradieren; (thought, feeling) auslöschen

eraser [ɪ'reɪzər] n Radiergummi m

erect [ɪ'rɛkt] adj aufrecht; (tail) hoch erhoben; (ears) gespitzt ▷ vt bauen; (assemble) aufstellen

erection [ɪ'rɛkʃən] n Bauen nt; (of statue) Errichten nt; (of tent, machinery etc) Aufstellen nt; (Physiol) Erektion f

ergonomics [əːgə'nɔmɪks] n sing Ergonomie f, Ergonomik f

ERISA (US) n abbr (= Employee Retirement Income Security Act) Gesetz zur Regelung der Rentenversicherung

Eritrea n abbr Eritrea nt

ERM n abbr (= Exchange Rate Mechanism) Wechselkursmechanismus m

ermine ['əːmɪn] n (fur) Hermelin m

Ernie, Ernie ['əːnɪ] (Brit) n abbr (= Electronic Random Number Indicator Equipment) Gerät zur Ermittlung von Gewinnnummern für Prämiensparer

erode [ɪ'rəud] vt erodieren, auswaschen; (metal) zerfressen; (confidence, power) untergraben

erogenous [ɪ'rɔdʒənəs] adj erogen

erosion [ɪ'rəuʒən] n (see vb) Erosion f, Auswaschen nt; Zerfressen nt; Untergraben nt

erotic [ɪ'rɔtɪk] adj erotisch

eroticism [ɪ'rɔtɪsɪzəm] n Erotik f

err [əːr] vi sich irren; **to ~ on the side of caution/simplicity** (im Zweifelsfall) zur Vorsicht/Vereinfachung neigen

errand ['ɛrənd] n Besorgung f; (to give a message etc) Botengang m; **to run ~s** Besorgungen/ Botengänge machen; **~ of mercy** Rettungsaktion f

erratic [ɪ'rætɪk] adj unberechenbar; (attempts) unkoordiniert; (noise) unregelmäßig

erroneous [ɪ'rəunɪəs] adj irrig

error ['ɛrər] n Fehler m; **typing/spelling ~** Tipp-/Rechtschreibfehler m; **in ~** irrtümlicherweise; **~s and omissions excepted** Irrtum vorbehalten

error message n Fehlermeldung f

erstwhile ['əːstwaɪl] adj einstig, vormalig

erudite ['ɛrjudaɪt] adj gelehrt

erupt [ɪ'rʌpt] vi ausbrechen

eruption [ɪ'rʌpʃən] n Ausbruch m

ESA n abbr (= European Space Agency) Europäische Weltraumbehörde f

escalate ['ɛskəleɪt] vi eskalieren, sich ausweiten

escalation [ɛskə'leɪʃən] n Eskalation f

escalator ['ɛskəleɪtəʳ] n Rolltreppe f

escalator clause n Gleitklausel f

escapade [ɛskə'peɪd] n Eskapade f

escape [ɪs'keɪp] n Flucht f; (Tech: of liquid) Ausfließen nt; (of gas) Ausströmen nt; (of air, heat) Entweichen nt ▷ vi entkommen; (from prison) ausbrechen; (liquid) ausfließen; (gas) ausströmen; (air, heat) entweichen ▷ vt (pursuers etc) entkommen +dat; (punishment etc) entgehen +dat; **his name ~s me** sein Name ist mir entfallen; **to ~ from** flüchten aus; (prison) ausbrechen aus; (person) entkommen +dat; **to ~ to Peru** nach Peru fliehen; **to ~ to safety** sich in Sicherheit bringen; **to ~ notice** unbemerkt bleiben

escape artist n Entfesselungskünstler(in) m(f)

escape clause n (in contract) Befreiungsklausel f

escapee [ɪskeɪ'piː] n entwichener Häftling m

escape hatch n Notluke f

escape key n (Comput) Escape-Taste f

escape route n Fluchtweg m

escapism [ɪs'keɪpɪzəm] n Wirklichkeitsflucht f, Eskapismus m

escapist [ɪs'keɪpɪst] adj eskapistisch

escapologist [ɛskə'pɒlədʒɪst] (Brit) n = **escape artist**

escarpment [ɪs'kɑːpmənt] n Steilhang m

eschew [ɪs'tʃuː] vt meiden

escort [n 'ɛskɔːt, vt ɪs'kɔːt] n Eskorte f; (companion) Begleiter(in) m(f) ▷ vt begleiten; **his ~** seine Begleiterin; **her ~** ihr Begleiter

escort agency n Agentur f für Begleiter(innen)

Eskimo ['ɛskɪməʊ] n Eskimo(frau) m(f)

ESL n abbr (Scol: = English as a Second Language) Englisch nt als Zweitsprache

esophagus [iː'sɒfəgəs] (US) n = **oesophagus**

esoteric [ɛsə'tɛrɪk] adj esoterisch

ESP n abbr = **extrasensory perception**; (Scol: = English for Specific (or Special) Purposes) Englischunterricht für spezielle Fachbereiche

esp. abbr = **especially**

especially [ɪs'pɛʃlɪ] adv besonders

espionage ['ɛspɪənɑːʒ] n Spionage f

esplanade [ɛsplə'neɪd] n Promenade f

espouse [ɪs'paʊz] vt eintreten für

Esquire [ɪs'kwaɪəʳ] n (abbr Esq.): **J. Brown, ~** Herrn J. Brown

essay ['ɛseɪ] n Aufsatz m; (Liter) Essay m or nt

essence ['ɛsns] n Wesen nt; (Culin) Essenz f; **in ~** im Wesentlichen; **speed is of the ~** Geschwindigkeit ist von entscheidender Bedeutung

essential [ɪ'sɛnʃl] adj notwendig; (basic) wesentlich ▷ n (see adj) Notwendigste(s) nt; Wesentliche(s) nt; **it is ~ that** es ist unbedingt or absolut erforderlich, dass

essentially [ɪ'sɛnʃəlɪ] adv im Grunde genommen

EST (US) abbr (= Eastern Standard Time) ostamerikanische Standardzeit

est. abbr = **established; estimate; estimated**

establish [ɪs'tæblɪʃ] vt gründen; (facts) feststellen; (proof) erstellen; (relations, contact) aufnehmen; (reputation) sich dat verschaffen

established [ɪs'tæblɪʃt] adj üblich; (business) eingeführt

establishment [ɪs'tæblɪʃmənt] n (see vb) Gründung f; Feststellung f; Erstellung f; Aufnahme f; (of reputation) Begründung f; (shop etc) Unternehmen nt; **the E~** das Establishment

estate [ɪs'teɪt] n Gut nt; (Brit: also: **housing estate**) Siedlung f; (Law) Nachlass m

estate agency (Brit) n Maklerbüro nt

estate agent (Brit) n Immobilienmakler(in) m(f)

estate car (Brit) n Kombiwagen m

esteem [ɪs'tiːm] n: **to hold sb in high ~** eine hohe Meinung von jdm haben

esthetic [ɪs'θɛtɪk] (US) adj = **aesthetic**

estimate ['ɛstɪmət] n Schätzung f; (assessment) Einschätzung f; (Comm) (Kosten)voranschlag m ▷ vt schätzen ▷ vi (Brit: Comm): **to ~ for** einen Kostenvoranschlag machen für; **to give sb an ~ of sth** jdm eine Vorstellung von etw geben; **to ~ for** einen Kostenvoranschlag machen für; **at a rough ~** grob geschätzt, über den Daumen gepeilt (inf); **I ~ that** ich schätze, dass

estimation [ɛstɪ'meɪʃən] n Schätzung f; (opinion) Einschätzung f; **in my ~** meiner Einschätzung nach

estimator ['ɛstɪmeɪtəʳ] n Schätzer(in) m(f)

Estonia [ɛs'təʊnɪə] n Estland nt

Estonian [ɛs'təʊnɪən] adj estnisch ▷ n Este m, Estin f; (Ling) Estnisch nt

estranged [ɪs'treɪndʒd] adj entfremdet; (from spouse) getrennt; (couple) getrennt lebend

estrangement [ɪs'treɪndʒmənt] n Entfremdung f; (from spouse) Trennung f

estrogen ['iːstrəʊdʒən] (US) n = **oestrogen**

estuary ['ɛstjuərɪ] n Mündung f

ET (Brit) n abbr (= Employment Training) Ausbildungsmaßnahmen für Arbeitslose

ETA n abbr (= estimated time of arrival) voraussichtliche Ankunftszeit f

et al. abbr (= et alii) u. a.

etc. abbr (= et cetera) etc.

etch [ɛtʃ] vt (design, surface: with needle) radieren; (: with acid) ätzen; (: with chisel) meißeln; **it will be ~ed on my memory** es wird sich tief in mein Gedächtnis eingraben

etching ['ɛtʃɪŋ] n Radierung f

ETD n abbr (= estimated time of departure) voraussichtliche Abflugzeit f

eternal [ɪ'təːnl] adj ewig

eternity [ɪ'təːnɪtɪ] n Ewigkeit f

ether ['iːθəʳ] n Äther m

ethereal [ɪ'θɪərɪəl] adj ätherisch

ethical ['ɛθɪkl] adj ethisch

ethics ['ɛθɪks] n Ethik f ▷ npl (morality) Moral f

Ethiopia [iːθɪ'əʊpɪə] n Äthiopien nt

Ethiopian [iːθɪ'əʊpɪən] adj äthiopisch ▷ n

e

543

Äthiopier(in) *m(f)*

ethnic ['εθnɪk] *adj* ethnisch; *(music)*
folkloristisch; *(culture etc)* urwüchsig

ethnic cleansing [-'klɛnzɪŋ] *n* ethnische
Säuberung *f*

ethnic minority *n* ethnische Minderheit *f*

ethnology [εθ'nɔlədʒɪ] *n* Ethnologie *f*,
Völkerkunde *f*

ethos ['i:θɔs] *n* Ethos *nt*

e-ticket ['i:tɪkɪt] *n abbr* (= *electronic ticket*)
E-Ticket *nt, elektronische Eintrittskarte/Fahrkarte
etc*

etiquette ['ɛtɪkɛt] *n* Etikette *f*

ETV (*US*) *n abbr* (= *educational television*)
*Fernsehsender, der Bildungs- und Kulturprogramme
ausstrahlt*

etymology [ɛtɪ'mɔlədʒɪ] *n* Etymologie *f*; (*of
word*) Herkunft *f*

EU *n abbr* (= *European Union*) EU *f*

eucalyptus [ju:kə'lɪptəs] *n* Eukalyptus *m*

Eucharist ['ju:kərɪst] *n*: **the ~** die Eucharistie,
das (heilige) Abendmahl

eulogy ['ju:lədʒɪ] *n* Lobrede *f*

euphemism ['ju:fəmɪzəm] *n* Euphemismus *m*

euphemistic [ju:fə'mɪstɪk] *adj* euphemistisch,
verhüllend

euphoria [ju:'fɔ:rɪə] *n* Euphorie *f*

Eurasia [juə'reɪʃə] *n* Eurasien *nt*

Eurasian [juə'reɪʃən] *adj* eurasisch ▷ *n*
Eurasier(in) *m(f)*

Euratom [juə'rætəm] *n abbr* (= *European Atomic
Energy Community*) Euratom *f*

euro ['juərəu] *n* (*Fin*) Euro *m*

Euro- ['juərəu] *pref* Euro-

euro cent ['juərəu-] *n* Eurocent *m*

Eurocrat ['juərəukræt] *n* Eurokrat(in) *m(f)*

Eurodollar ['juərəudɔləʳ] *n* Eurodollar *m*

Euroland ['juərəulænd] *n* (*Fin*) Eurozone *f*

Europe ['juərəp] *n* Europa *nt*

European [juərə'pi:ən] *adj* europäisch ▷ *n*
Europäer(in) *m(f)*

European Central Bank *n*: **the ~** die
Europäische Zentralbank

European Community *n*: **the ~** die
Europäische Gemeinschaft

European Convention *n* Europäische(r)
Konvent *m*, EU-Konvent *m*

European Court of Justice *n*: **the ~** der
Europäische Gerichtshof

European Economic Community
n (formerly): **the ~** die Europäische
Wirtschaftsgemeinschaft

Euro-sceptic ['juərəuskɛptɪk] *n*
Euroskeptiker(in) *m(f)*

euthanasia [ju:θə'neɪzɪə] *n* Euthanasie *f*

evacuate [ɪ'vækjueɪt] *vt* evakuieren; *(place)*
räumen

evacuation [ɪvækju'eɪʃən] *n* (*see verb*)
Evakuierung *f*; Räumung *f*

evacuee [ɪvækju'i:] *n* Evakuierte(r) *f(m)*

evade [ɪ'veɪd] *vt* (*person, question*) ausweichen
+*dat*; *(tax)* hinterziehen; *(duty, responsibility)* sich
entziehen +*dat*

evaluate [ɪ'væljueɪt] *vt* bewerten; *(situation)*
einschätzen

evangelical [i:væn'dʒɛlɪkl] *adj* evangelisch

evangelist [ɪ'vændʒəlɪst] *n* Evangelist(in)
m(f)

evangelize [ɪ'vændʒəlaɪz] *vi* evangelisieren

evaporate [ɪ'væpəreɪt] *vi* verdampfen; *(feeling,
attitude)* dahinschwinden

evaporated milk [ɪ'væpəreɪtɪd-] *n*
Kondensmilch *f*, Büchsenmilch *f*

evaporation [ɪvæpə'reɪʃən] *n* Verdampfung *f*

evasion [ɪ'veɪʒən] *n* Ausweichen *nt*; *(of tax)*
Hinterziehung *f*

evasive [ɪ'veɪsɪv] *adj* ausweichend; **to take ~
action** ein Ausweichmanöver machen

eve [i:v] *n*: **on the ~ of** am Tag vor +*dat*;
Christmas E~ Heiligabend *m*; **New Year's E~**
Silvester *m or nt*

even ['i:vn] *adj* (*level*) eben; *(smooth)* glatt;
(equal) gleich; *(number)* gerade ▷ *adv* sogar,
selbst; *(introducing a comparison)* sogar noch; **~
if, ~ though** selbst wenn; **~ more** sogar noch
mehr; **he loves her ~ more** er liebt sie umso
mehr; **it's going ~ faster now** es fährt jetzt
sogar noch schneller; **~ so** (aber) trotzdem;
not ~ nicht einmal; **~ he was there** sogar er
war da; **to break ~** die Kosten decken; **to get
~ with sb** es jdm heimzahlen

  ▶ **even out** *vi* sich ausgleichen ▷ *vt*
ausgleichen

even-handed ['i:vnhændɪd] *adj* gerecht

evening ['i:vnɪŋ] *n* Abend *m*; **in the ~** abends,
am Abend; **this ~** heute Abend; **tomorrow/
yesterday ~** morgen/gestern Abend

evening class *n* Abendkurs *m*

evening dress *n* (*no pl*) Abendkleidung *f*;
(woman's) Abendkleid *nt*

evenly ['i:vnlɪ] *adv* gleichmäßig

evensong ['i:vnsɔŋ] *n* Abendandacht *f*

event [ɪ'vɛnt] *n* Ereignis *nt*; *(Sport)*
Wettkampf *m*; **in the normal course of ~s**
normalerweise; **in the ~ of** im Falle +*gen*; **in
the ~** schließlich; **at all ~s** (*Brit*), **in any ~** auf
jeden Fall

eventful [ɪ'vɛntful] *adj* ereignisreich

eventing [ɪ'vɛntɪŋ] *n* (*Horseriding*) Military *f*

eventual [ɪ'vɛntʃuəl] *adj* schließlich; *(goal)*
letztlich

eventuality [ɪvɛntʃu'ælɪtɪ] *n* Eventualität *f*

eventually [ɪ'vɛntʃuəlɪ] *adv* endlich; *(in time)*
schließlich

ever ['ɛvəʳ] *adv* immer; *(at any time)* je(mals);
why ~ not? warum denn bloß nicht?; **the
best ~** der/die/das Allerbeste; **have you ~
seen it?** haben Sie es schon einmal gesehen?;
for ~ für immer; **hardly ~** kaum je(mals);
better than ~ besser als je zuvor; **~ since**
adv seitdem ▷ *conj* seit, seitdem; **~ so pretty**
unheimlich hübsch (*inf*); **thank you ~ so
much** ganz herzlichen Dank; **yours ~** (*Brit: in
letters*) alles Liebe

Everest ['ɛvərɪst] *n* (*also*: **Mount Everest**)
Mount Everest *m*

evergreen ['ɛvəgri:n] n (tree/bush)
immergrüner Baum/Strauch m
everlasting [ɛvə'lɑ:stɪŋ] adj ewig

○ KEYWORD

every ['ɛvrɪ] adj **1** jede(r, s); **every one of them**
(persons) jede(r) (Einzelne) von ihnen; (objects)
jedes einzelne Stück; **every day** jeden Tag;
every week jede Woche; **every other car**
jedes zweite Auto; **every other/third day**
alle zwei/drei Tage; **every shop in the town
was closed** alle Geschäfte der Stadt waren
geschlossen; **every now and then** ab und zu,
hin und wieder
2 (all possible): **I have every confidence in him**
ich habe volles Vertrauen in ihn; **we wish you
every success** wir wünschen Ihnen alles Gute

everybody ['ɛvrɪbɔdɪ] pron jeder, alle pl; ~
knows about it alle wissen es; ~ **else** alle
anderen pl
everyday ['ɛvrɪdeɪ] adj täglich; (usual, common)
alltäglich; (life, language) Alltags-
everyone ['ɛvrɪwʌn] pron = **everybody**
everything ['ɛvrɪθɪŋ] pron alles; **he did ~
possible** er hat sein Möglichstes getan
everywhere ['ɛvrɪwɛəʳ] adv überall; (wherever)
wo auch or immer; ~ **you go you meet ...** wo
man auch or wo immer man hingeht, trifft
man ...
evict [ɪ'vɪkt] vt zur Räumung zwingen
eviction [ɪ'vɪkʃən] n Ausweisung f
eviction notice n Räumungskündigung f
eviction order n Räumungsbefehl m
evidence ['ɛvɪdns] n Beweis m; (of witness)
Aussage f; (sign, indication) Zeichen nt, Spur f;
to give ~ (als Zeuge) aussagen; **to show ~ of**
zeigen; **in ~** sichtbar
evident ['ɛvɪdnt] adj offensichtlich
evidently ['ɛvɪdntlɪ] adv offensichtlich
evil ['i:vl] adj böse; (influence) schlecht ▷ n
Böse(s) nt; (unpleasant situation or activity) Übel nt
evocative [ɪ'vɔkətɪv] adj evokativ
evoke [ɪ'vəuk] vt hervorrufen; (memory) wecken
evolution [i:və'lu:ʃən] n Evolution f;
(development) Entwicklung f
evolve [ɪ'vɔlv] vt entwickeln ▷ vi sich
entwickeln
ewe [ju:] n Mutterschaf nt
ewer ['ju:əʳ] n (Wasser)krug m
ex- [ɛks] pref Ex-, frühere(r, s); **the price ex
works** der Preis ab Werk
exacerbate [ɛks'æsəbeɪt] vt verschärfen; (pain)
verschlimmern
exact [ɪg'zækt] adj genau; (word) richtig ▷ vt: **to
~ sth (from)** etw verlangen (von); (payment)
etw eintreiben (von)
exacting [ɪg'zæktɪŋ] adj anspruchsvoll
exactly [ɪg'zæktlɪ] adv genau; **~!** (ganz) genau!;
not ~ (hardly) nicht gerade
exaggerate [ɪg'zædʒəreɪt] vt, vi übertreiben
exaggerated [ɪg'zædʒəreɪtɪd] adj übertrieben

exaggeration [ɪgzædʒə'reɪʃən] n Übertreibung
f
exalt [ɪg'zɔ:lt] vt preisen
exalted [ɪg'zɔ:ltɪd] adj hoch; (elated) exaltiert
exam [ɪg'zæm] n abbr = **examination**
examination [ɪgzæmɪ'neɪʃən] n (see vb)
Untersuchung f; Prüfung f; Verhör nt; **to take
an ~, to sit an ~** (Brit) eine Prüfung machen;
the matter is under ~ die Angelegenheit
wird geprüft or untersucht
examine [ɪg'zæmɪn] vt untersuchen; (accounts,
candidate) prüfen; (witness) verhören
examiner [ɪg'zæmɪnəʳ] n Prüfer(in) m(f)
example [ɪg'zɑ:mpl] n Beispiel nt; **for ~** zum
Beispiel; **to set a good/bad ~** ein gutes/
schlechtes Beispiel geben
exasperate [ɪg'zɑ:spəreɪt] vt (annoy) verärgern;
(frustrate) zur Verzweiflung bringen; **~d by** or
with verärgert/verzweifelt über +acc
exasperating [ɪg'zɑ:spəreɪtɪŋ] adj ärgerlich;
(job) leidig
exasperation [ɪgzɑ:spə'reɪʃən] n Verzweiflung
f; **in ~** verzweifelt
excavate ['ɛkskəveɪt] vt ausgraben; (hole)
graben ▷ vi Ausgrabungen machen
excavation [ɛkskə'veɪʃən] n Ausgrabung f
excavator ['ɛkskəveɪtəʳ] n Bagger m
exceed [ɪk'si:d] vt übersteigen; (hopes)
übertreffen; (limit, budget, powers) überschreiten
exceedingly [ɪk'si:dɪŋlɪ] adv äußerst
excel [ɪk'sɛl] vt übertreffen ▷ vi: **to ~ (in** or **at)**
sich auszeichnen (in +dat); **to ~ o.s.** (Brit) sich
selbst übertreffen
excellence ['ɛksələns] n hervorragende
Leistung f
Excellency ['ɛksələnsɪ] n: **His ~** Seine Exzellenz
excellent ['ɛksələnt] adj ausgezeichnet,
hervorragend
except [ɪk'sɛpt] prep (also: **except for**) außer
+dat ▷ vt: **to ~ sb (from)** jdn ausnehmen (bei);
~ if, ~ when außer wenn; **~ that** nur dass
excepting [ɪk'sɛptɪŋ] prep außer +dat, mit
Ausnahme +gen
exception [ɪk'sɛpʃən] n Ausnahme f; **to take ~
to** Anstoß nehmen an +dat; **with the ~ of** mit
Ausnahme von
exceptional [ɪk'sɛpʃənl] adj außergewöhnlich
excerpt ['ɛksə:pt] n Auszug m
excess [ɪk'sɛs] n Übermaß nt; (Insurance)
Selbstbeteiligung f; **excesses** npl Exzesse
pl; **an ~ of £15, a £15 excess** eine
Selbstbeteiligung von £15; **in ~ of** über +dat
excess baggage n Übergepäck nt
excess fare (Brit) n Nachlösegebühr f
excessive [ɪk'sɛsɪv] adj übermäßig
excess supply n Überangebot nt
exchange [ɪks'tʃeɪndʒ] n Austausch m;
(conversation) Wortwechsel m; (also: **telephone
exchange**) Fernsprechamt nt ▷ vt: **to ~ (for)**
tauschen (gegen); (in shop) umtauschen
(gegen); **in ~ for** für; **foreign ~**
Devisenhandel m; (money) Devisen pl
exchange control n Devisenkontrolle f

exchange market n Devisenmarkt m
exchange rate n Wechselkurs m
Exchequer [ɪks'tʃɛkər] (Brit) n: **the ~** das Finanzministerium
excisable [ɪk'saɪzəbl] adj steuerpflichtig
excise ['ɛksaɪz] n Verbrauchssteuer f ▷ vt entfernen
excise duties npl Verbrauchssteuern pl
excitable [ɪk'saɪtəbl] adj (leicht) erregbar
excite [ɪk'saɪt] vt aufregen; (arouse) erregen; **to get ~d** sich aufregen
excitement [ɪk'saɪtmənt] n Aufregung f; (exhilaration) Hochgefühl nt
exciting [ɪk'saɪtɪŋ] adj aufregend
excl. abbr = **excluding; exclusive (of)**
exclaim [ɪks'kleɪm] vi aufschreien
exclamation [ɛkskla'meɪʃən] n Ausruf m; **~ of joy** Freudenschrei m
exclamation mark n Ausrufezeichen nt
exclude [ɪks'klu:d] vt ausschließen
excluding [ɪks'klu:dɪŋ] prep: **~ VAT** ohne Mehrwertsteuer
exclusion [ɪks'klu:ʒən] n Ausschluss m; **to concentrate on sth to the ~ of everything else** sich ausschließlich auf etw dat konzentrieren
exclusion clause n Freizeichnungsklausel f
exclusion zone n Sperrzone f
exclusive [ɪks'klu:sɪv] adj exklusiv; (story, interview) Exklusiv-; (use) ausschließlich ▷ n Exklusivbericht m ▷ adv: **from 1st to 15th March** ~ vom 1. bis zum 15. März ausschließlich; **~ of postage** ohne or exklusive Porto; **~ of tax** ausschließlich or exklusive Steuern; **to be mutually ~** sich or einander ausschließen
exclusively [ɪks'klu:sɪvlɪ] adv ausschließlich
exclusive rights npl Exklusivrechte pl
excommunicate [ɛkskə'mju:nɪkeɪt] vt exkommunizieren
excrement ['ɛkskrəmənt] n Kot m, Exkremente pl
excruciating [ɪks'kru:ʃɪeɪtɪŋ] adj grässlich, fürchterlich; (noise, embarrassment) unerträglich
excursion [ɪks'kə:ʃən] n Ausflug m
excursion ticket n verbilligte Fahrkarte f
excusable [ɪks'kju:zəbl] adj verzeihlich, entschuldbar
excuse [n ɪks'kju:s, vb ɪks'kju:z] n Entschuldigung f ▷ vt entschuldigen; (forgive) verzeihen; **to ~ sb from sth** jdm etw erlassen; **to ~ sb from doing sth** jdn davon befreien, etw zu tun; **~ me!** entschuldigen Sie!, Entschuldigung!; **if you will ~ me ...** entschuldigen Sie mich bitte ...; **to ~ o.s. for sth** sich für or wegen etw entschuldigen; **to ~ o.s. for doing sth** sich entschuldigen, dass man etw tut; **to make ~s for sb** jdn entschuldigen; **that's no ~!** das ist keine Ausrede!
ex-directory ['ɛksdɪ'rɛktərɪ] (Brit) adj (number) geheim; **she's ~** sie steht nicht im Telefonbuch
execrable ['ɛksɪkrəbl] adj scheußlich; (manners) abscheulich
execute ['ɛksɪkju:t] vt ausführen; (person) hinrichten
execution [ɛksɪ'kju:ʃən] n (see vb) Ausführung f; Hinrichtung f
executioner [ɛksɪ'kju:ʃnər] n Scharfrichter m
executive [ɪg'zɛkjutɪv] n leitende(r) Angestellte(r) f(m); (committee) Vorstand m ▷ adj geschäftsführend; (role) führend; (secretary) Chef-; (car, chair) für gehobene Ansprüche; (toys) Manager-; (plane) = Privat-
executive director n leitender Direktor m, leitende Direktorin f
executor [ɪg'zɛkjutər] n Testamentsvollstrecker(in) m(f)
exemplary [ɪg'zɛmplərɪ] adj vorbildlich, beispielhaft; (punishment) exemplarisch
exemplify [ɪg'zɛmplɪfaɪ] vt verkörpern; (illustrate) veranschaulichen
exempt [ɪg'zɛmpt] adj: **~ from** befreit von ▷ vt: **to ~ sb from** jdn befreien von
exemption [ɪg'zɛmpʃən] n Befreiung f
exercise ['ɛksəsaɪz] n Übung f; (no pl: keep-fit) Gymnastik f; (: energetic movement) Bewegung f; (: of authority etc) Ausübung f ▷ vt (patience) üben; (right) ausüben; (dog) ausführen; (mind) beschäftigen ▷ vi (also: **to take exercise**) Sport treiben
exercise book n (Schul)heft nt
exert [ɪg'zə:t] vt (influence) ausüben; (authority) einsetzen; **to ~ o.s.** sich anstrengen
exertion [ɪg'zə:ʃən] n Anstrengung f
ex gratia ['ɛks'greɪʃə] adj: **~ payment** freiwillige Zahlung f
exhale [ɛks'heɪl] vt, vi ausatmen
exhaust [ɪg'zɔ:st] n (also: **exhaust pipe**) Auspuff m; (fumes) Auspuffgase pl ▷ vt erschöpfen; (money) aufbrauchen; (topic) erschöpfend behandeln; **to ~ o.s.** sich verausgaben
exhausted [ɪg'zɔ:stɪd] adj erschöpft
exhausting [ɪg'zɔ:stɪŋ] adj anstrengend
exhaustion [ɪg'zɔ:stʃən] n Erschöpfung f; **nervous ~** nervöse Erschöpfung
exhaustive [ɪg'zɔ:stɪv] adj erschöpfend
exhibit [ɪg'zɪbɪt] n Ausstellungsstück nt; (Law) Beweisstück n ▷ vt zeigen, an den Tag legen; (paintings) ausstellen
exhibition [ɛksɪ'bɪʃən] n Ausstellung f; **to make an ~ of o.s.** sich unmöglich aufführen; **an ~ of bad manners** schlechte Manieren pl; **an ~ of draughtsmanship** zeichnerisches Können nt
exhibitionist [ɛksɪ'bɪʃənɪst] n Exhibitionist(in) m(f)
exhibitor [ɪg'zɪbɪtər] n Aussteller(in) m(f)
exhilarating [ɪg'zɪləreɪtɪŋ] adj erregend, berauschend; (news) aufregend
exhilaration [ɪgzɪlə'reɪʃən] n Hochgefühl nt
exhort [ɪg'zɔ:t] vt: **to ~ sb to do sth** jdn ermahnen, etw zu tun

exile ['ɛksaıl] n Exil nt; (person) Verbannte(r) f(m) ▷ vt verbannen; **in ~** im Exil

exist [ıg'zıst] vi existieren

existence [ıg'zıstəns] n Existenz f; **to be in ~** existieren

existentialism [ɛgzıs'tɛnʃlızəm] n Existenzialismus m

existing [ıg'zıstıŋ] adj bestehend

exit ['ɛksıt] n Ausgang m; (from motorway) Ausfahrt f; (departure) Abgang m ▷ vi (Theat) abgehen; (Comput: from program/file etc) das Programm/die Datei etc verlassen; **to ~ from** hinausgehen aus; (motorway etc) abfahren von

exit poll n bei Wählern unmittelbar nach Verlassen der Wahllokale durchgeführte Umfrage

exit ramp (US) n Ausfahrt f

exit visa n Ausreisevisum nt

exodus ['ɛksədəs] n Auszug m; **the ~ to the cities** die Abwanderung in die Städte

ex officio ['ɛksə'fıʃıəu] adj von Amts wegen ▷ adv kraft seines Amtes

exonerate [ıg'zɔnəreıt] vt: **to ~ from** entlasten von

exorbitant [ıg'zɔːbıtnt] adj (prices, rents) astronomisch, unverschämt; (demands) maßlos, übertrieben

exorcize ['ɛksɔːsaız] vt exorzieren; (spirit) austreiben

exotic [ıg'zɔtık] adj exotisch

expand [ıks'pænd] vt erweitern; (staff, numbers etc) vergrößern; (influence) ausdehnen ▷ vi expandieren; (population) wachsen; (gas, metal) sich ausdehnen; **to ~ on** weiter ausführen

expanse [ıks'pæns] n Weite f

expansion [ıks'pænʃən] n Expansion f; (of population) Wachstum nt; (of gas, metal) Ausdehnung f

expansionism [ıks'pænʃənızəm] n Expansionspolitik f

expansionist [ıks'pænʃənıst] adj Expansions-, expansionistisch

expatriate [ɛks'pætrıət] n im Ausland Lebende(r) f(m)

expect [ıks'pɛkt] vt erwarten; (suppose) denken, glauben; (count on) rechnen mit ▷ vi: **to be ~ing** ein Kind erwarten; **to ~ sb to do sth** erwarten, dass jd etw tut; **to ~ to do sth** vorhaben, etw zu tun; **as ~ed** wie erwartet; **I ~ so** ich glaube schon

expectancy [ıks'pɛktənsı] n Erwartung f; **life ~** Lebenserwartung f

expectant [ıks'pɛktənt] adj erwartungsvoll

expectantly [ıks'pɛktəntlı] adv erwartungsvoll

expectant mother n werdende Mutter f

expectation [ɛkspɛk'teıʃən] n Erwartung f; (hope) Hoffnung f; **in ~ of** in Erwartung +gen; **against** or **contrary to all ~(s)** wider Erwarten; **to come** or **live up to sb's ~s** jds Erwartungen dat entsprechen

expedience [ıks'piːdıəns] n = **expediency**

expediency [ıks'piːdıənsı] n Zweckmäßigkeit f; **for the sake of ~** aus Gründen der Zweckmäßigkeit

expedient [ıks'piːdıənt] adj zweckmäßig ▷ n Hilfsmittel nt

expedite ['ɛkspədaıt] vt beschleunigen

expedition [ɛkspə'dıʃən] n Expedition f; (for shopping etc) Tour f

expeditionary force [ɛkspə'dıʃənrı-] n Expeditionskorps nt

expeditious [ɛkspə'dıʃəs] adj schnell

expel [ıks'pɛl] vt (from school) verweisen; (from organization) ausschließen; (from place) vertreiben; (gas, liquid) ausstoßen

expend [ıks'pɛnd] vt ausgeben; (time, energy) aufwenden

expendable [ıks'pɛndəbl] adj entbehrlich

expenditure [ıks'pɛndıtʃər] n Ausgaben pl; (of energy, time) Aufwand m

expense [ıks'pɛns] n Kosten pl; (expenditure) Ausgabe f; **expenses** npl Spesen pl; **at the ~ of** auf Kosten +gen; **to go to the ~ of buying a new car** (viel) Geld für ein neues Auto anlegen; **at great/little ~** mit hohen/geringen Kosten

expense account n Spesenkonto nt

expensive [ıks'pɛnsıv] adj teuer; **to have ~ tastes** einen teuren Geschmack haben

experience [ıks'pıərıəns] n Erfahrung f; (event, activity) Erlebnis nt ▷ vt erleben; **by** or **from ~** aus Erfahrung; **to learn by ~** durch eigene Erfahrung lernen

experienced [ıks'pıərıənst] adj erfahren

experiment [ıks'pɛrımənt] n Experiment nt, Versuch m ▷ vi: **to ~ (with/on)** experimentieren (mit/an +dat); **to perform** or **carry out an ~** einen Versuch or ein Experiment durchführen; **as an ~** versuchsweise

experimental [ıkspɛrı'mɛntl] adj experimentell; **at the ~ stage** im Versuchsstadium

expert ['ɛkspəːt] adj ausgezeichnet, geschickt; (opinion, help etc) eines Fachmanns ▷ n Fachmann m, Fachfrau f, Experte m, Expertin f; **to be ~ in** or **at doing sth** etw ausgezeichnet können; **an ~ on sth/on the subject of sth** ein Experte für etw/auf dem Gebiet einer Sache gen; **~ witness** (Law) sachverständiger Zeuge m

expertise [ɛkspəː'tiːz] n Sachkenntnis f

expire [ıks'paıər] vi ablaufen

expiry [ıks'paıərı] n Ablauf m

expiry date n Ablauftermin m; (of voucher, special offer etc) Verfallsdatum nt

explain [ıks'pleın] vt erklären

▶ **explain away** vt eine Erklärung finden für

explanation [ɛksplə'neıʃən] n Erklärung f; **to find an ~ for sth** eine Erklärung für etw finden

explanatory [ıks'plænətrı] adj erklärend

expletive [ıks'pliːtıv] n Kraftausdruck m

explicable [ıks'plıkəbl] adj erklärbar; **for no ~ reason** aus unerfindlichen Gründen

explicit [ıks'plısıt] adj ausdrücklich; (sex,

violence) deutlich, unverhüllt; **to be ~** *(frank)* sich deutlich ausdrücken

explode [ɪks'pləud] *vi* explodieren; *(population)* sprunghaft ansteigen ▷ *vt* zur Explosion bringen; *(myth, theory)* zu Fall bringen

exploit ['eksplɔɪt] *n* Heldentat *f* ▷ *vt* ausnutzen; *(workers etc)* ausbeuten; *(resources)* nutzen

exploitation [eksplɔɪ'teɪʃən] *n (see vb)* Ausnutzung *f*; Ausbeutung *f*; Nutzung *f*

exploration [eksplə'reɪʃən] *n (see vb)* Erforschung *f*; Erkundung *f*; Untersuchung *f*

exploratory [ɪks'plɔrətrɪ] *adj* exploratorisch; *(expedition)* Forschungs-; **~ operation** *(Med)* Explorationsoperation *f*; **~ talks** Sondierungsgespräche *pl*

explore [ɪks'plɔːʳ] *vt* erforschen; *(with hands etc, idea)* untersuchen

explorer [ɪks'plɔːrəʳ] *n* Forschungsreisende(r) *f(m)*; *(of place)* Erforscher(in) *m(f)*

explosion [ɪks'pləuʒən] *n* Explosion *f*; *(outburst)* Ausbruch *m*

explosive [ɪks'pləusɪv] *adj* explosiv; *(device)* Spreng-; *(temper)* aufbrausend ▷ *n* Sprengstoff *m*; *(device)* Sprengkörper *m*

exponent [ɪks'pəunənt] *n* Vertreter(in) *m(f)*, Exponent(in) *m(f)*; *(Math)* Exponent *m*

exponential [ekspəu'nenʃl] *adj* exponentiell; *(Math: function etc)* Exponential-

export [eks'pɔːt] *vt* exportieren, ausführen; *(ideas, values)* verbreiten ▷ *n* Export *m*, Ausfuhr *f*; *(product)* Exportgut *nt* ▷ *cpd* Export-, Ausfuhr-

exportation [ekspɔː'teɪʃən] *n* Export *m*, Ausfuhr *f*

exporter [eks'pɔːtəʳ] *n* Exporteur *m*

expose [ɪks'pəuz] *vt* freilegen; *(to heat, radiation)* aussetzen; *(unmask)* entlarven; **to ~ o.s.** sich entblößen

exposé [ɪk'spəuzeɪ] *n* Enthüllung *f*

exposed [ɪks'pəuzd] *adj* ungeschützt; *(wire)* bloßliegend; **to be ~ to** *(radiation, heat etc)* ausgesetzt sein +*dat*

exposition [ekspə'zɪʃən] *n* Erläuterung *f*; *(exhibition)* Ausstellung *f*

exposure [ɪks'pəuʒəʳ] *n (to heat, radiation)* Aussetzung *f*; *(publicity)* Publicity *f*; *(of person)* Entlarvung *f*; *(Phot)* Belichtung *f*; *(: shot)* Aufnahme *f*; **to be suffering from ~** an Unterkühlung leiden; **to die from ~** erfrieren

exposure meter *n* Belichtungsmesser *m*

expound [ɪks'paund] *vt* darlegen, erläutern

express [ɪks'pres] *adj* ausdrücklich; *(intention)* bestimmt; *(Brit: letter etc)* Express-, Eil- ▷ *n* *(train)* Schnellzug *m*; *(bus)* Schnellbus *m* ▷ *adv* *(send)* per Express ▷ *vt* ausdrücken; *(view, emotion)* zum Ausdruck bringen; **to ~ o.s.** sich ausdrücken

expression [ɪks'preʃən] *n* Ausdruck *m*; *(on face)* (Gesichts)ausdruck *m*

expressionism [ɪks'preʃənɪzəm] *n* Expressionismus *m*

expressive [ɪks'presɪv] *adj* ausdrucksvoll; **~ ability** Ausdrucksfähigkeit *f*

expressly [ɪks'preslɪ] *adv* ausdrücklich; *(intentionally)* absichtlich

expressway [ɪks'preswei] *(US) n* Schnellstraße *f*

expropriate [eks'prəuprɪeɪt] *vt* enteignen

expulsion [ɪks'pʌlʃən] *n (Scol)* Verweisung *f*; *(Pol)* Ausweisung *f*; *(of gas, liquid etc)* Ausstoßen *nt*

expurgate ['ekspə:geɪt] *vt* zensieren; **the ~d version** die zensierte *or* bereinigte Fassung

exquisite [eks'kwɪzɪt] *adj* exquisit, erlesen; *(keenly felt)* köstlich

exquisitely [eks'kwɪzɪtlɪ] *adv* exquisit; *(carved)* kunstvoll; *(polite, sensitive)* äußerst

ex-serviceman ['eks'sə:vɪsmən] *(irreg: like* **man**) *n* ehemaliger Soldat *m*

ext. *abbr (Tel)* = **extension**

extemporize [ɪks'tempəraɪz] *vi* improvisieren

extend [ɪks'tend] *vt* verlängern; *(building)* anbauen an +*acc*; *(offer, invitation)* aussprechen; *(arm, hand)* ausstrecken; *(deadline)* verschieben ▷ *vi* sich erstrecken; *(period)* dauern

extension [ɪks'tenʃən] *n* Verlängerung *f*; *(of building)* Anbau *m*; *(of time)* Aufschub *m*; *(of campaign, rights)* Erweiterung *f*; *(Tel)* (Neben)anschluss *m*; **~ 3718** *(Tel)* Apparat 3718

extension cable *n* Verlängerungskabel *nt*

extension lead *n* Verlängerungsschnur *f*

extensive [ɪks'tensɪv] *adj* ausgedehnt; *(effect)* weitreichend; *(damage)* beträchtlich; *(coverage, discussion)* ausführlich; *(inquiries)* umfangreich; *(use)* häufig

extensively [ɪks'tensɪvlɪ] *adv*: **he's travelled ~** er ist viel gereist

extent [ɪks'tent] *n* Ausdehnung *f*; *(of problem, damage, loss etc)* Ausmaß *nt*; **to some ~** bis zu einem gewissen Grade; **to a certain ~** in gewissem Maße; **to a large ~** in hohem Maße; **to the ~ of ...** *(debts)* in Höhe von ...; **to go to the ~ of doing sth** so weit gehen, etw zu tun; **to such an ~ that ...** dermaßen, dass ...; **to what ~?** inwieweit?

extenuating [ɪks'tenjueɪtɪŋ] *adj*: **~ circumstances** mildernde Umstände *pl*

exterior [eks'tɪərɪəʳ] *adj (surface, angle, world)* Außen- ▷ *n* Außenseite *f*; *(appearance)* Äußere(s) *nt*

exterminate [ɪks'tə:mɪneɪt] *vt* ausrotten

extermination [ɪkstə:mɪ'neɪʃən] *n* Ausrottung *f*

external [eks'tə:nl] *adj (wall etc)* Außen-; *(use)* äußerlich; *(evidence)* unabhängig; *(examiner, auditor)* extern ▷ *n*: **the ~s** die Äußerlichkeiten *pl*; **for ~ use only** nur äußerlich (anzuwenden); **~ affairs** *(Pol)* auswärtige Angelegenheiten *pl*

externally [eks'tə:nəlɪ] *adv* äußerlich

extinct [ɪks'tɪŋkt] *adj* ausgestorben; *(volcano)* erloschen

extinction [ɪks'tɪŋkʃən] *n* Aussterben *nt*

extinguish [ɪks'tɪŋgwɪʃ] *vt* löschen; *(hope)* zerstören

extinguisher [ɪks'tɪŋgwɪʃəʳ] *n (also:* **fire**

extinguisher) Feuerlöscher *m*
extol, (*US*) **extoll** [ɪks'təul] *vt* preisen, rühmen
extort [ɪks'tɔːt] *vt* erpressen; (*confession*) erzwingen
extortion [ɪks'tɔːʃən] *n* (*see vb*) Erpressung *f*; Erzwingung *f*
extortionate [ɪks'tɔːʃnɪt] *adj* überhöht; (*price*) Wucher-
extra ['ɛkstrə] *adj* zusätzlich ▷ *adv* extra ▷ *n* Extra *nt*; (*surcharge*) zusätzliche Kosten *pl*; (*Cine, Theat*) Statist(in) *m(f)*; **wine will cost ~** Wein wird extra berechnet
extra ... ['ɛkstrə] *pref* außer-, extra-
extract [*vt* ɪks'trækt, *n* 'ɛkstrækt] *vt* (*tooth*) ziehen; (*mineral*) gewinnen ▷ *n* Auszug *m*; (*also*: **malt extract, vanilla extract** *etc*) Extrakt *m*; **to ~ (from)** (*object*) herausziehen (aus); (*money*) herausholen (aus); (*promise*) abringen +*dat*
extraction [ɪks'trækʃən] *n* (*see vb*) Ziehen *nt*; Gewinnung *f*; Herausziehen *nt*; Herausholen *nt*; Abringen *nt*; (*Dentistry*) Extraktion *f*; (*descent*) Herkunft *f*, Abstammung *f*; **to be of Scottish ~, to be Scottish by ~** schottischer Herkunft *or* Abstammung sein
extractor fan [ɪks'træktə-] *n* Sauglüfter *m*
extracurricular ['ɛkstrəkə'rɪkjuləʳ] *adj* außerhalb des Lehrplans
extradite ['ɛkstrədaɪt] *vt* ausliefern
extradition [ɛkstrə'dɪʃən] *n* Auslieferung *f* ▷ *cpd* Auslieferungs-
extramarital ['ɛkstrə'mærɪtl] *adj* außerehelich
extramural ['ɛkstrə'mjuərl] *adj* außerhalb der Universität; **~ classes** von der Universität veranstaltete Teilzeitkurse *pl*
extraneous [ɛks'treɪnɪəs] *adj* unwesentlich
extraordinary [ɪks'trɔːdnrɪ] *adj* ungewöhnlich; (*special*) außerordentlich; **the ~ thing is that ...** das Merkwürdige ist, dass ...
extraordinary general meeting *n* außerordentliche Hauptversammlung *f*
extrapolation [ɛkstræpə'leɪʃən] *n* Extrapolation *f*
extrasensory perception ['ɛkstrə'sɛnsərɪ-] *n* außersinnliche Wahrnehmung *f*
extra time *n* (*Football*) Verlängerung *f*
extravagance [ɪks'trævəgəns] *n* (*no pl*) Verschwendungssucht *f*; (*example of spending*) Luxus *m*
extravagant [ɪks'trævəgənt] *adj* extravagant; (*tastes, gift*) teuer; (*wasteful*) verschwenderisch; (*praise*) übertrieben; (*ideas*) ausgefallen
extreme [ɪks'triːm] *adj* extrem; (*point, edge, poverty*) äußerste(r, s) ▷ *n* Extrem *nt*; **the ~ right/left** (*Pol*) die äußerste *or* extreme Rechte/Linke; **~s of temperature** extreme Temperaturen *pl*
extremely [ɪks'triːmlɪ] *adv* äußerst, extrem
extremist [ɪks'triːmɪst] *n* Extremist(in) *m(f)* ▷ *adj* extremistisch

extremities [ɪks'trɛmɪtɪz] *npl* Extremitäten *pl*
extremity [ɪks'trɛmɪtɪ] *n* Rand *m*; (*end*) äußerstes Ende *nt*; (*of situation*) Ausmaß *nt*
extricate ['ɛkstrɪkeɪt] *vt*: **to ~ sb/sth (from)** jdn/etw befreien (aus)
extrovert ['ɛkstrəvəːt] *n* extravertierter Mensch *m*
exuberance [ɪg'zjuːbərns] *n* Überschwänglichkeit *f*
exuberant [ɪg'zjuːbərnt] *adj* überschwänglich; (*imagination etc*) lebhaft
exude [ɪg'zjuːd] *vt* ausstrahlen; (*liquid*) absondern; (*smell*) ausströmen
exult [ɪg'zʌlt] *vi*: **to ~ (in)** jubeln (über +*acc*)
exultant [ɪg'zʌltənt] *adj* jubelnd; (*shout*) Jubel-; **to be ~** jubeln
exultation [ɛgzʌl'teɪʃən] *n* Jubel *m*
eye [aɪ] *n* Auge *nt*; (*of needle*) Öhr *nt* ▷ *vt* betrachten; **to keep an ~ on** aufpassen auf +*acc*; **as far as the ~ can see** so weit das Auge reicht; **in the public ~** im Blickpunkt der Öffentlichkeit; **to have an ~ for sth** einen Blick für etw haben; **with an ~ to doing sth** (*Brit*) mit der Absicht, etw zu tun; **there's more to this than meets the ~** da steckt mehr dahinter(, als man auf den ersten Blick meint)
eyeball ['aɪbɔːl] *n* Augapfel *m*
eyebath ['aɪbɑːθ] (*Brit*) *n* Augenbadewanne *f*
eyebrow ['aɪbrau] *n* Augenbraue *f*
eyebrow pencil *n* Augenbrauenstift *m*
eye-catching ['aɪkætʃɪŋ] *adj* auffallend
eyecup ['aɪkʌp] (*US*) *n* = **eyebath**
eye drops *npl* Augentropfen *pl*
eyeful ['aɪful] *n*: **to get an ~ of sth** (*lit*) etw ins Auge bekommen; (*fig: have a good look*) einiges von etw zu sehen bekommen; **she's quite an ~** sie hat allerhand zu bieten
eyeglass ['aɪglɑːs] *n* Augenglas *nt*
eyelash ['aɪlæʃ] *n* Augenwimper *f*
eyelet ['aɪlɪt] *n* Öse *f*
eye level *n*: **at ~** in Augenhöhe
eyelevel ['aɪlɛvl] *adj* in Augenhöhe
eyelid ['aɪlɪd] *n* Augenlid *nt*
eyeliner ['aɪlaɪnəʳ] *n* Eyeliner *m*
eye-opener ['aɪəupnəʳ] *n* Überraschung *f*; **to be an ~ to sb** jdm die Augen öffnen
eye shadow *n* Lidschatten *m*
eyesight ['aɪsaɪt] *n* Sehvermögen *nt*
eyesore ['aɪsɔːʳ] *n* Schandfleck *m*
eyestrain ['aɪstreɪn] *n*: **to get ~** seine Augen überanstrengen
eyetooth ['aɪtuːθ] (*pl* **eyeteeth**) *n* Eckzahn *m*, Augenzahn *m*; **to give one's eyeteeth for sth** alles für etw geben; **to give one's eyeteeth to do sth** alles darum geben, etw zu tun
eyewash ['aɪwɔʃ] *n* Augenwasser *nt*; (*fig*) Gewäsch *nt*
eyewitness ['aɪwɪtnɪs] *n* Augenzeuge *m*, Augenzeugin *f*
eyrie ['ɪərɪ] *n* Horst *m*

Ff

F¹, f [ɛf] n (letter) F nt, f nt; **F for Frederick, F for Fox** (US) ≈ F wie Friedrich

F² [ɛf] n (Mus) F nt, f nt

F³ [ɛf] abbr (= Fahrenheit) F

FA (Brit) n abbr (= Football Association) englischer Fußball-Dachverband, ≈ DFB m

FAA (US) n abbr (= Federal Aviation Administration) amerikanische Luftfahrtbehörde

fable ['feɪbl] n Fabel f

fabric ['fæbrɪk] n Stoff m; (of society) Gefüge nt; (of building) Bausubstanz f

fabricate ['fæbrɪkeɪt] vt herstellen; (story) erfinden; (evidence) fälschen

fabrication [fæbrɪ'keɪʃən] n Herstellung f; (lie) Erfindung f

fabric ribbon n (for typewriter) Gewebefarbband nt

fabulous ['fæbjʊləs] adj fabelhaft, toll (inf); (extraordinary) sagenhaft; (mythical) legendär

façade [fə'sɑːd] n Fassade f

face [feɪs] n Gesicht nt; (expression) Gesichtsausdruck m; (grimace) Grimasse f; (of clock) Zifferblatt nt; (of mountain, cliff) (Steil)wand f; (of building) Fassade f; (side, surface) Seite f ▷ vt (subj: person) gegenübersitzen/-stehen +dat etc; (: building, street etc) liegen zu; (: north, south etc) liegen nach; (unpleasant situation) sich gegenübersehen +dat; (facts) ins Auge sehen +dat; **~ down** mit dem Gesicht nach unten; (card) mit der Bildseite nach unten; (object) mit der Vorderseite nach unten; **to lose/save ~** das Gesicht verlieren/wahren; **to make** or **pull a ~** das Gesicht verziehen; **in the ~ of** trotz +gen; **on the ~ of it** so, wie es aussieht; **to come ~ to ~ with sb** jdn treffen; **to come ~ to ~ with a problem** einem Problem gegenüberstehen; **to ~ each other** einander gegenüberstehen/-liegen/-sitzen etc; **to ~ the fact that ...** der Tatsache ins Auge sehen, dass ...; **the man facing me** der Mann mir gegenüber

▶ **face up to** vt fus (obligations, difficulty) auf sich acc nehmen; (situation, possibility) sich abfinden mit; (danger, fact) ins Auge sehen +dat

face cloth (Brit) n Waschlappen m

face cream n Gesichtscreme f

faceless ['feɪslɪs] adj (fig) anonym

face-lift ['feɪslɪft] n Facelifting nt; (of building

etc) Verschönerung f

face powder n Gesichtspuder m

face-saving ['feɪs'seɪvɪŋ] adj: **a ~ excuse/tactic** eine Entschuldigung/Taktik, um das Gesicht zu wahren

facet ['fæsɪt] n Seite f, Aspekt m; (of gem) Facette f

face time n (US) Zeit, die man mit jemandem im direkten persönlichen Gespräch verbringt

facetious [fə'siːʃəs] adj witzelnd

face-to-face [feɪstə'feɪs] adj persönlich; (confrontation) direkt

face value n Nennwert m; **to take sth at ~** (fig) etw für bare Münze nehmen

facia ['feɪʃə] n = **fascia**

facial ['feɪʃl] adj (expression, massage etc) Gesichts- ▷ n kosmetische Gesichtsbehandlung f

facile ['fæsaɪl] adj oberflächlich; (comment) nichtssagend

facilitate [fə'sɪlɪteɪt] vt erleichtern

facilities [fə'sɪlɪtɪz] npl Einrichtungen pl; **cooking ~** Kochgelegenheit f; **credit ~** Kreditmöglichkeiten pl

facility [fə'sɪlɪtɪ] n Einrichtung f; **to have a ~ for** (skill, aptitude) eine Begabung haben für

facing ['feɪsɪŋ] prep gegenüber +dat ▷ n (Sewing) Besatz m

facsimile [fæk'sɪmɪlɪ] n Faksimile nt; (also: **facsimile machine**) Fernkopierer m, (Tele)faxgerät nt; (transmitted document) Fernkopie f, (Tele)fax nt

fact [fækt] n Tatsache f; (truth) Wirklichkeit f; **in ~** eigentlich; (in reality) tatsächlich, in Wirklichkeit; **to know for a ~ that ...** ganz genau wissen, dass ...; **the ~ (of the matter) is that ...** die Sache ist die, dass ...; **it's a ~ of life that ...** es ist eine Tatsache, dass ...; **to tell sb the ~s of life** (sex) jdn aufklären

fact-finding ['fæktfaɪndɪŋ] adj: **a ~ tour** or **mission** eine Informationstour f

faction ['fækʃən] n Fraktion f

factional ['fækʃənl] adj (dispute, system) Fraktions-

factor ['fæktər] n Faktor m; (Comm) Kommissionär m; (: agent) Makler m; **safety ~** Sicherheitsfaktor m; **human ~** menschlicher Faktor

factory ['fæktərı] n Fabrik f
factory farming (Brit) n industriell betriebene Viehzucht f
factory floor n: **the ~** (workers) die Fabrikarbeiter pl; **on the ~** bei or unter den Fabrikarbeitern
factory ship n Fabrikschiff nt
factual ['fæktjuəl] adj sachlich; (information) Sach-
faculty ['fækəltı] n Vermögen nt, Kraft f; (ability) Talent nt; (of university) Fakultät f; (US: teaching staff) Lehrkörper m
fad [fæd] n Fimmel m, Tick m
fade [feɪd] vi verblassen; (light) nachlassen; (sound) schwächer werden; (flower) verblühen; (hope) zerrinnen; (smile) verschwinden
 ▶ **fade in** vt sep allmählich einblenden
 ▶ **fade out** vt sep ausblenden
faeces, (US) **feces** ['fiːsiːz] npl Kot m
fag [fæg] n (Brit: inf: cigarette) Glimmstängel m; (: chore) Schinderei f (inf), Plackerei f (inf); (US: inf: homosexual) Schwule(r) m
fail [feɪl] vt (exam) nicht bestehen; (candidate) durchfallen lassen; (subj: courage) verlassen; (: leader, memory) im Stich lassen ▷ vi (candidate) durchfallen; (attempt) fehlschlagen; (brakes) versagen; (also: **be failing**: health) sich verschlechtern; (: eyesight, light) nachlassen; **to ~ to do sth** etw nicht tun; (neglect) (es) versäumen, etw zu tun; **without ~** ganz bestimmt
failing ['feɪlɪŋ] n Schwäche f, Fehler m ▷ prep in Ermangelung +gen; **~ that** (oder) sonst, und wenn das nicht möglich ist
fail-safe ['feɪlseɪf] adj (ab)gesichert
failure ['feɪljəʳ] n Misserfolg m; (person) Versager(in) m(f); (of brakes, heart) Versagen nt; (of engine, power) Ausfall m; (of crops) Missernte f; (in exam) Durchfall m; **his ~ to turn up meant that we had to ...** weil er nicht kam, mussten wir ...; **it was a complete ~** es war ein totaler Fehlschlag
faint [feɪnt] adj schwach; (breeze, trace) leicht ▷ n Ohnmacht f ▷ vi ohnmächtig werden, in Ohnmacht fallen; **she felt ~** ihr wurde schwach
faintest ['feɪntɪst] adj, n: **I haven't the ~ (idea)** ich habe keinen blassen Schimmer
faint-hearted ['feɪnt'hɑːtɪd] adj zaghaft
faintly ['feɪntlı] adv schwach
fair [fɛəʳ] adj gerecht, fair; (size, number) ansehnlich; (chance, guess) recht gut; (hair) blond; (skin, complexion) hell; (weather) schön ▷ adv: **to play ~** fair spielen ▷ n (also: **trade fair**) Messe f; (Brit: funfair) Jahrmarkt m, Rummel m; **it's not ~!** das ist nicht fair!; **a ~ amount of** ziemlich viel
fair copy n Reinschrift f
fair game n: **to be ~ (for)** (for attack, criticism) Freiwild sein (für)
fairground ['fɛəgraund] n Rummelplatz m
fair-haired [fɛə'hɛəd] adj blond
fairly ['fɛəlı] adv gerecht; (quite) ziemlich; **I'm ~**

sure ich bin (mir) ziemlich sicher
fairness ['fɛənıs] n Gerechtigkeit f; **in all ~** gerechterweise, fairerweise
fair play n faires Verhalten nt, Fair Play nt
fairway ['fɛəweɪ] n (Golf): **the ~** das Fairway
fairy ['fɛərı] n Fee f
fairy godmother n gute Fee f
fairy lights (Brit) npl bunte Lichter pl
fairy tale n Märchen nt
faith [feɪθ] n Glaube m; (trust) Vertrauen nt; **to have ~ in sb** jdm vertrauen; **to have ~ in sth** Vertrauen in etw acc haben
faithful ['feɪθful] adj (account) genau; **~ (to)** (person) treu +dat
faithfully ['feɪθfəlı] adv (see adj) genau; treu
faith healer n Gesundbeter(in) m(f)
fake [feɪk] n Fälschung f; (person) Schwindler(in) m(f) ▷ adj gefälscht ▷ vt fälschen; (illness, emotion) vortäuschen; **his illness is a ~** er simuliert seine Krankheit nur
falcon ['fɔːlkən] n Falke m
Falkland Islands ['fɔːlklənd-] npl: **the ~** die Falklandinseln pl
fall [fɔːl] (pt **fell**, pp **~en**) n Fall m; (of price, temperature) Sinken nt; (: sudden) Sturz m; (US: autumn) Herbst m ▷ vi fallen; (night, darkness) hereinbrechen; (silence) eintreten; **falls** npl (waterfall) Wasserfall m; **a ~ of snow** ein Schneefall m; **a ~ of earth** ein Erdrutsch m; **to ~ flat** auf die Nase fallen; (plan) ins Wasser fallen; (joke) nicht ankommen; **to ~ in love (with sb/sth)** sich (in jdn/etw) verlieben; **to ~ short of sb's expectations** jds Erwartungen nicht erfüllen
 ▶ **fall apart** vi auseinanderfallen, kaputtgehen; (inf: emotionally) durchdrehen
 ▶ **fall back** vi zurückweichen
 ▶ **fall back on** vi zurückgreifen auf +acc; **to have sth to ~ back on** auf etw acc zurückgreifen können
 ▶ **fall behind** vi zurückbleiben; (fig: with payment) in Rückstand geraten
 ▶ **fall down** vi hinfallen; (building) einstürzen
 ▶ **fall for** vt fus (trick, story) hereinfallen auf +acc; (person) sich verlieben in +acc
 ▶ **fall in** vi einstürzen; (Mil) antreten
 ▶ **fall in with** vt fus eingehen auf +acc
 ▶ **fall off** vi herunterfallen; (takings, attendance) zurückgehen
 ▶ **fall out** vi (hair, teeth) ausfallen; **to ~ out with sb** sich mit jdm zerstreiten
 ▶ **fall over** vi hinfallen; (object) umfallen ▷ vt: **to ~ over o.s. to do sth** sich dat die größte Mühe geben, etw zu tun
 ▶ **fall through** vi (plan, project) ins Wasser fallen
fallacy ['fæləsı] n Irrtum m
fall-back ['fɔːlbæk] adj: **~ position** Rückzugsbasis f
fallen ['fɔːlən] pp of **fall**
fallible ['fæləbl] adj fehlbar
falling ['fɔːlıŋ] adj: **~ market** (Comm) Baissemarkt m
falling off n Rückgang m

falling-out ['fɔːlɪŋ'aut] n (break-up) Bruch m
Fallopian tube [fə'ləupɪən-] n Eileiter m
fallout ['fɔːlaut] n radioaktiver Niederschlag m
fallout shelter n Atombunker m
fallow ['fæləu] adj brach(liegend)
false [fɔːls] adj falsch; (imprisonment) widerrechtlich
false alarm n falscher or blinder Alarm m
falsehood ['fɔːlshud] n Unwahrheit f
falsely ['fɔːlslɪ] adv (accuse) zu Unrecht
false pretences npl: **under ~** unter Vorspiegelung falscher Tatsachen
false teeth (Brit) npl Gebiss nt
falsify ['fɔːlsɪfaɪ] vt fälschen
falter ['fɔːltər] vi stocken; (hesitate) zögern
fame [feɪm] n Ruhm m
familiar [fə'mɪlɪər] adj vertraut; (intimate) vertraulich; **to be ~ with** vertraut sein mit; **to make o.s. ~ with sth** sich mit etw vertraut machen; **to be on ~ terms with sb** mit jdm auf vertrautem Fuß stehen
familiarity [fəmɪlɪ'ærɪtɪ] n (see adj) Vertrautheit f; Vertraulichkeit f
familiarize [fə'mɪlɪəraɪz] vt: **to ~ o.s. with sth** sich mit etw vertraut machen
family ['fæmɪlɪ] n Familie f; (relations) Verwandtschaft f
family business, family company n Familienunternehmen nt or -betrieb m
family credit n Beihilfe für einkommensschwache Familien
family doctor n Hausarzt m, Hausärztin f
family life n Familienleben nt
family man n (home-loving) häuslich veranlagter Mann m; (with a family) Familienvater m
family planning n Familienplanung f; **~ clinic** ≈ Familienberatungsstelle f
family tree n Stammbaum m
famine ['fæmɪn] n Hungersnot f
famished ['fæmɪʃt] (inf) adj ausgehungert; **I'm ~** ich sterbe vor Hunger
famous ['feɪməs] adj berühmt
famously ['feɪməslɪ] adv (get on) prächtig
fan [fæn] n (person) Fan m; (object: folding) Fächer m; (: Elec) Ventilator m ▷ vt fächeln; (fire) anfachen; (quarrel) schüren
▶ **fan out** vi ausschwärmen; (unfurl) sich fächerförmig ausbreiten
fanatic [fə'nætɪk] n Fanatiker(in) m(f); (enthusiast) Fan m
fanatical [fə'nætɪkl] adj fanatisch
fan belt n (Aut) Keilriemen m
fanciful ['fænsɪful] adj (idea) abstrus, seltsam; (design, name) fantasievoll; (object) reich verziert
fan club n Fanklub m
fancy ['fænsɪ] n Laune f; (imagination) Fantasie f; (fantasy) Fantasievorstellung f ▷ adj (clothes, hat) toll, chic inv; (hotel) fein, vornehm; (food) ausgefallen ▷ vt mögen; (imagine) sich dat einbilden; (think) glauben; **to take a ~ to sth** Lust auf etw acc bekommen; **when the ~ takes him** wenn ihm gerade danach ist;

it took or caught my ~ es gefiel mir; **to ~ that ...** meinen, dass ...; **~ that!** (nein) so was!; **he fancies her** (inf) sie gefällt ihm
fancy dress n Verkleidung f, (Masken)kostüm nt
fancy-dress ball ['fænsɪdrɛs-] n Maskenball m
fancy goods npl Geschenkartikel pl
fanfare ['fænfɛər] n Fanfare f
fanfold paper ['fænfəuld-] n Endlospapier nt
fang [fæŋ] n (tooth) Fang m; (: of snake) Giftzahn m
fan heater (Brit) n Heizlüfter m
fanlight ['fænlaɪt] n Oberlicht nt
fanny ['fænɪ] n (US: inf: bottom) Po m; (Brit: inf!: genitals) Möse f (!)
fantasize ['fæntəsaɪz] vi fantasieren
fantastic [fæn'tæstɪk] adj fantastisch
fantasy ['fæntəsɪ] n Fantasie f; (dream) Traum m
fanzine ['fænziːn] n Fanmagazin nt
FAO n abbr (= Food and Agriculture Organization) FAO f
FAQ abbr (Comput: = frequently-asked questions) FAQ pl
far [fɑːʳ] adj: **at the ~ side** auf der anderen Seite ▷ adv weit; **at the ~ end** am anderen Ende; **the ~ left/right** die extreme Linke/Rechte; **~ away, ~ off** weit entfernt or weg; **her thoughts were ~ away** sie war mit ihren Gedanken weit weg; **~ from** (fig) alles andere als; **by ~** bei Weitem; **is it ~ to London?** ist es weit bis nach London?; **it's not ~ from here** es ist nicht weit von hier; **go as ~ as the church** gehen/fahren Sie bis zur Kirche; **as ~ back as the 13th century** schon im 13. Jahrhundert; **as ~ as I know** soweit ich weiß; **as ~ as possible** so weit wie möglich; **how ~?** wie weit?; **how ~ have you got with your work?** wie weit sind Sie mit Ihrer Arbeit (gekommen)?
faraway ['fɑːrəweɪ] adj weit entfernt; (look, voice) abwesend
farce [fɑːs] n Farce f
farcical ['fɑːsɪkl] adj absurd, grotesk
fare [fɛəʳ] n Fahrpreis m; (money) Fahrgeld nt; (passenger) Fahrgast m; (food) Kost f ▷ vi: **he ~d well/badly** es ging ihm gut/schlecht; **half/full ~** halber/voller Fahrpreis; **how did you ~?** wie ist es Ihnen ergangen?; **they ~d badly in the recent elections** sie haben bei den letzten Wahlen schlecht abgeschnitten
Far East n: **the ~** der Ferne Osten
farewell [fɛə'wɛl] excl lebe/lebt etc wohl! ▷ n Abschied m ▷ cpd Abschieds-
far-fetched ['fɑː'fɛtʃt] adj weit hergeholt
farm [fɑːm] n Bauernhof m ▷ vt bebauen
▶ **farm out** vt (work etc) vergeben
farmer ['fɑːməʳ] n Bauer m, Bäu(e)rin f, Landwirt(in) m(f)
farm hand n Landarbeiter(in) m(f)
farmhouse ['fɑːmhaus] n Bauernhaus nt
farming ['fɑːmɪŋ] n Landwirtschaft f; (of crops) Ackerbau m; (of animals) Viehzucht f;

sheep ~ Schafzucht *f*; **intensive** ~ (*of crops*) Intensivanbau *m*; (*of animals*) Intensivhaltung *f*

farm labourer *n* = **farm hand**

farmland ['fɑːmlænd] *n* Ackerland *nt*

farm produce *n* landwirtschaftliche Produkte *pl*

farm worker *n* = **farm hand**

farmyard ['fɑːmjɑːd] *n* Hof *m*

Faroe Islands ['fɛərəu-] *npl*: **the** ~ die Färöer *pl*

Faroes ['fɛərəuz] *npl* = **Faroe Islands**

far-reaching ['fɑːˈriːtʃɪŋ] *adj* weitreichend

far-sighted ['fɑːˈsaɪtɪd] *adj* weitsichtig; (*fig*) weitblickend

fart [fɑːt] *vi* furzen (*inf!*) ▷ *n* Furz *m* (*inf!*)

farther ['fɑːðəʳ] *adv* weiter ▷ *adj* weiter entfernt

farthest ['fɑːðɪst] *superl of* **far**

FAS, f.a.s. (*Brit*) *abbr* (= *free alongside ship*) frei Kai

fascia ['feɪʃə] *n* (*Aut*) Armaturenbrett *nt*

fascinate ['fæsɪneɪt] *vt* faszinieren

fascinating ['fæsɪneɪtɪŋ] *adj* faszinierend

fascination [fæsɪˈneɪʃən] *n* Faszination *f*

fascism ['fæʃɪzəm] *n* Faschismus *m*

fascist ['fæʃɪst] *adj* faschistisch ▷ *n* Faschist(in) *m(f)*

fashion ['fæʃən] *n* Mode *f*; (*manner*) Art *f* ▷ *vt* formen; **in** ~ modern; **out of** ~ unmodern; **after a** ~ recht und schlecht; **in the Greek** ~ im griechischen Stil

fashionable ['fæʃnəbl] *adj* modisch, modern; (*subject*) Mode-; (*club, writer*) in Mode

fashion designer *n* Modezeichner(in) *m(f)*

fashion show *n* Modenschau *f*

fashion victim *n* Modefreak *m*

fast [fɑːst] *adj* schnell; (*dye, colour*) farbecht ▷ *adv* schnell; (*stuck, held*) fest ▷ *n* Fasten *nt*; (*period of fasting*) Fastenzeit *f* ▷ *vi* fasten; **my watch is (5 minutes)** ~ meine Uhr geht (5 Minuten) vor; **to be** ~ **asleep** tief *or* fest schlafen; **as** ~ **as I can** so schnell ich kann; **to make a boat** ~ (*Brit*) ein Boot festmachen

fasten ['fɑːsn] *vt* festmachen; (*coat, belt etc*) zumachen ▷ *vi* (*see vt*) festgemacht werden; zugemacht werden

▸ **fasten (up)on** *vt fus* sich *dat* in den Kopf setzen

fastener ['fɑːsnəʳ] *n* Verschluss *m*

fastening ['fɑːsnɪŋ] *n* = **fastener**

fast food *n* Fast Food *nt*, Schnellgerichte *pl*

fast-food ['fɑːstfuːd] *cpd* (*industry, chain*) Fast-Food-; ~ **restaurant** Schnellimbiss *m*

fastidious [fæsˈtɪdɪəs] *adj* penibel

fast lane *n* (*Aut*): **the** ~ die Überholspur

fat [fæt] *adj* dick; (*person*) dick, fett (*pej*); (*animal*) fett; (*profit*) üppig ▷ *n* Fett *nt*; **that's a** ~ **lot of use** (*inf*) das hilft herzlich wenig; **to live off the** ~ **of the land** wie Gott in Frankreich *or* wie die Made im Speck leben

fatal ['feɪtl] *adj* tödlich; (*mistake*) verhängnisvoll

fatalistic [feɪtəˈlɪstɪk] *adj* fatalistisch

fatality [fəˈtælɪtɪ] *n* Todesopfer *nt*

fatally ['feɪtəlɪ] *adv* (*see adj*) tödlich; verhängnisvoll

fate [feɪt] *n* Schicksal *nt*; **to meet one's** ~ vom Schicksal ereilt werden

fated ['feɪtɪd] *adj* (*person*) unglückselig; (*project*) zum Scheitern verurteilt; (*governed by fate*) vorherbestimmt

fateful ['feɪtful] *adj* schicksalhaft

fat-free ['fætˈfriː] *adj* fettfrei

father ['fɑːðəʳ] *n* Vater *m*

Father Christmas *n* der Weihnachtsmann

fatherhood ['fɑːðəhud] *n* Vaterschaft *f*

father-in-law ['fɑːðərənlɔː] *n* Schwiegervater *m*

fatherland ['fɑːðəlænd] *n* Vaterland *nt*

fatherly ['fɑːðəlɪ] *adj* väterlich

fathom ['fæðəm] *n* (*Naut*) Faden *m* ▷ *vt* (*also:* **fathom out**) verstehen

fatigue [fəˈtiːg] *n* Erschöpfung *f*; **fatigues** *npl* (*Mil*) Arbeitsanzug *m*; **metal** ~ Metallermüdung *f*

fatness ['fætnɪs] *n* Dicke *f*

fatten ['fætn] *vt* mästen ▷ *vi* (*person*) dick werden; (*animal*) fett werden; **chocolate is** ~**ing** Schokolade macht dick

fatty ['fætɪ] *adj* fett ▷ *n* (*inf*) Dickerchen *nt*

fatuous ['fætjuəs] *adj* albern, töricht

faucet ['fɔːsɪt] (*US*) *n* (Wasser)hahn *m*

fault [fɔːlt] *n* Fehler *m*; (*blame*) Schuld *f*; (*in machine*) Defekt *m*; (*Geog*) Verwerfung *f* ▷ *vt* (*also:* **find fault with**) etwas auszusetzen haben an +*dat*; **it's my** ~ es ist meine Schuld; **at** ~ im Unrecht; **generous to a** ~ übermäßig großzügig

faultless ['fɔːltlɪs] *adj* fehlerlos

faulty ['fɔːltɪ] *adj* defekt

fauna ['fɔːnə] *n* Fauna *f*

faux pas ['fəuˈpɑː] *n inv* Fauxpas *m*

favor *etc* (*US*) = **favour** *etc*

favour, (US**) favor** ['feɪvəʳ] *n* (*approval*) Wohlwollen *nt*; (*help*) Gefallen *m* ▷ *vt* bevorzugen; (*be favourable for*) begünstigen; **to ask a** ~ **of sb** jdn um einen Gefallen bitten; **to do sb a** ~ jdm einen Gefallen tun; **to find** ~ **with sb** bei jdm Anklang finden; **in** ~ **of** (*biased*) zugunsten von; (*rejected*) zugunsten +*gen*; **to be in** ~ **of sth** für etw sein; **to be in** ~ **of doing sth** dafür sein, etw zu tun

favourable ['feɪvrəbl] *adj* günstig; (*reaction*) positiv; (*comparison*) vorteilhaft

favourably ['feɪvrəblɪ] *adv* (*react*) positiv; (*compare*) vorteilhaft

favourite ['feɪvrɪt] *adj* Lieblings- ▷ *n* Liebling *m*; (*in race*) Favorit(in) *m(f)*

favouritism ['feɪvrɪtɪzəm] *n* Günstlingswirtschaft *f*

fawn [fɔːn] *n* Rehkitz *nt* ▷ *adj* (*also:* **fawn-coloured**) hellbraun ▷ *vi*: **to** ~ **(up)on** sich einschmeicheln bei

fax [fæks] *n* Fax *nt*; (*machine*) Fax(gerät) *nt* ▷ *vt* faxen

FBI (*US*) *n abbr* (= *Federal Bureau of Investigation*) FBI *nt*

FCC (US) n abbr (= Federal Communications Commission) Aufsichtsbehörde im Medienbereich

FCO (Brit) n abbr (= Foreign and Commonwealth Office) ≈ Auswärtiges Amt nt

FD (US) n abbr = **fire department**

FDA (US) n abbr (= Food and Drug Administration) Nahrungs- und Arzneimittelbehörde

fear [fɪəʳ] n Furcht f, Angst f ▷ vt fürchten, Angst haben vor +dat; (be worried about) befürchten ▷ vi sich fürchten; ~ **of heights** Höhenangst f; **for** ~ **of doing sth** aus Angst, etw zu tun; **to** ~ **for** fürchten um; **to** ~ **that** ... befürchten, dass ...

fearful ['fɪəful] adj (frightening) furchtbar, schrecklich; (apprehensive) ängstlich; **to be** ~ **of** Angst haben vor +dat

fearfully ['fɪəfəlɪ] adv ängstlich; (inf: very) furchtbar, schrecklich

fearless ['fɪəlɪs] adj furchtlos

fearsome ['fɪəsəm] adj furchterregend

feasibility [fiːzə'bɪlɪtɪ] n Durchführbarkeit f

feasibility study n Machbarkeits- or Durchführbarkeitsstudie f

feasible ['fiːzəbl] adj machbar; (proposal, plan) durchführbar

feast [fiːst] n Festmahl nt; (Rel: also: **feast day**) Festtag m, Feiertag m ▷ vi schlemmen; **to** ~ **on** sich gütlich tun an +dat

feat [fiːt] n Leistung f

feather ['fɛðəʳ] n Feder f ▷ cpd Feder-; (mattress) Federkern- ▷ vt: **to** ~ **one's nest** (fig) sein Schäfchen ins Trockene bringen

featherweight ['fɛðəweɪt] n Leichtgewicht nt; (Boxing) Federgewicht nt

feature ['fiːtʃəʳ] n Merkmal nt; (Press, TV) Feature nt ▷ vt: **the film** ~**s Marlon Brando** Marlon Brando spielt in dem Film mit ▷ vi: **to** ~ **in** vorkommen in +dat; (film) mitspielen in +dat; **features** npl (of face) (Gesichts)züge pl; **it** ~**d prominently in** es spielte eine große Rolle in +dat; **a special** ~ **on sth/sb** ein Sonderbeitrag m über etw/jdn

feature film n Spielfilm m

featureless ['fiːtʃəlɪs] adj (landscape) eintönig

Feb. abbr (= February) Feb.

February ['fɛbruərɪ] n Februar m; see also **July**

feces ['fiːsiːz] (US) npl = **faeces**

feckless ['fɛklɪs] adj nutzlos

Fed [fɛd] (US: inf) n abbr: **the** ~ = **Federal Reserve Board**

Fed. (US) abbr = **federal; federation**

fed [fɛd] pt, pp of **feed**

federal ['fɛdərəl] adj föderalistisch

Federal Republic of Germany n Bundesrepublik f Deutschland

Federal Reserve Board (US) n Kontrollorgan der US-Zentralbank

Federal Trade Commission (US) n Handelskontrollbehörde

federation [fɛdə'reɪʃən] n Föderation f, Bund m

fed up adj: **to be** ~ **with** die Nase vollhaben von

fee [fiː] n Gebühr f; (of doctor, lawyer) Honorar nt; **school** ~**s** Schulgeld nt; **entrance** ~ Eintrittsgebühr f; **membership** ~ Mitgliedsbeitrag m; **for a small** ~ gegen eine geringe Gebühr

feeble ['fiːbl] adj schwach; (joke) lahm

feeble-minded ['fiːbl'maɪndɪd] adj dümmlich

feed [fiːd] (pt, pp **fed**) n Mahlzeit f; (of animal) Fütterung f; (on printer) Papiervorschub m ▷ vt füttern; (family etc) ernähren; (machine) versorgen; **to** ~ **sth into sth** etw in etw acc einfüllen or eingeben; (data, information) etw in etw acc eingeben; **to** ~ **material into sth** Material in etw acc eingeben
▶ **feed back** vt zurückleiten
▶ **feed on** vt fus sich nähren von

feedback ['fiːdbæk] n Feedback nt, Rückmeldung f; (from person) Reaktion f

feeder ['fiːdəʳ] n (road) Zubringer m; (railway line, air route) Zubringerlinie f; (baby's bottle) Flasche f

feeding bottle ['fiːdɪŋ-] (Brit) n Flasche f

feel [fiːl] (pt, pp **felt**) n (sensation, touch) Gefühl nt; (impression) Atmosphäre f ▷ vt fühlen; (desire, anger, grief) empfinden; (pain) spüren; (cold) leiden unter +dat; (think, believe): **I** ~ **that you ought to do it** ich meine or ich bin der Meinung, dass Sie es tun sollten; **it has a soft** ~ es fühlt sich weich an; **I** ~ **hungry** ich habe Hunger; **I** ~ **cold** mir ist kalt; **to** ~ **lonely/ better** sich einsam/besser fühlen; **I don't** ~ **well** mir geht es nicht gut; **I** ~ **sorry for him** er tut mir leid; **it** ~**s soft** es fühlt sich weich an; **it** ~**s colder here** es kommt mir hier kälter vor; **it** ~**s like velvet** es fühlt sich wie Samt an; **to** ~ **like** (desire) Lust haben auf +acc; **to** ~ **like doing sth** Lust haben, etw zu tun; **to get the** ~ **of sth** ein Gefühl für etw bekommen; **I'm still** ~**ing my way** ich versuche noch, mich zu orientieren
▶ **feel about** vi umhertasten; **to** ~ **about** or **around in one's pocket for** in seiner Tasche herumsuchen nach
▶ **feel around** vi = **feel about**

feelbad factor ['fiːlbæd-] n (inf) Frustfaktor m

feeler ['fiːləʳ] n Fühler m; **to put out a** ~ or **feelers** (fig) seine Fühler ausstrecken

feelgood ['fiːlgud] adj (film, song) Feelgood-

feeling ['fiːlɪŋ] n Gefühl nt; (impression) Eindruck m; ~**s ran high about it** man ereiferte sich sehr darüber; **what are your** ~**s about the matter?** was meinen Sie dazu?; **I have a** ~ **that** ... ich habe das Gefühl, dass ...; **my** ~ **is that** ... meine Meinung ist, dass ...; **to hurt sb's** ~**s** jdn verletzen

fee-paying ['fiːpeɪɪŋ] adj (school) Privat-; ~ **pupils** Schüler, deren Eltern Schulgeld zahlen

feet [fiːt] npl of **foot**

feign [feɪn] vt vortäuschen

feigned [feɪnd] adj vorgetäuscht

feint [feɪnt] n fein liniertes Papier nt

felicitous [fɪ'lɪsɪtəs] adj glücklich

feline ['fiːlaɪn] adj (eyes etc) Katzen-; (features, grace) katzenartig

fell [fɛl] pt of **fall** ▷ vt fällen; (opponent) niederstrecken ▷ n (Brit: mountain) Berg m;

(: *moorland*): **the ~s** das Moor(land) ▷ *adj*: **in one ~ swoop** auf einen Schlag

fellow ['fɛləu] *n* Mann *m*, Typ *m* (*inf*); (*comrade*) Kamerad *m*; (*of learned society*) Mitglied *nt*; (*of university*) Fellow *m*; **their ~ prisoners/students** ihre Mitgefangenen/Kommilitonen (und Kommilitoninnen); **his ~ workers** seine Kollegen (und Kolleginnen)

fellow citizen *n* Mitbürger(in) *m(f)*

fellow countryman (*irreg: like* **man**) *n* Landsmann *m*, Landsmännin *f*

fellow men *npl* Mitmenschen *pl*

fellowship ['fɛləuʃɪp] *n* Kameradschaft *f*; (*society*) Gemeinschaft *f*; (*Scol*) Forschungsstipendium *nt*

fell-walking ['fɛlwɔːkɪŋ] (*Brit*) *n* Bergwandern *nt*

felon ['fɛlən] *n* (*Law*) (Schwer)verbrecher *m*

felony ['fɛlənɪ] *n* (*Law*) (schweres) Verbrechen *nt*

felt [fɛlt] *pt, pp of* **feel** ▷ *n* Filz *m*

felt-tip pen ['fɛlttɪp-] *n* Filzstift *m*

female ['fiːmeɪl] *n* Weibchen *nt*; (*pej: woman*) Frau *f*, Weib *nt* (*pej*) ▷ *adj* weiblich; (*vote etc*) Frauen-; (*Elec: connector, plug*) Mutter-, Innen-; **male and ~ students** Studenten und Studentinnen

Femidom® ['fɛmɪdɔm] *n* Kondom *nt* für die Frau, Femidom® *nt*

feminine ['fɛmɪnɪn] *adj* weiblich, feminin ▷ *n* Femininum *nt*

femininity [fɛmɪ'nɪnɪtɪ] *n* Weiblichkeit *f*

feminism ['fɛmɪnɪzəm] *n* Feminismus *m*

feminist ['fɛmɪnɪst] *n* Feminist(in) *m(f)*

fen [fɛn] (*Brit*) *n*: **the F~s** *die Niederungen in East Anglia*

fence [fɛns] *n* Zaun *m*; (*Sport*) Hindernis *nt* ▷ *vt* (*also*: **fence in**) einzäunen ▷ *vi* (*Sport*) fechten; **to sit on the ~** (*fig*) neutral bleiben, nicht Partei ergreifen

fencing ['fɛnsɪŋ] *n* (*Sport*) Fechten *nt*

fend [fɛnd] *vi*: **to ~ for o.s.** für sich (selbst) sorgen, sich allein durchbringen

▸ **fend off** *vt* abwehren

fender ['fɛndə^r] *n* Kamingitter *nt*; (*on boat*) Fender *m*; (*US: of car*) Kotflügel *m*

fennel ['fɛnl] *n* Fenchel *m*

ferment [*vi* fə'mɛnt, *n* 'fəːmɛnt] *vi* gären ▷ *n* (*fig: unrest*) Unruhe *f*

fermentation [fəːmɛn'teɪʃən] *n* Gärung *f*

fern [fəːn] *n* Farn *m*

ferocious [fə'rəuʃəs] *adj* wild; (*behaviour*) heftig; (*competition*) scharf

ferocity [fə'rɔsɪtɪ] *n* (*see adj*) Wildheit *f*; Heftigkeit *f*; Schärfe *f*

ferret ['fɛrɪt] *n* Frettchen *nt*

▸ **ferret about** *vi* herumstöbern

▸ **ferret around** *vi* = **ferret about**

▸ **ferret out** *vt* aufspüren

ferry ['fɛrɪ] *n* (*also*: **ferryboat**) Fähre *f* ▷ *vt* transportieren; **to ~ sth/sb across** *or* **over** jdn/etw übersetzen

ferryman ['fɛrɪmən] (*irreg: like* **man**) *n* Fährmann *m*

fertile ['fəːtaɪl] *adj* fruchtbar; **~ period** fruchtbare Tage *pl*

fertility [fə'tɪlɪtɪ] *n* Fruchtbarkeit *f*

fertility drug *n* Fruchtbarkeitsmedikament *nt*

fertilization [fəːtɪlaɪ'zeɪʃən] *n* (*Biol*) Befruchtung *f*

fertilize ['fəːtɪlaɪz] *vt* düngen; (*Biol*) befruchten

fertilizer ['fəːtɪlaɪzə^r] *n* Dünger *m*

fervent ['fəːvənt] *adj* leidenschaftlich; (*admirer*) glühend

fervour, (*US*) **fervor** ['fəːvə^r] *n* Leidenschaft *f*

fester ['fɛstə^r] *vi* (*wound*) eitern; (*insult*) nagen; (*row*) sich verschlimmern

festival ['fɛstɪvəl] *n* Fest *nt*; (*Art, Mus*) Festival *nt*, Festspiele *pl*

festive ['fɛstɪv] *adj* festlich; **the ~ season** (*Brit: Christmas and New Year*) die Festzeit *f*

festivities [fɛs'tɪvɪtɪz] *npl* Feierlichkeiten *pl*

festoon [fɛs'tuːn] *vt*: **to ~ with** schmücken mit

fetch [fɛtʃ] *vt* holen; (*sell for*) (ein)bringen; **would you ~ me a glass of water please?** kannst du mir bitte ein Glas Wasser bringen?; **how much did it ~?** wie viel hat es eingebracht?

▸ **fetch up** (*inf*) *vi* landen (*inf*)

fetching ['fɛtʃɪŋ] *adj* bezaubernd, reizend

fête [feɪt] *n* Fest *nt*

fetid ['fɛtɪd] *adj* übel riechend

fetish ['fɛtɪʃ] *n* Fetisch *m*

fetter ['fɛtə^r] *vt* fesseln; (*horse*) anpflocken; (*fig*) in Fesseln legen

fetters ['fɛtəz] *npl* Fesseln *pl*

fettle ['fɛtl] (*Brit*) *n*: **in fine ~** in bester Form

fetus ['fiːtəs] (*US*) *n* = **foetus**

feud [fjuːd] *n* Streit *m* ▷ *vi* im Streit liegen; **a family ~** ein Familienstreit *m*

feudal ['fjuːdl] *adj* (*society etc*) Feudal-

feudalism ['fjuːdlɪzəm] *n* Feudalismus *m*

fever ['fiːvə^r] *n* Fieber *nt*; **he has a ~** er hat Fieber

feverish ['fiːvərɪʃ] *adj* fiebrig; (*activity, emotion*) fieberhaft

few [fjuː] *adj* wenige; **a ~** (*adj*) ein paar, einige; (*pron*) ein paar; **a ~ more (days)** noch ein paar (Tage); **they were ~** sie waren nur wenige; **~ succeed** nur wenigen gelingt es; **very ~ survive** nur sehr wenige überleben; **I know a ~** ich kenne einige; **a good ~, quite a ~** ziemlich viele; **in the next/past ~ days** in den nächsten/letzten paar Tagen; **every ~ days/months** alle paar Tage/Monate

fewer ['fjuːə^r] *adj* weniger; **there are ~ buses on Sundays** Sonntags fahren weniger Busse

fewest ['fjuːɪst] *adj* die wenigsten

FHA (*US*) *n abbr* (= *Federal Housing Administration*): **~ loan** Baudarlehen *nt*

fiancé [fɪ'ɑ̃ːŋseɪ] *n* Verlobte(r) *m*

fiancée [fɪ'ɑ̃ːŋseɪ] *n* Verlobte *f*

fiasco [fɪ'æskəu] *n* Fiasko *nt*

fib [fɪb] *n* Flunkerei *f* (*inf*)

fibre, (*US*) **fiber** ['faɪbə^r] *n* Faser *f*; (*cloth*) (Faser)stoff *m*; (*roughage*) Ballaststoffe *pl*; (*Anat: tissue*)

Gewebe nt

fibreboard, (US) **fiberboard** ['faɪbɔːd] n
Faserplatte f

fibreglass, (US) **fiberglass** ['faɪbəglɑːs] n
Fiberglas nt

fibrositis [faɪbrə'saɪtɪs] n
Bindegewebsentzündung f

FICA (US) n abbr (= Federal Insurance Contributions
Act) Abgabe zur Sozialversicherung

fickle ['fɪkl] adj unbeständig; (weather)
wechselhaft

fiction ['fɪkʃən] n Erfindung f; (Liter)
Erzählliteratur f, Prosaliteratur f

fictional ['fɪkʃənl] adj erfunden

fictionalize ['fɪkʃnəlaɪz] vt fiktionalisieren

fictitious [fɪk'tɪʃəs] adj (false) falsch; (invented)
fiktiv, frei erfunden

fiddle ['fɪdl] n Fiedel f (inf), Geige f; (fraud,
swindle) Schwindelei f ▷ vt (Brit: accounts)
frisieren (inf); **tax** ~ Steuermanipulation f; **to
work a** ~ ein krummes Ding drehen (inf)
  ▶ **fiddle with** vt fus herumspielen mit

fiddler ['fɪdlər] n Geiger(in) m(f)

fiddly ['fɪdlɪ] adj knifflig (inf); (object) fummelig

fidelity [fɪ'dɛlɪtɪ] n Treue f; (accuracy)
Genauigkeit f

fidget ['fɪdʒɪt] vi zappeln

fidgety ['fɪdʒɪtɪ] adj zappelig

fiduciary [fɪ'djuːʃɪərɪ] n (Law) Treuhänder m

field [fiːld] n Feld nt; (Sport: ground) Platz m;
(subject, area of interest) Gebiet nt; (Comput)
Datenfeld nt ▷ cpd Feld-; **to lead the** ~ das Feld
anführen; ~ **trip** Exkursion f

field day n: **to have a** ~ einen herrlichen Tag
haben

field glasses npl Feldstecher m

field hospital n Feldlazarett nt

field marshal n Feldmarschall m

field work n Feldforschung f; (Archaeology, Geog)
Arbeit f im Gelände

fiend [fiːnd] n Teufel m

fiendish ['fiːndɪʃ] adj teuflisch; (problem)
verzwickt

fierce [fɪəs] adj wild; (look) böse; (fighting, wind)
heftig; (loyalty) leidenschaftlich; (enemy)
erbittert; (heat) glühend

fiery ['faɪərɪ] adj glühend; (temperament) feurig,
hitzig

FIFA ['fiːfə] n abbr (= Fédération Internationale de
Football Association) FIFA f

fifteen [fɪf'tiːn] num fünfzehn

fifteenth [fɪf'tiːnθ] num fünfzehnte(r, s)

fifth [fɪfθ] num fünfte(r, s) ▷ n Fünftel nt

fiftieth ['fɪftɪɪθ] num fünfzigste(r, s)

fifty ['fɪftɪ] num fünfzig

fifty-fifty ['fɪftɪ'fɪftɪ] adj, adv halbe-halbe,
fifty-fifty; **to go/share** ~ **with sb** mit jdm
halbe-halbe or fifty-fifty machen; **we have a
** ~ **chance (of success)** unsere Chancen stehen
fifty-fifty

fig [fɪg] n Feige f

fight [faɪt] n (pt, pp **fought**) n Kampf m; (quarrel)
Streit m; (punch-up) Schlägerei f ▷ vt kämpfen

mit or gegen; (prejudice etc) bekämpfen; (election)
kandidieren bei; (emotion) ankämpfen gegen;
(Law: case) durchkämpfen, durchfechten ▷ vi
kämpfen; (quarrel) sich streiten; (punch-up)
sich schlagen; **to put up a** ~ sich zur Wehr
setzen; **to** ~ **one's way through a crowd/the
undergrowth** sich dat einen Weg durch die
Menge/das Unterholz bahnen; **to** ~ **against**
bekämpfen; **to** ~ **for one's rights** für seine
Rechte kämpfen
  ▶ **fight back** vi zurückschlagen; (Sport)
zurückkämpfen; (after illness) zu Kräften
kommen ▷ vt fus unterdrücken
  ▶ **fight down** vt unterdrücken
  ▶ **fight off** vt abwehren; (sleep, urge)
ankämpfen gegen
  ▶ **fight out** vt: **to** ~ **it out** es untereinander
ausfechten

fighter ['faɪtər] n Kämpfer(in) m(f); (plane)
Jagdflugzeug nt; (fig) Kämpfernatur f

fighter pilot n Jagdflieger m

fighting ['faɪtɪŋ] n Kämpfe pl; (brawl)
Schlägereien pl

figment ['fɪgmənt] n: **a** ~ **of the imagination**
ein Hirngespinst nt, pure Einbildung f

figurative ['fɪgjurətɪv] adj bildlich,
übertragen; (style) gegenständlich

figure ['fɪgər] n Figur f; (illustration) Abbildung
f; (number, statistic, cipher) Zahl f; (person) Gestalt
f; (personality) Persönlichkeit f ▷ vt (esp US)
glauben, schätzen ▷ vi eine Rolle spielen; **to
put a** ~ **on sth** eine Zahl für etw angeben;
public ~ Persönlichkeit f des öffentlichen
Lebens
  ▶ **figure out** vt ausrechnen

figurehead ['fɪgəhɛd] n Galionsfigur f

figure of speech n Redensart f, Redewendung f

figure skating n Eiskunstlaufen nt

Fiji ['fiːdʒiː] n, **Fiji Islands** npl Fidschi-Inseln
pl

filament ['fɪləmənt] n Glühfaden m; (Bot)
Staubfaden m

filch [fɪltʃ] (inf) vt filzen

file [faɪl] n Akte f; (folder) (Akten)ordner m;
(for loose leaf) (Akten)mappe f; (Comput) Datei
f; (row) Reihe f; (tool) Feile f ▷ vt ablegen,
abheften; (claim) einreichen; (wood,
metal, fingernails) feilen ▷ vi: **to** ~ **in/out**
nacheinander hereinkommen/hinausgehen;
to ~ **a suit against sb** eine Klage gegen
jdn erheben; **to** ~ **past** in einer Reihe
vorbeigehen; **to** ~ **for divorce** die Scheidung
einreichen

filename ['faɪlneɪm] n (Comput) Dateiname m

filibuster ['fɪlɪbʌstər] (esp US: Pol) n
(also: **filibusterer**) Dauerredner(in) m(f) ▷ vi
filibustern, Obstruktion betreiben

filing ['faɪlɪŋ] n Ablegen nt, Abheften nt

filing cabinet n Aktenschrank m

filing clerk n Angestellte(r) f(m) in der
Registratur

Filipino [fɪlɪ'piːnəu] n Filipino m, Filipina f;
(Ling) Philippinisch nt

fill [fɪl] vt füllen; (space, area) ausfüllen; (tooth) plombieren; (need) erfüllen ▷ vi sich füllen ▷ n: **to eat one's ~** sich satt essen; **we've already ~ed that vacancy** wir haben diese Stelle schon besetzt
▶ **fill in** vt füllen; (time) überbrücken; (form) ausfüllen ▷ vi: **to ~ in for sb** für jdn einspringen; **to ~ sb in on sth** (inf) jdn über etw acc ins Bild setzen
▶ **fill out** vt ausfüllen
▶ **fill up** vt füllen ▷ vi (Aut) tanken; **~ it up, please** (Aut) bitte volltanken
fillet ['fɪlɪt] n Filet nt ▷ vt filetieren
fillet steak n Filetsteak nt
filling ['fɪlɪŋ] n Füllung f; (for tooth) Plombe f
filling station n Tankstelle f
fillip ['fɪlɪp] n (stimulus) Ansporn m
filly ['fɪlɪ] n Stutfohlen nt
film [fɪlm] n Film m; (of powder etc) Schicht f; (for wrapping) Plastikfolie f ▷ vt, vi filmen
film star n Filmstar m
film strip n Filmstreifen m
film studio n Filmstudio nt
Filofax® ['faɪləʊfæks] n Filofax® nt, Terminplaner m
filter ['fɪltər] n Filter m ▷ vt filtern
▶ **filter in** vi durchsickern
▶ **filter through** vi = **filter in**
filter coffee n Filterkaffee m
filter lane (Brit) n Abbiegespur f
filter tip n Filter m
filter-tipped ['fɪltətɪpt] adj (cigarette) Filter-
filth [fɪlθ] n Dreck m, Schmutz m
filthy ['fɪlθɪ] adj dreckig, schmutzig; (language) unflätig
fin [fɪn] n Flosse f; (Tech) Seitenflosse f
final ['faɪnl] adj letzte(r, s); (ultimate) letztendlich; (definitive) endgültig ▷ n Finale nt, Endspiel nt; **finals** npl (Univ) Abschlussprüfung f
final demand n letzte Zahlungsaufforderung f
finale [fɪ'nɑːlɪ] n Finale nt; (Theat) Schlussszene f
finalist ['faɪnəlɪst] n Endrundenteilnehmer(in) m(f), Finalist(in) m(f)
finality [faɪ'nælɪtɪ] n Endgültigkeit f; **with an air of ~** mit Bestimmtheit
finalize ['faɪnəlaɪz] vt endgültig festlegen
finally ['faɪnəlɪ] adv endlich, schließlich; (lastly) schließlich, zum Schluss; (irrevocably) endgültig
finance [faɪ'næns] n Geldmittel pl; (money management) Finanzwesen nt ▷ vt finanzieren; **finances** npl (personal) Finanzen pl, Finanzlage f
financial [faɪ'nænʃəl] adj finanziell; **~ statement** Bilanz f
financially [faɪ'nænʃəlɪ] adv finanziell
financial year n Geschäftsjahr nt
financier [faɪ'nænsɪər] n Finanzier m
find [faɪnd] (pt, pp **found**) vt finden; (discover) entdecken ▷ n Fund m; **to ~ sb guilty** jdn für schuldig befinden; **to ~ (some) difficulty in doing sth** (einige) Schwierigkeiten haben, etw zu tun
▶ **find out** vt herausfinden; (person) erwischen ▷ vi: **to ~ out about** etwas herausfinden über +acc; (by chance) etwas erfahren über +acc
findings ['faɪndɪŋz] npl (Law) Urteil nt; (of report) Ergebnis nt
fine [faɪn] adj fein; (excellent) gut; (thin) dünn ▷ adv gut; (small) fein ▷ n Geldstrafe f ▷ vt mit einer Geldstrafe belegen; **he's ~** es geht ihm gut; **the weather is ~** das Wetter ist schön; **that's cutting it (a bit) ~** das ist aber (ein bisschen) knapp; **you're doing ~** das machen Sie gut
fine arts npl schöne Künste pl
finely ['faɪnlɪ] adv schön; (chop) klein; (slice) dünn; (adjust) fein
fine print n: **the ~** das Kleingedruckte
finery ['faɪnərɪ] n (of dress) Staat m
finesse [fɪ'nɛs] n Geschick nt
fine-tooth comb ['faɪntuːθ-] n: **to go through sth with a ~** (fig) etw genau unter die Lupe nehmen
finger ['fɪŋɡər] n Finger m ▷ vt befühlen; **little ~** kleiner Finger; **index ~** Zeigefinger m
fingernail ['fɪŋɡəneɪl] n Fingernagel m
fingerprint ['fɪŋɡəprɪnt] n Fingerabdruck m ▷ vt Fingerabdrücke abnehmen +dat
fingerstall ['fɪŋɡəstɔːl] n Fingerling m
fingertip ['fɪŋɡətɪp] n Fingerspitze f; **to have sth at one's ~s** (to hand) etw parat haben; (know well) etw aus dem Effeff kennen (inf)
finicky ['fɪnɪkɪ] adj pingelig
finish ['fɪnɪʃ] n Schluss m, Ende nt; (Sport) Finish nt; (polish etc) Verarbeitung f ▷ vt fertig sein mit; (work) erledigen; (book) auslesen; (use up) aufbrauchen ▷ vi enden; (person) fertig sein; **to ~ doing sth** mit etw fertig werden; **to ~ third** als Dritter durchs Ziel gehen; **to be ~ed with sth** mit etw fertig sein; **she's ~ed with him** sie hat mit ihm Schluss gemacht
▶ **finish off** vt fertig machen; (kill) den Gnadenstoß geben
▶ **finish up** vt (food) aufessen; (drink) austrinken ▷ vi (end up) landen
finished ['fɪnɪʃt] adj fertig; (performance) ausgereift; (inf: tired) erledigt
finishing line ['fɪnɪʃɪŋ-] n Ziellinie f
finishing school n höhere Mädchenschule f (in der auch Etikette und gesellschaftliches Verhalten gelehrt wird)
finishing touches npl: **the ~** der letzte Schliff
finite ['faɪnaɪt] adj begrenzt; (verb) finit
Finland ['fɪnlənd] n Finnland nt
Finn [fɪn] n Finne m, Finnin f
Finnish ['fɪnɪʃ] adj finnisch ▷ n (Ling) Finnisch nt
fiord [fjɔːd] n = **fjord**
fir [fəːr] n Tanne f
fire ['faɪər] n Feuer nt; (in hearth) (Kamin)feuer nt; (accidental fire) Brand m ▷ vt abschießen; (imagination) beflügeln; (enthusiasm) befeuern; (inf: dismiss) feuern ▷ vi feuern, schießen; **to ~ a gun** ein Gewehr abschießen; **to be**

on ~ brennen; **to set ~ to sth, set sth
on ~** etw anzünden; **insured against ~**
feuerversichert; **electric/gas ~** Elektro-/
Gasofen m; **to come/be under ~ (from)** unter
Beschuss (von) geraten/stehen

fire alarm n Feuermelder m

firearm ['faɪərɑːm] n Feuerwaffe f,
Schusswaffe f

fire brigade n Feuerwehr f

fire chief n Branddirektor m

fire department (US) n Feuerwehr f

fire door n Feuertür f

fire drill n Probealarm m

fire engine n Feuerwehrauto nt

fire escape n Feuertreppe f

fire-extinguisher ['faɪərɪk'stɪŋgwɪʃəʳ] n
Feuerlöscher m

fireguard ['faɪəgɑːd] (Brit) n (Schutz)gitter nt
(vor dem Kamin)

fire hazard n: **that's a ~** das ist
feuergefährlich

fire hydrant n Hydrant m

fire insurance n Feuerversicherung f

fireman ['faɪəmən] (irreg: like **man**) n
Feuerwehrmann m

fireplace ['faɪəpleɪs] n Kamin m

fireplug ['faɪəplʌg] (US) n = **fire hydrant**

fire practice n = **fire drill**

fireproof ['faɪəpruːf] adj feuerfest

fire regulations npl Brand-
schutzbestimmungen pl

fire screen n Ofenschirm m

fireside ['faɪəsaɪd] n: **by the ~** am Kamin

fire station n Feuerwache f

firewood ['faɪəwud] n Brennholz nt

fireworks ['faɪəwɜːks] npl Feuerwerkskörper pl;
(display) Feuerwerk nt

firing line ['faɪərɪŋ-] n Feuerlinie f, Schusslinie
f; **to be in the ~** (fig) in der Schusslinie sein

firing squad n Exekutionskommando nt

firm [fɜːm] adj fest; (mattress) hart; (measures)
durchgreifend ▷ n Firma f; **to be a ~ believer
in sth** fest von etw überzeugt sein

firmly ['fɜːmlɪ] adv (see adj) fest; hart; (definitely)
entschlossen

firmness ['fɜːmnɪs] n (see adj) Festigkeit f; Härte
f; (definiteness) Entschlossenheit f

first [fɜːst] adj erste(r, s) ▷ adv als Erste(r, s);
(before other things) zuerst; (when listing reasons
etc) erstens; (for the first time) zum ersten Mal
▷ n Erste(r, s); (Aut: also: **first gear**) der erste
Gang; (Brit: Scol) ≈ Eins f; **the ~ of January** der
erste Januar; **at ~** zuerst, zunächst; **~ of all** vor
allem; **in the ~ instance** zuerst or zunächst
einmal; **I'll do it ~ thing (tomorrow)** ich
werde es (morgen) als Erstes tun; **from the
very ~** gleich von Anfang an

first aid n erste Hilfe f

first-aid kit [fɜːst'eɪd-] n Erste-Hilfe-
Ausrüstung f

first-class ['fɜːst'klɑːs] adj erstklassig; (carriage,
ticket) Erste(r)-Klasse-; (post) bevorzugt
befördert ▷ adv (travel, send) erster Klasse

first-hand ['fɜːst'hænd] adj aus erster Hand

first lady (US) n First Lady f; **the ~ of jazz** die
Königin des Jazz

firstly ['fɜːstlɪ] adv erstens, zunächst einmal

first name n Vorname m

first night n Premiere f

first-rate ['fɜːst'reɪt] adj erstklassig

first-time buyer ['fɜːst'taɪm-] n jd, der zum ersten
Mal ein Haus/eine Wohnung kauft

fir tree n Tannenbaum m

fiscal ['fɪskl] adj (year) Steuer-; (policies) Finanz-

fish [fɪʃ] n inv Fisch m ▷ vt (area) fischen in +dat;
(river) angeln in +dat ▷ vi fischen; (as sport,
hobby) angeln; **to go ~ing** fischen/angeln
gehen

▶ **fish out** vt herausfischen

fish bone n (Fisch)gräte f

fish cake n Fischfrikadelle f

fisherman ['fɪʃəmən] (irreg: like **man**) n Fischer
m

fishery ['fɪʃərɪ] n Fischereigebiet nt

fish factory (Brit) n Fischfabrik f

fish farm n Fischzucht(anlage) f

fishfingers [fɪʃ'fɪŋgəz] (Brit) npl Fischstäbchen
pl

fish-hook ['fɪʃhuk] n Angelhaken m

fishing boat ['fɪʃɪŋ-] n Fischerboot nt

fishing line n Angelschnur f

fishing net n Fischnetz nt

fishing rod n Angelrute f

fishing tackle n Angelgeräte pl

fish market n Fischmarkt m

fishmonger ['fɪʃmʌŋgəʳ] (esp Brit) n
Fischhändler(in) m(f)

fishmonger's ['fɪʃmʌŋgəz], **fishmonger's
shop** (esp Brit) n Fischgeschäft nt

fish slice (Brit) n Fischvorlegemesser nt

fish sticks (US) npl = **fishfingers**

fishy ['fɪʃɪ] (inf) adj verdächtig, faul

fission ['fɪʃən] n Spaltung f; **atomic** or **nuclear
~** Atomspaltung f, Kernspaltung f

fissure ['fɪʃəʳ] n Riss m, Spalte f

fist [fɪst] n Faust f

fist fight n Faustkampf m

fit [fɪt] adj geeignet; (healthy) gesund; (Sport)
fit ▷ vt passen +dat; (adjust) anpassen; (match)
entsprechen +dat; (be suitable for) passen auf
+acc; (put in) einbauen; (attach) anbringen;
(equip) ausstatten ▷ vi passen; (parts)
zusammenpassen; (in space, gap) hineinpassen
▷ n (Med) Anfall m; **to ~ the description** der
Beschreibung entsprechen; **~ to** bereit zu; **~
to eat** essbar; **~ to drink** trinkbar; **to be ~
to keep** es wert sein, aufbewahrt zu werden;
~ for geeignet für; **~ for work** arbeitsfähig;
to keep ~ sich fit halten; **do as you think** or
see ~ tun Sie, was Sie für richtig halten; **a ~
of anger** ein Wutanfall m; **a ~ of pride** eine
Anwandlung von Stolz; **to have a ~** einen
Anfall haben; (inf, fig) einen Anfall kriegen;
this dress is a good ~ dieses Kleid sitzt or
passt gut; **by ~s and starts** unregelmäßig

▶ **fit in** vi (person) sich einfügen; (object)

hineinpassen ▷ vt (fig: appointment)
unterbringen, einschieben; (visitor) Zeit
finden für; **to ~ in with sb's plans** sich mit
jds Plänen vereinbaren lassen

fitful ['fɪtful] adj unruhig

fitment ['fɪtmənt] n Einrichtungsgegenstand
m

fitness ['fɪtnɪs] n Gesundheit f; (Sport) Fitness f

fitness instructor n Fitnesstrainer(in) m(f)

fitted carpet ['fɪtɪd-] n Teppichboden m

fitted cupboards npl Einbauschränke pl

fitted kitchen (Brit) n Einbauküche f

fitter ['fɪtəʳ] n Monteur m; (for machines)
(Maschinen)schlosser m

fitting ['fɪtɪŋ] adj passend; (thanks) gebührend
▷ n (of dress) Anprobe f; (of piece of equipment)
Installation f; **fittings** npl Ausstattung f

fitting room n Anprobe(kabine) f

five [faɪv] num fünf

five-day week ['faɪvdeɪ-] n Fünftagewoche f

fiver ['faɪvəʳ] (inf) n (Brit) Fünfpfundschein m;
(US) Fünfdollarschein m

fix [fɪks] vt (attach) befestigen; (arrange)
festsetzen, festlegen; (mend) reparieren; (meal,
drink) machen; (inf) manipulieren ▷ n: **to be
in a ~** in der Patsche or Klemme sitzen; **to ~
sth to/on sth** etw an/auf etw akk befestigen;
to ~ one's eyes/attention on seinen Blick/
seine Aufmerksamkeit richten auf +acc;
the fight was a ~ (inf) der Kampf war eine
abgekartete Sache

▶ **fix up** vt arrangieren; **to ~ sb up with sth**
jdm etw besorgen

fixation [fɪk'seɪʃən] n Fixierung f

fixative ['fɪksətɪv] n Fixativ nt

fixed [fɪkst] adj fest; (ideas) fix; (smile) starr;
~ charge Pauschale f; **how are you ~ for
money?** wie sieht es bei dir mit dem Geld aus?

fixed assets npl Anlagevermögen nt

fixture ['fɪkstʃəʳ] n Ausstattungsgegenstand
m; (Football etc) Spiel nt; (Athletics etc)
Veranstaltung f

fizz [fɪz] vi sprudeln; (firework) zischen

fizzle out ['fɪzl-] vi (plan) im Sande verlaufen;
(interest) sich verlieren

fizzy ['fɪzɪ] adj sprudelnd

fjord [fjɔːd] n Fjord m

FL, Fla. (US) abbr (Post) = Florida

flabbergasted ['flæbəgɑːstɪd] adj verblüfft

flabby ['flæbɪ] adj schwammig, wabbelig (inf)

flag [flæg] n Fahne f; (of country) Flagge f; (for
signalling) Signalflagge f; (also: **flagstone**)
(Stein)platte f ▷ vi erlahmen; **~ of
convenience** Billigflagge f; **to ~ down**
anhalten

flagon ['flægən] n Flasche f; (jug) Krug m

flagpole ['flægpəʊl] n Fahnenstange f

flagrant ['fleɪgrənt] adj flagrant; (injustice)
himmelschreiend

flagship ['flægʃɪp] n Flaggschiff nt

flagstone ['flægstəʊn] n (Stein)platte f

flag stop (US) n Bedarfshaltestelle f

flair [flɛəʳ] n Talent nt; (style) Flair nt

flak [flæk] n Flakfeuer nt; **to get a lot of ~ (for
sth)** (inf: criticism) (wegen etw) unter Beschuss
geraten

flake [fleɪk] n Splitter m; (of snow, soap powder)
Flocke f ▷ vi (also: **flake off**) abblättern,
absplittern

▶ **flake out** (inf) vi aus den Latschen kippen;
(go to sleep) einschlafen

flaky ['fleɪkɪ] adj brüchig; (skin) schuppig

flaky pastry n Blätterteig m

flamboyant [flæm'bɔɪənt] adj extravagant

flame [fleɪm] n Flamme f; **to burst into ~s** in
Flammen aufgehen; **an old ~** (inf) eine alte
Flamme

flaming ['fleɪmɪŋ] (inf!) adj verdammt

flamingo [flə'mɪŋgəʊ] n Flamingo m

flammable ['flæməbl] adj leicht entzündbar

flan [flæn] n Kuchen m; **~ case** Tortenboden m

Flanders ['flɑːndəz] n Flandern nt

flange [flændʒ] n Flansch m

flank [flæŋk] n Flanke f ▷ vt flankieren

flannel ['flænl] n Flanell m; (Brit: also: **face
flannel**) Waschlappen m; (: inf) Geschwafel nt;
flannels npl (trousers) Flanellhose f

flannelette [flænə'lɛt] n Baumwollflanell m,
Biber m or nt

flap [flæp] n Klappe f; (of envelope) Lasche f ▷ vt
schlagen mit ▷ vi flattern; (inf: also: **be in a
flap**) in heller Aufregung sein

flapjack ['flæpdʒæk] n (US: pancake)
Pfannkuchen m; (Brit: biscuit) Haferkeks m

flare [flɛəʳ] n Leuchtsignal nt; (in skirt etc) Weite
f

▶ **flare up** vi auflodern; (person) aufbrausen;
(fighting, violence, trouble) ausbrechen; see also
flared

flared ['flɛəd] adj (trousers) mit Schlag; (skirt)
ausgestellt

flash [flæʃ] n Aufblinken nt; (also: **newsflash**)
Eilmeldung f; (Phot) Blitz m, Blitzlicht nt;
(US: torch) Taschenlampe f ▷ vt aufleuchten
lassen; (news, message) durchgeben; (look, smile)
zuwerfen ▷ vi aufblinken; (light on ambulance)
blinken; (eyes) blitzen; **in a ~** im Nu; **quick as
a ~** blitzschnell; **~ of inspiration** Geistesblitz
m; **to ~ one's headlights** die Lichthupe
betätigen; **the thought ~ed through his
mind** der Gedanke schoss ihm durch den
Kopf; **to ~ by** or **past** vorbeiflitzen (inf)

flashback ['flæʃbæk] n Rückblende f

flashbulb ['flæʃbʌlb] n Blitzbirne f

flash card n Leselernkarte f

flashcube ['flæʃkjuːb] n Blitzwürfel m

flasher ['flæʃəʳ] n (Aut) Lichthupe f; (inf!: man)
Exhibitionist m

flashlight ['flæʃlaɪt] n Blitzlicht nt

flash point n (fig): **to be at ~** auf dem
Siedepunkt sein

flashy ['flæʃɪ] (pej) adj auffällig, protzig

flask [flɑːsk] n Flakon m; (Chem) Glaskolben m;
(also: **vacuum flask**) Thermosflasche® f

flat [flæt] adj flach; (surface) eben; (tyre) platt;
(battery) leer; (beer) schal; (refusal, denial) glatt;

559

(*note, voice*) zu tief; (*rate, fee*) Pauschal- ▷ *n*
(*Brit: apartment*) Wohnung *f*; (*Aut*) (Reifen)
panne *f*; (*Mus*) Erniedrigungszeichen *nt*; **to
work ~ out** auf Hochtouren arbeiten; **~ rate
of pay** Pauschallohn *m*

flat-footed ['flæt'futɪd] *adj*: **to be ~** Plattfüße
pl haben

flatly ['flætlɪ] *adv* (*refuse, deny*) glatt, kategorisch

flatmate ['flætmeɪt] (*Brit*) *n* Mitbewohner(in)
m(f)

flatness ['flætnɪs] *n* Flachheit *f*

flat screen *n* Flachbildschirm *m*

flat-screen monitor *n* Flachbildschirm *m*

flatten ['flætn] *vt* (*also*: **flatten out**) (ein)
ebnen; (*paper, fabric etc*) glätten; (*building, city*)
dem Erdboden gleichmachen; (*crop*) zu Boden
drücken; (*inf: person*) umhauen; **to ~ o.s.
against a wall/door** *etc* sich platt gegen *or* an
eine Wand/Tür *etc* drücken

flatter ['flætəʳ] *vt* schmeicheln +*dat*

flatterer ['flætərəʳ] *n* Schmeichler(in) *m(f)*

flattering ['flætərɪŋ] *adj* schmeichelhaft; (*dress
etc*) vorteilhaft

flattery ['flætərɪ] *n* Schmeichelei *f*

flatulence ['flætjuləns] *n* Blähungen *pl*

flaunt [flɔ:nt] *vt* zur Schau stellen, protzen mit

flavour, (*US*) **flavor** ['fleɪvəʳ] *n* Geschmack
m; (*of ice-cream etc*) Geschmacksrichtung *f* ▷ *vt*
Geschmack verleihen +*dat*; **to give** *or* **add ~
to** Geschmack verleihen +*dat*; **music with an
African ~** (*fig*) Musik mit einer afrikanischen
Note; **strawberry--ed** mit Erdbeergeschmack

flavouring ['fleɪvərɪŋ] *n* Aroma *nt*

flaw [flɔ:] *n* Fehler *m*

flawless ['flɔ:lɪs] *adj* (*performance*) fehlerlos;
(*complexion*) makellos

flax [flæks] *n* Flachs *m*

flaxen ['flæksən] *adj* (*hair*) flachsblond

flea [fli:] *n* Floh *m*

flea market *n* Flohmarkt *m*

fleck [flɛk] *n* Tupfen *m*, Punkt *m*; (*of dust*)
Flöckchen *nt*; (*of mud, paint, colour*) Fleck(en) *m*
▷ *vt* besprizten; **brown ~ed with white** braun
mit weißen Punkten

fled [flɛd] *pt, pp of* **flee**

fledgeling, **fledgling** ['flɛdʒlɪŋ] *n* Jungvogel *m*
▷ *adj* (*inexperienced: actor etc*) Nachwuchs-; (*newly
started: business etc*) jung

flee [fli:] (*pt, pp* **fled**) *vt* fliehen *or* flüchten
vor +*dat*; (*country*) fliehen *or* flüchten aus ▷ *vi*
fliehen, flüchten

fleece [fli:s] *n* Schafwolle *f*; (*sheep's coat*)
Schaffell *nt*, Vlies *nt* ▷ *vt* (*inf: cheat*) schröpfen

fleecy ['fli:sɪ] *adj* flauschig; (*cloud*) Schäfchen-

fleet [fli:t] *n* Flotte *f*; (*of lorries, cars*) Fuhrpark *m*

fleeting ['fli:tɪŋ] *adj* flüchtig

Flemish ['flɛmɪʃ] *adj* flämisch ▷ *n* (*Ling*)
Flämisch *nt*; **the Flemish** *npl* die Flamen

flesh [flɛʃ] *n* Fleisch *nt*; (*of fruit*) Fruchtfleisch *nt*
▶ **flesh out** *vt* ausgestalten

flesh wound [-wu:nd] *n* Fleischwunde *f*

flew [flu:] *pt of* **fly**

flex [flɛks] *n* Kabel *nt* ▷ *vt* beugen; (*muscles*)
spielen lassen

flexibility [flɛksɪ'bɪlɪtɪ] *n* (*see adj*) Flexibilität *f*;
Biegsamkeit *f*

flexible ['flɛksəbl] *adj* flexibel; (*material*)
biegsam

flexitime ['flɛksɪtaɪm] *n* gleitende Arbeitszeit
f, Gleitzeit *f*

flick [flɪk] *n* (*of finger*) Schnipsen *nt*; (*of hand*)
Wischen *nt*; (*of whip*) Schnalzen *nt*; (*of towel
etc*) Schlagen *nt*; (*of switch*) Knipsen *nt* ▷ *vt*
schnipsen; (*with hand*) wischen; (*whip*) knallen
mit; (*switch*) knipsen; **flicks** (*inf*) *npl* Kino *nt*;
to ~ a towel at sb mit einem Handtuch nach
jdm schlagen
▶ **flick through** *vt fus* durchblättern

flicker ['flɪkəʳ] *vi* flackern; (*eyelids*) zucken ▷ *n*
Flackern *nt*; (*of pain, fear*) Aufflackern *nt*; (*of
smile*) Anflug *m*; (*of eyelid*) Zucken *nt*

flick knife (*Brit*) *n* Klappmesser *nt*

flier ['flaɪəʳ] *n* Flieger(in) *m(f)*

flight [flaɪt] *n* Flug *m*; (*escape*) Flucht *f*;
(*also*: **flight of steps**) Treppe *f*; **to take ~** die
Flucht ergreifen; **to put to ~** in die Flucht
schlagen

flight attendant (*US*) *n* Flugbegleiter(in) *m(f)*

flight crew *n* Flugbesatzung *f*

flight deck *n* (*Aviat*) Cockpit *nt*; (*Naut*) Flugdeck
nt

flight path *n* Flugbahn *f*

flight recorder *n* Flugschreiber *m*

flimsy ['flɪmzɪ] *adj* leicht, dünn; (*building*) leicht
gebaut; (*excuse*) fadenscheinig; (*evidence*) nicht
stichhaltig

flinch [flɪntʃ] *vi* zusammenzucken; **to ~ from**
zurückschrecken vor +*dat*

fling [flɪŋ] (*pt, pp* **flung**) *vt* schleudern; (*arms*)
werfen; (*oneself*) stürzen ▷ *n* (flüchtige) Affäre
f

flint [flɪnt] *n* Feuerstein *m*

flip [flɪp] *vt* (*switch*) knipsen; (*coin*) werfen;
(*US: pancake*) umdrehen ▷ *vi*: **to ~ for sth** (*US*)
um etw mit einer Münze knobeln
▶ **flip through** *vt fus* durchblättern; (*records etc*)
durchgehen

flippant ['flɪpənt] *adj* leichtfertig

flipper ['flɪpəʳ] *n* Flosse *f*; (*for swimming*)
(Schwimm)flosse *f*

flip side *n* (*of record*) B-Seite *f*

flirt [flə:t] *vi* flirten; (*with idea*) liebäugeln
▷ *n*: **he/she is a ~** er/sie flirtet gern

flirtation [flə:'teɪʃən] *n* Flirt *m*

flit [flɪt] *vi* flitzen; (*expression, smile*) huschen

float [fləʊt] *n* Schwimmkork *m*; (*for fishing*)
Schwimmer *m*; (*lorry*) Festwagen *m*; (*money*)
Wechselgeld *nt* ▷ *vi* schwimmen; (*swimmer*)
treiben; (*through air*) schweben; (*currency*)
floaten ▷ *vt* (*currency*) freigeben, floaten lassen;
(*company*) gründen; (*idea, plan*) in den Raum
stellen
▶ **float around** *vi* im Umlauf sein; (*person*)
herumschweben (*inf*); (*object*) herumfliegen
(*inf*)

flock [flɔk] *n* Herde *f*; (*of birds*) Schwarm *m*

▷ vi: **to ~ to** (place) strömen nach; (event) in Scharen kommen zu
floe [fləʊ] n (also: **ice floe**) Eisscholle f
flog [flɒg] vt auspeitschen; (inf: sell) verscherbeln
flood [flʌd] n Überschwemmung f; (of letters, imports etc) Flut f ▷ vt überschwemmen; (Aut) absaufen lassen (inf) ▷ vi überschwemmt werden; **to be in ~** Hochwasser führen; **to ~ the market** den Markt überschwemmen; **to ~ into Hungary/the square/the palace** nach Ungarn/auf den Platz/in den Palast strömen
flooding ['flʌdɪŋ] n Überschwemmung f
floodlight ['flʌdlaɪt] n Flutlicht nt ▷ vt (mit Flutlicht) beleuchten; (building) anstrahlen
floodlit ['flʌdlɪt] pt, pp of **floodlight** ▷ adj (mit Flutlicht) beleuchtet; (building) angestrahlt
flood tide n Flut f
floodwater ['flʌdwɔːtə^r] n Hochwasser nt
floor [flɔː^r] n (Fuß)boden m; (storey) Stock nt; (of sea, valley) Boden m ▷ vt (subj: blow) zu Boden werfen; (: question, remark) die Sprache verschlagen +dat; **on the ~** auf dem Boden; **ground ~** (Brit), **first ~** (US) Erdgeschoss nt, Erdgeschoß nt (Österr); **first ~** (Brit), **second ~** (US) erster Stock m; **top ~** oberstes Stockwerk nt; **to have the ~** (speaker: at meeting) das Wort haben
floorboard ['flɔːbɔːd] n Diele f
flooring ['flɔːrɪŋ] n (Fuß)boden m; (covering) Fußbodenbelag m
floor lamp (US) n Stehlampe f
floor show n Show f, Vorstellung f
floorwalker ['flɔːwɔːkə^r] (esp US) n Ladenaufsicht f
floozy ['fluːzɪ] (inf) n Flittchen nt
flop [flɒp] n Reinfall m ▷ vi (play, book) durchfallen; (fall) sich fallen lassen; (scheme) ein Reinfall sein
floppy ['flɒpɪ] adj schlaff, schlapp ▷ n (also: **floppy disk**) Diskette f, Floppy Disk f; **~ hat** Schlapphut m
floppy disk n Diskette f, Floppy Disk f
flora ['flɔːrə] n Flora f
floral ['flɔːrl] adj geblümt
Florence ['flɔrəns] n Florenz nt
Florentine ['flɔrəntaɪn] adj florentinisch
florid ['flɒrɪd] adj (style) blumig; (complexion) kräftig
florist ['flɔrɪst] n Blumenhändler(in) m(f)
florist's ['flɔrɪsts], **florist's shop** n Blumengeschäft nt
flotation [fləʊ'teɪʃən] n (of shares) Auflegung f; (of company) Umwandlung f in eine Aktiengesellschaft
flotsam ['flɒtsəm] n (also: **flotsam and jetsam**) Strandgut nt; (floating) Treibgut nt
flounce [flaʊns] n Volant m
▶ **flounce out** vi hinausstolzieren
flounder ['flaʊndə^r] vi sich abstrampeln; (fig: speaker) ins Schwimmen kommen; (economy) in Schwierigkeiten geraten ▷ n

Flunder f
flour ['flaʊə^r] n Mehl nt
flourish ['flʌrɪʃ] vi gedeihen; (business) blühen, florieren ▷ vt schwenken ▷ n (in writing) Schnörkel m; (bold gesture): **with a ~** mit einer schwungvollen Bewegung
flourishing ['flʌrɪʃɪŋ] adj gut gehend, florierend
flout [flaʊt] vt sich hinwegsetzen über +acc
flow [fləʊ] n Fluss m; (of sea) Flut f ▷ vi fließen; (clothes, hair) wallen
flow chart n Flussdiagramm nt
flow diagram n = **flow chart**
flower ['flaʊə^r] n Blume f; (blossom) Blüte f ▷ vi blühen; **to be in ~** blühen
flowerbed ['flaʊəbed] n Blumenbeet nt
flowerpot ['flaʊəpɒt] n Blumentopf m
flowery ['flaʊərɪ] adj blumig; (pattern) Blumen-
flown [fləʊn] pp of **fly**
flu [fluː] n Grippe f
fluctuate ['flʌktjʊeɪt] vi schwanken; (opinions, attitudes) sich ändern
fluctuation [flʌktjʊ'eɪʃən] n: **~ (in)** Schwankung f (+gen)
flue [fluː] n Rauchfang m, Rauchabzug m
fluency ['fluːənsɪ] n Flüssigkeit f; **his ~ in German** sein flüssiges Deutsch
fluent ['fluːənt] adj flüssig; **he speaks ~ German, he's ~ in German** er spricht fließend Deutsch
fluently ['fluːəntlɪ] adv flüssig; (speak a language) fließend
fluff [flʌf] n Fussel m; (fur) Flaum m ▷ vt (inf: do badly) verpatzen; (also: **fluff out**) aufplustern
fluffy ['flʌfɪ] adj flaumig; (jacket etc) weich, kuschelig; **~ toy** Kuscheltier nt
fluid ['fluːɪd] adj fließend; (situation, arrangement) unklar ▷ n Flüssigkeit f
fluid ounce (Brit) n flüssige Unze f (= 28 ml)
fluke [fluːk] (inf) n Glücksfall m; **by a ~** durch einen glücklichen Zufall
flummox ['flʌməks] vt verwirren, durcheinanderbringen
flung [flʌŋ] pt, pp of **fling**
flunky ['flʌŋkɪ] n Lakai m
fluorescent [fluə'rɛsnt] adj fluoreszierend; (paint) Leucht-; (light) Neon-
fluoride ['fluəraɪd] n Fluorid nt
fluorine ['fluəriːn] n Fluor nt
flurry ['flʌrɪ] n (of snow) Gestöber nt; **a ~ of activity/excitement** hektische Aktivität/Aufregung
flush [flʌʃ] n Röte f; (fig: of beauty etc) Blüte f ▷ vt (durch)spülen, (aus)spülen ▷ vi erröten ▷ adj: **~ with** auf gleicher Ebene mit; **~ against** direkt an +dat; **in the first ~ of youth** in der ersten Jugendblüte; **in the first ~ of freedom** im ersten Freiheitstaumel; **hot ~es** (Brit) Hitzewallungen pl; **to ~ the toilet** spülen, die Wasserspülung betätigen
▶ **flush out** vt aufstöbern
flushed [flʌʃt] adj rot
fluster ['flʌstə^r] n: **in a ~** nervös; (confused)

durcheinander ▷ vt nervös machen; (confuse)
durcheinanderbringen

flustered ['flʌstəd] adj nervös; (confused)
durcheinander

flute [flu:t] n Querflöte f

fluted ['flu:tɪd] adj gerillt; (column) kanneliert

flutter ['flʌtəʳ] n Flattern nt; (of panic, nerves)
kurzer Anfall m; (of excitement) Beben nt
▷ vi flattern; (person) tänzeln; **to have a ~**
(Brit: inf: gamble) sein Glück (beim Wetten)
versuchen

flux [flʌks] n: **in a state of ~** im Fluss

fly [flaɪ] (pt **flew**, pp **flown**) n Fliege f; (on
trousers: also: **flies**) (Hosen)schlitz m ▷ vt
fliegen; (kite) steigen lassen ▷ vi fliegen;
(escape) fliehen; (flag) wehen; **to ~ open**
auffliegen; **to ~ off the handle** an die
Decke gehen (inf); **pieces of metal went
~ing everywhere** überall flogen Metallteile
herum; **she came ~ing into the room** sie
kam ins Zimmer gesaust; **her glasses flew
off** die Brille flog ihr aus dem Gesicht
▶ **fly away** vi wegfliegen
▶ **fly in** vi einfliegen; **he flew in yesterday** er
ist gestern mit dem Flugzeug gekommen
▶ **fly off** vi = **fly away**
▶ **fly out** vi ausfliegen; **he flew out yesterday**
er ist gestern hingeflogen

fly-fishing ['flaɪfɪʃɪŋ] n Fliegenfischen nt

flying ['flaɪɪŋ] n Fliegen nt ▷ adj: **a ~ visit** ein
Blitzbesuch m; **he doesn't like ~** er fliegt
nicht gerne; **with ~ colours** mit fliegenden
Fahnen

flying buttress n Strebebogen m

flying picket n mobiler Streikposten m

flying saucer n fliegende Untertasse f

flying squad n mobiles Einsatzkommando nt

flying start n: **to get off to a ~** (Sport)
hervorragend wegkommen; (fig) einen
glänzenden Start haben

flyleaf ['flaɪliːf] n Vorsatzblatt nt

flyover ['flaɪəuvəʳ] n (Brit) Überführung f; (US)
Luftparade f

fly-past ['flaɪpɑːst] n Luftparade f

flysheet ['flaɪʃiːt] n (for tent) Überzelt nt

flyweight ['flaɪweɪt] n Fliegengewicht nt

flywheel ['flaɪwiːl] n Schwungrad nt

FM abbr (Brit: Mil) = **field marshal**;
(Radio: = frequency modulation) FM, ≈ UKW

FMB (US) n abbr (= Federal Maritime Board)
Dachausschuss der Handelsmarine

FMCS (US) n abbr (= Federal Mediation and
Conciliation Service) Schlichtungsstelle für
Arbeitskonflikte

FO (Brit) n abbr = **Foreign Office**

foal [fəul] n Fohlen nt

foam [fəum] n Schaum m; (also: **foam rubber**)
Schaumgummi m ▷ vi schäumen

fob [fɔb] vt: **to ~ sb off** jdn abspeisen ▷ n
(also: **watch fob**) Uhrkette f

f.o.b. abbr (Comm: = free on board) frei Schiff

foc (Brit) abbr (Comm: = free of charge) gratis

focal point ['fəukl-] n Mittelpunkt m; (of

camera, telescope etc) Brennpunkt m

focus ['fəukəs] (pl **~es**) n Brennpunkt m; (of
storm) Zentrum nt ▷ vt einstellen; (light
rays) bündeln ▷ vi: **to ~ (on)** (with camera)
klar or scharf einstellen +acc; (person) sich
konzentrieren (auf +acc); **in/out of ~** (camera
etc) scharf/unscharf eingestellt; (photograph)
scharf/unscharf

focus group n (Pol) Fokusgruppe f

fodder ['fɔdəʳ] n Futter nt

FoE n abbr (= Friends of the Earth) Umwelt-
schutzorganisation

foe [fəu] n Feind(in) m(f)

foetus, (US) **fetus** ['fiːtəs] n Fötus m, Fetus m

fog [fɔg] n Nebel m

fogbound ['fɔgbaund] adj (airport) wegen Nebel
geschlossen

foggy ['fɔgɪ] adj neb(e)lig

fog lamp, (US) **fog light** n (Aut)
Nebelscheinwerfer m

foible ['fɔɪbl] n Eigenheit f

foil [fɔɪl] vt vereiteln ▷ n Folie f; (complement)
Kontrast m; (Fencing) Florett nt; **to act as a ~ to**
einen Kontrast darstellen zu

foist [fɔɪst] vt: **to ~ sth on sb** (goods) jdm etw
andrehen; (task) etw an jdn abschieben; (ideas,
views) jdm etw aufzwingen

fold [fəuld] n Falte f; (Agr) Pferch m; (fig)
Schoß m ▷ vt (zusammen)falten; (arms)
verschränken ▷ vi (business) eingehen (inf)
▶ **fold up** vi sich zusammenfalten lassen; (bed,
table) sich zusammenklappen lassen; (business)
eingehen (inf) ▷ vt zusammenfalten

folder ['fəuldəʳ] n Aktenmappe f; (binder) Hefter
m; (brochure) Informationsblatt nt

folding ['fəuldɪŋ] adj (chair, bed) Klapp-

foliage ['fəulɪɪdʒ] n Laubwerk nt

folk [fəuk] npl Leute pl ▷ cpd Volks-; **my ~s**
(parents) meine alten Herrschaften

folklore ['fəuklɔːʳ] n Folklore f

folk music n Volksmusik f; (contemporary) Folk m

folk song n Volkslied nt; (contemporary)
Folksong m

follow ['fɔləu] vt folgen +dat; (with eyes)
verfolgen; (advice, instructions) befolgen
▷ vi folgen; **to ~ in sb's footsteps** in jds
Fußstapfen acc treten; **I don't quite ~ you**
ich kann Ihnen nicht ganz folgen; **it ~s that**
daraus folgt, dass; **to ~ suit** (fig) jds Beispiel
dat folgen
▶ **follow on** vi (continue): **to ~ on from**
aufbauen auf +dat
▶ **follow out** vt (idea, plan) zu Ende verfolgen
▶ **follow through** vt = **follow out**
▶ **follow up** vt nachgehen +dat; (offer)
aufgreifen; (case) weiterverfolgen

follower ['fɔləuəʳ] n Anhänger(in) m(f)

following ['fɔləuɪŋ] adj folgend ▷ n
Anhängerschaft f

follow-up ['fɔləuʌp] n Weiterführung f ▷ adj: **~
treatment** Nachbehandlung f

folly ['fɔlɪ] n Torheit f; (building) exzentrisches
Bauwerk nt

fond [fɔnd] *adj* liebevoll; (*memory*) lieb; (*hopes, dreams*) töricht; **to be ~ of** mögen; **she's ~ of swimming** sie schwimmt gerne

fondle ['fɔndl] *vt* streicheln

fondly ['fɔndlɪ] *adv* liebevoll; (*naïvely*) törichterweise; **he ~ believed that ...** er war so naiv zu glauben, dass ...

fondness ['fɔndnɪs] *n* (*for things*) Vorliebe *f*; (*for people*) Zuneigung *f*; **a special ~ for** eine besondere Vorliebe für/Zuneigung zu

font [fɔnt] *n* Taufbecken *nt*; (*Typ*) Schrift *f*

food [fu:d] *n* Essen *nt*; (*for animals*) Futter *nt*; (*nourishment*) Nahrung *f*; (*groceries*) Lebensmittel *pl*

food chain *n* Nahrungskette *f*

food combining *n* Trennkost *f*

food mixer *n* Küchenmixer *m*

food poisoning *n* Lebensmittelvergiftung *f*

food processor *n* Küchenmaschine *f*

food stamp *n* Lebensmittelmarke *f*

foodstuffs ['fu:dstʌfs] *npl* Lebensmittel *pl*

fool [fu:l] *n* Dummkopf *m*; (*Culin*) Sahnespeise *aus Obstpüree* ▷ *vt* hereinlegen, täuschen ▷ *vi* herumalbern; **to make a ~ of sb** jdn lächerlich machen; (*trick*) jdn hereinlegen; **to make a ~ of o.s.** sich blamieren; **you can't ~ me** du kannst mich nicht zum Narren halten
▶ **fool about** (*pej*) *vi* herumtrödeln; (*behave foolishly*) herumalbern
▶ **fool around** *vi* = **fool about**

foolhardy ['fu:lhɑ:dɪ] *adj* tollkühn

foolish ['fu:lɪʃ] *adj* dumm

foolishly ['fu:lɪʃlɪ] *adv* dumm; **~, I forgot ...** dummerweise habe ich ... vergessen

foolishness ['fu:lɪʃnɪs] *n* Dummheit *f*

foolproof ['fu:lpru:f] *adj* idiotensicher

foolscap ['fu:lskæp] *n* ≈ Kanzleipapier *nt*

foot [fut] (*pl* **feet**) *n* Fuß *m*; (*of animal*) Pfote *f* ▷ *vt* (*bill*) bezahlen; **on ~** zu Fuß; **to find one's feet** sich eingewöhnen; **to put one's ~ down** (*Aut*) Gas geben; (*say no*) ein Machtwort sprechen

footage ['futɪdʒ] *n* Filmmaterial *nt*

foot-and-mouth [futənd'mauθ], **foot-and-mouth disease** *n* Maul- und Klauenseuche *f*

football ['futbɔ:l] *n* Fußball *m*; (*US*) Football *m*, amerikanischer Fußball *m*

footballer ['futbɔ:lə^r] (*Brit*) *n* Fußballspieler(in) *m(f)*

football ground *n* Fußballplatz *m*

football match (*Brit*) *n* Fußballspiel *nt*

football player *n* (*Brit*) Fußballspieler(in) *m(f)*; (*US*) Footballspieler(in) *m(f)*

FOOTBALL POOLS

Football pools, umgangssprachlich auch *the pools* genannt, ist das in Großbritannien sehr beliebte Fußballtoto, bei dem auf die Ergebnisse der samstäglichen Fußballspiele gewettet wird. Die Gewinne können sehr hoch sein und gelegentlich Millionen von Pfund betragen.

foot brake *n* Fußbremse *f*

footbridge ['futbrɪdʒ] *n* Fußgängerbrücke *f*

foothills ['futhɪlz] *npl* (Gebirgs)ausläufer *pl*

foothold ['futhəuld] *n* Halt *m*; **to get a ~** Fuß fassen

footing ['futɪŋ] *n* Stellung *f*; (*relationship*) Verhältnis *nt*; **to lose one's ~** den Halt verlieren; **on an equal ~** auf gleicher Basis

footlights ['futlaɪts] *npl* Rampenlicht *nt*

footman ['futmən] (*irreg: like* **man**) *n* Lakai *m*

footnote ['futnəut] *n* Fußnote *f*

footpath ['futpɑ:θ] *n* Fußweg *m*; (*in street*) Bürgersteig *m*

footprint ['futprɪnt] *n* Fußabdruck *m*; (*of animal*) Spur *f*

footrest ['futrest] *n* Fußstütze *f*

Footsie ['futsɪ] (*inf*) *n* = **FTSE 100 Index**

footsie ['futsɪ] (*inf*) *n*: **to play ~ with sb** mit jdm füßeln

footsore ['futsɔ:^r] *adj*: **to be ~** wunde Füße haben

footstep ['futstep] *n* Schritt *m*; (*footprint*) Fußabdruck *m*; **to follow in sb's ~s** in jds Fußstapfen *acc* treten

footwear ['futwɛə^r] *n* Schuhe *pl*, Schuhwerk *nt*

Ⓞ **KEYWORD**

for [fɔ:^r] *prep* **1** für *+acc*; **is this for me?** ist das für mich?; **the train for London** der Zug nach London; **it's time for lunch** es ist Zeit zum Mittagessen; **what's it for?** wofür ist das?; **he works for the government/a local firm** er arbeitet für die Regierung/eine Firma am Ort; **he's mature for his age** er ist reif für sein Alter; **I sold it for £20** ich habe es für £20 verkauft; **I'm all for it** ich bin ganz dafür; **G for George** = G wie Gustav
2 (*because of*): **for this reason** aus diesem Grund; **for fear of being criticised** aus Angst, kritisiert zu werden
3 (*referring to distance*): **there are roadworks for 5 km** die Straßenbauarbeiten erstrecken sich über 5 km; **we walked for miles** wir sind meilenweit gelaufen
4 (*referring to time*): **he was away for 2 years** er war 2 Jahre lang weg; **I have known her for years** ich kenne sie bereits seit Jahren
5 (*with infinitive clause*): **it is not for me to decide** es liegt nicht an mir, das zu entscheiden; **for this to be possible ...** um dies möglich zu machen, ...
6 (*in spite of*) trotz *+gen or dat*; **for all his complaints, he is very fond of her** trotz seiner vielen Klagen mag er sie sehr
▷ *conj* (*form: since, as*) denn; **she was very angry, for he was late again** sie war sehr böse, denn er kam wieder zu spät

f.o.r. *abbr* (*Comm*: = *free on rail*) frei Bahn

forage ['fɔrɪdʒ] *n* Futter *nt* ▷ *vi* herumstöbern; **to ~ (for food)** nach Futter suchen

forage cap *n* Schiffchen *nt*

foray ['fɔreɪ] n (Raub)überfall m

forbad, forbade [fə'bæd] pt of **forbid**

forbearing [fɔː'bɛərɪŋ] adj geduldig

forbid [fə'bɪd] (pt **forbade**, pp **~den**) vt verbieten; **to ~ sb to do sth** jdm verbieten, etw zu tun

forbidden [fə'bɪdn] pp of **forbid** ▷ adj verboten

forbidding [fə'bɪdɪŋ] adj (look) streng; (prospect) grauenhaft

force [fɔːs] n Kraft f; (violence) Gewalt f; (of blow, impact) Wucht f; (influence) Macht f ▷ vt zwingen; (push) drücken; (: person) drängen; (lock, door) aufbrechen; **the Forces** (Brit) npl die Streitkräfte pl; **in ~** (law etc) geltend; (people: arrive etc) zahlreich; **to come into ~** in Kraft treten; **to join ~s** sich zusammentun; **a ~ 5 wind** Windstärke 5; **the sales ~** das Verkaufspersonal; **to ~ o.s./sb to do sth** sich/jdn zwingen, etw zu tun

▸ **force back** vt zurückdrängen; (tears) unterdrücken

▸ **force down** vt (food) hinunterwürgen (inf)

forced [fɔːst] adj gezwungen; **~ labour** Zwangsarbeit f; **~ landing** Notlandung f

force-feed ['fɔːsfiːd] vt zwangsernähren; (animal) stopfen

forceful ['fɔːsful] adj energisch; (attack) wirkungsvoll; (point) überzeugend

forceps ['fɔːsɛps] npl Zange f

forcible ['fɔːsəbl] adj gewaltsam; (reminder, lesson) eindringlich

forcibly ['fɔːsəblɪ] adv mit Gewalt; (express) eindringlich

ford [fɔːd] n Furt f ▷ vt durchqueren; (on foot) durchwaten

fore [fɔːʳ] n: **to come to the ~** ins Blickfeld geraten

forearm ['fɔːrɑːm] n Unterarm m

forebear ['fɔːbɛəʳ] n Vorfahr(in) m(f), Ahn(e) m(f)

foreboding [fɔː'bəudɪŋ] n Vorahnung f

forecast ['fɔːkɑːst] (irreg: like **cast**) n Prognose f; (of weather) (Wetter)vorhersage f ▷ vt voraussagen

foreclose [fɔː'kləuz] vt (Law: also: **foreclose on**) kündigen; **to ~ sb** (on loan/mortgage) jds Darlehen/Hypothek kündigen

foreclosure [fɔː'kləuʒəʳ] n Zwangsvollstreckung f

forecourt ['fɔːkɔːt] n Vorplatz m

forefathers ['fɔːfɑːðəz] npl Vorfahren pl

forefinger ['fɔːfɪŋgəʳ] n Zeigefinger m

forefront ['fɔːfrʌnt] n: **in the ~ of** an der Spitze +gen

forego [fɔː'gəu] (irreg: like **go**) vt verzichten auf +acc

foregoing ['fɔːgəuɪŋ] adj vorhergehend ▷ n: **the ~** das Vorhergehende

foregone ['fɔːgɔn] pp of **forego** ▷ adj: **it's a ~ conclusion** es steht von vornherein fest

foreground ['fɔːgraund] n Vordergrund m

forehand ['fɔːhænd] n (Tennis) Vorhand f

forehead ['fɔrɪd] n Stirn f

foreign ['fɔrɪn] adj ausländisch; (holiday) im Ausland; (customs, appearance) fremdartig; (trade, policy) Außen-; (correspondent) Auslands-; (object, matter) fremd; **goods from ~ countries/a ~ country** Waren aus dem Ausland

foreign body n Fremdkörper m

foreign currency n Devisen pl

foreigner ['fɔrɪnəʳ] n Ausländer(in) m(f)

foreign exchange n Devisenhandel m; (money) Devisen pl

foreign exchange market n Devisenmarkt m

foreign exchange rate n Devisenkurs m

foreign investment n Auslandsinvestition f

foreign minister n Außenminister(in) m(f)

Foreign Office (Brit) n Außenministerium nt

Foreign Secretary (Brit) n Außenminister(in) m(f)

foreleg ['fɔːlɛg] n Vorderbein nt

foreman ['fɔːmən] (irreg: like **man**) n Vorarbeiter m; (of jury) Obmann m

foremost ['fɔːməust] adj führend ▷ adv: **first and ~** zunächst, vor allem

forename ['fɔːneɪm] n Vorname m

forensic [fə'rɛnsɪk] adj (test) forensisch; (medicine) Gerichts-; (expert) Spurensicherungs-

foreplay ['fɔːpleɪ] n Vorspiel nt

forerunner ['fɔːrʌnəʳ] n Vorläufer m

foresee [fɔː'siː] (irreg: like **see**) vt vorhersehen

foreseeable [fɔː'siːəbl] adj vorhersehbar; **in the ~ future** in absehbarer Zeit

foreseen [fɔː'siːn] pp of **foresee**

foreshadow [fɔː'ʃædəu] vt andeuten

foreshore ['fɔːʃɔːʳ] n Strand m

foreshorten [fɔː'ʃɔːtn] vt perspektivisch verkürzen

foresight ['fɔːsaɪt] n Voraussicht f, Weitblick m

foreskin ['fɔːskɪn] n (Anat) Vorhaut f

forest ['fɔrɪst] n Wald m

forestall [fɔː'stɔːl] vt zuvorkommen +dat; (discussion) im Keim ersticken

forestry ['fɔrɪstrɪ] n Forstwirtschaft f

foretaste ['fɔːteɪst] n: **a ~ of** ein Vorgeschmack von

foretell [fɔː'tɛl] (irreg: like **tell**) vt vorhersagen

forethought ['fɔːθɔːt] n Vorbedacht m

foretold [fɔː'təuld] pt, pp of **foretell**

forever [fə'rɛvəʳ] adv für immer; (endlessly) ewig; (consistently) dauernd, ständig; **you're ~ finding difficulties** du findest ständig or dauernd neue Schwierigkeiten

forewarn [fɔː'wɔːn] vt vorwarnen

forewent [fɔː'wɛnt] pt of **forego**

forewoman ['fɔːwumən] (irreg: like **woman**) n Vorarbeiterin f; (of jury) Obmännin f

foreword ['fɔːwəːd] n Vorwort nt

forfeit ['fɔːfɪt] n Strafe f, Buße f ▷ vt (right) verwirken; (friendship etc) verlieren; (one's happiness, health) einbüßen

forgave [fə'geɪv] pt of **forgive**

forge [fɔːdʒ] n Schmiede f ▷ vt fälschen; (wrought iron) schmieden

▸ **forge ahead** vi große or schnelle Fortschritte

machen

forger [ˈfɔːdʒəʳ] n Fälscher(in) m(f)

forgery [ˈfɔːdʒərɪ] n Fälschung f

forget [fəˈɡɛt] (pt **forgot**, pp **forgotten**) vt
vergessen ▷ vi es vergessen; **to ~ o.s.** sich
vergessen

forgetful [fəˈɡɛtful] adj vergesslich; **~ of sth**
(of duties etc) nachlässig gegenüber etw

forgetfulness [fəˈɡɛtfulnɪs] n Vergesslichkeit
f; (oblivion) Vergessenheit f

forget-me-not [fəˈɡɛtmɪnɔt] n
Vergissmeinnicht nt

forgive [fəˈɡɪv] (pt **forgave**, pp **~n**) vt verzeihen
+dat, vergeben +dat; **to ~ sb for sth** jdm etw
verzeihen or vergeben; **to ~ sb for doing sth**
jdm verzeihen or vergeben, dass er etw getan
hat; **~ me, but** ... entschuldigen Sie, aber ...;
they could be ~n for thinking that ... es ist
verständlich, wenn sie denken, dass ...

forgiveness [fəˈɡɪvnɪs] n Verzeihung f

forgiving [fəˈɡɪvɪŋ] adj versöhnlich

forgo [fɔːˈɡəu] (pt **forwent**, pp **~ne**) vt = **forego**

forgot [fəˈɡɔt] pt of **forget**

forgotten [fəˈɡɔtn] pp of **forget**

fork [fɔːk] n Gabel f; (in road, river, railway)
Gabelung f ▷ vi (road) sich gabeln
▶ **fork out** (inf) vt, vi (pay) blechen

forked [fɔːkt] adj (lightning) zickzackförmig

fork-lift truck [ˈfɔːklɪft-] n Gabelstapler m

forlorn [fəˈlɔːn] adj verlassen; (person) einsam
und verlassen; (attempt) verzweifelt; (hope)
schwach

form [fɔːm] n Form f; (Scol) Klasse f;
(questionnaire) Formular nt ▷ vt formen,
gestalten; (queue, organization, group) bilden;
(idea, habit) entwickeln; **in the ~ of** in Form
von or +gen; **in the ~ of Peter** in Gestalt von
Peter; **to be in good ~** gut in Form sein; **in
top ~** in Hochform; **on ~** in Form; **to ~ part of
sth** Teil von etw sein

formal [ˈfɔːməl] adj offiziell; (person, behaviour)
förmlich, formell; (occasion, dinner) feierlich;
(clothes) Gesellschafts-; (garden) formell
angelegt; (Art, Philosophy) formal; **~ dress**
Gesellschaftskleidung f

formalities [fɔːˈmælɪtɪz] npl Formalitäten pl

formality [fɔːˈmælɪtɪ] n Förmlichkeit f;
(procedure) Formalität f

formalize [ˈfɔːməlaɪz] vt formell machen

formally [ˈfɔːməlɪ] adv (see adj) offiziell;
förmlich, formell; feierlich; **to be ~ invited**
ausdrücklich eingeladen sein

format [ˈfɔːmæt] n Format nt; (form, style)
Aufmachung f ▷ vt (Comput) formatieren

formation [fɔːˈmeɪʃən] n Bildung f; (of theory)
Entstehung f; (of business) Gründung f;
(pattern: of rocks, clouds) Formation f

formative [ˈfɔːmətɪv] adj (influence) prägend;
(years) entscheidend

former [ˈfɔːməʳ] adj früher; **the ~ ... the
latter** ... Erstere(r, s) ... Letztere(r, s); **the ~
president** der ehemalige Präsident; **the ~
East Germany** die ehemalige DDR

formerly [ˈfɔːməlɪ] adv früher

form feed n (on printer) Papiervorschub m

Formica® [fɔːˈmaɪkə] n Resopal® nt

formidable [ˈfɔːmɪdəbl] adj (task) gewaltig,
enorm; (opponent) furchterregend

formula [ˈfɔːmjulə] (pl **formulae** or **~s**) n Formel
f; **F~ One** (Aut) Formel Eins

formulate [ˈfɔːmjuleɪt] vt formulieren

fornicate [ˈfɔːnɪkeɪt] vi Unzucht treiben

forsake [fəˈseɪk] (pt **forsook**, pp **~n**) vt im Stich
lassen; (belief) aufgeben

forsook [fəˈsuk] pt of **forsake**

fort [fɔːt] n Fort nt; **to hold the ~** die Stellung
halten

forte [ˈfɔːtɪ] n Stärke f, starke Seite f

forth [fɔːθ] adv aus; **back and ~** hin und her;
to go back and ~ auf und ab gehen; **to bring
~** hervorbringen; **and so ~** und so weiter

forthcoming [fɔːθˈkʌmɪŋ] adj (event)
bevorstehend; (person) mitteilsam; **to be ~**
(help) erfolgen; (evidence) geliefert werden

forthright [ˈfɔːθraɪt] adj offen

forthwith [ˈfɔːθˈwɪθ] adv umgehend

fortieth [ˈfɔːtɪɪθ] num vierzigste(r, s)

fortification [fɔːtɪfɪˈkeɪʃən] n Befestigung f,
Festungsanlage f

fortified wine [ˈfɔːtɪfaɪd-] n weinhaltiges
Getränk nt (Sherry, Portwein etc)

fortify [ˈfɔːtɪfaɪ] vt (city) befestigen; (person)
bestärken; (: subj: food, drink) stärken

fortitude [ˈfɔːtɪtjuːd] n innere Kraft or Stärke f

fortnight [ˈfɔːtnaɪt] (Brit) n vierzehn Tage
pl, zwei Wochen pl; **it's a ~ since** ... es ist
vierzehn Tage or zwei Wochen her, dass ...

fortnightly [ˈfɔːtnaɪtlɪ] adj vierzehntägig,
zweiwöchentlich ▷ adv alle vierzehn Tage,
alle zwei Wochen

FORTRAN [ˈfɔːtræn] n FORTRAN nt

fortress [ˈfɔːtrɪs] n Festung f

fortuitous [fɔːˈtjuːɪtəs] adj zufällig

fortunate [ˈfɔːtʃənɪt] adj glücklich; **to be ~**
Glück haben; **he is ~ to have** ... er kann sich
glücklich schätzen, ... zu haben; **it is ~ that** ...
es ist ein Glück, dass ...

fortunately [ˈfɔːtʃənɪtlɪ] adv glücklicherweise,
zum Glück

fortune [ˈfɔːtʃən] n Glück nt; (wealth) Vermögen
nt; **to make a ~** ein Vermögen machen; **to
tell sb's ~** jdm wahrsagen

fortune-teller [ˈfɔːtʃəntɛləʳ] n Wahrsager(in)
m(f)

forty [ˈfɔːtɪ] num vierzig

forum [ˈfɔːrəm] n Forum nt

forward [ˈfɔːwəd] adj vordere(r, s); (movement)
Vorwärts-; (not shy) dreist; (Comm: buying,
price) Termin- ▷ adv nach vorn; (movement)
vorwärts; (in time) voraus ▷ n (Sport) Stürmer
m ▷ vt (letter etc) nachsenden; (career, plans)
voranbringen; **~ planning** Vorausplanung
f; **to move ~** vorwärtskommen; **"please ~"**
„bitte nachsenden"

forwards [ˈfɔːwədz] adv nach vorn; (movement)
vorwärts; (in time) voraus

fossil ['fɒsl] n Fossil nt
fossil fuel n fossiler Brennstoff m
foster ['fɒstər] vt (child) in Pflege nehmen; (idea, activity) fördern
foster child n Pflegekind nt
foster mother n Pflegemutter f
fought [fɔːt] pt, pp of **fight**
foul [faul] adj abscheulich; (taste, smell, temper) übel; (water) faulig; (air) schlecht; (language) unflätig ▷ n (Sport) Foul nt ▷ vt beschmutzen; (Sport) foulen; (entangle) sich verheddern in +dat
foul play n unnatürlicher or gewaltsamer Tod m; ~ **is not suspected** es besteht kein Verdacht auf ein Verbrechen
found [faund] pt, pp of **find** ▷ vt gründen
foundation [faun'deɪʃən] n Gründung f; (base: also: fig) Grundlage f; (organization) Stiftung f; (also: **foundation cream**) Grundierungscreme f; **foundations** npl (of building) Fundament nt; **the rumours are without** ~ die Gerüchte entbehren jeder Grundlage; **to lay the ~s** (fig) die Grundlagen schaffen
foundation stone n Grundstein m
founder ['faundər] n Gründer(in) m(f) ▷ vi (ship) sinken
founder member n Gründungsmitglied nt
founding ['faundɪŋ] adj: ~ **fathers** (esp US) Väter pl
foundry ['faundrɪ] n Gießerei f
fount [faunt] n Quelle f; (Typ) Schrift f
fountain ['fauntɪn] n Brunnen m
fountain pen n Füllfederhalter m, Füller m
four [fɔːr] num vier; **on all ~s** auf allen vieren
four-letter word ['fɔːletə-] n Vulgärausdruck m
four-poster ['fɔː'pəustər] n (also: **four-poster bed**) Himmelbett nt
foursome ['fɔːsəm] n Quartett nt; **in** or **as a ~** zu viert
fourteen ['fɔː'tiːn] num vierzehn
fourteenth ['fɔː'tiːnθ] num vierzehnte(r, s)
fourth [fɔːθ] num vierte(r, s) ▷ n (Aut: also: **fourth gear**) der vierte (Gang)
four-wheel drive ['fɔːwiːl-] n (Aut): **with** ~ mit Vierradantrieb m
fowl [faul] n Vogel m (besonders Huhn, Gans, Ente etc)
fox [fɒks] n Fuchs m ▷ vt verblüffen
foxglove ['fɒksglʌv] n (Bot) Fingerhut m
fox-hunting ['fɒkshʌntɪŋ] n Fuchsjagd f
foxtrot ['fɒkstrɒt] n Foxtrott m
foyer ['fɔɪeɪ] n Foyer nt
FPA (Brit) n abbr (= Family Planning Association) Organisation für Familienplanung
Fr. abbr (Rel) = **father; friar**
fr. abbr (= franc) Fr.
fracas ['frækɑː] n Aufruhr m, Tumult m
fraction ['frækʃən] n Bruchteil m; (Math) Bruch m
fractionally ['frækʃnəlɪ] adv geringfügig
fractious ['frækʃəs] adj verdrießlich

fracture ['fræktʃər] n Bruch m ▷ vt brechen
fragile ['frædʒaɪl] adj zerbrechlich; (economy) schwach; (health) zart; (person) angeschlagen
fragment [n 'frægmənt, vb fræg'mɛnt] n Stück nt ▷ vt aufsplittern ▷ vi sich aufsplittern
fragmentary ['frægməntərɪ] adj fragmentarisch, bruchstückhaft
fragrance ['freɪgrəns] n Duft m
fragrant ['freɪgrənt] adj duftend
frail [freɪl] adj schwach, gebrechlich; (structure) zerbrechlich
frame [freɪm] n Rahmen m; (of building) (Grund) gerippe nt; (of human, animal) Gestalt f; (of spectacles: also: **frames**) Gestell nt ▷ vt (picture) rahmen; (reply) formulieren; (law, theory) entwerfen; ~ **of mind** Stimmung f, Laune f; **to** ~ **sb** (inf) jdm etwas anhängen
framework ['freɪmwəːk] n Rahmen m
France [frɑːns] n Frankreich nt
franchise ['fræntʃaɪz] n Wahlrecht nt; (Comm) Konzession f, Franchise f
franchisee [fræntʃaɪ'ziː] n Franchisenehmer(in) m(f)
franchiser ['fræntʃaɪzər] n Franchisegeber(in) m(f)
frank [fræŋk] adj offen ▷ vt (letter) frankieren
Frankfurt ['fræŋkfəːt] n Frankfurt nt
frankfurter ['fræŋkfəːtər] n (Frankfurter) Würstchen nt
franking machine ['fræŋkɪŋ-] n Frankiermaschine f
frankly ['fræŋklɪ] adv ehrlich gesagt; (candidly) offen
frankness ['fræŋknɪs] n Offenheit f
frantic ['fræntɪk] adj verzweifelt; (hectic) hektisch; (desperate) übersteigert
frantically ['fræntɪklɪ] adv verzweifelt; (hectically) hektisch
fraternal [frə'təːnl] adj brüderlich
fraternity [frə'təːnɪtɪ] n Brüderlichkeit f; (US: Univ) Verbindung f; **the legal/medical/golfing** ~ die Juristen/Mediziner/Golfer pl
fraternize ['frætənaɪz] vi Umgang haben
fraud [frɔːd] n Betrug m; (person) Betrüger(in) m(f)
fraudulent ['frɔːdjulənt] adj betrügerisch
fraught [frɔːt] adj (person) nervös; **to be ~ with danger/problems** voller Gefahren/Probleme sein
fray [freɪ] n: **the ~** der Kampf m ▷ vi (cloth) ausfransen; (rope) sich durchscheuern; **to return to the ~** sich wieder ins Getümmel stürzen; **tempers were ~ed** die Gemüter erhitzten sich; **her nerves were ~ed** sie war mit den Nerven am Ende
FRB (US) n abbr = **Federal Reserve Board**
FRCM (Brit) n abbr (= Fellow of the Royal College of Music) Qualifikationsnachweis in Musik
FRCO (Brit) n abbr (= Fellow of the Royal College of Organists) Qualifikationsnachweis für Organisten
FRCP (Brit) n abbr (= Fellow of the Royal College of Physicians) Qualifikationsnachweis für Ärzte
FRCS (Brit) n abbr (= Fellow of the Royal College of

Surgeons) Qualifikationsnachweis *für Chirurgen*
freak [fri:k] *n* Irre(r) *f(m)*; *(in appearance)* Missgeburt *f*; *(event, accident)* außergewöhnlicher Zufall *m*; *(pej: fanatic)*: **health** ~ Gesundheitsapostel *m*
▶ **freak out** *(inf)* *vi* aussteigen; *(on drugs)* ausflippen
freakish ['fri:kıʃ] *adj* verrückt
freckle ['frɛkl] *n* Sommersprosse *f*
freckled ['frɛkld] *adj* sommersprossig
free [fri:] *adj* frei; *(costing nothing)* kostenlos, gratis ▷ *vt* freilassen, frei lassen; *(jammed object)* lösen; **to give sb a ~ hand** jdm freie Hand lassen; **~ and easy** ungezwungen; **admission** ~ Eintritt frei; **~ (of charge), for free** umsonst, gratis
free agent *n*: **to be a** ~ sein eigener Herr sein
freebie ['fri:bɪ] *(inf)* *n* *(promotional gift)* Werbegeschenk *nt*
freedom ['fri:dəm] *n* Freiheit *f*
freedom fighter *n* Freiheitskämpfer(in) *m(f)*
free enterprise *n* freies Unternehmertum *nt*
Freefone® ['fri:fəun] *n*: **call ~ o800** rufen Sie gebührenfrei o800 an
free-for-all ['fri:fərɔ:l] *n* Gerangel *nt*; **the fight turned into a** ~ schließlich beteiligten sich alle an der Schlägerei
free gift *n* Werbegeschenk *nt*
freehold ['fri:həuld] *n* *(of property)* Besitzrecht *nt*
free kick *n* Freistoß *m*
freelance ['fri:lɑ:ns] *adj* *(journalist etc)* frei(schaffend), freiberuflich tätig
freelance work *n* freiberufliche Arbeit *f*
freeloader ['fri:ləudə^r] *(pej)* *n* Schmarotzer(in) *m(f)*
freely ['fri:lɪ] *adv* frei; *(spend)* mit vollen Händen; *(liberally)* großzügig; **drugs are ~ available in the city** Drogen sind in der Stadt frei erhältlich
free-market economy ['fri:'mɑ:kɪt-] *n* freie Marktwirtschaft *f*
Freemason ['fri:meɪsn] *n* Freimaurer *m*
Freemasonry ['fri:meɪsnrɪ] *n* Freimaurerei *f*
Freepost® ['fri:pəust] *n* ≈ „Gebühr zahlt Empfänger"
free-range ['fri:'reɪndʒ] *adj* *(eggs)* von frei laufenden Hühnern
free sample *n* Gratisprobe *f*
freesia ['fri:zɪə] *n* Freesie *f*
free speech *n* Redefreiheit *f*
freestyle ['fri:staɪl] *n* Freistil *m*
free trade *n* Freihandel *m*
freeway ['fri:weɪ] *(US)* *n* Autobahn *f*
freewheel [fri:'wi:l] *vi* im Freilauf fahren
free will *n* freier Wille *m*; **of one's own ~** aus freien Stücken
freeze [fri:z] *(pt* **froze**, *pp* **frozen**) *vi* frieren; *(liquid)* gefrieren; *(pipe)* einfrieren; *(person: stop moving)* erstarren ▷ *vt* einfrieren; *(water, lake)* gefrieren ▷ *n* Frost *m*; *(on arms, wages)* Stopp *m*
▶ **freeze over** *vi* *(river)* überfrieren; *(windscreen, windows)* vereisen
▶ **freeze up** *vi* zufrieren

freeze-dried ['fri:zdraɪd] *adj* gefriergetrocknet
freezer ['fri:zə^r] *n* Tiefkühltruhe *f*; *(upright)* Gefrierschrank *m*; *(in fridge: also:* **freezer compartment***)* Gefrierfach *nt*
freezing ['fri:zɪŋ] *adj*: ~ **(cold)** eiskalt ▷ *n*: **3 degrees below** ~ 3 Grad unter null; **I'm ~** mir ist eiskalt
freezing point *n* Gefrierpunkt *m*
freight [freɪt] *n* Fracht *f*; *(money charged)* Frachtkosten *pl*; ~ **forward** Fracht gegen Nachnahme; ~ **inward** Eingangsfracht *f*
freight car *(US)* *n* Güterwagen *m*
freighter ['freɪtə^r] *n* *(Naut)* Frachter *m*, Frachtschiff *nt*; *(Aviat)* Frachtflugzeug *nt*
freight forwarder [-'fɔ:wədə^r] *n* Spediteur *m*
freight train *(US)* *n* Güterzug *m*
French [frɛntʃ] *adj* französisch ▷ *n* *(Ling)* Französisch *nt*; **the French** *npl* die Franzosen *pl*
French bean *(Brit)* *n* grüne Bohne *f*
French Canadian *adj* frankokanadisch ▷ *n* Frankokanadier(in) *m(f)*
French dressing *n* Vinaigrette *f*
French fried potatoes *npl* Pommes frites *pl*
French fries [-fraɪz] *(US)* *npl* = **French fried potatoes**
French Guiana [-gaɪ'ænə] *n* Französisch-Guyana *nt*
Frenchman ['frɛntʃmən] *(irreg: like* **man***)* *n* Franzose *m*
French Riviera *n*: **the** ~ die französische Riviera
French stick *n* Stangenbrot *nt*
French window *n* Verandatür *f*
Frenchwoman ['frɛntʃwumən] *(irreg: like* **woman***)* *n* Französin *f*
frenetic [frə'nɛtɪk] *adj* frenetisch, rasend
frenzied ['frɛnzɪd] *adj* rasend
frenzy ['frɛnzɪ] *n* Raserei *f*; *(of joy, excitement)* Taumel *m*; **to drive sb into a** ~ jdn zum Rasen bringen; **to be in a** ~ in wilder Aufregung sein
frequency ['fri:kwənsɪ] *n* Häufigkeit *f*; *(Radio)* Frequenz *f*
frequency modulation *n* Frequenzmodulation *f*
frequent [*adj* 'fri:kwənt, *vt* frɪ'kwɛnt] *adj* häufig ▷ *vt* *(pub, restaurant)* oft *or* häufig besuchen
frequently ['fri:kwəntlɪ] *adv* oft, häufig
fresco ['frɛskəu] *n* Fresko *nt*
fresh [frɛʃ] *adj* frisch; *(instructions, approach, start)* neu; *(cheeky)* frech; **to make a ~ start** einen neuen Anfang machen
freshen ['frɛʃən] *vi* *(wind)* auffrischen; *(air)* frisch werden
▶ **freshen up** *vi* sich frisch machen
freshener ['frɛʃnə^r] *n*: **skin ~** Gesichtswasser *nt*; **air ~** Raumspray *m or nt*
fresher ['frɛʃə^r] *(Brit: inf)* *n* Erstsemester(in) *m(f)*
freshly ['frɛʃlɪ] *adv* frisch
freshman ['frɛʃmən] *(US: irreg: like* **man***)* *n* = **fresher**

freshness ['frɛʃnɪs] n Frische f
freshwater ['frɛʃwɔːtəʳ] adj (fish etc) Süßwasser-
fret [frɛt] vi sich dat Sorgen machen
fretful ['frɛtful] adj (child) quengelig
Freudian ['frɔɪdɪən] adj freudianisch,
  freudsch; **~ slip** freudscher Versprecher m
FRG n abbr (Hist: = Federal Republic of Germany)
  BRD f
Fri. abbr (= Friday) Fr.
friar ['fraɪəʳ] n Mönch m, (Ordens)bruder m
friction ['frɪkʃən] n Reibung f; (between people)
  Reibereien pl
friction feed n (on printer) Friktionsvorschub m
Friday ['fraɪdɪ] n Freitag m; see also **Tuesday**
fridge [frɪdʒ] (Brit) n Kühlschrank m
fridge-freezer ['frɪdʒ'friːzəʳ] n Kühl- und
  Gefrierkombination f
fried [fraɪd] pt, pp of **fry** ▷ adj gebraten; **~ egg**
  Spiegelei nt; **~ fish** Bratfisch m
friend [frɛnd] n Freund(in) m(f); (less intimate)
  Bekannte(r) f(m) ▷ vt (Internet): **to ~ sb** einen
  Freund/eine Freundin hinzufügen; **to make
  ~s with** sich anfreunden mit
friendliness ['frɛndlɪnɪs] n Freundlichkeit f
friendly ['frɛndlɪ] adj freundlich; (government)
  befreundet; (game, match) Freundschafts- ▷ n
  (also: **friendly match**) Freundschaftsspiel nt;
  to be ~ with befreundet sein mit; **to be ~ to**
  freundlich or nett sein zu
friendly fire n Beschuss m durch die eigene
  Seite
friendly society n Versicherungsverein m auf
  Gegenseitigkeit
friendship ['frɛndʃɪp] n Freundschaft f
frieze [friːz] n Fries m
frigate ['frɪgɪt] n Fregatte f
fright [fraɪt] n Schreck(en) m; **to take ~** es mit
  der Angst zu tun bekommen; **she looks a ~**
  sie sieht verboten or zum Fürchten aus (inf)
frighten ['fraɪtn] vt erschrecken
  ▸ **frighten away** or **off** vt verscheuchen
frightened ['fraɪtnd] adj ängstlich; **to be ~ (of)**
  Angst haben (vor +dat)
frightening ['fraɪtnɪŋ] adj furchterregend
frightful ['fraɪtful] adj schrecklich, furchtbar
frightfully ['fraɪtfəlɪ] adv schrecklich, furchtbar;
  I'm ~ sorry es tut mir schrecklich leid
frigid ['frɪdʒɪd] adj frigide
frigidity [frɪ'dʒɪdɪtɪ] n Frigidität f
frill [frɪl] n Rüsche f; **without ~s** (fig) schlicht
fringe [frɪndʒ] n (Brit: of hair) Pony m; (decoration)
  Fransen pl; (edge, also fig) Rand m
fringe benefits npl zusätzliche Leistungen pl
fringe theatre n avantgardistisches Theater nt
Frisbee® ['frɪzbɪ] n Frisbee® nt
frisk [frɪsk] vt durchsuchen, filzen (inf) ▷ vi
  umhertollen
frisky ['frɪskɪ] adj lebendig, ausgelassen
fritter ['frɪtəʳ] n Schmalzgebackenes nt no pl mit
  Füllung
  ▸ **fritter away** vt vergeuden
frivolity [frɪ'vɔlɪtɪ] n Frivolität f
frivolous ['frɪvələs] adj frivol; (activity)

leichtfertig
frizzy ['frɪzɪ] adj kraus
fro [frəu] adv: **to and ~** hin und her; (walk) auf
  und ab
frock [frɔk] n Kleid nt
frog [frɔg] n Frosch m; **to have a ~ in one's
  throat** einen Frosch im Hals haben
frogman ['frɔgmən] (irreg: like **man**) n
  Froschmann m
frogmarch ['frɔgmɑːtʃ] (Brit) vt: **to ~ sb in/out**
  jdn herein-/herausschleppen
frolic ['frɔlɪk] vi umhertollen ▷ n
  Ausgelassenheit f; (fun) Spaß m

 KEYWORD

from [frɔm] prep **1** (indicating starting place, origin)
  von +dat; **where do you come from?** woher
  kommen Sie?; **from London to Glasgow** von
  London nach Glasgow; **a letter/telephone
  call from my sister** ein Brief/Anruf von
  meiner Schwester; **to drink from the bottle**
  aus der Flasche trinken
  2 (indicating time) von (... an); **from one o'clock
  to** or **until** or **till now** von ein Uhr bis jetzt;
  from January (on) von Januar an, ab Januar
  3 (indicating distance) von ... entfernt; **the hotel
  is 1 km from the beach** das Hotel ist 1 km
  vom Strand entfernt
  4 (indicating price, number etc): **trousers from
  £20** Hosen ab £20; **prices range from £10 to
  £50** die Preise liegen zwischen £10 und £50
  5 (indicating difference): **he can't tell red
  from green** er kann Rot und Grün nicht
  unterscheiden; **to be different from sb/sth**
  anders sein als jd/etw
  6 (because of, on the basis of): **from what he
  says** nach dem, was er sagt; **to act from
  conviction** aus Überzeugung handeln; **weak
  from hunger** schwach vor Hunger

frond [frɔnd] n Wedel m
front [frʌnt] n Vorderseite f; (of dress)
  Vorderteil nt; (promenade: also: **sea front**)
  Strandpromenade f; (Mil, Met) Front f;
  (fig: appearances) Fassade f ▷ adj vorderste(r,
  s); (wheel, tooth, view) Vorder- ▷ vi: **to ~ onto
  sth** (house) auf etw acc hinausliegen; (window)
  auf etw acc hinausgehen; **in ~** vorne; **in ~ of**
  vor; **at the ~ of the coach/train/car** vorne
  im Bus/Zug/Auto; **on the political ~, little
  progress has been made** an der politischen
  Front sind kaum Fortschritte gemacht worden
frontage ['frʌntɪdʒ] n Vorderseite f, Front f; (of
  shop) Front
frontal ['frʌntl] adj (attack etc) Frontal-
front bench (Brit) n (Pol) vorderste or erste
  Reihe f

◉ **FRONT BENCH**
◉
◉ Front Bench bezeichnet im britischen
◉ Unterhaus die vorderste Bank auf der

Regierungs- und Oppositionsseite zur Rechten und Linken des Sprechers. Im weiteren Sinne bezieht sich front bench auf die Spitzenpolitiker der verschiedenen Parteien, die auf dieser Bank sitzen (auch „frontbenchers" genannt), d. h. die Minister auf der einen Seite und die Mitglieder des Schattenkabinetts auf der anderen.

front desk (US) n Rezeption f
front door n Haustür f
frontier [ˈfrʌntɪəʳ] n Grenze f
frontispiece [ˈfrʌntɪspiːs] n Frontispiz nt
front page n erste Seite f, Titelseite f
front room (Brit) n Wohnzimmer nt
frontrunner [ˈfrʌntrʌnəʳ] n Spitzenreiter m
front-wheel drive [ˈfrʌntwiːl-] n (Aut) Vorderradantrieb m
frost [frɒst] n Frost m; (also: **hoarfrost**) Raureif m
frostbite [ˈfrɒstbaɪt] n Erfrierungen pl
frosted [ˈfrɒstɪd] adj (glass) Milch-; (esp US) glasiert, mit Zuckerguss überzogen
frosting [ˈfrɒstɪŋ] (esp US) n Zuckerguss m
frosty [ˈfrɒstɪ] adj frostig; (look) eisig; (window) bereift
froth [frɒθ] n Schaum m
frothy [ˈfrɒθɪ] adj schäumend
frown [fraun] n Stirnrunzeln nt ▷ vi die Stirn runzeln
  ▶ **frown on** vt fus missbilligen
froze [frəuz] pt of **freeze**
frozen [ˈfrəuzn] pp of **freeze** ▷ adj tiefgekühlt; (food) Tiefkühl-; (Comm) eingefroren
FRS n abbr (Brit: = Fellow of the Royal Society) Auszeichnung für Naturwissenschaftler; (US: = Federal Reserve System) amerikanische Zentralbank
frugal [ˈfruːɡl] adj genügsam; (meal) einfach
fruit [fruːt] n inv Frucht f; (collectively) Obst nt; (fig: results) Früchte pl
fruiterer [ˈfruːtərəʳ] (esp Brit) n Obsthändler(in) m(f)
fruit fly n Fruchtfliege f
fruitful [ˈfruːtful] adj fruchtbar
fruition [fruːˈɪʃən] n: **to come to ~** (plan) Wirklichkeit werden; (efforts) Früchte tragen; (hope) in Erfüllung gehen
fruit juice n Fruchtsaft m
fruitless [ˈfruːtlɪs] adj fruchtlos, ergebnislos
fruit machine (Brit) n Spielautomat m
fruit salad n Obstsalat m
fruity [ˈfruːtɪ] adj (taste, smell etc) Frucht-, Obst-; (wine) fruchtig; (voice, laugh) volltönend
frump [frʌmp] n: **to feel a ~** sich dat wie eine Vogelscheuche vorkommen
frustrate [frʌsˈtreɪt] vt frustrieren; (attempt) vereiteln; (plan) durchkreuzen
frustrated [frʌsˈtreɪtɪd] adj frustriert
frustrating [frʌsˈtreɪtɪŋ] adj frustrierend
frustration [frʌsˈtreɪʃən] n Frustration f; (of attempt) Vereitelung f; (of plan) Zerschlagung f
fry [fraɪ] (pt, pp **fried**) vt braten; see also **small**

frying pan [ˈfraɪɪŋ-] n Bratpfanne f
FT (Brit) n abbr (= Financial Times) Wirtschaftszeitung; **the FT index** der Aktienindex der „Financial Times"
ft. abbr = **foot; feet**
FTC (US) n abbr = **Federal Trade Commission**
FTSE 100 Index n Aktienindex der "Financial Times"
fuchsia [ˈfjuːʃə] n Fuchsie f
fuck [fʌk] (inf!) vt, vi ficken (!); **~ off!** (inf!) verpiss dich! (!)
fuddled [ˈfʌdld] adj verwirrt
fuddy-duddy [ˈfʌdɪdʌdɪ] (pej) n Langweiler m
fudge [fʌdʒ] n Fondant m ▷ vt (issue, problem) ausweichen +dat, aus dem Weg gehen +dat
fuel [ˈfjuəl] n Brennstoff m; (for vehicle) Kraftstoff m; (: petrol) Benzin nt; (for aircraft, rocket) Treibstoff m ▷ vt (furnace etc) betreiben; (aircraft, ship etc) antreiben
fuel oil n Gasöl nt
fuel poverty n durch hohe Energiekosten verursachte Armut
fuel pump n (Aut) Benzinpumpe f
fuel tank n Öltank m; (in vehicle) (Benzin)tank m
fug [fʌɡ] (Brit: inf) n Mief m (inf)
fugitive [ˈfjuːdʒɪtɪv] n Flüchtling m
fulfil, (US) **fulfill** [fulˈfɪl] vt erfüllen; (order) ausführen
fulfilled [fulˈfɪld] adj ausgefüllt
fulfilment, (US) **fulfillment** [fulˈfɪlmənt] n Erfüllung f
full [ful] adj voll; (complete) vollständig; (skirt) weit; (life) ausgefüllt ▷ adv: **to know ~ well that ...** sehr wohl wissen, dass ...; **~ up** (hotel etc) ausgebucht; **I'm ~ (up)** ich bin satt; **a ~ two hours** volle zwei Stunden; **~ marks** die beste Note, ≈ eine Eins; (fig) höchstes Lob nt; **at ~ speed** in voller Fahrt; **in ~** ganz, vollständig; **to pay in ~** den vollen Betrag bezahlen; **to write one's name** etc **in ~** seinen Namen etc ausschreiben
fullback [ˈfulbæk] n (Rugby, Football) Verteidiger m
full-blooded [ˈfulˈblʌdɪd] adj (vigorous) kräftig; (virile) vollblütig
full board n Vollpension f
full-cream [ˈfulˈkriːm] adj: **~ milk** (Brit) Vollmilch f
full employment n Vollbeschäftigung f
full grown adj ausgewachsen
full-length [ˈfulˈleŋθ] adj (film) abendfüllend; (coat) lang; (portrait) lebensgroß; (mirror) groß
full moon n Vollmond m
fullness [ˈfulnɪs] n: **in the ~ of time** zu gegebener Zeit
full-page [ˈfulpeɪdʒ] adj ganzseitig
full-scale [ˈfulskeɪl] adj (war) richtig; (attack) Groß-; (model) in Originalgröße; (search) groß angelegt
full-sized [ˈfulsaɪzd] adj lebensgroß
full stop n Punkt m
full-time [ˈfulˈtaɪm] adj (work) Ganztags-; (study) Voll- ▷ adv ganztags
fully [ˈfulɪ] adv völlig; **~ as big as** mindestens

f

so groß wie

fully fledged [-'flɛdʒd] *adj* richtiggehend; (*doctor etc*) voll qualifiziert; (*member*) Voll-; (*bird*) flügge

fulsome ['fulsəm] (*pej*) *adj* übertrieben

fumble ['fʌmbl] *vi*: **to ~ with** herumfummeln an +*dat* ▷ *vt* (*ball*) nicht sicher fangen

fume [fju:m] *vi* wütend sein, kochen (*inf*)

fumes [fju:mz] *npl* (*of fire*) Rauch *m*; (*of fuel*) Dämpfe *pl*; (*of car*) Abgase *pl*

fumigate ['fju:mɪɡeɪt] *vt* ausräuchern

fun [fʌn] *n* Spaß *m*; **he's good ~ (to be with)** es macht viel Spaß, mit ihm zusammen zu sein; **for ~** aus *or* zum Spaß; **it's not much ~** es macht keinen Spaß; **to make ~ of, to poke ~ at** sich lustig machen über +*acc*

function ['fʌŋkʃən] *n* Funktion *f*; (*social occasion*) Veranstaltung *f*, Feier *f* ▷ *vi* funktionieren; **to ~ as** (*thing*) dienen als; (*person*) fungieren als

functional ['fʌŋkʃənl] *adj* (*operational*) funktionsfähig; (*practical*) funktionell, zweckmäßig

functional food *adj* Functional Food *nt*, Funktionsnahrung *f*

function key *n* (*Comput*) Funktionstaste *f*

fund [fʌnd] *n* (*of money*) Fonds *m*; (*source, store*) Schatz *m*, Vorrat *m*; **funds** *npl* (*money*) Mittel *pl*, Gelder *pl*

fundamental [fʌndə'mɛntl] *adj* fundamental, grundlegend

fundamentalism [fʌndə'mɛntəlɪzəm] *n* Fundamentalismus *m*

fundamentalist [fʌndə'mɛntəlɪst] *n* Fundamentalist(in) *m(f)*

fundamentally [fʌndə'mɛntəlɪ] *adv* im Grunde; (*radically*) von Grund auf

fundamentals [fʌndə'mɛntlz] *npl* Grundbegriffe *pl*

funding ['fʌndɪŋ] *n* Finanzierung *f*

fund-raising ['fʌndreɪzɪŋ] *n* Geldbeschaffung *f*

funeral ['fju:nərəl] *n* Beerdigung *f*

funeral director *n* Beerdigungsunternehmer(in) *m(f)*

funeral parlour *n* Leichenhalle *f*

funeral service *n* Trauergottesdienst *m*

funereal [fju:'nɪərɪəl] *adj* traurig, trübselig

funfair ['fʌnfɛə*r*] (*Brit*) *n* Jahrmarkt *m*

fungi ['fʌnɡaɪ] *npl of* **fungus**

fungus ['fʌnɡəs] (*pl* **fungi**) *n* Pilz *m*; (*mould*) Schimmel(pilz) *m*

funicular [fju:'nɪkjulə*r*] *n* (*also:* **funicular railway**) Seilbahn *f*

funky ['fʌŋkɪ] *adj* (*music*) Funk-

funnel ['fʌnl] *n* Trichter *m*; (*of ship*) Schornstein *m*

funnily ['fʌnɪlɪ] *adv* komisch; **~ enough** komischerweise

funny ['fʌnɪ] *adj* komisch; (*strange*) seltsam, komisch

funny bone *n* Musikantenknochen *m*

fun run *n* = Volkslauf *m*

fur [fə:*r*] *n* Fell *nt*, Pelz *m*; (*Brit: in kettle etc*) Kesselstein *m*

fur coat *n* Pelzmantel *m*

furious ['fjuərɪəs] *adj* wütend; (*exchange, argument*) heftig; (*effort*) riesig; (*speed*) rasend; **to be ~ with sb** wütend auf jdn sein

furiously ['fjuərɪəslɪ] *adv* (*see adj*) wütend; (*struggle etc*) heftig; (*run*) schnell

furl [fə:l] *vt* (*Naut*) einrollen

furlong ['fə:lɔŋ] *n* Achtelmeile *f* (= 201,17 m)

furlough ['fə:ləu] *n* (*Mil*) Urlaub *m*

furnace ['fə:nɪs] *n* (*in foundry*) Schmelzofen *m*; (*in power plant*) Hochofen *m*

furnish ['fə:nɪʃ] *vt* einrichten; (*room*) möblieren; **to ~ sb with sth** jdm etw liefern; **~ed flat, ~ed apartment** (*US*) möblierte Wohnung *f*

furnishings ['fə:nɪʃɪŋz] *npl* Einrichtung *f*

furniture ['fə:nɪtʃə*r*] *n* Möbel *pl*; **piece of ~** Möbelstück *nt*

furniture polish *n* Möbelpolitur *f*

furore [fjuə'rɔ:rɪ] *n* (*protests*) Proteste *pl*; (*enthusiasm*) Furore *f or nt*

furrier ['fʌrɪə*r*] *n* Kürschner(in) *m(f)*

furrow ['fʌrəu] *n* Furche *f*; (*in skin*) Runzel *f* ▷ *vt* (*brow*) runzeln

furry ['fə:rɪ] *adj* (*coat, tail*) flauschig; (*animal*) Pelz-; (*toy*) Plüsch-

further ['fə:ðə*r*] *adj* weitere(r, s) ▷ *adv* weiter; (*moreover*) darüber hinaus ▷ *vt* fördern; **until ~ notice** bis auf Weiteres; **how much ~ is it?** wie weit ist es noch?; **~ to your letter of ...** (*Comm*) Bezug nehmend auf Ihr Schreiben vom ...

further education (*Brit*) *n* Weiterbildung *f*, Fortbildung *f*

furthermore [fə:ðə'mɔ:*r*] *adv* außerdem

furthermost ['fə:ðəməust] *adj* äußerste(r, s)

furthest ['fə:ðɪst] *superl of* **far**

furtive ['fə:tɪv] *adj* verstohlen

furtively ['fə:tɪvlɪ] *adv* verstohlen

fury ['fjuərɪ] *n* Wut *f*; **to be in a ~** in Rage sein

fuse, (*US*) **fuze** [fju:z] *n* (*Elec*) Sicherung *f*; (*for bomb etc*) Zündschnur *f* ▷ *vt* (*pieces of metal*) verschmelzen; (*fig*) vereinigen ▷ *vi* (*pieces of metal*) sich verbinden; (*fig*) sich vereinigen; **to ~ the lights** (*Brit*) die Sicherung durchbrennen lassen; **a ~ has blown** eine Sicherung ist durchgebrannt

fuse box *n* Sicherungskasten *m*

fuselage ['fju:zəlɑ:ʒ] *n* Rumpf *m*

fuse wire *n* Schmelzdraht *m*

fusillade [fju:zɪ'leɪd] *n* Salve *f*

fusion ['fju:ʒən] *n* Verschmelzung *f*; (*also:* **nuclear fusion**) Kernfusion *f*

fuss [fʌs] *n* Theater *nt* (*inf*) ▷ *vi* sich (unnötig) aufregen ▷ *vt* keine Ruhe lassen +*dat*; **to make a ~** Krach schlagen (*inf*); **to make a ~ of sb** viel Getue um jdn machen (*inf*)
▶ **fuss over** *vt fus* bemuttern

fusspot ['fʌspɔt] *n* Nörgler(in) *m(f)*

fussy ['fʌsɪ] *adj* kleinlich, pingelig (*inf*); (*clothes, room etc*) verspielt; **I'm not ~** es ist mir egal

fusty ['fʌstɪ] *adj* muffig

futile ['fju:taɪl] *adj* vergeblich; (*existence*)

sinnlos; *(comment)* zwecklos
futility [fju:'tɪlɪtɪ] *n (see adj)* Vergeblichkeit *f*;
  Sinnlosigkeit *f*; Zwecklosigkeit *f*
futon ['fu:tɔn] *n* Futon *m*
future ['fju:tʃə'] *adj* zukünftig ▷ *n* Zukunft
  f; *(Ling)* Futur *nt*; **futures** *npl (Comm)*
  Termingeschäfte *pl*; **in (the)** ~ in Zukunft;
  in the near ~ in der nahen Zukunft; **in the
  immediate** ~ sehr bald

futuristic [fju:tʃə'rɪstɪk] *adj* futuristisch
fuze [fju:z] *(US) n, vt, vi* = **fuse**
fuzz [fʌz] *(inf) n (police)*: **the** ~ die Bullen *pl*
fuzzy ['fʌzɪ] *adj* verschwommen; *(hair)* kraus;
  (thoughts) verworren
fwd. *abbr* = **forward**
fwy *(US) abbr* = **freeway**
FYI *abbr (= for your information)* zu Ihrer
  Information

f

Gg

G¹, g¹ [dʒiː] n (letter) G nt, g nt; **G for George** = G wie Gustav

G² [dʒiː] n (Mus) G nt, g nt

G³ [dʒiː] n abbr (Brit: Scol) = **good**; (US: Cine: = general (audience)) Klassifikation für jugendfreie Filme; (Phys): **G-force** g-Druck m

g² abbr (= gram(me)) g; (Phys) = **gravity**

G8 n abbr (Pol: = Group of Eight) G8 f

G20 n abbr (Pol: = Group of Twenty) G20 f

GA (US) n abbr (Post) = Georgia

gab [gæb] (inf) n: **to have the gift of the ~** reden können, nicht auf den Mund gefallen sein

gabble ['gæbl] vi brabbeln (inf)

gaberdine [gæbə'diːn] n Gabardine m

gable ['geɪbl] n Giebel m

Gabon [gə'bɔn] n Gabun nt

gad about [gæd-] (inf) vi herumziehen

gadget ['gædʒɪt] n Gerät nt

gadgetry ['gædʒɪtrɪ] n Geräte pl

Gaelic ['geɪlɪk] adj gälisch ▷ n (Ling) Gälisch nt

gaffe [gæf] n Fauxpas m

gaffer ['gæfəʳ] (Brit: inf) n (boss) Chef m; (foreman) Vorarbeiter m; (old man) Alte(r) m

gag [gæg] n Knebel m; (joke) Gag m ▷ vt knebeln ▷ vi würgen

gaga ['gaːgaː] (inf) adj: **to go ~** verkalken

gage [geɪdʒ] (US) n, vt = **gauge**

gaiety ['geɪɪtɪ] n Fröhlichkeit f

gaily ['geɪlɪ] adv fröhlich; **~ coloured** farbenfroh, farbenprächtig

gain [geɪn] n Gewinn m ▷ vt gewinnen ▷ vi (clock, watch) vorgehen; **to do sth for ~** etw aus Berechnung tun; (for money) etw des Geldes wegen tun; **~ (in)** (increase) Zunahme f (an +dat); (in rights, conditions) Verbesserung f +gen; **to ~ ground** (an) Boden gewinnen; **to ~ speed** schneller werden; **to ~ weight** zunehmen; **to ~ 3lbs (in weight)** 3 Pfund zunehmen; **to ~ (in) confidence** sicherer werden; **to ~ from sth** von etw profitieren; **to ~ in strength** stärker werden; **to ~ by doing sth** davon profitieren, etw zu tun; **to ~ on sb** jdn einholen

gainful ['geɪnful] adj: **~ employment** Erwerbstätigkeit f

gainfully ['geɪnfəlɪ] adv: **~ employed** erwerbstätig

gainsay [geɪn'seɪ] (irreg: like **say**) vt widersprechen +dat; (fact) leugnen

gait [geɪt] n Gang m; **to walk with a slow/ confident ~** mit langsamen Schritten/ selbstbewusst gehen

gal. abbr = **gallon**

gala ['gaːlə] n Galaveranstaltung f; **swimming ~** großes Schwimmfest nt

Galapagos [gə'læpəgəs] n die Galapagosinseln pl

Galapagos Islands npl: **(the) ~** = **Galapagos**

galaxy ['gæləksɪ] n Galaxis f, Sternsystem nt

gale [geɪl] n Sturm m; **~ force 10** Sturmstärke 10

gall [gɔːl] n Galle f; (fig: impudence) Frechheit f ▷ vt maßlos ärgern

gall. abbr = **gallon**

gallant ['gælənt] adj tapfer; (polite) galant

gallantry ['gæləntrɪ] n (see adj) Tapferkeit f; Galanterie f

gall bladder n Gallenblase f

galleon ['gælɪən] n Galeone f

gallery ['gælərɪ] n (also: **art gallery**) Galerie f, Museum nt; (private) (Privat)galerie f; (in hall, church) Galerie f; (in theatre) oberster Rang m, Balkon m

galley ['gælɪ] n Kombüse f; (ship) Galeere f; (also: **galley proof**) Fahne f, Fahnenabzug m

Gallic ['gælɪk] adj gallisch; (French) französisch

galling ['gɔːlɪŋ] adj äußerst ärgerlich

gallon ['gælən] n Gallone f (Brit = 4,5 l, US = 3,8 l)

gallop ['gæləp] n Galopp m ▷ vi galoppieren; **~ing inflation** galoppierende Inflation f

gallows ['gæləuz] n Galgen m

gallstone ['gɔːlstəun] n Gallenstein m

Gallup poll ['gæləp-] n Meinungsumfrage f

galore [gə'lɔːʳ] adv in Hülle und Fülle

galvanize ['gælvənaɪz] vt (fig) mobilisieren; **to ~ sb into action** jdn plötzlich aktiv werden lassen

galvanized ['gælvənaɪzd] adj (metal) galvanisiert

Gambia ['gæmbɪə] n Gambia nt

gambit ['gæmbɪt] n: **(opening) ~** (einleitender) Schachzug m; (in conversation) (einleitende) Bemerkung f

gamble ['gæmbl] n Risiko nt ▷ vt einsetzen ▷ vi ein Risiko eingehen; (bet) spielen; (on horses etc) wetten; **to ~ on the Stock Exchange** an

der Börse spekulieren; **to ~ on sth** (*horses, race*)
auf etw *acc* wetten; (*success, outcome etc*) sich auf
etw *acc* verlassen

gambler ['gæmblə'] *n* Spieler(in) *m(f)*

gambling ['gæmblɪŋ] *n* Spielen *nt*; (*on horses etc*)
Wetten *nt*

gambol ['gæmbl] *vi* herumtollen

game [geɪm] *n* Spiel *nt*; (*sport*) Sport *m*; (*strategy,
scheme*) Vorhaben *nt*; (*Culin, Hunting*) Wild *nt*
▷ *adj*: **to be ~ (for)** mitmachen (bei); **games**
npl (*Scol*) Sport *m*; **to play a ~ of football/
tennis** Fußball/(eine Partie) Tennis spielen;
big ~ Großwild *nt*

game bird *n* Federwild *nt no pl*

gamekeeper ['geɪmkiːpə'] *n* Wildhüter(in)
m(f)

gamely ['geɪmlɪ] *adv* mutig

gamer ['geɪmə'] *n* Gamer(in) *m(f)*,
Computerspieler(in) *m(f)*

game reserve *n* Wildschutzreservat *nt*

games console ['geɪmz-] *n* (*Comput*)
Gameboy® *m*, Konsole *f*

game show *n* (*TV*) Spielshow *f*

gamesmanship ['geɪmzmənʃɪp] *n*
Gerissenheit *f* beim Spiel

gaming ['geɪmɪŋ] *n* (*gambling*) Spielen *nt*;
(*Comput*) Computerspielen *nt*

gammon ['gæmən] *n* Schinken *m*

gamut ['gæmət] *n* Skala *f*; **to run the ~ of** die
ganze Skala +*gen* durchlaufen

gander ['gændə'] *n* Gänserich *m*

gang [gæŋ] *n* Bande *f*; (*of friends*) Haufen *m*; (*of
workmen*) Kolonne *f*
▶ **gang up** *vi*: **to ~ up on sb** sich gegen jdn
zusammentun

Ganges ['gændʒiːz] *n*: **the ~** der Ganges

gangland ['gæŋlænd] *adj* (*killer, boss*)
Unterwelt-

gangling ['gæŋglɪŋ], **gangly** ['gæŋglɪ] *adj*
schlaksig, hoch aufgeschossen

gangplank ['gæŋplæŋk] *n* Laufplanke *f*

gangrene ['gæŋgriːn] *n* (*Med*) Brand *m*

gangster ['gæŋstə'] *n* Gangster *m*

gangway ['gæŋweɪ] *n* Laufplanke *f*, Gangway
f; (*in cinema, bus, plane etc*) Gang *m*

gantry ['gæntrɪ] *n* (*for crane*) Portal *nt*; (*for
railway signal*) Signalbrücke *f*; (*for rocket*)
Abschussrampe *f*

GAO (*US*) *n abbr* (= *General Accounting Office*)
Rechnungshof *der USA*

gaol [dʒeɪl] (*Brit*) *n, vt* = **jail**

gap [gæp] *n* Lücke *f*; (*in time*) Pause *f*;
(*difference*): **~ (between)** Kluft *f* (zwischen +*dat*)

gape [geɪp] *vi* starren, gaffen; (*hole*) gähnen;
(*shirt*) offen stehen

gaping ['geɪpɪŋ] *adj* (*hole*) gähnend; (*shirt*) offen

garage ['gæraːʒ] *n* Garage *f*; (*for car repairs*)
(Reparatur)werkstatt *f*; (*petrol station*)
Tankstelle *f*

garb [gaːb] *n* Gewand *nt*, Kluft *f*

garbage ['gaːbɪdʒ] *n* (*US: rubbish*) Abfall *m*,
Müll *m*; (*inf: nonsense*) Blödsinn *m*, Quatsch *m*;
(*fig: film, book*) Schund *m*

garbage can (*US*) *n* Mülleimer *m*, Abfalleimer
m

garbage collector (*US*) *n* Müllmann *m*

garbage disposal, **garbage disposal unit** *n*
Müllschlucker *m*

garbage truck (*US*) *n* Müllwagen *m*

garbled ['gaːbld] *adj* (*account*) wirr; (*message*)
unverständlich

garden ['gaːdn] *n* Garten *m* ▷ *vi* gärtnern;
gardens *npl* (*public park*) Park *m*; (*private*)
Gartenanlagen *pl*; **she was ~ing** sie arbeitete
im Garten

garden centre *n* Gartencenter *nt*

garden city *n* Gartenstadt *f*

gardener ['gaːdnə'] *n* Gärtner(in) *m(f)*

gardening ['gaːdnɪŋ] *n* Gartenarbeit *f*

gargle ['gaːgl] *vi* gurgeln ▷ *n* Gurgelwasser *nt*

gargoyle ['gaːgɔɪl] *n* Wasserspeier *m*

garish ['gɛərɪʃ] *adj* grell

garland ['gaːlənd] *n* Kranz *m*

garlic ['gaːlɪk] *n* Knoblauch *m*

garment ['gaːmənt] *n* Kleidungsstück *nt*

garner ['gaːnə'] *vt* sammeln

garnish ['gaːnɪʃ] *vt* garnieren

garret ['gærɪt] *n* Dachkammer *f*, Mansarde *f*

garrison ['gærɪsn] *n* Garnison *f*

garrulous ['gærʊləs] *adj* geschwätzig

garter ['gaːtə'] *n* Strumpfband *nt*;
(*US: suspender*) Strumpfhalter *m*

garter belt (*US*) *n* Strumpfgürtel *m*

gas [gæs] *n* Gas *nt*; (*US: gasoline*) Benzin *nt* ▷ *vt*
mit Gas vergiften; (*Mil*) vergasen; **to be given
~** (*as anaesthetic*) Lachgas bekommen

gas cooker (*Brit*) *n* Gasherd *m*

gas cylinder *n* Gasflasche *f*

gaseous ['gæsɪəs] *adj* gasförmig

gas fire (*Brit*) *n* Gasofen *m*

gas-fired ['gæsfaɪəd] *adj* (*heater etc*) Gas-

gash [gæʃ] *n* klaffende Wunde *f*; (*tear*) tiefer
Schlitz *m* ▷ *vt* aufschlitzen

gasket ['gæskɪt] *n* Dichtung *f*

gas mask *n* Gasmaske *f*

gas meter *n* Gaszähler *m*

gasoline ['gæsəliːn] (*US*) *n* Benzin *nt*

gasp [gaːsp] *n* tiefer Atemzug *m* ▷ *vi* keuchen;
(*in surprise*) nach Luft schnappen; **to give a ~
(of shock)** (vor Schreck) die Luft anhalten; **to
be ~ing for** sich sehnen nach +*dat*
▶ **gasp out** *vt* hervorstoßen

gas permeable *adj* (*lenses*) luftdurchlässig

gas ring *n* Gasbrenner *m*

gas station (*US*) *n* Tankstelle *f*

gas stove *n* (*cooker*) Gasherd *m*; (*for camping*)
Gaskocher *m*

gassy ['gæsɪ] *adj* (*drink*) kohlensäurehaltig

gas tank *n* Benzintank *m*

gastric ['gæstrɪk] *adj* (*upset, ulcer etc*) Magen-

gastric flu *n* Darmgrippe *f*

gastroenteritis ['gæstrəʊentə'raɪtɪs] *n* Magen-
Darm-Katarrh *m*

gastronomy [gæs'trɒnəmɪ] *n* Gastronomie *f*

gasworks ['gæswəːks] *n* Gaswerk *nt*

gate [geɪt] *n* (*of garden*) Pforte *f*; (*of field*) Gatter

g

nt; (of building) Tor nt; (at airport) Flugsteig m; (of level crossing) Schranke f; (of lock) Tor nt

gateau ['gætəʊ] (pl **-x**) n Torte f

gate-crash ['geɪtkræʃ] (Brit) vt (party) ohne Einladung besuchen; (concert) eindringen in +acc ▷ vi ohne Einladung hingehen; eindringen

gate-crasher ['geɪtkræʃəʳ] n ungeladener Gast m

gatehouse ['geɪthaʊs] n Pförtnerhaus nt

gateway ['geɪtweɪ] n (also fig) Tor nt

gather ['gæðəʳ] vt sammeln; (flowers, fruit) pflücken; (understand) schließen; (Sewing) kräuseln ▷ vi (assemble) sich versammeln; (dust) sich ansammeln; (clouds) sich zusammenziehen; **to - (from)** schließen (aus); **to - (that)** annehmen(, dass); **as far as I can ~** so wie ich es sehe; **to ~ speed** schneller werden

gathering ['gæðərɪŋ] n Versammlung f

GATT [gæt] n abbr (= General Agreement on Tariffs and Trade) GATT nt

gauche [gəʊʃ] adj linkisch

gaudy ['gɔːdɪ] adj knallig

gauge [geɪdʒ], (US) **gage** [geɪdʒ] n Messgerät nt, Messinstrument nt; (Rail) Spurweite f ▷ vt messen; (fig) beurteilen; **petrol ~, fuel ~, gas gage** (US) Benzinuhr f; **to ~ the right moment** den richtigen Moment abwägen

Gaul [gɔːl] n Gallien nt; (person) Gallier(in) m(f)

gaunt [gɔːnt] adj (haggard) hager; (bare, stark) öde

gauntlet ['gɔːntlɪt] n (Stulpen)handschuh m; (fig): **to run the ~** Spießruten laufen; **to throw down the ~** den Fehdehandschuh hinwerfen

gauze [gɔːz] n Gaze f

gave [geɪv] pt of **give**

gavel ['gævl] n Hammer m

gawk [gɔːk] (inf) vi gaffen, glotzen

gawky ['gɔːkɪ] adj schlaksig

gawp [gɔːp] vi: **to ~ at** angaffen, anglotzen (inf)

gay [geɪ] adj (homosexual) schwul; (cheerful) fröhlich; (dress) bunt

gay marriage adj gleichgeschlechtliche Ehe f, Homoehe f (inf)

gaze [geɪz] n Blick m ▷ vi: **to ~ at sth** etw anstarren

gazelle [gə'zɛl] n Gazelle f

gazette [gə'zɛt] n Zeitung f; (official) Amtsblatt nt

gazetteer [gæzə'tɪəʳ] n alphabetisches Ortsverzeichnis nt

gazump [gə'zʌmp] (Brit) vt: **to be ~ed** ein mündlich zugesagtes Haus an einen Höherbietenden verlieren

GB abbr (= Great Britain) GB

GBH (Brit) n abbr (Law) = **grievous bodily harm**

GC (Brit) n abbr (= George Cross) britische Tapferkeitsmedaille

GCE (Brit) n abbr (= General Certificate of Education) Schulabschlusszeugnis, ≈ Abitur nt

GCHQ (Brit) n abbr (= Government Communications Headquarters) Zentralstelle des britischen Nachrichtendienstes

GCSE (Brit) n abbr (= General Certificate of Secondary Education) Schulabschlusszeugnis, ≈ mittlere Reife f

Gdns abbr (in street names: = Gardens) ≈ Str.

GDP n abbr = **gross domestic product**

GDR n abbr (Hist: = German Democratic Republic) DDR f

gear [gɪəʳ] n (equipment) Ausrüstung f; (belongings) Sachen pl; (Tech) Getriebe nt; (Aut) Gang m; (on bicycle) Gangschaltung f ▷ vt (fig: adapt): **to ~ sth to** etw ausrichten auf +acc; **top/low/bottom ~, high/low/bottom ~** (US) hoher/niedriger/erster Gang; **to put a car into ~** einen Gang einlegen; **to leave the car in ~** den Gang eingelegt lassen; **to leave out of ~** im Leerlauf lassen; **our service is ~ed to meet the needs of the disabled** unser Betrieb ist auf die Bedürfnisse von Behinderten eingerichtet

▶ **gear up** vt, vi: **to ~ (o.s.) up (to)** sich vorbereiten (auf +acc) ▷ vt: **to ~ o.s. up to do sth** sich darauf vorbereiten, etw zu tun

gearbox ['gɪəbɒks] n Getriebe nt

gear lever, (US) **gear shift** n Schalthebel m

GED (US) n abbr (Scol: = general educational development) allgemeine Lernentwicklung

geek-speak ['giːkspiːk] n (US: inf) Fachchinesisch nt

geese [giːs] npl of **goose**

geezer ['giːzəʳ] (inf) n Kerl m, Typ m

Geiger counter ['gaɪgə-] n Geigerzähler m

gel [dʒɛl] n Gel nt

gelatin, **gelatine** ['dʒɛləti:n] n Gelatine f

gelignite ['dʒɛlɪgnaɪt] n Plastiksprengstoff m

gem [dʒɛm] n Edelstein m; **she/the house is a ~** (fig) sie/das Haus ist ein Juwel; **a ~ of an idea** eine ausgezeichnete Idee

Gemini ['dʒɛmɪnaɪ] n (Astrol) Zwillinge pl; **to be ~** (ein) Zwilling sein

gen [dʒɛn] (Brit: inf) n: **to give sb the ~ on sth** jdn über etw acc informieren

Gen. abbr (Mil: = General) Gen.

gen. abbr = **general, generally**

gender ['dʒɛndəʳ] n Geschlecht nt

gene [dʒiːn] n Gen nt

genealogy [dʒiːnɪ'ælədʒɪ] n Genealogie f, Stammbaumforschung f; (family history) Stammbaum m

general ['dʒɛnərl] n General m ▷ adj allgemein; (widespread) weitverbreitet; (non-specific) generell; **in ~** im Allgemeinen; **the ~ public** die Öffentlichkeit, die Allgemeinheit; **~ audit** (Comm) Jahresabschlussprüfung f

general anaesthetic n Vollnarkose f

general delivery (US) n: **to send sth ~** etw postlagernd schicken

general election n Parlamentswahlen pl

generalization ['dʒɛnrəlaɪ'zeɪʃən] n Verallgemeinerung f

generalize ['dʒɛnrəlaɪz] vi verallgemeinern

generally ['dʒɛnrəlɪ] adv im Allgemeinen

general manager n Hauptgeschäftsführer(in)

m(f)

general practitioner *n* praktischer Arzt *m*,
praktische Ärztin *f*
general strike *n* Generalstreik *m*
generate ['dʒɛnəreɪt] *vt* erzeugen; *(jobs)*
schaffen; *(profits)* einbringen
generation [dʒɛnə'reɪʃən] *n* Generation *f*; *(of
electricity etc)* Erzeugung *f*
generator ['dʒɛnəreɪtəʳ] *n* Generator *m*
generic [dʒɪ'nɛrɪk] *adj* allgemein; **~ term**
Oberbegriff *m*
generosity [dʒɛnə'rɒsɪtɪ] *n* Großzügigkeit *f*
generous ['dʒɛnərəs] *adj* großzügig; *(measure,
remuneration)* reichlich
genesis ['dʒɛnɪsɪs] *n* Entstehung *f*
genetic [dʒɪ'nɛtɪk] *adj* genetisch
genetically *adv* genetisch; **~ modified**
genmanipuliert
genetic engineering *n* Gentechnologie *f*
genetic fingerprint *n* genetischer
Fingerabdruck *m*
genetics [dʒɪ'nɛtɪks] *n* Genetik *f*
Geneva [dʒɪ'niːvə] *n* Genf *nt*
genial ['dʒiːnɪəl] *adj* freundlich; *(climate)*
angenehm
genitals ['dʒɛnɪtlz] *npl* Genitalien *pl*,
Geschlechtsteile *pl*
genitive ['dʒɛnɪtɪv] *n* Genitiv *m*
genius ['dʒiːnɪəs] *n* Talent *nt*; *(person)* Genie *nt*
Genoa ['dʒɛnəʊə] *n* Genua *nt*
genocide ['dʒɛnəʊsaɪd] *n* Völkermord *m*
Genoese [dʒɛnəʊ'iːz] *adj* genuesisch ▷ *n inv*
Genuese *m*, Genuesin *f*
gent [dʒɛnt] *(Brit: inf)* *n abbr* = **gentleman**
genteel [dʒɛn'tiːl] *adj* vornehm, fein
gentle ['dʒɛntl] *adj* sanft; *(movement, breeze)*
leicht; **a ~ hint** ein zarter Hinweis
gentleman ['dʒɛntlmən] *(irreg: like* **man***)* *n*
Herr *m*; *(referring to social position or good manners)*
Gentleman *m*; **~'s agreement** Vereinbarung *f*
auf Treu und Glauben
gentlemanly ['dʒɛntlmənlɪ] *adj*
zuvorkommend
gentleness ['dʒɛntlnɪs] *n (see adj)* Sanftheit *f*;
Leichtheit *f*; Zartheit *f*
gently ['dʒɛntlɪ] *adv (see adj)* sanft; leicht; zart
gentry ['dʒɛntrɪ] *n inv:* **the ~** die Gentry, der
niedere Adel
gents [dʒɛnts] *n:* **the ~** die Herrentoilette
genuine ['dʒɛnjuɪn] *adj* echt; *(person)* natürlich,
aufrichtig
genuinely ['dʒɛnjuɪnlɪ] *adv* wirklich
geographer [dʒɪ'ɒgrəfəʳ] *n* Geograf(in) *m(f)*
geographic [dʒɪə'græfɪk], **geographical**
[dʒɪə'græfɪkl] *adj* geografisch
geography [dʒɪ'ɒgrəfɪ] *n* Geografie *f*; *(Scol)*
Erdkunde *f*
geological [dʒɪə'lɒdʒɪkl] *adj* geologisch
geologist [dʒɪ'ɒlədʒɪst] *n* Geologe *m*, Geologin *f*
geology [dʒɪ'ɒlədʒɪ] *n* Geologie *f*
geometric [dʒɪə'mɛtrɪk], **geometrical**
[dʒɪə'mɛtrɪkl] *adj* geometrisch
geometry [dʒɪ'ɒmətrɪ] *n* Geometrie *f*

Geordie ['dʒɔːdɪ] *(inf)* *n aus dem Gebiet von
Newcastle stammende oder dort wohnhafte Person*
Georgia ['dʒɔːdʒə] *n (in Eastern Europe)* Georgien
nt
Georgian ['dʒɔːdʒən] *adj* georgisch ▷ *n*
Georgier(in) *m(f)*; *(Ling)* Georgisch *nt*
geranium [dʒɪ'reɪnɪəm] *n* Geranie *f*
geriatric [dʒɛrɪ'ætrɪk] *adj* geriatrisch ▷ *n*
Greis(in) *m(f)*
germ [dʒɜːm] *n* Bazillus *m*; *(Biol: fig)* Keim *m*
German ['dʒɜːmən] *adj* deutsch ▷ *n* Deutsche(r)
f(m); *(Ling)* Deutsch *nt*
German Democratic Republic *n (formerly)*
Deutsche Demokratische Republik *f*
germane [dʒɜː'meɪn] *adj:* **~ (to)** von Belang
(für)
German measles *(Brit)* *n* Röteln *pl*
German Shepherd, German Shepherd dog
(esp US) *n* Schäferhund *m*
Germany ['dʒɜːmənɪ] *n* Deutschland *nt*
germinate ['dʒɜːmɪneɪt] *vi* keimen; *(fig)*
aufkeimen
germination [dʒɜːmɪ'neɪʃən] *n* Keimung *f*
germ warfare *n* biologische Kriegsführung *f*,
Bakterienkrieg *m*
gerrymandering ['dʒɛrɪmændərɪŋ] *n*
Wahlkreisschiebungen *pl*
gestation [dʒɛs'teɪʃən] *n (of animals)*
Trächtigkeit *f*; *(of humans)* Schwangerschaft *f*
gesticulate [dʒɛs'tɪkjuleɪt] *vi* gestikulieren
gesture ['dʒɛstjəʳ] *n* Geste *f*; **as a ~ of
friendship** als Zeichen der Freundschaft

 KEYWORD

get [gɛt] *(pt, pp* **got**, *US pp* **gotten***)* *vi* **1** *(become,
be)* werden; **to get old/tired/cold** alt/müde/
kalt werden; **to get dirty** sich schmutzig
machen; **to get killed** getötet werden; **to get
married** heiraten
2 *(go):* **to get (from ...) to ...** (von ...) nach ...
kommen; **how did you get here?** wie sind Sie
hierhin gekommen?
3 *(begin):* **to get to know sb** jdn kennenlernen;
let's get going *or* **started** fangen wir an!
▷ *modal aux vb:* **you've got to do it** du musst
es tun
▷ *vt* **1: to get sth done** *(do oneself)* etw gemacht
bekommen; *(have done)* etw machen lassen;
to get one's hair cut sich *dat* die Haare
schneiden lassen; **to get the car going** *or* **to
go** das Auto in Gang bringen; **to get sb to do
sth** etw von jdm machen lassen; *(persuade)* jdn
dazu bringen, etw zu tun
2 *(obtain: money, permission, results)* erhalten;
(find: job, flat) finden; *(fetch: person, doctor, object)*
holen; **to get sth for sb** jdm etw besorgen;
can I get you a drink? kann ich Ihnen etwas
zu trinken anbieten?
3 *(receive, acquire: present, prize)* bekommen; **how
much did you get for the painting?** wie viel
haben Sie für das Bild bekommen?
4 *(catch)* bekommen, kriegen *(inf)*; *(hit: target*

575

etc) treffen; **to get sb by the arm/throat** jdn am Arm/Hals packen; **the bullet got him in the leg** die Kugel traf ihn ins Bein

5 (*take, move*) bringen; **to get sth to sb** jdm etw zukommen lassen

6 (*plane, bus etc: take*) nehmen; (: *catch*) bekommen

7 (*understand: joke etc*) verstehen; **I get it** ich verstehe

8 (*have, possess*): **to have got** haben; **how many have you got?** wie viele hast du?

▶ **get about** *vi* (*person*) herumkommen; (*news, rumour*) sich verbreiten

▶ **get across** *vt* (*message, meaning*) klarmachen

▶ **get along** *vi* (*be friends*) (miteinander) auskommen; (*depart*) sich auf den Weg machen

▶ **get around** *vt fus* = **get round**

▶ **get at** *vt fus* (*attack, criticize*) angreifen; (*reach*) herankommen an +*acc*; **what are you getting at?** worauf willst du hinaus?

▶ **get away** *vi* (*leave*) wegkommen; (*on holiday*) verreisen; (*escape*) entkommen

▶ **get away with** *vt fus* (*stolen goods*) entkommen mit; **he'll never get away with it!** damit kommt er nicht durch

▶ **get back** *vi* (*return*) zurückkommen

▷ *vt* (*regain*) zurückbekommen; **get back!** zurück!

▶ **get back at** (*inf*) *vt fus*: **to get back at sb for sth** jdm etw heimzahlen

▶ **get back to** *vt fus* (*return to*) zurückkehren zu; (*contact again*) zurückkommen auf +*acc*; **to get back to sleep** wieder einschlafen

▶ **get by** *vi* (*pass*) vorbeikommen; (*manage*) zurechtkommen; **I can get by in German** ich kann mich auf Deutsch verständlich machen

▶ **get down** *vi* (*from tree, ladder etc*) heruntersteigen; (*from horse*) absteigen; (*leave table*) aufstehen; (*bend down*) sich bücken; (*duck*) sich ducken

▷ *vt* (*depress: person*) fertigmachen; (*write*) aufschreiben

▶ **get down to** *vt fus*: **to get down to sth** (*work*) etw in Angriff nehmen; (*find time*) zu etw kommen; **to get down to business** (*fig*) zur Sache kommen

▶ **get in** *vi* (*be elected: candidate, party*) gewählt werden; (*arrive*) ankommen

▷ *vt* (*bring in: harvest*) einbringen; (: *shopping, supplies*) (herein)holen

▶ **get into** *vt fus* (*conversation, argument, fight*) geraten in +*acc*; (*vehicle*) einsteigen in +*acc*; (*clothes*) hineinkommen in +*acc*; **to get into bed** ins Bett gehen; **to get into the habit of doing sth** sich *dat* angewöhnen, etw zu tun

▶ **get off** *vi* (*from train etc*) aussteigen; (*escape punishment*) davonkommen

▷ *vt* (*remove: clothes*) ausziehen; (: *stain*) herausbekommen

▷ *vt fus* (*leave: train, bus*) aussteigen aus; **we get 3 days off at Christmas** zu Weihnachten bekommen wir 3 Tage frei; **to get off to a**

good start (*fig*) einen guten Anfang machen

▶ **get on** *vi* (*be friends*) (miteinander) auskommen

▷ *vt fus* (*bus, train*) einsteigen in +*acc*; **how are you getting on?** wie kommst du zurecht?; **time is getting on** es wird langsam spät

▶ **get on to** (*Brit*) *vt fus* (*subject, topic*) übergehen zu; (*contact: person*) sich in Verbindung setzen mit

▶ **get on with** *vt fus* (*person*) auskommen mit; (*meeting, work etc*) weitermachen mit

▶ **get out** *vi* (*leave: on foot*) hinausgehen; (*of vehicle*) aussteigen; (*news etc*) herauskommen

▷ *vt* (*take out: book etc*) herausholen; (*remove: stain*) herausbekommen

▶ **get out of** *vt fus* (*money: bank etc*) abheben von; (*avoid: duty etc*) herumkommen um

▷ *vt* (*extract: confession etc*) herausbekommen aus; (*derive: pleasure*) haben an +*dat*; (: *benefit*) haben von

▶ **get over** *vt fus* (*overcome*) überwinden; (: *illness*) sich erholen von; (*communicate: idea etc*) verständlich machen

▷ *vt*: **to get it over with** (*finish*) es hinter sich *acc* bringen

▶ **get round** *vt fus* (*law, rule*) umgehen; (*person*) herumkriegen

▶ **get round to** *vt fus*: **to get round to doing sth** dazu kommen, etw zu tun

▶ **get through** *vi* (*Tel*) durchkommen

▷ *vt fus* (*finish: work*) schaffen; (: *book*) lesen

▶ **get through to** *vt fus* (*Tel*) durchkommen zu; (*make o.s. understood*) durchdringen zu

▶ **get together** *vi* (*people*) zusammenkommen

▷ *vt* (*people*) zusammenbringen; (*project, plan etc*) zusammenstellen

▶ **get up** *vi* (*rise*) aufstehen

▷ *vt*: **to get up enthusiasm for sth** Begeisterung für etw aufbringen

▶ **get up to** *vt fus* (*prank etc*) anstellen

getaway ['gɛtəweɪ] *n*: **to make a/one's ~** sich davonmachen

getaway car *n* Fluchtauto *nt*

get-together ['gɛttəgɛðə^r] *n* Treffen *nt*; (*party*) Party *f*

get-up ['gɛtʌp] (*inf*) *n* Aufmachung *f*

get-well card [gɛt'wɛl-] *n* Karte *f* mit Genesungswünschen

geyser ['giːzə^r] *n* Geiser *m*; (*Brit: water heater*) Durchlauferhitzer *m*

Ghana ['gɑːnə] *n* Ghana *nt*

Ghanaian [gɑːˈneɪən] *adj* ghanaisch ▷ *n* Ghanaer(in) *m(f)*

ghastly ['gɑːstlɪ] *adj* grässlich; (*complexion*) totenblass; **you look ~!** (*ill*) du siehst grässlich aus!

gherkin ['gɜːkɪn] *n* Gewürzgurke *f*

ghetto ['gɛtəu] *n* G(h)etto *nt*

ghetto blaster [-ˈblɑːstə^r] (*inf*) *n* Gettoblaster *m*

ghost [gəust] *n* Geist *m*, Gespenst *nt* ▷ *vt* für jdn (als Ghostwriter) schreiben; **to give up the ~**

den Geist aufgeben

ghost town n Geisterstadt f

ghostwriter ['gəustraɪtə'] n Ghostwriter(in) m(f)

ghoul [gu:l] n böser Geist m

ghoulish ['gu:lɪʃ] adj makaber

GHQ n abbr (Mil: = General Headquarters) Hauptquartier nt

GHz abbr (= gigahertz) GHz

GI (US: inf) n abbr (= government issue) GI m

giant ['dʒaɪənt] n (also fig) Riese m ▷ adj riesig, riesenhaft; **~ (size) packet** Riesenpackung f

giant killer n (fig) Goliathbezwinger(in) m(f)

gibber ['dʒɪbə'] vi brabbeln

gibberish ['dʒɪbərɪʃ] n Quatsch m

gibe [dʒaɪb] n spöttische Bemerkung f ▷ vi: **to ~ at** spöttische Bemerkungen machen über +acc

giblets ['dʒɪblɪts] npl Geflügelinnereien pl

Gibraltar [dʒɪ'brɔ:ltə'] n Gibraltar nt

giddiness ['gɪdɪnɪs] n Schwindelgefühl nt

giddy ['gɪdɪ] adj: **I am/feel ~** mir ist schwind(e)lig; (height) schwindelerregend; **~ with excitement** vor Aufregung ganz ausgelassen

gift [gɪft] n Geschenk nt; (donation) Spende f; (Comm: also: **free gift**) (Werbe)geschenk nt; (ability) Gabe f; **to have a ~ for sth** ein Talent für etw haben

gift card n (US) elektronische Guthabenkarte f, Gift Card f (häufig in Form eines Gutscheins)

gifted ['gɪftɪd] adj begabt

gift token n Geschenkgutschein m

gift voucher n = **gift token**

gig [gɪg] (inf) n Konzert nt

gigabyte ['dʒɪgəbaɪt] n Gigabyte nt

gigantic [dʒaɪ'gæntɪk] adj riesig, riesengroß

giggle ['gɪgl] vi kichern ▷ n Spaß m; **to do sth for a ~** etw aus Spaß tun

GIGO ['gaɪgəu] (inf) abbr (Comput: = garbage in, garbage out) GIGO

gild [gɪld] vt vergolden

gill [dʒɪl] n Gill nt (Brit = 15 cl, US = 12 cl)

gills [gɪlz] npl Kiemen pl

gilt [gɪlt] adj vergoldet ▷ n Vergoldung f; **gilts** npl (Comm) mündelsichere Wertpapiere pl

gilt-edged ['gɪltedʒd] adj (stocks, securities) mündelsicher

gimlet ['gɪmlɪt] n Handbohrer m

gimmick ['gɪmɪk] n Gag m; **sales ~** Verkaufsmasche f, Verkaufstrick m

gin [dʒɪn] n Gin m

ginger ['dʒɪndʒə'] n Ingwer m ▷ adj (hair) rötlich; (cat) rötlich gelb

ginger ale n Gingerale nt

ginger beer n Ingwerbier nt

gingerbread ['dʒɪndʒəbred] n (cake) Ingwerkuchen m; (biscuit) ≈ Pfefferkuchen m

ginger group (Brit) n Aktionsgruppe f

gingerly ['dʒɪndʒəlɪ] adv vorsichtig

gingham ['gɪŋəm] n Gingan m, Gingham m

ginseng ['dʒɪnsɛŋ] n Ginseng m

gipsy ['dʒɪpsɪ] n Zigeuner(in) m(f)

gipsy caravan n Zigeunerwagen m

giraffe [dʒɪ'rɑ:f] n Giraffe f

girder ['gə:də'] n Träger m

girdle ['gə:dl] n Hüftgürtel m, Hüfthalter m ▷ vt (fig) umgeben

girl [gə:l] n Mädchen nt; (young unmarried woman) (junges) Mädchen nt; (daughter) Tochter f; **this is my little ~** das ist mein Töchterchen; **an English ~** eine Engländerin

girlfriend ['gə:lfrend] n Freundin f

Girl Guide n Pfadfinderin f

girlish ['gə:lɪʃ] adj mädchenhaft

Girl Scout (US) n Pfadfinderin f

Giro ['dʒaɪrəu] n: **the National ~** (Brit) der Postscheckdienst

giro ['dʒaɪrəu] n Giro nt, Giroverkehr m; (post office giro) Postscheckverkehr m; (Brit: welfare cheque) Sozialhilfescheck m

girth [gə:θ] n Umfang m; (of horse) Sattelgurt m

gist [dʒɪst] n Wesentliche(s) nt

 KEYWORD

give [gɪv] (pt **gave**, pp **given**) vt **1** (hand over): **to give sb sth, give sth to sb** jdm etw geben; **I'll give you £5 for it** ich gebe dir £5 dafür

2 (used with noun to replace a verb): **to give a sigh/cry/laugh** etc seufzen/schreien/lachen etc; **to give a speech/a lecture** eine Rede/einen Vortrag halten; **to give three cheers** ein dreifaches Hoch ausbringen

3 (tell, deliver: news, message etc) mitteilen; (: advice, answer) geben

4 (supply, provide: opportunity, job etc) geben; (: surprise) bereiten; (bestow: title, honour, right) geben, verleihen; **that's given me an idea** dabei kommt mir eine Idee

5 (devote: time, one's life) geben; (: attention) schenken

6 (organize: party, dinner etc) geben

▷ vi **1** (also: **give way**: break, collapse) nachgeben

2 (stretch: fabric) sich dehnen

▶ **give away** vt (money, opportunity) verschenken; (secret, information) verraten; (bride) zum Altar führen; **that immediately gave him away** dadurch verriet er sich sofort

▶ **give back** vt (money, book etc) zurückgeben

▶ **give in** vi (yield) nachgeben ▷ vt (essay etc) abgeben

▶ **give off** vt (heat, smoke) abgeben

▶ **give out** vt (prizes, books, drinks etc) austeilen ▷ vi (be exhausted: supplies) zu Ende gehen; (fail) versagen

▶ **give up** vt, vi aufgeben; **to give up smoking** das Rauchen aufgeben; **to give o.s. up** sich stellen; (after siege etc) sich ergeben

▶ **give way** vi (yield, collapse) nachgeben; (Brit: Aut) die Vorfahrt achten

give-and-take ['gɪvənd'teɪk] n (gegenseitiges) Geben und Nehmen nt

giveaway ['gɪvəweɪ] (inf) n: **her expression was a ~** ihr Gesichtsausdruck verriet alles; **the exam was a ~!** die Prüfung war geschenkt!; **~ prices** Schleuderpreise pl

given ['gɪvn] *pp of* **give** ▷ *adj* (*time, amount*) bestimmt ▷ *conj:* ~ **the circumstances …** unter den Umständen …; ~ **that …** angesichts der Tatsache, dass …

glacial ['gleɪsɪəl] *adj* (*landscape etc*) Gletscher-; (*fig*) eisig

glacier ['glæsɪər] *n* Gletscher *m*

glad [glæd] *adj* froh; **to be ~ about sth** sich über etw *acc* freuen; **to be ~ that** sich freuen, dass; **I was ~ of his help** ich war froh über seine Hilfe

gladden ['glædn] *vt* erfreuen

glade [gleɪd] *n* Lichtung *f*

gladioli [glædɪ'əʊlaɪ] *npl* Gladiolen *pl*

gladly ['glædlɪ] *adv* gern(e)

glamorous ['glæmərəs] *adj* reizvoll; (*model etc*) glamourös

glamour ['glæmər] *n* Glanz *m*, Reiz *m*

glance [glɑːns] *n* Blick *m* ▷ *vi:* **to ~ at** einen Blick werfen auf +*acc*
   ▶ **glance off** *vt fus* abprallen von

glancing ['glɑːnsɪŋ] *adj:* **to strike sth a ~ blow** etw streifen

gland [glænd] *n* Drüse *f*

glandular fever ['glændjʊlə-] (*Brit*) *n* Drüsenfieber *nt*

glare [glɛər] *n* wütender Blick *m*; (*of light*) greller Schein *m*; (*of publicity*) grelles Licht *nt* ▷ *vi* (*light*) grell scheinen; **to ~ at** (wütend) anstarren

glaring ['glɛərɪŋ] *adj* eklatant

glasnost ['glæznɒst] *n* Glasnost *f*

glass [glɑːs] *n* Glas *nt*; **glasses** *npl* (*spectacles*) Brille *f*

glass-blowing ['glɑːsbləʊɪŋ] *n* Glasbläserei *f*

glass ceiling *n* (*fig*) gläserne Decke *f*

glass fibre *n* Glasfaser *f*

glasshouse ['glɑːshaʊs] *n* Gewächshaus *nt*

glassware ['glɑːswɛər] *n* Glaswaren *pl*

glassy ['glɑːsɪ] *adj* glasig

Glaswegian [glæs'wiːdʒən] *adj* Glasgower ▷ *n* Glasgower(in) *m(f)*

glaze [gleɪz] *vt* (*door, window*) verglasen; (*pottery*) glasieren ▷ *n* Glasur *f*

glazed [gleɪzd] *adj* (*eyes*) glasig; (*pottery, tiles*) glasiert

glazier ['gleɪzɪər] *n* Glaser(in) *m(f)*

gleam [gliːm] *vi* (*light*) schimmern; (*polished surface, eyes*) glänzen ▷ *n:* **a ~ of hope** ein Hoffnungsschimmer *m*

gleaming ['gliːmɪŋ] *adj* schimmernd, glänzend

glean [gliːn] *vt* (*information*) herausbekommen, ausfindig machen

glee [gliː] *n* Freude *f*

gleeful ['gliːfʊl] *adj* fröhlich

glen [glɛn] *n* Tal *nt*

glib [glɪb] *adj* (*person*) glatt; (*promise, response*) leichthin gemacht

glibly ['glɪblɪ] *adv* (*talk*) gewandt; (*answer*) leichthin

glide [glaɪd] *vi* gleiten ▷ *n* Gleiten *nt*

glider ['glaɪdər] *n* Segelflugzeug *nt*

gliding ['glaɪdɪŋ] *n* Segelfliegen *nt*

glimmer ['glɪmər] *n* Schimmer *m*; (*of interest, hope*) Funke *m* ▷ *vi* schimmern

glimpse [glɪmps] *n* Blick *m* ▷ *vt* einen Blick werfen auf +*acc*; **to catch a ~ (of)** einen flüchtigen Blick erhaschen (von +*dat*)

glint [glɪnt] *vi* glitzern; (*eyes*) funkeln ▷ *n* (*see vb*) Glitzern *nt*; Funkeln *nt*

glisten ['glɪsn] *vi* glänzen

glitter ['glɪtər] *vi* glitzern; (*eyes*) funkeln ▷ *n* (*see vb*) Glitzern *nt*; Funkeln *nt*

glittering ['glɪtərɪŋ] *adj* glitzernd; (*eyes*) funkelnd; (*career*) glänzend

glitz [glɪts] (*inf*) *n* Glanz *m*

gloat [gləʊt] *vi:* **to ~ (over)** (*own success*) sich brüsten (mit); (*sb's failure*) sich hämisch freuen (über +*acc*)

global ['gləʊbl] *adj* global

globalization [gləʊblaɪ'zeɪʃn] *n* (*Pol, Econ*) Globalisierung *f*

global player *n* (*Econ*) Weltfirma *f*, Global Player *m*

global warming [-'wɔːmɪŋ] *n* Erwärmung *f* der Erdatmosphäre

globe [gləʊb] *n* Erdball *m*; (*model*) Globus *m*; (*shape*) Kugel *f*

globetrotter ['gləʊbtrɒtər] *n* Globetrotter(in) *m(f)*, Weltenbummler(in) *m(f)*

globule ['glɒbjuːl] *n* Tröpfchen *nt*

gloom [gluːm] *n* Düsterkeit *f*; (*sadness*) düstere *or* gedrückte Stimmung *f*

gloomily ['gluːmɪlɪ] *adv* düster

gloomy ['gluːmɪ] *adj* düster; (*person*) bedrückt; (*situation*) bedrückend

glorification [glɔːrɪfɪ'keɪʃən] *n* Verherrlichung *f*

glorify ['glɔːrɪfaɪ] *vt* verherrlichen

glorious ['glɔːrɪəs] *adj* herrlich; (*victory*) ruhmreich; (*future*) glanzvoll

glory ['glɔːrɪ] *n* Ruhm *m*; (*splendour*) Herrlichkeit *f* ▷ *vi:* **to ~ in** sich sonnen in +*dat*

glory hole (*inf*) *n* Rumpelkammer *f*

Glos (*Brit*) *abbr* (*Post*) = *Gloucestershire*

gloss [glɒs] *n* Glanz *m*; (*also:* **gloss paint**) Lack *m*, Lackfarbe *f*
   ▶ **gloss over** *vt fus* vom Tisch wischen

glossary ['glɒsərɪ] *n* Glossar *nt*

glossy ['glɒsɪ] *adj* glänzend; (*photograph, magazine*) Hochglanz- ▷ *n* (*also:* **glossy magazine**) (Hochglanz)magazin *nt*

glove [glʌv] *n* Handschuh *m*

glove compartment *n* Handschuhfach *nt*

glow [gləʊ] *vi* glühen; (*stars, eyes*) leuchten ▷ *n* (*see vb*) Glühen *nt*; Leuchten *nt*

glower ['glaʊər] *vi:* **to ~ at sb** jdn finster ansehen

glowing ['gləʊɪŋ] *adj* glühend; (*complexion*) blühend; (*fig: report, description etc*) begeistert

glow-worm ['gləʊwɜːm] *n* Glühwürmchen *nt*

glucose ['gluːkəʊs] *n* Traubenzucker *m*

glue [gluː] *n* Klebstoff *m* ▷ *vt:* **to ~ sth onto sth** etw an etw *acc* kleben; **to ~ sth into place** etw festkleben

glue-sniffing ['gluːsnɪfɪŋ] *n* (Klebstoff-)

Schnüffeln *nt*

glum [glʌm] *adj* bedrückt, niedergeschlagen

glut [glʌt] *n*: ~ **(of)** Überangebot *nt* (an +*dat*)
▷ *vt*: **to be ~ted (with)** überschwemmt sein (mit); **a ~ of pears** eine Birnenschwemme

glutinous ['glu:tɪnəs] *adj* klebrig

glutton ['glʌtn] *n* Vielfraß *m*; **a ~ for work** ein Arbeitstier *nt*; **a ~ for punishment** ein Masochist *m*

gluttonous ['glʌtənəs] *adj* gefräßig

gluttony ['glʌtənɪ] *n* Völlerei *f*

glycerin, glycerine ['glɪsəri:n] *n* Glyzerin *nt*

GM *abbr* = **genetically modified**

gm *abbr* (= *gram(me)*) g

GMAT (US) *n abbr* (= *Graduate Management Admissions Test*) Zulassungsprüfung für Handelsschulen

GMT *abbr* (= *Greenwich Mean Time*) WEZ *f*

gnarled [nɑ:ld] *adj* (*tree*) knorrig; (*hand*) knotig

gnash [næʃ] *vt*: **to ~ one's teeth** mit den Zähnen knirschen

gnat [næt] *n* (Stech)mücke *f*

gnaw [nɔ:] *vt* nagen an +*dat* ▷ *vi* (*fig*): **to ~ at** quälen

gnome [nəum] *n* Gnom *m*; (*in garden*) Gartenzwerg *m*

GNP *n abbr* (= *gross national product*) BSP *nt*

GNVQ (Brit) *n abbr* (= *General National Vocational Qualification*) allgemeine, auf die Arbeitswelt bezogene Qualifikation

go [gəu] (*pt* **went**, *pp* **gone**) *vi* **1** gehen; (*travel*) fahren; **a car went by** ein Auto fuhr vorbei **2** (*depart*) gehen; **"I must go," she said** „ich muss gehen", sagte sie; **she has gone to Sheffield/Australia** (*permanently*) sie ist nach Sheffield/Australien gegangen **3** (*attend, take part in activity*) gehen; **she went to university in Oxford** sie ist in Oxford zur Universität gegangen; **to go for a walk** spazieren gehen; **to go dancing** tanzen gehen **4** (*work*) funktionieren; **the tape recorder was still going** das Tonband lief noch **5** (*become*): **to go pale/mouldy** blass/schimmelig werden **6** (*be sold*): **to go for £100** für £100 weggehen *or* verkauft werden **7** (*be about to, intend to*): **we're going to stop in an hour** wir hören in einer Stunde auf; **are you going to come?** kommst du?, wirst du kommen? **8** (*time*) vergehen **9** (*event, activity*) ablaufen; **how did it go?** wie wars? **10** (*be given*): **the job is to go to someone else** die Stelle geht an jemand anders **11** (*break etc*) kaputtgehen; **the fuse went** die Sicherung ist durchgebrannt **12** (*be placed*) hingehören; **the milk goes in the fridge** die Milch kommt in den Kühlschrank
▷ *n* **1** (*try*): **to have a go at sth** etw versuchen; **I'll have a go at mending it** ich will

versuchen, es zu reparieren; **to have a go** es versuchen

2 (*turn*): **whose go is it?** wer ist dran *or* an der Reihe?

3 (*move*): **to be on the go** auf Trab sein

▶ **go about** *vi* (*also:* **go around**: *rumour*) herumgehen
▷ *vt fus*: **how do I go about this?** wie soll ich vorgehen?; **to go about one's business** seinen eigenen Geschäften nachgehen

▶ **go after** *vt fus* (*pursue: person*) nachgehen +*dat*; (*: job etc*) sich bemühen um; (*: record*) erreichen wollen

▶ **go against** *vt fus* (*be unfavourable to*) ungünstig verlaufen für; (*disregard: advice, wishes etc*) handeln gegen

▶ **go ahead** *vi* (*proceed*) weitergehen; **to go ahead with** weitermachen mit

▶ **go along** *vi* gehen

▶ **go along with** *vt fus* (*agree with*) zustimmen +*dat*; (*accompany*) mitgehen mit

▶ **go away** *vi* (*leave*) weggehen

▶ **go back** *vi* zurückgehen

▶ **go back on** *vt fus* (*promise*) zurücknehmen

▶ **go by** *vi* (*years, time*) vergehen
▷ *vt fus* (*rule etc*) sich richten nach

▶ **go down** *vi* (*descend*) hinuntergehen; (*ship, sun*) untergehen; (*price, level*) sinken
▷ *vt fus* (*stairs, ladder*) hinuntergehen; **his speech went down well** seine Rede kam gut an

▶ **go for** *vt fus* (*fetch*) holen (gehen); (*like*) mögen; (*attack*) losgehen auf +*acc*; (*apply to*) gelten für

▶ **go in** *vi* (*enter*) hineingehen

▶ **go in for** *vt fus* (*competition*) teilnehmen an +*dat*; (*favour*) stehen auf +*acc*

▶ **go into** *vt fus* (*enter*) hineingehen in +*acc*; (*investigate*) sich befassen mit; (*career*) gehen in +*acc*

▶ **go off** *vi* (*leave*) weggehen; (*food*) schlecht werden; (*bomb, gun*) losgehen; (*event*) verlaufen; (*lights etc*) ausgehen
▷ *vt fus* (*inf*): **I've gone off it/him** ich mache mir nichts mehr daraus/aus ihm; **the gun went off** das Gewehr ging los; **to go off to sleep** einschlafen; **the party went off well** die Party verlief gut

▶ **go on** *vi* (*continue*) weitergehen; (*happen*) vor sich gehen; (*lights*) angehen
▷ *vt fus* (*be guided by*) sich stützen auf +*acc*; **to go on doing sth** mit etw weitermachen; **what's going on here?** was geht hier vor?, was ist hier los?

▶ **go on at** (*inf*) *vt fus* (*nag*) herumnörgeln an +*dat*

▶ **go on with** *vt fus* weitermachen mit

▶ **go out** *vt fus* (*leave*) hinausgehen
▷ *vi* (*for entertainment*) ausgehen; (*fire, light*) ausgehen; (*couple*): **they went out for 3 years** sie gingen 3 Jahre lang miteinander

▶ **go over** *vi* hinübergehen
▷ *vt* (*check*) durchgehen; **to go over sth in**

one's mind etw überdenken

▶ **go round** vi (circulate: news, rumour) umgehen; (revolve) sich drehen; (suffice) ausreichen; (visit): **to go round (to sb's)** (bei jdm) vorbeigehen; **there's not enough to go round** es reicht nicht (für alle)

▶ **go through** vt fus (place) gehen durch; (by car) fahren durch; (undergo) durchmachen; (search through: files, papers) durchsuchen; (describe: list, book, story) durchgehen; (perform) durchgehen

▶ **go through with** vt fus (plan, crime) durchziehen; **I couldn't go through with it** ich brachte es nicht fertig

▶ **go under** vi (sink: person) untergehen; (fig: business, project) scheitern

▶ **go up** vi (ascend) hinaufgehen; (price, level) steigen; **to go up in flames** in Flammen aufgehen

▶ **go with** vt fus (suit) passen zu

▶ **go without** vt fus (food, treats) verzichten auf +acc

goad [gəud] vt aufreizen

▶ **goad on** vt anstacheln

go-ahead ['gəuəhed] adj zielstrebig; (firm) fortschrittlich ▷ n grünes Licht nt; **to give sb the ~** jdm grünes Licht geben

goal [gəul] n Tor nt; (aim) Ziel nt; **to score a ~** ein Tor schießen or erzielen

goal difference n Tordifferenz f

goalie ['gəulɪ] (inf) n Tormann m

goalkeeper ['gəulkiːpəʳ] n Torwart m

goal post n Torpfosten m

goat [gəut] n Ziege f

gobble ['gɔbl] vt (also: **gobble down, gobble up**) verschlingen

go-between ['gəubɪtwiːn] n Vermittler(in) m(f)

Gobi Desert ['gəubɪ-] n: **the ~** die Wüste Gobi

goblet ['gɔblɪt] n Pokal m

goblin ['gɔblɪn] n Kobold m

go-cart ['gəukɑːt] n Gokart m

God [gɔd] n Gott m ▷ excl o Gott!

god [gɔd] n Gott m

god-awful [gɔd'ɔːfəl] (inf) adj beschissen (!)

godchild ['gɔdtʃaɪld] n Patenkind nt

goddamn ['gɔddæm], **goddamned** ['gɔddæmd] (US: inf) adj gottverdammt

goddaughter ['gɔddɔːtəʳ] n Patentochter f

goddess ['gɔdɪs] n Göttin f

godfather ['gɔdfɑːðəʳ] n Pate m

God-fearing ['gɔdfɪərɪŋ] adj gottesfürchtig

godforsaken ['gɔdfəseɪkən] adj gottverlassen

godmother ['gɔdmʌðəʳ] n Patin f

godparent ['gɔdpɛərənt] n Pate m, Patin f

godsend ['gɔdsɛnd] n Geschenk nt des Himmels

godson ['gɔdsʌn] n Patensohn m

goes [gəuz] vb see **go**

gofer ['gəufəʳ] (inf) n Mädchen nt für alles

go-getter ['gəugɛtəʳ] (inf) n Ellbogentyp (pej, inf) m

goggle ['gɔgl] (inf) vi: **to ~ at** anstarren, anglotzen

goggles ['gɔglz] npl Schutzbrille f

going ['gəuɪŋ] n: **it was slow/hard ~** (fig) es ging nur langsam/schwer voran ▷ adj: **the ~ rate** der gängige Preis; **when the ~ gets tough** wenn es schwierig wird; **a ~ concern** ein gut gehendes Unternehmen

going-over [gəuɪŋ'əuvəʳ] (inf) n (check) Untersuchung f; (beating-up) Abreibung f; **to give sb a good ~** jdm eine tüchtige Abreibung verpassen

goings-on ['gəuɪŋz'ɔn] (inf) npl Vorgänge pl, Dinge pl

go-kart ['gəukɑːt] n = **go-cart**

gold [gəuld] n Gold nt; (also: **gold medal**) Gold nt, Goldmedaille f ▷ adj golden; (reserves, jewellery, tooth) Gold-

golden ['gəuldən] adj (also fig) golden

golden age n Blütezeit f

golden handshake (Brit) n Abstandssumme f

golden rule n goldene Regel f

goldfish ['gəuldfɪʃ] n Goldfisch m

gold leaf n Blattgold nt

gold medal n Goldmedaille f

gold mine n (also fig) Goldgrube f

gold-plated ['gəuld'pleɪtɪd] adj vergoldet

goldsmith ['gəuldsmɪθ] n Goldschmied(in) m(f)

gold standard n Goldstandard m

golf [gɔlf] n Golf nt

golf ball n (for game) Golfball m; (on typewriter) Kugelkopf m

golf club n Golfklub m; (stick) Golfschläger m

golf course n Golfplatz m

golfer ['gɔlfəʳ] n Golfspieler(in) m(f), Golfer(in) m(f)

golfing ['gɔlfɪŋ] n Golf(spielen) nt; **he does a lot of ~** er spielt viel Golf ▷ cpd Golf-

gondola ['gɔndələ] n Gondel f

gondolier [gɔndə'lɪəʳ] n Gondoliere m

gone [gɔn] pp of **go** ▷ adj weg; (days) vorbei

goner ['gɔnəʳ] (inf) n: **to be a ~** hinüber sein

gong [gɔŋ] n Gong m

good [gud] adj gut; (well-behaved) brav, lieb ▷ n (virtue, morality) Gute(s) nt; (benefit) Wohl nt; **goods** npl (Comm) Güter pl; **to have a ~ time** sich (gut) amüsieren; **to be ~ at sth** (swimming, talking etc) etw gut können; (science, sports etc) gut in etw dat sein; **to be ~ for sb/sth** gut für jdn/zu etw dat sein; **it's ~ for you** das tut dir gut; **it's a ~ thing you were there** gut, dass Sie da waren; **she is ~ with children** sie kann gut mit Kindern umgehen; **she is ~ with her hands** sie ist geschickt; **to feel ~** sich wohlfühlen; **it's ~ to see you** (es ist) schön, Sie zu sehen; **would you be ~ enough to …?** könnten Sie bitte …?; **that's very ~ of you** das ist wirklich nett von Ihnen; **a ~ deal (of)** ziemlich viel; **a ~ many** ziemlich viele; **take a ~ look** sieh dir das genau or gut an; **a ~ while ago** vor einiger Zeit; **to make ~** (damage) wiedergutmachen; (loss) ersetzen; **it's no ~ complaining** es ist sinnlos or es nützt nichts, sich zu beklagen; **~ morning/ afternoon/evening!** guten Morgen/Tag/ Abend!; **~ night!** gute Nacht!; **he's up to no ~** er führt nichts Gutes im Schilde; **for the common ~** zum Wohle aller; **is this any ~?** (will it help you?) können Sie das gebrauchen?; (is it good enough?) reicht das?; **is the book/ film any ~?** was halten Sie von dem Buch/ Film?; **for ~** für immer; **~s and chattels** Hab und Gut nt

goodbye [gud'baɪ] excl auf Wiedersehen!; **to say ~** sich verabschieden

good-for-nothing ['gudfənʌθɪŋ] adj nichtsnutzig

Good Friday n Karfreitag m

good-humoured ['gud'hju:məd] adj gut gelaunt; (good-natured) gutmütig; (remark, joke) harmlos

good-looking ['gud'lukɪŋ] adj gut aussehend

good-natured ['gud'neɪtʃəd] adj gutmütig; (discussion) freundlich

goodness ['gudnɪs] n Güte f; **for ~ sake!** um Himmels willen!; **~ gracious!** ach du liebe or meine Güte!

goods train (Brit) n Güterzug m

goodwill [gud'wɪl] n Wohlwollen nt; (Comm) Goodwill m

goody ['gudɪ] (inf) n Gute(r) m, Held m

goody-goody ['gudɪgudɪ] (pej) n Tugendlamm nt, Musterkind (inf) nt

gooey ['gu:ɪ] (inf) adj (sticky) klebrig; (cake) üppig; (fig: sentimental) rührselig

goose [gu:s] (pl **geese**) n Gans f

gooseberry ['guzbərɪ] n Stachelbeere f; **to play ~** (Brit) das fünfte Rad am Wagen sein

goose flesh n = **goose pimples**

goose pimples npl Gänsehaut f

goose step n Stechschritt m

GOP (US: inf) n abbr (Pol: = Grand Old Party) Republikanische Partei

gopher ['gəufər] n (Zool) Taschenratte f

gore [gɔːr] vt aufspießen ▷ n Blut nt

gorge [gɔːdʒ] n Schlucht f ▷ vt: **to ~ o.s. (on)** sich vollstopfen (mit)

gorgeous ['gɔːdʒəs] adj herrlich; (person) hinreißend

gorilla [gə'rɪlə] n Gorilla m

gormless ['gɔːmlɪs] (Brit: inf) adj doof

gorse [gɔːs] n Stechginster m

gory ['gɔːrɪ] adj blutig

go-slow ['gəu'sləu] (Brit) n Bummelstreik m

gospel ['gɔspl] n Evangelium nt; (doctrine) Lehre f

gossamer ['gɔsəmər] n Spinnfäden pl; (light fabric) hauchdünne Gaze f

gossip ['gɔsɪp] n (rumours) Klatsch m, Tratsch m; (chat) Schwatz m; (person) Klatschbase f ▷ vi schwatzen; **a piece of ~** eine Neuigkeit

gossip column n Klatschkolumne f, Klatschspalte f

got [gɔt] pt, pp of **get**

Gothic ['gɔθɪk] adj gotisch

gotten ['gɔtn] (US) pp of **get**

gouge [gaudʒ] vt (also: **gouge out**: hole etc) bohren; (: initials) eingravieren; **to ~ sb's eyes out** jdm die Augen ausstechen

gourd [guəd] n (container) Kürbisflasche f

gourmet ['guəmeɪ] n Feinschmecker(in) m(f), Gourmet m

gout [gaut] n Gicht f

govern ['gʌvən] vt (also Ling) regieren; (event, conduct) bestimmen

governess ['gʌvənɪs] n Gouvernante f

governing ['gʌvənɪŋ] adj (Pol) regierend

governing body n Vorstand m

government ['gʌvnmənt] n Regierung f ▷ cpd Regierungs-; **local ~** Kommunalverwaltung f, Gemeindeverwaltung f

governmental [gʌvn'mɛntl] adj Regierungs-

government stocks npl Staatspapiere pl, Staatsanleihen pl

governor ['gʌvənər] n Gouverneur(in) m(f); (of bank, hospital, Brit: of prison) Direktor(in) m(f); (of school) ≈ Mitglied nt des Schulbeirats

Govt abbr = **government**

gown [gaun] n (Abend)kleid nt; (of teacher, Brit: of judge) Robe f

GP n abbr = **general practitioner**

GPMU (Brit) n abbr (= Graphical Paper and Media Union) Mediengewerkschaft

GPO n abbr (Brit: formerly: = general post office) Postbehörde f; (US: = Government Printing Office) regierungsamtliche Druckanstalt

gr. abbr (Comm) = **gross**; (= gram(me)) g

grab [græb] vt packen; (chance, opportunity) (beim Schopf) ergreifen ▷ vi: **to ~ at** greifen or grapschen nach +dat; **to ~ some food** schnell etwas essen; **to ~ a few hours sleep** ein paar Stunden schlafen

grace [greɪs] n Gnade f; (gracefulness) Anmut f ▷ vt (honour) beehren; (adorn) zieren; **5 days' ~** 5 Tage Aufschub; **with (a) good ~** anstandslos; **with (a) bad ~** widerwillig; **his sense of humour is his saving ~** was einen mit ihm versöhnt, ist sein Sinn für Humor; **to say ~** das Tischgebet sprechen

graceful ['greɪsful] adj anmutig; (style, shape) gefällig; (refusal, behaviour) charmant

gracious ['greɪʃəs] adj (kind, courteous) liebenswürdig; (compassionate) gnädig; (smile) freundlich; (house, mansion etc) stilvoll; (living etc) kultiviert ▷ excl: **(good) ~!** (ach) du meine Güte!, (ach du) lieber Himmel!

gradation [grə'deɪʃən] n Abstufung f

grade [greɪd] n (Comm) (Güte)klasse f; (in hierarchy) Rang m; (Scol: mark) Note f; (US: school class) Klasse f; (: gradient: upward) Neigung f, Steigung f; (: downward) Neigung f, Gefälle nt ▷ vt klassifizieren; (work, student) einstufen; **to make the ~** (fig) es schaffen

grade crossing (US) n Bahnübergang m

grade school (US) n Grundschule f

gradient ['greɪdɪənt] n (upward) Neigung f, Steigung f; (downward) Neigung f, Gefälle nt; (Geom) Gradient m

gradual ['grædjuəl] adj allmählich

g

gradually ['grædjʊəlɪ] *adv* allmählich
graduate [*n* 'grædjʊɪt, *vi* 'grædjʊeɪt] *n* (*of university*) Hochschulabsolvent(in) *m(f)*; (*US: of high school*) Schulabgänger(in) *m(f)* ▷ *vi* (*from university*) graduieren; (*US*) die (Schul)abschlussprüfung bestehen
graduated pension ['grædjʊeɪtɪd-] *n* gestaffelte Rente *f*
graduation [grædjʊ'eɪʃən] *n* (Ab)schlussfeier *f*
graffiti [grə'fiːtɪ] *n, npl* Graffiti *pl*
graft [grɑːft] *n* (*Agr*) (Pfropf)reis *nt*; (*Med*) Transplantat *nt*; (*Brit: inf: hard work*) Schufterei *f*; (*bribery*) Schiebung *f* ▷ *vt*: **to ~** (*Agr*) (auf)pfropfen (auf *+acc*); (*Med*) übertragen (auf *+acc*), einpflanzen (in *+acc*); (*fig*) aufpfropfen *+dat*
grain [greɪn] *n* Korn *nt*; (*no pl: cereals*) Getreide *nt*; (*US: corn*) Getreide *nt*, Korn; (*of wood*) Maserung *f*; **it goes against the ~** (*fig*) es geht einem gegen den Strich
gram [græm] *n* Gramm *nt*
grammar ['græmə'] *n* Grammatik *f*, Sprachlehre *f*
grammar school (*Brit*) *n* ≈ Gymnasium *nt*
grammatical [grə'mætɪkl] *adj* grammat(ikal)isch
gramme [græm] *n* = **gram**
gramophone ['græməfəʊn] (*Brit*) *n* Grammofon *nt*
granary ['grænərɪ] *n* Kornspeicher *m*; **G~®bread/loaf** Körnerbrot *nt*
grand [grænd] *adj* großartig; (*inf: wonderful*) fantastisch ▷ *n* (*inf*) ≈ Riese *m* (*1000 Pfund/Dollar*)
grandchild ['græntʃaɪld] (*irreg: like* **child**) *n* Enkelkind *nt*, Enkel(in) *m(f)*
granddad ['grændæd] (*inf*) *n* Opa *m*
granddaughter ['grændɔːtə'] *n* Enkelin *f*
grandeur ['grændjə'] *n* (*of scenery etc*) Erhabenheit *f*; (*of building*) Vornehmheit *f*
grandfather ['grændfɑːðə'] *n* Großvater *m*
grandiose ['grændɪəʊs] (*also pej*) *adj* grandios
grand jury (*US*) *n* Großes Geschworenengericht *nt*
grandma ['grænmɑː] (*inf*) *n* Oma *f*
grandmother ['grænmʌðə'] *n* Großmutter *f*
grandpa ['grænpɑː] (*inf*) *n* Opa *m*
grandparents ['grændpɛərənts] *npl* Großeltern *pl*
grand piano *n* Flügel *m*
Grand Prix ['grɑ̃ːˈpriː] *n* (*Aut*) Grand Prix *m*
grandson ['grænsʌn] *n* Enkel *m*
grandstand ['grændstænd] *n* Haupttribüne *f*
grand total *n* Gesamtsumme *f*, Endsumme *f*
granite ['grænɪt] *n* Granit *m*
granny ['grænɪ] (*inf*) *n* Oma *f*
grant [grɑːnt] *vt* (*money*) bewilligen; (*request etc*) gewähren; (*visa*) erteilen; (*admit*) zugeben ▷ *n* Stipendium *nt*; (*subsidy*) Subvention *f*; **to take sth for ~ed** etw für selbstverständlich halten; **to take sb for ~ed** jdn als selbstverständlich hinnehmen; **to ~ that** zugeben, dass
granulated sugar ['grænjʊleɪtɪd-] *n* (Zucker)raffinade *f*

granule ['grænjuːl] *n* Körnchen *nt*
grape [greɪp] *n* (Wein)traube *f*; **a bunch of ~s** eine (ganze) Weintraube
grapefruit ['greɪpfruːt] (*pl ~* or **grapefruits**) *n* Pampelmuse *f*, Grapefruit *f*
grapevine ['greɪpvaɪn] *n* Weinstock *m*; **I heard it on the ~** (*fig*) es ist mir zu Ohren gekommen
graph [grɑːf] *n* (*diagram*) grafische Darstellung *f*, Schaubild *nt*
graphic ['græfɪk] *adj* plastisch, anschaulich; (*art, design*) grafisch; *see also* **graphics**
graphic designer *n* Grafiker(in) *m(f)*
graphic equalizer [-iːkwəlaɪzə'] *n* (Graphic) Equalizer *m*
graphics ['græfɪks] *n* Grafik *f* ▷ *npl* (*drawings*) Zeichnungen *pl*, grafische Darstellungen *pl*
graphite ['græfaɪt] *n* Grafit *m*
graph paper *n* Millimeterpapier *nt*
grapple ['græpl] *vi*: **to ~ with sb/sth** mit jdm/etw kämpfen; **to ~ with a problem** sich mit einem Problem herumschlagen
grasp [grɑːsp] *vt* (*seize*) ergreifen; (*hold*) festhalten; (*understand*) begreifen ▷ *n* Griff *m*; (*understanding*) Verständnis *nt*; **it slipped from my ~** es entglitt mir; **to have sth within one's ~** etw in greifbarer Nähe haben; **to have a good ~ of sth** (*fig*) etw gut beherrschen
▶ **grasp at** *vt fus* greifen nach; (*fig: opportunity*) ergreifen
grasping ['grɑːspɪŋ] *adj* habgierig
grass [grɑːs] *n* Gras *nt*; (*lawn*) Rasen *m*; (*Brit: inf: informer*) (Polizei)spitzel *m*
grasshopper ['grɑːshɔpə'] *n* Grashüpfer *m*, Heuschrecke *f*
grass-roots ['grɑːsruːts] *npl* (*of party etc*) Basis *f* ▷ *adj* (*opinion*) des kleinen Mannes; **at ~ level** an der Basis
grass snake *n* Ringelnatter *f*
grassy ['grɑːsɪ] *adj* Gras-, grasig
grate [greɪt] *n* (Feuer)rost *m* ▷ *vt* reiben; (*carrots etc*) raspeln ▷ *vi*: **to ~ (on)** kratzen (auf *+dat*)
grateful ['greɪtful] *adj* dankbar; (*thanks*) aufrichtig
gratefully ['greɪtfəlɪ] *adv* dankbar
grater ['greɪtə'] *n* Reibe *f*
gratification [grætɪfɪ'keɪʃən] *n* (*pleasure*) Genugtuung *f*; (*satisfaction*) Befriedigung *f*
gratify ['grætɪfaɪ] *vt* (*please*) erfreuen; (*satisfy*) befriedigen
gratifying ['grætɪfaɪɪŋ] *adj* (*see vt*) erfreulich; befriedigend
grating ['greɪtɪŋ] *n* Gitter *nt* ▷ *adj* (*noise*) knirschend; (*voice*) schrill
gratitude ['grætɪtjuːd] *n* Dankbarkeit *f*
gratuitous [grə'tjuːɪtəs] *adj* unnötig
gratuity [grə'tjuːɪtɪ] *n* Trinkgeld *nt*
grave [greɪv] *n* Grab *nt* ▷ *adj* (*decision, mistake*) schwer (wiegend), schwerwiegend; (*expression, person*) ernst
grave digger *n* Totengräber *m*
gravel ['grævl] *n* Kies *m*
gravely ['greɪvlɪ] *adv* (*see adj*) schwer, ernst; **~ ill** schwer krank

gravestone ['greɪvstəun] n Grabstein m
graveyard ['greɪvjɑ:d] n Friedhof m
gravitas ['grævɪtæs] n Seriosität f
gravitate ['grævɪteɪt] vi: **to ~ towards** angezogen werden von
gravity ['grævɪtɪ] n Schwerkraft f; (seriousness) Ernst m, Schwere f
gravy ['greɪvɪ] n (juice) (Braten)saft m; (sauce) (Braten)soße f
gravy boat n Sauciere f, Soßenschüssel f
gravy train (inf) n: **to ride the ~** leichtes Geld machen
gray [greɪ] (US) adj = **grey**
graze [greɪz] vi grasen, weiden ▷ vt streifen; (scrape) aufschürfen ▷ n (Med) Abschürfung f
grazing ['greɪzɪŋ] n Weideland nt
grease [gri:s] n (lubricant) Schmiere f; (fat) Fett nt ▷ vt (see n) schmieren; fetten; **to ~ the skids** (US: fig) die Maschinerie in Gang halten
grease gun n Fettspritze f, Fettpresse f
greasepaint ['gri:speɪnt] n (Fett)schminke f
greaseproof paper ['gri:spru:f-] (Brit) n Pergamentpapier nt
greasy ['gri:sɪ] adj fettig; (food: containing grease) fett; (tools) schmierig, ölig; (clothes) speckig; (Brit: road, surface) glitschig, schlüpfrig
great [greɪt] adj groß; (city) bedeutend; (inf: terrific) prima, toll; **they're ~ friends** sie sind gute Freunde; **we had a ~ time** wir haben uns glänzend amüsiert; **it was ~!** es war toll!; **the ~ thing is that …** das Wichtigste ist, dass …
Great Barrier Reef n: **the ~** das Große Barriereriff
Great Britain n Großbritannien nt
greater ['greɪtə^r] adj (see **great**) größer; bedeutender; **people in G~ Calcutta** die Leute in Kalkutta und Umgebung; **G~ Manchester** Groß-Manchester nt
great-grandchild [greɪt'græntʃaɪld] (irreg: like **child**) n Urenkel(in) m(f)
great-grandfather [greɪt'grænfɑ:ðə^r] n Urgroßvater m
great-grandmother [greɪt'grænmʌðə^r] n Urgroßmutter f
Great Lakes npl: **the ~** die Großen Seen pl
greatly ['greɪtlɪ] adv sehr; (influenced) stark
greatness ['greɪtnɪs] n Bedeutung f
Grecian ['gri:ʃən] adj griechisch
Greece [gri:s] n Griechenland nt
greed [gri:d] n (also: **greediness**): **~ for** Gier f nach; **~ for power** Machtgier f; **~ for money** Geldgier f
greedily ['gri:dɪlɪ] adv gierig
greedy ['gri:dɪ] adj gierig
Greek [gri:k] adj griechisch ▷ n Grieche m, Griechin f; (Ling) Griechisch nt; **ancient/ modern ~** Alt-/Neugriechisch nt
green [gri:n] adj (also ecological) grün ▷ n (also Golf) Grün nt; (stretch of grass) Rasen m, Grünfläche f; (also: **village green**) Dorfwiese f, Anger m; **greens** npl (vegetables) Grüngemüse nt; (Pol): **the G~s** die Grünen pl; **to have ~**

fingers, to have a ~ thumb (US) eine Hand für Pflanzen haben; **to give sb the ~ light** jdm grünes Licht geben
green belt n Grüngürtel m
green card n (Aut) grüne (Versicherungs)karte f; (US) ≈ Aufenthaltserlaubnis f
greenery ['gri:nərɪ] n Grün nt
greenfly ['gri:nflaɪ] (Brit) n Blattlaus f
greengage ['gri:ngeɪdʒ] n Reneklode f
greengrocer ['gri:ngrəusə^r] (Brit) n Obst- und Gemüsehändler(in) m(f)
greenhouse ['gri:nhaus] n Gewächshaus nt, Treibhaus nt; **~ effect** Treibhauseffekt m; **~ gas** Treibhausgas nt
greenish ['gri:nɪʃ] adj grünlich
Greenland ['gri:nlənd] n Grönland nt
Greenlander ['gri:nləndə^r] n Grönländer(in) m(f)
green light n grünes Licht nt; **to give sb the ~** jdm grünes Licht or freie Fahrt geben
Green Party n (Pol): **the ~** die Grünen pl
green pepper n grüne Paprikaschote f
green pound n grünes Pfund nt
greet [gri:t] vt begrüßen; (news) aufnehmen
greeting ['gri:tɪŋ] n Gruß m; (welcome) Begrüßung f; **Christmas ~s** Weihnachtsgrüße pl; **birthday ~s** Geburtstagsglückwünsche pl; **Season's ~s** frohe Weihnachten und ein glückliches neues Jahr
greeting card, greetings card n Grußkarte f; (congratulating) Glückwunschkarte f
gregarious [grə'gɛərɪəs] adj gesellig
grenade [grə'neɪd] n (also: **hand grenade**) (Hand)granate f
grew [gru:] pt of **grow**
grey, (US) **gray** [greɪ] adj grau; (dismal) trüb, grau; **to go ~** grau werden
grey-haired [greɪ'hɛəd] adj grauhaarig
greyhound ['greɪhaund] n Windhund m
grid [grɪd] n Gitter nt; (Elec) (Verteiler)netz nt; (US: Aut: intersection) Kreuzung f
griddle [grɪdl] n gusseiserne Pfanne zum Braten und Pfannkuchenbacken
gridiron ['grɪdaɪən] n Bratrost m
gridlock ['grɪdlɔk] n (esp US: on road) totaler Stau m; (stalemate) Patt nt ▷ vt: **to be ~ed** (roads) total verstopft sein; (talks etc) festgefahren sein
grief [gri:f] n Kummer m, Trauer f; **to come to ~** (plan) scheitern; (person) zu Schaden kommen; **good ~!** ach du liebe Güte!
grievance ['gri:vəns] n Beschwerde f; (feeling of resentment) Groll m
grieve [gri:v] vi trauern ▷ vt Kummer bereiten +dat, betrüben; **to ~ for** trauern um
grievous ['gri:vəs] adj (mistake) schwer; (situation) betrüblich; **~ bodily harm** (Law) schwere Körperverletzung f
grill [grɪl] n Grill m; (grilled food: also: **mixed grill**) Grillgericht nt; (restaurant) = **grillroom** ▷ vt (Brit) grillen; (inf: question) in die Zange nehmen, ausquetschen

grille [grɪl] n (screen) Gitter nt; (Aut) Kühlergrill m

grillroom ['grɪlrum] n Grillrestaurant nt

grim [grɪm] adj trostlos; (serious, stern) grimmig

grimace [grɪ'meɪs] n Grimasse f ▷ vi Grimassen schneiden

grime [graɪm] n Dreck m, Schmutz m

grimy ['graɪmɪ] adj dreckig, schmutzig

grin [grɪn] n Grinsen nt ▷ vi grinsen; **to ~ at sb** jdn angrinsen

grind [graɪnd] (pt, pp **ground**) vt zerkleinern; (coffee, pepper etc) mahlen; (US: meat) hacken, durch den Fleischwolf drehen; (knife) schleifen, wetzen; (gem, lens) schleifen ▷ vi (car gears) knirschen ▷ n (work) Schufterei f; **to ~ one's teeth** mit den Zähnen knirschen; **to ~ to a halt** (vehicle) quietschend zum Stehen kommen; (fig: talks, scheme) sich festfahren; (work) stocken; (production) zum Erliegen kommen; **the daily ~** (inf) der tägliche Trott

grinder ['graɪndə'] n (for coffee) Kaffeemühle f; (for waste disposal etc) Müllzerkleinerungsanlage f

grindstone ['graɪndstəun] n: **to keep one's nose to the ~** hart arbeiten

grip [grɪp] n Griff m; (of tyre, shoe) Halt m; (holdall) Reisetasche f ▷ vt packen; (audience, attention) fesseln; **to come to ~s with sth** etw in den Griff bekommen; **to lose one's ~** den Halt verlieren; (fig) nachlassen; **to ~ the road** (car) gut auf der Straße liegen

gripe [graɪp] (inf) n (complaint) Meckerei f ▷ vi meckern; **the ~s** (Med) Kolik f, Bauchschmerzen pl

gripping ['grɪpɪŋ] adj fesselnd, packend

grisly ['grɪzlɪ] adj grässlich, grausig

grist [grɪst] n (fig): **it's all ~ to the mill** das kann man alles verwerten

gristle ['grɪsl] n Knorpel m

grit [grɪt] n (for icy roads: sand) Sand m; (crushed stone) Splitt m; (determination, courage) Mut m ▷ vt (road) streuen; **grits** npl (US) Grütze f; **I've got a piece of ~ in my eye** ich habe ein Staubkorn im Auge; **to ~ one's teeth** die Zähne zusammenbeißen

grizzle ['grɪzl] (Brit) vi quengeln

grizzly ['grɪzlɪ] n (also: **grizzly bear**) Grizzlybär m

groan [grəun] n Stöhnen nt ▷ vi stöhnen; (tree, floorboard etc) ächzen, knarren

grocer ['grəusə'] n Lebensmittelhändler(in) m(f)

groceries ['grəusərɪz] npl Lebensmittel pl

grocer's, grocer's shop n Lebensmittelgeschäft nt

grog [grɔg] n Grog m

groggy ['grɔgɪ] adj angeschlagen

groin [grɔɪn] n Leistengegend f

groom [gru:m] n Stallbursche m; (also: **bridegroom**) Bräutigam m ▷ vt (horse) striegeln; (fig): **to ~ sb for** (job) jdn aufbauen für; **well-~ed** gepflegt

groove [gru:v] n Rille f

grope [grəup] vi: **to ~ for** tasten nach; (fig: try to think of) suchen nach

grosgrain ['grəugreɪn] n grob gerippter Stoff m

gross [grəus] adj (neglect) grob; (injustice) krass; (behaviour, speech) grob, derb; (Comm: income, weight) Brutto- ▷ n inv Gros nt ▷ vt: **to ~ £500,000** £500 000 brutto einnehmen

gross domestic product n Bruttoinlandsprodukt nt

grossly ['grəuslɪ] adv äußerst; (exaggerated) grob

gross national product n Bruttosozialprodukt nt

grotesque [grə'tɛsk] adj grotesk

grotto ['grɔtəu] n Grotte f

grotty ['grɔtɪ] (inf) adj mies

grouch [grautʃ] (inf) vi schimpfen ▷ n (person) Miesepeter m, Muffel m

ground [graund] pt, pp of **grind** ▷ n Boden m, Erde f; (land) Land nt; (Sport) Platz m, Feld nt; (US: Elec: also **ground wire**) Erde f; (reason: gen pl) Grund m ▷ vt (plane) aus dem Verkehr ziehen; (US: Elec) erden ▷ adj (coffee etc) gemahlen ▷ vi (ship) auflaufen; **grounds** npl (of coffee etc) Satz m; (gardens etc) Anlagen pl; **below ~** unter der Erde; **to gain/lose ~** Boden gewinnen/ verlieren; **common ~** Gemeinsame(s) nt; **on the ~s that** mit der Begründung, dass

ground cloth (US) n = **groundsheet**

ground control n (Aviat, Space) Bodenkontrolle f

ground floor n Erdgeschoss nt, Erdgeschoß nt (Österr)

grounding ['graundɪŋ] n (in education) Grundwissen nt

groundless ['graundlɪs] adj grundlos, unbegründet

groundnut ['graundnʌt] n Erdnuss f

ground rent (Brit) n Erbbauzins m

ground rule n Grundregel f

groundsheet ['graundʃi:t] (Brit) n Zeltboden m

groundskeeper ['graundzki:pə'] (US) n = **groundsman**

groundsman ['graundzmən] (irreg: like **man**) n (Sport) Platzwart m

ground staff n (Aviat) Bodenpersonal nt

groundswell n: **there was a ~ of public opinion against him** die Öffentlichkeit wandte sich gegen ihn

ground-to-air missile ['graundtə'εə'-] n Boden-Luft-Rakete f

ground-to-ground missile ['graundtə'graund-] n Boden-Boden-Rakete f

groundwork ['graundwə:k] n Vorarbeit f

group [gru:p] n Gruppe f; (Comm) Konzern m ▷ vt (also: **group together**) zusammentun; (: in several groups) in Gruppen einteilen ▷ vi (also: **group together**) sich zusammentun

groupie [gru:pɪ] (inf) n Groupie nt

group therapy n Gruppentherapie f

grouse [graus] n inv schottisches Moorhuhn nt ▷ vi (complain) schimpfen

grove [grəuv] n Hain m, Wäldchen nt

grovel ['grɒvl] vi (crawl) kriechen; (fig): **to ~ (before)** kriechen (vor +dat)

grow [grəʊ] (pt **grew**, pp **~n**) vi wachsen; (increase) zunehmen; (become) werden ▷ vt (roses) züchten; (vegetables) anbauen, ziehen; (beard) sich dat wachsen lassen; **to ~ tired of waiting** das Warten leid sein; **to ~ (out of or from)** (develop) entstehen (aus)

▸ **grow apart** vi (fig) sich auseinanderentwickeln

▸ **grow away from** vt fus (fig) sich entfremden +dat

▸ **grow on** vt fus: **that painting is ~ing on me** allmählich finde ich Gefallen an dem Bild

▸ **grow out of** vt fus (clothes) herauswachsen aus; (habit) ablegen; **he'll ~ out of it** diese Phase geht auch vorbei

▸ **grow up** vi aufwachsen; (mature) erwachsen werden; (idea, friendship) entstehen

grower ['grəʊəʳ] n (Bot) Züchter(in) m(f); (Agr) Pflanzer(in) m(f)

growing ['grəʊɪŋ] adj wachsend; (number) zunehmend; **~ pains** Wachstumsschmerzen pl; (fig) Kinderkrankheiten pl, Anfangsschwierigkeiten pl

growl [graʊl] vi knurren

grown [grəʊn] pp of **grow**

grown-up [grəʊn'ʌp] n Erwachsene(r) f(m)

growth [grəʊθ] n Wachstum nt; (what has grown: of weeds, beard etc) Wuchs m; (of person, character) Entwicklung f; (Med) Gewächs nt, Wucherung f

growth rate n Wachstumsrate f, Zuwachsrate f

grub [grʌb] n (larva) Larve f; (inf: food) Fressalien pl, Futter nt ▷ vi: **to ~ about** or **around (for)** (herum)wühlen (nach)

grubby ['grʌbɪ] adj (dirty) schmuddelig; (fig) schmutzig

grudge [grʌdʒ] n Groll m ▷ vt: **to ~ sb sth** jdm etw nicht gönnen; **to bear sb a ~** jdm böse sein, einen Groll gegen jdn hegen

grudging ['grʌdʒɪŋ] adj widerwillig

grudgingly ['grʌdʒɪŋlɪ] adv widerwillig

gruelling, (US) **grueling** ['gruəlɪŋ] adj (encounter) aufreibend; (trip, journey) äußerst strapaziös

gruesome ['gru:səm] adj grauenhaft

gruff [grʌf] adj barsch, schroff

grumble ['grʌmbl] vi murren, schimpfen

grumpy ['grʌmpɪ] adj mürrisch, brummig

grunge [grʌndʒ] (inf) n Grunge nt

grunt [grʌnt] vi grunzen ▷ n Grunzen nt

G-string ['dʒi:strɪŋ] n Minislip m, Tangaslip m

GT abbr (Aut: = gran turismo) GT

GU (US) abbr (Post) = Guam

guarantee [gærən'ti:] n Garantie f ▷ vt garantieren; **he can't ~ (that) he'll come** er kann nicht dafür garantieren, dass er kommt

guarantor [gærən'tɔːʳ] n (Comm) Bürge m

guard [gɑːd] n Wache f; (Boxing, Fencing) Deckung f; (Brit: Rail) Schaffner(in) m(f); (on machine) Schutz m, Schutzvorrichtung f;

(also: **fireguard**) (Schutz)gitter nt ▷ vt (prisoner) bewachen; (protect): **to ~ (against)** (be)schützen (vor +dat); (secret) hüten (vor +dat); **to be on one's ~** auf der Hut sein

▸ **guard against** vt fus (disease) vorbeugen +dat; (damage, accident) verhüten

guard dog n Wachhund m

guarded ['gɑːdɪd] adj vorsichtig, zurückhaltend

guardian ['gɑːdɪən] n Vormund m; (defender) Hüter m

guardrail ['gɑːdreɪl] n (Schutz)geländer nt

guard's van (Brit) n (Rail) Schaffnerabteil nt, Dienstwagen m

Guatemala [gwɑːtɪ'mɑːlə] n Guatemala nt

Guatemalan [gwɑːtɪ'mɑːlən] adj guatemaltekisch, aus Guatemala

Guernsey ['gə:nzɪ] n Guernsey nt

guerrilla [gə'rɪlə] n Guerilla m, Guerillakämpfer(in) m(f)

guerrilla warfare n Guerillakrieg m

guess [gɛs] vt schätzen; (answer) (er)raten; (US: think) schätzen (inf) ▷ vi (see vt) schätzen; raten ▷ n Vermutung f; **I ~ you're right** da haben Sie wohl recht; **to keep sb ~ing** jdn im Ungewissen lassen; **to take** or **have a ~** raten; (estimate) schätzen; **my ~ is that ...** ich schätze or vermute, dass ...

guesstimate ['gɛstɪmɪt] (inf) n grobe Schätzung f

guesswork ['gɛswə:k] n Vermutungen pl; **I got the answer by ~** ich habe die Antwort nur geraten

guest [gɛst] n Gast m; **be my ~** (inf) nur zu!

guesthouse ['gɛsthaʊs] n Pension f

guest room n Gästezimmer nt

guff [gʌf] (inf) n Quatsch m, Käse m

guffaw [gʌ'fɔː] vi schallend lachen ▷ n schallendes Lachen nt

guidance ['gaɪdəns] n Rat m, Beratung f; **under the ~ of** unter der Leitung von; **vocational ~** Berufsberatung f; **marriage ~** Eheberatung f

guide [gaɪd] n (person) Führer(in) m(f); (book) Führer m; (Brit: also **girl guide**) Pfadfinderin f ▷ vt führen; (direct) lenken; **to be ~d by sb/sth** sich von jdm/etw leiten lassen

guidebook ['gaɪdbʊk] n Führer m

guided missile n Lenkwaffe f

guide dog n Blindenhund m

guidelines ['gaɪdlaɪnz] npl Richtlinien pl

guild [gɪld] n Verein m

guildhall ['gɪldhɔːl] (Brit) n Gildehaus nt

guile [gaɪl] n Arglist f

guileless ['gaɪllɪs] adj arglos

guillotine ['gɪləti:n] n Guillotine f, Fallbeil nt; (for paper) (Papier)schneidemaschine f

guilt [gɪlt] n Schuld f; (remorse) Schuldgefühl nt

guilty ['gɪltɪ] adj schuldig; (expression) schuldbewusst; (secret) dunkel; **to plead ~/ not ~** sich schuldig/nicht schuldig bekennen; **to feel ~ about doing sth** ein schlechtes Gewissen haben, etw zu tun

g

Guinea ['gɪnɪ] n: **Republic of** ~ Guinea nt
guinea ['gɪnɪ] (Brit) n (old) Guinee f
guinea pig n Meerschweinchen nt; (fig: person)
Versuchskaninchen nt
guise [gaɪz] n: **in** or **under the** ~ **of** in der Form
+gen, in Gestalt +gen
guitar [gɪ'tɑːʳ] n Gitarre f
guitarist [gɪ'tɑːrɪst] n Gitarrist(in) m(f)
gulch [gʌltʃ] (US) n Schlucht f
gulf [gʌlf] n Golf m; (abyss) Abgrund m;
(fig: difference) Kluft f; **the (Persian) G**~ der
(Persische) Golf
Gulf States npl: **the** ~ die Golfstaaten pl
Gulf Stream n: **the** ~ der Golfstrom
Gulf War n: **the** ~ der Golfkrieg
gull [gʌl] n Möwe f
gullet ['gʌlɪt] n Speiseröhre f
gullibility [gʌlɪ'bɪlɪtɪ] n Leichtgläubigkeit f
gullible ['gʌlɪbl] adj leichtgläubig
gully ['gʌlɪ] n Schlucht f
gulp [gʌlp] vi schlucken ▷ vt (also: **gulp down**)
hinunterschlucken ▷ n: **at one** ~ mit einem
Schluck
gum [gʌm] n (Anat) Zahnfleisch nt; (glue)
Klebstoff m; (also: **gumdrop**) Weingummi nt;
(also: **chewing-gum**) Kaugummi m ▷ vt: **to** ~
(together) (zusammen)kleben
▶ **gum up** vt: **to** ~ **up the works** (inf) alles
vermasseln
gumboots ['gʌmbuːts] (Brit) npl Gummistiefel
pl
gumption ['gʌmpʃən] n Grips m (inf)
gumtree ['gʌmtriː] n: **to be up a** ~ (fig: inf)
aufgeschmissen sein
gun [gʌn] n (small) Pistole f; (medium-sized)
Gewehr nt; (large) Kanone f ▷ vt (also: **gun
down**) erschießen; **to stick to one's** ~**s** (fig)
nicht nachgeben, festbleiben
gunboat ['gʌnbəut] n Kanonenboot nt
gun dog n Jagdhund m
gunfire ['gʌnfaɪəʳ] n Geschützfeuer nt
gunge [gʌndʒ] (inf) n Schmiere f
gung ho ['gʌŋ'həu] (inf) adj übereifrig
gunman ['gʌnmən] (irreg: like **man**) n
bewaffneter Verbrecher m
gunner ['gʌnəʳ] n Kanonier m, Artillerist m
gunpoint ['gʌnpɔɪnt] n: **at** ~ mit vorgehaltener
Pistole; mit vorgehaltenem Gewehr
gunpowder ['gʌnpaudəʳ] n Schießpulver nt
gunrunner ['gʌnrʌnəʳ] n Waffen-
schmuggler(in) m(f), Waffenschieber(in) m(f)
gunrunning ['gʌnrʌnɪŋ] n Waffenschmuggel
m, Waffenschieberei f
gunshot ['gʌnʃɒt] n Schuss m
gunsmith ['gʌnsmɪθ] n Büchsenmacher m
gurgle ['gəːgl] vi (baby) glucksen; (water)
gluckern
guru ['guruː] n Guru m
gush [gʌʃ] vi hervorquellen, hervorströmen;
(person) schwärmen ▷ n Strahl m
gushing ['gʌʃɪŋ] adj (fig) überschwänglich

gusset ['gʌsɪt] n Keil m, Zwickel m
gust [gʌst] n Windstoß m, Bö(e) f; (of smoke)
Wolke f
gusto ['gʌstəu] n: **with** ~ mit Genuss, mit
Schwung
gusty ['gʌstɪ] adj (wind) böig; (day) stürmisch
gut [gʌt] n (Anat) Darm m; (for violin, racket)
Darmsaiten pl ▷ vt (poultry, fish) ausnehmen;
(building) ausräumen; (by fire) ausbrennen;
guts npl (Anat) Eingeweide pl; (inf: courage)
Mumm m; **to hate sb's** ~**s** jdn auf den Tod
nicht ausstehen können
gut reaction n rein gefühlsmäßige Reaktion f
gutsy ['gʌtsɪ] (inf) adj (vivid) rasant; (courageous)
mutig
gutter ['gʌtəʳ] n (in street) Gosse f, Rinnstein m;
(of roof) Dachrinne f
gutter press n Boulevardpresse f
guttural ['gʌtərl] adj guttural
guy [gaɪ] n (inf: man) Typ m, Kerl m;
(also: **guyrope**) Halteau nt, Halteseil nt; (for
Guy Fawkes' night) (Guy-Fawkes-)Puppe f

GUY FAWKES' NIGHT

Guy Fawkes' Night, auch „bonfire night"
genannt, erinnert an den „Gunpowder
Plot", einen Attentatsversuch auf James
I. und sein Parlament am 5. November
1605. Einer der Verschwörer, Guy Fawkes,
wurde auf frischer Tat ertappt, als er das
Parlamentsgebäude in die Luft sprengen
wollte. Vor der Guy Fawkes' Night
basteln Kinder in Großbritannien eine
Puppe des Guy Fawkes, mit der sie Geld
für Feuerwerkskörper von Passanten
erbetteln, und die dann am 5. November
auf einem Lagerfeuer mit Feuerwerk
verbrannt wird.

Guyana [gaɪ'ænə] n Guyana nt
guzzle ['gʌzl] vt (food) futtern; (drink) saufen
(inf)
gym [dʒɪm] n (also: **gymnasium**) Turnhalle f;
(also: **gymnastics**) Gymnastik f, Turnen nt
gymkhana [dʒɪm'kɑːnə] n Reiterfest nt
gymnasium [dʒɪm'neɪzɪəm] n Turnhalle f
gymnast ['dʒɪmnæst] n Turner(in) m(f)
gymnastics [dʒɪm'næstɪks] n Gymnastik f,
Turnen nt
gym shoes npl Turnschuhe pl
gymslip ['dʒɪmslɪp] (Brit) n (Schul)trägerrock m
gynaecologist, (US) **gynecologist**
[gaɪnɪ'kɒlədʒɪst] n Gynäkologe m, Gynäkologin
f, Frauenarzt m, Frauenärztin f
gynaecology, (US) **gynecology** [gaɪnɪ'kɒlədʒɪ]
n Gynäkologie f, Frauenheilkunde f
gypsy ['dʒɪpsɪ] n = **gipsy**
gyrate [dʒaɪ'reɪt] vi kreisen, sich drehen
gyroscope ['dʒaɪərəskəup] n Gyroskop nt

Hh

H, h [eɪtʃ] n (letter) H, h nt; **H for Harry, H for How** (US) ≈ H wie Heinrich

habeas corpus ['heɪbɪəs'kɔ:pəs] n Habeaskorpusakte f

haberdashery [hæbə'dæʃərɪ] (Brit) n Kurzwaren pl

habit ['hæbɪt] n Gewohnheit f; (esp undesirable) Angewohnheit f; (addiction) Sucht f; (Rel) Habit m or nt; **to get out of/into the ~ of doing sth** sich abgewöhnen/angewöhnen, etw zu tun; **to be in the ~ of doing sth** die (An)gewohnheit haben, etw zu tun

habitable ['hæbɪtəbl] adj bewohnbar

habitat ['hæbɪtæt] n Heimat f; (of animals) Lebensraum m, Heimat f

habitation [hæbɪ'teɪʃən] n Wohnstätte f; **fit for human ~** für Wohnzwecke geeignet, bewohnbar

habitual [hə'bɪtjuəl] adj (action) gewohnt; (drinker) Gewohnheits-; (liar) gewohnheitsmäßig

habitually [hə'bɪtjuəlɪ] adv ständig

hack [hæk] vt, vi (also Comput) hacken ▷ n (pej: writer) Schreiberling m; (horse) Mietpferd nt

hacker ['hækər] n (Comput) Hacker m

hackles ['hæklz] npl: **to make sb's ~ rise** (fig) jdn auf die Palme bringen (inf)

hackney cab ['hæknɪ-] n Taxi nt

hackneyed ['hæknɪd] adj abgedroschen

hacksaw ['hæksɔ:] n Metallsäge f

had [hæd] pt, pp of **have**

haddock ['hædək] (pl ~ or **haddocks**) n Schellfisch m

hadn't ['hædnt] = **had not**

haematology, (US) **hematology** ['hi:mə'tɔlədʒɪ] n Hämatologie f

haemoglobin, (US) **hemoglobin** ['hi:mə'gləubɪn] n Hämoglobin nt

haemophilia, (US) **hemophilia** ['hi:mə'fɪlɪə] n Bluterkrankheit f

haemorrhage, (US) **hemorrhage** ['hɛmərɪdʒ] n Blutung f

haemorrhoids, (US) **hemorrhoids** ['hɛmərɔɪdz] npl Hämorr(ho)iden pl

hag [hæg] n alte Hexe f; (witch) Hexe f

haggard ['hægəd] adj ausgezehrt; (from worry) abgehärmt; (from tiredness) abgespannt

haggis ['hægɪs] (Scot) n Gericht aus gehackten Schafsinnereien und Haferschrot, im Schafsmagen gekocht

haggle ['hægl] vi: **to ~ (over)** feilschen (um)

haggling ['hæglɪŋ] n Feilschen nt

Hague [heɪg] n: **The ~** Den Haag m

hail [heɪl] n Hagel m ▷ vt (person) zurufen +dat; (taxi) herbeiwinken, anhalten; (acclaim: person) zujubeln +dat; (: event etc) bejubeln ▷ vi hageln; **he ~s from Scotland** er kommt or stammt aus Schottland

hailstone ['heɪlstəun] n Hagelkorn nt

hailstorm ['heɪlstɔ:m] n Hagelschauer m

hair [hɛər] n (collectively: of person) Haar nt, Haare pl; (: of animal) Fell nt; (single hair) Haar nt; **to do one's ~** sich frisieren; **by a ~'s breadth** um Haaresbreite

hairbrush ['hɛəbrʌʃ] n Haarbürste f

haircut ['hɛəkʌt] n Haarschnitt m; (style) Frisur f

hairdo ['hɛədu:] n Frisur f

hairdresser ['hɛədrɛsər] n Friseur m, Friseuse f

hairdresser's ['hɛədrɛsəz] n Friseursalon m

hair dryer n Haartrockner m, Föhn f, Fön® m

-haired [hɛəd] suff: **fair-~** blond; **long-~** langhaarig

hairgrip ['hɛəgrɪp] n Haarklemme f

hairline ['hɛəlaɪn] n Haaransatz m

hairline fracture n Haarriss m

hairnet ['hɛənɛt] n Haarnetz nt

hair oil n Haaröl nt

hairpiece ['hɛəpi:s] n Haarteil nt; (for men) Toupet nt

hairpin ['hɛəpɪn] n Haarnadel f

hairpin bend, (US) **hairpin curve** n Haarnadelkurve f

hair-raising ['hɛəreɪzɪŋ] adj haarsträubend

hair remover n Enthaarungscreme f

hair slide n Haarspange f

hair spray n Haarspray nt

hairstyle ['hɛəstaɪl] n Frisur f

hairy ['hɛərɪ] adj behaart; (inf: situation) brenzlig, haarig

Haiti ['heɪtɪ] n Haiti nt

hake [heɪk] (pl ~ or **hakes**) n Seehecht m

halcyon ['hælsɪən] adj glücklich

hale [heɪl] adj: **~ and hearty** gesund und munter

half [hɑ:f] (pl **halves**) n Hälfte f; (of beer etc)

kleines Bier *nt etc*; (*Rail, bus*) Fahrkarte *f* zum halben Preis ▷ *adj, adv* halb; **first/second ~** (*Sport*) erste/zweite Halbzeit *f*; **two and a ~** zweieinhalb; **~-an-hour** eine halbe Stunde; **~ a dozen/pound** ein halbes Dutzend/Pfund; **a week and a ~** eineinhalb *or* anderthalb Wochen; **~ (of it)** die Hälfte; **~ (of)** die Hälfte (von *or* +gen); **~ the amount of** die halbe Menge an +dat; **to cut sth in ~** etw halbieren; **~ past three** halb vier; **to go halves (with sb)** (mit jdm) halbe-halbe machen; **she never does things by halves** sie macht keine halben Sachen; **he's too clever by ~** er ist ein richtiger Schlaumeier; **~ empty** halb leer; **~ closed** halb geschlossen
half-baked ['hɑːf'beɪkt] *adj* blödsinnig (*inf*)
half board *n* Halbpension *f*
half-breed ['hɑːfbriːd] *n* (*pej*) = **half-caste**
half-brother ['hɑːfbrʌðə*] *n* Halbbruder *m*
half-caste ['hɑːfkɑːst] *n* (*pej*) Mischling *m*
half-day [hɑːf'deɪ] *n* halber freier Tag *m*
half-hearted ['hɑːf'hɑːtɪd] *adj* halbherzig, lustlos
half-hour [hɑːf'auə*] *n* halbe Stunde *f*
half-life ['hɑːflaɪf] *n* (*Tech*) Halbwertszeit *f*
half-mast ['hɑːf'mɑːst]: **at ~** *adv* (auf) halbmast
halfpenny ['heɪpnɪ] (*Brit*) *n* halber Penny *m*
half-price ['hɑːf'praɪs] *adj, adv* zum halben Preis
half-sister ['hɑːfsɪstə*] *n* Halbschwester *f*
half term (*Brit*) *n* kleine Ferien *pl* (*in der Mitte des Trimesters*)
half-timbered [hɑːf'tɪmbəd] *adj* (*house*) Fachwerk-
half-time [hɑːf'taɪm] *n* (*Sport*) Halbzeit *f*
halfway ['hɑːf'weɪ] *adv*: **~ to** auf halbem Wege nach; **~ through** mitten in +dat; **to meet sb ~** (*fig*) jdm auf halbem Wege entgegenkommen
halfway house *n* (*hostel*) offene Anstalt *f*; (*fig*) Zwischending *nt*; (*: compromise*) Kompromiss *m*
halfwit ['hɑːfwɪt] *n* Schwachsinnige(r) *f(m)*; (*fig: inf*) Schwachkopf *m*
half-yearly [hɑːf'jɪəlɪ] *adv* halbjährlich, jedes halbe Jahr ▷ *adj* halbjährlich
halibut ['hælɪbət] *n inv* Heilbutt *m*
halitosis [hælɪ'təusɪs] *n* schlechter Atem *m*, Mundgeruch *m*
hall [hɔːl] *n* Diele *f*, (Haus)flur *m*; (*corridor*) Korridor *m*, Flur *m*; (*mansion*) Herrensitz *m*, Herrenhaus *nt*; (*for concerts etc*) Halle *f*; **to live in ~** (*Brit*) im Wohnheim wohnen
hallmark ['hɔːlmɑːk] *n* (*on gold, silver*) (Feingehalts)stempel *m*; (*of writer, artist etc*) Kennzeichen *nt*
hallo [hə'ləu] *excl* = **hello**
hall of residence (*pl* **halls of residence**) (*Brit*) *n* Studentenwohnheim *nt*
hallowed ['hæləud] *adj* (*ground*) heilig; (*fig: respected, revered*) geheiligt
Hallowe'en ['hæləu'iːn] *n* der Tag vor Allerheiligen

○ **HALLOWE'EN**
○
○ *Hallowe'en* ist der 31. Oktober, der Vorabend
○ von Allerheiligen und nach altem Glauben
○ der Abend, an dem man Geister und
○ Hexen sehen kann. In Großbritannien
○ und vor allem in den USA feiern die Kinder
○ Hallowe'en, indem sie sich verkleiden
○ und mit selbst gemachten Laternen aus
○ Kürbissen von Tür zu Tür ziehen.

hallucination [həluː'neɪʃən] *n* Halluzination *f*
hallucinogenic [həluː'sɪnəu'dʒenɪk] *adj* (*drug*) halluzinogen ▷ *n* Halluzinogen *nt*
hallway ['hɔːlweɪ] *n* Diele *f*, (Haus)flur *m*
halo ['heɪləu] *n* Heiligenschein *m*; (*circle of light*) Hof *m*
halt [hɔːlt] *vt* anhalten; (*progress etc*) zum Stillstand bringen ▷ *vi* anhalten, zum Stillstand kommen ▷ *n*: **to come to a ~** zum Stillstand kommen; **to call a ~ to sth** (*fig*) einer Sache *dat* ein Ende machen
halter ['hɔːltə*] *n* Halfter *nt*
halter-neck ['hɔːltənɛk] *adj* (*dress*) rückenfrei mit Nackenverschluss
halve [hɑːv] *vt* halbieren
halves [hɑːvz] *pl of* **half**
ham [hæm] *n* Schinken *m*; (*inf: also:* **radio ham**) Funkamateur *m*; (*: actor*) Schmierenkomödiant(in) *m(f)*
Hamburg ['hæmbəːg] *n* Hamburg *nt*
hamburger ['hæmbəːgə*] *n* Hamburger *m*
ham-fisted ['hæm'fɪstɪd], (*US*) **ham-handed** ['hæm'hændɪd] *adj* ungeschickt
hamlet ['hæmlɪt] *n* Weiler *m*, kleines Dorf *nt*
hammer ['hæmə*] *n* Hammer *m* ▷ *vt* hämmern; (*fig: criticize*) vernichtend kritisieren; (*: defeat*) vernichtend schlagen ▷ *vi* hämmern; **to ~ sth into sb, to ~ sth across to sb** jdm etw einhämmern *or* einbläuen ▷ **hammer out** *vt* hämmern; (*solution, agreement*) ausarbeiten
hammock ['hæmək] *n* Hängematte *f*
hamper ['hæmpə*] *vt* behindern ▷ *n* Korb *m*
hamster ['hæmstə*] *n* Hamster *m*
hamstring ['hæmstrɪŋ] *n* Kniesehne *f* ▷ *vt* einengen
hand [hænd] *n* Hand *f*; (*of clock*) Zeiger *m*; (*handwriting*) Hand(schrift) *f*; (*worker*) Arbeiter(in) *m(f)*; (*of cards*) Blatt *nt*; (*measurement: of horse*) ≈ 10 cm ▷ *vt* geben, reichen; **to give** *or* **lend sb a ~** jdm helfen; **at ~** (*place*) in der Nähe; (*time*) unmittelbar bevorstehend; **by ~** von Hand; **in ~** (*time*) zur Verfügung; (*job*) anstehend; (*situation*) unter Kontrolle; **we have the matter in ~** wir haben die Sache im Griff; **on ~** zur Verfügung; **out of ~** *adj* außer Kontrolle ▷ *adv* (*reject etc*) rundweg; **to ~** zur Hand; **on the one ~ ..., on the other ~ ...** einerseits ... andererseits ...;

to force sb's ~ jdn zwingen; **to have a free ~** freie Hand haben; **to change ~s** den Besitzer wechseln; **to have in one's ~** (also fig) in der Hand halten; **"~s off!"** „Hände weg!"
▸ **hand down** vt (knowledge) weitergeben; (possessions) vererben; (Law: judgement, sentence) fällen
▸ **hand in** vt abgeben, einreichen
▸ **hand out** vt verteilen; (information) austeilen; (punishment) verhängen
▸ **hand over** vt übergeben
▸ **hand round** vt (Brit) verteilen; (chocolates etc) herumreichen
handbag ['hændbæg] n Handtasche f
hand baggage n Handgepäck nt
handball ['hændbɔ:l] n Handball m
hand basin n Handwaschbecken nt
handbook ['hændbuk] n Handbuch nt
handbrake ['hændbreɪk] n Handbremse f
h & c (Brit) abbr (= hot and cold (water)) h. u. k.
hand cream n Handcreme f
handcuff ['hændkʌf] vt Handschellen anlegen +dat
handcuffs ['hændkʌfs] npl Handschellen pl
handful ['hændful] n Handvoll f
hand-held ['hænd'hɛld] adj (camera) Hand-
handicap ['hændɪkæp] n Behinderung f; (disadvantage) Nachteil m; (Sport) Handicap nt ▸ vt benachteiligen; **mentally/physically ~ped** geistig/körperlich behindert
handicraft ['hændɪkrɑ:ft] n Kunsthandwerk nt; (object) Kunsthandwerksarbeit f
handiwork ['hændɪwə:k] n Arbeit f; **this looks like his ~** (pej) das sieht nach seiner Arbeit aus
handkerchief ['hæŋkətʃɪf] n Taschentuch nt
handle ['hændl] n Griff m; (of door) Klinke f; (of cup) Henkel m; (of broom, brush etc) Stiel m; (for winding) Kurbel f; (CB Radio: name) Sendezeichen nt ▸ vt anfassen, berühren; (problem etc) sich befassen mit; (: successfully) fertig werden mit; (people) umgehen mit; **"~ with care"** „Vorsicht – zerbrechlich"; **to fly off the ~** an die Decke gehen; **to get a ~ on a problem** (inf) ein Problem in den Griff bekommen
handlebar ['hændlbɑ:ʳ] n, **handlebars** ['hændlbɑ:z] ▸ npl Lenkstange f
handling ['hændlɪŋ] n: ~ **(of)** (of plant, animal, issue etc) Behandlung f +gen; (of person, tool, machine etc) Umgang m (mit); (Admin) Bearbeitung f +gen
handling charges npl Bearbeitungsgebühr f; (Banking) Kontoführungsgebühr f
hand luggage n Handgepäck nt
handmade ['hænd'meɪd] adj handgearbeitet
hand-out ['hændaut] n (money, food etc) Unterstützung f; (publicity leaflet) Flugblatt nt; (summary) Informationsblatt nt
hand-picked ['hænd'pɪkt] adj von Hand geerntet; (staff etc) handverlesen
handrail ['hændreɪl] n Geländer nt
handset ['hændset] n (Tel) Hörer m
hands-free ['hændzfri:] adj (telephone, microphone) Freisprech-

handshake ['hændʃeɪk] n Händedruck m
handsome ['hænsəm] adj gut aussehend; (building) schön; (gift) großzügig; (profit, return) ansehnlich
hands-on ['hændzɔn] adj (training) praktisch; (approach etc) aktiv; ~ **experience** praktische Erfahrung
handstand ['hændstænd] n: **to do a ~** einen Handstand machen
hand-to-mouth ['hændtə'mauθ] adj: **to lead a ~ existence** von der Hand in den Mund leben
handwriting ['hændraɪtɪŋ] n Handschrift f
handwritten ['hændrɪtn] adj handgeschrieben
handy ['hændɪ] adj praktisch; (skilful) geschickt; (close at hand) in der Nähe; **to come in ~** sich als nützlich erweisen
handyman ['hændɪmæn] (irreg: like **man**) n (at home) Heimwerker m; (in hotel etc) Faktotum nt
hang [hæŋ] (pt, pp **hung**) vt aufhängen; (criminal: pt, pp **~ed**) hängen; (head) hängen lassen ▷ vi hängen; (hair, drapery) fallen ▷ n: **to get the ~ of sth** (inf) den richtigen Dreh (bei etw) herauskriegen
▸ **hang about** vi herumlungern
▸ **hang around** vi = **hang about**
▸ **hang back** vi: **to ~ back (from doing sth)** zögern(, etw zu tun)
▸ **hang on** vi warten ▷ vt fus (depend on) abhängen von; **to ~ on to** festhalten; (for protection, support) sich festhalten an +dat; (hope, position) sich klammern an +acc; (ideas) festhalten an +dat; (keep) behalten
▸ **hang out** vt draußen aufhängen ▷ vi heraushängen; (inf: live) wohnen
▸ **hang together** vi (argument) folgerichtig or zusammenhängend sein; (story, explanation) zusammenhängend sein; (statements) zusammenpassen
▸ **hang up** vt aufhängen ▷ vi (Tel): **to ~ up (on sb)** einfach auflegen
hangar ['hæŋəʳ] n Hangar m, Flugzeughalle f
hangdog ['hæŋdɔg] adj zerknirscht
hanger ['hæŋəʳ] n Bügel m
hanger-on [hæŋər'ɔn] n (parasite) Trabant m (inf); **the hangers-on** der Anhang
hang-glide ['hæŋglaɪd] vi drachenfliegen
hang-glider ['hæŋglaɪdəʳ] n (Flug)drachen m
hang-gliding ['hæŋglaɪdɪŋ] n Drachenfliegen nt
hanging ['hæŋɪŋ] n (execution) Hinrichtung f durch den Strang; (for wall) Wandbehang m
hangman ['hæŋmən] (irreg: like **man**) n Henker m
hangover ['hæŋəuvəʳ] n Kater m; (from past) Überbleibsel nt
hang-up ['hæŋʌp] n Komplex m
hank [hæŋk] n Strang m
hanker ['hæŋkəʳ] vi: **to ~ after** sich sehnen nach
hankering ['hæŋkərɪŋ] n: ~ **(for)** Verlangen nt (nach)
hankie, hanky ['hæŋkɪ] (pl **~s**) n = **handkerchief**

h

589

haphazard [hæp'hæzəd] *adj* planlos, wahllos

hapless ['hæplɪs] *adj* glücklos

happen ['hæpən] *vi* geschehen; **to ~ to do sth** zufällig(erweise) etw tun; **as it ~s** zufälligerweise; **what's ~ing?** was ist los?; **she ~ed to be free** sie hatte zufällig(erweise) gerade Zeit; **if anything ~ed to him** wenn ihm etwas zustoßen *or* passieren sollte
► **happen (up)on** *vt fus* zufällig stoßen auf *+acc*; *(person)* zufällig treffen

happening ['hæpnɪŋ] *n* Ereignis *nt*, Vorfall *m*

happily ['hæpɪlɪ] *adv (luckily)* glücklicherweise; *(cheerfully)* fröhlich

happiness ['hæpɪnɪs] *n* Glück *nt*

happy ['hæpɪ] *adj* glücklich; *(cheerful)* fröhlich; **to be ~ (with)** zufrieden sein (mit); **to be ~ to do sth** etw gerne tun; **~ birthday!** herzlichen Glückwunsch zum Geburtstag!

happy-go-lucky ['hæpɪgəu'lʌkɪ] *adj* unbekümmert

happy hour *n* Zeit, in der Bars, Pubs usw Getränke zu ermäßigten Preisen anbieten

harangue [hə'ræŋ] *vt* predigen *+dat (inf)*

harass ['hærəs] *vt* schikanieren

harassed ['hærəst] *adj* geplagt

harassment ['hærəsmənt] *n* Schikanierung *f*; **sexual ~** sexuelle Belästigung *f*

harbour, *(US)* **harbor** ['hɑːbəʳ] *n* Hafen *m* ▷ *vt (hope, fear, grudge etc)* hegen; *(criminal, fugitive)* Unterschlupf gewähren *+dat*

harbour dues *npl* Hafengebühren *pl*

harbour master *n* Hafenmeister *m*

hard [hɑːd] *adj* hart; *(question, problem)* schwierig; *(evidence)* gesichert ▷ *adv (work)* hart, schwer; *(think)* scharf; *(try)* sehr; **~ luck!** Pech!; **no ~ feelings!** ich nehme es dir nicht übel; **to be ~ of hearing** schwerhörig sein; **to be ~ done by** ungerecht behandelt werden; **I find it ~ to believe that ...** ich kann es kaum glauben, dass ...; **to look ~ at sth** *(object)* sich *+dat* etw genau ansehen; *(idea)* etw gründlich prüfen

hard-and-fast ['hɑːdən'fɑːst] *adj* fest

hardback ['hɑːdbæk] *n* gebundene Ausgabe *f*

hardboard ['hɑːdbɔːd] *n* Hartfaserplatte *f*

hard-boiled egg ['hɑːd'bɔɪld-] *n* hart gekochtes Ei *nt*

hard cash *n* Bargeld *nt*

hard copy *n (Comput)* Ausdruck *m*

hard core *n* harter Kern *m*

hard-core ['hɑːd'kɔːʳ] *adj (pornography)* hart; *(supporters)* zum harten Kern gehörend

hard court *n (Tennis)* Hartplatz *m*

hard disk *n (Comput)* Festplatte *f*

harden ['hɑːdn] *vt* härten; *(attitude, person)* verhärten ▷ *vi* hart werden, sich verhärten

hardened ['hɑːdnd] *adj (criminal)* Gewohnheits-; **to be ~ to sth** gegen etw abgehärtet sein

hardening ['hɑːdnɪŋ] *n* Verhärtung *f*

hard graft *n:* **by sheer ~** durch harte Arbeit

hard-headed ['hɑːd'hedɪd] *adj* nüchtern

hardhearted ['hɑːd'hɑːtɪd] *adj* hartherzig

hard-hitting ['hɑːd'hɪtɪŋ] *adj (fig: speech,**

journalist etc) knallhart

hard labour *n* Zwangsarbeit *f*

hardliner [hɑːd'laɪnəʳ] *n* Vertreter(in) *m(f)* der harten Linie

hard-luck story ['hɑːdlʌk-] *n* Leidensgeschichte *f*

hardly ['hɑːdlɪ] *adv* kaum; *(harshly)* hart, streng; **it's ~ the case** *(ironic)* das ist wohl kaum der Fall; **I can ~ believe it** ich kann es kaum glauben

hard-nosed [hɑːd'nəuzd] *adj* abgebrüht

hard-pressed [hɑːd'prest] *adj:* **to be ~** unter Druck sein; **~ for money** in Geldnot

hard sell *n* aggressive Verkaufstaktik *f*

hardship ['hɑːdʃɪp] *n* Not *f*

hard shoulder *(Brit) n (Aut)* Seitenstreifen *m*

hard up *(inf) adj* knapp bei Kasse

hardware ['hɑːdwɛəʳ] *n* Eisenwaren *pl*; *(household goods)* Haushaltswaren *pl*; *(Comput)* Hardware *f*; *(Mil)* Waffen *pl*

hardware shop *n* Eisenwarenhandlung *f*

hard-wearing [hɑːd'wɛərɪŋ] *adj* strapazierfähig

hard-won [hɑːd'wʌn] *adj* schwer erkämpft

hard-working [hɑːd'wəːkɪŋ] *adj* fleißig

hardy ['hɑːdɪ] *adj (animals)* zäh; *(people)* abgehärtet; *(plant)* winterhart

hare [hɛəʳ] *n* Hase *m*

harebrained ['hɛəbreɪnd] *adj* verrückt

harelip ['hɛəlɪp] *n* Hasenscharte *f*

harem [hɑː'riːm] *n* Harem *m*

hark back [hɑːk-] *vi:* **to ~ to** zurückkommen auf *+acc*

harm [hɑːm] *n* Schaden *m*; *(injury)* Verletzung *f* ▷ *vt* schaden *+dat*; *(person: physically)* verletzen; **to mean no ~** es nicht böse meinen; **out of ~'s way** in Sicherheit; **there's no ~ in trying** es kann nicht schaden, es zu versuchen

harmful ['hɑːmful] *adj* schädlich

harmless ['hɑːmlɪs] *adj* harmlos

harmonic [hɑː'mɔnɪk] *adj* harmonisch

harmonica [hɑː'mɔnɪkə] *n* Harmonika *f*

harmonics [hɑː'mɔnɪks] *npl* Harmonik *f*

harmonious [hɑː'məunɪəs] *adj* harmonisch

harmonium [hɑː'məunɪəm] *n* Harmonium *nt*

harmonize ['hɑːmənaɪz] *vi (Mus)* mehrstimmig singen/spielen; *(: one person)* die zweite Stimme singen/spielen; *(colours, ideas)* harmonieren

harmony ['hɑːmənɪ] *n* Einklang *m*; *(Mus)* Harmonie *f*

harness ['hɑːnɪs] *n (for horse)* Geschirr *nt*; *(for child)* Laufgurt *m*; *(also:* **safety harness***)* Sicherheitsgurt *m* ▷ *vt (resources, energy etc)* nutzbar machen; *(horse, dog)* anschirren

harp [hɑːp] *n* Harfe *f* ▷ *vi:* **to ~ on about** *(pej)* herumreiten auf *+dat*

harpist ['hɑːpɪst] *n* Harfenspieler(in) *m(f)*

harpoon [hɑː'puːn] *n* Harpune *f*

harpsichord ['hɑːpsɪkɔːd] *n* Cembalo *nt*

harried ['hærɪd] *adj* bedrängt

harrow ['hærəu] *n* Egge *f*

harrowing ['hærəuɪŋ] *adj (film)* erschütternd;

(*experience*) grauenhaft

harry ['hærɪ] *vt* bedrängen, zusetzen +*dat*

harsh [hɑːʃ] *adj* (*sound, light*) grell; (*judge, winter*) streng; (*criticism, life*) hart

harshly ['hɑːʃlɪ] *adv* (*judge*) streng; (*say*) barsch; (*criticize*) hart

harshness ['hɑːʃnɪs] *n* (*see adj*) Grelle *f*; Strenge *f*; Härte *f*

harvest ['hɑːvɪst] *n* Ernte *f* ▷ *vt* ernten

harvester ['hɑːvɪstəʳ] *n* (*also*: **combine harvester**) Mähdrescher *m*

has [hæz] *vb see* **have**

has-been ['hæzbiːn] (*inf*) *n*: **he's/she's a** ~ er/ sie ist eine vergangene *or* vergessene Größe

hash [hæʃ] *n* (*Culin*) Haschee *nt*; (*fig*): **to make a** ~ **of sth** etw verpfuschen (*inf*) ▷ *n abbr* (*inf*) (= *hashish*) Hasch *nt*

hashish ['hæʃɪʃ] *n* Haschisch *nt*

hasn't ['hæznt] = **has not**

hassle ['hæsl] (*inf*) *n* (*bother*) Theater *nt* ▷ *vt* schikanieren

haste [heɪst] *n* Hast *f*; (*speed*) Eile *f*; **in** ~ in Eile

hasten ['heɪsn] *vt* beschleunigen ▷ *vi*: **to** ~ **to do sth** sich beeilen, etw zu tun; **I** ~ **to add ...** ich muss allerdings hinzufügen, ...; **she** ~**ed back to the house** sie eilte zum Haus zurück

hastily ['heɪstɪlɪ] *adv* (*see adj*) hastig, eilig; vorschnell

hasty ['heɪstɪ] *adj* hastig, eilig; (*rash*) vorschnell

hat [hæt] *n* Hut *m*; **to keep sth under one's** ~ etw für sich behalten

hatbox ['hætbɔks] *n* Hutschachtel *f*

hatch [hætʃ] *n* (*Naut: also*: **hatchway**) Luke *f*; (*also*: **service hatch**) Durchreiche *f* ▷ *vi* (*bird*) ausschlüpfen ▷ *vt* ausbrüten; **the eggs** ~**ed after 10 days** nach 10 Tagen schlüpften die Jungen aus

hatchback ['hætʃbæk] *n* (*Aut: car*) Heckklappenmodell *nt*

hatchet ['hætʃɪt] *n* Beil *nt*; **to bury the** ~ das Kriegsbeil begraben

hatchet job (*inf*) *adj*: **to do a** ~ **on sb** jdn fertigmachen

hatchet man (*inf*) *n* (*fig*) Vollstrecker *m*

hate [heɪt] *vt* hassen ▷ *n* Hass *m*; **I** ~ **him/milk** ich kann ihn/ Milch nicht ausstehen; **to** ~ **to do/doing sth** es hassen, etw zu tun; (*weaker*) etw ungern tun; **I** ~ **to trouble you, but ...** es ist mir sehr unangenehm, dass ich Sie belästigen muss, aber ...

hateful ['heɪtful] *adj* abscheulich

hater ['heɪtəʳ] *n* Hasser(in) *m(f)*; **cop-** ~ Bullenhasser(in) *m(f)*; **woman-**~ Frauenhasser *m*

hatred ['heɪtrɪd] *n* Hass *m*; (*dislike*) Abneigung *f*

hat trick *n* Hattrick *m*

haughty ['hɔːtɪ] *adj* überheblich

haul [hɔːl] *vt* ziehen; (*by lorry*) transportieren; (*Naut*) den Kurs ändern +*gen* ▷ *n* Beute *f*; (*of fish*) Fang *m*; **he** ~**ed himself out of the pool** er stemmte sich aus dem Schwimmbecken

haulage ['hɔːlɪdʒ] *n* (*cost*) Transportkosten *pl*; (*business*) Transport *m*

haulage contractor (*Brit*) *n* Transportunternehmen *nt*, Spedition *f*; (*person*) Transportunternehmer(in) *m(f)*, Spediteur *m*

hauler ['hɔːləʳ] (*US*) *n* Transportunternehmer(in) *m(f)*, Spediteur *m*

haulier ['hɔːlɪəʳ] (*Brit*) *n* Transportunternehmer(in) *m(f)*, Spediteur *m*

haunch [hɔːntʃ] *n* Hüftpartie *f*; (*of meat*) Keule *f*

haunt [hɔːnt] *vt* (*place*) spuken in +*dat*, umgehen in +*dat*; (*person, fig*) verfolgen ▷ *n* Lieblingsplatz *m*; (*of crooks etc*) Treffpunkt *m*

haunted ['hɔːntɪd] *adj* (*expression*) gehetzt, gequält; **this building/room is** ~ in diesem Gebäude/Zimmer spukt es

haunting ['hɔːntɪŋ] *adj* (*music*) eindringlich; **a** ~ **sight** ein Anblick, der einen nicht loslässt

Havana [hə'vænə] *n* Havanna *nt*

⊙ KEYWORD

have [hæv] (*pt, pp* **had**) *aux vb* **1** haben; (*with verbs of motion*) sein; **to have arrived/gone** angekommen/gegangen sein; **to have eaten/slept** gegessen/geschlafen haben; **he has been promoted** er ist befördert worden; **having eaten** *or* **when he had eaten, he left** nachdem er gegessen hatte, ging er

2 (*in tag questions*): **you've done it, haven't you?** du hast es gemacht, nicht wahr?; **he hasn't done it, has he?** er hat es nicht gemacht, oder?

3 (*in short answers and questions*): **you've made a mistake — no I haven't/so I have** du hast einen Fehler gemacht — nein(, das habe ich nicht)/ja, stimmt; **we haven't paid — yes we have!** wir haben nicht bezahlt — doch!; **I've been there before — have you?** ich war schon einmal da — wirklich *or* tatsächlich? ▷ *modal aux vb* (*be obliged*): **to have (got) to do sth** etw tun müssen; **this has (got) to be a mistake** das muss ein Fehler sein ▷ *vt* **1** (*possess*) haben; **she has (got) blue eyes/ dark hair** sie hat blaue Augen/dunkle Haare; **I have (got) an idea** ich habe eine Idee

2 (*referring to meals etc*): **to have breakfast** frühstücken; **to have lunch/dinner** zu Mittag/Abend essen; **to have a drink** etwas trinken; **to have a cigarette** eine Zigarette rauchen

3 (*receive, obtain etc*) haben; **may I have your address?** kann ich Ihre Adresse haben *or* bekommen?; **to have a baby** ein Kind bekommen

4 (*allow*): **I won't have this nonsense** dieser Unsinn kommt nicht infrage!; **we can't have that** das kommt nicht infrage

5: **to have sth done** etw machen lassen; **to have one's hair cut** sich *dat* die Haare schneiden lassen; **to have sb do sth** (*order*) jdn etw tun lassen; **he soon had them all laughing/working** bald hatte er alle zum Lachen/Arbeiten gebracht

h

591

6 (*experience, suffer*): **to have a cold/flu** eine Erkältung/die Grippe haben; **she had her bag stolen** ihr *dat* wurde die Tasche gestohlen **7** (+ *noun: take, hold etc*): **to have a swim** schwimmen gehen; **to have a walk** spazieren gehen; **to have a rest** sich ausruhen; **to have a meeting** eine Besprechung haben; **to have a party** eine Party geben **8** (*inf: dupe*): **you've been had** man hat dich hereingelegt

▸ **have in** (*inf*) *vt*: **to have it in for sb** jdn auf dem Kieker haben

▸ **have on** *vt* (*wear*) anhaben; (*Brit: inf: tease*) auf den Arm nehmen; **I don't have any money on me** ich habe kein Geld bei mir; **do you have** *or* **have you anything on tomorrow?** haben Sie morgen etwas vor?

▸ **have out** *vt*: **to have it out with sb** (*settle a problem etc*) ein Wort mit jdm reden

haven ['heɪvn] *n* Hafen *m*; (*safe place*) Zufluchtsort *m*
haven't ['hævnt] = **have not**
haversack ['hævəsæk] *n* Rucksack *m*
haves [hævz] (*inf*) *npl*: **the ~ and the have-nots** die Betuchten und die Habenichtse
havoc ['hævək] *n* Verwüstung *f*; (*confusion*) Chaos *nt*; **to play ~ with sth** (*disrupt*) etw völlig durcheinanderbringen
Hawaii [hə'waɪiː] *n* Hawaii *nt*
Hawaiian [hə'waɪjən] *adj* hawaiisch ▷ *n* Hawaiianer(in) *m(f)*; (*Ling*) Hawaiisch *nt*
hawk [hɔːk] *n* Habicht *m*
hawker ['hɔːkəʳ] *n* Hausierer(in) *m(f)*
hawkish ['hɔːkɪʃ] *adj* (*person, approach*) knallhart
hawthorn ['hɔːθɔːn] *n* Weißdorn *m*, Rotdorn *m*
hay [heɪ] *n* Heu *nt*
hay fever *n* Heuschnupfen *m*
haystack ['heɪstæk] *n* Heuhaufen *m*
haywire ['heɪwaɪəʳ] (*inf*) *adj*: **to go ~** (*machine*) verrücktspielen; (*plans etc*) über den Haufen geworfen werden
hazard ['hæzəd] *n* Gefahr *f* ▷ *vt* riskieren; **to be a health/fire ~** eine Gefahr für die Gesundheit/feuergefährlich sein; **to ~ a guess** (es) wagen, eine Vermutung anzustellen
hazard lights (*Aut*) Warnblinkanlage *f*
hazardous ['hæzədəs] *adj* gefährlich
hazard pay (*US*) *n* Gefahrenzulage *f*
hazard warning lights *npl* = **hazard lights**
haze [heɪz] *n* Dunst *m*
hazel ['heɪzl] *n* Hasel(nuss)strauch *m*, Haselbusch *m* ▷ *adj* haselnussbraun
hazelnut ['heɪzlnʌt] *n* Haselnuss *f*
hazy ['heɪzɪ] *adj* dunstig, diesig; (*idea, memory*) unklar, verschwommen; **I'm rather ~ about the details** an die Einzelheiten kann ich mich nur vage *or* verschwommen erinnern; (*ignorant*) die genauen Einzelheiten sind mir nicht bekannt
H-bomb ['eɪtbɔm] *n* H-Bombe *f*
HD *n abbr* (= *high definition*) hochauflösend

HDTV *n abbr* (= *high definition television*) hochauflösendes Fernsehen
HE *abbr* (*Rel, Diplomacy*: = *His/Her Excellency*) Seine/Ihre Exzellenz; (= *high explosive*) hochexplosiver Sprengstoff *m*
he [hiː] *pron* er ▷ *pref* männlich; **he who ...** wer ...
head [hɛd] *n* Kopf *m*; (*of table*) Kopfende *nt*; (*of queue*) Spitze *f*; (*of company, organization*) Leiter(in) *m(f)*; (*of school*) Schulleiter(in) *m(f)*; (*on coin*) Kopfseite *f*; (*on tape recorder*) Tonkopf *m* ▷ *vt* anführen, an der Spitze stehen von; (*group, company*) leiten; (*Football: ball*) köpfen; **~s (or tails)** Kopf (oder Zahl); **~ over heels** Hals über Kopf; (*in love*) bis über beide Ohren; **£10 a** *or* **per ~** 10 Pfund pro Kopf; **at the ~ of the list** oben auf der Liste; **to have a ~ for business** einen guten Geschäftssinn haben; **to have no ~ for heights** nicht schwindelfrei sein; **to come to a ~** sich zuspitzen; **they put their ~s together** sie haben sich zusammengesetzt; **off the top of my** *etc* **~** ohne lange zu überlegen; **on your own ~ be it!** auf Ihre eigene Verantwortung *or* Kappe (*inf*)!; **to bite** *or* **snap sb's ~ off** jdn grob anfahren; **he won't bite your ~ off** er wird dir schon nicht den Kopf abreißen; **it went to my ~** es ist mir in den Kopf *or* zu Kopf gestiegen; **to lose/keep one's ~** den Kopf verlieren/nicht verlieren; **I can't make ~ nor tail of this** hieraus werde ich nicht schlau; **he's off his ~!** (*inf*) er ist nicht (ganz) bei Trost!

▸ **head for** *vt fus* (*on foot*) zusteuern auf +*acc*; (*by car*) in Richtung ... fahren; (*plane, ship*) Kurs nehmen auf +*acc*; **you are ~ing for trouble** du wirst Ärger bekommen

▸ **head off** *vt* abwenden

headache ['hɛdeɪk] *n* Kopfschmerzen *pl*, Kopfweh *nt*; (*fig*) Problem *nt*; **to have a ~** Kopfschmerzen *or* Kopfweh haben
headband ['hɛdbænd] *n* Stirnband *nt*
headboard ['hɛdbɔːd] *n* Kopfteil *nt*
head cold *n* Kopfgrippe *f*
headdress ['hɛddrɛs] (*Brit*) *n* Kopfschmuck *m*
headed notepaper ['hɛdɪd-] *n* Schreibpapier *nt* mit Briefkopf
header ['hɛdəʳ] (*Brit: inf*) *n* (*Football*) Kopfball *m*
headfirst ['hɛd'fɜːst] *adv* (*lit*) kopfüber; (*fig*) Hals über Kopf
head-hunt ['hɛdhʌnt] *vt* abwerben
head-hunter ['hɛdhʌntəʳ] *n* (*Comm*) Kopfjäger(in) *m(f)*
heading ['hɛdɪŋ] *n* Überschrift *f*
headlamp ['hɛdlæmp] (*Brit*) *n* = **headlight**
headland ['hɛdlənd] *n* Landspitze *f*
headlight ['hɛdlaɪt] *n* Scheinwerfer *m*
headline ['hɛdlaɪn] *n* Schlagzeile *f*; (*Radio, TV*): **(news) ~s** Nachrichtenüberblick *m*
headlong ['hɛdlɔŋ] *adv* kopfüber; (*rush*) Hals über Kopf
headmaster [hɛd'mɑːstəʳ] *n* Schulleiter *m*
headmistress [hɛd'mɪstrɪs] *n* Schulleiterin *f*
head office *n* Zentrale *f*

head of state (*pl* **heads of state**) *n*
Staatsoberhaupt *nt*
head-on ['hɛd'ɔn] *adj* (*collision*) frontal;
(*confrontation*) direkt
headphones ['hɛdfəunz] *npl* Kopfhörer *pl*
headquarters ['hɛdkwɔ:təz] *npl* Zentrale *f*;
(*Mil*) Hauptquartier *nt*
headrest ['hɛdrɛst] *n* (*Aut*) Kopfstütze *f*
headroom ['hɛdrum] *n* (*in car*) Kopfraum *m*;
(*under bridge*) lichte Höhe *f*
headscarf ['hɛdskɑ:f] *n* Kopftuch *nt*
headset ['hɛdsɛt] *n* = **headphones**
head start *n* Vorsprung *m*
headstone ['hɛdstəun] *n* Grabstein *m*
headstrong ['hɛdstrɔŋ] *adj* eigensinnig
head waiter *n* Oberkellner *m*
headway ['hɛdweɪ] *n*: **to make ~**
vorankommen
headwind ['hɛdwɪnd] *n* Gegenwind *m*
heady ['hɛdɪ] *adj* (*experience etc*) aufregend;
(*drink, atmosphere*) berauschend
heal [hi:l] *vt, vi* heilen
health [hɛlθ] *n* Gesundheit *f*
health care *n* Gesundheitsfürsorge *f*
health centre (*Brit*) *n* Ärztezentrum *nt*
health food *n* Reformkost *f*, Naturkost *f*
health food shop *n* Reformhaus *nt*,
Naturkostladen *m*
health hazard *n* Gefahr *f* für die Gesundheit
health service (*Brit*) *n*: **the Health Service**
das Gesundheitswesen
healthy ['hɛlθɪ] *adj* gesund; (*profit*) ansehnlich
heap [hi:p] *n* Haufen *m* ▷ *vt*: **to ~ (up)** (auf)
häufen; **~s of** (*inf*) jede Menge; **to ~ sth with**
etw beladen mit; **to ~ sth on** etw häufen auf
+*acc*; **to ~ favours/gifts** *etc* **on sb** jdn mit
Gefälligkeiten/Geschenken *etc* überhäufen;
to ~ praises on sb jdn mit Lob überschütten
hear [hɪər] (*pt, pp* **~d**) *vt* hören; (*Law: case*)
verhandeln; (: *witness*) vernehmen; **to ~ about**
hören von; **to ~ from sb** von jdm hören; **I've
never ~d of that book** von dem Buch habe
ich noch nie etwas gehört; **I wouldn't ~ of it!**
davon will ich nichts hören
▶ **hear out** *vt* ausreden lassen
heard [hə:d] *pt, pp of* **hear**
hearing ['hɪərɪŋ] *n* Gehör *nt*; (*of facts,
by committee*) Anhörung *f*; (*of witnesses*)
Vernehmung *f*; (*of a case*) Verhandlung *f*; **to
give sb a ~** (*Brit*) jdn anhören
hearing aid *n* Hörgerät *nt*
hearsay ['hɪəseɪ] *n* Gerüchte *pl*; **by ~** vom
Hörensagen
hearse [hə:s] *n* Leichenwagen *m*
heart [hɑ:t] *n* Herz *nt*; (*of problem*) Kern *m*;
hearts *npl* (*Cards*) Herz *nt*; **to lose ~** den Mut
verlieren; **to take ~** Mut fassen; **at ~** im
Grunde; **by ~** auswendig; **to set one's ~ on**
sth sein Herz an etw *acc* hängen; **to set one's
~ on doing sth** alles daransetzen, etw zu tun;
the ~ of the matter der Kern der Sache
heartache ['hɑ:teɪk] *n* Kummer *m*
heart attack *n* Herzanfall *m*

heartbeat ['hɑ:tbi:t] *n* Herzschlag *m*
heartbreak ['hɑ:tbreɪk] *n* großer Kummer *m*,
Leid *nt*
heartbreaking ['hɑ:tbreɪkɪŋ] *adj*
herzzerreißend
heartbroken ['hɑ:tbrəukən] *adj*: **to be ~**
todunglücklich sein
heartburn ['hɑ:tbə:n] *n* Sodbrennen *nt*
-hearted ['hɑ:tɪd] *suff*: **kind-~** gutherzig
heartening ['hɑ:tnɪŋ] *adj* ermutigend
heart failure *n* Herzversagen *nt*
heartfelt ['hɑ:tfɛlt] *adj* tief empfunden
hearth [hɑ:θ] *n* = Kamin *m*
heartily ['hɑ:tɪlɪ] *adv* (*see adj*) (laut und)
herzlich; herzhaft; tief; ungeteilt
heartland ['hɑ:tlænd] *n* Herz *nt*;
Britain's industrial ~ Großbritanniens
Industriezentrum *nt*
heartless ['hɑ:tlɪs] *adj* herzlos
heartstrings ['hɑ:tstrɪŋz] *npl*: **to tug at sb's ~**
bei jdm auf die Tränendrüsen drücken
heart-throb ['hɑ:tθrɔb] (*inf*) *n* Schwarm *m*
heart-to-heart ['hɑ:t'tə'hɑ:t] *adj, adv* ganz im
Vertrauen
heart transplant *n* Herztransplantation *f*,
Herzverpflanzung *f*
heart-warming ['hɑ:twɔ:mɪŋ] *adj*
herzerfreuend
hearty ['hɑ:tɪ] *adj* (*person*) laut und herzlich;
(*laugh, appetite*) herzhaft; (*welcome*) herzlich;
(*dislike*) tief; (*support*) ungeteilt
heat [hi:t] *n* Hitze *f*; (*warmth*) Wärme
f; (*temperature*) Temperatur *f*; (*Sport: also*:
qualifying heat) Vorrunde *f* ▷ *vt* erhitzen,
heiß machen; (*room, house*) heizen; **in ~, on ~**
(*Brit: Zool*) brünstig, läufig
▶ **heat up** *vi* sich erwärmen, warm werden
▷ *vt* aufwärmen; (*water, room*) erwärmen
heated ['hi:tɪd] *adj* geheizt; (*pool*) beheizt;
(*argument*) hitzig
heater ['hi:tər] *n* (Heiz)ofen *m*; (*in car*) Heizung *f*
heath [hi:θ] (*Brit*) *n* Heide *f*
heathen ['hi:ðn] *n* Heide *m*, Heidin *f*
heather ['hɛðər] *n* Heidekraut *nt*, Erika *f*
heating ['hi:tɪŋ] *n* Heizung *f*
heat-resistant ['hi:trɪzɪstənt] *adj*
hitzebeständig
heat-seeking ['hi:tsi:kɪŋ] *adj* Wärme suchend
heatstroke ['hi:tstrəuk] *n* Hitzschlag *m*
heat wave *n* Hitzewelle *f*
heave [hi:v] *vt* (*pull*) ziehen; (*push*) schieben;
(*lift*) (hoch)heben ▷ *vi* sich heben und senken;
(*retch*) sich übergeben ▷ *n* (*see vt*) Zug *m*; Stoß *m*;
Heben *nt*; **to ~ a sigh** einen Seufzer ausstoßen
▶ **heave to** (*pt, pp* **hove**) *vi* (*Naut*) beidrehen
heaven ['hɛvn] *n* Himmel *m*; **thank ~!** Gott sei
Dank!; **~ forbid!** bloß nicht!; **for ~'s sake!** um
Himmels *or* Gottes willen!
heavenly ['hɛvnlɪ] *adj* himmlisch
heaven-sent [hɛvn'sɛnt] *adj* ideal
heavily ['hɛvɪlɪ] *adv* schwer; (*drink, smoke,
depend, rely*) stark; (*sleep, sigh*) tief; (*say*) mit
schwerer Stimme

h

593

heavy ['hɛvɪ] *adj* schwer; (*clothes*) dick; (*rain, snow, drinker, smoker*) stark; (*build, frame*) kräftig; (*breathing, sleep*) tief; (*schedule, week*) anstrengend; (*weather*) drückend, schwül; **the conversation was ~ going** die Unterhaltung war mühsam; **the book was ~ going** das Buch las sich schwer

heavy cream (*US*) *n Sahne mit hohem Fettgehalt,* ≈ Schlagsahne *f*

heavy-duty ['hɛvɪ'dju:tɪ] *adj* strapazierfähig

heavy goods vehicle *n* Lastkraftwagen *m*

heavy-handed ['hɛvɪ'hændɪd] *adj* schwerfällig, ungeschickt

heavy industry *n* Schwerindustrie *f*

heavy metal *n* (*Mus*) Heavymetal *nt*

heavyset ['hɛvɪ'sɛt] (*esp US*) *adj* kräftig gebaut

heavyweight ['hɛvɪweɪt] *n* (*Sport*) Schwergewicht *nt*

Hebrew ['hi:bru:] *adj* hebräisch ▷ *n* (*Ling*) Hebräisch *nt*

Hebrides ['hɛbrɪdi:z] *npl*: **the ~** die Hebriden *pl*

heck [hɛk] (*inf*) *interj*: **oh ~!** zum Kuckuck! ▷ *n*: **a ~ of a lot** irrsinnig viel

heckle ['hɛkl] *vt* durch Zwischenrufe stören

heckler ['hɛklə'] *n* Zwischenrufer(in) *m(f)*, Störer(in) *m(f)*

hectare ['hɛktɑ:'] (*Brit*) *n* Hektar *nt or m*

hectic ['hɛktɪk] *adj* hektisch

hector ['hɛktə'] *vt* tyrannisieren

he'd [hi:d] = **he would; he had**

hedge [hɛdʒ] *n* Hecke *f* ▷ *vi* ausweichen, sich nicht festlegen ▷ *vt*: **to ~ one's bets** (*fig*) sich absichern; **as a ~ against inflation** als Absicherung *or* Schutz gegen die Inflation
  ▸ **hedge in** *vt* (*person*) (in seiner Freiheit) einschränken; (*proposals etc*) behindern

hedgehog ['hɛdʒhɔg] *n* Igel *m*

hedgerow ['hɛdʒrəu] *n* Hecke *f*

hedonism ['hi:dənɪzəm] *n* Hedonismus *m*

heed [hi:d] *vt* (*also*: **take heed of**) beachten ▷ *n*: **to pay (no) ~ to, take (no) ~ of** (nicht) beachten

heedless ['hi:dlɪs] *adj* achtlos; **~ of sb/sth** ohne auf jdn/etw zu achten

heel [hi:l] *n* Ferse *f*; (*of shoe*) Absatz *m* ▷ *vt* (*shoe*) mit einem neuen Absatz versehen; **to bring to ~** (*dog*) bei Fuß gehen lassen; (*fig: person*) an die Kandare nehmen; **to take to one's ~s** (*inf*) sich aus dem Staub machen

hefty ['hɛftɪ] *adj* kräftig; (*parcel etc*) schwer; (*profit*) ansehnlich

heifer ['hɛfə'] *n* Färse *f*

height [haɪt] *n* Höhe *f*; (*of person*) Größe *f*; (*fig: of luxury, good taste etc*) Gipfel *m*; **what ~ are you?** wie groß bist du?; **of average ~** durchschnittlich groß; **to be afraid of ~s** nicht schwindelfrei sein; **it's the ~ of fashion** das ist die neueste Mode; **at the ~ of the tourist season** in der Hauptsaison

heighten ['haɪtn] *vt* erhöhen

heinous ['heɪnəs] *adj* abscheulich, verabscheuungswürdig

heir [ɛə'] *n* Erbe *m*; **the ~ to the throne** der Thronfolger

heir apparent *n* gesetzlicher Erbe *m*

heiress ['ɛərɛs] *n* Erbin *f*

heirloom ['ɛəlu:m] *n* Erbstück *nt*

heist [haɪst] (*US: inf*) *n* Raubüberfall *m*

held [hɛld] *pt, pp of* **hold**

helicopter ['hɛlɪkɔptə'] *n* Hubschrauber *m*

heliport ['hɛlɪpɔ:t] *n* Hubschrauberflugplatz *m*, Heliport *m*

helium ['hi:lɪəm] *n* Helium *nt*

hell [hɛl] *n* Hölle *f*; **~!** (*inf!*) verdammt! (*infl*); **a ~ of a lot** (*inf*) verdammt viel (*inf*); **a ~ of a mess** (*inf*) ein wahnsinniges Chaos (*inf*); **a ~ of a noise** (*inf*) ein Höllenlärm *m*; **a ~ of a nice guy** ein wahnsinnig netter Typ

he'll [hi:l] = **he will; he shall**

hellbent ['hɛl'bɛnt] *adj*: **~ (on)** versessen (auf +*acc*)

hellish ['hɛlɪʃ] (*inf*) *adj* höllisch

hello [hə'ləu] *excl* hallo; (*expressing surprise*) nanu, he

Hell's Angels *npl* Hell's Angels *pl*

helm [hɛlm] *n* Ruder *nt*, Steuer *nt*; **at the ~** am Ruder

helmet ['hɛlmɪt] *n* Helm *m*

helmsman ['hɛlmzmən] (*irreg: like* **man**) *n* Steuermann *m*

help [hɛlp] *n* Hilfe *f*; (*charwoman*) (Haushalts)hilfe *f* ▷ *vt* helfen +*dat*; **with the ~ of** (*person*) mit (der) Hilfe +*gen*; (*tool etc*) mithilfe +*gen*; **to be of ~ to sb** jdm behilflich sein, jdm helfen; **can I ~ you?** (*in shop*) womit kann ich Ihnen dienen?; **~ yourself** bedienen Sie sich; **he can't ~ it** er kann nichts dafür; **I can't ~ thinking that ...** ich kann mir nicht helfen, ich glaube, dass ...

helper ['hɛlpə'] *n* Helfer(in) *m(f)*

helpful ['hɛlpful] *adj* hilfsbereit; (*advice, suggestion*) nützlich, hilfreich

helping ['hɛlpɪŋ] *n* Portion *f*

helping hand *n*: **to give** *or* **lend sb a ~** jdm behilflich sein

helpless ['hɛlplɪs] *adj* hilflos

helplessly ['hɛlplɪslɪ] *adv* hilflos

helpline ['hɛlplaɪn] *n* (*for emergencies*) Notruf *m*; (*for information*) Informationsdienst *m*

Helsinki ['hɛlsɪŋkɪ] *n* Helsinki *nt*

helter-skelter ['hɛltə'skɛltə'] (*Brit*) *n* Rutschbahn *f*

hem [hɛm] *n* Saum *m* ▷ *vt* säumen
  ▸ **hem in** *vt* einschließen, umgeben; **to feel ~med in** (*fig*) sich eingeengt fühlen

hematology ['hi:mə'tɔlədʒɪ] (*US*) *n* = **haematology**

hemisphere ['hɛmɪsfɪə'] *n* Hemisphäre *f*; (*of sphere*) Halbkugel *f*

hemlock ['hɛmlɔk] *n* Schierling *m*

hemoglobin ['hi:mə'gləubɪn] (*US*) *n* = **haemoglobin**

hemophilia ['hi:mə'fɪlɪə] (*US*) *n* = **haemophilia**

hemorrhage ['hɛmərɪdʒ] (*US*) *n* = **haemorrhage**

hemorrhoids ['hɛmərɔɪdz] (*US*) *npl* =

haemorrhoids

hemp [hɛmp] n Hanf m

hen [hɛn] n Henne f, Huhn nt; (female bird) Weibchen nt

hence [hɛns] adv daher; **2 years** ~ in zwei Jahren

henceforth [hɛns'fɔ:θ] adv von nun an; (from that time on) von da an

henchman ['hɛntʃmən] (irreg: like **man**) (pej) n Spießgeselle m

henna ['hɛnə] n Henna nt

hen night, **hen party** (inf) n Damenkränzchen nt; siehe Info-Artikel

⬤ **HEN NIGHT**

⬤ Als hen night bezeichnet man eine
⬤ feuchtfröhliche Frauenparty, die kurz vor
⬤ einer Hochzeit von der Braut und ihren
⬤ Freundinnen meist in einem Gasthaus
⬤ oder Nachtklub abgehalten wird und bei
⬤ der die Freundinnen dafür sorgen, dass vor
⬤ allem die Braut große Mengen an Alkohol
⬤ konsumiert. Siehe auch stag night.

henpecked ['hɛnpɛkt] adj: **to be** ~ unter dem Pantoffel stehen; ~ **husband** Pantoffelheld m

hepatitis [hɛpə'taɪtɪs] n Hepatitis f

her [hə:ʳ] pron sie; (indirect) ihr ▷ adj ihr; **I see** ~ ich sehe sie; **give** ~ **a book** gib ihr ein Buch; **after** ~ nach ihr; see also **me**; **my**

herald ['hɛrəld] n (Vor)bote m ▷ vt ankündigen

heraldic [he'rældɪk] adj heraldisch, Wappen-

heraldry ['hɛrəldrɪ] n Wappenkunde f, Heraldik f; (coats of arms) Wappen pl

herb [hə:b] n Kraut nt

herbaceous [hə:'beɪʃəs] adj: ~ **border** Staudenrabatte f; ~ **plant** Staude f

herbal ['hə:bl] adj (tea, medicine) Kräuter-

herbicide ['hə:bɪsaɪd] n Unkrautvertilgungsmittel nt, Herbizid nt

herd [hə:d] n Herde f; (of wild animals) Rudel nt ▷ vt treiben; (gather) zusammentreiben; ~**ed together** zusammengetrieben

here [hɪəʳ] adv hier; **she left** ~ **yesterday** sie ist gestern von hier abgereist; ~ **is/are** ..., ~ **you are** (giving) (hier,) bitte; ~ **we are!** (finding sth) da ist es ja!; ~ **she is!** da ist sie ja!; ~ **she comes** da kommt sie ja; **come** ~! komm hierher or hierhin!; ~ **and there** hier und da; "~'**s to** ..." „auf ... acc"

hereabouts ['hɪərə'baʊts] adv hier

hereafter [hɪər'ɑ:ftəʳ] adv künftig

hereby [hɪə'baɪ] adv hiermit

hereditary [hɪ'rɛdɪtrɪ] adj erblich, Erb-

heredity [hɪ'rɛdɪtɪ] n Vererbung f

heresy ['hɛrəsɪ] n Ketzerei f

heretic ['hɛrətɪk] n Ketzer(in) m(f)

heretical [hɪ'rɛtɪkl] adj ketzerisch

herewith [hɪə'wɪð] adv hiermit

heritage ['hɛrɪtɪdʒ] n Erbe nt; **our national** ~ unser nationales Erbe

hermetically [hə:'mɛtɪklɪ] adv: ~ **sealed**

hermetisch verschlossen

hermit ['hə:mɪt] n Einsiedler(in) m(f)

hernia ['hə:nɪə] n Bruch m

hero ['hɪərəʊ] (pl ~**es**) n Held m; (idol) Idol nt

heroic [hɪ'rəʊɪk] adj heroisch; (figure, person) heldenhaft

heroin ['hɛrəʊɪn] n Heroin nt

heroin addict n Heroinsüchtige(r) f(m)

heroine ['hɛrəʊɪn] n Heldin f; (idol) Idol nt

heroism ['hɛrəʊɪzəm] n Heldentum nt

heron ['hɛrən] n Reiher m

hero worship n Heldenverehrung f

herring ['hɛrɪŋ] n Hering m

hers [hə:z] pron ihre(r, s); **a friend of** ~ ein Freund von ihr; **this is** ~ das gehört ihr; see also **mine**

herself [hə:'sɛlf] pron sich; (emphatic) (sie) selbst; see also **oneself**

Herts [hɑ:ts] (Brit) abbr (Post) = Hertfordshire

he's [hi:z] = **he is**; **he has**

hesitant ['hɛzɪtənt] adj zögernd; **to be** ~ **about doing sth** zögern, etw zu tun

hesitate ['hɛzɪteɪt] vi zögern; (be unwilling) Bedenken haben; **to** ~ **about** Bedenken haben wegen; **don't** ~ **to see a doctor if you are worried** gehen Sie ruhig zum Arzt, wenn Sie sich Sorgen machen

hesitation [hɛzɪ'teɪʃən] n Zögern nt; Bedenken pl; **to have no** ~ **in saying sth** etw ohne Weiteres sagen können

hessian ['hɛsɪən] n Sackleinwand f, Rupfen m

heterogenous [hɛtə'rɒdʒɪnəs] adj heterogen

heterosexual ['hɛtərəʊ'sɛksjʊəl] adj heterosexuell ▷ n Heterosexuelle(r) f(m)

het up [hɛt-] (inf) adj: **to get** ~ **(about)** sich aufregen (über +acc)

HEW (US) n abbr (= Department of Health, Education and Welfare) Ministerium für Gesundheit, Erziehung und Sozialfürsorge

hew [hju:] (pt, pp **hewed** or ~**n**) vt (stone) behauen; (wood) hacken

hex [hɛks] (US) n Fluch m ▷ vt verhexen

hexagon ['hɛksəgən] n Sechseck nt

hexagonal [hɛk'sægənl] adj sechseckig

hey [heɪ] excl he; (to attract attention) he du/Sie

heyday ['heɪdeɪ] n: **the** ~ **of** (person) die Glanzzeit +gen; (nation, group etc) die Blütezeit +gen

HF n abbr (= high frequency) HF

HGV (Brit) n abbr (Hist: = heavy goods vehicle) Lkw m

HI (US) abbr (Post) = Hawaii

hi [haɪ] excl hallo

hiatus [haɪ'eɪtəs] n Unterbrechung f

hibernate ['haɪbəneɪt] vi Winterschlaf halten or machen

hibernation [haɪbə'neɪʃən] n Winterschlaf m

hiccough ['hɪkʌp] vi hicksen

hiccoughs ['hɪkʌps] npl Schluckauf m; **to have (the)** ~ den Schluckauf haben

hiccup ['hɪkʌp] vi = **hiccough**

hiccups ['hɪkʌps] npl = **hiccoughs**

hick [hɪk] (US: inf) n Hinterwäldler m

hid [hɪd] pt of **hide**

hidden ['hɪdn] *pp of* **hide** ▷ *adj* (*advantage, danger*) unsichtbar; (*place*) versteckt; **there are no ~ extras** es gibt keine versteckten Extrakosten

hide [haɪd] (*pt* **hid**, *pp* **hidden**) *n* Haut *f*, Fell *nt*; (*of birdwatcher etc*) Versteck *nt* ▷ *vt* verstecken; (*feeling, information*) verbergen; (*obscure*) verdecken ▷ *vi*: **to ~ (from sb)** sich (vor jdm) verstecken; **to ~ sth (from sb)** etw (vor jdm) verstecken

hide-and-seek ['haɪdən'siːk] *n* Versteckspiel *nt*; **to play ~** Verstecken spielen

hideaway ['haɪdəweɪ] *n* Zufluchtsort *m*

hideous ['hɪdɪəs] *adj* scheußlich; (*conditions*) furchtbar

hideously ['hɪdɪəslɪ] *adv* furchtbar

hide-out ['haɪdaut] *n* Versteck *nt*

hiding ['haɪdɪŋ] *n* Tracht *f* Prügel; **to be in ~** (*concealed*) sich versteckt halten

hiding place *n* Versteck *nt*

hierarchy ['haɪəraːkɪ] *n* Hierarchie *f*

hieroglyphics [haɪərə'glɪfɪks] *npl* Hieroglyphen *pl*

hi-fi ['haɪfaɪ] *n abbr* (= *high fidelity*) Hi-Fi *nt* ▷ *adj* (*equipment etc*) Hi-Fi-

higgledy-piggledy ['hɪgldɪ'pɪgldɪ] *adj* durcheinander

high [haɪ] *adj* hoch; (*wind*) stark; (*risk*) groß; (*quality*) gut; (*inf: on drugs*) high; (: *on drink*) blau; (*Brit: food*) schlecht; (: *game*) anbrüchig ▷ *adv* hoch ▷ *n*: **exports have reached a new ~** der Export hat einen neuen Höchststand erreicht; **to pay a ~ price for sth** etw teuer bezahlen; **it's ~ time you did it** es ist *or* wird höchste Zeit, dass du es machst; **~ in the air** hoch oben in der Luft

highball ['haɪbɔːl] (*US*) *n* Highball *m*

highboy ['haɪbɔɪ] (*US*) *n* hohe Kommode *f*

highbrow ['haɪbrau] *adj* intellektuell; (*book, discussion etc*) anspruchsvoll

highchair ['haɪtʃɛəʳ] *n* Hochstuhl *m*

high-class ['haɪ'klaːs] *adj* erstklassig; (*neighbourhood*) vornehm

⊛ **HIGH COURT**

⊚ High Court ist in England und Wales
⊚ die Kurzform für „High Court of
⊚ Justice" und bildet zusammen mit
⊚ dem Berufungsgericht den Obersten
⊚ Gerichtshof. In Schottland ist es die
⊚ Kurzform für „High Court of Justiciary",
⊚ das höchste Strafgericht in Schottland, das
⊚ in Edinburgh und anderen Großstädten
⊚ (immer mit Richter und Geschworenen)
⊚ zusammentritt und für Verbrechen wie
⊚ Mord, Vergewaltigung und Hochverrat
⊚ zuständig ist. Weniger schwere
⊚ Verbrechen werden vor dem „sheriff
⊚ court" verhandelt und leichtere Vergehen
⊚ vor dem „district court".

higher ['haɪəʳ] *adj* (*form of study, life etc*) höher (entwickelt) ▷ *adv* höher ▷ *n* (*Scot: Scol*): **H~** mit

„Higher" wird die vorgeschrittenenstufe des „Scottish certificate of education" und auch der Abschluss dieses Ausbildungsjahr bezeichnet

higher education *n* Hochschulbildung *f*

highfalutin [haɪfə'luːtɪn] (*inf*) *adj* hochtrabend

high finance *n* Hochfinanz *f*

high-flier, high-flyer [haɪ'flaɪəʳ] *n* Senkrechtstarter(in) *m(f)*

high-flying [haɪ'flaɪɪŋ] *adj* (*person*) erfolgreich; (*lifestyle*) exklusiv

high-handed [haɪ'hændɪd] *adj* eigenmächtig

high-heeled [haɪ'hiːld] *adj* hochhackig

high heels *npl* hochhackige Schuhe *pl*

high jump *n* Hochsprung *m*

Highlands ['haɪləndz] *npl*: **the ~** das Hochland

high-level ['haɪlɛvl] *adj* (*talks etc*) auf höchster Ebene; **~ language** (*Comput*) höhere Programmiersprache *f*

highlight ['haɪlaɪt] *n* (*of event*) Höhepunkt *m*; (*in hair*) Strähnchen *nt* ▷ *vt* (*problem, need*) ein Schlaglicht werfen auf +*acc*

highlighter ['haɪlaɪtəʳ] *n* Textmarker *m*

highly ['haɪlɪ] *adv* hoch-; **to speak ~ of** sich sehr positiv äußern über +*acc*; **to think ~ of** eine hohe Meinung haben von

highly strung *adj* nervös

High Mass *n* Hochamt *nt*

highness ['haɪnɪs] *n*: **Her/His/Your H~** Ihre/Seine/Eure Hoheit *f*

high-pitched [haɪ'pɪtʃt] *adj* hoch

high point *n* Höhepunkt *m*

high-powered ['haɪ'pauəd] *adj* (*engine*) Hochleistungs-; (*job*) Spitzen-; (*businessman*) dynamisch; (*person*) äußerst fähig; (*course*) anspruchsvoll

high-pressure ['haɪprɛʃəʳ] *adj* (*area, system*) Hochdruck-; (*inf: sales technique*) aggressiv

high-rise ['haɪraɪz] *adj* (*apartment, block*) Hochhaus-; **~ building/flats** Hochhaus *nt*

high school *n* ≈ Oberschule *f*

⊛ **HIGH SCHOOL**

⊚ High school ist eine weiterführende Schule
⊚ in den USA. Man unterscheidet zwischen
⊚ „junior high school" (im Anschluss
⊚ an die Grundschule, umfasst des 7.,
⊚ 8. und 9. Schuljahr) und „senior high
⊚ school" (10., 11. und 12. Schuljahr, mit
⊚ akademischen und berufsbezogenen
⊚ Fächern). Weiterführende Schulen in
⊚ Großbritannien werden manchmal auch
⊚ als high school bezeichnet. Siehe auch
⊚ „elementary school".

high season (*Brit*) *n* Hochsaison *f*

high spirits *npl* Hochstimmung *f*

high street (*Brit*) *n* Hauptstraße *f*

high strung (*US*) *adj* = **highly strung**

high tide *n* Flut *f*

highway ['haɪweɪ] (*US*) *n* Straße *f*; (*between towns, states*) Landstraße *f*; **information ~** Datenautobahn *f*

Highway Code (Brit) n
Straßenverkehrsordnung f
highwayman ['haɪweɪmən] (irreg: like **man**) n
Räuber m, Wegelagerer m
hijack ['haɪdʒæk] vt entführen ▷ n
(also: **hijacking**) Entführung f
hijacker ['haɪdʒækə'] n Entführer(in) m(f)
hike [haɪk] vi wandern ▷ n Wanderung f; (inf: in
prices etc) Erhöhung f ▷ vt (inf) erhöhen
hiker ['haɪkə'] n Wanderer m, Wanderin f
hiking ['haɪkɪŋ] n Wandern nt
hilarious [hɪ'lɛərɪəs] adj urkomisch
hilarity [hɪ'lærɪtɪ] n übermütige
Ausgelassenheit f
hill [hɪl] n Hügel m; (fairly high) Berg m; (slope)
Hang m; (on road) Steigung f
hillbilly ['hɪlbɪlɪ] (US) n Hillbilly m; (pej)
Hinterwäldler(in) m(f), Landpomeranze f
hillock ['hɪlək] n Hügel m, Anhöhe f
hillside ['hɪlsaɪd] n Hang m
hill start n (Aut) Anfahren nt am Berg
hilltop ['hɪltɔp] n Gipfel m
hill walking n Bergwandern nt
hilly ['hɪlɪ] adj hügelig
hilt [hɪlt] n (of sword, knife) Heft nt; **to the ~** voll
und ganz
him [hɪm] pron ihn; (indirect) ihm; see also **me**
Himalayas [hɪmə'leɪəz] npl: **the ~** der
Himalaja
himself [hɪm'sɛlf] pron sich; (emphatic) (er)
selbst; see also **oneself**
hind [haɪnd] adj (legs) Hinter- ▷ n (female deer)
Hirschkuh f
hinder ['hɪndə'] vt behindern; **to ~ sb from
doing sth** jdn daran hindern, etw zu tun
hindquarters ['haɪnd'kwɔːtəz] npl Hinterteil nt
hindrance ['hɪndrəns] n Behinderung f
hindsight ['haɪndsaɪt] n: **with ~** im
Nachhinein
Hindu ['hɪnduː] adj hinduistisch, Hindu-
hinge [hɪndʒ] n (on door) Angel f ▷ vi: **to ~ on**
anhängen von
hint [hɪnt] n Andeutung f; (advice) Tipp m;
(sign, glimmer) Spur f ▷ vt: **to ~ that** andeuten,
dass ▷ vi: **to ~ at** andeuten; **to drop a ~** eine
Andeutung machen; **give me a ~** geben Sie
mir einen Hinweis; **white with a ~ of pink**
weiß mit einem Hauch von Rosa
hip [hɪp] n Hüfte f
hip flask n Taschenflasche f, Flachmann m (inf)
hip-hop ['hɪphɔp] n Hip-Hop nt
hippie ['hɪpɪ] n Hippie m
hippo ['hɪpəu] n Nilpferd nt
hip pocket n Gesäßtasche f
hippopotamus [hɪpə'pɔtəməs] (pl **-es** or
hippopotami) n Nilpferd nt
hippy ['hɪpɪ] n = **hippie**
hire ['haɪə'] vt (Brit) mieten; (worker) einstellen
▷ n (Brit) Mieten nt; **for ~** (taxi) frei; (boat) zu
vermieten; **on ~** gemietet
▸ **hire out** vt vermieten
hire car, hired car (Brit) n Mietwagen m,
Leihwagen m

hire-purchase [haɪə'pəːtʃɪs] (Brit) n Ratenkauf
m; **to buy sth on ~** etw auf Raten kaufen
his [hɪz] pron seine(r, s) ▷ adj sein; see also **my**;
mine²
hiss [hɪs] vi zischen; (cat) fauchen ▷ n Zischen
nt; (of cat) Fauchen nt
histogram ['hɪstəgræm] n Histogramm nt
historian [hɪ'stɔːrɪən] n Historiker(in) m(f)
historic [hɪ'stɔrɪk] adj historisch
historical [hɪ'stɔrɪkl] adj historisch
history ['hɪstərɪ] n Geschichte f; **there's a ~
of heart disease in his family** Herzleiden
liegen bei ihm in der Familie; **medical ~**
Krankengeschichte f
hit [hɪt] n (pt, pp **~**) vt schlagen; (reach,
affect) treffen; (vehicle: another vehicle)
zusammenstoßen mit; (: wall, tree) fahren
gegen; (: more violently) prallen gegen; (: person)
anfahren ▷ n Schlag m; (success) Erfolg m; (song)
Hit m; **to ~ it off with sb** sich gut mit jdm
verstehen; **to ~ the headlines** Schlagzeilen
machen; **to ~ the road** (inf) sich auf den Weg
or die Socken (inf) machen; **to ~ the roof** (inf)
an die Decke or in die Luft gehen
▸ **hit back** vi: **to ~ back at sb** jdn
zurückschlagen; (fig) jdm Kontra geben
▸ **hit out at** vt fus auf jdn losschlagen; (fig) jdn
scharf angreifen
▸ **hit (up)on** vt fus stoßen auf +acc, finden
hit-and-miss ['hɪtən'mɪs] adj = **hit-or-miss**
hit-and-run driver ['hɪtən'rʌn-] n
unfallflüchtiger Fahrer m, unfallflüchtige
Fahrerin f
hitch [hɪtʃ] vt festmachen, anbinden;
(also: **hitch up**) trousers, skirt) hochziehen
▷ n Schwierigkeit f, Problem nt; **to ~ a lift**
trampen, per Anhalter fahren; **technical ~**
technische Panne f
▸ **hitch up** vt anspannen; see also **hitch**
hitchhike ['hɪtʃhaɪk] vi trampen, per Anhalter
fahren
hitchhiker ['hɪtʃhaɪkə'] n Tramper(in) m(f),
Anhalter(in) m(f)
hi-tech ['haɪ'tɛk] adj Hightech-, hoch
technisiert ▷ n Hightech nt, Hochtechnologie f
hitherto [hɪðə'tuː] adv bisher, bis jetzt
hit list n Abschussliste f
hit man (inf) n Killer m
hit-or-miss ['hɪtə'mɪs] adj ungeplant; **to be
a ~ affair** eine unsichere Sache sein; **it's ~
whether ...** es ist nicht zu sagen, ob ...
hit parade n Hitparade f
hits counter n (on website) Zugriffs- or
Besucherzähler m, Counter m
HIV n abbr (= human immunodeficiency virus) HIV;
~-negative HIV-negativ; **~-positive** HIV-
positiv
hive [haɪv] n Bienenkorb m; **to be a ~ of
activity** einem Bienenhaus gleichen
▸ **hive off** (inf) vt ausgliedern, abspalten
hl abbr (= hectolitre) hl
HM abbr (= His/Her Majesty) S./I.M.
HMG (Brit) abbr (= His/Her Majesty's Government)

h

597

die Regierung Seiner/Ihrer Majestät

HMI (Brit) n abbr (Scol: = His/Her Majesty's Inspector) regierungsamtlicher Schulaufsichtsbeauftragter

HMO (US) n abbr (= Health Maintenance Organization) Organisation zur Gesundheitsfürsorge

HMS (Brit) abbr (= His (or Her) Majesty's Ship) Namensteil von Schiffen der Kriegsmarine

HNC (Brit) n abbr (= Higher National Certificate) Berufsschulabschluss

HND (Brit) n abbr (= Higher National Diploma) Qualifikationsnachweis in technischen Fächern

hoard [hɔːd] n (of food) Vorrat m; (of money etc) Schatz m ⊳ vt (food) hamstern; (money) horten

hoarding ['hɔːdɪŋ] (Brit) n Plakatwand f

hoarfrost ['hɔːfrɔst] n (Rau)reif m

hoarse [hɔːs] adj heiser

hoax [həʊks] n (false alarm) blinder Alarm m

hob [hɔb] n Kochmulde f

hobble ['hɔbl] vi humpeln

hobby ['hɔbɪ] n Hobby nt, Steckenpferd nt

hobbyhorse ['hɔbɪhɔːs] n (fig) Lieblingsthema nt

hobnail boot ['hɔbneɪl-] n Nagelschuh m

hobnob ['hɔbnɔb] vi: **to ~ with** auf Du und Du stehen mit

hobo ['həʊbəʊ] (US) n Penner m (inf)

hock [hɔk] n (Brit) weißer Rheinwein m; (of animal) Sprunggelenk nt; (US: Culin) Gelenkstück nt; (inf): **to be in ~** (person: in debt) in Schulden stecken; (object) verpfändet or im Leihhaus sein

hockey ['hɔkɪ] n Hockey nt

hocus-pocus ['həʊkəs'pəʊkəs] n Hokuspokus m; (trickery) faule Tricks pl; (jargon) Jargon m

hod [hɔd] n (for bricks etc) Tragemulde f

hodgepodge ['hɔdʒpɔdʒ] (US) n = **hotchpotch**

hoe [həʊ] n Hacke f ⊳ vt hacken

hog [hɔg] n (Mast)schwein nt ⊳ vt (road) für sich beanspruchen; (telephone etc) in Beschlag nehmen; **to go the whole ~** Nägel mit Köpfen machen

Hogmanay [hɔgmə'neɪ] (Scot) n Silvester nt

hogwash ['hɔgwɔʃ] (inf) n (nonsense) Quatsch m

ho hum ['həʊ'hʌm] interj na gut

hoist [hɔɪst] n Hebevorrichtung f ⊳ vt hochheben; (flag, sail) hissen

hoity-toity [hɔɪtɪ'tɔɪtɪ] (inf: pej) adj hochnäsig

hold [həʊld] (pt, pp **held**) vt halten; (contain) enthalten; (power, qualification) haben; (opinion) vertreten; (meeting) abhalten; (conversation) führen; (prisoner, hostage) festhalten ⊳ vi halten; (be valid) gelten; (weather) sich halten ⊳ n (grasp) Griff m; (of ship, plane) Laderaum m; **to ~ one's head up** den Kopf hochhalten; **to ~ sb responsible/liable** etc jdn verantwortlich/haftbar etc machen; **~ the line!** (Tel) bleiben Sie am Apparat!; **~ it!** Moment mal!; **to ~ one's own** sich behaupten; **he ~s the view that ...** er ist der Meinung or er vertritt die Ansicht, dass ...; **to ~ firm** or **fast** halten; **~ still!**, **~ steady!** stillhalten!; **his luck held** das Glück blieb ihm treu; **I don't ~ with ...** ich bin gegen ...; **to catch** or **get (a) ~ of** sich

festhalten an +dat; **to get ~ of** (fig) finden, auftreiben; **to get ~ of o.s.** sich in den Griff bekommen; **to have a ~ over** in der Hand haben

▶ **hold back** vt zurückhalten; (tears, laughter) unterdrücken; (secret) verbergen; (information) geheim halten

▶ **hold down** vt niederhalten; (job) sich halten in +dat

▶ **hold forth** vi: **to ~ forth (about)** sich ergehen or sich auslassen (über +acc)

▶ **hold off** vt abwehren ⊳ vi: **if the rain ~s off** wenn es nicht regnet

▶ **hold on** vi sich festhalten; (wait) warten; **~ on!** (Tel) einen Moment bitte!

▶ **hold on to** vt fus sich festhalten an; (keep) behalten

▶ **hold out** vt (hand) ausstrecken; (hope) haben; (prospect) bieten ⊳ vi nicht nachgeben

▶ **hold over** vt vertagen

▶ **hold up** vt hochheben; (support) stützen; (delay) aufhalten; (rob) überfallen

holdall ['həʊldɔːl] (Brit) n Tasche f; (for clothes) Reisetasche f

holder ['həʊldəʳ] n Halter m; (of ticket, record, office, title etc) Inhaber(in) m(f)

holding ['həʊldɪŋ] n (share) Anteil m; (small farm) Gut nt ⊳ adj (operation, tactic) zur Schadensbegrenzung

holding company n Dachgesellschaft f, Holdinggesellschaft f

hold-up ['həʊldʌp] n bewaffneter Raubüberfall m; (delay) Verzögerung f; (Brit: in traffic) Stockung f

hole [həʊl] n Loch nt; (unpleasant town) Kaff nt (inf) ⊳ vt (ship) leckschlagen; (building etc) durchlöchern; **~ in the heart** Loch im Herz(en); **to pick ~s** (fig) (über)kritisch sein; **to pick ~s in sth** (fig) an etw dat herumkritisieren

▶ **hole up** vi sich verkriechen

holiday ['hɔlɪdeɪ] n (Brit) Urlaub m; (Scol) Ferien pl; (day off) freier Tag m; (also: **public holiday**) Feiertag m; **on ~** im Urlaub, in den Ferien

holiday camp (Brit) n (also: **holiday centre**) Feriendorf nt

holiday home n Ferienhaus nt

holiday-maker ['hɔlɪdɪmeɪkəʳ] (Brit) n Urlauber(in) m(f)

holiday pay n Lohn-/Gehaltsfortzahlung während des Urlaubs

holiday resort n Ferienort m

holiday season n Urlaubszeit f

holiness ['həʊlɪnɪs] n Heiligkeit f

holistic [həʊ'lɪstɪk] adj holistisch

Holland ['hɔlənd] n Holland nt

holler ['hɔləʳ] (inf) vi brüllen ⊳ n Schrei m

hollow ['hɔləʊ] adj hohl; (eyes) tief liegend; (laugh) unecht; (sound) dumpf; (fig) leer; (: victory, opinion) wertlos ⊳ n Vertiefung f ⊳ vt: **to ~ out** aushöhlen

holly ['hɔlɪ] n Stechpalme f, Ilex m; (leaves) Stechpalmenzweige pl

hollyhock ['hɒlɪhɒk] n Malve f
Hollywood ['hɒlɪwʊd] n Hollywood nt
holocaust ['hɒləkɔ:st] n Inferno nt; (in Third Reich) Holocaust m
hologram ['hɒləgræm] n Hologramm nt
hols [hɒlz] (inf) npl Ferien pl
holster ['həʊlstə^r] n Pistolenhalfter m or nt
holy ['həʊlɪ] adj heilig
Holy Communion n heilige Kommunion f
Holy Father n Heiliger Vater m
Holy Ghost n Heiliger Geist m
Holy Land n: **the ~** das Heilige Land
holy orders npl Priesterweihe f
Holy Spirit n Heiliger Geist m
homage ['hɒmɪdʒ] n Huldigung f; **to pay ~ to** huldigen +dat
home [həʊm] n Heim nt; (house, flat) Zuhause nt; (area, country) Heimat f; (institution) Anstalt f ▷ cpd Heim-; (Econ, Pol) Innen- ▷ adv (go etc) nach Hause, heim; **at ~** zu Hause (Österr, Schweiz); (in country) im Inland; **to be** or **feel at ~** (fig) sich wohlfühlen; **make yourself at ~** machen Sie es sich dat gemütlich or bequem; **to make one's ~ somewhere** sich irgendwo niederlassen; **the ~ of free enterprise/jazz** etc die Heimat des freien Unternehmertums/ Jazz etc; **when will you be ~?** wann bist du wieder zu Hause?; **a ~ from home** ein zweites Zuhause nt; **~ and dry** aus dem Schneider; **to drive a nail ~** einen Nagel einschlagen; **to bring sth ~ to sb** jdm etw klarmachen
▶ **home in on** vt fus (missiles) sich ausrichten auf +acc
home address n Heimatanschrift f
home-brew [həʊm'bru:] n selbst gebrautes Bier nt
homecoming ['həʊmkʌmɪŋ] n Heimkehr f
home computer n Heimcomputer m
Home Counties (Brit) npl: **the ~** die Grafschaften, die an London angrenzen
home economics n Hauswirtschaft(slehre) f
home ground n (Sport) eigener Platz m; **to be on ~** (fig) sich auf vertrautem Terrain bewegen
home-grown ['həʊmgrəʊn] adj (not foreign) einheimisch; (from garden) selbst gezogen
home help n Haushaltshilfe f
homeland ['həʊmlænd] n Heimat f, Heimatland nt
homeless ['həʊmlɪs] adj obdachlos; (refugee) heimatlos
home loan n Hypothek f
homely ['həʊmlɪ] adj einfach; (US: plain) unscheinbar
home-made [həʊm'meɪd] adj selbst gemacht
Home Office (Brit) n Innenministerium nt
homeopath ['həʊmɪəʊpæθ] (US) n = **homoeopath**
homeopathy [həʊmɪ'ɒpəθɪ] (US) n = **homoeopathy**
home page n (Comput) Homepage f
home rule n Selbstbestimmung f, Selbstverwaltung f

Home Secretary (Brit) n Innenminister(in) m(f)
homesick ['həʊmsɪk] adj heimwehkrank; **to be ~** Heimweh haben
homestead ['həʊmstɛd] n Heimstätte f; (farm) Gehöft nt
home town n Heimatstadt f
home truth n bittere Wahrheit f; **to tell sb some ~s** jdm deutlich die Meinung sagen
homeward ['həʊmwəd] adj (journey) Heim- ▷ adv = **homewards**
homewards ['həʊmwədz] adv nach Hause, heim
homework ['həʊmwə:k] n Hausaufgaben pl
homicidal [hɒmɪ'saɪdl] adj gemeingefährlich
homicide ['hɒmɪsaɪd] (US) n Mord m
homily ['hɒmɪlɪ] n Predigt f
homing ['həʊmɪŋ] adj (device, missile) mit Zielsucheinrichtung; **~ pigeon** Brieftaube f
homoeopath, (US) **homeopath** ['həʊmɪəʊpæθ] n Homöopath(in) m(f)
homoeopathy, (US) **homeopathy** [həʊmɪ'ɒpəθɪ] n Homöopathie f
homogeneous [hɒməʊ'dʒi:nɪəs] adj homogen
homogenize [hə'mɒdʒənaɪz] vt homogenisieren
homosexual [hɒməʊ'sɛksjʊəl] adj homosexuell ▷ n Homosexuelle(r) f(m)
Hon. abbr = **honourable; honorary**
Honduras [hɒn'djʊərəs] n Honduras nt
hone [həʊn] n Schleifstein m ▷ vt schleifen; (fig: groom) erziehen
honest ['ɒnɪst] adj ehrlich; (trustworthy) redlich; (sincere) aufrichtig; **to be quite ~ with you ...** um ehrlich zu sein, ...
honestly ['ɒnɪstlɪ] adv (see adj) ehrlich; redlich; aufrichtig
honesty ['ɒnɪstɪ] n (see adj) Ehrlichkeit f; Redlichkeit f; Aufrichtigkeit f
honey ['hʌnɪ] n Honig m; (US: inf) Schätzchen nt
honeycomb ['hʌnɪkəʊm] n Bienenwabe f; (pattern) Wabe f ▷ vt: **to ~ with** durchlöchern mit
honeymoon ['hʌnɪmu:n] n Flitterwochen pl; (trip) Hochzeitsreise f
honeysuckle ['hʌnɪsʌkl] n Geißblatt nt
Hong Kong ['hɒŋ'kɒŋ] n Hongkong nt
honk [hɒŋk] vi (Aut) hupen
Honolulu [hɒnə'lu:lu:] n Honolulu nt
honor etc ['ɒnə^r] (US) = **honour** etc
honorary ['ɒnərərɪ] adj ehrenamtlich; (title, degree) Ehren-
honour, (US) **honor** ['ɒnə^r] vt ehren; (commitment, promise) stehen zu ▷ n Ehre f; (tribute) Auszeichnung f; **in ~ of** zu Ehren von or +gen
honourable ['ɒnərəbl] adj (person) ehrenwert; (action, defeat) ehrenvoll
honour-bound ['ɒnə'baʊnd] adj: **to be ~ to do sth** moralisch verpflichtet sein, etw zu tun
honours degree ['ɒnəz-] n akademischer Grad mit

h

Prüfung im Spezialfach; siehe Info-Artikel

● **HONOURS DEGREE**
●
● *Honours degree* ist ein Universitätsabschluss
● mit einer guten Note, also der Note I (first
● class), II:1 (upper second class), II:2 (lower
● second class), oder III (third class). Wer
● ein honours degree erhalten hat, darf die
● Abkürzung *Hons* nach seinem Namen und
● Titel führen, z. B. Mary Smith MA Hons.
● Heute sind fast alle Universitätsabschlusse
● in Großbritannien honours degrees. Siehe
● auch *ordinary degree*.

honours list n Liste verliehener/zu verleihender
Ehrentitel; siehe Info-Artikel

● **HONOURS LIST**
●
● *Honours list* ist eine Liste von Adelstiteln
● und Orden, die der britische Monarch
● zweimal jährlich (zu Neujahr und am
● offiziellen Geburtstag des Monarchen)
● an Bürger in Großbritannien und im
● Commonwealth verleiht. Die Liste wird
● vom Premierminister zusammengestellt,
● aber drei Orden (der Hosenbandorden, der
● Verdienstorden und der Victoria-Orden)
● werden vom Monarchen persönlich
● vergeben. Erfolgreiche Geschäftsleute,
● Militärangehörige, Sportler und andere
● Prominente, aber auch im sozialen Bereich
● besonders aktive Bürger werden auf diese
● Weise geehrt.

Hons. abbr (Univ) = **Honours degree**
hood [hud] n (of coat etc) Kapuze f; (of cooker)
Abzugshaube f; (Aut: Brit: folding roof) Verdeck
nt; (: US: bonnet) (Motor)haube f
hooded ['hudɪd] adj maskiert; (jacket etc) mit
Kapuze
hoodlum ['hu:dləm] n Gangster m
hoodwink ['hudwɪŋk] vt (he)reinlegen
hoof [hu:f] (pl **hooves**) n Huf m
hook [huk] n Haken m ▷ vt festhaken; (fish) an
die Angel bekommen; **by ~ or by crook** auf
Biegen und Brechen; **to be ~ed on** (inf: film,
exhibition, etc) fasziniert sein von; (: drugs)
abhängig sein von; (: person) stehen auf +acc
▶ **hook up** vt (Radio, TV etc) anschließen
hook and eye (pl **hooks and eyes**) n Haken und
Öse pl
hooligan ['hu:lɪgən] n Rowdy m
hooliganism ['hu:lɪgənɪzəm] n Rowdytum nt
hoop [hu:p] n Reifen m; (for croquet: arch) Tor nt
hooray [hu:'reɪ] excl = **hurrah**
hoot [hu:t] vi hupen; (siren) heulen; (owl)
schreien, rufen; (person) johlen ▷ vt (horn)
drücken auf +acc ▷ n (see vi) Hupen nt; Heulen
nt; Schreien nt, Rufen nt; Johlen nt; **to ~ with
laughter** in johlendes Gelächter ausbrechen
hooter ['hu:tər] n (Brit: Aut) Hupe f; (Naut, of

factory) Sirene f
Hoover® ['hu:vər] (Brit) n Staubsauger m
▷ vt: **hoover** (carpet) saugen
hooves [hu:vz] npl of **hoof**
hop [hɔp] vi hüpfen ▷ n Hüpfer m; see also **hops**
hope [həup] vi hoffen ▷ n Hoffnung f
▷ vt: **to ~ that** hoffen, dass; **I ~ so** ich hoffe
es, hoffentlich; **I ~ not** ich hoffe nicht,
hoffentlich nicht; **to ~ for the best** das Beste
hoffen; **to have no ~ of sth/doing sth** keine
Hoffnung auf etw +acc haben/darauf haben,
etw zu tun; **in the ~ of/that** in der Hoffnung
auf/, dass; **to ~ to do sth** hoffen, etw zu tun
hopeful ['həupful] adj hoffnungsvoll;
(situation) vielversprechend; **I'm ~ that she'll
manage** ich hoffe, dass sie es schafft
hopefully ['həupfulɪ] adv hoffnungsvoll;
(one hopes) hoffentlich; **~, he'll come back**
hoffentlich kommt er wieder
hopeless ['həuplɪs] adj hoffnungslos; (situation)
aussichtslos; (useless): **to be ~ at sth** etw
überhaupt nicht können
hopper ['hɔpər] n Einfülltrichter m
hops [hɔps] npl Hopfen m
horde [hɔ:d] n Horde f
horizon [hə'raɪzn] n Horizont m
horizontal [hɔrɪ'zɔntl] adj horizontal
hormone ['hɔ:məun] n Hormon nt
hormone replacement therapy n
Hormonersatztherapie f
horn [hɔ:n] n Horn nt; (Aut) Hupe f
horned [hɔ:nd] adj (animal) mit Hörnern
hornet ['hɔ:nɪt] n Hornisse f
horn-rimmed ['hɔ:n'rɪmd] adj (spectacles) Horn-
horny ['hɔ:nɪ] (inf) adj (aroused) scharf, geil
horoscope ['hɔrəskəup] n Horoskop nt
horrendous [hə'rendəs] adj abscheulich,
entsetzlich
horrible ['hɔrɪbl] adj fürchterlich, schrecklich;
(scream, dream) furchtbar
horrid ['hɔrɪd] adj entsetzlich, schrecklich
horrific [hɔ'rɪfɪk] adj entsetzlich, schrecklich
horrify ['hɔrɪfaɪ] vt entsetzen
horrifying ['hɔrɪfaɪɪŋ] adj schrecklich,
fürchterlich, entsetzlich
horror ['hɔrər] n Entsetzen nt, Grauen nt; **~ (of
sth)** (abhorrence) Abscheu m (vor etw dat); the
~s of war die Schrecken pl des Krieges
horror film n Horrorfilm m
horror-stricken ['hɔrəstrɪkn] adj = **horror-
struck**
horror-struck ['hɔrəstrʌk] adj von Entsetzen or
Grauen gepackt
hors d'œuvre [ɔ:'də:vrə] n Hors d'œuvre nt,
Vorspeise f
horse [hɔ:s] n Pferd nt
horseback ['hɔ:sbæk]: **on ~** adj, adv zu Pferd
horsebox ['hɔ:sbɔks] n Pferdetransporter m
horse chestnut n Rosskastanie f
horse-drawn ['hɔ:sdrɔ:n] adj von Pferden
gezogen
horsefly ['hɔ:sflaɪ] n (Pferde)bremse f
horseman ['hɔ:smən] (irreg: like **man**) n

Reiter *m*
horsemanship ['hɔːsmənʃɪp] *n* Reitkunst *f*
horseplay ['hɔːspleɪ] *n* Alberei *f*, Balgerei *f*
horsepower ['hɔːspauə'] *n* Pferdestärke *f*
horse racing *n* Pferderennen *nt*
horseradish ['hɔːsrædɪʃ] *n* Meerrettich *m*
horseshoe ['hɔːsʃuː] *n* Hufeisen *nt*
horse show *n* Reitturnier *nt*
horse trading *n* Kuhhandel *m*
horse trials *npl* = **horse show**
horsewhip ['hɔːswɪp] *n* Reitpeitsche *f* ▷ *vt*
auspeitschen
horsewoman ['hɔːswumən] (*irreg: like* **woman**)
n Reiterin *f*
horsey ['hɔːsɪ] *adj* pferdenärrisch; (*appearance*)
pferdeähnlich
horticulture ['hɔːtɪkʌltʃə'] *n* Gartenbau *m*
hose [həuz] *n* (*also:* **hose pipe**) Schlauch *m*
▶ **hose down** *vt* abspritzen
hosiery ['həuzɪərɪ] *n* Strumpfwaren *pl*
hospice ['hɔspɪs] *n* Pflegeheim *nt* (*für unheilbar*
Kranke)
hospitable ['hɔspɪtəbl] *adj* gastfreundlich;
(*climate*) freundlich
hospital ['hɔspɪtl] *n* Krankenhaus *nt*; **in ~, in**
the ~ (*US*) im Krankenhaus
hospitality [hɔspɪ'tælɪtɪ] *n* Gastfreundschaft
f
hospitalize ['hɔspɪtəlaɪz] *vt* ins Krankenhaus
einweisen
host [həust] *n* Gastgeber *m*; (*Rel*) Hostie *f* ▷ *adj*
Gast- ▷ *vt* Gastgeber sein bei; **a ~ of** eine
Menge
hostage ['hɔstɪdʒ] *n* Geisel *f*; **to be taken/**
held ~ als Geisel genommen/festgehalten
werden
hostel ['hɔstl] *n* (Wohn)heim *nt*; (*also:* **youth**
hostel) Jugendherberge *f*
hostelling ['hɔstlɪŋ] *n*: **to go (youth) ~** in
Jugendherbergen übernachten
hostess ['həustɪs] *n* Gastgeberin *f*; (*Brit: also:* **air**
hostess) Stewardess *f*; (*in night-club*) Hostess *f*
hostile ['hɔstaɪl] *adj* (*conditions*) ungünstig;
(*environment*) unwirtlich; (*person*): **~ (to or**
towards) feindselig (gegenüber +*dat*)
hostility [hɔ'stɪlɪtɪ] *n* Feindseligkeit *f*;
hostilities *npl* (*fighting*) Feindseligkeiten *pl*
hot [hɔt] *adj* heiß; (*moderately hot*) warm; (*spicy*)
scharf; (*temper*) hitzig; **I am** *or* **feel ~** mir ist
heiß; **to be ~ on sth** (*knowledgeable etc*) sich
gut mit etw auskennen; (*strict*) sehr auf etw
acc achten
▶ **hot up** (*Brit: inf*) *vi* (*situation*) sich verschärfen
or zuspitzen; (*party*) in Schwung kommen ▷ *vt*
(*pace*) steigern; (*engine*) frisieren
hot air *n* leeres Gerede *nt*
hot-air balloon [hɔt'ɛə'-] *n* Heißluftballon *m*
hotbed ['hɔtbɛd] *n* (*fig*) Brutstätte *f*
hot-blooded [hɔt'blʌdɪd] *adj* heißblütig
hotchpotch ['hɔtʃpɔtʃ] (*Brit*) *n* Durcheinander
nt, Mischmasch *m*
hot dog *n* Hotdog *m or nt*
hotel [həu'tɛl] *n* Hotel *nt*

hotelier [həu'tɛlɪə'] *n* Hotelier(in) *m(f)*
hotel industry *n* Hotelgewerbe *nt*
hotel room *n* Hotelzimmer *nt*
hot flash (*US*) *n* = **hot flush**
hot flush *n* (*Med*) Hitzewallung *f*
hotfoot ['hɔtfut] *adv* eilends
hothead ['hɔthɛd] *n* Hitzkopf *m*
hot-headed [hɔt'hɛdɪd] *adj* hitzköpfig
hothouse ['hɔthaus] *n* Treibhaus *nt*
hot line *n* (*Pol*) heißer Draht *m*
hotly ['hɔtlɪ] *adv* (*contest*) heiß; (*speak, deny*)
heftig
hotplate ['hɔtpleɪt] *n* Kochplatte *f*
hotpot ['hɔtpɔt] (*Brit*) *n* Fleischeintopf *m*
hot potato (*fig: inf*) *n* heißes Eisen *nt*; **to drop**
sb like a ~ jdn wie eine heiße Kartoffel fallen
lassen
hot seat *n*: **to be in the ~** auf dem
Schleudersitz sitzen
hotspot ['hɔtspɔt] *n* (*Comput*) Hotspot *m*
hot spot *n* (*fig*) Krisenherd *m*
hot spring *n* heiße Quelle *f*, Thermalquelle *f*
hot stuff *n* große Klasse *f*
hot-tempered ['hɔt'tɛmpəd] *adj* leicht
aufbrausend, jähzornig
hot-water bottle [hɔt'wɔːtə'-] *n* Wärmflasche
f
hot-wire (*inf*) *vt* (*car*) kurzschließen
hound [haund] *vt* hetzen, jagen ▷ *n* Jagdhund
m; **the ~s** die Meute
hour ['auə'] *n* Stunde *f*; (*time*) Zeit *f*; **at 60**
miles an ~ mit 60 Meilen in der Stunde;
lunch ~ Mittagspause *f*; **to pay sb by the ~**
jdn stundenweise bezahlen
hourly ['auəlɪ] *adj* stündlich; (*rate*) Stunden-
▷ *adv* stündlich, jede Stunde; (*soon*) jederzeit
house [haus] *n* Haus *nt*; (*household*)
Haushalt *m*; (*dynasty*) Geschlecht *nt*, Haus
nt; (*Theat: performance*) Vorstellung *f* ▷ *vt*
unterbringen; **at my ~** bei mir (zu Hause); **to**
my ~ zu mir (nach Hause); **on the ~** (*fig*) auf
Kosten des Hauses; **the H~ (of Commons)**
(*Brit*) das Unterhaus; **the H~ (of Lords)** (*Brit*)
das Oberhaus; **the H~ (of Representatives)**
(*US*) das Repräsentantenhaus; *siehe Info-Artikel*
house arrest *n* Hausarrest *m*
houseboat ['hausbəut] *n* Hausboot *nt*
housebound ['hausbaund] *adj* ans Haus
gefesselt
housebreaking ['hausbreɪkɪŋ] *n* Einbruch *m*
house-broken ['hausbrəukn] (*US*) *adj* = **house-**
trained
housecoat ['hauskəut] *n* Morgenrock *m*
household ['haushəuld] *n* Haushalt *m*; **to be a**
~ name ein Begriff sein
householder ['haushəuldə'] *n* Hausinhaber(in)
m(f); (*of flat*) Wohnungsinhaber(in) *m(f)*
house-hunting ['haushʌntɪŋ] *n*: **to go ~** nach
einem Haus suchen
housekeeper ['hauskiːpə'] *n* Haushälterin *f*
housekeeping ['hauskiːpɪŋ] *n* Hauswirtschaft
f; (*money*) Haushaltsgeld *nt*, Wirtschaftsgeld *nt*
houseman ['hausmən] (*Brit: irreg: like* **man**) *n*

h

(Med) Assistenzarzt m, Assistenzärztin f

HOUSE OF COMMONS

Das House of Commons ist das Unterhaus des britischen Parlaments, mit 651 Abgeordneten, die in Wahlkreisen in allgemeiner Wahl gewählt werden. Das Unterhaus hat die Regierungsgewalt inne und tagt etwa 175 Tage im Jahr unter Vorsitz des Sprechers. Als House of Lords wird das Oberhaus des britischen Parlaments bezeichnet. Die Mitglieder sind nicht gewählt, sondern werden auf Lebenszeit ernannt („life peers") oder sie haben ihren Oberhaussitz geerbt („hereditary peers"). Das House of Lords setzt sich aus Kirchenmännern und Adeligen zusammen („Lords Spiritual/Temporal"). Es hat im Grunde keine Regierungsgewalt, kann aber vom Unterhaus erlassene Gesetze abändern und ist das oberste Berufungsgericht in Großbritannien (außer Schottland).

HOUSE OF REPRESENTATIVES

Das House of Representatives bildet zusammen mit dem Senat die amerikanische gesetzgebende Versammlung (den Kongress). Es besteht aus 435 Abgeordneten, die entsprechend den Bevölkerungszahlen auf die einzelnen Bundesstaaten verteilt sind und jeweils für 2 Jahre direkt vom Volk gewählt werden. Es tritt im „Capitol" in Washington zusammen. Siehe auch „Congress".

house owner n Hausbesitzer(in) m(f)
house party n mehrtägige Einladung f; (people) Gesellschaft f
house plant n Zimmerpflanze f
house-proud ['hauspraud] adj auf Ordnung und Sauberkeit im Haushalt bedacht
house-to-house ['haustə'haus] adj von Haus zu Haus
house-trained ['haustreɪnd] (Brit) adj (animal) stubenrein
house-warming ['hauswɔːmɪŋ], **house-warming party** n Einzugsparty f
housewife ['hauswaɪf] (irreg: like **wife**) n Hausfrau f
housework ['hauswəːk] n Hausarbeit f
housing ['hauzɪŋ] n Wohnungen pl; (provision) Wohnungsbeschaffung f ▷ cpd Wohnungs-
housing association n Wohnungsbaugesellschaft f
housing benefit n ≈ Wohngeld nt
housing conditions npl Wohnbedingungen pl, Wohnverhältnisse pl
housing development n (Wohn)siedlung f

housing estate n (Wohn)siedlung f
hovel ['hɔvl] n (armselige) Hütte f
hover ['hɔvə^r] vi schweben; (person) herumstehen; **to ~ round sb** jdm nicht von der Seite weichen
hovercraft ['hɔvəkrɑːft] n Hovercraft nt, Luftkissenfahrzeug nt
hoverport ['hɔvəpɔːt] n Anlegestelle f für Hovercrafts

○ KEYWORD

how [hau] adv **1** (in what way) wie; **how was the film?** wie war der Film?; **how is school?** was macht die Schule?; **how are you?** wie geht es Ihnen?
2 (to what degree): **how much milk?** wie viel Milch?; **how many people?** wie viele Leute?; **how long have you been here?** wie lange sind Sie schon hier?; **how old are you?** wie alt bist du?; **how lovely/awful!** wie schön/furchtbar!

however [hau'ɛvə^r] conj jedoch, aber ▷ adv wie … auch; (in questions) wie … bloß or nur
howl [haul] vi heulen; (animal) jaulen; (baby, person) schreien ▷ n (see vb) Heulen nt; Jaulen nt; Schreien nt
howler ['haulə^r] (inf) n (mistake) Schnitzer m
howling ['haulɪŋ] adj (wind, gale) heulend
HP (Brit) n abbr = **hire-purchase**
h.p. abbr (Aut: = horsepower) PS
HQ abbr = **headquarters**
HR (US) n abbr (Pol: = House of Representatives) Repräsentantenhaus nt; = Human Resources
hr abbr (= hour) Std.
HRH (Brit) abbr (= His/Her Royal Highness) Seine/Ihre Königliche Hoheit
hrs abbr (= hours) Std.
HST (US) abbr (= Hawaiian Standard Time) Normalzeit in Hawaii
HTML (Comput) abbr (= hypertext markup language) HTML f
hub [hʌb] n (Rad)nabe f; (fig: centre) Mittelpunkt m, Zentrum nt
hubbub ['hʌbʌb] n Lärm m; (commotion) Tumult m
hubcap ['hʌbkæp] n Radkappe f
HUD (US) n abbr (= Department of Housing and Urban Development) Ministerium für Wohnungsbau und Stadtentwicklung
huddle ['hʌdl] vi: **to ~ together** sich zusammendrängen ▷ n: **in a ~** dicht zusammengedrängt
hue [hjuː] n Farbton m
hue and cry n großes Geschrei nt
huff [hʌf] n: **in a ~** beleidigt, eingeschnappt ▷ vi: **to ~ and puff** sich aufregen
huffy ['hʌfɪ] (inf) adj beleidigt
hug [hʌg] vt umarmen; (thing) umklammern ▷ n Umarmung f; **to give sb a ~** jdn umarmen
huge [hjuːdʒ] adj riesig
hugely ['hjuːdʒlɪ] adv ungeheuer

hulk [hʌlk] n (wrecked ship) Wrack nt; (person, building etc) Klotz m
hulking ['hʌlkɪŋ] adj: ~ **great** massig
hull [hʌl] n Schiffsrumpf m; (of nuts) Schale f; (of fruit) Blättchen nt ▷ vt (fruit) entstielen
hullaballoo [hʌləbə'lu:] (inf) n Spektakel m
hullo [hə'ləu] excl = **hello**
hum [hʌm] vt summen ▷ vi summen; (machine) brummen ▷ n Summen nt; (of traffic) Brausen nt; (of machines) Brummen nt; (of voices) Gemurmel nt
human ['hju:mən] adj menschlich ▷ n (also: **human being**) Mensch m
humane [hju:'meɪn] adj human
humanism ['hju:mənɪzəm] n Humanismus m
humanitarian [hju:mænɪ'tɛərɪən] adj humanitär
humanity [hju:'mænɪtɪ] n Menschlichkeit f; (mankind) Menschheit f; (humaneness) Humanität f; **humanities** npl (Scol): **the humanities** die Geisteswissenschaften pl
humanly ['hju:mənlɪ] adv menschlich; **if (at all) ~ possible** wenn es irgend möglich ist
humanoid ['hju:mənɔɪd] adj menschenähnlich ▷ n menschenähnliches Wesen nt
human rights npl Menschenrechte pl
humble ['hʌmbl] adj bescheiden ▷ vt demütigen
humbly ['hʌmblɪ] adv bescheiden
humbug ['hʌmbʌg] n Humbug m, Mumpitz m; (Brit: sweet) Pfefferminzbonbon m or nt
humdrum ['hʌmdrʌm] adj eintönig, langweilig
humid ['hju:mɪd] adj feucht
humidifier [hju:'mɪdɪfaɪəʳ] n Luftbefeuchter m
humidity [hju:'mɪdɪtɪ] n Feuchtigkeit f
humiliate [hju:'mɪlɪeɪt] vt demütigen
humiliating [hju:'mɪlɪeɪtɪŋ] adj demütigend
humiliation [hju:mɪlɪ'eɪʃən] n Demütigung f
humility [hju:'mɪlɪtɪ] n Bescheidenheit f
humor etc (US) = **humour** etc
humorist ['hju:mərɪst] n Humorist(in) m(f)
humorous ['hju:mərəs] adj (remark) witzig; (book) lustig; (person) humorvoll
humour, (US) **humor** ['hju:məʳ] n Humor m; (mood) Stimmung f ▷ vt seinen Willen lassen +dat; **sense of ~** (Sinn m für) Humor; **to be in good/bad ~** gute/schlechte Laune haben
humourless ['hju:məlɪs] adj humorlos
hump [hʌmp] n Hügel m; (of camel) Höcker m; (deformity) Buckel m
humpbacked ['hʌmpbækt] adj: ~ **bridge** gewölbte Brücke f
humus ['hju:məs] n Humus m
hunch [hʌntʃ] n Gefühl nt, Ahnung f; **I have a ~ that …** ich habe den (leisen) Verdacht, dass …
hunchback ['hʌntʃbæk] n Bucklige(r) f(m)
hunched [hʌntʃt] adj gebeugt; (shoulders) hochgezogen; (back) krumm
hundred ['hʌndrəd] num hundert; **a** or **one ~ books/people/dollars** (ein)hundert Bücher/

Personen/Dollar; **~s of** Hunderte von; **I'm a ~ per cent sure** ich bin absolut sicher
hundredth ['hʌndrədθ] num hundertste(r, s)
hundredweight ['hʌndrɪdweɪt] n Gewichtseinheit (Brit = 50,8 kg; US = 45,3 kg) ≈ Zentner m
hung [hʌŋ] pt, pp of **hang**
Hungarian [hʌŋ'gɛərɪən] adj ungarisch ▷ n Ungar(in) m(f); (Ling) Ungarisch nt
Hungary ['hʌŋgərɪ] n Ungarn nt
hunger ['hʌŋgəʳ] n Hunger m ▷ vi: **to ~ for** hungern nach
hunger strike n Hungerstreik m
hung over (inf) adj verkatert
hungrily ['hʌŋgrəlɪ] adv hungrig
hungry ['hʌŋgrɪ] adj hungrig; **to be ~** Hunger haben; **to be ~ for** hungern nach; (news) sehnsüchtig warten auf; **to go ~** hungern
hung up (inf) adj: **to be ~ on** (person) ein gestörtes Verhältnis haben zu; **to be ~ about** nervös sein wegen
hunk [hʌŋk] n großes Stück nt; (inf: man) (großer, gut aussehender) Mann m
hunt [hʌnt] vt jagen; (criminal, fugitive) fahnden nach ▷ vi (Sport) jagen ▷ n (see vb) Jagd f; Fahndung f; (search) Suche f; **to ~ for** (search) suchen (nach)
▶ **hunt down** vt Jagd machen auf +acc
hunter ['hʌntəʳ] n Jäger(in) m(f)
hunting ['hʌntɪŋ] n Jagd f, Jagen nt
hurdle ['hə:dl] n Hürde f
hurl [hə:l] vt schleudern; **to ~ sth at sb** (also fig) jdm etw entgegenschleudern
hurling ['hə:lɪŋ] n (Sport) Hurling nt, irische Hockeyart
hurly-burly ['hə:lɪ'bə:lɪ] n Rummel m
hurrah [hu'rɑ:] n Hurra nt ▷ excl hurra
hurray [hu'reɪ] n = **hurrah**
hurricane ['hʌrɪkən] n Orkan m
hurried ['hʌrɪd] adj eilig; (departure) überstürzt
hurriedly ['hʌrɪdlɪ] adv eilig
hurry ['hʌrɪ] n Eile f ▷ vi eilen; (to do sth) sich beeilen ▷ vt (zur Eile) antreiben; (work) beschleunigen; **to be in a ~** es eilig haben; **to do sth in a ~** etw schnell tun; **there's no ~** es eilt nicht; **what's the ~?** warum so eilig?; **they hurried to help him** sie eilten ihm zu Hilfe; **to ~ home** nach Hause eilen
▶ **hurry along** vi sich beeilen
▶ **hurry away** vi schnell weggehen, forteilen
▶ **hurry off** vi = **hurry away**
▶ **hurry up** vt (zur Eile) antreiben ▷ vi sich beeilen
hurt [hə:t] (pt, pp ~) vt wehtun +dat; (injure, fig) verletzen ▷ vi wehtun ▷ adj verletzt; **I've ~ my arm** ich habe mir am Arm wehgetan; (injured) ich habe mir den Arm verletzt; **where does it ~?** wo tut es weh?
hurtful ['hə:tful] adj verletzend
hurtle ['hə:tl] vi: **to ~ past** vorbeisausen; **to ~ down** (fall) hinunterfallen
husband ['hʌzbənd] n (Ehe)mann m
hush [hʌʃ] n Stille f ▷ vt zum Schweigen

bringing; ~! pst!

▶ **hush up** vt vertuschen

hushed [hʌʃt] adj still; (voice) gedämpft

hush-hush [hʌʃ'hʌʃ] (inf) adj streng geheim

husk [hʌsk] n Schale f; (of wheat) Spelze f; (of maize) Hüllblatt nt

husky ['hʌskɪ] adj (voice) rau ▷ n Schlittenhund m

hustings ['hʌstɪŋz] (Brit) npl (Pol) Wahlkampf m

hustle ['hʌsl] vt drängen ▷ n: ~ **and bustle** Geschäftigkeit f

hut [hʌt] n Hütte f

hutch [hʌtʃ] n (Kaninchen)stall m

hyacinth ['haɪəsɪnθ] n Hyazinthe f

hybrid ['haɪbrɪd] n (plant, animal) Kreuzung f; (mixture) Mischung f ▷ adj Misch-

hybrid car, hybrid vehicle n Hybridfahrzeug nt or -auto nt

hydrant ['haɪdrənt] n (also: **fire hydrant**) Hydrant m

hydraulic [haɪ'drɔːlɪk] adj hydraulisch

hydraulics [haɪ'drɔːlɪks] n Hydraulik f

hydrochloric acid ['haɪdrəu'klɔrɪk-] n Salzsäure f

hydroelectric ['haɪdrəuɪ'lɛktrɪk] adj hydroelektrisch

hydrofoil ['haɪdrəfɔɪl] n Tragflächenboot nt, Tragflügelboot nt

hydrogen ['haɪdrədʒən] n Wasserstoff m

hydrogen bomb n Wasserstoffbombe f

hydrophobia ['haɪdrə'fəubɪə] n Hydrophobie f, Wasserscheu f

hydroplane ['haɪdrəpleɪn] n Gleitboot nt; (plane) Wasserflugzeug nt ▷ vi (boat) abheben

hyena [haɪ'iːnə] n Hyäne f

hygiene ['haɪdʒiːn] n Hygiene f

hygienic [haɪ'dʒiːnɪk] adj hygienisch

hymn [hɪm] n Kirchenlied nt

hype [haɪp] (inf) n Rummel m

hyperactive ['haɪpər'æktɪv] adj überaktiv

hyperinflation ['haɪpərɪn'fleɪʃən] n galoppierende Inflation f

hypermarket ['haɪpəmɑːkɪt] (Brit) n Verbrauchermarkt m

hypertension ['haɪpə'tɛnʃən] n Hypertonie f, Bluthochdruck m

hypertext ['haɪpətɛkst] n (Comput) Hypertext m

hyphen ['haɪfn] n Bindestrich m; (at end of line) Trennungsstrich m

hyphenated ['haɪfəneɪtɪd] adj mit Bindestrich (geschrieben)

hypnosis [hɪp'nəusɪs] n Hypnose f

hypnotic [hɪp'nɒtɪk] adj hypnotisierend; (trance) hypnotisch

hypnotism ['hɪpnətɪzəm] n Hypnotismus m

hypnotist ['hɪpnətɪst] n Hypnotiseur m, Hypnotiseuse f

hypnotize ['hɪpnətaɪz] vt hypnotisieren

hypoallergenic ['haɪpəuælə'dʒɛnɪk] adj für äußerst empfindliche Haut

hypochondriac [haɪpə'kɒndrɪæk] n Hypochonder m

hypocrisy [hɪ'pɒkrɪsɪ] n Heuchelei f

hypocrite ['hɪpəkrɪt] n Heuchler(in) m(f)

hypocritical [hɪpə'krɪtɪkl] adj heuchlerisch

hypodermic [haɪpə'dəːmɪk] adj (injection) subkutan ▷ n (Injektions)spritze f

hypotenuse [haɪ'pɒtɪnjuːz] n Hypotenuse f

hypothermia [haɪpə'θəːmɪə] n Unterkühlung f

hypothesis [haɪ'pɒθɪsɪs] (pl **hypotheses**) n Hypothese f

hypothesize [haɪ'pɒθɪsaɪz] vi Hypothesen aufstellen ▷ vt annehmen

hypothetic [haɪpə'θɛtɪk], **hypothetical** [haɪpəu'θɛtɪkl] adj hypothetisch

hysterectomy [hɪstə'rɛktəmɪ] n Hysterektomie f

hysteria [hɪ'stɪərɪə] n Hysterie f

hysterical [hɪ'stɛrɪkl] adj hysterisch; (situation) wahnsinnig komisch; **to become ~** hysterisch werden

hysterically [hɪ'stɛrɪklɪ] adv hysterisch; ~ **funny** wahnsinnig komisch

hysterics [hɪ'stɛrɪks] npl: **to be in** or **to have ~** einen hysterischen Anfall haben; (laughter) einen Lachanfall haben

Hz abbr (= hertz) Hz.

I¹, i [aɪ] *n* (*letter*) I *nt*, i *nt*; **I for Isaac, I for Item**
(*US*) ≈ I wie Ida
I² [aɪ] *pron* ich
I. *abbr* = **island; isle**
IA (*US*) *abbr* (*Post*) = Iowa
IAEA *n abbr* = **International Atomic Energy
Agency**
ib *abbr* (= *ibidem*) ib(id).
Iberian [aɪˈbɪərɪən] *adj:* **the ~ Peninsula** die
Iberische Halbinsel
ibid *abbr* (= *ibidem*) ib(id).
i/c (*Brit*) *abbr* (= *in charge (of)*) *see* **charge**
ICBM *n abbr* (= *intercontinental ballistic missile*)
Interkontinentalrakete *f*
ICC *n abbr* = **International Chamber of
Commerce**; (*US:* = *Interstate Commerce
Commission*) Kommission zur Regelung des
Warenverkehrs zwischen den US-Bundesstaaten
ice [aɪs] *n* Eis *nt*; (*on road*) Glatteis *nt* ▷ *vt* (*cake*)
mit Zuckerguss überziehen, glasieren ▷ *vi*
(*also:* **ice over, ice up**) vereisen; (*puddle etc*)
zufrieren; **to put sth on ~** (*fig*) etw auf Eis
legen
Ice Age *n* Eiszeit *f*
ice axe *n* Eispickel *m*
iceberg [ˈaɪsbəːg] *n* Eisberg *m*; **the tip of the ~**
(*fig*) die Spitze des Eisbergs
icebox [ˈaɪsbɒks] *n* (*US: fridge*) Kühlschrank
m; (*Brit: compartment*) Eisfach *nt*; (*insulated box*)
Kühltasche *f*
icebreaker [ˈaɪsbreɪkəʳ] *n* Eisbrecher *m*
ice bucket *n* Eiskühler *m*
icecap [ˈaɪskæp] *n* Eisdecke *f*; (*polar*) Eiskappe *f*
ice-cold [ˈaɪsˈkəʊld] *adj* eiskalt
ice cream *n* Eis *nt*
ice-cream soda [ˈaɪskriːm-] *n* Eisbecher mit Sirup
und Sodawasser
ice cube *n* Eiswürfel *m*
iced [aɪst] *adj* (*cake*) mit Zuckerguss überzogen,
glasiert; (*beer etc*) eisgekühlt; (*tea, coffee*) Eis-
ice hockey *n* Eishockey *nt*
Iceland [ˈaɪslənd] *n* Island *nt*
Icelander [ˈaɪsləndəʳ] *n* Isländer(in) *m(f)*
Icelandic [aɪsˈlændɪk] *adj* isländisch ▷ *n* (*Ling*)
Isländisch *nt*
ice lolly (*Brit*) *n* Eis *nt* am Stiel
ice pick *n* Eispickel *m*
ice rink *n* (*Kunst*)eisbahn *f*, Schlittschuhbahn *f*

ice skate *n* Schlittschuh *m*
ice-skate [ˈaɪsskeɪt] *vi* Schlittschuh laufen
ice-skating [ˈaɪsskeɪtɪŋ] *n* Eislauf *m*,
Schlittschuhlaufen *nt*
icicle [ˈaɪsɪkl] *n* Eiszapfen *m*
icing [ˈaɪsɪŋ] *n* (*Culin*) Zuckerguss *m*; (*Aviat etc*)
Vereisung *f*
icing sugar (*Brit*) *n* Puderzucker *m*
ICJ *n abbr* = **International Court of Justice**
icon [ˈaɪkɒn] *n* Ikone *f*; (*Comput*) Ikon *nt*
ICR (*US*) *n abbr* (= *Institute for Cancer Research*)
Krebsforschungsinstitut
ICT (*Brit*) *n abbr* (*Scol*) = **information and
communication technology**
ICU *n abbr* (*Med*) = **intensive care unit**
icy [ˈaɪsɪ] *adj* eisig; (*road*) vereist
ID, Ida. (*US*) *abbr* (*Post*) = Idaho; = **identification**
(*document*)
I'd [aɪd] = **I would; I had**
ID card *n* = **identity card**
IDD (*Brit*) *n abbr* (*Tel:* = *international direct dialling*)
Selbstwählferndienst ins Ausland
idea [aɪˈdɪə] *n* Idee *f*; (*opinion*) Ansicht *f*; (*notion*)
Vorstellung *f*; (*objective*) Ziel *nt*; **good ~!** gute
Idee!; **to have a good ~ that** sich *dat* ziemlich
sicher sein, dass; **I haven't the least ~** ich
habe nicht die leiseste Ahnung
ideal [aɪˈdɪəl] *n* Ideal *nt* ▷ *adj* ideal
idealist [aɪˈdɪəlɪst] *n* Idealist(in) *m(f)*
ideally [aɪˈdɪəlɪ] *adv* ideal; **~ the book
should ...** idealerweise or im Idealfall sollte
das Buch ...; **she's ~ suited for ...** sie eignet
sich hervorragend für ...
identical [aɪˈdɛntɪkl] *adj* identisch; (*twins*)
eineiig
identification [aɪdɛntɪfɪˈkeɪʃən]
n Identifizierung *f*; **(means of) ~**
Ausweispapiere *pl*
identify [aɪˈdɛntɪfaɪ] *vt* (*recognize*) erkennen;
(*distinguish*) identifizieren; **to ~ sb/sth with**
jdn/etw identifizieren mit
Identikit® [aɪˈdɛntɪkɪt] *n:* **~ (picture)**
Phantombild *nt*
identity [aɪˈdɛntɪtɪ] *n* Identität *f*
identity card *n* (*Personal*)ausweis *m*
identity papers *npl* Ausweispapiere *pl*
identity parade (*Brit*) *n* Gegenüberstellung *f*
ideological [aɪdɪəˈlɒdʒɪkl] *adj* ideologisch,

weltanschaulich

ideology [aɪdɪ'ɔlədʒɪ] n Ideologie f, Weltanschauung f

idiocy ['ɪdɪəsɪ] n Idiotie f, Dummheit f

idiom ['ɪdɪəm] n (style) Ausdrucksweise f; (phrase) Redewendung f

idiomatic [ɪdɪə'mætɪk] adj idiomatisch

idiosyncrasy [ɪdɪəu'sɪŋkrəsɪ] n Eigenheit f, Eigenart f

idiosyncratic [ɪdɪəusɪn'krætɪk] adj eigenartig; (way, method, style) eigen

idiot ['ɪdɪət] n Idiot(in) m(f), Dummkopf m

idiotic [ɪdɪ'ɔtɪk] adj idiotisch, blöd(sinnig)

idle ['aɪdl] adj untätig; (lazy) faul; (unemployed) unbeschäftigt; (machinery, factory) stillstehend; (question) müßig; (conversation, pleasure) leer ▷ vi leerlaufen, im Leerlauf sein; **to lie ~** (machinery) außer Betrieb sein; (factory) die Arbeit eingestellt haben

▸ **idle away** vt (time) vertrödeln, verbummeln

idleness ['aɪdlnɪs] n Untätigkeit f; (laziness) Faulheit f

idler ['aɪdləʳ] n Faulenzer(in) m(f)

idle time n (Comm) Leerlaufzeit f

idly ['aɪdlɪ] adv untätig; (glance) abwesend

idol ['aɪdl] n Idol nt; (Rel) Götzenbild nt

idolize ['aɪdəlaɪz] vt vergöttern

idyllic [ɪ'dɪlɪk] adj idyllisch

i.e. abbr (= id est) d. h.

○ **KEYWORD**

if [ɪf] conj **1** (given that, providing that etc) wenn, falls; **if anyone comes in** wenn or falls jemand hereinkommt; **if necessary** wenn or falls nötig; **if I were you** wenn ich Sie wäre, an Ihrer Stelle

2 (whenever) wenn

3 (although): **(even) if** auch or selbst wenn; **I like it, (even) if you don't** mir gefällt es, auch wenn du es nicht magst

4 (whether) ob; **ask him if he can come** frag ihn, ob er kommen kann

5: **if so/not** falls ja/nein; **if only** wenn nur; see also **as**

iffy ['ɪfɪ] (inf) adj (uncertain) unsicher; (plan, proposal) fragwürdig; **he was a bit ~ about it** er hat sich sehr vage ausgedrückt

igloo ['ɪglu:] n Iglu m or nt

ignite [ɪg'naɪt] vt entzünden ▷ vi sich entzünden

ignition [ɪg'nɪʃən] n (Aut) Zündung f

ignition key n (Aut) Zündschlüssel m

ignoble [ɪg'nəubl] adj schändlich, unehrenhaft

ignominious [ɪgnə'mɪnɪəs] adj schmachvoll

ignoramus [ɪgnə'reɪməs] n Ignorant(in) m(f)

ignorance ['ɪgnərəns] n Unwissenheit f, Ignoranz f; **to keep sb in ~ of sth** jdn in Unkenntnis über etw acc lassen

ignorant ['ɪgnərənt] adj unwissend, ignorant; **to be ~ of** (subject) sich nicht auskennen in +dat; (events) nicht informiert sein über +acc

ignore [ɪg'nɔːʳ] vt ignorieren; (fact) außer Acht lassen

ikon ['aɪkɔn] n = **icon**

IL (US) abbr (Post) = Illinois

I'll [aɪl] = **I will; I shall**

ill [ɪl] adj krank; (effects) schädlich ▷ n Übel nt; (trouble) Schlechte(s) nt ▷ adv: **to speak ~ of sb** Schlechtes über jdn sagen; **to be taken ~** krank werden; **to think ~ of sb** schlecht von jdm denken

ill-advised [ɪləd'vaɪzd] adj unklug; (person) schlecht beraten

ill at ease adj unbehaglich

ill-considered [ɪlkən'sɪdəd] adj unüberlegt

ill-disposed [ɪldɪs'pəuzd] adj: **to be ~ toward sb/sth** jdm/etw nicht wohlgesinnt sein

illegal [ɪ'liːgl] adj illegal

illegally [ɪ'liːgəlɪ] adv illegal

illegible [ɪ'lɛdʒɪbl] adj unleserlich

illegitimate [ɪlɪ'dʒɪtɪmət] adj (child) unehelich; (activity, treaty) unzulässig

ill-fated [ɪl'feɪtɪd] adj unglückselig

ill-favoured, (US) **ill-favored** [ɪl'feɪvəd] adj ungestalt (liter), hässlich

ill feeling n Verstimmung f

ill-gotten ['ɪlgɔtn] adj: **~ gains** unrechtmäßig erworbener Gewinn m

ill health n schlechter Gesundheitszustand m

illicit [ɪ'lɪsɪt] adj verboten

ill-informed [ɪlɪn'fɔːmd] adj (judgement) wenig sachkundig; (person) schlecht informiert or unterrichtet

illiterate [ɪ'lɪtərət] adj (person) des Lesens und Schreibens unkundig; (letter) voller Fehler

ill-mannered [ɪl'mænəd] adj unhöflich

illness ['ɪlnɪs] n Krankheit f

illogical [ɪ'lɔdʒɪkl] adj unlogisch

ill-suited [ɪl'suːtɪd] adj nicht zusammenpassend; **he is ~ to the job** er ist für die Stelle ungeeignet

ill-timed [ɪl'taɪmd] adj ungelegen, unpassend

ill-treat [ɪl'triːt] vt misshandeln

ill-treatment [ɪl'triːtmənt] n Misshandlung f

illuminate [ɪ'luːmɪneɪt] vt beleuchten

illuminated sign [ɪ'luːmɪneɪtɪd-] n Leuchtzeichen nt

illuminating [ɪ'luːmɪneɪtɪŋ] adj aufschlussreich

illumination [ɪluːmɪ'neɪʃən] n Beleuchtung f; **illuminations** npl (decorative lights) festliche Beleuchtung f, Illumination f

illusion [ɪ'luːʒən] n Illusion f; (trick) (Zauber) trick m; **to be under the ~ that ...** sich dat einbilden, dass ...

illusive [ɪ'luːsɪv] adj = **illusory**

illusory [ɪ'luːsərɪ] adj illusorisch, trügerisch

illustrate ['ɪləstreɪt] vt veranschaulichen; (book) illustrieren

illustration [ɪlə'streɪʃən] n Illustration f; (example) Veranschaulichung f

illustrator ['ɪləstreɪtəʳ] n Illustrator(in) m(f)

illustrious [ɪ'lʌstrɪəs] adj (career) glanzvoll; (predecessor) berühmt

ill will n böses Blut nt
ILO n abbr = **International Labour Organization**
IM n abbr (= instant messaging) IM nt
I'm [aɪm] = **I am**
image ['ɪmɪdʒ] n Bild nt; (public face) Image nt; (reflection) Abbild nt
image-building campaign ['ɪmɪdʒbɪldɪŋ-] n Imagekampagne f
imagery ['ɪmɪdʒərɪ] n (in writing) Metaphorik f; (in painting etc) Symbolik f
imaginable [ɪ'mædʒɪnəbl] adj vorstellbar, denkbar; **we've tried every ~ solution** wir haben jede denkbare Lösung ausprobiert; **she had the prettiest hair ~** sie hatte das schönste Haar, das man sich vorstellen kann
imaginary [ɪ'mædʒɪnərɪ] adj erfunden; (being) Fantasie-; (danger) eingebildet
imagination [ɪmædʒɪ'neɪʃən] n Fantasie f; (illusion) Einbildung f; **it's just your ~** das bildest du dir nur ein
imaginative [ɪ'mædʒɪnətɪv] adj fantasievoll; (solution) einfallsreich
imagine [ɪ'mædʒɪn] vt sich dat vorstellen; (dream) sich dat träumen lassen; (suppose) vermuten
imbalance [ɪm'bæləns] n Unausgeglichenheit f
imbecile ['ɪmbəsiːl] n Schwachkopf m, Idiot m
imbue [ɪm'bjuː] vt: **to ~ sb/sth with** jdn/etw durchdringen mit
IMF n abbr (= International Monetary Fund) IWF m
imitate ['ɪmɪteɪt] vt imitieren; (mimic) nachahmen
imitation [ɪmɪ'teɪʃən] n Imitation f, Nachahmung f
imitator ['ɪmɪteɪtər] n Imitator(in) m(f), Nachahmer(in) m(f)
immaculate [ɪ'mækjulət] adj makellos; (appearance, piece of work) tadellos; (Rel) unbefleckt
immaterial [ɪmə'tɪərɪəl] adj unwichtig, unwesentlich
immature [ɪmə'tjuər] adj unreif; (organism) noch nicht voll entwickelt
immaturity [ɪmə'tjuərɪtɪ] n Unreife f
immeasurable [ɪ'mɛʒrəbl] adj unermesslich groß
immediacy [ɪ'miːdɪəsɪ] n Unmittelbarkeit f, Direktheit f; (of needs) Dringlichkeit f
immediate [ɪ'miːdɪət] adj sofortig; (need) dringend; (neighbourhood, family) nächste(r, s)
immediately [ɪ'miːdɪətlɪ] adv sofort; (directly) unmittelbar; **~ next to** direkt neben
immense [ɪ'mɛns] adj riesig, enorm
immensely [ɪ'mɛnslɪ] adv unheimlich; (grateful, complex etc) äußerst
immensity [ɪ'mɛnsɪtɪ] n ungeheure Größe f, Unermesslichkeit f; (of problems etc) gewaltiges Ausmaß nt
immerse [ɪ'məːs] vt eintauchen; **to ~ sth in** etw tauchen in +acc; **to be ~d in** (fig) vertieft sein in +acc
immersion heater [ɪ'məːʃən-] (Brit) n

elektrischer Heißwasserboiler m
immigrant ['ɪmɪgrənt] n Einwanderer m, Einwanderin f
immigration [ɪmɪ'greɪʃən] n Einwanderung f; (at airport etc) Einwanderungsstelle f
imminent ['ɪmɪnənt] adj bevorstehend
immobile [ɪ'məubaɪl] adj unbeweglich
immobilize [ɪ'məubɪlaɪz] vt (person) handlungsunfähig machen; (machine) zum Stillstand bringen
immobilizer [ɪ'məubɪlaɪzər] n (Aut) Wegfahrsperre f
immoderate [ɪ'mɔdərət] adj unmäßig; (opinion, reaction) extrem; (demand) maßlos
immodest [ɪ'mɔdɪst] adj unanständig; (boasting) unbescheiden
immoral [ɪ'mɔrl] adj unmoralisch; (behaviour) unsittlich
immorality [ɪmɔ'rælɪtɪ] n (see adj) Unmoral f; Unsittlichkeit f
immortal [ɪ'mɔːtl] adj unsterblich
immortality [ɪmɔː'tælɪtɪ] n Unsterblichkeit f
immortalize [ɪ'mɔːtlaɪz] vt unsterblich machen
immovable [ɪ'muːvəbl] adj unbeweglich; (person, opinion) fest
immune [ɪ'mjuːn] adj: **~ (to)** (disease) immun (gegen); (flattery) unempfänglich (für); (criticism) unempfindlich (gegen); (attack) sicher (vor +dat)
immune system n Immunsystem nt
immunity [ɪ'mjuːnɪtɪ] n (see adj) Immunität f; Unempfänglichkeit f; Unempfindlichkeit f; Sicherheit f; (of diplomat, from prosecution) Immunität f
immunization [ɪmjunaɪ'zeɪʃən] n Immunisierung f
immunize ['ɪmjunaɪz] vt: **to ~ (against)** immunisieren (gegen)
imp [ɪmp] n Kobold m; (child) Racker m (inf)
impact ['ɪmpækt] n Aufprall m; (of crash) Wucht f; (of law, measure) (Aus)wirkung f
impair [ɪm'pɛər] vt beeinträchtigen
impaired [ɪm'pɛəd] adj beeinträchtigt; (hearing) schlecht; **~ vision** schlechte Augen pl
impale [ɪm'peɪl] vt: **to ~ sth (on)** etw aufspießen (auf +dat)
impart [ɪm'pɑːt] vt: **to ~ (to)** (information) mitteilen +dat; (flavour) verleihen +dat
impartial [ɪm'pɑːʃl] adj unparteiisch
impartiality [ɪmpɑːʃɪ'ælɪtɪ] n Unparteilichkeit f
impassable [ɪm'pɑːsəbl] adj unpassierbar
impasse [æm'pɑːs] n Sackgasse f
impassive [ɪm'pæsɪv] adj gelassen
impatience [ɪm'peɪʃəns] n Ungeduld f
impatient [ɪm'peɪʃənt] adj ungeduldig; **to get** or **grow ~** ungeduldig werden; **to be ~ to do sth** es nicht erwarten können, etw zu tun
impatiently [ɪm'peɪʃəntlɪ] adv ungeduldig
impeach [ɪm'piːtʃ] vt anklagen; (public official) eines Amtsvergehens anklagen
impeachment [ɪm'piːtʃmənt] n Anklage f

607

wegen eines Amtsvergehens, Impeachment *nt*

impeccable [ɪm'pɛkəbl] *adj* (*dress*) untadelig; (*manners*) tadellos

impecunious [ɪmpɪ'kjuːnɪəs] *adj* mittellos

impede [ɪm'piːd] *vt* behindern

impediment [ɪm'pɛdɪmənt] *n* Hindernis *nt*; (*also*: **speech impediment**) Sprachfehler *m*

impel [ɪm'pɛl] *vt*: **to ~ sb to do sth** jdn (dazu) nötigen, etw zu tun

impending [ɪm'pɛndɪŋ] *adj* bevorstehend; (*catastrophe*) drohend

impenetrable [ɪm'pɛnɪtrəbl] *adj* undurchdringlich; (*fig*) unergründlich

imperative [ɪm'pɛrətɪv] *adj* dringend; (*tone*) Befehls- ▷ *n* (*Ling*) Imperativ *m*, Befehlsform *f*

imperceptible [ɪmpə'sɛptɪbl] *adj* nicht wahrnehmbar, unmerklich

imperfect [ɪm'pəːfɪkt] *adj* mangelhaft; (*goods*) fehlerhaft ▷ *n* (*Ling*: *also*: **imperfect tense**) Imperfekt *nt*, Vergangenheit *f*

imperfection [ɪmpə'fɛkʃən] *n* Fehler *m*

imperial [ɪm'pɪərɪəl] *adj* kaiserlich; (*Brit*: *measure*) britisch

imperialism [ɪm'pɪərɪəlɪzəm] *n* Imperialismus *m*

imperil [ɪm'pɛrɪl] *vt* gefährden

imperious [ɪm'pɪərɪəs] *adj* herrisch, gebieterisch

impersonal [ɪm'pəːsənl] *adj* unpersönlich

impersonate [ɪm'pəːsəneɪt] *vt* sich ausgeben als; (*Theat*) imitieren

impersonation [ɪmpəːsə'neɪʃən] *n* (*Theat*) Imitation *f*; **~ of** (*Law*) Auftreten *nt* als

impertinent [ɪm'pəːtɪnənt] *adj* unverschämt

imperturbable [ɪmpə'təːbəbl] *adj* unerschütterlich

impervious [ɪm'pəːvɪəs] *adj*: **~ to** (*criticism*, *pressure*) unberührt von; (*charm*, *influence*) unempfänglich für

impetuous [ɪm'pɛtjuəs] *adj* ungestüm, stürmisch; (*act*) impulsiv

impetus ['ɪmpətəs] *n* Schwung *m*; (*fig*: *driving force*) treibende Kraft *f*

impinge [ɪm'pɪndʒ]: **to ~ on** *vt fus* sich auswirken auf +*acc*; (*rights*) einschränken

impish ['ɪmpɪʃ] *adj* schelmisch

implacable [ɪm'plækəbl] *adj* unerbittlich, erbittert

implant [ɪm'plɑːnt] *vt* (*Med*) einpflanzen; (*fig*: *idea*, *principle*) einimpfen

implausible [ɪm'plɔːzɪbl] *adj* unglaubwürdig

implement [*n* 'ɪmplɪmənt, *vt* 'ɪmplɪmɛnt] *n* Gerät *nt*, Werkzeug *nt* ▷ *vt* durchführen

implicate ['ɪmplɪkeɪt] *vt* verwickeln

implication [ɪmplɪ'keɪʃən] *n* Auswirkung *f*; (*involvement*) Verwicklung *f*; **by ~** implizit

implicit [ɪm'plɪsɪt] *adj* (*inferred*) implizit, unausgesprochen; (*unquestioning*) absolut

implicitly [ɪm'plɪsɪtlɪ] *adv* (*see adj*) implizit; absolut

implore [ɪm'plɔːr] *vt* anflehen

imply [ɪm'plaɪ] *vt* andeuten; (*mean*) bedeuten

impolite [ɪmpə'laɪt] *adj* unhöflich

imponderable [ɪm'pɒndərəbl] *adj* unberechenbar ▷ *n* unberechenbare Größe *f*

import [*vt* ɪm'pɔːt, *n* 'ɪmpɔːt] *vt* importieren, einführen ▷ *n* Import *m*, Einfuhr *f*; (*article*) Importgut *nt* ▷ *cpd* Import-, Einfuhr-

importance [ɪm'pɔːtns] *n* (*see adj*) Wichtigkeit *f*; Bedeutung *f*; **to be of little/great ~** nicht besonders wichtig/sehr wichtig sein

important [ɪm'pɔːtənt] *adj* wichtig; (*influential*) bedeutend; **it's not ~** es ist unwichtig

importantly [ɪm'pɔːtəntlɪ] *adv* wichtigtuerisch; **but more ~ ...** aber was noch wichtiger ist, ...

importation [ɪmpɔː'teɪʃən] *n* Import *m*, Einfuhr *f*

imported [ɪm'pɔːtɪd] *adj* importiert, eingeführt

importer [ɪm'pɔːtər] *n* Importeur *m*

impose [ɪm'pəuz] *vt* auferlegen; (*sanctions*) verhängen ▷ *vi*: **to ~ on sb** jdm zur Last fallen

imposing [ɪm'pəuzɪŋ] *adj* eindrucksvoll

imposition [ɪmpə'zɪʃən] *n* (*of tax etc*) Auferlegung *f*; **to be an ~ on** eine Zumutung sein für

impossibility [ɪmpɒsə'bɪlɪtɪ] *n* Unmöglichkeit *f*

impossible [ɪm'pɒsɪbl] *adj* unmöglich; **it's ~ for me to leave now** ich kann jetzt unmöglich gehen

impossibly [ɪm'pɒsɪblɪ] *adv* unmöglich

imposter [ɪm'pɒstər] *n* = **impostor**

impostor [ɪm'pɒstər] *n* Hochstapler(in) *m(f)*

impotence ['ɪmpətns] *n* (*see adj*) Machtlosigkeit *f*; Impotenz *f*

impotent ['ɪmpətnt] *adj* machtlos; (*Med*) impotent

impound [ɪm'paund] *vt* beschlagnahmen

impoverished [ɪm'pɒvərɪʃt] *adj* verarmt

impracticable [ɪm'præktɪkəbl] *adj* (*idea*) undurchführbar; (*solution*) unbrauchbar

impractical [ɪm'præktɪkl] *adj* (*plan*) undurchführbar; (*person*) unpraktisch

imprecise [ɪmprɪ'saɪs] *adj* ungenau

impregnable [ɪm'prɛgnəbl] *adj* uneinnehmbar; (*fig*) unerschütterlich

impregnate ['ɪmprɛgneɪt] *vt* tränken

impresario [ɪmprɪ'sɑːrɪəu] *n* (*Theat*) Impresario *m*

impress [ɪm'prɛs] *vt* beeindrucken; (*mark*) aufdrücken; **to ~ sth on sb** jdm etw einschärfen

impression [ɪm'prɛʃən] *n* Eindruck *m*; (*of stamp*, *seal*) Abdruck *m*; (*imitation*) Nachahmung *f*, Imitation *f*; **to make a good/bad ~ on sb** einen guten/schlechten Eindruck auf jdn machen; **to be under the ~ that ...** den Eindruck haben, dass ...

impressionable [ɪm'prɛʃnəbl] *adj* leicht zu beeindrucken

impressionist [ɪm'prɛʃənɪst] *n* Impressionist(in) *m(f)*; (*entertainer*) Imitator(in) *m(f)*

impressive [ɪm'prɛsɪv] *adj* beeindruckend

imprint ['ɪmprɪnt] *n* (*of hand etc*) Abdruck *m*;

(*Publishing*) Impressum *nt*
imprinted [ɪm'prɪntɪd] *adj*: **it is ~ on my memory/mind** es hat sich mir eingeprägt
imprison [ɪm'prɪzn] *vt* inhaftieren, einsperren
imprisonment [ɪm'prɪznmənt] *n* Gefangenschaft *f*; **three years' ~** drei Jahre Gefängnis *or* Freiheitsstrafe
improbable [ɪm'prɔbəbl] *adj* unwahrscheinlich
impromptu [ɪm'prɔmptju:] *adj* improvisiert
improper [ɪm'prɔpəʳ] *adj* ungehörig; (*procedure*) unrichtig; (*dishonest*) unlauter
impropriety [ɪmprə'praɪətɪ] *n* (*see adj*) Ungehörigkeit *f*; Unrichtigkeit *f*; Unlauterkeit *f*
improve [ɪm'pru:v] *vt* verbessern ▷ *vi* sich bessern; **the patient is improving** dem Patienten geht es besser
  ▶ **improve (up)on** *vt fus* verbessern
improvement [ɪm'pru:vmənt] *n*: **~ (in)** Verbesserung *f* (+*gen*); **to make ~s to** Verbesserungen durchführen an +*dat*
improvisation [ɪmprəvaɪ'zeɪʃən] *n* Improvisation *f*
improvise ['ɪmprəvaɪz] *vt, vi* improvisieren
imprudence [ɪm'pru:dns] *n* Unklugheit *f*
imprudent [ɪm'pru:dnt] *adj* unklug
impudent ['ɪmpjudnt] *adj* unverschämt
impugn [ɪm'pju:n] *vt* angreifen; (*sincerity, motives, reputation*) in Zweifel ziehen
impulse ['ɪmpʌls] *n* Impuls *m*; (*urge*) Drang *m*; **to act on ~** aus einem Impuls heraus handeln
impulse buy *n* Impulsivkauf *m*
impulsive [ɪm'pʌlsɪv] *adj* impulsiv, spontan; (*purchase*) Impulsiv-
impunity [ɪm'pju:nɪtɪ] *n*: **with ~** ungestraft
impure [ɪm'pjuəʳ] *adj* unrein; (*adulterated*) verunreinigt
impurity [ɪm'pjuərɪtɪ] *n* Verunreinigung *f*
IN (*US*) *abbr* (*Post*) = **Indiana**

○ **KEYWORD**

in [ɪn] *prep* **1** (*indicating place, position*) in +*dat*; (*with motion*) in +*acc*; **in the house/garden** im Haus/Garten; **in town** in der Stadt; **in the country** auf dem Land; **in here** hierin; **in there** darin
2 (*with place names: of town, region, country*) in +*dat*; **in London/Bavaria** in London/Bayern
3 (*indicating time*) in +*dat*; **in spring/summer/May** im Frühling/Sommer/Mai; **in 1994** 1994; **in the afternoon** am Nachmittag; **at 4 o'clock in the afternoon** um 4 Uhr nachmittags; **I did it in 3 hours/days** ich habe es in 3 Stunden/Tagen gemacht; **in 2 weeks** *or* **2 weeks' time** in 2 Wochen
4 (*indicating manner, circumstances, state*) in +*dat*; **in a loud/soft voice** mit lauter/weicher Stimme; **in English/German** auf Englisch/Deutsch; **in the sun** in der Sonne; **in the rain** im Regen; **in good condition** in guter Verfassung

5 (*with ratios, numbers*): **1 in 10** eine(r, s) von 10; **20 pence in the pound** 20 Pence pro Pfund; **they lined up in twos** sie stellten sich in Zweierreihen auf
6 (*referring to people, works*): **the disease is common in children** die Krankheit ist bei Kindern verbreitet; **in (the works of) Dickens** bei Dickens; **they have a good leader in him** in ihm haben sie einen guten Führer
7 (*indicating profession etc*): **to be in teaching/the army** Lehrer(in)/beim Militär sein
8 (*with present participle*): **in saying this, I ...** wenn ich das sage, ...
  ▷ *adv*: **to be in** (*person: at home, work*) da sein; (*train, ship, plane*) angekommen sein; (*in fashion*) in sein; **to ask sb in** jdn hereinbitten; **to run/limp** *etc* **in** hereinlaufen/-humpeln *etc*
  ▷ *n*: **the ins and outs** (*of proposal, situation etc*) die Einzelheiten *pl*

in. *abbr* = **inch**
inability [ɪnə'bɪlɪtɪ] *n* Unfähigkeit *f*
inaccessible [ɪnək'sɛsɪbl] *adj* unzugänglich
inaccuracy [ɪn'ækjurəsɪ] *n* (*see adj*) Ungenauigkeit *f*; Unrichtigkeit *f*; (*mistake*) Fehler *m*
inaccurate [ɪn'ækjurət] *adj* ungenau; (*not correct*) unrichtig
inaction [ɪn'ækʃən] *n* Untätigkeit *f*
inactive [ɪn'æktɪv] *adj* untätig
inactivity [ɪnæk'tɪvɪtɪ] *n* Untätigkeit *f*
inadequacy [ɪn'ædɪkwəsɪ] *n* Unzulänglichkeit *f*
inadequate [ɪn'ædɪkwət] *adj* unzulänglich
inadmissible [ɪnəd'mɪsəbl] *adj* unzulässig
inadvertently [ɪnəd'və:tntlɪ] *adv* ungewollt
inadvisable [ɪnəd'vaɪzəbl] *adj* unratsam; **it is ~ to ...** es ist nicht ratsam, zu ...
inane [ɪ'neɪn] *adj* dumm
inanimate [ɪn'ænɪmət] *adj* unbelebt
inapplicable [ɪn'æplɪkəbl] *adj* unzutreffend
inappropriate [ɪnə'prəuprɪət] *adj* unpassend; (*word, expression*) unangebracht
inapt [ɪn'æpt] *adj* unpassend
inarticulate [ɪnɑ:'tɪkjulət] *adj* (*speech*) unverständlich; **he is ~** er kann sich nur schlecht ausdrücken
inasmuch as [ɪnəz'mʌtʃ-] *adv* da, weil; (*in so far as*) insofern als
inattention [ɪnə'tɛnʃən] *n* Unaufmerksamkeit *f*
inattentive [ɪnə'tɛntɪv] *adj* unaufmerksam
inaudible [ɪn'ɔ:dɪbl] *adj* unhörbar
inaugural [ɪ'nɔ:gjurəl] *adj* (*speech, meeting*) Eröffnungs-
inaugurate [ɪ'nɔ:gjureɪt] *vt* einführen; (*president, official*) (feierlich) in sein/ihr Amt einführen
inauguration [ɪnɔ:gju'reɪʃən] *n* (*see vb*) Einführung *f*; (feierliche) Amtseinführung *f*
inauspicious [ɪnɔ:s'pɪʃəs] *adj* Unheil verheißend

in-between [ɪnbɪ'twiːn] *adj* Mittel-, Zwischen-
inborn [ɪn'bɔːn] *adj* angeboren
inbred [ɪn'brɛd] *adj* angeboren; **an ~ family**
eine Familie, in der Inzucht herrscht
inbreeding [ɪn'briːdɪŋ] *n* Inzucht *f*
in-built ['ɪnbɪlt] *adj* (*quality*) ihm/ihr *etc* eigen;
(*feeling etc*) angeboren
Inc. *abbr* = **incorporated company**
Inca ['ɪŋkə] *adj* (*also*: **Incan**) Inka-, inkaisch ▷ *n*
Inka *mf*
incalculable [ɪn'kælkjuləbl] *adj* (*effect*)
unabsehbar; (*loss*) unermesslich
incapable [ɪn'keɪpəbl] *adj* hilflos; **to be ~ of
sth** unfähig zu etw sein; **to be ~ of doing sth**
unfähig sein, etw zu tun
incapacitate [ɪnkə'pæsɪteɪt] *vt*: **to ~ sb** jdn
unfähig machen
incapacitated [ɪnkə'pæsɪteɪtɪd] *adj* (*Law*)
entmündigt
incapacity [ɪnkə'pæsɪtɪ] *n* Hilflosigkeit *f*;
(*inability*) Unfähigkeit *f*
incarcerate [ɪn'kɑːsəreɪt] *vt* einkerkern
incarnate [ɪn'kɑːnɪt] *adj* leibhaftig, in Person;
evil ~ das leibhaftige Böse
incarnation [ɪnkɑː'neɪʃən] *n* Inbegriff *m*; (*Rel*)
Menschwerdung *f*
incendiary [ɪn'sɛndɪərɪ] *adj* (*bomb*) Brand-; ~
device Brandsatz *m*
incense [*n* 'ɪnsɛns, *vt* ɪn'sɛns] *n* Weihrauch *m*;
(*perfume*) Duft *m* ▷ *vt* wütend machen
incense burner *n* Weihrauchschwenker *m*
incentive [ɪn'sɛntɪv] *n* Anreiz *m*
inception [ɪn'sɛpʃən] *n* Beginn *m*, Anfang *m*
incessant [ɪn'sɛsnt] *adj* unablässig
incessantly [ɪn'sɛsntlɪ] *adv* unablässig
incest ['ɪnsɛst] *n* Inzest *m*
inch [ɪntʃ] *n* Zoll *m*; **to be within an ~ of sth**
kurz vor etw *dat* stehen; **he didn't give an ~**
(*fig*) er gab keinen Fingerbreit nach
▶ **inch forward** *vi* sich millimeterweise
vorwärtsschieben
incidence ['ɪnsɪdns] *n* Häufigkeit *f*
incident ['ɪnsɪdnt] *n* Vorfall *m*; (*diplomatic etc*)
Zwischenfall *m*
incidental [ɪnsɪ'dɛntl] *adj* zusätzlich;
(*unimportant*) nebensächlich; ~ **to** verbunden
mit; ~ **expenses** Nebenkosten *pl*
incidentally [ɪnsɪ'dɛntəlɪ] *adv* übrigens
incidental music *n* Begleitmusik *f*
incident room *n* Einsatzzentrale *f*
incinerate [ɪn'sɪnəreɪt] *vt* verbrennen
incinerator [ɪn'sɪnəreɪtər] *n* (*for waste, refuse*)
(Müll)verbrennungsanlage *f*
incipient [ɪn'sɪpɪənt] *adj* einsetzend
incision [ɪn'sɪʒən] *n* Einschnitt *m*
incisive [ɪn'saɪsɪv] *adj* treffend
incisor [ɪn'saɪzər] *n* Schneidezahn *m*
incite [ɪn'saɪt] *vt* (*rioters*) aufhetzen; (*violence,
hatred*) schüren
incl. *abbr* = **including; inclusive (of)**
inclement [ɪn'klɛmənt] *adj* (*weather*) rau,
unfreundlich
inclination [ɪnklɪ'neɪʃən] *n* Neigung *f*

incline [*n* 'ɪnklaɪn, *vb* ɪn'klaɪn] *n* Abhang *m* ▷ *vt*
neigen ▷ *vi* sich neigen; **to be ~d to** neigen
zu; **to be well ~d towards sb** jdm geneigt *or*
gewogen sein
include [ɪn'kluːd] *vt* einbeziehen; (*in price*)
einschließen; **the tip is not ~d in the price**
Trinkgeld ist im Preis nicht inbegriffen
including [ɪn'kluːdɪŋ] *prep* einschließlich; ~
service charge inklusive Bedienung
inclusion [ɪn'kluːʒən] *n* (*see vb*) Einbeziehung *f*;
Einschluss *m*
inclusive [ɪn'kluːsɪv] *adj* (*terms*) inklusive;
(*price*) Inklusiv-, Pauschal-; ~ **of** einschließlich
+gen
incognito [ɪnkɔg'niːtəu] *adv* inkognito
incoherent [ɪnkəu'hɪərənt] *adj*
zusammenhanglos; (*speech*) wirr; (*person*) sich
unklar *or* undeutlich ausdrückend
income ['ɪnkʌm] *n* Einkommen *nt*; (*from
property, investment, pension*) Einkünfte *pl*;
gross/net ~ Brutto-/Nettoeinkommen
nt; ~ **and expenditure account** Gewinn-
und Verlustrechnung *f*; ~ **bracket**
Einkommensklasse *f*
income support *n* ≈ Sozialhilfe *f*
income tax *n* Einkommensteuer *f* ▷ *cpd*
Steuer-
incoming ['ɪnkʌmɪŋ] *adj* (*passenger*)
ankommend; (*flight*) landend; (*call, mail*)
eingehend; (*government, official*) neu; (*wave*)
hereinbrechend; ~ **tide** Flut *f*
incommunicado ['ɪnkəmjunɪ'kɑːdəu] *adj*: **to
hold sb ~** jdn ohne jede Verbindung zur
Außenwelt halten
incomparable [ɪn'kɔmpərəbl] *adj*
unvergleichlich
incompatible [ɪnkəm'pætɪbl] *adj* unvereinbar
incompetence [ɪn'kɔmpɪtns] *n* Unfähigkeit *f*
incompetent [ɪn'kɔmpɪtnt] *adj* unfähig; (*job*)
unzulänglich
incomplete [ɪnkəm'pliːt] *adj* unfertig; (*partial*)
unvollständig
incomprehensible [ɪnkɔmprɪ'hɛnsɪbl] *adj*
unverständlich
inconceivable [ɪnkən'siːvəbl] *adj*: **it is ~
(that ...)** es ist unvorstellbar *or* undenkbar(,
dass ...)
inconclusive [ɪnkən'kluːsɪv] *adj* (*experiment,
discussion*) ergebnislos; (*evidence, argument*) nicht
überzeugend; (*result*) unbestimmt
incongruous [ɪn'kɔŋgruəs] *adj* (*strange*) absurd;
(*inappropriate*) unpassend
inconsequential [ɪnkɔnsɪ'kwɛnʃl] *adj*
unbedeutend, unwichtig
inconsiderable [ɪnkən'sɪdərəbl] *adj*: **not ~**
beachtlich; (*sum*) nicht unerheblich
inconsiderate [ɪnkən'sɪdərət] *adj*
rücksichtslos
inconsistency [ɪnkən'sɪstənsɪ] *n* (*see adj*)
Widersprüchlichkeit *f*; Inkonsequenz *f*;
Unbeständigkeit *f*
inconsistent [ɪnkən'sɪstnt] *adj*
widersprüchlich; (*person*) inkonsequent; (*work*)

unbeständig; **to be ~ with** im Widerspruch stehen zu

inconsolable [ɪnkən'səuləbl] *adj* untröstlich

inconspicuous [ɪnkən'spɪkjuəs] *adj* unauffällig; **to make o.s. ~** sich unauffällig benehmen

incontinence [ɪn'kɔntɪnəns] *n* (*Med*) Unfähigkeit *f*, Stuhl und/oder Harn zurückzuhalten, Inkontinenz *f*

incontinent [ɪn'kɔntɪnənt] *adj* (*Med*) unfähig, Stuhl und/oder Harn zurückzuhalten, inkontinent

inconvenience [ɪnkən'viːnjəns] *n* Unannehmlichkeit *f*; (*trouble*) Umstände *pl* ▷ *vt* Umstände bereiten +*dat*; **don't ~ yourself** machen Sie sich keine Umstände

inconvenient [ɪnkən'viːnjənt] *adj* (*time, place*) ungünstig; (*house*) unbequem, unpraktisch; (*visitor*) ungelegen

incorporate [ɪn'kɔːpəreɪt] *vt* aufnehmen; (*contain*) enthalten; **safety features have been ~d in the design** in der Konstruktion sind auch Sicherheitsvorkehrungen enthalten

incorporated company [ɪn'kɔːpəreɪtɪd-] (*US*) *n* eingetragene Gesellschaft *f*

incorrect [ɪnkə'rɛkt] *adj* falsch

incorrigible [ɪn'kɔrɪdʒɪbl] *adj* unverbesserlich

incorruptible [ɪnkə'rʌptɪbl] *adj* unbestechlich

increase [*vb* ɪn'kriːs, *n* 'ɪnkriːs] *vi* (*level etc*) zunehmen; (*price*) steigen; (*in size*) sich vergrößern; (*in number, quantity*) sich vermehren ▷ *vt* vergrößern; (*price*) erhöhen ▷ *n:* **~ (in)** Zunahme *f* (+*gen*); (*in wages, spending etc*) Erhöhung *f* (+*gen*); **an ~ of 5%** eine Erhöhung von 5%, eine Zunahme um 5%; **to be on the ~** zunehmen

increasing [ɪn'kriːsɪŋ] *adj* zunehmend

increasingly [ɪn'kriːsɪŋlɪ] *adv* zunehmend

incredible [ɪn'krɛdɪbl] *adj* unglaublich; (*amazing, wonderful*) unwahrscheinlich (*inf*), sagenhaft (*inf*)

incredulity [ɪnkrɪ'djuːlɪtɪ] *n* Ungläubigkeit *f*

incredulous [ɪn'krɛdjuləs] *adj* ungläubig

increment ['ɪnkrɪmənt] *n* (*in salary*) Erhöhung *f*, Zulage *f*

incriminate [ɪn'krɪmɪneɪt] *vt* belasten

incriminating [ɪn'krɪmɪneɪtɪŋ] *adj* belastend

incrusted [ɪn'krʌstɪd] *adj* = **encrusted**

incubate ['ɪnkjubeɪt] *vt* ausbrüten ▷ *vi* ausgebrütet werden; (*disease*) zum Ausbruch kommen

incubation [ɪnkju'beɪʃən] *n* Ausbrüten *nt*; (*of illness*) Inkubation *f*

incubation period *n* Inkubationszeit *f*

incubator ['ɪnkjubeɪtəʳ] *n* (*for babies*) Brutkasten *m*, Inkubator *m*

inculcate ['ɪnkʌlkeɪt] *vt:* **to ~ sth in(to) sb** jdm etw einprägen

incumbent [ɪn'kʌmbənt] *n* Amtsinhaber(in) *m(f)* ▷ *adj:* **it is ~ on him to ...** es obliegt ihm *or* es ist seine Pflicht, zu ...

incur [ɪn'kəːʳ] *vt* (*expenses, debt*) machen; (*loss*)

erleiden; (*disapproval, anger*) sich *dat* zuziehen

incurable [ɪn'kjuərəbl] *adj* unheilbar

incursion [ɪn'kəːʃən] *n* (*Mil*) Einfall *m*

Ind. (*US*) *abbr* (*Post*) = Indiana

indebted [ɪn'dɛtɪd] *adj:* **to be ~ to sb** jdm (zu Dank) verpflichtet sein

indecency [ɪn'diːsnsɪ] *n* Unanständigkeit *f*, Anstößigkeit *f*

indecent [ɪn'diːsnt] *adj* unanständig, anstößig; (*haste*) ungebührlich

indecent assault (*Brit*) *n* Sexualverbrechen *nt*

indecent exposure *n* Erregung *f* öffentlichen Ärgernisses

indecipherable [ɪndɪ'saɪfərəbl] *adj* unleserlich; (*expression, glance etc*) unergründlich

indecision [ɪndɪ'sɪʒən] *n* Unentschlossenheit *f*

indecisive [ɪndɪ'saɪsɪv] *adj* unentschlossen

indeed [ɪn'diːd] *adv* aber sicher; (*in fact*) tatsächlich, in der Tat; (*furthermore*) sogar; **yes ~!** oh ja!, das kann man wohl sagen!

indefatigable [ɪndɪ'fætɪgəbl] *adj* unermüdlich

indefensible [ɪndɪ'fɛnsɪbl] *adj* (*conduct*) unentschuldbar

indefinable [ɪndɪ'faɪnəbl] *adj* undefinierbar

indefinite [ɪn'dɛfɪnɪt] *adj* unklar, vage; (*period, number*) unbestimmt

indefinite article *n* (*Ling*) unbestimmter Artikel *m*

indefinitely [ɪn'dɛfɪnɪtlɪ] *adv* (*continue*) endlos; (*wait*) unbegrenzt (lange); (*postpone*) auf unbestimmte Zeit

indelible [ɪn'dɛlɪbl] *adj* (*mark, stain*) nicht zu entfernen; **~ pen** Tintenstift *m*; **~ ink** Wäschetinte *f*

indelicate [ɪn'dɛlɪkɪt] *adj* taktlos; (*not polite*) ungehörig

indemnify [ɪn'dɛmnɪfaɪ] *vt* entschädigen

indemnity [ɪn'dɛmnɪtɪ] *n* (*insurance*) Versicherung *f*; (*compensation*) Entschädigung *f*

indent [ɪn'dɛnt] *vt* (*text*) einrücken, einziehen

indentation [ɪndɛn'teɪʃən] *n* Einkerbung *f*; (*Typ*) Einrückung *f*, Einzug *m*; (*on metal*) Delle *f*

indenture [ɪn'dɛntʃəʳ] *n* Ausbildungsvertrag *m*, Lehrvertrag *m*

independence [ɪndɪ'pɛndns] *n* Unabhängigkeit *f*

INDEPENDENCE DAY

Independence Day (der 4. Juli) ist in den USA ein gesetzlicher Feiertag zum Gedenken an die Unabhängigkeitserklärung vom 4. Juli 1776, mit der die 13 amerikanischen Kolonien ihre Freiheit und Unabhängigkeit von Großbritannien erklärten.

independent [ɪndɪ'pɛndnt] *adj* unabhängig

independently [ɪndɪ'pɛndntlɪ] *adv* unabhängig

in-depth ['ɪndɛpθ] *adj* eingehend

indescribable [ɪndɪs'kraɪbəbl] *adj* unbeschreiblich

indestructible [ɪndɪs'trʌktəbl] *adj*
unzerstörbar

indeterminate [ɪndɪ'tə:mɪnɪt] *adj* unbestimmt

index ['ɪndɛks] (*pl* **~es**) *n* (*in book*) Register *nt*; (*in library etc*) Katalog *m*; (*also*: **card index**) Kartei *f* (*pl* **indices**: *ratio*) Index *m*; (: *sign*) (An)zeichen *nt*

index card *n* Karteikarte *f*

indexed ['ɪndɛkst] (*US*) *adj* = **index-linked**

index finger *n* Zeigefinger *m*

index-linked ['ɪndɛks'lɪŋkt] *adj* der Inflationsrate *dat* angeglichen

India ['ɪndɪə] *n* Indien *nt*

Indian ['ɪndɪən] *adj* indisch; (*American Indian*) indianisch ▷ *n* Inder(in) *m(f)*; **American ~** Indianer(in) *m(f)*

Indian Ocean *n*: **the ~** der Indische Ozean

Indian summer *n* Altweibersommer *m*

India paper *n* Dünndruckpapier *nt*

India rubber *n* Gummi *m*, Kautschuk *m*

indicate ['ɪndɪkeɪt] *vt* (an)zeigen; (*point to*) deuten auf +*acc*; (*mention*) andeuten ▷ *vi* (*Brit*: *Aut*): **to ~ left/right** links/rechts blinken

indication [ɪndɪ'keɪʃən] *n* (An)zeichen *nt*

indicative [ɪn'dɪkətɪv] *n* (*Ling*) Indikativ *m*, Wirklichkeitsform *f* ▷ *adj*: **to be ~ of sth** auf etw *acc* schließen lassen

indicator ['ɪndɪkeɪtər] *n* (*instrument, gauge*) Anzeiger *m*; (*fig*) (An)zeichen *nt*; (*Aut*) Richtungsanzeiger *m*, Blinker *m*

indices ['ɪndɪsi:z] *npl of* **index**

indict [ɪn'daɪt] *vt* anklagen

indictable [ɪn'daɪtəbl] *adj* (*person*) strafrechtlich verfolgbar; **~ offence** strafbare Handlung *f*

indictment [ɪn'daɪtmənt] *n* Anklage *f*; **to be an ~ of sth** (*fig*) ein Armutszeugnis *nt* für etw sein

indifference [ɪn'dɪfrəns] *n* Gleichgültigkeit *f*

indifferent [ɪn'dɪfrənt] *adj* gleichgültig; (*mediocre*) mittelmäßig

indigenous [ɪn'dɪdʒɪnəs] *adj* einheimisch

indigestible [ɪndɪ'dʒɛstɪbl] *adj* unverdaulich

indigestion [ɪndɪ'dʒɛstʃən] *n* Magenverstimmung *f*

indignant [ɪn'dɪgnənt] *adj*: **to be ~ at sth/ with sb** entrüstet über etw/jdn sein

indignation [ɪndɪg'neɪʃən] *n* Entrüstung *f*

indignity [ɪn'dɪgnɪti] *n* Demütigung *f*

indigo ['ɪndɪgəʊ] *n* Indigo *nt or m*

indirect [ɪndɪ'rɛkt] *adj* indirekt; **~ way** *or* **route** Umweg *m*

indirectly [ɪndɪ'rɛktlɪ] *adv* indirekt

indiscreet [ɪndɪs'kri:t] *adj* indiskret

indiscretion [ɪndɪs'krɛʃən] *n* Indiskretion *f*

indiscriminate [ɪndɪs'krɪmɪnət] *adj* wahllos; (*taste*) unkritisch

indispensable [ɪndɪs'pɛnsəbl] *adj* unentbehrlich

indisposed [ɪndɪs'pəʊzd] *adj* unpässlich

indisputable [ɪndɪs'pju:təbl] *adj* unbestreitbar

indistinct [ɪndɪs'tɪŋkt] *adj* undeutlich; (*image*) verschwommen; (*noise*) schwach

indistinguishable [ɪndɪs'tɪŋgwɪʃəbl] *adj*: **~**

from nicht zu unterscheiden von

individual [ɪndɪ'vɪdjuəl] *n* Individuum *nt*, Einzelne(r) *f(m)* ▷ *adj* eigen; (*single*) einzeln; (*case, portion*) Einzel-; (*particular*) individuell

individualist [ɪndɪ'vɪdjuəlɪst] *n* Individualist(in) *m(f)*

individuality [ɪndɪvɪdju'ælɪti] *n* Individualität *f*

individually [ɪndɪ'vɪdjuəlɪ] *adv* einzeln, individuell

indivisible [ɪndɪ'vɪzɪbl] *adj* unteilbar

Indochina [ɪndəʊ'tʃaɪnə] *n* Indochina *nt*

indoctrinate [ɪn'dɒktrɪneɪt] *vt* indoktrinieren

indoctrination [ɪndɒktrɪ'neɪʃən] *n* Indoktrination *f*

indolence ['ɪndələns] *n* Trägheit *f*

indolent ['ɪndələnt] *adj* träge

Indonesia [ɪndə'ni:zɪə] *n* Indonesien *nt*

Indonesian [ɪndə'ni:zɪən] *adj* indonesisch ▷ *n* Indonesier(in) *m(f)*; (*Ling*) Indonesisch *nt*

indoor ['ɪndɔ:r] *adj* (*plant, aerial*) Zimmer-; (*clothes, shoes*) Haus-; (*swimming pool, sport*) Hallen-; (*games*) im Haus

indoors [ɪn'dɔ:z] *adv* drinnen; **to go ~** hineingehen

indubitable [ɪn'dju:bɪtəbl] *adj* unzweifelhaft

indubitably [ɪn'dju:bɪtəblɪ] *adv* zweifellos

induce [ɪn'dju:s] *vt* herbeiführen; (*persuade*) dazu bringen; (*Med*: *birth*) einleiten; **to ~ sb to do sth** jdn dazu bewegen *or* bringen, etw zu tun

inducement [ɪn'dju:smənt] *n* Anreiz *m*; (*pej*: *bribe*) Bestechung *f*

induct [ɪn'dʌkt] *vt* (in sein/ihr *etc* Amt) einführen

induction [ɪn'dʌkʃən] *n* (*Med*: *of birth*) Einleitung *f*

induction course (*Brit*) *n* Einführungskurs *m*

indulge [ɪn'dʌldʒ] *vt* nachgeben +*dat*; (*person, child*) verwöhnen ▷ *vi*: **to ~ in** sich hingeben +*dat*

indulgence [ɪn'dʌldʒəns] *n* (*pleasure*) Luxus *m*; (*leniency*) Nachgiebigkeit *f*

indulgent [ɪn'dʌldʒənt] *adj* nachsichtig

industrial [ɪn'dʌstrɪəl] *adj* industriell; (*accident*) Arbeits-; (*city*) Industrie-

industrial action *n* Arbeitskampfmaßnahmen *pl*

industrial design *n* Industriedesign *nt*

industrial estate (*Brit*) *n* Industriegebiet *nt*

industrialist [ɪn'dʌstrɪəlɪst] *n* Industrielle(r) *f(m)*

industrialize [ɪn'dʌstrɪəlaɪz] *vt* industrialisieren

industrial park (*US*) *n* = **industrial estate**

industrial relations *npl* Beziehungen *zwischen Arbeitgebern, Arbeitnehmern und Gewerkschaften*

industrial tribunal (*Brit*) *n* Arbeitsgericht *nt*

industrial unrest (*Brit*) *n* Arbeitsunruhen *pl*

industrious [ɪn'dʌstrɪəs] *adj* fleißig

industry ['ɪndəstrɪ] *n* Industrie *f*; (*diligence*) Fleiß *m*

inebriated [ɪ'ni:brɪeɪtɪd] *adj* betrunken

inedible [ɪnˈɛdɪbl] adj ungenießbar
ineffective [ɪnɪˈfɛktɪv] adj wirkungslos; (government) unfähig
ineffectual [ɪnɪˈfɛktʃuəl] adj = ineffective
inefficiency [ɪnɪˈfɪʃənsɪ] n (see adj) Ineffizienz f; Leistungsunfähigkeit f
inefficient [ɪnɪˈfɪʃənt] adj ineffizient; (machine) leistungsunfähig
inelegant [ɪnˈɛlɪgənt] adj unelegant
ineligible [ɪnˈɛlɪdʒɪbl] adj (candidate) nicht wählbar; to be ~ for sth zu etw nicht berechtigt sein
inept [ɪˈnɛpt] adj (politician) unfähig; (management) stümperhaft
ineptitude [ɪˈnɛptɪtjuːd] n (see adj) Unfähigkeit f; Stümperhaftigkeit f
inequality [ɪnɪˈkwɒlɪtɪ] n Ungleichheit f
inequitable [ɪnˈɛkwɪtəbl] adj ungerecht
inert [ɪˈnɜːt] adj unbeweglich; ~ gas Edelgas nt
inertia [ɪˈnɜːʃə] n Trägheit f
inertia-reel seat belt [ɪˈnɜːʃəˈriːl-] n Automatikgurt m
inescapable [ɪnɪˈskeɪpəbl] adj unvermeidlich; (conclusion) zwangsläufig
inessential [ɪnɪˈsɛnʃl] adj unwesentlich; (furniture etc) entbehrlich
inessentials [ɪnɪˈsɛnʃlz] npl Nebensächlichkeiten pl
inestimable [ɪnˈɛstɪməbl] adj unschätzbar
inevitability [ɪnevɪtəˈbɪlɪtɪ] n Unvermeidlichkeit f; it is an ~ es ist nicht zu vermeiden
inevitable [ɪnˈɛvɪtəbl] adj unvermeidlich; (result) zwangsläufig
inevitably [ɪnˈɛvɪtəblɪ] adv zwangsläufig; ~, he was late es konnte ja nicht ausbleiben, dass er zu spät kam; as ~ happens ... wie es immer so ist ...
inexact [ɪnɪgˈzækt] adj ungenau
inexcusable [ɪnɪksˈkjuːzəbl] adj unentschuldbar, unverzeihlich
inexhaustible [ɪnɪgˈzɔːstɪbl] adj unerschöpflich
inexorable [ɪnˈɛksərəbl] adj unaufhaltsam
inexpensive [ɪnɪkˈspɛnsɪv] adj preisgünstig
inexperience [ɪnɪkˈspɪərɪəns] n Unerfahrenheit f
inexperienced [ɪnɪkˈspɪərɪənst] adj unerfahren; (swimmer etc) ungeübt; to be ~ in sth wenig Erfahrung mit etw haben
inexplicable [ɪnɪksˈplɪkəbl] adj unerklärlich
inexpressible [ɪnɪkˈsprɛsɪbl] adj unbeschreiblich
inextricable [ɪnɪkˈstrɪkəbl] adj unentwirrbar; (dilemma) unlösbar
inextricably [ɪnɪkˈstrɪkəblɪ] adv unentwirrbar; (linked) untrennbar
infallibility [ɪnfæləˈbɪlɪtɪ] n Unfehlbarkeit f
infallible [ɪnˈfælɪbl] adj unfehlbar
infamous [ˈɪnfəməs] adj niederträchtig
infamy [ˈɪnfəmɪ] n Verrufenheit f
infancy [ˈɪnfənsɪ] n frühe Kindheit f; (of movement, firm) Anfangsstadium nt

infant [ˈɪnfənt] n Säugling m; (young child) Kleinkind nt ▷ cpd Säuglings-
infantile [ˈɪnfəntaɪl] adj kindisch, infantil; (disease) Kinder-
infantry [ˈɪnfəntrɪ] n Infanterie f
infantryman [ˈɪnfəntrɪmən] (irreg: like man) n Infanterist m
infant school (Brit) n Grundschule f (für die ersten beiden Jahrgänge)
infatuated [ɪnˈfætjueɪtɪd] adj: ~ with vernarrt in +acc; to become ~ with sich vernarren in +acc
infatuation [ɪnfætjuˈeɪʃən] n Vernarrtheit f
infect [ɪnˈfɛkt] vt anstecken (also fig), infizieren; (food) verseuchen; to become ~ed (wound) sich entzünden
infection [ɪnˈfɛkʃən] n Infektion f, Entzündung f; (contagion) Ansteckung f
infectious [ɪnˈfɛkʃəs] adj ansteckend
infer [ɪnˈfɜːʳ] vt schließen; (imply) andeuten
inference [ˈɪnfərəns] n (see vb) Schluss m; Andeutung f
inferior [ɪnˈfɪərɪəʳ] adj (in rank) untergeordnet, niedriger; (in quality) minderwertig; (in quantity, number) geringer ▷ n Untergebene(r) f(m); to feel ~ (to sb) sich (jdm) unterlegen fühlen
inferiority [ɪnfɪərɪˈɒrətɪ] n (see adj) untergeordnete Stellung f, niedriger Rang m; Minderwertigkeit f; geringere Zahl f
inferiority complex n Minderwertigkeitskomplex m
infernal [ɪnˈfɜːnl] adj höllisch; (temper) schrecklich
inferno [ɪnˈfɜːnəu] n (blaze) Flammenmeer nt
infertile [ɪnˈfɜːtaɪl] adj unfruchtbar
infertility [ɪnfɜːˈtɪlɪtɪ] n Unfruchtbarkeit f
infested [ɪnˈfɛstɪd] adj: ~ (with) verseucht (mit)
infidelity [ɪnfɪˈdɛlɪtɪ] n Untreue f
infighting [ˈɪnfaɪtɪŋ] n interne Machtkämpfe pl
infiltrate [ˈɪnfɪltreɪt] vt (organization etc) infiltrieren, unterwandern; (: to spy) einschleusen
infinite [ˈɪnfɪnɪt] adj unendlich; (time, money) unendlich viel
infinitely [ˈɪnfɪnɪtlɪ] adv unendlich viel
infinitesimal [ɪnfɪnɪˈtɛsɪməl] adj unendlich klein, winzig
infinitive [ɪnˈfɪnɪtɪv] n (Ling) Infinitiv m, Grundform f
infinity [ɪnˈfɪnɪtɪ] n Unendlichkeit f; (Math, Phot) Unendliche nt; an ~ of ... unendlich viel(e) ...
infirm [ɪnˈfɜːm] adj schwach, gebrechlich
infirmary [ɪnˈfɜːmərɪ] n Krankenhaus nt
infirmity [ɪnˈfɜːmɪtɪ] n Schwäche f, Gebrechlichkeit f
inflame [ɪnˈfleɪm] vt aufbringen
inflamed [ɪnˈfleɪmd] adj entzündet
inflammable [ɪnˈflæməbl] adj feuergefährlich
inflammation [ɪnfləˈmeɪʃən] n Entzündung f

i

inflammatory [ɪn'flæmətərɪ] adj (speech) aufrührerisch, Hetz-

inflatable [ɪn'fleɪtəbl] adj aufblasbar; (dinghy) Schlauch-

inflate [ɪn'fleɪt] vt aufpumpen; (balloon) aufblasen; (price) hochtreiben; (expectation) steigern; (position, ideas etc) hochspielen

inflated [ɪn'fleɪtɪd] adj (value, price) überhöht

inflation [ɪn'fleɪʃən] n Inflation f

inflationary [ɪn'fleɪʃənərɪ] adj inflationär; (spiral) Inflations-

inflexible [ɪn'flɛksɪbl] adj inflexibel; (rule) starr

inflict [ɪn'flɪkt] vt: **to ~ sth on sb** (damage, suffering, wound) jdm etw zufügen; (punishment) jdm etw auferlegen; (fig: problems) jdn mit etw belasten

infliction [ɪn'flɪkʃən] n (see vb) Zufügen nt; Auferlegung f; Belastung f

in-flight ['ɪnflaɪt] adj während des Fluges

inflow ['ɪnfləu] n Zustrom m

influence ['ɪnfluəns] n Einfluss m ▷ vt beeinflussen; **under the ~ of alcohol** unter Alkoholeinfluss

influential [ɪnflu'ɛnʃl] adj einflussreich

influenza [ɪnflu'ɛnzə] n (Med) Grippe f

influx ['ɪnflʌks] n (of refugees) Zustrom m; (of funds) Zufuhr f

inform [ɪn'fɔːm] vt: **to ~ sb of sth** jdn von etw unterrichten, jdn über etw acc informieren ▷ vi: **to ~ on sb** jdn denunzieren

informal [ɪn'fɔːml] adj ungezwungen; (manner, clothes) leger; (unofficial) inoffiziell; (announcement, invitation) informell

informality [ɪnfɔː'mælɪtɪ] n (see adj) Ungezwungenheit f; legere Art f; inoffizieller Charakter m; informeller Charakter m

informally [ɪn'fɔːməlɪ] adv (see adj) ungezwungen; leger; inoffiziell; informell

informant [ɪn'fɔːmənt] n Informant(in) m(f)

information [ɪnfə'meɪʃən] n Informationen pl, Auskunft f; (knowledge) Wissen nt; **to get ~ on** sich informieren über +acc; **a piece of ~** eine Auskunft or Information; **for your ~** zu Ihrer Information

information and communication technology (Brit) n (Scol) ≈ Informations- und Kommunikationstechnologie

information bureau n Auskunftsbüro nt

information desk n Auskunftsschalter m

information office n Auskunftsbüro nt

information processing n Informationsverarbeitung f

information retrieval n Informationsabruf m, Datenabruf m

information science n Informatik f

information superhighway n (Comput) Datenautobahn f

information technology n Informationstechnik f

informative [ɪn'fɔːmətɪv] adj aufschlussreich

informed [ɪn'fɔːmd] adj informiert; (guess, opinion) wohlbegründet; **to be well/better ~** gut/besser informiert sein

informer [ɪn'fɔːməʳ] n Informant(in) m(f); (also: **police informer**) Polizeispitzel m

infra dig ['ɪnfrə'dɪg] (inf) adj abbr (= infra dignitatem) unter meiner/seiner etc Würde

infrared [ɪnfrə'rɛd] adj infrarot

infrastructure ['ɪnfrəstrʌktʃəʳ] n Infrastruktur f

infrequent [ɪn'friːkwənt] adj selten

infringe [ɪn'frɪndʒ] vt (law) verstoßen gegen, übertreten ▷ vi: **to ~ on** (rights) verletzen

infringement [ɪn'frɪndʒmənt] n (see vb) Verstoß m, Übertretung f; Verletzung f

infuriate [ɪn'fjuərɪeɪt] vt wütend machen

infuriating [ɪn'fjuərɪeɪtɪŋ] adj äußerst ärgerlich

infuse [ɪn'fjuːz] vt (tea etc) aufgießen; **to ~ sb with sth** (fig) jdm etw einflößen

infusion [ɪn'fjuːʒən] n (tea etc) Aufguss m

ingenious [ɪn'dʒiːnjəs] adj genial

ingenuity [ɪndʒɪ'njuːɪtɪ] n Einfallsreichtum m; (skill) Geschicklichkeit f

ingenuous [ɪn'dʒɛnjuəs] adj offen, aufrichtig; (innocent) naiv

ingot ['ɪŋgət] n Barren m

ingrained [ɪn'greɪnd] adj (habit) fest; (belief) unerschütterlich

ingratiate [ɪn'greɪʃɪeɪt] vt: **to ~ o.s. with sb** sich bei jdm einschmeicheln

ingratiating [ɪn'greɪʃɪeɪtɪŋ] adj schmeichlerisch

ingratitude [ɪn'grætɪtjuːd] n Undank m

ingredient [ɪn'griːdɪənt] n (of cake etc) Zutat f; (of situation) Bestandteil m

ingrowing ['ɪngrəuɪŋ] adj: **~ toenail** eingewachsener Zehennagel m

inhabit [ɪn'hæbɪt] vt bewohnen, wohnen in +dat

inhabitant [ɪn'hæbɪtnt] n Einwohner(in) m(f); (of street, house) Bewohner(in) m(f)

inhale [ɪn'heɪl] vt einatmen ▷ vi einatmen; (when smoking) inhalieren

inhaler [ɪn'heɪləʳ] n Inhalationsapparat m

inherent [ɪn'hɪərənt] adj: **~ in** or **to** eigen +dat

inherently [ɪn'hɪərəntlɪ] adv von Natur aus

inherit [ɪn'hɛrɪt] vt erben

inheritance [ɪn'hɛrɪtəns] n Erbe nt

inhibit [ɪn'hɪbɪt] vt hemmen

inhibited [ɪn'hɪbɪtɪd] adj gehemmt

inhibiting [ɪn'hɪbɪtɪŋ] adj hemmend; **~ factor** Hemmnis nt

inhibition [ɪnhɪ'bɪʃən] n Hemmung f

inhospitable [ɪnhɔs'pɪtəbl] adj ungastlich; (place, climate) unwirtlich

in-house ['ɪn'haus] adj, adv hausintern

inhuman [ɪn'hjuːmən] adj (behaviour) unmenschlich; (appearance) nicht menschlich

inhumane [ɪnhju'meɪn] adj inhuman; (treatment) menschenunwürdig

inimitable [ɪ'nɪmɪtəbl] adj unnachahmlich

iniquitous [ɪ'nɪkwɪtəs] adj (unfair) ungerecht

iniquity [ɪ'nɪkwɪtɪ] n Ungerechtigkeit f; (wickedness) Ungeheuerlichkeit f

initial [ɪ'nɪʃl] adj anfänglich; (stage) Anfangs-

▷ *n* Initiale *f*, Anfangsbuchstabe *m* ▷ *vt* (*document*) abzeichnen; **initials** *npl* Initialen *pl*; (*as signature*) Namenszeichen *nt*

initialize [ɪˈnɪʃəlaɪz] *vt* initialisieren

initially [ɪˈnɪʃəlɪ] *adv* zu Anfang; (*first*) zuerst

initiate [ɪˈnɪʃɪeɪt] *vt* (*talks*) eröffnen; (*process*) einleiten; (*new member*) feierlich aufnehmen; **to ~ sb into a secret** jdn in ein Geheimnis einweihen; **to ~ proceedings against sb** (*Law*) einen Prozess gegen jdn anstrengen

initiation [ɪnɪʃɪˈeɪʃən] *n* (*beginning*) Einführung *f*; (*into secret etc*) Einweihung *f*

initiative [ɪˈnɪʃətɪv] *n* Initiative *f*; **to take the ~** die Initiative ergreifen

inject [ɪnˈdʒɛkt] *vt* (ein)spritzen; (*fig: funds*) hineinpumpen; **to ~ sb with sth** jdm etw spritzen *or* injizieren; **to ~ money into sth** (*fig*) Geld in etw *acc* pumpen

injection [ɪnˈdʒɛkʃən] *n* Spritze *f*, Injektion *f*; **to give/have an ~** eine Spritze *or* Injektion geben/bekommen; **an ~ of money/funds** (*fig*) eine Finanzspritze

injudicious [ɪndʒuˈdɪʃəs] *adj* unklug

injunction [ɪnˈdʒʌŋkʃən] *n* (*Law*) gerichtliche Verfügung *f*

injure [ˈɪndʒəʳ] *vt* verletzen; (*reputation*) schaden +*dat*; **to ~ o.s.** sich verletzen

injured [ˈɪndʒəd] *adj* verletzt; (*tone*) gekränkt; **~ party** (*Law*) Geschädigte(r) *f(m)*

injurious [ɪnˈdʒuərɪəs] *adj*: **to be ~ to** schaden +*dat*, schädlich sein +*dat*

injury [ˈɪndʒərɪ] *n* Verletzung *f*; **to escape without ~** unverletzt davonkommen

injury time *n* (*Sport*) Nachspielzeit *f*; **to play ~** nachspielen

injustice [ɪnˈdʒʌstɪs] *n* Ungerechtigkeit *f*; **you do me an ~** Sie tun mir unrecht

ink [ɪŋk] *n* Tinte *f*; (*in printing*) Druckfarbe *f*

ink-jet printer [ˈɪŋkdʒɛt-] *n* Tintenstrahldrucker *m*

inkling [ˈɪŋklɪŋ] *n* (dunkle) Ahnung *f*; **to have an ~ of** ahnen

ink pad *n* Stempelkissen *nt*

inky [ˈɪŋkɪ] *adj* tintenschwarz; (*fingers*) tintenbeschmiert

inlaid [ˈɪnleɪd] *adj* eingelegt

inland [ˈɪnlənd] *adj* (*port, sea, waterway*) Binnen- ▷ *adv* (*travel*) landeinwärts

Inland Revenue (*Brit*) *n* ≈ Finanzamt *nt*

in-laws [ˈɪnlɔːz] *npl* (*parents-in-law*) Schwiegereltern *pl*; (*other relatives*) angeheiratete Verwandte *pl*

inlet [ˈɪnlɛt] *n* (schmale) Bucht *f*

inlet pipe *n* Zuleitung *f*, Zuleitungsrohr *nt*

inmate [ˈɪnmeɪt] *n* Insasse *m*, Insassin *f*

inmost [ˈɪnməʊst] *adj* innerst

inn [ɪn] *n* Gasthaus *nt*

innards [ˈɪnədz] (*inf*) *npl* Innereien *pl*

innate [ɪˈneɪt] *adj* angeboren

inner [ˈɪnəʳ] *adj* innere(r, s); (*courtyard*) Innen-

inner city *n* Innenstadt *f*

innermost [ˈɪnəməʊst] *adj* = **inmost**

inner tube *n* (*of tyre*) Schlauch *m*

innings [ˈɪnɪŋz] *n* (*Cricket*) Innenrunde *f*; **he's had a good ~** (*fig*) er kann auf ein langes, ausgefülltes Leben zurückblicken

innocence [ˈɪnəsns] *n* Unschuld *f*

innocent [ˈɪnəsnt] *adj* unschuldig

innocuous [ɪˈnɔkjuəs] *adj* harmlos

innovation [ɪnəʊˈveɪʃən] *n* Neuerung *f*

innuendo [ɪnjuˈɛndəʊ] (*pl* **-es**) *n* versteckte Andeutung *f*

innumerable [ɪˈnjuːmrəbl] *adj* unzählig

inoculate [ɪˈnɔkjuleɪt] *vt*: **to ~ sb against sth** jdn gegen etw impfen; **to ~ sb with sth** jdm etw einimpfen

inoculation [ɪnɔkjuˈleɪʃən] *n* Impfung *f*

inoffensive [ɪnəˈfɛnsɪv] *adj* harmlos

inopportune [ɪnˈɔpətjuːn] *adj* unangebracht; (*moment*) ungelegen

inordinate [ɪˈnɔːdɪnət] *adj* (*thirst etc*) unmäßig; (*amount, pleasure*) ungeheuer

inordinately [ɪˈnɔːdɪnətlɪ] *adv* (*proud*) unmäßig; (*long, large etc*) ungeheuer

inorganic [ɪnɔːˈgænɪk] *adj* anorganisch

inpatient [ˈɪnpeɪʃənt] *n* stationär behandelter Patient *m*, stationär behandelte Patientin *f*

input [ˈɪnpʊt] *n* (*of capital, manpower*) Investition *f*; (*of energy*) Zufuhr *f*; (*Comput*) Eingabe *f*, Input *m or nt* ▷ *vt* (*Comput*) eingeben

inquest [ˈɪnkwɛst] *n* gerichtliche Untersuchung *f* der Todesursache

inquire [ɪnˈkwaɪəʳ] *vi*: **to ~ about** sich erkundigen nach, fragen nach ▷ *vt* sich erkundigen nach, fragen nach; **to ~ when/ where/whether** fragen *or* sich erkundigen, wann/wo/ob

▸ **inquire after** *vt fus* sich erkundigen nach

▸ **inquire into** *vt fus* untersuchen

inquiring [ɪnˈkwaɪərɪŋ] *adj* wissensdurstig

inquiry [ɪnˈkwaɪərɪ] *n* Untersuchung *f*; (*question*) Anfrage *f*; **to hold an ~ into sth** eine Untersuchung +*gen* durchführen

inquiry desk (*Brit*) *n* Auskunft *f*, Auskunftsschalter *m*

inquiry office (*Brit*) *n* Auskunft *f*, Auskunftsbüro *nt*

inquisition [ɪnkwɪˈzɪʃən] *n* Untersuchung *f*; (*Rel*): **the I~** die Inquisition

inquisitive [ɪnˈkwɪzɪtɪv] *adj* neugierig

inroads [ˈɪnrəʊdz] *npl*: **to make ~ into** (*savings, supplies*) angreifen

ins *abbr* (= *inches*) *see* **inch**

insane [ɪnˈseɪn] *adj* wahnsinnig; (*Med*) geisteskrank

insanitary [ɪnˈsænɪtərɪ] *adj* unhygienisch

insanity [ɪnˈsænɪtɪ] *n* Wahnsinn *m*; (*Med*) Geisteskrankheit *f*

insatiable [ɪnˈseɪʃəbl] *adj* unersättlich

inscribe [ɪnˈskraɪb] *vt* (*on ring*) eingravieren; (*on stone*) einmeißeln; (*on banner*) schreiben; **to ~ a ring/stone/banner with sth** etw in einen Ring eingravieren/in einen Stein einmeißeln/auf ein Spruchband schreiben; **to ~ a book** eine Widmung in ein Buch schreiben

inscription [ɪnˈskrɪpʃən] n Inschrift f; (in book) Widmung f

inscrutable [ɪnˈskruːtəbl] adj (comment) unergründlich; (expression) undurchdringlich

inseam measurement [ˈɪnsiːm-] (US) n innere Beinlänge f

insect [ˈɪnsɛkt] n Insekt nt

insect bite n Insektenstich m

insecticide [ɪnˈsɛktɪsaɪd] n Insektizid nt, Insektengift nt

insect repellent n Insektenbekämpfungsmittel nt

insecure [ɪnsɪˈkjuəʳ] adj unsicher

insecurity [ɪnsɪˈkjuərɪtɪ] n Unsicherheit f

insemination [ɪnsɛmɪˈneɪʃən] n: **artificial ~** künstliche Besamung f

insensible [ɪnˈsɛnsɪbl] adj bewusstlos; **~ to** unempfindlich gegen; **~ of** nicht bewusst +gen

insensitive [ɪnˈsɛnsɪtɪv] adj gefühllos

insensitivity [ɪnsɛnsɪˈtɪvɪtɪ] n Gefühllosigkeit f

inseparable [ɪnˈsɛprəbl] adj untrennbar; (friends) unzertrennlich

insert [vt ɪnˈsəːt, n ˈɪnsəːt] vt einfügen; (into sth) hineinstecken ▷ n (in newspaper etc) Beilage f; (in shoe) Einlage f

insertion [ɪnˈsəːʃən] n Hineinstecken nt; (of needle) Einstechen nt; (of comment) Einfügen nt

in-service [ˈɪnˈsəːvɪs] adj: **~ training** (berufsbegleitende) Fortbildung f; **~ course** Fortbildungslehrgang m

inshore [ˈɪnˈʃɔːʳ] adj (fishing, waters) Küsten- ▷ adv in Küstennähe; (move) auf die Küste zu

inside [ɪnˈsaɪd] n Innere(s) nt, Innenseite f; (of road: in Britain) linke Spur f; (: in US, Europe etc) rechte Spur f ▷ adj innere(r, s); (pocket, cabin, light) Innen- ▷ adv (go) nach innen, hinein; (be) drinnen ▷ prep (location) in +dat; (motion) in +acc; **~ 10 minutes** innerhalb von 10 Minuten; **insides** npl (inf) Bauch m; (innards) Eingeweide pl

inside forward n (Sport) Halbstürmer m

inside information n Insiderinformation f

inside knowledge n Insiderwissen nt

inside lane n (Brit) linke Spur f; (in US, Europe etc) rechte Spur f

inside leg measurement (Brit) n innere Beinlänge f

inside out adv (know) in- und auswendig; (piece of clothing: be) links or verkehrt herum; (: turn) nach links

insider [ɪnˈsaɪdəʳ] n Insider m, Eingeweihte(r) f(m)

insider dealing, insider trading n (Stock Exchange) Insiderhandel m or -geschäfte pl

inside story n Insidestory f, Inside Story f

insidious [ɪnˈsɪdɪəs] adj heimtückisch

insight [ˈɪnsaɪt] n Verständnis nt; **to gain (an) ~ into** einen Einblick gewinnen in +acc

insignia [ɪnˈsɪɡnɪə] npl Insignien pl

insignificant [ɪnsɪɡˈnɪfɪknt] adj belanglos

insincere [ɪnsɪnˈsɪəʳ] adj unaufrichtig, falsch

insincerity [ɪnsɪnˈsɛrɪtɪ] n Unaufrichtigkeit f,

Falschheit f

insinuate [ɪnˈsɪnjueɪt] vt anspielen auf +acc

insinuation [ɪnsɪnjuˈeɪʃən] n Anspielung f

insipid [ɪnˈsɪpɪd] adj fad(e); (person) geistlos; (colour) langweilig

insist [ɪnˈsɪst] vi bestehen; **to ~ on** bestehen auf +dat; **to ~ that** darauf bestehen, dass; (claim) behaupten, dass

insistence [ɪnˈsɪstəns] n (determination) Bestehen nt

insistent [ɪnˈsɪstənt] adj (determined) hartnäckig; (continual) andauernd, penetrant (pej)

in so far as adv insofern als

insole [ˈɪnsəul] n Einlegesohle f

insolence [ˈɪnsələns] n Frechheit f, Unverschämtheit f

insolent [ˈɪnsələnt] adj frech, unverschämt

insoluble [ɪnˈsɔljubl] adj unlösbar

insolvency [ɪnˈsɔlvənsɪ] n Zahlungsunfähigkeit f

insolvent [ɪnˈsɔlvənt] adj zahlungsunfähig

insomnia [ɪnˈsɔmnɪə] n Schlaflosigkeit f

insomniac [ɪnˈsɔmnɪæk] n: **to be an ~** an Schlaflosigkeit leiden

inspect [ɪnˈspɛkt] vt kontrollieren; (examine) prüfen; (troops) inspizieren

inspection [ɪnˈspɛkʃən] n (see vb) Kontrolle f; Prüfung f; Inspektion f

inspector [ɪnˈspɛktəʳ] n Inspektor(in) m(f); (Brit: on buses, trains) Kontrolleur(in) m(f); (: Police) Kommissar(in) m(f)

inspiration [ɪnspəˈreɪʃən] n Inspiration f; (idea) Eingebung f

inspire [ɪnˈspaɪəʳ] vt inspirieren; (confidence, hope etc) (er)wecken

inspired [ɪnˈspaɪəd] adj genial; **in an ~ moment** in einem Augenblick der Inspiration

inspiring [ɪnˈspaɪərɪŋ] adj inspirierend

inst. (Brit) abbr (Comm: = instant): **of the 16th ~** vom 16. d. M.

instability [ɪnstəˈbɪlɪtɪ] n Instabilität f; (of person) Labilität f

install [ɪnˈstɔːl] vt installieren; (telephone) anschließen; (official) einsetzen; **to ~ o.s.** sich niederlassen

installation [ɪnstəˈleɪʃən] n Installation f; (of telephone) Anschluss m; (Industry, Mil: plant) Anlage f

installment plan (US) n Ratenzahlung f

instalment, (US) **installment** [ɪnˈstɔːlmənt] n Rate f; (of story) Fortsetzung f; (of TV serial etc) (Sende)folge f; **in ~s** in Raten

instance [ˈɪnstəns] n Beispiel nt; **for ~** zum Beispiel; **in that ~** in diesem Fall; **in many ~s** in vielen Fällen; **in the first ~** zuerst or zunächst (einmal)

instant [ˈɪnstənt] n Augenblick m ▷ adj (reaction) unmittelbar; (success) sofortig; **~ food** Schnellgerichte pl; **~ coffee** Instantkaffee m; **the 10th ~** (Comm, Admin) der 10. dieses Monats

instantaneous [ɪnstənˈteɪnɪəs] adj

unmittelbar

instantly ['ɪnstəntlɪ] *adv* sofort

instant messaging [-'mɛsɪdʒɪŋ] *n* Instant Messaging *nt*

instant replay *n* (TV) Wiederholung *f*

instead [ɪn'stɛd] *adv* stattdessen; ~ **of** statt +*gen*; ~ **of sb** an jds Stelle *dat*; ~ **of doing sth** anstatt *or* anstelle etw zu tun

instep ['ɪnstɛp] *n* Spann *m*; (*of shoe*) Blatt *nt*

instigate ['ɪnstɪgeɪt] *vt* anstiften, anzetteln; (*talks etc*) initiieren

instigation [ɪnstɪ'geɪʃən] *n* (*see vb*) Anstiftung *f*, Anzettelung *f*; Initiierung *f*; **at sb's** ~ auf jds Betreiben *acc*

instil [ɪn'stɪl] *vt*: **to ~ sth into sb** (*confidence, fear etc*) jdm etw einflößen

instinct ['ɪnstɪŋkt] *n* Instinkt *m*; (*reaction, inclination*) instinktive Reaktion *f*

instinctive [ɪn'stɪŋktɪv] *adj* instinktiv

institute ['ɪnstɪtjuːt] *n* Institut *nt*; (*for teaching*) Hochschule *f*; (*professional body*) Bund *m*, Verband *m* ▷ *vt* einführen; (*inquiry, course of action*) einleiten; (*proceedings*) anstrengen

institution [ɪnstɪ'tjuːʃən] *n* Einführung *f*; (*organization*) Institution *f*, Einrichtung *f*; (*hospital, mental home*) Anstalt *f*, Heim *nt*

institutional [ɪnstɪ'tjuːʃənl] *adj* (*education*) institutionell; (*value, quality etc*) institutionalisiert; ~ **care** Unterbringung *f* in einem Heim *or* einer Anstalt; **to be in ~ care** in einem Heim *or* einer Anstalt sein

instruct [ɪn'strʌkt] *vt*: **to ~ sb in sth** jdn in etw *dat* unterrichten; **to ~ sb to do sth** jdn anweisen, etw zu tun

instruction [ɪn'strʌkʃən] *n* Unterricht *m*; **instructions** *npl* (*orders*) Anweisungen *pl*; ~**s (for use)** Gebrauchsanweisung *f*, Gebrauchsanleitung *f*; ~ **book/manual/ leaflet** *etc* Bedienungsanleitung *f*

instructive [ɪn'strʌktɪv] *adj* lehrreich; (*response*) aufschlussreich

instructor [ɪn'strʌktə'] *n* Lehrer(in) *m(f)*

instrument ['ɪnstrʊmənt] *n* Instrument *nt*; (*Mus*) (Musik)instrument *nt*

instrumental [ɪnstrʊ'mɛntl] *adj* (*Mus: music, accompaniment*) Instrumental-; **to be ~ in** eine bedeutende Rolle spielen bei

instrumentalist [ɪnstrʊ'mɛntəlɪst] *n* Instrumentalist(in) *m(f)*

instrument panel *n* Armaturenbrett *nt*

insubordination [ɪnsəbɔːdɪ'neɪʃən] *n* Gehorsamsverweigerung *f*

insufferable [ɪn'sʌfrəbl] *adj* unerträglich

insufficient [ɪnsə'fɪʃənt] *adj* unzureichend

insufficiently [ɪnsə'fɪʃəntlɪ] *adv* unzureichend

insular ['ɪnsjʊlə'] *adj* engstirnig

insulate ['ɪnsjʊleɪt] *vt* isolieren; (*person, group*) abschirmen

insulating tape ['ɪnsjʊleɪtɪŋ-] *n* Isolierband *nt*

insulation [ɪnsjʊ'leɪʃən] *n* (*see vb*) Isolierung *f*; Abschirmung *f*

insulator ['ɪnsjʊleɪtə'] *n* Isolierstoff *m*

insulin ['ɪnsjʊlɪn] *n* Insulin *nt*

insult [*n* 'ɪnsʌlt, *vt* ɪn'sʌlt] *n* Beleidigung *f* ▷ *vt* beleidigen

insulting [ɪn'sʌltɪŋ] *adj* beleidigend

insuperable [ɪn'sjuːprəbl] *adj* unüberwindlich

insurance [ɪn'ʃʊərəns] *n* Versicherung *f*; **fire/life** ~ Brand-/Lebensversicherung *f*; **to take out** ~ **(against)** eine Versicherung abschließen (gegen)

insurance agent *n* Versicherungsvertreter(in) *m(f)*

insurance broker *n* Versicherungsmakler(in) *m(f)*

insurance policy *n* Versicherungspolice *f*

insurance premium *n* Versicherungsprämie *f*

insure [ɪn'ʃʊə'] *vt* versichern; **to ~ o.s./ sth against sth** sich/etw gegen etw versichern; **to ~ o.s.** *or* **one's life** eine Lebensversicherung abschließen; **to ~ (o.s.) against sth** (*fig*) sich gegen etw absichern; **to be ~d for £5,000** für £5000 versichert sein

insured [ɪn'ʃʊəd] *n*: **the ~** der/die Versicherte

insurer [ɪn'ʃʊərə'] *n* Versicherer *m*

insurgent [ɪn'səːdʒənt] *adj* aufständisch ▷ *n* Aufständische(r) *f(m)*

insurmountable [ɪnsə'maʊntəbl] *adj* unüberwindlich

insurrection [ɪnsə'rɛkʃən] *n* Aufstand *m*

intact [ɪn'tækt] *adj* intakt; (*whole*) ganz; (*unharmed*) unversehrt

intake ['ɪnteɪk] *n* (*of food*) Aufnahme *f*; (*of air*) Zufuhr *f*; (*Brit: Scol*): **an ~ of 200 a year** 200 neue Schüler pro Jahr

intangible [ɪn'tændʒɪbl] *adj* unbestimmbar; (*idea*) vage; (*benefit*) immateriell

integer ['ɪntɪdʒə'] *n* (*Math*) ganze Zahl *f*

integral ['ɪntɪgrəl] *adj* wesentlich

integrate ['ɪntɪgreɪt] *vt* integrieren ▷ *vi* sich integrieren

integrated circuit ['ɪntɪgreɪtɪd-] *n* (*Comput*) integrierter Schaltkreis *m*

integration [ɪntɪ'greɪʃən] *n* Integration *f*; **racial** ~ Rassenintegration *f*

integrity [ɪn'tɛgrɪtɪ] *n* Integrität *f*; (*of group*) Einheit *f*; (*of culture, text*) Unversehrtheit *f*

intellect ['ɪntəlɛkt] *n* Intellekt *m*

intellectual [ɪntə'lɛktjʊəl] *adj* intellektuell, geistig ▷ *n* Intellektuelle(r) *f(m)*

intelligence [ɪn'tɛlɪdʒəns] *n* Intelligenz *f*; (*information*) Informationen *pl*

intelligence quotient *n* Intelligenzquotient *m*

intelligence service *n* Nachrichtendienst *m*, Geheimdienst *m*

intelligence test *n* Intelligenztest *m*

intelligent [ɪn'tɛlɪdʒənt] *adj* intelligent; (*decision*) klug

intelligently [ɪn'tɛlɪdʒəntlɪ] *adv* intelligent

intelligentsia [ɪntɛlɪ'dʒɛntsɪə] *n*: **the ~** die Intelligenz

intelligible [ɪn'tɛlɪdʒɪbl] *adj* verständlich

intemperate [ɪn'tɛmpərət] *adj* unmäßig; (*remark*) überzogen

intend [ɪn'tɛnd] *vt*: **to be ~ed for sb** für jdn gedacht sein; **to ~ to do sth** beabsichtigen, etw zu tun

intended [ɪnˈtɛndɪd] *adj (effect, victim)* beabsichtigt; *(journey)* geplant; *(insult)* absichtlich

intense [ɪnˈtɛns] *adj* intensiv; *(anger, joy)* äußerst groß; *(person)* ernsthaft

intensely [ɪnˈtɛnslɪ] *adv* äußerst; **I dislike him ~** ich verabscheue ihn

intensify [ɪnˈtɛnsɪfaɪ] *vt* intensivieren, verstärken

intensity [ɪnˈtɛnsɪtɪ] *n* Intensität *f*; *(of anger)* Heftigkeit *f*

intensive [ɪnˈtɛnsɪv] *adj* intensiv

intensive care *n*: **to be in ~** auf der Intensivstation sein

intensive care unit *n* Intensivstation *f*

intent [ɪnˈtɛnt] *n* Absicht *f* ▷ *adj (attentive)* aufmerksam; *(absorbed):* **~ (on)** versunken (in +*acc*); **to all ~s and purposes** im Grunde; **to be ~ on doing sth** entschlossen sein, etw zu tun

intention [ɪnˈtɛnʃən] *n* Absicht *f*

intentional [ɪnˈtɛnʃənl] *adj* absichtlich

intentionally [ɪnˈtɛnʃnəlɪ] *adv* absichtlich

intently [ɪnˈtɛntlɪ] *adv* konzentriert

inter [ɪnˈtəːʳ] *vt* bestatten

interact [ɪntərˈækt] *vi (people)* interagieren; *(things)* aufeinander einwirken; *(ideas)* sich gegenseitig beeinflussen; **to ~ with** interagieren mit; einwirken auf +*acc*; beeinflussen

interaction [ɪntərˈækʃən] *n (see vb)* Interaktion *f*; gegenseitige Einwirkung *f*; gegenseitige Beeinflussung *f*

interactive [ɪntərˈæktɪv] *adj (also Comput)* interaktiv

intercede [ɪntəˈsiːd] *vi*: **to ~ (with sb/on behalf of sb)** sich (bei jdm/für jdn) einsetzen

intercept [ɪntəˈsɛpt] *vt* abfangen

interception [ɪntəˈsɛpʃən] *n* Abfangen *nt*

interchange [ˈɪntətʃeɪndʒ] *n* Austausch *m*; *(on motorway)* (Autobahn)kreuz *nt*

interchangeable [ɪntəˈtʃeɪndʒəbl] *adj* austauschbar

intercity [ɪntəˈsɪtɪ] *adj*: **~ train** Intercityzug *m*

intercom [ˈɪntəkɔm] *n* (Gegen)sprechanlage *f*

interconnect [ɪntəkəˈnɛkt] *vi (rooms)* miteinander verbunden sein

intercontinental [ˈɪntəkɔntɪˈnɛntl] *adj (flight, missile)* Interkontinental-

intercourse [ˈɪntəkɔːs] *n (sexual)* (Geschlechts) verkehr *m*; *(social, verbal)* Verkehr *m*

intercultural [ɪntəˈkʌltʃərəl] *adj* interkulturell

interdependence [ɪntədɪˈpɛndəns] *n* gegenseitige Abhängigkeit *f*

interdependent [ɪntədɪˈpɛndənt] *adj* voneinander abhängig

interest [ˈɪntrɪst] *n* Interesse *nt*; *(Comm: in company)* Anteil *m*; *(: sum of money)* Zinsen *pl* ▷ *vt* interessieren; **compound ~** Zinseszins *m*; **simple ~** einfache Zinsen; **British ~s in the Middle East** britische Interessen im Nahen Osten; **his main ~ is ...** er interessiert sich

hauptsächlich für ...

interested [ˈɪntrɪstɪd] *adj* interessiert; *(party, body etc)* beteiligt; **to be ~ in sth** sich für etw interessieren; **to be ~ in doing sth** daran interessiert sein, etw zu tun

interest-free [ˈɪntrɪstˈfriː] *adj, adv* zinslos

interesting [ˈɪntrɪstɪŋ] *adj* interessant

interest rate *n* Zinssatz *m*

interface [ˈɪntəfeɪs] *n* Verbindung *f*; *(Comput)* Schnittstelle *f*

interfere [ɪntəˈfɪəʳ] *vi*: **to ~ in** sich einmischen in +*acc*; **to ~ with** *(object)* sich zu schaffen machen an +*dat*; *(plans)* durchkreuzen; *(career, duty, decision)* beeinträchtigen; **don't ~** misch dich nicht ein

interference [ɪntəˈfɪərəns] *n* Einmischung *f*; *(Radio, TV)* Störung *f*

interfering [ɪntəˈfɪərɪŋ] *adj (person)* sich ständig einmischend

interim [ˈɪntərɪm] *adj (agreement, government etc)* Übergangs- ▷ *n*: **in the ~** in der Zwischenzeit

interim dividend *n (Comm)* Abschlagsdividende *f*

interior [ɪnˈtɪərɪəʳ] *n* Innere(s) *nt*; *(decor etc)* Innenausstattung *f* ▷ *adj* Innen-

interior decorator *n* Innenausstatter(in) *m(f)*

interior designer *n* Innenarchitekt(in) *m(f)*

interjection [ɪntəˈdʒɛkʃən] *n* Einwurf *m*; *(Ling)* Interjektion *f*

interlock [ɪntəˈlɔk] *vi* ineinandergreifen

interloper [ˈɪntələupəʳ] *n* Eindringling *m*

interlude [ˈɪntəluːd] *n* Unterbrechung *f*, Pause *f*; *(Theat)* Zwischenspiel *nt*

intermarry [ɪntəˈmærɪ] *vi* untereinander heiraten

intermediary [ɪntəˈmiːdɪərɪ] *n* Vermittler(in) *m(f)*

intermediate [ɪntəˈmiːdɪət] *adj (stage)* Zwischen-; **an ~ student** ein fortgeschrittener Anfänger

interment [ɪnˈtəːmənt] *n* Bestattung *f*

interminable [ɪnˈtəːmɪnəbl] *adj* endlos

intermission [ɪntəˈmɪʃən] *n* Pause *f*

intermittent [ɪntəˈmɪtnt] *adj (noise)* periodisch auftretend; *(publication)* in unregelmäßigen Abständen veröffentlicht

intermittently [ɪntəˈmɪtntlɪ] *adv (see adj)* periodisch; in unregelmäßigen Abständen

intern [*vt* ɪnˈtəːn, *n* ˈɪntəːn] *vt* internieren ▷ *n (US)* Assistenzarzt *m*, Assistenzärztin *f*

internal [ɪnˈtəːnl] *adj* innere(r, s); *(pipes)* im Haus; *(politics)* Innen-; *(dispute, reform, memo, structure etc)* intern

internally [ɪnˈtəːnəlɪ] *adv*: **"not to be taken ~"** „nicht zum Einnehmen"

Internal Revenue Service *(US) n* ≈ Finanzamt *nt*

international [ɪntəˈnæʃənl] *adj* international ▷ *n (Brit: Sport)* Länderspiel *nt*

International Atomic Energy Agency *n* Internationale Atomenergiebehörde

International Chamber of Commerce *n* Internationale Handelskammer *f*

International Court of Justice n
Internationaler Gerichtshof m

international date line n Datumsgrenze f

International Labour Organization n
Internationale Arbeitsorganisation f

internationally [ɪntə'næʃnəlɪ] adv
international

International Monetary Fund n
Internationaler Währungsfonds m

international relations npl
zwischenstaatliche Beziehungen pl

internecine [ɪntə'niːsaɪn] adj mörderisch;
(war) Vernichtungs-

internee [ɪntəː'niː] n Internierte(r) f(m)

Internet ['ɪntənɛt] n Internet nt

Internet café n Internetcafé nt

internment [ɪn'təːnmənt] n Internierung f

interplay ['ɪntəpleɪ] n: ~ **(of** or **between)**
Zusammenspiel nt (von)

Interpol ['ɪntəpɔl] n Interpol f

interpret [ɪn'təːprɪt] vt auslegen,
interpretieren; (translate) dolmetschen ▷ vi
dolmetschen

interpretation [ɪntəːprɪ'teɪʃən] n (see vb)
Auslegung f, Interpretation f; Dolmetschen nt

interpreter [ɪn'təːprɪtər] n Dolmetscher(in)
m(f)

interpreting [ɪn'təːprɪtɪŋ] n Dolmetschen nt

interrelated [ɪntərɪ'leɪtɪd] adj
zusammenhängend

interrogate [ɪn'tɛrəugeɪt] vt verhören;
(witness) vernehmen

interrogation [ɪntɛrəu'geɪʃən] n (see vb) Verhör
nt; Vernehmung f

interrogative [ɪntə'rɔgətɪv] adj (Ling: pronoun)
Interrogativ-, Frage-

interrogator [ɪn'tɛrəgeɪtər] n (Police)
Vernehmungsbeamte(r) m; **the hostage's** ~
derjenige, der die Geisel verhörte

interrupt [ɪntə'rʌpt] vt, vi unterbrechen

interruption [ɪntə'rʌpʃən] n Unterbrechung
f

intersect [ɪntə'sɛkt] vi sich kreuzen ▷ vt
durchziehen; (Math) schneiden

intersection [ɪntə'sɛkʃən] n Kreuzung f; (Math)
Schnittpunkt m

intersperse [ɪntə'spəːs] vt: **to be ~d with**
durchsetzt sein mit; **he ~d his lecture
with ...** er spickte seine Rede mit ...

intertwine [ɪntə'twaɪn] vi sich ineinander
verschlingen

interval ['ɪntəvl] n Pause f; (Mus) Intervall nt;
bright ~s (in weather) Aufheiterungen pl; **at ~s**
in Abständen

intervene [ɪntə'viːn] vi eingreifen; (event)
dazwischenkommen; (time) dazwischenliegen

intervening [ɪntə'viːnɪŋ] adj (period, years)
dazwischenliegend

intervention [ɪntə'vɛnʃən] n Eingreifen nt

interview ['ɪntəvjuː] n (for job)
Vorstellungsgespräch nt; (for place at college etc)
Auswahlgespräch nt; (Radio, TV etc) Interview
nt ▷ vt (see n) ein Vorstellungsgespräch/

Auswahlgespräch führen mit; interviewen

interviewee [ɪntəvjuːˈiː] n (for job)
Stellenbewerber(in) m(f); (TV etc)
Interviewgast m

interviewer ['ɪntəvjuər] n Leiter(in) m(f) des
Vorstellungsgesprächs/Auswahlgesprächs;
(Radio, TV etc) Interviewer(in) m(f)

intestate [ɪn'tɛsteɪt] adv: **to die** ~ ohne
Testament sterben

intestinal [ɪn'tɛstɪnl] adj (infection etc) Darm-

intestine [ɪn'tɛstɪn] n Darm m

intimacy ['ɪntɪməsɪ] n Vertrautheit f

intimate [adj 'ɪntɪmət, vt 'ɪntɪmeɪt] adj eng;
(sexual, also restaurant, dinner, atmosphere)
intim; (conversation, matter, detail) vertraulich;
(knowledge) gründlich ▷ vt andeuten; (make
known) zu verstehen geben

intimately ['ɪntɪmətlɪ] adv (see adj) eng; intim;
vertraulich; gründlich

intimation [ɪntɪ'meɪʃən] n Andeutung f

intimidate [ɪn'tɪmɪdeɪt] vt einschüchtern

intimidation [ɪntɪmɪ'deɪʃən] n
Einschüchterung f

 KEYWORD

into ['ɪntu] prep **1** (indicating motion or direction) in
+acc; **to go into town** in die Stadt gehen; **he
worked late into the night** er arbeitete bis
spät in die Nacht; **the car bumped into the
wall** der Wagen fuhr gegen die Mauer
2 (indicating change of condition, result): **it broke
into pieces** es zerbrach in Stücke; **she
translated into English** sie übersetzte ins
Englische; **to change pounds into dollars**
Pfund in Dollar wechseln; **5 into 25** 25 durch 5

intolerable [ɪn'tɔlərəbl] adj unerträglich

intolerance [ɪn'tɔlərns] n Intoleranz f

intolerant [ɪn'tɔlərnt] adj: ~ **(of)** intolerant
(gegenüber)

intonation [ɪntəu'neɪʃən] n Intonation f

intoxicated [ɪn'tɔksɪkeɪtɪd] adj betrunken;
(fig) berauscht

intoxication [ɪntɔksɪ'keɪʃən] n (Be)
trunkenheit f; (fig) Rausch m

intractable [ɪn'træktəbl] adj hartnäckig; (child)
widerspenstig; (temper) unbeugsam

intranet ['ɪntrənet] n (Comput) Intranet nt

intransigence [ɪn'trænsɪdʒəns] n
Unnachgiebigkeit f

intransigent [ɪn'trænsɪdʒənt] adj
unnachgiebig

intransitive [ɪn'trænsɪtɪv] adj (Ling) intransitiv

intrauterine device ['ɪntrə'juːtəraɪn-] n (Med)
Intrauterinpessar nt, Spirale f (inf)

intravenous [ɪntrə'viːnəs] adj intravenös

in-tray ['ɪntreɪ] n Ablage f für Eingänge

intrepid [ɪn'trɛpɪd] adj unerschrocken

intricacy ['ɪntrɪkəsɪ] n Kompliziertheit
f

intricate ['ɪntrɪkət] adj kompliziert

intrigue [ɪn'triːg] n Intrigen pl ▷ vt faszinieren

intriguing [ɪn'tri:gɪŋ] *adj* faszinierend

intrinsic [ɪn'trɪnsɪk] *adj* wesentlich

introduce [ɪntrə'dju:s] *vt* (*sth new*) einführen; (*speaker, TV show etc*) ankündigen; **to ~ sb (to sb)** jdn (jdm) vorstellen; **to ~ sb to** (*pastime, technique*) jdn einführen in +*acc*; **may I ~ ...?** darf ich ... vorstellen?

introduction [ɪntrə'dʌkʃən] *n* Einführung *f*; (*of person*) Vorstellung *f*; (*to book*) Einleitung *f*; **a letter of ~** ein Einführungsschreiben *nt*

introductory [ɪntrə'dʌktərɪ] *adj* Einführungs-; **~ remarks** einführende Bemerkungen *pl*; **~ offer** Einführungsangebot *nt*

introspection [ɪntrəu'spɛkʃən] *n* Selbstbeobachtung *f*, Introspektion *f*

introspective [ɪntrəu'spɛktɪv] *adj* in sich gekehrt

introvert ['ɪntrəuvə:t] *n* Introvertierte(r) *f(m)* ▷ *adj* (*also:* **introverted**) introvertiert

intrude [ɪn'tru:d] *vi* eindringen; **to ~ on** stören; (*conversation*) sich einmischen in +*acc*; **am I intruding?** störe ich?

intruder [ɪn'tru:dəʳ] *n* Eindringling *m*

intrusion [ɪn'tru:ʒən] *n* Eindringen *nt*

intrusive [ɪn'tru:sɪv] *adj* aufdringlich

intuition [ɪntju:'ɪʃən] *n* Intuition *f*

intuitive [ɪn'tju:ɪtɪv] *adj* intuitiv; (*feeling*) instinktiv

inundate ['ɪnʌndeɪt] *vt*: **to ~ with** überschwemmen mit

inure [ɪn'juəʳ] *vt*: **to ~ o.s. to** sich gewöhnen an +*acc*

invade [ɪn'veɪd] *vt* einfallen in +*acc*; (*fig*) heimsuchen

invader [ɪn'veɪdəʳ] *n* Invasor *m*

invalid [*n* 'ɪnvəlɪd, *adj* ɪn'vælɪd] *n* Kranke(r) *f(m)*; (*disabled*) Invalide *m* ▷ *adj* ungültig

invalidate [ɪn'vælɪdeɪt] *vt* entkräften; (*law, marriage, election*) ungültig machen

invaluable [ɪn'væljuəbl] *adj* unschätzbar

invariable [ɪn'vɛərɪəbl] *adj* unveränderlich

invariably [ɪn'vɛərɪəblɪ] *adv* ständig, unweigerlich; **she is ~ late** sie kommt immer zu spät

invasion [ɪn'veɪʒən] *n* Invasion *f*; **an ~ of privacy** ein Eingriff *m* in die Privatsphäre

invective [ɪn'vɛktɪv] *n* Beschimpfungen *pl*

inveigle [ɪn'vi:gl] *vt*: **to ~ sb into sth/doing sth** jdn zu etw verleiten/dazu verleiten, etw zu tun

invent [ɪn'vɛnt] *vt* erfinden

invention [ɪn'vɛnʃən] *n* Erfindung *f*

inventive [ɪn'vɛntɪv] *adj* erfinderisch

inventiveness [ɪn'vɛntɪvnɪs] *n* Einfallsreichtum *m*

inventor [ɪn'vɛntəʳ] *n* Erfinder(in) *m(f)*

inventory ['ɪnvəntrɪ] *n* Inventar *nt*

inventory control *n* (*Comm*) Bestandskontrolle *f*

inverse [ɪn'və:s] *adj* umgekehrt; **in ~ proportion (to)** im umgekehrten Verhältnis (zu)

invert [ɪn'və:t] *vt* umdrehen

invertebrate [ɪn'və:tɪbrət] *n* wirbelloses Tier *nt*

inverted commas [ɪn'və:tɪd-] (*Brit*) *npl* Anführungszeichen *pl*

invest [ɪn'vɛst] *vt* investieren ▷ *vi*: **~ in** investieren in +*acc*; (*fig*) sich *dat* anschaffen; **to ~ sb with sth** jdm etw verleihen

investigate [ɪn'vɛstɪgeɪt] *vt* untersuchen

investigation [ɪnvɛstɪ'geɪʃən] *n* Untersuchung *f*

investigative [ɪn'vɛstɪgeɪtɪv] *adj*: **~ journalism** Enthüllungsjournalismus *m*

investigator [ɪn'vɛstɪgeɪtəʳ] *n* Ermittler(in) *m(f)*; **private ~** Privatdetektiv(in) *m(f)*

investiture [ɪn'vɛstɪtʃəʳ] *n* (*of chancellor*) Amtseinführung *f*; (*of prince*) Investitur *f*

investment [ɪn'vɛstmənt] *n* Investition *f*

investment income *n* Kapitalerträge *pl*

investment trust *n* Investmenttrust *m*

investor [ɪn'vɛstəʳ] *n* (Kapital)anleger(in) *m(f)*

inveterate [ɪn'vɛtərət] *adj* unverbesserlich

invidious [ɪn'vɪdɪəs] *adj* (*task, job*) unangenehm; (*comparison, decision*) ungerecht

invigilator [ɪn'vɪdʒɪleɪtəʳ] *n* Aufsicht *f*

invigorating [ɪn'vɪgəreɪtɪŋ] *adj* belebend; (*experience etc*) anregend

invincible [ɪn'vɪnsɪbl] *adj* unbesiegbar; (*belief, conviction*) unerschütterlich

inviolate [ɪn'vaɪələt] *adj* sicher; (*truth*) unantastbar

invisible [ɪn'vɪzɪbl] *adj* unsichtbar

invisible mending *n* Kunststopfen *nt*

invitation [ɪnvɪ'teɪʃən] *n* Einladung *f*; **by ~ only** nur auf Einladung; **at sb's ~** auf jds Aufforderung *acc* (hin)

invite [ɪn'vaɪt] *vt* einladen; (*discussion*) auffordern zu; (*criticism*) herausfordern; **to ~ sb to do sth** jdn auffordern, etw zu tun; **to ~ sb to dinner** jdn zum Abendessen einladen ▶ **invite out** *vt* einladen

inviting [ɪn'vaɪtɪŋ] *adj* einladend; (*desirable*) verlockend

invoice ['ɪnvɔɪs] *n* Rechnung *f* ▷ *vt* in Rechnung stellen; **to ~ sb for goods** jdm für Waren eine Rechnung ausstellen

invoke [ɪn'vəuk] *vt* anrufen; (*feelings, memories etc*) heraufbeschwören

involuntary [ɪn'vɔləntrɪ] *adj* unbeabsichtigt; (*reflex*) unwillkürlich

involve [ɪn'vɔlv] *vt* (*person*) beteiligen; (*thing*) verbunden sein mit; (*concern, affect*) betreffen; **to ~ sb in sth** jdn in etw *acc* verwickeln

involved [ɪn'vɔlvd] *adj* kompliziert; **the work/problems ~** die damit verbundene Arbeit/verbundenen Schwierigkeiten; **to be ~ in** beteiligt sein an +*dat*; (*be engrossed*) engagiert sein in +*dat*; **to become ~ with sb** Umgang mit jdm haben; (*emotionally*) mit jdm eine Beziehung anfangen

involvement [ɪn'vɔlvmənt] *n* Engagement *nt*; (*participation*) Beteiligung *f*

invulnerable [ɪn'vʌlnərəbl] *adj* unverwundbar; (*ship, building etc*) uneinnehmbar

inward ['ɪnwəd] *adj* innerste(r, s); (*movement*)

nach innen ▷ adv nach innen
inwardly ['ɪnwədlɪ] adv innerlich
inwards ['ɪnwədz] adv nach innen
I/O abbr (Comput: = input/output) E/A
IOC n abbr (= International Olympic Committee) IOC nt, IOK nt
iodine ['aɪəudiːn] n Jod nt
IOM (Brit) abbr (Post) = Isle of Man
ion ['aɪən] n Ion nt
Ionian Sea [aɪ'əʊnɪən-] n: **the ~** das Ionische Meer
ionizer ['aɪənaɪzər] n Ionisator m
iota [aɪ'əʊtə] n Jota nt
IOU n abbr (= I owe you) Schuldschein m
IOW (Brit) abbr (Post) = Isle of Wight
IP abbr (Comput: = Internet Protocol) IP
IPA n abbr (= International Phonetic Alphabet) internationale Lautschrift f
iPod® ['aɪpɔd] n iPod® m
IQ n abbr (= intelligence quotient) IQ m
IRA n abbr (= Irish Republican Army) IRA f; (US: = individual retirement account) privates Rentensparkonto
Iran [ɪ'rɑːn] n (der) Iran
Iranian [ɪ'reɪnɪən] adj iranisch ▷ n Iraner(in) m(f); (Ling) Iranisch nt
Iraq [ɪ'rɑːk] n (der) Irak
Iraqi [ɪ'rɑːkɪ] adj irakisch ▷ n Iraker(in) m(f)
irascible [ɪ'ræsɪbl] adj jähzornig
irate [aɪ'reɪt] adj zornig
Ireland ['aɪələnd] n Irland nt; **the Republic of ~** die Republik Irland
iris ['aɪrɪs] (pl **~es**) n (Anat) Iris f, Regenbogenhaut f; (Bot) Iris, Schwertlilie f
Irish ['aɪrɪʃ] adj irisch ▷ npl: **the ~** die Iren pl, die Irländer pl
Irishman ['aɪrɪʃmən] (irreg: like **man**) n Ire m, Irländer m
Irish Sea n: **the ~** die Irische See
Irishwoman ['aɪrɪʃwʊmən] (irreg: like **woman**) n Irin f, Irländerin f
irk [əːk] vt ärgern
irksome ['əːksəm] adj lästig
IRN n abbr (= Independent Radio News) Nachrichtendienst des kommerziellen Rundfunks
iron ['aɪən] n Eisen nt; (for clothes) Bügeleisen nt ▷ cpd Eisen-; (will, discipline etc) eisern ▷ vt bügeln
▷ **iron out** vt (fig) aus dem Weg räumen
Iron Curtain n: **the ~** der Eiserne Vorhang
ironic [aɪ'rɔnɪk], **ironical** [aɪ'rɔnɪkl] adj ironisch; (situation) paradox, witzig
ironically [aɪ'rɔnɪklɪ] adv ironisch; **~, the intelligence chief was the last to find out** witzigerweise war der Geheimdienstchef der Letzte, der es erfuhr
ironing ['aɪənɪŋ] n Bügeln nt; (clothes) Bügelwäsche f
ironing board n Bügelbrett nt
iron lung n (Med) eiserne Lunge f
ironmonger ['aɪənmʌŋɡər] (Brit) n Eisen- und Haushaltswarenhändler(in) m(f); **ironmonger's (shop)** (Brit) Eisen- und

Haushaltswarenhandlung f
iron ore n Eisenerz nt
irons ['aɪəns] npl Hand- und Fußschellen pl; **to clap sb in ~** jdn in Eisen legen
irony ['aɪrənɪ] n Ironie f; **the ~ of it is that ...** das Ironische daran ist, dass ...
irrational [ɪ'ræʃənl] adj irrational
irreconcilable [ɪrekən'saɪləbl] adj unvereinbar
irredeemable [ɪrɪ'diːməbl] adj (Comm) nicht einlösbar; (loan) unkündbar; (fault, character) unverbesserlich
irrefutable [ɪrɪ'fjuːtəbl] adj unwiderlegbar
irregular [ɪ'rɛɡjulər] adj unregelmäßig; (surface) uneben; (behaviour) ungehörig
irregularity [ɪrɛɡju'lærɪtɪ] n (see adj) Unregelmäßigkeit f; Unebenheit f; Ungehörigkeit f
irrelevance [ɪ'rɛləvəns] n Irrelevanz f
irrelevant [ɪ'rɛləvənt] adj unwesentlich, irrelevant
irreligious [ɪrɪ'lɪdʒəs] adj unreligiös
irreparable [ɪ'rɛprəbl] adj nicht wiedergutzumachen
irreplaceable [ɪrɪ'pleɪsəbl] adj unersetzlich
irrepressible [ɪrɪ'prɛsəbl] adj (good humour) unerschütterlich; (enthusiasm etc) unbändig; (person) nicht unterzukriegen
irreproachable [ɪrɪ'prəʊtʃəbl] adj untadelig
irresistible [ɪrɪ'zɪstɪbl] adj unwiderstehlich
irresolute [ɪ'rɛzəluːt] adj unentschlossen
irrespective [ɪrɪ'spɛktɪv]: **~ of** prep ungeachtet +gen
irresponsible [ɪrɪ'spɔnsɪbl] adj verantwortungslos; (action) unverantwortlich
irretrievable [ɪrɪ'triːvəbl] adj (object) nicht mehr wiederzubekommen; (loss) unersetzlich; (damage) nicht wiedergutzumachen
irreverent [ɪ'rɛvərnt] adj respektlos
irrevocable [ɪ'rɛvəkəbl] adj unwiderruflich
irrigate ['ɪrɪɡeɪt] vt bewässern
irrigation [ɪrɪ'ɡeɪʃən] n Bewässerung f
irritable ['ɪrɪtəbl] adj reizbar
irritant ['ɪrɪtənt] n Reizerreger m; (situation etc) Ärgernis nt
irritate ['ɪrɪteɪt] vt ärgern, irritieren; (Med) reizen
irritating ['ɪrɪteɪtɪŋ] adj ärgerlich, irritierend; **he is ~** er kann einem auf die Nerven gehen
irritation [ɪrɪ'teɪʃən] n Ärger m; (Med) Reizung f; (annoying thing) Ärgernis nt
IRS (US) n abbr (= Internal Revenue Service) Steuereinzugsbehörde
is [ɪz] vb see **be**
ISA ['aɪsə] n abbr (= individual savings account) steuerfreies Sparsystem mit begrenzter Einlagenhöhe
ISBN n abbr (= International Standard Book Number) ISBN f
ISDN n abbr (= Integrated Services Digital Network) ISDN nt
Islam ['ɪzlɑːm] n der Islam; (Islamic countries) die islamischen Länder pl
Islamic [ɪz'læmɪk] adj islamisch
island ['aɪlənd] n Insel f; (also: **traffic island**)

621

Verkehrsinsel f

islander ['aɪləndə'] n Inselbewohner(in) m(f)

isle [aɪl] n Insel f

isn't ['ɪznt] = **is not**

isobar ['aɪsəʊbaː'] n Isobare f

isolate ['aɪsəleɪt] vt isolieren

isolated ['aɪsəleɪtɪd] adj isoliert; (place) abgelegen; ~ **incident** Einzelfall m

isolation [aɪsə'leɪʃən] n Isolierung f

isolationism [aɪsə'leɪʃənɪzəm] n Isolationismus m

isotope ['aɪsəʊtəʊp] n Isotop nt

ISP (Comput) n abbr (= Internet Service Provider) Provider m

Israel ['ɪzreɪl] n Israel nt

Israeli [ɪz'reɪlɪ] adj israelisch ▷ n Israeli mf

issue ['ɪʃjuː] n Frage f; (subject) Thema nt; (problem) Problem nt; (of book, stamps etc) Ausgabe f; (offspring) Nachkommenschaft f ▷ vt ausgeben; (statement) herausgeben; (documents) ausstellen ▷ vi: **to ~ (from)** dringen (aus); (liquid) austreten (aus); **the point at ~** der Punkt, um den es geht; **to avoid the ~** ausweichen; **to confuse** or **obscure the ~** es unnötig kompliziert machen; **to ~ sth to sb** or ~ **sb with sth** jdm etw geben; (documents) jdm etw ausstellen; (gun etc) jdn mit etw ausstatten; **to take ~ with sb (over)** jdm widersprechen (in +dat); **to make an ~ of sth** etw aufbauschen

isthmus ['ɪsməs] n Landenge f, Isthmus m

IT n abbr = **information technology**

KEYWORD

it [ɪt] pron **1** (specific: subject) er/sie/es; (: direct object) ihn/sie/es; (: indirect object) ihm/ihr/ihm; **it's on the table** es ist auf dem Tisch; **I can't find it** ich kann es nicht finden; **give it to me** gib es mir; **about it** darüber; **from it** davon; **in it** darin; **of it** davon; **what did you learn from it?** was hast du daraus gelernt?; **I'm proud of it** ich bin stolz darauf

2 (impersonal) es; **it's raining** es regnet; **it's Friday tomorrow** morgen ist Freitag; **who is it?** — **it's me** wer ist da? — ich bins

ITA, (Brit) **i.t.a.** n abbr (= initial teaching alphabet) Alphabet zum Lesenlernen

Italian [ɪ'tæljən] adj italienisch ▷ n Italiener(in) m(f); (Ling) Italienisch nt; **the ~s** die Italiener pl

italics [ɪ'tælɪks] npl Kursivschrift f

Italy ['ɪtəlɪ] n Italien nt

ITC (Brit) n abbr (= Independent Television Commission) Fernseh-Aufsichtsgremium

itch [ɪtʃ] n Juckreiz m ▷ vi jucken; **I am ~ing all over** mich juckt es überall; **to ~ to do sth** darauf brennen, etw zu tun

itchy ['ɪtʃɪ] adj juckend; **my back is ~** mein Rücken juckt

it'd ['ɪtd] = **it would; it had**

item ['aɪtəm] n Punkt m; (of collection) Stück nt; (also: **news item**) Meldung f; (: in newspaper) Zeitungsnotiz f; **~s of clothing** Kleidungsstücke pl

itemize ['aɪtəmaɪz] vt einzeln aufführen

itemized bill ['aɪtəmaɪzd-] n Rechnung, auf der die Posten einzeln aufgeführt sind

itinerant [ɪ'tɪnərənt] adj (labourer, priest etc) Wander-; (salesman) reisend

itinerary [aɪ'tɪnərərɪ] n Reiseroute f

it'll ['ɪtl] = **it will; it shall**

ITN (Brit) n abbr (TV: = Independent Television News) Nachrichtendienst des kommerziellen Fernsehens

its [ɪts] adj sein(e), ihr(e) ▷ pron seine(r, s), ihre(r, s)

it's [ɪts] = **it is; it has**

itself [ɪt'sɛlf] pron sich; (emphatic) selbst

ITV (Brit) n abbr (TV: = Independent Television) kommerzieller Fernsehsender; siehe Info-Artikel

○ ITV

ITV steht für „Independent Television" und ist ein landesweiter privater Fernsehsender in Großbritannien. Unter der Oberaufsicht einer unabhängigen Rundfunkbehörde produzieren Privatfirmen die Programme für die verschiedenen Sendegebiete. ITV, das seit 1955 Programme ausstrahlt, wird ganz durch Werbung finanziert und bietet etwa ein Drittel Informationssendungen (Nachrichten, Dokumentarfilme, Aktuelles) und ansonsten Unterhaltung (Sport, Komödien, Drama, Spielshows, Filme).

IUD n abbr = **intrauterine device**

I've [aɪv] = **I have**

ivory ['aɪvərɪ] n Elfenbein nt

Ivory Coast n Elfenbeinküste f

ivory tower n (fig) Elfenbeinturm m

ivy ['aɪvɪ] n Efeu m

Ivy League (US) n Eliteuniversitäten der USA

○ IVY LEAGUE

Als Ivy League bezeichnet man die acht renommiertesten Universitäten im Nordosten der Vereinigten Staaten (Brown, Columbia, Cornell, Dartmouth College, Harvard, Princeton, University of Pennsylvania, Yale), die untereinander Sportwettkämpfe austragen. Der Name bezieht sich auf die efeubewachsenen Mauern der Universitätsgebäude.

Jj

J, j [dʒeɪ] n (letter) J nt, j nt; **J for Jack, J for Jig** (US) ≈ J wie Julius
JA n abbr = **judge advocate; joint account**
J/A abbr = **joint account**
jab [dʒæb] vt stoßen; (with finger, needle) stechen ▷ n (inf) Spritze f ▷ vi: **to ~ at** einstechen auf +acc; **to ~ sth into sth** etw in etw acc stoßen/stechen
jack [dʒæk] n (Aut) Wagenheber m; (Bowls) Zielkugel f; (Cards) Bube m
▶ **jack in** (inf) vt aufgeben
▶ **jack up** vt (Aut) aufbocken
jackal ['dʒækl] n Schakal m
jackass ['dʒækæs] (inf) n (person) Esel m
jackdaw ['dʒækdɔː] n Dohle f
jacket ['dʒækɪt] n Jackett nt; (of book) Schutzumschlag m; **potatoes in their ~s, ~ potatoes** in der Schale gebackene Kartoffeln pl
jack-in-the-box ['dʒækɪnðəbɒks] n Schachtelteufel m, Kastenteufel m
jack-knife ['dʒæknaɪf] n Klappmesser nt ▷ vi: **the lorry ~d** der Anhänger (des Lastwagens) hat sich quer gestellt
jack-of-all-trades ['dʒækəvˈɔːltreɪdz] n Alleskönner m
jack plug n Bananenstecker m
jackpot ['dʒækpɒt] n Hauptgewinn m; **to hit the ~** (fig) das große Los ziehen
Jacuzzi® [dʒəˈkuːzɪ] n Whirlpool m
jade [dʒeɪd] n Jade m or f
jaded ['dʒeɪdɪd] adj abgespannt; **to get ~** die Nase vollhaben
JAG n abbr = **Judge Advocate General**
jagged ['dʒægɪd] adj gezackt
jaguar ['dʒægjuəʳ] n Jaguar m
jail [dʒeɪl] n Gefängnis nt ▷ vt einsperren
jailbird ['dʒeɪlbɜːd] n Knastbruder m (inf)
jailbreak ['dʒeɪlbreɪk] n (Gefängnis)ausbruch m
jalopy [dʒəˈlɒpɪ] (inf) n alte (Klapper)kiste f or Mühle f
jam [dʒæm] n Marmelade f, Konfitüre f; (also: **traffic jam**) Stau m; (inf: difficulty) Klemme f ▷ vt blockieren; (mechanism, drawer etc) verklemmen; (Radio) stören ▷ vi klemmen; (gun) Ladehemmung haben; **I'm in a real ~** (inf) ich stecke wirklich in der Klemme; **to get**

sb out of a ~ (inf) jdm aus der Klemme helfen; **to ~ sth into sth** etw in etw acc stopfen; **the telephone lines are ~med** die Leitungen sind belegt
Jamaica [dʒəˈmeɪkə] n Jamaika nt
Jamaican [dʒəˈmeɪkən] adj jamaikanisch ▷ n Jamaikaner(in) m(f)
jamb [dʒæm] n (of door) (Tür)pfosten m; (of window) (Fenster)pfosten m
jamboree [dʒæmbəˈriː] n Fest nt
jam-packed [dʒæmˈpækt] adj: **~ (with)** vollgestopft (mit)
jam session n (Mus) Jamsession f
Jan. abbr (= January) Jan.
jangle ['dʒæŋgl] vi klimpern
janitor ['dʒænɪtəʳ] n Hausmeister(in) m(f)
January ['dʒænjuərɪ] n Januar m; see also **July**
Japan [dʒəˈpæn] n Japan nt
Japanese [dʒæpəˈniːz] adj japanisch ▷ n inv Japaner(in) m(f); (Ling) Japanisch nt
jar [dʒɑːʳ] n Topf m, Gefäß nt; (glass) Glas nt ▷ vi (sound) gellen; (colours) nicht harmonieren, sich beißen ▷ vt erschüttern; **to ~ on sb** jdm auf die Nerven gehen
jargon ['dʒɑːgən] n Jargon m
jarring ['dʒɑːrɪŋ] adj (sound) gellend, schrill; (colour) schreiend
jasmine ['dʒæzmɪn] n Jasmin m
jaundice ['dʒɔːndɪs] n Gelbsucht f
jaundiced ['dʒɔːndɪst] adj (view, attitude) zynisch
jaunt [dʒɔːnt] n Spritztour f
jaunty ['dʒɔːntɪ] adj munter; (step) schwungvoll
Java ['dʒɑːvə] n Java nt
javelin ['dʒævlɪn] n Speer m
jaw [dʒɔː] n Kiefer m
jawbone ['dʒɔːbəun] n Kieferknochen m
jay [dʒeɪ] n Eichelhäher m
jaywalker ['dʒeɪwɔːkəʳ] n unachtsamer Fußgänger m, unachtsame Fußgängerin f
jazz [dʒæz] n Jazz m
▶ **jazz up** vt aufpeppen (inf)
jazz band n Jazzband f
JCB® n Erdräummaschine f
JCS (US) n abbr (= Joint Chiefs of Staff) Stabschefs pl
JD (US) n abbr (= Doctor of Laws) ≈ Dr. jur.; (= Justice Department), ≈ Justizministerium nt
jealous ['dʒɛləs] adj eifersüchtig; (envious)

neidisch
jealously ['dʒɛləslɪ] *adv* eifersüchtig; *(enviously)* neidisch; *(watchfully)* sorgsam
jealousy ['dʒɛləsɪ] *n* Eifersucht *f*; *(envy)* Neid *m*
jeans [dʒiːnz] *npl* Jeans *pl*
Jeep® [dʒiːp] *n* Jeep® *m*
jeer [dʒɪər] *vi* höhnische Bemerkungen machen; **to ~ at** verhöhnen
jeering ['dʒɪərɪŋ] *adj* höhnisch; *(crowd)* johlend ▷ *n* Johlen *nt*
jeers ['dʒɪəz] *npl* Buhrufe *pl*
jelly ['dʒɛlɪ] *n* Götterspeise *f*; *(jam)* Gelee *m or nt*
jelly baby *(Brit)* *n* Gummibärchen *nt*
jellyfish ['dʒɛlɪfɪʃ] *n* Qualle *f*
jeopardize ['dʒɛpədaɪz] *vt* gefährden
jeopardy ['dʒɛpədɪ] *n*: **to be in ~** gefährdet sein
jerk [dʒəːk] *n* Ruck *m*; *(inf: idiot)* Trottel *m* ▷ *vt* reißen ▷ *vi (vehicle)* ruckeln
jerkin ['dʒəːkɪn] *n* Wams *nt*
jerky ['dʒəːkɪ] *adj* ruckartig
jerry-built ['dʒɛrɪbɪlt] *adj* schlampig gebaut
jerry can ['dʒɛrɪ-] *n* großer Blechkanister *m*
Jersey ['dʒəːzɪ] *n* Jersey *nt*
jersey ['dʒəːzɪ] *n* Pullover *m*; *(fabric)* Jersey *m*
Jerusalem [dʒəˈruːsləm] *n* Jerusalem *nt*
jest [dʒɛst] *n* Scherz *m*
jester ['dʒɛstər] *n* Narr *m*
Jesus ['dʒiːzəs] *n* Jesus *m*; **~ Christ** Jesus Christus *m*
jet [dʒɛt] *n* Strahl *m*; *(Aviat)* Düsenflugzeug *nt*; *(Mineralogy, Jewellery)* Jett *m or nt*, Gagat *m*
jet-black ['dʒɛt'blæk] *adj* pechschwarz
jet engine *n* Düsentriebwerk *nt*
jet lag *n* Jetlag *nt*
jet-propelled ['dʒɛtprə'pɛld] *adj* Düsen-, mit Düsenantrieb
jetsam ['dʒɛtsəm] *n* Strandgut *nt*; *(floating)* Treibgut *nt*
jet-setter ['dʒɛtsɛtər] *n*: **to be a ~** zum Jetset gehören
jettison ['dʒɛtɪsn] *vt* abwerfen; *(from ship)* über Bord werfen
jetty ['dʒɛtɪ] *n* Landesteg *m*, Pier *m*
Jew [dʒuː] *n* Jude *m*, Jüdin *f*
jewel ['dʒuːəl] *n* Edelstein *m*, Juwel *nt (also fig)*; *(in watch)* Stein *m*
jeweller, *(US)* **jeweler** ['dʒuːələr] *n* Juwelier *m*
jeweller's, jeweller's shop *n* Juwelier *m*, Juweliergeschäft *nt*
jewellery, *(US)* **jewelry** ['dʒuːəlrɪ] *n* Schmuck *m*
Jewess ['dʒuːɪs] *n* Jüdin *f*
Jewish ['dʒuːɪʃ] *adj* jüdisch
JFK *(US)* *n abbr* (= *John Fitzgerald Kennedy International Airport*) John-F.-Kennedy-Flughafen *m*
jib [dʒɪb] *n (Naut)* Klüver *m*; *(of crane)* Ausleger *m* ▷ *vi (horse)* scheuen, bocken; **to ~ at doing sth** sich dagegen sträuben, etw zu tun
jibe [dʒaɪb] *n* = **gibe**
jiffy ['dʒɪfɪ] *(inf) n*: **in a ~** sofort
jig [dʒɪɡ] *n lebhafter Volkstanz*
jigsaw ['dʒɪɡsɔː] *n (also:* **jigsaw puzzle**)

Puzzle(spiel) *nt*; *(tool)* Stichsäge *f*
jilt [dʒɪlt] *vt* sitzen lassen
jingle ['dʒɪŋɡl] *n (tune)* Jingle *m* ▷ *vi (bracelets)* klimpern; *(bells)* bimmeln
jingoism ['dʒɪŋɡəuɪzəm] *n* Hurrapatriotismus *m*
jinx [dʒɪŋks] *(inf) n* Fluch *m*; **there's a ~ on it** es ist verhext
jitters ['dʒɪtəz] *(inf) npl*: **to get the ~** das große Zittern bekommen
jittery ['dʒɪtərɪ] *(inf) adj* nervös, rappelig
jiujitsu [dʒuːˈdʒɪtsuː] *n* Jiu-Jitsu *nt*
job [dʒɔb] *n* Arbeit *f*; *(post, employment)* Stelle *f*, Job *m*; **it's not my ~** es ist nicht meine Aufgabe; **a part-time ~** eine Teilzeitbeschäftigung; **a full-time ~** eine Ganztagsstelle; **he's only doing his ~** er tut nur seine Pflicht; **it's a good ~ that ...** nur gut, dass ...; **just the ~!** genau das Richtige!
jobber ['dʒɔbər] *(Brit) n* Börsenhändler *m*
jobbing ['dʒɔbɪŋ] *(Brit) adj* Gelegenheits-
job centre *(Brit) n* Arbeitsamt *nt*
job creation scheme *n* Arbeits-beschaffungsmaßnahmen *pl*
job description *n* Tätigkeitsbeschreibung *f*
job interview *n* Vorstellungs- *or* Bewerbungsgespräch *nt*
jobless ['dʒɔblɪs] *adj* arbeitslos ▷ *npl*: **the ~** die Arbeitslosen *pl*
job lot *n* (Waren)posten *m*
job satisfaction *n* Zufriedenheit *f* am Arbeitsplatz
job security *n* Sicherheit *f* des Arbeitsplatzes
job sharing *n* Jobsharing *nt*, Arbeitsplatzteilung *f*
job specification *n* Tätigkeitsbeschreibung *f*
Jock [dʒɔk] *(inf) n* Schotte *m*
jockey ['dʒɔkɪ] *n* Jockey *m* ▷ *vi*: **to ~ for position** um eine gute Position rangeln
jockey box *(US) n (Aut)* Handschuhfach *nt*
jocular ['dʒɔkjulər] *adj* spaßig, witzig
jog [dʒɔɡ] *vt* (an)stoßen ▷ *vi* joggen, Dauerlauf machen; **to ~ sb's memory** jds Gedächtnis *dat* nachhelfen
▶ **jog along** *vi* entlangzuckeln *(inf)*
jogger ['dʒɔɡər] *n* Jogger(in) *m(f)*
jogging ['dʒɔɡɪŋ] *n* Jogging *nt*, Joggen *nt*
john [dʒɔn] *(US: inf) n (toilet)* Klo *nt*
join [dʒɔɪn] *vt (club, party)* beitreten +*dat*; *(queue)* sich stellen in +*acc*; *(things, places)* verbinden; *(group of people)* sich anschließen +*dat* ▷ *vi (roads)* sich treffen; *(rivers)* zusammenfließen ▷ *n* Verbindungsstelle *f*; **to ~ forces (with)** *(fig)* sich zusammentun (mit); **will you ~ us for dinner?** wollen Sie mit uns zu Abend essen?; **I'll ~ you later** ich komme später
▶ **join in** *vi* mitmachen ▷ *vt fus* sich beteiligen an +*dat*
▶ **join up** *vi* sich treffen; *(Mil)* zum Militär gehen
joiner ['dʒɔɪnər] *(Brit) n* Schreiner(in) *m(f)*
joinery ['dʒɔɪnərɪ] *(Brit) n* Schreinerei *f*
joint [dʒɔɪnt] *n (in woodwork)* Fuge *f*; *(in pipe*

etc) Verbindungsstelle *f*; (*Anat*) Gelenk *nt*;
(*Brit: Culin*) Braten *m*; (*inf: place*) Laden *m*; (: *of cannabis*) Joint *m* ▷ *adj* gemeinsam; (*combined*) vereint

joint account *n* gemeinsames Konto *nt*

jointly ['dʒɔɪntlɪ] *adv* gemeinsam

joint ownership *n* Miteigentum *nt*

joint-stock company ['dʒɔɪnt'stɔk-] *n* Aktiengesellschaft *f*

joint venture *n* Gemeinschaftsunternehmen *nt*, Joint Venture *nt*

joist [dʒɔɪst] *n* Balken *m*, Träger *m*

joke [dʒəuk] *n* Witz *m*; (*also:* **practical joke**) Streich *m* ▷ *vi* Witze machen; **to play a ~ on sb** jdm einen Streich spielen

joker ['dʒəukə^r] *n* (*Cards*) Joker *m*

joking ['dʒəukɪŋ] *adj* scherzhaft

jokingly ['dʒəukɪŋlɪ] *adv* scherzhaft, im Spaß

jollity ['dʒɔlɪtɪ] *n* Fröhlichkeit *f*

jolly ['dʒɔlɪ] *adj* fröhlich; (*enjoyable*) lustig ▷ *adv* (*Brit: inf: very*) ganz (schön) ▷ *vt* (*Brit*): **to ~ sb along** jdm aufmunternd zureden; **~ good!** prima!

jolt [dʒəult] *n* Ruck *m*; (*shock*) Schock *m* ▷ *vt* schütteln; (*subj: bus etc*) durchschütteln; (*emotionally*) aufrütteln

Jordan ['dʒɔːdən] *n* Jordanien *nt*; (*river*) Jordan *m*

Jordanian [dʒɔː'deɪnɪən] *adj* jordanisch ▷ *n* Jordanier(in) *m(f)*

joss stick [dʒɔs-] *n* Räucherstäbchen *nt*

jostle ['dʒɔsl] *vt* anrempeln ▷ *vi* drängeln

jot [dʒɔt] *n*: **not one ~** kein bisschen
▶ **jot down** *vt* notieren

jotter ['dʒɔtə^r] (*Brit*) *n* Notizbuch *nt*; (*pad*) Notizblock *m*

journal ['dʒɜːnl] *n* Zeitschrift *f*; (*diary*) Tagebuch *nt*

journalese [dʒɜːnə'liːz] (*pej*) *n* Pressejargon *m*

journalism ['dʒɜːnəlɪzəm] *n* Journalismus *m*

journalist ['dʒɜːnəlɪst] *n* Journalist(in) *m(f)*

journey ['dʒɜːnɪ] *n* Reise *f* ▷ *vi* reisen; **a 5-hour ~** eine Fahrt von 5 Stunden; **return ~** Rückreise *f*; (*both ways*) Hin- und Rückreise *f*

jovial ['dʒəuvɪəl] *adj* fröhlich; (*atmosphere*) freundlich, herzlich

jowl [dʒaul] *n* Backe *f*

joy [dʒɔɪ] *n* Freude *f*

joyful ['dʒɔɪful] *adj* freudig

joyride ['dʒɔɪraɪd] *n* Spritztour *in einem gestohlenen Auto*

joyrider ['dʒɔɪraɪdə^r] *n* Autodieb, *der den Wagen nur für eine Spritztour benutzt*

joystick ['dʒɔɪstɪk] *n* (*Aviat*) Steuerknüppel *m*; (*Comput*) Joystick *m*

JP *n abbr* = **Justice of the Peace**

Jr *abbr* (*in names*: = *junior*) jun.

JTPA (*US*) *n abbr* (= *Job Training Partnership Act*) *Arbeitsbeschaffungsprogramm für benachteiligte Bevölkerungsteile und Minderheiten*

jubilant ['dʒuːbɪlnt] *adj* überglücklich

jubilation [dʒuːbɪ'leɪʃən] *n* Jubel *m*

jubilee ['dʒuːbɪliː] *n* Jubiläum *nt*; **silver ~** 25-jähriges Jubiläum; **golden ~** 50-jähriges Jubiläum

judge [dʒʌdʒ] *n* Richter(in) *m(f)*; (*in competition*) Preisrichter(in) *m(f)*; (*fig: expert*) Kenner(in) *m(f)* ▷ *vt* (*Law: person*) über die Verhandlung führen über +*acc*; (: *case*) verhandeln; (*competition*) Preisrichter(in) sein bei; (*person etc*) beurteilen; (*consider*) halten für; (*estimate*) einschätzen ▷ *vi*: **judging by** *or* **to ~ by his expression** seinem Gesichtsausdruck nach zu urteilen; **she's a good ~ of character** sie ist ein guter Menschenkenner; **I'll be the ~ of that** das müssen Sie mich schon selbst beurteilen lassen; **as far as I can ~** soweit ich es beurteilen kann; **I ~d it necessary to inform him** ich hielt es für nötig, ihn zu informieren

judge advocate *n* (*Mil*) Beisitzer(in) *m(f)* bei einem Kriegsgericht

Judge Advocate General *n* (*Mil*) *Vorsitzender des obersten Militärgerichts*

judgment, judgement ['dʒʌdʒmənt] *n* Urteil *nt*; (*Rel*) Gericht *nt*; (*view, opinion*) Meinung *f*; (*discernment*) Urteilsvermögen *nt*; **in my ~** meiner Meinung nach; **to pass ~ (on)** (*Law*) das Urteil sprechen (über +*acc*); (*fig*) ein Urteil fällen (über +*acc*)

judicial [dʒuː'dɪʃl] *adj* gerichtlich, Justiz-; (*fig*) kritisch; **~ review** gerichtliche Überprüfung *f*

judiciary [dʒuː'dɪʃɪərɪ] *n*: **the ~** die Gerichtsbehörden *pl*

judicious [dʒuː'dɪʃəs] *adj* klug

judo ['dʒuːdəu] *n* Judo *nt*

jug [dʒʌg] *n* Krug *m*

jugged hare ['dʒʌgd-] (*Brit*) *n* ≈ Hasenpfeffer *m*

juggernaut ['dʒʌgənɔːt] (*Brit*) *n* Fernlastwagen *m*

juggle ['dʒʌgl] *vi* jonglieren

juggler ['dʒʌglə^r] *n* Jongleur *m*

Jugoslav *etc* ['juːgəu'slɑːv] = **Yugoslav** *etc*

jugular ['dʒʌgjulə^r] *adj*: **~ (vein)** Drosselvene *f*

juice [dʒuːs] *n* Saft *m*; (*inf: petrol*): **we've run out of ~** wir haben keinen Sprit mehr

juicy ['dʒuːsɪ] *adj* saftig

jukebox ['dʒuːkbɔks] *n* Musikbox *f*

Jul. *abbr* = **July**

July [dʒuː'laɪ] *n* Juli *m*; **the first of ~** der erste Juli; **on the eleventh of ~** am elften Juli; **in the month of ~** im (Monat) Juli; **at the beginning/end of ~** Anfang/Ende Juli; **in the middle of ~** Mitte Juli; **during ~** im Juli; **in ~ of next year** im Juli nächsten Jahres; **each** *or* **every ~** jedes Jahr im Juli; **~ was wet this year** der Juli war dieses Jahr ein nasser Monat

jumble ['dʒʌmbl] *n* Durcheinander *nt*; (*items for sale*) gebrauchte Sachen *pl; siehe Info-Artikel* ▷ *vt* (*also:* **jumble up**) durcheinanderbringen

● **JUMBLE SALE**

Jumble sale ist ein Wohltätigkeitsbasar, meist in einer Aula oder einem Gemeindehaus abgehalten, bei dem alle möglichen Gebrauchtwaren (vor allem Kleidung, Spielzeug, Bücher,

J

Geschirr und Möbel) verkauft werden. Der Erlös fließt entweder einer Wohltätigkeitsorganisation zu oder wird für örtliche Zwecke verwendet, z. B. die Pfadfinder, die Grundschule, Reparatur der Kirche usw.

jumbo ['dʒʌmbəu]

jumbo jet n Jumbo(jet) m

jumbo-size ['dʒʌmbəusaɪz] adj (packet etc) Riesen-

jump [dʒʌmp] vi springen; (with fear, surprise) zusammenzucken; (increase) sprunghaft ansteigen ▷ vt springen über +acc ▷ n (see vb) Sprung m; Zusammenzucken nt; sprunghafter Anstieg m; **to ~ the queue** (Brit) sich vordrängeln
▶ **jump about** vi herumspringen
▶ **jump at** vt fus (idea) sofort aufgreifen; (chance) sofort ergreifen; **he ~ed at the offer** er griff bei dem Angebot sofort zu
▶ **jump down** vi herunterspringen
▶ **jump up** vi hochspringen; (from seat) aufspringen

jumped-up ['dʒʌmptʌp] (Brit: pej) adj eingebildet

jumper ['dʒʌmpə'] n (Brit) Pullover m; (US: dress) Trägerkleid nt; (Sport) Springer(in) m(f)

jumper cables (US) npl = **jump leads**

jumping jack n Knallfrosch m

jump jet n Senkrechtstarter m

jump leads (Brit) npl Starthilfekabel nt

jump-start ['dʒʌmpstɑːt] vt (Aut: engine) durch Anschieben des Wagens in Gang bringen

jump suit n Overall m

jumpy ['dʒʌmpɪ] adj nervös

Jun. abbr = **June**

junction ['dʒʌŋkʃən] (Brit) n Kreuzung f; (Rail) Gleisanschluss m

juncture ['dʒʌŋktʃə'] n: **at this ~** zu diesem Zeitpunkt

June [dʒuːn] n Juni m; see also **July**

jungle ['dʒʌŋgl] n Urwald m, Dschungel m (also fig)

junior ['dʒuːnɪə'] adj jünger; (subordinate) untergeordnet ▷ n Jüngere(r) f(m); (young person) Junior m; **he's ~ to me (by 2 years)**, **he's my ~ (by 2 years)** (younger) er ist (2 Jahre) jünger als ich; **he's ~ to me** (subordinate) er steht unter mir

junior executive n Zweiter Geschäftsführer m, Zweite Geschäftsführerin f

junior high school (US) n ≈ Mittelschule f

junior minister (Brit) n Staatssekretär(in) m(f)

junior partner n Juniorpartner(in) m(f)

junior school (Brit) n ≈ Grundschule f

junior sizes npl (Comm) Kindergrößen pl

juniper ['dʒuːnɪpə'] n: **~ berry** Wacholderbeere f

junk [dʒʌŋk] n (rubbish) Gerümpel nt; (cheap goods) Ramsch m; (ship) Dschunke f ▷ vt (inf) ausrangieren

junk bond n (Fin) niedrig eingestuftes Wertpapier mit hohen Ertragschancen bei erhöhtem Risiko

junket ['dʒʌŋkɪt] n Dickmilch f; (inf: pej: free trip): **to go on a ~** eine Reise auf Kosten des Steuerzahlers machen

junk food n ungesundes Essen nt

junkie ['dʒʌŋkɪ] (inf) n Fixer(in) m(f)

junk mail n (Post)wurfsendungen pl

junk room n Rumpelkammer f

junk shop n Trödelladen m

Junr abbr (in names: = junior) jun.

junta ['dʒʌntə] n Junta f

Jupiter ['dʒuːpɪtə'] n Jupiter m

jurisdiction [dʒuərɪs'dɪkʃən] n Gerichtsbarkeit f; (Admin) Zuständigkeit f, Zuständigkeitsbereich m; **it falls** or **comes within/outside my ~** dafür bin ich zuständig/nicht zuständig

jurisprudence [dʒuərɪs'pruːdəns] n Jura no art, Rechtswissenschaft f

juror ['dʒuərə'] n Schöffe m, Schöffin f; (for capital crimes) Geschworene(r) f(m); (in competition) Preisrichter(in) m(f)

jury ['dʒuərɪ] n: **the ~** die Schöffen pl; (for capital crimes) die Geschworenen pl; (for competition) die Jury, das Preisgericht

jury box n Schöffenbank f; Geschworenenbank f

juryman ['dʒuərɪmən] (irreg: like **man**) n = **juror**

just [dʒʌst] adj gerecht ▷ adv (exactly) genau; (only) nur; **he's ~ done it/left** er hat es gerade getan/ist gerade gegangen; **~ as I expected** genau wie ich erwartet habe; **~ right** genau richtig; **~ two o'clock** erst zwei Uhr; **we were ~ going** wir wollten gerade gehen; **I was ~ about to phone** ich wollte gerade anrufen; **she's ~ as clever as you** sie ist genauso klug wie du; **it's ~ as well (that ...)** nur gut, dass ...; **~ as he was leaving** gerade als er gehen wollte; **~ before** gerade noch; **~ enough** gerade genug; **~ here** genau hier, genau an dieser Stelle; **he ~ missed** er hat genau danebengetroffen; **it's ~ me** ich bin's nur; **it's ~ a mistake** es ist nur ein Fehler; **~ listen** hör mal; **~ ask someone the way** frage doch einfach jemanden nach dem Weg; **not ~ now** nicht gerade jetzt; **~ a minute!**, **~ one moment!** einen Moment, bitte!

justice ['dʒʌstɪs] n Justiz f; (of cause, complaint) Berechtigung f; (fairness) Gerechtigkeit f; (US: judge) Richter(in) m(f); **Lord Chief J~** (Brit) oberster Richter in Großbritannien; **to do ~ to** (fig) gerecht werden +dat

Justice of the Peace n Friedensrichter(in) m(f)

justifiable [dʒʌstɪ'faɪəbl] adj gerechtfertigt, berechtigt

justifiably [dʒʌstɪ'faɪəblɪ] adv zu Recht, berechtigterweise

justification [dʒʌstɪfɪ'keɪʃən] n Rechtfertigung f; (Typ) Justierung f

justify ['dʒʌstɪfaɪ] vt rechtfertigen; (text) justieren; **to be justified in doing sth** etw zu or mit Recht tun

justly ['dʒʌstlɪ] *adv* zu *or* mit Recht; (*deservedly*) gerecht

jut [dʒʌt] *vi* (*also*: **jut out**) vorstehen

jute [dʒuːt] *n* Jute *f*

juvenile ['dʒuːvənaɪl] *adj* (*crime, offenders*) Jugend-; (*humour, mentality*) kindisch, unreif ▷ *n* Jugendliche(r) *f(m)*

juvenile delinquency *n* Jugendkriminalität *f*

juvenile delinquent *n* jugendlicher Straftäter *m*, jugendliche Straftäterin *f*

juxtapose ['dʒʌkstəpəuz] *vt* nebeneinanderstellen

juxtaposition ['dʒʌkstəpə'zɪʃən] *n* Nebeneinanderstellung *f*

Kk

K¹, k [keɪ] *n* (*letter*) K *nt*, k *nt*; **K for King** = K wie Kaufmann

K² [keɪ] *abbr* (= *one thousand*) K; (*Comput:* = *kilobyte*) KB; (*Brit: in titles*) = **knight**

kaftan ['kæftæn] *n* Kaftan *m*

Kalahari Desert [kælə'hɑːrɪ-] *n*: **the ~** die Kalahari

kale [keɪl] *n* Grünkohl *m*

kaleidoscope [kə'laɪdəskəup] *n* Kaleidoskop *nt*

kamikaze ['kæmɪ'kɑːzɪ] *adj* (*mission etc*) Kamikaze-, Selbstmord-

Kampala [kæm'pɑːlə] *n* Kampala *nt*

Kampuchea [kæmpu'tʃɪə] *n* Kampuchea *nt*

Kampuchean [kæmpu'tʃɪən] *adj* kampucheanisch

kangaroo [kæŋgə'ruː] *n* Känguru *nt*

Kans. (*US*) *abbr* (*Post*) = **Kansas**

kaput [kə'put] (*inf*) *adj*: **to be ~** kaputt sein

karaoke [kɑːrə'əukɪ] *n* Karaoke *nt*

karate [kə'rɑːtɪ] *n* Karate *nt*

Kashmir [kæʃ'mɪəʳ] *n* Kaschmir *nt*

kayak ['kaɪæk] *n* Kajak *m or nt*

Kazakhstan [kæzæk'stɑːn] *n* Kasachstan *nt*

KC (*Brit*) *n abbr* (*Law*: = *King's Counsel*) Kronanwalt *m*

kebab [kə'bæb] *n* Kebab *m*

keel [kiːl] *n* Kiel *m*; **on an even ~** (*fig*) stabil
▶ **keel over** *vi* kentern; (*person*) umkippen

keen [kiːn] *adj* begeistert, eifrig; (*interest*) groß; (*desire*) heftig; (*eye, intelligence, competition, edge*) scharf; **to be ~ to do** *or* **on doing sth** scharf darauf sein, etw zu tun (*inf*); **to be ~ on sth** an etw *dat* sehr interessiert sein; **to be ~ on sb** von jdm sehr angetan sein; **I'm not ~ on going** ich brenne nicht gerade darauf, zu gehen

keenly ['kiːnlɪ] *adv* (*enthusiastically*) begeistert; (*feel*) leidenschaftlich; (*look*) aufmerksam

keenness ['kiːnnɪs] *n* Begeisterung *f*, Eifer *m*; **his ~ to go is suspicious** dass er so unbedingt gehen will, ist verdächtig

keep [kiːp] (*pt, pp* **kept**) *vt* behalten; (*preserve, store*) aufbewahren; (*house, shop, accounts, diary*) führen; (*garden etc*) pflegen; (*chickens, bees, promise*) halten; (*family etc*) versorgen, unterhalten; (*detain*) aufhalten; (*prevent*) abhalten ▷ *vi* (*remain*) bleiben; (*food*) sich halten ▷ *n* (*food etc*) Unterhalt *m*; (*of castle*) Bergfried *m*; **to ~ doing sth** etw immer wieder tun; **to ~ sb happy** jdn zufriedenstellen; **to ~ a room tidy** ein Zimmer in Ordnung halten; **to ~ sb waiting** jdn warten lassen; **to ~ an appointment** eine Verabredung einhalten; **to ~ a record of sth** über etw *acc* Buch führen; **to ~ sth for o.s.** etw für sich behalten; **to ~ sth (back) from sb** etw vor jdm geheim halten; **to ~ sb from doing sth** jdn davon abhalten, etw zu tun; **to ~ sth from happening** etw verhindern; **to ~ time** (*clock*) genau gehen; **enough for his ~** genug für seinen Unterhalt
▶ **keep away** *vt* fernhalten ▷ *vi*: **to ~ away (from)** wegbleiben (von)
▶ **keep back** *vt* zurückhalten; (*tears*) unterdrücken; (*money*) einbehalten ▷ *vi* zurückbleiben
▶ **keep down** *vt* (*prices*) niedrig halten; (*spending*) einschränken; (*food*) bei sich behalten ▷ *vi* unten bleiben
▶ **keep in** *vt* im Haus behalten; (*at school*) nachsitzen lassen ▷ *vi* (*inf*): **to ~ in with sb** sich mit jdm gut stellen
▶ **keep off** *vt* fernhalten ▷ *vi* wegbleiben; **"~ off the grass"** „Betreten des Rasens verboten"; **~ your hands off** Hände weg
▶ **keep on** *vi*: **to ~ on doing sth** (*continue*) etw weiter tun; **to ~ on (about sth)** unaufhörlich (von etw) reden
▶ **keep out** *vt* fernhalten; **"~ out"** „Zutritt verboten"
▶ **keep up** *vt* (*payments*) weiterbezahlen; (*standards etc*) aufrechterhalten ▷ *vi*: **to ~ up (with)** mithalten können (mit)

keeper ['kiːpəʳ] *n* Wärter(in) *m(f)*

keep fit *n* Fitnesstraining *nt*

keeping ['kiːpɪŋ] *n* (*care*) Obhut *f*; **in ~ with** in Übereinstimmung mit; **out of ~ with** nicht im Einklang mit; **I'll leave this in your ~** ich vertraue dies deiner Obhut an

keeps [kiːps] *n*: **for ~** (*inf*) für immer

keepsake ['kiːpseɪk] *n* Andenken *nt*

keg [kɛg] *n* Fässchen *nt*; **~ beer** Bier *nt* vom Fass

Ken. (*US*) *abbr* (*Post*) = **Kentucky**

kennel ['kɛnl] *n* Hundehütte *f*

kennels ['kɛnlz] *n* Hundeheim *nt*; **we had to leave our dog in ~ over Christmas** wir mussten unseren Hund über Weihnachten in ein Heim geben

Kenya ['kɛnjə] n Kenia nt

Kenyan ['kɛnjən] adj kenianisch ▷ n Kenianer(in) m(f)

kept [kɛpt] pt, pp of **keep**

kerb [kɜːb] (Brit) n Bordstein m

kerb crawler [-'krɔːlə^r] (inf) n Freier m im Autostrich

kernel ['kɜːnl] n Kern m

kerosene ['kɛrəsiːn] n Kerosin nt

kestrel ['kɛstrəl] n Turmfalke m

ketchup ['kɛtʃəp] n Ket(s)chup m or nt

kettle ['kɛtl] n Kessel m

kettledrum ['kɛtldrʌm] n (Kessel)pauke f

key [kiː] n Schlüssel m; (Mus) Tonart f; (of piano, computer, typewriter) Taste f ▷ cpd (issue etc) Schlüssel- ▷ vt (also: **key in**) eingeben

keyboard ['kiːbɔːd] n Tastatur f

keyboarder ['kiːbɔːdə^r] n Datentypist(in) m(f)

keyed up [kiːd-] adj: **to be (all) ~** (ganz) aufgedreht sein (inf)

keyhole ['kiːhəul] n Schlüsselloch nt

keyhole surgery n Schlüssellochchirurgie f, minimal invasive Chirurgie f

keynote ['kiːnəut] n Grundton m; (of speech) Leitgedanke m

keypad ['kiːpæd] n Tastenfeld nt

key ring n Schlüsselring m

keystroke ['kiːstrəuk] n Anschlag m

kg abbr (= kilogram) kg

KGB n abbr (Pol: formerly) KGB m

khaki ['kɑːkɪ] n K(h)aki nt

kHz abbr (= kilohertz) kHz

kibbutz [kɪ'buts] n Kibbuz m

kick [kɪk] vt treten; (table, ball) treten gegen +acc; (inf: habit) ablegen; (: addiction) wegkommen von ▷ vi (horse) ausschlagen ▷ n Tritt m; (to ball) Schuss m; (of rifle) Rückstoß m; (thrill): **he does it for ~s** er macht es zum Spaß
  ▸ **kick around** (inf) vi (person) rumhängen; (thing) rumliegen
  ▸ **kick off** vi (Sport) anstoßen

kickoff ['kɪkɔf] n (Sport) Anstoß m

kick start n (Aut: also: **kick starter**) Kickstarter m

kid [kɪd] n (inf: child) Kind nt; (animal) Kitz nt; (leather) Ziegenleder nt, Glacéleder nt ▷ vi (inf) Witze machen; **~ brother** kleiner Bruder m; **~ sister** kleine Schwester f

kid gloves npl: **to treat sb with ~** (fig) jdn mit Samthandschuhen anfassen

kidnap ['kɪdnæp] vt entführen, kidnappen

kidnapper ['kɪdnæpə^r] n Entführer(in) m(f), Kidnapper(in) m(f)

kidnapping ['kɪdnæpɪŋ] n Entführung f, Kidnapping nt

kidney ['kɪdnɪ] n Niere f

kidney bean n Gartenbohne f

kidney machine n (Med) künstliche Niere f

Kilimanjaro [kɪlɪmən'dʒɑːrəu] n: **Mount ~** der Kilimandscharo

kill [kɪl] vt töten; (murder) ermorden, umbringen; (plant) eingehen lassen; (proposal) zu Fall bringen; (rumour) ein Ende machen +dat ▷ n Abschuss m; **to ~ time** die Zeit totschlagen; **to ~ o.s. to do sth** (fig) sich fast umbringen, um etw zu tun; **to ~ o.s. (laughing)** (fig) sich totlachen
  ▸ **kill off** vt abtöten; (fig: romance) beenden

killer ['kɪlə^r] n Mörder(in) m(f)

killer instinct n (fig) Tötungsinstinkt m

killing ['kɪlɪŋ] n Töten nt; (instance) Mord m; **to make a ~** (inf) einen Riesengewinn machen

killjoy ['kɪldʒɔɪ] n Spielverderber(in) m(f)

kiln [kɪln] n Brennofen m

kilo ['kiːləu] n Kilo nt

kilobyte ['kiːləubaɪt] n Kilobyte nt

kilogram, kilogramme ['kɪləugræm] n Kilogramm nt

kilohertz ['kɪləuhəːts] n inv Kilohertz nt

kilometre, (US) **kilometer** ['kɪləmiːtə^r] n Kilometer m

kilowatt ['kɪləuwɔt] n Kilowatt nt

kilt [kɪlt] n Kilt m, Schottenrock m

kilter ['kɪltə^r] n: **out of ~** nicht in Ordnung

kimono [kɪ'məunəu] n Kimono m

kin [kɪn] n see **kith**; **next**

kind [kaɪnd] adj freundlich ▷ n Art f; (sort) Sorte f; **would you be ~ enough to ...?, would you be so ~ as to ...?** wären Sie (vielleicht) so nett und ...?; **it's very ~ of you (to do ...)** es ist wirklich nett von Ihnen(, ... zu tun); **in ~** (Comm) in Naturalien; **a ~ of ...** eine Art ...; **they are two of a ~** sie sind beide von der gleichen Art; (people) sie sind vom gleichen Schlag

kindergarten ['kɪndəgɑːtn] n Kindergarten m

kind-hearted [kaɪnd'hɑːtɪd] adj gutherzig

kindle ['kɪndl] vt anzünden; (emotion) wecken

kindling ['kɪndlɪŋ] n Anzündholz nt

kindly ['kaɪndlɪ] adj, adv freundlich, nett; **will you ~** ... würden Sie bitte ...; **he didn't take it ~** er konnte sich damit nicht anfreunden

kindness ['kaɪndnɪs] n Freundlichkeit f

kindred ['kɪndrɪd] adj: **~ spirit** Gleichgesinnte(r) f(m)

kinetic [kɪ'netɪk] adj kinetisch

king [kɪŋ] n (also fig) König m

kingdom ['kɪŋdəm] n Königreich nt

kingfisher ['kɪŋfɪʃə^r] n Eisvogel m

kingpin ['kɪŋpɪn] n (Tech) Bolzen m; (Aut) Achsschenkelbolzen m; (fig) wichtigste Stütze f

king-size ['kɪŋsaɪz], **king-sized** ['kɪŋsaɪzd] adj extragroß; (cigarette) Kingsize-

kink [kɪŋk] n Knick m; (in hair) Welle f; (fig) Schrulle f

kinky ['kɪŋkɪ] (pej) adj schrullig; (sexually) abartig

kinship ['kɪnʃɪp] n Verwandtschaft f

kinsman ['kɪnzmən] (irreg: like **man**) n Verwandte(r) m

kinswoman ['kɪnzwumən] (irreg: like **woman**) n Verwandte f

kiosk ['kiːɔsk] n Kiosk m; (Brit) (Telefon)zelle f; (also: **newspaper kiosk**) (Zeitungs)kiosk m

k

kipper ['kɪpəʳ] n Räucherhering m

Kirghizia [kəˈgɪzɪə] n Kirgistan nt

kiss [kɪs] n Kuß m ▷ vt küssen ▷ vi sich küssen; **to ~ (each other)** sich küssen; **to ~ sb goodbye** jdm einen Abschiedskuss geben

kissagram ['kɪsəgræm] n durch eine(n) Angestellte(n) einer Agentur persönlich übermittelter Kuss

kiss of life (Brit) n: **the ~** Mund-zu-Mund-Beatmung f

kit [kɪt] n Zeug nt, Sachen pl; (equipment, also Mil) Ausrüstung f; (set of tools) Werkzeug nt; (for assembly) Bausatz m
  ▸ **kit out** (Brit) vt ausrüsten, ausstatten

kitbag ['kɪtbæg] n Seesack m

kitchen ['kɪtʃɪn] n Küche f

kitchen garden n Küchengarten m

kitchen sink n Spüle f

kitchen unit (Brit) n Küchenschrank m

kitchenware ['kɪtʃɪnwɛəʳ] n Küchengeräte pl

kite [kaɪt] n Drachen m; (Zool) Milan m

kith [kɪθ] n: **~ and kin** Freunde und Verwandte pl

kitten ['kɪtn] n Kätzchen nt

kitty ['kɪtɪ] n (gemeinsame) Kasse f

kiwi ['kiːwiː], **kiwi fruit** n Kiwi(frucht) f

KKK (US) n abbr (= Ku Klux Klan) Ku-Klux-Klan m

Kleenex® ['kliːnɛks] n Tempo(taschentuch)® nt

kleptomaniac [klɛptəʊ'meɪnɪæk] n Kleptomane m, Kleptomanin f

km abbr (= kilometre) km

km/h abbr (= kilometres per hour) km/h

knack [næk] n: **to have the ~ of doing sth** es heraushaben, wie man etw macht; **there's a ~ to doing this** da ist ein Trick or Kniff dabei

knackered ['nækəd] (Brit: inf) adj kaputt

knapsack ['næpsæk] n Rucksack m

knead [niːd] vt kneten

knee [niː] n Knie nt

kneecap ['niːkæp] n Kniescheibe f

kneecapping ['niːkæpɪŋ] n Durchschießen nt der Kniescheibe

knee-deep ['niːˈdiːp] adj, adv: **the water was ~** das Wasser ging mir etc bis zum Knie; **~ in mud** knietief or bis zu den Knien im Schlamm

kneejerk reaction ['niːdʒɜːk-] n (fig) instinktive Reaktion f

kneel [niːl] (pt, pp **knelt**) vi knien; (also: **kneel down**) niederknien

kneepad ['niːpæd] n Knieschützer m

knell [nɛl] n Totengeläut(e) nt; (fig) Ende nt

knelt [nɛlt] pt, pp of **kneel**

knew [njuː] pt of **know**

knickers ['nɪkəz] (Brit) npl Schlüpfer m

knick-knacks ['nɪknæks] npl Nippsachen pl

knife [naɪf] n (pl **knives**) n Messer nt ▷ vt (injure, attack) einstechen auf +acc; **~, fork and spoon** Messer, Gabel und Löffel

knife edge n: **to be balanced on a ~** (fig) auf Messers Schneide stehen

knight [naɪt] n (Brit) Ritter m; (Chess) Springer m, Pferd nt

knighthood ['naɪthʊd] (Brit) n: **to get a ~** in den Adelsstand erhoben werden

knit [nɪt] vt stricken ▷ vi stricken; (bones) zusammenwachsen; **to ~ one's brows** die Stirn runzeln

knitted ['nɪtɪd] adj gestrickt, Strick-

knitting ['nɪtɪŋ] n Stricken nt; (garment being made) Strickzeug nt

knitting machine n Strickmaschine f

knitting needle n Stricknadel f

knitting pattern n Strickmuster nt

knitwear ['nɪtwɛəʳ] n Strickwaren pl

knives [naɪvz] npl of **knife**

knob [nɔb] n Griff m; (of stick) Knauf m; (on radio, TV etc) Knopf m; **a ~ of butter** (Brit) ein Stückchen nt Butter

knobbly ['nɔblɪ], (US) **knobby** adj (wood) knorrig; (surface) uneben; **~ knees** Knubbelknie pl (inf)

knock [nɔk] vt schlagen; (bump into) stoßen gegen +acc; (inf: criticize) runtermachen ▷ vi klopfen ▷ n Schlag m; (bump) Stoß m; (on door) Klopfen nt; **to ~ a nail into sth** einen Nagel in etw acc schlagen; **to ~ some sense into sb** jdn zur Vernunft bringen; **to ~ at/on** klopfen an/auf +acc; **he ~ed at the door** er klopfte an, er klopfte an die Tür
  ▸ **knock about** (inf) vt schlagen, verprügeln ▷ vi rumziehen; **~ about with** sich rumtreiben mit
  ▸ **knock around** vt, vi = **knock about**
  ▸ **knock back** (inf) vt (drink) sich dat hinter die Binde kippen
  ▸ **knock down** vt anfahren; (fatally) überfahren; (building etc) abreißen; (price: buyer) herunterhandeln; (: seller) heruntergehen mit
  ▸ **knock off** vi (inf) Feierabend machen ▷ vt (from price) nachlassen; (inf: steal) klauen; **to ~ off £10** £10 nachlassen
  ▸ **knock out** vt bewusstlos schlagen; (subj: drug) bewusstlos werden lassen; (Boxing) k. o. schlagen; (in game, competition) besiegen
  ▸ **knock over** vt umstoßen; (with car) anfahren

knockdown ['nɔkdaʊn] adj: **~ price** Schleuderpreis m

knocker ['nɔkəʳ] n Türklopfer m

knock-for-knock ['nɔkfə'nɔk] (Brit) adj: **~ agreement** Vereinbarung, bei der jede Versicherungsgesellschaft den Schaden am von ihr versicherten Fahrzeug übernimmt

knocking ['nɔkɪŋ] n Klopfen nt

knock-kneed [nɔk'niːd] adj x-beinig; **to be ~** X-Beine haben

knockout ['nɔkaʊt] n (Boxing) K.-o.-Schlag m, Ko.-Schlag m ▷ cpd (competition etc) Ausscheidungs-

knock-up ['nɔkʌp] n (Tennis): **to have a ~** ein paar Bälle schlagen

knot [nɔt] n Knoten m; (in wood) Ast m ▷ vt einen Knoten machen in +acc; (knot together) verknoten; **to tie a ~** einen Knoten machen

knotty ['nɔtɪ] adj (fig: problem) verwickelt

know [nəʊ] (pt **knew**, pp **~n**) vt kennen; (facts)

wissen; (*language*) können ▷ *vi*: **to ~ about** *or*
of sth/sb von etw/jdm gehört haben; **to ~
how to swim** schwimmen können; **to get to
~ sth** etw erfahren; (*place*) etw kennenlernen;
I don't ~ him ich kenne ihn nicht; **to ~ right
from wrong** Gut und Böse unterscheiden
können; **as far as I ~** soviel ich weiß; **yes, I ~**
ja, ich weiß; **I don't ~** ich weiß (es) nicht
know-all ['nəuɔːl] (*Brit*: *pej*) *n* Alleswisser
m

know-how ['nəuhau] *n* Know-how *nt*,
Sachkenntnis *f*
knowing ['nəuɪŋ] *adj* wissend
knowingly ['nəuɪŋlɪ] *adv* (*purposely*) bewusst;
(*smile, look*) wissend
know-it-all ['nəuɪtɔːl] (*US*) *n* = **know-all**
knowledge ['nɒlɪdʒ] *n* Wissen *nt*, Kenntnis
f; (*learning, things learnt*) Kenntnisse *pl*; **to
have no ~ of** nichts wissen von; **not to my
~** nicht, dass ich wüsste; **without my ~**
ohne mein Wissen; **it is common ~ that ...**
es ist allgemein bekannt, dass ...; **it has
come to my ~ that ...** ich habe erfahren,
dass ...; **to have a working ~ of French**
Grundkenntnisse in Französisch haben
knowledgeable ['nɒlɪdʒəbl] *adj* informiert
known [nəun] *pp of* **know** ▷ *adj* bekannt;
(*expert*) anerkannt
knuckle ['nʌkl] *n* (Finger)knöchel *m*

▸ **knuckle down** (*inf*) *vi* sich dahinter
klemmen; **to ~ down to work** sich an die
Arbeit machen
▸ **knuckle under** (*inf*) *vi* sich fügen, spuren
knuckle-duster ['nʌkl'dʌstəʳ] *n* Schlagring *m*
KO *n abbr* (= *knockout*) K. o. *m* ▷ *vt* k. o. schlagen
koala [kəu'ɑːlə] *n* (*also*: **koala bear**) Koala(bär)
m
kook [kuːk] (*US*: *inf*) *n* Spinner *m*
Koran [kɔ'rɑːn] *n*: **the ~** der Koran
Korea [kə'rɪə] *n* Korea *nt*; **North ~** Nordkorea
nt; **South ~** Südkorea *nt*
Korean [kə'rɪən] *adj* koreanisch ▷ *n*
Koreaner(in) *m(f)*
kosher ['kəuʃəʳ] *adj* koscher
kowtow ['kau'tau] *vi*: **to ~ to sb** vor jdm
dienern *or* einen Kotau machen
Kremlin ['krɛmlɪn] *n*: **the ~** der Kreml
KS (*US*) *abbr* (*Post*) = *Kansas*
Kt (*Brit*) *abbr* (*in titles*) = **knight**
Kuala Lumpur ['kwɑːlə'lumpuəʳ] *n* Kuala
Lumpur *nt*
kudos ['kjuːdɔs] *n* Ansehen *nt*, Ehre *f*
Kurd [kəːd] *n* Kurde *m*, Kurdin *f*
Kuwait [ku'weɪt] *n* Kuwait *nt*
Kuwaiti [ku'weɪtɪ] *adj* kuwaitisch ▷ *n*
Kuwaiter(in) *m(f)*
kW *abbr* (= *kilowatt*) kW
KY (*US*) *abbr* (*Post*) = *Kentucky*

k

L l

L¹, l¹ [ɛl] n (letter) L nt, l nt; **L for Lucy, L for Love** (US) ≈ L wie Ludwig

L² [ɛl] abbr (Brit: Aut: = learner) am Auto angebrachtes Kennzeichen für Fahrschüler; = **lake**; (= large) gr.; (= left) l.

l² abbr (= litre) l

LA (US) n abbr = Los Angeles ▷ abbr (Post) = Louisiana

La. (US) abbr (Post) = Louisiana

lab [læb] n abbr = **laboratory**

label ['leɪbl] n Etikett nt; (brand: of record) Label nt ▷ vt etikettieren; (fig: person) abstempeln

labor etc ['leɪbə^r] (US) n = **labour** etc

laboratory [lə'bɔrətərɪ] n Labor nt

● **LABOR DAY**
●
● Labor Day ist in den USA und Kanada der
● Name für den Tag der Arbeit. Er wird dort
● als gesetzlicher Feiertag am ersten Montag
● im September begangen.

laborious [lə'bɔːrɪəs] adj mühsam

labor union (US) n Gewerkschaft f

labour, (US) **labor** ['leɪbə^r] n Arbeit f; (work force) Arbeitskräfte pl; (Med): **to be in ~** in den Wehen liegen ▷ vi: **to ~ (at sth)** sich (mit etw) abmühen ▷ vt: **to ~ a point** auf einem Thema herumreiten; **L~, the ~ Party** (Brit) die Labour Party; **hard ~** Zwangsarbeit f

labour camp n Arbeitslager nt

labour cost n Lohnkosten pl

labour dispute n Arbeitskampf m

laboured ['leɪbəd] adj (breathing) schwer; (movement, style) schwerfällig

labourer ['leɪbərə^r] n Arbeiter(in) m(f); **farm ~** Landarbeiter(in) m(f)

labour force n Arbeiterschaft f

labour intensive adj arbeitsintensiv

labour market n Arbeitsmarkt m

labour pains npl Wehen pl

labour relations npl Beziehungen pl zwischen Arbeitnehmern, Arbeitgebern und Gewerkschaften

labour-saving ['leɪbəseɪvɪŋ] adj arbeitssparend

laburnum [lə'bəːnəm] n (Bot) Goldregen m

labyrinth ['læbɪrɪnθ] n Labyrinth nt

lace [leɪs] n (fabric) Spitze f; (of shoe etc) (Schuh)band nt, Schnürsenkel m ▷ vt (also: **lace up**) (zu)schnüren; **to ~ a drink** einen Schuss Alkohol in ein Getränk geben

lacemaking ['leɪsmeɪkɪŋ] n Klöppelei f

lacerate ['læsəreɪt] vt zerschneiden

laceration [læsə'reɪʃən] n Schnittwunde f

lace-up ['leɪsʌp] adj (shoes etc) Schnür-

lack [læk] n Mangel m ▷ vt, vi: **sb ~s sth, sb is ~ing in sth** jdm fehlt es an etw dat; **through** or **for ~ of** aus Mangel an +dat; **to be ~ing** fehlen

lackadaisical [lækə'deɪzɪkl] adj lustlos

lackey ['lækɪ] (pej) n Lakai m

lacklustre, (US) **lackluster** ['læklʌstə^r] adj farblos, langweilig

laconic [lə'kɔnɪk] adj lakonisch

lacquer ['lækə^r] n Lack m; (also: **hair lacquer**) Haarspray nt

lacrosse [lə'krɔs] n Lacrosse nt

lacy ['leɪsɪ] adj Spitzen-; (like lace) spitzenartig

lad [læd] n Junge m

ladder ['lædə^r] n (also fig) Leiter f; (Brit: in tights) Laufmasche f ▷ vt (Brit) Laufmaschen bekommen in +dat ▷ vi (Brit) Laufmaschen bekommen

laden ['leɪdn] adj: **~ (with)** beladen (mit); **fully ~** vollbeladen

ladle ['leɪdl] n Schöpflöffel m, (Schöpf)kelle f ▷ vt schöpfen

▶ **ladle out** vt (fig) austeilen

lady ['leɪdɪ] n (woman) Frau f; (: dignified, graceful etc) Dame f; (Brit: title) Lady f; **ladies and gentlemen ...** meine Damen und Herren ...; **young ~** junge Dame; **the ladies' (room)** die Damentoilette

ladybird ['leɪdɪbəːd], (US) **ladybug** ['leɪdɪbʌg] n Marienkäfer m

lady-in-waiting ['leɪdɪɪn'weɪtɪŋ] n Hofdame f

lady-killer ['leɪdɪkɪlə^r] n Herzensbrecher m

ladylike ['leɪdɪlaɪk] adj damenhaft

ladyship ['leɪdɪʃɪp] n: **your L~** Ihre Ladyschaft

lag [læg] n (period of time) Zeitabstand m ▷ vi (also: **lag behind**) zurückbleiben; (trade, investment etc) zurückgehen ▷ vt (pipes etc) isolieren; **old ~** (inf: prisoner) (ehemaliger) Knacki m

lager ['lɑːgə^r] n helles Bier nt

lager lout (Brit: inf) n betrunkener Rowdy m

lagging ['lægɪŋ] n Isoliermaterial nt

lagoon [ləˈguːn] n Lagune f
Lagos [ˈleɪɡɔs] n Lagos nt
laid [leɪd] pt, pp of **lay**
laid-back [leɪdˈbæk] (inf) adj locker
laid up adj: **to be ~ (with)** im Bett liegen (mit)
lain [leɪn] pp of **lie**
lair [lɛəʳ] n Lager nt; (cave) Höhle f; (den) Bau m
laissez faire [lɛseɪˈfɛəʳ] n Laisser-faire nt
laity [ˈleɪətɪ] n or npl Laien pl
lake [leɪk] n See m
Lake District (Brit) n: **the ~** der Lake Distrikt, Seengebiet im NW Englands
lamb [læm] n Lamm nt; (meat) Lammfleisch nt
lamb chop n Lammkotelett nt
lambskin [ˈlæmskɪn] n Lammfell nt
lamb's wool n Lammwolle f
lame [leɪm] adj lahm; (argument, answer) schwach
lame duck n (person) Niete f; (business) unwirtschaftliche Firma f
lamely [ˈleɪmlɪ] adv lahm
lament [ləˈmɛnt] n Klage f ▷ vt beklagen
lamentable [ˈlæməntəbl] adj beklagenswert
laminated [ˈlæmɪneɪtɪd] adj laminiert; (metal) geschichtet; **~ glass** Verbundglas nt; **~ wood** Sperrholz nt
lamp [læmp] n Lampe f
lamplight [ˈlæmplaɪt] n: **by ~** bei Lampenlicht
lampoon [læmˈpuːn] n Schmähschrift f ▷ vt verspotten
lamppost [ˈlæmppəʊst] (Brit) n Laternenpfahl m
lampshade [ˈlæmpʃeɪd] n Lampenschirm m
lance [lɑːns] n Lanze f ▷ vt (Med) aufschneiden
lance corporal (Brit) n Obergefreite(r) m
lancet [ˈlɑːnsɪt] n (Med) Lanzette f
Lancs [læŋks] (Brit) abbr (Post) = Lancashire
land [lænd] n Land nt; (as property) Grund und Boden m ▷ vi (Aviat, fig) landen; (from ship) an Land gehen ▷ vt (passengers) absetzen; (goods) an Land bringen; **to own ~** Land besitzen; **to go** or **travel by ~** auf dem Landwege reisen; **to ~ on one's feet** (fig) auf die Füße fallen; **to ~ sb with sth** (inf) jdm etw aufhalsen
  ▶ **land up** vi: **to ~ up in/at** landen in +dat
landed gentry [ˈlændɪd-] n Landadel m
landfill site [ˈlændfɪl-] n ≈ Mülldeponie f
landing [ˈlændɪŋ] n (of house) Flur m; (outside flat door) Treppenabsatz m; (Aviat) Landung f
landing card n Einreisekarte f
landing craft n inv Landungsboot nt
landing gear n (Aviat) Fahrgestell nt
landing stage n Landesteg m
landing strip n Landebahn f
landlady [ˈlændleɪdɪ] n Vermieterin f; (of pub) Wirtin f
landlocked [ˈlændlɒkt] adj von Land eingeschlossen; **~ country** Binnenstaat m
landlord [ˈlændlɔːd] n Vermieter m; (of pub) Wirt m
landlubber [ˈlændlʌbəʳ] (old) n Landratte f
landmark [ˈlændmɑːk] n Orientierungspunkt m; (famous building) Wahrzeichen nt; (fig)

Meilenstein m
landowner [ˈlændəʊnəʳ] n Grundbesitzer(in) m(f)
landscape [ˈlændskeɪp] n Landschaft f ▷ vt landschaftlich or gärtnerisch gestalten
landscape architect n Landschaftsarchitekt(in) m(f)
landscape gardener n Landschaftsgärtner(in) m(f)
landscape painting n Landschaftsmalerei f
landslide [ˈlændslaɪd] n Erdrutsch m; (fig: electoral) Erdrutschsieg m
lane [leɪn] n (in country) Weg m; (in town) Gasse f; (of carriageway) Spur f; (of race course, swimming pool) Bahn f; **shipping ~** Schifffahrtsweg m
language [ˈlæŋgwɪdʒ] n Sprache f; **bad ~** Kraftausdrücke pl
language laboratory n Sprachlabor nt
languid [ˈlæŋgwɪd] adj träge, matt
languish [ˈlæŋgwɪʃ] vi schmachten; (project, case) erfolglos bleiben
lank [læŋk] adj (hair) strähnig
lanky [ˈlæŋkɪ] adj schlaksig
lanolin, lanoline [ˈlænəlɪn] n Lanolin nt
lantern [ˈlæntən] n Laterne f
Laos [laus] n Laos nt
lap [læp] n Schoß m; (in race) Runde f ▷ vt (also: **lap up**) aufschlecken ▷ vi (water) plätschern
  ▶ **lap up** vt (fig) genießen
lapdog [ˈlæpdɒg] (pej) n (fig) Schoßhund m
lapel [ləˈpɛl] n Aufschlag m, Revers nt or m
Lapland [ˈlæplænd] n Lappland nt
Lapp [læp] adj lappländisch ▷ n Lappe m, Lappin f; (Ling) Lappländisch nt
lapse [læps] n (bad behaviour) Fehltritt m; (of memory etc) Schwäche f; (of time) Zeitspanne f ▷ vi ablaufen; (law) ungültig werden; **to ~ into bad habits** in schlechte Gewohnheiten verfallen
laptop [ˈlæptɒp] (Comput) n Laptop m ▷ cpd Laptop-
larceny [ˈlɑːsənɪ] n Diebstahl m
larch [lɑːtʃ] n Lärche f
lard [lɑːd] n Schweineschmalz nt
larder [ˈlɑːdəʳ] n Speisekammer f; (cupboard) Speiseschrank m
large [lɑːdʒ] adj groß; (person) korpulent; **to make ~r** vergrößern; **a ~ number of people** eine große Anzahl von Menschen; **on a ~ scale** im großen Rahmen; (extensive) weitreichend; **at ~** (as a whole) im Allgemeinen; (at liberty) auf freiem Fuß; **by and ~** im Großen und Ganzen
large goods vehicle n Lastkraftwagen m
largely [ˈlɑːdʒlɪ] adv (mostly) zum größten Teil; (mainly) hauptsächlich
large-scale [ˈlɑːdʒˈskeɪl] adj im großen Rahmen; (extensive) weitreichend; (map, diagram) in einem großen Maßstab
largesse [lɑːˈʒɛs] n Großzügigkeit f
lark [lɑːk] n (bird) Lerche f; (joke) Spaß m, Jux m
  ▶ **lark about** vi herumalbern

larva ['lɑːvə] (*pl* **~e**) *n* Larve *f*
larvae ['lɑːviː] *npl of* **larva**
laryngitis [lærɪn'dʒaɪtɪs] *n* Kehlkopfentzündung *f*
larynx ['lærɪŋks] *n* Kehlkopf *m*
lasagne [lə'zænjə] *n* Lasagne *pl*
lascivious [lə'sɪvɪəs] *adj* lüstern
laser ['leɪzəʳ] *n* Laser *m*
laser beam *n* Laserstrahl *m*
laser printer *n* Laserdrucker *m*
lash [læʃ] *n* (*also:* **eyelash**) Wimper *f*; (*blow with whip*) Peitschenhieb *m* ▷ *vt* peitschen; (*rain, wind*) peitschen gegen; (*tie*): **to ~ to** festbinden an +*dat*; **to ~ together** zusammenbinden
  ▸ **lash down** *vt* festbinden ▷ *vi* (*rain*) niederprasseln
  ▸ **lash out** *vi* um sich schlagen; **to ~ out at sb** auf jdn losschlagen; **to ~ out at** *or* **against sb** (*criticize*) gegen jdn wettern
lashing ['læʃɪŋ] *n*: **~s of** (*Brit: inf*) massenhaft
lass [læs] (*Brit*) *n* Mädchen *nt*
lasso [læ'suː] *n* Lasso *nt* ▷ *vt* mit dem Lasso einfangen
last [lɑːst] *adj* letzte(r, s) ▷ *adv* (*most recently*) zuletzt, das letzte Mal; (*finally*) als Letztes ▷ *vi* (*continue*) dauern; (: *in good condition*) sich halten; (*money, commodity*) reichen; **~ week** letzte Woche; **~ night** gestern Abend; **~ but one** vorletzte(r, s); **the ~ time** das letzte Mal; **at ~** endlich; **it ~s (for) 2 hours** es dauert 2 Stunden
last-ditch ['lɑːst'dɪtʃ] *adj* (*attempt*) allerletzte(r, s)
lasting ['lɑːstɪŋ] *adj* dauerhaft
lastly ['lɑːstlɪ] *adv* (*finally*) schließlich; (*last of all*) zum Schluss
last-minute ['lɑːstmɪnɪt] *adj* in letzter Minute
latch [lætʃ] *n* Riegel *m*; **to be on the ~** nur eingeklinkt sein
  ▸ **latch on to** *vt fus* (*person*) sich anschließen +*dat*; (*idea*) abfahren auf +*acc* (*inf*)
latchkey ['lætʃkiː] *n* Hausschlüssel *m*
latchkey child *n* Schlüsselkind *nt*
late [leɪt] *adj* spät; (*not on time*) verspätet ▷ *adv* spät; (*behind time*) zu spät; (*recently*): **~ of Glasgow** bis vor Kurzem in Glasgow wohnhaft; **the ~ Mr X** (*deceased*) der verstorbene Herr X; **in ~ May** Ende Mai; **to be (10 minutes) ~** (10 Minuten) zu spät kommen; (*train etc*) (10 Minuten) Verspätung haben; **to work ~** länger arbeiten; **~ in life** relativ spät (im Leben); **of ~** in letzter Zeit
latecomer ['leɪtkʌməʳ] *n* Nachzügler(in) *m(f)*
lately ['leɪtlɪ] *adv* in letzter Zeit
lateness ['leɪtnɪs] *n* (*of person*) Zuspätkommen *nt*; (*of train, event*) Verspätung *f*
latent ['leɪtnt] *adj* (*energy*) ungenutzt; (*skill, ability*) verborgen
later ['leɪtəʳ] *adj, adv* später; **~ on** nachher
lateral ['lætərəl] *adj* seitlich; **~ thinking** kreatives Denken *nt*
latest ['leɪtɪst] *adj* neueste(r, s) ▷ *n*: **at the ~** spätestens

latex ['leɪtɛks] *n* Latex *m*
lathe [leɪð] *n* Drehbank *f*
lather ['lɑːðəʳ] *n* (Seifen)schaum *m* ▷ *vt* einschäumen
Latin ['lætɪn] *n* Latein *nt*; (*person*) Südländer(in) *m(f)* ▷ *adj* lateinisch; (*temperament etc*) südländisch
Latin America *n* Lateinamerika *nt*
Latin American *adj* lateinamerikanisch ▷ *n* Lateinamerikaner(in) *m(f)*
Latino [læ'tiːnəʊ] (*US*) *adj* aus Lateinamerika stammend ▷ *n* Latino *mf*, in den USA lebende(r) Lateinamerikaner(in)
latitude ['lætɪtjuːd] *n* (*Geog*) Breite *f*; (*fig: freedom*) Freiheit *f*
latrine [lə'triːn] *n* Latrine *f*
latter ['lætəʳ] *adj* (*of two*) letztere(r, s); (*later*) spätere(r, s); (*second part of period*) zweite(r, s); (*recent*) letzte(r, s) ▷ *n*: **the ~** der/die/das Letztere, die Letzteren
latter-day ['lætədeɪ] *adj* modern
latterly ['lætəlɪ] *adv* in letzter Zeit
lattice ['lætɪs] *n* Gitter *nt*
lattice window *n* Gitterfenster *nt*
Latvia ['lætvɪə] *n* Lettland *nt*
Latvian ['lætvɪən] *adj* lettisch ▷ *n* Lette *m*, Lettin *f*; (*Ling*) Lettisch *nt*
laudable ['lɔːdəbl] *adj* lobenswert
laudatory ['lɔːdətrɪ] *adj* (*comments*) lobend; (*speech*) Lob-
laugh [lɑːf] *n* Lachen *nt* ▷ *vi* lachen; **(to do sth) for a ~** (etw) aus Spaß (tun)
  ▸ **laugh at** *vt fus* lachen über +*acc*
  ▸ **laugh off** *vt* mit einem Lachen abtun
laughable ['lɑːfəbl] *adj* lächerlich, lachhaft
laughing gas ['lɑːfɪŋ-] *n* Lachgas *nt*
laughing matter *n*: **this is no ~** das ist nicht zum Lachen
laughing stock *n*: **to be the ~ of** zum Gespött +*gen* werden
laughter ['lɑːftəʳ] *n* Lachen *nt*, Gelächter *nt*
launch [lɔːntʃ] *n* (*of rocket, missile*) Abschuss *m*; (*of satellite*) Start *m*; (*Comm: of product*) Einführung *f*; (: *with publicity*) Lancierung *f*; (*motorboat*) Barkasse *f* ▷ *vt* (*ship*) vom Stapel lassen; (*rocket, missile*) abschießen; (*satellite*) starten; (*fig: start*) beginnen mit; (*Comm*) auf den Markt bringen; (: *with publicity*) lancieren
  ▸ **launch into** *vt fus* (*speech*) vom Stapel lassen; (*activity*) in Angriff nehmen
  ▸ **launch out** *vi*: **to ~ out (into)** beginnen (mit)
launching ['lɔːntʃɪŋ] *n* (*of ship*) Stapellauf *m*; (*of rocket, missile*) Abschuss *m*; (*of satellite*) Start *m*; (*fig: start*) Beginn *m*; (*Comm: of product*) Einführung *f*; (: *with publicity*) Lancierung *f*
launching pad, launch pad *n* Startrampe *f*, Abschussrampe *f*
launder ['lɔːndəʳ] *vt* waschen und bügeln; (*pej: money*) waschen
laundrette [lɔːn'drɛt] (*Brit*) *n* Waschsalon *m*
Laundromat® ['lɔːndrəmæt] (*US*) *n* Waschsalon *m*

laundry ['lɔ:ndrɪ] n Wäsche f; (dirty) (schmutzige) Wäsche; (business) Wäscherei f; (room) Waschküche f; **to do the ~** (Wäsche) waschen

laureate ['lɔ:rɪət] adj see **poet laureate**

laurel ['lɔrl] n (tree) Lorbeer(baum) m; **to rest on one's ~s** sich auf seinen Lorbeeren ausruhen

Lausanne [ləʊ'zæn] n Lausanne nt

lava ['lɑ:və] n Lava f

lavatory ['lævətərɪ] n Toilette f

lavatory paper n Toilettenpapier nt

lavender ['lævəndər] n Lavendel m

lavish ['lævɪʃ] adj großzügig; (meal) üppig; (surroundings) feudal; (wasteful) verschwenderisch ▷ vt: **to ~ sth on sb** jdn mit etw überhäufen

lavishly ['lævɪʃlɪ] adv (generously) großzügig; (sumptuously) aufwendig

law [lɔ:] n Recht nt; (a rule: also of nature, science) Gesetz nt; (professions connected with law) Rechtswesen nt; (Scol) Jura no art; **against the ~** rechtswidrig; **to study ~** Jura or Recht(swissenschaft) studieren; **to go to ~** vor Gericht gehen; **to break the ~** gegen das Gesetz verstoßen

law-abiding ['lɔ:əbaɪdɪŋ] adj gesetzestreu

law and order n Ruhe und Ordnung f

lawbreaker ['lɔ:breɪkər] n Rechtsbrecher(in) m(f)

law court n Gerichtshof m, Gericht nt

lawful ['lɔ:fʊl] adj rechtmäßig

lawfully ['lɔ:fəlɪ] adv rechtmäßig

lawless ['lɔ:lɪs] adj gesetzwidrig

Law Lord (Brit) n Mitglied des Oberhauses mit besonderem Verantwortungsbereich in Rechtsfragen

lawn [lɔ:n] n Rasen m

lawn mower n Rasenmäher m

lawn tennis n Rasentennis nt

law school (US) n juristische Hochschule f

law student n Jurastudent(in) m(f)

lawsuit ['lɔ:su:t] n Prozess m

lawyer ['lɔ:jər] n (Rechts)anwalt m, (Rechts)anwältin f

lax [læks] adj lax

laxative ['læksətɪv] n Abführmittel nt

laxity ['læksɪtɪ] n Laxheit f; **moral ~** lockere or laxe Moral f

lay [leɪ] (pt, pp **laid**) pt of **lie** ▷ adj (Rel: preacher etc) Laien- ▷ vt legen; (table) decken; (carpet, cable etc) verlegen; (plans) schmieden; (trap) stellen; **the ~ person** (not expert) der Laie; **to ~ facts/proposals before sb** jdm Tatsachen vorlegen/Vorschläge unterbreiten; **to ~ one's hands on sth** (fig) etw in die Finger bekommen; **to get laid** (inf!) bumsen (!)

▶ **lay aside** vt weglegen, zur Seite legen

▶ **lay by** vt beiseitelegen, auf die Seite legen

▶ **lay down** vt hinlegen; (rules, laws etc) festlegen; **to ~ down the law** Vorschriften machen; **to ~ down one's life** sein Leben geben

▶ **lay in** vt (supply) anlegen

▶ **lay into** vt fus losgehen auf +acc; (criticize) herunterputzen

▶ **lay off** vt (workers) entlassen

▶ **lay on** vt (meal) auftischen; (entertainment etc) sorgen für; (water, gas) anschließen; (paint) auftragen

▶ **lay out** vt ausbreiten; (inf: spend) ausgeben

▶ **lay up** vt (illness) außer Gefecht setzen; see also **lay by**

layabout ['leɪəbaʊt] (inf: pej) n Faulenzer m

lay-by ['leɪbaɪ] (Brit) n Parkbucht f

lay days npl Liegezeit f

layer ['leɪər] n Schicht f

layette [leɪ'et] n Babyausstattung f

layman ['leɪmən] (irreg: like **man**) n Laie m

lay-off ['leɪɔf] n Entlassung f

layout ['leɪaʊt] n (of garden) Anlage f; (of building) Aufteilung f; (Typ) Layout nt

laze [leɪz] vi (also: **laze about**) (herum)faulenzen

laziness ['leɪzɪnɪs] n Faulheit f

lazy ['leɪzɪ] adj faul; (movement, action) langsam, träge

LB (Canada) abbr = **Labrador**

lb abbr (= pound (weight)) britisches Pfund (0,45 kg), ≈ Pfd.

lbw abbr (Cricket: = leg before wicket) Regelverletzung beim Kricket

LC (US) n abbr (= Library of Congress) Bibliothek des US-Parlaments

L/C abbr = **letter of credit**

lc abbr (Typ: = lower case) see **case**

lcd, LCD n abbr (= liquid-crystal display) LCD nt

Ld (Brit) abbr (in titles) = **lord**

LDS n abbr (Brit: = Licentiate in Dental Surgery) ≈ Dr. med. dent. ▷ n abbr (= Latter-day Saints) Heilige pl der Letzten Tage

LEA (Brit) n abbr (= Local Education Authority) örtliche Schulbehörde

lead¹ [li:d] (pt, pp **led**) n (Sport, fig) Führung f; (clue) Spur f; (in play, film) Hauptrolle f; (for dog) Leine f; (Elec) Kabel nt ▷ vt anführen; (guide) führen; (organization, orchestra) leiten ▷ vi führen; **to be in the ~** (Sport, fig) in Führung liegen; **to take the ~** (Sport) in Führung gehen; **to ~ the way** vorangehen; **to ~ sb astray** jdn vom rechten Weg abführen; (mislead) jdn irreführen; **to ~ sb to believe that ...** jdm den Eindruck vermitteln, dass ...; **to ~ sb to do sth** jdn dazu bringen, etw zu tun

▶ **lead away** vt wegführen; (prisoner etc) abführen

▶ **lead back** vt zurückführen

▶ **lead off** vi (in conversation etc) den Anfang machen; (room, road) abgehen ▷ vt fus abgehen von

▶ **lead on** vt (tease) aufziehen

▶ **lead to** vt fus führen zu

▶ **lead up to** vt fus (events) vorangehen +dat; (in conversation) hinauswollen auf +acc

lead² [led] n Blei nt; (in pencil) Mine f

leaded ['ledɪd] adj (window) bleiverglast; (petrol) verbleit

635

leaden ['lɛdn] adj (sky, sea) bleiern; (movements) bleischwer

leader ['li:dəʳ] n Führer(in) m(f); (Sport) Erste(r) f(m); (in newspaper) Leitartikel m; **the L~ of the House (of Commons/of Lords)** (Brit) der Führer des Unterhauses/des Oberhauses

leadership ['li:dəʃɪp] n Führung f; (position) Vorsitz m; (quality) Führungsqualitäten pl

lead-free ['lɛdfri:] (old) adj bleifrei

leading ['li:dɪŋ] adj führend; (role) Haupt-; (first, front) vorderste(r, s)

leading lady n (Theat) Hauptdarstellerin f

leading light n führende Persönlichkeit f

leading man n (Theat) Hauptdarsteller m

leading question n Suggestivfrage f

lead pencil [lɛd-] n Bleistift m

lead poisoning [lɛd-] n Bleivergiftung f

lead singer [li:d-] n Leadsänger(in) m(f)

lead time [li:d-] n (Comm: for production) Produktionszeit f; (: for delivery) Lieferzeit f

lead-up ['li:dʌp] n: **the ~ to sth** die Zeit vor etw dat

leaf [li:f] (pl **leaves**) n Blatt nt; (of table) Ausziehplatte f; **to turn over a new ~** einen neuen Anfang machen; **to take a ~ out of sb's book** sich dat von jdm eine Scheibe abschneiden
  ▶ **leaf through** vt fus durchblättern

leaflet ['li:flɪt] n Informationsblatt nt

leafy ['li:fɪ] adj (tree, branch) belaubt; (lane, suburb) grün

league [li:g] n (of people, clubs) Verband m; (of countries) Bund m; (Football) Liga f; **to be in ~ with sb** mit jdm gemeinsame Sache machen

league table n Tabelle f

leak [li:k] n Leck nt; (in roof, pipe etc) undichte Stelle f; (piece of information) zugespielte Information f ▷ vi (shoes, roof, pipe) undicht sein; (ship) lecken; (liquid) auslaufen; (gas) ausströmen ▷ vt (information) durchsickern lassen; **to ~ sth to sb** jdm etw zuspielen
  ▶ **leak out** vi (liquid) auslaufen; (news, information) durchsickern

leakage ['li:kɪdʒ] n (of liquid) Auslaufen nt; (of gas) Ausströmen nt

leaky ['li:kɪ] adj (roof, container) undicht

lean [li:n] (pt, pp **leaned** or **~t**) adj (person) schlank; (meat, time) mager ▷ vt: **to ~ sth on sth** etw an etw acc lehnen; (rest) etw auf etw acc stützen ▷ vi (slope) sich neigen; **to ~ against** sich lehnen gegen; **to ~ on** sich stützen auf +acc; **to ~ forward/back** sich vorbeugen/zurücklehnen; **to ~ towards** tendieren zu
  ▶ **lean out** vi sich hinauslehnen
  ▶ **lean over** vi sich vorbeugen

leaning ['li:nɪŋ] n Hang m, Neigung f

leant [lɛnt] pt, pp of **lean**

lean-to ['li:ntu:] n Anbau m

leap [li:p] (pt, pp **leaped** or **~t**) n Sprung m; (in price, number etc) sprunghafter Anstieg m ▷ vi springen; (price, number etc) sprunghaft (an) steigen

  ▶ **leap at** vt fus (offer) sich stürzen auf +acc; (opportunity) beim Schopf ergreifen
  ▶ **leap up** vi aufspringen

leapfrog ['li:pfrɔg] n Bockspringen nt

leapt [lɛpt] pt, pp of **leap**

leap year n Schaltjahr nt

learn [lə:n] (pt, pp **learned** or **~t**) vt lernen; (facts) erfahren ▷ vi lernen; **to ~ about or of sth** von etw erfahren; **to ~ about sth** (study) etw lernen; **to ~ that ...** (hear, read) erfahren, dass ...; **to ~ to do sth** etw lernen

learned ['lə:nɪd] adj gelehrt; (book, paper) wissenschaftlich

learner ['lə:nəʳ] (Brit) n (also: **learner driver**) Fahrschüler(in) m(f)

learning ['lə:nɪŋ] n Gelehrsamkeit f

learnt [lə:nt] pt, pp of **learn**

lease [li:s] n Pachtvertrag m ▷ vt: **to ~ sth (to sb)** etw (an jdn) verpachten; **on ~ (to)** verpachtet (an +acc); **to ~ sth (from sb)** etw (von jdm) pachten
  ▶ **lease back** vt rückmieten

leaseback ['li:sbæk] n Verkauf und Rückmiete pl

leasehold ['li:shəuld] n Pachtbesitz m ▷ adj gepachtet

leash [li:ʃ] n Leine f

least [li:st] adv am wenigsten ▷ adj: **the ~** (+ noun) der/die/das wenigste; (: slightest) der/die/das geringste; **the ~ expensive car** das billigste Auto; **at ~** mindestens; (still, rather) wenigstens; **you could at ~ have written** du hättest wenigstens schreiben können; **not in the ~** nicht im Geringsten; **it was the ~ I could do** das war das wenigste, was ich tun konnte

leather ['lɛðəʳ] n Leder nt

leave [li:v] (pt, pp **left**) vt verlassen; (leave behind) zurücklassen; (mark, stain) hinterlassen; (object: accidentally) liegen lassen, stehen lassen; (food) übrig lassen; (space, time etc) lassen ▷ vi (go away) (weg)gehen; (bus, train) abfahren ▷ n Urlaub m; **to ~ sth to sb** (money etc) jdm etw hinterlassen; **to ~ sb with sth** (impose) jdm etw aufhalsen; (possession) jdm etw lassen; **they were left with nothing** ihnen blieb nichts; **to be left** übrig sein; **to be left over** (remain) übrig (geblieben) sein; **to ~ for** gehen/fahren nach; **to take one's ~ of sb** sich von jdm verabschieden; **on ~** auf Urlaub
  ▶ **leave behind** vt zurücklassen; (object: accidentally) liegen lassen, stehen lassen
  ▶ **leave off** vt (cover, lid) ablassen; (heating, light) auslassen ▷ vi (inf: stop) aufhören
  ▶ **leave on** vt (light, heating) anlassen
  ▶ **leave out** vt auslassen

leave of absence n Beurlaubung f

leaves [li:vz] npl of **leaf**

Lebanese [lɛbə'ni:z] adj libanesisch ▷ n inv Libanese m, Libanesin f

Lebanon ['lɛbənən] n Libanon m

lecherous ['lɛtʃərəs] (pej) adj lüstern

lectern ['lɛktə:n] *n* Rednerpult *nt*
lecture ['lɛktʃə^r] *n* Vortrag *m*; (*Univ*) Vorlesung *f* ▷ *vi* Vorträge/Vorlesungen halten ▷ *vt* (*scold*): **to ~ sb on** *or* **about sth** jdm wegen etw eine Strafpredigt halten; **to give a ~ on** einen Vortrag/eine Vorlesung halten über +*acc*
lecture hall *n* Hörsaal *m*
lecturer ['lɛktʃərə^r] (*Brit*) *n* Dozent(in) *m(f)*; (*speaker*) Redner(in) *m(f)*
LED *n abbr* (*Elec*: = *light-emitting diode*) LED *f*
led [lɛd] *pt, pp of* **lead**¹
ledge [lɛdʒ] *n* (*of mountain*) (Fels)vorsprung *m*; (*of window*) Fensterbrett *nt*; (*on wall*) Leiste *f*
ledger ['lɛdʒə^r] *n* (*Comm*) Hauptbuch *nt*
lee [li:] *n* Windschatten *m*; (*Naut*) Lee *f*
leech [li:tʃ] *n* Blutegel *m*; (*fig*) Blutsauger *m*
leek [li:k] *n* Porree *m*, Lauch *m*
leer [lɪə^r] *vi*: **to ~ at** jdm lüsterne Blicke zuwerfen
leeward ['li:wəd] (*Naut*) *adj* (*side etc*) Lee- ▷ *adv* leewärts ▷ *n*: **to ~** an der Leeseite; (*direction*) nach der Leeseite
leeway ['li:weɪ] *n* (*fig*): **to have some ~** etwas Spielraum haben; **there's a lot of ~ to make up** ein großer Rückstand muss aufgeholt werden
left [lɛft] *pt, pp of* **leave** ▷ *adj* (*remaining*) übrig; (*of position*) links; (*of direction*) nach links ▷ *n* linke Seite *f* ▷ *adv* links; nach links; **on the ~, to the ~** links; **the L~** (*Pol*) die Linke
left-click ['lɛftklɪk] (*Comput*) *vt* links klicken ▷ *vi* links klicken auf +*acc*
left-hand drive ['lɛfthænd-] *adj* mit Linkssteuerung
left-handed [lɛft'hændɪd] *adj* linkshändig
left-hand side ['lɛfthænd-] *n* linke Seite *f*
leftie ['lɛftɪ] (*inf*) *n* = **leftist**
leftist ['lɛftɪst] (*Pol*) *n* Linke(r) *f(m)* ▷ *adj* linke(r, s)
left-luggage [lɛft'lʌgɪdʒ], **left-luggage office** (*Brit*) *n* Gepäckaufbewahrung *f*
leftovers ['lɛftəuvəz] *npl* Reste *pl*
left-wing ['lɛft'wɪŋ] *adj* (*Pol*) linke(r, s)
left-winger ['lɛft'wɪŋə^r] *n* (*Pol*) Linke(r) *f(m)*
lefty ['lɛftɪ] *n* = **leftie**
leg [lɛg] *n* Bein *nt*; (*Culin*) Keule *f*; (*Sport*) Runde *f*; (: *of relay race*) Teilstrecke *f*; (*of journey etc*) Etappe *f*; **to stretch one's ~s** sich *dat* die Beine vertreten; **to get one's ~ over** (*inf*) bumsen
legacy ['lɛgəsɪ] *n* Erbschaft *f*; (*fig*) Erbe *nt*
legal ['li:gl] *adj* (*requirement*) rechtlich, gesetzlich; (*system*) Rechts-; (*allowed by law*) legal, rechtlich zulässig; **to take ~ action** *or* **proceedings against sb** jdn verklagen
legal adviser *n* juristischer Berater *m*
legal holiday (*US*) *n* gesetzlicher Feiertag *m*
legality [lɪ'gælɪtɪ] *n* Legalität *f*
legalize ['li:gəlaɪz] *vt* legalisieren
legally ['li:gəlɪ] *adv* rechtlich, gesetzlich; (*in accordance with the law*) rechtmäßig; **~ binding** rechtsverbindlich
legal tender *n* gesetzliches Zahlungsmittel *nt*

legation [lɪ'geɪʃən] *n* Gesandtschaft *f*
legend ['lɛdʒənd] *n* Legende *f*, Sage *f*; (*fig: person*) Legende *f*
legendary ['lɛdʒəndərɪ] *adj* legendär; (*very famous*) berühmt
-legged ['lɛgɪd] *suff* -beinig
leggings ['lɛgɪnz] *npl* Leggings *pl*, Leggins *pl*
leggy ['lɛgɪ] *adj* langbeinig
legibility [lɛdʒɪ'bɪlɪtɪ] *n* Lesbarkeit *f*
legible ['lɛdʒəbl] *adj* leserlich
legibly ['lɛdʒəblɪ] *adv* leserlich
legion ['li:dʒən] *n* Legion *f* ▷ *adj* zahlreich
legionnaire [li:dʒə'nɛə^r] *n* Legionär *m*
legionnaire's disease *n* Legionärskrankheit *f*
legislate ['lɛdʒɪsleɪt] *vi* Gesetze/ein Gesetz erlassen
legislation [lɛdʒɪs'leɪʃən] *n* Gesetzgebung *f*; (*laws*) Gesetze *pl*
legislative ['lɛdʒɪslətɪv] *adj* gesetzgebend; **~ reforms** Gesetzesreformen *pl*
legislator ['lɛdʒɪsleɪtə^r] *n* Gesetzgeber *m*
legislature ['lɛdʒɪslətʃə^r] *n* Legislative *f*
legitimacy [lɪ'dʒɪtɪməsɪ] *n* (*validity*) Berechtigung *f*; (*legality*) Rechtmäßigkeit *f*
legitimate [lɪ'dʒɪtɪmət] *adj* (*reasonable*) berechtigt; (*excuse*) begründet; (*legal*) rechtmäßig
legitimize [lɪ'dʒɪtɪmaɪz] *vt* legitimieren
legless ['lɛglɪs] (*inf*) *adj* (*drunk*) sternhagelvoll
legroom ['lɛgru:m] *n* Beinfreiheit *f*
Leics (*Brit*) *abbr* (*Post*) = *Leicestershire*
leisure ['lɛʒə^r] *n* Freizeit *f*; **at ~** in Ruhe
leisure centre *n* Freizeitzentrum *nt*
leisurely ['lɛʒəlɪ] *adj* geruhsam
leisure suit *n* Freizeitanzug *m*
lemon ['lɛmən] *n* Zitrone *f*; (*colour*) Zitronengelb *nt*
lemonade [lɛmə'neɪd] *n* Limonade *f*
lemon cheese *n* = **lemon curd**
lemon curd *n* zähflüssiger Brotaufstrich mit Zitronengeschmack
lemon juice *n* Zitronensaft *m*
lemon squeezer *n* Zitronenpresse *f*
lemon tea *n* Zitronentee *m*
lend [lɛnd] (*pt, pp* **lent**) *vt*: **to ~ sth to sb** jdm etw leihen; **to ~ sb a hand (with sth)** jdm (bei etw) helfen; **it ~s itself to ...** es eignet sich für ...
lender ['lɛndə^r] *n* Verleiher(in) *m(f)*
lending library ['lɛndɪŋ-] *n* Leihbücherei *f*
length [lɛŋθ] *n* Länge *f*; (*piece*) Stück *nt*; (*amount of time*) Dauer *f*; **the ~ of the island** (*all along*) die ganze Insel entlang; **2 metres in ~** 2 Meter lang; **at ~** (*at last*) schließlich; (*for a long time*) lange; **to go to great ~s to do sth** sich *dat* sehr viel Mühe geben, etw zu tun; **to fall full-~** lang hinfallen; **to lie full-~** in voller Länge daliegen
lengthen ['lɛŋθən] *vt* verlängern ▷ *vi* länger werden
lengthways ['lɛŋθweɪz] *adv* der Länge nach
lengthy ['lɛŋθɪ] *adj* lang
leniency ['li:nɪənsɪ] *n* Nachsicht *f*

637

lenient ['liːnɪənt] adj nachsichtig
leniently ['liːnɪəntlɪ] adv nachsichtig
lens [lɛnz] n (of spectacles) Glas nt; (of camera) Objektiv nt; (of telescope) Linse f
Lent [lɛnt] n Fastenzeit f
lent [lɛnt] pt, pp of **lend**
lentil ['lɛntɪl] n Linse f
Leo ['liːəu] n Löwe m; **to be ~** Löwe sein
leopard ['lɛpəd] n Leopard m
leotard ['liːətaːd] n Gymnastikanzug m
leper ['lɛpəʳ] n Leprakranke(r) f(m)
leper colony n Leprasiedlung f
leprosy ['lɛprəsɪ] n Lepra f
lesbian ['lɛzbɪən] adj lesbisch ▷ n Lesbierin f
lesion ['liːʒən] n Verletzung f
Lesotho [lɪ'suːtuː] n Lesotho nt
less [lɛs] adj, pron, adv weniger ▷ prep: **~ tax/10% discount** abzüglich Steuer/10% Rabatt; **~ than half** weniger als die Hälfte; **~ than ever** weniger denn je; **~ and less** immer weniger; **the ~ he works ...** je weniger er arbeitet ...; **the Prime Minister, no ~** kein Geringerer als der Premierminister
lessee [lɛ'siː] n Pächter(in) m(f)
lessen ['lɛsn] vi nachlassen, abnehmen ▷ vt verringern
lesser ['lɛsəʳ] adj geringer; **to a ~ extent** in geringerem Maße
lesson ['lɛsn] n (class) Stunde f; (example, warning) Lehre f; **to teach sb a ~** (fig) jdm eine Lektion erteilen
lessor ['lɛsɔːʳ] n Verpächter(in) m(f)
lest [lɛst] conj damit ... nicht
let [lɛt] (pt, pp **~**) vt (allow) lassen; (Brit: lease) vermieten; **to ~ sb do sth** jdn etw tun lassen, jdm erlauben, etw zu tun; **to ~ sb know sth** jdn etw wissen lassen; **~'s go** gehen wir!; **~ him come** lassen Sie ihn kommen; **"to ~"** „zu vermieten"
  ▶ **let down** vt (tyre etc) die Luft herauslassen aus; (person) im Stich lassen; (dress etc) länger machen; (hem) auslassen; **to ~ one's hair down** (fig) aus sich herausgehen
  ▶ **let go** vi loslassen ▷ vt (release) freilassen; **to ~ go of** loslassen; **to ~ o.s. go** aus sich herausgehen; (neglect o.s.) sich gehen lassen
  ▶ **let in** vt hereinlassen; (water) durchlassen
  ▶ **let off** vt (culprit) laufen lassen; (firework, bomb) hochgehen lassen; (gun) abfeuern; **to ~ sb off sth** (excuse) jdm etw erlassen; **to ~ off steam** (inf: fig) sich abreagieren
  ▶ **let on** vi verraten
  ▶ **let out** vt herauslassen; (sound) ausstoßen; (house, room) vermieten
  ▶ **let up** vi (cease) aufhören; (diminish) nachlassen
letdown ['lɛtdaun] n Enttäuschung f
lethal ['liːθl] adj tödlich
lethargic [lɛ'θaːdʒɪk] adj träge, lethargisch
lethargy ['lɛθədʒɪ] n Trägheit f, Lethargie f
letter ['lɛtəʳ] n Brief m; (of alphabet) Buchstabe m; **small/capital ~** Klein-/Großbuchstabe m
letter bomb n Briefbombe f

letter box (Brit) n Briefkasten m
letterhead ['lɛtəhɛd] n Briefkopf m
lettering ['lɛtərɪŋ] n Beschriftung f
letter of credit n Akkreditiv nt
letter opener n Brieföffner m
letterpress ['lɛtəprɛs] n Hochdruck m
letter-quality printer ['lɛtəkwɔlɪtɪ-] n Schönschreibdrucker m
letters patent npl Patent nt, Patenturkunde f
lettuce ['lɛtɪs] n Kopfsalat m
let-up ['lɛtʌp] n Nachlassen nt; **there was no ~** es ließ nicht nach
leukaemia, (US) **leukemia** [luː'kiːmɪə] n Leukämie f
level ['lɛvl] adj eben ▷ n (on scale, of liquid) Stand m; (of lake, river) Wasserstand m; (height) Höhe f; (fig: standard) Niveau nt; (also: **spirit level**) Wasserwaage f ▷ vt (building) abreißen; (forest etc) einebnen ▷ vi: **to ~ with sb** (inf) ehrlich mit jdm sein ▷ adv: **to draw ~ with** einholen; **to be ~ with** auf gleicher Höhe sein mit; **to do one's ~ best** sein Möglichstes tun; **"A" ~s** (Brit) = Abitur nt; **"O" ~s** (Brit) = mittlere Reife f; **on the ~** (fig: honest) ehrlich, reell; **to ~ a gun at sb** ein Gewehr auf jdn richten; **to ~ an accusation at** or **against sb** eine Anschuldigung gegen jdn erheben; **to ~ a criticism at** or **against sb** Kritik an jdm üben
  ▶ **level off** vi (prices etc) sich beruhigen
  ▶ **level out** vi = **level off**
level crossing (Brit) n (beschrankter) Bahnübergang m
level-headed [lɛvl'hɛdɪd] adj (calm) ausgeglichen
levelling ['lɛvlɪŋ] n Nivellierung f
level playing field n Chancengleichheit f; **to compete on a ~** unter gleichen Bedingungen antreten
lever ['liːvəʳ] n Hebel m; (bar) Brechstange f; (fig) Druckmittel nt ▷ vt: **to ~ up** hochhieven; **to ~ out** heraushieven
leverage ['liːvərɪdʒ] n Hebelkraft f; (fig: influence) Einfluss m
levity ['lɛvɪtɪ] n Leichtfertigkeit f
levy ['lɛvɪ] n (tax) Steuer f; (charge) Gebühr f ▷ vt erheben
lewd [luːd] adj (look etc) lüstern; (remark) anzüglich
lexicographer [lɛksɪ'kɔgrəfəʳ] n Lexikograf(in) m(f)
lexicography [lɛksɪ'kɔgrəfɪ] n Lexikografie f
LGV (Brit) n abbr (= large goods vehicle) Lkw m
LI (US) abbr = **Long Island**
liability [laɪə'bɪlətɪ] n Belastung f; (Law) Haftung f; **liabilities** npl (Comm) Verbindlichkeiten pl
liable ['laɪəbl] adj: **to be ~ to** (subject to) unterliegen +dat; (prone to) anfällig sein für; **~ for** (responsible) haftbar für; **to be ~ to do sth** dazu neigen, etw zu tun
liaise [liː'eɪz] vi: **to ~ (with)** sich in Verbindung setzen (mit)
liaison [liː'eɪzɔn] n Zusammenarbeit f; (sexual

relationship) Liaison f
liar ['laɪəʳ] n Lügner(in) m(f)
libel ['laɪbl] n Verleumdung f ▷ vt verleumden
libellous, (US) **libelous** ['laɪbləs] adj
verleumderisch
liberal ['lɪbərl] adj (Pol) liberal; (tolerant)
aufgeschlossen; (generous: offer) großzügig;
(: amount etc) reichlich ▷ n (tolerant person)
liberal eingestellter Mensch m; (Pol): **L~**
Liberale(r) f(m); **~ with** großzügig mit
Liberal Democrat n Liberaldemokrat(in) m(f)
liberalize ['lɪbərəlaɪz] vt liberalisieren
liberally ['lɪbrəlɪ] adv großzügig
liberal-minded ['lɪbərl'maɪndɪd] adj liberal
(eingestellt)
liberate ['lɪbəreɪt] vt befreien
liberation [lɪbə'reɪʃən] n Befreiung f
liberation theology n Befreiungstheologie f
Liberia [laɪ'bɪərɪə] n Liberia nt
Liberian [laɪ'bɪərɪən] adj liberianisch ▷ n
Liberianer(in) m(f)
liberty ['lɪbətɪ] n Freiheit f; **to be at ~** (criminal)
auf freiem Fuß sein; **to be at ~ to do sth** etw
tun dürfen; **to take the ~ of doing sth** sich
dat erlauben, etw zu tun
libido [lɪ'biːdəu] n Libido f
Libra ['liːbrə] n Waage f; **to be ~** Waage sein
librarian [laɪ'brɛərɪən] n Bibliothekar(in) m(f)
library ['laɪbrərɪ] n Bibliothek f; (institution)
Bücherei f
library book n Buch nt aus der Bücherei
libretto [lɪ'brɛtəu] n Libretto nt
Libya ['lɪbɪə] n Libyen nt
Libyan ['lɪbɪən] adj libysch ▷ n Libyer(in) m(f)
lice [laɪs] npl of **louse**
licence, (US) **license** ['laɪsns] n (document)
Genehmigung f; (also: **driving licence**)
Führerschein m; (Comm) Lizenz f; (excessive
freedom) Zügellosigkeit f; **to get a TV ~** ≈
Fernsehgebühren bezahlen; **under ~** (Comm)
in Lizenz
license ['laɪsns] n (US) = **licence** ▷ vt (person,
organization) eine Lizenz vergeben an +acc;
(activity) eine Genehmigung erteilen für
licensed ['laɪsnst] adj: **the car is ~** die
Kfz-Steuer für das Auto ist bezahlt; **~
hotel/restaurant** Hotel/Restaurant mit
Schankerlaubnis
licensee [laɪsən'siː] n (of bar) Inhaber(in) m(f)
einer Schankerlaubnis
license plate (US) n Nummernschild nt
licensing hours ['laɪsnsɪŋ-] (Brit) npl
Ausschankzeiten pl
licentious [laɪ'sɛnʃəs] adj ausschweifend,
zügellos
lichen ['laɪkən] n Flechte f
lick [lɪk] vt lecken; (stamp etc) lecken an +dat;
(inf: defeat) in die Pfanne hauen ▷ n Lecken nt;
to ~ one's lips sich dat die Lippen lecken; (fig)
sich dat die Finger lecken; **a ~ of paint** ein
Anstrich m
licorice ['lɪkərɪs] (US) n = **liquorice**
lid [lɪd] n Deckel m; (eyelid) Lid nt; **to take the ~**

off sth (fig) etw enthüllen or aufdecken
lido ['laɪdəu] (Brit) n Freibad nt
lie¹ [laɪ] (pt, pp **~d**) vi lügen ▷ n Lüge f; **to tell
~s** lügen
lie² [laɪ] (pt **lay**, pp **lain**) vi (lit, fig) liegen; **to ~
low** (fig) untertauchen
   ▶ **lie about** vi herumliegen
   ▶ **lie around** vi = **lie about**
   ▶ **lie back** vi sich zurücklehnen; (fig: accept the
   inevitable) sich fügen
   ▶ **lie down** vi sich hinlegen
   ▶ **lie up** vi (hide) untertauchen; (rest) im Bett
   bleiben
Liechtenstein ['lɪktənstaɪn] n Liechtenstein nt
lie detector n Lügendetektor m
lie-down ['laɪdaun] (Brit) n: **to have a ~** ein
Schläfchen machen
lie-in ['laɪɪn] (Brit) n: **to have a ~** (sich)
ausschlafen
lieu [luː]: **in ~ of** prep anstelle von, anstatt +gen
Lieut. abbr (Mil: = lieutenant) Lt.
lieutenant [lɛf'tɛnənt, (US) luː'tɛnənt] n
Leutnant m
lieutenant colonel n Oberstleutnant m
life [laɪf] (pl **lives**) n Leben nt; (of machine etc)
Lebensdauer f; **true to ~** lebensecht; **painted
from ~** aus dem Leben gegriffen; **to be sent
to prison for ~** zu einer lebenslänglichen
Freiheitsstrafe verurteilt werden; **such is ~** so
ist das Leben; **to come to ~** (fig: person) munter
werden; (: party etc) in Schwung kommen
life annuity n Leibrente f
life assurance (Brit) n = **life insurance**
life belt (Brit) n Rettungsgürtel m
lifeblood ['laɪfblʌd] n (fig) Lebensnerv m
lifeboat ['laɪfbəut] n Rettungsboot nt
life buoy n Rettungsring m
life expectancy n Lebenserwartung f
lifeguard ['laɪfɡɑːd] n (at beach)
Rettungsschwimmer(in) m(f); (at swimming
pool) Bademeister(in) m(f)
life imprisonment n lebenslängliche
Freiheitsstrafe f
life insurance n Lebensversicherung f
life jacket n Schwimmweste f
lifeless ['laɪflɪs] adj leblos; (fig: person, party etc)
langweilig
lifelike ['laɪflaɪk] adj lebensecht; (painting)
naturgetreu
lifeline ['laɪflaɪn] n (fig) Rettungsanker m; (rope)
Rettungsleine f
lifelong ['laɪflɔŋ] adj lebenslang
life preserver (US) n = **life belt; life jacket**
lifer ['laɪfəʳ] (inf) n Lebenslängliche(r) f(m)
life raft n Rettungsfloß nt
life-saver ['laɪfseɪvəʳ] n Lebensretter(in) m(f)
life sciences npl Biowissenschaften pl
life sentence n lebenslängliche Freiheitsstrafe
f
life-size ['laɪfsaɪz], **life-sized** ['laɪfsaɪzd] adj in
Lebensgröße
life span n Lebensdauer f; (of person) Lebenszeit
f

I

life style ['laɪfstaɪl] n Lebensstil m

life-support system ['laɪfsəpɔːt-] n (Med) Lebenserhaltungssystem nt

lifetime ['laɪftaɪm] n Lebenszeit f; (of thing) Lebensdauer f; (of parliament) Legislaturperiode f; **in my ~** während meines Lebens; **the chance of a ~** eine einmalige Chance

lift [lɪft] vt (raise) heben; (end: ban etc) aufheben; (plagiarize) abschreiben; (inf: steal) mitgehen lassen, klauen ▷ vi (fog) sich auflösen ▷ n (Brit) Aufzug m, Fahrstuhl m; **to take the ~** mit dem Aufzug or Fahrstuhl fahren; **to give sb a ~** (Brit) jdn (im Auto) mitnehmen
  ▶ **lift off** vi abheben
  ▶ **lift up** vt hochheben

liftoff ['lɪftɔf] n Abheben nt

ligament ['lɪgəmənt] n (Anat) Band nt

light [laɪt] (pt, pp **lit**) n Licht nt ▷ vt (candle, cigarette, fire) anzünden; (room) beleuchten ▷ adj leicht; (pale, bright) hell; (traffic etc) gering; (music) Unterhaltungs- ▷ adv: **to travel ~** mit leichtem Gepäck reisen; **lights** npl (Aut: also: **traffic lights**) Ampel f; **the ~s** (of car) die Beleuchtung; **have you got a ~?** haben Sie Feuer?; **to turn the ~ on/off** das Licht an-/ ausmachen; **to come to ~** ans Tageslicht kommen; **to cast** or **shed** or **throw ~ on** (fig) Licht bringen in +acc; **in the ~ of** angesichts +gen; **to make ~ of sth** (fig) etw auf die leichte Schulter nehmen; **~ blue/green** etc hellblau/-grün etc
  ▶ **light up** vi (face) sich erhellen ▷ vt (illuminate) beleuchten, erhellen

light bulb n Glühbirne f

lighten ['laɪtn] vt (make less heavy) leichter machen ▷ vi (become less dark) sich aufhellen

lighter ['laɪtər] n (also: **cigarette lighter**) Feuerzeug nt

light-fingered [laɪt'fɪŋgəd] (inf) adj langfingerig

light-headed [laɪt'hɛdɪd] adj (dizzy) benommen; (excited) ausgelassen

light-hearted [laɪt'hɑːtɪd] adj unbeschwert; (question, remark etc) scherzhaft

lighthouse ['laɪthaus] n Leuchtturm m

lighting ['laɪtɪŋ] n Beleuchtung f

lighting-up time [laɪtɪŋ'ʌp-] n Zeitpunkt, zu dem die Fahrzeugbeleuchtung eingeschaltet werden muss

lightly ['laɪtlɪ] adv leicht; (not seriously) leichthin; **to get off ~** glimpflich davonkommen

light meter n Belichtungsmesser m

lightness ['laɪtnɪs] n (in weight) Leichtigkeit f

lightning ['laɪtnɪŋ] n Blitz m ▷ adj (attack etc) Blitz-; **with ~ speed** blitzschnell

lightning conductor n Blitzableiter m

lightning rod (US) n = **lightning conductor**

light pen n Lichtstift m, Lichtgriffel m

lightship ['laɪtʃɪp] n Feuerschiff nt

lightweight ['laɪtweɪt] adj leicht ▷ n (Boxing) Leichtgewichtler m

light year n Lichtjahr nt

like [laɪk] vt mögen ▷ prep wie; (such as) wie (zum Beispiel) ▷ n: **and the ~** und dergleichen; **I would ~, I'd ~** ich hätte or möchte gern; **would you ~ a coffee?** möchten Sie einen Kaffee?; **if you ~** wenn Sie wollen; **to be/look ~ sb/sth** jdm/etw ähnlich sein/ sehen; **something ~ that** so etwas Ähnliches; **what does it look/taste/sound ~?** wie sieht es aus/schmeckt es/hört es sich an?; **what's he/the weather ~?** wie ist er/das Wetter?; **I feel ~ a drink** ich möchte gerne etwas trinken; **there's nothing ~ ...** es geht nichts über +acc; **that's just ~ him** das sieht ihm ähnlich; **do it ~ this** mach es so; **it is nothing ~** (+noun) es ist ganz anders als; (+adj) es ist alles andere als; **it is nothing ~ as ...** es ist bei Weitem nicht so ...; **his ~s and dislikes** seine Vorlieben und Abneigungen

likeable ['laɪkəbl] adj sympathisch

likelihood ['laɪklɪhud] n Wahrscheinlichkeit f; **there is every ~ that ...** es ist sehr wahrscheinlich, dass ...; **in all ~** aller Wahrscheinlichkeit nach

likely ['laɪklɪ] adj wahrscheinlich; **to be ~ to do sth** wahrscheinlich etw tun; **not ~!** (inf) wohl kaum!

like-minded [laɪk'maɪndɪd] adj gleich gesinnt

liken ['laɪkən] vt: **to ~ sth to sth** etw mit etw vergleichen

likeness ['laɪknɪs] n Ähnlichkeit f; **that's a good ~** (photo, portrait) das ist ein gutes Bild von ihm/ihr etc

likewise ['laɪkwaɪz] adv ebenso; **to do ~** das Gleiche tun

liking ['laɪkɪŋ] n: **~ (for)** (person) Zuneigung f (zu); (thing) Vorliebe f (für); **to be to sb's ~** nach jds Geschmack sein; **to take a ~ to sb** an jdm Gefallen finden

lilac ['laɪlək] n (Bot) Flieder m ▷ adj fliederfarben, (zart)lila

Lilo® ['laɪləu] n Luftmatratze f

lilt [lɪlt] n singender Tonfall m

lilting ['lɪltɪŋ] adj singend

lily ['lɪlɪ] n Lilie f

lily of the valley n Maiglöckchen nt

Lima ['liːmə] n Lima nt

limb [lɪm] n Glied nt; (of tree) Ast m; **to be out on a ~** (fig) (ganz) allein (da)stehen

limber up ['lɪmbər-] vi Lockerungsübungen machen

limbo ['lɪmbəu] n: **to be in ~** (fig: plans etc) in der Schwebe sein; (: person) in der Luft hängen (inf)

lime [laɪm] n (fruit) Limone f; (tree) Linde f; (also: **lime juice**) Limonensaft m; (for soil) Kalk m; (rock) Kalkstein m

limelight ['laɪmlaɪt] n: **to be in the ~** im Rampenlicht stehen

limerick ['lɪmərɪk] n Limerick m

limestone ['laɪmstəun] n Kalkstein m

limit ['lɪmɪt] n Grenze f; (restriction) Beschränkung f ▷ vt begrenzen, einschränken; **within ~s** innerhalb gewisser Grenzen

limitation [lɪmɪ'teɪʃən] n Einschränkung f;
  limitations npl (shortcomings) Grenzen pl
limited ['lɪmɪtɪd] adj begrenzt, beschränkt; **to
  be ~ to** beschränkt sein auf +acc
limited edition n beschränkte Ausgabe f
limited company, limited liability company
  (Brit) n ≈ Gesellschaft f mit beschränkter
  Haftung
limitless ['lɪmɪtlɪs] adj grenzenlos
limousine ['lɪməzi:n] n Limousine f
limp [lɪmp] adj schlaff; (material etc) weich ▷ vi
  hinken ▷ n: **to have a ~** hinken
limpet ['lɪmpɪt] n Napfschnecke f
limpid ['lɪmpɪd] adj klar
limply ['lɪmplɪ] adv schlaff
linchpin ['lɪntʃpɪn] n (fig) wichtigste Stütze f
Lincs [lɪŋks] (Brit) abbr (Post) = Lincolnshire
line [laɪn] n Linie f; (written, printed) Zeile f;
  (wrinkle) Falte f; (row: of people) Schlange f;
  (: of things) Reihe f; (for fishing, washing) Leine
  f; (wire, Tel) Leitung f; (railway track) Gleise pl;
  (fig: attitude) Standpunkt m; (: business) Branche
  f; (Comm: of product(s)) Art f ▷ vt (road) säumen;
  (container) auskleiden; (clothing) füttern; **hold
  the ~ please!** (Tel) bleiben Sie am Apparat!;
  to cut in ~ (US) sich vordrängeln; **in ~** in
  einer Reihe; **in ~ with** im Einklang mit, in
  Übereinstimmung mit; **to be in ~ for sth** mit
  etw an der Reihe sein; **to bring sth into ~
  with sth** etw auf die gleiche Linie wie etw acc
  bringen; **on the right ~s** auf dem richtigen
  Weg; **I draw the ~ at that** da mache ich nicht
  mehr mit; **to ~ sth with sth** etw mit etw
  auskleiden; (drawers etc) etw mit etw auslegen;
  to ~ the streets die Straßen säumen
  ▶ **line up** vi sich aufstellen ▷ vt (in a row)
  aufstellen; (engage) verpflichten; (prepare)
  arrangieren; **to have sb ~d up** jdn
  verpflichtet haben; **to have sth ~d up** etw
  geplant haben
linear ['lɪnɪə^r] adj linear; (shape, form) gerade
lined [laɪnd] adj (face) faltig; (paper) liniert;
  (skirt, jacket) gefüttert
line editing n (Comput) zeilenweise
  Aufbereitung f
line feed n (Comput) Zeilenvorschub m
lineman ['laɪnmən] (US: irreg: like **man**) n
  (Football) Stürmer m
linen ['lɪnɪn] n (cloth) Leinen nt; (tablecloths,
  sheets etc) Wäsche f
line printer n (Comput) Zeilendrucker m
liner ['laɪnə^r] n (ship) Passagierschiff nt;
  (also: **bin liner**) Müllbeutel m
linesman ['laɪnzmən] (irreg: like **man**) n (Sport)
  Linienrichter m
line-up ['laɪnʌp] n (US: queue) Schlange f; (Sport)
  Aufstellung f; (at concert etc) Künstleraufgebot
  nt; (identity parade) Gegenüberstellung f
linger ['lɪŋgə^r] vi (smell) sich halten; (tradition
  etc) fortbestehen; (person) sich aufhalten
lingerie ['lænʒəriː] n (Damen)unterwäsche f
lingering ['lɪŋgərɪŋ] adj bleibend
lingo ['lɪŋgəʊ] (pl **~es**) (inf) n Sprache f

linguist ['lɪŋgwɪst] n (person who speaks several
  languages) Sprachkundige(r) f(m)
linguistic [lɪŋ'gwɪstɪk] adj sprachlich
linguistics [lɪŋ'gwɪstɪks] n
  Sprachwissenschaft f
liniment ['lɪnɪmənt] n Einreibemittel nt
lining ['laɪnɪŋ] n (cloth) Futter nt; (Anat: of
  stomach) Magenschleimhaut f; (Tech)
  Auskleidung f; (of brakes) (Brems)belag m
link [lɪŋk] n Verbindung f, Beziehung f;
  (communications link) Verbindung; (of a chain)
  Glied nt; (Comput) Link m ▷ vi (Comput): **to
  ~ to a site** einen Link zu einer Website
  haben ▷ vt (join) verbinden; (Comput) per Link
  verbinden; **links** npl (Golf) Golfplatz m; **rail ~**
  Bahnverbindung f
  ▶ **link up** vt verbinden ▷ vi verbunden werden
linkup ['lɪŋkʌp] n Verbindung f; (of spaceships)
  Koppelung f
lino ['laɪnəʊ] n = **linoleum**
linoleum [lɪ'nəʊlɪəm] n Linoleum nt
linseed oil ['lɪnsiːd-] n Leinöl nt
lint [lɪnt] n Mull m
lintel ['lɪntl] n (Archit) Sturz m
lion ['laɪən] n Löwe m
lion cub n Löwenjunge(s) nt
lioness ['laɪənɪs] n Löwin f
lip [lɪp] n (Anat) Lippe f; (of cup etc) Rand m;
  (inf: insolence) Frechheiten pl
liposuction ['lɪpəʊsʌkʃən] n Liposuktion f
lip-read ['lɪpriːd] vi von den Lippen ablesen
lip salve n Fettstift m
lip service (pej) n: **to pay ~ to sth** ein
  Lippenbekenntnis nt zu etw ablegen
lipstick ['lɪpstɪk] n Lippenstift m
liquefy ['lɪkwɪfaɪ] vt verflüssigen ▷ vi sich
  verflüssigen
liqueur [lɪ'kjʊə^r] n Likör m
liquid ['lɪkwɪd] adj flüssig ▷ n Flüssigkeit f
liquid assets npl flüssige Vermögenswerte pl
liquidate ['lɪkwɪdeɪt] vt liquidieren
liquidation [lɪkwɪ'deɪʃən] n Liquidation f
liquidation sale (US) n Verkauf m wegen
  Geschäftsaufgabe
liquidator ['lɪkwɪdeɪtə^r] n Liquidator m
liquid-crystal display ['lɪkwɪd'krɪstl-] n
  Flüssigkristallanzeige f
liquidity [lɪ'kwɪdɪtɪ] n Liquidität f
liquidize ['lɪkwɪdaɪz] vt (im Mixer) pürieren
liquidizer ['lɪkwɪdaɪzə^r] n Mixer m
liquor ['lɪkə^r] n Spirituosen pl, Alkohol m; **hard
  ~** harte Drinks pl
liquorice ['lɪkərɪs] (Brit) n Lakritze f
liquor store (US) n Spirituosengeschäft nt
Lisbon ['lɪzbən] n Lissabon nt
lisp [lɪsp] n Lispeln nt ▷ vi lispeln
list [lɪst] n Liste f ▷ vt aufführen; (Comput)
  auflisten; (write down) aufschreiben ▷ vi (ship)
  Schlagseite haben
listed building ['lɪstɪd-] (Brit) n unter
  Denkmalschutz stehendes Gebäude nt
listed company n börsennotierte Firma f
listen ['lɪsn] vi hören; **to ~ (out) for** horchen

I

641

auf +*acc*; **to ~ to sb** jdm zuhören; **to ~ to sth**
etw hören; **~!** hör zu!
listener ['lɪsnəʳ] *n* Zuhörer(in) *m(f)*; (*Radio*)
Hörer(in) *m(f)*
listeria [lɪs'tɪərɪə] *n* Listeriose *f*
listing ['lɪstɪŋ] *n* Auflistung *f*; (*entry*) Eintrag *m*
listless ['lɪstlɪs] *adj* lustlos
listlessly ['lɪstlɪslɪ] *adv* lustlos
list price *n* Listenpreis *m*
lit [lɪt] *pt, pp of* **light**
litany ['lɪtənɪ] *n* Litanei *f*
liter ['liːtəʳ] (*US*) *n* = **litre**
literacy ['lɪtərəsɪ] *n* die Fähigkeit, lesen und
schreiben zu können
literacy campaign *n* Kampagne *f* gegen das
Analphabetentum
literal ['lɪtərəl] *adj* wörtlich, eigentlich;
(*translation*) (wort)wörtlich
literally ['lɪtrəlɪ] *adv* buchstäblich
literary ['lɪtərərɪ] *adj* literarisch
literate ['lɪtərət] *adj* (*educated*) gebildet; **to be ~**
lesen und schreiben können
literature ['lɪtrɪtʃəʳ] *n* Literatur *f*; (*printed
information*) Informationsmaterial *nt*
lithe [laɪð] *adj* gelenkig; (*animal*) geschmeidig
lithography [lɪ'θɒɡrəfɪ] *n* Lithografie *f*
Lithuania [lɪθju'eɪnɪə] *n* Litauen *nt*
Lithuanian [lɪθju'eɪnɪən] *adj* litauisch ▷ *n*
Litauer(in) *m(f)*; (*Ling*) Litauisch *nt*
litigation [lɪtɪ'ɡeɪʃən] *n* Prozess *m*
litmus paper ['lɪtməs-] *n* Lackmuspapier *nt*
litre, (*US*) **liter** ['liːtəʳ] *n* Liter *m or nt*
litter ['lɪtəʳ] *n* (*rubbish*) Abfall *m*; (*young animals*)
Wurf *m*
litter bin (*Brit*) *n* Abfalleimer *m*
litterbug ['lɪtəbʌɡ] *n* Dreckspatz *m*
littered ['lɪtəd] *adj*: **~ with** (*scattered*) übersät
mit
litter lout *n* Dreckspatz *m*
little ['lɪtl] *adj* klein; (*short*) kurz ▷ *adv* wenig; **a
~** ein wenig, ein bisschen; **a ~ bit** ein kleines
bisschen; **to have ~ time/money** wenig Zeit/
Geld haben; **~ by little** nach und nach
little finger *n* kleiner Finger *m*
little-known ['lɪtl'nəun] *adj* wenig bekannt
liturgy ['lɪtədʒɪ] *n* Liturgie *f*
live [*vi* lɪv, *adj* laɪv] *vi* leben; (*in house, town*)
wohnen ▷ *adj* lebend; (*TV, Radio*) live;
(*performance, pictures etc*) Live-; (*Elec*) Strom
führend; (*bullet, bomb etc*) scharf; **to ~ with sb**
mit jdm zusammenleben
▶ **live down** *vt* hinwegkommen über +*acc*
▶ **live for** *vt* leben für
▶ **live in** *vi* (*student/servant*) im Wohnheim/
Haus wohnen
▶ **live off** *vt fus* leben von; (*parents etc*) auf
Kosten +*gen* leben
▶ **live on** *vt fus* leben von
▶ **live out** *vi* (*Brit: student/servant*) außerhalb
(des Wohnheims/Hauses) wohnen ▷ *vt*: **to ~
out one's days** *or* **life** sein Leben verbringen
▶ **live together** *vi* zusammenleben
▶ **live up** *vt*: **to ~ it up** einen draufmachen (*inf*)

▶ **live up to** *vt fus* erfüllen, entsprechen +*dat*
live-in ['lɪvɪn] *adj* (*cook, maid*) im Haus
wohnend; **her ~ lover** ihr Freund, der bei ihr
wohnt
livelihood ['laɪvlɪhud] *n* Lebensunterhalt *m*
liveliness ['laɪvlɪnɪs] *n* (*see adj*) Lebhaftigkeit *f*;
Lebendigkeit *f*
lively ['laɪvlɪ] *adj* lebhaft; (*place, event, book etc*)
lebendig
liven up ['laɪvn-] *vt* beleben, Leben bringen
in +*acc*; (*person*) aufmuntern ▷ *vi* (*person*)
aufleben; (*discussion, evening etc*) in Schwung
kommen
liver ['lɪvəʳ] *n* (*Anat, Culin*) Leber *f*
liverish ['lɪvərɪʃ] *adj*: **to be ~** sich unwohl
fühlen
Liverpudlian [lɪvə'pʌdlɪən] *adj* Liverpooler ▷ *n*
Liverpooler(in) *m(f)*
livery ['lɪvərɪ] *n* Livree *f*
lives [laɪvz] *npl of* **life**
livestock ['laɪvstɒk] *n* Vieh *nt*
live wire (*inf*) *n* (*person*) Energiebündel *nt*
livid ['lɪvɪd] *adj* (*colour*) bleifarben; (*inf: furious*)
fuchsteufelswild
living ['lɪvɪŋ] *adj* lebend ▷ *n*: **to earn** *or* **make a
~** sich *dat* seinen Lebensunterhalt verdienen;
within ~ memory seit Menschengedenken;
the cost of ~ die Lebenshaltungskosten *pl*
living conditions *npl* Wohnverhältnisse *pl*
living expenses *npl* Lebenshaltungskosten *pl*
living room *n* Wohnzimmer *nt*
living standards *npl* Lebensstandard *m*
living wage *n* ausreichender Lohn *m*
lizard ['lɪzəd] *n* Eidechse *f*
llama ['lɑːmə] *n* Lama *nt*
LLB *n abbr* (= *Bachelor of Laws*) akademischer Grad
für Juristen
LLD *n abbr* (= *Doctor of Laws*) ≈ Dr. jur.
LMT (*US*) *abbr* (= *Local Mean Time*) Ortszeit
load [ləud] *n* Last *f*; (*of vehicle*) Ladung *f*; (*weight,
Elec*) Belastung *f* ▷ *vt* (*also*: **load up**) beladen;
(*gun, program, data*) laden; **that's a ~ of
rubbish** (*inf*) das ist alles Blödsinn; **~s of, a ~
of** (*fig*) jede Menge; **to ~ a camera** einen Film
einlegen
loaded ['ləudɪd] *adj* (*inf: rich*) steinreich; (*dice*)
präpariert; (*vehicle*): **to be ~ with** beladen sein
mit; **a ~ question** eine Fangfrage
loading bay ['ləudɪŋ-] *n* Ladeplatz *m*
loaf [ləuf] (*pl* **loaves**) *n* Brot *nt*, Laib *m* ▷ *vi*
(*also*: **loaf about, loaf around**) faulenzen; **use
your ~!** (*inf*) streng deinen Grips an!
loam [ləum] *n* Lehmerde *f*
loan [ləun] *n* Darlehen *nt* ▷ *vt*: **to ~ sth to sb**
jdm etw leihen; **on ~** geliehen
loan account *n* Darlehenskonto *nt*
loan capital *n* Anleihekapital *nt*
loan shark (*inf*) *n* Kredithai *m*
loath [ləuθ] *adj*: **to be ~ to do sth** etw ungern
tun
loathe [ləuð] *vt* verabscheuen
loathing ['ləuðɪŋ] *n* Abscheu *m*
loathsome ['ləuðsəm] *adj* abscheulich

loaves [ləʊvz] npl of **loaf**

lob [lɒb] vt (ball) lobben

lobby ['lɒbɪ] n (of building) Eingangshalle f; (Pol: pressure group) Interessenverband m ▷ vt Einfluss nehmen auf +acc

lobbyist ['lɒbɪɪst] n Lobbyist(in) m(f)

lobe [ləʊb] n Ohrläppchen nt

lobster ['lɒbstə^r] n Hummer m

lobster pot n Hummer(fang)korb m

local ['ləʊkl] adj örtlich; (council) Stadt-, Gemeinde-; (paper) Lokal- ▷ n (pub) Stammkneipe f; **the locals** npl (local inhabitants) die Einheimischen pl

local anaesthetic n örtliche Betäubung f

local authority n Gemeindeverwaltung f, Stadtverwaltung f

local call n Ortsgespräch nt

local government n Kommunalverwaltung f

locality [ləʊ'kælɪtɪ] n Gegend f

localize ['ləʊkəlaɪz] vt lokalisieren

locally ['ləʊkəlɪ] adv am Ort

locate [ləʊ'keɪt] vt (find) ausfindig machen; **to be ~d in** sich befinden in +dat

location [ləʊ'keɪʃən] n Ort m; (position) Lage f; (Cine) Drehort m; **he's on ~ in Mexico** er ist bei Außenaufnahmen in Mexiko; **to be filmed on ~** als Außenaufnahme gedreht werden

loch [lɒx] n (Scot) See m

lock [lɒk] n (of door etc) Schloss nt; (on canal) Schleuse f; (also: **lock of hair**) Locke f ▷ vt (door etc) abschließen; (steering wheel) sperren; (Comput: keyboard) verriegeln ▷ vi (door etc) sich abschließen lassen; (wheels, mechanism etc) blockieren; **on full ~** (Aut) voll eingeschlagen; **~, stock and barrel** mit allem Drum und Dran; **his jaw ~ed** er hatte Mundsperre
▶ **lock away** vt wegschließen; (criminal) einsperren
▶ **lock in** vt einschließen
▶ **lock out** vt aussperren
▶ **lock up** vt (criminal etc) einsperren; (house) abschließen ▷ vi abschließen

locker ['lɒkə^r] n Schließfach nt

locker room n Umkleideraum m

locket ['lɒkɪt] n Medaillon nt

lockjaw ['lɒkdʒɔː] n Wundstarrkrampf m

lockout ['lɒkaʊt] n Aussperrung f

locksmith ['lɒksmɪθ] n Schlosser m

lockup ['lɒkʌp] n (US: inf: jail) Gefängnis nt; (also: **lock-up garage**) Garage f

locomotive [ləʊkə'məʊtɪv] n Lokomotive f

locum ['ləʊkəm] n (Med) Vertreter(in) m(f)

locust ['ləʊkəst] n Heuschrecke f

lodge [lɒdʒ] n Pförtnerhaus nt; (also: **hunting lodge**) Hütte f; (Freemasonry) Loge f ▷ vt (complaint, protest etc) einlegen ▷ vi (bullet) stecken bleiben; (person): **to ~ (with)** zur Untermiete wohnen (bei)

lodger ['lɒdʒə^r] n Untermieter(in) m(f)

lodging ['lɒdʒɪŋ] n Unterkunft f

lodging house n Pension f

lodgings ['lɒdʒɪŋz] npl möbliertes Zimmer nt; (several rooms) Wohnung f

loft [lɒft] n Boden m, Speicher m

lofty ['lɒftɪ] adj (noble) hoch(fliegend); (self-important) hochmütig; (high) hoch

log [lɒg] n (of wood) Holzblock m, Holzklotz m; (written account) Log nt ▷ n abbr (Math: = logarithm) log ▷ vt (ins Logbuch) eintragen
▶ **log in** vi (Comput) sich anmelden
▶ **log off** vi (Comput) sich abmelden
▶ **log on** vi (Comput) = **log in**
▶ **log out** vi (Comput) = **log off**

logarithm ['lɒgərɪðm] n Logarithmus m

logbook ['lɒgbʊk] n (Naut) Logbuch nt; (Aviat) Bordbuch nt; (of car) Kraftfahrzeugbrief m; (of lorry driver) Fahrtenbuch nt; (of events) Tagebuch nt; (of movement of goods etc) Dienstbuch nt

log fire n Holzfeuer nt

logger ['lɒgə^r] n (lumberjack) Holzfäller m

loggerheads ['lɒgəhedz] npl: **to be at ~** Streit haben

logic ['lɒdʒɪk] n Logik f

logical ['lɒdʒɪkl] adj logisch

logically ['lɒdʒɪkəlɪ] adv logisch; (reasonably) logischerweise

login ['lɒgɪn] n (Comput) Log-in nt, Ammeldung f

logistics [lɒ'dʒɪstɪks] n Logistik f

logjam n (fig) Blockierung f; **to break the ~** freie Bahn schaffen

logo ['ləʊgəʊ] n Logo nt

loin [lɔɪn] n Lende f

loincloth ['lɔɪnklɒθ] n Lendenschurz m

loiter ['lɔɪtə^r] vi sich aufhalten

lol abbr (Internet, Tel: = laugh out loud) lol (lautes Lachen)

loll [lɒl] vi (also: **loll about**: person) herumhängen; (head) herunterhängen; (tongue) heraushängen

lollipop ['lɒlɪpɒp] n Lutscher m

lollipop lady (Brit) n ≈ Schülerlotsin f

lollipop man (Brit) n ≈ Schülerlotse m; siehe Info-Artikel

● **LOLLIPOP MAN/LADY**
●
● Lollipop man/lady heißen in Großbritannien
● die Männer bzw. Frauen, die mithilfe
● eines runden Stoppschildes den Verkehr
● anhalten, damit Schulkinder die Straße
● gefahrlos überqueren können. Der Name
● bezieht sich auf die Form des Schildes, die
● an einen Lutscher erinnert.

lollop ['lɒləp] vi zockeln

lolly ['lɒlɪ] (inf) n (lollipop) Lutscher m; (money) Mäuse pl

London ['lʌndən] n London nt

Londoner ['lʌndənə^r] n Londoner(in) m(f)

lone [ləʊn] adj einzeln, einsam; (only) einzig

loneliness ['ləʊnlɪnɪs] n Einsamkeit f

lonely ['ləʊnlɪ] adj einsam

lonely hearts adj: **~ ad** Kontaktanzeige f; **the ~ column** die Kontaktanzeigen pl

lone parent n Alleinerziehende(r) f(m)

loner ['ləʊnə^r] n Einzelgänger(in) m(f)

long [lɒŋ] adj lang ▷ adv lang(e) ▷ vi: **to ~ for sth** sich nach etw sehnen; **in the ~ run** auf die Dauer; **how ~ is the lesson?** wie lange dauert die Stunde?; **6 metres/months ~** 6 Meter/Monate lang; **so** or **as ~ as** (on condition that) solange; (while) während; **don't be ~!** bleib nicht so lange!; **all night ~** die ganze Nacht; **he no ~er comes** er kommt nicht mehr; **~ ago** vor langer Zeit; **~ before/after** lange vorher/danach; **before ~** bald; **at ~ last** schließlich und endlich; **the ~ and the short of it is that ...** kurz gesagt, ...

long-distance [lɒŋ'dɪstəns] adj (travel, phone call) Fern-; (race) Langstrecken-

longevity [lɒn'dʒevɪtɪ] n Langlebigkeit f

long-haired ['lɒŋ'hɛəd] adj langhaarig; (animal) Langhaar-

longhand ['lɒŋhænd] n Langschrift f

longing ['lɒŋɪŋ] n Sehnsucht f

longingly ['lɒŋɪŋlɪ] adv sehnsüchtig

longitude ['lɒŋgɪtjuːd] n Länge f

long johns [-dʒɒnz] npl lange Unterhose f

long jump n Weitsprung m

long-life ['lɒŋlaɪf] adj (batteries etc) mit langer Lebensdauer; **~ milk** H-Milch f

long-lost ['lɒŋlɒst] adj verloren geglaubt

long-playing record ['lɒŋpleɪɪŋ-] n Langspielplatte f

long-range ['lɒŋ'reɪndʒ] adj (plan, forecast) langfristig; (missile, plane etc) Langstrecken-

longshoreman ['lɒŋʃɔːmən] (US: irreg: like **man**) n Hafenarbeiter m

long-sighted ['lɒŋ'saɪtɪd] adj weitsichtig

long-standing ['lɒŋ'stændɪŋ] adj langjährig

long-suffering [lɒŋ'sʌfərɪŋ] adj schwer geprüft

long-term ['lɒŋtɜːm] adj langfristig

long wave n Langwelle f

long-winded [lɒŋ'wɪndɪd] adj umständlich, langatmig

loo [luː] (Brit: inf) n Klo nt

loofah ['luːfə] n Luffa(schwamm) m

look [luk] vi sehen, schauen, gucken (inf); (seem, appear) aussehen ▷ n (glance) Blick m; (appearance) Aussehen nt; (expression) Miene f; (Fashion) Look m; **looks** npl (good looks) (gutes) Aussehen; **to ~ (out) onto the sea/south** (building etc) Blick aufs Meer/nach Süden haben; **~ (here)!** (expressing annoyance) hör (mal) zu!; **~!** (expressing surprise) sieh mal!; **to ~ like sb/sth** wie jd/etw aussehen; **it ~s like him** es sieht ihm ähnlich; **it ~s about 4 metres long** es scheint etwa 4 Meter lang zu sein; **it ~s all right to me** es scheint mir in Ordnung zu sein; **to ~ ahead** vorausschauen; **to have a ~ at sth** sich etw dat ansehen; **let me have a ~** lass mich mal sehen; **to have a ~ for sth** nach etw suchen

▶ **look after** vt fus sich kümmern um

▶ **look at** vt fus ansehen; (read quickly) durchsehen; (study, consider) betrachten

▶ **look back** vi: **to ~ back (on)** zurückblicken (auf +acc); **to ~ back at sth/sb** sich nach jdm/etw umsehen

▶ **look down on** vt fus (fig) herabsehen auf +acc

▶ **look for** vt fus suchen

▶ **look forward to** vt fus sich freuen auf +acc; **we ~ forward to hearing from you** (in letters) wir hoffen, bald von Ihnen zu hören

▶ **look in** vi: **to ~ in on sb** bei jdm vorbeikommen

▶ **look into** vt fus (investigate) untersuchen

▶ **look on** vi (watch) zusehen

▶ **look out** vi (beware) aufpassen

▶ **look out for** vt fus Ausschau halten nach

▶ **look over** vt (essay etc) durchsehen; (house, town etc) sich ansehen; (person) mustern

▶ **look round** vi sich umsehen

▶ **look through** vt fus durchsehen

▶ **look to** vt fus (rely on) sich verlassen auf +acc

▶ **look up** vi aufsehen; (situation) sich bessern ▷ vt (word etc) nachschlagen; **things are ~ing up** es geht bergauf

▶ **look up to** vt fus aufsehen zu

lookalike ['lukəlaɪk] n Doppelgänger(in) m(f)

look-in ['lukɪn] n: **to get a ~** (inf) eine Chance haben

lookout ['lukaut] n (tower etc) Ausguck m; (person) Wachtposten m; **to be on the ~ for sth** nach etw Ausschau halten

loom [luːm] vi (also: **loom up**: object, shape) sich abzeichnen; (event) näher rücken ▷ n Webstuhl m

loony ['luːnɪ] (inf) adj verrückt ▷ n Verrückte(r) f(m)

loop [luːp] n Schlaufe f; (Comput) Schleife f ▷ vt: **to ~ sth around sth** etw um etw schlingen

loophole ['luːphəʊl] n Hintertürchen nt; **a ~ in the law** eine Lücke im Gesetz

loose [luːs] adj lose, locker; (clothes etc) weit; (long hair) offen; (not strictly controlled, promiscuous) locker; (definition) ungenau; (translation) frei ▷ vt (animal) loslassen; (prisoner) freilassen; (set off, unleash) entfesseln ▷ n: **to be on the ~** frei herumlaufen

loose change n Kleingeld nt

loose chippings npl Schotter m

loose end n: **to be at a ~**, **to be at ~s** (US) nichts mit sich dat anzufangen wissen; **to tie up ~s** die offenstehenden Probleme lösen

loose-fitting ['luːsfɪtɪŋ] adj weit

loose-leaf ['luːsliːf] adj Loseblatt-; **~ binder** Ringbuch nt

loose-limbed [luːs'lɪmd] adj gelenkig, beweglich

loosely ['luːslɪ] adv lose, locker

loosely-knit ['luːslɪ'nɪt] adj (fig) locker

loosen ['luːsn] vt lösen, losmachen; (clothing, belt etc) lockern

loosen up vi (before game) sich auflockern; (relax) auftauen

loot [luːt] n (inf) Beute f ▷ vt plündern

looter ['luːtə'] n Plünderer m

looting ['luːtɪŋ] n Plünderung f

lop off [lɒp-] vt abhacken

lopsided ['lɒp'saɪdɪd] adj schief

lord [lɔːd] n (Brit) Lord m; **L~ Smith** Lord Smith; **the L~** (Rel) der Herr; **my ~** (to bishop) Exzellenz; (to noble) Mylord; (to judge) Euer Ehren; **good L~!** ach, du lieber Himmel!; **the (House of) L~s** (Brit) das Oberhaus

lordly ['lɔːdlɪ] adj hochmütig

lordship ['lɔːdʃɪp] n: **your L~** Eure Lordschaft

lore [lɔːʳ] n Überlieferungen pl

lorry ['lɒrɪ] (Brit) n Lastwagen m, Lkw m

lorry driver (Brit) n Lastwagenfahrer m

lose [luːz] (pt, pp **lost**) vt verlieren; (opportunity) verpassen; (pursuers) abschütteln ▷ vi verlieren; **to ~ (time)** (clock) nachgehen; **to ~ weight** abnehmen; **to ~ 5 pounds** 5 Pfund abnehmen; **to ~ sight of sth** (also fig) etw aus den Augen verlieren

loser ['luːzəʳ] n Verlierer(in) m(f); (inf: failure) Versager m; **to be a good/bad ~** ein guter/ schlechter Verlierer sein

loss [lɒs] n Verlust m; **to make a ~ (of £1,000)** (1000 Pfund) Verlust machen; **to sell sth at a ~** etw mit Verlust verkaufen; **heavy ~es** schwere Verluste pl; **to cut one's ~es** aufgeben, bevor es noch schlimmer wird; **to be at a ~** nicht mehr weiterwissen

loss adjuster n Schadenssachverständige(r) f(m)

loss leader n (Comm) Lockvogelangebot nt

lost [lɒst] pt, pp of **lose** ▷ adj (person, animal) vermisst; (object) verloren; **to be ~** sich verlaufen/verfahren haben; **to get ~** sich verlaufen/verfahren; **get ~!** (inf) verschwinde!; **~ in thought** in Gedanken verloren

lost and found (US) n = **lost property**

lost cause n aussichtslose Sache f

lost property (Brit) n Fundsachen pl; (also: **lost property office**) Fundbüro nt

lot [lɒt] n (kind) Art f; (group) Gruppe f; (at auctions, destiny) Los nt; **to draw ~s** losen, Lose ziehen; **the ~** alles; **a ~ (of)** (a large number (of)) viele; (a great deal (of)) viel; **~s of** viele; **I read a ~** ich lese viel; **this happens a ~** das kommt oft vor

loth [ləʊθ] adj = **loath**

lotion ['ləʊʃən] n Lotion f

lottery ['lɒtərɪ] n Lotterie f

loud [laʊd] adj laut; (clothes) schreiend ▷ adv laut; **to be ~ in one's support of sb/sth** jdn/ etw lautstark unterstützen; **out ~** (read, laugh etc) laut

loud-hailer [laʊd'heɪləʳ] (Brit) n Megafon nt

loudly ['laʊdlɪ] adv laut

loudmouthed ['laʊdmaʊθt] adj großmäulig

loudspeaker [laʊd'spiːkəʳ] n Lautsprecher m

lounge [laʊndʒ] n (in house) Wohnzimmer nt; (in hotel) Lounge f; (at airport, station) Wartehalle f; (Brit: also: **lounge bar**) Salon m ▷ vi faulenzen
▸ **lounge about** vi herumliegen, herumsitzen, herumstehen
▸ **lounge around** vi = **lounge about**

lounge suit (Brit) n Straßenanzug m

louse [laʊs] (pl **lice**) n Laus f

▸ **louse up** (inf) vt vermasseln

lousy ['laʊzɪ] (inf) adj (bad-quality) lausig, mies; (despicable) fies, gemein; (ill): **to feel ~** sich miserabel or elend fühlen

lout [laʊt] n Lümmel m, Flegel m

louvre, (US) **louver** ['luːvəʳ] adj (door, window) Lamellen-

lovable ['lʌvəbl] adj liebenswert

love [lʌv] n Liebe f ▷ vt lieben; (thing, activity etc) gern mögen; **"~ (from) Anne"** (on letter) „mit herzlichen Grüßen, Anne"; **to be in ~ with** verliebt sein in +acc; **to fall in ~ with** sich verlieben in +acc; **to make ~** sich lieben; **~ at first sight** Liebe auf den ersten Blick; **to send one's ~ to sb** jdn grüßen lassen; **"fifteen ~"** (Tennis) „fünfzehn null"; **to ~ doing sth** etw gern tun; **I'd ~ to come** ich würde sehr gerne kommen; **I ~ chocolate** ich esse Schokolade liebend gern

love affair n Verhältnis nt, Liebschaft f

love child n uneheliches Kind nt, Kind nt der Liebe

loved ones ['lʌvdwʌnz] npl enge Freunde und Verwandte pl

love-hate relationship ['lʌvheɪt-] n Hassliebe f

love letter n Liebesbrief m

love life n Liebesleben nt

lovely ['lʌvlɪ] adj (beautiful) schön; (delightful) herrlich; (person) sehr nett

lover ['lʌvəʳ] n Geliebte(r) f(m); (person in love) Liebende(r) f(m); **~ of art/music** Kunst-/ Musikliebhaber(in) m(f); **to be ~s** ein Liebespaar sein

lovesick ['lʌvsɪk] adj liebeskrank

love song n Liebeslied nt

loving ['lʌvɪŋ] adj liebend; (actions) liebevoll

low [ləʊ] adj niedrig; (bow, curtsey) tief; (quality) schlecht; (sound: deep) tief; (: quiet) leise; (depressed) niedergeschlagen, bedrückt ▷ adv (sing) leise; (fly) tief ▷ n (Met) Tief nt; **to be/run ~** knapp sein/werden; **sb is running ~ on sth** jdm wird etw knapp; **to reach a new or an all-time ~** einen neuen Tiefstand erreichen

low-alcohol ['ləʊ'ælkəhɒl] adj alkoholarm

lowbrow ['ləʊbraʊ] adj (geistig) anspruchslos

low-calorie ['ləʊ'kælərɪ] adj kalorienarm

low-carb [ləʊ'kɑːb] adj low-carb, kohlenhydratarm; **~ bread** kohlenhydratarmes Brot

low-cut ['ləʊkʌt] adj (dress) tief ausgeschnitten

lowdown ['ləʊdaʊn] (inf) n: **he gave me the ~ on it** er hat mich darüber informiert

lower ['ləʊəʳ] adj untere(r, s); (lip, jaw, arm) Unter- ▷ vt senken

low-fat ['ləʊ'fæt] adj fettarm

low-key ['ləʊ'kiː] adj zurückhaltend; (not obvious) unaufdringlich

lowlands ['ləʊləndz] npl Flachland nt

low-level language ['ləʊlevl-] n (Comput) niedere Programmiersprache f

low-loader ['ləʊ'ləʊdəʳ] n Tieflader m

lowly ['ləʊlɪ] adj (position) niedrig; (origin)

bescheiden
low-lying ['ləʊ'laɪɪŋ] adj tief gelegen
low-paid [ləʊ'peɪd] adj schlecht bezahlt
low-rise ['ləʊraɪz] adj niedrig (gebaut)
low-tech ['ləʊtɛk] adj nicht mit Hightech
  ausgestattet
loyal ['lɔɪəl] adj treu; (support) loyal
loyalist ['lɔɪəlɪst] n Loyalist(in) m(f)
loyalty ['lɔɪəltɪ] n (see adj) Treue f; Loyalität f
loyalty card (Brit) n (Comm) Paybackkarte f
lozenge ['lɒzɪndʒ] n Pastille f; (shape) Raute f
LP n abbr (= long player) LP f; see also **long-playing
  record**
LPG n abbr (= liquefied petroleum gas) Flüssiggas nt

L-PLATES

Als *L-plates* werden in Großbritannien
die weißen Schilder mit einem roten
„L" bezeichnet, die vorne und hinten an
jedem von einem Fahrschüler geführten
Fahrzeug befestigt werden müssen.
Fahrschüler müssen einen vorläufigen
Führerschein beantragen und dürfen
damit unter der Aufsicht eines erfahrenen
Autofahrers auf allen Straßen außer
Autobahnen fahren.

LPN (US) n abbr (= Licensed Practical Nurse)
  staatlich anerkannte Krankenschwester f,
  staatlich anerkannter Krankenpfleger m
LRAM (Brit) n abbr (= Licentiate of the Royal Academy
  of Music) Qualifikationsnachweis in Musik
LSAT (US) n abbr (= Law School Admissions Test)
  Zulassungsprüfung für juristische Hochschulen
LSD n abbr (= lysergic acid diethylamide) LSD nt;
  (Brit: also: **L.S.D.**: = pounds, shillings and pence)
  früheres britisches Währungssystem
LSE (Brit) n abbr (= London School of Economics)
  Londoner Wirtschaftshochschule
Lt abbr (Mil: = lieutenant) Lt.
Ltd abbr (Comm: = limited (liability)) ≈ GmbH f
lubricant ['lu:brɪkənt] n Schmiermittel nt
lubricate ['lu:brɪkeɪt] vt schmieren, ölen
lucid ['lu:sɪd] adj klar; (person) bei klarem
  Verstand
lucidity [lu:'sɪdɪtɪ] n Klarheit f
luck [lʌk] n (esp good luck) Glück nt; **bad ~**
  Unglück nt; **good ~!** viel Glück!; **bad** or **hard**
  or **tough ~!** so ein Pech!; **hard** or **tough ~!**
  (showing no sympathy) Pech gehabt!; **to be in ~**
  Glück haben; **to be out of ~** kein Glück haben
luckily ['lʌkɪlɪ] adv glücklicherweise
luckless ['lʌklɪs] adj glücklos
lucky ['lʌkɪ] adj (situation, event) glücklich;
  (object) Glück bringend; (person): **to be ~** Glück
  haben; **to have a ~ escape** noch einmal
  davonkommen; **~ charm** Glücksbringer m
lucrative ['lu:krətɪv] adj einträglich
ludicrous ['lu:dɪkrəs] adj grotesk
ludo ['lu:dəʊ] n Mensch, ärgere dich nicht nt
lug [lʌg] (inf) vt schleppen
luggage ['lʌgɪdʒ] n Gepäck nt

luggage car (US) n = **luggage van**
luggage rack n Gepäckträger m; (in train)
  Gepäckablage f
luggage van (Brit) n (Rail) Gepäckwagen m
lugubrious [lʊ'gu:brɪəs] adj schwermütig
lukewarm ['lu:kwɔ:m] adj lauwarm; (fig: person,
  reaction etc) lau
lull [lʌl] n Pause f ▷ vt: **to ~ sb to sleep** jdn
  einlullen or einschläfern; **to be ~ed into
  a false sense of security** in trügerische
  Sicherheit gewiegt werden
lullaby ['lʌləbaɪ] n Schlaflied nt
lumbago [lʌm'beɪgəʊ] n Hexenschuss m
lumber ['lʌmbər] n (wood) Holz nt; (junk)
  Gerümpel nt ▷ vi: **to ~ about/along** herum-/
  entlangtapsen
  ▶ **lumber with** vt: **to be/get ~ed with sth** etw
  am Hals haben/aufgehalst bekommen
lumberjack ['lʌmbədʒæk] n Holzfäller m
lumber room (Brit) n Rumpelkammer f
lumberyard ['lʌmbəjɑ:d] (US) n Holzlager nt
luminous ['lu:mɪnəs] adj leuchtend, Leucht-
lump [lʌmp] n Klumpen m; (on body) Beule f;
  (in breast) Knoten m; (also: **sugar lump**) Stück
  nt (Zucker) ▷ vt: **to ~ together** in einen Topf
  werfen; **a ~ sum** eine Pauschalsumme
lumpy ['lʌmpɪ] adj klumpig
lunacy ['lu:nəsɪ] n Wahnsinn m
lunar ['lu:nər] adj Mond-
lunatic ['lu:nətɪk] adj wahnsinnig ▷ n
  Wahnsinnige(r) f(m), Irre(r) f(m)
lunatic asylum n Irrenanstalt f
lunatic fringe n: **the ~** die Extremisten pl
lunch [lʌntʃ] n Mittagessen nt; (time)
  Mittagszeit f ▷ vi zu Mittag essen
lunch break n Mittagspause f
luncheon ['lʌntʃən] n Mittagessen nt
luncheon meat n Frühstücksfleisch nt
luncheon voucher (Brit) n Essensmarke f
lunch hour n Mittagspause f
lunch time n Mittagszeit f
lung [lʌŋ] n Lunge f
lunge [lʌndʒ] vi (also: **lunge forward**) sich nach
  vorne stürzen; **to ~ at** sich stürzen auf +acc
lupin ['lu:pɪn] n Lupine f
lurch [lɜ:tʃ] vi ruckeln; (person) taumeln ▷ n
  Ruck m; (of person) Taumeln nt; **to leave sb in
  the ~** jdn im Stich lassen
lure [lʊər] n Verlockung f ▷ vt locken
lurid ['lʊərɪd] adj (story etc) reißerisch;
  (pej: brightly coloured) grell, in grellen Farben
lurk [lɜ:k] vi (also fig) lauern
luscious ['lʌʃəs] adj (attractive) fantastisch;
  (food) köstlich, lecker
lush [lʌʃ] adj (fields) saftig; (gardens) üppig;
  (luxurious) luxuriös
lust [lʌst] n (pej) n (sexual) (sinnliche) Begierde f;
  (for money, power etc) Gier f
  ▶ **lust after** vt fus (sexually) begehren; (crave)
  gieren nach
  ▶ **lust for** vt fus = **lust after**
lustful ['lʌstful] adj lüstern
lustre, (US) **luster** ['lʌstər] n Schimmer m,

Glanz *m*
lusty ['lʌstɪ] *adj* gesund und munter
lute [luːt] *n* Laute *f*
luvvie, luvvy ['lʌvɪ] (*inf*) *n* Schätzchen *nt*
Luxembourg ['lʌksəmbəːg] *n* Luxemburg *nt*
luxuriant [lʌg'zjuərɪənt] *adj* üppig
luxuriate [lʌg'zjuərɪeɪt] *vi*: **to ~ in sth** sich in etw *dat* aalen
luxurious [lʌg'zjuərɪəs] *adj* luxuriös
luxury ['lʌkʃərɪ] *n* Luxus *m* (*no pl*) ▷ *cpd* (*hotel, car etc*) Luxus-; **little luxuries** kleine Genüsse

LV (*Brit*) *n abbr* = **luncheon voucher**
LW *abbr* (*Radio*: = *long wave*) LW
Lycra® ['laɪkrə] *n* Lycra *nt*
lying ['laɪɪŋ] *n* Lügen *nt* ▷ *adj* verlogen
lynch [lɪntʃ] *vt* lynchen
lynx [lɪŋks] *n* Luchs *m*
lyric ['lɪrɪk] *adj* lyrisch
lyrical ['lɪrɪkl] *adj* lyrisch; (*fig: praise etc*) schwärmerisch
lyricism ['lɪrɪsɪzəm] *n* Lyrik *f*
lyrics ['lɪrɪks] *npl* (*of song*) Text *m*

Mm

M¹, m¹ [ɛm] n (letter) M nt, m nt; **M for Mary, M for Mike** (US) ≈ M wie Martha

M² [ɛm] n abbr (Brit: = motorway): **the M8** ≈ die A8 ▷ abbr = **medium**

m² abbr (= metre) m; = **mile**; (= million) Mio.

MA n abbr (= Master of Arts) akademischer Grad für Geisteswissenschaftler; (= military academy) Militärakademie f ▷ abbr (US: Post) = Massachusetts

mac [mæk] (Brit) n Regenmantel m

macabre [mə'kɑ:brə] adj makaber

macaroni [mækə'rəʊnɪ] n Makkaroni pl

macaroon [mækə'ru:n] n Makrone f

mace [meɪs] n (weapon) Keule f; (ceremonial) Amtsstab m; (spice) Muskatblüte f

Macedonia [mæsɪ'dəʊnɪə] n Makedonien nt

Macedonian [mæsɪ'dəʊnɪən] adj makedonisch ▷ n Makedonier(in) m(f); (Ling) Makedonisch nt

machinations [mækɪ'neɪʃənz] npl Machenschaften pl

machine [mə'ʃi:n] n Maschine f; (fig: party machine etc) Apparat m ▷ vt (Tech) maschinell herstellen or bearbeiten; (dress etc) mit der Maschine nähen

machine code n Maschinencode m

machine gun n Maschinengewehr nt

machine language n Maschinensprache f

machine-readable [mə'ʃi:nri:dəbl] adj maschinenlesbar

machinery [mə'ʃi:nərɪ] n Maschinen pl; (fig: of government) Apparat m

machine shop n Maschinensaal m

machine tool n Werkzeugmaschine f

machine washable adj waschmaschinenfest

machinist [mə'ʃi:nɪst] n Maschinist(in) m(f)

macho ['mætʃəʊ] adj Macho-; **a ~ man** ein Macho m

mackerel ['mækrl] n inv Makrele f

mackintosh ['mækɪntɔʃ] (Brit) n Regenmantel m

macro ... ['mækrəʊ] pref Makro-, makro-

macroeconomics ['mækrəʊi:kə'nɒmɪks] npl Makroökonomie f

mad [mæd] adj wahnsinnig, verrückt; (angry) böse, sauer (inf); **to be ~ about** verrückt sein auf +acc; **to be ~ at sb** böse or sauer auf jdn sein; **to go ~** (insane) verrückt or wahnsinnig werden; (angry) böse or sauer werden

madam ['mædəm] n gnädige Frau f; **yes, ~** ja(wohl); **M~ Chairman** Frau Vorsitzende

madcap ['mædkæp] adj (idea) versponnen; (tricks) toll

mad cow disease n Rinderwahn m

madden ['mædn] vt ärgern, fuchsen (inf)

maddening ['mædnɪŋ] adj unerträglich

made [meɪd] pt, pp of **make**

Madeira [mə'dɪərə] n Madeira nt; (wine) Madeira m

made-to-measure ['meɪdtə'mɛʒəʳ] (Brit) adj maßgeschneidert

madhouse ['mædhaus] n (also fig) Irrenhaus nt

madly ['mædlɪ] adv wie verrückt; **~ in love** bis über beide Ohren verliebt

madman ['mædmən] (irreg: like **man**) n Verrückte(r) m, Irre(r) m

madness ['mædnɪs] n Wahnsinn m

Madrid [mə'drɪd] n Madrid nt

Mafia ['mæfɪə] n Mafia f

mag [mæg] (Brit: inf) n = **magazine**

magazine [mægə'zi:n] n Zeitschrift f; (Radio, TV) Magazin nt; (Radio, TV, of firearm) Magazin nt; (Mil: store) Depot nt

maggot ['mægət] n Made f

magic ['mædʒɪk] n Magie f; (conjuring) Zauberei f ▷ adj magisch; (formula) Zauber-; (fig: place, moment etc) zauberhaft

magical ['mædʒɪkl] adj magisch; (experience, evening) zauberhaft

magician [mə'dʒɪʃən] n (wizard) Magier m; (conjurer) Zauberer m

magistrate ['mædʒɪstreɪt] n Friedensrichter(in) m(f)

magnanimous [mæg'nænɪməs] adj großmütig

magnate ['mægneɪt] n Magnat m

magnesium [mæg'ni:zɪəm] n Magnesium nt

magnet ['mægnɪt] n Magnet m

magnetic [mæg'nɛtɪk] adj magnetisch; (field, compass, pole etc) Magnet-; (personality) anziehend

magnetic disk n (Comput) Magnetplatte f

magnetic tape n Magnetband nt

magnetism ['mægnɪtɪzəm] n Magnetismus m; (of person) Anziehungskraft f

magnetize ['mægnɪtaɪz] vt magnetisieren

magnification [mægnɪfɪ'keɪʃən] n

Vergrößerung f

magnificence [mæg'nɪfɪsns] n Großartigkeit f; (of robes) Pracht f

magnificent [mæg'nɪfɪsnt] adj großartig; (robes) prachtvoll

magnify ['mægnɪfaɪ] vt vergrößern; (sound) verstärken; (fig: exaggerate) aufbauschen

magnifying glass ['mægnɪfaɪɪŋ-] n Vergrößerungsglas nt, Lupe f

magnitude ['mægnɪtjuːd] n (size) Ausmaß nt, Größe f; (importance) Bedeutung f

magnolia [mæg'nəʊlɪə] n Magnolie f

magpie ['mægpaɪ] n Elster f

mahogany [mə'hɔgənɪ] n Mahagoni nt ▷ cpd Mahagoni-

maid [meɪd] n Dienstmädchen nt; old ~ (pej) alte Jungfer

maiden ['meɪdn] n (liter) Mädchen nt ▷ adj unverheiratet; (speech, voyage) Jungfern-

maiden name n Mädchenname m

mail [meɪl] n Post f ▷ vt aufgeben; by ~ mit der Post

mailbox ['meɪlbɔks] n (US) Briefkasten m; (Comput) Mailbox f, elektronischer Briefkasten m

mailing list ['meɪlɪŋ-] n Anschriftenliste f

mailman ['meɪlmæn] (US: irreg: like **man**) n Briefträger m, Postbote m

mail order n (system) Versand m ▷ cpd: **mail-order firm** or **business** Versandhaus nt; by ~ durch Bestellung per Post

mailshot ['meɪlʃɔt] (Brit) n Werbebrief m

mail train n Postzug m

mail truck (US) n Postauto nt

mail van (Brit) n (Aut) Postauto nt; (Rail) Postwagen m

maim [meɪm] vt verstümmeln

main [meɪn] adj Haupt-, wichtigste(r, s); (door, entrance, meal) Haupt- ▷ n Hauptleitung f; **the mains** npl (Elec) das Stromnetz; (gas, water) die Hauptleitung; **in the ~** im Großen und Ganzen

main course n (Culin) Hauptgericht nt

mainframe ['meɪnfreɪm] n (Comput) Großrechner m

mainland ['meɪnlənd] n Festland nt

mainline ['meɪnlaɪn] adj: ~ **station** Fernbahnhof m ▷ vt (drugs slang) spritzen ▷ vi (drugs slang) fixen

main line n Hauptstrecke f

mainly ['meɪnlɪ] adv hauptsächlich

main road n Hauptstraße f

mainstay ['meɪnsteɪ] n (foundation) (wichtigste) Stütze f; (chief constituent) Hauptbestandteil m

mainstream ['meɪnstriːm] n Hauptrichtung f ▷ adj (cinema etc) populär; (politics) der Mitte

maintain [meɪn'teɪn] vt (preserve) aufrechterhalten; (keep up) beibehalten; (provide for) unterhalten; (look after: building) instand halten; (: equipment) warten; (affirm: opinion) vertreten; (: innocence) beteuern; **to ~ that** ... behaupten, dass ...

maintenance ['meɪntənəns] n (of building)

Instandhaltung f; (of equipment) Wartung f; (preservation) Aufrechterhaltung f; (Law: alimony) Unterhalt m

maintenance contract n Wartungsvertrag m

maintenance order n (Law) Unterhaltsurteil nt

maisonette [meɪzə'net] (Brit) n Maisonettewohnung f

maize [meɪz] n Mais m

Maj. abbr (Mil) = **major**

majestic [mə'dʒestɪk] adj erhaben

majesty ['mædʒɪstɪ] n (title): **Your M~** Eure Majestät; (splendour) Erhabenheit f

major ['meɪdʒər] n Major m ▷ adj bedeutend; (Mus) Dur ▷ vi (US): **to ~ in French** Französisch als Hauptfach belegen; **a ~ operation** eine größere Operation

Majorca [mə'jɔːkə] n Mallorca nt

major general n Generalmajor m

majority [mə'dʒɔrɪtɪ] n Mehrheit f ▷ cpd (verdict, holding) Mehrheits-

make [meɪk] (pt, pp **made**) vt machen; (clothes) nähen; (cake) backen; (speech) halten; (manufacture) herstellen; (earn) verdienen; (cause to be): **to ~ sb sad** jdn traurig machen; (force): **to ~ sb do sth** jdn zwingen, etw zu tun; (cause) jdn dazu bringen, etw zu tun; (equal): **2 and 2 ~ 4** 2 und 2 ist or macht 4 ▷ n Marke f, Fabrikat nt; **to ~ a fool of sb** jdn lächerlich machen; **to ~ a profit/loss** Gewinn/Verlust machen; **to ~ it** (arrive) es schaffen; (succeed) Erfolg haben; **what time do you ~ it?** wie spät hast du?; **to ~ good** erfolgreich sein; (threat) wahr machen; (promise) einlösen; (damage) wiedergutmachen; (loss) ersetzen; **to ~ do with** auskommen mit

▸ **make for** vt fus (place) zuhalten auf +acc

▸ **make off** vi sich davonmachen

▸ **make out** vt (decipher) entziffern; (understand) verstehen; (see) ausmachen; (write: cheque) ausstellen; (claim, imply) behaupten; (pretend) so tun, als ob; **to ~ out a case for sth** für etw argumentieren

▸ **make over** vt: **to ~ over (to)** überschreiben (+dat)

▸ **make up** vt (constitute) bilden; (invent) erfinden; (prepare: bed) zurechtmachen; (: parcel) zusammenpacken ▷ vi (after quarrel) sich versöhnen; (with cosmetics) sich schminken; **to be made up of** bestehen aus

▸ **make up for** vt fus (loss) ersetzen; (disappointment etc) ausgleichen

make-believe ['meɪkbɪliːv] n Fantasie f; **a world of ~** eine Fantasiewelt; **it's just ~** es ist nicht wirklich

makeover ['meɪkəʊvər] n grundlegende Veränderung des Aussehens; **to give sb a ~** jdm ein neues Aussehen verpassen

maker ['meɪkər] n Hersteller m; **film ~** Filmemacher(in) m(f)

makeshift ['meɪkʃɪft] adj behelfsmäßig

make-up ['meɪkʌp] n Make-up nt, Schminke f

make-up bag n Kosmetiktasche f

make-up remover n Make-up-Entferner m

m

making ['meɪkɪŋ] n (fig): **in the ~** im Entstehen; **to have the ~s of** das Zeug haben zu

maladjusted [mælə'dʒʌstɪd] adj verhaltensgestört

maladroit [mælə'drɔɪt] adj ungeschickt

malaise [mæ'leɪz] n Unbehagen nt

malaria [mə'lɛərɪə] n Malaria f

Malawi [mə'lɑːwɪ] n Malawi nt

Malay [mə'leɪ] adj malaiisch ▷ n Malaie m, Malaiin f; (Ling) Malaiisch nt

Malaya [mə'leɪə] n Malaya nt

Malayan [mə'leɪən] adj, n = **Malay**

Malaysia [mə'leɪzɪə] n Malaysia nt

Malaysian [mə'leɪzɪən] adj malaysisch ▷ n Malaysier(in) m(f)

Maldives ['mɔːldiːvz] npl Malediven pl

male [meɪl] n (animal) Männchen nt; (man) Mann m ▷ adj männlich; (Elec): ~ **plug** Stecker m; **because he is ~** weil er ein Mann/Junge ist; **~ and female students** Studenten und Studentinnen; **a ~ child** ein Junge

male chauvinist n Chauvinist m

male nurse n Krankenpfleger m

malevolence [mə'levələns] n Boshaftigkeit f; (of action) Böswilligkeit f

malevolent [mə'levələnt] adj boshaft; (intention) böswillig

malfunction [mæl'fʌŋkʃən] n (of computer) Funktionsstörung f; (of machine) Defekt m ▷ vi (computer) eine Funktionsstörung haben; (machine) defekt sein

malice ['mælɪs] n Bosheit f

malicious [mə'lɪʃəs] adj boshaft; (Law) böswillig

malign [mə'laɪn] vt verleumden ▷ adj (influence) schlecht; (interpretation) böswillig

malignant [mə'lɪgnənt] adj bösartig; (intention) böswillig

malingerer [mə'lɪŋgərər] n Simulant(in) m(f)

mall [mɔːl] n (also: **shopping mall**) Einkaufszentrum nt

malleable ['mælɪəbl] adj (lit, fig) formbar

mallet ['mælɪt] n Holzhammer m

malnutrition [mælnjuː'trɪʃən] n Unterernährung f

malpractice [mæl'præktɪs] n Berufsvergehen nt

malt [mɔːlt] n Malz nt; (also: **malt whisky**) Malt Whisky m

Malta ['mɔːltə] n Malta nt

Maltese [mɔːl'tiːz] adj maltesisch ▷ n inv Malteser(in) m(f); (Ling) Maltesisch nt

maltreat [mæl'triːt] vt schlecht behandeln; (violently) misshandeln

mammal ['mæml] n Säugetier nt

mammoth ['mæməθ] n Mammut nt ▷ adj (task) Mammut-

man [mæn] (pl **men**) n Mann m; (mankind) der Mensch, die Menschen pl; (Chess) Figur f ▷ vt (ship) bemannen; (gun, machine) bedienen; (post) besetzen; **~ and wife** Mann und Frau

manage ['mænɪdʒ] vi: **to ~ to do sth** es

schaffen, etw zu tun; (get by financially) zurechtkommen ▷ vt (business, organization) leiten; (control) zurechtkommen mit; **to ~ without sb/sth** ohne jdn/etw auskommen; **well ~d** (business, shop etc) gut geführt

manageable ['mænɪdʒəbl] adj (task) zu bewältigen; (number) überschaubar

management ['mænɪdʒmənt] n Leitung f, Führung f; (persons) Unternehmensleitung f; **"under new ~"** „unter neuer Leitung"

management accounting n Kosten- und Leistungsrechnung f

management consultant n Unternehmensberater(in) m(f)

manager ['mænɪdʒər] n (of business) Geschäftsführer(in) m(f); (of institution etc) Direktor(in) m(f); (of department) Leiter(in) m(f); (of pop star) Manager(in) m(f); (Sport) Trainer(in) m(f); **sales ~** Verkaufsleiter(in) m(f)

manageress [mænɪdʒə'rɛs] n (of shop, business) Geschäftsführerin f; (of office, department etc) Leiterin f

managerial [mænɪ'dʒɪərɪəl] adj (role, post) leitend; (decisions) geschäftlich; **~ staff/skills** Führungskräfte pl/-qualitäten pl

managing director ['mænɪdʒɪŋ-] n Geschäftsführer(in) m(f)

Mancunian [mæŋ'kjuːnɪən] n Bewohner(in) m(f) Manchesters

mandarin ['mændərɪn] n (also: **mandarin orange**) Mandarine f; (official: Chinese) Mandarin m; (: gen) Funktionär m

mandate ['mændeɪt] n Mandat nt; (task) Auftrag m

mandatory ['mændətərɪ] adj obligatorisch

mandolin, mandoline ['mændəlɪn] n Mandoline f

mane [meɪn] n Mähne f

maneuver etc [mə'nuːvər] (US) = **manoeuvre** etc

manfully ['mænfəlɪ] adv mannhaft, beherzt

manganese [mæŋgə'niːz] n Mangan nt

mangetout ['mɔnʒ'tuː] (Brit) n Zuckererbse f

mangle ['mæŋgl] vt (übel) zurichten ▷ n Mangel f

mango ['mæŋgəu] (pl **~es**) n Mango f

mangrove ['mæŋgrəuv] n Mangrove(n)baum m

mangy ['meɪndʒɪ] adj (animal) räudig

manhandle ['mænhændl] vt (mistreat) grob behandeln; (move by hand) (von Hand) befördern

manhole ['mænhəul] n Kanalschacht m

manhood ['mænhud] n Mannesalter nt

man-hour ['mænauər] n Arbeitsstunde f

manhunt ['mænhʌnt] n Fahndung f

mania ['meɪnɪə] n Manie f; (craze) Sucht f; **persecution ~** Verfolgungswahn m

maniac ['meɪnɪæk] n Wahnsinnige(r) f(m), Verrückte(r) f(m); (fig) Fanatiker(in) m(f)

manic ['mænɪk] adj (behaviour) manisch; (activity) rasend

manic-depressive ['mænɪkdɪ'presɪv] n Manisch-Depressive(r) f(m) ▷ adj manisch-

depressiv
manicure ['mænɪkjuəʳ] n Maniküre f ▷ vt
manikuren
manicure set n Nageletui nt, Maniküreetui nt
manifest ['mænɪfɛst] vt zeigen, bekunden
▷ adj offenkundig ▷ n Manifest nt
manifestation [mænɪfɛs'teɪʃən] n Anzeichen
nt
manifesto [mænɪ'fɛstəu] n Manifest nt
manifold ['mænɪfəuld] adj vielfältig
▷ n: **exhaust** ~ Auspuffkrümmer m
Manila [mə'nɪlə] n Manila nt
manila [mə'nɪlə] adj: ~ **envelope** brauner
Briefumschlag m
manipulate [mə'nɪpjuleɪt] vt manipulieren
manipulation [mənɪpju'leɪʃən] n
Manipulation f
mankind [mæn'kaɪnd] n Menschheit f
manliness ['mænlɪnɪs] n Männlichkeit f
manly ['mænlɪ] adj männlich
man-made ['mæn'meɪd] adj künstlich; (fibre)
synthetisch
manna ['mænə] n Manna nt
mannequin ['mænɪkɪn] n (dummy)
Schaufensterpuppe f; (fashion model)
Mannequin nt
manner ['mænəʳ] n (way) Art f, Weise f;
(behaviour) Art f; (type, sort): **all** ~ **of things** die
verschiedensten Dinge; **manners** pl (conduct)
Manieren pl, Umgangsformen pl; **bad** ~**s**
schlechte Manieren; **that's bad** ~**s** das gehört
sich nicht
mannerism ['mænərɪzəm] n Eigenheit f
mannerly ['mænəlɪ] adj wohlerzogen
manning ['mænɪŋ] n Besatzung f
manoeuvrable, (US) **maneuverable**
[mə'nu:vrəbl] adj manövrierfähig
manoeuvre, (US) **maneuver** [mə'nu:vəʳ]
vt manövrieren; (situation) manipulieren
▷ vi manövrieren ▷ n (skilful move) Manöver
nt; **manoeuvres** npl (Mil) Manöver nt,
Truppenübungen pl; **to** ~ **sb into doing sth**
jdn dazu bringen, etw zu tun
manor ['mænəʳ] n (also: **manor house**)
Herrenhaus nt
manpower ['mænpauəʳ] n Personal nt,
Arbeitskräfte pl
Manpower Services Commission (Brit) n
Behörde für Arbeitsbeschaffung, Arbeitsvermittlung
und Berufsausbildung
manservant ['mænsə:vənt] (pl **menservants**)
n Diener m
mansion ['mænʃən] n Villa f
manslaughter ['mænslɔ:təʳ] n Totschlag m
mantelpiece ['mæntlpi:s] n Kaminsims nt or m
mantle ['mæntl] n Decke f; (fig) Deckmantel m
man-to-man ['mæntə'mæn] adj, adv von Mann
zu Mann
manual ['mænjuəl] adj manuell, Hand-;
(controls) von Hand ▷ n Handbuch nt
manufacture [mænju'fæktʃəʳ] vt herstellen
▷ n Herstellung f
manufactured goods npl Fertigerzeugnisse pl

manufacturer [mænju'fæktʃərəʳ] n Hersteller
m
manufacturing [mænju'fæktʃərɪŋ] n
Herstellung f
manure [mə'njuəʳ] n Dung m
manuscript ['mænjuskrɪpt] n Manuskript nt;
(old document) Handschrift f
many ['mɛnɪ] adj, pron viele; **a great** ~ eine
ganze Reihe; **how** ~**?** wie viele?; **too** ~
difficulties zu viele Schwierigkeiten; **twice**
as ~ doppelt so viele; ~ **a time** so manches Mal
Maori ['mauri] adj maorisch ▷ n Maori mf
map [mæp] n (Land)karte f; (of town) Stadtplan
m ▷ vt eine Karte anfertigen von
▶ **map out** vt planen; (plan) entwerfen; (essay)
anlegen
maple ['meɪpl] n (tree, wood) Ahorn m
Mar. abbr = **March**
mar [mɑ:ʳ] vt (appearance) verunstalten; (day)
verderben; (event) stören
marathon ['mærəθən] n Marathon m ▷ adj: **a** ~
session eine Marathonsitzung
marathon runner n Marathonläufer(in) m(f)
marauder [mə'rɔ:dəʳ] n (robber) Plünderer m;
(killer) Mörder m
marble ['mɑ:bl] n Marmor m; (toy) Murmel f
marbles ['mɑ:blz] n (game) Murmeln pl
March [mɑ:tʃ] n März m; see also **July**
march [mɑ:tʃ] vi marschieren; (protesters)
ziehen ▷ n Marsch m; (demonstration)
Demonstration f; **to** ~ **out of/into** (heraus)
marschieren aus +dat/(herein)marschieren
in +acc
marcher ['mɑ:tʃəʳ] n Demonstrant(in) m(f)
marching orders ['mɑ:tʃɪŋ-] npl: **to give sb**
his/her ~ (employee) jdn entlassen; (lover) jdm
den Laufpass geben
march past n Vorbeimarsch m
mare [mɛəʳ] n Stute f
margarine [mɑ:dʒə'ri:n] n Margarine f
marge [mɑ:dʒ] (Brit: inf) n = **margarine**
margin ['mɑ:dʒɪn] n Rand m; (of votes) Mehrheit
f; (for safety, error etc) Spielraum m; (Comm)
Gewinnspanne f
marginal ['mɑ:dʒɪnl] adj geringfügig; (note)
Rand-
marginally ['mɑ:dʒɪnəlɪ] adv nur wenig,
geringfügig
marginal (seat) n (Pol) mit knapper Mehrheit
gewonnener Wahlkreis
marigold ['mærɪɡəuld] n Ringelblume f
marijuana [mærɪ'wɑ:nə] n Marihuana nt
marina [mə'ri:nə] n Jachthafen m
marinade [mærɪ'neɪd] n Marinade f ▷ vt =
marinate
marinate ['mærɪneɪt] vt marinieren
marine [mə'ri:n] adj (plant, biology) Meeres- ▷ n
(Brit: soldier) Marineinfanterist m; (US: sailor)
Marinesoldat m; ~ **engineer** Schiff(s)
bauingenieur m; ~ **engineering** Schiff(s)
bau m
marine insurance n Seeversicherung f
marital ['mærɪtl] adj ehelich; (problem) Ehe-;

651

~ **status** Familienstand *m*
maritime ['mærɪtaɪm] *adj* (*nation*) Seefahrer-;
(*museum*) Seefahrts-; (*law*) See-
marjoram ['mɑːdʒərəm] *n* Majoran *m*
mark [mɑːk] *n* Zeichen *nt*; (*stain*) Fleck *m*; (*in*
snow, mud etc) Spur *f*; (Brit: *Scol*) Note *f*; (*level,*
point): **the halfway ~** die Hälfte *f*; (*currency*)
Mark *f*; (Brit: *Tech*): **M~ 2/3** Version *f* 2/3 ▷ *vt*
(*with pen*) beschriften; (*with shoes etc*) schmutzig
machen; (*with tyres etc*) Spuren hinterlassen
auf +*dat*; (*damage*) beschädigen; (*stain*) Flecken
machen auf +*dat*; (*indicate*) markieren;
(: *price*) auszeichnen; (*commemorate*) begehen;
(*characterize*) kennzeichnen; (Brit: *Scol*)
korrigieren (und benoten); (*Sport: player*)
decken; **punctuation ~s** Satzzeichen *pl*;
to be quick off the ~ (in doing sth) (*fig*)
blitzschnell reagieren (und etw tun); **to be up**
to the ~ den Anforderungen entsprechen; **to**
~ time auf der Stelle treten
▶ **mark down** *vt* (*prices, goods*) herabsetzen,
heruntersetzen
▶ **mark off** *vt* (*tick off*) abhaken
▶ **mark out** *vt* markieren; (*person*) auszeichnen
▶ **mark up** *vt* (*price*) heraufsetzen
marked [mɑːkt] *adj* deutlich
markedly ['mɑːkɪdlɪ] *adv* deutlich
marker ['mɑːkər] *n* Markierung *f*; (*bookmark*)
Lesezeichen *nt*
market ['mɑːkɪt] *n* Markt *m* ▷ *vt* (*sell*)
vertreiben; (*new product*) auf den Markt
bringen; **to be on the ~** auf dem Markt sein;
on the open ~ auf dem freien Markt; **to play**
the ~ (*Stock Exchange*) an der Börse spekulieren
marketable ['mɑːkɪtəbl] *adj* marktfähig
market analysis *n* Marktanalyse *f*
market day *n* Markttag *m*
market demand *n* Marktbedarf *m*
market economy *n* Marktwirtschaft *f*
market expert *n* Marktexperte *m*,
Marktexpertin *f*
market forces *npl* Marktkräfte *pl*
market garden (Brit) *n* Gemüseanbaubetrieb
m
marketing ['mɑːkɪtɪŋ] *n* Marketing *nt*
marketing manager *n*
Marketingmanager(in) *m(f)*
marketplace ['mɑːkɪtpleɪs] *n* Marktplatz *m*;
(*Comm*) Markt *m*
market price *n* Marktpreis *m*
market research *n* Marktforschung *f*
market sector *n* Marktsegment *nt or* -sektor *m*
market value *n* Marktwert *m*
marking ['mɑːkɪŋ] *n* (*on animal*) Zeichnung *f*;
(*on road*) Markierung *f*
marksman ['mɑːksmən] (*irreg: like* **man**) *n*
Scharfschütze *m*
marksmanship ['mɑːksmənʃɪp] *n*
Treffsicherheit *f*
mark-up ['mɑːkʌp] *n* (*Comm: margin*)
Handelsspanne *f*; (: *increase*) (Preis)aufschlag *m*
marmalade ['mɑːməleɪd] *n*
Orangenmarmelade *f*

maroon [mə'ruːn] *vt*: **to be ~ed** festsitzen ▷ *adj*
kastanienbraun
marquee [mɑː'kiː] *n* Festzelt *nt*
marquess, marquis ['mɑːkwɪs] *n* Marquis *m*
Marrakech, Marrakesh [mærə'kɛʃ] *n*
Marrakesch *nt*
marriage ['mærɪdʒ] *n* Ehe *f*; (*institution*) die
Ehe; (*wedding*) Hochzeit *f*; ~ **of convenience**
Vernunftehe *f*
marriage bureau *n* Ehevermittlung *f*
marriage certificate *n* Heiratsurkunde *f*
marriage guidance, (US) **marriage**
counseling *n* Eheberatung *f*
married ['mærɪd] *adj* verheiratet; (*life*) Ehe-;
(*love*) ehelich; **to get ~** heiraten
marrow ['mærəu] *n* (*vegetable*) Kürbis *m*;
(*also:* **bone marrow**) (Knochen)mark *nt*
marry ['mærɪ] *vt* heiraten; (*father*) verheiraten;
(*priest*) trauen ▷ *vi* heiraten
Mars [mɑːz] *n* Mars *m*
Marseilles [mɑː'seɪlz] *n* Marseilles *nt*
marsh [mɑːʃ] *n* Sumpf *m*; (*also:* **salt marsh**)
Salzsumpf *m*
marshal ['mɑːʃl] *n* (Mil: *also:* **field marshal**)
(Feld)marschall *m*; (*official*) Ordner *m*; (US: *of*
police) Bezirkspolizeichef *m* ▷ *vt* (*thoughts*)
ordnen; (*support*) auftreiben; (*soldiers*)
aufstellen
marshalling yard ['mɑːʃlɪŋ-] *n* (Rail)
Rangierbahnhof *m*
marshmallow [mɑːʃ'mæləu] *n* (Bot) Eibisch *m*;
(*sweet*) Marshmallow *nt*
marshy ['mɑːʃɪ] *adj* sumpfig
marsupial [mɑː'suːpɪəl] *n* Beuteltier *nt*
martial ['mɑːʃl] *adj* kriegerisch
martial arts *npl* Kampfsport *m*; **the ~** die
Kampfkunst *sing*
martial law *n* Kriegsrecht *nt*
Martian ['mɑːʃən] *n* Marsmensch *m*
martin ['mɑːtɪn] *n* (*also:* **house martin**)
Schwalbe *f*
martyr ['mɑːtər] *n* Märtyrer(in) *m(f)* ▷ *vt*
martern
martyrdom ['mɑːtədəm] *n* Martyrium *nt*
marvel ['mɑːvl] *n* Wunder *nt* ▷ *vi*: **to ~ (at)**
staunen (über +*acc*)
marvellous, (US) **marvelous** ['mɑːvləs] *adj*
wunderbar
Marxism ['mɑːksɪzəm] *n* Marxismus *m*
Marxist ['mɑːksɪst] *adj* marxistisch ▷ *n*
Marxist(in) *m(f)*
marzipan ['mɑːzɪpæn] *n* Marzipan *nt*
mascara [mæs'kɑːrə] *n* Wimperntusche *f*
mascot ['mæskət] *n* Maskottchen *nt*
masculine ['mæskjulɪn] *adj* männlich;
(*atmosphere, woman*) maskulin; (Ling) männlich,
maskulin
masculinity [mæskju'lɪnɪtɪ] *n* Männlichkeit
f
MASH [mæʃ] (US) *n abbr* (= *mobile army surgical*
hospital) mobiles Lazarett *nt*
mash [mæʃ] *vt* zerstampfen
mashed potatoes [mæʃt-] *npl* Kartoffelpüree

nt, Kartoffelbrei *m*

mask [mɑːsk] *n* Maske *f* ▷ *vt (cover)* verdecken; *(hide)* verbergen; **surgical ~** Mundschutz *m*

masking tape ['mɑːskɪŋ-] *n* Abdeckband *nt*

masochism ['mæsəʊkɪzəm] *n* Masochismus *m*

masochist ['mæsəʊkɪst] *n* Masochist(in) *m(f)*

mason ['meɪsn] *n (also:* **stone mason***)* Steinmetz *m*; *(also:* **freemason***)* Freimaurer *m*

masonic [mə'sɒnɪk] *adj (lodge etc)* Freimaurer-

masonry ['meɪsnrɪ] *n* Mauerwerk *nt*

masquerade [mæskə'reɪd] *vi:* **to ~ as** sich ausgeben als ▷ *n* Maskerade *f*

Mass. *(US) abbr (Post)* = *Massachusetts*

mass [mæs] *n* Masse *f*; *(of people)* Menge *f*; *(large amount)* Fülle *f*; *(Rel):* **M~** Messe *f* ▷ *cpd* Massen- ▷ *vi (troops)* sich massieren; *(protesters)* sich versammeln; **the masses** *npl (ordinary people)* die Masse, die Massen *pl*; **to go to M~** zur Messe gehen; **~es of** *(inf)* massenhaft, jede Menge

massacre ['mæsəkəʳ] *n* Massaker *nt* ▷ *vt* massakrieren

massage ['mæsɑːʒ] *n* Massage *f* ▷ *vt* massieren

masseur [mæ'səːʳ] *n* Masseur *m*

masseuse [mæ'səːz] *n* Masseurin *f*

massive ['mæsɪv] *adj (furniture, person)* wuchtig; *(support)* massiv; *(changes, increase)* enorm

mass market *n* Massenmarkt *m*

mass media *npl* Massenmedien *pl*

mass meeting *n* Massenveranstaltung *f*; *(of everyone concerned)* Vollversammlung *f*; *(Pol)* Massenkundgebung *f*

mass-produce ['mæsprə'djuːs] *vt* in Massenproduktion herstellen

mass-production ['mæsprə'dʌkʃən] *n* Massenproduktion *f*

mast [mɑːst] *n (Naut)* Mast *m*; *(Radio etc)* Sendeturm *m*

mastectomy [mæs'tektəmɪ] *n* Brustamputation *f*

master ['mɑːstəʳ] *n* Herr *m*; *(teacher)* Lehrer *m*; *(title):* **M~ X** (der junge) Herr X; *(Art, Mus, of craft etc)* Meister *m* ▷ *cpd:* **~ baker/plumber** *etc* Bäcker-/Klempnermeister *etc m* ▷ *vt* meistern; *(feeling)* unter Kontrolle bringen; *(skill, language)* beherrschen

master disk *n (Comput)* Stammdiskette *f*

masterful ['mɑːstəful] *adj* gebieterisch; *(skilful)* meisterhaft

master key *n* Hauptschlüssel *m*

masterly ['mɑːstəlɪ] *adj* meisterhaft

mastermind ['mɑːstəmaɪnd] *n* (führender) Kopf *m* ▷ *vt* planen und ausführen

Master of Arts *n* Magister *m* der philosophischen Fakultät

Master of Ceremonies *n* Zeremonienmeister *m*; *(for variety show etc)* Conférencier *m*

Master of Science *n* Magister *m* der naturwissenschaftlichen Fakultät

masterpiece ['mɑːstəpiːs] *n* Meisterwerk *nt*

master plan *n* kluger Plan *m*

Master's Degree ist ein höherer akademischer Grad, den man in der Regel nach dem *bachelor's degree* erwerben kann. Je nach Universität erhält man ein master's degree nach einem entsprechenden Studium und/oder einer Dissertation. Die am häufigsten verliehenen Grade sind *MA* (= Master of Arts) und *MSc* (= Master of Science), die beide Studium und Dissertation erfordern, während für *MLitt* (= Master of Letters) und *MPhil* (= Master of Philosophy) meist nur eine Dissertation nötig ist. Siehe auch *bachelor's degree, doctorate.*

masterstroke ['mɑːstəstrəʊk] *n* Meisterstück *nt*

mastery ['mɑːstərɪ] *n (of language etc)* Beherrschung *f*; *(skill)* (meisterhaftes) Können *nt*

mastiff ['mæstɪf] *n* Dogge *f*

masturbate ['mæstəbeɪt] *vi* masturbieren, onanieren

masturbation [mæstə'beɪʃən] *n* Masturbation *f*, Onanie *f*

mat [mæt] *n* Matte *f*; *(also:* **doormat***)* Fußmatte *f*; *(also:* **table mat***)* Untersetzer *m*; *(: of cloth)* Deckchen *nt* ▷ *adj* = **matt**

match [mætʃ] *n* Wettkampf *m*; *(team game)* Spiel *nt*; *(Tennis)* Match *nt*; *(for lighting fire etc)* Streichholz *nt*; *(equivalent):* **to be a good/ perfect ~** gut/perfekt zusammenpassen ▷ *vt (go well with)* passen zu; *(equal)* gleichkommen +*dat*; *(correspond to)* entsprechen +*dat*; *(suit)* sich anpassen +*dat*; *(also:* **match up***: pair)* passend zusammenbringen ▷ *vi* zusammenpassen; **to be no ~ for** sich nicht messen können mit; **with shoes to ~** mit (dazu) passenden Schuhen

▶ **match up** *vi* zusammenpassen

matchbox ['mætʃbɒks] *n* Streichholzschachtel *f*

matching ['mætʃɪŋ] *adj* (dazu) passend

matchless ['mætʃlɪs] *adj* unvergleichlich

mate [meɪt] *n (inf: friend)* Freund(in) *m(f)*, Kumpel *m*; *(animal)* Männchen *nt*, Weibchen *nt*; *(assistant)* Gehilfe *m*, Gehilfin *f*; *(in merchant navy)* Maat *m* ▷ *vi (animals)* sich paaren

material [mə'tɪərɪəl] *n* Material *nt*; *(cloth)* Stoff *m* ▷ *adj (possessions, existence)* materiell; *(relevant)* wesentlich; **materials** *npl (equipment)* Material *nt*

materialistic [mətɪərɪə'lɪstɪk] *adj* materialistisch

materialize [mə'tɪərɪəlaɪz] *vi (event)* zustande kommen; *(plan)* verwirklicht werden; *(hope)* sich verwirklichen; *(problem)* auftreten; *(crisis, difficulty)* eintreten

maternal [mə'təːnl] *adj* mütterlich, Mutter-

m

maternity [məˈtəːnɪtɪ] n Mutterschaft f ▷ cpd (ward etc) Entbindungs-; (care) für werdende und junge Mütter

maternity benefit n Mutterschaftsgeld nt

maternity dress n Umstandskleid nt

maternity hospital n Entbindungsheim nt

maternity leave n Mutterschaftsurlaub m

matey [ˈmeɪtɪ] (Brit: inf) adj kumpelhaft

math [mæθ] (US) n = **maths**

mathematical [mæθəˈmætɪkl] adj mathematisch

mathematician [mæθəməˈtɪʃən] n Mathematiker(in) m(f)

mathematics [mæθəˈmætɪks] n Mathematik f

maths [mæθs], (US) **math** [mæθ] n Mathe f

matinée [ˈmætɪneɪ] n Nachmittagsvorstellung f

mating [ˈmeɪtɪŋ] n Paarung f

mating call n Lockruf m

mating season n Paarungszeit f

matriarchal [meɪtrɪˈɑːkl] adj matriarchalisch

matrices [ˈmeɪtrɪsiːz] npl of **matrix**

matriculation [mətrɪkjuˈleɪʃən] n Immatrikulation f

matrimonial [mætrɪˈməʊnɪəl] adj Ehe-

matrimony [ˈmætrɪmənɪ] n Ehe f

matrix [ˈmeɪtrɪks] (pl **matrices**) n (Math) Matrix f; (framework) Gefüge nt

matron [ˈmeɪtrən] n (in hospital) Oberschwester f; (in school) Schwester f

matronly [ˈmeɪtrənlɪ] adj matronenhaft

matt [mæt] adj matt; (paint) Matt-

matted [ˈmætɪd] adj verfilzt

matter [ˈmætəʳ] n (event, situation) Sache f, Angelegenheit f; (Phys) Materie f; (substance, material) Stoff m; (Med: pus) Eiter m ▷ vi (be important) wichtig sein; **matters** npl (affairs) Angelegenheiten pl, Dinge pl; (situation) Lage f; **what's the ~?** was ist los?; **no ~ what** egal was (passiert); **that's another ~** das ist etwas anderes; **as a ~ of course** selbstverständlich; **as a ~ of fact** eigentlich; **it's a ~ of habit** es ist eine Gewohnheitssache; **vegetable ~** pflanzliche Stoffe pl; **printed ~** Drucksachen pl; **reading ~** (Brit) Lesestoff m; **it doesn't ~** es macht nichts

matter-of-fact [ˈmætərəvˈfækt] adj sachlich

matting [ˈmætɪŋ] n Matten pl; **rush ~** Binsenmatten pl

mattress [ˈmætrɪs] n Matratze f

mature [məˈtjʊəʳ] adj reif; (wine) ausgereift ▷ vi reifen; (Comm) fällig werden

mature student n älterer Student m, ältere Studentin f

maturity [məˈtjʊərɪtɪ] n Reife f; **to have reached ~** (person) erwachsen sein; (animal) ausgewachsen sein

maudlin [ˈmɔːdlɪn] adj gefühlsselig

maul [mɔːl] vt (anfallen und) übel zurichten

Mauritania [mɔːrɪˈteɪnɪə] n Mauritanien nt

Mauritius [məˈrɪʃəs] n Mauritius nt

mausoleum [mɔːsəˈlɪəm] n Mausoleum nt

mauve [məʊv] adj mauve

maverick [ˈmævrɪk] n (dissenter) Abtrünnige(r) m; (independent thinker) Querdenker m

mawkish [ˈmɔːkɪʃ] adj rührselig

max. abbr = **maximum**

maxim [ˈmæksɪm] n Maxime f

maxima [ˈmæksɪmə] npl of **maximum**

maximize [ˈmæksɪmaɪz] vt maximieren

maximum [ˈmæksɪməm] (pl **maxima** or **~s**) adj (amount, speed etc) Höchst-; (efficiency) maximal ▷ n Maximum nt

May [meɪ] n Mai m; see also **July**

may [meɪ] (conditional **might**) vi (be possible) können; (have permission) dürfen; **he ~ come** vielleicht kommt er; **~ I smoke?** darf ich rauchen?; **~ God bless you!** (wish) Gott segne dich!; **~ I sit here?** kann ich mich hier hinsetzen?; **he might be there** er könnte da sein; **you might like to try** vielleicht möchten Sie es mal versuchen; **you ~ as well go** Sie können ruhig gehen

maybe [ˈmeɪbiː] adv vielleicht; **~ he'll ...** es kann sein, dass er ...; **~ not** vielleicht nicht

Mayday [ˈmeɪdeɪ] n Maydaysignal nt, ≈ SOS-Ruf m

May Day n der 1. Mai

mayhem [ˈmeɪhɛm] n Chaos nt

mayonnaise [meɪəˈneɪz] n Mayonnaise f

mayor [mɛəʳ] n Bürgermeister m

mayoress [ˈmɛərɛs] n Bürgermeisterin f; (partner) Frau f des Bürgermeisters

maypole [ˈmeɪpəʊl] n Maibaum m

maze [meɪz] n Irrgarten m; (fig) Wirrwarr m

MB abbr (Comput: = megabyte) MB; (Canada) = Manitoba

MBA n abbr (= Master of Business Administration) akademischer Grad in Betriebswirtschaft

MBE (Brit) n abbr (= Member of (the Order of) the British Empire) britischer Ordenstitel

MC n abbr = **Master of Ceremonies**

MCAT (US) n abbr (= Medical College Admissions Test) Zulassungsprüfung für medizinische Fachschulen

m-commerce [ˈɛmˈkɒmɜːs] n (Comm) M-Commerce m, mobiler Handel m

MD n abbr (= Doctor of Medicine) ≈ Dr. med.; (Comm) = **managing director** ▷ abbr (US: Post) = Maryland

MDT (US) abbr (= Mountain Daylight Time) amerikanische Sommerzeitzone

ME n abbr (US) = **medical examiner**; (Med: = myalgic encephalomyelitis) krankhafter Energiemangel (oft nach Viruserkrankungen) ▷ abbr (US: Post) = Maine

○ **KEYWORD**

me [miː] pron 1 (direct) mich; **can you hear me?** können Sie mich hören?; **it's me** ich bins 2 (indirect) mir; **he gave me the money, he gave the money to me** er gab mir das Geld 3 (after prep): **it's for me** es ist für mich; **with me** mit mir; **give them to me** gib sie mir; **without me** ohne mich

meadow ['mɛdəu] *n* Wiese *f*
meagre, (*US*) **meager** ['mi:gər] *adj* (*amount*)
  kläglich; (*meal*) dürftig
meal [mi:l] *n* Mahlzeit *f*; (*food*) Essen *nt*; (*flour*)
  Schrotmehl *nt*; **to go out for a ~** essen
  gehen; **to make a ~ of sth** (*fig*) etw auf sehr
  umständliche Art machen
meals on wheels *n sing* Essen *nt* auf Rädern
mealtime ['mi:ltaɪm] *n* Essenszeit *f*
mealy-mouthed ['mi:lɪmauðd] *adj*
  unaufrichtig; (*politician*) schönfärberisch
mean [mi:n] (*pt, pp* **~t**) *adj* (*with money*) geizig;
  (*unkind*) gemein; (*US: inf: animal*) bösartig;
  (*shabby*) schäbig; (*average*) Durchschnitts-,
  mittlere(r, s) ▷ *vt* (*signify*) bedeuten; (*refer to*)
  meinen; (*intend*) beabsichtigen ▷ *n* (*average*)
  Durchschnitt *m*; **means** *npl* (*way*) Möglichkeit
  f; (*money*) Mittel *pl*; **by ~s of** durch; **by all ~s!**
  aber natürlich *or* selbstverständlich!; **do you
  ~ it?** meinst du das ernst?; **what do you ~?**
  was willst du damit sagen?; **to be ~t for sb/
  sth** für jdn/etw bestimmt sein; **to ~ to do sth**
  etw tun wollen
meander [mɪˈændər] *vi* (*river*) sich schlängeln;
  (*person: walking*) schlendern; (*: talking*)
  abschweifen
meaning ['mi:nɪŋ] *n* Sinn *m*; (*of word, gesture*)
  Bedeutung *f*
meaningful ['mi:nɪŋful] *adj* sinnvoll; (*glance,
  remark*) vielsagend, bedeutsam; (*relationship*)
  tiefer gehend
meaningless ['mi:nɪŋlɪs] *adj* sinnlos; (*word,
  song*) bedeutungslos
meanness ['mi:nnɪs] *n* (*with money*) Geiz
  m; (*unkindness*) Gemeinheit *f*; (*shabbiness*)
  Schäbigkeit *f*
means test [mi:nz-] *n* Überprüfung *f* der
  Einkommens- und Vermögensverhältnisse
means-tested ['mi:nztestɪd] *adj* von den
  Einkommens- und Vermögensverhältnissen
  abhängig
meant [mɛnt] *pt, pp of* **mean**
meantime ['mi:ntaɪm] *adv* (*also:* **in the
  meantime**) inzwischen
meanwhile ['mi:nwaɪl] *adv* = **meantime**
measles ['mi:zlz] *n* Masern *pl*
measly ['mi:zlɪ] (*inf*) *adj* mick(e)rig
measurable ['mɛʒərəbl] *adj* messbar
measure ['mɛʒər] *vt, vi* messen ▷ *n* (*amount*)
  Menge *f*; (*ruler*) Messstab *m*; (*of achievement*)
  Maßstab *m*; (*action*) Maßnahme *f*; **a litre ~** ein
  Messbecher *m*, der einen Liter fasst; **a/some ~
  of** ein gewisses Maß an +*dat*; **to take ~s to do
  sth** Maßnahmen ergreifen, um etw zu tun
  ▶ **measure up** *vi*: **to ~ up to** herankommen
  an +*acc*
measured ['mɛʒəd] *adj* (*tone*) bedächtig; (*step*)
  gemessen
measurement ['mɛʒəmənt] *n* (*measure*) Maß
  nt; (*act*) Messung *f*; **chest/hip ~** Brust-/
  Hüftumfang *m*
measurements ['mɛʒəmənts] *npl* Maße *pl*; **to
  take sb's ~** bei jdm Maß nehmen

meat [mi:t] *n* Fleisch *nt*; **cold ~s** (*Brit*)
  Aufschnitt *m*; **crab ~** Krabbenfleisch *nt*
meatball ['mi:tbɔ:l] *n* Fleischkloß *m*
meat pie *n* Fleischpastete *f*
meaty ['mi:tɪ] *adj* (*meal, dish*) mit viel
  Fleisch; (*fig: satisfying: book etc*) gehaltvoll;
  (*: brawny: person*) kräftig (gebaut)
Mecca ['mɛkə] *n* (*Geog, fig*) Mekka *nt*
mechanic [mɪˈkænɪk] *n* Mechaniker(in) *m(f)*
mechanical [mɪˈkænɪkl] *adj* mechanisch
mechanical engineering *n* Maschinenbau *m*
mechanics [mɪˈkænɪks] *n* (*Phys*) Mechanik *f*
  ▷ *npl* (*of reading etc*) Technik *f*; (*of government etc*)
  Mechanismus *m*
mechanism ['mɛkənɪzəm] *n* Mechanismus *m*
mechanization [mɛkənaɪˈzeɪʃən] *n*
  Mechanisierung *f*
mechanize ['mɛkənaɪz] *vt, vi* mechanisieren
MEd *n abbr* (= *Master of Education*) akademischer
  Grad für Lehrer
medal ['mɛdl] *n* Medaille *f*; (*decoration*) Orden *m*
medallion [mɪˈdæliən] *n* Medaillon *nt*
medallist, (*US*) **medalist** ['mɛdlɪst] *n*
  Medaillengewinner(in) *m(f)*
meddle ['mɛdl] *vi*: **to ~ (in)** sich einmischen
  (in +*acc*); **to ~ with sb** sich mit jdm einlassen;
  to ~ with sth (*tamper*) sich *dat* an etw *dat* zu
  schaffen machen
meddlesome ['mɛdlsəm], **meddling** ['mɛdlɪŋ]
  adj sich ständig einmischend
media ['mi:dɪə] *npl* Medien *pl*
media bashing (*inf*) *n* Medienschelte *f*
media circus *n* Medienrummel *m*
mediaeval [mɛdɪˈi:vl] *adj* = **medieval**
median ['mi:dɪən] (*US*) *n* (*also:* **median strip**)
  Mittelstreifen *m*
mediate ['mi:dɪeɪt] *vi* vermitteln
mediation [mi:dɪˈeɪʃən] *n* Vermittlung *f*
mediator ['mi:dɪeɪtər] *n* Vermittler(in) *m(f)*
Medicaid ['mɛdɪkeɪd] (*US*) *n* staatliche
  *Krankenversicherung und Gesundheitsfürsorge für
  Einkommensschwache*
medical ['mɛdɪkl] *adj* (*care*) medizinisch;
  (*treatment*) ärztlich ▷ *n* (ärztliche)
  Untersuchung *f*
medical certificate *n* (*confirming health*)
  ärztliches Gesundheitszeugnis *nt*; (*confirming
  illness*) ärztliches Attest *nt*
medical examiner (*US*) *n* ≈
  Gerichtsmediziner(in) *m(f)*; (*performing autopsy*)
  Leichenbeschauer *m*
medical student *n* Medizinstudent(in) *m(f)*
Medicare ['mɛdɪkeər] (*US*) *n* staatliche
  *Krankenversicherung und Gesundheitsfürsorge für
  ältere Bürger*
medicated ['mɛdɪkeɪtɪd] *adj* medizinisch
medication [mɛdɪˈkeɪʃən] *n* Medikamente *pl*
medicinal [mɛˈdɪsɪnl] *adj* (*substance*) Heil-;
  (*qualities*) heilend; (*purposes*) medizinisch
medicine ['mɛdsɪn] *n* Medizin *f*; (*drug*) Arznei *f*
medicine ball *n* Medizinball *m*
medicine chest *n* Hausapotheke *f*
medicine man *n* Medizinmann *m*

m

medieval [mɛdɪ'iːvl] *adj* mittelalterlich
mediocre [miːdɪ'əʊkəʳ] *adj* mittelmäßig
mediocrity [miːdɪ'ɔkrɪtɪ] *n* Mittelmäßigkeit *f*
meditate ['mɛdɪteɪt] *vi* nachdenken; (*Rel*)
meditieren
meditation [mɛdɪ'teɪʃən] *n* Nachdenken *nt*;
(*Rel*) Meditation *f*
Mediterranean [mɛdɪtə'reɪnɪən] *adj* (*country,
climate etc*) Mittelmeer-; **the ~ (Sea)** das
Mittelmeer
medium ['miːdɪəm] (*pl* **media** *or* **~s**) *adj*
mittlere(r, s) ▷ *n* (*means*) Mittel *nt*; (*substance,
material*) Medium *nt* (*pl* **~s**) (*person*) Medium *nt*;
of ~ height mittelgroß; **to strike a happy ~**
den goldenen Mittelweg finden
medium-dry ['miːdɪəm'draɪ] *adj* (*wine, sherry*)
halbtrocken
medium-sized ['miːdɪəm'saɪzd] *adj* mittelgroß
medium wave *n* (*Radio*) Mittelwelle *f*
medley ['mɛdlɪ] *n* Gemisch *nt*; (*Mus*) Medley *nt*
meek [miːk] *adj* sanft(mütig), duldsam
meet [miːt] (*pt, pp* **met**) *vt* (*encounter*) treffen;
(*by arrangement*) sich treffen mit; (*for the first
time*) kennenlernen; (*go and fetch*) abholen;
(*opponent*) treffen auf +*acc*; (*condition, standard*)
erfüllen; (*need, expenses*) decken; (*problem*)
stoßen auf +*acc*; (*challenge*) begegnen +*dat*;
(*bill*) begleichen; (*join: line*) sich schneiden
mit; (*: road etc*) treffen auf +*acc* ▷ *vi* (*encounter*)
sich begegnen; (*by arrangement*) sich treffen;
(*for the first time*) sich kennenlernen; (*for
talks etc*) zusammenkommen; (*committee*)
tagen; (*join: lines*) sich schneiden; (*: roads etc*)
aufeinandertreffen ▷ *n* (*Brit: Hunting*) Jagd
f; (*US: Sport*) Sportfest *nt*; **pleased to ~ you!**
(sehr) angenehm!
▶ **meet up** *vi*: **to ~ up with sb** sich mit jdm
treffen
▶ **meet with** *vt fus* (*difficulty, success*) haben
meeting ['miːtɪŋ] *n* (*assembly, people assembling*)
Versammlung *f*; (*Comm, of committee
etc*) Sitzung *f*; (*also*: **business meeting**)
Besprechung *f*; (*encounter*) Begegnung *f*;
(*: arranged*) Treffen *nt*; (*Pol*) Gespräch *nt*; (*Sport*)
Veranstaltung *f*; **she's at** *or* **in a ~** (*Comm*) sie
ist bei einer Besprechung; **to call a ~** eine
Sitzung/Versammlung einberufen
meeting-place ['miːtɪŋpleɪs] *n* Treffpunkt *m*
megabyte ['mɛgəbaɪt] *n* Megabyte *nt*
megalomaniac [mɛgələ'meɪnɪæk] *n*
Größenwahnsinnige(r) *f(m)*
megaphone ['mɛgəfəʊn] *n* Megafon *nt*
megawatt ['mɛgəwɔt] *n* Megawatt *nt*
melancholy ['mɛlənkəlɪ] *n* Melancholie
f, Schwermut *f* ▷ *adj* melancholisch,
schwermütig
mellow ['mɛləʊ] *adj* (*sound*) voll, weich; (*light,
colour, stone*) warm; (*weathered*) verwittert;
(*person*) gesetzt; (*wine*) ausgereift ▷ *vi* (*person*)
gesetzter werden
melodious [mɪ'ləʊdɪəs] *adj* melodisch
melodrama ['mɛləʊdrɑːmə] *n* Melodrama *nt*
melodramatic [mɛlədrə'mætɪk] *adj*
melodramatisch
melody ['mɛlədɪ] *n* Melodie *f*
melon ['mɛlən] *n* Melone *f*
melt [mɛlt] *vi* (*lit, fig*) schmelzen ▷ *vt*
schmelzen; (*butter*) zerlassen
▶ **melt down** *vt* einschmelzen
meltdown ['mɛltdaʊn] *n* (*in nuclear reactor*)
Kernschmelze *f*
melting point ['mɛltɪŋ-] *n* Schmelzpunkt *m*
melting pot *n* (*lit, fig*) Schmelztiegel *m*; **to be
in the ~** in der Schwebe sein
member ['mɛmbəʳ] *n* Mitglied *nt*; (*Anat*)
Glied *nt* ▷ *cpd*: **~ country** Mitgliedsland *nt*; **~
state** Mitgliedsstaat *m*; **M~ of Parliament**
(*Brit*) Abgeordnete(r) *f(m)* (*des Unterhauses*);
M~ of the European Parliament (*Brit*)
Abgeordnete(r) *f(m)* des Europaparlaments
membership ['mɛmbəʃɪp] *n* Mitgliedschaft
f; (*members*) Mitglieder *pl*; (*number of members*)
Mitgliederzahl *f*
membership card *n* Mitgliedsausweis *m*
membrane ['mɛmbreɪn] *n* Membran(e) *f*
memento [mə'mɛntəʊ] *n* Andenken *nt*
memo ['mɛməʊ] *n* Memo *nt*, Mitteilung *f*
memoir ['mɛmwɑːʳ] *n* Kurzbiografie *f*
memoirs ['mɛmwɑːz] *npl* Memoiren *pl*
memo pad *n* Notizblock *m*
memorable ['mɛmərəbl] *adj* denkwürdig;
(*unforgettable*) unvergesslich
memorandum [mɛmə'rændəm] (*pl
memoranda) *n* Mitteilung *f*
memorial [mɪ'mɔːrɪəl] *n* Denkmal *nt* ▷ *adj*
(*service, prize*) Gedenk-
Memorial Day (*US*) *n* ≈ Volkstrauertag *m*; *siehe
Info-Artikel*

⬤ **MEMORIAL DAY**
⬤
⬤ *Memorial Day* ist in den USA ein gesetzlicher
⬤ Feiertag am letzten Montag im Mai
⬤ zum Gedenken an die in allen Kriegen
⬤ gefallenen amerikanischen Soldaten.
⬤ Siehe auch *Remembrance Sunday*

memorize ['mɛmər) aɪz] *vt* sich *dat* einprägen
memory ['mɛmərɪ] *n* Gedächtnis *nt*; (*sth
remembered*) Erinnerung *f*; (*Comput*) Speicher
m; **in ~ of** zur Erinnerung an +*acc*; **to have a
good/bad ~** ein gutes/schlechtes Gedächtnis
haben; **loss of ~** Gedächtnisschwund *m*
memory stick *n* (*Comput*) Memorystick® *nt*
men [mɛn] *npl of* **man**
menace ['mɛnɪs] *n* Bedrohung *f*; (*nuisance*)
(Land)plage *f* ▷ *vt* bedrohen; **a public ~** eine
Gefahr für die Öffentlichkeit
menacing ['mɛnɪsɪŋ] *adj* drohend
mend [mɛnd] *vt* reparieren; (*darn*) flicken
▷ *n*: **to be on the ~** auf dem Wege der
Besserung sein; **to ~ one's ways** sich bessern
mending ['mɛndɪŋ] *n* Reparaturen *pl*; (*clothes*)
Flickarbeiten *pl*
menial ['miːnɪəl] (*often pej*) *adj* niedrig,
untergeordnet

meningitis [mɛnɪn'dʒaɪtɪs] n Hirnhautentzündung f

menopause ['mɛnəupɔːz] n: **the ~** die Wechseljahre pl

menservants ['mɛnsəːvənts] npl of **manservant**

men's room (US) n Herrentoilette f

menstrual ['mɛnstruəl] adj (Biol: cycle etc) Menstruations-; **~ period** Monatsblutung f

menstruate ['mɛnstrueɪt] vi die Menstruation haben

menstruation [mɛnstru'eɪʃən] n Menstruation f

menswear ['mɛnzwɛəʳ] n Herren(be)kleidung f

mental ['mɛntl] adj geistig; (illness) Geistes-; **~ arithmetic** Kopfrechnen nt

mental hospital n psychiatrische Klinik f

mentality [mɛn'tælɪtɪ] n Mentalität f

mentally ['mɛntlɪ] adv: **to be ~ handicapped** geistig behindert sein

menthol ['mɛnθɔl] n Menthol nt

mention ['mɛnʃən] n Erwähnung f ▷ vt erwähnen; **don't ~ it!** (bitte,) gern geschehen!; **not to ~ …** von … ganz zu schweigen

mentor ['mɛntɔːʳ] n Mentor m

menu ['mɛnjuː] n Menü nt; (printed) Speisekarte f

menu-driven ['mɛnjuːdrɪvn] adj (Comput) menügesteuert

MEP (Brit) n abbr (= Member of the European Parliament) Abgeordnete(r) f(m) des Europaparlaments

mercantile ['məːkəntaɪl] adj (class, society) Handel treibend; (law) Handels-

mercenary ['məːsɪnərɪ] adj (person) geldgierig ▷ n Söldner m

merchandise ['məːtʃəndaɪz] n Ware f

merchandiser ['məːtʃəndaɪzəʳ] n Verkaufsförderungsexperte m

merchant ['məːtʃənt] n Kaufmann m; **timber/ wine ~** Holz-/Weinhändler m

merchant bank (Brit) n Handelsbank f

merchantman ['məːtʃəntmən] (irreg: like **man**) n Handelsschiff nt

merchant navy, (US) **merchant marine** n Handelsmarine f

merciful ['məːsɪful] adj gnädig; **a ~ release** eine Erlösung

mercifully ['məːsɪflɪ] adv glücklicherweise

merciless ['məːsɪlɪs] adj erbarmungslos

mercurial [məː'kjuərɪəl] adj (unpredictable) sprunghaft, wechselhaft; (lively) quecksilbrig

mercury ['məːkjurɪ] n Quecksilber nt

mercy ['məːsɪ] n Gnade f; **to have ~ on sb** Erbarmen mit jdm haben; **at the ~ of** ausgeliefert +dat

mercy killing n Euthanasie f

mere [mɪəʳ] adj bloß; **his ~ presence irritates her** schon or allein seine Anwesenheit ärgert sie; **she is a ~ child** sie ist noch ein Kind; **it's a ~ trifle** es ist eine Lappalie; **by ~ chance** rein durch Zufall

merely ['mɪəlɪ] adv lediglich, bloß

merge [məːdʒ] vt (combine) vereinen; (Comput: files) mischen ▷ vi (Comm) fusionieren; (colours, sounds, shapes) ineinander übergehen; (roads) zusammenlaufen

merger ['məːdʒəʳ] n (Comm) Fusion f

meridian [mə'rɪdɪən] n Meridian m

meringue [mə'ræŋ] n Baiser nt

merit ['mɛrɪt] n (worth, value) Wert m; (advantage) Vorzug m; (achievement) Verdienst nt ▷ vt verdienen

meritocracy [mɛrɪ'tɔkrəsɪ] n Leistungsgesellschaft f

mermaid ['məːmeɪd] n Seejungfrau f, Meerjungfrau f

merrily ['mɛrɪlɪ] adv vergnügt

merriment ['mɛrɪmənt] n Heiterkeit f

merry ['mɛrɪ] adj vergnügt; (music) fröhlich; **M~ Christmas!** fröhliche or frohe Weihnachten!

merry-go-round ['mɛrɪgəuraund] n Karussell nt

mesh [mɛʃ] n Geflecht nt; **wire ~** Maschendraht m

mesmerize ['mɛzməraɪz] vt (fig) faszinieren

mess [mɛs] n Durcheinander nt; (dirt) Dreck m; (Mil) Kasino nt; **to be in a ~** (untidy) unordentlich sein; (in difficulty) in Schwierigkeiten stecken; **to be a ~** (fig: life) verkorkst sein; **to get o.s. in a ~** in Schwierigkeiten geraten

▶ **mess about** (inf) vi (fool around) herumalbern

▶ **mess about with** (inf) vt fus (play around with) herumfummeln an +dat

▶ **mess around** (inf) vi = **mess about**

▶ **mess around with** (inf) vt fus = **mess about with**

▶ **mess up** vt durcheinanderbringen; (dirty) verdrecken

message ['mɛsɪdʒ] n Mitteilung f, Nachricht f; (meaning) Aussage f; **to get the ~** (inf: fig) kapieren

message switching [-'swɪtʃɪŋ] n (Comput) Speichervermittlung f

messenger ['mɛsɪndʒəʳ] n Bote m

Messiah [mɪ'saɪə] n Messias m

Messrs ['mɛsəz] abbr (on letters: = messieurs) An (die Herren)

messy ['mɛsɪ] adj (dirty) dreckig; (untidy) unordentlich

Met [mɛt] (US) n abbr (= Metropolitan Opera) Met f

met [mɛt] pt, pp of **meet**

met. abbr (= meteorological): **the M~ Office** das Wetteramt

metabolism [mɛ'tæbəlɪzəm] n Stoffwechsel m

metal ['mɛtl] n Metall nt

metal fatigue n Metallermüdung f

metalled ['mɛtld] adj (road) asphaltiert

metallic [mɪ'tælɪk] adj metallisch; (made of metal) aus Metall

metallurgy [mɛ'tælədʒɪ] n Metallurgie f

metalwork ['mɛtlwəːk] n Metallarbeit f

metamorphosis [mɛtə'mɔːfəsɪs] (pl

metamorphoses) n Verwandlung f
metaphor ['mɛtəfəʳ] n Metapher f
metaphorical [mɛtə'fɒrɪkl] adj metaphorisch
metaphysics [mɛtə'fɪzɪks] n Metaphysik f
meteor ['miːtɪəʳ] n Meteor m
meteoric [miːtɪ'ɒrɪk] adj (fig) kometenhaft
meteorite ['miːtɪəraɪt] n Meteorit m
meteorological [miːtɪərə'lɒdʒɪkl] adj
(conditions, office etc) Wetter-
meteorology [miːtɪə'rɒlədʒɪ] n Wetterkunde f,
Meteorologie f
mete out [miːt-] vt austeilen; **to ~ justice**
Recht sprechen
meter ['miːtəʳ] n Zähler m; (also: **water meter**)
Wasseruhr f; (also: **parking meter**) Parkuhr f;
(US: unit) = **metre**
methane ['miːθeɪn] n Methan nt
method ['mɛθəd] n Methode f; **~ of payment**
Zahlungsweise f
methodical [mɪ'θɒdɪkl] adj methodisch
Methodist ['mɛθədɪst] n Methodist(in) m(f)
methodology [mɛθə'dɒlədʒɪ] n Methodik f
meths [mɛθs] (Brit) n = **methylated spirit**
methylated spirit ['mɛθɪleɪtɪd-] (Brit) n
(Brenn)spiritus m
meticulous [mɪ'tɪkjuləs] adj sorgfältig; (detail)
genau
metre, (US) **meter** ['miːtəʳ] n Meter m or nt
metric ['mɛtrɪk] adj metrisch; **to go ~** auf das
metrische Maßsystem umstellen
metrical ['mɛtrɪkl] adj metrisch
metrication [mɛtrɪ'keɪʃən] n Umstellung f auf
das metrische Maßsystem
metric system n metrisches Maßsystem nt
metric ton n Metertonne f
metronome ['mɛtrənəum] n Metronom nt
metropolis [mɪ'trɒpəlɪs] n Metropole f
metropolitan [mɛtrə'pɒlɪtn] adj großstädtisch
Metropolitan Police (Brit) n: **the ~** die
Londoner Polizei
mettle ['mɛtl] n: **to be on one's ~** auf dem
Posten sein
mew [mjuː] vi miauen
mews [mjuːz] (Brit) n Gasse f mit ehemaligen
Kutscherhäuschen
Mexican ['mɛksɪkən] adj mexikanisch ▷ n
Mexikaner(in) m(f)
Mexico ['mɛksɪkəu] n Mexiko nt
Mexico City n Mexico City f
mezzanine ['mɛtsəniːn] n Mezzanin nt
MFA (US) n abbr (= Master of Fine Arts) akademischer
Grad in Kunst
mfr abbr = **manufacture; manufacturer**
mg abbr (= milligram(me)) mg
Mgr abbr (= Monseigneur, Monsignor) Mgr.; (Comm)
= **manager**
MHR (US, Australia) n abbr (= Member of the House
of Representatives) Abgeordnete(r) f(m) des
Repräsentantenhauses
MHz abbr (= megahertz) MHz
MI (US) abbr (Post) = Michigan
MI5 (Brit) n abbr (= Military Intelligence, section five)
britischer Spionageabwehrdienst

MI6 (Brit) n abbr (= Military Intelligence, section six)
britischer Geheimdienst
MIA abbr (Mil: = missing in action) vermisst
miaow [miː'au] vi miauen
mice [maɪs] npl of **mouse**
Mich. (US) abbr (Post) = Michigan
micro ['maɪkrəu] n = **microcomputer**
micro ... ['maɪkrəu] pref mikro-, Mikro-
microbe ['maɪkrəub] n Mikrobe f
microbiology [maɪkrəubaɪ'ɒlədʒɪ] n
Mikrobiologie f
microchip ['maɪkrəutʃɪp] n Mikrochip m
microcomputer ['maɪkrəukəm'pjuːtəʳ] n
Mikrocomputer m
microcosm ['maɪkrəukɒzəm] n Mikrokosmos
m
microeconomics ['maɪkrəuiːkə'nɒmɪks] n
Mikroökonomie f
microelectronics ['maɪkrəuɪlɛk'trɒnɪks] n
Mikroelektronik f
microfiche ['maɪkrəufiːʃ] n Mikrofiche m or nt
microfilm ['maɪkrəufɪlm] n Mikrofilm m
microlight ['maɪkrəulaɪt] n
Ultraleichtflugzeug nt
micrometer [maɪ'krɒmɪtəʳ] n Messschraube f
microphone ['maɪkrəfəun] n Mikrofon nt
microprocessor ['maɪkrəu'prəusɛsəʳ] n
Mikroprozessor m
microscope ['maɪkrəskəup] n Mikroskop nt;
under the ~ unter dem Mikroskop
microscopic [maɪkrə'skɒpɪk] adj
mikroskopisch; (creature) mikroskopisch klein
microwave ['maɪkrəuweɪv] n Mikrowelle f;
(also: **microwave oven**) Mikrowellenherd m
mid [mɪd] adj: **in ~May** Mitte Mai; **in
~afternoon** (mitten) am Nachmittag; **in ~air**
(mitten) in der Luft; **he's in his ~thirties** er
ist Mitte dreißig
midday [mɪd'deɪ] n Mittag m
middle ['mɪdl] n Mitte f ▷ adj mittlere(r, s); **in
the ~ of the night** mitten in der Nacht; **I'm
in the ~ of reading it** ich bin mittendrin; **a ~
course** ein Mittelweg m
middle age n mittleres Lebensalter nt
middle-aged [mɪdl'eɪdʒd] adj mittleren Alters
Middle Ages npl Mittelalter nt
middle-class ['mɪdl'klɑːs] adj mittelständisch
middle class(es) n(pl) Mittelstand m
Middle East n Naher Osten m
middleman ['mɪdlmæn] (irreg: like **man**) n
Zwischenhändler m
middle management n mittleres
Management nt
middle name n zweiter Vorname m
middle-of-the-road ['mɪdləvðə'rəud] adj
gemäßigt; (politician) der Mitte; (Mus) leicht
middleweight ['mɪdlweɪt] n (Boxing)
Mittelgewicht nt
middling ['mɪdlɪŋ] adj mittelmäßig
Middx (Brit) abbr (Post) = Middlesex
midge [mɪdʒ] n Mücke f
midget ['mɪdʒɪt] n Liliputaner(in) m(f)
midi system ['mɪdɪ-] n Midi-System nt

Midlands ['mɪdləndz] (*Brit*) *npl*: **the ~** Mittelengland *nt*

midnight ['mɪdnaɪt] *n* Mitternacht *f* ▷ *cpd* Mitternachts-; **at ~** um Mitternacht

midriff ['mɪdrɪf] *n* Taille *f*

midst [mɪdst] *n*: **in the ~ of** mitten in +*dat*; **to be in the ~ of doing sth** mitten dabei sein, etw zu tun

midsummer [mɪd'sʌmə^r] *n* Hochsommer *m*; **M~('s) Day** Sommersonnenwende *f*

midway [mɪd'weɪ] *adj*: **we have reached the ~ point** wir haben die Hälfte hinter uns *dat* ▷ *adv* auf halbem Weg; **~ between** (*in space*) auf halbem Weg zwischen; **~ through** (*in time*) mitten in +*dat*

midweek [mɪd'wiːk] *adv* mitten in der Woche ▷ *adj* Mitte der Woche

midwife ['mɪdwaɪf] (*pl* **midwives**) *n* Hebamme *f*

midwifery ['mɪdwɪfərɪ] *n* Geburtshilfe *f*

midwinter [mɪd'wɪntə^r] *n*: **in ~** im tiefsten Winter

miffed [mɪft] (*inf*) *adj*: **to be ~** eingeschnappt sein

might [maɪt] *vb see* **may** ▷ *n* Macht *f*; **with all one's ~** mit aller Kraft

mighty ['maɪtɪ] *adj* mächtig

migraine ['miːgreɪn] *n* Migräne *f*

migrant ['maɪgrənt] *adj* (*bird*) Zug-; (*worker*) Wander- ▷ *n* (*bird*) Zugvogel *m*; (*worker*) Wanderarbeiter(in) *m(f)*

migrate [maɪ'greɪt] *vi* (*bird*) ziehen; (*person*) abwandern

migration [maɪ'greɪʃən] *n* Wanderung *f*; (*to cities*) Abwanderung *f*; (*of birds*) (Vogel)zug *m*

mike [maɪk] *n* = **microphone**

Milan [mɪ'læn] *n* Mailand *nt*

mild [maɪld] *adj* mild; (*gentle*) sanft; (*slight: infection etc*) leicht; (: *interest*) gering

mildew ['mɪldjuː] *n* Schimmel *m*

mildly ['maɪldlɪ] *adv* (*say*) sanft; (*slight*) leicht; **to put it ~** gelinde gesagt

mildness ['maɪldnɪs] *n* Milde *f*; (*gentleness*) Sanftheit *f*; (*of infection etc*) Leichtigkeit *f*

mile [maɪl] *n* Meile *f*; **to do 30 ~s per gallon** ≈ 9 Liter auf 100 km verbrauchen

mileage ['maɪlɪdʒ] *n* Meilenzahl *f*; (*fig*) Nutzen *m*; **to get a lot of ~ out of sth** etw gründlich ausnutzen; **there is a lot of ~ in the idea** aus der Idee lässt sich viel machen

mileage allowance *n* ≈ Kilometergeld *nt*

mileometer [maɪ'lɒmɪtə^r] *n* ≈ Kilometerzähler *m*

milestone ['maɪlstəʊn] *n* (*lit, fig*) Meilenstein *m*

milieu ['miːljəː] *n* Milieu *nt*

militant ['mɪlɪtnt] *adj* militant ▷ *n* Militante(r) *f(m)*

militarism ['mɪlɪtərɪzəm] *n* Militarismus *m*

militaristic [mɪlɪtə'rɪstɪk] *adj* militaristisch

military ['mɪlɪtərɪ] *adj* (*history, leader etc*) Militär- ▷ *n*: **the ~** das Militär

military police *n* Militärpolizei *f*

military service *n* Militärdienst *m*

militate ['mɪlɪteɪt] *vi*: **to ~ against** negative Auswirkungen haben auf +*acc*

militia [mɪ'lɪʃə] *n* Miliz *f*

milk [mɪlk] *n* Milch *f* ▷ *vt* (*lit, fig*) melken

milk chocolate *n* Vollmilchschokolade *f*

milk float (*Brit*) *n* Milchwagen *m*

milking ['mɪlkɪŋ] *n* Melken *nt*

milkman ['mɪlkmən] (*irreg: like* **man**) *n* Milchmann *m*

milk shake *n* Milchmixgetränk *nt*

milk tooth *n* Milchzahn *m*

milk truck (*US*) *n* = **milk float**

milky ['mɪlkɪ] *adj* milchig; (*drink*) mit viel Milch; **~ coffee** Milchkaffee *m*

Milky Way *n* Milchstraße *f*

mill [mɪl] *n* Mühle *f*; (*factory*) Fabrik *f*; (*woollen mill*) Spinnerei *f* ▷ *vt* mahlen ▷ *vi* (*also*: **mill about**) umherlaufen

millennium [mɪ'lɛnɪəm] (*pl* **~s** or **millennia**) *n* Jahrtausend *nt*

millennium bug *n* (*Comput*) Jahrtausendfehler *m*

miller ['mɪlə^r] *n* Müller *m*

millet ['mɪlɪt] *n* Hirse *f*

milli... ['mɪlɪ] *pref* Milli-

milligram, milligramme ['mɪlɪgræm] *n* Milligramm *nt*

millilitre, (*US*) **milliliter** ['mɪlɪliːtə^r] *n* Milliliter *m* or *nt*

millimetre, (*US*) **millimeter** ['mɪlɪmiːtə^r] *n* Millimeter *m* or *nt*

millinery ['mɪlɪnərɪ] *n* Hüte *pl*

million ['mɪljən] *n* Million *f*; **a ~ times** (*fig*) tausend Mal, x-mal

millionaire [mɪljə'nɛə^r] *n* Millionär *m*

millipede ['mɪlɪpiːd] *n* Tausendfüßler *m*

millstone ['mɪlstəʊn] *n* (*fig*): **it's a ~ round his neck** es ist für ihn ein Klotz am Bein

millwheel ['mɪlwiːl] *n* Mühlrad *nt*

milometer [maɪ'lɒmɪtə^r] *n* = **mileometer**

mime [maɪm] *n* Pantomime *f*; (*actor*) Pantomime *m* ▷ *vt* pantomimisch darstellen

mimic ['mɪmɪk] *n* Imitator *m* ▷ *vt* (*for amusement*) parodieren; (*animal, person*) imitieren, nachahmen

mimicry ['mɪmɪkrɪ] *n* Nachahmung *f*

Min. (*Brit*) *abbr* (*Pol*) = **ministry**

min. *abbr* (= *minute*) Min. = **minimum**

minaret [mɪnə'rɛt] *n* Minarett *nt*

mince [mɪns] *vt* (*meat*) durch den Fleischwolf drehen ▷ *vi* (*in walking*) trippeln ▷ *n* (*Brit: meat*) Hackfleisch *nt*; **he does not ~ (his) words** er nimmt kein Blatt vor den Mund

mincemeat ['mɪnsmiːt] *n* süße Gebäckfüllung aus Dörrobst und Sirup; (*US: meat*) Hackfleisch *nt*; **to make ~ of sb** (*inf*) Hackfleisch aus jdm machen

mince pie *n* mit Mincemeat gefülltes Gebäck

mincer ['mɪnsə^r] *n* Fleischwolf *m*

mincing ['mɪnsɪŋ] *adj* (*walk*) trippelnd; (*voice*) geziert

mind [maɪnd] *n* Geist *m*, Verstand *m*; (*thoughts*) Gedanken *pl*; (*memory*) Gedächtnis *nt* ▷ *vt*

aufpassen auf +*acc*; (*office etc*) nach dem
Rechten sehen in +*dat*; (*object to*) etwas haben
gegen; **to my ~** meiner Meinung nach; **to be
out of one's ~** verrückt sein; **it is on my ~** es
beschäftigt mich; **to keep** *or* **bear sth in ~**
etw nicht vergessen, an etw denken; **to make
up one's ~** sich entscheiden; **to change
one's ~** es sich *dat* anders überlegen; **to be in
two ~s about sth** sich *dat* über etw *acc* nicht
im Klaren sein; **to have it in ~ to do sth**
die Absicht haben, etw zu tun; **to have sb/
sth in ~** an jdn/etw denken; **it slipped my
~** ich habe es vergessen; **to bring** *or* **call sth
to ~** etw in Erinnerung rufen; **I can't get it
out of my ~** es geht mir nicht aus dem Kopf;
his ~ was on other things er war mit den
Gedanken woanders; **"~ the step"** „Vorsicht
Stufe"; **do you ~ if …?** macht es Ihnen etwas
aus, wenn …?; **I don't ~** es ist mir egal; **~
you, …** allerdings …; **never ~!** (*it makes no odds*)
ist doch egal!; (*don't worry*) macht nichts!

mind-boggling ['maɪndbɒglɪŋ] (*inf*) *adj*
atemberaubend

-minded ['maɪndɪd] *adj*: **fair~** gerecht; **an
industrially~ nation** ein auf Industrie
ausgerichtetes Land

minder ['maɪndə^r] *n* Betreuer(in) *m(f)*;
(*inf: bodyguard*) Aufpasser(in) *m(f)*

mindful ['maɪndful] *adj*: **~ of** unter
Berücksichtigung +*gen*

mindless ['maɪndlɪs] *adj* (*violence*) sinnlos;
(*work*) geistlos

mine¹ [maɪn] *n* (*also:* **coal mine, gold mine**)
Bergwerk *nt*; (*bomb*) Mine *f* ⊳ *vt* (*coal*) abbauen;
(*beach etc*) verminen; (*ship*) eine Mine
befestigen an +*dat*

mine² [maɪn] *pron* meine(r, s); **that book
is ~** das Buch ist mein(e)s, das Buch gehört
mir; **this is ~** das ist meins; **a friend of ~** ein
Freund/eine Freundin von mir

mine detector *n* Minensuchgerät *nt*

minefield ['maɪnfiːld] *n* Minenfeld *nt*; (*fig*)
brisante Situation *f*

miner ['maɪnə^r] *n* Bergmann *m*, Bergarbeiter *m*

mineral ['mɪnərəl] *adj* (*deposit, resources*)
Mineral- ⊳ *n* Mineral *nt*; **minerals** *npl* (*Brit: soft
drinks*) Erfrischungsgetränke *pl*

mineralogy [mɪnə'rælədʒɪ] *n* Mineralogie *f*

mineral water *n* Mineralwasser *nt*

minesweeper ['maɪnswiːpə^r] *n*
Minensuchboot *nt*

mingle ['mɪŋgl] *vi*: **to ~ (with)** sich vermischen
(mit); **to ~ with** (*people*) Umgang haben
mit; (*at party etc*) sich unterhalten mit; **you
should ~ a bit** du solltest dich unter die Leute
mischen

mingy ['mɪndʒɪ] (*inf*) *adj* knick(e)rig; (*amount*)
mick(e)rig

mini… ['mɪnɪ] *pref* Mini-

miniature ['mɪnətʃə^r] *adj* winzig; (*version etc*)
Miniatur- ⊳ *n* Miniatur *f*; **in ~** im Kleinen, im
Kleinformat

minibus ['mɪnɪbʌs] *n* Kleinbus *m*

minicab ['mɪnɪkæb] *n* Kleintaxi *nt*

minicomputer ['mɪnɪkəm'pjuːtə^r] *n*
Minicomputer *m*

minim ['mɪnɪm] *n* (*Mus*) halbe Note *f*

minima ['mɪnɪmə] *npl of* **minimum**

minimal ['mɪnɪml] *adj* minimal

minimalist ['mɪnɪməlɪst] *adj* minimalistisch

minimize ['mɪnɪmaɪz] *vt* auf ein Minimum
reduzieren; (*play down*) herunterspielen

minimum ['mɪnɪməm] (*pl* **minima**) *n*
Minimum *nt* ⊳ *adj* (*income, speed*) Mindest-;
to reduce to a ~ auf ein Mindestmaß
reduzieren; **~ wage** Mindestlohn *m*

minimum lending rate *n* Diskontsatz *m*

mining ['maɪnɪŋ] *n* Bergbau *m* ⊳ *cpd* Bergbau-

minion ['mɪnjən] (*pej*) *n* Untergebene(r) *f(m)*

miniseries ['mɪnɪsɪərɪːz] *n* Miniserie *f*

miniskirt ['mɪnɪskəːt] *n* Minirock *m*

minister ['mɪnɪstə^r] *n* (*Brit: Pol*) Minister(in)
m(f); (*Rel*) Pfarrer *m* ⊳ *vi*: **to ~ to** sich kümmern
um; (*needs*) befriedigen

ministerial [mɪnɪs'tɪərɪəl] (*Brit*) *adj* (*Pol*)
ministeriell

ministry ['mɪnɪstrɪ] *n* (*Brit: Pol*) Ministerium *nt*;
to join the ~ (*Rel*) Geistliche(r) werden

Ministry of Defence (*Brit*) *n*
Verteidigungsministerium *nt*

mink [mɪŋk] (*pl* **minks** *or* **~**) *n* Nerz *m*

mink coat *n* Nerzmantel *m*

Minn. (*US*) *abbr* (*Post*) = Minnesota

minnow ['mɪnəu] *n* Elritze *f*

minor ['maɪnə^r] *adj* kleinere(r, s); (*poet*)
unbedeutend; (*planet*) klein; (*Mus*) Moll ⊳ *n*
Minderjährige(r) *f(m)*

Minorca [mɪ'nɔːkə] *n* Menorca *nt*

minority [maɪ'nɔrɪtɪ] *n* Minderheit *f*; **to be in
a ~** in der Minderheit sein

minster ['mɪnstə^r] *n* Münster *nt*

minstrel ['mɪnstrəl] *n* Spielmann *m*

mint [mɪnt] *n* Minze *f*; (*sweet*)
Pfefferminz(bonbon) *nt*; (*place*): **the M~**
die Münzanstalt ⊳ *vt* (*coins*) prägen; **in ~
condition** neuwertig

mint sauce *n* Minzsoße *f*

minuet [mɪnju'ɛt] *n* Menuett *nt*

minus ['maɪnəs] *n* (*also:* **minus sign**)
Minuszeichen *nt* ⊳ *prep* minus, weniger; **~
24°C** 24 Grad unter null

minuscule ['mɪnəskjuːl] *adj* winzig

minute¹ [maɪ'njuːt] *adj* winzig; (*search*)
peinlich genau; (*detail*) kleinste(r, s); **in ~
detail** in allen Einzelheiten

minute² ['mɪnɪt] *n* Minute *f*; (*fig*) Augenblick
m, Moment *m*; **minutes** *npl* (*of meeting*)
Protokoll *nt*; **it is 5 ~s past 3** es ist 5 Minuten
nach 3; **wait a ~!** einen Augenblick *or*
Moment!; **up-to-the-~** (*news*) hochaktuell;
(*technology*) allerneueste(r, s); **at the last ~** in
letzter Minute

minute book *n* Protokollbuch *nt*

minute hand *n* Minutenzeiger *m*

minutely [maɪ'njuːtlɪ] *adv* (*in detail*)
genauestens; (*by a small amount*) ganz

geringfügig

minutiae [mɪˈnjuːʃiː] *npl* Einzelheiten *pl*

miracle [ˈmɪrəkl] *n* (*Rel, fig*) Wunder *nt*

miraculous [mɪˈrækjuləs] *adj* wunderbar; (*powers, effect, cure*) Wunder-; (*success, change*) unglaublich; **to have a ~ escape** wie durch ein Wunder entkommen

mirage [ˈmɪrɑːʒ] *n* Fata Morgana *f*; (*fig*) Trugbild *nt*

mire [ˈmaɪəʳ] *n* Morast *m*

mirror [ˈmɪrəʳ] *n* Spiegel *m* ▷ *vt* (*lit, fig*) widerspiegeln

mirror image *n* Spiegelbild *nt*

mirth [məːθ] *n* Heiterkeit *f*

misadventure [mɪsədˈventʃəʳ] *n* Missgeschick *nt*; **death by ~** (*Brit*) Tod *m* durch Unfall

misanthropist [mɪˈzænθrəpɪst] *n* Misanthrop *m*, Menschenfeind *m*

misapply [mɪsəˈplaɪ] *vt* (*term*) falsch verwenden; (*rule*) falsch anwenden

misapprehension [ˈmɪsæprɪˈhenʃən] *n* Missverständnis *nt*; **you are under a ~** Sie befinden sich im Irrtum

misappropriate [mɪsəˈprəʊprɪeɪt] *vt* veruntreuen

misappropriation [ˈmɪsəprəʊprɪˈeɪʃən] *n* Veruntreuung *f*

misbehave [mɪsbɪˈheɪv] *vi* sich schlecht benehmen

misbehaviour, (*US*) **misbehavior** [mɪsbɪˈheɪvjəʳ] *n* schlechtes Benehmen *nt*

misc. *abbr* = **miscellaneous**

miscalculate [mɪsˈkælkjuleɪt] *vt* falsch berechnen; (*misjudge*) falsch einschätzen

miscalculation [ˈmɪskælkjuˈleɪʃən] *n* Rechenfehler *m*; (*misjudgement*) Fehleinschätzung *f*

miscarriage [ˈmɪskærɪdʒ] *n* (*Med*) Fehlgeburt *f*; **~ of justice** (*Law*) Justizirrtum *m*

miscarry [mɪsˈkærɪ] *vi* (*Med*) eine Fehlgeburt haben; (*fail: plans*) fehlschlagen

miscellaneous [mɪsɪˈleɪnɪəs] *adj* verschieden; (*subjects, items*) divers; **~ expenses** sonstige Unkosten *pl*

mischance [mɪsˈtʃɑːns] *n* unglücklicher Zufall *m*

mischief [ˈmɪstʃɪf] *n* (*bad behaviour*) Unfug *m*; (*playfulness*) Verschmitztheit *f*; (*harm*) Schaden *m*; (*pranks*) Streiche *pl*; **to get into ~** etwas anstellen; **to do sb a ~** jdm etwas antun

mischievous [ˈmɪstʃɪvəs] *adj* (*naughty*) ungezogen; (*playful*) verschmitzt

misconception [ˈmɪskənˈsepʃən] *n* fälschliche Annahme *f*

misconduct [mɪsˈkɒndʌkt] *n* Fehlverhalten *nt*; **professional ~** Berufsvergehen *nt*

misconstrue [mɪskənˈstruː] *vt* missverstehen

miscount [mɪsˈkaunt] *vt* falsch zählen ▷ *vi* sich verzählen

misdemeanour, (*US*) **misdemeanor** [mɪsdɪˈmiːnəʳ] *n* Vergehen *nt*

misdirect [mɪsdɪˈrekt] *vt* (*person*) in die falsche Richtung schicken; (*talent*) vergeuden

miser [ˈmaɪzəʳ] *n* Geizhals *m*

miserable [ˈmɪzərəbl] *adj* (*unhappy*) unglücklich; (*wretched*) erbärmlich, elend; (*unpleasant: weather*) trostlos; (: *person*) gemein; (*contemptible: offer, donation*) armselig; (: *failure*) kläglich; **to feel ~** sich elend fühlen

miserably [ˈmɪzərəblɪ] *adv* (*fail*) kläglich; (*live*) elend; (*smile, speak*) unglücklich; (*small*) jämmerlich

miserly [ˈmaɪzəlɪ] *adj* geizig; (*amount*) armselig

misery [ˈmɪzərɪ] *n* (*unhappiness*) Kummer *m*; (*wretchedness*) Elend *nt*; (*inf: person*) Miesepeter *m*

misfire [mɪsˈfaɪəʳ] *vi* (*plan*) fehlschlagen; (*car engine*) fehlzünden

misfit [ˈmɪsfɪt] *n* Außenseiter(in) *m(f)*

misfortune [mɪsˈfɔːtʃən] *n* Pech *nt*, Unglück *nt*

misgiving [mɪsˈgɪvɪŋ] *n* Bedenken *pl*; **to have ~s about sth** sich bei etw nicht wohlfühlen

misguided [mɪsˈgaɪdɪd] *adj* töricht; (*opinion, view*) irrig; (*misplaced*) unangebracht

mishandle [mɪsˈhændl] *vt* falsch handhaben

mishap [ˈmɪshæp] *n* Missgeschick *nt*

mishear [mɪsˈhɪəʳ] (*irreg: like* **hear**) *vt* falsch hören ▷ *vi* sich verhören

misheard [mɪsˈhəːd] *pt, pp of* **mishear**

mishmash [ˈmɪʃmæʃ] (*inf*) *n* Mischmasch *m*

misinform [mɪsɪnˈfɔːm] *vt* falsch informieren

misinterpret [mɪsɪnˈtəːprɪt] *vt* (*gesture, situation*) falsch auslegen; (*comment*) falsch auffassen

misinterpretation [ˈmɪsɪntəːprɪˈteɪʃən] *n* falsche Auslegung *f*

misjudge [mɪsˈdʒʌdʒ] *vt* falsch einschätzen

mislay [mɪsˈleɪ] (*irreg: like* **lay**) *vt* verlegen

mislead [mɪsˈliːd] (*irreg: like* **lead**) *vt* irreführen

misleading [mɪsˈliːdɪŋ] *adj* irreführend

misled [mɪsˈled] *pt, pp of* **mislead**

mismanage [mɪsˈmænɪdʒ] *vt* (*business*) herunterwirtschaften; (*institution*) schlecht führen

mismanagement [mɪsˈmænɪdʒmənt] *n* Misswirtschaft *f*

misnomer [mɪsˈnəuməʳ] *n* unzutreffende Bezeichnung *f*

misogynist [mɪˈsɒdʒɪnɪst] *n* Frauenfeind *m*

misplaced [mɪsˈpleɪst] *adj* (*misguided*) unangebracht; (*wrongly positioned*) an der falschen Stelle

misprint [ˈmɪsprɪnt] *n* Druckfehler *m*

mispronounce [mɪsprəˈnauns] *vt* falsch aussprechen

misquote [mɪsˈkwəut] *vt* falsch zitieren

misread [mɪsˈriːd] (*irreg: like* **read**) *vt* falsch lesen; (*misinterpret*) falsch verstehen

misrepresent [mɪsreprɪˈzent] *vt* falsch darstellen; **he was ~ed** seine Worte wurden verfälscht wiedergegeben

Miss [mɪs] *n* Fräulein *nt*; **Dear ~ Smith** Liebe Frau Smith

miss [mɪs] *vt* (*train etc, chance, opportunity*) verpassen; (*target*) verfehlen; (*notice loss of, regret absence of*) vermissen; (*class, meeting*) fehlen bei ▷ *vi* danebentreffen; (*missile, object*) danebengehen ▷ *n* Fehltreffer *m*; **you can't ~**

m

it du kannst es nicht verfehlen; **the bus just
~ed the wall** der Bus wäre um ein Haar gegen
die Mauer gefahren; **you're ~ing the point**
das geht an der Sache vorbei
▸ **miss out** (Brit) vt auslassen
▸ **miss out on** vt fus (party) verpassen; (fun) zu
kurz kommen bei
missal ['mɪsl] n Messbuch nt
misshapen [mɪs'ʃeɪpən] adj missgebildet
missile ['mɪsaɪl] n (Mil) Rakete f; (object thrown)
(Wurf)geschoss nt, (Wurf)geschoß nt (Öster)
missile base n Raketenbasis f
missile launcher [-'lɔːntʃəʳ] n Startrampe f
missing ['mɪsɪŋ] adj (lost: person) vermisst;
(: object) verschwunden; (absent, removed)
fehlend; **to be ~** fehlen; **to go ~**
verschwinden; **~ person** Vermisste(r) f(m)
mission ['mɪʃən] n (task) Mission f, Auftrag m;
(representatives) Gesandtschaft f; (Mil) Einsatz
m; (Rel) Mission f; **on a ~ to ...** (to place/people)
im Einsatz in +dat/bei ...
missionary ['mɪʃənrɪ] n Missionar(in) m(f)
missive ['mɪsɪv] (form) n Schreiben nt
misspell ['mɪs'spɛl] (irreg: like **spell**) vt falsch
schreiben
misspent ['mɪs'spɛnt] adj (youth) vergeudet
mist [mɪst] n Nebel m; (light) Dunst m ▷ vi
(also: **mist over**: eyes) sich verschleiern;
(Brit: also: **mist over, mist up**: windows)
beschlagen
mistake [mɪs'teɪk] (irreg: like **take**) n Fehler
m ▷ vt sich irren in +dat; (intentions) falsch
verstehen; **by ~** aus Versehen; **to make a ~**
(in writing, calculation) sich vertun; **to make a ~
(about sb/sth)** sich (in jdm/etw) irren; **to ~ A
for B** A mit B verwechseln
mistaken [mɪs'teɪkən] pp of **mistake** ▷ adj
falsch; **to be ~** sich irren
mistaken identity n Verwechslung f
mistakenly [mɪs'teɪkənlɪ] adv
irrtümlicherweise
mister ['mɪstəʳ] (inf) n (sir) not translated; see **Mr**
mistletoe ['mɪsltəu] n Mistel f
mistook [mɪs'tuk] pt of **mistake**
mistranslation [mɪstræns'leɪʃən] n falsche
Übersetzung f
mistreat [mɪs'triːt] vt schlecht behandeln
mistress ['mɪstrɪs] n (lover) Geliebte f; (of house,
servant, situation) Herrin f; (Brit: teacher) Lehrerin
f
mistrust [mɪs'trʌst] vt misstrauen +dat ▷ n: ~
(of) Misstrauen nt (gegenüber)
mistrustful [mɪs'trʌstful] adj: ~ **(of)**
misstrauisch (gegenüber)
misty ['mɪstɪ] adj (day etc) neblig; (glasses,
windows) beschlagen
misty-eyed ['mɪstɪ'aɪd] adj mit verschleiertem
Blick
misunderstand [mɪsʌndə'stænd] (irreg:
like **understand**) vt missverstehen, falsch
verstehen ▷ vi es falsch verstehen
misunderstanding ['mɪsʌndə'stændɪŋ]
n Missverständnis nt; (disagreement)

Meinungsverschiedenheit f
misunderstood [mɪsʌndə'stud] pt, pp of
misunderstand
misuse [n mɪs'juːs, vt mɪs'juːz] n Missbrauch m
▷ vt missbrauchen; (word) falsch gebrauchen
MIT (US) n abbr (= Massachusetts Institute of
Technology) private technische Fachhochschule
mite [maɪt] n (small quantity) bisschen nt;
(Brit: small child) Würmchen nt
miter ['maɪtəʳ] (US) n = **mitre**
mitigate ['mɪtɪgeɪt] vt mildern; **mitigating
circumstances** mildernde Umstände pl
mitigation [mɪtɪ'geɪʃən] n Milderung f
mitre, (US) **miter** ['maɪtəʳ] n (of bishop) Mitra f;
(Carpentry) Gehrung f
mitt ['mɪt], **mitten** ['mɪtn] n Fausthandschuh
m
mix [mɪks] vt mischen; (drink) mixen; (sauce,
cake) zubereiten; (ingredients) verrühren ▷ vi: **to
~ (with)** verkehren (mit) ▷ n Mischung f; **to
~ sth with sth** etw mit etw vermischen; **to
~ business with pleasure** das Angenehme
mit dem Nützlichen verbinden; **cake ~**
Backmischung f
▸ **mix in** vt (eggs etc) unterrühren
▸ **mix up** vt (people) verwechseln; (things)
durcheinanderbringen; **to be ~ed up in sth**
in etw acc verwickelt sein
mixed [mɪkst] adj gemischt; **~ marriage**
Mischehe f
mixed-ability ['mɪkstə'bɪlɪtɪ] adj (group etc) mit
unterschiedlichen Fähigkeiten
mixed bag n (of things, problems) Sammelsurium
nt; (of people) gemischter Haufen m
mixed blessing n: **it's a ~** das ist ein
zweischneidiges Schwert
mixed doubles npl gemischtes Doppel nt
mixed economy n gemischte
Wirtschaftsform f
mixed grill (Brit) n Grillteller m
mixed-up [mɪkst'ʌp] adj durcheinander
mixer ['mɪksəʳ] n (for food) Mixer m; (drink) Tonic
etc zum Auffüllen von alkoholischen Mixgetränken;
to be a good ~ (sociable person) kontaktfreudig
sein
mixer tap n Mischbatterie f
mixture ['mɪkstʃəʳ] n Mischung f; (Culin)
Gemisch nt; (: for cake) Teig m; (Med) Mixtur f
mix-up ['mɪksʌp] n Durcheinander nt
MK (Brit) abbr (Tech) = **mark**
mkt abbr = **market**
MLA (Brit) n abbr (Pol: = Member of the Legislative
Assembly (of Northern Ireland)) Abgeordnete(r) f(m)
der gesetzgebenden Versammlung
MLitt n abbr (= Master of Literature, Master of Letters)
akademischer Grad in Literaturwissenschaft
MLR (Brit) n abbr = **minimum lending rate**
mm abbr (= millimetre) mm
MMS n abbr (= Multimedia Messaging Service)
MMS® m
MN abbr (Brit) = **merchant navy**;
(US: Post) = Minnesota
MO n abbr (= medical officer) Sanitätsoffizier m;

(US: inf) = **modus operandi**

moan [məʊn] n Stöhnen nt ▷ vi stöhnen; (inf: complain): **to ~ (about)** meckern (über +acc)

moaner ['məʊnəʳ] (inf) n Miesmacher(in) m(f)

moat [məʊt] n Wassergraben m

mob [mɒb] n Mob m; (organized) Bande f ▷ vt herfallen über +acc

mobile ['məʊbaɪl] adj beweglich; (workforce, society) mobil ▷ n (decoration) Mobile nt; **applicants must be ~** Bewerber müssen motorisiert sein

mobile home n Wohnwagen m

mobile (phone) n Funktelefon nt, Handy nt

mobility [məʊ'bɪlɪtɪ] n Beweglichkeit f; (of workforce etc) Mobilität f

mobility allowance n Beihilfe für Gehbehinderte

mobilize ['məʊbɪlaɪz] vt mobilisieren; (Mil) mobil machen ▷ vi (Mil) mobil machen

moccasin ['mɒkəsɪn] n Mokassin m

mock [mɒk] vt sich lustig machen über +acc ▷ adj (fake: Elizabethan etc) Pseudo-; (exam) Probe-; (battle) Schein-

mockery ['mɒkərɪ] n Spott m; **to make a ~ of sb** jdn zum Gespött machen; **to make a ~ of sth** etw zur Farce machen

mocking ['mɒkɪŋ] adj spöttisch groß

mockingbird ['mɒkɪŋbɜːd] n Spottdrossel f

mock-up ['mɒkʌp] n Modell nt

MOD (Brit) n abbr = **Ministry of Defence**

mod cons ['mɒd'kɒnz] (Brit) npl (= modern conveniences) Komfort m

mode [məʊd] n Form f; (Comput, Tech) Betriebsart f; **~ of life** Lebensweise f; **~ of transport** Transportmittel nt

model ['mɒdl] n Modell nt; (also: **fashion model**) Mannequin nt; (example) Muster nt ▷ adj (excellent) vorbildlich; (small scale: railway etc) Modell- ▷ vt (clothes) vorführen; (with clay etc) modellieren, formen ▷ vi (for designer, photographer etc) als Modell arbeiten; **to ~ o.s. on sb** sich dat jdn zum Vorbild nehmen

modeller, (US) **modeler** ['mɒdləʳ] n Modellbauer m

model railway n Modelleisenbahn f

modem ['məʊdɛm] n Modem nt

moderate [adj 'mɒdərət, vb 'mɒdəreɪt] adj gemäßigt; (amount) nicht allzu groß; (change) leicht ▷ n Gemäßigte(r) f(m) ▷ vi (storm, wind etc) nachlassen ▷ vt (tone, demands) mäßigen

moderately ['mɒdərətlɪ] adv mäßig; (expensive, difficult) nicht allzu; (pleased, happy) einigermaßen; **~ priced** nicht allzu teuer

moderation [mɒdə'reɪʃən] n Mäßigung f; **in ~** in or mit Maßen

moderator ['mɒdəreɪtəʳ] n (Eccl) Synodalpräsident m

modern ['mɒdən] adj modern; **~ languages** moderne Fremdsprachen pl

modernization [mɒdənaɪ'zeɪʃən] n Modernisierung f

modernize ['mɒdənaɪz] vt modernisieren

modest ['mɒdɪst] adj bescheiden; (chaste) schamhaft

modestly ['mɒdɪstlɪ] adv bescheiden; (behave) schamhaft; (to a moderate extent) mäßig

modesty ['mɒdɪstɪ] n Bescheidenheit f; (chastity) Schamgefühl nt

modicum ['mɒdɪkəm] n: **a ~ of** ein wenig or bisschen

modification [mɒdɪfɪ'keɪʃən] n Änderung f; (to policy etc) Modifizierung f; **to make ~s to** (Ver)änderungen vornehmen an +dat, modifizieren

modify ['mɒdɪfaɪ] vt (ver)ändern; (policy etc) modifizieren

modish ['məʊdɪʃ] adj (fashionable) modisch

Mods [mɒdz] (Brit) n abbr (Scol: = (Honour) Moderations) akademische Prüfung an der Universität Oxford

modular ['mɒdjʊləʳ] adj (unit, furniture) aus Bauelementen (zusammengesetzt); (Comput) modular

modulate ['mɒdjʊleɪt] vt modulieren; (process, activity) umwandeln

modulation [mɒdju'leɪʃən] n Modulation f; (modification) Veränderung f

module ['mɒdjuːl] n (Bau)element nt; (Space) Raumkapsel f; (Scol) Kurs m

modus operandi ['məʊdəsɔpə'rændiː] n Modus Operandi m

Mogadishu [mɒgə'dɪʃuː] n Mogadischu nt

mogul ['məʊgl] n (fig) Mogul m

MOH (Brit) n abbr (= Medical Officer of Health) Amtsarzt m, Amtsärztin f

mohair ['məʊhɛəʳ] n Mohair m

Mohammed [mə'hæmɛd] n Mohammed m

moist [mɔɪst] adj feucht

moisten ['mɔɪsn] vt anfeuchten

moisture ['mɔɪstʃəʳ] n Feuchtigkeit f

moisturize ['mɔɪstʃəraɪz] vt (skin) mit einer Feuchtigkeitscreme behandeln

moisturizer ['mɔɪstʃəraɪzəʳ] n Feuchtigkeitscreme f

molar ['məʊləʳ] n Backenzahn m

molasses [mə'læsɪz] n Melasse f

mold etc [məʊld] (US) n, vt = **mould** etc

Moldavia [mɒl'deɪvɪə] n Moldawien nt

Moldavian [mɒl'deɪvɪən] adj moldawisch

Moldova [mɒl'dəʊvə] n Moldawien nt

Moldovan adj moldawisch

mole [məʊl] n (on skin) Leberfleck m; (Zool) Maulwurf m; (fig: spy) Spion(in) m(f)

molecular [məʊ'lɛkjʊləʳ] adj molekular; (biology) Molekular-

molecule ['mɒlɪkjuːl] n Molekül nt

molehill ['məʊlhɪl] n Maulwurfshaufen m

molest [mə'lɛst] vt (assault sexually) sich vergehen an +dat; (harass) belästigen

mollusc ['mɒləsk] n Weichtier nt

mollycoddle ['mɒlɪkɒdl] vt verhätscheln

Molotov cocktail ['mɒlətɔf-] n Molotowcocktail m

molt [məʊlt] (US) vi = **moult**

molten ['məʊltən] adj geschmolzen, flüssig

mom [mɒm] (US) n = **mum**

moment ['məʊmənt] n Moment m, Augenblick m; (importance) Bedeutung f; **for a**

~ (für) einen Moment or Augenblick; **at that**
~ in diesem Moment or Augenblick; **at the ~**
momentan; **for the ~** vorläufig; **in a ~** gleich;
"one ~ please" (Tel) „bleiben Sie am Apparat"
momentarily ['məuməntrılı] adv für einen
Augenblick or Moment; (US: very soon) jeden
Augenblick or Moment
momentary ['məuməntərı] adj (brief) kurz
momentous [məu'mɛntəs] adj (occasion)
bedeutsam; (decision) von großer Tragweite
momentum [məu'mɛntəm] n (Phys) Impuls m;
(fig: of movement) Schwung m; (: of events, change)
Dynamik f; **to gather ~** schneller werden; (fig)
richtig in Gang kommen
mommy ['mɔmɪ] (US) n = **mummy**
Mon. abbr (= Monday) Mo.
Monaco ['mɔnəkəu] n Monaco nt
monarch ['mɔnək] n Monarch(in) m(f)
monarchist ['mɔnəkɪst] n Monarchist(in) m(f)
monarchy ['mɔnəkı] n Monarchie f; **the M~**
(royal family) die königliche Familie
monastery ['mɔnəstərı] n Kloster nt
monastic [mə'næstık] adj Kloster-, klösterlich;
(fig) mönchisch, klösterlich einfach
Monday ['mʌndı] n Montag m; see also **Tuesday**
Monegasque [mɔnə'gæsk] adj monegassisch
▷ n Monegasse m, Monegassin f
monetarist ['mʌnıtərıst] n Monetarist(in) m(f)
▷ adj monetaristisch
monetary ['mʌnıtərı] adj (system, union)
Währungs-
money ['mʌnı] n Geld nt; **to make ~** (person)
Geld verdienen; (business) etwas einbringen;
danger ~ (Brit) Gefahrenzulage f; **I've got no
~ left** ich habe kein Geld mehr
moneyed ['mʌnıd] (form) adj begütert
moneylender ['mʌnılɛndəʳ] n
Geldverleiher(in) m(f)
moneymaker ['mʌnımeıkəʳ] n (person)
Finanzgenie nt; (idea) einträgliche Sache f;
(product) Verkaufserfolg m
moneymaking ['mʌnımeıkıŋ] adj einträglich
money market n Geldmarkt m
money order n Zahlungsanweisung f
money-spinner ['mʌnıspınəʳ] (inf) n
Verkaufsschlager m; (person, business)
Goldgrube f
money supply n Geldvolumen nt
Mongol ['mɔŋgəl] n Mongole m, Mongolin f;
(Ling) Mongolisch nt
mongol ['mɔŋgəl] (offensive) n Mongoloide(r)
f(m)
Mongolia [mɔŋ'gəulıə] n die Mongolei
Mongolian [mɔŋ'gəulıən] adj mongolisch ▷ n
Mongole m, Mongolin f; (Ling) Mongolisch nt
mongoose ['mɔŋguːs] n Mungo m
mongrel ['mʌŋgrəl] n Promenadenmischung f
monitor ['mɔnıtəʳ] n Monitor m ▷ vt
überwachen; (broadcasts) mithören
monk [mʌŋk] n Mönch m
monkey ['mʌŋkı] n Affe m
monkey business (inf) n faule Sachen pl
monkey nut (Brit) n Erdnuss f

monkey tricks npl = **monkey business**
monkey wrench n verstellbarer
Schraubenschlüssel m
mono ['mɔnəu] adj (recording etc) Mono-
monochrome ['mɔnəkrəum] adj (photograph,
television) Schwarzweiß-; (Comput: screen)
Monochrom-
monogamous [mə'nɔgəməs] adj monogam
monogamy [mə'nɔgəmı] n Monogamie f
monogram ['mɔnəgræm] n Monogramm nt
monolith ['mɔnəlıθ] n Monolith m
monolithic [mɔnə'lıθık] adj monolithisch
monologue ['mɔnəlɔg] n Monolog m
monoplane ['mɔnəpleın] n Eindecker m
monopolize [mə'nɔpəlaız] vt beherrschen;
(person) mit Beschlag belegen; (conversation) an
sich acc reißen
monopoly [mə'nɔpəlı] n Monopol nt; **to have
a ~ on** or **of sth** (fig: domination) etw für sich
gepachtet haben; **Monopolies and Mergers
Commission** (Brit) ≈ Kartellamt nt
monorail ['mɔnəureıl] n Einschienenbahn f
monosodium glutamate [mɔnə'səudıəm-
'gluːtəmeıt] n Glutamat nt
monosyllabic [mɔnəsı'læbık] adj einsilbig
monosyllable ['mɔnəsıləbl] n einsilbiges
Wort nt
monotone ['mɔnətəun] n: **in a ~** monoton
monotonous [mə'nɔtənəs] adj monoton,
eintönig
monotony [mə'nɔtənı] n Monotonie f,
Eintönigkeit f
monsoon [mɔn'suːn] n Monsun m
monster ['mɔnstəʳ] n Ungetüm nt, Monstrum
nt; (imaginary creature) Ungeheuer nt, Monster
nt; (person) Unmensch m
monstrosity [mɔn'strɔsıtı] n Ungetüm nt,
Monstrum nt
monstrous ['mɔnstrəs] adj (huge) riesig; (ugly)
abscheulich; (atrocious) ungeheuerlich
Mont. (US) abbr (Post) = Montana
montage [mɔn'taːʒ] n Montage f
Mont Blanc [mɔ̃'blɑ̃] n Montblanc m
month [mʌnθ] n Monat m; **every ~** jeden
Monat; **300 dollars a ~** 300 Dollar im Monat
monthly ['mʌnθlı] adj monatlich; (ticket,
magazine) Monats- ▷ adv monatlich; **twice ~**
zweimal im Monat
Montreal [mɔntrı'ɔːl] n Montreal nt
monument ['mɔnjumənt] n Denkmal nt
monumental [mɔnju'mɛntl] adj (building,
statue) gewaltig, monumental; (book, piece of
work) unsterblich; (storm, row) ungeheuer
moo [muː] vi muhen
mood [muːd] n Stimmung f; (of person) Laune
f, Stimmung f; **to be in a good/bad ~** gut/
schlecht gelaunt sein; **to be in the ~ for**
aufgelegt sein zu
moodily ['muːdılı] adv launisch; (sullenly)
schlecht gelaunt
moody ['muːdı] adj launisch; (sullen) schlecht
gelaunt
moon [muːn] n Mond m

moonlight ['mu:nlaɪt] n Mondschein m ▷ vi (inf) schwarzarbeiten
moonlighting ['mu:nlaɪtɪŋ] (inf) n Schwarzarbeit f
moonlit ['mu:nlɪt] adj (night) mondhell
moonshot ['mu:nʃɒt] n Mondflug m
moor [muər] n (Hoch)moor nt, Heide f ▷ vt vertäuen ▷ vi anlegen
mooring ['muərɪŋ] n Anlegeplatz m; **moorings** npl (chains) Verankerung f
Moorish ['muərɪʃ] adj maurisch
moorland ['muələnd] n Moorlandschaft f, Heidelandschaft f
moose [mu:s] n inv Elch m
moot [mu:t] vt: **to be ~ed** vorgeschlagen werden ▷ adj: **it's a ~ point** das ist fraglich
mop [mɒp] n (for floor) Mop m; (for dishes) Spülbürste f; (of hair) Mähne f ▷ vt (floor) wischen; (face) abwischen; (eyes) sich dat wischen; **to ~ the sweat from one's brow** sich dat den Schweiß von der Stirn wischen
 ▶ **mop up** vt aufwischen
mope [məup] vi Trübsal blasen
 ▶ **mope about** vi mit einer Jammermiene herumlaufen
 ▶ **mope around** vi = **mope about**
moped ['məupɛd] n Moped nt
moquette [mɒ'kɛt] n Mokett m
MOR adj abbr (Mus) = **middle-of-the-road**
moral ['mɒrl] adj moralisch; (welfare, values) sittlich; (behaviour) moralisch einwandfrei ▷ n Moral f; **morals** npl (principles, values) Moralvorstellungen pl; **~ support** moralische Unterstützung f
morale [mɒ'rɑ:l] n Moral f
morality [mə'rælɪtɪ] n Sittlichkeit f; (system of morals) Moral f, Ethik f; (correctness) moralische Richtigkeit f
moralize ['mɒrəlaɪz] vi moralisieren; **to ~ about** sich moralisch entrüsten über +acc
morally ['mɒrəlɪ] adv moralisch; (live, behave) moralisch einwandfrei
moral victory n moralischer Sieg m
morass [mə'ræs] n Morast m, Sumpf m, Sumpf m (also fig)
moratorium [mɒrə'tɔ:rɪəm] n Stopp m; Moratorium nt
morbid ['mɔ:bɪd] adj (imagination) krankhaft; (interest) unnatürlich; (comments, behaviour) makaber

⊙ KEYWORD

more [mɔ:ʳ] adj 1 (greater in number etc) mehr; **more people/work/letters than we expected** mehr Leute/Arbeit/Briefe, als wir erwarteten; **I have more wine/money than you** ich habe mehr Wein/Geld als du
 2 (additional): **do you want (some) more tea?** möchten Sie noch mehr Tee?; **is there any more wine?** ist noch Wein da?; **I have no more money, I don't have any more money** ich habe kein Geld mehr

 ▷ pron 1 (greater amount) mehr; **more than 10** mehr als 10; **it cost more than we expected** es kostete mehr, als wir erwarteten
 2 (further or additional amount): **is there any more?** gibt es noch mehr?; **there's no more** es ist nichts mehr da; **many/much more** viel mehr

 ▷ adv mehr; **more dangerous/difficult/easily** etc (than) gefährlicher/schwerer/leichter etc (als); **more and more** mehr und mehr, immer mehr; **more and more excited/expensive** immer aufgeregter/teurer; **more or less** mehr oder weniger; **more than ever** mehr denn je, mehr als jemals zuvor; **more beautiful than ever** schöner denn je; **no more, not any more** nicht mehr

moreover [mɔ:'rəuvəʳ] adv außerdem, zudem
morgue [mɔ:g] n Leichenschauhaus nt
MORI ['mɔ:rɪ] (Brit) n abbr (= Market and Opinion Research Institute) Markt- und Meinungsforschungsinstitut
moribund ['mɒrɪbʌnd] adj dem Untergang geweiht
Mormon ['mɔ:mən] n Mormone m, Mormonin f
morning ['mɔ:nɪŋ] n Morgen m; (as opposed to afternoon) Vormittag m ▷ cpd Morgen-; **in the ~** morgens; vormittags; (tomorrow) morgen früh; **7 o'clock in the ~** 7 Uhr morgens; **this ~** heute Morgen
morning-after pill ['mɔ:nɪŋ'ɑ:ftə-] n Pille f danach
morning market n (Econ) Vormittagsmarkt m
morning sickness n (Schwangerschafts) übelkeit f
Moroccan [mə'rɒkən] adj marokkanisch ▷ n Marokkaner(in) m(f)
Morocco [mə'rɒkəu] n Marokko nt
moron ['mɔ:rɒn] (inf) n Schwachkopf m
moronic [mə'rɒnɪk] (inf) adj schwachsinnig
morose [mə'rəus] adj missmutig
morphine ['mɔ:fi:n] n Morphium nt
morris dancing ['mɒrɪs-] n Moriskentanz m, alter englischer Volkstanz
Morse [mɔ:s] n (also: **Morse code**) Morsealphabet nt
morsel ['mɔ:sl] n Stückchen nt
mortal ['mɔ:tl] adj sterblich; (wound, combat) tödlich; (danger) Todes-; (sin, enemy) Tod- ▷ n (human being) Sterbliche(r) f(m)
mortality [mɔ:'tælɪtɪ] n Sterblichkeit f; (number of deaths) Todesfälle pl
mortality rate n Sterblichkeitsziffer f
mortar ['mɔ:təʳ] n (Mil) Minenwerfer m; (Constr) Mörtel m; (Culin) Mörser m
mortgage ['mɔ:gɪdʒ] n Hypothek f ▷ vt mit einer Hypothek belasten; **to take out a ~** eine Hypothek aufnehmen
mortgage company (US) n Hypothekenbank f
mortgagee [mɔ:gə'dʒi:] n Hypothekengläubiger m

m

mortgagor ['mɔ:gədʒəʳ] n Hypotheken-schuldner m

mortician [mɔ:'tɪʃn] (US) n Bestattungs-unternehmer m

mortified ['mɔ:tɪfaɪd] adj: **he was ~** er empfand das als beschämend; (embarrassed) es war ihm schrecklich peinlich

mortify ['mɔ:tɪfaɪ] vt beschämen

mortise lock ['mɔ:tɪs-] n Einsteckschloss nt

mortuary ['mɔ:tjuərɪ] n Leichenhalle f

mosaic [məu'zeɪɪk] n Mosaik nt

Moscow ['mɔskəu] n Moskau nt

Moslem ['mɔzləm] adj, n = **Muslim**

mosque [mɔsk] n Moschee f

mosquito [mɔs'ki:təu] (pl **~es**) n Stechmücke f; (in tropics) Moskito m

mosquito net n Moskitonetz nt

moss [mɔs] n Moos nt

mossy ['mɔsɪ] adj bemoost

 KEYWORD

most [məust] adj **1** (almost all: people, things etc) meiste(r, s); **most people** die meisten Leute **2** (largest, greatest: interest, money etc) meiste(r, s); **who has (the) most money?** wer hat das meiste Geld?
▷ pron (greatest quantity, number) der/die/das meiste; **most of it** das meiste (davon); **most of them** die meisten von ihnen; **most of the time/work** die meiste Zeit/Arbeit; **most of the time he's very helpful** er ist meistens sehr hilfsbereit; **to make the most of sth** das Beste aus etw machen; **at the (very) most** (aller)höchstens
▷ adv (+ vb: spend, eat, work etc) am meisten; (+ adv: carefully, easily etc) äußerst; (very: polite, interesting etc) höchst; (+ adj): **the most intelligent/expensive** etc der/die/das intelligenteste/teuerste etc; **a most interesting book** ein höchst interessantes Buch

mostly ['məustlɪ] adv (chiefly) hauptsächlich; (usually) meistens

MOT (Brit) n abbr (= Ministry of Transport): **~ (test)** ≈ TÜV m; **the car failed its ~** das Auto ist nicht durch den TÜV gekommen

motel [məu'tɛl] n Motel nt

moth [mɔθ] n Nachtfalter m; (also: **clothes moth**) Motte f

mothball ['mɔθbɔ:l] n Mottenkugel f

moth-eaten ['mɔθi:tn] (pej) adj mottenzerfressen

mother ['mʌðəʳ] n Mutter f ▷ adj (country) Heimat-; (company) Mutter- ▷ vt großziehen; (pamper, protect) bemuttern

motherboard ['mʌðəbɔ:d] n (Comput) Hauptplatine f

motherhood ['mʌðəhud] n Mutterschaft f

mother-in-law ['mʌðərɪnlɔ:] n Schwiegermutter f

motherly ['mʌðəlɪ] adj mütterlich

mother-of-pearl ['mʌðərəv'pə:l] n Perlmutt nt

mother's help n Haushaltshilfe f

mother-to-be ['mʌðətə'bi:] n werdende Mutter f

mother tongue n Muttersprache f

mothproof ['mɔθpru:f] adj mottenfest

motif [məu'ti:f] n Motiv nt

motion ['məuʃən] n Bewegung f; (proposal) Antrag m; (Brit: also: **bowel motion**) Stuhlgang m ▷ vt, vi: **to ~ (to) sb to do sth** jdm ein Zeichen geben, dass er/sie etw tun solle; **to be in ~** (vehicle) fahren; **to set in ~** in Gang bringen; **to go through the ~s (of doing sth)** (fig) etw der Form halber tun; (pretend) so tun, als ob (man etw täte)

motionless ['məuʃənlɪs] adj reg(ungs)los

motion picture n Film m

motivate ['məutɪveɪt] vt motivieren

motivated ['məutɪveɪtɪd] adj motiviert; **~ by** getrieben von

motivation [məutɪ'veɪʃən] n Motivation f

motive ['məutɪv] n Motiv nt, Beweggrund m ▷ adj (power, force) Antriebs-; **from the best (of) ~s** mit den besten Absichten

motley ['mɔtlɪ] adj bunt (gemischt)

motor ['məutəʳ] n Motor m; (Brit: inf: car) Auto nt ▷ cpd (industry, trade) Auto(mobil)-

motorbike ['məutəbaɪk] n Motorrad nt

motorboat ['məutəbəut] n Motorboot nt

motorcade ['məutəkeɪd] n Fahrzeugkolonne f

motorcar ['məutəka:] (Brit) n (Personenkraft) wagen m

motorcoach ['məutəkəutʃ] (Brit) n Reisebus m

motorcycle ['məutəsaɪkl] n Motorrad nt

motorcycle racing n Motorradrennen nt

motorcyclist ['məutəsaɪklɪst] n Motorradfahrer(in) m(f)

motoring ['məutərɪŋ] (Brit) n Autofahren nt ▷ cpd Auto-; (offence, accident) Verkehrs-

motorist ['məutərɪst] n Autofahrer(in) m(f)

motorized ['məutəraɪzd] adj motorisiert

motor oil n Motorenöl nt

motor racing (Brit) n Autorennen nt

motor scooter n Motorroller m

motor vehicle n Kraftfahrzeug nt

motorway ['məutəweɪ] (Brit) n Autobahn f

mottled ['mɔtld] adj gesprenkelt

motto ['mɔtəu] (pl **~es**) n Motto nt

mould, (US) **mold** [məuld] n (cast) Form f; (: for metal) Gussform f; (mildew) Schimmel m ▷ vt (lit, fig) formen

moulder, (US) **molder** ['məuldəʳ] vi (decay) vermodern

moulding, (US) **molding** ['məuldɪŋ] n (Archit) Zierleiste f

mouldy, (US) **moldy** ['məuldɪ] adj schimmelig; (smell) moderig

moult, (US) **molt** [məult] vi (animal) sich haaren; (bird) sich mausern

mound [maund] n (of earth) Hügel m; (heap) Haufen m

mount [maunt] n (in proper names): **M~ Carmel** der Berg Karmel; (horse) Pferd nt; (for picture)

Passepartout *nt* ▷ *vt* (*horse*) besteigen; (*exhibition etc*) vorbereiten; (*jewel*) (ein)fassen; (*picture*) mit einem Passepartout versehen; (*staircase*) hochgehen; (*stamp*) aufkleben; (*attack, campaign*) organisieren ▷ *vi* (*increase*) steigen; (: *problems*) sich häufen; (*on horse*) aufsitzen

▶ **mount up** *vi* (*costs, savings*) sich summieren, sich zusammenläppern (*inf*)

mountain ['mauntɪn] *n* Berg *m* ▷ *cpd* (*road, stream*) Gebirgs-; **to make a ~ out of a molehill** aus einer Mücke einen Elefanten machen

mountain bike *n* Mountainbike *nt*

mountaineer [mauntɪ'nɪə^r] *n* Bergsteiger(in) *m(f)*

mountaineering [mauntɪ'nɪərɪŋ] *n* Bergsteigen *nt*; **to go ~** bergsteigen gehen

mountainous ['mauntɪnəs] *adj* gebirgig

mountain range *n* Gebirgskette *f*

mountain rescue team *n* Bergwacht *f*

mountainside ['mauntɪnsaɪd] *n* (Berg)hang *m*

mounted ['mauntɪd] *adj* (*police*) beritten

Mount Everest *n* Mount Everest *m*

mourn [mɔːn] *vt* betrauern ▷ *vi*: **to ~ (for)** trauern (um)

mourner ['mɔːnə^r] *n* Trauernde(r) *f(m)*

mournful ['mɔːnful] *adj* traurig

mourning ['mɔːnɪŋ] *n* Trauer *f*; **to be in ~** trauern; (*wear special clothes*) Trauer tragen

mouse [maus] (*pl* **mice**) *n* (*Zool, Comput*) Maus *f*; (*fig: person*) schüchternes Mäuschen *nt*

mouse potato *n* (*inf*) Computerjunkie *m*, Mouse Potato *f*

mousetrap ['maustræp] *n* Mausefalle *f*

moussaka [muːˈsɑːkə] *n* Moussaka *f*

mousse [muːs] *n* (*Culin*) Mousse *f*; (*cosmetic*) Schaumfestiger *m*

moustache, (*US*) **mustache** [məsˈtɑːʃ] *n* Schnurrbart *m*

mousy ['mausɪ] *adj* (*hair*) mausgrau

mouth [mauθ] (*pl* **~s**) *n* Mund *m*; (*of cave, hole, bottle*) Öffnung *f*; (*of river*) Mündung *f*

mouthful ['mauθful] *n* (*of food*) Bissen *m*; (*of drink*) Schluck *m*

mouth organ *n* Mundharmonika *f*

mouthpiece ['mauθpiːs] *n* Mundstück *nt*; (*spokesman*) Sprachrohr *nt*

mouth-to-mouth ['mauθtə'mauθ] *adj*: **~ resuscitation** Mund-zu-Mund-Beatmung *f*

mouthwash ['mauθwɔʃ] *n* Mundwasser *nt*

mouth-watering ['mauθwɔːtərɪŋ] *adj* appetitlich

movable ['muːvəbl] *adj* beweglich; **~ feast** beweglicher Feiertag *m*

move [muːv] *n* (*movement*) Bewegung *f*; (*in game*) Zug *m*; (*change: of house*) Umzug *m*; (: *of job*) Stellenwechsel *m* ▷ *vt* bewegen; (*furniture*) (ver)rücken; (*car*) umstellen; (*in game*) ziehen mit; (*emotionally*) bewegen, ergreifen; (*Pol: resolution etc*) beantragen ▷ *vi* sich bewegen; (*traffic*) vorankommen; (*in game*) ziehen; (*also*: **move house**) umziehen; (*develop*) sich entwickeln;

it's my ~ ich bin am Zug; **to get a ~ on** sich beeilen; **to ~ sb to do sth** jdn (dazu) veranlassen, etw zu tun; **to ~ towards** sich nähern +*dat*

▶ **move about** *vi* sich (hin- und her) bewegen; (*travel*) unterwegs sein; (*from place to place*) umherziehen; (*change residence*) umziehen; (*change job*) die Stelle wechseln; **I can hear him moving about** ich höre ihn herumlaufen

▶ **move along** *vi* weitergehen

▶ **move around** *vi* = **move about**

▶ **move away** *vi* (*from town, area*) wegziehen

▶ **move back** *vi* (*return*) zurückkommen

▶ **move forward** *vi* (*advance*) vorrücken

▶ **move in** *vi* (*to house*) einziehen; (*police, soldiers*) anrücken

▶ **move off** *vi* (*car*) abfahren

▶ **move on** *vi* (*leave*) weitergehen; (*travel*) weiterfahren ▷ *vt* (*onlookers*) zum Weitergehen auffordern

▶ **move out** *vi* (*of house*) ausziehen

▶ **move over** *vi* (*to make room*) (zur Seite) rücken

▶ **move up** *vi* (*employee*) befördert werden; (*pupil*) versetzt werden; (*deputy*) aufrücken

moveable ['muːvəbl] *adj* = **movable**

movement ['muːvmənt] *n* (*action, group*) Bewegung *f*; (*freedom to move*) Bewegungsfreiheit *f*; (*transportation*) Beförderung *f*; (*shift*) Trend *m*; (*Mus*) Satz *m*; (*Med: also*: **bowel movement**) Stuhlgang *m*

mover ['muːvə^r] *n* (*of proposal*) Antragsteller(in) *m(f)*

movie ['muːvɪ] *n* Film *m*; **to go to the ~s** ins Kino gehen

movie camera *n* Filmkamera *f*

moviegoer ['muːvɪɡəuə^r] (*US*) *n* Kinogänger(in) *m(f)*

moving ['muːvɪŋ] *adj* beweglich; (*emotional*) ergreifend; (*instigating*): **the ~ spirit/force** die treibende Kraft

mow [məu] (*pt* **~ed**, *pp* **mowed** *or* **~n**) *vt* mähen

▶ **mow down** *vt* (*kill*) niedermähen

mower ['məuə^r] *n* (*also*: **lawnmower**) Rasenmäher *m*

Mozambique [məuzəm'biːk] *n* Mosambik *nt*

MP *n abbr* (= *Member of Parliament*) ≈ MdB; = **military police**; (*Canada*: = *Mounted Police*) berittene Polizei *f*

MP3 *abbr* (*Comput*) MP3

MP3 player *n* (*Comput*) MP3-Spieler *m*

mpg *n abbr* (= *miles per gallon*) *see* **mile**

mph *abbr* (= *miles per hour*) Meilen pro Stunde

MPhil *n abbr* (= *Master of Philosophy*) ≈ M.A.

MPS (*Brit*) *n abbr* (= *Member of the Pharmaceutical Society*) *Qualifikationsnachweis für Pharmazeuten*

Mr, (*US*) **Mr.** ['mɪstə^r] *n*: **Mr Smith** Herr Smith

MRC (*Brit*) *n abbr* (= *Medical Research Council*) *medizinischer Forschungsausschuss*

MRCP (*Brit*) *n abbr* (= *Member of the Royal College of Physicians*) *höchster akademischer Grad in Medizin*

MRCS (*Brit*) *n abbr* (= *Member of the Royal College of Surgeons*) *höchster akademischer Grad für Chirurgen*

m

MRCVS (Brit) n abbr (= Member of the Royal College of Veterinary Surgeons) höchster akademischer Grad für Tiermediziner

Mrs, (US) **Mrs.** ['mɪsɪz] n: ~ **Smith** Frau Smith

MS n abbr (= multiple sclerosis) MS f; (US: = Master of Science) akademischer Grad in Naturwissenschaften ▷ abbr (US: Post) = Mississippi

MS. (pl **MSS.**) n abbr (= manuscript) Ms.

Ms, (US) **Ms.** [mɪz] n (= Miss or Mrs): **Ms Smith** Frau Smith

MSA n abbr (= Master of Science in Agriculture) akademischer Grad in Agronomie

MSc n abbr (= Master of Science) akademischer Grad in Naturwissenschaften

MSG n abbr = **monosodium glutamate**

MSP (Brit) n abbr (Pol: = Member of the Scottish Parliament) Abgeordnete(r) f(m) des schottischen Parlaments

MST (US) abbr (= Mountain Standard Time) amerikanische Standardzeitzone

MSW (US) n abbr (= Master of Social Work) akademischer Grad in Sozialwissenschaft

MT n abbr (Comput, Ling: = machine translation) maschinelle Übersetzung f

Mt abbr (Geog) = **mount**

MTV (esp US) n abbr (= music television) MTV nt

 KEYWORD

much [mʌtʃ] adj (time, money, effort) viel; **how much money/time do you need?** wie viel Geld/Zeit brauchen Sie?; **he's done so much work for us** er hat so viel für uns gearbeitet; **as much as** so viel wie; **I have as much money/intelligence as you** ich besitze genauso viel Geld/Intelligenz wie du ▷ pron viel; **how much is it?** was kostet es? ▷ adv **1** (greatly, a great deal) sehr; **thank you very much** vielen Dank, danke sehr; **I read as much as I can** ich lese so viel wie ich kann **2** (by far) viel; **I'm much better now** mir geht es jetzt viel besser **3** (almost) fast; **how are you feeling? — much the same** wie fühlst du dich? — fast genauso; **the two books are much the same** die zwei Bücher sind sich sehr ähnlich

muck [mʌk] n (dirt) Dreck m
▶ **muck about** (inf) vi (fool about) herumalbern ▷ vt: **to ~ sb about** mit jdm beliebig umspringen
▶ **muck around** vi, vt = **muck about**
▶ **muck in** (Brit: inf) vi mit anpacken
▶ **muck out** vt (stable) ausmisten
▶ **muck up** (inf) vt (exam etc) verpfuschen

muckraking ['mʌkreɪkɪŋ] (fig: inf) n Sensationsmache f ▷ adj sensationslüstern

mucky ['mʌkɪ] adj (dirty) dreckig; (field) matschig

mucus ['mjuːkəs] n Schleim m

mud [mʌd] n Schlamm m

muddle ['mʌdl] n (mess) Durcheinander nt; (confusion) Verwirrung f ▷ vt (person) verwirren; (also: **muddle up**) durcheinanderbringen; **to be in a ~** völlig durcheinander sein; **to get in a ~** (person) konfus werden; (things) durcheinandergeraten
▶ **muddle along** vi vor sich acc hin wursteln
▶ **muddle through** vi (get by) sich durchschlagen

muddle-headed [mʌdl'hedɪd] adj zerstreut

muddy ['mʌdɪ] adj (floor) schmutzig; (field) schlammig

mud flats npl Watt(enmeer) nt

mudguard ['mʌdgɑːd] (Brit) n Schutzblech nt

mudpack ['mʌdpæk] n Schlammpackung f

mud-slinging ['mʌdslɪŋɪŋ] n (fig) Schlechtmacherei f

muesli ['mjuːzlɪ] n Müsli nt

muffin ['mʌfɪn] n (Brit) weiches, flaches Milchbrötchen, meist warm gegessen; (US) kleiner runder Rührkuchen

muffle ['mʌfl] vt (sound) dämpfen; (against cold) einmummeln

muffled ['mʌfld] adj (see vt) gedämpft; eingemummelt

muffler ['mʌflər] n (US: Aut) Auspufftopf m; (scarf) dicker Schal m

mufti ['mʌftɪ] n: **in ~** in Zivil

mug [mʌg] n (cup) Becher m; (for beer) Krug m; (inf: face) Visage f; (: fool) Trottel m ▷ vt (auf der Straße) überfallen; **it's a ~'s game** (Brit) das ist doch Schwachsinn
▶ **mug up** (Brit: inf) vt (also: **mug up on**) pauken

mugger ['mʌgər] n Straßenräuber m

mugging ['mʌgɪŋ] n Straßenraub m

muggins ['mʌgɪnz] (Brit: inf) n Dummkopf m; ... **and ~ does all the work** ... und ich bin mal wieder der/die Dumme und mache die ganze Arbeit

muggy ['mʌgɪ] adj (weather, day) schwül

mug shot (inf) n (of criminal) Verbrecherfoto nt; (for passport) Passbild nt

mulatto [mjuːˈlætəu] (pl **~es**) n Mulatte m, Mulattin f

mulberry ['mʌlbrɪ] n (fruit) Maulbeere f; (tree) Maulbeerbaum m

mule [mjuːl] n Maultier nt

mulled [mʌld] adj: ~ **wine** Glühwein m

mullioned ['mʌlɪənd] adj (windows) längs unterteilt

mull over [mʌl-] vt sich dat durch den Kopf gehen lassen

multi... ['mʌltɪ] pref multi-, Multi-

multi-access [mʌltɪ'ækses] adj (Comput: system etc) Mehrplatz-

multicoloured, (US) **multicolored** ['mʌltɪkʌləd] adj mehrfarbig

multifarious [mʌltɪ'feərɪəs] adj vielfältig

multifocals ['mʌltɪfəuklz] npl Gleitsichtgläser pl

multilateral [mʌltɪ'lætərl] adj multilateral

multi-level ['mʌltɪlevl] (US) adj = **multistorey**

multimillionaire [mʌltɪmɪljə'nɛəʳ] n
Multimillionär m
multinational [mʌltɪ'næʃənl] adj
multinational ▷ n multinationaler Konzern
m, Multi m (inf)
multiple ['mʌltɪpl] adj (injuries) mehrfach;
(interests, causes) vielfältig ▷ n Vielfache(s) nt; ~
collision Massenkarambolage f
multiple-choice ['mʌltɪpltʃɔɪs] adj (question etc)
Multiple-Choice-
multiple sclerosis n multiple Sklerose f
multiplex ['mʌltɪplɛks] n: ~ **transmitter**
Multiplexsender m; ~ **(cinema)** Multiplexkino
nt ▷ adj (Tech) Mehrfach- ▷ vt (Tel) gleichzeitig
senden
multiplication [mʌltɪplɪ'keɪʃən] n
Multiplikation f; (increase) Vervielfachung
f
multiplication table n Multiplikationstabelle
f
multiplicity [mʌltɪ'plɪsɪtɪ] n: **a ~ of** eine
Vielzahl von
multiply ['mʌltɪplaɪ] vt multiplizieren ▷ vi
(increase: problems) stark zunehmen; (: number)
sich vervielfachen; (breed) sich vermehren
multiracial [mʌltɪ'reɪʃl] adj gemischtrassig;
(school) ohne Rassentrennung; ~ **policy** Politik
f der Rassenintegration
multistorey [mʌltɪ'stɔːrɪ] (Brit) adj (building, car
park) mehrstöckig
multitude ['mʌltɪtjuːd] n Menge f; **a ~ of** eine
Vielzahl von, eine Menge
mum [mʌm] (Brit: inf) n Mutti f, Mama f
▷ adj: **to keep ~** den Mund halten; ~**'s the
word** nichts verraten!
mumble ['mʌmbl] vt, vi (indistinctly) nuscheln;
(quietly) murmeln
mumbo jumbo ['mʌmbəʊ-] n (nonsense)
Geschwafel nt
mummify ['mʌmɪfaɪ] vt mumifizieren
mummy ['mʌmɪ] n (Brit: mother) Mami f;
(embalmed body) Mumie f
mumps [mʌmps] n Mumps m or f
munch [mʌntʃ] vt, vi mampfen
mundane [mʌn'deɪn] adj (life) banal; (task)
stumpfsinnig
Munich ['mjuːnɪk] n München nt
municipal [mjuː'nɪsɪpl] adj städtisch, Stadt-;
(elections, administration) Kommunal-
municipality [mjuːnɪsɪ'pælɪtɪ] n Gemeinde f,
Stadt f
munitions [mjuː'nɪʃənz] npl Munition f
mural ['mjʊərl] n Wandgemälde nt
murder ['məːdəʳ] n Mord m ▷ vt ermorden;
(spoil: piece of music, language) verhunzen; **to
commit ~** einen Mord begehen
murderer ['məːdərəʳ] n Mörder m
murderess ['məːdərɪs] n Mörderin f
murderous ['məːdərəs] adj blutrünstig; (attack)
Mord-; (fig: look, attack) vernichtend; (: pace,
heat) mörderisch
murk [məːk] n Düsternis f
murky ['məːkɪ] adj düster; (water) trübe

murmur ['məːməʳ] n (of voices) Murmeln nt;
(of wind, waves) Rauschen nt ▷ vt, vi murmeln;
heart ~ Herzgeräusche pl
MusB, MusBac n abbr (= Bachelor of Music)
akademischer Grad in Musikwissenschaft
muscle ['mʌsl] n Muskel m; (fig: strength) Macht
f
▷ **muscle in** vi: **to ~ in (on sth)** (bei etw)
mitmischen
muscular ['mʌskjʊləʳ] adj (pain, dystrophy)
Muskel-; (person, build) muskulös
muscular dystrophy n Muskeldystrophie f
MusD, MusDoc n abbr (= Doctor of Music) Doktorat
in Musikwissenschaft
muse [mjuːz] vi nachgrübeln ▷ n Muse f
museum [mjuː'zɪəm] n Museum nt
mush [mʌʃ] n Brei m; (pej) Schmalz m
mushroom ['mʌʃrʊm] n (edible) (essbarer) Pilz
m; (poisonous) Giftpilz m; (button mushroom)
Champignon m ▷ vi (fig: buildings etc) aus
dem Boden schießen; (: town, organization)
explosionsartig wachsen
mushroom cloud n Atompilz m
mushy ['mʌʃɪ] adj matschig; (consistency) breiig;
(inf: sentimental) rührselig; ~ **peas** Erbsenbrei m
music ['mjuːzɪk] n Musik f; (written music, score)
Noten pl
musical ['mjuːzɪkl] adj musikalisch; (sound,
tune) melodisch ▷ n Musical nt
musical box n = **music box**
musical chairs n die Reise f nach Jerusalem
musical instrument n Musikinstrument nt
music box n Spieldose f
music centre n Musikcenter nt
music hall n Varieté nt
musician [mjuː'zɪʃən] n Musiker(in) m(f)
music stand n Notenständer m
musk [mʌsk] n Moschus m
musket ['mʌskɪt] n Muskete f
muskrat ['mʌskræt] n Bisamratte f
musk rose n Moschusrose f
Muslim ['mʌzlɪm] adj moslemisch ▷ n Moslem
m, Moslime f
muslin ['mʌzlɪn] n Musselin m
musquash ['mʌskwɒʃ] n Bisamratte f; (fur)
Bisam m
mussel ['mʌsl] n (Mies)muschel f
must [mʌst] aux vb müssen; (in negative)
dürfen ▷ n Muss nt; **I ~ do it** ich muss es
tun; **you ~ not do that** das darfst du nicht
tun; **he ~ be there by now** jetzt müsste er
schon dort sein; **you ~ come and see me
soon** Sie müssen mich bald besuchen; **why
~ he behave so badly?** warum muss er sich
so schlecht benehmen?; **I ~ have made a
mistake** ich muss mich geirrt haben; **the
film is a ~** den Film muss man unbedingt
gesehen haben
mustache ['mʌstæʃ] (US) n = **moustache**
mustard ['mʌstəd] n Senf m
mustard gas n (Mil) Senfgas nt
muster ['mʌstəʳ] vt (support)
zusammenbekommen; (also: **muster

m

669

up: *energy, strength, courage*) aufbringen; (*troops, members*) antreten lassen ▷ *n*: **to pass** ~ den Anforderungen genügen

mustiness ['mʌstɪnɪs] *n* Muffigkeit *f*

mustn't ['mʌsnt] = **must not**

musty ['mʌstɪ] *adj* muffig; (*building*) moderig

mutant ['mjuːtənt] *n* Mutante *f*

mutate [mjuːˈteɪt] *vi* (*Biol*) mutieren

mutation [mjuːˈteɪʃən] *n* (*Biol*) Mutation *f*; (*alteration*) Veränderung *f*

mute [mjuːt] *adj* stumm

muted ['mjuːtɪd] *adj* (*colour*) gedeckt; (*reaction, criticism*) verhalten; (*sound, trumpet, Mus*) gedämpft

mutilate ['mjuːtɪleɪt] *vt* verstümmeln

mutilation [mjuːtɪˈleɪʃən] *n* Verstümmelung *f*

mutinous ['mjuːtɪnəs] *adj* meuterisch; (*attitude*) rebellisch

mutiny ['mjuːtɪnɪ] *n* Meuterei *f* ▷ *vi* meutern

mutter ['mʌtəʳ] *vt, vi* murmeln

mutton ['mʌtn] *n* Hammelfleisch *nt*

mutual ['mjuːtʃuəl] *adj* (*feeling, attraction*) gegenseitig; (*benefit*) beiderseitig; (*interest, friend*) gemeinsam; **the feeling was** ~ das beruhte auf Gegenseitigkeit

mutually ['mjuːtʃuəlɪ] *adv* (*beneficial, satisfactory*) für beide Seiten; (*accepted*) von beiden Seiten; **to be** ~ **exclusive** einander ausschließen; ~ **incompatible** nicht miteinander vereinbar

Muzak® ['mjuːzæk] *n* Berieselungsmusik *f* (*inf*)

muzzle ['mʌzl] *n* (*of dog*) Maul *nt*; (*of gun*) Mündung *f*; (*guard: for dog*) Maulkorb *m* ▷ *vt* (*dog*) einen Maulkorb anlegen +*dat*; (*fig: press, person*) mundtot machen

MV *abbr* (= *motor vessel*) MS

MVP (US) *n abbr* (*Sport*: = *most valuable player*) wertvollster Spieler *m*, wertvollste Spielerin *f*

MW *abbr* (*Radio*: = *medium wave*) MW

 **KEYWORD**

my [maɪ] *adj* mein(e); **this is my brother/ sister/house** das ist mein Bruder/meine Schwester/mein Haus; **I've washed my hair/cut my finger** ich habe mir die Haare gewaschen/mir in den Finger geschnitten; **is this my pen or yours?** ist das mein Stift oder deiner?

Myanmar ['maɪænmaːʳ] *n* Myanmar *nt*

myopic [maɪˈɔpɪk] *adj* (*Med, fig*) kurzsichtig

myriad ['mɪrɪəd] *n* Unzahl *f*

myrrh [məːʳ] *n* Myrr(h)e *f*

myself [maɪˈself] *pron* (*acc*) mich; (*dat*) mir; (*emphatic*) selbst; *see also* **oneself**

mysterious [mɪsˈtɪərɪəs] *adj* geheimnisvoll, mysteriös

mysteriously [mɪsˈtɪərɪəslɪ] *adv* auf mysteriöse Weise; (*smile*) geheimnisvoll

mystery ['mɪstərɪ] *n* (*puzzle*) Rätsel *nt*; (*strangeness*) Rätselhaftigkeit *f* ▷ *cpd* (*guest, voice*) mysteriös; ~ **tour** Fahrt *f* ins Blaue

mystery caller *n* Testanrufer(in) *m(f)*

mystery calling *n* Testanruf *m*

mystery shopper *n* Testkäufer(in) *m(f)*

mystery story *n* Kriminalgeschichte *f*

mystery visitor *n* Testbesucher(in) *m(f)*

mystic ['mɪstɪk] *n* Mystiker(in) *m(f)* ▷ *adj* mystisch

mystical ['mɪstɪkl] *adj* mystisch

mystify ['mɪstɪfaɪ] *vt* vor ein Rätsel stellen

mystique [mɪsˈtiːk] *n* geheimnisvoller Nimbus *m*

myth [mɪθ] *n* Mythos *m*; (*fallacy*) Märchen *nt*

mythical ['mɪθɪkl] *adj* mythisch; (*jobs, opportunities etc*) fiktiv

mythological [mɪθəˈlɔdʒɪkl] *adj* mythologisch

mythology [mɪˈθɔlədʒɪ] *n* Mythologie *f*

Nn

N¹, n [ɛn] n (letter) N nt, n nt; **N for Nellie, N for Nan** (US) = N wie Nordpol

N² [ɛn] abbr (= north) N

NA (US) n abbr (= Narcotics Anonymous) Hilfsorganisation für Drogensüchtige; (= National Academy) Dachverband verschiedener Forschungsunternehmen

n/a abbr (= not applicable) entf.

NAACP (US) n abbr (= National Association for the Advancement of Colored People) Vereinigung zur Förderung Farbiger

NAAFI ['næfɪ] (Brit) n abbr (= Navy, Army, & Air Force Institutes) Laden für britische Armeeangehörige

NACU (US) n abbr (= National Association of Colleges and Universities) Fachhochschul- und Universitätsverband

nadir ['neɪdɪəʳ] n (fig) Tiefstpunkt m; (Astron) Nadir m

NAFTA n abbr (= North Atlantic Free Trade Agreement) amerikanische Freihandelszone

nag [næg] vt herumnörgeln an +dat ▷ vi nörgeln ▷ n (pej: horse) Gaul m; (: person) Nörgler(in) m(f); **to ~ at sb** jdn plagen, jdm keine Ruhe lassen

nagging ['nægɪŋ] adj (doubt, suspicion) quälend; (pain) dumpf

nail [neɪl] n Nagel m ▷ vt (inf: thief etc) drankriegen; (: fraud) aufdecken; **to ~ sth to sth** etw an etw acc nageln; **to ~ sb down (to sth)** jdn (auf etw acc) festnageln

nailbrush ['neɪlbrʌʃ] n Nagelbürste f

nailfile ['neɪlfaɪl] n Nagelfeile f

nail polish n Nagellack m

nail polish remover n Nagellackentferner m

nail scissors npl Nagelschere f

nail varnish (Brit) n = **nail polish**

Nairobi [naɪˈrəʊbɪ] n Nairobi nt

naive [naɪˈiːv] adj naiv

naïveté [naːiːvˈteɪ] n = **naivety**

naivety [naɪˈiːvtɪ] n Naivität f

naked ['neɪkɪd] adj nackt; (flame, light) offen; **with the ~ eye** mit bloßem Auge; **to the ~ eye** für das bloße Auge

nakedness ['neɪkɪdnɪs] n Nacktheit f

NAM (US) n abbr (= National Association of Manufacturers) nationaler Verband der verarbeitenden Industrie

name [neɪm] n Name m ▷ vt nennen; (ship)

taufen; (identify) (beim Namen) nennen; (date etc) bestimmen, festlegen; **what's your ~?** wie heißen Sie?; **my ~ is Peter** ich heiße Peter; **by ~** mit Namen; **in the ~ of** im Namen +gen; **to give one's ~ and address** Namen und Adresse angeben; **to make a ~ for o.s.** sich dat einen Namen machen; **to give sb a bad ~** jdn in Verruf bringen; **to call sb ~s** jdn beschimpfen; **to be ~d after sb/sth** nach jdm/etw benannt werden

name-dropping ['neɪmdrɔpɪŋ] n Angeberei f mit berühmten Namen

nameless ['neɪmlɪs] adj namenlos; **who/ which shall remain ~** der/die/das ungenannt bleiben soll

namely ['neɪmlɪ] adv nämlich

nameplate ['neɪmpleɪt] n Namensschild nt

namesake ['neɪmseɪk] n Namensvetter(in) m(f)

nan bread [naːn-] n Nan-Brot nt, fladenförmiges Weißbrot als Beilage zu indischen Gerichten

nanny ['nænɪ] n Kindermädchen nt

nanny-goat ['nænɪɡəʊt] n Geiß f

nap [næp] n Schläfchen nt; (of fabric) Strich m ▷ vi: **to be caught ~ping** (fig) überrumpelt werden; **to have a ~** ein Schläfchen or ein Nickerchen (inf) machen

NAPA (US) n abbr (= National Association of Performing Artists) Künstlergewerkschaft

napalm ['neɪpaːm] n Napalm nt

nape [neɪp] n: **the ~ of the neck** der Nacken

napkin ['næpkɪn] n (also: **table napkin**) Serviette f

Naples ['neɪplz] n Neapel nt

Napoleonic [nəpəʊlɪˈɔnɪk] adj napoleonisch

nappy ['næpɪ] (Brit) n Windel f

nappy liner (Brit) n Windeleinlage f

nappy rash n Wundsein nt

narcissistic [naːsɪˈsɪstɪk] adj narzisstisch

narcissus [naːˈsɪsəs] (pl **narcissi**) n Narzisse f

narcotic [naːˈkɔtɪk] adj narkotisch ▷ n Narkotikum nt; **narcotics** npl (drugs) Drogen pl; **~ drug** Rauschgift nt

nark [naːk] (Brit: inf) vt: **to be ~ed at sth** sauer über etw acc sein

narrate [nəˈreɪt] vt erzählen; (film, programme) kommentieren

narration [nəˈreɪʃən] n Kommentar m

narrative ['nærətɪv] n Erzählung f; (of journey etc) Schilderung f

narrator [nə'reɪtə'] n Erzähler(in) m(f); (in film etc) Kommentator(in) m(f)

narrow ['nærəu] adj eng; (ledge etc) schmal; (majority, advantage, victory, defeat) knapp; (ideas, view) engstirnig ▷ vi sich verengen; (gap, difference) sich verringern ▷ vt (gap, difference) verringern; (eyes) zusammenkneifen; **to have a ~ escape** mit knapper Not davonkommen; **to ~ sth down (to sth)** etw (auf etw acc) beschränken

narrow gauge ['nærəugeɪdʒ] adj (Rail) Schmalspur-

narrowly ['nærəulɪ] adv knapp; (escape) mit knapper Not

narrow-minded [nærəu'maɪndɪd] adj engstirnig

NAS (US) n abbr (= National Academy of Sciences) Akademie der Wissenschaften

NASA ['næsə] (US) n abbr (= National Aeronautics and Space Administration) NASA f

nasal ['neɪzl] adj Nasen-; (voice) näselnd

Nassau ['næsɔː] n Nassau nt

nastily ['nɑːstɪlɪ] adv gemein; (say) gehässig

nastiness ['nɑːstɪnɪs] n Gemeinheit f; (of remark) Gehässigkeit f; (of smell, taste etc) Ekelhaftigkeit f

nasturtium [nəs'təːʃəm] n Kapuzinerkresse f

nasty ['nɑːstɪ] adj (remark) gehässig; (person) gemein; (taste, smell) ekelhaft; (wound, disease, accident, shock) schlimm; (problem, question) schwierig; (weather, temper) abscheulich; **to turn ~** unangenehm werden; **it's a ~ business** es ist schrecklich; **he's got a ~ temper** mit ihm ist nicht gut Kirschen essen

NAS/UWT (Brit) n abbr (= National Association of Schoolmasters/Union of Women Teachers) Lehrergewerkschaft

nation ['neɪʃən] n Nation f; (people) Volk nt

national ['næʃənl] adj (character, flag) National-; (interests) Staats-; (newspaper) überregional ▷ n Staatsbürger(in) m(f); **foreign ~** Ausländer(in) m(f)

national anthem n Nationalhymne f

National Curriculum n zentraler Lehrplan für Schulen in England und Wales

national debt n Staatsverschuldung f

national dress n Nationaltracht f

National Guard (US) n Nationalgarde f

National Health Service (Brit) n Staatlicher Gesundheitsdienst m

National Insurance (Brit) n Sozial-versicherung f

nationalism ['næʃnəlɪzəm] n Nationalismus m

nationalist ['næʃnəlɪst] adj nationalistisch ▷ n Nationalist(in) m(f)

nationality [næʃə'nælɪtɪ] n Staats-angehörigkeit f, Nationalität f

nationalization [næʃnəlaɪ'zeɪʃən] n Verstaatlichung f

nationalize ['næʃnəlaɪz] vt verstaatlichen

National Lottery n ≈ Lotto nt

nationally ['næʃnəlɪ] adv landesweit

national park n Nationalpark m

national press n überregionale Presse f

National Security Council (US) n Nationaler Sicherheitsrat m

national service n Wehrdienst m

National Trust (Brit) n Organisation zum Schutz historischer Bauten und Denkmäler sowie zum Landschaftsschutz; siehe Info-Artikel

NATIONAL TRUST

Der National Trust ist ein 1895 gegründeter Natur- und Denkmalschutzverband in Großbritannien, der Gebäude und Gelände von besonderem historischem oder ästhetischem Interesse erhält und der Öffentlichkeit zugänglich macht. Viele Gebäude im Besitz des National Trust sind (z. T. gegen ein Eintrittsgeld) zu besichtigen.

nationwide ['neɪʃənwaɪd] adj, adv landesweit

native ['neɪtɪv] n Einheimische(r) f(m) ▷ adj einheimisch; (country) Heimat-; (language) Mutter-; (innate) angeboren; **a ~ of Germany, a ~ German** ein gebürtiger Deutscher, eine gebürtige Deutsche; **~ to** beheimatet in +dat

Native American adj indianisch, der Ureinwohner Amerikas ▷ n Ureinwohner(in) m(f) Amerikas

native speaker n Muttersprachler(in) m(f)

Nativity [nə'tɪvɪtɪ] n: **the ~** Christi Geburt f

nativity play n Krippenspiel nt

NATO ['neɪtəu] n abbr (= North Atlantic Treaty Organization) NATO f

natter ['nætə'] (Brit) vi quatschen (inf) ▷ n: **to have a ~** einen Schwatz halten

natural ['nætʃrəl] adj natürlich; (disaster) Natur-; (innate) angeboren; (born) geboren; (Mus) ohne Vorzeichen; **to die of ~ causes** eines natürlichen Todes sterben; **~ foods** Naturkost f; **she played F ~ not F sharp** sie spielte f statt fis

natural childbirth n natürliche Geburt f

natural gas n Erdgas nt

natural history n Naturkunde f; **the ~ of England** die Naturgeschichte Englands

naturalist ['nætʃrəlɪst] n Naturforscher(in) m(f)

naturalize ['nætʃrəlaɪz] vt: **to become ~d** eingebürgert werden

naturally ['nætʃrəlɪ] adv natürlich; (happen) auf natürlichem Wege; (die) eines natürlichen Todes; (cheerful, talented, blonde) von Natur aus

naturalness ['nætʃrəlnɪs] n Natürlichkeit f

natural resources npl Naturschätze pl

natural selection n natürliche Auslese f

natural wastage n natürliche Personalreduzierung f

nature ['neɪtʃə'] n (Nature) Natur f; (kind, sort) Art f; (character) Wesen nt; **by ~** von Natur aus; **by its (very) ~** naturgemäß; **documents of a**

confidential ~ Unterlagen vertraulicher Art

-natured ['neɪtʃəd] *suff*: **good~** gutmütig; **ill~** bösartig

nature reserve (*Brit*) *n* Naturschutzgebiet *nt*

nature trail *n* Naturlehrpfad *m*

naturist ['neɪtʃərɪst] *n* Anhänger(in) *m(f)* der Freikörperkultur

naught [nɔːt] *n* = **nought**

naughtiness ['nɔːtɪnɪs] *n* (*see adj*) Unartigkeit *f*, Ungezogenheit *f*; Unanständigkeit *f*

naughty ['nɔːtɪ] *adj* (*child*) unartig, ungezogen; (*story, film, words*) unanständig

nausea ['nɔːsɪə] *n* Übelkeit *f*

nauseate ['nɔːsɪeɪt] *vt* Übelkeit verursachen +*dat*; (*fig*) anwidern

nauseating ['nɔːsɪeɪtɪŋ] *adj* ekelerregend; (*fig*) widerlich

nauseous ['nɔːsɪəs] *adj* ekelhaft; **I feel** ~ mir ist übel

nautical ['nɔːtɪkl] *adj* (*chart*) See-; (*uniform*) Seemanns-

nautical mile *n* Seemeile *f*

naval ['neɪvl] *adj* Marine-; (*battle, forces*) See-

naval officer *n* Marineoffizier *m*

nave [neɪv] *n* Hauptschiff *nt*, Mittelschiff *nt*

navel ['neɪvl] *n* Nabel *m*

navel piercing ['neɪvl] *n* Nabelpiercing *nt*

navigable ['nævɪɡəbl] *adj* schiffbar

navigate ['nævɪɡeɪt] *vt* (*river*) befahren; (*path*) begehen ▷ *vi* navigieren; (*Aut*) den Fahrer dirigieren

navigation [nævɪ'ɡeɪʃən] *n* Navigation *f*

navigator ['nævɪɡeɪtəʳ] *n* (*Naut*) Steuermann *m*; (*Aviat*) Navigator(in) *m(f)*; (*Aut*) Beifahrer(in) *m(f)*

navvy ['nævɪ] (*Brit*) *n* Straßenarbeiter *m*

navy ['neɪvɪ] *n* (Kriegs)marine *f*; (*ships*) (Kriegs) flotte *f* ▷ *adj* marineblau; **Department of the N~** (*US*) Marineministerium *nt*

navy-blue ['neɪvɪ'bluː] *adj* marineblau

Nazareth ['næzərɪθ] *n* Nazareth *nt*

Nazi ['nɑːtsɪ] *n* Nazi *m*

NB *abbr* (= *nota bene*) NB; (*Canada*) = *New Brunswick*

NBA (*US*) *n abbr* (= *National Basketball Association*) Basketball-Dachverband; (= *National Boxing Association*) Boxsport-Dachverband

NBC (*US*) *n abbr* (= *National Broadcasting Company*) Fernsehsender

NBS (*US*) *n abbr* (= *National Bureau of Standards*) amerikanischer Normenausschuss

NC *abbr* (*Comm etc*: = *no charge*) frei; (*US: Post*) = *North Carolina*

NCC (*US*) *n abbr* (= *National Council of Churches*) Zusammenschluss protestantischer und orthodoxer Kirchen

NCCL (*Brit*) *n abbr* (= *National Council for Civil Liberties*) Organisation zum Schutz von Freiheitsrechten

NCO *n abbr* (*Mil*: = *noncommissioned officer*) Uffz.

ND (*US*) *abbr* (*Post*) = *North Dakota*

N.Dak. (*US*) *abbr* (*Post*) = *North Dakota*

NE *abbr* = **north-east**; (*US: Post*) = *New England*; *Nebraska*

NEA (*US*) *n abbr* (= *National Education Association*) Verband für das Erziehungswesen

neap [niːp] *n* (*also*: **neap tide**) Nippflut *f*

Neapolitan [nɪə'pɒlɪtən] *adj* neapolitanisch ▷ *n* Neapolitaner(in) *m(f)*

near [nɪəʳ] *adj* nahe ▷ *adv* nahe; (*almost*) fast, beinahe ▷ *prep* also: **near to**: (*in space*) nahe an +*dat*; (: *in time*) um *acc* ... herum; (: *in situation, in intimacy*) nahe +*dat* ▷ *vt* sich nähern +*dat*; (*state, situation*) kurz vor +*dat* stehen; **Christmas is** ~ bald ist Weihnachten; **£25,000 or ~est offer** (*Brit*) £25.000 oder das nächstbeste Angebot; **in the** ~ **future** in naher Zukunft, bald; **in** ~ **darkness** fast im Dunkeln; **a** ~ **tragedy** beinahe eine Tragödie; ~ **here/there** hier/ dort in der Nähe; **to be** ~ **(to) doing sth** nahe daran sein, etw zu tun; **the building is** ~**ing completion** der Bau steht kurz vor dem Abschluss

nearby [nɪə'baɪ] *adj* nahe gelegen ▷ *adv* in der Nähe

Near East *n*: **the** ~ der Nahe Osten

nearer ['nɪərəʳ] *adj comp, adv comp of* **near**

nearest ['nɪərəst] *adj superl, adv superl of* **near**

nearly ['nɪəlɪ] *adv* fast; **I** ~ **fell** ich wäre beinahe gefallen; **it's not** ~ **big enough** es ist bei Weitem nicht groß genug; **she was** ~ **crying** sie war den Tränen nahe

near miss *n* Beinahezusammenstoß *m*; **that was a** ~ (*shot*) das war knapp daneben

nearness ['nɪənɪs] *n* Nähe *f*

nearside ['nɪəsaɪd] (*Aut*) *adj* (*when driving on left*) linksseitig; (*when driving on right*) rechtsseitig ▷ *n*: **the** ~ (*when driving on left*) die linke Seite; (*when driving on right*) die rechte Seite

near-sighted [nɪə'saɪtɪd] *adj* kurzsichtig

neat [niːt] *adj* ordentlich; (*handwriting*) sauber; (*plan, solution*) elegant; (*description*) prägnant; (*spirits*) pur; **I drink it** ~ ich trinke es pur

neatly ['niːtlɪ] *adv* ordentlich; (*conveniently*) sauber

neatness ['niːtnɪs] *n* Ordentlichkeit *f*; (*of solution, plan*) Sauberkeit *f*

Nebr. (*US*) *abbr* (*Post*) = *Nebraska*

nebulous ['nɛbjuləs] *adj* vage, unklar

necessarily ['nɛsɪsrɪlɪ] *adv* notwendigerweise; **not** ~ nicht unbedingt

necessary ['nɛsɪsrɪ] *adj* notwendig, nötig; (*inevitable*) unausweichlich; **if** ~ wenn nötig, nötigenfalls; **it is** ~ **to** ... man muss ...

necessitate [nɪ'sɛsɪteɪt] *vt* erforderlich machen

necessity [nɪ'sɛsɪtɪ] *n* Notwendigkeit *f*; **of** ~ notgedrungen; **out of** ~ aus Not; **the necessities (of life)** das Notwendigste (zum Leben)

neck [nɛk] *n* Hals *m*; (*of shirt, dress, jumper*) Ausschnitt *m* ▷ *vi* (*inf*) knutschen; ~ **and neck** Kopf an Kopf; **to stick one's** ~ **out** (*inf*) seinen Kopf riskieren

necklace ['nɛklɪs] *n* (Hals)kette *f*

neckline ['nɛklaɪn] *n* Ausschnitt *m*

n

673

necktie ['nɛktaɪ] (*esp US*) *n* Krawatte *f*
nectar ['nɛktə'] *n* Nektar *m*
nectarine ['nɛktərɪn] *n* Nektarine *f*
née [neɪ] *prep*: **~ Scott** geborene Scott
need [niːd] *n* Bedarf *m*; (*necessity*)
Notwendigkeit *f*; (*requirement*) Bedürfnis
nt; (*poverty*) Not *f* ▷ *vt* brauchen; (*could do
with*) nötig haben; **in ~** nötig haben; **to be in
~ of sth** etw nötig haben; **£10 will meet
my immediate ~s** mit £ 10 komme ich erst
einmal aus; **(there's) no ~** (das ist) nicht
nötig; **there's no ~ to get so worked up
about it** du brauchst dich darüber nicht so
aufzuregen; **he had no ~ to work** er hatte es
nicht nötig zu arbeiten; **I ~ to do it** ich muss
es tun; **you don't ~ to go, you needn't go** du
brauchst nicht zu gehen; **a signature is ~ed**
das bedarf einer Unterschrift *gen*
needle ['niːdl] *n* Nadel *f* ▷ *vt* (*fig: inf: goad*)
ärgern, piesacken
needless ['niːdlɪs] *adj* unnötig; **~ to say**
natürlich
needlessly ['niːdlɪslɪ] *adv* unnötig
needlework ['niːdlwəːk] *n* Handarbeit *f*
needn't ['niːdnt] = **need not**
needy ['niːdɪ] *adj* bedürftig ▷ *npl*: **the ~** die
Bedürftigen *pl*
negation [nɪ'geɪʃən] *n* Verweigerung *f*
negative ['nɛgətɪv] *adj* negativ; (*answer*)
abschlägig ▷ *n* (*Phot*) Negativ *nt*; (*Ling*)
Verneinungswort *nt*, Negation *f*; **to answer
in the ~** eine verneinende Antwort geben
negative equity *n* Differenz zwischen gefallenem
Wert und hypothekarischer Belastung eines
Wohnungseigentums
neglect [nɪ'glɛkt] *vt* vernachlässigen; (*writer,
artist*) unterschätzen ▷ *n* Vernachlässigung *f*
neglected [nɪ'glɛktɪd] *adj* vernachlässigt;
(*writer, artist*) unterschätzt
neglectful [nɪ'glɛktful] *adj* nachlässig;
(*father*) pflichtvergessen; **to be ~ of sth** etw
vernachlässigen
negligee ['nɛglɪʒeɪ] *n* Negligee *nt*, Negligé *nt*
negligence ['nɛglɪdʒəns] *n* Nachlässigkeit *f*;
(*Law*) Fahrlässigkeit *f*
negligent ['nɛglɪdʒənt] *adj* nachlässig; (*Law*)
fahrlässig; (*casual*) lässig
negligently ['nɛglɪdʒəntlɪ] *adv* (*see adj*)
nachlässig; fahrlässig; lässig
negligible ['nɛglɪdʒɪbl] *adj* geringfügig
negotiable [nɪ'gəuʃɪəbl] *adj*
verhandlungsfähig; (*path, river*) passierbar;
not ~ (*on cheque etc*) nicht übertragbar
negotiate [nɪ'gəuʃɪeɪt] *vi* verhandeln ▷ *vt*
aushandeln; (*obstacle, hill*) überwinden; (*bend*)
nehmen; **to ~ with sb (for sth)** mit jdm (über
etw *acc*) verhandeln
negotiating table [nɪ'gəuʃɪeɪtɪŋ-] *n*
Verhandlungstisch *m*
negotiation [nɪgəuʃɪ'eɪʃən] *n* Verhandlung *f*;
the matter is still under ~ über die Sache
wird noch verhandelt
negotiator [nɪ'gəuʃɪeɪtə'] *n* Unterhändler(in)

m(f)
Negress ['niːgrɪs] *n* Negerin *f*
Negro ['niːgrəu] (*pl* **N~es**) *adj* (*boy, slave*) Neger-
▷ *n* Neger *m*
neigh [neɪ] *vi* wiehern
neighbour, (*US*) **neighbor** ['neɪbə'] *n*
Nachbar(in) *m(f)*
neighbourhood ['neɪbəhud] *n* (*place*) Gegend *f*;
(*people*) Nachbarschaft *f*; **in the ~ of ...** in der
Nähe von ...; (*sum of money*) so um die ...
neighbourhood watch *n* Vereinigung von
Bürgern, die Straßenwachen etc zur Unterstützung der
Polizei bei der Verbrechensbekämpfung organisiert
neighbouring ['neɪbərɪŋ] *adj* benachbart,
Nachbar-
neighbourly ['neɪbəlɪ] *adj* nachbarlich
neither ['naɪðə'] *conj*: **I didn't move and ~ did
John** ich bewegte mich nicht und John auch
nicht ▷ *pron* keine(r, s) (von beiden) ▷ *adv*: **~ ...
nor ...** weder ... noch ...; **~ story is true** keine
der beiden Geschichten stimmt; **~ is true**
beides stimmt nicht; **~ do I/have I** ich auch
nicht
neo ... ['niːəu] *pref* neo-, Neo-
neolithic [nɪə'lɪθɪk] *adv* jungsteinzeitlich,
neolithisch
neologism [nɪ'ɔlədʒɪzəm] *n* (Wort)neubildung
f, Neologismus *m*
neon ['niːɔn] *n* Neon *nt*
neon light *n* Neonlampe *f*
neon sign *n* Neonreklame *f*
Nepal [nɪ'pɔːl] *n* Nepal *nt*
nephew ['nɛvjuː] *n* Neffe *m*
nepotism ['nɛpətɪzəm] *n* Vetternwirtschaft *f*
nerd [nəːd] (*inf*) *n* Schwachkopf *m*
nerve [nəːv] *n* (*Anat*) Nerv *m*; (*courage*) Mut *m*;
(*impudence*) Frechheit *f*; **nerves** *npl* (*anxiety*)
Nervosität *f*; (*emotional strength*) Nerven *pl*; **he
gets on my ~s** er geht mir auf die Nerven; **to
lose one's ~** die Nerven verlieren
nerve-centre, (*US*) **nerve-center** ['nəːvsɛntə']
n (*fig*) Schaltzentrale *f*
nerve gas *n* Nervengas *nt*
nerve-racking ['nəːvrækɪŋ] *adj* nervenaufreibend
nervous ['nəːvəs] *adj* Nerven-, nervlich;
(*anxious*) nervös; **to be ~ of/about** Angst
haben vor +*dat*
nervous breakdown *n*
Nervenzusammenbruch *m*
nervously ['nəːvəslɪ] *adv* nervös
nervousness ['nəːvəsnɪs] *n* Nervosität *f*
nervous system *n* Nervensystem *nt*
nervous wreck (*inf*) *n* Nervenbündel *nt*; **to be
a ~** mit den Nerven völlig am Ende sein
nervy ['nəːvɪ] (*inf*) *adj* (*Brit: tense*) nervös;
(*US: cheeky*) dreist
nest [nɛst] *n* Nest *nt* ▷ *vi* nisten; **a ~ of tables**
ein Satz Tische *or* von Tischen
nest egg *n* Notgroschen *m*
nestle ['nɛsl] *vi* sich kuscheln; (*house*)
eingebettet sein
nestling ['nɛstlɪŋ] *n* Nestling *m*

Net [nɛt] n: **the ~** (Comput) das Internet
net [nɛt] n Netz nt; (fabric) Tüll m ▷ adj (Comm)
Netto-; (final: result, effect) End- ▷ vt (mit einem
Netz) fangen; (profit) einbringen; (deal, sale,
fortune) an Land ziehen; **~ of tax** steuerfrei; **he
earns £10,000 ~ per year** er verdient £10.000
netto im Jahr; **it weighs 250g ~** es wiegt 250
g netto
netball ['nɛtbɔ:l] n Netzball m
net curtains npl Gardinen pl, Stores pl
Netherlands ['nɛðələndz] npl: **the ~** die
Niederlande pl
netiquette ['nɛtɪkɛt] n Netiquette f
nett [nɛt] adj = **net**
netting ['nɛtɪŋ] n (for fence etc) Maschendraht
m; (fabric) Netzgewebe nt, Tüll m
nettle ['nɛtl] n Nessel f
network ['nɛtwə:k] n Netz nt; (TV, Radio)
Sendenetz nt ▷ vt (Radio, TV) im ganzen
Netzbereich ausstrahlen; (computers) in einem
Netzwerk zusammenschließen
neuralgia [njuə'rældʒə] n Neuralgie f,
Nervenschmerzen pl
neurological [njuərə'lɔdʒɪkl] adj neurologisch
neurotic [njuə'rɔtɪk] adj neurotisch ▷ n
Neurotiker(in) m(f)
neuter ['nju:tə'] adj (Ling) sächlich ▷ vt
kastrieren; (female) sterilisieren
neutral ['nju:trəl] adj neutral ▷ n (Aut) Leerlauf
m
neutrality [nju:'trælɪtɪ] n Neutralität f
neutralize ['nju:trəlaɪz] vt neutralisieren,
aufheben
neutron bomb n Neutronenbombe f
Nev. (US) abbr (Post) = Nevada
never ['nɛvə'] adv nie; (not) nicht; **~ in my life**
noch nie; **~ again** nie wieder; **well I ~!** nein, so
was!; see also **mind**
never-ending [nɛvər'ɛndɪŋ] adj endlos
nevertheless [nɛvəðə'lɛs] adv trotzdem,
dennoch
new [nju:] adj neu; (mother) jung; **as good as ~**
so gut wie neu; **to be ~ to sb** jdm neu sein
New Age n New Age nt
newbie ['nju:bɪ] (inf) n Neuling m
newborn ['nju:bɔ:n] adj neugeboren
newcomer ['nju:kʌmə'] n Neuankömmling m;
(in job) Neuling m
new-fangled ['nju:'fæŋgld] (pej) adj
neumodisch
new-found ['nju:faund] adj neu entdeckt;
(confidence) neu geschöpft
Newfoundland ['nju:fənlənd] n Neufundland
nt
New Guinea n Neuguinea nt
newly ['nju:lɪ] adv neu
newly-weds ['nju:lɪwedz] npl Neuvermählte
pl, Frischvermählte pl
new moon n Neumond m
newness ['nju:nɪs] n Neuheit f; (of cheese, bread
etc) Frische f
New Orleans [-'ɔ:li:ənz] n New Orleans nt
news [nju:z] n Nachricht f; **a piece of ~** eine

Neuigkeit; **the ~** (Radio, TV) die Nachrichten
pl; **good/bad ~** gute/schlechte Nachrichten
news agency n Nachrichtenagentur f
newsagent ['nju:zeɪdʒənt] (Brit) n
Zeitungshändler(in) m(f)
news bulletin n Bulletin nt
newscaster ['nju:zkɑ:stə'] n
Nachrichtensprecher(in) m(f)
newsdealer ['nju:zdi:lə'] (US) n = **newsagent**
newsflash ['nju:zflæʃ] n Kurzmeldung f
newsletter ['nju:zletə'] n Rundschreiben nt,
Mitteilungsblatt nt
newspaper ['nju:zpeɪpə'] n Zeitung f; **daily/
weekly ~** Tages-/Wochenzeitung f
newsprint ['nju:zprɪnt] n Zeitungspapier nt
newsreader ['nju:zri:də'] n = **newscaster**
newsreel ['nju:zri:l] n Wochenschau f
newsroom ['nju:zru:m] n
Nachrichtenredaktion f; (Radio, TV)
Nachrichtenstudio nt
newsstand ['nju:zstænd] n Zeitungsstand m
newsworthy ['nju:zwə:ðɪ] adj: **to be ~**
Neuigkeitswert haben
newt [nju:t] n Wassermolch m
new town (Brit) n neue, teilweise mit
Regierungsgeldern errichtete städtische Siedlung
New Year n neues Jahr nt; (New Year's Day)
Neujahr nt; **Happy ~!** (ein) glückliches or
frohes neues Jahr!
New Year's Day n Neujahr nt, Neujahrstag m
New Year's Eve n Silvester nt
New York [-'jɔ:k] n New York nt; (also: **New
York State**) der Staat New York
New Zealand [-'zi:lənd] n Neuseeland nt ▷ adj
neuseeländisch
New Zealander [-'zi:ləndə'] n
Neuseeländer(in) m(f)
next [nɛkst] adj nächste(r, s); (room) Neben-
▷ adv dann; (do, happen) als Nächstes;
(afterwards) danach; **the ~ day** am nächsten
or folgenden Tag; **~ time** das nächste Mal;
~ year nächstes Jahr; **~ please!** der Nächste
bitte!; **who's ~?** wer ist der Nächste?; **"turn
to the ~ page"** „bitte umblättern"; **the week
after ~** übernächste Woche; **the ~ on the
right/left** der/die/das Nächste rechts/links;
the ~ thing I knew das Nächste, woran ich
mich erinnern konnte; **~ to** neben +dat; **~ to
nothing** so gut wie nichts; **when do we meet
~?** wann treffen wir uns wieder or das nächste
Mal?; **the ~ best** der/die/das Nächstbeste
next door adv nebenan ▷ adj: **next-door**
nebenan; **the house ~** das Nebenhaus; **to
go ~** nach nebenan gehen; **my next-door
neighbour** mein direkter Nachbar
next-of-kin ['nɛkstəv'kɪn] n nächster
Verwandter m, nächste Verwandte f
NF n abbr (Brit: Pol: = National Front) rechtsradikale
Partei f (Canada) = Newfoundland
NFL (US) n abbr (= National Football League) Fußball-
Nationalliga
NG (US) abbr = **National Guard**
NGO n abbr (= nongovernmental organization)

n

675

nichtstaatliche Organisation

NH (US) *abbr* (Post) = New Hampshire

NHL (US) *n abbr* (= National Hockey League) Hockey-Nationalliga

NHS (Brit) *n abbr* = **National Health Service**

NI *abbr* = **Northern Ireland**; (Brit) = **National Insurance**

Niagara Falls [naɪˈægərə-] *npl* Niagarafälle *pl*

nib [nɪb] *n* Feder *f*

nibble [ˈnɪbl] *vt* knabbern; (bite) knabbern an +dat ▷ *vi*: **to ~ at** knabbern an +dat

Nicaragua [nɪkəˈrægjuə] *n* Nicaragua *nt*

Nicaraguan [nɪkəˈrægjuən] *adj* nicaraguanisch ▷ *n* Nicaraguaner(in) *m(f)*

Nice [niːs] *n* Nizza *nt*

nice [naɪs] *adj* nett; (holiday, weather, picture etc) schön; (taste) gut; (person, clothes etc) hübsch

nicely [ˈnaɪslɪ] *adv* (attractively) hübsch; (politely) nett; (satisfactorily) gut; **that will do ~** das reicht (vollauf)

niceties [ˈnaɪsɪtɪz] *npl*: **the ~** die Feinheiten *pl*

niche [niːʃ] *n* Nische *f*; (job, position) Plätzchen *nt*

nick [nɪk] *n* Kratzer *m*; (in metal, wood etc) Kerbe *f* ▷ *vt* (Brit: inf: steal) klauen; (: arrest) einsperren, einlochen; (cut): **to ~ o.s.** sich schneiden; **in good ~** (Brit: inf) gut in Schuss; **in the ~** (Brit: inf: in prison) im Knast; **in the ~ of time** gerade noch rechtzeitig

nickel [ˈnɪkl] *n* Nickel *nt*; (US) Fünfcentstück *nt*

nickname [ˈnɪkneɪm] *n* Spitzname *m* ▷ *vt* betiteln, taufen (inf)

Nicosia [nɪkəˈsiːə] *n* Nikosia *nt*

nicotine [ˈnɪkətiːn] *n* Nikotin *nt*

nicotine patch *n* Nikotinpflaster *nt*

niece [niːs] *n* Nichte *f*

nifty [ˈnɪftɪ] (inf) *adj* flott; (gadget, tool) schlau

Niger [ˈnaɪdʒəʳ] *n* Niger *m*

Nigeria [naɪˈdʒɪərɪə] *n* Nigeria *nt*

Nigerian [naɪˈdʒɪərɪən] *adj* nigerianisch ▷ *n* Nigerianer(in) *m(f)*

niggardly [ˈnɪgədlɪ] *adj* knauserig; (allowance, amount) armselig

nigger [ˈnɪgəʳ] (offensive) *n* Nigger *m* (inf!)

niggle [ˈnɪgl] *vt* plagen, zu schaffen machen +dat ▷ *vi* herumkritisieren

niggling [ˈnɪglɪŋ] *adj* quälend; (pain, ache) bohrend

night [naɪt] *n* Nacht *f*; (evening) Abend *m*; **the ~ before last** vorletzte Nacht, vorgestern Abend; **at ~, by ~** nachts, abends; **nine o'clock at ~** neun Uhr abends; **in the ~, during the ~** in der Nacht; **~ and day** Tag und Nacht

nightcap [ˈnaɪtkæp] *n* Schlaftrunk *m*

nightclub [ˈnaɪtklʌb] *n* Nachtlokal *nt*

nightdress [ˈnaɪtdrɛs] *n* Nachthemd *nt*

nightfall [ˈnaɪtfɔːl] *n* Einbruch *m* der Dunkelheit

nightgown [ˈnaɪtgaun] *n* = **nightdress**

nightie [ˈnaɪtɪ] *n* = **nightdress**

nightingale [ˈnaɪtɪŋgeɪl] *n* Nachtigall *f*

nightlife [ˈnaɪtlaɪf] *n* Nachtleben *nt*

nightly [ˈnaɪtlɪ] *adj* (all)nächtlich, Nacht-;

nightmare [ˈnaɪtmɛəʳ] *n* Albtraum *m*

night porter *n* Nachtportier *m*

night safe *n* Nachtsafe *m*

night school *n* Abendschule *f*

nightshade [ˈnaɪtʃeɪd] *n*: **deadly ~** Tollkirsche *f*

night shift *n* Nachtschicht *f*

night-time [ˈnaɪttaɪm] *n* Nacht *f*

night watchman *n* Nachtwächter *m*

nihilism [ˈnaɪɪlɪzəm] *n* Nihilismus *m*

nil [nɪl] *n* Nichts *nt*; (Brit: Sport) Null *f*

Nile [naɪl] *n*: **the ~** der Nil

nimble [ˈnɪmbl] *adj* flink; (mind) beweglich

nine [naɪn] *num* neun

nineteen [ˈnaɪnˈtiːn] *num* neunzehn

nineteenth [naɪnˈtiːnθ] *num* neunzehnte(r, s)

ninety [ˈnaɪntɪ] *num* neunzig

ninth [naɪnθ] *num* neunte(r, s) ▷ *n* Neuntel *nt*

nip [nɪp] *vt* zwicken ▷ *n* Biss *m*; (drink) Schlückchen *nt* ▷ *vi* (Brit: inf): **to ~ out/down/up** kurz raus-/runter-/raufgehen; **to ~ into a shop** (Brit: inf) kurz in einen Laden gehen

nipple [ˈnɪpl] *n* (Anat) Brustwarze *f*

nippy [ˈnɪpɪ] (Brit) *adj* (quick: person) flott; (: car) spritzig; (cold) frisch

nit [nɪt] *n* Nisse *f*; (inf: idiot) Dummkopf *m*

nitpicking [ˈnɪtpɪkɪŋ] (inf) *n* Kleinigkeitskrämerei *f*

nitrogen [ˈnaɪtrədʒən] *n* Stickstoff *m*

nitroglycerin, nitroglycerine [ˈnaɪtrəʊˈglɪsəriːn] *n* Nitroglyzerin *nt*

nitty-gritty [ˈnɪtɪˈgrɪtɪ] (inf) *n*: **to get down to the ~** zur Sache kommen

nitwit [ˈnɪtwɪt] (inf) *n* Dummkopf *m*

NJ (US) *abbr* (Post) = New Jersey

NLF *n abbr* (= National Liberation Front) vietnamesische Befreiungsbewegung während des Vietnamkrieges

NLRB (US) *n abbr* (= National Labor Relations Board) Ausschuss zur Regelung der Beziehungen zwischen Arbeitgebern und Arbeitnehmern

NM, N.Mex. (US) *abbr* (Post) = New Mexico

 KEYWORD

no [nəʊ] (pl **noes**) *adv* (opposite of "yes") nein; **no thank you** nein danke
▷ *adj* (not any) kein(e); **I have no money/time/books** ich habe kein Geld/keine Zeit/keine Bücher; **"no entry"** „kein Zutritt"; **"no smoking"** „Rauchen verboten"
▷ *n* Nein *nt*; **there were 20 noes and one abstention** es gab 20 Neinstimmen und eine Enthaltung; **I won't take no for an answer** ich bestehe darauf

no. *abbr* (= number) Nr.

nobble [ˈnɔbl] (Brit: inf) *vt* (bribe) (sich dat) kaufen; (grab) sich dat schnappen; (Racing: horse, dog) lahmlegen

Nobel Prize [nəʊˈbɛl-] *n* Nobelpreis *m*

nobility [nəʊˈbɪlɪtɪ] *n* Adel *m*; (quality) Edelmut

m

noble ['nəʊbl] *adj* edel, nobel; *(aristocratic)* ad(e)lig; *(impressive)* prächtig

nobleman ['nəʊblmən] *(irreg: like* **man***)* *n* Ad(e)lige(r) *f(m)*

nobly ['nəʊblɪ] *adv* edel

nobody ['nəʊbədɪ] *pron* niemand, keiner ▷ *n:* **he's a ~** er ist ein Niemand *m*

no-claims bonus [nəʊ'kleɪmz-] *n* Schadenfreiheitsrabatt *m*

nocturnal [nɔk'tɜːnl] *adj* nächtlich; *(animal)* Nacht-

nod [nɔd] *vi* nicken; *(fig: flowers etc)* wippen ▷ *vt:* **to ~ one's head** mit dem Kopf nicken ▷ *n* Nicken *nt;* **they ~ded their agreement** sie nickten zustimmend

▶ **nod off** *vi* einnicken

no-fly zone [nəʊ'flaɪ-] *n* Sperrzone *f* für den Flugverkehr

noise [nɔɪz] *n* Geräusch *nt;* *(din)* Lärm *m*

noiseless ['nɔɪzlɪs] *adj* geräuschlos

noisily ['nɔɪzɪlɪ] *adv* laut

noisy ['nɔɪzɪ] *adj* laut

nomad ['nəʊmæd] *n* Nomade *m*, Nomadin *f*

nomadic [nəʊ'mædɪk] *adj* Nomaden-, nomadisch

no-man's-land ['nəʊmænzlænd] *n* Niemandsland *nt*

nominal ['nɔmɪnl] *adj* nominell

nominate ['nɔmɪneɪt] *vt* nominieren; *(appoint)* ernennen

nomination [nɔmɪ'neɪʃən] *n* Nominierung *f;* *(appointment)* Ernennung *f*

nominee [nɔmɪ'niː] *n* Kandidat(in) *m(f)*

non- [nɔn] *pref* nicht-, Nicht-

non-alcoholic [nɔnælkə'hɔlɪk] *adj* alkoholfrei

non-aligned [nɔnə'laɪnd] *adj* blockfrei

non-breakable [nɔn'breɪkəbl] *adj* unzerbrechlich

nonce word ['nɔns-] *n* Ad-hoc-Bildung *f*

nonchalant ['nɔnʃələnt] *adj* lässig, nonchalant

noncommissioned officer [nɔnkə'mɪʃənd-] *n* Unteroffizier *m*

non-committal [nɔnkə'mɪtl] *adj* zurückhaltend; *(answer)* unverbindlich

nonconformist [nɔnkən'fɔːmɪst] *n* Nonkonformist(in) *m(f)* ▷ *adj* nonkonformistisch

non-cooperation ['nɔnkəʊɔpə'reɪʃən] *n* unkooperative Haltung *f*

nondescript ['nɔndɪskrɪpt] *adj* unauffällig; *(colour)* unbestimmbar

none [nʌn] *pron (not one)* kein(e, er, es); *(not any)* nichts; **~ of us** keiner von uns; **I've ~ left** *(not any)* ich habe nichts übrig; *(not one)* ich habe kein(e, en, es) übrig; **~ at all** *(not any)* überhaupt nicht; *(not one)* überhaupt kein(e, er, es); **I was ~ the wiser** ich war auch nicht klüger; **she would have ~ of it** sie wollte nichts davon hören; **it was ~ other than X** es war kein anderer als X

nonentity [nɔ'nɛntɪtɪ] *n (person)* Nichts *nt*, unbedeutende Figur *f*

non-essential [nɔnɪ'sɛnʃl] *adj* unnötig ▷ *n:* **~s** nicht (lebens)notwendige Dinge *pl*

nonetheless ['nʌnðə'lɛs] *adv* nichtsdestoweniger, trotzdem

nonevent [nɔnɪ'vɛnt] *n* Reinfall *m*

non-existent [nɔnɪg'zɪstənt] *adj* nicht vorhanden

non-fiction [nɔn'fɪkʃən] *n* Sachbücher *pl* ▷ *adj* *(book)* Sach-; *(prize)* Sachbuch-

non-flammable [nɔn'flæməbl] *adj* nicht entzündbar

non-intervention ['nɔnɪntə'vɛnʃən] *n* Nichteinmischung *f*, Nichteingreifen *nt*

no-no ['nəʊnəʊ] *n:* **it's a ~** *(inf)* das kommt nicht infrage

non obst. *abbr (= non obstante)* dennoch

no-nonsense [nəʊ'nɔnsəns] *adj (approach, look)* nüchtern

non-payment [nɔn'peɪmənt] *n* Nichtzahlung *f*, Zahlungsverweigerung *f*

nonplussed [nɔn'plʌst] *adj* verdutzt, verblüfft

non-profit making ['nɔn'prɔfɪt-] *adj (organization)* gemeinnützig

nonreturnable [nɔnrə'tɜːnəbl] *adj:* **~ bottle** Einwegflasche *f*

nonsense ['nɔnsəns] *n* Unsinn *m;* **~!** Unsinn!, Quatsch!; **it is ~ to say that …** es ist dummes Gerede zu sagen, dass …; **to make (a) ~ of sth** etw ad absurdum führen

nonsensical [nɔn'sɛnsɪkl] *adj (idea, action etc)* unsinnig

non-shrink [nɔn'ʃrɪŋk] *(Brit) adj* nicht einlaufend

non-smoker [nɔn'sməʊkəʳ] *n* Nichtraucher(in) *m(f)*

nonstarter [nɔn'stɑːtəʳ] *n (fig):* **it's a ~** *(idea etc)* es hat keine Erfolgschance

non-stick ['nɔn'stɪk] *adj* kunststoffbeschichtet, Teflon-®

non-stop ['nɔn'stɔp] *adj* ununterbrochen; *(flight)* Nonstop-, Non-Stop- ▷ *adv* ununterbrochen; *(fly)* nonstop

non-taxable [nɔn'tæksəbl] *adj* nicht steuerpflichtig

non-U [nɔn'juː] *(Brit: inf) adj abbr (= non-upper class)* nicht vornehm

non-white ['nɔn'waɪt] *adj* farbig ▷ *n* Farbige(r) *f(m)*

noodles ['nuːdlz] *npl* Nudeln *pl*

nook [nuk] *n:* **every ~ and cranny** jeder Winkel

noon [nuːn] *n* Mittag *m*

no-one ['nəʊwʌn] *pron* = **nobody**

noose [nuːs] *n* Schlinge *f*

nor [nɔːʳ] *conj, adv* = **neither**

Norf *(Brit) abbr (Post)* = Norfolk

norm [nɔːm] *n* Norm *f*

normal ['nɔːməl] *adj* normal ▷ *n:* **to return to ~** sich wieder normalisieren

normality [nɔː'mælɪtɪ] *n* Normalität *f*

normally ['nɔːməlɪ] *adv* normalerweise; *(act, behave)* normal

Normandy ['nɔːməndɪ] *n* Normandie *f*

n

north [nɔːθ] *n* Norden *m* ▷ *adj* nördlich, Nord-
▷ *adv* nach Norden; ~ **of** nördlich von

North Africa *n* Nordafrika *nt*

North African *adj* nordafrikanisch ▷ *n*
Nordafrikaner(in) *m(f)*

North America *n* Nordamerika *nt*

North American *adj* nordamerikanisch ▷ *n*
Nordamerikaner(in) *m(f)*

Northants [nɔːˈθænts] (*Brit*) *abbr*
(*Post*) = Northamptonshire

northbound [ˈnɔːθbaund] *adj* in Richtung
Norden; (*carriageway*) nach Norden (führend)

Northd (*Brit*) *abbr* (*Post*) = Northumberland

north-east [nɔːθˈiːst] *n* Nordosten *m* ▷ *adj*
nordöstlich, Nordost- ▷ *adv* nach Nordosten; ~
of nordöstlich von

northerly [ˈnɔːðəlɪ] *adj* nördlich

northern [ˈnɔːðən] *adj* nördlich, Nord-

Northern Ireland *n* Nordirland *nt*

North Korea *n* Nordkorea *nt*

North Pole *n*: **the ~** der Nordpol

North Sea *n*: **the ~** die Nordsee *f*

North Sea oil *n* Nordseeöl *nt*

northward [ˈnɔːθwəd], **northwards**
[ˈnɔːθwədz] *adv* nach Norden, nordwärts

north-west [nɔːθˈwɛst] *n* Nordwesten *m*
▷ *adj* nordwestlich, Nordwest- ▷ *adv* nach
Nordwesten; ~ **of** nordwestlich von

Norway [ˈnɔːweɪ] *n* Norwegen *nt*

Norwegian [nɔːˈwiːdʒən] *adj* norwegisch ▷ *n*
Norweger(in) *m(f)*; (*Ling*) Norwegisch *nt*

nos. *abbr* (= numbers) Nrn.

nose [nəuz] *n* Nase *f*; (*of car*) Schnauze *f* ▷ *vi*
(*also*: **nose one's way**) sich schieben; **to follow
one's ~** immer der Nase nach gehen; **to get
up one's ~** (*inf*) auf die Nerven gehen +*dat*; **to
have a (good) ~ for sth** eine (gute) Nase für
etw haben; **to keep one's ~ clean** (*inf*) eine
saubere Weste behalten; **to look down one's
~ at sb/sth** (*inf*) auf jdn/etw herabsehen; **to
pay through the ~ (for sth)** (*inf*) (für etw)
viel blechen; **to rub sb's ~ in sth** (*inf*) jdm
etw unter die Nase reiben; **to turn one's ~
up at sth** (*inf*) die Nase über etw *acc* rümpfen;
under sb's ~ vor jds Augen
▸ **nose about** *vi* herumschnüffeln
▸ **nose around** *vi* = **nose about**

nosebleed [ˈnəuzbliːd] *n* Nasenbluten *nt*

nose-dive [ˈnəuzdaɪv] *n* (*of plane*) Sturzflug *m*
▷ *vi* (*plane*) im Sturzflug herabgehen

nose drops *npl* Nasentropfen *pl*

nosey [ˈnəuzɪ] (*inf*) *adj* = **nosy**

nostalgia [nɔsˈtældʒɪə] *n* Nostalgie *f*

nostalgic [nɔsˈtældʒɪk] *adj* nostalgisch

nostril [ˈnɔstrɪl] *n* Nasenloch *nt*; (*of animal*)
Nüster *f*

nosy [ˈnəuzɪ] (*inf*) *adj* neugierig

KEYWORD

not [nɔt] *adv* nicht; **he is not** *or* **isn't here** er
ist nicht hier; **you must not** *or* **you mustn't
do that** das darfst du nicht tun; **it's too late,**
isn't it? es ist zu spät, nicht wahr?; **not that I
don't like him** nicht, dass ich ihn nicht mag;
not yet noch nicht; **not now** nicht jetzt; *see
also* **all; only**

notable [ˈnəutəbl] *adj* bemerkenswert

notably [ˈnəutəblɪ] *adv* hauptsächlich;
(*markedly*) bemerkenswert

notary [ˈnəutərɪ] *n* (*also*: **notary public**)
Notar(in) *m(f)*

notation [nəuˈteɪʃən] *n* Notation *f*; (*Mus*)
Notenschrift *f*

notch [nɔtʃ] *n* Kerbe *f*; (*in blade, saw*) Scharte *f*;
(*fig*) Klasse *f*
▸ **notch up** *vt* erzielen; (*victory*) erringen

note [nəut] *n* Notiz *f*; (*of lecturer*) Manuskript
nt; (*of student etc*) Aufzeichnung *f*; (*in book etc*)
Anmerkung *f*; (*letter*) paar Zeilen *pl*; (*banknote*)
Note *f*, Schein *m*; (*Mus: sound*) Ton *m*; (*: symbol*)
Note *f*; (*tone*) Ton *m*, Klang *m* ▷ *vt* beachten;
(*point out*) anmerken; (*also*: **note down**)
notieren; **of ~** bedeutend; **to make a ~ of
sth** sich *dat* etw notieren; **to take ~s** Notizen
machen, mitschreiben; **to take ~ of sth** etw
zur Kenntnis nehmen

notebook [ˈnəutbuk] *n* Notizbuch *nt*; (*for
shorthand*) Stenoblock *m*

notecase [ˈnəutkeɪs] (*Brit*) *n* Brieftasche *f*

noted [ˈnəutɪd] *adj* bekannt

notepad [ˈnəutpæd] *n* Notizblock *m*

notepaper [ˈnəutpeɪpəʳ] *n* Briefpapier *nt*

noteworthy [ˈnəutwəːðɪ] *adj* beachtenswert

nothing [ˈnʌθɪŋ] *n* nichts; ~ **new/worse** *etc*
nichts Neues/Schlimmeres *etc*; ~ **much** nicht
viel; ~ **else** sonst nichts; **for ~** umsonst; ~ **at
all** überhaupt nichts

notice [ˈnəutɪs] *n* Bekanntmachung *f*; (*sign*)
Schild *nt*; (*warning*) Ankündigung *f*; (*dismissal*)
Kündigung *f*; (*Brit: review*) Kritik *f*, Rezension *f*
▷ *vt* bemerken; **to bring sth to sb's ~** jdn auf
etw *acc* aufmerksam machen; **to take no ~ of**
ignorieren, nicht beachten; **to escape sb's ~**
jdm entgehen; **it has come to my ~ that ...**
es ist mir zu Ohren gekommen, dass ...; **to
give sb ~ of sth** jdm von etw Bescheid geben;
without ~ ohne Ankündigung; **advance ~**
Vorankündigung *f*; **at short/a moment's ~**
kurzfristig/innerhalb kürzester Zeit; **until
further ~** bis auf Weiteres; **to hand in one's
~** kündigen; **to be given one's ~** gekündigt
werden +*dat*

noticeable [ˈnəutɪsəbl] *adj* deutlich

noticeboard [ˈnəutɪsbɔːd] (*Brit*) *n*
Anschlagbrett *nt*

notification [nəutɪfɪˈkeɪʃən] *n*
Benachrichtigung *f*

notify [ˈnəutɪfaɪ] *vt*: **to ~ sb (of sth)** jdn (von
etw) benachrichtigen

notion [ˈnəuʃən] *n* Vorstellung *f*; **notions** (*US*)
npl (*haberdashery*) Kurzwaren *pl*

notoriety [nəutəˈraɪətɪ] *n* traurige
Berühmtheit *f*

notorious [nəuˈtɔːrɪəs] *adj* berüchtigt

notoriously [nəu'tɔ:rɪəslɪ] adv notorisch

Notts [nɔts] (Brit) abbr (Post) = Nottinghamshire

notwithstanding [nɔtwɪθ'stændɪŋ] adv trotzdem ▷ prep trotz +dat

nougat ['nu:gɑ:] n Nugat m

nought [nɔ:t] n Null f

noughties ['nɔ:tɪz] npl (inf) das erste Jahrzehnt des dritten Jahrtausends, Nullerjahre pl

noun [naun] n Hauptwort nt, Substantiv nt

nourish ['nʌrɪʃ] vt nähren

nourishing ['nʌrɪʃɪŋ] adj nahrhaft

nourishment ['nʌrɪʃmənt] n Nahrung f

Nov. abbr (= November) Nov.

Nova Scotia ['nəuvə'skəuʃə] n Neuschottland nt

novel ['nɔvl] n Roman m ▷ adj neu(artig)

novelist ['nɔvəlɪst] n Romanschriftsteller(in) m(f)

novelty ['nɔvəltɪ] n Neuheit f; (object) Kleinigkeit f

November [nəu'vɛmbə^r] n November m; see also **July**

novice ['nɔvɪs] n Neuling m, Anfänger(in) m(f); (Rel) Novize m, Novizin f

NOW [nau] (US) n abbr (= National Organization for Women) Frauenvereinigung

now [nau] adv jetzt; (these days) heute ▷ conj: ~ **(that)** jetzt, wo; **right** ~ gleich, sofort; **by** ~ inzwischen, mittlerweile; **that's the fashion just** ~ das ist gerade modern; **I saw her just** ~ ich habe sie gerade gesehen; **(every)** ~ **and then, (every)** ~ **and again** ab und zu, gelegentlich; **from** ~ **on** von nun an; **in 3 days from** ~ (heute) in 3 Tagen; **between** ~ **and Monday** bis Montag; **that's all for** ~ das ist erst einmal alles; **any day** ~ jederzeit; ~ **then** also

nowadays ['nauədeɪz] adv heute

nowhere ['nəuwɛə^r] adv (be) nirgends, nirgendwo; (go) nirgendwohin; ~ **else** nirgendwo anders

no-win situation [nəu'wɪn-] n aussichtslose Lage f

noxious ['nɔkʃəs] adj (gas, fumes) schädlich; (smell) übel

nozzle ['nɔzl] n Düse f

NP n abbr (Law) = **notary public**

NS (Canada) abbr = Nova Scotia

NSC (US) n abbr = **National Security Council**

NSF (US) n abbr (= National Science Foundation) Organisation zur Förderung der Wissenschaft

NSPCC (Brit) n abbr (= National Society for the Prevention of Cruelty to Children) Kinderschutzbund m

NSW (Australia) abbr (Post) = New South Wales

NT n abbr (Bible: = New Testament) NT

nth [ɛnθ] (inf) adj: **to the** ~ **degree** in der n-ten Potenz

nuance ['nju:ɑ̃ns] n Nuance f

nubile ['nju:baɪl] adj gut entwickelt

nuclear ['nju:klɪə^r] adj (bomb, industry etc) Atom-; ~ **physics** Kernphysik f; ~ **war** Atomkrieg m

nuclear disarmament n nukleare or atomare Abrüstung f

nuclear family n Kleinfamilie f, Kernfamilie f

nuclear-free zone ['nju:klɪə'fri:-] n atomwaffenfreie Zone f

nuclei ['nju:klɪaɪ] npl of **nucleus**

nucleus ['nju:klɪəs] (pl **nuclei**) n Kern m

NUCPS (Brit) n abbr (= National Union of Civil and Public Servants) Gewerkschaft für Beschäftigte im öffentlichen Dienst

nude [nju:d] adj nackt ▷ n (Art) Akt m; **in the** ~ nackt

nudge [nʌdʒ] vt anstoßen

nudist ['nju:dɪst] n Nudist(in) m(f)

nudist colony n FKK-Kolonie f

nudity ['nju:dɪtɪ] n Nacktheit f

nugget ['nʌgɪt] n (of gold) Klumpen m; (fig: of information) Brocken m

nuisance ['nju:sns] n: **to be a** ~ lästig sein; (situation) ärgerlich sein; **he's a** ~ er geht einem auf die Nerven; **what a** ~! wie ärgerlich/lästig!

NUJ (Brit) n abbr (= National Union of Journalists) Journalistengewerkschaft

null [nʌl] adj: ~ **and void** null und nichtig

nullify ['nʌlɪfaɪ] vt zunichtemachen; (claim, law) für null und nichtig erklären

NUM (Brit) n abbr (= National Union of Mineworkers) Bergarbeitergewerkschaft

numb [nʌm] adj taub, gefühllos; (fig: with fear etc) wie betäubt ▷ vt taub or gefühllos machen; (pain, mind) betäuben

number ['nʌmbə^r] n Zahl f; (quantity) (An)zahl f; (of house, bank account, bus etc) Nummer f ▷ vt (pages etc) nummerieren; (amount to) zählen; **a** ~ **of** einige; **any** ~ **of** beliebig viele; (reasons) alle möglichen; **wrong** ~ (Tel) falsch verbunden; **to be** ~**ed among** zählen zu

number plate (Brit) n (Aut) Nummernschild nt

Number Ten (Brit) n (Pol: = 10 Downing Street) Nummer zehn f (Downing Street)

numbness ['nʌmnɪs] n Taubheit f, Starre f; (fig) Benommenheit f, Betäubung f

numbskull ['nʌmskʌl] n = **numskull**

numeral ['nju:mərəl] n Ziffer f

numerate ['nju:mərɪt] (Brit) adj: **to be** ~ rechnen können

numerical [nju:'mɛrɪkl] adj numerisch

numerous ['nju:mərəs] adj zahlreich

numskull ['nʌmskʌl] (inf) n Holzkopf m

nun [nʌn] n Nonne f

nunnery ['nʌnərɪ] n (Nonnen)kloster nt

nuptial ['nʌpʃəl] adj (feast, celebration) Hochzeits-; ~ **bliss** Eheglück nt

nurse [nə:s] n Krankenschwester f; (also: **nursemaid**) Kindermädchen nt ▷ vt pflegen; (cold, toothache etc) auskurieren; (baby) stillen; (fig: desire, grudge) hegen

nursery ['nə:sərɪ] n Kindergarten m; (room) Kinderzimmer nt; (for plants) Gärtnerei f

nursery rhyme n Kinderreim m

nursery school n Kindergarten m

nursery slope (Brit) n (Ski) Anfängerhügel m

nursing ['nə:sɪŋ] n Krankenpflege f; (care)

n

Pflege f
nursing home n Pflegeheim nt
nursing mother n stillende Mutter f
nurture ['nə:tʃə'] vt hegen und pflegen;
(fig: ideas, creativity) fördern
NUS (Brit) n abbr (= National Union of Students)
Studentengewerkschaft
NUT (Brit) n abbr (= National Union of Teachers)
Lehrergewerkschaft
nut [nʌt] n (Tech) (Schrauben)mutter f; (Bot)
Nuss f; (inf: lunatic) Spinner(in) m(f)
nutcase ['nʌtkeɪs] (inf) n Spinner(in) m(f)
nutcrackers ['nʌtkrækəz] npl Nussknacker m
nutmeg ['nʌtmeg] n Muskat m, Muskatnuss f
nutrient ['nju:trɪənt] n Nährstoff m
nutrition [nju:'trɪʃən] n Ernährung f;
(nourishment) Nahrung f
nutritionist [nju:'trɪʃnɪst] n
Ernährungswissenschaftler(in) m(f)
nutritious [nju:'trɪʃəs] adj nahrhaft

nuts [nʌts] (inf) adj verrückt; **he's** ~ er spinnt
nutshell ['nʌtʃɛl] n Nussschale f; **in a** ~ (fig)
kurz gesagt
nutty ['nʌtɪ] adj (flavour) Nuss-; (inf: idea etc)
bekloppt
nuzzle ['nʌzl] vi: **to** ~ **up to** sich drücken or
schmiegen an +acc
NV (US) abbr (Post) = Nevada
NVQ n abbr (= National Vocational Qualification)
Qualifikation für berufsbegleitende Ausbildungsinhalte
NW abbr = **north-west**
NY (US) abbr (Post) = New York
nylon ['naɪlɒn] n Nylon nt ▷ adj Nylon-; **nylons**
npl (stockings) Nylonstrümpfe pl
nymph [nɪmf] n Nymphe f
nymphomaniac ['nɪmfəʊ'meɪnɪæk] n
Nymphomanin f
NYSE (US) n abbr (= New York Stock Exchange) New
Yorker Börse
NZ abbr = **New Zealand**

Oo

O, o [əʊ] *n* (*letter*) O *nt*, o *nt*; (*US: Scol: outstanding*) ≈ Eins *f*; (*Tel etc*) Null *f*; **O for Olive, O for Oboe** (*US*) ≈ O wie Otto
oaf [əʊf] *n* Trottel *m*
oak [əʊk] *n* (*tree, wood*) Eiche *f* ▷ *adj* (*furniture, door*) Eichen-
O & M *n abbr* (= *organization and method*) Organisation und Arbeitsweise *pl*
OAP (*Brit*) *n abbr* = **old age pensioner**
oar [ɔːʳ] *n* Ruder *nt*; **to put** *or* **shove one's ~ in** (*inf: fig*) mitmischen, sich einmischen
oarsman ['ɔːzmən] (*irreg: like* **man**) *n* Ruderer *m*
oarswoman ['ɔːzwumən] (*irreg: like* **woman**) *n* Ruderin *f*
OAS *n abbr* (= *Organization of American States*) OAS *f*
oasis [əʊ'eɪsɪs] (*pl* **oases**) *n* (*lit, fig*) Oase *f*
oath [əʊθ] *n* (*promise*) Eid *m*, Schwur *m*; (*swear word*) Fluch *m*; **on ~** (*Brit*): **under ~** unter Eid; **to take the ~** (*Law*) vereidigt werden
oatmeal ['əʊtmiːl] *n* Haferschrot *m*; (*colour*) Hellbeige *nt*
oats [əʊts] *npl* Hafer *m*; **he's getting his ~** (*Brit: inf: fig*) er kommt im Bett auf seine Kosten
obdurate ['ɒbdjʊrɪt] *adj* unnachgiebig
OBE (*Brit*) *n abbr* (= *Officer of (the order of) the British Empire*) britischer Ordenstitel
obedience [ə'biːdɪəns] *n* Gehorsam *m*; **in ~ to** gemäß +*dat*
obedient [ə'biːdɪənt] *adj* gehorsam; **to be ~ to sb** jdm gehorchen
obelisk ['ɒbɪlɪsk] *n* Obelisk *m*
obese [əʊ'biːs] *adj* fettleibig
obesity [əʊ'biːsɪtɪ] *n* Fettleibigkeit *f*
obey [ə'beɪ] *vt* (*person*) gehorchen +*dat*, folgen +*dat*; (*orders, law*) befolgen ▷ *vi* gehorchen
obituary [ə'bɪtjʊərɪ] *n* Nachruf *m*
object [*n* 'ɒbdʒɪkt, *vi* əb'dʒɛkt] *n* (*also Ling*) Objekt *nt*; (*aim, purpose*) Ziel *nt*, Zweck *m* ▷ *vi* dagegen sein; **to be an ~ of ridicule** (*person*) sich lächerlich machen; (*thing*) lächerlich wirken; **money is no ~** Geld spielt keine Rolle; **he ~ed that ...** er wandte ein, dass ...; **I ~!** ich protestiere!; **do you ~ to my smoking?** haben Sie etwas dagegen, wenn ich rauche?
objection [əb'dʒɛkʃən] *n* (*argument*) Einwand *m*; **I have no ~ to ...** ich habe nichts dagegen, dass ...; **if you have no ~** wenn Sie nichts dagegen haben; **to raise** *or* **voice an ~** einen

Einwand erheben *or* vorbringen
objectionable [əb'dʒɛkʃənəbl] *adj* (*language, conduct*) anstößig; (*person*) unausstehlich
objective [əb'dʒɛktɪv] *adj* objektiv ▷ *n* Ziel *nt*
objectively [əb'dʒɛktɪvlɪ] *adv* objektiv
objectivity [ɒbdʒɪk'tɪvɪtɪ] *n* Objektivität *f*
object lesson *n*: **an ~ in** ein Paradebeispiel *nt* für
objector [əb'dʒɛktəʳ] *n* Gegner(in) *m(f)*
obligation [ɒblɪ'geɪʃən] *n* Pflicht *f*; **to be under an ~ to do sth** verpflichtet sein, etw zu tun; **to be under an ~ to sb** jdm verpflichtet sein; **"no ~ to buy"** (*Comm*) „kein Kaufzwang"
obligatory [ə'blɪgətərɪ] *adj* obligatorisch
oblige [ə'blaɪdʒ] *vt* (*compel*) zwingen; (*do a favour for*) einen Gefallen tun +*dat*; **I felt ~d to invite him in** ich fühlte mich verpflichtet, ihn hereinzubitten; **to be ~d to sb for sth** (*grateful*) jdm für etw dankbar sein; **anything to ~!** (*inf*) stets zu Diensten!
obliging [ə'blaɪdʒɪŋ] *adj* entgegenkommend
oblique [ə'bliːk] *adj* (*line, angle*) schief; (*reference, compliment*) indirekt, versteckt ▷ *n* (*Brit: also:* **oblique stroke**) Schrägstrich *m*
obliterate [ə'blɪtəreɪt] *vt* (*village etc*) vernichten; (*fig: memory, error*) auslöschen
oblivion [ə'blɪvɪən] *n* (*unconsciousness*) Bewusstlosigkeit *f*; (*being forgotten*) Vergessenheit *f*; **to sink into ~** (*event etc*) in Vergessenheit geraten
oblivious [ə'blɪvɪəs] *adj*: **he was ~ of** *or* **to it** er war sich dessen nicht bewusst
oblong ['ɒblɒŋ] *adj* rechteckig ▷ *n* Rechteck *nt*
obnoxious [əb'nɒkʃəs] *adj* widerwärtig, widerlich
o.b.o. (*US*) *abbr* (*in classified ads*: = *or best offer*) bzw. Höchstgebot
oboe ['əʊbəʊ] *n* Oboe *f*
obscene [əb'siːn] *adj* obszön; (*fig: wealth*) unanständig; (*income etc*) unverschämt
obscenity [əb'sɛnɪtɪ] *n* Obszönität *f*
obscure [əb'skjʊəʳ] *adj* (*little known*) unbekannt, obskur; (*difficult to understand*) unklar ▷ *vt* (*obstruct, conceal*) verdecken
obscurity [əb'skjʊərɪtɪ] *n* (*of person, book*) Unbekanntheit *f*; (*of remark etc*) Unklarheit *f*
obsequious [əb'siːkwɪəs] *adj* unterwürfig

o

observable [əb'zə:vəbl] *adj* wahrnehmbar; (*noticeable*) erkennbar

observance [əb'zə:vəns] *n* (*of law etc*) Befolgung *f*; **religious ~s** religiöse Feste *pl*

observant [əb'zə:vənt] *adj* aufmerksam

observation [ɔbzə'veɪʃən] *n* (*remark*) Bemerkung *f*; (*act of observing*, *Med*) Beobachtung *f*; **she's in hospital under ~** sie ist zur Beobachtung im Krankenhaus

observation post *n* Beobachtungsposten *m*

observatory [əb'zə:vətrɪ] *n* Observatorium *nt*

observe [əb'zə:v] *vt* (*watch*) beobachten; (*notice*, *comment*) bemerken; (*abide by: rule etc*) einhalten

observer [əb'zə:vəʳ] *n* Beobachter(in) *m(f)*

obsess [əb'sɛs] *vt* verfolgen; **to be ~ed by** *or* **with sb/sth** von jdm/etw besessen sein

obsession [əb'sɛʃən] *n* Besessenheit *f*

obsessive [əb'sɛsɪv] *adj* (*person*) zwanghaft; (*interest, hatred, tidiness*) krankhaft; **to be ~ about cleaning/tidying up** einen Putz-/Ordnungsfimmel haben (*inf*)

obsolescence [ɔbsə'lɛsns] *n* Veralten *nt*; **built-in** *or* **planned ~** (*Comm*) geplanter Verschleiß *m*

obsolete ['ɔbsəli:t] *adj* veraltet

obstacle ['ɔbstəkl] *n* (*lit*, *fig*) Hindernis *nt*

obstacle race *n* Hindernisrennen *nt*

obstetrician [ɔbstə'trɪʃən] *n* Geburtshelfer(in) *m(f)*

obstetrics [ɔb'stɛtrɪks] *n* Geburtshilfe *f*

obstinacy ['ɔbstɪnəsɪ] *n* (*of person*) Starrsinn *m*

obstinate ['ɔbstɪnɪt] *adj* (*person*) starrsinnig, stur; (*refusal, cough etc*) hartnäckig

obstruct [əb'strʌkt] *vt* (*road, path*) blockieren; (*traffic, fig*) behindern

obstruction [əb'strʌkʃən] *n* (*object*) Hindernis *nt*; (*of plan, law*) Behinderung *f*

obstructive [əb'strʌktɪv] *adj* hinderlich, obstruktiv (*esp Pol*); **she's being ~** sie macht Schwierigkeiten

obtain [əb'teɪn] *vt* erhalten, bekommen ▷ *vi* (*form: exist, be the case*) gelten

obtainable [əb'teɪnəbl] *adj* erhältlich

obtrusive [əb'tru:sɪv] *adj* aufdringlich; (*conspicuous*) auffällig

obtuse [əb'tju:s] *adj* (*person, remark*) einfältig; (*Math*) stumpf

obverse ['ɔbvə:s] *n* (*of situation, argument*) Kehrseite *f*

obviate ['ɔbvɪeɪt] *vt* (*need, problem etc*) vorbeugen +*dat*

obvious ['ɔbvɪəs] *adj* offensichtlich; (*lie*) klar; (*predictable*) naheliegend

obviously ['ɔbvɪəslɪ] *adv* (*clearly*) offensichtlich; (*of course*) natürlich; **~!** selbstverständlich!; **~ not** offensichtlich nicht; **he was ~ not drunk** er war natürlich nicht betrunken; **he was not ~ drunk** offenbar war er nicht betrunken

OCAS *n abbr* (= *Organization of Central American States*) *mittelamerikanischer Staatenbund*

occasion [ə'keɪʒən] *n* Gelegenheit *f*; (*celebration etc*) Ereignis *nt* ▷ *vt* (*form: cause*) verursachen; **on ~** (*sometimes*) gelegentlich; **on that ~** bei der Gelegenheit; **to rise to the ~** sich der Lage gewachsen zeigen

occasional [ə'keɪʒənl] *adj* gelegentlich; **he likes the ~ cigar** er raucht gelegentlich gern eine Zigarre

occasionally [ə'keɪʒənəlɪ] *adv* gelegentlich; **very ~** sehr selten

occasional table *n* Beistelltisch *m*

occult [ɔ'kʌlt] *n*: **the ~** der Okkultismus ▷ *adj* okkult

occupancy ['ɔkjupənsɪ] *n* (*of room etc*) Bewohnen *nt*

occupant ['ɔkjupənt] *n* (*of house etc*) Bewohner(in) *m(f)*; (*temporary: of car*) Insasse *m*, Insassin *f*; **the ~ of this table/office** derjenige, der an diesem Tisch sitzt/in diesem Büro arbeitet

occupation [ɔkju'peɪʃən] *n* (*job*) Beruf *m*; (*pastime*) Beschäftigung *f*; (*of building, country etc*) Besetzung *f*

occupational guidance [ɔkju'peɪʃənl-] (*Brit*) *n* Berufsberatung *f*

occupational hazard *n* Berufsrisiko *nt*

occupational pension scheme *n* betriebliche Altersversorgung *f*

occupational therapy *n* Beschäftigungstherapie *f*

occupier ['ɔkjupaɪəʳ] *n* Bewohner(in) *m(f)*

occupy ['ɔkjupaɪ] *vt* (*house, office*) bewohnen; (*place etc*) belegen; (*building, country etc*) besetzen; (*time, attention*) beanspruchen; (*position, space*) einnehmen; **to ~ o.s. (in** *or* **with sth)** sich (mit etw) beschäftigen; **to ~ o.s. in** *or* **with doing sth** sich damit beschäftigen, etw zu tun; **to be occupied in** *or* **with sth** mit etw beschäftigt sein; **to be occupied in** *or* **with doing sth** damit beschäftigt sein, etw zu tun

occur [ə'kə:ʳ] *vi* (*take place*) geschehen, sich ereignen; (*exist*) vorkommen; **to ~ to sb** jdm einfallen

occurrence [ə'kʌrəns] *n* (*event*) Ereignis *nt*; (*incidence*) Auftreten *nt*

ocean ['əʊʃən] *n* Ozean *m*, Meer *nt*; **~s of** (*inf*) jede Menge

ocean bed *n* Meeresgrund *m*

ocean-going ['əʊʃəngəʊɪŋ] *adj* (*ship, vessel*) Hochsee-

Oceania [əʊʃɪ'eɪnɪə] *n* Ozeanien *nt*

ocean liner *n* Ozeandampfer *m*

ochre, (*US*) **ocher** ['əʊkəʳ] *adj* ockerfarben

o'clock [ə'klɔk] *adv*: **it is 5 ~** es ist 5 Uhr

OCR *n abbr* (*Comput*) = **optical character reader**; **optical character recogniton**

Oct. *abbr* (= *October*) Okt.

octagonal [ɔk'tægənl] *adj* achteckig

octane ['ɔkteɪn] *n* Oktan *nt*; **high-~ petrol**, **high-~ gas** (*US*) Benzin *nt* mit hoher Oktanzahl

octave ['ɔktɪv] *n* Oktave *f*

October [ɔk'təʊbəʳ] *n* Oktober *m*; *see also* **July**

octogenarian ['ɔktəudʒɪ'nɛərɪən] *n* Achtzigjährige(r) *f(m)*

octopus ['ɔktəpəs] *n* Tintenfisch *m*
odd [ɔd] *adj* (*person*) sonderbar, komisch;
(*behaviour, shape*) seltsam; (*number*) ungerade;
(*sock, shoe etc*) einzeln; (*occasional*) gelegentlich;
60-~ etwa 60; **at ~ times** ab und zu; **to be the
~ one out** der Außenseiter/die Außenseiterin
sein; **add meat or the ~ vegetable to the
soup** fügen Sie der Suppe Fleisch oder auch
etwas Gemüse bei
oddball ['ɔdbɔːl] (*inf*) *n* komischer Kauz *m*
oddity ['ɔdɪtɪ] *n* (*person*) Sonderling *m*; (*thing*)
Merkwürdigkeit *f*
odd-job man [ɔd'dʒɔb-] *n* Mädchen *nt* für alles
odd jobs *npl* Gelegenheitsarbeiten *pl*
oddly ['ɔdlɪ] *adv* (*behave, dress*) seltsam; *see also*
enough
oddments ['ɔdmənts] *npl* (*Comm*) Restposten *m*
odds [ɔdz] *npl* (*in betting*) Gewinnquote *f*; (*fig*)
Chancen *pl*; **the ~ are in favour of/against
his coming** es sieht so aus, als ob er kommt/
nicht kommt; **to succeed against all the ~**
allen Erwartungen zum Trotz erfolgreich sein;
it makes no ~ es spielt keine Rolle; **to be at ~
(with)** (*in disagreement*) uneinig sein (mit); (*at
variance*) sich nicht vertragen (mit)
odds and ends *npl* Kleinigkeiten *pl*
odds-on [ɔdz'ɔn] *adj*: **the ~ favourite** der klare
Favorit ▷ *adv*: **it's ~ that she'll win** es ist so
gut wie sicher, dass sie gewinnt
ode [əud] *n* Ode *f*
odious ['əudɪəs] *adj* widerwärtig
odometer [ɔ'dɔmɪtəʳ] (*US*) *n* Tacho(meter) *m*
odor *etc* (*US*) = **odour** *etc*
odour, (*US*) **odor** ['əudəʳ] *n* Geruch *m*
odourless ['əudəlɪs] *adj* geruchlos
OECD *n abbr* (= *Organization for Economic
Cooperation and Development*) OECD *f*
oesophagus, (*US*) **esophagus** [iː'sɔfəgəs] *n*
Speiseröhre *f*
oestrogen, (*US*) **estrogen** ['iːstrəudʒən] *n*
Östrogen *nt*

 KEYWORD

of [ɔv] *prep* **1** von; **the history of Germany** die
Geschichte Deutschlands; **a friend of ours**
ein Freund von uns; **a boy of ten** ein Junge
von zehn Jahren, ein zehnjähriger Junge;
that was kind of you das war nett von Ihnen;
the city of New York die Stadt New York
2 (*expressing quantity, amount, dates etc*): **a kilo of
flour** ein Kilo Mehl; **how much of this do
you need?** wie viel brauchen Sie davon?; **3 of
them** (*people*) 3 von ihnen; (*objects*) 3 davon; **a
cup of tea** eine Tasse Tee; **a vase of flowers**
eine Vase mit Blumen; **the 5th of July** der
5. Juli
3 (*from, out of*) aus; **a bracelet of solid gold** ein
Armband aus massivem Gold; **made of wood**
aus Holz (gemacht)

Ofcom ['ɔfkɔm] (*Brit*) *n abbr* (= *Office of
Communications Regulation*) Regulierungsbehörde für

die Kommunikationsindustrie

 KEYWORD

off [ɔf] *adv* **1** (*referring to distance, time*): **it's a long
way off** es ist sehr weit weg; **the game is 3
days off** es sind noch 3 Tage bis zum Spiel
2 (*departure*): **to go off to Paris/Italy** nach
Paris/Italien fahren; **I must be off** ich muss
gehen
3 (*removal*): **to take off one's coat/clothes**
seinen Mantel/sich ausziehen; **the button
came off** der Knopf ging ab; **10 % off** (*Comm*)
10% Nachlass
4: **to be off** (*on holiday*) im Urlaub sein; (*due
to sickness*) krank sein; **I'm off on Fridays**
freitags habe ich frei; **he was off on Friday**
Freitag war er nicht da; **to have a day off**
(*from work*) einen Tag freihaben; **to be off sick**
wegen Krankheit fehlen
▷ *adj* **1** (*not turned on: machine, light, engine etc*) aus;
(*: water, gas*) abgedreht; (*: tap*) zu
2: **to be off** (*meeting, match*) ausfallen;
(*agreement*) nicht mehr gelten
3 (*Brit: not fresh*) verdorben, schlecht
4: **on the off chance that ...** für den Fall,
dass ...; **to have an off day** (*not as good as
usual*) nicht in Form sein; **to be badly off** sich
schlecht stehen
▷ *prep* **1** (*indicating motion, removal etc*) von +*dat*;
to fall off a cliff von einer Klippe fallen; **to
take a picture off the wall** ein Bild von der
Wand nehmen
2 (*distant from*): **5 km off the main road** 5 km
von der Hauptstraße entfernt; **an island off
the coast** eine Insel vor der Küste
3: **I'm off meat/beer** (*no longer eat/drink it*)
ich esse kein Fleisch/trinke kein Bier mehr;
(*no longer like it*) ich kann kein Fleisch/Bier *etc*
mehr sehen

offal ['ɔfl] *n* (*Culin*) Innereien *pl*
off-beat ['ɔfbiːt] *adj* (*clothes, ideas*) ausgefallen
off-centre, (*US*) **off-center** [ɔf'sɛntəʳ] *adj* nicht
genau in der Mitte, links/rechts von der Mitte
▷ *adv* asymmetrisch
off-colour ['ɔf'kʌləʳ] (*Brit*) *adj* (*ill*) unpässlich;
to feel ~ sich unwohl fühlen
offence, (*US*) **offense** [ə'fɛns] *n* (*crime*)
Vergehen *nt*; (*insult*) Beleidigung *f*, Kränkung
f; **to commit an ~** eine Straftat begehen; **to
take ~ (at)** Anstoß nehmen (an +*dat*); **to give
~ (to)** Anstoß erregen (bei); **"no ~"** „nichts für
ungut"
offend [ə'fɛnd] *vt* (*upset*) kränken; **to ~ against**
(*law, rule*) verstoßen gegen
offender [ə'fɛndəʳ] *n* Straftäter(in) *m*(*f*)
offending [ə'fɛndɪŋ] *adj* (*item etc*)
anstoßerregend
offense [ə'fɛns] (*US*) *n* = **offence**
offensive [ə'fɛnsɪv] *adj* (*remark, behaviour*)
verletzend; (*smell etc*) übel; (*weapon*) Angriffs-
▷ *n* (*Mil*) Offensive *f*

o

offer ['ɔfəʳ] *n* Angebot *nt* ▷ *vt* anbieten; (*money, opportunity, service*) bieten; (*reward*) aussetzen; **to make an ~ for sth** ein Angebot für etw machen; **on ~** (*Comm: available*) erhältlich; (: *cheaper*) im Angebot; **to ~ sth to sb** jdm etw anbieten; **to ~ to do sth** anbieten, etw zu tun

offering ['ɔfərɪŋ] *n* Darbietung *f*; (*Rel*) Opfergabe *f*

off-hand [ɔf'hænd] *adj* (*casual*) lässig; (*impolite*) kurz angebunden ▷ *adv* auf Anhieb; **I can't tell you ~** das kann ich Ihnen auf Anhieb nicht sagen

office ['ɔfɪs] *n* Büro *nt*; (*position*) Amt *nt*; **doctor's ~** (*US*) Praxis *f*; **to take ~** das Amt antreten; **in ~** (*minister etc*) im Amt; **through his good ~s** durch seine guten Dienste; **O~ of Fair Trading** (*Brit*) Behörde *f* gegen unlauteren Wettbewerb

office block, (*US*) **office building** *n* Bürogebäude *nt*

office boy *n* Bürogehilfe *m*

office holder *n* Amtsinhaber(in) *m(f)*

office hours *npl* (*Comm*) Bürostunden *pl*; (*US: Med*) Sprechstunde *f*

office manager *n* Büroleiter(in) *m(f)*

officer ['ɔfɪsəʳ] *n* (*Mil etc*) Offizier *m*; (*also*: **police officer**) Polizeibeamte(r) *m*, Polizeibeamtin *f*; (*of organization*) Funktionär *m*

office work *n* Büroarbeit *f*

office worker *n* Büroangestellte(r) *f(m)*

official [ə'fɪʃl] *adj* offiziell ▷ *n* (*in government*) Beamte(r) *m*, Beamtin *f*; (*in trade union etc*) Funktionär *m*

officialdom [ə'fɪʃldəm] (*pej*) *n* Bürokratie *f*

officially [ə'fɪʃəlɪ] *adv* offiziell

official receiver *n* (*Comm*) Konkursverwalter *m*

officiate [ə'fɪʃɪeɪt] *vi* amtieren; **to ~ at a marriage** eine Trauung vornehmen

officious [ə'fɪʃəs] *adj* übereifrig

offing ['ɔfɪŋ] *n*: **in the ~** in Sicht

off-key [ɔf'kiː] *adj* (*Mus: sing, play*) falsch; (*instrument*) verstimmt

off-licence ['ɔflaɪsns] (*Brit*) *n* ≈ Wein- und Spirituosenhandlung *f; siehe Info-Artikel*

● **OFF-LICENCE**

● *Off-licence* ist ein Geschäft (oder eine Theke
● in einer Gaststätte), wo man alkoholische
● Getränke kaufen kann, die aber anderswo
● konsumiert werden müssen. In solchen
● Geschäften, die oft von landesweiten
● Ketten betrieben werden, kann man auch
● andere Getränke, Süßigkeiten, Zigaretten
● und Knabbereien kaufen.

off-limits [ɔf'lɪmɪts] *adj* verboten

off-line [ɔf'laɪn] (*Comput*) *adj* Offline- ▷ *adv* offline; (*switched off*) abgetrennt

off-load ['ɔfləud] *vt* abladen

off-peak ['ɔf'piːk] *adj* (*heating*) Nachtspeicher-; (*electricity*) Nacht-; (*train*) außerhalb der Stoßzeit; **~ ticket** Fahrkarte *f* zur Fahrt außerhalb der Stoßzeit

off-putting ['ɔfputɪŋ] (*Brit*) *adj* (*remark, behaviour*) abstoßend

off-season ['ɔf'siːzn] *adj, adv* außerhalb der Saison

offset ['ɔfsɛt] (*irreg: like* **set**) *vt* (*counteract*) ausgleichen

offshoot ['ɔfʃuːt] *n* (*Bot, fig*) Ableger *m*

offshore ['ɔfʃɔːʳ] *adj* (*breeze*) ablandig; (*oil rig, fishing*) küstennah

offside ['ɔf'saɪd] *adj* (*Sport*) im Abseits; (*Aut: when driving on left*) rechtsseitig; (: *when driving on right*) linksseitig ▷ *n*: **the ~** (*Aut: when driving on left*) die rechte Seite; (: *when driving on right*) die linke Seite

offspring ['ɔfsprɪŋ] *n inv* Nachwuchs *m*

offstage [ɔf'steɪdʒ] *adv* hinter den Kulissen

off-the-cuff [ɔfðə'kʌf] *adj* (*remark*) aus dem Stegreif

off-the-job ['ɔfðə'dʒɔb] *adj*: **~ training** außerbetriebliche Weiterbildung *f*

off-the-peg ['ɔfðə'pɛg], (*US*) **off-the-rack** ['ɔfðə'ræk] *adv* von der Stange

off-the-record ['ɔfðə'rekɔːd] *adj* (*conversation, briefing*) inoffiziell; **that's strictly ~** das ist ganz im Vertrauen

off-white ['ɔfwaɪt] *adj* gebrochen weiß

Ofgem ['ɔfgɛm] *n* Überwachungsgremium zum Verbraucherschutz nach Privatisierung der Stromindustrie

often ['ɔfn] *adv* oft; **how ~?** wie oft?; **more ~ than not** meistens; **as ~ as not** ziemlich oft; **every so ~** ab und zu

Ofwat ['ɔfwɔt] *n* Überwachungsgremium zum Verbraucherschutz nach Privatisierung der Wasserindustrie

ogle ['əugl] *vt* schielen nach, begaffen (*pej*)

ogre ['əugəʳ] *n* (*monster*) Menschenfresser *m*

OH (*US*) *abbr* (*Post*) = Ohio

oh [əu] *excl* oh

ohm [əum] *n* Ohm *nt*

OHMS (*Brit*) *abbr* (= *On His/Her Majesty's Service*) *Aufdruck auf amtlichen Postsendungen*

oil [ɔɪl] *n* Öl *nt*; (*petroleum*) (Erd)öl *nt* ▷ *vt* ölen

oilcan ['ɔɪlkæn] *n* Ölkanne *f*

oil change *n* Ölwechsel *m*

oilcloth ['ɔɪlklɔθ] *n* Wachstuch *nt*

oilfield ['ɔɪlfiːld] *n* Ölfeld *nt*

oil filter *n* Ölfilter *m*

oil-fired ['ɔɪlfaɪəd] *adj* (*boiler, central heating*) Öl-

oil gauge *n* Ölstandsmesser *m*

oil painting *n* Ölgemälde *nt*

oil refinery *n* Ölraffinerie *f*

oil rig *n* Ölförderturm *m*; (*at sea*) Bohrinsel *f*

oilskins ['ɔɪlskɪnz] *npl* Ölzeug *nt*

oil slick *n* Ölteppich *m*

oil tanker *n* (*ship*) (Öl)tanker *m*; (*truck*) Tankwagen *m*

oil well *n* Ölquelle *f*

oily ['ɔɪlɪ] *adj* (*substance*) ölig; (*rag*) öldurchtränkt; (*food*) fettig

ointment ['ɔɪntmənt] *n* Salbe *f*

OK (*US*) *abbr* (*Post*) = Oklahoma

O.K. ['əu'keɪ] (*inf*) *excl* okay; (*granted*) gut ▷ *adj* (*average*) einigermaßen; (*acceptable*) in Ordnung ▷ *vt* genehmigen ▷ *n*: **to give sb/ sth the ~** jdm/etw seine Zustimmung geben; **is it ~?** ist es in Ordnung?; **are you ~?** bist du in Ordnung?; **are you ~ for money?** hast du (noch) genug Geld?; **it's ~ with** *or* **by me** mir ist es recht

okay ['əu'keɪ] *excl* = **O.K.**

Okla. (*US*) *abbr* (*Post*) = Oklahoma

old [əuld] *adj* alt; **how ~ are you?** wie alt bist du?; **he's 10 years ~** er ist 10 Jahre alt; **~er brother** ältere(r) Bruder; **any ~ thing will do for him** ihm ist alles recht

old age *n* Alter *nt*

old age pension *n* Rente *f*

old age pensioner (*Brit*) *n* Rentner(in) *m(f)*

old-fashioned ['əuld'fæʃnd] *adj* altmodisch

old hand *n* alter Hase *m*

old hat *adj*: **to be ~** ein alter Hut sein

old maid *n* alte Jungfer *f*

old people's home *n* Altersheim *nt*

old-style ['əuldstaɪl] *adj* im alten Stil

old-time dancing ['əuldtaɪm-] *n* Tänze *pl* im alten Stil

old-timer [əuld'taɪməʳ] (*esp US*) *n* Veteran *m*

old wives' tale *n* Ammenmärchen *nt*

oleander [əulɪ'ændəʳ] *n* Oleander *m*

O level (*Brit*) *n* (*formerly*) ≈ Abschluss *m* der Sekundarstufe 1 ≈ mittlere Reife *f*

olive ['ɒlɪv] *n* Olive *f*; (*tree*) Olivenbaum *m* ▷ *adj* (*also*: **olive-green**) olivgrün; **to offer an ~ branch to sb** (*fig*) jdm ein Friedensangebot machen

olive oil *n* Olivenöl *nt*

Olympic [əu'lɪmpɪk] *adj* olympisch

Olympic Games *npl*: **the ~** (*also*: **the Olympics**) die Olympischen Spiele *pl*

OM (*Brit*) *n abbr* (= *Order of Merit*) britischer Verdienstorden

Oman [əu'mɑːn] *n* Oman *nt*

OMB (*US*) *n abbr* (= *Office of Management and Budget*) Regierungsbehörde für Verwaltung und Etat

ombudsman ['ɒmbudzmən] *n* Ombudsmann *m*

omelette, (*US*) **omelet** ['ɒmlɪt] *n* Omelett *nt*; **ham/cheese omelet(te)** Schinken-/ Käseomelett *nt*

omen ['əumən] *n* Omen *nt*

ominous ['ɒmɪnəs] *adj* (*silence, warning*) ominös; (*clouds, smoke*) bedrohlich

omission [əu'mɪʃən] *n* (*thing omitted*) Auslassung *f*; (*act of omitting*) Auslassen *nt*

omit [əu'mɪt] *vt* (*deliberately*) unterlassen; (*by mistake*) auslassen ▷ *vi*: **to ~ to do sth** es unterlassen, etw zu tun

omnivorous [ɒm'nɪvrəs] *adj*: **to be ~** Allesfresser sein

ON (*Canada*) *abbr* = Ontario

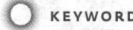 KEYWORD

on [ɒn] *prep* **1** (*indicating position*) auf +*dat*; (*with vb of motion*) auf +*acc*; **it's on the table** es ist auf dem Tisch; **she put the book on the table** sie legte das Buch auf den Tisch; **on the left** links; **on the right** rechts; **the house is on the main road** das Haus liegt an der Hauptstraße

2 (*indicating means, method, condition etc*): **on foot** (*go, be*) zu Fuß; **to be on the train/plane** im Zug/Flugzeug sein; **to go on the train/ plane** mit dem Zug/Flugzeug reisen; (**to be wanted**) **on the telephone** am Telefon (verlangt werden); **on the radio/television** im Radio/Fernsehen; **to be on drugs** Drogen nehmen; **to be on holiday** im Urlaub sein; **I'm here on business** ich bin geschäftlich hier

3 (*referring to time*): **on Friday** am Freitag; **on Fridays** freitags; **on June 20th** am 20. Juni; **on Friday, June 20th** am Freitag, dem 20. Juni; **a week on Friday** Freitag in einer Woche; **on (his) arrival he went straight to his hotel** bei seiner Ankunft ging er direkt in sein Hotel; **on seeing this he ... ** als er das sah, ... er ...

4 (*about, concerning*) über +*acc*; **a book on physics** ein Buch über Physik

▷ *adv* **1** (*referring to dress*): **to have one's coat on** seinen Mantel anhaben; **what's she got on?** was hat sie an?

2 (*referring to covering*): **screw the lid on tightly** dreh den Deckel fest zu

3 (*further, continuously*): **to walk/drive/read on** weitergehen/-fahren/-lesen

▷ *adj* **1** (*functioning, in operation: machine, radio, TV, light*) an; (: *tap*) auf; (: *handbrake*) angezogen; **there's a good film on at the cinema** im Kino läuft ein guter Film

2: **that's not on!** (*inf: of behaviour*) das ist nicht drin!

once [wʌns] *adv* (*on one occasion*) einmal; (*formerly*) früher; (*a long time ago*) früher einmal ▷ *conj* (*as soon as*) sobald; **at ~** (*immediately*) sofort; (*simultaneously*) gleichzeitig; **~ a week** einmal pro Woche; **~ more** *or* **again** noch einmal; **~ and for all** ein für alle Mal; **~ upon a time** es war einmal; **~ in a while** ab und zu; **all at ~** (*suddenly*) plötzlich; **for ~ ausnahmsweise** (einmal); **~ or twice** ein paarmal; **~ he had left** sobald er gegangen war; **~ it was done** nachdem es getan war

oncoming ['ɒnkʌmɪŋ] *adj* (*traffic etc*) entgegenkommend

 KEYWORD

one [wʌn] *num* ein(e); (*counting*) eins; **one hundred and fifty** (ein)hundert(und)fünfzig; **one day there was a sudden knock at the door** eines Tages klopfte es plötzlich an der Tür; **one by one** einzeln

▷ *adj* **1** (*sole*) einzige(r, s); **the one book which ...** das einzige Buch, das ...

2 (*same*): **they came in the one car** sie kamen

in demselben Wagen; **they all belong to the one family** sie alle gehören zu ein und derselben Familie
▷ *pron* **1**: **this one** diese(r, s); **that one** der/die/das (da); **which one?** welcher/welche/welches?; **he is one of us** er ist einer von uns; **I've already got one/a red one** ich habe schon eins/ein rotes
2: **one another** einander; **do you two ever see one another?** seht ihr zwei euch jemals?
3 (*impersonal*) man; **one never knows** man weiß nie; **to cut one's finger** sich *dat* in den Finger schneiden

one-day excursion ['wʌndeɪ-] (*US*) *n* (*day return*) Tagesrückfahrkarte *f*
one-man ['wʌn'mæn] *adj* (*business, show*) Einmann-
one-man band *n* Einmannkapelle *f*
one-off [wʌn'ɔf] (*Brit: inf*) *n* einmaliges Ereignis *nt*
one-parent family ['wʌnpɛərənt-] *n* Familie *f* mit nur einem Elternteil
one-piece ['wʌnpiːs] *adj*: **~ swimsuit** einteiliger Badeanzug *m*
onerous ['ɔnərəs] *adj* (*duty etc*) schwer

 KEYWORD

oneself [wʌn'self] *pron* (*reflexive: after prep*) sich; (*emphatic*) selbst; **to hurt oneself** sich *dat* wehtun; **to keep sth for oneself** etw für sich behalten; **to talk to oneself** Selbstgespräche führen

one-shot ['wʌnʃɔt] (*US*) *n* = **one-off**
one-sided [wʌn'saɪdɪd] *adj* einseitig
one-time ['wʌntaɪm] *adj* ehemalig
one-to-one ['wʌntəwʌn] *adj* (*relationship, tuition*) Einzel-
one-upmanship [wʌn'ʌpmənʃɪp] *n*: **the art of ~** die Kunst, anderen um einen Schritt voraus zu sein
one-way ['wʌnweɪ] *adj* (*street, traffic*) Einbahn-; (*ticket*) Einzel-
ongoing ['ɔngəʊɪŋ] *adj* (*project*) laufend; (*situation etc*) andauernd
onion ['ʌnjən] *n* Zwiebel *f*
on-line ['ɔnlaɪn] (*Comput*) *adj* (*printer, database*) Online-; (*switched on*) gekoppelt ▷ *adv* online
onlooker ['ɔnlukəʳ] *n* Zuschauer(in) *m(f)*
only ['əʊnlɪ] *adv* nur ▷ *adj* einzige(r, s) ▷ *conj* nur, bloß; **I ~ took one** ich nahm nur eins; **I saw her ~ yesterday** ich habe sie erst gestern gesehen; **I'd be ~ too pleased to help** ich würde allzu gern helfen; **not ~ ... but (also) ...** nicht nur ..., sondern auch ...; **an ~ child** ein Einzelkind *nt*; **I would come, ~ I'm too busy** ich würde kommen, wenn ich nicht so viel zu tun hätte
ono (*Brit*) *abbr* (*in classified ads*: = *or near(est) offer*) see **near**
onset ['ɔnsɛt] *n* Beginn *m*

onshore ['ɔnʃɔːʳ] *adj* (*wind*) auflandig, See-
onslaught ['ɔnslɔːt] *n* Attacke *f*
on-the-job ['ɔnðə'dʒɔb] *adj*: **~ training** Ausbildung *f* am Arbeitsplatz
onto ['ɔntu] *prep* = **on to**
onus ['əʊnəs] *n* Last *f*, Pflicht *f*; **the ~ is on him to prove it** er trägt die Beweislast
onward ['ɔnwəd], **onwards** ['ɔnwədz] *adv* weiter; **from that time ~(s)** von der Zeit an ▷ *adj* fortschreitend
onyx ['ɔnɪks] *n* Onyx *m*
ooze [uːz] *vi* (*mud, water etc*) triefen
opacity [əʊ'pæsɪtɪ] *n* (*of substance*) Undurchsichtigkeit *f*
opal ['əʊpl] *n* Opal *m*
opaque [əʊ'peɪk] *adj* (*substance*) undurchsichtig, trüb
OPEC ['əʊpɛk] *n abbr* (= *Organization of Petroleum-Exporting Countries*) OPEC *f*
open ['əʊpn] *adj* offen; (*packet, shop, museum*) geöffnet; (*view*) frei; (*meeting, debate*) öffentlich; (*ticket, return*) unbeschränkt; (*vacancy*) verfügbar ▷ *vt* öffnen, aufmachen; (*book, paper etc*) aufschlagen; (*account*) eröffnen; (*blocked road*) frei machen ▷ *vi* (*door, eyes, mouth*) sich öffnen; (*shop, bank etc*) aufmachen; (*commence*) beginnen; (*film, play*) Premiere haben; (*flower*) aufgehen; **in the ~ (air)** im Freien; **the ~ sea** das offene Meer; **to have an ~ mind on sth** etw *dat* aufgeschlossen gegenüberstehen; **to be ~ to** (*ideas etc*) offen sein für; **to be ~ to criticism** der Kritik *dat* ausgesetzt sein; **to be ~ to the public** für die Öffentlichkeit zugänglich sein; **to ~ one's mouth** (*speak*) den Mund aufmachen
▶ **open on to** *vt fus* (*room, door*) führen auf +*acc*
▶ **open up** *vi* (*unlock*) aufmachen; (*confide*) sich äußern
open-air [əʊpn'ɛəʳ] *adj* im Freien; **~ concert** Open-Air-Konzert *nt*; **~ swimming pool** Freibad *nt*
open-and-shut ['əʊpnən'ʃʌt] *adj*: **~ case** klarer Fall *m*
open day *n* Tag *m* der offenen Tür
open-ended [əʊpn'endɪd] *adj* (*question etc*) mit offenem Ausgang; (*contract*) unbefristet
opener ['əʊpnəʳ] *n* (*also*: **tin opener, can opener**) Dosenöffner *m*
open-heart [əʊpn'hɑːt] *adj*: **~ surgery** Eingriff *m* am offenen Herzen
opening ['əʊpnɪŋ] *adj* (*commencing: stages, scene*) erste(r, s); (*remarks, ceremony etc*) Eröffnungs- ▷ *n* (*gap, hole*) Öffnung *f*; (*of play etc*) Anfang *m*; (*of new building etc*) Eröffnung *f*; (*opportunity*) Gelegenheit *f*
opening hours *npl* Öffnungszeiten *pl*
opening night *n* (*Theat*) Eröffnungsabend *m*
open learning *n Weiterbildungssystem auf Teilzeitbasis*
openly ['əʊpnlɪ] *adv* offen
open-minded [əʊpn'maɪndɪd] *adj* aufgeschlossen
open-necked ['əʊpnnɛkt] *adj* (*shirt*) mit

offenem Kragen

openness ['əupnnɪs] n (frankness) Offenheit f

open-plan ['əupn'plæn] adj (office) Großraum-

open prison n offenes Gefängnis nt

open sandwich n belegtes Brot nt

open shop n Unternehmen ohne Gewerkschaftszwang

Open University (Brit) n ≈ Fernuniversität f; siehe Info-Artikel

---

OPEN UNIVERSITY

Open University ist eine 1969 in Großbritannien gegründete Fernuniversität für Spätstudierende. Der Unterricht findet durch Fernseh- und Radiosendungen statt, schriftliche Arbeiten werden mit der Post verschickt, und der Besuch von Sommerkursen ist Pflicht. Die Studenten müssen eine bestimmte Anzahl von Unterrichtseinheiten in einem bestimmten Zeitraum absolvieren und für die Verleihung eines akademischen Grades eine Mindestzahl von Scheinen machen.

---

open verdict n (Law) Todesfeststellung ohne Angabe der Todesursache

opera ['ɔpərə] n Oper f

opera glasses npl Opernglas nt

opera house n Opernhaus nt

opera singer n Opernsänger(in) m(f)

operate ['ɔpəreɪt] vt (machine etc) bedienen ▷ vi (machine etc) funktionieren; (company) arbeiten; (laws, forces) wirken; (Med) operieren; **to ~ on sb** jdn operieren

operatic [ɔpə'rætɪk] adj (singer etc) Opern-

operating room ['ɔpəreɪtɪŋ-] (US) n Operationssaal m

operating system n (Comput) Betriebssystem nt

operating table n (Med) Operationstisch m

operating theatre n (Med) Operationssaal m

operation [ɔpə'reɪʃən] n (activity) Unternehmung f; (of machine etc) Betrieb m; (Mil, Med) Operation f; (Comm) Geschäft nt; **to be in ~** (law, scheme) in Kraft sein; **to have an ~** (Med) operiert werden; **to perform an ~** (Med) eine Operation vornehmen

operational [ɔpə'reɪʃənl] adj (machine etc) einsatzfähig

operative ['ɔpərətɪv] adj (measure, system) wirksam; (law) gültig ▷ n (in factory) Maschinenarbeiter(in) m(f); **the ~ word** das entscheidende Wort

operator ['ɔpəreɪtəʳ] n (Tel) Vermittlung f; (of machine) Bediener(in) m(f)

operetta [ɔpə'retə] n Operette f

ophthalmic [ɔf'θælmɪk] adj (department) Augen-

ophthalmic optician n Augenoptiker(in) m(f)

ophthalmologist [ɔfθæl'mɔlədʒɪst] n Augenarzt m, Augenärztin f

opinion [ə'pɪnjən] n Meinung f; **in my ~** meiner Meinung nach; **to have a good/ high ~ of sb/o.s.** eine gute/hohe Meinung von jdm/sich haben; **to be of the ~ that ...** der Ansicht or Meinung sein, dass ...; **to get a second ~** (Med etc) ein zweites Gutachten einholen

opinionated [ə'pɪnjəneɪtɪd] (pej) adj rechthaberisch

opinion poll n Meinungsumfrage f

opium ['əupɪəm] n Opium nt

opponent [ə'pəunənt] n Gegner(in) m(f)

opportune ['ɔpətjuːn] adj (moment) günstig

opportunism [ɔpə'tjuːnɪsəm] (pej) n Opportunismus m

opportunist [ɔpə'tjuːnɪst] (pej) n Opportunist(in) m(f)

opportunity [ɔpə'tjuːnɪtɪ] n Gelegenheit f, Möglichkeit f; (prospects) Chance f; **to take the ~ of doing sth** die Gelegenheit ergreifen, etw zu tun

oppose [ə'pəuz] vt (opinion, plan) ablehnen; **to be ~d to sth** gegen etw sein; **as ~d to** im Gegensatz zu

opposing [ə'pəuzɪŋ] adj (side, team) gegnerisch; (ideas, tendencies) entgegengesetzt

opposite ['ɔpəzɪt] adj (house, door) gegenüberliegend; (end, direction) entgegengesetzt; (point of view, effect) gegenteilig ▷ adv gegenüber ▷ prep (in front of) gegenüber; (next to: on list, form etc) neben ▷ n: **the ~** das Gegenteil; **the ~ sex** das andere Geschlecht; **"see ~ page"** „siehe gegenüber"

opposite number n (person) Gegenspieler(in) m(f)

opposition [ɔpə'zɪʃən] n (resistance) Widerstand m; (Sport) Gegner pl; **the O~** (Pol) die Opposition

oppress [ə'pres] vt unterdrücken

oppressed [ə'prest] adj unterdrückt

oppression [ə'preʃən] n Unterdrückung f

oppressive [ə'presɪv] adj (weather, heat) bedrückend; (political regime) repressiv

opprobrium [ə'prəubrɪəm] n (form) Schande f, Schmach f

opt [ɔpt] vi: **to ~ for** sich entscheiden für; **to ~ to do sth** sich entscheiden, etw zu tun
  ▶ **opt out (of)** vi (not participate) sich nicht beteiligen (an +dat); (of insurance scheme etc) kündigen; **to ~ out (of local authority control)** (Pol: hospital, school) aus der Kontrolle der Gemeindeverwaltung austreten

optical ['ɔptɪkl] adj optisch

optical character reader n optischer Klarschriftleser m

optical character recognition n optische Zeichenerkennung f

optical illusion n optische Täuschung f

optician [ɔp'tɪʃən] n Optiker(in) m(f)

optics ['ɔptɪks] n Optik f

optimism ['ɔptɪmɪzəm] n Optimismus m

optimist ['ɔptɪmɪst] n Optimist(in) m(f)

optimistic [ɔptɪ'mɪstɪk] adj optimistisch

O

optimum ['ɔptɪməm] *adj* optimal
option ['ɔpʃən] *n* (*choice*) Möglichkeit *f*; (*Scol*) Wahlfach *nt*; (*Comm*) Option *f*; **to keep one's ~s open** sich *dat* alle Möglichkeiten offenhalten; **to have no ~** keine (andere) Wahl haben
optional ['ɔpʃənl] *adj* freiwillig; **~ extras** (*Comm*) Extras *pl*
opulence ['ɔpjuləns] *n* Reichtum *m*
opulent ['ɔpjulənt] *adj* (*very wealthy*) reich, wohlhabend
OR (*US*) *abbr* (*Post*) = *Oregon*
or [ɔːʳ] *conj* oder; **he hasn't seen or heard anything** er hat weder etwas gesehen noch gehört; **or else** (*otherwise*) sonst; **fifty or sixty people** fünfzig bis sechzig Leute
oracle ['ɔrəkl] *n* Orakel *nt*
oral ['ɔːrəl] *adj* (*test, report*) mündlich; (*Med: vaccine, contraceptive*) zum Einnehmen ▷ *n* (*exam*) mündliche Prüfung *f*
orange ['ɔrɪndʒ] *n* Orange *f*, Apfelsine *f* ▷ *adj* (*colour*) orange
orangeade [ɔrɪndʒ'eɪd] *n* Orangenlimonade *f*
oration [ɔː'reɪʃən] *n* Ansprache *f*
orator ['ɔrətəʳ] *n* Redner(in) *m(f)*
orb [ɔːb] *n* Kugel *f*
orbit ['ɔːbɪt] *n* (*of planet etc*) Umlaufbahn *f* ▷ *vt* umkreisen
orbital motorway ['ɔːbɪtəl-] *n* Ringautobahn *f*
orchard ['ɔːtʃəd] *n* Obstgarten *m*; **apple ~** Obstgarten mit Apfelbäumen
orchestra ['ɔːkɪstrə] *n* Orchester *nt*; (*US: stalls*) Parkett *nt*
orchestral [ɔː'kestrəl] *adj* (*piece, musicians*) Orchester-
orchestrate ['ɔːkɪstreɪt] *vt* orchestrieren
orchid ['ɔːkɪd] *n* Orchidee *f*
ordain [ɔː'deɪn] *vt* (*Rel*) ordinieren; (*decree*) verfügen
ordeal [ɔː'diːl] *n* Qual *f*
order ['ɔːdəʳ] *n* (*command*) Befehl *m*; (*Comm, in restaurant*) Bestellung *f*; (*sequence*) Reihenfolge *f*; (*discipline, organization*) Ordnung *f*; (*Rel*) Orden *m* ▷ *vt* (*command*) befehlen; (*Comm, in restaurant*) bestellen; (*also:* **put in order**) ordnen; **in ~** (*permitted*) in Ordnung; **in (working) ~** betriebsfähig; **in ~ to do sth** um etw zu tun; **in ~ of size** nach Größe (geordnet); **on ~** (*Comm*) bestellt; **out of ~** (*not working*) außer Betrieb; (*in the wrong sequence*) durcheinander; (*motion, proposal*) nicht zulässig; **to place an ~ for sth with sb** eine Bestellung für etw bei jdm aufgeben; **made to ~** (*Comm*) auf Bestellung (gemacht); **to be under ~s to do sth** die Anweisung haben, etw zu tun; **to take ~s** Befehle entgegennehmen; **a point of ~** (*in debate etc*) eine Verfahrensfrage; **"pay to the ~ of …"** „zahlbar an +*dat* …"; **of** *or* **in the ~ of** in der Größenordnung von; **to ~ sb to do sth** jdn anweisen, etw zu tun
▶ **order around** *vt* (*also:* **order about**) herumkommandieren

order book *n* (*Comm*) Auftragsbuch *nt*
order form *n* Bestellschein *m*
orderly ['ɔːdəlɪ] *n* (*Mil*) Offiziersbursche *m*; (*Med*) Pfleger(in) *m(f)* ▷ *adj* (*manner*) ordentlich; (*sequence, system*) geordnet
order number *n* (*Comm*) Bestellnummer *f*
ordinal ['ɔːdɪnl] *adj*: **~ number** Ordinalzahl *f*
ordinarily ['ɔːdnrɪlɪ] *adv* normalerweise
ordinary ['ɔːdnrɪ] *adj* (*everyday*) gewöhnlich, normal; (*pej: mediocre*) mittelmäßig; **out of the ~** außergewöhnlich

ORDINARY DEGREE

Ordinary degree ist ein Universitätsabschluss, der an Studenten vergeben wird, die entweder die für ein *honours degree* nötige Note nicht erreicht haben, aber trotzdem nicht durchgefallen sind, oder die sich nur für ein ordinary degree eingeschrieben haben, wobei das Studium meist kürzer ist.

ordinary seaman (*Brit*) *n* Leichtmatrose *m*
ordinary shares *npl* Stammaktien *pl*
ordination [ɔːdɪ'neɪʃən] *n* (*Rel*) Ordination *f*
ordnance ['ɔːdnəns] *n* (*unit*) Technische Truppe *f* ▷ *adj* (*factory, supplies*) Munitions-
Ordnance Survey (*Brit*) *n* Landesvermessung *f*
ore [ɔːʳ] *n* Erz *nt*
Ore. (*US*) *abbr* (*Post*) = *Oregon*
organ ['ɔːgən] *n* (*Anat*) Organ *nt*; (*Mus*) Orgel *f*
organic [ɔː'gænɪk] *adj* organisch; (*farming, vegetables*) Bio-, Öko-; **~ food** Biokost *f*
organism ['ɔːgənɪzəm] *n* Organismus *m*
organist ['ɔːgənɪst] *n* Organist(in) *m(f)*
organization [ɔːgənaɪ'zeɪʃən] *n* Organisation *f*
organization chart *n* Organisationsplan *m*
organize ['ɔːgənaɪz] *vt* organisieren; **to get ~d** sich fertig machen
organized crime *n* organisiertes Verbrechen *nt*
organized labour *n* organisierte Arbeiterschaft *f*
organizer ['ɔːgənaɪzəʳ] *n* (*of conference etc*) Organisator *m*, Veranstalter *m*
orgasm ['ɔːgæzəm] *n* Orgasmus *m*
orgy ['ɔːdʒɪ] *n* Orgie *f*; **an ~ of destruction** eine Zerstörungsorgie
Orient ['ɔːrɪənt] *n*: **the ~** der Orient
orient ['ɔːrɪənt] *vt*: **to ~ o.s. (to)** sich orientieren (in +*dat*); **to be ~ed towards** ausgerichtet sein auf +*acc*
oriental [ɔːrɪ'entl] *adj* orientalisch
orientate ['ɔːrɪənteɪt] *vt*: **to ~ o.s.** sich orientieren; (*fig*) sich zurechtfinden; **to be ~d towards** ausgerichtet sein auf +*acc*
orifice ['ɔrɪfɪs] *n* (*Anat*) Öffnung *f*
origin ['ɔrɪdʒɪn] *n* Ursprung *m*; (*of person*) Herkunft *f*; **country of ~** Herkunftsland *nt*
original [ə'rɪdʒɪnl] *adj* (*first*) ursprünglich; (*genuine*) original; (*imaginative*) originell ▷ *n* Original *nt*

originality [ərɪdʒɪ'nælɪtɪ] *n* Originalität *f*

originally [ə'rɪdʒɪnəlɪ] *adv* (*at first*) ursprünglich

originate [ə'rɪdʒɪneɪt] *vi:* **to ~ in** (*idea, custom etc*) entstanden sein in +*dat;* **to ~ with** *or* **from** stammen von

originator [ə'rɪdʒɪneɪtə^r] *n* (*of idea, custom*) Urheber(in) *m(f)*

Orkneys ['ɔːknɪz] *npl:* **the ~** (*also:* **the Orkney Islands**) die Orkneyinseln *pl*

ornament ['ɔːnəmənt] *n* (*object*) Ziergegenstand *m;* (*decoration*) Verzierungen *pl*

ornamental [ɔːnə'mɛntl] *adj* (*garden, pond*) Zier-

ornamentation [ɔːnəmɛn'teɪʃən] *n* Verzierungen *pl*

ornate [ɔː'neɪt] *adj* (*necklace, design*) kunstvoll

ornithologist [ɔːnɪ'θɒlədʒɪst] *n* Ornithologe *m,* Ornithologin *f*

ornithology [ɔːnɪ'θɒlədʒɪ] *n* Ornithologie *f,* Vogelkunde *f*

orphan ['ɔːfn] *n* Waise *f,* Waisenkind *nt* ▷ *vt:* **to be ~ed** zur Waise werden

orphanage ['ɔːfənɪdʒ] *n* Waisenhaus *nt*

orthodox ['ɔːθədɒks] *adj* orthodox; **~ medicine** die konventionelle Medizin

orthodoxy ['ɔːθədɒksɪ] *n* Orthodoxie *f*

orthopaedic, (US) **orthopedic** [ɔːθə'piːdɪk] *adj* orthopädisch

OS *abbr* (*Brit*) = **Ordnance Survey;** (*Naut*) = **ordinary seaman;** (*Dress*) = **outsize**

o.s. *abbr* (*Comm:* = *out of stock*) nicht auf Lager

Oscar ['ɒskə^r] *n* Oscar *m*

oscillate ['ɒsɪleɪt] *vi* (*Elec, Phys*) schwingen, oszillieren; (*fig*) schwanken

OSHA (US) *n abbr* (= *Occupational Safety and Health Administration*) Regierungsstelle für Arbeitsschutzvorschriften

Oslo ['ɒzləʊ] *n* Oslo *nt*

OST *n abbr* (= *Office of Science and Technology*) Ministerium für Wissenschaft und Technologie

ostensible [ɒs'tɛnsɪbl] *adj* vorgeblich, angeblich

ostensibly [ɒs'tɛnsɪblɪ] *adv* angeblich

ostentation [ɒstɛn'teɪʃən] *n* Pomp *m,* Protz *m*

ostentatious [ɒstɛn'teɪʃəs] *adj* (*building, car etc*) pompös; (*person*) protzig

osteopath ['ɒstɪəpæθ] *n* Osteopath(in) *m(f)*

ostracize ['ɒstrəsaɪz] *vt* ächten

ostrich ['ɒstrɪtʃ] *n* Strauß *m*

OT *abbr* (*Bible:* = *Old Testament*) AT

OTB (US) *n abbr* (= *offtrack betting*) Wetten außerhalb des Rennbahngeländes

OTE *abbr* (*Comm:* = *on-target earnings*) Einkommensziel *nt*

other ['ʌðə^r] *adj* andere(r, s) ▷ *pron:* **the ~ (one)** der/die/das andere; **~s** andere *pl;* **the ~s** die anderen *pl;* **~ than** (*apart from*) außer; **the ~ day** (*recently*) neulich; **some actor or ~** irgendein Schauspieler; **somebody or ~** irgendjemand; **the car was none ~ than Robert's** das Auto gehörte keinem anderen als Robert

otherwise ['ʌðəwaɪz] *adv* (*differently*) anders; (*apart from that, if not*) sonst, ansonsten; **an ~**

good piece of work eine im Übrigen gute Arbeit

OTT (*inf*) *abbr* (= *over the top*) *see* **top**

otter ['ɒtə^r] *n* Otter *m*

OU (*Brit*) *n abbr* = **Open University**

ouch [autʃ] *excl* autsch

ought [ɔːt] (*pt* ~) *aux vb:* **I ~ to do it** ich sollte es tun; **this ~ to have been corrected** das hätte korrigiert werden müssen; **he ~ to win** (*he probably will win*) er dürfte wohl gewinnen; **you ~ to go and see it** das solltest du dir ansehen

ounce [auns] *n* Unze *f;* (*fig: small amount*) bisschen *nt*

our ['auə^r] *adj* unsere(r, s); *see also* **my**

ours [auəz] *pron* unsere(r, s); *see also* **mine**¹

ourselves [auə'sɛlvz] *pron pl* uns (selbst); (*emphatic*) selbst; **we did it (all) by ~** wir haben alles selbst gemacht; *see also* **oneself**

oust [aust] *vt* (*forcibly remove*) verdrängen

 KEYWORD

out¹ [aut] *adv* **1** (*not in*) draußen; **out in the rain/snow** draußen im Regen/Schnee; **out here** hier; **out there** dort; **to go/come** *etc* **out** hinausgehen/-kommen *etc;* **to speak out loud** laut sprechen

2 (*not at home, absent*) nicht da

3 (*indicating distance*): **the boat was 10 km out** das Schiff war 10 km weit draußen; **3 days out from Plymouth** 3 Tage nach dem Auslaufen von Plymouth

4 (*Sport*) aus; **the ball is out/has gone out** der Ball ist aus

▷ *adj* **1: to be out** (*person: unconscious*) bewusstlos sein; (*: out of game*) ausgeschieden sein; (*out of fashion: style, singer*) out sein

2 (*have appeared: flowers*) da; (*: news, secret*) heraus

3 (*extinguished, finished: fire, light, gas*) aus; **before the week was out** ehe die Woche zu Ende war

4: to be out to do sth (*intend*) etw tun wollen

5 (*wrong*): **to be out in one's calculations** sich in seinen Berechnungen irren

out² [aut] *vt* (*inf: expose as homosexual*) outen

outage ['autɪdʒ] (*esp US*) *n* (*power failure*) Stromausfall *m*

out-and-out ['autəndaut] *adj* (*liar, thief etc*) ausgemacht

outback ['autbæk] *n* (*in Australia*): **the ~** das Hinterland

outbid [aut'bɪd] *vt* überbieten

outboard ['autbɔːd] *n* (*also:* **outboard motor**) Außenbordmotor *m*

outbound ['autbaund] *adj* (*ship*) auslaufend

outbreak ['autbreɪk] *n* (*of war, disease etc*) Ausbruch *m*

outbuilding ['autbɪldɪŋ] *n* Nebengebäude *nt*

outburst ['autbəːst] *n* (*of anger etc*) Gefühlsausbruch *m*

outcast ['autkɑːst] *n* Ausgestoßene(r) *f(m)*

outclass [aut'klɑːs] *vt* deklassieren

outcome ['autkʌm] *n* Ergebnis *nt,* Resultat *nt*

o

outcrop ['autkrɔp] n (of rock) Block m

outcry ['autkraɪ] n Aufschrei m

outdated [aut'deɪtɪd] adj (custom, idea) veraltet

outdo [aut'duː] (irreg: like **do**) vt übertreffen

outdoor [aut'dɔːʳ] adj (activities) im Freien; (clothes) für draußen; **~ swimming pool** Freibad nt; **she's an ~ person** sie liebt die freie Natur

outdoors [aut'dɔːz] adv (play, sleep) draußen, im Freien

outer ['autəʳ] adj äußere(r, s); **~ suburbs** (äußere) Vorstädte pl; **the ~ office** das Vorzimmer

outer space n der Weltraum

outfit ['autfɪt] n (clothes) Kleidung f; (inf: team) Verein m

outfitter's ['autfɪtəz] (Brit) n (shop) Herrenausstatter m

outgoing ['autɡəʊɪŋ] adj (extrovert) kontaktfreudig; (retiring: president etc) scheidend; (mail etc) ausgehend

outgoings ['autɡəʊɪŋz] (Brit) npl Ausgaben pl

outgrow [aut'ɡrəʊ] (irreg: like **grow**) vt (clothes) herauswachsen aus; (habits etc) ablegen

outhouse ['authaus] n Nebengebäude nt

outing ['autɪŋ] n Ausflug m

outlandish [aut'lændɪʃ] adj eigenartig, seltsam

outlast [aut'lɑːst] vt überleben

outlaw ['autlɔː] n Geächtete(r) f(m) ▷ vt verbieten

outlay ['autleɪ] n Auslagen pl

outlet ['autlet] n (hole, pipe) Abfluss m; (US: Elec) Steckdose f; (Comm: also: **retail outlet**) Verkaufsstelle f; (fig: for grief, anger etc) Ventil nt

outline ['autlaɪn] n (shape) Umriss m; (brief explanation) Abriss m; (rough sketch) Skizze f ▷ vt (fig: theory, plan etc) umreißen, skizzieren

outlive [aut'lɪv] vt (survive) überleben

outlook ['autluk] n (attitude) Einstellung f; (prospects) Aussichten pl; (for weather) Vorhersage f

outlying ['autlaɪɪŋ] adj (area, town etc) entlegen

outmanoeuvre, (US) **outmaneuver** [autmə'nuːvəʳ] vt ausmanövrieren

outmoded [aut'məudɪd] adj veraltet

outnumber [aut'nʌmbəʳ] vt zahlenmäßig überlegen sein +dat; **to be ~ed (by) 5 to 1** im Verhältnis 5 zu 1 in der Minderheit sein

 **KEYWORD**

out of prep **1** (outside, beyond: position) nicht in +dat; (: motion) aus +dat; **to look out of the window** aus dem Fenster blicken; **to be out of danger** außer Gefahr sein

2 (cause, origin) aus +dat; **out of curiosity/fear/greed** aus Neugier/Angst/Habgier; **to drink sth out of a cup** etw aus einer Tasse trinken

3 (from among) von +dat; **one out of every three smokers** einer von drei Rauchern

4 (without): **to be out of sugar/milk/petrol** etc keinen Zucker/keine Milch/kein Benzin etc mehr haben

out of bounds adj: **to be ~** verboten sein

out-of-court [autəv'kɔːt] adj (settlement) außergerichtlich; see also **court**

out-of-date [autəv'deɪt] adj (passport, ticket etc) abgelaufen; (clothes, idea) veraltet

out-of-doors [autəv'dɔːz] adv (play, stay etc) im Freien

out-of-the-way ['autəvðə'weɪ] adj (place) entlegen; (pub, restaurant etc) kaum bekannt

out-of-work ['autəvwɜːk] adj arbeitslos

outpatient ['autpeɪʃənt] n ambulanter Patient m, ambulante Patientin f

outpost ['autpəust] n (Mil, Comm) Vorposten m

outpouring ['autpɔːrɪŋ] n (of emotion etc) Erguss m

output ['autput] n (production: of factory, writer etc) Produktion f; (Comput) Output m, Ausgabe f ▷ vt (Comput) ausgeben

outrage ['autreɪdʒ] n (scandal) Skandal m; (atrocity) Verbrechen nt, Ausschreitung f; (anger) Empörung f ▷ vt (shock, anger) empören

outrageous [aut'reɪdʒəs] adj (remark etc) empörend; (clothes) unmöglich; (scandalous) skandalös

outrider ['autraɪdəʳ] n (on motorcycle) Kradbegleiter m

outright [aut'raɪt] adv (kill) auf der Stelle; (win) überlegen; (buy) auf einen Schlag; (ask, refuse) ohne Umschweife ▷ adj (winner, victory) unbestritten; (refusal, hostility) total

outrun [aut'rʌn] (irreg: like **run**) vt schneller laufen als

outset ['autset] n Anfang m, Beginn m; **from the ~** von Anfang an; **at the ~** am Anfang

outshine [aut'ʃaɪn] (irreg: like **shine**) vt (fig) in den Schatten stellen

outside [aut'saɪd] n (of building etc) Außenseite f ▷ adj (wall, lavatory) Außen- ▷ adv (be, wait) draußen; (go) nach draußen ▷ prep außerhalb +gen; (door etc) vor +dat; **at the ~** (at the most) höchstens; (at the latest) spätestens; **an ~ chance** eine geringe Chance

outside broadcast n außerhalb des Studios produzierte Sendung f

outside lane n Überholspur f

outside line n (Tel) Amtsanschluss m

outsider [aut'saɪdəʳ] n (stranger) Außenstehende(r) f(m); (odd one out, in race etc) Außenseiter(in) m(f)

outsize ['autsaɪz] adj (clothes) übergroß

outskirts ['autskɜːts] npl (of town) Stadtrand m

outsmart [aut'smɑːt] vt austricksen (inf)

outspoken [aut'spəukən] adj offen

outspread [aut'spred] adj (wings, arms etc) ausgebreitet

outstanding [aut'stændɪŋ] adj (exceptional) hervorragend; (remaining) ausstehend; **your account is still ~** Ihr Konto weist noch Außenstände auf

outstay [aut'steɪ] vt: **to ~ one's welcome** länger bleiben als erwünscht

outstretched [aut'stretʃt] adj ausgestreckt

outstrip [aut'strıp] vt (competitors, supply): **to ~ (in)** übertreffen (an +dat)
out tray n Ablage f für Ausgänge
outvote [aut'vəut] vt überstimmen
outward ['autwəd] adj (sign, appearances) äußere(r, s) ▷ adv (move, face) nach außen; **~ journey** Hinreise f
outwardly ['autwədlı] adv (on the surface) äußerlich
outwards ['autwədz] adv (move, face) nach außen
outweigh [aut'weı] vt schwerer wiegen als
outwit [aut'wıt] vt überlisten
ova ['əuvə] npl of **ovum**
oval ['əuvl] adj oval ▷ n Oval nt

> ● OVAL OFFICE
>
> *Oval Office*, ein großer ovaler Raum im Weißen Haus, ist das private Büro des amerikanischen Präsidenten. Im weiteren Sinne bezieht sich dieser Begriff oft auf die Präsidentschaft selbst.

ovarian [əu'vɛərıən] adj (Anat) des Eierstocks/der Eierstöcke; **~ cyst** Zyste f im Eierstock
ovary ['əuvərı] n (Anat, Med) Eierstock m
ovation [əu'veıʃən] n Ovation f
oven ['ʌvn] n (Culin) Backofen m
ovenproof ['ʌvnpru:f] adj (dish etc) feuerfest
oven-ready ['ʌvnrɛdı] adj backfertig
ovenware ['ʌvnwɛər] n feuerfestes Geschirr nt

○ KEYWORD

over ['əuvər] adv **1** (across: walk, jump, fly etc) hinüber; **over here** hier; **over there** dort (drüben); **to ask sb over** (to one's house) jdn zu sich einladen
2 (indicating movement): **to fall over** (person) hinfallen; (object) umfallen; **to knock sth over** etw umstoßen; **to turn over** (in bed) sich umdrehen; **to bend over** sich bücken
3 (finished): **to be over** (game, life, relationship etc) vorbei sein, zu Ende sein
4 (excessively: clever, rich, fat etc) übermäßig
5 (remaining: money, food etc) übrig; **is there any cake (left) over?** ist noch Kuchen übrig?
6: all over (everywhere) überall
7 (repeatedly): **over and over (again)** immer (und immer) wieder; **five times over** fünfmal
▷ prep **1** (on top of, above) über +dat; (with vb of motion) über +acc; **to spread a sheet over sth** ein Laken über etw acc breiten
2 (on the other side of): **the pub over the road** die Kneipe gegenüber; **he jumped over the wall** er sprang über die Mauer
3 (more than) über +acc; **over 200 people** über 200 Leute; **over and above my normal duties** über meine normalen Pflichten hinaus; **over and above that** darüber hinaus

4 (during) während; **let's discuss it over dinner** wir sollten es beim Abendessen besprechen

over ... ['əuvər] pref über-
overact [əuvər'ækt] vi übertreiben
overall ['əuvərɔ:l] adj (length, cost etc) Gesamt-; (impression, view) allgemein ▷ adv (measure, cost) insgesamt; (generally) im Allgemeinen ▷ n (Brit) Kittel m; **overalls** npl Overall m
overall majority n absolute Mehrheit f
overanxious [əuvər'æŋkʃəs] adj überängstlich
overawe [əuvər'ɔ:] vt: **to be ~d (by)** überwältigt sein (von)
overbalance [əuvə'bæləns] vi das Gleichgewicht verlieren
overbearing [əuvə'bɛərıŋ] adj (person, manner) aufdringlich
overboard ['əuvəbɔ:d] adv (Naut) über Bord; **to go ~** (fig) es übertreiben, zu weit gehen
overbook [əuvə'buk] vt überbuchen
overcame [əuvə'keım] pt of **overcome**
overcapitalize [əuvə'kæpıtəlaız] vt überkapitalisieren
overcast ['əuvəka:st] adj (day, sky) bedeckt
overcharge [əuvə'tʃa:dʒ] vt zu viel berechnen +dat
overcoat ['əuvəkəut] n Mantel m
overcome [əuvə'kʌm] (irreg: like **come**) vt (problem, fear) überwinden ▷ adj überwältigt; **she was ~ with grief** der Schmerz übermannte sie
overconfident [əuvə'kɔnfıdənt] adj zu selbstsicher
overcrowded [əuvə'kraudıd] adj überfüllt
overcrowding [əuvə'kraudıŋ] n Überfüllung f
overdo [əuvə'du:] (irreg: like **do**) vt übertreiben; **to ~ it** es übertreiben
overdose ['əuvədəus] n Überdosis f
overdraft ['əuvədra:ft] n Kontoüberziehung f; **to have an ~** sein Konto überziehen
overdrawn [əuvə'drɔ:n] adj (account) überzogen; **I am ~** ich habe mein Konto überzogen
overdrive ['əuvədraıv] n (Aut) Schongang m
overdue [əuvə'dju:] adj überfällig; **that change was long ~** diese Änderung war schon lange fällig
overemphasis [əuvər'ɛmfəsıs] n: **~ on** Überbetonung +gen
overestimate [əuvər'ɛstımeıt] vt überschätzen
overexcited [əuvərık'saıtıd] adj ganz aufgeregt
overexertion [əuvərıg'zə:ʃən] n Überanstrengung f
overexpose [əuvərık'spəuz] vt (Phot) überbelichten
overflow [əuvə'fləu] vi (river) über die Ufer treten; (bath, jar etc) überlaufen ▷ n (also: **overflow pipe**) Überlaufrohr nt
overgenerous [əuvə'dʒɛnərəs] adj allzu großzügig

O

overgrown [əuvə'grəun] *adj* (*garden*) verwildert; **he's just an ~ schoolboy** er ist nur ein großes Kind

overhang ['əuvə'hæŋ] (*irreg: like* **hang**) *vt* herausragen über +*acc* ▷ *vi* überhängen ▷ *n* Überhang *m*

overhaul [əuvə'hɔːl] *vt* (*equipment, car etc*) überholen ▷ *n* Überholung *f*

overhead [əuvə'hɛd] *adv* (*above*) oben; (*in the sky*) in der Luft ▷ *adj* (*lighting*) Decken-; (*cables, wires*) Überland- ▷ *n* (*US*) = **overheads**

overheads *npl* allgemeine Unkosten *pl*

overhear [əuvə'hɪəʳ] (*irreg: like* **hear**) *vt* (*zufällig*) mit anhören

overheat [əuvə'hiːt] *vi* (*engine*) heißlaufen

overjoyed [əuvə'dʒɔɪd] *adj* überglücklich; **to be ~ (at)** überglücklich sein (über +*acc*)

overkill ['əuvəkɪl] *n* (*fig*): **it would be ~** das wäre zu viel des Guten

overland ['əuvəlænd] *adj* (*journey*) Überland- ▷ *adv* (*travel*) über Land

overlap [əuvə'læp] *vi* (*figures, ideas etc*) sich überschneiden

overleaf [əuvə'liːf] *adv* umseitig, auf der Rückseite

overload [əuvə'ləud] *vt* (*vehicle*) überladen; (*Elec*) überbelasten; (*fig: with work etc*) überlasten

overlook [əuvə'luk] *vt* (*have view over*) überblicken; (*fail to notice*) übersehen; (*excuse, forgive*) hinwegsehen über +*acc*

overlord ['əuvəlɔːd] *n* oberster Herr *m*

overmanning [əuvə'mænɪŋ] *n* Überbesetzung *f*

overnight [əuvə'naɪt] *adv* über Nacht ▷ *adj* (*bag, clothes*) Reise-; (*accommodation, stop*) für die Nacht; **to travel ~** nachts reisen; **he'll be away ~** (*tonight*) er kommt erst morgen zurück; **to stay ~** über Nacht bleiben; **~ stay** Übernachtung *f*

overpass ['əuvəpɑːs] (*esp US*) *n* Überführung *f*

overpay [əuvə'peɪ] *vt*: **to ~ sb by £50** jdm £ 50 zu viel bezahlen

overplay [əuvə'pleɪ] *vt* (*overact*) übertrieben darstellen; **to ~ one's hand** den Bogen überspannen

overpower [əuvə'pauəʳ] *vt* überwältigen

overpowering [əuvə'pauərɪŋ] *adj* (*heat*) unerträglich; (*stench*) durchdringend; (*feeling, desire*) überwältigend

overproduction ['əuvəprə'dʌkʃən] *n* Überproduktion *f*

overrate [əuvə'reɪt] *vt* überschätzen

overreach [əuvə'riːtʃ] *vt*: **to ~ o.s.** sich übernehmen

overreact [əuvəriː'ækt] *vi* übertrieben reagieren

override [əuvə'raɪd] (*irreg: like* **ride**) *vt* (*order etc*) sich hinwegsetzen über +*acc*

overriding [əuvə'raɪdɪŋ] *adj* vorrangig

overrule [əuvə'ruːl] *vt* (*claim, person*) zurückweisen; (*decision*) aufheben

overrun [əuvə'rʌn] (*irreg: like* **run**) *vt* (*country,*

continent) einfallen in +*acc* ▷ *vi* (*meeting etc*) zu lange dauern; **the town is ~ with tourists** die Stadt ist von Touristen überlaufen

overseas [əuvə'siːz] *adv* (*live, work*) im Ausland; (*travel*) ins Ausland ▷ *adj* (*market, trade*) Übersee-; (*student, visitor*) aus dem Ausland

oversee [əuvə'siː] *vt* (*supervise*) beaufsichtigen, überwachen

overseer ['əuvəsɪəʳ] *n* Aufseher(in) *m(f)*

overshadow [əuvə'ʃædəu] *vt* (*place, building etc*) überschatten; (*fig*) in den Schatten stellen

overshoot [əuvə'ʃuːt] (*irreg: like* **shoot**) *vt* (*target, runway*) hinausschießen über +*acc*

oversight ['əuvəsaɪt] *n* Versehen *nt*; **due to an ~** aus Versehen

oversimplify [əuvə'sɪmplɪfaɪ] *vt* zu stark vereinfachen

oversleep [əuvə'sliːp] (*irreg: like* **sleep**) *vi* verschlafen

overspend [əuvə'spɛnd] (*irreg: like* **spend**) *vi* zu viel ausgeben; **we have overspent by 5,000 dollars** wir haben 5000 Dollar zu viel ausgegeben

overspill ['əuvəspɪl] *n* (*excess population*) Bevölkerungsüberschuss *m*

overstaffed [əuvə'stɑːft] *adj*: **to be ~** überbesetzt sein

overstate [əuvə'steɪt] *vt* (*exaggerate*) zu sehr betonen

overstatement [əuvə'steɪtmənt] *n* Übertreibung *f*

overstay [əuvə'steɪ] *vt see* **outstay**

overstep [əuvə'stɛp] *vt*: **to ~ the mark** zu weit gehen

overstock [əuvə'stɔk] *vt* zu große Bestände anlegen in +*dat*

overstretched [əuvə'strɛtʃt] *adj* (*person, resources*) überfordert

overstrike ['əuvəstraɪk] (*irreg: like* **strike**) *n* (*on printer*) Mehrfachdruck *m* ▷ *vt* mehrfachdrucken

oversubscribed [əuvəsəb'skraɪbd] *adj* (*Comm etc*) überzeichnet

overt [əu'vəːt] *adj* offen

overtake [əuvə'teɪk] (*irreg: like* **take**) *vt* (*Aut*) überholen; (*event, change*) hereinbrechen über +*acc*; (*emotion*) befallen ▷ *vi* (*Aut*) überholen

overtaking [əuvə'teɪkɪŋ] *n* (*Aut*) Überholen *nt*

overtax [əuvə'tæks] *vt* (*Econ*) zu hoch besteuern; (*strength, patience*) überfordern; **to ~ o.s.** sich übernehmen

overthrow [əuvə'θrəu] (*irreg: like* **throw**) *vt* (*government etc*) stürzen

overtime ['əuvətaɪm] *n* Überstunden *pl*; **to do** *or* **work ~** Überstunden machen

overtime ban *n* Überstundenverbot *nt*

overtone ['əuvətəun] *n* (*fig: also:* **overtones**): **~s of** Untertöne *pl* von

overture ['əuvətʃuəʳ] *n* (*Mus*) Ouvertüre *f*; (*fig*) Annäherungsversuch *m*

overturn [əuvə'təːn] *vt* (*car, chair*) umkippen; (*fig: decision*) aufheben; (*: government*) stürzen ▷ *vi* (*train etc*) umkippen; (*car*) sich

überschlagen; (*boat*) kentern
overview ['əʊvəvjuː] *n* Überblick *m*
overweight [əʊvə'weɪt] *adj* (*person*)
übergewichtig
overwhelm [əʊvə'wɛlm] *vt* überwältigen
overwhelming [əʊvə'wɛlmɪŋ] *adj*
überwältigend; **one's ~ impression is of
heat/noise** man bemerkt vor allem die Hitze/
den Lärm
overwhelmingly [əʊvə'wɛlmɪŋlɪ] *adv* (*vote,
reject*) mit überwältigender Mehrheit;
(*appreciative, generous etc*) über alle Maßen;
(*opposed etc*) überwiegend
overwork [əʊvə'wəːk] *n* Überarbeitung *f* ▷ *vt*
(*person*) (mit Arbeit) überlasten; (*cliché etc*)
überstrapazieren ▷ *vi* sich überarbeiten
overwrite [əʊvə'raɪt] *vt* (*Comput*) überschreiben
overwrought [əʊvə'rɔːt] *adj* (*person*) überreizt
ovulate ['ɔvjuleɪt] *vi* ovulieren
ovulation [ɔvju'leɪʃən] *n* Eisprung *m*,
Ovulation *f*
ovum ['əʊvəm] (*pl* **ova**) *n* Eizelle *f*
owe [əʊ] *vt*: **to ~ sb sth, to ~ sth to sb** (*lit, fig*)
jdm etw schulden; (*life, talent, good looks etc*)
jdm etw verdanken
owing to ['əʊɪŋ-] *prep* (*because of*) wegen +*gen*,
aufgrund +*gen*
owl [aʊl] *n* Eule *f*
own [əʊn] *vt* (*possess*) besitzen ▷ *vi* (*Brit: form*): **to
~ up to sth** etw zugeben ▷ *adj* eigen; **a room
of my ~** mein eigenes Zimmer; **to get one's
~ back** (*take revenge*) sich rächen; **on one's ~**
allein; **to come into one's ~** sich entfalten
▷ **own up** *vi* gestehen, es zugeben
own brand *n* (*Comm*) Hausmarke *f*
owner ['əʊnə^r] *n* Besitzer(in) *m(f)*,
Eigentümer(in) *m(f)*
owner-occupier ['əʊnər'ɔkjupaɪə^r] *n* (*Admin,*

Law) Bewohner(in) *m(f)* im eigenen Haus
ownership ['əʊnəʃɪp] *n* Besitz *m*; **under new ~**
(*shop etc*) unter neuer Leitung
own goal *n* (*also fig*) Eigentor *nt*
ox [ɔks] (*pl* **oxen**) *n* Ochse *m*

OXFAM (*Brit*) *n abbr* (= *Oxford Committee for Famine
Relief*) karitative Vereinigung zur Hungerhilfe
oxide ['ɔksaɪd] *n* Oxid *nt*
oxidize ['ɔksɪdaɪz] *vi* oxidieren
Oxon. ['ɔksn] (*Brit*) *abbr* (*Post*) = *Oxfordshire*; (*in
degree titles*: = *Oxoniensis*) der Universität Oxford
oxtail ['ɔksteɪl] *n*: **~ soup**
Ochsenschwanzsuppe *f*
oxyacetylene ['ɔksɪə'sɛtɪliːn] *adj*
(*flame*) Azetylensauerstoff-; **~ burner**
Schweißbrenner *m*; **~ welding**
Autogenschweißen *nt*
oxygen ['ɔksɪdʒən] *n* Sauerstoff *m*
oxygen mask *n* Sauerstoffmaske *f*
oxygen tent *n* Sauerstoffzelt *nt*
oyster ['ɔɪstə^r] *n* Auster *f*
oz *abbr* = **ounce**
ozone ['əʊzəʊn] *n* Ozon *nt*
ozone hole *n* Ozonloch *nt*
ozone layer *n*: **the ~** die Ozonschicht

O

Pp

P, p¹ [pi:] n (letter) P nt, p nt; **P for Peter** ≈ P wie Paula

P. abbr = **president; prince**

p² (Brit) abbr = **penny; pence**

p. abbr (= page) S.

PA n abbr = **personal assistant; public-address system** ▷ abbr (US: Post) = Pennsylvania

pa [pɑ:] (inf) n Papa m

p.a. abbr (= per annum) p.a.

PAC (US) n abbr (= political action committee) politisches Aktionskomitee

pace [peɪs] n (step) Schritt m; (speed) Tempo nt ▷ vi: **to ~ up and down** auf und ab gehen; **to keep ~ with** Schritt halten mit; **to set the ~** das Tempo angeben; **to put sb through his/her ~s** (fig) jdn auf Herz und Nieren prüfen

pacemaker ['peɪsmeɪkər] n (Med) (Herz) schrittmacher m; (Sport: pacesetter) Schrittmacher m

pacesetter ['peɪssetər] n (Sport) = **pacemaker**

Pacific [pə'sɪfɪk] n (Geog): **the ~ (Ocean)** der Pazifik, der Pazifische Ozean

pacific [pə'sɪfɪk] adj (intentions etc) friedlich

pacifier ['pæsɪfaɪər] (US) n (dummy) Schnuller m

pacifist ['pæsɪfɪst] n Pazifist(in) m(f)

pacify ['pæsɪfaɪ] vt (person, fears) beruhigen

pack [pæk] n (packet) Packung f; (US: of cigarettes) Schachtel f; (of people, hounds) Meute f; (also: **back pack**) Rucksack m; (of cards) (Karten)spiel nt ▷ vt (clothes etc) einpacken; (suitcase etc, Comput) packen; (press down) pressen ▷ vi packen; **to ~ one's bags** (fig) die Koffer packen; **to ~ into** (cram: people, objects) hineinstopfen in +acc; **to send sb ~ing** (inf) jdn kurz abfertigen

▶ **pack in** (Brit: inf) vt (job) hinschmeißen; **~ it in!** hör auf!

▶ **pack off** vt schicken

▶ **pack up** vi (Brit: inf: machine) den Geist aufgeben; (: person) Feierabend machen ▷ vt (belongings) zusammenpacken

package ['pækɪdʒ] n (parcel, Comput) Paket nt; (also: **package deal**) Pauschalangebot nt ▷ vt verpacken

package holiday (Brit), **package tour** (US) n Pauschalreise f

packaging ['pækɪdʒɪŋ] n Verpackung f

packaging industry n Verpackungsindustrie f

packed [pækt] adj (crowded) randvoll

packed lunch (Brit) n Lunchpaket nt

packer ['pækər] n Packer(in) m(f)

packet ['pækɪt] n Packung f; (of cigarettes) Schachtel m; **to make a ~** (Brit: inf) einen Haufen Geld verdienen

packet switching n (Comput) Paketvermittlung f

pack ice ['pækaɪs] n Packeis nt

packing ['pækɪŋ] n (act) Packen nt; (material) Verpackung f

packing case n Kiste f

pact [pækt] n Pakt m

pad [pæd] n (paper) Block m; (to prevent damage) Polster nt; (inf: home) Bude f ▷ vt (upholstery etc) polstern ▷ vi: **to ~ about/in** herum-/ hereintrotten

padded cell ['pædɪd-] n Gummizelle f

padding ['pædɪŋ] n (material) Polsterung f; (fig) Füllwerk nt

paddle ['pædl] n (oar) Paddel nt; (US: for table tennis) Schläger m ▷ vt paddeln ▷ vi (at seaside) plan(t)schen

paddle steamer n Raddampfer m

paddling pool ['pædlɪŋ-] (Brit) n Plan(t) schbecken nt

paddock ['pædək] n (small field) Koppel f; (at race course) Sattelplatz m

paddy field ['pædɪ-] n Reisfeld nt

padlock ['pædlɒk] n Vorhängeschloss nt ▷ vt (mit einem Vorhängeschloss) verschließen

padre ['pɑ:drɪ] n (Rel) Feldgeistliche(r) m

paediatrician [pi:dɪə'trɪʃən] n Kinderarzt m, Kinderärztin f

paediatrics, (US) **pediatrics** [pi:dɪ'ætrɪks] n Kinderheilkunde f, Pädiatrie f

paedophile ['pi:dəufaɪl] n Pädophile(r) f(m) ▷ adj pädophil

paedophilia [pi:dəu'fɪlɪə] n Pädophilie f

pagan ['peɪgən] adj heidnisch ▷ n Heide m, Heidin f

page [peɪdʒ] n (of book etc) Seite f; (also: **pageboy**: in hotel) Page m ▷ vt (in hotel etc) ausrufen lassen

pageant ['pædʒənt] n (historical procession) Festzug m; (show) Historienspiel nt

pageantry ['pædʒəntrɪ] n Prunk m

pageboy ['peɪdʒbɔɪ] n see **page**

pager ['peɪdʒər] n Funkrufempfänger m,
Piepser m (inf)
paginate ['pædʒɪneɪt] vt paginieren
pagination [pædʒɪ'neɪʃən] n Paginierung f
pagoda [pə'gəudə] n Pagode f
paid [peɪd] pt, pp of **pay** ▷ adj bezahlt; **to put ~
to** (Brit) zunichtemachen
paid-up ['peɪdʌp], (US) **paid-in** adj (member)
zahlend; (Comm: shares) eingezahlt; ~ **capital**
eingezahltes Kapital nt
pail [peɪl] n Eimer m
pain [peɪn] n Schmerz m; (also: **pain in the
neck**: inf: nuisance) Plage f; **to have a ~ in
the chest/arm** Schmerzen in der Brust/im
Arm haben; **to be in ~** Schmerzen haben;
to take ~s to do sth (make an effort) sich dat
Mühe geben, etw zu tun; **on ~ of death** bei
Todesstrafe; **he is/it is a right ~ (in the
neck)** (inf) er/das geht einem auf den Wecker
pained [peɪnd] adj (expression) gequält
painful ['peɪnful] adj (back, injury etc)
schmerzhaft; (sight, decision etc) schmerzlich;
(laborious) mühsam; (embarrassing) peinlich
painfully ['peɪnfəlɪ] adv (fig: extremely) furchtbar
painkiller ['peɪnkɪlər] n schmerzstillendes
Mittel nt
painless ['peɪnlɪs] adj schmerzlos
painstaking ['peɪnzteɪkɪŋ] adj (work, person)
gewissenhaft
paint [peɪnt] n Farbe f ▷ vt (door, house etc)
anstreichen; (person, picture) malen; (fig)
zeichnen; **a tin of ~** eine Dose Farbe; **to ~ the
door blue** die Tür blau streichen; **to ~ in oils**
in Öl malen
paintbox ['peɪntbɔks] n Farbkasten m,
Malkasten m
paintbrush ['peɪntbrʌʃ] n Pinsel m
painter ['peɪntər] n (artist) Maler(in) m(f);
(decorator) Anstreicher(in) m(f)
painting ['peɪntɪŋ] n (activity: of artist) Malerei
f; (: of decorator) Anstreichen nt; (picture) Bild nt,
Gemälde nt
paint stripper n Abbeizmittel nt
paintwork ['peɪntwəːk] n (of wall etc) Anstrich
m; (of car) Lack m
pair [peər] n Paar nt; **a ~ of scissors** eine
Schere; **a ~ of trousers** eine Hose
▶ **pair off** vi: **to ~ off with sb** sich jdm
anschließen
pajamas [pə'dʒɑːməz] (US) npl Schlafanzug m,
Pyjama m
Pakistan [pɑːkɪ'stɑːn] n Pakistan nt
Pakistani [pɑːkɪ'stɑːnɪ] adj pakistanisch ▷ n
Pakistani m, Pakistaner(in) m(f)
PAL n abbr (TV: = phase alternation line) PAL nt
pal [pæl] (inf) n (friend) Kumpel m, Freund(in)
m(f)
palace ['pæləs] n Palast m
palaeontology [pælɪɔn'tɔlədʒɪ] n
Paläontologie f
palatable ['pælɪtəbl] adj (food, drink) genießbar;
(fig: idea, fact etc) angenehm
palate ['pælɪt] n (Anat) Gaumen m; (sense of

taste) Geschmackssinn m
palatial [pə'leɪʃəl] adj (residence etc) prunkvoll
palaver [pə'lɑːvər] (inf) n (fuss) Theater nt
pale [peɪl] adj blass; (light) fahl ▷ vi erblassen
▷ n: **beyond the ~** (unacceptable: behaviour)
indiskutabel; **to grow** or **turn ~**
erblassen, blass werden; ~ **blue** zartblau;
to ~ into insignificance (beside) zur
Bedeutungslosigkeit herabsinken (gegenüber
+dat)
paleness ['peɪlnɪs] n Blässe f
Palestine ['pælɪstaɪn] n Palästina nt
Palestinian [pælɪs'tɪnɪən] adj palästinensisch
▷ n Palästinenser(in) m(f)
palette ['pælɪt] n Palette f
palings ['peɪlɪŋz] npl (fence) Lattenzaun m
palisade [pælɪ'seɪd] n Palisade f
pall [pɔːl] n (cloud of smoke) (Rauch)wolke f ▷ vi
an Reiz verlieren
pallet ['pælɪt] n (for goods) Palette f
palliative ['pælɪətɪv] n (Med) Linderungsmittel
nt; (fig) Beschönigung f
pallid ['pælɪd] adj bleich
pallor ['pælər] n Bleichheit f
pally ['pælɪ] (inf) adj: **they're very ~** sie sind
dicke Freunde
palm [pɑːm] n (also: **palm tree**) Palme f; (of
hand) Handteller m ▷ vt: **to ~ sth off on sb**
(inf) jdm etw andrehen
palmistry ['pɑːmɪstrɪ] n Handlesekunst f
Palm Sunday n Palmsonntag m
palpable ['pælpəbl] adj (obvious) offensichtlich
palpitations [pælpɪ'teɪʃənz] npl (Med)
Herzklopfen nt
paltry ['pɔːltrɪ] adj (amount, wage) armselig
pamper ['pæmpər] vt verwöhnen
pamphlet ['pæmflət] n Broschüre f; (political)
Flugschrift f
pan [pæn] n (also: **saucepan**) Topf m;
(also: **frying pan**) Pfanne f ▷ vi (Cine, TV)
schwenken ▷ vt (inf: book, film) verreißen; **to ~
for gold** Gold waschen
panacea [pænə'sɪə] n Allheilmittel nt
panache [pə'næʃ] n Elan m, Schwung m
Panama ['pænəmɑː] n Panama nt
panama [pænə'mɑː] n (also: **panama hat**)
Panamahut m
Panama Canal n: **the ~** der Panamakanal
Panamanian [pænə'meɪnɪən] adj panamaisch
▷ n Panamaer(in) m(f)
pancake ['pænkeɪk] n Pfannkuchen m
Pancake Day (Brit) n Fastnachtsdienstag m
pancake roll n gefüllte Pfannkuchenrolle
pancreas ['pæŋkrɪəs] n Bauchspeicheldrüse f
panda ['pændə] n Panda m
panda car (Brit) n Streifenwagen m
pandemic [pæn'dɛmɪk] n Pandemie f
pandemonium [pændɪ'məunɪəm] n Chaos nt
pander ['pændər] vi: **to ~ to** (person, desire etc)
sich richten nach, entgegenkommen +dat
p & h (US) abbr (= postage and handling) Porto und
Bearbeitungsgebühr
P & L abbr (= profit and loss) Gewinn und Verlust;

P

see also **profit**

p & p (*Brit*) *abbr* (= *postage and packing*) Porto und Verpackung

pane [peɪn] *n* (*of glass*) Scheibe *f*

panel ['pænl] *n* (*wood, metal, glass etc*) Platte *f*, Tafel *f*; (*group of experts etc*) Diskussionsrunde *f*; ~ **of judges** Jury *f*

panel game (*Brit*) *n* Ratespiel *nt*

panelling, (*US*) **paneling** ['pænəlɪŋ] *n* Täfelung *f*

panellist, (*US*) **panelist** ['pænəlɪst] *n* Diskussionsteilnehmer(in) *m(f)*

pang [pæŋ] *n*: **to have** *or* **feel a ~ of regret** Reue empfinden; **hunger ~s** quälender Hunger *m*; **~s of conscience** Gewissensbisse *pl*

panhandler ['pænhændlə^r] (*US: inf*) *n* Bettler(in) *m(f)*

panic ['pænɪk] *n* Panik *f* ▷ *vi* in Panik geraten

panic buying [-baɪɪŋ] *n* Panikkäufe *pl*

panicky ['pænɪkɪ] *adj* (*person*) überängstlich; (*feeling*) Angst-; (*reaction*) Kurzschluss-

panic-stricken ['pænɪkstrɪkən] *adj* (*person, face*) von Panik erfasst

pannier ['pænɪə^r] *n* (*on bicycle*) Satteltasche *f*; (*on animal*) (Trage)korb *m*

panorama [pænə'rɑ:mə] *n* (*view*) Panorama *nt*

panoramic [pænə'ræmɪk] *adj* (*view*) Panorama-

pansy ['pænzɪ] *n* (*Bot*) Stiefmütterchen *nt*; (*inf: pej: sissy*) Tunte *f*

pant [pænt] *vi* (*person*) keuchen; (*animal*) hecheln

pantechnicon [pæn'tɛknɪkən] (*Brit*) *n* Möbelwagen *m*

panther ['pænθə^r] *n* Pant(h)er *m*

panties ['pæntɪz] *npl* Höschen *nt*

panto ['pæntəu] *n*, **pantomime** ['pæntəumaɪm] *n siehe* Info-Artikel

PANTOMIME

Pantomime oder umgangssprächlich *panto* ist in Großbritannien ein zur Weihnachtszeit aufgeführtes Märchenspiel mit possenhaften Elementen, Musik, Standardrollen (ein als Frau verkleideter Mann, ein Junge, ein Bösewicht) und aktuellen Witzen. Publikumsbeteiligung wird gern gesehen (z. B. warnen die Kinder den Helden mit dem Ruf „He's behind you" vor einer drohenden Gefahr), und viele der Witze sprechen vor allem Erwachsene an, sodass pantomimes Unterhaltung für die ganze Familie bieten.

pantry ['pæntrɪ] *n* (*cupboard*) Vorratsschrank *m*; (*room*) Speisekammer *f*

pants [pænts] *npl* (*Brit: woman's*) Höschen *nt*; (: *man's*) Unterhose *f*; (*US: trousers*) Hose *f*

panty hose (*US*) *npl* Strumpfhose *f*

papacy ['peɪpəsɪ] *n* Papsttum *nt*; **during the ~ of Paul VI** während der Amtszeit von Papst Paul VI

papal ['peɪpəl] *adj* päpstlich

paparazzi [pæpə'rætsi:] *npl* Pressefotografen *pl*, Paparazzi *pl*

paper ['peɪpə^r] *n* Papier *nt*; (*also*: **newspaper**) Zeitung *f*; (*exam*) Arbeit *f*; (*academic essay*) Referat *nt*; (*document*) Dokument *nt*, Papier; (*wallpaper*) Tapete *f* ▷ *adj* (*made from paper: hat, plane etc*) Papier-, aus Papier ▷ *vt* (*room*) tapezieren; **papers** *npl* (*also*: **identity papers**) Papiere *pl*; **a piece of ~** (*odd bit*) ein Stück *nt* Papier, ein Zettel *m*; (*sheet*) ein Blatt *nt* Papier; **to put sth down on ~** etw schriftlich festhalten

paper advance *n* (*on printer*) Papiervorschub *m*

paperback ['peɪpəbæk] *n* Taschenbuch *nt*, Paperback *nt* ▷ *adj*: **~ edition** Taschenbuchausgabe *f*

paper bag *n* Tüte *f*

paperboy ['peɪpəbɔɪ] *n* Zeitungsjunge *m*

paperclip ['peɪpəklɪp] *n* Büroklammer *f*

paper hankie *n* Tempotaschentuch® *nt*

paper mill *n* Papierfabrik *f*

paper money *n* Papiergeld *nt*

paper shop *n* Zeitungsladen *m*

paperweight ['peɪpəweɪt] *n* Briefbeschwerer *m*

paperwork ['peɪpəwə:k] *n* Schreibarbeit *f*

papier-mâché [pæpjeɪ'mæʃeɪ] *n* Papiermaschee *nt*

paprika ['pæprɪkə] *n* Paprika *m*

Pap Smear, Pap Test *n* (*Med*) Abstrich *m*

par [pɑ:^r] *n* (*Golf*) Par *nt*; **to be on a ~ with** sich messen können mit; **at ~** (*Comm*) zum Nennwert; **above/below ~** (*Comm*) über/unter dem Nennwert; **above** *or* **over ~** (*Golf*) über dem Par; **below** *or* **under ~** (*Golf*) unter dem Par; **to feel below** *or* **under ~** sich nicht auf der Höhe fühlen; **to be ~ for the course** (*fig*) zu erwarten sein

parable ['pærəbl] *n* Gleichnis *nt*

parabola [pə'ræbələ] *n* (*Math*) Parabel *f*

parachute ['pærəʃu:t] *n* Fallschirm *m*

parachute jump *n* Fallschirmabsprung *m*

parachutist ['pærəʃu:tɪst] *n* Fallschirmspringer(in) *m(f)*

parade [pə'reɪd] *n* (*procession*) Parade *f*; (*ceremony*) Zeremonie *f* ▷ *vt* (*people*) aufmarschieren lassen; (*wealth, knowledge etc*) zur Schau stellen ▷ *vi* (*Mil*) aufmarschieren; **fashion ~** Modenschau *f*

parade ground *n* Truppenübungsplatz *m*, Exerzierplatz *m*

paradise ['pærədaɪs] *n* (*also fig*) Paradies *nt*

paradox ['pærədɔks] *n* Paradox *nt*

paradoxical [pærə'dɔksɪkl] *adj* (*situation*) paradox

paradoxically [pærə'dɔksɪklɪ] *adv* paradoxerweise

paraffin ['pærəfɪn] (*Brit*) *n* (*also*: **paraffin oil**) Petroleum *nt*; **liquid ~** Paraffinöl *nt*

paraffin heater (*Brit*) *n* Petroleumofen *m*

paraffin lamp (*Brit*) *n* Petroleumlampe *f*

paragon ['pærəgən] *n*: **a ~ of** (*honesty, virtue etc*) ein Muster *nt* an +*dat*

paragraph ['pærəgrɑːf] *n* Absatz *m*, Paragraf *m*; **to begin a new ~** einen neuen Absatz beginnen

parallel ['pærəlɛl] *adj* (*also Comput*) parallel; (*fig: similar*) vergleichbar ▷ *n* Parallele *f*; (*Geog*) Breitenkreis *m*; **to run ~ (with** *or* **to)** (*lit, fig*) parallel verlaufen (zu); **to draw ~s between/ with** Parallelen ziehen zwischen/mit; **in ~** (*Elec*) parallel

paralyse ['pærəlaɪz] (*Brit*) *vt* (*also fig*) lähmen

paralysis [pə'rælɪsɪs] (*pl* **paralyses**) *n* Lähmung *f*

paralytic [pærə'lɪtɪk] *adj* paralytisch, Lähmungs-; (*Brit: inf: drunk*) sternhagelvoll

paralyze ['pærəlaɪz] (*US*) *vt* = **paralyse**

paramedic [pærə'mɛdɪk] *n* Sanitäter(in) *m(f)*; (*in hospital*) medizinisch-technischer Assistent *m*, medizinisch-technische Assistentin *f*

parameter [pə'ræmɪtər] *n* (*Math*) Parameter *m*; (*fig: factor*) Faktor *m*; (*: limit*) Rahmen *m*

paramilitary [pærə'mɪlɪtərɪ] *adj* paramilitärisch

paramount ['pærəmaunt] *adj* vorherrschend; **of ~ importance** von höchster *or* größter Wichtigkeit

paranoia [pærə'nɔɪə] *n* Paranoia *f*

paranoid ['pærənɔɪd] *adj* paranoid

paranormal [pærə'nɔːml] *adj* übersinnlich, paranormal ▷ *n*: **the ~** das Übersinnliche

parapet ['pærəpɪt] *n* Brüstung *f*

paraphernalia [pærəfə'neɪlɪə] *n* Utensilien *pl*

paraphrase ['pærəfreɪz] *vt* umschreiben

paraplegic [pærə'pliːdʒɪk] *n* Paraplegiker(in) *m(f)*, doppelseitig Gelähmte(r) *f(m)*

parapsychology [pærəsaɪ'kɔlədʒɪ] *n* Parapsychologie *f*

parasite ['pærəsaɪt] *n* (*also fig*) Parasit *m*

parasol ['pærəsɔl] *n* Sonnenschirm *m*

paratrooper ['pærətruːpər] *n* Fallschirmjäger *m*

parcel ['pɑːsl] *n* Paket *nt* ▷ *vt* (*also:* **parcel up**) verpacken
▶ **parcel out** *vt* aufteilen

parcel bomb (*Brit*) *n* Paketbombe *f*

parcel post *n* Paketpost *f*

parch [pɑːtʃ] *vt* ausdörren, austrocknen

parched [pɑːtʃt] *adj* ausgetrocknet; **I'm ~** (*inf: thirsty*) ich bin am Verdursten

parchment ['pɑːtʃmənt] *n* Pergament *nt*

pardon ['pɑːdn] *n* (*Law*) Begnadigung *f* ▷ *vt* (*forgive*) verzeihen +*dat*, vergeben +*dat*; (*Law*) begnadigen; **~ me!, I beg your pardon!** (*I'm sorry!*) verzeihen Sie bitte!; **(I beg your) ~?, ~ me?** (*US: what did you say?*) bitte?

pare [pɛər] *vt* (*Brit: nails*) schneiden; (*fruit etc*) schälen; (*fig: costs etc*) reduzieren

parent ['pɛərənt] *n* (*mother*) Mutter *f*; (*father*) Vater *m*; **parents** *npl* (*mother and father*) Eltern *pl*

parentage ['pɛərəntɪdʒ] *n* Herkunft *f*; **of unknown ~** unbekannter Herkunft

parental [pə'rɛntl] *adj* (*love, control etc*) elterlich

parent company *n* Mutterunternehmen *nt*

parentheses [pə'rɛnθɪsiːz] *npl of* **parenthesis**

parenthesis [pə'rɛnθɪsɪs] (*pl* **parentheses**) *n* Klammer *f*; **in ~** in Klammern

parenthood ['pɛərənthud] *n* Elternschaft *f*

parenting ['pɛərəntɪŋ] *n* elterliche Pflege *f*

Paris ['pærɪs] *n* Paris *nt*

parish ['pærɪʃ] *n* Gemeinde *f*

parish council (*Brit*) *n* Gemeinderat *m*

parishioner [pə'rɪʃənər] *n* Gemeindemitglied *nt*

Parisian [pə'rɪzɪən] *adj* Pariser *inv*, paris(er)isch ▷ *n* Pariser(in) *m(f)*

parity ['pærɪtɪ] *n* (*equality*) Gleichstellung *f*

park [pɑːk] *n* Park *m* ▷ *vt, vi* (*Aut*) parken

parka ['pɑːkə] *n* Parka *m*

parking ['pɑːkɪŋ] *n* Parken *nt*; **"no ~"** „Parken verboten"

parking lights *npl* Parklicht *nt*

parking lot (*US*) *n* Parkplatz *m*

parking meter *n* Parkuhr *f*

parking offence (*Brit*) *n* Parkvergehen *nt*

parking place *n* Parkplatz *m*

parking ticket *n* Strafzettel *m*

parking violation (*US*) *n* = **parking offence**

Parkinson's ['pɑːkɪnsənz], **Parkinson's disease** *n* parkinsonsche Krankheit *f*

parkway ['pɑːkweɪ] (*US*) *n* Allee *f*

parlance ['pɑːləns] *n*: **in common/modern ~** im allgemeinen/modernen Sprachgebrauch

parliament ['pɑːləmənt] *n* Parlament *nt*

○ **PARLIAMENT**
○
○
○ *Parliament* ist die höchste gesetzgebende
○ Versammlung in Großbritannien und
○ tritt im Parlamentsgebäude in London
○ zusammen. Die Legislaturperiode beträgt
○ normalerweise 5 Jahre von einer Wahl zur
○ nächsten. Das Parlament besteht aus zwei
○ Kammern, dem Oberhaus (siehe *House of*
○ *Lords* und dem Unterhaus (siehe *House of*
○ *Commons*).

---

parliamentary [pɑːlə'mɛntərɪ] *adj* parlamentarisch

parlour, (*US*) **parlor** ['pɑːlər] *n* Salon *m*

parlous ['pɑːləs] *adj* (*state*) prekär

Parmesan [pɑːmɪ'zæn] *n* (*also:* **Parmesan cheese**) Parmesan(käse) *m*

parochial [pə'rəukɪəl] (*pej*) *adj* (*person, attitude*) engstirnig

parody ['pærədɪ] *n* Parodie *f* ▷ *vt* parodieren

parole [pə'rəul] *n* (*Law*) Bewährung *f*; **on ~** auf Bewährung

paroxysm ['pærəksɪzəm] *n* (*also Med*) Anfall *m*

parquet ['pɑːkeɪ] *n* (*also:* **parquet floor(ing)**) Parkettboden *m*

parrot ['pærət] *n* Papagei *m*

parrot-fashion ['pærətfæʃən] *adv* (*say, learn*) mechanisch; (*repeat*) wie ein Papagei

parry ['pærɪ] *vt* (*blow, argument*) parieren, abwehren

parsimonious [pɑːsɪ'məunɪəs] *adj* geizig

parsley ['pɑːslɪ] *n* Petersilie *f*

parsnip ['pɑːsnɪp] *n* Pastinake *f*

p

parson ['pɑːsn] *n* Pfarrer *m*
part [pɑːt] *n* Teil *m*; (*Tech*) Teil *nt*; (*Theat, Cine etc: role*) Rolle *f*; (*US: in hair*) Scheitel *m*; (*Mus*) Stimme *f* ▷ *adv* = **partly** ▷ *vt* (*separate*) trennen; (*hair*) scheiteln ▷ *vi* (*roads, people*) sich trennen; (*crowd*) sich teilen; **to take ~ in** teilnehmen an +*dat*; **to take sth in good ~** etw nicht übel nehmen; **to take sb's ~** (*support*) sich auf jds Seite *acc* stellen; **on his ~** seinerseits; **for my ~** für meinen Teil; **for the most ~** (*generally*) zumeist; **for the better** *or* **best ~ of the day** die meiste Zeit des Tages; **to be ~ and parcel of** dazugehören zu; **~ of speech** (*Ling*) Wortart *f*
▶ **part with** *vt fus* sich trennen von
partake [pɑːˈteɪk] (*irreg: like* **take**) *vi* (*form*): **to ~ of sth** etw zu sich nehmen
part exchange (*Brit*) *n*: **to give/take sth in ~** etw in Zahlung geben/nehmen
partial ['pɑːʃl] *adj* (*victory, solution*) Teil-; (*support*) teilweise; (*biassed*) parteiisch; **to be ~ to** (*person, drink etc*) eine Vorliebe haben für
partially ['pɑːʃəlɪ] *adv* (*to some extent*) teilweise, zum Teil
participant [pɑːˈtɪsɪpənt] *n* Teilnehmer(in) *m(f)*
participate [pɑːˈtɪsɪpeɪt] *vi* sich beteiligen; **to ~ in** teilnehmen an +*dat*
participation [pɑːtɪsɪˈpeɪʃən] *n* Teilnahme *f*
participle ['pɑːtɪsɪpl] *n* Partizip *nt*
particle ['pɑːtɪkl] *n* Teilchen *nt*, Partikel *f*
particular [pəˈtɪkjʊləʳ] *adj* (*distinct: person, time, place etc*) bestimmt, speziell; (*special*) speziell, besondere(r, s) ▷ *n*: **in ~** insbesondere, besonders; **particulars** *npl* Einzelheiten *pl*; (*name, address etc*) Personalien *pl*; **to be very ~ about sth** (*fussy*) in Bezug auf etw *acc* sehr eigen sein
particularly [pəˈtɪkjʊləlɪ] *adv* besonders
parting ['pɑːtɪŋ] *n* (*action*) Teilung *f*; (*farewell*) Abschied *m*; (*Brit: in hair*) Scheitel *m* ▷ *adj* (*words, gift etc*) Abschieds-; **his ~ shot was ...** (*fig*) seine Bemerkung zum Abschied war ...
partisan [pɑːtɪˈzæn] *adj* (*politics, views*) voreingenommen ▷ *n* (*supporter*) Anhänger(in) *m(f)*; (*fighter*) Partisan *m*
partition [pɑːˈtɪʃən] *n* (*wall, screen*) Trennwand *f*; (*of country*) Teilung *f* ▷ *vt* (*room, office*) aufteilen; (*country*) teilen
partly ['pɑːtlɪ] *adv* teilweise, zum Teil
partner ['pɑːtnəʳ] *n* Partner(in) *m(f)*; (*Comm*) Partner(in), Teilhaber(in) *m(f)* ▷ *vt* (*at dance, cards etc*) als Partner(in) haben
partnership ['pɑːtnəʃɪp] *n* (*Pol etc*) Partnerschaft *f*; (*Comm*) Teilhaberschaft *f*; **to go into ~ (with sb), form a ~ (with sb)** (mit jdm) eine Partnerschaft eingehen
part payment *n* Anzahlung *f*
partridge ['pɑːtrɪdʒ] *n* Rebhuhn *nt*
part-time ['pɑːt'taɪm] *adj* (*work, staff*) Teilzeit-, Halbtags- ▷ *adv*: **to work ~** Teilzeit arbeiten; **to study ~** Teilzeitstudent(in) *m(f)* sein
part-timer [pɑːt'taɪməʳ] *n* (*also:* **part-time**

worker) Teilzeitbeschäftigte(r) *f(m)*
party ['pɑːtɪ] *n* (*Pol, Law*) Partei *f*; (*celebration, social event*) Party *f*, Fete *f*; (*group of people*) Gruppe *f*, Gesellschaft *f* ▷ *cpd* (*Pol*) Partei-; **dinner ~** Abendgesellschaft *f*; **to give** *or* **throw a ~** eine Party geben, eine Fete machen; **we're having a ~ next Saturday** bei uns ist nächsten Samstag eine Party; **our son's birthday ~** die Geburtstagsfeier unseres Sohnes; **to be a ~ to a crime** an einem Verbrechen beteiligt sein
party dress *n* Partykleid *nt*
party line *n* (*Tel*) Gemeinschaftsanschluss *m*; (*Pol*) Parteilinie *f*
party piece (*inf*) *n*: **to do one's ~** auf einer Party etwas zum Besten geben
party political *adj* parteipolitisch
party political broadcast *n* parteipolitische Sendung *f*
par value *n* (*Comm: of share, bond*) Nennwert *m*
pass [pɑːs] *vt* (*spend: time*) verbringen; (*hand over*) reichen, geben; (*go past*) vorbeikommen an +*dat*; (*: in car*) vorbeifahren an +*dat*; (*overtake*) überholen; (*fig: exceed*) übersteigen; (*exam*) bestehen; (*law, proposal*) genehmigen ▷ *vi* (*go past*) vorbeigehen; (*: in car*) vorbeifahren; (*in exam*) bestehen ▷ *n* (*permit*) Ausweis *m*; (*in mountains, Sport*) Pass *m*; **to ~ sth through sth** etw durch etw führen; **to ~ the ball to** den Ball zuspielen +*dat*; **could you ~ the vegetables round?** könnten Sie das Gemüse herumreichen?; **to get a ~ in ...** (*Scol*) die Prüfung in ... bestehen; **things have come to a pretty ~ when ...** (*Brit: inf*) so weit ist es schon gekommen, dass ...; **to make a ~ at sb** (*inf*) jdn anmachen
▶ **pass away** *vi* (*die*) dahinscheiden
▶ **pass by** *vi* (*go past*) vorbeigehen; (*: in car*) vorbeifahren ▷ *vt* (*ignore*) vorbeigehen an +*dat*
▶ **pass down** *vt* (*customs, inheritance*) weitergeben
▶ **pass for** *vt*: **she could ~ for 25** sie könnte für 25 durchgehen
▶ **pass on** *vi* (*die*) verscheiden ▷ *vt*: **to ~ on (to)** weitergeben (an +*acc*)
▶ **pass out** *vi* (*faint*) ohnmächtig werden; (*Brit: Mil*) die Ausbildung beenden
▶ **pass over** *vt* (*ignore*) übergehen ▷ *vi* (*die*) entschlafen
▶ **pass up** *vt* (*opportunity*) sich *dat* entgehen lassen
passable ['pɑːsəbl] *adj* (*road*) passierbar; (*acceptable*) passabel
passage ['pæsɪdʒ] *n* Gang *m*; (*in book*) Passage *f*; (*way through crowd etc, Anat*) Weg *m*; (*act of passing: of train etc*) Durchfahrt *f*; (*journey: on boat*) Überfahrt *f*
passageway ['pæsɪdʒweɪ] *n* Gang *m*
passenger ['pæsɪndʒəʳ] *n* (*in boat, plane*) Passagier *m*; (*in car*) Fahrgast *m*
passer-by [pɑːsəˈbaɪ] (*pl* **passers-by**) *n* Passant(in) *m(f)*
passing ['pɑːsɪŋ] *adj* (*moment, thought etc*)

flüchtig; **in ~** (*incidentally*) beiläufig, nebenbei; **to mention sth in ~** etw beiläufig *or* nebenbei erwähnen

passing place *n* (*Aut*) Ausweichstelle *f*

passion ['pæʃən] *n* Leidenschaft *f*; **to have a ~ for sth** eine Leidenschaft für etw haben

passionate ['pæʃənɪt] *adj* leidenschaftlich

passion fruit *n* Passionsfrucht *f*, Maracuja *f*

Passion play *n* Passionsspiel *nt*

passive ['pæsɪv] *adj* passiv; (*Ling*) Passiv- ▷ *n* (*Ling*) Passiv *nt*

passive smoking *n* passives Rauchen, Passivrauchen *nt*

passkey ['pɑːskiː] *n* Hauptschlüssel *m*

Passover ['pɑːsəuvəʳ] *n* Passah(fest) *nt*

passport ['pɑːspɔːt] *n* Pass *m*; (*fig: to success etc*) Schlüssel *m*

passport control *n* Passkontrolle *f*

passport office *n* Passamt *nt*

password ['pɑːswəːd] *n* Kennwort *nt*; (*Comput*) Passwort *nt*

past [pɑːst] *prep* (*in front of*) vorbei an +*dat*; (*beyond*) hinter +*dat*; (*later than*) nach ▷ *adj* (*government etc*) früher, ehemalig; (*week, month etc*) vergangen ▷ *n* Vergangenheit *f* ▷ *adv*: **to run ~** vorbeilaufen; **he's ~ 40** er ist über 40; **it's ~ midnight** es ist nach Mitternacht; **ten/quarter ~ eight** zehn/Viertel nach acht; **he ran ~ me** er lief an mir vorbei; **I'm ~ caring** es kümmert mich nicht mehr; **to be ~ it** (*Brit: inf: person*) es nicht mehr bringen; **for the ~ few/3 days** während der letzten Tage/3 Tage; **in the ~** (*also Ling*) in der Vergangenheit

pasta ['pæstə] *n* Nudeln *pl*

paste [peɪst] *n* (*wet mixture*) Teig *m*; (*glue*) Kleister *m*; (*jewellery*) Strass *m*; (*fish, tomato paste*) Paste *f* ▷ *vt* (*stick*) kleben

pastel ['pæstl] *adj* (*colour*) Pastell-

pasteurized ['pæstʃəraɪzd] *adj* pasteurisiert

pastille ['pæstɪl] *n* Pastille *f*

pastime ['pɑːstaɪm] *n* Zeitvertreib *m*, Hobby *nt*

past master (*Brit*) *n*: **to be a ~ at sth** ein Experte *m* in etw *dat* sein

pastor ['pɑːstəʳ] *n* Pastor(in) *m(f)*

pastoral ['pɑːstərl] *adj* (*Rel: duties etc*) als Pastor

pastry ['peɪstrɪ] *n* (*dough*) Teig *m*; (*cake*) Gebäckstück *nt*

pasture ['pɑːstʃəʳ] *n* Weide *f*

pasty [*n* 'pæstɪ, *adj* 'peɪstɪ] *n* (*pie*) Pastete *f* ▷ *adj* (*complexion*) bläßlich

pat [pæt] *vt* (*with hand*) tätscheln ▷ *adj* (*answer, remark*) glatt ▷ *n*: **to give sb/o.s. a ~ on the back** (*fig*) jdm/sich auf die Schulter klopfen; **he knows it off ~, he has it down ~** (*US*) er kennt das in- und auswendig

patch [pætʃ] *n* (*piece of material*) Flicken *m*; (*also*: **eye patch**) Augenklappe *f*; (*damp, bald etc*) Fleck *m*; (*of land*) Stück *nt*; (: *for growing vegetables etc*) Beet *nt* ▷ *vt* (*clothes*) flicken; **(to go through) a bad ~** eine schwierige Zeit (durchmachen)

▶ **patch up** *vt* (*clothes etc*) flicken; (*quarrel*) beilegen

patchwork ['pætʃwəːk] *n* (*Sewing*) Patchwork *nt*

patchy ['pætʃɪ] *adj* (*colour*) ungleichmäßig; (*information, knowledge etc*) lückenhaft

pate [peɪt] *n*: **a bald ~** eine Glatze

pâté ['pæteɪ] *n* Pastete *f*

patent ['peɪtnt] *n* Patent *nt* ▷ *vt* patentieren lassen ▷ *adj* (*obvious*) offensichtlich

patent leather *n* Lackleder *nt*

patently ['peɪtntlɪ] *adv* (*obvious, wrong*) vollkommen

patent medicine *n* patentrechtlich geschütztes Arzneimittel *nt*

Patent Office *n* Patentamt *nt*

paternal [pə'təːnl] *adj* väterlich; **my ~ grandmother** meine Großmutter väterlicherseits

paternalistic [pətəːnə'lɪstɪk] *adj* patriarchalisch

paternity [pə'təːnɪtɪ] *n* Vaterschaft *f*

paternity leave *n* Vaterschaftsurlaub *m*

paternity suit *n* Vaterschaftsprozess *m*

path [pɑːθ] *n* (*also fig*) Weg *m*; (*trail, track*) Pfad *m*; (*trajectory: of bullet, aircraft, planet*) Bahn *f*

pathetic [pə'θetɪk] *adj* (*pitiful*) mitleiderregend; (*very bad*) erbärmlich

pathological [pæθə'lɔdʒɪkl] *adj* (*liar, hatred*) krankhaft; (*Med*) pathologisch

pathologist [pə'θɔlədʒɪst] *n* Pathologe *m*, Pathologin *f*

pathology [pə'θɔlədʒɪ] *n* Pathologie *f*

pathos ['peɪθɔs] *n* Pathos *nt*

pathway ['pɑːθweɪ] *n* Pfad *m*, Weg *m*; (*fig*) Weg

patience ['peɪʃns] *n* Geduld *f*; (*Brit: Cards*) Patience *f*; **to lose (one's) ~** die Geduld verlieren

patient ['peɪʃnt] *n* Patient(in) *m(f)* ▷ *adj* geduldig; **to be ~ with sb** Geduld mit jdm haben

patiently ['peɪʃntlɪ] *adv* geduldig

patio ['pætɪəu] *n* Terrasse *f*

patriot ['peɪtrɪət] *n* Patriot(in) *m(f)*

patriotic [pætrɪ'ɔtɪk] *adj* patriotisch

patriotism ['pætrɪətɪzəm] *n* Patriotismus *m*

patrol [pə'trəul] *n* (*Mil*) Patrouille *f*; (*Police*) Streife *f* ▷ *vt* (*Mil, Police: city, streets etc*) patrouillieren; **to be on ~** (*Mil*) auf Patrouille sein; (*Police*) auf Streife sein

patrol boat *n* Patrouillenboot *nt*

patrol car *n* Streifenwagen *m*

patrolman [pə'trəulmən] (*US: irreg: like* **man**) *n* (*Police*) (Streifen)polizist *m*

patron ['peɪtrən] *n* (*customer*) Kunde *m*, Kundin *f*; (*benefactor*) Förderer *m*; **~ of the arts** Kunstmäzen *m*

patronage ['pætrənɪdʒ] *n* (*of artist, charity etc*) Förderung *f*

patronize ['pætrənaɪz] *vt* (*pej: look down on*) von oben herab behandeln; (*artist etc*) fördern; (*shop, club*) besuchen

patronizing ['pætrənaɪzɪŋ] *adj* herablassend

patron saint *n* Schutzheilige(r) *f(m)*

patter ['pætəʳ] *n* (*of feet*) Trappeln *nt*; (*of rain*) Prasseln *nt*; (*sales talk etc*) Sprüche *pl* ▷ *vi*

(*footsteps*) trappeln; (*rain*) prasseln
pattern ['pætən] *n* Muster *nt*; (*Sewing*)
Schnittmuster *nt*; **behaviour ~s**
Verhaltensmuster *pl*
patterned ['pætənd] *adj* gemustert; **~ with
flowers** mit Blumenmuster
paucity ['pɔːsɪtɪ] *n*: **a ~ of** ein Mangel *m* an +*dat*
paunch [pɔːntʃ] *n* Bauch *m*, Wanst *m*
pauper ['pɔːpər] *n* Arme(r) *f(m)*; **~'s grave**
Armengrab *nt*
pause [pɔːz] *n* Pause *f* ▷ *vi* eine Pause machen;
(*hesitate*) innehalten; **to ~ for breath** eine
Verschnaufpause einlegen
pave [peɪv] *vt* (*street, yard etc*) pflastern; **to ~
the way for** (*fig*) den Weg bereiten *or* bahnen
für
pavement ['peɪvmənt] *n* (*Brit*) Bürgersteig *m*;
(*US: roadway*) Straße *f*
pavilion [pə'vɪlɪən] *n* (*Sport*) Klubhaus *nt*
paving ['peɪvɪŋ] *n* (*material*) Straßenbelag *m*
paving stone *n* Pflasterstein *m*
paw [pɔː] *n* (*of cat, dog etc*) Pfote *f*; (*of lion, bear etc*)
Tatze *f*, Pranke *f* ▷ *vt* (*pej: touch*) betatschen; **to
~ the ground** (*animal*) scharren
pawn [pɔːn] *n* (*Chess*) Bauer *m*; (*fig*) Schachfigur
f ▷ *vt* versetzen
pawnbroker ['pɔːnbrəukər] *n* Pfandleiher *m*
pawnshop ['pɔːnʃɔp] *n* Pfandhaus *nt*
pay [peɪ] (*pt, pp* **paid**) *n* (*wage*) Lohn *m*; (*salary*)
Gehalt *nt* ▷ *vt* (*sum of money, wage*) zahlen;
(*bill, person*) bezahlen ▷ *vi* (*be profitable*) sich
bezahlt machen; (*fig*) sich lohnen; **how
much did you ~ for it?** wie viel hast du dafür
bezahlt?; **I paid 10 pounds for that book**
ich habe 10 Pfund für das Buch bezahlt, das
Buch hat mich 10 Pfund gekostet; **to ~ one's
way** seinen Beitrag leisten; **to ~ dividends**
(*fig*) sich bezahlt machen; **to ~ the price/
penalty for sth** (*fig*) den Preis/die Strafe
für etw zahlen; **to ~ sb a compliment** jdm
ein Kompliment machen; **to ~ attention
(to)** achtgeben (auf+*acc*); **to ~ sb a visit** jdn
besuchen; **to ~ one's respects to sb** jdm
seine Aufwartung machen
▶ **pay back** *vt* zurückzahlen; **I'll ~ you back
next week** ich gebe dir das Geld nächste
Woche zurück
▶ **pay for** *vt fus* (*also fig*) (be)zahlen für
▶ **pay in** *vt* einzahlen
▶ **pay off** *vt* (*debt*) abbezahlen; (*person*)
auszahlen; (*creditor*) befriedigen; (*mortgage*)
tilgen ▷ *vi* sich auszahlen; **to ~ sth off in
instalments** etw in Raten (ab)zahlen
▶ **pay out** *vt* (*money*) ausgeben; (*rope*) ablaufen
lassen
▶ **pay up** *vi* zahlen
payable ['peɪəbl] *adj* zahlbar; **to make
a cheque ~ to sb** einen Scheck auf jdn
ausstellen
pay award *n* Lohn-/Gehaltserhöhung *f*
payday ['peɪdeɪ] *n* Zahltag *m*
PAYE (*Brit*) *n abbr* (= *pay as you earn*)
Lohnsteuerabzugsverfahren

payee [peɪ'iː] *n* Zahlungsempfänger *m*
pay envelope (*US*) *n* = **pay packet**
paying guest ['peɪɪŋ-] *n* zahlender Gast *m*
payload ['peɪləud] *n* Nutzlast *f*
payment ['peɪmənt] *n* (*act*) Zahlung *f*,
Bezahlung *f*; (*of bill*) Begleichung *f*; (*sum
of money*) Zahlung *f*; **advance ~** (*part sum*)
Anzahlung *f*; (*total sum*) Vorauszahlung
f; **deferred payment, ~ by instalments**
Ratenzahlung *f*; **monthly ~** (*sum of money*)
Monatsrate *f*; **on ~ of** gegen Zahlung von
pay packet (*Brit*) *n* Lohntüte *f*
pay-per-click ['peɪpə'klɪk] *n* (*Comput*) Pay-per-
Click *nt*
payphone ['peɪfəun] *n* Münztelefon *nt*; (*card
phone*) Kartentelefon *nt*
payroll ['peɪrəul] *n* Lohnliste *f*; **to be on a
firm's ~** bei einer Firma beschäftigt sein
pay slip (*Brit*) *n see* **pay** Lohnstreifen *m*;
Gehaltsstreifen *m*
pay station (*US*) *n* = **payphone**
PBS (*US*) *n abbr* (= *Public Broadcasting Service*)
öffentliche Rundfunkanstalt
PC *n abbr* (= *personal computer*) PC *m*; (*Brit*) = **police
constable** ▷ *adj abbr* = **politically correct** ▷ *abbr*
(*Brit*) = **Privy Councillor**
pc *abbr* = **per cent; postcard**
p/c *abbr* = **petty cash**
PCB *n abbr* (*Elec., Comput*) = **printed circuit board**;
(= *polychlorinated biphenyl*) PCB *nt*
pcm *abbr* (= *per calendar month*) pro Monat
PD (*US*) *n abbr* = **police department**
pd *abbr* (= *paid*) bez.
PDA *abbr* (*Comput*) *of* **personal digital assistant**
PDA *m*
pdq (*inf*) *adv abbr* (= *pretty damn quick*) verdammt
schnell
PDSA (*Brit*) *n abbr* (= *People's Dispensary for Sick
Animals*) kostenloses Behandlungszentrum für
Haustiere
PDT (*US*) *abbr* (= *Pacific Daylight Time*) pazifische
Sommerzeit
PE *n abbr* (*Scol*) = **physical education**
pea [piː] *n* Erbse *f*
peace [piːs] *n* Frieden *m*; **to be at ~ with sb/
sth** mit jdm/etw in Frieden leben; **to keep
the ~** (*policeman*) die öffentliche Ordnung
aufrechterhalten; (*citizen*) den Frieden wahren
peaceable ['piːsəbl] *adj* friedlich
peaceful ['piːsful] *adj* friedlich
peacekeeper ['piːskiːpər] *n*
Friedenswächter(in) *m(f)*
peacekeeping force ['piːskiːpɪŋ-] *n*
Friedenstruppen *pl*
peace offering *n* Friedensangebot *nt*
peach [piːtʃ] *n* Pfirsich *m*
peacock ['piːkɔk] *n* Pfau *m*
peak [piːk] *n* (*of mountain*) Spitze *f*, Gipfel *m*; (*of
cap*) Schirm *m*; (*fig*) Höhepunkt *m*
peak hours *npl* Stoßzeit *f*
peak period *n* Spitzenzeit *f*, Stoßzeit *f*
peak rate *n* Höchstrate *f*
peaky ['piːkɪ] (*Brit: inf*) *adj* blass

peal [piːl] n (of bells) Läuten nt; **~s of laughter** schallendes Gelächter nt

peanut ['piːnʌt] n Erdnuss f

peanut butter n Erdnussbutter f

pear [pɛəʳ] n Birne f

pearl [pəːl] n Perle f

peasant ['pɛznt] n Bauer m

peat [piːt] n Torf m

pebble ['pɛbl] n Kieselstein m

peck [pɛk] vt (bird) picken; (also: **peck at**) picken an +dat ▷ n (of bird) Schnabelhieb m; (kiss) Küsschen nt

pecking order ['pɛkɪŋ-] n (fig) Hackordnung f

peckish ['pɛkɪʃ] (Brit: inf) adj (hungry) leicht hungrig; **I'm feeling ~** ich könnte was zu essen gebrauchen

peculiar [pɪ'kjuːlɪəʳ] adj (strange) seltsam; **~ to** (exclusive to) charakteristisch für

peculiarity [pɪkjuːlɪ'ærɪtɪ] n (strange habit) Eigenart f; (distinctive feature) Besonderheit f, Eigentümlichkeit f

peculiarly [pɪ'kjuːlɪəlɪ] adv (oddly) seltsam; (distinctively) unverkennbar

pecuniary [pɪ'kjuːnɪərɪ] adj finanziell

pedal ['pɛdl] n Pedal nt ▷ vi in die Pedale treten

pedal bin (Brit) n Treteimer m

pedant ['pɛdənt] n Pedant(in) m(f)

pedantic [pɪ'dæntɪk] adj pedantisch

peddle ['pɛdl] vt (goods) feilbieten, verkaufen; (drugs) handeln mit; (gossip) verbreiten

peddler ['pɛdləʳ] n (also: **drug peddler**) Pusher m

pedestal ['pɛdəstl] n Sockel m

pedestrian [pɪ'dɛstrɪən] n Fußgänger(in) m(f) ▷ adj Fußgänger-; (fig) langweilig

pedestrian crossing (Brit) n Fußgängerüberweg m

pedestrian mall (US) n Fußgängerzone f

pedestrian precinct (Brit) n Fußgängerzone f

pediatrics [piːdɪ'ætrɪks] (US) n = **paediatrics**

pedigree ['pɛdɪgriː] n (of animal) Stammbaum m; (fig: background) Vorgeschichte f ▷ cpd (dog) Rasse-, reinrassig

pee [piː] (inf) vi pinkeln

peek [piːk] vi: **to ~ at/over/into** etc gucken nach/über +acc/in +acc etc ▷ n: **to have** or **take a ~ (at)** einen (kurzen) Blick werfen (auf +acc)

peel [piːl] n Schale f ▷ vt schälen ▷ vi (paint) abblättern; (wallpaper) sich lösen; (skin, back etc) sich schälen

▶ **peel back** vt abziehen

peeler ['piːləʳ] n (potato peeler etc) Schälmesser nt

peelings ['piːlɪŋz] npl Schalen pl

peep [piːp] n (look) kurzer Blick m; (sound) Pieps m ▷ vi (look) gucken; **to have** or **take a ~ (at)** einen kurzen Blick werfen (auf +acc)

▶ **peep out** vi (be visible) hervorgucken

peephole ['piːphəul] n Guckloch nt

peer [pɪəʳ] n (noble) Peer m; (equal) Gleichrangige(r) f(m); (contemporary) Gleichaltrige(r) f(m) ▷ vi: **to ~ at** starren auf +acc

peerage ['pɪərɪdʒ] n (title) Adelswürde f; (position) Adelsstand m; **the ~** (all the peers) der Adel

peerless ['pɪəlɪs] adj unvergleichlich

peeved [piːvd] adj verärgert, sauer (inf)

peevish ['piːvɪʃ] adj (bad-tempered) mürrisch

peg [pɛg] n (hook, knob) Haken m; (Brit: also: **clothes peg**) Wäscheklammer f; (also: **tent peg**) Zeltpflock m, Hering m ▷ vt (washing) festklammern; (prices) festsetzen; **off the ~** von der Stange

pejorative [pɪ'dʒɔrətɪv] adj abwertend

Pekin [piː'kɪn] n = **Peking**

Pekinese [piːkɪ'niːz] n = **Pekingese**

Peking [piː'kɪŋ] n Peking nt

Pekingese [piːkɪ'niːz] n (dog) Pekinese m

pelican ['pɛlɪkən] n Pelikan m

pelican crossing (Brit) n (Aut) Fußgängerüberweg m mit Ampel

pellet ['pɛlɪt] n (of paper etc) Kügelchen nt; (of mud etc) Klümpchen nt; (for shotgun) Schrotkugel f

pell-mell ['pɛl'mɛl] adv in heillosem Durcheinander

pelmet ['pɛlmɪt] n (wooden) Blende f; (fabric) Querbehang m

pelt [pɛlt] vi (rain: also: **pelt down**) niederprasseln; (inf: run) rasen ▷ n (animal skin) Pelz m, Fell nt ▷ vt: **to ~ sb with sth** jdn mit etw bewerfen

pelvis ['pɛlvɪs] n Becken nt

pen [pɛn] n (also: **fountain pen**) Füller m; (also: **ballpoint pen**) Kugelschreiber m; (also: **felt-tip pen**) Filzstift m; (enclosure: for sheep, pigs etc) Pferch m; (US: inf: prison) Knast m; **to put ~ to paper** zur Feder greifen

penal ['piːnl] adj (Law: colony, institution) Straf-; (: system, reform) Strafrechts-; **~ code** Strafgesetzbuch nt

penalize ['piːnəlaɪz] vt (punish) bestrafen; (fig) benachteiligen

penal servitude [-'səːvɪtjuːd] n Zwangsarbeit f

penalty ['pɛnltɪ] n Strafe f; (Sport) Strafstoß m; (: Football) Elfmeter m

penalty area (Brit) n (Sport) Strafraum m

penalty clause n Strafklausel f

penalty kick n (Rugby) Strafstoß m; (Football) Elfmeter m

penalty shoot-out [-'ʃuːtaut] n (Football) Elfmeterschießen nt

penance ['pɛnəns] n (Rel): **to do ~ for one's sins** für seine Sünden Buße tun

pence [pɛns] npl of **penny**

penchant ['pãːʃãːŋ] n Vorliebe f, Schwäche f; **to have a ~ for** eine Schwäche haben für

pencil ['pɛnsl] n Bleistift m ▷ vt: **to ~ sb/sth in** jdn/etw vormerken

pencil case n Federmäppchen nt

pencil sharpener n Bleistiftspitzer m

pendant ['pɛndnt] n Anhänger m

pending ['pɛndɪŋ] adj anstehend ▷ prep: **~ his return** bis zu seiner Rückkehr; **~ a decision** bis eine Entscheidung getroffen ist

pendulum ['pɛndjuləm] n Pendel nt

penetrate ['pɛnɪtreɪt] vt (person: territory etc)

p

durchdringen; (*light, water, sound*) eindringen in +*acc*
penetrating ['pɛnɪtreɪtɪŋ] *adj* (*sound, gaze*) durchdringend; (*mind, observation*) scharf
penetration [pɛnɪ'treɪʃən] *n* Durchdringen *nt*
pen friend (*Brit*) *n* Brieffreund(in) *m(f)*
penguin ['pɛŋgwɪn] *n* Pinguin *m*
penicillin [pɛnɪ'sɪlɪn] *n* Penizillin *nt*
peninsula [pə'nɪnsjulə] *n* Halbinsel *f*
penis ['piːnɪs] *n* Penis *m*
penitence ['pɛnɪtns] *n* Reue *f*
penitent ['pɛnɪtnt] *adj* reuig
penitentiary [pɛnɪ'tɛnʃərɪ] (*US*) *n* Gefängnis *nt*
penknife ['pɛnnaɪf] *n* Taschenmesser *nt*
Penn. (*US*) *abbr* (*Post*) = **Pennsylvania**
pen name *n* Pseudonym *nt*
pennant ['pɛnənt] *n* (*Naut*) Wimpel *m*
penniless ['pɛnɪlɪs] *adj* mittellos
Pennines ['pɛnaɪnz] *npl*: **the ~** die Pennines *pl*
penny ['pɛnɪ] (*Brit*) (*pl* **pence**) *n* Penny *m*; (*US*) Cent *m*; **it was worth every ~** es war jeden Pfennig wert; **it won't cost you a ~** es kostet dich keinen Pfennig
pen pal *n* Brieffreund(in) *m(f)*
penpusher ['pɛnpuʃəʳ] *n* Schreiberling *m*
pension ['pɛnʃən] *n* Rente *f*
▸ **pension off** *vt* (vorzeitig) pensionieren
pensionable ['pɛnʃnəbl] *adj* (*age*) Pensions-; (*job*) mit Pensionsberechtigung
pensioner ['pɛnʃənəʳ] (*Brit*) *n* Rentner(in) *m(f)*
pension scheme *n* Rentenversicherung *f*
pensive ['pɛnsɪv] *adj* nachdenklich
pentagon ['pɛntəgən] (*US*) *n*: **the P~** das Pentagon; *siehe Info-Artikel*

⊚ **PENTAGON**
⊚
⊚ *Pentagon heißt das fünfeckige Gebäude*
⊚ *in Arlington, Virginia, in dem das*
⊚ *amerikanische Verteidigungsministerium*
⊚ *untergebracht ist. Im weiteren Sinne*
⊚ *bezieht sich dieses Wort auf die*
⊚ *amerikanische Militärführung.*

Pentecost ['pɛntɪkɔst] *n* (*in Judaism*) Erntefest *nt*; (*in Christianity*) Pfingsten *nt*
penthouse ['pɛnthaus] *n* Penthouse *nt*
pent-up ['pɛntʌp] *adj* (*feelings*) aufgestaut
penultimate [pɛ'nʌltɪmət] *adj* vorletzte(r, s)
penury ['pɛnjurɪ] *n* Armut *f*, Not *f*
people ['piːpl] *npl* (*persons*) Leute *pl*; (*inhabitants*) Bevölkerung *f* ▸ *n* (*nation, race*) Volk *nt*; **old ~** alte Menschen *or* Leute; **young ~** junge Leute; **the room was full of ~** das Zimmer war voller Leute *or* Menschen; **several ~ came** mehrere (Leute) kamen; **~ say that ...** man sagt, dass ...; **the ~** (*Pol*) das Volk; **a man of the ~** ein Mann des Volkes
PEP *n abbr* (= *personal equity plan*) *steuerbegünstigte Kapitalinvestition*
pep [pɛp] (*inf*) *n* Schwung *m*, Pep *m*
▸ **pep up** *vt* (*person*) aufmöbeln; (*food*) pikanter machen

pepper ['pɛpəʳ] *n* (*spice*) Pfeffer *m*; (*vegetable*) Paprika *m* ▸ *vt*: **to ~ with** (*fig*) übersäen mit; **two ~s** zwei Paprikaschoten
peppercorn ['pɛpəkɔːn] *n* Pfefferkorn *nt*
pepper mill *n* Pfeffermühle *f*
peppermint ['pɛpəmɪnt] *n* (*sweet*) Pfefferminz *nt*; (*plant*) Pfefferminze *f*
pepperoni [pɛpə'rəunɪ] *n* ≈ Pfeffersalami *f*
pepper pot *n* Pfefferstreuer *m*
pep talk (*inf*) *n* aufmunternde Worte *pl*
per [pəːʳ] *prep* (*for each*) pro; **~ day/person/ kilo** pro Tag/Person/Kilo; **~ annum** pro Jahr; **as ~ your instructions** gemäß Ihren Anweisungen
per capita [-'kæpɪtə] *adj* (*income*) Pro-Kopf-
▸ *adv* pro Kopf
perceive [pə'siːv] *vt* (*see*) wahrnehmen; (*view, understand*) verstehen
per cent *n* Prozent *nt*; **a 20 ~ discount** 20 Prozent Rabatt
percentage [pə'sɛntɪdʒ] *n* Prozentsatz *m*; **on a ~ basis** auf Prozentbasis
percentage point *n* Prozent *nt*
perceptible [pə'sɛptɪbl] *adj* (*difference, change*) wahrnehmbar, merklich
perception [pə'sɛpʃən] *n* (*insight*) Einsicht *f*; (*opinion, understanding*) Erkenntnis *f*; (*faculty*) Wahrnehmung *f*
perceptive [pə'sɛptɪv] *adj* (*person*) aufmerksam; (*analysis etc*) erkenntnisreich
perch [pəːtʃ] *n* (*for bird*) Stange *f*; (*fish*) Flussbarsch *m* ▸ *vi*: **to ~ (on)** (*bird*) sitzen (auf +*dat*); (*person*) hocken (auf +*dat*)
percolate ['pəːkəleɪt] *vt* (*coffee*) (mit einer Kaffeemaschine) zubereiten ▸ *vi* (*coffee*) durchlaufen; **to ~ through/into** (*idea, light etc*) durchsickern durch/in +*acc*
percolator ['pəːkəleɪtəʳ] *n* (*also*: **coffee percolator**) Kaffeemaschine *f*
percussion [pə'kʌʃən] *n* (*Mus*) Schlagzeug *nt*
peremptory [pə'rɛmptərɪ] (*pej*) *adj* (*person*) herrisch; (*order*) kategorisch
perennial [pə'rɛnɪəl] *adj* (*plant*) mehrjährig; (*fig: problem, feature etc*) immer wiederkehrend ▸ *n* (*Bot*) mehrjährige Pflanze *f*
perfect [*adj, n* 'pəːfɪkt, *vt* pə'fɛkt] *adj* perfekt; (*nonsense, idiot etc*) ausgemacht ▸ *vt* (*technique*) perfektionieren ▸ *n*: **the ~** (*also*: **the perfect tense**) das Perfekt; **he's a ~ stranger to me** er ist mir vollkommen fremd
perfection [pə'fɛkʃən] *n* Perfektion *f*, Vollkommenheit *f*
perfectionist [pə'fɛkʃənɪst] *n* Perfektionist(in) *m(f)*
perfectly ['pəːfɪktlɪ] *adv* vollkommen; (*faultlessly*) perfekt; **I'm ~ happy with the situation** ich bin mit der Lage vollkommen zufrieden; **you know ~ well that ...** Sie wissen ganz genau, dass ...
perforate ['pəːfəreɪt] *vt* perforieren
perforated ulcer ['pəːfəreɪtəd-] *n* durchgebrochenes Geschwür *nt*
perforation [pəːfə'reɪʃən] *n* (*small hole*) Loch *nt*;

(*line of holes*) Perforation *f*

perform [pə'fɔːm] *vt* (*operation, ceremony etc*) durchführen; (*task*) erfüllen; (*piece of music, play etc*) aufführen ▷ *vi* auftreten; **to ~ well/ badly** eine gute/schlechte Leistung zeigen

performance [pə'fɔːməns] *n* Leistung *f*; (*of play, show*) Vorstellung *f*; **the team put up a good ~** die Mannschaft zeigte eine gute Leistung

performer [pə'fɔːmə^r] *n* Künstler(in) *m(f)*

performing [pə'fɔːmɪŋ] *adj* (*animal*) dressiert

performing arts *npl*: **the ~** die darstellenden Künste *pl*

perfume ['pəːfjuːm] *n* Parfüm *nt*; (*fragrance*) Duft *m* ▷ *vt* parfümieren

perfunctory [pə'fʌŋktərɪ] *adj* flüchtig

perhaps [pə'hæps] *adv* vielleicht; **~ he'll come** er kommt vielleicht; **~ not** vielleicht nicht

peril ['pɛrɪl] *n* Gefahr *f*

perilous ['pɛrɪləs] *adj* gefährlich

perilously ['pɛrɪləslɪ] *adv*: **they came ~ close to being caught** sie wären um ein Haar gefangen worden

perimeter [pə'rɪmɪtə^r] *n* Umfang *m*

perimeter fence *n* Umzäunung *f*

period ['pɪərɪəd] *n* (*length of time*) Zeitraum *m*, Periode *f*; (*era*) Zeitalter *nt*; (*Scol*) Stunde *f*; (*esp US: full stop*) Punkt *m*; (*Med: also:* **menstrual period**) Periode ▷ *adj* (*costume etc*) zeitgenössisch; **for a ~ of 3 weeks** für eine Dauer *or* einen Zeitraum von 3 Wochen; **the holiday ~** (*Brit*) die Urlaubszeit; **I won't do it. P~.** ich mache das nicht, und damit basta!

periodic [pɪərɪ'ɒdɪk] *adj* periodisch

periodical [pɪərɪ'ɒdɪkl] *n* Zeitschrift *f* ▷ *adj* periodisch

periodically [pɪərɪ'ɒdɪklɪ] *adv* periodisch

period pains (*Brit*) *npl* Menstruationsschmerzen *pl*

peripatetic [pɛrɪpə'tɛtɪk] *adj* (*Brit: teacher*) an mehreren Schulen tätig; **~ life** Wanderleben *nt*

peripheral [pə'rɪfərəl] *adj* (*feature, issue*) Rand-, nebensächlich; (*vision*) peripher ▷ *n* (*Comput*) Peripheriegerät *nt*

periphery [pə'rɪfərɪ] *n* Peripherie *f*

periscope ['pɛrɪskəup] *n* Periskop *nt*

perish ['pɛrɪʃ] *vi* (*die*) umkommen; (*rubber, leather etc*) verschleißen

perishable ['pɛrɪʃəbl] *adj* (*food*) leicht verderblich

perishables ['pɛrɪʃəblz] *npl* leicht verderbliche Waren *pl*

perishing ['pɛrɪʃɪŋ] (*Brit: inf*) *adj*: **it's ~ (cold)** es ist eisig kalt

peritonitis [pɛrɪtə'naɪtɪs] *n* Bauchfellentzündung *f*

perjure ['pəːdʒə^r] *vt*: **to ~ o.s.** einen Meineid leisten

perjury ['pəːdʒərɪ] *n* (*in court*) Meineid *m*; (*breach of oath*) Eidesverletzung *f*

perks [pəːks] (*inf*) *npl* (*extras*) Vergünstigungen *pl*

perk up *vi* (*cheer up*) munter werden

perky ['pəːkɪ] *adj* (*cheerful*) munter

perm [pəːm] *n* Dauerwelle *f* ▷ *vt*: **to have one's hair ~ed** sich *dat* eine Dauerwelle machen lassen

permanence ['pəːmənəns] *n* Dauerhaftigkeit *f*

permanent ['pəːmənənt] *adj* dauerhaft; (*job, position*) fest; **~ address** ständiger Wohnsitz *m*; **I'm not ~ here** ich bin hier nicht fest angestellt

permanently ['pəːmənəntlɪ] *adv* (*damage*) dauerhaft; (*stay, live*) ständig; (*locked, open, frozen etc*) dauernd

permeable ['pəːmɪəbl] *adj* durchlässig

permeate ['pəːmɪeɪt] *vt* durchdringen ▷ *vi*: **to ~ through** dringen durch

permissible [pə'mɪsɪbl] *adj* zulässig

permission [pə'mɪʃən] *n* Erlaubnis *f*, Genehmigung *f*; **to give sb ~ to do sth** jdm die Erlaubnis geben, etw zu tun

permissive [pə'mɪsɪv] *adj* permissiv

permit [*n* 'pəːmɪt, *vt* pə'mɪt] *n* Genehmigung *f* ▷ *vt* (*allow*) erlauben; (*make possible*) gestatten; **fishing ~** Angelschein *m*; **to ~ sb to do sth** jdm erlauben, etw zu tun; **weather ~ting** wenn das Wetter es zulässt

permutation [pəːmju'teɪʃən] *n* Permutation *f*; (*fig*) Variation *f*

pernicious [pəː'nɪʃəs] *adj* (*lie, nonsense*) bösartig; (*effect*) schädlich

pernickety [pə'nɪkɪtɪ] (*inf*) *adj* pingelig

perpendicular [pəːpən'dɪkjulə^r] *adj* senkrecht ▷ *n*: **the ~** die Senkrechte; **~ to** senkrecht zu

perpetrate ['pəːpɪtreɪt] *vt* (*crime*) begehen

perpetual [pə'pɛtjuəl] *adj* ständig, dauernd

perpetuate [pə'pɛtjueɪt] *vt* (*custom, belief etc*) bewahren; (*situation*) aufrechterhalten

perpetuity [pəːpɪ'tjuːɪtɪ] *n*: **in ~** auf ewig

perplex [pə'plɛks] *vt* verblüffen

perplexing [pəː'plɛksɪŋ] *adj* verblüffend

perquisites ['pəːkwɪzɪts] (*form*) *npl* Vergünstigungen *pl*

per se [-seɪ] *adv* an sich

persecute ['pəːsɪkjuːt] *vt* verfolgen

persecution [pəːsɪ'kjuːʃən] *n* Verfolgung *f*

perseverance [pəːsɪ'vɪərns] *n* Beharrlichkeit *f*, Ausdauer *f*

persevere [pəːsɪ'vɪə^r] *vi* durchhalten, beharren

Persia ['pəːʃə] *n* Persien *nt*

Persian ['pəːʃən] *adj* persisch ▷ *n* (*Ling*) Persisch *nt*; **the (persian) Gulf** der (Persische) Golf

Persian cat *n* Perserkatze *f*

persist [pə'sɪst] *vi*: **to ~ (with** *or* **in)** beharren (auf +*dat*), festhalten (an +*dat*); **to ~ in doing sth** darauf beharren, etw zu tun

persistence [pə'sɪstəns] *n* Beharrlichkeit *f*

persistent [pə'sɪstənt] *adj* (*person, noise*) beharrlich; (*smell, cough etc*) hartnäckig; (*lateness, rain*) andauernd; **~ offender** Wiederholungstäter(in) *m(f)*

persnickety [pə'snɪkɪtɪ] (*US: inf*) *adj* = **pernickety**

person ['pəːsn] *n* Person *f*, Mensch *m*; **in ~**

p

persönlich; **on** or **about one's** ~ bei sich; ~ **to** ~ **call** (Tel) Gespräch nt mit Voranmeldung

personable ['pəːsnəbl] adj von angenehmer Erscheinung

personal ['pəːsnl] adj persönlich; (life) Privat-; **nothing** ~! nehmen Sie es nicht persönlich!

personal allowance n (Tax) persönlicher Steuerfreibetrag m

personal assistant n persönlicher Referent m, persönliche Referentin f

personal column n private Kleinanzeigen pl

personal computer n Personal Computer m

personal details npl Personalien pl

personal hygiene n Körperhygiene f

personal identification number n Geheimnummer f, PIN-Nummer f

personality [pəːsə'nælɪtɪ] n (character, person) Persönlichkeit f

personal loan n Personaldarlehen nt

personally ['pəːsnlɪ] adv persönlich; **to take sth** ~ etw persönlich nehmen

personal organizer n Terminplaner m

personal, social and health education (Brit) n (Scol) ≈ persönlichkeits-, gesellschafts- und gesundheitsbezogene Erziehung

personal stereo n Walkman® m

personal trainer n (persönlicher) Fitnesstrainer m, (persönliche) Fitnesstrainerin f

personify [pəː'sɒnɪfaɪ] vt personifizieren; (embody) verkörpern

personnel [pəːsə'nɛl] n Personal nt

personnel department n Personalabteilung f

personnel manager n Personalleiter(in) m(f)

perspective [pə'spɛktɪv] n (also fig) Perspektive f; **to get sth into** ~ (fig) etw in Relation zu anderen Dingen sehen

Perspex® ['pəːspɛks] n Acrylglas nt

perspicacity [pəːspɪ'kæsɪtɪ] n Scharfsinn m

perspiration [pəːspɪ'reɪʃən] n Transpiration f

perspire [pə'spaɪəʳ] vi transpirieren

persuade [pə'sweɪd] vt: **to** ~ **sb to do sth** jdn dazu überreden, etw zu tun; **to** ~ **sb that** jdn davon überzeugen, dass; **to be** ~**d of sth** von etw überzeugt sein

persuasion [pə'sweɪʒən] n (act) Überredung f; (creed) Überzeugung f

persuasive [pə'sweɪsɪv] adj (person, argument) überzeugend

pert [pəːt] adj (person) frech; (nose, buttocks) keck; (hat) kess

pertaining [pəː'teɪnɪŋ]: ~ **to** prep betreffend +acc

pertinent ['pəːtɪnənt] adj relevant

perturb [pə'təːb] vt beunruhigen

Peru [pə'ruː] n Peru nt

perusal [pə'ruːzl] n Durchsicht f

peruse [pə'ruːz] vt durchsehen

Peruvian [pə'ruːvjən] adj peruanisch ▷ n Peruaner(in) m(f)

pervade [pə'veɪd] vt (smell, feeling) erfüllen

pervasive [pə'veɪzɪv] adj (smell) durchdringend; (influence) weitreichend; (mood, atmosphere)

allumfassend

perverse [pə'vəːs] adj (person) borniert; (behaviour) widernatürlich, pervers

perversion [pə'vəːʃən] n (sexual) Perversion f; (of truth, justice) Verzerrung f, Pervertierung f

perversity [pə'vəːsɪtɪ] n Widernatürlichkeit f

pervert [n pə'vəːt, vt pə'vəːt] n (sexual deviant) perverser Mensch m ▷ vt (person, mind) verderben; (distort: truth, custom) verfälschen

pessimism ['pɛsɪmɪzəm] n Pessimismus m

pessimist ['pɛsɪmɪst] n Pessimist(in) m(f)

pessimistic [pɛsɪ'mɪstɪk] adj pessimistisch

pest [pɛst] n (insect) Schädling m; (fig: nuisance) Plage f

pest control n Schädlingsbekämpfung f

pester ['pɛstəʳ] vt belästigen

pesticide ['pɛstɪsaɪd] n Schädlingsbekämpfungsmittel nt, Pestizid nt

pestilence ['pɛstɪləns] n Pest f

pestle ['pɛsl] n Stößel m

pet [pɛt] n (animal) Haustier nt ▷ adj (theory etc) Lieblings- ▷ vt (stroke) streicheln ▷ vi (inf: sexually) herumknutschen; **teacher's** ~ (favourite) Lehrers Liebling m; **a** ~ **rabbit/ snake** etc ein Kaninchen/eine Schlange etc (als Haustier); **that's my** ~ **hate** das hasse ich besonders

petal ['pɛtl] n Blütenblatt nt

peter out ['piːtə-] vi (road etc) allmählich aufhören, zu Ende gehen; (conversation, meeting) sich totlaufen

petite [pə'tiːt] adj (woman) zierlich

petition [pə'tɪʃən] n (signed document) Petition f; (Law) Klage f ▷ vt ersuchen ▷ vi: **to** ~ **for divorce** die Scheidung einreichen

pet name (Brit) n Kosename m

petrified ['pɛtrɪfaɪd] adj (fig: terrified) starr vor Angst

petrify ['pɛtrɪfaɪ] vt (fig: terrify) vor Angst erstarren lassen

petrochemical [pɛtrə'kɛmɪkl] adj petrochemisch

petrodollars ['pɛtrəudɒləz] npl Petrodollar pl

petrol ['pɛtrəl] (Brit) n Benzin nt; **two-star** ~ Normalbenzin nt; **four-star** ~ Super(benzin) nt; **unleaded** ~ bleifreies or unverbleites Benzin

petrol bomb n Benzinbombe f

petrol can (Brit) n Benzinkanister m

petrol engine (Brit) n Benzinmotor m

petroleum [pə'trəuljəm] n Petroleum nt

petroleum jelly n Vaseline f

petrol pump (Brit) n (in garage) Zapfsäule f; (in engine) Benzinpumpe f

petrol station (Brit) n Tankstelle f

petrol tank (Brit) n Benzintank m

petticoat ['pɛtɪkəut] n (underskirt: full-length) Unterkleid nt; (: waist) Unterrock m

pettifogging ['pɛtɪfɒgɪŋ] adj kleinlich

pettiness ['pɛtɪnɪs] n Kleinlichkeit f

petty ['pɛtɪ] adj (trivial) unbedeutend; (small-minded) kleinlich; (crime) geringfügig; (official) untergeordnet; (excuse) billig; (remark) spitz

petty cash n (in office) Portokasse f
petty officer n Maat m
petulant ['pɛtjulənt] adj (person, expression) gereizt
pew [pju:] n (in church) Kirchenbank f
pewter ['pju:təʳ] n Zinn nt
PG n abbr (Cine: = parental guidance) Klassifikation für Filme, die Kinder nur in Begleitung Erwachsener sehen dürfen
PGA n abbr (= Professional Golfers' Association) Golf-Profiverband
PGA 13 (US) abbr (Cine: = Parental Guidance 13) Klassifikation für Kinofilme, welche Kinder unter 13 Jahren nur in Begleitung Erwachsener sehen dürfen
pH n abbr (= potential of hydrogen) pH
PHA (US) n abbr (= Public Housing Administration) Regierungsbehörde für sozialen Wohnungsbau
phallic ['fælɪk] adj phallisch; (symbol) Phallus-
phantom ['fæntəm] n Phantom nt ▷ adj (fig) Phantom-
Pharaoh ['feərəu] n Pharao m
pharmaceutical [fɑ:məˈsju:tɪkl] adj pharmazeutisch
pharmaceuticals [fɑ:məˈsju:tɪklz] npl Arzneimittel pl, Pharmaka pl
pharmacist ['fɑ:məsɪst] n Apotheker(in) m(f)
pharmacy ['fɑ:məsɪ] n (shop) Apotheke f; (science) Pharmazie f
phase [feɪz] n Phase f ▷ vt: **to ~ sth in/out** etw stufenweise einführen/abschaffen
phat [fæt] adj (inf) abgefahren, geil
PhD n abbr (= Doctor of Philosophy) ≈ Dr. phil.
pheasant ['fɛznt] n Fasan m
phenomena [fəˈnɒmɪnə] npl of **phenomenon**
phenomenal [fəˈnɒmɪnl] adj phänomenal
phenomenon [fəˈnɒmɪnən] (pl **phenomena**) n Phänomen nt
phew [fju:] excl puh!
phial ['faɪəl] n Fläschchen nt
philanderer [fɪˈlændərəʳ] n Schwerenöter m
philanthropic [fɪlənˈθrɒpɪk] adj philanthropisch
philanthropist [fɪˈlænθrəpɪst] n Philanthrop(in) m(f)
philatelist [fɪˈlætəlɪst] n Philatelist(in) m(f)
philately [fɪˈlætəlɪ] n Philatelie f
Philippines ['fɪlɪpi:nz] npl: **the ~** die Philippinen pl
Philistine ['fɪlɪstaɪn] n (boor) Banause m
philosopher [fɪˈlɒsəfəʳ] n Philosoph(in) m(f)
philosophical [fɪləˈsɒfɪkl] adj philosophisch; (fig: calm, resigned) gelassen
philosophize [fɪˈlɒsəfaɪz] vi philosophieren
philosophy [fɪˈlɒsəfɪ] n Philosophie f
phlegm [flɛm] n (Med) Schleim m
phlegmatic [flɛɡˈmætɪk] adj phlegmatisch
phobia ['fəubjə] n Phobie f
phone [fəun] n Telefon nt ▷ vt anrufen ▷ vi anrufen, telefonieren; **to be on the ~** (possess a phone) Telefon haben; (be calling) telefonieren
▶ **phone back** vt, vi zurückrufen
▶ **phone up** vt, vi anrufen
phone book n Telefonbuch nt

phone booth n Telefonzelle f
phone box (Brit) n Telefonzelle f
phone call n Anruf m
phonecard ['fəunkɑ:d] n Telefonkarte f
phone-in ['fəunɪn] (Brit) n (Radio, TV) Radio-/Fernsehsendung mit Hörer-/Zuschauerbeteiligung per Telefon, Phone-in ▷ adj mit Hörer-/Zuschaueranrufen
phone tapping [-tæpɪŋ] n Abhören nt von Telefonleitungen
phonetics [fəˈnɛtɪks] n Phonetik f
phoney ['fəunɪ] adj (address) falsch; (accent) unecht; (person) unaufrichtig
phonograph ['fəunəɡrɑ:f] (US) n Grammofon nt
phony ['fəunɪ] adj = **phoney**
phosphate ['fɒsfeɪt] n Phosphat nt
phosphorus ['fɒsfərəs] n Phosphor m
photo ['fəutəu] n Foto nt
photo ... ['fəutəu] pref Foto-
photocopier ['fəutəukɒpɪəʳ] n Fotokopierer m
photocopy ['fəutəukɒpɪ] n Fotokopie f ▷ vt fotokopieren
photoelectric [fəutəuɪˈlɛktrɪk] adj (effect) fotoelektrisch; (cell) Photo-
photo finish n Fotofinish nt
Photofit® ['fəutəufɪt] n, **Photofit® picture** ▷ n Phantombild nt
photogenic [fəutəuˈdʒɛnɪk] adj fotogen
photograph ['fəutəɡræf] n Fotografie f ▷ vt fotografieren; **to take a ~ of sb** jdn fotografieren
photographer [fəˈtɒɡrəfəʳ] n Fotograf(in) m(f)
photographic [fəutəˈɡræfɪk] adj (equipment etc) fotografisch, Foto-
photography [fəˈtɒɡrəfɪ] n Fotografie f
photo opportunity n Fototermin m; (accidental) Fotogelegenheit f
photostat ['fəutəustæt] n Fotokopie f
photosynthesis [fəutəuˈsɪnθəsɪs] n Fotosynthese f
phrase [freɪz] n Satz m; (Ling) Redewendung f; (Mus) Phrase f ▷ vt ausdrücken; (letter) formulieren
phrase book n Sprachführer m
physical ['fɪzɪkl] adj (bodily) körperlich; (geography, properties) physikalisch; (law, explanation) natürlich; **~ examination** ärztliche Untersuchung f; **the ~ sciences** die Naturwissenschaften
physical education n Sportunterricht m
physically ['fɪzɪklɪ] adv (fit, attractive) körperlich
physician [fɪˈzɪʃən] n Arzt m, Ärztin f
physicist ['fɪzɪsɪst] n Physiker(in) m(f)
physics ['fɪzɪks] n Physik f
physiological ['fɪzɪəˈlɒdʒɪkl] adj physiologisch
physiology [fɪzɪˈɒlədʒɪ] n Physiologie f
physiotherapist [fɪzɪəuˈθɛrəpɪst] n Physiotherapeut(in) m(f)
physiotherapy [fɪzɪəuˈθɛrəpɪ] n Physiotherapie f
physique [fɪˈzi:k] n Körperbau m

P

pianist ['pi:ənɪst] n Pianist(in) m(f)
piano [pɪ'ænəu] n Klavier nt, Piano nt
piano accordion (Brit) n Akkordeon nt
piccolo ['pɪkələu] n Piccoloflöte f
pick [pɪk] n (also: **pickaxe**) Spitzhacke f ▷ vt (select) aussuchen; (gather: fruit, mushrooms) sammeln; (: flowers) pflücken; (remove, take out) herausnehmen; (lock) knacken; (scab, spot) kratzen an +dat; **take your ~** (choose) Sie haben die Wahl; **the ~ of** (best) das Beste +gen; **to ~ one's nose** in der Nase bohren; **to ~ one's teeth** in den Zähnen stochern; **to ~ sb's brains** jdn als Informationsquelle nutzen; **to ~ sb's pocket** jdn bestehlen; **to ~ a quarrel (with sb)** einen Streit (mit jdm) anfangen
▶ **pick at** vt fus (food) herumstochern in +dat
▶ **pick off** vt (shoot) abschießen
▶ **pick on** vt fus (criticize) herumhacken auf +dat
▶ **pick out** vt (distinguish) ausmachen; (select) aussuchen
▶ **pick up** vi (health) sich verbessern; (economy) sich erholen ▷ vt (from floor etc) aufheben; (arrest) festnehmen; (collect: person, parcel etc) abholen; (hitchhiker) mitnehmen; (for sexual encounter) aufreißen; (learn: skill etc) mitbekommen; (Radio) empfangen; **to ~ up where one left off** da weitermachen, wo man aufgehört hat; **to ~ up speed** schneller werden; **to ~ o.s. up** (after falling etc) sich aufrappeln
pickaxe, (US) **pickax** ['pɪkæks] n Spitzhacke f
picket ['pɪkɪt] n (in strike) Streikposten m ▷ vt (factory etc) Streikposten aufstellen vor +dat
picketing ['pɪkɪtɪŋ] n Aufstellen nt von Streikposten
picket line n Streikpostenkette f
pickings ['pɪkɪŋz] npl: **there are rich ~ to be had here** hier ist die Ausbeute gut
pickle ['pɪkl] n (also: **pickles**: as condiment) Pickles pl ▷ vt einlegen; **to be in a ~** in der Klemme sitzen; **to get in a ~** in eine Klemme geraten
pick-me-up ['pɪkmiːʌp] n Muntermacher m
pickpocket ['pɪkpɔkɪt] n Taschendieb(in) m(f)
pick-up ['pɪkʌp] n (also: **pick-up truck**) offener Kleintransporter m; (Brit: on record player) Tonabnehmer m
picnic ['pɪknɪk] n Picknick nt ▷ vi picknicken
picnicker ['pɪknɪkəʳ] n Picknicker(in) m(f)
pictorial [pɪk'tɔːrɪəl] adj (record, coverage etc) bildlich
picture ['pɪktʃəʳ] n Bild nt; (film) Film m ▷ vt (imagine) sich dat vorstellen; **the ~s** (Brit: inf: the cinema) das Kino; **to take a ~ of sb** ein Bild von jdm machen; **to put sb in the ~** jdn ins Bild setzen
picture book n Bilderbuch nt
picture messaging n Picture Messaging nt
picturesque [pɪktʃə'resk] adj malerisch
picture window n Aussichtsfenster nt
piddling ['pɪdlɪŋ] (inf) adj lächerlich
pidgin ['pɪdʒɪn] adj: ~ **English** Pidginenglisch nt
pie [paɪ] n (vegetable, meat) Pastete f; (fruit) Torte f

piebald ['paɪbɔːld] adj (horse) scheckig
piece [piːs] n Stück nt; (Draughts etc) Stein m; (Chess) Figur f; **in ~s** (broken) kaputt; (taken apart) auseinandergenommen, in Einzelteilen; **a ~ of clothing/furniture/ music** ein Kleidungs-/Möbel-/Musikstück nt; **a ~ of machinery** eine Maschine; **a ~ of research** eine Forschungsarbeit; **a ~ of advice** ein Rat m; **to take sth to ~s** etw auseinandernehmen; **in one ~** (object) unbeschädigt; (person) wohlbehalten; **a 10p ~** (Brit) ein 10-Pence-Stück nt; **~ by piece** Stück für Stück; **a six-~ band** eine sechsköpfige Band; **let her say her ~** lass sie ausreden
▶ **piece together** vt zusammenfügen
piecemeal ['piːsmiːl] adv stückweise, Stück für Stück
piecework ['piːswəːk] n Akkordarbeit f
pie chart n Tortendiagramm nt
pier [pɪəʳ] n Pier m
pierce [pɪəs] vt durchstechen; **to have one's ears ~d** sich dat die Ohrläppchen durchstechen lassen
piercing ['pɪəsɪŋ] adj (fig: cry, eyes, stare) durchdringend; (wind) schneidend
piety ['paɪətɪ] n Frömmigkeit f
piffling ['pɪflɪŋ] (inf) adj lächerlich
pig [pɪg] n (also pej) Schwein nt; (greedy person) Vielfraß m
pigeon ['pɪdʒən] n Taube f
pigeonhole ['pɪdʒənhəul] n (for letters etc) Fach nt; (fig) Schublade f ▷ vt (fig: person) in eine Schublade stecken
pigeon-toed ['pɪdʒəntəud] adj mit einwärtsgerichteten Zehen
piggy bank ['pɪgɪ-] n Sparschwein nt
pig-headed ['pɪg'hedɪd] (pej) adj dickköpfig
piglet ['pɪglɪt] n Schweinchen nt, Ferkel nt
pigment ['pɪgmənt] n Pigment nt
pigmentation [pɪgmən'teɪʃən] n Pigmentierung f, Färbung f
pigmy ['pɪgmɪ] n = **pygmy**
pigskin ['pɪgskɪn] n Schweinsleder nt
pigsty ['pɪgstaɪ] n (also fig) Schweinestall m
pigtail ['pɪgteɪl] n Zopf m
pike [paɪk] n (fish) Hecht m; (spear) Spieß m
pilchard ['pɪltʃəd] n Sardine f
pile [paɪl] n (heap) Haufen m; (stack) Stapel m; (of carpet, velvet) Flor m; (pillar) Pfahl m ▷ vt (also: **pile up**) (auf)stapeln; **in a ~** in einem Haufen; **to ~ into/out of** (vehicle) sich drängen in +acc/aus
▶ **pile on** vt: **to ~ it on** (inf) zu dick auftragen
▶ **pile up** vi sich stapeln
piles [paɪlz] npl (Med) Hämorr(ho)iden pl
pile-up ['paɪlʌp] n (Aut) Massenkarambolage f
pilfer ['pɪlfəʳ] vt, vi stehlen
pilfering ['pɪlfərɪŋ] n Diebstahl m
pilgrim ['pɪlgrɪm] n Pilger(in) m(f)
pilgrimage ['pɪlgrɪmɪdʒ] n Pilgerfahrt f, Wallfahrt f
pill [pɪl] n Tablette f, Pille f; **the ~** (contraceptive) die Pille; **to be on the ~** die Pille nehmen

pillage ['pɪlɪdʒ] *n* Plünderung *f* ▷ *vt* plündern
pillar ['pɪlə'] *n* Säule *f*; **a ~ of society** (*fig*) eine Säule *or* Stütze der Gesellschaft
pillar box (*Brit*) *n* Briefkasten *m*
pillion ['pɪljən] *n*: **to ride ~** (*on motorcycle*) auf dem Soziussitz mitfahren; (*on horse*) hinten auf dem Pferd mitreiten
pillory ['pɪlərɪ] *vt* (*criticize*) anprangern ▷ *n* Pranger *m*
pillow ['pɪləʊ] *n* (Kopf)kissen *nt*
pillowcase ['pɪləʊkeɪs] *n* (Kopf)kissenbezug *m*
pillowslip ['pɪləʊslɪp] *n* = **pillowcase**
pilot ['paɪlət] *n* (*Aviat*) Pilot(in) *m(f)*; (*Naut*) Lotse *m* ▷ *adj* (*scheme, study etc*) Pilot- ▷ *vt* (*aircraft*) steuern; (*fig: new law, scheme*) sich zum Fürsprecher machen +*gen*
pilot boat *n* Lotsenboot *nt*
pilot light *n* (*on cooker, boiler*) Zündflamme *f*
pilot test *n* (*Test*) Pilot- *od* Modellversuch *m*
pimento [pɪ'mɛntəʊ] *n* (*spice*) Piment *nt*
pimp [pɪmp] *n* Zuhälter *m*
pimple ['pɪmpl] *n* Pickel *m*
pimply ['pɪmplɪ] *adj* pick(e)lig
PIN *n abbr* (= *personal identification number*) PIN; **~ number** PIN-Nummer *f*
pin [pɪn] *n* (*metal: for clothes, papers*) Stecknadel *f*; (*Tech*) Stift *m*; (*Brit: also:* **drawing pin**) Heftzwecke *f*; (*in grenade*) Sicherungsstift *m*; (*Brit: Elec*) Pol *m* ▷ *vt* (*fasten with pin*) feststecken; **~s and needles** (*in arms, legs etc*) Kribbeln *nt*; **to ~ sb against/to sth** jdn gegen/an etw *acc* pressen; **to ~ sth on sb** (*fig*) jdm etw anhängen
▶ **pin down** *vt* (*fig: person*) festnageln; **there's something strange here but I can't quite ~ it down** hier stimmt etwas nicht, aber ich weiß nicht genau was
pinafore ['pɪnəfɔ:'] (*Brit*) *n* (*also:* **pinafore dress**) Trägerkleid *nt*
pinball ['pɪnbɔ:l] *n* (*game*) Flippern *nt*; (*machine*) Flipper *m*
pincers ['pɪnsəz] *npl* (*tool*) Kneifzange *f*; (*of crab, lobster etc*) Schere *f*
pinch [pɪntʃ] *n* (*of salt etc*) Prise *f* ▷ *vt* (*with finger and thumb*) zwicken, kneifen; (*inf: steal*) klauen ▷ *vi* (*shoe*) drücken; **at a ~** zur Not; **to feel the ~** (*fig*) die schlechte Lage zu spüren bekommen
pinched [pɪntʃt] *adj* (*face*) erschöpft; **~ with cold** verfroren
pincushion ['pɪnkʊʃən] *n* Nadelkissen *nt*
pine [paɪn] *n* (*also:* **pine tree**) Kiefer *f*; (*wood*) Kiefernholz *nt* ▷ *vi*: **to ~ for** sich sehnen nach
▶ **pine away** *vi* sich (vor Kummer) verzehren
pineapple ['paɪnæpl] *n* Ananas *f*
pine cone *n* Kiefernzapfen *m*
pine needles *npl* Kiefernnadeln *pl*
ping [pɪŋ] *n* (*noise*) Klingeln *nt*
Ping-Pong® ['pɪŋpɔŋ] *n* Pingpong *nt*
pink [pɪŋk] *adj* rosa *inv* ▷ *n* (*colour*) Rosa *nt*; (*Bot*) Gartennelke *f*
pinking shears *npl* Zickzackschere *f*
pin money (*Brit: inf*) *n* Nadelgeld *nt*
pinnacle ['pɪnəkl] *n* (*of building, mountain*) Spitze

f; (*fig*) Gipfel *m*
pinpoint ['pɪnpɔɪnt] *vt* (*identify*) genau festlegen, identifizieren; (*position of sth*) genau aufzeigen
pinstripe ['pɪnstraɪp] *adj*: **~ suit** Nadelstreifenanzug *m*
pint [paɪnt] *n* (*Brit: = 568 cc*) (britisches) Pint *nt*; (*US: = 473 cc*) (amerikanisches) Pint; **a ~** (*Brit: inf: of beer*) ≈ eine Halbe
pin-up ['pɪnʌp] *n* (*picture*) Pin-up-Foto *nt*
pioneer [paɪə'nɪə'] *n* (*lit, fig*) Pionier *m* ▷ *vt* (*invention etc*) Pionierarbeit leisten für
pious ['paɪəs] *adj* fromm
pip [pɪp] *n* (*of apple, orange*) Kern *m* ▷ *vt*: **to be ~ped at the post** (*Brit: fig*) um Haaresbreite geschlagen werden; **the pips** *npl* (*Brit: Radio*) das Zeitzeichen
pipe [paɪp] *n* (*for water, gas*) Rohr *nt*; (*for smoking*) Pfeife *f*; (*Mus*) Flöte *f* ▷ *vt* (*water, gas, oil*) (durch Rohre) leiten; **pipes** *npl* (*also:* **bagpipes**) Dudelsack *m*
▶ **pipe down** (*inf*) *vi* (*be quiet*) ruhig sein
pipe cleaner *n* Pfeifenreiniger *m*
piped music [paɪpt-] *n* Berieselungsmusik *f*
pipe dream *n* Hirngespinst *nt*
pipeline ['paɪplaɪn] *n* Pipeline *f*; **it's in the ~** (*fig*) es ist in Vorbereitung
piper ['paɪpə'] *n* (*bagpipe player*) Dudelsackspieler(in) *m(f)*
pipe tobacco *n* Pfeifentabak *m*
piping ['paɪpɪŋ] *adv*: **~ hot** kochend heiß
piquant ['pi:kənt] *adj* (*also fig*) pikant
pique ['pi:k] *n*: **in a fit of ~** eingeschnappt, pikiert
piracy ['paɪərəsɪ] *n* Piraterie *f*, Seeräuberei *f*; (*Comm*): **to commit ~** ein Plagiat *nt* begehen
pirate ['paɪərət] *n* Pirat *m*, Seeräuber *m* ▷ *vt* (*Comm: video tape, cassette etc*) illegal herstellen
pirate radio station (*Brit*) *n* Piratensender *m*
pirouette [pɪru'ɛt] *n* Pirouette *f* ▷ *vi* Pirouetten drehen
Pisces ['paɪsi:z] *n* Fische *pl*; **to be ~** Fische *or* (ein) Fisch sein
piss [pɪs] (*inf!*) *vi* pissen ▷ *n* Pisse *f*; **~ off!** verpiss dich!; **to be ~ed off** (**with sb/sth**) (von jdm/etw) die Schnauze vollhaben; **it's ~ing down** (*Brit: raining*) es schifft; **to take the ~ out of sb** (*Brit*) jdn verarschen
pissed [pɪst] (*inf!*) *adj* (*drunk*) besoffen
pistol ['pɪstl] *n* Pistole *f*
piston ['pɪstən] *n* Kolben *m*
pit [pɪt] *n* Grube *f*; (*in surface of road*) Schlagloch *nt*; (*coal mine*) Zeche *f*; (*also:* **orchestra pit**) Orchestergraben *m* ▷ *vt*: **to ~ one's wits against sb** seinen Verstand mit jdm messen; **the pits** *npl* (*Aut*) die Box; **to ~ o.s. against sth** den Kampf gegen etw aufnehmen; **to ~ sb against sb** jdn gegen jdn antreten lassen; **the ~ of one's stomach** die Magengrube
pitapat ['pɪtə'pæt] (*Brit*) *adv*: **to go ~** (*heart*) pochen, klopfen; (*rain*) prasseln
pitch [pɪtʃ] *n* (*Brit: Sport: field*) Spielfeld *nt*; (*Mus*) Tonhöhe *f*; (*fig: level, degree*) Grad *m*; (*tar*) Pech

p

nt; (also: **sales pitch**) Verkaufsmasche f; (Naut)
Stampfen nt ▷ vt (throw) werfen, schleudern;
(set: price, message) ansetzen ▷ vi (fall forwards)
hinschlagen; (Naut) stampfen; **to ~ a tent**
ein Zelt aufschlagen; **to be ~ed forward**
vornüber geworfen werden

pitch-black ['pɪtʃ'blæk] adj pechschwarz

pitched battle [pɪtʃt-] n offene Schlacht f

pitcher ['pɪtʃəʳ] n (jug) Krug m; (US: Baseball)
Werfer m

pitchfork ['pɪtʃfɔːk] n Heugabel f

piteous ['pɪtɪəs] adj kläglich, erbärmlich

pitfall ['pɪtfɔːl] n Falle f

pith [pɪθ] n (of orange etc) weiße Haut f; (of plant)
Mark nt; (fig) Kern m

pithead ['pɪthed] n Schachtanlagen pl über
Tage

pithy ['pɪθɪ] adj (comment etc) prägnant

pitiable ['pɪtɪəbl] adj mitleiderregend

pitiful ['pɪtɪful] adj (sight etc) mitleiderregend;
(excuse, attempt) jämmerlich, kläglich

pitifully ['pɪtɪfəlɪ] adv (thin, frail) jämmerlich;
(inadequate, ill-equipped) fürchterlich

pitiless ['pɪtɪlɪs] adj mitleidlos

pittance ['pɪtns] n Hungerlohn m

pitted ['pɪtɪd] adj: **~ with** übersät mit; **~ with
rust** voller Rost

pity ['pɪtɪ] n Mitleid nt ▷ vt bemitleiden,
bedauern; **what a ~!** wie schade!; **it is a ~
that you can't come** schade, dass du nicht
kommen kannst; **to take ~ on sb** Mitleid mit
jdm haben

pitying ['pɪtɪɪŋ] adj mitleidig

pivot ['pɪvət] n (Tech) Drehpunkt m; (fig) Dreh-
und Angelpunkt m ▷ vi sich drehen
▶ **pivot on** (depend on) abhängen von

pixel ['pɪksl] n (Comput) Pixel nt

pixie ['pɪksɪ] n Elf m, Elfe f

pizza ['piːtsə] n Pizza f

placard ['plækɑːd] n Plakat nt, Aushang m; (in
march etc) Transparent nt

placate [plə'keɪt] vt beschwichtigen,
besänftigen

placatory [plə'keɪtərɪ] adj beschwichtigend,
besänftigend

place [pleɪs] n Platz m; (position) Stelle f, Ort m;
(seat: on committee etc) Sitz m; (home) Wohnung
f; (in street names) = Straße f ▷ vt (put: object)
stellen, legen; (identify: person) unterbringen;
~ of birth Geburtsort m; **to take ~** (happen)
geschehen, passieren; **at/to his ~** (home) bei/
zu ihm; **from ~ to place** von Ort zu Ort; **all
over the ~** überall; **in ~s** stellenweise; **in
sb's/sth's ~** anstelle von jdm/etw; **to take
sb's/sth's ~** an die Stelle von jdm/etw treten,
jdn/etw ersetzen; **out of ~** (inappropriate)
unangebracht; **I feel out of ~ here** ich fühle
mich hier fehl am Platze; **in the first ~** (first
of all) erstens; **to change ~s with sb** mit jdm
den Platz tauschen; **to put sb in his ~** (fig)
jdn in seine Schranken weisen; **he's going
~s** er bringt es noch mal weit; **it's not my ~
to do it** es ist nicht an mir, das zu tun; **to be
~d** (in race, exam) platziert sein; **to be ~d third**
den dritten Platz belegen; **to ~ an order with
sb (for sth)** eine Bestellung bei jdm (für etw)
aufgeben; **how are you ~d next week?** wie
sieht es bei Ihnen nächste Woche aus?

placebo [plə'siːbəʊ] n Placebo nt; (fig)
Beruhigungsmittel nt

place mat n Set nt or m

placement ['pleɪsmənt] n Platzierung f

place name n Ortsname m

placenta [plə'sentə] n Plazenta f

place setting n Gedeck nt

placid ['plæsɪd] adj (person) ruhig, gelassen;
(place, river etc) friedvoll

plagiarism ['pleɪdʒərɪzəm] n Plagiat nt

plagiarist ['pleɪdʒərɪst] n Plagiator(in) m(f)

plagiarize ['pleɪdʒəraɪz] vt (idea, work)
kopieren, plagiieren

plague [pleɪg] n (Med) Seuche f; (fig: of locusts
etc) Plage f ▷ vt (fig: problems etc) plagen; **to ~ sb
with questions** jdn mit Fragen quälen

plaice [pleɪs] n inv Scholle f

plaid [plæd] n Plaid nt

plain [pleɪn] adj (unpatterned) einfarbig; (simple)
einfach, schlicht; (clear, easily understood) klar;
(not beautiful) unattraktiv; (frank) offen ▷ adv
(wrong, stupid etc) einfach ▷ n (area of land) Ebene
f; (Knitting) rechte Masche f; **to make sth ~ to
sb** jdm etw klarmachen

plain chocolate n Bitterschokolade f

plain-clothes ['pleɪnkləʊðz] adj (police officer)
in Zivil

plainly ['pleɪnlɪ] adv (obviously) eindeutig;
(clearly) deutlich, klar

plainness ['pleɪnnɪs] n (of person) Reizlosigkeit f

plain speaking n Offenheit f; **a bit of ~** ein
paar offene Worte

plain-spoken ['pleɪn'spəʊkn] adj offen

plaintiff ['pleɪntɪf] n Kläger(in) m(f)

plaintive ['pleɪntɪv] adj (cry, voice) klagend;
(song) schwermütig; (look) traurig

plait [plæt] n (of hair) Zopf m; (of rope, leather)
Geflecht nt ▷ vt flechten

plan [plæn] n Plan m ▷ vt planen; (building,
schedule) entwerfen ▷ vi planen; **to ~ to do
sth** planen or vorhaben, etw zu tun; **how long
do you ~ to stay?** wie lange haben Sie vor, zu
bleiben?; **to ~ for or on** (expect) sich einstellen
auf +acc; **to ~ on doing sth** vorhaben, etw
zu tun

plane [pleɪn] n (Aviat) Flugzeug nt; (Math)
Ebene f; (fig: level) Niveau nt; (tool) Hobel m;
(also: **plane tree**) Platane f ▷ vt (wood) hobeln
▷ vi (Naut, Aut) gleiten

planet ['plænɪt] n Planet m

planetarium [plænɪ'teərɪəm] n Planetarium nt

plank [plæŋk] n (of wood) Brett nt; (fig: of policy
etc) Schwerpunkt m

plankton ['plæŋktən] n Plankton nt

planned economy ['plænd-] n Planwirtschaft
f

planner ['plænəʳ] n Planer(in) m(f)

planning ['plænɪŋ] n Planung f

planning permission (*Brit*) *n*
Baugenehmigung *f*
plant [plɑːnt] *n* (*Bot*) Pflanze *f*; (*machinery*)
Maschinen *pl*; (*factory*) Anlage *f* ⊳ *vt* (*seed*,
plant, crops) pflanzen; (*field, garden*) bepflanzen;
(*microphone, bomb etc*) anbringen; (*incriminating
evidence*) schleusen; (*fig: object*) stellen; (: *kiss*)
drücken
plantation [plæn'teɪʃən] *n* Plantage *f*; (*wood*)
Anpflanzung *f*
plant pot (*Brit*) *n* Blumentopf *m*
plaque [plæk] *n* (*on building etc*) Tafel *f*, Plakette
f; (*on teeth*) Zahnbelag *m*
plasma ['plæzmə] *n* Plasma *nt*
plaster ['plɑːstəʳ] *n* (*for walls*) Putz *m*;
(*also:* **plaster of Paris**) Gips *m*; (*Brit: also:*
sticking plaster) Pflaster *nt* ⊳ *vt* (*wall, ceiling*)
verputzen; **in ~** (*Brit*) in Gips; **to ~ with** (*cover*)
bepflastern mit
plasterboard ['plɑːstəbɔːd] *n* Gipskarton *m*
plaster cast *n* (*Med*) Gipsverband *m*; (*model,
statue*) Gipsform *f*
plastered ['plɑːstəd] (*inf*) *adj* (*drunk*)
sturzbesoffen
plasterer ['plɑːstərəʳ] *n* Gipser *m*
plastic ['plæstɪk] *n* Plastik *nt* ⊳ *adj* (*bucket, cup
etc*) Plastik-; (*flexible*) formbar; **the ~ arts** die
bildende Kunst
plastic bag *n* Plastiktüte *f*
plastic bullet *n* Plastikgeschoss *nt*
plastic explosive *n* Plastiksprengstoff *m*
Plasticine® ['plæstɪsiːn] *n* Plastilin *nt*
plastic surgery *n* plastische Chirurgie *f*
plate [pleɪt] *n* (*dish*) Teller *m*; (*metal cover*) Platte *f*;
(*Typ*) Druckplatte *f*; (*Aut*) Nummernschild
nt; (*in book: picture*) Tafel *f*; (*also:* **dental plate**)
Gaumenplatte *f*; (*on door*) Schild *nt*; **gold/
silver ~** vergoldeter/versilberter Artikel *m*;
that necklace is just ~ die Halskette ist nur
vergoldet/versilbert
plateau ['plætəʊ] (*pl* **plateaus** *or* **~x**) *n* (*Geog*)
Plateau *nt*, Hochebene *f*; (*fig*) stabiler Zustand
m
plateful ['pleɪtful] *n* Teller *m*
plate glass *n* Tafelglas *nt*
platen ['plætən] *n* (*on typewriter, printer*) (Schreib)
walze *f*
plate rack *n* Geschirrständer *m*
platform ['plætfɔːm] *n* (*stage*) Podium *nt*; (*for
landing, loading on etc, Brit: of bus*) Plattform *f*;
(*Rail*) Bahnsteig *m*; (*Pol*) Programm *nt*; **the
train leaves from ~ 7** der Zug fährt von Gleis
7 ab
platform ticket (*Brit*) *n* (*Rail*) Bahnsteigkarte *f*
platinum ['plætɪnəm] *n* Platin *nt*
platitude ['plætɪtjuːd] *n* Plattitüde *f*,
Gemeinplatz *m*
platonic [plə'tɔnɪk] *adj* (*relationship*) platonisch
platoon [plə'tuːn] *n* Zug *m*
platter ['plætəʳ] *n* Platte *f*
plaudits ['plɔːdɪts] *npl* Ovationen *pl*
plausible ['plɔːzɪbl] *adj* (*theory, excuse*) plausibel;
(*liar etc*) glaubwürdig

play [pleɪ] *n* (*Theat*) (Theater)stück *nt*; (*TV*)
Fernsehspiel *nt*; (*Radio*) Hörspiel *nt*; (*activity*)
Spiel *nt* ⊳ *vt* spielen; (*team, opponent*) spielen
gegen ⊳ *vi* spielen; **to bring into ~** ins Spiel
bringen; **a ~ on words** ein Wortspiel *nt*; **to ~
a trick on sb** jdn hereinlegen; **to ~ a part** *or*
role in sth (*fig*) eine Rolle bei etw spielen; **to
~ for time** (*fig*) auf Zeit spielen, Zeit gewinnen
wollen; **to ~ safe** auf Nummer sicher gehen;
to ~ into sb's hands jdm in die Hände spielen
▶ **play about with** *vt fus* = **play around with**
▶ **play along with** *vt fus* (*person*) sich richten
nach; (*plan, idea*) eingehen auf +*acc*
▶ **play around with** *vt fus* (*fiddle with*)
herumspielen mit
▶ **play at** *vt fus* (*do casually*) spielen mit; **to ~ at
being sb/sth** jdn/etw spielen
▶ **play back** *vt* (*recording*) abspielen
▶ **play down** *vt* herunterspielen
▶ **play on** *vt fus* (*sb's feelings etc*) ausnutzen; **to ~
on sb's mind** jdm im Kopf herumgehen
▶ **play up** *vi* (*machine, knee etc*) Schwierigkeiten
machen; (*children*) frech werden
play-act ['pleɪækt] *vi* Theater spielen
playboy ['pleɪbɔɪ] *n* Playboy *m*
player ['pleɪəʳ] *n* (*Sport, Mus*) Spieler(in) *m(f)*;
(*Theat*) Schauspieler(in) *m(f)*
playful ['pleɪful] *adj* (*person, gesture*) spielerisch;
(*animal*) verspielt
playgoer ['pleɪɡəʊəʳ] *n* Theaterbesucher(in)
m(f)
playground ['pleɪɡraʊnd] *n* (*in park*) Spielplatz
m; (*in school*) Schulhof *m*
playgroup ['pleɪɡruːp] *n* Spielgruppe *f*
playing card ['pleɪŋ-] *n* Spielkarte *f*
playing field *n* Sportplatz *m*
playmaker ['pleɪmeɪkəʳ] *n* (*Sport*)
Spielmacher(in) *m(f)*
playmate ['pleɪmeɪt] *n* Spielkamerad(in) *m(f)*
play-off ['pleɪɔf] *n* Ausscheidungsspiel *nt*,
Play-off *nt*
playpen ['pleɪpen] *n* Laufstall *m*
playroom ['pleɪruːm] *n* Spielzimmer *nt*
playschool ['pleɪskuːl] *n* = **playgroup**
plaything ['pleɪθɪŋ] *n* (*also fig*) Spielzeug *nt*
playtime ['pleɪtaɪm] *n* (kleine) Pause *f*
playwright ['pleɪraɪt] *n* Dramatiker(in) *m(f)*
plc (*Brit*) *n abbr* (= *public limited company*) ≈ AG *f*
plea [pliː] *n* (*request*) Bitte *f*; (*Law*): **to enter
a ~ of guilty/not guilty** sich schuldig/
unschuldig erklären; (*excuse*) Vorwand *m*
plea bargaining *n* Verhandlungen zwischen
Anklage und Verteidigung mit dem Ziel, bestimmte
Anklagepunkte fallen zu lassen, wenn der Angeklagte
sich in anderen Punkten schuldig bekennt
plead [pliːd] *vi* (*Law*) vor Gericht eine Schuld-/
Unschuldserklärung abgeben ⊳ *vt* (*Law*): **to ~ sb's
case** jdn vertreten; (*give as excuse: ignorance, ill
health etc*) vorgeben, sich berufen auf +*acc*; **to
~ with sb** (*beg*) jdn inständig bitten; **to ~ for
sth** um etw nachsuchen; **to ~ guilty/not
guilty** sich schuldig/nicht schuldig bekennen
pleasant ['plɛznt] *adj* angenehm; (*smile*)

P

freundlich

pleasantly ['plɛzntlɪ] *adv* (*surprised*) angenehm; (*say, behave*) freundlich

pleasantries ['plɛzntrɪz] *npl* Höflichkeiten *pl*, Nettigkeiten *pl*

please [pliːz] *excl* bitte ▷ *vt* (*satisfy*) zufriedenstellen ▷ *vi* (*give pleasure*) gefällig sein; **~ Miss/Sir!** (*to attract teacher's attention*) = Frau/Herr X!; **yes,** ~ ja, bitte; **my bill,** ~ die Rechnung, bitte; **~ don't cry!** bitte wein doch nicht!; **~ yourself!** (*inf*) wie du willst!; **do as you** ~ machen Sie, was Sie für richtig halten

pleased [pliːzd] *adj* (*happy*) erfreut; (*satisfied*) zufrieden; **~ to meet you** freut mich(, Sie kennenzulernen); **~ with** zufrieden mit; **we are ~ to inform you that ...** wir freuen uns, Ihnen mitzuteilen, dass ...

pleasing ['pliːzɪŋ] *adj* (*remark, picture etc*) erfreulich; (*person*) sympathisch

pleasurable ['plɛʒərəbl] *adj* angenehm

pleasure ['plɛʒəʳ] *n* (*happiness, satisfaction*) Freude *f*; (*fun, enjoyable experience*) Vergnügen *nt*; **it's a ~, my ~** gern geschehen; **with ~** gern, mit Vergnügen; **is this trip for business or ~?** ist diese Reise geschäftlich oder zum Vergnügen?

pleasure boat *n* Vergnügungsschiff *nt*

pleasure cruise *n* Vergnügungsfahrt *f*

pleat [pliːt] *n* Falte *f*

pleb [plɛb] (*inf: pej*) *n* Prolet *m*

plebiscite ['plɛbɪsɪt] *n* Volksentscheid *m*, Plebiszit *nt*

plectrum ['plɛktrəm] *n* Plektron *nt*, Plektrum *nt*

pledge [plɛdʒ] *n* (*promise*) Versprechen *nt* ▷ *vt* (*promise*) versprechen; **to ~ sb to secrecy** jdn zum Schweigen verpflichten

plenary ['pliːnərɪ] *adj* (*powers*) unbeschränkt; **~ session** Plenarsitzung *f*; **~ meeting** Vollversammlung *f*

plentiful ['plɛntɪful] *adj* reichlich

plenty ['plɛntɪ] *n* (*lots*) eine Menge; (*sufficient*) reichlich; **~ of** eine Menge; **we've got ~ of time to get there** wir haben jede Menge Zeit, dorthin zu kommen

plethora ['plɛθərə] *n*: **a ~ of** eine Fülle von, eine Unmenge an +*dat*

pleurisy ['pluərɪsɪ] *n* Rippenfellentzündung *f*

Plexiglas® ['plɛksɪɡlɑːs] (*US*) *n* Plexiglas® *nt*

pliable ['plaɪəbl] *adj* (*material*) biegsam; (*fig: person*) leicht beeinflussbar

pliant ['plaɪənt] *adj* = **pliable**

pliers ['plaɪəz] *npl* Zange *f*

plight [plaɪt] *n* (*of person, country*) Not *f*

plimsolls ['plɪmsəlz] (*Brit*) *npl* Turnschuhe *pl*

plinth [plɪnθ] *n* Sockel *m*

PLO *n abbr* (= *Palestine Liberation Organization*) PLO *f*

plod [plɒd] *vi* (*walk*) trotten; (*fig*) sich abplagen

plodder ['plɒdəʳ] (*pej*) *n* (*slow worker*) zäher Arbeiter *m*, zähe Arbeiterin *f*

plonk [plɒŋk] (*inf*) *n* (*Brit: wine*) (billiger) Wein *m* ▷ *vt*: **to ~ sth down** etw hinknallen

plot [plɒt] *n* (*secret plan*) Komplott *nt*,

Verschwörung *f*; (*of story, play, film*) Handlung *f* ▷ *vt* (*sb's downfall etc*) planen; (*on chart, graph*) markieren ▷ *vi* (*conspire*) sich verschwören; **a ~ of land** ein Grundstück *nt*; **a vegetable ~** (*Brit*) ein Gemüsebeet *nt*

plotter ['plɒtəʳ] *n* (*instrument, Comput*) Plotter *m*

plough, (*US*) **plow** [plau] *n* Pflug *m* ▷ *vt* pflügen; **to ~ money into sth** (*project etc*) Geld in etw *acc* stecken

▶ **plough back** *vt* (*Comm*) reinvestieren

▶ **plough into** *vt fus* (*crowd*) rasen in +*acc*

ploughman, (*US*) **plowman** ['plaumən] (*irreg: like* **man**) *n* Pflüger *m*

ploughman's lunch ['plaumənz-] (*Brit*) *n* Imbiss aus Brot, Käse und Pickles

plow *etc* (*US*) = **plough** *etc*

ploy [plɔɪ] *n* Trick *m*

pls *abbr* (= *please*) b.

pluck [plʌk] *vt* (*fruit, flower, leaf*) pflücken; (*musical instrument, eyebrows*) zupfen; (*bird*) rupfen ▷ *n* (*courage*) Mut *m*; **to ~ up courage** allen Mut zusammennehmen

plucky ['plʌkɪ] (*inf*) *adj* (*person*) tapfer

plug [plʌg] *n* (*Elec*) Stecker *m*; (*stopper*) Stöpsel *m*; (*Aut: also:* **spark(ing) plug**) Zündkerze *f* ▷ *vt* (*hole*) zustopfen; (*inf: advertise*) Reklame machen für; **to give sb/sth a ~** für jdn/etw Reklame machen

▶ **plug in** *vt* (*Elec*) einstöpseln, anschließen ▷ *vi* angeschlossen werden

plughole ['plʌghəul] (*Brit*) *n* Abfluss *m*

plum [plʌm] *n* (*fruit*) Pflaume *f* ▷ *adj* (*inf*): **a ~ job** ein Traumjob *m*

plumage ['pluːmɪdʒ] *n* Gefieder *nt*

plumb [plʌm] *vt*: **to ~ the depths of despair/ humiliation** die tiefste Verzweiflung/ Erniedrigung erleben

▶ **plumb in** *vt* anschließen, installieren

plumber ['plʌməʳ] *n* Installateur *m*, Klempner *m*

plumbing ['plʌmɪŋ] *n* (*piping*) Installationen *pl*, Rohrleitungen *pl*; (*trade*) Klempnerei *f*; (*work*) Installationsarbeiten *pl*

plumb line *n* Lot *nt*, Senkblei *nt*

plume [pluːm] *n* (*of bird*) Feder *f*; (*on helmet, horse's head*) Federbusch *m*; **~ of smoke** Rauchfahne *f*

plummet ['plʌmɪt] *vi* (*bird, aircraft*) (hinunter) stürzen; (*price, rate*) rapide absacken

plump [plʌmp] *adj* (*person*) füllig, mollig

▶ **plump for** (*inf*) *vt fus* sich entscheiden für

▶ **plump up** *vt* (*cushion*) aufschütteln

plunder ['plʌndəʳ] *n* (*activity*) Plünderung *f*; (*stolen things*) Beute *f* ▷ *vt* (*city, tomb*) plündern

plunge [plʌndʒ] *n* (*of bird, person*) Sprung *m*; (*fig: of prices, rates etc*) Sturz *m* ▷ *vt* (*hand, knife*) stoßen ▷ *vi* (*thing*) stürzen; (*bird, person*) sich stürzen; (*fig: prices, rates etc*) abfallen, stürzen; **to take the ~** (*fig*) den Sprung wagen; **the room was ~d into darkness** das Zimmer war in Dunkelheit getaucht

plunger ['plʌndʒəʳ] *n* (*for sink*) Sauger *m*

plunging ['plʌndʒɪŋ] *adj*: **~ neckline** tiefer

Ausschnitt *m*

pluperfect [pluːˈpəːfɪkt] *n*: **the ~** das Plusquamperfekt

plural [ˈpluərl] *adj* Plural- ⊳ *n* Plural *m*, Mehrzahl *f*

plus [plʌs] *n* (*also*: **plus sign**) Pluszeichen *nt* ⊳ *prep, adj* plus; **it's a ~** (*fig*) es ist ein Vorteil *or* ein Pluspunkt; **ten/twenty ~** (*more than*) über zehn/zwanzig; **B ~** (*Scol*) ≈ Zwei plus

plus fours *npl* Überfallhose *f*

plush [plʌʃ] *adj* (*car, hotel etc*) feudal ⊳ *n* (*fabric*) Plüsch *m*

plutonium [pluːˈtəʊnɪəm] *n* Plutonium *nt*

ply [plaɪ] *vt* (*a trade*) ausüben, nachgehen +*dat*; (*tool*) gebrauchen, anwenden ⊳ *vi* (*ship*) verkehren ⊳ *n* (*of wool, rope*) Stärke *f*; (*also*: **plywood**) Sperrholz *nt*; **to ~ sb with drink** jdn ausgiebig bewirten; **two-/three-~ wool** zwei-/dreifädige Wolle

plywood [ˈplaɪwʊd] *n* Sperrholz *nt*

PM (*Brit*) *abbr* = **Prime Minister**

p.m. *adv abbr* (= *post meridiem*) nachmittags; (*later*) abends

PMT *abbr* = **premenstrual tension**

pneumatic [njuːˈmætɪk] *adj* pneumatisch

pneumatic drill *n* Pressluftbohrer *m*

pneumonia [njuːˈməʊnɪə] *n* Lungenentzündung *f*

PO *n abbr* = **Post Office**; (*Mil*) = **petty officer**

p.o. *abbr* = **postal order**

POA (*Brit*) *n abbr* (= *Prison Officers' Association*) Gewerkschaft der Gefängnisbeamten

poach [pəʊtʃ] *vt* (*steal: fish, animals, birds*) illegal erbeuten, wildern; (*Culin: egg*) pochieren; (: *fish*) dünsten ⊳ *vi* (*steal*) wildern

poached [pəʊtʃt] *adj*: **~ eggs** verlorene Eier

poacher [ˈpəʊtʃəʳ] *n* Wilderer *m*

PO Box *n abbr* (= *Post Office Box*) Postf.

pocket [ˈpɔkɪt] *n* Tasche *f*; (*fig: small area*) vereinzelter Bereich *m* ⊳ *vt* (*put in one's pocket, steal*) einstecken; **to be out of ~** (*Brit*) Verlust machen; **~ of resistance** Widerstandsnest *nt*

pocketbook [ˈpɔkɪtbʊk] *n* (*notebook*) Notizbuch *nt*; (*US: wallet*) Brieftasche *f*; (: *handbag*) Handtasche *f*

pocket calculator *n* Taschenrechner *m*

pocketknife [ˈpɔkɪtnaɪf] *n* Taschenmesser *nt*

pocket money *n* Taschengeld *nt*

pocket-sized [ˈpɔkɪtsaɪzd] *adj* im Taschenformat

pockmarked [ˈpɔkmɑːkt] *adj* (*face*) pockennarbig

pod [pɔd] *n* Hülse *f*

podcast [ˈpɔdkɑːst] *n* Podcast *m*

podgy [ˈpɔdʒɪ] (*inf*) *adj* rundlich, pummelig

podiatrist [pɔˈdiːətrɪst] (*US*) *n* Fußspezialist(in) *m(f)*

podiatry [pɔˈdiːətrɪ] (*US*) *n* Fußpflege *f*

podium [ˈpəʊdɪəm] *n* Podium *nt*

POE *n abbr* (= *port of embarkation*) Ausgangshafen *m*; (= *port of entry*) Eingangshafen *m*

poem [ˈpəʊɪm] *n* Gedicht *nt*

poet [ˈpəʊɪt] *n* Dichter(in) *m(f)*

poetic [pəʊˈɛtɪk] *adj* poetisch, dichterisch; (*fig*) malerisch

poetic justice *n* ausgleichende Gerechtigkeit *f*

poetic licence *n* dichterische Freiheit *f*

poet laureate *n* Hofdichter *m*; *siehe Info-Artikel*

◉ **POET LAUREATE**
◉
◉ *Poet laureate* ist in Großbritannien ein
◉ Dichter, der ein Gehalt als Hofdichter
◉ bezieht und kraft seines Amtes ein
◉ lebenslanges Mitglied des britischen
◉ Königshofes ist. Der Poet Laureate schrieb
◉ traditionellerweise ausführliche Gedichte
◉ zu Staatsanlässen; ein Brauch, der heute
◉ kaum noch befolgt wird. Der erste Poet
◉ Laureate 1616 war Ben Jonson.

---

poetry [ˈpəʊɪtrɪ] *n* (*poems*) Gedichte *pl*; (*writing*) Poesie *f*

poignant [ˈpɔɪnjənt] *adj* ergreifend; (*situation*) herzzerreißend

point [pɔɪnt] *n* Punkt *m*; (*of needle, knife etc*) Spitze *f*; (*purpose*) Sinn *m*, Zweck *m*; (*significant part*) Entscheidende(s) *nt*; (*moment*) Zeitpunkt *m*; (*Elec: also*: **power point**) Steckdose *f*; (*also*: **decimal point**) ≈ Komma *nt* ⊳ *vt* (*show, mark*) deuten auf +*acc* ⊳ *vi* (*with finger, stick etc*) zeigen, deuten; **points** *npl* (*Aut*) (Unterbrecher)kontakte *pl*; (*Rail*) Weichen *pl*; **two ~ five** (= 2.5) zwei Komma fünf; **good/ bad ~s** (*of person*) gute/schlechte Seiten *or* Eigenschaften; **the train stops at Carlisle and all ~s south** der Zug hält in Carlisle und allen Orten weiter südlich; **to be on the ~ of doing sth** im Begriff sein, etw zu tun; **to make a ~ of doing sth** besonders darauf achten, etw zu tun; (*make a habit of*) Wert darauf legen, etw zu tun; **to get/miss the ~** verstehen/nicht verstehen, worum es geht; **to come** *or* **get to the ~** zur Sache kommen; **to make one's ~** seinen Standpunkt klarmachen; **that's the whole ~!** darum geht es ja gerade!; **what's the ~?** was solls?; **to be beside the ~** unwichtig *or* irrelevant sein; **there's no ~ talking to you** es ist sinnlos, mit dir zu reden; **you've got a ~ there!** da könnten Sie recht haben!; **in ~ of fact** in Wirklichkeit; **~ of sale** (*Comm*) Verkaufsstelle *f*; **to ~ sth at sb** (*gun etc*) etw auf jdn richten; (*finger*) mit etw auf jdn *acc* zeigen; **to ~ at** zeigen auf +*acc*; **to ~ to** zeigen auf +*acc*; (*fig*) hinweisen auf +*acc*

▸ **point out** *vt* hinweisen auf +*acc*

▸ **point to** *vt fus* hindeuten auf +*acc*

point-blank [ˈpɔɪntˈblæŋk] *adv* (*say, ask*) direkt; (*refuse*) glatt; (*also*: **at point-blank range**) aus unmittelbarer Entfernung

point duty (*Brit*) *n*: **to be on ~** Verkehrsdienst haben

pointed [ˈpɔɪntɪd] *adj* spitz; (*fig: remark*) spitz, scharf

pointedly [ˈpɔɪntɪdlɪ] *adv* (*ask, reply etc*) spitz,

scharf

pointer ['pɔɪntə^r] n (on chart, machine) Zeiger m; (fig: piece of information or advice) Hinweis m; (stick) Zeigestock m; (dog) Pointer m

pointing ['pɔɪntɪŋ] n (Constr) Ausfugung f

pointless ['pɔɪntlɪs] adj sinnlos, zwecklos

point of view n Ansicht f, Standpunkt m; **from a practical ~** von einem praktischen Standpunkt aus

poise [pɔɪz] n (composure) Selbstsicherheit f; (balance) Haltung f ▷ vt: **to be ~d for sth** (fig) bereit zu etw sein

poison ['pɔɪzn] n Gift nt ▷ vt vergiften

poisoning ['pɔɪznɪŋ] n Vergiftung f

poisonous ['pɔɪznəs] adj (animal, plant) Gift-; (fumes, chemicals etc) giftig; (fig: rumours etc) zersetzend

poison-pen letter [pɔɪzn'pɛn] n anonymer Brief m (mit Indiskretionen)

poke [pəʊk] vt (with finger, stick etc) stoßen; (fire) schüren ▷ n (jab) Stoß m, Schubs m (inf); **to ~ sth in(to)** (put) etw stecken in +acc; **to ~ one's head out of the window** seinen Kopf aus dem Fenster strecken; **to ~ fun at sb** sich über jdn lustig machen

  ▶ **poke about** vi (search) herumstochern

  ▶ **poke out** vi (stick out) vorstehen

poker ['pəʊkə^r] n (metal bar) Schürhaken m; (Cards) Poker nt

poker-faced ['pəʊkə'feɪst] adj mit unbewegter Miene, mit Pokergesicht

poky ['pəʊkɪ] (pej) adj (room, house) winzig

Poland ['pəʊlənd] n Polen nt

polar ['pəʊlə^r] adj (icecap) polar; (region) Polar-

polar bear n Eisbär m

polarize ['pəʊləraɪz] vt polarisieren

Pole [pəʊl] n Pole m, Polin f

pole [pəʊl] n (post, stick) Stange f; (flag pole, telegraph pole etc) Mast m; (Geog, Elec) Pol m; **to be ~s apart** (fig) durch Welten (voneinander) getrennt sein

poleaxe, (US) **poleax** ['pəʊlæks] vt (fig) umhauen

pole bean (US) n (runner bean) Stangenbohne f

polecat ['pəʊlkæt] n Iltis m

Pol. Econ. ['pɒlɪkɒn] n abbr (= political economy) Volkswirtschaft f

polemic [pɒ'lɛmɪk] n Polemik f

Pole Star n Polarstern m

pole vault ['pəʊlvɔːlt] n Stabhochsprung m

police [pə'liːs] npl (organization) Polizei f; (members) Polizisten pl, Polizeikräfte pl ▷ vt (street, area, town) kontrollieren; **a large number of ~ were hurt** viele Polizeikräfte wurden verletzt

police car n Polizeiauto nt

police constable (Brit) n Polizist(in) m(f), Polizeibeamte(r) m, Polizeibeamtin f

police department (US) n Polizei f

police force n Polizei f

policeman [pə'liːsmən] (irreg: like man) n Polizist m

police officer n = **police constable**

police record n: **to have a ~** vorbestraft sein

police state n (Pol) Polizeistaat m

police station n Polizeiwache f

policewoman [pə'liːswʊmən] (irreg: like woman) n Polizistin f

policy ['pɒlɪsɪ] n (Pol, Econ) Politik f; (also: **insurance policy**) (Versicherungs)police f; (of newspaper) Grundsatz m; **to take out a ~** (Insurance) eine Versicherung abschließen

policyholder ['pɒlɪsɪ'həʊldə^r] n (Insurance) Versicherungsnehmer(in) m(f)

policy making n Strategieplanung f

polio ['pəʊlɪəʊ] n Kinderlähmung f, Polio f

Polish ['pəʊlɪʃ] adj polnisch ▷ n (Ling) Polnisch nt

polish ['pɒlɪʃ] n (for shoes) Creme f; (for furniture) Politur f; (for floors) Bohnerwachs nt; (shine: on shoes, floor etc) Glanz m; (fig: refinement) Schliff m ▷ vt (shoes) putzen; (floor, furniture etc) polieren

  ▶ **polish off** vt (work) erledigen; (food) verputzen

polished ['pɒlɪʃt] adj (fig: person) mit Schliff; (: style) geschliffen

polite [pə'laɪt] adj höflich; (company, society) fein; **it's not ~ to do that** es gehört sich nicht, das zu tun

politely [pə'laɪtlɪ] adv höflich

politeness [pə'laɪtnɪs] n Höflichkeit f

politic ['pɒlɪtɪk] adj klug, vernünftig

political [pə'lɪtɪkl] adj politisch

political asylum n politisches Asyl nt

politically [pə'lɪtɪklɪ] adv politisch; **~ correct** politisch korrekt

politician [pɒlɪ'tɪʃən] n Politiker(in) m(f)

politics ['pɒlɪtɪks] n Politik f ▷ npl (beliefs, opinions) politische Ansichten pl

polka ['pɒlkə] n Polka f

poll [pəʊl] n (also: **opinion poll**) (Meinungs) umfrage f; (election) Wahl f ▷ vt (in opinion poll) befragen; (number of votes) erhalten; **to go to the ~s** (voters) zur Wahl gehen; (government) sich den Wählern stellen

pollen ['pɒlən] n Pollen m, Blütenstaub m

pollen count n Pollenkonzentration f

pollinate ['pɒlɪneɪt] vt bestäuben

polling booth ['pəʊlɪŋ-] (Brit) n Wahlkabine f

polling day (Brit) n Wahltag m

polling station (Brit) n Wahllokal nt

pollster ['pəʊlstə^r] n Meinungsforscher(in) m(f)

poll tax n Kopfsteuer f

pollutant [pə'luːtənt] n Schadstoff m

pollute [pə'luːt] vt verschmutzen

pollution [pə'luːʃən] n (process) Verschmutzung f; (substances) Schmutz m

polo ['pəʊləʊ] n Polo nt

polo neck n (jumper) Rollkragenpullover m

polo-necked ['pəʊləʊnɛkt] adj (jumper, sweater) Rollkragen-

poltergeist ['pɔːltəgaɪst] n Poltergeist m

poly ['pɒlɪ] (Brit) n = **polytechnic**

poly bag (inf) n Plastiktüte f

polyester [pɒlɪ'ɛstə^r] n Polyester m

polygamy [pə'lɪɡəmɪ] n Polygamie f
polygraph ['pɒlɪɡrɑːf] (US) n (lie detector)
Lügendetektor m
Polynesia [pɒlɪ'niːzɪə] n Polynesien nt
Polynesian [pɒlɪ'niːzɪən] adj polynesisch ▷ n
Polynesier(in) m(f)
polyp ['pɒlɪp] n Polyp m
polystyrene [pɒlɪ'staɪriːn] n ≈ Styropor® nt
polytechnic [pɒlɪ'tɛknɪk] n technische
Hochschule f
polythene ['pɒlɪθiːn] n Polyäthylen nt
polythene bag n Plastiktüte f
polyurethane [pɒlɪ'jʊərɪθeɪn] n Polyurethan
nt
pomegranate ['pɒmɪɡrænɪt] n Granatapfel m
pommel ['pɒml] n (on saddle) Sattelknopf m ▷ vt
(US) = **pummel**
po-mo ['pəʊməʊ] abbr (= postmodern)
postmodern; (= postmodernism) Postmoderne f
pomp [pɒmp] n Pomp m, Prunk m
pompom ['pɒmpɒm] n Troddel f
pompous ['pɒmpəs] (pej) adj (person)
aufgeblasen; (piece of writing) geschwollen
pond [pɒnd] n Teich m
ponder ['pɒndər] vt nachdenken über +acc ▷ vi
nachdenken
ponderous ['pɒndərəs] adj (style, language)
schwerfällig
pong [pɒŋ] (Brit: inf) n Gestank m ▷ vi stinken
pontiff ['pɒntɪf] n Papst m
pontificate [pɒn'tɪfɪkeɪt] vi dozieren
pontoon [pɒn'tuːn] n (floating platform) Ponton
m; (Cards) Siebzehnundvier nt
pony ['pəʊnɪ] n Pony nt
ponytail ['pəʊnɪteɪl] n Pferdeschwanz m; **to
have one's hair in a ~** einen Pferdeschwanz
tragen
pony trekking (Brit) n Ponytrecken nt
poodle ['puːdl] n Pudel m
pooh-pooh ['puː'puː] vt verächtlich abtun
pool [puːl] n (pond) Teich m; (also: **swimming
pool**) Schwimmbad nt; (of blood) Lache f;
(Sport) Poolbillard nt; (of cash, workers) Bestand
m; (Cards: kitty) Kasse f; (Comm: consortium)
Interessengemeinschaft f ▷ vt (money)
zusammenlegen; (knowledge, resources)
vereinigen; **pools** npl (also: **football pools**)
≈ Fußballtoto nt; **a ~ of sunlight/shade**
eine sonnige/schattige Stelle; **car ~**
Fahrgemeinschaft f; **typing ~, secretary ~**
(US) Schreibzentrale f; **to do the (football) ~s**
≈ im Fußballtoto spielen
poor [pʊər] adj arm; (bad) schlecht ▷ npl: **the ~**
die Armen pl; **~ in** (resources etc) arm an +dat; **~
Bob** der arme Bob
poorly ['pʊəlɪ] adj (ill) elend, krank ▷ adv
(badly: designed, paid, furnished) schlecht
pop [pɒp] n (Mus) Pop m; (fizzy drink) Limonade
f; (US: inf: father) Papa m; (sound) Knall m ▷ vi
(balloon) platzen; (cork) knallen ▷ vt: **to ~ sth
into/onto sth** etw schnell in etw acc stecken/
auf etw acc legen; **his eyes ~ped out of his
head** (inf) ihm fielen fast die Augen aus dem

Kopf; **she ~ped her head out of the window**
sie streckte den Kopf aus dem Fenster
 ▸ **pop in** vi vorbeikommen
 ▸ **pop out** vi kurz weggehen
 ▸ **pop up** vi auftauchen; (Comput: window)
aufpoppen
popcorn ['pɒpkɔːn] n Popcorn nt
pope [pəʊp] n Papst m
poplar ['pɒplər] n Pappel f
poplin ['pɒplɪn] n Popeline f
popper ['pɒpər] (Brit: inf) n (for fastening)
Druckknopf m
poppy ['pɒpɪ] n Mohn m
poppycock ['pɒpɪkɒk] (inf) n Humbug m,
dummes Zeug nt
Popsicle® ['pɒpsɪkl] (US) n Eis nt am Stiel
pop star n Popstar m
populace ['pɒpjʊləs] n: **the ~** die Bevölkerung,
das Volk
popular ['pɒpjʊlər] adj (well-liked, fashionable)
beliebt, populär; (general, non-specialist)
allgemein; (idea) weitverbreitet;
(Pol: movement) Volks-; (: cause) des Volkes; **to
be ~ with** beliebt sein bei; **the ~ press** die
Boulevardpresse
popularity [pɒpjʊ'lærɪtɪ] n Beliebtheit f,
Popularität f
popularize ['pɒpjʊləraɪz] vt (sport, music, fashion)
populär machen; (science, ideas) popularisieren
popularly ['pɒpjʊləlɪ] adv (commonly) allgemein
population [pɒpjʊ'leɪʃən] n Bevölkerung
f; (of a species) Zahl f, Population f; **a
prison ~ of 44,000** (eine Zahl von) 44.000
Gefängnisinsassen; **the civilian ~** die
Zivilbevölkerung
population explosion n
Bevölkerungsexplosion f
populous ['pɒpjʊləs] adj dicht besiedelt
pop-up window ['pɒpʌp-] n (Comput) Popup-
Fenster nt
porcelain ['pɔːslɪn] n Porzellan nt
porch [pɔːtʃ] n (entrance) Vorbau m; (US)
Veranda f
porcupine ['pɔːkjʊpaɪn] n Stachelschwein nt
pore [pɔːr] n Pore f ▷ vi: **to ~ over** (book etc)
gründlich studieren
pork [pɔːk] n Schweinefleisch nt
pork chop n Schweinekotelett nt
porn [pɔːn] (inf) n Porno m; **~ channel/
magazine/shop** Pornokanal m/-magazin
nt/-laden m
pornographic [pɔːnə'ɡræfɪk] adj
pornografisch
pornography [pɔː'nɒɡrəfɪ] n Pornografie f
porous ['pɔːrəs] adj porös
porpoise ['pɔːpəs] n Tümmler m
porridge ['pɒrɪdʒ] n Haferbrei m, Porridge nt
port [pɔːt] n (harbour) Hafen m; (Naut: left side)
Backbord nt; (wine) Portwein m; (Comput)
Port m ▷ adj (Naut) Backbord-; **to ~** (Naut) an
Backbord; **~ of call** (Naut) Anlaufhafen nt
portable ['pɔːtəbl] adj (television, typewriter etc)
tragbar, portabel

p

713

portal ['pɔːtl] n Portal nt
portaloo ['pɔːtəluː] n Mobiltoilette f
portcullis [pɔːt'kʌlɪs] n Fallgitter nt
portent ['pɔːtɛnt] n Vorzeichen nt
porter ['pɔːtə'] n (for luggage) Gepäckträger m; (doorkeeper) Pförtner m; (US: Rail) Schlafwagenschaffner(in) m(f)
portfolio [pɔːt'fəʊlɪəʊ] n (case) Aktenmappe f; (Pol) Geschäftsbereich m; (Fin) Portefeuille nt; (of artist) Kollektion f
porthole ['pɔːthəʊl] n Bullauge nt
portico ['pɔːtɪkəʊ] n Säulenhalle f
portion ['pɔːʃən] n (part) Teil m; (helping of food) Portion f
portly ['pɔːtlɪ] adj beleibt, korpulent
portrait ['pɔːtreɪt] n Porträt nt
portray [pɔː'treɪ] vt darstellen
portrayal [pɔː'treɪəl] n Darstellung f
Portugal ['pɔːtjʊgl] n Portugal nt
Portuguese [pɔːtjʊ'giːz] adj portugiesisch ▷ n inv (person) Portugiese m, Portugiesin f; (Ling) Portugiesisch nt
Portuguese man-of-war [-mænəv'wɔː'] n (Zool) Röhrenqualle f, Portugiesische Galeere f
pose [pəʊz] n Pose f ▷ vt (question, problem) aufwerfen; (danger) mit sich bringen ▷ vi: ~ as (pretend) sich ausgeben als; to strike a ~ sich in Positur werfen; to ~ for (painting etc) Modell sitzen für, posieren für
poser ['pəʊzə'] n (problem, puzzle) harte Nuss f (inf); (person) = poseur
poseur [pəʊ'zɜː'] (pej) n Angeber(in) m(f)
posh [pɔʃ] (inf) adj vornehm; to talk ~ vornehm daherreden
position [pə'zɪʃən] n (place: of thing, person) Position f, Lage f; (of person's body) Stellung f; (job) Stelle f; (in race etc) Platz m; (attitude) Haltung f, Standpunkt m; (situation) Lage f ▷ vt (person, thing) stellen; to be in a ~ to do sth in der Lage sein, etw zu tun
positive ['pɔzɪtɪv] adj positiv; (certain) sicher; (decisive: action, policy) konstruktiv
positively ['pɔzɪtɪvlɪ] adv (emphatic: rude, stupid etc) eindeutig; (encouragingly, Elec) positiv; the body has been ~ identified die Leiche ist eindeutig identifiziert worden
posse ['pɔsɪ] (US) n (Polizei)truppe f
possess [pə'zɛs] vt besitzen; (subj: feeling, belief) Besitz ergreifen von; like a man ~ed wie besessen; whatever ~ed you to do it? was ist in dich gefahren, das zu tun?
possession [pə'zɛʃən] n Besitz m; possessions npl (belongings) Besitz m; to take ~ of Besitz ergreifen von
possessive [pə'zɛsɪv] adj (nature etc) besitzergreifend; (Ling: pronoun) Possessiv-; (: adjective) besitzanzeigend; to be ~ about sb/sth Besitzansprüche an jdn/etw acc stellen
possessiveness [pə'zɛsɪvnɪs] n besitzergreifende Art f
possessor [pə'zɛsə'] n Besitzer(in) m(f)
possibility [pɔsɪ'bɪlɪtɪ] n Möglichkeit f
possible ['pɔsɪbl] adj möglich; it's ~ (maybe

true) es ist möglich, es kann sein; it's ~ to do it es ist machbar or zu machen; as far as ~ so weit wie möglich; if ~ falls or wenn möglich; as soon as ~ so bald wie möglich
possibly ['pɔsɪblɪ] adv (perhaps) möglicherweise, vielleicht; (conceivably) überhaupt; if you ~ can falls überhaupt möglich; what could they ~ want? was um alles in der Welt wollen sie?; I cannot ~ come ich kann auf keinen Fall kommen
post [pəʊst] n (Brit) Post f; (pole, goal post) Pfosten m; (job) Stelle f; (Mil) Posten m; (also: trading post) Handelsniederlassung f; (on internet forum) Posting n ▷ vt (Brit: letter) aufgeben; (Mil) aufstellen; (to internet) posten; by ~ (Brit) per Post; by return of ~ (Brit) postwendend, umgehend; to keep sb ~ed (informed) jdn auf dem Laufenden halten; to ~ sb to (town, country) jdn versetzen nach; (embassy, office) jdn versetzen zu; (Mil) jdn abkommandieren nach
  ▶ **post up** vt anschlagen
post ... [pəʊst] pref Post-, post-; **~-1990** nach 1990
postage ['pəʊstɪdʒ] n Porto nt
postage stamp n Briefmarke f
postal ['pəʊstl] adj (charges, service) Post-
postal order (Brit) n Postanweisung f
postbag ['pəʊstbæg] (Brit) n Postsack m; (letters) Posteingang m
postbox ['pəʊstbɔks] n Briefkasten m
postcard ['pəʊstkɑːd] n Postkarte f
postcode ['pəʊstkəʊd] (Brit) n Postleitzahl f
postdate ['pəʊst'deɪt] vt (cheque) vordatieren
poster ['pəʊstə'] n Poster nt, Plakat nt
poste restante [pəʊst'rɛstɑːnt] (Brit) n Stelle f für postlagernde Sendungen ▷ adv postlagernd
posterior [pɔs'tɪərɪə'] (hum) n Allerwerteste(r) m
posterity [pɔs'tɛrɪtɪ] n die Nachwelt
poster paint n Plakatfarbe f
post exchange (US) n (Mil) Laden für US-Militärpersonal
post-free [pəʊst'friː] (Brit) adj, adv portofrei
postgraduate ['pəʊst'grædjuət] n Graduierte(r) f(m) (im Weiterstudium)
posthumous ['pɔstjuməs] adj posthum
posthumously ['pɔstjuməslɪ] adv posthum
posting ['pəʊstɪŋ] n (job) Stelle f
postman ['pəʊstmən] (irreg: like man) n Briefträger m, Postbote m
postmark ['pəʊstmɑːk] n Poststempel m
postmaster ['pəʊstmɑːstə'] n Postmeister m
Postmaster General n ≈ Postminister(in) m(f)
postmistress ['pəʊstmɪstrɪs] n Postmeisterin f
postmortem [pəʊst'mɔːtəm] n (Med) Obduktion f; (fig) nachträgliche Erörterung f
postnatal ['pəʊst'neɪtl] adj nach der Geburt, postnatal
post office n (building) Post f, Postamt nt; the Post Office (organization) die Post
Post Office Box n Postfach nt

post-paid ['pəʊst'peɪd] *adj, adv* = **post-free**

postpone [pəʊs'pəʊn] *vt* verschieben

postponement [pəʊs'pəʊnmənt] *n* Aufschub *m*

postscript ['pəʊstskrɪpt] *n* (*to letter*) Nachschrift *f*, PS *nt*

postulate ['pɔstjʊleɪt] *vt* ausgehen von, postulieren

posture ['pɔstʃəʳ] *n* (*also fig*) Haltung *f* ▷ *vi* (*pej*) posieren

postwar [pəʊst'wɔːʳ] *adj* Nachkriegs-

posy ['pəʊzɪ] *n* Blumensträußchen *nt*

pot [pɔt] *n* Topf *m*; (*teapot, coffee pot, potful*) Kanne *f*; (*inf: marijuana*) Pot *nt* ▷ *vt* (*plant*) eintopfen; **to go to ~** (*inf*) auf den Hund kommen; **~s of** (*Brit: inf*) jede Menge

potash ['pɔtæʃ] *n* Pottasche *f*

potassium [pə'tæsɪəm] *n* Kalium *nt*

potato [pə'teɪtəʊ] (*pl* **-es**) *n* Kartoffel *f*

potato chips (US) *npl* = **potato crisps**

potato crisps *npl* Kartoffelchips *pl*

potato flour *n* Kartoffelmehl *nt*

potato peeler *n* Kartoffelschäler *m*

potbellied ['pɔtbɛlɪd] *adj* (*from overeating*) dickbäuchig; (*from malnutrition*) blähbäuchig

potency ['pəʊtnsɪ] *n* (*sexual*) Potenz *f*; (*of drink, drug*) Stärke *f*

potent ['pəʊtnt] *adj* (*powerful*) stark; (*sexually*) potent

potentate ['pəʊtnteɪt] *n* Machthaber *m*, Potentat *m*

potential [pə'tenʃl] *adj* potenziell ▷ *n* Potenzial *nt*; **to have ~** (*person, machine*) Fähigkeiten or Potenzial haben; (*idea, plan*) ausbaufähig sein

potentially [pə'tenʃəlɪ] *adv* potentziell; **it's ~ dangerous** es könnte gefährlich sein

pothole ['pɔthəʊl] *n* (*in road*) Schlagloch *nt*; (*cave*) Höhle *f*

potholing ['pɔthəʊlɪŋ] (*Brit*) *n*: **to go ~** Höhlenforschung betreiben

potion ['pəʊʃən] *n* Elixier *nt*

potluck [pɔt'lʌk] *n*: **to take ~** sich überraschen lassen

potpourri [pəʊ'pʊriː] *n* (*dried petals*) Duftsträußchen *nt*; (*fig*) Sammelsurium *nt*

pot roast *n* Schmorbraten *m*

pot shot *n*: **to take a ~ at** aufs Geratewohl schießen auf +*acc*

potted ['pɔtɪd] *adj* (*food*) eingemacht; (*plant*) Topf-; (*abbreviated: history etc*) Kurz-, kurz gefasst

potter ['pɔtəʳ] *n* Töpfer(in) *m(f)* ▷ *vi*: **to ~ around**, **~ about** (*Brit*) herumhantieren; **to ~ around the house** im Haus herumwerkeln

potter's wheel *n* Töpferscheibe *f*

pottery ['pɔtərɪ] *n* (*pots, dishes etc*) Keramik *f*, Töpferwaren *pl*; (*work, hobby*) Töpfern *nt*; (*factory, workshop*) Töpferei *f*; **a piece of ~** ein Töpferstück *nt*

potty ['pɔtɪ] *adj* (*inf: mad*) verrückt ▷ *n* (*for child*) Töpfchen *nt*

potty-training ['pɔtɪtreɪnɪŋ] *n* Entwöhnung *f* vom Windeltragen

pouch [paʊtʃ] *n* Beutel *m* (*also Zool*)

pouf, pouffe [puːf] *n* (*stool*) gepolsterter Hocker *m*

poultice ['pəʊltɪs] *n* Umschlag *m*

poultry ['pəʊltrɪ] *n* Geflügel *nt*

poultry farm *n* Geflügelfarm *f*

poultry farmer *n* Geflügelzüchter(in) *m(f)*

pounce [paʊns] *vi*: **to ~ on** (*also fig*) sich stürzen auf +*acc*

pound [paʊnd] *n* (*unit of money*) Pfund *nt*; (*unit of weight*) (britisches) Pfund (= 453,6g); (*for dogs*) Zwinger *m*; (*for cars*) Abholstelle *f* (*für abgeschleppte Fahrzeuge*) ▷ *vt* (*beat: table, wall etc*) herumhämmern auf +*dat*; (*crush: grain, spice etc*) zerstoßen; (*bombard*) beschießen ▷ *vi* (*heart*) klopfen, pochen; (*head*) dröhnen; **half a ~ of butter** ein halbes Pfund Butter; **a five-~ note** ein Fünfpfundschein *m*

pounding ['paʊndɪŋ] *n*: **to take a ~** (*fig*) schwer angegriffen werden; (*team*) eine Schlappe einstecken müssen

pound sterling *n* Pfund Sterling

pour [pɔːʳ] *vt* (*tea, wine etc*) gießen; (*cereal etc*) schütten ▷ *vi* strömen; **to ~ sb a glass of wine/a cup of tea** jdm ein Glas Wein/eine Tasse Tee einschenken; **to ~ with rain** in Strömen gießen

▶ **pour away** *vt* wegschütten

▶ **pour in** *vi* (*people*) hereinströmen; (*letters etc*) massenweise eintreffen

▶ **pour out** *vi* (*people*) herausströmen ▷ *vt* (*tea, wine etc*) eingießen; (*fig: thoughts, feelings, etc*) freien Lauf lassen +*dat*

pouring ['pɔːrɪŋ] *adj*: **~ rain** strömender Regen *m*

pout [paʊt] *vi* einen Schmollmund ziehen

poverty ['pɔvətɪ] *n* Armut *f*

poverty line *n* Armutsgrenze *f*

poverty risk *n* Armutsrisiko *f*

poverty-stricken ['pɔvətɪstrɪkn] *adj* verarmt, Not leidend

poverty trap (*Brit*) *n* gleichbleibend schlechte wirtschaftliche Situation aufgrund des Wegfalls von Sozialleistungen bei verbessertem Einkommen, Armutsfalle *f*

POW *n abbr* = **prisoner of war**

powder ['paʊdəʳ] *n* Pulver *nt* ▷ *vt*: **to ~ one's face** sich *dat* das Gesicht pudern; **to ~ one's nose** (*euph*) kurz mal verschwinden

powder compact *n* Puderdose *f*

powdered milk ['paʊdəd-] *n* Milchpulver *nt*

powder keg *n* (*also fig*) Pulverfass *nt*

powder puff *n* Puderquaste *f*

powder room (*euph*) *n* Damentoilette *f*

power ['paʊəʳ] *n* (*control, legal right*) Macht *f*; (*ability*) Fähigkeit *f*; (*of muscles, ideas, words*) Kraft *f*; (*of explosion, engine*) Gewalt *f*; (*electricity*) Strom *m*; **2 to the ~ (of) 3** (*Math*) 2 hoch 3; **to do everything in one's ~ to help** alles in seiner Macht Stehende tun, um zu helfen; **a world ~** eine Weltmacht; **the ~s that be** (*authority*) diejenigen, die das Sagen haben; **~ of attorney** Vollmacht *f*; **to be in ~** (*Pol etc*) an

p

715

der Macht sein

powerboat ['pauəbəut] *n* schnelles Motorboot *nt*, Rennboot *nt*

power cut *n* Stromausfall *m*

powered ['pauəd] *adj*: ~ **by** angetrieben von; **nuclear-~ submarine** atomgetriebenes U-Boot

power failure *n* Stromausfall *m*

powerful ['pauəful] *adj* (*person, organization*) mächtig; (*body, voice, blow etc*) kräftig; (*engine*) stark; (*unpleasant: smell*) streng; (*emotion*) überwältigend; (*argument, evidence*) massiv

powerhouse ['pauəhaus] *n*: **he is a ~ of ideas** er hat ständig neue Ideen

powerless ['pauəlis] *adj* machtlos; **to be ~ to do sth** nicht die Macht haben, etw zu tun

power line *n* Stromkabel *nt*

power point (*Brit*) *n* Steckdose *f*

power station *n* Kraftwerk *nt*

power steering *n* (*Aut*) Servolenkung *f*

powwow ['pauwau] *n* Besprechung *f*

pp *abbr* (= *per procurationem*) ppa.

pp. *abbr* (= *pages*) S.

PPE (*Brit*) *n abbr* (*Univ*: = *philosophy, politics, and economics*) *Studiengang bestehend aus Philosophie, Politologie und Volkswirtschaft*

PPS *n abbr* (= *post postscriptum*) PPS; (*Brit*: = *parliamentary private secretary*) Privatsekretär eines Ministers

PQ (*Canada*) *abbr* (= *Province of Quebec*)

PR *n abbr* = **public relations**; (*Pol*) = **proportional representation** ▷ *abbr* (*US: Post*) = *Puerto Rico*

Pr. *abbr* = **prince**

practicability [præktɪkə'bɪlɪtɪ] *n* Durchführbarkeit *f*

practicable ['præktɪkəbl] *adj* (*scheme, idea*) durchführbar

practical ['præktɪkl] *adj* praktisch; (*person: good with hands*) praktisch veranlagt; (*ideas, methods*) praktikabel

practicality [præktɪ'kælɪtɪ] *n* (*of person*) praktische Veranlagung *f*; **practicalities** *npl* (*of situation etc*) praktische Einzelheiten *pl*

practical joke *n* Streich *m*

practically ['præktɪklɪ] *adv* praktisch

practice ['præktɪs] *n* (*also Med, Law*) Praxis *f*; (*custom*) Brauch *m*; (*exercise*) Übung *f* ▷ *vt, vi* (*US*) = **practise**; **in ~** in der Praxis; **out of ~** aus der Übung; **2 hours' piano ~** 2 Stunden Klavierübungen; **it's common** *or* **standard ~** es ist allgemein üblich; **to put sth into ~** etw in die Praxis umsetzen; **target ~** Zielschießen *nt*

practice match *n* Übungsspiel *nt*

practise, (*US*) **practice** ['præktɪs] *vt* (*train at*) üben; (*carry out: custom*) pflegen; (: *activity etc*) ausüben; (*profession*) praktizieren ▷ *vi* (*train*) üben; (*lawyer, doctor etc*) praktizieren

practised ['præktɪst] (*Brit*) *adj* (*person, liar*) geübt; (*performance*) gekonnt; **with a ~ eye** mit geschultem Auge

practising ['præktɪsɪŋ] *adj* praktizierend

practitioner [præk'tɪʃənə^r] *n*: **medical ~**

praktischer Arzt *m*, praktische Ärztin *f*; **legal ~** Rechtsanwalt *m*, Rechtsanwältin *f*

pragmatic [præg'mætɪk] *adj* pragmatisch

pragmatism ['prægmətɪzəm] *n* Pragmatismus *m*

Prague [prɑːg] *n* Prag *nt*

prairie ['prɛərɪ] *n* (*Gras*)steppe *f*; **the ~s** (*US*) die Prärien

praise [preɪz] *n* Lob *nt* ▷ *vt* loben; (*Rel*) loben, preisen

praiseworthy ['preɪzwəːðɪ] *adj* lobenswert

pram [præm] (*Brit*) *n* Kinderwagen *m*

prance [prɑːns] *vi* (*horse*) tänzeln; **to ~ about/in/out** (*person*) herum-/hinein-/hinausstolzieren

prank [præŋk] *n* Streich *m*

prat [præt] (*Brit: inf*) *n* (*idiot*) Trottel *m*

prattle ['prætl] *vi*: **to ~ on (about)** pausenlos plappern (über +*acc*)

prawn [prɔːn] *n* (*Culin, Zool*) Garnele *f*, Krabbe *f*; **~ cocktail** Krabbencocktail *m*

pray [preɪ] *vi* beten; **to ~ for sb/sth** (*Rel, fig*) für jdn/um etw beten

prayer [prɛə^r] *n* Gebet *nt*; **to say one's ~s** beten

prayer book *n* Gebetbuch *nt*

pre ... [priː] *pref* Prä-, prä-; **~-1970** vor 1970

preach [priːtʃ] *vi* (*Rel*) predigen; (*pej: moralize*) Predigten halten ▷ *vt* (*sermon*) direkt halten; (*fig: advocate*) predigen, verkünden; **to ~ at sb** (*fig*) jdm Moralpredigten halten; **to ~ to the converted** (*fig*) offene Türen einrennen

preacher ['priːtʃə^r] *n* Prediger(in) *m(f)*

preamble [prɪ'æmbl] *n* Vorbemerkung *f*

prearranged [priːə'reɪndʒd] *adj* (vorher) vereinbart

precarious [prɪ'kɛərɪəs] *adj* prekär

precaution [prɪ'kɔːʃən] *n* Vorsichtsmaßnahme *f*; **to take ~s** Vorsichtsmaßnahmen treffen

precautionary [prɪ'kɔːʃənrɪ] *adj* (*measure*) vorbeugend, Vorsichts-

precede [prɪ'siːd] *vt* (*event*) vorausgehen +*dat*; (*person*) vorangehen +*dat*; (*words, sentences*) vorangestellt sein +*dat*

precedence ['presɪdəns] *n* (*priority*) Vorrang *m*; **to take ~ over** Vorrang haben vor +*dat*

precedent ['presɪdənt] *n* (*Law*) Präzedenzfall *m*; **without ~** noch nie da gewesen; **to establish** *or* **set a ~** einen Präzedenzfall schaffen

preceding [prɪ'siːdɪŋ] *adj* vorhergehend

precept ['priːsɛpt] *n* Grundsatz *m*, Regel *f*

precinct ['priːsɪŋkt] *n* (*US: part of city*) Bezirk *m*; **precincts** *npl* (*of cathedral, palace*) Gelände *nt*; **shopping ~** (*Brit*) Einkaufsviertel *nt*; (*under cover*) Einkaufscenter *nt*

precious ['prɛʃəs] *adj* wertvoll, kostbar; (*pej: person, writing*) geziert; (*ironic: damned*) heiß geliebt, wundervoll ▷ *adv* (*inf*): **~ little/few** herzlich wenig/wenige

precious stone *n* Edelstein *m*

precipice ['prɛsɪpɪs] *n* (*also fig*) Abgrund *m*

precipitate [*vt* prɪ'sɪpɪteɪt, *adj* prɪ'sɪpɪtɪt] *vt* (*event*) heraufbeschwören ▷ *adj* (*hasty*) überstürzt, übereilt

precipitation [prɪsɪpɪ'teɪʃən] n (rain) Niederschlag m

precipitous [prɪ'sɪpɪtəs] adj (steep) steil; (hasty) übereilt

précis ['preɪsiː] n inv Zusammenfassung f

precise [prɪ'saɪs] adj genau, präzise; **at 4 o'clock to be ~** um 4 Uhr, um genau zu sein

precisely [prɪ'saɪslɪ] adv genau, exakt; (emphatic) ganz genau; **~!** genau!

precision [prɪ'sɪʒən] n Genauigkeit f, Präzision f

preclude [prɪ'kluːd] vt ausschließen; **to ~ sb from doing sth** jdn daran hindern, etw zu tun

precocious [prɪ'kəʊʃəs] adj (child, behaviour) frühreif

preconceived [priːkən'siːvd] adj (idea) vorgefasst

preconception ['priːkən'sepʃən] n vorgefasste Meinung f

precondition ['priːkən'dɪʃən] n Vorbedingung f

precursor [priː'kɜːsə'] n Vorläufer m

predate ['priː'deɪt] vt (precede) vorausgehen +dat

predator ['predətə'] n (Zool) Raubtier nt; (fig) Eindringling m

predatory ['predətərɪ] adj (animal) Raub-; (person, organization) auf Beute lauernd

predecessor ['priːdɪsesə'] n Vorgänger(in) m(f)

predestination [priːdestɪ'neɪʃən] n Vorherbestimmung f

predetermine [priːdɪ'tɜːmɪn] vt vorherbestimmen

predicament [prɪ'dɪkəmənt] n Notlage f, Dilemma nt; **to be in a ~** in einer Notlage or einem Dilemma stecken

predicate ['predɪkɪt] n (Ling) Prädikat nt

predict [prɪ'dɪkt] vt vorhersagen

predictable [prɪ'dɪktəbl] adj vorhersagbar

predictably [prɪ'dɪktəblɪ] adv (behave, react) wie vorherzusehen; **~ she didn't come** wie vorherzusehen war, kam sie nicht

prediction [prɪ'dɪkʃən] n Voraussage f

predispose ['priːdɪs'pəʊz] vt: **to ~ sb to sth** jdn zu etw veranlassen; **to be ~d to do sth** geneigt sein, etw zu tun

predominance [prɪ'dɒmɪnəns] n Vorherrschaft f

predominant [prɪ'dɒmɪnənt] adj vorherrschend; **to become ~** vorherrschend werden

predominantly [prɪ'dɒmɪnəntlɪ] adv überwiegend

predominate [prɪ'dɒmɪneɪt] vi (in number, size) vorherrschen; (in strength, influence) überwiegen

pre-eminent [priː'emɪnənt] adj herausragend

pre-empt [priː'emt] vt zuvorkommen +dat

pre-emptive [priː'emtɪv] adj: **~ strike** Präventivschlag m

preen [priːn] vt: **to ~ itself** (bird) sich putzen; **to ~ o.s.** sich herausputzen

prefab ['priːfæb] n Fertighaus nt

prefabricated [priː'fæbrɪkeɪtɪd] adj vorgefertigt

preface ['prefəs] n Vorwort nt ▷ vt: **to ~ with/by** (speech, action) einleiten mit/durch

prefect ['priːfekt] (Brit) n (in school) Aufsichtsschüler(in) m(f)

prefer [prɪ'fɜː'] vt (like better) vorziehen; **to ~ charges** (Law) Anklage erheben; **to ~ doing** or **to do sth** (es) vorziehen, etw zu tun; **I ~ tea to coffee** ich mag lieber Tee als Kaffee

preferable ['prefrəbl] adj: **to be ~ (to)** vorzuziehen sein (+dat)

preferably ['prefrəblɪ] adv vorzugsweise, am besten

preference ['prefrəns] n: **to have a ~ for** (liking) eine Vorliebe haben für; **I drink beer in ~ to wine** ich trinke lieber Bier als Wein; **to give ~ to** (priority) vorziehen, Vorrang einräumen +dat

preference shares (Brit) npl (Comm) Vorzugsaktien pl

preferential [prefə'renʃəl] adj: **~ treatment** bevorzugte Behandlung f; **to give sb ~ treatment** jdn bevorzugt behandeln

preferred stock [prɪ'fɜːd-] (US) npl = **preference shares**

prefix ['priːfɪks] n (Ling) Präfix nt

pregnancy ['pregnənsɪ] n (of woman) Schwangerschaft f; (of female animal) Trächtigkeit f

pregnancy test n Schwangerschaftstest m

pregnant ['pregnənt] adj (woman) schwanger; (female animal) trächtig; (fig: pause, remark) bedeutungsschwer; **3 months ~** im vierten Monat (schwanger)

prehistoric [priːhɪs'tɒrɪk] adj prähistorisch, vorgeschichtlich

prehistory [priː'hɪstərɪ] n Vorgeschichte f

prejudge [priː'dʒʌdʒ] vt vorschnell beurteilen

prejudice ['predʒʊdɪs] n (bias against) Vorurteil nt; (bias in favour) Voreingenommenheit f ▷ vt beeinträchtigen; **without ~ to** (form) unbeschadet +gen, ohne Beeinträchtigung +gen; **to ~ sb in favour of/against sth** jdn für/gegen etw einnehmen

prejudiced ['predʒʊdɪst] adj (person, view) voreingenommen

prelate ['prelət] n Prälat m

preliminaries [prɪ'lɪmɪnərɪz] npl Vorbereitungen pl; (of competition) Vorrunde f

preliminary [prɪ'lɪmɪnərɪ] adj (step, arrangements) vorbereitend; (remarks) einleitend

pre-loaded [prɪ'ləʊdɪd] adj (Comput: program etc) vorinstalliert

prelude ['preljuːd] n (Mus) Präludium nt; (: as introduction) Vorspiel nt; **a ~ to** (fig) ein Vorspiel or ein Auftakt zu

premarital ['priː'mærɪtl] adj vorehelich

premature ['premətʃʊə'] adj (earlier than expected) vorzeitig; (too early) verfrüht; **you are being a little ~** Sie sind etwas voreilig; **~ baby** Frühgeburt f

premeditated [priː'medɪteɪtɪd] adj vorsätzlich

premeditation [priːmedɪ'teɪʃən] n Vorsatz m

premenstrual tension [pri:'mɛnstruəl-] *n*
prämenstruelles Syndrom *nt*
premier ['prɛmɪəʳ] *adj* (*best*) beste(r,
s), bedeutendste(r, s) ▷ *n* (*Pol*)
Premierminister(in) *m(f)*
premiere ['prɛmɪəʳ] *n* Premiere *f*
premise ['prɛmɪs] *n* (*of argument*)
Voraussetzung *f*; **premises** *npl* (*of business etc*)
Räumlichkeiten *pl*; **on the ~s** im Hause
premium ['pri:mɪəm] *n* (*Comm, Insurance*)
Prämie *f*; **to be at a ~** (*expensive*) zum
Höchstpreis gehandelt werden; (*hard to get*)
Mangelware sein
premium bond (*Brit*) *n* Prämienanleihe *f*; *siehe*
Info-Artikel

 PREMIUM BONDS

Premium bonds, eigentlich *premium savings
bonds*, sind Lotterieaktien, die seit 1956
vom britischen Finanzministerium
ausgegeben werden und keine Zinsen
bringen, sondern stattdessen an einer
monatlichen Auslosung teilnehmen. Die
Gewinnnummern für die verschiedenen
Geldpreise werden in Blackpool von einem
Computer namens „ERNIE" (Electronic
Random Number Indicator Equipment)
ermittelt.

premium gasoline (*US*) *n* Super(benzin) *nt*
premonition [prɛmə'nɪʃən] *n* Vorahnung *f*
preoccupation [pri:ɔkju'peɪʃən] *n*: **~ with**
(*vorrangige*) Beschäftigung mit
preoccupied [pri:'ɔkjupaɪd] *adj* (*thoughtful*)
gedankenverloren; (*with work, family*)
beschäftigt
prep [prɛp] (*Scol*) *adj* (= *preparatory*) *see*
prep school ▷ *n* (= *preparation*) Hausaufgaben
pl
prepaid [pri:'peɪd] *adj* (*paid in advance*) im Voraus
bezahlt; (*envelope*) frankiert
preparation [prɛpə'reɪʃən] *n* Vorbereitung
f; (*food, medicine, cosmetic*) Zubereitung *f*;
preparations *npl* Vorbereitungen *pl*; **in ~ for
sth** als Vorbereitung für etw
preparatory [prɪ'pærətərɪ] *adj* vorbereitend;
~ to sth/to doing sth als Vorbereitung für
etw/, um etw zu tun
prepare [prɪ'peəʳ] *vt* vorbereiten; (*food, meal*)
zubereiten ▷ *vi*: **to ~ for** sich vorbereiten auf
+*acc*
prepared [prɪ'peəd] *adj*: **to be ~ to do sth**
(*willing*) bereit sein, etw zu tun; **to be ~ for sth**
(*ready*) auf etw *acc* vorbereitet sein
preponderance [prɪ'pɔndərns] *n* Übergewicht
nt
preposition [prɛpə'zɪʃən] *n* Präposition *f*
prepossessing [pri:pə'zɛsɪŋ] *adj* von
angenehmer Erscheinung
preposterous [prɪ'pɔstərəs] *adj* grotesk,
widersinnig
prep school *n* = **prep(aratory) school**; *siehe*

 PREP(ARATORY) SCHOOL

Prep(aratory) school ist in Großbritannien
eine meist private Schule für Kinder
im Alter von 7 bis 13 Jahren, die auf eine
weiterführende Privatschule vorbereiten
soll.

prerecorded ['pri:rɪ'kɔ:dɪd] *adj* (*broadcast*)
aufgezeichnet; (*cassette, video*) bespielt
prerequisite [pri:'rɛkwɪzɪt] *n* Vorbedingung *f*,
Grundvoraussetzung *f*
prerogative [prɪ'rɔgətɪv] *n* Vorrecht *nt*,
Privileg *nt*
Presbyterian [prɛzbɪ'tɪərɪən] *adj*
presbyterianisch ▷ *n* Presbyterianer(in) *m(f)*
presbytery ['prɛzbɪtərɪ] *n* Pfarrhaus *nt*
preschool ['pri:'sku:l] *adj* (*age, child, education*)
Vorschul-
prescribe [prɪ'skraɪb] *vt* (*Med*) verschreiben;
(*demand*) anordnen, vorschreiben
prescribed *adj* (*duties, period*) vorgeschrieben
prescription [prɪ'skrɪpʃən] *n* (*Med: slip of
paper*) Rezept *nt*; (: *medicine*) Medikament
nt; **to make up a ~, to fill a ~** (*US*) ein
Medikament zubereiten; **"only available on
~"** „rezeptpflichtig"
prescription charges (*Brit*) *npl* Rezeptgebühr *f*
prescriptive [prɪ'skrɪptɪv] *adj* normativ
presence ['prɛzns] *n* Gegenwart *f*,
Anwesenheit *f*; (*fig: personality*) Ausstrahlung *f*;
(*spirit, invisible being*) Erscheinung *f*; **in sb's
~** in jds *dat* Gegenwart *or* Beisein; **~ of mind**
Geistesgegenwart *f*
present [*adj, n* 'prɛznt, *vt* prɪ'zɛnt] *adj* (*current*)
gegenwärtig, derzeitig; (*in attendance*)
anwesend ▷ *n* (*gift*) Geschenk *nt*; (*Ling: also:*
present tense) Präsens *nt*, Gegenwart *f* ▷ *vt*
(*give: prize etc*) überreichen; (*plan, report*)
vorlegen; (*cause, provide, portray*) darstellen;
(*information, view*) darlegen; (*Radio, TV*) leiten;
to be ~ at anwesend *or* zugegen sein bei;
those ~ die Anwesenden; **to give sb a ~**
jdm ein Geschenk geben; **the ~** (*actuality*)
die Gegenwart; **at ~** gegenwärtig, im
Augenblick; **to ~ sth to sb, ~ sb with sth**
jdm etw übergeben *or* überreichen; **to ~ sb
(to)** (*formally: introduce*) jdn vorstellen +*dat*; **to ~
itself** (*opportunity*) sich bieten
presentable [prɪ'zɛntəbl] *adj* (*person*)
präsentabel, ansehnlich
presentation [prɛzn'teɪʃən] *n* (*of prize*)
Überreichung *f*; (*of plan, report etc*) Vorlage *f*;
(*appearance*) Erscheinungsbild *nt*; (*talk*) Vortrag
m; **on ~ of** (*voucher etc*) gegen Vorlage +*gen*
present-day ['prɛzntdeɪ] *adj* heutig,
gegenwärtig
presenter [prɪ'zɛntəʳ] *n* (*on radio, TV*)
Moderator(in) *m(f)*
presently ['prɛzntlɪ] *adv* (*soon after*) gleich
darauf; (*soon*) bald, in Kürze; (*currently*) derzeit,

gegenwärtig

present participle n Partizip nt Präsens

preservation [prezə'veɪʃən] n (of peace, standards etc) Erhaltung f; (of furniture, building) Konservierung f

preservative [prɪ'zə:vətɪv] n Konservierungsmittel nt

preserve [prɪ'zə:v] vt erhalten; (peace) wahren; (wood) schützen; (food) konservieren ▷ n (often pl: jam, chutney etc) Eingemachte(s) nt; (for game, fish) Revier nt; **a male ~** (fig) eine männliche Domäne; **a working class ~** (fig) eine Domäne der Arbeiterklasse

preshrunk ['pri:'ʃrʌŋk] adj (jeans etc) vorgewaschen

preside [prɪ'zaɪd] vi: **to ~ over** (meeting etc) vorsitzen +dat, den Vorsitz haben bei

presidency ['prezɪdənsɪ] n (Pol) Präsidentschaft f; (US: of company) Vorsitz m

president ['prezɪdənt] n (Pol) Präsident(in) m(f); (of organization) Vorsitzende(r) f(m)

presidential [prezɪ'denʃl] adj (election, campaign etc) Präsidentschafts-; (adviser, representative etc) des Präsidenten

press [pres] n (also: **printing press**) Presse f; (of switch, bell) Druck m; (for wine) Kelter f ▷ vt drücken, pressen; (button, sb's hand etc) drücken; (iron: clothes) bügeln; (put pressure on: person) drängen; (pursue: idea, claim) vertreten ▷ vi (squeeze) drücken, pressen; **the P~** (newspapers, journalists) die Presse; **to go to ~** (newspaper) in Druck gehen; **to be in ~** (at the printer's) im Druck sein; **to be in the ~** (in the newspapers) in der Zeitung stehen; **at the ~ of a button** auf Knopfdruck; **to ~ sth (up) on sb** (force) jdm etw aufdrängen; **we are ~ed for time/money** wir sind in Geldnot/Zeitnot; **to ~ sb for an answer** auf jds acc Antwort drängen; **to ~ sb to do or into doing sth** jdn drängen, etw zu tun; **to ~ charges (against sb)** (Law) Klage (gegen jdn) erheben; **to ~ for** (changes etc) drängen auf +acc

▶ **press ahead** vi weitermachen; **to ~ ahead with sth** etw durchziehen

▶ **press on** vi weitermachen

press agency n Presseagentur f

press clipping n Zeitungsausschnitt m

press conference n Pressekonferenz f

press cutting n = **press clipping**

press-gang ['presgæŋ] vt: **to ~ sb into doing sth** jdn bedrängen, etw zu tun

pressing ['presɪŋ] adj (urgent) dringend

press officer n Pressesprecher(in) m(f)

press release n Pressemitteilung f

press stud (Brit) n Druckknopf m

press-up ['presʌp] (Brit) n Liegestütz m

pressure ['preʃə'] n (also fig) Druck m ▷ vt: **to ~ sb to do sth** jdn dazu drängen, etw zu tun; **to put ~ on sb (to do sth)** Druck auf jdn ausüben(, etw zu tun); **high/low ~** (Tech, Met) Hoch-/Tiefdruck m

pressure cooker n Schnellkochtopf m

pressure gauge n Druckmesser m, Manometer nt

pressure group n Interessenverband m, Pressuregroup f

pressurize ['preʃəraɪz] vt: **to ~ sb (to do sth** or **into doing sth)** jdn unter Druck setzen(, etw zu tun)

pressurized ['preʃəraɪzd] adj (cabin, container etc) Druck-

Prestel® ['prestel] n ≈ Bildschirmtext m, Btx nt

prestige [pres'ti:ʒ] n Prestige nt

prestigious [pres'tɪdʒəs] adj (institution, appointment) mit hohem Prestigewert

presumably [prɪ'zju:məblɪ] adv vermutlich; **~ he did it** vermutlich or wahrscheinlich hat er es getan

presume [prɪ'zju:m] vt: **to ~ (that)** (assume) annehmen(, dass); **to ~ to do sth** (dare) sich anmaßen, etw zu tun; **I ~ so** das nehme ich an

presumption [prɪ'zʌmpʃən] n (supposition) Annahme f; (audacity) Anmaßung f

presumptuous [prɪ'zʌmpʃəs] adj anmaßend

presuppose [pri:sə'pəuz] vt voraussetzen

presupposition [pri:sʌpə'zɪʃən] n Voraussetzung f

pretax [pri:'tæks] adj (profit) vor (Abzug der) Steuern

pretence, (US) **pretense** [prɪ'tens] n (false appearance) Vortäuschung f; **under false ~s** unter Vorspiegelung falscher Tatsachen; **she is devoid of all ~** sie ist völlig natürlich; **to make a ~ of doing sth** vortäuschen, etw zu tun

pretend [prɪ'tend] vt (feign) vorgeben ▷ vi (feign) sich verstellen, so tun, als ob; **I don't ~ to understand it** (claim) ich erhebe nicht den Anspruch, es zu verstehen

pretense [prɪ'tens] (US) n = **pretence**

pretentious [prɪ'tenʃəs] adj anmaßend

preterite ['pretərɪt] n Imperfekt nt, Präteritum nt

pretext ['pri:tekst] n Vorwand m; **on** or **under the ~ of doing sth** unter dem Vorwand, etw zu tun

pretty ['prɪtɪ] adj hübsch, nett ▷ adv: **~ clever** ganz schön schlau; **~ good** ganz gut

prevail [prɪ'veɪl] vi (be current) vorherrschen; (triumph) siegen; **to ~ (up)on sb to do sth** (persuade) jdn dazu bewegen or überreden, etw zu tun

prevailing [prɪ'veɪlɪŋ] adj (wind, fashion etc) vorherrschend

prevalent ['prevələnt] adj (belief, custom) vorherrschend

prevaricate [prɪ'værɪkeɪt] vi (by saying sth) Ausflüchte machen; (by doing sth) Ausweichmanöver machen

prevarication [prɪværɪ'keɪʃən] n (see vi) Ausflucht f; Ausweichmanöver nt

prevent [prɪ'vent] vt verhindern; **to ~ sb from doing sth** jdn daran hindern, etw zu tun; **to ~ sth from happening** verhindern, dass etw geschieht

preventable [prɪ'ventəbl] adj verhütbar,

P

vermeidbar

preventative [prɪˈvɛntətɪv] adj = **preventive**

prevention [prɪˈvɛnʃən] n Verhütung f

preventive [prɪˈvɛntɪv] adj (measures, medicine) vorbeugend

preview [ˈpriːvjuː] n (of film) Vorpremiere f; (of exhibition) Vernissage f

previous [ˈpriːvɪəs] adj (earlier) früher; (preceding) vorhergehend; ~ **to** vor +dat

previously [ˈpriːvɪəslɪ] adv (before) zuvor; (formerly) früher

prewar [priːˈwɔːʳ] adj (period) Vorkriegs-

prey [preɪ] n Beute f; **to fall ~ to** (fig) zum Opfer fallen +dat

▸ **prey on** vt fus (animal) Jagd machen auf +acc; **it was ~ing on his mind** es ließ ihn nicht los

price [praɪs] n (also fig) Preis m ▸ vt (goods) auszeichnen; **what is the ~ of ...?** was kostet ...?; **to go up** or **rise in ~** im Preis steigen, teurer werden; **to put a ~ on sth** (also fig) einen Preis für etw festsetzen; **what ~ his promises now?** wie steht es jetzt mit seinen Versprechungen?; **he regained his freedom, but at a ~** er hat seine Freiheit wieder, aber zu welchem Preis!; **to be ~d at £30** £30 kosten; **to ~ o.s. out of the market** durch zu hohe Preise konkurrenzunfähig werden

price control n Preiskontrolle f

price-cutting [ˈpraɪskʌtɪŋ] n Preissenkungen pl

priceless [ˈpraɪslɪs] adj (diamond, painting) von unschätzbarem Wert; (inf: amusing) unbezahlbar, köstlich

price list n Preisliste f

price range n Preisklasse f; **it's within my ~** ich kann es mir leisten

price tag n Preisschild nt; (fig) Preis m

price war n Preiskrieg m

pricey [ˈpraɪsɪ] (inf) adj kostspielig

prick [prɪk] n (sting) Stich m; (inf!: penis) Schwanz m; (: idiot) Arsch m ▸ vt stechen; (sausage, balloon) einstechen; **to ~ up one's ears** die Ohren spitzen

prickle [ˈprɪkl] n (of plant) Dorn m, Stachel m; (sensation) Prickeln nt

prickly [ˈprɪklɪ] adj (plant) stachelig; (fabric) kratzig

prickly heat n Hitzebläschen pl

prickly pear n Feigenkaktus m

pride [praɪd] n Stolz m; (pej: arrogance) Hochmut m ▸ vt: **to ~ o.s. on** sich rühmen +gen; **to take (a) ~** in stolz sein auf +acc; **to take a ~ in doing sth** etw mit Stolz tun; **to have** or **take ~ of place** (Brit) die Krönung sein

priest [priːst] n Priester m

priestess [ˈpriːstɪs] n Priesterin f

priesthood [ˈpriːsthud] n Priestertum nt

prig [prɪg] n: **he's a ~** er hält sich für ein Tugendlamm

prim [prɪm] (pej) adj (person) etepetete

primacy [ˈpraɪməsɪ] n (supremacy) Vorrang m; (position) Vorrangstellung f

prima-facie [ˈpraɪməˈfeɪʃɪ] adj: **to have a ~**

case (Law) eine gute Beweisgrundlage haben

primal [ˈpraɪməl] adj ursprünglich; **~ scream** Urschrei m

primarily [ˈpraɪmərɪlɪ] adv in erster Linie, hauptsächlich

primary [ˈpraɪmərɪ] adj (principal) Haupt-, hauptsächlich; (education, teacher) Grundschul- ▸ n (US: election) Vorwahl f; siehe Info-Artikel

primary colour n Primärfarbe f

primary school (Brit) n Grundschule f; siehe Info-Artikel

primate [ˈpraɪmɪt] n (Zool) Primat m; (Rel) Primas m

prime [praɪm] adj (most important) oberste(r, s); (best quality) erstklassig ▸ n (of person's life) die besten Jahre pl ▸ vt (wood) grundieren; (fig: person) informieren; (gun) schussbereit machen; (pump) auffüllen; **~ example** erstklassiges Beispiel; **in the ~ of life** im besten Alter

Prime Minister n Premierminister(in) m(f)

primer [ˈpraɪməʳ] n (paint) Grundierung f; (book) Einführung f

prime time n (Radio, TV) Hauptsendezeit f

primeval [praɪˈmiːvl] adj (beast) urzeitlich; (fig: feelings) instinktiv; **~ forest** Urwald m

primitive [ˈprɪmɪtɪv] adj (tribe, tool, conditions etc) primitiv; (life form, machine etc) frühzeitlich; (man) der Urzeit

primrose [ˈprɪmrəuz] n Primel f, gelbe Schlüsselblume f

primula [ˈprɪmjulə] n Primel f

Primus® [ˈpraɪməs], **Primus stove** (Brit) n Primuskocher m

prince [prɪns] n Prinz m

Prince Charming (*hum*) *n* Märchenprinz *m*
princess ['prɪn'ses] *n* Prinzessin *f*
principal ['prɪnsɪpl] *adj* (*most important*) Haupt-,
wichtigste(r, s) ▷ *n* (*of school, college*) Rektor(in)
m(f); (*Theat*) Hauptdarsteller(in) *m(f)*; (*Fin*)
Kapitalsumme *f*
principality [prɪnsɪ'pælɪtɪ] *n* Fürstentum *nt*
principally ['prɪnsɪplɪ] *adv* vornehmlich
principle ['prɪnsɪpl] *n* Prinzip *nt*; **in** ~ im
Prinzip, prinzipiell; **on** ~ aus Prinzip
print [prɪnt] *n* (*Art*) Druck *m*; (*Phot*) Abzug
m; (*fabric*) bedruckter Stoff *m* ▷ *vt* (*produce*)
drucken; (*publish*) veröffentlichen; (*cloth,
pattern*) bedrucken; (*write in capitals*) in
Druckschrift schreiben; **prints** *npl* (*fingerprints
etc*) Abdrücke *pl*; **out of** ~ vergriffen; **in**
~ erhältlich; **the fine** *or* **small** ~ das
Kleingedruckte
 ▶ **print out** *vt* (*Comput*) ausdrucken
printed circuit ['prɪntɪd-] *n* gedruckte
Schaltung *f*
printed circuit board *n* Leiterplatte *f*
printed matter *n* Drucksache *f*
printer ['prɪntə'] *n* (*person*) Drucker(in) *m(f)*;
(*firm*) Druckerei *f*; (*machine*) Drucker *m*
printhead ['prɪnthed] *n* Druckkopf *m*
printing ['prɪntɪŋ] *n* (*activity*) Drucken *nt*
printing press *n* Druckerpresse *f*
print-out ['prɪntaut] (*Comput*) *n* Ausdruck *m*
print run *n* Auflage *f*
printwheel ['prɪntwiːl] *n* (*Comput*) Typenrad *nt*
prior ['praɪə'] *adj* (*previous: knowledge, warning*)
vorherig; (*: engagement*) früher; (*more
important: claim, duty*) vorrangig ▷ *n* (*Rel*)
Prior *m*; **without** ~ **notice** ohne vorherige
Ankündigung; **to have a** ~ **claim on sth** ein
Vorrecht auf etw *acc* haben; ~ **to** vor+*dat*
priority [praɪ'ɒrɪtɪ] *n* vorrangige
Angelegenheit *f*; **priorities** *npl* Prioritäten
pl; **to take** *or* **have** ~ **(over sth)** Vorrang (vor
etw *dat*) haben; **to give** ~ **to sb/sth** jdm/etw
Vorrang einräumen
priory ['praɪərɪ] *n* Kloster *nt*
prise [praɪz] (*Brit*) *vt*: **to** ~ **open** aufbrechen
prism ['prɪzəm] *n* Prisma *nt*
prison ['prɪzn] *n* Gefängnis *nt* ▷ *cpd* (*officer, food,
cell etc*) Gefängnis-
prison camp *n* Gefangenenlager *nt*
prisoner ['prɪznə'] *n* Gefangene(r) *f(m)*; **the** ~
at the bar (*Law*) der/die Angeklagte; **to take
sb** ~ jdn gefangen nehmen
prisoner of war *n* Kriegsgefangene(r) *f(m)*
prissy ['prɪsɪ] (*pej*) *adj* zimperlich
pristine ['prɪstiːn] *adj* makellos; **in** ~
condition in makellosem Zustand
privacy ['prɪvəsɪ] *n* Privatsphäre *f*
private ['praɪvɪt] *adj* privat; (*life*) Privat-;
(*thoughts, plans etc*) persönlich; (*place*)
abgelegen; (*secretive: person*) verschlossen
▷ *n* (*Mil*) Gefreite(r) *m*; "~" (*on envelope*)
„vertraulich"; (*on door*) „privat"; **in** ~ privat;
in (his) ~ **life** in seinem Privatleben; **to be
in** ~ **practice** (*Med*) Privatpatienten haben; ~

hearing (*Law*) nicht öffentliche Verhandlung
f
private enterprise *n* Privatunternehmen *nt*
private eye *n* Privatdetektiv *m*
private limited company (*Brit*) *n* (*Comm*) =
Aktiengesellschaft *f*
privately ['praɪvɪtlɪ] *adv* privat; (*secretly*)
insgeheim; **a** ~ **owned company** eine Firma
im Privatbesitz
private parts *npl* (*Anat*) Geschlechtsteile *pl*
private property *n* Privatbesitz *m*
private school *n* (*fee-paying*) Privatschule *f*
privation [praɪ'veɪʃən] *n* Not *f*
privatize ['praɪvɪtaɪz] *vt* privatisieren
privet ['prɪvɪt] *n* Liguster *m*
privilege ['prɪvɪlɪdʒ] *n* (*advantage*) Privileg *nt*;
(*honour*) Ehre *f*
privileged ['prɪvɪlɪdʒd] *adj* privilegiert; **to be**
~ **to do sth** das Privileg *or* die Ehre haben, etw
zu tun
privy ['prɪvɪ] *adj*: **to be** ~ **to** eingeweiht sein
in +*acc*

Privy Councillor (*Brit*) *n* Geheimer Rat *m*
prize [praɪz] *n* Preis *m* ▷ *adj* (*prize-winning*)
preisgekrönt; (*classic: example*) erstklassig ▷ *vt*
schätzen; ~ **idiot** (*inf*) Vollidiot *m*
prizefighter ['praɪzfaɪtə'] *n* Preisboxer *m*
prizegiving ['praɪzgɪvɪŋ] *n* Preisverleihung *f*
prize money *n* Geldpreis *m*
prizewinner ['praɪzwɪnə'] *n* Preisträger(in)
m(f)
prizewinning ['praɪzwɪnɪŋ] *adj* preisgekrönt
PRO *n abbr* = **public relations officer**
pro [prəu] *n* (*Sport*) Profi *m* ▷ *prep* (*in favour of*) pro
+*acc*, für +*acc*; **the** ~**s and cons** das Für und
Wider
pro- [prəu] *pref* (*in favour of*) Pro-, pro-;
~**disarmament campaign** Kampagne *f* für
Abrüstung
proactive [prəu'æktɪv] *adj* proaktiv
probability [prɒbə'bɪlɪtɪ] *n*
Wahrscheinlichkeit *f*; **in all** ~ aller
Wahrscheinlichkeit nach
probable ['prɒbəbl] *adj* wahrscheinlich; **it
seems** ~ **that** ... es ist wahrscheinlich, dass ...
probably ['prɒbəblɪ] *adv* wahrscheinlich
probate ['prəubɪt] *n* gerichtliche
Testamentsbestätigung *f*
probation [prə'beɪʃən] *n*: **on** ~ (*lawbreaker*) auf
Bewährung; (*employee*) auf Probe
probationary [prə'beɪʃənrɪ] *adj* (*period*) Probe-

probationer [prə'beɪʃənəʳ] n (nurse: female) Lernschwester f; (: male) Lernpfleger m

probation officer n Bewährungshelfer(in) m(f)

probe [prəub] n (Med, Space) Sonde f; (enquiry) Untersuchung f ▷ vt (investigate) untersuchen; (poke) bohren in +dat

probity ['prəubɪtɪ] n Rechtschaffenheit f

problem ['prɒbləm] n Problem nt; **to have ~s with the car** Probleme or Schwierigkeiten mit dem Auto haben; **what's the ~?** wo fehlts?; **I had no ~ finding her** ich habe sie ohne Schwierigkeiten gefunden; **no ~!** kein Problem!

problematic [prɒblə'mætɪk], **problematical** [prɒblə'mætɪkl] adj problematisch

problem-solving ['prɒbləmsɒlvɪŋ] adj (skills, ability) zur Problemlösung ▷ n Problemlösung f

procedural [prə'siːdjurəl] adj (agreement, problem) verfahrensmäßig

procedure [prə'siːdʒəʳ] n Verfahren nt

proceed [prə'siːd] vi (carry on) fortfahren; (person: go) sich bewegen; **to ~ to do sth** etw tun; **to ~ with** fortfahren mit; **I am not sure how to ~** ich bin nicht sicher über die weitere Vorgehensweise; **to ~ against sb** (Law) gegen jdn gerichtlich vorgehen

proceedings [prə'siːdɪŋz] npl (organized events) Vorgänge pl; (Law) Verfahren nt; (records) Protokoll nt

proceeds ['prəusiːdz] npl Erlös m

process ['prəusɛs] n (series of actions) Verfahren nt; (Biol, Chem) Prozess m ▷ vt (raw materials, food, Comput: data) verarbeiten; (application) bearbeiten; (Phot) entwickeln; **in the ~** dabei; **to be in the ~ of doing sth** (gerade) dabei sein, etw zu tun

processed cheese ['prəusɛst-], (US) **process cheese** n Schmelzkäse m

processing ['prəusɛsɪŋ] n (Phot) Entwickeln nt

procession [prə'sɛʃən] n Umzug m, Prozession f; **wedding/funeral ~** Hochzeits-/Trauerzug m

proclaim [prə'kleɪm] vt verkünden, proklamieren

proclamation [prɒklə'meɪʃən] n Proklamation f

proclivity [prə'klɪvɪtɪ] (form) n Vorliebe f

procrastinate [prəu'kræstɪneɪt] vi zögern, zaudern

procrastination [prəukræstɪ'neɪʃən] n Zögern nt, Zaudern nt

procreation [prəukrɪ'eɪʃən] n Fortpflanzung f

procurator fiscal ['prɒkjureɪtə-] n (pl **procurators fiscal**) (Scot) ≈ Staatsanwalt m, ≈ Staatsanwältin f

procure [prə'kjuəʳ] vt (obtain) beschaffen

procurement [prə'kjuəmənt] n (Comm) Beschaffung f

prod [prɒd] vt (push: with finger, stick etc) stoßen, stupsen (inf); (fig: urge) anspornen ▷ n (with finger, stick etc) Stoß m, Stups m (inf); (fig: reminder) mahnender Hinweis m

prodigal ['prɒdɪgl] adj: **~ son** verlorener Sohn m

prodigious [prə'dɪdʒəs] adj (cost, memory) ungeheuer

prodigy ['prɒdɪdʒɪ] n (person) Naturtalent nt; **child ~** Wunderkind nt

produce [n 'prɒdjuːs, vt prə'djuːs] n (Agr) (Boden)produkte pl ▷ vt (result etc) hervorbringen; (goods, commodity) produzieren, herstellen; (Biol, Chem) erzeugen; (fig: evidence etc) liefern; (: passport etc) vorlegen; (play, film, programme) produzieren

producer [prə'djuːsəʳ] n (person) Produzent(in) m(f); (country, company) Produzent m, Hersteller m

product ['prɒdʌkt] n Produkt nt

production [prə'dʌkʃən] n Produktion f; (Theat) Inszenierung f; **to go into ~** (goods) in Produktion gehen; **on ~ of** gegen Vorlage +gen

production agreement (US) n Produktivitätsabkommen nt

production line n Fließband nt, Fertigungsstraße f

production manager n Produktionsleiter(in) m(f)

productive [prə'dʌktɪv] adj produktiv

productivity [prɒdʌk'tɪvɪtɪ] n Produktivität f

productivity agreement (Brit) n Produktivitätsabkommen nt

productivity bonus n Leistungszulage f

Prof. n abbr (= professor) Prof.

profane [prə'feɪn] adj (language etc) profan; (secular) weltlich

profess [prə'fɛs] vt (claim) vorgeben; (express: feeling, opinion) zeigen, bekunden; **I do not ~ to be an expert** ich behaupte nicht, ein Experte zu sein

professed [prə'fɛst] adj (self-declared) erklärt

profession [prə'fɛʃən] n Beruf m; (people) Berufsstand m; **the ~s** die gehobenen Berufe

professional [prə'fɛʃənl] adj (organization, musician etc) Berufs-; (misconduct, advice) beruflich; (skilful) professionell ▷ n (doctor, lawyer, teacher etc) Fachmann m, Fachfrau f; (Sport) Profi m; (skilled person) Experte m, Expertin f; **to seek ~ advice** fachmännischen Rat einholen

professionalism [prə'fɛʃnəlɪzəm] n fachliches Können nt

professionally [prə'fɛʃnəlɪ] adv beruflich; (for a living) berufsmäßig; **I only know him ~** ich kenne ihn nur beruflich

professor [prə'fɛsəʳ] n (Brit) Professor(in) m(f); (US, Canada) Dozent(in) m(f)

professorship [prə'fɛsəʃɪp] n Professur f

proffer ['prɒfəʳ] vt (advice, drink, one's hand) anbieten; (apologies) aussprechen; (plate etc) hinhalten

proficiency [prə'fɪʃənsɪ] n Können nt, Fertigkeiten pl

proficient [prə'fɪʃənt] adj fähig; **to be ~ at** or **in** gut sein in +dat

profile ['prəufaɪl] n (of person's face) Profil nt; (fig: biography) Porträt nt; **to keep a low ~** (fig) sich zurückhalten; **to have a high ~** (fig) eine große Rolle spielen

profit ['prɔfɪt] n (Comm) Gewinn m, Profit m ▷ vi: **to ~ by** or **from** (fig) profitieren von; **~ and loss account** Gewinn-und-Verlust-Rechnung; **to make a ~** einen Gewinn machen; **to sell (sth) at a ~** (etw) mit Gewinn verkaufen

profitability [prɔfɪtə'bɪlɪtɪ] n Rentabilität f

profitable ['prɔfɪtəbl] adj (business, deal) rentabel, einträglich; (fig: useful) nützlich

profit centre n Bilanzabteilung f

profiteering [prɔfɪ'tɪərɪŋ] (pej) n Profitmacherei f

profit-making ['prɔfɪtmeɪkɪŋ] adj (organization) gewinnorientiert

profit margin n Gewinnspanne f

profit-sharing ['prɔfɪtʃɛərɪŋ] n Gewinnbeteiligung f

profits tax (Brit) n Ertragssteuer f

profligate ['prɔflɪgɪt] adj (person, spending) verschwenderisch; (waste) sinnlos; **~ with** (extravagant) verschwenderisch mit

pro forma ['prəu'fɔːmə] adj: **~ invoice** Pro-forma-Rechnung f

profound [prə'faund] adj (shock) schwer, tief; (effect, differences) weitreichend; (idea, book) tief schürfend

profuse [prə'fjuːs] adj (apologies) überschwänglich

profusely [prə'fjuːslɪ] adv (apologise, thank) vielmals; (sweat, bleed) stark

profusion [prə'fjuːʒən] n Überfülle f

progeny ['prɔdʒɪnɪ] n Nachkommenschaft f

prognoses [prɔg'nəusiːz] npl of **prognosis**

prognosis [prɔg'nəusɪs] (pl **prognoses**) n (Med, fig) Prognose f

program ['prəugræm] (Comput) n Programm nt ▷ vt programmieren

programme, (US) **program** ['prəugræm] n Programm nt ▷ vt (machine, system) programmieren

programmer ['prəugræmər] n Programmierer(in) m(f)

programming, (US) **programing** ['prəugræmɪŋ] n Programmierung f

programming language n Programmiersprache f

progress [n 'prəugrɛs, vi prə'grɛs] n Fortschritt m; (improvement) Fortschritte pl ▷ vi (advance) vorankommen; (become higher in rank) aufsteigen; (continue) sich fortsetzen; **in ~** (meeting, battle, match) im Gange; **to make ~** Fortschritte machen

progression [prə'grɛʃən] n (development) Fortschritt m, Entwicklung f; (series) Folge f

progressive [prə'grɛsɪv] adj (enlightened) progressiv, fortschrittlich; (gradual) fortschreitend

progressively [prə'grɛsɪvlɪ] adv (gradually) zunehmend

progress report n (Med) Fortschrittsbericht m; (Admin) Tätigkeitsbericht m

prohibit [prə'hɪbɪt] vt (ban) verbieten; **to ~ sb from doing sth** jdm verbieten or untersagen, etw zu tun; **"smoking ~ed"** „Rauchen verboten"

prohibition [prəuɪ'bɪʃən] n Verbot nt; **P~** (US) Prohibition f

prohibitive [prə'hɪbɪtɪv] adj (cost etc) untragbar

project [n 'prɔdʒɛkt, vt, vi prə'dʒɛkt] n (plan, scheme) Projekt nt; (Scol) Referat nt ▷ vt (plan) planen; (estimate) schätzen, voraussagen; (light, film, picture) projizieren ▷ vi (stick out) hervorragen

projectile [prə'dʒɛktaɪl] n Projektil nt, Geschoss nt, Geschoß nt (Österr)

projection [prə'dʒɛkʃən] n (estimate) Schätzung f, Voraussage f; (overhang) Vorsprung m; (Cine) Projektion f

projectionist [prə'dʒɛkʃənɪst] n Filmvorführer(in) m(f)

projection room n Vorführraum m

projector [prə'dʒɛktər] n Projektor m

proletarian [prəulɪ'tɛərɪən] adj proletarisch

proletariat [prəulɪ'tɛərɪət] n: **the ~** das Proletariat

proliferate [prə'lɪfəreɪt] vi sich vermehren

proliferation [prəlɪfə'reɪʃən] n Vermehrung f, Verbreitung f

prolific [prə'lɪfɪk] adj (artist, writer) produktiv

prologue, (US) **prolog** ['prəulɔg] n (of play, book) Prolog m

prolong [prə'lɔŋ] vt verlängern

prom [prɔm] n abbr = **promenade**; (Mus) = **promenade concert**; (US: college ball) Studentenball m; siehe Info-Artikel

○ **PROM**

○ Prom (promenade concert) ist in
○ Großbritannien ein Konzert, bei dem
○ ein Teil der Zuhörer steht (ursprünglich
○ spazieren ging). Die seit 1895 alljährlich
○ stattfindenden Proms (seit 1941 immer in
○ der Londoner Royal Albert Hall) zählen zu
○ den bedeutendsten Musikereignissen in
○ England. Der letzte Abend der Proms steht
○ ganz im Zeichen des Patriotismus und
○ gipfelt im Singen des Lieds „Land of Hope
○ and Glory". In den USA und Kanada steht
○ das Wort für promenade, ein Ball an einer
○ high school oder einem college.

promenade [prɔmə'nɑːd] n Promenade f

promenade concert (Brit) n Promenadenkonzert nt

promenade deck n Promenadendeck nt

prominence ['prɔmɪnəns] n (importance) Bedeutung f; **to rise to ~** bekannt werden

prominent ['prɔmɪnənt] adj (person) prominent; (thing) bedeutend; (very noticeable) herausragend; **he is ~ in the field of science** er ist eine führende Persönlichkeit im naturwissenschaftlichen Bereich

prominently ['prɔmɪnəntlɪ] adv (display, set)

p

deutlich sichtbar; **he figured ~ in the case** er spielte in dem Fall eine bedeutende Rolle

promiscuity [prɔmɪsˈkjuːɪtɪ] n Promiskuität f

promiscuous [prəˈmɪskjuəs] adj promisk

promise [ˈprɔmɪs] n (vow) Versprechen nt; (potential, hope) Hoffnung f ▷ vi versprechen ▷ vt: **to ~ sb sth, ~ sth to sb** jdm etw versprechen; **to make/break/keep a ~** ein Versprechen geben/brechen/halten; **a young man of ~** ein vielversprechender junger Mann; **she shows ~** sie gibt zu Hoffnungen Anlass; **it ~s to be lively** es verspricht lebhaft zu werden; **to ~ (sb) to do sth** (jdm) versprechen, etw zu tun

promising [ˈprɔmɪsɪŋ] adj vielversprechend

promissory note [ˈprɔmɪsərɪ-] n Schuldschein m

promontory [ˈprɔməntrɪ] n Felsvorsprung m

promote [prəˈməut] vt (employee) befördern; (advertise) werben für; (encourage: peace etc) fördern; **the team was ~d to the first division** (Brit: Football) die Mannschaft stieg in die erste Division auf

promoter [prəˈməutəʳ] n (of concert, event) Veranstalter(in) m(f); (of cause, idea) Förderer m, Förderin f

promotion [prəˈməuʃən] n (at work) Beförderung f; (of product, event) Werbung f; (of idea) Förderung f; (publicity campaign) Werbekampagne f

prompt [prɔmpt] adj prompt, sofortig ▷ adv (exactly) pünktlich ▷ n (Comput) Prompt m ▷ vt (cause) veranlassen; (when talking) auf die Sprünge helfen +dat; (Theat) soufflieren +dat; **they're very ~** (punctual) sie sind sehr pünktlich; **he was ~ to accept** er nahm unverzüglich an; **at 8 o'clock ~** (um) Punkt 8 Uhr; **to ~ sb to do sth** jdn dazu veranlassen, etw zu tun

prompter [ˈprɔmptəʳ] n (Theat) Souffleur m, Souffleuse f

promptly [ˈprɔmptlɪ] adv (immediately) sofort; (exactly) pünktlich

promptness [ˈprɔmptnɪs] n Promptheit f

promulgate [ˈprɔməlgeɪt] vt (policy) bekannt machen, verkünden; (idea) verbreiten

prone [prəun] adj (face down) in Bauchlage; **to be ~ to sth** zu etw neigen; **she is ~ to burst into tears if ...** sie neigt dazu, in Tränen auszubrechen, wenn ...

prong [prɔŋ] n (of fork) Zinke f

pronoun [ˈprəunaun] n Pronomen nt, Fürwort nt

pronounce [prəˈnauns] vt (word) aussprechen; (give verdict, opinion) erklären ▷ vi: **to ~ (up)on** sich äußern zu; **they ~d him dead/unfit to drive** sie erklärten ihn für tot/fahruntüchtig

pronounced [prəˈnaunst] adj (noticeable) ausgeprägt, deutlich

pronouncement [prəˈnaunsmənt] n Erklärung f

pronto [ˈprɔntəu] (inf) adv fix

pronunciation [prənʌnsɪˈeɪʃən] n Aussprache f

proof [pruːf] n (evidence) Beweis m; (Typ) (Korrektur)fahne f ▷ adj: **~ against** sicher vor +dat; **to be 70 % ~** (alcohol) ≈ einen Alkoholgehalt von 40% haben

proofreader [ˈpruːfriːdəʳ] n Korrektor(in) m(f)

Prop. abbr (Comm: = proprietor) Inh.

prop [prɔp] n (support) Stütze f ▷ vt (lean): **to ~ sth against sth** etw an etw acc lehnen
   ▸ **prop up** vt sep (thing) (ab)stützen; (fig: government, industry) unterstützen

propaganda [prɔpəˈgændə] n Propaganda f

propagate [ˈprɔpəgeɪt] vt (plants) züchten; (ideas etc) propagieren ▷ vi (plants, animals) sich fortpflanzen

propagation [prɔpəˈgeɪʃən] n (of ideas etc) Propagierung f; (of plants, animals) Fortpflanzung f

propel [prəˈpɛl] vt (vehicle, machine) antreiben; (person) schubsen; (fig: person) treiben

propeller [prəˈpɛləʳ] n Propeller m

propelling pencil [prəˈpɛlɪŋ-] (Brit) n Drehbleistift m

propensity [prəˈpɛnsɪtɪ] n: **a ~ for** or **to sth** ein Hang m or eine Neigung zu etw; **to have a ~ to do sth** dazu neigen, etw zu tun

proper [ˈprɔpəʳ] adj (genuine, correct) richtig; (socially acceptable) schicklich; (inf: real) echt; **the town/city ~** die Stadt selbst; **to go through the ~ channels** den Dienstweg einhalten

properly [ˈprɔpəlɪ] adv (eat, work) richtig; (behave) anständig

proper noun n Eigenname m

property [ˈprɔpətɪ] n (possessions) Eigentum nt; (building and its land) Grundstück nt; (quality) Eigenschaft f; **it's their ~** es gehört ihnen

property developer n ≈ Grundstücksmakler(in) m(f)

property market n Immobilienmarkt m

property owner n Grundbesitzer(in) m(f)

property tax n Vermögenssteuer f

prophecy [ˈprɔfɪsɪ] n Prophezeiung f

prophesy [ˈprɔfɪsaɪ] vt prophezeien ▷ vi Prophezeiungen machen

prophet [ˈprɔfɪt] n Prophet m; **~ of doom** Unheilsprophet(in) m(f)

prophetic [prəˈfɛtɪk] adj prophetisch

proportion [prəˈpɔːʃən] n (part) Teil m; (number: of people, things) Anteil m; (ratio) Verhältnis nt; **in ~ to** im Verhältnis zu; **to be out of all ~ to sth** in keinem Verhältnis zu etw stehen; **to get sth in/out of ~** etw im richtigen/falschen Verhältnis sehen; **a sense of ~** (fig) ein Sinn für das Wesentliche

proportional [prəˈpɔːʃənl] adj: **~ to** proportional zu

proportional representation n Verhältniswahlrecht nt

proportionate [prəˈpɔːʃənɪt] adj **= proportional**

proposal [prəˈpəuzl] n (plan) Vorschlag m; **~ (of marriage)** Heiratsantrag m

propose [prəˈpəuz] vt (plan, idea) vorschlagen; (motion) einbringen; (toast) ausbringen ▷ vi *(offer marriage)* einen Heiratsantrag machen; **to ~ to do sth** *or* **doing sth** *(intend)* die Absicht haben, etw zu tun

proposer [prə'pəuzə'] *n (of motion etc)* Antragsteller(in) *m(f)*

proposition [prɔpə'zɪʃən] *n (statement)* These *f*; *(offer)* Angebot *nt*; **to make sb a ~** jdm ein Angebot machen

propound [prə'paund] *vt (idea etc)* darlegen

proprietary [prə'praɪətərɪ] *adj (brand, medicine)* Marken-; *(tone, manner)* besitzergreifend

proprietor [prə'praɪətə'] *n (of hotel, shop etc)* Inhaber(in) *m(f)*; *(of newspaper)* Besitzer(in) *m(f)*

propriety [prə'praɪətɪ] *n (seemliness)* Schicklichkeit *f*

props [prɔps] *npl (Theat)* Requisiten *pl*

propulsion [prə'pʌlʃən] *n* Antrieb *m*

pro rata [prəu'rɑ:tə] *adj, adv* anteilmäßig; **on a ~ basis** anteilmäßig

prosaic [prəu'zeɪɪk] *adj* prosaisch, nüchtern

Pros. Atty. *(US) abbr = **prosecuting attorney**

proscribe [prə'skraɪb] *(form) vt* verbieten, untersagen

prose [prəuz] *n (not poetry)* Prosa *f*; *(Brit: Scol: translation)* Übersetzung *f* in die Fremdsprache

prosecute ['prɔsɪkju:t] *vt (Law: person)* strafrechtlich verfolgen; *(: case)* die Anklage vertreten in *+dat*

prosecuting attorney ['prɔsɪkju:tɪŋ-] *(US) n* Staatsanwalt *m*, Staatsanwältin *f*

prosecution [prɔsɪ'kju:ʃən] *n (Law: action)* strafrechtliche Verfolgung *f*; *(: accusing side)* Anklage(vertretung) *f*

prosecutor ['prɔsɪkju:tə'] *n* Anklagevertreter(in) *m(f)*; *(also: **public prosecutor**)* Staatsanwalt *m*, Staatsanwältin *f*

prospect [*n* 'prɔspekt, *vi* prə'spekt] *n* Aussicht *f* ⊳ *vi*: **to ~ (for)** suchen (nach); **prospects** *npl (for work etc)* Aussichten *pl*, Chancen *pl*; **we are faced with the ~ of higher unemployment** wir müssen mit der Möglichkeit rechnen, dass die Arbeitslosigkeit steigt

prospecting ['prɔspektɪŋ] *n (for gold, oil etc)* Suche *f*

prospective [prə'spektɪv] *adj (son-in-law)* zukünftig; *(customer, candidate)* voraussichtlich

prospectus [prə'spektəs] *n (of college, company)* Prospekt *m*

prosper ['prɔspə'] *vi (person)* Erfolg haben; *(business, city etc)* gedeihen, florieren

prosperity [prɔ'sperɪtɪ] *n* Wohlstand *m*

prosperous ['prɔspərəs] *adj (person)* wohlhabend; *(business, city etc)* blühend

prostate ['prɔsteɪt] *n (also: **prostate gland**)* Prostata *f*

prostitute ['prɔstɪtju:t] *n (female)* Prostituierte *f*; *(male)* männliche(r) Prostituierte(r) *m*, Strichjunge *m (inf)* ⊳ *vt*: **to ~ o.s.** *(fig)* sich prostituieren, sich unter Wert verkaufen

prostitution [prɔstɪ'tju:ʃən] *n* Prostitution *f*

prostrate ['prɔstreɪt] *adj (face down)* ausgestreckt (liegend); *(fig)*

niedergeschmettert ⊳ *vt*: **to ~ o.s. before** sich zu Boden werfen vor *+dat*

protagonist [prə'tægənɪst] *n (of idea, movement)* Verfechter(in) *m(f)*; *(Theat, Liter)* Protagonist(in) *m(f)*

protect [prə'tekt] *vt* schützen

protection [prə'tekʃən] *n* Schutz *m*; **police ~** Polizeischutz *m*

protectionism [prə'tekʃənɪzəm] *n* Protektionismus *m*

protection racket *n* Organisation *f* zur Erpressung von Schutzgeld

protective [prə'tektɪv] *adj (clothing, layer etc)* Schutz-; *(person)* fürsorglich; **~ custody** Schutzhaft *f*

protector [prə'tektə'] *n (person)* Beschützer(in) *m(f)*; *(device)* Schutz *m*

protégé, protégée ['prəutɪʒeɪ] *n* Schützling *m*

protein ['prəuti:n] *n* Protein *nt*, Eiweiß *nt*

pro tem [prəu'tem] *adv abbr (= pro tempore)* vorläufig

protest [*n* 'prəutest, *vi*, *vt* prə'test] *n* Protest *m* ⊳ *vi*: **to ~ about** *or* **against** *or* **at sth** gegen etw protestieren ⊳ *vt*: **to ~ (that)** *(insist)* beteuern(, dass)

Protestant ['prɔtɪstənt] *adj* protestantisch ⊳ *n* Protestant(in) *m(f)*

protester [prə'testə'] *n (in demonstration)* Demonstrant(in) *m(f)*

protest march *n* Protestmarsch *m*

protestor [prə'testə'] *n =* **protester**

protocol ['prəutəkɔl] *n* Protokoll *nt*

prototype ['prəutətaɪp] *n* Prototyp *m*

protracted [prə'træktɪd] *adj (meeting etc)* langwierig, sich hinziehend; *(absence)* länger

protractor [prə'træktə'] *n (Geom)* Winkelmesser *m*

protrude [prə'tru:d] *vi (rock, ledge, teeth)* vorstehen

protuberance [prə'tju:bərəns] *n* Auswuchs *m*

proud [praud] *adj* stolz; *(arrogant)* hochmütig; **~ of sb/sth** stolz auf jdn/etw; **to be ~ to do sth** stolz (darauf) sein, etw zu tun; **to do sb/o.s. ~** *(inf)* jdn/sich verwöhnen

proudly ['praudlɪ] *adv* stolz

prove [pru:v] *vt* beweisen ⊳ *vi*: **to ~ (to be) correct** sich als richtig herausstellen *or* erweisen; **to ~ (o.s./itself) (to be) useful** sich als nützlich erweisen; **he was ~d right in the end** er hat schließlich recht behalten

proverb ['prɔvə:b] *n* Sprichwort *nt*

proverbial [prə'və:bɪəl] *adj* sprichwörtlich

provide [prə'vaɪd] *vt (food, money, shelter etc)* zur Verfügung stellen; *(answer, example etc)* liefern; **to ~ sb with sth** jdm etw zur Verfügung stellen
  ▸ **provide for** *vt fus (person)* sorgen für; *(future event)* vorsorgen für

provided [prə'vaɪdɪd] *conj*: **~ (that)** vorausgesetzt(, dass)

Providence ['prɔvɪdəns] *n* die Vorsehung

providing [prə'vaɪdɪŋ] *conj*: **~ (that)** vorausgesetzt(, dass)

P

province ['prɔvɪns] *n* (*of country*) Provinz *f*; (*responsibility etc*) Bereich *m*, Gebiet *nt*; **provinces** *npl*: **the ~s** außerhalb der Hauptstadt liegende Landesteile, Provinz *f*

provincial [prə'vɪnʃəl] *adj* (*town, newspaper etc*) Provinz-; (*pej: parochial*) provinziell

provision [prə'vɪʒən] *n* (*supplying*) Bereitstellung *f*; (*preparation*) Vorsorge *f*, Vorkehrungen *pl*; (*stipulation, clause*) Bestimmung *f*; **provisions** *npl* (*food*) Proviant *m*; **to make ~ for** vorsorgen für; (*for people*) sorgen für; **there's no ~ for this in the contract** dies ist im Vertrag nicht vorgesehen

provisional [prə'vɪʒənl] *adj* vorläufig, provisorisch ▷ *n*: **P~** (*Irish: Pol*) *Mitglied der provisorischen Irisch-Republikanischen Armee*

provisional licence (*Brit*) *n* (*Aut*) vorläufige Fahrerlaubnis *f*

provisionally [prə'vɪʒnəlɪ] *adv* vorläufig

proviso [prə'vaɪzəu] *n* Vorbehalt *m*; **with the ~ that ...** unter dem Vorbehalt, dass ...

Provo ['prɔvəu] (*Irish: inf*) *n abbr* (*Pol*) = **Provisional**

provocation [prɔvə'keɪʃən] *n* Provokation *f*, Herausforderung *f*; **to be under ~** provoziert werden

provocative [prə'vɔkətɪv] *adj* provozierend, herausfordernd; (*sexually stimulating*) aufreizend

provoke [prə'vəuk] *vt* (*person*) provozieren, herausfordern; (*fight*) herbeiführen; (*reaction etc*) hervorrufen; **to ~ sb to do** *or* **into doing sth** jdn dazu provozieren, etw zu tun

provost ['prɔvəst] *n* (*Brit: of university*) Dekan *m*; (*Scot*) Bürgermeister(in) *m(f)*

prow [prau] *n* (*of boat*) Bug *m*

prowess ['prauɪs] *n* Können *nt*, Fähigkeiten *pl*; **his ~ as a footballer** sein fußballerisches Können

prowl [praul] *vi* (*also*: **prowl about, prowl around**) schleichen ▷ *n*: **on the ~** auf Streifzug

prowler ['praulə'] *n* Herumtreiber *m*

proximity [prɔk'sɪmɪtɪ] *n* Nähe *f*

proxy ['prɔksɪ] *n*: **by ~** durch einen Stellvertreter

prude [pru:d] *n*: **to be a ~** prüde sein

prudence ['pru:dns] *n* Klugheit *f*, Umsicht *f*

prudent ['pru:dnt] *adj* (*sensible*) klug

prudish ['pru:dɪʃ] *adj* prüde

prune [pru:n] *n* Backpflaume *f* ▷ *vt* (*plant*) stutzen, beschneiden

pry [praɪ] *vi*: **to ~ (into)** seine Nase hineinstecken (in +*acc*), herumschnüffeln (in +*dat*)

PS *abbr* (= *postscript*) PS

psalm [sɑ:m] *n* Psalm *m*

PSAT® (*US*) *n abbr* (= *Preliminary Scholastic Aptitude Test*) *Schuleignungstest*

PSBR (*Brit*) *n abbr* (*Econ*: = *public sector borrowing requirement*) *staatlicher Kreditbedarf m*

pseud [sju:d] (*Brit: inf: pej*) *n* Angeber(in) *m(f)*

pseudo- ['sju:dəu] *pref* Pseudo-

pseudonym ['sju:dənɪm] *n* Pseudonym *nt*

PSHE (*Brit*) *n abbr* (*Scol*) = **personal, social and health education**

PST (*US*) *abbr* (= *Pacific Standard Time*) *pazifische Standardzeit*

psyche ['saɪkɪ] *n* Psyche *f*

psychedelic [saɪkə'dɛlɪk] *adj* (*drug*) psychedelisch; (*clothes, colours*) in psychedelischen Farben

psychiatric [saɪkɪ'ætrɪk] *adj* psychiatrisch

psychiatrist [saɪ'kaɪətrɪst] *n* Psychiater(in) *m(f)*

psychiatry [saɪ'kaɪətrɪ] *n* Psychiatrie *f*

psychic ['saɪkɪk] *adj* (*person*) übersinnlich begabt; (*damage, disorder*) psychisch ▷ *n* Mensch *m* mit übersinnlichen Fähigkeiten

psycho ['saɪkəu] (*US: inf*) *n* Verrückte(r) *f(m)*

psychoanalyse [saɪkəu'ænəlaɪz] *vt* psychoanalytisch behandeln, psychoanalysieren

psychoanalysis [saɪkəuə'nælɪsɪs] *n* Psychoanalyse *f*

psychoanalyst [saɪkəu'ænəlɪst] *n* Psychoanalytiker(in) *m(f)*

psychological [saɪkə'lɔdʒɪkl] *adj* psychologisch

psychologist [saɪ'kɔlədʒɪst] *n* Psychologe *m*, Psychologin *f*

psychology [saɪ'kɔlədʒɪ] *n* (*science*) Psychologie *f*; (*character*) Psyche *f*

psychopath ['saɪkəupæθ] *n* Psychopath(in) *m(f)*

psychoses [saɪ'kəusi:z] *npl of* **psychosis**

psychosis [saɪ'kəusɪs] (*pl* **psychoses**) *n* Psychose *f*

psychosomatic ['saɪkəusə'mætɪk] *adj* psychosomatisch

psychotherapy [saɪkəu'θɛrəpɪ] *n* Psychotherapie *f*

psychotic [saɪ'kɔtɪk] *adj* psychotisch

PT (*Brit*) *n abbr* (*Scol*: = *physical training*) Turnen *nt*

Pt *abbr* (*in place names*: = *Point*) Pt.

pt *abbr* = **pint; point**

PTA *n abbr* (= *Parent-Teacher Association*) *Lehrer- und Elternverband*

Pte (*Brit*) *abbr* (*Mil*) = **private**

PTO *abbr* (= *please turn over*) b. w.

PTV (*US*) *n abbr* (= *pay television*) Pay-TV *nt*; (= *public television*) öffentliches Fernsehen *nt*

pub [pʌb] *n* = **public house**; *siehe Info-Artikel*

● **PUB**

  Pub ist ein Gasthaus mit einer Lizenz
  zum Ausschank von alkoholischen
  Getränken. Ein Pub besteht meist aus
  verschiedenen gemütlichen (lounge, snug)
  oder einfacheren Räumen (public bar),
  in der oft auch Spiele wie Darts, Domino
  und Poolbillard zur Verfügung stehen.
  In Pubs werden vor allem mittags oft
  auch Mahlzeiten angeboten. Pubs sind
  normalerweise von 11 bis 23 Uhr geöffnet,
  aber manchmal nachmittags geschlossen.

pub-crawl ['pʌbkrɔ:l] (inf) n: **to go on a** ~ eine Kneipentour machen

puberty ['pju:bətɪ] n Pubertät f

pubic ['pju:bɪk] adj (hair) Scham-; ~ **bone** Schambein nt

public ['pʌblɪk] adj öffentlich ▷ n: **the** ~ (in general) die Öffentlichkeit; (particular set of people) das Publikum; **to be** ~ **knowledge** allgemein bekannt sein; **to make sth** ~ etw bekannt machen; **to go** ~ (Comm) in eine Aktiengesellschaft umgewandelt werden; **in** ~ in aller Öffentlichkeit; **the general** ~ die Allgemeinheit

public-address system [pʌblɪkə'drɛs-] n Lautsprecheranlage f

publican ['pʌblɪkən] n Gastwirt(in) m(f)

publication [pʌblɪ'keɪʃən] n Veröffentlichung f

public company n Aktiengesellschaft f

public convenience (Brit) n öffentliche Toilette f

public holiday n gesetzlicher Feiertag m

public house (Brit) n Gaststätte f

publicity [pʌb'lɪsɪtɪ] n (information) Werbung f; (attention) Publicity f

publicity tour n Werbetour f; **to be on a** ~ auf Werbetour sein

publicize ['pʌblɪsaɪz] vt (fact) bekannt machen; (event) Publicity machen für

public limited company n ≈ Aktiengesellschaft f

publicly ['pʌblɪklɪ] adv öffentlich; **to be** ~ **owned** (Comm) in Staatsbesitz sein

public opinion n die öffentliche Meinung

public ownership n: **to be taken into** ~ verstaatlicht werden

Public Prosecutor n Staatsanwalt m, Staatsanwältin f

public relations n Public Relations pl, Öffentlichkeitsarbeit f

public relations officer n Beauftragte(r) f(m) für Öffentlichkeitsarbeit

public school n (Brit) Privatschule f; (US) staatliche Schule f; siehe Info-Artikel

---

PUBLIC SCHOOL

Public school bezeichnet vor allem in England eine weiterführende Privatschule, meist eine Internatsschule mit hohem Prestige, an die oft auch eine preparatory school angeschlossen ist. Public schools werden von einem Schulbeirat verwaltet und durch Stiftungen und Schulgelder, die an den bekanntesten Schulen wie Eton, Harrow und Westminster sehr hoch sein können, finanziert. Die meisten Schüler einer public school gehen zur Universität, oft nach Oxford oder Cambridge. Viele Industrielle, Abgeordnete und hohe Beamte haben eine public school besucht.

In Schottland und den USA bedeutet public school eine öffentliche, vom Steuerzahler finanzierte Schule.

public sector n: **the** ~ der öffentliche Sektor

public-service vehicle [pʌblɪk'sə:vɪs-] (Brit) n öffentliches Verkehrsmittel nt

public-spirited [pʌblɪk'spɪrɪtɪd] adj gemeinsinnig

public transport n öffentliche Verkehrsmittel pl

public utility n öffentlicher Versorgungsbetrieb m

public works npl öffentliche Bauprojekte pl

publish ['pʌblɪʃ] vt veröffentlichen

publisher ['pʌblɪʃər] n (person) Verleger(in) m(f); (company) Verlag m

publishing ['pʌblɪʃɪŋ] n (profession) das Verlagswesen

publishing company n Verlag m, Verlagshaus nt

pub lunch n in Pubs servierter Imbiss

puce [pju:s] adj (face) hochrot

puck [pʌk] n (Ice Hockey) Puck m

pucker ['pʌkər] vi (lips, face) sich verziehen; (fabric etc) Falten werfen ▷ vt (lips, face) verziehen; (fabric etc) Falten machen in +acc

pudding ['pudɪŋ] n (cooked sweet food) Süßspeise f; (Brit: dessert) Nachtisch m; **rice** ~ Milchreis m; **black** ~, **blood** ~ (US) ≈ Blutwurst f

puddle ['pʌdl] n (of rain) Pfütze f; (of blood) Lache f

puerile ['pjuəraɪl] adj kindisch

Puerto Rico ['pwə:təʊ'ri:kəʊ] n Puerto Rico nt

puff [pʌf] n (of cigarette, pipe) Zug m; (gasp) Schnaufer m; (of air) Stoß m; (of smoke) Wolke f ▷ vt (also: **puff on, puff at**: cigarette, pipe) ziehen an +dat ▷ vi (gasp) keuchen, schnaufen
▶ **puff out** vt (one's chest) herausdrücken; (one's cheeks) aufblasen

puffed [pʌft] (inf) adj außer Puste

puffin ['pʌfɪn] n Papageientaucher m

puff pastry, (US) **puff paste** n Blätterteig m

puffy ['pʌfɪ] adj (eye) geschwollen; (face) aufgedunsen

pugnacious [pʌg'neɪʃəs] adj (person) streitsüchtig

pull [pʊl] vt (rope, handle etc) ziehen an +dat; (cart etc) ziehen; (close: curtain) zuziehen; (: blind) herunterlassen; (inf: attract: people) anlocken; (: sexual partner) aufreißen; (pint of beer) zapfen ▷ vi ziehen ▷ n (also fig: attraction) Anziehungskraft f; **to** ~ **the trigger** abdrücken; **to** ~ **a face** ein Gesicht schneiden; **to** ~ **a muscle** sich dat einen Muskel zerren; **not to** ~ **one's** or **any punches** (fig) sich dat keine Zurückhaltung auferlegen; **to** ~ **to pieces** (fig) zerreißen; **to** ~ **one's weight** (fig) sich ins Zeug legen; **to** ~ **o.s. together** sich zusammenreißen; **to** ~ **sb's leg** (fig) jdn auf den Arm nehmen; **to** ~ **strings (for sb)** seine Beziehungen (für jdn) spielen lassen; **to give sth a** ~ an etw dat ziehen

P

▶ **pull apart** *vt* (*separate*) trennen
▶ **pull away** *vi* (*Aut*) losfahren
▶ **pull back** *vi* (*retreat*) sich zurückziehen; (*fig*) einen Rückzieher machen (*inf*)
▶ **pull down** *vt* (*building*) abreißen
▶ **pull in** *vi* (*Aut: at kerb*) anhalten; (*Rail*) einfahren ▷ *vt* (*inf: money*) einsacken; (*crowds, people*) anlocken; (*police: suspect*) sich *dat* schnappen (*inf*)
▶ **pull off** *vt* (*clothes etc*) ausziehen; (*fig: difficult thing*) schaffen, bringen (*inf*)
▶ **pull out** *vi* (*Aut: from kerb*) losfahren; (: *when overtaking*) ausscheren; (*Rail*) ausfahren; (*withdraw*) sich zurückziehen ▷ *vt* (*extract*) herausziehen
▶ **pull over** *vi* (*Aut*) an den Straßenrand fahren
▶ **pull through** *vi* (*Med*) durchkommen
▶ **pull up** *vi* (*Aut, Rail: stop*) anhalten ▷ *vt* (*raise*) hochziehen; (*uproot*) herausreißen; (*chair*) heranrücken
pullback ['pulbæk] *n* (*retreat*) Rückzug *m*
pulley ['pulɪ] *n* Flaschenzug *m*
pull-out ['pulaut] *n* (*in magazine*) Beilage *f* (*zum Heraustrennen*)
pullover ['puləuvəʳ] *n* Pullover *m*
pulp [pʌlp] *n* (*of fruit*) Fruchtfleisch *nt*; (*for paper*) (Papier)brei *m*; (*Liter: pej*) Schund *m* ▷ *adj* (*pej: magazine, novel*) Schund-; **to reduce sth to a ~** etw zu Brei machen
pulpit ['pulpɪt] *n* Kanzel *f*
pulsate [pʌl'seɪt] *vi* (*heart*) klopfen; (*music*) pulsieren
pulse [pʌls] *n* (*Anat*) Puls *m*; (*rhythm*) Rhythmus *m*; **pulses** *npl* (*Bot*) Hülsenfrüchte *pl*; (*Tech*) Impuls *m* ▷ *vi* pulsieren; **to take** *or* **feel sb's ~** jdm den Puls fühlen; **to have one's finger on the ~ (of sth)** (*fig*) den Finger am Puls (einer Sache *gen*) haben
pulverize ['pʌlvəraɪz] *vt* pulverisieren; (*fig: destroy*) vernichten
puma ['pju:mə] *n* Puma *m*
pumice ['pʌmɪs] *n* (*also:* **pumice stone**) Bimsstein *m*
pummel ['pʌml] *vt* mit Faustschlägen bearbeiten
pump [pʌmp] *n* Pumpe *f*; (*also:* **petrol pump**) Zapfsäule *f*; (*shoe*) Turnschuh *m* ▷ *vt* pumpen; **to ~ sb for information** jdn aushorchen; **she had her stomach ~ed** ihr wurde der Magen ausgepumpt
▶ **pump up** *vt* (*inflate*) aufpumpen
pumpkin ['pʌmpkɪn] *n* Kürbis *m*
pun [pʌn] *n* Wortspiel *nt*
punch [pʌntʃ] *n* (*blow*) Schlag *m*; (*fig: force*) Schlagkraft *f*; (*tool*) Locher *m*; (*drink*) Bowle *f*, Punsch *m* ▷ *vt* (*hit*) schlagen; (*make a hole in*) lochen; **to ~ a hole in sth** ein Loch in etw *acc* stanzen
▶ **punch in** (*US*) *vi* (bei Arbeitsbeginn) stempeln
▶ **punch out** (*US*) *vi* (bei Arbeitsende) stempeln
Punch and Judy show *n* ≈ Kasper(le)theater *nt*

punch card, (*US*) **punched card** [pʌntʃt-] *n* Lochkarte *f*
punch-drunk ['pʌntʃdrʌŋk] (*Brit*) *adj* (*boxer*) angeschlagen
punch line *n* Pointe *f*
punch-up ['pʌntʃʌp] (*Brit: inf*) *n* Schlägerei *f*
punctual ['pʌŋktjuəl] *adj* pünktlich
punctuality [pʌŋktju'ælɪtɪ] *n* Pünktlichkeit *f*
punctually ['pʌŋktjuəlɪ] *adv* pünktlich; **it will start ~ at 6** es beginnt um Punkt 6 *or* pünktlich um 6
punctuation [pʌŋktju'eɪʃən] *n* Zeichensetzung *f*
punctuation mark *n* Satzzeichen *nt*
puncture ['pʌŋktʃəʳ] *n* (*Aut*) Reifenpanne *f* ▷ *vt* durchbohren; **I have a ~** ich habe eine Reifenpanne
pundit ['pʌndɪt] *n* Experte *m*, Expertin *f*
pungent ['pʌndʒənt] *adj* (*smell, taste*) scharf; (*fig: speech, article etc*) spitz, scharf
punish ['pʌnɪʃ] *vt* bestrafen; **to ~ sb for sth** jdn für etw bestrafen; **to ~ sb for doing sth** jdn dafür bestrafen, dass er etw getan hat
punishable ['pʌnɪʃəbl] *adj* strafbar
punishing ['pʌnɪʃɪŋ] *adj* (*fig: exercise, ordeal*) hart
punishment ['pʌnɪʃmənt] *n* (*act*) Bestrafung *f*; (*way of punishing*) Strafe *f*; **to take a lot of ~** (*fig: car, person etc*) viel abbekommen
punitive ['pju:nɪtɪv] *adj* (*action*) Straf-, zur Strafe; (*measure*) (*extrem*) hart
punk [pʌŋk] *n* (*also:* **punk rocker**) Punker(in) *m(f)*; (*also:* **punk rock**) Punk *m*; (*US: inf: hoodlum*) Gangster *m*
punnet ['pʌnɪt] *n* (*of raspberries etc*) Körbchen *nt*
punt[1] [pʌnt] *n* (*boat*) Stechkahn *m* ▷ *vi* mit dem Stechkahn fahren
punt[2] [pʌnt] (*Irish*) *n* (*currency*) irisches Pfund *nt*
punter ['pʌntəʳ] (*Brit*) *n* (*gambler*) Wetter(in) *m(f)*; **the ~s** (*inf: customers*) die Leute; **the average ~** (*inf*) Otto Normalverbraucher
puny ['pju:nɪ] *adj* (*person, arms etc*) schwächlich; (*efforts*) kläglich, kümmerlich
pup [pʌp] *n* (*young dog*) Welpe *m*, junger Hund *m*; **seal ~** Welpenjunge(s) *nt*
pupil ['pju:pl] *n* (*Scol*) Schüler(in) *m(f)*; (*of eye*) Pupille *f*
puppet ['pʌpɪt] *n* Handpuppe *f*; (*with strings, fig: person*) Marionette *f*
puppet government *n* Marionettenregierung *f*
puppy ['pʌpɪ] *n* (*young dog*) Welpe *m*, junger Hund *m*
purchase ['pə:tʃɪs] *n* Kauf *m*; (*grip*) Halt *m* ▷ *vt* kaufen; **to get** *or* **gain (a) ~ on** (*grip*) Halt finden an +*dat*
purchase order *n* Bestellung *f*
purchase price *n* Kaufpreis *m*
purchaser ['pə:tʃɪsəʳ] *n* Käufer(in) *m(f)*
purchase tax *n* Kaufsteuer *f*
purchasing power ['pə:tʃɪsɪŋ-] *n* Kaufkraft *f*
pure [pjuəʳ] *adj* rein; **a ~ wool jumper** ein Pullover aus reiner Wolle; **it's laziness ~ and simple** es ist nichts als reine Faulheit

purebred ['pjuəbrɛd] adj reinrassig
puree ['pjuəreɪ] n Püree nt
purely ['pjuəlɪ] adv rein
purgatory ['pə:gətərɪ] n (Rel) das Fegefeuer; (fig) die Hölle
purge [pə:dʒ] n (Pol) Säuberung f ▷ vt (Pol: organization) säubern; (: extremists etc) entfernen; (fig: thoughts, mind etc) befreien
purification [pjuərɪfɪ'keɪʃən] n Reinigung f
purify ['pjuərɪfaɪ] vt reinigen
purist ['pjuərɪst] n Purist(in) m(f)
puritan ['pjuərɪtən] n Puritaner(in) m(f)
puritanical [pjuərɪ'tænɪkl] adj puritanisch
purity ['pjuərɪtɪ] n Reinheit f
purl [pə:l] (Knitting) n linke Masche f ▷ vt links stricken
purloin [pə:'lɔɪn] (form) vt entwenden
purple ['pə:pl] adj violett
purport [pə:'pɔ:t] vi: **to ~ to be/do sth** vorgeben, etw zu sein/tun
purpose ['pə:pəs] n (reason) Zweck m; (aim) Ziel nt, Absicht f; **on ~** absichtlich; **for illustrative ~s** zu Illustrationszwecken; **for all practical ~s** praktisch (gesehen); **for the ~s of this meeting** zum Zweck dieses Treffens; **to little ~** mit wenig Erfolg; **to no ~** ohne Erfolg; **a sense of ~** ein Zielbewusstsein nt
purpose-built ['pə:pəs'bɪlt] (Brit) adj speziell angefertigt, Spezial-
purposeful ['pə:pəsful] adj entschlossen
purposely ['pə:pəslɪ] adv absichtlich, bewusst
purr [pə:ʳ] vi (cat) schnurren
purse [pə:s] n (Brit: for money) Geldbörse f, Portemonnaie nt; (US: handbag) Handtasche f ▷ vt (lips) kräuseln
purser ['pə:səʳ] n (Naut) Zahlmeister m
purse-snatcher ['pə:ssnætʃəʳ] (US) n Handtaschendieb m
pursue [pə'sju:] vt (person, vehicle, plan, aim) verfolgen; (fig: interest etc) nachgehen +dat
pursuer [pə'sju:əʳ] n Verfolger(in) m(f)
pursuit [pə'sju:t] n (chase) Verfolgung f; (pastime) Beschäftigung f; (fig): **~ of** (of happiness etc) Streben nt nach; **in ~ of** (person, car etc) auf der Jagd nach; (fig: happiness etc) im Streben nach
purveyor [pə'veɪəʳ] (form) n (of goods etc) Lieferant m
pus [pʌs] n Eiter m
push [puʃ] n Stoß m, Schub m ▷ vt (press) drücken; (shove) schieben; (fig: put pressure on: person) bedrängen; (: promote: product) werben für; (inf: sell: drugs) pushen ▷ vi (press) drücken; (shove) schieben; **at the ~ of a button** auf Knopfdruck; **at a ~** (Brit: inf) notfalls; **to ~ a door open/shut** eine Tür auf-/zudrücken; **"~"** (on door) „drücken"; (on bell) „klingeln"; **to be ~ed for time/money** (inf) in Zeitnot/Geldnot sein; **she is ~ing fifty** (inf) sie geht auf die fünfzig zu; **to ~ for** (demand) drängen auf +acc
▶ **push around** vt (bully) herumschubsen

▶ **push aside** vt beiseiteschieben
▶ **push in** vi sich dazwischendrängeln
▶ **push off** (inf) vi abhauen
▶ **push on** vi (continue) weitermachen
▶ **push over** vt umstoßen
▶ **push through** vt (measure etc) durchdrücken
▶ **push up** vt (total, prices) hochtreiben
push-bike ['puʃbaɪk] (Brit) n Fahrrad nt
push-button ['puʃbʌtn] adj (machine, calculator) Drucktasten-
pushchair ['puʃtʃeəʳ] (Brit) n Sportwagen m
pusher ['puʃəʳ] n (drug dealer) Pusher m
pushover ['puʃəuvəʳ] (inf) n: **it's a ~** das ist ein Kinderspiel
push-up ['puʃʌp] (US) n Liegestütz m
pushy ['puʃɪ] (pej) adj aufdringlich
puss [pus] (inf) n Miez e f
pussy ['pusɪ], **pussycat** ['pusɪkæt] (inf) n Mieze(katze) f
put [put] (pt, pp ~) vt (thing) tun; (: upright) stellen; (: flat) legen; (person: in room, institution etc) stecken; (: in state, situation) versetzen; (express: idea etc) ausdrücken; (present: case, view) vorbringen; (ask: question) stellen; (classify) einschätzen; (write, type) schreiben; **to ~ sb in a good/bad mood** jdn gut/schlecht stimmen; **to ~ sb to bed** jdn ins Bett bringen; **to ~ sb to a lot of trouble** jdm viele Umstände machen; **how shall I ~ it?** wie soll ich es sagen or ausdrücken?; **to ~ a lot of time into sth** viel Zeit auf etw acc verwenden; **to ~ money on a horse** Geld auf ein Pferd setzen; **the cost is now ~ at 2 million pounds** die Kosten werden jetzt auf 2 Millionen Pfund geschätzt; **I ~ it to you that ...** (Brit) ich behaupte, dass ...; **to stay ~** (an Ort und Stelle) bleiben
▶ **put about** vi (Naut) den Kurs ändern ▷ vt (rumour) verbreiten
▶ **put across** vt (ideas etc) verständlich machen
▶ **put around** vt = **put about**
▶ **put aside** vt (work) zur Seite legen; (idea, problem) unbeachtet lassen; (sum of money) zurücklegen
▶ **put away** vt (store) wegräumen; (inf: consume) verdrücken; (save: money) zurücklegen; (imprison) einsperren
▶ **put back** vt (replace) zurücktun; (: upright) zurückstellen; (: flat) zurücklegen; (postpone) verschieben; (delay) zurückwerfen
▶ **put by** vt (money, supplies etc) zurücklegen
▶ **put down** vt (upright) hinstellen; (flat) hinlegen; (cup, glass) absetzen; (in writing) aufschreiben; (riot, rebellion) niederschlagen; (humiliate) demütigen; (kill) töten
▶ **put down to** vt (attribute) zurückführen auf +acc
▶ **put forward** vt (ideas etc) vorbringen; (watch, clock) vorstellen; (date, meeting) vorverlegen
▶ **put in** vt (application, complaint) einreichen; (time, effort) investieren; (gas, electricity etc) installieren ▷ vi (Naut) einlaufen
▶ **put in for** vt fus (promotion) sich bewerben um; (leave) beantragen

P

▶ **put off** vt (delay) verschieben; (distract) ablenken; **to ~ sb off sth** (discourage) jdn von etw abbringen

▶ **put on** vt (clothes, brake) anziehen; (glasses, kettle) aufsetzen; (make-up, ointment etc) auftragen; (light, TV) anmachen; (play etc) aufführen; (record, tape, video) auflegen; (dinner etc) aufsetzen; (assume: look, behaviour etc) annehmen; (inf: tease) auf den Arm nehmen; (extra bus, train etc) einsetzen; **to ~ on airs** sich zieren; **to ~ on weight** zunehmen

▶ **put on to** vt (tell about) vermitteln

▶ **put out** vt (fire, light) ausmachen; (take out: rubbish) herausbringen; (: cat etc) vor die Tür setzen; (one's hand) ausstrecken; (story, announcement) verbreiten; (Brit: dislocate: shoulder etc) verrenken; (inf: inconvenience) Umstände machen +dat ▷ vi (Naut): **to ~ out to sea** in See stechen; **to ~ out from Plymouth** von Plymouth auslaufen

▶ **put through** vt (Tel: person) verbinden; (: call) durchstellen; (plan, agreement) durchbringen; **~ me through to Ms Blair** verbinden Sie mich mit Frau Blair

▶ **put together** vt (furniture etc) zusammenbauen; (plan, campaign) ausarbeiten; **more than the rest of them ~ together** mehr als alle anderen zusammen

▶ **put up** vt (fence, building) errichten; (tent) aufstellen; (umbrella) aufspannen; (hood) hochschlagen; (poster, sign etc) anbringen; (price, cost) erhöhen; (accommodate) unterbringen; **to ~ up resistance** Widerstand leisten; **to ~ up a fight** sich zur Wehr setzen; **to ~ sb up to sth** jdn zu etw anstiften; **to ~ sb up to doing sth** jdn dazu anstiften, etw zu tun; **to ~ sth up for sale** etw zum Verkauf anbieten

▶ **put upon** vt fus: **to be ~ upon** (imposed on) ausgenutzt werden

▶ **put up with** vt fus sich abfinden mit

putative ['pjuːtətɪv] adj mutmaßlich

putrid ['pjuːtrɪd] adj (mess, meat) faul

putt [pʌt] n Putt m

putter ['pʌtəʳ] n (Golf) Putter m ▷ vi (US) = **potter**

putting green ['pʌtɪŋ-] n kleiner Golfplatz m zum Putten

putty ['pʌtɪ] n Kitt m

put-up ['putʌp] adj: **a ~ job** ein abgekartetes Spiel nt

puzzle ['pʌzl] n (game, toy) Geschicklichkeitsspiel nt; (mystery) Rätsel nt ▷ vt verwirren ▷ vi: **to ~ over sth** sich dat über etw acc den Kopf zerbrechen; **to be ~d as to why ...** vor einem Rätsel stehen, warum ...

puzzling ['pʌzlɪŋ] adj verwirrend; (mysterious) rätselhaft

PVC n abbr (= polyvinyl chloride) PVC nt

Pvt. (US) abbr (Mil) = **private**

p.w. abbr (= per week) pro Woche

pygmy ['pɪgmɪ] n Pygmäe m

pyjamas, (US) **pajamas** [pə'dʒɑːməz] npl Pyjama m, Schlafanzug m; **a pair of ~** ein Schlafanzug

pylon ['paɪlən] n Mast m

pyramid ['pɪrəmɪd] n Pyramide f

Pyrenean [pɪrə'niːən] adj pyrenäisch

Pyrenees [pɪrə'niːz] npl: **the ~** die Pyrenäen pl

Pyrex® ['paɪreks] n ≈ Jenaer Glas® nt ▷ adj (dish, bowl) aus Jenaer Glas®

python ['paɪθən] n Pythonschlange f

Qq

Q, q [kju:] *n (letter)* Q *nt*, q *nt*; **Q for Queen** ≈ Q wie Quelle

Qatar [kæ'tɑːʳ] *n* Katar *nt*

QC (Brit) *n abbr (Law: = Queen's Counsel)* Kronanwalt *m; siehe Info-Artikel*

QCA (Brit) *n abbr* (= *Qualifications and Curriculum Authority*) *Behörde, die in England für die Entwicklung von Lehrplänen und deren Beachtung zuständig ist*

QED *abbr* (= *quod erat demonstrandum*) q. e. d.

QM *n abbr* (Mil) = **quartermaster**

q.t. *n abbr* (inf) (= *quiet*): **on the ~** heimlich

quack [kwæk] *n (of duck)* Schnattern *nt*, Quaken *nt*; *(inf: pej: doctor)* Quacksalber *m* ▷ *vi* schnattern, quaken

quad [kwɒd] *abbr* = **quadrangle**; (= *quadruplet*) Vierling *m*

quadrangle ['kwɒdræŋgl] *n (courtyard)* Innenhof *m*

quadrilateral [kwɒdrɪ'lætərəl] *n* Viereck *nt*

quadruped ['kwɒdruped] *n* Vierfüßer *m*

quadruple [kwɒ'druːpl] *vt* vervierfachen ▷ *vi* sich vervierfachen

quadruplets [kwɒ'druːplɪts] *npl* Vierlinge *pl*

quagmire ['kwægmaɪəʳ] *n (also fig)* Sumpf *m*

quail [kweɪl] *n* Wachtel *f* ▷ *vi*: **he ~ed at the thought/before her anger** ihm schauderte bei dem Gedanken/vor ihrem Zorn

quaint [kweɪnt] *adj (house, village)* malerisch; *(ideas, customs)* urig, kurios

quake [kweɪk] *vi* beben, zittern ▷ *n* = **earthquake**

Quaker ['kweɪkəʳ] *n* Quäker(in) *m(f)*

qualification [kwɒlɪfɪ'keɪʃən] *n (often pl: degree etc)* Qualifikation *f*; *(attribute)* Voraussetzung *f*; *(reservation)* Vorbehalt *m*; **what are your ~s?**

welche Qualifikationen haben Sie?

qualified ['kwɒlɪfaɪd] *adj (trained: doctor etc)* qualifiziert, ausgebildet; *(limited: agreement, praise)* bedingt; **to be/feel ~ to do sth** *(fit, competent)* qualifiziert sein/sich qualifiziert fühlen, etw zu tun; **it was a ~ success** es war kein voller Erfolg; **he's not ~ for the job** ihm fehlen die Qualifikationen für die Stelle

qualify ['kwɒlɪfaɪ] *vt (entitle)* qualifizieren; *(modify: statement)* einschränken ▷ *vi (pass examination)* sich qualifizieren; **to ~ for** *(be eligible)* die Berechtigung erlangen für; *(in competition)* sich qualifizieren für; **to ~ as an engineer** die Ausbildung zum Ingenieur abschließen

qualifying ['kwɒlɪfaɪɪŋ] *adj*: **~ exam** Auswahlprüfung *f*; **~ game** Vorrunden- *or* Qualifikationsspiel *f*; **~ group** Vorrunden- *or* Qualifikationsgruppe *f*; **~ round** Qualifikationsrunde *f*

qualitative ['kwɒlɪtətɪv] *adj* qualitativ

quality ['kwɒlɪtɪ] *n* Qualität *f*; *(characteristic)* Eigenschaft *f* ▷ *cpd* Qualitäts-; **of good/poor ~** von guter/schlechter Qualität; **~ of life** Lebensqualität *f*

quality control *n* Qualitätskontrolle *f*

quality papers (Brit) *npl*: **the ~** die seriösen Zeitungen *pl; siehe Info-Artikel*

qualm [kwɑːm] *n* Bedenken *pl*; **to have ~s about sth** Bedenken wegen etw haben

quandary ['kwɒndrɪ] *n*: **to be in a ~** in einem Dilemma sein

quango ['kwæŋgəʊ] (Brit) *n abbr* (= *quasi-autonomous nongovernmental organization*) ≈ (regierungsunabhängige) Kommission *f*

quantifiable ['kwɒntɪfaɪəbl] *adj*

q

quantifizierbar

quantitative [ˈkwɒntɪtətɪv] *adj* quantitativ

quantity [ˈkwɒntɪtɪ] *n* (*amount*) Menge *f*; **in large/small quantities** in großen/kleinen Mengen; **in ~** (*in bulk*) in großen Mengen; **an unknown ~** (*fig*) eine unbekannte Größe

quantity surveyor *n* Baukostenkalkulator(in) *m(f)*

quantum leap [ˈkwɒntəm-] *n* (*Phys*) Quantensprung *m*; (*fig*) Riesenschritt *m*

quarantine [ˈkwɒrntiːn] *n* Quarantäne *f*; **in ~** in Quarantäne

quark [kwɑːk] *n* (*cheese*) Quark *m*; (*Phys*) Quark *nt*

quarrel [ˈkwɒrl] *n* (*argument*) Streit *m* ▷ *vi* sich streiten; **to have a ~ with sb** sich mit jdm streiten; **I've no ~ with him** ich habe nichts gegen ihn; **I can't ~ with that** dagegen kann ich nichts einwenden

quarrelsome [ˈkwɒrəlsəm] *adj* streitsüchtig

quarry [ˈkwɒrɪ] *n* (*for stone*) Steinbruch *m*; (*prey*) Beute *f* ▷ *vt* (*marble etc*) brechen

quart [kwɔːt] *n* Quart *nt*

quarter [ˈkwɔːtəʳ] *n* Viertel *nt*; (*US: coin*) 25-Cent-Stück *nt*; (*of year*) Quartal *nt*; (*district*) Viertel *nt* ▷ *vt* (*divide*) vierteln; (*Mil: lodge*) einquartieren; **quarters** *npl* (*Mil*) Quartier *nt*; (*also*: **living quarters**) Unterkünfte *pl*; **a ~ of an hour** eine viertel Stunde; **it's a ~ to three, it's a ~ of three** (*US*) es ist Viertel vor drei; **it's a ~ past three, it's a ~ after three** (*US*) es ist Viertel nach drei; **from all ~s** aus allen Richtungen; **at close ~s** aus unmittelbarer Nähe

quarterback [ˈkwɔːtəbæk] *n* (*American Football*) Quarterback *m*

quarterdeck [ˈkwɔːtədɛk] *n* (*Naut*) Quarterdeck *nt*

quarterfinal [ˈkwɔːtəˈfaɪnl] *n* Viertelfinale *nt*

quarterly [ˈkwɔːtəlɪ] *adj, adv* vierteljährlich ▷ *n* Vierteljahresschrift *f*

quartermaster [ˈkwɔːtəmɑːstəʳ] *n* (*Mil*) Quartiermeister *m*

quartet [kwɔːˈtɛt] *n* (*Mus*) Quartett *nt*

quarto [ˈkwɔːtəʊ] *n* (*size of paper*) Quartformat *nt*; (*book*) im Quartformat

quartz [kwɔːts] *n* Quarz *m* ▷ *cpd* (*watch, clock*) Quarz-

quash [kwɒʃ] *vt* (*verdict*) aufheben

quasi- [ˈkweɪzaɪ] *pref* quasi-

quaver [ˈkweɪvəʳ] *n* (*Brit: Mus*) Achtelnote *f* ▷ *vi* (*voice*) beben, zittern

quay [kiː] *n* Kai *m*

quayside [ˈkiːsaɪd] *n* Kai *m*

queasiness [ˈkwiːzɪnɪs] *n* Übelkeit *f*

queasy [ˈkwiːzɪ] *adj* (*nauseous*) übel; **I feel ~** mir ist übel *or* schlecht

Quebec [kwɪˈbɛk] *n* Quebec *nt*

queen [kwiːn] *n* (*also Zool*) Königin *f*; (*Cards, Chess*) Dame *f*

queen mother *n* Königinmutter *f*

Queen's speech (*Brit*) *n*
≈ Regierungserklärung *f*; *siehe Info-Artikel*

queer [kwɪəʳ] *adj* (*odd*) sonderbar, seltsam ▷ *n* (*infl: pej: male homosexual*) Schwule(r) *m*; **I feel ~** (*Brit: unwell*) mir ist ganz komisch

quell [kwɛl] *vt* (*riot*) niederschlagen; (*fears*) überwinden

quench [kwɛntʃ] *vt*: **to ~ one's thirst** seinen Durst stillen

querulous [ˈkwɛruləs] *adj* nörglerisch

query [ˈkwɪərɪ] *n* Anfrage *f* ▷ *vt* (*check*) nachfragen bezüglich +*gen*; (*express doubt about*) bezweifeln

quest [kwɛst] *n* Suche *f*

question [ˈkwɛstʃən] *n* Frage *f* ▷ *vt* (*interrogate*) befragen; (*doubt*) bezweifeln; **to ask sb a question, put a ~ to sb** jdm eine Frage stellen; **to bring** *or* **call sth into ~** etw infrage stellen; **the ~ is ...** die Frage ist ...; **there's no ~ of him playing for England** es ist ausgeschlossen, dass er für England spielt; **the person/night in ~** die fragliche Person/ Nacht; **to be beyond ~** außer Frage stehen; **to be out of the ~** nicht infrage kommen

questionable [ˈkwɛstʃənəbl] *adj* fraglich

questioner [ˈkwɛstʃənəʳ] *n* Fragesteller(in) *m(f)*

questioning [ˈkwɛstʃənɪŋ] *adj* (*look*) fragend; (*mind*) forschend ▷ *n* (*Police*) Vernehmung *f*

question mark *n* Fragezeichen *nt*

questionnaire [kwɛstʃəˈnɛəʳ] *n* Fragebogen *m*

queue [kjuː] (*Brit*) *n* Schlange *f* ▷ *vi* (*also*: **queue up**) Schlange stehen

quibble [ˈkwɪbl] *vi*: **to ~ about** *or* **over** sich streiten über +*acc*; **to ~ with** herumnörgeln an +*dat* ▷ *n* Krittelei *f*

quiche [kiːʃ] *n* Quiche *f*

quick [kwɪk] *adj* schnell; (*mind, wit*) wach; (*look, visit*) flüchtig ▷ *adv* schnell ▷ *n*: **to cut sb to the ~** (*fig*) jdn tief verletzen; **be ~!** mach schnell!; **to be ~ to act** schnell handeln; **she was ~ to see that ...** sie begriff schnell, dass ...; **she has a ~ temper** sie wird leicht hitzig

quicken [ˈkwɪkən] *vt* beschleunigen ▷ *vi* schneller werden, sich beschleunigen

quick-fire [ˈkwɪkfaɪəʳ] *adj* (*questions*) wie aus der Pistole

quick fix *n* Sofortlösung *f*

quicklime [ˈkwɪklaɪm] *n* ungelöschter Kalk *m*

quickly [ˈkwɪklɪ] *adv* schnell

quickness [ˈkwɪknɪs] *n* Schnelligkeit *f*; **~ of mind** Scharfsinn *m*

quicksand ['kwɪksænd] *n* Treibsand *m*

quickstep ['kwɪkstɛp] *n* Quickstepp *m*

quick-tempered [kwɪk'tɛmpəd] *adj* hitzig, leicht erregbar

quick-witted [kwɪk'wɪtɪd] *adj* schlagfertig

quid [kwɪd] (*Brit: inf*) *n inv* Pfund *nt*

quid pro quo ['kwɪdprəʊ'kwəʊ] *n* Gegenleistung *f*

quiet ['kwaɪət] *adj* leise; (*place*) ruhig, still; (*silent, reserved*) still; (*business, day*) ruhig; (*without fuss etc: wedding*) in kleinem Rahmen ▷ *n* (*peacefulness*) Stille *f*, Ruhe *f*; (*silence*) Ruhe *f* ▷ *vt, vi* (*US*) = **quieten**; **keep** *or* **be ~!** sei still!; **I'll have a ~ word with him** ich werde mal unter vier Augen mit ihm reden; **on the ~** (*in secret*) heimlich

quieten ['kwaɪətn] (*Brit: also:* **quieten down**) *vi* ruhiger werden ▷ *vt* (*person, animal*) beruhigen

quietly ['kwaɪətlɪ] *adv* leise; (*silently*) still; (*calmly*) ruhig; **~ confident** insgeheim sicher

quietness ['kwaɪətnɪs] *n* (*peacefulness*) Ruhe *f*; (*silence*) Stille *f*

quill [kwɪl] *n* (*pen*) Feder *f*; (*of porcupine*) Stachel *m*

quilt [kwɪlt] *n* Decke *f*; (*also:* **continental quilt**) Federbett *nt*

quin [kwɪn] (*Brit*) *n abbr* (= **quintuplet**) Fünfling *m*

quince [kwɪns] *n* Quitte *f*

quinine [kwɪ'ni:n] *n* Chinin *nt*

quintet [kwɪn'tɛt] *n* (*Mus*) Quintett *nt*

quintuplets [kwɪn'tju:plɪts] *npl* Fünflinge *pl*

quip [kwɪp] *n* witzige *or* geistreiche Bemerkung *f* ▷ *vt* witzeln

quire ['kwaɪəʳ] *n* (*of paper*) 24 Bogen Papier

quirk [kwɜːk] *n* Marotte *f*; **a ~ of fate** eine Laune des Schicksals

quit [kwɪt] (*pt, pp* **~** *or* **quitted**) *vt* (*smoking*) aufgeben; (*job*) kündigen; (*premises*) verlassen ▷ *vi* (*give up*) aufgeben; (*resign*) kündigen; **to ~**

doing sth aufhören, etw zu tun; **~ stalling!** (*US: inf*) weichen Sie nicht ständig aus!; **notice to ~** (*Brit*) Kündigung *f*

quite [kwaɪt] *adv* (*rather*) ziemlich; (*entirely*) ganz; **not ~** nicht ganz; **I ~ like it** ich mag es ganz gern; **I ~ understand** ich verstehe; **I don't ~ remember** ich erinnere mich nicht genau; **not ~ as many as the last time** nicht ganz so viele wie das letzte Mal; **that meal was ~ something!** das Essen konnte sich sehen lassen!; **it was ~ a sight** das war vielleicht ein Anblick; **~ a few of them** eine ganze Reihe von Ihnen; **~ (so)!** ganz recht!

quits [kwɪts] *adj*: **we're ~** wir sind quitt; **let's call it ~** lassen wirs dabei

quiver ['kwɪvəʳ] *vi* zittern

quiz [kwɪz] *n* (*game*) Quiz *nt* ▷ *vt* (*question*) befragen

quizzical ['kwɪzɪkl] *adj* (*look, smile*) wissend

quoits [kwɔɪts] *npl* (*game*) Wurfspiel mit Ringen

quorum ['kwɔːrəm] *n* Quorum *nt*

quota ['kwəʊtə] *n* (*allowance*) Quote *f*

quotation [kwəʊ'teɪʃən] *n* (*from book etc*) Zitat *nt*; (*estimate*) Preisangabe *f*; (*Comm*) Kostenvoranschlag *m*

quotation marks *npl* Anführungszeichen *pl*

quote [kwəʊt] *n* (*from book etc*) Zitat *nt*; (*estimate*) Kostenvoranschlag *m* ▷ *vt* zitieren; (*fact, example*) anführen; (*price*) nennen; **quotes** *npl* (*quotation marks*) Anführungszeichen *pl*; **in ~s** in Anführungszeichen; **the figure ~d for the repairs** die für die Reparatur genannte Summe; **~ ... unquote** Zitat Anfang ... Zitat Ende

quotient ['kwəʊʃənt] *n* Quotient *m*

qv *abbr* (= *quod vide*) s.d.

qwerty keyboard ['kwɜːtɪ-] *n* Qwerty-Tastatur *f*

q

Rr

R¹, r [ɑːʳ] *n* (*letter*) R *nt*, r *nt*; **R for Robert, R for Roger** (*US*) ≈ R wie Richard

R² [ɑːʳ] *abbr* (= *Réaumur (scale)*) R; (*US: Cine: = restricted*) *Klassifikation für nicht jugendfreie Filme*

R. *abbr* (= *right*) r. = **river**; (*US: Pol*) = **republican**; (*Brit: = Rex*) *König*; (= *Regina*) *Königin*

RA *abbr* (*Mil*) = **rear admiral** ▷ *n abbr* (*Brit*: = *Royal Academy*) *Gesellschaft zur Förderung der Künste*; (= *Royal Academician*) *Mitglied der Royal Academy*

RAAF *n abbr* (*Mil*: = *Royal Australian Air Force*) *australische Luftwaffe f*

Rabat [rəˈbɑːt] *n* Rabat *nt*

rabbi [ˈræbaɪ] *n* Rabbi *m*

rabbit [ˈræbɪt] *n* Kaninchen *nt* ▷ *vi* (*Brit: inf: also:* **to rabbit on**) quatschen, schwafeln

rabbit hole *n* Kaninchenbau *m*

rabbit hutch *n* Kaninchenstall *m*

rabble [ˈræbl] (*pej*) *n* Pöbel *m*

rabid [ˈræbɪd] *adj* (*animal*) tollwütig; (*fig: fanatical*) fanatisch

rabies [ˈreɪbiːz] *n* Tollwut *f*

RAC (*Brit*) *n abbr* (= *Royal Automobile Club*) *Autofahrerorganisation*, ≈ ADAC *m*

raccoon [rəˈkuːn] *n* Waschbär *m*

race [reɪs] *n* (*species*) Rasse *f*; (*competition*) Rennen *nt*; (*for power, control*) Wettlauf *m* ▷ *vt* (*horse, pigeon*) an Wettbewerben teilnehmen lassen; (*car etc*) ins Rennen schicken; (*person*) um die Wette laufen mit ▷ *vi* (*compete*) antreten; (*hurry*) rennen; (*pulse, heart*) rasen; (*engine*) durchdrehen; **the human ~** die Menschheit; **a ~ against time** ein Wettlauf mit der Zeit; **he ~d across the road** er raste über die Straße; **to ~ in/out** hinein-/hinausstürzen

race car (*US*) *n* = **racing car**

race car driver (*US*) *n* = **racing driver**

racecourse [ˈreɪskɔːs] *n* Rennbahn *f*

racehorse [ˈreɪshɔːs] *n* Rennpferd *nt*

race meeting *n* Rennveranstaltung *f*

race relations *npl* Beziehungen *pl* zwischen den Rassen

racetrack [ˈreɪstræk] *n* Rennbahn *f*; (*US*) = **racecourse**

racial [ˈreɪʃl] *adj* Rassen-

racialism [ˈreɪʃlɪzəm] *n* Rassismus *m*

racialist [ˈreɪʃlɪst] *adj* rassistisch ▷ *n* (*pej*)

Rassist(in) *m(f)*

racing [ˈreɪsɪŋ] *n* (*also:* **horse racing**) Pferderennen *nt*; (*also:* **motor racing**) Rennsport *m*

racing car (*Brit*) *n* Rennwagen *m*

racing driver (*Brit*) *n* Rennfahrer(in) *m(f)*

racism [ˈreɪsɪzəm] *n* Rassismus *m*

racist [ˈreɪsɪst] *adj* rassistisch ▷ *n* (*pej*) Rassist(in) *m(f)*

rack [ræk] *n* (*also:* **luggage rack**) Gepäckablage *f*; (*also:* **roof rack**) Dachgepäckträger *m*; (*for dresses etc*) Ständer *m*; (*for dishes*) Gestell *nt* ▷ *vt*: **~ed by** (*pain etc*) gemartert von; **magazine/toast ~** Zeitungs-/Toastständer *m*; **to ~ one's brains** sich *dat* den Kopf zerbrechen; **to go to ~ and ruin** (*building*) zerfallen; (*business, country*) herunterkommen

racket [ˈrækɪt] *n* (*for tennis etc*) Schläger *m*; (*noise*) Krach *m*, Radau *m*; (*swindle*) Schwindel *m*

racketeer [rækɪˈtɪəʳ] (*esp US*) *n* Gangster *m*

racoon [rəˈkuːn] *n* = **raccoon**

racquet [ˈrækɪt] *n* (*for tennis etc*) Schläger *m*

racy [ˈreɪsɪ] *adj* (*book, story*) rasant

RADA [ˈrɑːdə] (*Brit*) *n abbr* (= *Royal Academy of Dramatic Art*) *Schauspielschule*

radar [ˈreɪdɑːʳ] *n* Radar *m or nt* ▷ *cpd* Radar-

radar trap *n* Radarfalle *f*

radial [ˈreɪdɪəl] *adj* (*roads*) strahlenförmig verlaufend; (*pattern*) strahlenförmig ▷ *n* (*also:* **radial tyre**) Gürtelreifen *m*

radiance [ˈreɪdɪəns] *n* Glanz *m*

radiant [ˈreɪdɪənt] *adj* strahlend; (*Phys: heat*) Strahlungs-

radiate [ˈreɪdɪeɪt] *vt* (*lit, fig*) ausstrahlen ▷ *vi* (*lines, roads*) strahlenförmig verlaufen

radiation [reɪdɪˈeɪʃən] *n* (*radioactivity*) radioaktive Strahlung *f*; (*from sun etc*) Strahlung *f*

radiation sickness *n* Strahlenkrankheit *f*

radiator [ˈreɪdɪeɪtəʳ] *n* (*heater*) Heizkörper *m*; (*Aut*) Kühler *m*

radiator cap *n* (*Aut*) Kühlerdeckel *m*

radiator grill *n* (*Aut*) Kühlergrill *m*

radical [ˈrædɪkl] *adj* radikal ▷ *n* (*person*) Radikale(r) *f(m)*

radii [ˈreɪdɪaɪ] *npl of* **radius**

radio [ˈreɪdɪəu] *n* (*broadcasting*) Radio *nt*, Rundfunk *m*; (*device: for receiving broadcasts*)

Radio nt; (: for transmitting and receiving)
Funkgerät nt ▷ vi: **to ~ to sb** mit jdm per Funk
sprechen ▷ vt (person) per Funk verständigen;
(message, position) per Funk durchgeben; **on the**
~ im Radio
radio ... ['reɪdɪəu] pref Radio ..., radio ...
radioactive ['reɪdɪəu'æktɪv] adj radioaktiv
radioactivity ['reɪdɪəuæk'tɪvɪtɪ] n
Radioaktivität f
radio announcer n Rundfunksprecher(in) m(f)
radio-controlled ['reɪdɪəukən'trəuld] adj
ferngesteuert
radiographer [reɪdɪ'ɒgrəfəʳ] n Röntgenologe
m, Röntgenologin f
radiography [reɪdɪ'ɒgrəfɪ] n Röntgenografie f
radiologist [reɪdɪ'ɒlədʒɪst] n Radiologe m,
Radiologin f
radiology [reɪdɪ'ɒlədʒɪ] n Radiologie f
radio station n Radiosender m
radio taxi n Funktaxi nt
radiotelephone ['reɪdɪəu'telɪfəun] n
Funksprechgerät nt
radio telescope n Radioteleskop nt
radiotherapist ['reɪdɪəu'θerəpɪst] n
Strahlentherapeut(in) m(f)
radiotherapy ['reɪdɪəu'θerəpɪ] n
Strahlentherapie f
radish ['rædɪʃ] n Radieschen nt; (long white
variety) Rettich m
radium ['reɪdɪəm] n Radium nt
radius ['reɪdɪəs] (pl **radii**) n Radius m; (area)
Umkreis m; **within a ~ of 50 miles** in einem
Umkreis von 50 Meilen
RAF (Brit) n abbr = **Royal Air Force**
raffia ['ræfɪə] n Bast m
raffish ['ræfɪʃ] adj (person) verwegen; (place)
verkommen
raffle ['ræfl] n Verlosung f, Tombola f ▷ vt (prize)
verlosen; ~ **ticket** Los nt
raft [rɑːft] n Floß nt; (also: **life raft**)
Rettungsfloß nt
rafter ['rɑːftəʳ] n Dachsparren m
rag [ræg] n (piece of cloth) Lappen m; (torn
cloth) Fetzen m; (pej: newspaper) Käseblatt nt;
(Brit: Univ) studentische Wohltätigkeitsveranstaltung
▷ vt (Brit: tease) aufziehen; **rags** npl (torn
clothes) Lumpen pl; **in ~s** (person) zerlumpt; **his
was a ~s-to-riches story** er brachte es vom
Tellerwäscher zum Millionär
rag-and-bone man [rægən'bəun-] (Brit) n
Lumpensammler m
ragbag ['rægbæg] n (assortment)
Sammelsurium nt

rag doll n Stoffpuppe f
rage [reɪdʒ] n (fury) Wut f, Zorn m ▷ vi toben,
wüten; **it's all the ~** (fashionable) es ist der
letzte Schrei; **to fly into a ~** einen Wutanfall
bekommen
ragged ['rægɪd] adj (jagged) zackig; (clothes,
person) zerlumpt; (beard) ausgefranst
raging ['reɪdʒɪŋ] adj (sea, storm, torrent) tobend,
tosend; (fever) heftig; (thirst) brennend;
(toothache) rasend
rag trade (inf) n: **the ~** die Modebranche f
raid [reɪd] n (Mil) Angriff m, Überfall m; (by
police) Razzia f; (by criminal: forcefully) Überfall
m; (: secretly) Einbruch m ▷ vt (Mil) angreifen,
überfallen; (police) stürmen; (criminal: forcefully)
überfallen; (: secretly) einbrechen in +acc
rail [reɪl] n Geländer nt; (on deck of ship) Reling
f; **rails** npl (for train) Schienen pl; **by ~** mit der
Bahn
railcard ['reɪlkɑːd] (Brit) n (for young people) ≈
Juniorenpass m; (for pensioners) ≈ Seniorenpass
m
railing ['reɪlɪŋ] n, **railings** ['reɪlɪŋz] ▷ npl (fence)
Zaun m
railroad ['reɪlrəud] (US) n = **railway**
railway ['reɪlweɪ] (Brit) n Eisenbahn f; (track)
Gleis nt; (company) Bahn f
railway engine (Brit) n Lokomotive f
railway line (Brit) n Bahnlinie f; (track) Gleis nt
railwayman ['reɪlweɪmən] (irreg: like **man**);
(Brit) n Eisenbahner m
railway station (Brit) n Bahnhof m
rain [reɪn] n Regen m ▷ vi regnen; **in the ~** im
Regen; **as right as ~** voll auf der Höhe; **it's
~ing** es regnet; **it's ~ing cats and dogs** es
regnet in Strömen
rainbow ['reɪnbəu] n Regenbogen m
rainbow family n gleichgeschlechtliches Paar mit
Kind/Kindern, Regenbogenfamilie f
rainbow flag n Regenbogenfahne f or -flagge f
rain check (US) n: **to take a ~ on sth** sich dat
etw noch einmal überlegen
raincoat ['reɪnkəut] n Regenmantel m
raindrop ['reɪndrɒp] n Regentropfen m
rainfall ['reɪnfɔːl] n Niederschlag m
rainforest ['reɪnfɒrɪst] n Regenwald m
rainproof ['reɪnpruːf] adj wasserfest
rainstorm ['reɪnstɔːm] n schwere Regenfälle pl
rainwater ['reɪnwɔːtəʳ] n Regenwasser nt
rainy ['reɪnɪ] adj (day) regnerisch, verregnet;
(area) regenreich; ~ **season** Regenzeit f; **to
save sth for a ~ day** etw für schlechte Zeiten
aufheben
raise [reɪz] n (pay rise) Gehaltserhöhung f ▷ vt
(lift: hand) hochheben; (: window) hochziehen;
(siege) beenden; (embargo) aufheben; (increase)

r

erhöhen; (*improve*) verbessern; (*question etc*) zur Sprache bringen; (*doubts etc*) vorbringen; (*child, cattle*) aufziehen; (*crop*) anbauen; (*army*) aufstellen; (*funds*) aufbringen; (*loan*) aufnehmen; **to ~ a glass to sb/sth** das Glas auf jdn/etw erheben; **to ~ one's voice** die Stimme erheben; **to ~ sb's hopes** jdm Hoffnungen machen; **to ~ a laugh/smile** Gelächter/ein Lächeln hervorrufen; **this ~s the question** ... das wirft die Frage auf ...

raisin ['reɪzn] *n* Rosine *f*

Raj [rɑːdʒ] *n*: **the ~** *britische Regierung in Indien vor 1947*

rajah ['rɑːdʒə] *n* Radscha *m*

rake [reɪk] *n* Harke *f*; (*old: person*) Schwerenöter *m* ▷ *vt* harken; (*light, gun: area*) bestreichen; **he's raking it in** (*inf*) er scheffelt das Geld nur so

rake-off ['reɪkɔf] (*inf*) *n* Anteil *m*

rally ['rælɪ] *n* (*Pol etc*) Kundgebung *f*; (*Aut*) Rallye *f*; (*Tennis etc*) Ballwechsel *m* ▷ *vt* (*support*) sammeln ▷ *vi* (*sick person, Stock Exchange*) sich erholen

▶ **rally round** *vi* sich zusammentun ▷ *vt fus* zu Hilfe kommen +*dat*

rallying point ['rælɪɪŋ-] *n* Sammelstelle *f*

RAM [ræm] *n abbr* (*Comput: = random access memory*) RAM

ram [ræm] *n* Widder *m* ▷ *vt* rammen

ramble ['ræmbl] *n* Wanderung *f* ▷ *vi* wandern; (*also:* **ramble on**: *talk*) schwafeln

rambler ['ræmblər] *n* Wanderer *m*, Wanderin *f*; (*Bot*) Kletterrose *f*

rambling ['ræmblɪŋ] *adj* (*speech, letter*) weitschweifig; (*house*) weitläufig; (*Bot*) rankend, Kletter-

rambunctious [ræm'bʌŋkʃəs] (*US*) *adj* = **rumbustious**

RAMC (*Brit*) *n abbr* (= *Royal Army Medical Corps*) *Verband zur Versorgung der Armee mit Stabsärzten und Sanitätern*

ramifications [ræmɪfɪ'keɪʃənz] *npl* Auswirkungen *pl*

ramp [ræmp] *n* Rampe *f*; (*in garage*) Hebebühne *f*; **on ~** (*US: Aut*) Auffahrt *f*; **off ~** (*US: Aut*) Ausfahrt *f*

rampage [ræm'peɪdʒ] *n*: **to be/go on the ~** randalieren ▷ *vi*: **they went rampaging through the town** sie zogen randalierend durch die Stadt

rampant ['ræmpənt] *adj*: **to be ~** (*crime, disease etc*) wild wuchern

rampart ['ræmpɑːt] *n* Schutzwall *m*

ram raiding [-reɪdɪŋ] *n* *Einbruchdiebstahl, wobei die Diebe mit einem Wagen in die Schaufensterfront eines Ladens eindringen*

ramshackle ['ræmʃækl] *adj* (*house*) baufällig; (*cart*) klapprig; (*table*) altersschwach

RAN *n abbr* (= *Royal Australian Navy*) australische Marine *f*

ran [ræn] *pt of* **run**

ranch [rɑːntʃ] *n* Ranch *f*

rancher ['rɑːntʃər] *n* Rancher(in) *m(f)*; (*worker*) Farmhelfer(in) *m(f)*

rancid ['rænsɪd] *adj* ranzig

rancour, (*US*) **rancor** ['ræŋkər] *n* Verbitterung *f*

R & B *n abbr* (= *rhythm and blues*) R & B

R & D *n abbr* = **research and development**

random ['rændəm] *adj* (*arrangement*) willkürlich; (*selection*) zufällig; (*Comput*) wahlfrei; (*Math*) Zufalls- ▷ *n*: **at ~** aufs Geratewohl

random access *n* (*Comput*) wahlfreier Zugriff *m*

random access memory *n* (*Comput*) Schreib-Lese-Speicher *m*

R & R (*US*) *n abbr* (*Mil: = rest and recreation*) Urlaub *m*

randy ['rændɪ] (*Brit: inf*) *adj* geil, scharf

rang [ræŋ] *pt of* **ring**

range [reɪndʒ] *n* (*of mountains*) Kette *f*; (*of missile*) Reichweite *f*; (*of voice*) Umfang *m*; (*series*) Reihe *f*; (*of products*) Auswahl *f*; (*Mil: also:* **rifle range**) Schießstand *m*; (*also:* **kitchen range**) Herd *m* ▷ *vt* (*place in a line*) anordnen ▷ *vi*: **to ~ over** (*extend*) sich erstrecken über +*acc*; **price ~** Preisspanne *f*; **do you have anything else in this price ~?** haben Sie noch etwas anderes in dieser Preisklasse?; **within (firing) ~** in Schussweite; **at close ~** aus unmittelbarer Entfernung; **~d left/right** (*text*) links-/rechtsbündig; **to ~ from ... to ...** sich zwischen ... und ... bewegen

ranger ['reɪndʒər] *n* Förster(in) *m(f)*

Rangoon [ræŋ'guːn] *n* Rangun *nt*

rank [ræŋk] *n* (*row*) Reihe *f*; (*Mil*) Rang *m*; (*social class*) Schicht *f*; (*Brit: also:* **taxi rank**) Taxistand *m* ▷ *vi*: **to ~ as/among** zählen zu ▷ *vt*: **he is ~ed third in the world** er steht weltweit an dritter Stelle ▷ *adj* (*stinking*) stinkend; (*sheer: hypocrisy etc*) rein; **the ranks** *npl* (*Mil*) die Mannschaften *pl*; **the ~ and file** (*ordinary members*) die Basis *f*; **to close ~s** (*Mil, fig*) die Reihen schließen

rankle ['ræŋkl] *vi* (*insult*) nachwirken; **to ~ with sb** jdn wurmen

rank outsider *n* totaler Außenseiter *m*, totale Außenseiterin *f*

ransack ['rænsæk] *vt* (*search*) durchwühlen; (*plunder*) plündern

ransom ['rænsəm] *n* (*money*) Lösegeld *nt*; **to hold sb to ~** (*hostage*) jdn als Geisel halten; (*fig*) jdn erpressen

rant [rænt] *vi* schimpfen, wettern; **to ~ and rave** herumwettern

ranting ['ræntɪŋ] *n* Geschimpfe *nt*

rap [ræp] *vi* klopfen ▷ *vt*: **to ~ sb's knuckles** jdm auf die Finger klopfen ▷ *n* (*at door*) Klopfen *nt*; (*also:* **rap music**) Rap *m*

rape [reɪp] *n* Vergewaltigung *f*; (*Bot*) Raps *m* ▷ *vt* vergewaltigen

rape oil, rapeseed oil ['reɪpsiːd-] *n* Rapsöl *nt*

rapid ['ræpɪd] *adj* schnell; (*growth, change*) schnell, rapid

rapidity [rə'pɪdɪtɪ] *n* Schnelligkeit *f*

rapidly ['ræpɪdlɪ] *adv* schnell; (*grow, change*) schnell, rapide

rapids ['ræpɪdz] *npl* Stromschnellen *pl*
rapist ['reɪpɪst] *n* Vergewaltiger *m*
rapport [ræ'pɔːʳ] *n* enges Verhältnis *nt*
rapprochement [ræ'prɔʃmɑ̃ːŋ] *n* Annäherung *f*
rapt [ræpt] *adj* (*attention*) gespannt; **to be ~ in thought** in Gedanken versunken sein
rapture ['ræptʃəʳ] *n* Entzücken *nt*; **to go into ~s over** ins Schwärmen geraten über +*acc*
rapturous ['ræptʃərəs] *adj* (*applause, welcome*) stürmisch
rare [rɛəʳ] *adj* selten; (*steak*) nur angebraten, englisch (gebraten); **it is ~ to find that ...** es kommt nur selten vor, dass ...
rarebit ['rɛəbɪt] *n see* **Welsh rarebit**
rarefied ['rɛərɪfaɪd] *adj* (*air, atmosphere*) dünn; (*fig*) exklusiv
rarely ['rɛəlɪ] *adv* selten
raring ['rɛərɪŋ] *adj*: **~ to go** (*inf*) in den Startlöchern
rarity ['rɛərɪtɪ] *n* Seltenheit *f*
rascal ['rɑːskl] *n* (*child*) Frechdachs *m*; (*rogue*) Schurke *m*
rash [ræʃ] *adj* (*person*) unbesonnen; (*promise, act*) übereilt ▷ *n* (*Med*) Ausschlag *m*; (*of events etc*) Flut *f*; **to come out in a ~** einen Ausschlag bekommen
rasher ['ræʃəʳ] *n* (*of bacon*) Scheibe *f*
rashly ['ræʃlɪ] *adv* (*promise etc*) voreilig
rasp [rɑːsp] *n* (*tool*) Raspel *f*; (*sound*) Kratzen *nt* ▷ *vt, vi* krächzen
raspberry ['rɑːzbərɪ] *n* Himbeere *f*; **~ bush** Himbeerstrauch *m*; **to blow a ~** (*inf*) verächtlich schnauben
rasping ['rɑːspɪŋ] *adj*: **a ~ noise** ein kratzendes Geräusch
Rastafarian *n* Rastafarier *m*
rat [ræt] *n* Ratte *f*
ratable ['reɪtəbl] *adj* = **rateable**
ratchet ['rætʃɪt] *n* Sperrklinke *f*; **~ wheel** Sperrad *nt*
rate [reɪt] *n* (*speed: of change etc*) Tempo *nt*; (*of inflation, unemployment etc*) Rate *f*; (*of interest, taxation*) Satz *m*; (*price*) Preis *m* ▷ *vt* einschätzen; **rates** *npl* (*Brit: property tax*) Kommunalabgaben *pl*; **at a ~ of 60 kph** mit einem Tempo von 60 km/h; **~ of growth** (*Econ*) Wachstumsrate *f*; **~ of return** (*Fin*) Rendite *f*; **pulse ~** Pulszahl *f*; **at this/that ~** wenn es so weitergeht; **at any ~** auf jeden Fall; **to ~ sb/sth as** jdn/etw einschätzen als; **to ~ sb/sth among** jdn/etw zählen zu; **to ~ sb/sth highly** jdn/etw hoch einschätzen
rateable ['reɪtəbl] *adj*: **~ value** (*Brit*) ▷ *n* steuerbarer Wert *m*
ratepayer ['reɪtpeɪəʳ] (*Brit*) *n* Steuerzahler(in) *m(f)*
rather ['rɑːðəʳ] *adv* (*somewhat*) etwas; (*very*) ziemlich; **~ a lot** ziemlich *or* recht viel; **I would ~ go** ich würde lieber gehen; **~ than** (*instead of*) anstelle von; **or ~** (*more accurately*) oder vielmehr; **I'd ~ not say** das möchte ich lieber nicht sagen; **I ~ think he won't come**

ich glaube eher, dass er nicht kommt
ratification [rætɪfɪ'keɪʃən] *n* Ratifikation *f*
ratify ['rætɪfaɪ] *vt* (*treaty etc*) ratifizieren
rating ['reɪtɪŋ] *n* (*score*) Rate *f*; (*assessment*) Beurteilung *f*; (*Naut: Brit: sailor*) Matrose *m*; **ratings** *npl* (*Radio, TV*) Einschaltquote *f*; **~s hit** Quotenhit *m*
ratio ['reɪʃɪəu] *n* Verhältnis *nt*; **a ~ of 5 to 1** ein Verhältnis von 5 zu 1
ration ['ræʃən] *n* Ration *f* ▷ *vt* rationieren; **rations** *npl* (*Mil*) Rationen *pl*
rational ['ræʃənl] *adj* rational, vernünftig
rationale [ræʃə'nɑːl] *n* Grundlage *f*
rationalization [ræʃnəlaɪ'zeɪʃən] *n* (*justification*) Rechtfertigung *f*; (*of company, system*) Rationalisierung *f*
rationalize ['ræʃnəlaɪz] *vt* (*see n*) rechtfertigen, rationalisieren
rationally ['ræʃnəlɪ] *adv* vernünftig, rational
rationing ['ræʃnɪŋ] *n* Rationierung *f*
ratpack (*Brit: inf*) *n* (*reporters*) Pressemeute *f*
rat poison *n* Rattengift *nt*
rat race *n*: **the ~** der ständige *or* tägliche Konkurrenzkampf *m*
rattan [ræ'tæn] *n* Rattan *nt*, Peddigrohr *nt*
rattle ['rætl] *n* (*of door, window, snake*) Klappern *nt*; (*of train, car etc*) Rattern *nt*; (*of chain*) Rasseln *nt*; (*toy*) Rassel *f* ▷ *vi* (*chains*) rasseln; (*windows*) klappern; (*bottles*) klirren ▷ *vt* (*shake noisily*) rütteln an +*dat*; (*fig: unsettle*) nervös machen; **to ~ along** (*car, bus*) dahinrattern
rattlesnake ['rætlsneɪk] *n* Klapperschlange *f*
ratty ['rætɪ] (*inf*) *adj* gereizt
raucous ['rɔːkəs] *adj* (*voice etc*) rau
raucously ['rɔːkəslɪ] *adv* rau
raunchy ['rɔːntʃɪ] *adj* (*voice, song*) lüstern, geil
ravage ['rævɪdʒ] *vt* verwüsten
ravages ['rævɪdʒɪz] *npl* (*of war*) Verwüstungen *pl*; (*of weather*) zerstörende Auswirkungen *pl*; (*of time*) Spuren *pl*
rave [reɪv] *vi* (*in anger*) toben ▷ *adj* (*inf: review*) glänzend; (*scene, culture*) Rave- ▷ *n* (*Brit: inf: party*) Rave *m*, Fete *f* ▷ **rave about** schwärmen von
raven ['reɪvən] *n* Rabe *m*
ravenous ['rævənəs] *adj* (*person*) ausgehungert; (*appetite*) unersättlich
ravine [rə'viːn] *n* Schlucht *f*
raving ['reɪvɪŋ] *adj*: **a ~ lunatic** ein total verrückter Typ
ravings ['reɪvɪŋz] *npl* Fantastereien *pl*
ravioli [rævɪ'əulɪ] *n* Ravioli *pl*
ravishing ['rævɪʃɪŋ] *adj* hinreißend
raw [rɔː] *adj* roh; (*sore*) wund; (*inexperienced*) unerfahren; (*weather, day*) rau; **to get a ~ deal** ungerecht behandelt werden
Rawalpindi [rɔːl'pɪndɪ] *n* Rawalpindi *nt*
raw material *n* Rohmaterial *nt*
ray [reɪ] *n* Strahl *m*; **~ of hope** Hoffnungsschimmer *m*
rayon ['reɪɔn] *n* Reyon *nt*
raze [reɪz] *vt* (*also*: **to raze to the ground**) dem Erdboden gleichmachen

r

razor ['reɪzə'] n Rasierapparat m; (open razor) Rasiermesser nt

razor blade n Rasierklinge f

razzle ['ræzl] (Brit: inf) n: **to be/go on the ~** einen draufmachen

razzmatazz ['ræzmə'tæz] (inf) n Trubel m

RC abbr (= Roman Catholic) r.-k.

RCAF n abbr (= Royal Canadian Air Force) kanadische Luftwaffe f

RCMP n abbr (= Royal Canadian Mounted Police) kanadische berittene Polizei

RCN n abbr (= Royal Canadian Navy) kanadische Marine

RD (US) abbr (Post) = rural delivery Landpostzustellung f

Rd abbr (= road) Str.

RDC (Brit) n abbr = **rural district council**

RE (Brit) n abbr (Scol) = **religious education** (Mil: = Royal Engineers) Königliches Pionierkorps

re [riː] prep (with regard to) bezüglich +gen

reach [riːtʃ] n (range) Reichweite f ▷ vt erreichen; (conclusion, decision) kommen zu; (be able to touch) kommen an +acc ▷ vi (stretch out one's arm) langen; **reaches** npl (of river) Gebiete pl; **within/out of ~** in/außer Reichweite; **within easy ~ of the supermarket/station** ganz in der Nähe des Supermarkts/Bahnhofs; **beyond the ~ of sb/sth** außerhalb der Reichweite von jdm/etw; **"keep out of the ~ of children"** „von Kindern fernhalten"; **can I ~ you at your hotel?** kann ich Sie in Ihrem Hotel erreichen?

▶ **reach out** vt (hand) ausstrecken ▷ vi die Hand ausstrecken; **to ~ out for sth** nach etw greifen

react [riː'ækt] vi: **to ~ (to)** (also Med) reagieren (auf +acc); (Chem): **to ~ (with)** reagieren (mit); **to ~ (against)** (rebel) sich wehren (gegen)

reaction [riː'ækʃən] n Reaktion f; **reactions** npl (reflexes) Reaktionen pl; **a ~ against sth** Widerstand gegen etw

reactionary [riː'ækʃənrɪ] adj reaktionär ▷ n Reaktionär(in) m(f)

reactor [riː'æktə'] n (also: **nuclear reactor**) Kernreaktor m

read [riːd] (pt, pp **~**) [rɛd] vi lesen; (piece of writing etc) sich lesen ▷ vt lesen; (meter, thermometer etc) ablesen; (understand: mood, thoughts) sich versetzen in +acc; (meter, thermometer etc: measurement) anzeigen; (study) studieren; **to ~ sb's lips** jdm von den Lippen ablesen; **to ~ sb's mind** jds Gedanken lesen; **to ~ between the lines** zwischen den Zeilen lesen; **to take sth as ~** (self-evident) etw für selbstverständlich halten; **you can take it as ~ that ...** Sie können davon ausgehen, dass ...; **do you ~ me?** (Tel) verstehen Sie mich?; **to ~ sth into sb's remarks** etw in jds Bemerkungen hineininterpretieren

▶ **read out** vt vorlesen

▶ **read over** vt durchlesen

▶ **read through** vt durchlesen

▶ **read up on** vt fus sich informieren über +acc

readable ['riːdəbl] adj (legible) lesbar; (book, author etc) lesenswert

reader ['riːdə'] n (person) Leser(in) m(f); (book) Lesebuch nt; (Brit: at university) ≈ Dozent(in) m(f); **to be an avid/slow ~** eifrig/langsam lesen

readership ['riːdəʃɪp] n (of newspaper etc) Leserschaft f

readily ['rɛdɪlɪ] adv (without hesitation) bereitwillig; (easily) ohne Weiteres

readiness ['rɛdɪnɪs] n Bereitschaft f; **in ~ for** bereit für

reading ['riːdɪŋ] n Lesen nt; (understanding) Verständnis nt; (from bible, of poetry etc) Lesung f; (on meter, thermometer etc) Anzeige f

reading lamp n Leselampe f

reading matter n Lesestoff m

reading room n Lesesaal m

readjust [riːə'dʒʌst] vt (position, knob, instrument etc) neu einstellen ▷ vi: **to ~ (to)** sich anpassen (an +acc)

readjustment [riːə'dʒʌstmənt] n (fig) Neuorientierung f

ready ['rɛdɪ] adj (prepared) bereit, fertig; (willing) bereit; (easy) leicht; (available) fertig ▷ n: **at the ~** (Mil) einsatzbereit; (fig) griffbereit; **~ for use** gebrauchsfertig; **to be ~ to do sth** bereit sein, etw zu tun; **to get ~** sich fertig machen; **to get sth ~** etw bereitmachen

ready cash n Bargeld nt

ready-cooked ['rɛdɪkukt] adj vorgekocht

ready-made ['rɛdɪ'meɪd] adj (clothes) von der Stange, Konfektions-; **~ meal** Fertiggericht nt

ready-mix ['rɛdɪmɪks] n (for cakes etc) Backmischung f; (concrete) Fertigbeton m

ready money n = **ready cash**

ready reckoner [-'rɛkənə'] (Brit) n Rechentabelle f

ready-to-wear ['rɛdɪtə'wɛə'] adj (clothes) von der Stange, Konfektions-

reaffirm [riːə'fəːm] vt bestätigen

reagent [riː'eɪdʒənt] n: **chemical ~** Reagens nt, Reagenz nt

real [rɪəl] adj (reason, result etc) wirklich; (leather, gold etc) echt; (life, feeling) wahr; (for emphasis) echt ▷ adv (US: inf: very) echt; **in ~ life** im wahren or wirklichen Leben; **in ~ terms** effektiv

real ale n Real Ale nt

real estate n Immobilien pl ▷ cpd (US: agent, business etc) Immobilien-

realign vt neu ausrichten

realism ['rɪəlɪzəm] n (also Art) Realismus m

realist ['rɪəlɪst] n Realist(in) m(f)

realistic [rɪə'lɪstɪk] adj realistisch

reality [riː'ælɪtɪ] n Wirklichkeit f, Realität f; **in ~** in Wirklichkeit

realization [rɪələ'zeɪʃən] n (understanding) Erkenntnis f; (fulfilment) Verwirklichung f, Realisierung f; (Fin: of asset) Realisation f

realize ['rɪəlaɪz] vt (understand) verstehen; (fulfil) verwirklichen, realisieren; (Fin: amount, profit) realisieren; **I ~ that ...** es ist mir klar, dass ...

really ['rɪəlɪ] *adv* wirklich; **what ~ happened**
was wirklich geschah; **~?** wirklich?; **~!**
(*indicating annoyance*) also wirklich!

realm [rɛlm] *n* (*fig: field*) Bereich *m*; (*kingdom*)
Reich *nt*

real-time ['ri:ltaɪm] *adj* (*Comput: processing etc*)
Echtzeit-

Realtor® ['rɪəltɔ:ʳ] (*US*) *n*
Immobilienmakler(in) *m(f)*

ream [ri:m] *n* (*of paper*) Ries *nt*; **reams** (*inf: fig*)
Bände *pl*

reap [ri:p] *vt* (*crop*) einbringen, ernten;
(*fig: benefits*) ernten; (*: rewards*) bekommen

reaper ['ri:pəʳ] *n* (*machine*) Mähdrescher *m*

reappear [ri:ə'pɪəʳ] *vi* wieder auftauchen

reappearance [ri:ə'pɪərəns] *n*
Wiederauftauchen *nt*

reapply [ri:ə'plaɪ] *vi*: **to ~ for** sich erneut
bewerben um

reappoint [ri:ə'pɔɪnt] *vt* (*to job*)
wiedereinstellen

reappraisal [ri:ə'preɪzl] *n* (*of idea etc*)
Neubeurteilung *f*

rear [rɪəʳ] *adj* hintere(r, s); (*wheel etc*) Hinter- ▷ *n*
Rückseite *f*; (*buttocks*) Hinterteil *nt* ▷ *vt* (*family,
animals*) aufziehen ▷ *vi* (*also*: **rear up**: *horse*) sich
aufbäumen

rear admiral *n* Konteradmiral *m*

rear-engined ['rɪər'ɛndʒɪnd] *adj* mit
Heckmotor

rearguard ['rɪəɡɑ:d] *n* (*Mil*) Nachhut *f*; **to fight
a ~ action** (*fig*) sich erbittert wehren

rearm [ri:'ɑ:m] *vi* (*country*) wiederaufrüsten ▷ *vt*
wiederbewaffnen

rearmament [ri:'ɑ:məmənt] *n*
Wiederaufrüstung *f*

rearrange [ri:ə'reɪndʒ] *vt* (*furniture*) umstellen;
(*meeting*) den Termin ändern +*gen*

rear-view mirror ['rɪəvju:-] *n* Rückspiegel *m*

reason ['ri:zn] *n* (*cause*) Grund *m*; (*rationality*)
Verstand *m*; (*common sense*) Vernunft *f* ▷ *vi*: **to
~ with sb** vernünftig mit jdm reden; **the ~
for/why** der Grund für/, warum; **we have ~
to believe that ...** wir haben Grund zu der
Annahme, dass ...; **it stands to ~ that ...**
es ist zu erwarten, dass ...; **she claims with
good ~ that ...** sie behauptet mit gutem
Grund *or* mit Recht, dass ...; **all the more ~
why ...** ein Grund mehr, warum ...; **yes, but
within ~** ja, solange es sich im Rahmen hält

reasonable ['ri:znəbl] *adj* vernünftig; (*number,
amount*) angemessen; (*not bad*) ganz ordentlich;
be ~! sei doch vernünftig!

reasonably ['ri:znəblɪ] *adv* (*fairly*) ziemlich;
(*sensibly*) vernünftig; **one could ~ assume
that ...** man könnte durchaus annehmen,
dass ...

reasoned ['ri:znd] *adj* (*argument*) durchdacht

reasoning ['ri:znɪŋ] *n* Argumentation *f*

reassemble [ri:ə'sɛmbl] *vt* (*machine*)
wieder zusammensetzen ▷ *vi* sich wieder
versammeln

reassert [ri:ə'sə:t] *vt*: **to ~ oneself/one's**

authority seine Autorität wieder geltend
machen

reassurance [ri:ə'ʃuərəns] *n* (*comfort*)
Beruhigung *f*; (*guarantee*) Bestätigung *f*

reassure [ri:ə'ʃuəʳ] *vt* beruhigen

reassuring [ri:ə'ʃuərɪŋ] *adj* beruhigend

reawakening [ri:ə'weɪknɪŋ] *n*
Wiedererwachen *nt*

rebate ['ri:beɪt] *n* (*on tax etc*) Rückerstattung *f*;
(*discount*) Ermäßigung *f*

rebel ['rɛbl] *n* Rebell(in) *m(f)* ▷ *vi* rebellieren

rebellion [rɪ'bɛljən] *n* Rebellion *f*

rebellious [rɪ'bɛljəs] *adj* rebellisch

rebirth [ri:'bə:θ] *n* Wiedergeburt *f*

rebound [rɪ'baund] *vi* (*ball*) zurückprallen
▷ *n*: **on the ~** (*fig*) als Tröstung

rebuff [rɪ'bʌf] *n* Abfuhr *f* ▷ *vt* zurückweisen

rebuild [ri:'bɪld] (*irreg: like* **build**) *vt*
wiederaufbauen; (*confidence*) wiederherstellen

rebuke [rɪ'bju:k] *vt* zurechtweisen, tadeln ▷ *n*
Zurechtweisung *f*, Tadel *m*

rebut [rɪ'bʌt] (*form*) *vt* widerlegen

rebuttal [rɪ'bʌtl] (*form*) *n* Widerlegung *f*

recalcitrant [rɪ'kælsɪtrənt] *adj* aufsässig

recall [rɪ'kɔ:l] *vt* (*remember*) sich erinnern
an +*acc*; (*ambassador*) abberufen; (*product*)
zurückrufen ▷ *n* (*of memories*) Erinnerung *f*; (*of
ambassador*) Abberufung *f*; (*of product*) Rückruf
m; **beyond ~** unwiederbringlich

recant [rɪ'kænt] *vi* widerrufen

recap ['ri:kæp] *vt, vi* zusammenfassen ▷ *n*
Zusammenfassung *f*

recapitulate [ri:kə'pɪtjuleɪt] *vt, vi* = **recap**

recapture [ri:'kæptʃəʳ] *vt* (*town*)
wiedereinnehmen; (*prisoner*) wiederergreifen;
(*atmosphere etc*) heraufbeschwören

rec'd *abbr* (*Comm*: = *received*) erh.

recede [rɪ'si:d] *vi* (*tide*) zurückgehen; (*lights
etc*) verschwinden; (*memory, hope*) schwinden;
his hair is beginning to ~ er bekommt eine
Stirnglatze

receding [rɪ'si:dɪŋ] *adj* (*hairline*)
zurückweichend; (*chin*) fliehend

receipt [rɪ'si:t] *n* (*document*) Quittung *f*; (*act
of receiving*) Erhalt *m*; **receipts** *npl* (*Comm*)
Einnahmen *pl*; **on ~ of** bei Erhalt +*gen*; **to be
in ~ of sth** etw erhalten

receivable [rɪ'si:vəbl] *adj* (*Comm*) zulässig;
(*owing*) ausstehend

receive [rɪ'si:v] *vt* erhalten, bekommen; (*injury*)
erleiden; (*treatment*) erhalten; (*visitor, guest*)
empfangen; **to be on the receiving end of
sth** der/die Leidtragende von etw sein; **"~d
with thanks"** (*Comm*) „dankend erhalten"

r

receiver [rɪ'siːvəʳ] n (Tel) Hörer m; (Radio, TV) Empfänger m; (of stolen goods) Hehler(in) m(f); (Comm) Empfänger(in) m(f)

receivership [rɪ'siːvəʃɪp] n: **to go into ~** in Konkurs gehen

recent ['riːsnt] adj (event) kürzlich; (times) letzte(r, s); **in ~ years** in den letzten Jahren

recently ['riːsntlɪ] adv (not long ago) kürzlich; (lately) in letzter Zeit; **as ~ as** erst; **until ~** bis vor Kurzem

receptacle [rɪ'septɪkl] n Behälter m

reception [rɪ'sepʃən] n (in hotel, office etc) Rezeption f; (party, Radio, TV) Empfang m; (welcome) Aufnahme f

reception centre (Brit) n Aufnahmelager nt
reception desk n Rezeption f

receptionist [rɪ'sepʃənɪst] n (in hotel) Empfangschef m, Empfangsdame f; (in doctor's surgery) Sprechstundenhilfe f

receptive [rɪ'septɪv] adj aufnahmebereit

recess [rɪ'ses] n (in room) Nische f; (secret place) Winkel m; (Pol etc: holiday) Ferien pl; (US: Law: short break) Pause f; (esp US: Scol) Pause f

recession [rɪ'seʃən] n (Econ) Rezession f

recessionista [rɪseʃə'nɪstə] n modebewusste Person, die in Zeiten der Rezession auf die Kosten ihres Lebensstils achtet

recharge [riː'tʃɑːdʒ] vt (battery) aufladen

rechargeable [riː'tʃɑːdʒəbl] adj aufladbar

recipe ['resɪpɪ] n Rezept nt; **a ~ for success** ein Erfolgsrezept nt; **to be a ~ for disaster** in die Katastrophe führen

recipient [rɪ'sɪpɪənt] n Empfänger(in) m(f)

reciprocal [rɪ'sɪprəkl] adj gegenseitig

reciprocate [rɪ'sɪprəkeɪt] vt (invitation, feeling) erwidern ▷ vi sich revanchieren

recital [rɪ'saɪtl] n (concert) Konzert nt

recite [rɪ'saɪt] vt (poem) vortragen; (complaints etc) aufzählen

reckless ['rekləs] adj (driving, driver) rücksichtslos; (spending) leichtsinnig

recklessly ['rekləslɪ] adv (drive) rücksichtslos; (spend, gamble) leichtsinnig

reckon ['rekən] vt (consider) halten für; (calculate) berechnen ▷ vi: **he is somebody to be ~ed with** mit ihm muss man rechnen; **I ~ that ...** (think) ich schätze, dass ...; **to ~ without sb/sth** nicht mit jdm/etw rechnen
▶ **reckon on** vt fus rechnen mit

reckoning ['rekniŋ] n (calculation) Berechnung f; **the day of ~** der Tag der Abrechnung

reclaim [rɪ'kleɪm] vt (luggage) abholen; (tax etc) zurückfordern; (land) gewinnen; (waste materials) zur Wiederverwertung sammeln

reclamation [reklə'meɪʃən] n (of land) Gewinnung f

recline [rɪ'klaɪn] vi (sit or lie back) zurückgelehnt sitzen

reclining [rɪ'klaɪnɪŋ] adj (seat) Liege-

recluse [rɪ'kluːs] n Einsiedler(in) m(f)

recognition [rekəg'nɪʃən] n (of person, place) Erkennen nt; (of problem, fact) Erkenntnis f; (of achievement) Anerkennung f; **in ~ of** in

Anerkennung +gen; **to gain ~** Anerkennung finden; **she had changed beyond ~** sie war nicht wieder zu erkennen

recognizable ['rekəgnaɪzəbl] adj erkennbar

recognize ['rekəgnaɪz] vt (person, place, voice) wiedererkennen; (sign, problem) erkennen; (qualifications, government, achievement) anerkennen; **to ~ sb by/as** jdn erkennen an +dat/als

recoil [rɪ'kɔɪl] vi (person): **to ~ from** zurückweichen vor +dat; (fig) zurückschrecken vor +dat ▷ n (of gun) Rückstoß m

recollect [rekə'lekt] vt (remember) sich erinnern an +acc

recollection [rekə'lekʃən] n Erinnerung f; **to the best of my ~** soweit ich mich erinnern or entsinnen kann

recommend [rekə'mend] vt empfehlen; **she has a lot to ~ her** es spricht sehr viel für sie

recommendation [rekəmen'deɪʃən] n Empfehlung f

recommended retail price (Brit) n (Comm) unverbindlicher Richtpreis m

recompense ['rekəmpens] n (reward) Belohnung f; (compensation) Entschädigung f

reconcilable ['rekənsaɪləbl] adj (ideas) (miteinander) vereinbar

reconcile ['rekənsaɪl] vt (people) versöhnen; (facts, beliefs) (miteinander) vereinbaren, in Einklang bringen; **to ~ o.s. to sth** sich mit etw abfinden

reconciliation [rekənsɪlɪ'eɪʃən] n (of people) Versöhnung f; (of facts, beliefs) Vereinbarung f

recondite [rɪ'kɒndaɪt] adj obskur

recondition [riːkən'dɪʃən] vt (machine) überholen

reconditioned [riːkən'dɪʃənd] adj (engine, TV) generalüberholt

reconnaissance [rɪ'kɒnɪsns] n (Mil) Aufklärung f

reconnoitre, (US) reconnoiter [rekə'nɔɪtəʳ] vt (Mil) erkunden

reconsider [riːkən'sɪdəʳ] vt (noch einmal) überdenken ▷ vi es sich dat noch einmal überlegen

reconstitute [riː'kɒnstɪtjuːt] vt (organization) neu bilden; (food) wiederherstellen

reconstruct [riːkən'strʌkt] vt (building) wiederaufbauen; (policy, system) neu organisieren; (event, crime) rekonstruieren

reconstruction [riːkən'strʌkʃən] n Wiederaufbau m; (of crime) Rekonstruktion f

reconvene [riːkən'viːn] vi (meet again) wieder zusammenkommen ▷ vt (meeting etc) wiedereinberufen

record ['rekɔːd] n (written account) Aufzeichnung f; (of meeting) Protokoll nt; (of decision) Beleg m; (Comput) Datensatz m; (file) Akte f; (Mus: disc) Schallplatte f; (history) Vorgeschichte f; (also: **criminal record**) Vorstrafen pl; (Sport) Rekord m ▷ vt aufzeichnen; (song etc) aufnehmen; (temperature, speed etc) registrieren ▷ adj (sales, profits) Rekord-; **~ of attendance**

Anwesenheitsliste f; **public ~s** Urkunden pl des Nationalarchivs; **to keep a ~ of sth** etw schriftlich festhalten; **to have a good/poor ~** gute/schlechte Leistungen vorzuweisen haben; **to have a (criminal) ~** vorbestraft sein; **to set** or **put the ~ straight** (fig) Klarheit schaffen; **he is on ~ as saying that ...** er hat nachweislich gesagt, dass ...; **off the ~** (remark) inoffiziell ▷ adv (speak) im Vertrauen; **in ~ time** in Rekordzeit

recorded delivery [rɪ'kɔ:dɪd-] (Brit) n (Post) Einschreiben nt; **to send sth (by) ~** etw per Einschreiben senden

recorder [rɪ'kɔ:dər] n (Mus) Blockflöte f; (Law) nebenamtlich als Richter tätiger Rechtsanwalt

record holder n (Sport) Rekordinhaber(in) m(f)

recording [rɪ'kɔ:dɪŋ] n Aufnahme f

recording studio n Aufnahmestudio nt

record library n Schallplattenverleih m

record player n Plattenspieler m

recount [rɪ'kaunt] vt (story etc) erzählen

re-count ['ri:kaunt] n (of votes) Nachzählung f ▷ vt (votes) nachzählen

recoup [rɪ'ku:p] vt: **to ~ one's losses** seine Verluste ausgleichen

recourse [rɪ'kɔ:s] n: **to have ~ to sth** Zuflucht zu etw nehmen

recover [rɪ'kʌvər] vt (get back) zurückbekommen; (stolen goods) sicherstellen; (wreck, body) bergen; (financial loss) ausgleichen ▷ vi sich erholen

re-cover [ri:'kʌvər] vt (chair etc) neu beziehen

recovery [rɪ'kʌvərɪ] n (from illness etc) Erholung f; (in economy) Aufschwung m; (of lost items) Wiederfinden nt; (of stolen goods) Sicherstellung f; (of wreck, body) Bergung f; (of financial loss) Ausgleich m

re-create [ri:krɪ'eɪt] vt (atmosphere, situation) wiederherstellen

recreation [rɛkrɪ'eɪʃən] n (leisure) Erholung f, Entspannung f

recreational [rɛkrɪ'eɪʃənl] adj (facilities etc) Freizeit-

recreational drug n Freizeitdroge f

recreational vehicle (US) n Caravan m

recrimination [rɪkrɪmɪ'neɪʃən] n gegenseitige Anschuldigungen pl

recruit [rɪ'kru:t] n (Mil) Rekrut m; (in company) neuer Mitarbeiter m, neue Mitarbeiterin f ▷ vt (Mil) rekrutieren; (staff, new members) anwerben

recruiting office [rɪ'kru:tɪŋ-] n (Mil) Rekrutierungsbüro nt

recruitment [rɪ'kru:tmənt] n (of staff) Anwerbung f

rectangle ['rɛktæŋgl] n Rechteck nt

rectangular [rɛk'tæŋgjulər] adj (shape) rechteckig

rectify ['rɛktɪfaɪ] vt (mistake etc) korrigieren

rector ['rɛktər] n (Rel) Pfarrer(in) m(f)

rectory ['rɛktərɪ] n Pfarrhaus nt

rectum ['rɛktəm] n Rektum nt, Mastdarm m

recuperate [rɪ'kju:pəreɪt] vi (recover) sich erholen

recur [rɪ'kə:r] vi (error, event) sich wiederholen; (pain etc) wiederholt auftreten

recurrence [rɪ'kə:rns] n (see vi) Wiederholung f; wiederholtes Auftreten nt

recurrent [rɪ'kə:rnt] adj (see vi) sich wiederholend; wiederholt auftretend

recurring [rɪ'kə:rɪŋ] adj (problem, dream) sich wiederholend; (Math): **six point five four ~** sechs Komma fünf Periode vier

recycle [ri:'saɪkl] vt (waste, paper etc) recyceln, wiederverwerten

recycling [ri:'saɪklɪŋ] n Recycling nt; **~ site** Recycling- or Wertstoffhof m

red [rɛd] n Rot nt; (pej, Pol) Rote(r) f(m) ▷ adj rot; **to be in the ~** (business etc) in den roten Zahlen sein

red alert n: **to be on ~** in höchster Alarmbereitschaft sein

red-blooded ['rɛd'blʌdɪd] adj heißblütig

● **REDBRICK UNIVERSITY**

Als *redbrick university* werden die jüngeren britischen Universitäten bezeichnet, die im späten 19. und Anfang des 20. Jh. in Städten wie Manchester, Liverpool und Bristol gegründet wurden. Der Name steht im Gegensatz zu Oxford und Cambridge und bezieht sich auf die roten Backsteinmauern der Universitätsgebäude.

red carpet treatment n: **to give sb the ~** den roten Teppich für jdn ausrollen

Red Cross n Rotes Kreuz nt

redcurrant ['rɛdkʌrənt] n Rote Johannisbeere f

redden ['rɛdn] vt röten ▷ vi (blush) erröten

reddish ['rɛdɪʃ] adj rötlich

redecorate [ri:'dɛkəreɪt] vt, vi renovieren

redecoration [ri:dɛkə'reɪʃən] n Renovierung f

redeem [rɪ'di:m] vt (situation etc) retten; (voucher, sth in pawn) einlösen; (loan) abzahlen; (Rel) erlösen; **to ~ oneself for sth** etw wiedergutmachen

redeemable [rɪ'di:məbl] adj (voucher etc) einlösbar

redeeming [rɪ'di:mɪŋ] adj (feature, quality) versöhnend

redefine [ri:dɪ'faɪn] vt neu definieren

redemption [rɪ'dɛmʃən] n (Rel) Erlösung f; **past** or **beyond ~** nicht mehr zu retten

redeploy [ri:dɪ'plɔɪ] vt (resources, staff) umverteilen; (Mil) verlegen

redeployment [ri:dɪ'plɔɪmənt] n (see vt) Umverteilung f; Verlegung f

redevelop [ri:dɪ'vɛləp] vt (area) sanieren

redevelopment [ri:dɪ'vɛləpmənt] n Sanierung f

red-handed [rɛd'hændɪd] adj: **to be caught ~** auf frischer Tat ertappt werden

redhead ['rɛdhɛd] n Rotschopf m

red herring n (fig) falsche Spur f

red-hot [rɛd'hɔt] adj (metal) rot glühend

r

redirect [riːdaɪˈrɛkt] vt (*mail*) nachsenden; (*traffic*) umleiten

rediscover [riːdɪsˈkʌvəʳ] vt wiederentdecken

redistribute [riːdɪsˈtrɪbjuːt] vt umverteilen

red-letter day [ˈrɛdlɛtə-] n besonderer Tag m

red light n (*Aut*): **to go through a ~** eine Ampel bei Rot überfahren

red-light district [ˈrɛdlaɪt-] n Rotlichtviertel nt

red meat n Rind- und Lammfleisch

redness [ˈrɛdnɪs] n Röte f

redo [riːˈduː] (*irreg: like* **do**) vt noch einmal machen

redolent [ˈrɛdələnt] adj: **to be ~ of sth** nach etw riechen; (*fig*) an etw erinnern

redouble [riːˈdʌbl] vt: **to ~ one's efforts** seine Anstrengungen verdoppeln

redraft [riːˈdrɑːft] vt (*agreement*) neu abfassen

redraw [riːˈdrɔː] vt neu zeichnen

redress [rɪˈdrɛs] n (*compensation*) Wiedergutmachung f ▷ vt (*error etc*) wiedergutmachen; **to ~ the balance** das Gleichgewicht wiederherstellen

Red Sea n: **the ~** das Rote Meer

redskin [ˈrɛdskɪn] (*old: offensive*) n Rothaut f

red tape n (*fig*) Bürokratie f

reduce [rɪˈdjuːs] vt (*spending, numbers, risk etc*) vermindern, reduzieren; **to ~ sth by/to 5%** etw um/auf 5% acc reduzieren; **to ~ sb to tears/silence** jdn zum Weinen/Schweigen bringen; **to ~ sb to begging/stealing** jdn zur Bettelei/zum Diebstahl zwingen; **"~ speed now"** (*Aut*) „langsam fahren"

reduced [rɪˈdjuːst] adj (*goods, ticket etc*) ermäßigt; **"greatly ~ prices"** „Preise stark reduziert"

reduction [rɪˈdʌkʃən] n (*in price etc*) Ermäßigung, Reduzierung f; (*in numbers*) Verminderung f

redundancy [rɪˈdʌndənsɪ] (*Brit*) n (*dismissal*) Entlassung f; (*unemployment*) Arbeitslosigkeit f; **compulsory ~** Entlassung f; **voluntary ~** freiwilliger Verzicht m auf den Arbeitsplatz

redundancy payment (*Brit*) n Abfindung f

redundant [rɪˈdʌndnt] adj (*Brit: worker*) arbeitslos; (*word, object*) überflüssig; **to be made ~** (*worker*) den Arbeitsplatz verlieren

reed [riːd] n (*Bot*) Schilf nt; (*Mus: of clarinet etc*) Rohrblatt nt

re-educate [riːˈɛdjukeɪt] vt umerziehen

reedy [ˈriːdɪ] adj (*voice*) Fistel-

reef [riːf] n (*at sea*) Riff nt

reek [riːk] vi: **to ~ (of)** (*lit, fig*) stinken (nach)

reel [riːl] n (*of thread etc, on fishing-rod*) Rolle f; (*Cine: scene*) Szene f; (*of film, tape*) Spule f; (*dance*) Reel m ▷ vi (*sway*) taumeln; **my head is ~ing** mir dreht sich der Kopf
▸ **reel in** vt (*fish, line*) einholen
▸ **reel off** vt (*say*) herunterrasseln

re-election [riːɪˈlɛkʃən] n Wiederwahl f

re-enter [riːˈɛntəʳ] vt (*country*) wieder einreisen in +acc; (*Space*) wieder eintreten in +acc

re-entry [riːˈɛntrɪ] n Wiedereinreise f; (*Space*) Wiedereintritt m

re-examine [riːɪgˈzæmɪn] vt (*proposal etc*) nochmals prüfen; (*witness*) nochmals vernehmen

re-export [ˈriːɪksˈpɔːt] vt wiederausführen ▷ n Wiederausfuhr f; (*commodity*) wiederausgeführte Ware f

ref [rɛf] (*inf*) n abbr (*Sport*) = **referee**

ref. abbr (*Comm*: = *with reference to*) betr.; **your ~** Ihr Zeichen;

refectory [rɪˈfɛktərɪ] n (*in university*) Mensa f

refer [rɪˈfəːʳ] vt: **to ~ sb to** (*book etc*) jdn verweisen auf +acc; (*doctor, hospital*) jdn überweisen zu; **to ~ sth to** (*task, problem*) etw übergeben an +acc; **he ~red me to the manager** er verwies mich an den Geschäftsführer
▸ **refer to** vt fus (*mention*) erwähnen; (*relate to*) sich beziehen auf +acc; (*consult*) hinzuziehen

referee [rɛfəˈriː] n (*Sport*) Schiedsrichter(in) m(f); (*Brit: for job application*) Referenz f ▷ vt als Schiedsrichter(in) leiten

reference [ˈrɛfrəns] n (*mention*) Hinweis m; (*in book, article*) Quellenangabe f; (*for job application, person*) Referenz f; **with ~ to** mit Bezug auf +acc; **"please quote this ~"** (*Comm*) „bitte dieses Zeichen angeben"

reference book n Nachschlagewerk nt

reference library n Präsenzbibliothek f

reference number n Aktenzeichen nt

referenda [rɛfəˈrɛndə] npl of **referendum**

referendum [rɛfəˈrɛndəm] (*pl* **referenda**) n Referendum nt, Volksentscheid m

referral [rɪˈfəːrəl] n (*of matter, problem*) Weiterleitung f; (*to doctor, specialist*) Überweisung f

refill [riːˈfɪl] vt nachfüllen ▷ n (*for pen etc*) Nachfüllmine f; (*drink*) Nachfüllung f

refine [rɪˈfaɪn] vt (*sugar, oil*) raffinieren; (*theory, idea*) verfeinern

refined [rɪˈfaɪnd] adj (*person*) kultiviert; (*taste*) fein, vornehm; (*sugar, oil*) raffiniert

refinement [rɪˈfaɪnmənt] n (*of person*) Kultiviertheit f; (*of system, ideas*) Verfeinerung f

refinery [rɪˈfaɪnərɪ] n (*for oil etc*) Raffinerie f

refit [riːˈfɪt] (*Naut*) n Überholung f ▷ vt (*ship*) überholen

reflate [riːˈfleɪt] vt (*economy*) ankurbeln

reflation [riːˈfleɪʃən] n (*Econ*) Reflation f

reflationary [riːˈfleɪʃənrɪ] adj (*Econ*) reflationär

reflect [rɪˈflɛkt] vt reflektieren; (*fig*) widerspiegeln ▷ vi (*think*) nachdenken
▸ **reflect on** vt fus (*discredit*) ein schlechtes Licht werfen auf +acc

reflection [rɪˈflɛkʃən] n (*image*) Spiegelbild nt; (*of light, heat*) Reflexion f; (*fig*) Widerspiegelung f; (: *thought*) Gedanke m; **on ~** nach genauerer Überlegung; **this is a ~ on ...** (*criticism*) das sagt einiges über ...

reflector [rɪˈflɛktəʳ] n (*Aut etc*) Rückstrahler m; (*for light, heat*) Reflektor m

reflex [ˈriːflɛks] adj Reflex-; **reflexes** npl (*Physiol, Psych*) Reflexe pl

reflexive [rɪˈflɛksɪv] adj (*Ling*) reflexiv

reform [rɪ'fɔːm] n Reform f ▷ vt reformieren ▷ vi (criminal etc) sich bessern

reformat [riː'fɔːmæt] vt (Comput) neu formatieren

Reformation [rɛfə'meɪʃən] n: **the ~** die Reformation

reformatory [rɪ'fɔːmətərɪ] (US) n Besserungsanstalt f

reformed [rɪ'fɔːmd] adj (character, alcoholic) gewandelt

refrain [rɪ'freɪn] vi: **to ~ from doing sth** etw unterlassen ▷ n (of song) Refrain m

refresh [rɪ'frɛʃ] vt erfrischen; **to ~ one's memory** sein Gedächtnis auffrischen

refresher course [rɪ'frɛʃə-] n Auffrischungskurs m

refreshing [rɪ'frɛʃɪŋ] adj erfrischend; (sleep) wohltuend; (idea etc) angenehm

refreshment [rɪ'frɛʃmənt] n Erfrischung f

refreshments [rɪ'frɛʃmənts] npl (food and drink) Erfrischungen pl

refrigeration [rɪfrɪdʒə'reɪʃən] n Kühlung f

refrigerator [rɪ'frɪdʒəreɪtəʳ] n Kühlschrank m

refuel [riː'fjuəl] vt, vi auftanken

refuelling [riː'fjuəlɪŋ] n Auftanken nt

refuge ['rɛfjuːdʒ] n Zuflucht f; **to seek/take ~ in** Zuflucht suchen/nehmen in +dat

refugee [rɛfju'dʒiː] n Flüchtling m; **a political ~** ein politischer Flüchtling

refugee camp n Flüchtlingslager nt

refund ['riːfʌnd] n Rückerstattung f ▷ vt (money) zurückerstatten

refurbish [riː'fəːbɪʃ] vt (shop etc) renovieren

refurbishment [riː'fəːbɪʃmənt] n (of shop etc) Renovierung f

refurnish [riː'fəːnɪʃ] vt neu möblieren

refusal [rɪ'fjuːzəl] n Ablehnung f; **a ~ to do sth** eine Weigerung, etw zu tun; **to give sb first ~ on sth** jdm etw zuerst anbieten

refuse[1] [rɪ'fjuːz] vt (request, offer etc) ablehnen; (gift) zurückweisen; (permission) verweigern ▷ vi ablehnen; (horse) verweigern; **to ~ to do sth** sich weigern, etw zu tun

refuse[2] ['rɛfjuːs] n (rubbish) Abfall m, Müll m

refuse collection n Müllabfuhr f

refuse disposal n Müllbeseitigung f

refusenik [rɪ'fjuːznɪk] n (inf) Verweigerer(in) m(f); (in former USSR) sowjetischer Jude, dem die Emigration nach Israel verweigert wurde

refute [rɪ'fjuːt] vt (argument) widerlegen

regain [rɪ'geɪn] vt wiedererlangen

regal ['riːgl] adj königlich

regale [rɪ'geɪl] vt: **to ~ sb with sth** jdn mit etw verwöhnen

regalia [rɪ'geɪlɪə] n (costume) Amtstracht f

regard [rɪ'gaːd] n (esteem) Achtung f ▷ vt (consider) ansehen, betrachten; (view) betrachten; **to give one's ~s to sb** jdm Grüße bestellen; **"with kindest ~s"** „mit freundlichen Grüßen"; **as regards, with ~ to** bezüglich +gen

regarding [rɪ'gaːdɪŋ] prep bezüglich +gen

regardless [rɪ'gaːdlɪs] adv trotzdem ▷ adj: **~ of**

ohne Rücksicht auf +acc

regatta [rɪ'gætə] n Regatta f

regency ['riːdʒənsɪ] n Regentschaft f ▷ adj: **R~** (furniture etc) Regency-

regenerate [rɪ'dʒɛnəreɪt] vt (inner cities, arts) erneuern; (person, feelings) beleben ▷ vi (Biol) sich regenerieren

regent ['riːdʒənt] n Regent(in) m(f)

reggae ['rɛgeɪ] n Reggae m

regime [reɪ'ʒiːm] n (government) Regime nt; (diet etc) Kur f

regiment ['rɛdʒɪmənt] n (Mil) Regiment nt ▷ vt reglementieren

regimental [rɛdʒɪ'mɛntl] adj Regiments-

regimentation [rɛdʒɪmɛn'teɪʃən] n Reglementierung f

region ['riːdʒən] n (of land) Gebiet nt; (of body) Bereich m; (administrative division of country) Region f; **in the ~ of** (approximately) im Bereich von

regional ['riːdʒənl] adj regional

regional development n regionale Entwicklung f

regionalize ['riːdʒənəlaɪz] vt regionalisieren

register ['rɛdʒɪstəʳ] n (list, Mus) Register nt; (also: **electoral register**) Wählerverzeichnis nt; (Scol) Klassenbuch nt ▷ vt registrieren; (car) anmelden; (letter) als Einschreiben senden; (amount, measurement) verzeichnen ▷ vi (person) sich anmelden; (: at doctor's) sich (als Patient) eintragen; (amount etc) registriert werden; (make impression) (einen) Eindruck machen; **to ~ a protest** Protest anmelden

registered ['rɛdʒɪstəd] adj (letter, parcel) eingeschrieben; (drug addict, childminder etc) (offiziell) eingetragen

registered company n eingetragene Gesellschaft f

registered nurse (US) n staatlich geprüfte Krankenschwester f, staatlich geprüfter Krankenpfleger m

registered trademark n eingetragenes Warenzeichen nt

register office n = **registry office**

registrar ['rɛdʒɪstraːʳ] n (in registry office) Standesbeamte(r) m, Standesbeamtin f; (in college etc) Kanzler m; (Brit: in hospital) Krankenhausarzt m, Krankenhausärztin f

registration [rɛdʒɪs'treɪʃən] n Registrierung f; (of students, unemployed etc) Anmeldung f

registration number (Brit) n (Aut) polizeiliches Kennzeichen nt

registry ['rɛdʒɪstrɪ] n Registratur f

registry office (Brit) n Standesamt nt; **to get married in a ~** standesamtlich heiraten

regret [rɪ'grɛt] n Bedauern nt ▷ vt bedauern; **with ~** mit Bedauern; **to have no ~s** nichts bereuen; **we ~ to inform you that ...** wir müssen Ihnen leider mitteilen, dass ...

regretfully [rɪ'grɛtfəlɪ] adv mit Bedauern

regrettable [rɪ'grɛtəbl] adj bedauerlich

regrettably [rɪ'grɛtəblɪ] adv bedauerlicherweise; **~, he said ...**

r

743

bedauerlicherweise sagte er ...

Regt abbr (Mil: = regiment) Rgt.

regular ['rɛgjʊləʳ] adj (also Ling) regelmäßig; (usual: time, doctor) üblich; (: customer) Stamm-; (soldier) Berufs-; (Comm: size) normal ▷ n (client) Stammkunde m, Stammkundin f

regularity [rɛgjʊ'lærɪtɪ] n Regelmäßigkeit f

regularly ['rɛgjʊləlɪ] adv regelmäßig; (breathe, beat: evenly) gleichmäßig

regulate ['rɛgjʊleɪt] vt regulieren

regulation [rɛgjʊ'leɪʃən] n Regulierung f; (rule) Vorschrift f

regulatory [rɛgjʊ'leɪtrɪ] adj (system) Regulierungs-; (body, agency) Überwachungs-

rehabilitate [riːə'bɪlɪteɪt] vt (criminal, drug addict) (in die Gesellschaft) wiedereingliedern; (invalid) rehabilitieren

rehabilitation ['riːəbɪlɪ'teɪʃən] n (see vt) Wiedereingliederung f (in die Gesellschaft); Rehabilitation f

rehash [riː'hæʃ] (inf) vt (idea etc) aufwärmen

rehearsal [rɪ'həːsəl] n (Theat) Probe f; **dress ~** Generalprobe f

rehearse [rɪ'həːs] vt (play, speech etc) proben

rehouse [riː'haʊz] vt neu unterbringen

reign [reɪn] n (lit, fig) Herrschaft f ▷ vi (lit, fig) herrschen

reigning ['reɪnɪŋ] adj regierend; (champion) amtierend

reimburse [riːɪm'bəːs] vt die Kosten erstatten +dat

rein [reɪn] n Zügel m; **to give sb free ~** (fig) jdm freie Hand lassen; **to keep a tight ~ on sth** (fig) bei etw die Zügel kurz halten

reincarnation [riːɪnkaː'neɪʃən] n (belief) die Wiedergeburt f; (person) Reinkarnation f

reindeer ['reɪndɪəʳ] n inv Ren(tier) nt

reinforce [riːɪn'fɔːs] vt (strengthen) verstärken; (support: idea etc) stützen; (: prejudice) stärken

reinforced concrete n Stahlbeton m

reinforcement [riːɪn'fɔːsmənt] n (strengthening) Verstärkung f; (of attitude etc) Stärkung f; **reinforcements** npl (Mil) Verstärkung f

reinstate [riːɪn'steɪt] vt (employee) wiedereinstellen; (tax, law) wiedereinführen; (text) wiedereinfügen

reinstatement [riːɪn'steɪtmənt] n (of employee) Wiedereinstellung f

reissue [riː'ɪʃjuː] vt neu herausgeben

reiterate [riː'ɪtəreɪt] vt wiederholen

reject ['riːdʒɛkt] n (Comm) Ausschuss m no pl ▷ vt ablehnen; (admirer) abweisen; (goods) zurückweisen; (machine: coin) nicht annehmen; (Med: heart, kidney) abstoßen

rejection [rɪ'dʒɛkʃən] n Ablehnung f; (of admirer) Abweisung f; (Med) Abstoßung f

rejoice [rɪ'dʒɔɪs] vi: **to ~ at** or **over** jubeln über +acc

rejoinder [rɪ'dʒɔɪndəʳ] n Erwiderung f

rejuvenate [rɪ'dʒuːvəneɪt] vt (person) verjüngen; (organization etc) beleben

rekindle [riː'kɪndl] vt (interest, emotion etc) wiedererwecken

relapse [rɪ'læps] n (Med) Rückfall m ▷ vi: **to ~ into** zurückfallen in +acc

relate [rɪ'leɪt] vt (tell) berichten; (connect) in Verbindung bringen ▷ vi: **to ~ to** (empathize with: person, subject) eine Beziehung finden zu; (connect with) zusammenhängen mit

related [rɪ'leɪtɪd] adj: **to be ~** (miteinander) verwandt sein; (issues etc) zusammenhängen

relating to [rɪ'leɪtɪŋ-] prep bezüglich +gen, mit Bezug auf +acc

relation [rɪ'leɪʃən] n (member of family) Verwandte(r) f(m); (connection) Beziehung f; **relations** npl (connection) Beziehungen pl; **diplomatic/international ~s** diplomatische/internationale Beziehungen; **in ~ to** im Verhältnis zu; **to bear no ~ to** in keinem Verhältnis stehen zu

relationship [rɪ'leɪʃənʃɪp] n Beziehung f; (between countries) Beziehungen pl; (affair) Verhältnis nt; **they have a good ~** sie haben ein gutes Verhältnis zueinander

relative ['rɛlətɪv] n Verwandte(r) f(m) ▷ adj relativ; **all her ~s** ihre ganze Verwandtschaft; **~ to** im Vergleich zu; **it's all ~** es ist alles relativ

relatively ['rɛlətɪvlɪ] adv relativ

relative pronoun n Relativpronomen nt

relax [rɪ'læks] vi (person, muscle) sich entspannen; (calm down) sich beruhigen ▷ vt (one's grip) lockern; (mind, person) entspannen; (control etc) lockern

relaxation [riːlæk'seɪʃən] n Entspannung f; (of control etc) Lockern nt

relaxed [rɪ'lækst] adj (person, atmosphere) entspannt; (discussion) locker

relaxing [rɪ'læksɪŋ] adj entspannend

relay ['riːleɪ] n (race) Staffel f, Staffellauf m ▷ vt (message etc) übermitteln; (broadcast) übertragen

release [rɪ'liːs] n (from prison) Entlassung f; (from obligation, situation) Befreiung f; (of documents, funds etc) Freigabe f; (of gas etc) Freisetzung f; (of film, book, record) Herausgabe f; (record, film) Veröffentlichung f; (Tech: device) Auslöser m ▷ vt (from prison) entlassen; (person: from obligation, from wreckage) befreien; (gas etc) freisetzen; (Tech, Aut: catch, brake etc) lösen; (record, film) herausbringen; (news, figures) bekannt geben; **on general ~** (film) überall in den Kinos; see also **press release**

relegate ['rɛləgeɪt] vt (downgrade) herunterstufen; (Brit: Sport): **to be ~d** absteigen

relent [rɪ'lɛnt] vi (give in) nachgeben

relentless [rɪ'lɛntlɪs] adj (heat, noise) erbarmungslos; (enemy etc) unerbittlich

relevance ['rɛləvəns] n Relevanz f, Bedeutung f; **the ~ of religion to society** die Relevanz or Bedeutung der Religion für die Gesellschaft

relevant ['rɛləvənt] adj relevant; (chapter, area) entsprechend; **~ to** relevant für

reliability [rɪlaɪə'bɪlɪtɪ] n Zuverlässigkeit f

reliable [rɪ'laɪəbl] adj zuverlässig

reliably [rɪˈlaɪəblɪ] *adv*: **to be ~ informed that ...** zuverlässige Informationen darüber haben, dass ...

reliance [rɪˈlaɪəns] *n*: **~ (on)** *(person)* Angewiesenheit *f* (auf +*acc*); *(drugs, financial support)* Abhängigkeit *f* (von)

reliant [rɪˈlaɪənt] *adj*: **to be ~ on sth/sb** auf etw/jdn angewiesen sein

relic [ˈrɛlɪk] *n* (*Rel*) Reliquie *f*; *(of the past)* Relikt *nt*

relief [rɪˈliːf] *n* *(from pain etc)* Erleichterung *f*; *(aid)* Hilfe *f*; (*Art, Geog*) Relief *nt* ▷ *cpd* *(bus)* Entlastungs-; *(driver)* zur Ablösung; **light ~** leichte Abwechslung *f*

relief map *n* Reliefkarte *f*

relief road (*Brit*) *n* Entlastungsstraße *f*

relieve [rɪˈliːv] *vt* *(pain)* lindern; *(fear, worry)* mildern; *(take over from)* ablösen; **to ~ sb of sth** *(load)* jdm etw abnehmen; *(duties, post)* jdn einer Sache *gen* entheben; **to ~ o.s.** *(euphemism)* sich erleichtern

relieved [rɪˈliːvd] *adj* erleichtert; **I'm ~ to hear it** es erleichtert mich, das zu hören

religion [rɪˈlɪdʒən] *n* Religion *f*

religious [rɪˈlɪdʒəs] *adj* religiös

religious education *n* Religionsunterricht *m*

religiously [rɪˈlɪdʒəslɪ] *adv* *(regularly, thoroughly)* gewissenhaft

relinquish [rɪˈlɪŋkwɪʃ] *vt* *(control etc)* aufgeben; *(claim)* verzichten auf +*acc*

relish [ˈrɛlɪʃ] *n* (*Culin*) würzige Soße *f*, Relish *nt*; *(enjoyment)* Genuss *m* ▷ *vt* *(enjoy)* genießen; **to ~ doing sth** etw mit Genuss tun

relive [riːˈlɪv] *vt* noch einmal durchleben

reload [riːˈləʊd] *vt* *(gun)* neu laden

relocate [riːləʊˈkeɪt] *vt* verlegen ▷ *vi* den Standort wechseln; **to ~ in** seinen Standort verlegen nach

reluctance [rɪˈlʌktəns] *n* Widerwille *m*

reluctant [rɪˈlʌktənt] *adj* unwillig, widerwillig; **I'm ~ to do that** es widerstrebt mir, das zu tun

reluctantly [rɪˈlʌktəntlɪ] *adv* widerwillig, nur ungern

rely on [rɪˈlaɪ-] *vt fus* *(be dependent on)* abhängen von; *(trust)* sich verlassen auf +*acc*

remain [rɪˈmeɪn] *vi* bleiben; *(survive)* übrig bleiben; **to ~ silent** weiterhin schweigen; **to ~ in control** die Kontrolle behalten; **much ~s to be done** es ist noch viel zu tun; **the fact ~s that ...** Tatsache ist und bleibt, dass ...; **it ~s to be seen whether ...** es bleibt abzuwarten, ob ...

remainder [rɪˈmeɪndəʳ] *n* Rest *m* ▷ *vt* (*Comm*) zu ermäßigtem Preis anbieten

remaining [rɪˈmeɪnɪŋ] *adj* übrig

remains [rɪˈmeɪnz] *npl* *(of meal)* Überreste *pl*; *(of building etc)* Ruinen *pl*; *(of body)* sterbliche Überreste *pl*

remand [rɪˈmɑːnd] *n*: **to be on ~** in Untersuchungshaft sein ▷ *vt*: **to be ~ed in custody** in Untersuchungshaft bleiben müssen

remand home *(formerly: Brit)* *n* Untersuchungsgefängnis *nt* für Jugendliche

remark [rɪˈmɑːk] *n* Bemerkung *f* ▷ *vt* bemerken ▷ *vi*: **to ~ on sth** Bemerkungen über etw *acc* machen; **to ~ that** die Bemerkung machen, dass

remarkable [rɪˈmɑːkəbl] *adj* bemerkenswert

remarry [riːˈmærɪ] *vi* wieder heiraten

remedial [rɪˈmiːdɪəl] *adj* *(tuition, classes)* Förder-; **~ exercise** Heilgymnastik *f*

remedy [ˈrɛmədɪ] *n* *(lit, fig)* (Heil)mittel *nt* ▷ *vt* *(mistake, situation)* abhelfen +*dat*

remember [rɪˈmɛmbəʳ] *vt* *(call back to mind)* sich erinnern an +*acc*; *(bear in mind)* denken an +*acc*; **~ me to him** *(send greetings)* grüße ihn von mir; **I ~ seeing it, I ~ having seen it** ich erinnere mich (daran), es gesehen zu haben; **she ~ed to do it** sie hat daran gedacht, es zu tun

remembrance [rɪˈmɛmbrəns] *n* Erinnerung *f*; **in ~ of sb/sth** im Gedenken an +*acc*

Remembrance Sunday (*Brit*) *n* ≈ Volkstrauertag *m*; *siehe Info-Artikel*

⬤ **REMEMBRANCE SUNDAY**
⬤
⬤ *Remembrance Sunday* oder *Remembrance*
⬤ *Day* ist der britische Gedenktag für
⬤ die Gefallenen der beiden Weltkriege
⬤ und anderer Konflikte. Er fällt auf
⬤ einen Sonntag vor oder nach dem 11.
⬤ November (am 11. November 1918 endete
⬤ der Erste Weltkrieg) und wird mit einer
⬤ Schweigeminute, Kranzniederlegungen
⬤ an Kriegerdenkmälern und dem Tragen
⬤ von Ansteckbnadeln in Form einer
⬤ Mohnblume begangen.

remind [rɪˈmaɪnd] *vt*: **to ~ sb to do sth** jdn daran erinnern, etw zu tun; **to ~ sb of sth** jdn an etw *acc* erinnern; **to ~ sb that ...** jdn daran erinnern, dass ...; **she ~s me of her mother** sie erinnert mich an ihre Mutter; **that ~s me!** dabei fällt mir etwas ein!

reminder [rɪˈmaɪndəʳ] *n* *(of person, place etc)* Erinnerung *f*; *(letter)* Mahnung *f*

reminisce [rɛmɪˈnɪs] *vi*: **to ~ (about)** sich in Erinnerungen ergehen (über +*acc*)

reminiscences [rɛmɪˈnɪsnsɪz] *npl* Erinnerungen *pl*

reminiscent [rɛmɪˈnɪsnt] *adj*: **to be ~ of sth** an etw *acc* erinnern

remiss [rɪˈmɪs] *adj* nachlässig; **it was ~ of him** es war nachlässig von ihm

remission [rɪˈmɪʃən] *n* *(of sentence)* Straferlass *m*; *(Med)* Remission *f*; *(Rel)* Erlass *m*

remit [rɪˈmɪt] *vt* *(money)* überweisen ▷ *n* *(of official etc)* Aufgabenbereich *m*

remittance [rɪˈmɪtns] *n* Überweisung *f*

remnant [ˈrɛmnənt] *n* Überrest *m*; *(Comm: of cloth)* Rest *m*

remonstrate [ˈrɛmənstreɪt] *vi*: **to ~ (with sb about sth)** sich beschweren (bei jdm wegen etw)

r

remorse [rɪ'mɔːs] n Reue f
remorseful [rɪ'mɔːsful] adj reumütig
remorseless [rɪ'mɔːslɪs] adj (noise, pain) unbarmherzig
remote [rɪ'məut] adj (distant: place, time) weit entfernt; (aloof) distanziert; (slight: chance etc) entfernt; **there is a ~ possibility that ...** es besteht eventuell die Möglichkeit, dass ...
remote control n Fernsteuerung f; (TV etc) Fernbedienung f
remote-controlled [rɪ'məutkən'trəuld] adj ferngesteuert
remotely [rɪ'məutlɪ] adv (slightly) entfernt
remoteness [rɪ'məutnɪs] n (of place) Entlegenheit f; (of person) Distanziertheit f
remould ['riːməuld] (Brit) n (Aut) runderneuerter Reifen m
removable [rɪ'muːvəbl] adj (detachable) abnehmbar
removal [rɪ'muːvəl] n (of object etc) Entfernung f; (of threat etc) Beseitigung f; (Brit: from house) Umzug m; (dismissal) Entlassung f; (Med: of kidney etc) Entfernung f
removal man (Brit) n Möbelpacker m
removal van (Brit) n Möbelwagen m
remove [rɪ'muːv] vt entfernen; (clothing) ausziehen; (bandage etc) abnehmen; (employee) entlassen; (name: from list) streichen; (doubt, threat, obstacle) beseitigen; **my first cousin once ~d** mein Vetter ersten Grades
remover [rɪ'muːvə] n (for paint, varnish) Entferner m; **stain ~** Fleckentferner m; **make-up ~** Make-up-Entferner m
remunerate [rɪ'mjuːnəreɪt] vt vergüten
remuneration [rɪmjuːnə'reɪʃən] n Vergütung f
Renaissance [rɪ'neɪsɑːs] n: **the ~** die Renaissance
renal ['riːnl] adj (Med) Nieren-
renal failure n Nierenversagen nt
rename [riː'neɪm] vt umbenennen
rend [rɛnd] (pt, pp **rent**) vt (air, silence) zerreißen
render ['rɛndə'] vt (give: assistance, aid) leisten; (cause to become: unconscious, harmless, useless) machen; (submit) vorlegen
rendering ['rɛndərɪŋ] (Brit) n = **rendition**
rendezvous ['rɔndɪvuː] n (meeting) Rendezvous nt; (place) Treffpunkt m ▷ vi (people) sich treffen; (spacecraft) ein Rendezvousmanöver durchführen; **to ~ with sb** sich mit jdm treffen
rendition [rɛn'dɪʃən] n (of song etc) Vortrag m
renegade ['rɛnɪgeɪd] n Renegat(in) m(f), Überläufer(in) m(f)
renew [rɪ'njuː] vt erneuern; (attack, negotiations) wiederaufnehmen; (loan, contract etc) verlängern; (relationship etc) wiederaufleben lassen
renewable [rɪ'njuːəbl] vt (energy) erneuerbar
renewables npl erneuerbare Energien pl
renewal [rɪ'njuːəl] n Erneuerung f; (of conflict) Wiederaufnahme f; (of contract etc) Verlängerung f
renounce [rɪ'nauns] vt verzichten auf +acc;

(belief) aufgeben
renovate ['rɛnəveɪt] vt (building) restaurieren; (machine) überholen
renovation [rɛnə'veɪʃən] n (see vb) Restaurierung f; Überholung f
renown [rɪ'naun] n Ruf m
renowned [rɪ'naund] adj berühmt
rent [rɛnt] pt, pp of **rend** ▷ n (for house) Miete f ▷ vt mieten; (also: **rent out**) vermieten
rental ['rɛntl] n (for television, car) Mietgebühr f
rent boy (inf) n Strichjunge m
rent strike n Mietstreik m
renunciation [rɪnʌnsɪ'eɪʃən] n Verzicht m; (of belief) Aufgabe f; (self-denial) Selbstverleugnung f
reopen [riː'əupən] vt (shop etc) wiedereröffnen; (negotiations, legal case etc) wiederaufnehmen
reopening [riː'əupnɪŋ] n (see vt) Wiedereröffnung f; Wiederaufnahme f
reorder [riː'ɔːdə'] vt (rearrange) umordnen
reorganization [riːɔːgənaɪ'zeɪʃən] n Umorganisation f
reorganize [riː'ɔːgənaɪz] vt umorganisieren
Rep. (US) abbr (Pol) = **representative; Republican**
rep [rɛp] n abbr (Comm) = **representative**; (Theat) = **repertory**
repair [rɪ'pɛə'] n Reparatur f ▷ vt reparieren; (clothes, road) ausbessern; **in good/bad ~** in gutem/schlechtem Zustand; **beyond ~** nicht mehr zu reparieren; **to be under ~** (road) ausgebessert werden
repair kit n (for bicycle) Flickzeug nt
repair man n Handwerker m
repair shop n Reparaturwerkstatt f
repartee [rɛpɑː'tiː] n (exchange) Schlagabtausch m; (reply) schlagfertige Bemerkung f
repast [rɪ'pɑːst] n (form) n Mahl nt
repatriate [riː'pætrɪeɪt] vt repatriieren
repay [riː'peɪ] (irreg: like **pay**) vt zurückzahlen; (sb's efforts, attention) belohnen; (favour) erwidern
repayment [riː'peɪmənt] n Rückzahlung f
repeal [rɪ'piːl] n (of law) Aufhebung f ▷ vt (law) aufheben
repeat [rɪ'piːt] n (Radio, TV) Wiederholung f ▷ vt, vi wiederholen ▷ cpd (performance) Wiederholungs-; (order) Nach-; **to ~ o.s./itself** sich wiederholen; **to ~ an order for sth** etw nachbestellen
repeatedly [rɪ'piːtɪdlɪ] adv wiederholt
repel [rɪ'pɛl] vt (drive away) zurückschlagen; (disgust) abstoßen
repellent [rɪ'pɛlənt] adj abstoßend ▷ n: **insect ~** Insekten(schutz)mittel nt
repent [rɪ'pɛnt] vi: **to ~ of sth** etw bereuen
repentance [rɪ'pɛntəns] n Reue f
repercussions [riːpə'kʌʃənz] npl Auswirkungen pl
repertoire ['rɛpətwɑː'] n (Mus, Theat) Repertoire nt; (fig) Spektrum nt
repertory ['rɛpətərɪ] n (also: **repertory theatre**) Repertoiretheater nt

repertory company n Repertoire-Ensemble nt

repetition [rɛpɪ'tɪʃən] n (repeat) Wiederholung f

repetitious [rɛpɪ'tɪʃəs] adj (speech etc) voller Wiederholungen

repetitive [rɪ'pɛtɪtɪv] adj eintönig, monoton

replace [rɪ'pleɪs] vt (put back: upright) zurückstellen; (: flat) zurücklegen; (take the place of) ersetzen; **to ~ X with Y** X durch Y ersetzen; **"~ the receiver"** (Tel) „Hörer auflegen"

replacement [rɪ'pleɪsmənt] n Ersatz m

replacement part n Ersatzteil nt

replay ['ri:pleɪ] n (of match) Wiederholungsspiel nt ▷ vt (match) wiederholen; (track, song: on tape) nochmals abspielen

replenish [rɪ'plɛnɪʃ] vt (glass, stock etc) auffüllen

replete [rɪ'pli:t] adj (after meal) gesättigt; **~ with** reichlich ausgestattet mit

replica ['rɛplɪkə] n (of object) Nachbildung f

reply [rɪ'plaɪ] n Antwort f ▷ vi: **to ~ (to sb/sth)** (jdm/auf etw acc) antworten; **in ~ to** als Antwort auf +acc; **there's no ~** (Tel) es meldet sich niemand

reply coupon n Antwortschein m

report [rɪ'pɔ:t] n Bericht m; (Brit: also: **school report**) Zeugnis nt; (of gun) Knall m ▷ vt berichten; (casualties, damage, theft etc) melden; (person: to police) anzeigen ▷ vi (make a report) Bericht erstatten; **to ~ to sb** (present o.s. to) sich bei jdm melden; (be responsible to) jdm unterstellt sein; **to ~ on sth** über etw acc Bericht erstatten; **to ~ sick** sich krankmelden; **it is ~ed that** es wird berichtet or gemeldet, dass ...

report card (US, Scot) n Zeugnis nt

reportedly [rɪ'pɔ:tɪdlɪ] adv: **she is ~ living in Spain** sie lebt angeblich in Spanien

reported speech n (Ling) indirekte Rede f

reporter [rɪ'pɔ:tər] n Reporter(in) m(f)

repose [rɪ'pəuz] n: **in ~** in Ruhestellung

repository [rɪ'pɒzɪtərɪ] n (person: of knowledge) Quelle f; (place: of collection etc) Lager nt

repossess ['ri:pə'zɛs] vt (wieder) in Besitz nehmen

repossession order [ri:pə'zɛʃən-] n Beschlagnahmungsverfügung f

reprehensible [rɛprɪ'hɛnsɪbl] adj verwerflich

represent [rɛprɪ'zɛnt] vt (person, nation) vertreten; (show: view, opinion) darstellen; (symbolize: idea) symbolisieren, verkörpern; **to ~ sth as** (describe) etw darstellen als

representation [rɛprɪzɛn'teɪʃən] n (state of being represented) Vertretung f; (picture etc) Darstellung f; **representations** npl (protest) Proteste pl

representative [rɛprɪ'zɛntətɪv] n (also Comm) Vertreter(in) m(f); (US: Pol) Abgeordnete(r) f(m) des Repräsentantenhauses ▷ adj repräsentativ; **~ of** repräsentativ für

repress [rɪ'prɛs] vt unterdrücken

repression [rɪ'prɛʃən] n Unterdrückung f

repressive [rɪ'prɛsɪv] adj repressiv

reprieve [rɪ'pri:v] n (cancellation) Begnadigung f; (postponement) Strafaufschub m; (fig) Gnadenfrist f ▷ vt: **he was ~d** (see n) er wurde begnadigt; ihm wurde Strafaufschub gewährt

reprimand ['rɛprɪmɑːnd] n Tadel m ▷ vt tadeln

reprint ['ri:prɪnt] n Nachdruck m ▷ vt nachdrucken

reprisal [rɪ'praɪzl] n Vergeltung f; **reprisals** npl Repressalien pl; (in war) Vergeltungsaktionen pl; **to take ~s** zu Repressalien greifen; (in war) Vergeltungsaktionen durchführen

reproach [rɪ'prəutʃ] n (rebuke) Vorwurf m ▷ vt: **to ~ sb for sth** jdm etw zum Vorwurf machen; **beyond ~** über jeden Vorwurf erhaben; **to ~ sb with sth** jdm etw vorwerfen

reproachful [rɪ'prəutʃful] adj vorwurfsvoll

reproduce [ri:prə'dju:s] vt reproduzieren ▷ vi (Biol) sich vermehren

reproduction [ri:prə'dʌkʃən] n Reproduktion f; (Biol) Fortpflanzung f

reproductive [ri:prə'dʌktɪv] adj (system, organs) Fortpflanzungs-

reproof [rɪ'pru:f] n (rebuke) Tadel m; **with ~** tadelnd

reprove [rɪ'pru:v] vt tadeln; **to ~ sb for sth** jdn wegen etw tadeln

reproving [rɪ'pru:vɪŋ] adj tadelnd

reptile ['rɛptaɪl] n Reptil nt

Repub. (US) abbr (Pol) = **Republican**

republic [rɪ'pʌblɪk] n Republik f

republican [rɪ'pʌblɪkən] adj republikanisch ▷ n Republikaner(in) m(f); **the R~s** (US: Pol) die Republikaner

repudiate [rɪ'pju:dɪeɪt] vt (accusation) zurückweisen; (violence) ablehnen; (old: friend, wife etc) verstoßen

repugnance [rɪ'pʌgnəns] n Abscheu m

repugnant [rɪ'pʌgnənt] adj abstoßend

repulse [rɪ'pʌls] vt (attack etc) zurückschlagen; (sight, picture etc) abstoßen

repulsion [rɪ'pʌlʃən] n Abscheu m

repulsive [rɪ'pʌlsɪv] adj widerwärtig, abstoßend

reputable ['rɛpjutəbl] adj (make, company etc) angesehen

reputation [rɛpju'teɪʃən] n Ruf m; **to have a ~ for** einen Ruf haben für; **he has a ~ for being awkward** er gilt als schwierig

repute [rɪ'pju:t] n: **of ~** angesehen; **to be held in high ~** in hohem Ansehen stehen

reputed [rɪ'pju:tɪd] adj angeblich; **he is ~ to be rich** er ist angeblich reich

reputedly [rɪ'pju:tɪdlɪ] adv angeblich

request [rɪ'kwɛst] n (polite) Bitte f; (formal) Ersuchen nt; (Radio) Musikwunsch m ▷ vt (politely) bitten um; (formally) ersuchen; **at the ~ of** auf Wunsch von; **"you are ~ed not to smoke"** „bitte nicht rauchen"

request stop (Brit) n Bedarfshaltestelle f

requiem ['rɛkwɪəm] n (Rel: also: **requiem mass**) Totenmesse f; (Mus) Requiem nt

require [rɪ'kwaɪər] vt (need) benötigen; (: situation) erfordern; (demand) verlangen; **to ~ sb to do sth** von jdm verlangen, etw zu tun;

r

if ~d falls nötig; **what qualifications are ~d?**
welche Qualifikationen werden verlangt?; **~d
by law** gesetzlich vorgeschrieben

required [rɪ'kwaɪəd] *adj* erforderlich

requirement [rɪ'kwaɪəmənt] *n* (*need*) Bedarf *m*;
(*condition*) Anforderung *f*; **to meet sb's ~s** jds
Anforderungen erfüllen

requisite ['rɛkwɪzɪt] *adj* erforderlich;
requisites *npl*: **toilet/travel ~s** Toiletten-/
Reiseartikel *pl*

requisition [rɛkwɪ'zɪʃən] *n*: **~ (for)**
(*demand*) Anforderung *f* (von) ▷ *vt* (*Mil*)
beschlagnahmen

reroute [riː'ruːt] *vt* (*train etc*) umleiten

resale [riː'seɪl] *n* Weiterverkauf *m*; **"not for ~"**
„nicht zum Weiterverkauf bestimmt"

resale price maintenance *n* Preisbindung *f*

rescind [rɪ'sɪnd] *vt* (*law, order*) aufheben;
(*decision*) rückgängig machen; (*agreement*)
widerrufen

rescue ['rɛskjuː] *n* Rettung *f* ▷ *vt* retten; **to
come to sb's ~** jdm zu Hilfe kommen

rescue party *n* Rettungsmannschaft *f*

rescuer ['rɛskjuəʳ] *n* Retter(in) *m(f)*

research [rɪ'sɜːtʃ] *n* Forschung *f* ▷ *vt* erforschen
▷ *vi*: **to ~ into sth** etw erforschen; **to do
~** Forschung betreiben; **a piece of ~** eine
Forschungsarbeit; **~ and development**
Forschung und Entwicklung

researcher [rɪ'sɜːtʃəʳ] *n* Forscher(in) *m(f)*

research work *n* Forschungsarbeit *f*

research worker *n* = **researcher**

resell [riː'sɛl] (*irreg: like* **sell**) *vt* weiterverkaufen

resemblance [rɪ'zɛmbləns] *n* Ähnlichkeit
f; **to bear a strong ~ to** starke Ähnlichkeit
haben mit; **it bears no ~ to ...** es hat keine
Ähnlichkeit mit ...

resemble [rɪ'zɛmbl] *vt* ähneln *+dat*, gleichen
+dat

resent [rɪ'zɛnt] *vt* (*attitude, treatment*)
missbilligen; (*person*) ablehnen

resentful [rɪ'zɛntful] *adj* (*person*) gekränkt;
(*attitude*) missbilligend

resentment [rɪ'zɛntmənt] *n* Verbitterung *f*

reservation [rɛzə'veɪʃən] *n* (*booking*)
Reservierung *f*; (*doubt*) Vorbehalt *m*; (*land*)
Reservat *nt*; **to make a ~** (*in hotel etc*) eine
Reservierung vornehmen; **with ~(s)** (*doubts*)
unter Vorbehalt

reservation desk *n* Reservierungsschalter *m*

reserve [rɪ'zɜːv] *n* Reserve *f*, Vorrat *m*; (*fig: of
talent etc*) Reserve *f*; (*Sport*) Reservespieler(in)
m(f); (*also:* **nature reserve**) Naturschutzgebiet
nt; (*restraint*) Zurückhaltung *f* ▷ *vt* reservieren;
(*table, ticket*) reservieren lassen; **reserves** *npl*
(*Mil*) Reserve *f*; **in ~** in Reserve

reserve currency *n* Reservewährung *f*

reserved [rɪ'zɜːvd] *adj* (*restrained*)
zurückhaltend; (*seat*) reserviert

reserve price (*Brit*) *n* Mindestpreis *m*

reserve team (*Brit*) *n* Reservemannschaft *f*

reservist [rɪ'zɜːvɪst] *n* (*Mil*) Reservist *m*

reservoir ['rɛzəvwɑːʳ] *n* (*lit, fig*) Reservoir *nt*

reset [riː'sɛt] (*irreg: like* **set**) *vt* (*watch*) neu
stellen; (*broken bone*) wieder einrichten;
(*Comput*) zurückstellen

reshape [riː'ʃeɪp] *vt* (*policy, view*) umgestalten

reshuffle [riː'ʃʌfl] *n*: **cabinet ~**
Kabinettsumbildung *f*

reside [rɪ'zaɪd] *vi* (*live: person*) seinen/ihren
Wohnsitz haben
▶ **reside in** *vt fus* (*exist*) liegen in *+dat*

residence ['rɛzɪdəns] *n* (*form: home*) Wohnsitz
m; (*length of stay*) Aufenthalt *m*; **to take up ~**
sich niederlassen; **in ~** (*queen etc*) anwesend;
writer/artist in ~ *Schriftsteller/Künstler, der in
einer Ausbildungsstätte bei freier Unterkunft lehrt und
arbeitet*

residence permit (*Brit*) *n*
Aufenthaltserlaubnis *f*

resident ['rɛzɪdənt] *n* (*of country, town*)
Einwohner(in) *m(f)*; (*in hotel*) Gast *m* ▷ *adj* (*in
country, town*) wohnhaft; (*population*) ansässig;
(*doctor*) hauseigen; (*landlord*) im Hause
wohnend

residential [rɛzɪ'dɛnʃəl] *adj* (*area*) Wohn-;
(*course*) mit Wohnung am Ort; (*staff*) im Hause
wohnend

residue ['rɛzɪdjuː] *n* (*Chem*) Rückstand *m*; (*fig*)
Überrest *m*

resign [rɪ'zaɪn] *vt* (*one's post*) zurücktreten
von ▷ *vi* (*from post*) zurücktreten; **to ~ o.s. to**
(*situation etc*) sich abfinden mit

resignation [rɛzɪg'neɪʃən] *n* (*from post*)
Rücktritt *m*; (*state of mind*) Resignation *f*; **to
tender one's ~** seine Kündigung einreichen

resigned [rɪ'zaɪnd] *adj*: **to be ~ to sth** sich mit
etw abgefunden haben

resilience [rɪ'zɪlɪəns] *n* (*of material*)
Widerstandsfähigkeit *f*; (*of person*)
Unverwüstlichkeit *f*

resilient [rɪ'zɪlɪənt] *adj* (*see n*)
widerstandsfähig; unverwüstlich

resin ['rɛzɪn] *n* Harz *nt*

resist [rɪ'zɪst] *vt* (*change, demand*) sich
widersetzen *+dat*; (*attack etc*) Widerstand
leisten *+dat*; (*urge etc*) widerstehen *+dat*; **I
couldn't ~ (doing) it** ich konnte nicht
widerstehen(, es zu tun)

resistance [rɪ'zɪstəns] *n* (*also Elec*) Widerstand
m; (*to illness*) Widerstandsfähigkeit *f*

resistant [rɪ'zɪstənt] *adj*: **~ (to)** (*to change etc*)
widerstandsfähig (gegenüber); (*to antibiotics
etc*) resistent (gegen)

resolute ['rɛzəluːt] *adj* (*person*) entschlossen,
resolut; (*refusal*) entschieden

resolution [rɛzə'luːʃən] *n* (*decision*) Beschluss *m*;
(*determination*) Entschlossenheit *f*; (*of problem*)
Lösung *f*; **to make a ~** einen Entschluss
fassen

resolve [rɪ'zɔlv] *n* (*determination*)
Entschlossenheit *f* ▷ *vt* (*problem*) lösen;
(*difficulty*) beseitigen ▷ *vi*: **to ~ to do sth**
beschließen, etw zu tun

resolved [rɪ'zɔlvd] *adj* (*determined*) entschlossen

resonance ['rɛzənəns] *n* Resonanz *f*

resonant ['rɛzənənt] *adj* (*sound, voice*)
volltönend; (*place*) widerhallend
resort [rɪ'zɔːt] *n* (*town*) Urlaubsort *m*; (*recourse*)
Zuflucht *f* ▷ *vi*: **to ~ to** Zuflucht nehmen
zu; **seaside ~** Seebad *nt*; **winter sports ~**
Wintersportort *m*; **as a last ~** als letzter
Ausweg; **in the last ~** schlimmstenfalls
resound [rɪ'zaund] *vi*: **to ~ (with)** widerhallen
(von)
resounding [rɪ'zaundɪŋ] *adj* (*noise*)
widerhallend; (*voice*) schallend; (*fig: success*)
durchschlagend; (: *victory*) überlegen
resource [rɪ'sɔːs] *n* (*raw material*) Bodenschatz
m; **resources** *npl* (*coal, oil etc*) Energiequellen
pl; (*money*) Mittel *pl*, Ressourcen *pl*; **natural ~s**
Naturschätze *pl*
resourceful [rɪ'sɔːsful] *adj* einfallsreich
resourcefulness [rɪ'sɔːsfulnɪs] *n*
Einfallsreichtum *m*
respect [rɪs'pɛkt] *n* (*consideration, esteem*)
Respekt *m* ▷ *vt* respektieren; **respects** *npl*
(*greetings*) Grüße *pl*; **to have ~ for sb/sth**
Respekt vor jdm/etw haben; **to show sb/sth**
~ Respekt vor jdm/etw zeigen; **out of ~ for**
aus Rücksicht auf +*acc*; **with ~ to, in ~ of** in
Bezug auf +*acc*; **in this ~** in dieser Hinsicht;
in some/many ~s in gewisser/vielfacher
Hinsicht; **with (all due) ~** bei allem Respekt
respectability [rɪspɛktə'bɪlɪtɪ] *n*
Anständigkeit *f*
respectable [rɪs'pɛktəbl] *adj* anständig;
(*amount, income*) ansehnlich; (*standard, mark etc*)
ordentlich
respected [rɪs'pɛktɪd] *adj* angesehen
respectful [rɪs'pɛktful] *adj* respektvoll
respectfully [rɪs'pɛktfəlɪ] *adv* (*behave*)
respektvoll
respective [rɪs'pɛktɪv] *adj* jeweilig
respectively [rɪs'pɛktɪvlɪ] *adv*
beziehungsweise; **Germany and**
Britain were 3rd and 4th ~ Deutschland
und Großbritannien belegten den 3.
beziehungsweise 4. Platz
respiration [rɛspɪ'reɪʃən] *n see* **artificial**
respirator ['rɛspɪreɪtəʳ] *n* Respirator *m*,
Beatmungsgerät *nt*
respiratory ['rɛspərətərɪ] *adj* (*system, failure*)
Atmungs-
respite ['rɛspaɪt] *n* (*rest*) Ruhepause *f*
resplendent [rɪs'plɛndənt] *adj* (*clothes*)
prächtig
respond [rɪs'pɔnd] *vi* (*answer*) antworten; (*react*)
reagieren
respondent [rɪs'pɔndənt] *n* (*Law*) Beklagte(r)
f(m)
response [rɪs'pɔns] *n* (*to question*) Antwort *f*;
(*to event etc*) Reaktion *f*; **in ~ to** als Antwort/
Reaktion auf +*acc*
responsibility [rɪspɔnsɪ'bɪlɪtɪ] *n*
Verantwortung *f*; **to take ~ for sth/sb** die
Verantwortung für etw/jdn übernehmen
responsible [rɪs'pɔnsɪbl] *adj* verantwortlich;
(*reliable, important*) verantwortungsvoll; **to be**

~ for sth für etw verantwortlich sein; **to be**
~ for doing sth dafür verantwortlich sein,
etw zu tun; **to be ~ to sb** jdm gegenüber
verantwortlich sein
responsibly [rɪs'pɔnsɪblɪ] *adv*
verantwortungsvoll
responsive [rɪs'pɔnsɪv] *adj* (*person*) ansprechbar
rest [rɛst] *n* (*relaxation*) Ruhe *f*; (*pause*)
Ruhepause *f*; (*remainder*) Rest *m*; (*support*)
Stütze *f*; (*Mus*) Pause *f* ▷ *vi* (*relax*) sich ausruhen
▷ *vt* (*eyes, legs etc*) ausruhen; **the ~ of them**
die Übrigen; **to put** *or* **set sb's mind at ~**
jdn beruhigen; **to come to ~** (*object*) zum
Stillstand kommen; **to lay sb to ~** jdn zur
letzten Ruhe betten; **to ~ on sth** (*lit, fig*) sich
auf etw *acc* stützen; **to let the matter ~** die
Sache auf sich beruhen lassen; **~ assured**
that … seien Sie versichert, dass …; **I won't**
~ until … ich werde nicht ruhen, bis …; **may**
he/she ~ in peace möge er/sie in Frieden
ruhen; **to ~ sth on/against sth** (*lean*) etw an
acc/gegen etw lehnen; **to ~ one's eyes** *or* **gaze**
on sth den Blick auf etw heften; **I ~ my case**
mehr brauche ich dazu wohl nicht zu sagen
restart [riː'stɑːt] *vt* (*engine*) wieder anlassen;
(*work*) wiederaufnehmen
restaurant ['rɛstərɔŋ] *n* Restaurant *nt*
restaurant car (*Brit*) *n* (*Rail*) Speisewagen *m*
rest cure *n* Erholung *f*
restful ['rɛstful] *adj* (*music*) ruhig; (*lighting*)
beruhigend; (*atmosphere*) friedlich
rest home *n* Pflegeheim *nt*
restitution [rɛstɪ'tjuːʃən] *n*: **to make ~ to**
sb of sth jdm etw zurückerstatten; (*as*
compensation) jdn für etw entschädigen
restive ['rɛstɪv] *adj* (*person, crew*) unruhig; (*horse*)
störrisch
restless ['rɛstlɪs] *adj* rastlos; (*audience*) unruhig;
to get ~ unruhig werden
restlessly ['rɛstlɪslɪ] *adv* (*walk around*) rastlos;
(*turn over*) unruhig
restock [riː'stɔk] *vt* (*shop, freezer*) wieder
auffüllen; (*lake, river: with fish*) wieder besetzen
restoration [rɛstə'reɪʃən] *n* (*of painting etc*)
Restauration *f*; (*of law and order, health, sight etc*)
Wiederherstellung *f*; (*of land, rights*) Rückgabe
f; (*Hist*): **the R~** die Restauration
restorative [rɪ'stɔrətɪv] *adj* (*power, treatment*)
stärkend ▷ *n* (*old: drink*) Stärkungsmittel *nt*
restore [rɪ'stɔːʳ] *vt* (*painting etc*) restaurieren;
(*law and order, faith, health etc*) wiederherstellen;
(*property*) zurückgeben; **to ~ sth to** (*to former*
state) etw zurückverwandeln in +*acc*; **to ~ sb**
to power jdn wieder an die Macht bringen
restorer [rɪ'stɔːrəʳ] *n* (*Art etc*) Restaurator(in)
m(f)
restrain [rɪs'treɪn] *vt* (*person*) zurückhalten;
(*feeling*) unterdrücken; (*growth, inflation*)
dämpfen; **to ~ sb from doing sth** jdn davon
abhalten, etw zu tun; **to ~ o.s. from doing**
sth sich beherrschen, etw nicht zu tun
restrained [rɪs'treɪnd] *adj* (*person*) beherrscht;
(*style etc*) zurückhaltend

r

749

restraint [rɪs'treɪnt] n (restriction)
Einschränkung f; (moderation) Zurückhaltung
f; **wage ~** Zurückhaltung f bei
Lohnforderungen
restrict [rɪs'trɪkt] vt beschränken
restricted area (Brit) n (Aut) Bereich m mit
Geschwindigkeitsbeschränkung
restriction [rɪs'trɪkʃən] n Beschränkung f
restrictive [rɪs'trɪktɪv] adj (law, measure)
restriktiv; (clothing) beengend
restrictive practices (Brit) npl (Industry)
wettbewerbshemmende Geschäftspraktiken
pl
rest room (US) n Toilette f
restructure [riː'strʌktʃəʳ] vt umstrukturieren
result [rɪ'zʌlt] n Resultat nt; (of match, election,
exam etc) Ergebnis nt ▷ vi: **to ~ in** führen zu;
as a ~ of the accident als Folge des Unfalls;
he missed the train as a ~ of sleeping in er
verpasste den Zug, weil er verschlafen hatte;
to ~ from resultieren or sich ergeben aus; **as a
~ it is too expensive** folglich ist es zu teuer
resultant [rɪ'zʌltənt] adj resultierend, sich
ergebend
resume [rɪ'zjuːm] vt (work, journey)
wiederaufnehmen; (seat) wieder einnehmen
▷ vi (start again) von Neuem beginnen
résumé ['reɪzjuːmeɪ] n Zusammenfassung f;
(US: curriculum vitae) Lebenslauf m
resumption [rɪ'zʌmpʃən] n (of work etc)
Wiederaufnahme f
resurgence [rɪ'sɜːdʒəns] n Wiederaufleben nt
resurrection [rɛzə'rɛkʃən] n (of hopes,
fears) Wiederaufleben nt; (of custom etc)
Wiederbelebung f; (Rel): **the R~** die
Auferstehung f
resuscitate [rɪ'sʌsɪteɪt] vt (Med, fig)
wiederbeleben
resuscitation [rɪsʌsɪ'teɪʃən] n Wiederbelebung
f
retail ['riːteɪl] adj (trade, department) Verkaufs-;
(shop, goods) Einzelhandels- ▷ adv im
Einzelhandel ▷ vt (sell) (im Einzelhandel)
verkaufen ▷ vi: **to ~ at** (im Einzelhandel)
kosten; **this product ~s at £25** dieses Produkt
kostet im Laden £25
retailer ['riːteɪləʳ] n Einzelhändler(in) m(f)
retail outlet n Einzelhandelsverkaufsstelle f
retail price n Einzelhandelspreis m
retail price index n Einzelhandelspreisindex
m
retain [rɪ'teɪn] vt (keep) behalten; (: heat,
moisture) zurückhalten
retainer [rɪ'teɪnəʳ] n (fee) Vorauszahlung f
retaliate [rɪ'tælieɪt] vi Vergeltung üben
retaliation [rɪtælɪ'eɪʃən] n Vergeltung f; **in ~
for** als Vergeltung für
retaliatory [rɪ'tælɪətərɪ] adj (move, attack)
Vergeltungs-
retarded [rɪ'tɑːdɪd] adj zurückgeblieben;
mentally ~ geistig zurückgeblieben
retch [rɛtʃ] vi würgen
retention [rɪ'tɛnʃən] n (of tradition etc)

Beibehaltung f; (of land, memories) Behalten nt;
(of heat, fluid etc) Zurückhalten nt
retentive [rɪ'tɛntɪv] adj (memory) merkfähig
rethink ['riː'θɪŋk] vt noch einmal überdenken
reticence ['rɛtɪsns] n Zurückhaltung f
reticent ['rɛtɪsnt] adj zurückhaltend
retina ['rɛtɪnə] n Netzhaut f
retinue ['rɛtɪnjuː] n Gefolge nt
retire [rɪ'taɪəʳ] vi (give up work) in den Ruhestand
treten; (withdraw, go to bed) sich zurückziehen
retired [rɪ'taɪəd] adj (person) im Ruhestand
retirement [rɪ'taɪəmənt] n (state) Ruhestand
m; (act) Pensionierung f
retirement age n Rentenalter nt
retiring [rɪ'taɪərɪŋ] adj (leaving) ausscheidend;
(shy) zurückhaltend
retort [rɪ'tɔːt] vi erwidern ▷ n (reply)
Erwiderung f
retrace [riː'treɪs] vt: **to ~ one's steps** (lit, fig)
seine Schritte zurückverfolgen
retract [rɪ'trækt] vt (promise) zurücknehmen;
(confession) zurückziehen; (claws, undercarriage)
einziehen
retractable [rɪ'træktəbl] adj (undercarriage,
aerial) einziehbar
retrain [riː'treɪn] vt umschulen ▷ vi
umgeschult werden
retraining [riː'treɪnɪŋ] n Umschulung f
retread ['riːtred] n (tyre) runderneuerter Reifen
m
retreat [rɪ'triːt] n (place) Zufluchtsort m;
(withdrawal, also Mil) Rückzug m ▷ vi sich
zurückziehen; **to beat a hasty ~** schleunigst
den Rückzug antreten
retrial [riː'traɪəl] n erneute Verhandlung f
retribution [rɛtrɪ'bjuːʃən] n Strafe f
retrieval [rɪ'triːvəl] n (of object) Zurückholen nt;
(Comput) Abruf m
retrieve [rɪ'triːv] vt (object) zurückholen;
(situation) retten; (error) wiedergutmachen;
(dog) apportieren; (Comput) abrufen
retriever [rɪ'triːvəʳ] n (dog) Apportierhund m
retroactive [rɛtrəu'æktɪv] adj rückwirkend
retrograde ['rɛtrəgreɪd] adj (step) Rück-
retrospect ['rɛtrəspɛkt] n: **in ~** rückblickend,
im Rückblick
retrospective [rɛtrə'spɛktɪv] adj (opinion etc) im
Nachhinein; (law, tax) rückwirkend ▷ n (Art)
Retrospektive f
return [rɪ'tɜːn] n (going or coming back) Rückkehr
f; (of sth stolen etc) Rückgabe f; (also: **return
ticket**: Brit) Rückfahrkarte f; (Fin: from
investment etc) Ertrag m; (of merchandise)
Rücksendung f; (official report) Erklärung
f ▷ cpd (journey) Rück- ▷ vi (person etc: come or
go back) zurückkehren; (feelings, symptoms
etc) wiederkehren ▷ vt (favour, greetings
etc) erwidern; (sth stolen etc) zurückgeben;
(Law: verdict) fällen; (Pol: candidate) wählen;
(ball) zurückspielen; **returns** npl (Comm)
Gewinne pl; **in ~ (for)** als Gegenleistung (für);
by ~ of post postwendend; **many happy ~s
(of the day)!** herzlichen Glückwunsch zum

Geburtstag!; ~ **match** Rückspiel nt
▶ **return to** vt fus (regain: consciousness, power)
wiedererlangen

returnable [rɪ'tə:nəbl] adj (bottle etc) Mehrweg-

returner n jd, der nach längerer Abwesenheit wieder in die Arbeitswelt zurückkehrt

returning officer [rɪ'tə:nɪŋ-] (Brit) n Wahlleiter(in) m(f)

return key n (Comput) Return-Taste f

reunion [ri:'ju:nɪən] n Treffen nt; (after long separation) Wiedervereinigung f

reunite [ri:ju:'naɪt] vt wiedervereinigen

Rev. abbr (Rel) = **Reverend**

rev [rɛv] n abbr (Aut: = revolution per minute) Umdrehung f pro Minute, U/min. ▷ vt (also: **rev up**: engine) aufheulen lassen

revaluation [ri:vælju'eɪʃən] n (of property) Neuschätzung f; (of currency) Aufwertung f; (of attitudes) Neubewertung f

revamp [ri:'væmp] vt (company, system) auf Vordermann bringen

rev counter (Brit) n (Aut) Drehzahlmesser m

Revd. abbr (Rel) = **Reverend**

reveal [rɪ'vi:l] vt (make known) enthüllen; (make visible) zum Vorschein bringen

revealing [rɪ'vi:lɪŋ] adj (comment, action) aufschlussreich; (dress) tief ausgeschnitten

reveille [rɪ'vælɪ] n (Mil) Wecksignal nt

revel ['rɛvl] vi: **to ~ in sth** in etw schwelgen; **to ~ in doing sth** es genießen, etw zu tun

revelation [rɛvə'leɪʃən] n (disclosure) Enthüllung f

reveller ['rɛvlə'] n Zecher(in) m(f)

revelry ['rɛvlrɪ] n Gelage nt

revenge [rɪ'vɛndʒ] n (for insult etc) Rache f ▷ vt rächen; **to get one's ~ (for sth)** seine Rache (für etw) bekommen; **to ~ o.s.** or **take one's ~ (on sb)** sich (an jdm) rächen

revengeful [rɪ'vɛndʒful] adj rachsüchtig

revenue ['rɛvənju:] n (of person, company) Einnahmen pl; (of government) Staatseinkünfte pl

reverberate [rɪ'və:bəreɪt] vi (sound etc) widerhallen; (fig: shock etc) Nachwirkungen haben

reverberation [rɪvə:bə'reɪʃən] n (of sound) Widerhall m; (fig: of event etc) Nachwirkungen pl

revere [rɪ'vɪə'] vt verehren

reverence ['rɛvərəns] n Ehrfurcht f

Reverend ['rɛvərənd] adj (in titles) Pfarrer; **the ~ John Smith** Pfarrer John Smith

reverent ['rɛvərənt] adj ehrfürchtig

reverie ['rɛvərɪ] n Träumerei f

reversal [rɪ'və:sl] n (of policy, trend) Umkehr f; **a ~ of roles** ein Rollentausch m

reverse [rɪ'və:s] n (opposite) Gegenteil nt; (back: of cloth) linke Seite f; (: of coin, paper) Rückseite f; (Aut: also: **reverse gear**) Rückwärtsgang m; (side) Rück-; (process) umgekehrt ▷ vt (position, trend etc) umkehren; (Law: verdict) revidieren; (roles) vertauschen; (car) zurücksetzen ▷ vi

(Brit: Aut) zurücksetzen; **in ~** umgekehrt; **to go into ~** den Rückwärtsgang einlegen; **in ~ order** in umgekehrter Reihenfolge; **to ~ direction** sich um 180 Grad drehen

reverse-charge call [rɪ'və:stʃɑ:dʒ-] (Brit) n R-Gespräch nt

reverse video n (Comput) invertierte Darstellung f

reversible [rɪ'və:səbl] adj (garment) auf beiden Seiten tragbar; (decision, operation) umkehrbar

reversing lights [rɪ'və:sɪŋ-] (Brit) npl Rückfahrscheinwerfer m

reversion [rɪ'və:ʃən] n: **~ to** Rückfall in +acc; (Zool) Rückentwicklung f

revert [rɪ'və:t] vi: **to ~ to** (former state) zurückkehren zu, zurückfallen in +acc; (Law: money, property) zurückfallen an +acc

review [rɪ'vju:] n (magazine) Zeitschrift f; (Mil) Inspektion f; (of book, film etc) Kritik f, Besprechung f, Rezension f; (of policy etc) Überprüfung f ▷ vt (Mil: troops) inspizieren; (book, film etc) besprechen, rezensieren; (policy etc) überprüfen; **to be/come under ~** überprüft werden

reviewer [rɪ'vju:ə'] n Kritiker(in) m(f), Rezensent(in) m(f)

revile [rɪ'vaɪl] vt schmähen

revise [rɪ'vaɪz] vt (manuscript) überarbeiten, revidieren; (opinion etc) ändern; (price, procedure) revidieren ▷ vi (study) wiederholen; **~d edition** überarbeitete Ausgabe

revision [rɪ'vɪʒən] n (of manuscript, law etc) Überarbeitung f, Revision f; (for exam) Wiederholung f

revitalize [ri:'vaɪtəlaɪz] vt neu beleben

revival [rɪ'vaɪvəl] n (recovery) Aufschwung m; (of interest, faith) Wiederaufleben nt; (Theat) Wiederaufnahme f

revive [rɪ'vaɪv] vt (person) wiederbeleben; (economy etc) Auftrieb geben +dat; (custom) wiederaufleben lassen; (hope, interest etc) neu beleben; (play) wiederaufnehmen ▷ vi (person) wieder zu sich kommen; (activity, economy etc) wieder aufblühen; (hope, interest etc) wiedererweckt werden

revoke [rɪ'vəuk] vt (law etc) aufheben; (title, licence) entziehen +dat; (promise, decision) widerrufen

revolt [rɪ'vəult] n Revolte f, Aufstand m ▷ vi rebellieren ▷ vt abstoßen; **to ~ against sb/ sth** gegen jdn/etw rebellieren

revolting [rɪ'vəultɪŋ] adj (disgusting) abscheulich, ekelhaft

revolution [rɛvə'lu:ʃən] n (Pol etc) Revolution f; (rotation) Umdrehung f

revolutionary [rɛvə'lu:ʃənrɪ] adj revolutionär; (leader, army) Revolutions- ▷ n Revolutionär(in) m(f)

revolutionize [rɛvə'lu:ʃənaɪz] vt revolutionieren

revolve [rɪ'vɔlv] vi sich drehen; **to ~ (a)round** sich drehen um

revolver [rɪ'vɔlvə'] n Revolver m

r

revolving [rɪ'vɔlvɪŋ] *adj* (*chair*) Dreh-; (*sprinkler etc*) drehbar

revolving door *n* Drehtür *f*

revue [rɪ'vju:] *n* (*Theat*) Revue *f*

revulsion [rɪ'vʌlʃən] *n* Abscheu *m*, Ekel *m*

reward [rɪ'wɔ:d] *n* Belohnung *f*; (*satisfaction*) Befriedigung *f* ▷ *vt* belohnen

reward card *n* Kundenkarte *f*, Pay-back-Karte® *f*

rewarding [rɪ'wɔ:dɪŋ] *adj* lohnend; **financially ~** einträglich

rewind [ri:'waɪnd] (*irreg: like* **wind**) *vt* (*tape etc*) zurückspulen

rewire [ri:'waɪər] *vt* neu verkabeln

reword [ri:'wɔ:d] *vt* (*message, note*) umformulieren

rework [ri:'wɜ:k] *vt* (*use again: theme etc*) wiederverarbeiten; (*revise*) neu fassen

rewritable [ri:'raɪtəbl] *adj* (*CD, DVD*) wiederbeschreibbar

rewrite [ri:'raɪt] (*irreg: like* **write**) *vt* neu schreiben

Reykjavik ['reɪkjəvi:k] *n* Reykjavik *nt*

RFD (*US*) *abbr* (*Post: = rural free delivery*) *freie* Landpostzustellung

RGN (*Brit*) *n abbr* (*= Registered General Nurse*) staatlich geprüfte Krankenschwester *f*, staatlich geprüfter Krankenpfleger *m*

Rh *abbr* (*Med: = rhesus*) Rh.

rhapsody ['ræpsədɪ] *n* (*Mus*) Rhapsodie *f*

rhesus negative *adj* Rhesus negativ

rhesus positive *adj* Rhesus positiv

rhetoric ['retərɪk] *n* Rhetorik *f*

rhetorical [rɪ'tɔrɪkl] *adj* rhetorisch

rheumatic [ru:'mætɪk] *adj* rheumatisch

rheumatism ['ru:mətɪzəm] *n* Rheuma *nt*, Rheumatismus *m*

rheumatoid arthritis ['ru:mətɔɪd-] *n* Gelenkrheumatismus *m*

Rhine [raɪn] *n*: **the ~** der Rhein

rhinestone ['raɪnstəun] *n* Rheinkiesel *m*

rhinoceros [raɪ'nɔsərəs] *n* Rhinozeros *nt*

Rhodes [rəudz] *n* Rhodos *nt*

Rhodesia [rəu'di:ʒə] (*formerly*) *n* (*Geog*) Rhodesien *nt*

rhododendron [rəudə'dendrən] *n* Rhododendron *m or nt*

rhubarb ['ru:bɑ:b] *n* Rhabarber *m*

rhyme [raɪm] *n* Reim *m*; (*verse*) Verse *pl* ▷ *vi*: **to ~ (with)** sich reimen (mit); **without ~ or reason** ohne Sinn und Verstand

rhythm ['rɪðm] *n* Rhythmus *m*

rhythmic ['rɪðmɪk], **rhythmical** ['rɪðmɪkl] *adj* rhythmisch

rhythmically ['rɪðmɪklɪ] *adv* (*move, beat*) rhythmisch, im Rhythmus

rhythm method *n* Knaus-Ogino-Methode *f*

RI *n abbr* (*Brit: Scol: = religious instruction*) Religionsunterricht *m* ▷ *abbr* (*US: Post*) = Rhode Island

rib [rɪb] *n* Rippe *f* ▷ *vt* (*mock*) aufziehen

ribald ['rɪbəld] *adj* (*laughter, joke*) rüde; (*person*) anzüglich

ribbed [rɪbd] *adj* (*socks, sweater*) gerippt

ribbon ['rɪbən] *n* (*for hair, decoration*) Band *nt*; (*of typewriter*) Farbband *nt*; **in ~s** (*torn*) in Fetzen

rice [raɪs] *n* Reis *m*

ricefield ['raɪsfi:ld] *n* Reisfeld *nt*

rice pudding *n* Milchreis *m*

rich [rɪtʃ] *adj* reich; (*soil*) fruchtbar; (*food*) schwer; (*diet*) reichhaltig; (*colour*) satt; (*voice*) volltönend; (*tapestries, silks*) prächtig ▷ *npl*: **the ~** die Reichen; **~ in** reich an +*dat*

riches ['rɪtʃɪz] *npl* Reichtum *m*

richly ['rɪtʃlɪ] *adv* (*decorated, carved*) reich; (*reward, benefit*) reichlich; **~ deserved/earned** wohlverdient

richness ['rɪtʃnɪs] *n* (*wealth*) Reichtum *m*; (*of life, culture, food*) Reichhaltigkeit *f*; (*of soil*) Fruchtbarkeit *f*; (*of costumes, furnishings*) Pracht *f*

rickets ['rɪkɪts] *n* Rachitis *f*

rickety ['rɪkɪtɪ] *adj* (*chair etc*) wackelig

rickshaw ['rɪkʃɔ:] *n* Rikscha *f*

ricochet ['rɪkəʃeɪ] *vi* abprallen ▷ *n* Abpraller *m*

rid [rɪd] (*pt, pp* **~**) *vt*: **to ~ sb/sth of** jdn/ etw befreien von; **to get ~ of** loswerden; (*inhibitions, illusions etc*) sich befreien von

riddance ['rɪdns] *n*: **good ~!** gut, dass wir den/die/das los sind!

ridden ['rɪdn] *pp of* **ride**

riddle ['rɪdl] *n* Rätsel *nt* ▷ *vt*: **to be ~d with** (*guilt, doubts*) geplagt sein von; (*holes, corruption*) durchsetzt sein von

ride [raɪd] (*pt* **rode**, *pp* **ridden**) *n* (*in car, on bicycle*) Fahrt *f*; (*on horse*) Ritt *m*; (*path*) Reitweg *m* ▷ *vi* (*on horse*) reiten; (*on bicycle, bus etc*) fahren ▷ *vt* (*see vi*) reiten; fahren; **car ~** Autofahrt *f*; **to go for a ~** eine Fahrt/einen Ausritt machen; **to take sb for a ~** (*fig*) jdn hereinlegen; **we rode all day/all the way** wir sind den ganzen Tag/den ganzen Weg geritten/gefahren; **to ~ at anchor** (*Naut*) vor Anker liegen; **can you ~ a bike?** kannst du Fahrrad fahren?

▷ **ride out** *vt*: **to ~ out the storm** (*fig*) den Sturm überstehen

rider ['raɪdər] *n* (*on horse*) Reiter(in) *m(f)*; (*on bicycle etc*) Fahrer(in) *m(f)*; (*in document etc*) Zusatz *m*

ridge [rɪdʒ] *n* (*of hill*) Grat *m*; (*of roof*) First *m*; (*in sand etc*) Rippelmarke *f*

ridicule ['rɪdɪkju:l] *n* Spott *m* ▷ *vt* (*person*) verspotten; (*proposal, system etc*) lächerlich machen; **she was the object of ~** alle machten sich über sie lustig

ridiculous [rɪ'dɪkjuləs] *adj* lächerlich

riding ['raɪdɪŋ] *n* Reiten *nt*

riding school *n* Reitschule *f*

rife [raɪf] *adj*: **to be ~** (*corruption, disease etc*) grassieren; **to be ~ with** (*rumours etc*) durchsetzt sein von

riffraff ['rɪfræf] *n* Gesindel *nt*

rifle ['raɪfl] *n* (*gun*) Gewehr *nt* ▷ *vt* (*wallet etc*) plündern

▷ **rifle through** *vt fus* (*papers etc*) durchwühlen

rifle range *n* Schießstand *m*

rift [rɪft] *n* Spalt *m*; (*fig*) Kluft *f*

rig [rɪg] n (also: **oil rig**: at sea) Bohrinsel f; (: on land) Bohrturm m ▷ vt (election, game etc) manipulieren
▶ **rig out** (Brit) vt: **to ~ sb out as/in** jdn ausstaffieren als/in +dat
▶ **rig up** vt (device) montieren
rigging ['rɪgɪŋ] n (Naut) Takelage f
right [raɪt] adj (correct) richtig; (not left) rechte(r, s) ▷ n Recht nt ▷ adv (correctly, properly) richtig; (directly, exactly) genau; (not on the left) rechts ▷ vt (ship, car etc) aufrichten; (fault, situation) korrigieren, berichtigen ▷ excl okay; **the ~ time** (exact) die genaue Zeit; (most suitable) die richtige Zeit; **to be ~** (person) recht haben; (answer, fact) richtig sein; (clock) genau gehen; (reading etc) korrekt sein; **to get sth ~** etw richtig machen; **let's get it ~ this time!** diesmal machen wir es richtig!; **you did the ~ thing** du hast das Richtige getan; **to put sth ~** (mistake etc) etw berichtigen; **on/to the ~** rechts; **the R~** (Pol) die Rechte; **by ~s** richtig genommen; **to be in the ~** im Recht sein; **you're within your ~s (to do that)** es ist dein gutes Recht(, das zu tun); **he is a well-known author in his own ~** er ist selbst auch ein bekannter Autor; **film ~s** Filmrechte pl; **~ now** im Moment; **~ before/after the party** gleich vor/nach der Party; **~ against the wall** unmittelbar an der Wand; **~ ahead** geradeaus; **~ away** (immediately) sofort; **~ in the middle** genau in der Mitte; **he went ~ to the end of the road** er ging bis ganz ans Ende der Straße
right angle n rechter Winkel m
right-click ['raɪtklɪk] (Comput) vi rechts klicken ▷ vt rechts klicken auf +acc
righteous ['raɪtʃəs] adj (person) rechtschaffen; (indignation) gerecht
righteousness ['raɪtʃəsnɪs] n Rechtschaffenheit f
rightful ['raɪtful] adj rechtmäßig
rightfully ['raɪtfəlɪ] adv von Rechts wegen
right-hand drive adj (vehicle) mit Rechtssteuerung
right-handed [raɪt'hændɪd] adj rechtshändig
right-hand man n rechte Hand f
right-hand side n rechte Seite f
rightly ['raɪtlɪ] adv (with reason) zu Recht; **if I remember ~** (Brit) wenn ich mich recht entsinne
right-minded [raɪt'maɪndɪd] adj vernünftig
right of way n (on path etc) Durchgangsrecht f; (Aut) Vorfahrt f
rights issue n (Stock Exchange) Bezugsrechtsemission f
right wing n (Pol, Sport) rechter Flügel m
right-wing [raɪt'wɪŋ] adj (Pol) rechtsgerichtet
right-winger [raɪt'wɪŋər] n (Pol) Rechte(r) f(m); (Sport) Rechtsaußen m
rigid ['rɪdʒɪd] adj (structure, views) starr; (principle, control etc) streng
rigidity [rɪ'dʒɪdɪtɪ] n (of structure etc) Starrheit f; (of attitude, views etc) Strenge f

rigidly ['rɪdʒɪdlɪ] adv (hold, fix etc) starr; (control, interpret) streng
rigmarole ['rɪgmərəul] n Gedöns nt (inf)
rigor ['rɪgər] (US) n = **rigour**
rigor mortis ['rɪgə'mɔːtɪs] n Totenstarre f
rigorous ['rɪgərəs] adj (control etc) streng; (training) gründlich
rigorously ['rɪgərəslɪ] adv (test, assess etc) streng
rigour, (US) **rigor** ['rɪgər] n (of argument, law) Strenge f; (of research) Gründlichkeit f; **the ~s of life/winter** die Härten des Lebens/des Winters
rig-out ['rɪgaut] (Brit: inf) n Aufzug m
rile [raɪl] vt ärgern
rim [rɪm] n (of glass, spectacles) Rand m; (of wheel) Felge f, Radkranz m
rimless ['rɪmlɪs] adj (spectacles) randlos
rimmed [rɪmd] adj: **~ with** umrandet von; **gold-~ spectacles** Brille f mit Goldfassung or Goldrand
rind [raɪnd] n (of bacon) Schwarte f; (of lemon, melon) Schale f; (of cheese) Rinde f
ring [rɪŋ] (pt **rang**, pp **rung**) n Ring m; (of people, objects) Kreis m; (of circus) Manege f; (bullring) Arena f; (sound of telephone) Klingeln nt; (sound of bell) Läuten nt; (on cooker) Kochstelle m ▷ vi (Tel: person) anrufen; (telephone, doorbell) klingeln; (bell) läuten; (also: **ring out**) ertönen ▷ vt (Brit: Tel) anrufen; (bell etc) läuten; (encircle) einen Kreis machen um; **to give sb a ~** (Brit: Tel) jdn anrufen; **that has a ~ of truth about it** das könnte stimmen; **to run ~s round sb** (inf: fig) jdn in die Tasche stecken; **to ~ true/false** wahr/falsch klingen; **my ears are ~ing** mir klingen die Ohren; **to ~ the doorbell** klingeln; **the name doesn't ~ a bell (with me)** der Name sagt mir nichts
▶ **ring back** (Brit) vt, vi (Tel) zurückrufen
▶ **ring off** (Brit) vi (Tel) (den Hörer) auflegen
▶ **ring up** (Brit) vt (Tel) anrufen
ring binder n Ringbuch nt
ring finger n Ringfinger m
ringing ['rɪŋɪŋ] n (of telephone) Klingeln nt; (of bell) Läuten nt; (in ears) Klingen nt
ringing tone (Brit) n (Tel) Rufzeichen nt
ringleader ['rɪŋliːdər] n Rädelsführer(in) m(f)
ringlets ['rɪŋlɪts] npl Ringellocken pl; **in ~** in Ringellocken
ring road (Brit) n Ringstraße f
ringtone ['rɪŋtəun] n (of mobile phone) Klingelton m
rink [rɪŋk] n (also: **ice rink**) Eisbahn f; (also: **roller skating rink**) Rollschuhbahn f
rinse [rɪns] n Spülen nt; (of hands) Abspülen nt; (hair dye) Tönung f ▷ vt spülen; (hands) abspülen; (also: **rinse out**: clothes) auswaschen; (: mouth) ausspülen; **to give sth a ~** etw spülen; (dishes) etw abspülen
Rio ['riːəu], **Rio de Janeiro** ['riːəudədʒə'nɪərəu] n Rio (de Janeiro) nt
riot ['raɪət] n (disturbance) Aufruhr m ▷ vi randalieren; **a ~ of colours** ein Farbenmeer nt; **to run ~** randalieren

r

753

rioter ['raɪətəʳ] n Randalierer m

riot gear n Schutzausrüstung f

riotous ['raɪətəs] adj (crowd) randalierend; (nights, party) ausschweifend; (welcome etc) tumultartig

riotously ['raɪətəslɪ] adv: ~ **funny** or **comic** urkomisch

riot police n Bereitschaftspolizei f; **hundreds of** ~ Hunderte von Bereitschaftspolizisten

RIP abbr (= requiescat or requiescant in pace) R.I.P.

rip [rɪp] n (tear) Riss m ▷ vt zerreißen ▷ vi reißen
▸ **rip off** vt (clothes) herunterreißen; (inf: swindle) übers Ohr hauen
▸ **rip up** vt zerreißen

ripcord ['rɪpkɔːd] n Reißleine f

ripe [raɪp] adj reif; **to be ~ for sth** (fig) reif für etw sein; **he lived to a ~ old age** er erreichte ein stolzes Alter

ripen ['raɪpn] vt reifen lassen ▷ vi reifen

ripeness ['raɪpnɪs] n Reife f

rip-off ['rɪpɔf] (inf) n: **it's a ~!** das ist Wucher!

riposte [rɪ'pɔst] n scharfe Entgegnung f

ripple ['rɪpl] n (wave) kleine Welle f; (of laughter, applause) Welle f ▷ vi (water) sich kräuseln; (muscles) spielen ▷ vt (surface) kräuseln

rise [raɪz] (pt **rose**, pp **~n**) n (incline) Steigung f; (Brit: salary increase) Gehaltserhöhung f; (in prices, temperature etc) Anstieg m; (fig: to fame etc) Aufstieg m ▷ vi (prices, water) steigen; (sun, moon) aufgehen; (wind) aufkommen; (from bed, chair) aufstehen; (sound, voice) ansteigen; (also: **rise up**: tower, rebel) sich erheben; (in rank) aufsteigen; **to give ~ to** Anlass geben zu; **to ~ to power** an die Macht kommen

risen ['rɪzn] pp of **rise**

rising ['raɪzɪŋ] adj (increasing) steigend; (up-and-coming) aufstrebend

rising damp n aufsteigende Feuchtigkeit f

rising star n (fig: person) Aufsteiger(in) m(f)

risk [rɪsk] n (danger, chance) Gefahr f; (deliberate) Risiko nt ▷ vt riskieren; **to take a ~** ein Risiko eingehen; **to run the ~ of sth** etw zu fürchten haben; **to run the ~ of doing sth** Gefahr laufen, etw zu tun; **at ~** in Gefahr; **at one's own ~** auf eigene Gefahr; **at the ~ of sounding rude** ... auf die Gefahr hin, unhöflich zu klingen, ...; **it's a fire/health ~** es ist ein Feuer-/Gesundheitsrisiko; **I'll ~ it** ich riskiere es

risk capital n Risikokapital nt

risky ['rɪskɪ] adj riskant

risqué ['riːskeɪ] adj (joke) gewagt

rissole ['rɪsəʊl] n (of meat, fish etc) Frikadelle f

rite [raɪt] n Ritus m; **last ~s** (Rel) Letzte Ölung f

ritual ['rɪtjʊəl] adj (law, murder) Ritual-; (dance) rituell ▷ n Ritual nt

rival ['raɪvl] n Rivale m, Rivalin f ▷ adj (firm, newspaper etc) Konkurrenz-; (teams, groups etc) rivalisierend ▷ vt (match) sich messen können mit; **to ~ sth/sb in sth** sich mit etw/jdm in Bezug auf etw messen können

rivalry ['raɪvlrɪ] n Rivalität f

river ['rɪvəʳ] n Fluss m; (fig: of blood etc) Strom m ▷ cpd (port, traffic) Fluss-; **up/down ~** flussaufwärts/-abwärts

river bank n Flussufer nt

river bed n Flussbett nt

riverside ['rɪvəsaɪd] n = **river bank**

rivet ['rɪvɪt] n Niete f ▷ vt (fig: attention) fesseln; (: eyes) heften

riveting ['rɪvɪtɪŋ] adj (fig) fesselnd

Riviera [rɪvɪ'ɛərə] n: **the (French) ~** die (französische) Riviera; **the Italian ~** die italienische Riviera

Riyadh [rɪ'jɑːd] n Riad nt

RMT n abbr (= National Union of Rail, Maritime and Transport Workers) Gewerkschaft der Eisenbahner, Seeleute und Transportarbeiter

RN n abbr (Brit) = **Royal Navy**; (US) = **registered nurse**

RNA n abbr (= ribonucleic acid) RNS f

RNLI (Brit) n abbr (= Royal National Lifeboat Institution) durch Spenden finanzierter Seenot-Rettungsdienst, ≈ DLRG f

RNZAF n abbr (= Royal New Zealand Air Force) neuseeländische Luftwaffe f

RNZN n abbr (= Royal New Zealand Navy) neuseeländische Marine f

road [rəʊd] n Straße f; (fig) Weg m ▷ cpd (accident, sense) Verkehrs-; **main ~** Hauptstraße f; **it takes four hours by ~** man braucht vier Stunden mit dem Auto; **let's hit the ~** machen wir uns auf den Weg!; **to be on the ~** (salesman etc) unterwegs sein; (pop group etc) auf Tournee sein; **on the ~ to success** auf dem Weg zum Erfolg; **major/minor ~** Haupt-/Nebenstraße f

road accident n Verkehrsunfall m

roadblock ['rəʊdblɔk] n Straßensperre f

road haulage n Spedition f

roadhog ['rəʊdhɔg] n Verkehrsrowdy m

road map n Straßenkarte f

road rage n Aggressivität f im Straßenverkehr

road safety n Verkehrssicherheit f

roadside ['rəʊdsaɪd] n Straßenrand m ▷ cpd (building, sign etc) am Straßenrand; **by the ~** am Straßenrand

road sign n Verkehrszeichen nt

roadsweeper ['rəʊdswiːpəʳ] (Brit) n (person) Straßenkehrer(in) m(f); (vehicle) Straßenkehrmaschine f

road user n Verkehrsteilnehmer(in) m(f)

roadway ['rəʊdweɪ] n Fahrbahn f

road works npl Straßenbauarbeiten pl

roadworthy ['rəʊdwəːðɪ] adj verkehrstüchtig

roam [rəʊm] vi wandern, streifen ▷ vt (streets, countryside) durchstreifen

roar [rɔːʳ] n (of animal, crowd) Brüllen nt; (of vehicle) Getöse nt; (of storm) Heulen nt ▷ vi (animal, person) brüllen; (engine, wind etc) heulen; **~s of laughter** brüllendes Gelächter; **to ~ with laughter** vor Lachen brüllen

roaring ['rɔːrɪŋ] adj: **a ~ fire** ein prasselndes Feuer; **a ~ success** ein Bombenerfolg m; **to do a ~ trade (in sth)** ein Riesengeschäft (mit etw) machen

roast [rəʊst] *n* Braten *m* ▷ *vt* (*meat, potatoes*) braten; (*coffee*) rösten

roast beef *n* Roastbeef *nt*

roasting ['rəʊstɪŋ] (*inf*) *adj* (*hot*) knallheiß ▷ *n* (*criticism*) Verriss *m*; (*telling-off*) Standpauke *f*; **to give sb a ~** (*criticize*) jdn verreißen; (*scold*) jdm eine Standpauke halten

rob [rɒb] *vt* (*person*) bestehlen; (*house, bank*) ausrauben; **to ~ sb of sth** jdm etw rauben; (*fig: deprive*) jdm etw vorenthalten

robber ['rɒbəʳ] *n* Räuber(in) *m(f)*

robbery ['rɒbərɪ] *n* Raub *m*

robe [rəʊb] *n* (*for ceremony etc*) Gewand *nt*; (*also:* **bath robe**) Bademantel *m*; (*US*) Morgenrock *m* ▷ *vt*: **to be ~d in** (*form*) (festlich) in etw *acc* gekleidet sein

robin ['rɒbɪn] *n* Rotkehlchen *nt*

robot ['rəʊbɒt] *n* Roboter *m*

robotics [rə'bɒtɪks] *n* Robotik *f*

robust [rəʊ'bʌst] *adj* robust; (*appetite*) gesund

rock [rɒk] *n* (*substance*) Stein *m*; (*boulder*) Felsen *m*; (*US: small stone*) Stein *m*; (*Brit: sweet*) ≈ Zuckerstange *f*; (*Mus: also:* **rock music**) Rock *m*, Rockmusik *f* ▷ *vt* (*swing gently: cradle*) schaukeln; (*: child*) wiegen; (*shake: also fig*) erschüttern ▷ *vi* (*object*) schwanken; (*person*) schaukeln; **on the ~s** (*drink*) mit Eis; (*ship*) (auf Felsen) aufgelaufen; (*marriage etc*) gescheitert; **to ~ the boat** (*fig*) Unruhe stiften

rock and roll *n* Rock and Roll *m*

rock bottom ['rɒk'bɒtəm] *adj* (*prices*) Tiefst- ▷ *n*: **to reach** *or* **touch** *or* **hit ~** (*person, prices*) den Tiefpunkt erreichen

rock cake *n* ≈ Rosinenbrötchen *nt*

rock climber *n* Felsenkletterer(in) *m(f)*

rock climbing *n* Felsenklettern *nt*

rockery ['rɒkərɪ] *n* Steingarten *m*

rocket ['rɒkɪt] *n* Rakete *f* ▷ *vi* (*prices*) in die Höhe schießen

rocket launcher *n* Raketenwerfer *m*

rock face *n* Felswand *f*

rock fall *n* Steinschlag *m*

rocking chair ['rɒkɪŋ-] *n* Schaukelstuhl *m*

rocking horse *n* Schaukelpferd *nt*

rocky ['rɒkɪ] *adj* (*path, ground*) felsig; (*fig: business, marriage*) wackelig

Rocky Mountains *npl*: **the ~** die Rocky Mountains *pl*

rod [rɒd] *n* (*also Tech*) Stange *f*; (*also:* **fishing rod**) Angelrute *f*

rode [rəʊd] *pt of* **ride**

rodent ['rəʊdnt] *n* Nagetier *nt*

rodeo ['rəʊdɪəʊ] (*US*) *n* Rodeo *nt*

roe [rəʊ] *n* (*Culin*): **hard ~** Rogen *m*; **soft ~** Milch *f*

roe deer *n inv* Reh *nt*

rogue [rəʊg] *n* Gauner *m*

roguish ['rəʊgɪʃ] *adj* schelmisch

role [rəʊl] *n* Rolle *f*

role model *n* Rollenmodell *nt*

role play *n* Rollenspiel *nt*

roll [rəʊl] *n* (*of paper*) Rolle *f*; (*of cloth*) Ballen *m*; (*of banknotes*) Bündel *nt*; (*also:* **bread roll**) Brötchen *nt*; (*register, list*) Verzeichnis *nt*; (*of drums etc*) Wirbel *m* ▷ *vt* rollen; (*also:* **roll up**: *string*) aufrollen; (*: sleeves*) aufkrempeln; (*cigarette*) drehen; (*also:* **roll out**: *pastry*) ausrollen; (*flatten: lawn, road*) walzen ▷ *vi* rollen; (*drum*) wirbeln; (*thunder*) grollen; (*ship*) schlingern; (*tears, sweat*) fließen; (*camera, printing press*) laufen; **cheese/ham ~** Käse-/Schinkenbrötchen *nt*; **he's ~ing in it** (*inf: rich*) er schwimmt im Geld

▸ **roll about** *vi* sich wälzen

▸ **roll around** *vi* = **roll about**

▸ **roll in** *vi* (*money, invitations*) hereinströmen

▸ **roll over** *vi* sich umdrehen

▸ **roll up** *vi* (*inf: arrive*) aufkreuzen ▷ *vt* (*carpet, umbrella etc*) aufrollen; **to ~ o.s. up into a ball** sich zusammenrollen

roll call *n* namentlicher Aufruf *m*

rolled gold [rəʊld-] *n* Doublégold *nt*

roller ['rəʊləʳ] *n* Rolle *f*; (*for lawn, road*) Walze *f*; (*for hair*) Lockenwickler *m*

Rollerblades® *npl* Rollerblades *pl*

roller blind *n* Rollo *nt*

roller coaster *n* Achterbahn *f*

roller skates *npl* Rollschuhe *pl*

rollicking ['rɒlɪkɪŋ] *adj* toll, Mords-; **to have a ~ time** sich ganz toll amüsieren

rolling ['rəʊlɪŋ] *adj* (*hills*) wellig

rolling mill *n* Walzwerk *nt*

rolling pin *n* Nudelholz *nt*

rolling stock *n* (*Rail*) Fahrzeuge *pl*

roll-on-roll-off ['rəʊlɒn'rəʊlɒf] (*Brit*) *adj* (*ferry*) Roll-on-roll-off-

roly-poly ['rəʊlɪ'pəʊlɪ] (*Brit*) *n* ≈ Strudel *m*

ROM [rɒm] *n abbr* (*Comput:* = *read only memory*) ROM

Roman ['rəʊmən] *adj* römisch ▷ *n* (*person*) Römer(in) *m(f)*

Roman Catholic *adj* römisch-katholisch ▷ *n* Katholik(in) *m(f)*

romance [rə'mæns] *n* (*love affair*) Romanze *f*; (*romanticism*) Romantik *f*; (*novel*) fantastische Erzählung *f*

Romanesque [rəʊmə'nɛsk] *adj* romanisch

Romania [rəʊ'meɪnɪə] *n* Rumänien *nt*

Romanian [rəʊ'meɪnɪən] *adj* rumänisch ▷ *n* (*person*) Rumäne *m*, Rumänin *f*; (*Ling*) Rumänisch *nt*

Roman numeral *n* römische Ziffer *f*

romantic [rə'mæntɪk] *adj* romantisch

romanticism [rə'mæntɪsɪzəm] *n* (*also Art, Liter*) Romantik *f*

Romany ['rɒmənɪ] *adj* Roma- ▷ *n* (*person*) Roma *mf*; (*Ling*) Romani *nt*

Rome [rəʊm] *n* Rom *nt*

romp [rɒmp] *n* Klamauk *m* ▷ *vi* (*also:* **romp about**) herumtollen; **to ~ home** (*horse*) spielend gewinnen

rompers ['rɒmpəz] *npl* (*clothing*) einteiliger Spielanzug für Babys

rondo ['rɒndəʊ] *n* (*Mus*) Rondo *nt*

roof [ru:f] (*pl* **~s**) *n* Dach *nt* ▷ *vt* (*house etc*) überdachen; **the ~ of the mouth** der Gaumen

r

roof garden n Dachgarten m

roofing ['ru:fɪŋ] n Deckung f; **~ felt** Dachpappe f

roof rack n Dachgepäckträger m

rook [ruk] n (bird) Saatkrähe f; (Chess) Turm m

rookie ['ruki:] (inf) n (esp Mil) Grünschnabel m

room [ru:m] n (in house, hotel) Zimmer nt; (space) Raum m, Platz m; (scope: for change etc) Raum m ▷ vi: **to ~ with sb** (esp US) ein Zimmer mit jdm teilen; **rooms** npl (lodging) Zimmer pl; **"~s to let"**, **"~s for rent"** (US) „Zimmer zu vermieten"; **single/double ~** Einzel-/Doppelzimmer nt; **is there ~ for this?** ist dafür Platz vorhanden?; **to make ~ for sb** für jdn Platz machen; **there is ~ for improvement** es gibt Möglichkeiten zur Verbesserung

rooming house ['ru:mɪŋ-] (US) n Mietshaus nt

roommate ['ru:mmeɪt] n Zimmergenosse m, Zimmergenossin f

room service n Zimmerservice m

room temperature n Zimmertemperatur f

roomy ['ru:mɪ] adj (building, car) geräumig

roost [ru:st] vi (birds) sich niederlassen

rooster ['ru:stə'] (esp US) n Hahn m

root [ru:t] n (also Math) Wurzel f ▷ vi (plant) Wurzeln schlagen ▷ vt: **to be ~ed in** verwurzelt sein in +dat; **roots** npl (family origins) Wurzeln pl; **to take ~** (plant, idea) Wurzeln schlagen; **the ~ cause of the problem** die Wurzel des Problems
  ▶ **root about** vi (search) herumwühlen
  ▶ **root for** vt fus (support) anfeuern
  ▶ **root out** vt ausrotten

root beer (US) n kohlensäurehaltiges Getränk aus Wurzel- und Kräuterextrakten

rope [rəup] n Seil nt; (Naut) Tau nt ▷ vt (tie) festbinden; (also: **rope together**) zusammenbinden; **to know the ~s** (fig) sich auskennen
  ▶ **rope in** vt (fig: person) einspannen
  ▶ **rope off** vt (area) mit einem Seil absperren

rope ladder n Strickleiter f

ropey, ropy ['rəupɪ] (inf) adj (ill, poor quality) miserabel

rosary ['rəuzərɪ] n Rosenkranz m

rose [rəuz] pt of **rise** ▷ n (flower) Rose f; (also: **rosebush**) Rosenstrauch m; (on watering can) Brause f ▷ adj rosarot

rosé ['rəuzeɪ] n (wine) Rosé m

rosebed ['rəuzbed] n Rosenbeet nt

rosebud ['rəuzbʌd] n Rosenknospe f

rosebush ['rəuzbuʃ] n Rosenstrauch m

rosemary ['rəuzmərɪ] n Rosmarin m

rosette [rəu'zet] n Rosette f

ROSPA ['rɒspə] (Brit) n abbr (= Royal Society for the Prevention of Accidents) Verband, der Maßnahmen zur Unfallverhütung propagiert

roster ['rɒstə'] n: **duty ~** Dienstplan m

rostrum ['rɒstrəm] n Rednerpult nt

rosy ['rəuzɪ] adj (colour) rosarot; (face, situation) rosig; **a ~ future** eine rosige Zukunft

rot [rɒt] n (decay) Fäulnis f; (fig: rubbish) Quatsch m ▷ vt verfaulen lassen ▷ vi (teeth, wood, fruit etc) verfaulen; **to stop the ~** (Brit: fig) den Verfall stoppen; **dry ~** Holzschwamm m; **wet ~** Nassfäule f

rota ['rəutə] n Dienstplan m; **on a ~ basis** reihum nach Plan

rotary ['rəutərɪ] adj (cutter) rotierend; (motion) Dreh-

rotate [rəu'teɪt] vt (spin) drehen, rotieren lassen; (crops) im Wechsel anbauen; (jobs) turnusmäßig wechseln ▷ vi (revolve) rotieren, sich drehen

rotating [rəu'teɪtɪŋ] adj (revolving) rotierend; (drum, mirror) Dreh-

rotation [rəu'teɪʃən] n (of planet, drum etc) Rotation f, Drehung f; (of crops) Wechsel m; (of jobs) turnusmäßiger Wechsel m; **in ~** der Reihe nach

rote [rəut] n: **by ~** auswendig

rotor ['rəutə'] n (also: **rotor blade**) Rotor m

rotten ['rɒtn] adj (decayed) faul, verfault; (inf: person, situation) gemein; (: film, weather, driver etc) mies; **to feel ~** sich elend fühlen

rotund [rəu'tʌnd] adj (person) rundlich

rouble, (US) **ruble** ['ru:bl] n Rubel m

rouge [ru:ʒ] n Rouge nt

rough [rʌf] adj rau; (terrain, road) uneben; (person, plan, drawing, guess) grob; (life, conditions, journey) hart; (sea, crossing) stürmisch ▷ n (Golf): **in the ~** im Rough ▷ vt: **to ~ it** primitiv or ohne Komfort leben; **the sea is ~ today** die See ist heute stürmisch; **to have a ~ time** eine harte Zeit durchmachen; **can you give me a ~ idea of the cost?** können Sie mir eine ungefähre Vorstellung von den Kosten geben?; **to feel ~** (Brit) sich elend fühlen; **to sleep ~** (Brit) im Freien übernachten; **to play ~** (fig) auf die grobe Tour kommen
  ▶ **rough out** vt (drawing, idea etc) skizzieren

roughage ['rʌfɪdʒ] n Ballaststoffe pl

rough-and-ready ['rʌfən'redɪ] adj provisorisch

rough-and-tumble ['rʌfən'tʌmbl] n (fighting) Balgerei f; (fig) Schlachtfeld nt

roughcast ['rʌfkɑ:st] n Rauputz m

rough copy n Entwurf m

rough draft n = **rough copy**

rough justice n Justizwillkür f

roughly ['rʌflɪ] adv grob; (approximately) ungefähr; **~ speaking** grob gesagt

roughness ['rʌfnɪs] n Rauheit f; (of manner) Grobheit f

roughshod ['rʌfʃɒd] adv: **to ride ~ over** sich rücksichtslos hinwegsetzen über +acc

roulette [ru:'let] n Roulette nt

Roumania etc [ru:'meɪnɪə] n = **Romania** etc

round [raund] adj rund ▷ n Runde f; (of ammunition) Ladung f ▷ vt (corner) biegen um; (cape) umrunden ▷ prep um ▷ adv: **all ~** rundherum; **in ~ figures** rund gerechnet; **the daily ~** (fig) der tägliche Trott; **a ~ of applause** Beifall m; **a ~ (of drinks)** eine Runde; **a ~ of sandwiches** ein Butterbrot; **a ~ of toast** (Brit) eine Scheibe Toast; **it's just ~ the corner** (fig)

es steht vor der Tür; **to go ~ the back** hinten herum gehen; **to go ~ (an obstacle)** (um ein Hindernis) herumgehen; **~ the clock** rund um die Uhr; **~ his neck/the table** um seinen Hals/den Tisch; **to sail ~ the world** die Welt umsegeln; **to walk ~ the room/park** im Zimmer/Park herumgehen; **~ about 300** (approximately) ungefähr 300; **the long way ~** auf Umwegen; **all (the) year ~** das ganze Jahr über; **the wrong way ~** falsch herum; **to ask sb ~** jdn zu sich einladen; **I'll be ~ at 6 o'clock** ich komme um 6 Uhr; **to go ~** (rotate) sich drehen; **to go ~ to sb's (house)** jdn (zu Hause) besuchen; **enough to go ~** genug für alle
- ▶ **round off** vt abrunden
- ▶ **round up** vt (cattle etc) zusammentreiben; (people) versammeln; (figure) aufrunden

roundabout ['raundəbaut] (Brit) n (Aut) Kreisverkehr m; (at fair) Karussell nt ▷ adj: **by a ~ route** auf Umwegen; **in a ~ way** auf Umwegen

rounded ['raundɪd] adj (hill, figure etc) rundlich

rounders ['raundəz] n ≈ Schlagball m

roundly ['raundlɪ] adv (fig: criticize etc) nachdrücklich

round robin (esp US) n (Sport) Wettkampf, bei dem jeder gegen jeden spielt

round-shouldered ['raund'ʃəuldəd] adj mit runden Schultern

round trip n Rundreise f

roundup ['raundʌp] n (of news etc) Zusammenfassung f; (of animals) Zusammentreiben nt; (of criminals) Aufgreifen nt; **a ~ of the latest news** ein Nachrichtenüberblick m

rouse [rauz] vt (wake up) aufwecken; (stir up) reizen

rousing ['rauzɪŋ] adj (speech) mitreißend; (welcome) stürmisch

rout [raut] (Mil) n totale Niederlage f ▷ vt (defeat) vernichtend schlagen

route [ruːt] n Strecke f; (of bus, train, shipping) Linie f; (of procession, fig) Weg m; **"all ~s"** (Aut) „alle Richtungen"; **the best ~ to London** der beste Weg nach London

route map (Brit) n Streckenkarte f

routine [ruː'tiːn] adj (work, check etc) Routine- ▷ n (habits) Routine f; (drudgery) Stumpfsinn m; (Theat) Nummer f; **~ procedure** Routinesache f

rove [rəuv] vt (area, streets) ziehen durch

roving reporter ['rəuvɪŋ-] n Reporter(in) m(f) im Außendienst

row¹ [rəu] n (line) Reihe f ▷ vi (in boat) rudern ▷ vt (boat) rudern; **three times in a ~** dreimal hintereinander

row² [rau] n (din) Krach m, Lärm m; (dispute) Streit m ▷ vi (argue) sich streiten; **to have a ~** sich streiten

rowboat ['rəubəut] (US) n = **rowing boat**

rowdiness ['raudɪnɪs] n Rowdytum nt

rowdy ['raudɪ] adj (person) rüpelhaft; (party etc) lärmend

rowdyism ['raudɪɪzəm] n = **rowdiness**

rowing ['rəuɪŋ] n (sport) Rudern nt

rowing boat (Brit) n Ruderboot nt

rowlock ['rɔlək] (Brit) n Dolle f

royal ['rɔɪəl] adj königlich; **the ~ family** die königliche Familie

Die Royal Academy oder Royal Academy of Arts, eine Akademie zur Förderung der Malerei, Bildhauerei und Architektur, wurde 1768 unter der Schirmherrschaft von George II. gegründet und befindet sich seit 1869 in Burlington House, Piccadilly, London. Jeden Sommer findet dort eine Ausstellung mit Werken zeitgenössischer Künstler statt. Die Royal Academy unterhält auch Schulen, an denen Malerei, Bildhauerei und Architektur unterrichtet wird.

Royal Air Force (Brit) n: **the ~** die Königliche Luftwaffe

royal blue adj königsblau

royalist ['rɔɪəlɪst] n Royalist(in) m(f) ▷ adj royalistisch

Royal Navy (Brit) n: **the ~** die Königliche Marine

royalty ['rɔɪəltɪ] n (royal persons) die königliche Familie; **royalties** npl (to author) Tantiemen pl; (to inventor) Honorar nt

RP (Brit) n abbr (= received pronunciation) Standardaussprache des Englischen; see also **receive**

rpm abbr (= revolutions per minute) U/min.

RR (US) abbr = **railroad**

RRP (Brit) n abbr = **recommended retail price**

RSA (Brit) n abbr (= Royal Society of Arts) akademischer Verband zur Vergabe von Diplomen; (= Royal Scottish Academy) Kunstakademie

RSI n abbr (Med: = repetitive strain injury) RSI nt, Schmerzempfindung durch ständige Wiederholung bestimmter Bewegungen

RSPB (Brit) n abbr (= Royal Society for the Protection of Birds) Vogelschutzorganisation

RSPCA (Brit) n abbr (= Royal Society for the Prevention of Cruelty to Animals) Tierschutzverein m

RSVP abbr (= répondez s'il vous plaît) u. A. w. g.

RTA n abbr (= road traffic accident) Verkehrsunfall m

Rt Hon. (Brit) abbr (= Right Honourable) Titel für Abgeordnete des Unterhauses

Rt Rev. abbr (Rel: = Right Reverend) Titel für Bischöfe

rub [rʌb] vt reiben ▷ n: **to give sth a ~** (polish) etw polieren; **he ~bed his hands together** er rieb sich dat die Hände; **to ~ sb up the wrong way, to ~ sb the wrong way** (US) bei jdm anecken
- ▶ **rub down** vt (body, horse) abreiben
- ▶ **rub in** vt (ointment) einreiben; **don't ~ it in!** (fig) reite nicht so darauf herum!
- ▶ **rub off** vi (paint) abfärben
- ▶ **rub off on** vt fus abfärben auf +acc

▸ **rub out** vt (with eraser) ausradieren
rubber ['rʌbəʳ] n (also inf: condom) Gummi nt or m; (Brit: eraser) Radiergummi m
rubber band n Gummiband nt
rubber bullet n Gummigeschoss nt
rubber plant n Gummibaum m
rubber ring n (for swimming) Schwimmreifen m
rubber stamp n Stempel m
rubber-stamp [rʌbə'stæmp] vt (fig: decision) genehmigen
rubbery ['rʌbərɪ] adj (material) gummiartig; (meat, food) wie Gummi
rubbish ['rʌbɪʃ] (Brit) n (waste) Abfall m; (fig: junk) Schrott m; (: pej: nonsense) Quatsch m ▷ vt (inf) heruntermachen; ~! Quatsch!
rubbish bin (Brit) n Abfalleimer m
rubbish dump (Brit) n Müllabladeplatz m
rubbishy ['rʌbɪʃɪ] (Brit: inf) adj miserabel, mies
rubble ['rʌbl] n (debris) Trümmer pl; (Constr) Schutt m
ruble ['ru:bl] (US) n = **rouble**
ruby ['ru:bɪ] n (gem) Rubin m ▷ adj (red) rubinrot
RUC (Brit) n abbr (= Royal Ulster Constabulary) nordirische Polizeibehörde
rucksack ['rʌksæk] n Rucksack m
ructions ['rʌkʃənz] (inf) npl Krach m, Ärger m
rudder ['rʌdəʳ] n (of ship, plane) Ruder nt
ruddy ['rʌdɪ] adj (complexion etc) rötlich; (inf: damned) verdammt
rude [ru:d] adj (impolite) unhöflich; (naughty) unanständig; (unexpected: shock etc) böse; (crude: table, shelter etc) primitiv; **to be ~ to sb** unhöflich zu jdm sein; **a ~ awakening** ein böses Erwachen
rudely ['ru:dlɪ] adv (interrupt) unhöflich; (say, push) grob
rudeness ['ru:dnɪs] n (impoliteness) Unhöflichkeit f
rudimentary [ru:dɪ'mɛntərɪ] adj (equipment) primitiv; (knowledge) Grund-
rudiments ['ru:dɪmənts] npl Grundlagen pl
rue [ru:] vt bereuen
rueful ['ru:ful] adj (expression, person) reuevoll
ruff [rʌf] n (collar) Halskrause f
ruffian ['rʌfɪən] n Rüpel m
ruffle ['rʌfl] vt (hair, feathers) zerzausen; (water) kräuseln; (fig: person) aus der Fassung bringen
rug [rʌg] n (on floor) Läufer m; (Brit: blanket) Decke f
rugby ['rʌgbɪ] n (also: **rugby football**) Rugby nt
rugged ['rʌgɪd] adj (landscape) rau; (man) robust; (features, face) markig; (determination, independence) wild
rugger ['rʌgəʳ] (Brit: inf) n Rugby nt
ruin ['ru:ɪn] n (destruction, downfall) Ruin m; (remains) Ruine f ▷ vt ruinieren; (building) zerstören; (clothes, carpet etc) verderben; **ruins** npl (of castle) Ruinen pl; (of building) Trümmer pl; **in ~s** (lit, fig) in Trümmern
ruination [ru:ɪ'neɪʃən] n (of building etc) Zerstörung f; (of person, life) Ruinierung f
ruinous ['ru:ɪnəs] adj (expense, interest) ruinös
rule [ru:l] n (norm) Regel f; (regulation) Vorschrift

f; (government) Herrschaft f; (ruler) Lineal nt ▷ vt (country, people) herrschen über +acc ▷ vi (monarch etc) herrschen; **it's against the ~s** das ist nicht gestattet; **as a ~ of thumb** als Faustregel; **under British ~** unter britischer Herrschaft; **as a ~** in der Regel; **to ~ in favour of/against/on sth** (Law) für/gegen/über etw acc entscheiden; **to ~ that ...** (umpire, judge etc) entscheiden, dass ...
▸ **rule out** vt (possibility etc) ausschließen; **murder cannot be ~d out** Mord ist nicht auszuschließen
ruled [ru:ld] adj (paper) liniert
ruler ['ru:ləʳ] n (sovereign) Herrscher(in) m(f); (for measuring) Lineal nt
ruling ['ru:lɪŋ] adj (party) Regierungs-; (body) maßgebend ▷ n (Law) Entscheidung f; **the ~ class** die herrschende Klasse
rum [rʌm] n Rum m ▷ adj (Brit: inf: peculiar) komisch
Rumania etc n = **Romania** etc
rumble ['rʌmbl] n (of thunder) Grollen nt; (of traffic) Rumpeln nt; (of guns) Donnern nt; (of voices) Gemurmel nt ▷ vi (stomach) knurren; (thunder) grollen; (traffic) rumpeln; (guns) donnern
rumbustious [rʌm'bʌstʃəs] adj (person) ungebärdig
ruminate ['ru:mɪneɪt] vi (person) grübeln; (cow, sheep etc) wiederkäuen
rummage ['rʌmɪdʒ] vi herumstöbern
rummage sale (US) n Trödelmarkt m
rumour, (US) **rumor** ['ru:məʳ] n Gerücht nt ▷ vt: **it is ~ed that ...** man sagt, dass ...
rump [rʌmp] n (of animal) Hinterteil nt; (of group etc) Rumpf m
rumple ['rʌmpl] vt (clothes etc) zerknittern; (hair) zerzausen
rump steak n Rumpsteak nt
rumpus ['rʌmpəs] n Krach m; **to kick up a ~** Krach schlagen
run [rʌn] (pt **ran**, pp **~**) n (as exercise, sport) Lauf m; (in car, train etc) Fahrt f; (series) Serie f; (Ski) Abfahrt f; (Cricket, Baseball) Run m; (Theat) Spielzeit f; (in tights etc) Laufmasche f ▷ vt (race, distance) laufen, rennen; (operate: business) leiten; (: hotel, shop) führen; (: competition, course) durchführen; (Comput: program) laufen lassen; (hand, fingers) streichen mit; (water, bath) einlaufen lassen; (Press: feature, article) bringen ▷ vi laufen, rennen; (flee) weglaufen; (bus, train) fahren; (river, tears) fließen; (colours) auslaufen; (jumper) färben; (in election) antreten; (road, railway etc) verlaufen; **to go for a ~** (as exercise) einen Dauerlauf machen; **to break into a ~** zu laufen or rennen beginnen; **a ~ of good/bad luck** eine Glücks-/Pechsträhne; **to have the ~ of sb's house** jds Haus zur freien Verfügung haben; **there was a ~ on ...** (meat, tickets) es gab einen Ansturm auf +acc; **in the long ~** langfristig; **in the short ~** kurzfristig; **to make a ~ for it** die Beine in die Hand nehmen; **on the ~** (fugitive)

auf der Flucht; **I'll ~ you to the station** ich fahre dich zum Bahnhof; **to ~ the risk of doing sth** Gefahr laufen, etw zu tun; **she ran her finger down the list** sie ging die Liste mit dem Finger durch; **it's very cheap to ~** (*car, machine*) es ist sehr billig im Verbrauch; **to ~ a bath** das Badewasser einlaufen lassen; **to be ~ off one's feet** (*Brit*) ständig auf Trab sein; **the baby's nose was ~ning** dem Baby lief die Nase; **the train ~s between Gatwick and Victoria** der Zug verkehrt zwischen Gatwick und Victoria; **the bus ~s every 20 minutes** der Bus fährt alle 20 Minuten; **to ~ on petrol/off batteries** mit Benzin/auf Batterie laufen; **to ~ for president** für das Amt des Präsidenten kandidieren; **to ~ dry** (*well etc*) austrocknen; **tempers were ~ning high** alle waren sehr erregt; **unemployment is ~ning at 20 per cent** die Arbeitslosigkeit beträgt 20 Prozent; **blonde hair ~s in the family** blonde Haare liegen in der Familie

▸ **run across** *vt fus* (*find*) stoßen auf +*acc*
▸ **run after** *vt fus* nachlaufen +*dat*
▸ **run away** *vi* weglaufen
▸ **run down** *vt* (*production*) verringern; (*factory*) allmählich stilllegen; (*Aut: person*) überfahren; (*criticize*) schlechtmachen ▷ *vi* (*battery*) leer werden
▸ **run in** (*Brit*) *vt* (*car*) einfahren
▸ **run into** *vt fus* (*meet: person*) begegnen +*dat*; (*: trouble etc*) bekommen; (*collide with*) laufen/fahren gegen; **to ~ into debt** in Schulden geraten; **their losses ran into millions** ihre Schulden gingen in die Millionen
▸ **run off** *vt* (*liquid*) ablassen; (*copies*) machen ▷ *vi* weglaufen
▸ **run out** *vi* (*time, passport*) ablaufen; (*money*) ausgehen; (*luck*) zu Ende gehen
▸ **run out of** *vt fus*: **we're ~ning out of money/petrol** uns geht das Geld/das Benzin aus; **we're ~ning out of time** wir haben keine Zeit mehr
▸ **run over** *vt* (*Aut*) überfahren ▷ *vt fus* (*repeat*) durchgehen ▷ *vi* (*bath, water*) überlaufen
▸ **run through** *vt fus* (*instructions, lines*) durchgehen
▸ **run up** *vt* (*debt*) anhäufen
▸ **run up against** *vt fus* (*difficulties*) stoßen auf +*acc*

runabout ['rʌnəbaut] *n* (*Aut*) Flitzer *m*
run-around ['rʌnəraund] (*inf*) *n*: **to give sb the ~** jdn an der Nase herumführen
runaway ['rʌnəweɪ] *adj* (*horse*) ausgerissen; (*truck, train*) außer Kontrolle geraten; (*child, slave*) entlaufen; (*fig: inflation*) unkontrollierbar; (*: success*) überwältigend
rundown ['rʌndaun] *n* (*of industry etc*) allmähliche Stillegung *f* ▷ *adj*: **to be run-down** (*person*) total erschöpft sein; (*building, area*) heruntergekommen
rung [rʌŋ] *pp of* **ring** ▷ *n* (*also fig*) Sprosse *f*
run-in ['rʌnɪn] (*inf*) *n* Auseinandersetzung *f*
runner ['rʌnəʳ] *n* Läufer(in) *m(f)*; (*horse*)

Rennpferd *nt*; (*on sledge, drawer etc*) Kufe *f*
runner bean (*Brit*) *n* Stangenbohne *f*
runner-up [rʌnər'ʌp] *n* Zweitplatzierte(r) *f(m)*
running ['rʌnɪŋ] *n* (*sport*) Laufen *nt*; (*of business etc*) Leitung *f*; (*of machine etc*) Betrieb *m* ▷ *adj* (*water, stream*) laufend; **to be in/out of the ~ for sth** bei etw im Rennen liegen/aus dem Rennen sein; **to make the ~** (*in race, fig*) das Rennen machen; **6 days ~** 6 Tage hintereinander; **to have a ~ battle with sb** ständig im Streit mit jdm liegen; **to give a ~ commentary on sth** etw fortlaufend kommentieren; **a ~ sore** eine nässende Wunde
running costs *npl* (*of car, machine*) Unterhaltskosten *pl*
running head *n* (*Typ, Comput*) Kolumnentitel *m*
running mate (*US*) *n* (*Pol*) Vizepräsidentschaftskandidat *m*
runny ['rʌnɪ] *adj* (*egg, butter*) dünnflüssig; (*nose, eyes*) triefend
run-off ['rʌnɔf] *n* (*in contest, election*) Entscheidungsrunde *f*; (*extra race*) Entscheidungsrennen *nt*
run-of-the-mill ['rʌnəvðə'mɪl] *adj* gewöhnlich
runt [rʌnt] *n* (*animal*) kleinstes und schwächstes Tier eines Wurfs; (*pej: person*) Zwerg *m*
run-through ['rʌnθru:] *n* (*rehearsal*) Probe *f*
run-up ['rʌnʌp] *n*: **the ~ to** (*election etc*) die Zeit vor +*dat*
runway ['rʌnweɪ] *n* (*Aviat*) Start- und Landebahn *f*
rupee [ru:'pi:] *n* Rupie *f*
rupture ['rʌptʃəʳ] *n* (*Med*) Bruch *m*; (*conflict*) Spaltung *f* ▷ *vt*: **to ~ o.s.** (*Med*) sich *dat* einen Bruch zuziehen
rural ['ruərl] *adj* ländlich; (*crime*) auf dem Lande
rural district council (*Brit*) *n* Landbezirksverwaltung *f*
ruse [ru:z] *n* List *f*
rush [rʌʃ] *n* (*hurry*) Eile *f*, Hetze *f*; (*Comm: sudden demand*) starke Nachfrage *f*; (*of water, air*) Stoß *m*; (*of feeling*) Woge *f* ▷ *vt* (*lunch, job etc*) beeilen bei; (*person, supplies etc*) schnellstens bringen ▷ *vi* (*person*) sich beeilen; (*air, water*) strömen; **rushes** *npl* (*Bot*) Schilf *nt*; (*for chair, basket etc*) Binsen *pl*; **is there any ~ for this?** eilt das?; **we've had a ~ of orders** wir hatten einen Zustrom von Bestellungen; **I'm in a ~ (to do sth)** ich habe es eilig (, etw zu tun); **gold ~** Goldrausch *m*; **don't ~ me!** drängen Sie mich nicht!; **to ~ sth off** (*send*) etw schnellstens abschicken; **to ~ sb into doing sth** jdn dazu drängen, etw zu tun
▸ **rush through** *vt fus* (*order, application*) schnellstens erledigen
rush hour *n* Hauptverkehrszeit *f*, Rushhour *f*
rush job *n* Eilauftrag *m*
rush matting *n* Binsenmatte *f*
rusk [rʌsk] *n* Zwieback *m*
Russia ['rʌʃə] *n* Russland *nt*
Russian ['rʌʃən] *adj* russisch ▷ *n* (*person*) Russe

r

759

m, Russin *f*; (*Ling*) Russisch *nt*
rust [rʌst] *n* Rost *m* ▷ *vi* rosten
rustic ['rʌstɪk] *adj* (*style, furniture*) rustikal ▷ *n*
(*pej: person*) Bauer *m*
rustle ['rʌsl] *vi* (*paper, leaves*) rascheln ▷ *vt* (*paper*)
rascheln mit; (*US: cattle*) stehlen
rustproof ['rʌstpru:f] *adj* nicht rostend
rustproofing ['rʌstpru:fɪŋ] *n* Rostschutz *m*
rusty ['rʌstɪ] *adj* (*car*) rostig; (*fig: skill etc*)
eingerostet
rut [rʌt] *n* (*in path etc*) Furche *f*; (*Zool: season*)
Brunft *f*, Brunst *f*; **to be in a ~** (*fig*) im Trott

stecken
rutabaga [ru:tə'beɪgə] (*US*) *n* Steckrübe *f*
ruthless ['ru:θlɪs] *adj* rücksichtslos
ruthlessness ['ru:θlɪsnɪs] *n*
Rücksichtslosigkeit *f*
RV *abbr* (*Bible:* = *revised version*) englische
Bibelübersetzung von 1885 ▷ *n abbr* (*US*) =
recreational vehicle
Rwanda [ru'ændə] *n* Ruanda *nt*
Rwandan [ru'ændən] *adj* ruandisch
rye [raɪ] *n* (*cereal*) Roggen *m*
rye bread *n* Roggenbrot *nt*

Ss

S¹, s [ɛs] n (letter) S nt, s nt; (US: Scol: satisfactory) ≈ 3; **S for Sugar** ≈ S wie Samuel
S² [ɛs] abbr (= saint) St.; (= small) kl.; (= south) S
SA abbr = **South Africa**; **South America**; (= South Australia) Südaustralien nt
Sabbath ['sæbəθ] n (Jewish) Sabbat m; (Christian) Sonntag m
sabbatical [sə'bætɪkl] n (also: **sabbatical year**) Forschungsjahr nt
sabotage ['sæbətɑːʒ] n Sabotage f ▷ vt einen Sabotageakt verüben auf +acc; (plan, meeting) sabotieren
sabre ['seɪbə'] n Säbel m
sabre-rattling ['seɪbərætlɪŋ] n Säbelrasseln nt
saccharin, saccharine ['sækərɪn] n Sa(c) charin nt ▷ adj (fig) zuckersüß
sachet ['sæʃeɪ] n (of shampoo) Beutel m; (of sugar etc) Tütchen nt
sack [sæk] n Sack m ▷ vt (dismiss) entlassen; (plunder) plündern; **to get the ~** rausfliegen (inf); **to give sb the ~** jdn rausschmeißen (inf)
sackful ['sækful] n: **a ~ of** ein Sack
sacking ['sækɪŋ] n (dismissal) Entlassung f; (material) Sackleinen nt
sacrament ['sækrəmənt] n Sakrament nt
sacred ['seɪkrɪd] adj heilig; (music, history) geistlich; (memory) geheiligt; (building) sakral
sacred cow n (lit, fig) heilige Kuh f
sacrifice ['sækrɪfaɪs] n Opfer nt ▷ vt opfern; **to make ~s (for sb)** (für jdn) Opfer bringen
sacrilege ['sækrɪlɪdʒ] n Sakrileg nt; **that would be ~** das wäre ein Sakrileg
sacrosanct ['sækrəʊsæŋkt] adj (lit, fig) sakrosankt
sad [sæd] adj traurig; **he was ~ to see her go** er war traurig (darüber), dass sie wegging
sadden ['sædn] vt betrüben
saddle ['sædl] n Sattel m ▷ vt (horse) satteln; **to be ~d with sb/sth** (inf) jdn/etw am Hals haben
saddlebag ['sædlbæg] n Satteltasche f
sadism ['seɪdɪzəm] n Sadismus m
sadist ['seɪdɪst] n Sadist(in) m(f)
sadistic [sə'dɪstɪk] adj sadistisch
sadly ['sædlɪ] adv traurig, betrübt; (unfortunately) leider, bedauerlicherweise; (seriously) schwer; **he is ~ lacking in humour** ihm fehlt leider jeglicher Humor

sadness ['sædnɪs] n Traurigkeit f
sadomasochism [seɪdəʊ'mæsəkɪzəm] n Sadomasochismus m
s.a.e. (Brit) abbr (= stamped addressed envelope) see **stamp**
safari [sə'fɑːrɪ] n Safari f; **to go on ~** auf Safari gehen
safari park n Safaripark m
safe [seɪf] adj sicher; (out of danger) in Sicherheit ▷ n Safe m or nt, Tresor m; **~ from** sicher vor +dat; **~ and sound** gesund und wohlbehalten; **(just) to be on the ~ side** (nur) um sicherzugehen; **to play ~** auf Nummer sicher gehen (inf); **it is ~ to say that ...** man kann wohl sagen, dass ...; **~ journey!** gute Fahrt or Reise!
safe bet n: **it's a ~ that ...** es ist sicher, dass ...
safe-breaker ['seɪfbreɪkə'] (Brit) n Safeknacker m (inf)
safe-conduct [seɪf'kɒndʌkt] n freies or sicheres Geleit nt
safe-cracker ['seɪfkrækə'] n = **safe-breaker**
safe-deposit ['seɪfdɪpɒzɪt] n (vault) Tresorraum m; (also: **safe-deposit box**) Banksafe m
safeguard ['seɪfgɑːd] n Schutz m ▷ vt schützen; (interests) wahren; (future) sichern; **as a ~ against** zum Schutz gegen
safe haven n Zufluchtsort m
safe house n geheimer Unterschlupf m
safekeeping ['seɪf'kiːpɪŋ] n sichere Aufbewahrung f
safely ['seɪflɪ] adv sicher; (assume, say) wohl, ruhig; (arrive) wohlbehalten; **I can ~ say ...** ich kann wohl sagen ...
safe passage n sichere Durchreise f
safe sex n Safer Sex m
safety ['seɪftɪ] n Sicherheit f; **~ first!** Sicherheit geht vor!
safety belt n Sicherheitsgurt m
safety catch n (on gun) Sicherung f; (on window, door) Sperre f
safety net n Sprungnetz nt, Sicherheitsnetz nt; (fig) Sicherheitsvorkehrung f
safety pin n Sicherheitsnadel f
safety valve n Sicherheitsventil nt
saffron ['sæfrən] n Safran m
sag [sæg] vi durchhängen; (breasts) hängen; (fig: spirits, demand) sinken

S

saga ['sɑːɡə] n Saga f; (fig) Geschichte f
sage [seɪdʒ] n (herb) Salbei m; (wise man) Weise(r) m
Sagittarius [sædʒɪ'tɛərɪəs] n Schütze m; **to be ~** Schütze sein
sago ['seɪɡəu] n Sago m
Sahara [sə'hɑːrə] n: **the ~ (Desert)** die (Wüste) Sahara
Sahel [sæ'hɛl] n Sahel m, Sahelzone f
said [sɛd] pt, pp of **say**
Saigon [saɪ'ɡɔn] n Saigon nt
sail [seɪl] n Segel nt ▷ vt segeln ▷ vi fahren; (Sport) segeln; (begin voyage: ship) auslaufen; (: passenger) abfahren; (fig: ball etc) fliegen, segeln; **to go for a ~** segeln gehen; **to set ~** losfahren, abfahren
  ▶ **sail through** vt fus (fig: exam etc) spielend schaffen
sailboat ['seɪlbəut] (US) n = **sailing boat**
sailing ['seɪlɪŋ] n (Sport) Segeln nt; (voyage) Überfahrt f; **to go ~** segeln gehen
sailing boat n Segelboot nt
sailing ship n Segelschiff nt
sailor ['seɪlə'] n Seemann m, Matrose m
saint [seɪnt] n (lit, fig) Heilige(r) f(m)
saintly ['seɪntlɪ] adj heiligmäßig; (expression) fromm
sake [seɪk] n: **for the ~ of sb/sth, for sb's/ sth's sake** um jds/einer Sache gen willen; (out of consideration for) jdm/etw zuliebe; **he enjoys talking for talking's ~** er redet gerne, nur damit etwas gesagt wird; **for the ~ of argument** rein theoretisch; **art for art's ~** Kunst um der Kunst willen; **for heaven's ~!** um Gottes willen!
salad ['sæləd] n Salat m; **tomato ~** Tomatensalat m; **green ~** grüner Salat m
salad bowl n Salatschüssel f
salad cream (Brit) n ≈ Mayonnaise f
salad dressing n Salatsoße f
salami [sə'lɑːmɪ] n Salami f
salaried ['sælərɪd] adj: **~ staff** Gehaltsempfänger pl
salary ['sælərɪ] n Gehalt nt
salary scale n Gehaltsskala f
sale [seɪl] n Verkauf m; (at reduced prices) Ausverkauf m; (auction) Auktion f; **sales** npl (total amount sold) Absatz m ▷ cpd (campaign) Verkaufs-; (conference) Vertreter-; (figures) Absatz-; **"for ~"** „zu verkaufen"; **on ~** im Handel; **on ~ or return** auf Kommissionsbasis; **closing-down ~, liquidation ~** (US) Räumungsverkauf m
sale and lease back n (Comm) Verkauf m mit Rückmiete
saleroom ['seɪlruːm] n Auktionsraum m
sales assistant, (US) **sales clerk** [seɪlz-] n Verkäufer(in) m(f)
sales force n Vertreterstab m
salesman ['seɪlzmən] (irreg: like **man**) n Verkäufer m; (representative) Vertreter m
sales manager n Verkaufsleiter m
salesmanship ['seɪlzmənʃɪp] n

Verkaufstechnik f
sales tax (US) n Verkaufssteuer f
saleswoman ['seɪlzwumən] (irreg: like **woman**) n Verkäuferin f; (representative) Vertreterin f
salient ['seɪlɪənt] adj (features) hervorstehend; (points) Haupt-
saline ['seɪlaɪn] adj (solution etc) Salz-
saliva [sə'laɪvə] n Speichel m
sallow ['sæləu] adj (complexion) fahl
sally forth ['sælɪ-] (old) vi sich aufmachen
sally out vi = **sally forth**
salmon ['sæmən] n inv Lachs m
salmon trout n Lachsforelle f
salon ['sælɔn] n Salon m
saloon [sə'luːn] n (US: bar) Saloon m; (Brit: Aut) Limousine f; (ship's lounge) Salon m
SALT [sɔːlt] n abbr (= Strategic Arms Limitation Talks/Treaty) SALT
salt [sɔːlt] n Salz nt ▷ vt (preserve) einsalzen; (put salt on) salzen; (road) mit Salz streuen ▷ cpd Salz-; (pork, beef) gepökelt; **the ~ of the earth** (fig) das Salz der Erde; **to take sth with a pinch** or **grain of ~** (fig) etw nicht ganz so ernst nehmen
salt cellar n Salzstreuer m
salt-free ['sɔːlt'friː] adj salzlos
salt mine n Salzbergwerk nt
saltwater ['sɔːlt'wɔːtə'] adj (fish, plant) Meeres-
salty ['sɔːltɪ] adj salzig
salubrious [sə'luːbrɪəs] adj (district etc) fein; (air, living conditions) gesund
salutary ['sæljutərɪ] adj heilsam
salute [sə'luːt] n (Mil, greeting) Gruß m; (Mil: with guns) Salut m ▷ vt (Mil) grüßen, salutieren vor +dat; (fig) begrüßen
salvage ['sælvɪdʒ] n Bergung f; (things saved) Bergungsgut nt ▷ vt bergen; (fig) retten
salvage vessel n Bergungsschiff nt
salvation [sæl'veɪʃən] n (Rel) Heil nt; (economic etc) Rettung f
Salvation Army n Heilsarmee f
salver ['sælvə'] n Tablett nt
salvo ['sælvəu] (pl **~es**) n Salve f
Samaritan [sə'mærɪtən] n: **the ~s** ≈ die Telefonseelsorge
same [seɪm] adj (similar) gleiche(r, s); (identical) selbe(r, s) ▷ pron: **the ~** (similar) der/die/das Gleiche; (identical) derselbe/dieselbe/dasselbe; **the ~ book as** das gleiche Buch wie; **they are the ~ age** sie sind gleichaltrig; **they are exactly the ~** sie sind genau gleich; **on the ~ day** am gleichen or selben Tag; **at the ~ time** (simultaneously) gleichzeitig, zur gleichen Zeit; (yet) doch; **they're one and the ~** (person) das ist doch ein und derselbe/dieselbe; (thing) das ist doch dasselbe; **~ again** (in bar etc) das Gleiche noch mal; **all** or **just the ~** trotzdem; **to do the ~ (as sb)** das Gleiche (wie jd) tun; **the ~ to you!** (danke) gleichfalls!; **~ here!** ich/wir etc auch!; **thanks all the ~** trotzdem vielen Dank; **it's all the ~ to me** es ist mir egal
same-sex marriage ['seɪmsɛks-] n

gleichgeschlechtliche Ehe f, Homoehe f (inf)
same-sex relationship ['seɪmsɛks-] n
gleichgeschlechtliche Beziehung f
sample ['sɑːmpl] n Probe f; (of merchandise)
Probe f, Muster nt ▷ vt probieren; **to take a ~**
eine Stichprobe machen; **free ~** kostenlose
Probe
sanatorium [sænəˈtɔːrɪəm] (pl **sanatoria**) n
Sanatorium nt
sanctify ['sæŋktɪfaɪ] vt heiligen
sanctimonious [sæŋktɪˈməʊnɪəs] adj
scheinheilig
sanction ['sæŋkʃən] n Zustimmung f ▷ vt
sanktionieren; **sanctions** npl (Pol) Sanktionen
pl; **to impose economic ~s on** or **against**
Wirtschaftssanktionen verhängen gegen
sanctity ['sæŋktɪtɪ] n (holiness) Heiligkeit f;
(inviolability) Unantastbarkeit f
sanctuary ['sæŋktjuərɪ] n (for birds/animals)
Schutzgebiet nt; (place of refuge) Zuflucht f;
(Rel: in church) Altarraum m
sand [sænd] n Sand m ▷ vt (also: **sand down**)
abschmirgeln; see also **sands**
sandal ['sændl] n Sandale f
sandbag ['sændbæg] n Sandsack m
sandblast ['sændblɑːst] vt sandstrahlen
sandbox ['sændbɒks] (US) n Sandkasten m;
(Comput: antivirus software) Sandbox f
sandcastle ['sændkɑːsl] n Sandburg f
sand dune n Sanddüne f
sander ['sændər] n (tool) Schleifmaschine f
S & M (US) n abbr (= sadomasochism) S/M
sandpaper ['sændpeɪpər] n Schmirgelpapier nt
sandpit ['sændpɪt] n Sandkasten m;
(Comput: antivirus software) Sandbox f
sands [sændz] npl (beach) Sandstrand m
sandstone ['sændstəun] n Sandstein m
sandstorm ['sændstɔːm] n Sandsturm m
sandwich ['sændwɪtʃ] n Sandwich nt ▷ vt: **~ed**
between eingequetscht zwischen; **cheese/**
ham ~ Käse-/Schinkenbrot nt
sandwich board n Reklametafel f
sandwich course (Brit) n Ausbildungsgang, bei
dem sich Theorie und Praxis abwechseln
sandwich man n Sandwichmann m,
Plakatträger m
sandy ['sændɪ] adj sandig; (beach) Sand-; (hair)
rotblond
sane [seɪn] adj geistig gesund; (sensible)
vernünftig
sang [sæŋ] pt of **sing**
sanguine ['sæŋgwɪn] adj zuversichtlich
sanitarium [sænɪˈtɛərɪəm] (US) (pl **sanitaria**) n
= **sanatorium**
sanitary ['sænɪtərɪ] adj hygienisch; (facilities)
sanitär; (inspector) Gesundheits-
sanitary towel, (US) **sanitary napkin** n
Damenbinde f
sanitation [sænɪˈteɪʃən] n Hygiene f; (toilets etc)
sanitäre Anlagen pl; (drainage) Kanalisation f
sanitation department (US) n
Stadtreinigung f
sanity ['sænɪtɪ] n geistige Gesundheit f;

(common sense) Vernunft f
sank [sæŋk] pt of **sink**
Santa Claus [sæntəˈklɔːz] n ≈ der
Weihnachtsmann
Santiago [sæntɪˈɑːgəu] n (also: **Santiago de**
Chile) Santiago (de Chile) nt
sap [sæp] n Saft m ▷ vt (strength) zehren an +dat;
(confidence) untergraben
sapling ['sæplɪŋ] n junger Baum m
sapphire ['sæfaɪər] n Saphir m
sarcasm ['sɑːkæzm] n Sarkasmus m
sarcastic [sɑːˈkæstɪk] adj sarkastisch
sarcophagus [sɑːˈkɒfəgəs] (pl **sarcophagi**) n
Sarkophag m
sardine [sɑːˈdiːn] n Sardine f
Sardinia [sɑːˈdɪnɪə] n Sardinien nt
Sardinian [sɑːˈdɪnɪən] adj sardinisch, sardisch
▷ n (person) Sardinier(in) m(f); (Ling) Sardinisch
nt
sardonic [sɑːˈdɒnɪk] adj (smile) süffisant
sari ['sɑːrɪ] n Sari m
SARS [sɑːz] n abbr (= severe acute respiratory
syndrome) SARS nt
sartorial [sɑːˈtɔːrɪəl] adj: **his ~ elegance** seine
elegante Art, sich zu kleiden
SAS (Brit) n abbr (Mil: = Special Air Service)
Spezialeinheit der britischen Armee
SASE (US) n abbr (= self-addressed stamped envelope)
frankierter Rückumschlag m
sash [sæʃ] n Schärpe f; (of window)
Fensterrahmen m
sash window n Schiebefenster nt
SAT (US) n abbr (= Scholastic Aptitude Test)
Hochschulaufnahmeprüfung f
sat [sæt] pt, pp of **sit**
Sat. abbr (= Saturday) Sa.
Satan ['seɪtn] n Satan m
satanic [səˈtænɪk] adj satanisch
satanism ['seɪtnɪzəm] n Satanismus m
satchel ['sætʃl] n (child's) Schultasche f
sated ['seɪtɪd] adj gesättigt; **to be ~ with sth**
(fig) von etw übersättigt sein
satellite ['sætəlaɪt] n Satellit m; (also: **satellite**
state) Satellitenstaat m
satellite dish n Satellitenantenne f,
Parabolantenne f
satellite receiver n Satellitenempfänger m
satellite television n Satellitenfernsehen nt
satiate ['seɪʃɪeɪt] vt (food) sättigen; (fig: pleasure
etc) übersättigen
satin ['sætɪn] n Satin m ▷ adj (dress etc) Satin-;
with a ~ finish mit Seidenglanz
satire ['sætaɪər] n Satire f
satirical [səˈtɪrɪkl] adj satirisch
satirist ['sætɪrɪst] n Satiriker(in) m(f)
satirize ['sætɪraɪz] vt satirisch darstellen
satisfaction [sætɪsˈfækʃən] n Befriedigung
f; **to get ~ from sb** (refund, apology etc)
Genugtuung von jdm erhalten; **has it been**
done to your ~? sind Sie damit zufrieden?
satisfactorily [sætɪsˈfæktərɪlɪ] adv
zufriedenstellend
satisfactory [sætɪsˈfæktərɪ] adj

S

763

zufriedenstellend

satisfied ['sætɪsfaɪd] *adj* zufrieden

satisfy ['sætɪsfaɪ] *vt* zufriedenstellen; *(needs, demand)* befriedigen; *(requirements, conditions)* erfüllen; **to ~ sb/o.s. that ...** jdn/sich davon überzeugen, dass ...

satisfying ['sætɪsfaɪɪŋ] *adj* befriedigend; *(meal)* sättigend

satsuma [sæt'su:mə] *n* Satsuma *f*

saturate ['sætʃəreɪt] *vt*: **to ~ (with)** durchnässen (mit); *(Chem: market)* sättigen; *(fig: area etc)* überschwemmen

saturated fat ['sætʃəreɪtɪd-] *n* gesättigtes Fett *nt*

saturation [sætʃə'reɪʃən] *n* *(Chem)* Sättigung *f*; **~ advertising** flächendeckende Werbung *f*; **~ bombing** Flächenbombardierung *f*

Saturday ['sætədɪ] *n* Samstag *m*; *see also* **Tuesday**

sauce [sɔ:s] *n* Soße *f*

saucepan ['sɔ:spən] *n* Kochtopf *m*

saucer ['sɔ:səʳ] *n* Untertasse *f*

saucy ['sɔ:sɪ] *adj* frech

Saudi ['saudi-] *adj* (*also*: **Saudi Arabian**) saudisch, saudi-arabisch

Saudi Arabia ['saudi-] *n* Saudi-Arabien *nt*

sauna ['sɔ:nə] *n* Sauna *f*

saunter ['sɔ:ntəʳ] *vi* schlendern

sausage ['sɒsɪdʒ] *n* Wurst *f*

sausage roll *n* Wurst *f* im Schlafrock

sauté ['səuteɪ] *vt* kurz anbraten ▷ *adj*: **~ed potatoes** Bratkartoffeln *pl*

savage ['sævɪdʒ] *adj* *(attack etc)* brutal; *(dog)* gefährlich; *(criticism)* schonungslos ▷ *n* *(old: pej)* Wilde(r) *f(m)* ▷ *vt* *(maul)* zerfleischen; *(fig: criticize)* verreißen

savagely ['sævɪdʒlɪ] *adv* *(attack etc)* brutal; *(criticize)* schonungslos

savagery ['sævɪdʒrɪ] *n* *(of attack)* Brutalität *f*

save [seɪv] *vt* *(rescue)* retten; *(money, time)* sparen; *(food etc)* aufheben; *(work, trouble)* (er)sparen; *(keep: receipts etc)* aufbewahren; *(: seat etc)* frei halten; *(Comput: file)* abspeichern; *(Sport: shot, ball)* halten ▷ *vi* (*also*: **save up**) sparen ▷ *n* *(Sport)* (Ball)abwehr *f* ▷ *prep* *(form)* außer +*dat*; **it will ~ me an hour** dadurch spare ich eine Stunde; **to ~ face** das Gesicht wahren; **God ~ the Queen!** Gott schütze die Königin!

saving ['seɪvɪŋ] *n* *(on price etc)* Ersparnis *f* ▷ *adj*: **the ~ grace of sth** das einzig Gute an etw *dat*; **savings** *npl* *(money)* Ersparnisse *pl*; **to make ~s** sparen

savings account *n* Sparkonto *nt*

savings bank *n* Sparkasse *f*

saviour, *(US)* **savior** ['seɪvjəʳ] *n* Retter(in) *m(f)*; *(Rel)* Erlöser *m*

savoir-faire ['sævwɑ:feəʳ] *n* Gewandtheit *f*

savour, *(US)* **savor** ['seɪvəʳ] *vt* genießen ▷ *n* *(of food)* Geschmack *m*

savoury, *(US)* **savory** ['seɪvərɪ] *adj* pikant

savvy ['sævɪ] *n* *(inf)* Grips *m*; **he hasn't got much ~** er hat keine Ahnung

saw [sɔ:] *(pt* **~ed**, *pp* **sawed** *or* **~n**) *vt* sägen ▷ *n* Säge *f* ▷ *pt of* **see**; **to ~ sth up** etw zersägen

sawdust ['sɔ:dʌst] *n* Sägemehl *nt*

sawmill ['sɔ:mɪl] *n* Sägewerk *nt*

sawn [sɔ:n] *pp of* **saw**

sawn-off ['sɔ:nɔf], *(US)* **sawed-off** ['sɔ:dɔf] *adj*: **~ shotgun** Gewehr *nt* mit abgesägtem Lauf

saxophone ['sæksəfəun] *n* Saxofon *nt*

say [seɪ] *(pt, pp* **said**) *vt* sagen ▷ *n*: **to have one's ~** seine Meinung äußern; **could you ~ that again?** können Sie das wiederholen?; **my watch ~s 3 o'clock** auf meiner Uhr ist es 3 Uhr; **it ~s on the sign "No Smoking"** auf dem Schild steht „Rauchen verboten"; **shall we ~ Tuesday?** sagen wir Dienstag?; **come for dinner at, ~, 8 o'clock** kommt um, sagen wir mal 8 Uhr, zum Essen; **that doesn't ~ much for him** das spricht nicht gerade für ihn; **when all is said and done** letzten Endes; **there is something/a lot to be said for it** es spricht einiges/vieles dafür; **you can ~ that again!** das kann man wohl sagen!; **that is to ~** das heißt; **that goes without ~ing** das versteht sich von selbst; **to ~ nothing of ...** von ... ganz zu schweigen; **~ (that) ...** angenommen, (dass) ...; **to have a** *or* **some ~ in sth** ein Mitspracherecht bei etw haben

saying ['seɪɪŋ] *n* Redensart *f*

say-so ['seɪsəu] *n* Zustimmung *f*; **to do sth on sb's ~** etw auf jds Anweisung *acc* hin tun

SBA *(US) n abbr* (= *Small Business Administration*) *Regierungsstelle zur Unterstützung kleiner und mittelständischer Betriebe*

SC *(US) n abbr* = **Supreme Court** ▷ *abbr (Post)* = *South Carolina*

s/c *abbr* = **self-contained**

scab [skæb] *n* *(on wound)* Schorf *m*; *(pej)* Streikbrecher(in) *m(f)*

scabby ['skæbɪ] *(pej) adj* *(hands, skin)* schorfig

scaffold ['skæfəld] *n* *(for execution)* Schafott *nt*

scaffolding ['skæfəldɪŋ] *n* Gerüst *nt*

scald [skɔ:ld] *n* Verbrühung *f* ▷ *vt* *(burn)* verbrühen

scalding ['skɔ:ldɪŋ] *adj* (*also*: **scalding hot**) siedend heiß

scale [skeɪl] *n* Skala *f*; *(of fish)* Schuppe *f*; *(Mus)* Tonleiter *f*; *(size, extent)* Ausmaß *nt*, Umfang *m*; *(of map, model)* Maßstab *m* ▷ *vt* *(cliff, tree)* erklettern; **(pair of) scales** *npl* *(for weighing)* Waage *f*; **pay ~** Lohnskala *f*; **to draw sth to ~** etw maßstabgetreu zeichnen; **a small-~ model** ein Modell in verkleinertem Maßstab; **on a large ~** im großen Rahmen; **~ of charges** Gebührenordnung *f*

▷ **scale down** *vt* verkleinern; *(fig)* verringern

scaled-down [skeɪld'daun] *adj* verkleinert; *(project, forecast)* eingeschränkt

scale drawing *n* maßstabgetreue Zeichnung *f*

scallion ['skæljən] *n* Frühlingszwiebel *f*; *(US: shallot)* Schalotte *f*; *(: leek)* Lauch *m*

scallop ['skɒləp] *n* *(Zool)* Kammmuschel *f*;

(*Sewing*) Bogenkante *f*

scalp [skælp] *n* Kopfhaut *f* ▷ *vt* skalpieren

scalpel ['skælpl] *n* Skalpell *nt*

scalper ['skælpəʳ] (*US: inf*) *n* (*ticket tout*) (Karten)schwarzhändler(in) *m(f)*

scam [skæm] (*inf*) *n* Betrug *m*

scamp [skæmp] (*inf*) *n* Frechdachs *m*

scamper ['skæmpəʳ] *vi*: **to ~ away** *or* **off** verschwinden

scampi ['skæmpɪ] (*Brit*) *npl* Scampi *pl*

scan [skæn] *vt* (*horizon*) absuchen; (*newspaper etc*) überfliegen; (*TV, Radar*) abtasten ▷ *vi* (*poetry*) das richtige Versmaß haben ▷ *n* (*Med*) Scan *m*

scandal ['skændl] *n* Skandal *m*; (*gossip*) Skandalgeschichten *pl*

scandalize ['skændəlaɪz] *vt* schockieren

scandalous ['skændələs] *adj* skandalös

Scandinavia [skændɪ'neɪvɪə] *n* Skandinavien *nt*

Scandinavian [skændɪ'neɪvɪən] *adj* skandinavisch ▷ *n* Skandinavier(in) *m(f)*

scanner ['skænəʳ] *n* (*Med*) Scanner *m*; (*Radar*) Richtantenne *f*

scant [skænt] *adj* wenig

scantily ['skæntɪlɪ] *adv*: **~ clad** *or* **dressed** spärlich bekleidet

scanty ['skæntɪ] *adj* (*information*) dürftig; (*meal*) kärglich; (*bikini*) knapp

scapegoat ['skeɪpgəut] *n* Sündenbock *m*

scar [skɑ:] *n* Narbe *f*; (*fig*) Wunde *f* ▷ *vt* eine Narbe hinterlassen auf *+dat*; (*fig*) zeichnen

scarce [skɛəs] *adj* knapp; **to make o.s. ~** (*inf*) verschwinden

scarcely ['skɛəslɪ] *adv* kaum; (*certainly not*) wohl kaum; **~ anybody** kaum jemand; **I can ~ believe it** ich kann es kaum glauben

scarcity ['skɛəsɪtɪ] *n* Knappheit *f*; **~ value** Seltenheitswert *m*

scare [skɛəʳ] *n* (*fright*) Schreck(en) *m*; (*public fear*) Panik *f* ▷ *vt* (*frighten*) erschrecken; (*worry*) Angst machen *+dat*; **to give sb a ~** jdm einen Schrecken einjagen; **bomb ~** Bombendrohung *f*

▶ **scare away** *vt* (*animal*) verscheuchen; (*investor, buyer*) abschrecken

▶ **scare off** *vt* = **scare away**

scarecrow ['skɛəkrəu] *n* Vogelscheuche *f*

scared ['skɛəd] *adj*: **to be ~** Angst haben; **to be ~ stiff** fürchterliche Angst haben

scaremonger ['skɛəmʌŋgəʳ] *n* Panikmacher *m*

scarf [skɑ:f] (*pl* **~s** *or* **scarves**) *n* Schal *m*; (*headscarf*) Kopftuch *nt*

scarlet ['skɑ:lɪt] *adj* (scharlach)rot

scarlet fever *n* Scharlach *m*

scarper ['skɑ:pəʳ] (*Brit: inf*) *vi* abhauen

scarred [skɑ:d] *adj* narbig; (*fig*) gezeichnet

SCART socket ['skɑ:tsɔkɪt] *n* (*Comput*) SCART-Büchse *f*

scarves [skɑ:vz] *npl of* **scarf**

scary ['skɛərɪ] (*inf*) *adj* unheimlich; (*film*) gruselig

scathing ['skeɪðɪŋ] *adj* (*comments*) bissig;

(*attack*) scharf; **to be ~ about sth** bissige Bemerkungen über etw *acc* machen

scatter ['skætəʳ] *vt* verstreuen; (*flock of birds*) aufscheuchen; (*crowd*) zerstreuen ▷ *vi* (*crowd*) sich zerstreuen

scatterbrained ['skætəbreɪnd] (*inf*) *adj* schusselig

scattered ['skætəd] *adj* verstreut; **~ showers** vereinzelte Regenschauer *pl*

scatty ['skætɪ] (*Brit: inf*) *adj* schusselig

scavenge ['skævəndʒ] *vi*: **to ~ for sth** nach etw suchen

scavenger ['skævəndʒəʳ] *n* (*person*) Aasgeier *m* (*inf*); (*animal, bird*) Aasfresser *m*

SCE *n abbr* (= *Scottish Certificate of Education*) Schulabschlusszeugnis in Schottland

scenario [sɪ'nɑ:rɪəu] *n* (*Theat, Cine*) Szenarium *nt*; (*fig*) Szenario *nt*

scene [si:n] *n* (*lit, fig*) Szene *f*; (*of crime*) Schauplatz *m*; (*of accident*) Ort *m*; (*sight*) Anblick *m*; **behind the ~s** (*fig*) hinter den Kulissen; **to make a ~** (*inf: fuss*) eine Szene machen; **to appear on the ~** (*fig*) auftauchen, auf der Bildfläche erscheinen; **the political ~** die politische Landschaft

scenery ['si:nərɪ] *n* (*Theat*) Bühnenbild *nt*; (*landscape*) Landschaft *f*

scenic ['si:nɪk] *adj* malerisch, landschaftlich schön

scent [sɛnt] *n* (*fragrance*) Duft *m*; (*track*) Fährte *f*; (*fig*) Spur *f*; (*liquid perfume*) Parfüm *nt*; **to put** *or* **throw sb off the ~** (*fig*) jdn von der Spur abbringen

sceptic, (*US*) **skeptic** ['skɛptɪk] *n* Skeptiker(in) *m(f)*

sceptical, (*US*) **skeptical** ['skɛptɪkl] *adj* skeptisch

scepticism, (*US*) **skepticism** ['skɛptɪsɪzəm] *n* Skepsis *f*

sceptre, (*US*) **scepter** ['sɛptəʳ] *n* Zepter *nt*

schedule ['ʃɛdju:l, (*US*) 'skɛdju:l] *n* (*of trains, buses*) Fahrplan *m*; (*of events*) Programm *nt*; (*of prices, details etc*) Liste *f* ▷ *vt* planen; (*visit, meeting etc*) ansetzen; **on ~** wie geplant, pünktlich; **we are working to a very tight ~** wir arbeiten nach einem sehr knappen Zeitplan; **everything went according to ~** alles ist planmäßig verlaufen; **to be ahead of/behind ~** dem Zeitplan voraus sein/im Rückstand sein; **he was ~d to leave yesterday** laut Zeitplan hätte er gestern abfahren sollen

scheduled ['ʃɛdju:ld, (*US*) 'skɛdju:ld] *adj* (*date, time*) vorgesehen; (*visit, event*) geplant; (*train, bus, stop*) planmäßig

scheduled flight *n* Linienflug *m*

schematic [skɪ'mætɪk] *adj* schematisch

scheme [ski:m] *n* (*personal plan*) Plan *m*; (*plot*) raffinierter Plan *m*, Komplott *nt*; (*formal plan*) Programm *nt* ▷ *vi* Pläne schmieden, intrigieren; **colour ~** Farbzusammenstellung *f*; **pension ~** Rentenversicherung *f*

scheming ['ski:mɪŋ] *adj* intrigierend ▷ *n*

S

Machenschaften *pl*

schism ['skɪzəm] *n* Spaltung *f*

schizophrenia [skɪtsə'fri:nɪə] *n* Schizophrenie *f*

schizophrenic [skɪtsə'frenɪk] *adj* schizophren ▷ *n* Schizophrene(r) *f(m)*

scholar ['skɔlər] *n* Gelehrte(r) *f(m)*; (*pupil*) Student(in) *m(f)*, Schüler(in) *m(f)*; (*scholarship holder*) Stipendiat(in) *m(f)*

scholarly ['skɔləlɪ] *adj* gelehrt; (*text, approach*) wissenschaftlich

scholarship ['skɔləʃɪp] *n* Gelehrsamkeit *f*; (*grant*) Stipendium *nt*

school [sku:l] *n* Schule *f*; (*US: inf: university*) Universität *f*; (*of whales, porpoises etc*) Schule *f*, Schwarm *m* ▷ *cpd* Schul-

school age *n* Schulalter *nt*

schoolbook ['sku:lbuk] *n* Schulbuch *nt*

schoolboy ['sku:lbɔɪ] *n* Schuljunge *m*, Schüler *m*

schoolchildren ['sku:ltʃɪldrən] *npl* Schulkinder *pl*, Schüler *pl*

schooldays ['sku:ldeɪz] *npl* Schulzeit *f*

schooled [sku:ld] *adj* geschult; **to be ~ in sth** über etw *acc* gut Bescheid wissen

schoolgirl ['sku:lgə:l] *n* Schulmädchen *nt*, Schülerin *f*

schooling ['sku:lɪŋ] *n* Schulbildung *f*

school-leaver [sku:l'li:vər] (*Brit*) *n* Schulabgänger(in) *m(f)*

schoolmaster ['sku:lmɑ:stər] *n* Lehrer *m*

schoolmistress ['sku:lmɪstrɪs] *n* Lehrerin *f*

school report (*Brit*) *n* Zeugnis *nt*

schoolroom ['sku:lru:m] *n* Klassenzimmer *nt*

schoolteacher ['sku:lti:tʃər] *n* Lehrer(in) *m(f)*

schoolyard ['sku:ljɑ:d] *n* Schulhof *m*

schooner ['sku:nər] *n* (*ship*) Schoner *m*; (*Brit: for sherry*) großes Sherryglas *nt*; (*US etc: for beer*) großes Bierglas *nt*

sciatica [saɪ'ætɪkə] *n* Ischias *m or nt*

science ['saɪəns] *n* Naturwissenschaft *f*; (*branch of knowledge*) Wissenschaft *f*; **the ~s** Naturwissenschaften *pl*

science fiction *n* Science-Fiction *f*

scientific [saɪən'tɪfɪk] *adj* wissenschaftlich

scientist ['saɪəntɪst] *n* Wissenschaftler(in) *m(f)*

sci-fi ['saɪfaɪ] (*inf*) *n abbr* (= *science fiction*) SF

Scillies ['sɪlɪz] *npl* = **Scilly Isles**

Scilly Isles ['sɪlɪ'aɪlz] *npl*: **the ~** die Scillyinseln *pl*

scintillating ['sɪntɪleɪtɪŋ] *adj* (*fig: conversation*) faszinierend; (*wit*) sprühend

scissors ['sɪzəz] *npl* Schere *f*; **a pair of ~** eine Schere

sclerosis [sklɪ'rəusɪs] *n* Sklerose *f*

scoff [skɔf] *vt* (*Brit: inf: eat*) futtern, verputzen ▷ *vi*: **to ~ (at)** (*mock*) spotten (über +*acc*), sich lustig machen (über +*acc*)

scold [skəuld] *vt* ausschimpfen

scolding ['skəuldɪŋ] *n* Schelte *f*; **to get a ~** ausgeschimpft werden

scone [skɔn] *n* brötchenartiges Teegebäck

scoop [sku:p] *n* (*for flour etc*) Schaufel *f*; (*for ice*

cream etc*) Portionierer *m*; (*amount*) Kugel *f*; (*Press*) Knüller *m*
▶ **scoop out** *vt* aushöhlen
▶ **scoop up** *vt* aufschaufeln; (*liquid*) aufschöpfen

scooter ['sku:tər] *n* (*also*: **motor scooter**) Motorroller *m*; (*toy*) (Tret)roller *m*

scope [skəup] *n* (*opportunity*) Möglichkeiten *pl*; (*range*) Ausmaß *nt*, Umfang *m*; (*freedom*) Freiheit *f*; **within the ~ of** im Rahmen +*gen*; **there is plenty of ~ for improvement** (*Brit*) es könnte noch viel verbessert werden

scorch [skɔ:tʃ] *vt* versengen; (*earth, grass*) verbrennen

scorched earth policy *n* (*Mil*) Politik *f* der verbrannten Erde

scorcher ['skɔ:tʃər] (*inf*) *n* heißer Tag *m*

scorching ['skɔ:tʃɪŋ] *adj* (*day, weather*) brütend heiß

score [skɔ:r] *n* (*number of points*) (Punkte)stand *m*; (*of game*) Spielstand *m*; (*Mus*) Partitur *f*; (*twenty*) zwanzig ▷ *vt* (*goal*) schießen; (*point, success*) erzielen; (*mark*) einkerben; (*cut*) einritzen ▷ *vi* (*in game*) einen Punkt/Punkte erzielen; (*Football etc*) ein Tor schießen; (*keep score*) (Punkte) zählen; **to settle an old ~ with sb** (*fig*) eine alte Rechnung mit jdm begleichen; **what's the ~?** (*Sport*) wie stehts?; **~s of** Hunderte von; **on that ~** in dieser Hinsicht; **to ~ well** gut abschneiden; **to ~ 6 out of 10** 6 von 10 Punkten erzielen; **to ~ (a point) over sb** (*fig*) jdn ausstechen
▶ **score out** *vt* ausstreichen

scoreboard ['skɔ:bɔ:d] *n* Anzeigetafel *f*

scorecard ['skɔ:kɑ:d] *n* (*Sport*) Spielprotokoll *nt*

score line *n* (*Sport*) Spielstand *m*; (: *final score*) Endergebnis *nt*

scorer ['skɔ:rər] *n* (*Football etc*) Torschütze *m*, Torschützin *f*; (*person keeping score*) Anschreiber(in) *m(f)*

scorn [skɔ:n] *n* Verachtung *f* ▷ *vt* verachten; (*reject*) verschmähen

scornful ['skɔ:nful] *adj* verächtlich, höhnisch

Scorpio ['skɔ:pɪəu] *n* Skorpion *m*; **to be ~** Skorpion sein

scorpion ['skɔ:pɪən] *n* Skorpion *m*

Scot [skɔt] *n* Schotte *m*, Schottin *f*

Scotch [skɔtʃ] *n* Scotch *m*

scotch [skɔtʃ] *vt* (*rumour*) aus der Welt schaffen; (*plan, idea*) unterbinden

Scotch tape® *n* ≈ Tesafilm® *m*

scot-free ['skɔt'fri:] *adv*: **to get off ~** ungeschoren davonkommen

Scotland ['skɔtlənd] *n* Schottland *nt*

Scots [skɔts] *adj* schottisch

Scotsman ['skɔtsmən] (*irreg: like* **man**) *n* Schotte *m*

Scotswoman ['skɔtswumən] (*irreg: like* **woman**) *n* Schottin *f*

Scottish ['skɔtɪʃ] *adj* schottisch

Scottish National Party *n* Partei, *die für die Unabhängigkeit Schottlands eintritt*

scoundrel ['skaundrl] *n* Schurke *m*

scour ['skauə^r] vt (search) absuchen; (clean) scheuern

scourer ['skauərə^r] n Topfkratzer m

scourge [skə:dʒ] n (lit, fig) Geißel f

scout [skaut] n (Mil) Kundschafter m, Späher m; (also: **boy scout**) Pfadfinder m; **girl ~** (US) Pfadfinderin f
▶ **scout around** vi sich umsehen

scowl [skaul] vi ein böses Gesicht machen ▷ n böses Gesicht nt; **to ~ at sb** jdn böse ansehen

scrabble ['skræbl] vi (also: **scrabble around**) herumtasten ▷ n: **S~®** Scrabble® nt; **to ~ at sth** nach etw krallen; **to ~ about** or **around for sth** nach etw herumsuchen

scraggy ['skrægɪ] adj (animal) mager; (body, neck etc) dürr

scram [skræm] (inf) vi abhauen, verschwinden

scramble ['skræmbl] n (climb) Kletterpartie f; (rush) Hetze f; (struggle) Gerangel nt ▷ vi: **to ~ up/over** klettern auf/über +acc; **to ~ for** sich drängeln um; **to go scrambling** (Sport) Querfeldeinrennen fahren

scrambled eggs ['skræmbld-] n Rührei nt

scrap [skræp] n (bit) Stückchen nt; (fig: of truth, evidence) Spur f; (fight) Balgerei f; (also: **scrap metal**) Altmetall nt, Schrott m ▷ vt (machines etc) verschrotten; (fig: plans etc) fallen lassen ▷ vi (fight) sich balgen; **scraps** npl (leftovers) Reste pl; **to sell sth for ~** etw als Schrott or zum Verschrotten verkaufen

scrapbook ['skræpbuk] n Sammelalbum nt

scrap dealer n Schrotthändler(in) m(f)

scrape [skreɪp] vt abkratzen; (hand etc) abschürfen; (car) verschrammen ▷ n: **to get into a ~** (difficult situation) in Schwulitäten pl kommen (inf)
▶ **scrape through** vt (exam etc) durchrutschen durch (inf)
▶ **scrape together** vt (money) zusammenkratzen

scraper ['skreɪpə^r] n Kratzer m

scrap heap n: **to be on the ~** (fig) zum alten Eisen gehören

scrap merchant (Brit) n Schrotthändler(in) m(f)

scrap metal n Altmetall nt, Schrott m

scrap paper n Schmierpapier nt

scrappy ['skræpɪ] adj zusammengestoppelt (inf)

scrap yard n Schrottplatz m

scratch [skrætʃ] n Kratzer m ▷ vt kratzen; (one's nose etc) sich kratzen an +dat; (paint, car, record) verkratzen; (Comput) löschen ▷ vi sich kratzen ▷ cpd (team, side) zusammengewürfelt; **to start from ~** ganz von vorne anfangen; **to be up to ~** den Anforderungen entsprechen; **to ~ the surface** (fig) an der Oberfläche bleiben

scratch pad (US) n Notizblock m

scrawl [skrɔ:l] n Gekritzel nt; (handwriting) Klaue f (inf) ▷ vt hinkritzeln

scrawny ['skrɔ:nɪ] adj dürr

scream [skri:m] n Schrei m ▷ vi schreien; **to be a ~** (inf) zum Schreien sein; **to ~ at sb (to do sth)** jdn anschreien(, etw zu tun)

scree [skri:] n Geröll nt

screech [skri:tʃ] vi kreischen; (tyres, brakes) quietschen ▷ n Kreischen nt; (of tyres, brakes) Quietschen nt

screen [skri:n] n (Cine) Leinwand f; (TV, Comput) Bildschirm m; (movable barrier) Wandschirm m; (fig: cover) Tarnung f; (also: **windscreen**) Windschutzscheibe f ▷ vt (protect) abschirmen; (from the wind etc) schützen; (conceal) verdecken; (film) zeigen, vorführen; (programme) senden; (candidates etc) überprüfen; (for illness): **to ~ sb for sth** jdn auf etw acc (hin) untersuchen

screen editing n (Comput) Bildschirmaufbereitung f

screening ['skri:nɪŋ] n (Med) Untersuchung f; (of film) Vorführung f; (TV) Sendung f; (for security) Überprüfung f

screen memory n (Comput) Bildschirmspeicher m

screenplay ['skri:npleɪ] n Drehbuch nt

screen saver n (Comput) Bildschirmschoner m

screen test n Probeaufnahmen pl

screw [skru:] n Schraube f ▷ vt schrauben; (inf!) bumsen (!); **to ~ sth in** etw einschrauben; **to ~ sth to the wall** etw an der Wand festschrauben; **to have one's head ~ed on** (fig) ein vernünftiger Mensch sein
▶ **screw up** vt (paper etc) zusammenknüllen; (inf: ruin) vermasseln; **to ~ up one's eyes** die Augen zusammenkneifen

screwdriver ['skru:draɪvə^r] n Schraubenzieher m

screwed-up ['skru:d'ʌp] (inf) adj: **to be/get ~ about sth** sich wegen etw ganz verrückt machen

screwy ['skru:ɪ] (inf) adj verrückt

scribble ['skrɪbl] n Gekritzel nt ▷ vt, vi kritzeln; **to ~ sth down** etw hinkritzeln

scribe [skraɪb] n Schreiber m

script [skrɪpt] n (Cine) Drehbuch nt; (of speech, play etc) Text m; (alphabet) Schrift f; (in exam) schriftliche Arbeit f

scripted ['skrɪptɪd] adj vorbereitet

scripture ['skrɪptʃə^r] n, **scriptures** ['skrɪptʃəz] ▷ npl (heilige) Schrift f; **the S~(s)** (the Bible) die Heilige Schrift f

scriptwriter ['skrɪptraɪtə^r] n (Radio, TV) Autor(in) m(f); (Cine) Drehbuchautor(in) m(f)

scroll [skrəul] n Schriftrolle f ▷ vi (Comput) scrollen

scroll bar n (Comput) Bildlaufleiste f

scrotum ['skrəutəm] n Hodensack m

scrounge [skraundʒ] (inf) vt: **to ~ sth off sb** etw bei jdm schnorren ▷ vi schnorren ▷ n: **on the ~** am Schnorren

scrounger ['skraundʒə^r] (inf) n Schnorrer(in) m(f)

scrub [skrʌb] n Gestrüpp nt ▷ vt (floor etc) schrubben; (inf: idea, plan) fallen lassen

scrubbing brush ['skrʌbɪŋ-] n Scheuerbürste f

scruff [skrʌf] n: **by the ~ of the neck** am Genick

S

scruffy ['skrʌfɪ] adj gammelig, verwahrlost
scrum ['skrʌm], **scrummage** ['skrʌmɪdʒ] n (Rugby) Gedränge nt
scruple ['skru:pl] n (gen pl) Skrupel m, Bedenken nt; **to have no ~s about doing sth** keine Skrupel or Bedenken haben, etw zu tun
scrupulous ['skru:pjuləs] adj gewissenhaft; (honesty) unbedingt
scrupulously ['skru:pjuləslɪ] adv gewissenhaft; (honest, fair) äußerst; (clean) peinlich
scrutinize ['skru:tɪnaɪz] vt prüfend ansehen; (data, records etc) genau prüfen or untersuchen
scrutiny ['skru:tɪnɪ] n genaue Untersuchung f; **under the ~ of sb** unter jds prüfendem Blick
scuba ['sku:bə] n (Schwimm)tauchgerät nt
scuba diving n Sporttauchen nt
scuff [skʌf] vt (shoes, floor) abwetzen
scuffle ['skʌfl] n Handgemenge nt
scull [skʌl] n Skull nt
scullery ['skʌlərɪ] n (old) Spülküche f
sculptor ['skʌlptə'] n Bildhauer(in) m(f)
sculpture ['skʌlptʃə'] n (art) Bildhauerei f; (object) Skulptur f
scum [skʌm] n (on liquid) Schmutzschicht f; (pej) Abschaum m
scupper ['skʌpə'] (Brit: inf) vt (plan, idea) zerschlagen
scurrilous ['skʌrɪləs] adj verleumderisch
scurry ['skʌrɪ] vi huschen
▸ **scurry off** vi forthasten
scurvy ['skə:vɪ] n Skorbut m
scuttle ['skʌtl] n (also: **coal scuttle**) Kohleneimer m ▸ vt (ship) versenken ▸ vi: **to ~ away** or **off** verschwinden
scythe [saɪð] n Sense f
SD, S.Dak. (US) abbr (Post) = South Dakota
SDI (US) n abbr (Mil: = Strategic Defense Initiative) SDI f
SDLP (Brit) n abbr (Pol: = Social Democratic and Labour Party) sozialdemokratische Partei in Nordirland
SE abbr (= south-east) SO
sea [si:] n Meer nt, See f; (fig) Meer nt ▸ cpd See-; **by ~** (travel) mit dem Schiff; **beside** or **by the ~** (holiday) am Meer, an der See; (village) am Meer; **on the ~** (boat) auf See; **at ~** auf See; **to be all at ~** (fig) nicht durchblicken (inf); **out to ~** aufs Meer (hinaus); **to look out to ~** aufs Meer hinausblicken; **heavy/rough ~(s)** schwere/raue See f
sea anemone n Seeanemone f
sea bed n Meeresboden m
seaboard ['si:bɔ:d] n Küste f
seafarer ['si:fɛərə'] n Seefahrer m
seafaring ['si:fɛərɪŋ] adj (life, nation) Seefahrer-
seafood ['si:fu:d] n Meeresfrüchte pl
seafront ['si:frʌnt] n Strandpromenade f
seagoing ['si:gəʊɪŋ] adj hochseetüchtig
seagull ['si:gʌl] n Möwe f
seal [si:l] n (animal) Seehund m; (official stamp) Siegel nt; (in machine etc) Dichtung f; (on bottle etc) Verschluss m ▸ vt (envelope) zukleben; (crack, opening) abdichten; (with seal) versiegeln;

(agreement, sb's fate) besiegeln; **to give sth one's ~ of approval** einer Sache dat seine offizielle Zustimmung geben
▸ **seal off** vt (place) abriegeln
sea level n Meeresspiegel m; **2,000 ft above/below ~** 2000 Fuß über/unter dem Meeresspiegel
sealing wax ['si:lɪŋ-] n Siegelwachs nt
sea lion n Seelöwe m
sealskin ['si:lskɪn] n Seehundfell nt
seam [si:m] n Naht f; (lit, fig: where edges join) Übergang m; (of coal etc) Flöz nt; **the hall was bursting at the ~s** der Saal platzte aus allen Nähten
seaman ['si:mən] (irreg: like **man**) n Seemann m
seamanship ['si:mənʃɪp] n Seemannschaft f
seamless ['si:mlɪs] adj (lit, fig) nahtlos
seamy ['si:mɪ] adj zwielichtig; **the ~ side of life** die Schattenseite des Lebens
séance ['seɪɒns] n spiritistische Sitzung f
seaplane ['si:pleɪn] n Wasserflugzeug nt
seaport ['si:pɔ:t] n Seehafen m
search [sə:tʃ] n Suche f; (inspection) Durchsuchung f; (Comput) Suchlauf m ▸ vt durchsuchen; (mind, memory) durchforschen ▸ vi: **to ~ for** suchen nach; **"~ and replace"** (Comput) „suchen und ersetzen"; **in ~ of** auf der Suche nach
▸ **search through** vt fus durchsuchen
searcher ['sə:tʃə'] n Suchende(r) f(m)
searching ['sə:tʃɪŋ] adj (question) bohrend; (look) prüfend; (examination) eingehend
searchlight ['sə:tʃlaɪt] n Suchscheinwerfer m
search party n Suchtrupp m; **to send out a ~** einen Suchtrupp ausschicken
search warrant n Durchsuchungsbefehl m
searing ['sɪərɪŋ] adj (heat) glühend; (pain) scharf
seashore ['si:ʃɔ:'] n Strand m; **on the ~** am Strand
seasick ['si:sɪk] adj seekrank
seasickness ['si:sɪknɪs] n Seekrankheit f
seaside ['si:saɪd] n Meer nt, See f; **to go to the ~** ans Meer or an die See fahren; **at the ~** am Meer, an die See
seaside resort n Badeort m
season ['si:zn] n Jahreszeit f; (Agr) Zeit f; (Sport, of films etc) Saison f; (Theat) Spielzeit f ▸ vt (food) würzen; **strawberries are in ~/out of ~** für Erdbeeren ist jetzt die richtige Zeit/nicht die richtige Zeit; **the busy ~** die Hochsaison f; **the open ~** (Hunting) die Jagdzeit f
seasonal ['si:znl] adj (work) Saison-
seasoned ['si:znd] adj (fig: traveller) erfahren; (wood) abgelagert; **she's a ~ campaigner** sie ist eine alte Kämpferin
seasoning ['si:znɪŋ] n Gewürz nt
season ticket n (Rail) Zeitkarte f; (Sport) Dauerkarte f; (Theat) Abonnement nt
seat [si:t] n (chair, of government, Pol) Sitz m; (place) Platz m; (buttocks) Gesäß nt; (of trousers) Hosenboden m; (of learning) Stätte f ▸ vt setzen; (have room for) Sitzplätze bieten für; **are there**

any ~s left? sind noch Plätze frei?; **to take one's ~** sich setzen; **please be ~ed** bitte nehmen Sie Platz; **to be ~ed** sitzen

seat belt n Sicherheitsgurt m

seating arrangements ['si:tɪŋ-] npl Sitzordnung f

seating capacity n Sitzplätze pl

SEATO ['si:təu] n abbr (= Southeast Asia Treaty Organization) SEATO f

sea urchin n Seeigel m

sea water n Meerwasser nt

seaweed ['si:wi:d] n Seetang m

seaworthy ['si:wə:ðɪ] adj seetüchtig

SEC (US) n abbr (= Securities and Exchange Commission) amerikanische Börsenaufsichtsbehörde

sec. abbr (= second) Sek.

secateurs [sɛkə'tə:z] npl Gartenschere f

secede [sɪ'si:d] vi (Pol) **to ~ (from)** sich abspalten (von)

secluded [sɪ'klu:dɪd] adj (place) abgelegen; (life) zurückgezogen

seclusion [sɪ'klu:ʒən] n Abgeschiedenheit f; **in ~** zurückgezogen

second¹ [sɪ'kɒnd] (Brit) vt (employee) abordnen

second² ['sɛkənd] adj (place, r, s) ▷ adv (come, be placed) Zweite(r, s); (when listing) zweitens ▷ n (time) Sekunde f; (Aut: also: **second gear**) der zweite Gang; (person) Zweite(r) f(m); (Comm: imperfect) zweite Wahl f ▷ vt (motion) unterstützen; **upper/lower** = (Brit: Univ) ≈ Zwei plus/minus; **Charles the S~** Karl der Zweite; **just a ~!** einen Augenblick!; **~ floor** (Brit) zweiter Stock m; (US) erster Stock m; **to ask for a ~ opinion** ein zweites Gutachten einholen

secondary ['sɛkəndərɪ] adj weniger wichtig

secondary education n höhere Schulbildung f

secondary picketing n Aufstellung von Streikposten bei nur indirekt beteiligten Firmen

secondary school n höhere Schule f; siehe Info-Artikel

- SECONDARY SCHOOL
-
- Secondary school ist in Großbritannien eine
- weiterführende Schule für Kinder von
- 11 bis 18 Jahren. Manche Schüler gehen
- schon mit 16 Jahren, wenn die allgemeine
- Schulpflicht endet, von der Schule ab.
- Die meisten secondary schools sind
- heute Gesamtschulen, obwohl es auch
- noch selektive Schulen gibt. Siehe auch
- comprehensive school, primary school.

second-best [sɛkənd'bɛst] adj zweitbeste(r, s) ▷ n: **as a ~** als Ausweichlösung; **don't settle for ~** gib dich nur mit dem Besten zufrieden

second-class ['sɛkənd'klɑ:s] adj zweitklassig; (citizen) zweiter Klasse; (Rail, Post) Zweite-Klasse- ▷ adv (Rail, Post) zweiter Klasse; **to send sth ~** etw zweiter Klasse schicken; **to travel ~** zweiter Klasse reisen

second cousin n Cousin m/Cousine f zweiten Grades f

seconder ['sɛkəndə'] n Befürworter(in) m(f)

second-guess ['sɛkənd'gɛs] vt vorhersagen; **to ~ sb** vorhersagen, was jd machen wird

second-hand ['sɛkənd'hænd] adj gebraucht; (clothing) getragen ▷ adv (buy) gebraucht; **to hear sth secondhand** etw aus zweiter Hand haben; **~ car** Gebrauchtwagen m; **~ smoking** (US) Passivrauchen nt

second hand n (on clock) Sekundenzeiger m

second-in-command ['sɛkəndɪnkə'mɑ:nd] n (Mil) stellvertretender Kommandeur m; (Admin) stellvertretender Leiter m

secondly ['sɛkəndlɪ] adv zweitens

secondment [sɪ'kɒndmənt] (Brit) n Abordnung f; **to be on ~** abgeordnet sein

second-rate ['sɛkənd'reɪt] adj zweitklassig

second thoughts npl: **on ~, on second thought** (US) wenn ich es mir (recht) überlege; **to have ~ (about doing sth)** es sich dat anders überlegen (und etw doch nicht tun)

Second World War n: **the ~** der Zweite Weltkrieg

secrecy ['si:krəsɪ] n Geheimhaltung f; (of person) Verschwiegenheit f; **in ~** heimlich

secret ['si:krɪt] adj geheim; (admirer) heimlich ▷ n Geheimnis nt; **in ~** heimlich; **~ passage** Geheimgang m; **to keep sth ~ from sb** etw vor jdm geheim halten; **can you keep a ~?** kannst du schweigen?; **to make no ~ of sth** kein Geheimnis or keinen Hehl aus etw machen

secret agent n Geheimagent(in) m(f)

secretarial [sɛkrɪ'tɛərɪəl] adj (work) Büro-; (course) Sekretärinnen-; (staff) Sekretariats-

secretariat [sɛkrɪ'tɛərɪət] n (Pol, Admin) Sekretariat nt

secretary ['sɛkrətərɪ] n (Comm) Sekretär(in) m(f); (of club) Schriftführer(in) m(f); **S~ of State (for)** (Brit: Pol) Minister(in) m(f) (für); **S~ of State** (US: Pol) Außenminister(in) m(f)

secretary-general ['sɛkrətərɪ'dʒɛnərl] (pl **secretaries-general**) n Generalsekretär(in) m(f)

secrete [sɪ'kri:t] vt (Anat, Biol, Med) absondern; (hide) verbergen

secretion [sɪ'kri:ʃən] n (substance) Sekret nt

secretive ['si:krətɪv] adj verschlossen; (pej) geheimnistuerisch

secretly ['si:krɪtlɪ] adv heimlich; (hope) insgeheim

secret police n Geheimpolizei f

secret service n Geheimdienst m

sect [sɛkt] n Sekte f

sectarian [sɛk'tɛərɪən] adj (killing etc) konfessionell motiviert; **~ violence** gewalttätige Konfessionsstreitigkeiten pl

section ['sɛkʃən] n (part) Teil m; (department) Abteilung f; (of document) Absatz m; (cross-section) Schnitt m ▷ vt (divide) teilen; **the business/sport ~** (Press) der Wirtschafts-/ Sportteil

S

sectional ['sɛkʃənl] *adj*: ~ **drawing** Darstellung *f* im Schnitt

sector ['sɛktəʳ] *n* Sektor *m*

secular ['sɛkjuləʳ] *adj* weltlich

secure [sɪ'kjuəʳ] *adj* sicher; (*firmly fixed*) fest ▷ *vt* (*fix*) festmachen; (*votes etc*) erhalten; (*contract etc*) (sich *dat*) sichern; (*Comm: loan*) (ab)sichern; **to make sth** ~ etw sichern; **to** ~ **sth for sb** jdm etw sichern

secured creditor [sɪ'kjuəd-] *n* (*Comm*) abgesicherter Gläubiger *m*

securely [sɪ'kjuəlɪ] *adv* (*firmly*) fest; (*safely*) sicher

security [sɪ'kjuərɪtɪ] *n* Sicherheit *f*; (*freedom from anxiety*) Geborgenheit *f*; **securities** *npl* (*Stock Exchange*) Effekten *pl*, Wertpapiere *pl*; **securities market** Wertpapiermarkt *m*; **to increase/tighten** ~ die Sicherheitsvorkehrungen verschärfen; ~ **of tenure** Kündigungsschutz *m*

Security Council *n* Sicherheitsrat *m*

security forces *npl* Sicherheitskräfte *pl*

security guard *n* Sicherheitsbeamte(r) *m*; (*transporting money*) Wachmann *m*

security risk *n* Sicherheitsrisiko *nt*

secy. *abbr* = **secretary**

sedan [sə'dæn] (*US*) *n* (*Aut*) Limousine *f*

sedate [sɪ'deɪt] *adj* (*person*) ruhig, gesetzt; (*life*) geruhsam; (*pace*) gemächlich ▷ *vt* (*Med*) Beruhigungsmittel geben +*dat*

sedation [sɪ'deɪʃən] *n* (*Med*) Beruhigungsmittel *pl*; **to be under** ~ unter dem Einfluss von Beruhigungsmitteln stehen

sedative ['sɛdɪtɪv] *n* (*Med*) Beruhigungsmittel *nt*

sedentary ['sɛdntrɪ] *adj* (*occupation, work*) sitzend

sediment ['sɛdɪmənt] *n* (*in bottle*) (Boden)satz *m*; (*in lake etc*) Ablagerung *f*

sedimentary [sɛdɪ'mɛntərɪ] *adj* (*Geog*) sedimentär; ~ **rock** Sedimentgestein *nt*

sedition [sɪ'dɪʃən] *n* Aufwiegelung *f*

seduce [sɪ'djuːs] *vt* verführen; **to** ~ **sb into doing sth** jdn dazu verleiten, etw zu tun

seduction [sɪ'dʌkʃən] *n* (*attraction*) Verlockung *f*; (*act of seducing*) Verführung *f*

seductive [sɪ'dʌktɪv] *adj* verführerisch; (*fig: offer*) verlockend

see [siː] (*pt* **saw**, *pp* ~**n**) *vt* sehen; (*look at*) sich *dat* ansehen; (*understand*) verstehen, (ein)sehen; (*doctor etc*) aufsuchen ▷ *vi* sehen ▷ *n* (*Rel*) Bistum *nt*; **to** ~ **that** (*ensure*) dafür sorgen, dass; **to** ~ **sb to the door** jdn zur Tür bringen; **there was nobody to be** ~**n** es war niemand zu sehen; **to go and** ~ **sb** jdn besuchen (gehen); **to** ~ **a doctor** zum Arzt gehen; ~ **you!** tschüss! (*inf*); ~ **you soon!** bis bald!; **let me** ~ (*show me*) lass mich mal sehen; (*let me think*) lass mich mal überlegen; **I** ~ ich verstehe, aha; (*annoyed*) ach so; **you** ~ weißt du, siehst du; ~ **for yourself** überzeug dich doch selbst; **I don't know what she** ~**s in him** ich weiß nicht, was sie an ihm findet; **as far as I can** ~ so wie ich das sehe

▶ **see about** *vt fus* sich kümmern um +*acc*

▶ **see off** *vt* verabschieden

▶ **see through** *vt fus* durchschauen ▷ *vt*: **to** ~ **sb through sth** jdm in etw *dat* beistehen; **to** ~ **sth through to the end** etw zu Ende bringen; **this should** ~ **you through** das müsste dir reichen

▶ **see to** *vt fus* sich kümmern um +*acc*

seed [siːd] *n* Samen *m*; (*of fruit*) Kern *m*; (*fig: usu pl*) Keim *m*; (*Tennis*) gesetzter Spieler *m*, gesetzte Spielerin *f*; **to go to** ~ (*plant*) Samen bilden; (*lettuce etc*) schießen; (*fig: person*) herunterkommen

seedless ['siːdlɪs] *adj* kernlos

seedling ['siːdlɪŋ] *n* (*Bot*) Sämling *m*

seedy ['siːdɪ] *adj* (*person, place*) zwielichtig, zweifelhaft

seeing ['siːɪŋ] *conj*: ~ **as** *or* **that** da

seek [siːk] (*pt, pp* **sought**) *vt* suchen; **to** ~ **advice from sb** jdn um Rat fragen; **to** ~ **help from sb** jdn um Hilfe bitten

▶ **seek out** *vt* ausfindig machen

seem [siːm] *vi* scheinen; **there** ~**s to be a mistake** da scheint ein Fehler zu sein; **it** ~**s (that)** es scheint(, dass); **it** ~**s to me that ...** mir scheint, dass ...; **what** ~**s to be the trouble?** worum geht es denn?; (*doctor*) was fehlt Ihnen denn?

seemingly ['siːmɪŋlɪ] *adv* anscheinend

seemly ['siːmlɪ] *adj* schicklich

seen [siːn] *pp of* **see**

seep [siːp] *vi* sickern

seersucker ['sɪəsʌkəʳ] *n* Krepp *m*, Seersucker *m*

seesaw ['siːsɔː] *n* Wippe *f*

seethe [siːð] *vi*: **to** ~ **with** (*place*) wimmeln von; **to** ~ **with anger** vor Wut kochen

see-through ['siːθruː] *adj* durchsichtig

segment ['sɛgmənt] *n* Teil *m*; (*of orange*) Stück *nt*

segregate ['sɛgrɪgeɪt] *vt* trennen, absondern

segregation [sɛgrɪ'geɪʃən] *n* Trennung *f*

Seine [seɪn] *n*: **the** ~ die Seine *f*

seismic shock *n* Erdstoß *m*

seize [siːz] *vt* packen, ergreifen; (*fig: opportunity*) ergreifen; (*power, control*) an sich *acc* reißen; (*territory, airfield*) besetzen; (*hostage*) nehmen; (*Law*) beschlagnahmen

▶ **seize up** *vi* (*engine*) sich festfressen

▶ **seize (up)on** *vt fus* sich stürzen auf +*acc*

seizure ['siːʒəʳ] *n* (*Med*) Anfall *m*; (*of power*) Ergreifung *f*; (*Law*) Beschlagnahmung *f*

seldom ['sɛldəm] *adv* selten

select [sɪ'lɛkt] *adj* exklusiv ▷ *vt* (aus)wählen; (*Sport*) aufstellen; **a** ~ **few** wenige Auserwählte *pl*

selection [sɪ'lɛkʃən] *n* (*being chosen*) Wahl *f*; (*range*) Auswahl *f*

selection committee *n* Auswahlkomitee *nt*

selective [sɪ'lɛktɪv] *adj* wählerisch; (*not general*) selektiv

selector [sɪ'lɛktəʳ] *n* (*Sport*) Mannschaft-saufsteller(in) *m(f)*; (*Tech*) Wählschalter *m*;

(: *button*) Taste *f*

self [sɛlf] (*pl* **selves**) *n* Selbst *nt*, Ich *nt*; **she was her normal ~ again** sie war wieder ganz die Alte

self ... [sɛlf] *pref* selbst-, Selbst-

self-addressed ['sɛlfə'drɛst] *adj*: **~ envelope** addressierter Rückumschlag *m*

self-adhesive [sɛlfəd'hi:zɪv] *adj* selbstklebend

self-appointed [sɛlfə'pɔɪntɪd] *adj* selbst ernannt

self-assertive [sɛlfə'sə:tɪv] *adj* selbstbewusst

self-assurance [sɛlfə'ʃuərəns] *n* Selbstsicherheit *f*

self-assured [sɛlfə'ʃuəd] *adj* selbstsicher

self-catering [sɛlf'keɪtərɪŋ] (*Brit*) *adj* (*holiday, flat*) für Selbstversorger

self-centred, (*US*) **self-centered** [sɛlf'sɛntəd] *adj* egozentrisch, ichbezogen

self-cleaning [sɛlf'kli:nɪŋ] *adj* selbstreinigend

self-confessed [sɛlfkən'fɛst] *adj* erklärt

self-confidence [sɛlf'kɒnfɪdns] *n* Selbstbewusstsein *nt*, Selbstvertrauen *nt*

self-confident [sɛlf'kɒnfɪdənt] *adj* selbstbewusst, selbstsicher

self-conscious [sɛlf'kɒnʃəs] *adj* befangen, gehemmt

self-contained [sɛlfkən'teɪnd] (*Brit*) *adj* (*flat*) abgeschlossen; (*person*) selb(st)ständig

self-control [sɛlfkən'trəul] *n* Selbstbeherrschung *f*

self-defeating [sɛlfdɪ'fi:tɪŋ] *adj* unsinnig

self-defence, (*US*) **self-defense** [sɛlfdɪ'fɛns] *n* Selbstverteidigung *f*; (*Law*) Notwehr *f*; **in ~ zu** seiner/ihrer *etc* Verteidigung; (*Law*) in Notwehr

self-discipline [sɛlf'dɪsɪplɪn] *n* Selbstdisziplin *f*

self-employed [sɛlfɪm'plɔɪd] *adj* selbstständig

self-esteem [sɛlfɪs'ti:m] *n* Selbstachtung *f*

self-evident [sɛlf'ɛvɪdnt] *adj* offensichtlich

self-explanatory [sɛlfɪks'plænətrɪ] *adj* unmittelbar verständlich

self-financing [sɛlffaɪ'nænsɪŋ] *adj* selbstfinanzierend

self-governing [sɛlf'gʌvənɪŋ] *adj* selbst verwaltet

self-help ['sɛlf'hɛlp] *n* Selbsthilfe *f*

self-importance [sɛlfɪm'pɔ:tns] *n* Aufgeblasenheit *f*

self-indulgent [sɛlfɪn'dʌldʒənt] *adj* genießerisch; **to be ~** sich verwöhnen

self-inflicted [sɛlfɪn'flɪktɪd] *adj* selbst zugefügt

self-interest [sɛlf'ɪntrɪst] *n* Eigennutz *m*

selfish ['sɛlfɪʃ] *adj* egoistisch, selbstsüchtig

selfishly ['sɛlfɪʃlɪ] *adv* egoistisch, selbstsüchtig

selfishness ['sɛlfɪʃnɪs] *n* Egoismus *m*, Selbstsucht *f*

selfless ['sɛlflɪs] *adj* selbstlos

selflessly ['sɛlflɪslɪ] *adv* selbstlos

selflessness ['sɛlflɪsnɪs] *n* Selbstlosigkeit *f*

self-made ['sɛlfmeɪd] *adj*: **~ man** Selfmademan *m*

self-pity [sɛlf'pɪtɪ] *n* Selbstmitleid *nt*

self-portrait [sɛlf'pɔ:treɪt] *n* Selbstporträt *nt*,

Selbstbildnis *nt*

self-possessed [sɛlfpə'zɛst] *adj* selbstbeherrscht

self-preservation ['sɛlfprɛzə'veɪʃən] *n* Selbsterhaltung *f*

self-raising ['sɛlf'reɪzɪŋ], (*US*) **self-rising** ['sɛlf'raɪzɪŋ] *adj*: **~ flour** Mehl *mit bereits beigemischtem Backpulver*

self-reliant [sɛlfrɪ'laɪənt] *adj* selb(st)ständig

self-respect [sɛlfrɪs'pɛkt] *n* Selbstachtung *f*

self-respecting [sɛlfrɪs'pɛktɪŋ] *adj* mit Selbstachtung; (*genuine*) der/die/das etwas auf sich hält

self-righteous [sɛlf'raɪtʃəs] *adj* selbstgerecht

self-rising [sɛlf'raɪzɪŋ] (*US*) *adj* = **self-raising**

self-sacrifice [sɛlf'sækrɪfaɪs] *n* Selbstaufopferung *f*

self-same ['sɛlfseɪm] *adj*: **the ~** genau derselbe/dieselbe/dasselbe

self-satisfied [sɛlf'sætɪsfaɪd] *adj* selbstzufrieden

self-sealing [sɛlf'si:lɪŋ] *adj* selbstklebend

self-service [sɛlf'sə:vɪs] *adj* (*shop, restaurant etc*) Selbstbedienungs-

self-styled ['sɛlfstaɪld] *adj* selbst ernannt

self-sufficient [sɛlfsə'fɪʃənt] *adj* (*country*) autark; (*person*) selb(st)ständig, unabhängig; **to be ~ in coal** seinen Kohlebedarf selbst decken können

self-supporting [sɛlfsə'pɔ:tɪŋ] *adj* (*business*) sich selbst tragend

self-taught [sɛlf'tɔ:t] *adj*: **to be ~** Autodidakt sein; **he is a ~ pianist** er hat sich das Klavierspielen selbst beigebracht

self-test ['sɛlftɛst] *n* (*Comput*) Selbsttest *m*

sell [sɛl] (*pt, pp* **sold**) *vt* verkaufen; (*shop: goods*) führen, haben (*inf*); (*fig: idea*) schmackhaft machen +*dat*, verkaufen (*inf*) ▷ *vi* sich verkaufen (lassen); **to ~ at** *or* **for 10 pounds** für 10 Pfund verkauft werden; **to ~ sb sth** jdm etw verkaufen; **to ~ o.s.** sich verkaufen

▶ **sell off** *vt* verkaufen

▶ **sell out** *vi*: **we/the tickets are sold out** wir/die Karten sind ausverkauft; **we have sold out of ...** wir haben kein ... mehr, ... ist ausverkauft

▶ **sell up** *vi* sein Haus/seine Firma *etc* verkaufen

sell-by date ['sɛlbaɪ-] *n* ≈ Haltbarkeitsdatum *nt*

seller ['sɛlə^r] *n* Verkäufer(in) *m(f)*; **~'s market** Verkäufermarkt *m*

selling point ['sɛlɪŋ-] *n* Verkaufsanreiz *m* or -argument *nt*

selling price ['sɛlɪŋ-] *n* Verkaufspreis *m*

sellotape® ['sɛləuteɪp] (*Brit*) *n* Klebeband ≈ Tesafilm® *m*

sellout ['sɛlaut] *n* (*inf: betrayal*) Verrat *m*; **the match was a ~** das Spiel war ausverkauft

selves [sɛlvz] *pl of* **self**

semantic [sɪ'mæntɪk] *adj* semantisch

semantics [sɪ'mæntɪks] *n* (*Ling*) Semantik *f*

semaphore ['sɛməfɔ:^r] *n* Flaggenalphabet *nt*

semblance ['sɛmblns] *n* Anschein *m*

semen ['si:mən] n Samenflüssigkeit f, Sperma nt

semester [sɪ'mɛstəʳ] (esp US) n Semester nt

semi ['sɛmɪ] n = **semidetached house**

semi ... ['sɛmɪ] pref halb-, Halb-

semibreve ['sɛmɪbri:v] (Brit) n (Mus) ganze Note f

semicircle ['sɛmɪsə:kl] n Halbkreis m

semicircular ['sɛmɪ'sə:kjuləʳ] adj halbkreisförmig

semicolon [sɛmɪ'kəʊlən] n Strichpunkt m, Semikolon nt

semiconductor [sɛmɪkən'dʌktəʳ] n Halbleiter m

semiconscious [sɛmɪ'kɒnʃəs] adj halb bewusstlos

semidetached

semidetached house (Brit) n Doppelhaushälfte f

semifinal [sɛmɪ'faɪnl] n Halbfinale nt

seminar ['sɛmɪnɑ:ʳ] n Seminar nt

seminary ['sɛmɪnərɪ] n (Rel) Priesterseminar nt

semi-precious stone n Halbedelstein m

semiquaver ['sɛmɪkweɪvəʳ] (Brit) n (Mus) Sechzehntelnote f

semiskilled [sɛmɪ'skɪld] adj (work) Anlern-; (worker) angelernt

semi-skimmed [sɛmɪ'skɪmd] adj (milk) teilentrahmt, Halbfett-

semitone ['sɛmɪtəʊn] n (Mus) Halbton m

semolina [sɛmə'li:nə] n Grieß m

Sen., sen. abbr (US) = **senator**; (in names: = senior) sen.

senate ['sɛnɪt] n Senat m; siehe Info-Artikel

◉ **SENATE**

◉ Senate ist das Oberhaus des
◉ amerikanischen Kongresses (das
◉ Unterhaus ist das House of Representatives.
◉ Der Senat besteht aus 100 Senatoren,
◉ zwei für jeden Bundesstaat, die für sechs
◉ Jahre gewählt werden, wobei ein Drittel
◉ alle zwei Jahre neu gewählt wird. Die
◉ Senatoren werden in direkter Wahl vom
◉ Volk gewählt. Siehe auch congress.

senator ['sɛnɪtəʳ] n Senator(in) m(f)

send [sɛnd] (pt, pp **sent**) vt schicken; (transmit) senden; **to ~ sth by post, to ~ sth by mail** (US) etw mit der Post schicken; **to ~ sb for sth** (for check-up etc) jdn zu etw schicken; **to ~ word that ...** Nachricht geben, dass ...; **she ~s (you) her love** sie lässt dich grüßen; **to ~ sb to Coventry** (Brit) jdn schneiden (inf); **to ~ sb to sleep** jdn einschläfern; **to ~ sth flying** etw umwerfen

▸ **send away** vt wegschicken

▸ **send away for** vt fus (per Post) anfordern

▸ **send back** vt zurückschicken

▸ **send for** vt fus (per Post) anfordern; (doctor, police) rufen

▸ **send in** vt einsenden, einschicken

▸ **send off** vt abschicken; (Brit: player) vom Platz weisen

▸ **send on** vt (Brit: letter) nachsenden; (luggage etc) vorausschicken

▸ **send out** vt verschicken; (light, heat) abgeben; (signal) aussenden

▸ **send round** vt schicken; (circulate) zirkulieren lassen

▸ **send up** vt (astronaut) hochschießen; (price, blood pressure) hochtreiben; (Brit: parody) verulken (inf)

sender ['sɛndəʳ] n Absender(in) m(f)

sending-off ['sɛndɪŋɒf] n (Sport) Platzverweis m

send-off ['sɛndɒf] n: **a good ~** eine große Verabschiedung

send-up ['sɛndʌp] n Verulkung f (inf)

Senegal [sɛnɪ'gɔ:l] n Senegal nt

Senegalese [sɛnɪgə'li:z] adj senegalesisch ▷ n inv Senegalese m, Senegalesin f

senile ['si:naɪl] adj senil

senility [sɪ'nɪlɪtɪ] n Senilität f

senior ['si:nɪəʳ] adj (staff, manager) leitend; (officer) höher; (post, position) leitend ▷ n (Scol): **the ~s** die Oberstufenschüler pl; **to be ~ to sb** jdm übergeordnet sein; **she is 15 years his ~** sie ist 15 Jahre älter als er; **P. Jones ~** P. Jones senior

senior citizen n Senior(in) m(f)

senior high school (US) n Oberstufe f

seniority [si:nɪ'ɒrɪtɪ] n (in service) (längere) Betriebszugehörigkeit f; (in rank) (höhere) Position f

sensation [sɛn'seɪʃən] n (feeling) Gefühl nt; (great success) Sensation f; **to cause a ~** großes Aufsehen erregen

sensational [sɛn'seɪʃənl] adj (wonderful) wunderbar; (result) sensationell; (headlines etc) reißerisch

sense [sɛns] n Sinn m; (feeling) Gefühl nt; (good sense) Verstand m, gesunder Menschenverstand m; (meaning) Bedeutung f, Sinn m ▷ vt spüren; **~ of smell** Geruchssinn m; **it makes ~** (can be understood) es ergibt einen Sinn; (is sensible) es ist vernünftig or sinnvoll; **there's no ~ in that** das hat keinen Sinn; **there is no ~ in doing that** es hat keinen Sinn, das zu tun; **to come to one's ~s** Vernunft annehmen; **to take leave of one's ~s** den Verstand verlieren

senseless ['sɛnslɪs] adj (pointless) sinnlos; (unconscious) besinnungslos, bewusstlos

sense of humour n Sinn m für Humor

sensibility [sɛnsɪ'brlɪtɪ] n Empfindsamkeit f; (sensitivity) Empfindlichkeit f; **to offend sb's sensibilities** jds Zartgefühl verletzen

sensible ['sɛnsɪbl] adj vernünftig; (shoes, clothes) praktisch

sensitive ['sɛnsɪtɪv] adj empfindlich; (understanding) einfühlsam; (touchy: person) sensibel; (: issue) heikel; **to be ~ to sth** in Bezug auf etw acc empfindlich sein; **he is very ~ about it/to criticism** er reagiert sehr empfindlich darauf/auf Kritik

sensitivity [sɛnsɪ'tɪvɪtɪ] *n* Empfindlichkeit *f*; (*understanding*) Einfühlungsvermögen *nt*; (*of issue etc*) heikle Natur *f*; **an issue of great ~** ein sehr heikles Thema

sensual ['sɛnsjuəl] *adj* sinnlich; (*person, life*) sinnenfroh

sensuous ['sɛnsjuəs] *adj* sinnlich

sent [sɛnt] *pt, pp of* **send**

sentence ['sɛntns] *n* (*Ling*) Satz *m*; (*Law: judgement*) Urteil *nt*; (*: punishment*) Strafe *f* ▷ *vt*: **to ~ sb to death/to 5 years in prison** jdn zum Tode/zu 5 Jahren Haft verurteilen; **to pass ~ on sb** das Urteil über jdn verkünden; (*fig*) jdn verurteilen; **to serve a life ~** eine lebenslängliche Freiheitsstrafe verbüßen

sentiment ['sɛntɪmənt] *n* Sentimentalität *f*; (*also pl: opinion*) Ansicht *f*

sentimental [sɛntɪ'mɛntl] *adj* sentimental

sentimentality [sɛntɪmen'tælɪtɪ] *n* Sentimentalität *f*

sentry ['sɛntrɪ] *n* Wachtposten *m*

sentry duty *n*: **to be on ~** auf Wache sein

Seoul [səul] *n* Seoul *nt*

separable ['sɛprəbl] *adj*: **to be ~ from** trennbar sein von

separate ['sɛprɪt] *adj* getrennt; (*occasions*) verschieden; (*rooms*) separat ▷ *vt* trennen ▷ *vi* sich trennen; **~ from** getrennt von; **to go ~ ways** getrennte Wege gehen; **under ~ cover** (*Comm*) mit getrennter Post; **to ~ into** aufteilen in +*acc*; *see also* **separates**

separately ['sɛprɪtlɪ] *adv* getrennt

separates ['sɛprɪts] *npl* (*clothes*) kombinierbare Einzelteile *pl*

separation [sɛpə'reɪʃən] *n* Trennung *f*

sepia ['si:pjə] *adj* sepiafarben

Sept. *abbr* (= *September*) Sept.

September [sɛp'tɛmbəʳ] *n* September *m*; *see also* **July**

septic ['sɛptɪk] *adj* vereitert, septisch; **to go ~** eitern

septicaemia, (US) **septicemia** [sɛptɪ'si:mɪə] *n* Blutvergiftung *f*

septic tank *n* Faulbehälter *m*

sequel ['si:kwl] *n* (*follow-up*) Nachspiel *nt*; (*of film, story*) Fortsetzung *f*

sequence ['si:kwəns] *n* Folge *f*; (*dance/film sequence*) Sequenz *f*; **in ~** der Reihe nach

sequential [sɪ'kwɛnʃəl] *adj* aufeinanderfolgend; **~ access** (*Comput*) sequenzieller Zugriff *m*

sequestrate [sɪ'kwɛstreɪt] *vt* (*Law, Comm*) sequestrieren, beschlagnahmen

sequin ['si:kwɪn] *n* Paillette *f*

Serbia ['sə:bɪə] *n* Serbien *nt*

Serbian ['sə:bɪən] *adj* serbisch ▷ *n* Serbier(in) *m(f)*; (*Ling*) Serbisch *nt*

Serbo-Croat ['sə:bəu'krəuæt] *n* (*Ling*) Serbokroatisch *nt*

serenade [sɛrə'neɪd] *n* Serenade *f* ▷ *vt* ein Ständchen *nt* bringen +*dat*

serene [sɪ'ri:n] *adj* (*landscape etc*) friedlich; (*expression*) heiter; (*person*) gelassen

serenity [sə'rɛnɪtɪ] *n* (*of landscape*) Friedlichkeit *f*; (*of expression*) Gelassenheit *f*

sergeant ['sa:dʒənt] *n* (*Mil etc*) Feldwebel *m*; (*Police*) Polizeimeister *m*

sergeant-major ['sa:dʒənt'meɪdʒəʳ] *n* Oberfeldwebel *m*

serial ['sɪərɪəl] *n* (*TV*) Serie *f*; (*Radio*) Sendereihe *f*; (*in magazine*) Fortsetzungsroman *m* ▷ *adj* (*Comput*) seriell

serialize ['sɪərɪəlaɪz] *vt* in Fortsetzungen veröffentlichen; (*TV, Radio*) in Fortsetzungen senden

serial killer *n* Serienmörder(in) *m(f)*

serial number *n* Seriennummer *f*

series ['sɪərɪz] *n inv* (*group*) Serie *f*, Reihe *f*; (*of books*) Reihe *f*; (*TV*) Serie *f*

serious ['sɪərɪəs] *adj* ernst; (*important*) wichtig; (*: illness*) schwer; (*: condition*) bedenklich; **are you ~ (about it)?** meinst du das ernst?

seriously ['sɪərɪəslɪ] *adv* ernst; (*talk, interested*) ernsthaft; (*ill, hurt, damaged*) schwer; (*not jokingly*) im Ernst; **to take sb/sth ~** jdn/etw ernst nehmen; **do you ~ believe that ...** glauben Sie ernsthaft *or* im Ernst, dass ...

seriousness ['sɪərɪəsnɪs] *n* Ernst *m*, Ernsthaftigkeit *f*; (*of problem*) Bedenklichkeit *f*

sermon ['sə:mən] *n* Predigt *f*; (*fig*) Moralpredigt *f*

serrated [sɪ'reɪtɪd] *adj* gezackt; **~ knife** Sägemesser *nt*

serum ['sɪərəm] *n* Serum *nt*

servant ['sə:vənt] *n* (*lit, fig*) Diener(in) *m(f)*; (*domestic*) Hausangestellte(r) *f(m)*

serve [sə:v] *vt* dienen +*dat*; (*in shop, with food/drink*) bedienen; (*food, meal*) servieren; (*purpose*) haben; (*apprenticeship*) durchmachen; (*prison term*) verbüßen ▷ *vi* (*at table*) auftragen, servieren; (*Tennis*) aufschlagen; (*soldier*) dienen; (*be useful*): **to ~ as/for** dienen als ▷ *n* (*Tennis*) Aufschlag *m*; **are you being ~d?** werden Sie schon bedient?; **to ~ its purpose** seinen Zweck erfüllen; **to ~ sb's purpose** jds Zwecken dienen; **it ~s him right** das geschieht ihm recht; **to ~ on a committee** einem Ausschuss angehören; **to ~ on a jury** Geschworene(r) *f(m)* sein; **it's my turn to ~** (*Tennis*) ich habe Aufschlag; **it ~s to show/explain ...** das zeigt/erklärt ...

▸ **serve out** *vt* (*food*) auftragen, servieren

▸ **serve up** *vt* = **serve out**

service ['sə:vɪs] *n* Dienst *m*; (*commercial*) Dienstleistung *f*; (*in hotel, restaurant*) Bedienung *f*, Service *m*; (*also:* **train service**) Bahnverbindung *f*; (*: generally*) Zugverkehr *m*; (*Rel*) Gottesdienst *m*; (*Aut*) Inspektion *f*; (*Tennis*) Aufschlag *m*; (*plates etc*) Service *nt* ▷ *vt* (*car, machine*) warten; **the Services** *npl* (*army, navy etc*) die Streitkräfte *pl*; **military/national ~** Militärdienst *m*; **to be of ~ to sb** jdm nützen; **to do sb a ~** jdm einen Dienst erweisen; **to put one's car in for a ~** sein Auto zur Inspektion geben; **dinner ~** Essservice *nt*

serviceable ['sə:vɪsəbl] *adj* zweckmäßig

S

773

service area n (on motorway) Raststätte f
service charge (Brit) n Bedienungsgeld nt
service contract n Wartungsvertrag m
service industry n Dienstleistungsbranche f
serviceman ['sɜːvɪsmən] (irreg: like **man**) n Militärangehörige(r) m
service station n Tankstelle f
serviette [sɜːvɪˈɛt] (Brit) n Serviette f
servile ['sɜːvaɪl] adj unterwürfig
session ['sɛʃən] n Sitzung f; (US, Scot: Scol) Studienjahr nt; (: term) Semester nt; **recording ~** Aufnahme f; **to be in ~** tagen
session musician n Session-Musiker(in) m(f)
set [sɛt] (pt, pp **~**) n (of saucepans, books, keys etc) Satz m; (group) Reihe f; (of cutlery) Garnitur f; (: also: **radio set**) Radio(gerät) nt; (also: **TV set**) Fernsehgerät nt; (Tennis) Satz m; (group of people) Kreis m; (Math) Menge f; (Theat: stage) Bühne f; (: scenery) Bühnenbild nt; (Cine) Drehort m; (Hairdressing) (Ein)legen nt ▷ adj (fixed) fest; (ready) fertig, bereit ▷ vt (table) decken; (place) auflegen; (time, price, rules etc) festsetzen; (record) aufstellen; (alarm, watch, task) stellen; (exam) zusammenstellen; (Typ) setzen ▷ vi (sun) untergehen; (jam, jelly, concrete) fest werden; (bone) zusammenwachsen; **a ~ of false teeth** ein Gebiss nt; **a ~ of dining-room furniture** eine Esszimmergarnitur; **a chess ~** ein Schachspiel nt; **to be ~ on doing sth** etw unbedingt tun wollen; **to be all ~ to do sth** bereit sein, etw zu tun; **he's ~ in his ways** er ist in seinen Gewohnheiten festgefahren; **a ~ phrase** eine feste Redewendung; **a novel ~ in Rome** ein Roman, der in Rom spielt; **to ~ to music** vertonen; **to ~ on fire** anstecken; **to ~ free** freilassen; **to ~ sail** losfahren

▶ **set about** vt fus (task) anpacken; **to ~ about doing sth** sich daranmachen, etw zu tun
▶ **set aside** vt (money etc) beiseitelegen; (time) einplanen
▶ **set back** vt: **to ~ sb back 5 pounds** jdn 5 Pfund kosten; **to ~ sb back (by)** (in time) jdn zurückwerfen (um); **a house ~ back from the road** ein Haus, das etwas von der Straße abliegt
▶ **set in** vi (bad weather) einsetzen; (infection) sich einstellen; **the rain has ~ in for the day** es hat sich für heute eingeregnet
▶ **set off** vi (depart) aufbrechen ▷ vt (bomb) losgehen lassen; (alarm, chain of events) auslösen; (show up well) hervorheben
▶ **set out** vi (depart) aufbrechen ▷ vt (goods etc) ausbreiten; (chairs etc) aufstellen; (arguments) darlegen; **to ~ out to do sth** sich dat vornehmen, etw zu tun; **to ~ out from home** zu Hause aufbrechen
▶ **set up** vt (organization) gründen; (monument) errichten; **to ~ up shop** ein Geschäft eröffnen; (fig) sich selb(st)ständig machen
setback ['sɛtbæk] n Rückschlag m
set menu n Menü nt
set square n Zeichendreieck nt
settee [sɛˈtiː] n Sofa nt

setting ['sɛtɪŋ] n (background) Rahmen m; (position) Einstellung f; (of jewel) Fassung f
setting lotion n (Haar)festiger m
settle ['sɛtl] vt (matter) regeln; (argument) beilegen; (accounts) begleichen; (affairs, business) in Ordnung bringen; (colonize: land) besiedeln ▷ vi (also: **settle down**) sich niederlassen; (sand, dust etc) sich legen; (sediment) sich setzen; (calm down) sich beruhigen; **to ~ one's stomach** den Magen beruhigen; **that's ~d then!** das ist also abgemacht!; **to ~ down to work** sich an die Arbeit setzen; **to ~ down to watch TV** es sich dat vor dem Fernseher gemütlich machen
▶ **settle for** vt fus sich zufriedengeben mit
▶ **settle in** vi sich einleben; (in job etc) sich eingewöhnen
▶ **settle on** vt fus sich entscheiden für
▶ **settle up** vi: **to ~ up with sb** mit jdm abrechnen
settlement ['sɛtlmənt] n (payment) Begleichung f; (Law) Vergleich m; (agreement) Übereinkunft f; (of conflict) Beilegung f; (village etc) Siedlung f, Niederlassung f; (colonization) Besiedelung f; **in ~ of our account** (Comm) zum Ausgleich unseres Kontos
settler ['sɛtlər] n Siedler(in) m(f)
setup, set-up ['sɛtʌp] n (organization) Organisation f; (system) System nt; (Comput) Setup nt
seven ['sɛvn] num sieben
seventeen [sɛvnˈtiːn] num siebzehn
seventh ['sɛvnθ] num siebte(r, s)
seventy ['sɛvntɪ] num siebzig
sever ['sɛvər] vt durchtrennen; (fig: relations) abbrechen; (: ties) lösen
several ['sɛvərl] adj einige, mehrere ▷ pron einige; **~ of us** einige von uns; **~ times** einige Male, mehrmals
severance ['sɛvərəns] n (of relations) Abbruch m
severance pay n Abfindung f
severe [sɪˈvɪər] adj (damage, shortage) schwer; (pain) stark; (person, expression, dress, winter) streng; (punishment) hart; (climate) rau
severely [sɪˈvɪəlɪ] adv (damage) stark; (punish) hart; (wounded, ill) schwer
severity [sɪˈvɛrɪtɪ] n (gravity: of punishment) Härte f; (: of manner, voice, winter) Strenge f; (: of weather) Rauheit f; (austerity) Strenge f
sew [səu] (pt **~ed**, pp **~n**) vt, vi nähen
▶ **sew up** vt (zusammen)nähen; **it is all ~n up** (fig) es ist unter Dach und Fach
sewage ['suːɪdʒ] n Abwasser nt
sewage works n Kläranlage f
sewer ['suːər] n Abwasserkanal m
sewing ['səuɪŋ] n Nähen nt; (items) Näharbeit f
sewing machine n Nähmaschine f
sewn [səun] pp of **sew**
sex [sɛks] n (gender) Geschlecht nt; (lovemaking) Sex m; **to have ~ with sb** (Geschlechts)verkehr mit jdm haben
sex act n Geschlechtsakt m
sex appeal n Sex-Appeal m
sex education n Sexualerziehung f

sexism ['sɛksɪzəm] n Sexismus m
sexist ['sɛksɪst] adj sexistisch
sex life n Sexualleben nt
sex object n Sexualobjekt nt
sextet [sɛks'tɛt] n Sextett nt
sexual ['sɛksjuəl] adj sexuell; (reproduction) geschlechtlich; (equality) der Geschlechter
sexual assault n Vergewaltigung f
sexual harassment n sexuelle Belästigung f
sexual intercourse n Geschlechtsverkehr m
sexually ['sɛksjuəlɪ] adv sexuell; (segregate) nach Geschlechtern; (discriminate) aufgrund des Geschlechts; (reproduce) geschlechtlich
sexual orientation n sexuelle Orientierung f
sexy ['sɛksɪ] adj sexy; (pictures, underwear) sexy, aufreizend
Seychelles [seɪ'ʃɛl(z)] npl: **the ~** die Seychellen pl
SF n abbr (= science fiction) SF
SG (US) n abbr (Mil, Med) = **Surgeon General**
Sgt abbr (Police, Mil) = **sergeant**
shabbiness ['ʃæbɪnɪs] n Schäbigkeit f
shabby ['ʃæbɪ] adj schäbig
shack [ʃæk] n Hütte f
  ▶ **shack up** (inf) vi: **to ~ up (with sb)** (mit jdm) zusammenziehen
shackles ['ʃæklz] npl Ketten pl; (fig) Fesseln pl
shade [ʃeɪd] n Schatten m; (for lamp) (Lampen)schirm m; (of colour) (Farb)ton m; (US: also: **window shade**) Jalousie f, Rollo nt ▷ vt beschatten; (eyes) abschirmen; **shades** npl (inf: sunglasses) Sonnenbrille f; **in the ~** im Schatten; **a ~ of blue** ein Blauton; **a ~ (more/too large)** (small quantity) etwas or eine Spur (mehr/zu groß)
shadow ['ʃædəu] n Schatten m ▷ vt (follow) beschatten; **without** or **beyond a ~ of a doubt** ohne den geringsten Zweifel
shadow cabinet (Brit) n Schattenkabinett nt
shadow economy n (Econ) Schattenwirtschaft f
shadowy ['ʃædəuɪ] adj schattig; (figure, shape) schattenhaft
shady ['ʃeɪdɪ] adj schattig; (fig: dishonest) zwielichtig; **~ deals** dunkle Geschäfte
shaft [ʃɑːft] n (of arrow, spear) Schaft m; (Aut, Tech) Welle f; (of mine, lift) Schacht m; (of light) Strahl m; **ventilation ~** Luftschacht m
shaggy ['ʃægɪ] adj zottelig; (dog, sheep) struppig
shake [ʃeɪk] (pt **shook**, pp ~**n**) vt schütteln; (weaken, upset, surprise) erschüttern; (weaken: resolve) ins Wanken bringen ▷ vi zittern, beben; (building, table) wackeln; (earth) beben ▷ n Schütteln nt; **to ~ one's head** den Kopf schütteln; **to ~ hands with sb** jdm die Hand schütteln; **to ~ one's fist (at sb)** (jdm) mit der Faust drohen; **give it a good ~** schütteln Sie es gut durch; **a ~ of the head** ein Kopfschütteln
  ▶ **shake off** vt (lit, fig) abschütteln
  ▶ **shake up** vt schütteln; (fig: upset) erschüttern
shake-out ['ʃeɪkaut] n Freisetzung f von Arbeitskräften

shake-up ['ʃeɪkʌp] n (radikale) Veränderung f
shakily ['ʃeɪkɪlɪ] adv (reply) mit zittriger Stimme; (walk, stand) unsicher, wackelig
shaky ['ʃeɪkɪ] adj (hand, voice) zittrig; (memory) schwach; (knowledge, prospects, future, start) unsicher
shale [ʃeɪl] n Schiefer m
shall [ʃæl] aux vb: **I ~ go** ich werde gehen; **~ I open the door?** soll ich die Tür öffnen?; **I'll go, ~ I?** soll ich gehen?
shallot [ʃə'lɔt] (Brit) n Schalotte f
shallow ['ʃæləu] adj flach; (fig) oberflächlich; **the shallows** npl die Untiefen pl
sham [ʃæm] n Heuchelei f; (person) Heuchler(in) m(f); (object) Attrappe f ▷ adj unecht; (fight) Schein- ▷ vt vortäuschen
shambles ['ʃæmblz] n heilloses Durcheinander nt; **the economy is (in) a complete ~** die Wirtschaft befindet sich in einem totalen Chaos
shambolic [ʃæm'bɔlɪk] (inf) adj chaotisch
shame [ʃeɪm] n Scham f; (disgrace) Schande f ▷ vt beschämen; **it is a ~ that ...** es ist eine Schande, dass ...; **what a ~!** wie schade!; **to bring ~ on** Schande bringen über +acc; **to put sb/sth to ~** jdn/etw in den Schatten stellen
shamefaced ['ʃeɪmfeɪst] adj betreten
shameful ['ʃeɪmful] adj schändlich
shameless ['ʃeɪmlɪs] adj schamlos
shampoo [ʃæm'puː] n Shampoo(n) nt ▷ vt waschen
shampoo and set n Waschen und Legen nt
shamrock ['ʃæmrɔk] n (plant) Klee m; (leaf) Kleeblatt nt
shandy ['ʃændɪ] n Bier nt mit Limonade, Radler m
shan't [ʃɑːnt] = **shall not**
shantytown ['ʃæntɪtaun] n Elendsviertel nt
SHAPE [ʃeɪp] n abbr (Mil: = Supreme Headquarters Allied Powers, Europe) Hauptquartier der alliierten Streitkräfte in Europa während des 2. Weltkriegs
shape [ʃeɪp] n Form f ▷ vt gestalten; (form) formen; (sb's ideas) prägen; (sb's life) bestimmen; **to take ~** Gestalt annehmen; **in the ~ of a heart** in Herzform; **I can't bear gardening in any ~ or form** ich kann Gartenarbeit absolut nicht ausstehen; **to get (o.s.) into ~** in Form kommen
  ▶ **shape up** vi sich entwickeln
-shaped [ʃeɪpt] suff: **heart~** herzförmig
shapeless ['ʃeɪplɪs] adj formlos
shapely ['ʃeɪplɪ] adj (woman) wohlproportioniert; (legs) wohlgeformt
share [ʃɛəʳ] n (part) Anteil m; (contribution) Teil m; (Comm) Aktie f ▷ vt teilen; (room, bed, taxi) sich dat teilen; (have in common) gemeinsam haben; **to ~ in** (joy, sorrow) teilen; (profits) beteiligt sein an +dat; (work) sich beteiligen an +dat
  ▶ **share out** vt aufteilen
share capital n Aktienkapital nt
share certificate n Aktienurkunde f
shareholder ['ʃɛəhəuldəʳ] n Aktionär(in) m(f)
share index n Aktienindex m; **the 100 Share**

S

Index *Aktienindex der Financial Times*

share issue n Aktienemission f

shark [ʃɑːk] n Hai(fisch) m

sharp [ʃɑːp] adj scharf; (point, nose, chin) spitz; (pain) heftig; (cold) schneidend; (Mus) zu hoch; (increase) stark; (person: quick-witted) clever; (: dishonest) gerissen ▷ n (Mus) Kreuz nt ▷ adv: **at 2 o'clock** ~ um Punkt 2 Uhr; **turn** ~ **left** biegen Sie scharf nach links ab; **to be** ~ **with sb** schroff mit jdm sein; ~ **practices** (Comm) unsaubere Geschäfte pl; **C** ~ (Mus) Cis nt; **look** ~**!** (ein bisschen) dalli! (inf)

sharpen [ʃɑːpn] vt schleifen, schärfen; (pencil, stick etc) (an)spitzen; (fig: appetite) anregen

sharpener [ʃɑːpnəʳ] n (also: **pencil sharpener**) (Bleistift)spitzer m; (also: **knife sharpener**) Schleifgerät nt

sharp-eyed [ʃɑːpˈaɪd] adj scharfsichtig

sharpish [ʃɑːpɪʃ] (inf) adj (instantly) auf der Stelle

sharply [ʃɑːplɪ] adv scharf; (stop) plötzlich; (retort) schroff

sharp-tempered [ʃɑːpˈtɛmpəd] adj jähzornig

sharp-witted [ʃɑːpˈwɪtɪd] adj scharfsinnig

shatter [ʃætəʳ] vt zertrümmern; (fig: hopes, dreams) zunichtemachen; (: confidence) zerstören ▷ vi zerbrechen, zerspringen

shattered [ʃætəd] adj erschüttert; (inf: exhausted) fertig, kaputt

shattering [ʃætərɪŋ] adj erschütternd, niederschmetternd; (exhausting) äußerst anstrengend

shatterproof [ʃætəpruːf] adj splitterfest, splitterfrei

shave [ʃeɪv] vt rasieren ▷ vi sich rasieren ▷ n: **to have a** ~ sich rasieren

shaven [ʃeɪvn] adj (head) kahl geschoren

shaver [ʃeɪvəʳ] n (also: **electric shaver**) Rasierapparat m

shaving [ʃeɪvɪŋ] n Rasieren nt; **shavings** npl (of wood etc) Späne pl

shaving brush n Rasierpinsel m

shaving cream n Rasiercreme f

shaving foam n Rasierschaum m

shaving point n Steckdose f für Rasierapparate

shaving soap n Rasierseife f

shawl [ʃɔːl] n (Woll)tuch nt

she [ʃiː] pron sie ▷ pref weiblich; ~**-bear** Bärin f; **there** ~ **is** da ist sie

sheaf [ʃiːf] (pl **sheaves**) n (of corn) Garbe f; (of papers) Bündel nt

shear [ʃɪəʳ] (pt ~**ed**, pp **shorn**) vt scheren ▶ **shear off** vi abbrechen

shears [ʃɪəz] npl (for hedge) Heckenschere f

sheath [ʃiːθ] n (of knife) Scheide f; (contraceptive) Kondom nt

sheathe [ʃiːð] vt ummanteln; (sword) in die Scheide stecken

sheath knife n Fahrtenmesser nt

sheaves [ʃiːvz] npl of **sheaf**

shed [ʃed] (pt, pp ~) n Schuppen m; (Industry, Rail) Halle f ▷ vt (tears, blood) vergießen; (load) verlieren; (workers) entlassen; **to** ~ **its skin**

sich häuten; **to** ~ **light on** (problem) erhellen

she'd [ʃiːd] = **she had; she would**

sheen [ʃiːn] n Glanz m

sheep [ʃiːp] n inv Schaf nt

sheepdog [ʃiːpdɒg] n Hütehund m

sheep farmer n Schaffarmer m

sheepish [ʃiːpɪʃ] adj verlegen

sheepskin [ʃiːpskɪn] n Schaffell nt ▷ cpd Schaffell-

sheer [ʃɪəʳ] adj (utter) rein; (steep) steil; (almost transparent) (hauch)dünn ▷ adv (straight up) senkrecht; **by** ~ **chance** rein zufällig

sheet [ʃiːt] n (on bed) (Bett)laken nt; (of paper) Blatt nt; (of glass, metal) Platte f; (of ice) Fläche f

sheet feed n (on printer) Papiereinzug m

sheet lightning n Wetterleuchten nt

sheet metal n Walzblech nt

sheet music n Notenblätter pl

sheik, sheikh [ʃeɪk] n Scheich m

shelf [ʃelf] (pl **shelves**) n Brett nt, Bord nt; **set of shelves** Regal nt

shelf life n Lagerfähigkeit f

shell [ʃel] n (on beach) Muschel f; (of egg, nut etc) Schale f; (explosive) Granate f; (of building) Mauern pl ▷ vt (peas) enthülsen; (Mil: fire on) (mit Granaten) beschießen ▶ **shell out** (inf) vt: **to** ~ **out (for)** blechen (für)

she'll [ʃiːl] = **she will; she shall**

shellfish [ʃelfɪʃ] n inv Schalentier nt; (scallop etc) Muschel f; (as food) Meeresfrüchte pl

shelter [ʃeltəʳ] n (building) Unterstand m; (refuge) Schutz m; (also: **bus shelter**) Wartehäuschen nt; (also: **night shelter**) Obdachlosenasyl nt ▷ vt (protect) schützen; (homeless, refugees) aufnehmen; (wanted man) Unterschlupf gewähren +dat ▷ vi sich unterstellen; (from storm) Schutz suchen; **to take** ~ **(from)** (from danger) sich in Sicherheit bringen (vor +dat); (from storm etc) Schutz suchen (vor +dat)

sheltered [ʃeltəd] adj (life) behütet; (spot) geschützt; ~ **housing** (for old people) Altenwohnungen pl; (for handicapped people) Behindertenwohnungen pl

shelve [ʃelv] vt (fig: plan) ad acta legen

shelves [ʃelvz] npl of **shelf**

shelving [ʃelvɪŋ] n Regale pl

shepherd [ʃepəd] n Schäfer m ▷ vt (guide) führen

shepherdess [ʃepədɪs] n Schäferin f

shepherd's pie (Brit) n Auflauf aus Hackfleisch und Kartoffelbrei

sherbet [ʃəːbət] n (Brit: powder) Brausepulver nt; (US: water ice) Fruchteis nt

sheriff [ʃerɪf] (US) n Sheriff m

sherry [ʃerɪ] n Sherry m

she's [ʃiːz] = **she is; she has**

Shetland [ʃetlənd] n (also: **the Shetland Islands**) die Shetlandinseln pl

Shetland pony n Shetlandpony nt

shield [ʃiːld] n (Mil) Schild m; (trophy) Trophäe f; (fig: protection) Schutz m ▷ vt: **to** ~ **(from)** schützen (vor +dat)

shift [ʃɪft] n (change) Änderung f; (work-

period, workers) Schicht f ▷ vt (move)
bewegen; (furniture) (ver)rücken; (stain)
herausbekommen ▷ vi (move) sich bewegen;
(wind) drehen; **a ~ in demand** (Comm) eine
Nachfrageverschiebung

shift key n Umschalttaste f

shiftless ['ʃɪftlɪs] adj träge

shift work n Schichtarbeit f; **to do ~** Schicht
arbeiten

shifty ['ʃɪftɪ] adj verschlagen

Shiite ['ʃiːaɪt] adj schiitisch ▷ n Schiit(in)
m(f)

shilling ['ʃɪlɪŋ] (Brit: old) n Shilling m

shilly-shally ['ʃɪlɪʃælɪ] vi unschlüssig sein

shimmer ['ʃɪmə'] vi schimmern

shimmering ['ʃɪmərɪŋ] adj schimmernd

shin [ʃɪn] n Schienbein nt ▷ vi: **to ~ up a tree**
einen Baum hinaufklettern

shindig ['ʃɪndɪg] (inf) n Remmidemmi nt

shine [ʃaɪn] (pt, pp **shone**) n Glanz m ▷ vi (sun,
light) scheinen; (eyes) leuchten; (hair: fig: person)
glänzen ▷ vt (polish: pt, pp shined) polieren; **to ~
a torch on sth** etw mit einer Taschenlampe
anleuchten

shingle ['ʃɪŋgl] n (on beach) Kiesel(steine) pl; (on
roof) Schindel f

shingles ['ʃɪŋglz] npl (Med) Gürtelrose f

shining ['ʃaɪnɪŋ] adj glänzend; (example)
leuchtend

shiny ['ʃaɪnɪ] adj glänzend

ship [ʃɪp] n Schiff nt ▷ vt verschiffen; (send)
versenden; (water) übernehmen; **on board ~**
an Bord

shipbuilder ['ʃɪpbɪldə'] n Schiffbauer m

shipbuilding ['ʃɪpbɪldɪŋ] n Schiffbau m

ship canal n Seekanal m

ship chandler [-'tʃɑːndlə'] n Schiffsausrüster m

shipment ['ʃɪpmənt] n (of goods) Versand m;
(amount) Sendung f

shipowner ['ʃɪpəunə'] n Schiffseigner m; (of
many ships) Reeder m

shipper ['ʃɪpə'] n (person) Spediteur m; (company)
Spedition f

shipping ['ʃɪpɪŋ] n (transport) Versand m; (ships)
Schiffe pl

shipping agent n Reeder m

shipping company n Schifffahrtslinie f,
Reederei f

shipping lane n Schifffahrtsstraße f

shipping line n = **shipping company**

shipshape ['ʃɪpʃeɪp] adj tipptopp (inf)

shipwreck ['ʃɪprɛk] n Schiffbruch m; (ship)
Wrack nt ▷ vt: **to be ~ed** schiffbrüchig sein

shipyard ['ʃɪpjɑːd] n Werft f

shire ['ʃaɪə'] (Brit) n Grafschaft f

shirk [ʃəːk] vt sich drücken vor +dat

shirt [ʃəːt] n (Ober)hemd nt; (woman's) (Hemd)
bluse f; **in (one's) ~ sleeves** in Hemdsärmeln

shirty ['ʃəːtɪ] (Brit: inf) adj sauer (inf)

shit [ʃɪt] (inf!) excl Scheiße (!)

shiver ['ʃɪvə'] n Schauer m ▷ vi zittern; **to ~
with cold** vor Kälte zittern

shoal [ʃəul] n (of fish) Schwarm m;

(also: **shoals**: fig) Scharen pl

shock [ʃɒk] n Schock m; (impact) Erschütterung
f; (also: **electric shock**) Schlag m ▷ vt (upset)
erschüttern; (offend) schockieren; **to be
suffering from ~** (Med) einen Schock haben;
to be in ~ unter Schock stehen; **it gave us a ~**
es hat uns erschreckt; **it came as a ~ to hear
that ...** wir hörten mit Bestürzung, dass ...

shock absorber n (Aut) Stoßdämpfer m

shocker ['ʃɒkə'] (inf) n (film etc) Schocker m,
Reißer m; **that's a real ~** (event etc) das haut
einen echt um

shocking ['ʃɒkɪŋ] adj schrecklich, fürchterlich;
(outrageous) schockierend

shockproof ['ʃɒkpruːf] adj stoßfest

shock therapy n Schocktherapie f

shock treatment n = **shock therapy**

shock wave n (lit) Druckwelle f; (fig)
Schockwelle f

shod [ʃɒd] pt, pp of **shoe**

shoddy ['ʃɒdɪ] adj minderwertig

shoe [ʃuː] (pt, pp **shod**) n Schuh m; (for horse)
Hufeisen nt; (also: **brake shoe**) Bremsbacke f
▷ vt (horse) beschlagen

shoebrush ['ʃuːbrʌʃ] n Schuhbürste f

shoehorn ['ʃuːhɔːn] n Schuhanzieher m

shoelace ['ʃuːleɪs] n Schnürsenkel m

shoemaker ['ʃuːmeɪkə'] n Schuhmacher m,
Schuster m

shoe polish n Schuhcreme f

shoe shop n Schuhgeschäft nt

shoestring ['ʃuːstrɪŋ] n (fig): **on a ~** mit ganz
wenig Geld

shoetree ['ʃuːtriː] n Schuhspanner m

shone [ʃɒn] pt, pp of **shine**

shoo [ʃuː] excl (to dog etc) pfui ▷ vt (also: **shoo
away, shoo off,** etc) verscheuchen; (somewhere)
scheuchen

shook [ʃuk] pt of **shake**

shoot [ʃuːt] (pt, pp **shot**) n (on branch) Trieb m;
(seedling) Sämling m; (Sport) Jagd f ▷ vt (gun)
abfeuern; (arrow, goal) schießen; (kill, execute)
erschießen; (wound) anschießen; (Brit: game
birds) schießen; (film) drehen ▷ vi: **to ~ (at)**
schießen (auf +acc); **to ~ past (sb/sth)** (an
jdm/etw) vorbeischießen
  ▶ **shoot down** vt abschießen
  ▶ **shoot in** vi hereingeschossen kommen
  ▶ **shoot out (of)** vi herausgeschossen
  kommen (aus +dat)
  ▶ **shoot up** vi (fig: increase) in die Höhe
  schnellen

shooting ['ʃuːtɪŋ] n Schießen nt, Schüsse pl;
(attack) Schießerei f; (murder) Erschießung f;
(Cine) Drehen nt; (Hunting) Jagen nt

shooting range n Schießplatz m

shooting star n Sternschnuppe f

shop [ʃɒp] n Geschäft nt, Laden m; (workshop)
Werkstatt f ▷ vi (also: **go shopping**) einkaufen
(gehen); **repair ~** Reparaturwerkstatt f; **to
talk ~** (fig) über die Arbeit reden
  ▶ **shop around** vi Preise vergleichen; (fig) sich
  umsehen

S

shopaholic ['ʃɒpə'hɒlɪk] (inf) n: **to be a ~** einen Einkaufsfimmel haben

shop assistant (Brit) n Verkäufer(in) m(f)

shop floor (Brit) n (workers) Arbeiter pl; **on the ~** bei or unter den Arbeitern

shopkeeper ['ʃɒpkiːpəʳ] n Geschäftsinhaber(in) m(f), Ladenbesitzer(in) m(f)

shoplifter ['ʃɒplɪftəʳ] n Ladendieb(in) m(f)

shoplifting ['ʃɒplɪftɪŋ] n Ladendiebstahl m

shopper ['ʃɒpəʳ] n Käufer(in) m(f)

shopping ['ʃɒpɪŋ] n (goods) Einkäufe pl

shopping bag n Einkaufstasche f

shopping centre, (US) **shopping center** n Einkaufszentrum nt

shopping mall n Shoppingcenter nt

shop-soiled ['ʃɒpsɔɪld] adj angeschmutzt

shop steward (Brit) n gewerkschaftlicher Vertrauensmann m

shop window n Schaufenster nt

shore [ʃɔːʳ] n Ufer nt; (beach) Strand m ▷ vt: **to ~ (up)** abstützen; **on ~** an Land

shore leave n (Naut) Landurlaub m

shorn [ʃɔːn] pp of **shear**; **to be ~ of** (power etc) entkleidet sein +gen

short [ʃɔːt] adj kurz; (person) klein; (curt) schroff, kurz angebunden (inf); (scarce) knapp ▷ n (also: **short film**) Kurzfilm m; **to be ~ of ...** zu wenig ... haben; **I'm 3 ~** ich habe 3 zu wenig, mir fehlen 3; **in ~** kurz gesagt; **to be in ~ supply** knapp sein; **it is ~ for ...** es ist die Kurzform von ...; **a ~ time ago** vor Kurzem; **in the ~ term** auf kurze Sicht; **~ of doing sth** außer etw zu tun; **to cut ~** abbrechen; **everything ~ of ...** alles außer ... +dat; **to fall ~ of sth** etw nicht erreichen; (expectations) etw nicht erfüllen; **to run ~ of ...** nicht mehr viel ... haben; **to stop ~** plötzlich innehalten; **to stop ~ of** haltmachen vor +dat; see also **shorts**

shortage ['ʃɔːtɪdʒ] n: **a ~ of** ein Mangel m an +dat

shortbread ['ʃɔːtbrɛd] n Mürbegebäck nt

short-change [ʃɔːt'tʃeɪndʒ] vt: **to ~ sb** jdm zu wenig Wechselgeld geben

short circuit n Kurzschluss m

shortcoming ['ʃɔːtkʌmɪŋ] n Fehler m, Mangel m

shortcrust pastry (Brit) n Mürbeteig m

short cut n Abkürzung f; (fig) Schnellverfahren nt

shorten ['ʃɔːtn] vt verkürzen

shortening ['ʃɔːtnɪŋ] n (Back)fett nt

shortfall ['ʃɔːtfɔːl] n Defizit nt

shorthand ['ʃɔːthænd] n Kurzschrift f, Stenografie f; (fig) Kurzform f; **to take sth down in ~** etw stenografieren

shorthand notebook (Brit) n Stenoblock m

shorthand typist (Brit) n Stenotypist(in) m(f)

short list (Brit) n Auswahlliste f; **to be on the ~** in der engeren Wahl sein

short-list ['ʃɔːtlɪst] (Brit) vt in die engere Wahl ziehen; **to be ~ed** in die engere Wahl kommen

short-lived ['ʃɔːt'lɪvd] adj kurzlebig; **to be ~** nicht von Dauer sein

shortly ['ʃɔːtlɪ] adv bald

shorts [ʃɔːts] npl: **(a pair of) ~** Shorts pl

short-sighted [ʃɔːt'saɪtɪd] (Brit) adj (lit, fig) kurzsichtig

short-sightedness [ʃɔːt'saɪtɪdnɪs] n Kurzsichtigkeit f

short-staffed [ʃɔːt'staːft] adj: **to be ~** zu wenig Personal haben

short story n Kurzgeschichte f

short-tempered [ʃɔːt'tɛmpəd] adj gereizt

short-term ['ʃɔːttəːm] adj kurzfristig

short time n: **to work ~, to be on ~** kurzarbeiten, Kurzarbeit haben

short-wave ['ʃɔːtweɪv] (Radio) adj auf Kurzwelle ▷ n Kurzwelle f

shot [ʃɒt] pt, pp of **shoot** ▷ n Schuss m; (shotgun pellets) Schrot m; (injection) Spritze f; (Phot) Aufnahme f; **to fire a ~ at sb/sth** einen Schuss auf jdn/etw abgeben; **to have a ~ at (doing) sth** etw mal versuchen; **to get ~ of sb/sth** (inf) jdn/etw loswerden; **a big ~** (inf) ein hohes Tier; **a good/poor ~** (person) ein guter/schlechter Schütze; **like a ~** sofort

shotgun ['ʃɒtɡʌn] n Schrotflinte f

should [ʃʊd] aux vb: **I ~ go now** ich sollte jetzt gehen; **he ~ be there now** er müsste eigentlich schon da sein; **I ~ go if I were you** an deiner Stelle würde ich gehen; **I ~ like to** ich möchte gerne, ich würde gerne; **~ he phone ...** falls er anruft ...

shoulder ['ʃəʊldəʳ] n Schulter f ▷ vt (fig) auf sich acc nehmen; **to rub ~s with sb** (fig) mit jdm in Berührung kommen; **to give sb the cold ~** (fig) jdm die kalte Schulter zeigen

shoulder bag n Umhängetasche f

shoulder blade n Schulterblatt nt

shoulder strap n (on clothing) Träger m; (on bag) Schulterriemen m

shouldn't ['ʃʊdnt] = **should not**

shout [ʃaʊt] n Schrei m, Ruf m ▷ vt schreien, rufen ▷ vi (also: **shout out**) aufschreien; **to give sb a ~** jdn rufen

▶ **shout down** vt niederbrüllen

shouting ['ʃaʊtɪŋ] n Geschrei nt

shouting match (inf) n: **to have a ~** sich gegenseitig anschreien

shove [ʃʌv] vt schieben; (with one push) stoßen, schubsen (inf) ▷ n: **to give sb a ~** jdn stoßen or schubsen (inf); **to give sth a ~** etw verrücken; (door) gegen etw stoßen; **to ~ sth in sth** (inf: put) etw in etw acc stecken; **he ~d me out of the way** er stieß mich zur Seite

▶ **shove off** (inf) vi abschieben

shovel ['ʃʌvl] n Schaufel f; (mechanical) Bagger m ▷ vt schaufeln

show [ʃəʊ] (pt **~ed**, pp **~n**) n (exhibition) Ausstellung f, Schau f; (Theat) Aufführung f; (TV) Show f; (Cine) Vorstellung f ▷ vt zeigen; (exhibit) ausstellen ▷ vi: **it ~s** man sieht es; (is evident) man merkt es; **to ask for a ~ of hands** um Handzeichen bitten; **without any ~ of**

emotion ohne jede Gefühlsregung; **it's just
for ~** es ist nur zur Schau; **on ~** ausgestellt,
zu sehen; **who's running the ~ here?** (*inf*)
wer ist hier verantwortlich?; **to ~ sb to his
seat/to the door** jdn an seinen Platz/zur Tür
bringen; **to ~ a profit/loss** Gewinn/Verlust
aufweisen; **it just goes to ~ that ...** da sieht
mans mal wieder, dass
▶ **show in** *vt* hereinführen
▶ **show off** (*pej*) *vi* angeben ▷ *vt* vorführen
▶ **show out** *vt* hinausbegleiten
▶ **show up** *vi* (*stand out*) sich abheben;
(*inf: turn up*) auftauchen ▷ *vt* (*uncover*) deutlich
erkennen lassen; (*shame*) blamieren
showbiz *n* = **show business**
show business *n* Showgeschäft *nt*
showcase ['ʃəʊkeɪs] *n* Schaukasten *m*; (*fig*)
Werbung *f*
showdown ['ʃəʊdaʊn] *n* Kraftprobe *f*
shower ['ʃaʊə^r] *n* (*of rain*) Schauer *m*; (*of stones
etc*) Hagel *m*; (*for bathing in*) Dusche *f*; (*US: party*)
Party, bei der jeder an seinen Geschenk für den Ehrengast
mitbringt ▷ *vi* duschen ▷ *vt*: **to ~ sb with** (*gifts
etc*) jdn überschütten mit; (*missiles, abuse etc*)
auf jdn niederhageln lassen; **to have** *or* **take
a ~** duschen; **a ~ of sparks** ein Funkenregen *m*
showercap ['ʃaʊəkæp] *n* Duschhaube *f*
showergel *n* Duschgel *nt*
showerproof ['ʃaʊəpruːf] *adj* regenfest
showery ['ʃaʊərɪ] *adj* regnerisch
showground ['ʃəʊgraʊnd] *n*
Ausstellungsgelände *nt*
showing ['ʃəʊɪŋ] *n* (*of film*) Vorführung *f*
show jumping *n* Springreiten *nt*
showman ['ʃəʊmən] (*irreg: like* **man**) *n* (*at
fair*) Schausteller *m*; (*at circus*) Artist *m*; (*fig*)
Schauspieler *m*
showmanship ['ʃəʊmənʃɪp] *n* Talent *nt* für
effektvolle Darbietung
shown [ʃəʊn] *pp of* **show**
show-off ['ʃəʊɔf] (*inf*) *n* Angeber(in) *m(f)*
showpiece ['ʃəʊpiːs] *n* (*of exhibition etc*)
Schaustück *nt*; (*best example*) Paradestück *nt*;
(*prime example*) Musterbeispiel *nt*
showroom ['ʃəʊrʊm] *n* Ausstellungsraum *m*
show trial *n* Schauprozess *m*
showy ['ʃəʊ] *adj* auffallend
shrank [ʃræŋk] *pt of* **shrink**
shrapnel ['ʃræpnl] *n* Schrapnell *nt*
shred [ʃred] *n* (*gen pl*) Fetzen *m*; (*fig*): **not a ~
of truth** kein Fünkchen Wahrheit; **not a ~
of evidence** keine Spur eines Beweises ▷ *vt*
zerfetzen; (*Culin*) raspeln
shredder ['ʃredə^r] *n* (*also*: **vegetable shredder**)
Raspel *f*; (*also*: **document shredder**) Reißwolf
m; (*also*: **garden shredder**) Häcksler *m*
shrew [ʃruː] *n* (*Zool*) Spitzmaus *f*; (*pej: woman*)
Xanthippe *f*
shrewd [ʃruːd] *adj* klug
shrewdness ['ʃruːdnɪs] *n* Klugheit *f*
shriek [ʃriːk] *n* schriller Schrei *m* ▷ *vi* schreien;
to ~ with laughter vor Lachen quietschen
shrift [ʃrɪft] *n*: **to give sb short ~** jdn kurz

abfertigen
shrill [ʃrɪl] *adj* schrill
shrimp [ʃrɪmp] *n* Garnele *f*
shrine [ʃraɪn] *n* Schrein *m*; (*fig*) Gedenkstätte *f*
shrink [ʃrɪŋk] (*pt* **shrank**, *pp* **shrunk**) *vi* (*cloth*)
einlaufen; (*profits, audiences*) schrumpfen;
(*forests*) schwinden; (*also*: **shrink away**)
zurückweichen ▷ *vt* (*cloth*) einlaufen lassen
▷ *n* (*inf: pej*) Klapsdoktor *m*; **to ~ from sth** vor
etw *dat* zurückschrecken; **to ~ from doing
sth** davor zurückschrecken, etw zu tun
shrinkage ['ʃrɪŋkɪdʒ] *n* (*of clothes*) Einlaufen *nt*
shrink-wrap ['ʃrɪŋkræp] *vt* einschweißen
shrivel ['ʃrɪvl] (*also*: **shrivel up**) *vt* austrocknen
▷ *vi* austrocknen, verschrumpeln
shroud [ʃraʊd] *n* Leichentuch *nt* ▷ *vt*: **~ed in
mystery** von einem Geheimnis umgeben
Shrove Tuesday ['ʃrəʊv-] *n*
Fastnachtsdienstag *m*
shrub [ʃrʌb] *n* Strauch *m*, Busch *m*
shrubbery ['ʃrʌbərɪ] *n* Gebüsch *nt*
shrug [ʃrʌg] *n* Achselzucken *nt* ▷ *vi, vt*: **to ~
(one's shoulders)** mit den Achseln zucken
▶ **shrug off** *vt* (*criticism*) auf die leichte Schulter
nehmen; (*illness*) abschütteln
shrunk [ʃrʌŋk] *pp of* **shrink**
shrunken ['ʃrʌŋkn] *adj* (ein)geschrumpft
shudder ['ʃʌdə^r] *n* Schauder *m* ▷ *vi* schaudern;
I ~ to think of it (*fig*) mir graut, wenn ich nur
daran denke
shuffle ['ʃʌfl] *vt* (*cards*) mischen ▷ *vi* schlurfen;
to ~ (one's feet) mit den Füßen scharren
shun [ʃʌn] *vt* meiden; (*publicity*) scheuen
shunt [ʃʌnt] *vt* rangieren
shunting yard ['ʃʌntɪŋ-] *n* Rangierbahnhof *m*
shush [ʃʊʃ] *excl* pst!, sch!
shut [ʃʌt] (*pt, pp ~*) *vt* schließen, zumachen (*inf*)
▷ *vi* sich schließen, zugehen; (*shop*) schließen,
zumachen (*inf*)
▶ **shut down** *vt* (*factory etc*) schließen; (*machine*)
abschalten ▷ *vi* schließen, zumachen (*inf*)
▶ **shut off** *vt* (*gas, electricity*) abstellen; (*oil
supplies etc*) abschneiden
▶ **shut out** *vt* (*person*) aussperren; (*cold, noise*)
nicht hereinlassen; (*view*) versperren; (*memory,
thought*) verdrängen
▶ **shut up** *vi* (*inf: keep quiet*) den Mund halten
▷ *vt* (*silence*) zum Schweigen bringen
shutdown ['ʃʌtdaʊn] *n* Schließung *f*
shutter ['ʃʌtə^r] *n* Fensterladen *m*; (*Phot*)
Verschluss *m*
shuttle ['ʃʌtl] *n* (*plane*) Pendelflugzeug *nt*;
(*train*) Pendelzug *m*; (*also*: **space shuttle**)
Raumtransporter *m*; (*also*: **shuttle service**)
Pendelverkehr *m*; (*for weaving*) Schiffchen
nt ▷ *vi*: **to ~ to and fro** pendeln; **to ~
between** pendeln zwischen ▷ *vt* (*passengers*)
transportieren
shuttlecock ['ʃʌtlkɔk] *n* Federball *m*
shuttle diplomacy *n* Reisediplomatie *f*
shy [ʃaɪ] *adj* schüchtern; (*animal*) scheu
▷ *vi*: **to ~ away from doing sth** (*fig*) davor
zurückschrecken, etw zu tun; **to fight ~ of**

S

779

aus dem Weg gehen +dat; **to be ~ of doing sth**
Hemmungen haben, etw zu tun

shyly ['ʃaɪlɪ] adv schüchtern, scheu

shyness ['ʃaɪnɪs] n Schüchternheit f, Scheu f

Siam [saɪ'æm] n Siam nt

Siamese [saɪə'mi:z] adj: **~ cat** Siamkatze f; **~ twins** siamesische Zwillinge pl

Siberia [saɪ'bɪərɪə] n Sibirien nt

sibling ['sɪblɪŋ] n Geschwister nt

Sicilian [sɪ'sɪlɪən] adj sizilianisch ▷ n Sizilianer(in) m(f)

Sicily ['sɪsɪlɪ] n Sizilien nt

sick [sɪk] adj krank; (humour, joke) makaber; **to be ~** (vomit) brechen, sich übergeben; **I feel ~** mir ist schlecht; **to fall ~** krank werden; **to be (off) ~** wegen Krankheit fehlen; **a ~ person** ein Kranker, eine Kranke; **to be ~ of** (fig) satthaben +acc

sickbag ['sɪkbæg] n Spucktüte f

sickbay ['sɪkbeɪ] n Krankenrevier nt

sickbed ['sɪkbed] n Krankenbett nt

sick building syndrome n Kopfschmerzen, Allergien etc, die in modernen, vollklimatisierten Bürogebäuden entstehen

sicken ['sɪkn] vt (disgust) anwidern ▷ vi: **to be ~ing for a cold/flu** eine Erkältung/Grippe bekommen

sickening ['sɪknɪŋ] adj (fig) widerlich, ekelhaft

sickle ['sɪkl] n Sichel f

sick leave n: **to be on ~** krankgeschrieben sein

sickle-cell anaemia n Sichelzellenanämie f

sick list n: **to be on the ~** auf der Krankenliste stehen

sickly ['sɪklɪ] adj kränklich; (causing nausea) widerlich, ekelhaft

sickness ['sɪknɪs] n Krankheit f; (vomiting) Erbrechen nt

sickness benefit n Krankengeld nt

sick note n Krankmeldung f

sick pay n Lohnfortzahlung f im Krankheitsfall; (paid by insurance) Krankengeld nt

sickroom ['sɪkru:m] n Krankenzimmer nt

side [saɪd] n Seite f; (team) Mannschaft f; (in conflict etc) Partei f, Seite f; (of hill) Hang m ▷ adj (door, entrance) Seiten-, Neben- ▷ vi: **to ~ with sb** jds Partei ergreifen; **by the ~ of** neben +dat; **~ by side** Seite an Seite; **the right/wrong ~** (of cloth) die rechte/linke Seite; **they are on our ~** sie stehen auf unserer Seite; **she never left my ~** sie wich mir nicht von der Seite; **to put sth to one ~** etw beiseitelegen; **from ~ to side** von einer Seite zur anderen; **to take ~s (with)** Partei ergreifen (für); **a ~ of beef** ein halbes Rind; **a ~ of bacon** eine Speckseite

sideboard ['saɪdbɔ:d] n Sideboard nt; **sideboards** (Brit) npl = **sideburns**

sideburns ['saɪdbə:nz] npl Koteletten pl

sidecar ['saɪdkɑ:ʳ] n Beiwagen m

side dish n Beilage f

side drum n kleine Trommel f

side effect n (Med, fig) Nebenwirkung f

sidekick ['saɪdkɪk] (inf) n Handlanger m

sidelight ['saɪdlaɪt] n (Aut) Begrenzungsleuchte f

sideline ['saɪdlaɪn] n (Sport) Seitenlinie f; (fig: job) Nebenerwerb m; **to stand on the ~s** (fig) unbeteiligter Zuschauer sein; **to wait on the ~s** (fig) in den Kulissen warten

sidelong ['saɪdlɔŋ] adj (glance) Seiten-; (: surreptitious) verstohlen; **to give sb a ~ glance** jdn kurz aus den Augenwinkeln ansehen

side plate n kleiner Teller m

side road n Nebenstraße f

side-saddle ['saɪdsædl] adv (ride) im Damensitz

sideshow ['saɪdʃəu] n Nebenattraktion f

sidestep ['saɪdstep] vt (problem) umgehen; (question) ausweichen +dat ▷ vi (Boxing etc) seitwärts ausweichen

side street n Seitenstraße f

sidetrack ['saɪdtræk] vt (fig) ablenken

sidewalk ['saɪdwɔ:k] (US) n Bürgersteig m

sideways ['saɪdweɪz] adv seitwärts; (lean, look) zur Seite

siding ['saɪdɪŋ] n Abstellgleis nt

sidle ['saɪdl] vi: **to ~ up (to)** sich heranschleichen (an +acc)

SIDS n abbr (Med: = sudden infant death syndrome) plötzlicher Kindstod m

siege [si:dʒ] n Belagerung f; **to be under ~** belagert sein; **to lay ~ to** belagern

siege economy n Belagerungswirtschaft f

siege mentality n Belagerungsmentalität f

Sierra Leone [sɪ'erəlɪ'əun] n Sierra Leone f

siesta [sɪ'estə] n Siesta f

sieve [sɪv] n Sieb nt ▷ vt sieben

sift [sɪft] vt sieben; (also: **sift through**) durchgehen

sigh [saɪ] n Seufzer m ▷ vi seufzen; **to breathe a ~ of relief** erleichtert aufseufzen

sight [saɪt] n (faculty) Sehvermögen nt, Augenlicht nt; (spectacle) Anblick m; (on gun) Visier nt ▷ vt sichten; **in ~** in Sicht; **on ~** (shoot) sofort; **out of ~** außer Sicht; **at ~** (Comm) bei Sicht; **at first ~** auf den ersten Blick; **I know her by ~** ich kenne sie vom Sehen; **to catch ~ of sb/sth** jdn/etw sehen; **to lose ~ of sth** (fig) etw aus den Augen verlieren; **to set one's ~s on sth** ein Auge auf etw werfen

sighted ['saɪtɪd] adj sehend; **partially ~** sehbehindert

sightseeing ['saɪtsi:ɪŋ] n Besichtigungen pl; **to go ~** auf Besichtigungstour gehen

sightseer ['saɪtsi:əʳ] n Tourist(in) m(f)

sign [saɪn] n Zeichen nt; (notice) Schild nt; (evidence) Anzeichen nt; (also: **road sign**) Verkehrsschild nt ▷ vt unterschreiben; (player) verpflichten; **a ~ of the times** ein Zeichen unserer Zeit; **it's a good/bad ~** es ist ein gutes/schlechtes Zeichen; **plus/minus ~** Plus-/Minuszeichen nt; **there's no ~ of her changing her mind** nichts deutet darauf hin, dass sie es sich anders überlegen wird; **he was showing ~s of improvement** er ließ Anzeichen einer Verbesserung erkennen; **to ~**

one's name unterschreiben; **to ~ sth over to sb** jdm etw überschreiben

▸ **sign away** vt (rights etc) verzichten auf +acc
▸ **sign in** vi sich eintragen
▸ **sign off** vi (Radio, TV) sich verabschieden; (in letter) Schluss machen
▸ **sign on** vi (Mil) sich verpflichten; (Brit: as unemployed) sich arbeitslos melden; (for course) sich einschreiben ▷ vt (Mil) verpflichten; (employee) anstellen
▸ **sign out** vi (from hotel etc) sich (aus dem Hotelgästebuch etc) austragen
▸ **sign up** vi (Mil) sich verpflichten; (for course) sich einschreiben ▷ vt (player, recruit) verpflichten

signal ['sɪgnl] n Zeichen nt; (Rail) Signal nt ▷ vi (Aut) Zeichen/ein Zeichen geben ▷ vt ein Zeichen geben +dat; **to ~ a right/left turn** (Aut) rechts/links blinken

signal box n Stellwerk nt

signalman ['sɪgnlmən] (irreg: like **man**) n Stellwerkswärter m

signatory ['sɪgnətərɪ] n Unterzeichner m; (state) Signatarstaat m

signature ['sɪgnətʃər] n Unterschrift f; (Zool, Biol) Kennzeichen nt

signature tune n Erkennungsmelodie f

signet ring ['sɪgnət-] n Siegelring m

significance [sɪg'nɪfɪkəns] n Bedeutung f; **that is of no ~** das ist belanglos or bedeutungslos

significant [sɪg'nɪfɪkənt] adj bedeutend, wichtig; (look, smile) vielsagend, bedeutsam; **it is ~ that** ... es ist bezeichnend, dass ...

significantly [sɪg'nɪfɪkəntlɪ] adv bedeutend; (smile) vielsagend, bedeutsam

signify ['sɪgnɪfaɪ] vt bedeuten; (person) zu erkennen geben

sign language n Zeichensprache f

signpost ['saɪnpəust] n (lit, fig) Wegweiser m

Sikh [siːk] n Sikh mf ▷ adj (province etc) Sikh-

silage ['saɪlɪdʒ] n Silage f, Silofutter nt

silence ['saɪləns] n Stille f; (of person) Schweigen nt ▷ vt zum Schweigen bringen; **in ~** still; (not talking) schweigend

silencer ['saɪlənsər] n (on gun) Schalldämpfer m; (Brit: Aut) Auspufftopf m

silent ['saɪlənt] adj still; (machine) ruhig; **~ film** Stummfilm m; **to remain ~** still bleiben; (about sth) sich nicht äußern

silently ['saɪləntlɪ] adv lautlos; (not talking) schweigend

silent partner n stiller Teilhaber m

silhouette [sɪluː'ɛt] n Sihouette f, Umriss m ▷ vt: **to be ~d against sth** sich als Silhouette gegen etw abheben

silicon ['sɪlɪkən] n Silizium nt

silicon chip n Silikonchip m

silicone ['sɪlɪkəun] n Silikon nt

silk [sɪlk] n Seide f ▷ adj (dress etc) Seiden-

silky ['sɪlkɪ] adj seidig

sill [sɪl] n (also: **window sill**) (Fenster)sims m or nt; (of door) Schwelle f; (Aut) Türleiste f

silly ['sɪlɪ] adj (person) dumm; **to do something**

~ etwas Dummes tun

silo ['saɪləu] n Silo nt; (for missile) Raketensilo nt

silt [sɪlt] n Schlamm m, Schlick m
▸ **silt up** vi verschlammen ▷ vt verschlämmen

silver ['sɪlvər] n Silber nt; (coins) Silbergeld nt ▷ adj silbern

silver foil (Brit) n Alufolie f

silver paper (Brit) n Silberpapier nt

silver-plated [sɪlvə'pleɪtɪd] adj versilbert

silversmith ['sɪlvəsmɪθ] n Silberschmied(in) m(f)

silverware ['sɪlvəwɛər] n Silber nt

silver wedding, silver wedding anniversary n Silberhochzeit f

silvery ['sɪlvrɪ] adj silbern; (sound) silberhell

SIM card ['sɪmkɑːd] n (Tel: = Subscriber Identity Module card) SIM-Karte f

similar ['sɪmɪlər] adj: **~ (to)** ähnlich (wie or +dat)

similarity [sɪmɪ'lærɪtɪ] n Ähnlichkeit f

similarly ['sɪmɪləlɪ] adv ähnlich; (likewise) genauso

simile ['sɪmɪlɪ] n (Ling) Vergleich m

simmer ['sɪmər] vi auf kleiner Flamme kochen
▸ **simmer down** (inf) vi (fig) sich abregen

simper ['sɪmpər] vi geziert lächeln

simpering ['sɪmpərɪŋ] adj geziert

simple ['sɪmpl] adj einfach; (dress) einfach, schlicht; (foolish) einfältig; **the ~ truth is that** ... es ist einfach so, dass ...

simple interest n Kapitalzinsen pl

simple-minded [sɪmpl'maɪndɪd] (pej) adj einfältig

simpleton ['sɪmpltən] (pej) n Einfaltspinsel m

simplicity [sɪm'plɪsɪtɪ] n Einfachheit f; (of dress) Schlichtheit f

simplification [sɪmplɪfɪ'keɪʃən] n Vereinfachung f

simplify ['sɪmplɪfaɪ] vt vereinfachen

simply ['sɪmplɪ] adv (just, merely) nur, bloß; (in a simple way) einfach

simulate ['sɪmjuleɪt] vt vortäuschen, spielen; (illness) simulieren

simulated ['sɪmjuleɪtɪd] adj (hair, fur) imitiert; (Tech) simuliert

simulation [sɪmju'leɪʃən] n Vortäuschung f; (simulated object) Imitation f; (Tech) Simulation f

simultaneous [sɪməl'teɪnɪəs] adj gleichzeitig; (translation, interpreting) Simultan-

simultaneously [sɪməl'teɪnɪəslɪ] adv gleichzeitig

sin [sɪn] n Sünde f ▷ vi sündigen

since [sɪns] adv inzwischen, seitdem ▷ prep seit ▷ conj (time) seit(dem); (because) da; **~ then, ever since** seitdem

sincere [sɪn'sɪər] adj aufrichtig, offen; (apology, belief) aufrichtig

sincerely [sɪn'sɪəlɪ] adv aufrichtig, offen; **yours ~** (in letter) mit freundlichen Grüßen

sincerity [sɪn'sɛrɪtɪ] n Aufrichtigkeit f

sine [saɪn] n Sinus m

sine qua non [sɪnɪkwɑː'nɔn] n unerlässliche Voraussetzung f

sinew ['sɪnjuː] n Sehne f

S

sinful ['sɪnful] *adj* sündig, sündhaft
sing [sɪŋ] (*pt* **sang**, *pp* **sung**) *vt, vi* singen
Singapore [sɪŋɡə'pɔːʳ] *n* Singapur *nt*
singe [sɪndʒ] *vt* versengen; (*lightly*) ansengen
singer ['sɪŋəʳ] *n* Sänger(in) *m(f)*
Singhalese [sɪŋə'liːz] *adj* = **Sinhalese**
singing ['sɪŋɪŋ] *n* Singen *nt*, Gesang *m*; **a ~ in the ears** ein Dröhnen in den Ohren
single ['sɪŋɡl] *adj* (*solitary*) einzige(r, s); (*individual*) einzeln; (*unmarried*) ledig, unverheiratet; (*not double*) einfach ▷ *n* (*Brit: also:* **single ticket**) Einzelfahrschein *m*; (*record*) Single *f*; **not a ~ one was left** es war kein Einziges mehr übrig; **every ~ day** jeden Tag; **~ spacing** einfacher Zeilenabstand *m*
  ▶ **single out** *vt* auswählen; **to ~ out for praise** lobend erwähnen
single bed *n* Einzelbett *nt*
single-breasted ['sɪŋɡlbrestɪd] *adj* einreihig
Single European Market *n:* **the ~** der Europäische Binnenmarkt
single file *n:* **in ~** im Gänsemarsch
single-handed [sɪŋɡl'hændɪd] *adv* ganz allein
single-minded [sɪŋɡl'maɪndɪd] *adj* zielstrebig
single parent *n* Alleinerziehende(r) *f(m)*
single parent family *n* Einelternfamilie *f*
single room *n* Einzelzimmer *nt*
singles ['sɪŋɡlz] *npl* (*Tennis*) Einzel *nt*
singles bar *n* Singles-Bar *f*
single-sex school *n* reine Jungen-/ Mädchenschule *f*; **education in ~s** nach Geschlechtern getrennte Schulerziehung
singly ['sɪŋɡlɪ] *adv* einzeln
singsong ['sɪŋsɒŋ] *adj* (*tone*) singend ▷ *n:* **to have a ~** zusammen singen
singular ['sɪŋɡjuləʳ] *adj* (*odd*) eigenartig; (*outstanding*) einzigartig; (*Ling: form etc*) Singular- ▷ *n* (*Ling*) Singular *m*, Einzahl *f*; **in the ~** im Singular
singularly ['sɪŋɡjuləlɪ] *adv* außerordentlich
Sinhalese [sɪnhə'liːz] *adj* singhalesisch
sinister ['sɪnɪstəʳ] *adj* unheimlich
sink [sɪŋk] (*pt* **sank**, *pp* **sunk**) *n* Spülbecken *nt* ▷ *vt* (*ship*) versenken; (*well*) bohren; (*foundations*) absenken ▷ *vi* (*ship*) sinken, untergehen; (*ground*) sich senken; (*person*) sinken; **to ~ one's teeth/claws into sth** die Zähne/seine Klauen in etw *acc* schlagen; **his heart/spirits sank at the thought** bei dem Gedanken verließ ihn der Mut; **he sank into the mud/a chair** er sank in den Schlamm ein/in einen Sessel
  ▶ **sink back** *vi* (zurück)sinken
  ▶ **sink down** *vi* (nieder)sinken
  ▶ **sink in** *vi* (*fig*) verstanden werden; **it's only just sunk in** ich begreife es erst jetzt
sinking ['sɪŋkɪŋ] *n* (*of ship*) Untergang *m*; (*: deliberate*) Versenkung *f* ▷ *adj:* **~ feeling** flaues Gefühl *nt* (im Magen)
sinking fund *n* Tilgungsfonds *m*
sink unit *n* Spüle *f*
sinner ['sɪnəʳ] *n* Sünder(in) *m(f)*

Sinn Féin [ʃɪn'feɪn] *n* republikanisch-nationalistische irische Partei
Sino- ['saɪnəu] *pref* chinesisch-
sinuous ['sɪnjuəs] *adj* (*snake*) gewunden; (*dance*) geschmeidig
sinus ['saɪnəs] *n* (Nasen)nebenhöhle *f*
sip [sɪp] *n* Schlückchen *nt* ▷ *vt* nippen an +*dat*
siphon ['saɪfən] *n* Heber *m*; (*also:* **soda siphon**) Siphon *m*
  ▶ **siphon off** *vt* absaugen; (*petrol*) abzapfen
SIPS *n abbr* (= *side impact protection system*) Seitenaufprallschutz *m*
sir [səʳ] *n* mein Herr, Herr X; **S~ John Smith** Sir John Smith; **yes, ~** ja(, Herr X); **Dear S~ (or Madam)** (*in letter*) Sehr geehrte (Damen und) Herren!
siren ['saɪərn] *n* Sirene *f*
sirloin ['səːlɔɪn] *n* (*also:* **sirloin steak**) Filetsteak *nt*
sirocco [sɪ'rɔkəu] *n* Schirokko *m*
sisal ['saɪsəl] *n* Sisal *m*
sissy ['sɪsɪ] (*inf: pej*) *n* Waschlappen *m* ▷ *adj* weichlich
sister ['sɪstəʳ] *n* Schwester *f*; (*nun*) (Ordens) schwester *f*; (*Brit: nurse*) Oberschwester *f* ▷ *cpd:* **~ organization** Schwesterorganisation *f*; **~ ship** Schwesterschiff *nt*
sister-in-law ['sɪstərɪnlɔː] *n* Schwägerin *f*
sit [sɪt] (*pt, pp* **sat**) *vi* (*sit down*) sich setzen; (*be sitting*) sitzen; (*assembly*) tagen; (*for painter*) Modell sitzen ▷ *vt* (*exam*) machen; **to ~ on a committee** in einem Ausschuss sitzen; **to ~ tight** abwarten
  ▶ **sit about** *vi* herumsitzen
  ▶ **sit around** *vi* = **sit about**
  ▶ **sit back** *vi* sich zurücklehnen
  ▶ **sit down** *vi* sich (hin)setzen; **to be ~ting down** sitzen
  ▶ **sit in on** *vt fus* dabei sein bei
  ▶ **sit up** *vi* sich aufsetzen; (*straight*) sich gerade hinsetzen; (*not go to bed*) aufbleiben
sitcom ['sɪtkɔm] *n abbr* (*TV*) = **situation comedy**
sit-down ['sɪtdaun] *adj:* **a ~ strike** ein Sitzstreik *m*; **a ~ meal** eine richtige Mahlzeit
site [saɪt] *n* (*place*) Platz *m*; (*of crime*) Ort *m*; (*also:* **building site**) Baustelle *f*; (*Comput*) Site *f* ▷ *vt* (*factory*) legen; (*missiles*) stationieren
sit-in ['sɪtɪn] *n* Sit-in *nt*
siting ['saɪtɪŋ] *n* (*location*) Lage *f*
sits vac *abbr* (= *situations vacant*) Stellenangebote *pl*
sitter ['sɪtəʳ] *n* (*for painter*) Modell *nt*; (*also:* **baby-sitter**) Babysitter *m*
sitting ['sɪtɪŋ] *n* Sitzung *f*; **we have two ~s for lunch** bei uns wird das Mittagessen in zwei Schüben serviert; **at a single ~** auf einmal
sitting member *n* (*Pol*) (derzeitiger) Abgeordnete(r) *m*, (derzeitige) Abgeordnete *f*
sitting room *n* Wohnzimmer *nt*
sitting tenant *n* (*Brit*) *n* (derzeitiger) Mieter *m*
situate ['sɪtjueɪt] *vt* legen
situated ['sɪtjueɪtɪd] *adj* gelegen; **to be ~** liegen

situation [sɪtjuˈeɪʃən] n Situation f, Lage f; (job) Stelle f; (location) Lage f; **"~s vacant** or **wanted"** „Stellenangebote"
situation comedy n (TV) Situationskomödie f
six [sɪks] num sechs
six-pack [ˈsɪkspæk] n Sechserpack m
sixteen [sɪksˈtiːn] num sechzehn
sixth [sɪksθ] num sechste(r, s); **the upper/ lower ~** (Brit: Scol) ≈ die Ober-/Unterprima
sixty [ˈsɪkstɪ] num sechzig
size [saɪz] n Größe f; (extent) Ausmaß nt; **I take ~ 14** ich habe Größe 14; **the small/large ~** (of soap powder etc) die kleine/große Packung; **it's the ~ of ...** es ist so groß wie ...; **cut to ~** auf die richtige Größe zurechtgeschnitten
▶ **size up** vt einschätzen
sizeable [ˈsaɪzəbl] adj ziemlich groß; (income etc) ansehnlich
sizzle [ˈsɪzl] vi brutzeln
SK (Canada) abbr (= Saskatchewan)
skate [skeɪt] n (also: **ice skate**) Schlittschuh m; (also: **roller skate**) Rollschuh m; (fish: pl inv) Rochen m ▷ vi Schlittschuh laufen
▶ **skate around** vt fus (problem, issue) einfach übergehen
▶ **skate over** vt fus = **skate around**
skateboard [ˈskeɪtbɔːd] n Skateboard nt
skater [ˈskeɪtəʳ] n Schlittschuhläufer(in) m(f)
skating [ˈskeɪtɪŋ] n Eislauf m
skating rink n Eisbahn f
skeleton [ˈskelɪtn] n Skelett nt ▷ attrib (plan, outline) skizzenhaft
skeleton key n Dietrich m; Nachschlüssel m
skeleton staff n Minimalbesetzung f
skeptic etc [ˈskeptɪk] (US) = **sceptic** etc
sketch [sketʃ] n Skizze f; (Theat, TV) Sketch m ▷ vt skizzieren; (also: **sketch out**: ideas) umreißen
sketchbook [ˈsketʃbuk] n Skizzenbuch nt
sketchpad [ˈsketʃpæd] n Skizzenblock m
sketchy [ˈsketʃɪ] adj (coverage) oberflächlich; (notes etc) bruchstückhaft
skew [skjuː] adj schief
skewed [skjuːd] adj (distorted) verzerrt
skewer [ˈskjuːəʳ] n Spieß m
ski [skiː] n Ski m ▷ vi Ski laufen or fahren
ski boot n Skistiefel m
skid [skɪd] n (Aut) Schleudern nt ▷ vi rutschen; (Aut) schleudern; **to go into a ~** ins Schleudern geraten or kommen
skid marks npl Reifenspuren pl; (from braking) Bremsspuren pl
skier [ˈskiːəʳ] n Skiläufer(in) m(f), Skifahrer(in) m(f)
skiing [ˈskiːɪŋ] n Skilaufen nt, Skifahren nt; **to go ~** Ski laufen or Ski fahren gehen
ski instructor n Skilehrer(in) m(f)
ski jump n (event) Skispringen nt; (ramp) Sprungschanze f
skilful, (US) **skillful** [ˈskɪlful] adj geschickt
skilfully adv geschickt
ski lift n Skilift m
skill [skɪl] n (ability) Können nt; (dexterity)

Geschicklichkeit f; **skills** (acquired abilities) Fähigkeiten pl; **computer/language ~s** Computer-/Sprachkenntnisse pl; **to learn a new ~** etwas Neues lernen
skilled [skɪld] adj (skilful) geschickt; (trained) ausgebildet; (work) qualifiziert
skillet [ˈskɪlɪt] n Bratpfanne f
skillful etc [ˈskɪlful] (US) = **skilful** etc
skim [skɪm] vt (also: **skim off**: cream, fat) abschöpfen; (glide over) gleiten über +acc
▷ vi: **to ~ through** (book etc) überfliegen
skimmed milk [skɪmd-] n Magermilch f
skimp [skɪmp] (also: **skimp on**) vt (work etc) nachlässig machen; (cloth etc) sparen an +dat
skimpy [ˈskɪmpɪ] adj (meagre) dürftig; (too small) knapp
skin [skɪn] n Haut f; (fur) Fell nt; (of fruit) Schale f ▷ vt (animal) häuten; **wet** or **soaked to the ~** nass bis auf die Haut
skin cancer n Hautkrebs m
skin-deep [skɪnˈdiːp] adj oberflächlich
skin diver n Sporttaucher(in) m(f)
skin diving n Sporttauchen nt
skinflint [ˈskɪnflɪnt] n Geizkragen m
skin graft n Hautverpflanzung f
skinhead [ˈskɪnhed] n Skinhead m
skinny [ˈskɪnɪ] adj dünn
skin test n Hauttest m
skintight [ˈskɪntaɪt] adj hauteng
skip [skɪp] n Sprung m, Hüpfer m; (Brit: container) (Müll)container m ▷ vi springen, hüpfen; (with rope) seilspringen ▷ vt überspringen; (miss: lunch, lecture) ausfallen lassen; **to ~ school** (esp US) die Schule schwänzen
ski pants npl Skihose f
ski pass n Skipass nt
ski pole n Skistock m
skipper [ˈskɪpəʳ] n (Naut) Kapitän m; (inf, Sport) Mannschaftskapitän m ▷ vt: **to ~ a boat/team** Kapitän eines Schiffes/einer Mannschaft sein
skipping rope [ˈskɪpɪŋ-] (Brit) n Sprungseil nt
ski resort n Wintersportort m
skirmish [ˈskəːmɪʃ] n (Mil) Geplänkel nt; (political etc) Zusammenstoß m
skirt [skəːt] n Rock m ▷ vt (fig) umgehen
skirting board [ˈskəːtɪŋ-] (Brit) n Fußleiste f
ski run n Skipiste f
ski slope n Skipiste f
ski suit n Skianzug m
skit [skɪt] n Parodie f
ski tow n Schlepplift m
skittle [ˈskɪtl] n Kegel m
skittles [ˈskɪtlz] n (game) Kegeln nt
skive [skaɪv] (Brit: inf) vi blaumachen; (from school) schwänzen
skulk [skʌlk] vi sich herumdrücken
skull [skʌl] n Schädel m
skullcap [ˈskʌlkæp] n Scheitelkäppchen nt
skunk [skʌŋk] n Skunk m, Stinktier nt; (fur) Skunk m
sky [skaɪ] n Himmel m; **to praise sb to the skies** jdn in den Himmel heben

S

783

sky-blue [skaɪˈbluː] *adj* himmelblau
skydiving [ˈskaɪdaɪvɪŋ] *n* Fallschirmspringen *nt*
sky-high [ˈskaɪˈhaɪ] *adj* (*prices, confidence*) himmelhoch ▷ *adv*: **to blow a bridge** ~ eine Brücke in die Luft sprengen
skylark [ˈskaɪlɑːk] *n* Feldlerche *f*
skylight [ˈskaɪlaɪt] *n* Dachfenster *nt*
skyline [ˈskaɪlaɪn] *n* (*horizon*) Horizont *m*; (*of city*) Skyline *f*, Silhouette *f*
Skype® [skaɪp] *n* (*Internet, Tel*) Skype *nt* ▷ *vt* skypen
skyscraper [ˈskaɪskreɪpəʳ] *n* Wolkenkratzer *m*
slab [slæb] *n* (*stone*) Platte *f*; (*of wood*) Tafel *f*; (*of cake, cheese*) großes Stück *nt*
slack [slæk] *adj* (*loose*) locker; (*rope*) durchhängend; (*skin*) schlaff; (*careless*) nachlässig; (*Comm: market*) flau; (: *demand*) schwach; (*period*) ruhig ▷ *n* (*in rope etc*) durchhängendes Teil *nt*; **slacks** *npl* (*trousers*) Hose *f*; **business is** ~ das Geschäft geht schlecht
slacken [ˈslækn] *vi* (*also:* **slacken off**: *speed, rain*) nachlassen; (: *pace*) langsamer werden; (: *demand*) zurückgehen ▷ *vt* (*grip*) lockern; (*speed*) verringern; (*pace*) verlangsamen
slag heap [slæg-] *n* Schlackenhalde *f*
slag off (*Brit: inf*) *vt* (*criticize*) (he)runtermachen
slain [sleɪn] *pp of* **slay**
slake [sleɪk] *vt* (*thirst*) stillen
slam [slæm] *vt* (*door*) zuschlagen, zuknallen (*inf*); (*throw*) knallen (*inf*); (*criticize*) verreißen ▷ *vi* (*door*) zuschlagen, zuknallen (*inf*)
slammer [ˈslæməʳ] *n* (*inf*) *n* (*prison*) Knast *m*
slander [ˈslɑːndəʳ] *n* (*Law*) Verleumdung *f*; (*insult*) Beleidigung *f* ▷ *vt* verleumden
slanderous [ˈslɑːndrəs] *adj* verleumderisch
slang [slæŋ] *n* Slang *m*; (*jargon*) Jargon *m*
slanging match [ˈslæŋɪŋ-] *n* gegenseitige Beschimpfungen *pl*
slant [slɑːnt] *n* Neigung *f*, Schräge *f*; (*fig: approach*) Perspektive *f* ▷ *vi* (*floor*) sich neigen; (*ceiling*) schräg sein
slanted [ˈslɑːntɪd] *adj* (*roof*) schräg; (*eyes*) schräg gestellt
slanting [ˈslɑːntɪŋ] *adj* = **slanted**
slap [slæp] *n* Schlag *m*, Klaps *m* ▷ *vt* schlagen ▷ *adv* (*inf: directly*) direkt; **to** ~ **sth on sth** etw auf etw *acc* klatschen
slapdash [ˈslæpdæʃ] *adj* nachlässig, schludrig (*inf*)
slapstick [ˈslæpstɪk] *n* Klamauk *m*
slap-up [ˈslæpʌp] *adj*: **a** ~ **meal** (*Brit*) ein Essen mit allem Drum und Dran
slash [slæʃ] *vt* aufschlitzen; (*fig: prices*) radikal senken; **to** ~ **one's wrists** sich *dat* die Pulsadern aufschneiden
slat [slæt] *n* Leiste *f*, Latte *f*
slate [sleɪt] *n* Schiefer *m*; (*piece*) Schieferplatte *f* ▷ *vt* (*criticize*) verreißen
slaughter [ˈslɔːtəʳ] *n* (*of animals*) Schlachten *nt*; (*of people*) Gemetzel *nt* ▷ *vt* (*animals*) schlachten; (*people*) abschlachten

slaughterhouse [ˈslɔːtəhaus] *n* Schlachthof *m*
Slav [slɑːv] *adj* slawisch ▷ *n* Slawe *m*, Slawin *f*
slave [sleɪv] *n* Sklave *m*, Sklavin *f* ▷ *vi* (*also:* **slave away**) sich abplagen, schuften (*inf*); **to** ~ **(away) at sth** sich mit etw herumschlagen
slave-driver [ˈsleɪvdraɪvəʳ] *n* Sklaventreiber(in) *m(f)*
slave labour *n* Sklavenarbeit *f*; **it's just** ~ (*fig*) es ist die reinste Sklavenarbeit
slaver [ˈslævəʳ] *vi* (*dribble*) geifern
slavery [ˈsleɪvərɪ] *n* Sklaverei *f*
Slavic [ˈslævɪk] *adj* slawisch
slavish [ˈsleɪvɪʃ] *adj* sklavisch
slavishly [ˈsleɪvɪʃlɪ] *adv* sklavisch
Slavonic [sləˈvɔnɪk] *adj* slawisch
slay [sleɪ] (*pt* **slew**, *pp* **slain**) *vt* (*liter*) erschlagen
sleazy [ˈsliːzɪ] *adj* schäbig
sledge [slɛdʒ] *n* Schlitten *m*
sledgehammer [ˈslɛdʒhæməʳ] *n* Vorschlaghammer *m*
sleek [sliːk] *adj* glatt, glänzend; (*car, boat etc*) schnittig
sleep [sliːp] (*pt, pp* **slept**) *n* Schlaf *m* ▷ *vi* schlafen ▷ *vt*: **we can** ~ **4** bei uns können 4 Leute schlafen; **to go to** ~ einschlafen; **to have a good night's** ~ sich richtig ausschlafen; **to put to** ~ (*euph: kill*) einschläfern; **to** ~ **lightly** einen leichten Schlaf haben; **to** ~ **with sb** (*euph: have sex*) mit jdm schlafen
  ▶ **sleep around** *vi* mit jedem/jeder schlafen
  ▶ **sleep in** *vi* (*oversleep*) verschlafen; (*rise late*) lange schlafen
sleeper [ˈsliːpəʳ] *n* (*train*) Schlafwagenzug *m*; (*berth*) Platz *m* im Schlafwagen; (*Brit: on track*) Schwelle *f*; (*person*) Schläfer(in) *m(f)*
sleepily [ˈsliːpɪlɪ] *adv* müde, schläfrig
sleeping accommodation *n* (*beds etc*) Schlafgelegenheiten *pl*
sleeping arrangements *npl* Bettenverteilung *f*
sleeping bag *n* Schlafsack *m*
sleeping car *n* Schlafwagen *m*
sleeping partner (*Brit*) = **silent partner**
sleeping pill *n* Schlaftablette *f*
sleeping sickness *n* Schlafkrankheit *f*
sleepless [ˈsliːplɪs] *adj* (*night*) schlaflos
sleeplessness [ˈsliːplɪsnɪs] *n* Schlaflosigkeit *f*
sleepover [ˈsliːpəuvəʳ] *n* Übernachtung *f* (*bei Freunden etc*)
sleepwalk [ˈsliːpwɔːk] *vi* schlafwandeln
sleepwalker [ˈsliːpwɔːkəʳ] *n* Schlafwandler(in) *m(f)*
sleepy [ˈsliːpɪ] *adj* müde, schläfrig; (*fig: village etc*) verschlafen; **to be** *or* **feel** ~ müde sein
sleet [sliːt] *n* Schneeregen *m*
sleeve [sliːv] *n* Ärmel *m*; (*of record*) Hülle *f*; **to have sth up one's** ~ (*fig*) etw in petto haben
sleeveless [ˈsliːvlɪs] *adj* (*garment*) ärmellos
sleigh [sleɪ] *n* (*Pferde*)schlitten *m*
sleight [slaɪt] *n*: ~ **of hand** Fingerfertigkeit *f*
slender [ˈslɛndəʳ] *adj* schlank, schmal; (*small*) knapp

slept [slɛpt] *pt, pp of* **sleep**

sleuth [slu:θ] *n* Detektiv *m*

slew [slu:] *vi* (*Brit: also:* **slew round**) herumschwenken; **the bus ~ed across the road** der Bus rutschte über die Straße ▷ *pt of* **slay**

slice [slaɪs] *n* Scheibe *f*; (*utensil*) Wender *m* ▷ *vt* (in Scheiben) schneiden; **~d bread** aufgeschnittenes Brot *nt*; **the best thing since ~d bread** der/die/das Allerbeste

slick [slɪk] *adj* professionell; (*pej*) glatt ▷ *n* (*also:* **oil slick**) Ölteppich *m*

slid [slɪd] *pt, pp of* **slide**

slide [slaɪd] (*pt, pp* **slid**) *n* (*on ice etc*) Rutschen *nt*; (*fig: to ruin etc*) Abgleiten *nt*; (*in playground*) Rutschbahn *f*; (*Phot*) Dia *nt*; (*Brit: also:* **hair slide**) Spange *f*; (*microscope slide*) Objektträger *m*; (*in prices*) Preisrutsch *m* ▷ *vt* schieben ▷ *vi* (*slip*) rutschen; (*glide*) gleiten; **to let things ~** (*fig*) die Dinge schleifen lassen

slide projector *n* Diaprojektor *m*

slide rule *n* Rechenschieber *m*

sliding ['slaɪdɪŋ] *adj* (*door, window etc*) Schiebe-

sliding roof *n* (*Aut*) Schiebedach *nt*

sliding scale *n* gleitende Skala *f*

slight [slaɪt] *adj* zierlich; (*small*) gering; (*error, accent, pain etc*) leicht; (*trivial*) leicht ▷ *n*: **a ~ (on sb/sth)** ein Affront *m* (gegen jdn/etw); **the ~est noise** der geringste Lärm; **the ~est problem** das kleinste Problem; **I haven't the ~est idea** ich habe nicht die geringste Ahnung; **not in the ~est** nicht im Geringsten

slightly ['slaɪtlɪ] *adv* etwas, ein bisschen; **~ built** zierlich

slim [slɪm] *adj* schlank; (*chance*) gering ▷ *vi* eine Schlankheitskur machen, abnehmen

slime [slaɪm] *n* Schleim *m*

slimming ['slɪmɪŋ] *n* Abnehmen *nt*

slimy ['slaɪmɪ] *adj* (*lit, fig*) schleimig

sling [slɪŋ] (*pt, pp* **slung**) *n* Schlinge *f*; (*for baby*) Tragetuch *nt*; (*weapon*) Schleuder *f* ▷ *vt* schleudern; **to have one's arm in a ~** den Arm in der Schlinge tragen

slingshot ['slɪŋʃɒt] *n* Steinschleuder *f*

slink [slɪŋk] (*pt, pp* **slunk**) *vi*: **to ~ away** *or* **off** sich davonschleichen

slinky ['slɪŋkɪ] *adj* (*dress*) eng anliegend

slip [slɪp] *n* (*fall*) Ausrutschen *nt*; (*mistake*) Fehler *m*, Schnitzer *m*; (*underskirt*) Unterrock *m*; (*also:* **slip of paper**) Zettel *m* ▷ *vt* (*slide*) stecken ▷ *vi* ausrutschen; (*decline*) fallen; **he had a nasty ~** er ist ausgerutscht und böse gefallen; **to give sb the ~** jdm entwischen; **a ~ of the tongue** ein Versprecher *m*; **to ~ into/out of sth, to ~ sth on/off** in etw *acc*/ aus etw schlüpfen; **to let a chance ~ by** eine Gelegenheit ungenutzt lassen; **it ~ped from her hand** es rutschte ihr aus der Hand

▶ **slip away** *vi* sich davonschleichen

▶ **slip in** *vt* stecken in +*acc*

▶ **slip out** *vi* kurz weggehen

▶ **slip up** *vi* sich vertun (*inf*)

slip-on ['slɪpɒn] *adj* zum Überziehen; **~ shoes**

Slipper *pl*

slipped disc [slɪpt-] *n* Bandscheibenschaden *m*

slipper ['slɪpə] *n* Pantoffel *m*, Hausschuh *m*

slippery ['slɪpərɪ] *adj* (*lit, fig*) glatt; (*fish etc*) schlüpfrig

slippy ['slɪpɪ] *adj* (*slippery*) glatt

slip road (*Brit*) *n* (*to motorway etc*) Auffahrt *f*; (*from motorway etc*) Ausfahrt *f*

slipshod ['slɪpʃɒd] *adj* schludrig (*inf*)

slipstream ['slɪpstriːm] *n* (*Tech*) Sog *m*; (*Aut*) Windschatten *m*

slip-up ['slɪpʌp] *n* Fehler *m*, Schnitzer *m*

slipway ['slɪpweɪ] *n* (*Naut*) Ablaufbahn *f*

slit [slɪt] (*pt, pp* **~**) *n* Schlitz *m*; (*tear*) Riss *m* ▷ *vt* aufschlitzen; **to ~ sb's throat** jdm die Kehle aufschlitzen

slither ['slɪðə] *vi* rutschen; (*snake etc*) gleiten

sliver ['slɪvə] *n* (*of glass, wood*) Splitter *m*; (*of cheese etc*) Scheibchen *nt*

slob [slɒb] (*inf*) *n* Drecksau *f* (!)

slog [slɒg] (*Brit*) *vi* (*work hard*) schuften ▷ *n*: **it was a hard ~** es war eine ganz schöne Schufterei; **to ~ away at sth** sich mit etw abrackern

slogan ['sləugən] *n* Slogan *m*

slop [slɒp] *vi* schwappen ▷ *vt* verschütten

▶ **slop out** *vi* (*in prison etc*) den Toiletteneimer ausleeren

slope [sləup] *n* Hügel *m*; (*side of mountain*) Hang *m*; (*ski slope*) Piste *f*; (*slant*) Neigung *f* ▷ *vi*: **to ~ down** abfallen; **to ~ up** ansteigen

sloping ['sləupɪŋ] *adj* (*upwards*) ansteigend; (*downwards*) abfallend; (*roof, handwriting*) schräg

sloppy ['slɒpɪ] *adj* (*work*) nachlässig; (*appearance*) schlampig; (*sentimental*) rührselig

slops [slɒps] *npl* Abfallbrühe *f*

slosh [slɒʃ] (*inf*) *vi*: **to ~ around** *or* **about** (*person*) herumplan(t)schen; (*liquid*) herumschwappen

sloshed [slɒʃt] (*inf*) *adj* (*drunk*) blau

slot [slɒt] *n* Schlitz *m*; (*fig: in timetable*) Termin *m*; (: , *Radio, TV*) Sendezeit *f* ▷ *vt*: **to ~ sth in** etw hineinstecken ▷ *vi*: **to ~ into** sich einfügen lassen in +*acc*

sloth [sləuθ] *n* (*laziness*) Trägheit *f*, Faulheit *f*; (*Zool*) Faultier *nt*

slot machine *n* (*Brit*) Münzautomat *m*; (*for gambling*) Spielautomat *m*

slot meter (*Brit*) *n* Münzzähler *m*

slouch [slautʃ] *vi* eine krumme Haltung haben; (*when walking*) krumm gehen ▷ *n*: **he's no ~** hat etwas los (*inf*); **she was ~ed in a chair** sie hing auf einem Stuhl

Slovak ['sləuvæk] *adj* slowakisch ▷ *n* Slowake *m*, Slowakin *f*; (*Ling*) Slowakisch *nt*; **the ~ Republic** die Slowakische Republik

Slovakia [sləu'vækɪə] *n* die Slowakei

Slovakian [sləu'vækɪən] *adj, n* = **Slovak**

Slovene ['sləuviːn] *n* Slowene *m*, Slowenin *f*; (*Ling*) Slowenisch *nt* ▷ *adj* slowenisch

Slovenia [sləu'viːnɪə] *n* Slowenien *nt*

Slovenian [sləu'viːnɪən] *adj, n* = **Slovene**

slovenly ['slʌvənlɪ] *adj* schlampig; (*careless*)

S

nachlässig, schludrig (inf)

slow [sləʊ] adj langsam; (not clever) langsam, begriffsstutzig ▷ adv langsam ▷ vt (also: **slow down, slow up**) verlangsamen; (business) verschlechtern ▷ vi (also: **slow down, slow up**) sich verlangsamen; (business) schlechter gehen; **to be ~** (watch, clock) nachgehen; **"~"** „langsam fahren"; **at a ~ speed** langsam; **to be ~ to act** sich dat Zeit lassen; **to be ~ to decide** lange brauchen, um sich zu entscheiden; **my watch is 20 minutes ~** meine Uhr geht 20 Minuten nach; **business is ~** das Geschäft geht schlecht; **to go ~** (driver) langsam fahren; (Brit: in industrial dispute) einen Bummelstreik machen

slow-acting [sləʊˈæktɪŋ] adj mit Langzeitwirkung

slow food n Slow Food nt

slowly [ˈsləʊlɪ] adv langsam

slow motion n: **in ~** in Zeitlupe

slow-moving [sləʊˈmuːvɪŋ] adj langsam; (traffic) kriechend

slowness [ˈsləʊnɪs] n Langsamkeit f

sludge [slʌdʒ] n Schlamm m

slue [sluː] (US) vi = **slew**

slug [slʌg] n Nacktschnecke f; (US: inf: bullet) Kugel f

sluggish [ˈslʌgɪʃ] adj träge; (engine) lahm; (Comm) flau

sluice [sluːs] n Schleuse f; (channel) (Wasch)rinne f ▷ vt: **to ~ down** or **out** abspritzen

slum [slʌm] n Slum m, Elendsviertel nt

slumber [ˈslʌmbəʳ] n Schlaf m

slump [slʌmp] n Rezession f ▷ vi fallen; **~ in sales** Absatzflaute f; **~ in prices** Preissturz m; **he was ~ed over the wheel** er war über dem Steuer zusammengesackt

slung [slʌŋ] pt, pp of **sling**

slunk [slʌŋk] pt, pp of **slink**

slur [slɜːʳ] n (fig): **~ (on)** Beleidigung f (für) ▷ vt (words) undeutlich aussprechen; **to cast a ~ on** verunglimpfen

slurp [slɜːp] (inf) vt, vi schlürfen

slurred [slɜːd] adj (speech, voice) undeutlich

slush [slʌʃ] n (melted snow) Schneematsch m

slush fund n Schmiergelder pl, Schmiergeldfonds m

slushy [ˈslʌʃɪ] adj matschig; (Brit: fig) schmalzig

slut [slʌt] (pej) n Schlampe f

sly [slaɪ] adj (smile, expression) wissend; (remark) vielsagend; (person) schlau, gerissen; **on the ~** heimlich

S/M n abbr (= sadomasochism) S/M

smack [smæk] n Klaps m; (on face) Ohrfeige f ▷ vt (hit) schlagen; (: child) einen Klaps geben +dat; (: on face) ohrfeigen ▷ vi: **to ~ of** riechen nach ▷ adv: **it fell ~ in the middle** (inf) es fiel genau in die Mitte; **to ~ one's lips** schmatzen

smacker [ˈsmækəʳ] (inf) n (kiss) Schmatzer m

small [smɔːl] adj klein ▷ n: **the ~ of the back** das Kreuz; **to get** or **grow ~er** (thing) kleiner werden; (numbers) zurückgehen; **to make ~er** (amount, income) kürzen; (object, garment)

kleiner machen; **a ~ shopkeeper** der Inhaber eines kleinen Geschäfts; **a ~ business** ein Kleinunternehmen nt

small ads (Brit) npl Kleinanzeigen pl

small arms n Handfeuerwaffen pl

small business n Kleinunternehmen nt

small change n Kleingeld nt

small fry npl (unimportant people) kleine Fische pl

smallholder [ˈsmɔːlhəʊldəʳ] (Brit) n Kleinbauer m

smallholding [ˈsmɔːlhəʊldɪŋ] (Brit) n kleiner Landbesitz m

small hours npl: **in the ~** in den frühen Morgenstunden

smallish [ˈsmɔːlɪʃ] adj ziemlich klein

small-minded [smɔːlˈmaɪndɪd] adj engstirnig

smallpox [ˈsmɔːlpɒks] n Pocken pl

small print n: **the ~** das Kleingedruckte

small-scale [ˈsmɔːlskeɪl] adj (map, model) in verkleinertem Maßstab; (business, farming) klein angelegt

small talk n (oberflächliche) Konversation f

small-time [ˈsmɔːltaɪm] adj (farmer etc) klein; **a ~ thief** ein kleiner Ganove

small-town [ˈsmɔːltaʊn] adj kleinstädtisch

smarmy [ˈsmɑːmɪ] (Brit: pej) adj schmierig

smart [smɑːt] adj (neat) ordentlich, gepflegt; (fashionable) chic inv, elegant; (clever) intelligent, clever (inf); (quick) schnell ▷ vi (sting) brennen; (suffer) leiden; **the ~ set** die Schickeria (inf); **and look ~ (about it)!** und zwar ein bisschen plötzlich! (inf)

smart card n Chipkarte f

smarten up [ˈsmɑːtn-] vi sich fein machen ▷ vt verschönern

smartphone [ˈsmɑːtfəʊn] n (Tel) Smartphone nt, Internethandy nt

smash [smæʃ] n (also: **smash-up**) Unfall m; (sound) Krachen nt; (song, play, film) Superhit m; (Tennis) Schmetterball m ▷ vt (break) zerbrechen; (car etc) kaputt fahren; (hopes) zerschlagen; (Sport: record) haushoch schlagen ▷ vi (break) zerbrechen; (against wall, into sth etc) krachen

▶ **smash up** vt (car) kaputt fahren; (room) kurz und klein schlagen (inf)

smash hit n Superhit m

smashing [ˈsmæʃɪŋ] (inf) adj super, toll

smattering [ˈsmætərɪŋ] n: **a ~ of Greek** etc ein paar Brocken Griechisch etc

smear [smɪəʳ] n (trace) verschmierter Fleck m; (insult) Verleumdung f; (Med) Abstrich m ▷ vt (spread) verschmieren; (make dirty) beschmieren; **his hands were ~ed with oil** seine Hände waren mit Öl beschmiert

smear campaign n Verleumdungskampagne f

smear test n Abstrich m

smell [smɛl] (pt, pp **smelt** or **~ed**) n Geruch m; (sense) Geruchssinn m ▷ vt riechen ▷ vi riechen; (pej) stinken; (pleasantly) duften; **to ~ of** riechen nach

smelly [ˈsmɛlɪ] (pej) adj stinkend

smelt [smɛlt] pt, pp of **smell** ▷ vt schmelzen

smile [smaɪl] n Lächeln nt ▷ vi lächeln
smiling ['smaɪlɪŋ] adj lächelnd
smirk [smə:k] (pej) n Grinsen nt
smithy ['smɪðɪ] n Schmiede f
smitten ['smɪtn] adj: ~ **with** vernarrt in +acc
smock [smɔk] n Kittel m; (US: overall) Overall m
smog [smɔg] n Smog m
smoke [sməuk] n Rauch m ▷ vi, vt rauchen; **to have a ~** eine rauchen; **to go up in ~** in Rauch (und Flammen) aufgehen; (fig) sich in Rauch auflösen; **do you ~?** rauchen Sie?
smoked [sməukt] adj geräuchert, Räucher-; ~ **glass** Rauchglas nt
smokeless fuel ['sməuklɪs-] n rauchlose Kohle f
smokeless zone (Brit) n rauchfreie Zone f
smoker ['sməukəʳ] n Raucher(in) m(f); (Rail) Raucherabteil nt
smoke screen n Rauchvorhang m; (fig) Deckmantel m
smoke shop (US) n Tabakladen m
smoking ['sməukɪŋ] n Rauchen nt; **"no ~"** „Rauchen verboten"
smoking compartment, (US) **smoking car** n Raucherabteil nt
smoking room n Raucherzimmer nt
smoky ['sməukɪ] adj verraucht; (taste) rauchig
smolder ['sməuldəʳ] (US) vi = **smoulder**
smoochy ['smu:tʃɪ] adj (music, tape) zum Schmusen
smooth [smu:ð] adj (lit, fig: pej) glatt; (flavour, whisky) weich; (movement) geschmeidig; (flight) ruhig
▶ **smooth out** vt glätten; (fig: difficulties) aus dem Weg räumen
▶ **smooth over** vt: **to ~ things over** (fig) die Sache bereinigen
smoothly ['smu:ðlɪ] adv reibungslos, glatt; **everything went ~** alles ging glatt über die Bühne
smoothness ['smu:ðnɪs] n Glätte f; (of flight) Ruhe f
smother ['smʌðəʳ] vt (fire, person) ersticken; (repress) unterdrücken
smoulder, (US) **smolder** ['sməuldəʳ] vi (lit, fig) glimmen, schwelen
SMS n abbr (= Short Message Service) SMS m
smudge [smʌdʒ] n Schmutzfleck m ▷ vt verwischen
smug [smʌg] (pej) adj selbstgefällig
smuggle ['smʌgl] vt schmuggeln; **to ~ in/out** einschmuggeln/herausschmuggeln
smuggler ['smʌgləʳ] n Schmuggler(in) m(f)
smuggling ['smʌglɪŋ] n Schmuggel m
smut [smʌt] n (grain of soot) Rußflocke f; (in conversation etc) Schmutz m
smutty ['smʌtɪ] adj (fig: joke, book) schmutzig
snack [snæk] n Kleinigkeit f (zu essen); **to have a ~** eine Kleinigkeit essen
snack bar n Imbissstube f
snag [snæg] n Haken m, Schwierigkeit f
snail [sneɪl] n Schnecke f
snake [sneɪk] n Schlange f

snap [snæp] n Knacken nt; (photograph) Schnappschuss m; (card game) = Schnippschnapp n ▷ adj (decision) plötzlich, spontan ▷ vt (break) (zer)brechen ▷ vi (break) (zer)brechen; (rope, thread etc) reißen; **a cold ~** ein Kälteeinbruch m; **his patience ~ped** ihm riss der Geduldsfaden; **his temper ~ped** er verlor die Beherrschung; **to ~ one's fingers** mit den Fingern schnipsen or schnalzen; **to ~ open/shut** auf-/zuschnappen
▶ **snap at** vt fus (dog) schnappen nach; (fig: person) anschnauzen (inf)
▶ **snap off** vt (break) abbrechen
▶ **snap up** vt (bargains) wegschnappen
snap fastener n Druckknopf m
snappy ['snæpɪ] (inf) adj (answer) kurz und treffend; (slogan) zündend; **make it ~** ein bisschen dalli!; **he is a ~ dresser** er zieht sich flott an
snapshot ['snæpʃɔt] n Schnappschuss m
snare [snɛəʳ] n Falle f ▷ vt (lit, fig) fangen
snarl [snɑ:l] vi knurren ▷ vt: **to get ~ed up** (plans) durcheinanderkommen; (traffic) stocken
snarl-up ['snɑ:lʌp] n Verkehrschaos nt
snatch [snætʃ] n (of conversation) Fetzen m; (of song) paar Takte pl ▷ vt (grab) greifen; (steal) stehlen, klauen (inf); (child) entführen; (fig: opportunity) ergreifen; (: look) werfen ▷ vi: **don't ~!** nicht grapschen!; **to ~ a sandwich** schnell ein Butterbrot essen; **to ~ some sleep** etwas Schlaf ergattern
▶ **snatch up** vt schnappen
snazzy ['snæzɪ] (inf) adj flott
sneak [sni:k] (pt **snuck**) (US) vi: **to ~ in/out** sich einschleichen/sich hinausschleichen ▷ vt: **to ~ a look at sth** heimlich auf etw acc schielen ▷ n (inf: pej) Petze f
▶ **sneak up** vi: **to ~ up on sb** sich an jdn heranschleichen
sneakers ['sni:kəz] npl Freizeitschuhe pl
sneaking ['sni:kɪŋ] adj: **to have a ~ feeling/ suspicion that ...** das ungute Gefühl/den leisen Verdacht haben, dass ...
sneaky ['sni:kɪ] (pej) adj raffiniert
sneer [snɪəʳ] vi (smile nastily) spöttisch lächeln; (mock): **to ~ at** verspotten ▷ n (smile) spöttisches Lächeln nt; (remark) spöttische Bemerkung f
sneeze [sni:z] n Niesen nt ▷ vi niesen
▶ **sneeze at** vt fus: **it's not to be ~d at** es ist nicht zu verachten
snicker ['snɪkəʳ] vi see **snigger**
snide [snaɪd] (pej) adj abfällig
sniff [snɪf] n Schniefen nt; (smell) Schnüffeln nt ▷ vi schniefen ▷ vt riechen, schnuppern an +dat; (glue) schnüffeln
sniffer dog ['snɪfə-] n Spürhund m
snigger ['snɪgəʳ] vi kichern
snip [snɪp] n Schnitt m; (Brit: inf: bargain) Schnäppchen nt ▷ vt schnippeln; **to ~ sth off/through sth** etw abschnippeln/ durchschnippeln

S

sniper ['snaɪpə^r] n Heckenschütze m

snippet ['snɪpɪt] n (of information) Bruchstück nt; (of conversation) Fetzen m

snivelling, (US) **sniveling** ['snɪvlɪŋ] adj heulend

snob [snɔb] n Snob m

snobbery ['snɔbərɪ] n Snobismus m

snobbish ['snɔbɪʃ] adj snobistisch, versnobt (inf)

snog [snɔg] (Brit: inf) n Knutscherei f; **to have a ~ with sb** mit jdm (rum)knutschen ▷ vi (rum)knutschen

snooker ['snuːkə^r] n Snooker nt ▷ vt (Brit: inf): **to be ~ed** festsitzen

snoop [snuːp] vi: **to ~ about** herumschnüffeln; **to ~ on sb** jdm nachschnüffeln

snooper ['snuːpə^r] n Schnüffler(in) m(f)

snooty ['snuːtɪ] adj hochnäsig

snooze [snuːz] n Schläfchen nt ▷ vi ein Schläfchen machen

snore [snɔː^r] n Schnarchen nt ▷ vi schnarchen

snoring ['snɔːrɪŋ] n Schnarchen nt

snorkel ['snɔːkl] n Schnorchel m

snort [snɔːt] n Schnauben nt ▷ vi (animal) schnauben; (person) prusten ▷ vt (inf: cocaine) schnüffeln

snotty ['snɔtɪ] (inf) adj (handkerchief, nose) Rotz-; (pej: snobbish) hochnäsig

snout [snaut] n Schnauze f

snow [snəu] n Schnee m ▷ vi schneien ▷ vt: **to be ~ed under with work** mit Arbeit reichlich eingedeckt sein; **it's ~ing** es schneit

snowball ['snəubɔːl] n Schneeball m ▷ vi (fig: problem) eskalieren; (: campaign) ins Rollen kommen

snowbound ['snəubaund] adj eingeschneit

snow-capped ['snəukæpt] adj schneebedeckt

snowdrift ['snəudrɪft] n Schneewehe f

snowdrop ['snəudrɔp] n Schneeglöckchen nt

snowfall ['snəufɔːl] n Schneefall m

snowflake ['snəufleɪk] n Schneeflocke f

snowline ['snəulaɪn] n Schneegrenze f

snowman ['snəumæn] (irreg: like **man**) n Schneemann m

snowplough, (US) **snowplow** ['snəuplau] n Schneepflug m

snowshoe ['snəuʃuː] n Schneeschuh m

snowstorm ['snəustɔːm] n Schneesturm m

snowy ['snəuɪ] adj schneeweiß; (covered with snow) verschneit

SNP (Brit) n abbr (Pol) = **Scottish National Party**

snub [snʌb] vt (person) vor den Kopf stoßen ▷ n Abfuhr f

snub-nosed [snʌb'nəuzd] adj stupsnasig

snuff [snʌf] n Schnupftabak m ▷ vt (also: **snuff out**: candle) auslöschen

snuff movie n Pornofilm, in dem jemand tatsächlich stirbt

snug [snʌg] adj behaglich, gemütlich; (well-fitting) gut sitzend; **it's a ~ fit** es passt genau

snuggle ['snʌgl] vi: **to ~ up to sb** sich an jdn kuscheln; **to ~ down in bed** sich ins Bett kuscheln

snugly ['snʌglɪ] adv behaglich; **it fits ~** (object in pocket etc) es passt genau hinein; (garment) es passt wie angegossen

SO n abbr (Banking) = **standing order**

 KEYWORD

so [səu] adv **1** (thus, likewise) so; **so saying he walked away** mit diesen Worten ging er weg; **if so** falls ja; **I didn't do it — you did so!** ich hab es nicht getan — hast du wohl!; **so do I, so am I** etc ich auch; **it's 5 o'clock — so it is!** es ist 5 Uhr — tatsächlich!; **I hope/think so** ich hoffe/glaube ja; **so far** bis jetzt

2 (in comparisons etc: to such a degree) so; **so big/quickly (that)** so groß/schnell(, dass); **I'm so glad to see you** ich bin ja so froh, dich zu sehen

3: **so much** so viel; **I've got so much work** ich habe so viel Arbeit; **I love you so much** ich liebe dich so sehr; **so many** so viele

4 (phrases): **10 or so** 10 oder so; **so long!** (inf: goodbye) tschüss!

▷ conj **1** (expressing purpose): **so as to do sth** um etw zu tun; **so (that)** damit

2 (expressing result) also; **so I was right after all** ich hatte also doch Recht; **so you see, I could have gone** wie Sie sehen, hätte ich gehen können; **so (what)?** na und?

soak [səuk] vt (drench) durchnässen; (steep) einweichen ▷ vi einweichen; **to be ~ed through** völlig durchnässt sein

▶ **soak in** vi einziehen

▶ **soak up** vt aufsaugen

soaking ['səukɪŋ] adj (also: **soaking wet**) patschnass

so-and-so ['səuənsəu] n (somebody) Soundso no art; **Mr/Mrs ~** Herr/Frau Soundso; **the little ~!** (pej) das Biest!

soap [səup] n Seife f; (TV: also: **soap opera**) Fernsehserie f, Seifenoper f (inf)

soapbox ['səupbɔks] n (lit) Seifenkiste f; (fig: platform) Apfelsinenkiste f

soapflakes ['səupfleɪks] npl Seifenflocken pl

soap opera n (TV) Fernsehserie f, Seifenoper f (inf)

soap powder n Seifenpulver nt

soapsuds ['səupsʌdz] npl Seifenschaum m

soapy ['səupɪ] adj seifig; **~ water** Seifenwasser nt

soar [sɔː^r] vi aufsteigen; (price, temperature) hochschnellen; (building etc) aufragen

soaring ['sɔːrɪŋ] adj (prices) in die Höhe schnellend; (inflation) unaufhaltsam

sob [sɔb] n Schluchzer m ▷ vi schluchzen

s.o.b. (US: inf!) n abbr (= son of a bitch) Scheißkerl m

sober ['səubə^r] adj nüchtern; (serious) ernst; (colour) gedeckt; (style) schlicht

▶ **sober up** vt nüchtern machen ▷ vi nüchtern werden

sobriety [sə'braɪətɪ] n Nüchternheit f;

(seriousness) Ernst m

sobriquet ['səubrɪkeɪ] n Spitzname m

sob story n rührselige Geschichte f

Soc. abbr (= society) Ges.

so-called ['səu'kɔ:ld] adj sogenannt

soccer ['sɔkə^r] n Fußball m

soccer pitch n Fußballplatz m

soccer player n Fußballspieler(in) m(f)

sociable ['səuʃəbl] adj gesellig

social ['səuʃl] adj sozial; (history) Sozial-; (structure) Gesellschafts-; (event, contact) gesellschaftlich; (person) gesellig; (animal) gesellig lebend ▷ n (party) geselliger Abend m; ~ **life** gesellschaftliches Leben nt; **to have no ~ life** nicht mit anderen Leuten zusammenkommen

social climber (pej) n Emporkömmling m, sozialer Aufsteiger m

social club n Klub m für geselliges Beisammensein

Social Democrat n Sozialdemokrat(in) m(f)

social insurance (US) n Sozialversicherung f

socialism ['səuʃəlɪzəm] n Sozialismus m

socialist ['səuʃəlɪst] adj sozialistisch ▷ n Sozialist(in) m(f)

socialite ['səuʃəlaɪt] n Angehörige(r) f(m) der Schickeria

socialize ['səuʃəlaɪz] vi unter die Leute kommen; **to ~ with** (meet socially) gesellschaftlich verkehren mit; (chat to) sich unterhalten mit

socially ['səuʃəlɪ] adv (visit) privat; (acceptable) in Gesellschaft

social networking [-'netwə:kɪŋ] n Netzwerken nt

social science n Sozialwissenschaft f

social security (Brit) n Sozialhilfe f; **Department of Social Security** Ministerium nt für Soziales

social services npl soziale Einrichtungen pl

social welfare n soziales Wohl nt

social work n Sozialarbeit f

social worker n Sozialarbeiter(in) m(f)

society [sə'saɪətɪ] n Gesellschaft f; (people, their lifestyle) die Gesellschaft; (club) Verein m; (also: **high society**) High Society f ▷ cpd (party, lady) Gesellschafts-

socioeconomic ['səusɪəui:kə'nɔmɪk] adj sozioökonomisch

sociological [səusɪə'lɔdʒɪkl] adj soziologisch

sociologist [səusɪ'ɔlədʒɪst] n Soziologe m, Soziologin f

sociology [səusɪ'ɔlədʒɪ] n Soziologie f

sock [sɔk] n Socke f ▷ vt (inf: hit) hauen; **to pull one's ~s up** (fig) sich am Riemen reißen

socket ['sɔkɪt] n (of eye) Augenhöhle f; (of joint) Gelenkpfanne f; (Brit: Elec: also: **wall socket**) Steckdose f; (: for light bulb) Fassung f

sod [sɔd] n (earth) Sode f; (Brit: inf!) Sau f (!); **the poor ~** das arme Schwein
▷ **sod off** (Brit: inf!) vi: ~ **off!** verpiss dich!

soda ['səudə] n Soda nt; (also: **soda water**) Soda(wasser) nt; (US: also: **soda pop**) Brause f

sodden ['sɔdn] adj durchnässt

sodium ['səudɪəm] n Natrium nt

sodium chloride n Natriumchlorid nt, Kochsalz nt

sofa ['səufə] n Sofa nt

Sofia ['səufɪə] n Sofia nt

soft [sɔft] adj weich; (not rough) zart; (voice, music, light, colour) gedämpft; (lenient) nachsichtig; ~ **in the head** (inf) nicht ganz richtig im Kopf

soft benefits npl ▷ econ nicht monetäre (betriebliche) Leistungen pl

soft-boiled ['sɔftbɔɪld] adj (egg) weich (gekocht)

soft drink n alkoholfreies Getränk nt

soft drugs npl weiche Drogen pl

soften ['sɔfn] vt weich machen; (effect, blow) mildern ▷ vi weich werden; (voice, expression) sanfter werden

softener ['sɔfnə^r] n (also: **water softener**) Enthärtungsmittel nt; (also: **fabric softener**) Weichspüler m

soft fruit (Brit) n Beerenobst nt

soft furnishings npl Raumtextilien pl

soft-hearted [sɔft'hɑ:tɪd] adj weichherzig

softly ['sɔftlɪ] adv (gently) sanft; (quietly) leise

softness ['sɔftnɪs] n Weichheit f; (gentleness) Sanftheit f

soft option n Weg m des geringsten Widerstandes

soft sell n weiche Verkaufstaktik f

soft spot n: **to have a ~ for sb** eine Schwäche für jdn haben

soft target n leicht verwundbares Ziel nt

soft toy n Stofftier nt

software ['sɔftwεə^r] n (Comput) Software f

software package n (Comput) Softwarepaket nt

soft water n weiches Wasser nt

soggy ['sɔgɪ] adj (ground) durchweicht; (sandwiches etc) matschig

soil [sɔɪl] n Erde f, Boden m ▷ vt beschmutzen

soiled [sɔɪld] adj schmutzig

sojourn ['sɔdʒə:n] (form) n Aufenthalt m

solace ['sɔlɪs] n Trost m

solar ['səulə^r] adj (eclipse, power station etc) Sonnen-

solarium [sə'lεərɪəm] (pl **solaria**) n Solarium nt

solar panel n Sonnenkollektor m

solar plexus [-'plεksəs] n (Anat) Solarplexus m, Magengrube f

solar power n Sonnenenergie f

solar system n Sonnensystem nt

solar wind n Sonnenwind m

sold [səuld] pt, pp of **sell**

solder ['səuldə^r] vt löten ▷ n Lötmittel nt

soldier ['səuldʒə^r] n Soldat m ▷ vi: **to ~ on** unermüdlich weitermachen; **toy ~** Spielzeugsoldat m

sold out adj ausverkauft

sole [səul] n Sohle f; (fish: pl inv) Seezunge f ▷ adj einzig, Allein-; (exclusive) alleinig; **the ~ reason** der einzige Grund

solely ['səullɪ] adv nur, ausschließlich; **I will hold you ~ responsible** ich mache Sie allein

S

789

dafür verantwortlich

solemn ['sɔləm] *adj* feierlich; (*person*) ernst

sole trader *n* (*Comm*) Einzelunternehmer *m*

solicit [sə'lɪsɪt] *vt* (*request*) erbitten, bitten um ▷ *vi* (*prostitute*) Kunden anwerben

solicitor [sə'lɪsɪtəʳ] (*Brit*) *n* Rechtsanwalt *m*, Rechtsanwältin *f*

solid ['sɔlɪd] *adj* (*not hollow, pure*) massiv; (*not liquid*) fest; (*reliable*) zuverlässig; (*strong: structure*) stabil; (*: foundations*) solide; (*substantial: advice*) gut; (*: experience*) solide; (*unbroken*) ununterbrochen ▷ *n* (*solid object*) Festkörper *m*; **solids** *npl* (*food*) feste Nahrung *f*; **to be on ~ ground** (*fig*) sich auf festem Boden befinden; **I read for 2 hours ~** ich habe 2 Stunden ununterbrochen gelesen

solidarity [sɔlɪ'dærɪtɪ] *n* Solidarität *f*

solid fuel *n* fester Brennstoff *m*

solidify [sə'lɪdɪfaɪ] *vi* fest werden ▷ *vt* fest werden lassen

solidity [sə'lɪdɪtɪ] *n* (*of structure*) Stabilität *f*; (*of foundations*) Solidität *f*

solidly ['sɔlɪdlɪ] *adv* (*built*) solide; (*in favour*) geschlossen, einmütig; **a ~ respectable family** eine durch und durch respektable Familie

solid-state ['sɔlɪdsteɪt] *adj* (*Elec: equipment*) Halbleiter-

soliloquy [sə'lɪləkwɪ] *n* Monolog *m*

solitaire [sɔlɪ'tɛəʳ] *n* (*gem*) Solitär *m*; (*game*) Patience *f*

solitary ['sɔlɪtərɪ] *adj* einsam; (*single*) einzeln

solitary confinement *n* Einzelhaft *f*

solitude ['sɔlɪtjuːd] *n* Einsamkeit *f*; **to live in ~** einsam leben

solo ['səuləu] *n* Solo *nt* ▷ *adv* (*fly*) allein; (*play, perform*) solo; **~ flight** Alleinflug *m*

soloist ['səuləuɪst] *n* Solist(in) *m(f)*

Solomon Islands ['sɔləmən-] *npl*: **the ~** die Salomoninseln *pl*

solstice ['sɔlstɪs] *n* Sonnenwende *f*

soluble ['sɔljubl] *adj* löslich

solution [sə'luːʃən] *n* (*answer, liquid*) Lösung *f*; (*to crossword*) Auflösung *f*

solve [sɔlv] *vt* lösen; (*mystery*) enträtseln

solvency ['sɔlvənsɪ] *n* (*Comm*) Zahlungsfähigkeit *f*

solvent ['sɔlvənt] *adj* (*Comm*) zahlungsfähig ▷ *n* (*Chem*) Lösungsmittel *nt*

solvent abuse *n* Lösungsmittelmissbrauch *m*

Som. (*Brit*) *abbr* (*Post*) = *Somerset*

Somali [sə'mɑːlɪ] *adj* somalisch ▷ *n* Somalier(in) *m(f)*

Somalia [sə'mɑːlɪə] *n* Somalia *nt*

Somaliland (*formerly*) Somaliland *nt*

sombre, (*US*) **somber** ['sɔmbəʳ] *adj* (*dark*) dunkel, düster; (*serious*) finster

KEYWORD

some [sʌm] *adj* **1** (*a certain amount or number of*) einige; **some tea/water/money** etwas Tee/Wasser/Geld; **some biscuits** ein

paar Plätzchen; **some children came** einige Kinder kamen; **he asked me some questions** er stellte mir ein paar Fragen

2 (*certain: in contrasts*) manche(r, s); **some people say that ...** manche Leute sagen, dass ...; **some films were excellent** einige *or* manche Filme waren ausgezeichnet

3 (*unspecified*) irgendein(e); **some woman was asking for you** eine Frau hat nach Ihnen gefragt; **some day** eines Tages; **some day next week** irgendwann nächste Woche; **that's some house!** das ist vielleicht ein Haus!

▷ *pron* **1** (*a certain number*) einige; **I've got some** (*books etc*) ich habe welche

2 (*a certain amount*) etwas; **I've got some** (*money, milk*) ich habe welche(s); **I've read some of the book** ich habe das Buch teilweise gelesen

▷ *adv*: **some 10 people** etwa 10 Leute

somebody ['sʌmbədɪ] *pron* = **someone**

someday ['sʌmdeɪ] *adv* irgendwann

somehow ['sʌmhau] *adv* irgendwie

someone ['sʌmwʌn] *pron* (*irgend*)jemand; **there's ~ coming** es kommt jemand; **I saw ~ in the garden** ich habe jemanden im Garten gesehen

someplace ['sʌmpleɪs] (*US*) *adv* = **somewhere**

somersault ['sʌməsɔːlt] *n* Salto *m* ▷ *vi* einen Salto machen; (*vehicle*) sich überschlagen

something ['sʌmθɪŋ] *pron* etwas; **~ nice** etwas Schönes; **there's ~ wrong** da stimmt etwas nicht; **would you like ~ to eat/drink?** möchten Sie etwas zu essen/trinken?

sometime ['sʌmtaɪm] *adv* irgendwann; **~ last month** irgendwann letzten Monat; **I'll finish it ~** ich werde es irgendwann fertig machen

sometimes ['sʌmtaɪmz] *adv* manchmal

somewhat ['sʌmwɔt] *adv* etwas, ein wenig; **~ to my surprise** ziemlich zu meiner Überraschung

somewhere ['sʌmwɛəʳ] *adv* (*be*) irgendwo; (*go*) irgendwohin; **~ (or other) in Scotland** irgendwo in Schottland; **~ else** (*be*) woanders; (*go*) woandershin

son [sʌn] *n* Sohn *m*

sonar ['səunɑːʳ] *n* Sonar(gerät) *nt*, Echolot *nt*

sonata [sə'nɑːtə] *n* Sonate *f*

song [sɔŋ] *n* Lied *nt*; (*of bird*) Gesang *m*

songbook ['sɔŋbuk] *n* Liederbuch *nt*

songwriter ['sɔŋraɪtəʳ] *n* Liedermacher *m*

sonic ['sɔnɪk] *adj* (*speed*) Schall-; **~ boom** Überschallknall *m*

son-in-law ['sʌnɪnlɔː] *n* Schwiegersohn *m*

sonnet ['sɔnɪt] *n* Sonett *nt*

sonny ['sʌnɪ] (*inf*) *n* Junge *m*

soon [suːn] *adv* bald; (*a short time after*) bald, schnell; (*early*) früh; **~ afterwards** kurz *or* bald danach; **quite ~** ziemlich bald; **how ~ can you finish it?** bis wann haben Sie es fertig?; **how ~ can you come back?** wann können Sie frühestens wiederkommen?; **see you ~!** bis bald!; *see also* **as**

sooner ['suːnəʳ] *adv* (*time*) früher, eher; (*preference*) lieber; **I would ~ do that** das würde ich lieber tun; **~ or later** früher oder später; **the ~ the better** je eher, desto besser; **no ~ said than done** gesagt, getan; **no ~ had we left than ...** wir waren gerade gegangen, da ...

soot [sut] *n* Ruß *m*

soothe [suːð] *vt* beruhigen; (*pain*) lindern

soothing ['suːðɪŋ] *adj* beruhigend; (*ointment etc*) schmerzlindernd; (*drink*) wohltuend; (*bath*) entspannend

SOP *n abbr* (= *standard operating procedure*) normale Vorgehensweise *f*

sop [sɔp] *n*: **that's only a ~** das soll nur zur Beschwichtigung dienen

sophisticated [sə'fɪstɪkeɪtɪd] *adj* (*woman, lifestyle*) kultiviert; (*audience*) anspruchsvoll; (*machinery*) hoch entwickelt; (*arguments*) differenziert

sophistication [səfɪstɪ'keɪʃən] *n* (*of person*) Kultiviertheit *f*; (*of machine*) hoher Entwicklungsstand *m*; (*of argument etc*) Differenziertheit *f*

sophomore ['sɔfəmɔːʳ] (*US*) *n* Student(in) im 2. Studienjahr

soporific [sɔpə'rɪfɪk] *adj* einschläfernd ▷ *n* Schlafmittel *nt*

sopping ['sɔpɪŋ] *adj*: **~ (wet)** völlig durchnässt

soppy ['sɔpɪ] (*pej*) *adj* (*person*) sentimental; (*film*) schmalzig

soprano [sə'prɑːnəu] *n* Sopranist(in) *m(f)*

sorbet ['sɔːbeɪ] *n* Sorbet *nt* or *m*, Fruchteis *nt*

sorcerer ['sɔːsərəʳ] *n* Hexenmeister *m*

sordid ['sɔːdɪd] *adj* (*dirty*) verkommen; (*wretched*) elend

sore [sɔːʳ] *adj* wund; (*esp US: offended*) verärgert, sauer (*inf*) ▷ *n* wunde Stelle *f*; **to have a ~ throat** Halsschmerzen haben; **it's a ~ point** (*fig*) es ist ein wunder Punkt

sorely ['sɔːlɪ] *adv*: **I am ~ tempted (to)** ich bin sehr in Versuchung(, zu)

soreness ['sɔːnɪs] *n* (*pain*) Schmerz *m*

sorrel ['sɔrəl] *n* (*Bot*) (großer) Sauerampfer *m*

sorrow ['sɔrəu] *n* Trauer *f*; **sorrows** *npl* (*troubles*) Sorgen und Nöte *pl*

sorrowful ['sɔrəuful] *adj* traurig

sorry ['sɔrɪ] *adj* traurig; (*excuse*) faul; (*sight*) jämmerlich; **~!** Entschuldigung!, Verzeihung!; **~?** wie bitte?; **I feel ~ for him** er tut mir leid; **I'm ~ to hear that ...** es tut mir leid, dass ...; **I'm ~ about ...** es tut mir leid wegen ...

sort [sɔːt] *n* Sorte *f*; (*make: of car etc*) Marke *f* ▷ *vt* (*also*: **sort out**) sortieren; (: *problems*) ins Reine bringen; (*Comput*) sortieren; **all ~s of reasons** alle möglichen Gründe; **what ~ do you want?** welche Sorte möchten Sie?; **what ~ of car?** was für ein Auto?; **I'll do nothing of the ~!** das kommt überhaupt nicht infrage!; **it's ~ of awkward** (*inf*) es ist irgendwie schwierig; **to ~ sth out** etw in Ordnung bringen

sort code *n* Bankleitzahl *f*

sortie ['sɔːtɪ] *n* (*Mil*) Ausfall *m*; (*fig*) Ausflug *m*

sorting office ['sɔːtɪŋ-] *n* Postverteilstelle *f*

SOS *n abbr* (= *save our souls*) SOS *nt*

so-so ['səusəu] *adv*, *adj* so lala

soufflé ['suːfleɪ] *n* Soufflé *nt*

sought [sɔːt] *pt*, *pp of* **seek**

sought-after ['sɔːtɑːftəʳ] *adj* begehrt, gesucht; **a much ~ item** ein viel begehrtes Stück

soul [səul] *n* Seele *f*; (*Mus*) Soul *m*; **the poor ~ had nowhere to sleep** der Ärmste hatte keine Unterkunft; **I didn't see a ~** ich habe keine Menschenseele gesehen

soul-destroying ['səuldɪstrɔɪɪŋ] *adj* geisttötend

soulful ['səulful] *adj* (*eyes*) seelenvoll; (*music*) gefühlvoll

soulless ['səullɪs] *adj* (*place*) seelenlos; (*job*) eintönig

soul mate *n* Seelenfreund(in) *m(f)*

soul-searching ['səulsɑːtʃɪŋ] *n*: **after much ~** nach reiflicher Überlegung

sound [saund] *adj* (*healthy*) gesund; (*safe, secure*) sicher; (*not damaged*) einwandfrei; (*reliable*) solide; (*thorough*) gründlich; (*sensible, valid*) vernünftig ▷ *adv*: **to be ~ asleep** tief und fest schlafen ▷ *n* Geräusch *nt*; (*Mus*) Klang *m*; (*on TV etc*) Ton *m*; (*Geog*) Meerenge *f*, Sund *m* ▷ *vt*: **to ~ the alarm** Alarm schlagen ▷ *vi* (*alarm, horn*) ertönen; (*fig: seem*) sich anhören, klingen; **to be of ~ mind** bei klarem Verstand sein; **I don't like the ~ of it** das klingt gar nicht gut; **to ~ one's horn** (*Aut*) hupen; **to ~ like** sich anhören wie; **that ~s like them arriving** das hört sich so an, als ob sie ankommen; **it ~s as if ...** es klingt *or* es hört sich so an, als ob ...

  ▶ **sound off** (*inf*) *vi*: **to ~ off (about)** sich auslassen (über *+acc*)

  ▶ **sound out** *vt* (*person*) aushorchen; (*opinion*) herausbekommen

sound barrier *n* Schallmauer *f*

sound bite *n* prägnantes Zitat *nt*

sound effects *npl* Toneffekte *pl*

sound engineer *n* Toningenieur(in) *m(f)*

sounding ['saundɪŋ] *n* (*Naut*) Loten *nt*, Peilung *f*

sounding board *n* (*Mus*) Resonanzboden *m*; (*fig*): **to use sb as a ~ for one's ideas** seine Ideen an jdm testen

soundly ['saundlɪ] *adv* (*sleep*) tief und fest; (*beat*) tüchtig

soundproof ['saundpruːf] *adj* schalldicht ▷ *vt* schalldicht machen

sound system *n* Verstärkersystem *nt*

soundtrack ['saundtræk] *n* Filmmusik *f*

sound wave *n* Schallwelle *f*

soup [suːp] *n* Suppe *f*; **to be in the ~** (*fig*) in der Tinte sitzen

soup kitchen *n* Suppenküche *f*

soup plate *n* Suppenteller *m*

soupspoon ['suːpspuːn] *n* Suppenlöffel *m*

sour ['sauəʳ] *adj* sauer; (*fig: bad-tempered*) säuerlich; **to go** *or* **turn ~** (*milk, wine*) sauer

S

werden; (*fig: relationship*) sich trüben; **it's ~
grapes** (*fig*) die Trauben hängen zu hoch
source [sɔːs] n Quelle f; (*fig: of problem, anxiety*)
Ursache f; **I have it from a reliable ~ that ...**
ich habe es aus sicherer Quelle, dass ...
south [sauθ] n Süden m ▷ adj südlich, Süd-
▷ adv nach Süden; **(to the) ~ of** im Süden or
südlich von; **to travel ~** nach Süden fahren;
the S~ of France Südfrankreich nt
South Africa n Südafrika nt
South African adj südafrikanisch ▷ n
Südafrikaner(in) m(f)
South America n Südamerika nt
South American adj südamerikanisch ▷ n
Südamerikaner(in) m(f)
southbound ['sauθbaund] adj in Richtung
Süden; (*carriageway*) Richtung Süden
south-east [sauθ'iːst] n Südosten m
South-East Asia n Südostasien nt
southerly ['sʌðəlɪ] adj südlich; (*wind*) aus
südlicher Richtung
southern ['sʌðən] adj südlich, Süd-; **the
~ hemisphere** die südliche Halbkugel or
Hemisphäre
South Korea n Südkorea nt
South Pole n Südpol m
South Sea Islands npl Südseeinseln pl
South Seas npl Südsee f
southward ['sauθwəd], **southwards**
['sauθwədz] adv nach Süden, in Richtung
Süden
south-west [sauθ'wɛst] n Südwesten m
souvenir [suːvə'nɪəʳ] n Andenken nt, Souvenir
nt
sovereign ['sɔvrɪn] n Herrscher(in) m(f)
sovereignty ['sɔvrɪntɪ] n Oberhoheit f,
Souveränität f
soviet ['səuvɪət] (*formerly*) adj sowjetisch ▷ n
Sowjetbürger(in) m(f); **the S~ Union** die
Sowjetunion f
sow[1] [sau] n Sau f
sow[2] [səu] (pt **~ed**, pp **~n**) vt (*lit, fig*) säen
soya ['sɔɪə], **soy** [sɔɪ] (*US*) n: **~ bean** Sojabohne
f; **~ sauce** Sojasoße f
sozzled ['sɔzld] (*Brit: inf*) adj besoffen
spa [spaː] n (*town*) Heilbad nt; (*US: also:* **health
spa**) Fitnesszentrum nt
space [speɪs] n Platz m, Raum m; (*gap*) Lücke
f; (*beyond Earth*) der Weltraum; (*interval, period*)
Zeitraum m ▷ cpd Raum- ▷ vt (*also:* **space out**)
verteilen; **to clear a ~ for sth** für etw Platz
schaffen; **in a confined ~** auf engem Raum;
in a short ~ of time in kurzer Zeit; **(with)in
the ~ of an hour** innerhalb einer Stunde
space bar n (*on keyboard*) Leertaste f
spacecraft ['speɪskrɑːft] n Raumfahrzeug nt
spaceman ['speɪsmæn] (*irreg: like* **man**) n
Raumfahrer m
spaceship ['speɪsʃɪp] n Raumschiff nt
space shuttle n Raumtransporter m
spacesuit ['speɪssuːt] n Raumanzug m
spacewoman ['speɪswumən] (*irreg: like* **woman**)
n Raumfahrerin f

spacing ['speɪsɪŋ] n Abstand m; **single/double
~** einfacher/doppelter Zeilenabstand
spacious ['speɪʃəs] adj geräumig
spade [speɪd] n Spaten m; (*child's*) Schaufel f;
spades npl (*Cards*) Pik nt
spadework ['speɪdwəːk] n (*fig*) Vorarbeit f
spaghetti [spə'gɛtɪ] n Spag(h)etti pl
Spain [speɪn] n Spanien nt
spam [spæm] (*Comput*) n Spam m ▷ vt wit
Werbung bombardieren
span [spæn] n (*of bird, plane, arch*) Spannweite
f; (*in time*) Zeitspanne f ▷ vt überspannen;
(*fig: time*) sich erstrecken über +acc
Spaniard ['spænjəd] n Spanier(in) m(f)
spaniel ['spænjəl] n Spaniel m
Spanish ['spænɪʃ] adj spanisch ▷ n (*Ling*)
Spanisch nt; **the Spanish** npl die Spanier pl; **~
omelette** Omelett mit Paprikaschoten, Zwiebeln,
Tomaten etc
spank [spæŋk] vt: **to ~ sb's bottom** jdm den
Hintern versohlen (*inf*)
spanner ['spænəʳ] (*Brit*) n Schraubenschlüssel
m
spar [spaːʳ] n (*Naut*) Sparren m ▷ vi (*Boxing*) ein
Sparring nt machen
spare [spɛəʳ] adj (*free*) frei; (*extra: part, fuse etc*)
Ersatz- ▷ n = **spare part** ▷ vt (*save: trouble etc*)
(er)sparen; (*make available*) erübrigen; (*afford
to give*) (übrig) haben; (*refrain from hurting*)
verschonen; **these 2 are going ~** diese beiden
sind noch übrig; **to ~** (*surplus*) übrig; **to ~ no
expense** keine Kosten scheuen, an nichts
sparen; **can you ~ the time?** haben Sie Zeit?;
I've a few minutes to ~ ich habe ein paar
Minuten Zeit; **there is no time to ~** es ist
keine Zeit; **~ me the details** verschone mich
mit den Einzelheiten
spare part n Ersatzteil nt
spare room n Gästezimmer nt
spare time n Freizeit f
spare tyre n Reservereifen m
spare wheel n Reserverad nt
sparing ['spɛərɪŋ] adj: **to be ~ with** sparsam
umgehen mit
sparingly ['spɛərɪŋlɪ] adv sparsam
spark [spaːk] n (*lit, fig*) Funke m
sparking plug ['spaːkɪŋ-] n = **spark plug**
sparkle ['spaːkl] n Funkeln nt, Glitzern nt ▷ vi
funkeln, glitzern
sparkler ['spaːkləʳ] n (*firework*) Wunderkerze f
sparkling ['spaːklɪŋ] adj (*water*) mit
Kohlensäure; (*conversation*) vor Geist sprühend;
(*performance*) glänzend; **~ wine** Schaumwein m
spark plug n Zündkerze f
sparring partner ['spaːrɪŋ-] n (*also fig*)
Sparringspartner m
sparrow ['spærəu] n Spatz m
sparse [spaːs] adj spärlich; (*population*) dünn
spartan ['spaːtən] adj (*fig*) spartanisch
spasm ['spæzəm] n (*Med*) Krampf m; (*fig: of anger
etc*) Anfall m
spasmodic [spæz'mɔdɪk] adj (*fig*) sporadisch
spastic ['spæstɪk] (*old*) n Spastiker(in) m(f) ▷ adj

spastisch

spat [spæt] *pt, pp of* **spit** ▷ *n* (*US: quarrel*) Krach *m*

spate [speɪt] *n* (*fig*): **a ~ of** eine Flut von; **to be in full ~** (*river*) Hochwasser führen

spatial ['speɪʃl] *adj* räumlich

spatter ['spætər] *vt* (*liquid*) verspritzen; (*surface*) bespritzen ▷ *vi* spritzen

spatula ['spætjulə] *n* (*Culin*) Spachtel *m*; (*Med*) Spatel *m*

spawn [spɔːn] *vi* laichen ▷ *vt* hervorbringen, erzeugen ▷ *n* Laich *m*

SPCA (*US*) *n abbr* (= *Society for the Prevention of Cruelty to Animals*) Tierschutzverein *m*

SPCC (*US*) *n abbr* (= *Society for the Prevention of Cruelty to Children*) Kinderschutzbund *m*

speak [spiːk] (*pt* **spoke**, *pp* **spoken**) *vt* (*say*) sagen; (*language*) sprechen ▷ *vi* sprechen, reden; (*make a speech*) sprechen; **to ~ one's mind** seine Meinung sagen; **to ~ to sb/of** *or* **about sth** mit jdm/über etw *acc* sprechen *or* reden; **~ up!** sprich lauter!; **to ~ at a conference** bei einer Tagung einen Vortrag halten; **to ~ in a debate** in einer Debatte sprechen; **he has no money to ~ of** er hat so gut wie kein Geld; **so to ~** sozusagen
  ▶ **speak for** *vt fus*: **to ~ for sb** (*on behalf of*) in jds Namen *dat or* für jdn sprechen; **that picture is already spoken for** (*in shop*) das Bild ist schon verkauft *or* vergeben; **~ for yourself!** das meinst auch nur du!

speaker ['spiːkər] *n* (*in public*) Redner(in) *m(f)*; (*also*: **loudspeaker**) Lautsprecher *m*; (*Pol*): **the S~** (*Brit, US*) der Sprecher, die Sprecherin; **are you a Welsh ~?** sprechen Sie Walisisch?

speaking ['spiːkɪŋ] *adj* sprechend; **Italian-- people** Italienischsprechende *pl*; **to be on ~ terms** miteinander reden *or* sprechen; **~ clock** telefonische Zeitansage

spear [spɪər] *n* Speer *m* ▷ *vt* aufspießen

spearhead ['spɪəhɛd] *vt* (*Mil, fig*) anführen

spearmint ['spɪəmɪnt] *n* Grüne Minze *f*

spec [spɛk] (*inf*) *n*: **on ~** auf Verdacht, auf gut Glück; **to buy/go on ~** auf gut Glück kaufen/hingehen

spec. *n abbr* (*Tech*) = **specification**

special ['spɛʃl] *adj* besondere(r, s); (*service, performance, adviser, permission, school*) Sonder- ▷ *n* (*train*) Sonderzug *m*; **take ~ care** pass besonders gut auf; **nothing ~** nichts Besonderes; **today's ~** (*at restaurant*) Tagesgericht *nt*

special agent *n* Agent(in) *m(f)*

special correspondent *n* Sonderberichterstatter(in) *m(f)*

special delivery *n* (*Post*): **by ~** durch Eilzustellung

special effects *npl* Spezialeffekte *pl*

specialist ['spɛʃəlɪst] *n* Spezialist(in) *m(f)*; (*Med*) Facharzt *m*, Fachärztin *f*; **heart ~** Facharzt *m*/Fachärztin *f* für Herzkrankheiten

speciality [spɛʃɪ'ælɪtɪ] *n* Spezialität *f*; (*study*) Spezialgebiet *nt*

specialize ['spɛʃəlaɪz] *vi*: **to ~ (in)** sich

specialisieren (auf +*acc*)

specially ['spɛʃlɪ] *adv* besonders, extra

special offer *n* Sonderangebot *nt*

specialty ['spɛʃəltɪ] (*esp US*) = **speciality**

species ['spiːʃiːz] *n inv* Art *f*

specific [spə'sɪfɪk] *adj* (*fixed*) bestimmt; (*exact*) genau; **to be ~ to** eigentümlich sein für

specifically [spə'sɪfɪklɪ] *adv* (*specially*) speziell; (*exactly*) genau; **more ~** und zwar

specification [spɛsɪfɪ'keɪʃən] *n* genaue Angabe *f*; (*requirement*) Bedingung *f*; **specifications** *npl* (*Tech*) technische Daten *pl*

specify ['spɛsɪfaɪ] *vt* angeben; **unless otherwise specified** wenn nicht anders angegeben

specimen ['spɛsɪmən] *n* Exemplar *nt*; (*Med*) Probe *f*

specimen copy *n* Belegexemplar *nt*, Probeexemplar *nt*

specimen signature *n* Unterschriftsprobe *f*

speck [spɛk] *n* Fleckchen *nt*; (*of dust*) Körnchen *nt*

speckled ['spɛkld] *adj* gesprenkelt

specs [spɛks] (*inf*) *npl* Brille *f*

spectacle ['spɛktəkl] *n* (*scene*) Schauspiel *nt*; (*sight*) Anblick *m*; (*grand event*) Spektakel *nt*; **spectacles** *npl* (*glasses*) Brille *f*

spectacle case (*Brit*) *n* Brillenetui *nt*

spectacular [spɛk'tækjulər] *adj* sensationell; (*success*) spektakulär ▷ *n* (*Theat etc*) Show *f*

spectator [spɛk'teɪtər] *n* Zuschauer(in) *m(f)*; **~ sport** Publikumssport *m*

spectra ['spɛktrə] *npl of* **spectrum**

spectre, (*US*) **specter** ['spɛktər] *n* Gespenst *nt*; (*fig*) (Schreck)gespenst *nt*

spectrum ['spɛktrəm] (*pl* **spectra**) *n* (*lit, fig*) Spektrum *nt*

speculate ['spɛkjuleɪt] *vi* (*Fin*) spekulieren; **to ~ about** spekulieren *or* Vermutungen anstellen über +*acc*

speculation [spɛkju'leɪʃən] *n* Spekulation *f*

speculative ['spɛkjulətɪv] *adj* spekulativ

speculator ['spɛkjuleɪtər] *n* Spekulant(in) *m(f)*

sped [spɛd] *pt, pp of* **speed**

speech [spiːtʃ] *n* Sprache *f*; (*manner of speaking*) Sprechweise *f*; (*enunciation*) (Aus)sprache *f*; (*formal talk, Theat*) Rede *f*

speech day (*Brit*) *n* (*Scol*) = Schulfeier *f*

speech impediment *n* Sprachfehler *m*

speechless ['spiːtʃlɪs] *adj* sprachlos

speech recognition software *n* (*Comput*) Spracherkennungssoftware *f*

speech therapist *n* Logopäde *m*, Logopädin *f*, Sprachtherapeut(in) *m(f)*

speech therapy *n* Logopädie *f*, Sprachtherapie *f*

speed [spiːd] (*pt, pp* **sped**) *n* Geschwindigkeit *f*, Schnelligkeit *f* ▷ *vi* (*exceed speed limit*) zu schnell fahren; **to ~ along** dahinsausen; **to ~ by** (*car etc*) vorbeischießen; (*years*) verfliegen; **at ~** (*Brit*) mit hoher Geschwindigkeit; **at full** *or* **top ~** mit Höchstgeschwindigkeit; **at a ~ of 70km/h** mit (einer Geschwindigkeit *or* einem

S

Tempo von) 70 km/h; **shorthand/typing ~s** Silben/Anschläge pro Minute; **a five-~ gearbox** ein Fünfganggetriebe nt
▶ **speed up** (pt, pp **~ed up**) vi beschleunigen; (fig) sich beschleunigen ▷ vt beschleunigen
speedboat ['spiːdbəut] n Rennboot nt
speed dial (Tel) n Kurzwahl f ▷ adj Kurzwahl-; **~ button** Kurzwahltaste f
speedily ['spiːdɪlɪ] adv schnell
speeding ['spiːdɪŋ] n Geschwindigkeitsüberschreitung f
speed limit n Tempolimit nt, Geschwindigkeitsbegrenzung f
speedometer [spɪ'dɒmɪtəʳ] n Tachometer m
speed trap n Radarfalle f
speedway ['spiːdweɪ] n (also: **speedway racing**) Speedway-Rennen nt
speedy ['spiːdɪ] adj schnell; (reply, settlement) prompt
speleologist [spɛlɪ'ɒlədʒɪst] n Höhlenkundler(in) m(f)
spell [spɛl] (Brit) (pt, pp **~ed**) n (also: **magic spell**) Zauber m; (incantation) Zauberspruch m; (period of time) Zeit f, Weile f ▷ vt schreiben; (also: **spell out**: aloud) buchstabieren; (signify) bedeuten; **to cast a ~ on sb** jdn verzaubern; **cold ~** Kältewelle f; **how do you ~ your name?** wie schreibt sich Ihr Name?; **can you ~ it for me?** können Sie das bitte buchstabieren?; **he can't ~** er kann keine Rechtschreibung
spellbound ['spɛlbaund] adj gebannt
spelling ['spɛlɪŋ] n Schreibweise f; (ability) Rechtschreibung f; **~ mistake** Rechtschreibfehler m
spelt [spɛlt] pt, pp of **spell**
spend [spɛnd] (pt, pp **spent**) vt (money) ausgeben; (time, life) verbringen; **to ~ time/ money/effort on sth** Zeit/Geld/Mühe für etw aufbringen
spending ['spɛndɪŋ] n Ausgaben pl; **government ~** öffentliche Ausgaben pl
spending money n Taschengeld nt
spending power n Kaufkraft f
spendthrift ['spɛndθrɪft] n Verschwender(in) m(f)
spent [spɛnt] pt, pp of **spend** ▷ adj (patience) erschöpft; (cartridge, bullets) verbraucht; (match) abgebrannt
sperm [spəːm] n Samenzelle f, Spermium nt
sperm bank n Samenbank f
sperm whale n Pottwal m
spew [spjuː] vt (also: **spew up**) erbrechen; (fig) ausspucken
sphere [sfɪəʳ] n Kugel f; (area) Gebiet nt, Bereich m
spherical ['sfɛrɪkl] adj kugelförmig
sphinx [sfɪŋks] n Sphinx f
spice [spaɪs] n Gewürz nt ▷ vt würzen
spick-and-span ['spɪkən'spæn] adj blitzsauber
spicy ['spaɪsɪ] adj stark gewürzt
spider ['spaɪdəʳ] n Spinne f; **~'s web** Spinnengewebe nt, Spinnennetz nt
spidery ['spaɪdərɪ] adj (handwriting) krakelig

spiel [spiːl] (inf) n Sermon m
spike [spaɪk] n (point) Spitze f; (Bot) Ähre f; (Elec) Spannungsspitze f; **spikes** npl (Sport) Spikes pl
spike heel (US) n Pfennigabsatz m
spiky ['spaɪkɪ] adj stachelig; (branch) dornig
spill [spɪl] (pt, pp **spilt** or **~ed**) vt verschütten ▷ vi verschüttet werden; **to ~ the beans** (inf: fig) alles ausplaudern
▶ **spill out** vi (people) herausströmen
▶ **spill over** vi überlaufen; (fig: spread) sich ausbreiten; **to ~ over into** sich auswirken auf +acc
spillage ['spɪlɪdʒ] n (act) Verschütten nt; (quantity) verschüttete Menge f
spin [spɪn] (pt **spun**, **span**, pp **spun**) n (trip) Spritztour f; (revolution) Drehung f; (Aviat) Trudeln nt; (on ball) Drall m ▷ vt (wool etc) spinnen; (ball, coin) (hoch)werfen; (wheel) drehen; (Brit: also: **spin-dry**) schleudern ▷ vi (make thread) spinnen; (person) sich drehen; (car etc) schleudern; **to ~ a yarn** Seemannsgarn spinnen; **to ~ a coin** (Brit) eine Münze werfen; **my head is ~ning** mir dreht sich alles
▶ **spin out** vt (talk) ausspinnen; (job, holiday) in die Länge ziehen; (money) strecken
spina bifida ['spaɪnə'bɪfɪdə] n offene Wirbelsäule f, Spina bifida f
spinach ['spɪnɪtʃ] n Spinat m
spinal ['spaɪnl] adj (injury etc) Rückgrat-
spinal column n Wirbelsäule f
spinal cord n Rückenmark nt
spindly ['spɪndlɪ] adj spindeldürr
spin doctor n PR-Fachmann m, PR-Fachfrau f
spin-dry ['spɪn'draɪ] vt schleudern
spin-dryer [spɪn'draɪəʳ] (Brit) n (Wäsche)schleuder f
spine [spaɪn] n (Anat) Rückgrat nt; (thorn) Stachel m
spine-chilling ['spaɪntʃɪlɪŋ] adj schaurig, gruselig
spineless ['spaɪnlɪs] adj (fig) rückgratlos
spinner ['spɪnəʳ] n (of thread) Spinner(in) m(f)
spinning ['spɪnɪŋ] n (art) Spinnen nt
spinning top n Kreisel m
spinning wheel n Spinnrad nt
spin-off ['spɪnɔf] n (fig) Nebenprodukt nt
spinster ['spɪnstəʳ] n unverheiratete Frau; (pej) alte Jungfer
spiral ['spaɪərl] n Spirale f ▷ vi (fig: prices etc) in die Höhe klettern; **the inflationary ~** die Inflationsspirale
spiral staircase n Wendeltreppe f
spire ['spaɪəʳ] n Turmspitze f
spirit ['spɪrɪt] n Geist m; (soul) Seele f; (energy) Elan m, Schwung m; (courage) Mut m; (sense) Geist m, Sinn m; (frame of mind) Stimmung f; **spirits** npl (drink) Spirituosen pl; **in good ~s** guter Laune; **community ~** Gemeinschaftssinn m
spirited ['spɪrɪtɪd] adj (resistance, defence) mutig; (performance) lebendig
spirit level n Wasserwaage f
spiritual ['spɪrɪtjuəl] adj geistig, seelisch;

(*religious*) geistlich ▷ *n* (*also:* **Negro spiritual**) Spiritual *nt*

spiritualism ['spɪrɪtjuəlɪzəm] *n* Spiritismus *m*

spit [spɪt] (*pt, pp* **spat**) *n* (*for roasting*) Spieß *m*; (*saliva*) Spucke *f* ▷ *vi* spucken; (*fire*) Funken sprühen; (*cooking*) spritzen; (*inf: rain*) tröpfeln

spite [spaɪt] *n* Boshaftigkeit *f* ▷ *vt* ärgern; **in ~ of** trotz +*gen*

spiteful ['spaɪtful] *adj* boshaft, gemein

spitroast ['spɪtrəust] *n* Spießbraten *m*

spitting ['spɪtɪŋ] *n:* "~ **prohibited**" „Spucken verboten" ▷ *adj:* **to be the ~ image of sb** jdm wie aus dem Gesicht geschnitten sein

spittle ['spɪtl] *n* Speichel *m*, Spucke *f*

spiv [spɪv] (*Brit: inf: pej*) *n* schmieriger Typ *m*

splash [splæʃ] *n* (*sound*) Platschen *nt*; (*of colour*) Tupfer *m* ▷ *excl* platsch! ▷ *vi* (*also:* **splash about**) herumplan(t)schen; (*water, rain*) spritzen; **to ~ paint on the floor** den Fußboden mit Farbe bespritzen

splashdown ['splæʃdaun] *n* (*Space*) Wasserung *f*

splayfooted ['spleɪfutɪd] *adj* mit nach außen gestellten Füßen

spleen [spli:n] *n* Milz *f*

splendid ['splɛndɪd] *adj* hervorragend, ausgezeichnet; (*impressive*) prächtig

splendour, (*US*) **splendor** ['splɛndə'] *n* Pracht *f*; **splendours** *npl* Pracht *f*

splice [splaɪs] *vt* spleißen, kleben

splint [splɪnt] *n* Schiene *f*

splinter ['splɪntə'] *n* Splitter *m* ▷ *vi* (zer)splittern

splinter group *n* Splittergruppe *f*

split [splɪt] (*pt, pp* ~) *n* (*tear*) Riss *m*; (*fig: division*) Aufteilung *f*; (: *difference*) Kluft *f*; (*Pol*) Spaltung *f* ▷ *vt* (*divide*) aufteilen; (*party*) spalten; (*share equally*) teilen ▷ *vi* (*divide*) sich aufteilen; (*tear*) reißen; **to do the ~s** (einen) Spagat machen; **let's ~ the difference** teilen wir uns die Differenz

▶ **split up** *vi* sich trennen; (*meeting*) sich auflösen

split-level ['splɪtlɛvl] *adj* mit versetzten Geschossen

split peas *npl* getrocknete (halbe) Erbsen *pl*

split personality *n* gespaltene Persönlichkeit *f*

split second *n* Bruchteil *m* einer Sekunde

splitting ['splɪtɪŋ] *adj:* **a ~ headache** rasende Kopfschmerzen *pl*

splutter ['splʌtə'] *vi* (*engine etc*) stottern; (*person*) prusten

spoil [spɔɪl] (*pt, pp* **spoilt** *or* ~**ed**) *vt* verderben; (*child*) verwöhnen; (*ballot paper, vote*) ungültig machen ▷ *vi:* **to be ~ing for a fight** Streit suchen

spoils [spɔɪlz] *npl* Beute *f*; (*fig*) Gewinn *m*

spoilsport ['spɔɪlspɔ:t] (*pej*) *n* Spielverderber *m*

spoilt [spɔɪlt] *pt, pp of* **spoil** ▷ *adj* (*child*) verwöhnt; (*ballot paper*) ungültig

spoke [spəuk] *pt of* **speak** ▷ *n* Speiche *f*

spoken ['spəukn] *pp of* **speak**

spokesman ['spəuksmən] (*irreg: like* **man**) *n*

Sprecher *m*

spokesperson ['spəukspə:sn] *n* Sprecher(in) *m(f)*

spokeswoman ['spəukswumən] (*irreg: like* **woman**) *n* Sprecherin *f*

sponge [spʌndʒ] *n* Schwamm *m*; (*also:* **sponge cake**) Biskuit(kuchen) *m* ▷ *vt* mit einem Schwamm waschen ▷ *vi:* **to ~ off** *or* **on sb** jdm auf der Tasche liegen

sponge bag (*Brit*) *n* Waschbeutel *m*, Kulturbeutel *m*

sponger ['spʌndʒə'] (*pej*) *n* Schmarotzer *m*

spongy ['spʌndʒɪ] *adj* schwammig

sponsor ['sponsə'] *n* Sponsor(in) *m(f)*, Geldgeber(in) *m(f)*; (*Brit: for charitable event*) Sponsor(in) *m(f)*; (*for application, bill etc*) Befürworter(in) *m(f)* ▷ *vt* sponsern, finanziell unterstützen; (*fund-raiser*) sponsern; (*applicant*) unterstützen; (*proposal, bill etc*) befürworten; **I ~ed him at 3p a mile** (*in fund-raising race*) ich habe mich verpflichtet, ihm 3 Pence pro Meile zu geben

sponsorship ['sponsəʃɪp] *n* finanzielle Unterstützung *f*

spontaneity [spontə'neɪɪtɪ] *n* Spontaneität *f*

spontaneous [spon'teɪnɪəs] *adj* spontan; **~ combustion** Selbstentzündung *f*

spoof [spu:f] *n* (*parody*) Parodie *f*; (*hoax*) Ulk *m*

spooky ['spu:kɪ] (*inf*) *adj* gruselig

spool [spu:l] *n* Spule *f*

spoon [spu:n] *n* Löffel *m*

spoon-feed ['spu:nfi:d] *vt* (mit dem Löffel) füttern; (*fig*) gängeln

spoonful ['spu:nful] *n* Löffel *m*

sporadic [spə'rædɪk] *adj* sporadisch, vereinzelt

sport [spɔ:t] *n* Sport *m*; (*type*) Sportart *f*; (*also:* **good sport:** *person*) feiner Kerl *m* ▷ *vt* (*wear*) tragen; **indoor ~s** Hallensport *m*; **outdoor ~s** Sport *m* im Freien

sporting ['spɔ:tɪŋ] *adj* (*event etc*) Sport-; (*generous*) großzügig; **to give sb a ~ chance** jdm eine faire Chance geben

sport jacket (*US*) *n* = **sports jacket**

sports car *n* Sportwagen *m*

sports centre *n* Sportzentrum *nt*

sports ground *n* Sportplatz *m*

sports jacket (*Brit*) *n* Sakko *m*

sportsman ['spɔ:tsmən] (*irreg: like* **man**) *n* Sportler *m*

sportsmanship ['spɔ:tsmənʃɪp] *n* Sportlichkeit *f*

sports page *n* Sportseite *f*

sportswear ['spɔ:tsweə'] *n* Sportkleidung *f*

sportswoman ['spɔ:tswumən] (*irreg: like* **woman**) *n* Sportlerin *f*

sporty ['spɔ:tɪ] *adj* sportlich

spot [spot] *n* (*mark*) Fleck *m*; (*dot*) Punkt *m*; (*on skin*) Pickel *m*; (*place*) Stelle *f*, Platz *m*; (*Radio, TV*) Nummer *f*, Auftritt *m*; (*also:* **spot advertisement**) Werbespot *m*; (*small amount*): **a ~ of** ein bisschen ▷ *vt* entdecken; **on the ~** (*in that place*) an Ort und Stelle; (*immediately*) auf der Stelle; **to be in a ~** in der Klemme sitzen; **to put sb on the ~** jdn in Verlegenheit bringen; **to come out in ~s** Pickel bekommen

spot check n Stichprobe f

spotless ['spɒtlɪs] adj makellos sauber

spotlight ['spɒtlaɪt] n Scheinwerfer m; (in room) Strahler m

spot-on [spɒt'ɒn] (Brit: inf) adj genau richtig

spot price n Kassapreis m

spotted ['spɒtɪd] adj gepunktet

spotty ['spɒtɪ] adj pickelig

spouse [spaʊs] n (male) Gatte m; (female) Gattin f

spout [spaʊt] n (of jug, teapot) Tülle f; (of pipe) Ausfluss m; (of liquid) Strahl m ▷ vi spritzen; (flames) sprühen

sprain [spreɪn] n Verstauchung f ▷ vt: **to ~ one's ankle/wrist** sich dat den Knöchel/das Handgelenk verstauchen

sprang [spræŋ] pt of **spring**

sprawl [sprɔːl] vi (person) sich ausstrecken; (place) wild wuchern ▷ n: **urban ~** wild wuchernde Ausbreitung des Stadtgebietes; **to send sb ~ing** jdn zu Boden werfen

spray [spreɪ] n (small drops) Sprühnebel m; (sea spray) Gischt m or f; (container) Sprühdose f; (garden spray) Sprühgerät nt; (of flowers) Strauß m ▷ vt sprühen, spritzen; (crops) spritzen ▷ cpd (deodorant) Sprüh-; **~ can** Sprühdose f

spread [spred] (pt, pp ~) n (range) Spektrum nt; (selection) Auswahl f; (distribution) Verteilung f; (for bread) (Brot)aufstrich m; (inf: food) Festessen nt; (Press, Typ: two pages) Doppelseite f ▷ vt ausbreiten; (butter) streichen; (workload, wealth, repayments etc) verteilen; (scatter) verstreuen; (rumour, disease) verbreiten ▷ vi (disease, news) sich verbreiten; (also: **spread out**: stain) sich ausbreiten; **to get a middle-age ~** in den mittleren Jahren Speck ansetzen
   ▶ **spread out** vi (move apart) sich verteilen

spread-eagled ['spredi:gld] adj mit ausgestreckten Armen und Beinen; **to be** or **lie ~** mit ausgestreckten Armen und Beinen daliegen

spreadsheet ['spredʃi:t] n (Comput) Tabellenkalkulation f

spree [spri:] n: **to go on a ~** (drinking) eine Zechtour machen; (spending) groß einkaufen gehen

sprig [sprɪg] n Zweig m

sprightly ['spraɪtlɪ] adj rüstig

spring [sprɪŋ] (pt **sprang**, pp **sprung**) n (coiled metal) Sprungfeder f; (season) Frühling m, Frühjahr nt; (of water) Quelle f ▷ vi (leap) springen ▷ vt: **to ~ a leak** (pipe etc) undicht werden; **in ~** im Frühling or Frühjahr; **to walk with a ~ in one's step** mit federnden Schritten gehen; **to ~ from** (result) herrühren von; **to ~ into action** aktiv werden; **he sprang the news on me** er hat mich mit der Nachricht überrascht
   ▶ **spring up** vi (building, plant) aus dem Boden schießen

springboard ['sprɪŋbɔːd] n (Sport, fig)

Sprungbrett nt

spring-clean [sprɪŋ'kli:n], **spring-cleaning** [sprɪŋ'kli:nɪŋ] n Frühjahrsputz m

spring onion (Brit) n Frühlingszwiebel f

spring roll n Frühlingsrolle f

springtime ['sprɪŋtaɪm] n Frühling m

springy ['sprɪŋɪ] adj federnd; (mattress) weich gefedert

sprinkle ['sprɪŋkl] vt (liquid) sprenkeln; (salt, sugar) streuen; **to ~ water on, ~ with water** mit Wasser besprengen; **to ~ sugar etc on, ~ with sugar** etc mit Zucker etc bestreuen

sprinkler ['sprɪŋklə^r] n (for lawn) Rasensprenger m; (to put out fire) Sprinkler m

sprinkling ['sprɪŋklɪŋ] n: **a ~ of** (water) ein paar Tropfen; (salt, sugar) eine Prise; (fig) ein paar ...

sprint [sprɪnt] n Sprint m ▷ vi rennen; (Sport) sprinten; **the 200 metres ~** der 200-Meter-Lauf

sprinter ['sprɪntə^r] n Sprinter(in) m(f)

sprite [spraɪt] n Kobold m

spritzer ['sprɪtsə^r] n Schorle f

sprocket ['sprɒkɪt] n Kettenzahnrad nt

sprout [spraʊt] vi sprießen; (vegetable) keimen

sprouts [spraʊts] npl (also: **Brussels sprouts**) Rosenkohl m

spruce [spru:s] n inv Fichte f ▷ adj gepflegt, adrett
   ▶ **spruce up** vt auf Vordermann bringen (inf); **to ~ o.s. up** sein Äußeres pflegen

sprung [sprʌn] pp of **spring**

spry [spraɪ] adj rüstig

SPUC n abbr (= Society for the Protection of the Unborn Child) Gesellschaft zum Schutz des ungeborenen Lebens

spud [spʌd] (inf) n Kartoffel f

spun [spʌn] pt, pp of **spin**

spur [spə:^r] n Sporn m; (fig) Ansporn m ▷ vt (also: **spur on**: fig) anspornen; **on the ~ of the moment** ganz spontan

spurious ['spjʊərɪəs] adj falsch

spurn [spə:n] vt verschmähen

spurt [spə:t] n (of blood etc) Strahl m; (of energy) Anwandlung f ▷ vi (blood) (heraus)spritzen; **to put on a ~** (lit, fig) einen Spurt einlegen

sputter ['spʌtə^r] vi = **splutter**

spy [spaɪ] n Spion(in) m(f) ▷ vi: **to ~ on** nachspionieren +dat ▷ vt sehen ▷ cpd (film, story) Spionage-

spying ['spaɪɪŋ] n Spionage f

Sq. abbr (in address: = square) ≈ Pl.

sq. abbr = **square**

squabble ['skwɒbl] vi (sich) zanken ▷ n Streit m

squad [skwɒd] n (Mil) Trupp m; (Police) Kommando nt; (: drug/fraud squad) Dezernat nt; (Sport) Mannschaft f; **flying ~** (Police) Überfallkommando nt

squad car (Brit) n (Police) Streifenwagen m

squaddie ['skwɒdɪ] (Brit) n (private soldier) Gefreite(r) m

squadron ['skwɒdrn] n (Mil) Schwadron f; (Aviat) Staffel f; (Naut) Geschwader nt

squalid ['skwɒlɪd] adj verkommen; (conditions) elend; (sordid) erbärmlich

squall [skwɔ:l] *n* Bö(e) *f*
squalor ['skwɔlə^r] *n* Elend *nt*
squander ['skwɔndə^r] *vt* verschwenden;
(*chances*) vertun
square [skwɛə^r] *n* Quadrat *nt*; (*in town*) Platz *m*;
(*US: block of houses*) Block *m*; (*also:* **set square**)
Zeichendreieck *nt*; (*inf: person*) Spießer *m*
▷ *adj* quadratisch; (*inf: ideas, person*) spießig
▷ *vt* (*arrange*) ausrichten; (*Math*) quadrieren;
(*reconcile*) in Einklang bringen ▷ *vi* (*accord*)
übereinstimmen; **we're back to ~ one**
jetzt sind wir wieder da, wo wir angefangen
haben; **all ~** (*Sport*) unentschieden; (*fig*)
quitt; **a ~ meal** eine ordentliche Mahlzeit;
2 metres ~ 2 Meter im Quadrat; **2 ~ metres**
2 Quadratmeter; **I'll ~ it with him** (*inf*) ich
mache das mit ihm ab; **can you ~ it with
your conscience?** können Sie das mit Ihrem
Gewissen vereinbaren?
  ▷ **square up** (*Brit*) *vi* abrechnen
square bracket *n* eckige Klammer *f*
squarely ['skwɛəlɪ] *adv* (*directly*) direkt, genau;
(*firmly*) fest; (*honestly*) ehrlich; (*fairly*) gerecht,
fair
square root *n* Quadratwurzel *f*
squash [skwɔʃ] *n* (*Brit*): **lemon/orange
~** Zitronen-/Orangensaftgetränk *nt*;
(*US: marrow etc*) Kürbis *m*; (*Sport*) Squash *nt* ▷ *vt*
zerquetschen
squat [skwɔt] *adj* gedrungen ▷ *vi* (*also:* **squat
down**) sich (hin)hocken; (*on property*): **to ~ (in a
house)** ein Haus besetzen
squatter ['skwɔtə^r] *n* Hausbesetzer(in) *m(f)*
squawk [skwɔ:k] *vi* kreischen
squeak [skwi:k] *vi* quietschen; (*mouse etc*)
piepsen ▷ *n* Quietschen *nt*; (*of mouse etc*)
Piepsen *nt*
squeaky-clean [skwi:kɪˈkli:n] (*inf*) *adj*
blitzsauber
squeal [skwi:l] *vi* quietschen
squeamish ['skwi:mɪʃ] *adj* empfindlich
squeeze [skwi:z] *n* Drücken *nt*; (*Econ*)
Beschränkung *f*; (*also:* **credit squeeze**)
Kreditbeschränkung *f* ▷ *vt* drücken; (*lemon
etc*) auspressen ▷ *vi*: **to ~ past sth** sich an
etw *dat* vorbeidrücken; **to ~ under sth** sich
unter etw *dat* durchzwängen; **to give sth a
~** etw drücken; **a ~ of lemon** ein Spritzer *m*
Zitronensaft
  ▷ **squeeze out** *vt* (*juice etc*) (her)auspressen;
(*fig: exclude*) hinausdrängen
squelch [skwɛltʃ] *vi* (*mud etc*) quatschen
squib [skwɪb] *n* Knallfrosch *m*
squid [skwɪd] *n* Tintenfisch *m*
squiggle ['skwɪgl] *n* Schnörkel *m*
squint [skwɪnt] *vi* (*in the sunlight*) blinzeln ▷ *n*
(*Med*) Schielen *nt*; **he has a ~** er schielt
squire ['skwaɪə^r] (*Brit*) *n* Gutsherr *m*; (*inf*) Chef
m
squirm [skwə:m] *vi* (*lit, fig*) sich winden
squirrel ['skwɪrəl] *n* Eichhörnchen *nt*
squirt [skwə:t] *vi, vt* spritzen
Sr *abbr* (*in names:* = *senior*) sen.; (*Rel*) = **sister**

SRC (*Brit*) *n abbr* (= *Students' Representative Council*)
studentische Vertretung
Sri Lanka [srɪˈlæŋkə] *n* Sri Lanka *nt*
SRO (*US*) *abbr* (= *standing room only*) nur
Stehplätze
SS *abbr* = **steamship**
SSA (*US*) *n abbr* (= *Social Security Administration*)
Sozialversicherungsbehörde
SST (*US*) *n abbr* (= *supersonic transport*)
Überschallverkehr *m*
ST (*US*) *abbr* = **standard time**
St *abbr* (= *saint*) St.; (= *street*) Str.
stab [stæb] *n* Stich *m*, Stoß *m*; (*inf: try*): **to
have a ~ at sth** etw probieren ▷ *vt* (*person*)
niederstechen; (*body*) einstechen auf +*acc*; **a
~ of pain** ein stechender Schmerz; **to ~ sb to
death** jdn erstechen
stabbing ['stæbɪŋ] *n* Messerstecherei *f* ▷ *adj*
(*pain*) stechend
stability [stəˈbɪlɪtɪ] *n* Stabilität *f*
stabilization [steɪbəlaɪˈzeɪʃən] *n* Stabilisierung
f
stabilize ['steɪbəlaɪz] *vt* stabilisieren ▷ *vi* sich
stabilisieren
stabilizer ['steɪbəlaɪzə^r] *n* (*Aviat*)
Stabilisierungsfläche *f*; (*Naut, food additive*)
Stabilisator *m*
stable ['steɪbl] *adj* stabil; (*marriage*) dauerhaft
▷ *n* Stall *m*; **riding ~s** Reitstall *m*
staccato [stəˈkɑːtəu] *adv* (*Mus*) stakkato ▷ *adj*
abgehackt
stack [stæk] *n* Stapel *m*; (*of books etc*) Stoß
m ▷ *vt* (*also:* **stack up**) aufstapeln; **~s of
time** (*Brit: inf*) jede Menge Zeit; **to ~ with**
vollstapeln mit
stadia ['steɪdɪə] *npl of* **stadium**
stadium ['steɪdɪəm] (*pl* **stadia** *or* **~s**) *n* Stadion
nt
staff [stɑ:f] *n* (*workforce, servants*) Personal *nt*;
(*Brit: also:* **teaching staff**) (Lehrer)kollegium *nt*;
(*stick, Mil*) Stab *m* ▷ *vt* (mit Personal) besetzen;
one of his ~ einer seiner Mitarbeiter; **a
member of ~** ein(e) Mitarbeiter(in) *m(f)*; (*Scol*)
ein(e) Lehrer(in) *m(f)*
staffroom ['stɑ:fru:m] *n* (*Scol*) Lehrerzimmer *nt*
Staffs (*Brit*) *abbr* (*Post*) = **Staffordshire**
stag [stæg] *n* Hirsch *m*; (*Brit: Stock Exchange*)
Spekulant *m* (*der junge Aktien aufkauft*); **~ market**
(*Brit: Stock Exchange*) Spekulantenmarkt *m*
stage [steɪdʒ] *n* Bühne *f*; (*platform*) Podium *nt*;
(*point, period*) Stadium *nt* ▷ *vt* (*play*) aufführen;
(*demonstration*) organisieren; (*perform: recovery
etc*) schaffen; **the ~** das Theater, die Bühne; **in
~s** etappenweise; **to go through a difficult ~**
eine schwierige Phase durchmachen; **in the
early/final ~s** im Anfangs-/Endstadium
stagecoach ['steɪdʒkəutʃ] *n* Postkutsche *f*
stage door *n* Bühneneingang *m*
stage fright *n* Lampenfieber *nt*
stagehand ['steɪdʒhænd] *n*
Bühnenarbeiter(in) *m(f)*
stage-manage ['steɪdʒmænɪdʒ] *vt* (*fig*)
inszenieren

S

stage manager n Inspizient(in) m(f)

stagger ['stægə'] vi schwanken, taumeln ▷ vt (amaze) die Sprache verschlagen +dat; (hours, holidays) staffeln

staggering ['stægərɪŋ] adj (amazing) atemberaubend

staging post ['steɪdʒɪŋ-] n Zwischenstation f

stagnant ['stægnənt] adj (water) stehend; (economy etc) stagnierend

stagnate [stæg'neɪt] vi (economy etc) stagnieren; (person) verdummen

stagnation [stæg'neɪʃən] n Stagnation f

stag night, stag party n Herrenabend m; siehe Info-Artikel

⬡ **STAG NIGHT**

Als stag night bezeichnet man eine feuchtfröhliche Männerparty, die kurz vor einer Hochzeit vom Bräutigam und seinen Freunden meist in einem Gasthaus oder Nachtklub abgehalten wird. Diese Feiern sind oft sehr ausgelassen und können manchmal auch zu weit gehen (wenn dem betrunkenen Bräutigam ein Streich gespielt wird). Siehe auch hen night.

staid [steɪd] adj gesetzt

stain [steɪn] n Fleck m; (colouring) Beize f ▷ vt beflecken; (wood) beizen

stained glass window [steɪnd-] n buntes Glasfenster nt

stainless steel ['steɪnlɪs-] n (rostfreier) Edelstahl m

stain remover n Fleckentferner m

stair [stεə'] n (step) Stufe f; **stairs** npl (flight of steps) Treppe f; **on the ~s** auf der Treppe

staircase ['stεəkeɪs] n Treppe f

stairway ['stεəweɪ] n = **staircase**

stairwell ['stεəwεl] n Treppenhaus nt

stake [steɪk] n (post) Pfahl m, Pfosten m; (Comm) Anteil m; (Betting: gen pl) Einsatz m ▷ vt (money) setzen; (also: **stake out**: area) abstecken; **to be at ~** auf dem Spiel stehen; **to have a ~ in sth** einen Anteil an etw dat haben; **to ~ a claim (to sth)** sich dat ein Anrecht (auf etw acc) sichern; **to ~ one's life on sth** seinen Kopf auf etw acc wetten; **to ~ one's reputation on sth** sich für etw verbürgen

stakeout ['steɪkaut] n (surveillance) Überwachung f

stalactite ['stæləktaɪt] n Stalaktit m

stalagmite ['stæləgmaɪt] n Stalagmit m

stale [steɪl] adj (bread) altbacken; (food) alt; (smell) muffig; (air) verbraucht; (beer) schal

stalemate ['steɪlmeɪt] n (Chess) Patt nt; (fig) Sackgasse f

stalk [stɔːk] n Stiel m ▷ vt sich heranpirschen an +acc ▷ vi: **to ~ out/off** hinaus-/davonstolzieren

stall [stɔːl] n (Brit: in market etc) Stand m; (in stable) Box f ▷ vt (engine, car) abwürgen; (fig: person) hinhalten; (: decision etc)

hinauszögern ▷ vi (engine) absterben; (car) stehen bleiben; (fig: person) ausweichen; **stalls** npl (Brit: in cinema, theatre) Parkett nt; **a seat in the ~s** ein Platz im Parkett; **a clothes/flower ~** ein Kleidungs-/Blumenstand; **to ~ for time** versuchen, Zeit zu gewinnen

stallholder ['stɔːlhəuldə'] (Brit) n Standbesitzer(in) m(f)

stallion ['stæljən] n Hengst m

stalwart ['stɔːlwət] adj treu

stamen ['steɪmɛn] n Staubgefäß nt

stamina ['stæmɪnə] n Ausdauer f

stammer ['stæmə'] n Stottern nt ▷ vi stottern; **to have a ~** stottern

stamp [stæmp] n (lit, fig) Stempel m; (also: **postage stamp**) Briefmarke f ▷ vi stampfen; (also: **stamp one's foot**) (mit dem Fuß) aufstampfen ▷ vt stempeln; (with postage stamp) frankieren; **~ed addressed envelope** frankierter Rückumschlag

▶ **stamp out** vt (fire) austreten; (fig: crime) ausrotten; (: opposition) unterdrücken

stamp album n Briefmarkenalbum nt

stamp collecting n Briefmarkensammeln nt

stamp duty (Brit) n (Stempel)gebühr f

stampede [stæm'piːd] n (of animals) wilde Flucht f; (fig) Massenandrang m

stamp machine n Briefmarkenautomat m

stance [stæns] n Haltung f; (fig) Einstellung f

stand [stænd] (pt, pp **stood**) n (Comm) Stand m; (Sport) Tribüne f; (piece of furniture) Ständer m ▷ vi stehen; (rise) aufstehen; (remain) bestehen bleiben; (in election etc) kandidieren ▷ vt stellen; (tolerate, withstand) ertragen; **to make a ~ against sth** Widerstand gegen etw leisten; **to take a ~ on sth** einen Standpunkt zu etw vertreten; **to take the ~** (US: Law) in den Zeugenstand treten; **to ~ at** (value, score etc) betragen; (level) liegen bei; **to ~ for parliament** (Brit) in den Parlamentswahlen kandidieren; **to ~ to gain/lose sth** etw gewinnen/verlieren können; **it ~s to reason** es ist einleuchtend; **as things ~** nach Lage der Dinge; **to ~ sb a drink/meal** jdm einen Drink/ein Essen spendieren; **I can't ~ him** ich kann ihn nicht leiden or ausstehen; **we don't ~ a chance** wir haben keine Chance; **to ~ trial** vor Gericht stehen

▶ **stand by** vi (be ready) sich bereithalten; (fail to help) (unbeteiligt) danebenstehen ▷ vt fus (opinion, decision) stehen zu; (person) halten zu

▶ **stand down** vi zurücktreten

▶ **stand for** vt fus (signify) bedeuten; (represent) stehen für; (tolerate) sich dat gefallen lassen

▶ **stand in for** vt fus vertreten

▶ **stand out** vi hervorstechen

▶ **stand up** vi aufstehen

▶ **stand up for** vt fus eintreten für

▶ **stand up to** vt fus standhalten +dat; (person) sich behaupten gegenüber +dat

stand-alone ['stændələun] adj (Comput) selb(st)ständig

standard ['stændəd] n (level) Niveau nt; (norm)

Norm f; (criterion) Maßstab m; (flag) Standarte f ▷ adj (size, model, value etc) Standard-; (normal) normal; **standards** npl (morals) (sittliche) Maßstäbe pl; **to be** or **to come up to ~** den Anforderungen genügen; **to apply a double ~** mit zweierlei Maß messen

Standard Grade (Scot) n (Scol) Schulabschlusszeugnis, ≈ mittlere Reife f

standardization [stændədaɪ'zeɪʃən] n Vereinheitlichung f

standardize ['stændədaɪz] vt vereinheitlichen

standard lamp (Brit) n Stehlampe f

standard of living n Lebensstandard m

standard time n Normalzeit f

stand-by, standby ['stændbaɪ] n Reserve f; (also: **standby ticket**) Stand-by-Ticket nt ▷ adj (generator) Reserve-, Ersatz-; **to be on ~** (doctor) Bereitschaftsdienst haben; (crew, firemen etc) in Bereitschaft sein, einsatzbereit sein

stand-by ticket n Stand-by-Ticket nt

stand-in ['stændɪn] n Ersatz m

standing ['stændɪŋ] adj (permanent) ständig; (army) stehend ▷ n (status) Rang m, Stellung f; **a ~ ovation** stürmischer Beifall; **of many years' ~** von langjähriger Dauer; **a relationship of 6 months' ~** eine seit 6 Monaten bestehende Beziehung; **a man of some ~** ein angesehener Mann

standing joke n Standardwitz m

standing order (Brit) n (at bank) Dauerauftrag m

standing room n Stehplätze pl

standoff n (situation) ausweglose or verfahrene Situation f

stand-offish [stænd'ɒfɪʃ] adj distanziert

standpat ['stændpæt] (US) adj konservativ

standpipe ['stændpaɪp] n Steigrohr nt

standpoint ['stændpɔɪnt] n Standpunkt m

standstill ['stændstɪl] n: **to be at a ~** stillstehen; (fig: negotiations) in eine Sackgasse geraten sein; **to come to a ~** (traffic) zum Stillstand kommen

stank [stæŋk] pt of **stink**

stanza ['stænzə] n Strophe f

staple ['steɪpl] n (for papers) Heftklammer f; (chief product) Hauptartikel m ▷ adj (food, diet) Grund-, Haupt- ▷ vt heften

stapler ['steɪplə'] n Hefter m

star [stɑː'] n Stern m; (celebrity) Star m ▷ vt (Theat, Cine) in der Hauptrolle zeigen ▷ vi: **to ~ in** die Hauptrolle haben in; **the stars** npl (horoscope) das Horoskop; **4-~ hotel** 4-Sterne-Hotel nt; **2-~ petrol** (Brit) Normal(benzin) nt; **4-~ petrol** (Brit) Super(benzin) nt

star attraction n Hauptattraktion f

starboard ['stɑːbɔːd] adj (side) Steuerbord-; **to ~** (nach) Steuerbord

starch [stɑːtʃ] n Stärke f

starched [stɑːtʃt] adj gestärkt

starchy ['stɑːtʃɪ] adj (food) stärkehaltig; (pej: person) steif

stardom ['stɑːdəm] n Berühmtheit f

stare [steə'] n starrer Blick m ▷ vi: **to ~ at** anstarren

starfish ['stɑːfɪʃ] n Seestern m

stark [stɑːk] adj (bleak) kahl; (simplicity) schlicht; (colour) eintönig; (reality, poverty) nackt ▷ adv: **~ naked** splitternackt

starkers ['stɑːkəz] (inf) adj splitter(faser)nackt

starlet ['stɑːlɪt] n (Film)sternchen nt, Starlet nt

starlight ['stɑːlaɪt] n Sternenlicht nt

starling ['stɑːlɪŋ] n Star m

starlit ['stɑːlɪt] adj sternklar

starry ['stɑːrɪ] adj sternklar; **~ sky** Sternenhimmel m

starry-eyed [stɑːrɪ'aɪd] adj (innocent) arglos, blauäugig; (from wonder) verzückt

Stars and Stripes n sing Sternenbanner nt

star sign n Sternzeichen nt

star-studded ['stɑːstʌdɪd] adj: **a ~ cast** eine Starbesetzung f

START n abbr (Mil: = Strategic Arms Reduction Talks) START

start [stɑːt] n Beginn m, Anfang m; (departure) Aufbruch m; (advantage) Vorsprung m ▷ vt anfangen mit; (panic) auslösen; (fire) anzünden; (found) gründen; (: restaurant etc) eröffnen; (engine) anlassen; (car) starten ▷ vi anfangen; (with fright) zusammenfahren; (engine etc) anspringen; **at the ~** am Anfang, zu Beginn; **for a ~** erstens; **to make an early ~** frühzeitig aufbrechen; **to give a ~** zusammenfahren; **to wake up with a ~** aus dem Schlaf hochschrecken; **to ~ doing** or **to do sth** anfangen, etw zu tun; **to ~ (off) with ...** (firstly) erstens; (at the beginning) zunächst

‣ **start off** vi (begin) anfangen; (begin moving) losgehen/-fahren

‣ **start out** vi (leave) sich aufmachen

‣ **start over** (US) vi noch einmal von vorn anfangen

‣ **start up** vt (business) gründen; (restaurant etc) eröffnen; (car) starten; (engine) anlassen

starter ['stɑːtə'] n (Aut) Anlasser m; (Sport): official, runner, horse) Starter m; (Brit: Culin) Vorspeise f; **for ~s** (inf) für den Anfang

starting point ['stɑːtɪŋ-] n (lit, fig) Ausgangspunkt m

starting price n (at auction) Ausgangsangebot nt

startle ['stɑːtl] vt erschrecken

startling ['stɑːtlɪŋ] adj (news etc) überraschend

star turn (Brit) n Sensation f, Hauptattraktion f

starvation [stɑː'veɪʃən] n Hunger m; **to die of/from ~** verhungern

starve [stɑːv] vi hungern; (to death) verhungern ▷ vt hungern lassen; (fig: deprive): **to ~ sb of sth** jdm etw vorenthalten; **I'm starving** ich sterbe vor Hunger

Star Wars n Krieg m der Sterne

stash [stæʃ] vi (also: **stash away**) beiseiteschaffen ▷ n (secret store) geheimes Lager nt

state [steɪt] n (condition) Zustand m; (Pol) Staat m ▷ vt (say) feststellen; (declare) erklären; **the**

S

799

States npl (Geog) die (Vereinigten) Staaten pl; **to be in a ~** aufgeregt sein; (on edge) nervös sein; (in a mess) in einem schrecklichen Zustand sein; **to get into a ~** durchdrehen (inf); **in ~** feierlich; **to lie in ~** (feierlich) aufgebahrt sein; **~ of emergency** Notstand m; **~ of mind** Verfassung f

state control n staatliche Kontrolle f

stated ['steɪtɪd] adj erklärt

State Department (US) n Außenministerium nt

state education (Brit) n staatliche Erziehung f; (system) staatliches Bildungswesen nt

stateless ['steɪtlɪs] adj staatenlos

stately ['steɪtlɪ] adj würdevoll; (walk) gemessen; **~ home** Schloss nt

statement ['steɪtmənt] n (thing said) Feststellung f; (declaration) Erklärung f; (Fin) (Konto)auszug m; **official ~** (amtliche) Erklärung f; **bank ~** Kontoauszug m

state of the art n: **the ~** der neueste Stand der Technik ▷ adj: **state-of-the-art** auf dem neuesten Stand der Technik; (technology) Spitzen-

state-owned ['steɪtəʊnd] adj staatseigen

state school n öffentliche Schule f

state secret n Staatsgeheimnis nt

statesman ['steɪtsmən] (irreg: like man) n Staatsmann m

statesmanship ['steɪtsmənʃɪp] n Staatskunst f

static ['stætɪk] n (Radio, TV) atmosphärische Störungen pl ▷ adj (not moving) konstant

static electricity n Reibungselektrizität f

station ['steɪʃən] n (Rail) Bahnhof m; (also: **bus station**) Busbahnhof m; (also: **police station**) (Polizei)wache f; (Radio) Sender m ▷ vt (guards etc) postieren; (soldiers etc) stationieren; **action ~s** (Mil) Stellung f; **above one's ~** über seinem Stand

stationary ['steɪʃnərɪ] adj (vehicle) haltend; **to be ~** stehen

stationer ['steɪʃənəʳ] n Schreibwarenhändler(in) m(f)

stationer's, stationer's shop n Schreibwarenhandlung f

stationery ['steɪʃnərɪ] n Schreibwaren pl; (writing paper) Briefpapier nt

stationmaster ['steɪʃənmɑːstəʳ] n Bahnhofsvorsteher m

station wagon (US) n Kombi(wagen) m

statistic [stə'tɪstɪk] n Statistik f

statistical [stə'tɪstɪkl] adj statistisch

statistics [stə'tɪstɪks] n (science) Statistik f

statue ['stætjuː] n Statue f

statuesque [stætju'ɛsk] adj stattlich

statuette [stætju'ɛt] n Statuette f

stature ['stætʃəʳ] n Wuchs m, Statur f; (fig: reputation) Format nt

status ['steɪtəs] n Status m; (position) Stellung f; **the ~ quo** der Status quo

status line n (Comput) Statuszeile f

status symbol n Statussymbol nt

statute ['stætjuːt] n Gesetz nt; **statutes** npl (of club etc) Satzung f

statute book n: **to be on the ~** geltendes Recht sein

statutory ['stætjutrɪ] adj gesetzlich; **~ declaration** eidesstattliche Erklärung f

staunch [stɔːntʃ] adj treu ▷ vt (flow) stauen; (blood) stillen

stave [steɪv] n (Mus) Notensystem nt
▶ **stave off** vt (attack) abwehren; (threat) abwenden

stay [steɪ] n Aufenthalt m ▷ vi bleiben; (with sb, as guest) wohnen; (in hotel) übernachten; **~ of execution** (Law) Aussetzung f; **to ~ put** bleiben; **to ~ with friends** bei Freunden untergebracht sein; **to ~ the night** übernachten
▶ **stay behind** vi zurückbleiben
▶ **stay in** vi (at home) zu Hause bleiben
▶ **stay on** vi bleiben
▶ **stay out** vi (of house) wegbleiben; (remain on strike) weiterstreiken
▶ **stay up** vi (at night) aufbleiben

staying power ['steɪɪŋ-] n Stehvermögen nt, Durchhaltevermögen nt

STD n abbr (Brit: Tel: = subscriber trunk dialling) Selbstwählferndienst m; (Med: = sexually transmitted disease) durch Geschlechtsverkehr übertragene Krankheit f

stead [stɛd] n: **in sb's ~** an jds Stelle; **to stand sb in good ~** jdm zugute- or zustattenkommen

steadfast ['stɛdfɑːst] adj standhaft

steadily ['stɛdɪlɪ] adv (regularly) regelmäßig; (constantly) stetig; (fixedly) fest, unverwandt

steady ['stɛdɪ] adj (job, boyfriend, girlfriend, look) fest; (income) regelmäßig; (speed) gleichmäßig; (rise) stetig; (person, character) zuverlässig, solide; (voice, hand etc) ruhig ▷ vt (stabilize) ruhig halten; (nerves) beruhigen; **to ~ o.s. on sth** sich auf etw acc stützen; **to ~ o.s. against sth** sich an etw dat abstützen

steak [steɪk] n Steak nt; (fish) Filet nt

steakhouse ['steɪkhaʊs] n Steakrestaurant nt

steal [stiːl] (pt stole, pp stolen) vt stehlen ▷ vi stehlen; (move secretly) sich stehlen, schleichen
▶ **steal away** vi sich davonschleichen

stealth [stɛlθ] n: **by ~** heimlich

stealthy ['stɛlθɪ] adj heimlich, verstohlen

steam [stiːm] n Dampf m ▷ vt (Culin) dämpfen, dünsten ▷ vi dampfen; **covered with ~** (window etc) beschlagen; **under one's own ~** (fig) allein, ohne Hilfe; **to run out of ~** (fig) den Schwung verlieren; **to let off ~** (inf: fig) Dampf ablassen
▶ **steam up** vi (window) beschlagen; **to get ~ed up about sth** (inf: fig) sich über etw acc aufregen

steam engine n (Rail) Dampflok(omotive) f

steamer ['stiːməʳ] n Dampfer m; (Culin) Dämpfer m

steam iron n Dampfbügeleisen nt

steamroller ['stiːmrəʊləʳ] n Dampfwalze f

steamship ['stiːmʃɪp] n = **steamer**

steamy ['sti:mɪ] *adj (room)* dampfig; *(window)*
beschlagen; *(book, film)* heiß
steed [sti:d] *(liter) n* Ross *nt*
steel [sti:l] *n* Stahl *m* ▷ *adj (girder, wool etc)* Stahl-
steel band *n (Mus)* Steelband *f*
steel industry *n* Stahlindustrie *f*
steel mill *n* Stahlwalzwerk *nt*
steelworks ['sti:lwɜ:ks] *n* Stahlwerk *nt*
steely ['sti:lɪ] *adj (determination)* eisern; *(eyes,
gaze)* hart, stählern
steep [sti:p] *adj* steil; *(increase, rise)* stark; *(price,
fees)* gepfeffert ▷ *vt* einweichen; **to be ~ed in
history** geschichtsträchtig sein
steeple ['sti:pl] *n* Kirchturm *m*
steeplechase ['sti:pltʃeɪs] *n (for horses)*
Hindernisrennen *nt*; *(for runners)*
Hindernislauf *m*
steeplejack ['sti:pldʒæk] *n* Turmarbeiter *m*
steeply ['sti:plɪ] *adv* steil
steer [stɪə^r] *vt* steuern; *(car etc)* lenken; *(person)*
lotsen ▷ *vi* steuern; *(in car etc)* lenken; **to ~ for**
zusteuern auf +*acc*; **to ~ clear of sb** *(fig)* jdm
aus dem Weg gehen; **to ~ clear of sth** *(fig)*
etw meiden
steering ['stɪərɪŋ] *n (Aut)* Lenkung *f*
steering column *n (Aut)* Lenksäule *f*
steering committee *n* Lenkungsausschuss *m*
steering wheel *n (Aut)* Lenkrad *nt*, Steuer *nt*
stellar ['stɛlə^r] *adj* stellar
stem [stɛm] *n* Stiel *m*; *(of pipe)* Hals *m* ▷ *vt*
aufhalten; *(flow)* eindämmen; *(bleeding)* zum
Stillstand bringen
▶ **stem from** *vt fus* zurückgehen auf +*acc*
stench [stɛntʃ] *(pej) n* Gestank *m*
stencil ['stɛnsl] *n* Schablone *f* ▷ *vt* mit
Schablone zeichnen
stenographer [stɛ'nɔgrəfə^r] *(US) n*
Stenograf(in) *m(f)*
stenography [stɛ'nɔgrəfɪ] *(US) n* Stenografie *f*
step [stɛp] *n (lit, fig)* Schritt *m*; *(of stairs)* Stufe
f ▷ *vi*: **to ~ forward/back** vor-/zurücktreten;
steps *npl (Brit)* = **stepladder**; **- by step**
(fig) Schritt für Schritt; **in/out of ~ (with)**
im/nicht im Tritt (mit); *(fig)* im/nicht im
Gleichklang (mit)
▶ **step down** *vi (fig: resign)* zurücktreten
▶ **step in** *vi (fig)* eingreifen
▶ **step off** *vt fus* aussteigen aus +*dat*
▶ **step on** *vt fus* treten auf +*acc*
▶ **step over** *vt fus* steigen über +*acc*
▶ **step up** *vt (efforts)* steigern; *(pace etc)*
beschleunigen
stepbrother ['stɛpbrʌðə^r] *n* Stiefbruder *m*
stepchild ['stɛptʃaɪld] *n* Stiefkind *nt*
stepdaughter ['stɛpdɔ:tə^r] *n* Stieftochter *f*
stepfather ['stɛpfɑ:ðə^r] *n* Stiefvater *m*
stepladder ['stɛplædə^r] *(Brit) n* Trittleiter *f*
stepmother ['stɛpmʌðə^r] *n* Stiefmutter *f*
stepping stone ['stɛpɪŋ-] *n* Trittstein *m*; *(fig)*
Sprungbrett *nt*
stepsister ['stɛpsɪstə^r] *n* Stiefschwester *f*
stepson ['stɛpsʌn] *n* Stiefsohn *m*
stereo ['stɛrɪəu] *n (system)* Stereoanlage *f* ▷ *adj*

(sound etc) Stereo-; **in ~** in Stereo
stereotype ['stɪərɪətaɪp] *n* Klischee *nt*,
Klischeevorstellung *f* ▷ *vt* in ein Klischee
zwängen; **~d** stereotyp
sterile ['stɛraɪl] *adj* steril, keimfrei; *(barren)*
unfruchtbar; *(fig: debate)* fruchtlos
sterility [stɛ'rɪlɪtɪ] *n* Unfruchtbarkeit *f*
sterilization [stɛrɪlaɪ'zeɪʃən] *n* Sterilisation *f*,
Sterilisierung *f*
sterilize ['stɛrɪlaɪz] *vt* sterilisieren
sterling ['stɜ:lɪŋ] *adj (silver)* Sterling-; *(fig)*
gediegen ▷ *n (Econ)* das Pfund Sterling, das
englische Pfund; **one pound ~** ein Pfund
Sterling
sterling area *n (Econ)* Sterlingländer *pl*
stern [stɜ:n] *adj* streng ▷ *n* Heck *nt*
sternum ['stɜ:nəm] *n* Brustbein *nt*
steroid ['stɪərɔɪd] *n* Steroid *nt*
stethoscope ['stɛθəskəup] *n* Stethoskop *nt*
stevedore ['sti:vədɔ:^r] *n* Stauer *m*,
Schauermann *m*
stew [stju:] *n* Eintopf *m* ▷ *vt* schmoren; *(fruit,
vegetables)* dünsten ▷ *vi* schmoren; **~ed tea**
bitterer Tee *m*; **~ed fruit** (Obst)kompott *nt*
steward ['stju:əd] *n* Steward *m*; *(at public
event)* Ordner(in) *m(f)*; *(also:* **shop steward***)*
gewerkschaftliche Vertrauensperson *f*
stewardess ['stju:ədɛs] *n* Stewardess *f*
stewardship ['stju:ədʃɪp] *n* Verwaltung *f*
stewing steak, *(US)* **stew meat** ['stju:ɪŋ-] *n*
(Rinder)schmorfleisch *nt*
St. Ex. *abbr* = **stock exchange**
stg *abbr* = **sterling**
stick [stɪk] *(pt, pp* **stuck***) n* Zweig *m*; *(of dynamite)*
Stange *f*; *(of chalk etc)* Stück *nt*; *(as weapon)* Stock
m; *(also:* **walking stick***)* (Spazier)stock *m* ▷ *vt*
(with glue etc) kleben; *(inf: put)* tun, stecken;
(: tolerate) aushalten; *(thrust)* stoßen ▷ *vi*: **to
~ (to)** kleben (an +*dat*); *(remain)* (hängen)
bleiben; *(door etc)* klemmen; *(lift)* stecken
bleiben; **to get hold of the wrong end of
the ~** *(Brit: fig)* es falsch verstehen; **to ~ in sb's
mind** jdm im Gedächtnis (haften) bleiben
▶ **stick around** *(inf) vi* hier-/dableiben
▶ **stick out** *vi (ears etc)* abstehen ▷ *vt*: **to ~ it
out** *(inf)* durchhalten
▶ **stick to** *vt fus (one's word, promise)* halten;
(agreement, rules) sich halten an +*acc*; *(the truth,
facts)* bleiben bei
▶ **stick up** *vi* hochstehen
▶ **stick up for** *vt fus* eintreten für
sticker ['stɪkə^r] *n* Aufkleber *m*
sticking plaster ['stɪkɪŋ-] *n* Heftpflaster *nt*
sticking point *n* Hindernis *nt*; *(in discussion etc)*
strittiger Punkt *m*
stickleback ['stɪklbæk] *n* Stichling *m*
stickler ['stɪklə^r] *n*: **to be a ~ for sth** es mit etw
peinlich genau nehmen
stick shift *(US) n* Schaltknüppel *m*; *(car)* Wagen
m mit Handschaltung
stick-up ['stɪkʌp] *(inf) n* Überfall *m*
sticky ['stɪkɪ] *adj* klebrig; *(label, tape)* Klebe-;
(weather, day) schwül

S

stiff [stɪf] adj steif; (hard, firm) hart; (paste, egg-white) fest; (door, zip etc) schwer gehend; (competition) hart; (sentence) schwer; (drink) stark ▷ adv (bored, worried, scared) zu Tode; **to be** or **feel ~** steif sein; **to have a ~ neck** einen steifen Hals haben; **to keep a ~ upper lip** (Brit: fig) die Haltung bewahren

stiffen ['stɪfn] vi steif werden; (body) erstarren

stiffness ['stɪfnɪs] n Steifheit f

stifle ['staɪfl] vt unterdrücken; (heat) erdrücken

stifling ['staɪflɪŋ] adj (heat) drückend

stigma ['stɪgmə] n Stigma nt; (Bot) Narbe f, Stigma nt; **stigmata** npl (Med) Wundmal nt

stile [staɪl] n Zaunübertritt m

stiletto [stɪ'letəu] (Brit) n (also: **stiletto heel**) Bleistiftabsatz m

still [stɪl] adj (motionless) bewegungslos; (tranquil) ruhig; (air, water) still; (Brit: drink) ohne Kohlensäure ▷ adv (immer) noch; (yet, even) noch; (nonetheless) trotzdem ▷ n (Cine) Standfoto nt; **to stand ~** (machine, motor) stillstehen; (motionless) still stehen; **keep ~!** halte still!; **he ~ hasn't arrived** er ist immer noch nicht angekommen

stillborn ['stɪlbɔːn] adj tot geboren

still life n Stillleben nt

stilt [stɪlt] n (pile) Pfahl m; (for walking on) Stelze f

stilted ['stɪltɪd] adj gestelzt

stimulant ['stɪmjulənt] n Anregungsmittel nt

stimulate ['stɪmjuleɪt] vt anregen, stimulieren; (demand) ankurbeln

stimulating ['stɪmjuleɪtɪŋ] adj anregend, stimulierend

stimulation [stɪmju'leɪʃən] n Anregung f, Stimulation f

stimuli ['stɪmjulaɪ] npl of **stimulus**

stimulus ['stɪmjuləs] (pl **stimuli**) n (incentive) Anreiz m; (Biol) Reiz m; (Psych) Stimulus m

sting [stɪŋ] (pt, pp **stung**) n Stich m; (pain) Stechen nt; (organ: of insect) Stachel m; (inf: confidence trick) Ding nt ▷ vt stechen; (fig) treffen, verletzen ▷ vi stechen; (eyes, ointment, plant etc) brennen; **my eyes are ~ing** mir brennen die Augen

stingy ['stɪndʒɪ] (pej) adj geizig, knauserig

stink [stɪŋk] (pt **stank**, pp **stunk**) n Gestank m ▷ vi stinken

stinker ['stɪŋkər] (inf) n (problem) harter Brocken m; (person) Ekel nt

stinking ['stɪŋkɪŋ] (inf) adj (fig) beschissen (!); **a ~ cold** eine scheußliche Erkältung; **~ rich** stinkreich

stint [stɪnt] n (period) Zeit f; (batch of work) Pensum nt; (share) Teil m ▷ vi: **to ~ on** sparen mit

stipend ['staɪpend] n Gehalt nt

stipendiary [staɪ'pendɪərɪ] adj: **~ magistrate** bezahlter Friedensrichter m

stipulate ['stɪpjuleɪt] vt festsetzen; (condition) stellen

stipulation [stɪpju'leɪʃən] n Bedingung f, Auflage f

stir [stəːr] n (fig) Aufsehen nt ▷ vt umrühren;

(fig: emotions) aufwühlen; (: person) bewegen ▷ vi sich bewegen; **to give sth a ~** etw umrühren; **to cause a ~** Aufsehen erregen

▶ **stir up** vt: **to ~ up trouble** Unruhe stiften; **to ~ things up** stänkern

stir-fry ['stəː'fraɪ] vt unter Rühren kurz anbraten ▷ n Pfannengericht nt (das unter Rühren kurz angebraten wurde)

stirring ['stəːrɪŋ] adj bewegend

stirrup ['stɪrəp] n Steigbügel m

stitch [stɪtʃ] n (Sewing) Stich m; (Knitting) Masche f; (Med) Faden m; (pain) Seitenstiche pl ▷ vt nähen; **he had to have ~es** er musste genäht werden

stoat [stəut] n Wiesel nt

stock [stɔk] n Vorrat m; (Comm) Bestand m; (Agr) Vieh nt; (Culin) Brühe f; (descent, origin) Abstammung f, Herkunft f; (Fin) Wertpapiere pl; (Rail: also: **rolling stock**) rollendes Material nt ▷ adj (reply, excuse etc) Standard- ▷ vt (in shop) führen; **in/out of ~** vorrätig/nicht vorrätig; **~s and shares** (Aktien und) Wertpapiere pl; **government ~** Staatsanleihe f; **to take ~ of** (fig) Bilanz ziehen über +acc; **well-~ed** (shop) mit gutem Sortiment

▶ **stock up** vi: **to ~ up (with)** sich eindecken (mit)

stockade [stɔ'keɪd] n Palisade f

stockbroker ['stɔkbrəukər] n Börsenmakler m

stock control n Bestandsüberwachung f

stock cube (Brit) n Brühwürfel m

stock exchange n Börse f

stockholder ['stɔkhəuldər] (esp US) n Aktionär(in) m(f)

Stockholm ['stɔkhəum] n Stockholm nt

stocking ['stɔkɪŋ] n Strumpf m

stock-in-trade ['stɔkɪn'treɪd] n (fig): **it's his ~** es gehört zu seinem festen Repertoire

stockist ['stɔkɪst] (Brit) n Händler m

stock market (Brit) n Börse f

stock phrase n Standardsatz m

stockpile ['stɔkpaɪl] n Vorrat m; (of weapons) Lager nt ▷ vt horten

stockroom ['stɔkruːm] n Lager nt, Lagerraum m

stocktaking ['stɔkteɪkɪŋ] (Brit) n Inventur f

stocky ['stɔkɪ] adj stämmig

stodgy ['stɔdʒɪ] adj (food) pampig (inf), schwer

stoic ['stəuɪk] n Stoiker(in) m(f) ▷ adj stoisch

stoical ['stəuɪkl] adj stoisch

stoke [stəuk] vt (fire) schüren; (furnace, boiler) heizen

stoker ['stəukər] n Heizer m

stole [stəul] pt of **steal** ▷ n Stola f

stolen ['stəuln] pp of **steal**

stolid ['stɔlɪd] adj phlegmatisch, stur (inf)

stomach ['stʌmək] n Magen m; (belly) Bauch m ▷ vt (fig) vertragen

stomach ache n Magenschmerzen pl

stomach pump n Magenpumpe f

stomach ulcer n Magengeschwür nt

stomp [stɔmp] vi stapfen

stone [stəun] n Stein m; (Brit: weight) Gewichtseinheit (= 6,35 kg) ▷ adj (wall, jar etc)

Stein-, steinern ▷ vt (person) mit Steinen bewerfen; (fruit) entkernen, entsteinen; **within a ~'s throw of the station** nur einen Katzensprung vom Bahnhof entfernt

Stone Age n Steinzeit f

stone-cold ['stəun'kəuld] adj eiskalt

stoned [stəund] (inf) adj (on drugs) stoned; (drunk) total zu

stone-deaf ['stəun'dɛf] adj stocktaub

stonemason ['stəunmeısn] n Steinmetz m

stonewall [stəun'wɔ:l] vi mauern; (in answering questions) ausweichen

stonework ['stəunwɜ:k] n Mauerwerk nt

stony ['stəunı] adj steinig; (fig: silence etc) steinern

stood [stud] pt, pp of **stand**

stooge [stu:dʒ] n (inf) Handlanger(in) m(f); (Theat) Stichwortgeber(in) m(f)

stool [stu:l] n Hocker m

stoop [stu:p] vi (also: **stoop down**) sich bücken; (walk) gebeugt gehen; **to ~ to sth** (fig) sich zu etw herablassen; **to ~ to doing sth** sich dazu herablassen, etw zu tun

stop [stɔp] n Halt m; (short stay) Aufenthalt m; (in punctuation: also: **full stop**) Punkt m; (bus stop etc) Haltestelle f ▷ vt stoppen; (car etc) anhalten; (block) sperren; (prevent) verhindern ▷ vi (car etc) anhalten; (train) halten; (pedestrian, watch, clock) stehen bleiben; (end) aufhören; **to come to a ~** anhalten; **to put a ~ to** einen Riegel vorschieben +dat; **to ~ doing sth** aufhören, etw zu tun; **to ~ sb (from) doing sth** jdn davon abhalten, etw zu tun; **~ it!** lass das!, hör auf!

▶ **stop by** vi kurz vorbeikommen

▶ **stop off** vi kurz haltmachen, Zwischenstation machen

▶ **stop up** vt (hole) zustopfen

stopcock ['stɔpkɔk] n Absperrhahn m

stopgap ['stɔpgæp] n (person) Lückenbüßer m; (thing) Notbehelf m; **~ measure** Überbrückungsmaßnahme f

stop-go [stɔp'gəu] adj (economic cycle etc) mit ständigem Auf und Ab

stoplights ['stɔplaıts] npl (Aut) Bremslichter pl

stopover ['stɔpəuvə'] n Zwischenaufenthalt m; (Aviat) Zwischenlandung f

stoppage ['stɔpıdʒ] n (strike) Streik m; (blockage) Unterbrechung f; (of pay, cheque) Sperrung f; (deduction) Abzug m

stopper ['stɔpə'] n Stöpsel m

stop press n letzte Meldungen pl

stopwatch ['stɔpwɔtʃ] n Stoppuhr f

storage ['stɔ:rıdʒ] n Lagerung f; (also: **storage space**) Stauraum m; (Comput) Speicherung f

storage capacity n (Comput) Speicherkapazität f

storage heater (Brit) n (Nacht)speicherofen m

store [stɔ:'] n Vorrat m; (depot) Lager nt; (Brit: large shop) Geschäft nt, Kaufhaus nt; (US: shop) Laden m; (fig): **a ~ of** eine Fülle an +dat ▷ vt lagern; (information etc, Comput) speichern; (food, medicines etc) aufbewahren;

(in filing system) ablegen; **stores** npl (provisions) Vorräte pl; **in ~** eingelagert; **who knows what's in ~ for us?** wer weiß, was uns bevorsteht?; **to set great/little ~ by sth** viel/wenig von etw halten

▶ **store up** vt einen Vorrat anlegen von; (memories) im Gedächtnis bewahren

storehouse ['stɔ:haus] n (US: Comm) Lager(haus) nt; (fig) Fundgrube f

storekeeper ['stɔ:ki:pə'] (US) n Ladenbesitzer(in) m(f)

storeroom ['stɔ:ru:m] n Lagerraum m

storey, (US) **story** ['stɔ:rı] n Stock m, Stockwerk nt

stork [stɔ:k] n Storch m

storm [stɔ:m] n (lit, fig) Sturm m; (bad weather) Unwetter nt; (also: **electrical storm**) Gewitter nt ▷ vi (fig) toben ▷ vt (attack) stürmen

storm cloud n Gewitterwolke f

storm door n äußere Windfangtür f

stormy ['stɔ:mı] adj (lit, fig) stürmisch

story ['stɔ:rı] n Geschichte f; (Press) Artikel m; (lie) Märchen nt; (US) = **storey**

storybook ['stɔ:rıbuk] n Geschichtenbuch nt

storyteller ['stɔ:rıtelə'] n Geschichtenerzähler(in) m(f)

stout [staut] adj (strong) stark; (fat) untersetzt; (resolute) energisch ▷ n Starkbier nt

stove [stəuv] n Herd m; (small) Kocher m; (for heating) (Heiz)ofen m; **gas ~** Gasherd m

stow [stəu] vt (also: **stow away**) verstauen

stowaway ['stəuəweı] n blinder Passagier m

straddle ['strædl] vt (sitting) rittlings sitzen auf +dat; (standing) breitbeinig stehen über +dat; (jumping) grätschen über +acc; (fig) überspannen

strafe [strɑ:f] vt beschießen

straggle ['strægl] vi (houses etc) verstreut liegen; (people etc) zurückbleiben

straggler ['stræglə'] n Nachzügler m

straggly ['stræglı] adj (hair) unordentlich

straight [streıt] adj gerade; (hair) glatt; (honest) offen, direkt; (simple) einfach; (: fight) direkt; (Theat) ernst; (inf: heterosexual) hetero; (whisky etc) pur ▷ adv (in time) sofort; (in direction) direkt; (drink) pur ▷ n (Sport) Gerade f; **to put or get sth ~** (make clear) etw klären; (make tidy) etw in Ordnung bringen; **let's get this ~** das wollen wir mal klarstellen; **10 ~ wins** 10 Siege hintereinander; **to go ~ home** direkt nach Hause gehen; **~ out** rundheraus; **~ away, ~ off** sofort, gleich

straighten ['streıtn] vt (skirt, sheet etc) gerade ziehen

▶ **straighten out** vt (fig) klären

straighteners ['streıtnəz] npl (for hair) Haarglätter m

straight-faced [streıt'feıst] adj: **to be/remain ~** ernst bleiben ▷ adv ohne zu lachen

straightforward [streıt'fɔ:wəd] adj (simple) einfach; (honest) offen

straight sets npl (Tennis): **to win in ~** ohne Satzverlust gewinnen

S

strain [streɪn] n Belastung f; (Med: also: **back strain**) überanstrengter Rücken m; (: tension) Überlastung f; (of virus) Art f; (breed) Sorte f ▷ vt (back etc) überanstrengen; (resources) belasten; (Culin) abgießen ▷ vi: **to ~ to do sth** sich anstrengen, etw zu tun; **strains** npl (Mus) Klänge pl; **he's been under a lot of ~** er hat unter großem Stress gestanden

strained [streɪnd] adj (back) überanstrengt; (muscle) gezerrt; (forced) gezwungen; (relations) gespannt

strainer ['streɪnəʳ] n Sieb nt

strait [streɪt] n Meerenge f, Straße f; **straits** npl (fig): **to be in dire ~s** in großen Nöten sein

straitjacket ['streɪtdʒækɪt] n Zwangsjacke f

strait-laced [streɪt'leɪst] adj prüde, puritanisch

strand [strænd] n (lit, fig) Faden m; (of wire) Litze f; (of hair) Strähne f

stranded ['strændɪd] adj: **to be ~** (traveller) festsitzen; (ship, sea creature) gestrandet

strange [streɪndʒ] adj fremd; (odd) seltsam, merkwürdig

strangely ['streɪndʒlɪ] adv seltsam, merkwürdig; see also **enough**

stranger ['streɪndʒəʳ] n Fremde(r) f(m); **I'm a ~ here** ich bin hier fremd

strangle ['stræŋgl] vt erwürgen, erdrosseln; (fig: economy etc) ersticken

stranglehold ['stræŋglhəʊld] n (fig) absolute Machtposition f

strangulation [stræŋgju'leɪʃən] n Erwürgen nt, Erdrosseln nt

strap [stræp] n Riemen m; (of dress etc) Träger m ▷ vt (also: **strap in**) anschnallen; (also: **strap on**) umschnallen

straphanging ['stræphæŋɪŋ] n Pendeln nt (als stehender Fahrgast)

strapless ['stræplɪs] adj trägerlos, schulterfrei

strapped [stræpt] (inf) adj: **~ (for cash)** pleite

strapping ['stræpɪŋ] adj stramm

Strasbourg ['stræzbɔːg] n Straßburg nt

strata ['strɑːtə] npl of **stratum**

stratagem ['strætɪdʒəm] n List f

strategic [strə'tiːdʒɪk] adj strategisch; (error) taktisch

strategist ['strætɪdʒɪst] n Stratege m, Strategin f

strategy ['strætɪdʒɪ] n Strategie f

stratosphere ['strætəsfɪəʳ] n Stratosphäre f

stratum ['strɑːtəm] (pl **strata**) n Schicht f

straw [strɔː] n Stroh nt; (also: **drinking straw**) Strohhalm m; **that's the last ~!** das ist der Gipfel!

strawberry ['strɔːbərɪ] n Erdbeere f

stray [streɪ] adj (animal) streunend; (bullet) verirrt; (scattered) einzeln, vereinzelt ▷ vi (children) sich verirren; (animals) streunen; (thoughts) abschweifen

streak [striːk] n Streifen m; (in hair) Strähne f; (fig: of madness etc) Zug m ▷ vt streifen ▷ vi: **to ~ past** vorbeiflitzen; **a winning/losing ~** eine Glücks-/Pechsträhne

streaker ['striːkəʳ] (inf) n Blitzer(in) m(f)

streaky ['striːkɪ] adj (bacon) durchwachsen

stream [striːm] n (small river) Bach m; (current) Strömung f; (of people, vehicles) Strom m; (of questions, insults etc) Flut f, Schwall m; (of smoke) Schwaden m; (Scol) Leistungsgruppe f ▷ vt (Scol) in Leistungsgruppen einteilen ▷ vi strömen; **against the ~** gegen den Strom; **to come on ~** (new power plant etc) in Betrieb genommen werden

streamer ['striːməʳ] n Luftschlange f

stream feed n automatischer Papiereinzug m

streamline ['striːmlaɪn] vt Stromlinienform geben +dat; (fig) rationalisieren

streamlined ['striːmlaɪnd] adj stromlinienförmig; (Aviat, Aut) windschlüpfrig; (fig) rationalisiert

street [striːt] n Straße f; **the back ~s** die Seitensträßchen pl; **to be on the ~s** (homeless) obdachlos sein; (as prostitute) auf den Strich gehen

streetcar ['striːtkɑːʳ] (US) n Straßenbahn f

street cred [-krɛd] (inf) n Glaubwürdigkeit f

street lamp n Straßenlaterne f

street lighting n Straßenbeleuchtung f

street map n Stadtplan m

street market n Straßenmarkt m

street plan n Stadtplan m

streetwise ['striːtwaɪz] (inf) adj: **to be ~** wissen, wos langgeht

strength [strɛŋθ] n (lit, fig) Stärke f; (physical) Kraft f, Stärke f; (of girder etc) Stabilität f; (of knot etc) Festigkeit f; (of chemical solution) Konzentration f; (of wine) Schwere f; **on the ~ of** aufgrund +gen; **at full ~** vollzählig; **to be below ~** nicht die volle Stärke haben

strengthen ['strɛŋθən] vt (lit, fig) verstärken; (muscle) kräftigen; (economy, currency, relationship) festigen

strenuous ['strɛnjuəs] adj anstrengend; (determined) unermüdlich

strenuously ['strɛnjuəslɪ] adv energisch; **she ~ denied the rumour** sie leugnete das Gerücht hartnäckig

stress [strɛs] n Druck m; (mental) Belastung f, Stress m; (Ling) Betonung f; (emphasis) Akzent m, Gewicht nt ▷ vt betonen; **to lay great ~ on sth** großen Wert auf etw acc legen; **to be under ~** großen Belastungen ausgesetzt sein, unter Stress stehen

stressful ['strɛsful] adj anstrengend, stressig; (situation) angespannt

stretch [strɛtʃ] n (of sand, water etc) Stück nt; (of time) Zeit f ▷ vi (person, animal) sich strecken; (land, area) sich erstrecken ▷ vt (pull) spannen; (fig: job, task) fordern; **at a ~** an einem Stück, ohne Unterbrechung; **by no ~ of the imagination** beim besten Willen nicht; **to ~ to** or **as far as the frontier** (extend) sich bis zur Grenze erstrecken; **to ~ one's legs** sich dat die Beine vertreten

▶ **stretch out** vi sich ausstrecken ▷ vt ausstrecken

▸ **stretch to** vt fus (be enough) reichen für
stretcher ['strɛtʃəʳ] n (Trag)bahre f
stretcher-bearer ['strɛtʃəbɛərəʳ] n
  Krankenträger m
stretch marks npl Dehnungsstreifen pl;
  (through pregnancy) Schwangerschaftsstreifen pl
strewn [struːn] adj: ~ **with** übersät mit
stricken ['strɪkən] adj (person) leidend; (city,
  industry etc) Not leidend; ~ **with** (disease)
  geschlagen mit; (fear etc) erfüllt von
strict [strɪkt] adj streng; (precise) genau; **in the**
  ~est confidence streng vertraulich; **in the ~**
  sense of the word streng genommen
strictly ['strɪktlɪ] adv streng; (exactly) genau;
  (solely) ausschließlich; ~ **confidential** streng
  vertraulich; ~ **speaking** genau genommen;
  not ~ true nicht ganz richtig; ~ **between**
  ourselves ganz unter uns
strictness ['strɪktnɪs] n Strenge f
stridden ['strɪdn] pp of **stride**
stride [straɪd] (pt **strode**, pp **stridden**) n Schritt
  m ▷ vi schreiten; **to take sth in one's ~** (fig)
  mit etw spielend fertig werden
strident ['straɪdnt] adj schrill, durchdringend;
  (demands) lautstark
strife [straɪf] n Streit m, Zwietracht f
strike [straɪk] (pt, pp **struck**) n Streik m,
  Ausstand m; (Mil) Angriff m ▷ vt (hit) schlagen;
  (fig: idea, thought) in den Sinn kommen +dat;
  (oil etc) finden, stoßen auf +acc; (bargain,
  deal) aushandeln; (coin, medal) prägen ▷ vi
  streiken; (illness, killer) zuschlagen; (disaster)
  hereinbrechen; (clock) schlagen; **on ~**
  streikend; **to be on ~** streiken; **to ~ a balance**
  einen Mittelweg finden; **to be struck by**
  lightning vom Blitz getroffen werden; **to ~ a**
  match ein Streichholz anzünden
  ▸ **strike back** vi (Mil) zurückschlagen; (fig) sich
  wehren
  ▸ **strike down** vt niederschlagen
  ▸ **strike off** vt (from list) (aus)streichen; (doctor
  etc) die Zulassung entziehen +dat
  ▸ **strike out** vi losziehen, sich aufmachen ▷ vt
  (word, sentence) (aus)streichen
  ▸ **strike up** vt (Mus) anstimmen; (conversation)
  anknüpfen; (friendship) schließen
strikebreaker ['straɪkbreɪkəʳ] n Streikbrecher
  m
strike pay n Streikgeld nt
striker ['straɪkəʳ] n Streikende(r) f(m); (Sport)
  Stürmer m
striking ['straɪkɪŋ] adj auffallend; (attractive)
  attraktiv
strimmer ['strɪməʳ] n Rasentrimmer m
string [strɪŋ] (pt, pp **strung**) n Schnur f; (of
  islands) Kette f; (of people, cars) Schlange f; (series)
  Serie f; (Comput) Zeichenfolge f; (Mus) Saite
  f ▷ vt: **to ~ together** aneinanderreihen; **the**
  strings npl (Mus) die Streichinstrumente pl; **to**
  pull ~s (fig) Beziehungen spielen lassen; **with**
  no ~s attached (fig) ohne Bedingungen; **to ~**
  sth out etw verteilen
string bean n grüne Bohne f

stringed instrument n Saiteninstrument nt
stringent ['strɪndʒənt] adj streng; (measures)
  drastisch
string quartet n Streichquartett nt
strip [strɪp] n Streifen m; (of metal) Band
  nt; (Sport) Trikot nt, Dress m ▷ vt (undress)
  ausziehen; (paint) abbeizen; (also: **strip**
  down: machine etc) auseinandernehmen ▷ vi
  (undress) sich ausziehen
strip cartoon n Comic(strip) m
stripe [straɪp] n Streifen m; **stripes** npl (Mil,
  Police) (Ärmel)streifen pl
striped [straɪpt] adj gestreift
strip lighting (Brit) n Neonlicht nt
strip mall n Einkaufsmeile nt
stripper ['strɪpəʳ] n Stripper(in) m(f),
  Stripteasetänzer(in) m(f)
strip-search ['strɪpsɛtʃ] n Leibesvisitation f (bei
  der man sich ausziehen muss) ▷ vt: **to be ~ed** sich
  ausziehen müssen und durchsucht werden
striptease ['strɪptiːz] n Striptease m or nt
strive [straɪv] (pt **strove**, pp **~n**) vi: **to ~ for**
  sth nach etw streben; **to ~ to do sth** danach
  streben, etw zu tun
striven ['strɪvn] pp of **strive**
strobe [strəʊb] n (also: **strobe lights**)
  Stroboskoplicht nt
strode [strəʊd] pt of **stride**
stroke [strəʊk] n Schlag m, Hieb m;
  (Swimming: style) Stil m; (Med) Schlaganfall m;
  (of clock) Schlag m; (of paintbrush) Strich m ▷ vt
  (caress) streicheln; **at a ~** mit einem Schlag;
  on the ~ of 5 Punkt 5 (Uhr); **a ~ of luck** ein
  Glücksfall m; **a 2~ engine** ein Zweitaktmotor
  m
stroll [strəʊl] n Spaziergang m ▷ vi spazieren;
  to go for a ~, have or **take a ~** einen
  Spaziergang machen
stroller ['strəʊləʳ] (US) n (pushchair) Sportwagen
  m
strong [strɒŋ] adj stark; (person, arms, grip)
  stark, kräftig; (healthy) kräftig; (object, material)
  solide, stabil; (letter) geharnischt; (measure)
  drastisch; (language) derb; (nerves) gut; (taste,
  smell) streng ▷ adv: **to be going ~** (company)
  sehr erfolgreich sein; (person) gut in Schuss
  sein; **I have no ~ feelings about it** es ist
  mir ziemlich egal; **they are 50 ~** sie sind
  insgesamt 50
strong-arm ['strɒŋɑːm] adj brutal
strongbox ['strɒŋbɒks] n (Geld)kassette f
stronghold ['strɒŋhəʊld] n Festung f; (fig)
  Hochburg f
strongly ['strɒŋlɪ] adv (solidly) stabil; (forcefully)
  entschieden; (deeply) fest; **to feel ~ that ...**
  fest davon überzeugt sein, dass ...; **I feel ~**
  about it mir liegt sehr viel daran; (negatively)
  ich bin sehr dagegen
strongman ['strɒŋmæn] (irreg: like **man**) n (lit,
  fig) starker Mann m
strongroom ['strɒŋruːm] n Tresorraum m
stroppy ['strɒpɪ] (Brit: inf) adj pampig;
  (obstinate) stur

S

805

strove [strəuv] *pt of* **strive**

struck [strʌk] *pt, pp of* **strike**

structural ['strʌktʃrəl] *adj* strukturell; *(damage)* baulich; *(defect)* Konstruktions-

structurally ['strʌktʃrəlɪ] *adv*: ~ **sound** mit guter Bausubstanz

structure ['strʌktʃəʳ] *n* Struktur *f*, Aufbau *m*; *(building)* Gebäude *nt*

struggle ['strʌgl] *n* Kampf *m*; *(difficulty)* Anstrengung *f* ▷ *vi (try hard)* sich abmühen; *(fight)* kämpfen; *(in self-defence)* sich wehren; **to have a ~ to do sth** Mühe haben, etw zu tun; **to be a ~ for sb** jdm große Schwierigkeiten bereiten

strum [strʌm] *vt (guitar)* klimpern auf +*dat*

strung [strʌŋ] *pt, pp of* **string**

strut [strʌt] *n* Strebe *f*, Stütze *f* ▷ *vi* stolzieren

strychnine ['strɪkniːn] *n* Strychnin *nt*

stub [stʌb] *n (of cheque, ticket etc)* Abschnitt *m*; *(of cigarette)* Kippe *f* ▷ *vt*: **to ~ one's toe** sich *dat* den Zeh stoßen

▶ **stub out** *vt (cigarette)* ausdrücken

stubble ['stʌbl] *n* Stoppeln *pl*

stubborn ['stʌbən] *adj* hartnäckig; *(child)* störrisch

stubby ['stʌbɪ] *adj* kurz und dick

stucco ['stʌkəu] *n* Stuck *m*

stuck [stʌk] *pt, pp of* **stick** ▷ *adj*: **to be ~** *(jammed)* klemmen; *(unable to answer)* nicht klarkommen; **to get ~** stecken bleiben; *(fig)* nicht weiterkommen

stuck-up [stʌk'ʌp] *(inf) adj* hochnäsig

stud [stʌd] *n (on clothing etc)* Niete *f*; *(on collar)* Kragenknopf *m*; *(earring)* Ohrstecker *m*; *(on boot)* Stollen *m*; *(also:* **stud farm***)* Gestüt *nt*; *(also:* **stud horse***)* Zuchthengst *m* ▷ *vt (fig)*: **~ded with** übersät mit; *(with jewels)* dicht besetzt mit

student ['stjuːdənt] *n* Student(in) *m(f)*; *(at school)* Schüler(in) *m(f)* ▷ *cpd* Studenten-; **law/ medical ~** Jura-/Medizinstudent(in) *m(f)*; **~ nurse** Krankenpflegeschüler(in) *m(f)*; **~ teacher** Referendar(in) *m(f)*

student driver *(US) n* Fahrschüler(in) *m(f)*

students' union ['stjuːdənts-] *(Brit) n* Studentenvereinigung *f* ≈ AStA *m*; *(building)* Gebäude *nt* der Studentenvereinigung

studied ['stʌdɪd] *adj (expression)* einstudiert; *(attitude)* berechnet

studio ['stjuːdɪəu] *n* Studio *nt*; *(sculptor's etc)* Atelier *nt*

studio flat, *(US)* **studio apartment** *n* Einzimmerwohnung *f*

studious ['stjuːdɪəs] *adj* lernbegierig

studiously ['stjuːdɪəslɪ] *adv (carefully)* sorgsam

study ['stʌdɪ] *n* Studium *nt*, Lernen *nt*; *(room)* Arbeitszimmer *nt* ▷ *vt* studieren; *(face)* prüfend ansehen; *(evidence)* prüfen ▷ *vi* studieren, lernen; **studies** *npl (studying)* Studien *pl*; **to make a ~ of sth** etw untersuchen; *(academic)* etw studieren; **to ~ for an exam** sich auf eine Prüfung vorbereiten

stuff [stʌf] *n* Zeug *nt* ▷ *vt* ausstopfen; *(Culin)* füllen; *(inf: push)* stopfen; **my nose is ~ed up** ich habe eine verstopfte Nase; **get ~ed!** *(inf!)* du kannst mich mal!

stuffed toy [stʌft-] *n* Stofftier *nt*

stuffing ['stʌfɪŋ] *n* Füllung *f*; *(in sofa etc)* Polstermaterial *nt*

stuffy ['stʌfɪ] *adj (room)* stickig; *(person, ideas)* spießig

stumble ['stʌmbl] *vi* stolpern; **to ~ across** *or* **on** *(fig)* (zufällig) stoßen auf +*acc*

stumbling block ['stʌmblɪŋ-] *n* Hürde *f*, Hindernis *nt*

stump [stʌmp] *n* Stumpf *m* ▷ *vt*: **to be ~ed** überfragt sein

stun [stʌn] *vt* betäuben; *(news)* fassungslos machen

stung [stʌŋ] *pt, pp of* **sting**

stunk [stʌŋk] *pp of* **stink**

stunning ['stʌnɪŋ] *adj (news, event)* sensationell; *(girl, dress)* hinreißend

stunt [stʌnt] *n (in film)* Stunt *m*; *(publicity stunt)* (Werbe)gag *m*

stunted ['stʌntɪd] *adj* verkümmert

stuntman ['stʌntmæn] *(irreg: like* **man***) n* Stuntman *m*

stupefaction [stjuːpɪ'fækʃən] *n* Verblüffung *f*

stupefy ['stjuːpɪfaɪ] *vt* benommen machen; *(fig)* verblüffen

stupendous [stjuː'pɛndəs] *adj* enorm

stupid ['stjuːpɪd] *adj* dumm

stupidity [stjuː'pɪdɪtɪ] *n* Dummheit *f*

stupidly ['stjuːpɪdlɪ] *adv* dumm

stupor ['stjuːpəʳ] *n* Benommenheit *f*; **in a ~** benommen

sturdily ['stəːdɪlɪ] *adv*: ~ **built** *(person)* kräftig gebaut; *(thing)* stabil gebaut

sturdy ['stəːdɪ] *adj (person)* kräftig; *(thing)* stabil

sturgeon ['stəːdʒən] *n* Stör *m*

stutter ['stʌtəʳ] *n* Stottern *nt* ▷ *vi* stottern; **to have a ~** stottern

Stuttgart ['stutgɑːt] *n* Stuttgart *nt*

sty [staɪ] *n* Schweinestall *m*

stye [staɪ] *n* Gerstenkorn *nt*

style [staɪl] *n* Stil *m*; *(design)* Modell *nt*; **in the latest ~** nach der neuesten Mode; **hair ~** Frisur *f*

styli ['staɪlaɪ] *npl of* **stylus**

stylish ['staɪlɪʃ] *adj* elegant

stylist ['staɪlɪst] *n (hair stylist)* Friseur *m*, Friseuse *f*; *(literary stylist)* Stilist(in) *m(f)*

stylized ['staɪlaɪzd] *adj* stilisiert

stylus ['staɪləs] *(pl* **styli** *or* **~es***) n* Nadel *f*

Styrofoam® ['staɪrəfəum] *n* ≈ Styropor® *nt*

suave [swɑːv] *adj* zuvorkommend

sub [sʌb] *n abbr (Naut)* = **submarine**; *(Admin)* = **subscription**; *(Brit: Press)* = **subeditor**

sub ... [sʌb] *pref* Unter-, unter-

subcommittee ['sʌbkəmɪtɪ] *n* Unterausschuss *m*

subconscious [sʌb'kɔnʃəs] *adj* unterbewusst

subcontinent [sʌb'kɔntɪnənt] *n*: **the (Indian) ~** der (indische) Subkontinent

subcontract [*vt* 'sʌbkən'trækt, *n* 'sʌb'kɔntrækt]
vt (vertraglich) weitervergeben ▷ *n*
Nebenvertrag *m*

subcontractor ['sʌbkən'træktəʳ] *n*
Subunternehmer *m*

subdivide [sʌbdɪ'vaɪd] *vt* unterteilen

subdivision ['sʌbdɪvɪʒən] *n* Unterteilung *f*

subdue [səb'djuː] *vt* unterwerfen; (*emotions*)
dämpfen

subdued [səb'djuːd] *adj* (*light*) gedämpft;
(*person*) bedrückt

subeditor [sʌb'ɛdɪtəʳ] (*Brit*) *n* Redakteur(in)
m(f)

subject [*n* 'sʌbdʒɪkt, *vt* səb'dʒɛkt] *n* (*matter*)
Thema *nt*; (*Scol*) Fach *nt*; (*of country*)
Staatsbürger(in) *m(f)*; (*Gram*) Subjekt *nt* ▷ *vt*: **to
~ sb to sth** jdn einer Sache *dat* unterziehen;
(*expose*) jdn einer Sache *dat* aussetzen; **to
change the ~** das Thema wechseln; **to be ~ to**
(*law, tax*) unterworfen sein +*dat*; (*heart attacks
etc*) anfällig sein für; **~ to confirmation in
writing** vorausgesetzt, es wird schriftlich
bestätigt

subjection [səb'dʒɛkʃən] *n* Unterwerfung *f*

subjective [səb'dʒɛktɪv] *adj* subjektiv

subject matter *n* Stoff *m*; (*content*) Inhalt *m*

sub judice [sʌb'djuːdɪsɪ] *adj* (*Law*): **to be ~**
verhandelt werden

subjugate ['sʌbdʒugeɪt] *vt* unterwerfen

subjunctive [səb'dʒʌŋktɪv] *n* Konjunktiv *m*; **in
the ~** im Konjunktiv

sublet [sʌb'lɛt] *vt* untervermieten

sublime [sə'blaɪm] *adj* erhaben, vollendet;
that's going from the ~ to the ridiculous
das ist ein Abstieg ins Profane

subliminal [sʌb'lɪmɪnl] *adj* unterschwellig

submachine gun ['sʌbmə'ʃiːn-] *n*
Maschinenpistole *f*

submarine [sʌbmə'riːn] *n* Unterseeboot *nt*,
U-Boot *nt*

submerge [səb'mɜːdʒ] *vt* untertauchen; (*flood*)
überschwemmen ▷ *vi* tauchen; **~d** unter
Wasser

submersion [səb'mɜːʃən] *n* Untertauchen
nt; (*of submarine*) Tauchen *nt*; (*by flood*)
Überschwemmung *f*

submission [səb'mɪʃən] *n* (*subjection*)
Unterwerfung *f*; (*of plan, application etc*)
Einreichung *f*; (*proposal*) Vorlage *f*

submissive [səb'mɪsɪv] *adj* gehorsam; (*gesture*)
demütig

submit [səb'mɪt] *vt* (*proposal*) vorlegen;
(*application etc*) einreichen ▷ *vi*: **to ~ to sth** sich
einer Sache *dat* unterwerfen

subnormal [sʌb'nɔːml] *adj* (*below average*)
unterdurchschnittlich; (*old: child
etc*) minderbegabt; **educationally ~**
lernbehindert

subordinate [sə'bɔːdɪnət] *n* Untergebene(r)
f(m); (*Ling*): **~ clause** Nebensatz *m* ▷ *adj*
untergeordnet; **to be ~ to sb** jdm
untergeordnet sein

subpoena [səb'piːnə] *n* (*Law*) Vorladung *f* ▷ *vt*

vorladen

subroutine [sʌbruː'tiːn] *n* (*Comput*)
Unterprogramm *nt*

subscribe [səb'skraɪb] *vi* spenden; **to ~ to**
(*opinion, theory*) sich anschließen +*dat*; (*fund,
charity*) regelmäßig spenden an +*acc*; (*magazine
etc*) abonnieren

subscriber [səb'skraɪbəʳ] *n* (*to magazine*)
Abonnent(in) *m(f)*; (*Tel*) Teilnehmer(in) *m(f)*

subscript ['sʌbskrɪpt] *n* tiefgestelltes Zeichen
nt

subscription [səb'skrɪpʃən] *n* (*to magazine etc*)
Abonnement *nt*; (*membership dues*) (Mitglieds)
beitrag *m*; **to take out a ~ to** (*magazine etc*)
abonnieren

subsequent ['sʌbsɪkwənt] *adj* später,
nachfolgend; (*further*) weiter; **~ to** im
Anschluss an +*acc*

subsequently ['sʌbsɪkwəntlɪ] *adv* später

subservient [səb'sɜːvɪənt] *adj* unterwürfig;
(*less important*) untergeordnet; **to be ~ to**
untergeordnet sein +*dat*

subside [səb'saɪd] *vi* (*feeling, pain*) nachlassen;
(*flood*) sinken; (*earth*) sich senken

subsidence [səb'saɪdns] *n* Senkung *f*

subsidiarity [səbsɪdɪ'ærɪtɪ] *n* Subsidiarität *f*

subsidiary [səb'sɪdɪərɪ] *adj* (*question, role, Brit,
Scol: subject*) Neben- ▷ *n* (*also:* **subsidiary
company**) Tochtergesellschaft *f*

subsidize ['sʌbsɪdaɪz] *vt* subventionieren

subsidy ['sʌbsɪdɪ] *n* Subvention *f*

subsist [səb'sɪst] *vi*: **to ~ on sth** sich von etw
ernähren

subsistence [səb'sɪstəns] *n* Existenz *f*; **enough
for ~** genug zum (Über)leben

subsistence allowance *n* Unterhaltszuschuss
m

subsistence level *n* Existenzminimum *nt*

substance ['sʌbstəns] *n* Substanz *f*, Stoff
m; (*fig: essence*) Kern *m*; **a man of ~** ein
vermögender Mann; **to lack ~** (*book*)
keine Substanz haben; (*argument*) keine
Durchschlagskraft haben

substance abuse *n* Missbrauch von Alkohol,
Drogen, Arzneimitteln etc

substandard [sʌb'stændəd] *adj* minderwertig;
(*housing*) unzulänglich

substantial [səb'stænʃl] *adj* (*solid*) solide;
(*considerable*) beträchtlich, größere(r, s); (*meal*)
kräftig

substantially [səb'stænʃəlɪ] *adv* erheblich; (*in
essence*) im Wesentlichen

substantiate [səb'stænʃɪeɪt] *vt* erhärten,
untermauern

substitute ['sʌbstɪtjuːt] *n* Ersatz *m* ▷ *vt*: **to ~ A
for B** B durch A ersetzen

substitute teacher (*US*) *n* Vertretung *f*

substitution [sʌbstɪ'tjuːʃən] *n* Ersetzen *nt*;
(*Football*) Auswechseln *nt*

subterfuge ['sʌbtəfjuːdʒ] *n* Tricks *pl*; (*trickery*)
Täuschung *f*

subterranean [sʌbtə'reɪnɪən] *adj* unterirdisch

subtitle ['sʌbtaɪtl] *n* Untertitel *m*

subtle ['sʌtl] *adj* fein; (*indirect*) raffiniert
subtlety ['sʌtltɪ] *n* Feinheit *f*; (*art of being subtle*) Finesse *f*
subtly ['sʌtlɪ] *adv* (*change, vary*) leicht; (*different*) auf subtile Weise; (*persuade*) raffiniert
subtotal [sʌb'təʊtl] *n* Zwischensumme *f*
subtract [səb'trækt] *vt* abziehen, subtrahieren
subtraction [səb'trækʃən] *n* Abziehen *nt*, Subtraktion *f*
subtropical [sʌb'trɒpɪkl] *adj* subtropisch
suburb ['sʌbə:b] *n* Vorort *m*
suburban [sə'bə:bən] *adj* (*train etc*) Vorort-; (*lifestyle etc*) spießig, kleinbürgerlich
suburbia [sə'bə:bɪə] *n* die Vororte *pl*
subvention [səb'venʃən] *n* Subvention *f*
subversion [səb'və:ʃən] *n* Subversion *f*
subversive [səb'və:sɪv] *adj* subversiv
subway ['sʌbweɪ] *n* (*US*) Untergrundbahn *f*, U-Bahn *f*; (*Brit: underpass*) Unterführung *f*
sub-zero [sʌb'zɪərəʊ] *adj*: ~ **temperatures** Temperaturen unter null
succeed [sək'si:d] *vi* (*plan etc*) gelingen, erfolgreich sein; (*person*) erfolgreich sein, Erfolg haben ▷ *vt* (*in job*) Nachfolger werden +*gen*; (*in order*) folgen +*dat*; **sb ~s in doing sth** es gelingt jdm, etw zu tun
succeeding [sək'si:dɪŋ] *adj* folgend; ~ **generations** spätere *or* nachfolgende Generationen *pl*
success [sək'sɛs] *n* Erfolg *m*; **without** ~ ohne Erfolg, erfolglos
successful [sək'sɛsful] *adj* erfolgreich; **to be** ~ erfolgreich sein, Erfolg haben; **sb is ~ in doing sth** es gelingt jdm, etw zu tun
successfully [sək'sɛsfəlɪ] *adv* erfolgreich, mit Erfolg
succession [sək'sɛʃən] *n* Folge *f*, Serie *f*; (*to throne etc*) Nachfolge *f*; **3 years in** ~ 3 Jahre nacheinander *or* hintereinander
successive [sək'sɛsɪv] *adj* aufeinanderfolgend; **on 3 ~ days** 3 Tage nacheinander *or* hintereinander
successor [sək'sɛsə^r] *n* Nachfolger(in) *m(f)*
succinct [sək'sɪŋkt] *adj* knapp, prägnant
succulent ['sʌkjulənt] *adj* saftig ▷ *n* Fettpflanze *f*, Sukkulente *f*
succumb [sə'kʌm] *vi*: ~ **to** (*temptation*) erliegen +*dat*; (*illness: become affected by*) bekommen; (: *die of*) erliegen +*dat*
such [sʌtʃ] *adj* (*of that kind*): ~ **a book** so ein Buch; (*so much*): ~ **courage** so viel Mut; (*emphasizing similarity*): **or some** ~ **place/name** *etc* oder so ähnlich ▷ *adv* so; ~ **books** solche Bücher; ~ **a lot of** so viel; **she made** ~ **a noise that ...** sie machte so einen Lärm, dass ...; ~ **books as I have** was ich an Büchern habe; **I said no** ~ **thing** das habe ich nie gesagt; ~ **a long trip** so eine lange Reise; **as** ~ als wie (zum Beispiel); **as** ~ an sich
such-and-such ['sʌtʃənsʌtʃ] *adj* die und die, der und der, das und das
suchlike ['sʌtʃlaɪk] (*inf*) *pron*: **and** ~ und dergleichen

suck [sʌk] *vt* (*sweet etc*) lutschen; (*ice-lolly*) lutschen an +*dat*; (*baby*) saugen an +*dat*; (*pump, machine*) saugen
sucker ['sʌkə^r] *n* (*Zool*) Saugnapf *m*; (*Tech*) Saugfuß *m*; (*Bot*) unterirdischer Ausläufer *m*; (*inf*) Dummkopf *m*
suckle ['sʌkl] *vt* (*baby*) stillen; (*animal*) säugen
sucrose ['su:krəʊz] *n* (*pflanzlicher*) Zucker *m*
suction ['sʌkʃən] *n* Saugwirkung *f*
suction pump *n* Saugpumpe *f*
Sudan [su'dɑ:n] *n* der Sudan
Sudanese [su:də'ni:z] *adj* sudanesisch ▷ *n* Sudanese *m*, Sudanesin *f*
sudden ['sʌdn] *adj* plötzlich; **all of a** ~ ganz plötzlich
sudden death *n* (*also*: **sudden-death play-off**) Stichkampf *m*
suddenly ['sʌdnlɪ] *adv* plötzlich
sudoku [su'dəʊku:] *n* Sudoku *nt*
suds [sʌdz] *npl* Seifenschaum *m*
sue [su:] *vt* verklagen ▷ *vi* klagen, vor Gericht gehen; **to** ~ **sb for damages** jdn auf Schadenersatz verklagen; **to** ~ **for divorce** die Scheidung einreichen
suede [sweɪd] *n* Wildleder *nt* ▷ *cpd* Wildleder-
suet ['suɪt] *n* Nierenfett *nt*
Suez ['su:ɪz] *n*: **the** ~ **Canal** der Suezkanal
Suff. (*Brit*) *abbr* (*Post*) = **Suffolk**
suffer ['sʌfə^r] *vt* erleiden; (*rudeness etc*) ertragen ▷ *vi* leiden; **to** ~ **from** leiden an +*dat*; **to** ~ **the effects of sth** an den Folgen von etw leiden
sufferance ['sʌfərns] *n*: **he was only there on** ~ er wurde dort nur geduldet
sufferer ['sʌfərə^r] *n* Leidende(r) *f(m)*
suffering ['sʌfərɪŋ] *n* Leid *nt*
suffice [sə'faɪs] *vi* genügen
sufficient [sə'fɪʃənt] *adj* ausreichend; ~ **money** genug Geld
sufficiently [sə'fɪʃəntlɪ] *adv* genug, ausreichend; ~ **powerful** mächtig genug
suffix ['sʌfɪks] *n* Suffix *nt*, Nachsilbe *f*
suffocate ['sʌfəkeɪt] *vi* (*lit, fig*) ersticken
suffocation [sʌfə'keɪʃən] *n* Ersticken *nt*
suffrage ['sʌfrɪdʒ] *n* Wahlrecht *nt*
suffragette [sʌfrə'dʒɛt] *n* Suffragette *f*
suffused [sə'fju:zd] *adj*: ~ **with** erfüllt von; ~ **with light** lichtdurchflutet
sugar ['ʃugə^r] *n* Zucker *m* ▷ *vt* zuckern
sugar beet *n* Zuckerrübe *f*
sugar bowl *n* Zuckerdose *f*
sugar cane *n* Zuckerrohr *nt*
sugar-coated ['ʃugə'kəʊtɪd] *adj* mit Zucker überzogen
sugar lump *n* Zuckerstück *nt*
sugar refinery *n* Zuckerraffinerie *f*
sugary ['ʃugərɪ] *adj* süß; (*fig: smile, phrase*) süßlich
suggest [sə'dʒɛst] *vt* vorschlagen; (*indicate*) andeuten, hindeuten auf +*acc*; **what do you** ~ **I do?** was schlagen Sie vor?
suggestion [sə'dʒɛstʃən] *n* Vorschlag *m*; (*indication*) Anflug *m*; (*trace*) Spur *f*
suggestive [sə'dʒɛstɪv] (*pej*) *adj* anzüglich

suicidal [suɪ'saɪdl] *adj* selbstmörderisch; (*person*) selbstmordgefährdet; **to be** *or* **feel ~** Selbstmordgedanken haben

suicide ['suɪsaɪd] *n* (*lit, fig*) Selbstmord *m*; (*person*) Selbstmörder(in) *m(f)*; *see also* **commit**

suicide attack *n* Selbstmordanschlag *m*

suicide attacker *n* Selbstmordattentäter(in) *m(f)*

suicide attempt, suicide bid *n* Selbstmordversuch *m*

suicide bomber *n* Selbstmordattentäter(in) *m(f)*

suit [su:t] *n* (*man's*) Anzug *m*; (*woman's*) Kostüm *nt*; (*Law*) Prozess *m*, Verfahren *nt*; (*Cards*) Farbe *f* ▷ *vt* passen +*dat*; (*colour, clothes*) stehen +*dat*; **to bring a ~ against sb** (*Law*) gegen jdn Klage erheben *or* einen Prozess anstrengen; **to follow ~** (*fig*) das Gleiche tun; **to ~ sth to** etw anpassen an +*acc*; **to be ~ed to do sth** sich dafür eignen, etw zu tun; **~ yourself!** wie du willst!; **well ~ed** (*couple*) gut zusammenpassend

suitability [su:tə'bɪlɪtɪ] *n* Eignung *f*

suitable ['su:təbl] *adj* (*convenient*) passend; (*appropriate*) geeignet; **would tomorrow be ~?** würde Ihnen morgen passen?; **Monday isn't ~** Montag passt nicht; **we found somebody ~** wir haben jemand Passenden gefunden

suitably ['su:təblɪ] *adv* passend; (*impressed*) gebührend

suitcase ['su:tkeɪs] *n* Koffer *m*

suite [swi:t] *n* (*of rooms*) Suite *f*, Zimmerflucht *f*; (*Mus*) Suite *f*; **bedroom/dining room ~** Schlafzimmer-/Esszimmereinrichtung *f*; **a three-piece ~** eine dreiteilige Polstergarnitur

suitor ['su:tə'] *n* Kläger(in) *m(f)*

sulfate ['sʌlfeɪt] (*US*) *n* = **sulphate**

sulfur ['sʌlfə'] (*US*) *n* = **sulphur**

sulfuric [sʌl'fjuərɪk] (*US*) *adj* = **sulphuric**

sulk [sʌlk] *vi* schmollen

sulky ['sʌlkɪ] *adj* schmollend

sullen ['sʌlən] *adj* mürrisch, verdrossen

sulphate, (*US*) **sulfate** ['sʌlfeɪt] *n* Sulfat *nt*, schwefelsaures Salz *nt*

sulphur, (*US*) **sulfur** ['sʌlfə'] *n* Schwefel *m*

sulphur dioxide *n* Schwefeldioxid *nt*

sulphuric, (*US*) **sulfuric** [sʌl'fjuərɪk] *adj*: **~ acid** Schwefelsäure *f*

sultan ['sʌltən] *n* Sultan *m*

sultana [sʌl'tɑ:nə] *n* Sultanine *f*

sultry ['sʌltrɪ] *adj* schwül

sum [sʌm] *n* (*calculation*) Rechenaufgabe *f*; (*amount*) Summe *f*, Betrag *m*
▶ **sum up** *vt* zusammenfassen; (*evaluate rapidly*) einschätzen ▷ *vi* zusammenfassen

Sumatra [su'mɑ:trə] *n* Sumatra *nt*

summarize ['sʌməraɪz] *vt* zusammenfassen

summary ['sʌmərɪ] *n* Zusammenfassung *f* ▷ *adj* (*justice, executions*) im Schnellverfahren

summer ['sʌmə'] *n* Sommer *m* ▷ *cpd* Sommer-; **in ~** im Sommer

summer camp (*US*) *n* Ferienlager *nt*

summer holidays *npl* Sommerferien *pl*

summerhouse ['sʌməhaus] *n* (*in garden*) Gartenhaus *nt*, Gartenlaube *f*

summertime ['sʌmətaɪm] *n* Sommer *m*, Sommerszeit *f*

summer time *n* Sommerzeit *f*

summery ['sʌmərɪ] *adj* sommerlich

summing-up [sʌmɪŋ'ʌp] *n* (*Law*) Resümee *nt*

summit ['sʌmɪt] *n* Gipfel *m*; (*also:* **summit conference/meeting**) Gipfelkonferenz *f*/-treffen *nt*

summon ['sʌmən] *vt* rufen, kommen lassen; (*help*) holen; (*meeting*) einberufen; (*Law: witness*) vorladen
▶ **summon up** *vt* aufbringen

summons ['sʌmənz] *n* (*Law*) Vorladung *f*; (*fig*) Aufruf *m* ▷ *vt* (*Law*) vorladen; **to serve a ~ on sb** jdn vor Gericht laden

sumo ['su:məu], **sumo wrestling** *n* Sumo(-Ringen) *nt*

sump [sʌmp] (*Brit*) *n* Ölwanne *f*

sumptuous ['sʌmptjuəs] *adj* (*meal*) üppig; (*costume*) aufwendig

Sun. *abbr* (= *Sunday*) So.

sun [sʌn] *n* Sonne *f*; **to catch the ~** einen Sonnenbrand bekommen; **everything under the ~** alles Mögliche

sunbathe ['sʌnbeɪð] *vi* sich sonnen

sunbeam ['sʌnbi:m] *n* Sonnenstrahl *m*

sunbed ['sʌnbed] *n* (*with sun lamp*) Sonnenbank *f*

sunblock *n* Sonnenschutzcreme *f*

sunburn ['sʌnbə:n] *n* Sonnenbrand *m*

sunburned ['sʌnbə:nd] *adj* = **sunburnt**

sunburnt ['sʌnbə:nt] *adj* sonnenverbrannt, sonnengebräunt; **to be ~** (*painfully*) einen Sonnenbrand haben

sun-cream ['sʌnkri:m] *n* Sonnencreme *f*

sundae ['sʌndeɪ] *n* Eisbecher *m*

Sunday ['sʌndɪ] *n* Sonntag *m*; *see also* **Tuesday**

Sunday paper *n* Sonntagszeitung *f*; *siehe Info-Artikel*

● **SUNDAY PAPERS**
●
● Die *Sunday papers* umfassen sowohl
● Massenblätter als auch seriöse
● Zeitungen. „The Observer" ist die
● älteste überregionale Sonntagszeitung
● der Welt. Die Sonntagszeitungen sind
● alle sehr umfangreich mit vielen Farb-
● und Sonderbeilagen. Zu den meisten
● Tageszeitungen gibt es parallele
● Sonntagsblätter, die aber separate
● Redaktionen haben.

Sunday school *n* Sonntagsschule *f*

sundial ['sʌndaɪəl] *n* Sonnenuhr *f*

sundown ['sʌndaun] (*esp US*) *n* Sonnenuntergang *m*

sundries ['sʌndrɪz] *npl* Verschiedenes *nt*

sundry ['sʌndrɪ] *adj* verschieden; **all and ~** jedermann

sunflower ['sʌnflauə'] *n* Sonnenblume *f*

sunflower oil *n* Sonnenblumenöl *nt*

sung [sʌŋ] pp of **sing**
sunglasses ['sʌnglɑ:sɪz] npl Sonnenbrille f
sunk [sʌŋk] pp of **sink**
sunken ['sʌŋkn] adj versunken; (eyes) tief liegend; (cheeks) eingefallen; (bath) eingelassen
sunlamp ['sʌnlæmp] n Höhensonne f
sunlight ['sʌnlaɪt] n Sonnenlicht nt
sunlit ['sʌnlɪt] adj sonnig, sonnenbeschienen
sunny ['sʌnɪ] adj sonnig; (fig) heiter
sunrise ['sʌnraɪz] n Sonnenaufgang m
sun roof n (Aut) Schiebedach nt; (on building) Sonnenterrasse f
sun screen n Sonnenschutzmittel nt
sunset ['sʌnsɛt] n Sonnenuntergang m
sunshade ['sʌnʃeɪd] n Sonnenschirm m
sunshine ['sʌnʃaɪn] n Sonnenschein m
sunspot ['sʌnspɒt] n Sonnenfleck m
sunstroke ['sʌnstrəʊk] n Sonnenstich m
suntan ['sʌntæn] n (Sonnen)bräune f; **to get a ~** braun werden
suntan lotion n Sonnenmilch f
suntanned ['sʌntænd] adj braun (gebrannt)
suntan oil n Sonnenöl nt
suntrap ['sʌntræp] n sonniges Eckchen nt
super ['su:pə^r] (inf) adj fantastisch, toll
superannuation [su:pəræenju'eɪʃən] n Beitrag m zur Rentenversicherung
superb [su:'pə:b] adj ausgezeichnet, großartig; (meal) vorzüglich
Super Bowl n Superbowl m, Super Bowl m, American-Football-Turnier zwischen den Spitzenreitern der Nationalligen
supercilious [su:pə'sɪlɪəs] adj herablassend
superconductor [su:pəkən'dʌktə^r] n (Phys) Superleiter m
superficial [su:pə'fɪʃəl] adj oberflächlich
superficially [su:pə'fɪʃəlɪ] adv oberflächlich; (from a superficial point of view) oberflächlich gesehen
superfluous [su'pə:fluəs] adj überflüssig
superglue ['su:pəglu:] n Sekundenkleber m
superhighway (US) n ≈ Autobahn f; **information ~** Datenautobahn f
superhuman [su:pə'hju:mən] adj übermenschlich
superimpose ['su:pərɪm'pəʊz] vt (two things) übereinanderlegen; **to ~ on** legen auf +acc; **to ~ with** überlagern mit
superintend [su:pərɪn'tɛnd] vt beaufsichtigen, überwachen
superintendent [su:pərɪn'tɛndənt] n Aufseher(in) m(f); (Police) Kommissar(in) m(f)
superior [su'pɪərɪə^r] adj besser, überlegen +dat; (more senior) höhergestellt; (smug) überheblich; (: smile) überlegen ▷ n Vorgesetzte(r) f(m); **Mother S~** (Rel) Mutter Oberin
superiority [supɪərɪ'ɒrɪtɪ] n Überlegenheit f
superlative [su'pə:lətɪv] n Superlativ m ▷ adj überragend
superman ['su:pəmæn] (irreg: like **man**) n Übermensch m
supermarket ['su:pəmɑ:kɪt] n Supermarkt m

supermodel ['su:pəmɔdl] n Supermodell nt
supernatural [su:pə'næetʃərəl] adj übernatürlich ▷ n: **the ~** das Übernatürliche
supernova [su:pə'nəʊvə] n Supernova f
superpower ['su:pəpaʊə^r] n Supermacht f
superscript ['su:pəskrɪpt] n hochgestelltes Zeichen nt
supersede [su:pə'si:d] vt ablösen, ersetzen
supersonic ['su:pə'sɒnɪk] adj (aircraft etc) Überschall-
superstar ['su:pəstɑ:^r] n Superstar m
superstition [su:pə'stɪʃən] n Aberglaube m
superstitious [su:pə'stɪʃəs] adj abergläubisch
superstore ['su:pəstɔ:^r] (Brit) n Großmarkt m
supertanker ['su:pətæŋkə^r] n Supertanker m
supertax ['su:pətæks] n Höchststeuer f
supervise ['su:pəvaɪz] vt beaufsichtigen
supervision [su:pə'vɪʒən] n Beaufsichtigung f; **under medical ~** unter ärztlicher Aufsicht
supervisor ['su:pəvaɪzə^r] n Aufseher(in) m(f); (of students) Tutor(in) m(f)
supervisory ['su:pəvaɪzərɪ] adj beaufsichtigend, Aufsichts-
supine ['su:paɪn] adj: **to be ~** auf dem Rücken liegen ▷ adv auf dem Rücken
supper ['sʌpə^r] n Abendessen nt; **to have ~** zu Abend essen
supplant [sə'plɑ:nt] vt ablösen, ersetzen
supple ['sʌpl] adj geschmeidig; (person) gelenkig
supplement ['sʌplɪmənt] n Zusatz m; (of book) Ergänzungsband m; (of newspaper etc) Beilage f ▷ vt ergänzen
supplementary [sʌplɪ'mɛntərɪ] adj zusätzlich, ergänzend
supplementary benefit (Brit: old) n ≈ Sozialhilfe f
supplementary budget n (Pol) ≈ Nachtragshaushalt m or -etat m
supplier [sə'plaɪə^r] n Lieferant(in) m(f)
supply [sə'plaɪ] vt liefern; (provide) sorgen für; (a need) befriedigen ▷ n Vorrat m; (supplying) Lieferung f; **supplies** npl (food) Vorräte pl; (Mil) Nachschub m; **to ~ sth to sb** jdm etw liefern; **to ~ sth with sth** etw mit etw versorgen; **it comes supplied with an adaptor** es wird mit einem Adapter geliefert; **office supplies** Bürobedarf m; **to be in short ~** knapp sein; **the electricity/water/gas ~** die Strom-/Wasser-/Gasversorgung f; **~ and demand** Angebot nt und Nachfrage
supply teacher (Brit) n Vertretung f
support [sə'pɔ:t] n Unterstützung f; (Tech) Stütze f ▷ vt unterstützen, eintreten für; (financially: family etc) unterhalten; (: party etc) finanziell unterstützen; (Tech) (ab)stützen; (theory etc) untermauern; **they stopped work in ~ of ...** sie sind in den Streik getreten, um für ... einzutreten; **to ~ o.s.** (financially) finanziell unabhängig sein; **to ~ Arsenal** Arsenal-Fan sein
supporter [sə'pɔ:tə^r] n (Pol etc) Anhänger(in) m(f); (Sport) Fan m

supporting [sə'pɔːtɪŋ] *adj*: ~ **role** Nebenrolle *f*; ~ **actor** Schauspieler *m* in einer Nebenrolle; ~ **film** Vorfilm *m*

supportive [sə'pɔːtɪv] *adj* hilfreich; **to be ~ of sb/sth** jdn/etw unterstützen

suppose [sə'pəʊz] *vt* annehmen, glauben; (*imagine*) sich *dat* vorstellen; **to be ~d to do sth** etw tun sollen; **it was worse than she'd ~d** es war schlimmer, als sie es sich vorgestellt hatte; **I don't ~ she'll come** ich glaube kaum, dass sie kommt; **he's about sixty, I ~** er muss wohl so um die Sechzig sein; **he's an expert** er ist angeblich ein Experte; **I ~ so/not** ich glaube schon/nicht

supposedly [sə'pəʊzɪdlɪ] *adv* angeblich

supposing [sə'pəʊzɪŋ] *conj* angenommen

supposition [sʌpə'zɪʃən] *n* Annahme *f*

suppository [sə'pɒzɪtrɪ] *n* Zäpfchen *nt*

suppress [sə'prɛs] *vt* unterdrücken; (*publication*) verbieten

suppression [sə'prɛʃən] *n* Unterdrückung *f*

suppressor [sə'prɛsəʳ] *n* (*Elec etc*) Entstörungselement *nt*

supremacy [su'prɛməsɪ] *n* Vormachtstellung *f*

supreme [su'priːm] *adj* Ober-, oberste(r, s); (*effort*) äußerste(r, s); (*achievement*) höchste(r, s)

Supreme Court (*US*) *n* Oberster Gerichtshof *m*

supremo [su'priːməʊ] (*Brit: inf*) *n* Boss *m*

Supt *abbr* (*Police*) = **superintendent**

surcharge ['səːtʃɑːdʒ] *n* Zuschlag *m*

sure [ʃʊəʳ] *adj* sicher; (*reliable*) zuverlässig, sicher ▷ *adv* (*inf: esp US*): **that ~ is pretty, that's ~ pretty** das ist aber schön; **to make ~ of sth** sich einer Sache *gen* vergewissern; **to make ~ that** sich vergewissern, dass; **I'm ~ of it** ich bin mir da sicher; **I'm not ~ how/ why/when** ich bin mir nicht sicher or ich weiß nicht genau, wie/warum/wann; **to be ~ of o.s.** selbstsicher sein; **~!** klar!; **~ enough** tatsächlich

sure-fire ['ʃʊəfaɪəʳ] (*inf*) *adj* todsicher

sure-footed [ʃʊə'futɪd] *adj* trittsicher

surely ['ʃʊəlɪ] *adv* sicherlich, bestimmt; ~ **you don't mean that!** das meinen Sie doch bestimmt *or* sicher nicht (so)!

surety ['ʃʊərətɪ] *n* Bürgschaft *f*, Sicherheit *f*; **to go** *or* **stand ~ for sb** für jdn bürgen

surf [səːf] *n* Brandung *f*

surface ['səːfɪs] *n* Oberfläche *f* ▷ *vt* (*road*) mit einem Belag versehen ▷ *vi* (*lit, fig*) auftauchen; (*feeling*) hochkommen; (*rise from bed*) hochkommen; **on the ~** (*fig*) oberflächlich betrachtet

surface area *n* Fläche *f*

surface mail *n* Post *f* auf dem Land-/Seeweg

surface-to-surface ['səːfɪstə'səːfɪs] *adj* (*missile*) Boden-Boden-

surfboard ['səːfbɔːd] *n* Surfbrett *nt*

surfeit ['səːfɪt] *n*: **a ~ of** ein Übermaß an +*dat*

surfer ['səːfəʳ] *n* Surfer(in) *m(f)*

surfing ['səːfɪŋ] *n* Surfen *nt*; **to go ~** surfen gehen

surge [səːdʒ] *n* Anstieg *m*; (*fig: of emotion*) Woge *f*; (*Elec*) Spannungsstoß *m* ▷ *vi* (*water*) branden; (*people*) sich drängen; (*vehicles*) sich wälzen; (*emotion*) aufwallen; (*Elec: power*) ansteigen; **to ~ forward** nach vorne drängen

surgeon ['səːdʒən] *n* Chirurg(in) *m(f)*

Surgeon General (*US*) *n* (*Med*) ≈ Gesundheitsminister(in) *m(f)*; (*Mil*) Sanitätsinspekteur *m*

surgery ['səːdʒərɪ] *n* Chirurgie *f*; (*Brit: room*) Sprechzimmer *nt*; (: *building*) Praxis *f*; (*also:* **surgery hours**): *of doctor, MP etc*) Sprechstunde *f*; **to have ~** operiert werden; **to need ~** operiert werden müssen

surgical ['səːdʒɪkl] *adj* chirurgisch; (*treatment*) operativ

surgical spirit (*Brit*) *n* Wundbenzin *nt*

surly ['səːlɪ] *adj* verdrießlich, mürrisch

surmise [səː'maɪz] *vt* vermuten, mutmaßen

surmount [səː'maunt] *vt* (*fig*) überwinden

surname ['səːneɪm] *n* Nachname *m*

surpass [səː'pɑːs] *vt* übertreffen

surplus ['səːpləs] *n* Überschuss *m* ▷ *adj* überschüssig; **it is ~ to our requirements** das benötigen wir nicht

surprise [sə'praɪz] *n* Überraschung *f* ▷ *vt* überraschen; (*astonish*) erstaunen; (*army*) überrumpeln; (*thief*) ertappen; **to take sb by ~** jdn überraschen

surprising [sə'praɪzɪŋ] *adj* überraschend; (*situation*) erstaunlich; **it is ~ how/that** es ist erstaunlich, wie/dass

surprisingly [sə'praɪzɪŋlɪ] *adv* überraschend, erstaunlich; (*somewhat*) ~, **he agreed** erstaunlicherweise war er damit einverstanden

surrealism [sə'rɪəlɪzəm] *n* Surrealismus *m*

surrealist [sə'rɪəlɪst] *adj* surrealistisch

surrender [sə'rɛndəʳ] *n* Kapitulation *f* ▷ *vi* sich ergeben ▷ *vt* aufgeben

surrender value *n* Rückkaufswert *m*

surreptitious [sʌrəp'tɪʃəs] *adj* heimlich, verstohlen

surrogate ['sʌrəgɪt] *n* Ersatz *m* ▷ *adj* (*parents*) Ersatz-

surrogate mother *n* Leihmutter *f*

surround [sə'raund] *vt* umgeben; (*Mil, Police etc*) umstellen

surrounding [sə'raundɪŋ] *adj* umliegend; **the ~ area** die Umgebung

surroundings [sə'raundɪŋz] *npl* Umgebung *f*

surtax ['səːtæks] *n* Steuerzuschlag *m*

surveillance [səː'veɪləns] *n* Überwachung *f*; **to be under ~** überwacht werden

survey ['səːveɪ] *n* (*of land*) Vermessung *f*; (*of house*) Begutachtung *f*; (*investigation*) Untersuchung *f*; (*report*) Gutachten *nt*; (*comprehensive view*) Überblick *m* ▷ *vt* (*land*) vermessen; (*house*) inspizieren; (*look at*) betrachten

surveying [sə'veɪɪŋ] *n* (*of land*) Vermessung *f*

surveyor [sə'veɪəʳ] *n* (*of land*) Landvermesser(in) *m(f)*; (*of house*) Baugutachter(in) *m(f)*

S

811

survival [sə'vaɪvl] n Überleben nt;
(relic) Überbleibsel nt; ~ **course/kit**
Überlebenstraining nt/-ausrüstung f; ~ **bag**
Expeditionsschlafsack m

survive [sə'vaɪv] vi überleben; (custom etc)
weiter bestehen ▷ vt überleben

survivor [sə'vaɪvəʳ] n Überlebende(r) f(m)

susceptible [sə'septəbl] adj: ~ **(to)** anfällig
(für); (influenced by) empfänglich (für)

suspect ['sʌspɛkt] adj verdächtig ▷ n
Verdächtige(r) f(m) ▷ vt: **to ~ sb of** jdn
verdächtigen +gen; (think) vermuten; (doubt)
bezweifeln

suspected [səs'pɛktɪd] adj (terrorist etc)
mutmaßlich; **he is a ~ member of this
organization** er steht im Verdacht, Mitglied
dieser Organisation zu sein

suspend [səs'pɛnd] vt (hang) (auf)hängen;
(delay, stop) einstellen; (from employment)
suspendieren; **to be ~ed (from)** (hang)
hängen (an +dat)

suspended animation [səs'pɛndɪd-] n
vorübergehender Stillstand aller Körperfunktionen

suspended sentence n (Law) zur Bewährung
ausgesetzte Strafe f

suspender belt [səs'pɛndəʳ-] n Strumpfgürtel
m

suspenders [səs'pɛndəz] npl (Brit)
Strumpfhalter pl; (US) Hosenträger pl

suspense [səs'pɛns] n Spannung f; (uncertainty)
Ungewissheit f; **to keep sb in ~** jdn auf die
Folter spannen

suspension [səs'pɛnʃən] n (from job)
Suspendierung f; (from team) Sperrung f; (Aut)
Federung f; (of driving licence) zeitweiliger
Entzug m; (of payment) zeitweilige Einstellung f

suspension bridge n Hängebrücke f

suspicion [səs'pɪʃən] n Verdacht m; (distrust)
Misstrauen nt; (trace) Spur f; **to be under
~** unter Verdacht stehen; **arrested on
~ of murder** wegen Mordverdacht(s)
festgenommen

suspicious [səs'pɪʃəs] adj (suspecting)
misstrauisch; (causing suspicion) verdächtig;
to be ~ of or **about sb/sth** jdn/etw mit
Misstrauen betrachten

suss out [sʌs-] (Brit: inf) vt (discover)
rauskriegen; (understand) durchschauen

sustain [səs'teɪn] vt (continue)
aufrechterhalten; (food, drink) bei Kräften
halten; (suffer: injury) erleiden

sustainable [səs'teɪnəbl] adj: **to be ~**
aufrechtzuerhalten sein; **~ growth** stetiges
Wachstum nt

sustained [səs'teɪnd] adj (effort) ausdauernd;
(attack) anhaltend

sustenance ['sʌstɪnəns] n Nahrung f

suture ['suːtʃəʳ] n Naht f

SUV n abbr (= sport utility vehicle) SUV m,
Geländewagen m

SVQ n abbr (= Scottish Vocational Qualification)
Qualifikation für berufsbegleitende Ausbildungsinhalte
in Schottland

SW abbr (= south-west) SW; (Radio: = short-wave)
KW

swab [swɔb] n (Med) Tupfer m ▷ vt (Naut: also:
swab down) wischen

swagger ['swægəʳ] vi stolzieren

swallow ['swɔləu] n (bird) Schwalbe f; (of food,
drink etc) Schluck m ▷ vt (herunter)schlucken;
(fig: story, insult, one's pride) schlucken
▶ **swallow up** vt verschlingen

swam [swæm] pt of **swim**

swamp [swɔmp] n Sumpf m ▷ vt (lit, fig)
überschwemmen

swampy ['swɔmpɪ] adj sumpfig

swan [swɔn] n Schwan m

swank [swæŋk] (inf) vi angeben

swan song (fig) Schwanengesang m

swap [swɔp] n Tausch m ▷ vt: **to ~ (for)** (ein)
tauschen (gegen)

SWAPO ['swɑːpəu] n abbr (= South-West Africa
People's Organization) SWAPO f

swarm [swɔːm] n Schwarm m; (of people) Schar
f ▷ vi (bees, people) schwärmen; **to be ~ing with**
wimmeln von

swarthy ['swɔːðɪ] adj (person, face)
dunkelhäutig; (complexion) dunkel

swastika ['swɔstɪkə] n Hakenkreuz nt

SWAT (US) n abbr (= Special Weapons and Tactics): ~
team = schnelle Eingreiftruppe f

swat [swɔt] vt totschlagen ▷ n (Brit: also: **fly
swat**) Fliegenklatsche f

swathe [sweɪð] vt: **to ~ in** wickeln in +acc

swatter ['swɔtəʳ] n (also: **fly swatter**)
Fliegenklatsche f

sway [sweɪ] vi schwanken ▷ vt (influence)
beeinflussen ▷ n: **to hold ~** herrschen; **to
hold ~ over sb** jdn beherrschen or in seiner
Macht haben

swear [sweəʳ] (pt **swore**, pp **sworn**) vi (curse)
fluchen ▷ vt (promise) schwören; **to ~ an oath**
einen Eid ablegen
▶ **swear in** vt vereidigen

swearword ['sweəwəːd] n Fluch m,
Kraftausdruck m

sweat [swɛt] n Schweiß m ▷ vi schwitzen; **to
be in a ~** schwitzen

sweatband ['swɛtbænd] n Schweißband nt

sweater ['swɛtəʳ] n Pullover m

sweatshirt ['swɛtʃəːt] n Sweatshirt nt

sweatshop ['swɛtʃɔp] (pej) n Ausbeuterbetrieb
m

sweaty ['swɛtɪ] adj verschwitzt; (hands)
schweißig

Swede [swiːd] n Schwede m, Schwedin f

swede [swiːd] (Brit) n Steckrübe f

Sweden ['swiːdn] n Schweden nt

Swedish ['swiːdɪʃ] adj schwedisch ▷ n
Schwedisch nt

sweep [swiːp] (pt, pp **swept**) n (curve) Bogen
m; (range) Bereich m; (also: **chimney sweep**)
Kaminkehrer m, Schornsteinfeger m ▷ vt
fegen, kehren; (current) reißen ▷ vi (through air)
gleiten; (wind) fegen; **to give sth a ~** etw fegen
or kehren

▸ **sweep away** vt hinwegfegen

▸ **sweep past** vi vorbeirauschen

▸ **sweep up** vi zusammenfegen, zusammenkehren

sweeper ['swi:pə'] n (Football) Ausputzer m

sweeping ['swi:pɪŋ] adj (gesture) weit ausholend; (changes, reforms) weitreichend; (statement) verallgemeinernd

sweepstake ['swi:psteɪk] n Pferdewette, bei der der Preis aus der Summe der Einsätze besteht

sweet [swi:t] n (candy) Bonbon nt or m; (Brit: Culin) Nachtisch m ⊳ adj süß; (air, water) frisch; (kind) lieb ⊳ adv: **to smell/taste ~** süß duften/schmecken; **~ and sour** süß-sauer

sweetbread ['swi:tbrɛd] n Bries nt

sweetcorn ['swi:tkɔ:n] n Mais m

sweeten ['swi:tn] vt süßen; (temper) bessern; (person) gnädig stimmen

sweetener ['swi:tnə'] n Süßstoff m

sweetheart ['swi:thɑ:t] n Freund(in) m(f); (in speech, writing) Schatz m, Liebling m

sweetness ['swi:tnɪs] n Süße f; (kindness) Liebenswürdigkeit f

sweet pea n (Garten)wicke f

sweet potato n Süßkartoffel f, Batate f

sweet shop (Brit) n Süßwarengeschäft nt

sweet tooth n: **to have a ~** gern Süßes essen

swell [swɛl] (pt **~ed**, pp **swollen** or **~ed**) n Seegang m ⊳ adj (US: inf) toll, prima m ⊳ vi (increase) anwachsen; (sound) anschwellen; (feeling) stärker werden; (also: **swell up**) anschwellen

swelling ['swɛlɪŋ] n Schwellung f

sweltering ['swɛltərɪŋ] adj (heat) glühend; (weather, day) glühend heiß

swept [swɛpt] pt, pp of **sweep**

swerve [swəːv] vi (animal) ausbrechen; (driver, vehicle) ausschwenken; **to ~ off the road** ausschwenken und von der Straße abkommen

swift [swɪft] n Mauersegler m ⊳ adj schnell

swiftly ['swɪftlɪ] adv schnell

swiftness ['swɪftnɪs] n Schnelligkeit f

swig [swɪg] (inf) n Schluck m ⊳ vt herunterkippen

swill [swɪl] vt (also: **swill out**) ausspülen; (also: **swill down**) abspülen ⊳ n (for pigs) Schweinefutter nt

swim [swɪm] (pt **swam**, pp **swum**) vi schwimmen; (before one's eyes) verschwimmen ⊳ vt (the Channel etc) durchschwimmen; (a length) schwimmen ⊳ n: **to go for a ~** schwimmen gehen; **to go ~ming** schwimmen gehen; **my head is ~ming** mir dreht sich der Kopf

swimmer ['swɪmə'] n Schwimmer(in) m(f)

swimming ['swɪmɪŋ] n Schwimmen nt

swimming baths (Brit) npl Schwimmbad nt

swimming cap n Badekappe f, Bademütze f

swimming costume n Badeanzug m

swimmingly ['swɪmɪŋlɪ] (inf) adv glänzend

swimming pool n Schwimmbad nt

swimming trunks npl Badehose f

swimsuit ['swɪmsuːt] n Badeanzug m

swindle ['swɪndl] n Schwindel m, Betrug m ⊳ vt: **to ~ sb (out of sth)** jdn (um etw) betrügen or beschwindeln

swindler ['swɪndlə'] n Schwindler(in) m(f)

swine [swaɪn] (inf!) n Schwein nt

swine flu n Schweinegrippe f

swing [swɪŋ] (pt, pp **swung**) n (in playground) Schaukel f; (movement) Schwung m; (change) Umschwung m; (Mus) Swing m ⊳ vt (arms, legs) schwingen (mit); (also: **swing round**) herumschwenken ⊳ vi schwingen; (also: **swing round**) sich umdrehen; (vehicle) herumschwenken; **a ~ to the left** (Pol) ein Linksruck m; **to get into the ~ of things** richtig reinkommen; **to be in full ~** (party etc) in vollem Gang sein

swing bridge n Drehbrücke f

swing door, (US) **swinging door** n Pendeltür f

swingeing ['swɪndʒɪŋ] (Brit) adj (blow) hart; (attack) scharf; (cuts, increases) extrem

swinging ['swɪŋɪŋ] adj (music) schwungvoll; (movement) schaukelnd

swipe [swaɪp] vt (also: **swipe at**) schlagen nach; (inf: steal) klauen ⊳ n Schlag m

swirl [swəːl] vi wirbeln ⊳ n Wirbeln nt

swish [swɪʃ] vi rauschen; (tail) schlagen ⊳ n Rauschen nt; (of tail) Schlagen nt ⊳ adj (inf) chic inv, schick

Swiss [swɪs] adj schweizerisch, Schweizer ⊳ n inv Schweizer(in) m(f)

Swiss French adj französischschweizerisch

Swiss German adj deutsch-schweizerisch

Swiss roll n Biskuitrolle f

switch [swɪtʃ] n Schalter m; (change) Änderung f ⊳ vt (change) ändern; (exchange) tauschen, wechseln; **to ~ (round** or **over)** vertauschen

▸ **switch off** vt abschalten; (light) ausschalten ⊳ vi (fig) abschalten

▸ **switch on** vt einschalten; (radio) anstellen; (engine) anlassen

switchback ['swɪtʃbæk] (Brit) n (road) auf und ab führende Straße f; (roller-coaster) Achterbahn f

switchblade ['swɪtʃbleɪd] n Schnappmesser nt

switchboard ['swɪtʃbɔːd] n Vermittlung f, Zentrale f

switchboard operator n Telefonist(in) m(f)

Switzerland ['swɪtsələnd] n die Schweiz f

swivel ['swɪvl] vi (also: **swivel round**) sich (herum)drehen

swollen ['swəʊlən] pp of **swell** ⊳ adj geschwollen; (lake etc) angeschwollen

swoon [swuːn] vi beinahe ohnmächtig werden ⊳ n Ohnmacht f

swoop [swuːp] n (by police etc) Razzia f; (of bird etc) Sturzflug m ⊳ vi (also: **swoop down**: bird) herabstoßen; (plane) einen Sturzflug machen

swop [swɔp] = **swap**

sword [sɔːd] n Schwert nt

swordfish ['sɔːdfɪʃ] n Schwertfisch m

swore [swɔː'] pt of **swear**

sworn [swɔːn] pp of **swear** ⊳ adj (statement) eidlich; (evidence) unter Eid; (enemy)

S

geschworen

swot [swɔt] vi pauken ▷ n (pej) Streber(in) m(f)
▶ **swot up** vt: **to ~ up (on)** pauken (+acc)

swum [swʌm] pp of **swim**

swung [swʌŋ] pt, pp of **swing**

sycamore ['sɪkəmɔːʳ] n Bergahorn m

sycophant ['sɪkəfænt] n Kriecher m,
Speichellecker m

sycophantic [sɪkə'fæntɪk] adj kriecherisch

Sydney ['sɪdnɪ] n Sydney nt

syllable ['sɪləbl] n Silbe f

syllabus ['sɪləbəs] n Lehrplan m; **on the ~** im
Lehrplan

symbol ['sɪmbl] n Symbol nt

symbolic [sɪm'bɔlɪk], **symbolical** [sɪm'bɔlɪkl]
adj symbolisch; **to be ~(al) of sth** etw
symbolisieren, ein Symbol für etw sein

symbolism ['sɪmbəlɪzəm] n Symbolismus m

symbolize ['sɪmbəlaɪz] vt symbolisieren

symmetrical [sɪ'mɛtrɪkl] adj symmetrisch

symmetry ['sɪmɪtrɪ] n Symmetrie f

sympathetic [sɪmpə'θɛtɪk] adj (understanding)
verständnisvoll; (showing pity) mitfühlend;
(likeable) sympathisch; (supportive)
wohlwollend; **to be ~ to a cause** (well-
disposed) einer Sache wohlwollend
gegenüberstehen

sympathetically [sɪmpə'θɛtɪklɪ] adv (showing
understanding) verständnisvoll; (showing support)
wohlwollend

sympathize ['sɪmpəθaɪz] vi: **to ~ with** (person)
Mitleid haben mit; (feelings) Verständnis
haben für; (cause) sympathisieren mit

sympathizer ['sɪmpəθaɪzəʳ] n (Pol)
Sympathisant(in) m(f)

sympathy ['sɪmpəθɪ] n Mitgefühl nt;
sympathies npl (support, tendencies) Sympathien
pl; **with our deepest ~** mit aufrichtigem or
herzlichem Beileid; **to come out in ~** (workers)
in einen Sympathiestreik treten

symphonic [sɪm'fɔnɪk] adj sinfonisch

symphony ['sɪmfənɪ] n Sinfonie f

symphony orchestra n Sinfonieorchester nt

symposia [sɪm'pəuzɪə] npl of **symposium**

symposium [sɪm'pəuzɪəm] (pl **~s** or **symposia**)
n Symposium nt

symptom ['sɪmptəm] n (Med, fig) Symptom nt,
Anzeichen nt

symptomatic [sɪmptə'mætɪk] adj: **~ of**
symptomatisch für

synagogue ['sɪnəgɔg] n Synagoge f

sync [sɪŋk] n abbr (= synchronization): **in ~**

synchron; **out of ~** nicht synchron

synchromesh [sɪŋkrəu'mɛʃ] n
Synchrongetriebe nt

synchronize ['sɪŋkrənaɪz] vt (watches)
gleichstellen; (movements) aufeinander
abstimmen; (sound) synchronisieren ▷ vi: **to ~
with** (sound) synchron sein mit

synchronized swimming ['sɪŋkrənaɪzd-] n
Synchronschwimmen nt

syncopated ['sɪŋkəpeɪtɪd] adj synkopiert

syndicate ['sɪndɪkɪt] n
Interessengemeinschaft f; (of businesses)
Verband m; (of newspapers) Pressezentrale f

syndrome ['sɪndrəum] n Syndrom nt; (fig)
Phänomen nt

synonym ['sɪnənɪm] n Synonym nt

synonymous [sɪ'nɒnɪməs] adj (fig): **~ (with)**
gleichbedeutend (mit)

synopses [sɪ'nɒpsiːz] npl of **synopsis**

synopsis [sɪ'nɒpsɪs] (pl **synopses**) n Abriss m,
Zusammenfassung f

syntactic [sɪn'tæktɪk] adj syntaktisch

syntax ['sɪntæks] n Syntax f

syntax error n (Comput) Syntaxfehler m

syntheses ['sɪnθəsiːz] npl of **synthesis**

synthesis ['sɪnθəsɪs] (pl **syntheses**) n Synthese
f

synthesizer ['sɪnθəsaɪzəʳ] n Synthesizer m

synthetic [sɪn'θɛtɪk] adj synthetisch; (speech)
künstlich; **synthetics** npl (man-made fabrics)
Synthetik f

syphilis ['sɪfɪlɪs] n Syphilis f

syphon ['saɪfən] = **siphon**

Syria ['sɪrɪə] n Syrien nt

Syrian ['sɪrɪən] adj syrisch ▷ n Syrer(in)
m(f)

syringe [sɪ'rɪndʒ] n Spritze f

syrup ['sɪrəp] n Sirup m; (also: **golden syrup**)
(gelber) Sirup m

syrupy ['sɪrəpɪ] adj sirupartig;
(pej: fig: sentimental) schmalzig

system ['sɪstəm] n System nt; (body) Körper m;
(Anat) Apparat m, System nt; **it was a shock to
his ~** er hatte schwer damit zu schaffen

systematic [sɪstə'mætɪk] adj systematisch

system disk n (Comput) Systemdiskette f

systems administrator ['sɪstəmz-] n (Comput)
Systembetreuer(in) m(f)

systems analyst ['sɪstəmz-] n (Comput)
Systemanalytiker(in) m(f)

systems engineer ['sɪstəmz-] n (Comput)
Systemtechniker(in) m(f)

Tt

T, t [tiː] *n* (*letter*) T *nt*, t *nt*; **T for Tommy** ≈ T wie Theodor

TA (*Brit*) *n abbr* = **Territorial Army**

ta [taː] (*Brit: inf*) *interj* danke

tab [tæb] *n* (*on drinks can*) Ring *m*; (*on garment*) Etikett *nt*; **to keep ~s on sb/sth** (*fig*) jdn/etw im Auge behalten

tab [tæb] *n abbr* = **tabulator** ▷ *n* (*on drinks can*) Ring *m*; (*on garment*) Etikett *nt*; **to keep ~s on sb/sth** (*fig*) jdn/etw im Auge behalten

tabby ['tæbɪ] *n* (*also:* **tabby cat**) getigerte Katze *f*

tabernacle ['tæbənækl] *n* Tabernakel *nt*

table ['teɪbl] *n* Tisch *m*; (*Math, Chem etc*) Tabelle *f* ▷ *vt* (*Brit: Parl: motion etc*) einbringen; **to lay** *or* **set the ~** den Tisch decken; **to clear the ~** den Tisch abräumen; **league ~** (*Brit: Sport*) Tabelle *f*

tablecloth ['teɪblklɒθ] *n* Tischdecke *f*

table d'hôte [taːblˈdəʊt] *adj* (*menu, meal*) Tagesmenü *nt*

table lamp *n* Tischlampe *f*

tablemat ['teɪblmæt] *n* (*of cloth*) Set *nt or m*; (*for hot dish*) Untersatz *m*

table of contents *n* Inhaltsverzeichnis *nt*

table salt *n* Tafelsalz *nt*

tablespoon ['teɪblspuːn] *n* Esslöffel *m*; (*also:* **tablespoonful**) Esslöffel(voll) *m*

tablet ['tæblɪt] *n* (*Med*) Tablette *f*; (*Hist: for writing*) Tafel *f*; (*plaque*) Plakette *f*; **~ of soap** (*Brit*) Stück *nt* Seife

table tennis *n* Tischtennis *nt*

table wine *n* Tafelwein *m*

tabloid ['tæblɔɪd] *n* (*newspaper*) Boulevardzeitung *f*; **the ~s** die Boulevardpresse

TABLOID PRESS

Des Ausdruck *tabloid press* bezieht sich auf kleinformatige Zeitungen (ca 30 x 40 cm); diese sind in Großbritannien fast ausschließlich Massenblätter. Im Gegensatz zur *quality press* verwenden sie viele Fotos und einen knappen, oft reißerischen Stil. Sie kommen denjenigen Lesern entgegen, die mehr Wert auf Unterhaltung legen.

taboo [təˈbuː] *n* Tabu *nt* ▷ *adj* tabu; **a ~ subject/word** ein Tabuthema/Tabuwort

tabulate ['tæbjuleɪt] *vt* tabellarisieren

tabulator ['tæbjuleɪtə^r] *n* (*on typewriter*) Tabulator *m*

tachograph ['tækəɡrɑːf] *n* Fahrtenschreiber *m*

tachometer [tæˈkɒmɪtə^r] *n* Tachometer *m*

tacit ['tæsɪt] *adj* stillschweigend

taciturn ['tæsɪtəːn] *adj* schweigsam

tack [tæk] *n* (*nail*) Stift *m* ▷ *vt* (*nail*) anheften; (*stitch*) heften ▷ *vi* (*Naut*) kreuzen; **to change ~** (*fig*) den Kurs ändern; **to ~ sth on to (the end of) sth** etw (hinten) an etw *acc* anheften

tackle ['tækl] *n* (*for fishing*) Ausrüstung *f*; (*for lifting*) Flaschenzug *m*; (*Football, Rugby*) Angriff *m* ▷ *vt* (*deal with: difficulty*) in Angriff nehmen; (*challenge: person*) zur Rede stellen; (*physically, also Sport*) angreifen

tacky ['tækɪ] *adj* (*sticky*) klebrig; (*pej: cheap-looking*) schäbig

tact [tækt] *n* Takt *m*

tactful ['tæktful] *adj* taktvoll; **to be ~** taktvoll sein

tactfully ['tæktfəlɪ] *adv* taktvoll

tactical ['tæktɪkl] *adj* taktisch; **~ error** taktischer Fehler; **~ voting** taktische Stimmabgabe

tactician [tækˈtɪʃən] *n* Taktiker(in) *m(f)*

tactics ['tæktɪks] *npl* Taktik *f*

tactless ['tæktlɪs] *adj* taktlos

tactlessly ['tæktlɪslɪ] *adv* taktlos

tadpole ['tædpəʊl] *n* Kaulquappe *f*

taffy ['tæfɪ] (*US*) *n* (*toffee*) Toffee *nt*, Sahnebonbon *nt*

tag [tæɡ] *n* (*label*) Anhänger *m*; **price/name ~** Preis-/Namensschild *nt*; **(electronic) ~** (elektronische) Fußfessel *f*
▶ **tag along** *vi* sich anschließen

Tahiti [taːˈhiːtɪ] *n* Tahiti *nt*

tail [teɪl] *n* (*of animal*) Schwanz *m*; (*of plane*) Heck *nt*; (*of shirt, coat*) Schoß *m* ▷ *vt* (*follow*) folgen +*dat*; **tails** *npl* (*formal suit*) Frack *m*; **to turn ~** die Flucht ergreifen; *see also* **head**
▶ **tail off** *vi* (*in size etc*) abnehmen; (*voice*) schwächer werden

tailback ['teɪlbæk] (*Brit*) *n* (*Aut*) Stau *m*

tail coat *n* = **tails**

tail end *n* Ende *nt*

tailgate ['teɪlgeɪt] n (Aut) Heckklappe f
taillight ['teɪllaɪt] n (Aut) Rücklicht nt
tailor ['teɪlə'] n Schneider(in) m(f) ▷ vt: **to ~ sth (to)** etw abstimmen (auf +acc); **~'s shop** Schneiderei f
tailoring ['teɪlərɪŋ] n (craft) Schneiderei f; (cut) Verarbeitung f
tailor-made ['teɪlə'meɪd] adj (also fig) maßgeschneidert
tailwind ['teɪlwɪnd] n Rückenwind m
taint [teɪnt] vt (meat, food) verderben; (fig: reputation etc) beschmutzen
tainted ['teɪntɪd] adj (food, water, air) verdorben; (fig: profits, reputation etc): **~ with** behaftet mit
Taiwan ['taɪ'wɑːn] n Taiwan nt
Tajikistan [tɑːdʒɪkɪ'stɑːn] n Tadschikistan nt
take [teɪk] (pt **took**, pp **~n**) vt nehmen; (photo, notes) machen; (decision) fällen; (require: courage, time) erfordern; (tolerate: pain etc) ertragen; (hold: passengers etc) fassen; (accompany: person) begleiten; (carry, bring) mitnehmen; (exam, test) machen; (conduct: meeting) leiten; (: class) unterrichten ▷ vi (have effect: drug) wirken; (: dye) angenommen werden ▷ n (Cine) Aufnahme f; **to ~ sth from** (drawer etc) etw nehmen aus +dat; **I ~ it (that)** ich nehme an(, dass); **I took him for a doctor** (mistake) ich hielt ihn für einen Arzt; **to ~ sb's hand** jds Hand nehmen; **to ~ sb for a walk** mit jdm spazieren gehen; **to be ~n ill** krank werden; **to ~ it upon o.s. to do sth** es auf sich nehmen, etw zu tun; **~ the first (street) on the left** nehmen Sie die erste Straße links; **to ~ Russian at university** Russisch studieren; **it won't ~ long** es dauert nicht lange; **I was quite ~n with her/it** (attracted to) ich war von ihr/davon recht angetan
▶ **take after** vt fus (resemble) ähneln +dat, ähnlich sein +dat
▶ **take apart** vt auseinandernehmen
▶ **take away** vt wegnehmen; (carry off) wegbringen; (Math) abziehen ▷ vi: **to ~ away from** (detract from) schmälern, beeinträchtigen
▶ **take back** vt (return) zurückbringen; (one's words) zurücknehmen
▶ **take down** vt (write down) aufschreiben; (dismantle) abreißen
▶ **take in** vt (deceive: person) hereinlegen, täuschen; (understand) begreifen; (include) einschließen; (lodger) aufnehmen; (orphan, stray dog) zu sich nehmen; (dress, waistband) enger machen
▶ **take off** vi (Aviat) starten; (go away) sich absetzen ▷ vt (clothes) ausziehen; (glasses) abnehmen; (make-up) entfernen; (time) freinehmen; (imitate: person) nachmachen
▶ **take on** vt (work, responsibility) übernehmen; (employee) einstellen; (compete against) antreten gegen
▶ **take out** vt (invite) ausgehen mit; (remove: tooth) herausnehmen; (licence) erwerben; **to ~ sth out of sth** (drawer, pocket

etc) etw aus etw nehmen; **don't ~ it out on me!** lass es nicht an mir aus!
▶ **take over** vt (business) übernehmen; (country) Besitz ergreifen von ▷ vi (replace): **to ~ over from sb** jdn ablösen
▶ **take to** vt fus (person, thing) mögen; (activity) Gefallen finden an +dat; (form habit of): **to ~ to doing sth** sich dat angewöhnen, etw zu tun
▶ **take up** vt (hobby, sport) anfangen mit; (job) antreten; (idea etc) annehmen; (time, space) beanspruchen; (continue: task, story) fortfahren mit; (shorten: hem, garment) kürzer machen ▷ vi (befriend): **to ~ up with sb** sich mit jdm anfreunden; **to ~ sb up on an offer/a suggestion** auf jds Angebot/Vorschlag eingehen
takeaway ['teɪkəweɪ] (Brit) n (shop, restaurant) = Schnellimbiss m; (food) Imbiss m (zum Mitnehmen)
take-home pay ['teɪkhəum-] n Nettolohn m
taken ['teɪkən] pp of **take**
takeoff ['teɪkɔf] n (Aviat) Start m
takeout ['teɪkaut] (US) n = **takeaway**
takeover ['teɪkəuvə'] n (Comm) Übernahme f; (of country) Inbesitznahme f
takeover bid n Übernahmeangebot nt
takings ['teɪkɪŋz] npl Einnahmen pl
talc [tælk] n (also: **talcum powder**) Talkumpuder nt
tale [teɪl] n Geschichte f; **to tell ~s (to sb)** (child) (jdm) Geschichten erzählen
talent ['tælnt] n Talent nt
talented ['tælntɪd] adj talentiert, begabt
talent scout n Talentsucher(in) m(f)
talisman ['tælɪzmən] n Talisman m
talk [tɔːk] n (speech) Vortrag m; (conversation, discussion) Gespräch nt; (gossip) Gerede nt ▷ vi (speak) sprechen; (chat) reden; (gossip) klatschen; **talks** npl (Pol etc) Gespräche pl; **to give a ~** einen Vortrag halten; **to ~ about** (discuss) sprechen or reden über; **~ing of films, have you seen ...?** da wir gerade von Filmen sprechen: hast du ... gesehen?; **to ~ sb into doing sth** jdn zu etw überreden; **to ~ sb out of doing sth** jdm etw ausreden
▶ **talk over** vt (problem etc) besprechen, bereden
talkative ['tɔːkətɪv] adj gesprächig
talker ['tɔːkə'] n: **to be a good/entertaining/fast** etc ~ gut/amüsant/schnell etc reden können
talking point ['tɔːkɪŋ-] n Gesprächsthema nt
talking-to ['tɔːkɪŋtu] n: **to give sb a (good) ~** jdm eine (ordentliche) Standpauke halten (inf)
talk show n Talkshow f
tall [tɔːl] adj (person) groß; (glass, bookcase, tree, building) hoch; (ladder) lang; **to be 6 feet ~** (person) = 1,80m groß sein; **how ~ are you?** wie groß bist du?
tallboy ['tɔːlbɔɪ] (Brit) n Kommode f
tallness ['tɔːlnɪs] n (of person) Größe f; (of tree, building etc) Höhe f
tall story n unglaubliche Geschichte f

tally ['tælɪ] n (of marks, amounts etc) aktueller Stand m ▷ vi: **to ~ (with)** (figures, stories etc) übereinstimmen mit; **to keep a ~ of sth** über etw acc Buch führen

talon ['tælən] n Kralle f

tambourine [tæmbə'ri:n] n Tamburin nt

tame [teɪm] adj (animal, bird) zahm; (fig: story, party, performance) lustlos, lahm (inf)

Tamil ['tæmɪl] adj tamilisch ▷ n Tamile m, Tamilin f; (Ling) Tamil nt

tamper ['tæmpəʳ] vi: **to ~ with sth** an etw dat herumpfuschen (inf)

tampon ['tæmpɔn] n Tampon m

tan [tæn] n (also: **suntan**) (Sonnen)bräune f ▷ vi (person, skin) braun werden ▷ vt (hide) gerben; (skin) bräunen ▷ adj (colour) hellbraun; **to get a ~** braun werden

tandem ['tændəm] n Tandem nt; (together): **in ~** (fig) zusammen

tandoori [tæn'dʊərɪ] n: **~ oven** Tandoori-Ofen m; **~ chicken** im Tandoori-Ofen gebratenes Huhn

tang [tæŋ] n (smell) Geruch m; (taste) Geschmack m

tangent ['tændʒənt] n (Math) Tangente f; **to go off at a ~** (fig) vom Thema abschweifen

tangerine [tændʒə'ri:n] n (fruit) Mandarine f; (colour) Orangerot nt

tangible ['tændʒəbl] adj greifbar; **~ assets** (Comm) Sachanlagevermögen nt

Tangier [tæn'dʒɪəʳ] n Tanger nt

tangle ['tæŋgl] n (of branches, wire etc) Gewirr nt; **to be in a ~** verheddert sein; (fig) durcheinander sein; **to get in a ~** sich verheddern; (fig) durcheinandergeraten

tango ['tæŋgəʊ] n Tango m

tank [tæŋk] n Tank m; (for photographic processing) Wanne f; (also: **fish tank**) Aquarium nt; (Mil) Panzer m

tankard ['tæŋkəd] n Bierkrug m

tanker ['tæŋkəʳ] n (ship) Tanker m; (truck) Tankwagen m

tankini [tæŋ'ki:nɪ] n Tankini m

tanned [tænd] adj (person) braun gebrannt; (hide) gegerbt

tannin ['tænɪn] n Tannin nt

tanning ['tænɪŋ] n (of leather) Gerben nt

Tannoy® ['tænɔɪ] (Brit) n Lautsprechersystem nt; **over the ~** über Lautsprecher

tantalizing ['tæntəlaɪzɪŋ] adj (smell) verführerisch; (possibility) verlockend

tantamount ['tæntəmaʊnt] adj: **~ to** gleichbedeutend mit

tantrum ['tæntrəm] n Wutanfall m; **to throw a ~** einen Wutanfall bekommen

Tanzania [tænzə'nɪə] n Tansania nt

Tanzanian [tænzə'nɪən] adj tansanisch ▷ n (person) Tansanier(in) m(f)

tap [tæp] n (on sink, gas tap) Hahn m; (gentle blow) leichter Schlag m, Klaps m ▷ vt (hit gently) klopfen; (exploit: resources, energy) nutzen; (telephone) abhören, anzapfen; **on ~** (fig: resources) zur Verfügung; (beer) vom Fass

tap-dancing ['tæpdɑ:nsɪŋ] n Stepptanz m

tape [teɪp] n (also: **magnetic tape**) Tonband nt; (cassette) Kassette f; (also: **sticky tape**) Klebeband nt; (for tying) Band nt ▷ vt (record, conversation) aufnehmen, aufzeichnen; (stick with tape) mit Klebeband befestigen; **on ~** (song etc) auf Band

tape deck n Tapedeck nt

tape measure n Bandmaß nt

taper ['teɪpəʳ] n (candle) lange, dünne Kerze ▷ vi sich verjüngen

tape recorder n Tonband(gerät) nt

tape recording n Tonbandaufnahme f

tapered ['teɪpəd] adj (skirt, jacket) nach unten enger werdend

tapering ['teɪpərɪŋ] adj spitz zulaufend

tapestry ['tæpɪstrɪ] n (on wall) Wandteppich m; (fig) Kaleidoskop nt

tapeworm ['teɪpwə:m] n Bandwurm m

tapioca [tæpɪ'əʊkə] n Tapioka f

tappet ['tæpɪt] n (Aut) Stößel m

tar [tɑ:] n Teer m; **low/middle ~ cigarettes** Zigaretten mit niedrigem/mittlerem Teergehalt

tarantula [tə'ræntjulə] n Tarantel f

tardy ['tɑ:dɪ] adj (reply, letter) verspätet; (progress) langsam

target ['tɑ:gɪt] n Ziel nt; (fig: of joke, criticism etc) Zielscheibe f; **to be on ~** (project, work) nach Plan verlaufen

target practice n Zielschießen nt

tariff ['tærɪf] n (tax on goods) Zoll m; (Brit: in hotels etc) Preisliste f

tariff barrier n Zollschranke f

tarmac® ['tɑ:mæk] n (Brit: on road) Asphalt m; (Aviat): **on the ~** auf dem Rollfeld ▷ vt (Brit: road etc) asphaltieren

tarn [tɑ:n] n Bergsee m

tarnish ['tɑ:nɪʃ] vt (silver, brass etc) stumpf werden lassen; (fig: reputation etc) beflecken, in Mitleidenschaft ziehen

tarot ['tærəʊ] n Tarot nt or m

tarpaulin [tɑ:'pɔ:lɪn] n Plane f

tarragon ['tærəgən] n Estragon m

tart [tɑ:t] n (Culin) Torte f; (: small) Törtchen nt; (Brit: inf: prostitute) Nutte f ▷ adj (apple, grapefruit etc) säuerlich
▶ **tart up** (Brit: inf) vt (room, building) aufmotzen; **to ~ o.s. up** sich fein machen; (pej) sich auftakeln

tartan ['tɑ:tn] n Tartan m, Schottenstoff m ▷ adj (scarf etc) mit Schottenmuster

tartar ['tɑ:təʳ] n (on teeth) Zahnstein m; (pej: person) Tyrann(in) m(f)

tartar sauce, tartare sauce ['tɑ:tə-] n Remouladensoße f

task [tɑ:sk] n Aufgabe f; **to take sb to ~** jdn ins Gebet nehmen

task force n (Mil) Sonderkommando nt; (Police) Spezialeinheit f

taskmaster ['tɑ:skmɑ:stəʳ] n: **a hard ~** ein strenger Lehrmeister

Tasmania [tæz'meɪnɪə] n Tasmanien nt

tassel ['tæsl] n Quaste f

t

taste [teɪst] n Geschmack m; (sample) Kostprobe f; (fig: of suffering, freedom etc) Vorgeschmack m ▷ vt (get flavour of) schmecken; (test) probieren, versuchen ▷ vi: **to ~ of/like sth** nach/wie etw schmecken; **sense of ~** Geschmackssinn m; **to have a ~ of sth** (sample) etw probieren; **to acquire a ~ for sth** (liking) Geschmack an etw dat finden; **to be in good/bad ~** (joke etc) geschmackvoll/geschmacklos sein; **you can ~ the garlic (in it)** (detect) man schmeckt den Knoblauch durch; **what does it ~ like?** wie schmeckt es?

taste buds npl Geschmacksknospen pl

tasteful ['teɪstful] adj geschmackvoll

tastefully ['teɪstfəlɪ] adv geschmackvoll

tasteless ['teɪstlɪs] adj geschmacklos

tasty ['teɪstɪ] adj schmackhaft

tattered ['tætəd] adj (clothes, paper etc) zerrissen; (fig: hopes etc) angeschlagen

tatters ['tætəz] npl: **to be in ~** (clothes) in Fetzen sein

tattoo [tə'tuː] n (on skin) Tätowierung f; (spectacle) Zapfenstreich m ▷ vt: **to ~ sth on sth** etw auf etw acc tätowieren

tatty ['tætɪ] (Brit: inf) adj schäbig

taught [tɔːt] pt, pp of **teach**

taunt [tɔːnt] n höhnische Bemerkung f ▷ vt (person) verhöhnen

Taurus ['tɔːrəs] n Stier m; **to be ~** (ein) Stier sein

taut [tɔːt] adj (skin, thread etc) straff

tavern ['tævən] n Taverne f

tawdry ['tɔːdrɪ] adj billig

tawny ['tɔːnɪ] adj gelbbraun

tawny owl n Waldkauz m

tax [tæks] n Steuer f ▷ vt (earnings, goods etc) besteuern; (fig: memory, knowledge) strapazieren; (: patience etc) auf die Probe stellen; **before/after ~** vor/nach Abzug der Steuern; **free of ~** steuerfrei

taxable ['tæksəbl] adj steuerpflichtig; (income) steuerbar

tax allowance n Steuerfreibetrag m

taxation [tæk'seɪʃən] n (system) Besteuerung f; (money paid) Steuern pl

tax avoidance n Steuerumgehung f

tax collector n Steuerbeamte(r) m, Steuerbeamtin f

tax disc (Brit) n (Aut) Steuerplakette f

tax evasion n Steuerhinterziehung f

tax exemption n Steuerbefreiung f

tax exile (person) n Steuerflüchtling m

tax-free ['tæksfriː] adj steuerfrei

tax haven n Steuerparadies nt

taxi ['tæksɪ] n Taxi nt ▷ vi (Aviat: plane) rollen

taxidermist ['tæksɪdəːmɪst] n Taxidermist(in) m(f), Tierpräparator(in) m(f)

taxi driver n Taxifahrer(in) m(f)

taxi inspector (Brit) n Steuerinspektor(in) m(f)

taxi rank (Brit) n Taxistand m

taxi stand n = **taxi rank**

taxpayer ['tækspeɪər] n Steuerzahler(in) m(f)

tax rebate n Steuerrückvergütung f

tax relief n Steuernachlass m

tax return n Steuererklärung f

tax shelter n (Comm) System zur Verhinderung von Steuerbelastung

tax year n Steuerjahr nt

TB n abbr (= tuberculosis) Tb f, Tbc f

tbc abbr (= to be confirmed) noch zu bestätigen

TD (US) n abbr = **Treasury Department**; (Football) = **touchdown**

tea [tiː] n (drink) Tee m; (Brit: evening meal) Abendessen nt; **afternoon ~** (Brit) Nachmittagstee m

tea bag n Teebeutel m

tea break (Brit) n Teepause f

teacake ['tiːkeɪk] (Brit) n Rosinenbrötchen nt

teach [tiːtʃ] (pt, pp **taught**) vt: **to ~ sb sth, ~ sth to sb** (instruct) jdm etw beibringen; (in school) jdn in etw dat unterrichten ▷ vi unterrichten; **it taught him a lesson** (fig) er hat seine Lektion gelernt

teacher ['tiːtʃər] n Lehrer(in) m(f); **German ~** Deutschlehrer(in) m(f)

teacher training college n (for primary schools) ≈ pädagogische Hochschule f; (for secondary schools) ≈ Studienseminar nt

teaching ['tiːtʃɪŋ] n (work of teacher) Unterricht m

teaching aids npl Lehrmittel pl

teaching hospital (Brit) n Ausbildungskrankenhaus nt

teaching staff (Brit) n Lehrerkollegium nt

tea cosy n Teewärmer m

teacup ['tiːkʌp] n Teetasse f

teak [tiːk] n Teak nt

tea leaves npl Teeblätter pl

team [tiːm] n (of experts etc) Team nt; (Sport) Mannschaft f, Team nt; (of horses, oxen) Gespann nt

▶ **team up** vi: **to ~ up (with)** sich zusammentun (mit)

team game n Mannschaftsspiel nt

team spirit n Teamgeist m

teamwork ['tiːmwəːk] n Teamwork nt, Teamarbeit f

tea party n Teegesellschaft f

teapot ['tiːpɔt] n Teekanne f

tear¹ [tɛər] (pt **tore**, pp **torn**) n (hole) Riss m ▷ vt (rip) zerreißen ▷ vi (become torn) reißen; **to ~ sth to pieces** or **bits** or **shreds** (lit, fig) etw in Stücke reißen; **to ~ sb to pieces** jdn fertigmachen

▶ **tear along** vi (rush: driver, car) entlangrasen

▶ **tear apart** vt (book, clothes, people) auseinanderreißen; (upset: person) hin- und herreißen

▶ **tear away** vt: **to ~ o.s. away (from sth)** (fig) sich (von etw) losreißen

▶ **tear out** vt (sheet of paper etc) herausreißen

▶ **tear up** vt (sheet of paper etc) zerreißen

tear² [tɪər] n (in eye) Träne f; **in ~s** in Tränen; **to burst into ~s** in Tränen ausbrechen

tearaway ['tɛərəweɪ] (Brit: inf) n Rabauke m

teardrop ['tɪədrɔp] n Träne f

tearful ['tɪəful] *adj* (*person*) weinend; (*face*) tränenüberströmt

tear gas *n* Tränengas *nt*

tearing ['tɛərɪŋ] *adj*: **to be in a ~ hurry** es unheimlich eilig haben

tearoom ['tiːruːm] *n* = **teashop**

tease [tiːz] *vt* necken; (*unkindly*) aufziehen ▷ *n*: **she's a real ~** sie zieht einen ständig auf

tea set *n* Teeservice *nt*

teashop ['tiːʃɔp] (*Brit*) *n* Teestube *f*

Teasmade® ['tiːzmeɪd] *n* Teemaschine *f* (*mit Zeiteinstellung*)

teaspoon ['tiːspuːn] *n* Teelöffel *m*; (*also*: **teaspoonful**: *measure*) Teelöffel(voll) *m*

tea strainer *n* Teesieb *nt*

teat [tiːt] *n* (*on bottle*) Sauger *m*

teatime ['tiːtaɪm] *n* Teestunde *f*

tea towel (*Brit*) *n* Geschirrtuch *nt*

tea urn *n* Teespender *m*

tech [tɛk] (*inf*) *n abbr* = **technical college; technology**

technical ['tɛknɪkl] *adj* technisch; (*terms, language*) Fach-

technical college (*Brit*) *n* technische Fachschule *f*

technicality [tɛknɪ'kælɪtɪ] *n* (*point of law*) Formalität *f*; (*detail*) technische Einzelheit *f*; **on a (legal) ~** aufgrund einer (juristischen) Formalität

technically ['tɛknɪklɪ] *adv* (*strictly speaking*) genau genommen; (*regarding technique*) technisch (gesehen)

technician [tɛk'nɪʃən] *n* Techniker(in) *m(f)*

technique [tɛk'niːk] *n* Technik *f*

techno ['tɛknəʊ] *n* (*Mus*) Techno *nt*

technocrat ['tɛknəkræt] *n* Technokrat(in) *m(f)*

technological [tɛknə'lɔdʒɪkl] *adj* technologisch

technologist [tɛk'nɔlədʒɪst] *n* Technologe *m*, Technologin *f*

technology [tɛk'nɔlədʒɪ] *n* Technologie *f*

technology college *n* Oberstufenkolleg *mit technischem Schwerpunkt*

teddy ['tɛdɪ], **teddy bear** *n* Teddy(bär) *m*

tedious ['tiːdɪəs] *adj* langweilig

tedium ['tiːdɪəm] *n* Langeweile *f*

tee [tiː] *n* (*Golf*) Tee *nt*
  ▶ **tee off** *vi* (*vom Tee*) abschlagen

teem [tiːm] *vi*: **to ~ with** (*tourists etc*) wimmeln von; **it is ~ing down** es gießt in Strömen

teenage ['tiːneɪdʒ] *adj* (*fashions etc*) Jugend-; (*children*) im Teenageralter

teenager ['tiːneɪdʒə'] *n* Teenager *m*, Jugendliche(r) *f(m)*

teens [tiːnz] *npl*: **to be in one's ~** im Teenageralter sein

tee shirt *n* = **T-shirt**

teeter ['tiːtə'] *vi* (*also fig*) schwanken, taumeln

teeth [tiːθ] *npl of* **tooth**

teethe [tiːð] *vi* Zähne bekommen, zahnen

teething ring ['tiːðɪŋ-] *n* Beißring *m*

teething troubles *npl* (*fig*) Kinderkrankheiten *pl*

teetotal ['tiː'təʊtl] *adj* (*person*) abstinent

teetotaller, (*US*) **teetotaler** ['tiː'təʊtlə'] *n* Abstinenzler(in) *m(f)*, Antialkoholiker(in) *m(f)*

TEFL ['tɛfl] *n abbr* (= *Teaching of English as a Foreign Language*) Unterricht in Englisch als Fremdsprache

Teflon® ['tɛflɔn] *n* Teflon® *nt*

Teheran [tɛə'rɑːn] *n* Teheran *nt*

tel. *abbr* (= *telephone*) Tel.

Tel Aviv ['tɛlə'viːv] *n* Tel Aviv *nt*

telecast ['tɛlɪkɑːst] *n* Fernsehsendung *f*

telecommunications ['tɛlɪkəmjuːnɪ'keɪʃənz] *n* Nachrichtentechnik *f*

teleconferencing [tɛlɪ'kɔnfərənsɪŋ] *n* Telekonferenzen *pl*

telegram ['tɛlɪgræm] *n* Telegramm *nt*

telegraph ['tɛlɪgrɑːf] *n* (*system*) Telegraf *m*

telegraphic [tɛlɪ'græfɪk] *adj* (*equipment*) telegrafisch

telegraph pole *n* Telegrafenmast *m*

telegraph wire *n* Telegrafenleitung *f*

telepathic [tɛlɪ'pæθɪk] *adj* telepathisch

telepathy [tə'lɛpəθɪ] *n* Telepathie *f*

telephone ['tɛlɪfəʊn] *n* Telefon *nt* ▷ *vt* (*person*) anrufen ▷ *vi* anrufen, telefonieren; **to be on the ~** (*talking*) telefonieren; (*possessing phone*) ein Telefon haben

telephone box, (*US*) **telephone booth** *n* Telefonzelle *f*

telephone call *n* Anruf *m*

telephone directory *n* Telefonbuch *nt*

telephone exchange *n* Telefonzentrale *f*

telephone number *n* Telefonnummer *f*

telephone operator *n* Telefonist(in) *m(f)*

telephone tapping *n* Abhören *nt* von Telefonleitungen

telephonist [tə'lɛfənɪst] (*Brit*) *n* Telefonist(in) *m(f)*

telephoto ['tɛlɪ'fəʊtəʊ] *adj*: **~ lens** Teleobjektiv *nt*

teleprinter ['tɛlɪprɪntə'] *n* Fernschreiber *m*

Teleprompter® ['tɛlɪprɔmptə'] (*US*) *n* Teleprompter *m*

telesales ['tɛlɪseɪlz] *n* Verkauf *m* per Telefon

telescope ['tɛlɪskəʊp] *n* Teleskop *nt* ▷ *vi* (*fig: bus, lorry*) sich ineinanderschieben ▷ *vt* (*make shorter*) zusammenschieben

telescopic [tɛlɪ'skɔpɪk] *adj* (*legs, aerial*) ausziehbar; **~ lens** Fernrohrlinse *f*

Teletext® ['tɛlɪtɛkst] *n* Videotext *m*

telethon ['tɛlɪθɔn] *n* Spendenaktion *für wohltätige Zwecke in Form einer vielstündigen Fernsehsendung*

televise ['tɛlɪvaɪz] *vt* (*im Fernsehen*) übertragen

television ['tɛlɪvɪʒən] *n* Fernsehen *nt*; (*set*) Fernseher *m*, Fernsehapparat *m*; **to be on ~** im Fernsehen sein

television licence (*Brit*) *n* Fernsehgenehmigung *f*

television programme *n* Fernsehprogramm *nt*

television set *n* Fernseher *m*, Fernsehapparat *m*

teleworking ['tɛlɪwəːkɪŋ] *n* Telearbeit *f*

t

telex ['tɛlɛks] n (system, machine, message) Telex nt ▷ vt (message) telexen; (person) ein Telex schicken +dat ▷ vi telexen

tell [tɛl] (pt, pp **told**) vt (say) sagen; (relate: story) erzählen; (distinguish): **to ~ sth from** etw unterscheiden von; (be sure) wissen ▷ vi (have an effect) sich auswirken; **to ~ sb to do sth** jdm sagen, etw zu tun; **to ~ sb of** or **about sth** jdm von etw erzählen; **to be able to ~ the time** (know how to) die Uhr kennen; **can you ~ me the time?** können Sie mir sagen, wie spät es ist?; **(I) ~ you what, let's go to the cinema** weißt du was? Lass uns ins Kino gehen!; **I can't ~ them apart** ich kann sie nicht unterscheiden

▸ **tell off** vt: **to ~ sb off** jdn ausschimpfen
▸ **tell on** vt fus (inform against) verpetzen

teller ['tɛlə^r] n (in bank) Kassierer(in) m(f)
telling ['tɛlɪŋ] adj (remark etc) verräterisch
telltale ['tɛlteɪl] adj verräterisch ▷ n (pej) Petzer m, Petze f
telly ['tɛlɪ] (Brit: inf) n abbr = **television**
temerity [tə'mɛrɪtɪ] n Unverschämtheit f
temp [tɛmp] (Brit: inf) n abbr (= temporary office worker) Zeitarbeitskraft f ▷ vi als Zeitarbeitskraft arbeiten
temper ['tɛmpə^r] n (nature) Naturell nt; (mood) Laune f ▷ vt (moderate) mildern; **a (fit of) ~** ein Wutanfall m; **to be in a ~** gereizt sein; **to lose one's ~** die Beherrschung verlieren
temperament ['tɛmprəmənt] n Temperament nt
temperamental [tɛmprə'mɛntl] adj (person, car) launisch
temperate ['tɛmprət] adj gemäßigt
temperature ['tɛmprətʃə^r] n Temperatur f; **to have** or **run a ~** Fieber haben; **to take sb's ~** bei jdm Fieber messen
temperature chart n (Med) Fiebertabelle f
tempered ['tɛmpəd] adj (steel) gehärtet
tempest ['tɛmpɪst] n Sturm m
tempestuous [tɛm'pɛstjuəs] adj (also fig) stürmisch; (person) leidenschaftlich
tempi ['tɛmpi:] npl of **tempo**
template ['tɛmplɪt] n Schablone f
temple ['tɛmpl] n (building) Tempel m; (Anat) Schläfe f
tempo ['tɛmpəu] (pl **~s** or **tempi**) n (Mus, fig) Tempo nt
temporal ['tɛmpərl] adj (non-religious) weltlich; (relating to time) zeitlich
temporarily ['tɛmpərərɪlɪ] adv vorübergehend; (unavailable, alone etc) zeitweilig
temporary ['tɛmpərərɪ] adj (arrangement) provisorisch; (worker, job) Aushilfs-; **~ refugee** Flüchtling m mit zeitlich begrenzter Aufenthaltserlaubnis; **~ secretary** Sekretärin zur Aushilfe; **~ teacher** Aushilfslehrer(in) m(f)
temporize ['tɛmpəraɪz] vi ausweichen
tempt [tɛmpt] vt in Versuchung führen; **to ~ sb into doing sth** jdn dazu verleiten, etw zu tun; **to be ~ed to do sth** versucht sein, etw

temptation [tɛmp'teɪʃən] n Versuchung f
tempting ['tɛmptɪŋ] adj (offer) verlockend; (food) verführerisch
ten [tɛn] num zehn ▷ n: **~s of thousands** Zehntausende pl
tenable ['tɛnəbl] adj (argument, position) haltbar
tenacious [tə'neɪʃəs] adj zäh, hartnäckig
tenacity [tə'næsɪtɪ] n Zähigkeit f, Hartnäckigkeit f
tenancy ['tɛnənsɪ] n (of room) Mietverhältnis nt; (of land) Pachtverhältnis nt
tenant ['tɛnənt] n (of room) Mieter(in) m(f); (of land) Pächter(in) m(f)
tend [tɛnd] vt (crops, sick person) sich kümmern um ▷ vi: **to ~ to do sth** dazu neigen or tendieren, etw zu tun
tendency ['tɛndənsɪ] n (of person) Neigung f; (of thing) Tendenz f
tender ['tɛndə^r] adj (person, care) zärtlich; (heart) gut; (sore) empfindlich; (meat, age) zart ▷ n (Comm) Angebot nt; (money): **legal ~** gesetzliches Zahlungsmittel nt ▷ vt (offer) vorlegen; (resignation) einreichen; (apology) anbieten; **to put in a ~ (for)** ein Angebot vorlegen (für); **to put work out to ~** (Brit) Arbeiten ausschreiben
tenderize ['tɛndəraɪz] vt (meat) zart machen
tenderly ['tɛndəlɪ] adv zärtlich, liebevoll
tenderness ['tɛndənɪs] n (affection) Zärtlichkeit f; (of meat) Zartheit f
tendon ['tɛndən] n Sehne f
tendril ['tɛndrɪl] n (Bot) Ranke f; (of hair etc) Strähne f
tenement ['tɛnəmənt] n Mietshaus nt
Tenerife [tɛnə'ri:f] n Teneriffa nt
tenet ['tɛnət] n Prinzip nt
Tenn. (US) abbr (Post) = Tennessee
tenner ['tɛnə^r] (Brit: inf) n Zehner m
tennis ['tɛnɪs] n Tennis nt
tennis ball n Tennisball m
tennis club n Tennisklub m
tennis court n Tennisplatz m
tennis elbow n (Med) Tennisell(en)bogen m
tennis match n Tennismatch nt
tennis player n Tennisspieler(in) m(f)
tennis racket n Tennisschläger m
tennis shoes npl Tennisschuhe pl
tenor ['tɛnə^r] n (Mus) Tenor m; (of speech etc) wesentlicher Gehalt m
tenpin bowling ['tɛnpɪn-] (Brit) n Bowling nt
tense [tɛns] adj (person, muscle) angespannt; (smile) verkrampft; (period, situation) gespannt ▷ n (Ling) Zeit f, Tempus nt ▷ vt (muscles) anspannen
tenseness ['tɛnsnɪs] n Gespanntheit f
tension ['tɛnʃən] n (nervousness) Angespanntheit f; (between ropes etc) Spannung f
tent [tɛnt] n Zelt nt
tentacle ['tɛntəkl] n (Zool) Fangarm m; (fig) Klaue f
tentative ['tɛntətɪv] adj (person, smile) zögernd;

(step) unsicher; *(conclusion, plans)* vorläufig

tentatively ['tɛntətɪvlɪ] *adv (suggest)* versuchsweise; *(wave etc)* zögernd

tenterhooks ['tɛntəhʊks] *npl*: **to be on ~** wie auf glühenden Kohlen sitzen

tenth [tɛnθ] *num* zehnte(r, s) ▷ *n* Zehntel *nt*

tent peg *n* Hering *m*

tent pole *n* Zeltstange *f*

tenuous ['tɛnjuəs] *adj (hold, links etc)* schwach

tenure ['tɛnjuə'] *n (of land etc)* Nutzungsrecht *nt*; *(of office)* Amtszeit *f*; *(Univ)*: **to have ~** eine Dauerstellung haben

tepid ['tɛpɪd] *adj (also fig)* lauwarm

Ter. *abbr (in street names: = terrace)* ≈ Str.

term [tə:m] *n (word)* Ausdruck *m*; *(period in power etc)* Amtszeit *f*; *(Scol: three per year)* Trimester *nt* ▷ *vt (call)* nennen; **terms** *npl (also Comm)* Bedingungen *pl*; **in economic/political ~s** wirtschaftlich/politisch gesehen; **in ~s of business** was das Geschäft angeht *or* betrifft; **~ of imprisonment** Gefängnisstrafe *f*; **"easy ~s"** *(Comm)* „günstige Bedingungen"; **in the short/long ~** auf kurze/lange Sicht; **to be on good ~s with sb** sich mit jdm gut verstehen; **to come to ~s with** *(problem)* sich abfinden mit

terminal ['tə:mɪnl] *adj (disease, patient)* unheilbar ▷ *n (Aviat, Comm, Comput)* Terminal *nt*; *(Elec)* Anschluss *m*; *(Brit: also: **bus terminal**)* Endstation *f*

terminate ['tə:mɪneɪt] *vt* beenden ▷ *vi*: **to ~ in** enden in +*dat*

termination [tə:mɪ'neɪʃən] *n* Beendigung *f*; *(expiry: of contract)* Ablauf *m*; *(Med: of pregnancy)* Abbruch *m*

termini ['tə:mɪnaɪ] *npl of* **terminus**

terminology [tə:mɪ'nɔlədʒɪ] *n* Terminologie *f*

terminus ['tə:mɪnəs] *n (pl* **termini** *) (for buses, trains)* Endstation *f*

termite ['tə:maɪt] *n* Termite *f*

term paper *(US) n (Univ)* ≈ Semesterarbeit *f*

Terr. *abbr (in street names: = terrace)* ≈ Str.

terrace ['tɛrəs] *n (Brit: row of houses)* Häuserreihe *f*; *(Agr, patio)* Terrasse *f*; **the terraces** *npl (Brit: Sport)* die Ränge *pl*

terraced ['tɛrəst] *adj (house)* Reihen-; *(garden)* terrassenförmig angelegt

terracotta ['tɛrə'kɔtə] *n (clay)* Terrakotta *f*; *(colour)* Braunrot *nt* ▷ *adj (pot, roof etc)* Terrakotta-

terrain [tɛ'reɪn] *n* Gelände *nt*, Terrain *nt*

terrible ['tɛrɪbl] *adj* schrecklich, furchtbar

terribly ['tɛrɪblɪ] *adv (very)* furchtbar; *(very badly)* entsetzlich

terrier ['tɛrɪə'] *n* Terrier *m*

terrific [tə'rɪfɪk] *adj (very great: thunderstorm, speed)* unheimlich; *(time, party)* sagenhaft

terrify ['tɛrɪfaɪ] *vt* erschrecken; **to be terrified** schreckliche Angst haben

terrifying ['tɛrɪfaɪɪŋ] *adj* entsetzlich, grauenvoll

territorial [tɛrɪ'tɔ:rɪəl] *adj (boundaries, dispute)* territorial, Gebiets-; *(waters)* Hoheits- ▷ *n (Mil)* Soldat *m* der Territorialarmee

Territorial Army *(Brit) n (Mil)*: **the ~** die Territorialarmee

territorial waters *npl* Hoheitsgewässer *pl*

territory ['tɛrɪtərɪ] *n (also fig)* Gebiet *nt*

terror ['tɛrə'] *n (great fear)* panische Angst *f*

terrorism ['tɛrərɪzəm] *n* Terrorismus *m*

terrorist ['tɛrərɪst] *n* Terrorist(in) *m(f)*

terrorize ['tɛrəraɪz] *vt* terrorisieren

terse [tə:s] *adj* knapp

tertiary ['tə:ʃərɪ] *adj* tertiär; **~ education** *(Brit)* Universitätsausbildung *f*

Terylene® ['tɛrɪli:n] *n* Terylen® *nt* ▷ *adj* Terylen-

TESL ['tɛsl] *n abbr (= Teaching of English as a Second Language)* Unterricht in Englisch als Zweitsprache

TESSA ['tɛsə] *(Brit) n abbr (= Tax Exempt Special Savings Account)* steuerfreies Sparsystem mit begrenzter Einlagehöhe

test [tɛst] *n* Test *m*; *(of courage etc)* Probe *f*; *(Scol)* Prüfung *f*; *(also: **driving test**)* Fahrprüfung *f* ▷ *vt* testen; *(check: „Scol)* prüfen; **to put sth to the ~** etw auf die Probe stellen; **to ~ sth for sth** etw auf etw *acc* prüfen

testament ['tɛstəmənt] *n* Zeugnis *nt*; **the Old/New T~** das Alte/Neue Testament; **last will and ~** Testament *nt*

test ban *n (also: **nuclear test ban**)* Teststopp *m*

test card *n (TV)* Testbild *nt*

test case *n (Law)* Musterfall *m*; *(fig)* Musterbeispiel *nt*

testes ['tɛsti:z] *npl* Testikel *pl*, Hoden *pl*

test flight *n* Testflug *m*

testicle ['tɛstɪkl] *n* Hoden *m*

testify ['tɛstɪfaɪ] *vi (Law)* aussagen; **to ~ to sth** *(Law, fig)* etw bezeugen

testimonial [tɛstɪ'məʊnɪəl] *n (Brit: reference)* Referenz *f*; *(Sport: also: **testimonial match**)* Benefizspiel, dessen Erlös einem verdienten Spieler zugutekommt

testimony ['tɛstɪmənɪ] *n (statement)* Aussage *f*; *(clear proof)*: **to be (a) ~ to** ein Zeugnis *nt* sein für

testing ['tɛstɪŋ] *adj* schwierig

test match *n (Cricket, Rugby)* Testmatch *nt*, Test Match *nt*, Länderspiel *nt*

testosterone [tɛs'tɔstərəʊn] *n* Testosteron *nt*

test paper *n (Scol)* Klassenarbeit *f*

test pilot *n* Testpilot(in) *m(f)*

test tube *n* Reagenzglas *nt*

test-tube baby ['tɛsttju:b-] *n* Retortenbaby *nt*

testy ['tɛstɪ] *adj* gereizt

tetanus ['tɛtənəs] *n* Tetanus *m*

tetchy ['tɛtʃɪ] *adj* gereizt

tether ['tɛðə'] *vt (animal)* festbinden ▷ *n*: **to be at the end of one's ~** völlig am Ende sein

text [tɛkst] *n* Text *m*; *(sent by mobile phone)* SMS *f* ▷ *vt (on mobile phone)* **to ~ sb** jdm eine SMS schreiben

textbook ['tɛkstbʊk] *n* Lehrbuch *nt*

textiles ['tɛkstaɪlz] *npl* Textilien *pl*

text message *n (Tel)* SMS *f*

t

text messaging n (Tel) Textnachrichten pl

textual ['tɛkstjʊəl] adj (analysis etc) Text-

texture ['tɛkstʃəʳ] n Beschaffenheit f, Struktur f

TGWU (Brit) n abbr (= Transport and General Workers' Union) Transportarbeitergewerkschaft

Thai [taɪ] adj thailändisch ▷ n Thailänder(in) m(f)

Thailand ['taɪlænd] n Thailand nt

thalidomide® [θə'lɪdəmaɪd] n Contergan® nt

Thames [tɛmz] n: **the ~** die Themse

than [ðæn] conj (in comparisons) als; **more ~ 10** mehr als 10; **she is older ~ you think** sie ist älter, als Sie denken; **more ~ once** mehr als einmal

thank [θæŋk] vt danken +dat; **~ you** danke; **~ you very much** vielen Dank; **~ God!** Gott sei Dank!

thankful ['θæŋkful] adj: **~ (for/that)** dankbar (für/, dass)

thankfully ['θæŋkfəlɪ] adv dankbar; **~ there were few victims** zum Glück gab es nur wenige Opfer

thankless ['θæŋklɪs] adj undankbar

thanks [θæŋks] npl Dank m ▷ excl (also: **many thanks, thanks a lot**) danke, vielen Dank; **~ to** dank +gen

Thanksgiving ['θæŋksgɪvɪŋ], **Thanksgiving Day** (US) n Thanksgiving Day m

   ● Thanksgiving (Day) ist ein Feiertag in den
   ● USA, der auf den vierten Donnerstag im
   ● November fällt. Er soll daran erinnern,
   ● wie die Pilgerväter die gute Ernte im Jahre
   ● 1621 feierten. In Kanada gibt es einen
   ● ähnlichen Erntedanktag (der aber nichts
   ● mit den Pilgervätern zu tun hat) am
   ● zweiten Montag im Oktober.

○ KEYWORD

that [ðæt, ðət] (pl **those**) adj (demonstrative) der/die/das; **that man** der Mann; **that woman** die Frau; **that book** das Buch; **that one** der/die/das da; **I want this one, not that one** ich will dieses (hier), nicht das (da)
  ▷ pron **1** (demonstrative) das; **who's/what's that?** wer/was ist das?; **is that you?** bist du das?; **will you eat all that?** isst du das alles?; **that's what he said** das hat er gesagt; **what happened after that?** was geschah danach?; **that is (to say)** das heißt; **and that's that!** und damit Schluss!
  2 (relative: subject) der/die/das; (: (: pl) die; (: direct object) den/die/das; (: (: pl) die; (: indirect object) dem/der/dem; (: (: pl) denen; **the man that I saw** der Mann, den ich gesehen habe; **all that I have** alles was ich habe; **the people that I spoke to** die Leute, mit denen ich geredet habe
  3 (relative: of time): **the day that he came** der

Tag, an dem er kam; **the winter that he came to see us** der Winter, in dem er uns besuchte
  ▷ conj dass; **he thought that I was ill** er dachte, dass ich krank sei, er dachte, ich sei krank
  ▷ adv (demonstrative) so; **I can't work that much** ich kann nicht so viel arbeiten; **that high** so hoch

thatched [θætʃt] adj strohgedeckt

Thatcherism ['θætʃərɪzəm] n Thatcherismus m

Thatcherite ['θætʃəraɪt] adj thatcheristisch ▷ n Thatcher-Anhänger(in) m(f)

thaw [θɔː] n Tauwetter nt ▷ vi (ice) tauen; (food) auftauen ▷ vt (also: **thaw out**) auftauen; **it's ~ing** es taut

○ KEYWORD

the [ðiː, ðə] def art **1** (before masculine noun) der; (before feminine noun) die; (before neuter noun) das; (before plural noun) die; **to play the piano/violin** Klavier/Geige spielen; **I'm going to the butcher's/the cinema** ich gehe zum Metzger/ins Kino
  2 (+ adj to form noun): **the rich and the poor** die Reichen und die Armen; **to attempt the impossible** das Unmögliche versuchen
  3 (in titles): **Elizabeth the First** Elisabeth die Erste; **Peter the Great** Peter der Große
  4 (in comparisons): **the more he works the more he earns** je mehr er arbeitet, desto mehr verdient er; **the sooner the better** je eher, desto besser

theatre, (US) **theater** ['θɪətəʳ] n Theater nt; (also: **lecture theatre**) Hörsaal m; (also: **operating theatre**) Operationsaal m

theatre-goer ['θɪətəgəʊəʳ] n Theaterbesucher(in) m(f)

theatrical [θɪ'ætrɪkl] adj (event, production) Theater-; (gestures etc) theatralisch

theft [θeft] n Diebstahl m

their [ðɛəʳ] adj ihr

theirs [ðɛəz] pron ihre(r, s); **it is ~** es gehört ihnen; **a friend of ~** ein Freund/eine Freundin von ihnen; see also **my; mine¹**

them [ðɛm] pron (direct) sie; (indirect) ihnen; **I see ~** ich sehe sie; **give ~ the book** gib ihnen das Buch; **give me a few of ~** geben Sie mir ein paar davon; **with ~** mit ihnen; **without ~** ohne sie; see also **me**

theme [θiːm] n (also Mus) Thema nt

theme park n Themenpark m

theme song n Titelmusik f

theme tune n Titelmelodie f

themselves [ðəm'sɛlvz] pl pron (reflexive, after prep) sich; (emphatic, alone) selbst; **between ~** unter sich

then [ðɛn] adv (at that time) damals; (next, later) dann ▷ conj (therefore) also ▷ adj: **the ~ president** der damalige Präsident; **by ~** (past) bis dahin; *(future)* bis dann; **from ~ on** von da an; **before ~** davor; **until ~** bis dann; **and ~ what?** und was dann?; **what do you want me to do ~?** was soll ich dann machen?; **... but ~ (again) he's the boss** ... aber er ist ja der Chef

theologian [θɪə'ləʊdʒən] *n* Theologe *m*, Theologin *f*

theological [θɪə'lɒdʒɪkl] *adj* theologisch

theology [θɪ'ɒlədʒɪ] *n* Theologie *f*

theorem ['θɪərəm] *n* Lehrsatz *m*

theoretical [θɪə'rɛtɪkl] *adj* theoretisch

theorize ['θɪəraɪz] *vi* theoretisieren

theory ['θɪərɪ] *n* Theorie *f*; **in ~** theoretisch

therapeutic [θɛrə'pjuːtɪk] *adj* therapeutisch

therapist ['θɛrəpɪst] *n* Therapeut(in) *m(f)*

therapy ['θɛrəpɪ] *n* Therapie *f*

◯ KEYWORD

there [ðɛəʳ] *adv* **1**: **there is/are** da ist/sind; *(there exist(s))* es gibt; **there are 3 of them** es gibt 3 davon; **there has been an accident** da war ein Unfall; **there will be a meeting tomorrow** morgen findet ein Treffen statt **2** *(referring to place)* da, dort; **down/over there** da unten/drüben; **put it in/on there** leg es dorthinein/-hinauf; **I want that book there** ich möchte das Buch da; **there he is!** da ist er ja! **3**: **there, there** *(esp to child)* ist ja gut

thereabouts ['ðɛərə'baʊts] *adv*: **or ~** *(place)* oder dortherum; *(amount, time)* oder so

thereafter [ðɛər'ɑːftəʳ] *adv* danach

thereby ['ðɛəbaɪ] *adv* dadurch

therefore ['ðɛəfɔːʳ] *adv* daher, deshalb

there's [ðɛəz] = **there is; there has**

thereupon [ðɛərə'pɒn] *adv* (*at that point*) darauf(hin)

thermal ['θɜːml] *adj* *(springs)* Thermal-; *(underwear, paper, printer)* Thermo-

thermodynamics ['θɜːmədaɪ'næmɪks] *n* Thermodynamik *f*

thermometer [θə'mɒmɪtəʳ] *n* Thermometer *nt*

thermonuclear ['θɜːməʊ'njuːklɪəʳ] *adj* thermonuklear

Thermos® ['θɜːməs] *n* (*also:* **Thermos flask**) Thermosflasche® *f*

thermostat ['θɜːməʊstæt] *n* Thermostat *m*

thesaurus [θɪ'sɔːrəs] *n* Synonymwörterbuch *nt*

these [ðiːz] *pl adj, pl pron* diese

theses ['θiːsiːz] *npl of* **thesis**

thesis ['θiːsɪs] (*pl* **theses**) *n* These *f*; *(for doctorate etc)* Dissertation *f*, Doktorarbeit *f*

they [ðeɪ] *pl pron* sie; **~ say that ...** (*it is said that*) man sagt, dass ...

they'd [ðeɪd] = **they had**; = **they would**

they'll [ðeɪl] = **they shall; they will**

they're [ðɛəʳ] = **they are**

they've [ðeɪv] = **they have**

thick [θɪk] *adj* dick; *(sauce etc)* dickflüssig; *(fog, forest, hair etc)* dicht; *(inf: stupid)* blöd ▷ *n*: **in the ~ of the battle** mitten im Gefecht; **it's 20 cm**

~ es ist 20 cm dick

thicken ['θɪkn] *vi* *(fog etc)* sich verdichten ▷ *vt* *(sauce etc)* eindicken; **the plot ~s** die Sache wird immer verwickelter

thicket ['θɪkɪt] *n* Dickicht *nt*

thickly ['θɪklɪ] *adv* *(spread, cut)* dick; **~ populated** dicht bevölkert

thickness ['θɪknɪs] *n* *(of rope, wire)* Dicke *f*; *(layer)* Lage *f*

thickset [θɪk'sɛt] *adj* *(person, body)* gedrungen

thick-skinned [θɪk'skɪnd] *adj* *(also fig)* dickhäutig

thief [θiːf] *(pl* **thieves**) *n* Dieb(in) *m(f)*

thieves [θiːvz] *npl of* **thief**

thieving ['θiːvɪŋ] *n* Stehlen *nt*

thigh [θaɪ] *n* Oberschenkel *m*

thighbone ['θaɪbəʊn] *n* Oberschenkelknochen *m*

thimble ['θɪmbl] *n* Fingerhut *m*

thin [θɪn] *adj* dünn; *(fog)* leicht; *(hair, crowd)* spärlich ▷ *vt*: **to ~ (down)** *(sauce, paint)* verdünnen ▷ *vi* *(fog, crowd)* sich lichten; **his hair is ~ning** sein Haar lichtet sich

thing [θɪŋ] *n* Ding *nt*; *(matter)* Sache *f*; *(inf)*: **to have a ~ about sth** *(be fascinated by)* wie besessen sein von etw; *(hate)* etw nicht ausstehen können; **things** *npl (belongings)* Sachen *pl*; **to do sth first ~ (every morning/ tomorrow morning)** etw morgens/morgen früh als Erstes tun; **I look awful first ~ in the morning** ich sehe frühmorgens immer furchtbar aus; **to do sth last ~ (at night)** etw als Letztes (am Abend) tun; **the ~ is ...** die Sache ist die: ...; **for one ~** zunächst mal; **don't worry about a ~** du brauchst dir überhaupt keine Sorgen zu machen; **you'll do no such ~!** das lässt du schön bleiben!; **poor ~** armes Ding; **the best ~ would be to ...** das Beste wäre, zu ...; **how are ~s?** wie gehts?

think [θɪŋk] (*pt, pp* **thought**) *vi* *(reflect)* nachdenken; *(reason)* denken ▷ *vt* *(be of the opinion)* denken; *(believe)* glauben; **to ~ of** denken an +*acc*; *(recall)* sich erinnern an +*acc*; **what did you ~ of them?** was hielten Sie von ihnen?; **to ~ about sth/sb** *(ponder)* über etw/ jdn nachdenken; **I'll ~ about it** ich werde es mir überlegen; **to ~ of doing sth** daran denken, etw zu tun; **to ~ highly of sb** viel von jdm halten; **to ~ aloud** laut nachdenken; **~ again!** denk noch mal nach!; **I ~ so/not** ich glaube ja/nein

▶ **think over** *vt* *(offer, suggestion)* überdenken; **I'd like to ~ things over** ich möchte mir die Sache noch einmal überlegen

▶ **think through** *vt* durchdenken

▶ **think up** *vt* sich *dat* ausdenken

thinking ['θɪŋkɪŋ] *n* Denken *nt*; **to my (way of) ~** meiner Meinung *or* Ansicht nach

think-tank ['θɪŋktæŋk] *n* Expertengremium *nt*

thinly ['θɪnlɪ] *adv* dünn; *(disguised, veiled)* kaum

thinness ['θɪnnɪs] *n* Dünne *f*

third [θɜːd] *num* dritte(r, s) ▷ *n* *(fraction)* Drittel *nt*; *(Aut: also:* **third gear**) dritter Gang *m*;

t

(Brit: Scol: degree) ≈ Ausreichend nt; **a ~ of** ein Drittel +gen

third-degree burns ['θəːddɪɡriː-] npl Verbrennungen pl dritten Grades

thirdly ['θəːdlɪ] adv drittens

third party insurance (Brit) n ≈ Haftpflichtversicherung f

third-rate ['θəːd'reɪt] (pej) adj drittklassig

Third World n: **the ~** die Dritte Welt ▷ adj der Dritten Welt

thirst [θəːst] n Durst m

thirsty ['θəːstɪ] adj durstig; **to be ~** Durst haben; **gardening is ~ work** Gartenarbeit macht durstig

thirteen [θəː'tiːn] num dreizehn

thirteenth ['θəː'tiːnθ] num dreizehnte(r, s)

thirtieth ['θəːtɪɪθ] num dreißigste(r, s)

thirty ['θəːtɪ] num dreißig

 KEYWORD

this [ðɪs] (pl **these**) adj (demonstrative) diese(r, s); **this man** dieser Mann; **this woman** diese Frau; **this book** dieses Buch; **this one** diese(r, s) (hier)
▷ pron (demonstrative) dies, das; **who/what is this?** wer/was ist das?; **this is where I live** hier wohne ich; **this is what he said** das hat er gesagt; **this is Mr Brown** (in introductions, photo) das ist Herr Brown; (on telephone) hier ist Herr Brown
▷ adv (demonstrative): **this high/long** etc so hoch/lang etc

thistle ['θɪsl] n Distel f

thong [θɒŋ] n Riemen m

thorn [θɔːn] n Dorn m

thorny ['θɔːnɪ] adj dornig; (fig: problem) heikel

thorough ['θʌrə] adj gründlich

thoroughbred ['θʌrəbred] n (horse) Vollblüter m

thoroughfare ['θʌrəfɛəʳ] n (road) Durchgangsstraße f; **"no ~"** (Brit) „Durchfahrt verboten"

thoroughgoing ['θʌrəgəuɪŋ] adj (changes, reform) grundlegend; (investigation) gründlich

thoroughly ['θʌrəlɪ] adv gründlich; (very) äußerst; **I ~ agree** ich stimme vollkommen zu

thoroughness ['θʌrənɪs] n Gründlichkeit f

those [ðəuz] pl adj, pl pron die (da); **~ (of you) who ...** diejenigen (von Ihnen), die ...

though [ðəu] conj obwohl ▷ adv aber; **even ~** obwohl; **it's not easy, ~** es ist aber nicht einfach

thought [θɔːt] pt, pp of **think** ▷ n Gedanke m; **thoughts** npl (opinion) Gedanken pl; **after much ~** nach langer Überlegung; **I've just had a ~** mir ist gerade etwas eingefallen; **to give sth some ~** sich dat Gedanken über etw acc machen

thoughtful ['θɔːtful] adj (deep in thought) nachdenklich; (considerate) aufmerksam

thoughtfully ['θɔːtfəlɪ] adv (look etc)

nachdenklich; (behave etc) rücksichtsvoll; (provide) rücksichtsvollerweise

thoughtless ['θɔːtlɪs] adj gedankenlos

thoughtlessly ['θɔːtlɪslɪ] adv gedankenlos

thoughtlessness ['θɔːtlɪsnɪs] n Gedankenlosigkeit f

thought-out [θɔːt'aut] adj durchdacht

thought-provoking ['θɔːtprəvəukɪŋ] adj: **to be ~** Denkanstöße geben

thousand ['θauzənd] num (ein)tausend; **two ~** zweitausend; **~s of** Tausende von

thousandth ['θauzəntθ] num tausendste(r, s)

thrash [θræʃ] vt (beat) verprügeln; (defeat) (vernichtend) schlagen
▶ **thrash about** vi um sich schlagen
▶ **thrash around** vi = **thrash about**
▶ **thrash out** vt (problem) ausdiskutieren

thrashing ['θræʃɪŋ] n: **to give sb a ~** jdn verprügeln

thread [θred] n (yarn) Faden m; (of screw) Gewinde nt ▷ vt (needle) einfädeln; **to ~ one's way between** sich hindurchschlängeln zwischen

threadbare ['θredbɛəʳ] adj (clothes) abgetragen; (carpet) abgelaufen

threat [θret] n Drohung f; (fig): **~ (to)** Gefahr f (für); **to be under ~ of** (closure etc) bedroht sein von

threaten ['θretn] vi bedrohen ▷ vt: **to ~ sb with sth** jdm mit etw drohen; **to ~ to do sth** (damit) drohen, etw zu tun

threatening ['θretnɪŋ] adj drohend, bedrohlich

three [θriː] num drei

three-dimensional [θriːdɪ'mensənl] adj dreidimensional

threefold ['θriːfəuld] adv: **to increase ~** dreifach or um das Dreifache ansteigen

three-piece suit ['θriːpiːs-] n dreiteiliger Anzug m

three-piece suite n dreiteilige Polstergarnitur f

three-ply [θriː'plaɪ] adj (wool) dreifädig; (wood) dreilagig

three-quarters [θriː'kwɔːtəz] npl drei Viertel pl; **~ full** drei viertel voll

three-wheeler ['θriː'wiːləʳ] n (car) Dreiradwagen m

thresh [θreʃ] vt dreschen

threshing machine ['θreʃɪŋ-] n Dreschmaschine f

threshold ['θreʃhəuld] n Schwelle f; **to be on the ~ of sth** (fig) an der Schwelle zu etw sein or stehen

threshold agreement n (Econ) Tarifvereinbarung über der Inflationsrate angeglichene Lohnerhöhungen

threw [θruː] pt of **throw**

thrift [θrɪft] n Sparsamkeit f

thrifty ['θrɪftɪ] adj sparsam

thrill [θrɪl] n (excitement) Aufregung f; (shudder) Erregung f ▷ vi zittern ▷ vt (person, audience) erregen; **to be ~ed** (with gift etc) sich riesig freuen

thriller ['θrɪlə^r] *n* Thriller *m*

thrilling ['θrɪlɪŋ] *adj* (*ride, performance etc*) erregend; (*news*) aufregend

thrive [θraɪv] (*pt* **~d** *or* **throve**, *pp* **~d**) *vi* gedeihen; **to ~ on sth** von etw leben

thriving ['θraɪvɪŋ] *adj* (*business, community*) blühend, florierend

throat [θrəut] *n* Kehle *f*; **to have a sore ~** Halsschmerzen haben

throb [θrɔb] *n* (*of heart*) Klopfen *nt*; (*pain*) Pochen *nt*; (*of engine*) Dröhnen *nt* ▷ *vi* (*heart*) klopfen; (*pain*) pochen; (*machine*) dröhnen; **my head is ~bing** ich habe rasende Kopfschmerzen

throes [θrəuz] *npl*: **in the ~ of** (*war, moving house etc*) mitten in +*dat*; **death ~** Todeskampf *m*

thrombosis [θrɔm'bəusɪs] *n* Thrombose *f*

throne [θrəun] *n* Thron *m*; **on the ~** auf dem Thron

throng ['θrɔŋ] *n* Masse *f* ▷ *vt* (*streets etc*) sich drängen in +*dat* ▷ *vi*: **to ~ to** strömen zu; **a ~ of people** eine Menschenmenge; **to be ~ed with** wimmeln von

throttle ['θrɔtl] *n* (*in car*) Gaspedal *nt*; (*on motorcycle*) Gashebel *m* ▷ *vt* (*strangle*) erdrosseln

through [θru:] *prep* durch; (*time*) während; (*owing to*) infolge +*gen* ▷ *adj* (*ticket, train*) durchgehend ▷ *adv* durch; **(from) Monday ~ Friday** (*US*) von Montag bis Freitag; **to be ~** (*Tel*) verbunden sein; **to be ~ with sb/sth** mit jdm/etw fertig sein; **we're ~!** es ist aus zwischen uns!; **"no ~ road", "no ~ traffic"** (*US*) „keine Durchfahrt"; **to let sb ~** jdn durchlassen; **to put sb ~ to sb** (*Tel*) jdn mit jdm verbinden

throughout [θru:'aut] *adv* (*everywhere*) überall; (*the whole time*) die ganze Zeit über ▷ *prep* (*place*) überall in +*dat*; (*time*): **~ the morning/ afternoon** während des ganzen Morgens/ Nachmittags; **~ her life** ihr ganzes Leben lang

throughput ['θru:put] *n* (*also Comput*) Durchsatz *m*

throve [θrəuv] *pt of* **thrive**

throw [θrəu] (*pt* **threw**, *pp* **~n**) *n* Wurf *m* ▷ *vt* werfen; (*rider*) abwerfen; (*fig: confuse*) aus der Fassung bringen; (*pottery*) töpfern; **to ~ a party** eine Party geben; **to ~ open** (*doors, windows*) aufreißen; (*debate*) öffnen

▶ **throw about** *vt* (*money*) herumwerfen mit

▶ **throw around** *vt* = **throw about**

▶ **throw away** *vt* wegwerfen; (*waste*) verschwenden

▶ **throw off** *vt* (*get rid of: burden*) abwerfen

▶ **throw out** *vt* (*rubbish*) wegwerfen; (*idea*) verwerfen; (*person*) hinauswerfen

▶ **throw together** *vt* (*meal*) hinhauen; (*clothes*) zusammenpacken

▶ **throw up** *vi* (*vomit*) sich übergeben

throwaway ['θrəuəweɪ] *adj* (*cutlery etc*) Einweg-; (*line, remark*) beiläufig

throwback ['θrəubæk] *n*: **it's a ~ to** (*reminder*) es erinnert an +*acc*

throw-in ['θrəuɪn] *n* (*Football*) Einwurf *m*

thrown [θrəun] *pp of* **throw**

thru [θru:] (*US*) *prep, adj, adv* = **through**

thrush [θrʌʃ] *n* (*bird*) Drossel *f*; (*Med: esp in children*) Soor *m*; (*: Brit: in women*) vaginale Pilzerkrankung *f*

thrust [θrʌst] (*pt, pp* **~**) *n* (*Tech*) Schubkraft *f*; (*push*) Stoß *m*; (*fig: impetus*) Stoßkraft *f* ▷ *vt* stoßen

thud [θʌd] *n* dumpfes Geräusch *nt*

thug [θʌg] *n* Schlägertyp *m*

thumb [θʌm] *n* Daumen *m* ▷ *vt*: **to ~ a lift** per Anhalter fahren; **to give sb/sth the ~s up** (*approve*) jdm/etw grünes Licht geben; **to give sb/sth the ~s down** (*disapprove*) jdn/etw ablehnen

▶ **thumb through** *vt fus* (*book*) durchblättern

thumb index *n* Daumenregister *nt*

thumbnail ['θʌmneɪl] *n* Daumennagel *m*

thumbnail sketch *n* kurze Darstellung *f*

thumbtack ['θʌmtæk] (*US*) *n* Heftzwecke *f*

thump [θʌmp] *n* (*blow*) Schlag *m*; (*sound*) dumpfer Schlag *m* ▷ *vt* schlagen auf +*acc* ▷ *vi* (*heart etc*) heftig pochen

thumping ['θʌmpɪŋ] *adj* (*majority, victory etc*) Riesen-; (*headache, cold*) fürchterlich

thunder ['θʌndə^r] *n* Donner *m* ▷ *vi* donnern; (*shout angrily*) brüllen; **to ~ past** (*train etc*) vorbeidonnern

thunderbolt ['θʌndəbəult] *n* Blitzschlag *m*

thunderclap ['θʌndəklæp] *n* Donnerschlag *m*

thunderous ['θʌndrəs] *adj* donnernd

thunderstorm ['θʌndəstɔ:m] *n* Gewitter *nt*

thunderstruck ['θʌndəstrʌk] *adj*: **to be ~** (*shocked*) wie von Donner gerührt sein

thundery ['θʌndərɪ] *adj* (*weather*) gewitterig

Thur., Thurs. *abbr* (= *Thursday*) Do.

Thursday ['θə:zdɪ] *n* Donnerstag *m*; *see also* **Tuesday**

thus [ðʌs] *adv* (*in this way*) so; (*consequently*) somit

thwart [θwɔ:t] *vt* (*person*) einen Strich durch die Rechnung machen +*dat*; (*plans*) vereiteln

thyme [taɪm] *n* Thymian *m*

thyroid ['θaɪrɔɪd] *n* (*also:* **thyroid gland**) Schilddrüse *f*

tiara [tɪ'ɑ:rə] *n* Diadem *nt*

Tiber ['taɪbə^r] *n*: **the ~** der Tiber

Tibet [tɪ'bɛt] *n* Tibet *nt*

Tibetan [tɪ'bɛtən] *adj* tibetanisch ▷ *n* (*person*) Tibetaner(in) *m(f)*; (*Ling*) Tibetisch *nt*

tibia ['tɪbɪə] *n* Schienbein *nt*

tic [tɪk] *n* nervöse Zuckung *f*, Tic *m*, Tick *m*

tick [tɪk] *n* (*sound*) Ticken *nt*; (*mark*) Häkchen *nt*; (*Zool*) Zecke *f*; (*Brit: inf: moment*) Augenblick *m*; (*: credit*): **to buy sth on ~** etw auf Pump kaufen ▷ *vi* (*clock, watch*) ticken ▷ *vt* (*item on list*) abhaken; **to put a ~ against sth** etw abhaken; **what makes him ~?** was ist er für ein Mensch?

▶ **tick off** *vt* (*item on list*) abhaken; (*person*) rüffeln

▶ **tick over** *vi* (*engine*) im Leerlauf sein; (*fig: business etc*) sich über Wasser halten

ticker tape ['tɪkəteɪp] *n* Lochstreifen *m*; (*US: in*

t

celebrations) ≈ Luftschlangen *pl*

ticket ['tɪkɪt] *n* (*for public transport*) Fahrkarte *f*; (*for theatre etc*) Eintrittskarte *f*; (*in shop: on goods*) Preisschild *nt*; (: *from cash register*) Kassenbon *m*; (*for raffle*) Los *nt*; (*for library*) Ausweis *m*; (*also:* **parking ticket**: *fine*) Strafzettel *m*; (*US: Pol*) Wahlliste *f*; **to get a (parking)** ~ (*Aut*) einen Strafzettel bekommen

ticket agency *n* (*Theat*) Vorverkaufsstelle *f*

ticket collector *n* (*Rail: at station*) Fahrkartenkontrolleur(in) *m(f)*; (*on train*) Schaffner(in) *m(f)*

ticket holder *n* Karteninhaber(in) *m(f)*

ticket inspector *n* Fahrkartenkontrolleur(in) *m(f)*

ticket office *n* (*Rail*) Fahrkartenschalter *m*; (*Theat*) Theaterkasse *f*

tickle ['tɪkl] *vt* kitzeln; (*fig: amuse*) amüsieren ▷ *vi* kitzeln; **it ~s!** das kitzelt!

ticklish ['tɪklɪʃ] *adj* (*person, situation*) kitzlig

tidal ['taɪdl] *adj* (*force*) Gezeiten-, der Gezeiten; (*river*) Tide-

tidal wave *n* Flutwelle *f*

tidbit ['tɪdbɪt] (*US*) *n* = **titbit**

tiddlywinks ['tɪdlɪwɪŋks] *n* Flohhüpfen *nt*

tide [taɪd] *n* (*in sea*) Gezeiten *pl*; (*fig: of events, opinion etc*) Trend *m*; **high** ~ Flut *f*; **low** ~ Ebbe *f*; **the** ~ **is in/out** es ist Flut/Ebbe; **the** ~ **is coming in** die Flut kommt

▶ **tide over** *vt* über die Runden helfen +*dat*

tidily ['taɪdɪlɪ] *adv* ordentlich

tidiness ['taɪdɪnɪs] *n* Ordentlichkeit *f*

tidy ['taɪdɪ] *adj* (*room, desk*) ordentlich, aufgeräumt; (*person*) ordnungsliebend; (*sum, income*) ordentlich ▷ *vt* (*also:* **tidy up**) aufräumen

tie [taɪ] *n* (*Brit: also:* **necktie**) Krawatte *f*; (*string etc*) Band *nt*; (*fig: link*) Verbindung *f*; (*Sport: match*) Spiel *nt*; (*in competition: draw*) Unentschieden *nt* ▷ *vt* (*parcel*) verschnüren; (*shoelaces*) zubinden; (*ribbon*) binden ▷ *vi* (*Sport etc*): **to** ~ **with sb for first place** sich mit jdm den ersten Platz teilen; **"black** ~**"** „Abendanzug"; **"white** ~**"** „Frackzwang"; **family** ~**s** familiäre Bindungen; **to** ~ **sth in a bow** etw zu einer Schleife binden; **to** ~ **a knot in sth** einen Knoten in etw *acc* machen

▶ **tie down** *vt* (*fig: restrict*) binden; (: *to date, price etc*) festlegen

▶ **tie in** *vi*: **to** ~ **in with** zusammenpassen mit

▶ **tie on** *vt* (*Brit*) anbinden

▶ **tie up** *vt* (*parcel*) verschnüren; (*dog*) anbinden; (*boat*) festmachen; (*person*) fesseln; (*arrangements*) unter Dach und Fach bringen; **to be ~d up** (*busy*) zu tun haben, beschäftigt sein

tie-break ['taɪbreɪk], **tie-breaker** ['taɪbreɪkə'] *n* (*Tennis*) Tiebreak *m*; (*in quiz*) Entscheidungsfrage *f*

tie-on ['taɪɒn] (*Brit*) *adj* (*label*) Anhänge-

tiepin ['taɪpɪn] (*Brit*) *n* Krawattennadel *f*

tier [tɪə'] *n* (*of stadium etc*) Rang *m*; (*of cake*) Lage *f*

tie-tack ['taɪtæk] (*US*) *n* = **tiepin**

tiff [tɪf] *n* Krach *m*

tiger ['taɪgə'] *n* Tiger *m*

tiger economy *n* (*Econ*) Tigerstaat *m*

tight [taɪt] *adj* (*screw, knot, grip*) fest; (*shoes, clothes, bend*) eng; (*security*) streng; (*budget, money*) knapp; (*schedule*) gedrängt; (*inf: drunk*) voll; (: *stingy*) knickerig ▷ *adv* fest; **to be packed** ~ (*suitcase*) prallvoll sein; (*room*) gerammelt voll sein; **everybody hold** ~**!** alle festhalten!

tighten ['taɪtn] *vt* (*rope, strap*) straffen; (*screw, bolt*) anziehen; (*grip*) festigen; (*security*) verschärfen ▷ *vi* (*grip*) sich festigen; (*rope etc*) sich spannen

tightfisted [taɪt'fɪstɪd] *adj* knickerig (*inf*)

tight-lipped ['taɪt'lɪpt] *adj* (*fig: silence*) eisern; **to be** ~ **about sth** über etw *acc* schweigen

tightly ['taɪtlɪ] *adv* fest

tightrope ['taɪtrəʊp] *n* Seil *nt*; **to be on** *or* **walking a** ~ (*fig*) einen Balanceakt vollführen

tightrope walker *n* Seiltänzer(in) *m(f)*

tights [taɪts] (*Brit*) *npl* Strumpfhose *f*

tigress ['taɪgrɪs] *n* Tigerin *f*

tilde ['tɪldə] *n* Tilde *f*

tile [taɪl] *n* (*on roof*) Ziegel *m*; (*on floor*) Fliese *f*; (*on wall*) Kachel *f* ▷ *vt* (*floor*) mit Fliesen auslegen; (*bathroom*) kacheln

tiled [taɪld] *adj* (*floor*) mit Fliesen ausgelegt; (*wall*) gekachelt

till [tɪl] *n* (*in shop etc*) Kasse *f* ▷ *vt* (*land*) bestellen ▷ *prep, conj* = **until**

tiller ['tɪlə'] *n* (*Naut*) Ruderpinne *f*

tilt [tɪlt] *vt* sich neigen ▷ *vi* sich neigen ▷ *n* (*slope*) Neigung *f*; **to wear one's hat at a** ~ den Hut schief aufhaben; (**at**) **full** ~ mit Volldampf

timber ['tɪmbə'] *n* (*material*) Holz *nt*; (*trees*) Nutzholz *nt*

time [taɪm] *n* Zeit *f*; (*occasion*) Gelegenheit *f*, Mal *nt*; (*Mus*) Takt *m* ▷ *vt* (*measure time of*) die Zeit messen bei; (*runner*) stoppen; (*fix moment for: visit etc*) den Zeitpunkt festlegen für; **a long** ~ eine lange Zeit; **for the** ~ **being** vorläufig; **4 at a** ~ 4 auf einmal; **from** ~ **to time** von Zeit zu Zeit; ~ **after time,** ~ **and again** immer (und immer) wieder; **at** ~**s** manchmal, zuweilen; **in** ~ (*soon enough*) rechtzeitig; (*eventually*) mit der Zeit; (*Mus*) im Takt; **in a week's** ~ in einer Woche; **in no** ~ im Handumdrehen; **any** ~ jederzeit; **on** ~ rechtzeitig; **to be 30 minutes behind/ahead of** ~ 30 Minuten zurück/voraus sein; **by the** ~ **he arrived** als er ankam; **5** ~**s 5** 5 mal 5; **what** ~ **is it?** wie spät ist es?; **to have a good** ~ sich amüsieren; **we/they** *etc* **had a hard** ~ wir/sie *etc* hatten es schwer; ~**'s up!** die Zeit ist um!; **I've no** ~ **for it** (*fig*) dafür habe ich nichts übrig; **he'll do it in his own (good)** ~ (*without being hurried*) er macht es, ohne sich hetzen zu lassen; **he'll do it in his own** ~, **he'll do it on his own** ~ (*US: out of working hours*) er macht es in seiner Freizeit; **to be behind the** ~**s** rückständig sein; **to** ~ **sth well/badly** den richtigen/falschen Zeitpunkt für etw wählen;

the bomb was ~d to go off 5 minutes later die Bombe war so eingestellt, dass sie 5 Minuten später explodieren sollte

time-and-motion study ['taɪmənd'məuʃən-] *n* Arbeitsstudie *f*

time bomb *n* (*also fig*) Zeitbombe *f*

time card *n* Stechkarte *f*

time clock *n* (*in factory etc*) Stechuhr *f*

time-consuming ['taɪmkənsju:mɪŋ] *adj* zeitraubend

time difference *n* Zeitunterschied *m*

time frame *n* zeitlicher Rahmen *m*

time-honoured, (US) **time-honored** ['taɪmɔnəd] *adj* althergebracht

timekeeper ['taɪmki:pəʳ] *n*: **she's a good ~** sie erfüllt ihr Zeitsoll

time-lag ['taɪmlæg] *n* Verzögerung *f*

timeless ['taɪmlɪs] *adj* zeitlos

time limit *n* zeitliche Grenze *f*

timely ['taɪmlɪ] *adj* (*arrival*) rechtzeitig; (*reminder*) zur rechten Zeit

time management *n* Zeitmanagement *nt*

time off *n*: **to take ~** sich *dat* freinehmen

timer ['taɪməʳ] *n* (*time switch*) Schaltuhr *f*; (*on cooker*) Zeitmesser *m*; (*on video*) Timer *m*

time-saving ['taɪmseɪvɪŋ] *adj* zeitsparend

timescale ['taɪmskeɪl] (*Brit*) *n* Zeitspanne *f*

time-share ['taɪmʃɛəʳ] *n* Ferienwohnung *f* auf Timesharingbasis

time-sharing ['taɪmʃɛərɪŋ] *n* (*of property*, *Comput*) Timesharing *nt*

time sheet *n* = **time card**

time signal *n* (*Radio*) Zeitzeichen *nt*

time switch *n* Zeitschalter *m*

timetable ['taɪmteɪbl] *n* (*Rail etc*) Fahrplan *m*; (*Scol*) Stundenplan *m*; (*programme of events*) Programm *nt*

time zone *n* Zeitzone *f*

timid ['tɪmɪd] *adj* (*person*) schüchtern; (*animal*) scheu

timidity [tɪ'mɪdɪtɪ] *n* (*shyness*) Schüchternheit *f*

timing ['taɪmɪŋ] *n* (*Sport*) Timing *nt*; **the ~ of his resignation** der Zeitpunkt seines Rücktritts

timing device *n* (*on bomb*) Zeitzünder *m*

timpani ['tɪmpənɪ] *npl* Kesselpauken *pl*

tin [tɪn] *n* (*metal*) Blech *nt*; (*container*) Dose *f*; (: *for baking*) Form *f*; (: *Brit*: *can*) Büchse *f*, Dose *f*; **two ~s of paint** zwei Dosen Farbe

tinfoil ['tɪnfɔɪl] *n* Alufolie *f*

tinge [tɪndʒ] *n* (*of colour*) Färbung *f*; (*fig*: *of emotion etc*) Anflug *m*, Anstrich *m* ▷ *vt*: **~d with blue/red** leicht blau/rot gefärbt; **to be ~d with sth** (*fig*: *emotion etc*) einen Anstrich von etw haben

tingle ['tɪŋgl] *vi* prickeln; (*from cold*) kribbeln; **I was tingling with excitement** ich zitterte vor Aufregung

tinker ['tɪŋkəʳ] *n* (*gipsy*) Kesselflicker *m*
  ▶ **tinker with** *vt fus* herumbasteln an +*dat*

tinkle ['tɪŋkl] *vi* klingeln ▷ *n* (*inf*): **to give sb a ~** (*Tel*) bei jdm anklingeln

tin mine *n* Zinnbergwerk *nt*

tinned [tɪnd] (*Brit*) *adj* (*food, peas*) Dosen-, in Dosen

tinnitus ['tɪnɪtəs] *n* Tinnitus *m*, Ohrensummen *nt*

tinny ['tɪnɪ] (*pej*) *adj* (*sound*) blechern; (*car etc*) Schrott-

tin-opener ['tɪnəupnəʳ] (*Brit*) *n* Dosenöffner *m*

tinsel ['tɪnsl] *n* Rauschgoldgirlanden *pl*

tint [tɪnt] *n* (*colour*) Ton *m*; (*for hair*) Tönung *f* ▷ *vt* (*hair*) tönen

tinted ['tɪntɪd] *adj* getönt

tiny ['taɪnɪ] *adj* winzig

tip [tɪp] *n* (*end*) Spitze *f*; (*gratuity*) Trinkgeld *nt*; (*Brit*: *for rubbish*) Müllkippe *f*; (: *for coal*) Halde *f*; (*advice*) Tipp *m*, Hinweis *m* ▷ *vt* (*waiter*) ein Trinkgeld geben +*dat*; (*tilt*) kippen; (*also*: **tip over**: *overturn*) umkippen; (*also*: **tip out**: *empty*) leeren; (*predict*: *winner etc*) tippen *or* setzen auf +*acc*; **he ~ped out the contents of the box** er kippte den Inhalt der Kiste aus
  ▶ **tip off** *vt* einen Tipp *or* Hinweis geben +*dat*

tip-off ['tɪpɔf] *n* Hinweis *m*

tipped ['tɪpt] *adj* (*Brit*: *cigarette*) Filter-; **steel-~** mit Stahlspitze

Tipp-Ex® ['tɪpɛks] *n* Tipp-Ex® *nt*

tipple ['tɪpl] (*Brit*) *vi* picheln ▷ *n*: **to have a ~** einen trinken

tipster ['tɪpstəʳ] *n jd*, *der bei Pferderennen*, *Börsengeschäften etc Tipps gegen Bezahlung weitergibt*

tipsy ['tɪpsɪ] (*inf*) *adj* beschwipst

tiptoe ['tɪptəu] *n*: **on ~** auf Zehenspitzen

tip-top ['tɪp'tɔp] *adj*: **in ~ condition** tipptopp

tirade [taɪ'reɪd] *n* Tirade *f*

tire ['taɪəʳ] *n* (*US*) = **tyre** ▷ *vt* müde machen, ermüden ▷ *vi* (*become tired*) müde werden; **to ~ of sth** genug von etw haben
  ▶ **tire out** *vt* erschöpfen

tired ['taɪəd] *adj* müde; **to be/look ~** müde sein/aussehen; **to feel ~** sich müde fühlen; **to be ~ of sth** etw satthaben; **to be ~ of doing sth** es satthaben, etw zu tun

tiredness ['taɪədnɪs] *n* Müdigkeit *f*

tireless ['taɪəlɪs] *adj* unermüdlich

tiresome ['taɪəsəm] *adj* lästig

tiring ['taɪərɪŋ] *adj* ermüdend, anstrengend

tissue ['tɪʃu:] *n* (*Anat*, *Biol*) Gewebe *nt*; (*paper handkerchief*) Papiertaschentuch *nt*

tissue paper *n* Seidenpapier *nt*

tit [tɪt] *n* (*bird*) Meise *f*; (*inf*: *breast*) Titte *f*; **~ for tat** wie du mir, so ich dir

titanium [tɪ'teɪnɪəm] *n* Titan *nt*

titbit, (US) **tidbit** ['tɪtbɪt] *n* (*food*, *news*) Leckerbissen *m*

titillate ['tɪtɪleɪt] *vt* erregen, reizen

titivate ['tɪtɪveɪt] *vt* fein machen

title ['taɪtl] *n* Titel *m*; (*Law*): **~ to** Anspruch auf +*acc*

title deed *n* Eigentumsurkunde *f*

title page *n* Titelseite *f*

title role *n* Titelrolle *f*

title track *n* Titelstück *nt*

titter ['tɪtəʳ] *vi* kichern

tittle-tattle ['tɪtltætl] (*inf*) *n* Klatsch *m*, Gerede *nt*

t

827

tizzy ['tɪzɪ] *n*: **to be in a ~** aufgeregt sein; **to get in a ~** sich aufregen

T-junction ['tiː'dʒʌŋkʃən] *n* T-Kreuzung *f*

TM *abbr* (= *trademark*) Wz = **transcendental meditation**

TN (*US*) *abbr* (*Post*) = *Tennessee*

TNT *n abbr* (= *trinitrotoluene*) TNT *nt*

 **KEYWORD**

to [tuː] *prep* **1** (*direction*) nach +*dat*, zu +*dat*; **to go to France/London/school/the station** nach Frankreich/nach London/zur Schule/zum Bahnhof gehen; **to the left/right** nach links/rechts; **I have never been to Germany** ich war noch nie in Deutschland

2 (*as far as*) bis; **to count to 10** bis 10 zählen

3 (*with expressions of time*) vor +*dat*; **a quarter to 5** (*Brit*) Viertel vor 5

4 (*for, of*): **the key to the front door** der Schlüssel für die Haustür; **a letter to his wife** ein Brief an seine Frau

5 (*expressing indirect object*): **to give sth to sb** jdm etw geben; **to talk to sb** mit jdm sprechen; **I sold it to a friend** ich habe es an einen Freund verkauft; **you've done something to your hair** du hast etwas mit deinem Haar gemacht

6 (*in relation to*) zu; **A is to B as C is to D** A verhält sich zu B wie C zu D; **3 goals to 2** 3 zu 2 Tore; **40 miles to the gallon** 40 Meilen pro Gallone

7 (*purpose, result*) zu; **to sentence sb to death** jdn zum Tode verurteilen; **to my surprise** zu meiner Überraschung

▷ *with vb* **1** (*simple infinitive*): **to go** gehen; **to eat** essen

2 (*following another vb*): **to want to do sth** etw tun wollen; **to try/start to do sth** versuchen/anfangen, etw zu tun

3 (*with vb omitted*): **I don't want to** ich will nicht; **you ought to** du solltest es tun

4 (*purpose, result*) (um …) zu; **I did it to help you** ich habe es getan, um dir zu helfen

5 (*equivalent to relative clause*) zu; **he has a lot to lose** er hat viel zu verlieren; **the main thing is to try** die Hauptsache ist, es zu versuchen

6 (*after adjective etc*): **ready to use** gebrauchsfertig; **too old/young to …** zu alt/jung, um zu …; **it's too heavy to lift** es ist zu schwer zu heben

▷ *adv*: **to push/pull the door to** die Tür zudrücken/zuziehen; **to and fro** hin und her

toad [təʊd] *n* Kröte *f*

toadstool ['təʊdstuːl] *n* Giftpilz *m*

toady ['təʊdɪ] (*pej*) *vi*: **to ~ to sb** vor jdm kriechen

toast [təʊst] *n* (*bread, drink*) Toast *m* ▷ *vt* (*bread etc*) toasten; (*drink to*) einen Toast *or* Trinkspruch ausbringen auf +*acc*; **a piece** *or* **slice of ~** eine Scheibe Toast

toaster ['təʊstəʳ] *n* Toaster *m*

toastmaster ['təʊstmɑːstəʳ] *n* Zeremonienmeister *m*

toast rack *n* Toastständer *m*

tobacco [tə'bækəʊ] *n* Tabak *m*; **pipe ~** Pfeifentabak *m*

tobacconist [tə'bækənɪst] *n* Tabakhändler(in) *m(f)*

tobacconist's [tə'bækənɪsts], **tobacconist's shop** *n* Tabakwarenladen *m*

Tobago [tə'beɪgəʊ] *n see* **Trinidad**

toboggan [tə'bɔgən] *n* Schlitten *m*

today [tə'deɪ] *adv, n* heute; **what day is it ~?** welcher Tag ist heute?; **what date is it ~?** der Wievielte ist heute?; **~ is the 4th of March** heute ist der 4. März; **a week ago ~** heute vor einer Woche; **~'s paper** die Zeitung von heute

toddle ['tɔdl] (*inf*) *vi*: **to ~ in/off/along** herein-/davon-/entlangwatscheln

toddler ['tɔdləʳ] *n* Kleinkind *nt*

to-do [tə'duː] *n* Aufregung *f*, Theater *nt*

toe [təʊ] *n* Zehe *f*, Zeh *m*; (*of shoe, sock*) Spitze *f*; **to ~ the line** (*fig*) auf Linie bleiben; **big/little ~** großer/kleiner Zeh

toehold ['təʊhəʊld] *n* (*in climbing*) Halt *m* für die Fußspitzen; (*fig*): **to get/gain a ~ (in)** einen Einstieg bekommen/sich *dat* einen Einstieg verschaffen (in +*dat*)

toenail ['təʊneɪl] *n* Zehennagel *m*

toffee ['tɔfɪ] *n* Toffee *m*

toffee apple (*Brit*) *n* ≈ kandierter Apfel *m*

tofu ['təʊfuː] *n* Tofu *m*

toga ['təʊgə] *n* Toga *f*

together [tə'geðəʳ] *adv* zusammen; (*at the same time*) gleichzeitig; **~ with** gemeinsam mit

togetherness [tə'geðənɪs] *n* Beisammensein *nt*

toggle switch ['tɔgl-] *n* (*Comput*) Toggle-Schalter *m*

Togo ['təʊgəʊ] *n* Togo *nt*

togs [tɔgz] (*inf*) *npl* Klamotten *pl*

toil [tɔɪl] *n* Mühe *f* ▷ *vi* sich abmühen

toilet ['tɔɪlət] *n* Toilette *f* ▷ *cpd* (*kit, accessories etc*) Toiletten-; **to go to the ~** auf die Toilette gehen

toilet bag (*Brit*) *n* Kulturbeutel *m*

toilet bowl *n* Toilettenbecken *nt*

toilet paper *n* Toilettenpapier *nt*

toiletries ['tɔɪlətrɪz] *npl* Toilettenartikel *pl*

toilet roll *n* Rolle *f* Toilettenpapier

toilet soap *n* Toilettenseife *f*

toilet water *n* Toilettenwasser *nt*

to-ing and fro-ing ['tuːɪŋən'frəʊɪŋ] (*Brit*) *n* Hin und Her *nt*

token ['təʊkən] *n* (*sign, souvenir*) Zeichen *nt*; (*substitute coin*) Wertmarke *f* ▷ *adj* (*strike, payment etc*) symbolisch; **by the same ~** (*fig*) in gleicher Weise; **book/record/gift ~** (*Brit*) Bücher-/Platten-/Geschenkgutschein *m*

tokenism ['təʊkənɪzəm] *n*: **to be (pure) ~** (nur) eine Alibifunktion haben

Tokyo ['təʊkjəʊ] *n* Tokio *nt*

told [təʊld] *pt, pp of* **tell**

tolerable ['tɔlərəbl] *adj* (*bearable*) erträglich;

(*fairly good*) passabel

tolerably ['tɔlərəblɪ] *adv*: ~ **good** ganz annehmbar *or* passabel

tolerance ['tɔlərns] *n* Toleranz *f*

tolerant ['tɔlərnt] *adj* tolerant; **to be ~ of sth** tolerant gegenüber etw sein

tolerate ['tɔləreɪt] *vt* (*pain, noise*) erdulden, ertragen; (*injustice*) tolerieren

toleration [tɔlə'reɪʃən] *n* (*of person, pain etc*) Duldung *f*; (*Rel, Pol*) Toleranz *f*

toll [təʊl] *n* (*of casualties, deaths*) (Gesamt)zahl *f*; (*tax, charge*) Gebühr *f* ▷ *vi* (*bell*) läuten; **the work took its ~ on us** die Arbeit blieb nicht ohne Auswirkungen auf uns

tollbridge ['təʊlbrɪdʒ] *n* gebührenpflichtige Brücke *f*, Mautbrücke *f*

toll call (*US*) *n* Ferngespräch *nt*

toll-free ['təʊlfriː] (*US*) *adj* gebührenfrei

toll road *n* gebührenpflichtige Straße *f*, Mautstraße *f*

tomato [tə'mɑːtəʊ] (*pl* **~es**) *n* Tomate *f*

tomato purée *n* Tomatenmark *nt*

tomb [tuːm] *n* Grab *nt*

tombola [tɔm'bəʊlə] *n* Tombola *f*

tomboy ['tɔmbɔɪ] *n* Wildfang *m*

tombstone ['tuːmstəʊn] *n* Grabstein *m*

tomcat ['tɔmkæt] *n* Kater *m*

tome [təʊm] (*form*) *n* Band *m*

tomorrow [tə'mɔrəʊ] *adv* morgen ▷ *n* morgen; (*future*) Zukunft *f*; **the day after ~** übermorgen; **a week ~** morgen in einer Woche; **~ morning** morgen früh

ton [tʌn] *n* (*Brit*) (britische) Tonne *f*; (*US: also*: **short ton**) (US-)Tonne *f* (*ca. 907 kg*); (*also*: **metric ton**) (metrische) Tonne *f*; **~s of** (*inf*) Unmengen von

tonal ['təʊnl] *adj* (*Mus*) klanglich, tonal

tone [təʊn] *n* Ton *m* ▷ *vi* (*also*: **tone in**: *colours*) (farblich) passen
  ▶ **tone down** *vt* (*also fig*) abschwächen
  ▶ **tone up** *vt* (*muscles*) kräftigen

tone-deaf [təʊn'dɛf] *adj* ohne Gefühl für Tonhöhen

toner ['təʊnə'] *n* (*for photocopier*) Toner *m*

Tonga ['tɔŋə] *n* Tonga *nt*

tongs [tɔŋz] *npl* Zange *f*; (*also*: **curling tongs**) Lockenstab *m*

tongue [tʌŋ] *n* Zunge *f*; (*form*: *language*) Sprache *f*; **~-in-cheek** (*speak, say*) ironisch

tongue-tied ['tʌŋtaɪd] *adj* (*fig*) sprachlos

tongue-twister ['tʌŋtwɪstə'] *n* Zungenbrecher *m*

tonic ['tɔnɪk] *n* (*Med*) Tonikum *nt*; (*fig*) Wohltat *f*; (*also*: **tonic water**) Tonic *nt*; (*Mus*) Tonika *f*, Grundton *m*

tonight [tə'naɪt] *adv* (*this evening*) heute Abend; (*this night*) heute Nacht ▷ *n* (*this evening*) der heutige Abend; (*this night*) die kommende Nacht; (**I'll**) **see you ~!** bis heute Abend!

tonnage ['tʌnɪdʒ] *n* Tonnage *f*

tonne [tʌn] (*Brit*) *n* (*metric ton*) Tonne *f*

tonsil ['tɔnsl] *n* Mandel *f*; **to have one's ~s out** sich *dat* die Mandeln herausnehmen lassen

tonsillitis [tɔnsɪ'laɪtɪs] *n* Mandelentzündung *f*

too [tuː] *adv* (*excessively*) zu; (*also*) auch; **it's ~ sweet** es ist zu süß; **I went ~** ich bin auch mitgegangen; ~ **much** (*adj*) zu viel; (*adv*) zu sehr; ~ **many** zu viele; ~ **bad!** das ist eben Pech!

took [tʊk] *pt of* **take**

tool [tuːl] *n* (*also fig*) Werkzeug *nt*

tool box *n* Werkzeugkasten *m*

tool kit *n* Werkzeugsatz *m*

toot [tuːt] *n* (*of horn*) Hupton *m*; (*of whistle*) Pfeifton *m* ▷ *vi* (*with car-horn*) hupen

tooth [tuːθ] (*pl* **teeth**) *n* (*also Tech*) Zahn *m*; **to have a ~ out**, **to have a ~ pulled** (*US*) sich *dat* einen Zahn ziehen lassen; **to brush one's teeth** sich *dat* die Zähne putzen; **by the skin of one's teeth** (*fig*) mit knapper Not

toothache ['tuːθeɪk] *n* Zahnschmerzen *pl*; **to have ~** Zahnschmerzen haben

toothbrush ['tuːθbrʌʃ] *n* Zahnbürste *f*

toothpaste ['tuːθpeɪst] *n* Zahnpasta *f*

toothpick ['tuːθpɪk] *n* Zahnstocher *m*

tooth powder *n* Zahnpulver *nt*

top [tɔp] *n* (*of mountain, tree, ladder*) Spitze *f*; (*of cupboard, table, box*) Oberseite *f*; (*of street*) Ende *nt*; (*lid*) Verschluss *m*; (*Aut: also*: **top gear**) höchster Gang *m*; (*also*: **spinning top**: *toy*) Kreisel *m*; (*blouse etc*) Oberteil *nt*; (*of pyjamas*) Jacke *f* ▷ *adj* höchste(r, s); (*highest in rank*) oberste(r, s); (: *golfer etc*) Top- ▷ *vt* (*poll, vote, list*) anführen; (*estimate etc*) übersteigen; **at the ~ of the stairs/page** oben auf der Treppe/ Seite; **at the ~ of the street** am Ende der Straße; **on ~ of** (*above*) auf +*dat*; (*in addition to*) zusätzlich zu; **from ~ to bottom** von oben bis unten; **from ~ to toe** (*Brit*) von Kopf bis Fuß; **at the ~ of the list** oben auf der Liste; **at the ~ of his voice** so laut er konnte; **over the ~** (*inf*: *behaviour*) übertrieben; **to go over the ~** (*inf*) übertreiben; **at ~ speed** bei Höchstgeschwindigkeit
  ▶ **top up**, (*US*) **top off** *vt* (*drink*) nachfüllen; (*salary*) aufbessern

topaz ['təʊpæz] *n* Topas *m*

top-class ['tɔp'klɑːs] *adj* erstklassig; (*hotel, player etc*) Spitzen-

topcoat ['tɔpkəʊt] *n* (*overcoat*) Mantel *m*; (*of paint*) Deckanstrich *m*

top floor *n* oberster Stock *m*

top hat *n* Zylinder *m*

top-heavy [tɔp'hɛvɪ] *adj* (*also fig*) kopflastig

topic ['tɔpɪk] *n* Thema *nt*

topical ['tɔpɪkl] *adj* (*issue etc*) aktuell

topless ['tɔplɪs] *adj* (*waitress*) Oben-ohne-; (*bather*) barbusig ▷ *adv* oben ohne

top-level ['tɔplɛvl] *adj* auf höchster Ebene

topmost ['tɔpməʊst] *adj* oberste(r, s)

top-notch ['tɔp'nɔtʃ] *adj* erstklassig

topography [tə'pɔgrəfɪ] *n* Topografie *f*

topping ['tɔpɪŋ] *n* (*Culin*) Überzug *m*

topple ['tɔpl] *vt* (*government etc*) stürzen ▷ *vi* (*person*) stürzen; (*object*) fallen

top-ranking ['tɔpræŋkɪŋ] *adj* (*official*)

t

hochgestellt

top-secret ['tɒp'siːkrɪt] *adj* streng geheim

top-security ['tɒpsə'kjuərɪtɪ] (*Brit*) *adj* (*prison, wing*) Hochsicherheits-

topsy-turvy ['tɒpsɪ'tɜːvɪ] *adj* auf den Kopf gestellt ▷ *adv* durcheinander; (*fall, land*) verkehrt herum

top-up ['tɒpʌp] *n*: **would you like a ~?** darf ich Ihnen nachschenken?

top-up loan *n* Ergänzungsdarlehen *nt*

torch [tɔːtʃ] *n* Fackel *f*; (*Brit: electric*) Taschenlampe *f*

tore [tɔː^r] *pt of* **tear**

torment [*n* 'tɔːmɛnt, *vt* tɔː'mɛnt] *n* Qual *f* ▷ *vt* quälen; (*annoy*) ärgern

torn [tɔːn] *pp of* **tear**¹ ▷ *adj*: **~ between** (*fig*) hin- und hergerissen zwischen

tornado [tɔː'neɪdəʊ] (*pl* **~es**) *n* (*storm*) Tornado *m*

torpedo [tɔː'piːdəʊ] (*pl* **~es**) *n* Torpedo *m*

torpedo boat *n* Torpedoboot *nt*

torpor ['tɔːpə^r] *n* Trägheit *f*

torrent ['tɒrnt] *n* (*flood*) Strom *m*; (*fig*) Flut *f*

torrential [tɒ'rɛnʃl] *adj* (*rain*) wolkenbruchartig

torrid ['tɒrɪd] *adj* (*weather, love affair*) heiß

torso ['tɔːsəʊ] *n* Torso *m*

tortoise ['tɔːtəs] *n* Schildkröte *f*

tortoiseshell ['tɔːtəʃɛl] *adj* (*jewellery, ornaments*) aus Schildpatt; (*cat*) braungelbschwarz, braun-gelb-schwarz

tortuous ['tɔːtjuəs] *adj* (*path*) gewunden; (*argument, mind*) umständlich

torture ['tɔːtʃə^r] *n* Folter *f*; (*fig*) Qual *f* ▷ *vt* foltern; (*fig: torment*) quälen

torturer ['tɔːtʃərə^r] *n* Folterer *m*

Tory ['tɔːrɪ] (*Brit: Pol*) *adj* konservativ ▷ *n* Tory *m*, Konservative(r) *f(m)*

toss [tɒs] *vt* (*throw*) werfen; (*one's head*) zurückwerfen; (*salad*) anmachen; (*pancake*) wenden ▷ *n*: **with a ~ of her head** mit einer Kopfbewegung; **to ~ a coin** eine Münze werfen; **to win/lose the ~** die Entscheidung per Münzwurf gewinnen/verlieren; **to ~ up for sth** etw per Münzwurf entscheiden; **to ~ and turn** (*in bed*) sich hin und her wälzen

tot [tɒt] *n* (*Brit: drink*) Schluck *m*; (*child*) Knirps *m*
  ▶ **tot up** (*Brit*) *vt* (*figures*) zusammenzählen

total ['təʊtl] *adj* (*number etc*) gesamt; (*failure, wreck etc*) völlig, total ▷ *n* Gesamtzahl *f* ▷ *vt* (*add up*) zusammenzählen; (*add up to*) sich belaufen auf; **in ~** insgesamt

totalitarian [təʊtælɪ'tɛərɪən] *adj* totalitär

totality [təʊ'tælɪtɪ] *n* Gesamtheit *f*

totally ['təʊtəlɪ] *adv* völlig

totem pole ['təʊtəm-] *n* Totempfahl *m*

totter ['tɒtə^r] *vi* (*person*) wanken, taumeln; (*fig: government*) ins Wanken sein

touch [tʌtʃ] *n* (*sense of touch*) Gefühl *nt*; (*contact*) Berührung *f*; (*skill: of pianist etc*) Hand *f* ▷ *vt* berühren; (*tamper with*) anrühren; (*emotionally*) rühren ▷ *vi* (*make contact*) sich berühren; **the personal ~** die persönliche Note; **to put the finishing ~es to sth** letzte Hand an etw *acc* legen; **a ~ of** (*fig: frost etc*) etwas,

ein Hauch von; **in ~ with** (*person, group*) in Verbindung mit; **to get in ~ with sb** mit jdm in Verbindung treten; **I'll be in ~** ich melde mich; **to lose ~** (*friends*) den Kontakt verlieren; **to be out of ~ with events** nicht auf dem Laufenden sein
  ▶ **touch on** *vt fus* (*topic*) berühren
  ▶ **touch up** *vt* (*car etc*) ausbessern

touch-and-go ['tʌtʃən'gəʊ] *adj* (*situation*) auf der Kippe; **it was ~ whether we'd succeed** es war völlig offen, ob wir Erfolg haben würden

touchdown ['tʌtʃdaʊn] *n* (*of rocket, plane*) Landung *f*; (*US: Football*) Touchdown *m*

touched [tʌtʃt] *adj* (*moved*) gerührt; (*inf: mad*) plemplem

touching ['tʌtʃɪŋ] *adj* rührend

touchline ['tʌtʃlaɪn] *n* (*Sport*) Seitenlinie *f*

touch screen *n* (*Tech*) Berührungsbildschirm *m*, Touchscreen *m*

touch screen mobile *n* Touchscreen-Handy *nt*

touch screen technology *n* Touchscreentechnologie *f*

touch-sensitive ['tʌtʃ'sɛnsɪtɪv] *adj* berührungsempfindlich; (*switch*) Kontakt-

touch-type ['tʌtʃtaɪp] *vi* blindschreiben

touchy ['tʌtʃɪ] *adj* (*person, subject*) empfindlich

tough [tʌf] *adj* (*strong, firm, difficult*) hart; (*resistant*) widerstandsfähig; (*meat, animal, person*) zäh; (*rough*) rau; **~ luck!** Pech!

toughen ['tʌfn] *vt* (*sb's character*) hart machen; (*glass etc*) härten

toughness ['tʌfnɪs] *n* Härte *f*

toupee ['tuːpeɪ] *n* Toupet *nt*

tour ['tʊə^r] *n* (*journey*) Reise *f*, Tour *f*; (*of factory, museum etc*) Rundgang *m*; (: *also*: **guided tour**) Führung *f*; (*by pop group etc*) Tournee *f* ▷ *vt* (*country, factory etc: on foot*) ziehen durch; (: *in car*) fahren durch; **to go on a ~ of a museum/castle** an einer Museums-/Schlossführung teilnehmen; **to go on a ~ of the Highlands** die Highlands bereisen; **to go on ~** (*pop group, theatre company etc*) auf Tournee gehen

tour guide *n* Reiseleiter(in) *m(f)*

touring ['tʊərɪŋ] *n* Umherreisen *nt*

tourism ['tʊərɪzm] *n* Tourismus *m*

tourist ['tʊərɪst] *n* Tourist(in) *m(f)* ▷ *cpd* (*attractions, season*) Touristen-; **the ~ trade** die Tourismusbranche

tourist class *n* Touristenklasse *f*

tourist information centre (*Brit*) *n* Touristen-Informationszentrum *nt*

tourist office *n* Verkehrsamt *nt*

tournament ['tʊənəmənt] *n* Turnier *nt*

tourniquet ['tʊənɪkeɪ] *n* Aderpresse *f*

tour operator (*Brit*) *n* Reiseveranstalter *m*

tousled ['taʊzld] *adj* (*hair*) zerzaust

tout [taʊt] *vi*: **to ~ for business** die Reklametrommel schlagen; **to ~ for custom** auf Kundenfang gehen ▷ *n* (*also*: **ticket tout**) Schwarzhändler, der Eintrittskarten zu überhöhten Preisen verkauft

tow [təʊ] *vt* (*vehicle*) abschleppen; (*caravan, trailer*) ziehen ▷ *n*: **to give sb a ~** (*Aut*) jdn abschleppen; **"on ~", "in ~"** (US) „Fahrzeug wird abgeschleppt"

▶ **tow away** vt (vehicle) abschleppen

toward [tə'wɔːd], **towards** [tə'wɔːdz] prep (direction) zu; (attitude) gegenüber +dat; (purpose) für; (in time) gegen; **~(s) noon/the end of the year** gegen Mittag/Ende des Jahres; **to feel friendly ~(s) sb** jdm freundlich gesinnt sein

towel ['tauəl] n Handtuch nt; **to throw in the ~** (fig) das Handtuch werfen

towelling ['tauəlıŋ] n Frottee nt or m

towel rail, (US) **towel rack** n Handtuchstange f

tower ['tauə'] n Turm m ▷ vi aufragen; **to ~ above** or **over sb/sth** über jdm/etw aufragen

tower block (Brit) n Hochhaus nt

towering ['tauərıŋ] adj hoch aufragend

towline ['təulaın] n Abschleppseil nt

town [taun] n Stadt f; **to go (in)to ~** in die Stadt gehen; **to go to ~ on sth** (fig) sich bei etw ins Zeug legen; **in ~** in der Stadt; **to be out of ~** (person) nicht in der Stadt sein

town centre n Stadtzentrum nt

town clerk n Stadtdirektor(in) m(f)

town council n Stadtrat m

town crier [-'kraıə'] n Ausrufer m

town hall n Rathaus nt

townie ['taunı] (inf) n (town-dweller) Städter(in) m(f)

town plan n Stadtplan m

town planner n Stadtplaner(in) m(f)

town planning n Stadtplanung f

township ['taunʃıp] n Stadt(gemeinde) f; (formerly: in South Africa) Township f

townspeople ['taunzpiːpl] npl Stadtbewohner pl

towpath ['təupɑːθ] n Leinpfad m

towrope ['təurəup] n Abschleppseil nt

tow truck (US) n Abschleppwagen m

toxic ['tɔksık] adj giftig, toxisch

toxic asset n (Econ) faule Wertpapiere pl

toxic bank n (Econ) Bad Bank f

toxin ['tɔksın] n Gift nt, Giftstoff m

toy [tɔı] n Spielzeug nt

▶ **toy with** vt fus (object, idea) spielen mit

toyshop ['tɔıʃɔp] n Spielzeugladen m

trace [treıs] n (sign, small amount) Spur f ▷ vt (draw) nachzeichnen; (follow) verfolgen; (locate) aufspüren; **without ~** (disappear) spurlos; **there was no ~ of it** es war spurlos verschwunden

trace element n Spurenelement nt

tracer ['treısə'] n (Mil: also: **tracer bullet**) Leuchtspurgeschoss nt; (Med) Indikator m

trachea [trə'kıə] n Luftröhre f

tracing paper ['treısıŋ-] n Pauspapier nt

track [træk] n Weg m; (of comet, Sport) Bahn f; (of suspect, animal) Spur f; (Rail) Gleis nt; (on tape, record) Stück nt, Track m ▷ vt (follow) verfolgen; **to keep ~ of sb/sth** (fig) jdn/etw im Auge behalten; **to be on the right ~** (fig) auf der richtigen Spur sein

▶ **track down** vt aufspüren

tracker dog ['trækə-] (Brit) n Spürhund m

track events npl Laufwettbewerbe f

tracking station ['trækıŋ-] n Bodenstation f

track meet (US) n (Sport) Leichtathletikwettkampf m

track record n: **to have a good ~** (fig) gute Leistungen vorzuweisen haben

tracksuit ['træksuːt] n Trainingsanzug m

tract [trækt] n (Geog) Gebiet nt; (pamphlet) Traktat m or nt; **respiratory ~** Atemwege pl

traction ['trækʃən] n (power) Zugkraft f; (Aut: grip) Bodenhaftung f; (Med): **in ~** im Streckverband

traction engine n Zugmaschine f

tractor ['træktə'] n Traktor m

trade [treıd] n (activity) Handel m; (skill, job) Handwerk nt ▷ vi (do business) handeln ▷ vt: **to ~ sth (for sth)** etw (gegen etw) eintauschen; **foreign ~** Außenhandel m; **Department of T~ and Industry** (Brit) ≈ Wirtschaftsministerium nt; **to ~ with** Handel treiben mit; **to ~ in** (merchandise) handeln in +dat

▶ **trade in** vt in Zahlung geben

trade barrier n Handelsschranke f

trade deficit n Handelsdefizit nt

Trade Descriptions Act (Brit) n Gesetz über korrekte Warenbeschreibungen

trade discount n Händlerrabatt m

trade fair n Handelsmesse f

trade figures npl Handelsziffern pl

trade-in ['treıdın] n: **to take sth as a ~** etw in Zahlung nehmen

trade-in value n Gebrauchtwert m

trademark ['treıdmɑːk] n Warenzeichen nt

trade mission n Handelsmission f

trade name n Handelsname m

trade-off ['treıdɔf] n Handel m; **there's bound to be a ~ between speed and quality** es gibt entweder Einbußen bei der Schnelligkeit oder bei der Qualität

trader ['treıdə'] n Händler(in) m(f)

trade secret n (also fig) Betriebsgeheimnis nt

tradesman ['treıdzmən] (irreg: like **man**) n (shopkeeper) Händler m

trade union n Gewerkschaft f

trade unionist [-'juːnjənıst] n Gewerkschaftler(in) m(f)

trade wind n Passat m

trading ['treıdıŋ] n Handel m

trading estate (Brit) n Industriegelände nt

trading stamp n Rabattmarke f

tradition [trə'dıʃən] n Tradition f

traditional [trə'dıʃənl] adj traditionell

traditionally [trə'dıʃnəlı] adv traditionell

traffic ['træfık] n Verkehr m; (in drugs etc) Handel m ▷ vi: **to ~ in** handeln mit

traffic calming n Verkehrsberuhigung f

traffic circle (US) n Kreisverkehr m

traffic island n Verkehrsinsel f

traffic jam n Verkehrsstauung f, Stau m

trafficker ['træfıkə'] n Händler(in) m(f)

traffic lights npl Ampel f

t

traffic offence (Brit) n Verkehrsdelikt nt
traffic sign n Verkehrszeichen nt
traffic violation (US) n = **traffic offence**
traffic warden n Verkehrspolizist für Parkvergehen; (woman) ≈ Politesse f
tragedy ['trædʒədɪ] n Tragödie f
tragic ['trædʒɪk] adj tragisch
trail [treɪl] n (path) Weg m; (track) Spur f; (of smoke, dust) Wolke f ▷ vt (drag) schleifen; (follow) folgen +dat ▷ vi (hang loosely) schleifen; (in game, contest) zurückliegen; **to be on sb's ~** jdm auf der Spur sein
  ▸ **trail away** vi (sound, voice) sich verlieren
  ▸ **trail behind** vi hinterhertrotten
  ▸ **trail off** vi = **trail away**
trailer ['treɪlə^r] n (Aut) Anhänger m; (US: caravan) Caravan m, Wohnwagen m; (Cine, TV) Trailer m
trailer truck (US) n Sattelschlepper m
train [treɪn] n (Rail) Zug m; (of dress) Schleppe f ▷ vt (apprentice etc) ausbilden; (dog) abrichten; (athlete) trainieren; (mind) schulen; (plant) ziehen; (point: camera, gun etc): **to ~ on** richten auf +acc ▷ vi (learn a skill) ausgebildet werden; (Sport) trainieren; **~ of thought** Gedankengang m; **to go by ~** mit dem Zug fahren; **~ of events** Ereignisfolge f; **to ~ sb to do sth** jdn dazu ausbilden, etw zu tun
train attendant (US) n Schlafwagenschaffner m
trained [treɪnd] adj (worker) gelernt; (teacher) ausgebildet; (animal) dressiert; (eye) geschult
trainee [treɪ'niː] n Auszubildende(r) f(m)
trainer ['treɪnə^r] n (Sport: coach) Trainer(in) m(f); (: shoe) Trainingsschuh m; (of animals) Dresseur(in) m(f)
training ['treɪnɪŋ] n (for occupation) Ausbildung f; (Sport) Training nt; **in ~** (Sport) im Training
training college n (for teachers) ≈ pädagogische Hochschule f
training course n Ausbildungskurs m
train wreck n (fig) unabwendbare Katastrophe; **he's a complete ~** er ist ein Wrack
traipse [treɪps] vi: **to ~ in/out** hinein-/herauslatschen
trait [treɪt] n Zug m, Eigenschaft f
traitor ['treɪtə^r] n Verräter(in) m(f)
trajectory [trə'dʒɛktərɪ] n Flugbahn f
tram [træm] (Brit) n (also: **tramcar**) Straßenbahn f
tramline ['træmlaɪn] n Straßenbahnschiene f
tramp [træmp] n Landstreicher m; (pej: woman) Flittchen nt ▷ vi stapfen ▷ vt (walk through: town, streets) latschen durch
trample ['træmpl] vt: **to ~ (underfoot)** niedertrampeln ▷ vi (also fig): **to ~ on** herumtrampeln auf +dat
trampoline ['træmpəliːn] n Trampolin nt
trance [trɑːns] n Trance f; **to go into a ~** in Trance verfallen
tranquil ['træŋkwɪl] adj ruhig, friedlich
tranquillity, (US) **tranquility** [træŋ'kwɪlɪtɪ] n Ruhe f

tranquillizer, (US) **tranquilizer** ['træŋkwɪlaɪzə^r] n Beruhigungsmittel nt
transact [træn'zækt] vt (business) abwickeln
transaction [træn'zækʃən] n Geschäft nt; **cash ~** Bargeldtransaktion f
transatlantic ['trænzət'læntɪk] adj transatlantisch; (phone-call) über den Atlantik
transcend [træn'sɛnd] vt überschreiten
transcendental [trænsɛn'dɛntl] adj: **~ meditation** transzendentale Meditation f
transcribe [træn'skraɪb] vt transkribieren
transcript ['trænskrɪpt] n Niederschrift f, Transkription f
transcription [træn'skrɪpʃən] n Transkription f
transept ['trænsɛpt] n Querschiff nt
transfer ['trænsfə^r] n (of employees) Versetzung f; (of money) Überweisung f; (of power) Übertragung f; (Sport) Transfer m; (picture, design) Abziehbild nt ▷ vt (employees) versetzen; (money) überweisen; (power, ownership) übertragen; **by bank ~** per Banküberweisung; **to ~ the charges** (Brit: Tel) ein R-Gespräch führen
transferable [træns'fəːrəbl] adj übertragbar; **"not ~"** „nicht übertragbar"
transfix [træns'fɪks] vt aufspießen; **~ed with fear** (fig) starr vor Angst
transform [træns'fɔːm] vt umwandeln
transformation [trænsfə'meɪʃən] n Umwandlung f
transformer [træns'fɔːmə^r] n (Elec) Transformator m
transfusion [træns'fjuːʒən] n (also: **blood transfusion**) Bluttransfusion f
transgress [træns'grɛs] vt (go beyond) überschreiten; (violate: rules, law) verletzen
transient ['trænzɪənt] adj vorübergehend
transistor [træn'zɪstə^r] n (Elec) Transistor m; (also: **transistor radio**) Transistorradio nt
transit ['trænzɪt] n: **in ~** unterwegs
transit camp n Durchgangslager nt
transition [træn'zɪʃən] n Übergang m
transitional [træn'zɪʃənl] adj Übergangs-
transitive ['trænzɪtɪv] adj (verb) transitiv
transit lounge n Transithalle f
transitory ['trænzɪtərɪ] adj (emotion, arrangement etc) vorübergehend
transit visa n Transitvisum nt
translate [trænz'leɪt] vt übersetzen; **to ~ (from/into)** übersetzen (aus/in +acc)
translation [trænz'leɪʃən] n Übersetzung f; **in ~** als Übersetzung
translator [trænz'leɪtə^r] n Übersetzer(in) m(f)
translucent [trænz'luːsnt] adj (object) lichtdurchlässig
transmission [trænz'mɪʃən] n (also TV) Übertragung f; (of information) Übermittlung f; (Aut) Getriebe nt
transmission rate n (Tel, Comput) Übertragungsrate f
transmit [trænz'mɪt] vt (also TV) übertragen; (message, signal) übermitteln

transmitter [trænz'mɪtə^r] n (TV, Radio) Sender m

transparency [træns'pɛərnsɪ] n (of glass etc) Durchsichtigkeit f; (Brit: Phot) Dia nt

transparent [træns'pærnt] adj durchsichtig; (fig: obvious) offensichtlich

transpire [træns'paɪə^r] vi (turn out) bekannt werden; (happen) passieren; **it finally ~d that** ... schließlich sickerte durch, dass ...

transplant [vt træns'plɑːnt, n 'trɑːnsplɑːnt] vt (organ, seedlings) verpflanzen ▷ n (Med) Transplantation f; **to have a heart ~** sich einer Herztransplantation unterziehen

transport ['trænspɔːt] n Transport m, Beförderung f ▷ vt transportieren; **do you have your own ~?** haben Sie ein Auto?; **public ~** öffentliche Verkehrsmittel pl; **Department of T~** (Brit) Verkehrsministerium nt

transportation ['trænspɔː'teɪʃən] n Transport m, Beförderung f; (means of transport) Beförderungsmittel nt; **Department of T~** (US) Verkehrsministerium nt

transport café (Brit) n Fernfahrerlokal nt

transpose [træns'pəuz] vt versetzen

transsexual [trænz'sɛksuəl] adj transsexuell ▷ n Transsexuelle(r) f(m)

transverse ['trænzvɜːs] adj (beam etc) Quer-

transvestite [trænz'vɛstaɪt] n Transvestit m

trap [træp] n (also fig) Falle f; (carriage) zweirädriger Pferdewagen m ▷ vt (animal) (mit einer Falle) fangen; (person: trick) in die Falle locken; (: confine) gefangen halten; (immobilize) festsetzen; (capture: energy) stauen; **to set** or **lay a ~ (for sb)** (jdm) eine Falle stellen; **to shut one's ~** (inf) die Klappe halten; **to ~ one's finger in the door** sich dat den Finger in der Tür einklemmen

trap door n Falltür f

trapeze [trə'piːz] n Trapez nt

trapper ['træpə^r] n Fallensteller m, Trapper m

trappings ['træpɪŋz] npl äußere Zeichen pl; (of power) Insignien pl

trash [træʃ] n (rubbish) Abfall m, Müll m; (pej: nonsense) Schund m, Mist m

trash can (US) n Mülleimer m

trashy ['træʃɪ] adj (goods) minderwertig, wertlos; (novel etc) Schund-

trauma ['trɔːmə] n Trauma nt

traumatic [trɔː'mætɪk] adj traumatisch

traumatize ['trɔːmətaɪz] vt traumatisieren

travel ['trævl] n (travelling) Reisen nt ▷ vi reisen; (short distance) fahren; (move: car, aeroplane) sich bewegen; (sound etc) sich fortpflanzen; (news) sich verbreiten ▷ vt (distance) zurücklegen; **travels** npl (journeys) Reisen pl; **this wine doesn't ~ well** dieser Wein verträgt den Transport nicht

travel agency n Reisebüro nt

travel agent n Reisebürokaufmann m, Reisebürokauffrau f

travel brochure n Reiseprospekt m

traveling etc (US) = **travelling** etc

traveller, (US) **traveler** ['trævlə^r] n Reisende(r)

f(m); (Comm) Vertreter(in) m(f)

traveller's cheque, (US) **traveler's check** n Reisescheck m

travelling, (US) **traveling** ['trævlɪŋ] n Reisen nt ▷ cpd (circus, exhibition) Wander-; (bag, clock) Reise-; **~ expenses** Reisespesen pl

travelling salesman n Vertreter m

travelogue ['trævəlɒg] n Reisebericht m

travel sickness n Reisekrankheit f

traverse ['trævəs] vt durchqueren

travesty ['trævəstɪ] n Travestie f

trawler ['trɔːlə^r] n Fischdampfer m

tray [treɪ] n (for carrying) Tablett nt; (also: **in-tray/out-tray**: on desk) Ablage f für Eingänge/Ausgänge

treacherous ['trɛtʃərəs] adj (person, look) verräterisch; (ground, tide) tückisch; **road conditions are ~** die Straßen sind in gefährlichem Zustand

treachery ['trɛtʃərɪ] n Verrat m

treacle ['triːkl] n Sirup m

tread [trɛd] (pt **trod**, pp **trodden**) n (of tyre) Profil nt; (footstep) Schritt m; (of stair) Stufe f ▷ vi gehen

▷ **tread on** vt fus treten auf +acc

treadle ['trɛdl] n Pedal nt

treas. abbr = **treasurer**

treason ['triːzn] n Verrat m

treasure ['trɛʒə^r] n (also fig) Schatz m ▷ vt schätzen; **treasures** npl (art treasures etc) Schätze pl, Kostbarkeiten pl

treasure hunt n Schatzsuche f

treasurer ['trɛʒərə^r] n Schatzmeister(in) m(f)

treasury ['trɛʒərɪ] n: **the T~, the T~ Department** (US) das Finanzministerium

treasury bill n kurzfristiger Schatzwechsel m

treat [triːt] n (present) (besonderes) Vergnügen nt ▷ vt (also Med, Tech) behandeln; **it came as a ~** es war eine besondere Freude; **to ~ sth as a joke** etw als Witz ansehen; **to ~ sb to sth** jdm etw spendieren

treatment ['triːtmənt] n Behandlung f; **to have ~ for sth** wegen etw in Behandlung sein

treaty ['triːtɪ] n Vertrag m

treble ['trɛbl] adj (triple) dreifach; (Mus: voice, part) (Knaben)sopran-; (instrument) Diskant- ▷ n (singer) (Knaben)sopran m; (on hi-fi, radio etc) Höhen pl ▷ vt verdreifachen ▷ vi sich verdreifachen; **to be ~ the amount/size of sth** dreimal so viel/so groß wie etw sein

treble clef n Violinschlüssel m

tree [triː] n Baum m

tree-lined ['triːlaɪnd] adj baumbestanden

treetop ['triːtɒp] n Baumkrone f

tree trunk n Baumstamm m

trek [trɛk] n Treck m; (tiring walk) Marsch m ▷ vi trecken

trellis ['trɛlɪs] n Gitter nt

tremble ['trɛmbl] vi (voice, body, trees) zittern; (ground) beben

trembling ['trɛmblɪŋ] n (of ground) Beben nt, Erschütterung f; (of trees) Zittern nt ▷ adj (hand, voice etc) zitternd

t

tremendous [trɪ'mɛndəs] adj (amount, success etc) gewaltig, enorm; (holiday, view etc) fantastisch

tremendously [trɪ'mɛndəslɪ] adv (difficult, exciting) ungeheuer; **he enjoyed it** ~ es hat ihm ausgezeichnet gefallen

tremor ['trɛmə'] n Zittern nt; (also: **earth tremor**) Beben nt, Erschütterung f

trench [trɛntʃ] n Graben m

trench coat n Trenchcoat m

trench warfare n Stellungskrieg m

trend [trɛnd] n Tendenz f; (fashion) Trend m; **a** ~ **towards/away from sth** eine Tendenz zu/weg von etw; **to set a/the** ~ richtungsweisend sein

trendy ['trɛndɪ] adj modisch

trepidation [trɛpɪ'deɪʃən] n (apprehension) Beklommenheit f; **in** ~ beklommen

trespass ['trɛspəs] vi: **to** ~ **on** (private property) unbefugt betreten; **"no ~ing"** „Betreten verboten"

trespasser ['trɛspəsə'] n Unbefugte(r) f(m); **"~s will be prosecuted"** „widerrechtliches Betreten wird strafrechtlich verfolgt"

tress [trɛs] n (of hair) Locke f

trestle ['trɛsl] n Bock m

trestle table n Klapptisch m

trial ['traɪəl] n (Law) Prozess m; (test: of machine, drug etc) Versuch m; (worry) Plage f; **trials** npl (unpleasant experiences) Schwierigkeiten pl; ~ **by jury** Schwurgerichtsverfahren nt; **to be sent for** ~ vor Gericht gestellt werden; **to be/go on** ~ (Law) angeklagt sein/werden; **by** ~ **and error** durch Ausprobieren

trial balance n Probebilanz f

trial basis n: **on a** ~ probeweise

trial period n Probezeit f

trial run n Versuch m

triangle ['traɪæŋgl] n Dreieck nt; (US: set square) (Zeichen)dreieck nt; (Mus) Triangel f

triangular [traɪ'æŋgjulə'] adj dreieckig

triathlon [traɪ'æθlən] n Triathlon nt

tribal ['traɪbl] adj (warrior, warfare, dance) Stammes-

tribe [traɪb] n Stamm m

tribesman ['traɪbzmən] (irreg: like **man**) n Stammesangehörige(r) m

tribulations [trɪbju'leɪʃənz] npl Kümmernisse pl

tribunal [traɪ'bju:nl] n Gericht nt

tributary ['trɪbjutərɪ] n (of river) Nebenfluss m

tribute ['trɪbju:t] n Tribut m; **to pay** ~ **to** Tribut zollen +dat

trice [traɪs] n: **in a** ~ im Handumdrehen

trick [trɪk] n Trick m; (Cards) Stich m ▷ vt hereinlegen; **to play a** ~ **on sb** jdm einen Streich spielen; **it's a** ~ **of the light** das Licht täuscht; **that should do the** ~ das müsste hinhauen; **to** ~ **sb into doing sth** jdn (mit einem Trick) dazu bringen, etw zu tun; **to** ~ **sb out of sth** jdn um etw prellen

trickery ['trɪkərɪ] n Tricks pl, Betrügerei f

trickle ['trɪkl] n (of water etc) Rinnsal nt ▷ vi

(water, rain etc) rinnen; (people) sich langsam bewegen

trick photography n Trickfotografie f

trick question n Fangfrage f

trickster ['trɪkstə'] n Betrüger(in) m(f)

tricky ['trɪkɪ] adj (job, problem) schwierig

tricycle ['traɪsɪkl] n Dreirad nt

trifle ['traɪfl] n (detail) Kleinigkeit f; (Culin) Trifle nt ▷ adv: **a** ~ **long** ein bisschen lang ▷ vi: **to** ~ **with sb/sth** jdn/etw nicht ernst nehmen; **he is not (someone) to be ~d with** mit ihm ist nicht zu spaßen

trifling ['traɪflɪŋ] adj (detail) unbedeutend

trigger ['trɪgə'] n Abzug m
▶ **trigger off** vt fus auslösen

trigonometry [trɪgə'nɔmətrɪ] n Trigonometrie f

trilby ['trɪlbɪ] (Brit) n (also: **trilby hat**) Filzhut m

trill [trɪl] n (Mus) Triller m; (of birds) Trillern nt

trilogy ['trɪlədʒɪ] n Trilogie f

trim [trɪm] adj (house, garden) gepflegt; (figure, person) schlank ▷ n (haircut etc): **to have a** ~ sich dat die Haare nachschneiden lassen; (on clothes, car) Besatz m ▷ vt (hair, beard) nachschneiden; (decorate): **to** ~ **(with)** besetzen (mit); (Naut: a sail) trimmen mit; **to keep o.s. in (good)** ~ (gut) in Form bleiben

trimmings ['trɪmɪŋz] npl (Culin): **with all the** ~ mit allem Drum und Dran; (cuttings: of pastry etc) Reste pl

Trinidad and Tobago ['trɪnɪdæd-] n Trinidad und Tobago nt

trinity ['trɪnɪtɪ] n (Rel) Dreieinigkeit f

trinket ['trɪŋkɪt] n (ornament) Schmuckgegenstand m; (piece of jewellery) Schmuckstück nt

trio ['tri:əu] n Trio nt

trip [trɪp] n (journey) Reise f; (outing) Ausflug m ▷ vi (stumble) stolpern; (go lightly) trippeln; **on a** ~ auf Reisen
▶ **trip over** vt fus stolpern über +acc
▶ **trip up** vi stolpern ▷ vt (person) zu Fall bringen

tripartite [traɪ'pɑ:taɪt] adj (agreement, talks) dreiseitig

tripe [traɪp] n (Culin) Kaldaunen pl; (pej: rubbish) Stuss m

triple ['trɪpl] adj dreifach ▷ adv: ~ **the distance/the speed** dreimal so weit/schnell; ~ **the amount** dreimal so viel

triple jump n Dreisprung m

triplets ['trɪplɪts] npl Drillinge pl

triplicate ['trɪplɪkət] n: **in** ~ in dreifacher Ausfertigung

tripod ['traɪpɔd] n (Phot) Stativ nt

Tripoli ['trɪpəlɪ] n Tripolis nt

tripper ['trɪpə'] (Brit) n Ausflügler(in) m(f)

tripwire ['trɪpwaɪə'] n Stolperdraht m

trite [traɪt] (pej) adj (comment, idea etc) banal

triumph ['traɪʌmf] n Triumph m ▷ vi: **to** ~ **(over)** triumphieren (über +acc)

triumphal [traɪ'ʌmfl] adj (return) triumphal

triumphant [traɪ'ʌmfənt] adj triumphal;

(victorious) siegreich

triumphantly [traɪˈʌmfəntlɪ] *adv*
triumphierend

trivia [ˈtrɪvɪə] *(pej) npl* Trivialitäten *pl*

trivial [ˈtrɪvɪəl] *adj* trivial

triviality [trɪvɪˈælɪtɪ] *n* Trivialität *f*

trivialize [ˈtrɪvɪəlaɪz] *vt* trivialisieren

trod [trɒd] *pt of* **tread**

trodden [ˈtrɒdn] *pp of* **tread**

trolley [ˈtrɒlɪ] *n (for luggage)* Kofferkuli
m; (for shopping) Einkaufswagen *m; (table
on wheels)* Teewagen *m; (also:* **trolley bus***)*
Oberleitungsomnibus *m*, Obus *m*

trollop [ˈtrɒləp] *(pej) n (woman)* Schlampe *f*

trombone [trɒmˈbəʊn] *n* Posaune *f*

troop [tru:p] *n (of people, monkeys etc)* Gruppe
f ▷ vi: **to ~ in/out** hinein-/hinausströmen;
troops *npl (Mil)* Truppen *pl*

troop carrier *n* Truppentransporter *m;
(Naut: also:* **troopship***)* Truppentransportschiff
nt

trooper [ˈtru:pəʳ] *n (Mil)* Kavallerist *m;
(US: policeman)* Polizist *m*

trooping the colour [ˈtru:pɪŋ-] *(Brit) n
(ceremony)* Fahnenparade *f*

troopship [ˈtru:pʃɪp] *n* Truppentransportschiff
nt

trophy [ˈtrəʊfɪ] *n* Trophäe *f*

tropic [ˈtrɒpɪk] *n* Wendekreis *m;* **the tropics**
npl die Tropen *pl;* **T~ of Cancer/Capricorn**
Wendekreis des Krebses/Steinbocks

tropical [ˈtrɒpɪkl] *adj* tropisch

trot [trɒt] *n (fast pace)* Trott *m; (of horse)* Trab *m*
▷ vi (horse) traben; *(person)* trotten; **on the ~**
(Brit: fig) hintereinander
▶ **trot out** *vt (facts, excuse etc)* vorbringen

trouble [ˈtrʌbl] *n* Schwierigkeiten *pl; (bother,
effort)* Umstände *pl; (unrest)* Unruhen *pl ▷ vt
(worry)* beunruhigen; *(disturb: person)* belästigen
▷ vi: **to ~ to do sth** sich *dat* die Mühe
machen, etw zu tun; **troubles** *npl (personal)*
Probleme *pl; (Pol etc)* Unruhen *pl;* **to be in ~**
in Schwierigkeiten sein; **to have ~ doing
sth** Schwierigkeiten *or* Probleme haben, etw
zu tun; **to go to the ~ of doing sth** sich *dat*
die Mühe machen, etw zu tun; **it's no ~!**
das macht mir nichts aus!; **the ~ is ...** das
Problem ist ...; **what's the ~?** wo fehlts?;
stomach *etc ~* Probleme mit dem Magen *etc;*
please don't ~ yourself bitte bemühen Sie
sich nicht

troubled [ˈtrʌbld] *adj (person)* besorgt; *(country,
life, era)* von Problemen geschüttelt

trouble-free [ˈtrʌblfri:] *adj* problemlos

troublemaker [ˈtrʌblmeɪkəʳ] *n*
Unruhestifter(in) *m(f)*

troubleshooter [ˈtrʌblʃu:təʳ] *n* Vermittler(in)
m(f)

troublesome [ˈtrʌblsəm] *adj (child)* schwierig;
(cough etc) lästig

trouble spot *n (Mil)* Unruheherd *m*

troubling [ˈtrʌblɪŋ] *adj (question etc)*
beunruhigend

trough [trɒf] *n (also:* **drinking trough***)*
Wassertrog *m; (also:* **feeding trough***)*
Futtertrog *m; (channel)* Rinne *f; (low point)* Tief
nt; **a ~ of low pressure** ein Tiefdruckkeil *m*

trounce [traʊns] *vt (defeat)* vernichtend
schlagen

troupe [tru:p] *n* Truppe *f*

trouser press [ˈtraʊzə-] *n* Hosenpresse *f*

trousers [ˈtraʊzəz] *npl* Hose *f;* **short ~** kurze
Hose; **a pair of ~** eine Hose

trouser suit *(Brit) n* Hosenanzug *m*

trousseau [ˈtru:səʊ] *(pl* **trousseaux** *or* **~s***) n*
Aussteuer *f*

trout [traʊt] *n inv* Forelle *f*

trowel [ˈtraʊəl] *n (garden tool)* Pflanzkelle *f;
(builder's tool)* (Maurer)kelle *f*

truant [ˈtruːənt] *(Brit) n:* **to play ~** die Schule
schwänzen

truce [tru:s] *n* Waffenstillstand *m*

truck [trʌk] *n (lorry)* Lastwagen *m; (Rail)*
Güterwagen *m; (for luggage)* Gepäckwagen *m;*
to have no ~ with sb nichts mit jdm zu tun
haben

truck driver *n* Lkw-Fahrer(in) *m(f)*

trucker [ˈtrʌkəʳ] *(US) n* Lkw-Fahrer(in) *m(f)*

truck farm *(US) n* Gemüsefarm *f*

trucking [ˈtrʌkɪŋ] *(US) n* Transport *m*

trucking company *(US) n* Spedition *f*

truculent [ˈtrʌkjʊlənt] *adj* aufsässig

trudge [trʌdʒ] *vi (also:* **trudge along***)* sich
dahinschleppen

true [tru:] *adj* wahr; *(accurate)* genau; *(genuine)*
echt; *(faithful: friend)* treu; *(wall, beam)* gerade;
(circle) rund; **to come ~** wahr werden; **~ to life**
lebensecht

truffle [ˈtrʌfl] *n (fungus, sweet)* Trüffel *f*

truly [ˈtru:lɪ] *adv* wahrhaft, wirklich; *(truthfully)*
wirklich; **yours ~** *(in letter)* mit freundlichen
Grüßen

trump [trʌmp] *n (also:* **trump card***; also: fig)*
Trumpf *m;* **to turn up ~s** *(fig)* sich als Retter
in der Not erweisen

trumped-up *adj:* **a ~ charge** eine erfundene
Anschuldigung

trumpet [ˈtrʌmpɪt] *n* Trompete *f*

truncated [trʌŋˈkeɪtɪd] *adj (message, object)*
verstümmelt

truncheon [ˈtrʌntʃən] *(Brit) n* Gummiknüppel
m

trundle [ˈtrʌndl] *vt (trolley etc)* rollen *▷ vi:* **to
~ along** *(person)* dahinschlendern; *(vehicle)*
dahinrollen

trunk [trʌŋk] *n (of tree)* Stamm *m; (of person)*
Rumpf *m; (of elephant)* Rüssel *m; (case)*
Schrankkoffer *m; (US: Aut)* Kofferraum *m;*
trunks *npl (also:* **swimming trunks***)* Badehose *f*

trunk call *(Brit) n* Ferngespräch *nt*

trunk road *(Brit) n* Fernstraße *f*

truss [trʌs] *n (Med)* Bruchband *nt*
▶ **truss (up)** *vt (Culin)* dressieren; *(person)*
fesseln

trust [trʌst] *n* Vertrauen *nt; (Comm: for charity
etc)* Stiftung *f ▷ vt* vertrauen +*dat;* **to take sth**

t

835

etc) etw einfach glauben; **to be in**
uhänderisch verwaltet werden; **to ~**
pe) hoffen(, dass)
pany *n* Trust *m*
['trʌstɪd] *adj (friend, servant)* treu
[trʌs'tiː] *n (Law)* Treuhänder(in) *m(f)*;
ol etc) Aufsichtsratsmitglied *nt*
ul ['trʌstful] *adj* vertrauensvoll
.fund *n* Treuhandvermögen *nt*
ting ['trʌstɪŋ] *adj* vertrauensvoll
stworthy ['trʌstwəːðɪ] *adj (person)*
ertrauenswürdig
usty ['trʌstɪ] *adj* getreu
ruth [truːθ] *(pl* **~s)** *n:* **the ~** die Wahrheit *f*
truthful ['truːθful] *adj (person)* ehrlich; *(answer etc)* wahrheitsgemäß
truthfully ['truːθfəlɪ] *adv (answer)* wahrheitsgemäß
truthfulness ['truːθfəlnɪs] *n* Ehrlichkeit *f*
try [traɪ] *n (also Rugby)* Versuch *m* ▷ *vt (attempt)* versuchen; *(test)* probieren; *(Law)* vor Gericht stellen; *(strain: patience)* auf die Probe stellen ▷ *vi* es versuchen; **to have a ~** es versuchen, einen Versuch machen; **to ~ to do sth** versuchen, etw zu tun; **to ~ one's (very) best** or **hardest** sein Bestes versuchen *or* tun
▶ **try on** *vt (clothes)* anprobieren; **she's ~ing it on** *(fig)* sie probiert, wie weit sie gehen kann
▶ **try out** *vt* ausprobieren
trying ['traɪɪŋ] *adj (person)* schwierig; *(experience)* schwer
tsar [zɑːʳ] *n* Zar *m*
T-shirt ['tiːʃəːt] *n* T-Shirt *nt*
T-square ['tiːskweəʳ] *n (Tech)* Reißschiene *f*
TT *adj abbr (Brit: inf)* = **teetotal** ▷ *abbr* *(US: Post:* = *Trust Territories)* der US-Verwaltungshoheit unterstellte Gebiete
tub [tʌb] *n (container)* Kübel *m*; *(bath)* Wanne *f*
tuba ['tjuːbə] *n* Tuba *f*
tubby ['tʌbɪ] *adj* rundlich
tube [tjuːb] *n (pipe)* Rohr *nt*; *(container)* Tube *f*; *(Brit: underground)* U-Bahn *f*; *(US: inf):* **the ~** *(television)* die Röhre
tubeless ['tjuːblɪs] *adj (tyre)* schlauchlos
tuber ['tjuːbəʳ] *n (Bot)* Knolle *f*
tuberculosis [tjubəːkjuˈləusɪs] *n* Tuberkulose *f*
tube station *(Brit)* *n* U-Bahn-Station *f*
tubing ['tjuːbɪŋ] *n* Schlauch *m*; **a piece of ~** ein Schlauch
tubular ['tjuːbjuləʳ] *adj* röhrenförmig
TUC *(Brit)* *n abbr (= Trades Union Congress)* britischer Gewerkschafts-Dachverband
tuck [tʌk] *vt (put)* stecken ▷ *n (Sewing)* Biese *f*
▶ **tuck away** *vt (money)* wegstecken; **to be ~ed away** *(building)* versteckt liegen
▶ **tuck in** *vt (clothing)* feststecken; *(child)* zudecken ▷ *vi (eat)* zulangen
▶ **tuck up** *vt (invalid, child)* zudecken
tuck shop *n* Süßwarenladen *m*
Tue., Tues. *abbr (= Tuesday)* Di.
Tuesday ['tjuːzdɪ] *n* Dienstag *m*; **it is ~ 23rd March** heute ist Dienstag, der 23. März; **on ~** am Dienstag; **on ~s** dienstags; **every ~**

jeden Dienstag; **every other ~** jeden zweiten Dienstag; **last/next ~** letzten/nächsten Dienstag; **the following ~** am Dienstag darauf; **~'s newspaper** die Zeitung von Dienstag; **a week/fortnight on ~** Dienstag in einer Woche/in vierzehn Tagen; **the ~ before last** der vorletzte Dienstag; **the ~ after next** der übernächste Dienstag; **~ morning/ lunchtime/afternoon/evening** Dienstag Morgen/Mittag/Nachmittag/Abend; **~ night** *(overnight)* Dienstag Nacht
tuft [tʌft] *n* Büschel *nt*
tug [tʌg] *n (ship)* Schlepper *m* ▷ *vt* zerren
tug of love *n* Tauziehen *nt (um das Sorgerecht für Kinder)*
tug-of-war [tʌgəvˈwɔːʳ] *n (also fig)* Tauziehen *nt*
tuition [tjuːˈɪʃən] *n (Brit)* Unterricht *m*; *(US: school fees)* Schulgeld *nt*
tulip ['tjuːlɪp] *n* Tulpe *f*
tumble ['tʌmbl] *n (fall)* Sturz *m* ▷ *vi (fall)* stürzen
▶ **tumble to** *(inf)* *vt fus* kapieren
tumbledown ['tʌmbldaun] *adj (building)* baufällig
tumble dryer *(Brit)* *n* Wäschetrockner *m*
tumbler ['tʌmbləʳ] *n (glass)* Trinkglas *nt*
tummy ['tʌmɪ] *(inf)* *n* Bauch *m*
tumour, *(US)* **tumor** ['tjuːməʳ] *n (Med)* Tumor *m*, Geschwulst *f*
tumult ['tjuːmʌlt] *n* Tumult *m*
tumultuous [tjuːˈmʌltjuəs] *adj (welcome, applause etc)* stürmisch
tuna ['tjuːnə] *n inv (also:* **tuna fish)** T(h)unfisch *m*
tune [tjuːn] *n (melody)* Melodie *f* ▷ *vt (Mus)* stimmen; *(Radio, TV, Aut)* einstellen; **to be in/out of ~** *(instrument)* richtig gestimmt/ verstimmt sein; *(singer)* richtig/falsch singen; **to be in/out of ~ with** *(fig)* in Einklang/nicht in Einklang stehen mit; **she was robbed to the ~ of 10,000 pounds** sie wurde um einen Betrag in Höhe von 10.000 Pfund beraubt
▶ **tune in** *vi (Radio, TV)* einschalten; **to ~ in to BBC1** BBC1 einschalten
▶ **tune up** *vi (Mus)* (das Instrument/die Instrumente) stimmen
tuneful ['tjuːnful] *adj* melodisch
tuner ['tjuːnəʳ] *n:* **piano ~** Klavierstimmer(in) *m(f)*; *(radio set)* Tuner *m*
tuner amplifier *n* Steuergerät *nt*
tungsten ['tʌŋstən] *n* Wolfram *nt*
tunic ['tjuːnɪk] *n* Hemdbluse *f*
tuning fork ['tjuːnɪŋ-] *n* Stimmgabel *f*
Tunis ['tjuːnɪs] *n* Tunis *nt*
Tunisia [tjuːˈnɪzɪə] *n* Tunesien *nt*
Tunisian [tjuːˈnɪzɪən] *adj* tunesisch ▷ *n (person)* Tunesier(in) *m(f)*
tunnel ['tʌnl] *n* Tunnel *m*; *(in mine)* Stollen *m* ▷ *vi* einen Tunnel bauen
tunnel vision *n (Med)* Gesichtsfeldeinengung *f*; *(fig)* Engstirnigkeit *f*
tunny ['tʌnɪ] *n* T(h)unfisch *m*
turban ['təːbən] *n* Turban *m*

turbid ['tə:bɪd] *adj* (*water*) trüb; (*air*) schmutzig

turbine ['tə:baɪn] *n* Turbine *f*

turbo ['tə:bəu] *n* Turbo *m*; **~ engine** Turbomotor *m*

turbojet [tə:bəu'dʒɛt] *n* Düsenflugzeug *nt*

turboprop [tə:bəu'prɔp] *n* (*engine*) Turbo-Prop-Turbine *f*

turbot ['tə:bət] *n inv* Steinbutt *m*

turbulence ['tə:bjuləns] *n* (*Aviat*) Turbulenz *f*

turbulent ['tə:bjulənt] *adj* (*water, seas*) stürmisch; (*fig: career, period*) turbulent

tureen [tə'ri:n] *n* Terrine *f*

turf [tə:f] *n* (*grass*) Rasen *m*; (*clod*) Sode *f* ▷ *vt* (*area*) mit Grassoden bedecken; **the T~** (*horseracing*) der Pferderennsport

▸ **turf out** (*inf*) *vt* (*person*) rausschmeißen

turf accountant (*Brit*) *n* Buchmacher *m*

turgid ['tə:dʒɪd] *adj* geschwollen

Turin ['tjuə'rɪn] *n* Turin *nt*

Turk [tə:k] *n* Türke *m*, Türkin *f*

Turkey ['tə:kɪ] *n* die Türkei *f*

turkey ['tə:kɪ] *n* (*bird*) Truthahn *m*, Truthenne *f*; (*meat*) Puter *m*

Turkish ['tə:kɪʃ] *adj* türkisch ▷ *n* (*Ling*) Türkisch *nt*

Turkish bath *n* türkisches Bad *nt*

Turkish delight *n* geleeartige Süßigkeit, mit Puderzucker oder Schokolade überzogen

turmeric ['tə:mərɪk] *n* Kurkuma *f*

turmoil ['tə:mɔɪl] *n* Aufruhr *m*; **in ~** in Aufruhr

turn [tə:n] *n* (*change*) Wende *f*; (*in road*) Kurve *f*; (*rotation*) Drehung *f*; (*performance*) Nummer *f*; (*inf, Med*) Anfall *m* ▷ *vt* (*handle, key*) drehen; (*collar, steak*) wenden; (*page*) umblättern; (*shape: wood*) drechseln; (: *metal*) drehen ▷ *vi* (*object*) sich drehen; (*person*) sich umdrehen; (*change direction*) abbiegen; (*milk*) sauer werden; **to do sb a good ~** jdm einen guten Dienst erweisen; **a ~ of events** eine Wendung der Dinge; **it gave me quite a ~** (*inf*) das hat mir einen schönen Schrecken eingejagt; **"no left ~"** (*Aut*) „Linksabbiegen verboten"; **it's your ~** du bist dran; **in ~** der Reihe nach; **to take ~s (at)** sich abwechseln (bei); **at the ~ of the century/year** zur Jahrhundertwende/Jahreswende; **to take a ~ for the worse** (*events*) sich zum Schlechten wenden; **his health** *or* **he has taken a ~ for the worse** sein Befinden hat sich verschlechtert; **to ~ nasty/forty/grey** unangenehm/vierzig/grau werden

▸ **turn against** *vt fus* sich wenden gegen

▸ **turn around** *vi* sich umdrehen; (*in car*) wenden

▸ **turn away** *vi* sich abwenden ▷ *vt* (*applicants*) abweisen; (*business*) zurückweisen

▸ **turn back** *vi* umkehren ▷ *vt* (*person, vehicle*) zurückweisen

▸ **turn down** *vt* (*request*) ablehnen; (*heating*) kleiner stellen; (*radio etc*) leiser stellen; (*bedclothes*) aufschlagen

▸ **turn in** *vi* (*inf: go to bed*) sich hinhauen ▷ *vt* (*to police*) anzeigen; **to ~ o.s. in** sich stellen

▸ **turn into** *vt fus* (*change*) sich verwandeln in +*acc* ▷ *vt* machen zu

▸ **turn off** *vi* (*from road*) abbiegen ▷ *vt* (*light, radio etc*) ausmachen; (*tap*) zudrehen; (*engine*) abstellen

▸ **turn on** *vt* (*light, radio etc*) anmachen; (*tap*) aufdrehen; (*engine*) anstellen

▸ **turn out** *vt* (*light*) ausmachen; (*gas*) abstellen ▷ *vi* (*appear, attend*) erscheinen; **to ~ out to be** (*prove to be*) sich erweisen als; **to ~ out well/badly** (*situation*) gut/schlecht enden

▸ **turn over** *vi* (*person*) sich umdrehen ▷ *vt* (*object*) umdrehen, wenden; (*page*) umblättern; **to ~ sth over to** (*to sb*) etw übertragen +*dat*; (*to sth*) etw verlagern zu

▸ **turn round** *vi* sich umdrehen; (*vehicle*) wenden

▸ **turn up** *vi* (*person*) erscheinen; (*lost object*) wieder auftauchen ▷ *vt* (*collar*) hochklappen; (*heater*) höher stellen; (*radio etc*) lauter stellen

turnabout ['tə:nəbaut] *n* (*fig*) Kehrtwendung *f*

turnaround ['tə:nəraund] *n* = **turnabout**

turncoat ['tə:nkəut] *n* Überläufer(in) *m(f)*

turned-up ['tə:ndʌp] *adj*: **~ nose** Stupsnase *f*

turning ['tə:nɪŋ] *n* (*in road*) Abzweigung *f*; **the first ~ on the right** die erste Straße rechts

turning circle (*Brit*) *n* (*Aut*) Wendekreis *m*

turning point *n* (*fig*) Wendepunkt *m*

turning radius (*US*) *n* = **turning circle**

turnip ['tə:nɪp] *n* Rübe *f*

turnout ['tə:naut] *n* (*of voters etc*) Beteiligung *f*

turnover ['tə:nəuvə'] *n* (*Comm: amount of money*) Umsatz *m*; (: *of staff*) Fluktuation *f*; (*Culin*): **apple ~** Apfeltasche *f*; **there is a rapid ~ in staff** der Personalbestand wechselt ständig

turnpike ['tə:npaɪk] (*US*) *n* gebührenpflichtige Autobahn *f*

turnstile ['tə:nstaɪl] *n* Drehkreuz *nt*

turntable ['tə:nteɪbl] *n* (*on record player*) Plattenteller *m*

turn-up ['tə:nʌp] (*Brit*) *n* (*on trousers*) Aufschlag *m*; **that's a ~ for the books!** (*inf*) das ist eine echte Überraschung!

turpentine ['tə:pəntaɪn] *n* (*also:* **turps**) Terpentin *nt*

turquoise ['tə:kwɔɪz] *n* (*stone*) Türkis *m* ▷ *adj* (*colour*) türkis

turret ['tʌrɪt] *n* Turm *m*

turtle ['tə:tl] *n* Schildkröte *f*

turtleneck ['tə:tlnɛk], **turtleneck sweater** *n* Pullover *m* mit rundem Kragen

Tuscan ['tʌskən] *adj* toskanisch ▷ *n* (*person*) Toskaner(in) *m(f)*

Tuscany ['tʌskənɪ] *n* die Toskana

tusk [tʌsk] *n* (*of elephant*) Stoßzahn *m*

tussle ['tʌsl] *n* Gerangel *nt*

tutor ['tju:tə'] *n* Tutor(in) *m(f)*; (*private tutor*) Privatlehrer(in) *m(f)*

tutorial [tju:'tɔ:rɪəl] *n* Kolloquium *nt*

tuxedo [tʌk'si:dəu] (*US*) *n* Smoking *m*

TV [ti:'vi:] *n abbr* (= *television*) TV *nt*

TV dinner *n* Fertiggericht *nt*

t

l] (inf) n dummes Zeug nt
n (of instrument) singender
:e) näselnder Ton m ▷ vi einen
on von sich geben ▷ vt (guitar)

k] vt kneifen
:d] n Tweed m
'twi:zəz] npl Pinzette f
welfθ] num zwölfte(r, s) ▷ n Zwölftel

Night n = Dreikönige nt
twelv] num zwölf; **at ~ (o'clock)**
) um zwölf Uhr (mittags); (midnight) um
Uhr nachts
eth ['twentıθ] num zwanzigste(r, s)
y ['twenti] num zwanzig
ty-four seven ['twentıfɔː'sevn] n (store)
:häft, das an sieben Tagen die Woche und
itunden am Tag geöffnet hat ▷ adj rund um
Uhr; ~ **service** Service, der rund um die
r zur Verfügung steht
erp [twəːp] (inf) n Schwachkopf m
Jice [twaıs] adv zweimal; ~ **as much**
zweimal so viel; ~ **a week** zweimal die Woche;
she is ~ your age sie ist doppelt so alt wie du
:widdle ['twıdl] vt drehen an +dat ▷ vi: **to ~
(with)** herumdrehen (an +dat); **to ~ one's
thumbs** (fig) Däumchen drehen

twig [twıg] n Zweig m ▷ vi, vt (Brit: inf: realize)
kapieren
twilight ['twaılaıt] n Dämmerung f; **in the ~**
in der Dämmerung
twill [twıl] n (cloth) Köper m
twin [twın] adj (sister, brother) Zwillings-;
(towers) Doppel- ▷ n Zwilling m; (room in hotel
etc) Zweibettzimmer nt ▷ vt (towns etc): **to be
~ned with ... ...** als Partnerstadt haben
twin-bedded room ['twın'bedıd-] n
Zweibettzimmer nt
twin beds npl zwei (gleiche) Einzelbetten pl
twin-carburettor ['twınkɑ:bju'retər] adj
Doppelvergaser-
twine [twaın] n Bindfaden m ▷ vi sich winden
twin-engined [twın'endʒınd] adj zweimotorig
twinge [twındʒ] n (of pain) Stechen nt; **a ~ of
conscience** Gewissensbisse pl; **a ~ of fear/
guilt** ein Angst-/Schuldgefühl nt
twinkle ['twıŋkl] vi funkeln ▷ n Funkeln nt
twin town n Partnerstadt f
twirl [twəːl] vt herumwirbeln ▷ vi wirbeln ▷ n
Wirbel m
twist [twıst] n (action) Drehung f; (in road)
Kurve; (in coil, flex) Biegung f; (in story)
Wendung f ▷ vt (turn) drehen; (injure: ankle etc)
verrenken; (twine) wickeln; (fig: meaning etc)
verdrehen ▷ vi (road, river) sich winden; ~ **my
arm!** (inf) überreden Sie mich einfach!
twisted ['twıstıd] adj (wire, rope) gedreht; (ankle)
verrenkt; (fig: logic, mind) verdreht
twit [twıt] (inf) n Trottel m
twitch [twıtʃ] n (jerky movement) Zucken nt ▷ vi
zucken
Twitter® ['twıtər] n Twitter nt ▷ vi twittern

two [tuː] num zwei; ~ **by** ~, **in ~s** zu zweit; **to
put ~ and ~ together** (fig) zwei und zwei
zusammenzählen
two-bit [tuː'bıt] (inf) adj (worthless) mies
two-door [tuː'dɔːʳ] adj zweitürig
two-faced [tuː'feıst] (pej) adj scheinheilig
twofold ['tuːfəuld] adv: **to increase** ~ um das
Doppelte ansteigen ▷ adj (increase) um das
Doppelte; (aim, value etc) zweifach
two-piece ['tuːpiːs] n (also: **two-piece suit**)
Zweiteiler m; (also: **two-piece swimsuit**)
zweiteiliger Badeanzug m
two-ply ['tuːplaı] adj (wool) zweifädig; (tissues)
zweilagig
two-seater ['tuː'siːtəʳ] n (car) Zweisitzer m
twosome ['tuːsəm] n (people) Paar nt
two-stroke ['tuːstrəuk] n (also: **two-stroke
engine**) Zweitakter m ▷ adj (engine) Zweitakt-
two-tone ['tuː'təun] adj (in colour) zweifarbig
two-way ['tuːweı] adj: ~ **traffic** Verkehr m in
beiden Richtungen; ~ **radio** Funksprechgerät
nt
TX (US) abbr (Post) = Texas
tycoon [taı'kuːn] n Magnat m
type [taıp] n (category, model, example) Typ m;
(Typ) Schrift f ▷ vt (letter etc) tippen, (mit der)
Maschine schreiben; **a ~ of** eine Art von;
what ~ do you want? welche Sorte möchten
Sie?; **in bold/italic ~** in Fett-/Kursivdruck
typecast ['taıpkɑːst] (irreg: like **cast**) vt (actor)
(auf eine Rolle) festlegen
typeface ['taıpfeıs] n Schrift f, Schriftbild nt
typescript ['taıpskrıpt] n
(maschinengeschriebenes) Manuskript nt
typeset ['taıpset] (irreg: like **set**) vt setzen
typesetter ['taıpsetəʳ] n Setzer(in) m(f)
typewriter ['taıpraıtəʳ] n Schreibmaschine f
typewritten ['taıprıtn] adj maschine(n)
geschrieben
typhoid ['taıfɔıd] n Typhus m
typhoon [taı'fuːn] n Taifun m
typhus ['taıfəs] n Fleckfieber nt
typical ['tıpıkl] adj typisch; ~ **(of)** typisch (für);
that's ~! das ist typisch!
typify ['tıpıfaı] vt typisch sein für
typing ['taıpıŋ] n Maschine(n)schreiben nt
typing error n Tippfehler m
typing pool n Schreibzentrale f
typist ['taıpıst] n Schreibkraft f
typo ['taıpəu] (inf) n abbr (= typographical error)
Druckfehler m
typography [tı'pɔgrəfı] n Typografie f
tyranny ['tırənı] n Tyrannei f
tyrant ['taıərnt] n Tyrann(in) m(f)
tyre, (US) **tire** ['taıəʳ] n Reifen m
tyre pressure n Reifendruck m
Tyrol [tı'rəul] n Tirol nt
Tyrolean [tırə'liːən] adj Tiroler ▷ n (person)
Tiroler(in) m(f)
Tyrolese [tırə'liːz] = **Tyrolean**
Tyrrhenian Sea [tı'riːnıən-] n: **the ~** das
Tyrrhenische Meer
tzar [zɑːʳ] n = **tsar**

Uu

U¹, u [juː] *n (letter)* U *nt*, u *nt*; **U for Uncle** = U wie Ulrich

U² [juː] *(Brit) n abbr (Cine: = universal)* Klassifikation für jugendfreie Filme

UAW *(US) n abbr (= United Automobile Workers)* Automobilarbeitergewerkschaft

UB40 *(Brit) n abbr (= unemployment benefit form 40)* Arbeitslosenausweis *m*

U-bend ['juːbɛnd] *n (in pipe)* U-Krümmung *f*

ubiquitous [juːˈbɪkwɪtəs] *adj* allgegenwärtig

UCCA ['ʌkə] *(Brit) n abbr (= Universities Central Council on Admissions)* akademische Zulassungsstelle, = ZVS *f*

UDA *(Brit) n abbr (= Ulster Defence Association)* paramilitärische protestantische Organisation in Nordirland

UDC *(Brit) n abbr (= Urban District Council)* Stadtverwaltung *f*

udder ['ʌdəʳ] *n* Euter *nt*

UDI *(Brit) n abbr (Pol: = unilateral declaration of independence)* einseitige Unabhängigkeitserklärung *f*

UDR *(Brit) n abbr (= Ulster Defence Regiment)* Regiment aus Teilzeitsoldaten zur Unterstützung der britischen Armee und Polizei in Nordirland

UEFA [juːˈeɪfə] *n abbr (= Union of European Football Associations)* UEFA *f*

UFO ['juːfəʊ] *n abbr (= unidentified flying object)* UFO *nt*

Uganda [juːˈɡændə] *n* Uganda *nt*

Ugandan [juːˈɡændən] *adj* ugandisch ▷ *n* Ugander(in) *m(f)*

UGC *(Brit) n abbr (= University Grants Committee)* Ausschuss zur Verteilung von Geldern an Universitäten

ugh [əːh] *excl* igitt

ugliness ['ʌɡlɪnɪs] *n* Hässlichkeit *f*

ugly ['ʌɡlɪ] *adj* hässlich; *(nasty)* schlimm

UHF *abbr (= ultrahigh frequency)* UHF

UHT *abbr (= ultra heat treated):* ~ **milk** H-Milch *f*

UK *n abbr* = **United Kingdom**

Ukraine [juːˈkreɪn] *n* Ukraine *f*

Ukrainian [juːˈkreɪnɪən] *adj* ukrainisch ▷ *n* Ukrainer(in) *m(f)*; *(Ling)* Ukrainisch *nt*

ulcer ['ʌlsəʳ] *n (stomach ulcer etc)* Geschwür *nt*; *(also:* **mouth ulcer)** Abszess *m* im Mund

Ulster ['ʌlstəʳ] *n* Ulster *nt*

ulterior [ʌlˈtɪərɪəʳ] *adj:* ~ **motive** Hintergedanke *m*

ultimata [ʌltɪˈmeɪtə] *npl of* **ultimatum**

ultimate ['ʌltɪmət] *adj (final)* letztendlich; *(greatest)* größte(r, s); *(: deterrent)* äußerste(r, s); *(: authority)* höchste(r, s) ▷ *n:* **the ~ in luxury** das Äußerste or Höchste an Luxus

ultimately ['ʌltɪmətlɪ] *adv (in the end)* schließlich, letzten Endes; *(basically)* im Grunde (genommen)

ultimatum [ʌltɪˈmeɪtəm] *(pl* ~**s** *or* **ultimata)** *n* Ultimatum *nt*

ultrasonic [ʌltrəˈsɒnɪk] *adj (sound)* Ultraschall-

ultrasound ['ʌltrəsaʊnd] *n* Ultraschall *m*

ultraviolet ['ʌltrəˈvaɪəlɪt] *adj* ultraviolett

umbilical cord [ʌmˈbɪlɪkl-] *n* Nabelschnur *f*

umbrage ['ʌmbrɪdʒ] *n:* **to take ~ at** Anstoß nehmen an +*dat*

umbrella [ʌmˈbrɛlə] *n (for rain)* (Regen)schirm *m*; *(for sun)* Sonnenschirm *m*; *(fig):* **under the ~ of** unter der Leitung von

umlaut ['umlaut] *n* Umlaut *m*; *(mark)* Umlautzeichen *nt*

umpire ['ʌmpaɪəʳ] *n* Schiedsrichter(in) *m(f)* ▷ *vt (game)* als Schiedsrichter leiten

umpteen [ʌmpˈtiːn] *adj* zig

umpteenth [ʌmpˈtiːnθ] *adj:* **for the ~ time** zum x-ten Mal

UMWA *n abbr (= United Mineworkers of America)* amerikanische Bergarbeitergewerkschaft

UN *n abbr (= United Nations)* UNO *f*

unabashed [ʌnəˈbæʃt] *adj:* **to be/seem ~** unbeeindruckt sein/scheinen

unabated [ʌnəˈbeɪtɪd] *adj* unvermindert ▷ *adv:* **to continue ~** nicht nachlassen

unable [ʌnˈeɪbl] *adj:* **to be ~ to do sth** etw nicht tun können

unabridged [ʌnəˈbrɪdʒd] *adj* ungekürzt

unacceptable [ʌnəkˈsɛptəbl] *adj* unannehmbar, nicht akzeptabel

unaccompanied [ʌnəˈkʌmpənɪd] *adj (child, song)* ohne Begleitung; *(luggage)* unbegleitet

unaccountably [ʌnəˈkaʊntəblɪ] *adv* unerklärlich

unaccounted [ʌnəˈkaʊntɪd] *adj:* **to be ~ for** *(passengers, money etc)* (noch) fehlen

unaccustomed [ʌnəˈkʌstəmd] *adj:* **to be ~ to** nicht gewöhnt sein an +*acc*

unacquainted [ʌnəˈkweɪntɪd] *adj:* **to be ~ with** nicht vertraut sein mit

u

unadulterated [ʌnə'dʌltəreɪtɪd] adj rein
unaffected [ʌnə'fɛktɪd] adj (person, behaviour) natürlich, ungekünstelt; **to be ~ by sth** von etw nicht berührt werden
unafraid [ʌnə'freɪd] adj: **to be ~** keine Angst haben
unaided [ʌn'eɪdɪd] adv ohne fremde Hilfe
unanimity [juːnə'nɪmɪtɪ] n Einstimmigkeit f
unanimous [juː'nænɪməs] adj einstimmig
unanimously [juː'nænɪməslɪ] adv einstimmig
unanswered [ʌn'ɑːnsəd] adj unbeantwortet
unappetizing [ʌn'æpɪtaɪzɪŋ] adj (food) unappetitlich
unappreciative [ʌnə'priːʃɪətɪv] adj (person) undankbar; (audience) verständnislos
unarmed [ʌn'ɑːmd] adj unbewaffnet; **~ combat** Nahkampf m ohne Waffen
unashamed [ʌnə'ʃeɪmd] adj (pleasure, greed etc) unverhohlen
unassisted [ʌnə'sɪstɪd] adv ohne fremde Hilfe
unassuming [ʌnə'sjuːmɪŋ] adj bescheiden
unattached [ʌnə'tætʃt] adj (single: person) ungebunden; (unconnected) ohne Verbindung
unattended [ʌnə'tɛndɪd] adj (car, luggage, child) unbeaufsichtigt
unattractive [ʌnə'træktɪv] adj unattraktiv
unauthorized [ʌn'ɔːθəraɪzd] adj (visit, use) unbefugt; (version) nicht unautorisiert
unavailable [ʌnə'veɪləbl] adj (article, room) nicht verfügbar; (person) nicht zu erreichen; **~ for comment** nicht zu sprechen
unavoidable [ʌnə'vɔɪdəbl] adj unvermeidlich
unavoidably [ʌnə'vɔɪdəblɪ] adv (delayed etc) auf unvermeidliche Weise
unaware [ʌnə'wɛəʳ] adj: **he was ~ of it** er war sich dat dessen nicht bewusst
unawares [ʌnə'wɛəz] adv (catch, take) unerwartet
unbalanced [ʌn'bælənst] adj (report) unausgewogen; **(mentally) ~** geistig gestört
unbearable [ʌn'bɛərəbl] adj unerträglich
unbeatable [ʌn'biːtəbl] adj unschlagbar
unbeaten [ʌn'biːtn] adj ungeschlagen
unbecoming [ʌnbɪ'kʌmɪŋ] adj (language, behaviour) unpassend; (garment) unvorteilhaft
unbeknown [ʌnbɪ'nəʊn], **unbeknownst** [ʌnbɪ'nəʊnst] adv: **~(st) to me/Peter** ohne mein/Peters Wissen
unbelief [ʌnbɪ'liːf] n Ungläubigkeit f
unbelievable [ʌnbɪ'liːvəbl] adj unglaublich
unbelievably [ʌnbɪ'liːvəblɪ] adv unglaublich
unbend [ʌn'bɛnd] (irreg: like **bend**) vi (relax) aus sich herausgehen ▷ vt (wire etc) gerade biegen
unbending [ʌn'bɛndɪŋ] adj (person, attitude) unnachgiebig
unbiased, unbiassed [ʌn'baɪəst] adj unvoreingenommen
unblemished [ʌn'blɛmɪʃt] adj (also fig) makellos
unblock [ʌn'blɒk] vt (pipe) frei machen
unborn [ʌn'bɔːn] adj ungeboren
unbounded [ʌn'baʊndɪd] adj grenzenlos
unbreakable [ʌn'breɪkəbl] adj (object) unzerbrechlich

unbridled [ʌn'braɪdld] adj ungezügelt
unbroken [ʌn'brəʊkən] adj (seal) unversehrt; (silence) ununterbrochen; (record, series) ungebrochen
unbuckle [ʌn'bʌkl] vt aufschnallen
unburden [ʌn'bəːdn] vt: **to ~ o.s. (to sb)** (jdm) sein Herz ausschütten
unbusinesslike [ʌn'bɪznɪslaɪk] adj ungeschäftsmäßig
unbutton [ʌn'bʌtn] vt aufknöpfen
uncalled-for [ʌn'kɔːldfɔːʳ] adj (remark etc) unnötig
uncanny [ʌn'kænɪ] adj unheimlich
unceasing [ʌn'siːsɪŋ] adj (search, flow etc) unaufhörlich; (loyalty) unermüdlich
unceremonious [ʌnsɛrɪ'məʊnɪəs] adj (abrupt, rude) brüsk, barsch
uncertain [ʌn'səːtn] adj (person) unsicher; (future, outcome) ungewiss; **to be ~ about sth** unsicher über etw acc sein; **in no ~ terms** unzweideutig
uncertainty [ʌn'səːtntɪ] n Ungewissheit f; **uncertainties** npl (doubts) Unsicherheiten pl
unchallenged [ʌn'tʃælɪndʒd] adj unbestritten ▷ adv (walk, enter) ungehindert; **to go ~** unangefochten bleiben
unchanged [ʌn'tʃeɪndʒd] adj unverändert
uncharitable [ʌn'tʃærɪtəbl] adj (remark, behaviour etc) unfreundlich
uncharted [ʌn'tʃɑːtɪd] adj (land, sea) unverzeichnet
unchecked [ʌn'tʃɛkt] adv (grow, continue) ungehindert
uncivil [ʌn'sɪvɪl] adj (person) grob
uncivilized [ʌn'sɪvɪlaɪzd] adj unzivilisiert
uncle ['ʌŋkl] n Onkel m
unclear [ʌn'klɪəʳ] adj unklar; **I'm still ~ about what I'm supposed to do** mir ist immer noch nicht klar, was ich tun soll
uncoil [ʌn'kɔɪl] vt (rope, wire) abwickeln ▷ vi (snake) sich strecken
uncomfortable [ʌn'kʌmfətəbl] adj (person, chair) unbequem; (room) ungemütlich; (nervous) unbehaglich; (unpleasant: situation, fact) unerfreulich
uncomfortably [ʌn'kʌmfətəblɪ] adv (sit) unbequem; (smile) unbehaglich
uncommitted [ʌnkə'mɪtɪd] adj nicht engagiert; **~ to** nicht festgelegt auf +acc
uncommon [ʌn'kɒmən] adj ungewöhnlich
uncommunicative [ʌnkə'mjuːnɪkətɪv] adj (person) schweigsam
uncomplicated [ʌn'kɒmplɪkeɪtɪd] adj unkompliziert
uncompromising [ʌn'kɒmprəmaɪzɪŋ] adj (person, belief) kompromisslos
unconcerned [ʌnkən'səːnd] adj (person) unbekümmert; **to be ~ about sth** sich nicht um etw kümmern
unconditional [ʌnkən'dɪʃənl] adj bedingungslos; (acceptance) vorbehaltlos
uncongenial [ʌnkən'dʒiːnɪəl] adj (surroundings) unangenehm

unconnected [ʌnkə'nɛktɪd] *adj (unrelated)* ohne Verbindung; **to be ~ with sth** nicht mit etw in Beziehung stehen

unconscious [ʌn'kɒnʃəs] *adj (in faint)* bewusstlos; *(unaware)*: **~ of** nicht bewusst *+gen* ▷ *n*: **the ~** das Unbewusste; **to knock sb ~** jdn bewusstlos schlagen

unconsciously [ʌn'kɒnʃəslɪ] *adv* unbewusst

unconsciousness [ʌn'kɒnʃəsnɪs] *n* Bewusstlosigkeit *f*

unconstitutional ['ʌnkɒnstɪ'tjuːʃənl] *adj* verfassungswidrig

uncontested [ʌnkən'tɛstɪd] *adj (Pol: seat, election)* ohne Gegenkandidat; *(divorce)* ohne Einwände der Gegenseite

uncontrollable [ʌnkən'trəʊləbl] *adj* unkontrollierbar; *(laughter)* unbändig

uncontrolled [ʌnkən'trəʊld] *adj (behaviour)* ungezähmt; *(price rises etc)* ungehindert

unconventional [ʌnkən'vɛnʃənl] *adj* unkonventionell

unconvinced [ʌnkən'vɪnst] *adj*: **to be/remain ~** nicht überzeugt sein/bleiben

unconvincing [ʌnkən'vɪnsɪŋ] *adj* nicht überzeugend

uncork [ʌn'kɔːk] *vt (bottle)* entkorken

uncorroborated [ʌnkə'rɒbəreɪtɪd] *adj (evidence)* unbestätigt

uncouth [ʌn'kuːθ] *adj (person, behaviour)* ungehobelt

uncover [ʌn'kʌvəʳ] *vt* aufdecken

unctuous ['ʌŋktjʊəs] *(form) adj (person, behaviour)* salbungsvoll

undamaged [ʌn'dæmɪdʒd] *adj* unbeschädigt

undaunted [ʌn'dɔːntɪd] *adj (person)* unverzagt; **~, she struggled on** sie kämpfte unverzagt weiter

undecided [ʌndɪ'saɪdɪd] *adj (person)* unentschlossen; *(question)* unentschieden

undelivered [ʌndɪ'lɪvəd] *adj (goods)* nicht geliefert; *(letters)* nicht zugestellt; **if ~ return to sender** *(on envelope)* falls unzustellbar, zurück an Absender

undeniable [ʌndɪ'naɪəbl] *adj* unbestreitbar

undeniably [ʌndɪ'naɪəblɪ] *adv (true)* zweifellos; *(handsome)* unbestreitbar

under ['ʌndəʳ] *prep (position)* unter *+dat*; *(motion)* unter *+acc*; *(according to: law etc)* nach, gemäß *+dat* ▷ *adv (go, fly etc)* darunter; **to come from ~ sth** unter etw *dat* hervorkommen; **~ there** darunter; **in ~ 2 hours** in weniger als 2 Stunden; **~ anaesthetic** unter Narkose; **to be ~ discussion** diskutiert werden; **~ repair** in Reparatur; **~ the circumstances** unter den Umständen

under ... ['ʌndəʳ] *pref* Unter-, unter-

underage [ʌndər'eɪdʒ] *adj (person)* minderjährig; **~ drinking** Alkoholgenuss *m* von Minderjährigen

underarm ['ʌndərɑːm] *adv (bowl, throw)* von unten ▷ *adj (throw, shot)* von unten; *(deodorant)* Achselhöhlen-

undercapitalized ['ʌndə'kæpɪtəlaɪzd] *adj* unterkapitalisiert

undercarriage ['ʌndəkærɪdʒ] *n (Aviat)* Fahrgestell *nt*

undercharge [ʌndə'tʃɑːdʒ] *vt* zu wenig berechnen *+dat*

underclass ['ʌndəklɑːs] *n* Unterklasse *f*

underclothes ['ʌndəkləʊðz] *npl* Unterwäsche *f*

undercoat ['ʌndəkəʊt] *n (paint)* Grundierung *f*

undercover [ʌndə'kʌvəʳ] *adj (duty, agent)* Geheim- ▷ *adv (work)* insgeheim

undercurrent ['ʌndəkʌrnt] *n (also fig)* Unterströmung *f*

undercut [ʌndə'kʌt] *(irreg: like **cut**) vt (person, prices)* unterbieten

underdeveloped ['ʌndədɪ'vɛləpt] *adj* unterentwickelt

underdog ['ʌndədɒg] *n*: **the ~** der/die Benachteiligte

underdone [ʌndə'dʌn] *adj (food)* nicht gar; *(: meat)* nicht durchgebraten

underemployment ['ʌndərɪm'plɔɪmənt] *n* Unterbeschäftigung *f*

underestimate ['ʌndər'ɛstɪmeɪt] *vt* unterschätzen

underexposed ['ʌndərɪks'pəʊzd] *adj (Phot)* unterbelichtet

underfed [ʌndə'fɛd] *adj* unterernährt

underfoot [ʌndə'fut] *adv*: **to crush sth ~** etw am Boden zerdrücken; **to trample sth ~** auf etw *dat* herumtrampeln

underfunded ['ʌndə'fʌndɪd] *adj* unterfinanziert

undergo [ʌndə'gəʊ] *(irreg: like **go**) vt (change)* durchmachen; *(test, operation)* sich unterziehen; **the car is ~ing repairs** das Auto wird gerade repariert

undergraduate [ʌndə'grædjuɪt] *n* Student(in) *m(f)* ▷ *cpd*: **~ courses** Kurse *pl* für nicht graduierte Studenten

underground ['ʌndəgraund] *adj* unterirdisch; *(Pol: newspaper, activities)* Untergrund- ▷ *adv (work)* unterirdisch; *(: miners)* unter Tage; *(Pol)*: **to go ~** untertauchen ▷ *n*: **the ~** *(Brit)* die U-Bahn; *(Pol)* die Untergrundbewegung; **~ car park** Tiefgarage *f*

undergrowth ['ʌndəgrəʊθ] *n* Unterholz *nt*

underhand [ʌndə'hænd], **underhanded** [ʌndə'hændɪd] *adj (fig: behaviour, person)* hinterhältig

underinsured [ʌndərɪn'ʃuəd] *adj* unterversichert

underlay [ʌndə'leɪ] *n* Unterlage *f*

underlie [ʌndə'laɪ] *(irreg: like **lie**) vt (fig: be basis of)* zugrunde liegen *+dat*; **the underlying cause** der eigentliche Grund

underline [ʌndə'laɪn] *vt* unterstreichen; *(fig: emphasize)* betonen

underling ['ʌndəlɪŋ] *(pej) n* Befehlsempfänger(in) *m(f)*

undermanning [ʌndə'mænɪŋ] *n* Personalmangel *m*

undermentioned [ʌndə'mɛnʃənd] *adj* unten genannt

u

841

undermine [ʌndə'maɪn] *vt* unterminieren, unterhöhlen

underneath [ʌndə'niːθ] *adv* darunter ▷ *prep* (*position*) unter +*dat*; (*motion*) unter +*acc*

undernourished [ʌndə'nʌrɪʃt] *adj* unterernährt

underpaid [ʌndə'peɪd] *adj* unterbezahlt

underpants ['ʌndəpænts] *npl* Unterhose *f*

underpass ['ʌndəpɑːs] (*Brit*) *n* Unterführung *f*

underpin [ʌndə'pɪn] *vt* (*argument*) untermauern

underplay [ʌndə'pleɪ] (*Brit*) *vt* herunterspielen

underpopulated [ʌndə'pɒpjuleɪtɪd] *adj* unterbevölkert

underprice [ʌndə'praɪs] *vt* (*goods*) zu billig anbieten

underprivileged [ʌndə'prɪvɪlɪdʒd] *adj* unterprivilegiert

underrate [ʌndə'reɪt] *vt* unterschätzen

underscore [ʌndə'skɔːr] *vt* unterstreichen

underseal [ʌndə'siːl] (*Brit*) *vt* (*car*) mit Unterbodenschutz versehen ▷ *n* (*of car*) Unterbodenschutz *m*

undersecretary ['ʌndə'sɛkrətərɪ] *n* (*Pol*) Staatssekretär(in) *m(f)*

undersell [ʌndə'sɛl] (*irreg: like* **sell**) *vt* (*competitors*) unterbieten

undershirt ['ʌndəʃəːt] (*US*) *n* Unterhemd *nt*

undershorts ['ʌndəʃɔːts] (*US*) *npl* Unterhose *f*

underside ['ʌndəsaɪd] *n* Unterseite *f*

undersigned ['ʌndəsaɪnd] *adj* unterzeichnet ▷ *n*: **the ~** der/die Unterzeichnete; **we the ~ agree that …** wir, die Unterzeichneten, kommen überein, dass …

underskirt ['ʌndəskəːt] (*Brit*) *n* Unterrock *m*

understaffed [ʌndə'stɑːft] *adj* unterbesetzt

understand [ʌndə'stænd] (*irreg: like* **stand**) *vt, vi* verstehen; **I ~ (that) you have …** (*believe*) soweit ich weiß, haben Sie …; **to make o.s. understood** sich verständlich machen

understandable [ʌndə'stændəbl] *adj* verständlich

understanding [ʌndə'stændɪŋ] *adj* verständnisvoll ▷ *n* Verständnis *nt*; **to come to an ~ with sb** mit jdm übereinkommen; **on the ~ that …** unter der Voraussetzung, dass …

understate [ʌndə'steɪt] *vt* herunterspielen

understatement ['ʌndəsteɪtmənt] *n* Understatement *nt*, Untertreibung *f*; **that's an ~!** das ist untertrieben!

understood [ʌndə'stud] *pt, pp of* **understand** ▷ *adj* (*agreed*) abgemacht; (*implied*) impliziert

understudy ['ʌndəstʌdɪ] *n* zweite Besetzung *f*

undertake [ʌndə'teɪk] (*irreg: like* **take**) *vt* (*task*) übernehmen ▷ *vi*: **to ~ to do sth** es übernehmen, etw zu tun

undertaker ['ʌndəteɪkər] *n* (Leichen)bestatter *m*

undertaking ['ʌndəteɪkɪŋ] *n* (*job*) Unternehmen *nt*; (*promise*) Zusicherung *f*

undertone ['ʌndətəun] *n* (*of criticism etc*) Unterton *m*; **in an ~** mit gedämpfter Stimme

undervalue [ʌndə'væljuː] *vt* (*person, work etc*) unterbewerten

underwater ['ʌndə'wɔːtər] *adv* (*swim etc*) unter Wasser ▷ *adj* (*exploration, camera etc*) Unterwasser-

underwear ['ʌndəwɛər] *n* Unterwäsche *f*

underweight [ʌndə'weɪt] *adj*: **to be ~** Untergewicht haben

underworld ['ʌndəwəːld] *n* Unterwelt *f*

underwrite [ʌndə'raɪt] *vt* (*Fin*) garantieren; (*Insurance*) versichern

underwriter ['ʌndəraɪtər] *n* (*Insurance*) Versicherer(in) *m(f)*

undeserved [ʌndɪ'zəːvd] *adj* unverdient

undesirable [ʌndɪ'zaɪərəbl] *adj* unerwünscht

undeveloped [ʌndɪ'vɛləpt] *adj* (*land*) unentwickelt; (*resources*) ungenutzt

undies ['ʌndɪz] (*inf*) *npl* Unterwäsche *f*

undiluted ['ʌndaɪ'luːtɪd] *adj* (*substance*) unverdünnt; (*emotion*) unverfälscht

undiplomatic ['ʌndɪplə'mætɪk] *adj* undiplomatisch

undischarged ['ʌndɪs'tʃɑːdʒd] *adj*: **~ bankrupt** nicht entlasteter Konkursschuldner *m*, nicht entlastete Konkursschuldnerin *f*

undisciplined [ʌn'dɪsɪplɪnd] *adj* undiszipliniert

undiscovered ['ʌndɪs'kʌvəd] *adj* unentdeckt

undisguised ['ʌndɪs'gaɪzd] *adj* (*dislike, amusement etc*) unverhohlen

undisputed ['ʌndɪs'pjuːtɪd] *adj* unbestritten

undistinguished ['ʌndɪs'tɪŋgwɪʃt] *adj* (*career, person*) mittelmäßig; (*appearance*) durchschnittlich

undisturbed [ʌndɪs'təːbd] *adj* ungestört; **to leave sth ~** etw unberührt lassen

undivided [ʌndɪ'vaɪdɪd] *adj*: **you have my ~ attention** Sie haben meine ungeteilte Aufmerksamkeit

undo [ʌn'duː] (*irreg: like* **do**) *vt* (*unfasten*) aufmachen; (*spoil*) zunichtemachen

undoing [ʌn'duːɪŋ] *n* Verderben *nt*

undone [ʌn'dʌn] *pp of* **undo** ▷ *adj*: **to come ~** (*shoelace etc*) aufgehen

undoubted [ʌn'dautɪd] *adj* unzweifelhaft

undoubtedly [ʌn'dautɪdlɪ] *adv* zweifellos

undress [ʌn'drɛs] *vi* sich ausziehen ▷ *vt* ausziehen

undrinkable [ʌn'drɪŋkəbl] *adj* (*unpalatable*) ungenießbar; (*poisonous*) nicht trinkbar

undue [ʌn'djuː] *adj* (*excessive*) übertrieben

undulating ['ʌndjuleɪtɪŋ] *adj* (*movement*) Wellen-; (*hills*) sanft

unduly [ʌn'djuːlɪ] *adv* (*excessively*) übermäßig

undying [ʌn'daɪɪŋ] *adj* (*love, loyalty etc*) ewig

unearned [ʌn'əːnd] *adj* (*praise*) unverdient; **~ income** Kapitaleinkommen *nt*

unearth [ʌn'əːθ] *vt* (*skeleton etc*) ausgraben; (*fig: secrets etc*) ausfindig machen

unearthly [ʌn'əːθlɪ] *adj* (*eerie*) unheimlich; **at some ~ hour** zu nachtschlafender Zeit

unease [ʌn'iːz] *n* Unbehagen *nt*

uneasy [ʌn'iːzɪ] *adj* (*person*) unruhig; (*feeling*) unbehaglich; (*peace, truce*) unsicher; **to feel ~ about doing sth** ein ungutes Gefühl dabei haben, etw zu tun

uneconomic [ˈʌniːkəˈnɔmɪk] *adj*
unwirtschaftlich

uneconomical [ˈʌniːkəˈnɔmɪkl] *adj*
unwirtschaftlich

uneducated [ʌnˈedjukeɪtɪd] *adj* ungebildet

unemployed [ʌnɪmˈplɔɪd] *adj* arbeitslos
▷ *npl*: **the ~** die Arbeitslosen *pl*

unemployment [ʌnɪmˈplɔɪmənt] *n*
Arbeitslosigkeit *f*

unemployment benefit (*Brit*) *n*
Arbeitslosenunterstützung *f*

unemployment compensation (*US*) *n* =
unemployment benefit

unending [ʌnˈendɪŋ] *adj* endlos

unenviable [ʌnˈenvɪəbl] *adj* (*task, conditions etc*)
wenig beneidenswert

unequal [ʌnˈiːkwəl] *adj* ungleich; **to feel ~ to**
sich nicht gewachsen fühlen +*dat*

unequalled, (*US*) **unequaled** [ʌnˈiːkwəld] *adj*
unübertroffen

unequivocal [ʌnɪˈkwɪvəkl] *adj* (*answer*)
unzweideutig; **to be ~ about sth** eine klare
Haltung zu etw haben

unerring [ʌnˈəːrɪŋ] *adj* unfehlbar

UNESCO [juːˈneskəu] *n abbr* (= *United Nations
Educational, Scientific and Cultural Organization*)
UNESCO *f*

unethical [ʌnˈeθɪkl] *adj* (*methods*) unlauter;
(*doctor's behaviour*) unethisch

uneven [ʌnˈiːvn] *adj* (*teeth, road etc*) uneben;
(*performance*) ungleichmäßig

uneventful [ʌnɪˈventful] *adj* ereignislos

unexceptional [ʌnɪkˈsepʃənl] *adj*
durchschnittlich

unexciting [ʌnɪkˈsaɪtɪŋ] *adj* (*film, news*) wenig
aufregend

unexpected [ʌnɪksˈpektɪd] *adj* unerwartet

unexpectedly [ʌnɪksˈpektɪdlɪ] *adv* unerwartet

unexplained [ʌnɪksˈpleɪnd] *adj* (*mystery, failure*)
ungeklärt

unexploded [ʌnɪksˈpləudɪd] *adj* nicht
explodiert

unfailing [ʌnˈfeɪlɪŋ] *adj* (*support, energy*)
unerschöpflich

unfair [ʌnˈfeəʳ] *adj* unfair, ungerecht;
(*advantage*) ungerechtfertigt; **~ to** unfair *or*
ungerecht zu

unfair dismissal *n* ungerechtfertigte
Entlassung *f*

unfairly [ʌnˈfeəlɪ] *adv* (*treat*) unfair, ungerecht;
(*dismiss*) ungerechtfertigt

unfaithful [ʌnˈfeɪθful] *adj* (*lover, spouse*) untreu

unfamiliar [ʌnfəˈmɪlɪəʳ] *adj* ungewohnt;
(*person*) fremd; **to be ~ with sth** mit etw nicht
vertraut sein

unfashionable [ʌnˈfæʃnəbl] *adj* (*clothes, ideas*)
unmodern; (*place*) unbeliebt

unfasten [ʌnˈfaːsn] *vt* (*seat belt, strap*) lösen

unfathomable [ʌnˈfæðəməbl] *adj*
unergründlich

unfavourable, (*US*) **unfavorable** [ʌnˈfeɪvrəbl]
adj (*circumstances, weather*) ungünstig; (*opinion,

report*) negativ

unfavourably, (*US*) **unfavorably** [ʌnˈfeɪvrəblɪ]
adv: **to compare ~ (with sth)** im Vergleich
(mit etw) ungünstig sein; **to compare ~
(with sb)** im Vergleich (mit jdm) schlechter
abschneiden; **to look ~ on** (*suggestion etc*)
ablehnend gegenüberstehen +*dat*

unfeeling [ʌnˈfiːlɪŋ] *adj* gefühllos

unfinished [ʌnˈfɪnɪʃt] *adj* unvollendet

unfit [ʌnˈfɪt] *adj* (*physically*) nicht fit;
(*incompetent*) unfähig; **~ for work**
arbeitsunfähig; **~ for human consumption**
zum Verzehr ungeeignet

unflagging [ʌnˈflægɪŋ] *adj* (*attention, energy*)
unermüdlich

unflappable [ʌnˈflæpəbl] *adj* unerschütterlich

unflattering [ʌnˈflætərɪŋ] *adj* (*dress, hairstyle*)
unvorteilhaft; (*remark*) wenig schmeichelhaft

unflinching [ʌnˈflɪntʃɪŋ] *adj* unerschrocken

unfold [ʌnˈfəuld] *vt* (*sheets, map*)
auseinanderfalten ▷ *vi* (*situation, story*) sich
entfalten

unforeseeable [ʌnfɔːˈsiːəbl] *adj*
unvorhersehbar

unforeseen [ˈʌnfɔːˈsiːn] *adj* unvorhergesehen

unforgettable [ʌnfəˈgetəbl] *adj* unvergesslich

unforgivable [ʌnfəˈgɪvəbl] *adj* unverzeihlich

unformatted [ʌnˈfɔːmætɪd] *adj* (*disk, text*)
unformatiert

unfortunate [ʌnˈfɔːtʃənət] *adj* (*unlucky*)
unglücklich; (*regrettable*) bedauerlich; **it is ~
that ...** es ist bedauerlich, dass ...

unfortunately [ʌnˈfɔːtʃənətlɪ] *adv* leider

unfounded [ʌnˈfaundɪd] *adj* (*allegations, fears*)
unbegründet

unfriendly [ʌnˈfrendlɪ] *adj* unfreundlich

unfulfilled [ʌnfulˈfɪld] *adj* (*ambition, prophecy*)
unerfüllt; (*person*) unausgefüllt

unfurl [ʌnˈfəːl] *vt* (*flag etc*) entrollen

unfurnished [ʌnˈfəːnɪʃt] *adj* unmöbliert

ungainly [ʌnˈgeɪnlɪ] *adj* (*person*) unbeholfen

ungodly [ʌnˈgɔdlɪ] *adj* (*annoying*) heillos; **at
some ~ hour** zu nachtschlafender Zeit

ungrateful [ʌnˈgreɪtful] *adj* undankbar

unguarded [ʌnˈgaːdɪd] *adj*: **in an ~ moment**
in einem unbedachten Augenblick

unhappily [ʌnˈhæpɪlɪ] *adv* (*miserably*)
unglücklich; (*unfortunately*) leider

unhappiness [ʌnˈhæpɪnɪs] *n* Traurigkeit
f

unhappy [ʌnˈhæpɪ] *adj* unglücklich; **~ about/
with** (*dissatisfied*) unzufrieden über +*acc*/mit

unharmed [ʌnˈhaːmd] *adj* (*person, animal*)
unversehrt

UNHCR *n abbr* (= *United Nations High Commission
for Refugees*) Flüchtlingskommission der Vereinten
Nationen

unhealthy [ʌnˈhelθɪ] *adj* (*person*) nicht gesund;
(*place*) ungesund; (*fig: interest*) krankhaft

unheard-of [ʌnˈhəːdɔv] *adj* (*unknown*)
unbekannt; (*outrageous*) unerhört

unhelpful [ʌnˈhelpful] *adj* (*person*) nicht
hilfreich; (*advice*) nutzlos

u

unhesitating [ʌnˈhɛzɪteɪtɪŋ] adj (loyalty) bereitwillig; (reply, offer) prompt

unholy [ʌnˈhəʊlɪ] (inf) adj (fig: alliance) übel; (: mess) heillos; (: row) furchtbar

unhook [ʌnˈhuk] vt (unfasten) losmachen

unhurt [ʌnˈhəːt] adj unverletzt

unhygienic [ˈʌnhaɪˈdʒiːnɪk] adj unhygienisch

UNICEF [ˈjuːnɪsɛf] n abbr (= United Nations International Children's Emergency Fund) UNICEF f

unicorn [ˈjuːnɪkɔːn] n Einhorn nt

unidentified [ʌnaɪˈdɛntɪfaɪd] adj (unknown) unbekannt; (unnamed) ungenannt; see also **UFO**

unification [juːnɪfɪˈkeɪʃən] n Vereinigung f

unification process n Einigungsprozess m

uniform [ˈjuːnɪfɔːm] n Uniform f ▷ adj (length, width etc) einheitlich

uniformity [juːnɪˈfɔːmɪtɪ] n Einheitlichkeit f

unify [ˈjuːnɪfaɪ] vt vereinigen

unilateral [juːnɪˈlætərəl] adj einseitig

unimaginable [ʌnɪˈmædʒɪnəbl] adj unvorstellbar

unimaginative [ʌnɪˈmædʒɪnətɪv] adj fantasielos

unimpaired [ʌnɪmˈpɛəd] adj unbeeinträchtigt

unimportant [ʌnɪmˈpɔːtənt] adj unwichtig

unimpressed [ʌnɪmˈprɛst] adj unbeeindruckt

uninhabited [ʌnɪnˈhæbɪtɪd] adj unbewohnt

uninhibited [ʌnɪnˈhɪbɪtɪd] adj (person) ohne Hemmungen; (behaviour) hemmungslos

uninjured [ʌnˈɪndʒəd] adj unverletzt

uninspiring [ʌnɪnˈspaɪərɪŋ] adj wenig aufregend; (person) trocken, nüchtern

unintelligent [ʌnɪnˈtɛlɪdʒənt] adj unintelligent

unintentional [ʌnɪnˈtɛnʃənəl] adj unbeabsichtigt

unintentionally [ʌnɪnˈtɛnʃnəlɪ] adv unabsichtlich

uninvited [ʌnɪnˈvaɪtɪd] adj (guest) ungeladen

uninviting [ʌnɪnˈvaɪtɪŋ] adj (food) unappetitlich; (place) wenig einladend

union [ˈjuːnjən] n (unification) Vereinigung f; (also: **trade union**) Gewerkschaft f ▷ cpd (activities, leader etc) Gewerkschafts-; **the U~** (US) die Vereinigten Staaten

unionize [ˈjuːnjənaɪz] vt (employees) gewerkschaftlich organisieren

Union Jack n Union Jack m

union shop n gewerkschaftspflichtiger Betrieb m

unique [juːˈniːk] adj (object etc) einmalig; (ability, skill) einzigartig; **to be ~ to** charakteristisch sein für

unisex [ˈjuːnɪsɛks] adj (clothes) Unisex-; (hairdresser) für Damen und Herren

UNISON [ˈjuːnɪsn] n Gewerkschaft der Angestellten im öffentlichen Dienst

unison [ˈjuːnɪsn] n: **in ~** (say, sing) einstimmig; (act) in Übereinstimmung

unit [ˈjuːnɪt] n Einheit f; **production ~** Produktionsabteilung f; **kitchen ~** Küchen-Einbauelement nt

unitary [ˈjuːnɪtrɪ] adj (state, system etc) einheitlich

unit cost n (Comm) Stückkosten pl

unite [juːˈnaɪt] vt vereinigen ▷ vi sich zusammenschließen

united [juːˈnaɪtɪd] adj (agreed) einig; (country, party) vereinigt

United Arab Emirates npl: **the ~** die Vereinigten Arabischen Emirate pl

United Kingdom n: **the ~** das Vereinigte Königreich

United Nations npl: **the ~** die Vereinten Nationen pl

United States n: **the ~ (of America)** die Vereinigten Staaten pl (von Amerika)

unit price n (Comm) Einzelpreis m

unit trust (Brit) n (Comm) Investmenttrust m

unity [ˈjuːnɪtɪ] n Einheit f

Univ. abbr = **university**

universal [juːnɪˈvəːsl] adj allgemein

universe [ˈjuːnɪvəːs] n Universum nt

university [juːnɪˈvəːsɪtɪ] n Universität f ▷ cpd (student, professor) Universitäts-; (education, year) akademisch

university degree n Universitätsabschluss m

unjust [ʌnˈdʒʌst] adj ungerecht; (society) unfair

unjustifiable [ˈʌndʒʌstɪˈfaɪəbl] adj nicht zu rechtfertigen

unjustified [ʌnˈdʒʌstɪfaɪd] adj (belief, action) ungerechtfertigt; (text) nicht bündig

unkempt [ʌnˈkɛmpt] adj ungepflegt

unkind [ʌnˈkaɪnd] adj (person, comment etc) unfreundlich

unkindly [ʌnˈkaɪndlɪ] adv unfreundlich

unknown [ʌnˈnəʊn] adj unbekannt; **~ to me, ...** ohne dass ich es wusste, ...; **~ quantity** (fig) unbekannte Größe

unladen [ʌnˈleɪdn] adj (ship) ohne Ladung; (weight) Leer-

unlawful [ʌnˈlɔːful] adj gesetzwidrig

unleaded [ˈʌnˈlɛdɪd] adj (petrol) bleifrei, unverbleit; **I use ~** ich fahre bleifrei

unleash [ʌnˈliːʃ] vt (fig: feeling, forces etc) entfesseln

unleavened [ʌnˈlɛvnd] adj (bread) ungesäuert

unless [ʌnˈlɛs] conj es sei denn; **~ he comes** wenn er nicht kommt; **~ otherwise stated** wenn nicht anders angegeben; **~ I am mistaken** wenn ich mich nicht irre; **there will be a strike ~ ...** es wird zum Streik kommen, es sei denn, ...

unlicensed [ʌnˈlaɪsnst] (Brit) adj (restaurant) ohne Schankkonzession

unlike [ʌnˈlaɪk] adj (not alike) unähnlich ▷ prep (different from) verschieden von; **~ me, she is very tidy** im Gegensatz zu mir ist sie sehr ordentlich

unlikelihood [ʌnˈlaɪklɪhʊd] n Unwahrscheinlichkeit f

unlikely [ʌnˈlaɪklɪ] adj unwahrscheinlich; (combination etc) merkwürdig; **in the ~ event of/that ...** im unwahrscheinlichen Fall +gen/dass ...

unlimited [ʌnˈlɪmɪtɪd] adj unbeschränkt

unlisted [ˈʌnˈlɪstɪd] *adj* (*Stock Exchange*) nicht notiert; (*US: Tel:*) **to be ~** nicht im Telefonbuch stehen

unlit [ʌnˈlɪt] *adj* (*room etc*) unbeleuchtet

unload [ʌnˈləʊd] *vt* (*box etc*) ausladen; (*car etc*) entladen

unlock [ʌnˈlɔk] *vt* aufschließen

unlucky [ʌnˈlʌkɪ] *adj* (*object*) Unglück bringend; (*number*) Unglücks-; **to be ~** (*person*) Pech haben

unmanageable [ʌnˈmænɪdʒəbl] *adj* (*tool, vehicle*) kaum zu handhaben; (*person, hair*) widerspenstig; (*situation*) unkontrollierbar

unmanned [ʌnˈmænd] *adj* (*station, spacecraft etc*) unbemannt

unmarked [ʌnˈmɑːkt] *adj* (*unstained*) fleckenlos; (*unscarred*) nicht gezeichnet; (*unblemished*) makellos; **~ police car** nicht gekennzeichneter Streifenwagen *m*

unmarried [ʌnˈmærɪd] *adj* unverheiratet

unmarried mother *n* ledige Mutter *f*

unmask [ʌnˈmɑːsk] *vt* (*reveal*) enthüllen

unmatched [ʌnˈmætʃt] *adj* unübertroffen

unmentionable [ʌnˈmɛnʃnəbl] *adj* (*topic, word*) Tabu-; **to be ~** tabu sein

unmerciful [ʌnˈməːsɪful] *adj* erbarmungslos

unmistakable, unmistakeable [ʌnmɪsˈteɪkəbl] *adj* unverkennbar

unmistakably, unmistakeably [ʌnmɪsˈteɪkəblɪ] *adv* unverkennbar

unmitigated [ʌnˈmɪtɪɡeɪtɪd] *adj* (*disaster etc*) total

unnamed [ʌnˈneɪmd] *adj* (*nameless*) namenlos; (*anonymous*) ungenannt

unnatural [ʌnˈnætʃrəl] *adj* unnatürlich; (*against nature: habit*) widernatürlich

unnecessarily [ʌnˈnɛsəsərɪlɪ] *adv* (*worry etc*) unnötigerweise; (*severe etc*) übertrieben

unnecessary [ʌnˈnɛsəsərɪ] *adj* unnötig

unnerve [ʌnˈnəːv] *vt* entnerven

unnoticed [ʌnˈnəʊtɪst] *adj*: **to go** *or* **pass ~** unbemerkt bleiben

UNO [ˈjuːnəʊ] *n abbr* (= *United Nations Organization*) UNO *f*

unobservant [ʌnəbˈzəːvənt] *adj* unaufmerksam

unobtainable [ʌnəbˈteɪnəbl] *adj* (*item*) nicht erhältlich; **this number is ~** (*Tel*) kein Anschluss unter dieser Nummer

unobtrusive [ʌnəbˈtruːsɪv] *adj* unauffällig

unoccupied [ʌnˈɔkjupaɪd] *adj* (*seat*) frei; (*house*) leer (stehend)

unofficial [ʌnəˈfɪʃl] *adj* inoffiziell

unopened [ʌnˈəʊpənd] *adj* ungeöffnet

unopposed [ʌnəˈpəʊzd] *adj*: **to be ~** (*suggestion*) nicht auf Widerstand treffen; (*motion, bill*) ohne Gegenstimmen angenommen werden

unorthodox [ʌnˈɔːθədɔks] *adj* (*also Rel*) unorthodox

unpack [ʌnˈpæk] *vt, vi* auspacken

unpaid [ʌnˈpeɪd] *adj* unbezahlt

unpalatable [ʌnˈpælətəbl] *adj* (*meal*) ungenießbar; (*truth*) bitter

unparalleled [ʌnˈpærəlɛld] *adj* beispiellos

unpatriotic [ˈʌnpætrɪˈɔtɪk] *adj* unpatriotisch

unplanned [ʌnˈplænd] *adj* ungeplant

unpleasant [ʌnˈplɛznt] *adj* unangenehm; (*person, manner*) unfreundlich

unplug [ʌnˈplʌɡ] *vt* (*iron, record player etc*) den Stecker herausziehen +*gen*

unpolluted [ʌnpəˈluːtɪd] *adj* unverschmutzt

unpopular [ʌnˈpɔpjuləʳ] *adj* unpopulär; **to make o.s. ~ (with)** sich unbeliebt machen (bei)

unprecedented [ʌnˈprɛsɪdɛntɪd] *adj* noch nie da gewesen; (*decision*) einmalig

unpredictable [ʌnprɪˈdɪktəbl] *adj* (*person, weather*) unberechenbar; (*reaction*) unvorhersehbar

unprejudiced [ʌnˈprɛdʒudɪst] *adj* unvoreingenommen

unprepared [ʌnprɪˈpɛəd] *adj* unvorbereitet

unprepossessing [ˈʌnpriːpəˈzɛsɪŋ] *adj* (*person, place*) unattraktiv

unpretentious [ʌnprɪˈtɛnʃəs] *adj* (*building, person*) schlicht

unprincipled [ʌnˈprɪnsɪpld] *adj* (*person*) charakterlos

unproductive [ʌnprəˈdʌktɪv] *adj* (*land*) unfruchtbar, ertragsarm; (*discussion*) unproduktiv

unprofessional [ʌnprəˈfɛʃənl] *adj* unprofessionell

unprofitable [ʌnˈprɔfɪtəbl] *adj* nicht profitabel, unrentabel

UNPROFOR *n abbr* (= *United Nations Protection Force*) UNPROFOR *f*; **~ troops** UNPROFOR-Truppen, UNO-Schutztruppen

unprotected [ˈʌnprəˈtɛktɪd] *adj* ungeschützt

unprovoked [ʌnprəˈvəʊkt] *adj* (*attack*) grundlos

unpunished [ʌnˈpʌnɪʃt] *adj*: **to go ~** straflos bleiben

unqualified [ʌnˈkwɔlɪfaɪd] *adj* unqualifiziert; (*disaster, success*) vollkommen

unquestionably [ʌnˈkwɛstʃənəblɪ] *adv* fraglos

unquestioning [ʌnˈkwɛstʃənɪŋ] *adj* bedingungslos

unravel [ʌnˈrævl] *vt* (*also fig*) entwirren

unreal [ʌnˈrɪəl] *adj* (*artificial*) unecht; (*peculiar*) unwirklich

unrealistic [ˈʌnrɪəˈlɪstɪk] *adj* unrealistisch

unreasonable [ʌnˈriːznəbl] *adj* (*person, attitude*) unvernünftig; (*demand, length of time*) unzumutbar

unrecognizable [ʌnˈrɛkəɡnaɪzəbl] *adj* nicht zu erkennen

unrecognized [ʌnˈrɛkəɡnaɪzd] *adj* (*talent etc*) unerkannt; (*Pol: regime*) nicht anerkannt

unreconstructed [ˈʌnriːkənˈstrʌktɪd] (*esp US*) *adj* (*unwilling to accept change*) unverbesserlich

unrecorded [ʌnrəˈkɔːdɪd] *adj* (*piece of music etc*) nicht aufgenommen; (*incident, statement*) nicht schriftlich festgehalten

unrefined [ʌnrəˈfaɪnd] *adj* (*sugar, petroleum*) nicht raffiniert

unrehearsed [ʌnrɪˈhəːst] *adj* (*Theat etc*) nicht

u

geprobt; (*spontaneous*) spontan

unrelated [ʌnrɪˈleɪtɪd] *adj* (*incidents*) ohne
Beziehung; (*people*) nicht verwandt

unrelenting [ʌnrɪˈlentɪŋ] *adj* (*person, behaviour
etc*) unnachgiebig

unreliable [ʌnrɪˈlaɪəbl] *adj* unzuverlässig

unrelieved [ʌnrɪˈliːvd] *adj* ungemindert

unremitting [ʌnrɪˈmɪtɪŋ] *adj* (*efforts, attempts*)
unermüdlich

unrepeatable [ʌnrɪˈpiːtəbl] *adj* (*offer*) einmalig;
(*comment*) nicht wiederholbar

unrepentant [ʌnrɪˈpentənt] *adj*: **to be ~ about
sth** etw nicht bereuen; **he's an ~ Marxist** er
bereut es nicht, nach wie vor Marxist zu sein

unrepresentative [ˈʌnreprɪˈzentətɪv] *adj*: **~ (of)**
nicht repräsentativ (für)

unrepresented [ˈʌnreprɪˈzentɪd] *adj* nicht
vertreten

unreserved [ʌnrɪˈzəːvd] *adj* (*seat*) unreserviert;
(*approval etc*) uneingeschränkt, vorbehaltlos

unreservedly [ʌnrɪˈzəːvɪdlɪ] *adv* ohne
Vorbehalt

unresponsive [ʌnrɪsˈpɒnsɪv] *adj*
unempfänglich

unrest [ʌnˈrest] *n* Unruhen *pl*

unrestricted [ʌnrɪˈstrɪktɪd] *adj* unbeschränkt;
to have ~ access to ungehinderten Zugang
haben zu

unrewarded [ʌnrɪˈwɔːdɪd] *adj* unbelohnt

unripe [ʌnˈraɪp] *adj* unreif

unrivalled, (US) **unrivaled** [ʌnˈraɪvəld] *adj*
unübertroffen

unroll [ʌnˈrəʊl] *vt* entrollen ▷ *vi* sich entrollen

unruffled [ʌnˈrʌfld] *adj* unbewegt; (*hair*)
unzerzaust

unruly [ʌnˈruːlɪ] *adj* (*child, behaviour*)
ungebärdig; (*hair*) widerspenstig

unsafe [ʌnˈseɪf] *adj* unsicher; (*machine,
bridge, car etc*) gefährlich; **~ to eat/drink**
ungenießbar

unsaid [ʌnˈsed] *adj*: **to leave sth ~** etw
ungesagt lassen

unsaleable, (US) **unsalable** [ʌnˈseɪləbl] *adj*
unverkäuflich

unsatisfactory [ˈʌnsætɪsˈfæktərɪ] *adj*
unbefriedigend

unsatisfied [ʌnˈsætɪsfaɪd] *adj* unzufrieden

unsavoury, (US) **unsavory** [ʌnˈseɪvərɪ] *adj*
(*fig: person, place*) widerwärtig

unscathed [ʌnˈskeɪðd] *adj* unversehrt

unscientific [ˈʌnsaɪənˈtɪfɪk] *adj*
unwissenschaftlich

unscrew [ʌnˈskruː] *vt* losschrauben

unscrupulous [ʌnˈskruːpjuləs] *adj* skrupellos

unseat [ʌnˈsiːt] *vt* (*rider*) abwerfen; (*from office*)
aus dem Amt drängen

unsecured [ˈʌnsɪˈkjuəd] *adj*: **~ creditor** nicht
gesicherter Gläubiger *m*; **~ loan** Blankokredit
m

unseeded [ʌnˈsiːdɪd] *adj* (*player*) nicht gesetzt

unseemly [ʌnˈsiːmlɪ] *adj* unschicklich

unseen [ʌnˈsiːn] *adj* (*person, danger*) unsichtbar

unselfish [ʌnˈselfɪʃ] *adj* selbstlos

unsettled [ʌnˈsetld] *adj* (*person*) unruhig;
(*future*) unsicher; (*question*) ungeklärt; (*weather*)
unbeständig

unsettling [ʌnˈsetlɪŋ] *adj* beunruhigend

unshakable, unshakeable [ʌnˈʃeɪkəbl] *adj*
unerschütterlich

unshaven [ʌnˈʃeɪvn] *adj* unrasiert

unsightly [ʌnˈsaɪtlɪ] *adj* unansehnlich

unskilled [ʌnˈskɪld] *adj* (*work, worker*) ungelernt

unsociable [ʌnˈsəʊʃəbl] *adj* ungesellig

unsocial [ʌnˈsəʊʃl] *adj*: **to work ~ hours**
außerhalb der normalen Arbeitszeit arbeiten

unsold [ʌnˈsəʊld] *adj* unverkauft

unsolicited [ʌnsəˈlɪsɪtɪd] *adj* unerbeten

unsophisticated [ʌnsəˈfɪstɪkeɪtɪd] *adj* (*person*)
anspruchslos; (*method, device*) simpel

unsound [ʌnˈsaund] *adj* (*floor, foundations*)
unsicher; (*policy, advice*) unklug; **of ~ mind**
unzurechnungsfähig

unspeakable [ʌnˈspiːkəbl] *adj* (*indescribable*)
unsagbar; (*awful*) abscheulich

unspoken [ʌnˈspəʊkn] *adj* (*word*)
unausgesprochen; (*agreement etc*)
stillschweigend

unstable [ʌnˈsteɪbl] *adj* (*piece of furniture*) nicht
stabil; (*government*) instabil; (*person: mentally*)
labil

unsteady [ʌnˈstedɪ] *adj* (*step, voice, legs*)
unsicher; (*ladder*) wack(e)lig

unstinting [ʌnˈstɪntɪŋ] *adj* (*support*)
vorbehaltlos; (*generosity*) unbegrenzt

unstuck [ʌnˈstʌk] *adj*: **to come ~** (*label etc*) sich
lösen; (*fig: plan, idea etc*) versagen

unsubstantiated [ˈʌnsəbˈstænʃɪeɪtɪd] *adj*
(*rumour*) unbestätigt; (*accusation*) unbegründet

unsuccessful [ʌnsəkˈsesful] *adj* erfolglos;
(*marriage*) gescheitert; **to be ~** keinen Erfolg
haben

unsuccessfully [ʌnsəkˈsesfəlɪ] *adv* ohne Erfolg,
vergeblich

unsuitable [ʌnˈsuːtəbl] *adj* (*time*) unpassend;
(*clothes, person*) ungeeignet

unsuited [ʌnˈsuːtɪd] *adj*: **to be ~ for** *or* **to sth**
für etw ungeeignet sein

unsung [ˈʌnsʌŋ] *adj*: **an ~ hero** ein
unbesungener Held

unsure [ʌnˈʃuəʳ] *adj* unsicher; **to be ~ of o.s.**
unsicher sein

unsuspecting [ʌnsəsˈpektɪŋ] *adj* ahnungslos

unsweetened [ʌnˈswiːtnd] *adj* ungesüßt

unswerving [ʌnˈswəːvɪŋ] *adj* unerschütterlich

unsympathetic [ˈʌnsɪmpəˈθetɪk] *adj* (*showing
little understanding*) abweisend; (*unlikeable*)
unsympathisch; **to be ~ to(wards) sth** einer
Sache *dat* ablehnend gegenüberstehen

untangle [ʌnˈtæŋgl] *vt* entwirren

untapped [ʌnˈtæpt] *adj* (*resources*) ungenutzt

untaxed [ʌnˈtækst] *adj* (*goods, income*) steuerfrei

unthinkable [ʌnˈθɪŋkəbl] *adj* undenkbar

unthinking [ʌnˈθɪŋkɪŋ] *adj* (*uncritical*)
bedenkenlos; (*thoughtless*) gedankenlos

untidy [ʌnˈtaɪdɪ] *adj* unordentlich

untie [ʌnˈtaɪ] *vt* (*knot, parcel*) aufschnüren;

(*prisoner, dog*) losbinden

until [ən'tɪl] *prep* bis +*acc*; (*after negative*) vor +*dat*
▷ *conj* bis; (*after negative*) bevor; **~ now** bis jetzt;
~ then bis dann; **from morning ~ night**
von morgens bis abends; **~ he comes** bis er
kommt

untimely [ʌn'taɪmlɪ] *adj* (*moment*) unpassend;
(*arrival*) ungelegen; (*death*) vorzeitig

untold [ʌn'təuld] *adj* (*joy, suffering, wealth*)
unermesslich; **the ~ story** die Hintergründe

untouched [ʌn'tʌtʃt] *adj* unberührt;
(*undamaged*) unversehrt; **~ by** (*unaffected*)
unberührt von

untoward [ʌntə'wɔːd] *adj* (*events, effects etc*)
ungünstig

untrained ['ʌn'treɪnd] *adj* unausgebildet; (*eye,
hands*) ungeschult

untrammelled [ʌn'træmld] *adj* (*person*)
ungebunden; (*behaviour*) unbeschränkt

untranslatable [ʌntrænz'leɪtəbl] *adj*
unübersetzbar

untried [ʌn'traɪd] *adj* (*policy, remedy*) unerprobt;
(*prisoner*) noch nicht vor Gericht gestellt

untrue [ʌn'truː] *adj* unwahr

untrustworthy [ʌn'trʌstwəːðɪ] *adj*
unzuverlässig

unusable [ʌn'juːzəbl] *adj* (*object*) unbrauchbar;
(*room*) nicht benutzbar

unused¹ [ʌn'juːzd] *adj* (*new*) unbenutzt

unused² [ʌn'juːst] *adj*: **to be ~ to sth** an etw
acc nicht gewöhnt sein; **to be ~ to doing sth**
nicht daran gewöhnt sein, etw zu tun

unusual [ʌn'juːʒuəl] *adj* ungewöhnlich;
(*exceptional*) außergewöhnlich

unusually [ʌn'juːʒuəlɪ] *adv* (*large, high etc*)
ungewöhnlich

unveil [ʌn'veɪl] *vt* (*also fig*) enthüllen

unwanted [ʌn'wɒntɪd] *adj* unerwünscht

unwarranted [ʌn'wɒrəntɪd] *adj*
ungerechtfertigt

unwary [ʌn'wɛərɪ] *adj* unachtsam

unwavering [ʌn'weɪvərɪŋ] *adj* (*faith, support*)
unerschütterlich; (*gaze*) fest

unwelcome [ʌn'wɛlkəm] *adj* (*guest*)
unwillkommen; (*news*) unerfreulich; **to feel ~**
sich nicht willkommen fühlen

unwell [ʌn'wɛl] *adj*: **to be ~, to feel ~** sich
nicht wohlfühlen

unwieldy [ʌn'wiːldɪ] *adj* (*object*) unhandlich;
(*system*) schwerfällig

unwilling [ʌn'wɪlɪŋ] *adj*: **to be ~ to do sth** etw
nicht tun wollen

unwillingly [ʌn'wɪlɪŋlɪ] *adv* widerwillig

unwind [ʌn'waɪnd] (*irreg: like* **wind**) *vt*
abwickeln ▷ *vi* sich abwickeln; (*relax*) sich
entspannen

unwise [ʌn'waɪz] *adj* unklug

unwitting [ʌn'wɪtɪŋ] *adj* (*accomplice*)
unwissentlich; (*victim*) ahnungslos

unworkable [ʌn'wəːkəbl] *adj* (*plan*)
undurchführbar

unworthy [ʌn'wəːðɪ] *adj* unwürdig; **to be ~
of sth** einer Sache *gen* nicht wert *or* würdig

sein; **to be ~ to do sth** es nicht wert sein,
etw zu tun; **that remark is ~ of you** diese
Bemerkung ist unter deiner Würde

unwrap [ʌn'ræp] *vt* auspacken

unwritten [ʌn'rɪtn] *adj* (*law*) ungeschrieben;
(*agreement*) stillschweigend

unzip [ʌn'zɪp] *vt* aufmachen

 KEYWORD

up [ʌp] *prep*: **to be up sth** (oben) auf etw *dat*
sein; **to go up sth** (auf) etw *acc* hinaufgehen;
go up that road and turn left gehen Sie die
Straße hinauf und biegen Sie links ab
▷ *adv* **1** (*upwards, higher*) oben; **put it a bit
higher up** stelle es etwas höher; **up there**
dort oben; **up above** hoch oben
2: **to be up** (*out of bed*) auf sein; (*prices, level*)
gestiegen sein; (*building, tent*) stehen; **time's
up** die Zeit ist um *or* vorbei
3: **up to** (*as far as*) bis; **up to now** bis jetzt
4: **to be up to** (*depending on*) abhängen von;
it's up to you das hängt von dir ab; **it's not
up to me to decide** es liegt nicht bei mir, das
zu entscheiden
5: **to be up to** (*equal to*) gewachsen sein +*dat*;
he's not up to it (*job, task etc*) er ist dem
nicht gewachsen; **his work is not up to the
required standard** seine Arbeit entspricht
nicht dem gewünschten Niveau
6: **to be up to** (*inf: be doing*) vorhaben; **what
is he up to?** (*showing disapproval, suspicion*) was
führt er im Schilde?
▷ *n*: **ups and downs** (*in life, career*) Höhen und
Tiefen *pl*
▷ *vi* (*inf*): **she upped and left** sie sprang auf
und rannte davon
▷ *vt* (*inf: price*) heraufsetzen

up-and-coming [ʌpənd'kʌmɪŋ] *adj* (*actor,
company etc*) kommend

upbeat ['ʌpbiːt] *n* (*Mus*) Auftakt *m*; (*in
economy etc*) Aufschwung *m* ▷ *adj* (*optimistic*)
optimistisch

upbraid [ʌp'breɪd] *vt* tadeln

upbringing ['ʌpbrɪŋɪŋ] *n* Erziehung *f*

upcoming ['ʌpkʌmɪŋ] (*esp US*) *adj* kommend

update [ʌp'deɪt] *vt* aktualisieren

upend [ʌp'ɛnd] *vt* auf den Kopf stellen

upfront [ʌp'frʌnt] *adj* (*person*) offen ▷ *adv*: **20%
~** 20% (als) Vorschuss, 20% im Voraus

upgrade [ʌp'greɪd] *vt* (*house*) Verbesserungen
durchführen in +*dat*; (*job*) verbessern;
(*employee*) befördern; (*Comput*) nachrüsten

upheaval [ʌp'hiːvl] *n* Unruhe *f*

uphill ['ʌp'hɪl] *adj* bergaufwärts (führend);
(*fig: task*) mühsam ▷ *adv* (*push, move*)
bergaufwärts; (*go*) bergauf

uphold [ʌp'həuld] (*irreg: like* **hold**) *vt* (*law,
principle*) wahren; (*decision*) unterstützen

upholstery [ʌp'həulstərɪ] *n* Polsterung *f*

upkeep ['ʌpkiːp] *n* (*maintenance*)
Instandhaltung *f*

u

847

up-market | use

up-market [ʌp'mɑ:kɪt] adj anspruchsvoll

upon [ə'pɒn] prep (position) auf +dat; (motion) auf +acc

upper ['ʌpə'] adj obere(r, s) ▷ n (of shoe) Oberleder nt

upper class n: the ~ die Oberschicht

upper-class ['ʌpə'klɑ:s] adj vornehm

uppercut ['ʌpəkʌt] n Uppercut m

upper hand n: to have the ~ die Oberhand haben

Upper House n (Pol) Oberhaus nt

uppermost ['ʌpəməust] adj oberste(r, s); what was ~ in my mind woran ich in erster Linie dachte

Upper Volta [-'vɒltə] n (formerly) Obervolta nt

upright ['ʌpraɪt] adj (vertical) vertikal; (fig: honest) rechtschaffen ▷ adv (sit, stand) aufrecht ▷ n (Constr) Pfosten m

uprising ['ʌpraɪzɪŋ] n Aufstand m

uproar ['ʌprɔ:'] n Aufruhr m

uproarious [ʌp'rɔ:rɪəs] adj (laughter) brüllend; (joke) brüllend komisch; (mirth) überwältigend

uproot [ʌp'ru:t] vt (tree) entwurzeln; (fig: people) aus der gewohnten Umgebung reißen; (: in war etc) entwurzeln

upset [vt, adj ʌp'sɛt, n 'ʌpsɛt] (irreg: like set) vt (knock over) umstoßen; (person: offend, make unhappy) verletzen; (routine, plan) durcheinanderbringen ▷ adj (unhappy) aufgebracht; (stomach) verstimmt ▷ n: to have/get a stomach ~ (Brit) eine Magenverstimmung haben/bekommen; to get ~ sich aufregen

upset price n (US, Scot) n Mindestpreis m

upsetting [ʌp'sɛtɪŋ] adj (distressing) erschütternd

upshot ['ʌpʃɒt] n Ergebnis nt; the ~ of it all was that ... es lief schließlich darauf hinaus, dass ...

upside down ['ʌpsaɪd-] adv verkehrt herum; to turn a room ~ (fig) ein Zimmer auf den Kopf stellen

upstage ['ʌp'steɪdʒ] adv (Theat) im Bühnenhintergrund ▷ vt: to ~ sb (fig) jdn ausstechen, jdm die Schau stehlen (inf)

upstairs [ʌp'stɛəz] adv (be) oben; (go) nach oben ▷ adj (room) obere(r, s); (window) im oberen Stock ▷ n oberes Stockwerk nt; there's no ~ das Haus hat kein Obergeschoss

upstart ['ʌpstɑ:t] (pej) n Emporkömmling m

upstream [ʌp'stri:m] adv, adj flussaufwärts

upsurge ['ʌpsə:dʒ] n (of enthusiasm etc) Schwall m

uptake ['ʌpteɪk] n: to be quick on the ~ schnell kapieren; to be slow on the ~ schwer von Begriff sein

uptight [ʌp'taɪt] (inf) adj nervös

up-to-date ['ʌptə'deɪt] adj (modern) modern; (person) up to date

upturn ['ʌptə:n] n (in economy) Aufschwung m

upturned ['ʌptə:nd] adj: ~ nose Stupsnase f

upward ['ʌpwəd] adj (movement) Aufwärts-; (glance) nach oben gerichtet

upwardly mobile ['ʌpwədlɪ-] adj: to be ~ ein Aufsteigertyp m sein

upwards ['ʌpwədz] adv (move) aufwärts; (glance) nach oben; ~ of (more than) über +acc

URA (US) n abbr (= Urban Renewal Administration) Stadtsanierungsbehörde

Ural Mountains ['juərəl-] npl: the ~ (also: the Urals) der Ural

uranium [juə'reɪnɪəm] n Uran nt

Uranus [juə'reɪnəs] n Uranus m

urban ['ə:bən] adj städtisch; (unemployment) in den Städten

urbane [ə:'beɪn] adj weltgewandt

urbanization ['ə:bənaɪ'zeɪʃən] n Urbanisierung f, Verstädterung f

urchin ['ə:tʃɪn] (pej) n Gassenkind nt

Urdu ['uədu:] n Urdu nt

urge [ə:dʒ] n (need, desire) Verlangen nt ▷ vt: to ~ sb to do sth jdn eindringlich bitten, etw zu tun; to ~ caution zur Vorsicht mahnen
▶ urge on vt antreiben

urgency ['ə:dʒənsɪ] n Dringlichkeit f

urgent ['ə:dʒənt] adj dringend; (voice) eindringend

urgently ['ə:dʒəntlɪ] adv dringend

urinal ['juərɪnl] n (building) Pissoir nt; (vessel) Urinal nt

urinate ['juərɪneɪt] vi urinieren

urine ['juərɪn] n Urin m

URL n abbr (Comput: = uniform resource locator) URL-Adresse f, Internetadresse f

urn [ə:n] n Urne f; (also: tea urn) Teekessel m

Uruguay ['juərəgwaɪ] n Uruguay nt

Uruguayan [juərə'gwaɪən] adj uruguayisch ▷ n (person) Uruguayer(in) m(f)

US n abbr (= United States) USA pl

us [ʌs] pl pron uns; (emphatic) wir; see also me

USA n abbr (= United States of America) USA f; (Mil: = United States Army) US-Armee f

usable ['ju:zəbl] adj brauchbar

USAF n abbr (= United States Air Force) US-Luftwaffe f

usage ['ju:zɪdʒ] n (Ling) (Sprach)gebrauch m

USB abbr of universal serial bus

USCG n abbr (= United States Coast Guard) Küstenwache der USA

USDA n abbr (= United States Department of Agriculture) US-Landwirtschaftsministerium

USDAW ['ʌzdɔ:] (Brit) n abbr (= Union of Shop, Distributive, and Allied Workers) Einzelhandelsgewerkschaft

USDI n abbr (= United States Department of the Interior) US-Innenministerium

use [n ju:s, vt ju:z] n (using) Gebrauch m, Verwendung f; (usefulness, purpose) Nutzen m ▷ vt benutzen, gebrauchen; (phrase) verwenden; in ~ in Gebrauch; out of ~ außer Gebrauch; to be of ~ nützlich or von Nutzen sein; to make ~ of sth Gebrauch von etw machen; it's no ~ es hat keinen Zweck; to have the ~ of sth über etw acc verfügen können; what's this ~d for? wofür wird das gebraucht?; to be ~d to sth etw

gewohnt sein; **to get ~d to sth** sich an etw *acc*
gewöhnen; **she ~d to do it** sie hat es früher
gemacht
▶ **use up** *vt* (*food, leftovers*) aufbrauchen;
(*money*) verbrauchen
used [juːzd] *adj* gebraucht; (*car*) Gebraucht-
useful ['juːsful] *adj* nützlich; **to come in ~** sich
als nützlich erweisen
usefulness ['juːsfəlnɪs] *n* Nützlichkeit *f*
useless ['juːslɪs] *adj* nutzlos; (*person: hopeless*)
hoffnungslos
user ['juːzəʳ] *n* Benutzer(in) *m(f)*; (*of petrol, gas
etc*) Verbraucher(in) *m(f)*
user-friendly ['juːzə'frendlɪ] *adj*
benutzerfreundlich
usher ['ʌʃəʳ] *n* (*at wedding*) Platzanweiser *m*
▷ *vt*: **to ~ sb in** jdn hineinführen
usherette [ʌʃə'rɛt] *n* Platzanweiserin *f*
USIA *n abbr* (= *United States Information Agency*) US-
Informations- und Kulturinstitut
USM *n abbr* (= *United States Mint*) US-Münzanstalt;
(= *United States Mail*) US-Postbehörde
USN *n abbr* (= *United States Navy*) US-Marine *f*
USPHS *n abbr* (= *United States Public Health Service*)
US-Gesundheitsbehörde
USPO *n abbr* (= *United States Post Office*) US-
Postbehörde
USS *abbr* (= *United States Ship*) Namensteil von
Schiffen der Kriegsmarine
USSR *n abbr* (*formerly*: = *Union of Soviet Socialist
Republics*) UdSSR *f*
usu. *abbr* = **usually**
usual ['juːʒuəl] *adj* üblich, gewöhnlich; **as ~**
wie gewöhnlich
usually ['juːʒuəlɪ] *adv* gewöhnlich
usurer ['juːʒərəʳ] *n* Wucherer *m*
usurp [juː'zəːp] *vt* (*title, position*) an sich *acc*
reißen
usury ['juːʒurɪ] *n* Wucher *m*
UT (*US*) *abbr* (*Post*) = *Utah*
utensil [juː'tɛnsl] *n* Gerät *nt*; **kitchen ~s**
Küchengeräte *pl*
uterus ['juːtərəs] *n* Gebärmutter *f*, Uterus *m*
utilitarian [juːtɪlɪ'tɛərɪən] *adj* (*building, object*)
praktisch; (*Philosophy*) utilitaristisch
utility [juː'tɪlɪtɪ] *n* (*usefulness*) Nützlichkeit *f*;
(*public utility*) Versorgungsbetrieb *m*
utility room *n* ≈ Hauswirtschaftsraum *m*
utilization [juːtɪlaɪ'zeɪʃən] *n* Verwendung *f*
utilize ['juːtɪlaɪz] *vt* verwenden
utmost ['ʌtməust] *adj* äußerste(r, s) ▷ *n*: **to
do one's ~** sein Möglichstes tun; **of the ~
importance** von äußerster Wichtigkeit
utter ['ʌtəʳ] *adj* (*amazement*) äußerste(r, s);
(*rubbish, fool*) total ▷ *vt* (*sounds, words*)
äußern
utterance ['ʌtərəns] *n* Äußerung *f*
utterly ['ʌtəlɪ] *adv* (*totally*) vollkommen
U-turn ['juː'təːn] *n* (*also fig*) Kehrtwendung *f*
Uzbekistan [ʌzbɛkɪ'stɑːn] *n* Usbekistan *nt*

u

Vv

V¹, v [viː] n (letter) V nt, v nt; **V for Victor** ≈ V wie Viktor

V² abbr (= volt) V

v. abbr = verse; (= versus) vs.; (= vide) s.

VA (US) abbr (Post) = Virginia

vac [væk] (Brit: inf) n = **vacation**

vacancy ['veɪkənsɪ] n (Brit: job) freie Stelle f; (room in hotel etc) freies Zimmer nt; **"no vacancies"** „belegt"; **have you any vacancies?** (hotel) haben Sie Zimmer frei?; (office) haben Sie freie Stellen?

vacant ['veɪkənt] adj (room, seat, job) frei; (look) leer

vacant lot (US) n unbebautes Grundstück nt

vacate [vəˈkeɪt] vt (house) räumen; (one's seat) frei machen; (job) aufgeben

vacation [vəˈkeɪʃən] n (esp US) n (holiday) Urlaub m; (Scol) Ferien pl; **to take a ~** Urlaub machen; **on ~** im Urlaub

vacation course n Ferienkurs m

vaccinate ['væksɪneɪt] vt: **to ~ sb (against sth)** jdn (gegen etw) impfen

vaccination [væksɪˈneɪʃən] n Impfung f

vaccine ['væksiːn] n Impfstoff m

vacuum ['vækjum] n (empty space) Vakuum nt

vacuum cleaner n Staubsauger m

vacuum flask (Brit) n Thermosflasche® f

vacuum-packed ['vækjum'pækt] adj vakuumverpackt

vagabond ['væɡəbɒnd] n Vagabund m

vagary ['veɪɡərɪ] n: **the vagaries of** die Launen +gen

vagina [vəˈdʒaɪnə] n Scheide f, Vagina f

vagrancy ['veɪɡrənsɪ] n Landstreicherei f; (in towns, cities) Stadtstreicherei f

vagrant ['veɪɡrənt] n Landstreicher(in) m(f); (in town, city) Stadtstreicher(in) m(f)

vague [veɪɡ] adj (memory) vage; (outline) undeutlich; (look, idea, instructions) unbestimmt; (person: not precise) unsicher; (: evasive) unbestimmt; **to look ~** (absent-minded) zerstreut aussehen; **I haven't the ~st idea** ich habe nicht die leiseste Ahnung

vaguely ['veɪɡlɪ] adv (unclearly) vage, unbestimmt; (slightly) in etwa

vagueness ['veɪɡnɪs] n Unbestimmtheit f

vain [veɪn] adj (person) eitel; (attempt, action) vergeblich; **in ~** vergebens; **to die in ~**

umsonst sterben

vainly ['veɪnlɪ] adv vergebens

valance ['væləns] n (of bed) Volant m

valedictorian [vælɪdɪk'tɔːrɪən] (US) n (Scol) Abschiedsredner(in) bei der Schulentlassungsfeier

valedictory [vælɪ'dɪktərɪ] adj (speech) Abschieds-; (remarks) zum Abschied

valentine ['væləntaɪn] n (also: **valentine card**) Valentinsgruß m; (person) Freund/Freundin, dem/der man am Valentinstag einen Gruß schickt

valet ['vælɪt] n Kammerdiener m

valet parking n Einparken nt (durch Hotelangestellte etc)

valet service n Reinigungsdienst m

valiant ['vælɪənt] adj (effort) tapfer

valid ['vælɪd] adj (ticket, document) gültig; (argument, reason) stichhaltig

validate ['vælɪdeɪt] vt (contract, document) für gültig erklären; (argument, claim) bestätigen

validity [vəˈlɪdɪtɪ] n (soundness) Gültigkeit f

valise [vəˈliːz] n kleiner Koffer m

valley ['vælɪ] n Tal nt

valour, (US) **valor** ['vælər] n Tapferkeit f

valuable ['væljuəbl] adj wertvoll; (time) kostbar

valuables ['væljuəblz] npl Wertsachen pl

valuation [væljuˈeɪʃən] n (of house etc) Schätzung f; (judgement of quality) Einschätzung f

value ['væljuː] n Wert m; (usefulness) Nutzen m ▷ vt schätzen; **values** npl (principles, beliefs) Werte pl; **you get good ~ (for money) in that shop** in dem Laden bekommt man etwas für sein Geld; **to lose (in) ~** an Wert verlieren; **to gain (in) ~** im Wert steigen; **to be of great ~ (to sb)** (fig) von großem Wert (für jdn) sein

value-added tax [vælju:'ædɪd-] (Brit) n Mehrwertsteuer f

valued ['væljuːd] adj (customer, advice) geschätzt

valuer ['væljuər] n Schätzer(in) m(f)

valve [vælv] n Ventil nt; (Med) Klappe f

vampire ['væmpaɪər] n Vampir m

van [væn] n (Aut) Lieferwagen m; (Brit: Rail) Wa(g)gon m

V and A (Brit) n abbr (= Victoria and Albert Museum) Londoner Museum

vandal ['vændl] n Rowdy m

vandalism ['vændəlɪzəm] n Vandalismus m

vandalize ['vændəlaɪz] vt mutwillig zerstören

vanguard ['væŋgɑːd] n (fig): **in the ~ of** an der Spitze +gen

vanilla [və'nɪlə] n Vanille f

vanilla ice cream n Vanilleeis nt

vanish ['vænɪʃ] vi verschwinden

vanity ['vænɪtɪ] n (of person) Eitelkeit f

vanity case n Kosmetikkoffer m

vantage point ['vɑːntɪdʒ-] n Aussichtspunkt m; (fig): **from our ~** aus unserer Sicht

vaporize ['veɪpəraɪz] vt verdampfen ▷ vi verdunsten

vapour, (US) **vapor** ['veɪpəʳ] n (gas, steam) Dampf m; (mist) Dunst m

vapour trail n (Aviat) Kondensstreifen m

variable ['veərɪəbl] adj (likely to change: mood, quality, weather) veränderlich, wechselhaft; (able to be changed: temperature, height, speed) variabel ▷ n veränderlicher Faktor m; (Math) Variable f

variance ['veərɪəns] n: **to be at ~ (with)** nicht übereinstimmen (mit)

variant ['veərɪənt] n Variante f

variation [veərɪ'eɪʃən] n (change) Veränderung f; (different form: of plot, theme etc) Variation f

varicose ['værɪkəus] adj: **~ veins** Krampfadern pl

varied ['veərɪd] adj (diverse) unterschiedlich; (full of changes) abwechslungsreich

variety [və'raɪətɪ] n (diversity) Vielfalt f; (varied collection) Auswahl f; (type) Sorte f; **a wide ~ of ...** eine Vielfalt an +acc ...; **for a ~ of reasons** aus verschiedenen Gründen

variety show n Varietévorführung f

various ['veərɪəs] adj (reasons, people) verschiedene; **at ~ times** (different) zu verschiedenen Zeiten; (several) mehrmals, mehrfach

varnish ['vɑːnɪʃ] n Lack m ▷ vt (wood, one's nails) lackieren

vary ['veərɪ] vt verändern ▷ vi (be different) variieren; **to ~ with** (weather, season etc) sich ändern mit

varying ['veərɪɪŋ] adj unterschiedlich

vase [vɑːz] n Vase f

vasectomy [væ'sektəmɪ] n Vasektomie f

Vaseline® ['væsɪliːn] n Vaseline f

vast [vɑːst] adj (knowledge) enorm; (expense, area) riesig

vastly ['vɑːstlɪ] adv (superior, improved) erheblich

vastness ['vɑːstnɪs] n ungeheure Größe f

VAT [væt] (Brit) n abbr (= value-added tax) MwSt f

vat [væt] n Fass nt

Vatican ['vætɪkən] n: **the ~** der Vatikan

vatman ['vætmæn] (inf: irreg: like **man**) n ≈ Fiskus m (bezüglich Einbehaltung der Mehrwertsteuer)

vaudeville ['vəudəvɪl] n Varieté nt

vault [vɔːlt] n (of roof) Gewölbe nt; (tomb) Gruft f; (in bank) Tresorraum m; (jump) Sprung m ▷ vt (also: **vault over**) überspringen

vaunted ['vɔːntɪd] adj: **much-~** viel gepriesen

VC n abbr = **vice-chairman**; (Brit: = Victoria Cross) Viktoriakreuz nt, höchste britische Tapferkeitsauszeichnung

VCR n abbr = **video cassette recorder**

VD n abbr = **venereal disease**

VDU n abbr (Comput) = **visual display unit**

veal [viːl] n Kalbfleisch nt

veer [vɪəʳ] vi (wind) sich drehen; (vehicle) ausscheren

veg (Brit: inf) n abbr = **vegetable; vegetables**

vegan ['viːgən] n Veganer(in) m(f) ▷ adj radikal vegetarisch

vegeburger ['vedʒɪbəːgəʳ] n vegetarischer Hamburger m

vegetable ['vedʒtəbl] n (plant) Gemüse nt; (plant life) Pflanzen pl ▷ cpd (oil etc) Pflanzen-; (garden, plot) Gemüse-

vegetarian [vedʒɪ'teərɪən] n Vegetarier(in) m(f) ▷ adj vegetarisch

vegetate ['vedʒɪteɪt] vi (fig: person) dahinvegetieren

vegetation [vedʒɪ'teɪʃən] n (plants) Vegetation f

vegetative ['vedʒɪtətɪv] adj vegetativ

veggieburger ['vedʒɪbəːgəʳ] n = **vegeburger**

vehemence ['viːɪməns] n Vehemenz f, Heftigkeit f

vehement ['viːɪmənt] adj heftig

vehicle ['viːɪkl] n (machine) Fahrzeug nt; (fig: means) Mittel nt

vehicular [vɪ'hɪkjuləʳ] adj: **"no ~ traffic"** „kein Fahrzeugverkehr"

veil [veɪl] n Schleier m ▷ vt (also fig) verschleiern; **under a ~ of secrecy** unter einem Schleier von Geheimnissen

veiled [veɪld] adj (also fig: threat) verschleiert

vein [veɪn] n Ader f; (fig: mood, style) Stimmung f

Velcro® ['velkrəu] n (also: **Velcro fastener** or **fastening**) Klettverschluss m

vellum ['veləm] n (writing paper) Pergament nt

velocity [vɪ'lɔsɪtɪ] n Geschwindigkeit f

velours [və'luəʳ] n Velours m

velvet ['velvɪt] n Samt m ▷ adj (skirt, jacket) Samt-

vendetta [ven'detə] n Vendetta f; (between families) Blutrache f

vending machine ['vendɪŋ-] n Automat m

vendor ['vendəʳ] n Verkäufer(in) m(f); **street ~** Straßenhändler(in) m(f)

veneer [və'nɪəʳ] n (on furniture) Furnier nt; (fig) Anstrich m

venerable ['venərəbl] adj ehrwürdig; (Rel) hochwürdig

venereal [vɪ'nɪərɪəl] adj: **~ disease** Geschlechtskrankheit f

Venetian [vɪ'niːʃən] adj (Geog) venezianisch ▷ n (person) Venezianer(in) m(f)

Venetian blind n Jalousie f

Venezuela [venɛ'zweɪlə] n Venezuela nt

Venezuelan [venɛ'zweɪlən] adj venezolanisch ▷ n (person) Venezolaner(in) m(f)

vengeance ['vendʒəns] n Rache f; **with a ~** (fig: fiercely) gewaltig; **he broke the rules with a ~** er verstieß die Regeln – und nicht zu knapp

vengeful ['vendʒful] adj rachsüchtig

851

Venice ['vɛnɪs] n Venedig nt
venison ['vɛnɪsn] n Rehfleisch nt
venom ['vɛnəm] n (poison) Gift nt; (bitterness, anger) Gehässigkeit f
venomous ['vɛnəməs] adj (snake, insect) giftig; (look) gehässig
vent [vɛnt] n (also: **air vent**) Abzug m; (in jacket) Schlitz m ▷ vt (fig: feelings) abreagieren
ventilate ['vɛntɪleɪt] vt (building) belüften; (room) lüften
ventilation [vɛntɪ'leɪʃən] n Belüftung f
ventilation shaft n Luftschacht m
ventilator ['vɛntɪleɪtə'] n (Tech) Ventilator m; (Med) Beatmungsgerät nt
ventriloquist [vɛn'trɪləkwɪst] n Bauchredner(in) m(f)
venture ['vɛntʃə'] n Unternehmung f ▷ vt (opinion) zu äußern wagen ▷ vi (dare to go) sich wagen; **a business ~** ein geschäftliches Unternehmen; **to ~ to do sth** es wagen, etw zu tun
venture capital n Risikokapital nt
venue ['vɛnjuː] n (for meeting) Treffpunkt m; (for big events) Austragungsort m
Venus ['viːnəs] n Venus f
veracity [və'ræsɪtɪ] n (of person) Aufrichtigkeit f; (of evidence etc) Richtigkeit f
veranda, verandah [və'rændə] n Veranda f
verb [vɜːb] n Verb nt
verbal ['vɜːbl] adj verbal; (skills) sprachlich; (translation) wörtlich
verbally ['vɜːbəlɪ] adv (communicate etc) mündlich, verbal
verbatim [vɜː'beɪtɪm] adj wörtlich ▷ adv Wort für Wort
verbose [vɜː'bəus] adj (person) wortreich; (writing) weitschweifig
verdict ['vɜːdɪkt] n (Law, fig) Urteil nt; **~ of guilty/not guilty** Schuld-/Freispruch m
verge [vɜːdʒ] (Brit) n (of road) Rand m, Bankett nt; **"soft ~s"** (Brit: Aut) „Seitenstreifen nicht befahrbar"; **to be on the ~ of doing sth** im Begriff sein, etw zu tun
▷ **verge on** vt fus grenzen an +acc
verger ['vɜːdʒə'] n (Rel) Küster m
verification [vɛrɪfɪ'keɪʃən] n (see vt) Bestätigung f; Überprüfung f
verify ['vɛrɪfaɪ] vt (confirm) bestätigen; (check) überprüfen
veritable ['vɛrɪtəbl] adj (real) wahr
vermin ['vɜːmɪn] npl Ungeziefer nt
vermouth ['vɜːməθ] n Wermut m
vernacular [və'nækjulə'] n (of country) Landessprache f; (of region) Dialekt m
versatile ['vɜːsətaɪl] adj vielseitig
versatility [vɜːsə'tɪlɪtɪ] n Vielseitigkeit f
verse [vɜːs] n (poetry) Poesie f; (stanza) Strophe f; (in bible) Vers m; **in ~** in Versform
versed [vɜːst] adj: **(well-)~ in** (gut) bewandert in +dat
version ['vɜːʃən] n Version f
versus ['vɜːsəs] prep gegen
vertebra ['vɜːtɪbrə] (pl **-e**) n Rückenwirbel m

vertebrae ['vɜːtɪbriː] npl of **vertebra**
vertebrate ['vɜːtɪbrɪt] n Wirbeltier nt
vertical ['vɜːtɪkl] adj vertikal, senkrecht ▷ n Vertikale f
vertically ['vɜːtɪklɪ] adv vertikal
vertigo ['vɜːtɪgəu] n Schwindelgefühle pl; **to suffer from ~** leicht schwindlig werden
verve [vɜːv] n Schwung m
very ['vɛrɪ] adv sehr ▷ adj: **the ~ book which ...** genau das Buch, das ...; **the ~ last** der/die/das Allerletzte; **at the ~ least** allerwenigstens; **~ well/little** sehr gut/wenig; **~ much** sehr viel; (like, hope) sehr; **the ~ thought (of it) alarms me** der bloße Gedanke (daran) beunruhigt mich; **at the ~ end** ganz am Ende
vespers ['vɛspəz] npl (Rel) Vesper f
vessel ['vɛsl] n Gefäß nt; (Naut) Schiff nt; see **blood**
vest [vɛst] n (Brit: underwear) Unterhemd nt; (US: waistcoat) Weste f ▷ vt: **to ~ sb with sth, ~ sth in sb** jdm etw verleihen
vested interest ['vɛstɪd-] n (Comm) finanzielles Interesse nt; **to have a ~ in doing sth** ein besonderes Interesse daran haben, etw zu tun
vestibule ['vɛstɪbjuːl] n Vorhalle f
vestige ['vɛstɪdʒ] n Spur f
vestment ['vɛstmənt] n (Rel) Ornat nt
vestry ['vɛstrɪ] n Sakristei f
Vesuvius [vɪ'suːvɪəs] n Vesuv m
vet [vɛt] (Brit) n = **veterinary surgeon**; (US) = **veteran** ▷ vt (examine) überprüfen
veteran ['vɛtərn] n Veteran(in) m(f) ▷ adj: **she's a ~ campaigner for ...** sie ist eine altgediente Kämpferin für ...
veteran car n Oldtimer m (vor 1919 gebaut)
veterinarian [vɛtrɪ'nɛərɪən] (US) n = **veterinary surgeon**
veterinary ['vɛtrɪnərɪ] adj (practice, medicine) Veterinär-; (care, training) tierärztlich
veterinary surgeon (Brit) n Tierarzt m, Tierärztin f
veto ['viːtəu] (pl **-es**) n Veto nt ▷ vt ein Veto einlegen gegen; **to put a ~ on sth** gegen etw ein Veto einlegen
vetting ['vɛtɪŋ] n Überprüfung f
vex [vɛks] vt (irritate, upset) ärgern
vexed [vɛkst] adj (upset) verärgert; (question) umstritten
VFD (US) n abbr (= volunteer fire department) ≈ freiwillige Feuerwehr f
VG (Brit) n abbr (Scol etc: = very good) ≈ "sehr gut"
VHF abbr (Radio: = very high frequency) VHF
VI (US) abbr (Post) = Virgin Islands
via ['vaɪə] prep über +acc
viability [vaɪə'bɪlɪtɪ] n (see adj) Durchführbarkeit f; Rentabilität f
viable ['vaɪəbl] adj (project) durchführbar; (company) rentabel
viaduct ['vaɪədʌkt] n Viadukt m
vial ['vaɪəl] n Fläschchen nt
vibes [vaɪbz] npl (Mus) see **vibraphone** (inf: vibrations): **I get good/bad ~ from it/him** das/er macht mich an/nicht an

vibrant ['vaɪbrnt] adj (lively) dynamisch; (bright) lebendig; (full of emotion: voice) volltönend
vibraphone ['vaɪbrəfəʊn] n Vibrafon nt
vibrate [vaɪ'breɪt] vi (house) zittern, beben; (machine, sound etc) vibrieren
vibration [vaɪ'breɪʃən] n (act of vibrating) Vibrieren nt; (instance) Vibration f
vibrator [vaɪ'breɪtə^r] n Vibrator m
vicar ['vɪkə^r] n Pfarrer m
vicarage ['vɪkərɪdʒ] n Pfarrhaus nt
vicarious [vɪ'kɛərɪəs] adj (pleasure, experience) indirekt
vice [vaɪs] n (moral fault) Laster nt; (Tech) Schraubstock m
vice- [vaɪs] pref Vize-
vice-chairman [vaɪs'tʃɛəmən] n stellvertretender Vorsitzender m
vice chancellor (Brit) n (of university) ≈ Rektor m
vice president n Vizepräsident(in) m(f)
viceroy ['vaɪsrɔɪ] n Vizekönig m
vice squad n (Police) Sittendezernat nt
vice versa ['vaɪsɪ'və:sə] adv umgekehrt
vicinity [vɪ'sɪnɪtɪ] n: **in the ~ (of)** in der Nähe or Umgebung (+gen)
vicious ['vɪʃəs] adj (attack, blow) brutal; (words, look) gemein; (horse, dog) bösartig
vicious circle n Teufelskreis m
viciousness ['vɪʃəsnɪs] n Bösartigkeit f, Gemeinheit f
vicissitudes [vɪ'sɪsɪtjuːdz] npl Wechselfälle pl
victim ['vɪktɪm] n Opfer nt; **to be the ~ of an attack** einem Angriff zum Opfer fallen
victimization ['vɪktɪmaɪ'zeɪʃən] n Schikanierung f
victimize ['vɪktɪmaɪz] vt schikanieren
victor ['vɪktə^r] n Sieger(in) m(f)
Victorian [vɪk'tɔːrɪən] adj viktorianisch
victorious [vɪk'tɔːrɪəs] adj (team) siegreich; (shout) triumphierend
victory ['vɪktərɪ] n Sieg m; **to win a ~ over sb** einen Sieg über jdn erringen
video ['vɪdɪəʊ] n (film, cassette, recorder) Video nt ▷ vt auf Video aufnehmen ▷ cpd Video-
video camera n Videokamera f
video cassette n Videokassette f
video cassette recorder n Videorekorder m
videodisc, videodisk ['vɪdɪəʊdɪsk] n Bildplatte f
video game n Videospiel nt, Telespiel nt
video nasty n Video mit übertriebenen Gewaltszenen und/oder pornografischem Inhalt
videophone ['vɪdɪəʊfəʊn] n Bildtelefon nt
video recorder n Videorekorder m
video recording n Videoaufnahme f
video tape n Videoband nt
vie [vaɪ] vi: **to ~ with sb/for sth** mit jdm/um etw wetteifern
Vienna [vɪ'ɛnə] n Wien nt
Viennese [vɪə'niːz] adj Wiener
Vietnam ['vjɛt'næm] n Vietnam nt
Viet Nam ['vjɛt'næm] n = **Vietnam**
Vietnamese [vjɛtnə'miːz] adj vietnamesisch ▷ n inv (person) Vietnamese m, Vietnamesin f;

(Ling) Vietnamesisch nt
view [vjuː] n (from window etc) Aussicht f; (sight) Blick m; (outlook) Sicht f; (opinion) Ansicht f ▷ vt betrachten; (house) besichtigen; **to be on ~** (in museum etc) ausgestellt sein; **in full ~ of** vor den Augen +gen; **to take the ~ that ...** der Ansicht sein, dass ...; **in ~ of the weather/ the fact that** in Anbetracht des Wetters/der Tatsache, dass ...; **in my ~** meiner Ansicht nach; **an overall ~ of the situation** ein allgemeiner Überblick über die Lage; **with a ~ to doing sth** mit der Absicht, etw zu tun
viewdata® ['vjuːdeɪtə] (Brit) n Bildschirmtext m
viewer ['vjuː:ə^r] n (person) Zuschauer(in) m(f); (viewfinder) Sucher m
viewfinder ['vjuːfaɪndə^r] n Sucher m
viewpoint ['vjuːpɔɪnt] n (attitude) Standpunkt m; (place) Aussichtspunkt m
vigil ['vɪdʒɪl] n Wache f; **to keep ~** Wache halten
vigilance ['vɪdʒɪləns] n Wachsamkeit f
vigilance committee (US) n Bürgerwehr f
vigilant ['vɪdʒɪlənt] adj wachsam
vigilante [vɪdʒɪ'læntɪ] n Mitglied einer Selbstschutzorganisation oder Bürgerwehr ▷ adj (group, patrol) Bürgerwehr-, Selbstschutz-
vigorous ['vɪgərəs] adj (action, campaign) energisch, dynamisch; (plant) kräftig
vigour, (US) **vigor** ['vɪgə^r] n (of person, campaign) Energie f, Dynamik f
vile [vaɪl] adj abscheulich
vilify ['vɪlɪfaɪ] vt diffamieren
villa ['vɪlə] n Villa f
village ['vɪlɪdʒ] n Dorf nt
villager ['vɪlɪdʒə^r] n Dorfbewohner(in) m(f)
villain ['vɪlən] n (scoundrel) Schurke m; (in novel etc) Bösewicht m; (Brit: criminal) Verbrecher(in) m(f)
VIN (US) n abbr (= vehicle identification number) amtliches Kennzeichen nt
vinaigrette [vɪneɪ'grɛt] n Vinaigrette f
vindicate ['vɪndɪkeɪt] vt (person) rehabilitieren; (action) rechtfertigen
vindication [vɪndɪ'keɪʃən] n Rechtfertigung f
vindictive [vɪn'dɪktɪv] adj (person) nachtragend; (action) aus Rache
vine [vaɪn] n (Bot: producing grapes) Weinrebe f; (: in jungle) Rebengewächs nt
vinegar ['vɪnɪgə^r] n Essig m
vine grower n Weinbauer m
vine-growing ['vaɪngrəʊɪŋ] adj (region) Weinbau- ▷ n Weinbau m
vineyard ['vɪnjɑːd] n Weinberg m
vintage ['vɪntɪdʒ] n (of wine) Jahrgang m ▷ cpd (classic) klassisch; **the 1980 ~** (of wine) der Jahrgang 1980
vintage car n Oldtimer m (zwischen 1919 und 1930 gebaut)
vintage wine n erlesener Wein m
vinyl ['vaɪnl] n Vinyl nt; (records) Schallplatten pl
viola [vɪ'əʊlə] n Bratsche f

V

853

violate ['vaɪəleɪt] vt (agreement) verletzen; (peace) stören; (graveyard) schänden

violation [vaɪə'leɪʃən] n (of agreement etc) Verletzung f; **in ~ of** (rule, law) unter Verletzung +gen

violence ['vaɪələns] n Gewalt f; (strength) Heftigkeit f

violent ['vaɪələnt] adj (behaviour) gewalttätig; (death) gewaltsam; (explosion, criticism, emotion) heftig; **a ~ dislike of sb/sth** eine heftige Abneigung gegen jdn/etw

violently ['vaɪələntlɪ] adv heftig; (ill) schwer; (angry) äußerst

violet ['vaɪələt] adj violett ▷ n (colour) Violett nt; (plant) Veilchen nt

violin [vaɪə'lɪn] n Geige f, Violine f

violinist [vaɪə'lɪnɪst] n Violinist(in) m(f), Geiger(in) m(f)

VIP n abbr (= very important person) VIP m

viper ['vaɪpəʳ] n Viper f

viral ['vaɪərəl] adj (disease, infection) Virus-

virgin ['vɜːdʒɪn] n Jungfrau f ▷ adj (snow, forest etc) unberührt; **she is a ~** sie ist Jungfrau; **the Blessed V~** die Heilige Jungfrau

virgin birth n unbefleckte Empfängnis f; (Biol) Jungfernzeugung f

virginity [vəː'dʒɪnɪtɪ] n (of person) Jungfräulichkeit f

Virgo ['vɜːgəu] n (sign) Jungfrau f; **to be ~** Jungfrau sein

virile ['vɪraɪl] adj (person) männlich

virility [vɪ'rɪlɪtɪ] n (masculine qualities) Männlichkeit f

virtual ['vɜːtjuəl] adj (Comput, Phys) virtuell; **it's a ~ impossibility** es ist so gut wie unmöglich; **to be the ~ leader** eigentlich or praktisch der Führer sein

virtually ['vɜːtjuəlɪ] adv praktisch, nahezu; **it is ~ impossible** es ist so gut wie unmöglich

virtual reality n virtuelle Realität f

virtue ['vɜːtjuː] n Tugend f; (advantage) Vorzug m; **by ~ of** aufgrund +gen

virtuosi [vɜːtju'əuzi] npl of **virtuoso**

virtuosity [vɜːtju'ɒsɪtɪ] n Virtuosität f

virtuoso [vɜːtju'əuzəu] (pl **~s** or **virtuosi**) n Virtuose m

virtuous ['vɜːtjuəs] adj tugendhaft

virulence ['vɪruləns] n (of disease) Bösartigkeit f; (hatred) Feindseligkeit f

virulent ['vɪrulənt] adj (disease) bösartig; (actions, feelings) feindselig

virus ['vaɪərəs] n (Med, Comput) Virus m or nt

visa ['viːzə] n Visum nt

vis-à-vis [viːzə'viː] prep gegenüber

viscose ['vɪskəus] n (also Chem) Viskose f

viscount ['vaɪkaunt] n Viscount m

viscous ['vɪskəs] adj zähflüssig

vise [vaɪs] (US) n (Tech) = **vice**

visibility [vɪzɪ'bɪlɪtɪ] n (range of vision) Sicht(weite) f

visible ['vɪzəbl] adj sichtbar; **~ exports/ imports** sichtbare Ausfuhren/Einfuhren

visibly ['vɪzəblɪ] adv sichtlich

vision ['vɪʒən] n (sight) Sicht f; (foresight) Weitblick m; (in dream) Vision f

visionary ['vɪʒənrɪ] adj (with foresight) vorausblickend

visit ['vɪzɪt] n Besuch m ▷ vt besuchen; **a private/official ~** ein privater/offizieller Besuch

visiting ['vɪzɪtɪŋ] adj (speaker, team) Gast-

visiting card n Visitenkarte f

visiting hours npl Besuchszeiten pl

visiting professor n Gastprofessor(in) m(f)

visitor ['vɪzɪtəʳ] n Besucher(in) m(f)

visitors' book ['vɪzɪtəz-] n Gästebuch nt

visor ['vaɪzəʳ] n (of helmet etc) Visier nt

VISTA ['vɪstə] (US) n abbr (= Volunteers In Service To America) staatliches Förderprogramm für strukturschwache Gebiete

vista ['vɪstə] n Aussicht f

visual ['vɪzjuəl] adj (image etc) visuell; **the ~ arts** die darstellenden Künste

visual aid n Anschauungsmaterial nt

visual display unit n (Daten)sichtgerät nt

visualize ['vɪzjuəlaɪz] vt sich dat vorstellen

visually ['vɪzjuəlɪ] adv visuell; **~ appealing** optisch ansprechend; **~ handicapped** sehbehindert

vital ['vaɪtl] adj (essential) unerlässlich; (organ) lebenswichtig; (full of life) vital; **of ~ importance (to sb/sth)** von größter Wichtigkeit (für jdn/etw)

vitality [vaɪ'tælɪtɪ] n (liveliness) Vitalität f

vitally ['vaɪtəlɪ] adv: **~ important** äußerst wichtig

vital statistics npl (fig: of woman) Körpermaße pl; (of population) Bevölkerungsstatistik f

vitamin ['vɪtəmɪn] n Vitamin nt ▷ cpd (pill, deficiencies) Vitamin-

vitiate ['vɪʃɪeɪt] vt (spoil) verunreinigen

vitreous ['vɪtrɪəs] adj: **~ china** Porzellanemail nt; **~ enamel** Glasemail nt

vitriolic [vɪtrɪ'ɒlɪk] adj (fig: language, behaviour) hasserfüllt

viva ['vaɪvə] n (Scol: also: **viva voce** [-'vəutʃɪ]) mündliche Prüfung f

vivacious [vɪ'veɪʃəs] adj lebhaft

vivacity [vɪ'væsɪtɪ] n Lebendigkeit f

vivid ['vɪvɪd] adj (description) lebendig; (memory, imagination) lebhaft; (colour) leuchtend; (light) hell

vividly ['vɪvɪdlɪ] adv (describe) lebendig; (remember) lebhaft

vivisection [vɪvɪ'sɛkʃən] n Vivisektion f

vixen ['vɪksn] n (Zool) Füchsin f; (pej: woman) Drachen m

viz [vɪz] abbr (= videlicet) nämlich

VLF abbr (Radio: = very low frequency) VLF

V-neck ['viːnɛk] n (also: **V-neck jumper** or **pullover**) Pullover m mit V-Ausschnitt

VOA n abbr (= Voice of America) Stimme f Amerikas

vocabulary [vəu'kæbjulərɪ] n (words known) Vokabular nt, Wortschatz m

vocal ['vəukl] adj (of the voice) stimmlich;

(*articulate*) lautstark
vocal cords *npl* Stimmbänder *pl*
vocalist ['vəukəlɪst] *n* Sänger(in) *m(f)*
vocals ['vəuklz] *npl* (*Mus*) Gesang *m*
vocation [vəu'keɪʃən] *n* (*calling*) Berufung *f*;
(*profession*) Beruf *m*
vocational [vəu'keɪʃənl] *adj* (*training, guidance etc*) Berufs-
vociferous [və'sɪfərəs] *adj* (*protesters, demands*) lautstark
vodka ['vɔdkə] *n* Wodka *m*
vogue [vəug] *n* (*fashion*) Mode *f*; (*popularity*) Popularität *f*; **in ~** in Mode
voice [vɔɪs] *n* (*also fig*) Stimme *f* ▷ *vt* (*opinion*) zum Ausdruck bringen; **in a loud/soft ~** mit lauter/leiser Stimme; **to give ~ to** Ausdruck verleihen +*dat*
voice mail *n* (*Comput*) Voicemail *f*
voice-over ['vɔɪsəuvəʳ] *n* (*Film*)kommentar *m*
void [vɔɪd] *n* (*hole*) Loch *nt*; (*fig: emptiness*) Leere *f* ▷ *adj* (*invalid*) ungültig; **~ of** (*empty*) ohne
voile [vɔɪl] *n* Voile *m*
vol. *abbr* (= *volume*) Bd.
volatile ['vɔlətaɪl] *adj* (*person*) impulsiv; (*situation*) unsicher; (*liquid etc*) flüchtig
volcanic [vɔl'kænɪk] *adj* (*rock, eruption*) vulkanisch, Vulkan-
volcano [vɔl'keɪnəu] (*pl* **-es**) *n* Vulkan *m*
volition [və'lɪʃən] *n*: **of one's own ~** aus freiem Willen
volley ['vɔlɪ] *n* (*of gunfire*) Salve *f*; (*of stones, questions*) Hagel *m*; (*Tennis etc*) Volley *m*
volleyball ['vɔlɪbɔːl] *n* Volleyball *m*
volt [vəult] *n* Volt *nt*
voltage ['vəultɪdʒ] *n* Spannung *f*; **high/low ~** Hoch-/Niederspannung *f*
volte-face ['vɔlt'fɑːs] *n* Kehrtwendung *f*
voluble ['vɔljubl] *adj* (*person*) redselig; (*speech*) wortreich
volume ['vɔljuːm] *n* (*space*) Volumen *nt*; (*amount*) Umfang *m*, Ausmaß *nt*; (*book*) Band *m*; (*sound level*) Lautstärke *f*; **~ one/two** (*of book*) Band eins/zwei; **his expression spoke ~s** sein Gesichtsausdruck sprach Bände
volume control *n* (*Radio, TV*) Lautstärkeregler *m*
volume discount *n* (*Comm*) Mengenrabatt *m*
voluminous [və'luːmɪnəs] *adj* (*clothes*) sehr weit; (*correspondence, notes*) umfangreich
voluntarily ['vɔləntrɪlɪ] *adv* freiwillig
voluntary ['vɔləntərɪ] *adj* freiwillig
voluntary liquidation *n* freiwillige Liquidation *f*
volunteer [vɔlən'tɪəʳ] *n* Freiwillige(r) *f(m)* ▷ *vt* (*information*) vorbringen ▷ *vi* (*for army etc*) sich freiwillig melden; **to ~ to do sth** sich

anbieten, etw zu tun
voluptuous [və'lʌptjuəs] *adj* sinnlich, wollüstig
vomit ['vɔmɪt] *n* Erbrochene(s) *nt* ▷ *vt* erbrechen ▷ *vi* sich übergeben
voracious [və'reɪʃəs] *adj* (*person*) gefräßig; **~ appetite** Riesenappetit *m*
vortal ['vɔːtl] *n* (*Comput*) Vortal *nt*
vote [vəut] *n* Stimme *f*; (*votes cast*) Stimmen *pl*; (*right to vote*) Wahlrecht *nt*; (*ballot*) Abstimmung *f* ▷ *vt* (*elect*): **to be ~d chairman etc** zum Vorsitzenden *etc* gewählt werden; (*propose*): **to ~ that** vorschlagen, dass ▷ *vi* (*in election etc*) wählen; **to put sth to the vote, (take a) ~ on sth** über etw *acc* abstimmen; **~ of censure** Tadelsantrag *m*; **to pass a ~ of confidence/no confidence** ein Vertrauens-/ Misstrauensvotum annehmen; **to ~ to do sth** dafür stimmen, etw zu tun; **to ~ yes/no** mit Ja/Nein stimmen; **to ~ Labour/Green etc** Labour/die Grünen *etc* wählen; **to ~ for** *or* **in favour of sth/against sth** für/gegen etw stimmen
vote of thanks *n* Danksagung *f*
voter ['vəutəʳ] *n* Wähler(in) *m(f)*
voting ['vəutɪŋ] *n* Wahl *f*
voting paper (*Brit*) *n* Stimmzettel *m*
voting right *n* Stimmrecht *nt*
vouch [vautʃ]: **~ for** *vt fus* bürgen für
voucher ['vautʃəʳ] *n* Gutschein *m*; (*receipt*) Beleg *m*; **gift ~** Geschenkgutschein *m*; **luncheon ~** Essensmarke *f*; **travel ~** Reisegutschein *m*
vow [vau] *n* Versprechen *nt* ▷ *vt*: **to ~ to do sth/that** geloben, etw zu tun/dass; **to take** *or* **make a ~ to do sth** geloben, etw zu tun
vowel ['vauəl] *n* Vokal *m*
voyage ['vɔɪɪdʒ] *n* Reise *f*
voyeur [vwaː'jəːʳ] *n* Voyeur(in) *m(f)*
voyeurism [vwaː'jəːrɪzəm] *n* Voyeurismus *m*
VP *n abbr* = **vice president**
vs *abbr* (= *versus*) vs.
V-sign ['viːsaɪn] (*Brit*) *n*: **to give sb the ~** jdm den Vogel zeigen
VSO (*Brit*) *n abbr* (= *Voluntary Service Overseas*) britischer Entwicklungsdienst
VT (*US*) *abbr* (*Post*) = *Vermont*
vulgar ['vʌlgəʳ] *adj* (*remarks, gestures*) vulgär; (*decor, ostentation*) geschmacklos
vulgarity [vʌl'gærɪtɪ] *n* (*see adj*) Vulgarität *f*; Geschmacklosigkeit *f*
vulnerability [vʌlnərə'bɪlɪtɪ] *n* Verletzlichkeit *f*
vulnerable ['vʌlnərəbl] *adj* (*person, position*) verletzlich
vulture ['vʌltʃəʳ] *n* (*also fig*) Geier *m*
vulva ['vʌlvə] *n* Vulva *f*

v

855

W¹, w ['dʌblju:] n (letter) W nt, w nt; **W for William** = W wie Wilhelm

W² ['dʌblju:] abbr (Elec: = watt) W; (= west) W

WA abbr (US: Post) = Washington; (Australia) = Western Australia

wad [wɔd] n (of cotton wool) Bausch m; (of paper, banknotes) Bündel nt

wadding ['wɔdɪŋ] n Füllmaterial nt

waddle ['wɔdl] vi watscheln

wade [weɪd] vi: **to ~ across** (a river, stream) waten durch; **to ~ through** (fig: a book) sich durchkämpfen durch

wafer ['weɪfər] n (biscuit) Waffel f

wafer-thin ['weɪfə'θɪn] adj hauchdünn

waffle ['wɔfl] n (Culin) Waffel f; (inf: empty talk) Geschwafel nt ▷ vi (in speech etc) schwafeln

waffle iron n Waffeleisen nt

waft [wɔft] vt, vi wehen

wag [wæg] vt (tail) wedeln mit; (finger) drohen mit ▷ vi (tail) wedeln; **the dog ~ged its tail** der Hund wedelte mit dem Schwanz

wage [weɪdʒ] n (also: **wages**) Lohn m ▷ vt: **to ~ war** Krieg führen; **a day's ~s** ein Tageslohn

wage claim n Lohnforderung f

wage differential n Lohnunterschied m

wage earner [-əːnər] n Lohnempfänger(in) m(f)

wage freeze n Lohnstopp m

wage packet n Lohntüte f

wager ['weɪdʒər] n Wette f ▷ vt wetten

waggle ['wægl] vt (ears etc) wackeln mit ▷ vi wackeln

wagon, waggon ['wægən] n (horse-drawn) Fuhrwerk nt; (Brit: Rail) Wa(g)gon m

wail [weɪl] n (of person) Jammern nt; (of siren) Heulen nt ▷ vi (person) jammern; (siren) heulen

waist [weɪst] n (Anat, of clothing) Taille f

waistcoat ['weɪskəut] (Brit) n Weste f

waistline ['weɪstlaɪn] n Taille f

wait [weɪt] n Wartezeit f ▷ vi warten; **to lie in ~ for sb** jdm auflauern; **to keep sb ~ing** jdn warten lassen; **I can't ~ to ...** (fig) ich kann es kaum erwarten, zu ...; **to ~ for sb/sth** auf jdn/etw warten; **~ a minute!** Moment mal!; **"repairs while you ~"** „Reparaturen sofort"

▸ **wait behind** vi zurückbleiben

▸ **wait on** vt fus (serve) bedienen

▸ **wait up** vi aufbleiben; **don't ~ up for me**

warte nicht auf mich

waiter ['weɪtər] n Kellner m

waiting ['weɪtɪŋ] n: **"no ~"** (Brit: Aut) „Halten verboten"

waiting list n Warteliste f

waiting room n (in surgery) Wartezimmer nt; (in railway station) Wartesaal m

waitress ['weɪtrɪs] n Kellnerin f

waive [weɪv] vt (rule) verzichten auf +acc

waiver ['weɪvər] n Verzicht m

wake [weɪk] (pt **woke, ~d**, pp **woken, ~d**) vt (also: **wake up**) wecken ▷ vi (also: **wake up**) aufwachen ▷ n (for dead person) Totenwache f; (Naut) Kielwasser nt; **to ~ up to** (fig) sich dat bewusst werden +gen; **in the ~ of** (fig) unmittelbar nach, im Gefolge +gen; **to follow in sb's ~** (fig) hinter jdm herziehen

waken ['weɪkn] vt = **wake**

Wales [weɪlz] n Wales nt; **the Prince of ~** der Prinz von Wales

walk [wɔːk] n (hike) Wanderung f; (shorter) Spaziergang m; (gait) Gang m; (path) Weg m; (in park, along coast etc) (Spazier)weg m ▷ vi gehen; (instead of driving) zu Fuß gehen; (for pleasure, exercise) spazieren gehen ▷ vt (distance) gehen, laufen; (dog) ausführen; **it's 10 minutes' ~ from here** es ist 10 Minuten zu Fuß von hier; **to go for a ~** spazieren gehen; **to slow to a ~** im Schritttempo weitergehen; **people from all ~s of life** Leute aus allen Gesellschaftsschichten; **to ~ in one's sleep** schlafwandeln; **I'd rather ~ than take the bus** ich gehe lieber zu Fuß als mit dem Bus zu fahren; **I'll ~ you home** ich bringe dich nach Hause

▸ **walk out** vi (audience) den Saal verlassen; (workers) in Streik treten

▸ **walk out on** (inf) vt fus (family etc) verlassen

walkabout ['wɔːkəbaut] n: **the Queen/ president went on a ~** die Königin/der Präsident mischte sich unters Volk or nahm ein Bad in der Menge

walker ['wɔːkər] n (person) Spaziergänger(in) m(f)

walkie-talkie ['wɔːkɪ'tɔːkɪ] n Walkie-Talkie nt

walking ['wɔːkɪŋ] n Wandern nt; **it's within ~ distance** es ist zu Fuß erreichbar

walking holiday n Wanderurlaub m

walking shoes npl Wanderschuhe pl
walking stick n Spazierstock m
Walkman® ['wɔːkmən] n Walkman® m
walk-on ['wɔːkɔn] adj (Theat): ~ **part** Statistenrolle f
walkout ['wɔːkaʊt] n (of workers) Streik m
walkover ['wɔːkəʊvəʳ] (inf) n (competition, exam etc) Kinderspiel nt
walkway ['wɔːkweɪ] n Fußweg m
wall [wɔːl] n Wand f; (exterior, city wall etc) Mauer f; **to go to the ~** (fig: firm etc) kaputtgehen
▸ **wall in** vt (enclose) ummauern
wall cupboard n Wandschrank m
walled [wɔːld] adj von Mauern umgeben
wallet ['wɔlɪt] n Brieftasche f
wallflower ['wɔːlflaʊəʳ] n (Bot) Goldlack m; **to be a ~** (fig) ein Mauerblümchen sein
wall hanging n Wandbehang m
wallop ['wɔləp] (Brit: inf) vt verprügeln
wallow ['wɔləʊ] vi (in mud, water) sich wälzen; (in guilt, grief) schwelgen
wallpaper ['wɔːlpeɪpəʳ] n Tapete f ▸ vt tapezieren
wall-to-wall ['wɔːltə'wɔːl] adj: ~ **carpeting** Teppichboden m
wally [wɔlɪ] (inf) n Trottel m
walnut ['wɔːlnʌt] n (nut) Walnuss f; (tree) Walnussbaum m; (wood) Nussbaumholz nt
walrus ['wɔːlrəs] (pl ~ or **walruses**) n Walross nt
waltz [wɔːlts] n Walzer m ▸ vi Walzer tanzen
wan [wɔn] adj bleich; (smile) matt
wand [wɔnd] n (also: **magic wand**) Zauberstab m
wander ['wɔndəʳ] vi (person) herumlaufen; (mind, thoughts) wandern ▸ vt (the streets, the hills etc) durchstreifen
wanderer ['wɔndərəʳ] n Wandervogel m
wandering ['wɔndrɪŋ] adj (tribe) umherziehend; (minstrel, actor) fahrend
wane [weɪn] vi (moon) abnehmen; (influence etc) schwinden
wangle ['wæŋgl] (Brit: inf) vt sich dat verschaffen
wanker ['wæŋkəʳ] (inf!) n Wichser m
wannabe, wannabee ['wɔnəbiː] (inf) n Möchtegern m; **James Bond ~(e)** Möchtegern-James-Bond m
want [wɔnt] vt (wish for) wollen; (need) brauchen ▸ n (lack): **for ~ of** aus Mangel an +dat; **wants** npl (needs) Bedürfnisse pl; **to ~ to do sth** etw tun wollen; **to ~ sb to do sth** wollen, dass jd etw tut; **to ~ in/out** herein-/hinauswollen; **you're ~ed on the phone** Sie werden am Telefon verlangt; **he is ~ed by the police** er wird von der Polizei gesucht; **a ~ of foresight** ein Mangel m an Voraussicht
want ads (US) npl Kaufgesuche pl
wanted ['wɔntɪd] adj (criminal etc) gesucht; **"cook ~"** „Koch/Köchin gesucht"
wanting ['wɔntɪŋ] adj: **to be found ~** sich als unzulänglich erweisen
wanton ['wɔntn] adj (violence) mutwillig; (promiscuous: woman) schamlos

WAP [wæp] n abbr (Comput: = wireless application protocol) WAP nt
war [wɔːʳ] n Krieg m; **to go to ~** (start) einen Krieg anfangen; **to be at ~ (with)** im Kriegszustand befinden (mit); **to make ~ (on)** Krieg führen (gegen); **a ~ on drugs/crime** ein Feldzug gegen Drogen/das Verbrechen
warble ['wɔːbl] n Trällern nt ▸ vi trällern
war cry n Kriegsruf m; (fig: slogan) Schlachtruf m
ward [wɔːd] n (in hospital) Station f; (Pol) Wahlbezirk m; (Law: also: **ward of court**) Mündel nt unter Amtsvormundschaft
▸ **ward off** vt (attack, enemy, illness) abwehren
warden ['wɔːdn] n (of park etc) Aufseher(in) m(f); (of jail) Wärter(in) m(f); (Brit: of youth hostel) Herbergsvater m, Herbergsmutter f; (: in university) Wohnheimleiter(in) m(f); (: also: **traffic warden**) Verkehrspolizist(in) m(f)
warder ['wɔːdəʳ] (Brit) n Gefängniswärter(in) m(f)
wardrobe ['wɔːdrəʊb] n (for clothes) Kleiderschrank m; (collection of clothes) Garderobe f; (Cine, Theat) Kostüme pl
warehouse ['wɛəhaʊs] n Lager nt
wares [wɛəz] npl Waren pl
warfare ['wɔːfɛəʳ] n Krieg m
war game n Kriegsspiel nt
warhead ['wɔːhɛd] n Sprengkopf m
warily ['wɛərɪlɪ] adv vorsichtig
Warks (Brit) abbr (Post) = Warwickshire
warlike ['wɔːlaɪk] adj kriegerisch
warm [wɔːm] adj warm; (thanks, applause, welcome, person) herzlich; **it's ~** es ist warm; **I'm ~** mir ist warm; **to keep sth ~** etw warm halten; **with my ~est thanks/ congratulations** mit meinem herzlichsten Dank/meinen herzlichsten Glückwünschen
▸ **warm up** vi warm werden; (athlete) sich aufwärmen ▸ vt aufwärmen
warm-blooded ['wɔːm'blʌdɪd] adj warmblütig
war memorial n Kriegerdenkmal nt
warm-hearted [wɔːm'hɑːtɪd] adj warmherzig
warmly ['wɔːmlɪ] adv (applaud, welcome) herzlich; (dress) warm
warmonger ['wɔːmʌŋgəʳ] (pej) n Kriegshetzer m
warmongering ['wɔːmʌŋgrɪŋ] (pej) n Kriegshetze f
warmth [wɔːmθ] n Wärme f; (friendliness) Herzlichkeit f
warm-up ['wɔːmʌp] n Aufwärmen nt; ~ **exercise** Aufwärmübung f
warn [wɔːn] vt: **to ~ sb that ...** jdn warnen, dass ...; **to ~ sb of sth** jdn vor etw dat warnen; **to ~ sb not to do sth** or **against doing sth** jdn davor warnen, etw zu tun
warning ['wɔːnɪŋ] n Warnung f; **without (any) ~** (suddenly) unerwartet; (without notifying) ohne Vorwarnung; **gale ~** Sturmwarnung f
warning light n Warnlicht nt
warning triangle n (Aut) Warndreieck nt
warp [wɔːp] vi (wood etc) sich verziehen ▸ vt

w

857

(fig: character) entstellen ▷ *n (Textiles)* Kette *f*

warpath ['wɔːpɑːθ] *n*: **to be on the ~** auf dem Kriegspfad sein

warped [wɔːpt] *adj (wood)* verzogen; *(fig: character, sense of humour etc)* abartig

warrant ['wɔrnt] *n (Law: for arrest)* Haftbefehl *m*; *(: also:* **search warrant**) Durchsuchungsbefehl *m* ▷ *vt (justify, merit)* rechtfertigen

warrant officer *n (Mil)* Dienstgrad zwischen Offizier und Unteroffizier

warranty ['wɔrəntɪ] *n* Garantie *f*; **under ~** *(Comm)* unter Garantie

warren ['wɔrən] *n (of rabbits)* Bau *m*; *(fig: of passages, streets)* Labyrinth *nt*

warring ['wɔːrɪŋ] *adj (nations)* Krieg führend; *(interests)* gegensätzlich; *(factions)* verfeindet

warrior ['wɔrɪəʳ] *n* Krieger *m*

Warsaw ['wɔːsɔː] *n* Warschau *nt*

warship ['wɔːʃɪp] *n* Kriegsschiff *nt*

wart [wɔːt] *n* Warze *f*

wartime ['wɔːtaɪm] *n*: **in ~** im Krieg

wary ['wɛərɪ] *adj (person)* vorsichtig; **to be ~ about** *or* **of doing sth** Bedenken haben, etw zu tun

was [wɔz] *pt of* **be**

wash [wɔʃ] *vt* waschen; *(dishes)* spülen, abwaschen; *(remove grease, paint etc)* ausspülen ▷ *vi (person)* sich waschen ▷ *n (clothes etc)* Wäsche *f*; *(washing programme)* Waschgang *m*; *(of ship)* Kielwasser *nt*; **he was ~ed overboard** er wurde über Bord gespült; **to ~ over/against sth** *(sea etc)* über/gegen etw *acc* spülen; **to have a ~** sich waschen; **to give sth a ~** etw waschen

▸ **wash away** *vt* wegspülen

▸ **wash down** *vt (wall, car)* abwaschen; *(food: with wine etc)* hinunterspülen

▸ **wash off** *vi* sich herauswaschen ▷ *vt* abwaschen

▸ **wash out** *vt (stain)* herauswaschen

▸ **wash up** *vi (Brit: wash dishes)* spülen, abwaschen; *(US: have a wash)* sich waschen

Wash. *(US) abbr (Post)* = Washington

washable ['wɔʃəbl] *adj (fabric)* waschbar; *(wallpaper)* abwaschbar

washbasin ['wɔʃbeɪsn], *(US)* **washbowl** ['wɔʃbəul] *n* Waschbecken *nt*

washcloth ['wɔʃklɔθ] *(US) n* Waschlappen *m*

washer ['wɔʃəʳ] *n (on tap etc)* Dichtungsring *m*

washing ['wɔʃɪŋ] *n* Wäsche *f*

washing line *(Brit) n* Wäscheleine *f*

washing machine *n* Waschmaschine *f*

washing powder *(Brit) n* Waschpulver *nt*

Washington ['wɔʃɪŋtən] *n* Washington *nt*

washing-up [wɔʃɪŋ'ʌp] *n* Abwasch *m*; **to do the ~** spülen, abwaschen

washing-up liquid *(Brit) n* (Geschirr)spülmittel *nt*

wash-out ['wɔʃaut] *(inf) n (failed event)* Reinfall *m*

washroom ['wɔʃrum] *(US) n* Waschraum *m*

wasn't ['wɔznt] = **was not**

WASP, Wasp [wɔsp] *(US: inf) n abbr (=* White Anglo-Saxon Protestant) weißer angelsächsischer Protestant *m*

wasp [wɔsp] *n* Wespe *f*

waspish ['wɔspɪʃ] *adj* giftig

wastage ['weɪstɪdʒ] *n* Verlust *m*; **natural ~** natürliche Personalreduzierung

waste [weɪst] *n* Verschwendung *f*; *(rubbish)* Abfall *m* ▷ *adj (material)* Abfall-; *(left over: paper etc)* ungenutzt ▷ *vt* verschwenden; *(opportunity)* vertun; **wastes** *npl (area of land)* Wildnis *f*; **it's a ~ of money** das ist Geldverschwendung; **to go to ~** umkommen; **to lay ~** *(area, town)* verwüsten

▸ **waste away** *vi* verkümmern

wastebasket ['weɪstbɑːskɪt] *(US) n* = **wastepaper basket**

waste disposal unit *(Brit) n* Müllschlucker *m*

wasteful ['weɪstful] *adj (person)* verschwenderisch; *(process)* aufwendig

waste ground *(Brit) n* unbebautes Grundstück *nt*

wasteland ['weɪstlənd] *n* Ödland *nt*; *(in town)* ödes Gebiet *nt*; *(fig)* Einöde *f*

wastepaper basket ['weɪstpeɪpə-] *(Brit) n* Papierkorb *m*

waste pipe *n* Abflussrohr *nt*

waste products *npl* Abfallprodukte *pl*

waster ['weɪstəʳ] *n* Verschwender(in) *m(f)*; *(good-for-nothing)* Taugenichts *m*

watch [wɔtʃ] *n (also:* **wristwatch**) (Armband)uhr *f*; *(surveillance)* Bewachung *f*; *(Mil, Naut: group of guards)* Wachmannschaft *f*; *(Naut: spell of duty)* Wache *f* ▷ *vt (look at)* betrachten; *(: match, programme)* sich *dat* ansehen; *(spy on, guard)* beobachten; *(be careful of)* aufpassen auf +*acc* ▷ *vi (look)* zusehen; **to be on ~** Wache halten; **to keep a close ~ on sb/sth** jdn/etw genau im Auge behalten; **to ~ TV** fernsehen; **~ what you're doing!** pass auf!; **~ how you drive!** fahr vorsichtig!

▸ **watch out** *vi* aufpassen; **~ out!** Vorsicht!

watchband ['wɔtʃbænd] *(US) n* = **watchstrap**

watchdog ['wɔtʃdɔg] *n (dog)* Wachhund *m*; *(fig)* Aufpasser(in) *m(f)*

watchful ['wɔtʃful] *adj* wachsam

watchmaker ['wɔtʃmeɪkəʳ] *n* Uhrmacher(in) *m(f)*

watchman ['wɔtʃmən] *(irreg: like* **man**) *n see* **night watchman**

watch stem *(US) n (winder)* Krone *f*, Aufziehrädchen *nt*

watchstrap ['wɔtʃstræp] *n* Uhrarmband *nt*

watchword ['wɔtʃwəːd] *n* Parole *f*

water ['wɔːtəʳ] *n* Wasser *nt* ▷ *vt (plant)* gießen; *(garden)* bewässern ▷ *vi (eyes)* tränen; **a drink of ~** ein Schluck Wasser; **in British ~s** in britischen (Hoheits)gewässern; **to pass ~** *(urinate)* Wasser lassen; **my mouth is ~ing** mir läuft das Wasser im Mund zusammen; **to make sb's mouth ~** jdm den Mund wässrig machen

▸ **water down** *vt (also fig)* verwässern

water biscuit *n* Cracker *m*

water cannon n Wasserwerfer m
water closet (Brit: old) n Wasserklosett nt
watercolour, (US) **watercolor** ['wɔ:təkʌlə'] n (picture) Aquarell nt; **watercolours** npl (paints) Wasserfarben pl
water-cooled ['wɔ:təku:ld] adj wassergekühlt
water-cooler ['wɔ:təku:lə'] n Wasserkühler m; **~ talks** (inf) Flurfunk m
watercress ['wɔ:təkrɛs] n Brunnenkresse f
waterfall ['wɔ:təfɔ:l] n Wasserfall m
waterfront ['wɔ:təfrʌnt] n (at seaside) Ufer nt; (at docks) Hafengegend f
water heater n Heißwassergerät nt
water hole n Wasserloch nt
water ice n Fruchteis nt (auf Wasserbasis)
watering can ['wɔ:tərɪŋ-] n Gießkanne f
water level n Wasserstand m; (of flood) Pegelstand m
water lily n Seerose f
water line n Wasserlinie f
waterlogged ['wɔ:təlɔgd] adj (ground) unter Wasser
water main n Hauptwasserleitung f
watermark ['wɔ:təmɑ:k] n (on paper) Wasserzeichen nt
watermelon ['wɔ:təmɛlən] n Wassermelone f
waterproof ['wɔ:təpru:f] adj (trousers, jacket etc) wasserdicht
water-repellent ['wɔ:tərɪ'pɛlnt] adj Wasser abstoßend
watershed ['wɔ:təʃɛd] n (Geog) Wasserscheide f; (fig) Wendepunkt m
water-skiing ['wɔ:təski:ɪŋ] n Wasserski nt
water softener n Wasserenthärter m
water tank n Wassertank m
watertight ['wɔ:tətaɪt] adj wasserdicht; (fig: excuse, case, agreement etc) hieb- und stichfest
water vapour n Wasserdampf m
waterway ['wɔ:təweɪ] n Wasserstraße f
waterworks ['wɔ:təwə:ks] n Wasserwerk nt; (inf: fig: bladder) Blase f
watery ['wɔ:tərɪ] adj (coffee, soup etc) wässrig; (eyes) tränend
watt [wɔt] n Watt nt
wattage ['wɔtɪdʒ] n Wattleistung f
wattle ['wɔtl] n Flechtwerk nt
wattle and daub n Lehmgeflecht nt
wave [weɪv] n (also fig) Welle f; (of hand) Winken nt ▷ vi (signal) winken; (branches) sich hin und her bewegen; (grass) wogen; (flag) wehen ▷ vt (hand, flag etc) winken mit; (gun, stick) schwenken; (hair) wellen; **short/medium/long ~** (Radio) Kurz-/Mittel-/Langwelle f; **the new ~** (Cine, Mus) die neue Welle f; **he ~d us over to his table** er winkte uns zu seinem Tisch hinüber; **to ~ goodbye to sb** jdm zum Abschied winken
▶ **wave aside** vt (fig: suggestion etc) zurückweisen
waveband ['weɪvbænd] n (Radio) Wellenbereich m
wavelength ['weɪvlɛŋθ] n (Radio) Wellenlänge

f; **on the same ~** (fig) auf derselben Wellenlänge
waver ['weɪvə'] vi (voice) schwanken; (eyes) zucken; (love, person) wanken
wavy ['weɪvɪ] adj (line) wellenförmig; (hair) wellig
wax [wæks] n Wachs nt; (for sealing) Siegellack m; (in ear) Ohrenschmalz nt ▷ vt (floor) bohnern; (car, skis) wachsen ▷ vi (moon) zunehmen
waxed [wækst] adj (jacket) gewachst
waxen ['wæksn] adj (face) wachsbleich
waxworks ['wækswə:ks] npl (models) Wachsfiguren pl ▷ n (place) Wachsfigurenkabinett nt
way [weɪ] n Weg m; (distance) Strecke f; (direction) Richtung f; (manner) Art f; (method) Art und Weise f; (habit) Gewohnheit f; **which ~ to ...?** wo geht es zu ...?; **this ~, please** hier entlang, bitte; **on the ~** (en route) auf dem Weg, unterwegs; **to be on one's ~** auf dem Weg sein; **to fight one's ~ through a crowd** sich acc durch die Menge kämpfen; **to lie one's ~ out of sth** sich aus etw herauslügen; **to keep out of sb's ~** jdm aus dem Weg gehen; **it's a long ~ away** es ist weit entfernt; (event) das ist noch lange hin; **the village is rather out of the ~** das Dorf ist recht abgelegen; **to go out of one's ~ to do sth** sich sehr bemühen, etw zu tun; **to be in the ~** im Weg sein; **to lose one's ~** sich verirren; **under ~** (project etc) im Gang; **the ~ back** der Rückweg; **to make ~ (for sb/sth)** (für jdn/etw) Platz machen; **to get one's own ~** seinen Willen bekommen; **put it the right ~ up** (Brit) stell es richtig herum hin; **to be the wrong ~ round** verkehrt herum sein; **he's in a bad ~** ihm geht es schlecht; **in a ~** in gewisser Weise; **in some ~s** in mancher Hinsicht; **no ~!** (inf) kommt nicht infrage!; **by the ~ ...** übrigens ...; **"~ in"** (Brit) „Eingang"; **"~ out"** (Brit) „Ausgang"; **"give ~"** (Brit: Aut) „Vorfahrt beachten"; **~ of life** Lebensstil m
waybill ['weɪbɪl] n Frachtbrief m
waylay [weɪ'leɪ] (irreg: like lay) vt auflauern +dat; **to get waylaid** (fig) abgefangen werden
wayside ['weɪsaɪd] adj am Straßenrand ▷ n Straßenrand m; **to fall by the ~** (fig) auf der Strecke bleiben
way station (US) n (Rail) kleiner Bahnhof m; (fig) Zwischenstation f
wayward ['weɪwəd] adj (behaviour) eigenwillig; (child) eigensinnig
WC (Brit) n abbr (= water closet) WC nt
WCC n abbr (= World Council of Churches) Weltkirchenrat m
we [wi:] pl pron wir; **here we are** (arriving) da sind wir; (finding sth) na bitte
weak [wi:k] adj schwach; (tea, coffee) dünn; **to grow ~(er)** schwächer werden
weaken ['wi:kn] vi (resolve, person) schwächer werden; (influence, power) nachlassen ▷ vt schwächen

w

weak-kneed ['wi:k'ni:d] *adj* (*fig*) schwächlich

weakling ['wi:klɪŋ] *n* Schwächling *m*

weakly ['wi:klɪ] *adv* schwach

weakness ['wi:knɪs] *n* Schwäche *f*; **to have a ~ for** eine Schwäche haben für

wealth [wɛlθ] *n* Reichtum *m*; (*of details, knowledge etc*) Fülle *f*

wealth tax *n* Vermögenssteuer *f*

wealthy ['wɛlθɪ] *adj* wohlhabend, reich

wean [wi:n] *vt* (*also fig*) entwöhnen

weapon ['wɛpən] *n* Waffe *f*; **~s of mass destruction** Massenvernichtungswaffen *pl*

wear [wɛəʳ] (*pt* **wore**, *pp* **worn**) *vt* (*clothes, shoes, beard*) tragen; (*put on*) anziehen ▷ *vi* (*last*) halten; (*become old: carpet, jeans*) sich abnutzen ▷ *n* (*damage*) Verschleiß *m*; (*use*): **I got a lot of/very little ~ out of the coat** der Mantel hat lange/nicht sehr lange gehalten; **baby~** Babykleidung *f*; **sports~** Sportkleidung *f*; **evening ~** Kleidung für den Abend; **to ~ a hole in sth** (*coat etc*) etw durchwetzen

▶ **wear away** *vt* verschleißen ▷ *vi* (*inscription etc*) verwittern

▶ **wear down** *vt* (*heels*) abnutzen; (*person, strength*) zermürben

▶ **wear off** *vi* (*pain etc*) nachlassen

▶ **wear on** *vi* sich hinziehen

▶ **wear out** *vt* (*shoes, clothing*) verschleißen; (*person, strength*) erschöpfen

wearable ['wɛərəbl] *adj* tragbar

wear and tear [-tɛəʳ] *n* Verschleiß *m*

wearer ['wɛərəʳ] *n* Träger(in) *m(f)*

wearily ['wɪərɪlɪ] *adv* (*say, sit*) lustlos, müde

weariness ['wɪərɪnɪs] *n* (*tiredness*) Müdigkeit *f*

wearisome ['wɪərɪsəm] *adj* (*boring*) langweilig; (*tiring*) ermüdend

weary ['wɪərɪ] *adj* (*tired*) müde; (*dispirited*) lustlos ▷ *vi*: **to ~ of sb/sth** jds/etw *gen* überdrüssig werden

weasel ['wi:zl] *n* Wiesel *nt*

weather ['wɛðəʳ] *n* Wetter *nt* ▷ *vt* (*storm, crisis*) überstehen; (*rock, wood*) verwittern; **what's the ~ like?** wie ist das Wetter?; **under the ~** (*fig: ill*) angeschlagen

weather-beaten ['wɛðəbi:tn] *adj* (*face*) vom Wetter gegerbt; (*building, stone*) verwittert

weathercock ['wɛðəkɔk] *n* Wetterhahn *m*

weather forecast *n* Wettervorhersage *f*

weatherman ['wɛðəmæn] *n* (*irreg: like* **man**) *n* Mann *m* vom Wetteramt, Wetterfrosch *m* (*hum inf*)

weatherproof ['wɛðəpru:f] *adj* wetterfest

weather report *n* Wetterbericht *m*

weather vane [-veɪn] *n* = **weathercock**

weave [wi:v] (*pt* **wove**, *pp* **woven**) *vt* (*cloth*) weben; (*basket*) flechten ▷ *vi* (*fig: pt, pp* **weaved**: *move in and out*) sich schlängeln

weaver ['wi:vəʳ] *n* Weber(in) *m(f)*

weaving ['wi:vɪŋ] *n* Weberei *f*

web [wɛb] *n* (*also fig*) Netz *nt*; (*Comput*) **the Web** das Web, das Internet; (*on duck's foot*) Schwimmhaut *f*

webbed ['wɛbd] *adj* (*foot*) Schwimm-

webbing ['wɛbɪŋ] *n* (*on chair*) Gewebe *nt*

website ['wɛbsaɪt] *n* (*Comput*) Website *f*, Webseite *f*

wed [wɛd] (*pt, pp* **~ded**) *vt, vi* heiraten ▷ *n*: **the newly-~s** die Jungvermählten *pl*

Wed. *abbr* (= *Wednesday*) Mi.

we'd [wi:d] = **we had; we would**

wedded ['wɛdɪd] *pt, pp of* **wed** ▷ *adj*: **to be ~ to sth** (*idea etc*) mit etw eng verbunden sein

wedding ['wɛdɪŋ] *n* Hochzeit *f*; **silver/golden ~** silberne/goldene Hochzeit

wedding day *n* Hochzeitstag *m*

wedding dress *n* Hochzeitskleid *nt*

wedding present *n* Hochzeitsgeschenk *nt*

wedding ring *n* Trauring *m*

wedge [wɛdʒ] *n* Keil *m*; (*of cake*) Stück *nt* ▷ *vt* (*fasten*) festklemmen; (*pack tightly*) einkeilen

wedge-heeled shoes ['wɛdʒhi:ld-] *npl* Schuhe *pl* mit Keilabsätzen

wedlock ['wɛdlɔk] *n* Ehe *f*

Wednesday ['wɛdnzdɪ] *n* Mittwoch *m*; *see also* **Tuesday**

wee [wi:] (*Scot*) *adj* klein

weed [wi:d] *n* (*Bot*) Unkraut *nt*; (*pej: person*) Schwächling *m* ▷ *vt* (*garden*) jäten

▶ **weed out** *vt* (*fig*) aussondern

weedkiller ['wi:dkɪləʳ] *n* Unkrautvertilger *m*

weedy ['wi:dɪ] *adj* (*person*) schwächlich

week [wi:k] *n* Woche *f*; **once/twice a ~** einmal/zweimal die Woche; **in two ~s' time** in zwei Wochen; **a ~ today/on Friday** heute/Freitag in einer Woche

weekday ['wi:kdeɪ] *n* Wochentag *m*; (*Comm: Monday to Saturday*) Werktag *m*; **on ~s** an Wochentagen/Werktagen

weekend [wi:k'ɛnd] *n* Wochenende *nt*; **this/next/last ~** an diesem/am nächsten/am letzten Wochenende; **what are you doing at the ~?** was machen Sie am Wochenende?; **open at ~s** an Wochenenden geöffnet

weekly ['wi:klɪ] *adv* wöchentlich ▷ *adj* (*newspaper*) Wochen- ▷ *n* (*newspaper*) Wochenzeitung *f*; (*magazine*) Wochenzeitschrift *f*

weep [wi:p] (*pt, pp* **wept**) *vi* (*person*) weinen; (*wound*) nässen

weeping willow ['wi:pɪŋ-] *n* (*tree*) Trauerweide *f*

weepy ['wi:pɪ] *adj* (*person*) weinerlich; (*film*) rührselig ▷ *n* (*film etc*) Schmachtfetzen *m*

weigh [weɪ] *vt* wiegen; (*fig: evidence, risks*) abwägen ▷ *vi* wiegen; **to ~ anchor** den Anker lichten

▶ **weigh down** *vt* niederdrücken

▶ **weigh out** *vt* (*goods*) auswiegen

▶ **weigh up** *vt* (*person, offer, risk*) abschätzen

weighbridge ['weɪbrɪdʒ] *n* Brückenwaage *f*

weighing machine ['weɪɪŋ-] *n* Waage *f*

weight [weɪt] *n* Gewicht *nt* ▷ *vt* (*fig*): **to be ~ed in favour of sb/sth** jdn/etw begünstigen; **to be sold by ~** nach Gewicht verkauft werden; **to lose ~** abnehmen; **to put on ~** zunehmen; **~s and measures** Maße und Gewichte

weighting ['weɪtɪŋ] n (allowance) Zulage f
weightlessness ['weɪtlɪsnɪs] n
  Schwerelosigkeit f
weightlifter ['weɪtlɪftə'] n Gewichtheber m
weight limit n Gewichtsbeschränkung f
weight training n Krafttraining nt
weighty ['weɪtɪ] adj schwer; (fig: important)
  gewichtig
weir [wɪə'] n (in river) Wehr nt
weird [wɪəd] adj (object, situation, effect) komisch;
  (person) seltsam
weirdo ['wɪədəu] (inf) n verrückter Typ m
welcome ['wɛlkəm] adj willkommen ▷ n
  Willkommen nt ▷ vt begrüßen, willkommen
  heißen; **~ to London!** willkommen in
  London!; **to make sb ~** jdn freundlich
  aufnehmen; **you're ~ to try** du kannst es
  gern versuchen; **thank you — you're ~!**
  danke — nichts zu danken!
welcoming ['wɛlkəmɪŋ] adj (smile, room)
  einladend; (person) freundlich
weld [wɛld] n Schweißnaht f ▷ vt schweißen
welder ['wɛldə'] n (person) Schweißer(in) m(f)
welding ['wɛldɪŋ] n Schweißen nt
welfare ['wɛlfɛə'] n (well-being) Wohl nt; (social
  aid) Sozialhilfe f
welfare state n Wohlfahrtsstaat m
welfare work n Fürsorgearbeit f
well [wɛl] n (for water) Brunnen m; (oil well)
  Quelle f ▷ adv gut; (for emphasis with adj)
  durchaus ▷ adj: **to be ~** (person) gesund sein
  ▷ excl nun!, na!; **as ~** (in addition) ebenfalls;
  you might as ~ tell me sag es mir ruhig; **he
  did as ~ as he could** er machte es so gut er
  konnte; **pretty as ~ as rich** sowohl hübsch
  als auch reich; **~ done!** gut gemacht!; **to
  do ~** (person) gut vorankommen; (business)
  gut gehen; **~ before dawn** lange vor
  Tagesanbruch; **~ over 40** weit über 40; **I
  don't feel ~** ich fühle mich nicht gut or wohl;
  get ~ soon! gute Besserung!; **~, as I was
  saying** ... also, wie ich bereits sagte, ...
  ▷ **well up** vi (tears, emotions) aufsteigen
we'll [wi:l] = **we will; we shall**
well-behaved ['wɛlbɪ'heɪvd] adj wohlerzogen
well-being ['wɛl'bi:ɪŋ] n Wohl(ergehen) nt
well-bred ['wɛl'brɛd] adj (person) gut erzogen
well-built ['wɛl'bɪlt] adj gut gebaut
well-chosen ['wɛl'tʃəuzn] adj gut gewählt
well-deserved ['wɛldɪ'zə:vd] adj wohlverdient
well-developed ['wɛldɪ'vɛləpt] adj gut
  entwickelt
well-disposed ['wɛl'dɪspəuzd] adj: **~ to(wards)**
  freundlich gesonnen +dat
well-dressed ['wɛl'drɛst] adj gut gekleidet
well-earned ['wɛl'ə:nd] adj (rest) wohlverdient
well-groomed ['wɛl'gru:md] adj gepflegt
well-heeled ['wɛl'hi:ld] (inf) adj betucht
well-informed ['wɛlɪn'fɔ:md] adj gut
  informiert
Wellington ['wɛlɪŋtən] n (Geog) Wellington nt
wellingtons ['wɛlɪŋtənz] npl (also: **wellington
  boots**) Gummistiefel pl

well-kept ['wɛl'kɛpt] adj (house, grounds)
  gepflegt; (secret) gut gehütet
well-known ['wɛl'nəun] adj wohlbekannt
well-mannered ['wɛl'mænəd] adj
  wohlerzogen
well-meaning ['wɛl'mi:nɪŋ] adj (person)
  wohlmeinend; (offer etc) gut gemeint
well-nigh ['wɛl'naɪ] adv: **~ impossible**
  geradezu unmöglich
well-off ['wɛl'ɔf] adj (rich) begütert
well-read ['wɛl'rɛd] adj belesen
well-spoken ['wɛl'spəukn] adj: **to be ~** sich gut
  or gewandt ausdrücken
well-stocked ['wɛl'stɔkt] adj gut bestückt
well-timed ['wɛl'taɪmd] adj gut abgepasst
well-to-do ['wɛltə'du:] adj wohlhabend
well-wisher ['wɛlwɪʃə'] n (friend, admirer)
  wohlmeinender Mensch m; **scores of ~s
  had gathered** eine große Gefolgschaft hatte
  sich versammelt; **letters from ~s** Briefe von
  Leuten, die es gut meinen
well-woman clinic ['wɛlwumən-] n ≈
  Frauensprechstunde f
Welsh [wɛlʃ] adj walisisch ▷ n (Ling) Walisisch
  nt; **the Welsh** npl die Waliser pl
Welshman ['wɛlʃmən] (irreg: like **man**) n
  Waliser m
Welsh rarebit n überbackenes Käsebrot nt
Welshwoman ['wɛlʃwumən] (irreg: like **woman**)
  n Waliserin f
welter ['wɛltə'] n: **a ~ of** eine Flut von
went [wɛnt] pt of **go**
wept [wɛpt] pt, pp of **weep**
were [wə:'] pt of **be**
we're [wɪə'] = **we are**
weren't [wə:nt] = **were not**
werewolf ['wɪəwulf] (pl **werewolves**) n
  Werwolf m
werewolves ['wɪəwulvz] npl of **werewolf**
west [wɛst] n Westen m ▷ adj (wind, side, coast)
  West-, westlich ▷ adv (to or towards the west)
  westwärts; **the W~** (Pol) der Westen
westbound ['wɛstbaund] adj (traffic,
  carriageway) in Richtung Westen
West Country (Brit) n: **the ~** Südwestengland
  nt
westerly ['wɛstəlɪ] adj westlich
western ['wɛstən] adj westlich ▷ n (Cine)
  Western m
westerner ['wɛstənə'] n Abendländer(in) m(f)
westernized ['wɛstənaɪzd] adj (society etc)
  verwestlicht
West German adj westdeutsch ▷ n (person)
  Westdeutsche(r) f(m)
West Germany n (formerly) Bundesrepublik f
  Deutschland
West Indian adj westindisch ▷ n (person)
  Westinder(in) m(f)
West Indies [-'ɪndɪz] npl: **the ~** Westindien nt
Westminster ['wɛstmɪnstə'] n Westminster
  nt; (parliament) das britische Parlament
westward ['wɛstwəd], **westwards**
  ['wɛstwədz] adv westwärts

W

wet [wɛt] *adj* nass ⊳ *n* (Brit: Pol) Gemäßigte(r) *f(m)*, Waschlappen *m* (*pej*); **to get ~** nass werden; **"~ paint"** „frisch gestrichen"; **to be a ~ blanket** (*fig: pej: person*) ein(e) Spielverderber(in) *m(f)* sein; **to ~ one's pants/o.s.** sich *dat* in die Hosen machen

wetness ['wɛtnɪs] *n* Nässe *f*; (*of climate*) Feuchtigkeit *f*

wet suit *n* Taucheranzug *m*

we've [wi:v] = **we have**

whack [wæk] *vt* schlagen

whacked [wækt] (Brit: *inf*) *adj* (*exhausted*) erschlagen

whale [weɪl] *n* Wal *m*

whaler ['weɪlər] *n* Walfänger *m*

whaling ['weɪlɪŋ] *n* Walfang *m*

wharf [wɔ:f] (*pl* **wharves**) *n* Kai *m*

wharves [wɔ:vz] *npl of* **wharf**

⬤ KEYWORD

what [wɔt] *adj* **1** (*in direct/indirect questions*) welche(r, s); **what colour/shape is it?** welche Farbe/Form hat es?; **for what reason?** aus welchem Grund?
2 (*in exclamations*) was für ein(e); **what a mess!** was für ein Durcheinander!; **what a fool I am!** was bin ich doch (für) ein Idiot!
⊳ *pron* (*interrogative, relative*) was; **what are you doing?** was machst du?; **what are you talking about?** wovon redest du?; **what is it called?** wie heißt das?; **what about me?** und ich?; **what about a cup of tea?** wie wärs mit einer Tasse Tee?; **what about going to the cinema?** sollen wir ins Kino gehen?; **I saw what you did/what was on the table** ich habe gesehen, was du getan hast/was auf dem Tisch war; **tell me what you're thinking about** sag mir, woran du denkst
⊳ *excl* (*disbelieving*) was, wie; **what, no coffee!** was *or* wie, kein Kaffee?

whatever [wɔt'ɛvər] *adj*: **~ book** welches Buch auch immer ⊳ *pron*: **do ~ is necessary/you want** tun Sie, was nötig ist/was immer Sie wollen; **~ happens** was auch passiert; **no reason ~ or whatsoever** überhaupt kein Grund; **nothing ~ or whatsoever** überhaupt nichts

whatsoever [wɔtsəu'ɛvər] *adj* = **whatever**

wheat [wi:t] *n* Weizen *m*

wheatgerm ['wi:tdʒə:m] *n* Weizenkeim *m*

wheatmeal ['wi:tmi:l] *n* Weizenmehl *nt*

wheedle ['wi:dl] *vt*: **to ~ sb into doing sth** jdn beschwatzen, etw zu tun; **to ~ sth out of sb** jdm etw abluchsen

wheel [wi:l] *n* Rad *nt*; (*also*: **steering wheel**) Lenkrad *nt*; (*Naut*) Steuer *nt* ⊳ *vt* (*pram etc*) schieben ⊳ *vi* (*birds*) kreisen; (*also*: **wheel round**: *person*) sich herumdrehen

wheelbarrow ['wi:lbærəu] *n* Schubkarre *f*

wheelbase ['wi:lbeɪs] *n* Radstand *m*

wheelchair ['wi:ltʃɛər] *n* Rollstuhl *m*

wheel clamp *n* Parkkralle *f*

wheeler-dealer ['wi:lə'di:lər] (*pej*) *n* Geschäftemacher(in) *m(f)*

wheelie-bin ['wi:lɪbɪn] *n* Mülltonne *f* auf Rädern

wheeling ['wi:lɪŋ] *n*: **~ and dealing** (*pej*) Geschäftemacherei *f*

wheeze [wi:z] *vi* (*person*) keuchen ⊳ *n* (*idea, joke etc*) Scherz *m*

wheezy ['wi:zɪ] *adj* (*person*) mit pfeifendem Atem; (*cough*) keuchend; (*breath*) pfeifend; (*laugh*) asthmatisch

⬤ KEYWORD

when [wɛn] *adv* wann
⊳ *conj* **1** (*at, during, after the time that*) wenn; **she was reading when I came in** als ich hereinkam, las sie gerade; **be careful when you cross the road** sei vorsichtig, wenn du die Straße überquerst
2 (*on, at which*) als; **on the day when I met him** am Tag, als ich ihn traf
3 (*whereas*) wo ... doch, obwohl; **why did you buy that when you can't afford it?** warum hast du das gekauft, obwohl du es dir nicht leisten kannst?

whenever [wɛn'ɛvər] *adv, conj* (*any time that*) wann immer; (*every time that*) (jedes Mal,) wenn; **I go ~ I can** ich gehe, wann immer ich kann

where [wɛər] *adv, conj* wo; **this is ~ ...** hier ...; **~ possible** so weit möglich; **~ are you from?** woher kommen Sie?

whereabouts [wɛərə'bauts] *adv* wo
⊳ *n*: **nobody knows his ~** keiner weiß, wo er ist

whereas [wɛər'æz] *conj* während

whereby [wɛə'baɪ] (*form*) *adv* wonach

whereupon [wɛərə'pɔn] *conj* worauf

wherever [wɛər'ɛvər] *conj* (*position*) wo (auch) immer; (*motion*) wohin (auch) immer ⊳ *adv* (*surprise*) wo (um alles in der Welt); **sit ~ you like** nehmen Sie Platz, wo immer Sie wollen

wherewithal ['wɛəwɪðɔ:l] *n*: **the ~ (to do sth)** (*money*) das nötige Kleingeld(, um etw zu tun)

whet [wɛt] *vt* (*appetite*) anregen; (*tool*) schleifen

whether ['wɛðər] *conj* ob; **I don't know ~ to accept or not** ich weiß nicht, ob ich annehmen soll oder nicht; **~ you go or not** du gehst oder nicht; **it's doubtful ~ ...** es ist zweifelhaft, ob ...

whey ['weɪ] *n* Molke *f*

⬤ KEYWORD

which [wɪtʃ] *adj* **1** (*interrogative: direct, indirect*) welche(r, s); **which picture?** welches Bild?; **which books?** welche Bücher?; **which one?** welche(r, s)?
2: **in which case** in diesem Fall; **by which time** zu dieser Zeit

▷ *pron* **1** (*interrogative*) welche(r, s); **which of you are coming?** wer von Ihnen kommt?; **I don't mind which** mir ist gleich, welche(r, s) **2** (*relative*) der/die/das; **the apple which you ate/which is on the table** der Apfel, den du gegessen hast/der auf dem Tisch liegt; **the chair on which you are sitting** der Stuhl, auf dem Sie sitzen; **the book of which you spoke** das Buch, wovon *or* von dem Sie sprachen; **he said he saw her, which is true** er sagte, er habe sie gesehen, was auch stimmt; **after which** wonach

whichever [wɪtʃˈɛvəʳ] *adj*: **take ~ book you want** nehmen Sie irgendein *or* ein beliebiges Buch; **~ book you take** welches Buch Sie auch nehmen

whiff [wɪf] *n* (*of perfume*) Hauch *m*; (*of petrol, smoke*) Geruch *m*; **to catch a ~ of sth** den Geruch von etw wahrnehmen

while [waɪl] *n* Weile *f* ▷ *conj* während; **for a ~** eine Weile (lang); **in a ~** gleich; **all the ~** die ganze Zeit (über); **I'll/we'll** *etc* **make it worth your ~** es wird sich für Sie lohnen
▶ **while away** *vt* (*time*) sich *dat* vertreiben

whilst [waɪlst] *conj* = **while**

whim [wɪm] *n* Laune *f*

whimper [ˈwɪmpəʳ] *n* (*cry, moan*) Wimmern *nt* ▷ *vi* wimmern

whimsical [ˈwɪmzɪkəl] *adj* wunderlich, seltsam; (*story*) kurios

whine [waɪn] *n* (*of pain*) Jammern *nt*; (*of engine, siren*) Heulen *nt* ▷ *vi* (*person*) jammern; (*dog*) jaulen; (*engine, siren*) heulen

whip [wɪp] *n* Peitsche *f*; (*Pol*) ≈ Fraktionsführer *m* ▷ *vt* (*person, animal*) peitschen; (*cream, eggs*) schlagen; (*move quickly*): **to ~ sth out/off** etw blitzschnell hervorholen/wegbringen
▶ **whip up** *vt* (*cream*) schlagen; (*inf: meal*) hinzaubern; (*arouse: support*) anheizen; (: *people*) mitreißen

○ **WHIP**
○
○ Der Ausdruck *whip* bezieht sich in der
○ Politik auf einen Abgeordneten, der für die
○ Einhaltung der Parteidisziplin zuständig
○ ist, besonders für die Anwesenheit und
○ das Wahlverhalten der Abgeordneten
○ im Unterhaus. Die whips fordern die
○ Abgeordneten ihrer Partei schriftlich
○ zur Anwesenheit auf und deuten
○ die Wichtigkeit der Abstimmungen
○ durch ein-, zwei-, oder dreimaliges
○ Unterstreichen an, wobei dreimaliges
○ Unterstreichen (3-line whip) strengsten
○ Fraktionszwang bedeutet.

whiplash [ˈwɪplæʃ] *n* (*Med: also*: **whiplash injury**) Schleudertrauma *nt*

whipped cream [wɪpt-] *n* Schlagsahne *f*

whipping boy [ˈwɪpɪŋ-] *n* (*fig*) Prügelknabe *m*

whip-round [ˈwɪpraund] (*Brit: inf*) *n* (*Geld*)

sammlung *f*

whirl [wəːl] *vt* (*arms, sword etc*) herumwirbeln ▷ *vi* wirbeln ▷ *n* (*of activity, pleasure*) Wirbel *m*; **to be in a ~** (*mind, person*) völlig verwirrt sein

whirlpool [ˈwəːlpuːl] *n* (*lit*) Strudel *m*

whirlwind [ˈwəːlwɪnd] *n* (*lit*) Wirbelwind *m*

whirr [wəːʳ] *vi* (*motor etc*) surren

whisk [wɪsk] *n* (*Culin*) Schneebesen *m* ▷ *vt* (*cream, eggs*) schlagen; **to ~ sb away** *or* **off** jdn in Windeseile wegbringen

whiskers [ˈwɪskəz] *npl* (*of animal*) Barthaare *pl*; (*of man*) Backenbart *m*

whisky, (*US, Ireland*) **whiskey** [ˈwɪskɪ] *n* Whisky *m*

whisper [ˈwɪspəʳ] *n* Flüstern *nt*; (*fig: of wind*) Wispern *nt* ▷ *vt, vi* flüstern; **to ~ sth to sb** jdm etw zuflüstern

whispering [ˈwɪspərɪŋ] *n* Geflüster *nt*

whist [wɪst] (*Brit*) *n* Whist *nt*

whistle [ˈwɪsl] *n* (*sound*) Pfiff *m*; (*object*) Pfeife *f* ▷ *vi, vt* pfeifen

whistle-stop [ˈwɪslstɔp] *adj*: **to make a ~ tour of** (*fig*) eine Rundreise machen durch; (*Pol*) eine Wahlkampfreise machen durch

Whit [wɪt] *n* = **Whitsun**

white [waɪt] *adj* weiß ▷ *n* (*colour*) Weiß *nt*; (*person*) Weiße(r) *f(m)*; (*of egg, eye*) Weiße(s) *nt*; **to turn** *or* **go ~** (*person: with fear*) weiß *or* bleich werden; (: *with age*) weiße Haare bekommen; (*hair*) weiß werden; **the ~s** (*washing*) die Weißwäsche *f*; **tennis/cricket ~s** weiße Tennis-/Krickettrikots

whitebait [ˈwaɪtbeɪt] *n* essbare Jungfische (*Heringe, Sprotten etc*)

whiteboard [ˈwaɪtbɔːd] *n* Weißwandtafel *f*; **interactive ~** interaktive Weißwandtafel

white coffee (*Brit*) *n* Kaffee *m* mit Milch

white-collar worker [ˈwaɪtkɔlə-] *n* Schreibtischarbeiter(in) *m(f)*

white elephant *n* (*fig: venture*) Fehlinvestition *f*

white food *n* weiße Lebensmittel *pl*, weißes Essen *nt*

white goods *npl* (*appliances*) große Haushaltsgeräte *pl*; (*linen etc*) Weißwaren *pl*

white-hot [waɪtˈhɔt] *adj* (*metal*) weiß glühend

○ **WHITE HOUSE**
○
○ *White House*, eine weiß gestrichene Villa in
○ Washington, ist der offizielle Wohnsitz
○ des amerikanischen Präsidenten. Im
○ weiteren Sinne bezieht sich dieser Begriff
○ auf die Exekutive der amerikanischen
○ Regierung.

white lie *n* Notlüge *f*

whiteness [ˈwaɪtnɪs] *n* Weiß *nt*

white noise *n* weißes Rauschen *nt*

whiteout [ˈwaɪtaut] *n* starkes Schneegestöber *nt*

white paper *n* (*Pol*) Weißbuch *nt*

whitewash [ˈwaɪtwɔʃ] *n* (*paint*) Tünche *f*; (*inf, Sport*) totale Niederlage *f* ▷ *vt* (*building*)

w

tünchen; (*fig: incident, reputation*) reinwaschen

white water *n*: **white-water rafting** Wildwasserflößen *nt*

whiting ['waɪtɪŋ] *n inv* (*fish*) Weißling *m*

Whit Monday *n* Pfingstmontag *m*

Whitsun ['wɪtsn] *n* Pfingsten *nt*

whittle ['wɪtl] *vt*: **to ~ away** *or* **down** (*costs etc*) verringern

whizz [wɪz] *vi*: **to ~ past** *or* **by** vorbeisausen

whizz kid (*inf*) *n* Senkrechtstarter(in) *m(f)*

WHO *n abbr* (= *World Health Organization*) Weltgesundheitsorganisation *f*, WHO *f*

○ KEYWORD

who [huː] *pron* **1** (*interrogative*) wer; (*: acc*) wen; (*: dat*) wem; **who is it?, who's there?** wer ist da?; **who did you give it to?** wem hast du es gegeben?

2 (*relative*) der/die/das; **the man/woman who spoke to me** der Mann, der/die Frau, die mit mir gesprochen hat

---

whodunit, whodunnit [huːˈdʌnɪt] (*inf*) *n* Krimi *m*

whoever [huːˈɛvəʳ] *pron*: **~ finds it** wer (auch immer) es findet; **ask ~ you like** fragen Sie, wen Sie wollen; **~ he marries** ganz gleich *or* egal, wen er heiratet; **~ told you that?** wer um alles in der Welt hat dir das erzählt?

whole [həʊl] *adj* (*entire*) ganz; (*not broken*) heil ▷ *n* Ganze(s) *nt*; **the ~ lot (of it)** alles; **the ~ lot (of them)** alle; **the ~ (of the) time** die ganze Zeit; **~ villages were destroyed** ganze Dörfer wurden zerstört; **the ~ of** der/die/das ganze; **the ~ of Glasgow/Europe** ganz Glasgow/Europa; **the ~ of the town** die ganze Stadt; **on the ~** im Ganzen (gesehen)

wholefood ['həʊlfuːd] *n*, **wholefoods** ['həʊlfuːdz] ▷ *npl* Vollwertkost *f*

wholefood shop *n* ≈ Reformhaus *nt*

wholehearted [həʊlˈhɑːtɪd] *adj* (*agreement etc*) rückhaltlos

wholeheartedly [həʊlˈhɑːtɪdlɪ] *adv* (*agree etc*) rückhaltlos

wholemeal ['həʊlmiːl] (*Brit*) *adj* (*bread, flour*) Vollkorn-

whole note (*US*) *n* ganze Note *f*

wholesale ['həʊlseɪl] *n* (*business*) Großhandel *m* ▷ *adj* (*price*) Großhandels-; (*destruction etc*) umfassend ▷ *adv* (*buy, sell*) im Großhandel

wholesaler ['həʊlseɪləʳ] *n* Großhändler *m*

wholesome ['həʊlsəm] *adj* (*food*) gesund; (*effect*) zuträglich; (*attitude*) positiv

wholewheat ['həʊlwiːt] *adj* = **wholemeal**

wholly ['həʊlɪ] *adv* ganz und gar

○ KEYWORD

whom [huːm] *pron* **1** (*interrogative: acc*) wen; (*: dat*) wem; **whom did you see?** wen hast du gesehen?; **to whom did you give it?** wem hast du es gegeben?

2 (*relative: acc*) den/die/das; (*: dat*) dem/der/dem; **the man whom I saw/to whom I spoke** der Mann, den ich gesehen habe/mit dem ich gesprochen habe

---

whooping cough ['huːpɪŋ-] *n* Keuchhusten *m*

whoosh [wuʃ] *vi*: **to ~ along/past/down** entlang-/vorbei-/hinuntersausen ▷ *n* Sausen *nt*; **the skiers ~ed past, skiers came by with a ~** die Skifahrer sausten vorbei

whopper ['wɒpəʳ] (*inf*) *n* (*lie*) faustdicke Lüge *f*; (*large thing*) Mordsding *nt*

whopping ['wɒpɪŋ] (*inf*) *adj* Riesen-, riesig

whore [hɔːʳ] (*inf: pej*) *n* Hure *f*

○ KEYWORD

whose [huːz] *adj* **1** (*possessive: interrogative*) wessen; **whose book is this?, whose is this book?** wessen Buch ist das?, wem gehört das Buch?; **I don't know whose it is** ich weiß nicht, wem es gehört

2 (*possessive: relative*) dessen/deren/dessen; **the man whose son you rescued** der Mann, dessen Sohn du gerettet hast; **the woman whose car was stolen** die Frau, deren Auto gestohlen worden war

▷ *pron*: **whose is this?** wem gehört das?; **I know whose it is** ich weiß, wem es gehört

---

Who's Who ['huːzˈhuː] *n* (*book*) Who's who *nt*

○ KEYWORD

why [waɪ] *adv* warum; **why not?** warum nicht?

▷ *conj* warum; **I wonder why he said that** ich frage mich, warum er das gesagt hat; **that's not why I'm here** ich bin nicht deswegen hier; **the reason why** der Grund, warum *or* weshalb

▷ *excl* (*expressing surprise, shock*) na so was; (*expressing annoyance*) ach; **why, yes (of course)** aber ja doch; **why, it's you!** na so was, du bists!

WI *n abbr* (*Brit: = Women's Institute*) britischer Frauenverband ▷ *abbr* = **West Indies**; (*US: Post*) = Wisconsin

wick [wɪk] *n* Docht *m*; **he gets on my ~** (*Brit: inf*) er geht mir auf den Geist

wicked ['wɪkɪd] *adj* (*crime, person*) böse; (*smile, wit*) frech; (*inf: prices*) unverschämt; (*: weather*) schrecklich

wicker ['wɪkəʳ] *adj* (*chair etc*) Korb-; (*basket*) Weiden-

wickerwork ['wɪkəʳwɜːk] *adj* (*chair etc*) Korb-; (*basket*) Weiden- ▷ *n* (*objects*) Korbwaren *pl*

wicket ['wɪkɪt] *n* (*Cricket: stumps*) Tor *nt*, Wicket *nt*; (*: grass area*) Spielbahn *f*

wicket-keeper ['wɪkɪtkiːpəʳ] *n* Torwächter *m*

wide [waɪd] *adj* breit; (*area*) weit; (*publicity*) umfassend ▷ *adv*: **to open sth ~** etw weit

---

öffnen; **it is 3 metres ~** es ist 3 Meter breit; **to go ~** vorbeigehen

wide-angle lens ['waɪdæŋgl-] n Weitwinkelobjektiv nt

wide-awake [waɪdə'weɪk] adj hellwach

wide-eyed [waɪd'aɪd] adj mit großen Augen; (fig) unschuldig, naiv

widely ['waɪdlɪ] adv (differ, vary) erheblich; (travel) ausgiebig, viel; (spaced) weit; (believed, known) allgemein; **to be ~ read** (reader) sehr belesen sein

widen ['waɪdn] vt (road, river) verbreitern; (one's experience) erweitern ▷ vi sich verbreitern

wideness ['waɪdnɪs] n (of road, river, gap) Breite f

wide open adj weit geöffnet

wide-ranging [waɪd'reɪndʒɪŋ] adj (effects) weitreichend; (interview, survey) umfassend

widespread ['waɪdspred] adj weitverbreitet

widget ['wɪdʒɪt] n (Comput) Minianwendung f, Widget nt

widow ['wɪdəʊ] n Witwe f

widowed ['wɪdəʊd] adj verwitwet

widower ['wɪdəʊəʳ] n Witwer m

width [wɪdθ] n Breite f; (in swimming pool) (Quer) bahn f; **it's 7 metres in ~** es ist 7 Meter breit

widthways ['wɪdθweɪz] adv der Breite nach

wield [wi:ld] vt (sword) schwingen; (power) ausüben

wife [waɪf] (pl **wives**) n Frau f

Wi-Fi ['waɪfaɪ] n Wi-Fi nt

wig [wɪg] n Perücke f

wigging ['wɪgɪŋ] (Brit: inf) n Standpauke f

wiggle ['wɪgl] vt wackeln mit

wiggly ['wɪglɪ] adj: **~ line** Schlangenlinie f

wild [waɪld] adj wild; (weather) rau, stürmisch; (person, behaviour) ungestüm; (idea) weit hergeholt; (applause) stürmisch ▷ n: **the ~** (natural surroundings) die freie Natur f; **the wilds** npl die Wildnis; **I'm not ~ about it** ich bin nicht versessen or scharf darauf

wild card n (Comput) Wildcard f, Ersatzzeichen nt

wildcat ['waɪldkæt] n Wildkatze f

wildcat strike n wilder Streik m

wilderness ['wɪldənɪs] n Wildnis f

wildfire ['waɪldfaɪəʳ] n: **to spread like ~** sich wie ein Lauffeuer ausbreiten

wild-goose chase [waɪld'gu:s-] n aussichtslose Suche f

wildlife ['waɪldlaɪf] n (animals) die Tierwelt f

wildly ['waɪldlɪ] adv wild; (very: romantic) wild-; (: inefficient) furchtbar

wiles [waɪlz] npl List f

wilful, (US) **willful** ['wɪlful] adj (obstinate) eigensinnig; (deliberate) vorsätzlich

○ KEYWORD

will [wɪl] aux vb **1** (forming future tense): **I will finish it tomorrow** ich werde es morgen fertig machen, ich mache es morgen fertig; **will you do it?** — **yes I will/no I won't** machst du es? — ja/nein

2 (in conjectures, predictions): **that will be the postman** das ist bestimmt der Briefträger

3 (in commands, requests, offers): **will you sit down** bitte nehmen Sie Platz; (angrily) nun setz dich doch; **will you be quiet!** seid jetzt still!; **will you help me?** hilfst du mir?; **will you have a cup of tea?** möchten Sie eine Tasse Tee?; **I won't put up with it!** das lasse ich mir nicht gefallen!

▷ vt (pt, pp **willed**) **to will sb to do sth** jdn durch Willenskraft dazu bewegen, etw zu tun; **he willed himself to go on** er zwang sich dazu, weiterzumachen

▷ n (volition) Wille m; (testament) Testament nt; **he did it against his will** er tat es gegen seinen Willen

willful ['wɪlful] (US) adj = **wilful**

willing ['wɪlɪŋ] adj (having no objection) gewillt; (enthusiastic) bereitwillig; **he's ~ to do it** er ist bereit, es zu tun; **to show ~** guten Willen zeigen

willingly ['wɪlɪŋlɪ] adv bereitwillig

willingness ['wɪlɪŋnɪs] n (readiness) Bereitschaft f; (enthusiasm) Bereitwilligkeit f

will-o'-the-wisp ['wɪləðə'wɪsp] n Irrlicht nt; (fig) Trugbild nt

willow ['wɪləʊ] n (tree) Weide f; (wood) Weidenholz nt

willpower ['wɪl'paʊəʳ] n Willenskraft f

willy-nilly ['wɪlɪ'nɪlɪ] adv (willingly or not) wohl oder übel

wilt [wɪlt] vi (plant) welken

Wilts [wɪlts] (Brit) abbr (Post) = **Wiltshire**

wily ['waɪlɪ] adj listig, raffiniert

wimp [wɪmp] (inf: pej) n Waschlappen m

wimpish ['wɪmpɪʃ] (inf) adj weichlich

win [wɪn] (pt, pp **won**) n Sieg m ▷ vt gewinnen ▷ vi siegen, gewinnen

▶ **win over** vt (persuade) gewinnen

▶ **win round** (Brit) vt = **win over**

wince [wɪns] vi zusammenzucken

winch [wɪntʃ] n Winde f

Winchester disk ['wɪntʃɪstə-] n Winchesterplatte f

wind¹ [wɪnd] n (air) Wind m; (Med) Blähungen pl; (breath) Atem m ▷ vt (take breath away from) den Atem nehmen +dat; **the winds** npl (Mus) die Bläser pl; **into** or **against the ~** gegen den Wind; **to get ~ of sth** (fig) von etw Wind bekommen; **to break ~** Darmwind entweichen lassen

wind² [waɪnd] (pt, pp **wound**) vt (thread, rope, bandage) wickeln; (clock, toy) aufziehen ▷ vi (road, river) sich winden

▶ **wind down** vt (car window) herunterdrehen; (fig: production) zurückschrauben

▶ **wind up** vt (clock, toy) aufziehen; (debate) abschließen

windbreak ['wɪndbreɪk] n Windschutz m

windcheater ['wɪndtʃi:təʳ], (US) **windbreaker** n Windjacke f

865

winder ['waɪndəʳ] (Brit) n (on watch) Krone f, Aufziehrädchen nt

windfall ['wɪndfɔːl] n (money) unverhoffter Glücksfall m; (apple) Fallobst nt

wind farm n Windpark m

winding ['waɪndɪŋ] adj gewunden

wind instrument ['wɪnd-] n Blasinstrument nt

windmill ['wɪndmɪl] n Windmühle f

window ['wɪndəʊ] n (also Comput) Fenster nt; (in shop) Schaufenster nt

window box n Blumenkasten m

window cleaner n Fensterputzer(in) m(f)

window dresser n Schaufensterdekorateur(in) m(f)

window envelope n Fensterumschlag m

window frame n Fensterrahmen m

window ledge n Fenstersims m

window pane n Fensterscheibe f

window-shopping ['wɪndəʊʃɒpɪŋ] n Schaufensterbummel m; **to go ~** einen Schaufensterbummel machen

windowsill ['wɪndəʊsɪl] n Fensterbank f

windpipe ['wɪndpaɪp] n Luftröhre f

wind power ['wɪnd-] n Windkraft f, Windenergie f

windscreen ['wɪndskriːn] n Windschutzscheibe f

windscreen washer n Scheibenwaschanlage f

windscreen wiper [-waɪpəʳ] n Scheibenwischer m

windshield ['wɪndʃiːld] (US) n = **windscreen**

windsurfing ['wɪndsɜːfɪŋ] n Windsurfen nt

windswept ['wɪndswɛpt] adj (place) vom Wind gepeitscht; (person) vom Wind zerzaust

wind tunnel ['wɪnd-] n Windkanal m

windy ['wɪndɪ] adj windig; **it's ~** es ist windig

wine [waɪn] n Wein m ▷ vt: **to ~ and dine sb** jdm zu einem guten Essen ausführen

wine bar n Weinlokal nt

wine cellar n Weinkeller m

wine glass n Weinglas nt

wine list n Weinkarte f

wine merchant n Weinhändler(in) m(f)

wine tasting [-teɪstɪŋ] n Weinprobe f

wine waiter n Weinkellner m

wing [wɪŋ] n (of bird, insect, plane) Flügel m; (of building) Trakt m; (of car) Kotflügel m; **the wings** npl (Theat) die Kulissen pl

winger ['wɪŋəʳ] n (Sport) Flügelspieler(in) m(f)

wing mirror (Brit) n Seitenspiegel m

wing nut n Flügelmutter f

wingspan ['wɪŋspæn] n Flügelspannweite f

wingspread ['wɪŋsprɛd] n = **wingspan**

wink [wɪŋk] n (of eye) Zwinkern nt ▷ vi (with eye) zwinkern; (light etc) blinken

winkle [wɪŋkl] n Strandschnecke f

winner ['wɪnəʳ] n (of race, competition) Sieger(in) m(f); (of prize) Gewinner(in) m(f)

winning ['wɪnɪŋ] adj (team, entry) siegreich; (shot, goal) entscheidend; (smile) einnehmend; see also **winnings**

winning post n (lit) Zielpfosten m; (fig) Ziel nt

winnings ['wɪnɪŋz] npl Gewinn m

winsome ['wɪnsəm] adj (expression) gewinnend; (person) reizend

winter ['wɪntəʳ] n Winter m ▷ vi (birds) überwintern; **in ~** im Winter

winter sports npl Wintersport m

wintry ['wɪntrɪ] adj (weather, day) winterlich, Winter-

wipe [waɪp] vt wischen; (dry) abtrocknen; (clean) abwischen; (erase: tape) löschen; **to ~ one's nose** sich dat die Nase putzen ▷ n: **to give sth a ~** etw abwischen
  ▶ **wipe off** vt abwischen
  ▶ **wipe out** vt (destroy: city etc) auslöschen
  ▶ **wipe up** vt (mess) aufwischen

wire ['waɪəʳ] n Draht m; (US: telegram) Telegramm nt ▷ vt (US): **to ~ sb** jdm telegrafieren; (also: **wire up**: electrical fitting) anschließen

wire brush n Drahtbürste f

wire cutters npl Drahtschere f

wireless ['waɪəlɪs] (Brit: old) n Funk m; (set) Rundfunkgerät nt

wireless phone n schnurloses Telefon nt

wire netting n Maschendraht m

wire service (US) n Nachrichtenagentur f

wire-tapping ['waɪətæpɪŋ] n Anzapfen nt von Leitungen

wiring ['waɪərɪŋ] n elektrische Leitungen pl

wiry ['waɪərɪ] adj (person) drahtig; (hair) borstig

Wis. (US) abbr (Post) = Wisconsin

wisdom ['wɪzdəm] n (of person) Weisheit f; (of action, remark) Klugheit f

wisdom tooth n Weisheitszahn m

wise adj (person) weise; (action, remark) klug; **I'm none the ~r** ich bin genauso klug wie vorher
  ▶ **wise up** (inf) vi: **to ~ up to sth** hinter etw acc kommen

...wise [waɪz] suff: **timewise/moneywise** etc zeitmäßig/geldmäßig etc

wisecrack ['waɪzkræk] n Witzelei f

wisely ['waɪzlɪ] adv klug, weise

wish [wɪʃ] n Wunsch m ▷ vt wünschen; **best ~es** (for birthday etc) herzliche Grüße, alle guten Wünsche; **with best ~es** (in letter) mit den besten Wünschen or Grüßen; **give her my best ~es** grüßen Sie sie herzlich von mir; **to make a ~** sich dat etw wünschen; **to ~ sb goodbye** jdm Auf Wiedersehen sagen; **he ~ed me well** er wünschte mir alles Gute; **to ~ to do sth** etw tun wollen; **to ~ sth on sb** jdm etw wünschen; **to ~ for sth** sich dat etw wünschen

wishbone ['wɪʃbəʊn] n Gabelbein nt

wishful ['wɪʃful] adj: **it's ~ thinking** das ist reines Wunschdenken

wishy-washy ['wɪʃɪwɒʃɪ] (inf) adj (colour) verwaschen; (person) farblos; (ideas) nichtssagend

wisp [wɪsp] n (of grass) Büschel nt; (of hair) Strähne f; (of smoke) Fahne f

wistful ['wɪstful] adj wehmütig

wit [wɪt] n (wittiness) geistreiche Art f; (person) geistreicher Mensch m; (presence of mind) Verstand m; **wits** npl (intelligence) Verstand m;

to be at one's ~s' end mit seinem Latein am Ende sein; to have one's ~s about one einen klaren Kopf haben; to ~ (namely) und zwar
witch [wɪtʃ] n Hexe f
witchcraft ['wɪtʃkrɑːft] n Hexerei f
witch doctor n Medizinmann m
witch-hunt ['wɪtʃhʌnt] n (fig) Hexenjagd f

🔘 KEYWORD

with [wɪð] prep 1 (accompanying, in the company of) mit; we stayed with friends wir wohnten bei Freunden; I'll be with you in a minute einen Augenblick, ich bin sofort da; I'm with you (I understand) ich verstehe; to be with it (inf: up-to-date) auf dem Laufenden sein; (: alert) da sein
2 (descriptive, indicating manner) mit; the man with the grey hat/blue eyes der Mann mit dem grauen Hut/den blauen Augen; with tears in her eyes mit Tränen in den Augen; red with anger rot vor Wut

withdraw [wɪð'drɔː] (irreg: like draw) vt (object, offer) zurückziehen; (remark) zurücknehmen ▷ vi (troops) abziehen; (person) sich zurückziehen; to ~ money (from bank) Geld abheben; to ~ into o.s. sich in sich acc selbst zurückziehen
withdrawal [wɪð'drɔːəl] n (of offer, remark) Zurücknahme f; (of troops) Abzug m; (of participation) Ausstieg m; (of services) Streichung f; (of money) Abhebung f
withdrawal symptoms npl Entzugserscheinungen pl
withdrawn [wɪð'drɔːn] pp of withdraw ▷ adj (person) verschlossen
wither ['wɪðəʳ] vi (plant) verwelken
withered ['wɪðəd] adj (plant) verwelkt; (limb) verkümmert
withhold [wɪð'həʊld] (irreg: like hold) vt vorenthalten
within [wɪð'ɪn] prep (place) innerhalb +gen; (time, distance) innerhalb von ▷ adv innen; ~ reach in Reichweite; ~ sight (of) in Sichtweite (+gen); ~ the week vor Ende der Woche; ~ a mile of weniger als eine Meile entfernt von; ~ an hour innerhalb einer Stunde; ~ the law im Rahmen des Gesetzes
without [wɪð'aʊt] prep ohne; ~ a coat ohne Mantel; ~ speaking ohne zu sprechen; it goes ~ saying das versteht sich von selbst; ~ anyone knowing ohne dass jemand davon wusste
withstand [wɪð'stænd] (irreg: like stand) vt widerstehen +dat
witness ['wɪtnɪs] n Zeuge m, Zeugin f ▷ vt (event) sehen, Zeuge/Zeugin sein +gen; (fig) miterleben; ~ to bear ~ to sth Zeugnis für etw ablegen; ~ for the prosecution/defence Zeuge/Zeugin der Anklage/Verteidigung; to ~ to sth etw bezeugen; to ~ having seen sth bezeugen, etw gesehen zu haben

witness box n Zeugenstand m
witness stand (US) n = witness box
witticism ['wɪtɪsɪzəm] n geistreiche Bemerkung f
witty ['wɪtɪ] adj geistreich
wives [waɪvz] npl of wife
wizard ['wɪzəd] n Zauberer m
wizened ['wɪznd] adj (person) verhutzelt; (fruit, vegetable) verschrumpelt
wk abbr = week
Wm. abbr = William
WO n abbr (Mil) = warrant officer
wobble ['wɒbl] vi wackeln; (legs) zittern
wobbly ['wɒblɪ] adj (hand, voice) zitt(e)rig; (table, chair) wack(e)lig; to feel ~ sich wack(e)lig fühlen
woe [wəʊ] n (sorrow) Jammer m; (misfortune) Kummer m
woeful ['wəʊful] adj traurig
wok [wɒk] n Wok m
woke [wəʊk] pt of wake
woken ['wəʊkn] pp of wake
wolf [wʊlf] (pl wolves) n Wolf m
wolves [wʊlvz] npl of wolf
woman ['wʊmən] (pl women) n Frau f; ~ friend Freundin f; ~ teacher Lehrerin f; young ~ junge Frau; women's page Frauenseite f
woman doctor n Ärztin f
womanize ['wʊmənaɪz] (pej) vi hinter Frauen her sein
womanly ['wʊmənlɪ] adj (virtues etc) weiblich
womb [wuːm] n Mutterleib m; (Med) Gebärmutter f
women ['wɪmɪn] npl of woman
women's lib ['wɪmɪnz-] (inf) n Frauenbefreiung f
Women's Liberation Movement, Women's Movement n Frauenbewegung f
won [wʌn] pt, pp of win
wonder ['wʌndəʳ] n (miracle) Wunder nt; (awe) Verwunderung f ▷ vi: to ~ whether/why etc sich fragen, ob/warum etc; it's no ~ (that) es ist kein Wunder(, dass); to ~ at (marvel at) staunen über +acc; to ~ about sich dat Gedanken machen über +acc; I ~ if you could help me könnten Sie mir vielleicht helfen
wonderful ['wʌndəful] adj wunderbar
wonderfully ['wʌndəfəlɪ] adv wunderbar
wonky ['wɒŋkɪ] (Brit: inf) adj wack(e)lig
wont [wəʊnt] n: as is his ~ wie er zu tun pflegt
won't [wəʊnt] = will not
woo [wuː] vt (woman, audience) umwerben
wood [wʊd] n (timber) Holz nt; (forest) Wald m ▷ cpd Holz-
woodcarving ['wʊdkɑːvɪŋ] n (act, object) Holzschnitzerei f
wooded ['wʊdɪd] adj bewaldet
wooden ['wʊdn] adj (also fig) hölzern
woodland ['wʊdlənd] n Waldland nt
woodpecker ['wʊdpekəʳ] n Specht m
wood pigeon n Ringeltaube f
woodwind ['wʊdwɪnd] adj (instrument)

w

Holzblasinstrument nt; **the ~** die Holzbläser pl
woodwork ['wudwɜːk] n (skill) Holzarbeiten pl
woodworm ['wudwɜːm] n Holzwurm m
woof [wuf] n (of dog) Wau nt ▷ vi kläffen; **~, ~!**
wau, wau!
wool [wul] n Wolle f; **to pull the ~ over sb's
eyes** (fig) jdn hinters Licht führen
woollen, (US) **woolen** ['wulən] adj (hat) Woll-,
wollen
woollens ['wulənz] npl Wollsachen pl
woolly, (US) **wooly** ['wulɪ] adj (socks, hat
etc) Woll-; (fig: ideas) schwammig; (person)
verworren ▷ n (pullover) Wollpullover m
woozy ['wuːzɪ] (inf) adj duselig
Worcs (Brit) abbr (Post) = Worcestershire
word [wɜːd] n Wort nt; (news) Nachricht f
▷ vt (letter, message) formulieren; **~ for word**
Wort für Wort, (wort)wörtlich; **what's the
~ for "pen" in German?** was heißt „pen"
auf Deutsch?; **to put sth into ~s** etw in
Worte fassen; **in other ~s** mit anderen
Worten; **to break/keep one's ~** sein Wort
brechen/halten; **to have ~s with sb** eine
Auseinandersetzung mit jdm haben; **to have
a ~ with sb** mit jdm sprechen; **I'll take your
~ for it** ich verlasse mich auf Sie; **to send ~ of
sth** etw verlauten lassen; **to leave ~ (with sb/
for sb) that ...** (bei jdm/für jdn) die Nachricht
hinterlassen, dass ...; **by ~ of mouth** durch
mündliche Überlieferung
wording ['wɜːdɪŋ] n (of message, contract etc)
Wortlaut m, Formulierung f
word-perfect ['wɜːd'pɜːfɪkt] adj: **to be ~** den
Text perfekt beherrschen
word processing n Textverarbeitung f
word processor [-prəusesəʳ] n
Textverarbeitungssystem nt
wordwrap ['wɜːdræp] n (Comput)
(automatischer) Zeilenumbruch m
wordy ['wɜːdɪ] adj (book) langatmig; (person)
wortreich
wore [wɔːʳ] pt of **wear**
work [wɜːk] n Arbeit f; (Art, Liter) Werk nt ▷ vi
arbeiten; (mechanism) funktionieren; (be
successful: medicine etc) wirken ▷ vt (clay, wood,
land) bearbeiten; (mine) arbeiten in; (machine)
bedienen; (create: effect, miracle) bewirken;
to go to ~ zur Arbeit gehen; **to set to ~, to
start ~** sich an die Arbeit machen; **to be at ~
(on sth)** (an etw dat) arbeiten; **to be out of ~**
arbeitslos sein; **to be in ~** eine Stelle haben;
to ~ hard hart arbeiten; **to ~ loose** (part, knot)
sich lösen; **to ~ on the assumption that ...**
von der Annahme ausgehen, dass ...
▶ **work on** vt fus (task) arbeiten an +dat;
(person: influence) bearbeiten; **he's ~ing on his
car** er arbeitet an seinem Auto
▶ **work out** vi (plans etc) klappen; (Sport)
trainieren ▷ vt (problem) lösen; (plan)
ausarbeiten; **it ~s out at 100 pounds** es
ergibt 100 Pfund
▶ **work up** vt: **to get ~ed up** sich aufregen
workable ['wɜːkəbl] adj (system) durchführbar;

(solution) brauchbar
workaholic [wɜːkə'hɒlɪk] n Arbeitstier nt
workbench ['wɜːkbentʃ] n Werkbank f
worker ['wɜːkəʳ] n Arbeiter(in) m(f); **office ~**
Büroarbeiter(in) m(f)
workforce ['wɜːkfɔːs] n Arbeiterschaft f
work-in ['wɜːkɪn] (Brit) n Fabrikbesetzung f
working ['wɜːkɪŋ] adj (day, conditions) Arbeits-;
(population) arbeitend; (mother) berufstätig;
a ~ knowledge of English (adequate)
Grundkenntnisse in Englisch
working capital n Betriebskapital nt
working class n Arbeiterklasse f
working-class ['wɜːkɪŋ'klɑːs] adj (family, town)
Arbeiter-
working man n Arbeiter m
working order n: **in ~** in betriebsfähigem
Zustand
working party (Brit) n Ausschuss m
working relationship n Arbeitsbeziehung f
working week n Arbeitswoche f
work-in-progress ['wɜːkɪn'prəugres] n
laufende Arbeiten pl
workload ['wɜːkləud] n Arbeitsbelastung f
workman ['wɜːkmən] (irreg: like **man**) n
Arbeiter m
workmanship ['wɜːkmənʃɪp] n Arbeitsqualität
f
workmate ['wɜːkmeɪt] n Arbeitskollege m,
Arbeitskollegin f
workout ['wɜːkaut] n Fitnesstraining nt
work permit n Arbeitserlaubnis f
works [wɜːks] (Brit) n (factory) Fabrik f, Werk nt
▷ npl (of clock) Uhrwerk nt; (of machine) Getriebe
nt
work sheet n Arbeitsblatt nt
workshop ['wɜːkʃɒp] n (building) Werkstatt f;
(practical session) Workshop nt
work station n Arbeitsplatz m; (Comput)
Workstation f
work-study ['wɜːkstʌdɪ] n Arbeitsstudie f
worktop ['wɜːktɒp] n Arbeitsfläche f
work-to-rule ['wɜːktə'ruːl] (Brit) n Dienst m
nach Vorschrift
world [wɜːld] n Welt f ▷ cpd (champion, power,
war) Welt-; **all over the ~** auf der ganzen
Welt; **to think the ~ of sb** große Stücke auf
jdn halten; **what in the ~ is he doing?** was
um alles in der Welt macht er?; **to do sb
a** or **the ~ of good** jdm unwahrscheinlich
guttun; **W~ War One/Two** der Erste/Zweite
Weltkrieg; **out of this ~** fantastisch
World Cup n: **the ~** (Football) die
Fußballweltmeisterschaft f
world-famous [wɜːld'feɪməs] adj weltberühmt
worldly ['wɜːldlɪ] adj weltlich; (knowledgeable)
weltgewandt
world music n World Music f, Richtung der
Popmusik, die musikalische Stilelemente der Dritten
Welt verwendet
World Series (US) n Endrunde der Baseball-
Weltmeisterschaft zwischen den Tabellenführern der
Spitzenligen

worldwide ['wə:ld'waɪd] *adj, adv* weltweit
worm [wə:m] *n* Wurm *m*
  ▶ **worm out** *vt*: **to ~ sth out of sb** jdm etw
  entlocken
worn [wɔ:n] *pp of* **wear** ▷ *adj* (*carpet*) abgenutzt;
  (*shoe*) abgetragen
worn-out ['wɔ:naut] *adj* (*object*) abgenutzt;
  (*person*) erschöpft
worried ['wʌrɪd] *adj* besorgt; **to be ~ about
  sth** sich wegen etw Sorgen machen
worrier ['wʌrɪəʳ] *n*: **to be a ~** sich ständig
  Sorgen machen
worrisome ['wʌrɪsəm] *adj* besorgniserregend
worry ['wʌrɪ] *n* Sorge *f* ▷ *vt* beunruhigen ▷ *vi*
  sich *dat* Sorgen machen; **to ~ about** *or* **over
  sth/sb** sich um etw/jdn Sorgen machen
worrying ['wʌrɪɪŋ] *adj* beunruhigend
worse [wə:s] *adj* schlechter, schlimmer
  ▷ *adv* schlechter ▷ *n* Schlechtere(s) *nt*,
  Schlimmere(s) *nt*; **to get ~** (*situation etc*)
  sich verschlechtern *or* verschlimmern; **he
  is none the ~ for it** er hat keinen Schaden
  dabei erlitten; **so much the ~ for you!** um so
  schlimmer für dich!; **a change for the ~** eine
  Wendung zum Schlechten
worsen ['wə:sn] *vt* verschlimmern ▷ *vi* sich
  verschlechtern
worse off *adj* (*also fig*) schlechter dran; **he is
  now ~ than before** er ist jetzt schlechter dran
  als zuvor
worship ['wə:ʃɪp] *n* (*act*) Verehrung *f* ▷ *vt* (*god*)
  anbeten; (*person, thing*) verehren; **Your W~**
  (*Brit: to mayor*) verehrter Herr Bürgermeister;
  (: *to judge*) Euer Ehren
worshipper ['wə:ʃɪpəʳ] *n* (*in church etc*)
  Kirchgänger(in) *m(f)*; (*fig*) Anbeter(in) *m(f)*,
  Verehrer(in) *m(f)*
worst [wə:st] *adj* schlechteste(r, s),
  schlimmste(r, s) ▷ *adv* am schlimmsten ▷ *n*
  Schlimmste(s) *nt*; **at ~** schlimmstenfalls; **if
  the ~ comes to the worst** wenn alle Stricke
  reißen
worst-case scenario ['wə:stkeɪs-] *n*
  Schlimmstfallszenario *nt*
worsted ['wustɪd] *n* Kammgarn *nt*
worth [wə:θ] *n* Wert *m* ▷ *adj*: **to be ~** wert sein;
  £2 ~ of apples Äpfel für £ 2; **how much is it
  ~?** was *or* wie viel ist es wert?; **it's ~ it** (*effort,
  time*) es lohnt sich; **it's ~ every penny** es ist
  sein Geld wert
worthless ['wə:θlɪs] *adj* wertlos
worthwhile ['wə:θ'waɪl] *adj* lohnend
worthy [wə:ðɪ] *adj* (*person*) würdig; (*motive*)
  ehrenwert; **~ of** wert +*gen*

KEYWORD

would [wud] *aux vb* **1** (*conditional tense*): **if you
  asked him he would do it** wenn du ihn
  fragtest, würde er es tun; **if you had asked
  him he would have done it** wenn du ihn
  gefragt hättest, hätte er es getan
2 (*in offers, invitations, requests*): **would you like a**

biscuit? möchten Sie ein Plätzchen?; **would
  you ask him to come in?** würden Sie ihn
  bitten hereinzukommen?
3 (*in indirect speech*): **I said I would do it** ich
  sagte, ich würde es tun
4 (*emphatic*): **it WOULD have to snow today!**
  ausgerechnet heute musste es schneien!
5 (*insistence*): **she wouldn't behave** sie wollte
  sich partout nicht benehmen
6 (*conjecture*): **it would have been midnight**
  es mochte etwa Mitternacht gewesen sein; **it
  would seem so** so scheint es wohl
7 (*indicating habit*): **he would go there on
  Mondays** er ging montags immer dorthin;
  he would spend every day on the beach er
  verbrachte jeden Tag am Strand

would-be ['wudbi:] *adj* (*singer, writer*)
  Möchtegern-
wouldn't ['wudnt] = **would not**
wound¹ [waund] *pt, pp of* **wind²**
wound² [wu:nd] *n* Wunde *f* ▷ *vt* verwunden;
  ~ed in the leg am Bein verletzt
wove [wəuv] *pt of* **weave**
woven ['wəuvn] *pp of* **weave**
WP *n abbr* = **word processing; word processor**
  ▷ *abbr* (*Brit: inf: = weather permitting*) bei
  günstiger Witterung
WPC (*Brit*) *n abbr* (= *woman police constable*)
  Polizistin *f*
wpm *abbr* (= *words per minute*) Worte pro Minute
  (*beim Maschineschreiben*)
WRAC (*Brit*) *n abbr* (= *Women's Royal Army Corps*)
  Frauenkorps der Armee
WRAF (*Brit*) *n abbr* (= *Women's Royal Air Force*)
  Frauenkorps der Luftwaffe
wrangle ['ræŋgl] *n* Gerangel *nt* ▷ *vi*: **to ~ with
  sb over sth** sich mit jdm um etw zanken
wrap [ræp] *n* (*shawl*) Umhang *m*; (*cape*) Cape
  nt ▷ *vt* einwickeln; (*also*: **wrap up**: *pack*)
  einpacken; (*wind: tape etc*) wickeln; **under ~s**
  (*fig: plan*) geheim
wrapper ['ræpəʳ] *n* (*on chocolate*) Papier *nt*;
  (*Brit: of book*) Umschlag *m*
wrapping paper ['ræpɪŋ-] *n* (*brown*) Packpapier
  nt; (*fancy*) Geschenkpapier *nt*
wrath [rɔθ] *n* Zorn *m*
wreak [ri:k] *vt*: **to ~ havoc (on)** verheerenden
  Schaden anrichten (bei); **to ~ vengeance** *or*
  revenge on sb Rache an jdm üben
wreath [ri:θ] *n* (*pl* **~s**) *n* Kranz *m*
wreck [rɛk] *n* Wrack *nt*; (*vehicle*) Schrotthaufen
  m ▷ *vt* kaputt machen; (*car*) zu Schrott fahren;
  (*chances*) zerstören
wreckage ['rɛkɪdʒ] *n* (*of car, plane, building*)
  Trümmer *pl*; (*of ship*) Wrackteile *pl*
wrecker ['rɛkəʳ] (*US*) *n* (*breakdown van*)
  Abschleppwagen *m*
Wren (*Brit*) *n abbr* weibliches Mitglied der britischen
  Marine
wren [rɛn] *n* (*Zool*) Zaunkönig *m*
wrench [rɛntʃ] *n* (*Tech*) Schraubenschlüssel *m*;
  (*tug*) Ruck *m*; (*fig*) schmerzhaftes Erlebnis *nt*

w

▷ vt (pull) reißen; (injure: arm, back) verrenken;
to ~ sth from sb jdm etw entreißen
wrest [rɛst] vt: **to ~ sth from sb** jdm etw
abringen
wrestle ['rɛsl] vi: **to ~ (with sb)** (mit jdm)
ringen; **to ~ with a problem** mit einem
Problem kämpfen
wrestler ['rɛslə'] n Ringer(in) m(f)
wrestling ['rɛslɪŋ] n Ringen nt; (also: **all-in
wrestling**) Freistilringen nt
wrestling match n Ringkampf m
wretch [rɛtʃ] n: **poor ~** (man) armer Schlucker
m; (woman) armes Ding nt; **little ~!** (often
humorous) kleiner Schlingel!
wretched ['rɛtʃɪd] adj (poor) erbärmlich;
(unhappy) unglücklich; (inf: damned) elend
wriggle ['rɪgl] vi (also: **wriggle about**: person)
zappeln; (fish) sich winden; (snake etc) sich
schlängeln ▷ n Zappeln nt
wring [rɪŋ] (pt, pp **wrung**) vt (wet clothes)
auswringen; (hands) wringen; (neck)
umdrehen; **to ~ sth out of sth/sb** (fig) etw/
jdm etw abringen
wringer ['rɪŋə'] n Mangel f
wringing ['rɪŋɪŋ] adj (also: **wringing wet**)
tropfnass
wrinkle ['rɪŋkl] n Falte f ▷ vt (nose, forehead etc)
runzeln ▷ vi (skin, paint etc) sich runzeln
wrinkled ['rɪŋkld] adj (fabric, paper) zerknittert;
(surface) gekräuselt; (skin) runzlig
wrinkly ['rɪŋklɪ] adj = **wrinkled**
wrist [rɪst] n Handgelenk nt
wristband ['rɪstbænd] (Brit) n (of shirt)
Manschette f; (of watch) Armband nt
wristwatch ['rɪstwɒtʃ] n Armbanduhr f
writ [rɪt] n (Law) (gerichtliche) Verfügung f;
to issue a ~ against sb, serve a ~ on sb eine
Verfügung gegen jdn erlassen
write [raɪt] (pt **wrote**, pp **written**) vt schreiben;
(cheque) ausstellen ▷ vi schreiben; **to ~ to sb**
jdm schreiben
▸ **write away** vi: **to ~ away for sth** etw
anfordern
▸ **write down** vt aufschreiben
▸ **write off** vt (debt, project) abschreiben;
(wreck: car etc) zu Schrott fahren ▷ vi = **write
away**
▸ **write out** vt (put in writing) schreiben; (cheque,
receipt etc) ausstellen
▸ **write up** vt (report etc) schreiben
write-off ['raɪtɒf] n (Aut) Totalschaden m
write-protected ['raɪtprə'tɛktɪd] adj (Comput)

schreibgeschützt
writer ['raɪtə'] n (author) Schriftsteller(in) m(f);
(of report, document etc) Verfasser(in) m(f)
write-up ['raɪtʌp] n (review) Kritik f
writhe [raɪð] vi sich krümmen
writing ['raɪtɪŋ] n Schrift f; (of author) Arbeiten
pl; (activity) Schreiben nt; **in ~** schriftlich; **in
my own ~** in meiner eigenen Handschrift
writing case n Schreibmappe f
writing desk n Schreibtisch m
writing paper n Schreibpapier nt
written ['rɪtn] pp of **write**
WRNS (Brit) n abbr (= Women's Royal Naval Service)
Frauenkorps der Marine
wrong [rɒŋ] adj falsch; (morally bad) unrecht;
(unfair) ungerecht ▷ adv falsch ▷ n (injustice)
Unrecht nt; (evil): **right and ~** Gut und Böse
▷ vt (treat unfairly) unrecht or ein Unrecht tun
+dat; **to be ~** (answer) falsch sein; (in doing,
saying sth) unrecht haben; **you are ~ to do it**
es ist ein Fehler von dir, das zu tun; **it's ~ to
steal, stealing is wrong** Stehlen ist unrecht;
you are ~ about that, you've got it wrong
da hast du unrecht; **what's ~?** wo fehlts?;
there's nothing ~ es ist alles in Ordnung;
to go ~ (person) einen Fehler machen; (plan)
schiefgehen; (machine) versagen; **to be in the
~** im Unrecht sein
wrongdoer ['rɒŋduːə'] n Übeltäter(in) m(f)
wrong-foot [rɒŋ'fut] vt: **to ~ sb** (Sport) jdn
auf dem falschen Fuß erwischen; (fig) jdn im
falschen Moment erwischen
wrongful ['rɒŋful] adj unrechtmäßig
wrongly ['rɒŋlɪ] adv falsch; (unjustly) zu
Unrecht
wrong number n (Tel): **you've got the ~** Sie
sind falsch verbunden
wrong side n: **the ~** (of material) die linke
Seite
wrote [rəut] pt of **write**
wrought [rɔːt] adj: **~ iron** Schmiedeeisen nt
wrung [rʌŋ] pt, pp of **wring**
WRVS (Brit) n abbr (= Women's Royal Voluntary
Service) karitativer Frauenverband
wry [raɪ] adj (smile, humour) trocken
wt. abbr = **weight**
WV (US) abbr (Post) = West Virginia
W.Va. (US) abbr (Post) = West Virginia
WWW n abbr (= World Wide Web) WWW nt
WY, Wyo. (US) abbr (Post) = Wyoming
WYSIWYG ['wɪzɪwɪg] abbr (Comput: = what you see
is what you get) WYSIWYG nt

X, x [ɛks] n (letter) X nt, x nt; (Brit: Cine: formerly) Klassifikation für nicht jugendfreie Filme; **X for Xmas** ≈ X wie Xanthippe
Xerox® ['zɪərɔks] n (also: **Xerox machine**) Xerokopierer m; (photocopy) Xerokopie f ▷ vt xerokopieren
XL abbr (= extra large) XL
Xmas ['ɛksməs] n abbr = **Christmas**

XML abbr (Comput: = extensible markup language) XML
X-rated ['ɛks'reɪtɪd] (US) adj (film) nicht jugendfrei
X-ray ['ɛksreɪ] n Röntgenstrahl m; (photo) Röntgenbild nt ▷ vt röntgen; **to have an ~** sich röntgen lassen
xylophone ['zaɪləfəun] n Xylofon nt

Yy

Y, y [waɪ] n (letter) Y nt, y nt; **Y for Yellow, Y for Yoke** (US) ≈ Y wie Ypsilon

yacht [jɔt] n Jacht f

yachting ['jɔtɪŋ] n Segeln nt

yachtsman ['jɔtsmən] (irreg: like **man**) n Segler m

yam [jæm] n Jamswurzel f, Yamswurzel f

Yank [jæŋk] (pej) n Ami m

yank [jæŋk] vt reißen ▷ n Ruck m; **to give sth a ~** mit einem Ruck an etw dat ziehen

Yankee ['jæŋkɪ] (pej) n = **Yank**

yap [jæp] vi (dog) kläffen

yard [jɑːd] n (of house etc) Hof m; (US: garden) Garten m; (measure) Yard nt (= 0,91 m); **builder's ~** Bauhof m

yardstick ['jɑːdstɪk] n (fig) Maßstab m

yarn [jɑːn] n (thread) Garn nt; (tale) Geschichte f

yawn [jɔːn] n Gähnen nt ▷ vi gähnen

yawning ['jɔːnɪŋ] adj (gap) gähnend

yd abbr = **yard**

yeah [jɛə] (inf) adv ja

year [jɪəʳ] n Jahr nt; (referring to wine) Jahrgang m; **every ~** jedes Jahr; **this ~** dieses Jahr; **a** or **per ~** pro Jahr; **~ in, ~ out** jahrein, jahraus; **to be 8 ~s old** 8 Jahre alt sein; **an eight-~-old child** ein achtjähriges Kind

yearbook ['jɪəbuk] n Jahrbuch nt

yearling ['jɪəlɪŋ] n (horse) Jährling m

yearly ['jɪəlɪ] adj, adv (once a year) jährlich; **twice ~** zweimal jährlich or im Jahr

yearn [jəːn] vi: **to ~ for sth** sich nach etwas sehnen; **to ~ to do sth** sich danach sehnen, etw zu tun

yearning ['jəːnɪŋ] n: **to have a ~ for sth** ein Verlangen nach etw haben; **to have a ~ to do sth** ein Verlangen danach haben, etw zu tun

yeast [jiːst] n Hefe f

yell [jɛl] n Schrei m ▷ vi schreien

yellow ['jɛləu] adj gelb ▷ n Gelb nt

yellow fever n Gelbfieber nt

yellowish ['jɛləuɪʃ] adj gelblich

Yellow Pages® npl: **the Yellow Pages** die gelben Seiten pl, das Branchenverzeichnis

Yellow Sea n: **the ~** das Gelbe Meer

yelp [jɛlp] n Jaulen nt ▷ vi jaulen

Yemen ['jɛmən] n: **(the) ~** (der) Jemen

Yemeni ['jɛmənɪ] adj jemenitisch ▷ n Jemenit(in) m(f)

yen [jɛn] n (currency) Yen m; (craving): **to have a ~ for** Lust auf etw haben; **to have a ~ to do sth** Lust darauf haben, etw zu tun

yeoman ['jəumən] (irreg: like **man**) n: **Y~ of the Guard** (königlicher) Leibgardist m

yes [jɛs] adv ja; (in reply to negative) doch ▷ n Ja nt; **to say ~** Ja sagen; **to answer ~** mit Ja antworten

yes-man ['jɛsmæn] (irreg: like **man**) (pej) n Jasager m

yesterday ['jɛstədɪ] adv gestern ▷ n Gestern nt; **~ morning/evening** gestern Morgen/Abend; **~'s paper** die Zeitung von gestern; **the day before ~** vorgestern; **all day ~** gestern den ganzen Tag (lang)

yet [jɛt] adv noch ▷ conj jedoch; **it is not finished ~** es ist noch nicht fertig; **must you go just ~?** musst du schon gehen?; **the best ~** der/die/das bisher Beste; **as ~** bisher; **it'll be a few days ~** es wird noch ein paar Tage dauern; **not for a few days ~** nicht in den nächsten paar Tagen; **~ again** wiederum

yew [juː] n (tree) Eibe f; (wood) Eibenholz nt

Y-fronts® ['waɪfrʌnts] npl (Herren-)Slip m (mit y-förmiger Vorderseite)

YHA (Brit) n abbr (= Youth Hostels Association) britischer Jugendherbergsverband

Yiddish ['jɪdɪʃ] n Jiddisch nt

yield [jiːld] n (Agr) Ertrag m; (Comm) Gewinn m ▷ vt (surrender: control etc) abtreten; (produce: results, profit) hervorbringen ▷ vi (surrender, give way) nachgeben; (US: Aut) die Vorfahrt achten; **a ~ of 5%** ein Ertrag or Gewinn von 5%

YMCA n abbr (organization: = Young Men's Christian Association) CVJM m

yob ['jɔb], **yobbo** ['jɔbəu] (Brit: inf: pej) n Rowdy m

yodel ['jəudl] vi jodeln

yoga ['jəugə] n Yoga m or nt

yoghourt, yogourt ['jəugət] n = **yoghurt**

yoghurt, yogurt ['jəugət] n Joghurt m or nt

yoke [jəuk] n (also fig) Joch nt ▷ vt (also: **yoke together**) oxen) einspannen

yolk [jəuk] n (of egg) Dotter m, Eigelb nt

yonder ['jɔndəʳ] adv: **(over) ~** dort drüben ▷ adj: **from ~ house** von dem Haus dort drüben

yonks [jɔŋks] (*inf*) *n*: **for** ~ seit einer Ewigkeit
Yorks [jɔːks] (*Brit*) *abbr* (*Post*) = Yorkshire

 KEYWORD

you [juː] *pron* **1** (*subject: familiar: singular*) du;
(*: plural*) ihr; (*: polite*) Sie; **you Germans enjoy
your food** ihr Deutschen esst gern gut
2 (*object: direct: familiar: singular*) dich; (*: plural*)
euch; (*: polite*) Sie; (*: indirect: familiar: singular*)
dir; (*: plural*) euch; (*: polite*) Ihnen; **I know you**
ich kenne dich/euch/Sie; **I gave it to you** ich
habe es dir/euch/Ihnen gegeben; **if I were
you I would** ... an deiner/eurer/Ihrer Stelle
würde ich ...
3 (*after prep, in comparisons*): **it's for you** es ist für
dich/euch/Sie; **she's younger than you** sie
ist jünger als du/ihr/Sie
4 (*impersonal: one*) man; **you never know** man
weiß nie

you'd [juːd] = **you had; you would**
you'll [juːl] = **you will; you shall**
young [jʌŋ] *adj* jung; **the young** *npl* (*of animal*)
die Jungen *pl*; (*people*) die jungen Leute *pl*; **a**
~ **man** ein junger Mann; **a** ~ **lady** eine junge
Dame
younger [jʌŋgəʳ] *adj* jünger; **the** ~ **generation**
die jüngere Generation
youngish [ˈjʌŋɪʃ] *adj* recht jung
youngster [ˈjʌŋstəʳ] *n* Kind *nt*
your [jɔːʳ] *adj* (*familiar: sing*) dein/deine/dein;
(*: pl*) euer/eure/euer; (*polite*) Ihr/Ihre/Ihr;
(*one's*) sein; **you mustn't eat with** ~ **fingers**
man darf nicht mit den Fingern essen; *see
also* **my**
you're [juəʳ] = **you are**
yours [jɔːz] *pron* (*familiar: sing*) deiner/deine/

dein(e)s; (*: pl*) eurer/eure/eures; (*polite*)
Ihrer/Ihre/Ihres; **a friend of** ~ ein Freund
von dir/Ihnen; **is it** ~? gehört es dir/Ihnen?;
~ **sincerely/faithfully** mit freundlichen
Grüßen; *see also* **mine¹**
yourself [jɔːˈsɛlf] *pron* (*reflexive: familiar: sing: acc*)
dich; (*: dat*) dir; (*: pl*) euch; (*: polite*) sich;
(*emphatic*) selbst; **you** ~ **told me** das haben Sie
mir selbst gesagt
yourselves [jɔːˈsɛlvz] *pl pron* (*reflexive: familiar*)
euch; (*: polite*) sich; (*emphatic*) selbst; *see also*
oneself
youth [juːθ] *n* Jugend *f*; (*young man: pl youths*)
Jugendliche(r) *m*; **in my** ~ in meiner Jugend
youth club *n* Jugendklub *m*
youthful [ˈjuːθful] *adj* jugendlich
youthfulness [ˈjuːθfəlnɪs] *n* Jugendlichkeit
f
youth hostel *n* Jugendherberge *f*
youth movement *n* Jugendbewegung *f*
you've [juːv] = **you have**
yowl [jaul] *n* (*of animal*) Jaulen *nt*; (*of person*)
Heulen *nt*
yr *abbr* (= *year*) J.
YT (*Canada*) *abbr* = Yukon Territory
yuck factor [ˈjʌkfæktəʳ] *n* (*inf*) Igitt-Faktor *m*
Yugoslav [ˈjuːgəslɑːv] (*formerly*) *adj*
jugoslawisch ▷ *n* Jugoslawe *m*, Jugoslawin *f*
Yugoslavia [ˈjuːgəuˈslɑːvɪə] (*formerly*) *n*
Jugoslawien *nt*
Yugoslavian [ˈjuːgəuˈslɑːvɪən] (*formerly*) *adj*
jugoslawisch
Yule log [juːl-] *n* Biskuitrolle mit Überzug, die zu
Weihnachten gegessen wird
yuppie [ˈjʌpɪ] (*inf*) *n* Yuppie *m* ▷ *adj* yuppiehaft;
(*job, car*) Yuppie-
YWCA *n abbr* (*organization*): = Young Women's
Christian Association) CVJF *m*

Zz

Z, z [zɛd, (US) ziː] n (letter) Z nt, z nt; **Z for Zebra**
≈ Z wie Zacharias
Zaire [zɑːˈiːəʳ] n Zaire nt
Zambia [ˈzæmbɪə] n Sambia nt
Zambian [ˈzæmbɪən] adj sambisch ▷ n
Sambier(in) m(f)
zany [ˈzeɪnɪ] adj verrückt
zap [zæp] vt (Comput: delete) löschen
zeal [ziːl] n Eifer m
zealot [ˈzɛlət] n Fanatiker(in) m(f)
zealous [ˈzɛləs] adj eifrig
zebra [ˈziːbrə] n Zebra nt
zebra crossing (Brit) n Zebrastreifen m
zenith [ˈzɛnɪθ] n (also fig) Zenit m
zero [ˈzɪərəʊ] n (number) Null f ▷ vi: **to ~ in on
sth** (target) etw einkreisen; **5 degrees below ~**
5 Grad unter null
zero hour n die Stunde X
zero option n (esp Pol) Nulllösung f
zero-rated [ˈziːrəʊreɪtɪd] (Brit) adj (Tax)
mehrwertsteuerfrei
zest [zɛst] n (for life) Begeisterung f; (of orange)
Orangenschale f
zigzag [ˈzɪgzæg] n Zickzack m ▷ vi sich im
Zickzack bewegen
Zimbabwe [zɪmˈbɑːbwɪ] n Zimbabwe nt
Zimbabwean [zɪmˈbɑːbwɪən] adj zimbabwisch
zimmer® [ˈzɪməʳ] n (also: **zimmer frame**)
Laufgestell nt

zinc [zɪŋk] n Zink nt
Zionism [ˈzaɪənɪzəm] n Zionismus m
Zionist [ˈzaɪənɪst] adj zionistisch ▷ n
Zionist(in) m(f)
zip [zɪp] n (also: **zip fastener**) Reißverschluss m
▷ vt (also: **zip up**: dress etc) den Reißverschluss
zumachen an +dat
zip code (US) n Postleitzahl f
zipper [ˈzɪpəʳ] (US) n = **zip**
zither [ˈzɪðəʳ] n Zither f
zodiac [ˈzəʊdɪæk] n Tierkreis m
zombie [ˈzɒmbɪ] n (fig) Schwachkopf m
zone [zəʊn] n (also Mil) Zone f, Gebiet nt; (in
town) Bezirk m
zonked [zɒŋkt] (inf) adj (tired) total geschafft;
(high on drugs) high; (drunk) voll
zoo [zuː] n Zoo m
zoological [zuəˈlɒdʒɪkl] adj zoologisch
zoologist [zuˈɒlədʒɪst] n Zoologe m, Zoologin
f
zoology [zuːˈɒlədʒɪ] n Zoologie f
zoom [zuːm] vi: **to ~ past** vorbeisausen; **to
~ in (on sth/sb)** (Phot, Cine) (etw/jdn) näher
heranholen
zoom lens n Zoomobjektiv nt
zucchini [zuːˈkiːnɪ] (US) n(pl) Zucchini pl
Zulu [ˈzuːluː] adj (tribe, culture) Zulu- ▷ n (person)
Zulu m/f; (Ling) Zulu nt
Zürich [ˈzjʊərɪk] n Zürich nt

Grammar
Grammatik

Using the grammar

The Grammar section deals systematically and comprehensively with all the information you will need in order to communicate accurately in German. The user-friendly layout explains the grammar point on a left-hand page, leaving the facing page free for illustrative examples. The numbers, → ● etc, direct you to the relevant example in every case.

The Grammar section also provides invaluable guidance on the danger of translating English structures by identical structures in German. Use of Numbers and Punctuation are important areas covered towards the end of the section. Finally, the index lists the main words and grammatical terms in both English and German.

Abbreviations

acc	feminine
ctd	continued
dat	dative
fem	feminine
intr	intransitive
masc	masculine
neut	neuter
nom	nominative
tr	transitive

Contents

Tense Formation

Tenses are either simple or compound. Once you know how to form the past participle, compound tenses are similar for all verbs (see pages 22–29). To form simple tenses you need to know whether a verb is weak, strong or mixed.

In German these are:

> Present indicative → ❶
> Imperfect indicative → ❷
> Present subjunctive → ❸
> Imperfect subjunctive → ❹

Subjunctive forms are widely used in German, especially for indirect or reported speech (see pages 66–67).

The simple tenses are formed by adding endings to a verb stem. The endings show the number, person and tense of the subject of the verb → ❺

The types of verb you need to know to form simple tenses are:

Strong verbs (pages 12–15), those whose vowel usually changes in forming the imperfect indicative → ❻

Weak verbs (pages 8–11), which are usually completely regular and have no vowel changes. Their endings differ from those of strong verbs → ❼

Mixed verbs (pages 16–17), which have a vowel change like strong verbs, but the endings of weak verbs → ❽

Examples

1	ich hole	I fetch
		I am fetching
		I do fetch
2	ich holte	I fetched
		I was fetching
		I used to fetch
3	(dass) ich hole	(that) I fetch / I fetched
4	(dass) ich holte	(that) I fetched
5	ich hole	I fetch
	wir holen	we fetch
	du holtest	you fetched
6	singen	to sing
	er singt	he sings
	er sang	he sang
7	holen	to fetch
	er holt	he fetches
	er holte	he fetched
8	bringen	to bring
	er bringt	he brings
	er bringte	he brought

Weak Verbs

Weak verbs are usually regular in conjugation. Their simple tenses are formed as follows:

Present and imperfect tenses are formed by adding the endings shown below to the verb stem. This stem is formed by removing the **–en** ending of the infinitive (the form found in the dictionary) → ❶

Where the infinitive of a weak verb ends in **–eln** or **–ern**, only the **–n** is removed to form the verb stem → ❷

The endings are as follows:

	PRESENT INDICATIVE	PRESENT SUBJUNCTIVE	
1st singular	-e	-e	
2nd	-st	-est	
3rd	-t	-e	→ ❸
1st plural	-en	-en	
2nd	-t	-et	
3rd	-en	-en	

	IMPERFECT INDICATIVE	IMPERFECT SUBJUNCTIVE	
1st singular	-te	-te	
2nd	-test	-test	
3rd	-te	-te	→ ❸
1st plural	-ten	-ten	
2nd	-tet	-tet	
3rd	-ten	-ten	

① INFINITIVE | | STEM

holen	to fetch	**hol-**
machen	to make	**mach-**
kauen	to chew	**kau-**

② INFINITIVE | | STEM

| wandern | to roam | **wander-** |
| handeln | to trade, to act | **handel-** |

③ holen to fetch

PRESENT INDICATIVE	PRESENT SUBJUNCTIVE	
ich hol**e**	ich hol**e**	I fetch
du hol**st**	du hol**est**	you fetch
er/sie/es hol**t**	er/sie/es hol**e**	he/she/it fetches
wir hol**en**	wir hol**en**	we fetch
ihr hol**t**	ihr hol**et**	you (*plural*) fetch
sie/Sie hol**en**	sie/Sie hol**en**	they/you (*polite*) fetch

IMPERFECT INDICATIVE AND IMPERFECT SUBJUNCTIVE
(*These tenses are identical for weak verbs*)

ich hol**te**	I fetched
du hol**test**	you fetched
er/sie/es hol**te**	he/she/it fetched
wir hol**ten**	we fetched
ihr hol**tet**	you (*plural*) fetched
sie/Sie hol**ten**	they/you (*polite*) fetched

Weak Verbs *continued*

Where the stem of a weak verb ends in -d or -t, an extra -e- is inserted before those endings where this will ease pronunciation → ❶

Weak verbs whose stems end in -m or -n may take this extra -e-, or not, depending on whether its addition is necessary for pronunciation. If the -m or -n is preceded by a consonant other than l, r or h, the -e- is inserted → ❷

Weak (and strong) verbs whose stem ends in a sibilant sound (-s, -z, -ss, -ß) normally lose the -s- of the second person singular ending (the du form) in the present indicative → ❸

NOTE: When this sibilant is -sch, the -s- of the ending remains → ❹

1 reden to speak   arbeiten to work

PRESENT	IMPERFECT	PRESENT	IMPERFECT
ich rede	ich redete	ich arbeite	ich arbeitete
du redest	du redetest	du arbeitest	du arbeitetest
er redet	er redete	er arbeitet	er arbeitete
wir reden	wir redeten	wir arbeiten	wir arbeiteten
ihr redet	ihr redetet	ihr arbeitet	ihr arbeitetet
sie reden	sie redeten	sie arbeiten	sie arbeiteten

2 atmen to breathe   segnen to bless

PRESENT	IMPERFECT	PRESENT	IMPERFECT
ich atme	ich atmete	ich segne	ich segnete
du atmest	du atmetest	du segnest	du segnetest
er atmet	er atmete	er segnet	er segnete
wir atmen	wir atmeten	wir segnen	wir segneten
ihr atmet	ihr atmetet	ihr segnet	ihr segnetet
sie atmen	sie atmeten	sie segnen	sie segneten

BUT:

umarmen to embrace   lernen to learn

PRESENT	IMPERFECT	PRESENT	IMPERFECT
ich umarme	ich umarmte	ich lerne	ich lernte
du umarmst	du umarmtest	du lernst	du lerntest
er umarmt	er umarmte	er lernt	er lernte
wir umarmen	wir umarmten	wir lernen	wir lernten
ihr umarmt	ihr umarmtet	ihr lernt	ihr lerntet
sie umarmen	sie umarmten	sie lernen	sie lernten

3 grüßen to greet   **4** löschen to extinguish

PRESENT	PRESENT
ich grüße	ich lösche
du **grüßt**	du löschst
er grüßt	er löscht
wir grüßen	wir löschen
ihr grüßt	ihr löscht
sie grüßen	sie löschen

Strong Verbs

A table of the most useful strong verbs is given on pages 86–97.

What differentiates strong verbs from weak ones is that when forming their imperfect indicative tense, strong verbs undergo a vowel change and have a different set of endings → ❶

Their past participles are also formed differently (see page 24).

To form the imperfect subjunctive of strong verbs, the endings from the appropriate table below are added to the stem of the imperfect indicative, but the vowel is modified by an umlaut where this is possible, i.e. **a ä, o ö, u ü**. Exceptions to this are clearly shown in the table of strong verbs → ❷

The endings for the simple tenses of strong verbs are as follows:

	PRESENT INDICATIVE	PRESENT SUBJUNCTIVE	
1st singular	-e	-e	
2nd	-st	-est	
3rd	-t	-e	→ ❸
1st plural	-en	-en	
2nd	-t	-et	
3rd	-en	-en	

	IMPERFECT INDICATIVE	IMPERFECT SUBJUNCTIVE	
1st singular	—	-e	
2nd	-st	-(e)st	
3rd	—	-e	→ ❸
1st plural	-en	-en	
2nd	-t	-(e)t	
3rd	-en	-en	

1 Compare:

	INFINITIVE	PRESENT	IMPERFECT
WEAK	sagen to say	er sagt	er sagte
STRONG	rufen to shout	er ruft	er rief

2

	IMPERFECT INDICATIVE	IMPERFECT SUBJUNCTIVE
	er gab he gave	er gäbe (*umlaut added*)
BUT:	er rief he shouted	er riefe (*no umlaut possible*)

3 singen to sing

PRESENT INDICATIVE	PRESENT SUBJUNCTIVE
ich singe	ich singe
du singst	du singest
er singt	er singe
wir singen	wir singen
ihr singt	ihr singet
sie singen	sie singen
Sie singen	Sie singen

IMPERFECT INDICATIVE	IMPERFECT SUBJUNCTIVE
ich sang	ich sänge
du sangst	du säng(e)st
er sang	er sänge
wir sangen	wir sängen
ihr sangt	ihr säng(e)t
sie sangen	sie sängen
Sie sangen	Sie sängen

Strong Verbs *continued*

In the present tense of strong verbs, the vowel also often changes for the second and third persons singular (the du and er/sie/es forms). The pattern of possible changes is as follows:

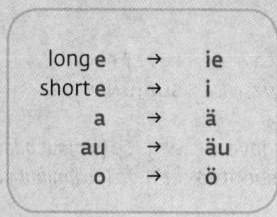

long e	→	ie
short e	→	i
a	→	ä
au	→	äu
o	→	ö

Verbs which undergo these changes are clearly shown in the table on page 86 → **1**

Strong (and weak) verbs whose stem ends with a sibilant sound (-s, -z, -ss, -ß) normally lose the -s- of the second person singular ending (the du form) in the *present indicative*, unless the sibilant is -sch, when it remains → **2**

In the second person singular of the *imperfect* tense of strong verbs whose stem ends in a sibilant sound (including -sch) the sibilant remains, and an -e- is inserted between it and the appropriate ending → **3**

❶

sehen to see	helfen to help	fahren to drive
ich sehe	ich helfe	ich fahre
du **sie**hst	du **hi**lfst	du **fä**hrst
er/sie/es **sie**ht	er/sie/es **hi**lft	er **fä**hrt
wir sehen	wir helfen	wir fahren
ihr seht	ihr helft	ihr fahrt
sie sehen	sie helfen	sie fahren

saufen to booze	stoßen to push
ich saufe	ich stoße
du **säu**fst	du st**öß**t
er **säu**ft	er st**öß**t
wir saufen	wir stoßen
ihr sauft	ihr stoßt
sie saufen	sie stoßen

❷

wachsen to grow	waschen to wash
ich wachse	ich wasche
du **wäch**st	du **wäsch**st
er **wäch**st	er **wäsch**t
wir wachsen	wir waschen
ihr wachst	ihr wascht
sie wachsen	sie waschen

❸

lesen to read	schließen to close	waschen to wash
ich las	ich schloss	ich wusch
du las**est**	du schloss**est**	du wusch**est**
er las	er schloss	er wusch
wir lasen	wir schlossen	wir wuschen
ihr last	ihr schlosst	ihr wuscht
sie lasen	sie schlossen	sie wuschen

Mixed Verbs

There are nine mixed verbs in German, and, as their name implies, they are formed according to a mixture of the rules already outlined for weak and strong verbs.

The mixed verbs are:

brennen to burn	kennen to know	senden to send
bringen to bring	nennen to name	wenden to turn
denken to think	rennen to run	wissen to know

Full details of their principal parts are given in the verb table beginning on page 86.

Mixed verbs form their imperfect tense by adding the weak verb endings to a stem whose vowel has been changed as for a strong verb → ❶

NOTE: Bringen and denken have a consonant change too in their imperfect forms → ❷

The imperfect subjunctive forms of mixed verbs are unusual and should be noted → ❸

Other tenses of mixed verbs are formed as for strong verbs.

The past participle of mixed verbs has characteristics of both weak and strong verbs, as shown on page 24.

①   IMPERFECT INDICATIVE

kennen to know	senden to send	wissen to know
ich kannte	ich sandte	ich wusste
du kanntest	du sandtest	du wusstest
er kannte	er sandte	er wusste
wir kannten	wir sandten	wir wussten
ihr kanntet	ihr sandtet	ihr wusstet
sie kannten	sie sandten	sie wussten

②   IMPERFECT INDICATIVE

bringen to bring	denken to think
ich brachte	ich dachte
du brachtest	du dachtest
er brachte	er dachte
wir brachten	wir dachten
ihr brachtet	ihr dachtet
sie brachten	sie dachten

③   IMPERFECT SUBJUNCTIVE

brennen	kennen	senden
ich brennte	ich kennte	ich sendete
du brenntest	du kenntest	du sendetest
er brennte *etc*	er kennte *etc*	er sendete *etc*

bringen	nennen	wenden
ich brächte	ich nennte	ich wendete
du brächtest	du nenntest	du wendetest
er brächte *etc*	er nennte *etc*	er wendete *etc*

denken	rennen	wissen
ich dächte	ich rennte	ich wüsste
du dächtest	du renntest	du wüsstest
er dächte *etc*	er rennte *etc*	er wüsste *etc*

17

The Imperative

Ths is the form of a verb used to give an order or a command, or to make a request:

> Come here/Stand up/Please bring me a beer → **①**

German has three main imperative forms. These correspond to the three ways of addressing people - **Sie**, **du** and **ihr** (see page 160)

	FORMATION	EXAMPLES	
SINGULAR	stem (+e)	hol(e)!	fetch!
PLURAL	stem +t	holt	fetch!
POLITE (*sing* and *pl*)	stem +en Sie	holen Sie!	fetch!

The **-e** of the singular form is often dropped, BUT not where the verb stem ends in **-chn**, **-ckn**, **-dn**, **-fn**, **-gn** or **-tm** → **②**

Weak verbs ending in **-eln** or **-ern** take the **-e** ending in the singular form, but the additional **-e-** within the stem may be dropped → **③**

Any vowel change in the present tense of a strong verb (see page 14) occurs also in its singular imperative form and no **-e** is added → **④**

BUT: If the vowel modification in the present tense of a strong verb is the addition of an umlaut, this is not added in the singular form of the imperative → **⑤**

In the imperative form of a reflexive verb (see page 30) the pronoun is placed immediately after the verb → **⑥**

Separable prefixes (see page 72) are placed at the end of an imperative statement → **⑦**

1

SINGULAR	Komm mal her!	Come here!
PLURAL	Steht auf!	Stand up!
POLITE	Kommen Sie herein!	Do come in!

2

Hör zu!	Listen!
Hol es!	Fetch it!

BUT:

Öffne die Tür!	Open the door!

3

wandern to walk	handeln to act
wand(e)re! walk!	hand(e)le! act!

4

nehmen to take	helfen to help
du nimmst you take	du hilfst you help
nimm! take!	hilf! help!

BUT:

sehen to see
sieh(e)! see!

5

laufen to run	stoßen to push
du läufst you run	du stößt you push
lauf(e)! run!	stoß(e)! push!

6

sich setzen to sit down
Setz dich! Sit down!
Setzt euch! Sit down!
Setzen Sie sich! Do sit down!

7

zumachen to close	aufhören to stop
Mach die Tür zu!	Hör aber endlich auf!
Close the door!	Do stop it!

The Imperative *continued*

Imperatives are followed in German by an exclamation mark, unless the imperative is not intended as a command → ❶

Du and **ihr**, though not normally present in imperative forms, may be included for emphasis → ❷

An imperative form also exists for the **wir** form of the verb. It consists of the normal present tense form, but with the pronoun **wir** following the verb. It is used for making suggestions → ❸

The imperative forms of **sein** (to be) are irregular → ❹

The particles **auch**, **nur**, **mal**, **doch** are frequently used with imperatives. They heighten or soften the imperative effect, or add a note of encouragement to a request or command. Often they have no direct equivalent in English and are therefore not always translated → ❺

Some alternatives to the imperative in German

Infinitives are often used instead of the imperative in written instructions or public announcements → ❻

The impersonal passive (see page 34) may be used → ❼

Nouns, adjectives or adverbs can also be used with imperative effect → ❽

Some of these have become set expressions → ❾

❶ Lass ihn in Ruhe!
Leave him alone!
Sagen Sie mir bitte, wie spät es ist.
What's the time please?

❷ Geht ihr voran! You go on ahead.
Sag du ihm, was los ist. You tell him what's wrong.

❸ Nehmen wir an, dass ...
Let's assume that ...
Sagen wir mal, es habe 2.000 Euro gekostet.
Let's just say it cost 2,000 euros.

❹ sein to be
sei!
seid!
seien wir!
seien Sie!

❺ Geh doch! Go on!/Get going!
Sag mal, ... Tell me ...
Versuchen Sie es mal! Do give it a try!
Komm schon! Do come/Please come!
Mach es auch richtig! Be sure to do it properly.

❻ Einsteigen!
All aboard!
Zwiebeln abziehen und in Ringe schneiden.
Peel the onions and slice them.

❼ Jetzt wird aufgeräumt!
You're going to clear up now!

❽ Ruhe! Be quiet!/Silence!
Vorsicht! Careful!/Look out!

❾ Achtung! Listen!/Attention!
Rauchen verboten! No smoking.

Compound Tenses

The present and imperfect tenses in German are simple tenses, as described on pages 6–17.

All other tenses, called compound tenses, are formed for all types of verb by using the appropriate tense of an auxiliary verb plus a part of the main verb.

There are three auxiliary verbs:

haben	for past tenses
sein	also for past tenses
werden	for future and conditional tenses

The compound past tenses in German are:

Perfect indicative → ❶
Perfect subjunctive → ❷
Pluperfect indicative → ❸
Pluperfect subjunctive → ❹

These are dealt with on pages 24–27.

The future and conditional tenses in German are all compound tenses.

They are:

Future indicative → ❺
Future subjunctive → ❻
Future perfect → ❼
Conditional → ❽
Conditional perfect → ❾

These are dealt with on pages 28–29.

Examples

	WITH haben	WITH sein
❶	er hat geholt he (has) fetched	er ist gereist he (has) travelled
❷	er habe geholt he (has) fetched	er sei gereist he (has) travelled
❸	er hatte geholt he had fetched	er war gereist he had travelled
❹	er hätte geholt he had fetched	er wäre gereist he had travelled
❺	er wird holen he will fetch	er wird reisen he will travel
❻	er werde holen he will fetch	er werde reisen he will travel
❼	er wird geholt haben he will have fetched	er wird gereist sein he will have travelled
❽	er würde holen he would fetch	er würde reisen he would travel
❾	er würde geholt haben he would have fetched	er würde gereist sein he would have travelled

Compound Past Tenses: Formation

Compound past tenses are normally formed by using the auxiliary verb haben, plus the past participle of the main verb (see below) → ❶

Certain types of verb take sein instead of haben, and this is clearly indicated in the verb table starting on page 86. They fall into three main types:

- intransitive verbs (those that take no direct object, often showing a change of state or place) → ❷

- certain verbs meaning "to happen" → ❸

- miscellaneous others, including:
  begegnen to meet, bleiben to remain,
  gelingen to succeed, sein to be, werden to become → ❹

In some cases the verb can be conjugated with either haben or sein, depending on whether it is used transitively (with a direct object) or intransitively (where no direct object is possible) → ❺

The past participle: formation (see also page 50)

Weak verbs add the prefix ge- and suffix -t to the verb stem → ❻

Verbs ending in -ieren or -eien omit the ge- → ❼

Strong verbs add the prefix ge- and the suffix -en to the verb stem → ❽
The vowel of the stem may be modified (see verb table, page 86) → ❾

Mixed verbs add the prefix ge- and the "weak" suffix -t to the stem. The stem vowel is modified as for many strong verbs → ❿

1   Haben Sie gut geschlafen?
Did you sleep well?
Die Kinder hatten fleißig gearbeitet.
The children had worked hard.

2   Wir sind nach Bonn gefahren.
We went to Bonn.
Er ist schnell eingeschlafen.
He quickly fell asleep.

3   Was ist geschehen?
What happened?

4   Er ist zu Hause geblieben.   Er ist krank gewesen.
He stayed at home.   **He has been ill.**
Es ist uns nicht gelungen.   Sie ist krank geworden.
We did not succeed.   **She became ill.**
Er ist einem Freund begegnet.
He met a friend.

5   Er hat den Wagen nach Köln gefahren.
He drove the car to Cologne.
Er ist nach Köln gefahren.
He went to Cologne.

6   holen **to fetch**   **9**   singen **to sing**
geholt **fetched**   gesungen **sung**

7   studieren **to study**   **10**   enden **to send**
studiert **studied**   gesandt **sent**
prophezeien **to prophesy**   bringen **to bring**
prophezeit **prophesied**   gebracht **brought**

8   laufen **to run**
gelaufen **run**

For a full list of strong and mixed verbs see page 86.

Compound Past Tenses: Formation *continued*

The formation of past participles for weak, strong and mixed verbs is described on page 24, and a comprehensive list of the principal parts of the most commonly used strong and mixed verbs is provided for reference on pages 86–97.

How to form the compound past tenses:

Perfect indicative   the present tense of haben or sein plus the past participle of the verb → ❶

Perfect subjunctive   (used in indirect or reported speech) the present subjunctive of haben or sein plus the past participle → ❷

Pluperfect indicative   imperfect indicative of haben or sein plus the past participle → ❸

Pluperfect subjunctive   (for indirect or reported speech) imperfect subjunctive of haben or sein plus the past participle → ❹

NOTE: The pluperfect subjunctive is a frequently used tense in German, since it can replace the much clumsier conditional perfect tense shown on page 28.

Examples

	WITH haben	**WITH** sein

① PERFECT INDICATIVE

ich habe geholt	ich bin gereist
du hast geholt	du bist gereist
er/sie/es hat geholt	er/sie/es ist gereist
wir haben geholt	wir sind gereist
ihr habt geholt	ihr seid gereist
sie/Sie haben geholt	sie/Sie sind gereist

② PERFECT SUBJUNCTIVE

ich habe geholt	ich sei gereist
du habest geholt	du sei(e)st gereist
er/sie/es habe geholt	er/sie/es sei gereist
wir haben geholt	wir seien gereist
ihr habet geholt	ihr seiet gereist
sie/Sie haben geholt	sie/Sie seien gereist

③ PLUPERFECT INDICATIVE

ich hatte geholt	ich war gereist
du hattest geholt	du warst gereist
er/sie/es hatte geholt	er/sie/es war gereist
wir hatten geholt	wir waren gereist
ihr hattet geholt	ihr wart gereist
sie/Sie hatten geholt	sie/Sie waren gereist

④ PLUPERFECT SUBJUNCTIVE

ich hätte geholt	ich wäre gereist
du hättest geholt	du wär(e)st gereist
er/sie/es hätte geholt	er/sie/es wäre gereist
wir hätten geholt	wir wären gereist
ihr hättet geholt	ihr wär(e)t gereist
sie/Sie hätten geholt	sie/Sie wären gereist

Future and Conditional Tenses: Formation

The future and conditional tenses are formed in the same way for all verbs, whether weak, strong or mixed.

The auxiliary werden is used for all verbs together with the infinitive of the main verb.

The infinitive is usually placed at the end of the clause (see page 224).

How to form the future and conditional tenses:

Future indicative	present tense of werden plus the infinitive of the verb → ➊
Future subjunctive	present subjunctive of werden plus the infinitive → ➋
Future perfect	present indicative of werden plus the perfect infinitive (see below) → ➌
Conditional imperfect	subjunctive of werden plus the infinitive → ➍
Conditional perfect	imperfect subjunctive of werden plus the perfect infinitive (see below) → ➎

NOTE: The conditional perfect is often replaced by the pluperfect subjunctive.

The perfect infinitive consists of the infinitive of haben/sein plus the past participle of the verb.

Examples

❶ FUTURE INDICATIVE

ich werde holen	wir werden holen
du wirst holen	ihr werdet holen
er/sie/es wird holen	sie/Sie werden holen

❷ FUTURE SUBJUNCTIVE

ich werde holen	wir werden holen
du werdest holen	ihr werdet holen
er/sie/es werde holen	sie/Sie werden holen

❸ FUTURE PERFECT

ich werde geholt haben	wir werden geholt haben
du wirst geholt haben	ihr werdet geholt haben
er wird geholt haben	sie/Sie werden geholt haben

❹ CONDITIONAL IMPERFECT

ich würde holen	wir würden holen
du würdest holen	ihr würdet holen
er/sie/es würde holen	sie/Sie würden holen

❺ CONDITIONAL PERFECT

ich würde geholt haben	wir würden geholt haben
du würdest geholt haben	ihr würdet geholt haben
er würde geholt haben	sie/Sie würden geholt haben

NOTE: The conditional perfect is often replaced by the pluperfect subjunctive (see page 26).

Reflexive Verbs

A verb whose action is reflected back to its subject may be termed reflexive:

she washes *herself*

Reflexive verbs in German are recognized in the infinitive by the preceding reflexive pronoun sich → ❶

German has many reflexive verbs, a great number of which are not reflexive in English → ❶

Reflexive verbs are composed of the verb and a reflexive pronoun (see page 170). This pronoun may be either the direct object (and therefore in the accusative case) or the indirect object (and therefore in the dative case) → ❷

Many verbs in German which are not essentially reflexive may become reflexive by the addition of a reflexive pronoun → ❸
When a verb with an indirect object is made reflexive (see page 170) the pronoun is usually dative → ❹

A direct object reflexive pronoun changes to the dative if another direct object is present → ❺

In a main clause the reflexive pronoun follows the verb → ❻
After inversion (see page 226), or in a subordinate clause, the reflexive pronoun must come after the subject if the subject is a personal pronoun → ❼
It may precede or follow a noun subject → ❽

Reflexive verbs are always conjugated with haben *except* where the pronoun is used to mean *each other*. Then the verb is normally conjugated with sein.

The imperative forms are shown on page 19.

Examples

①   sich beeilen   wir beeilen uns
    to hurry   we are hurrying

②   sich (*accusative*) erinnern to remember

ich erinnere mich	wir erinnern uns
du erinnerst dich	ihr erinnert euch
er/sie/es erinnert sich	sie/Sie erinnern sich

    sich (*dative*) erlauben to allow oneself

ich erlaube mir	wir erlauben uns
du erlaubst dir	ihr erlaubt euch
er/sie/es erlaubt sich	sie/Sie erlauben sich

③   etwas melden to report something
    sich melden   Ich habe mich gemeldet.
    to report/to volunteer   I volunteered.

④   wehtun to hurt
    sich wehtun   Hast du dir wehgetan?
    to get hurt   Have you hurt yourself?

    kaufen to buy
    Er kaufte ihr einen Mantel.   Er kaufte sich (*dative*)
    He bought her a coat.   einen neuen Mantel.
                                   He bought himself a new coat.

⑤   Ich wasche mich.   Ich wasche mir die Hände.
    I am having a wash.   I am washing my hands.

⑥   Er wird sich darüber freuen.
    He'll be pleased about that.

⑦   Darüber wird er sich freuen.
    He'll be pleased about that.
    Ich frage mich, ob er sich darüber freuen wird.
    I wonder if he'll be pleased about that.

⑧   Langsam drehten sich die Kinder um. OR:
    Langsam drehten die Kinder sich um.
    The children slowly turned round.

Reflexive Verbs *continued*

Some examples of verbs which can be used with a reflexive pronoun in the accusative case:

> sich anziehen to get dressed → ①
> sich aufregen to get excited → ②
> sich beeilen to hurry → ③
> sich beschäftigen mit[1] to be occupied with → ④
> sich bewerben um[1] to apply for → ⑤
> sich erinnern an[1] to remember → ⑥
> sich freuen auf[1] to look forward to → ⑦
> sich interessieren für[1] to be interested in → ⑧
> sich irren to be wrong → ⑨
> sich melden to report (for duty *etc*)/to volunteer
> sich rasieren to shave
> sich (hin)setzen to sit down → ⑩
> sich trauen[2] to trust oneself
> sich umsehen to look around → ⑪

Some examples of verbs which can be used with a reflexive pronoun in the dative case:

> sich abgewöhnen to give up (something) → ⑫
> sich aneignen to appropriate
> sich ansehen to have a look at
> sich einbilden to imagine (wrongly) → ⑬
> sich erlauben to allow oneself → ⑭
> sich leisten to treat oneself → ⑮
> sich nähern to get close to
> sich vornehmen to plan to do → ⑯
> sich vorstellen to imagine → ⑰
> sich wünschen to want → ⑱

[1] For verbs normally followed by a preposition, see pages 76–79.

[2] trauen when non-reflexive takes the dative case.

① Du sollst dich sofort anziehen.
You are to get dressed immediately.

② Reg dich doch nicht so auf!
Calm down!

③ Wir müssen uns beeilen.
We must hurry.

④ Sie beschäftigen sich sehr mit den Kindern.
They spend a lot of time with the children.

⑤ Hast du dich um diese Stelle beworben?
Have you applied for this post?

⑥ Ich erinnere mich nicht daran.
I can't remember it.

⑦ Ich freue mich auf die Fahrt.
I am looking forward to the journey.

⑧ Interessierst du dich für Musik?
Are you interested in music?

⑨ Er hat sich geirrt.
He was wrong.

⑩ Bitte, setzt euch hin!
Please sit down!

⑪ Die Kinder sahen sich erstaunt um.
The children looked around in amazement.

⑫ Eigentlich müsste man sich das Rauchen abgewöhnen.
One really ought to give up smoking.

⑬ Bilde dir doch nichts ein!
Don't kid yourself!

⑭ Eins könntest du dir doch erlauben.
You could surely allow yourself one.

⑮ Wenn ich mir nur einen Mercedes leisten könnte!
If only I could afford a Mercedes!

⑯ Du hast dir wieder zu viel vorgenommen!
You've taken on too much again!

⑰ So hatte ich es mir oft vorgestellt.
I had often imagined it like this.

⑱ Was wünscht ihr euch zu Weihnachten?
What do you want for Christmas?

The Passive

In active tenses, the subject of a verb carries out the action of the verb, but in passive tenses the subject of the verb has something done to it.

Compare the following:

> Peter kicked the cat (subject: Peter)
> The cat was kicked by Peter (subject: the cat)

English uses the verb "to be" to form its passive tenses. German uses werden → ❶

A sample verb is conjugated in the passive on pages 39–41.

In English, the word "by" usually introduces the agent through which the action of a passive tense is performed. In German this agent is introduced by:

> von for the performer of the action
> durch for an inanimate cause → ❷

The passive can be used to add impersonality or distance to an event → ❸

It may also be used where the identity of the cause of the deed is unknown or not important → ❹

In general, however, the passive is used less in German than in English. The following are common replacements for the passive:

- an active tense with the impersonal pronoun man as subject (meaning they/one). This resembles the use of *on* in French, and man is not always translated as one or they → ❺

- sich lassen plus a verb in the infinitive → ❻

1   Das Auto wurde gekauft.
The car was bought.

2   Das ist von seinem Onkel geschickt worden.
It was sent by his uncle.

Das Kind wurde von einem Hund gebissen.
The child was bitten by a dog.

Seine Bewerbung ist von der Firma abgelehnt worden.
(*the firm is viewed as a human agent*)
His application was turned down by the firm.

Die Tür wurde durch den Wind geöffnet.
The door was opened by the wind.

Das Getreide wurde durch den Sturm niedergeschlagen.
The crop was flattened by the storm.

3   Die Praxis ist von Dr. Disselkamp übernommen worden.
The practice has been taken over by Dr Disselkamp.

Anfang 1993 wurde ein weiterer Anschlag auf sein
Leben verübt.
Another attempt was made on his life early in 1993.

4   In letzter Zeit sind neue Gesetze eingeführt worden.
New laws have recently been introduced.

5   Man hatte es schon verkauft.
It had already been sold.

Man wird es verkauft haben.
It will have been sold.

6   Das lässt sich schnell herausfinden.
We'll/You'll/One will be able to find that out quickly.

The Passive *continued*

In English the indirect object of an active tense can become the subject of a passive statement e.g.

> Peter gave *him* a car (*him* = to him)
> *He* was given a car by Peter

This is not possible in German, where the indirect object (*him*) must remain in the dative case (see page 110). There are two ways of handling this in German:

1. with the direct object (*car*) as the subject of a passive verb → ❶
2. by means of an impersonal passive construction, with or without the impersonal subject *es* → ❶

These constructions would however normally be avoided in favour of an active tense, when the agent of the action is known → ❷

Verbs which are normally followed by the dative case in German and so have only an indirect object (see page 80) should therefore be especially noted, as they can only adopt the impersonal or man-forms of the passive → ❸

Some passive tenses are avoided in German, as they are inelegant (and difficult to use!). For instance, the future perfect passives should be replaced by an active tense or a construction using man → ❹

The conditional perfect passives are also rarely used, past conditional being shown by the pluperfect subjunctives, either passive or active → ❺

English passive constructions such as

> he was heard whistling/they were thought to be dying

are not possible in German → ❻

① Ein Auto wurde ihm von Peter geschenkt.
OR:
Es wurde ihm von Peter ein Auto geschenkt.
OR:
Ihm wurde von Peter ein Auto geschenkt.
He was given a car by Peter.

② Peter schenkte ihm ein Auto.
Peter gave him a car.

③ helfen (+ *dative*) to help
Sie half mir.   Mir wurde von ihr geholfen.
She helped me.   OR:
                                            Es wurde mir von ihr geholfen.
                                            I was helped by her.

④ Er meint, es werde schon gesehen worden sein.
He thinks that it will already have been seen.

BETTER: Er meint, man werde es schon gesehen haben.

⑤ Es würde geholt worden sein / Man würde es geholt haben.
It would have been fetched.

BETTER: Es wäre geholt worden / Man hätte es geholt.

⑥ Man hörte ihn singen.
He was heard singing.
Man sah sie ankommen.
She was seen arriving.
Man glaubte, er sei betrunken.
He was thought to be drunk.

Passive Tenses: Conjugation

Simple tenses

Present passive indicative e.g. *it is seen*	present indicative of werden + past participle of the verb → ❶
Present passive subjunctive	present subjunctive of werden + past participle of the verb → ❷
Imperfect passive indicative e.g. *it was seen*	imperfect indicative of werden + past participle of the verb → ❸
Imperfect passive subjunctive	imperfect subjunctive of werden + past participle of the verb → ❹

Compound tenses

Perfect passive indicative e.g. *it has been seen*	present indicative of sein + e.g. past participle of the verb + worden → ❺
Perfect passive subjunctive	present subjunctive of sein + past participle of the verb + worden → ❻
Pluperfect passive indicative e.g. *it had been seen*	imperfect indicative of sein + past participle of the verb + worden → ❼

Examples

① PRESENT PASSIVE INDICATIVE

ich werde gesehen wir werden gesehen
du wirst gesehen ihr werdet gesehen
er/sie/es wird gesehen sie/Sie werden gesehen
OR: man sieht mich/man sieht dich *etc*

② PRESENT PASSIVE SUBJUNCTIVE

ich werde gesehen wir werden gesehen
du werdest gesehen ihr werdet gesehen
er/sie/es werde gesehen sie/Sie werden gesehen
OR: man sehe mich/man sehe dich *etc*

③ IMPERFECT PASSIVE INDICATIVE

ich wurde gesehen/wir wurden gesehen *etc*
OR: man sah mich/man sah uns *etc*

④ IMPERFECT PASSIVE SUBJUNCTIVE

ich würde gesehen/wir würden gesehen *etc*
OR: man sähe mich/man sähe uns *etc*

⑤ PERFECT PASSIVE INDICATIVE

ich bin gesehen worden/wir sind gesehen worden *etc*
OR: man hat mich/uns gesehen *etc*

⑥ PERFECT PASSIVE SUBJUNCTIVE

ich sei gesehen worden/wir seien gesehen worden *etc*
OR: man habe mich/uns gesehen *etc*

⑦ PLUPERFECT PASSIVE INDICATIVE

ich war gesehen worden/wir waren gesehen worden *etc*
OR: man hatte mich/uns gesehen *etc*

Passive Tenses: Conjugation *continued*

Pluperfect passive subjunctive	imperfect subjunctive of sein + past participle of the verb + worden → **❶**
Present passive infinitive e.g. *to be seen*	infinitive of werden + past participle of the verb → **❷**
Future passive indicative e.g. *it will be seen*	present indicative of werden + present passive infinitive of the verb → **❸**
Future passive subjunctive	present subjunctive of werden + present passive infinitive of the verb → **❹**
Perfect passive infinitive e.g. *to have been seen*	past participle of the verb + worden sein → **❺**
Future perfect passive e.g. *it will have been seen*	present indicative of werden + perfect passive infinitive of the verb → **❻**
Conditional passive e.g. *it would be seen*	imperfect subjunctive of werden + present passive infinitive of the verb → **❼**
Conditional perfect passive e.g. *it would have been seen*	imperfect subjunctive of werden + perfect passive infinitive of the verb → **❽**

1   PLUPERFECT PASSIVE SUBJUNCTIVE

ich wäre gesehen worden/wir wären gesehen worden *etc*
OR: man hätte mich/uns gesehen *etc*

2   PRESENT PASSIVE INFINITIVE

gesehen werden

3   FUTURE PASSIVE INDICATIVE

ich werde gesehen werden/wir werden gesehen werden *etc*
OR: man wird mich/uns sehen *etc*

4   FUTURE PASSIVE SUBJUNCTIVE

ich werde gesehen werden/wir werden gesehen werden *etc*
OR: man werde mich/uns sehen *etc*

5   PERFECT PASSIVE INFINITIVE

gesehen worden sein

6   FUTURE PERFECT PASSIVE

ich werde/wir werden gesehen worden sein *etc*
OR: man wird mich/uns gesehen haben *etc*

7   CONDITIONAL PASSIVE

ich würde gesehen werden/wir würden gesehen werden
OR: man würde mich/uns sehen *etc*

8   CONDITIONAL PERFECT PASSIVE

ich würde/wir würden gesehen worden sein *etc*
OR: man würde mich/uns gesehen haben *etc*
OR: pluperfect subjunctive: man hätte mich/uns gesehen *etc*

Impersonal Verbs

These verbs are used only in the third person singular, usually with the subject es meaning *it* → ❶

Intransitive verbs (verbs with no direct object) are often made impersonal in the passive to describe activity of a general nature → ❷

When the verb and subject are inverted (see page 226), the es is omitted → ❸

Impersonal verbs in the passive can also be used as an imperative form (see page 20) → ❹

In certain expressions in the active, the impersonal pronoun es can be omitted. In this case, a personal pronoun object begins the clause → ❺

In the following lists * indicates that es may be omitted in this way:

Some common impersonal verbs and expressions

es donnert	it's thundering
es fällt mir ein, dass/zu*	it occurs to me that/to → ❻
es fragt sich, ob	one wonders whether → ❼
es freut mich, dass/zu	I am glad that/to → ❽
es friert	it is freezing → ❾
es gefällt mir	I like it → ❿
es geht mir gut/schlecht	I'm fine/not too good
es geht nicht	it's not possible
es geht um	it's about
es gelingt mir (zu)	I succeed (in) → ⓫
es geschieht	it happens → ⓬
es gießt	it's pouring
es handelt sich um	it's a question of

①   Es regnet.
It's raining.

②   Es wurde viel gegessen und getrunken.
There was a lot of eating and drinking.

③   Auf der Hochzeit wurde viel gegessen und getrunken.
There was a lot of eating and drinking at the wedding.

④   Jetzt wird gearbeitet!
Now you're/we're going to work!

⑤   Mir ist warm.
I'm warm.

⑥   Nachher fiel (es) mir ein, dass der Mann ziemlich
komisch angezogen war.
Afterwards it occurred to me that the man was rather oddly
dressed.

⑦   Es fragt sich, ob es sich lohnt, das zu machen.
One wonders if that's worth doing.

⑧   Es freut mich sehr, dass du gekommen bist.
I'm so pleased that you have come.

⑨   Heute Nacht hat es gefroren.
It was below freezing last night.

⑩   Ihm hat es gar nicht gefallen.
He didn't like it at all.

⑪   Es war ihnen gelungen, die letzten Karten zu kriegen.
They had succeeded in getting the last tickets.

⑫   Und so geschah es, dass …
And so it came about that …

Impersonal Verbs and Expressions *continued*

es hängt davon ab	it depends
es hat keinen Zweck (zu)	there's no point (in) → ❶
es interessiert mich, dass/zu*	I am interested that/to
es ist mir egal (ob)*	it's all the same to me (if) → ❷
es ist möglich(, dass)	it's possible (that) → ❸
es ist nötig	it's necessary → ❹
es ist mir, als ob*	I feel as if
es ist mir gut/schlecht *etc* zumute	I feel good/bad *etc* → ❺
es ist schade(, dass)	it's a pity (that)
es ist (mir) wichtig*	it's important (to me)
es ist mir warm/kalt*	I'm warm/cold
es ist warm/kalt	it's *or* the weather is warm/cold
es ist zu hoffen/bedauern *etc*￼*	it is to be hoped/regretted *etc*
es klingelt	someone's ringing the bell → ❻
es klopft	someone's knocking
es kommt darauf an(, ob)	it all depends (whether)
es kommt mir vor(, als ob)	it seems to me (as if)
es läutet	the bell is ringing → ❼
es liegt an	it is because of → ❽
es lohnt sich (nicht)	it's (not) worth it → ❾
es macht nichts	it doesn't matter
es macht nichts aus	it makes no difference → ❿
es macht mir (keinen) Spaß(, zu)	it's (no) fun (to) → ⓫
es passiert	it happens → ⓬
es regnet	it's raining → ⓭
es scheint mir, dass/als ob*	it seems to me that/as if
es schneit	it's snowing
es stellt sich heraus, dass	it turns out that
es stimmt (nicht), dass	it's (not) true that
es tut mir leid(, dass)	I'm sorry (that)
wie geht es (dir)?	how are you? → ⓮
mir wird schlecht	I feel sick

1 Es hat keinen Zweck, weiter darüber zu diskutieren.
There's no point in discussing this any further.

2 Es ist mir egal, ob du kommst oder nicht.
I don't care if you come or not.

3 Es ist doch möglich, dass der Zug Verspätung hat.
It's always possible the train has been delayed.

4 Es wird nicht nötig sein, uns darüber zu informieren.
It won't be necessary to inform us of it.

5 Mir ist heute seltsam zumute.
I feel strange today.

6 Es hat gerade geklingelt.
The bell just went/The phone just rang.

7 Es hat schon geläutet.   **8** Woran liegt es?
The bell has gone.   Why is that?

9 Ich weiß nicht, ob es sich lohnt oder nicht.
I don't know if it's worth it or not.

10 Mir macht es nichts aus.
It makes no difference to me.
Macht es Ihnen etwas aus, wenn ...?
Would you mind if ...?

11 Hauptsache, es macht Spaß.
The main thing is to enjoy yourself.

12 Ihm ist bestimmt etwas passiert.
Something must have happened to him.

13 Es hat den ganzen Tag geregnet.
It rained the whole day.

14 Wie gehts denn? — Danke, es geht.
How are things? — All right, thank you.

The Infinitive

Forms

There are four forms of the infinitive → ❶.
These forms are used in certain compound tenses (see page 28). The present active infinitive is the most widely used and is the form found in dictionaries.

Uses

Preceded by zu (*to*)

- as in English, after other verbs ("I tried *to come*") → ❷

- as in English, after adjectives ("it was easy *to see*") → ❸

- where the English equivalent is not always an infinitive:

- after nouns, where English may use an "-ing" form → ❹

- after sein, where the English equivalent may be a passive tense → ❺

Without zu, the infinitive is used after the following:

modal verbs → ❻
lassen → ❼
heißen → ❽
bleiben → ❾
gehen → ❿
verbs of perception → ⓫

NOTE: Verbs of perception can also be followed by a subordinate clause beginning with wie or dass, especially if the sentence is long or involved → ⓬

Examples

1   INFINITIVES:

PRESENT ACTIVE	PERFECT ACTIVE
holen	geholt haben
to fetch	to have fetched

PRESENT PASSIVE	PERFECT PASSIVE
geholt werden	geholt worden sein
to be fetched	to have been fetched

2   Ich versuchte zu kommen.   I tried to come.

3   Es war leicht zu sehen.   It was easy to see.

4   Ich liebe es, Musik zu hören.
I love listening to music.

5   Er ist zu bedauern.   He is to be pitied.

6   Er kann schwimmen.   He can swim.

7   Sie ließen uns warten.   They kept us waiting.

8   Er hieß ihn kommen.   He bade him come.

9   Er blieb sitzen.   He remained seated.

10   Sie ging einkaufen.   She went shopping.

11   Ich sah ihn kommen.   I saw him coming.
Er hörte sie singen.   He heard her singing.

12   Er sah, wie sie langsam auf und ab schlenderte.
He watched her strolling slowly up and down.

The Infinitive *continued*

Used as an imperative

The infinitive can be used as an imperative (see page 20) → ❶

Used as a noun

The infinitive can be made into a noun by giving it a capital letter. Its gender is always neuter → ❷

Used with modal verbs (see page 52)

An infinitive used with a modal verb is always placed at the end of a clause (see page 56) → ❸

If the modal verb is in a compound tense, its auxiliary will follow the subject in a main clause in the normal way, and the modal participle comes after the infinitive.

BUT: In a subordinate clause, the auxiliary immediately precedes the infinitive and the modal participle, instead of coming at the end → ❹

An infinitive expressing change of place may be omitted entirely after a modal verb (see page 56) → ❺

Used in infinitive phrases

Infinitive phrases can be formed with:

zu	ohne ... zu
um ... zu	anstatt ... zu → ❻

The infinitive comes at the end of its phrase → ❼

In separable verbs, zu is inserted *between* the verb and its prefix in the present infinitive → ❽

A reflexive pronoun comes first, immediately following an introductory word if there is one → ❾

① Einsteigen und Türen schließen!
All aboard! Close the doors!

② rauchen to smoke
Er hat das Rauchen aufgegeben.
He's given up smoking.

③ Wir müssen morgen einkaufen gehen.
We have to go shopping tomorrow.

④ Sie haben gestern aufräumen müssen.
They had to tidy up yesterday.

BUT:

Da sie gestern haben aufräumen müssen, durften sie nicht
kommen.
They couldn't come as they had to tidy up yesterday.

⑤ Er will jetzt nach Hause.
He wants to go home now.

⑥ es zu tun   to do it
es getan zu haben   to have done it
um es zu tun   in order to do it
um es getan zu haben   in order to have done it
ohne es zu tun   without doing it
ohne es getan zu haben   without having done it
anstatt es zu tun   instead of doing it
anstatt es getan zu haben   instead of having done it

⑦ Ohne ein Wort zu sagen, verließ er das Haus.
He left the house without saying a word.
Er ging nach Hause, ohne mit ihr gesprochen zu haben.
He went home without having spoken to her.

⑧ aufgeben   to give up
um es aufzugeben   in order to give it up

⑨ Sie gingen weg, ohne sich zu verabschieden.
They left without saying goodbye.

The Present Participle

The present participle for all verbs is formed by adding -d to the infinitive form → ❶

The present participle may be used as an adjective. As with all adjectives, it is declined if used attributively (see page 140) → ❷

The present participle may also be used as an adjectival noun (see page 148) → ❸

The past participle

For weak verbs, the past participle is formed by prefixing **ge-** and adding -t to the verb stem → ❹

For strong verbs, the past participle is formed by adding the prefix **ge-** and the ending **-en** to the verb stem → ❺
The vowel is often modified too → ❻
(See table of strong and mixed verbs beginning on page 86)

Mixed verbs form their past participle by adding the **ge-** and -t of weak verbs, but they change their vowel as for strong verbs. (See table on page 86) → ❼

The past participles of *separable* verbs are formed according to the above rules and are joined on to the separable prefix → ❽

For *inseparable* verbs, past participles are formed without the **ge-** prefix → ❾

Many past participles can also be used as adjectives and adjectival nouns → ❿

❶
| lachen | to laugh | singen | to sing |
| lachend | laughing | singend | singing |

❷
| ein lachendes Kind | a laughing child |
| mit klopfendem Herzen | with beating heart |

❸
| der Vorsitzende/ein Vorsitzender | the/a chairman |

❹
| machen | to do/make |
| gemacht | done/made |

❺
| sehen | to see |
| gesehen | seen |

❻
| singen | to sing |
| gesungen | sung |

❼
| wissen | to know |
| gewusst | known |

❽
| aufstehen | to get up | nachmachen | to copy/ imitate |
| aufgestanden | got up | nachgemacht | copied/ imitated |

❾
| bestellen | to order | entscheiden | to decide |
| bestellt | ordered | entschieden | decided |

❿
| seine verlorene Brille | his lost spectacles |
| Wir aßen Gebratenes. | We ate fried food. |

Modal Auxiliary Verbs

Modal verbs, sometimes called modal auxiliaries, are used to modify other verbs (to show e.g. possibility, ability, willingness, permission, necessity) much as in English:

> he *can* swim
> *may* I come?
> we *shouldn't* go

In German the modal auxiliary verbs are: dürfen, können, mögen, müssen, sollen and wollen.

Modal verbs have some important differences in their uses and in their conjugation from other verbs, and these are clearly shown in the verb tables on pages 86–97.

Modal verbs have the following meanings:

dürfen   *to be allowed to/may* → ❶
           used negatively: *must not/may not* → ❷
           to show probability → ❸
           also used in some polite expressions → ❹

können   *to be able to/can* → ❺
           in its subjunctive forms:
           would be able to/could → ❻
           as an informal alternative to dürfen with the meaning:
           to be allowed to/can → ❼
           to show possibility → ❽

mögen   *to like/to like to* → ❾
           most common in its imperfect subjunctive form which expresses polite inquiry or request: *should like to/ would like to* → ❿
           to show possibility or probability → ⓫

1. Darfst du mit ins Kino kommen?
   Are you allowed to/can you come with us to the cinema?
   Darf ich bitte mitkommen?
   May I come with you please?
   Ich dürfte schon, aber ich will nicht.
   I could/would be allowed to, but I don't want to.

2. Hier darf man nicht rauchen.
   Smoking is prohibited here.

3. Das dürfte wohl das Beste sein.
   That's probably the best thing.

4. Was darf es sein?
   Can I help you?/What would you like?

5. Wir konnten es nicht schaffen.
   We couldn't/weren't able to do it.

6. Er könnte noch früher kommen.
   He could/would be able to come even earlier.
   Er meinte, er könne noch früher kommen.
   He thought he could come earlier.
   Wir könnten vielleicht morgen hinfahren?
   Perhaps we could go there tomorrow?

7. Kann ich/darf ich ein Eis haben?
   Can I/may I have an ice cream?

8. Wer könnte es gewesen sein?   Das kann sein.
   Who could it have been?   **That may be so.**

                 BUT: Das kann nicht sein.
                      That cannot be so.

9. Magst du Butter?
   Do you like butter?

10. Wir möchten bitte etwas trinken.
    We should like something to drink.
    Möchtest du sie besuchen?
    Would you like to visit her?

11. Wie alt mag sie sein?
    How old might she be?

Modal Auxiliary Verbs *continued*

müssen

to have to/must/need to → ❶

certain idiomatic uses → ❷

NOTE: For *must have …*, use the relevant tense of müssen + past participle of main verb + the auxiliary haben or sein → ❸

For *don't have to/need not*, a negative form of brauchen (*to need*) may be used instead of müssen → ❹

sollen

ought to/should → ❺

to be (supposed) to where the demand is not self-imposed → ❻

to be said to be → ❼

as a command, either direct or indirect → ❽

wollen

to want/want to → ❾

used as a less formal version of mögen to mean: *to want/wish* → ❿

to be willing to → ⓫

to show previous intention → ⓬

to claim or pretend → ⓭

①   Er hatte jeden Tag um sechs aufstehen müssen.
       He had to get up at six o'clock every day.
       Man musste lachen.
       One had to laugh/One couldn't help laughing.

②   Muss das sein? Is that really necessary?
       Ein Millionär müsste man sein! Oh to be a millionaire!
       Den Film muss man gesehen haben.
       That film is worth seeing.

③   Es muss geregnet haben. It must have been raining.
       Er meinte, es müsse am vorigen Abend passiert sein.
       He thought it must have happened the previous evening.

④   Das brauchtest du nicht zu sagen.
       You didn't have to say that.

⑤   Man sollte immer die Wahrheit sagen.
       One should always tell the truth.
       Er wusste nicht, was er tun sollte.
       He didn't know what to do. (*what he should do*)

⑥   Ich soll dir helfen.
       I am to help you. (*I have been told to help you*)
       Du sollst sofort deine Frau anrufen.
       You are to phone your wife at once. (*She has left a message asking you to ring*)

⑦   Er soll sehr reich sein.
       I've heard he's very rich/He is said to be very rich.

⑧   Es soll niemand sagen, dass die Schotten geizig sind!
       Let no-one say the Scots are mean!
       Sie sagte mir, ich solle damit aufhören.
       She told me to stop it.

⑨   Das Kind will Lkw-Fahrer werden.
       The child wants to become a lorry driver.

⑩   Willst du eins? Do you want one?
       Willst du/möchtest du etwas trinken?
       Do you want/would you like something to drink?

⑪   Er wollte nichts sagen. He refused to say anything.

⑫   Ich wollte gerade anrufen. I was just about to phone.

⑬   Keiner will es gewesen sein. No-one admits to doing it.

Modal Auxiliary Verbs *continued*

Conjugation and use

Modal verbs have unusual present tenses → ❶

Their principal parts are given in the verb tables on pages 86–97.

Each modal verb has two past participles.

The first, which is the more common, is the same as the infinitive form and is used where the modal is modifying a verb → ❷

The second resembles a normal weak past participle and is used only where no verb is being modified (see the verb tables on page 86) → ❸

The verb modified by the modal is placed in its infinitive form at the end of a clause → ❹

Where the modal is used in a compound tense, its past participle in the form of the infinitive is also placed at the end of a clause, immediately after the modified verb → ❺

If the modal verb is modifying a verb, and if the modal is used in a compound tense in a subordinate clause, then the normal word order for subordinate clauses (see p 228) does not apply. The auxiliary used to form the compound tense of the modal is not placed right at the end of the subordinate clause, but instead comes before both infinitives → ❻

Such constructions are usually avoided in German, by using a simple tense in place of a compound. (For notes on the use of tenses in German, see pages 58–61) → ❼

A modified verb which expresses motion may be omitted entirely if an adverb or adverbial phrase is present to indicate the movement or destination → ❽

❶

dürfen	können
ich/er/sie/es darf	ich/er/sie/es kann
du darfst	du kannst
wir/sie/Sie dürfen	wir/sie/Sie können
ihr dürft	ihr könnt
mögen	müssen
ich/er/sie/es mag	ich/er/sie/es muss
du magst	du musst
wir/sie/Sie mögen	wir/sie/Sie müssen
ihr mögt	ihr müsst
sollen	wollen
ich/er/sie/es soll	ich/er/sie/es will
du sollst	du willst
wir/sie/Sie sollen	wir/sie/Sie wollen
ihr sollt	ihr wollt

❷ wollen: **past participle** wollen
Er hat kommen wollen.
He wanted to come.

❸ wollen: **past participle** gewollt
Hast du es gewollt?
Did you want it?

❹ Er kann gut schwimmen.
He can swim well.

❺ Wir haben das Haus nicht kaufen wollen.
We didn't want to buy the house.
Sie wird dich bald sehen wollen.
She will want to see you soon.

❻ COMPARE:
Obwohl wir das Haus gekauft haben, ...
Although we bought the house ...
Obwohl wir das Haus haben kaufen wollen, ...
Although we wanted to buy the house ...

❼ Obwohl wir das Haus kaufen wollten ...
Although we wanted to buy the house ...

❽ Ich muss nach Hause.
I must go home.
Die Kinder sollen jetzt ins Bett.
The children have to go to bed now.

Use of Tenses

Continuous forms

Unlike English, the German verb does not distinguish between its
simple and continuous forms → ❶
To emphasize continuity, the following may be used:

        simple tense plus an adverb or adverbial phrase → ❷
        am or beim plus an infinitive used as a noun → ❸
        eben/gerade dabei sein zu plus an infinitive → ❹

The present

The present tense is used in German with seit or seitdem where English
uses a past tense to show an action which began in the past and still
continues → ❺
If the action is finished, or does not continue, a past tense is used → ❻
The present is commonly used with future meaning → ❼

The future

The present is often used as a future tense → ❼
The future tense is used however to:

        emphasize the future → ❽
        express doubt or supposition about the future → ❾
        express future intention → ❿

The future perfect

The future perfect is used as in English to mean *shall/will have done* → ⓫
It is used in German to express a supposition → ⓬
In conversation it is replaced by the perfect → ⓭

The conditional

The conditional may be used in place of the imperfect subjunctive to
express improbable condition (see page 62) → ⓮
It is used in indirect statements or questions to replace the future
subjunctive in conversation or where the subjunctive form is not
distinctive → ⓯

1 ich tue I do (*simple form*) OR: I am doing (*continuous*)
er rauchte he smoked OR: he was smoking
sie hat gelesen she has read OR: she has been reading
es ist geschickt worden it is sent OR: it is being sent

2 Er kochte gerade das Abendessen.
He was cooking the supper.
Nun spricht sie mit ihm.
Now she's talking to him.

3 Ich bin am Bügeln.
I am ironing.

4 Wir waren eben dabei, einige Briefe zu schreiben.
We were just writing a few letters.

5 Ich wohne seit drei Jahren hier.
I have been living here for three years.

6 Seit er krank ist, hat er uns nicht besucht.
He hasn't visited us since he's been ill.
Seit seiner Verlobung habe ich ihn nicht geehen.
I haven't seen him since his engagement.

7 Wir fahren nächstes Jahr nach Griechenland.
We're going to Greece next year.

8 Das werde ich erst nächstes Jahr machen können.
I won't be able to do that until next year.

9 Wenn er zurückkommt, wird er mir bestimmt helfen.
He's sure to help me when he returns.

10 Ich werde ihm helfen.
I'm going to help him.

11 Bis Sonntag wird er es gelesen haben.
He will have read it by Sunday.

12 Das wird Herr Keute gewesen sein.
That must have been Herr Keute.

13 Bis du zurückkommst, haben wir alles aufgeräumt.
We'll have tidied up by the time you get back.

14 Wenn ich eins hätte, würde ich es dir geben.
If I had one I would give it to you.
Wenn er jetzt bloß kommen würde!
If only he would get here!

15 Er fragte, ob wir fahren würden.
He asked if we were going to go.

Use of Tenses *continued*

The conditional perfect

May be used in place of the pluperfect subjunctive in a sentence
containing a wenn-clause → ❶
But the pluperfect subjunctive is preferred → ❷

The imperfect

Is used in German with seit or seitdem where the pluperfect is used
in English to show an action which began in the remote past and
continued to a point in the more recent past → ❸
For discontinued actions the pluperfect is used → ❹
Is used to describe past actions which have no link with the present as
far as the speaker is concerned → ❺
Is used for narrative purposes → ❻
Is used for repeated, habitual or prolonged past action → ❼
See also the NOTE on The perfect (below).

The perfect

Is used to translate the English perfect tense, eg:
  I have spoken, *he has been reading* → ❽
Describes past actions or events which still have a link with the present
or the speaker → ❾
Is used in conversation and similar communication → ❿

NOTE: In practice however the perfect and imperfect are often
interchangeable in German usage, and in spoken German a mixture of
both is common.

The pluperfect

Is used to translate *had done/had been doing*, except in conjunction with
seit/seitdem (see The imperfect above) → ⓫

The subjunctive

For uses of the subjunctive tenses, see pages 62–67.

① Wenn du es gesehen hättest, würdest dus geglaubt haben.
You would have believed it if you'd seen it.

② Hättest du es gesehen, so hättest du es geglaubt.
If you had seen it, you'd have believed it.
Wenn ich das nur nicht gemacht hätte!
If only I hadn't done it!
Wäre ich nur da gewesen!
If I'd only been there!

③ Sie war seit ihrer Heirat als Lehrerin beschäftigt.
She had been working as a teacher since her marriage.

④ Ihren Sohn hatten sie seit zwölf Jahren nicht gesehen.
They hadn't seen their son for twelve years.

⑤ Er kam zu spät, um teilnehmen zu können.
He arrived too late to take part.

⑥ Das Mädchen stand auf, wusch sich das Gesicht und verließ das Haus.
The girl got up, washed her face and went out.

⑦ Wir machten jeden Tag einen kleinen Spaziergang.
We went/We used to go for a little walk every day.

⑧ Ich habe ihn heute nicht gesehen.
I haven't seen him today.

⑨ Ich habe ihr nichts davon erzählt.
I didn't tell her anything about it.
Gestern sind wir in die Stadt gefahren und haben uns ein
paar Sachen gekauft.
Yesterday we went into town and bought ourselves a few things.

⑩ Hast du den Krimi gestern Abend im Fernsehen gesehen?
Did you see the thriller on television last night?

⑪ Sie waren schon weggefahren.
They had already left.
Diese Bücher hatten sie schon gelesen.
They had already read these books.

The Subjunctive: when to use it

The subjunctive form in English has almost died out, leaving only a few examples such as:

> if I *were* rich
> if only he *were* to come
> so *be* it

German however makes much wider use of subjunctive forms, especially in formal, educated or literary contexts. Although there is a growing tendency to use indicatives in spoken German, subjunctives are still very common.

The indicative tenses in German display fact or certainty. The subjunctives show unreality, uncertainty, speculation about a situation or any doubt in the speaker's mind → ❶

Subjunctives are also used in indirect speech, as shown on pages 66–67.

For how to form all tenses of the subjunctive, the reader is referred to the relevant sections on Simple Tenses (pages 6–17) and Compound Tenses (pages 22–29). See also the Subjunctive in Reported Speech (page 66).

The imperfect subjunctive is very common. It is important to note that the imperfect subjunctive form does not always represent actions performed in the past → ❷

Uses of the subjunctive in German

To show improbable condition (e.g. if he *came*, he would ...).

The wenn-clause has a verb in the imperfect subjunctive and the main clause can have either an imperfect subjunctive or a conditional → ❸

Examples

①

INDICATIVE

Das stimmt.	Es ist eine Unverschämtheit.
That's true.	It's a scandal.

SUBJUNCTIVE

Es könnte doch war sein.
It could well be true.
Sie meint, es sei eine Unverschämtheit.
She thinks it's a scandal.
(*speaker not necessarily in agreement with her*)

②

imperfect subjunctive expressing the future:
Wenn ich morgen nur da sein könnte!
If only I could be there tomorrow!

expressing the present/immediate future:
Wenn er jetzt nur käme!
If only he would come now!

speaker's opinion, referring to present or future:
Sie wäre die Beste.
She's the best.

③

Wenn du kämest, wäre ich froh.
OR:
Wenn du kämest, würde ich froh sein.
I should be happy if you came.

Wenn es mir nicht gefiele, würde ich es nicht bezahlen.
OR:
Wenn es mir nicht gefiele, bezahlte ich es nicht.
If I wasn't happy with it, I wouldn't pay for it.

(*The second form is less likely, as the imperfect subjunctive and imperfect indicative forms of* bezahlen *are identical*)

63

The Subjunctive: when to use it *continued*

The imperfect of sollen or wollen, or a conditional tense might be used in the wenn-clause to replace an uncommon imperfect subjunctive, or a subjunctive which is not distinct from the same tense of the indicative → ❶

To show unfulfilled condition (if he *had come*, he would have ...)

The wenn-clause requires a pluperfect subjunctive, the main clause a pluperfect subjunctive or conditional perfect → ❷

NOTE: The indicative is used to express a *probable* condition, as in English → ❸

Wenn can be omitted from conditional clauses. The verb must then follow the subject and dann or so usually begins the main clause → ❹

With selbst wenn (*even if/even though*) → ❺

With wenn ... nur (*if only ...*) → ❻

To speculate or make assumptions → ❼

After als (*as if/as though*) → ❽

Where there is uncertainty or doubt → ❾

To make a polite enquiry → ❿

To indicate theoretical possibility or unreality → ⓫

As an alternative to the conditional perfect → ⓬

1. Wenn er mich so sehen würde, würde er mich für verrückt halten!
   OR:
   Wenn er mich so sehen würde, hielte er mich für verrückt!
   OR:
   Wenn er mich so sehen sollte, würde er mich für verrückt halten!
   If he saw me like this, he would think I was mad!
   (Wenn er mich so sähe *would sound rather stilted*)

2. Wenn du pünktlich gekommen wärest, hättest du ihn gesehen.
   OR:

3. Wenn du pünktlich gekommen wärest, würdest du ihn gesehen haben.
   If you had been on time, you would have seen him.
   Wenn ich ihn sehe, gebe ich es ihm.
   If I see him I'll give him it.

4. Hättest du mich nicht gesehen, so wäre ich schon weg.
   If you hadn't seen me, I would have been gone by now.

5. Selbst wenn er etwas wüsste, würde er nichts sagen.
   Even if he knew about it, he wouldn't say anything.

6. Wenn wir nur erfolgreich wären!
   If only we were successful!

7. Und wenn er recht hätte?
   What if he were right?
   Eine Frau, die das sagen würde (OR: die das sagte), müsste Feministin sein!
   Any woman who would say that must be a feminist!

8. Er sah aus, als sei er krank.
   He looked as if he were ill.

9. Er wusste nicht, wie es ihr jetzt ginge.
   He didn't know how she was.

10. Wäre da sonst noch etwas?
    Will there be anything else?

11. Er stellte sich vor, wie gut er in dem Anzug aussähe.
    He imagined how good he would look in the suit.

12. Ich hätte ihn gesehen.
    OR:
    Ich würde ihn gesehen haben.
    I would have seen him.

The Subjunctive in Indirect Speech

What a person asks or thinks can be reported in one of two ways, either directly:

> Tom said, "I have been on holiday"

OR indirectly:

> Tom said (that) he had been on holiday

In English, indirect (or reported) speech can be indicated by a change in tense of what has been reported:

> He said, "I know your sister"
> He said (that) he knew my sister

In German the change is not in tense, but from indicative to subjunctive → ①

There are two ways of introducing indirect speech in German, similar to the parallel English constructions:

- The clause which reports what is said may be introduced by dass (that). The finite verb or auxiliary comes at the end of the clause → ②

- dass may be omitted. The verb in this case must stand in second position in the clause, instead of being placed at the end → ③

Forms of the subjunctive in indirect speech

For conjugation of verbs in the subjunctive, see pages 8–15 and 26–31. In indirect (or reported) speech, wherever the present subjunctive is identical to the present indicative form, the imperfect subjunctive is used instead → ④

❶   Er sagte: „Sie kennt deine Schwester".
He said, "She knows your sister".

Er sagte, sie kenne meine Schwester.
He said she knew my sister.

„Habe ich zu viel gesagt?", fragte er.
"Have I said too much?", he asked.

Er fragte, ob er zu viel gesagt habe.
He asked if he had said too much.

❷   Er hat uns gesagt, dass er Italienisch spreche.
He told us that he spoke Italian.

❸   Er hat uns gesagt, er spreche Italienisch.
He told us he spoke Italian.

❹   **PRESENT SUBJUNCTIVE IN INDIRECT SPEECH**

WEAK VERBS

holen **to fetch**

ich holte	wir holten
du holest	ihr holet
er hole	sie holten

STRONG VERBS

singen **to sing**

ich sänge	wir sängen
du singest	ihr singet
er singe	sie sängen

Verbs with Prefixes

Many verbs in German begin with a prefix. A prefix is a word or part of a word which precedes the verb stem → ❶

Often the addition of a prefix changes the meaning of the basic verb → ❷

Prefixes may be found in strong, weak or mixed verbs. Adding a prefix may occasionally change the verb conjugation → ❸

There are four kinds of prefix and each behaves in a slightly different way, as shown on the following pages. Prefixes may be inseparable, separable, double or variable (i.e. either separable or inseparable depending on the verb).

Inseparable prefixes

The eight inseparable prefixes are:

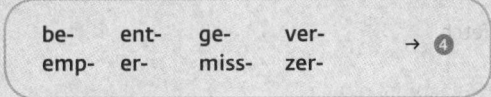

| be- | ent- | ge- | ver- |
| emp- | er- | miss- | zer- | → ❹

These exist only as prefixes, and cannot be words in their own right.

They are never separated from the verb stem, whatever tense of the verb is used → ❺

Inseparable prefixes are always unstressed → ❻

① zu + geben = zugeben
an + ziehen = anziehen

② nehmen to take
zunehmen to put on weight/to increase
sich benehmen to behave

③

WEAK		STRONG	
suchen	to look for	stehen	to stand
versuchen	to try	verstehen	to understand
besuchen	to visit	aufstehen	to get up

WEAK		STRONG	
löschen	to extinguish	erlöschen	to go out

WEAK		STRONG	
fehlen	to be missing	empfehlen	to recommend

④ beschreiben to describe
empfangen to receive
enttäuschen to disappoint
erhalten to contain
gehören to belong
misstrauen to mistrust
verlieren to lose
zerlegen to dismantle

⑤ besuchen to visit

Er besucht uns regelmäßig.	He visits us regularly.
Er besuchte uns jeden Tag.	He used to visit us every day.
Er hat uns jeden Tag besucht.	He visited us every day.
Er wird uns morgen besuchen.	He will visit us tomorrow.
Besuche sofort deine Tante!	Visit your aunt at once!

⑥ erlauben, verstehen, empfangen, vergessen

Verbs with Prefixes *continued*

Separable prefixes

Some common examples are:

ab	fest	herunter	mit
an	frei	hervor	nach
auf	her	hin	nieder
aus	herab	hinab	vor
bei	heran	hinauf	vorbei
da(r)	herauf	hinaus	vorüber
davon	heraus	hindurch	weg
dazu	herbei	hinein	zu
ein	herein	hinüber	zurecht
empor	herüber	hinunter	zurück
entgegen	herum	los	zusammen

Unlike inseparable prefixes, separable prefixes may be words in their own right. Indeed, nouns, adjectives and adverbs are often used as separable prefixes → **1**

The past participle of a verb with a separable prefix is formed with **ge-**. It comes between the verb and the prefix → **2**

In main clauses, the prefix is placed at the end of the clause if the verb is in a simple tense (i.e. present, imperfect or imperative form) → **3**

In subordinate clauses, whatever the tense of the verb, the prefix is attached to the verb and the resulting whole placed at the end of the clause → **4**

Where an infinitive construction requiring zu is used (see page 48), the zu is placed between the infinitive and prefix to form one word → **5**

① *noun + verb*:   teilnehmen   to take part
adjective + verb: loswerden   to get free of
adverb + verb: niederlegen   to lay down

② Er hat nicht teilgenommen.
He did not participate.
Wir sind an der Grenze zurückgewiesen worden.
We were turned back at the border.

③ wegbringen to take for repair/to take away

PRESENT
Wir bringen das Auto weg

IMPERFECT
Wir brachten das Auto weg

IMPERATIVE
Bringt das Auto weg!

FUTURE
Wir werden das Auto wegbringen

CONDITIONAL
Wir würden das Auto wegbringen

PERFECT
Wir haben das Auto weggebracht

PERFECT PASSIVE
Das Auto ist weggebracht worden

PLUPERFECT SUBJUNCTIVE
Wir hätten das Auto weggebracht

④ **PRESENT**
Weil wir das Auto wegbringen, ...

IMPERFECT
Dass wir das Auto wegbrachten, ...

PERFECT
Nachdem wir das Auto weggebracht haben, ...

PLUPERFECT SUBJUNCTIVE
Wenn wir das Auto weggebracht hätten, ...

FUTURE
Obwohl wir das Auto wegbringen werden, ...

⑤ Um das Auto rechtzeitig wegzubringen, müssen wir morgen früh aufstehen.
In order to take the car in on time we shall have to get up early tomorrow.

Verbs with Prefixes *continued*

Variable prefixes

These are:

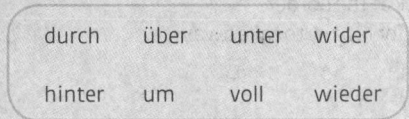

durch	über	unter	wider
hinter	um	voll	wieder

These can be separable or inseparable → ❶

Often they are used separably and inseparably with the same verb. In such cases the verb and prefix will tend to retain their basic meanings if the prefix is used separably, but adopt figurative meanings when the prefix is used inseparably → ❷

Variable prefixes behave as separable prefixes when used separably, and as inseparable prefixes when used inseparably → ❸

Double prefixes

These occur where a verb with an inseparable prefix is preceded by a separable prefix → ❹

The separable prefix behaves as described on page 70, the verb plus inseparable prefix representing the basic verb to which the separable prefix is attached → ❺

Unlike other separable verbs, however, verbs with double prefixes have no **ge-** in their past participles → ❻

1   unternehmen (*inseparable*) to undertake, take on
Wir haben in den Ferien vieles unternommen.
We did a great deal in the holidays.
Du unternimmst zu viel.
You take on too much.

untergehen (*separable*) to sink, go down
Die Sonne geht unter.
The sun is going down/is setting.
Die Sonne ist untergangen.
The sun has gone down/has set.

2   etwas wiederholen (*separable*)   to retrieve something
etwas wiederholen (*inseparable*)   to repeat something

3   Er holte ihr die Tasche wieder.
He brought her back her bag.
Er wiederholte den Satz.
He repeated the sentence.

4   ausverkaufen to sell off

5   Er verkauft alles aus.
He's selling everything off.
Um alles auszuverkaufen ...
In order to sell everything off ...
Er wird alles ausverkaufen.
He'll be selling everything off.

6   Aber er hat doch alles ausverkauft.
But he's sold everything off.

Verb Combinations

Noun + verb combinations are normally written separately → ❶

BUT: Compound verbs if they are written as one word are almost exclusively used in the infinitive or as participles → ❷

OR: if the noun element has lost its distinctive meaning → ❸

Infinitive + verb combinations are normally written separately but many may also be written as one word → ❹

Participle + verb combinations are normally written separately → ❺

Adjective/adverb + verb combinations are written as one word if the first component of the compound is not a word in its own right → ❻

Adjective + verb combinations are normally written separately but writing them as one word is also acceptable → ❼

BUT: In figurative usage, such combinations are always written as one word → ❽

Verb combinations with **-ander** are written as one word → ❾

Verb combinations with **-seits** and **-wärts** are written as one word → ❿

Verb combinations with sein are written separately → ⓫

Examples

①   Ski fahren, Schlange stehen, Klavier spielen

②   bergsteigen, brustschwimmen, kopfrechnen, sonnenbaden

③   eislaufen, kopfstehen, teilhaben

④   baden gehen, sitzen bleiben *or* sitzenbleiben, spazieren gehen *or* spazierengehen

⑤   gefangen nehmen, getrennt schreiben

⑥   abhandenkommen, fehlschlagen, kundgeben

⑦   bekannt machen *or* bekanntmachen, blau färben *or* blaufärben, klein schneiden *or* kleinschneiden

⑧   freihalten, leichtfallen, nahebringen, satthaben

⑨   aneinanderlegen, auseinanderlaufen, durcheinanderreden

⑩   abseitsstehen, abwärtsgehen

⑪   auf sein, zu sein

Verbs followed by Prepositions

Some verbs in English usage require a preposition (*for/with/by* etc) for their completion.

This also happens in German, though the prepositions used with German verbs may not be those expected from their English counterparts → ❶

The preposition used may significantly alter the meaning of a verb in German → ❷

Occasionally German verbs use a preposition where their English equivalents do not → ❸

Prepositions used with verbs behave as normal prepositions and affect the *case* of the following noun (see page 198).

A verb plus preposition may be followed by a clause containing another verb rather than by a noun or pronoun. This often corresponds to an *-ing* construction in English:

> Thank you for *coming*

In German, this is dealt with in two ways:

- Where the "verb-plus-preposition" construction has the same subject as the following verb, the preposition is preceded by **da-** or **dar-** and the following verb becomes an infinitive used with zu → ❹

- Where the subject of the "verb-plus-preposition" is not the same as for the following verb, a dass clause is used → ❺

Following clauses may also be introduced by interrogatives (ob, wie etc) if the meaning demands them → ❻

①   COMPARE:

sich sehnen **nach**	to long *for*
warten **auf**	to wait *for*
bitten **um**	to ask *for*

②

bestehen	to pass (an examination/a test *etc*)
bestehen aus	to consist of
bestehen auf	to insist on
sich freuen auf	to look forward to
sich freuen über	to be pleased about

③   diskutieren über   to discuss

④   Ich freue mich sehr darauf, mal wieder mit ihm zu arbeiten.
I am looking forward to working with him again.

⑤   Ich freue mich sehr darauf, dass du morgen kommst.
I am looking forward to your coming tomorrow.

Er sorgte dafür, dass die Kinder immer gut gepflegt waren.
He saw to it that the children were always well cared for.

⑥   Er dachte lange darüber nach, ob er es wirklich kaufen wollte.
He thought for ages about whether he really wanted to buy it.

Sie freut sich darüber, wie schnell ihre Schüler gelernt haben.
She is pleased at how quickly her students have learned.

Verbs followed by Prepositions *continued*

COMMON VERBS FOLLOWED BY PREPOSITION PLUS **ACCUSATIVE CASE**:

achten auf	to pay attention to, keep an eye on → ①
sich amüsieren über	to laugh at, smile about
sich ärgern über	to get annoyed about/with
sich bewerben um	to apply for → ②
bitten um	to ask for → ③
denken an	to be thinking of → ④
denken über	to hold an opinion of, think about → ⑤
sich erinnern an	to remember
sich freuen auf	to look forward to
sich freuen über	to be pleased about → ⑥
sich gewöhnen an	to get used to → ⑦
sich interessieren für	to be interested in → ⑧
kämpfen um	to fight for
sich kümmern um	to take care of, see to
nachdenken über	to ponder, reflect on → ⑨
sich unterhalten über	to talk about
sich verlassen auf	to rely on, depend on → ⑩
warten auf	to wait for

COMMON VERBS FOLLOWED BY PREPOSITION PLUS **DATIVE CASE**:

abhängen von	to be dependent on → ⑪
sich beschäftigen mit	to occupy oneself with → ⑫
bestehen aus	to consist of → ⑬
leiden an/unter	to suffer from → ⑭
neigen zu	to be inclined to
riechen nach	to smell of → ⑮
schmecken nach	to taste of
sich sehnen nach	to long for
sterben an	to die of
teilnehmen an	to take part in → ⑯
träumen von	to dream of → ⑰
sich verabschieden von	to say goodbye to
sich verstehen mit	to get along with, get on with
zittern vor	to tremble with → ⑱

1. Er musste auf die Kinder achten.
   He had to keep an eye on the children.
2. Sie hat sich um die Stelle als Sekretärin beworben.
   She applied for the post of secretary.
3. Die Kinder baten ihre Mutter um Plätzchen.
   The children asked their mother for some biscuits.
4. Woran denkst du?
   What are you thinking about?
   Daran habe ich gar nicht mehr gedacht.
   I'd forgotten about that.
5. Wie denkt ihr darüber?
   What do you think about it?
6. Ich freute mich sehr darüber, Johannes besucht zu haben.
   I was very glad I had visited Johannes.
7. Man gewöhnt sich an alles. One gets used to anything.
8. Sie interessiert sich sehr für Politik.
   She is very interested in politics.
9. Er hatte schon lange darüber nachgedacht.
   He had been thinking about it for a long time.
10. Er verlässt sich darauf, dass seine Frau alles tut.
    He relies on his wife to do everything.
11. Das hängt davon ab.
    It all depends.
12. Sie sind im Moment sehr damit beschäftigt, ihr neues Haus in Ordnung zu bringen.
    They are very busy sorting out their new house at the moment.
13. Dieser Kuchen besteht aus Eiern, Mehl und Zucker.
    This cake is made from eggs, flour and sugar.
14. Sie hat lange an dieser Krankheit gelitten.
    She suffered from this illness for a long time.
    Alte Leute können sehr unter der Einsamkeit leiden.
    Old people can suffer from dreadful loneliness.
15. Der Kuchen roch nach Zimt.
    The cake smelled of cinnamon.
16. Sie hat an der Bonner Tagung teilnehmen müssen.
    She had to attend the Bonn conference.
17. Er hat von seinem Urlaub geträumt.
    He dreamt of his holiday.
18. Er zitterte vor Freude.
    He was trembling with joy.

Verbs followed by the Dative

Some verbs have a direct object and an indirect object. In the English
sentence "*He gave me a book*", *a book* is the direct object of *gave* and would
be in the accusative and *me* (= *to me*) is the indirect object and would
appear in the dative case in German → ❶

In German, as in English, this type of verb is usually concerned with
giving or telling something to someone, or with performing an action
for someone → ❷

The normal word order after such verbs is for the direct object to follow
the indirect, *except* where the direct object is a personal pronoun (see
page 224) → ❷

This order may be reversed for emphasis → ❸

Some examples of verbs followed by the dative in this way:

anbieten	gönnen	schicken	
bringen	kaufen	schreiben	
beweisen	leihen	schulden	→ ❹
erzählen	mitteilen	verkaufen	
geben	schenken	zeigen	

Certain verbs in German however can be followed *only* by an indirect
object in the dative case. These should be noted especially, since most of
them are quite different from their English equivalents:

begegnen	gratulieren	schmeicheln	
danken	helfen	trauen	
fehlen	imponieren	trotzen	
gefallen	misstrauen	vorangehen	→ ❺
gehören	nachgehen	wehtun	
gelingen	schaden	widersprechen	
gleichen	schmecken	widerstehen	

For how to form the passive of such verbs, see page 36.

❶   Er gab mir ein Buch.   He gave me a book.

❷   Er wusch dem Kind (*indirect*) das Gesicht (*direct*).
       He washed the child's face.
       Er erzählte ihm (*indirect*) eine Geschichte (*direct*).
       He told him a story.
       BUT:
       Er hat sie (*direct*) meiner Mutter (*indirect*) gezeigt.
       He showed it to my mother.
       Kaufst du es (*direct*) mir (*indirect*)?
       Will you buy it for me?

❸   Er wollte das Buch (*direct*) seiner Mutter (*indirect*) geben.
       (*This emphasises* seiner Mutter)
       He wanted to give the book to his mother.

❹   Er bot ihr die Arbeitsstelle an.   He offered her the job.
       Bringst du mir eins?   Will you bring me one?
       Ich gönne dir das neue Kleid.
       I want you to have the new dress.
       Er hat ihr mitgeteilt, dass ...   He told her that ...
       Ich schenke meiner Mutter Parfüm zum Geburtstag.
       I am giving my mother perfume for her birthday.
       Das schulde ich ihm.   I owe him that.
       Zeig es mir!   Show me it!

❺   Er ist seinem Freund in der Stadt begegnet.
       He bumped into his friend in town.
       Mir fehlt der Mut dazu.   I don't have the courage.
       Es ist ihnen gelungen.   They succeeded.
       Wem gehört dieses Buch?   Whose book is this?
       Er wollte ihr nicht helfen.   He refused to help her.
       Ich gratuliere dir!   Congratulations!
       Rauchen schadet der Gesundheit.
       Smoking is bad for your health.
       Das Essen hat ihnen gut geschmeckt.
       They enjoyed the meal.

There is/There are

There are three ways of expressing this in German:

Es gibt

This is always used in the singular form, and is followed by an accusative object which may be either singular or plural → ❶

Es gibt is used to refer to things of a general nature or location → ❷

It also has some idiomatic usages → ❸

Es ist/es sind

The es here merely introduces the real subject. The verb therefore becomes plural where the real subject is plural. The real subject is in the nominative case → ❹

The es is not required and is therefore omitted when the verb and real subject come together. This happens when inversion of subject and verb occurs (see page 226) and in subordinate clauses → ❺

Es ist or es sind are used to refer to:

- subjects with a specific and confined location.
  This location must always be mentioned either by name or by
  da, darauf, darin *etc* → ❻
- temporary existence → ❼
- as a beginning to a story → ❽

The passive voice

Often *there is/there are* in English will be rendered by a verb in the passive voice in German → ❾

Examples

① Es gibt zu viele Probleme dabei.
There are too many problems with it.
Es gibt kein besseres Bier.
There's no better beer.

② Es gibt bestimmt Regen.
It's definitely going to rain.
Ruhe hat es bei uns nie gegeben.
There has never been any peace here.

③ Was gibts (= gibt es) zum Essen? What is there to eat?
Was gibts? What's wrong?, What's up?
So was gibts doch nicht! That's impossible!

④ Es waren zwei ältere Leute unten im Hof.
There were two elderly people down in the yard.
Es sind so viele Touristen da.
There are so many tourists there.

⑤ Unten im Hof waren zwei ältere Leute.
Down in the yard were two elderly people.
Wenn so viele Touristen da sind, ...
If there are so many tourists there, ...

⑥ Es waren viele Flaschen Sekt im Keller.
There were a lot of bottles of champagne in the cellar.
Ein Brief lag auf dem Tisch. Es waren auch zwei
Bücher darauf.
A letter lay on the table. There were also two books on it.

⑦ Es war niemand da.
There was no-one there.

⑧ Es war einmal ein König ...
Once upon a time there was a king ...

⑨ Es wurde auf der Party viel getrunken.
There was a lot of drinking at the party.

Use of "**es**" as an Anticipatory Object

Many verbs can have as their object a dass clause or an infinitive with zu → ❶

With some verbs es is used as an object to anticipate this clause or infinitive phrase → ❷

When the clause or infinitive phrase begins the sentence, es is not used in the main clause but its place may be taken by an optional das → ❸

COMMON VERBS WHICH *USUALLY* HAVE THE "**ES**" OBJECT:

es ablehnen, zu	to refuse to
es aushalten, zu tun/dass	to stand doing → ❹
es ertragen, zu tun/dass	to endure doing
es leicht haben, zu	to find it easy to → ❺
es nötig haben, zu	to need to → ❻
es satt haben, zu	to have had enough of (doing)
es verstehen, zu	to know how to → ❼

COMMON VERBS WHICH *OFTEN* HAVE THE "**ES**" OBJECT:

es jemandem anhören/ansehen, dass	to tell by listening to/ looking at someone that → ❽
es begreifen, dass/warum/wie	to understand that/why/ how
es bereuen, zu tun/dass	to regret having done/that
es leugnen, dass	to deny that → ❾
es unternehmen, zu	to undertake to
es jemandem verbieten, zu	to forbid someone to
es jemandem vergeben, dass	to forgive someone for (doing)
es jemandem verschweigen, dass	not to tell someone that
es jemandem verzeihen, dass	to forgive someone for (doing)
es wagen zu	to dare to

1   Er wusste, dass wir pünktlich kommen würden.
He knew that we would come on time.
Sie fing an zu lachen.
She began to laugh.

2   Er hatte es abgelehnt mitzufahren.
He had refused to come.

3   Dass es Wolfgang war, das haben wir ihr verschwiegen.
OR:
Dass es Wolfgang war, haben wir ihr verschwiegen.
We didn't tell her that it was Wolfgang.

4   Ich halte es nicht mehr aus, bei ihnen zu arbeiten.
I can't stand working for them any longer.

5   Er hatte es nicht leicht, sie zu überreden.
He didn't have an easy job persuading them.

6   Ich habe es nicht nötig, mit dir darüber zu reden.
I don't have to talk to you about it.

7   Er versteht es, Autos zu reparieren.
He knows about repairing cars.

8   Man hörte es ihm sofort an, dass er kein Deutscher war.
OR:
Dass er kein Deutscher war, (das) hörte man ihm sofort an.
One could tell immediately (from the way he spoke) that he
wasn't German.

Man sieht es ihm sofort an, dass er dein Bruder ist.
OR:
Dass er dein Bruder ist, (das) sieht man ihm sofort an.
One can tell at a glance that he's your brother.

9   Er hat es nie geleugnet, das Geld genommen zu haben.
He has never denied taking the money.

Verb Table

Strong and Mixed Verbs – Principal Parts

INFINITIVE	TRANSLATION	3RD PERSON PRESENT
backen	to bake	er bäckt
befehlen	to command	er befiehlt
beginnen	to begin	er beginnt
beißen	to bite	er beißt
bergen	to rescue	er birgt
bersten	to burst *intr*	er birst
betrügen	to deceive	er betrügt
biegen	to bend *tr*/to turn *intr*	er biegt
bieten	to offer	er bietet
binden	to tie	er bindet
bitten	to ask for	er bittet
blasen	to blow	er bläst
bleiben	to remain	er bleibt
braten	to fry	er brät
brechen	to break	er bricht
brennen	to burn	er brennt
bringen	to bring	er bringt
denken	to think	er denkt
dreschen	to thresh	er drischt
dringen	to penetrate	er dringt
dürfen	to be allowed to	er darf
empfehlen	to recommend	er empfiehlt
erlöschen	to go out (*fire, light*)	er erlischt
erschallen	to resound	er erschallt
erschrecken[1]	to be startled	er erschrickt
erwägen	to weigh up	er erwägt
essen	to eat	er isst
fahren	to travel	er fährt

[1] erschrecken meaning "to frighten" is weak:
erschrecken, erschreckt, erschreckte, hat erschreckt

3RD PERSON IMPERFECT	PERFECT	IMPERFECT SUBJUNCTIVE
er backte	er hat gebacken	er backte
er befahl	er hat befohlen	er befähle
er begann	er hat begonnen	er begänne
er biss	er hat gebissen	er bisse
er barg	er hat geborgen	er bärge
er barst	er ist geborsten	er bärste
er betrog	er hat betrogen	er betröge
er bog	er hat/ist gebogen	er böge
er bot	er hat geboten	er böte
er band	er hat gebunden	er bände
er bat	er hat gebeten	er bäte
er blies	er hat geblasen	er bliese
er blieb	er ist geblieben	er bliebe
er briet	er hat gebraten	er briete
er brach	er hat/ist gebrochen	er bräche
er brannte	er hat gebrannt	er brennte
er brachte	er hat gebracht	er brächte
er dachte	er hat gedacht	er dächte
er drosch	er hat gedroschen	er drösche
er drang	er ist gedrungen	er dränge
er durfte	er hat gedurft/dürfen[1]	er dürfte
er empfahl	er hat empfohlen	er empfähle
er erlosch	er ist erloschen	er erlösche
er erschallte	er ist erschollen	er erschölle
er erschrak	er ist erschrocken	er erschräke
er erwog	er hat erwogen	er erwöge
er aß	er hat gegessen	er äße
er fuhr	er ist gefahren	er führe

[1] The second (infinitive) form is used when combined with an infinitive construction (see page 56).

Strong and Mixed Verbs *continued*

INFINITVE	TRANSLATION	3RD PERSON PRESENT
fallen	to fall	er fällt
fangen	to catch	er fängt
fechten	to fight	er ficht
finden	to find	er findet
fliegen	to fly	er fliegt
fliehen	to flee *tr/intr*	er flieht
fließen	to flow	er fließt
fressen	to eat (*of animals*)	er frisst
frieren	to be cold/to freeze over	er friert
gebären	to give birth to	sie gebärt
geben	to give	er gibt
gedeihen	to thrive	er gedeiht
gehen	to go	er geht
gelingen	to succeed	es gelingt
gelten	to be valid	er gilt
genesen	to get well	er genest
genießen	to enjoy	er genießt
geraten	to get into (*a state etc*)	er gerät
geschehen	to happen	es geschieht
gewinnen	to win	er gewinnt
gießen	to pour	er gießt
gleichen	to resemble/to equal	er gleicht
gleiten	to glide	er gleitet
glimmen	to glimmer	er glimmt
graben	to dig	er gräbt
greifen	to grip	er greift
haben	to have	er hat
halten	to hold/to stop	er hält
hängen[1]	to hang *intr*	er hängt
heben	to lift	er hebt
heißen	to be called	er heißt

[1] hängen is weak when used transitively:
hängen, hängt, hängte, hat gehängt

3RD PERSON IMPERFECT	PERFECT	IMPERFECT SUBJUNCTIVE
er fiel	er ist gefallen	er fiele
er fing	er hat gefangen	er finge
er focht	er hat gefochten	er föchte
er fand	er hat gefunden	er fände
er flog	er hat/ist geflogen	er flöge
er floh	er hat/ist geflohen	er flöhe
er floss	er ist geflossen	er flösse
er fraß	er hat gefressen	er fräße
er fror	er hat/ist gefroren	er fröre
sie gebar	sie hat geboren	sie gebäre
er gab	er hat gegeben	er gäbe
er gedieh	er ist gediehen	er gediehe
er ging	er ist gegangen	er ginge
es gelang	es ist gelungen	es gelänge
er galt	er hat gegolten	er gälte
er genas	er ist genesen	er genäse
er genoss	er hat genossen	er genösse
er geriet	er ist geraten	er geriete
es geschah	es ist geschehen	es geschähe
er gewann	er hat gewonnen	er gewönne
er goss	er hat gegossen	er gösse
er glich	er hat geglichen	er gliche
er glitt	er ist geglitten	er glitte
er glomm	er hat geglommen	er glömme
er grub	er hat gegraben	er grübe
er griff	er hat gegriffen	er griffe
er hatte	er hat gehabt	er hätte
er hielt	er hat gehalten	er hielte
er hing	er hat gehangen	er hinge
er hob	er hat gehoben	er höbe
er hieß	er hat geheißen	er hieße

Strong and Mixed Verbs *continued*

INFINITVE	TRANSLATION	3RD PERSON PRESENT
helfen	to help	er hilft
kennen	to know (*someone etc*)	er kennt
klingen	to sound	er klingt
kommen	to come	er kommt
kneifen	to pinch	er kneift
können	to be able to	er kann
kriechen	to crawl	er kriecht
laden	to load	er lädt
lassen	to allow	er lässt
laufen	to walk/to run	er läuft
leiden	to suffer	er leidet
leihen	to lend	er leiht
lesen	to read	er liest
liegen	to lie	er liegt
lügen	to tell a lie	er lügt
mahlen	to grind	er mahlt
messen	to measure	er misst
misslingen	to fail	es misslingt
mögen	to like to	er mag
müssen	to have to	er muss
nehmen	to take	er nimmt
nennen	to call	er nennt
pfeifen	to whistle	er pfeift
preisen	to praise	er preist
quellen	to gush	er quillt
raten	to advise/to guess	er rät
reiben	to rub	er reibt
reißen	to tear *tr/intr*	er reißt
reiten	to ride *tr/intr*	er reitet

3RD PERSON IMPERFECT	PERFECT	IMPERFECT SUBJUNCTIVE
er half	er hat geholfen	er hülfe
er kannte	er hat gekannt	er kennte
er klang	er hat geklungen	er klänge
er kam	er ist gekommen	er käme
er kniff	er hat gekniffen	er kniffe
er konnte	er hat gekonnt/können[1]	er könnte
er kroch	er ist gekrochen	er kröche
er lud	er hat geladen	er lüde
er ließ	er hat gelassen	er ließe
er lief	er ist gelaufen	er liefe
er litt	er hat gelitten	er litte
er lieh	er hat geliehen	er liehe
er las	er hat gelesen	er läse
er lag	er hat gelegen	er läge
er log	er hat gelogen	er löge
er mahlte	er hat gemahlen	er mahlte
er maß	er hat gemessen	er mäße
es misslang	es ist misslungen	es misslänge
er mochte	er hat gemocht/mögen[1]	er möchte
er musste	er hat gemusst/müssen[1]	er müsste
er nahm	er hat genommen	er nähme
er nannte	er hat genannt	er nennte
er pfiff	er hat gepfiffen	er pfiffe
er pries	er hat gepriesen	er priese
er quoll	er ist gequollen	er quölle
er riet	er hat geraten	er riete
er rieb	er hat gerieben	er riebe
er riss	er hat/ist gerissen	er risse
er ritt	er hat/ist geritten	er ritte

[1] The second (infinitive) form is used when combined with an infinitive construction (see page 56).

Strong and Mixed Verbs *continued*

INFINITVE	TRANSLATION	3RD PERSON PRESENT
rennen	to run	er rennt
riechen	to smell	er riecht
ringen	to wrestle	er ringt
rinnen	to flow	er rinnt
rufen	to shout	er ruft
salzen	to salt	er salzt
saufen	to booze/to drink	er säuft
saugen	to suck	er saugt
schaffen[1]	to create	er schafft
scheiden	to separate *tr/intr*	er scheidet
scheinen	to seem/to shine	er scheint
schelten	to scold	er schilt
scheren	to shear	er schert
schieben	to shove	er schiebt
schießen	to shoot	er schießt
schlafen	to sleep	er schläft
schlagen	to hit	er schlägt
schleichen	to creep	er schleicht
schleifen	to grind	er schleift
schließen	to close	er schließt
schlingen	to wind	er schlingt
schmeißen	to fling	er schmeißt
schmelzen	to melt *tr/intr*	er schmilzt
schneiden	to cut	er schneidet
schreiben	to write	er schreibt
schreien	to shout	er schreit
schreiten	to stride	er schreitet
schweigen	to be silent	er schweigt

[1]schaffen meaning "to work hard/to manage" is weak:
  schaffen, schafft, schaffte, hat geschafft

3RD PERSON IMPERFECT	PERFECT	IMPERFECT SUBJUNCTIVE
er rannte	er ist gerannt	er rennte
er roch	er hat gerochen	er röche
er rang	er hat gerungen	er ränge
er rann	er ist geronnen	er ränne
er rief	er hat gerufen	er riefe
er salzte	er hat gesalzen	er salzte
er soff	er hat gesoffen	er söffe
er sog	er hat gesogen	er söge
er schuf	er hat geschaffen	er schüfe
er schied	er hat/ist geschieden	er schiede
er schien	er hat geschienen	er schiene
er schalt	er hat gescholten	er schölte
er schor	er hat geschoren	er schöre
er schob	er hat geschoben	er schöbe
er schoss	er hat geschossen	er schösse
er schlief	er hat geschlafen	er schliefe
er schlug	er hat geschlagen	er schlüge
er schlich	er ist geschlichen	er schliche
er schliff	er hat geschliffen	er schliffe
er schloss	er hat geschlossen	er schlösse
er schlang	er hat geschlungen	er schlänge
er schmiss	er hat geschmissen	er schmisse
er schmolz	er hat/ist geschmolzen	er schmölze
er schnitt	er hat geschnitten	er schnitte
er schrieb	er hat geschrieben	er schriebe
er schrie	er hat geschrien	er schrie
er schritt	er ist geschritten	er schritte
er schwieg	er hat geschwiegen	er schwiege

Strong and Mixed Verbs *continued*

INFINITVE	TRANSLATION	3RD PERSON PRESENT
schwellen[1]	to swell *intr*	er schwillt
schwimmen	to swim	er schwimmt
schwingen	to swing	er schwingt
schwören	to vow	er schwört
sehen	to see	er sieht
sein	to be	er ist
senden[2]	to send	er sendet
singen	to sing	er singt
sinken	to sink	er sinkt
sinnen	to ponder	er sinnt
sitzen	to sit	er sitzt
sollen	to be supposed to be	er soll
spalten	to split *tr/intr*	er spaltet
speien	to spew	er speit
spinnen	to spin	er spinnt
sprechen	to speak	er spricht
sprießen	to sprout	er sprießt
springen	to jump	er springt
stechen	to sting/to prick	er sticht
stehen	to stand	er steht
stehlen	to steal	er stiehlt
steigen	to climb	er steigt
sterben	to die	er stirbt
stinken	to stink	er stinkt
stoßen	to push	er stößt
streichen	to stroke/to wander	er streicht
streiten	to quarrel	er streitet

[1] schwellen is weak when used transitively:
schwellen, schwellt, schwellte, hat geschwellt
[2] senden meaning "to broadcast" is weak:
senden, sendet, sendete, hat gesendet

3RD PERSON IMPERFECT	PERFECT	IMPERFECT SUBJUNCTIVE
er schwoll	er ist geschwollen	er schwölle
er schwamm	er ist geschwommen	er schwömme
er schwang	er hat geschwungen	er schwänge
er schwor	er hat geschworen	er schwüre
er sah	er hat gesehen	er sähe
er war	er ist gewesen	er wäre
er sandte	er hat gesandt	er sendete
er sang	er hat gesungen	er sänge
er sank	er ist gesunken	er sänke
er sann	er hat gesonnen	er sänne
er saß	er hat gesessen	er säße
er sollte	er hat gesollt/sollen[1]	er sollte
er spaltete	er hat/ist gespalten	er spaltete
er spie	er hat gespien	er spie
er spann	er hat gesponnen	er spönne
er sprach	er hat gesprochen	er spräche
er spross	er ist gesprossen	er sprösse
er sprang	er ist gesprungen	er spränge
er stach	er hat gestochen	er stäche
er stand	er hat gestanden	er stünde
er stahl	er hat gestohlen	er stähle
er stieg	er ist gestiegen	er stiege
er starb	er ist gestorben	er stürbe
er stank	er hat gestunken	er stänke
er stieß	er hat/ist gestoßen	er stieße
er strich	er hat/ist gestrichen	er striche
er stritt	er hat gestritten	er stritte

[1] The second (infinitive) form is used when combined with an infinitive construction (see page 56).

Strong and Mixed Verbs *continued*

INFINITVE	TRANSLATION	3RD PERSON PRESENT
tragen	to carry/to wear	er trägt
treffen	to meet	er trifft
treiben	to drive/to engage in	er treibt
treten	to kick/step	er tritt
trinken	to drink	er trinkt
tun	to do	er tut
verderben	to spoil/to go bad	er verdirbt
verdrießen	to irritate	er verdrießt
vergessen	to forget	er vergisst
verlieren	to lose	er verliert
vermeiden	to avoid	er vermeidet
verschwinden	to disappear	er verschwindet
verzeihen	to pardon	er verzeiht
wachsen	to grow	er wächst
waschen	to wash	er wäscht
weichen	to yield	er weicht
weisen	to point	er weist
wenden	to turn	er wendet
werben	to recruit	er wirbt
werden	to become	er wird
werfen	to throw	er wirft
wiegen[1]	to weigh	er wiegt
winden	to wind	er windet
wissen	to know	er weiß
wollen	to want to	er will
ziehen	to pull	er zieht
zwingen	to force	er zwingt

[1] wiegen meaning "to rock" is weak:
wiegen, wiegt, wiegte, hat gewiegt

3RD PERSON IMPERFECT	PERFECT	IMPERFECT SUBJUNCTIVE
er trug	er hat getragen	er trüge
er traf	er hat getroffen	er träfe
er trieb	er hat getrieben	er triebe
er trat	er hat/ist getreten	er träte
er trank	er hat getrunken	er tränke
er tat	er hat getan	er täte
er verdarb	er hat/ist verdorben	er verdürbe
er verdross	er hat verdrossen	er verdrösse
er vergaß	er hat vergessen	er vergäße
er verlor	er hat verloren	er verlöre
er vermied	er hat vermieden	er vermiede
er verschwand	er ist verschwunden	er verschwände
er verzieh	er hat verziehen	er verziehe
er wuchs	er ist gewachsen	er wüchse
er wusch	er hat gewaschen	er wüsche
er wich	er ist gewichen	er wiche
er wies	er hat gewiesen	er wiese
er wandte	er hat gewandt	er wendete
er warb	er hat geworben	er würbe
er wurde	er ist geworden	er würde
er warf	er hat geworfen	er würfe
er wog	er hat gewogen	er wöge
er wand	er hat gewunden	er wände
er wusste	er hat gewusst	er wüsste
er wollte	er hat gewollt/wollen[1]	er wollte
er zog	er hat gezogen	er zöge
er zwang	er hat gezwungen	er zwänge

[1] The second (infinitive) form is used when combined with an infinitive construction (see page 56).

The Declension of Nouns

In German, all nouns may be declined. This means that they may change their form according to their:

> *gender* (i.e. masculine, feminine or neuter) → ❶

> *case* (i.e. their function in the sentence) → ❷

> *number* (i.e. singular or plural) → ❸

Nearly all *feminine* nouns change in the *plural* form by adding -n or -en. Many *masculine* and *neuter* nouns also change → ❹

Masculine and *neuter* nouns, with a few exceptions, add -s (-s or -es for nouns of one syllable) in the *genitive singular* (but see page 110) → ❺

All nouns end in -n or -en in the *dative plural*. This is added to the nominative plural form, where this does not already end in -n → ❻

A good dictionary will provide guidance on how to decline a noun:

The nominative singular form is given in full, followed by the gender of the noun, then the genitive singular and nominative plural endings are shown where appropriate → ❼

Adjectives used as nouns are declined as adjectives rather than nouns. Their declension endings are therefore dictated by the preceding article, as well as by number, case and gender (see page 140) → ❽

❶

der Tisch (*masculine*)	the table
die Gabel (*feminine*)	the fork
das Mädchen (*neuter*)	the girl

❷

des Tisches	of the table
auf den Tischen	on the tables

❸

die Tische	the tables
die Gabeln	the forks
die Mädchen	the girls

❹

	NOM SING	NOM PLURAL
MASC	der Apfel	die Äpfel
FEM	die Schule	die Schulen
NEUT	das Kind	die Kinder

❺

	NOM SING	GEN SING
MASC	der Apfel	des Apfels
FEM	die Schule	der Schule
NEUT	das Kind	des Kind(e)s

❻

	DAT PLURAL
MASC	den Äpfeln
FEM	den Schulen
NEUT	den Kindern

❼

Tiger *m* -s, -

NOM SING	der Tiger	the tiger
GEN SING	des Tigers	of the tiger, the tiger's
NOM PLURAL	die Tiger	the tigers

❽

der Angestellte	the employee
ein Angestellter	an employee
(die) Angestellten	(the) employees

The Gender of Nouns

In German a noun may be masculine, feminine or neuter. Gender is relatively unpredictable and has to be learned for each noun. This is best done by learning each noun with its definite article, i.e.

der Teppich
die Zeit
das Bild

The following are intended therefore only as guidelines in helping decide the gender of a word:

Nouns denoting male people and animals are masculine → ❶

Nouns denoting the female of the species, as shown on page 104, are feminine → ❷

But nouns denoting an entire species can be of any gender → ❸

Makes of cars identify with der Wagen and so are usually masculine → ❹

Makes of aeroplane identify with die Maschine and so are usually feminine → ❺

Seasons, months, days of the week, weather features and points of the compass are masculine → ❻

Names of objects that perform an action are usually masculine → ❼

Foreign nouns ending in **-ant**, **-ast**, **-ismus**, **-or** are masculine → ❽

Nouns ending in **-ich**, **-ig**, **-ing**, **-ling** are masculine → ❾

❶	der Hörer	(male) listener
	der Löwe	(male) lion
	der Onkel	uncle
	der Vetter	(male) cousin
❷	die Hörerin	(female) listener
	die Löwin	lioness
	die Tante	aunt
	die Kusine	(female) cousin
❸	der Hund	dog
	die Schlange	snake
	das Vieh	cattle
❹	der Mercedes	Mercedes
	der VW	VW, Volkswagen
❺	die Boeing	Boeing
	die Concorde	Concorde
❻	der Sommer	summer
	der Winter	winter
	der August	August
	der Freitag	Friday
	der Wind	wind
	der Schnee	snow
	der Norden	north
	der Osten	east
❼	der Wecker	alarm clock
	der Computer	computer
❽	der Ballast	ballast
	der Chauvinismus	chauvinism
❾	der Essig	vinegar
	der Schmetterling	butterfly

The Gender of Nouns *continued*

Cardinal numbers are mostly feminine, but fractions are neuter → ❶

Most nouns ending in -e are feminine → ❷

> BUT: Male people or animals are masculine → ❸
> Nouns beginning with Ge– are normally neuter (*see below*)

Nouns ending in -heit, -keit, -schaft, -ung, -ei are feminine → ❹

Foreign nouns ending in -anz, -enz, -ie, -ik, -ion, -tät, -ur are generally feminine → ❺

Nouns denoting the young of a species are neuter → ❻

Infinitives used as nouns are neuter → ❼

Most nouns beginning with Ge– are neuter → ❽

-chen or -lein may be added to many words to give a diminutive form. These words are then neuter → ❾

NOTE: The vowel adds an umlaut where possible (i.e. on a, o, u or au) and a final -e is dropped before these endings → ❿

Nouns ending in -nis or -tum are neuter → ⑪

Foreign nouns ending in -at, -ett, -fon, -ma, -ment, -um, -ium are mainly neuter → ⑫

Adjectives and participles may be used as masculine, feminine or neuter nouns (see page 148) → ⑬

①	Er hat eine Drei gekriegt.	He got a three (*mark*).
	ein Drittel davon	a third of it
②	die Falte	crease, wrinkle
	die Brücke	bridge
③	der Löwe	lion
	der Matrose	sailor
④	die Eitelkeit	vanity
	die Gewerkschaft	trade union
	die Scheidung	divorce
	die Druckerei	printing works
⑤	die Distanz	distance
	die Konkurrenz	rivalry
	die Theorie	theory
	die Panik	panic
	die Union	union
	die Elektrizität	electricity
	die Partitur	score (*musical*)
⑥	das Baby	baby
	das Kind	child
⑦	das Schwimmen	swimming
⑧	das Geschirr	crockery, dishes
	das Geschöpf	creature
⑨	das Getreide	crop
	das Kindlein	child
⑩	das Bächlein (*from* der Bach)	(small) stream
	das Kätzchen (*from* die Katze)	kitten
⑪	das Ereignis	event
	das Altertum	antiquity
⑫	das Tablett	tray
	das Telefon	telephone
	das Testament	will
	das Podium	platform, podium
⑬	der Verwandte	(male) relative
	die Verwandte	(female) relative
	das Gehackte	minced meat

The Gender of Nouns *continued*

The following are some common exceptions to the gender guidelines shown on pages 100–103:

das Weib	woman, wife
die Person	person
die Waise	orphan
das Mitglied	member
das Genie	genius
die Wache	sentry, guard
das Restaurant	restaurant

The formation of feminine nouns

As in English, male and female forms are sometimes shown by two completely different words e.g.

mother/father

→ **1**

uncle/aunt etc

Where such separate forms do not exist, however, German often differentiates between male and female forms in one of two ways:

- The masculine form may sometimes be made feminine by the addition of **-in** in the singular and **-innen** in the plural → **2**

- An adjective may be used as a feminine noun (see page 148). It has feminine adjective endings which change according to the article which precedes it (see page 140) → **3**

①

der Vater	die Mutter
father	mother

der Bulle	die Kuh
bull	cow

der Mann	die Frau
man	woman

②

der Lehrer	die Lehrerin
(male) teacher	(female) teacher

der König	die Königin
king	queen

der Hörer	die Hörerin
(male) listener	(female) listener

Liebe Hörer und Hörerinnen!
Dear listeners!

unsere Leser und Leserinnen
our readers

③

eine Deutsche
a German woman
Er ist mit einer Deutschen verheiratet.
He is married to a German.

die Abgeordnete
the female MP
Nur Abgeordnete durften dabei sein.
Only MPs were allowed in.

The Gender of Nouns: Miscellaneous Points

Compound nouns

Compound nouns, i.e. nouns composed of two or more nouns put together, are a regular feature of German.

They normally take their gender and declension from the last noun of the compound word → ❶

Exceptions to this are compounds ending in -mut, -scheu and -wort, which do not always have the same gender as the last word when it stands alone → ❷

Nouns with more than one gender

A few nouns have two genders, one of which may only be used in certain regions → ❸

Other nouns have two genders, each of which gives the noun a different meaning → ❹

Abbreviations

These take the gender of their principal noun → ❺

❶

die Armbanduhr	wristwatch
(*from* die Uhr)	
der Tomatensalat	tomato salad
(*from* der Salat)	
der Fußballspieler	footballer
(*from* der Spieler)	

❷

der Mut	courage
die Armut	poverty
die Demut	humility
die Scheu	fear, shyness, timidity
der Abscheu	repugnance, abhorrence
das Wort	word
die Antwort	reply

❸

das/der Marzipan	marzipan
das/der Keks	biscuit

❹

der Band	volume, book
das Band	ribbon, band, tape, bond
der See	lake
die See	sea
der Leiter	leader, manager
die Leiter	ladder
der Tau	dew
das Tau	rope, hawser

❺

der DGB	the Federation of German Trade Unions
(*from* der Deutsche Gewerkschaftsbund)	
die EU	the EU
(*from* die Europäische Gemeinschaft)	
das AKW	nuclear power station
(*from* das Atomkraftwerk)	

The Cases

There are four grammatical *cases* – nominative, accusative, genitive and dative – which are generally shown by the form of the article used before the noun (see page 118).

The nominative case

The nominative singular is the form shown in full in dictionary entries.

The nominative plural is formed as described on page 98.

The nominative case is used for:

- the subject of a verb → ❶

- the complement of sein or werden → ❷

The accusative case

The noun in the accusative case usually has the same form as in the nominative → ❸

Exceptions to this are "weak" masculine nouns (see page 115) and adjectives used as nouns (see page 148).

It is used:

- for the direct object of the verb → ❹

- after those prepositions which always take the accusative case (see pages 206–209) → ❺

- to show change of location after prepositions of place (see page 210) → ❻

- in many expressions of time and place which do not contain a preposition → ❼

- in certain fixed expressions → ❽

Examples

1 Das Mädchen singt. The girl is singing.

2 Er ist ein guter Lehrer. He's a good teacher.
Das wird ein Pullover. It's going to be a jumper.

3
| das Lied | the song | (*nominative*) |
| das Lied | the song | (*accusative*) |

| der Wagen | the car | (*nominative*) |
| den Wagen | the car | (*accusative*) |

| die Dose | the tin | (*nominative*) |
| die Dose | the tin | (*accusative*) |

4 Er hat ein Lied gesungen. He sang a song.

5 für seine Freundin for his girlfriend
ohne diesen Wagen without this car
durch das Rauchen through smoking

6 in die Stadt (*accusative*) into town
BUT:
in der Stadt (*dative*) in town

7 Das macht sie jeden Donnerstag.
She does that every Thursday.
Die Schule ist einen Kilometer entfernt.
The school is a kilometre away.

8 Guten Abend! Good evening!
Vielen Dank! Thank you very much!

The Cases *continued*

The genitive case

In the genitive singular, *masculine* and *neuter* nouns take endings as follows:

- -s is added to nouns ending in -en, -el, -er → ❶
- -es is added to nouns ending in -tz, -sch, -st, -ss or -ß → ❷
- for nouns of one syllable, either -s or -es may be added → ❸

Feminine singular and all *plural* nouns have the same form as their nominative.

The genitive is used:

- to show possession → ❸
- after prepositions taking the genitive (see page 212) → ❹
- in expressions of time when the exact occasion is not specified → ❺

The dative case

Singular nouns in the dative have the same form as in the nominative → ❻
-e may be added to the dative singular of *masculine* and *neuter* nouns if the sentence rhythm needs it → ❼
This -e is always used in certain set phrases → ❽
Dative plural forms for all genders end in -n → ❾
The only exceptions to this are some nouns of foreign origin that end in -s in all plural forms, including the dative plural (see page 114) → ❿

The dative is used:

- as the indirect object → ⓫
- after verbs taking the dative (see page 80) → ⓬
- after prepositions taking the dative (see page 202) → ⓭
- in certain idiomatic expressions → ⓮
- instead of the possessive adjective to refer to parts of the body and items of clothing (see page 122) → ⓯

①

der Wagen car	► des Wagens of the car
das Rauchen smoking	► des Rauchens of smoking
der Computer computer	► des Computers of the computer
der Reiter rider	► des Reiters of the rider

②

der Sitz seat; residence	► des Sitzes of the seat/residence
der Arzt doctor	► des Arztes of the doctor
das Schloss castle	► des Schlosses of the castle

③

Die Zähne des Kindes waren faul geworden.
The child's teeth had decayed.
Der Name des Kinds war ihm unbekannt.
The child's name was not known to him.

④

wegen seiner Krankheit	because of his illness
trotz ihrer Bemühungen	despite her efforts

⑤

eines Tages	one day

⑥

dem Wagen	to the car
der Frau	to the woman
dem Mädchen	to the girl

⑦

zu welchem Zwecke?	to what purpose?

⑧

nach Hause	home

sich zu Tode trinken/arbeiten
to drink/work oneself to death

⑨

mit den Anwälten	with the lawyers
nach den Kindern	after the children

⑩

SINGULAR	PLURAL
das Auto	die Autos
das Auto	die Autos
des Autos	der Autos
dem Auto	den Autos

⑪ Er gab dem Mann das Buch. He gave the man the book.
⑫ Sie half ihrer Mutter. She helped her mother.
⑬ Nach dem Essen ... After eating ...
⑭ Mir ist kalt. I'm cold
⑮ Ich habe mir die Hände gewaschen. I've washed my hands.

The Formation of Plurals

The following pages show full noun declensions in all their singular and plural forms.
Those nouns shown represent the most common types of plural.

Most feminine nouns add -n, -en or -nen to form their plurals:

	SINGULAR	PLURAL
NOM	die Frau	die Frauen
ACC	die Frau	die Frauen
GEN	der Frau	der Frauen
DAT	der Frau	den Frauen

Many nouns have no plural ending.
These are mainly masculine or neuter nouns ending in -en, -er, -el:

	SINGULAR	PLURAL
NOM	der Onkel	die Onkel
ACC	den Onkel	die Onkel
GEN	des Onkels	der Onkel
DAT	dem Onkel	den Onkeln

An umlaut is sometimes added to the vowel in the plural forms:

	SINGULAR	PLURAL
NOM	der Apfel	die Äpfel
ACC	den Apfel	die Äpfel
GEN	des Apfels	der Äpfel
DAT	dem Apfel	die Äpfeln

The Formation of Plurals *continued*

Many nouns form their plurals by adding ⸚e:

	SINGULAR	PLURAL
NOM	der Stuhl	die Stühle
ACC	den Stuhl	die Stühle
GEN	des Stuhl(e)s	der Stühle
DAT	dem Stuhl	den Stühlen

	SINGULAR	PLURAL
NOM	die Angst	die Ängste
ACC	die Angst	die Ängste
GEN	der Angst	der Ängste
DAT	der Angst	den Ängsten

Masculine and neuter nouns often add -e in the plural:

	SINGULAR	PLURAL
NOM	das Schicksal	die Schicksale
ACC	das Schicksal	die Schicksale
GEN	des Schicksals	der Schicksale
DAT	dem Schicksal	den Schicksalen

Masculine and neuter nouns sometimes add ⸚er or -er:

	SINGULAR	PLURAL
NOM	das Dach	die Dächer
ACC	das Dach	die Dächer
GEN	des Dach(e)s	der Dächer
DAT	dem Dach	den Dächern

The Formation of Plurals *continued*

Some unusual plurals

SINGULAR	TRANSLATION	PLURAL
das Ministerium	department	die Ministerien
das Prinzip	principle	die Prinzipien
das Thema	theme, topic, subject	die Themen
das Drama	drama	die Dramen
der Firma	firm	die Firmen
das Konto	bank account	die Konten
das Risiko	risk	die Risiken
das Komma	comma/decimal point	die Kommas *or* Kommata
das Baby	baby	die Babys
der Klub	club	die Klubs
der Streik	strike	die Streiks
der Park	park	die Parks
der Chef	boss, chief, head	die Chefs
der Israeli	Israeli	die Israelis
das Restaurant	restaurant	die Restaurants
das Bonbon	sweet	die Bonbons
das Hotel	hotel	die Hotels
das Niveau	standard, level	die Niveaus

German singular/English plural nouns

Some nouns are always plural in English, but singular in German.

Some of the most common examples are:

eine Brille	glasses, spectacles
eine Schere	scissors
eine Hose	trousers

They are only used in the plural in German to mean more than one pair,
e.g. zwei Hosen *two pairs of trousers*

The Declension of Nouns

"Weak" masculine nouns

Some masculine nouns have a weak declension, which means that in all cases apart from the nominative singular, they end in -en or, if the word ends in a vowel, in -n.

The dictionary will often show such nouns as:

>   Junge *m* -n, -n boy
>   Held *m* -en, -en hero

Weak masculine nouns are declined as follows:

	SINGULAR	PLURAL
NOM	der Junge	die Jungen
ACC	den Jungen	die Jungen
GEN	des Jungen	der Jungen
DAT	dem Jungen	den Jungen

Masculine nouns falling into this category include:

-   those ending in -og(e) referring to males:
    der Psychologe, der Geologe, der Astrologe
-   those ending in -aph (*in many cases now spelt -af*) or -oph:
    der Graph, der Paragraf, der Philosoph
-   those ending in -nom referring to males:
    der Astronom, der Gastronom
-   those ending in -ant:
    der Elefant, der Diamant
-   those ending in -t referring to males:
    der Astronaut, der Komponist, der Architekt
-   miscellaneous others:
    der Bauer, der Chirurg, der Franzose, der Katholik, der Kollege, der Mensch, der Ochse, der Spatz

der Name (*name*) has a different ending in the genitive singular, -ns: des Namens. Otherwise it is the same as der Junge shown above. Others in this category are: der Buchstabe, der Funke, der Gedanke, der Glaube.

The Declension of Proper Nouns

Names of people and places add **-s** in the genitive singular unless they are preceded by the definite article or a demonstrative → **1**

Where proper names end in a sibilant (**-s**, **-sch**, **-ss**, **-ß**, **-x**, **-z**, **-tz**) and this makes the genitive form with **-s** almost impossible to pronounce, they are best avoided altogether by using von followed by the dative case → **2**

Personal names can be given diminutive forms if desired. These may be used as a sign of affection as well as with diminutive meaning → **3**

Herr (*Mr*) is always declined where it occurs as part of a proper name → **4**

When articles or adjectives form part of a proper name (e.g. in the names of books, plays, hotels, restaurants etc), these are declined in the normal way (see pages 118 and 140) → **5**

Surnames usually form their plurals by adding **-s**, unless they end in a sibilant, in which case they sometimes add **-ens**. They are often preceded by the definite article → **6**

Nouns of measurement and quantity

These usually remain singular, even if preceded by a plural number → **7**

The substance which they measure follows in the same case as the noun of quantity, and not in the genitive case as in English → **8**

①
Annas Buch	Anna's book
Klaras Mantel	Klara's coat
die Werke Goethes	Goethe's works
BUT: die Versenkung der Bismarck	
the sinking of the Bismarck	

②
das Buch von Hans	Hans' book
die Werke von Marx	the works of Marx
die Freundin von Klaus	Klaus's girlfriend

③

von deinem Sabinchen   from your Sabine
Das kleine Kläuschen hat uns dann ein Lied gesungen.
Then little Klaus sang us a song.

④
an Herrn Schmidt	to Mr Schmidt
Sehr geehrte Herren	Dear Sirs

⑤

im Weißen Schwan   in the White Swan
Er hat den „Zauberberg" schon gelesen.
He has already read "The Magic Mountain".

nach Karl dem Großen   after Charlemagne

⑥

Die Schmidts haben uns eingeladen.
The Schmidts have invited us.
Die Zeißens haben uns eingeladen.
Mr and Mrs Zeiß have invited us.

⑦

Möchten Sie zwei Stück?
Would you like two?

⑧

Er wollte zwei Kilo Kartoffeln.
He wanted two kilos of potatoes.
Sie hat drei Tassen Kaffee getrunken.
She drank three cups of coffee.
Drei Glas Weißwein, bitte!
Three glasses of white wine please.

The Definite Article

In English the definite article *the* always keeps the same form:

> *the* book
> *the* books
> with *the* books

In German, however, the definite article has many forms:

In its singular form it changes for masculine, feminine and neuter nouns → **1**

In its plural forms it is the same for all genders → **2**

The definite article is also used to show the function of the noun in the sentence by showing which case it is.

There are four cases, as explained more fully on page 108:

1. *nominative* for the subject or complement of the verb → **3**
2. *accusative* for the object of the verb and after some prepositions → **4**
3. *genitive* to show possession and after some prepositions → **5**
4. *dative* for an indirect object (*to* or *for*) and after some prepositions and certain verbs → **6**

The forms of the definite article are as follows:

| | SINGULAR | | | PLURAL |
	MASC	FEM	NEUT	ALL GENDERS
NOM	der	die	das	die
ACC	den	die	das	die
GEN	des	der	des	der
DAT	dem	der	dem	den

→ **7**

Examples

1   MASCULINE: der Mann   the man
                                der Wagen   the car
         FEMININE: die Frau   the wife/woman
                                die Blume   the flower
         NEUTER: das Ding   the thing
                                das Mädchen   the girl

2   die Männer   the men
       die Frauen   the women
       die Dinge   the things

3   Der Mann ist jung.   The man is young.
       Die Frau/das Kind ist jung.   The woman/the child is young.

4   Ich kenne den Mann/die Frau/das Kind.
       I know the man/the woman/the child.

5   der Kopf des Mannes/der Frau/des Kindes
       the man's/woman's/child's head
       wegen des Mannes/der Frau/des Kindes
       because of the man/the woman/the child

6   Ich gab es dem Mann/der Frau/dem Kind.
       I gave it to the man/to the woman/to the child.

7

SINGULAR

	MASC	FEM	NEUT
NOM	der Mann	die Frau	das Kind
ACC	den Mann	die Frau	das Kind
GEN	des Mann(e)s	der Frau	des Kind(e)s
DAT	dem Mann	der Frau	dem Kind

PLURAL

	MASC	FEM	NEUT
NOM	die Männer	die Frauen	die Kinder
ACC	die Männer	die Frauen	die Kinder
GEN	der Männer	der Frauen	der Kinder
DAT	den Männern	den Frauen	den Kindern

Uses of the Definite Article

When to use and when not to use the definite article in German is one of the most difficult areas for the learner. The following guidelines show where German practice varies from English.

The definite article is used with:

abstract and other nouns where something is being referred to as a whole or as a general idea → ❶

Where these nouns are quantified or modified, the article is not used → ❷

the genitive, unless the noun is a proper name or is acting as a proper name → ❸

occasionally with proper names to make the sex or case clearer → ❹

always with proper names preceded by an adjective → ❺

sometimes with proper names in familiar contexts or for slight emphasis → ❻

with masculine and feminine countries and districts → ❼

with geographical names preceded by an adjective → ❽

with names of seasons → ❾

often with meals → ❿

with the names of roads → ⓫

❶	Das Leben ist schön.	Life is wonderful.
❷	Es braucht Mut.	It needs (some) courage.
	Gibt es dort Leben?	Is there (any) life there?
❸	das Auto des Lehrers	the teacher's car
	Günters Auto	Günter's car
	Muttis Auto	Mummy's car

❹   Er hat es Frau Lehmann gegeben.
Er hat es der Frau Lehmann gegeben.
He gave it to Frau Lehmann.

❺   Der alte Herr Brockhaus ist gestorben.
Old Mr Brockhaus has died.

❻   Ich habe heute den Christoph gesehen.
I saw Christoph today.
Du hast es aber nicht der Petra geschenkt!
You haven't given it to *Petra*!

❼	Deutschland is sehr schön.	Germany is very beautiful.
	Die Schweiz ist auch schön.	Switzerland is also lovely.

❽   im (= in dem) heutigen Deutschland
in today's Germany

❾   Im (= in dem) Sommer gehen wir schwimmen.
We go swimming in summer.
Der Winter kommt bald.
Soon it will be winter.

❿   Das Abendessen wird ab acht Uhr serviert.
Dinner is served from eight o'clock.
Was gibts zum (= zu dem) Mittagessen?
What's for lunch?
BUT:
Um acht Uhr ist Frühstück.
Breakfast is at eight o'clock.

⓫   Sie wohnt jetzt in der Geisener Straße.
She lives in Geisener Road now.

Uses of the Definite Article *continued*

with months of the year except after seit/nach/vor → ❶

instead of the possessive adjective to refer to parts of the body and items of clothing → ❷

A reflexive pronoun or noun in the dative case is used if it is necessary to clarify to whom the parts of the body belong → ❸

in expressions of price, to mean *each/per/a* → ❹

with certain common expressions → ❺

Other uses

The definite article can be used with demonstrative meaning → ❻

After certain prepositions, forms of the definite article can be shortened (see pages 198–201).
Some of these forms are best used in informal situations → ❼
Others are commonly and correctly used in formal contexts → ❶ → ❺
→ ❽

Omitting the definite article

The definite article may be omitted in German:

in certain set expressions → ❾

in *preposition + adjective + noun* combinations → ❿

For the declension of adjectives without the article see page 142.

Examples

❶   Wir fahren im (= in dem) September weg.
    We are going away in September.
    Wir sind seit September hier.
    We have been here since September.

❷   Er legte den Hut auf den Tisch.
    He laid his hat on the table.
    Ich drücke Ihnen die Daumen.
    I'm keeping my fingers crossed for you.

❸   Er hat sich die Hände schon gewaschen.
    He has already washed his hands.
    Er hat dem Kind schon die Hände gewaschen.
    He has already washed the child's hands.

❹

Die kosten …	They cost …
… fünf Euro das Pfund	**… five euros a pound**
… sechs Euro das Stück	**… six euros each**

❺

in die Stadt fahren	**to go into town**
zur (= zu der) Schule gehen	**to go to school**
mit der Post	**by post**
mit dem Zug/Bus/Auto	**by train/bus/car**
im (= in dem) Gefängnis	**in prison**

❻   Du willst **das** Buch lesen!
    You want to read *that* book!

❼   für das ► fürs   vor dem ► vorm   um das ► ums *etc*

❽   an dem ► am   zu dem ► zum   zu der ► zur *etc*

❾

von Beruf	**by profession**
nach Wunsch	**as desired**
Nachrichten hören	**to listen to the news**

❿   Mit gebeugtem Rücken …   **Bending his back, …**

The Indefinite Article

Like the definite article, the form of the indefinite article varies depending on the gender and case of the noun → ❶

It has no plural forms → ❷

The indefinite article is declined as follows:

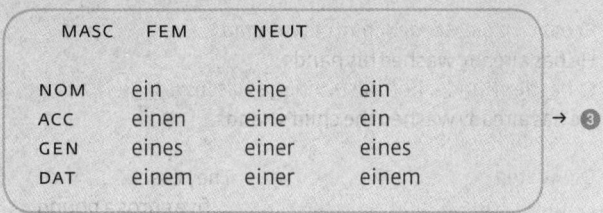

	MASC	FEM	NEUT
NOM	ein	eine	ein
ACC	einen	eine	ein
GEN	eines	einer	eines
DAT	einem	einer	einem

→ ❸

The indefinite article is omitted in the following:

- descriptions of people by profession, religion, nationality etc → ❹

BUT: Note that the article is included when an adjective precedes the noun → ❺

- in certain fixed expressions → ❻

- after als (*as a*) → ❼

①

Da ist ein Auto.	There's a car.
Er hat eine Wohnung.	He has a flat.
Sie gab es einem Kind.	She gave it to a child.

②

Autos sind in letzter Zeit teurer geworden.
Cars have become more expensive recently.

③

	SINGULAR		
	MASC	FEM	NEUT
NOM	ein Mann	eine Frau	ein Kind
ACC	einen Mann	eine Frau	ein Kind
GEN	eines Mann(e)s	einer Frau	eines Kind(e)s
DAT	einem Mann	einer Frau	einem Kind

④

| Sie ist Kinderärztin. | She's a paediatrician. |
| Sie ist Deutsche. | She's (a) German. |

⑤

Sie ist eine sehr geschickte Kinderärztin.
She's a very clever paediatrician.

⑥

| Es ist Geschmacksache . | It's a question of taste. |
| Tatsache ist ... | It's a fact ... |

⑦

Als Ausländer ist er hier nicht wahlberechtigt.
As a foreigner he doesn't have the vote here.

... und ich rede nun als Vater von vier Kindern
... and I'm talking now as a father of four

The Indefinite Article *continued*

In German, a separate negative form of the indefinite article exists. It is declined exactly like ein in the singular, and also has plural forms:

| | SINGULAR | | | PLURAL |
	MASC	FEM	NEUT	ALL GENDERS
NOM	kein	keine	kein	keine
ACC	keinen	keine	kein	keine
GEN	keines	keiner	keines	keiner
DAT	keinem	keiner	keinem	keinen

→ ❶

It has the meaning *no/not a/not one/not any* → ❷

It is used even where the equivalent *positive* phrase has no article → ❸

It is also used in many idiomatic expressions → ❹

Nicht ein may be used instead of kein where the ein is to be emphasized → ❺

Examples

❶

SINGULAR

	MASC	FEM	NEUT
NOM	kein Mann	keine Frau	kein Kind
ACC	keinen Mann	keine Frau	kein Kind
GEN	keines Mann(e)s	keiner Frau	keines Kind(e)s
DAT	keinem Mann	keiner Frau	keinem Kind

PLURAL

	MASC	FEM	NEUT
NOM	keine Männer	keine Frauen	keine Kinder
ACC	keine Männer	keine Frauen	keine Kinder
GEN	keiner Männer	keiner Frauen	keiner Kinder
DAT	keinen Männern	keinen Frauen	keinen Kindern

❷

Er hatte keine Geschwister.	He had no brothers or sisters.
Ich sehe keinen Unterschied.	I don't see any difference.
Das ist keine richtige Antwort.	That's no answer.
Kein Mensch hat es gesehen.	Not one person has seen it.

❸

Er hatte Angst davor.	He was frightened.
Er hatte keine Angst davor.	He wasn't frightened.

❹

Er hatte kein Geld mehr.   All his money was gone.
Es waren keine drei Monate vergangen, als ...
It was less than three months later that ...
Es hat mich keine zehn Euro gekostet.
It cost me less than ten euros.

❺

Nicht ein Kind hat es singen können.
Not *one* child could sing it.

Words declined like the definite article

The following have endings similar to those of the definite article shown on page 118:

aller, alle, alles	all, all of them
beide	both (*plural only*)
dieser, diese, dieses	this, this one, these
einiger, einige, einiges	some, a few, a little
irgendwelcher, -e, -es	some or other
jeder, jede, jedes	each, each one, every
jener, jene, jenes	that, that one, those
mancher, manche, manches	many a/some
sämtliche	all, entire (*usually plural*)
solcher, solche, solches	such/such a
welcher, welche, welches	which, which one

These words can be used as:

- articles → ❶
- pronouns → ❷

They have the following endings:

	SINGULAR			PLURAL
	MASC	FEM	NEUT	ALL GENDERS
NOM	-er	-e	-es	-e
ACC	-en	-e	-es	-e
GEN	-es/-en	-er	-es/-en	-er
DAT	-em	-er	-em	-en

Example declensions are shown on pages 134–135.

einiger and irgendwelcher use the **-en** genitive ending before masculine or neuter nouns ending in **-s** → ❸

jeder, welcher, mancher and solcher may also do so → ❹

❶ Dieser Mann kommt aus Südamerika.
This man comes from South America.

Er geht jeden Tag ins Büro.
He goes to the office every day.

Manche Leute können das nicht.
A good many people can't do it.

❷ Willst du diesen?
Do you want this one?

In manchem hat er recht.
He's right about some things.

Man kann ja nicht alles wissen.
You can't know everything.

Es gibt manche, die keinen Alkohol mögen.
There are some people who don't like alcohol.

❸ wegen irgendwelchen Geredes
on account of some gossip

❹ der Besitz solchen Reichtums
the possession of such wealth

trotz jeden Versuchs
despite all attempts

Words declined like the definite article *continued*

Adjectives following these words have the weak declension
(see page 140) → ❶

Exceptions are the plural forms of einige, which are followed by the
strong declension (see page 142) → ❷

Further points

Solcher, beide, sämtliche may be used after another article or possessive
adjective. They then take weak (see page 140) or mixed (see page 142)
adjectival endings, as appropriate → ❸

Although beide generally has plural forms only, one singular form does
exist. This is in the neuter nominative and accusative: beides → ❹

Dies often replaces the nominative and accusative dieses and diese
when used as a pronoun → ❺

A fixed form all exists which is used together with other articles or
possessive pronouns → ❻

Ganz can also be used to replace both the inflected form aller/alle/alles
and the uninflected all das/dieses/sein *etc.* It is declined as a normal
adjective (see page 140) → ❼

It must be used with collective nouns, in time phrases and geographical
references → ❽

1   dieses alte Auto
   this old car
   aus irgendwelchem dummen Grund
   for some stupid reason or other
   Welche neuen Waren?
   Which new goods?

2   Dies sind einige gute Freunde von mir.
   These are some good friends of mine.

3   Ein solches Kleid habe ich früher auch getragen.
   I used to wear a dress like that too.
   Diese beiden Männer haben es gesehen.
   Both of these men have seen it.

4   Beides ist richtig.
   Both are right.
   Sie hat beides genommen.
   She took both.

5   Hast du dies schon gelesen?
   Have you already read this?
   Dies sind meine neuen Sachen.
   These are my new things.

6   All sein Mut war verschwunden.
   All his courage had vanished.
   mit all diesem Geld
   with all this money

7   mit dem ganzen Geld
   with all the money

8   die ganze Gesellschaft
   the entire company
   Es hat den ganzen Tag geschneit.
   It snowed the whole day long.
   Im ganzen Land gab es keinen besseren Wein.
   There wasn't a better wine in the whole country.

Words declined like the definite article *continued*

derjenige/diejenige/dasjenige (*the one*, *those*) is declined exactly as the definite article plus an adjective in the weak declension (see page 140) → ❶

derselbe/dieselbe/dasselbe (*the same*, *the same one*) is declined in the same way as derjenige → ❷

After prepositions, however, the normal contracted forms of the definite article are used for the appropriate parts of derselbe → ❸

①

SINGULAR

MASC FEM	NEUT	
derjenige Mann	**die**jenige Frau	**das**jenige Kind
denjenigen Mann	**die**jenige Frau	**das**jenige Kind
desjenigen Mann(e)s	**der**jenigen Frau	**des**jenigen Kind(e)s
demjenigen Mann	**der**jenigen Frau	**dem**jenigen Kind

PLURAL

MASC	FEM	NEUT
diejenigen Männer	**die**jenigen Frauen	**die**jenigen Kinder
diejenigen Männer	**die**jenigen Frauen	**die**jenigen Kinder
derjenigen Männer	**der**jenigen Frauen	**der**jenigen Kinder
denjenigen Männern	**den**jenigen Frauen	**den**jenigen Kindern

②

SINGULAR

MASC	FEM	NEUT
derselbe Mann	**die**selbe Frau	**das**selbe Kind
denselben Mann	**die**selbe Frau	**das**selbe Kind
desselben Mann(e)s	**der**selben Frau	**des**selben Kind(e)s
demselben Mann	**der**selben Frau	**dem**selben Kind

PLURAL

MASC	FEM	NEUT
dieselben Männer	**die**selben Frauen	**die**selben Kinder
dieselben Männer	**die**selben Frauen	**die**selben Kinder
derselben Männer	**der**selben Frauen	**der**selben Kinder
denselben Männern	**den**selben Frauen	**den**selben Kindern

③   zur selben (= zu derselben) Zeit   at the same time
im selben (= in demselben) Zimmer   in the same room

Words declined like the definite article *continued*

Sample declensions in full

dieser, diese, dieses this, this one:

| | SINGULAR | | |
	MASC	FEM	NEUT
NOM	dieser Mann	diese Frau	dieses Kind
ACC	diesen Mann	diese Frau	dieses Kind
GEN	dieses Mann(e)s	dieser Frau	dieses Kind(e)s
DAT	diesem Mann	dieser Frau	diesem Kind

| | PLURAL | | |
	MASC	FEM	NEUT
NOM	diese Männer	diese Frauen	diese Kinder
ACC	diese Männer	diese Frauen	diese Kinder
GEN	dieser Männer	dieser Frauen	dieser Kinder
DAT	diesen Männern	diesen Frauen	diesen Kindern

jener, jene, jenes that, that one:

| | SINGULAR | | |
	MASC	FEM	NEUT
NOM	jener Mann	jene Frau	jenes Kind
ACC	jenen Mann	jene Frau	jenes Kind
GEN	jenes Mann(e)s	jener Frau	jenes Kind(e)s
DAT	jenem Mann	jener Frau	jenem Kind

| | PLURAL | | |
	MASC	FEM	NEUT
NOM	jene Männer	jene Frauen	jene Kinder
ACC	jene Männer	jene Frauen	jene Kinder
GEN	jener Männer	jener Frauen	jener Kinder
DAT	jenen Männern	jenen Frauen	jenen Kindern

jeder, jede, jedes **each, every, everybody:**

SINGULAR

	MASC	FEM	NEUT
NOM	jed**er** Wagen	jed**e** Minute	jed**es** Bild
ACC	jed**en** Wagen	jed**e** Minute	jed**es** Bild
GEN	jed**es** Wagens	jed**er** Minute	jed**es** Bild(e)s
	(jed**en** Wagens)		(jed**en** Bild(e)s)
DAT	jed**em** Wagen	jed**er** Minute	jed**em** Bild

welcher, welche, welches **which?, which:**

SINGULAR

	MASC	FEM	NEUT
NOM	welch**er** Preis	welch**e** Sorte	welch**es** Mädchen
ACC	welch**en** Preis	welch**e** Sorte	welch**es** Mädchen
GEN	welch**es** Preises	welch**er** Sorte	welch**es** Mädchens
	(welch**en** Preises)		(welch**en** Mädchens)
DAT	welch**em** Preis	welch**er** Sorte	welch**em** Mädchen

PLURAL

	MASC	FEM	NEUT
NOM	welch**e** Preise	welch**e** Sorten	welch**e** Mädchen
ACC	welch**e** Preise	welch**e** Sorten	welch**e** Mädchen
GEN	welch**er** Preise	welch**er** Sorten	welch**er** Mädchen
DAT	welch**en** Preisen	welch**en** Sorten	welch**en** Mädchen

135

Words declined like the indefinite article

The following have the same declension pattern as the indefinite articles
ein and kein (see pages 124 and 126):

The possessive adjectives

mein	my → ①
dein	your (*singular familiar*)
sein	his/its
ihr	her/its → ②
unser	our
euer	your (*plural familiar*)
ihr	their → ③
Ihr	your (*polite singular and plural*)

These words are declined as follows:

	SINGULAR			PLURAL
	MASC	FEM	NEUT	ALL GENDERS
NOM	—	-e	—	-e
ACC	-en	-e	—	-e
GEN	-es	-er	-es	-er
DAT	-em	-er	-em	-en

Adjectives following these determiners have the mixed declension
forms (see page 142), e.g.

> sein altes Auto his old car

irgendein (*some … or other*) also follows this declension pattern in the
singular. Its plural form is irgendwelche (see page 128).

Examples

❶   mein, meine, mein **my**

SINGULAR

	MASC	FEM	NEUT
NOM	mein Bruder	mein**e** Schwester	mein Kind
ACC	mein**en** Bruder	mein**e** Schwester	mein Kind
GEN	mein**es** Bruders	mein**er** Schwester	mein**es** Kind(e)s
DAT	mein**em** Bruder	mein**er** Schwester	mein**em** Kind

PLURAL

	MASC	FEM	NEUT
NOM	mein**e** Brüder	mein**e** Schwestern	mein**e** Kinder
ACC	mein**e** Brüder	mein**e** Schwestern	mein**e** Kinder
GEN	mein**er** Brüder	mein**er** Schwestern	mein**er** Kinder
DAT	mein**en** Brüdern	mein**en** Schwestern	mein**en** Kindern

❷   ihr, ihre, ihr **her/its/their**

SINGULAR

	MASC	FEM	NEUT
NOM	ihr Bruder	ihr**e** Schwester	ihr Kind
ACC	ihr**en** Bruder	ihr**e** Schwester	ihr Kind
GEN	ihr**es** Bruders	ihr**er** Schwester	ihr**es** Kind(e)s
DAT	ihr**em** Bruder	ihr**er** Schwester	ihr**em** Kind

PLURAL

	MASC	FEM	NEUT
NOM	ihr**e** Brüder	ihr**e** Schwestern	ihr**e** Kinder
ACC	ihr**e** Brüder	ihr**e** Schwestern	ihr**e** Kinder
GEN	ihr**er** Brüder	ihr**er** Schwestern	ihr**er** Kinder
DAT	ihr**en** Brüdern	ihr**en** Schwestern	ihr**en** Kindern

Indefinite Adjectives

These are adjectives used in place of, or together with, an article:

ander	other, different
mehrere *(plural only)*	several
viel	much, a lot, many
wenig	little, a little, few

After the definite article and words declined like it (see page 128) these adjectives have weak declension endings → **①**

Adjectives following the indefinite adjectives are also weak → **②**

After ein, kein, irgendein or the possessive adjectives they have mixed declension endings → **③**

Adjectives following the indefinite adjectives are also mixed in declension → **④**

When used without a preceding article, ander and mehrere have strong declension endings → **⑤**

When used without a preceding article, viel and wenig may be declined as follows, though in the singular they are usually undeclined → **⑥**

	SINGULAR			PLURAL
	MASC	FEM	NEUT	ALL GENDERS
NOM	viel	viel	viel	viele
ACC	viel	viel	viel	viele
GEN	vielen	vieler	vielen	vieler
DAT	viel(em)	vieler	viel(em)	vielen

Any adjective following viel or wenig has strong endings → **⑦**

①   Die wenigen Kuchen, die übrig geblieben waren …
        The few cakes which were left over …

②   die vielen interessanten Ideen, die ans Licht kamen
        the many interesting ideas which came to light

③   Ihr anderes Auto ist in der Werkstatt.
        Their other car is in for repair.

④   Mehrere gute Freunde waren gekommen.
        Several good friends had come.

⑤   Mehrere prominente Gäste sind eingeladen.
        Various prominent guests are invited.

        Er war anderer Meinung.
        He was of a different opinion.

⑥   Es wurde viel Bier getrunken.
        They drank a lot of beer.

        Sie essen nur wenig Obst.
        They don't eat a lot of fruit.

⑦   Er kaufte viele billige Sachen.
        He bought a lot of cheap things.

        Es wurde viel gutes Bier getrunken.
        They drank a lot of good beer.

        Sie essen wenig frisches Obst.
        They don't eat a lot of fresh fruit.

The Declension of Adjectives

There are two ways of using adjectives:

- They can be used attributively, where the adjective comes before the noun: *the new book*

- They can be used non-attributively, where the adjective comes after the verb: *the book is new*

In English the adjective does not change its form no matter how it is used.

In German, however, adjectives remain unchanged only when used non-attributively → **1**

Used attributively, adjectives change to show the number, gender and case of the noun they precede → **2**

The endings also depend on the nature of the article which precedes them → **3**

There are three sets of endings:

1) The weak declension

These are the endings used after der and those words declined like it as shown on page 128 → **4**

	SINGULAR			PLURAL
	MASC	FEM	NEUT	ALL GENDERS
NOM	-e	-e	-e	-en
ACC	-en	-e	-e	-en
GEN	-en	-en	-en	-en
DAT	-en	-en	-en	-en

❶

Das Buch ist neu.
The book is new.
Der Vortrag war sehr langweilig.
The lecture was very boring.

❷

Das neue Buch ist da.
The new book has arrived.
Während des langweiligen Vortrags sind wir alle
eingeschlafen.
We all fell asleep during the boring lecture.

❸

der junge Rechtsanwalt
the young lawyer
ein junger Rechtsanwalt
a young lawyer
manch junger Rechtsanwalt
many a young lawyer

❹

SINGULAR

	MASC	FEM	NEUT
NOM	der alte Mann	die alte Frau	das alte Haus
ACC	den alten Mann	die alte Frau	das alte Haus
GEN	des alten Mann(e)s	der alten Frau	des alten Hauses
DAT	dem alten Mann	der alten Frau	dem alten Haus

PLURAL

	MASC	FEM	NEUT
NOM	die alten Männer	die alten Frauen	die alten Häuser
ACC	die alten Männer	die alten Frauen	die alten Häuser
GEN	der alten Männer	der alten Frauen	der alten Häuser
DAT	den alten Männern	den alten Frauen	den alten Häusern

The Declension of Adjectives *continued*

2) The mixed declension

These are the endings used after ein, kein, irgendein and the possessive adjectives (see page 136) → ❶

	SINGULAR			PLURAL
	MASC	FEM	NEUT	ALL GENDERS
NOM	-er	-e	-es	-en
ACC	-en	-e	-es	-en
GEN	-en	-en	-en	-en
DAT	-en	-en	-en	-en

→ ❷

3) The strong declension

Strong declension endings:

	SINGULAR			PLURAL
	MASC	FEM	NEUT	ALL GENDERS
NOM	-er	-e	-es	-e
ACC	-en	-e	-es	-e
GEN	-en	-er	-en	-er
DAT	-em	-er	-em	-en

→ ❸

These endings are used where there is no preceding article. The article is omitted more frequently in German than in English, especially in *preposition + adjective + noun* combinations (see page 122).

These endings enable the adjective to do the work of the missing article by showing case, number and gender → ❹

1 Meine neue Stelle ist bei einer großen Druckerei.
My new job is with a large printing works.
Ihre frühere Theorie ist jetzt bestätigt worden.
Her earlier theory has now been proved true.

2

	SINGULAR		
	MASC	**FEM**	**NEUT**
NOM	ein langer Weg	eine lange Reise	ein langes Spiel
ACC	einen langen Weg	eine lange Reise	ein langes Spiel
GEN	eines langen Weg(e)s	einer langen Reise	eines langen Spiel(e)s
DAT	einem langen Weg	einer langen Reise	einem langen Spiel

PLURAL
ALL GENDERS

NOM	ihre langen Wege/Reisen/Spiele
ACC	ihre langen Wege/Reisen/Spiele
GEN	ihrer langen Wege/Reisen/Spiele
DAT	ihren langen Wegen/Reisen/Spielen

3

	SINGULAR		
	MASC	**FEM**	**NEUT**
NOM	guter Käse	gute Marmelade	gutes Bier
ACC	guten Käse	gute Marmelade	gutes Bier
GEN	guten Käses	guter Marmelade	guten Biers
DAT	gutem Käse	guter Marmelade	gutem Bier

PLURAL
ALL GENDERS

NOM	gute Käse/Marmeladen/Biere
ACC	gute Käse/Marmeladen/Biere
GEN	guter Käse/Marmeladen/Biere
DAT	guten Käsen/Marmeladen/Bieren

4

nach kurzer Fahrt	after a short journey
mit gleichem Gehalt	with the same salary

The Declension of Adjectives *continued*

Strong declension endings are also used after any of the following where they are not preceded by an article or other determiner:

ein bisschen	a little, a bit of
ein wenig	a little
ein paar	a few, a couple → ❶
weniger	fewer, less
einige (*plural forms only*)	some
allerlei/allerhand	all kinds of, all sorts of
keinerlei	no … whatsoever, no … at all
mancherlei	various, a number of
etwas	some, any (*singular*) → ❷
mehr	more
lauter	nothing but, sheer, pure
solch	such
vielerlei	various, all sorts of, many different
mehrerlei	several kinds of
was für	what, what kind of
(NOTE: Was für ein takes the mixed declension)	
welcherlei	what kind of, what sort of
viel	much, many, a lot of
wievielerlei	how many kinds of
welch …!	what …! what a …! → ❸
manch	many a
wenig	little, few, not much → ❹
zweierlei/dreierlei *etc*	two/three *etc* kinds of
zwei, drei *etc*	two, three *etc* → ❺
(NOTE: The mixed declension is used after ein)	

The strong declension is also required after possessives where no other word indicates the case, gender and number → ❻

① ein paar gute Tipps (*strong declension*)
a couple of good tips

② Etwas starken Pfeffer zugeben. (*strong*)
Add a little strong pepper.

③ Welch herrliches Wetter! (*strong*)
What splendid weather!

④ Es gab damals nur wenig frisches Obst. (*strong*)
At that time there was little fresh fruit.

BUT:

Das wenige frische Obst, das es damals gab ... (*weak*)
The little fresh fruit that was then available ...

⑤ Zwei große Jungen waren gekommen. (*strong*)
Two big boys had come along.

BUT:

die zwei großen Jungen, die gekommen waren (*weak*)
the two big boys who had come along

meine zwei großen Jungen (*mixed*)
my two big sons

⑥ Herberts altes Buch. (*strong*)
Herbert's old book.

Muttis neues Auto. (*strong*)
Mum's new car.

The Declension of Adjectives *continued*

Some spelling changes when adjectives are declined

When the adjective hoch (*high*) is declined, its stem changes to
hoh- → ①

Adjectives ending in **-el** lose the **-e-** when inflected, i.e. when endings are
added → ②

Adjectives with an **-er** ending often lose the **-e-** when inflected → ③

The participles as adjectives

The present participle can be used as an adjective with normal adjectival
endings (pages 140–143) → ④

The present participles of sein and haben cannot be used in this way.

The past participle can also be used as an adjective → ⑤

Adjectives followed by the dative case

The *dative case* is required after many adjectives e.g.

ähnlich	similar to
bekannt	familiar to
dankbar	grateful to
fremd	alien to
gleich	all the same to/like → ⑥
leicht	easy for
nah	close to
peinlich	painful for
unbekannt	unknown to

❶   Das Gebäude ist hoch.   **BUT:**   ein hohes Gebäude
The building is high.   a high building

❷   Das Zimmer ist dunkel.   **BUT:**   in dem dunklen Zimmer
The room is dark.   in the dark room

❸   Das Auto war teuer.   **BUT:**   Er kaufte ein teures Auto.
The car was expensive.   He bought an expensive car.

❹   die werdende Mutter
the mother-to-be

ein lachendes Kind
a laughing child

❺   meine verlorene Sachen
my lost things

die ausgebeuteten Arbeiter
the exploited workers

❻   Ist dir das bekannt?
Do you know about it?

Ich wäre Ihnen dankbar, wenn ...
I should be grateful to you if ...

Diese Sache ist mir etwas peinlich.
This matter is somewhat embarrassing for me.

Solche Gedanken waren ihm fremd.
Such thoughts were alien to him.

Adjectives

Adjectives used as Nouns

All adjectives in German, and those participles used as adjectives, can also be used as nouns. These are often called adjectival nouns.

Adjectives and participles used as nouns have:

- a capital letter like other nouns → **1**

- declension endings like other adjectives, depending on the preceding article, if any (see below) → **2**

Declension endings for adjectives used as nouns

After der, dieser and words like it shown on page 128, the normal *weak* adjective endings apply (see page 140) → **3**
Der Junge (*the boy*) is an exception, and is declined like a weak masculine noun, as shown on page 115.

After ein, kein, irgendein and the possessive adjectives shown on page 136, the *mixed* adjective endings apply (see page 142) → **4**

Where no article is present, or after those words shown on page 144, the *strong* adjective endings are used (see page 142) → **5**

When another adjective precedes the adjectival noun, the *strong* endings become *weak* in two instances:

- in the *dative singular* → **6**

- in the *nominative* and *accusative plural* after a possessive, where the strong endings might cause confusion with the singular feminine form → **7**

Examples

①   der Angestellte
        the employee

②   die Angestellte
        the (female) employee
        das Neue daran ist ...
        the new thing about it is ...
        Es bleibt beim Alten.
        Things remain as they were.
        Er hat den ersten Besten genommen.
        He took the first that came to hand.

③   für den Angeklagten
        for the accused
        mit dieser Bekannten
        with this (*female*) friend

④   Kein Angestellter darf hier rauchen.
        No employee may smoke here.
        Sie machten einen Ausflug mit ihren Bekannten zusammen.
        They went on a trip with their friends.

⑤   Etwas Besonderes ist geschehen.
        Something special has happened.

⑥   Ich hatte es Rudis jüngerem Verwandten versprochen.
        I had promised it to Rudi's young relative.

⑦   Rudis jüngere Verwandten wollten es haben.
        Rudi's young relatives wanted to have it.

Miscellaneous Points

Adjectives of nationality

These are not spelt with a capital letter in German except in public or official names → ①

However, when used as a noun to refer to the language, a capital letter is used → ②

In German, for expressions like *he is English/he is German etc* a noun or adjectival noun is used instead of an adjective → ③

Adjectives derived from place names

These are formed by adding -er to names of towns → ④

They are never inflected → ⑤

Adjectives from die Schweiz and from certain regions can also be formed in this way → ⑥

Such adjectives may be used as nouns denoting the inhabitants of a town.
They are then declined as normal nouns (see pages 98–99) → ⑦
The feminine form is made by adding -in in the singular and -innen in the plural → ⑧

Certain names ending in -en drop the -e- or the -en of their ending before adding -er → ⑨

A second type of adjective formed from place names exists, ending in -isch and spelt with a small letter. It is inflected as a normal adjective (see page 140).
It is used mainly where the speaker is referring to the mood of, or something typical of, that place → ⑩

1 die deutsche Sprache   das französische Volk
the German language   the French people
  BUT:
die Deutsche Bahn
the German railways

2 Sie sprechen kein Englisch.
They don't speak English.

3 Er ist Deutscher.   Sie ist Deutsche.
He is German.   She is German.

4 Kölner, Frankfurter, Leipziger *etc*

5 der Kölner Dom   ein Frankfurter Würstchen
Cologne cathedral   a frankfurter sausage

6 Schweizer Käse
Swiss cheese

7 Die Sprache des Kölners heißt Kölsch.
People from Cologne speak Kölsch.
von den Frankfurtern
of the people of Frankfurt

8 die Kölnerin, die Kölnerinnen
die Londonerin, die Londonerinnen

9 München   ▶   der Münchner
Bremen   ▶   der Bremer
Göttingen   ▶   der Göttinger

10 ein echt frankfurterischer Ausdruck
a real Frankfurt expression
Er spricht etwas münchnerisch.
He has something of a Munich accent.

The Comparison of Adjectives

Adjectives have three basic forms of comparison:

1) The simple form is used to describe something or someone.

e.g. a *little* house
the house is *little*

This form is fully dealt with on pages 140–147.

Simple forms are used in *as … as / not as … as* comparisons → ①

2) The comparative form is used to compare two things or persons.

e.g. he is *bigger* than his brother

In German, comparatives are formed by adding **-er** to the simple form → ②

Than in comparative statements is translated by als → ③

Unlike English, the vast majority of German adjectives, including those of several syllables, form their comparatives in this way → ④

Many adjectives modify the stem vowel when forming their comparatives → ⑤

Examples

① so ... wie as ... as
Er ist so gut wie sein Bruder.
He is as good as his brother.

ebenso ... wie just as ... as
Er war ebenso glücklich wie ich.
He was just as happy as I was.

zwei-/dreimal *etc* twice/three times *etc*
so ... wie as ... as

Er war zweimal so groß wie sein Bruder.
He was twice as big as his brother.

nicht so ... wie not as ... as
Er ist nicht so alt wie du
He is not as old as you

② klein/kleiner   small/smaller
schön/schöner   lovely/lovelier

③ Er ist kleiner als seine Schwester.
He is smaller than his sister.

④ bequem/bequemer   comfortable/more comfortable
gebildet/gebildeter   educated/more educated
effektiv/effektiver   effective/more effective

⑤ alt/älter   old/older
stark/stärker   strong/stronger
schwach/schwächer   weak/weaker
scharf/schärfer   sharp/sharper
lang/länger   long/longer
kurz/kürzer   short/shorter
warm/wärmer   warm/warmer
kalt/kälter   cold/colder
hart/härter   hard/harder
groß/größer   big/bigger

The Comparison of Adjectives *continued*

Adjectives whose simple form ends in **-el** lose the **-e-** before adding the comparative ending **-er** → ❶

Adjectives with a diphthong followed by **-er** in their simple forms also drop the **-e-** before adding **-er** → ❷

Adjectives whose simple form ends in **-en** or **-er** may drop the **-e-** of the simple form when adjectival endings are added to their comparative forms → ❸

With a few adjectives, comparative forms may be used not only for comparison, but also to render the idea of "-ish" or "rather ..." Some common examples are:

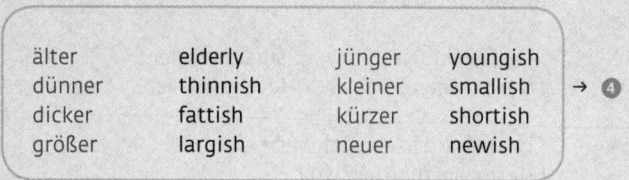

älter	elderly	jünger	youngish	
dünner	thinnish	kleiner	smallish	→ ❹
dicker	fattish	kürzer	shortish	
größer	largish	neuer	newish	

When used attributively (*before* the noun), comparative forms are declined in exactly the same way as simple adjectives (see pages 140–147) → ❹ → ❺

3) The superlative form is used to compare three or more persons or things.

> e.g. he is *the biggest/the best*

Superlatives are formed by adding **-st** to the simple adjective. The vowel is modified, as for comparative forms, where applicable.

Superlative forms are generally used with an article and take endings accordingly (see page 140) → ❻

①
eitel/eitler   vain/vainer
dunkel/dunkler   dark/darker

②
sauer/saurer   sour/more sour
die saurere Zitrone
the sourer lemon
Der Wein ist saurer geworden.
The wine has grown more sour.

teuer/teurer   expensive/more expensive
Das ist eine teurere Sorte.
That is a more expensive kind.
Die Neuen sind teurer.
The new ones are more expensive.

③
finster/finsterer   dark/darker
ein finstreres Gesicht
OR:
ein finstereres Gesicht
a grimmer face

④
ein älterer Herr
an elderly gentleman
eine größere Summe
a rather large sum
von jüngerem Aussehen
of youngish appearance

⑤
Die jüngere Schwester ist größer als die ältere.
The younger sister is bigger than the older one.
Mein kleinerer Bruder geht jetzt zur Schule.
My younger brother goes to school now.

⑥
Er ist der Jüngste.
He is the youngest.
Ihr erfolgreichster Versuch war im Herbst 2009.
Her most successful attempt was in the autumn of 2009.

The Comparison of Adjectives *continued*

Many adjectives form their superlative forms by adding **-est** instead of **-st** where pronunciation would otherwise be difficult or unaesthetic → ❶

The English superlative "*most*" meaning "*very*" can be shown in German by any of the following → ❷

> äußerst
>
> sehr
>
> besonders
>
> außerordentlich
>
> höchst (*not with monosyllabic words*)
>
> furchtbar (*conversational only*)
>
> richtig (*conversational only*)

Some irregular comparative and superlative forms

SIMPLE FORM	COMPARATIVE	SUPERLATIVE
gut	besser	der beste
hoch	höher	der höchste
viel	mehr	der meiste
nah	näher	der nächste

❶   der/die/das schlechteste
the worst

der/die/das schmerzhafteste
the most painful

der/die/das süßeste
the sweetest

der/die/das neueste
the newest

der/die/das stolzeste
the proudest

der/die/das frischeste
the freshest

❷   Er ist ein äußerst begabter Mensch.
He is a most gifted person.

Das Essen war besonders schlecht.
The food was really/most dreadful.

Der Wein war furchtbar teuer!
The wine was dreadfully/most expensive!

Das sieht richtig komisch aus.
That looks really/most funny.

Personal Pronouns

As in English, personal pronouns change their form depending on their function in the sentence:

> I saw *him*
> *He* saw *me* → 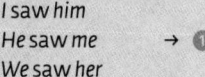 ❶
> *We* saw *her*

The personal pronouns are declined as follows:

NOMINATIVE		ACCUSATIVE		DATIVE	
ich	I	mich	me	mir	to/for me
du	you (*familiar*)	dich	you	dir	to/for you
er	he/it	ihn	him/it	ihm	to/for him/it
sie	she/it	sie	her/it	ihr	to/for her/it
es	it/he/she	es	it/him/her	ihm	to/for it/him/her → ❷
wir	we	uns	us	uns	to/for us
ihr	you (*plural*)	euch	you	euch	to/for you
sie	they	sie	them	ihnen	to/for them
Sie	you (*polite*)	Sie	you	Ihnen	to/for you
man	one	einen	one	einem	to/for one

As can be seen from the above table, there are three ways of addressing people in German – du, ihr or Sie.

All three forms are illustrated on page 160.

Personal pronouns in the dative require no preposition when acting as indirect object, i.e. *to* me, *to* him *etc* → ❸

Examples

❶
Ich sah ihn.
I saw him.

Er sah mich.
He saw me.

Wir sahen sie.
We saw her.

❷
Wir sind mit ihnen spazieren gegangen.
We went for a walk with them.

Sie haben uns eine tolle Geschichte erzählt.
They told us a great story.

Soll ich Ihnen etwas mitbringen?
Shall I bring something back for you?

❸
Er hat es ihr gegeben.
He gave it to her.

Ich habe ihm ein neues Buch gekauft.
I bought a new book for him.
OR:
I bought him a new book.

Personal Pronouns *continued*

Du is a singular form, used only when speaking to one person. It is used to talk to children, close friends and relatives, animals and objects of affection such as a toy, one's car etc.

When in doubt it is always best to use the more formal Sie form.

Ihr is simply the plural form of du and is used in exactly the same situations wherever more than one person is to be addressed → ❶

The familiar forms and their possessives are written with a small letter → ❷

Sie is the polite, or formal, way of addressing people. It is written in all its declined forms with a capital letter, including the possessive → ❸

Sie is used:

- by children talking to adults outside their immediate family.

- by adults talking to older children from mid-teens onwards. Teachers use it to their senior classes and bosses to their trainees etc.

- among adult strangers meeting for the first time.

- among colleagues, friends and acquaintances unless a suggestion has been formally made by one party and accepted by the other that the familiar forms should be used. Familiar forms must then continue to be used at all times, as a reversion to the formal might be considered insulting.

1	Kinder, was wollt ihr essen?
Children, what do you want to eat?

2	Er hat mir gesagt, du sollst deine Frau mitbringen.
He told me you were to bring your wife.

Gestern bin ich deinem Bruder begegnet.
I met your brother yesterday.

3	Was haben Sie gesagt?
What did you say?

Ich habe es Ihnen schon gegeben.
I have already given it to you.

Ja, Ihre Sachen sind jetzt fertig.
Yes, your things are ready now.

Personal Pronouns *continued*

Er/sie/es

All German nouns are masculine, feminine or neuter → ➊

The personal pronoun must agree in number and in gender with the noun which it represents.

Es is used only for neuter nouns, and not for all inanimate objects → ➋

Inanimate objects which are masculine use the pronoun er → ➌

Feminine inanimate objects use the pronoun sie → ➍

Neuter nouns referring to people have the neuter pronoun es → ➎

NOTE: A common error for English speakers is to call all objects es.

Man

This is used in much the same way as the pronoun one in English, but it is much more commonly used in German → ➏

It is also used to make an alternative passive form (see page 34) → ➐

The genitive personal pronoun

Genitive forms of the personal pronouns do exist → ➑

In practice, however, these are rarely used. Wherever possible, alternative expressions are found which do not require the genitive personal pronoun.

Special genitive forms exist for use with the prepositions wegen and willen → ➒

Examples

①
der Tisch	the table (*masculine*)
die Gardine	the curtain (*feminine*)
das Baby	the baby (*neuter*)

②
Das Bild ist schön.	►	Es ist schön.
The picture is beautiful.	►	It is beautiful.

③
Der Tisch ist groß.	►	Er ist groß.
The table is large.	►	It is large.

④
Die Gardine ist weiß.	►	Sie ist weiß.
The curtain is white.	►	It is white.

⑤
Das Kind stand auf.	►	Es stand auf.
The child stood up.	►	He/she stood up.

⑥
Es tut einem gut.
It does one good.

⑦
Man holt mich um sieben ab.
I am being picked up at seven.

⑧
meiner	of me	unser	of us
deiner	of you	euer	of you (*plural*)
seiner	of him/it	ihrer	of them
ihrer	of her/it	Ihrer	of you (*polite*)

⑨
meinetwegen	because of me, on my account
deinetwegen	because of you, on your account *etc*
seinetwegen	
ihretwegen	
unsertwegen	
euretwegen	
Ihretwegen	

meinetwillen	for my sake, for me *etc*
deinetwillen	
ihretwillen *etc*	

Personal Pronouns *continued*

The use of pronouns after prepositions

Personal pronouns used after prepositions and referring to a person are in the *case* required by the preposition in question (see pages 198–199) →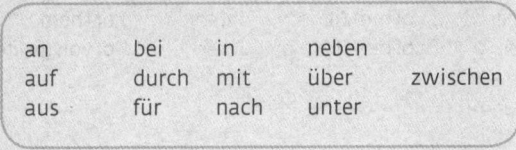

When, however, a *thing* rather than a person is referred to, the construction

> *preposition + pronoun*

becomes

> **da-** + *preposition* → ❷

Before a preposition beginning with a vowel, the form **dar-** + *preposition* is used → ❸

This affects the following prepositions:

an	bei	in	neben	
auf	durch	mit	über	zwischen
aus	für	nach	unter	

These contracted forms are used after verbs followed by a preposition (see pages 76–79) → ❹

After prepositions used to express motion the form with **da(r)-** is not felt to be sufficiently strong. Forms with hin and her are used as follows:

> aus: heraus/hinaus
> auf: herauf/hinauf → ❺
> in: herein/hinein

❶ Ich bin mit ihm spazieren gegangen.
I went for a walk with him.

❷ Klaus hatte ein Messer geholt und wollte damit den
Kuchen schneiden.
Klaus had brought a knife and was about to cut the cake
with it.

❸ Lege es bitte darauf.
Put it there please.

❹ Der Unterschied liegt darin, dass ...
The difference is that ...

Ich erinnere mich nicht daran.
I don't remember (it).

❺ Er sah eine Treppe und ging leise hinauf.
He saw some stairs and went up them quietly.

Endlich fand er unser Zelt und kam herein.
He finally found our tent and came in.

Er öffnete den Koffer und legte das Hemd hinein.
He opened his suitcase and put in his shirt.

Possessive Pronouns

meiner	mine
deiner	yours (*familiar*)
seiner	his/its
ihrer	hers/its
uns(e)rer	ours
eu(e)rer	yours (*plural*)
ihrer	theirs
Ihrer	yours (*polite*)

These have the same endings as dieser. Their declension is therefore the same as for possessive adjectives (see page 136) except in the masculine nominative singular and the neuter nominative and accusative singular:

		SINGULAR		PLURAL
	MASC	FEM	NEUT	ALL GENDERS
NOM	-er	-e	-(e)s	-e
ACC	-en	-e	-(e)s	-e
GEN	-es	-er	-es	-er
DAT	-em	-er	-em	-en

The bracketed **(e)** is often omitted, especially in spoken German.

Possessive pronouns must agree in number, gender and case with the noun they replace → **1**

Note the translation of *of mine, of yours* etc → **2**

meiner is declined in full opposite → **3**
Deiner, seiner and ihrer are declined like meiner.

Unserer and euerer are shown in full, since they have slightly different forms with an optional -e- → **4**

1 Der Wagen da drüben ist meiner. Er ist kleiner als deiner.
The car over there is mine. It is smaller than yours.

2 Er ist ein Bekannter von mir.
He is an acquaintance of mine.

3 meiner mine

	SINGULAR			PLURAL
	MASC	FEM	NEUT	ALL GENDERS
NOM	meiner	meine	mein(e)s	meine
ACC	meinen	meine	mein(e)s	meine
GEN	meines	meiner	meines	meiner
DAT	meinem	meiner	meinem	meinen

4 uns(e)rer ours

	SINGULAR			PLURAL
	MASC	FEM	NEUT	ALL GENDERS
NOM	uns(e)rer	uns(e)re	uns(e)res	uns(e)re
ACC	uns(e)ren	uns(e)re	uns(e)res	uns(e)re
GEN	uns(e)res	uns(e)rer	uns(e)res	uns(e)rer
DAT	uns(e)rem	uns(e)rer	uns(e)rem	uns(e)ren

eu(e)rer yours (*plural*)

	SINGULAR			PLURAL
	MASC	FEM	NEUT	ALL GENDERS
NOM	eu(e)rer	eu(e)re	eu(e)res	eu(e)re
ACC	eu(e)ren	eu(e)re	eu(e)res	eu(e)re
GEN	eu(e)res	eu(e)rer	eu(e)res	eu(e)rer
DAT	eu(e)rem	eu(e)rer	eu(e)rem	eu(e)ren

Possessive Pronouns *continued*

Alternative forms

There are two alternatives to the meiner/deiner *etc* forms shown on page 167:

der, die, das meinige *or* Meinige	mine
der, die, das deinige *or* Deinige	yours (*familiar*)
der, die, das seinige *or* Seinige	his/its
der, die, das ihrige *or* Ihrige	hers/its
der, die, das uns(e)rige *or* Uns(e)rige	ours
der, die, das eu(e)rige *or* Eu(e)rige	yours (*plural*)
der, die, das ihrige *or* Ihrige	theirs
der, die, das Ihrige	yours (*polite*)

These are not as common as the meiner/deiner *etc* forms → **❶**

These forms are declined as the definite article followed by a weak adjective (see page 140) → **❷**

The bracketed (e) of the first and second person plural is often omitted in spoken German.

der, die, das meine *or* Meine	mine
der, die, das deine *or* Deine	yours (*familiar*)
der, die, das seine *or* Seine	his/its
der, die, das ihre *or* Ihre	hers/its
der, die, das uns(e)re *or* Uns(e)re	ours
der, die, das eu(e)re *or* Eu(e)re	yours (*plural*)
der, die, das ihre *or* Ihre	theirs
der, die, das Ihre	yours (*polite*)

These forms are also less common than the meiner/deiner *etc* forms. They are declined as the definite article followed by a weak adjective (see page 140) → **❸**

① Ihr Auto ist aber neuer als das meinige *or* Meinige.
Your car is newer than mine.
Paul hat seiner Freundin Blumen gekauft. Ich habe der
meinigen *or* Meinigen Parfüm geschenkt.
Paul bought his girlfriend some flowers. I bought mine perfume.

②

	SINGULAR		
	MASC	**FEM**	**NEUT**
NOM	der meinige	die meinige	das meinige
ACC	den meinigen	die meinige	das meinige
GEN	des meinigen	der meinigen	des meinigen
DAT	dem meinigen	der meinigen	dem meinigen

PLURAL
ALL GENDERS

NOM	die meinigen
ACC	die meinigen
GEN	der meinigen
DAT	den meinigen

③

	SINGULAR		
	MASC	**FEM**	**NEUT**
NOM	der meine	die meine	das meine
ACC	den meinen	die meine	das meine
GEN	des meinen	der meinen	des meinen
DAT	dem meinen	der meinen	dem meinen

PLURAL
ALL GENDERS

NOM	die meinen
ACC	die meinen
GEN	der meinen
DAT	den meinen

NOTE: Der/die/das meinige *etc* can also be spelt der/die/das Meinige *etc*
and der/die/das meine *etc* can also be spelt der/die/das Meine *etc*.

Reflexive Pronouns

Reflexive pronouns, used to form reflexive verbs, have two forms, accusative and dative, as follows → ❶

ACCUSATIVE	DATIVE	
mich	mir	myself
dich	dir	yourself (*familiar*)
sich	sich	himself/herself/itself/themselves
uns	uns	ourselves
euch	euch	yourselves (*plural*)
sich	sich	yourself/yourselves (*polite*)

Unlike personal pronouns and possessives, the polite forms have no capital letter → ❷

For the position of reflexive pronouns within a sentence see page 30 (reflexive verbs) and pages 224–235 (sentence structure).

Reflexive pronouns are also used after prepositions when the pronoun has the function of "reflecting back" to the subject of the sentence → ❸

A further use of reflexive pronouns in German is with transitive verbs where the action is performed for the benefit of the subject, as in the English phrase:

> I bought *myself* a new hat

The pronoun is not always translated in English → ❹

Examples

❶   Er hat sich rasiert.
He had a shave.

Du hast dich gebadet.
You had a bath.

Ich will es mir zuerst überlegen.
I'll have to think about it first.

❷   Setzen Sie sich bitte.
Please take a seat.

❸   Er hatte nicht genug Geld bei sich. (NOT: bei ihm)
He didn't have enough money on him.

❹   Ich hole mir ein Bier.
I'm going to get a beer (for myself).

Er hat sich einen neuen Anzug gekauft.
He bought (himself) a new suit.

Reflexive Pronouns *continued*

Reflexive pronouns may be used for *reciprocal* actions, usually rendered by "each other" in English → ❶

Reciprocal actions may also be expressed by einander. This does not change in form → ❷

Einander is always used in place of the reflexive pronoun after prepositions. Note that the preposition and einander come together to form one word → ❸

Emphatic reflexive pronouns

In English, these have the same forms as the normal reflexive pronouns:

> The queen *herself* had given the order

> I haven't read it *myself*, but ...

In German, this idea is expressed not by the reflexive pronouns, but by selbst or (in colloquial speech) selber placed at some point in the sentence after the noun or pronoun to which they refer → ❹

selbst/selber do not change their form, regardless of number and gender of the noun to which they refer → ❹

They are always stressed, regardless of their position in the sentence.

①   Wir sind uns letzte Woche begegnet.
We met (each other) last week.

Sie hatten sich auf einer Tagung kennengelernt.
They had got to know each other at a conference.

②   Wir kennen uns schon.
OR:
Wir kennen einander schon.
We already know each other.

Sie kennen sich schon.
OR:
Sie kennen einander schon.
They already know each other.

③   Sie redeten miteinander.
They were talking to each other.

④   Die Königin selbst hat es befohlen.
The queen herself has given the order.

Ich selbst habe es nicht gelesen, aber ...
I haven't read it myself, but ...

Relative Pronouns

These have the same forms as the definite article, except in the dative plural and genitive cases.

They are declined as follows:

| | SINGULAR | | | PLURAL |
	MASC	FEM	NEUT	ALL GENDERS
NOM	der	die	das	die
ACC	den	die	das	die
GEN	dessen	deren	dessen	deren
DAT	dem	der	dem	denen

Relative pronouns must agree in gender and number with the noun to which they refer. They take their case however from the function they have in their own relative clause → **1**

The relative pronoun cannot be omitted in German as it sometimes is in English → **2**

The genitive forms are used in relative clauses in much the same way as in English → **3**

NOTE, however, the translation of certain phrases → **4**

When a preposition introduces the relative clause, the relative pronoun may be replaced by **wo-** or **wor-** if the noun or pronoun it stands for refers to an inanimate object or abstract concept → **5**

The full form of relative pronoun plus preposition is however stylistically better.

Relative clauses are always divided off by commas from the rest of the sentence → **1** - **5**

Examples

① Der Mann, den ich gestern gesehen habe, kommt aus Hamburg.
The man whom I saw yesterday comes from Hamburg.

② Die Frau, mit der ich gestern gesprochen habe, kennt deine Mutter.
The woman I spoke to yesterday knows your mother.

③ Das Kind, dessen Fahrrad gestohlen worden war, ...
The child whose bicycle had been stolen ...

④ Die Kinder, von denen einige schon lesen konnten, ...
The children, some of whom could read, ...

Meine Freunde, von denen einer ...
My friends, one of whom ...

⑤ Das Buch, woraus ich vorgelesen habe, ...
OR:
Das Buch, aus dem ich vorgelesen habe, ...
The book I read aloud from ...

Relative Pronouns *continued*

Welcher

A second relative pronoun exists. This has the same forms as the interrogative adjective welcher without the genitive forms:

| | | SINGULAR | | PLURAL |
	MASC	FEM	NEUT	ALL GENDERS
NOM	welcher	welche	welches	welche
ACC	welchen	welche	welches	welche
GEN	—	—	—	—
DAT	welchem	welcher	welchem	welchen

These forms are used only infrequently as relative pronouns, where sentence rhythm might benefit.

They are also useful used as articles or adjectives to connect a noun in the relative clause with the contents of the main clause → 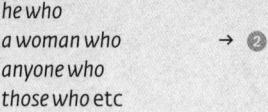 ❶

Wer, was

These are normally used as interrogative pronouns meaning *who?*, *what?* and are declined as such on page 178.

They may, however, also be used without interrogative meaning to replace both subject and relative pronoun in English:

> *he who*
> *a woman who*   → ❷
> *anyone who*
> *those who* etc

Was is the relative pronoun used in set expressions with certain neuter forms → ❸

❶ Er glaubte, mit der Hausarbeit nicht helfen zu brauchen, mit welcher Idee seine Mutter nicht einverstanden war!
He thought he didn't have to help in the house, an idea with which his mother was not in agreement!

❷ Wer das glaubt, ist verrückt.
Anyone who believes that is mad.

Was mich angeht, ...
For my part, ...

Was du gestern gekauft hast, steht dir ganz gut.
The things you bought yesterday suit you very well.

❸

alles, was ...	everything which
allerlei, was ...	all kinds of things that
das, was ...	that which
dasjenige, was ...	that which
dasselbe, was ...	the same one that
einiges, was ...	some that
Folgendes, was ...	the following which
manches, was ...	some which
nichts, was ...	nothing that
vieles, was ...	a lot that
wenig, was ...	little that

Nichts, was er sagte, hat gestimmt.
Nothing that he said was right.

Das, was du jetzt machst, ist reiner Unsinn!
What you are doing now is sheer nonsense!

Mit allem, was du gesagt hast, sind wir einverstanden.
We agree with everything you said.

Interrogative Pronouns

These are the pronouns used to ask questions.

As in English, they have few forms, singular and plural being the same.

They are declined as follows:

PERSONS		THINGS
NOM	wer?	was?
ACC	wen?	was?
GEN	wessen?	wessen?
DAT	wem?	—

They are used in direct questions → ❶

or in indirect questions → ❷

When used as the subject of a sentence, they are always followed by a singular verb → ❸

BUT: When followed by a verb and taking a noun complement, the verb may be plural if the sense demands it → ❹

The interrogative pronouns can be used in rhetorical questions or in exclamations → ❺

1   Wer hat es gemacht?
          Who did it?

          Mit wem bist du gekommen?
          Who did you come with?

2   Ich weiß nicht, wer es gemacht hat.
          I don't know who did it.

          Er wollte wissen, mit wem er fahren sollte.
          He wanted to know who he was to travel with.

3   Wer kommt heute?
          Who's coming today?

4   Wer sind diese Leute?
          Who are these people?

5   Was haben wir gelacht!
          How we laughed!

Interrogative Pronouns *continued*

When used with prepositions, was usually becomes wo- and is placed in front of the preposition to form one word → ❶

Where the preposition begins with a vowel, wor- is used instead → ❷

This construction is similar to da(r)- + *preposition* shown on page 164.

As with da(r)- + *preposition*, this construction is not used when the preposition is intended to convey movement.

Wohin (*where to*) and woher (*where from*) are used instead → ❸

Was für ein?, welcher?

These are used to mean *what kind of one?* and *which one?*

They are declined as shown on pages 124–128.

They are used to form either direct or indirect questions → ❹

They may refer either to persons or to things with the appropriate declension endings → ❺

①   Wonach sehnst du dich?
        What do you long for?

        Wodurch ist es zerstört worden?
        How was it destroyed?

②   Worauf kann man sich heutzutage noch verlassen?
        What is there left to rely on these days?

③   Wohin fährst du?
        Where are you going?

        Woher kommt das?
        Where has this come from?/How has this come about?

④   Was für eins hat er?
        What kind (of one) does he have?

        Welches hast du gewollt?
        Which one did you want?

⑤   Für welchen hat sie sich entschieden?
        Which one (*man/hat etc*) did she choose?

Indefinite Pronouns

(irgend)jemand someone, somebody

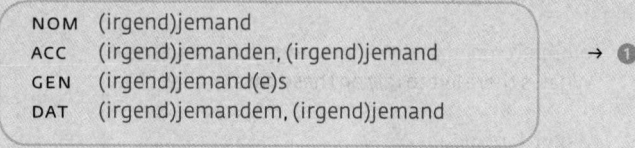

NOM (irgend)jemand
ACC (irgend)jemanden, (irgend)jemand
GEN (irgend)jemand(e)s
DAT (irgend)jemandem, (irgend)jemand

→ ❶

niemand no-one, nobody

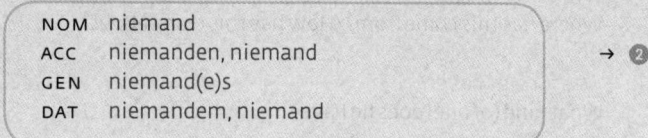

NOM niemand
ACC niemanden, niemand
GEN niemand(e)s
DAT niemandem, niemand

→ ❷

The forms without endings are used in conversational German, but the inflected forms are preferred in literary and written styles.

When niemand and (irgend)jemand are used with a following adjective, they are usually not declined, but the adjective takes a capital letter and is declined as follows:

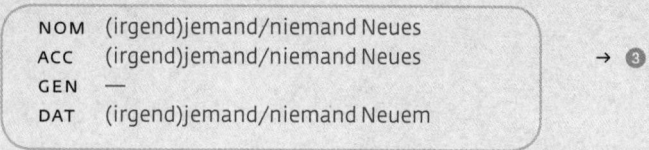

NOM (irgend)jemand/niemand Neues
ACC (irgend)jemand/niemand Neues
GEN —
DAT (irgend)jemand/niemand Neuem

→ ❸

When (irgend)jemand and niemand are followed by ander(e)s, this is written with a small letter, e.g. (irgend)jemand/niemand ander(e)s.

❶ Ich habe es (irgend)jemandem (*dat*) gegeben.
I gave it to someone.

(Irgend)jemand (*nom*) hat es genommen.
Someone has stolen it.

❷ Er hat niemanden (*acc*) gesehen.
He didn't see anyone.

Er ist unterwegs niemandem (*dat*) begegnet.
He encountered no-one on the way.

❸ Diese Aufgabe erfordert (irgend)jemand Intelligentes.
Someone intelligent is needed for this task.

Indefinite Pronouns *continued*

keiner none

| | | SINGULAR | | PLURAL |
	MASC	FEM	NEUT	ALL GENDERS
NOM	keiner	keine	keins	keine
ACC	keinen	keine	keins	keine
GEN	keines	keiner	keines	keiner
DAT	keinem	keiner	keinem	keinen

It is declined like the article kein, keine, kein (see page 126) except in
the nominative masculine and nominative and accusative neuter
forms → ❶

It may be used to refer to people or things → ❶

einer one

| | | SINGULAR | |
	MASC	FEM	NEUT
NOM	einer	eine	ein(e)s
ACC	einen	eine	ein(e)s
GEN	eines	einer	eines
DAT	einem	einer	einem

This pronoun may be used to refer to either people or things → ❷

It exists only in the singular forms.

❶ Keiner von ihnen hat es tun können.
Not one of them was able to do it.

Gibst du mir eine Zigarette? — Tut mir leid, ich habe keine.
Will you give me a cigarette? — Sorry, I haven't got any.

❷ Sie ist mit einem meiner Verwandten verlobt.
She is engaged to one of my relatives.

Wo sind die anderen Kinder? Ich sehe hier nur eins.
Where are the rest of the children? I can only see one here.

Gibst du mir einen? (e.g. *einen Whisky, einen Zehner* etc) OR:
Gibst du mir eine? (e.g. *eine Zigarette, eine Blume* etc) OR:
Gibst du mir eins? (e.g. *ein Buch, ein Butterbrot* etc)
Will you give me one?

Indefinite Pronouns *continued*

Certain adjectives and articles can be used as pronouns.

The following are all declined to agree in gender and number with the noun or pronoun they represent → ❶

aller	all
ander	other
beide	both
derjenige	that one
derselbe	the same one
dieser	this one
einiger	some
irgendwelcher	someone or other/something or other
jeder	each (one), every one
jener	that one
mancher	some, quite a few
mehrere	several
sämtliche	all, the lot
solcher	such as that, such a one
welcher	which one

The following do not change whatever the gender or number of the noun or pronoun they represent → ❷

ein bisschen	a bit, a little
ein paar	a few
ein wenig	a little, a few
(irgend)etwas	some, something
mehr	more
nichts	nothing, none

When an adjective follows etwas or nichts, it takes a capital letter and declension endings, e.g. etwas/nichts Gutes

➊   Andere machen es besser. (e.g. *Leute*, *Waschmaschinen* etc)
Others do it better.

Mit einem solchen kommst du nicht bis nach Hause.
(e.g. *Wagen* etc)
You won't make it home in one like that.

Alles, was er ihr schenkte, schickte sie sofort zurück.
Everything that he gave her she sent back at once.

Er war mit beiden zufrieden. (e.g. *Computern*, *Autos* etc)
He was satisfied with both.

➋   Ich muss dir etwas sagen.
I must tell you something.

(Irgend)etwas ist herausgefallen.
Something fell out.

Nichts ist geschehen.
Nothing happened.

Er ist mit nichts zufrieden.
Nothing ever satisfies him.

Gibst du mir bitte ein paar?
Will you give me a few?

Er hatte ein wenig bei sich.
He had a little with him.

Er braucht immer mehr um zu überleben.
He needs more and more to survive.

Use of Adverbs

Adverbs, or phrases which are used as adverbs, may:

- modify a verb → ❶

- modify an adjective → ❷

- modify another adverb → ❸

- modify a conjunction → ❹

- ask a question → ❺

- form verb prefixes (see page 72) → ❻

Adverbs are also used, in much the same way as in English, to make the meaning of certain tenses more precise e.g.

- with continuous tenses → ❼

- to show a future meaning where the tense used is not future → ❽

❶ Er ging langsam über die Brücke.
He walked slowly over the bridge.

❷ Er ist ein ziemlich großer Kerl.
He's quite a big chap.

❸ Sie arbeitet heute besonders tüchtig.
She's working exceptionally well today.

❹ Wenn er es nur aufgeben wollte!
If only he would give it up!

❺ Wann kommt er an?
When does he arrive?

❻ falsch spielen
to cheat (*at cards*)

hintragen
to carry (*to a place*)

❼ Er liest gerade die Zeitung.
He's just reading the paper.

❽ Er wollte gerade aufstehen, als ...
He was just about to get up when ...

Wir fahren morgen nach Köln.
We're driving to Cologne tomorrow.

The Formation of Adverbs

Many German adverbs are simply adjectives used as adverbs. Used in this way, unlike adjectives, they are not declined → **1**

Some adverbs are formed by adding **-weise** or **-sweise** to a noun → **2**

Some adverbs are also formed by adding **-erweise** to an uninflected adjective.

Such adverbs are used mainly to show the speaker's opinion → **3**

There is also a class of adverbs which are not formed from other parts of speech e.g. unten, oben, leider → **4**

For the position of adverbs within a clause or sentence, see the section on sentence structure, pages 224–235.

The following are some common adverbs of time:

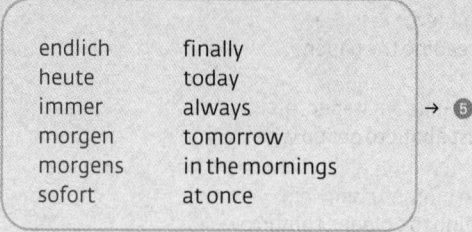

endlich	finally
heute	today
immer	always
morgen	tomorrow
morgens	in the mornings
sofort	at once

→ **5**

The following are some common adverbs of degree:

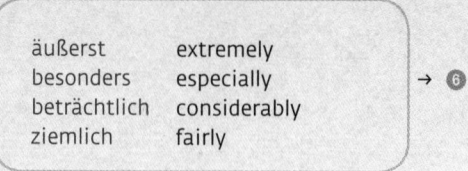

äußerst	extremely
besonders	especially
beträchtlich	considerably
ziemlich	fairly

→ **6**

Examples

1 Habe ich das richtig gehört?
Is it true what I've heard?

Sie war modern angezogen.
She was fashionably dressed.

2

beispielsweise	for example
beziehungsweise	or/or rather/that is to say
schrittweise	step by step
zeitweise	at times
zwangsweise	compulsorily

3

erstaunlicherweise	astonishingly enough
glücklicherweise	fortunately
komischerweise	strangely enough

4 Unten wohnte Frau Schmidt.
Mrs Schmidt lived downstairs.

Leider können wir nicht kommen.
Unfortunately we cannot come.

5 Ich kann erst morgen kommen.
I can't come till tomorrow.

Das Kind hat immer Hunger.
The child is always hungry.

6 Das Paket war besonders schwer.
The parcel was unusually heavy.

Diese Übung ist ziemlich leicht.
This exercise is quite easy.

Adverbs of place

In certain respects German adverbs of place behave very differently from their English counterparts:

Where no movement, or merely a movement within the same place, is involved, the adverb is used in its simple dictionary form →

Movement *away from the speaker* is shown by the presence of hin → ❷

The following compound adverbs are therefore often used when movement away from the original position is concerned, even though a simple adverb would be used in English:

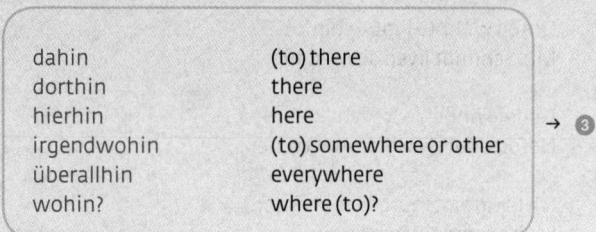

dahin	(to) there
dorthin	there
hierhin	here
irgendwohin	(to) somewhere or other
überallhin	everywhere
wohin?	where (to)?

→ ❸

Movement *towards the speaker* or central person is shown by the presence of her.

The following compound adverbs are therefore often used to show movement towards a person:

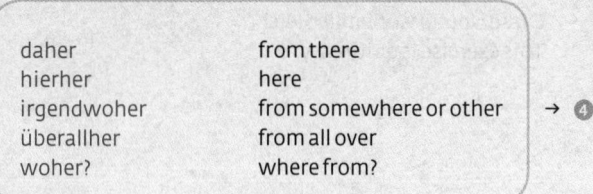

daher	from there
hierher	here
irgendwoher	from somewhere or other
überallher	from all over
woher?	where from?

→ ❹

❶ Wo ist er?
Where is he?

Er ist nicht da.
He isn't there.

Hier darf man nicht parken.
You can't park here.

❷ Klaus und Ulli geben heute eine Party. Gehen wir hin?
Klaus and Ulli are having a party today. Shall we go?

❸ Wohin fährst du?
Where are you going?

Sie liefen überallhin.
They ran everywhere.

❹ Woher kommst du?
Where do you come from?

Woher hast du das?
Where did you get that from?

Das habe ich irgendwoher gekriegt.
I got that from somewhere or other.

Comparison of Adverbs

The comparative form of the adverb is obtained in exactly the same way as that of adjectives, i.e. by adding **-er** → ➊

The superlative form is produced as follows:

> am + *adverb* + **-sten/-esten**

It is not declined → ➋

Note the use of the comparative adverb with immer to show progression → ➌

the more ... the more ... is expressed in German by:

> je ... desto ... or je ... umso ... → ➍

Some adverbial superlatives are used to show the extent of a quality rather than a comparison with others. These are as follows:

bestens	very well/very warmly
höchstens	at the most/at best
meistens	mostly/most often
spätestens	at the latest
strengstens	strictly, absolutely
wenigstens	at least

→ ➎

Two irregular comparatives and superlatives:

gern	▶	lieber	▶	am liebsten (used with haben) → ➏
well	▶	better	▶	best

bald	▶	eher	▶	am ehesten
soon	▶	sooner	▶	soonest

① Er läuft schneller als seine Schwester.
He runs faster than his sister.

Ich sehe ihn seltener als früher.
I see him less often than before.

② Wer von ihnen arbeitet am schnellsten?
Which of them works fastest?

Er isst am meisten.
He eats most.

③ Die Mädchen sprachen immer lauter.
The girls were talking more and more loudly.

Er fuhr immer langsamer.
He drove more and more slowly.

④ Je eher, desto besser.
The sooner the better.

⑤ Er kommt meistens zu spät an.
He usually arrives late.

Rauchen strengstens verboten!
Smoking strictly prohibited.

⑥ Welches hast du am liebsten?
Which do you like best?

Emphasizers

These are words commonly used in German, as indeed in English, especially in the spoken language, to emphasize or modify in some way the meaning of the sentence. The following are some of the most common:

aber

Used to lend emphasis to a statement → **1**

denn

As well as its uses as a conjunction (see page 214), denn is widely used to emphasize the meaning. It often cannot be directly translated → **2**

doch

Used as a positive reply in order to correct negative assumptions or impressions → **3**
It can strengthen an imperative → **4**
It can make a question out of a statement → **5**

mal

May be used with imperatives → **6**
It also has several idiomatic uses → **7**

ja

Strengthens a statement → **8**
It also has several idiomatic uses → **9**

schon

Is used familiarly with an imperative → **10**
It is also used in various idiomatic ways → **11**

Examples

❶   Das ist aber schön!   Aber ja!
Oh that's pretty!   Yes indeed!

❷   Was ist denn hier los?   Wo denn?
What's going on here then?   Where?

❸   Hat es dir nicht gefallen? — Doch!
Didn't you like it? — Oh yes, I did!

❹   Lass ihn doch!
Just leave him!

❺   Das schaffst du doch?
You'll manage it, won't you?

❻   Komm mal her!   Moment mal!
Come here!   Just a minute!

❼   Mal sehen.   Hören Sie mal …
We'll see.   Look here now …
Er soll es nur mal versuchen!
Just let him try it!

❽   Er sieht ja wie seine Mutter aus.
He looks like his mother.
Das kann ja sein.
That may well be.

❾   Ja und?   Das ist ja lächerlich.
So what?/What then?   That's ridiculous.
Das ist es ja.
That's just it.

❿   Mach schon!
Get on with it!

⓫   schon wieder   Schon gut!
again   Okay/Very well!

Prepositions

In English, a preposition does not affect the word or phrase which it introduces, e.g.

the women	a large meal	these events
with the women	*after* a large meal	*before* these events

In German, however, the noun following a preposition must be put in a certain *case*:

accusative → ❶

dative → ❷

genitive → ❸

It is therefore important to learn each preposition with the case, or cases, it governs.

The following guidelines will help you:

Prepositions which take the accusative or dative cases are much more common than those taking the genitive case.

Certain prepositions may take a dative or accusative case, depending on whether *movement* is involved or not. This is explained further on pages 202–211 → ❹

Prepositions are often used to complete the sense of certain verbs, as shown on pages 76–79 → ❺

After many prepositions, a shortened or *contracted* form of the definite article may be merged with the preposition to form one word, e.g.

auf + das	►	aufs
bei + dem	►	beim
zu + der	►	zur

Examples

❶   Es ist für dich.
It's for you.

      Wir sind durch die ganze Welt gereist.
We travelled all over the world.

❷   Er ist mit seiner Frau gekommen.
He came with his wife.

❸   Es ist ihm trotz seiner Bemühungen nicht gelungen.
Despite his efforts, he still didn't succeed.

❹   Es liegt auf dem Tisch.
It's on the table.
(*dative*: no movement implied)

      Lege es bitte auf den Tisch.
Please put it on the table.
(*accusative*: movement *onto* the table)

❺   Ich warte auf meinen Mann.
I'm waiting for my husband.

Contracted forms

Contractions are possible with the following prepositions:

PREPOSITION	+ das	+ den	+ dem	+ der
an	ans		am	
auf	aufs*			
bei			beim	
durch	durchs*			
für	fürs*			
hinter	hinters*	hintern*	hinterm*	
in	ins		im	
über	übers*	übern*	überm*	
um	ums*			
unter	unters*	untern*	unterm*	
vor	vors*		vorm*	
von			vom	
zu			zum	zur

> * NOTE: Those forms marked with an asterisk are suitable only for use in colloquial, spoken German.
> All other forms (not marked with an asterisk) may be safely used in any context, formal or informal → ❶

Contracted forms are not used where the article is to be stressed → ❷

Other contracted forms involving prepositions, as shown on pages 164 and 174, occur:

- in the introduction to relative clauses → ❸
- with personal pronouns representing inanimate objects → ❹

Examples

1 Wir gehen heute Abend ins Theater.
We are going to the theatre this evening.

Er geht zur Schule.
He goes to school.

Das kommt vom Trinken.
That comes from drinking.

2 In dem Anzug kann ich mich nicht sehen lassen!
I can't go out in that suit!

3 Die Bank, worauf wir saßen, war etwas wackelig.
The bench we were sitting on was rather wobbly.

4 Er war damit zufrieden.
He was satisfied with that.

Er hat es darauf gesetzt.
He put it on it.

Prepositions followed by the Dative Case

Some of the most common prepositions taking the dative case are:

aus	gegenüber	seit
außer	mit	von
bei	nach	zu

aus

as a preposition meaning: *out of/from* → ❶

as a separable verbal prefix (see page 72) → ❷

außer

as a preposition meaning: *out of* → ❸

                                   except → ❹

bei

as a preposition meaning: *at the home/shop/work* etc *of* → ❺

                                   near → ❻

                                   in the course of/during → ❼

as a separable verbal prefix (see page 72) → ❽

gegenüber

as a preposition meaning: *opposite* → ❾

                                   to(wards) → ❿

NOTE: When used as a preposition, gegenüber is placed *after a pronoun*, but may be placed *before or after a noun*.

as a separable verbal prefix → ⓫

Examples

① Er trinkt aus der Flasche.
   He is drinking out of the bottle.
   Er kommt aus Essen.
   He comes from Essen.

② aushalten to endure
   Ich halte es nicht mehr aus.
   I can't stand it any longer.

③ außer Gefahr/Betrieb
   out of danger/order

④ alle außer mir
   all except me

⑤ bei uns in Schottland
   at home in Scotland
   Er wohnt immer noch bei seinen Eltern.
   He still lives with his parents.

⑥ Er saß bei mir.
   He was sitting next to me.

⑦ Ich singe immer beim Arbeiten.
   I always sing when I'm working.
   Bei unserer Ankunft ...
   On our arrival ...

⑧ beistehen to stand by
   Er stand seinem Freund bei.
   He stood by his friend.

⑨ Er wohnt uns gegenüber.
   He lives opposite us.

⑩ Er ist mir gegenüber immer sehr freundlich gewesen.
   He has always been very friendly towards me.

⑪ gegenüberstehen to face/to have an attitude towards
   Er steht ihnen kritisch gegenüber.
   He takes a critical view of them.

Prepositions followed by the Dative Case *continued*

mit

as a preposition meaning: *with* → ❶

as a separable verbal prefix (see page 72) → ❷

nach

as a preposition meaning: *after* → ❸
                               to → ❹
                               according to (it can be placed after the noun with this meaning) → ❺

as a separable verbal prefix (see page 72) → ❻

seit

as a preposition meaning: *since* → ❼
                               for (of time) → ❽
                               NOTE: Beware of the tense!

von

as a preposition meaning: *from* → ❾
                               about → ❿

as an alternative, often preferred, to the genitive case → ⓫

as a preposition meaning: *by* (to introduce the agent of a passive action, see page 34) → ⓬

zu

as a preposition meaning: *to* → ⓭
                               for → ⓮

as a separable verbal prefix (see page 72) → ⓯

Examples

1. Er ging mit seinen Freunden spazieren.
   He went walking with his friends.
2. jemanden mitnehmen to give someone a lift
   Nimmst du mich bitte mit?
   Will you give me a lift please?
3. Nach zwei Stunden kam er wieder.
   He returned two hours later.
4. Er ist nach London gereist.
   He went to London.
5. Ihrer Sprache nach ist sie Süddeutsche.
   From the way she spoke I would say she is from southern
   Germany.
6. nachmachen to copy
   Sie macht mir alles nach.
   She copies everything I do.
7. Seit der Zeit ...
   Since then ...
8. Ich wohne seit zwei Jahren in Frankfurt.
   I've been living in Frankfurt for two years.
9. Von Frankfurt sind wir weiter nach München gefahren.
   From Frankfurt we went on to Munich.
10. Ich weiß nichts von ihm.
    I know nothing about him.
11. Die Mutter von diesen Mädchen ...
    The mother of these girls ...
    Sie ist eine Freundin von Horst.
    She is a friend of Horst's.
12. Er ist von unseren Argumenten überzeugt worden.
    He was convinced by our arguments.
13. Er ging zum Arzt.
    He went to the doctor's.
14. Wir sind zum Essen eingeladen.
    We're invited for dinner.
15. zumachen to shut
    Mach die Tür zu!
    Shut the door!

Prepositions followed by the Accusative Case

The most common of these are:

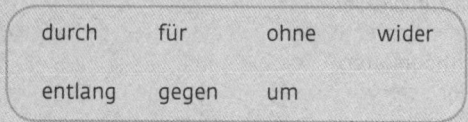

durch	für	ohne	wider
entlang	gegen	um	

durch

as a preposition meaning: *through* → ❶

preceding the inanimate agent of a passive action (see page 34) → ❷

as a separable verbal prefix

entlang

as a preposition meaning: *along* (it follows the noun with this meaning) → ❸

as a separable verbal prefix → ❹

für

as a preposition meaning: *for* → ❺
to → ❻

in was für/was für ein *what kind of/what* (see pages 144 and 180) → ❼

gegen

as a preposition meaning: *against* → ❽
towards/getting on for → ❾

as a separable verbal prefix

Examples

1   durch das Fenster blicken
to look through the window

2   Durch seine Bemühungen wurden alle gerettet.
Everyone was saved through his efforts.

3   die Straße entlang
along the street

4   entlanggehen to go along
Wir gingen die Straße entlang.
We went along the street.

5   Ich habe es für dich getan.
I did it for you.

6   Das ist für ihn sehr wichtig.
That is very important to him.

7   Was für Äpfel sind das?
What kind of apples are they?

8   Stelle es gegen die Mauer.
Put it against the wall.

    Haben Sie ein Mittel gegen Schnupfen?
Have you something for colds?

    Ich habe nichts dagegen.
I've got nothing against it.

9   Wir sind gegen vier angekommen.
We arrived at getting on for/around four o'clock.

Prepositions followed by the Accusative Case *continued*

ohne

as a preposition meaning: *without* → ❶

um

as a preposition meaning: *(a)round/round about* → ❷

at (in time expressions) → ❸

for (after certain verbs) → ❹

about (after certain verbs) → ❺

by (in expressions of quantity) → ❻

as a variable verbal prefix (see page 74) → ❼

wider

as a preposition meaning: *contrary to/against* → ❽

as a variable verbal prefix (see page 74) → ❾

① Ohne ihn gehts nicht.
It won't work without him.

② um die Ecke
(a)round the corner

③ Es fängt um neun Uhr an.
It begins at nine.

④ Sie baten ihre Mutter um Kekse.
They asked their mother for some biscuits.

⑤ Es handelt sich um dein Benehmen.
It's a question of your behaviour.

⑥ Es ist um zehn Euro billiger.
It is cheaper by ten euros.

⑦ umarmen to embrace (*inseparable*)
Er hat sie umarmt.
He gave her a hug.

umfallen to fall over (*separable*)
Er ist umgefallen.
He fell over.

⑧ Das geht mir wider die Natur.
That's against my nature.

⑨ widersprechen to go against (*inseparable*)
Das hat meinen Wünschen widersprochen.
That went against my wishes.

(sich) widerspiegeln to reflect (*separable*)
Der Baum spiegelt sich im Wasser wider.
The tree is reflected in the water.

Prepositions followed by the Accusative or the Dative Case

These prepositions are followed by:

- the accusative when *movement towards* a different place is involved.

- the dative when *position* is described as opposed to movement, or when the movement is *within* the same place.

The most common prepositions in this category are:

an	*on/at/to*
auf	*on/in/to/at*
hinter	*behind*
in	*in/into/to* → ❶
neben	*next to/beside*
über	*over/across/above*
unter	*under/among* → ❷
vor	*in front of/before*
zwischen	*between* → ❸

These prepositions may also be used with figurative meanings as part of a *verb + preposition* construction (see page 76).

The case following auf or an is then not the same after all verbs →

It is therefore best to learn such constructions together with the case which follows them.

Many of these prepositions are also used as verbal prefixes in the same way as the prepositions described on pages 202–209 → ❺

❶ Er ging ins Zimmer (*acc*).
He entered the room.

Im Zimmer (*dat*) warteten viele Leute auf ihn.
A lot of people were waiting for him in the room.

❷ Er stellte sich unter den Baum (*acc*).
He (came and) stood under the tree.

Er lebte dort unter Freunden (*dat*).
There he lived among friends.

❸ Er legte es zwischen die beiden Teller (*acc*).
He put it between the two plates.

Das Dorf liegt zwischen den Bergen (*dat*).
The village lies between the mountains.

❹ sich verlassen auf (+*acc*)   to depend on
bestehen auf (+*dat*)   to insist on

glauben an (+*acc*)   to believe in
leiden an (+*dat*)   to suffer from

❺ anrechnen to charge for (*separable*)
Das wird Ihnen später angerechnet.
You'll be charged for that later.

aufsetzen to put on (*separable*)
Sie setzte sich den Hut auf.
She put her hat on.

überqueren to cross (*inseparable*)
Sie hat die Straße überquert.
She crossed the street.

Prepositions followed by the Genitive Case

The following are some of the more common prepositions which take the genitive case:

außerhalb	*outside*
beiderseits	*on both sides of*
diesseits	*on this side of*
... halber	*for ... sake/because of ...*
hinsichtlich	*with regard to*
infolge	*as a result of*
innerhalb	*within/inside* → ❶
jenseits	*on the other side of* → ❷
statt*	*instead of*
trotz*	*in spite of* → ❸
um ... willen	*for ... sake/because of ...*
während*	*during* → ❹
wegen*	*on account of* → ❺

* NOTE: Those prepositions marked with an asterisk may also be followed by the dative case → ❻

NOTE: Special forms of the possessive and relative pronouns are used with wegen, halber and willen → ❼

Examples

① innerhalb dieses Zeitraums
within this period of time

② jenseits der Grenze
on the other side of the frontier

③ trotz seiner Befürchtungen
despite his fears

④ während der Vorstellung
during the performance

⑤ wegen der neuen Stelle
because of the new job

⑥ trotz allem
in spite of everything

wegen mir
because of me

⑦

meinetwegen	on my account, because of me
deinetwegen	on your account, because of you (*familiar*)
seinetwegen	on his account, because of him
ihretwegen	on her/their account, because of her/them
unsertwegen	on our account, because of us
euertwegen	on your account, because of you (*plural*)
Ihretwegen	on your account, because of you (*polite*)
derentwegen	for whose sake, for her/their/its sake
dessentwegen	for whose sake, for his/its sake
meinethalben *etc*	on my *etc* account
derenthalben	on whose account, on her/their/its account
dessenthalben	on whose account, on his/its account
meinetwillen *etc*	for my *etc* sake
derentwillen	for whose sake, for her/its/their sake
dessentwillen	for whose sake, for his/its sake

Co-ordinating Conjunctions

These are used to link words, phrases or clauses.

These are the main co-ordinating conjunctions:

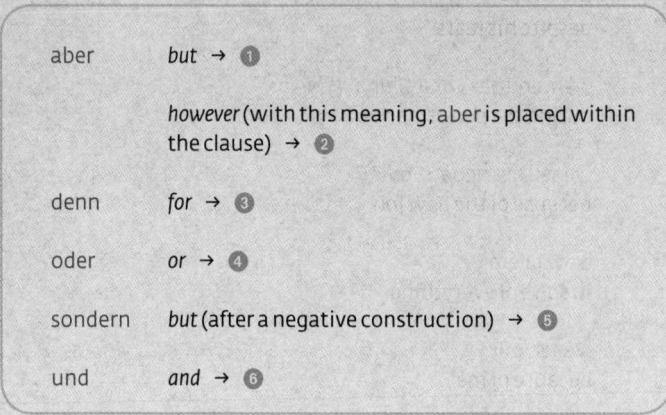

aber	*but* → ❶
	however (with this meaning, aber is placed within the clause) → ❷
denn	*for* → ❸
oder	*or* → ❹
sondern	*but* (after a negative construction) → ❺
und	*and* → ❻

These do not cause the inversion of subject and verb, i.e. the verb follows the subject in the normal way (see page 224) → ❶ – ❻

Inversion may however be caused by something other than the co-ordinating conjunction, e.g. dann, trotzdem, montags in the examples opposite → ❼

① Wir wollten ins Kino, aber wir hatten kein Geld.
We wanted to go to the cinema but we had no money.

② Ich wollte ins Theater; er aber wollte nicht mit.
I wanted to go to the theatre; however he wouldn't come.

③ Wir wollten heute fahren, denn montags ist weniger Verkehr.
We wanted to travel today because the traffic is lighter on Mondays.

④ Er hatte noch nie Whisky oder Schnaps getrunken.
He had never drunk whisky or schnapps.

Willst du eins oder hast du vielleicht keinen Hunger?
Do you want one or aren't you hungry?

⑤ Er ist nicht alt, sondern jung.
He isn't old, but young.

⑥ Horst und Veronika
Horst and Veronika

Er ging in die Stadt und kaufte sich ein neues Hemd.
He went into town and bought himself a new shirt.

⑦ Er hat sie besucht und dann ist er wieder nach Hause gegangen.
He paid her a visit and then went home again.

Wir wollten doch ins Kino, aber trotzdem sind wir zu Hause geblieben.
We wanted to go to the cinema, but even so we stayed at home.

Wir wollten heute fahren, denn montags ist der Verkehr geringer.
We wanted to travel today because there is less traffic on Mondays.

Double Co-ordinating Conjunctions

These conjunctions consist of two separate elements, like their English counterparts, e.g.

not only … but also …

The following are widely used:

> sowohl.. als auch
> *both … and*

This may link words or phrases → ❶

The verb is usually plural, whether the subjects are singular or plural → ❶

> weder … noch
> *neither … nor*

This may link words or phrases → ❷

It may also link clauses, and inversion of subject and verb then takes place in both clauses → ❸

The verb is plural unless both subjects are singular → ❹

❶ Sowohl sein Vater als auch seine Mutter haben sich darüber gefreut.
Both his father and his mother were pleased about it.

Sowohl unser Lehrkörper als auch unsere Schüler haben teilgenommen.
Both our staff and our pupils took part.

❷ Weder Georg noch sein Bruder kannte das Mädchen.
Neither Georg nor his brother knew the girl.

❸ Weder mag ich ihn noch respektiere ich ihn.
I neither like nor respect him.

❹ Weder die Befürworter noch die Gegner haben recht.
Neither the supporters nor the opponents are right.

Weder du noch ich würde es schaffen.
Neither you nor I would be able to do it.

Double Co-ordinating Conjunctions *continued*

> nicht nur … sondern auch
> *not only … but also*

This is used to link clauses as well as words and phrases → ❶

The word order is: inversion of subject and verb in the first clause, and normal order in the second → ❷

However, if nicht nur does not begin the clause, normal order prevails → ❸

The verb agrees in number with the subject nearest to it → ❹

> entweder … oder
> *either … or*

The verb agrees with the subject nearest it → ❺

The normal word order is: inversion in the first clause, and normal order in the second → ❻

However, it is possible to use normal order in the first clause, and this may lend a more threatening tone to the statement → ❼

> teils … teils
> *partly … partly*

The verb is normally plural unless both subjects are singular → ❽

Inversion of subject and verb takes place in both clauses → ❾

① Er ist nicht nur geschickt, sondern auch intelligent. OR:
Nicht nur ist er geschickt, sondern er ist auch intelligent.
He is not only skilful but also intelligent.

② Nicht nur hat es die ganze Zeit geregnet, sondern ich habe mir
auch noch das Bein gebrochen.
Not only did it rain the whole time, but I also broke my leg.

③ Es hat nicht nur die ganze Zeit geregnet, sondern ich habe mir
auch noch das Bein gebrochen.
Not only did it rain the whole time, but I also broke my leg.

④ Nicht nur ich, sondern auch die Mädchen sind dafür
verantwortlich.
It's not just me, but it's also the girls who are also responsible.

Nicht nur sie, sondern auch ich habe es gehört.
They weren't the only ones to hear it — I heard it too.

⑤ Entweder du oder Georg muss es getan haben.
It must have been either you or Georg who did it.

⑥ Entweder komme ich morgen vorbei, oder ich rufe dich an.
I'll either drop in tomorrow or I'll give you a ring.

⑦ Entweder du gibst das sofort auf, oder du kriegst kein
Taschengeld mehr.
Either you stop that immediately, or you get no more pocket
money.

⑧ Die Studenten waren teils Deutsche, teils Ausländer.
The students were partly German and partly from abroad.

⑨ Teils bin ich überzeugt, teils bleibe ich skeptisch.
Part of me is convinced, and part remains sceptical.

Subordinating Conjunctions

These are used to link clauses in such a way as to make one clause dependent on another for its meaning. The dependent clause is called a subordinate clause and the other a main clause.

The subordinate clause is always separated from the rest of the sentence by commas → ❶

The subordinate clause may precede the main clause. When this happens, the verb and subject of the main clause are inverted, i.e. they swap places, as shown on page 226 → ❷

The finite part of the verb (i.e. the conjugated part) is always at the end of a subordinate clause (see page 228) → ❸

For compound tenses in subordinate clauses, it is the auxiliary (the main part of the verb) which comes last, after the participle or infinitive used to form the compound tense (see pages 22–29) → ❹

Any modal verb (mögen, können etc, see pages 52–57) used in a subordinate clause is placed last in the clause → ❺

BUT: When the modal verb is in a compound tense, the order is as shown → ❻

MAIN CLAUSE   **SUBORDINATE CLAUSE**

Er ist zu Fuß gekommen, weil der Bus zu teuer ist.
He came on foot because the bus is too dear.

Ich trinke viel Bier, obwohl es nicht gesund ist.
I drink a lot of beer although it isn't good for me.

Wir haben weitergefeiert, nachdem sie gegangen waren.
We carried on with the party after they went.

② **SUBORDINATE CLAUSE**   **MAIN CLAUSE**

Weil der Bus zu teuer ist, ist er zu Fuß gekommen.

Obwohl es nicht gesund ist, trinke ich viel Bier.

Nachdem sie gegangen waren, haben wir weitergefeiert.

③ Als er uns sah, ist er davongelaufen. **OR:**
Er ist davongelaufen, als er uns sah.
He ran away when he saw us.

④ Nachdem er gegessen hatte, ging er hinaus.
He went out after he had eaten.

⑤ Da er nicht mit uns sprechen wollte, ist er davongelaufen.
Since he didn't want to speak to us he ran away.

⑥ Da er nicht mit uns hat sprechen wollen, ist er davongelaufen.
Since he didn't want to speak to us he ran away.

Subordinating conjunctions *continued*

Here are some common examples of subordinating conjunctions and their uses:

als	when → ❶
als ob	as if, as though
bevor	before
bis	until → ❷
da	as, since → ❸
damit	so (that)
indem	while
inwiefern	to what extent
nachdem	after → ❹
ob	whether, if
obwohl	although
wann	when (*interrogative*) → ❺
während	while → ❻
weil	because → ❼
wenn	when, whenever/if → ❽
wie	as, like
wo	where
wohin	to where
worauf	whereupon/on which
worin	in which
seitdem	since
so dass, sodass	such that, so that
sobald	as soon as
soweit	as far as

① Es regnete, als ich in Köln ankam. OR:
Als ich in Köln ankam, regnete es.
It was raining when I arrived in Cologne.

② Ich warte, bis du zurückkommst.
I'll wait till you get back.

③ Da er nicht kommen wollte, ...
Since he didn't want to come ...

④ Er wird uns Bescheid sagen können, nachdem er angerufen
hat. OR:
Nachdem er angerufen hat, wird er uns Bescheid sagen
können.
He will be able to let us know for certain once he has phoned.

⑤ Er möchte wissen, wann der Zug ankommt.
He would like to know when the train is due to arrive.

⑥ Während seine Frau die Koffer auspackte, machte er das
Abendessen. OR:
Er machte das Abendessen, während seine Frau die Koffer
auspackte.
He made the supper while his wife unpacked the cases.

⑦ Wir haben den Hund nicht mitgenommen, weil im
Auto nicht genug Platz war. OR:
Weil im Auto nicht genug Platz war, haben wir den Hund nicht
mitgenommen.
We didn't take the dog because there wasn't enough room in
the car.

⑧ Wenn ich ins Kino gehe ...
When(ever) I go to the cinema ...

Ich komme, wenn du willst.
I'll come if you like.

Word Order: Main Clauses

In a main clause the subject comes first and is followed by the verb, as in English:

> His mother (*subject*) drinks (*verb*) whisky → ❶

If the verb is in a compound or passive tense, the auxiliary follows the subject and the past participle or infinitive goes to the end of the clause → ❷

The verb is the second concept in a main clause. The first concept may be a word, phrase or clause (see page 226) → ❸

Any reflexive pronoun follows the main verb in simple tenses and the auxiliary in compound tenses → ❹

The order for articles, adjectives and nouns is as in English: *article + adjective(s) + noun* → ❺

A direct object usually follows an indirect, except where the direct object is a personal pronoun.

BUT: The indirect object can be placed last for emphasis, providing it is not a pronoun → ❻

The position of adverbial expressions (see page 188) is not fixed. As a general rule they are placed close to the words to which they refer.

Adverbial items of *time* often come first in the clause, but this is flexible → ❼

Adverbial items of *place* can be placed at the beginning of a clause when emphasis is required → ❽

Adverbial items of *manner* are more likely to be within the clause, close to the word to which they refer → ❾

Where there is more than one adverb, a useful rule of thumb is: "time, manner, place" → ❿

① Seine Mutter trinkt Whisky.
His mother drinks whisky.

② Sie wird dir etwas sagen.   Sie hat mir nichts gesagt.
She will tell you something.   She told me nothing.
Es ist für ihn gekauft worden.
It was bought for him.

③

1ST CONCEPT	2ND CONCEPT	
Die neuen Waren	kommen	morgen
(The new goods are coming tomorrow)		
Was du gesagt hast,	stimmt	nicht
(What you said isn't true)		

④ Er rasierte sich.   Er hat sich rasiert.
He shaved.   He (has) shaved.

⑤ ein alter Mann   diese alten Sachen
an old man   these old things

⑥ Ich gab dem Mann das Geld.
I gave the man the money.
Ich gab ihm das Geld.   Ich gab es ihm.
I gave him the money.   I gave him it/I gave it to him.
Er gab das Geld seiner Schwester.
He gave the money to his sister. (*not his brother*)

⑦ Gestern gingen wir ins Theater. OR:
Wir gingen gestern ins Theater.
We went to the theatre yesterday.

⑧ Dort haben sie Fußball gespielt. OR:
Sie haben dort Fußball gespielt.
They played football there.

⑨ Sie spielen gut Fußball.
They play football well.
Das war furchtbar teuer.
It was terribly expensive.

⑩ Wir haben gestern gut hierhin gefunden.
We found our way here all right yesterday.

225

Word Order: Main Clauses *continued*

A pronoun object precedes all adverbs → ❶

While the main verb must normally remain the second concept, the first concept need not always be the subject. Main clauses can begin with many things, including:

> an adverb → ❷
> a direct or indirect object → ❸
> an infinitive phrase → ❹
> a complement → ❺
> a past participle → ❻
> a prepositional phrase → ❼
> a clause acting as the object of the verb → ❽
> a subordinate clause → ❾

If the subject does not begin a main clause, the verb and subject must be turned around or "inverted" → ❷ – ❾

Beginning a sentence with something other than the subject is frequent in German.
It may however also be used for special effect to:

> • *highlight* whatever is placed first in the clause → ❿
>
> • *emphasize* the subject of the clause by forcing it from its initial position to the end of the clause → ⓫

After inversion, any reflexive pronoun precedes the subject, unless the subject is a pronoun → ⓬

The following do not cause inversion when placed at the beginning of a main clause, although inversion may be caused by something else placed after them:

> allein, denn, oder, sondern, und → ⓭
> ja and nein → ⓮
> certain exclamations: ach, also, nun *etc* → ⓯
> words or phrases qualifying the subject: auch, nur, sogar, *etc* → ⓰

① Sie haben es gestern sehr billig gekauft.
They bought it very cheaply yesterday.

② Gestern sind wir ins Theater gegangen.
We went to the theatre yesterday.

③ So ein Kind habe ich noch nie gesehen!
I've never seen such a child!
Seinen Freunden wollte er es nicht zeigen.
He wouldn't show it to his friends.

④ Seinen Freunden zu helfen, hat er nicht versucht.
He didn't try to help his friends.

⑤ Deine Schwester war es.　　　It was your sister.

⑥ Geraucht hatte er nie.　　　He had never smoked.

⑦ In diesem Haus ist Mozart auf die Welt gekommen.
Mozart was born in this house.

⑧ Was mit ihm los war, haben wir nicht herausgefunden.
We never discovered what was wrong with him.

⑨ Nachdem ich ihn gesehen hatte, ging ich nach Hause.
I went home after seeing him.

⑩ Dem würde ich nichts sagen!
I wouldn't tell *him* anything!

⑪ An der Ecke stand eine riesengroße Fabrik.
A huge factory stood on the corner.

⑫ Daran erinnerten sich die Zeugen nicht.
The witnesses didn't remember that.
Daran erinnerten sie sich nicht.
They didn't remember that.

⑬ Peter ging nach Hause und Elsa blieb auf der Party.
Peter went home and Elsa stayed at the party.
BUT:　Peter ging nach Hause und unterwegs sah er Kurt.
　　　Peter went home and on the way he saw Kurt.

⑭ Nein, ich will nicht.　　　No, I don't want to.
BUT:　Nein, das tue ich nicht.　　No, I won't do that.

⑮ Also, wir fahren nach Hamburg.
So we'll go to Hamburg.
BUT:　Also, nach Hamburg wollt ihr fahren.
　　　So you want to go to Hamburg.

⑯ Sogar seine Mutter wollte es ihm nicht glauben.
Even his mother wouldn't believe him.
BUT:　Sogar mit dem Zug ginge es nicht schneller.
　　　It would be no faster even by train.

Word Order: Subordinate Clauses

A subordinate clause may be introduced by:

- a relative pronoun (see page 174) → ①

- a subordinating conjunction (see page 222) → ② – ③

The subject follows the opening conjunction or relative pronoun – see wir and er → ① – ③

The main verb almost always goes to the end of a subordinate clause → ① – ③

The exceptions to this are:

- in a wenn clause where wenn is omitted (see page 64) → ④

- in an indirect statement without dass (see page 64) → ⑤

The order for articles, nouns, adjectives, adverbs, direct and indirect objects is the same as for main clauses (see page 224), but they are all placed between the subject of the clause and the verb → ⑥

If the subject of a reflexive verb in a subordinate clause is a pronoun, the order is *subject pronoun + reflexive pronoun* → ⑦

If the subject is a noun, the reflexive pronoun may follow or precede it → ⑧

Where one subordinate clause lies inside another, both still obey the order rule for subordinate clauses → ⑨

Examples

1. Die Kinder, die wir gesehen haben ...
   The children whom we saw ...
2. Da er nicht schwimmen wollte, ist er nicht mitgekommen.
   As he didn't want to swim he didn't come.
3. Ich weiß, dass er zur Zeit in London wohnt.
   I know he's living in London at the moment.
   Ich weiß nicht, ob er kommt.
   I don't know if he's coming.
4. Findest du meine Uhr, so ruf mich bitte an.
   (= Wenn du meine Uhr findest, ruf mich bitte an.)
   If you find my watch, please give me a ring.
5. Er meint, er werde es innerhalb einer Stunde schaffen.
   (= Er meint, dass er es innerhalb einer Stunde schaffen werde.)
   He thinks (that) he will manage it within an hour.

6. **MAIN CLAUSE**
   Er ist gestern mit seiner Mutter in die Stadt gefahren.
   He went to town with his mother yesterday.

   SUBORDINATE CLAUSES
   Da er gestern mit seiner Mutter in die Stadt gefahren ist, ...
   Since he went to town with his mother yesterday ...
   Der Junge, der gestern mit seiner Mutter in die Stadt gefahren ist, ...
   The boy who went to town with his mother yesterday ...
   Ich weiß, dass er gestern mit seiner Mutter in die Stadt gefahren ist.
   I know that he went to town with his mother yesterday.

7. Weil er sich nicht setzen wollte, ...
   Because he wouldn't sit down ...
8. Weil das Kind sich nicht setzen wollte, ... OR:
   Weil sich das Kind nicht setzen wollte, ...
   Because the child wouldn't sit down ...
9. Er wusste, dass der Mann, mit dem er gesprochen hatte, bei einer Baufirma arbeitete.
   He knew that the man he had been speaking to worked for a construction company.

Sentence structure

Word Order

In the imperative

- normal order → ❶

- with reflexive verbs → ❷

- with separable verbs → ❸

- with separable reflexive verbs → ❹

In direct and indirect speech

The verb of saying ("he replied/he said") must be inverted if it is placed within a quotation → ❺

The position of the verb in indirect speech depends on whether or not dass (see page 66) is used → ❻

Verbs with separable prefixes (see pages 72–75)

In main clauses the verb and prefix are separated in simple tenses and imperative forms → ❼

For compound tenses of main clauses and all tenses of subordinate clauses, the verb and its prefix are united at the end of the clause → ❽

In a present infinitive phrase (see page 46), the verb and prefix are joined together by zu and placed at the end of the phrase → ❾

1.   Hol mir das Buch! (*singular*)
    Holt mir das Buch! (*plural*)   Fetch me that book!
    Holen Sie mir das Buch! (*polite*)

2.   Wasch dich sofort! (*singular*)
    Wascht euch sofort! (*plural*)   Wash yourself/yourselves
    Waschen Sie sich sofort! (*polite*)   at once!

3.   Hör jetzt auf! (*singular*)
    Hört jetzt auf! (*plural*)   Stop it!
    Hören Sie jetzt auf! (*polite*)

4.   Dreh dich um! (*singular*)
    Dreht euch um! (*plural*)   Turn round!
    Drehen Sie sich um! (*polite*)

5.   „Meine Mutter" sagte er, „kommt erst morgen an".
    "My mother", he said, "won't arrive till tomorrow".

6.   Er sagte, dass sie erst am nächsten Tag ankomme.
    He said that she would not arrive until the next day.
    Er sagte, sie komme erst am nächsten Tag an.
    He said she would not arrive until the next day.

7.   Er machte die Tür zu.
    He closed the door.
    Ich räume zuerst auf.
    I'll clean up first.
    Hol mich um 7 ab!
    Pick me up at 7!

8.   Er hat die Tür zugemacht.
    He closed the door.
    Ich werde zuerst aufräumen.
    I'll clean up first.
    Er wurde um 7 abgeholt.
    He was picked up at 7.
    Wenn du mich um 7 abholst, ...
    If you pick me up at 7 ...
    Nachdem du mich abgeholt hast, ...
    After you've picked me up ...

9.   Um frühzeitig anzukommen, fuhren wir sofort ab.
    In order to arrive early we left immediately.

Question Forms

Direct questions

In German, a direct question is formed by simply inverting the verb and subject → ①

In compound tenses (see pages 22–27) the past participle or infinitive goes to the end of the clause → ②

A statement can be made into a question by the addition of nicht, nicht wahr or doch, as with "isn't it" in English → ③

Questions formed in this way normally expect the answer to be "yes".

When a question is put in the negative, doch can be used to answer it more positively than ja → ④

Questions formed using interrogative words

When questions are formed with interrogative adverbs, the subject and verb are inverted → ⑤

When questions are formed with interrogative pronouns and adjectives (see pages 144 and 176–178), the word order is that of direct statements:

- as the subject of the verb at the beginning of the clause they do not cause inversion → ⑥
- if *not* the subject of the verb *and* at the beginning of the clause they do cause inversion → ⑦

Indirect questions

These are questions following verbs of asking and wondering etc. The verb comes at the end of an indirect question → ⑧

Examples

❶ Magst du ihn?
Do you like him?

❷ Gehst du ins Kino?   Do you go to the cinema?
OR: Are you going to the cinema?

Hast du ihn gesehen?   Did you see him?
OR: Have you seen him?

Wird sie mit ihm kommen?
Will she come with him?

❸ Das stimmt, nicht (wahr)?
That's true, isn't it?

Das schaffst du doch?
You'll manage, won't you?

❹ Glaubst du mir nicht? — Doch!
Don't you believe me? — Yes I do!

❺ Wann ist er gekommen?
When did he come?

Wo willst du hin?
Where are you off to?

❻ Wer hat das gemacht?
Who did this?

❼ Wem hast du es geschenkt?
Who did you give it to?

❽ Er fragte, ob du mitkommen wolltest.
He asked if you wanted to come.

Er möchte wissen, warum du nicht gekommen bist.
He would like to know why you didn't come.

Negatives

A statement or question is made negative by adding:

> nicht (*not*) or nie (*never*)

The negative may be placed next to the phrase or word to which it refers. The negative meaning can be shifted from one element of the sentence to another in this way → **❶**

nie can be placed at the beginning of a sentence for added emphasis, in which case the subject and verb are inverted → **❷**

nicht comes at the end of a negative imperative, except when the verb is separable, in which case nicht *precedes* the separable prefix → **❸**

The combination nicht ein is usually replaced by forms of kein (see page 126) → **❹**

doch (see page 196) is used in place of ja to contradict a negative statement → **❺**

Negative comparison is made with nicht ... sondern (*not ... but*).

This construction is used to correct a previous false impression or idea → **❻**

①   Mit ihr wollte er nicht sprechen.
He didn't want to speak to *her*.
Er wollte nicht mit ihr sprechen.
He didn't *want* to speak to her.

Er will nicht morgen nach Hause.
OR: Morgen will er nicht nach Hause.
He doesn't want to go home *tomorrow*.
Er will morgen nicht nach Hause.
He doesn't want to go *home* tomorrow.

Wohnen Sie nicht in Dortmund?
Don't you live in Dortmund?
Warum ist er nicht mitgekommen?
Why didn't he come with you?
Waren Sie nie in Dortmund?
Have you never been to Dortmund?

②   Nie war sie glücklicher gewesen.
She had never been happier.

③   Iss das nicht!
Don't eat that!
Beeilen Sie sich nicht!
Don't hurry!
BUT: Geh nicht weg!
      Don't go away!

④   Gibt es keine Plätzchen?
Aren't there any biscuits?
Kein einziges Kind hatte die Arbeit geschrieben.
Not a single child had done the work.

⑤   Du kommst nicht mit. — Doch, ich komme mit.
You're not coming. — Yes I am.

⑥   Nicht Joachim, sondern sein Bruder war es.
It wasn't Joachim, but his brother.

Numbers

Cardinal
(one, two etc)

Ordinal
(first, second etc)

null	0		
eins	1	der erste [2]	1.
zwei [1]	2	der zweite [1]	2.
drei	3	der dritte	3.
vier	4	der vierte	4.
fünf	5	der fünfte	5.
sechs	6	der sechste	6.
sieben	7	der siebte	7.
acht	8	der achte	8.
neun	9	der neunte	9.
zehn	10	der zehnte	10.
elf	11	der elfte	11.
zwölf	12	der zwölfte	12.
dreizehn	13	der dreizehnte	13.
vierzehn	14	der vierzehnte	14.
fünfzehn	15	der fünfzehnte	15.
sechzehn	16	der sechzehnte	16.
siebzehn	17	der siebzehnte	17.
achtzehn	18	der achtzehnte	18.
neunzehn	19	der neunzehnte	19.
zwanzig	20	der zwanzigste	20.
einundzwanzig	21	der einundzwanzigste	21.
zweiundzwanzig [1]	22	der zweiundzwanzigste [1]	22.
dreißig	30	der dreißigste	30.
vierzig	40	der vierzigste	40.
fünfzig	50	der fünfzigste	50.
sechzig	60	der sechzigste	60.

[1] zwo **often replaces** zwei **in speech, to distinguish it clearly from** drei: zwo, zwoundzwanzig *etc.*

[2] The ordinal number and the preceding definite article (and adjective if there is one) are declined, e.g.:

bei seinem dritten Versuch   **at his third attempt**

siebzig	70	der siebzigste	70.
achtzig	80	der achtzigste	80.
neunzig	90	der neunzigste	90.
hundert	a hundred	der hundertste	100.
einhundert	one hundred		
hunderteins	101	der hunderterste	101.
hundertzwei	102	der hundertzweite	102.
hunderteinundzwanzig	121	der hunderteinundzwanzigste	121.
zweihundert	200	der zweihundertste	200.
tausend	a thousand	der tausendste	1000.
eintausend	one thousand		
tausendeins	1001	der tausenderste	1001.
zweitausend	2000	der zweitausendste	2000.
hunderttausend	100 000	der hunderttausendste	100 000.
eine Million	1 000 000	der millionste	1 000 000.

With large numbers, spaces or full stops are used where English uses a comma, e.g.:

1.000.000 or 1 000 000 for 1,000,000 (*a million*)

Decimals are written with a comma instead of a full stop, e.g.:

7,5 (sieben Komma fünf) for 7.5 (*seven point five*)

When ordinal numbers are used as nouns, they are written with a capital letter, e.g.:

sie ist die Zehnte   she's the tenth

Fractions

halb	die Hälfte	eine halbe Stunde
half (a)	half (the)	half an hour
das Drittel	zwei Drittel	das Viertel
third	two thirds	quarter
drei viertel	anderthalb, eineinhalb	zweieinhalb
three quarters	one and a half	two and a half

Wie spät ist es? / Wie viel Uhr ist es?
What time is it?

Es ist ...
It's ...

00.00	Mitternacht / null Uhr / vierundzwanzig Uhr / zwölf Uhr
00.10	zehn (Minuten) nach zwölf / null Uhr zehn
00.15	Viertel nach zwölf / null Uhr fünfzehn
00.30	halb eins / null Uhr dreißig
00.40	zwanzig (Minuten) vor eins / null Uhr vierzig
00.45	Viertel vor eins / drei viertel eins / null Uhr fünfundvierzig
01.00	ein Uhr
01.10	zehn (Minuten) nach eins / ein Uhr zehn
01.15	Viertel nach eins / ein Uhr fünfzehn
01.30	halb zwei / ein Uhr dreißig
01.40	zwanzig (Minuten) vor zwei / ein Uhr vierzig
01.45	Viertel vor zwei / drei viertel zwei / ein Uhr fünfundvierzig
01.50	zehn (Minuten) vor zwei / ein Uhr fünfzig
12.00	zwölf Uhr
12.30	halb eins / zwölf Uhr dreißig
13.00	ein Uhr / dreizehn Uhr
16.30	halb fünf / sechzehn Uhr dreißig
22.00	zehn Uhr / zweiundzwanzig Uhr / zwoundzwanzig Uhr

morgen um halb drei	um drei Uhr (nachmittags)
at half past two tomorrow	at three (pm)
kurz vor zehn Uhr	gegen vier Uhr (nachmittags)
just before ten o'clock	towards four o'clock (in the afternoon)
erst um halb neun	ab neun Uhr
not until half past eight	from nine o'clock onwards
morgen früh/Abend	
tomorrow morning/evening	

Dates

Der Wievielte ist heute? / Welches Datum haben wir heute?
What's the date today?

Heute ist …	It's …
der zwanzigste März	the twentieth of March
der Zwanzigste	the twentieth
Heute haben wir …	It's …
den zwanzigsten März	the twentieth of March
den Zwanzigsten	the twentieth

Am Wievielten findet es statt?	When does it take place?
Es findet am ersten April statt …	… on the first of April
Es findet am Ersten statt	… on the first

Es findet (am) Montag, den ersten April statt.
OR:
Es findet Montag, den 1. April statt.
It takes place on Monday, the first of April / April 1st.

Years

Er wurde 1980 geboren.	(im Jahre) 2010
He was born in 1980.	in 2010

Other expressions

im Dezember/Januar *etc*	im Winter/Sommer/Herbst/Frühling
in December/January *etc*	in winter/summer/autumn/spring
nächstes Jahr	Anfang September
next year	at the beginning of September

Punctuation

German punctuation differs from English in the following cases:

Commas

Decimal places are always shown by a comma → ①

Large numbers are separated off by means of a space or a full stop → ②

Subordinate clauses are always marked off from the rest of the sentence by a comma → ③

This applies to all types of subordinate clause, e.g.:

- clauses with an adverbial function → ③

- relative clauses → ④

- clauses containing indirect speech → ⑤

A comma is not required between two main clauses linked by und or oder → ⑥

Exclamation marks

Exclamation marks are used after imperative forms unless these are not intended as commands → ⑦

An exclamation mark is occasionally used after the name at the beginning of a letter, but this tends to be rather old-fashioned → ⑧

① 3,4 (drei Komma vier)
3.4 (three point four)

② 20 000
OR: 20.000 (zwanzigtausend)
20,000 (twenty thousand)

③ Als er nach Hause kam, war sie schon weg.
She had already gone when he came home.

Er bleibt gesund, obwohl er zu viel trinkt.
He stays healthy, even though he drinks too much.

④ Der Mann, mit dem sie verheiratet ist, soll sehr reich sein.
The man she is married to is said to be very rich.

⑤ Er sagt, es gefällt ihm nicht.
He says he doesn't like it.

⑥ Wir gehen ins Kino oder wir bleiben zu Hause.
We'll go to the cinema or stay at home.

⑦ Steh auf!
Get up!

Bitte nehmen Sie doch Platz.
Do please sit down.

⑧ Liebe Elke! ...
Dear Elke, ...

Sehr geehrter Herr Braun! ...
Dear Mr Braun, ...

Index

The following index lists comprehensively both grammatical terms and *key words* in **German** and English contained in this book.

Index

Index

Index

Index